A London
Bibliography of the
Social Sciences

BRITISH LIBRARY OF POLITICAL AND ECONOMIC SCIENCE

A London Bibliography of the Social Sciences

Twelfth Supplement

1977

VOLUME XXXV

MANSELL, LONDON, 1978

*This Bibliography has been computer typeset from
the machine-readable subject catalogue of the
British Library of Political and Economic Science by*
Mansell Information/Publishing Limited
3 Bloomsbury Place, London WC1A 2QA

ISBN 0 7201 0829 2
ISSN 0076-051X
Library of Congress Card Number 31-9970

Printed and bound in Great Britain at
The Scolar Press Ilkley Yorkshire

British Library Cataloguing in Publication Data

British Library of Political and Economic Science
    A London bibliography of the social sciences.
    Vol.35: 1977: 12th supplement.
    1. Social sciences – Bibliography
    I. Title
    016.3 Z7161

ISBN 0 7201 0829 2

Preface

This annual supplement to *A London Bibliography of the Social Sciences* is the fourth to be produced by means of computer typesetting.

Readers are again referred to the 'List of subject headings used in the Bibliography arranged under topics' as an essential guide to related headings in their field. This is to be found at the end of the volume.

D. A. Clarke   *August* 1978

Contents

VOLUMES I-XXXV

PERIODICALS LISTS

An alphabetical list of the periodicals in the British
Library of Political and Economic Science in 1929
is given in Volume IV; supplementary lists up to
1936 are given in Volumes V and VI, after which they
have been discontinued.

AUTHOR INDEX

Author indexes are given in Volumes IV (for Volumes
I–III), V, and VI, but not in later volumes.
Volumes I–XIV were published by the
British Library of Political and Economic Science,
Houghton Street, London WC2

A London
Bibliography of the
Social Sciences

AALST

— Social history.

BOON (LOUIS PAUL) De Zwarte Hand; of, Het anarchisme van de negentiende eeuw in het industriestadje Aalst. Amsterdam, 1976 repr. 1977. pp. 295.

ABD EL-KRIM.

ABD el-Krim et la République du Rif: actes du colloque international d'études historiques et sociologiques, 18-20 janvier 1973. Paris, 1976. pp. 536.

ABDUL RAZAK BIN HUSSEIN.

SHAW (WILLIAM) Author of Tun Razak. Tun Razak: his life and times. London, 1976. pp. 267. *bibliog.*

ABENDROTH (WOLFGANG).

ABENDROTH (WOLFGANG) Ein Leben in der Arbeiterbewegung: Gespräche, aufgezeichnet und herausgegeben von Barbara Dietrich und Joachim Perels. Frankfurt am Main, 1976. pp. 288. *bibliog.*

ABERDEEN

— Economic history.

KIBBLEWHITE (LIZ) and RIGBY (ANDREW) Aberdeen in the general strike. Aberdeen, 1977. pp. 32. *bibliog.*

ABOLITIONISTS.

MARSHALL (PETER D.) Bristol and the abolition of slavery: the politics of emancipation. Bristol, 1975. pp. 28,iv. *bibliog. (Historical Association. Bristol Branch. Local History Pamphlets. No. 37)*

SHYLLON (FOLARIN OLAWALE) James Ramsay: the unknown abolitionist. Edinburgh, 1977. pp. 144. *bibliog.*

ABORTION.

ANNUAL REVIEW OF POPULATION LAW; [pd. by] Fletcher School of Law and Diplomacy, Tufts University. a., 1974- Medford, Mass.

L'ABORTO nelle sentenze delle corti costituzionali: USA, Austria, Francia e Repubblica Federale Tedesca. Milano, 1976. pp. 333. *(Giurisprudenza Costituzionale. Quaderni. Nuova Serie. 5) In various languages.*

— Ireland (Republic).

ROSE (R.S.) An outline of fertility control, focusing on the element of abortion in the Republic of Ireland to 1976. Stockholm, 1976. pp. 249. *Ph.D. thesis, Stockholm - University of Stockholm.*

— Italy.

LEGISLAZIONE sull'aborto: prospettive di una riforma; interventi ed atti di un convegno, 20-21 febbraio 1975. [Camerino], 1975. pp. 432. *(Camerino. Università. Facoltà di Giurisprudenza. Pubblicazioni. 7)*

— United Kingdom.

ABORTION: the NHS and the charities; papers presented at a symposium held by the Co-ordinating Committee in Defence of the 1967 Abortion Act; edited by Helene Grahame. London, [1977]. pp. 31.

ABORTION rights: a socialist perspective; [by] Gill Crozier [and others]. London, [1977]. pp. 31. *(Socialist Woman. Pamphlets)*

ABSENTEEISM (LABOUR)

— United Kingdom.

CLARK (JILL) Time out?: a study of absenteeism among nurses. London, [1975]. pp. 68. *bibliog. (Royal College of Nursing and National Council of Nurses of the United Kingdom. Research Series)*

ABUSE OF ADMINISTRATIVE POWER

— Russia.

ZDRAVOMYSLOV (BORIS VIKTOROVICH) Dolzhnostnye prestupleniia: poniatie i kvalifikatsiia. Moskva, 1975. pp. 168.

ACCIDENTS

— Switzerland.

LAUBER (GISELA) Unfälle berufstätiger Frauen: sozialstatistische Untersuchung anhand von Akten der Schweizerischen Unfallsversicherungsanstalt des Jahres 1969. Zürich, 1976. pp. 276. *bibliog. Dissertation der Universität Zürich zur Erlangung der Würde eines Doktors der Wirtschaftswissenschaft.*

ACCION NACIONAL.

See PARTIDO ACCION NACIONAL.

ACCOUNTING.

CARTER (W.G.K.) and MORLAND (D.P.) Investigations and reports: guidelines for accountants investigating and reporting for the purpose of acquisitions, disposals and prospectuses. London, 1976. pp. 66.

KHOZIAISTVENNYI raschet v sotsialisticheskoi ekonomike: iz opyta stran SEV. Moskva, 1976. pp. 254.

SCOTT (MAURICE FITZGERALD) Some economic principles of accounting: a constructive critique of the Sandilands report. London, [1976]. 1 pamphlet (unpaged). *bibliog. (Institute for Fiscal Studies. Lecture Series. No. 7)*

CORREA (HECTOR) Integrated economic accounting: theory and applications to national, real, and financial economic planning. Lexington, Mass., [1977]. pp. 222.

ENTHOVEN (ADOLF JAN HENRI) Accountancy systems in third world economies; Ford Foundation sponsored study. Amsterdam, 1977 . pp. 359.

— Bibliography.

INSTITUTE OF CHARTERED ACCOUNTANTS OF SCOTLAND. An accountants' book collection, 1494-1930: catalogue of the antiquarian collection...; with an introduction by Anna B.G. Dunlop. 3rd ed. Edinburgh, 1976. pp. 113.

— United Kingdom.

INSTITUTE OF CHARTERED ACCOUNTANTS IN ENGLAND AND WALES. Accounting Standards Committee. Accounting standards, 1977; prepared by members of the staff of the Technical Directorate. London, [1977]. pp. 265.

ACCOUNTING AND PRICE FLUCTUATIONS.

ALOI (DELICE) Contabilità per l'inflazione. Milano, 1975. pp. 108. *bibliog.*

ACCULTURATION.

KINDERMANN (GOTTFRIED KARL) ed. Kulturen im Umbruch: Studien zur Problematik und Analyse des Kulturwandels in Entwicklungsländern. Freiburg im Breisgau, [1962]. pp. 422. *bibliogs.*

PRESS (IRWIN) Tradition and adaptation: life in a modern Yucatan Maya village. Westport, Conn., 1975. pp. 224.

JONES (DOROTHY MIRIAM) Aleuts in transition: a comparison of two villages. Seattle, [1976]. pp. 125. *bibliog.*

CONNOR (JOHN W.) Tradition and change in three generations of Japanese Americans. Chicago, [1977]. pp. 356. *bibliog.*

ACHESON (DEAN GOODERHAM).

McLELLAN (DAVID S.) Dean Acheson : the State Department years. New York, [1976]. pp. 466.

ACQUISITIONS (LIBRARIES).

LANCASTER. University. Library. Research Unit. The scope for automatic data processing in the British Library: supporting paper L: foreign books acquisitions study. [Lancaster?], 1971. fo. 11. *Photocopy.*

ACTION RESEARCH

— United Kingdom.

HATCH (STEPHEN) and others. Research and reform: the case of the Southwark Community Development Project, 1969-1972. London, Home Office, Urban Deprivation Unit, 1977. pp. 292.

ACTIONS AND DEFENCES

— Russia.

MARTYNCHIK (EVGENII GRIGOR'EVICH) Garantii prav obviniaemogo v sude pervoi instantsii; pod redaktsiei...P.S. Nikitiuka. Kishinev, 1975. pp. 219.

ADAMS (HENRY BROOKS).

KUCZYNSKI (JUERGEN) Die Muse und der Historiker: Studien über Jacob Burckhardt, Hyppolite[sic] Taine, Henry Adams; und eine Bibliographie sämtlicher Schriften von Jürgen Kuczynski, zusammengestellt von Erika Behm. Berlin, 1974. pp. 247. *bibliog. (Jahrbuch für Wirtschaftsgeschichte. Sonderbände)*

ADAPTABILITY (PSYCHOLOGY).

BINDRA (DALBIR) A theory of intelligent behavior. New York, [1976]. pp. 447. *bibliog.*

ADMINISTRATION.

REDFORD (EMMETTE SHELBURN) Ideal and practice in public administration. University, Ala., 1958 repr. 1975. pp. 155. *Presented as lectures in the annual lecture series in public administration at the University of Alabama.*

PETERS (J.) Author of Algemene beginselen van behoorlijk bestuur. Algemene beginselen van behoorlijk bestuur: debater: Prof. Mr. D. Simons: (voordracht gehouden op de Belastingconsulentendag 1971 georganiseerd door de Nederlandse Federatie van Belastingconsulenten). Deventer, 1971. pp. 47. *(Nederlandse Federatie van Belastingconsulenten. Serie Belastingconsulentendagen. Nr. 16)*

BALK (WALTER L.) Improving government productivity: some policy perspectives. Beverly Hills, [1975]. pp. 70. *bibliog.*

THOMPSON (VICTOR A.) Without sympathy or enthusiasm: the problem of administrative compassion. University, Ala., [1975]. pp. 137. *bibliog.*

DUNN (WILLIAM N.) and FOZOUNI (BAHMAN) Toward a critical administrative theory. Beverly Hills, [1976]. pp. 75. *bibliog.*

HILL (MICHAEL J.) The state, administration and the individual. London, 1976. pp. 256. *bibliog.*

JUN (JONG S.) Management by objectives in government: theory and practice. Beverly Hills, [1976]. pp. 80. *bibliog.*

MUNZEL (DIETER) Die Funktionsfähigkeit von Planungs- und Kontrollsystemen auf der Ebene von Bundesregierung und Bundesverwaltung. Hamburg, 1976. pp. 205. *bibliog. Dissertation zur Erlangung des Grades eines Doktors der Wirtschafts- und Sozialwissenschaften der Universität Hamburg.*

SELF (PETER J.O.) Administrative theories and politics: an enquiry into the structure and processes of modern government. 2nd ed. London, 1977. pp. 308. *bibliog.*

— Bibliography.

PALIC (VLADIMIR M.) compiler. Government publications: a guide to bibliographic tools; incorporating Government organization manuals: a bibliography. Oxford, [1977]. pp. 553.

ADMINISTRATION.(Cont.)

— Data processing.

UNION DOUANIERE ET ECONOMIQUE DE L'AFRIQUE CENTRALE. Département des Statistiques. 1970. Informatique et gestion de l'état. Brazzaville, 1970. 2 pts. *(Etudes Statistiques. Nos. 16, 18)*

— Decision making.

CORINA (LEWIS) Local government decision making: some influences on elected members' role playing. [York, 1975]. pp. 39. *(Papers in Community Studies. No. 2)*

GRUPPENINTERESSEN und Entscheidungsprozess in der Sowjetunion; herausgegeben von Boris Meissner und Georg Brunner. Köln, [1975]. pp. 264. *Papers based on the proceedings of a conference held in 1973.*

KIPPER (HEINZ) Entscheidungen in öffentlichen Organisationen: zur Problematik öffentlicher Investitionsentscheidungen und Beschaffungsprozesse. [Mannheim], 1975. pp. 355,xxxvi. *bibliog. Dissertation - Universität Mannheim.*

CAMPBELL (RITA RICARDO) Drug lag: federal government decision making. Stanford, Calif., 1976. pp. 62. *(Stanford University. Hoover Institution on War, Revolution and Peace. Hoover Institution Studies. 55)*

LERNER (ALLAN W.) The politics of decision-making: strategy, cooperation and conflict. Beverly Hills, [1976]. pp. 213. *bibliog.*

DECISION making in the European Community; [by] Christoph Sasse [and others]. New York, 1977. pp. 352. *bibliogs.*

— Research.

DEVELOPING research on African administration: some methodological issues; edited by Adebayo Adedeji and Goran Hyden. Ile Ife, 1974. pp. 201. *bibliogs. Based on informal discussions at the International Conference on Trends in University Teaching and Research in Public Administration in Africa, Institute of Administration, University of Ife, 1970.*

— Study and teaching — Africa.

AFRICAN TRAINING AND RESEARCH CENTRE IN ADMINISTRATION FOR DEVELOPMENT. Documentation Centre. 1976. Directory of institutions for the teaching of public administration and management in Africa. Tangier, 1976. pp. 16. *In English and French.*

ADMINISTRATION OF ESTATES

— United Kingdom — Ireland.

GREIG (WILLIAM) General report on the Gosford estates in county Armagh, 1821; with an introduction by F.M.L. Thompson and D. Tierney. Belfast, H.M.S.O., 1976. pp. 245.

ADMINISTRATIVE AGENCIES

— Australia.

AUSTRALIA. Social Welfare Commission. 1976. An idea before its time. [Canberra?], 1976. 1 vol. (various pagings) *bibliog. (Reference Papers)*

— Brazil.

BRAZIL. Superintendência da Borracha. Relatorio de atividades. a., 1972- [Rio de Janeiro].

— Ecuador.

ECUADOR. Junta Nacional de Planificacion y Coordinacion Economica. 1973. Guia institucional del sector publico ecuatoriano; (version preliminar). [Quito], 1973. pp. 410.

— United Kingdom.

TECHNICAL EDUCATION AND TRAINING ORGANISATION FOR OVERSEAS COUNTRIES [U.K.]. Annual report. a., 1973/74 [2nd]- London.

— United States.

AMERICAN ENTERPRISE INSTITUTE FOR PUBLIC POLICY RESEARCH. Legislative Analyses. 94th Congress. No. 16. Regulatory reform: a survey of proposals in the 94th Congress. Washington, D.C., 1976. pp. 60. *bibliog.*

ANNA (HENRY J.) Task groups and linkages in complex organizations: a case study of NASA. Beverly Hills, Calif., [1976]. pp. 64. *bibliog.*

ECONOMIC impact of large public programs: the NASA experience; [by] Eli Ginzberg [and others]. Salt Lake City, [1976]. pp. 176. *bibliogs.*

LOBE (THOMAS) United States national security policy and aid to the Thailand police. Denver, Col., [1977]. pp. 161. *(Denver. University. Social Science Foundation and Graduate School of International Studies. Monograph Series in World Affairs. vol. 14, no. 2)*

UNITED STATES. OSHA Task Force. 1977. OSHA safety regulation: report;...edited by Paul W. MacAvoy. Washington, D.C., [1977]. pp. 104. *(American Enterprise Institute for Public Policy Research. AEI Studies. 151)*

UNITED STATES. Task Force on Reform of Federal Energy Administration. 1977. Federal Energy Administration regulation: report of the Presidential Task Force; edited by Paul W. MacAvoy. Washington, D.C., [1977]. pp. 195. *(American Enterprise Institute for Public Policy Research. AEI Studies. 150)*

ADMINISTRATIVE AND POLITICAL DIVISIONS

See also subdivision Administrative and political divisions under countries, cities, etc.

ADMINISTRATIVE COURTS

— United Kingdom.

FROST (ANNE) and HOWARD (CORAL) Representation and administrative tribunals. London, 1977. pp. 94. *bibliog.*

ADMINISTRATIVE DISCRETION

— United States.

JOWELL (JEFFREY L.) Law and bureaucracy: administrative discretion and the limits of legal action. Port Washington, N.Y., [1975]. pp. 214.

ADMINISTRATIVE LAW.

AUSTRALIA. Commonwealth Administrative Review Committee. 1971. Report; [J.R. Kerr, chairman]. in AUSTRALIA. Parliament. Parliamentary papers, 1971, vol.1.

— Poland.

LITWIN (JOZEF) Les conflits d'attributions entre les organes administratifs et les tribunaux de droit commun d'après un projet de loi polonais de 1962. Warszawa, [1962]. pp. 24. *(Polska Akademia Nauk. Centre Scientifique à Paris. Conférences. Fascicule 28)*

STAROŚCIAK (JERZY) ed. Prawo administracyjne. Warszawa, 1966. pp. 582.

— Russia.

KOZLOV (IURII MARKOVICH) Administrativnye pravootnosheniia. Moskva, 1976. pp. 184.

— South Africa.

COCKRAM (GAIL MARYSE) Administrative law. Cape Town, 1976. pp. 92.

— United Kingdom.

FOULKES (DAVID) Introduction to administrative law. 4th ed. London, 1976. pp. 323.

WILSON (GEOFFREY PHILIP) Cases and materials on constitutional and administrative law. 2nd ed. Cambridge, 1976. pp. 803.

DE SMITH (STANLEY ALEXANDER) Constitutional and administrative law; third edition...revised by Harry Street [and others]. Harmondsworth, 1977. pp. 729.

— United States.

GELLHORN (WALTER) and BYSE (CLARK) Administrative law: cases and comments. 6th ed. Mineola, N.Y., 1974. pp. 1192.

ADMINISTRATIVE PROCEDURE

— United Kingdom.

PLANNING inquiry practice: papers from a conference organised by the Law Society [and others]. London, 1974. pp. 57. *(Journal of Planning and Environment Law. Occasional Papers)*

ADMINISTRATIVE REMEDIES

— United States.

JOWELL (JEFFREY L.) Law and bureaucracy: administrative discretion and the limits of legal action. Port Washington, N.Y., [1975]. pp. 214.

ADOLESCENCE.

MERELMAN (RICHARD M.) Political reasoning in adolescence: some bridging themes. Beverly Hills, [1976]. pp. 37. *bibliog.*

ADOPTION

— United Kingdom.

KORNITZER (MARGARET) Adoption. 5th ed. London, 1976. pp. 186. *bibliog.*

ADORNO (THEODOR WIESENGRUND).

TAR (ZOLTÁN) The Frankfurt School: the critical theories of Max Horkheimer and Theodor W. Adorno. New York, [1977]. pp. 243. *bibliog.*

ADVERTISING.

STEINER (ROBERT L.) Does advertising lower consumer prices?. Washington, 1976. pp. 18. *(American Enterprise Institute for Public Policy Research. Reprints. No. 37) (Reprinted from Journal of Marketing, vol. 37, no. 4, October 1973)*

The CONSUMER society; edited by I.R.C. Hirst and W. Duncan Reekie. London, 1977. pp. 198. *bibliogs. Papers of a seminar organised by the Faculty of Social Sciences, Edinburgh University, 1973.*

MERK (GERHARD) Zur Begrenzung der Offensivwerbung. Berlin, [1977]. pp. 116.

ORNSTEIN (STANLEY I.) Industrial concentration and advertising intensity. Los Angeles, [1977]. pp. 85. *(American Enterprise Institute for Public Policy Research. AEI Studies. 152)*

— Drugs — United States.

CADY (JOHN FRANK) Restricted advertising and competition: the case of retail drugs. Washington, [1976]. pp. 20. *(American Enterprise Institute for Public Policy Research. Domestic Affairs Studies. 44)*

— United Kingdom.

U.K. Central Office of Information. Reference Division. Reference Pamphlets. 146. Advertising and public relations in Britain. London, 1976. pp. 30. *bibliog.*

— United States.

ADVERTISING and the public interest; (a Round Table held on June 10,1976...); John Charles Daly, moderator, etc. Washington, [1976]. pp. 40. *(American Enterprise Institute for Public Policy Research. Round Tables)*

ADVERTISING, POLITICAL.

BENJAMIN (JACQUES) Comment on fabrique un premier ministre québécois: de 1960 à nos jours. Montréal, [1975]. pp. 190.

ADVERTISING LAWS

— United States.

CADY (JOHN FRANK) Restricted advertising and competition: the case of retail drugs. Washington, [1976]. pp. 20. (*American Enterprise Institute for Public Policy Research. Domestic Affairs Studies. 44*)

AERONAUTICS, COMMERCIAL

— Freight.

MEIER (ROLF HANS) Die Aufteilung des Frachttransportes auf Luft- und Oberflächenverkehr. Zürich, 1977. pp. 190. *bibliog. Dissertation der Universität Zürich zur Erlangung der Würde eines Doktors der Wirtschaftswissenschaft.*

— Canada — Statistics.

CANADA. Statistics Canada. Air carrier traffic at Canadian airports. q., 1976(1st)-. Ottawa. *[in English and French]. Supersedes CANADA. Statistics Canada. Airport activity statistics.*

— Europe.

BRITISH AIRWAYS. Civil air transport in Europe; (prepared for the British Civil Aviation Authority). [London], 1977. pp. (140).

— Netherlands.

NETHERLANDS. Rijksluchtvaartdienst. 1975. Revised forecast of airtraffic to and from the Netherlands, 1975-2000. [The Hague], 1975. fo. 13.

— United Kingdom.

U.K. Civil Aviation Authority. Annual report and accounts. a., 1972/73- London.

AIR TRANSPORT AND TRAVEL INDUSTRY TRAINING BOARD [U.K.]. Manpower in air transport and travel, 1973 to 1976. [Staines, 1974]. pp. 14.

— — Freight.

U.K. Civil Aviation Authority. 1977. Air freight demand: a survey of UK shippers. London, 1977. 1 pamphlet (various pagings). ([*Publications*]. CAP 401)

AERONAUTICS AND STATE.

THOMSON (ADAM) b. 1926. Air transport - government subsidies or commercially viable? Edinburgh, [1975]. pp. 23. (*Edinburgh. University. Commerce Graduates' Association. Jubilee Lectures. 1974*)

— United Kingdom.

U.K. Civil Aviation Authority. Annual report and accounts. a., 1972/73- London.

AEROPLANE INDUSTRY AND TRADE

— Germany.

HOMZE (EDWARD L.) Arming the Luftwaffe: the Reich Air Ministry and the German aircraft industry, 1919-39. Lincoln, Neb., [1976]. pp. 296. *bibliog.*

— United States.

SCHLOTTER (PETER) Rüstungspolitik in der Bundesrepublik Deutschland: die Beispiele Starfighter und Phantom. Frankfurt, [1975]. pp. 210.

NETHERLANDS. Commissie van Drie. 1976. Rapport...: onderzoek naar de juistheid van verklaringen over betalingen door een Amerikaanse vliegtuigfabriek. 's-Gravenhage, 1976. pp. 240.

AEROSPACE INDUSTRIES

— France.

FRANCE. Groupe sectoriel d'Analyse et de Prévision Industrie Aérospatiale. 1976. Rapport...: préparation du 7e Plan. Paris, 1976. pp. 167.

— United Kingdom.

ELLIOTT (DAVID) The Lucas Aerospace workers' campaign. London, 1977. pp. 20. (*Young Fabian Pamphlets. 46*)

— United States.

ECONOMIC impact of large public programs: the NASA experience; [by] Eli Ginzberg [and others]. Salt Lake City, [1976]. pp. 176. *bibliogs.*

AESTHETICS.

BROWN (RICHARD HARVEY) A poetic for sociology: toward a logic of discovery for the human sciences. Cambridge, 1977. pp. 302. *bibliog.*

AFAN VALLEY

— Industries.

ALDEN (JEREMY D.) State of the community report: job getting and holding capacities. [Port Talbot], Glamorgan-Glyncorrwg Community Development Project, 1972. fo. 58.

— Social conditions.

GLAMORGAN-GLYNCORRWG COMMUNITY DEVELOPMENT PROJECT. Director's report to the management committee. [Port Talbot], 1972. fo. (125).

GLAMORGAN-GLYNCORRWG COMMUNITY DEVELOPMENT PROJECT. State of the community report: community health and welfare. [Port Talbot], 1972. pp. 27.

GLAMORGAN-GLYNCORRWG COMMUNITY DEVELOPMENT PROJECT. Transport and the younger unemployed. [Port Talbot], 1973. pp. 14.

AFFIRMATIVE ACTION PROGRAMMES

— United States.

AFFIRMATIVE action: the answer to discrimination?; (an AEI Round Table held on May 28, 1975...[in] Washington...); Ralph K. Winter, Jr., moderator, etc. Washington, [1976]. pp. 40. (*American Enterprise Institute for Public Policy Research. Round Tables*)

— — Illinois.

KOCH (JAMES V.) and CHIZMAR (JOHN F.) The economics of affirmative action. Lexington, Mass., [1976]. pp. 158. *bibliog.*

AFGHANISTAN

— Constitution.

AFGHANISTAN. Constitution. 1964. Constitution of Afghanistan...1 October, 1964. [Kabul], 1964. pp. 62.

— Description and travel.

TOYNBEE (ARNOLD JOSEPH) Between Oxus and Jumna. London, 1961. pp. 211.

— Population.

BLANC (JEAN CHARLES) L'Afghanistan et ses populations. [Paris, 1976]. pp. 166. *bibliog.*

AFONSO I, King of the Congo.

FARINHA (ANTONIO LOURENÇO) D. Afonso I, rei do Congo. [2nd? ed.] Lisboa, Agência Geral do Ultramar, 1969. pp. 109. (*Figuras e Feitos de Alem-Mar. 3*)

AFRICA.

AFRICAN dimensions: essays in honor of William O. Brown; edited by Mark Karp. Brookline, Mass., 1975. pp. 213.

— Bibliography.

BAGANOVA (TAT'IANA ALEKSANDROVNA) and BULATOV (SERGEI SERAFIMOVICH) eds. Spravochnaia literatura po stranam Azii i Afriki: svodnyi katalog inostrannykh fondov Biblioteki Akademii nauk SSSR i Gosudarstvennoi publichnoi biblioteki im. M.E. Saltykova- Shchedrina, 1945-1968. Leningrad, 1972. pp. 534.

— Commerce.

OROSZ (ÁRPÁD) Trade of African developing countries up to 1970 and prognosis to 1980. Budapest, 1975. pp. 91. *bibliog. (Magyar Tudományos Akadémia. Világgazdasági Kutató Intézet. Studies on Developing Countries. No. 70)*

BAILEY (RICHARD) Africa's industrial future. Blandford, Dorset, [1976]. pp. 198.

— — Africa, Central.

UNION DOUANIERE ET ECONOMIQUE DE L'AFRIQUE CENTRALE. Département des Statistiques. 1970. Commerce interafricain des pays membres de l'U[nion] D[ouanière et] E[conomique de l'] A[frique] C[entrale], 1966-1968. [Brazzaville], 1970. fo. 66. (*Etudes Statistiques. No. 17*)

— — Europe, Eastern.

OROSZ (ÁRPÁD) Trade of African developing countries up to 1970 and prognosis to 1980. Budapest, 1975. pp. 91. *bibliog. (Magyar Tudományos Akadémia. Világgazdasági Kutató Intézet. Studies on Developing Countries. No. 70)*

— Economic conditions.

L'AFRIQUE de l'indépendance politique à l'indépendance économique; John D. Esseks, directeur de publication; [by] G. de Bernis [and others]; traduit par Nina Dessau. Grenoble, 1975. pp. 275.

METROWICH (F.R.) Africa survey: essays on contemporary African affairs. Pretoria, 1975. pp. 184. *Radio talks first broadcast on Springbok Radio.*

The POLITICAL economy of contemporary Africa; Peter C.W. Gutkind and Immanuel Wallerstein, editors. Beverly Hills, [1976]. pp. 313. *bibliogs.*

— Economic history.

The POLITICAL economy of contemporary Africa; Peter C.W. Gutkind and Immanuel Wallerstein, editors. Beverly Hills, [1976]. pp. 313. *bibliogs.*

— Economic policy.

BAILEY (RICHARD) Africa's industrial future. Blandford, Dorset, [1976]. pp. 198.

DAMACHI (UKANDI GODWIN) Leadership ideology in Africa: attitudes toward socioeconomic development. New York, 1976. pp. 112. *bibliog.*

OKWUOSA (EMANUEL A.) New direction for economic development in Africa. London, 1976. pp. 222.

— Foreign relations.

METROWICH (F.R.) Africa survey: essays on contemporary African affairs. Pretoria, 1975. pp. 184. *Radio talks first broadcast on Springbok Radio.*

AMERICAN ACADEMY OF POLITICAL AND SOCIAL SCIENCE. Annals. vol. 432. Africa in transition; special editor of this volume, Marvin E. Wolfgang. Philadelphia, 1977. pp. 204.

The FOREIGN policies of African states; edited by Olajide Aluko. London, 1977. pp. 243. *bibliogs.*

See also EUROPEAN ECONOMIC COMMUNITY — Africa.

— Government publications — Bibliography.

AFRICAN TRAINING AND RESEARCH CENTRE IN ADMINISTRATION FOR DEVELOPMENT. Documentation Centre. 1976. Bibliography on African government documents. [Tangier?, 1976]. 1 vol.(various pagings). *In English and French.*

— History.

AKINTOYE (STEPHEN ADEBANJI) Emergent African states: topics in twentieth century African history. London, 1976. pp. 250.

— Industries.

BAILEY (RICHARD) Africa's industrial future. Blandford, Dorset, [1976]. pp. 198.

— Nationalism.

BENOT (YVES) Indépendances africaines: idéologies et réalités. Paris, 1975. 2 vols. (in 1).

— Politics and government.

L'AFRIQUE de l'indépendance politique à l'indépendance économique; John D. Esseks, directeur de publication; [by] G. de Bernis [and others]; traduit par Nina Dessau. Grenoble, 1975. pp. 275.

BENOT (YVES) Indépendances africaines: idéologies et réalités. Paris, 1975. 2 vols. (in 1).

GOSUDARSTVO sotsialisticheskoi orientatsii. Moskva, 1975. pp. 376. *bibliog. (Akademiia Nauk SSSR. Institut Gosudarstva i Prava. Gosudarstvo i Pravo Stran, Osvobodivshikhsia ot Kolonial'noi Zavisimosti. [5])*

METROWICH (F.R.) Africa survey: essays on contemporary African affairs. Pretoria, 1975. pp. 184. *Radio talks first broadcast on Springbok Radio.*

NGUYEN VAN CHIEN. Les politiques d'unité africaine. Lubumbashi, 1975. pp. 401. *bibliog. Thèse (Doctorat d'Etat es-Lettres et Sciences Humaines) - Université de Paris V.*

DE VILLIERS (CAS) African problems and challenges: selected essays on contemporary African affairs. Sandton, 1976. pp. 210.

AMERICAN ACADEMY OF POLITICAL AND SOCIAL SCIENCE. Annals. vol. 432. Africa in transition; special editor of this volume, Marvin E. Wolfgang. Philadelphia, 1977. pp. 204.

MARKOVITZ (IRVING LEONARD) Power and class in Africa: an introduction to change and conflict in African politics. Englewood Cliffs, N.J., [1977]. pp. 398. *bibliog.*

— — Bibliography.

DRABEK (ANNE GORDON) and KNAPP (WILFRID FRANCIS) compilers. The politics of African and Middle Eastern states: an annotated bibliography. Oxford, 1976. pp. 192.

— — Research.

DEVELOPING research on African administration: some methodological issues; edited by Adebayo Adedeji and Goran Hyden. Ile Ife, 1974. pp. 201. *bibliogs. Based on informal discussions at the International Conference on Trends in University Teaching and Research in Public Administration in Africa, Institute of Administration, University of Ife, 1970.*

— Population.

MIGRANTS and strangers in Africa; guest editor: Niara Sudarkasa. East Lansing, [1975]. pp. 124. *bibliogs. (Michigan State University. African Studies Center. African Urban Notes. Series B, No. 1)*

Les MIGRATIONS africaines: réseaux et processus migratoires; par Michel Aghassian [and others]; sous la direction de Jean-Loup Amselle. Paris, 1976. pp. 126. *bibliog. (Paris. Ecole des Hautes Etudes en Sciences Sociales. Centre d'Etudes Africaines. Dossiers Africains)*

— Race question.

VAN DEN BERGHE (PIERRE LOUIS) ed. Race and ethnicity in Africa. Nairobi, 1975. pp. 357. *bibliog.*

DE VILLIERS (CAS) African problems and challenges: selected essays on contemporary African affairs. Sandton, 1976. pp. 210.

— Relations (general) with China.

FOMICHEVA (MARGARITA VASIL'EVNA) and KRASIL'NIKOV (ALEKSANDR SERGEEVICH) Kitai i Afrika: podryvnaia deiatel'nost' maoistov v Afrike; pod redaktsiei...G.V. Astaf'eva. Moskva, 1976. pp. 263.

— Rural conditions.

APTHORPE (RAYMOND J.) Rural co-operatives and planned change in Africa: an analytical overview. (UNRISD Reports. No.72.4). Geneva, United Nations Research Institute for Social Development, 1972. pp. 114. *(Rural Institutions and Planned Change. Vol.5)*

— Social conditions.

AMERICAN ACADEMY OF POLITICAL AND SOCIAL SCIENCE. Annals. vol. 432. Africa in transition; special editor of this volume, Marvin E. Wolfgang. Philadelphia, 1977. pp. 204.

— Social policy.

DAMACHI (UKANDI GODWIN) Leadership ideology in Africa: attitudes toward socioeconomic development. New York, 1976. pp. 112. *bibliog.*

AFRICA, CENTRAL

— Commerce — Africa.

UNION DOUANIERE ET ECONOMIQUE DE L'AFRIQUE CENTRALE. Département des Statistiques. 1970. Commerce interafricain des pays membres de l'U[nion] D[ouanière et] E[conomique de l'] A[frique] C[entrale], 1966-1968. [Brazzaville], 1970. fo. 66. *(Etudes Statistiques. No. 17)*

AFRICA, EAST

— Economic conditions.

GOVERNMENT and rural development in East Africa: essays on political penetration; edited by L. Cliffe [and others]. The Hague, 1977. pp. 330. *(Hague. Institute of Social Studies. Series on the Development of Societies. vol. 2)*

— Economic integration.

GHAI (YASH P.) Reflections on law and economic integration in East Africa. Uppsala, 1976. pp. 47. *(Nordiska Afrikainstitutet. Research Reports. No. 36)*

— Foreign relations.

FARER (TOM J.) War clouds on the Horn of Africa: a crisis for détente. New York, [1976]. pp. 157. *bibliog.*

— History.

FALLERS (LLOYD A.) The social anthropology of the nation-state. Chicago, 1974. pp. 171. *bibliog. (Rochester, N.Y. University. Lewis Henry Morgan Lectures. 1971)*

BOCA (ANGELO DEL) Gli italiani in Africa Orientale: dall'Unità alla marcia su Roma. Roma, 1976. pp. 909.

FARER (TOM J.) War clouds on the Horn of Africa: a crisis for détente. New York, [1976]. pp. 157. *bibliog.*

— Politics and government.

GOVERNMENT and rural development in East Africa: essays on political penetration; edited by L. Cliffe [and others]. The Hague, 1977. pp. 330. *(Hague. Institute of Social Studies. Series on the Development of Societies. vol. 2)*

— Rural conditions.

GOVERNMENT and rural development in East Africa: essays on political penetration; edited by L. Cliffe [and others]. The Hague, 1977. pp. 330. *(Hague. Institute of Social Studies. Series on the Development of Societies. vol. 2)*

AFRICA, NORTH

— Civilization — Roman influences.

BENABOU (MARCEL) La résistance africaine à la romanisation. Paris, 1976. pp. 635. *bibliog.*

— Foreign relations — Bibliography.

SCHULZ (ANN T.) compiler. International and regional politics in the Middle East and North Africa: a guide to information sources. Detroit, [1977]. pp. 244. *(Gale Research Company. Gale Information Guide Library. International Relations Information Guide Series. 6)*

— History.

BENABOU (MARCEL) La résistance africaine à la romanisation. Paris, 1976. pp. 635. *bibliog.*

AFRICA, SUBSAHARAN

— Biography.

EDIAFRIC-SERVICE Les élites africaines. 3rd ed. Paris, [1974]. pp. 490. *(Bulletin de l'Afrique Noire. Numéro Spécial)*

VENTER (ALBERTUS JOHANNES) Black leaders of southern Africa. Randburg, [1976]. pp. 208.

— Commerce.

BURGESS (JULIAN) Interdependence in southern Africa: trade and transport links in south, central and east Africa. London, 1976. pp. 93. *(Economist Intelligence Unit. EIU Special Reports. No. 32)*

— Constitutional law.

NWABUEZE (BENJAMIN OBI) Judicialism in Commonwealth Africa: the role of the courts in government. London, [1977]. pp. 324.

— Constitutions.

LAVROFF (DMITRI GEORGES) Les systèmes constitutionnels en Afrique noire: les états francophones. Paris, [1976]. pp. 438. *bibliog. (Bordeaux. Université. Centre d'Etude d'Afrique Noire. Bibliothèque. Série Afrique Noire. 7)*

— Description and travel.

KNIGHT (C. GREGORY) and NEWMAN (JAMES L.) eds. Contemporary Africa: geography and change. Englewood Cliffs, N.J., [1976]. pp. 546. *bibliog.*

— Economic conditions.

KNIGHT (C. GREGORY) and NEWMAN (JAMES L.) eds. Contemporary Africa: geography and change. Englewood Cliffs, N.J., [1976]. pp. 546. *bibliog.*

SZENTES (TAMÁS) The negative impact of the dualistic socio-economic structure on domestic market, capital formation and labour. Budapest, 1976. pp. 24. *(Magyar Tudományos Akadémia. Világgazdasági Kutató Intézet. Studies on Developing Countries. No. 86)*

— Economic history.

KONCZACKI (ZBIGNIEW A.) and KONCZACKI (JANINA M.) eds. An economic history of tropical Africa. London, 1977 in progress.

— Economic policy.

EDIAFRIC-SERVICE. Les plans de développement des pays d'Afrique noire. 3rd ed. Paris, [1975]. 1 vol. (various pagings). *(Bulletin de l'Afrique Noire. Numéro Spécial)*

BOETTCHER (DETLEV) Entwicklung durch Integration: das Verhältnis der Europäischen Gemeinschaft zu Schwarzafrika. Berlin, 1976. pp. 282. *bibliog. Inaugural-Dissertation zur Erlangung des Grades eines Doktors der Wirtschaftswissenschaften der Freien Universität Berlin.*

— **Foreign economic relations — United Kingdom.**

WODDIS (JACK) Southern Africa: which side is Britain on?. London, [1976]. pp. 12. *(Communist Party of Great Britain. Communist Party Pamphlets)*

— **Foreign relations.**

BALLINGER (RONALD B.) and OLIVIER (GERRIT) Détente in Southern Africa: two views. Braamfontein, 1976. pp. 29. *bibliog.*

BOZEMAN (ADDA BRUEMMER) Conflict in Africa: concepts and realities. Princeton, N.J., 1976. pp. 429. *bibliog.*

GEYSER (OCKERT) Détente in Southern Africa. Bloemfontein, 1976. pp. 59. *bibliog. (Universiteit van die Oranje-Vrystaat. Institute for Contemporary History. Focus on Politics. 2)*

SOUTHERN Africa in crisis; edited by Gwendolen M. Carter and Patrick O'Meara. Bloomington, Ind., [1977]. pp. 277. *bibliog.*

See also EUROPEAN ECONOMIC COMMUNITY — Africa, Subsaharan; UNITED NATIONS — Africa, Subsaharan.

— — **China.**

SCALAPINO (ROBERT A.) Africa and Peking's United Front: ten years of Chinese communist foreign policy in Africa. Berkeley, [1966?]. pp. 11. *(California University. Center for Chinese Studies. Reprints. No. 188) (Reprinted from Current Scene, vol.3, no. 26)*

— — **Ghana.**

GHANA. Ministry of Information. 1966. Nkrumah's subversion in Africa: documentary evidence of Nkrumah's interference in the affairs of other African States. [Accra, 1966]. pp. 91.

GHANA. Information Services Department. 1967. Nkrumah's deception of Africa. [Accra, 1967]. pp. 95.

— — **South Africa.**

METROWICH (F.R.) ed. Towards dialogue and détente. Sandton, S.A., 1975. pp. 139.

— — **United Kingdom.**

WODDIS (JACK) Southern Africa: which side is Britain on?. London, [1976]. pp. 12. *(Communist Party of Great Britain. Communist Party Pamphlets)*

— **History.**

WILSON (HENRY S.) The imperial experience in sub-Saharan Africa since 1870. Minneapolis, 1977. pp. 415. *bibliog.*

— **Industries.**

EDIAFRIC-SERVICE. L'industrie africaine en 1975. Paris, [1975]. 1 vol. (various pagings). *(Bulletin de l'Afrique Noire. Numéro Spécial)*

— **Military policy.**

VENTER (ALBERTUS JOHANNES) Vorster's Africa: friendship and frustration. Johannesburg, 1977. pp. 387.

— **Nationalism.**

VENTER (ALBERTUS JOHANNES) Vorster's Africa: friendship and frustration. Johannesburg, 1977. pp. 387.

WILSON (HENRY S.) The imperial experience in sub-Saharan Africa since 1870. Minneapolis, 1977. pp. 415. *bibliog.*

— **Politics and government.**

COLLINS (LEWIS JOHN) 'Detente' and the prospect for peace in Southern Africa. London, [1975]. pp. 7. *Opening address to the 12th annual conference of the International Defence and Aid Fund, Dublin, 1975.*

BAKER (DONALD G.) Rhodesia, settlement and Southern Africa. Braamfontein, 1976. pp. 14. *(South African Institute of International Affairs. Occasional Papers)*

EGELAND (LEIF) Report...[to the] meeting of the national executive council [of the South African Institute of International Affairs, Cape Town], 23 February, 1976. Braamfontein, [1976]. pp. 11.

LEGUM (COLIN) and HODGES (TONY) After Angola: the war over southern Africa. London, 1976. pp. 85.

SILVEIRA (ONESIMO) Africa south of the Sahara: party systems and ideologies of socialism. Uppsala, [1976]. pp. 212. *bibliog. (Uppsala, Statsvetenskapliga Föreningen. Skrifter. 71) Doctoral thesis, Uppsala University, 1976.*

HANNON (PETER) Southern Africa: what kind of change? Johannesburg, 1977. pp. 136.

MAIR (LUCY PHILIP) African kingdoms. Oxford, 1977. pp. 151. *bibliog.*

SOUTHERN Africa in crisis. London, [1977]. pp. 48. *bibliog. (Red Weekly. Pamphlets)*

SOUTHERN Africa in crisis; edited by Gwendolen M. Carter and Patrick O'Meara. Bloomington, Ind., [1977]. pp. 277. *bibliog.*

VENTER (ALBERTUS JOHANNES) Vorster's Africa: friendship and frustration. Johannesburg, 1977. pp. 387.

— **Race question.**

COLLINS (LEWIS JOHN) 'Detente' and the prospect for peace in Southern Africa. London, [1975]. pp. 7. *Opening address to the 12th annual conference of the International Defence and Aid Fund, Dublin, 1975.*

HANNON (PETER) Southern Africa: what kind of change? Johannesburg, 1977. pp. 136.

VENTER (ALBERTUS JOHANNES) Vorster's Africa: friendship and frustration. Johannesburg, 1977. pp. 387.

— **Relations (military) with Russia.**

REES (DAVID) Soviet strategic penetration of Africa. London, 1976. pp. 20. *(Institute for the Study of Conflict. Conflict Studies. No. 77).*

— **Religion.**

HANNON (PETER) Southern Africa: what kind of change? Johannesburg, 1977. pp. 136.

— **Rural conditions.**

KNIGHT (C. GREGORY) and NEWMAN (JAMES L.) eds. Contemporary Africa: geography and change. Englewood Cliffs, N.J., [1976]. pp. 546. *bibliog.*

MICKELWAIT (DONALD R.) and others. Women in rural development: a survey of the roles of women in Ghana, Lesotho, Kenya, Nigeria, Bolivia, Paraguay and Peru. Boulder, Col., 1976. pp. 224. *bibliog.*

— **Social conditions.**

SZENTES (TAMÁS) The structure of society and its changes in the African countries. Budapest, 1975. pp. 56. *(Magyar Tudományos Akadémia. Világgazdasági Kutató Intézet. Studies on Developing Countries. No. 76)*

MANGHEZI (ALPHEUS) Class, elite and community in African development. Uppsala, 1976. pp. 118. *bibliog.*

AFRICA, WEST

— **Commerce — Europe.**

WAPPAEUS (J.E.) Untersuchungen über die Negerländer der Araber und über den Seehandel der Italiener, Spanier und Portugiesen im Mittelalter. Amsterdam, 1966. pp. 365. *Reprint of work originally published in Göttingen in 1842.*

— — **Portugal.**

KUNSTMANN (FRIEDRICH) Die Handelsverbindungen der Portugiesen mit Timbuktu im XV. Jahrhunderte. [Munich, 1850]. pp. 171-235. *(Bayerische Akademie der Wissenschaften. 3. Classe. Abhandlungen. 6. Band, 1. Abth.)*

— **Constitutional history.**

ADIGWE (FRANCIS) Essentials of government for West Africa. Ibadan, 1974 repr. 1975. pp. 389. *bibliog.*

— **Social conditions.**

HRISTOV (ANGEL) Social structure and social development of West African countries (1900-1970). Budapest, 1976. pp. 70. *(Magyar Tudományos Akadémia. Világgazdasági Kutató Intézet. Studies on Developing Countries. No. 73)*

— **Social history.**

HRISTOV (ANGEL) Social structure and social development of West African countries (1900-1970). Budapest, 1976. pp. 70. *(Magyar Tudományos Akadémia. Világgazdasági Kutató Intézet. Studies on Developing Countries. No. 73)*

AFRICAN DRAMA.

INTERNATIONAL DEFENCE AND AID FUND. Fact Papers on Southern Africa. No. 2. Black theatre in South Africa. London, 1976. pp. 11.

AFRICAN STUDIES

— **Directories.**

AFRICAN TRAINING AND RESEARCH CENTRE IN ADMINISTRATION FOR DEVELOPMENT. Documentation Centre. 1976. Directory of institutions for the teaching of public administration and management in Africa. Tangier, 1976. pp. 16. *In English and French.*

— **Senegal.**

DAKAR. Université. Faculté des Lettres et Sciences Humaines. Enseignement et recherches africanistes propres à la Faculte, etc. [Dakar, 1963]. pp. 15.

AFRICANIZATION

— **Cameroun.**

CLIGNET (REMI) The Africanization of the labor market: educational and occupational segmentation in the Cameroun. Berkeley, Calif., [1976]. pp. 230.

— **Ghana.**

GHANA. 1968. Government policy on the promotion of Ghanaian business enterprises. [Accra], 1968. pp. 8.

AFRICANS IN EUROPE.

MAGGS (PETER B.) and LEE (LUKE TSUNG-CHOU) North African migrants under western European law. Medford, Mass., 1976. pp. 225-250. *(Tufts University. Fletcher School of Law and Diplomacy. Law and Population Monograph Series. No. 37) (Reprinted from Texas International Law Journal, vol. 11, no. 2)*

AGE AND EMPLOYMENT

— **Finland.**

LÄHTEINEN (MARTTI) Eri ikäisten teollisuuden työntekijäin koulutus, etc. Helsinki, 1977. pp. 123. *bibliog. (Finland. Suomen Virallinen Tilasto. Finlands Officiella Statistik. 32. Sosiaalisia Erikoistutkimuksia. 50) With English summary.*

— **Germany.**

KAEMPCHEN (HUBERT) Beschäftigungs- und Einkommenssicherung älterer Arbeitnehmer: zur Konzeption und Ausgestaltung der Arbeitsmarktpolitik in der Bundesrepublik Deutschland. Hamburg, 1975. pp. 438. *bibliog. Dissertation zur Erlangung des Grades eines Doktors der Wirtschafts- und Sozialwissenschaften der Universität Hamburg.*

— Germany, Eastern.

DEMMLER (HORST) and LOHSE (CHRISTA) Probleme der Arbeitsbedingungen für ältere Werktätige. Berlin, 1976. pp. 103. *bibliog.*

AGENCY (LAW)

— United Kingdom.

BOWSTEAD (WILLIAM) On agency; fourteenth edition by F.M.B. Reynolds and B.J. Davenport. London, 1976. pp. 461.

AGENTS PROVOCATEURS

— United Kingdom.

NATIONAL COUNCIL FOR CIVIL LIBERTIES. Entrapment and official instigation of crime: memorandum to the Law Commission on Working Paper 55. London, 1975. pp. 12.

AGGRESSION (INTERNATIONAL LAW).

MENZHINSKII (VIKTOR IVANOVICH) Neprimenenie sily v mezhdunarodnykh otnosheniiakh. Moskva, 1976. pp. 295.

AGGRESSIVENESS (PSYCHOLOGY).

GEEN (RUSSELL G.) and O'NEAL (EDGAR C.) eds. Perspectives on aggression. New York, 1976. pp. 273. *bibliog.*

AGRICULTURAL ADMINISTRATION

— Russia.

DENISOV (IURII PAVLOVICH) Razvitie kolkhoznoi demokratii, 1946-1970 gody. Rostov-na-Donu, 1975. pp. 183.

PROBLEMY sovershenstvovaniia upravleniia sotsialisticheskoi ekonomikoi. Moskva, 1976. pp. 272.

TAREL'NIK (BORIS IVANOVICH) Kolkhoznaia demokratiia razvitogo sotsialisticheskogo obshchestva. L'vov, 1976. pp. 154. *bibliog.*

— — Russia (RSFSR).

LOSEV (ALEKSANDR VISSARIONOVICH) and BURAKOV (MITROFAN EGOROVICH) Sovershenstvovanie form i metodov partiinoi raboty na sele. Voronezh, 1975. pp. 212.

AGRICULTURAL ASSISTANCE.

VALLIANATOS (E.G.) Fear in the countryside: the control of agricultural resources in the poor countries by nonpeasant elites. Cambridge, Mass., [1976]. pp. 180.

AGRICULTURAL COLONIES

— Sudan.

BORN (MARTIN) and others. Ländliche Siedlungen im nordöstlichen Sudan: Rural settlement in northeastern Sudan. Saarbrücken, 1971. pp. 100. *bibliog. (Saarbrücken. Universität. Geographisches Institut. Arbeiten. Band 14) In German, with English summary.*

AGRICULTURAL CREDIT

— European Economic Community countries.

EUROPEAN COMMUNITIES. Commission. Information on Agriculture. [Brussels], 1976 in progress. *[In various Community languages].*

— Ghana.

BROWN (C.K.) Some problems of investment and innovation confronting the Ghanaian food crop farmer. Legon, Ghana, 1972. pp. 95. *bibliog. (Ghana University. Institute of Statistical, Social and Economic Research. Technical Publication Series. No. 24)*

— Netherlands.

VRIES (JOH. DE) De Coöperatieve Raiffeisen- en Boerenleenbanken in Nederland 1948-1973: van exponent tot component. [Amsterdam], 1973. pp. 260. *bibliog.*

— Russia.

SCHWANEBACH (P.) Die Vorschuss-Vereine in Russland. St. Petersburg, 1874. 1 vol.(various pagings). *(Separatabdruck aus der Russischen Revue, Bd.III, Heft 12)*

EDEL'SHTEIN (ILLIA VOLODYMYROVYCH) and others. Finansy i kredytuvannia sil's'kohospodars'kykh pidpryiemstv. 3rd ed. Kyïv, 1969. pp. 359.

— Tanzania.

MSAMBICHAKA (L.A.) and MABELE (ROBERT B.) Agricultural credit and the development of Ujamaa villages in Tanzania. Dar es Salaam, [1974]. pp. 40. *bibliog. (Dar es Salaam. University. Economic Research Bureau. ERB Papers. 74.10)*

MOHELE (A.T.) The Ismani maize credit programme. Dar es Salaam, 1975. pp. 51. *(Dar es Salaam. University. Economic Research Bureau. ERB Papers. 75.2)*

AGRICULTURAL EXTENSION WORK

— Ghana.

BROWN (C.K.) Some problems of investment and innovation confronting the Ghanaian food crop farmer. Legon, Ghana, 1972. pp. 95. *bibliog. (Ghana University. Institute of Statistical, Social and Economic Research. Technical Publication Series. No. 24)*

— Italy.

CEMBALO (AGOSTINO) and COSENTINO (VINCENZO) Dieci anni di esperienza di assistenza tecnica del nucleo di Capua: un tentativo di valutazione. Portici, 1975. pp. 51. *bibliog. (Naples. Università. Centro di Specializzazione e Ricerche Economico-Agrarie per il Mezzogiorno. Assistenza Tecnica. 6) With English summary.*

— Kenya.

LEONARD (DAVID KING) Reaching the peasant farmer: organization theory and practice in Kenya. Chicago, 1977. pp. 297.

— Singapore.

SINGAPORE. Ministry of National Development. Annual report. a., 1975- Singapore.

AGRICULTURAL INDUSTRIES

— Russia.

KOLESOV (NIKOLAI DMITRIEVICH) and others. Agrarno-promyshlennye kompleksy: sotsial'no-ekonomicheskie aspekty formirovaniia i razvitiia; pod redaktsiei...A.F. Tarasova. Moskva, 1973. pp. 247.

AGRARNO-promyshlennye kompleksy: predpriiatiia, kombinaty, ob"edineniia. Moskva, 1974. pp. 223.

BLAZH (IL'IA DEMENT'EVICH) Optimal'noe planirovanie proizvodstva v agrarno-promyshlennykh kompleksakh. Moskva, 1974. pp. 216. *bibliog.*

PREVRASHCHENIE sel'skokhoziaistvennogo truda v raznovidnost' truda industrial'nogo. Minsk, 1974. pp. 239.

AGRARNO-promyshlennye kompleksy: osobennosti razmeshcheniia, planirovaniia i organizatsii ucheta. Moskva, 1975. pp. 280.

IVANOV (KUZ'MA IVANOVICH) Territorial'nye sistemy obshchestvennogo proizvodstva: geograficheskie aspekty agrarno-promyshlennogo kompleksirovaniia. Moskva, 1975. pp. 269. *bibliog.*

KARPOV (K.D.) ed. Agrarno-promyshlennye ob"edineniia: problema, opyt, puti resheniia. Ulan-Ude, 1975. pp. 390.

USTIIAN (I.) Agrarno-promyshlennoe kooperirovanie i khozraschetnye otnosheniia. Kishinev, 1975. pp. 219.

VOROTILO (ANDREI STEPANOVICH) and KODITSA (NIKOLAI VASIL'EVICH) Agrarno-promyshlennaia integratsiia i mezhkhoziaistvennaia kooperatsiia. Kishinev, 1975. pp. 136.

AGRARNO-promyshlennye kompleksy: problemy razvitiia i optimal'nogo funktsionirovaniia. Kiev, 1976. pp. 251. *bibliog.*

BONDARS (ARVID RIKHARDOVICH) and others. Raionnye agrarno-promyshlennye ob"edineniia. Riga, 1976. pp. 179.

EKONOMICHESKIE problemy agrarno-promyshlennoi integratsii. Moskva, 1976. pp. 384. *(Vsesoiuznaia Akademiia Sel'skokhoziaistvennykh Nauk. Nauchnye Trudy)*

— — Moldavian Republic.

BAZIN (MIKHAIL IAKOVLEVICH) Agrarno-promyshlennoe kooperirovanie: ob integratsionnykh protsessakh sel'skokhoziaistvennogo i promyshlennogo proizvodstva v Moldavii. Kishinev, 1975. pp. 158.

— United States.

DAHL (DALE C.) and HAMMOND (JEROME W.) Market and price analysis: the agricultural industries. New York, [1977]. pp. 323. *bibliogs.*

AGRICULTURAL INNOVATIONS.

SÁRKÁNY (PÁL) Sel'skoe khoziaistvo budushchego: na poroge tret'ego tysiacheletiia; perevod s vengerskogo Laslo Z. Partosha. Moskva, 1975. pp. 270.

— Brazil.

CONTADOR (CLAUDIO ROBERTO) ed. Tecnologia e desenvolvimento agricola. Rio de Janeiro, 1975. pp. 308. *(Brazil. Instituto de Planejamento Econômico e Social. Instituto de Pesquisas. Monografias. No. 17)*

— Ghana.

BROWN (C.K.) Some problems of investment and innovation confronting the Ghanaian food crop farmer. Legon, Ghana, 1972. pp. 95. *bibliog. (Ghana University. Institute of Statistical, Social and Economic Research. Technical Publication Series. No. 24)*

— India — Madras.

GREEN revolution?: technology and change in rice-growing areas of Tamil Nadu and Sri Lanka; edited by B.H. Farmer. London, 1977. pp. 429. *bibliogs.*

— Ireland (Republic).

HIGGINS (TOM) Research planning and innovation: a study of success and failure in innovation and the implications for R and D management and choice; (study...supported by An Foras Taluntais...and the National Science Council). Dublin, Stationery Office, 1977. pp. 283. *bibliog.*

— Russia.

KARLIUK (IPPOLIT IAKOVLEVICH) and SLOBODIN (V.M.) eds. Prognozirovanie razvitiia sel'skokhoziaistvennogo proizvodstva: nauchnye trudy. Moskva, 1975. pp. 232. *(Nauchno-Issledovatel'skii Ekonomicheskii Institut. Nauchnye Trudy)*

IAKIMOV (VITALII NIKOLAEVICH) Tekhnicheskii progress i vosproizvodstvo rabochei sily v kolkhozakh. Moskva, 1976. pp. 151.

ISAKHANOV (RAFAEL SERGEEVICH) Nauchno-tekhnicheskii progress i izmenenie kharaktera truda v sel'skom khoziaistve. Erevan, 1977. pp. 242.

— — Tajikistan.

KADYROV (DZHABAR) Osnovnye ekonomicheskie problemy razvitiia i povysheniia effektivnosti khlopkovodstva v usloviiakh tekhnicheskogo progressa. Dushanbe, 1976. pp. 416. *bibliog.*

— Sri Lanka.

GREEN revolution?: technology and change in rice-growing areas of Tamil Nadu and Sri Lanka; edited by B.H. Farmer. London, 1977. pp. 429. *bibliogs.*

AGRICULTURAL LABOURERS.

DAELEMANS (J.) Arbeidsorganisatie in de landbouw. Merelbeke, Rijksstation voor Landbouwtechniek, 1972. pp. 315. *bibliogs. Chart in end pocket.*

— Australia.

AUSTRALIA. Commonwealth Bureau of Census and Statistics. Rural land use, improvements, agricultural machinery and labour. a., 1971/72 [1st]- Canberra. *Formerly included in AUSTRALIA. Commonwealth Bureau of Census and Statistics. Rural land use and crop production.*

— Finland.

GEBHARD (HANNES) Jordbruksbefolkningen: dess förhållande till andra yrkesgrupper och dess sociala sammansättning i Finlands landskommuner år 1901. Helsingfors, 1913. pp. 151, 127. *(Finland. Subkomitén för den Obesuttna Befolkningen. Statistisk undersökning af socialekonomiska förhållenden i Finlands landskommuner år 1901. 1)*

— India.

INDIA. Labour Bureau, 1975. Rural labour enquiry, 1963-65: final report. [Delhi, 1975]. pp. 688.

— — Assam.

TAGORE (SAUMYENDRANATH) Teeplantagenkulis: eine indische Erzählung; (autorisierte Übersetzung aus dem Indischen). Berlin, [1932]. pp. 45.

— Russia.

PREVRASHCHENIE sel'skokhoziaistvennogo truda v raznovidnost' truda industrial'nogo. Minsk, 1974. pp. 239.

IAKIMOV (VITALII NIKOLAEVICH) Tekhnicheskii progress i vosproizvodstvo rabochei sily v kolkhozakh. Moskva, 1976. pp. 151.

ISAKHANOV (RAFAEL SERGEEVICH) Nauchno-tekhnicheskii progress i izmenenie kharaktera truda v sel'skom khoziaistve. Erevan, 1977. pp. 242.

— — Uzbekistan.

NURULLAEV (A.N.) Sel'skokhoziaistvennyi otriad rabochego klassa Uzbekistana v period stroitel'stva sotsializma, 1924-1941 gg. Tashkent, 1975. pp. 195.

— Spain.

La AGRICULTURA en el desarrollo capitalista español, 1940-1970; por Jose Luis Leal [and others]. Madrid, 1975. pp. 248.

— United Kingdom.

BRERETON (JOSEPH LLOYD) "Employers and employed". London, Ridgway, 1866. pp. 28.

UNITED KINGDOM. Parliament. House of Commons. Select Committee on Andover Union. 1846. Report. The north-west Hampshire agricultural labourer, 1846 (or "the new poor law"); edited by J.E.H. Spaul; and The north-west Hampshire agricultural labourer, 1867-1875; by George E. Brickell. Andover, 1975. pp. 30.

HORN (PAMELA) Labouring life in the Victorian countryside. Dublin, 1976. pp. 292. *bibliog.*

ECONOMIC DEVELOPMENT COMMITTEE FOR THE AGRICULTURAL INDUSTRY. Agriculture into the 1980s: manpower. London, National Economic Development Office, 1977. pp. 30.

NEWBY (HOWARD) The deferential worker: a study of farm workers in East Anglia. London, 1977. pp. 462.

— — Scotland.

FREE CHURCH OF SCOTLAND. Home Mission. Report on agricultural labourers. [Edinburgh, 1879]. pp. 15.

— United States.

MEISTER (DICK) and LOFTIS (ANNE) A long time coming: the struggle to unionize America's farm workers. New York, 1977. pp. 241.

AGRICULTURAL LAWS AND LEGISLATION

— Mexico.

LUNA ARROYO (ANTONIO) Derecho agrario mexicano. Mexico, 1975. pp. 827.

— Poland.

WPŁYW instrumentów prawnych na przestrzenną strukturę rolnictwa w Polsce; pod redakcją Andrzeja Stelmachowskiego. Warszawa, 1977. pp. 100. *(Polska Akademia Nauk. Komitet Przestrzennego Zagospodarowania Kraju. Studia. t.58) With Russian and English summaries.*

— Russia.

NEKIPELOV (PAVEL TROFIMOVICH) Ugolovno-pravovaia okhrana sel'skokhoziaistvennogo proizvodstva v SSSR. Rostov-na-Donu, 1973. pp. 171.

RUSSIA (USSR). Statutes, etc. 1965-1974. Resheniia partii i pravitel'stva po sel'skomu khoziaistvu, 1965- 1974 gg. Moskva, 1975. pp. 927.

ZENIN (VLADIMIR PETROVICH) Rabochii klass i kolkhoznoe krest'ianstvo: sblizhenie ikh pravovykh statusov. Kiev, 1976. pp. 155. *bibliog.*

AGRICULTURAL MACHINERY

— Trade and manufacture — United Kingdom.

GRACE (DAVID ROBERT) and PHILLIPS (DAVID COLIN) Ransomes of Ipswich: a history of the firm and guide to its records. Reading, Berks, 1975. pp. 64. *bibliog.*

— Australia.

AUSTRALIA. Commonwealth Bureau of Census and Statistics. Rural land use, improvements, agricultural machinery and labour. a., 1971/72 [1st]- Canberra. *Formerly included in AUSTRALIA. Commonwealth Bureau of Census and Statistics. Rural land use and crop production.*

AGRICULTURAL PRICE SUPPORTS

— European Economic Community countries.

IRVING (R.W.) and FEARN (H.A.) Green money and the common agricultural policy. Ashford, Kent, 1975. pp. 66. *(London. University. Wye College. Centre for European Agricultural Studies. Occasional Papers. No. 2)*

AGRICULTURAL PRICES

— Ecuador.

ECUADOR. Servicio de Informacion de Mercadeo Agropecuario. Anuario. a., 1973- Quito.

— European Economic Community countries.

EUROPEAN COMMUNITIES. Statistical Office. Agricultural price statistics. a., 1969/75- Luxembourg. *[in Community languages].*

U.K. Ministry of Agriculture, Fisheries and Food. Economics Division. 1976. EEC common and UK transition prices, 1975/76 to 1976/77: agricultural commodities. London, 1976. pp. 70.

— United Kingdom.

U.K. Ministry of Agriculture, Fisheries and Food. Economics Division. 1976. EEC common and UK transition prices, 1975/76 to 1976/77: agricultural commodities. London, 1976. pp. 70.

— United States.

DAHL (DALE C.) and HAMMOND (JEROME W.) Market and price analysis: the agricultural industries. New York, [1977]. pp. 323. *bibliogs.*

AGRICULTURAL RESEARCH.

FOOD: politics, economics, nutrition and research; edited by Philip H. Abelson. Washington, D.C., [1975]. pp. 202. *bibliog. The contents originally appeared in Science, weekly journal of the American Association for the Advancement of Science from January 1972 to March 1975.*

— Ireland (Republic).

AGRICULTURAL development: prospects and possibilities; (proceedings of conference). Dublin, 1976. pp. 145. *Proceedings of a conference organised by An Foras Talúntais, Economics and Rural Welfare Research Centre.*

AGRICULTURAL SOCIETIES

— Canada.

WOOD (LOUIS AUBREY) A history of farmers' movements in Canada;...[reprint of the 1924 edition with a new] introduction by Foster J.K. Griezic. Toronto, [1975]. pp. 372.

— Germany.

GESSNER (DIETER) Agrarverbände in der Weimarer Republik: wirtschaftliche und soziale Voraussetzungen agrarkonservativer Politik vor 1933. Düsseldorf, [1976]. pp. 304. *bibliog.*

AGRICULTURAL SURPLUS

— Russia.

MINBAEV (BARKY) and TOKTOBAEV (AZIZ) Proizvodstvo i raspredelenie kolkhoznogo pribavochnogo produkta. Tashkent, 1975. pp. 125.

AGRICULTURE.

BAADE (FRITZ) Welternährungswirtschaft. Hamburg, 1956. pp. 174. *bibliog.*

— Economic aspects.

INSTITUT NATIONAL DE LA RECHERCHE AGRONOMIQUE [FRANCE]. Département d'Economie et de Sociologie Rurales. Bulletin d'information. irreg., current issues only. Paris.

TUSHUNOV (ANATOLII VASIL'EVICH) Voprosy agrarnoi teorii. Moskva, 1976. pp. 318.

HILL (BRIAN E.) and INGERSENT (K.A.) An economic analysis of agriculture. London, 1977. pp. 296.

WORLD food prospects and agricultural potential; [by] Marylin Chou [and others]. New York, 1977. pp. 316. *Second of a series under the Hudson Institute's Prospects for Mankind program.*

— — Mathematical models.

MUKHOPADHYAY (SUDHIN K.) Sources of variation in agricultural productivity: a cross section time-series study in India. Delhi, 1976. pp. 121. *bibliog.*

RITSON (CHRISTOPHER) Agricultural economics: principles and policy. London, 1977. pp. 409. *bibliogs.*

— Africa.

OKWUOSA (EMANUEL A.) New direction for economic development in Africa. London, 1976. pp. 222.

— Africa, Subsaharan.

EDIAFRIC-SERVICE. L'agriculture africaine. Paris, [1975]. 1 vol. (various pagings). *(Bulletin de l'Afrique Noire. Numéro Spécial)*

AGRICULTURE.(Cont.)

— Africa, West.

GUILLAUME ( ) Agronomist. Rapport d'une mission d'études des aménagements hydroagricoles dans la vallée du Niger et de leurs possibilités d'extension. [Paris? 1959?]. 2 vols.

— Argentine Republic.

GASTIAZORO (EUGENIO) Argentina hoy: latifundio, dependencia y estructura de clases. 3rd ed. Buenos Aires, 1975. pp. 236.

— Australia — Statistics.

AUSTRALIA. Commonwealth Bureau of Census and Statistics. Crop statistics. a., 1971/72 [1st]- Canberra. *Formerly included in AUSTRALIA. Commonwealth Bureau of Census and Statistics. Rural land use and crop production.*

— — Queensland.

QUEENSLAND. Government Office, London. 1897. English farming in Australia: homes and homesteads on Darling Downs, etc. London, 1897. pp. 36. *Reprinted from The Queenslander, 20th November, 1897.*

— — Western Australia.

GLYNN (SEAN) Government policy and agricultural development: a study of the role of government in the development of the Western Australian wheat belt, 1900-1930. Nedlands, W.A., 1975. pp. 173. *bibliog.*

— Belgium.

BELGIUM. Institut Economique Agricole. La rentabilité de l'exploitation agricole. a., 1974/75- Bruxelles.

— Belize.

The AGRICULTURAL development potential of the Belize Valley; [by] R.N. Jenkin [and others]. Tolworth, 1976. pp. 344. *bibliog. (U.K. Ministry of Overseas Development. Land Resources Division. Land Resource Studies. 24) 8 maps in end pocket.*

— Brazil.

RIBEIRO (SYLVIO WANICK) Desempenho do setor agricola: decada 1960/70. Brasilia, 1973. pp. 176. *(Brazil. Instituto de Planejamento Econômico e Social. Instituto de Planejamento. Estudos para o Planejamento. No. 6)*

CONTADOR (CLAUDIO ROBERTO) ed. Tecnologia e desenvolvimento agricola. Rio de Janeiro, 1975. pp. 308. *(Brazil. Instituto de Planejamento Econômico e Social. Instituto de Pesquisas. Monografias. No. 17)*

— — Prices.

SÃO PAULO (STATE). Departamento da Produção Vegetal. Divisão de Economia Rural. Subdivisão de Economia Rural. Estudos de Economia Rural. A legislação federal de preços minimos par produtos agricolas; [by] Rubens Araujo Dias. São Paulo, 1950. pp. 30.

— — Statistics.

BRAZIL. Departamento de Censos. 1974-75. Censo agropecuario [1970: results by states and federal district]. [Rio de Janeiro, 1974-75]. 22 parts. *Tomos V, Maranhão, X, Pernambuco, XVI, Rio de Janeiro, XIX, Parana, out of print.*

BRAZIL. Departamento de Censos. 1975. Censo agropecuario [1970]: Brasil, [whole country]. [Rio de Janeiro, 1975]. pp. 299.

— — Para.

PENTEADO (ANTONIO ROCHA) O uso da terra na região Bragantina-Para. São Paulo, 1967. pp. 111. *bibliog. (São Paulo. Universidade. Instituto de Estudos Brasileiros. Publicações. 8)*

— Canada — Ontario.

ONTARIO. Economic Council. 1966. People and land in transition: opportunities for resource development on rural Ontario's marginal and abandoned acres. Toronto, 1966. pp. 36.

— China.

BANDYOPADHYAYA (KALYANI) Agricultural development in China and India: a comparative study. New Delhi, [1976]. pp. 204. *bibliog.*

KUO (LESLIE TSE-CHIU) Agriculture in the People's Republic of China: structural changes and technical transformation. New York, 1976. pp. 288.

— — History.

TISSIER (PATRICK) La Chine: transformations rurales et développement socialiste. Paris, 1976. pp. 325. *bibliog.*

— Colombia — Statistics.

COLOMBIA. Departamento Administrativo Nacional de Estadistica. Censo Agropecuario, 1970-1971. Censo nacional agropecuario [1970-1971]. [Bogota, 1974]. 8 vols. (in 1).

COLOMBIA. Departamento Administrativo Nacional de Estadistica. 1975. Memoria del sector agropecuario 1954-1974. [Bogota, 1975]. pp. 448.

— Communist countries.

AGRARNO-promyshlennaia integratsiia stran SEV. Moskva, 1976. pp. 286.

— Cuba.

CASTRO RUZ (FIDEL) Speech delivered...at the farewell ceremony for scholarship students who have completed various projects in the Guane-Mantua region and the inauguration of various projects at Guane, Pinar del Rio, sports stadium, April 29, 1967. London, Cuban Embassy, 1967. pp. 15. *(Cuba Information Bulletins. 1967. No. 5)*

AUROI (CLAUDE) La nouvelle agriculture cubaine. Paris, [1976]. pp. 259. *bibliog.*

— Ecuador — Statistics.

ESTIMACION DE LA SUPERFICIE COSECHADA Y DE LA PRODUCCION AGRICOLA DEL ECUADOR; [pd. by] Departamento de Estadisticas Agropecuarias. a., 1962/73- Quito.

— Ethiopia — Statistics.

ETHIOPIA. Central Statistical Office. 1974-1975. Results of the national sample survey, second round. Vols. 1,3-5. Addis Ababa, 1974-1975. 4 vols. *(Statistical Bulletins. 10)*

— Europe, Eastern.

The FUTURE of agriculture in the Soviet Union and Eastern Europe: the 1976-80 five year plans; edited by Roy D. Laird [and others]. Boulder, Colo., 1977. pp. 242. *Papers of two panels of the autumn 1976 meeting of the American Association for the Advancement of Slavic Studies.*

— European Economic Community countries.

FEDERAL TRUST FOR EDUCATION AND RESEARCH. Current agricultural proposals for Europe: report of a conference...January 1970. London, 1970. pp. 57.

EUROPEAN COMMUNITIES. Economic and Social Committee. 1975. Progress report on the common agricultural policy. Brussels, 1975. pp. 47. *(Studies)*

IRVING (R.W.) and FEARN (H.A.) Green money and the common agricultural policy. Ashford, Kent, 1975. pp. 66. *(London. University. Wye College. Centre for European Agricultural Studies. Occasional Papers. No. 2)*

EUROPEAN COMMUNITIES. Commission. Information on Agriculture. [Brussels], 1976 in progress. *[In various Community languages].*

HILL (BRIAN E.) and INGERSENT (K.A.) An economic analysis of agriculture. London, 1977. pp. 296.

— — Accounting.

EUROPEAN COMMUNITIES. Statistical Office. Agricultural accounts. a., 1976[1st]- Luxembourg. *[in Community languages]. Previously included in EUROPEAN COMMUNITIES. Statistical Office Agricultural. statistics.*

— — Statistics.

EUROPEAN COMMUNITIES. Statistical Office. Land use and production. a., 1976- Luxembourg. *[in Community languages] Earlier information included in various issues of EUROPEAN COMMUNITIES. Statistical Office. Agricultural statistics.*

— Finland.

WESTERMARCK (NILS) Lantbruksekonomiska utblickar. [Helsinki, 1975]. pp. 76. *(Ekonomiska Samfundet i Finland. Populärekonomiska Skrifter. Nr.7)*

— France.

FRANCE. Commission Agriculture-Environnement. 1975. Agriculture, environnement: éléments pour une évaluation de l'espace rural. Paris, La Documentation Française, 1975. pp. 191. *(Environnement. 43)*

FRANCE. Commission de l'Agriculture et de l'Alimentation. 1976. Rapport...: préparation du 7e Plan. Paris, 1976. pp. 152.

DUMONT (RENE) and RAVIGNAN (FRANÇOIS DE) Nouveaux voyages dans les campagnes françaises. Paris, [1977]. pp. 318. *bibliog.*

INSTITUT NATIONAL DE LA RECHERCHE AGRONOMIQUE [FRANCE]. Département d'Economie et de Sociologie Rurales. Bulletin d'information. irreg., current issues only. Paris.

— — History.

FRANCE. Ministère de l'Agriculture. Statistique agricole. Supplément. Série Etudes. No. 140. La statistique agricole française; par Maurice Alfroy. Paris, 1976 in progress.

— — Productivity.

FRANCE. Ministère de l'Agriculture. Statistique agricole. Supplément. Série Etudes. No. 138. Les gains de productivité de l'agriculture française de 1970 à 1974;...étude...rédigée par Maurice Desriers [and others]. Paris, 1975. pp. 71. *bibliog.*

— — Statistics.

FRANCE. Ministère de l'Agriculture. Statistique agricole. Supplément. Série Etudes. No. 138. Les gains de productivité de l'agriculture française de 1970 à 1974;...étude...rédigée par Maurice Desriers [and others]. Paris, 1975. pp. 71. *bibliog.*

FRANCE. Ministère de l'Agriculture. Statistique agricole. Supplément. Série Etudes. No. 140. La statistique agricole française; par Maurice Alfroy. Paris, 1976 in progress.

— Gambia.

The AGRICULTURAL development of the Gambia: an agricultural, environmental and socioeconomic analysis; [by] J.R. Dunsmore [and others]. Tolworth, 1976. pp. 445. *bibliog. (U.K. Ministry of Overseas Development. Land Resources Division. Land Resource Studies. 22) 4 maps in end pocket.*

— Germany.

BORSIG (ERNST VON) Reagrarisierung Deutschlands?: eine Untersuchung über ihre Möglichkeiten und Grenzen. Jena, 1934. pp. 94. *bibliog.*

WENDLER (DIETRICH) Die wirtschaftliche Bedeutung der Bereichsausnahme für die Landwirtschaft im GWB. Berlin, [1977]. pp. 266. *bibliog.*

— — History.

WOPFNER (HERMANN) ed. Urkunden zur deutschen Agrargeschichte. Aalen, 1969. pp. 386. *bibliog. Neudruck der Ausgabe Stuttgart 1928.*

WINTERNITZ (JOSEPH) Lenin und die Agrarfrage in Deutschland. Berlin, [1949]. pp. 48.

— — Bavaria — History.

HAUSMANN (FRIEDERIKE) Die Agrarpolitik der Regierung Montgelas: Untersuchungen zum gesellschaftlichen Strukturwandel Bayerns um die Wende vom 18. zum 19. Jahrhundert. Bern, 1975. pp. 288. *bibliog.*

— Germany, Eastern.

MUECKENBERGER (ERICH) Die politische Massenarbeit im Dorf und die nächsten Aufgaben in der Landwirtschaft: Referat auf der 17. Tagung des Zentralkomitees der Sozialistischen Einheitspartei Deutschlands am 22. Januar 1954. Berlin, 1954. pp. 112.

MUECKENBERGER (ERICH) Die Perspektive der Landwirtschaft und die Klassenverhältnisse auf dem Dorfe in der Deutschen Demokratischen Republik. Berlin, 1957. pp. 51. *(Berlin. Parteihochschule Karl Marx. Lektionen)*

— — History.

DEUTSCHES INSTITUT FÜR WIRTSCHAFTSFORSCHUNG. Sonderhefte. [Neue Folge]. 117. Die Landwirtschaft der DDR vor und nach ihrer Umgestaltung im Jahre 1960; ([by] Horst Lambrecht). Berlin, 1977. pp. 307. *bibliog. With English summary.*

— Grenada.

BRIERLEY (JOHN S.) Small farming in Grenada, West Indies. Winnipeg, 1974. pp. 308. *bibliog. (Manitoba University. Department of Geography. Manitoba Geographical Studies. 4)*

— Hungary.

ECONOMIC studies on Hungary's agriculture; edited by Iván Benet and János Gyenis; (translated from the Hungarian by Jenö Rácz). Budapest, 1977. pp. 194. *bibliogs.*

— India.

MUKERJEE (RADHAKAMAL) Food planning for four hundred millions. London, 1938. pp. 267.

SIVARAMAN (M.S.) Self-help in agriculture: a lecture. New Delhi, Planning Commission, [1958]. pp. 7.

RAMAKRISHNA AYYAR (VIRAVANALLUR GOPALIER) and others. Rural economics. Nagercoil, [imprint], 1964. pp. 448. *bibliog.*

LONDON (PAUL A.) Merchants as promoters of rural development: an Indian case study. New York, 1975. pp. 159. *bibliog.*

BANDYOPADHYAYA (KALYANI) Agricultural development in China and India: a comparative study. New Delhi, [1976]. pp. 204. *bibliog.*

MUKHOPADHYAY (SUDHIN K.) Sources of variation in agricultural productivity: a cross section time-series study in India. Delhi, 1976. pp. 121. *bibliog.*

— — Statistics.

THOMAS (PARAKUNNEL JOSEPH) and SASTRY (NARASIMHADEVARA SUNDARA RAMA) Indian agricultural statistics: an introductory study. Madras, 1939. pp. 144. *(Madras (City). University. Economics Series)*

INDIA. Department of Agriculture. 1975. All India report on agriculture census 1970-71. [Delhi, 1975]. pp. 287.

— — Assam — Statistics.

ASSAM. Directorate of Economics and Statistics. 1976. World agricultural census, 1970-71: Assam. Gauhati, [1976]. pp. 225.

— — Gujarat.

ADHVARYU (J.H.) and PARIKH (GOKUL O.) Studies in the economics of farm management in Surat and Bulsar districts, Gujarat: report for the year 1967-68. [Delhi, Controller of Publications], 1975. 2 vols. (in 1).

INDIA. Ministry of Agriculture and Irrigation. Directorate of Economics and Statistics. 1976. Studies in economics of farm management in I.A.D.P. region of Surat and Bulsar, Gujarat: combined report for the years 1966- 67 to 1968-69. Delhi, 1976. pp. 464.

— Iran.

RESEARCH CENTER FOR INDUSTRIAL AND TRADE DEVELOPMENT [IRAN] Agro-industry in Iran. Tehran, Ministry of Economy, 1971. fo. 24.

BERGMANN (HERBERT) and KHADEMADAM (NASSER) The impacts of large-scale farms on development in Iran: a case study of certain aspects of the Iranian agrarian reform. Saarbrücken, 1975. pp. 204. *bibliog. (Research Centre for International Agrarian Development. Publications. 4)*

ARESVIK (ODDVAR) The agricultural development of Iran. New York, 1976. pp. 271. *bibliog.*

— Ireland (Republic).

AGRICULTURAL development: prospects and possibilities; (proceedings of conference). Dublin, 1976. pp. 145. *Proceedings of a conference organised by An Foras Talúntais, Economics and Rural Welfare Research Centre.*

— Israel — Statistics.

ISRAEL. Agriculture and Settlement Planning and Development Center. 1976. Agriculture in Israel, 1959-1975: statistical series. Jerusalem, 1976. fo. 52. *(Israel. Central Bureau of Statistics. Special Series. No. 514) In English and Hebrew.*

— Japan.

SHIMPO (MITSURU) Three decades in Shiwa: economic development and social change in a Japanese farming community. Vancouver, [1976]. pp. 141. *bibliog.*

— Kenya.

AGRICULTURAL development in Kenya: an economic assessment; editors Judith Heyer [and others]. Nairobi, 1976. pp. 372.

— — Accounting.

SCOTT (MAURICE FITZGERALD) and others. Project appraisal in practice: the Little-Mirrlees method applied in Kenya. London, 1976. pp. 548. *bibliog.*

— Kuwait.

KUWAIT. Ministry of Guidance and Information. 1963. Agriculture in Kuwait. Kuwait, 1963. pp. 56.

— Malawi.

FARRINGTON (J.) Farm surveys in Malawi: the collection and analysis of labour data. Reading, 1975. 1 vol. (various pagings). *(Reading. University. Department of Agricultural Economics and Management. Development Studies. No.16)*

— Malaysia — Statistics.

FEDERATION OF MALAYSIA. Ministry of Agriculture and Rural Development. Economics and Statistics Section. Statistical digest: peninsular Malaysia. a., 1971, 1973- Kuala Lumpur. *[in English and Malay]*

— Mali (Republic).

ERNST (KLAUS) Tradition and progress in the African village: the non- capitalist transformation of rural communities in Mali; (translated from the German). London, 1976. pp. 262. *bibliog.*

— Mexico — Statistics.

MEXICO. Direccion General de Estadistica. Censo Agricola- Ganadero y Ejidal, 1970. V censos agricola-ganadero y ejidal, 1970: [state tables]. Mexico, 1975 in progress.

MEXICO. Direccion General de Estadistica. Censo Agricola- Ganadero y Ejidal, 1970. V Censos agricola-ganadero y ejidal, 1970: resumen general abreviado. Mexico, 1975. fo. 53.

— Nigeria.

IGBOZURIKE (MARTIN) Problem-generating structures in Nigeria's rural development. Uppsala, 1976. pp. 140. *bibliog.*

— Pakistan — Statistics.

PAKISTAN. Agricultural Census Organization. 1975- . Pakistan census of agriculture, 1972. Lahore, [1975 in progress].

— Palestine.

LOWDERMILK (WALTER CLAY) Palestine: land of promise. London, 1946. pp. 167.

— Peru.

KEITH (ROBERT G.) Conquest and agrarian change: the emergence of the hacienda system on the Peruvian coast. Cambridge, Mass., 1976. pp. 176. *bibliog. (Harvard University. Harvard Historical Studies. vol. 93)*

— — Statistics.

PERU. Ministerio de Agricultura. Oficina de Estadistica. Estadistica agraria. a., 1966(t.1,2), 1968(t.2), 1969/71- Lima.

PERU. Oficina Nacional de Estadistica y Censos. 1975- . II censo nacional agropecuario, 4 al 24 de setiembre 1972: [departmental results]. Lima, 1975 in progress.

PERU. Oficina Nacional de Estadistica y Censos. 1975. II censo nacional agropecuario, 4 al 24 de setiembre 1972: resultados definitivos; nivel nacional. Lima, 1975. pp. 415.

— Philippine Islands — Statistics.

PHILIPPINE ISLANDS. Bureau of Agricultural Economics. Crop statistics. a., 1974- Quezon City. *Supersedes in part PHILIPPINE ISLANDS. Agricultural Economics Division. Crop, livestock and natural resources statistics.*

— Poland.

WOŚ (AUGUSTYN) Związki rolnictwa z gospodarką narodową. Warszawa, 1975. pp. 304. *bibliog.*

KAPUSTA (FRANCISZEK) Zmiany struktury agrarnej i kierunków produkcji rolniczej w Legnicko-Głogowskim Okręgu Miedziowym. Warszawa, 1976. pp. 140. *bibliog. (Polska Akademia Nauk. Komitet i Zakład Badań Rejonów Uprzemysławianych. Problemy Rejonów Uprzemysławianych) With Russian and English summaries.*

RURAL social change in Poland; editors: Jan Turowski [and] Lili Maria Szwengrub. Wrocław, 1976. pp. 334. *bibliogs. Edited on the occasion of the Fourth World Congress for Rural Sociology, Toruń, Poland, 1976, and Ninth Congress of the European Society for Rural Sociology.*

— — History.

GÓRA (WŁADYSŁAW) Reforma rolna PKWN. Warszawa, 1969. pp. 276. *bibliog.*

— — Productivity.

FELBUR (STEFAN) Problemy wzrostu produkcji rolniczej w Polsce. Warszawa, 1972. pp. 300. *With Russian and English summaries.*

— Russia.

BAKHTIN (NIKOLAI IVANOVICH) Gorod i derevnia: ekonomicheskie aspekty. Minsk, 1974. pp. 191.

BLAZH (IL'IA DEMENT'EVICH) Optimal'noe planirovanie proizvodstva v agrarno-promyshlennykh kompleksakh. Moskva, 1974. pp. 216. *bibliog.*

IVANOV (KUZ'MA IVANOVICH) Territorial'nye sistemy obshchestvennogo proizvodstva: geograficheskie aspekty agrarno-promyshlennogo kompleksirovaniia. Moskva, 1975. pp. 269. *bibliog.*

AGRICULTURE.(Cont.)

KARLIUK (IPPOLIT IAKOVLEVICH) and SLOBODIN (V.M.) eds. Prognozirovanie razvitiia sel'skokhoziaistvennogo proizvodstva: nauchnye trudy. Moskva, 1975. pp. 232. *(Nauchno-Issledovatel'skii Ekonomicheskii Institut. Nauchnye Trudy)*

NOVYI etap v razvitii sel'skogo khoziaistva SSSR. Moskva, 1975. pp. 503.

VSESOIUZNAIA NAUCHNO-TEORETICHESKAIA KONFERENTSIIA, POSVIASHCHENNAIA 10-LETIIU MARTOVSKOGO PLENUMA TSK KPSS, 1975. Problemy agrarnoi politiki KPSS na sovremennom etape: materialy Vsesoiuznoi nauchno-teoreticheskoi konferentsii, posviashchennoi 10- letiiu martovskogo Plenuma TsK KPSS, 24-26 marta 1975 g. Moskva, 1975. 2 vols.

AGRARNAIA politika KPSS v usloviiakh razvitogo sotsializma. Moskva, 1976. pp. 336.

McCAULEY (MARTIN) Khrushchev and the development of Soviet agriculture: the Virgin Land Programme, 1953-1964. London, 1976. pp. 232. *bibliog. (London. University. School of Slavonic and East European Studies. Studies in Russian and East European History)*

SOWJET-Landwirtschaft heute; mit Beiträgen von Josef Breburda [and others]. Berlin, [1976]. pp. 221. *bibliog. (Giessen. Universität. Zentrum für Kontinentale Agrar- und Wirtschaftsforschung. Giessener Abhandlungen zur Agrar- und Wirtschaftsforschung des Europäischen Ostens. Band 78) With English summary.*

SPINDLER (BERND) Investitionsplanung in der sowjetischen Landwirtschaft. Berlin, 1976. pp. 202. *bibliog. (Giessen. Universität. Zentrum für Kontinentale Agrar- und Wirtschaftsforschung. Giessener Abhandlungen zur Agrar- und Wirtschaftsforschung des Europäischen Ostens. Band 77) With English summary.*

The FUTURE of agriculture in the Soviet Union and Eastern Europe: the 1976-80 five year plans; edited by Roy D. Laird [and others]. Boulder, Colo., 1977. pp. 242. *Papers of two panels of the autumn 1976 meeting of the American Association for the Advancement of Slavic Studies.*

RAZVITIE proizvodstvennykh otnoshenii v sel'skom khoziaistve. Kiev, 1977. pp. 283. *bibliog.*

— — Accounting.

AGRARNO-promyshlennye kompleksy: osobennosti razmeshcheniia, planirovaniia i organizatsii ucheta. Moskva, 1975. pp. 280.

USTIIAN (I.) Agrarno-promyshlennoe kooperirovanie i khozraschetnye otnosheniia. Kishinev, 1975. pp. 219.

— — History.

GROSSKOPF (SIGRID) L'alliance ouvrière et paysanne en U.R.S.S., 1921-1928: le problème du blé. Paris, 1976. pp. 459. *bibliog.*

DANILOV (VIKTOR PETROVICH) Sovetskaia dokolkhoznaia derevnia: naselenie, zemlepol'zovanie, khoziaistvo. Moskva, 1977. pp. 319.

SMITH (ROBERT ERNEST FREDERICK) Peasant farming in Muscovy. Cambridge, 1977. pp. 289. *bibliog.*

— — Mathematical models.

MODELI razmeshcheniia proizvodstva. Moskva, 1975. pp. 216. *(Akademiia Nauk SSSR. Problemy Sovetskoi Ekonomiki)*

— — Productivity.

CAIRNS (ANDREW) Agricultural production in Soviet Russia; a preliminary report as at May 1st, 1933. [London, Empire Marketing Board, 1933]. pp. 98.

SEMCHENKO (ANDREI PETROVICH) Problemy povysheniia effektivnosti kapital'nykh vlozhenii i osnovnykh fondov sel'skogo khoziaistva SSSR. Leningrad, 1976. pp. 127.

— — Estonia — History.

KAHK (JUHAN) and others. Beiträge zur marxistischen Agrargeschichte Estlands der Feudalzeit: neue Ergebnisse, neue Probleme, neue Methoden; [translated from the Russian]. Tallinn, 1974. pp. 152.

— — Mari Republic — History.

PO planu partii. Ioshkar-Ola, 1976. pp. 298.

— — Siberia — History.

ASALKHANOV (INNOKENTII ARSEN'EVICH) Sel'skoe khoziaistvo Sibiri kontsa XIX - nachala XX v. Novosibirsk, 1975. pp. 267.

GORIUSHKIN (LEONID MIKHAILOVICH) Agrarnye otnosheniia v Sibiri perioda imperializma, 1900-1917 gg.; otvetstvennyi redaktor...I.D. Koval'chenko. Novosibirsk, 1976. pp. 343. *bibliog.*

— — Soviet Far East — Productivity.

PANKRAT'EV (MAKSIM NIKIFOROVICH) Voprosy povysheniia effektivnosti proizvodstva v sovkhozakh Dal'nego Vostoka. Khabarovsk, 1975. pp. 174.

— — Tajikistan — History.

MUKHIDDINOV (IKROMIDDIN) Zemledelie pamirskikh tadzhikov Vakhana i Ishkashima v XIX - nachale XX v.: istoriko-etnograficheskii ocherk. Moskva, 1975. pp. 127. *bibliog.*

— — Tuva.

KONGAR (NIKOLAI MONZUELOVICH) Aktual'nye problemy razvitiia sel'skogo khoziaistva v Tuve. Kyzyl, 1974. pp. 110.

— — Ukraine — History.

LOS' (FEDIR IEVDOKYMOVYCH) and MYKHAILIUK (OLEKSII HRYHOROVYCH) Klasova borot'ba v ukraïns'komu seli, 1907-1914. Kyïv, 1976. pp. 283. *bibliog.*

— — White Russia — History.

KOZLOVSKII (PAVEL GRIGOR'EVICH) Magnatskoe khoziaistvo Belorussii vo vtoroi polovine XVIII v.: tsentral'naia i zapadnaia zony. Minsk, 1974. pp. 182. *bibliog.*

— Sierra Leone.

LEVI (JOHN) and others. African agriculture: economic action and reaction in Sierra Leone. Farnham Royal, Commonwealth Agricultural Bureau, 1976. pp. 428. *bibliog. (Commonwealth Bureau of Agricultural Economics. Miscellaneous Publications. No.2)*

— Singapore — Statistics.

SINGAPORE. Ministry of National Development. 1975. Report on the agricultural census of Singapore, 1973. Singapore, 1975. pp. 259.

— Spain.

La AGRICULTURA en el desarrollo capitalista español, 1940-1970; por Jose Luis Leal [and others]. Madrid, 1975. pp. 248.

— Sri Lanka.

SELVANAYAGAM (SOMASUNDARAM) The problem of economic holdings in the peasant agriculture of the dry zone of Ceylon. 1971. fo. 361. *bibliog. Typescript. Ph.D.(London) thesis: unpublished. 3 pamphlets in end pocket.*

ÖHRLING (STAFFAN) Rural change and spatial reorganization in Sri Lanka: barriers against development of traditional Sinhalese local communities. London, 1977. pp. 289. *bibliog. (Scandinavian Institute of Asian Studies. Monograph Series. No. 34).*

— Swaziland — Statistics.

SWAZILAND. Central Statistical Office. Annual census of individual tenure farms. a., 1972/73 (6th)- Mbabane.

SWAZILAND. Central Statistical Office. 1973. Agricultural sample census, Swazi Nation Land, 1971/72. Mbabane, [1973]. pp. 134.

— Sweden — History.

HELLSTRÖM (GUNNAR) Jordbrukspolitik i industrisamhället, med tyngdpunkt på 1920- och 30-talen. Stockholm, 1976. pp. 696. *bibliog. Akademisk avhandling för vinnande af filosofie doktorsgrad, Stockholms Universitet; with English summary.*

— — Kalmar (County).

SWEDEN. Lantbruksstyrelsen. 1974. Förändringar i jordbruket, 1956-71: Kalmarundersökningen; [report of a working group; chairman, Åke Anderson]. Stockholm, 1974. pp. 110. *(Meddelanden. Serie A. Nr. 16)*

— Switzerland — History.

PFISTER (CHRISTIAN) Climatologist. Agrarkonjunktur und Witterungsverlauf im westlichen Schweizer Mittelland zur Zeit der Ökonomischen Patrioten, 1755-1797: ein Beitrag zur Umwelt- und Wirtschaftsgeschichte des 18. Jahrhunderts. Bern, 1975. pp. 279. *bibliog.*

— — Aargau (Canton).

DETTWILER (E.) Die aargauische Landwirtschaft heute und morgen: eine Perspektiv- und Leitbildstudie. Tänikon, 1973. pp. 110. *(Station Fédérale de Recherches d'Economie d'Entreprise et de Génie Rural [Switzerland]. Comptes-rendus. 4)*

— Trinidad and Tobago.

FLOYD (BARRY NEIL) Small-scale agriculture in Trinidad: a Caribbean case study in the problems of transforming rural societies in the tropics. [Durham, 1977]. pp. 69. *bibliog. (Durham. University. Department of Geography. Occasional Publications (New Series). No. 10)*

— Tropics.

RUTHENBERG (HANS) Farming systems in the tropics. 2nd ed. Oxford, 1976. pp. 366. *bibliog.*

— Tunisia.

CHANGE in Tunisia: studies in the social sciences; edited by Russell A. Stone and John Simmons. Albany, N.Y., 1976. pp. 333. *bibliogs.*

— Underdeveloped areas.

See UNDERDEVELOPED AREAS — Agriculture.

— United Kingdom.

The CAUSE and cure of the dearness of provisions, etc., humbly offered to the consideration of the inhabitants of Great-Britain; by E.V. Market-Harborough, Harrod, 1800. pp. 12.

HESLOP (LUKE) A comparative statement of the food produced from arable and grass land, and the returns arising from each; with observations on the late inclosures, and the probable effect of a general act for inclosing commons or wastes, heaths, etc.; together with other matters; addressed to John Fane, Esq. M.P. London, Reynolds, 1801. pp. iv, 18.

[HALL (GEORGE WEBB)] The origin and proceedings of the agricultural associations in Great Britain, in which their claims to protection against foreign produce, duty-free, are fully and ably set forth, etc. London, Sherwood, Neely, and Jones, [1819]. pp. 39.

An EXPOSITION of the real causes and effective remedies of the agricultural distress; by an impartial looker-on. London, Sherwood, 1822. pp. 42.

ADVISORY COUNCIL FOR AGRICULTURE AND HORTICULTURE IN ENGLAND AND WALES. Report of an inquiry into agricultural exports. [London], 1976. pp. 61.

AGRICULTURAL DEVELOPMENT AND ADVISORY SERVICE [U.K.]. Agricultural land classification of England and Wales: the definition and identification of sub-grades within grade 3. [London], 1976. pp. 10. (Technical Reports. 11/1)

CAMBRIDGE. University. Department of Land Economy. Agricultural Economics Unit. Reports. No. 66. Report on farming, 1975-76: changes in the production and profitability of farming with standards for farm business analysis: eastern counties of England; [by] M.C. Thompson [and] F. G. Sturrock. Cambridge, 1976. 1 pamphlet (unpaged).

ECONOMIC DEVELOPMENT COMMITTEE FOR THE AGRICULTURAL INDUSTRY. Interim report to N[ational] E[conomic] D[evelopment] C[ouncil], October 1976. [London, National Economic Development Office, 1976]. pp. 11.

READING. University. Centre for Agricultural Strategy. CAS Reports. 1. Land for agriculture. Reading, 1976. pp. 100. bibliogs.

ECONOMIC DEVELOPMENT COMMITTEE FOR THE AGRICULTURAL INDUSTRY. Agriculture into the 1980s: finance. London, National Economic Development Office, 1977. pp. 32.

ECONOMIC DEVELOPMENT COMMITTEE FOR THE AGRICULTURAL INDUSTRY. Agriculture into the 1980s: land use. London, National Economic Development Office, 1977. pp. 32.

HILL (BRIAN E.) and INGERSENT (K.A.) An economic analysis of agriculture. London, 1977. pp. 296.

U.K. Central Office of Information. Reference Division. Reference Pamphlets. 43. Agriculture in Britain. 7th ed. London, 1977. pp. 71. bibliog.

— — Accounting.

AGRICULTURAL DEVELOPMENT AND ADVISORY SERVICE [U.K.]. An enquiry into the expenses of agricultural land ownership, England and Wales, 1973-74. [Pinner], 1976. pp. 69. bibliog. (Technical Reports. 25/1)

— — History.

ADAMS (IAN HUGH) Agrarian landscape terms: a glossary for historical geography. London, 1976. pp. 314. bibliog. (Institute of British Geographers. Special Publications. No.9)

— — — Sources.

MINGAY (GORDON EDMUND) ed. The agricultural revolution: changes in agriculture, 1650-1880. London, 1977. pp. 322.

— — Productivity.

ECONOMIC DEVELOPMENT COMMITTEE FOR THE AGRICULTURAL INDUSTRY. Agriculture into the 1980s: resources and strategy. London, National Economic Development Office, 1977. pp. 38.

— — Taxation.

ECONOMIC DEVELOPMENT COMMITTEE FOR THE AGRICULTURAL INDUSTRY. Agriculture into the 1980s: the impact of taxation. London, National Economic Development Office, 1977. pp. 44.

— — Buckinghamshire.

READING. University. Department of Agricultural Economics and Management. Miscellaneous Studies. No. 57. Milton Keynes 1973: case studies in a dwindling agriculture. Reading, 1974. pp. 25.

— — Devon.

DAVIES (E.T.) The Dartmoor and Exmoor National Parks: changes in farming structure 1952-1972. Exeter, 1976. pp. 33. (Exeter. University. Agricultural Economics Unit. Reports. No. 197)

— — Ireland — History.

GREIG (WILLIAM) General report on the Gosford estates in county Armagh, 1821; with an introduction by F.M.L. Thompson and D. Tierney. Belfast, H.M.S.O., 1976. pp. 245.

— — Scotland.

BRYDEN (JOHN M.) and HOUSTON (GEORGE F.B.) Agrarian change in the Scottish Highlands: the role of the Highlands and Islands Development Board in the agricultural economy of the crofting counties. London, 1976. pp. 152. bibliog. (Glasgow. University. Social and Economic Research Studies. 4.) Published in association with the Highlands and Islands Development Board.

— — Wales.

FROST (JOHN) of Newport. A second letter to Sir Charles Morgan of Tredegar, in the county of Monmouth, Baronet, M.P.;...also a letter to the farmers. Newport, the Author, 1822. pp. 39.

COLYER (RICHARD J.) The Welsh cattle drovers: agriculture and the Welsh cattle trade before and during the nineteenth century. Cardiff, 1976. pp. 155. bibliog.

— United States.

SHOVER (JOHN L.) First majority - last minority: the transforming of rural life in America. DeKalb, Ill., [1976]. pp. 338. bibliog.

AMERICAN ACADEMY OF POLITICAL AND SOCIAL SCIENCE. Annals. vol. 429. The new rural America; special editor of this volume Frank Clemente. Philadelphia, Pa., [1977]. pp. 208.

— — Alaska.

INDIANA STATE UNIVERSITY. Department of Geography and Geology. Professional Papers. No. 7. [Selected articles]. Terre Haute, Ind., 1975. pp. 56.

— Venezuela.

DUBUC PICON (ROBERTO) and UGALDE (LUIS) Evolucion historica del sector agropecuario y su crisis actual. Caracas, 1973 [or rather 1974]. pp. 139. bibliog.

— Yugoslavia.

KONTETZKI (HEINZ) Agrarpolitischer Wandel und Modernisierung in Jugoslawien: Zwischenbilanz einer sozialistischen Entwicklungsstrategie. Nürnberg, [1976]. pp. 563. bibliog. (Südosteuropa-Gesellschaft. Südosteuropa-Studien. 24)

— Zaire.

LUMUMBA (TOLENGA EMERY) Le rôle de l'agriculture dans les pays du Tiers Monde, particulièrement au Zaïre. Budapest, 1976. pp. 24. (Magyar Tudományos Akadémia. Világgazdasági Kutató Intézet. Studies on Developing Countries. No. 89)

— Zambia.

TENCH (ANDREW B.) Socio-economic factors influencing agricultural output, with special reference to Zambia. Saarbrücken, 1975. pp. 309. bibliog.

BATES (ROBERT H.) Rural responses to industrialization: a study of village Zambia. New Haven, 1976. pp. 380. bibliog.

AGRICULTURE, COOPERATIVE.

GROUP FARMING CONFERENCE, MADISON, WISCONSIN, 1975. Cooperative and commune: group farming in the economic development of agriculture; edited by Peter Dorner. Madison, Wis., 1977. 392. Papers of the conference sponsored by the Research and Training Network of the Agricultural Development Council and the Land Tenure Center of Wisconsin-Madison University.

— Mathematical models.

FEKETE (FERENC) and others. Economics of cooperative farming: objectives and optima in Hungary. Leyden, 1976. pp. 184. bibliog.

— America, Latin.

FALS BORDA (ORLANDO) El reformismo por dentro en America Latina. Mexico, 1972. pp. 211.

— Austria.

GRIMM (ALOIS) Das landwirtschaftliche Genossenschaftswesen in Tirol, mit vergleichender Darstellung...in den angrenzenden österreichischen Alpenländern, etc. Zürich, 1910. pp. 83. bibliog. Inaugural-Dissertation der Universität Zürich zur Erlangung der Würde eines Doctor oeconomiae publicae.

— Canada.

WOOD (LOUIS AUBREY) A history of farmers' movements in Canada;...[reprint of the 1924 edition with a new] introduction by Foster J.K. Griezic. Toronto, [1975]. pp. 372.

— Germany, Eastern.

GENOSSENSCHAFTSBAUERN, gestern, heute, morgen: ...im Prozess der Gestaltung der industriemässig produzierenden Landwirtschaft in der DDR; (Autorenkollektiv unter Leitung von Kurt Krambach). Berlin, 1977. pp. 284.

— Hungary.

HOLÁCS (IBOLYA) Some results of sociological research in co-operative and state farms. Keszthely, 1975. pp. 74. bibliog. (Keszthelyi Agrártudományi Egyetem. Studies. 6) .

FEKETE (FERENC) and others. Economics of cooperative farming: objectives and optima in Hungary. Leyden, 1976. pp. 184. bibliog.

— Italy.

STRUMENTI e linee di azione della C.I.S.L. in agricoltura: atti della tavola rotonda sul CeNaSCA, Roma, 29-30 gennaio 1969. Roma, 1969. pp. 47. (Centro Nazionale per lo Sviluppo della Cooperazione Agricola. [Publications]. 2)

BELTRAME (CARLO) Le cantine sociali in provincia di Alessandria: situazione, problemi, linee di azione; relazione introduttiva per un dibattito allargato. Alessandria, 1972. pp. 44. (Alessandria (Province). Centro Documentazione e Ricerche Economico-Sociali. Quaderni. n.68)

— Korea.

HISTORICAL experience of agricultural cooperation in our country. Pyongyang, 1975. pp. 172.

— Russia.

KOLESOV (NIKOLAI DMITRIEVICH) and others. Agrarno-promyshlennye kompleksy: sotsial'no-ekonomicheskie aspekty formirovaniia i razvitiia; pod redaktsiei...A.F. Tarasova. Moskva, 1973. pp. 247.

AGRARNO-promyshlennye kompleksy: predpriiatiia, kombinaty, ob"edineniia. Moskva, 1974. pp. 223.

AGRARNO-promyshlennye kompleksy: osobennosti razmeshcheniia, planirovaniia i organizatsii ucheta. Moskva, 1975. pp. 280.

KARPOV (K.D.) ed. Agrarno-promyshlennye ob"edineniia: problema, opyt, puti resheniia. Ulan-Ude, 1975. pp. 390.

USTIIAN (I.) Agrarno-promyshlennoe kooperirovanie i khozraschetnye otnosheniia. Kishinev, 1975. pp. 219.

VOROTILO (ANDREI STEPANOVICH) and KODITSA (NIKOLAI VASIL'EVICH) Agrarno-promyshlennaia integratsiia i mezhkhoziaistvennaia kooperatsiia. Kishinev, 1975. pp. 136.

AGRARNO-promyshlennye kompleksy: problemy razvitiia i optimal'nogo funktsionirovaniia. Kiev, 1976. pp. 251. bibliog.

BONDARS (ARVID RIKHARDOVICH) and others. Raionnye agrarno-promyshlennye ob"edineniia. Riga, 1976. pp. 179.

EKONOMICHESKIE problemy agrarno-promyshlennoi integratsii. Moskva, 1976. pp. 384. (Vsesoiuznaia Akademiia Sel'skokhoziaistvennykh Nauk. Nauchnye Trudy)

TUSHUNOV (ANATOLII VASIL'EVICH) Voprosy agrarnoi teorii. Moskva, 1976. pp. 318.

VYLTSAN (MIKHAIL AVGUSTOVICH) Vosstanovlenie i razvitie material'no-tekhnicheskoi bazy kolkhoznogo stroia, 1945-1958. Moskva, 1976. pp. 264.

— — Finance.

EDEL'SHTEIN (ILLIA VOLODYMYROVYCH) and others. Finansy i kredytuvannia sil's'kohospodars'kykh pidpryiemstv. 3rd ed. Kyïv, 1969. pp. 359.

KRUGLIAK (BRONISLAV STEPANOVICH) Effektivnost' kontsentratsii kapital'nykh vlozhenii v sel'skom khoziaistve. Moskva, 1976. pp. 143.

— — Moldavian Republic.

BAZIN (MIKHAIL IAKOVLEVICH) Agrarno-promyshlennoe kooperirovanie: ob integratsionnykh protsessakh sel'skokhoziaistvennogo i promyshlennogo proizvodstva v Moldavii. Kishinev, 1975. pp. 158.

SYTNIK (MIKHAIL KONDRAT'EVICH) Kollektivizatsiia sel'skogo khoziaistva i formirovanie klassa kolkhoznogo krest'ianstva v Moldavii. Kishinev, 1976. pp. 355. bibliog.

— — Russia (RSFSR).

FLORENT'EV (LEONID IAKOVLEVICH) ed. Mezhkhoziaistvennoe proizvodstvennoe kooperirovanie v sel'skom khoziaistve RSFSR. Moskva, 1975. pp. 413.

SELEZNEV (VALERII ALEKSANDROVICH) and GUTAROV (ALEKSANDR NIKOLAEVICH) Sovetskaia derevnia v predvoennye gody, 1938-1941: iz istorii kolkhoznogo stroitel'stva v osnovnykh raionakh Severo-Zapada RSFSR, Leningradskaia oblast'; kratkii istoricheskii ocherk. Leningrad, 1976. pp. 112.

— — Ukraine.

Z istoriï kolektyvizatsiï sil's'koho hospodarstva zakhidnykh oblastei Ukraïns'koï RSR: zbirnyk dokumentiv i materialiv. Kyïv, 1976. pp. 511.

— Tanzania.

SUMRA (SULEMAN) Problems of agricultural production in Ujamaa villages in Handeni districts. Dar es Salaam, 1975. pp. 19. (Dar es Salaam. University. Economic Research Bureau. ERB Papers. 75.3)

AGRICULTURE AND STATE

— Australia.

AUSTRALIA. Working Group on all Aspects of Rural Policy in Australia. 1974. The principles of rural policy in Australia; a discussion paper. 2nd ed. Canberra, 1974. pp. 323.

— — Western Australia.

GLYNN (SEAN) Government policy and agricultural development: a study of the role of government in the development of the Western Australian wheat belt, 1900-1930. Nedlands, W.A., 1975. pp. 173. bibliog.

— Brazil — São Paulo.

SÃO PAULO (STATE). Secretaria de Agricultura. 1972. Diretrizes de atuação da Secretaria...: desenvolvimento agricola: um grande desafio. [São Paulo, 1972]. pp. 139.

— Canada.

WOOD (LOUIS AUBREY) A history of farmers' movements in Canada;...[reprint of the 1924 edition with a new] introduction by Foster J.K. Griezic. Toronto, [1975]. pp. 372.

— China.

KUO (LESLIE TSE-CHIU) Agriculture in the People's Republic of China: structural changes and technical transformation. New York, 1976. pp. 288.

— Colombia.

COLOMBIA. Ministerio de Agricultura. Programas ganaderos. a., 1976(2nd)- Bogota.

— European Economic Community countries.

EUROPEAN COMMUNITIES. Commission. Information on Agriculture. [Brussels], 1976 in progress. [In various Community languages].

— Germany.

SOZIALDEMOKRATISCHE PARTEI DEUTSCHLANDS. Agrarpolitische Zentrale. Die Nachkriegshilfe für die deutsche Landwirtschaft; auf Grund amtlichen Materials und der Berichte der sozialdemokratischen Landtags- und Bürgerschaftsfraktionen zusammengestellt. [Berlin?, 1929?]. pp. 62.

AUSSCHUSS FÜR DEUTSCHE EINHEIT. Schwarzbuch über das Bauernlegen in Westdeutschland. Berlin, 1960. pp. 94.

FARQUHARSON (JOHN E.) The plough and the swastika: the NSDAP and agriculture in Germany, 1928-45. London, [1976]. pp. 312. bibliog.

GESSNER (DIETER) Agrarverbände in der Weimarer Republik: wirtschaftliche und soziale Voraussetzungen agrarkonservativer Politik vor 1933. Düsseldorf, [1976]. pp. 304. bibliog.

— India.

JOSHI (NARHAR SADASHIV) and DHEKNEY (B.R.) Irrigation and agriculture in the first five year plan: an appraisal. Poona, 1954. 2 vols.

INDIA. Department of Agriculture. Report. a., 1975/76- New Delhi.

— Mexico.

BARTRA (ROGER) Estructura agraria y clases sociales en Mexico. Mexico, 1974. pp. 182. bibliog.

— Nigeria.

WELLS (JEROME C.) Agricultural policy and economic growth in Nigeria, 1962-1968. Ibadan, 1974. pp. 490. bibliog. Published for the Nigerian Institute of Social and Economic Research.

— Peru.

ZUTTER (PIERRE DE) Campesinado y revolucion. Lima, 1975. pp. 312.

— Russia.

BRUCE (JAMES B.) The politics of Soviet policy formation: Khrushchev's innovative policies in education and agriculture. Denver, Colo., [1976]. pp. 138. (Denver. University. Social Science Foundation and Graduate School of International Studies. Monograph Series in World Affairs. vol. 13, no. 4)

PERRIE (MAUREEN) The agrarian policy of the Russian Socialist-Revolutionary Party from its origins through the revolution of 1905-1907. Cambridge, 1976. pp. 216. bibliog. (National Association for Soviet and East European Studies. Soviet and East European Studies)

— Spain.

INFORMACION AGRARIA: boletin de informacion; [pd. by] Ministerio de Agricultura [Spain]. s-a., primer semestre 1968 [num.O]- Madrid. num.0 is also the final (nums.129/131) issue of Boletin informativa del Ministerio de Agricultura, of which the Library has no file.

— Sudan.

SUDAN (SOUTHERN REGION). Regional Ministry of Agriculture, Irrigation, Forestry and Animal Production. 1973. A new outlook in agricultural, forestry and animal wealth in the Southern Region. rev. ed. Juba, 1973. pp. 33.

— United Kingdom.

DAVEY (BRIAN HUMPHREY) and others eds. Agriculture and the state: British policy in a world context. London, 1976. pp. 280. bibliog.

ECONOMIC DEVELOPMENT COMMITTEE FOR THE AGRICULTURAL INDUSTRY. Agriculture into the 1980s: resources and strategy. London, National Economic Development Office, 1977. pp. 38.

WILSON (GRAHAM K.) Special interests and policymaking: agricultural policies and politics in Britain and the United States of America, 1956-70. London, [1977]. pp. 205. bibliog.

— — Ireland, Northern.

NORTHERN IRELAND AGRICULTURAL TRUST. Annual report. a., 1971/72 (5th)- Belfast. 1967/68-1970/71 (1st-4th) included in IRELAND, NORTHERN. Parliament. House of Commons. [Papers].

— United States.

COCHRANE (WILLARD WESLEY) and RYAN (MARY E.) American farm policy, 1948-1973. Minneapolis, [1976]. pp. 431.

HALCROW (HAROLD GRAHAM) Food policy for America. New York, [1977]. pp. 564.

WILSON (GRAHAM K.) Special interests and policymaking: agricultural policies and politics in Britain and the United States of America, 1956-70. London, [1977]. pp. 205. bibliog.

— Venezuela.

DUBUC PICON (ROBERTO) and UGALDE (LUIS) Evolucion historica del sector agropecuario y su crisis actual. Caracas, 1973 [or rather 1974]. pp. 139. bibliog.

AGUARUNA INDIANS.

SIVERTS (HENNING) Tribal survival in the Atto Marañon: the Aguaruna case. Copenhagen, 1972. pp. 81. bibliog. (International Work Group for Indigenous Affairs. Documents. 10)

AIR

— Pollution — Economic aspects — United States.

SMITH (VINCENT KERRY) The economic consequences of air pollution. Cambridge, Mass., [1976]. pp. 113. bibliog.

— — Austria.

SCHEER (LORE) Atemgift und seine Messung: die Wiener Luft und Wiener Parks im Urteil der Wiener: objektive und subjektive Indikatoren. Wien, [1975]. pp. 29. *With English summary.*

— — United Kingdom.

U.K. Health and Safety Executive. Industrial air pollution. a., 1975(1st)- London. *Supersedes U.K. Department of the Environment. Annual report on alkali, etc., works.*

AIR CHARTER CONTRACTS.

KAMP (JAAP) Air charter regulation: a legal, economic and consumer study. New York, 1976. pp. 162. *bibliog.*

AIR LINES

— Finance.

THOMSON (ADAM) b. 1926. Air transport - government subsidies or commercially viable? Edinburgh, [1975]. pp. 23. *(Edinburgh. University. Commerce Graduates' Association. Jubilee Lectures. 1974)*

— European Economic Community countries.

DELEPIERE-NYS (CHRISTIANE) Air Europe: la politique de coopération entre les compagnies aériennes de l'Europe des six. Bruxelles, 1974. pp. 464. *bibliog. (Brussels. Université Libre. Institut d'Etudes Européennes. Thèses et Travaux Economiques)*

— United Kingdom — Rates.

AIRLINE USERS COMMITTEE [U.K.]. Sub-Committee on Passenger Fares. European air fares: a report...to the Civil Aviation Authority; [Sir Archibald Hope, chairman]. London, Civil Aviation Authority, 1976. pp. 52.

— United States — Rates.

REGULATION of passenger fares and competition among the airlines; edited by Paul W. MacAvoy and John W. Snow. Washington, D.C., [1977]. pp. 210. *(American Enterprise Institute for Public Policy Research. AEI Studies. 158)*

AIRPORTS

— Environmental aspects — United Kingdom.

PARKER (J.) Pollution from airports: Heathrow, 1970-71; paper given to Folkestone conference of the National Society for Clean Air, November 1971. [Stevenage?], Warren Spring Laboratory, [1972?]. pp. 33.

— Canada.

CANADA. Statistics Canada. Air carrier traffic at Canadian airports. q., 1976(1st)-. Ottawa. *[in English and French]. Supersedes CANADA. Statistics Canada. Airport activity statistics.*

— Netherlands.

NETHERLANDS. Plangroep Tweede Nationale Luchthaven. 1976. Second national airport in the Netherlands: (site-selection analysis). The Hague, 1976. pp. 139.

— — Cost effectiveness.

NETHERLANDS. Centraal Planbureau. 1975. Cost-benefit analysis: second national airport in the Netherlands; (with Deelstudies); (by J.B. Vermetten and V. P.C.F. Herzberg under the direction of R. Ruiter). 's-Gravenhage, 1975. 2 vols. (in 1) *(Monografieën. No. 18) The Deelstudies are in Dutch.*

— United Kingdom.

U.K. Civil Aviation Authority. 1976. Passengers at major airports in Scotland and central England: origin and destination survey, July-November 1975. London, 1976. pp. 72. *([Publications]. CAP 394)*

— — Planning.

LONDON. Greater London Council. Airport strategy for Great Britain, part 1: the London area: a consultation document; report. [London], 1976. pp. 59.

AKWE-SHAVANTE INDIANS.

GIACCARIA (BARTOLOMEU) and HEIDE (ADALBERTO) Xavante: auwe uptabi, povo autêntico; pesquisa historico- etnografica. São Paulo, 1972. pp. 304, 18 fold.leaves. *bibliog.*

ALABAMA

— Politics and government.

WIGGINS (SARAH WOOLFOLK) The scalawag in Alabama politics, 1865-1881. University, Ala., [1977]. pp. 220. *bibliog.*

ALASKA

— Climate.

INDIANA STATE UNIVERSITY. Department of Geography and Geology. Professional Papers. No. 7. [Selected articles]. Terre Haute, Ind., 1975. pp. 56.

— Economic history.

DOCUMENTS on the history of the Russian-American Company; translated by Marina Ramsay; edited by Richard A. Pierce. Kingston, Ont., [1976]. pp. 220.

ALBANIA

— History.

LOGORECI (ANTON) The Albanians: Europe's forgotten survivors. London, 1977. pp. 230. *bibliog.*

— Politics and government.

ALBANIA. Gazeta zyrtare. m., F 1977(no. 1)- [Tirana].

LOGORECI (ANTON) The Albanians: Europe's forgotten survivors. London, 1977. pp. 230. *bibliog.*

ALBANY

— Politics and government.

ROBINSON (FRANK S.) Machine politics: a study of Albany's O'Connells. New Brunswick, N.J., [1977]. pp. 262.

ALBERTA

— Industries.

PRINCIPAL MANUFACTURING STATISTICS, ALBERTA; [pd. by] Bureau of Statistics. a., 1974(2nd)- Edmonton.

ALBERTA. Business Services Branch. List of industrial projects. s-a., Ja/Je 1976- [Edmonton].

— Statistics.

ALBERTA STATISTICAL REVIEW; [pd. by] Bureau of Statistics. m., Ap 1977- Edmonton.

ALBIGENSES.

LE ROY LADURIE (EMMANUEL) Montaillou, village occitan de 1294 à 1324. [Paris, 1976]. pp. 642. *bibliog.*

ALCOHOL.

LIMA (OSWALDO GONÇALVES DE) Pulque, balchê e pajauaru na etnobiologia das bebidas e dos alimentos fermentados. Recife, 1975. pp. 405. *bibliog.*

ALCOHOLISM.

BOURNE (PETER GEOFFREY) and FOX (RUTH) eds. Alcoholism: progress in research and treatment. New York, 1973. pp. 439. *bibliogs.*

ALESSANDRIA (PROVINCE)

— Economic conditions.

BELTRAME (CARLO) Le cantine sociali in provincia di Alessandria: situazione, problemi, linee di azione; relazione introduttiva per un dibattito allargato. Alessandria, 1972. pp. 44. *(Alessandria (Province). Centro Documentazione e Ricerche Economico-Sociali. Quaderni. n.68)*

ALEUTS.

JONES (DOROTHY MIRIAM) Aleuts in transition: a comparison of two villages. Seattle, [1976]. pp. 125. *bibliog.*

ALGEBRA, ABSTRACT.

SHAPIRO (LOUIS W.) Introduction to abstract algebra. New York, [1975]. pp. 340.

ALGEBRAS, LINEAR.

LIPSCHUTZ (SEYMOUR) Schaum's outline of theory and problems of linear algebra. New York, [1968]. pp. 334.

ALGERIA

— Census.

ALGERIA. Census, 1966. Recensement général de la population et de l'habitat, 1966, etc. Oran, 1970 in progress.

— Commerce.

ALGERIA. Administration des Douanes. 1961. Le commerce extérieur de l'Algérie en 1960. [Alger, 1961]. pp. 101.

— Economic conditions.

TEMMAR (HAMID) Structures et modèle de développement de l'économie de l'Algérie. [Alger, 1974]. pp. 318.

— Economic policy.

BRACHEMI (KACIM) Planning in public enterprises in developing countries; (translated by Meri Radosević). Ljubljana, International Center for Public Enterprises, 1974. fo. 19. *(International Seminar 1974. National Papers)*

TEMMAR (HAMID) Structures et modèle de développement de l'économie de l'Algérie. [Alger, 1974]. pp. 318.

— Executive departments.

REMILI (ABDERRAHMANE) Les institutions administratives algériennes. 2nd ed. Alger, [1973]. pp. 356. *bibliog.*

— History — 1945-1962.

HORNE (ALISTAIR) A savage war of peace: Algeria, 1954-1962. London, 1977. pp. 604. *bibliog.*

— Industries.

L'INDUSTRIALISATION de l'est algérien: Bône, Constantine, Philippeville, Batna, Setif, Bougie. 3rd ed. n.p. 1961. 1 vol. (unpaged).

— Nationalism.

BEDJAOUI (MOHAMMED) Law and the Algerian revolution. Brussels, 1961. pp. 260.

LACHTAR (MOUSSA) La guillotine: journal d'un condamné à mort. Paris, [1962]. pp. 23.

TALEB (AHMED) Lettres de prison, (1957-1961). Alger, 1966. pp. 189.

SIVAN (EMMANUEL) Communisme et nationalisme en Algérie, 1920-1962. [Paris, 1976]. pp. 262. *(Fondation Nationale des Sciences Politiques. Travaux et Recherches de Science Politique. 41)*

ALGERIA(Cont.)

— Politics and government.

TALEB (AHMED) Lettres de prison, (1957-1961). Alger, 1966. pp. 189.

MAMERI (KHALFA) Orientations politiques de l'Algérie: analyse des discours du Président Boumediène, 1965-1970. Alger, [1973]. pp. 217. *bibliog.*

REMILI (ABDERRAHMANE) Les institutions administratives algériennes. 2nd ed. Alger, [1973]. pp. 356. *bibliog.*

FRANCE. Direction de la Documentation. La Documentation Française. Notes et Etudes Documentaires. Nos. 4,348-4, 349-4,350. La Charte nationale algérienne, 27 juin 1976; par Nicole Grimaud. Paris, 1976. pp. 106. *bibliog.*

JACKSON (HENRY F.) The FLN in Algeria: party development in a revolutionary society. Westport, Conn., 1977. pp. 255. *bibliog.*

— Race question.

KUPER (LEO) The pity of it all: polarisation of racial and ethnic relations. London, 1977. pp. 302. *bibliog.*

— Statistics, Vital.

TABUTIN (DOMINIQUE) Mortalité infantile et juvénile en Algérie. [Paris], 1976. pp. 275. *bibliog. (France. Institut National d'Etudes Démographiques. Travaux et Documents. Cahiers. No. 77)*

ALGERIANS IN FRANCE.

FRANCE. Direction de la Documentation. La Documentation Française. Notes et Etudes Documentaires. Nos. 4,275-4, 276. Les rapatriés d'Algérie en France; par Pierre Baillet. Paris, 1976. pp. 79. *bibliog.*

ALGORITHMS.

BELLMAN (RICHARD ERNEST) and others. Algorithms, graphs and computers. New York, 1970. pp. 246. *bibliogs.*

POWELL (SUSAN ELLEN) A product form of the reduced basis simplex algorithm for linear programming. 1976 [or rather 1977]. fo. 145. *bibliog. Typescript. Ph.D. (London) thesis: unpublished. This thesis is the property of London University and may not be removed from the Library.*

ALIANZA NACIONAL POPULAR.

MARTINEZ (JUAN PABLO) and IZQUIERDO (MARIA ISABEL) Anapo: oposicion o revolucion. Bogota, 1972. pp. 105.

ALIANZA POPULAR REVOLUCIONARIA AMERICANA.

VILLANUEVA (VICTOR) El APRA en busca del poder, 1930-1940. Lima, [1975]. pp. 234. *bibliog.*

ALIEN LABOUR

— Denmark.

MARTINSEN (HARALD R.) and ESTRUP (CHRISTIAN) Fremmedarbejdere som faktor i dansk økonomi: en cost-benefit analyse. København, 1973. pp. 49. *bibliog.*

— France.

ROCHCAU (GEORGES) and others. Ces étrangers parmi nous. Paris, [1975]. pp. 128. *bibliog.*

— Germany.

HAMMER (HANS) Wirkungen politischer Massnahmen zur Lenkung der Ausländerbeschäftigung: eine Studie zur Arbeitsmarktpolitik. Göttingen, [1976]. 1 vol.(various pagings). *bibliog. (Kommission für Wirtschaftlichen und Sozialen Wandel. Schriften. 117)*

INTEGRATION ausländischer Arbeitnehmer: Eingliederung, Einstellungen, Weiterbildung; mit Beiträgen von: Elisabeth Harder [and others]. Bonn, [1976]. pp. 339. *bibliog. (Institut für Kommunalwissenschaften [Bonn]. Studien zur Kommunalpolitik. Band 13)*

INTEGRATION ausländischer Arbeitnehmer: Verwaltung, Recht, Partizipation; [by] Dieter Grunow [and others]. Bonn, [1976]. pp. 391. *bibliog. (Institut für Kommunalwissenschaften [Bonn]. Studien zur Kommunalpolitik. Band 15)*

LAMBERTS (WILLI) Wachstum und Strukturbildung bei Ausländerbeschäftigung. Berlin, [1976]. pp. 116. *(Rheinisch- Westfälisches Institut für Wirtschaftsforschung, Essen. Schriftenreihe. Neue Folge. 38)*

RAUTE (RUDOLF) Lohn- und Verteilungswirkungen der Ausländerbeschäftigung. Bochum, 1976. pp. 214,xxxiv. *bibliog.*

— Russia.

MAKARENKO (OLEKSANDR ANDRIIOVYCH) Moguchaia sila proletarskoi solidarnosti: podderzhka zarubezhnym proletariatom Sovetskoi strany v 1921-1925 gg. Moskva, 1976. pp. 319.

— Switzerland.

CONTRO i movimenti xenofobi, per l'unità della classe operaia. Lugano-Breganzona, 1974. pp. 48.

HOFFMANN-NOWOTNY (HANS JOACHIM) Die Zukunft des Fremdarbeiter-Problems. Zürich, [1974]. pp. 17.

WIRTSCHAFTSFÖRDERUNG: GESELLSCHAFT ZUR FÖRDERUNG DER SCHWEIZERISCHEN WIRTSCHAFT. Fremdarbeiter, Überfremdung: Dokumentation zur Überfremdungsinitiative III. [Zürich?], 1974. pp. 27.

KAMMERMANN (JOHANN) Der Familiennachzug der ausländischen Arbeitskräfte: eine Überprüfung auf Verfassungsmässigkeit und Menschenrechte. Zürich, [1976]. pp. 217. *bibliog. (Zuerich. Universität. Rechts- und staatswissenschaftliche Fakultät. Zuercher Beiträge zur Rechtswissenschaft. Neue Folge. Heft 503)*

— United States.

PARLIN (BRADLEY W.) Immigrant professionals in the United States: discrimination in the scientific labor market. New York, 1976. pp. 97. *bibliog.*

ALIEN LABOUR, FILIPINO.

PHILIPPINE ISLANDS. Overseas Employment Development Board. Annual report. a., 1975/76 [1st]- Manila.

ALIEN LABOUR, MEXICAN

— United States.

REISLER (MARK) By the sweat of their brow: Mexican immigrant labor in the United States, 1900-1940. Westport, Conn., 1976. pp. 298. *bibliog.*

ALIENATION (PHILOSOPHY).

KAPLAN (MORTON A.) Alienation and identification. New York, [1976]. pp. 206.

ALIENATION (SOCIAL PSYCHOLOGY).

ALIENATION in contemporary society: a multidisciplinary examination; edited by Roy S. Bryce-Laporte, Claudewell S. Thomas. New York, 1976. pp. 394.

OLLMAN (BERTELL) Alienation: Marx's conception of man in capitalist society. 2nd ed. Cambridge, 1976. pp. 338. *bibliog.*

SENNETT (RICHARD) The fall of public man. Cambridge, 1977. pp. 386.

TORRANCE (JOHN) Estrangement, alienation and exploitation: a sociological approach to historical materialism. London, 1977. pp. 374.

ALIENS

— Finland — Bibliography.

SCHWARZ (DAVID) compiler. Invandrar- och minoritetsfrågor: nordisk bibliografi. Stockholm, [1976]. pp. 105. *With table of contents in English.*

— Poland.

ACKERBERG (ARMAND) Rechte und Pflichten der Ausländer in Polen: Gesetze, Verordnungen, zwischenstaatliche Abkommen, Gerichtsentscheidungen, etc. Berlin, 1933. pp. 263.

— Scandinavia — Bibliography.

SCHWARZ (DAVID) compiler. Invandrar- och minoritetsfrågor: nordisk bibliografi. Stockholm, [1976]. pp. 105. *With table of contents in English.*

ALL-RUSSIAN SOCIAL-CHRISTIAN UNION FOR THE LIBERATION OF THE PEOPLE.

See VSEROSSIISKII SOTSIAL-KHRISTIANSKII SOIUZ OSVOBOZHDENIIA NARODA.

ALLENDE (SALVADOR).

ROJAS (ROBINSON) The murder of Allende and the end of the Chilean way to socialism. New York, [1976]. pp. 274.

ALUMINIUM INDUSTRY AND TRADE

— United Kingdom.

JONES (COLIN) Political writer. The £200,000 jobe': a study of government intervention in aluminium smelting: the way the money goes. London, 1977. pp. 34.

AMAZON VALLEY

— Economic conditions.

LATIN AMERICAN CONFERENCE, 23RD, UNIVERSITY OF FLORIDA, 1973. Man in the Amazon: [proceedings]; edited by Charles Wagley. Gainesville, Fla., 1974. pp. 330. *bibliogs. Conference sponsored by the Center for Latin American Studies and the Center for Tropical Agriculture, University of Florida, and by the Conselho Federal de Cultura of the Ministry of Education and Culture of Brazil.*

LIMA (ARAUJO) Amazônia, a terra e o homem. São Paulo, 1975. pp. 151. *Text of the first edition of 1933, with the preface by Alcen de Amoroso Lima included in second and subsequent editions, and a new introduction.*

— Social conditions.

LATIN AMERICAN CONFERENCE, 23RD, UNIVERSITY OF FLORIDA, 1973. Man in the Amazon: [proceedings]; edited by Charles Wagley. Gainesville, Fla., 1974. pp. 330. *bibliogs. Conference sponsored by the Center for Latin American Studies and the Center for Tropical Agriculture, University of Florida, and by the Conselho Federal de Cultura of the Ministry of Education and Culture of Brazil.*

LIMA (ARAUJO) Amazônia, a terra e o homem. São Paulo, 1975. pp. 151. *Text of the first edition of 1933, with the preface by Alcen de Amoroso Lima included in second and subsequent editions, and a new introduction.*

AMERICA

— Discovery and exploration.

REUNION DE ANTROPOLOGOS ESPAÑOLES, 1a, Sevilla, 1973. Primera reunion de antropologos españoles: actas, comunicaciones, documentacion; edicion preparada por Alfredo Jimenez. Sevilla, [1975]. pp. 401. *bibliog.*

— **Economic policy.**

REPORT of the Inter-American Policy Research Group (Grupo para investigaciones de sistemas político-administrativos interamericanos). Austin, 1973. pp. 50. *bibliog. (American Society for Public Administration. Latin American Development Administration Committee and Texas University. Institute of Latin American Studies. LADAC Occasional Papers. Series 2. No. 8) Report of a workshop held in Rio de Janeiro in 1973.*

— **Politics and government.**

REPORT of the Inter-American Policy Research Group (Grupo para investigaciones de sistemas político-administrativos interamericanos). Austin, 1973. pp. 50. *bibliog. (American Society for Public Administration. Latin American Development Administration Committee and Texas University. Institute of Latin American Studies. LADAC Occasional Papers. Series 2. No. 8) Report of a workshop held in Rio de Janeiro in 1973.*

AMERICA, LATIN

— **Antiquities.**

REUNION DE ANTROPOLOGOS ESPAÑOLES, 1a, Sevilla, 1973. Primera reunion de antropologos españoles: actas, comunicaciones, documentacion; edicion preparada por Alfredo Jimenez. Sevilla, [1975]. pp. 401. *bibliog.*

The EARLY Mesoamerican village; edited by Kent V. Flannery. New York, [1976]. pp. 377. *bibliogs.*

— **Armed forces — Political activity.**

LOWENTHAL (ABRAHAM F.) ed. Armies and politics in Latin America. New York, 1976. pp. 356.

— — **Bibliography.**

LINDENBERG (KLAUS) compiler. Fuerzas armadas y politica en America Latina: bibliografia selecta. Santiago de Chile, 1972. pp. 199. *(Instituto Latinoamericano de Investigaciones Sociales. Estudios y Documentos. 15)*

— **Civilization.**

MAURO (FREDERIC) L'Amérique espagnole et portugaise de 1920 à nos jours. [Paris, 1975]. pp. 231. *bibliog.*

RANGEL (CARLOS) Du bon sauvage au bon révolutionnaire; traduit de l'espagnol par F.-M. Rosset. Paris, [1976]. pp. 398.

— **Commerce.**

INSTITUTE FOR LATIN AMERICAN INTEGRATION. 1973. Exportaciones de los paises de la ALALC: agrupadas segun la Clasificacion Uniforme para el Comercio Internacional (CUCI), modificada; año[s] 1953, (1961, 1969). [Buenos Aires, 1973?]. 3 vols. (in 1).

OROSZ (ÁRPÁD) The foreign trade turnover of Latin America till 1970, and its prospective development up to 1980. Budapest, 1976. pp. 121. *bibliog. (Magyar Tudományos Akadémia. Világgazdasági Kutató Intézet. Studies on Developing Countries. No. 81)*

— — **Europe, Eastern.**

OROSZ (ÁRPÁD) The foreign trade turnover of Latin America till 1970, and its prospective development up to 1980. Budapest, 1976. pp. 121. *bibliog. (Magyar Tudományos Akadémia. Világgazdasági Kutató Intézet. Studies on Developing Countries. No. 81)*

— **Economic conditions.**

MATOS MAR (JOSE) ed. La crisis del desarrollismo y la nueva dependencia. Buenos Aires, [1972]. pp. 189.

PROBLEMAS del subdesarrollo latinoamericano; [by] Sergio Bagu [and others]. Mexico, 1973. pp. 195. *Papers presented at a Seminar on Development Strategies in Africa and Latin America organized by the African Institute of Economic Development and Planning in Dakar, 1972.*

MAURO (FREDERIC) L'Amérique espagnole et portugaise de 1920 à nos jours. [Paris, 1975]. pp. 231. *bibliog.*

CEPAL REVIEW; [pd. by] Economic Commission for Latin America, United Nations. s-a., 1976 (1st)- [Santiago]. *Supersedes ECONOMIC BULLETIN FOR LATIN AMERICA.*

AMERICA Latina: ensaios de interpretação economica; coordenador Jose Serra; textos de Anibal Pinto [and others]; tradução dos ensaios de autores latino-americanos Celina Whately. Rio de Janeiro, 1976. pp. 403.

GUZMAN (GABRIEL) El desarrollo latinoamericano y la CEPAL. Barcelona, 1976. pp. 359. *bibliog.*

ORTIZ MENA (ANTONIO) Development in Latin America: a view from the IDB; addresses and documents, 1971-75. [Washington, Inter-American Development Bank, 1976?]. pp. 515.

— **Economic integration.**

CENTRAL AMERICAN BANK FOR ECONOMIC INTEGRATION. Memoria. a., 1968/69 (8th)- , with gap (1969/70, 9th) Tegucigalpa. *1972/73 in English.*

LANUS (JUAN ARCHIBALDO) La integracion economica de America Latina. Buenos Aires, [1972]. pp. 233. *bibliog.*

INSTITUTE FOR LATIN AMERICAN INTEGRATION. 1973. La dimension juridica de la integracion: America Latina. Buenos Aires, 1973. pp. 464.

CAMBRIDGE. University. Centre of Latin American Studies. Working Papers. No. 20. Regional integration in Central and Latin America: a progress report; by Allan R. Brewer-Carias. Cambridge, [1974]. pp. 14,10.

INOTAI (ANDRÁS) The possibilities and limits of a balanced and harmonious development in the Andean integration. Budapest, 1975. pp. 61. *(Magyar Tudományos Akadémia. Világgazdasági Kutató Intézet. Studies on Developing Countries. No. 80)*

KÁDÁR (BÉLA) Regional cooperation in Latin America. Budapest, 1975. pp. 40. *(Magyar Tudományos Akadémia. Világgazdasági Kutató Intézet. Studies on Developing Countries. No. 84)*

POLITICAS de transporte en esquemas de integración económica: con especial referencia al transporte vial. Buenos Aires, Instituto para la Integración de América Latina, [1975]. pp. 506.

ASOCIACION LATINOAMERICANA DE LIBRE COMERCIO. Newsletter. bi-m., Current issues only kept. Montevideo.

ICAP: administracion, desarrollo, integracion: organo informativo bimestral del Instituto Centroamericano de Administracion Publica. q. (formerly bi-m.) San Jose. *Current issues only kept.*

— **Economic policy.**

CIBOTTI (RICARDO) and SIERRA (ENRIQUE) El sector publico en la planificacion del desarrollo. Mexico, 1970. pp. 271. *bibliog.*

AMERICA Latina: ensaios de interpretação economica; coordenador Jose Serra; textos de Anibal Pinto [and others]; tradução dos ensaios de autores latino-americanos Celina Whately. Rio de Janeiro, 1976. pp. 403.

DELIBANES (DEMETRIOS) Economic development in South America. Thessalonika, 1976. pp. 39.

GUZMAN (GABRIEL) El desarrollo latinoamericano y la CEPAL. Barcelona, 1976. pp. 359. *bibliog.*

ORTIZ MENA (ANTONIO) Development in Latin America: a view from the IDB; addresses and documents, 1971-75. [Washington, Inter-American Development Bank, 1976?]. pp. 515.

The STATE and economic development in Latin America; proceedings of a conference held at Cambridge in December 1976; edited by E.V.K. Fitzgerald [and others]. Cambridge, 1977. pp. 342. *(Cambridge. University. Centre of Latin American Studies. Occasional Papers. 1) In English or Spanish.*

— **Foreign economic relations.**

CONSEJO LATINOAMERICANO EN CIENCIAS SOCIALES. Asamblea General. Reunion, 2a, Lima, 1968. La dependencia politico-economica de America Latina; por Helio Jaguaribe [and others]; (ponencias presentadas en la Reunion...con la transcripcion de sus discusiones). Mexico, 1970 repr. 1974. pp. 293.

MATOS MAR (JOSE) ed. La crisis del desarrollismo y la nueva dependencia. Buenos Aires, [1972]. pp. 189.

OCAMPO RODRIGUEZ (ESTEBAN) Imperialismo y Pacto Andino. Lima, 1973. pp. 246. *bibliog.*

BAMBIRRA (VANIA) El capitalismo dependiente latinoamericano. Mexico,.1974 repr. 1975. pp. 180.

THEBERGE (JAMES DANIEL) Latin America in the world system: the limits of internationalism. Beverly Hills, [1975]. pp. 65. *bibliog. (Georgetown University. Center for Strategic and International Studies. Washington Papers. vol. 3/27)*

LATIN America's new internationalism; the end of hemispheric isolation; edited by Roger W. Fontaine and James Daniel Theberge. New York, 1976. pp. 327. *Papers of the second Williamsburg conference held in 1975, and sponsored by the Center for Strategic and International Studie Georgetown University.*

INTERNATIONAL INSTITUTE FOR STRATEGIC STUDIES. Adelphi Papers. No. 137. Latin America in world politics: the next decade; by Gregory F. Treverton. London, 1977. pp. 45.

— — **Canada.**

OGELSBY (J.C.M.) Gringos from the far North: essays in the history of Canadian- Latin American relations, 1866-1968. Toronto, [1976]. pp. 346. *bibliog.*

— — **Spain.**

PRIMERAS jornadas hispano-andinas de cooperacion economica y tecnica; patrocinadas por Junta de Acuerdo de Cartagena, Instituto de Cultura Hispanica, Secretaria del Convenio "Andres Bello"; celebradas en el Instituto de Cultura Hispanica Madrid, 4 al 9 de junio, 1973. Madrid, 1975. pp. 395.

— — **United States.**

HANSEN (ROGER D.) U.S.-Latin American economic policy: bilateral, regional, or global? Washington, D.C., 1975. pp. 69. *(Overseas Development Council. Development Papers. 18)*

BAILY (SAMUEL L.) The United States and the development of South America, 1945-1975. New York, 1976. pp. 246. *bibliog.*

SWANSBROUGH (ROBERT H.) The embattled colossus: economic nationalism and United States investors in Latin America. Gainesville, Florida, 1976. pp. 261. *bibliog. (Florida University. School of Inter-American Studies. Latin American Monographs. 2nd Series. 16)*

UNITED States policy towards Latin America: antecedents and alternatives; Lewis A. Tambs, editor. Tempe, [1976]. pp. 220. *A collection of papers presented at a conference held at Arizona State University...,1975 and sponsored by the Center for Latin American Studies...and the American Graduate School of International Management.*

— **Foreign relations.**

BENAVIDES CORREA (ALFONSO) Habra guerra proximamente en el Cono Sur?: America Latina, explosiva caldera geopolitica. Mexico, 1974. pp. 170.

THEBERGE (JAMES DANIEL) Latin America in the world system: the limits of internationalism. Beverly Hills, [1975]. pp. 65. *bibliog. (Georgetown University. Center for Strategic and International Studies. Washington Papers. vol. 3/27)*

LATIN America's new internationalism: the end of hemispheric isolation; edited by Roger W. Fontaine and James Daniel Theberge. New York, 1976. pp. 327. *Papers of the second Williamsburg conference held in 1975, and sponsored by the Center for Strategic and International Studie Georgetown University.*

AMERICA, LATIN(Cont.)

ATKINS (G. POPE) Latin America in the international political system. New York, [1977]. pp. 448. *bibliog.*

INTERNATIONAL INSTITUTE FOR STRATEGIC STUDIES. Adelphi Papers. No. 137. Latin America in world politics: the next decade; by Gregory F. Treverton. London, 1977. pp. 45.

— — Treaties.

PACHECO QUINTERO (JORGE) El Congreso Anficionico de Panama y la politica internacional de los Estados Unidos. Bogota, 1971. pp. 170. *(Academia Colombiana de Historia. Coleccion de Bolsilibros. 18)*

— — Cuba.

MARQUEZ STERLING (MANUEL) La diplomacia en nuestra historia. La Habana, 1967. pp. 214. *First published in 1909.*

— — Germany.

POMMERIN (REINER) Das Dritte Reich und Lateinamerika: die deutsche Politik gegenüber Süd- und Mittelamerika, 1939-1942. Düsseldorf, [1977]. pp. 377. *bibliog.*

— — Mexico.

MEXICO y America Latina: la nueva politica exterior; [edited by Mario Ojeda Gomez]. Mexico, 1974. pp. 201. *(Mexico City. Colegio de Mexico. Centro e Estudios Internacionales. Coleccion. 11)*

— — United Kingdom.

LABOUR PARTY. National Executive Committee. Argentina, Chile and Brazil; a statement. London, 1977. pp. 7.

— — United States.

CASTRO RUZ (FIDEL) Speech delivered...at the ceremony held in the Chaplin Theatre, April 19, 1967, commemorating the anniversary of the defeat of Yankee imperialism at Playa Giron. London, Cuban Embassy, 1967. pp. 15. *(Cuba Information Bulletins. 1967. No. 4)*

GRIEB (KENNETH J.) The Latin American policy of Warren G. Harding. Fort Worth, Texas, [1976]. pp. 223. *bibliog.*

TARNOFF (CURTIS LEE) Evolving structures of great power blocs: the U.S.A. and Latin America, 1901-1975: the USSR and Eastern Europe, 1945-1975. 1976. fo. 529. *bibliog. Typescript. Ph.D. (London) thesis: unpublished. This thesis is the property of London University and may not be removed from the Library.*

UNITED States policy towards Latin America: antecedents and alternatives; Lewis A. Tambs, editor. Tempe, [1976]. pp. 220. *A collection of papers presented at a conference held at Arizona State University..., 1975 and sponsored by the Center for Latin American Studies...and the American Graduate School of International Management.*

— Industries.

NOLFF (MAX) ed. El desarrollo industrial latinoamericano. Mexico, 1974 [or rather 1975]. pp. 698. *(Trimestre Economico, El. Lecturas. 12)*

— Military policy.

BENAVIDES CORREA (ALFONSO) Habra guerra proximamente en el Cono Sur?: America Latina, explosiva caldera geopolitica. Mexico, 1974. pp. 170.

— Native races.

MARROQUIN (ALEJANDRO D.) Balance del indigenismo: informe sobre la politica indigenista en America. Mexico, 1972. pp. 300. *bibliog. (Inter-American Indian Institute. Ediciones Especiales. 62)*

— Politics and government.

ALMEIDA (JUAN) Speech delivered by Major Juan Almeida, member of the political bureau of the central committee of the Communist Party of Cuba, in commemoration of May 1, international workers' day: Plaza de la Revolucion, May 1, 1967, year of heroic Viet Nam. London, Cuban Embassy, 1967. pp. 15. *(Cuba Information Bulletins. 1967. No.6)*

JAGUARIBE (HELIO) Crisis y alternativas de America Latina: reforma o revolucion; desarrollo politico; una investigacion en teoria social y politica y un estudio del caso latinoamericano. Buenos Aires, 1972. pp. 211. *bibliog.*

SCHENKEL (PETER) La estructura de poder de los medios de comunicacion en cinco paises latinoamericanos. Santiago de Chile, 1973. pp. 104. *(Instituto Latinoamericano de Investigaciones Sociales. Estudios y Documentos. 20)*

BUSEY (JAMES LYNN) ed. Latin American political guide. 16th ed. Manitou Springs, Colo., [1975]. pp. 63.

MAURO (FREDERIC) L'Amérique espagnole et portugaise de 1920 à nos jours. [Paris, 1975]. pp. 231. *bibliog.*

RUSSELL TRIBUNAL II ON REPRESSION IN BRAZIL, CHILE AND LATIN AMERICA. 2nd session. Found guilty; the verdict of the Russell tribunal session in Brussels. Nottingham, [1975?]. pp. 36. *(Spokesman, The. Pamphlets. No. 51)*

DUNCAN (WALTER RAYMOND) Latin American politics: a developmental approach. New York, 1976. pp. 277. *bibliogs.*

LOWENTHAL (ABRAHAM F.) ed. Armies and politics in Latin America. New York, 1976. pp. 356.

RANGEL (CARLOS) Du bon sauvage au bon révolutionnaire; traduit de l'espagnol par F.-M. Rosset. Paris, [1976]. pp. 398.

AUTHORITARIANISM and corporatism in Latin America; James M. Malloy, editor. Pittsburgh, [1977]. pp. 549. *bibliog. Papers of a conference held at the University of Pittsburgh in April 1974, and sponsored by its Center for International Studies.*

INTERNATIONAL INSTITUTE FOR STRATEGIC STUDIES. Adelphi Papers. No. 137. Latin America in world politics: the next decade; by Gregory F. Treverton. London, 1977. pp. 45.

NEEDLER (MARTIN CYRIL) An introduction to Latin American politics: the structure of conflict. Englewood Cliffs, N.J., [1977]. pp. 358. *bibliog.*

TERMS of conflict: ideology in Latin American politics; editors: Morris J. Blachman and Ronald G. Hellman. Philadelphia, [1977]. pp. 275. *(Center for Inter-American Relations. Inter-American Politics Series. vol. 1) Based on a six-part seminar series in 1973-1974 sponsored by the Center.*

ICAP: administracion, desarrollo, integracion: organo informativo bimestral del Instituto Centroamericano de Administracion Publica. q. (formerly bi-m.) San Jose. *Current issues only kept.*

— Population.

MAURO (FREDERIC) L'Amérique espagnole et portugaise de 1920 à nos jours. [Paris, 1975]. pp. 231. *bibliog.*

VIEL VICUNA (BENJAMIN) The demographic explosion: the Latin American experience;... translated from the Spanish and updated by James Walls. New York, [1976]. pp. 249. *bibliog.*

— Relations (general) with the United States.

FALS-BORDA (ORLANDO) Ciencia propia y colonialismo intelectual. Bogota, 1971. pp. 138. *Reprint of 1st ed. published in Mexico in 1970.*

WHITAKER (ARTHUR PRESTON) The United States and the southern cone: Argentina, Chile, and Uruguay. Cambridge, Mass., 1976. pp. 464. *bibliog.*

— Religion.

EAGLESON (JOHN) ed. Christians and socialism: documentation of the Christians for Socialism movement in Latin America; translated by John Durry. Maryknoll, N.Y., [1975]. pp. 246.

— Rural conditions.

ESTUDIOS de la realidad campesina: cooperacion y cambio: informes y materiales de campo recogidos en Venezuela, Ecuador y Colombia; por R. Pugh [and others]. Ginebra, Instituto de Investigaciones de las Naciones Unidas para el Desarrollo Social, 1970. pp. 421. *(Rural Institutions and Planned Change. Vol.2) Summaries in French and English.*

MICKELWAIT (DONALD R.) and others. Women in rural development: a survey of the roles of women in Ghana, Lesotho, Kenya, Nigeria, Bolivia, Paraguay and Peru. Boulder, Col., 1976. pp. 224. *bibliog.*

— Social conditions.

STAVENHAGEN (RODOLFO) Sociologia y subdesarrollo. Mexico, 1971 repr. 1974. pp. 236. *bibliog.*

MATOS MAR (JOSE) ed. La crisis del desarrollismo y la nueva dependencia. Buenos Aires, [1972]. pp. 189.

PROBLEMAS del subdesarrollo latinoamericano; [by] Sergio Bagu [and others]. Mexico, 1973. pp. 195. *Papers presented at a Seminar on Development Strategies in Africa and Latin America organized by the African Institute of Economic Development and Planning in Dakar, 1972.*

LA BELLE (THOMAS J.) Nonformal education and social change in Latin America. Los Angeles, 1976. pp. 219. *bibliogs. (California University. Latin American Center. Latin American Studies. vol. 35)*

— Social policy.

STAVENHAGEN (RODOLFO) Sociologia y subdesarrollo. Mexico, 1971 repr. 1974. pp. 236. *bibliog.*

— Statistics.

STATISTICAL ABSTRACT OF LATIN AMERICA. Supplement Series. 6. Quantitative Latin American studies: methods and findings...; edited by James W. Wilkie [and] Kenneth Ruddle. Los Angeles, 1977. pp. 91. *bibliogs.*

AMERICAN CIVIL LIBERTIES UNION.

LAMSON (PEGGY) Roger Baldwin, founder of the American Civil Liberties Union: a portrait. Boston, [Mass]., 1976. pp. 304.

AMERICAN PARTY.

BAKER (JEAN H.) Ambivalent Americans: the Know-Nothing party in Maryland. Baltimore, [1977]. pp. 206. *bibliog.*

AMERICANS IN CANADA.

KASINSKY (RENÉE GOLDSMITH) Refugees from militarism: draft-age Americans in Canada. New Brunswick, N.J., [1976]. pp. 301.

AMIN (IDI).

CAMPBELL (HORACE) Four essays on neo-colonialism in Uganda: the military dictatorship of Idi Amin. Toronto, [1975]. pp. 56.

MELADY (THOMAS PATRICK) and MELADY (MARGARET BADUM) Uganda: the Asian exiles. Maryknoll, N.Y., [1976]. pp. 86. *bibliog.*

AMNESTY

— United States.

BASKIR (LAWRENCE M.) and STRAUSS (WILLIAM A.) Reconciliation after Vietnam: a program of relief for Vietnam era draft and military offenders. Notre Dame, Ind., [1977]. pp. 150. *bibliogs. A report of the Vietnam Offender Study Center for Civil Rights, University of Notre Dame.*

ANABAPTISTS

— Europe.

JANSMA (LAMMERT GOSSE) Melchiorieten, Munstersen en Batenburgers: een sociologische analyse van een millennistische beweging uit de 16e eeuw. 1977. pp. 348. *bibliog. Proefschrift (doctor) - Erasmus Universiteit Rotterdam.*

— Germany.

DUELMEN (RICHARD VAN) Reformation als Revolution: soziale Bewegung und religiöser Radikalismus in der deutschen Reformation. München, 1977. pp. 387. *bibliog.*

ANARCHISM AND ANARCHISTS.

MARR (WILHELM) Das junge Deutschland in der Schweiz: (ein Beitrag zur Geschichte der geheimen Verbindungen unserer Tage); Anhang: Anarchie oder Autorität?. Glashütten im Taunus, 1976. pp. 364,132. *Reprint of the works originally published in Leipzig in 1846 and in Hamburg in 1852.*

HERZBERG (WILHELM) Sozialdemokratie und Anarchismus. Ludwigshafen am Rhein, 1906. pp. 32.

GRAVE (JEAN) Di obshtorbende gezelshaft un di anarkhye; iberzetst fun R. Roker. London, 1908. pp. 280. *In Yiddish with Hebrew characters. Bound with Rudolf Rocker, Di geshikte fun der teroristisher bevegung in Frankraykh.*

PEUKERT (JOSEPH) Gerechtigkeit in der Anarchie. London, [1910?]. pp. 20. *(Gruppe Autonomie. Anarchistisch-Communistische Bibliothek. Heft 5)*

CAHN (BERTHOLD) Sollen sich Anarchisten organisieren?. Berlin, [1923]. pp. 8. *Text of lecture given in 1912, with additional footnotes.*

MELLA (RICARDO) Ideario. Gijon, 1926. pp. 335.

MUEHSAM (ERICH) Befreiung der Gesellschaft vom Staat; Vorwort: Zur Aktualität der anarchistischen Staatsauffassung; [by] Hans Jörg Viesel. 2nd ed. Berlin, 1975. pp. 131. *bibliog. 6 essays originally published 1927-32, mainly in Fanal.*

BONANNO (ALFREDO M.) Anarchism and the national liberation struggle. Port Glasgow, [1976]. pp. 16. *(Bratach Dubh Collective. Anarchist Pamphlets. No. 1)*

De VOLLE vrijheid: ideologie en geschiedenis van het anarchisme; [by] Frans Boenders [and others]. Brussel, [1976]. pp. 181. *bibliog.*

WOODCOCK (GEORGE) 1912- , ed. The anarchist reader. [Glasgow], 1977. pp. 383. *bibliog.*

— Biography.

BAKUNIN (MIKHAIL ALEKSANDROVICH) The confession of Mikhail Bakunin: with the marginal comments of Tsar Nicholas I; translated by Robert C. Howes; introduction and notes by Lawrence D. Orton. Ithaca, N.Y., 1977. pp. 200. *Translation of Ispoved'.*

— America, Latin — Bibliography.

NETTLAU (MAX) Contribucion a la bibliografia anarquista de la America Latina hasta 1914. London, 1975. *Originally published in Buenos Aires in 1927.*

— Austria.

BOTZ (GERHARD) and others. Im Schatten der Arbeiterbewegung: zur Geschichte des Anarchismus in Österreich und Deutschland. Wien, [1977]. pp. 190. *(Ludwig Boltzmann Institut für Geschichte der Arbeiterbewegung. Schriftenreihe. 6)*

— Belgium.

BOON (LOUIS PAUL) De Zwarte Hand; of, Het anarchisme van de negentiende eeuw in het industriestadje Aalst. Amsterdam, 1976 repr. 1977. pp. 295.

— France.

ROCKER (RUDOLF) Di geshikhte fun der teroristisher bevegung in Frankraykh. London, "Arbeyter Freynd" Drukerey, [190-?]. 2 vols. (in 1). *In Yiddish with Hebrew characters. Bound with Jean Grave, Di obshtorbende gezelshaft, etc.*

CARR (REG) Anarchism in France: the case of Octave Mirbeau. Manchester, 1977. pp. 190. *bibliog.*

— Germany.

LOOS (HANS) Die Anarchisten und die Nationalversammlung. Berlin, [1918?]. pp. 7.

LINSE (ULRICH) Die anarchistische und anarcho-syndikalistische Jugendbewegung, 1919-1933: zur Geschichte und Ideologie, etc. Frankfurt am Main, 1976. pp. 330. *bibliog.*

— Spain.

NOIR ET ROUGE: cahiers d'études anarchistes révolutionnaires. Brochures. Les collectivités anarchistes en Espagne révolutionnaire. Paris, 1964. pp. 38.

MONTSENY (FEDERICA) Cronicas de "CNT", 1960-1961; seleccion e introduccion de M. Celma. [Paris], 1974. pp. 183.

ALBEROLA (OCTAVIO) and GRANSAC (ARIANE) El anarquismo español y la accion revolucionaria, 1961-1974. [Paris, 1975]. pp. 381.

ENZENSBERGER (HANS MAGNUS) El corto verano de la anarquia: vida y muerte de Buenaventura Durruti; traduccion de Julio Forcat y Ulrike Hartmann. [Mexico, 1975]. pp. 334. *bibliog.*

SEMPRUN-MAURA (CARLOS) Ni dios ni amo ni C.N.T. [Paris], 1975. pp. 111.

ALVAREZ JUNCO (JOSE) La ideologia politica del anarquismo español, 1868-1910. Mexico, 1976. pp. 660. *bibliog.*

KAPLAN (TEMMA) Anarchists of Andalusia, 1868-1903. Princeton, N.J., [1977]. pp. 266. *bibliog.*

— — Bibliography.

TEORIA y practica del movimiento obrero en España, 1900-1936; (edicion a cargo de Albert Balcells). Valencia, [1977]. pp. 335.

— United Kingdom.

MELTZER (ALBERT) The anarchists in London, 1935-1955. Sanday, Orkney Islands, 1976. pp. 40.

— United States.

REICHERT (WILLIAM O.) Partisans of freedom: a study in American anarchism. Bowling Green, Ohio, [1976]. pp. 602. *bibliog.*

ANDALUSIA

— Description and travel.

CAMACHO ANSINO (JUAN) Andalucia: riqueza y diaspora. Jaen, 1974. pp. 179.

— History.

CAMACHO ANSINO (JUAN) Andalucia: riqueza y diaspora. Jaen, 1974. pp. 179.

RUIZ LAGOS (MANUEL) Politica y desarrollo social en la Baja Andalucia. Madrid, [1976]. pp. 373.

— Politics and government.

TUSELL GOMEZ (JAVIER) Oligarquia y caciquismo en Andalucia, 1890-1923. Barcelona, 1976. pp. 589.

KAPLAN (TEMMA) Anarchists of Andalusia, 1868-1903. Princeton, N.J., [1977]. pp. 266. *bibliog.*

— Social history.

BERNAL (ANTONIO MIGUEL) La propiedad de la tierra y las luchas agrarias andaluzas. Barcelona, [1974]. pp. 189.

CALERO AMOR (ANTONIO MARIA) Movimientos sociales en Andalucia, 1820-1936. Madrid, 1976. pp. 178. *bibliog.*

ANDEAN GROUP.

OCAMPO RODRIGUEZ (ESTEBAN) Imperialismo y Pacto Andino. Lima, 1973. pp. 246. *bibliog.*

CAMBRIDGE. University. Centre of Latin American Studies. Working Papers. No. 20. Regional integration in Central and Latin America: a progress report; by Allan R. Brewer-Carias. Cambridge, [1974]. pp. 14,10.

OCAMPO RODRIGUEZ (ESTEBAN) El Pacto Andino o Acuerdo de Cartagena. Lima, [1974]. pp. 187. *bibliog.*

FISCAL harmonization in the Andean countries; by Dr. Adolfo Atchabahian [and others]. Amsterdam, 1975. pp. 118. *bibliog. (International Bureau of Fiscal Documentation. International Fiscal Harmonization. No.3)*

INOTAI (ANDRÁS) The possibilities and limits of a balanced and harmonious development in the Andean integration. Budapest, 1975. pp. 61. *(Magyar Tudományos Akadémia. Világgazdasági Kutató Intézet. Studies on Developing Countries. No. 80)*

PRIMERAS jornadas hispano-andinas de cooperacion economica y tecnica; patrocinadas por Junta de Acuerdo de Cartagena, Instituto de Cultura Hispanica, Secretaria del Convenio "Andres Bello"; celebradas en el Instituto de Cultura Hispanica Madrid, 4 al 9 de junio, 1973. Madrid, 1975. pp. 395.

ANDERSEN NEXØ (MARTIN).

HOUMANN (BØRGE) Partifaelle Nexø: Martin Andersen Nexø mellem radikalisme og socialdemokratisme, 1910-1913. [Risskov], 1975. pp. 80.

ANDERSON (PERRY).

HOBSBAWM (ERIC JOHN ERNEST) and BOURN (DOUGLAS) Feudalism, capitalism and the absolute state; [2] reviews of Perry Anderson. London, 1976. pp. 18. *(Communist Party of Great Britain. History Group. Our History. No.66)*

ANDES REGION

— Economic conditions.

PIKE (FREDERICK BRAUN) The United States and the Andean Republics: Peru, Bolivia, and Ecuador. Cambridge, Mass., 1977. pp. 493. *bibliogs.*

— Foreign economic relations — United States.

PIKE (FREDERICK BRAUN) The United States and the Andean Republics: Peru, Bolivia, and Ecuador. Cambridge, Mass., 1977. pp. 493. *bibliogs.*

— Politics and government.

PIKE (FREDERICK BRAUN) The United States and the Andean Republics: Peru, Bolivia, and Ecuador. Cambridge, Mass., 1977. pp. 493. *bibliogs.*

— Social conditions.

PIKE (FREDERICK BRAUN) The United States and the Andean Republics: Peru, Bolivia, and Ecuador. Cambridge, Mass., 1977. pp. 493. *bibliogs.*

ANDRADE (VICTOR).

ANDRADE (VICTOR) My missions for revolutionary Bolivia, 1944-1962;...edited and with an introduction by Cole Blasier. Pittsburgh, Pa., [1976]. pp. 200.

ANGOLA

— Economic conditions.

INSTITUTO DE CREDITO DE ANGOLA. Conselho de Administração. Relatorio balanço e contas do Conselho de Administração e parecer do Conselho Fiscal. a., 1970-1972. [Luanda].

— Foreign relations.

LEGUM (COLIN) and HODGES (TONY) After Angola: the war over southern Africa. London, 1976. pp. 85.

— Industries.

ANGOLA. Serviços de Planeamento e Integração Economica de Angola. 1971. Trabalhos preparatorios do IV plano de fomento, 1974-1979: estrutura e planeamento industrial. Luanda, 1971. fo. 359.

— Nationalism.

MOVIMENTO POPULAR DE LIBERTAÇÃO DE ANGOLA. [Open letter]. [1972]. fo. 14. *Photocopy of typescript.*

GJERSTAD (OLE) The people in power: an account from Angola's second war of national liberation. Richmond, [1976]. pp. 108.

— Politics and government.

MOVIMENTO POPULAR DE LIBERTAÇÃO DE ANGOLA. [Open letter]. [1972]. fo. 14. *Photocopy of typescript.*

COFFEE for Britain means blood for Angola. Birmingham, [1973]. pp. 15.

BARRATT (JOHN) The Angolan conflict: internal and international aspects. Braamfontein, 1976. pp. 21.

GJERSTAD (OLE) The people in power: an account from Angola's second war of national liberation. Richmond, [1976]. pp. 108.

LEGUM (COLIN) and HODGES (TONY) After Angola: the war over southern Africa. London, 1976. pp. 85.

ANIMAL INDUSTRY

— Africa — Statistics.

SOCIETE D'ETUDES POUR LE DEVELOPPEMENT ECONOMIQUE ET SOCIAL. Recueil statistique de la production animale; (document...établi par G. Gouet). [Paris], 1975. pp. 1201.

— Colombia.

COLOMBIA. Ministerio de Agricultura. Programas ganaderos. a., 1976(2nd)- Bogota.

— South Africa.

OSTERHOFF (D.R.) Bakensyfers vir die reproduksie. Pretoria, 1974. pp. 69. *(Pretoria. University of Pretoria. Publications. New Series. No.83)*

ANIMALS, HABITS AND BEHAVIOUR OF.

DAWKINS (RICHARD) The selfish gene. Oxford, 1976. pp. 224. *bibliog.*

ANNE, Queen of Great Britain and Ireland.

[SWIFT (JONATHAN)] The management of the four last years vindicated: in which Her late Majesty, and her ministry, are fully cleared from the false aspersions cast on them in a late pamphlet [by Charles Povey], entituled An enquiry into the miscarriages of the four last years reign, etc. [London], Morphew, 1714. pp. 48. *Signed C.B.*

ANSO (MARIANO).

ANSO (MARIANO) Yo fin ministro de Negrin:...(memorias ineludibles). Barcelona, [1976]. pp. 347.

ANTARCTIC REGIONS.

BRAUN MENENDEZ (ARMANDO) Pequeña historia antartica. Buenos Aires, 1974. pp. 180. *bibliog.*

FITTE (ERNESTO J.) Cronicas del Atlantico sur: Patagonia, Malvinas y Antartida. Buenos Aires, 1974. pp. 469. *bibliog.*

ANTHROPOGEOGRAPHY.

COATES (BRYAN ELLIS) and others. Geography and inequality. Oxford, 1977. pp. 292. *bibliog.*

HAGGETT (PETER) and others. Locational analysis in human geography. 2nd ed. London, 1977. pp. 605. *bibliog.*

JONES (EMRYS) and EYLES (JOHN D.) An introduction to social geography. Oxford, 1977. pp. 273. *bibliog.*

SMITH (DAVID MARSHALL) Human geography: a welfare approach. London, 1977. pp. 402. *bibliog.*

— Brazil.

LIMA (ARAUJO) Amazônia, a terra e o homem. São Paulo, 1975. pp. 151. *Text of the first edition of 1933, with the preface by Alcen de Amoroso Lima included in second and subsequent editions, and a new introduction.*

— France — Research.

FRANCO-BRITISH CONFERENCE IN HUMAN GEOGRAPHY, LONDON, 1975. Human geography in France and Britain; edited by John I. Clarke and Philippe Pinchemel; papers presented to the... conference. London, Social Science Research Council, [1976]. pp. 77. *bibliogs. In English and French.*

— United Kingdom.

ADAMS (IAN HUGH) Agrarian landscape terms: a glossary for historical geography. London, 1976. pp. 314. *bibliog. (Institute of British Geographers. Special Publications. No.9)*

ROBERTS (BRIAN K.) Rural settlement in Britain. Folkestone, 1977. pp. 221. *bibliog.*

YATES (EDWARD MARSHALL) Tudor Greatham, a social geography of a Hampshire village. London, 1977. pp. 60. *(London. University. King's College. Geography Department. Occasional Papers. No. 4)*

— — Research.

FRANCO-BRITISH CONFERENCE IN HUMAN GEOGRAPHY, LONDON, 1975. Human geography in France and Britain; edited by John I. Clarke and Philippe Pinchemel; papers presented to the... conference. London, Social Science Research Council, [1976]. pp. 77. *bibliogs. In English and French.*

— — Ireland.

ORME (A.R.) Ireland. London, 1970 repr. 1976. pp. 276. *bibliog.*

— United States.

ESTALL (ROBERT CHARLES) A modern geography of the United States: aspects of life and economy. 2nd ed. Harmondsworth, 1976. pp. 466. *bibliog.*

ANTHROPOLOGICAL LINGUISTICS.

SOCIOCULTURAL dimensions of language change; edited by Ben G. Blount [and] Mary Sanches. New York, [1977]. pp. 293. *bibliogs.*

ANTHROPOLOGISTS, SPANISH.

REUNION DE ANTROPOLOGOS ESPAÑOLES, 1a, Sevilla, 1973. Primera reunion de antropologos españoles: actas, comunicaciones, documentacion; edicion preparada por Alfredo Jimenez. Sevilla, [1975]. pp. 401. *bibliog.*

ANTHROPOLOGY.

JOUSSE (MARCEL) La manducation de la parole. [Paris, 1975]. pp. 287. *(L'anthropologie du geste.2)*

FREEDOM and constraint: a memorial tribute to Max Gluckman; edited by Myron J. Aronoff. Assen, 1976. pp. 179. *bibliogs.*

SOUTHERN ANTHROPOLOGICAL SOCIETY. Annual Meeting, 10th, Clearwater Beach, Florida, 1975. Do applied anthropologists apply anthropology?: [proceedings; edited by] Michael V. Angrosino. Athens, Georgia, [1976]. pp. 133. *bibliogs. (Southern Anthropological Society. Proceedings. No. 10)*

BEALS (RALPH LEON) and others. An introduction to anthropology. 5th ed. New York, [1977]. pp. 749. *bibliogs.*

SOCIAL anthropology and law; edited by Ian Hamnett. London, 1977. pp. 234. *(Association of Social Anthropologists of the Commonwealth. A.S.A. Monographs. 14) Papers of a conference held at the University of Keele in March 1974.*

— Bibliography.

MEAD (MARGARET) Margaret Mead: the complete bibliography, 1925-1975; edited by Joan Gordan. The Hague, 1976. pp. 202. *bibliog. Introduction in English, French and Spanish.*

— Methodology.

LEACH (Sir EDMUND RONALD) Culture and communication, the logic by which symbols are connected: an introduction to the use of structuralist analysis in social anthropology. Cambridge, 1976. pp. 105. *bibliog.*

— America, Latin.

HANDBOOK of middle American Indians. vol. 6. Social anthropology; Manning Nash, volume editor. Austin, Texas, [1967] repr. 1975. pp. 597. *bibliog. Edited at Middle American Research Institute, Tulane University, under the sponsorship of the National Research Council Committee on Latin American Anthropology.*

ANTHROPOLOGY, STRUCTURAL.

See STRUCTURAL ANTHROPOLOGY.

ANTHROPOMETRY

— America, Latin.

COMAS CAMPS (JUAN) Antropologia de los pueblos iberoamericanos. Barcelona, 1974. pp. 223. *bibliog.*

ANTICLERICALISM

— France.

REMOND (RENE) L'anti-cléricalisme en France de 1815 à nos jours. Paris, [1976]. pp. 374. *bibliog.*

ANTICOMMUNIST MOVEMENTS

— Poland — Silesia.

JANAS (EUGENIUSZ) Działalność pohitlerowskiego zbrojnego podziemia na Śląsku odzyskanym w latach 1945-1947. Opole, 1975. pp. 100. *bibliog.*

— Russia.

DUNLOP (JOHN B.) The new Russian revolutionaries. Belmont, Mass., 1976. pp. 344. *bibliog.*

— — Russia (RSFSR).

KIRIENKO (IURII KONSTANTINOVICH) Krakh kaledinshchiny. Moskva, 1976. pp. 246. *bibliog.*

— — Ukraine.

DOBRETSOVA (VIOLLI VIACHESLAVIVNA) Natsionalizm i relihiia na sluzhbi antykomunizmu: pro kontrrevoliutsiinu diial'nist' burzhuazno-natsionalistychnykh i klerykal'nykh orhanizatsii na zakhidnoukraïns'kykh zemliakh u 20-30-kh rokakh ta borot'bu proty nykh prohresyvnykh syl. L'viv, 1976. pp. 204.

VARVARTSEV (MYKOLA MYKOLAIOVYCH) Burzhuazne "ukraïnoznavstvo" - znariaddia ideolohichnykh dyversii imperializmu. Kyïv, 1976. pp. 185. *bibliog.*

— Yugoslavia — Bosnia.

ŠEHIĆ (NUSRET) Četništvo u Bosni i Hercegovini, 1918-1941: politička uloga i oblici djelatnosti četničkih udruženja; Le mouvement des tchetniks en Bosnie-Herzegovine, etc.; uredník Hamdija Kapidžić. Sarajevo, 1971. pp. 239. bibliog. (Akademija Nauka i Umjetnosti Bosne i Hercegovine. Djela. kn.42 [being also] Odjeljenje Društvenih Nauka. kn.27) With German summary.

ANTINAZI MOVEMENT.

INSTITUT FÜR MARXISMUS-LENINISMUS (BERLIN). Schon damals kämpften wir gemeinsam: Erinnerungen deutscher und tschechoslowakischer Antifaschisten an ihre illegale Grenzarbeit, 1933 bis 1938; (zusammengestellt und bearbeitet von Ernst Krüger und Gertrud Glondajewski). Berlin, 1961. pp. 136.

VEREINIGUNG DER VERFOLGTEN DES NAZIREGIMES. Vom Häftlingskomitee zum Bund der Antifaschisten: der Weg der VVN; (Redaktion: Max Oppenheimer). Frankfurt/Main, [1972]. pp. 172.

MAUR (HANS) Mahn-, Gedenk- und Erinnerungsstätten der Arbeiterbewegung in Berlin-Köpenick: Beiträge zur Geschichte der Berliner Arbeiterbewegung. Berlin, [1973?]. pp. 48. bibliog.

OPPENHEIMER (MAX) Das kämpferische Leben der Johanna Kirchner: Porträt einer antifaschistischen Widerstandskämpferin. Frankfurt am Main, [1974]. pp. 48. bibliog.

NEUHAUS (BARBARA) Funksignale vom Wartabogen:...über den gemeinsamen Kampf deutscher Kommunisten, sowjetischer und polnischer Partisanen. Berlin, [1975 repr. 1977]. pp. 604.

BEER (HELMUT) Widerstand gegen den Nationalsozialismus in Nürnberg, 1933- 1945. Nürnberg, [1976]. pp. 398. bibliog. (Nuremberg. Stadtarchiv. Nürnberger Werkstücke zur Stadt- und Landesgeschichte. Band 20) Erlanger Phil. Dissertation 1976.

EBNETH (RUDOLF) Die österreichische Wochenschrift "Der Christliche Ständestaat": deutsche Emigration in Österreich, 1933- 1938. Mainz, [1976]. pp. 271. bibliog. (Kommission für Zeitgeschichte. Veröffentlichungen. Reihe B: Forschungen. Band 19)

GRASMANN (PETER) Sozialdemokraten gegen Hitler, 1933-1945. München, [1976]. pp. 163. bibliog.

MAUSBACH-BROMBERGER (BARBARA) Arbeiterwiderstand in Frankfurt am Main gegen den Faschismus, 1933-1945. Frankfurt am Main, [1976]. pp. 312. bibliog.

NIETHAMMER (LUTZ) and others, eds. Arbeiterinitiative 1945: antifaschistische Ausschüsse und Reorganisation der Arbeiterbewegung in Deutschland; Autoren: Ulrich Borsdorf [and others]. Wuppertal, [1976]. pp. 782. bibliog.

PEUKERT (DETLEV) Ruhrarbeiter gegen den Faschismus: Dokumentation über den Widerstand im Ruhrgebiet, 1933-1945. Frankfurt/Main, [1976]. pp. 412. bibliog.

TIDL (MARIE) Die Roten Studenten: Dokumente und Erinnerungen, 1938-1945. Wien, 1976. pp. 300. bibliog. (Ludwig-Boltzmann-Institut fur Geschichte der Arbeiterbewegung. Materialien zur Arbeiterbewegung. Nr. 3)

IM Kampf bewährt: Erinnerungen deutscher Genossen an den antifaschistischen Widerstand von 1933 bis 1945; eingeleitet und zusammengestellt von Heinz Vosske. 2nd ed. Berlin, 1977. pp. 616.

VOGL (FRIEDRICH) Widerstand im Waffenrock: österreichische Freiheitskämpfer in der Deutschen Wehrmacht, 1938-1945. Wien, 1977. pp. 258. bibliog. (Ludwig Boltzmann Institut für Geschichte der Arbeiterbewegung. Materialien zur Arbeiterbewegung. Nr. 7)

— Bibliography.

BUECHEL (REGINE) compiler. Der deutsche Widerstand im Spiegel von Fachliteratur und Publizistik seit 1945. München, 1975. pp. 215. (Bibliothek für Zeitgeschichte. Schriften. Heft 15)

LAAK (URSULA VAN) compiler. Bibliographie zur Geschichte von Widerstand und Verfolgung in Bayern, 1933-1945. München, 1975. fo. 77. (Institut für Zeitgeschichte. Widerstand und Verfolgung in Bayern, 1933-1945. Hilfsmittel)

ANTIPATHIES AND PREJUDICES

— Ireland (Republic).

MAC GRÉIL (MÍCHEÁL) Prejudice and tolerance in Ireland: based on a survey of intergroup attitudes of Dublin adults and other sources. Dublin, 1977. pp. 634. bibliog.

ANTISEMITISM

— Austria.

AMERONGEN (MARTIN VAN) Kreisky und seine unbewältigte Gegenwart; (ins Deutsche übertragen [from the Dutch] von Gerhard Hartmann). Graz, 1977. pp. 128.

— Germany.

ERGAENZUNG zum Antisemiten-Spiegel, zweite Auflage, 1900: die Antisemiten im Lichte des Christenthums, des Rechtes und der Wissenschaft. Berlin, 1903. pp. 34.

— Poland.

HELLER (CELIA STOPNICKA) On the edge of destruction: Jews of Poland between the two world wars. New York, 1977. pp. 369.

ANTONOV-OVSEENKO (VLADIMIR ALEKSANDROVICH).

RAKITIN (ANTON VLADIMIROVICH) V.A. Antonov-Ovseenko: dokumental'nyi biograficheskii ocherk. Leningrad, 1975. pp. 342.

ANTRIM (COUNTY)

— Economic policy.

IRELAND, NORTHERN. Department of the Environment. 1977. East Antrim area plan. Belfast, 1977. pp. 51. 3 maps in back pocket.

ANTWERP

— Economic history.

POHL (HANS) Die Portugiesen in Antwerpen, 1567-1648: zur Geschichte einer Minderheit. Wiesbaden, 1977. pp. 439. bibliog. (Vierteljahrschrift für Sozial- und Wirtschaftsgeschichte. Beihefte. Nr. 63) 1 map in end pocket.

— Social history.

POHL (HANS) Die Portugiesen in Antwerpen, 1567-1648: zur Geschichte einer Minderheit. Wiesbaden, 1977. pp. 439. bibliog. (Vierteljahrschrift für Sozial- und Wirtschaftsgeschichte. Beihefte. Nr. 63) 1 map in end pocket.

APARTMENT HOUSES

— Singapore.

HASSAN (RIAZ) Families in flats: a study of low income families in public housing. Singapore, [1977]. pp. 249. bibliog.

APPALACHIAN MOUNTAINS

— Economic conditions.

CAUDILL (HARRY M.) The watches of the night. Boston, [Mass.], [1976]. pp. 275.

— Social conditions.

CAUDILL (HARRY M.) The watches of the night. Boston, [Mass.], [1976]. pp. 275.

— Social life and customs.

HICKS (GEORGE LEON) Appalachian Valley. New York, [1976]. pp. 112. bibliog.

APPELLATE PROCEDURE

— South Africa.

SOUTH AFRICAN LAW COMMISSION. Report: inquiry into granting persons convicted in criminal cases an absolute right of appeal (R.P. 73/1977). in SOUTH AFRICA. Parliament. House of Assembly. Votes and proceedings; (with Printed annexures).

APPLICATIONS FOR POSITIONS.

CONSUMERS' ASSOCIATION. Dismissal, redundancy and job hunting. London, [1976]. pp. 137.

APULIA

— History.

GRAMEGNA (GIUSEPPE) Braccianti e popolo in Puglia, 1944-1971: cronache di un protagonista. Bari, [1976]. pp. 343.

ARAB COUNTRIES.

HATIM (MUHAMMAD ABD AL-QADIR) Land of the Arabs. London, 1977. pp. 323.

— Commerce — Europe.

WAPPAEUS (J.E.) Untersuchungen über die Negerländer der Araber und über den Seehandel der Italiener, Spanier und Portugiesen im Mittelalter. Amsterdam, 1966. pp. 365. Reprint of work originally published in Göttingen in 1842.

— Defences.

PRANGER (ROBERT JOHN) and TAHTINEN (DALE R.) Implications of the 1976 Arab-Israeli military status. Washington, 1976. pp. 49. (American Enterprise Institute for Public Policy Research. Foreign Affairs Studies. 34)

— Economic conditions.

DEMIR (SOLIMAN) The Kuwait Fund and the political economy of Arab regional development. New York, 1976. pp. 138. bibliog.

— Economic policy.

DEMIR (SOLIMAN) The Kuwait Fund and the political economy of Arab regional development. New York, 1976. pp. 138. bibliog.

— Foreign economic relations — Israel.

CHILL (DAN S.) The Arab boycott of Israel: economic aggression and world reaction. New York, 1976. pp. 121. bibliog.

— Foreign opinion, American.

ESSAYS on the American public opinion and the Palestine problem. Beirut, 1969. pp. 192. bibliog. (Palestine Research Center. Palestine Monographs. 53)

— Foreign opinion, Israeli.

HARKABI (YEHOSHAFAT) Arab strategies and Israel's response. New York, [1977]. pp. 194.

— Foreign relations — Germany.

ABEDISEID (MOHAMMAD) Die deutsch-arabischen Beziehungen: Probleme und Krisen. Stuttgart Degerloch, [1976]. pp. 303. bibliog.

— — Israel.

AL-ABID (IBRAHIM) Israel and negotiations. Beirut, 1970. pp. 29. (Palestine Research Center. Palestine Essays. No. 20)

— Nationalism.

SAYEGH (ANIS) Palestine and Arab nationalism. Beirut, 1970. pp. 86. (Palestine Research Center. Palestine Essays. No. 3)

— Social conditions.

CUISENIER (JEAN) Economie et parenté: leurs affinités de structure dans le domaine turc et dans le domaine arabe. Paris, [1975]. pp. 569. *bibliog. (Paris. Ecole Pratique des Hautes Etudes. Section des Sciences Economiques et Sociales. Le Monde d'Outre-Mer Passé et Présent. 1e Série. Etudes. 60)*

ARAKCHEEV (ALEKSEI ANDREEVICH) Graf.

GESSEN (SERGEI IAKOVLEVICH) Arakcheevskaia barshchina: istoricheskie zarisovki iz epokhi voennykh poselenii. Moskva, 1932. pp. 119.

ARAPESH TRIBE.

TUZIN (DONALD F.) The Ilahita Arapesh: dimensions of unity. Berkeley, Calif., [1976]. pp. 376. *bibliog.*

ARAWAKAN LANGUAGES.

NOBLE (GLADWYN KINGSLEY) Proto-Arawakan and its descendants. Bloomington, Ind., 1965. pp. 129. *bibliog. (Indiana University. Research Center in Anthropology, Folklore, and Linguistics. Publications. 38)*

ARBITRATION, INDUSTRIAL.

COMPULSORY arbitration: an international comparison; [by] J. Joseph Loewenberg [and others]. Lexington, Mass., [1976]. pp. 213.

— Jamaica.

GERSHENFELD (WALTER J.) Compulsory arbitration in Jamaica, 1952-1969. Kingston, Jamaica, 1974. pp. 187. *(West Indies, University of the. Institute of Social and Economic Research. Law and Society in the Caribbean. No. 4)*

— United States.

SUFFERN (ARTHUR ELLIOTT) Conciliation and arbitration in the coal industry of America. Boston, [Mass.], 1915; New York, 1976. pp. 376. *bibliog. (Hart, Schaffner and Marx Prize Essays. 18)*

POPS (GERALD M.) Emergence of the public sector arbitrator. Lexington, Mass., [1976]. pp. 136.

ARBITRATION, INTERNATIONAL.

HSIAO (GENE T.) Communist China's foreign trade contracts and means of settling disputes. Berkeley, Calif., [1969]. pp. 503-529. *(California University. Center for Chinese Studies. China Series Reprints. No. C-11) (Reprinted from Vanderbilt Law Review, 1969)*

ARBITRATION AND AWARD

— China.

LUBMAN (STANLEY) Mao and mediation: politics and dispute resolution in communist China. Berkeley, Calif., [1968]. pp. 1284-1359. *(California University. Centre for Chinese Studies. China Series Reprints. No. C-3) (Reprinted from California Law Review, 1967, vol. 55, no. 5)*

— Russia.

RUSSIA (USSR). Statutes, etc. 1974. Sbornik polozhenii ob organakh gosudarstvennogo arbitrazha. Moskva, 1975. pp. 183.

ARCHAEOLOGY

— Atlases.

WHITEHOUSE (DAVID) and WHITEHOUSE (RUTH) Archaeological atlas of the world. London, [1975]. pp. 272. *bibliogs.*

ARCHAEOLOGY, MEDIEVAL.

The PLANS and topography of medieval towns in England and Wales; edited by M.W. Barley. [London], 1976. pp. 92. *bibliog. (Council for British Archaeology. Research Reports. No. 14)*

ARCHITECTURE

— United Kingdom.

BETJEMAN (Sir JOHN) The English town in the last hundred years. Cambridge, 1956. pp. 28. *(Cambridge. University. Rede Lectures. 1956)*

ARCHITECTURE AND SOCIETY.

WARD (COLIN) ed. Vandalism. London, 1973. pp. 327. *bibliog.*

KIDD (WILLIAM JACQUES) People and the built environment;...an inaugural lecture delivered before the Queen's University of Belfast on 12th February 1975. Belfast, [1975]. pp. 16. *(Belfast. Queen's University. Lectures. New Series. No. 85)*

ARCHIVES

— Denmark.

DENMARK. Rigsarkivet. 1973. Danish Department of Foreign Affairs until 1770; by Arthur G. Hassø and Erik Kroman; translated by Mogens Møller. Copenhagen, 1973. pp. 196. *(Vejledende Arkivregistraturer. 16)*

— France.

HARTMANN (PETER CLAUS) Pariser Archive, Bibliotheken und Dokumentationszentren zur Geschichte des 19. und 20. Jahrhunderts: eine Einführung, etc. München, 1976. pp. 131. *(Deutsches Historisches Institut, Paris. Dokumentation Westeuropa. Band 1)*

— Germany.

GERMANY (BUNDESREPUBLIK). Bundesarchiv. Schriften. 10. Das Bundesarchiv und seine Bestände;...von Gerhard Granier [and others]. 3rd ed. Boppard am Rhein, [1977]. pp. 940.

— India.

RENFORD (RAYMOND K.) Archival and library sources for the study of the activities of the non-official British community in India: a brief survey. [London], 1976. pp. 25.

— Poland.

LEWANSKI (RICHARD CASIMIR) compiler. Guide to Polish libraries and archives. New York, 1974. pp. 209. *bibliog. (East European Quarterly. East European Monographs. 6)*

— Russia — Ukraine.

MITIUKOV (OLEKSANDR HEORHIIOVYCH) Radians'ke arkhivne budivnytstvo na Ukraïni, 1917-1973. Kyïv, 1975. pp. 271. *With Russian, English and French summaries.*

— United Kingdom.

U.K. British Transport Commission. 1977. British Transport Commission historical records: canal, dock, harbour, navigation and steamship companies: RAIL 800-887: class list. London, 1977. pp. 380. *(List and Index Society. [Publications]. vol.142)*

U.K. War Cabinet. 1939-45. Cabinet Office list of War Cabinet memoranda, CAB 66, W.P. and C.P. series, 1939 Sept. - 1945 July. London, 1977. pp. 211. *(List and Index Society. [Publications]. Vol. 136)*

— — Directories.

STOREY (RICHARD A.) and DRUKER (JANET) Guide to the Modern Records Centre, University of Warwick Library. Warwick, [1977]. pp. 152. *(University of Warwick. Library. Occasional Publications. No. 2)*

— United States.

STANFORD UNIVERSITY. Hoover Institution on War, Revolution and Peace. Archival and manuscript materials...; a checklist of major collections. Stanford, [1975]. pp. 22.

— Yugoslavia — Directories.

JOVANOVIĆ (SLOBODAN) and ROJNIĆ (MATKO) compilers. A guide to Yugoslav libraries and archives;...Paul L. Horecky chief editor; Elizabeth Beyerly, translator and associate editor. Columbus, Ohio, 1975. pp. 113. *bibliogs. (American Council of Learned Societies and Social Science Research Council. Joint Committee on Eastern Europe. Publication Series. 2)*

ARGENTINE REPUBLIC

— Boundaries — Chile.

U.K. Court of Arbitration of a Controversy between the Argentine Republic and the Republic of Chile. 1965-67. Argentine-Chile frontier case court of arbitration transcript of hearings [with memorials, counter memorials, documents, etc. submitted by Argentine and Chile]; [Lord McNair, president] . London, 1965-67. 20 vols. (in 15).

— Constitution.

ARGENTINE REPUBLIC. Constitution. 1810-1972. Las constituciones de la Argentina, 1810-1972; recopilacion, notas y estudio preliminar [by] Arturo Enrique Sampay. Buenos Aires, [1975]. pp. 661.

— Description and travel.

FITTE (ERNESTO J.) Cronicas del Atlantico sur: Patagonia, Malvinas y Antartida. Buenos Aires, 1974. pp. 469. *bibliog.*

— Economic conditions.

PEÑA (MILCIADES) Industria, burguesia industrial y liberacion nacional. Buenos Aires, 1974. pp. 195.

ROFMAN (ALEJANDRO BORIS) Desigualdades regionales y concentracion economica: el caso argentino. Buenos Aires, 1974. pp. 150.

GASTIAZORO (EUGENIO) Argentina hoy: latifundio, dependencia y estructura de clases. 3rd ed. Buenos Aires, 1975. pp. 236.

— Economic history.

CARRETERO (ANDRES M.) Origenes de la dependencia economica argentina. Buenos Aires, 1974. pp. 184.

— Economic policy.

WYNIA (GARY W.) Economic policy-making under stress: conflict and exchange in Argentina. Austin, 1974. pp. 69. *(American Society for Public Administration. Latin American Development Administration Committee and Texas University. Institute of Latin American Studies. LADAC Occasional Papers. Series 2. No. 11)*

— Emigration and immigration.

DIAZ (BENITO) Inmigracion y agricultura en la epoca de Rosas. Buenos Aires, [1975]. pp. 79.

— Foreign relations — United Kingdom.

FELL (BRIAN JOHN) Britain and the Argentine, 1914-1918. 1976. fo.379. *bibliog. Typescript. Ph.D.(London) thesis: unpublished. This thesis is the property of London University and may not be removed from the Library.*

— Historiography.

El REVISIONISMO historico socialista; [by] Jorge Enea Spilimbergo [and others]. Buenos Aires, 1974. pp. 315.

— History.

PEÑA (MILCIADES) Masas, caudillos y elites: la dependencia argentina de Yrigoyen a Peron. Buenos Aires, [1973]. pp. 136. *bibliog.*

CARRETERO (ANDRES M.) Origenes de la dependencia economica argentina. Buenos Aires, 1974. pp. 184.

MORENO (NAHUEL) Metodo de interpretacion de la historia argentina; con la colaboracion de Hugo Kasevich. Buenos Aires, [1975]. pp. 212.

WHITAKER (ARTHUR PRESTON) The United States and the southern cone: Argentina, Chile, and Uruguay. Cambridge, Mass., 1976. pp. 464. *bibliog.*

— — 1860-1910.

SABSAY (FERNANDO LEONIDAS) and CASABLANCA (ADOLFO) La sociedad argentina: en busca de la voluntad popular. Buenos Aires, 1974. pp. 343. *bibliog.*

— — 1943- .

BEARN (GEORGES) ed. La décade péroniste. [Paris, 1975]. pp. 253. *bibliog.*

SOBEL (LESTER A.) Argentina and Peron, 1970-75. New York, [1975]. pp. 167.

— Industries.

GASTIAZORO (EUGENIO) Argentina hoy: latifundio, dependencia y estructura de clases. 3rd ed. Buenos Aires, 1975. pp. 236.

— Politics and government.

MANUAL de doctrina nacional. Buenos Aires, 1953 repr. 1974. pp. 185. *Reprinted with a new prologue.*

NADRA (FERNANDO) Socialismo nacional. Buenos Aires, 1973. pp. 237.

RAMOS (JORGE ABELARDO) Marxismo para latinoamericanos. Buenos Aires, [1973]. pp. 341.

MERCIER VEGA (LUIS) Autopsia de Peron: balance del peronismo; [translated from the French by] Menene Gras. Barcelona, [1975]. pp. 270.

SOBEL (LESTER A.) Argentina and Peron, 1970-75. New York, [1975]. pp. 167.

ARGENTINA SUPPORT MOVEMENT. Argentina, 1976: repression and resistance. London, [1976]. 1 pamphlet (various pagings).

ARGENTINA SUPPORT MOVEMENT. Argentina: the trade union struggle. London, [1976]. 1 pamphlet (unpaged).

HODGES (DONALD CLARK) Argentina, 1943-1976: the national revolution and resistance. Albuquerque, [1976]. pp. 207. *bibliog.*

VILLAR ARAUJO (CARLOS) Argentina: de Peron al golpe militar. Madrid, 1976. pp. 220. *bibliog.*

— Popular culture.

La CULTURA popular del Peronismo; [by] Norman Briski [and others]. [Buenos Aires], 1973. pp. 155.

— Presidents.

SABSAY (FERNANDO LEONIDAS) and CASABLANCA (ADOLFO) La sociedad argentina: en busca de la voluntad popular. Buenos Aires, 1974. pp. 343. *bibliog.*

— Social conditions.

ROFMAN (ALEJANDRO BORIS) Desigualdades regionales y concentracion economica: el caso argentino. Buenos Aires, 1974. pp. 150.

ARID REGIONS.

ARID land irrigation in developing countries: environmental problems and effects; based on the international symposium, 16-21 February 1976, Alexandria, Egypt; editor E. Barton Worthington. Oxford, [1977]. pp. 463.

ARISTOTLE.

MORRALL (JOHN BRIMYARD) Aristotle. London, 1977. pp. 120. *bibliog.*

ARMAMENTS.

LUTTWAK (EDWARD) Strategic power: military capabilities and political utility. Beverly Hills, [1976]. pp. 70. *bibliog.* (*Georgetown University. Center for Strategic and International Studies. Washington Papers. vol. 4/38*)

ARMED FORCES

— Political activity.

WAYMAN (FRANK WHELON) Military involvement in politics: a causal model. Beverly Hills, [1975]. pp. 71. *bibliog.*

BURTON (ANTHONY M.) The destruction of loyalty: an examination of the threat of propaganda and subversion against the armed forces of the West. London, [1976]. pp. 63. *bibliog.*

NORDLINGER (ERIC A.) Soldiers in politics: military coups and governments. Englewood Cliffs, [1977]. pp. 224. *bibliog.*

PERLMUTTER (AMOS) The military and politics in modern times: on professionals, praetorians and revolutionary soldiers. New Haven, 1977. pp. 335. *Written under the auspices of the Center for International Affairs, Harvard University.*

WODDIS (JACK) Armies and politics. London, 1977. pp. 309.

— — Mathematical models.

CORTESE (CHARLES F.) Modernization, threat and the power of the military. Beverly Hills, [1976]. pp. 64. *bibliog.*

ARMENIANS.

LANG (DAVID MARSHALL) and WALKER (CHRISTOPHER J.) The Armenians. London, [1976]. pp. 24. *bibliog.* (*Minority Rights Group. Reports. No. 42*)

ARNOLD (MATTHEW).

COXALL (WILLIAM NORMAN) Two Victorian theorists of democracy: a comparative study of Sir Henry Maine and Matthew Arnold. 1977. fo. 347. *bibliog. Typescript. Ph.D. (London) thesis: unpublished. This thesis is the property of London University and may not be removed from the Library.*

ARNSBERG

— Economic history.

NOLL (ADOLF) Sozio-ökonomischer Strukturwandel des Handwerks in der zweiten Phase der Industrialisierung: unter besonderer Berücksichtigung der Regierungsbezirke Arnsberg und Münster. Göttingen, 1975. pp. 386. *bibliog. (Fritz Thyssen Stiftung. Neunzehntes Jahrhundert. Studien zum Wandel von Gesellschaft und Bildung im Neunzehnten Jahrhundert. Band 10)*

ARREST

— Russia.

BEKESHKO (SERGEI PETROVICH) and MATVIENKO (EVGENII ALEKSANDROVICH) Podozrevaemyi v sovetskom ugolovnom protsesse. Minsk, 1969. pp. 128.

ART AND SOCIETY.

MORRIS (WILLIAM) Selected writings and designs; edited with an introduction by Asa Briggs; with a supplement by Graeme Shankland on William Morris, designer, illustrated by twenty-four plates. Harmondsworth, 1962, repr. 1977. pp. 309. *bibliog.*

ROSENBERG (HAROLD) Discovering the present: three decades in art, culture, and politics. Chicago, 1973. pp. 336.

ARTESIAN BASINS

— Australia — Queensland.

QUEENSLAND. Geological Survey. Bulletins. No. 1. Artesian water in the western interior of Queensland; by Robert L. Jack. Brisbane, 1895. pp. 16.

ARTIFICIAL ISLANDS.

PAPADAKIS (NIKOS) The international legal regime of artificial islands. Leyden, 1977. pp. 277.

ARTIFICIAL SATELLITES IN TELECOMMUNICATION.

SIGNITZER (BENNO) Regulation of direct broadcasting from satellites: the U.N. involvement. New York, 1976. pp. 112. *bibliog.*

ARTISANS

— Germany.

NOLL (ADOLF) Sozio-ökonomischer Strukturwandel des Handwerks in der zweiten Phase der Industrialisierung: unter besonderer Berücksichtigung der Regierungsbezirke Arnsberg und Münster. Göttingen, 1975. pp. 386. *bibliog. (Fritz Thyssen Stiftung. Neunzehntes Jahrhundert. Studien zum Wandel von Gesellschaft und Bildung im Neunzehnten Jahrhundert. Band 10)*

SCHWARZ (KLAUS) Die Lage der Handwerksgesellen in Bremen während des 18. Jahrhunderts. Bremen, 1975. pp. 401. *bibliog. (Bremen. Staatsarchiv. Veröffentlichungen. Band 44)*

— Poland.

KWAPIEŃ (MARIA) and others. Studia nad produkcją rzemieślniczą w Polsce, XIV-XVIII w. Wrocław, 1976. pp. 244. *(Polska Akademia Nauk. Instytut Historii Kultury Materialnej. Studia i Materiały z Historii Kultury Materialnej. tom 51) With English summaries.*

— Russia — Uzbekistan.

MUKMINOVA (ROZIIA GALIEVNA) Ocherki po istorii remesla v Samarkande i Bukhare v XVI veke. Tashkent, 1976. pp. 234.

— — White Russia.

TITOV (VIKTOR STEPANOVICH) Narodnye derevoobrabatyvaiushchie promysly Belorussii, 1917-1941 gg.: etnograficheskie ocherki bondarnogo promysla i izgotovleniia transportnykh sredstv; redaktor... V.K. Bondarchik. Minsk, 1976. pp. 135.

— United Kingdom.

HARVEY (JOHN H.) Mediaeval craftsmen. London, 1975. pp. 231. *bibliog.*

ARTS

— Russia.

ISKUSSTVO i ideologicheskaia rabota partii. Moskva, 1976. pp. 351.

— United Kingdom.

U.K. Department of Education and Science. 1968. Report on the arts: a going concern. [London], 1968. pp. (4).

TRADES UNION CONGRESS. Working Party on the Arts. The TUC working party report on the arts. London, [1976]. pp. 44.

ASIA

— Bibliography.

BAGANOVA (TAT'IANA ALEKSANDROVNA) and BULATOV (SERGEI SERAFIMOVICH) eds. Spravochnaia literatura po stranam Azii i Afriki: svodnyi katalog inostrannykh fondov Biblioteki Akademii nauk SSSR i Gosudarstvennoi publichnoi biblioteki im. M.E. Saltykova- Shchedrina, 1945-1968. Leningrad, 1972. pp. 534.

— Commerce — Europe.

FURBER (HOLDEN) Rival empires of trade in the Orient, 1600-1800. Minneapolis, 1976. pp. 408. *bibliog.*

— Commercial policy.

VITTAL (NAGARAJAN) ed. Export processing zones in Asia: some dimensions. Tokyo, Asian Productivity Organization, [1977]. pp. 122.

— Economic conditions.

SOUTHERN Asia: the politics of poverty and peace; edited by Donald C. Hellmann. Lexington, Mass., [1976]. pp. 297. *(Commission on Critical Choices for Americans. Critical Choices for Americans. vol. 13)*

— Foreign relations — Russia.

KOVALENKO (IVAN IVANOVICH) Sovetskii Soiuz v bor'be za mir i kollektivnuiu bezopasnost' v Azii. Moskva, 1976. pp. 431. *bibliog.*

— — United States.

ROSE (LISLE ABBOTT) Roots of tragedy: the United States and the struggle for Asia, 1945-1953. Westport, Conn., 1976. pp. 262. *bibliog.*

SOUTHERN Asia: the politics of poverty and peace; edited by Donald C. Hellmann. Lexington, Mass., [1976]. pp. 297. *(Commission on Critical Choices for Americans. Critical Choices for Americans. vol. 13)*

— Full employment policies.

MEHTA (MADHAVA MAL) Industrialization and employment; with special reference to Asia and the Far East. Bombay, 1976. pp. 128.

— Industries.

MEHTA (MADHAVA MAL) Industrialization and employment; with special reference to Asia and the Far East. Bombay, 1976. pp. 128.

— Politics and government.

GOSUDARSTVO sotsialisticheskoi orientatsii. Moskva, 1975. pp. 376. *bibliog. (Akademiia Nauk SSSR. Institut Gosudarstva i Prava. Gosudarstvo i Pravo Stran, Osvobodivshikhsia ot Kolonial'noi Zavisimosti. [5])*

KOVALENKO (IVAN IVANOVICH) Sovetskii Soiuz v bor'be za mir i kollektivnuiu bezopasnost' v Azii. Moskva, 1976. pp. 431. *bibliog.*

SOUTHERN Asia: the politics of poverty and peace; edited by Donald C. Hellmann. Lexington, Mass., [1976]. pp. 297. *(Commission on Critical Choices for Americans. Critical Choices for Americans. vol. 13)*

— Population.

ASIA urbanizing: population growth and concentration and the problems thereof; a comparative symposium by Asian and Western experts in search of wise approaches; edited by Social Science Research Institute, International Christian University. Tokyo, [1976]. pp. 178. *Papers of an international symposium convened by the Institute and held May 6-7, 1975 in Tokyo.*

— Relations (general) with Europe.

DODGE (ERNEST S.) Islands and empires: western impact on the Pacific and East Asia. Minneapolis, Minn., 1976. pp. 364. *bibliog.*

— Relations (general) with Russia.

ATAMAMEDOV (N.V.) and GOLOVIN (IULII MIKHAILOVICH) eds. Lenin v sud'bakh narodov Vostoka. Ashkhabad, 1975. pp. 143.

— Rural conditions.

INAYATULLAH. Co-operatives and development in Asia: a study of co-operatives in fourteen rural communities of Iran, Pakistan and Ceylon. (UNRISD Reports. No.72.7). Geneva, United Nations Research Institute for Social Development, 1972. pp. 272. *(Rural Institutions and Planned Change. Vol.7)*

ASIA, SOUTHEAST

— Armed forces.

LEBRA (JOYCE CHAPMAN) Japanese-trained armies in southeast Asia: independence and volunteer forces in World War II. New York, 1977. pp. 226. *bibliog.*

— Economic conditions — Bibliography.

CWIK (HANS JUERGEN) and others, compilers. Entwicklungswirtschaftlich relevante Ressourcen in den A[ssociation of] S[outh]-E[ast] A[sian] N[ations]- Ländern, Auswahlbibliographie: A select bibliography, etc. Hamburg, 1974. pp. 133. *(Hamburg. Institut für Asienkunde. Dokumentations-Leitstelle Asien. Dokumentationsdienst Asien. Reihe A. 5)*

— Economic policy.

WONG (JOHN) The Asean economies: development outlook for the 1980s. Singapore, 1977. pp. 51. *(University of Singapore. Economic Research Centre. Occasional Paper Series. No. 1)*

— Foreign economic relations — Japan.

MANGLAPUS (RAUL S.) Japan in Southeast Asia: collision course. New York, [1976]. pp. 151. *bibliog.*

— Foreign relations — China.

TAYLOR (JAY) China and Southeast Asia: Peking's relations with revolutionary movements. 2nd ed. New York, 1976. pp. 400.

MARTIN (EDWIN W.) Southeast Asia and China: the end of containment. Boulder, Colo., 1977. pp. 114. *Prepared for the Center for Strategic and International Studies, Georgetown University.*

— — United States.

MARTIN (EDWIN W.) Southeast Asia and China: the end of containment. Boulder, Colo., 1977. pp. 114. *Prepared for the Center for Strategic and International Studies, Georgetown University.*

— Nationalism.

LEBRA (JOYCE CHAPMAN) Japanese-trained armies in southeast Asia: independence and volunteer forces in World War II. New York, 1977. pp. 226. *bibliog.*

— Native races.

ALATAS (SYED HUSSEIN) The myth of the lazy native: a study of the image of the Malays, Filipinos and Javanese from the 16th to the 20th century and its function in the ideology of colonial capitalism. London, 1977. pp. 267. *bibliog.*

— Politics and government.

TAYLOR (JAY) China and Southeast Asia: Peking's relations with revolutionary movements. 2nd ed. New York, 1976. pp. 400.

— Social conditions.

BROWN (D.E.) Principles of social structure: Southeast Asia. London, 1976. pp. 248. *bibliog.*

ASIATICS IN THE UNITED KINGDOM.

COMMUNITY RELATIONS COMMISSION. Between two cultures: a study of relationships between generations in the Asian community in Britain. London, 1976. pp. 73.

MOBBS (MICHAEL C.) Meeting their needs: an account of language tuition schemes for ethnic minority women. London, Community Relations Commission, 1977. pp. 64. *bibliog.*

ASQUITH (HERBERT HENRY) 1st Earl of Oxford and Asquith.

KOSS (STEPHEN E.) Asquith. New York, 1976. pp. 310. *bibliog.*

HOBHOUSE (Sir CHARLES EDWARD HENRY) Inside Asquith's Cabinet: from the diaries of Charles Hobhouse; edited by Edward David. London, [1977]. pp. 295.

ASSAM

— Statistics.

ASSAM. Directorate of Economics and Statistics. Municipal statistical year book. a., 1968-69/1969-70 (1st)- Gauhati.

ASSASSINATION

— Germany.

KOMMUNISTISCHE PARTEI DEUTSCHLANDS. Bezirk Wasserkante. Mord über Deutschland. [Hamburg?, 1931?]. pp. 24.

— Spain.

AGIRRE (JULEN) Opération "Ogro"...: comment et pourquoi nous avons exécuté Carrero Blanco, premier ministre espagnol; traduit de l'espagnol par Victoria Pueblos. Paris, [1974]. pp. 224.

AGIRRE (JULEN) Operation Ogro: the execution of Admiral Luis Carrero Blanco;...translated from the Spanish, adapted and with an introduction by Barbara Probst Solomon. New York, [1975]. pp. 196.

ASSEMBLER LANGUAGE (COMPUTER PROGRAM LANGUAGE).

BURIAN (BARBARA J.) A simplified approach to S/370 assembly language programming. Englewood Cliffs, [1977]. pp. 558.

ASSOCIATIONS, INSTITUTIONS, ETC.

ROSS (JACK C.) An assembly of good fellows: voluntary associations in history. Westport, Conn., 1976. pp. 325. *bibliog.*

— Germany.

WOLF (HEINRICH) of the Jungdeutscher Orden. Die Entstehung des Jungdeutschen Ordens und seine frühen Jahre, 1918-1922. München, 1970. pp. 47. *bibliog. (Jungdeutsches Archiv. Beiträge zur Geschichte des Jungdeutschen Ordens. Heft 1)*

VEREINIGUNG DER VERFOLGTEN DES NAZIREGIMES. Vom Häftlingskomitee zum Bund der Antifaschisten: der Weg der VVN; (Redaktion: Max Oppenheimer). Frankfurt/Main, [1972]. pp. 172.

WOLF (HEINRICH) of the Jungdeutscher Orden. Der Jungdeutsche Orden in seinen mittleren Jahren, 1922-1925. München, 1972. pp. 71. *bibliog. (Jungdeutsches Archiv. Beiträge zur Geschichte des Jungdeutschen Ordens. Heft 2)*

25 Jahre Deutscher Sportbund; [by] Willy Weyer [and others]. [Frankfurt/Main. 1975]. pp. 16.

BOLZ (WOLFGANG EBERHARD) Elitenselektion in Verbänden. Hamburg, 1976. pp. 331. *bibliog. Dissertation zur Erlangung des Grades eines Doktors der Wirtschafts- und Sozialwissenschaften der Universität Hamburg.*

KOESTLIN (KONRAD) Gilden in Schleswig-Holstein: die Bestimmung des Standes durch "Kultur". Göttingen, [1976]. pp. 320. *bibliog.*

WEBER (JUERGEN) Die Interessengruppen im politischen System der Bundesrepublik Deutschland. Stuttgart, [1977]. pp. 392. *bibliog.*

— — Directories.

HANDBUCH der deutschen wissenschaftlichen Akademien und Gesellschaften...; herausgegeben von Friedrich Domay. 2nd ed. Wiesbaden, 1977. pp. 1209.

— Russia.

DOBROVOL'NYE obshchestva pri sotsializme. Moskva, 1976. pp. 372.

— South Africa.

MITCHELL (M.L.) The Christian Institute: the United Party view. Johannesburg, [1975]. fo. 5. *In English and Afrikaans.*

— Sweden.

LINDROTH (BENGT) Bingo!: en kritisk granskning av folkrörelserna i Sverige, 1850-1975. [Stockholm, 1975]. pp. 225. *bibliog.*

— United Kingdom.

CIVIC TRUST. The local amenity movement; [including chapters by Anthony Barker]. London, 1976. pp. 36.

LANSLEY (JOHN) Voluntary organisations facing change: the report of a project to help Councils for Voluntary Service respond to local government reorganisation. London, 1976. pp. 96. *bibliog.*

MANLEY (ROY) and HASTINGS (HELEN) Influencing Europe: a guide for pressure groups. London, 1977. pp. 19. *bibliog. (Fabian Society. Research Series. [No.] 332)*

— — Directories.

COUNCILS, committees, and boards: a handbook of advisory, consultative, executive and similar bodies in British public life; edited by I.G. Anderson. 3rd ed. Beckenham, 1977. pp. 402.

— United States.

BERGER (PETER L.) and NEUHAUS (RICHARD JOHN) To empower people: the role of mediating structures in public policy. Washington, [1977]. pp. 45. *(American Enterprise Institute for Public Policy Research. AEI Studies. 139)*

ASTHMA.

OFFICE OF HEALTH ECONOMICS. [Studies in Current Health Problems]. No.57. Asthma. London, [1976]. pp. 47. *bibliog.*

ASTORGA

— Growth.

CABERO DIEGUEZ (VALENTIN) Evolucion y estructura urbana de Astorga. Leon, 1973. pp. 114.

— History.

CABERO DIEGUEZ (VALENTIN) Evolucion y estructura urbana de Astorga. Leon, 1973. pp. 114.

— Population.

CABERO DIEGUEZ (VALENTIN) Evolucion y estructura urbana de Astorga. Leon, 1973. pp. 114.

ASYLUM, RIGHT OF.

REINHARD (ERNST) Das schweizerische Asylrecht. Olten, [1919?]. pp. 44.

ATHEISM

— Dictionaries and encyclopaedias.

KARMANNYI slovar' ateista. Moskva, 1975. pp. 287.

ATHENS

— Social conditions.

RANKIN (H.D.) Pentheus and Plato: a study in social disintegration; an inaugural lecture delivered at the University [of Southampton] 20 November 1975. Southampton, 1975. pp. 32.

— Social history.

RANKIN (H.D.) Pentheus and Plato: a study in social disintegration; an inaugural lecture delivered at the University [of Southampton] 20 November 1975. Southampton, 1975. pp. 32.

CARLTON (ERIC JAMES) Ideology and social order. London, 1977. pp. 320. *bibliog.*

ATLANTIC COMMUNITY.

DANKERT (PETER) General report on Atlantic political problems [to the Political Committee of the North Atlantic Assembly]. [Brussels], 1974. fo. 31, 3.

ATLANTIC Europe?: the radical view; [papers presented at a conference convened in 1975 by the Transnational Institute]; edited by Tom Nairn. Amsterdam, 1976. pp. 126.

CONFERENCE ON AMERICAN FOREIGN POLICY AND THE NEW EUROPE, BLACKSBURG, 1974. America and European security; edited by Louis J. Mensonides and James A. Kuhlman. Leyden, 1976. pp. 170. *bibliog. (East-West Foundation. East-West Perspectives. 2)*

ATLASES.

ATLAS universalis; Encyclopaedia Universalis...éditeur à Paris. Paris, 1975. pp. 312, 222. *Produced in association with Encyclopaedia Britannica and Rand, McNally and Company.*

ATOMIC BOMB

— History.

THOMAS (GORDON) and MORGAN-WITTS (MAX) Rain from the air: the atomic mission to Hiroshima. London, 1977. pp. 386. *bibliog.*

ATOMIC ENERGY.

INTERNATIONAL ATOMIC ENERGY AGENCY. Annual report. a., 1960/61(4th)- [Vienna]. *1957/58-1959/60 (1st-3rd) included in INTERNATIONAL ATOMIC ENERGY AGENCY. General Conference. [Documents]. 2nd Session, 1958-1961.*

INTERNATIONAL ATOMIC ENERGY AGENCY. The Agency's budget (formerly Program and budget). a., 1962- [Vienna]. *From 1965-1968 in 2 pts; The Agency's programme and The Agency's budget. From 1969- every alternate issue of the Agency's budget included the Agency's programme.*

INTERNATIONAL ATOMIC ENERGY AGENCY. General Conference. Press release[s]. irreg., current issues only. Vienna.

ATOMIC POWER.

ATLANTIC COUNCIL OF THE UNITED STATES. Nuclear Fuels Policy Working Group. Nuclear fuels policy. Boulder, Col., 1976. pp. 136.

HAYES (DENIS) Environmentalist. Nuclear power: the fifth horseman. Washington, 1976. pp. 68. *(Worldwatch Institute. Worldwatch Papers. No. 6)*

INTERNATIONAL INSTITUTE FOR STRATEGIC STUDIES. Adelphi Papers. No. 130. Nuclear power and weapons proliferation; by Ted Greenwood, George W. Rathjens and Jack Ruina. London, 1976. pp. 51.

The NUCLEAR power controversy; [edited by Arthur W. Murphy]. Englewood Cliffs, [1976]. pp. 184. *Background papers for the 50th American Assembly, held at Arden House, Harriman, New York, 1976.*

— Security measures.

FLOOD (MICHAEL) and GROVE-WHITE (ROBIN) Nuclear prospects: a comment on the individual, the state and nuclear power. London, [1976]. pp. 64. *bibliog.*

ATOMIC POWER INDUSTRY

— Australia — Queensland.

STATE ELECTRICITY COMMISSION OF · QUEENSLAND. The economics of electricity generation in Queensland and the potential employment of nuclear reactors. Sydney, 1958. pp. 265-272. *bibliog. Reprinted from Australian Atomic Energy Symposium 1958.*

— United States.

DAWSON (FRANK G.) Nuclear power: development and management of a technology. Seattle, [1976]. pp. 320. *bibliog.*

NUCLEAR ENERGY POLICY STUDY GROUP. Nuclear power issues and choices; foreword by McGeorge Bundy ...Spurgeon M. Keeny, chairman. Cambridge, Mass., [1977]. pp. 418.

ATOMIC POWER PLANTS

— United Kingdom — Location.

FLOOD (MICHAEL) and GROVE-WHITE (ROBIN) Nuclear prospects: a comment on the individual, the state and nuclear power. London, [1976]. pp. 64. *bibliog.*

ATOMIC WEAPONS.

INTERNATIONAL INSTITUTE FOR STRATEGIC STUDIES. Adelphi Papers. No. 130. Nuclear power and weapons proliferation; by Ted Greenwood, George W. Rathjens and Jack Ruina. London, 1976. pp. 51.

POLMAR (NORMAN) Strategic weapons: an introduction. London, 1976. pp. 161.

AMERICAN ACADEMY OF POLITICAL AND SOCIAL SCIENCE. Annals. vol. 430. Nuclear proliferation: prospects, problems, and proposals; special editor of this volume, Joseph I. Coffey. Philadelphia, Pa., 1977. pp. 236.

BEYOND nuclear deterrence: new aims, new arms; edited by Johan J. Holst [and] Uwe Nerlich. New York, [1977]. pp. 314. *bibliog.*

HARKAVY (ROBERT E.) Spectre of a middle eastern holocaust: the strategic and diplomatic implications of the Israeli nuclear weapons program. Denver, [1977]. pp. 126. *(Denver. University. Social Science Foundation and Graduate School of International Studies. Monograph Series in World Affairs. vol. 14, no. 4)*

INTERNATIONAL INSTITUTE FOR STRATEGIC STUDIES. Adelphi Papers. No. 133. The diffusion of power: I. Proliferation of force; [papers presented at the 18th annual conference of the IISS at Baden bei Wien, 1976]. London, 1977. pp. 41.

STOCKHOLM INTERNATIONAL PEACE RESEARCH INSTITUTE. World armaments: the nuclear threat. Stockholm, [1977]. pp. 39.

— Testing.

KALIADIN (ALEKSANDR NIKOLAEVICH) Problemy zapreshcheniia ispytanii i rasprostraneniia iadernogo oruzhiia. Moskva, 1976. pp. 350.

ATOMIC WEAPONS AND DISARMAMENT.

ARMS, defense policy and arms control; essays by Franklin A. Long [and others]; edited by Franklin A. Long and George W. Rathjens. New York, [1976]. pp. 222.

KALIADIN (ALEKSANDR NIKOLAEVICH) Problemy zapreshcheniia ispytanii i rasprostraneniia iadernogo oruzhiia. Moskva, 1976. pp. 350.

PENTZ (MICHAEL) The nuclear arms race: new dangers: new possibilities of disarmament. London, [1976]. pp. 15.

STANFORD UNIVERSITY. Stanford Arms Control Group. International arms control: issues and agreements; edited by John H. Barton and Lawrence D. Weiler. Stanford, Calif., 1976. pp. 444. *bibliog.*

STOCKHOLM INTERNATIONAL PEACE RESEARCH INSTITUTE. Armaments and disarmament in the nuclear age: a handbook; (edited by...Marek Thee). Atlantic Highlands, N.J., [1976]. pp. 306. *bibliog.*

KENT (BRUCE) and others. Christians and nuclear disarmament. London, [1977]. pp. 17. *(Campaign for Nuclear Disarmament. Christian Group. Christian CND Pamphlets)*

LENS (SIDNEY) The day before doomsday: an anatomy of the nuclear arms race. New York, 1977. pp. 274.

ATTITUDE (PSYCHOLOGY).

FISHBEIN (MARTIN) and others. Voting behaviour in Britain: an attitudinal analysis. London, Social Science Research Council Survey Unit, [1976]. pp. 69, 19. *bibliog. (Occasional Papers in Survey Research. 7)*

ATTITUDE CHANGE.

STANFORTH (JOHN) Role conflict and attitude change: a study of the effects of teaching practice on third year students at a college of education. 1977. fo. 244. *bibliog. Typescript. Ph.D. (London) thesis: unpublished. This thesis is the property of London University and may not be removed from the Library.*

AUCKLAND

— City planning.

AUCKLAND. City Council. Objectives '76. Auckland, [N.Z.], [1976]. pp. 168.

AUDIO-VISUAL EDUCATION

— Cost effectiveness.

OATEY (MICHAEL JOHN) The cost-effectiveness of different media of instruction with special reference to industrial training. 1976. fo. 353. *bibliog. Typescript. Ph.D.(London) thesis: unpublished. This thesis is the property of London University and may not be removed from the Library.*

AUDITING.

MAIR (WILLIAM C.) Computer control and audit. 2nd ed. Altamonte Springs, Fla., 1976. pp. 489. *bibliog. Table in end pocket.*

AUDITORY PERCEPTION.

PLOMP (REINER) Aspects of tone sensation: a psychophysical study. London, 1976. pp. 167. *bibliog.*

AUSTRALIA

— Armed forces — Pay, allowances, etc.

AUSTRALIA. Committee of Inquiry into Financial Terms and Conditions of Service for Male and Female Members of the Regular Armed Forces. 1971. Report no.2. Other ranks' pay; [John R. Kerr, chairman]. in AUSTRALIA. Parliament. Parliamentary papers, 1971, vol.2.

— Constitution.

TASMANIA. Parliamentary Delegation to the Australian Constitutional Convention. 1975. Report to Parliament on the...Convention;...W.A. Neilson, leader. in TASMANIA. Parliament. Journals and Printed Papers. 1975, no.75.

LABOUR and the constitution, 1972-1975: essays and commentaries on the constitutional controversies of the Whitlam years in Australian government; edited by Gareth Evans. Melbourne, 1977. pp. 383. *Proceedings of a seminar sponsored by the Faculty of Law of the University of Melbourne in 1976 to commemorate the 75th Anniversary of the Australian Federation.*

— Defences.

MEANEY (NEVILLE KINGSLEY) A history of Australian defence and foreign policy, 1901-23. Sydney, 1976 in progress. *bibliog.*

— Economic conditions.

COMMONWEALTH BANKING CORPORATION [AUSTRALIA]. Annual report. a., (formerly s-a.) 1912 (1st)- Canberra. *Included in AUSTRALIA. Parliament. [Parliamentary papers].*

AUSTRALIA. 1968. Australia: [economic fact sheets]. [Canberra?, 1968]. 14 pts. (in 1 vol.).

— Emigration and immigration.

AUSTRALIA. Department of Education. Migrant education programme. Report. a., 1970/71 [1st]- Canberra. *Included in AUSTRALIA. Parliament. [Parliamentary papers].*

AUSTRALIA. Commonwealth Bureau of Census and Statistics. 1973. Assisted and unassisted migrants, August 1972. Canberra, 1973. pp. 7.

CHEDA (GIORGIO) L'emigrazione ticinese in Australia. [Locarno], 1976. 2 vols. *bibliog.*

— Foreign relations.

BELL (CORAL) Crises and Australian diplomacy. Canberra, 1973. pp. 34. *(Australian National University. Arthur F. Yencken Memorial Lectures. 1972)*

AUSTRALIA. Department of Foreign Affairs. 1975- . Documents on Australian foreign policy, 1937-49; [edited by] R.G. Neale [and others]. Canberra, 1975 in progress.

MEANEY (NEVILLE KINGSLEY) A history of Australian defence and foreign policy, 1901-23. Sydney, 1976 in progress. *bibliog.*

AUSTRALIA in the new world order: foreign policy in the 1970s. Melbourne, 1976. pp. 156. *Essays based on the discussions of a study group of the Victorian Branch of the Australian Institute of International Affairs, 1972-3.*

See also EUROPEAN ECONOMIC COMMUNITY — Australia.

— Military policy.

MEANEY (NEVILLE KINGSLEY) A history of Australian defence and foreign policy, 1901-23. Sydney, 1976 in progress. *bibliog.*

— Native races.

AUSTRALIA. Office of Aboriginal Affairs. Commonwealth Capital Fund for Aboriginal Enterprises. Annual report. a., 1968/69 (1st)- Canberra. *Included in AUSTRALIA. Parliament. [Parliamentary papers].*

HARRISON (BARBARA) Outside down under: the history, conditions and struggle of the Australian Aborigines. Denver, Colo., [1971]. pp. 29. *(Denver. University. Center on International Race Relations. Studies in Race and Nations. vol. 3, No. 1)*

— Officials and employees.

COMPENDIUM OF AUSTRALIAN PUBLIC SERVICE INFORMATION; [pd. by] Public Service Board. a., current issue only. Canberra.

— Parliament — Privileges and immunities.

AUSTRALIA. Parliament. House of Representatives. Committee of Privileges. 1971. Report relating to an article published in the Daily Telegraph, 27 August 1971, together with minutes of proceedings and minutes of evidence of the Committee; [E.N. Drury, chairman]. in AUSTRALIA. Parliament. Parliamentary papers, 1971, vol.11.

AUSTRALIA. Parliament. Senate. Committee of Privileges. 1971. Report upon articles in The Sunday Australian and The Sunday Review of 2 May 1971; [T.C. Drake-Brockman, chairman]. in AUSTRALIA. Parliament. Parliamentary papers, 1971, vol.11.

— — Salaries, allowances, etc.

AUSTRALIA. Inquiry into the Salaries and Allowances of Members of the Commonwealth Parliament. 1971. Salaries and allowances of members of the parliament of the commonwealth; report of inquiry by Mr. Justice Kerr. in AUSTRALIA. Parliament. Parliamentary papers, 1971, vol.7.

— Politics and government.

ROBERTSON (JOHN) Historian. J.H. Scullin: a political biography. Nedlands, W.A. 1974. pp. 495. *bibliog.*

AUSTRALIA. Task Force on a Regional Basis for Australian Government Administration. 1975. A regional basis for Australian government administration: Task Force report: report to the Royal Commission on Australian Government Administration by a Task Force appointed...to design a flexible basis for administration at regional and local levels. [Canberra], 1975. 2 vols. (in 1.). *bibliog.*

AITKIN (DONALD ALEXANDER) Stability and change in Australian politics. Canberra, 1977. pp. 301.

CONNELL (ROBERT WILLIAM) Ruling class, ruling culture: studies of conflict, power and hegemony in Australian life. Cambridge, 1977. pp. 250.

LABOUR and the constitution, 1972-1975: essays and commentaries on the constitutional controversies of the Whitlam years in Australian government; edited by Gareth Evans. Melbourne, 1977. pp. 383. *Proceedings of a seminar sponsored by the Faculty of Law of the University of Melbourne in 1976 to commemorate the 75th Anniversary of the Australian Federation.*

POWER (FRANCIS RENTON) The fight for "life", 1975. Sandringham, Victoria, [1977]. pp. 63.

REFORMING Australian government: the Coombs report and beyond; Cameron Hazlehurst and J.R. Nethercote, editors. Canberra, 1977. pp. 201. *Proceedings of a conference held by the Australian Capital Territory Regional Group of the Royal Institute of Public Administration.*

— Population.

AUSTRALIA. Commonwealth Bureau of Census and Statistics. 1974. Internal migration, 1969-70 to 1972-73. Canberra, 1974. pp. 18.

AUSTRALIA. Cities Commission. 1975. Studies of Australian internal migration 1966-1971. [Canberra], 1975. pp. 92. *(Occasional Papers. No.2)*

— Race question.

HARRISON (BARBARA) Outside down under: the history, conditions and struggle of the Australian Aborigines. Denver, Colo., [1971]. pp. 29. *(Denver. University. Center on International Race Relations. Studies in Race and Nations. vol. 3, No. 1)*

GALE (FAY) and BROOKMAN (ALISON) Race relations in Australia: the aborigines. Sydney, [1975]. pp. 138. *bibliog.*

PITTOCK (A. BARRIE) Beyond white Australia: a short history of race relations in Australia. Surry Hills, N.S.W., 1975. pp. 51.

— Relations (general) with Canada.

CORBETT (DAVID CHARLES) Looking at Canada. Melbourne, 1976. pp. 226. *bibliog.*

— Relations (general) with Papua New Guinea.

HASLUCK (Sir PAUL MEERNAA CAEDWALLA) A time for building: Australian administration in Papua and New Guinea 1951-1963. Melbourne, 1976. pp. 452.

— Relations (general) with the Indian Ocean Region.

AUSTRALIA. Parliament. Joint Committee on Foreign Affairs. 1971. Report...on the Indian Ocean region; [J.P. Sim, chairman]. in AUSTRALIA. Parliament. Parliamentary papers, 1971, vol.8.

— Relations (general) with the United States.

FOX (ANNETTE BAKER) The politics of attraction: four middle powers and the United States. New York, 1977. pp. 371.

— Social conditions.

SOCIALISATION in Australia; edited by F.J. Hunt. Sydney, 1972. pp. 317.

— Social history.

MENDELSOHN (RONALD SALI) The condition of the Australian people since federation. [Canberra], 1975. fo. 21. *(Australian National University. Department of History. Work in Progress Seminars. 1975)*

AUSTRALIAN ABORIGINES.

PITTOCK (A. BARRIE) Aboriginal land rights. Copenhagen, 1973. pp. 24. *(International Work Group for Indigenous Affairs. Documents. 3)*

GALE (FAY) and BROOKMAN (ALISON) Race relations in Australia: the aborigines. Sydney, [1975]. pp. 138. *bibliog.*

— Education.

SOMMERLAD (ELIZABETH ANN) Kormilda, the way to tomorrow?: a study in Aboriginal education. Canberra, 1976. pp. 187. *bibliog.*

AUSTRALIAN CAPITAL TERRITORY

— Politics and government.

AUSTRALIA. Department of the Capital Territory. 1973. Inquiry into self-government for the Australian Capital Territory: statement of evidence for presentation to the Joint Committee on the A[ustralian] C[apital] T[erritory]. Canberra, 1973. pp. 71. *bibliog.*

AUSTRALIA. Department of the Capital Territory. 1974. Inquiry into self-government for the Australian Capital Territory: second statement of evidence for presentation to the Joint Committee on the A[ustralian] C[apital] T[erritory]. Canberra, 1974. pp. 65.

AUSTRALIAN CAPITAL TERRITORY ADVISORY COUNCIL. Inquiry into self-government for the Australian Capital Territory: statement of evidence for presentation to the Joint Committee on the [Australian] C[apital] T[erritory]. [Canberra], 1974. pp. 34.

DALGARNO (ANN PATRICIA) Evidence given to the inquiry into self-government for the Australian Capital Territory; presented to the Joint Committee on the A[ustralian] C[apital] T[erritory]. [Canberra], Australian Capital Territory Advisory Council, 1974. pp. 9. *Cover title: Case against self-government for the Australian Capital Territory.*

— Statistics.

AUSTRALIAN CAPITAL TERRITORY STATISTICAL SUMMARY; (pd. by) Commonwealth Bureau of Census and Statistics. a., 1976 (13th)- Canberra.

AUSTRIA

— Annexation to Germany.

BOTZ (GERHARD) Die Eingliederung Österreichs in das Deutsche Reich: Planung und Verwirklichung des politisch-administrativen Anschlusses, 1938-1940. 2nd ed. Wien, [1976]. pp. 194. *bibliog. (Ludwig-Boltzmann-Institut für Geschichte der Arbeiterbewegung. Schriftenreihe. 1)*

— Civilization.

HOVORKA (NIKOLAUS) Der Kampf um die geistige Wiedergeburt Österreichs: Vortrag, gehalten...am 26. Jänner 1946. Wien, 1946. pp. 30. *(Kommunistische Partei Österreichs. Zentralstelle für Volksbildung. Vortragsreihe "Probleme der Zeit". Heft 3)*

KOTLAN-WERNER (HENRIETTE) Kunst und Volk: David Josef Bach, 1874-1947. Wien, 1977. pp. 174. *(Ludwig-Boltzmann-Institut für Geschichte der Arbeiterbewegung. Materialien zur Arbeiterbewegung. Nr. 6)*

— Constitutional history.

WALTER (FRIEDRICH) of Vienna. Die theresianische Staatsreform von 1749. München, [1958]. pp. 71. *(Arbeitskreis für Österreichische Geschichte. Österreich Archiv)*

HASIBA (GERNOT D.) Die zweite Bundes-Verfassungsnovelle von 1929: ihr Werdegang und wesentliche verfassungspolitische Ereignisse seit 1918. Wien, 1976. pp. 215. *bibliog. (Gesellschaft zur Förderung der Forschungen zur Europäischen und Vergleichenden Rechtsgeschichte. Forschungen zur Europäischen und Vergleichenden Rechtsgeschichte. Band 1)*

— Constitutional law.

HASIBA (GERNOT D.) Die zweite Bundes-Verfassungsnovelle von 1929: ihr Werdegang und wesentliche verfassungspolitische Ereignisse seit 1918. Wien, 1976. pp. 215. *bibliog. (Gesellschaft zur Förderung der Forschungen zur Europäischen und Vergleichenden Rechtsgeschichte. Forschungen zur Europäischen und Vergleichenden Rechtsgeschichte. Band 1)*

— Defences.

OESTERREICHISCHE VOLKSPARTEI. Konzeptive Grundlagen für die Landesverteidigungspolitik. [Vienna], 1975. pp. 12.

— Economic history.

GERSCHENKRON (ALEXANDER) An economic spurt that failed: four lectures in Austrian history. Princeton, N.J., 1977. pp. 171. *(Princeton University. Woodrow Wilson School of Public and International Affairs. Eliot Janeway Lectures on Historical Economics. 1973)*

MEJZLIK (HEINRICH) Die Eisenbewirtschaftung im Ersten Weltkrieg: die Planwirtschaft des k. u. k. Kriegsministeriums. Wien, [1977]. pp. 781. *bibliog.*

— Economic policy.

AUSCH (KARL) Die neue Wirtschaft im neuen Österreich;...mit einem Vorwort von Stefan Wirlandner. 2nd ed. Wien, [1947]. pp. 24.

— Foreign relations.

GRUBER (KARL) Ein politisches Leben: Österreichs Weg zwischen den Diktaturen. Wien, [1976]. pp. 300.

— — Germany.

BAGDASARIAN (NICHOLAS DER) The Austro-German rapprochement, 1870-1879: from the Battle of Sedan to the Dual Alliance. Rutherford, N.J., [1976]. pp. 334. *bibliog.*

— History — 1848-1849, Revolution — Bibliography.

HARVARD UNIVERSITY. Library. Houghton Library. 1848: Austrian revolutionary broadsides and pamphlets: a catalogue of the collection in the Houghton Library, Harvard University; compiled by James E. Walsh. Boston, Mass., [1976]. pp. 286.

— — 1918-1939.

BOTZ (GERHARD) Gewalt in der Politik: Attentate, Zusammenstösse, Putschversuche, Unruhen in Österreich, 1918 bis 1934. München, 1976. pp. 358. *bibliog.*

— — 1934, Socialist Uprising, February.

Das JAHR 1934: 12. Februar; Protokoll des Symposiums in Wien am 5. Februar 1974; (herausgegeben von Ludwig Jedlicka und Rudolf Neck). Wien, 1975. pp. 163. *bibliog. (Theodor-Körner-Stiftungsfonds and Leopold-Kunschak-Preis. Wissenschaftliche Kommission zur Erforschung der Österreichischen Geschichte der Jahre 1927 bis 1938. Veröffentlichungen. Band 2)*

— — 1938-1945.

BOTZ (GERHARD) Die Eingliederung Österreichs in das Deutsche Reich: Planung und Verwirklichung des politisch-administrativen Anschlusses, 1938-1940. 2nd ed. Wien, [1976]. pp. 194. *bibliog. (Ludwig-Boltzmann-Institut für Geschichte der Arbeiterbewegung. Schriftenreihe. 1)*

— Nationalrat.

OESTERREICHISCHER ARBEITER- UND ANGESTELLTENBUND. ÖAAB im Parlament. [Vienna, 1973]. pp. 75. *(Gesellschaftspolitische Informationen. 6)*

MACHUNZE (ERWIN) Vom Rechtlosen zum Gleichberechtigten: die Flüchtlings- und Vertriebenenfrage im Wiener Parlament. Salzburg, 1974-76. 2 vols.(in 1).

— Politics and government.

WALTER (FRIEDRICH) of Vienna. Die theresianische Staatsreform von 1749. München, [1958]. pp. 71. *(Arbeitskreis für Österreichische Geschichte. Österreich Archiv)*

KLUB DER SOZIALISTISCHEN ABGEORDNETEN UND BUNDESRÄTE. Die Bundesregierung informiert: verwirklicht und gehalten; ein Leistungsbericht der Regierung Kreisky. 2nd ed. Wien, 1971. pp. 104.

OESTERREICHISCHER ARBEITER- UND ANGESTELLTENBUND. ÖAAB im Parlament. [Vienna, 1973]. pp. 75. *(Gesellschaftspolitische Informationen. 6)*

KNOLL (REINHOLD) and MAYER (ANTON) Austrian political writer. Österreichische Konsensdemokratie in Theorie und Praxis: Staat, Interessenverbände, Parteien und die politische Wirklichkeit. Wien, 1976. pp. 198. *bibliog.*

MOMMSEN-REINDL (MARGARETA) Die österreichische Proporzdemokratie und der Fall Habsburg. Wien, 1976. pp. 264. *bibliog.*

VODOPIVEC (ALEXANDER) Die Dritte Republik: Machtstrukturen in Österreich. Wien, [1976?]. pp. 336.

— Statistics.

KAMMER FÜR ARBEITER UND ANGESTELLTE FÜR OBERÖSTERREICH. Die Lebenshaltung von Arbeitern und Angestellten in Linz, 1974. [Linz], 1976. fo.67. *(Statistik. Heft 48)* 120 tables appended.

AUSTRIA-HUNGARY

— Economic history.

RUDOLPH (RICHARD L.) Banking and industrialization in Austria-Hungary: the role of banks in the industrialization of the Czech Crownlands, 1873-1914. Cambridge, 1976. pp. 291. *bibliog.*

— History.

ANDICS (HELLMUT) Der Untergang der Donaumonarchie: Österreich-Ungarn von der Jahrhundertwende bis zum November 1918. Wien, [1976]. pp. 348.

— Nationalism.

ČESKÝ národ ve světové válce a vídeňská vláda: dotaz poslanců Františka Staňka...Zdeňka Tobolky a soudruhů na... ministerského předsedu v příčině chování se vládních kruhů k českému národu za války. Pardubice, 1917. pp. 129.

AUSTRIAN PERIODICALS.

EBNETH (RUDOLF) Die österreichische Wochenschrift "Der Christliche Ständestaat": deutsche Emigration in Österreich, 1933- 1938. Mainz, [1976]. pp. 271. *bibliog. (Kommission für Zeitgeschichte. Veröffentlichungen. Reihe B: Forschungen. Band 19)*

AUSTRIAN SCHOOL OF ECONOMISTS.

The FOUNDATIONS of modern Austrian economics; edited with an introduction by Edwin G. Dolan. Kansas City, [1976]. pp. 238. *bibliog. Proceedings of a conference sponsored by the Institute for Humane Studies and held at Royalton College, Vt., in June 1974.*

GERSCHENKRON (ALEXANDER) An economic spurt that failed: four lectures in Austrian history. Princeton, N.J., 1977. pp. 171. *(Princeton University. Woodrow Wilson School of Public and International Affairs. Eliot Janeway Lectures on Historical Economics. 1973)*

AUTHORITARIANISM.

KAUFMAN (ROBERT R.) Transitions to stable authoritarian-corporate regimes: the Chilean case?. Beverly Hills, [1976]. pp. 68. *bibliog.*

WHIMSTER (MICHAEL STEPHEN) Patrimonialism: its meaning for nineteenth century German historians with special reference to Max Weber's adoption and use of the term in his Herrschaftssoziologie. 1976. fo.172. *bibliog. Typescript. Ph.D. (London) thesis: unpublished. This thesis is the property of London University and may not be removed from the Library.*

AUTHORITARIANISM and corporatism in Latin America; James M. Malloy, editor. Pittsburgh, [1977]. pp. 549. *bibliog. Papers of a conference held at the University of Pittsburgh in April 1974, and sponsored by its Center for International Studies.*

AUTHORITY.

WISE (CHARLES R.) Clients evaluate authority: the view from the other side. Beverly Hills, [1976]. pp. 91. *bibliog.*

AUTHORITY.(Cont.)

KIECHL (ROLF) Zur Autorität in der Unternehmensführung: normative Überlegungen über die Autoritätsformen im kooperativen Führungsstil. [Zurich], 1977. pp. 221. *bibliog. Dissertation der Universität Zürich zur Erlangung der Würde eines Doktors der Wirtschaftswissenschaft.*

AUTHORS AND PUBLISHERS

— Yugoslavia.

YUGOSLAVIA. Statutes, etc. 1965. Zbirka zakona o štampi, novinskim i izdavačkim preduzećima i ustanovama, radio-saobraćaju i radio-difuznim ustanovama i autorskom pravu. Beograd, 1965. pp. 131. *(Zbirka Saveznih Propisa. br.31)*

AUTOMATION

— Underdeveloped areas.

See UNDERDEVELOPED AREAS — Automation.

AUTOMOBILE INDUSTRY AND TRADE

— America, Latin.

JENKINS (RHYS OWEN) Dependent industrialization in Latin America: the automotive industry in Argentina, Chile, and Mexico. New York, 1977. pp. 298.

— France.

FRIDENSON (PATRICK) Histoire des usines Renault: 1 : naissance de la grande entreprise, 1898-1939. Paris, [1972]. pp. 359. *bibliog.*

FRANCE. Groupe sectoriel d'Analyse et de Prévision Matériels de Transport. 1976. Rapport...: préparation du 7e Plan. Paris, 1976. pp. 96.

LAUX (JAMES M.) In first gear: the French automobile industry to 1914. Liverpool, 1976. pp. 239. *bibliog.*

— Germany.

DIEKMANN (ACHIM) Die Automobilnachfrage als Konjunkturund Wachstumsfaktor: eine Input-Output-Studie. Tübingen, [1975]. pp. 489. *bibliog. (Tübingen. Institut für Angewandte Wirtschaftsforschung. Schriftenreihe. Band 29)*

— Sweden.

LINDHOLM (ROLF) and NORSTEDT (JAN-PEDER) The Volvo report;...translated by David Jenkins. [Stockholm, 1975]. pp. 92.

— United Kingdom.

NOCKOLDS (HAROLD) Lucas: the first hundred years. Newton Abbot, [1976 in progress]. *bibliog.*

AMALGAMATED UNION OF ENGINEERING WORKERS. Technical and Supervisory Section. A policy for the British motor vehicle industry: a trade union response to the government White Paper (January 1976, Cmnd. 6377). Richmond, Surrey, 1976. pp. 28. *bibliog.*

FILBY (PETER) TVR: success against the odds. London, 1976. pp. 224.

OVERY (R.J.) William Morris, Viscount Nuffield. London, [1976]. pp. 151. *bibliog.*

RICHARDSON (KENNETH) The British motor industry, 1896-1939;...assisted by C. N. O'Gallagher. London, 1977. pp. 258. *bibliog.*

YOUNG (STEPHEN) and HOOD (NEIL) Chrysler U.K.: a corporation in transition. New York, 1977. pp. 342.

AUTOMOBILE INDUSTRY WORKERS

— Italy.

MOTOR industry study tour report; [edited by Ed Coker and Walter Kendall]. Oxford, [1976]. pp. 78.

— United States.

WIDICK (B.J.) ed. Auto work and its discontents. Baltimore, [1976]. pp. 112. *bibliog.*

AUTOMOBILES

— Apparatus and supplies.

NOCKOLDS (HAROLD) Lucas: the first hundred years. Newton Abbot, [1976 in progress]. *bibliog.*

— Laws and regulations — United States.

PELTZMAN (SAM) Regulation of automobile safety. Washington, 1975. pp. 53. *(American Enterprise Institute for Public Policy Research. Evaluative Studies. 26)*

— Safety measures.

PELTZMAN (SAM) Regulation of automobile safety. Washington, 1975. pp. 53. *(American Enterprise Institute for Public Policy Research. Evaluative Studies. 26)*

— Service stations — Ireland (Republic).

EIRE. Fair Trade Commission. 1971. Report of enquiry into the conditions which obtain in regard to the supply and distribution of motor spirit in so far as they effect the nature and growth in numbers of motor spirit retail outlets. Dublin, [1971]. pp. 83.

AVIGNON.

FRANCE. Direction de la Documentation. La Documentation Française. Notes et Etudes Documentaires. Nos. 4,359-4, 360-4,361. Les villes françaises: Avignon; par Christiane et Jean-Michel Spill. Paris, 1977. pp. 87. *bibliog.*

AVON

— Social conditions.

AVON. County Council. Planning Department. Avon County structure plan: situation reports. Bristol, 1976. 10 parts (in 1 vol.)

— Social policy.

AVON. County Council. Planning Department. Avon County structure plan: situation reports. Bristol, 1976. 10 parts (in 1 vol.)

AYRES (CLARENCE EDWIN).

SCIENCE and ceremony: the institutional economics of C.E. Ayres; edited by William Breit and William Patton Culbertson; foreword by John Kenneth Galbraith. Austin, Texas, [1976]. pp. 210. *bibliog.*

AYRSHIRE

— Economic history.

CZERKAWSKA (CATHERINE LUCY) Fisher-folk of Carrick: a history of the fishing industry in South Ayrshire. Glasgow, 1975. pp. 59. *bibliog.*

AZCARATE Y FLOREZ (PABLO DE).

AZCARATE Y FLOREZ (PABLO DE) Mi embajada en Londres durante la guerra civil española. Barcelona, 1976. pp. 403.

AZERBAIJAN

— History — Sources.

TSENTRAL'NAIA bol'shevistskaia pechat' ob Azerbaidzhane, 1905- 1907 gg.: sbornik materialov. Baku, 1976. pp. 200.

— Politics and government.

ALIEV (GEIDER ALIRZA) Otchetnyi doklad Tsentral'nogo Komiteta Kompartii Azerbaidzhana XXIX s"ezdu Kommunisticheskoi partii Azerbaidzhana, 28 ianvaria 1976 goda. Baku, 1976. pp. 101.

MESHADI Azizbekov, plamennyi borets za vlast' Sovetov: rechi, dokumenty i materialy. Baku, 1976. pp. 286.

— Social conditions.

ZEMTSOV (IL'IA GRIGOR'EVICH) Partiia ili mafiia?: razvorovannaia respublika. Paris, 1976. pp. 125.

— Statistics.

AZERBAIJAN. Tsentral'noe Statisticheskoe Upravlenie. 1975. Azerbaidzhan v tsifrakh v 1974 godu: kratkii statisticheskii sbornik. Baku, 1975. pp. 126.

AZERBAIJANI NEWSPAPERS.

TSENTRAL'NAIA bol'shevistskaia pechat' ob Azerbaidzhane, 1905- 1907 gg.: sbornik materialov. Baku, 1976. pp. 200.

AZIZBEKOV (MESHADI AZIM-BEK-OGLY).

MESHADI Azizbekov, plamennyi borets za vlast' Sovetov: rechi, dokumenty i materialy. Baku, 1976. pp. 286.

BACH (DAVID JOSEF).

KOTLAN-WERNER (HENRIETTE) Kunst und Volk: David Josef Bach, 1874-1947. Wien, 1977. pp. 174. *(Ludwig-Boltzmann-Institut für Geschichte der Arbeiterbewegung. Materialien zur Arbeiterbewegung. Nr. 6)*

BACON (FRANCIS) Viscount St. Albans.

EPSTEIN (JOEL J.) Francis Bacon: a political biography. Athens, Ohio, [1977]. pp. 187.

BADEN

— Politics and government.

THIEL (JUERGEN) Die Grossblockpolitik der Nationalliberalen Partei Badens, 1905 bis 1914: ein Beitrag zur Zusammenarbeit von Liberalismus und Sozialdemokratie in der Spätphase des Wilhelminischen Deutschlands. Stuttgart, 1976. pp. 283. *bibliog. (Kommission für Geschichtliche Landeskunde in Baden-Württemberg. Veröffentlichungen. Reihe B: Forschungen. 86. Band)*

BAEUMLER (ALFRED).

JOCH (WINFRIED) Politische Leibeserziehung und ihre Theorie im nationalsozialistischen Deutschland: Voraussetzungen, Begründungszusammenhang, Dokumentation. Bern, 1976. pp. 249. *bibliog.*

BAIKAL-AMUR RAILWAY.

SHABAD (THEODORE) and MOTE (VICTOR L.) Gateway to Siberian resources: the BAM. New York, 1977. pp. 189. *bibliogs.*

BAIL

— United States.

THOMAS (WAYNE H.) Bail reform in America. Berkeley, Calif., [1976]. pp. 272.

BAKERS AND BAKERIES

— Germany.

GOETTMANN (FRANK) Die Frankfurter Bäckerzunft im späten Mittelalter: Aufbau und Aufgaben städtischer Handwerkergenossenschaften. Frankfurt am Main, 1975. pp. 128. *bibliog. (Frankfurter Verein für Geschichte und Landeskunde. Studien zur Frankfurter Geschichte. Heft 10)*

BAKERY EMPLOYEES

— Switzerland.

MUELLER-TRENKA (J.) Fünfzig Jahre Bäcker und Konditoren, Sektion Zürich, V[erband der] H[andels-,] T[ransport- und] L[ebensmittelarbeiter], 1897-1947, etc. [Zürich, 1947?]. pp. 88.

— United Kingdom.

DITTON (JASON) Part-time crime: an ethnography of fiddling and pilferage. London, 1977. pp. 195. *bibliog.*

BAKU

— Industries.

ISMAILOV (MAKHMUD A.) Promyshlennost' Baku v nachale XX veka. Baku, 1976. pp. 153.

BAKUNIN (MIKHAIL ALEKSANDROVICH).

DAVE (VICTOR) Michel Bakounine et Karl Marx. [Bordeaux, 1970?]. pp. 55. *Originally published in Paris in 1900.*

HERZEN, Ogarev, Bakounine: lettres inédites; introduction, traductions et notes par Michel Mervaud. Paris, 1975. pp. 158. *With French translations of letters in German and Russian. Includes in addition eight letters from Victor Hugo to Herzen.*

MIKHAILOV (MIKHAIL IVANOVICH) Bor'ba protiv bakunizma v I Internatsionale. Moskva, 1976. pp. 351.

BAKUNIN (MIKHAIL ALEKSANDROVICH) The confession of Mikhail Bakunin: with the marginal comments of Tsar Nicholas I; translated by Robert C. Howes; introduction and notes by Lawrence D. Orton. Ithaca, N.Y., 1977. pp. 200. *Translation of Ispoved'.*

BALANCE OF PAYMENTS.

WEILLER (JEAN) La balance des paiements. 3rd ed. Paris, 1974. pp. 128. *bibliog.*

GRUBEL (HERBERT G.) Domestic origins of the monetary approach to the balance of payments. Princeton, 1976. pp. 18. *bibliog. (Princeton University. Department of Economics and Sociology. International Finance Section. Essays in International Finance. No. 117)*

— Mathematical models.

KYLE (JOHN F.) The balance of payments in a monetary economy. Princeton, N.J., [1976]. pp. 192. *bibliog. (Omicron Delta Epsilon. Irving Fisher Award Series)*

INTERNATIONAL MONETARY FUND. 1977. The monetary approach to the balance of payments: a collection of research papers by members of the staff of the International Monetary Fund. Washington, 1977. pp. 290. *bibliogs.*

— France.

FRANCE. Direction du Trésor. Règlements entre la France et l'extérieur. a., 1975- [Paris].

— United Kingdom.

BELYI (PAVEL FEDOROVICH) Platezhnyi balans Anglii: teorii i deistvitel'nost'. Leningrad, 1976. pp. 104.

ROBINSON (COLIN) and MORGAN (JON) Effects of North Sea oil on the United Kingdom's balance of payments. London, [1976]. fo. 39. *(University of Surrey. Department of Economics. Guest Papers. No. 5)*

U.K. Central Office of Information. Reference Division. 1976. Britain's overseas trade and payments. rev. ed. London, 1976. pp. 24. *bibliog.*

CASE studies in international economics; edited by Peter Maunder; [by] Peter Barker [and others]. London, 1977. pp. 87. *bibliogs. (Economics Association. Case Studies in Economic Analysis. 6)*

NATIONAL ECONOMIC DEVELOPMENT OFFICE. International price competitiveness, non-price factors and export performance. London, 1977. pp. 45. *bibliog.*

— United States.

MACHLUP (FRITZ) International payments, debts and gold; collected essays. 2nd ed. New York, 1976. pp. 514.

BALANCE OF POWER.

LUTTWAK (EDWARD) Strategic power: military capabilities and political utility. Beverly Hills, [1976]. pp. 70. *bibliog. (Georgetown University. Center for Strategic and International Studies. Washington Papers. vol. 4/38)*

QUESTER (GEORGE H.) Offense and defense in the international system. New York, [1977]. pp. 219.

BALANCE OF TRADE

— Bangladesh.

BANGLADESH. Provincial Statistical Board and Bureau of Commercial and Industrial Intelligence. Trade supplement: an account relating to the foreign trade, coastal trade, navigation, East Bengal Railway. Statistics and balance of trade of East Pakistan. m., Je 1958. Dacca.

BALDWIN (ROGER NASH).

LAMSON (PEGGY) Roger Baldwin, founder of the American Civil Liberties Union: a portrait. Boston, [Mass.], 1976. pp. 304.

BALKAN STATES

— Commerce.

CLARK (CAL) and FARLOW (ROBERT L.) Comparative patterns of foreign policy and trade: the communist Balkans and international trade. Bloomington, [1976]. pp. 152. *(Indiana University. International Development Research Center. Studies in East European and Soviet Planning, Development and Trade. No. 23)*

— Defences.

INTERNATIONAL INSTITUTE FOR STRATEGIC STUDIES. Adelphi Papers. No. 135. Balkan security; by F. Stephen Larrabee. London, 1977. pp. 44.

— Economic history.

ČUBRILOVIĆ (VASA) and others, eds. Svetska ekonomska kriza, 1929-1934 godine i njen odraz u zemljama jugoistočne Evrope; Crise économique mondiale, 1929-1934 et ses reflets dans les pays du Sud-Est européen. Beograd, 1976. pp. 424. *(Srpska Akademija Nauka i Umetnosti. Balkanološki Institut. Posebna Izdanja. knj.5) Articles in English or French with Serbo-Croat summaries, or in Serbo-Croat with French summaries.*

— Foreign economic relations.

Les GRANDES puissances et les Balkans à la veille et au début de la Deuxieme Guerre mondiale, 1937-1941; conférence internationale, Sofia, 21-16 avril, 1971; (rédaction, Nikolaj Todorov, Christina Mihova). Sofia, 1973. pp. 430. *(Bulgarska Akademiia na Naukite. Institut za Balkanistika. Studia Balcanica. 7) In various languages.*

— Foreign relations.

Les GRANDES puissances et les Balkans à la veille et au début de la Deuxieme Guerre mondiale, 1937-1941; conférence internationale, Sofia, 21-16 avril, 1971; (rédaction, Nikolaj Todorov, Christina Mihova). Sofia, 1973. pp. 430. *(Bulgarska Akademiia na Naukite. Institut za Balkanistika. Studia Balcanica. 7) In various languages.*

CLARK (CAL) and FARLOW (ROBERT L.) Comparative patterns of foreign policy and trade: the communist Balkans and international politics. Bloomington, [1976]. pp. 152. *(Indiana University. International Development Research Center. Studies in East European and Soviet Planning, Development and Trade. No. 23)*

INTERNATIONAL INSTITUTE FOR STRATEGIC STUDIES. Adelphi Papers. No. 135. Balkan security; by F. Stephen Larrabee. London, 1977. pp. 44.

— — France.

DAMIANOV (SIMEON) Frenskata politika na Balkanite, 1829-1853; La politique française aux Balkans, 1829-1853. Sofiia, 1977. pp. 324. *bibliog. With Russian and French summaries.*

— — Russia.

NOVIKOV (NIKOLAI VASIL'EVICH) Puti i pereput'ia diplomata: zapiski o 1943-1944 gg. Moskva, 1976. pp. 256.

— History — 1912-1913, War of.

SOZIALDEMOKRATISCHE PARTEI DEUTSCHLANDS. Vorstand. Die Greuel des Krieges. [Berlin, 1912]. pp. 16. *(Sozialdemokratische Flugschriften. 14) Wanting title-page.*

— Nationalism.

Les LUMIÈRES et la formation de la conscience nationale chez les peuples du Sud-Est européen: actes du Colloque international organisé par la Commission de l'AIESEE pour l'histoire des idées...Paris, 11-12 avril 1968. Bucarest, 1970. pp. 129.

BALLOT.

SYMONS (JELINGER COOKSON) Ought electors to elect?: ten minutes talk on the ballot; illustrated by diagrams. 2nd ed. London, Effingham Wilson and Henry Hetherington, [1837]. pp. (6).

BALTIC ENTENTE, 1934- .

KASLAS (BRONIS J.) The Baltic nations: the quest for regional integration and political liberty: Estonia, Latvia, Lithuania, Finland, Poland. Pittston, Penn., 1976. pp. 319. *bibliog.*

BALTIC STATES

— History.

KASLAS (BRONIS J.) The Baltic nations: the quest for regional integration and political liberty: Estonia, Latvia, Lithuania, Finland, Poland. Pittston, Penn., 1976. pp. 319. *bibliog.*

— Politics and government.

KASLAS (BRONIS J.) The Baltic nations: the quest for regional integration and political liberty: Estonia, Latvia, Lithuania, Finland, Poland. Pittston, Penn., 1976. pp. 319. *bibliog.*

BALTIMORE

— Politics and government.

KREFETZ (SHARON PERLMAN) Welfare policy making and city politics. New York, 1976. pp. 218.

BALUCHISTAN

— Appropriations and expenditures.

ANNUAL DEVELOPMENT PROGRAMME OF BALUCHISTAN; [pd. by] Finance Department. a., 1970/71- , with gap (1971/72) [Quetta].

— Economic policy.

ANNUAL DEVELOPMENT PROGRAMME OF BALUCHISTAN; [pd. by] Finance Department. a., 1970/71- , with gap (1971/72) [Quetta].

— Social policy.

ANNUAL DEVELOPMENT PROGRAMME OF BALUCHISTAN; [pd. by] Finance Department. a., 1970/71- , with gap (1971/72) [Quetta].

BAMBRZY.

PARADOWSKA (MARIA) Bambrzy: mieszkańcy dawnych wsi miasta Poznania. Warszawa, 1975. pp. 177. *(Poznań. Urząd Miasta. Wydział Kultury. Biblioteka Kroniki Miasta Poznania)*

BANABANS.

BINDER (PEARL) Treasure islands: the trials of the Ocean Islanders. London, 1977. pp. 192. *bibliog.*

BANANA TRADE

— America, Latin.

McCANN (THOMAS P.) An American company: the tragedy of United Fruit;...edited by Henry Scammell. New York, [1976]. pp. 244.

BANANA TRADE(Cont.)

— Jamaica.

NORTH LONDON HASLEMERE GROUP. Bananas: a study of the crisis in the Jamaican banana industry. London, [1970?]. 1 pamphlet (unpaged).

BANCO CENTROAMERICANO DE INTEGRACION ECONOMICA.

See CENTRAL AMERICAN BANK FOR ECONOMIC INTEGRATION.

BANCO DE MEXICO.

MEXICO. Statutes, etc. 1917-1953. Legislacion sobre el Banco de Mexico. Mexico, 1958. pp. 436.

BANCO DE PORTUGAL.

PORTUGAL. Statutes, etc. 1975. Banco de Portugal: organic law approved by decree-law No. 644/75 of November 15. Lisbon, 1976. pp. 31.

BANGLADESH.

NARODNAIA Respublika Bangladesh: spravochnik. Moskva, 1974. pp. 199.

— Commerce — Statistics.

BANGLADESH. Provincial Statistical Board and Bureau of Commercial and Industrial Intelligence. Trade supplement: an account relating to the foreign trade, coastal trade, navigation, East Bengal Railway. Statistics and balance of trade of East Pakistan. m., Je 1958. Dacca.

— Economic conditions.

BANGLADESH. Planning Commission. Economic review. a., 1974/75(1st)- Dacca. *Shorter review for 1972-73 and 1973-74 included in BANGLADESH. Planning Commission. Annual plan.*

— Economic policy.

BANGLADESH. Planning Commission. Annual plan. a., 1972/73(1st)- Dacca.

AHMAD (MUZAFFER) Planning and public sector enterprises in Bangladesh. Ljubljana, International Center for Public Enterprises, 1974. pp. 36. *(International Seminar 1974. National Papers)*

NURUL ISLAM. Development planning in Bangladesh: a study in political economy. London, [1977]. pp. 267.

— Emigration and immigration.

TINKER (HUGH) The banyan tree: overseas emigrants from India, Pakistan and Bangladesh. Oxford, 1977. pp. 204.

— Foreign relations — India.

INDIA. Ministry of External Affairs. 1971. Bangla Desh needs political solution: Foreign Minister Sardar Swaran Singh's address to the National Press Club, Washington, June 17, 1971. [New Delhi, 1971]. pp. 23.

INDIA. Prime Minister. 1971. India recognises Bangla Desh: Prime Minister's statement in Parliament and some important communications from Bangla Desh leaders. [Delhi, 1971]. pp. 17.

— History — 1971, Revolution.

CANADA. Parliamentary Delegation to India. 1971. Press conference by the Canadian parliamentary delegation. [New Delhi, Ministry of External Affairs, 1971]. pp. 14.

INDIA. Prime Minister. 1971. Refugees are international responsibility: statement of Prime Minister Shrimati Indira Gandhi in Rajya Sabha on June 15, 1971. [New Delhi, 1971]. pp. 7.

INTERNATIONAL MARXIST GROUP. The struggle in Bengal and the Fourth International. [London, 1971]. pp. 14.

— Industries.

ISLAM (RIZWANUL) Factor intensity and labour absorption in manufacturing industries: the case of Bangladesh. 1976. fo. 471. *bibliog. Typescript. Ph.D. (London) thesis: unpublished. This thesis is the property of London University and may not be removed from the Library.*

— Relations (general) with the United Kingdom.

SCOTT (GUTHRIE MICHAEL) A void of law: (Britain and Bangladesh). London, [1975]. pp. 98.

— Social policy.

BANGLADESH. Planning Commission. Annual plan. a., 1972/73(1st)- Dacca.

NURUL ISLAM. Development planning in Bangladesh: a study in political economy. London, [1977]. pp. 267.

— Statistics, Vital.

U.K. Ministry of Overseas Development. Population Bureau. 1977. Report on the 1974 Bangladesh retrospective survey of fertility and mortality. London, 1977. pp. 173.

BANGLADESHIS IN FOREIGN COUNTRIES.

TINKER (HUGH) The banyan tree: overseas emigrants from India, Pakistan and Bangladesh. Oxford, 1977. pp. 204.

BANK EMPLOYEES

— Germany.

RUDL (FRANZ GERHARD) Die Angestellten im Bankgewerbe, 1870 bis 1933: eine sozialstatistische Untersuchung. [Mannheim], 1975. pp. 319. *bibliog. Inaugural-Dissertation zur Erlangung der Würde eines Doktors der Wirtschaftswissenschaften der Universität Mannheim.*

BANK HOLDING COMPANIES

— United States.

LAWRENCE (ROBERT J.) Operating policies of bank holding companies. Part 1. [Washington, 1971]. pp. 82. *(United States. Board of Governors of the Federal Reserve System. Staff Economic Studies. No. 59)*

TALLEY (SAMUEL H.) The effect of holding company acquisitions on bank performance. [Washington, 1972]. pp. 25. *(United States. Board of Governors of the Federal Reserve System. Staff Economic Studies. No. 69)*

LAWRENCE (ROBERT J.) Operating policies of bank holding companies. Part 2: nonbanking subsidiaries. [Washington, 1974]. pp. 59. *(United States. Board of Governors of the Federal Reserve System. Staff Economic Studies. No. 81)*

TALLEY (SAMUEL H.) The impact of holding company acquisitions on aggregate concentration in banking. [Washington, 1974]. pp. 24. *(United States. Board of Governors of the Federal Reserve System. Staff Economic Studies. No. 80)*

BANK INVESTMENTS

— Mathematical models.

LAFRANCE (ROBERT ROLLAND) Optimal portfolio behaviour in imperfect financial markets: an econometric study of the Canadian chartered banks, 1961-73. 1977. fo.120. *bibliog. Typescript. Ph.D. (London) thesis: unpublished. This thesis is the property of London University and may not be removed from the Library.*

— Canada — Mathematical models.

LAFRANCE (ROBERT ROLLAND) Optimal portfolio behaviour in imperfect financial markets: an econometric study of the Canadian chartered banks, 1961-73. 1977. fo.120. *bibliog. Typescript. Ph.D. (London) thesis: unpublished. This thesis is the property of London University and may not be removed from the Library.*

BANK OF CANADA.

COURCHENE (THOMAS J.) Money, inflation and the Bank of Canada: an analysis of Canadian monetary policy from 1970 to early 1975. Montreal, [1976]. pp. 283. *bibliogs. (Howe (C.D.) Research Institute. Special Studies)*

BANK OF SCOTLAND.

See ROYAL BANK OF SCOTLAND.

BANK OF THE NETHERLANDS.

PALGRAVE (Sir ROBERT HARRY INGLIS) translator. Reports and transactions of the Banks of France, Germany, Belgium and the Netherlands, 1909-(1917). Great Yarmouth, 1912-17. 5 vols. *(Reprinted from the Bankers' Magazine) Collected and bound for the author's library.*

BANK RESERVES

— Spain.

VIÑAS MARTIN (ANGEL) El oro español en la guerra civil. [Madrid], Instituto de Estudios Fiscales, [1976]. pp. 618. *bibliog.*

BANKING LAW

— Mexico.

MEXICO. Statutes, etc. 1896-1957. Legislacion bancaria. Mexico, 1957. 4 vols. (in 2)

— United Kingdom — Guernsey.

INTER-BANK RESEARCH ORGANISATION. Prudential regulation of banks in Guernsey. London, 1976. fo.43. *bibliog.*

— — Isle of Man.

INTER-BANK RESEARCH ORGANISATION. Prudential regulation of banks in the Isle of Man. London, 1976. fo.44. *bibliog.*

— — Jersey.

INTER-BANK RESEARCH ORGANISATION. Prudential regulation of banks in Jersey. London, 1976. fo.43. *bibliog.*

BANKRUPTCY

— Germany — North Rhine-Westphalia.

NORTH RHINE-WESTPHALIA. Landesamt für Datenverarbeitung und Statistik. Beiträge zur Statistik des Landes Nordrhein- Westfalen. Heft 366. Zahlungsschwierigkeiten in Nordrhein-Westfalen, 1969 bis 1975. Düsseldorf, 1976. pp. 58.

— United Kingdom.

SALES (CHARLES ALLISON) The law relating to bankruptcy, liquidations and receiverships; sixth edition by J.H. Thompson. Plymouth, 1977. pp. 332.

BANKS AND BANKING.

LUCKETT (DUDLEY G.) Money and banking. New York, [1976]. pp. 585.

RANLETT (JOHN GRANT) Money and banking: an introduction to analysis and policy. 3rd ed. Santa Barbara, [1977]. pp. 614. *bibliogs.*

SAVAGE (DONALD T.) Money and banking. Santa Barbara, Calif., [1977]. pp. 491. *bibliogs.*

— State supervision.

REVELL (JACK) Solvency and regulation of banks: theoretical and practical implications. [Cardiff], 1975. pp. 145. *bibliog. (Wales. University. University College of North Wales. Bangor Occasional Papers in Economics. No. 5)*

— **Africa, Subsaharan.**

NWANKWO (GREEN ONYEKABA) New dimensions in banking in developing countries: collected essays. Lagos, [1977?]. pp. 304.

— **Australasia.**

SKULLY (MICHAEL T.) Merchant banking in the Far East: an examination of the development, operation, and future of merchant banking in Australia, Hong Kong, Indonesia, Japan, Malaysia, New Zealand, Philippines, Singapore, and Thailand. London, [1976]. pp. 284. *bibliog.*

— **Australia.**

COMMONWEALTH BANKING CORPORATION [AUSTRALIA]. Annual report. a., (formerly s-a.) 1912 (1st)- Canberra. *Included in AUSTRALIA. Parliament. [Parliamentary papers].*

— **Austria.**

MICHEL (BERNARD) Banques et banquiers en Autriche au début du 20e siècle. [Paris, 1976]. pp. 405. *bibliog. (Fondation Nationale des Sciences Politiques. Cahiers. 199)*

— **Austria-Hungary.**

RUDOLPH (RICHARD L.) Banking and industrialization in Austria-Hungary: the role of banks in the industrialization of the Czech Crownlands, 1873-1914. Cambridge, 1976. pp. 291. *bibliog.*

— **Communist countries.**

BUTAKOV (DANIIL DMITRIEVICH) Kredit i intensifikatsiia proizvodstva v stranakh SEV. Moskva, 1976. pp. 207.

— **Czechoslovakia.**

RUDOLPH (RICHARD L.) Banking and industrialization in Austria-Hungary: the role of banks in the industrialization of the Czech Crownlands, 1873-1914. Cambridge, 1976. pp. 291. *bibliog.*

— **East (Far East).**

SKULLY (MICHAEL T.) Merchant banking in the Far East: an examination of the development, operation, and future of merchant banking in Australia, Hong Kong, Indonesia, Japan, Malaysia, New Zealand, Philippines, Singapore, and Thailand. London, [1976]. pp. 284. *bibliog.*

— **Europe.**

TRITTEN (KURT) European banks: a comparative analysis of the leading European banks. 2nd ed. Berne, 1976. pp. 167.

— **France.**

BÉRARD (AUGUSTE SIMON LOUIS) Projet de banques départementales adressé à la Chambre des Députés et à celle des Pairs. [Paris, imprint, 1828]. pp. 12.

— **Germany.**

[GEFFCKEN (FRIEDRICH HEINRICH)] Zur Bankfrage. Hamburg, 1856. pp. 68.

SCHROEDER (UWE) Konzentrations- und Kooperationstendenzen bei den Girozentralen: eine Analyse...für den Zeitraum von 1965 bis 1973. Hamburg, 1976. pp. 311. *bibliog. Dissertation zur Erlangung des Grades eines Doktors der Wirtschafts- und Sozialwissenschaften der Universität Hamburg.*

— **Honduras.**

BANCO CENTRAL DE HONDURAS. Departamento de Estudios Economicos. Informe economico. a., 1975- Tegucigalpa, D.C.

— **Italy.**

REISS (LOTHAR) Das italienische Banksystem: eine Strukturanalyse. Hannover, 1976. pp. 300. *bibliog. Inaugural-Dissertation zur Erlangung des Grades eines Doktors der Wirtschaftswissenschaften der Freien Universität Berlin.*

— **Mexico.**

El BANCO de Avio y el fomento de la industria nacional. Mexico, 1966. pp. 350. *(Banco Nacional de Comercio Exterior. Coleccion de Documentos para la Historia del Comercio Exterior de Mexico. 2a Serie. 3)*

— **Nigeria.**

NWANKWO (GREEN ONYEKABA) New dimensions in banking in developing countries: collected essays. Lagos, [1977?]. pp. 304.

— **Poland.**

MŁYNARSKI (FELIKS JOHN) Wspomnienia. Warszawa, 1971. pp. 563.

— **South Africa.**

GOEDHUYS (D.W.) Money and banking. Johannesburg, [1975] repr. 1976. pp. 231. *bibliogs.*

— **Switzerland.**

DUPERREX (EMILE) 1869-1969: 100 Jahre Schweizerische Volksbank, Schweizer Wirtschaftsleben; herausgegeben...anlässlich der Hundertjahrfeier ihrer Gründung, etc. Bern, 1969. pp. 192.

MARBACHER (JOSEF) Das Zahlungsverkehrs-System der Schweiz: eine Analyse der Geschichte...des nationalen monetären Transfer-Systems. Bern, 1976. pp. 383. *bibliog. Dissertation der Universität Zürich zur Erlangung der Würde eines Doktors der Wirtschaftswissenschaft.*

BUECHENBACHER (CHRISTOPH) Tatsachen über das schweizerische Bankgeheimnis. Zürich, [1977]. pp. 336. *bibliog.*

— **Underdeveloped areas.**

See UNDERDEVELOPED AREAS — Banks and banking.

— **United Kingdom.**

PALGRAVE (Sir ROBERT HARRY INGLIS) Articles in the Quarterly Review...1878-1899. [Great Yarmouth], 1899. 1 vol. (various pagings). *Collected and bound for the author's library.*

BAILEY (MARTIN DAWSON) Barclays and South Africa. [Birmingham, 1975]. pp. 12.

The BANKS and industry; based on the seminar held at... Cambridge, 5-10 September, 1976. London, 1976. pp. 106. *bibliog.*

END LOANS TO SOUTHERN AFRICA. Letters and papers from Midland. [London, 1976]. pp. 12.

ROSE (HAROLD BERTRAM) Banking and finance; a reply to the Labour Party National Executive Committee's statement presented to the Labour Party annual conference, September 1976. [London, 1976]. pp. 25.

CHANNON (DEREK F.) British banking strategy and the international challenge. London, 1977. pp. 207.

HELLER (ROBERT) B.A. and WILLATT (NORRIS) Can you trust your bank? London, [1977]. pp. 298.

— — **Scotland.**

FORBES (R.N.) The history of the Institute of Bankers in Scotland, 1875-1975. Edinburgh, [1975]. pp. 52.

— **United States.**

TALLEY (SAMUEL H.) The effect of holding company acquisitions on bank performance. [Washington, 1972]. pp. 25. *(United States. Board of Governors of the Federal Reserve System. Staff Economic Studies. No. 69)*

U.S. financing of East-West trade: the political economy of government credits and the national interest; edited by Paul Marer. Bloomington, Ind., [1975]. pp. 442. *bibliog. (Indiana University. International Development Research Center. Studies in East European and Soviet Planning, Development and Trade. No. 22) Includes papers delivered at a panel discussion on "The political economy of subsidized credits in East-West trade", San Francisco, 1974.*

HELLER (ROBERT) B.A. and WILLATT (NORRIS) Can you trust your bank? London, [1977]. pp. 298.

RANLETT (JOHN GRANT) Money and banking: an introduction to analysis and policy. 3rd ed. Santa Barbara, [1977]. pp. 614. *bibliogs.*

BANKS AND BANKING, CENTRAL.

JOHNSON (HARRY GORDON) The problems of central bankers in a world of floating rates. [Elmont, N.Y.], 1973. fo. 3. *Reprinted from Euromoney, July 1973.*

— **Sweden.**

LINDGREN (TORGNY) Banko- och riksgäldsrevisionerna, 1782-1807: "de redliga män, som bewakade Ständers rätt". Uppsala, 1975. pp. 198. *bibliog. (Uppsala. Universitet. Historiska Institutionen. Studia Historica Upsaliensia. 72) With summaries in English and Finnish.*

BANKS AND BANKING, COOPERATIVE

— **Canada — Quebec.**

ROBY (YVES) Les caisses populaires: Alphonse Desjardins, 1900-1920. Québec, 1975. pp. 113. *bibliog.*

— **Netherlands.**

VRIES (JOH. DE) De Coöperatieve Raiffeisen- en Boerenleenbanken in Nederland 1948-1973: van exponent tot component. [Amsterdam], 1973. pp. 260. *bibliog.*

BANKS AND BANKING, FOREIGN

— **Colombia.**

BOYCE (JAMES E.) and LOMBARD (FRANÇOIS J.) Colombia's treatment of foreign banks: a precedent setting case?. Washington, D.C., 1976. pp. 56. *(American Enterprise Institute for Public Policy Research. Foreign Affairs Studies. 36)*

BANKS AND BANKING, INTERNATIONAL.

MOSCHETTO (BRUNO) and PLAGNOL (ANDRE) Les activités bancaires internationales. [Paris], 1976. pp. 125. *bibliog.*

BANKS AND BANKING, TRADE UNION

— **America, Latin.**

LEWERENZ (JUERGEN) Die Arbeiterbanken in Lateinamerika und in der Karibik. Frankfurt am Main, [1976]. pp. 62. *bibliog. (Bank für Gemeinwirtschaft. Schriftenreihe Gemeinwirtschaft. Nr.21)*

— **Caribbean area.**

LEWERENZ (JUERGEN) Die Arbeiterbanken in Lateinamerika und in der Karibik. Frankfurt am Main, [1976]. pp. 62. *bibliog. (Bank für Gemeinwirtschaft. Schriftenreihe Gemeinwirtschaft. Nr.21)*

— **Germany.**

LOESCH (ACHIM VON) Die deutschen Arbeitnehmerbanken in den zwanziger Jahren. Frankfurt am Main, 1974 repr. 1976. pp. 72. *(Bank für Gemeinwirtschaft. Schriftenreihe Gemeinwirtschaft. Nr.12)*

— **Japan.**

HOYNDEN (YOSHIO) Arbeiterbanken in Japan. Frankfurt am Main, [1974]. pp. 50. *(Bank für Gemeinwirtschaft. Schriftenreihe Gemeinwirtschaft. Nr.16)*

BANQUE DE FRANCE.

PALGRAVE (Sir ROBERT HARRY INGLIS) translator. Reports and transactions of the Bank of France and the Bank of Germany from 1876 to (1897). [Great Yarmouth, n.d.]. 2 vols. *Collected and bound for the author's library.*

PALGRAVE (Sir ROBERT HARRY INGLIS) Reports and transactions of the Bank of France, Germany, and Belgium, 1898-(1905). [Great Yarmouth, n.d.]. 3 vols. *(Reprinted from the Bankers' Magazine) Collected and bound for the author's library. Covering title-page lacking: title taken from the spine.*

PALGRAVE (Sir ROBERT HARRY INGLIS) translator. Reports and transactions of the Bank of France, Germany, Belgium and the Netherlands, 1909-(1917). Great Yarmouth, 1912-17. 5 vols. *(Reprinted from the Bankers' Magazine) Collected and bound for the author's library.*

BANQUE NATIONALE DE BELGIQUE.

PALGRAVE (Sir ROBERT HARRY INGLIS) Reports and transactions of the Bank of France, Germany, and Belgium, 1898-(1905). [Great Yarmouth, n.d.]. 3 vols. *(Reprinted from the Bankers' Magazine) Collected and bound for the author's library. Covering title-page lacking: title taken from the spine.*

PALGRAVE (Sir ROBERT HARRY INGLIS) translator. Reports and transactions of the Banks of France, Germany, Belgium and the Netherlands, 1909-(1917). Great Yarmouth, 1912-17. 5 vols. *(Reprinted from the Bankers' Magazine) Collected and bound for the author's library.*

BANTUS IN ZAIRE.

IYEKI (JEAN FRANÇOIS) Essai sur la psychologie du Bonto. Kinshasa, Office National de la Recherche et du Développement, 1970. pp. 47.

BARBADOS

— Economic conditions.

CENTRAL BANK OF BARBADOS. Quarterly report. a., Je 1977 (v.4, no.2)- Bridgetown.

— Economic policy.

BARBADOS. 1952. Five year plan of development and taxation. [Bridgetown, 1952?]. pp. 28.

— Emigration and immigration.

BARBADOS. 195-. Information booklet for intending emigrants to Britain. [rev.ed.]. [Bridgetown, 195-]. pp. 31.

BARBADOS. 195-. Informtation booklet for intending emigrants to Britain. [Bridgetown, 195-]. pp. 24.

— Nationalism.

MATTHEWS (HARRY G.) Multinational corporations and black power. Cambridge, Mass., [1976]. pp. 124.

— Parliament — Rules and practice.

BARBADOS. House of Assembly. 196-. Standing orders of the General Assembly of Barbados. [Bridgetown, 196-]. pp. 65.

— Social conditions.

BARBADOS. Commission appointed to Enquire into the Disturbances which took place in Barbados on the 27th July 1937 and subsequent days. 1937. Report; [G.C. Deane, chairman]. [Bridgetown, 1937]. pp. 41.

— Social policy.

BARBADOS. 1952. Five year plan of development and taxation. [Bridgetown, 1952?]. pp. 28.

BARCELONA

— History.

CRUELLS PIFARRE (MANUEL) La revolta del 1936 a Barcelona. Barcelona, 1976. pp. 364. *bibliog.*

BARGES.

WILLMOTT (FRANK G.) Cement, mud and 'muddies'. Rainham, Kent, 1977. pp. 141.

BARKER (JOSEPH).

TRUTH and reform against the world; or, Letters to W. Cooke in reply to his attack on Mr. Joseph Barker. [Newcastle-upon-Tyne, J. Barker, c. 1845]. 7 pts. (in 1 vol.). *Signed, A. Christian.*

BARNARD (Sir JOHN).

A FULL confutation of the gross misrepresentations and falsities contain'd in a scandalous pamphlet entitled, The court-broker: a description of an anti-patriot, etc. in a letter to Mr. Gideon. London, the Author, 1747. pp. 21.

[VENN (HENRY) Vicar of Huddersfield] Memoirs of the late Sir John Barnard, Knight, and Alderman of the City of London. London, Oliver, 1776. pp. 22.

BARRÈS (AUGUSTE MAURICE).

DOTY (CHARLES STEWART) From cultural rebellion to counterrevolution: the politics of Maurice Barrès. Athens, Ohio, [1976]. pp. 294. *bibliog.*

BARTHOLOMEW FAMILY.

GARDINER (LESLIE) Bartholomew: 150 years. Edinburgh, [1976]. pp. 111.

BARZEL (RAINER).

BARZEL (RAINER) Es ist noch nicht zu spät. München, 1977. pp. 191.

BASEL-LAND (CANTON)

— Economic history.

GSCHWIND (FRANZ) Bevölkerungsentwicklung und Wirtschaftsstruktur der Landschaft Basel im 18. Jahrhundert: ein historisch-demographischer Beitrag zur Sozial- und Wirtschaftsgeschichte mit besonderer Berücksichtigung der langfristigen Bevölkerungsentwicklung von Stadt (seit 1100) und Landschaft (seit 1500) Basel. Liestal, 1977. pp. 687. *(Basel-land (Canton). Quellen und Forschungen zur Geschichte und Landeskunde des Kantons Baselland. Bd.15)*

— Population.

GSCHWIND (FRANZ) Bevölkerungsentwicklung und Wirtschaftsstruktur der Landschaft Basel im 18. Jahrhundert: ein historisch-demographischer Beitrag zur Sozial- und Wirtschaftsgeschichte mit besonderer Berücksichtigung der langfristigen Bevölkerungsentwicklung von Stadt (seit 1100) und Landschaft (seit 1500) Basel. Liestal, 1977. pp. 687. *(Basel-land (Canton). Quellen und Forschungen zur Geschichte und Landeskunde des Kantons Baselland. Bd.15)*

— Social history.

GSCHWIND (FRANZ) Bevölkerungsentwicklung und Wirtschaftsstruktur der Landschaft Basel im 18. Jahrhundert: ein historisch-demographischer Beitrag zur Sozial- und Wirtschaftsgeschichte mit besonderer Berücksichtigung der langfristigen Bevölkerungsentwicklung von Stadt (seit 1100) und Landschaft (seit 1500) Basel. Liestal, 1977. pp. 687. *(Basel-land (Canton). Quellen und Forschungen zur Geschichte und Landeskunde des Kantons Baselland. Bd.15)*

BASHKIR REPUBLIC

— Industries.

NIKIFOROV (IURII NIKIFOROVICH) Shagi neftekhimii respubliki: istoriko-partiinyi ocherk. Ufa, 1974. pp. 215.

BASILDON

— Economic conditions.

BASILDON. District Council. Policy Planning Unit. Basildon district socio-economic profile. [Basildon], 1975. pp. 216.

— Social conditions.

BASILDON. District Council. Policy Planning Unit. Basildon district socio-economic profile. [Basildon], 1975. pp. 216.

BASQUE PROVINCES

— Economic conditions.

SEMANA INTERNACIONAL DE ANTROPOLOGIA VASCA, 3A, BILBAO, 1973. III Semana Internacional de Antropologia Vasca. Bilbao, 1976. 2 vols.

— Economic history.

SEMANA INTERNACIONAL DE ANTROPOLOGIA VASCA, 3A, BILBAO, 1973. III Semana Internacional de Antropologia Vasca. Bilbao, 1976. 2 vols.

— History.

BELTZA ( ) El nacionalismo vasco: de 1876 a 1937. Hendaye, [1974]. pp. 334. *bibliog.*

— Nationalism.

AGIRRE (JULEN) Opération "Ogro"...: comment et pourquoi nous avons exécuté Carrero Blanco, premier ministre espagnol; traduit de l'espagnol par Victoria Pueblos. Paris, [1974]. pp. 224.

BELTZA ( ) El nacionalismo vasco: de 1876 a 1937. Hendaye, [1974]. pp. 334. *bibliog.*

AGIRRE (JULEN) Operation Ogro: the execution of Admiral Luis Carrero Blanco;...translated from the Spanish, adapted and with an introduction by Barbara Probst Solomon. New York, [1975]. pp. 196.

— Politics and government.

ESTORNES ZUBIZARRETA (IDOIA) Carlismo y abolicion foral: en torno a un centenario, 1876-1976. San Sebastian, [1976]. pp. 250.

BASQUES.

SEMANA INTERNACIONAL DE ANTROPOLOGIA VASCA, 3A, BILBAO, 1973. III Semana Internacional de Antropologia Vasca. Bilbao, 1976. 2 vols.

BASQUES IN AMERICA.

DOUGLASS (WILLIAM A.) and BILBAO (JON) Amerikanuak: Basques in the New World. Reno, Nev., 1975. pp. 519. *bibliog.*

BASSA (LIBERIAN PEOPLE).

SIEGMANN (WILLIAM) Report on the Bassa. Robertsport, Liberia, 1969. fo. 39, 3. *bibliog. (Tubman Center of African Culture. Ethnographic Survey of Southeastern Liberia. Reports)*

BATLEY

— Social conditions.

McGRATH (MORAG) Batley East and West: a C[ommunty] D[evelopment] P[roject] survey. [York, 1976]. pp. 62. *(Papers in Community Studies. No. 6)*

BAUDELOT (CHRISTIAN).

SNYDERS (GEORGES) Ecole, classe et lutte des classes: une relecture critique de Baudelot-Establet, Bourdieu-Passeron et Illich. Paris, [1976]. pp. 379.

BAUER (BRUNO).

ROSEN (ZVI) Bruno Bauer and Karl Marx: the influence of Bruno Bauer on Marx's thought. The Hague, 1977. pp. 254. *bibliog. (International Institute of Social History. Studies in Social History. [No.]2)*

BAUXITE.

KAMP (A.F.) De standvastige tinnen soldaat: N.V. Billiton Maatschappij 's- Gravenhage (1860-1960). [The Hague, 1960]. pp. 296. *With English summary and English captions to illustrations.*

BAVARIA

— Economic history.

HAUSMANN (FRIEDERIKE) Die Agrarpolitik der Regierung Montgelas: Untersuchungen zum gesellschaftlichen Strukturwandel Bayerns um die Wende vom 18. zum 19. Jahrhundert. Bern, 1975. pp. 288. *bibliog.*

TAUSENDPFUND (ALFRED) Die Manufaktur im Fürstentum Neuburg: Studien zur Sozial- und Wirtschaftsgeschichte unter besonderer Berücksichtigung der grossbetrieblichen Entwicklung im Zeitalter des Merkantilismus. Nürnberg, 1975. pp. 430. *bibliog. (Nuremberg. Stadtarchiv. Nürnberger Werkstücke zur Stadt- und Landesgeschichte. Band 16) Erlanger Phil. Dissertation 1975.*

ECKARDT (GUENTHER) Industrie und Politik in Bayern, 1900-1919: der Bayerische Industriellen-Verband als Modell des Einflusses von Wirtschaftsverbänden. Berlin, [1976]. pp. 201. *bibliog. (Munich. Universität. Institut für Bayerische Geschichte. Beiträge zu einer Historischen Strukturanalyse Bayerns im Industriezeitalter. Band 15)*

— History.

MUEHSAM (ERICH) Von Eisner bis Leviné: die Entstehung und Niederlage der bayerischen Räterepublik: ein Bericht; mit einem Vorwort von H.J. Viesel, etc. Hamburg, [1976]. pp. 90. *Reprint of work originally published in Berlin in 1929.*

— — Sources.

KONGRESS DER ARBEITER-, BAUERN- UND SOLDATENRÄTE, MÜNCHEN, 1919. Stenographischer Bericht über die Verhandlungen...vom 25. Februar bis 8. März 1919 in München; eingeleitet von Gisela Kissel und Hiltrud Witt. Glashütten im Taunus, 1974. pp. 200. *Reprint of work originally published in Munich in 1919.*

— Politics and government.

WERNER (GEORGE S.) Bavaria in the German Confederation, 1820-1848. Rutherford, N.J., [1977]. pp. 270. *bibliog.*

BAYESIAN STATISTICAL DECISION THEORY.

TESFATSION (LEIGH) "Bayes' theorem" for utility. Minneapolis, 1976. fo. 33. *bibliog. (Minnesota University. Center for Economic Research. Discussion Papers. No. 65)*

BAYKAL-AMUR RAILWAY. See BAIKAL-AMUR RAILWAY.

BEANS

— Panama.

PANAMA. Direccion de Estadistica y Censo. Estadistica panameña. Superficie sembrada y cosecha de arroz, maiz y frijol de bejuco. a., 1975/76- Panama. *Supersedes in part PANAMA. Direccion de Estadistica y Censo. Estadistica panameña. Serie H. Informacion agropecuaria.*

BEAUFORT (Sir FRANCIS).

FRIENDLY (ALFRED) Beaufort of the Admiralty: the life of Sir Francis Beaufort, 1774-1857. London, 1977. pp. 362. *bibliog.*

BEBEL (AUGUST).

LORECK (JOCHEN) Wie man früher Sozialdemokrat wurde: das Kommunikationsverhalten in der deutschen Arbeiterbewegung und die Konzeption der sozialistischen Parteipublizistik durch August Bebel. Bonn-Bad Godesberg, [1977]. pp. 290. *(Friedrich-Ebert-Stiftung. Forschungsinstitut. Schriftenreihe. Band 130)*

BEDFORD PRISON.

STOCKDALE (ERIC) A study of Bedford prison, 1660-1878, in the context of social and penological developments. 1976. fo. 339. *Typescript. Ph.D. (London) thesis: unpublished. This thesis is the property of London University and may not be removed from the Library.*

BEEF

— Prices — Ireland (Republic).

EIRE. Review Body on Beef Intervention and Cattle Slaughter Premium Systems. 1976. Report. Dublin, 1976. pp. 74.

— Australia — Grading.

AUSTRALIA. Bureau of Agricultural Economics. 1976. Developments in beef carcass classification. Canberra, 1976. pp. 80. *bibliog. (Beef Research Reports. No. 19)*

BEEF CATTLE

— Prices — Ireland (Republic).

EIRE. Review Body on Beef Intervention and Cattle Slaughter Premium Systems. 1976. Report. Dublin, 1976. pp. 74.

— Australia.

AUSTRALIA. Bureau of Agricultural Economics. 1975. The Australian beef cattle industry: an examination of the current situation, future prospects and possible policy options. 2nd ed. Canberra, 1975. pp. 61. *(Occasional Papers. No. 25)*

— — Northern Territory.

AUSTRALIA. Bureau of Agricultural Economics. 1974. The Northern Territory and Kimberley region beef cattle industry: a summary of B.A.E. survey results, 1968-69 to 1970-71. Canberra, 1974. pp. 36. *(Beef Research Reports. No. 13)*

— — Queensland.

AUSTRALIA. Bureau of Agricultural Economics. 1974. The Queensland beef cattle industry: a summary of B.A.E. survey results, 1968-69 to 1970-71. Canberra, 1974. pp. 72. *(Beef Research Reports. No. 14)*

— — Victoria.

AUSTRALIA. Bureau of Agricultural Economics. 1974. The Victorian beef cattle industry: a summary of B.A.E. survey results, 1968-69 to 1970-71. Canberra, 1974. pp. 36. *(Beef Research Reports. No. 15)*

BEGGING

— Belgium.

LETTRE d'un patriote bruxellois, à un patriote gantois, sur la mendicité, les enfans trouvés, et un monument à élever à la gloire des auteurs de la révolution pour la liberté des Pays- Bas. Bruxelles, the Author, 1790. pp. 7.

— Portugal.

CARVALHO (MANOEL PEDRO HENRIQUES DE) Noticia historica sobre a origem da pobresa e da mendicidade, das suas causas mais influentes, dos seus espantosos progresos, finalmente dos meios que tem tentado em algumas nações para reprimir uma, e anniquillar a outra. Lisboa, Nery, 1835. pp. 46.

BELFAST

— History.

IRELAND, NORTHERN. Public Record Office. 1973. Problems of a growing city: Belfast 1780-1870. [Belfast], 1973. pp. 258.

— Social conditions.

SPENCER (ANTHONY E.C.W.) Ballymurphy: a tale of two surveys. Belfast, 1973. pp. 150.

IRELAND, NORTHERN. 1977. Belfast: areas of special social need; report by project team, 1976; [M.N. Hayes, chairman until March 1975; J.M.C. Parke, chairman from May 1975]. Belfast, 1977. pp. 85.

BELGIAN PERIODICALS.

VOS-GEVERS (LOUIS) and VOS-GEVERS (LIEVE) Dat volk moet herleven: het studententijdschrift De Vlaamsche Vlagge, 1875-1933. Leuven, [1976]. pp. 319. *bibliog.*

BELGIUM.

BELGIUM. Ministère des Affaires Etrangères, du Commerce Extérieur et de la Coopération au Développement. 1972. Basic facts about Belgium. Brussels, 1972. pp. 48. *bibliog. (Memo from Belgium. No.147)*

— Biography.

INSTITUT BELGE D'INFORMATION ET DE DOCUMENTATION. Walloons and Flemings in the world. [Brussels], Ministry of Foreign Affairs and External Trade, 1971. pp. 19. *(Belgian News. No.7a)*

— Constitution.

TINDEMANS (LEO) Dagboek van de Werkgroep-Eyskens. Lier, [1973]. pp. 216.

— Economic conditions.

BELGIUM. Ministère des Affaires Etrangères et du Commerce Extérieur. 1968. Idealism by all means, but a little more realism as well; by Raymond Scheyven, Minister for Co-operation in Development, [and] Events during the month and chronicles. Brussels, 1968. pp. 80. *(Memo from Belgium. No.107)*

BELGIUM. Ministère des Affaires Etrangères, du Commerce Extérieur et de la Coopération au Développement. 1971. Belgium's foreign policy; by Pierre Harmel, Minister of Foreign Affairs, [and] Chronicles. [Brussels], 1971. pp. 80. *(Memo from Belgium. No.135-136)*

BELGIUM. Ministère des Affaires Etrangères, du Commerce Extérieur et de la Coopération au Développement. 1971. Scientific policy of Belgium; by Theo Lefèvre, Minister for Scientific Policy and Planning, [and] chronicles. [Brussels], 1971. pp. 66. *(Memo from Belgium. No.139)*

— Economic history.

MOKYR (JOEL) Industrialization in the Low Countries, 1795-1850. New Haven, 1976. pp. 295. *bibliog.*

HOUTTE (JAN A. VAN) An economic history of the Low Countries, 800-1800. London, [1977]. pp. 342. *bibliog.*

— Foreign relations.

BELGIUM. Ministère des Affaires Etrangères, du Commerce Extérieur et de la Coopération au Développement. 1971. Belgium's foreign policy; by Pierre Harmel, Minister of Foreign Affairs, [and] Chronicles. [Brussels], 1971. pp. 80. *(Memo from Belgium. No.135-136)*

BELGIUM. Ministère des Affaires Etrangères, du Commerce Extérieur et de la Coopération au Développement. 1976. Belgium's foreign policy, 1973-1974-1975: [speeches]; by Renaat van Elslande, Minister of Foreign Affairs and Cooperation in Development. Brussels, 1976. pp. 411. *(Memo from Belgium. No.173)*

— History.

INSTITUT BELGE D'INFORMATION ET DE DOCUMENTATION. Walloons and Flemings in the world. [Brussels], Ministry of Foreign Affairs and External Trade, 1971. pp. 19. *(Belgian News. No.7a)*

KOSSMANN (ERNST HEINRICH) De Lage Landen 1780-1940: anderhalve eeuw Nederland en België. Amsterdam, 1976. pp. 618. *bibliog.*

BELGIUM.(Cont.)

— Industries.

DEFAY (JACQUES) La science facteur de production: recherche sur l'intégration de la recherche-développement dans la fonction de production. Bruxelles, Services de Programmation de la Politique Scientifique, 1973. pp. 268. *(Recherche et Croissance Economique. 3)*

MOKYR (JOEL) Industrialization in the Low Countries, 1795-1850. New Haven, 1976. pp. 295. *bibliog.*

— Languages.

WAUTIER (ANDRE) La question linguistique en Belgique. Nalinnes-lez-Charleroi, 1966. pp. 16. *(Institut Jules Destrée pour la Défense et l'Illustration de la Wallonie. Etudes et Documents)*

— Politics and government.

TINDEMANS (LEO) Dagboek van de Werkgroep-Eyskens. Lier, [1973]. pp. 216.

WILLEQUET (JACQUES) Paul-Henri Spaak: un homme, des combats. [Bruxelles, 1975]. pp. 283.

— Social conditions.

BELGIUM. Ministère des Affaires Etrangères et du Commerce Extérieur. 1968. Idealism by all means, but a little more realism as well; by Raymond Scheyven, Minister for Co-operation in Development, [and] Events during the month and chronicles. Brussels, 1968. pp. 80. *(Memo from Belgium. No.107)*

BELGIUM. Ministère des Affaires Etrangères, du Commerce Extérieur et de la Coopération au Développement. 1971. Belgium's foreign policy; by Pierre Harmel, Minister of Foreign Affairs, [and] Chronicles. [Brussels], 1971. pp. 80. *(Memo from Belgium. No.135-136)*

BELGIUM. Ministère des Affaires Etrangères, du Commerce Extérieur et de la Coopération au Développement. 1971. Scientific policy of Belgium; by Theo Lefèvre, Minister for Scientific Policy and Planning, [and] chronicles. [Brussels], 1971. pp. 66. *(Memo from Belgium. No.139)*

— Statistics.

ETUDES STATISTIQUES; [pd. by] Institut National de Statistique [Belgium]. irreg., 1974 (no.34)- Bruxelles.

BELINSKII (VISSARION GRIGOR'EVICH).

BEREZINA (VALENTINA GRIGOR'EVNA) Belinskii i voprosy istorii russkoi zhurnalistiki. Leningrad, 1973. pp. 144.

BELIZE

— Economic history.

BOLLAND (O. NIGEL) The formation of a colonial society: Belize, from conquest to crown colony. Baltimore, [1977]. pp. 240. *bibliog. (Johns Hopkins University. Johns Hopkins Studies in Atlantic History and Culture)*

— Politics and government.

GRANT (CEDRIC HILBURN) The making of modern Belize: politics, society and British colonialism in Central America. Cambridge, 1976. pp. 400. *bibliog.*

— Social history.

BOLLAND (O. NIGEL) The formation of a colonial society: Belize, from conquest to crown colony. Baltimore, [1977]. pp. 240. *bibliog. (Johns Hopkins University. Johns Hopkins Studies in Atlantic History and Culture)*

BELLO (ANDRÉS).

CALDERA RODRIGUEZ (RAFAEL) Andrés Bello: philosopher, poet, philologist, educator, legislator, statesman;...translated by John Street. London, 1977. pp. 165. *bibliog.*

BELLONA ISLAND

— Economic conditions.

MONBERG (TORBEN) The reactions of people of Bellona Island towards a mining project. Copenhagen, 1976. pp. 61. *bibliog. (International Work Group for Indigenous Affairs. Documents. 24)*

BELZU (MANUEL ISIDORO).

SALINAS MARIACA (RAMON) Viva Belzu: compendio de la vida y obra de este gran caudillo. La Paz, [1974]. pp. 196.

BENEDICT XIII, Antipope, 1399-1419.

SCOTTISH HISTORY SOCIETY. [Publications]. 4th Series. vol.13. Calendar of papal letters to Scotland of Benedict XIII of Avignon, 1394-1419; edited by Francis McGurk. Edinburgh, 1976. pp. 456.

BENGAL

— Commerce.

MARSHALL (PETER JAMES) East Indian fortunes: the British in Bengal in the eighteenth century. London, 1976. pp. 284. *bibliog.*

BENGAL, WEST

— Population.

MUKHERJEE (S.B.) Age composition of the population in the districts of West Bengal: 1872-1961. Delhi, 1975 [or rather 1976]. pp. 312. *(India. Census, 1971. Series 22. Part XI(i) Special Monographs)*

— Social conditions.

MITTER (SWASTI) Peasant movements in West Bengal: their impact on agrarian class relations since 1967. Cambridge, 1977. pp. 85. *bibliog. (Cambridge. University. Department of Land Economy. Occasional Papers. No. 8)*

BENIGNI (UMBERTO).

POULAT (EMILE) Catholicisme, démocratie et socialisme: le mouvement catholique et Mgr. Benigni de la naissance du socialisme à la victoire du fascisme. [Paris, 1977]. pp. 562. *bibliog.*

BENISZ (ADAM).

BENISZ (ADAM) W burzy 'zycia; do druku przygotował Mieczysław Wrzosek. Opole, 1976. pp. 200.

BENTHAM (JEREMY).

STEINTRAGER (JAMES) Bentham. London, 1977. pp. 133. *bibliog.*

BERDIAEV (NIKOLAI ALEKSANDROVICH).

KUVAKIN (VALERII ALEKSANDROVICH) Kritika ekzistentsializma Berdiaeva. Moskva, 1976. pp. 205.

BEREAVEMENT.

WILLANS (JOAN H.) Death and bereavement. London, [1974]. pp. 12. *bibliog. (Age Concern England. Manifesto Series. No. 17)*

BERGSON (HENRI LOUIS).

KENNEDY (ELLEN LEE) 'Freedom' and 'the open society': Henri Bergson's contribution to political philosophy. 1977. fo. 278. *bibliog. Typescript. Ph.D. (London) thesis: unpublished. This thesis is the property of London University and may not be removed from the Library.*

BERKSHIRE

— Economic policy.

BERKSHIRE. Planning Department. West Berkshire structure plan: report of survey. [Reading, Berks.], 1975. pp. 223.

BERKSHIRE. Planning Department. East Berkshire structure plan: report of survey. [Reading, Berks.], 1976. pp. 282.

— Social policy.

BERKSHIRE. Planning Department. West Berkshire structure plan: report of survey. [Reading, Berks.], 1975. pp. 223.

BERKSHIRE. Planning Department. East Berkshire structure plan: report of survey. [Reading, Berks.], 1976. pp. 282.

BERLIN

— Economic conditions.

LUNZE (ARNULF) ed. Berlin: Initiativen im Deutschen Bundestag in der 7. Wahlperiode. Bonn, 1977. pp. 72. *(Germany (Bundesrepublik). Deutscher Bundestag. Wissenschaftliche Dienste. Materialien. 48)*

— Economic history.

INDUSTRIALISIERUNG und Gewerbe in Raum Berlin/Brandenburg. Band II. Die Zeit um 1800/ die Zeit um 1875; herausgegeben von Otto Büsch; mit Textbeiträgen von Otto Büsch und Wolfgang Scharfe, und Kartenbeilagen zum "Gewerbe in Brandenburg..." bbearbeitet von Otto Büsch [and others]. Berlin, 1977. pp. 186. *(Historische Kommission zu Berlin. Einzelveröffentlichungen. Band 19)* 2 maps in end pocket.

— Economic policy.

DEUTSCHES INSTITUT FÜR WIRTSCHAFTSFORSCHUNG. Sonderhefte. [Neue Folge]. 118. Kriterien wirtschaftsfördernder Massnahmen für die verarbeitende Industrie in Berlin; ([by] Burkhard Dreher) . Berlin, 1977. pp. 50. *bibliog.*

— History.

PETZOLD (JOACHIM) Der 9. November 1918 in Berlin: Berliner Arbeiterveteranen berichten über die Vorbereitung der Novemberrevolution und ihren Ausbruch am 9. November 1918 in Berlin. Berlin, 1958. pp. 47. *(Sozialistische Einheitspartei Deutschlands. Bezirksleitung Gross-Berlin. Kommission zur Erforschung der Geschichte der Berliner Arbeiterbewegung. Die Novemberrevolution 1918/1919 in Berlin)*

WROBEL (KURT) Der Sieg der Arbeiter und Matrosen im Dezember 1918 in Berlin: Berliner Arbeiterveteranen berichten über ihren Kampf in der Novemberrevolution. Berlin, 1958. pp. 64. *(Sozialistische Einheitspartei Deutschlands. Bezirksleitung Gross-Berlin. Kommission zur Erforschung der Geschichte der Berliner Arbeiterbewegung. Die Novemberrevolution 1918/1919 in Berlin)*

— Monuments.

MAUR (HANS) Mahn-, Gedenk- und Erinnerungsstätten der Arbeiterbewegung in Berlin-Köpenick: Beiträge zur Geschichte der Berliner Arbeiterbewegung. Berlin, [1973?]. pp. 48. *bibliog.*

BERLIN (Sir ISAIAH).

ROTENSTREICH (NATHAN) Philosophy, history and politics: studies in contemporary English philosophy of history. The Hague, 1976. pp. 158. *bibliog.*

BERLIN QUESTION (1945-).

JENDRETZKY (HANS) Sie hetzen, wir bauen auf: für die Einheit Berlins, gegen die Spalterwahlen. Berlin, [1948]. pp. 31.

LUNZE (ARNULF) ed. Berlin: Initiativen im Deutschen Bundestag in der 7. Wahlperiode. Bonn, 1977. pp. 72. *(Germany (Bundesrepublik). Deutscher Bundestag. Wissenschaftliche Dienste. Materialien. 48)*

BERNAYS (KARL LUDWIG).

HIRSCH (HELMUT) Karl Ludwig Bernays und die Revolutionserwartung vor 1848, dargestellt am Mordfall Praslin. Trier, [1976]. pp. 54. *(Karl-Marx-Haus. Schriften. 17)*

BERNHARD, Prince of the Netherlands.

NETHERLANDS. Commissie van Drie. 1976. Rapport...: onderzoek naar de juistheid van verklaringen over betalingen door een Amerikaanse vliegtuigfabriek. 's-Gravenhage, 1976. pp. 240.

BERNSTEIN (EDUARD).

ZAGARI (EUGENIO) Marxismo e revisionismo: Bernstein, Sorel, Graziadei, Leone. Napoli, [1975]. pp. 357.

BERRIGAN (DANIEL).

The BURDEN of the Berrigans. Worcester, Mass., 1971. pp. 80. *(Holy Cross Quarterly. vol.4. no.1)*

BERRIGAN (PHILIP F.).

The BURDEN of the Berrigans. Worcester, Mass., 1971. pp. 80. *(Holy Cross Quarterly. vol.4. no.1)*

BESKROVNYI (LIUBOMIR GRIGOR'EVICH).

ISTORICHESKAIA geografiia Rossii, XII - nachalo xx v.: sbornik statei k 70-letiiu professora Liubomira Grigor'evicha Beskrovnogo. Moskva, 1975. pp. 347. *bibliog.*

BESSARABIA

— History — 1917-1921, Revolution — Sources.

KHOTINSKOE vosstanie: sbornik dokumentov i materialov. Kishinev, 1976. pp. 443.

BEVERIDGE (WILLIAM HENRY) 1st Baron Beveridge.

HARRIS (JOSÉ) William Beveridge: a biography. Oxford, 1977. pp. 488. *bibliog.*

BEZER (JOHN JAMES).

TESTAMENTS of radicalism: memoirs of working class politicians, 1790-1885; edited and introduced by David Vincent. London, [1977]. pp. 246. *bibliogs.*

BIBLE, NEW TESTAMENT

— Criticism, interpretation, etc.

DAVIDSON (JAMES WEST) The logic of millennial thought: eighteenth-century New England. New Haven, 1977. pp. 308. *bibliog. (Yale University. Yale Historical Publications. Miscellany. 112)*

BIBLIOGRAPHICAL SERVICES

— United Kingdom.

BRITISH LIBRARY. Bibliographic Services Division. Newsletter. irreg., current issues only. London.

BIBLIOGRAPHY

— Early printed books.

WING (DONALD GODARD) Short-title catalogue of books printed in England, Scotland, Ireland, Wales, and British America, and of English books printed in other countries, 1641-1700. 2nd ed. New York, 1972 in progress.

BIBLIOGRAPHY, NATIONAL

— Commonwealth.

COMMONWEALTH SECRETARIAT. Commonwealth national bibliographies: an annotated directory. London, 1977. pp. 98.

— Cuban.

BIBLIOGRAFIA CUBANA; [pd. by] Biblioteca Nacional José Marti. a., 1972- La Habana.

— English.

WING (DONALD GODARD) Short-title catalogue of books printed in England, Scotland, Ireland, Wales, and British America, and of English books printed in other countries, 1641-1700. 2nd ed. New York, 1972 in progress.

— Ivory Coast.

BIBLIOGRAPHIE DE LA CÔTE D'IVOIRE; [pd. by] Bibliothèque Nationale [Ivory Coast]. a., [1969, 1st issue]-Abidjan.

BICYCLE INDUSTRY

— France.

FRANCE. Groupe sectoriel d'Analyse et de Prévision Matériels de Transport. 1976. Rapport...: préparation du 7e Plan. Paris, 1976. pp. 96.

BIERMANN (WOLF).

STEIGERWALD (ROBERT REINHOLD) Der "wahre" oder konterrevolutionäre "Sozialismus": was wollen Havemann, Dutschke, Biermann?. Frankfurt am Main, 1977. pp. 145.

BIERUT (BOLESLAW).

RECHOWICZ (HENRYK) Bolesław Bierut, 1892-1956. 2nd ed. Warszawa, 1977. pp. 291.

BIG BUSINESS.

UFERMANN (PAUL) Die Internationale der Unternehmer: überstaatliche Verbindungen der Industrie, des Handels und des Verkehrs: ein erweiterter Vortrag. Lübeck, [1926]. pp. 42.

— Switzerland.

GIOVANOLI (FRIEDRICH) Unter der Herrschaft des Finanzkapitals. [Zurich?, 1934]. pp. 71.

HOEPFLINGER (FRANÇOIS) Das unheimliche Imperium: Wirtschaftsverflechtung in der Schweiz. Zürich, [1977]. pp. 251.

BIHAR

— History.

PRASAD (RAJENDRA) Mahatma Gandhi and Bihar: some reminiscences. Bombay, 1949. pp. 132.

— Social conditions.

MOSER (RUPERT R.) The situation of the Adivasis of Chotanagpur and Santal Parganas, Bihar, India. Copenhagen, 1972. pp. 11. *(International Work Group for Indigenous Affairs. Documents. 4)*

BILINGUALISM.

RAZVITIE natsional'no-russkogo dvuiazychiia. Moskva, 1976. pp. 368.

BILLITON

— Economic history.

KAMP (A.F.) De standvastige tinnen soldaat: N.V. Billiton Maatschappij 's- Gravenhage (1860-1960). [The Hague, 1960]. pp. 296. *With English summary and English captions to illustrations.*

BILLS OF LADING.

UNITED NATIONS. Conference on Trade and Development. 1971. Bills of lading: report, etc. (TD/B/C.4/ISL/6/Rev. 1). New York, 1971. pp. 78. *bibliog.*

BINGHAMTON METROPOLITAN AREA.

COWING (THOMAS G.) and HOLTMANN (ALPHONSE G.) The economics of public service consolidation. Lexington, Mass., [1976]. pp. 166. *bibliog.*

BIOLOGY

— Philosophy.

DISCOURS biologique et ordre social; ([by] Pierre Achard [and others]). Paris, [1977]. pp. 286.

— Social aspects.

DISCOURS biologique et ordre social; ([by] Pierre Achard [and others]). Paris, [1977]. pp. 286.

BIOMETRY.

BARTLETT (MAURICE STEVENSON) Stochastic population models in ecology and epidemiology. London, 1960 repr. 1970. pp. 90. *bibliog.*

BIRMINGHAM

— City planning.

CHERRY (GORDON E.) Urban and regional planning: promise and potential in the West Midlands; an inaugural lecture delivered in the University of Birmingham on 4th November 1976. Birmingham, 1976. pp. 22. *bibliog.*

LLEWELYN-DAVIES WEEKS [AND PARTNERS]. Inner area study: Birmingham: the management of urban renewal. [London], Department of the Environment, [1976]. pp. 85. *bibliog.*

LLEWELYN-DAVIES WEEKS [AND PARTNERS]. Unequal city: final report of the Birmingham inner area study. London, H.M.S.O., 1977. pp. 339. *bibliog.*

— Economic history.

The NINE days in Birmingham: the General Strike 4-12 May, 1926; [written by a working party of the Workers' Educational Association, the Birmingham Trades Council and the Social Sciences Department of the Reference Library]. Birmingham, 1976. pp. 43.

— Industries.

LLEWELYN-DAVIES WEEKS [AND PARTNERS]. Inner area study: Birmingham: industrial employment and property availability. [London], Department of the Environment, [1976]. pp. 85. *bibliog.*

— Politics and government.

LLEWELYN-DAVIES WEEKS [AND PARTNERS]. Inner area study: Birmingham: the management of urban renewal. [London], Department of the Environment, [1976]. pp. 85. *bibliog.*

— Social conditions.

BIRMINGHAM COMMUNITY DEVELOPMENT PROJECT. First report about the Saltley project area. [Birmingham], 1973. pp. 71. *Photocopy.*

BIRMINGHAM COMMUNITY DEVELOPMENT PROJECT. Second report: strategy. [Birmingham], 1973. pp. 18. *Photocopy.*

LLEWELYN-DAVIES WEEKS [AND PARTNERS]. Unequal city: final report of the Birmingham inner area study. London, H.M.S.O., 1977. pp. 339. *bibliog.*

— Social policy.

LLEWELYN-DAVIES WEEKS [AND PARTNERS]. Unequal city: final report of the Birmingham inner area study. London, H.M.S.O., 1977. pp. 339. *bibliog.*

BIRTH CONTROL.

NATIONAL SEMINAR ON GENERAL CONSEQUENCES OF POPULATION GROWTH, 2ND, KUALA LUMPUR, 1970. Proceedings of the...Seminar, etc. Kuala Lumpur, National Family Planning Board, [1970?]. pp. 189.

BERELSON (BERNARD) The great debate on population policy: an instructive entertainment. New York, [1975]. pp. 32. *(Population Council. Occasional Papers)*

SAI (FRED T.) Some ethical issues in family planning. London, 1976. pp. 35. *(International Planned Parenthood Federation. Occasional Essays. No. 1)*

VIEL VICUNA (BENJAMIN) The demographic explosion: the Latin American experience;... translated from the Spanish and updated by James Walls. New York, [1976]. pp. 249. *bibliog.*

— Bibliography.

EATON (PETER) and WARNICK (MARILYN) compilers. Marie Stopes: a checklist of her writings. London, [1977]. pp. 59.

— Law and legislation.

ANNUAL REVIEW OF POPULATION LAW; [pd. by] Fletcher School of Law and Diplomacy, Tufts University. a., 1974- Medford, Mass.

FARLEY (JOHN U.) and TOKARSKI (STEVEN S.) Legal restrictions on the distribution of contraceptives in the developing nations: some suggestions for determining priorities and estimating impact of change. Medford, Mass., 1975. pp. 415-445. *(Tufts University. Fletcher School of Law and Diplomacy. Law and Population Monograph Series. No. 27) (Reprinted from Columbia Human Rights Law Review, vol. 6)*

KELLOGG (EDMUND H.) Reform of laws affecting population growth: recent developments. Medford, Mass., 1975. pp. 36. *(Tufts University. Fletcher School of Law and Diplomacy. Law and Population Monograph Series. No. 36)*

PAXMAN (JOHN M.) and others. Expanded roles for non-physicians in fertility regulation: legal perspectives. Medford, Mass., 1976. pp. 117. *(Tufts University. Fletcher School of Law and Diplomacy. Law and Population Monograph Series. No. 41)*

— — Mexico.

LAW and population in Mexico; [by] Gerardo Cornejo [and others]. Medford, Mass., 1975. pp. 78. *(Tufts University. Fletcher School of Law and Diplomacy. Law and Population Monograph Series. No. 23)*

— — Sri Lanka.

JAYASURIYA (D.C.) Law and population in Sri Lanka. Medford, Mass., 1976. pp. 42. *bibliog. (Tufts University. Fletcher School of Law and Diplomacy. Law and Population Monograph Series. No. 40).*

— — Uganda.

KIAPI (ABRAHAM) Law and population in Uganda. Medford, Mass., 1977. pp. 53. *(Tufts University. Fletcher School of Law and Diplomacy. Law and Population Monograph Series. No. 42)*

— Research — Nigeria.

McWILLIAM (JOHN) and UCHE (CHUKWUDUM) Nigeria: selected studies: social science research for population and family planning policies and programme. London, 1976. pp. 50. *bibliog. (International Planned Parenthood Federation. Research for Action. No. 1)*

— America, Latin.

CARVAJAL (MANUEL J.) and GEITHMAN (DAVID T.) Family planning and family size determination: the evidence from seven Latin American cities. Gainesville, Fla., 1976. pp. 96. *bibliog. (Florida University. School of Inter-American Studies. Latin American Monographs. 2nd Series. 18)*

— Botswana.

COOK (SHEILA) Evaluation of family planning programmes: an example from Botswana. London, 1976. pp. 13. *(International Planned Parenthood Federation. Evaluation and Social Sciences Department. Research for Action. No. 2)*

— Denmark.

MØRKEBERG (HENRIK) Fødslers placering i familiens livsforløb, etc. København, 1976. pp. 158. *bibliog.(Socialforskningsinstituttet. Publikationer. 68) With English summary.*

— Ireland (Republic).

ROSE (R.S.) An outline of fertility control, focusing on the element of abortion in the Republic of Ireland to 1976. Stockholm, 1976. pp. 249. *Ph.D. thesis, Stockholm - University of Stockholm.*

— Malaysia.

NATIONAL FAMILY PLANNING BOARD, MALAYSIA. Annual report. a., 1970, 1972- [Kuala Lumpur]. *[in English and Malay].*

— Nigeria.

McWILLIAM (JOHN) and UCHE (CHUKWUDUM) Nigeria: selected studies: social science research for population and family planning policies and programme. London, 1976. pp. 50. *bibliog. (International Planned Parenthood Federation. Research for Action. No. 1)*

— Singapore.

SINGAPORE. Family Planning and Population Board. 1974. Report of the first national survey on family planning in Singapore, 1973. [Singapore], 1974. pp. 141, 1 map.

— Underdeveloped areas.

See UNDERDEVELOPED AREAS — Birth control.

— United Kingdom.

LANGFORD (C.M.) Birth control practice and marital fertility in Great Britain: a report on a survey carried out in 1967-68. London, 1976. pp. 141.

WALT (AUDREY GILLIAN) Policy making in Britain: a comparative study of fluoridation and family planning, 1960-1974. 1976. fo. 273. *bibliog. Typescript. Ph.D. (London) thesis: unpublished. This thesis is the property of London University and may not be removed from the Library.*

— — Scotland.

AITKEN-SWAN (JEAN) Fertility control and the medical profession. London, [1977]. pp. 238.

— United States.

CUTRIGHT (PHILLIPS) and JAFFE (FREDERICK S.) Impact of family planning programs on fertility: the U.S. experience. New York, 1977. pp. 150.

WESTOFF (CHARLES F.) and RYDER (NORMAN B.) The contraceptive revolution. Princeton, [1977]. pp. 388. *Published for the Office of Population Research, Princeton University.*

BISMARCK-SCHOENHAUSEN (OTTO EDUARD LEOPOLD VON) Prince.

BISMARCKS Sturz: zur Rolle der Klassen in der Endphase des preussisch-deutschen Bonapartismus 1884/85 bis 1890...; wissenschaftliche Redaktion: Gustav Seeber, Heinz Wolter; Autoren: Konrad Canis [and others]. Berlin, 1977. pp. 422. *bibliog. (Akademie der Wissenschaften der DDR. Zentralinstitut für Geschichte. Schriften. Band 52)*

STERN (FRITZ RICHARD) Gold and iron: Bismarck, Bleichröder, and the building of the German Empire. London, 1977. pp. 620.

BLACK (JOSEPH).

DONOVAN (ARTHUR L.) Philosophical chemistry in the Scottish Enlightenment: the doctrines and discoveries of William Cullen and Joseph Black. Edinburgh, [1975]. pp. 343. *bibliog.*

BLACK COUNTRY

— History.

BARNSBY (GEORGE) The working class movement in the Black Country, 1750 to 1867. Wolverhampton, 1977. pp. 233. *bibliog.*

BLACK DEATH.

DOLS (MICHAEL WALTERS) The Black Death in the Middle East. Princeton, N.J., [1977]. pp. 390. *bibliog.*

BLACK PANTHER PARTY.

HEATH (G. LOUIS) ed. The Black Panther leaders speak: Huey P. Newton, Bobby Seale, Eldridge Cleaver and company speak out through the Black Panther Party's official newspaper. Metuchen, N.J., 1976. pp. 165. *bibliog.*

HEATH (G. LOUIS) ed. Off the pigs!: the history and literature of the Black Panther Party. Metuchen, N.J., 1976. pp. 419. *bibliog.*

BLACK POWER

— Caribbean Area.

MATTHEWS (HARRY G.) Multinational corporations and black power. Cambridge, Mass., [1976]. pp. 124.

BLACKSMITHS

— Germany.

LEUNINGER (ALOIS) Die Nagelschmiede von Mengerskirchen: zur Geschichte eines ausgestorbenen Gewerbes. [Weilburg, 1972?]. pp. 24. *(Sonderdruck aus "Land und Leute im Oberlahnkreis", Heimatkundliche Beilage des "Weilburger Tageblatt")*

BLAENAVON

— History.

DAVIES (EDWARD JOHN) Sometime Chairman, Blaenavon Urban District Council. The Blaenavon story. 2nd ed. [Pontypool], Torfaen Borough Council, 1975. pp. 125.

BLAGA (LUCIAN).

BLAGA (LUCIAN) Aspecte antropologice; ediţie îngrijită şi prefaţă de Ion Maxim, postfaţă de Al. Tănase. [n.p.], 1976. pp. 203.

BLAKE (EDWARD).

SCHULL (JOHN JOSEPH) Edward Blake: leader and exile, 1881-1912. Toronto, [1976]. pp. 266. *bibliog.*

BLEICHROEDER (GERSON VON).

STERN (FRITZ RICHARD) Gold and iron: Bismarck, Bleichröder, and the building of the German Empire. London, 1977. pp. 620.

BLIND

— Nigeria.

NIGERIAN NATIONAL ADVISORY COUNCIL FOR THE BLIND. Tenth anniversary report, 1960-1970. [Lagos, Government Printer, 1970]. pp. 38.

BLOCH (ERNST).

UTOPIE - marxisme selon Ernst Bloch: un système de l'inconstructible; hommages à Ernst Bloch pour son 90e anniversaire publiés sous la direction de Gérard Raulet. Paris, 1976. pp. 334. *bibliog.*

BOCHUM

— History.

WAGNER (JOHANNES VOLKER) Nur Mut, sei Kämpfer!: Heinrich König, ein Leben für die Freiheit: Bochumer politische Lebensbilder aus der Zeit der Weimarer Republik und des Nationalsozialismus. Bochum, 1976. pp. 231. *bibliog. (Bochum. Stadtarchiv. Veröffentlichungen)*

BODY IMAGE.

FISHER (SEYMOUR) Body consciousness. Glasgow, 1976. pp. 221. *bibliog. First published in 1973.*

BOERS.

SCHREINER (OLIVE) Thoughts on South Africa. Johannesburg, 1976. pp. 398. *Reprint of the 1923 edition with new foreword and illustrations.*

BOGOMILES.

OBOLENSKY (DIMITRI) Prince. The Bogomils: a study in Balkan neo-Manichaeism. Twickenham, 1948 repr. 1972. pp. 317. *bibliog.*

BOLIVIA

— Commerce.

ANUARIO DE COMERCIO EXTERIOR DE LA REPUBLICA BOLIVIA; [pd. by] Instituto Nacional de Estadistica. a., 1972- La Paz.

— Economic conditions.

PUHLE (HANS JUERGEN) Tradicion y politica de reformas en Bolivia: economia, sociedad y politica en un pais sudamericano en desarrollo; (traductor: Leonardo Halpern). Santiago de Chile. 1972. pp. 146. *(Instituto Latinoamericano de Investigaciones Sociales. Estudios y Documentos. 19)*

MOLLOJA HOYOS (RANULFO) Enfoque socio-economico del sudeste. La Paz, 1973. pp. 499. *bibliog.*

— — Statistics.

ESTADISTICAS ECONOMICAS (formerly Economic and program statistics); [pd. by] USAID - Bolivia. [formerly in English and Spanish]. a., Oc 1964 (6)- , with gap (1968, 1969). [La Paz].

— Economic policy.

MOLLOJA HOYOS (RANULFO) Enfoque socio-economico del sudeste. La Paz, 1973. pp. 499. *bibliog.*

— Foreign economic relations.

ROMERO LOZA (JOSE) Bolivia: nacion en desarrollo. La Paz, 1974. pp. 457. *bibliog.*

— Foreign relations — United States.

ANDRADE (VICTOR) My missions for revolutionary Bolivia, 1944-1962;...edited and with an introduction by Cole Blasier. Pittsburgh, Pa., [1976]. pp. 200.

— History.

ROMERO LOZA (JOSE) Bolivia: nacion en desarrollo. La Paz, 1974. pp. 457. *bibliog.*

— — To 1809.

BARNADAS (JOSEP MARIA) Charcas: origenes historicos de una sociedad colonial. La Paz, 1973. pp. 635. *bibliog.*

— — 1825-1879.

SALINAS MARIACA (RAMON) Viva Belzu: compendio de la vida y obra de este gran caudillo. La Paz, [1974]. pp. 196.

— Industries.

BOLIVIA. Direccion General de Estadistica y Censos. Anuario industrial. a., 1965. La Paz.

BOLIVIA. Instituto Nacional de Estadistica. Estadisticas industriales. a., 1969/71- La Paz. *In 3 vols.*

— Politics and government.

PUHLE (HANS JUERGEN) Tradicion y politica de reformas en Bolivia: economia, sociedad y politica en un pais sudamericano en desarrollo; (traductor: Leonardo Halpern). Santiago de Chile. 1972. pp. 146. *(Instituto Latinoamericano de Investigaciones Sociales. Estudios y Documentos. 19)*

RAMOS (JORGE ABELARDO) Marxismo para latinoamericanos. Buenos Aires, [1973]. pp. 341.

— Social conditions.

PUHLE (HANS JUERGEN) Tradicion y politica de reformas en Bolivia: economia, sociedad y politica en un pais sudamericano en desarrollo; (traductor: Leonardo Halpern). Santiago de Chile. 1972. pp. 146. *(Instituto Latinoamericano de Investigaciones Sociales. Estudios y Documentos. 19)*

— Statistics.

BOLIVIA EN CIFRAS; [pd. by] Instituto Nacional de Estadistica. a., 1973- La Paz.

BOLTON

— Economic history.

DAVIES (TREVOR) Bolton, May 1926: a review of the General Strike as it affected Bolton and district. [Bolton, 1976]. pp. 19.

BOMBAY (CITY)

— Economic conditions.

JOSHI (HEATHER) and JOSHI (VIJAY CHANDRA) Surplus labour and the city: a study of Bombay. Delhi, 1976. pp. 189.

— Economic policy.

JOSHI (HEATHER) and JOSHI (VIJAY CHANDRA) Surplus labour and the city: a study of Bombay. Delhi, 1976. pp. 189.

BONNOT DE MABLY (GABRIEL).

BONNOT DE MABLY (GABRIEL) Sur la théorie du pouvoir politique; introduction et notes par Peter Friedmann. Paris, [1975]. pp. 288.

BOOK INDUSTRIES AND TRADE.

GRUNDMANN (HERBERT) Buch, Buchhandel und Politik. 2nd ed. Bonn, 1966 repr. 1974. pp. 35. *bibliog. (Bonn. Universität. Universitätsbibliothek. Forschungsstelle für Buchwissenschaft. Kleine Schriften. 5)*

GEDIN (PER) Literature in the marketplace; translated by George Bisset. London, 1977. pp. 211.

— Ghana.

GHANA. Committee of Enquiry into the affairs of the Distribution Division of the Ghana Publishing Corporation. 1967. Report; [K.S. Essah, chairman]. Accra, [1968]. pp. 64. *Bound with White Paper on the report.*

GHANA. 1969. White Paper on the report of the Committee of Enquiry into the affairs of the Distribution Division of the erstwhile State Publishing Corporation. [Accra, 1969]. pp. 8. *(W[hite] P[apers]. 1969. No. 1) Bound with the report.*

— India.

NATIONAL COUNCIL OF APPLIED ECONOMIC RESEARCH. Survey of Indian book industry. New Delhi, [1976]. 2 vols.

— United Kingdom.

STUDIES in the book trade in honour of Graham Pollard; [edited by R.W. Hunt and others]. Oxford, 1975. pp. 403. *bibliog. (Oxford. Oxford Bibliographical Society. Publications. New Series. vol. 18)*

MAXTED (IAN) The London book trades, 1775-1800: a preliminary checklist of members. Folkestone, Kent, 1977. pp. 257.

BOOKBINDERS

— Sweden.

EK (SVEN B.) 14 augusti 1894: en bok om arbetarna i bokbinderi och emballageindustri i Lund. Lund, 1974. pp. 135. *bibliog. (Etnologiska Sällskapet i Lund. Skrifter. 5) With English summary.*

BOOKS.

SPIRE (ANTOINE) and VIALA (JEAN PIERRE) La bataille du livre. Paris, [1976]. pp. 302.

— History — Russia.

LUPPOV (SERGEI PAVLOVICH) Kniga v Rossii v poslepetrovskoe vremia, 1725-1740. Leningrad, 1976. pp. 380.

— — — Tatar Republic.

KARIMULLIN (ABRAR GIBADULLOVICH) U istokov tatarskoi knigi: ot nachala vozniknoveniia do 60-kh godov XIX veka. Kazan', 1971. pp. 223. *bibliog.*

BOOKS AND READING.

GRUNDMANN (HERBERT) Buch, Buchhandel und Politik. 2nd ed. Bonn, 1966 repr. 1974. pp. 35. *bibliog. (Bonn. Universität. Universitätsbibliothek. Forschungsstelle für Buchwissenschaft. Kleine Schriften. 5)*

SPIRE (ANTOINE) and VIALA (JEAN PIERRE) La bataille du livre. Paris, [1976]. pp. 302.

— Bibliography.

MANN (MARGARET GWENDOLINE) compiler. The role of books in higher education: a select annotated bibliography. Sheffield, 1974. pp. 86.

BOOKSELLERS AND BOOKSELLING

— Germany.

[A COLLECTION of documents relating to book censorship and the book trade in Germany during the years immediately following World War II]. 1945-48. pp. various.

— Russia.

ARBUZOV (MIKHAIL FEDOROVICH) Knizhnaia torgovlia v SSSR: teoreticheskie osnovy i printsipy organizatsii. Moskva, 1976. pp. 156.

BOOTS AND SHOES

— Trade and manufacture — Nigeria.

NAFZIGER (E. WAYNE) African capitalism: a case study in Nigerian entrepreneurship. Stanford, Calif., 1977. pp. 293. *bibliog. (Stanford University. Hoover Institution on War, Revolution and Peace. Hoover Institution Publications. 169)*

— — United Kingdom.

U.K. Footwear Industry Study Steering Group. 1977. Report;...chairman: G.W. Marriott. London, 1977. 1 vol. (various pagings).

— — United States — Massachusetts.

DAWLEY (ALAN) Class and community: the industrial revolution in Lynn. Cambridge, Mass., 1976. pp. 301. *bibliog. (Harvard University. Harvard Studies in Urban History)*

BOPHUTHATSWANA

— Economic conditions.

SOUTH AFRICA. Bureau for Economic Research re Bantu Development. 1975. Bophuthatswana:...economic revue [sic], 1975, etc. Pretoria, 1975. pp. 66. *bibliog. In English and Afrikaans.*

BORDEAUX

— Commerce.

HUETZ DE LEMPS (CHRISTIAN) Géographie du commerce de Bordeaux à la fin du règne de Louis XIV. Paris, [1975]. pp. 661. *bibliog. (Paris. Ecole des Hautes Etudes en Sciences Sociales. Centre de Recherches Historiques. Civilisations et Sociétés. 49)*

— Economic history.

HUETZ DE LEMPS (CHRISTIAN) Géographie du commerce de Bordeaux à la fin du règne de Louis XIV. Paris, [1975]. pp. 661. *bibliog. (Paris. Ecole des Hautes Etudes en Sciences Sociales. Centre de Recherches Historiques. Civilisations et Sociétés. 49)*

BORDEN (ROBERT LAIRD).

BROWN (ROBERT CRAIG) Robert Laird Borden: a biography. Toronto, [1975 in progress]. *bibliog.*

BORDER PATROLS

— Russia.

POGRANICHNYE voiska SSSR v Velikoi Otechestvennoi voine, 1941: sbornik dokumentov i materialov. Moskva, 1976. pp. 944.

BORNEO

— Appropriations and expenditures.

NORTH BORNEO. Standing Finance Committee. Summary of supplementary provision. q., 1959-1960, with gaps (1959: no.1, 1960: no.4). [Jesselton].

BOSNIA

— Nationalism.

ŠEHIĆ (NUSRET) Četništvo u Bosni i Hercegovini, 1918-1941: politička uloga i oblici djelatnosti četničkih udruženja; Le mouvement des tchetniks en Bosnie-Herzegovine, etc.; urednik Hamdija Kapidžić. Sarajevo, 1971. pp. 239. *bibliog. (Akademija Nauka i Umjetnosti Bosne i Hercegovine. Djela. kn.42 [being also] Odjeljenje Društvenih Nauka. kn.27) With German summary.*

BOSTON, MASSACHUSETTS

— Schools.

HILLSON (JON) The battle of Boston. New York, [1977]. pp. 286.

— Social conditions.

DIFFERENT strokes: pathways to maturity in the Boston ghetto; a report to the Ford Foundation; ([by] Robert Rosenthal [and others]). Boulder, Colo., 1976. pp. 358. *bibliog.*

BOTSWANA

— Executive departments.

BOTSWANA. Department of Customs and Excise. Report. a., 1975/77[2nd]- Gaborone.

— Politics and government.

VENGROFF (RICHARD) Botswana: rural development in the shadow of apartheid. Rutherford, N.J., [1977]. pp. 205. *bibliog.*

BOURDIEU (PIERRE).

SNYDERS (GEORGES) Ecole, classe et lutte des classes: une relecture critique de Baudelot-Establet, Bourdieu-Passeron et Illich. Paris, [1976]. pp. 379.

BOYCOTT

— United Kingdom.

COFFEE for Britain means blood for Angola. Birmingham, [1973]. pp. 15.

BOYS

— Societies and clubs — United Kingdom.

HASELHURST (ALAN) A time for heroes. [London], 1976. pp. 12. *(National Association of Boys' Clubs. Basil Henriques Memorial Lectures. 1976)*

BRADLEY (FRANCIS HERBERT).

BRADLEY (FRANCIS HERBERT) The presuppositions of critical history; edited with introduction and commentary by Lionel Rubinoff. Chicago, [1968]. pp. 147. *bibliog.*

BRAIN.

BLAKEMORE (COLIN) Mechanics of the mind. Cambridge, 1977. pp. 208. *bibliog. (British Broadcasting Corporation. Reith Lectures. 1976)*

BRAIN DRAIN.

BRAIN drain statistics: empirical evidence and guidelines; (report on an international expert meeting in Stockholm 1973 and guidelines for future studies); editor, Göran Friborg. Stockholm, 1975. pp. 283. *(Sweden. Forskningsekonomiska Kommittén. Rapporter. 6)*

GRUBEL (HERBERT G.) and SCOTT (ANTHONY) The brain drain: determinants, measurement and welfare effects. Waterloo, Ont., [1977]. pp. 165. *bibliog. Brings together papers previously published during the period 1966 to 1970.*

— Nigeria.

NIGERIA. Ministerial Committee on the Nigerian Brain Drain. 1974. Report; [T.A. Otubanjo, Chairman]. Lagos, 1974. pp. 111.

BRANDENBURG (PROVINCE)

— Economic history.

INDUSTRIALISIERUNG und Gewerbe in Raum Berlin/Brandenburg. Band II. Die Zeit um 1800/ die Zeit um 1875; herausgegeben von Otto Büsch; mit Textbeiträgen von Otto Büsch und Wolfgang Scharfe, und Kartenbeilagen zum "Gewerbe in Brandenburg..." bearbeitet von Otto Büsch [and others]. Berlin, 1977. pp. 186. *(Historische Kommission zu Berlin. Einzelveröffentlichungen. Band 19)* 2 maps in end pocket.

BRANDT (WILLY).

LEHMANN (HANS GEORG) In Acht und Bann: politische Emigration, NS- Ausbürgerung und Wiedergutmachung am Beispiel Willy Brandts. München, [1976]. pp. 387. *bibliog.*

BRAUN (OTTO).

SCHULZE (HAGEN) Otto Braun; oder, Preussens demokratische Sendung: eine Biographie...; eine Veröffentlichung der Stiftung Preussischer Kulturbesitz. Frankfurt/M, [1977]. pp. 1095. *bibliog.*

BRAZIL

— Armed forces.

BLACK (JAN KNIPPERS) United States penetration of Brazil. [Philadelphia], 1977. pp. 313. *bibliog.*

— — Political activity.

HAUSEN (IVAN ZANONI) Brasil: por que os militarese? Rio de Janeiro, 1975. pp. 213. *bibliog.*

— Boundaries — Paraguay.

CARDOZO (EFRAIM) 20 preguntas sin respuesta sobre los Saltos del Guaira: recopilacion de articulos publicados en "El Radical". Asuncion, 1971. pp. 122.

— Census.

BRAZIL. Census, 1970. (VIII recenseamento geral, 1970): censo demografico: [states and federal district]. [Rio de Janeiro, 1972-73]. 26 parts. *Tomos XVI, Rio de Janeiro, XX Santa Catarina out of print.*

— Civilization.

RIBEIRO (DARCY) Los brasileños. Mexico, 1975. pp. 211. *bibliog.*

— Economic conditions.

BRAZIL DEVELOPMENT SERIES. No.3. São Paulo, 1972. 2 vols. *Vol. 2 entitled The National Housing Plan.*

ENSAIOS econômicos: ([in honour of] Octavio Gouvêa de Bulhões); [edited by Mircea Buescu]. Rio de Janeiro, [1972 repr.] 1974. pp. 549.

ANDRADE (MANUEL CORREIA DE) Cidade e campo no Brasil. São Paulo, 1974. pp. 223.

FURTADO (CELSO) El desarrollo economico: un mito. Mexico, 1975 repr. 1976. pp. 141.

BRAZIL in the seventies; Riordan Roett, editor. Washington, D.C., [1976]. pp. 118. *(American Enterprise Institute for Public Policy Research. AEI Studies. 132) Papers discussed at a series of seminars in March 1976.*

CAMBRIDGE. University. Centre of Latin American Studies. Working Papers. No.24. Underconsumption, market size and expenditure patterns in Brazil; by J.R. Wells. Cambridge, 1976. pp. 57.

SIMONSEN (MARIO HENRIQUE) and CAMPOS (ROBERTO DE OLIVEIRA) A nova economia Brasileira. 2nd ed. Rio de Janeiro, 1976. pp. 257.

SCHLAGHECK (JAMES L.) The political, economic and labor climate in Brazil. Philadelphia, [1977]. pp. 116. *(Pennsylvania University. Wharton School of Finance and Commerce. Industrial Research Unit. Multinational Industrial Relations Series. No.4a)*

SINGER (PAUL ISRAEL) Brazilian economist. A crise do "milagre": interpretação critica da economia brasileira. Rio de Janeiro, 1977. pp. 167.

— Economic history.

ANDRADE (MANUEL CORREIA DE) Historia econômica e administrativa do Brasil. São Paulo, 1976. pp. 193. *bibliog.*

LIMA (HEITOR FERREIRA) Historia do pensamento econômico no Brasil. São Paulo, 1976. pp. 198.

PELAEZ (CARLOS MANUEL) and BUESCU (MIRCEA) eds. A moderna historia econômica. Rio de Janeiro, [1976]. pp. 257.

— Economic policy.

BRAZIL DEVELOPMENT SERIES. No.3. São Paulo, 1972. 2 vols. *Vol. 2 entitled The National Housing Plan.*

HADDAD (PAULO ROBERTO) ed. Desequilibrios regionais e descentralização industrial. Rio de Janeiro, 1975. pp. 206. *(Brazil. Instituto de Planejamento Econômico e Social. Instituto de Pesquisas. Monografias. No. 16)*

PLANEJAMENTO; [pd.by] Fundação de Pesquisas-CPE, Secretaria do Planejamento, Ciencia e Tecnologia [Bahia(State)]. q., Ja/Mr 1976 (v.4,no1)- Salvador.

SIMONSEN (MARIO HENRIQUE) and CAMPOS (ROBERTO DE OLIVEIRA) A nova economia Brasileira. 2nd ed. Rio de Janeiro, 1976. pp. 257.

SINGER (PAUL ISRAEL) Brazilian economist. A crise do "milagre": interpretação critica da economia brasileira. Rio de Janeiro, 1977. pp. 167.

— Emigration and immigration.

DURHAM (EUNICE RIBEIRO) Assimilação e mobilidade: a historia do imigrante italiano num municipio paulista. São Paulo, 1966. pp. 67. *bibliog. (São Paulo. Universidade. Instituto de Estudos Brasileiros. Publicações. 3)*

DIEGUES (MANUEL) Etnias e culturas no Brasil. Rio de Janeiro, 1976. pp. 208. *bibliog.*

— Executive departments.

BRAZIL. Ministerio das Relações Exteriores. Relatorio. a., 1974- [Rio de Janeiro].

— Foreign economic relations.

BRAZIL in the seventies; Riordan Roett, editor. Washington, D.C., [1976]. pp. 118. (*American Enterprise Institute for Public Policy Research. AEI Studies. 132*) *Papers discussed at a series of seminars in March 1976.*

— Foreign relations.

BRAZIL. Ministerio das Relações Exteriores. Relatorio. a., 1974- [Rio de Janeiro].

BRAZIL in the seventies; Riordan Roett, editor. Washington, D.C., [1976]. pp. 118. (*American Enterprise Institute for Public Policy Research. AEI Studies. 132*) *Papers discussed at a series of seminars in March 1976.*

PERRY (WILLIAM) Writer on foreign policy. Contemporary Brazilian foreign policy: the international strategy of an emerging power. Beverly Hills, [1976]. pp. 89. (*Foreign Policy Research Institute. Foreign Policy Papers. Vol. 2/6*)

— — United States.

BLACK (JAN KNIPPERS) United States penetration of Brazil. [Philadelphia], 1977. pp. 313. *bibliog.*

— Historiography.

LAPA (JOSÉ ROBERTO DO AMARAL) A historia em questão: historiografia Brasileira contemporânea. Petrópolis, 1976. pp. 204. *bibliog.*

— History.

RIBEIRO (DARCY) Los brasileños. Mexico, 1975. pp. 211. *bibliog.*

ANDRADE (MANUEL CORREIA DE) Historia econômica e administrativa do Brasil. São Paulo, 1976. pp. 193. *bibliog.*

— — 1964, Revolution.

BLACK (JAN KNIPPERS) United States penetration of Brazil. [Philadelphia], 1977. pp. 313. *bibliog.*

— Industries.

BRAZIL. Departamento de Censos. 1974. Censo industrial [1970]: Brasil [whole country]. [Rio de Janeiro, 1974]. pp. 287.

BRAZIL. Departamento de Censos. 1975. Censo industrial [1970]: Brasil; produção fisica. [Rio de Janeiro, 1975]. pp. 303.

SILVA (SERGIO) Expansão cafeeira e origens da industria no Brasil. São Paulo, 1976. pp. 120. *bibliog.*

WIPPLINGER (GUENTER) Kleine und mittlere Industrieunternehmen in Brasilien: Strukturen, Probleme, Förderung. Tübingen, [1976]. pp. 170. (*Institut für Iberoamerika-Kunde. Schriftenreihe. Band 27*)

MARTINS (JOSÉ DE SOUZA) Agriculture and industry in Brazil: two studies. Cambridge, 1977. pp. 32. (*Cambridge. University. Centre of Latin American Studies. Working Papers. No. 27*)

— Politics and government.

ESTUDOS LEGISLATIVOS; [pd. by] Câmara dos Deputados [Brazil]. s-a., Ja/Je 1973 (v.1, no.1)- Brasilia.

HAUSEN (IVAN ZANONI) Brasil: por que os militarese? Rio de Janeiro, 1975. pp. 213. *bibliog.*

LAFER (CELSO) O sistema politico brasileiro: estrutura e processo. São Paulo, [1975]. pp. 130.

SCHLAGHECK (JAMES L.) The political, economic and labor climate in Brazil. Philadelphia, [1977]. pp. 116. (*Pennsylvania University. Wharton School of Finance and Commerce. Industrial Research Unit. Multinational Industrial Relations Series. No.4a*)

— Population.

HADDAD (PAULO ROBERTO) ed. Desequilibrios regionais e descentralização industrial. Rio de Janeiro, 1975. pp. 206. (*Brazil. Instituto de Planejamento Econômico e Social. Instituto de Pesquisas. Monografias. No. 16*)

— Relations (general) with the United States.

FOX (ANNETTE BAKER) The politics of attraction: four middle powers and the United States. New York, 1977. pp. 371.

— Rural conditions.

ANDRADE (MANUEL CORREIA DE) Cidade e campo no Brasil. São Paulo, 1974. pp. 223.

— Social conditions.

RIBEIRO (DARCY) Los brasileños. Mexico, 1975. pp. 211. *bibliog.*

— Social policy.

PLANEJAMENTO; [pd.by] Fundação de Pesquisas-CPE, Secretaria do Planejamento, Ciencia e Tecnologia [Bahia(State)]. q., Ja/Mr 1976 (v.4,no1)- Salvador.

— Statistics.

PORTO SEGURO ( ) Visconde de. Quelques renseignements statistiques sur le Brésil: tirés de sources officielles par le délégué au congrès de Bude-Pesth. Vienne, 1876. pp. 23. *Author's edition.*

BREAD.

IRELAND, NORTHERN. Working Party on Bread Costs and Prices. 1976. Report; [N.J. Gibson, chairman]. [Belfast], 1976. fo. 43.

BRECHT (BERTOLT).

ALBRECHT (RICHARD) Marxismus, bürgerliche Ideologie, Linksradikalismus: zur Ideologie und Sozialgeschichte des westeuropäischen Linksradikalismus. Frankfurt/Main, 1975. pp. 169.

BRECON BEACONS NATIONAL PARK.

BRECON BEACONS NATIONAL PARK COMMITTEE. Draft national park plan, for public discussion and consultation. Brecon, 1976. 1 vol. (unpaged).

BREMEN

— Commerce.

MEYER's Contor-Handbuch, 1827-1829: Faksimile-Ausgabe der Beiträge Altona, Bremen, Hamburg. Hamburg, 1977. 1 vol. (various pagings). (*Wirtschaftsgeschichtliche Forschungsstelle. Veröffentlichungen. Band 40*) With postscripts by Maria Möring and Heinz Sarkowski.

— Water supply.

OHL (ALFRED) Die Wasserversorgung der Freien Hansestadt Bremen: 100 Jahre zentrale Wasserversorgung, 1873 bis 1973. Bremen, 1973. pp. 275. *bibliog.*

BRESCIA

— History.

RUZZENENTI (MARINO) Il movimento operaio bresciano nella Resistenza. Roma, 1975. pp. 227.

BREWER (WAYNE).

SOMERSET. Area Review Committee for Non-accidental Injury to Children. Review Panel. Wayne Brewer; report of the review panel; [by] John Clark [and others]. Taunton, 1977. pp. 51.

BREZHNEV (LEONID IL'ICH).

BREZHNEV (LEONID IL'ICH) Voprosy upravleniia ekonomikoi razvitogo sotsialisticheskogo obshchestva: rechi, doklady, vystupleniia. Moskva, 1976. pp. 600.

DNEPROVSKIE ogni: kak iz ruin i pepla byl podniat posle voiny Zaporozhskii industrial'nyi kompleks. Kiev, 1976. pp. 190.

BRIAND (ARISTIDE PIERRE HENRI).

ROLO (PAUL JACQUES VICTOR) Britain and the Briand plan: the common market that never was: an inaugural lecture...given in the University of Keele, 1972. Keele, 1973. pp. 23.

BRIBERY

— Mathematical models.

YOUNG (H.P.) Power, prices, and incomes in voting systems. Laxenburg, 1977. pp. 28. *bibliog.* (*International Institute for Applied Systems Analysis. Research Memoranda. RM-77-5*)

— Netherlands.

NETHERLANDS. Commissie van Drie. 1976. Rapport...: onderzoek naar de juistheid van verklaringen over betalingen door een Amerikaanse vliegtuigfabriek. 's-Gravenhage, 1976. pp. 240.

BRICK TRADE

— United States.

McCOLLAM (C. HAROLD) The brick and tile industry in Stark County, 1809-1976: a history. Canton, Ohio, 1976. pp. 337.

BRIGANDS AND ROBBERS

— Switzerland.

HUGGER (PAUL) Sozialrebellen und Rechtsbrecher in der Schweiz: eine historisch-volkskundliche Studie. Zürich, [1976]. pp. 143. *bibliog.*

BRISTOL

— Docks.

NEALE (W.G.) The tides of war and the port of Bristol, 1914-1918. Bristol, Port of Bristol Authority, 1976. pp. 349. *bibliog. Continues his At the port of Bristol.*

— Politics and government.

MARSHALL (PETER D.) Bristol and the abolition of slavery: the politics of emancipation. Bristol, 1975. pp. 28,iv. *bibliog.* (*Historical Association. Bristol Branch. Local History Pamphlets. No. 37*)

BRISTOL. Bristol Record Society. Publications. vol. 29. Bristol and its municipal government, 1820-1851; by Graham Bush. Bristol, 1976. pp. 254. *bibliog.*

— Social history.

PRESS (JONATHAN) The merchant seamen of Bristol, 1747-1789. Bristol, 1976. pp. 23. *bibliog.* (*Historical Association. Bristol Branch. Local History Pamphlets. No. 38*)

BRITISH BROADCASTING CORPORATION.

BURNS (TOM) The BBC: public institution and private world. London, 1977. pp. 313.

BRITISH COLUMBIA

— Economic conditions.

BRITISH COLUMBIA. Bureau of Provincial Information. 1910. Handbook of British Columbia, Canada. [London], 1910. pp. 71. *Map in end pocket.*

BRITISH COLUMBIA. Bureau of Provincial Information. 1911. Columbia-Kootenay valley and its resources and capabilities. Victoria, 1911. pp. 97. (*Bulletins. No. 26*) *Map in end pocket.*

— Economic history.

ESSAYS in B.C. political economy; edited by Paul Knox and Philip Resnick. Vancouver, [1974]. pp. 81. *Essays mainly from the first conference of the British Columbia Committee on Socialist Studies, held at the University of British Columbia in January, 1973.*

BRITISH IN INDIA.

MARSHALL (PETER JAMES) East Indian fortunes: the British in Bengal in the eighteenth century. London, 1976. pp. 284. *bibliog.*

— Bibliography.

RENFORD (RAYMOND K.) Archival and library sources for the study of the activities of the non-official British community in India: a brief survey. [London], 1976. pp. 25.

BRITISH IN PARAGUAY.

PLA (JOSEFINA) The British in Paraguay, 1850-1870; translated from the Spanish by Brian Charles MacDermot. Richmond, Surrey, [1976]. pp. 277. *bibliog.*

BRITISH VIRGIN ISLANDS

— Statistics.

STATISTICAL ABSTRACT OF THE BRITISH VIRGIN ISLANDS; [pd. by] Statistics Office. a., 1974 (1st)- Tortola.

BRITTANY

— Nationalism.

DENIEL (ALAIN) Le mouvement breton, 1919-1945. Paris, 1976. pp. 451. *bibliog.*

REECE (JACK E.) The Bretons against France: ethnic minority nationalism in twentieth-century Brittany. Chapel Hill, [1977]. pp. 263. *bibliog.*

BROADCASTING

— Social aspects — United Kingdom.

BURNS (TOM) The BBC: public institution and private world. London, 1977. pp. 313.

BROADSIDES

— Bibliography.

HARVARD UNIVERSITY. Library. Houghton Library. 1848: Austrian revolutionary broadsides and pamphlets: a catalogue of the collection in the Houghton Library, Harvard University; compiled by James E. Walsh. Boston, Mass., [1976]. pp. 286.

BROCKWAY (ARCHIBALD FENNER) Baron Brockway.

BROCKWAY (ARCHIBALD FENNER) Baron Brockway. Towards tomorrow: the autobiography of Fenner Brockway. London, 1977. pp. 280.

BRODETSKY (SELIG).

FISHER (SAMUEL) Baron Fisher of Camden. Brodetsky: leader of the Anglo-Jewish community. Leeds, 1976. pp. 29. *(Leeds. University. Selig Brodetsky Memorial Lectures. No. 17)*

BROWNE (FRANCES WORSLEY STELLA).

ROWBOTHAM (SHEILA) A new world for women: Stella Browne: socialist feminist. London, 1977. pp. 128.

BRUCE (DAVID KIRKPATRICK ESTE).

DOUGLAS-HOME (ALEXANDER FREDERICK) Baron Home, and others. Diplomacy, détente and the democracies;... edited...by D.K. Adams. Keele, [1976]. pp. 48. *(Keele. University. David Bruce Centre for American Studies. Lectures. 1976)*

BRUCE (THOMAS) 7th Earl of Elgin and 11th Earl of Kincardine.

BRUCE (THOMAS) 7th Earl of Elgin and 11th Earl of Kincardine. Letter to the editor of the Edinburgh Review on the subject of an article in No. L. of that journal, on "The remains of John Tweddell". 3rd. ed. London, J. Murray, 1816. pp. 63.

BRUNEI

— Census.

BRUNEI. Census, 1971. Report on the census of population, 1971. Banda Seri Begawan, [1973]. pp. 260.

— Population — Bibliography.

SAW (SWEE-HOCK) and CHENG (SIOK-HWA) compilers. A bibliography of the demography of Malaysia and Brunei. Singapore, 1975. pp. 103.

— Statistics.

GERMANY (BUNDESREPUBLIK). Statistisches Bundesamt. Länderkurzberichte: Brunei. a., 1976- Wiesbaden.

BRUNO (GIORDANO).

BRUNO (GIORDANO) The Ash Wednesday supper: La cena de le Ceneri; translated with an introduction and notes by Stanley L. Jaki. The Hague, [1975]. pp. 174.

BRUSON

— Social conditions.

WEINBERG (DANIELA) Peasant wisdom: cultural adaptation in a Swiss village. Berkeley, Calif., [1975]. pp. 214. *bibliog.*

BUCIUMI.

BĂDINA (OVIDIU) and others. Buciumi: un sat din Ţara de Sub Munte, etc. Bucureşti, 1970. pp. 410. *(Centrul de Cercetări pentru Problemele Tineretului. Tineretul şi Lumea de Mîine) With English, French, German, Russian and Spanish tables of contents.*

BUCKINGHAMSHIRE

— Economic history.

TURNER (M.E.) Land shortage as a prelude to Parliamentary enclosure: the example of Buckinghamshire. Sheffield, 1975. pp. 22. *(Sheffield. University. Department of Economic and Social History. Studies in Economic and Social History. 1)*

BUDDHA AND BUDDHISM

— Thailand.

TAMBIAH (S.J.) World conqueror and world renouncer: a study of Buddhism and polity in Thailand against a historical background. Cambridge, 1976. pp. 557. *bibliog.*

SUKSAMRAN (SOMBOON) Political Buddhism in southeast Asia: the role of the Sangha in the modernization of Thailand;...edited with an introduction by Trevor O. Ling. London, [1977]. pp. 154. *bibliog.*

BUDDHISM AND STATE

— Sri Lanka.

PHADNIS (URMILA) Religion and politics in Sri Lanka. London, 1976. pp. 376. *bibliog.*

— Thailand.

TAMBIAH (S.J.) World conqueror and world renouncer: a study of Buddhism and polity in Thailand against a historical background. Cambridge, 1976. pp. 557. *bibliog.*

SUKSAMRAN (SOMBOON) Political Buddhism in southeast Asia: the role of the Sangha in the modernization of Thailand;...edited with an introduction by Trevor O. Ling. London, [1977]. pp. 154. *bibliog.*

BUDGET.

GENIERE (RENAUD DE LA) Le budget. [Paris, 1976]. pp. 405. *bibliog. (Fondation Nationale des Sciences Politiques. Cahiers. 201)*

BUDGETS and bureaucrats: the sources of government growth; edited by Thomas E. Borcherding. Durham, N.C., 1977. pp. 291. *bibliogs. Papers for the year 1972-73 of Workshop on Non- Market Bureaucracy of the Center for the Study of Public Choice, Virginia Polytechnic Institute.*

— Angola.

ANGOLA. [Direccão dos Serviços de Finanças]. Orçamento geral. a., 1970-1974. [Luanda]. *File includes Avaliação das receitas do Orçamento geral, 1973.*

— Austria.

HENSELER (PETER) Stabilisierungseffekte der Budgetpolitik des Bundes, 1956-1969. Wien, 1972. pp. 45. *bibliog. (Institut für Finanzwissenschaft und Steuerrecht. Sonderdrucke)*

— Belgium.

BELGIUM. Ministère des Affaires Economiques. Direction Générale des Etudes et de la Documentation. Budget économique. a., 1975- Bruxelles. *File includes Annexe statistique and Estimations révisées.*

— Brazil.

BRAZIL. Secretaria de Planejamento da Presidência da Republica. Subsecretaria de Orçamento e Finanças. 1975. Orçamento plurianual de investimentos, triênio 1975/77: Lei No. 6,188 de 16 de Dezembro de 1974. Brasilia, 1975. 2 vols.

BRAZIL. Secretaria de Planejamento da Presidencia da Republica. Subsecretaria de Orçamento e Finanças. Orçamento da união. a., 1976- Brasilia.

— Colombia.

BAILEY (JOHN J.) Public budgeting in Colombia: disjoined incrementalism in a dependent polity. Austin, 1974. pp. 46. *(American Society for Public Administration. Latin American Development Administration Committee and Texas University. Institute of Latin American Studies. LADAC Occasional Papers. Series 2. No. 10)*

— Cyprus.

CYPRUS. Ministry of Finance. 1972. Address before the House of Representatives on the 1972 budget, the achievements of the second and the targets and objectives of the third five-year plan; by the Minister of Finance Andreas Patsalides. Nicosia, 1972. pp. 39.

— Czechoslovakia.

CZECHOSLOVAKIA. [Ministerstvo Financí]. 1967. Statement on the state budget for 1967 delivered in the National Assembly of the Czechoslovak Socialist Republic. [Prague, 1967]. fo. 47.

— Denmark.

DENMARK. (Finansministeriet). Forslag til finanslov. a., 1977/78- [København]. *In 2 v.; v.1. Tekst; v.2, Anmaerkninger.*

— Gambia.

GAMBIA. Ministry of Finance and Trade. 1971. Budget speech by S.M. Dibba, Minister of Finance and Trade, 25th June, 1971 in the House of Representatives. Bathurst, 1971. pp. 20. *(Gambia. Sessional Papers. 1971. No. 3)*

— Norway.

NORWAY. Finansdepartementet. Budsjettene: nasjonalbudsjettet, statsbudsjettet. a., current issue only. *Oslo.*

— Russia.

BESCHEREVNYKH (VIKTOR VASIL'EVICH) Kompetentsiia Soiuza SSR v oblasti biudzheta. Moskva, 1976. pp. 176.

— Sweden.

SWEDISH BUDGET, THE: a summary pd. by the Budgetdepartementet. a., 1962/63 (1st), 1963/64 (2nd), 1970/71 (9th)- Stockholm.

— United Kingdom — Guernsey.

GUERNSEY. States Office. Budget report. a., 1977- [St. Peter Port]. *Formerly included in GUERNSEY. Billet D'état.*

— United States.

BALUTIS (ALAN P.) and BUTLER (DARON K.) eds. The political pursestrings: the role of the legislature in the budgetary process. New York, [1975]. pp. 221.

LYNN (JAMES T.) and SCHULTZE (CHARLES L.) The Federal budget: what are the nation's priorities?. Washington, [1976]. pp. 54. *(American Enterprise Institute for Public Policy Research. Rational Debate Series)*

OTT (DAVID J.) and OTT (ATTIAT F.) Federal budget policy. 3rd ed. Washington, D.C., [1977]. pp. 178. *(Brookings Institution. Studies of Government Finance)*

— Zaire.

AYINGOL (MBAKAR) Budgetprobleme des Zaire: eine Analyse der Probleme der Budgetpolitik in der wirtschaftlichen und sozialen Entwicklung. Zürich, 1976. pp. 180. *bibliog. Dissertation der Universität Zürich zur Erlangung der Würde eines Doktors der Wirtschaftswissenschaft.*

BUDGET IN BUSINESS.

OLVE (NILS-GÖRAN) Multiobjective budgetary planning: models for interactive planning in decentralized organizations. Stockholm, 1977. pp. 312. *bibliog.*

BUELOW (BERNHARD HEINRICH MARTIN KARL) Fürst von.

WINZEN (PETER) Bülows Weltmachtkonzept: Untersuchung zur Frühphase seiner Aussenpolitik, 1897-1901. Boppard am Rhein, [1977]. pp. 462. *bibliog. (Germany (Bundesrepublik). Bundesarchiv. Schriften. 22)*

BUENOS AIRES (PROVINCE)

— Economic conditions.

TADIOLI (PEDRO) Buenos Aires hoy y mañana: introduccion a un estudio socio- economico de la provincia de Buenos Aires. La Plata, 1974. pp. 173.

— Social conditions.

TADIOLI (PEDRO) Buenos Aires hoy y mañana: introduccion a un estudio socio- economico de la provincia de Buenos Aires. La Plata, 1974. pp. 173.

BUILDING

— France — Statistics.

FRANCE. Direction du Bâtiment et des Travaux Publics et de la Conjoncture. Service des Statistiques et des Etudes Economiques. 1972- . Annuaire statistique de l'équipement. Paris, [1972 in progress].

BUILDING, BRICK.

WIGHT (JANE A.) Brick building in England: from the middle ages to 1550. London, 1972. pp. 439. *bibliog.*

BUILDING MATERIALS INDUSTRY

— France.

FRANCE. Groupe sectoriel d'Analyse et de Prévision Matériaux et Produits pour la Construction. 1976. Rapport...: préparation du 7e Plan. Paris, 1976. pp. 174.

BUILDINGS

BRAZIL. Departamento de Censos. 1974. Censo predial [1970]: Brasil [whole country]. [Rio de Janeiro, 1974]. pp. 74.

BUJAK (FRANCISZEK).

BUJAK (FRANCISZEK) Wybór pism; przedmowa, komentarze, przypisy i ogólna redakcja naukowa Helena Madurowicz-Urbańska. Warszawa, 1976. 2 vols. *bibliog.*

BUKHARA

— Economic history.

MUKMINOVA (ROZIIA GALIEVNA) Ocherki po istorii remesla v Samarkande i Bukhare v XVI veke. Tashkent, 1976. pp. 234.

— History.

KHALFIN (NAFTULA ARONOVICH) Rossiia i Bukharskii emirat na Zapadnom Pamire, konets XIX - nachalo XX v. Moskva, 1975. pp. 127.

ISTORIIA Bukhary s drevneishikh vremen do nashikh dnei. Tashkent, 1976. pp. 383. *bibliog.*

— — Sources.

ISTORIIA Bukharskoi Narodnoi Sovetskoi Respubliki, 1920-1924 gg.: sbornik dokumentov. Tashkent, 1976. pp. 483.

BULGARIA

— Economic conditions.

DOBREV (KRUSTIU ZHELIAZKOV) Problemi na stroitelstvoto na sotsializma v NR Bulgariia: izbrani proizvedeniia; [with an introductory essay by Ivan Stefanov]. Sofiia, 1975. pp. 267. *bibliog.*

— Economic policy.

SOTSIALNO-ikonomicheski problemi na izgrazhdaneto na razvito sotsialistichesko obshtestvo v Bulgariia; Socio-economic problems in building a developed socialist society in Bulgaria. Sofiia, 1974. pp. 403. *With Russian and English summaries and tables of contents.*

FEIWEL (GEORGE R.) Growth and reforms in centrally planned economies: the lessons of the Bulgarian experience. New York, 1977. pp. 345. *bibliog.*

— Foreign relations — Russia.

SOVETSKO-bolgarskie otnosheniia i sviazi: dokumenty i materialy. Moskva, 1976 in progress. *bibliog.*

— Politics and government.

ZHIVKOV (TODOR) Izbrannye stat'i i rechi, 1965-1975; [perevod s bolgarskogo]. Moskva, 1975. pp. 583.

— Social conditions.

OSHAVKOV (ZHIVKO) ed. Sotsiologicheskata struktura na suvremennoto bulgarsko obshtestvo; Sociological structure of modern Bulgarian society. Sofiia, 1976. pp. 525. *bibliog. With Russian and English summaries and tables of contents.*

BULLER (ANNIE).

WATSON (LOUISE) She never was afraid: the biography of Annie Buller. Toronto, 1976. pp. 129.

BÜLOW.

See BUELOW.

BUND DER KOMMUNISTEN.

Die FRUEHSOZIALISTISCHEN Bünde in der Geschichte der deutschen Arbeiterbewegung: vom "Bund der Gerechten" zum "Bund der Kommunisten", 1836-1847: ein Tagungsbericht; bearbeitet und herausgegeben von Otto Büsch, Hans Herzfeld ...; mit Beiträgen von Frolinde Balser [and others]. Berlin, 1975. pp. 209. *(IWK: internationale wissenschaftliche Korrespondenz zur Geschichte der deutschen Arbeiterbewegung. Beihefte. 2)*

BURCKHARDT (JACOB).

KUCZYNSKI (JUERGEN) Die Muse und der Historiker: Studien über Jacob Burckhardt, Hyppolite[sic] Taine, Henry Adams; und eine Bibliographie sämtlicher Schriften von Jürgen Kuczynski, zusammengestellt von Erika Behm. Berlin, 1974. pp. 247. *bibliog. (Jahrbuch für Wirtschaftsgeschichte. Sonderbände)*

BURDEN OF PROOF

— United Kingdom.

CROSS (Sir RUPERT) The golden thread of the English criminal law: the burden of proof. Cambridge, 1976. pp. 19. *(Cambridge. University. Rede Lectures. 1976)*

BUREAUCRACY.

ESTUDIOS sobre la burocracia española. Madrid, 1974. pp. 285. *(Instituto de Estudios Politicos. Estudios de Administracion. 40) Papers presented at a seminar held by the Asociacion Española de Administracion Publica.*

DOWNS (GEORGE W.) Bureaucracy, innovation, and public policy. Lexington, Mass., [1976]. pp. 150. *bibliog.*

HEGEDÜS (ANDRÁS) Socialism and bureaucracy. London, 1976. pp. 193.

POLITICAL leadership in Korea; edited by Dae-Sook Suh and Chae-Jin Lee. Seattle, [1976]. pp. 272. *(Washington State University. Institute for Comparative and Foreign Area Studies. Publications on Asia. No. 27) Selected papers presented at two symposia held in Seoul during the summers of 1971 and 1972 under the auspices of the University of Washington, Seattle.*

SWINGLE (PAUL G.) The management of power. Hillsdale, N.J., 1976. pp. 178. *bibliog.*

BUDGETS and bureaucrats: the sources of government growth; edited by Thomas E. Borcherding. Durham, N.C., 1977. pp. 291. *bibliogs. Papers for the year 1972-73 of Workshop on Non-Market Bureaucracy of the Center for the Study of Public Choice, Virginia Polytechnic Institute.*

LEVI (MARGARET) Bureaucratic insurgency: the case of police unions. Lexington, Mass., [1977]. pp. 165.

LEWIS (EUGENE) American politics in a bureaucratic age: citizens, constituents, clients and victims. Cambridge, Mass., [1977]. pp. 182.

BURKE (EDMUND).

RITCHESON (CHARLES RAY) Edmund Burke and the American Revolution. Leicester, 1976. pp. 15. *(Sir George Watson Lectures. 1976)*

BURMA

— Foreign relations.

CADY (JOHN FRANK) The United States and Burma. Cambridge, Mass., 1976. pp. 303. *bibliog. A history of Burmese development from the pagan empire to the present.*

— History.

CADY (JOHN FRANK) The United States and Burma. Cambridge, Mass., 1976. pp. 303. *bibliog. A history of Burmese development from the pagan empire to the present.*

BURNS (JOHN).

BROWN (KENNETH D.) John Burns. London, 1977. pp. 217. *bibliog. (Royal Historical Society. Studies in History)*

BURUNDI

— Race question.

KUPER (LEO) The pity of it all: polarisation of racial and ethnic relations. London, 1977. pp. 302. *bibliog.*

BURYAT REPUBLIC

— Economic policy.

PROBLEMY povysheniia effektivnosti narodnogo khoziaistva Buriatskoi ASSR. Ulan-Ude, 1974. pp. 166. *(Akademiia Nauk SSSR. Sibirskoe Otdelenie. Buriatskii Filial. Otdel Ekonomicheskikh Issledovanii. Trudy. vyp. 6(10)).*

— History — Sources.

BURIATIIA v gody Velikoi Otechestvennoi voiny, 1941-1945 gg.: sbornik dokumentov. Ulan-Ude, 1975. pp. 452.

DEKABRISTY o Buriatii: stat'i, ocherki, pis'ma. Ulan-Ude, 1975. pp. 232.

BUSHMEN.

LEE (RICHARD B.) and DEVORE (IRVEN) eds. Kalahari hunter-gathers: studies of the !Kung San and their neighbors. Cambridge, Mass, 1976. pp. 408. *bibliog.*

MARSHALL (LORNA) The !Kung of Nyae Nyae. Cambridge, Mass., 1976. pp. 433.

BUSINESS.

BACKMAN (JULES) ed. Business and the American economy, 1776-2001. New York, 1976. pp. 196. *(New York (City). University. College of Business and Public Administration. Key Issues Lecture Series. 5)*

JOSEPH (Sir KEITH SINJOHN) The business of business. London, [1977]. pp. 8.

BUSINESS AND POLITICS

— France.

JEANNENEY (JEAN NOËL) François de Wendel en république: l'argent et le pouvoir, 1914-1940. Paris, [1976]. pp. 670.

— Germany.

STEIN (GUSTAV) ed. Unternehmer in der Politik;...verfasst von Herbert Gross [and others]. Düsseldorf, [1954]. pp. 330.

— United States.

NADEL (MARK V.) Corporations and political accountability. Lexington, Mass., [1976]. pp. 265.

GREENBERG (EDWARD S.) The American political system: a radical approach. Cambridge, Mass., [1977]. pp. 501. *bibliogs.*

BUSINESS CONSULTANTS.

PRODUCTIVITY through consultancy in small industrial enterprises. Tokyo, Asian Productivity Organization, [1974]. pp. 504.

— America, Latin.

UNITED NATIONS INDUSTRIAL DEVELOPMENT ORGANIZATION. 1972. The development of management consultancy in Latin America: report of UNIDO meeting held in Santiago, Chile 5-9 July 1971. (ID/89). New York, United Nations, 1972. pp. 27.

UNITED NATIONS INDUSTRIAL DEVELOPMENT ORGANIZATION. 1973. The development of management consultancy, with special reference to Latin America: a digest of papers presented to the UNIDO meeting held at Santiago, Chile, July 1971. (ID/95). New York, United Nations, 1973. pp. 132.

BUSINESS CYCLES.

BAIN (GEORGE SAYERS) and ELSHEIKH (FAROUK) Union growth and the business cycle: an econometric analysis. Oxford, [1976]. pp. 155. *(Warwick Studies in Industrial Relations)*

KLEIN (PHILIP A.) Business cycles in the postwar world: some reflections on recent research. Washington, 1976. pp. 51. *(American Enterprise Institute for Public Policy Research. Domestic Affairs Studies. 42)*

SPREE (REINHARD) Die Wachstumszyklen der deutschen Wirtschaft von 1840 bis 1880; mit einem konjunkturstatistischen Anhang. Berlin, [1977]. pp. 577.

— Mathematical models.

LOEF (HANS EDI) Ein monetäres Modell zyklischen Wachstums. Berlin, [1976]. pp. 151. *bibliog.*

BUSINESS EDUCATION

— United Kingdom.

BUSINESS EDUCATION COUNCIL. First policy statement. London, 1976. pp. 36.

BUSINESS FORECASTING.

DATA processing in 1980-1985: a study of potential limitations to progress; [by] T.A. Dolotta [and others]. New York, [1976]. pp. 191. *bibliogs.*

LUND (PHILIP J.) and others. Investment intentions, authorisations and expenditures. London, H.M.S.O., 1976. pp. 107. *bibliog. (Government Economic Service Occasional Papers. 12)*

BUSINESS LAW

— Peru.

CENTRO DE ESTUDIOS Y PROMOCION DEL DESARROLLO. Propiedad social: polemica. Lima, 1975. pp. 289.

TORRES Y TORRES LARA (CARLOS) La empresa de propiedad social: el modelo empresarial peruano; teoria y legislacion concordada, Decreto Ley 20598. Lima, 1975. pp. 216.

BUSINESS RECORDS

— Russia — Estonia.

TALLIN. Stadtkämmerei. Kämmereibuch der Stadt Reval, 1432-1463; bearbeitet von Reinhard Vogelsang. Köln, 1976. 2 vols. in 1. *bibliog. (Hansischer Geschichtsverein. Quellen und Darstellungen zur Hansischen Geschichte. Neue Folge. Band 22)*

BUSINESS TAX

— Germany — Hesse.

HESSE. Statistisches Landesamt. Beiträge zur Statistik Hessens. Neue Folge. Nr. 77. Gewerbeertrag, Gewerbekapital, Lohnsummen und ihre Besteuerung, 1970: Ergebnisse der Gewerbesteuerstatistik, 1970. Wiesbaden, 1976. pp. 181.

— — North Rhine-Westphalia.

NORTH RHINE-WESTPHALIA. Landesamt für Datenverarbeitung und Statistik. Beiträge zur Statistik des Landes Nordrhein- Westfalen. Heft 361. Die Gewerbesteuer in Nordrhein-Westfalen, 1970. Düsseldorf, 1976 in progress.

— United Kingdom.

MINTER (MICHAEL) Death by taxation: the threat to the smaller firm. London, [1976?]. pp. 11.

BUSINESSMEN

— Canada.

TULCHINSKY (GERALD J. J.) The river barons: Montreal businessmen and the growth of industry and transportation, 1837-53. Toronto, [1977]. pp. 310. *bibliog.*

— India.

LONDON (PAUL A.) Merchants as promoters of rural development: an Indian case study. New York,1975. pp. 159. *bibliog.*

— Mexico.

PENSAMIENTO empresarial mexicano; [by] Fernando Aranguren [and others]. Monterrey, 1975. pp. 239.

BUTLER (JOSEPH) successively Bishop of Bristol and of Durham.

BUTLER (JOSEPH) successively Bishop of Bristol and of Durham. A charge delivered to the clergy at the primary visitation of the diocese of Durham, in the year MDCCLI;...the second edition, with a preface, giving some account of the character and writings of the author, by Samuel, Lord Bishop of Gloucester. London, T. Cadell, 1786. pp. lxxxviii, 46.

BYZANTINE EMPIRE

— Civilization.

CAMERON (ALAN) Circus factions: Blues and Greens at Rome and Byzantium. Oxford, 1976. pp. 364. *bibliog.*

— Politics and government.

CAMERON (ALAN) Circus factions: Blues and Greens at Rome and Byzantium. Oxford, 1976. pp. 364. *bibliog.*

CABINET MINISTERS

— Brazil.

BRAZIL. Ministerio da Fazenda. 1972. Ministros da Fazenda, 1822-1972. Rio de Janeiro, 1972. pp. 238.

— Mexico.

SIERRA BRABATA (CARLOS J.) Historia de la administracion hacendaria en Mexico, 1911-1970. Vol. II. Mexico, Secretaria de Hacienda y Credito Publico, 1971. pp. 45. *(Boletin Bibliografico. Publicaciones)*

STANSFIELD (DAVID E.) The Mexican cabinet: an indicator of political change. Glasgow, 1973. pp. 20. *(Glasgow. University. Institute of Latin American Studies. Occasional Papers. No. 8)*

CABINET SYSTEM

— Canada.

MATHESON (WILLIAM A.) The Prime Minister and the cabinet. Toronto, [1976]. pp. 246.

— France.

SEARLS (ELLA) Political-administrative relations in the Fifth Republic: a study of ministerial cabinets, 1959-74. 1976 [or rather 1977]. fo. 409. *bibliog. Typescript. Ph.D. (London) thesis: unpublished. This thesis is the property of London University and may not be removed from the Library.*

— United Kingdom.

WILSON (Sir HAROLD) The governance of Britain. London, 1976. pp. 219.

CABRAL (AMILCAR).

FISAS ARMENGOL (VICENÇ) Amilcar Cabral y la independencia de Guinea-Bissau; [with two articles by Amilcar Cabral included as appendices]. Barcelona, 1974. pp. 132.

CAETANO (MARCELLO).

CAETANO (MARCELLO) Testimonio. Madrid, 1975. pp. 226. *bibliog.*

CALABRIA

— Social history.

MISÈFARI (ENZO) Storia sociale della Calabria: popolo, classi dominanti, forme di resistenza dagli inizi dell'età moderna al XIX secolo. Milano, 1976. pp. 464.

CALCULATING MACHINES.

RANDELL (BRIAN) 1936- , ed. The origins of digital computers: selected papers. 2nd ed. Berlin, 1975. pp. 464. *bibliog.*

CALCUTTA

— **Description.**

BLECHYNDEN (KATHLEEN) Calcutta past and present. London, 1905. pp. 245.

— **History.**

BLECHYNDEN (KATHLEEN) Calcutta past and present. London, 1905. pp. 245.

CALIFORNIA

— **Economic history.**

BLACKFORD (MANSEL G.) The politics of business in California, 1890-1920. Columbus, Ohio, [1977]. pp. 221. *bibliog.*

— **Economic policy.**

EMERGING issues in public policy: research reports and essays, 1960-1965: a collection of six years of Public Affairs Report, bulletin of the Institute of Governmental Studies. Berkeley, Calif., 1973. pp. 168.

EMERGING issues in public policy: research reports and essays, 1966-1972: a collection of seven years of Public Affairs Report, bulletin of the Institute of Governmental Studies; Harriet Nathan and Stanley Scott, editors. Berkeley, Calif., 1973. pp. 200.

— **Industries.**

BLACKFORD (MANSEL G.) The politics of business in California, 1890-1920. Columbus, Ohio, [1977]. pp. 221. *bibliog.*

— **Politics and government.**

EMERGING issues in public policy: research reports and essays, 1960-1965: a collection of six years of Public Affairs Report, bulletin of the Institute of Governmental Studies: Harriet Nathan and Stanley Scott, editors. Berkeley, Calif., 1973. pp. 168.

EMERGING issues in public policy: research reports and essays, 1966-1972: a collection of seven years of Public Affairs Report, bulletin of the Institute of Governmental Studies; Harriet Nathan and Stanley Scott, editors. Berkeley, Calif., 1973. pp. 200.

— **Social policy.**

EMERGING issues in public policy: research reports and essays, 1960-1965: a collection of six years of Public Affairs Report, bulletin of the Institute of Governmental Studies: Harriet Nathan and Stanley Scott, editors. Berkeley, Calif., 1973. pp. 168.

EMERGING issues in public policy: research reports and essays, 1966-1972: a collection of seven years of Public Affairs Report, bulletin of the Institute of Governmental Studies; Harriet Nathan and Stanley Scott, editors. Berkeley, Calif., 1973. pp. 200.

CAMACHO (MARCELINO).

CAMACHO (MARCELINO) Ecrits de la prison: le mouvement syndical espagnol et les Commissions ouvrières. Paris. [1976]. pp. 157.

CAMBODIA

— **History.**

BARRON (JOHN) and PAUL (ANTHONY) Peace with horror: the untold story of communist genocide in Cambodia. London, [1977]. pp. 234. *bibliogs.*

— **Politics and government.**

HILDEBRAND (GEORGE C.) and PORTER (GARETH) Cambodia: starvation and revolution. New York, [1976]. pp. 124.

— **Rural conditions.**

HILDEBRAND (GEORGE C.) and PORTER (GARETH) Cambodia: starvation and revolution. New York, [1976]. pp. 124.

CAMDEN

— **Economic conditions.**

CAMDEN. Town Clerk's Department. Policy Analysis Unit. Community profile. a., 1976- London.

— **Social conditions.**

CAMDEN. Town Clerk's Department. Policy Analysis Unit. Community profile. a., 1976- London.

CAMEROUN

— **Directories.**

CAMEROUN, LE: annuaire international: The Cameroon: international directory. a., 1974. Douala. *[in English and French].*

— **Economic conditions.**

LOGINOVA (V.P.) United Republic of Cameroon. Budapest, 1976. pp. 82. *bibliog. (Magyar Tudományos Akadémia. Világgazdasági Kutató Intézet. Studies on Developing Countries. No. 87)*

— **Economic policy.**

LOGINOVA (V.P.) United Republic of Cameroon. Budapest, 1976. pp. 82. *bibliog. (Magyar Tudományos Akadémia. Világgazdasági Kutató Intézet. Studies on Developing Countries. No. 87)*

— **Foreign relations.**

NDAM NJOYA (ADAMOU) Le Cameroun dans les relations internationales. Paris, 1976. pp. 414. *bibliog.*

— **History.**

JOSEPH (RICHARD A.) Radical nationalism in Cameroun: social origins of the U.P.C. rebellion. Oxford, 1977. pp. 383. *bibliog.*

— **Social history.**

AZARYA (VICTOR) Dominance and change in North Cameroon: the Fulbe aristocracy. Beverly Hills, [1976]. pp. 71. *bibliog.*

CAMP SITES, FACILITIES, ETC.

—**Netherlands.**

ECONOMISCH INSTITUUT VOOR HET MIDDEN- EN KLEINBEDRIJF. Bedrijfseconomische Publikaties. Resultaten van kampeerbedrijven: bedrijfsgegevens en enige ontwikkelingslijnen van campings, bungalowbedrijven en mengvormen van beide. 's-Gravenhage, 1972 repr.1973. pp. 94.

CAMPAIGN FUNDS.

PESONEN (PERTTI) Impact of public financing of political parties: the Finnish experience;...paper delivered at the IXth World Congress of th International Political Science Association, Montreal... 1973. Helsinki, 1974. pp. 28. *(Helsinki. Yliopisto. Yleisen Valtio-Opin Laitos. Tutkimuksia. 33/1974)*

AIMS FOR FREEDOM AND ENTERPRISE. Evidence to the Committee on Aid to Political Parties. London, [1975]. fo. 4.

CANADA.

CORBETT (DAVID CHARLES) Looking at Canada. Melbourne, 1976. pp. 226. *bibliog.*

— **Administrative and political divisions.**

CANADA. Statistics Canada. Changes to municipal boundaries, status and names. a., 1975- Ottawa. *[in English and French].*

— **Capital.**

KNIGHT (DAVID B.) A capital for Canada: conflict and compromise in the nineteenth century. Chicago, 1977. pp. 341. *bibliog. (Chicago. University. Department of Geography. Research Papers. No. 182)*

— **Church history.**

HANDY (ROBERT THEODORE) A history of the churches in the United States and Canada. Oxford, 1976. pp. 471. *bibliog.*

— **Constitution.**

ATLANTIC PROVINCES ECONOMIC COUNCIL. Submission to the maritime union study. Halifax, Nova Scotia, 1969. pp. 35.

— **Constitutional law.**

BROSSARD (JACQUES) Professor of Law, University of Montreal. L'accession à la souveraineté et le cas du Québec: conditions et modalités politico-juridiques. Montréal, 1976. pp. 799. *bibliog.*

— **Economic conditions.**

SAWYER (JOHN A.) Macroeconomics: theory and policy in the Canadian economy. Toronto, [1975]. pp. 406. *bibliogs.*

GREEN (ALAN G.) Immigration and the postwar Canadian economy. Toronto, [1976]. pp. 312. *bibliog.*

— **Economic policy.**

GORDON (WALTER LOCKHART) Storm signals: new economic policies for Canada. Toronto, [1975]. pp. 140.

CANADIAN LABOUR CONGRESS. Labour's manifesto for Canada. Ottawa, [1976]. pp. 14.

CARELESS (ANTHONY G.S.) Initiative and response: the adaptation of Canadian federalism to regional economic development. Montreal, 1977. pp. 244. *(Institute of Public Administration of Canada. Canadian Public Administration Series)*

— **Emigration and immigration.**

INTERNATIONAL AND INTERPROVINCIAL MIGRATION IN CANADA; [pd. by] Statistics Canada. a., 1961-62/1975-76- Ottawa. *[in English and French]*

CANADIAN LABOUR CONGRESS. Submission by the Canadian Labour Congress to the Honourable Robert Andras, Minister of Manpower and Immigration, on a new immigration policy for Canada. Ottawa, 1974. fo. 21.

HARNEY (ROBERT F.) and TROPER (HAROLD MARTIN) Immigrants: a portrait of the urban experience, 1890-1930. Toronto, [1975]. pp. 212.

GREEN (ALAN G.) Immigration and the postwar Canadian economy. Toronto, [1976]. pp. 312. *bibliog.*

— **Executive departments.**

LANGFORD (JOHN W.) Transport in transition: the reorganization of the federal transport portfolio. Montreal, 1976. pp. 267. *(Institute of Public Administration of Canada. Canadian Public Administration Series)*

— **Foreign economic relations — United States.**

DOSMAN (EDGAR J.) The national interest: the politics of Northern development, 1968-75. Toronto, [1975]. pp. 224.

— **Foreign relations.**

THOMSON (DALE C.) and SWANSON (ROGER FRANK) Canadian foreign policy: options and perspectives. Toronto, [1971]. pp. 170. *bibliog.*

INTERNATIONAL PERSPECTIVES: a jl. of the Department of External Affairs [Canada]. bi-m., Ja/F 1972 (1)- Ottawa. *Supersedes its External affairs.*

— — **United Kingdom.**

WIGLEY (PHILIP G.) Canada and the transition to Commonwealth: British-Canadian relations, 1917-1926. Cambridge, 1977. pp. 294. *bibliog.*

— Government publications — Bibliography.

PUBLICAT INDEX: a Canadian federal documents service. m., Ja/Mr 1977 (v.1, no.1)- Toronto. *[in English and French]. File includes annual cumulation.*

— — Indexes.

PUBLICAT INDEX: a Canadian federal documents service. m., Ja/Mr 1977 (v.1, no.1)- Toronto. *[in English and French]. File includes annual cumulation.*

— History — 1867- .

FUMOLEAU (RENE) As long as this land shall last: a history of Treaty 8 and Treaty 11, 1870-1939. Toronto, [1973?]. pp. 415. *bibliog.*

— Nationalism — Bibliography.

LAMBERT (RONALD D.) compiler. Nationalism and national ideologies in Canada and Quebec: a bibliography. rev. ed. Waterloo, Ont., 1975. fo. 144.

— Parliament — Elections.

MEISEL (JOHN) Working papers on Canadian politics. 2nd ed. Montreal, 1973. pp. 257.

— — House of Commons.

KORNBERG (ALLAN) and MISHLER (WILLIAM T.E.) Influence in parliament: Canada. Durham, N.C., 1976. pp. 403. *(Consortium for Comparative Legislative Studies. Publications)*

STEWART (JOHN BENJAMIN) The Canadian House of Commons: procedure and reform. Montreal, 1977. pp. 337. *bibliog.*

— Politics and government.

MEISEL (JOHN) Working papers on Canadian politics. 2nd ed. Montreal, 1973. pp. 257.

WAITE (PETER BUSBY) Macdonald: his life and world. Toronto, [1975]. pp. 224. *bibliog.*

KASHTAN (WILLIAM) Toward socialism:...selected writings, 1966-1976. Toronto, 1976. pp. 372.

MATHESON (WILLIAM A.) The Prime Minister and the cabinet. Toronto, [1976]. pp. 246.

PAMMETT (JON H.) and WHITTINGTON (MICHAEL S.) eds. Foundations of political culture: political socialization in Canada. Toronto, [1976]. pp. 318.

SCHULL (JOHN JOSEPH) Edward Blake: leader and exile, 1881-1912. Toronto, [1976]. pp. 266. *bibliog.*

STURSBERG (PETER) Diefenbaker: leadership lost, 1962-67. Toronto, [1976]. pp. 212. *Based on recorded interviews and discussions.*

SWEENY (ALASTAIR) George-Etienne Cartier: a biography. Toronto, [1976]. pp. 352. *bibliog.*

KNIGHT (DAVID B.) A capital for Canada: conflict and compromise in the nineteenth century. Chicago, 1977. pp. 341. *bibliog. (Chicago. University. Department of Geography. Research Papers. No. 182)*

— Population.

INTERNATIONAL AND INTERPROVINCIAL MIGRATION IN CANADA; [pd. by] Statistics Canada. a., 1961-62/1975-76- Ottawa. *[in English and French]*

CANADIAN INSTITUTE OF INTERNATIONAL AFFAIRS and others. Public consultation on population questions: a report to the government of Canada. Toronto, 1974. pp. 69.

CHARBONNEAU (HUBERT) Vie et mort de nos ancêtres: étude démographique. Montréal, 1975. pp. 267.

— Relations (general) with Australia.

CORBETT (DAVID CHARLES) Looking at Canada. Melbourne, 1976. pp. 226. *bibliog.*

— Relations (general) with the United States.

MORSE (RANDY) and PRATT (LARRY) Darkness at the end of the tunnel: a radical analysis of Canadian-American relations. Toronto, 1975. pp. 39.

CANADA-United States relations; edited by Harry Edward English. New York, 1976. pp. 180. *Papers of a conference sponsored by the Academy of Political Science and the Center of Canadian Studies, Johns Hopkins University, in Washington, D.C., 1975.*

FOX (ANNETTE BAKER) The politics of attraction: four middle powers and the United States. New York, 1977. pp. 371.

— Religion — Bibliography.

CRYSDALE (STEWART) and MONTMINY (JEAN PAUL) compilers. La religion au Canada: bibliographie annotée des travaux en sciences humaines des religions, 1945-1970; Religion in Canada: annotated inventory of scientific studies of religion, 1945-1972 [sic]. Downsview, Ont., 1974. pp. 189. *In French and English.*

— Social conditions.

FORCESE (DENNIS P.) The Canadian class structure. Toronto, [1975]. pp. 148. *bibliog.*

RAMU (G.N.) and JOHNSON (STUART D.) eds. Introduction to Canadian society: sociological analysis. Toronto, [1976]. pp. 530. *bibliog.*

— Social history.

WAITE (PETER BUSBY) Macdonald: his life and world. Toronto, [1975]. pp. 224. *bibliog.*

— Statistical services.

CANADA. Statistics Canada. Special Surveys Coordination Division. New surveys: notes on statistical survey activity within the federal government. q., current issues only. Ottawa. *[in English and French].*

— Statistics, Vital.

CANADA. Statistics Canada. Principal vital statistics by local areas. a., 1974 (1st)- Ottawa. *[in English and French].*

CANADIAN PACIFIC RAILWAY.

GILBERT (HEATHER) The end of the road: the life of Lord Mount Stephen, vol. II, 1891-1921. Aberdeen, 1977. pp. 442.

CANALS

— United Kingdom.

PORTEOUS (JOHN DOUGLAS) Canal ports: the urban achievement of the canal age. London, 1977. pp. 249.

U.K. British Transport Commission. 1977. British Transport Commission historical records: canal, dock, harbour, navigation and steamship companies: RAIL 800-887: class list. London, 1977. pp. 380. *(List and Index Society. [Publications]. vol.142)*

CANARIS (WILHELM).

HOEHNE (HEINZ) Canaris: Patriot im Zwielicht. München, [1976]. pp. 607. *bibliog.*

CANBERRA

— City planning.

AUSTRALIA. Parliament. Joint Committee on the Australian Capital Territory. 1971. Report on proposals for variations of the plan of lay-out of the city of Canberra and its environs, forty-seventh series; [John E. Marriott, chairman]. in AUSTRALIA. Parliament. Parliamentary papers, 1971, vol.8.

AUSTRALIA. Parliament. Joint Committee on the Australian Capital Territory. 1971. Report on proposals for variations of the plan of lay-out of the city of Canberra and its environs, forty-eighth series; [R.G. Withers, chairman]. in AUSTRALIA. Parliament. Parliamentary papers, 1971, vol.8.

CANCER RESEARCH

— United States.

HIXSON (JOSEPH R.) The patchwork mouse. Garden City, N.Y., 1976. pp. 228.

CANELOS INDIANS.

WHITTEN (NORMAN E.) and others. Sacha Runa: ethnicity and adaptation of Ecuadorian Jungle Quichua. Urbana, Ill., [1976]. pp. 348. *bibliog.*

CANNING TOWN

— Industries.

CANNING TOWN COMMUNITY DEVELOPMENT PROJECT. Canning Town's declining community income: case study: Tate and Lyle. [London, 1976]. pp. 33.

CANNON (JAMES PATRICK).

JAMES P. Cannon as we knew him: by thirty-three comrades, friends, and relatives. New York, 1976. pp. 288.

CANON LAW.

CHURCH and government in the Middle Ages: essays presented to C.R. Cheney on his 70th birthday;...edited by C.N.L. Brooke [and others]. Cambridge, 1976. pp. 312. *bibliog.*

CANTON

— Description.

SWISHER (EARL) Canton in revolution: the collected papers...1925-1928; edited by Kenneth W. Rea. Boulder, Colo., 1977. pp. 141.

— History — Sources.

SWISHER (EARL) Canton in revolution: the collected papers...1925-1928; edited by Kenneth W. Rea. Boulder, Colo., 1977. pp. 141.

CAPITAL.

JOHNSON (HARRY GORDON) International capital movement controls. [Elmont, N.Y.], 1973. fo. 2. *Reprinted from Euromoney, August 1973.*

HARCOURT (GEOFFREY COLIN) Capital theory: much ado about something. London, 1975. pp. 16. *bibliog. (Thames Polytechnic. School of Social Sciences. Thames Papers in Political Economy)*

— Mathematical models.

WARD (MICHAEL) The measurement of capital: the methodology of capital stock estimates in OECD countries. Paris, Organisation for Economic Co-operation and Development, 1976. pp. 148. *bibliog.*

— Bangladesh.

ISLAM (RIZWANUL) Factor intensity and labour absorption in manufacturing industries: the case of Bangladesh. 1976. fo. 471. *bibliog. Typescript. Ph.D. (London) thesis: unpublished. This thesis is the property of London University and may not be removed from the Library.*

— Russia.

KLOCHKO (VASILII STEPANOVICH) Vosproizvodstvo osnovnykh fondov promyshlennosti SSSR. Khar'kov, 1976. pp. 139. *bibliog.*

TOLPEKIN (S.Z.) Ekonomicheskie problemy kompleksnogo ispol'zovaniia osnovnykh sredstv proizvodstva: voprosy teorii, metodologii i metodov analiza. Moskva, 1976. pp. 536.

— — Tajikistan.

KAIUMOV (NURIDDIN) and PYSHNOGRAI (SVETLANA PAVLOVNA) Oborotnye proizvodstvennye fondy legkoi promyshlennosti Tadzhikistana i ikh ispol'zovanie; pod redaktsiei...L.I. Itina. Dushanbe, 1975. pp. 206.

— United Kingdom.

ROSE (HAROLD BERTRAM) The British capital market and the economy: villain or scapegoat? London, 1976. pp. 11. *One of the 1976 Stockton Lectures.*

MIDGLEY (KENNETH) and BURNS (RONALD) The capital market: its nature and significance. London, 1977. pp. 148. *bibliogs.*

CAPITAL ASSETS PRICING MODEL.

RISK and return in finance; edited by Irwin Friend [and] James L. Bicksler. Cambridge, Mass., [1977]. 2 vols. *bibliogs. Thirteen of the seventeen papers in these two volumes were originally presented at a Conference on Risk and the Rate of Return, sponsored by the American Telephone and Telegraph Company and held in Vail, Colorado, during August 5-10, 1973.*

CAPITAL BUDGET.

NORSTRÖM (CARL J.) Studies in capital budgeting. Bergen, 1975. pp. 95. *bibliogs.*

BROMWICH (MICHAEL) The economics of capital budgeting. Harmondsworth, 1976. pp. 395. *bibliog.*

WILKES (F.M.) Capital budgeting techniques. London, [1977]. pp. 424. *bibliogs.*

CAPITAL GAINS TAX

— United Kingdom.

CLARK (LAURENCE) Capital gains tax?: yes: - monetary gains tax?: no! Rickmansworth, [1972]. pp. 11. *(Veracity Ventures. Interim Papers. 8)*

CAPITAL INVESTMENTS.

MILLS (RODNEY H.) The regulation of short-term capital movements in major industrial countries. [Washington, 1972]. pp. 53. *(United States. Board of Governors of the Federal Reserve System. Staff Economic Studies. No. 74)*

— Ethiopia.

ETHIOPIA. Ministry of Planning and Development. 1967. Forms and explanations for the detailed guidance of the planning committees and units in the ministries and agencies: capital project inventory. Addis Ababa, 1967. 1 pamphlet (various foliations).

— European Economic Community countries.

EUROPEAN COMMUNITIES. Statistical Office. Annual investments in fixed assets in the industrial enterprises of the member countries of the European Communities. a., 1972/74- Luxembourg. *[in Community languages].*

— Poland.

WIT (ZBIGNIEW) Inwestycje, finansowanie i efektywność. Warszawa, 1976. pp. 116. *bibliog.*

— Russia.

FAL'TSMAN (VLADIMIR KONSTANTINOVICH) Potrebnost' v sredstvakh proizvodstva. Moskva, 1975. pp. 238.

KRUGLIAK (BRONISLAV STEPANOVICH) Effektivnost' kontsentratsii kapital'nykh vlozhenii v sel'skom khoziaistve. Moskva, 1976. pp. 143.

SEMCHENKO (ANDREI PETROVICH) Problemy povysheniia effektivnosti kapital'nykh vlozhenii i osnovnykh fondov sel'skogo khoziaistva SSSR. Leningrad, 1976. pp. 127.

SMYSHLIAEVA (LIUDMILA MATVEEVNA) Ekonomicheskii rost i proportsii kapital'nykh vlozhenii. Moskva, 1976. pp. 191.

— United Kingdom.

U.K. Board of Inland Revenue. 1973. Income tax and corporation tax: capital allowances on machinery or plant: new system. [London], 1973. pp. 26.

SCOTTISH COUNCIL (DEVELOPMENT AND INDUSTRY). International Forum, 5th, Aviemore, 1974. Investing in Scotland; (compiled by Jack McGill). Glasgow, [1975]. pp. 224. *bibliog.*

LUND (PHILIP J.) and others. Investment intentions, authorisations and expenditures. London, H.M.S.O., 1976. pp. 107. *bibliog. (Government Economic Service Occasional Papers. 12)*

CAPITAL LEVY

— United Kingdom.

U.K. Treasury. 1977. Capital taxation and the national heritage. [London], 1977. pp. 19.

CAPITAL MOVEMENTS.

KENEN (PETER BAIN) Capital mobility and financial integration: a survey. Princeton, 1976. pp. 78. *bibliog. (Princeton University. Department of Economics and Sociology. International Finance Section. Princeton Studies in International Finance. No. 39)*

— South Africa.

SOUTH AFRICA. Parliament. House of Assembly. Select Committee on Allegation by Member. 1977. Report...proceedings and evidence; (with Addendum) (S.C. 9 and 9A-1977). in SOUTH AFRICA. Parliament. House of Assembly. Select Committee reports.

CAPITAL PUNISHMENT

— Australia.

AUSTRALIA. Parliament. Senate. Standing Committee on Constitutional and Legal Affairs. 1971. Report on Death Penalty Abolition Bill 1970; [R.G. Withers, chairman]. in AUSTRALIA. Parliament. Parliamentary papers, 1971, vol.8.

— United Kingdom.

NATIONAL CAMPAIGN FOR THE ABOLITION OF CAPITAL PUNISHMENT and HOWARD LEAGUE FOR PENAL REFORM. Murder and capital punishment in England and Wales. London, 1974. pp. 17.

— United States.

BEDAU (HUGO ADAM) The case against the death penalty. New York, 1973. pp. 14. *bibliog.*

CAPITALISM.

ALSEGG (ROBERT) Die kapitalistische Wirtschaft. Wien, 1930. pp. 32. *(Wirtschaft und Politik. 1)*

LOEWENTHAL (RICHARD) Jenseits des Kapitalismus: ein Beitrag zur sozialistischen Neuorientierung; mit einer ausführlichen Einführung: nach 30 Jahren. Berlin, [1977]. pp. 268. *Reprint of work originally published at Lauf nr. Nuremberg in 1947 under the pseudonym Paul Sering.*

AIMS OF INDUSTRY. Economic Arguments. The pleasant face of capitalism. London, [1973]. pp. 9.

CAMBRIDGE. University. Centre of Latin American Studies. Working Papers. No. 16. The myth of economic development and the future of the third world; by Celso Furtado. Cambridge, 1974. fo. 22. *Photocopy.*

MBILINYI (MARJORIE J.) The transition to capitalism in rural Tanzania. Dar es Salaam, [1974]. pp. 49. *bibliog. (Dar es Salaam. University. Economic Research Bureau. ERB Papers. 74.7)*

DAS GUPTA (AMIYA KUMAR) The economics of austerity. Delhi, 1975. pp. 38. *(Benares Hindu University. Shastri Memorial Lectures. 1974)*

HOBSBAWM (ERIC JOHN ERNEST) The crisis and the outlook. London, [1975]. pp. 16. *Taken from a lecture given to Birkbeck College Socialist Society.*

KVIST (KENNETH) Den krisfria kapitalismen och andra myter: några drag i den svenska ekonomins utveckling. Stockholm, 1975. pp. 181.

MANDEL (ERNEST) The generalized recession of the international capitalist economy. Brussels, 1975. pp. 24.

POLITICHESKAIA ekonomiia sovremennogo monopolisticheskogo kapitalizma. 2nd ed. Moskva, 1975. 2 vols.

SHPIL'KO (GALINA ANTONOVNA) Teorii i metody regulirovaniia kapitalisticheskoi ekonomiki. Moskva, 1975. pp. 191.

WARREN (BILL) and PRIOR (MIKE) Advanced capitalism and backward socialism. Nottingham, [1975]. pp. 27. *(Spokesman, The. Pamphlets. No. 46)*

AMIN (SAMIR) Unequal development: an essay on the social formations of peripheral capitalism: translated [from the French] by Brian Pearce. Hassocks, [1976]. pp. 440. *bibliog.*

CULTURE ET LIBERTE. Les travailleurs face au capitalisme: initiation à l'économie. [Paris, 1976]. pp. 256. *bibliog.*

GURLEY (JOHN G.) China's economy and the Maoist strategy. New York, [1976]. pp. 325.

HARRISON (MARK) The economics of capitalism. London, 1976. pp. 41.

HOBSBAWM (ERIC JOHN ERNEST) and BOURN (DOUGLAS) Feudalism, capitalism and the absolute state; [2] reviews of Perry Anderson. London, 1976. pp. 18. *(Communist Party of Great Britain. History Group. Our History. No.66)*

INOZEMTSEV (NIKOLAI NIKOLAEVICH) and others, eds. Uglublenie obshchego krizisa kapitalizma. Moskva, 1976. pp. 358.

INSTITUT FÜR MARXISTISCHE STUDIEN UND FORSCHUNGEN. Kolloquium, 1976. Das Monopol: ökonomischer Kern des heutigen Kapitalismus: theoretische und aktuelle Gesichtspunkte der marxistisch-leninistischen Monopoltheorie: Referate...Frankfurt am Main vom 26./27. Juni 1976. Frankfurt am Main, 1976. pp. 322.

JOSEPH (Sir KEITH SINJOHN) Stranded on the middle ground?: reflections on circumstances and policies. London, 1976. pp. 80.

KLEIN (DIETER) Ökonomische Widersprüche im Kapitalismus. Berlin, [1976]. pp. 288.

The LABOUR process and class strategies. London, [1976]. pp. 129. *(Conference of Socialist Economists. Pamphlets. No. 1)*

RESOURCES and the environment: a socialist perspective; edited by Michael Barratt Brown [and others]. Nottingham, 1976. pp. 157. *Papers based on the materials prepared for a 1975 Spokesman conference on the environment.*

SCHUMPETER (JOSEPH ALOIS) Capitalism, socialism and democracy. 5th ed. London, 1952 repr. 1976. pp. 437. *Reprint contains a new introduction by Tom Bottomore.*

SIMMONS (D.A.) Economic power. Northolt, Middx., 1976. pp. 192. *bibliog.*

WAGNER (WOLF) Verelendungstheorie: die hilflose Kapitalismuskritik. Frankfurt am Main, 1976. pp. 253. *bibliog.*

WEBER (MAX) The Protestant ethic and the spirit of capitalism; translated by Talcott Parsons; introduction by Anthony Giddens. 2nd ed. London, 1976. pp. 292.

AURTHUR (JONATHAN) Socialism in the Soviet Union. Chicago, 1977. pp. 174. *bibliog.*

BOSQUET (MICHEL) Capitalism in crisis and everyday life; translated from the French by John Howe. Hassocks, Sussex, 1977. pp. 199.

BRAUDEL (FERNAND) Afterthoughts on material civilization and capitalism;... translated by Patricia M. Ranum. Baltimore, [1977]. pp. 120. *(Johns Hopkins University. Department of History. Johns Hopkins Symposia in Comparative History)*

BRITISH SOCIOLOGICAL ASSOCIATION. Annual Conference, 1975. Industrial society: class, cleavage and control; edited by Richard Scase. London, 1977. pp. 221. *bibliog. (British Sociological Association. Explorations in Sociology. 8)*

HADDEN (TOM) Company law and capitalism. 2nd ed. London, 1977. pp. 522.

HIRSCHMAN (ALBERT O.) The passions and the interests: political arguments for capitalism before its triumph. Princeton, N.J., [1977]. pp. 153.

LACLAU (ERNESTO) Politics and ideology in marxist theory: capitalism, fascism, populism. London, 1977. pp. 203.

LEWIS (W. RUSSELL) The survival of the capitalist system: challenge to the pluralist societies of the West; report of a study group of the Institute for the Study of Conflict. London, 1977. pp. 56. *(Institute for the Study of Conflict. Special Reports)*

NOBLE (DAVID F.) America by design: science, technology, and the rise of corporate capitalism. New York, 1977. pp. 384.

SPEISER (STUART M.) A piece of the action: a plan to provide every family with a [dollar]100,000 stake in the economy. New York, [1977]. pp. 390. *bibliog.*

The SUBTLE anatomy of capitalism; edited by Jesse Schwartz. Santa Monica, Calif., [1977]. pp. 503. *bibliogs.*

TELFORD (SHIRLEY) Economic and political peace, volume II. Portland, Or., [1977]. pp. 154. *Appears to be intended to be used with any edition of the author's earlier work with the same title.*

UNIVERSITY ASSOCIATION FOR CONTEMPORARY EUROPEAN STUDIES. Annual Conference, 7th, University of Sussex, 1977. Government, business and labour in European capitalism; papers presented at the...Conference...; edited by Richard T. Griffiths. London, 1977. pp. 229.

CAPITALISTS AND FINANCIERS

— Russia — Lithuania.

MATERIALY nauchnoi sessii po teme "Razlozhenie krepostnicheskoi sistemy i protsess formirovaniia kapitalisticheskogo uklada v sel'skom khoziaistve Belorussii i Litvy". Vil'nius, 1975. pp. 131.

— — White Russia.

MATERIALY nauchnoi sessii po teme "Razlozhenie krepostnicheskoi sistemy i protsess formirovaniia kapitalisticheskogo uklada v sel'skom khoziaistve Belorussii i Litvy". Vil'nius, 1975. pp. 131.

CAPRIVI (LEO VON) Graf.

WEITOWITZ (ROLF GUNTER) German trade policies and politics under the chancellorship of Count Leo von Caprivi, 1890-1894. 1977. fo.366. *bibliog. Typescript. Ph.D. (London) thesis: unpublished. This thesis is the property of London University and may not be removed from the Library.*

CARACAS (ARCHDIOCESE)

— Population.

LOMBARDI (JOHN V.) People and places in colonial Venezuela;...maps and figures by Cathryn L. Lombardi. Bloomington, Ind., [1976]. pp. 484.

CARBONARI.

ZAVALA (IRIS M.) Masones, comuneros y carbonarios. Madrid, 1971. pp. 363.

CARDENAS (LAZARO).

GILLY (ADOLFO) La revolucion interrumpida: Mexico, 1910-1920; una guerra campesina por la tierra y el poder. Mexico, [1971 repr. 1975]. pp. 397.

ANGUIANO (ARTURO) El Estado y la politica obrera del cardenismo. Mexico, 1975. pp. 187. *bibliog.*

CORONA (GUSTAVO) Lazaro Cardenas y la expropiacion de la industria petrolera en Mexico. Mexico, 1975. pp. 350.

SILVA HERZOG (JESUS) Lazaro Cardenas: su pensamiento economico, social y politico. Mexico, 1975. pp. 137.

CARDIFF

— Economic history.

WILLIAMS (ALLAN MORGAN) Social change and residential differentiation: a case study of nineteenth century Cardiff. 1976. fo. 525. *bibliog. Typescript. Ph.D. (London) thesis: unpublished. This thesis is the property of London University and may not be removed from the Library. Two transparencies in end pocket.*

— History.

DAUNTON (M.J.) Coal metropolis: Cardiff, 1870-1914. Leicester, 1977. pp. 260.

— Social history.

WILLIAMS (ALLAN MORGAN) Social change and residential differentiation: a case study of nineteenth century Cardiff. 1976. fo. 525. *bibliog. Typescript. Ph.D. (London) thesis: unpublished. This thesis is the property of London University and may not be removed from the Library. Two transparencies in end pocket.*

CARDS.

AUTENBOER (EUGEEN VAN) The Turnhout playing card industry, 1826-1976...: preceded by a History of Belgian playing cards from 1379 to 1826; by Louis Tummers; in collaboration with Jan Bauwens. Brussels, Ministry of Foreign Affairs, External Trade and Cooperation in Development, 1976. pp. 152. *bibliog. (Memo from Belgium. No.174)*

CARIBBEAN AREA

— Commerce.

JAINARAIN (ISERDEO) Trade and underdevelopment: a study of the small Caribbean countries and large multinational corporations. Guyana, 1976. pp. 390. *bibliog.*

— Economic conditions.

JAINARAIN (ISERDEO) Trade and underdevelopment: a study of the small Caribbean countries and large multinational corporations. Guyana, 1976. pp. 390. *bibliog.*

— Economic policy.

DEVELOPMENT prospects and options in the Commonwealth Caribbean; report of the conference jointly sponsored by the British-North American Research Association and the Overseas Development Institute at Ditchley Park, Oxfordshire, February 20-22, 1976; edited by Edith Hodgkinson. London, [1976]. pp. 85.

— Industries.

JAINARAIN (ISERDEO) Trade and underdevelopment: a study of the small Caribbean countries and large multinational corporations. Guyana, 1976. pp. 390. *bibliog.*

CARINTHIA

— Economic history.

KARNER (STEFAN) Kärntens Wirtschaft, 1938-1945, unter besonderer Berücksichtigung der Rüstungsindustrie. Klagenfurt, 1976. pp. 384. *bibliog. (Klagenfurt. Magistrat. Wissenschaftliche Veröffentlichungen der Landeshauptstadt Klagenfurt. Band 2)*

CARLISTS.

BARREIRO FERNANDEZ (JOSE RAMON) El carlismo gallego. Santiago de Compostela, 1976. pp. 359. *bibliog.*

ESTORNES ZUBIZARRETA (IDOIA) Carlismo y abolicion foral: en torno a un centenario, 1876-1976. San Sebastian, [1976]. pp. 250.

CAROLINE AMELIA ELIZABETH, Queen Consort of George IV, King of Great Britain and Ireland.

The ASSES' skin memorandum book, lost in St. Paul's; to which is added, a condolence with the ultras, etc. etc. etc.; (Old Tom, editor). London, Wright, 1820. pp. 15. *Verse satire on Alderman Matthew Wood, friend and adviser to Queen Caroline.*

[BAYLEY (PETER)] A Queen's appeal: Dieu et mon droit. London, R. Stodart, 1820. pp. 83.

[TOM, Old, of Oxford, pseud.] The new Christmas budget, etc. London, Wright, 1820. pp. 15. *Satires in verse on the Queen and her supporters.*

LETTER from the Queen in reply to the one from the King. London, J. Johnston, 1821. pp. 44. *Signed Caroline. A fictitious letter.*

CARRERO BLANCO (LUIS).

AGIRRE (JULEN) Opération "Ogro"...: comment et pourquoi nous avons exécuté Carrero Blanco, premier ministre espagnol; traduit de l'espagnol par Victoria Pueblos. Paris, [1974]. pp. 224.

CARRERO BLANCO (LUIS) Discursos y escritos, 1943-1973. [Madrid, 1974]. pp. 683.

AGIRRE (JULEN) Operation Ogro: the execution of Admiral Luis Carrero Blanco;...translated from the Spanish, adapted and with an introduction by Barbara Probst Solomon. New York, [1975]. pp. 196.

CARRIAGE AND WAGON MAKING

— Russia — White Russia.

TITOV (VIKTOR STEPANOVICH) Narodnye derevoobrabatyvaiushchie promysly Belorussii, 1917-1941 gg.: etnograficheskie ocherki bondarnogo promysla i izgotovleniia transportnykh sredstv; redaktor... V.K. Bondarchik. Minsk, 1976. pp. 135.

CARTER (JAMES EARL) President of the United States.

CARTER (JAMES EARL) President of the United States. Why not the best?. Nashville, Tenn., [1975]. pp. 156.

CARTER (JAMES EARL) President of the United States. A government as good as its people. New York, [1977]. pp. 262.

CARTIER (Sir GEORGES ETIENNE).

SWEENY (ALASTAIR) George-Etienne Cartier: a biography. Toronto, [1976]. pp. 352. *bibliog.*

CARTOGRAPHERS.

GARDINER (LESLIE) Bartholomew: 150 years. Edinburgh, [1976]. pp. 111.

CARTOGRAPHY.

MARGERISON (T.A.) Computers and the renaissance of cartography. London, Natural Environment Research Council, [1976]. pp. 20. *bibliog.*

— Africa.

UNITED NATIONS. Regional Cartographic Conference for Africa, [1st], Nairobi, 1963. United Nations Regional Cartographic Conference for Africa, 1-12 July, 1963, Nairobi, Kenya. vol. 2. Proceedings of the Conference and technical papers. (E/CONF. 43/106). New York, 1966. pp. 332.

UNITED NATIONS. Regional Cartographic Conference for Africa, 2nd, Tunis, 1966. Second...Conference...12-24 September 1966, Tunis, Tunisia. Report...(and Proceedings...and technical papers) (E/CN. 14/CART/240/Rev.1, E/CN.14/CART/242). New York, 1967. 2 vols (in 1). *bibliog.*

— Asia.

UNITED NATIONS. Regional Cartographic Conference for Asia and the Far East. 4th Conference, 1964. Fourth United Nations Regional Cartographic Conference for Asia and the Far East, 21 November-5 December, 1964, Manila, Philippines. vol.2. Proceedings of the Conference and technical papers. (E/CONF. 50/5). New York, 1966. pp. 505. *16 maps in end pocket.*

UNITED NATIONS. Regional Cartographic Conference for Asia and the Far East. 5th Conference, 1967. Fifth...Conference...8-22 March 1967, Canberra, Australia. Report...(and Proceedings...and technical papers) (E/CONF. 52/4, E/CONF. 52/5). New York, 1967-68. 2 vols. (in 1) *bibliog. 20 maps in end pocket.*

UNITED NATIONS. Regional Cartographic Conference for Asia and the Far East. 6th Conference, 1970. Sixth...Conference...24 October-7 November 1970, Tehran, Iran. Report...(and Technical papers) (E/CONF./57/2, E/CONF./57/3). New York, 1971-74. 2 vols (in 1). *bibliog. 22 maps in end pocket.*

— East (Far East).

UNITED NATIONS. Regional Cartographic Conference for Asia and the Far East. 4th Conference, 1964. Fourth United Nations Regional Cartographic Conference for Asia and the Far East, 21 November-5 December, 1964, Manila, Philippines. vol.2. Proceedings of the Conference and technical papers. (E/CONF. 50/5). New York, 1966. pp. 505. *16 maps in end pocket.*

CASTE

— India.

RAMU (G.N.) Family and caste in urban India: a case study. New Delhi, [1977]. pp. 224. *bibliog.*

— — Orissa.

FREEMAN (JAMES M.) Scarcity and opportunity in an Indian village. Menlo Park, Calif., [1977]. pp. 177. *bibliog.*

CASTILE

— Economic history.

LADERO QUESADA (MIGUEL ANGEL) La Hacienda real de Castilla en el siglo XV. La Laguna, Tenerife, 1973. pp. 384. *bibliog. (La Laguna. Universidad. Estudios de Historia. No. 1)*

CATALOGUES, LIBRARY.

UNITED STATES. Bureau of the Census. Library. 1976. Catalogs of the Bureau of the Census Library, Washington, D.C. Boston, 1976. 20 vols.

FONDAZIONE GIANGIACOMO FELTRINELLI. Catalogo dei periodici della biblioteca. Nendeln, 1977. 3 vols.

CATALOGUES, UNION.

WING (DONALD GODARD) Short-title catalogue of books printed in England, Scotland, Ireland, Wales, and British America, and of English books printed in other countries, 1641-1700. 2nd ed. New York, 1972 in progress.

LIST ECON: Förteckning över periodica inom ekonomi, handel, ekonomisk geografi och internationell statistik i nordiska bibliotek: List of periodicals in the fields of economics, trade, economic geography and international statistics in Nordic libraries; [pd. by] Biblioteket, Handelshögskolan, Stockholm. irreg., 1976- Stockholm.

WEBBER (ROSEMARY) compiler. World list of national newspapers: a union list of national newspapers in libraries in the British Isles. London, 1976. pp. 95. *bibliog.*

CATALOGUING.

PRUSSIA. Ministerium der Geistlichen, Unterrichts- und Medizinal-Angelegenheiten. 1915. Instruktionen für die alphabetischen Kataloge der preuszischen Bibliotheken vom 10. Mai 1899; zweite Ausgabe in der Fassung vom 10. August 1908. Berlin, 1915, repr. 1938. pp. 179.

CATALONIA

— Economic policy.

NADAL CAPARA (JOAQUIM DE) Catalunya i el Mercat Comu. Barcelona, 1975. pp. 304.

— History.

CRUELLS PIFARRE (MANUEL) La revolta del 1936 a Barcelona. Barcelona, 1976. pp. 364. *bibliog.*

ROMERO-MAURA (JOAQUIN) The Spanish army and Catalonia: the Cu-Cut incident and the Law of Jurisdictions, 1905-1906. Beverly Hills, [1976]. pp. 31.

— Nationalism.

ARNAU (ROGER) ed. Marxisme catala i questio nacional catalana, 1930-1936. Paris, 1974. 2 vols. (in 1).

CUCURULL (FELIX) Panoramica del nacionalisme catala. Paris, 1975 [or rather 1975-76]. 6 vols. *bibliog.*

LLULL (ANSELM) El mallorquinisme politic, 1840-1936: del regionalisme al nacionalisme. Paris, 1975. 2 vols. *bibliog.*

— Rural conditions.

HANSEN (EDWARD C.) Rural Catalonia under the Franco regime: the fate of regional culture since the Spanish Civil War. Cambridge, 1977. pp. 182. *bibliog.*

CATHOLIC CHURCH.

CARSON (HERBERT M.) Dawn or twilight?: a study of contemporary Roman Catholicism. rev. ed. Leicester, 1976. pp. 172. *bibliog. First published under the title Roman Catholicism today.*

— Government.

KONRAD, von Megenberg. Werke. Ökonomik. Buch I; herausgegeben von Sabine Krüger. Stuttgart, 1973. pp. 390. *bibliog. (Monumenta Germaniae Historica. Staatsschriften des Späteren Mittelalters. 3.Band. Die Werke des Konrad von Megenberg. 5. Stück. Yconomica) In Latin.*

— History — Modern period.

POULAT (EMILE) Catholicisme, démocratie et socialisme: le mouvement catholique et Mgr. Benigni de la naissance du socialisme à la victoire du fascisme. [Paris, 1977]. pp. 562. *bibliog.*

CATHOLIC CHURCH IN AFRICA.

KANGE (EWANE) Le politique dans le système religieux catholique romain en Afrique de 1815 à 1960. Lille, 1976. pp. 513. *bibliogs. Thèse - Université de Strasbourg II.*

CATHOLIC CHURCH IN FRANCE.

REMOND (RENE) L'anti-cléricalisme en France de 1815 à nos jours. Paris, [1976]. pp. 374. *bibliog.*

CATHOLIC CHURCH IN GERMANY.

RICHTER (AUG.) Vor dem Schwurgericht: Verteidigungsrede...am 30. Mai 1906 im Justizpalast zu München...wegen...Beschimpfung der katholischen Kirche. München, 1906. pp. 15.

— Charities.

CASSIANEUM. Festschrift hundert Jahre Cassianeum, Verlag und Druckerei Ludwig Auer, Donauwörth: 1875-1975. Donauwörth, [1975]. pp. 120.

CATHOLIC CHURCH IN IRELAND.

HUSSEY (THOMAS) Bishop of Waterford and Lismore. A pastoral letter to the Catholic clergy of the united dioceses of Waterford and Lismore. 7th ed. London, re-printed by J.P. Coghlan, 1797. pp. 12.

CATHOLIC CHURCH IN ITALY.

VALENTINI (NORBERTO) La politica in confessionale. Milano, [1974]. pp. 286.

MOLONY (JOHN NEYLON) The emergence of political catholicism in Italy: Partito Popolare 1919-1926. London, 1977. pp. 225. *bibliog.*

CATHOLIC CHURCH IN POLAND.

SOŁOMA (ANTONI) Za ka'zdą cenę: niemiecki kler katolicki wobec ludności polskiej na Warmii, Mazurach i Powiślu w latach 1919-1939. Warszawa, 1976. pp. 394. *bibliog.*

CATHOLIC CHURCH IN RWANDA.

LINDEN (IAN) Church and revolution in Rwanda. Manchester, [1977]. pp. 304. *bibliog.*

CATHOLIC CHURCH IN SCOTLAND.

SCOTTISH HISTORY SOCIETY. [Publications]. 4th Series. vol. 12. Calendar of papal letters to Scotland of Clement VII of Avignon, 1378-1394; edited by Charles Burns; [with] Annie I. Dunlop, 1897-1973: a memoir; by Ian B. Cowan. Edinburgh, 1976. pp. 240.

SCOTTISH HISTORY SOCIETY. [Publications]. 4th Series. vol.13. Calendar of papal letters to Scotland of Benedict XIII of Avignon, 1394-1419; edited by Francis McGurk. Edinburgh, 1976. pp. 456.

CATHOLIC CHURCH IN THE UNITED KINGDOM.

DOWDEN (RICHARD) Northern Ireland and the Catholic Church in Britain; published...for the Commission for International Justice and Peace of England and Wales as a contribution to public debate. Abbots Langley, [1975]. pp. 27.

CATHOLIC EMANCIPATION.

DUBLIN. Catholics. Proceedings at the Catholic meeting of Dublin, duly convened on Wednesday, October 31, 1792...with the letter of the Corporation of Dublin, to the Protestants of Ireland; annexed is the declaration adopted by the General Committee, etc. Dublin, printed by H. Fitzpatrick, 1792. pp. 72.

IRELAND. Parliament. House of Commons. Debates. 1795. A report of the debate...on the bill, presented by the Right Hon. Henry Grattan, For the further relief of his Majesty's Popish or Roman Catholic subjects, to which is annexed an appendix: containing the Catholic petition and an authentic copy of the bill, etc. Dublin, printed by J. Chambers, 1795. pp. 134.

JOHNSON (ROBERT) M.P. for Hillsborough. Speech...delivered in the House of Commons, Monday the 4th May 1795, on the motion, that the Bill, entitled A Bill for the further relief of his Majesty's popish or Roman Catholic subjects, be rejected. Dublin, printed for R.E. Mercier, 1795. pp. 98.

FOSTER (JOHN) 1st Baron Oriel. An accurate report of the speech of the Right Hon. John Foster, Speaker of the House of Commons, in the Committee on the Roman Catholic Bill, Feb. 27, 1793. Dublin, printed by R. Marchbank for J. Milliken, 1798. pp. 24.

CATHOLIC SCHOOLS

— United Kingdom.

NATIONAL CATHOLIC COMMISSION FOR RACIAL JUSTICE. Where creed and colour matter: a survey on black children and Catholic schools. London, [1975]. pp. 47.

— United States.

SANDERS (JAMES W.) The education of an urban minority: Catholics in Chicago, 1833-1965. New York, 1977. pp. 278. *bibliog.*

CATHOLICS IN IRELAND.

DUBLIN. Catholics. Proceedings at the Catholic meeting of Dublin, duly convened on Wednesday, October 31, 1792...with the letter of the Corporation of Dublin, to the Protestants of Ireland; annexed is the declaration adopted by the General Committee, etc. Dublin, printed by H. Fitzpatrick, 1792. pp. 72.

IRELAND. Parliament. House of Commons. Debates. 1795. A report of the debate...on the bill, presented by the Right Hon. Henry Grattan, For the further relief of his Majesty's Popish or Roman Catholic subjects, to which is annexed an appendix: containing the Catholic petition and an authentic copy of the bill, etc. Dublin, printed by J. Chambers, 1795. pp. 134.

JOHNSON (ROBERT) M.P. for Hillsborough. Speech...delivered in the House of Commons, Monday the 4th May 1795, on the motion, that the Bill, entitled A Bill for the further relief of his Majesty's popish or Roman Catholic subjects, be rejected. Dublin, printed for R.E. Mercier, 1795. pp. 98.

FOSTER (JOHN) 1st Baron Oriel. An accurate report of the speech of the Right Hon. John Foster, Speaker of the House of Commons, in the Committee on the Roman Catholic Bill, Feb. 27, 1793. Dublin, printed by R. Marchbank for J. Milliken, 1798. pp. 24.

CATHOLICS IN ITALY.

MOVIMENTO cattolico e sviluppo capitalistico: atti del Convegno su "Movimento...nel Veneto". Venezia, 1974. pp. 189. *Conference held in Padua in June 1973, with contributions by Emilio Franzina, and others.*

CATHOLICS IN NORTHERN IRELAND.

BURTON (FRANK PATRICK) The social meanings of Catholicism in Northern Ireland. 1976. fo. 311. *bibliog. Typescript. Ph.D. (London) thesis: unpublished. This thesis is the property of London University and may not be removed from the Library.*

CATHOLICS IN THE UNITED KINGDOM.

COMAN (PETER W.) Catholics and the welfare state. London, 1977. pp. 118. *bibliog.*

CATTLE

— Carcasses — Classification.

AUSTRALIA. Bureau of Agricultural Economics. 1976. Developments in beef carcass classification. Canberra, 1976. pp. 80. *bibliog. (Beef Research Reports. No. 19)*

— Australia.

AUSTRALIAN GRAZING INDUSTRY SURVEY, THE: incorporating former sheep industry survey; [pd. by] Bureau of Agricultural Economics. a., 1973/74(1st)- Canberra.

CATTLE TRADE

— Ireland (Republic).

EIRE. Review Body on Beef Intervention and Cattle Slaughter Premium Systems. 1976. Report. Dublin, 1976. pp. 74.

— United Kingdom — Wales.

COLYER (RICHARD J.) The Welsh cattle drovers: agriculture and the Welsh cattle trade before and during the nineteenth century. Cardiff, 1976. pp. 155. *bibliog.*

CATTLE TRAILS.

COLYER (RICHARD J.) The Welsh cattle drovers: agriculture and the Welsh cattle trade before and during the nineteenth century. Cardiff, 1976. pp. 155. *bibliog.*

CAUCA VALLEY

— Economic conditions.

KNIGHT (ROLF) Sugar plantations and labor patterns in the Cauca Valley, Colombia. Toronto, 1972. pp. 209. *bibliog. (Toronto. University. Department of Anthropology. Anthropological Series. No.12)*

CAUCASUS

— Constitutional history.

EBZEEVA (SOF'IA ESENOVNA) Stanovlenie sovetskoi natsional'noi gosudarstvennosti narodov Severnogo Kavkaza. Moskva, 1976. pp. 135.

— History — 1917-1921, Revolution.

IVANIDZE (KOBA MELKHISEDEKOVICH) Slavnye stranitsy bor'by i pobed: istoriia deiatel'nosti Kavkazskogo kraevogo komiteta RKP(b), 1917-1920 gody. Tbilisi, 1975. pp. 351.

TEVZADZE (GEORGII GEORGIEVICH) Bor'ba zheleznodorozhnikov Zakavkaz'ia za ustanovlenie i uprochenie Sovetskoi vlasti. Tbilisi, 1975. pp. 126.

AGAIAN (TSATUR PAVLOVICH) V.I. Lenin i sozdanie zakavkazskikh sovetskikh respublik. Erevan, 1976. pp. 263.

— Intellectual life.

PATSURIIA (LARISA B.) A.V. Lunacharskii i intelligentsiia Zakavkaz'ia. Tbilisi, 1976. pp. 144.

CAYMAN ISLANDS

— Economic conditions.

CAYMAN ISLANDS. Currency Board. Report. a., 1975- Grand Cayman.

CEAUSESCU (NICOLAE).

BRAUN (AUREL) Romanian foreign policy under Nicolae Ceausescu, 1965-1972: the political and military limits of autonomy. 1976. fo. 318. *bibliog. Typescript. Ph.D. (London) thesis: unpublished. This thesis is the property of London University and may not be removed from the Library.*

CEMENT INDUSTRIES

— Russia — Buryat Republic.

BAZHEEV (DANIIL GAVRILOVICH) Ocherki istorii Timliuiskikh tsementnogo i shifernogo zavodov. Ulan-Ude, 1973. pp. 88.

— Turkey.

TURKIYE SINAÎ KALKINMA BANKASI. Sector Research Publications. No. 7. Cement industry; [a] T.S.K.B. sector study. Istanbul, 1976. pp. 95. *bibliog.*

— United Kingdom.

FRANCIS (A.J.) The cement industry, 1796-1914: a history. Newton Abbot, [1977]. pp. 319.

WILLMOTT (FRANK G.) Cement, mud and 'muddies'. Rainham, Kent, 1977. pp. 141.

CENSORSHIP

— Germany.

[A COLLECTION of documents relating to book censorship and the book trade in Germany during the years immediately following World War II]. 1945-48. pp. various..

— United States.

NORWICK (KENNETH P.) Lobbying for freedom: censorship: a citizen's guide to state legislatures and how to make them respond on vital issues involving individual freedom. [New York, 1974]. pp. 72.

CENTRAL AMERICAN BANK FOR ECONOMIC INTEGRATION.

CENTRAL AMERICAN BANK FOR ECONOMIC INTEGRATION. Memoria. a., 1968/69 (8th)- , with gap (1969/70, 9th) Tegucigalpa. *1972/73 in English.*

CENTRAL AMERICAN COMMON MARKET.

McCALL (LOUIS A.) Regional integration: a comparison of European and Central American dynamics. Beverly Hills, [1976]. pp. 77. *bibliog.*

CENTRAL BUSINESS DISTRICTS.

ALEXANDER (IAN C.) The city centre: patterns and problems. Nedlands, W.A., 1974. pp. 216. *bibliog.*

— Sweden.

PERSSON (KENT) Sysselsättningen i centrum: sysselsättningsförändringar i stadscentrum, deras orsaker och verkan, med exempel från Göteborg. Göteborg, 1977. pp. 282. *bibliog. (Göteborgs Universitet. Geografiska Institutioner. Meddelanden. Ser.B. Nr.60) With English summary.*

CENTRAL PLACES.

BEAVON (KEITH SIDNEY ORROCK) Central place theory: a reinterpretation. London, 1977. pp. 157. *bibliog.*

BIRD (JAMES HAROLD) Centrality and cities. London, 1977. pp. 203. *bibliog.*

— Kenya.

OBUDHO (ROBERT) and WALLER (PETER P.) Periodic markets, urbanization, and regional planning: a case study from western Kenya. Westport, Conn., 1976. pp. 289. *bibliog.*

CENTRE PARTIES

— Germany.

WIRTSCHAFTSTAG, 1971. Soziale Marktwirtschaft: Gebot der Vernunft, Motor des Fortschritts; Protokoll; (herausgegeben vom Wirtschaftsrat der CDU). Bonn, 1971. pp. 179.

ADAMO (HANS) Die CDU/CSU: Wesen und Politik. Frankfurt am Main, 1976. pp. 285. *bibliog.*

MUECHLER (GUENTER) CDU/CSU: das schwierige Bündnis. München, 1976. pp. 250. *bibliog.*

MINTZEL (ALF) Geschichte der CSU: ein Überblick. Opladen, [1977]. pp. 498. *bibliog.*

— — Programme.

CHRISTLICH-DEMOKRATISCHE UNION DEUTSCHLANDS. Das Berliner Programm; mit Beschlüssen des Hamburger Parteitages 1973. [Bonn, 1974]. pp. 86.

— Germany, Eastern.

KRUBKE (ERWIN) Wirtschaftspolitik zwischen gestern und morgen: die Stellungnahme der CDU zur Herausbildung der sozialistischen Planwirtschaft in der DDR, etc. [Berlin], 1977. pp. 136. *bibliog. (Christlich-Demokratische Union [D.D.R.]. Beiträge zur Geschichte)*

— Peru.

CORNEJO CHAVEZ (HECTOR) Socialcristianismo y revolucion peruana. Lima, 1975. pp. 334.

— Switzerland.

KONSERVATIV-CHRISTLICHSOZIALE VOLKSPARTEI DER SCHWEIZ. Vers l'avenir: les 50 ans du Parti conservateur-chrétien- social suisse: discours en français et manifeste proclamés lors des Journées de jubilé du Parti les 20/21 octobre 1962 à Lucerne. [Lucerne?, 1962]. pp. 20.

CHACO DISPUTE.

ELIO (TOMAS MANUEL) La guerra y la paz del Chaco. La Paz, [1970?]. pp. 334.

CHAD

— Economic conditions.

CHAMBRE DE COMMERCE D'AGRICULTURE ET D'INDUSTRIE DU CHAD. Le Tchad 1962: aperçu général. Fort Lamy, 1962. fo.15.

FRANCE. Ministère de la Coopération. Service des Etudes Economiques et des Questions Internationales. 1976. Tchad: données statistiques sur les activités économiques, culturelles et sociales. Paris, 1976. pp. 179.

— **Economic policy.**

CHAMBRE DE COMMERCE D'AGRICULTURE ET D'INDUSTRIE DU CHAD. Les plans d'équipements. Fort Lamy, 1962. fo. 6.

— **Social conditions.**

FRANCE. Ministère de la Coopération. Service des Etudes Economiques et des Questions Internationales. 1976. Tchad: données statistiques sur les activités économiques, culturelles et sociales. Paris, 1976. pp. 179.

— **Social policy.**

CHAMBRE DE COMMERCE D'AGRICULTURE ET D'INDUSTRIE DU CHAD. Les plans d'équipements. Fort Lamy, 1962. fo. 6.

— **Statistics.**

FRANCE. Ministère de la Coopération. Service des Etudes Economiques et des Questions Internationales. 1976. Tchad: données statistiques sur les activités économiques, culturelles et sociales. Paris, 1976. pp. 179.

CHAMBERLAIN (JOSEPH).

JUDD (DENIS) Radical Joe: a life of Joseph Chamberlain. London, 1977. pp. 310. *bibliog.*

CHAMBERS OF COMMERCE

— **Germany.**

ZINNER (BERND) Die Handelskammer von Mittelfranken: Organisation und gutachtliche Tätigkeit, 1842-1889. Nürnberg, 1976. pp. 345. *bibliog. (Nuremberg. Stadtarchiv. Nürnberger Werkstücke zur Stadt- und Landesgeschichte. Band 19) Erlanger Phil. Dissertation 1976.*

CHANNEL TUNNEL.

UNION ROUTIERE DE FRANCE. Questions of the Day. 18. A comprehensive cross-Channel link. Paris, [1960?]. pp. 77.

CHARDZHOU (OBLAST')

— **Statistics.**

CHARDZHOU (OBLAST'). Statisticheskoe Upravlenie. Ekonomika i kul'tura Chardzhouskoi oblasti Turkmenskoi SSR: iubileinyi statisticheskii sbornik. Chardzhou, 1974. pp. 140.

CHARITABLE USES, TRUSTS AND FOUNDATIONS

— **United Kingdom.**

NATIONAL COUNCIL OF SOCIAL SERVICE. Committee of Inquiry into the Effect of Charity Law and Practice on Voluntary Organisations. Charity law and voluntary organisations: report of an independent committee...under the chairmanship of Lord Goodman, etc. London, [1976]. pp. 150.

CHARITIES.

SURINGAR (WILLEM HENDRIK DOMINICUS) Rede über das Bedürfniss einer zwechmässigern Armenpflege und der Errichtung eines Patronats sowie über das bei seiner Ausübung zu beobachtende Verfahren; gehalten zu Amsterdam am 22. Januar 1842, etc. Kitzingen, Dürr, [1842]. pp. 29.

— **Canada — Taxation.**

BIRD (RICHARD MILLER) and BUCOVETSKY (M.W.) Canadian tax reform and private philanthropy. Toronto, 1976. pp. 68. *(Canadian Tax Foundation. Canadian Tax Papers. No. 58)*

— **Switzerland — Vaud (Canton).**

BRIOD (ALICE) L'assistance des pauvres au moyen âge dans le Pays de Vaud. Lausanne, [1976]. pp. 120. *First published in 1926 under the title, L'assistance des pauvres dans le Pays de Vaud du commencement du moyen âge à la fin du XVIe siècle.*

— **United Kingdom.**

NATIONAL COUNCIL OF SOCIAL SERVICE. Committee of Inquiry into the Effect of Charity Law and Practice on Voluntary Organisations. Charity law and voluntary organisations: report of an independent committee...under the chairmanship of Lord Goodman, etc. London, [1976]. pp. 150.

— — **Ireland, Northern.**

IRELAND, NORTHERN. Department of Finance. Charities: report ...of proceedings under the Charities Act (Northern Ireland) 1964. a., 1971- Belfast. *1964/65 [1st]-1970 included in IRELAND, NORTHERN. Parliament. House of Commons. [Papers].*

— — **Scotland — Directories.**

EDINBURGH COUNCIL OF SOCIAL SERVICE. Directory of Scottish trusts, welfare societies and benevolent funds. Edinburgh, 1975. pp. 31.

CHARLES I, King of Great Britain and Ireland.

AIKIN (LUCY) Memoirs of the court of King Charles the First. 2nd ed. London, 1833. 2 vols.

FIREBRACE (CORDELL WILLIAM) Honest Harry: being the biography of Sir Henry Firebrace, Knight, 1619-1691. London, 1932. pp. 392. *bibliog.*

CHARTISM.

[HELPS (Sir ARTHUR)] A letter from one of the special constables in London on the late occasion of their being called out to keep the peace. London, W. Pickering, 1848. pp. 23.

BARNSBY (GEORGE) The working class movement in the Black Country, 1750 to 1867. Wolverhampton, 1977. pp. 233. *bibliog.*

CHEESE INDUSTRY

— **Switzerland.**

ROTH (ALFRED G.) Die Gründung der Käseunion GSK/SK, 1914: Referat vor dem Verwaltungsrat zum 60. Jahrestag. Bern, 1975. pp. 60. *bibliog.*

CHEMICAL INDUSTRIES.

UNITED NATIONS. Economic Commission for Europe. Annual bulletin of trade in chemical products. a., 1974 (v.1)- Geneva. *[in English with summaries in French and Russian].*

— **Russia — Ukraine.**

RAZVITIE khimicheskoi tekhnologii na Ukraine. Kiev, 1976. 2 vols. *bibliog.*

— **United Kingdom.**

HARDIE (DAVID WILLIAM FERGUSON) A history of the chemical industry in Widnes. Liverpool, 1950. pp. 250. *bibliog.*

CREMER AND WARNER. Cheshire chemical and allied industry survey: a county wide picture. [Chester?], Cheshire County Council and District Councils, 1976. pp. 345.

NICHOLS (THEO) and BEYNON (HUW) Living with capitalism: class relations and the modern factory. London, 1977. pp. 204.

CHEMICAL WARFARE.

VERWEY (WIL D.) Riot control agents and herbicides in war: their humanitarian, toxicological, ecological, military, polemological, and legal aspects. Leyden, 1977. pp. 377. *bibliog.*

CHEMICALS

— **Manufacture and industry — Iran.**

RESEARCH CENTER FOR INDUSTRIAL AND TRADE DEVELOPMENT [IRAN]. Chemical and petrochemical industries in Iran. Tehran, Ministry of Economy, 1971. fo.9.

CHEMISTRY

— **History — United Kingdom — Scotland.**

DONOVAN (ARTHUR L.) Philosophical chemistry in the Scottish Enlightenment: the doctrines and discoveries of William Cullen and Joseph Black. Edinburgh, [1975]. pp. 343. *bibliog.*

CHEREPANOV (ALEKSANDR IVANOVICH).

CHEREPANOV (ALEKSANDR IVANOVICH) Zapiski voennogo sovetnika v Kitae, [1925-1939]. [3rd ed., erroneously designated 2nd ed.]. Moskva, 1976. pp. 648.

CHEROKEE INDIANS.

GOODWIN (GARY C.) Cherokees in transition: a study of changing culture and environment prior to 1775. Chicago, 1977. pp. 207. *bibliog. (Chicago. University. Department of Geography. Research Papers. No. 181)*

CHESHIRE

— **Industries.**

CREMER AND WARNER. Cheshire chemical and allied industry survey: a county wide picture. [Chester?], Cheshire County Council and District Councils, 1976. pp. 345.

CHETVERIKOV (NIKOLAI SERGEEVICH).

CHETVERIKOV (NIKOLAI SERGEEVICH) Statisticheskie issledovaniia: teoriia i praktika. Moskva, 1975. pp. 388.

CHIANG (CHING).

WITKE (ROXANE) Comrade Chiang Ch'ing. London, 1977. pp. 54z.

CHIANG (KAI-SHEK).

LUMLEY (F.A.) The Republic of China under Chiang Kai-Shek: Taiwan today. London, 1976. pp. 167. *bibliog.*

CROZIER (BRIAN) The man who lost China: the first full biography of Chiang Kai-Shek. London, 1977. pp. 430.

CHICAGO

— **Schools.**

SANDERS (JAMES W.) The education of an urban minority: Catholics in Chicago, 1833- 1965. New York, 1977. pp. 278. *bibliog.*

— **Transit systems.**

ILLINOIS. Chicago Area Transportation Study. Annual report. a., 1975- Chicago.

CHILD DEVELOPMENT.

LEACH (PENELOPE JANE) Babyhood: infant development from birth to two years. Harmondsworth, 1974 repr. 1976. pp. 481. *bibliog.*

MILNER (DAVID) Children and race. Harmondsworth, 1975. pp. 281. *bibliog.*

BOWER (THOMAS GILLIE RUSSELL) The perceptual world of the child. London, 1977. pp. 93. *bibliog.*

DUSKA (RONALD) and WHELAN (MARIELLEN) Moral development: a guide to Piaget and Kohlberg. Dublin, 1977. pp. 128. *bibliog.*

CHILD PSYCHOLOGY.

NORBURN (VERONICA) and PUSHKIN (I.) Ethnic awareness in young children: a follow-up study into early adolescence. London, 1973. pp. 70, 66. *bibliog.*

FOSS (BRIAN MALZARD) ed. New perspectives in child development. Harmondsworth, 1974. pp. 266. *bibliogs.*

PEINE (HERMANN A.) and HOWARTH (ROY) Children and parents: everyday problems of behaviour. Harmondsworth, 1975. pp. 133.

CLARKE (ANN MARGARET) and CLARKE (ALAN DOUGLAS BENSON) eds. Early experience: myth and evidence. London, 1976. pp. 314. *bibliog.*

DUNN (JUDY) Distress and comfort. London, 1977. pp. 126. *bibliog.*

GARVEY (CATHERINE) Play. London, 1977. pp. 128. *bibliog.*

CHILD WELFARE

— Congresses.

INTERNATIONAL CONGRESS FOR THE WELFARE AND PROTECTION OF CHILDREN, PARIS, 1933. Congrès international pour la protection de l'enfance: [proceedings, with a summary volume]. Paris, Comité National de l'Enfance, 1933. 4 vols. (in 2) .

— Australia.

AUSTRALIA. Social Welfare Commission. 1974. Project care: children, parents, community. Canberra, 1974. pp. 255. *bibliog.*

— Canada — British Columbia.

BRITISH COLUMBIA. Department of Human Resources. Statistical reports and tables: annual report. a., 1972/73-Victoria.

— United Kingdom.

DAVIE (RONALD) Children and families with special needs; an inaugural lecture given on 22 January 1975 at University College, Cardiff. Cardiff, [1975]. pp. 17. *bibliog.*

DAVIES (HYWEL) and PLANK (DAVID) Children in the care of the London boroughs, 1967 to 1973. London, [1975]. pp. (159). *(London. Greater London Council. Research Memoranda. 480)*

LEWIS (PAUL) Child interim benefit: an interim guide. 2nd ed. London, 1976. pp. 20.

TIZARD (JACK) and others. All our children: pre-school services in a changing society. London, 1976. pp. 252. *bibliog.*

COMMUNITY RELATIONS COMMISSION. Caring for under-fives in a multi-racial society. London, 1977. pp. 60. *bibliog.*

— United States.

STEINER (GILBERT YALE) and MILIUS (PAULINE H.) The children's cause. Washington, D.C. [1976]. pp. 265.

CHILDBIRTH.

MACFARLANE (AIDAN) The psychology of childbirth. London, 1977. pp. 128. *bibliog.*

CHILDREN.

The VALUE of children: a cross-national study;...[by] Fred Arnold [and others]. Honolulu, 1975 in progress.

— Care and hygiene — Congress.

INTERNATIONAL CONGRESS FOR THE WELFARE AND PROTECTION OF CHILDREN, PARIS, 1933. Congrès international pour la protection de l'enfance: [proceedings, with a summary volume]. Paris, Comité National de l'Enfance, 1933. 4 vols. (in 2) .

— — Communist countries.

SOCIALIST CHILD CARE COLLECTIVE. Changing childcare: Cuba, China and the challenging of our own values. London, [1976]. pp. 24. *bibliog.*

— — Underdeveloped areas.

See UNDERDEVELOPED AREAS —
    Children — Care and hygiene.

— Hospital care.

HALL (DAVID J.) Social relations and innovation: changing the state of play in hospitals. London, 1977. pp. 222. *bibliog.*

— Institutional care — United Kingdom.

COMMUNITY RELATIONS COMMISSION. A home from home?: some policy considerations on black children in residential care. London, 1977. pp. 39. *bibliog.*

— Language.

GEORGETOWN UNIVERSITY ROUND TABLE ON LANGUAGES AND LINGUISTICS, 1975. Developmental psycholinguistics: theory and applications; Daniel P. Dato, editor. Washington, D.C., [1975]. pp. 297. *bibliogs.*

HALLIDAY (MICHAEL ALEXANDER KIRKWOOD) Learning how to mean: explorations in the development of language. London, 1975. pp. 164. *bibliog.*

BATES (ELIZABETH) Language and context: the acquisition of pragmatics. New York, [1976]. pp. 375. *bibliog.*

GREENFIELD (PATRICIA MARKS) and SMITH (JOSHUA H.) The structure of communication in early language development. New York, 1976. pp. 238. *bibliog.*

ADLAM (DIANA S.) Code in context. London, 1977. pp. 253. *bibliog.*

HAWKINS (PETER R.) Social class, the nominal group and verbal strategies. London, 1977. pp. 242. *bibliog.*

TALKING to children: language input and acquisition: papers from a conference sponsored by the Committee on Sociolinguistics of the Social Science Research Council (USA); edited by Catherine E. Snow and Charles A. Ferguson. Cambridge, 1977. pp. 369. *bibliog.*

— Law — Belgium.

COPPIETERS (FRANZ) The protection of youth. [Brussels], Ministry of Foreign Affairs, External Trade and Cooperation in Development, 1971. pp. 11. *(Belgian News. No.6d)*

— — Netherlands.

NETHERLANDS. Commissie voor de Herziening van het Kinderbeschermingsrecht. 1971. Jeugdbeschermingsrecht: rapport; [J.Wiarda, chairman]. 's-Gravenhage, 1971. pp. 285.

— — United Kingdom.

MUMFORD (GILBERT HENRY FRANCIS) and SELWOOD (TIMOTHY JOHN) A guide to the Children Act 1975. London, 1976. pp. 44.

— — United States.

STEINER (GILBERT YALE) and MILIUS (PAULINE H.) The children's cause. Washington, D.C. [1976]. pp. 265.

— Mortality.

TABUTIN (DOMINIQUE) Mortalité infantile et juvénile en Algérie. [Paris], 1976. pp. 275. *bibliog. (France. Institut National d'Etudes Démographiques. Travaux et Documents. Cahiers. No. 77)*

— — Mathematical models.

HELLER (PETER S.) Interactions of childhood mortality and fertility in W. Malaysia, 1947-1970. Ann Arbor, 1976. pp. 33. *bibliog. (Michigan University. Center for Research on Economic Development. Discussion Papers. No.57)*

— Nutrition — Underdeveloped areas.

See UNDERDEVELOPED AREAS —
    Children — Nutrition.

CHILDREN AND POLITICS.

MERELMAN (RICHARD M.) Political reasoning in adolescence: some bridging themes. Beverly Hills, [1976]. pp. 37. *bibliog.*

PAMMETT (JON H.) and WHITTINGTON (MICHAEL S.) eds. Foundations of political culture: political socialization in Canada. Toronto, [1976]. pp. 318.

CHILDREN IN AUSTRIA.

WINTER (MAX) Das Kind und der Sozialismus: eine Betrachtung. Berlin, 1924. pp. 135.

CHILDREN IN MALAYSIA.

HELLER (PETER S.) Interactions of childhood mortality and fertility in W. Malaysia, 1947-1970. Ann Arbor, 1976. pp. 33. *bibliog. (Michigan University. Center for Research on Economic Development. Discussion Papers. No.57)*

CHILDREN IN UNDERDEVELOPED AREAS.

See UNDERDEVELOPED AREAS —
    Children.

CHILDREN OF IMMIGRANTS

— Australia.

ISAACS (EVA) Greek children in Sydney. Canberra, 1976. pp. 128. *(Academy of the Social Sciences in Australia. Immigrants in Australia. 6)*

— United Kingdom.

COMMUNITY RELATIONS COMMISSION. Caring for under-fives in a multi-racial society. London, 1977. pp. 60. *bibliog.*

COMMUNITY RELATIONS COMMISSION. A home from home?: some policy considerations on black children in residential care. London, 1977. pp. 39. *bibliog.*

CHILDREN'S PERIODICALS, CHILEAN.

SOTO (FRANCISCO) Fascismo y Opus Dei en Chile: estudios de literatura e ideologia. Barcelona, 1976. pp. 261.

CHILE

— Boundaries — Argentine Republic.

U.K. Court of Arbitration of a Controversy between the Argentine Republic and the Republic of Chile. 1965-67. Argentine-Chile frontier case court of arbitration transcript of hearings [with memorials, counter memorials, documents, etc. submitted by Argentine and Chile]; [Lord McNair, president] . London, 1965-67. 20 vols. (in 15).

— Economic conditions.

DICKMAN (ENRIQUE) Visiones de Chile. Buenos Aires, 1936. pp. 78.

CHILE: the balanced view: a recopilation of articles about the Allende years and after; (edited by Francisco Orrego Vicuña). [Santiago, 1975]. pp. 298. *(Santiago de Chile. Universidad de Chile. Instituto de Estudios Internacionales. Estudios Internacionales)*

— Economic policy.

BRUNN (REINHARD VON) Chile: con leyes tradicionales hacia una nueva economia?; (traductor: Leonardo Halpern). Santiago de Chile, 1972. pp. 154. *(Instituto Latinoamericano de Investigaciones Sociales. Estudios y Documentos. 18)*

COLEGIO DE ARQUITECTOS DE CHILE. Plan nacional de desarrollo urbano, rural y de vivienda: planteamientos basicos, diagnosticos, estrategias. Santiago de Chile, 1973. pp. 255. *bibliog.*

ECONOMIA politica en la Unidad Popular: materiales de los Cuadernos de la Realidad Nacional, 1970-1973; presentacion, Manuel Antonio Garreton. Barcelona, 1975. pp. 341.

CHILE. Oficina de Planificacion Nacional. 1976. Estrategia nacional de desarrollo regional año 1975-1990: version preliminar corregida. [Santiago, 1976]. pp. 436.

FRANK (ANDRE GUNDER) Economic genocide in Chile: monetarist theory versus humanity; two open letters to Arnold Harberger and Milton Friedman. Nottingham, 1976. pp. 87.

BEHRMAN (JERE R.) Macroeconomic policy in a developing country: the Chilean experience. Amsterdam, 1977. pp. 340. *bibliog.*

— Emigration and immigration.

YOUNG (GEORGE F.W.) The Germans in Chile: immigration and colonization, 1849-1914. New York, [1974]. pp. 234. *bibliog.*

— Foreign relations — United States.

CHILE: the balanced view: a recopilation of articles about the Allende years and after; (edited by Francisco Orrego Vicuña). [Santiago, 1975]. pp. 298. *(Santiago de Chile. Universidad de Chile. Instituto de Estudios Internacionales. Estudios Internacionales)*

URIBE ARCE (ARMANDO) The black book of American intervention in Chile;...translated from the Spanish by Jonathan Casart. Boston, [Mass], [1975]. pp. 163.

— History.

WHITAKER (ARTHUR PRESTON) The United States and the southern cone: Argentina, Chile, and Uruguay. Cambridge, Mass., 1976. pp. 464. *bibliog.*

— — Sources.

HENFREY (COLIN) and SORJ (BERNARDO) eds. Chilean voices: activists describe their experiences of the Popular Unity period; recorded, edited and translated by Colin Henfrey and Bernardo Sorj. Hassocks, Sussex, 1977. pp. 196.

— — 1810- .

PALACIOS RODRIGUEZ (RAUL) La chilenizacion de Tacna y Arica, 1883-1929. Lima, [1974]. pp. 317. *bibliog.*

— — 1973, Coup d'état.

URIBE ARCE (ARMANDO) The black book of American intervention in Chile;...translated from the Spanish by Jonathan Casart. Boston, [Mass], [1975]. pp. 163.

— Politics and government.

CORDOVA CLAURE (LUIS EDUARDO) Chile si?: los primeros 800 dias. Buenos Aires, [1973]. pp. 159.

REVOLUCION y contrarrevolucion en Chile; [by] Volker Lühr y otros; (traducido de la edicion alemana por Francisco Zanutigh Nuñez). Buenos Aires, [1974]. pp. 195.

SELSER (GREGORIO) Chile para recordar. Buenos Aires, [1974]. pp. 315.

TAUFIC (CAMILO) Chile en la hoguera: cronica de la represion militar. Buenos Aires, [1974]. pp. 271.

CHILE: the balanced view: a recopilation of articles about the Allende years and after; (edited by Francisco Orrego Vicuña). [Santiago, 1975]. pp. 298. *(Santiago de Chile. Universidad de Chile. Instituto de Estudios Internacionales. Estudios Internacionales)*

EAGLESON (JOHN) ed. Christians and socialism: documentation of the Christians for Socialism movement in Latin America; translated by John Durry. Maryknoll, N.Y., [1975]. pp. 246.

KAUFMAN (ROBERT R.) Transitions to stable authoritarian-corporate regimes: the Chilean case?. Beverly Hills, [1976]. pp. 68. *bibliog.*

LETELIER (ORLANDO) Chile: economic freedom and political repression. London, [1976]. pp. 17. *(Spokesman, The. Pamphlets. No. 56)*

ROJAS (ROBINSON) The murder of Allende and the end of the Chilean way to socialism. New York, [1976]. pp. 274.

CUSACK (DAVID F.) Revolution and reaction: the internal dynamics of conflict and confrontation in Chile. Denver, [1977]. pp. 147. *(Denver. University. Social Science Foundation and Graduate School of International Studies. Monograph Series in World Affairs. vol. 14, no. 3)*

HENFREY (COLIN) and SORJ (BERNARDO) eds. Chilean voices: activists describe their experiences of the Popular Unity period; recorded, edited and translated by Colin Henfrey and Bernardo Sorj. Hassocks, Sussex, 1977. pp. 196.

ROXBOROUGH (IAN) and others. Chile: the state and revolution. London, 1977. pp. 304. *bibliog.*

— Religion.

EAGLESON (JOHN) ed. Christians and socialism: documentation of the Christians for Socialism movement in Latin America; translated by John Durry. Maryknoll, N.Y., [1975]. pp. 246.

— Social conditions.

DICKMAN (ENRIQUE) Visiones de Chile. Buenos Aires, 1936. pp. 78.

— Social policy.

COLEGIO DE ARQUITECTOS DE CHILE. Plan nacional de desarrollo urbano, rural y de vivienda: planteamientos basicos, diagnosticos, estrategias. Santiago de Chile, 1973. pp. 255. *bibliog.*

CHILE. Oficina de Planificacion Nacional. Informe social. s-a., 1976- [Santiago de Chile].

CHILE. Oficina de Planificacion Nacional. 1976. Estrategia nacional de desarrollo regional año 1975-1990: version preliminar corregida. [Santiago, 1976]. pp. 436.

CHIMBORAZO

— Economic conditions.

ECUADOR. Junta de Planificacion y Coordinacion Economica. 1974. Chimborazo: estudio socio-economico. Quito, [1974?]. 2 vols.

— Social conditions.

ECUADOR. Junta de Planificacion y Coordinacion Economica. 1974. Chimborazo: estudio socio-economico. Quito, [1974?]. 2 vols.

CHINA

— Army.

JOHNSON (CHALMERS) Lin Piao's army and its role in Chinese society. Berkeley, [1966?]. pp. 11. *(California University. Institute of International Studies. Reprint Series. No. 215) (Reprinted from Current Scene, vol. 4, no. 13)*

NELSEN (HARVEY W.) The Chinese military system: an organizational study of the Chinese People's Liberation Army. Boulder, Colo., 1977. pp. 266. *bibliog.*

— Boundaries — Russia.

PROKHOROV (A.) K voprosu o sovetsko-kitaiskoi granitse. Moskva, 1975. pp. 288.

— Civilization.

KITAI: traditsii i sovremennost': sbornik statei. Moskva, 1976. pp. 335.

— Commerce.

LAW and politics in China's foreign trade; edited by Victor H. Li. Seattle, [1977]. pp. 467. *(Washington University. School of Law. Asian Law Series. No. 4) Papers of a conference jointly sponsored by the Subcommittee on Chinese Law of the Joint Committee on Contemporary China of the Social Science Research Council and the American Council of Learned Societies and by the University of Illinois, and held in London in 1971.*

MOULDER (FRANCES V.) Japan, China and the modern world economy: toward a reinterpretation of East Asian development ca. 1600 to ca. 1918. Cambridge, 1977. pp. 255. *bibliog.*

— Commercial treaties.

HSIAO (GENE T.) Communist China's trade treaties and agreements, 1949-1964. Berkeley, Calif., [1968]. pp. 623-658. *(California University. Center for Chinese Studies. China Series Reprints. No. C-9) (Reprinted from Vanderbilt Law Review, 1968)*

— Congresses.

REFORM in nineteenth-century China; edited by Paul A. Cohen and John E. Schrecker. Cambridge, Mass., 1976. pp. 415. *(Harvard University. East Asian Research Center. Harvard East Asian Monographs. 72) Proceedings of a workshop held under the auspices of the Center at Harvard University, 1975.*

— Description and travel.

ALLEY (REWI) Travels in China, 1966-71. Peking, 1973. pp. 588.

— Economic conditions.

GURLEY (JOHN G.) China's economy and the Maoist strategy. New York, [1976]. pp. 325.

ECKSTEIN (ALEXANDER) Professor of Economics. China's economic revolution. Cambridge, 1977. pp. 340.

— Economic history.

SCHRAN (PETER) Guerrilla economy: the development of the Shensi-Kansu- Ninghsia border region, 1937-1945. New York, 1976. pp. 323. *bibliog.*

TISSIER (PATRICK) La Chine: transformations rurales et développement socialiste. Paris, 1976. pp. 325. *bibliog.*

HAWES (GRACE M.) The Marshall Plan for China: Economic Co-operation Administration, 1948-1949. Cambridge, Mass., [1977]. pp. 138. *bibliogs.*

MOULDER (FRANCES V.) Japan, China and the modern world economy: toward a reinterpretation of East Asian development ca. 1600 to ca. 1918. Cambridge, 1977. pp. 255. *bibliog.*

— Economic policy.

PRYBYLA (JAN S.) The political economy of communist China. Scranton, Penn., [1970]. pp. 605.

GURLEY (JOHN G.) China's economy and the Maoist strategy. New York, [1976]. pp. 325.

ECKSTEIN (ALEXANDER) Professor of Economics. China's economic revolution. Cambridge, 1977. pp. 340.

POULAIN (EDOUARD) Le mode d'industrialisation socialiste en Chine. Paris, 1977. pp. 261. *bibliog.*

— Foreign economic relations — Japan.

LEE (CHAE-JIN) Japan faces China: political and economic relations in the postwar era. Baltimore, [1976]. pp. 242.

— Foreign opinion.

RADIO FREE EUROPE. Audience and Public Opinion Research Department. The images of Polish, American, Russian, German and Chinese youth as seen by Poles. [Munich?], 1973. fo. 55.

— Foreign relations.

DOMES (JUERGEN) China after the Cultural Revolution: politics between two party congresses; with a contribution by Marie-Luise Näth; translated from the German by Annette Berg and David Goodman. London, [1976]. pp. 283.

DIMENSIONS of China's foreign relations; edited by Chün- tu Hsüeh. New York, 1977. pp. 293.

TUNG (WILLIAM L.) V.K. Wellington Koo and China's wartime diplomacy. New York, [1977]. pp. 179. *bibliog. (New York (City). St. John's University. Center of Asian Studies. Asia in the Modern World. No. 17)*

WANG (GUNG-WU) China and the world since 1949: the impact of independence, modernity and revolution. London, 1977. pp. 190. *bibliog.*

See also UNITED NATIONS — China.

— — Africa, Subsaharan.

SCALAPINO (ROBERT A.) Africa and Peking's United Front: ten years of Chinese communist foreign policy in Africa. Berkeley, [1966?]. pp. 11. *(California University. Center for Chinese Studies. Reprints. No. 188) (Reprinted from Current Scene, vol.3, no. 26)*

— — Asia, Southeast.

TAYLOR (JAY) China and Southeast Asia: Peking's relations with revolutionary movements. 2nd ed. New York, 1976. pp. 400.

MARTIN (EDWIN W.) Southeast Asia and China: the end of containment. Boulder, Colo., 1977. pp. 114. *Prepared for the Center for Strategic and International Studies, Georgetown University.*

— — — France.

ZARETSKAIA (SOF'IA IL'INICHNA) Vneshniaia politika Kitaia v 1856-1860 godakh: otnosheniia s Angliei i Frantsiei. Moskva, 1976. pp. 221. *bibliog.*

— — — Japan.

LEE (CHAE-JIN) Japan faces China: political and economic relations in the postwar era. Baltimore, [1976]. pp. 242.

— — — Philippine Islands.

HSIAO (SHI-CHING) Chinese-Philippine diplomatic relations, 1946-1975. Quezon City, 1975. pp. 317.

— — — Russia.

SCOTT (JACK) Two roads: the origin of the Sino-Soviet dispute. Vancouver, 1974. pp. 63.

BORISOV (OLEG BORISOVICH) Sovetskii Soiuz i Man'chzhurskaia revoliutsionnaia baza, 1945- 1949: k 30-letiiu razgroma militaristskoi Iaponii. Moskva, 1975. pp. 220.

LEONG (SOW-THENG) Sino-Soviet diplomatic relations, 1917-1926. Canberra, 1976. pp. 361. *bibliog.*

LOW (ALFRED D.) The Sino-Soviet dispute: an analysis of the polemics. Cranbury, N.J., [1976]. pp. 364. *bibliog.*

— — — United Kingdom.

ZARETSKAIA (SOF'IA IL'INICHNA) Vneshniaia politika Kitaia v 1856-1860 godakh: otnosheniia s Angliei i Frantsiei. Moskva, 1976. pp. 221. *bibliog.*

JAIN (JAGDISH PRASAD) China in world politics: a study of Sino-British relations, 1949-1975. London, 1977. pp. 373. *bibliog.*

JONES (ARTHUR PHILIP) Britain's search for Chinese cooperation in the First World War. 1976 [or rather 1977]. fo. 304. *bibliog. Typescript. Ph.D. (London) thesis: unpublished. This thesis is the property of London University and may not be removed from the Library.*

— — United States.

AMERICAN FRIENDS SERVICE COMMITTEE. Working Party on China Policy. A new China policy: some Quaker proposals. New Haven, Conn., [1965]. pp. 68. *bibliog.*

BACHRACK (STANLEY D.) The Committee of One Million: "China Lobby" politics, 1953-1971. New York, 1976. pp. 371. *bibliog.*

CHINA and Japan: a new balance of power; edited by Donald C. Hellmann. Lexington, Mass., [1976]. pp. 305. *(Commission on Critical Choices for Americans. Critical Choices for Americans. vol.12)*

HINTON (HAROLD CLENDENIN) Peking-Washington: Chinese foreign policy and the United States. Beverly Hills, [1976]. pp. 96. *bibliog. (Georgetown University. Center for Strategic and International Studies. Washington Papers. vol. 4/34)*

PURIFOY(LEWIS McCARROLL) Harry Truman's China policy: McCarthyism and the diplomacy of hysteria, 1947-1951. New York, 1976. pp. 316.

McKEE (DELBER L.) Chinese exclusion versus the open door policy, 1900-1906: clashes over China policy in the Roosevelt era. Detroit, 1977. pp. 292. *bibliog.*

— History.

FITZGERALD (CHARLES PATRICK) The birth of communist China. Harmondsworth, 1964. pp. 288. *A revised and updated edition of the work first published in 1952 under the title Revolution in China.*

KITAI: traditsii i sovremennost': sbornik statei. Moskva, 1976. pp. 335.

KITAI: gosudarstvo i obshchestvo: sbornik statei. Moskva, 1977. pp. 310. *bibliog.*

— — Sources.

SWISHER (EARL) Canton in revolution: the collected papers...1925-1928; edited by Kenneth W. Rea. Boulder, Colo., 1977. pp. 141.

— — 1800-1899.

HARRISON (JOHN ARMSTRONG) China since 1800. New York, [1967]. pp. 278.

NAQUIN (SUSAN) Millenarian rebellion in China: the Eight Trigams uprising of 1813. New Haven, Conn., 1976. pp. 384. *bibliog. (Yale University. Yale Historical Publications. Miscellany. 108)*

REFORM in nineteenth-century China; edited by Paul A. Cohen and John E. Schrecker. Cambridge, Mass., 1976. pp. 415. *(Harvard University. East Asian Research Center. Harvard East Asian Monographs. 72) Proceedings of a workshop held under the auspices of the Center at Harvard University, 1975.*

— — 1900- .

HARRISON (JOHN ARMSTRONG) China since 1800. New York, [1967]. pp. 278.

CROZIER (BRIAN) The man who lost China: the first full biography of Chiang Kai-Shek. London, 1977. pp. 430.

WITKE (ROXANE) Comrade Chiang Ch'ing. London, 1977. pp. 54z.

— — 1911-1912, Revolution.

ESHERICK (JOSEPH W.) Reform and revolution in China: the 1911 Revolution in Hunan and Hubei. Berkeley, Calif., [1976]. pp. 324. *bibliog. (Michigan University. Center for Chinese Studies. Michigan Studies on China)*

— — 1912-1949, Republic.

FITZGERALD (CHARLES PATRICK) The birth of communist China. Harmondsworth, 1964. pp. 288. *A revised and updated edition of the work first published in 1952 under the title Revolution in China.*

CHEREPANOV (ALEKSANDR IVANOVICH) Zapiski voennogo sovetnika v Kitae, [1925-1939]. [3rd ed., erroneously designated 2nd ed.]. Moskva, 1976. pp. 648.

— — 1912-1937.

CHINA in the 1920s: nationalism and revolution; editors: F. Gilbert Chan and Thomas H. Etzold. New York, 1976. pp. 249. *bibliog.*

NATHAN (ANDREW JAMES) Peking politics, 1918-1923: factionalism and the failure of constitutionalism. Berkeley, Calif., [1976]. pp. 299. *bibliog. (Michigan University. Center for Chinese Studies. Michigan Studies on China)*

TROTSKII (LEV DAVYDOVICH) Leon Trotsky on China; introduction by Peng Shu-tse; edited by Les Evans and Russell Block. New York, 1976. pp. 688.

— — 1926-1928, Northern Expedition.

JORDAN (DONALD A.) The northern expedition: China's national revolution of 1926- 1928. Honolulu, [1976]. pp. 341. *bibliog.*

— — 1945- .

BRUGGER (WILLIAM C.) Contemporary China. London, 1977. pp. 451. *bibliog.*

MILTON (DAVID) and others, eds. People's China: social experimentation, politics, entry on to the world scene, 1966-72. Harmondsworth, 1977. pp. 667. *bibliog. First published by Random House Inc., 1974.*

— Industries.

POULAIN (EDOUARD) Le mode d'industrialisation socialiste en Chine. Paris, 1977. pp. 261. *bibliog.*

SIGURDSON (JON) Rural industrialization in China. Cambridge, Mass., 1977. pp. 281. *bibliog. (Harvard University. East Asian Research Center. Harvard East Asian Monographs. 73)*

WANG (KUNG-PING) Mineral resources and basic industries in the People's Republic of China. Boulder, 1977. pp. 211.

— Nationalism.

VELIKODERZHAVNAIA politika maoistov v natsional'nykh raionakh KNR. Moskva, 1975. pp. 126.

— Politics and government.

CHINA. National People's Congress. 3rd Congress, 1st Session, 1964-65. Main documents of the...session. Peking, 1965. pp. 92.

JAN (GEORGE P.) ed. Government of communist China. San Francisco, [1966]. pp. 684. *bibliog.*

CHEN (THEODORE HSI-EN) ed. The Chinese communist regime: documents and commentary. New York, 1967. pp. 344. *bibliog.*

MAO (TSE-TUNG) and LIN (PIAO) Post-revolutionary writings; edited by K. Fan. Garden City, 1972. pp. 536.

KUL'PIN (EDUARD SAL'MANOVICH) Tekhniko-ekonomicheskaia politika rukovodstva KNR i rabochii klass Kitaia. Moskva, 1975. pp. 199. *bibliog.*

AHN (BYUNG-JOON) Chinese politics and the cultural revolution: dynamics of policy processes. Seattle, [1976]. pp. 392. *bibliog. (Washington State University. Institute for Comparative and Foreign Area Studies. Publications on Asia. No. 30)*

BENNETT (GORDON A.) Yundong: mass campaigns in Chinese communist leadership. Berkeley, [1976]. pp. 133. *bibliog. (California University. Center for Chinese Studies. China Research Monographs. No. 12)*

BOWDEN (TOM) and GOODMAN (DAVID S.G.) China: the politics of public security. London, 1976. pp. 22. bibliog. (Institute for the Study of Conflict. Conflict Studies. No. 78)

BURLATSKII (FEDOR MIKHAILOVICH) Mao Tsze-dun: "nash koronnyi nomer - eto voina, diktatura". Moskva, 1976. pp. 391.

CASSINELLI (CHARLES WILLIAM) Total revolution: a comparative study of Germany under Hitler, the Soviet Union under Stalin and China under Mao. Santa Barbara, Calif., [1976]. pp. 252.

CHINA in the 1920s: nationalism and revolution; editors: F. Gilbert Chan and Thomas H. Etzold. New York, 1976. pp. 249. bibliog.

DOMES (JUERGEN) China after the Cultural Revolution: politics between two party congresses; with a contribution by Marie-Luise Näth; translated from the German by Annette Berg and David Goodman. London, [1976]. pp. 283.

FITZGERALD (CHARLES PATRICK) Mao Tsetung and China. New York, 1976. pp. 166. bibliog.

GINNEKEN (JAAP VAN) The rise and fall of Lin Piao; translated by Danielle Adkinson. Harmondsworth, 1976. pp. 348. bibliog.

GUILLERMAZ (JACQUES) The Chinese Communist Party in power, 1949-1976;... translated by Anne Destenay. Boulder, Colo., 1976. pp. 614. bibliog.

NATHAN (ANDREW JAMES) Peking politics, 1918-1923: factionalism and the failure of constitutionalism. Berkeley, Calif., [1976]. pp. 299. bibliog. (Michigan University. Center for Chinese Studies. Michigan Studies on China)

RAMANENKO (O.M.) Antisotsialisticheskaia sushchnost' maoizma. Moskva, 1976. pp. 127.

TROTSKII (LEV DAVYDOVICH) Leon Trotsky on China; introduction by Peng Shu-tse; edited by Les Evans and Russell Block. New York, 1976. pp. 688.

WEST (PHILIP) Yenching University and Sino-Western relations, 1916-1952. Cambridge, Mass., 1976. pp. 327. bibliog. (Harvard University. East Asian Research Center. Harvard East Asian Series. 85)

WONG (PAUL) China's higher leadership in the socialist tradition. New York, [1976]. pp. 310. bibliog.

BRUGGER (WILLIAM C.) Contemporary China. London, 1977. pp. 451. bibliog.

CELL (CHARLES PRESTON) Revolution at work: mobilization campaigns in China. New York, [1977]. pp. 221. bibliog.

CROZIER (BRIAN) The man who lost China: the first full biography of Chiang Kai-Shek. London, 1977. pp. 430.

MILTON (DAVID) and others, eds. People's China: social experimentation, politics, entry on to the world scene, 1966-72. Harmondsworth, 1977. pp. 667. bibliog. First published by Random House Inc., 1974.

SOLINGER (DOROTHY J.) Regional government and political integration in Southwest China, 1949-1954: a case study. Berkeley, Calif., [1977]. pp. 291. bibliog.

WITKE (ROXANE) Comrade Chiang Ch'ing. London, 1977. pp. 54z.

— — Bibliography.

STARR (JOHN BRYAN) and DYER (NANCY ANNE) compilers. Post-liberation works of Mao Zedong: a bibliography and index. Berkeley, Calif., [1976]. pp. 222.

— Relations (general) with Africa.

FOMICHEVA (MARGARITA VASIL'EVNA) and KRASIL'NIKOV (ALEKSANDR SERGEEVICH) Kitai i Afrika: podryvnaia deiatel'nost' maoistov v Afrike; pod redaktsiei...G.V. Astaf'eva. Moskva, 1976. pp. 263.

— Relations (general) with the United States.

BARNETT (ARTHUR DOAK) China policy: old problems and new challenges. Washington, D.C., [1977]. pp. 131.

CHINA and America: the search for a new relationship; edited by William J. Barnds. New York, 1977. pp. 254. A Council on Foreign Relations Book.

— Religion.

POTTER (JACK M.) Wind, water, bones and souls: the religious world of the Cantonese peasant. Berkeley, [1970]. pp. 14. (California University. Center for Chinese Studies. China Reprint Series. No. C-18) (Reprinted from Journal of Oriental Studies, vol. 3, no. 1, 1970)

NAQUIN (SUSAN) Millenarian rebellion in China: the Eight Trigrams uprising of 1813. New Haven, Conn., 1976. pp. 384. bibliog. (Yale University. Yale Historical Publications. Miscellany. 108)

— Rural conditions.

SIGURDSON (JON) Rural industrialization in China. Cambridge, Mass., 1977. pp. 281. bibliog. (Harvard University. East Asian Research Center. Harvard East Asian Monographs. 73)

— Social conditions.

WHYTE (MARTIN KING) Small groups and political rituals in China. Berkeley, Calif., [1975]. pp. 271. (Michigan University. Center for Chinese Studies. Michigan Studies on China) First published in 1974.

ANDORS (STEPHEN) China's industrial revolution: politics, planning and management, 1949 to the present. London, [1977]. pp. 344. bibliog.

CHU (GODWIN C.) Radical change through communication in Mao's China. Honolulu, [1977]. pp. 340.

— Social life and customs.

CHANG (KWANG-CHIH) ed. Food in Chinese culture: anthropological and historical perspectives. New Haven, 1977. pp. 429. bibliog.

CHINESE IN INDONESIA.

MACKIE (J.A.C) ed. The Chinese in Indonesia: five essays. Melbourne, 1976. pp. 282. bibliog.

CHINESE IN MALAYSIA.

MAK (LAU-FONG) Chinese secret societies in Ipoh town, 1945-1969. Singapore, 1975. pp. 17. bibliog. (University of Singapore. Department of Sociology. Working Papers. No. 42)

LEE (EDWIN) The towkays of Sabah: Chinese leadership and indigenous challenge in the last phase of British rule. Singapore, [1976]. pp. 271. bibliog.

CHINESE IN THE UNITED STATES.

McKEE (DELBER L.) Chinese exclusion versus the open door policy, 1900-1906: clashes over China policy in the Roosevelt era. Detroit, 1977. pp. 292. bibliog.

CHINESE-JAPANESE WAR, 1894-1895.

DORWART (JEFFERY M.) The Pigtail War: American involvement in the Sino-Japanese War of 1894-1895. Amherst, Mass., 1975. pp. 168. bibliog.

CHINESE-JAPANESE WAR, 1937-1945.

SCHRAN (PETER) Guerrilla economy: the development of the Shensi-Kansu-Ninghsia border region, 1937-1945. New York, 1976. pp. 323. bibliog.

SHAI (ARON) Origins of the war in the east: Britain, China and Japan, 1937- 39. London, [1976]. pp. 267. bibliog.

TUNG (WILLIAM L.) V.K. Wellington Koo and China's wartime diplomacy. New York, [1977]. pp. 179. bibliog. (New York (City). St. John's University. Center of Asian Studies. Asia in the Modern World. No. 17)

CHINESE STUDIES

— United States.

LINDBECK (JOHN M.H.) Understanding China: an assessment of American scholarly resources;...a report to the Ford Foundation. New York, 1971. pp. 159.

CHINESE YOUTH PARTY.

CHAN (LAU KIT-CHING) The Chinese Youth Party, 1923-1945. Hong Kong, 1972. pp. 62. bibliog. (Hong Kong. University. Centre of Asian Studies. Occasional Papers and Monographs. No. 9)

CHOISEUL-PRASLIN (CHARLES LAURE HUGUES THEOBALD DE) Duc.

HIRSCH (HELMUT) Karl Ludwig Bernays und die Revolutionserwartung vor 1848, dargestellt am Mordfall Praslin. Trier, [1976]. pp. 54. (Karl-Marx-Haus. Schriften. 17)

CHOISEUL-PRASLIN (FANNY DE) Duchesse.

HIRSCH (HELMUT) Karl Ludwig Bernays und die Revolutionserwartung vor 1848, dargestellt am Mordfall Praslin. Trier, [1976]. pp. 54. (Karl-Marx-Haus. Schriften. 17)

CHOLERA, ASIATIC

— United Kingdom, 1832.

DUREY (MICHAEL) The first spasmodic cholera epidemic in York, 1832. York, 1974. pp. 29. (York. University. Borthwick Institute of Historical Research. Borthwick Papers. No. 46)

MORRIS (R.J.) Cholera, 1832: the social response to an epidemic. London, [1976]. pp. 235. bibliog.

CHOU (EN-LAI).

HSU (KAI-YU) Chou En-lai: China's gray eminence. Garden City, N.Y., 1968 repr. 1969. pp. 263. bibliog.

CHRISTENSEN (POUL).

CHRISTENSEN (POUL) Af en illegals erindringer; udgivet i samarbejde med Hans Kirchhoff. [Copenhagen], 1976. pp. 152. (Selskabet til Forskning i Arbejderbevaegelsens Historie. Publikationer. 4)

CHRISTIAN DEMOCRACY.

CORNEJO CHAVEZ (HECTOR) Democracia Cristiana y revolucion. [Lima, 1967]. pp. 38.

CHRISTIAN ETHICS.

TRUTH and reform against the world; or, Letters to W. Cooke in reply to his attack on Mr. Joseph Barker. [Newcastle-upon-Tyne, J. Barker, c. 1845]. 7 pts. (in 1 vol.). Signed, A. Christian.

CHRISTIAN LIFE.

BUTLER (JOSEPH) successively Bishop of Bristol and of Durham. A charge delivered to the clergy at the primary visitation of the diocese of Durham, in the year MDCCLI;...the second edition, with a preface, giving some account of the character and writings of the author, by Samuel, Lord Bishop of Gloucester. London, T. Cadell, 1786. pp. lxxxviii, 46.

WHITE (JOHN) Associate Professor of Psychiatry at the University of Manitoba. The cost of commitment. Leicester, 1976. pp. 91.

CHRISTIANITY

— Malawi.

McCRACKEN (K. JOHN) Politics and Christianity in Malawi 1875-1940: the impact of the Livingstonia Mission in the Northern Province. Cambridge, 1977. pp. 324. bibliog.

CHRISTIANITY AND ECONOMICS.

CHRISTIANITY AND ECONOMICS.

SLEEMAN (JOHN F.) Economic crisis: a Christian perspective. London, 1976. pp. 196. *bibliog.*

CHRISTIANITY AND EXISTENTIALISM.

KUVAKIN (VALERII ALEKSANDROVICH) Kritika ekzistentsializma Berdiaeva. Moskva, 1976. pp. 205.

CHRISTIANITY AND INTERNATIONAL AFFAIRS.

DOWDEN (RICHARD) Northern Ireland and the Catholic Church in Britain; published...for the Commission for International Justice and Peace of England and Wales as a contribution to public debate. Abbots Langley, [1975]. pp. 27.

SANSBURY (CYRIL KENNETH) Combating racism: the British churches and the WCC Programme to Combat Racism. London, [1975]. pp. 78. *bibliog.*

CATHOLIC CHURCH IN ENGLAND AND WALES. Bishops' Conference. Commission for International Justice and Peace. Christians and the arms trade. [Abbots Langley, 1976?]. pp. 19. *bibliog.*

FAHEY (JOSEPH J.) Peace, war and the Christian conscience. New York, [1976]. pp. 20.

CHRISTIANITY AND POLITICS.

FELIX (CELESTIN JOSEPH) Christianisme et socialisme. Paris, [1892]. pp. 36.

VALENTINI (NORBERTO) La politica in confessionale. Milano, [1974]. pp. 286.

EBNETH (RUDOLF) Die österreichische Wochenschrift "Der Christliche Ständestaat": deutsche Emigration in Österreich, 1933-1938. Mainz, [1976]. pp. 271. *bibliog.* *(Kommission für Zeitgeschichte. Veröffentlichungen. Reihe B: Forschungen. Band 19)*

CHRONICALLY ILL

— Australia.

AUSTRALIA. Commonwealth Bureau of Census and Statistics. 1976. Chronic illnesses, injuries and impairments, May 1974. Canberra, [1976]. pp. 32.

CHURCH.

THUNG (MADY A.) The precarious organisation: sociological explorations of the church's mission and structure. The Hague, [1976]. pp. 348. *bibliog.*

CHURCH AND LABOUR

— United States.

BETTEN (NEIL) Catholic activism and the industrial worker. Gainesville, Fla., [1976]. pp. 191. *bibliog.*

DAVIES (JOSEPH KENNETH) Deseret's sons of toil: a history of the worker movements of territorial Utah, 1852-1896. Salt Lake City, [1977]. pp. 264. *bibliogs.*

CHURCH AND RACE PROBLEMS.

SANSBURY (CYRIL KENNETH) Combating racism: the British churches and the WCC Programme to Combat Racism. London, [1975]. pp. 78. *bibliog.*

— South Africa.

STARES (RODNEY) Consolidated Gold Fields Limited: a review of activities and issues. London, [1975]. pp. 31. *bibliog.*

WAESBERGE (ROBERT VAN) Do we participate in apartheid?; reflections by black South Africans on themselves, us and our investments; translated [from the Dutch] by Esau du Plessis. Geneva, [1975]. pp. 56.

WINTER (COLIN O'BRIEN) Bishop of Damaraland. Namibia. Guildford, 1977. pp. 234.

— United Kingdom.

NATIONAL CATHOLIC COMMISSION FOR RACIAL JUSTICE. Where creed and colour matter: a survey on black children and Catholic schools. London, [1975]. pp. 47.

CHURCH AND SOCIAL PROBLEMS

— America, Latin — Catholic Church.

KRUMWIEDE (HEINRICH W.) La transformacion del papel sociopolitico de la iglesia catolica en America Latina. Santiago de Chile, 1971. pp. 70. *(Instituto Latinoamericano de Investigaciones Sociales. Estudios y Documentos. 12)*

— Ethiopia.

LUNDSTRÖM (KARL JOHAN) North-eastern Ethiopia: society in famine: a study of three social institutions in a period of severe strain. Uppsala, 1976. pp. 80. *bibliog.* *(Nordiska Afrikainstitutet. Research Reports. No. 34)*

— United Kingdom.

BARTLES-SMITH (DOUGLAS) and GERRARD (DAVID) Urban ghetto. Guildford, 1976. pp. 115.

COMMUNITY work and the churches;...report [of a working group set up by the Division of Community Affairs of the British Council of Churches]. London, [1976]. pp. 25.

— — Catholic Church.

NATIONAL CATHOLIC COMMISSION FOR RACIAL JUSTICE. Where creed and colour matter: a survey on black children and Catholic schools. London, [1975]. pp. 47.

— United States — Catholic Church.

BETTEN (NEIL) Catholic activism and the industrial worker. Gainesville, Fla., [1976]. pp. 191. *bibliog.*

CHURCH AND STATE

— Catholic Church.

COMAN (PETER W.) Catholics and the welfare state. London, 1977. pp. 118. *bibliog.*

CHURCH AND STATE IN AFRICA.

KANGE (EWANE) Le politique dans le système religieux catholique romain en Afrique de 1815 à 1960. Lille, 1976. pp. 513. *bibliogs. Thèse - Université de Strasbourg II.*

CHURCH AND STATE IN ITALY.

SPADOLINI (GIOVANNI) La questione del Concordato: con i documenti inediti della Commissione Gonella. Firenze, 1976. pp. 560.

CHURCH AND STATE IN LATIN AMERICA.

KRUMWIEDE (HEINRICH W.) La transformacion del papel sociopolitico de la iglesia catolica en America Latina. Santiago de Chile, 1971. pp. 70. *(Instituto Latinoamericano de Investigaciones Sociales. Estudios y Documentos. 12)*

CHURCH AND STATE IN POLAND.

GERMAN Polish dialogue: letters of the Polish and German bishops and international statements. Bonn, 1966. pp. 127.

CHURCH AND STATE IN RUSSIA.

GOL'ST (GEORGII ROBERTOVICH) Religiia i zakon. Moskva, 1975. pp. 110.

LUCHTERHANDT (OTTO) Der Sowjetstaat und die Russisch-Orthodoxe Kirche: eine rechtshistorische und rechtssystematische Untersuchung. Köln, [1976]. pp. 319. *bibliog. (Bundesinstitut für Ostwissenschaftliche und Internationale Studien. Abhandlungen. Band 30)*

CHURCH AND STATE IN SOUTH AFRICA.

MITCHELL (M.L.) The Christian Institute: the United Party view. Johannesburg, [1975]. fo. 5. *In English and Afrikaans.*

CHURCH AND STATE IN SPAIN.

GALLEGO (JOSE ANDRES) La politica religiosa en España, 1889-1913. Madrid, [1975]. pp. 521.

CHURCH AND STATE IN TANZANIA.

URFER (SYLVAIN) Socialisme et église en Tanzanie; suivi d'une étude de Jacques Van Nieuwenhove sur présence chrétienne en société socialiste. Paris, [1975]. pp. 168. *bibliog.*

CHURCH AND STATE IN THE ARGENTINE REPUBLIC.

GAMBINI (HUGO) El Peronismo y la iglesia. Buenos Aires, [1971]. pp. 116.

CHURCH AND STATE IN THE SUDAN.

ALL AFRICA CONFERENCE OF CHURCHES. The hard road to peace: a report to the churches in Africa on their part in the reconciliation in the Sudan and an appeal. Nairobi, [1972]. pp. 28.

CHURCH AND STATE IN THE UNITED KINGDOM.

SACHEVERELL (HENRY) The perils of false brethren, both in church, and state: set forth in a sermon preach'd before the Right Honourable the Lord- Mayor, aldermen, and citizens of London, at the cathedral-church of St. Paul, on the 5th November, 1709. London, Clements, 1709. pp. 24.

CHURCH AND UNDERDEVELOPED AREAS.

WORLD COUNCIL OF CHURCHES. Commission on the Churches' Participation in Development. CCPD activity report no.3. Geneva, 1975. pp. 58.

CHURCH CHARITIES.

MAGNUSON (NORRIS ALDEN) Salvation in the slums: evangelical social work, 1865-1920. Metuchen, N.J., 1977. pp. 299. *bibliog. (American Theological Library Association. ATLA Monograph Series. No. 10)*

CHURCH HISTORY.

JOHNSON (PAUL) A history of Christianity. London, [1976]. pp. 556. *bibliog.*

— 600-1500, Middle Ages.

CHURCH and government in the Middle Ages: essays presented to C.R. Cheney on his 70th birthday;...edited by C.N.L. Brooke [and others]. Cambridge, 1976. pp. 312. *bibliog.*

CHURCH LANDS

— Philippine Islands.

ROTH (DENNIS MORROW) The friar estates of the Philippines. Albuquerque, [1977]. pp. 197. *bibliog.*

CHURCH OF ENGLAND

— Government.

JENNINGS (DEREK ANDREW) The revival of the Convocation of York, 1837-1861. York, 1975. pp. 27. *(York. University. Borthwick Institute of Historical Research. Borthwick Papers. No. 47)*

CHURCH OF ENGLAND IN SOUTH AFRICA.

WINTER (COLIN O'BRIEN) Bishop of Damaraland. Namibia. Guildford, 1977. pp. 234.

CHURCH SCHOOLS

— United States — Finance.

ROBISON (JOSEPH B.) The case against parochiaid. New York, 1972. pp. 16.

CHURCHILL (Sir WINSTON LEONARD SPENCER).

ADAMIC (LOUIS) Dinner at the White House. New York, [1946]. pp. 276.

COLVILLE (Sir JOHN) Footprints in time. London, 1976. pp. 287.

LASH (JOSEPH P.) Roosevelt and Churchill, 1939-1941: the partnership that saved the West. New York, [1976]. pp. 528.

CIDER.

[HEATH (BENJAMIN)] The case of the county of Devon, with respect to the consequences of the new excise duty on cyder and perry: published by the direction of the committee appointed at a general meeting of that county to superintend the application for the repeal of that duty. London, Johnston, 1763. pp. 32.

CIRENCESTER

— History.

REECE (RICHARD) and CATLING (CHRISTOPHER) Cirencester: the development and buildings of a Cotswold town. Oxford, 1975. pp. 78. (British Archaeological Reports. 12)

CISKEI

— Appropriations and expenditures.

CISKEI. General Council. Proceedings and reports of select committees...and estimates of revenue and expenditure. a., 1955. King William's Town.

— Economic conditions.

SOUTH AFRICA. Bureau for Economic Research re Bantu Development. 1975. Ciskei:...economic revue [sic], 1975...compiled...at the request of the Ciskeian government. Pretoria, 1975. pp. 72. bibliog. In English and Afrikaans.

— Economic policy.

XHOSA DEVELOPMENT CORPORATION LIMITED. Annual report. a., 1975 (10th)- East London. [in English and Afrikaans].

— Politics and government.

CISKEI. General Council. Proceedings and reports of select committees...and estimates of revenue and expenditure. a., 1955. King William's Town.

CITIES AND TOWNS.

ALEXANDER (IAN C.) The city centre: patterns and problems. Nedlands, W.A., 1974. pp. 216. bibliog.

CARTER (HAROLD) The study of urban geography. 2nd ed. London, 1975. pp. 398. bibliogs.

HABITAT: UNITED NATIONS CONFERENCE ON HUMAN SETTLEMENTS, VANCOUVER, 1976. Global review of human settlements: a support paper for Habitat: United Nations Conference on Human Settlements; (with Statistical annex) (A/CONF.70/A/1 and A/CONF.70/A/1 Add.1). Oxford, 1976. 2 vols.

STRATEGIES for human settlements: habitat and environment; edited by Gwen Bell. Honolulu, [1976]. pp. 172.

BIRD (JAMES HAROLD) Centrality and cities. London, 1977. pp. 203. bibliog.

— Growth.

PROBLEMY urbanizatsii i rasseleniia: II sovetsko-pol'skii seminar po urbanizatsii. Moskva, 1976. pp. 269. With Polish and English tables of contents.

BERRY (BRIAN JOE LOBLEY) and KASARDA (JOHN D.) Contemporary urban ecology. New York, [1977]. pp. 497. bibliog.

CASTELLS (MANUEL) The urban question: a Marxist approach; translated by Alan Sheridan. London, 1977. pp. 502. bibliog.

PRED (ALLAN R.) City-systems in advanced economies: past growth, present processes and future development options. London, 1977. pp. 256. bibliog.

— Mathematical models.

BATTY (MICHAEL) Urban modelling: algorithms, calibrations; predictions. Cambridge, 1976. pp. 381. bibliog.

ROMANOS (MICHAEL C.) Residential spatial structure. Lexington, Mass., [1976]. pp. 197. bibliog.

— Planning.

See CITY PLANNING.

— America, Latin — Growth.

PARISI (LICIO) ed. Modo de produccion y metropolizacion en America Latina. Santiago de Chile, 1972. 2 vols. bibliog. (Instituto Latinoamericano de Investigaciones Sociales. Estudios y Documentos. 23, 24)

— Canada — Bibliography.

DIRECTORY OF CANADIAN URBAN INFORMATION SOURCES; [pd. by] Ministry of State for Urban Affairs. .a., current issue only. Ottawa.

— China.

The CITY in late imperialist China; edited by G. William Skinner. Stanford, Calif., 1977. pp. 820. (American Council of Learned Societies and Social Science Research Council. Joint Committee on Contemporary China. Subcommittee on Research on Chinese Society. Studies in Chinese Society) Includes papers presented at a conference held at Wentworth-by-the-Sea, Portsmouth, New Hampshire, 1968.

— Germany.

GERMANY (BUNDESREPUBLIK). Statistisches Bundesamt. 1972. Amtliches Gemeindeverzeichnis für die Bundesrepublik Deutschland: Ausgabe 1971, Bevölkerungsstand: 27.5.1970, Gebietsstand: 1.1.1971. Wiesbaden, 1972. pp. 772.

— India — Growth.

SATIN (LOWELL ROBERT) Towards a spatial strategy for Indian development. 1976. pp. 378. Typescript. Ph.D. (London) thesis: unpublished. This thesis is the property of London University and may not be removed from the Library.

— — Assam — Statistics.

ASSAM. Directorate of Economics and Statistics. Municipal statistical year book. a., 1968-69/1969-70 (1st)- Gauhati.

— Japan.

SOCIAL change and community politics in urban Japan; edited by James W. White and Frank Munger. Chapel Hill, N.C., 1976. pp. 132. bibliogs. (North Carolina University. Center for Urban and Regional Studies. Comparative Urban Studies. Monographs. No.4)

— Mexico.

ASENTAMIENTOS humanos: reforma constitucional, iniciativa de ley, comparecencia del C. Secretario de la Presidencia ante la H. Camara de Diputados. [Mexico, 1976]. fo. 94.

— Poland — Growth.

PROBLEMY urbanizatsii i rasseleniia: II sovetsko-pol'skii seminar po urbanizatsii. Moskva, 1976. pp. 269. With Polish and English tables of contents.

— Russia.

BAKHTIN (NIKOLAI IVANOVICH) Gorod i derevnia: ekonomicheskie aspekty. Minsk, 1974. pp. 191.

RUSSKII gorod: istoriko-metodologicheskii sbornik. Moskva, 1976. pp. 296.

— — Growth.

PIVOVAROV (IURII L'VOVICH) Sovremennaia urbanizatsiia: osnovnye tendentsii rasseleniia. Moskva, 1976. pp. 191.

PROBLEMY urbanizatsii i rasseleniia: II sovetsko-pol'skii seminar po urbanizatsii. Moskva, 1976. pp. 269. With Polish and English tables of contents.

— Underdeveloped areas.

See UNDERDEVELOPED AREAS — Cities and towns.

— United Kingdom.

BETJEMAN (Sir JOHN) The English town in the last hundred years. Cambridge, 1956. pp. 28. (Cambridge. University. Rede Lectures. 1956)

GOODEY (BRIAN) Urban walks and town trails: origins, principles and sources. Birmingham, 1974. 1 vol.(various pagings). bibliog. (Birmingham. University. Centre for Urban and Regional Studies. Research Memoranda. No.40)

U.K. Department of the Environment. 1975. Study of the inner areas of conurbations: supplement: analysis of 1971 census indicators. [London], 1975. pp. 72.

EYRE (REGINALD E.) Hope for our towns and cities: the right approach to urban affairs. London, 1977. pp. 24. (Conservative Political Centre. [Publications]. No. 606)

MIDDLE class housing in Britain; edited by M.A. Simpson and T.H. Lloyd. Newton Abbot, 1977. pp. 217.

U.K. Department of the Environment. 1977. Inner area studies: Liverpool, Birmingham and Lambeth: summaries of consultants' final reports. London, 1977. pp. 49.

WOHL (ANTHONY STEPHEN) The eternal slum: housing and social policy in Victorian London. London, 1977. pp. 386. bibliog.

— — Growth.

BATHER (NICHOLAS JOHN) The speculative residential developer and urban growth: the location decision in a planned environment. Reading, 1976. pp. 44. bibliog. (Reading. University. Department of Geography. Reading Geographical Papers. No. 47)

GROWTH and change in the future city region; edited by Tom Hancock. London, 1976. pp. 262. bibliogs. Based on papers given at an international symposium organised by the British Council in 1975.

— — History.

CLARK (PETER) and SLACK (PAUL) English towns in transition, 1500-1700. London, 1976. pp. 176. bibliog.

— — Ireland.

BUTLIN (ROBIN A.) ed. The development of the Irish town. Totowa, N.J., 1977. pp. 144.

— United States.

GLAAB (CHARLES NELSON) and BROWN (ANDREW THEODORE) A history of urban America;...revision prepared by Charles N. Glaab. 2nd ed. New York, [1976]. pp. 350. bibliogs.

CARALEY (DEMETRIOS) City governments and urban problems: a new introduction to urban politics. Englewood Cliffs, [1977]. pp. 448.

CURTIS (RICHARD FARNSWORTH) and JACKSON (ELTON F.) Inequality in American communities. New York, [1977]. pp. 354. bibliog.

CITIES AND TOWNS.(Cont.)

— — Growth.

WHEAT (LEONARD F.) Urban growth in the nonmetropolitan South. Lexington, Mass., [1976]. pp. 171.

— — North Carolina.

HAYES (CHARLES R.) The dispersed city: the case of Piedmont, North Carolina. Chicago, 1976. pp. 157. *bibliog.* (*Chicago. University. Department of Geography. Research Papers. No. 173*)

CITIES AND TOWNS, ANCIENT

— United Kingdom.

The 'SMALL towns' of Roman Britain: papers presented to a conference, Oxford 1975; edited by Warwick Rodwell and Trevor Rowley. Oxford, 1975. pp. 236. *bibliogs.* (*British Archaeological Reports. 15*)

CITIES AND TOWNS, MEDIEVAL

— United Kingdom.

The PLANS and topography of medieval towns in England and Wales; edited by M.W. Barley. [London], 1976. pp. 92. *bibliog.* (*Council for British Archaeology. Research Reports. No. 14*)

PLATT (COLIN) The English medieval town. London, 1976. pp. 219. *bibliog.*

REYNOLDS (SUSAN) An introduction to the history of English medieval towns. Oxford, 1977. pp. 234. *bibliog.*

CITIZENS' ASSOCIATIONS

— United States — Bibliography.

HUTCHESON (JOHN D.) and SHEVIN (JANN) compilers. Citizen groups in local politics: a bibliographic review. Santa Barbara, [1976]. pp. 275. *bibliogs.*

CITIZENSHIP.

BROOKS (LEONARD S.) World citizenship: rejection of political nationality: an appeal and a challenge to the Quaker conscience in Western Europe, North America, Southern Africa and Australasia. Eastbourne, [1975]. pp. 12.

— Germany.

STAATSANGEHOERIGKEIT, soziale Grundrechte, wirtschaftliche Zusammenarbeit nach dem Recht der Bundesrepublik Deutschland und der Volksrepublik Polen: Referate des Rechtscolloquiums 1974; herausgegeben von Józef Kokot und Krzysztof Skubiszewski. Berlin, 1976. pp. 293.

— Israel.

KRAINES (OSCAR) The impossible dilemma: who is a Jew in the state of Israel?. New York, [1976]. pp. 156. *bibliog.*

— Poland.

STAATSANGEHOERIGKEIT, soziale Grundrechte, wirtschaftliche Zusammenarbeit nach dem Recht der Bundesrepublik Deutschland und der Volksrepublik Polen: Referate des Rechtscolloquiums 1974; herausgegeben von Józef Kokot und Krzysztof Skubiszewski. Berlin, 1976. pp. 293.

— United Kingdom.

DUMMETT (ANN) Citizenship and nationality. London, 1976. pp. 88. *bibliog.*

U.K. Parliament. House of Commons. Library. Research Division. Reference Sheets. 76/17. East African Asians: their immigration and citizenship position. [London], 1976. pp. 19. *bibliog.*

CITIZENSHIP, LOSS OF

— Germany.

LEHMANN (HANS GEORG) In Acht und Bann: politische Emigration, NS-Ausbürgerung und Wiedergutmachung am Beispiel Willy Brandts. München, [1976]. pp. 387. *bibliog.*

CITRUS FRUITS

— Cyprus.

CYPRUS. 1975. Turks usurp Cyprus produce. [Nicosia?, 1975]. pp. 10.

CITY PLANNING.

CANAUX (JEAN) Ecrits d'urbanisme. [Paris, 1971]. pp. 287.

UNITED NATIONS. Ad Hoc Group of Experts on Social Programming of Housing in Urban Areas. 1971. Social programming of housing in urban areas: report of the Ad Hoc Group of Experts on (its meetings, held) New York, 17- 28 August 1970. (ST/SOA/109). New York, 1971. pp. 81.

WARD (COLIN) ed. Vandalism. London, 1973. pp. 327. *bibliog.*

BUCK (J. VINCENT) Politics and professionalism in municipal planning. Beverly Hills, [1976]. pp. 55. *bibliog.*

GOLANY (GIDEON) ed. Innovations for future cities. New York, 1976. pp. 264. *bibliogs.*

HABITAT: UNITED NATIONS CONFERENCE ON HUMAN SETTLEMENTS, VANCOUVER, 1976. Report of Habitat:...Vancouver, 31 May - 11 June 1976. (A/CONF.70/15). New York, 1976. pp. 183.

LOTTMAN (HERBERT R.) How cities are saved. New York, 1976. pp. 255.

PORTEOUS (JOHN DOUGLAS) Environment and behavior: planning and everyday urban life. Reading, Mass., [1977]. pp. 446. *bibliog.*

PRED (ALLAN R.) City-systems in advanced economies: past growth, present processes and future development options. London, 1977. pp. 256. *bibliog.*

— Bibliography.

VEAL (A.J.) and DUESBURY (W.K.) compilers. A first list of U.K. students theses and dissertations on planning and urban and regional studies. Birmingham, 1976. pp. 245. (*Birmingham. University. Centre for Urban and Regional Studies. Research Memoranda. No. 55*).

— Citizen participation.

FAGENCE (MICHAEL) Citizen participation in planning. Oxford, 1977. pp. 378.

PUBLIC participation in planning; edited by W.R. Derrick Sewell and J.T. Coppock. London, 1977. pp. 217. *Based on a joint seminar organized by the University of Edinburgh School of the Built Environment and Centre for Human Ecology, held in 1973.*

— Cost effectiveness.

SIMPSON (BARRY JOHN) The theoretical development and application of threshold analysis to assess land development costs. 1976 [or rather 1977]. fo. 342. *bibliog. Typescript. Ph.D. (London) thesis: unpublished. This thesis is the property of London University and may not be removed from the Library.*

— Mathematical models.

SAYER (R.A.) A dynamic Lowry model. Brighton, 1973. fo.38. *bibliog.* (*Brighton. University of Sussex. Sussex Working Papers in Urban and Regional Studies. 1*)

BATTY (MICHAEL) and MARCH (LIONEL) Dynamic urban models based on information-minimising. Reading, 1976. pp. 41. *bibliog.* (*Reading. University. Department of Geography. Reading Geographical Papers. No. 48*)

SAMMONS (ROGER) Zoning systems for spatial models. Reading, 1976. pp. 53. *bibliog.* (*Reading. University. Department of Geography. Reading Geographical Papers. No. 52*)

— Simulation methods.

PRETECEILLE (EDMOND) Jeux, modèles et simulations: critique des jeux urbains. Paris, [1974]. pp. 208. *bibliog.*

— America, Latin.

GALL (PIRIE M.) and others. Municipal development programs in Latin America: an intercounty evaluation. New York, 1976. pp. 124. *bibliog.*

— Asia.

INTERNATIONAL SEMINAR ON URBAN LAND USE POLICY, TAXATION AND ECONOMIC DEVELOPMENT, SINGAPORE, 1974. The cities of Asia: a study of urban solutions and urban finance; papers...edited by John Wong. Singapore, [1976]. pp. 450.

— Australia.

ALEXANDER (IAN C.) The city centre: patterns and problems. Nedlands, W.A., 1974. pp. 216. *bibliog.*

ARCHER (R.W.) Urban development and land prices: part I: planning and managing metropolitan development and land supply: rationalising the government roles in metropolitan development and land use. Melbourne, 1976. pp. 74. (*Committee for Economic Development of Australia. P Series. No. 19*)

— Canada — Citizen participation.

CANADIAN COUNCIL ON SOCIAL DEVELOPMENT. Integration of physical and social planning with special reference to neighbourhood services and citizen participation; report number two. Ottawa, [1968]. pp. 73. *bibliog. Report of a seminar held 28-29 March 1968 under the joint sponsorship of Special Project on Low-Income Housing and Community Funds and Councils Division of the Canadian Welfare Council.*

— Chile.

COLEGIO DE ARQUITECTOS DE CHILE. Plan nacional de desarrollo urbano, rural y de vivienda: planteamientos basicos, diagnosticos, estrategias. Santiago de Chile, 1973. pp. 255. *bibliog.*

— Europe.

COUNCIL OF EUROPE. Division of Local Authorities. Information bulletin: municipal and regional matters. s-a., 1974 (no. 6)- Strasbourg.

— France.

FRANCE. Direction de la Documentation. La Documentation Française. Notes et Etudes Documentaires. Nos. 4,234-4, 235-4,236. Le contrat d'aménagement de villes moyennes; par Philippe Leruste. Paris, 1975. pp. 85. *bibliog.*

BAUER (GERARD) and ROUX (JEAN MICHEL) La rurbanisation ou la ville éparpillée. Paris, [1976]. pp. 192. *bibliog.*

LABORIE (JEAN PAUL) Les petites villes en France. Paris, 1976. pp. 219. (*France. Délégation à l'Aménagement du Territoire et à l'Action Régionale. Travaux et Recherches de Prospective. 64) Map in end pocket.*

— Russia.

BORSHCHEVSKII (M.V.) and others. Gorod: metodologicheskie problemy kompleksnogo sotsial'nogo i ekonomicheskogo planirovaniia. Moskva, 1975. pp. 204.

NOVYE industrial'nye goroda: opyt proektirovaniia. Leningrad, 1975. pp. 94.

— — Siberia.

SOTSIAL'NYE problemy novykh gorodov Vostochnoi Sibiri. vyp.2. Irkutsk, 1974. pp. 181.

— — **White Russia.**

GRITSKEVICH (ANATOLII PETROVICH) Chastnovladel'cheskie goroda Belorussii v XVI-XVIII vv.: sotsial'no-ekonomicheskoe issledovanie istorii gorodov. Minsk, 1975. pp. 248.

— **Singapore.**

SINGAPORE. Ministry of National Development. Annual report. a., 1975- Singapore.

— **South Africa.**

SOUTH AFRICA. Parliament. House of Assembly. Select Committee on the Development Schemes Bill. 1977. Report...proceedings and evidence (S.C. 13-1977). in SOUTH AFRICA. Parliament. House of Assembly. Select Committee reports.

— **Underdeveloped areas.**

See UNDERDEVELOPED AREAS — City planning.

— **United Kingdom.**

LONDON. Greater London Council. Planned growth outside London; report. [London], 1975. pp. (31).

PAHL (RAYMOND EDWARD) Whose city?: and further essays on urban society. 2nd ed. Harmondsworth, 1975. pp. 306. bibliogs.

VEAL (A.J.) Recreation planning in new communities: a review of British experience. Birmingham, 1975. pp. 106. bibliog. (Birmingham. University. Centre for Urban and Regional Studies. Research Memoranda. No. 46)

BATHER (NICHOLAS JOHN) The speculative residential developer and urban growth: the location decision in a planned environment. Reading, 1976. pp. 44. bibliog. (Reading. University. Department of Geography. Reading Geographical Papers. No. 47)

GLADSTONE (FRANCIS) The politics of planning. London, 1976. pp. 128.

GROWTH and change in the future city region; edited by Tom Hancock. London, 1976. pp. 262. bibliogs. Based on papers given at an international symposium organised by the British Council in 1975.

LONDON. Greater London Council. Planned growth outside London: consultations; report. [London], 1976. 1 vol. (various pagings).

U.K. Department of the Environment. Housing Improvement Group. 1976. Environmental improvements: a report on a study of the problems and progress of environmental improvements in a sample of general improvement areas. London, 1976. pp. (64). bibliog. (Improvement Research Notes. 76-1)

BROADBENT (T.A.) Planning and profit in the urban economy. London, 1977. pp. 274. bibliog.

— — **Bibliography.**

JOHNSTONE (PAMELA) and LAMBERT (CLAIRE M.) compilers. Structure plans: list B: the literature and debate on structure plans and structure planning. [London, 1976]. pp. 33. (U.K. Department of the Environment. Library. Bibliographies. No. 152B) Bound with Structure plans: list A: structure plan documents.

LAMBERT (CLAIRE M.) compiler. Structure plans: list A: structure plan documents. London, 1976. pp. 63. (U.K. Department of the Environment. Library. Bibliographies. No. 152A) Bound with Structure plans: list B: the literature and debate on structure plans and structure planning.

McIVER (GLENYS) compiler. Planning: list A: basic list for the general library; list B: extended list of publications; list C: list for local authority planning departments; edited by Claire M. Lambert. [rev. ed.]. London, 1976. 3 pts. (in 1 vol.). (U.K. Department of the Environment. Library. Bibliographies. No. 160A, B and C).

— — **Citizen participation.**

JOWELL (ROGER) A review of public involvement in planning. London, 1975. pp. 35. (Social and Community Planning Research. Occasional Papers)

— — **Research.**

U.K. Social Science Research Council. Planning Committee. 1976. Research priorities of the SSRC Planning Committee. London, 1976. pp. 31. (Papers. No. 1)

CITY PLANNING AND REDEVELOPMENT LAW

— **United Kingdom.**

PLANNING inquiry practice: papers from a conference organised by the Law Society [and others]. London, 1974. pp. 57. (Journal of Planning and Environment Law. Occasional Papers)

RANDALL (SIMON JAMES CRAWFORD) Your land or theirs?: aspects of the Community Land Act 1975 and the Development Land Tax Bill. [Bromley?], 1976. pp. 31.

PURDUE (MICHAEL) Cases and materials on planning law. London, 1977. pp. 550.

CIVICS, RUSSIAN.

DEMOKRATIIA razvitogo sotsialisticheskogo obshchestva. Moskva, 1975. pp. 296.

DENISOV (ANDREI IVANOVICH) Obshchaia sistema sotsialisticheskoi demokratii. Moskva, 1975. pp. 247.

CIVIL LAW

— **International unification.**

Les INSTRUMENTS du rapprochement des législations dans la Communauté Economique Européenne; par D. De Ripainsel- Landy [and others]. Bruxelles, 1976. pp. 189. (Brussels. Université Libre. Institut d'Etudes Européennes. Thèses et Travaux Juridiques)

— **Russia.**

RECHI sovetskikh advokatov po grazhdanskim delam. Moskva, 1976. pp. 246.

VEBERS (IANIS ROBERTOVICH) Pravosub"ektivnost' grazhdan v sovetskom grazhdanskom i semeinom prave. Riga, 1976. pp. 231. bibliog.

— — **Azerbaijan.**

AZERBAIJAN. Statutes, etc. 1976. Grazhdanskii kodeks Azerbaidzhanskoi SSR; s izmeneniiami i dopolneniiami na 1 ianvaria 1976 g. Baku, 1976. pp. 201.

— — **Kirghizia.**

AL'CHIEV (KAARAGUL) Vozniknovenie i razvitie grazhdanskogo prava v Sovetskom Kirgizstane. Frunze, 1975. pp. 139.

— — **Russia (RSFSR).**

RUSSIA (RSFSR). Statutes, etc. 1975. Grazhdanskii kodeks RSFSR: s izmeneniiami i dopolneniiami na 1 dekabria 1975 goda, s prilozheniem postateino-sistematizirovannykh materialov. Moskva, 1976. pp. 295.

CIVIL PROCEDURE

— **Russia.**

BOLDYREV (EVGENII VLADIMIROVICH) and PERGAMENT (ALEKSANDRA IOSIFOVNA) eds. Nauchnyi kommentarii sudebnoi praktiki za 1972 god. Moskva, 1973. pp. 206.

— — **Lithuania.**

LITHUANIA. Statutes, etc. 1974. Grazhdanskii protsessual'nyi kodeks Litovskoi Sovetskoi Sotsialisticheskoi Respubliki: ofitsial'nyi tekst s izmeneniiami i dopolneniiami na 1 avgusta 1974 g. i s prilozheniem postateino-sistematizirovannykh materialov. Vil'nius, 1975. pp. 550.

LITHUANIA. Statutes, etc. 1974. Grazhdanskii protsessual'nyi kodeks Litovskoi Sovetskoi Sotsialisticheskoi Respubliki: ofitsial'nyi tekst s izmeneniiami i dopolneniiami na 1 avgusta 1974 g. i s prilozheniem postateino-sistematizirovannykh materialov. Vil'nius, 1975. pp. 550.

— — **Russia (RSFSR).**

RUSSIA (RSFSR). Statutes, etc. 1974. Grazhdanskii protsessual'nyi kodeks RSFSR: s izmeneniiami i dopolneniiami na 20 dekabria 1974 g., s prilozheniem postateino- sistematizirovannykh materialov. Moskva, 1975. pp. 310.

— **United Kingdom.**

LANGAN (PETER SAINT JOHN HEVEY) and LAWRENCE (DAVID GRANT) Civil procedure. 2nd ed. London, 1976. pp. 389.

CIVIL RIGHTS.

HOFER (WALTHER) Von der Freiheit und Würde des Menschen und ihrer Gefährdung: aus der Geschichte des Kampfes um die Menschenrechte. Bern, 1962. pp. 80.

FLATHMAN (RICHARD EARL) The practice of rights. Cambridge, [1976]. pp. 250.

INTERNATIONAL CONFEDERATION OF FREE TRADE UNIONS. World Congress, 11th, Mexico City, 1975. Human and trade union rights; [proceedings of the conference]. Brussels, 1976. pp. 47.

MAYER (DANIEL) Socialisme: le droit de l'homme au bonheur. [Paris, 1976]. pp. 171.

NAGEL (STUART S.) and NEEF (MARIAN) The application of mixed strategies: civil rights and other multiple-activity policies. Beverly Hills, [1976]. pp. 60.

DWORKIN (RONALD) Taking rights seriously. London, 1977. pp. 293.

— **America, Latin.**

RUSSELL TRIBUNAL II ON REPRESSION IN BRAZIL, CHILE AND LATIN AMERICA. 2nd session. Found guilty; the verdict of the Russell tribunal session in Brussels. Nottingham, [1975?]. pp. 36. (Spokesman, The. Pamphlets. No. 51)

— **European Economic Community countries.**

EUROPEAN COMMUNITIES. Commission. 1976. The protection of fundamental rights as Community law is created and developed: report of the Commission...to the European Parliament and the Council; the problems of drawing up a catalogue of fundamental rights for the European Communities;... study...drawn up by Professor R. Bernhardt. [Brussels], 1976. pp. 69. (Bulletin of the European Communities. Supplements. [1976/5])

— **France.**

FENET (ALAIN) ed. Les libertés publiques en France: documents pour une théorie générale. Paris, [1976]. pp. 352.

MACHELON (JEAN PIERRE) La République contre les libertés?...: les restrictions aux libertés publiques de 1879 à 1914. Paris, [1976]. pp. xvii, 462. (Fondation Nationale des Sciences Politiques. Cahiers. 206)

— **Germany.**

Die ZERSTOERUNG der Demokratie in der BRD durch Berufsverbote; herausgegeben von Horst Bethge [and others] . Köln, [1976]. pp. 396.

SCHEEL (WALTER) Vom Recht des anderen: Gedanken zur Freiheit. Düsseldorf, 1977. pp. 188. Speeches by the Federal German President, 1974-76.

— **India.**

INDIRA Gandhi's India: a political system reappraised; edited by Henry C. Hart. Boulder, Col., 1976. pp. 313.

— Israel.

AL-ABID (IBRAHIM) Israel and human rights. Beirut, 1969. pp. 172. *(Palestine Research Center. Palestine Books. No. 24)*

AL-ABID (IBRAHIM) Human rights in the occupied territories. Beirut, 1970. pp. 171. *(Palestine Research Center. Palestine Monographs. 73)*

— Nepal.

GYAWALI (S.P.) Towards rule of law. 2nd ed. Kathmandu, Department of Information, 1970. pp. 83.

— Russia.

SAKHAROV (ANDREI DMITRIEVICH) O strane i mire: sbornik proizvedenii. N'iu-Iork, 1976. pp. xxiv,183.

LAPENNA (IVO) Human rights: Soviet theory and practice; Helsinki and international law. London, 1977. pp. 15. *(Institute for the Study of Conflict. Conflict Studies. No. 83)*

— Switzerland.

SCHMID (MAX) Demokratie von Fall zu Fall: Repression in der Schweiz. Zürich, [1976]. pp. 461. *bibliog.*

— United Kingdom.

ZANDER (MICHAEL) A Bill of Rights?. Chichester, 1975. pp. 68.

GREENOAK (FRANCESCA) and others. What right have you got?: your rights and responsibilities as a citizen. London, 1976-77. 2 pts.(in 1 vol.). *bibliog. Part 2 edited by John Thomas.*

HILL (MICHAEL J.) The state, administration and the individual. London, 1976. pp. 256. *bibliog.*

SCORER (CATHERINE) The Prevention of Terrorism Acts 1974 and 1976: a report on the operation of the law. London, [1976]. pp. 39.

SOCIETY OF CONSERVATIVE LAWYERS. Bill of Rights Committee. Another bill of rights?; a report by the...committee...; [Alan Campbell, chairman]. London, 1976. pp. 23. *(Conservative Political Centre. [Publications]. No. 595)*

WALLINGTON (PETER) and McBRIDE (JEREMY) Civil liberties and a Bill of Rights. London, [1976]. pp. 148. *bibliog.*

— United States.

BERNS (WALTER) The First amendment and the future of American democracy. New York, [1976]. pp. 266.

LAMSON (PEGGY) Roger Baldwin, founder of the American Civil Liberties Union: a portrait. Boston, [Mass.], 1976. pp. 304.

McILHANY (WILLIAM H.) The ACLU on trial. New Rochelle, N.Y., [1976]. pp. 271.

VAUGHAN (PHILIP H.) The Truman administration's legacy for black America. Reseda, Calif., [1976]. pp. 116. *bibliog.*

WASBY (STEPHEN L.) ed. Civil liberties: policy and policy making. Lexington, Mass., [1976]. pp. 235. *bibliogs.*

WISE (DAVID) The American police state: the government against the people. New York, [1976]. pp. 437.

CIVIL RIGHTS (INTERNATIONAL LAW).

EUROPEAN COMMUNITIES. Commission. 1976. The protection of fundamental rights as Community law is created and developed: report of the Commission...to the European Parliament and the Council; the problems of drawing up a catalogue of fundamental rights for the European Communities;... study...drawn up by Professor R. Bernhardt. [Brussels], 1976. pp. 69. *(Bulletin of the European Communities. Supplements. [1976/5])*

KARTASHKIN (VLADIMIR ALEKSEEVICH) Mezhdunarodnaia zashchita prav cheloveka: osnovnye problemy sotrudnichestva gosudarstv. Moskva, 1976. pp. 223.

LAPENNA (IVO) Human rights: Soviet theory and practice; Helsinki and international law. London, 1977. pp. 15. *(Institute for the Study of Conflict. Conflict Studies. No. 83)*

La PROTECTION internationale des droits de l'homme. Bruxelles, 1977. pp. 207. *(Brussels. Université Libre. Institut de Sociologie. Centre de Droit International. [Publications]. 8)*

CIVIL SERVICE

— Africa — Research.

DEVELOPING research on African administration: some methodological issues; edited by Adebayo Adedeji and Goran Hyden. Ile Ife, 1974. pp. 201. *bibliogs. Based on informal discussions at the International Conference on Trends in University Teaching and Research in Public Administration in Africa, Institute of Administration, University of Ife, 1970.*

— Australia.

AUSTRALIA. Public Service Board. Statistical yearbook. a., 1976 (1st)- Canberra. *Incorporates AUSTRALIA. Public Service Board. Statistics of employment under the Public Service Act [at] 30th June*

COMPENDIUM OF AUSTRALIAN PUBLIC SERVICE INFORMATION; [pd. by] Public Service Board. a., current issue only. Canberra.

— India.

PUBLIC service commissions in India, 1926-1976; [by B.K. Basu and others]. [New Delhi], 1976. pp. 219.

— Kenya.

NYAMU (H.J.) The state of the civil service today: a critical appraisal. Nairobi, Kenya Institute of Administration, [1974]. pp. 19.

— Nigeria.

KATAGUM (ALHAJI SULE) The development of the Public Service Commission System and the problems of recruitment into the public service in a plural society: (text of a lecture at the Mid-West Public Service Forum, February 22, 1974). [Lagos, Government Printer, 1974]. pp. 14.

— Papua New Guinea.

PAPUA NEW GUINEA. Public Service Board. Annual report. a., 1968/69 [1st]- Port Moresby.

— Spain.

CARRASCO CANALS (CARLOS) La burocracia en la España del siglo XIX. Madrid, 1975. pp. 653.

— Sudan.

SUDAN. Terms of Service Commission. 1951. Report. London, 1951. 1 vol. (various pagings).

SUDAN. Ministry of Finance and Economics. Organisation and Methods Branch. 1958. Report on the civil service of the Sudan government. Khartoum, 1958. 1 vol. (various foliations).

SUDAN. Terms of Service Commission. 1959. Report..., 1958-59. [Khartoum, 1959]. 2 vols.(in 1).

— United Kingdom.

CUCKNEY (JOHN GRAHAM) The commercial approach to government operations; (transcript of lecture given on 13 June 1974). [London], Civil Service College, [1974]. pp. 17, 3. *(Lectures on Some Management Problems in the Civil Service. No. 6)*

MORRISON (Sir NICHOLAS) The Scottish Office: an example of administrative devolution; (transcript of lecture given on 22 April 1974). [London], Civil Service College, [1974]. pp. 11. *(Lectures on Some Management Problems in the Civil Service. No. 1)*

TRENAMAN (NANCY KATHLEEN) Some administrative consequences of the adoption of the Kilbrandon Commission recommendations: a personal view; (transcript of lecture given on 2 July 1974). [London], Civil Service College, [1974]. pp. 22. *(Lectures on Some Management Problems in the Civil Service. No. 7)*

SMITH (ANTHONY ROBERT) ed. Manpower planning in the civil service; [by] A.R. Smith [and others]. London, 1976. pp. 292. *bibliog. (U.K. Civil Service Department. Civil Service Studies. No. 3)*

U.K. Civil Service Department. Management Services. 1976. Management accounting in the civil service. [London], 1976. pp. 76. *bibliog. (Handbooks)*

— United States.

SEIDMAN (HAROLD) Politics, position and power: the dynamics of federal organization. 2nd ed. New York, 1975. pp. 354. *bibliog.*

CIVIL SERVICE RECRUITING

— United Kingdom.

MORRIS (B.R.) Statistical information for recruitment policy and management: a report of a review of statistical work in the Civil Service Commission. [London], 1969. pp. 49. *(U.K. Civil Service Department. Statistics Division. [Statistical Review Series]. R-02)*

CIVIL SUPREMACY OVER THE MILITARY.

CIVILIAN control of the military: theory and cases from developing countries; edited by Claude E. Welch. Albany, 1976. pp. 337. *bibliogs. Based on papers presented at a conference in October 1974.*

NORDLINGER (ERIC A.) Soldiers in politics: military coups and governments. Englewood Cliffs, [1977]. pp. 224. *bibliog.*

— Spain.

ROMERO-MAURA (JOAQUIN) The Spanish army and Catalonia: the Cu-Cut incident and the Law of Jurisdictions, 1905-1906. Beverly Hills, [1976]. pp. 31.

CIVILIZATION.

DAWSON (CHRISTOPHER HENRY) Enquiries into religion and culture. London, [1933]. pp. 347. *Consists mainly of reprinted essays.*

ROUSSEAU (JEAN JACQUES) The first and second discourses; edited, with introduction and notes, by Roger D. Masters; translated by Roger D. and Judith R. Masters. New York, [1964]. pp. 248.

CASCUDO (LUIS DA CAMARA) Civilização e cultura: pesquisas e notas de etnografia geral. Rio, 1973. 2 vols. *bibliog.*

CIVILIZATION, MODERN.

RESZLER (ANDRÉ) Le marxisme devant la culture. [Paris, 1975]. pp. 146. *bibliog.*

CAMILLERI (JOSEPH ANTHONY) Civilization in crisis: human prospects in a changing world. Cambridge, [1976]. pp. 303.

ENZENSBERGER (HANS MAGNUS) Raids and reconstructions: essays on politics, crime and culture; translations by Michael Roloff [and others]. London, 1976. pp. 312.

JOHNSON (PAUL) Enemies of society. London, [1977]. pp. 278. *bibliog.*

CIVILIZATION, OCCIDENTAL.

GREEN (CELIA) The decline and fall of science. London, 1976. pp. 184. *bibliog.*

CLASSIFICATION

— Books — Law.

COHEN (MORRIS L.) and others. Law and development classification plan. Medford, Mass., [1976]. pp. 14. *(Tufts University. Fletcher School of Law and Diplomacy. Law and Population Monograph Series. No. 38)*

CLASSIFICATION, LIBRARY OF CONGRESS.

IMMROTH (JOHN PHILLIP) A guide to the Library of Congress classification. 2nd ed. Littleton, Colo., 1971. pp. 335. *bibliog.*

CLAY

— Zambia.

REICHWALDER (P.) Brick-clay deposits at Kasondi Dambo, Ngwerere river and other localities near Lusaka. Lusaka, 1973. pp. 21. *(Zambia. Geological Survey Department. Economic Reports. No. 42)* 3 maps in end pocket.

CLAY INDUSTRIES

— United Kingdom.

WILLMOTT (FRANK G.) Cement, mud and 'muddies'. Rainham, Kent, 1977. pp. 141.

CLEANING COMPOUNDS

— Information services.

UNITED NATIONS INDUSTRIAL DEVELOPMENT ORGANIZATION. Guides to Information Sources. No. 24. Information sources on the soap and detergent industry. (ID/181) (UNIDO/LIB/SER.D/24). New York, United Nations, 1976. pp. 69. *bibliog.*

CLEAVER (ELDRIDGE).

HEATH (G. LOUIS) ed. The Black Panther leaders speak: Huey P. Newton, Bobby Seale, Eldridge Cleaver and company speak out through the Black Panther Party's official newspaper. Metuchen, N.J., 1976. pp. 165. *bibliog.*

CLEMENT VII, Antipope, 1378-1394.

SCOTTISH HISTORY SOCIETY. [Publications]. 4th Series. vol. 12. Calendar of papal letters to Scotland of Clement VII of Avignon, 1378-1394; edited by Charles Burns; [with] Annie I. Dunlop, 1897-1973: a memoir; by Ian B. Cowan. Edinburgh, 1976. pp. 240.

CLERGY

— Salaries, pensions, etc.

DOLE (GEORGES) Les ecclésiastiques et la sécurité sociale en droit comparé: intégration des clercs dans la cité. Paris, 1976. pp. 554. *bibliog.*

— United Kingdom.

WHITTET (JAMES) Letter to the ministers of the gospel on matters which deeply interest the working millions of Great Britain and Ireland. Perth, printed by G. Baxter, 1842. p. 16.

RANSON (STEWART) and others. Clergy, ministers and priests. London, 1977. pp. 204. *bibliog.*

CLERKS

— Switzerland.

FURRER (MILLY) and WALTER (HEDY) Die wirtschaftliche Lage und die Unterstützungsleistungen von Bürolistinnen und Verkäuferinnen der Stadt Zürich: Ergebnisse einer Umfrage, etc. Zürich, 1939. pp. 32.

— United Kingdom.

ANDERSON (GREGORY) Victorian clerks. Manchester, [1976]. pp. 145. *bibliog.*

CLEVELAND, OHIO

— Social conditions.

BRITTAIN (JOHN A.) The inheritance of economic status. Washington, D.C., [1977]. pp. 185. *(Brookings Institution. Studies in Social Economics)*

PETERSEN (GENE B.) and others. Southern newcomers to northern cities: work and social adjustment in Cleveland. New York, 1977. pp. 269.

CLINICAL PSYCHOLOGY.

REISMAN (JOHN M.) A history of clinical psychology. New York, [1976]. pp. 420. *bibliogs. Enlarged edition of his The development of clinical psychology.*

The ROLE of psychologists in the health services; report of the Sub-Committee; chairman: W.H. Trethowan. London, H.M.S.O., 1977. pp. 33.

CLINICS

— Location — Mathematical models.

LONDON. University. London School of Economics and Political Science. Graduate School of Geography. Discussion Papers. No. 60. Some thoughts on a model for the location of public facilities; [by] Mark Rosenberg. London, 1977. pp. 25. *bibliog.*

CLOCKS AND WATCHES

— Ireland (Republic).

EIRE. Fair Trade Commission. 1968. Report of enquiry into the conditions which obtain in regard to the supply and distribution to retailers of jewellery, watches and clocks. Dublin, [1968]. pp. 27.

CLOSTER-SEVEN, CONVENTION OF, 1757.

PARALLELE de la conduite du roi avec celle du roi d'Angleterre, electeur d'Hanovre, relativement aux affaires de l'Empire et nommément à la rupture de la capitulation de Closter-Seven par les Hanovriens. Amsterdam, Rey, 1758. pp. (iv), 192.

CLOTHING TRADE

— Czechoslovakia.

PASOLD (ERIC W.) Ladybird, Ladybird: a story of private enterprise. Manchester, [1977]. pp. 668.

— France.

FRANCE. Groupe sectoriel d'Analyse et de Prévision Textile-Habillement. 1976. Rapport...: préparation du 7e Plan. Paris, 1976. pp. 79.

— United Kingdom.

MAW (LEILA) and others. Immigrants and employment in the clothing industry. London, 1974. fo.26. *(Runnymede Trust. Industrial Publications)*

JOINT TEXTILE COMMITTEE [U.K.]. Textile trends 1966-75: an economic profile of the UK textile and clothing industries. London, National Economic Development Office, 1976. pp. 64. *bibliog.*

PASOLD (ERIC W.) Ladybird, Ladybird: a story of private enterprise. Manchester, [1977]. pp. 668.

CLOTHING WORKERS

— United States.

DUBINSKY (DAVID) and RASKIN (ABRAHAM HENRY) David Dubinsky: a life with labor. New York, [1977]. pp. 351.

CLWYD

— Statistics.

CLWYD. County Council. Abstract of statistics. a., 1976(3rd)- [Mold]. *[in English and Welsh].*

COAL

— Carbonization.

DRYDEN (I.G.C.). Carbonization and hydrogenation of coal. (ID/86). New York, United Nations, 1972. pp. 137. *bibliog.*

— European Economic Community countries.

EUROPEAN COMMUNITIES. Statistical Office. Coal: monthly bulletin. m., Mr 1977 (no. 1/3)- Luxembourg. *[In Community languages]. Supersedes in part EUROPEAN COMMUNITIES. Statistical Office. Quarterly bulletin of energy statistics.*

COMITE D'ETUDE DES PRODUCTEURS DE CHARBON D'EUROPE OCCIDENTALE. European coal 2000. [London, National Coal Board], 1977. pp. 7.

— France.

FRANCE. Direction de la Documentation. La Documentation Française. Notes et Etudes Documentaires. Nos. 4,280-4, 281-4,282. Le charbon en France; par Jules Lepidi. Paris, 1976. pp. 91. *bibliog.*

— United Kingdom.

COAL INDUSTRY TRIPARTITE GROUP [U.K.]. Coal for the future: progress with Plan for coal and prospects to the year 2000; [Tony Benn, chairman]. London, Department of Energy, [1976?]. pp. 23.

U.K. [Cabinet Office]. History of the Second World War: United Kingdom Civil Series. Coal; by W.H.B. Court. rev. ed. London, 1976. pp. 426,27. *Confidential version with full sources references.*

COAL MINERS.

SEKULES (EVA) The Miners' International Federation, 1945-1967: a case study of international trade unionism. 1977. fo.299. *bibliog. Typescript. M. Phil. (London) thesis: unpublished. This thesis is the property of London University and may not be removed from the Library.*

— Canada — Nova Scotia.

MACEWAN (PAUL) Miners and steelworkers: labour in Cape Breton. Toronto, 1976. pp. 400. *bibliog.*

— Germany — Ruhr.

TENFELDE (KLAUS) Sozialgeschichte der Bergarbeiterschaft an der Ruhr im 19. Jahrhundert. Bonn-Bad Godesberg, [1977]. pp. 738. *bibliog. (Friedrich-Ebert-Stiftung. Forschungsinstitut. Schriftenreihe. Band 125)*

— United Kingdom.

COLLS (ROBERT M.) The collier's rant: song and culture in the industrial village. London, [1977]. pp. 216.

— — Yorkshire.

BENSON (JOHN) and NEVILLE (ROBERT G.) eds. Studies in the Yorkshire coal industry. Manchester, [1976]. pp. 180. *bibliog.*

— United States.

SUFFERN (ARTHUR ELLIOTT) Conciliation and arbitration in the coal industry of America. Boston, [Mass.], 1915; New York, 1976. pp. 376. *bibliog. (Hart, Schaffner and Marx Prize Essays. 18)*

GRAEBNER (WILLIAM) Coal-mining safety in the Progressive period: the political economy of reform. Lexington, Ky., [1976]. pp. 244. *bibliog.*

LEVY (ELIZABETH) and RICHARDS (TAD) Struggle and lose, struggle and win: the United Mine Workers;...photo essay by Henry E.F. Gordillo. New York, [1977]. pp. 122. *bibliog.*

— — Diseases and hygiene.

MILLER (ARNOLD RAY) The wages of neglect: death and disease in the American workplace. San Francisco, 1975. pp. 8. *(National Conference on Social Welfare. 102nd Annual Forum, San Francisco, 1975)*

COAL MINES AND MINING

— Environmental aspects — United States.

LANDY (MARC KARNIS) The politics of environmental reform: controlling Kentucky strip mining. Washington, D.C., 1976. pp. 400. *bibliog. (Resources for the Future, Inc. Working Papers. PD-2)*

— Safety regulations — United States.

GRAEBNER (WILLIAM) Coal-mining safety in the Progressive period: the political economy of reform. Lexington, Ky., [1976]. pp. 244. *bibliog.*

— Germany.

KONZE (HEINZ) Entwicklung des Steinkohlenbergbaus im Ruhrgebiet, 1957-1974: Grundlagen und Strukturdaten für die Stadt- und Regionalplanung. Essen, 1975. pp. 64. *bibliog. (Siedlungsverband Ruhrkohlenbezirk. Schriftenreihe. Nr. 56) Includes supplement containing 18 maps.*

— — Government ownership.

HUE (OTTO) and WERNER (GEORG) Die Verstaatlichung des Bergbaues und die Grubenbeamten. [Stuttgart, 1919]. pp. 14. *(Wiederabdruck aus der "Neuen Zeit". 37. Jahrgang, Nr.15 und 18)*

— United Kingdom.

GRIFFIN (ALAN R.) The British coalmining industry: retrospect and prospect. Buxton, Derbys, [1977]. pp. 224. *bibliog.*

— United States.

SUFFERN (ARTHUR ELLIOTT) Conciliation and arbitration in the coal industry of America. Boston, [Mass.], 1915; New York, 1976. pp. 376. *bibliog. (Hart, Schaffner and Marx Prize Essays. 18)*

GRAEBNER (WILLIAM) Coal-mining safety in the Progressive period: the political economy of reform. Lexington, Ky., [1976]. pp. 244. *bibliog.*

COALITION (SOCIAL SCIENCES).

COALITIONS and time: cross-disciplinary studies; edited by Barbara Hinckley. Beverly Hills, 1976. pp. 143. *bibliogs.*

COALITION GOVERNMENTS.

LUTZ (DONALD S.) and WILLIAMS (JAMES R.) Minimum coalitions in legislatures: a review of the evidence. Beverly Hills, [1976]. pp. 45. *bibliog.*

— Austria.

MOMMSEN-REINDL (MARGARETA) Die österreichische Proporzdemokratie und der Fall Habsburg. Wien, 1976. pp. 264. *bibliog.*

— Germany.

THIEL (JUERGEN) Die Grossblockpolitik der Nationalliberalen Partei Badens, 1905 bis 1914: ein Beitrag zur Zusammenarbeit von Liberalismus und Sozialdemokratie in der Spätphase des Wilhelminischen Deutschlands. Stuttgart, 1976. pp. 283. *bibliog. (Kommission für Geschichtliche Landeskunde in Baden-Württemberg. Veröffentlichungen. Reihe B: Forschungen. 86. Band)*

COASTAL ZONE MANAGEMENT

— United Kingdom.

OCEANIC management: conflicting uses of the Celtic Sea and other western U.K. waters: report of a conference held at University College of Swansea, 19-22 September 1975; edited by M.M. Sibthorp, assisted by M. Unwin. London, [1977]. pp. 220. *Conference organised by the David Davies Memorial Institute of International Studies.*

— United States.

DITTON (ROBERT B.) and others. Coastal resources management: beyond bureaucracy and the market. Lexington, Mass., [1977]. pp. 196.

COBOL (COMPUTER PROGRAM LANGUAGE)

BOAR (B.H.) Abend debugging for COBOL programmers. New York, [1976]. pp. 321. *bibliog.*

COCOA

— Africa, West.

SIMMONS (JOHN) ed. Cocoa production: economic and botanical perspectives. New York, 1976. pp. 410.

— America, Latin.

CAMBRIDGE. University. Centre of Latin American Studies. Working Papers. No. 8. Britain and the cocoa trade in Latin America before 1914; [by Robert G. Greenhill]. Cambridge, [1973]. fo. 34. *Photocopy.*

SIMMONS (JOHN) ed. Cocoa production: economic and botanical perspectives. New York, 1976. pp. 410.

— Papua New Guinea.

GODYN (D.L.) An economic survey of cocoa in Papua New Guinea. Port Moresby, Department of Agriculture, Stock and Fisheries, 1974. 3 pts. (in 1 vol.).

COCOA TRADE.

CAMBRIDGE. University. Centre of Latin American Studies. Working Papers. No. 8. Britain and the cocoa trade in Latin America before 1914; [by Robert G. Greenhill]. Cambridge, [1973]. fo. 34. *Photocopy.*

REYSSET (BERNARD) Le marché du cacao. [Paris], Caisse Centrale de Coopération Economique, 1974. fo. 28.

SIMMONS (JOHN) ed. Cocoa production: economic and botanical perspectives. New York, 1976. pp. 410.

COFFEE

— Brazil.

DUQUE (HELIO MOACYR DE SOUZA) A luta pela modernização da economia cafeeira: assim agem as multinacionais. São Paulo, 1976. pp. 207. *bibliog.*

SILVA (SERGIO) Expansão cafeeira e origens da industria no Brasil. São Paulo, 1976. pp. 120. *bibliog.*

— — São Paulo.

MATOS (ODILON NOGUEIRA DE) Cafe e ferrovias: a evolução ferroviaria de São Paulo e o desenvolvimento da cultura cafeeira. São Paulo, 1974. pp. 135. *bibliog.*

— Panama.

PANAMA. Direccion de Estadistica y Censo. Estadistica panameña. Superficie sembrada y cosecha de café, tabaco y caña de azucar. a., 1975/76- Panama. *Supersedes in part* PANAMA. *Direccion de Estadistica y Censo. Estadistica panameña. Serie H. Informacion agropecuaria.*

COFFEE PLANTATION WORKERS

— Angola.

COFFEE for Britain means blood for Angola. Birmingham, [1973]. pp. 15.

COGNITION.

POSNER (MICHAEL I.) Cognition : an introduction. Glenview, Ill., [1973]. pp. 208. *bibliog.*

COGNITION (CHILD PSYCHOLOGY).

PICHE (DENISE) The geographical understanding of children aged 5 to 8 years. 1977. fo. 348. *bibliog. Typescript. Ph. D. (London) thesis: unpublished. This thesis is the property of London University and may not be removed from the Library.*

COIMBRA UNIVERSITY.

NAMORADO (RUI) Movimento estudantil e politica educacional. [Coimbra], 1972. pp. 168.

COINAGE

— United Kingdom.

EDWARDIAN monetary affairs, 1279-1344: a symposium held in Oxford, August 1976; edited by N.J. Mayhew. Oxford, 1977. pp. 186. *bibliog. (British Archaeological Reports. 36)*

— Uruguay.

ODICINI LEZAMA (ANTONIO) Monografia sobre el regimen monetario de la Republica Oriental del Uruguay, 1829-1955. Montevideo, 1958. pp. 239. *bibliog.*

COLDINGLEY PRISON.

[U.K. Prison Department. 1976]. Coldingley: an industrial prison. [London, 1976]. pp. 20.

COLEGIO DE SANTA CRUZ DE TLATELOLCO.

KOBAYASHI (JOSE MARIA) La educacion como conquista: empresa franciscana en Mexico. Mexico, 1974. pp. 423. *bibliog. (Mexico City. Colegio de Mexico. Centro de Estudios Historicos. Nueva Serie. 19)*

COLLECTIVE BARGAINING.

CLEGG (HUGH ARMSTRONG) Trade unionism under collective bargaining: a theory based on comparisons of six countries. Oxford, [1976]. pp. 121. *(Warwick Studies in Industrial Relations)*

FOLEY (BERNARD J.) and MAUNDERS (KEITH T.) Accounting information disclosure and collective bargaining. London, 1977. pp. 210.

MORLEY (IAN E.) and STEPHENSON (GEOFFREY M.) The social psychology of bargaining. London, 1977. pp. 317. *bibliog.*

— United Kingdom.

McCARTHY (WILLIAM EDWARD JOHN) Baron McCarthy. Making Whitley work: a review of the operation of the National Health Service Whitley Council system. [London, Department of Health and Social Security], 1976. pp. 144.

ADVISORY, CONCILIATION AND ARBITRATION SERVICE [U.K.] Disclosure of information to trade unions for collective bargaining purposes. [London, 1977]. pp. 5. *(Codes of Practice. 2)*

JENKINS (CLIVE) and SHERMAN (BARRIE) Collective bargaining: what you always wanted to know about trade unions and never dared to ask. London, 1977. pp. 156.

LABOUR RESEARCH DEPARTMENT. Guide to pay bargaining 1977-78. London, 1977. pp. 16.

— United States.

SUFFERN (ARTHUR ELLIOTT) Conciliation and arbitration in the coal industry of America. Boston, [Mass.], 1915; New York, 1976. pp. 376. *bibliog. (Hart, Schaffner and Marx Prize Essays. 18)*

ABEL (I.W.) Collective bargaining: labor relations in steel, then and now. New York, [1976]. pp. 62. *(Carnegie-Mellon University. Benjamin F. Fairless Memorial Lectures. 1975)*

RICHARDSON (REED COTT) Collective bargaining by objectives: positive approach. Englewood Cliffs, N.J., [1977]. pp. 387. *bibliogs.*

SCHICK (RICHARD P.) and COUTURIER (JEAN J.) The public interest in government labor relations. Cambridge, Mass., [1977]. pp. 264. *bibliog.*

COLLECTIVE LABOUR AGREEMENTS

— Switzerland.

BERUFSGEMEINSCHAFT IM SCHWEIZERISCHEN BUCHDRUCKERGEWERBE. Verhandlungs-Bericht über die Abänderungs-Anträge zum schweizerischen Buchdrucker-Tarif und über die Beratung der Berufs-Ordnung...August-Dezember 1917. Basel, 1918. pp. 238.

COLLECTIVE SETTLEMENTS

See COMMUNISTIC SETTLEMENTS.

COLLEGE COSTS

— United Kingdom.

U.K. Department of Education and Science. 1976. Undergraduate income and spending: summary report of a survey;...provisionally summarises the main findings of a survey of undergraduate student income and expenditure conducted in the 1974-75 academic year by the Social Survey Division of the Office of Population Censuses and Surveys. London, [1976]. pp. 12.

COLLINGWOOD (ROBIN GEORGE).

ROTENSTREICH (NATHAN) Philosophy, history and politics: studies in contemporary English philosophy of history. The Hague, 1976. pp. 158. *bibliog.*

COLOMBIA

— Appropriations and expenditures.

COLOMBIA. Contraloria General. Informe financiero sobre la Cuenta General del Presupuesto y de Tesoro y la gestion financiera de las entidades descentralizadas nacionales. a., 1973- Bogotá.

COLOMBIA. Contraloria General. Informe financiero vigencia. a., 1974- Bogota.

— Economic history.

RODRIGUEZ SALAZAR (OSCAR) Efectos de la gran depresion sobre la industria colombiana. Bogota, 1973. 1 vol.(various pagings).

— History.

IL'INA (NINA GEORGIEVNA) Kolumbiia: ot kolonii k nezavisimosti, 1781-1819 gg. Moskva, 1976. pp. 326. *bibliog.*

— Industries.

MISAS A. (GABRIEL) Contribucion al estudio del grado de concentracion en la industria colombiana. Santiago de Chile, 1973. pp. 111. *bibliog. (Instituto Latinoamericano de Investigaciones Sociales. Estudios y Documentos. 26)*

RODRIGUEZ SALAZAR (OSCAR) Efectos de la gran depresion sobre la industria colombiana. Bogota, 1973. 1 vol.(various pagings).

— Politics and government.

MARTINEZ (JUAN PABLO) and IZQUIERDO (MARIA ISABEL) Anapo: oposicion o revolucion. Bogota, 1972. pp. 105.

— Population.

FORNAGUERA (MIGUEL) and GUHL (ERNESTO) Colombia: ordenacion del territorio en base del epicentrismo regional. Bogota, 1969. pp. 175,(19).

— Statistics.

COLOMBIA. Departamento Administrativo Nacional de Estadistica. 1975. Estadisticas historicas. [Bogota, 1975]. pp. 200.

COLONIES.

BOTORAN (CONSTANTIN) and UNC (GHEORGHE) Tradiţii de solidaritate ale mişcării muncitoreşti şi democratice din România cu lupta de emancipare naţională şi socială a popoarelor din Asia, Africa şi America Latină. Bucureşti, 1977. pp. 255. *With English, French, German, Russian and Spanish tables of contents.*

UNITED NATIONS. Office of Public Information. 1977. The United Nations and decolonization: highlights of thirty years of United Nations efforts on behalf of colonial countries and peoples. New York, 1977. pp. 36.

COLONIES IN AFRICA.

WILSON (HENRY S.) The imperial experience in sub-Saharan Africa since 1870. Minneapolis, 1977. pp. 415. *bibliog.*

COLONIES IN WEST AFRICA.

HARGREAVES (JOHN DESMOND) The end of colonial rule in West Africa. London, [1976]. pp. 38. *bibliog. (Historical Association . General Series. G. 88)*

COLOURED PEOPLE (SOUTH AFRICA).

SOUTH AFRICA. Coloured Persons Representative Council. Debates and proceedings. sess., My/S 1975-(2nd council, 1st and 2nd sess.)- Pretoria. *[In English and Afrikaans].*

— Economic conditions.

OCCUPATIONAL and social change among coloured people in South Africa: proceedings of a workshop of the Centre for Intergroup Studies at the University of Cape Town; edited by Hendrik W. van der Merwe and C.J. Groenewald. Cape Town, 1976. pp. 278. *bibliog.*

— Education.

SOUTH AFRICA. Bureau of Statistics. Education: schools for Coloureds and Asians. a., 1971(5th)- Pretoria. *[in English and Afrikaans].*

— Social conditions.

OCCUPATIONAL and social change among coloured people in South Africa: proceedings of a workshop of the Centre for Intergroup Studies at the University of Cape Town; edited by Hendrik W. van der Merwe and C.J. Groenewald. Cape Town, 1976. pp. 278. *bibliog.*

COLUMBIA UNIVERSITY.

GOLD (ALICE ROSS) and others. Fists and flowers: a social psychological interpretation of student dissent. New York, 1976. pp. 204. *bibliog.*

COLUMBUS, OHIO

— Poor.

MONKKONEN (ERIC H.) The dangerous class: crime and poverty in Columbus, Ohio, 1860- 1885. Cambridge, Mass., 1975. pp. 186.

— Social history.

MONKKONEN (ERIC H.) The dangerous class: crime and poverty in Columbus, Ohio, 1860- 1885. Cambridge, Mass., 1975. pp. 186.

COLVILLE (Sir JOHN).

COLVILLE (Sir JOHN) Footprints in time. London, 1976. pp. 287.

COMMERCE.

MEMOIRE sur la question proposée en 1779, par la Société de bienfaisance et d'encouragement établie à Basle: savoir, jusqu'à quel point il est à propos de régler la dépense des citoyens dans une république, dont la prospérité est fondée sur le commerce. Basle, chez Jean-Jacques Flick, 1781. pp. 40.

REUSS (INGO) Ökonomie des Aussenhandels: Sicherheit durch Beteiligung am Welthandel und Weltverkehr. Baden-Baden, [1956]. pp. 204.

ECONOMISTS ADVISORY GROUP. World invisible trade;...prepared by Professor John H. Dunning and Mr. David Robertson. London, 1973. pp. 25.

SANDERSON (FRED H.) and CLEVELAND (HAROLD VAN BUREN) Strains in international finance and trade. Beverly Hills, [1974]. pp. 71. *bibliogs. (Georgetown University. Center for Strategic and International Studies. Washington Papers. vol. 2/14)*

WEILLER (JEAN) and COUSSY (JEAN) Economie internationale. Paris, [1975 in progress]. *(Paris. Ecole des Hautes Etudes en Sciences Sociales. Textes de Sciences Sociales. 13)*

ERICKSON (BONNIE H.) International networks: the structured webs of diplomacy and trade. Beverly Hills, [1975]. pp. 56. *bibliog.*

FRANCE. Direction de la Documentation. La Documentation Française. Notes et Etudes Documentaires. Nos. 4,226-4, 227-4,228. Le financement du commerce international; per Jacques Blanc. Paris, 1975. pp. 53. *bibliog.*

UNILEVER LIMITED. The outlook for world trade; (speech delivered in Frankfurt by David A. Orr...28th October, 1975). London, 1975. pp. 11.

DANIELS (JOHN D.) and others. International business: environments and operations. Reading, Mass., [1976]. pp. 554. *bibliogs.*

GANS (OSKAR) Beiträge zur Analyse von Welthandelsstrukturen, mit empirischen Untersuchungen zum Aussenhandel der Entwicklungs- und Industrieländer, 1960/1969. Berlin, [1976]. pp. 232. *bibliog.*

SOUBEYRAN (ANTOINE) Essai de reconstruction et de généralisation de la théorie pure du commerce international. Paris, 1976. pp. 465. *bibliog.*

GRUBEL (HERBERT G.) International economics. Homewood, Ill., 1977. pp. 657. *bibliog.*

MITRA (ASHOK) Terms of trade and class relations: an essay in political economy. London, 1977. pp. 193.

— Bibliography.

STERN (ROBERT M.) and others, compilers. Price elasticities in international trade: an annotated bibliography. London, 1976. pp. 363. *bibliog.*

— Congresses.

UNITED NATIONS. Conference on Trade and Development, 2nd, New Delhi, 1968. Rules of procedure. (TD/63/Rev.1). New York, 1968. pp. 23.

— Mathematical models.

DROLLAS (LEONIDAS) The foreign trade sector in disequilibrium: a comparative study of sixteen developed countries. 1976. fo.330. *Typescript. Ph.D. (London) thesis: unpublished. This thesis is the property of London University and may not be removed from the Library.*

JONES (RONALD W.) "Two-ness" in trade theory: costs and benefits. Princeton, 1977. pp. 43. *bibliog. (Princeton University. Department of Economics and Sociology. International Finance Section. Special Papers in International Economics. No. 12)*

KRUEGER (ANNE O.) Growth, distortions, and patterns of trade among many countries. Princeton, 1977. pp. 45. *bibliog. (Princeton University. Department of Economics and Sociology. International Finance Section. Princeton Studies in International Finance. No. 40)*

— Periodicals.

LIST ECON: Förteckning över periodica inom ekonomi, handel, ekonomisk geografi och internationell statistik i nordiska bibliotek: List of periodicals in the fields of economics, trade, economic geography and international statistics in Nordic libraries; [pd. by] Biblioteket, Handelshögskolan, Stockholm. irreg., 1976- Stockholm.

COMMERCIAL FINANCE COMPANIES

— Australia.

AUSTRALIA. Commonwealth Bureau of Census and Statistics. 1975. Foreign ownership and control of finance companies, 1973. Canberra, 1975. pp. 40.

COMMERCIAL LAW

— Russia.

LEBAHN (AXEL) Sozialistische Wirtschaftsintegration und Ost-West-Handel im sowjetischen internationalen Recht: Theorie und Praxis des Offenheitsprinzips, etc. Berlin, [1976]. pp. 495. *bibliog.*

COMMERCIAL LAW(Cont.)

— United Kingdom.

CHARLESWORTH (JOHN) LL.D. Mercantile law; thirteenth edition by Clive M. Schmitthoff and David A.G. Sarre. London, 1977. pp. 564. *bibliogs.*

SCHMITTHOFF (CLIVE MACMILLAN) Commercial law in a changing economic climate. London, 1977. pp. 49. *(Gresham Lectures. 1976)*

COMMERCIAL POLICY.

SEMINAR ON SHIPPING ECONOMICS, GENEVA, 1966. Shipping and the world economy: report of a seminar...(held in Geneva from 1-12 August, 1966). (TD/14) (TD/B/C.4/17/Rev.1) . New York, United Nations, 1966. pp. 36.

HUDEC (ROBERT E.) The GATT legal system and world trade diplomacy. New York, [1975]. pp. 399.

— Mathematical models.

RAY (ALOK) Trade, protection and economic policy: essays in international economics. Delhi, 1976. pp. 73. *bibliogs.*

MICHAELY (MICHAEL) Theory of commercial policy: trade and protection. Oxford, 1977. pp. 247. *bibliog.*

COMMERCIAL PRODUCTS.

PRIMARY commodity prices: analysis and forecasting; edited by W. Driehuis. Rotterdam, [1976]. pp. 346. *bibliogs. Selected papers of the Working Group on Primary Commodities of the Association of European Conjuncture-Institutes.*

U.K. Ministry of Overseas Development. Statistics Division. Commodity price charts. irreg., Current issue only. London.

— Classification.

EUROPEAN COMMUNITIES. Statistical Office. Common nomenclature of industrial products: NIPRO. irreg., 1975 (1st)- Luxembourg.

— Canada.

CANADA. Statistics Canada. Industry price indexes. m., 1971/1975 (1st)- Ottawa. *[in English and French]. Supersedes in part CANADA. Statistics Canada. Prices and price indexes.*

WILLIAMS (JAMES RALLA) Resources, tariffs, and trade: Ontario's stake. Toronto, 1976. pp. 117. *bibliog. (Ontario. Economic Council. Research Studies. No. 6)*

— Malaysia.

THOBURN (JOHN T.) Primary commodity exports and economic development: theory, evidence and a study of Malaysia. London, [1977]. pp. 310. *bibliog.*

— Russia.

MALAFEEV (ALEKSEI NIKOLAEVICH) Proshloe i nastoiashchee teorii tovarnogo proizvodstva pri sotsializme. Moskva, 1975. pp. 191.

COMMERCIAL VEHICLES.

FRYER (J.A.) and others. Goods vehicle activity in Greater London. London, [1977]. pp. 31. *(London. Greater London Council. Research Memoranda. 491)*

COMMISSIONS OF INQUIRY, INTERNATIONAL.

BENSALAH (TABRIZI) L'enquête internationale dans le règlement des conflits: règles juridiques applicables. Paris, 1976. pp. 269. *bibliog.*

COMMODITY CONTROL.

U.K. Empire Marketing Board. Statistics and Intelligence Branch. 1933. Regulation of supply: notes on schemes for regulating production, exports and stocks of certain primary products; prepared for the British commonwealth delegations, (Monetary and Economic Conference). [London], 1933. pp. 94.

O'NEILL (HELEN B.) A common interest in a common fund: proposals for new structures in international commodity markets. (TAD/INF/PUB/77.1). New York, United Nations, 1977. pp. 48.

COMMODITY EXCHANGES.

COMMODITY ANALYSIS LIMITED. Trading in London commodity futures. London, 1973. pp. 30.

GOSS (BARRY ANDREW) and YAMEY (BASIL SELIG) eds. The economics of futures trading: readings. New York, 1976. pp. 236. *bibliog.*

O'NEILL (HELEN B.) A common interest in a common fund: proposals for new structures in international commodity markets. (TAD/INF/PUB/77.1). New York, United Nations, 1977. pp. 48.

— Russia.

D'IACHENKO (VASILII PETROVICH) Tovarno-denezhnye otnosheniia i finansy pri sotsializme; (raboty... , opublikovannye v 1946-1970 gg.). Moskva, 1974. pp. 495. *bibliog.*

— United Kingdom.

BRACKENBURY (M.C.) AND COMPANY. Dealing on the London Metal Exchange and commodity markets. London, [1975?]. pp. 117. *Lacks title page. Title from cover.*

COMMON LAW MARRIAGE

— United Kingdom.

LISTER (RUTH) As man and wife?: a study of the cohabitation rule. London, [1973]. pp. 56. *(Child Poverty Action Group. Poverty Research Series. 2)*

COMMONWEALTH SECRETARIAT.

COMMONWEALTH SECRETARIAT. Information Division. The Commonwealth Secretariat. London, 1974. pp. 40.

COMMUNES (CHINA).

BURKI (SHAHID JAVED) A study of Chinese communes, 1965. Cambridge, Mass., [1969] repr. 1970. pp. 101. *(Harvard University. East Asian Research Center. Harvard East Asian Monographs. 29)*

COMMUNICATION.

BRETZ (RUDOLPH) A taxonomy of communication media. Englewood Cliffs, N.J., [1971] repr. 1974. pp. 165.

JOUSSE (MARCEL) La manducation de la parole. [Paris, 1975]. pp. 287. *(L'anthropologie du geste.2)*

KING (STEPHEN W.) Communication and social influence. Reading, Mass., [1975]. pp. 169. *bibliog.*

DIAZ BORDENAVE (JUAN E.) Communication and rural development. Paris, Unesco, 1977. pp. 109. *bibliog.*

— Social aspects.

VARIATIONS in black and white perceptions of the social environment; edited by Harry C. Triandis. Urbana, [1976]. pp. 202. *bibliog. Tables on microfiche (3 cards).*

— — China.

CHU (GODWIN C.) Radical change through communication in Mao's China. Honolulu, [1977]. pp. 340.

— — Malaysia — Pahang.

WILDER (WILLIAM DEAN) Social structure and the communications systems in a Malay village in Pahang, Malaya. 1976. fo. 406. *bibliog. 6 offprints in front pocket. Typescript. Ph.D. (London) thesis: unpublished. This thesis is the property of London University and may not be removed from the Library.*

— — Sweden.

HEDEBRO (GÖRAN) Information och engagemang: individuella och miljömässiga förutsättningar för deltagande i det lokala samhällslivet: exemplet skola. Stockholm, 1976. pp. 237. *bibliog. With English summary.*

— America, Latin.

SCHENKEL (PETER) La estructura de poder de los medios de comunicacion en cinco paises latinoamericanos. Santiago de Chile, 1973. pp. 104. *(Instituto Latinoamericano de Investigaciones Sociales. Estudios y Documentos. 20)*

— Rhodesia.

O'CALLAGHAN (MARION) Southern Rhodesia: the effects of a conquest society on education, culture and information;...with a contribution by Reginald Austin. Paris, Unesco, 1977. pp. 293.

— Russia.

SOTSIOLOGICHESKIE problemy obshchestvennogo mneniia i sredstv massovoi informatsii. Moskva, 1975. pp. 202.

— Underdeveloped areas.

See UNDERDEVELOPED AREAS — Communication.

— United States.

PORAT (MARC URI) The information economy. Ann Arbor, Mich., [1976]. 2 vols. *Ph.D. dissertation, Stanford University.*

COMMUNICATION AND TRAFFIC

— Africa.

ARNOLD (GUY) and WEISS (RUTH) Strategic highways of Africa. London, 1977. pp. 178. *bibliog.*

— France.

FRANCE. Commission des Transports et des Communications. 1976. Rapport...: préparation du 7e Plan. Paris, 1976. pp. 264.

COMMUNICATION IN MANAGEMENT

— United Kingdom.

GRAVES (DESMOND JAMES TURNER) Organisational change in a port operating authority. London, National Ports Council, 1976. fo. 88.

ADVISORY, CONCILIATION AND ARBITRATION SERVICE [U.K.] Disclosure of information to trade unions for collective bargaining purposes. [London, 1977]. pp. 5. *(Codes of Practice. 2)*

COMMUNICATION IN POLITICS.

KRAUS (SIDNEY) and DAVIS (DENNIS) The effects of mass communication on political behavior. University Park, Pa., [1976]. pp. 308.

— China.

CHU (GODWIN C.) Radical change through communication in Mao's China. Honolulu, [1977]. pp. 340.

COMMUNICATION IN SCIENCE.

LUNDQVIST (LENNART J.) The case of mercury pollution in Sweden: scientific information and public response. Stockholm, 1974. pp. 55. *bibliog. (Sweden. Forskningsekonomiska Kommittén. Rapporter. 4)*

COMMUNICATION IN THE SOCIAL SCIENCES.

FRIEDMANN (JOHN REMBERT PETER) Retracking America: the theory of transactive planning. Garden City, N.Y., 1973. pp. 289. *bibliog.*

ROBERTS (NORMAN) ed. Use of social sciences literature. London, 1977. pp. 326. *bibliogs.*

COMMUNISM.

RAPPOPORT (CHARLES) Précis du communisme. 4th ed. Strasbourg, [1929?]. pp. 32.

PARTI COMMUNISTE FRANÇAIS. Pour la victoire de la liberté. Paris, [195-?]. pp. 14.

KOLNAI (AUREL) Errores del anticomunismo. Madrid, 1952. pp. 167. *Photocopy.*

TROTSKII (LEV DAVYDOVICH) Bolchévisme et stalinisme: ([with] Le régime communiste aux U.S.A.); avant-propos de G. Bloch. [Paris, La Vérité, 1956]. pp. 28. *First published in 1937 and 1935 respectively.*

REISBERG (ARNOLD) Lenins Idee der Koexistenz wird triumphieren. Berlin, 1960. pp. 48.

MATVEEVA (TAMARA STEPANOVNA) Internatsional'nyi dolg i sovremennost': na materialakh Turkmenskoi SSR. Ashkhabad, 1970. pp. 141.

FEJTÖ (FRANÇOIS) L'héritage de Lénine: introduction à l'histoire du communisme mondial. [Paris, 1973]. pp. 397.

THAELMANN (ERNST) Geschichte und Politik: Artikel und Reden, 1925 bis 1933. Frankfurt am Main, 1974. pp. 238.

BRITISH AND IRISH COMMUNIST ORGANISATION. Policy Statements. No. 8. Imperialism. Belfast, 1975. pp. 63.

GOSUDARSTVO sotsialisticheskoi orientatsii. Moskva, 1975. pp. 376. *bibliog.* (*Akademiia Nauk SSSR. Institut Gosudarstva i Prava. Gosudarstvo i Pravo Stran, Osvobodivshikhsia ot Kolonial'noi Zavisimosti.* [5])

SEROVA (IRINA IVANOVNA) Sila, splachivaiushchaia voedino: internatsional'noe vospitanie trudiashchikhsia v razvitom sotsialisticheskom obshchestve. Minsk, 1975. pp. 262. *bibliog.*

MEZHDUNARODNOE rabochee dvizhenie: voprosy istorii i teorii. Moskva, 1976 in progress.

AKADEMIIA OBSHCHESTVENNYKH NAUK. Kafedra Teorii i Metodov Ideologicheskoi Raboty. Voprosy Teorii i Metodov Ideologicheskoi Raboty. vyp.5. Mirnoe sosushchestvovanie gosudarstv s razlichnym sotsial'nym stroem i sovremennaia ideologicheskaia bor'ba. Moskva, 1976. pp. 309.

DISCUSSION on socialist democracy: a Marxism Today supplement containing further contributions to a discussion on John Gollan's article "Socialist democracy: some problems". London, [1976]. pp. 34. (*Communist Party of Great Britain. Communist Party Pamphlets*)

The HUMANISATION of socialism: writings of the Budapest school; [by] Andras Hegedus [and others]. London, 1976. pp. 177. *Articles translated from various Hungarian journals published during the period 1967-1972.*

JANICKI (JANUSZ) and MUSZYŃSKI (JERZY) eds. Ideologia i polityka współczesnego lewactwa. Warszawa, 1976. pp. 387.

KOMMUNISTICHESKOE dvizhenie v avangarde bor'by za mir, natsional'noe i sotsial'noe osvobozhdenie: k 40-letiiu VII kongressa Kommunisticheskogo Internatsionala. Moskva, 1976. pp. 366.

LARIN (V.) Mezhdunarodnye otnosheniia i ideologicheskaia bor'ba, 60-70-e gody. Moskva, 1976. pp. 247. *bibliog.*

MITIN (MARK BORISOVICH) Problemy sovremennoi ideologicheskoi bor'by: kritika sotsiologicheskikh i sotsial'no-politicheskikh kontseptsii. Moskva, 1976. pp. 319.

POSADAS (J.) The process of partial regeneration in the workers' states; selection of articles 1975. [London], 1976. pp. 20. (*European Marxist Review. Publications*)

SOLZHENITSYN (ALEKSANDR ISAEVICH) Détente: prospects for democracy and dictatorship;...with commentary by Alex Simirenko [and others]. New Brunswick, [1976]. pp. 112. *Based on addresses given in Washington, D.C. and New York in 1975.*

SOTSIALISTICHESKII obraz zhizni i sovremennaia ideologicheskaia bor'ba. Moskva, 1976. pp. 350.

TODD (EMMANUEL) La chute finale: essai sur la décomposition de la sphère soviétique. Paris, 1976. pp. 324.

TSAGA (VIKTORIIA FRANTSEVNA) Antikommunismus heute: zu bürgerlichen ökonomischen Theorien; (ins Deutsche übertragen von Leon Nebenzahl). Berlin, [1976]. pp. 159.

BOTORAN (CONSTANTIN) and UNC (GHEORGHE) Tradiţii de solidaritate ale mişcării muncitoreşti şi democratice din România cu lupta de emancipare naţională şi socială a popoarelor din Asia, Africa şi America Latină. Bucureşti, 1977. pp. 255. *With English, French, German, Russian and Spanish tables of contents.*

PROBLEMY sotsialisticheskogo obrza zhizni. Moskva, 1977. pp. 288.

STEIGERWALD (ROBERT REINHOLD) Der "wahre" oder konterrevolutionäre "Sozialismus": was wollen Havemann, Dutschke, Biermann?. Frankfurt am Main, 1977. pp. 145.

WILHELM (DONALD) Creative alternatives to communism: guidelines for tomorrow's world. London, 1977. pp. 173.

— Bibliography.

GENERALSEKRETARIAT ZUM STUDIUM UND ZUR BEKÄMPFUNG DES BOLSCHEWISMUS. Führer durch die bolschewistische und antibolschewistische Literatur. London, 1975. pp. 24. (*Generalsekretariat zum Studium und zur Bekämpfung des Bolschewismus. Sammlung von Quellen zum Studium des Bolschewismus. 1. Heft) Reprint of work originally published in Berlin in 1919.*

STARR (JOHN BRYAN) and DYER (NANCY ANNE) compilers. Post-liberation works of Mao Zedong: a bibliography and index. Berkeley, Calif., [1976]. pp. 222.

WHETTEN (LAWRENCE L.) Current research in comparative communism: an analysis and bibliographic guide to the Soviet system. New York, 1976. pp. 159.

SHAFFER (HARRY GEORGE) Periodicals on the socialist countries and on marxism: a new annotated index of English-language publications. [rev. ed.] New York, 1977. pp. 134. *Edition of 1971 published under title: English language periodic publications on communism.*

— Congresses.

ZAKARIADZE (NODAR EZHIFANESOVICH) Razvitie leninskoi strategii i taktiki v dokumentakh i materialakh Soveshchaniia kommunisticheskikh i rabochikh partii 1969 goda. Tbilisi, 1975. pp. 144.

COMMUNIST INTERNATIONAL. World Congress, 2nd, 1920. Second congress of the Communist International: minutes of the proceedings; [translated by R.A. Archer]. London, [1977]. 2 vols. *bibliog.*

— History.

KOCH (HANS) 1894-1959, ed. Theorie, Taktik, Technik des Weltkommunismus: eine Zitatensammlung von Marx bis Chruschtschow;...bearbeitet von Eugen Wieber. Pfaffenhofen/Ilm, 1959. pp. 504. *bibliog.*

STALINISM: essays in historical interpretation; edited by Robert C. Tucker,...with contributions by Wlodzimierz Brus [and others]. New York, 1977. pp. 332. *Based on papers presented at a conference on "Stalinism and communist political culture" held at Bellagio, Italy, July 25-31, 1975 and sponsored by the Planning Group on Comparative Communist Studies of the American Council of Learned Societies.*

YOUNG (NIGEL) An infantile disorder?: the crisis and decline of the New Left. London, 1977. pp. 490. *bibliog.*

— Algeria.

SIVAN (EMMANUEL) Communisme et nationalisme en Algérie, 1920-1962. [Paris, 1976]. pp. 262. (*Fondation Nationale des Sciences Politiques. Travaux et Recherches de Science Politique. 41*)

— America, Latin.

RATLIFF (WILLIAM E.) Castroism and communism in Latin America, 1959-1976: the varieties of Marxist-Leninist experience. Stanford, Calif., 1976. pp. 240. (*American Enterprise Institute for Public Policy Research and Stanford University. Hoover Institution on War, Revolution and Peace. AEI-Hoover Policy Studies. 19*)

— Argentine Republic.

NADRA (FERNANDO) Socialismo nacional. Buenos Aires, 1973. pp. 237.

— Asia.

TAYLOR (JAY) China and Southeast Asia: Peking's relations with revolutionary movements. 2nd ed. New York, 1976. pp. 400.

— Bulgaria.

SOTSIALNO-ikonomicheski problemi na izgrazhdaneto na razvito sotsialistichesko obshtestvo v Bulgariia; Socio-economic problems in building a developed socialist society in Bulgaria. Sofiia, 1974. pp. 403. *With Russian and English summaries and tables of contents.*

DOBREV (KRUSTIU ZHELIAZKOV) Problemi na stroitelstvoto na sotsializma v NR Bulgariia: izbrani proizvedeniia; [with an introductory essay by Ivan Stefanov]. Sofiia, 1975. pp. 267. *bibliog.*

ZHIVKOV (TODOR) Izbrannye stat'i i rechi, 1965-1975; [perevod s bolgarskogo]. Moskva, 1975. pp. 583.

— Cambodia.

BARRON (JOHN) and PAUL (ANTHONY) Peace with horror: the untold story of communist genocide in Cambodia. London, [1977]. pp. 234. *bibliogs.*

— Canada.

LEAGUE FOR SOCIALIST ACTION. The socialist alternative for Canada; edited, with an introduction by George Addison. Toronto, [1974]. pp. 11.

OUT of the driver's seat: Marxism in North America today. Windsor, Ont., [1974]. pp. 75.

KASHTAN (WILLIAM) Toward socialism:...selected writings, 1966-1976. Toronto, 1976. pp. 372.

WATSON (LOUISE) She never was afraid: the biography of Annie Buller. Toronto, 1976. pp. 129.

— China.

FITZGERALD (CHARLES PATRICK) The birth of communist China. Harmondsworth, 1964. pp. 288. *A revised and updated edition of the work first published in 1952 under the title Revolution in China.*

CHINA. National People's Congress. 3rd Congress, 1st Session, 1964-65. Main documents of the...session. Peking, 1965. pp. 92.

PRYBYLA (JAN S.) The political economy of communist China. Scranton, Penn., [1970]. pp. 605.

MAO (TSE-TUNG) and LIN (PIAO) Post-revolutionary writings; edited by K. Fan. Garden City, 1972. pp. 536.

WHYTE (MARTIN KING) Small groups and political rituals in China. Berkeley, Calif., [1975]. pp. 271. (*Michigan University. Center for Chinese Studies. Michigan Studies on China*) First published in 1974.

BURLATSKII (FEDOR MIKHAILOVICH) Mao Tsze-dun: "nash koronnyi nomer - eto voina, diktatura". Moskva, 1976. pp. 391.

MARMOR (FRANÇOIS) Le maoïsme: philosophie et politique. [Paris, 1976]. pp. 127. *bibliog.*

RAMANENKO (O.M.) Antisotsialisticheskaia sushchnost' maoizma. Moskva, 1976. pp. 127.

TISSIER (PATRICK) La Chine: transformations rurales et développement socialiste. Paris, 1976. pp. 325. *bibliog.*

TROTSKII (LEV DAVYDOVICH) Leon Trotsky on China; introduction by Peng Shu-tse; edited by Les Evans and Russell Block. New York, 1976. pp. 688.

CHU (GODWIN C.) Radical change through communication in Mao's China. Honolulu, [1977]. pp. 340.

POULAIN (EDOUARD) Le mode d'industrialisation socialiste en Chine. Paris, 1977. pp. 261. *bibliog.*

— Cuba.

ALMEIDA (JUAN) Speech delivered by Major Juan Almeida, member of the political bureau of the central committee of the Communist Party of Cuba, in commemoration of May 1, international workers' day: Plaza de la Revolucion, May 1, 1967, year of heroic Viet Nam. London, Cuban Embassy, 1967. pp. 15. *(Cuba Information Bulletins. 1967. No.6)*

MATTHEWS (HERBERT LIONEL) Revolution in Cuba: an essay in understanding. New York, [1975]. pp. 468. *bibliog.*

FARBER (SAMUEL) Revolution and reaction in Cuba, 1933-1960: a political sociology from Machado to Castro. Middletown, Conn., [1976]. pp. 283. *bibliog.*

— Czechoslovakia.

HUSÁK (GUSTÁV) Projevy a stati, duben 1969 - leden 1970. Praha, 1970. pp. 403.

HUSÁK (GUSTÁV) Vybrané projevy, květen 1970 - prosinec 1971. Praha, 1972. pp. 511.

KAVAN (JAN) and DANIEL (JAN) pseud., eds. Sotsialisticheskaia oppozitsiia v Chekhoslovakii, 1973-75: podborka dokumentov; perevod [s cheshskogo] Iriny Khenkinoi. London, 1976. pp. 342. *bibliog.*

— East (Near East).

BAKHEIT (JAAFAR MUHAMMAD ALI) Communist activities in the Middle East between 1919-1927 with special reference to Egypt and the Sudan. [Khartoum], 1968, repr. 1975. pp. 34. *(Khartoum University. Institute of African and Asian Studies. African Studies Seminar Series. No. 3)*

— Egypt.

BAKHEIT (JAAFAR MUHAMMAD ALI) Communist activities in the Middle East between 1919-1927 with special reference to Egypt and the Sudan. [Khartoum], 1968, repr. 1975. pp. 34. *(Khartoum University. Institute of African and Asian Studies. African Studies Seminar Series. No. 3)*

— Europe.

BERLINGUER (ENRICO) and others. La via europea al socialismo; con contributi di N. Ceausescu [and others]; a cura di Ignazio Delogu. Roma, 1976. pp. 266.

McINNES (NEIL) Euro-Communism. Beverly Hills, [1976]. pp. 80. *bibliog. (Georgetown University. Center for Strategic and International Studies. Washington Papers. vol. 4/37)*

POSADAS (J.) Eurocommunism, the progress of Europe and socialism. [London], 1976. pp. 20. *(European Marxist Review. Publications)*

CARRILLO (SANTIAGO) Eurocomunismo y estado. Barcelona, [1977]. pp. 219.

— Europe, Eastern.

LENDVAI (PAUL) Die Grenzen des Wandels: Spielarten des Kommunismus im Donauraum. Wien, [1977]. pp. 398. *Collection of previously published articles and essays.*

STAAR (RICHARD FELIX) Communist regimes in Eastern Europe. 3rd ed. Stanford, Calif., 1977. pp. 302. *bibliog. (Stanford University. Hoover Institution on War, Revolution and Peace. Hoover Institution Publications. No. 171)*

STALINISM: essays in historical interpretation; edited by Robert C. Tucker,...with contributions by Wlodzimierz Brus [and others]. New York, 1977. pp. 332. *Based on papers presented at a conference on "Stalinism and communist political culture" held at Bellagio, Italy, July 25-31, 1975 and sponsored by the Planning Group on Comparative Communist Studies of the American Council of Learned Societies.*

— — Bibliography.

WHETTEN (LAWRENCE L.) Current research in comparative communism: an analysis and bibliographic guide to the Soviet system. New York, 1976. pp. 159.

— France.

DORIOT (JACQUES) La jeunesse communiste;...conférence faite à la première Ecole nationale du propagandiste de la jeunesse sur le but et le rôle de la jeunesse. Paris, [192-?]. pp. 39.

PARTI COMMUNISTE FRANÇAIS. Ce que veulent les communistes. Paris, [1946?]. pp. 16.

MANDEL (ERNEST) The lessons of May 1968: [and] The commune lives. London, [1971]. pp. 29.

GINSBURG (SHAUL) Raymond Lefebvre et les origines du communisme français. Paris, 1975. pp. 261. *bibliog.*

— Germany.

KONGRESS DER ARBEITER-, BAUERN- UND SOLDATENRÄTE DEUTSCHLANDS, 2., BERLIN, 1919. II. Kongress...8. bis 14. April 1919 im Herrenhaus zu Berlin: stenographisches Protokoll; Anhang: Vom 1. Rätekongress zur Nationalversammlung: die Tätigkeit des Zentralrates der sozialistischen Republik Deutschlands. Glashütten im Taunus, 1975. pp. 278, 47. *Reprint of works originally published in Berlin in 1919.*

LAUFENBERG (HEINRICH) and WOLFFHEIM (FRITZ) Moskau und die deutsche Revolution: eine kritische Erledigung der bolschewistischen Methoden. Hamburg, [1920]. pp. 48.

MUEHSAM (ERICH) Gerechtigkeit für Max Hoelz! 3rd ed. Berlin, 1976. pp. 77. *Reprint of work originally published in Berlin in 1926.*

LENZ (JOSEPH) Was wollen die Kommunisten? Berlin, 1927. pp. 61.

REMMELE (HERMANN) Sowjetstern oder Hakenkreuz: die Rettung Deutschlands aus der Youngsklaverei und Kapitalsknechtschaft. [Berlin, 1930]. pp. 24.

ROTE FAHNE, DIE: Zentralorgan der Kommunistischen Partei Deutschlands (Sektion der Kommunistischen Internationale). Die Rote Fahne: Kritik, Theorie, Feuilleton, 1918-1933; ([edited by] Manfred Brauneck). München, [1973]. pp. 513.

AUTHIER (DENIS) and BARROT (JEAN) La gauche communiste en Allemagne, 1918-1921; avec des textes de H. Laufenberg, F. Wolffheim, H. Gorter, H. Roland-Holst, A. Pannekoek; traduits par Denis Authier. Paris, 1976. pp. 390.

GERNS (WILLI) Krise der bürgerlichen Ideologie und ideologischer Kampf in der BRD. Frankfurt/Main, 1976. pp. 268.

REISSNER (LARISSA) Hamburg at the barricades, and other writings on Weimar Germany; translated from the Russian and edited by Richard Chappell. London, 1977. pp. 209.

— — Bavaria.

KONGRESS DER ARBEITER-, BAUERN- UND SOLDATENRÄTE, MÜNCHEN, 1919. Stenographischer Bericht über die Verhandlungen...vom 25. Februar bis 8. März 1919 in München; eingeleitet von Gisela Kissel und Hiltrud Witt. Glashütten im Taunus, 1974. pp. 200. *Reprint of work originally published in Munich in 1919.*

MUEHSAM (ERICH) Von Eisner bis Levliné: die Entstehung und Niederlage der bayerischen Räterepublik: ein Bericht; mit einem Vorwort von H.J. Viesel, etc. Hamburg, [1976]. pp. 90. *Reprint of work originally published in Berlin in 1929.*

— Germany, Eastern.

GELOEBNIS zur Einheit: Kundgebungen für die antifaschistisch-demokratische Einheit anlässlich des 70. Geburtstages von Wilhelm Pieck. Berlin, 1946. pp. 79.

HANKE (HELMUT) and ROSSOW (GERD) Sozialistische Kulturrevolution. Berlin, 1977. pp. 272.

HAVEMANN (ROBERT) Berliner Schriften; herausgegeben von Andreas W. Mytze. 3rd ed. Berlin, 1977. pp. 152.

LEENEN (WOLF RAINER) Zur Frage der Wachstumsorientierung der marxistisch-leninistischen Sozialpolitik in der DDR. Berlin, [1977]. pp. 225. *bibliog.*

MUECKENBERGER (ERICH) Im festen Bündnis mit der Partei und dem Lande Lenins: ausgewälte Reden. Berlin, 1977. pp. 477.

— India.

ROY (ASISH KUMAR) The spring thunder and after: a survey of the Maoist and ultra-leftist movements in India, 1962-75. Calcutta, 1975. pp. 303. *bibliog.*

— Italy.

MONTANARA (DINO) Illegal durch Italien; (autorisierte Übersetzung aus dem Italienischen von Lisa Dome). Berlin, [1932]. pp. 47.

NAPOLITANO (GIORGIO) I comunisti nella battaglia delle idee. Roma, [1975]. pp. 65. *"Relazione tenuta il 13.1.1975 alla sessione del Comitato centrale e della Commissione centrale di controllo del Partito comunista italiano".*

POLVERINI (GIORGIO) Benedetto Croce e il comunismo. Como, 1975. pp. 209.

GRAMSCI (ANTONIO) La rivoluzione italiana; introduzione e cura di Dino Ferreri. Roma, 1976. pp. 260.

CLARK (MARTIN) Antonio Gramsci and the revolution that failed. New Haven, 1977. pp. 255. *bibliog.*

— Japan.

KOBAYASHI (TAKIJI) Der 15. März 1928: eine japanische Arbeiter-Erzählung; (autorisierte Übersetzung aus dem Japanischen). Berlin, [1931]. pp. 47.

— Korea.

KONOVALOV (EVGENII ALEKSANDROVICH) and others, eds. Koreiskaia Narodno-Demokraticheskaia Respublika. Moskva, 1975. pp. 156. *(Akademiia Nauk SSSR. Institut Ekonomiki Mirovoi Sotsialisticheskoi Sistemy. Ekonomika i Politika Zarubezhnykh Stran Sotsializma)*

POLITICAL leadership in Korea; edited by Dae-Sook Suh and Chae-Jin Lee. Seattle, [1976]. pp. 272. *(Washington State University. Institute for Comparative and Foreign Area Studies. Publications on Asia. No. 27) Selected papers presented at two symposia held in Seoul during the summers of 1971 and 1972 under the auspices of the University of Washington, Seattle.*

— Mongolia.

NAMSARAI (TSOGTYN) Sotsialisticheskaia nadstroika v stranakh, minovavshikh kapitalizm: na opyte MNR. Moskva, 1976. pp. 246. *bibliog.*

— Poland.

LIPIŃSKI (EDWARD) Open letter to Comrade Edward Gierek. Warsaw, 1976. pp. 11.

NA LEWO. zeszyt nr.1. Kłamstwo, fałsz, prawda: 'nowy styl' polskiej biurokracji. n.p., [1976?]. pp. 21. *Reproduced from typescript.*

— Romania.

LEBEDEV (NIKOLAI IVANOVICH) Krakh fashizma v Rumynii. Moskva, 1976. pp. 632. *bibliog.*

— Russia.

UNITED STATES. Committee on Public Information. 1919. Die deutsch-bolschewistische Verschwörung: 70 Dokumente über die Beziehungen der Bolschewiki zur deutschen Heeresleitung, Grossindustrie und Finanz, nebst einer Anzahl photographischer Reproduktionen. Bern, 1919. pp. 123. *German translation of the Committee's War Information Series. No.20.*

HARDING (Mrs. STAN) The underworld of state;...with an introduction by Bertrand Russell. London, 1925. pp. 256.

KLOTZ (HENRY) La Russie des Soviets: faits et documents: qu'y a-t-il de vrai dans la formule: le communisme, voilà l'ennemi. Paris, 1928. pp. 189. *bibliog.*

MALEVSKII-MALEVICH (PETR NIKOLAEVICH) A new party in Russia. London, 1928. pp. 119.

KALNINS (BRUNO) Ist die Sowjetunion ein sozialistischer Staat? Wien, [1948]. pp. 45.

THAELMANN (ERNST) Geschichte und Politik: Artikel und Reden, 1925 bis 1933. Frankfurt am Main, 1974. pp. 238.

CHEKHARIN (EVGENII MIKHAILOVICH) Sovetskaia politicheskaia sistema v usloviiakh razvitogo sotsializma. Moskva, 1975. pp. 351.

DEMOKRATIIA razvitogo sotsialisticheskogo obshchestva. Moskva, 1975. pp. 296.

KALININ (MIKHAIL IVANOVICH) Stat'i i rechi, 1941-1946 gg. Moskva, 1975. pp. 672.

RABOCHII klass SSSR i ego vedushchaia rol' v stroitel'stve kommunizma. Moskva, 1975. pp. 568.

SOTSIALISTICHESKOE obshchestvo: sotsial'no-filosofskie problemy sovremennogo sovetskogo obshchestva. Moskva, 1975. pp. 343. *With English, Spanish, German and French summaries.*

DISCUSSION on socialist democracy: a Marxism Today supplement containing further contributions to a discussion on John Gollan's article "Socialist democracy: some problems". London, [1976]. pp. 34. *(Communist Party of Great Britain. Communist Party Pamphlets)*

KAS'IANENKO (VASILII IGNAT'EVICH) Razvitoi sotsializm: istoriografiia i metodologiia problemy. Moskva, 1976. pp. 270. *bibliog.*

PAKHOMOV (IURII NIKOLAEVICH) Proizvodstvennye otnosheniia razvitogo sotsializma. Kiev, 1976. pp. 338.

PERLMAN (SELIG) Selig Perlman's lectures on capitalism and socialism; [edited by] A.L. Riesch Owen. Madison, 1976. pp. 183. *bibliog.*

POLITICHESKAIA organizatsiia razvitogo sotsialisticheskogo obshchestva: pravovye problemy. Kiev, 1976. pp. 516.

SOTSIAL'NAIA struktura sotsialisticheskogo obshchestva v SSSR. Moskva, 1976. pp. 224.

SOTSIAL'NO-ekonomicheskie problemy istorii razvitogo sotsializma v SSSR. Moskva, 1976. pp. 487. *bibliog.*

SOVETY deputatov trudiashchikhsia i razvitie sotsialisticheskoi demokratii. Moskva, 1976. pp. 431.

SVERDLOV (IAKOV MIKHAILOVICH) Izbrannye proizvedeniia: stat'i, rechi, pis'ma; (sostaviteli M.M. Vasser i L.V. Ivanova). Moskva, 1976. pp. 367.

ZAKONOMERNOSTI sozdaniia material'no-tekhnicheskoi bazy kommunizma. Moskva, 1976. pp. 367.

BARTSCH (GUENTER) Trotzkismus als eigentlicher Sowjetkommunismus?: die IV. Internationale und ihre Konkurrenzverbände. Berlin, [1977]. pp. 194.

BORCKE (ASTRID VON) Die Ursprünge des Bolschewismus: die jakobinische Tradition in Russland und die Theorie der revolutionären Diktatur. München, [1977]. pp. 646. *bibliog.*

CHERKOVETS (VIKTOR NIKITICH) ed. Problemy razvitogo sotsializma v politicheskoi ekonomii, etc. Moskva, 1977. pp. 335. *(Akademiia Nauk SSSR. Problemy Sovetskoi Ekonomiki)*

EKONOMICHESKIE problemy razvitogo sotsializma i ego pererastaniia v kommunizm. Moskva, 1977. pp. 311.

MUECKENBERGER (ERICH) Im festen Bündnis mit der Partei und dem Lande Lenins: ausgewälte Reden. Berlin, 1977. pp. 477.

PROBLEMY razvitiia material'no-tekhnicheskoi bazy sotsializma. Moskva, 1977. pp. 271.

STALINISM: essays in historical interpretation; edited by Robert C. Tucker,...with contributions by Wlodzimierz Brus [and others]. New York, 1977. pp. 332. *Based on papers presented at a conference on "Stalinism and communist political culture" held at Bellagio, Italy, July 25-31, 1975 and sponsored by the Planning Group on Comparative Communist Studies of the American Council of Learned Societies.*

— — Bibliography.

GENERALSEKRETARIAT ZUM STUDIUM UND ZUR BEKÄMPFUNG DES BOLSCHEWISMUS. Führer durch die bolschewistische und antibolschewistische Literatur. London, 1975. pp. 24. *(Generalsekretariat zum Studium und zur Bekämpfung des Bolschewismus. Sammlung von Quellen zum Studium des Bolschewismus. 1. Heft) Reprint of work originally published in Berlin in 1919.*

WHETTEN (LAWRENCE L.) Current research in comparative communism: an analysis and bibliographic guide to the Soviet system. New York, 1976. pp. 159.

— — Study and teaching.

DYMSHITS (ALEKSANDR L'VOVICH) Nishcheta sovetologii i revizionizma: [sbornik statei]. Moskva, 1975. pp. 350.

— — Caucasus.

EBZEEVA (SOF'IA ESENOVNA) Stanovlenie sovetskoi natsional'noi gosudarstvennosti narodov Severnogo Kavkaza. Moskva, 1976. pp. 135.

— — Latvia.

ZILE (LIUBOV' IAKOVLEVNA) Periody i etapy stroitel'stva sotsializma i izmenenie sotsial'noi struktury obshchestva: na materialakh Latviiskoi SSR. Riga, 1975. pp. 198.

— Scandinavia.

PETERSEN (CARL HEINRICH) Fra klassekampens slagmark i Norden. [Århus], 1973. pp. 252. *bibliog. Selection of broadcasts, articles and essays.*

— Singapore.

NAIR (C.V. DEVAN) ed. Socialism that works: the Singapore way. Singapore, [1976]. pp. 267.

— Sudan.

BAKHEIT (JAAFAR MUHAMMAD ALI) Communist activities in the Middle East between 1919-1927 with special reference to Egypt and the Sudan. [Khartoum], 1968, repr. 1975. pp. 34. *(Khartoum University. Institute of African and Asian Studies. African Studies Seminar Series. No. 3)*

— Switzerland.

ENDERLI (HANS) Herunter mit der Maskee' Kampf den Schweizer Bolschewistene': ein Wort der Aufklärung und Mahnung an die schweizerische Arbeiterschaft. Zürich, 1918. pp. 31. *(Separat-Abdruck aus dem "Grütlianer")*

JOST (HANS ULRICH) Die Altkommunisten: Linksradikalismus und Sozialismus in der Schweiz, 1919 bis 1921. Frauenfeld, [1977]. pp. 232. *bibliog.*

— United Kingdom.

BRITISH AND IRISH COMMUNIST ORGANISATION. The cult of the individual: the controversy within British communism, 1956-58. Belfast, 1975. pp. 96.

WOODHOUSE (MICHAEL) and PEARCE (BRIAN LEONARD) Essays on the history of communism in Britain. London, [1975]. pp. 248. *Includes articles originally published in Fourth International and Labour Review.*

HACKNEY COMMUNIST PARTY. Hackney needs socialism. London, 1976. pp. 36.

CHALLINOR (RAYMOND) The origins of British bolshevism. London, 1977. pp. 291. *bibliogs.*

— — Scotland.

REID (JIMMY) Reflections of a Clyde-built man. London, 1976. pp. 166.

— United States.

HALL (GUS) The crisis of U.S. capitalism and the fight-back: report to the 21st Convention of the Communist Party, U.S.A. New York, 1975. pp. 93.

MYERS (CONSTANCE ASHTON) The prophet's army: Trotskyists in America, 1928-1941. Westport, Conn., 1977. pp. 281. *bibliog.*

WEISBORD (VERA BUCH) A radical life. Bloomington, Ind., [1977]. pp. 330.

— Vietnam.

DUIKER (WILLIAM J.) The Comintern and Vietnamese communism. Athens, Ohio, 1975. pp. 42. *(Ohio University. Center for International Studies. Papers in International Studies. Southeast Asia Series. No. 37)*

OGNETOV (I.A.) and others, eds. Demokraticheskaia Respublika V'etnam. Moskva, 1975. pp. 144. *(Akademiia Nauk SSSR. Institut Ekonomiki Mirovoi Sotsialisticheskoi Sistemy. Ekonomika i Politika Zarubezhnykh Stran Sotsializma).*

— — Bibliography.

PHAN (THIEN CHAU) Vietnamese communism: a research bibliography. Westport, Conn., 1975. pp. 359.

— Yugoslavia.

LAZITCH (BRANKO) Titov pokret i režim u Jugoslaviji, 1941-1946. [n.p.], 1946. pp. 219.

RADONJIĆ (RADOVAN) Sukob KPJ sa Kominformom i društveni razvoj Jugoslavije, 1948-1950. 2nd ed. Zagreb, 1976. pp. 276. *bibliog. (Zagreb. Narodno Sveučilište. Centar za Aktualni Politički Studij. Političke Teme: Biblioteka Suvremene Političke Misli)*

RUSINOW (DENNISON I.) The Yugoslav experiment, 1948-1974. London, 1977. pp. 410. *bibliog.*

COMMUNISM AND CHRISTIANITY.

RACKWITZ (ARTHUR) Der Marxismus im Lichte des Evangeliums: Untersuchungen über das Kommunistische Manifest. Berlin, 1948. pp. 23.

STEPUN (FEDOR) Der Bolschewismus und die christliche Existenz. Munchen, [1959]. pp. 298.

CHAPUIS (ROBERT) Les Chrétiens et le socialisme: témoignage et bilan. [Paris, 1976]. pp. 270.

VREE (DALE) On synthesizing Marxism and Christianity. New York, [1976]. pp. 206. *bibliog.*

COMMUNISM AND EDUCATION.

SNYDERS (GEORGES) Ecole, classe et lutte des classes: une relecture critique de Baudelot-Establet, Bourdieu-Passeron et Illich. Paris, [1976]. pp. 379.

COMMUNISM AND INTELLECTUALS.

NAPOLITANO (GIORGIO) I comunisti nella battaglia delle idee. Roma, [1975]. pp. 65. *"Relazione tenuta il 13.1.1975 alla sessione del Comitato centrale e della Commissione centrale di controllo del Partito comunista italiano".*

COMMUNISM AND ISLAM.

COMMUNISM AND ISLAM.

ASHIROV (NUGMAN) Islam i natsii. Moskva, 1975. pp. 144.

COMMUNISM AND LITERATURE.

EAGLETON (TERRY) Criticism and ideology: a study in Marxist literary theory. London, [1976]. pp. 191.

SERGE (VICTOR) pseud. [i.e. Viktor L'vovich KIBAL'CHICH] Littérature et révolution; suivi de Littérature prolétarienne?, et Une littérature prolétarienne est-elle possible?. Paris, 1976. pp. 122.

WEAPONS of criticism: marxism in America and the literary tradition; edited by Norman Rudich. Palo Alto, [1976]. pp. 389.

WILLIAMS (RAYMOND) Marxism and literature. Oxford, 1977. pp. 217. *bibliog.*

COMMUNISM AND MEDICINE.

NAVARRO (VICENTE) Social security and medicine in the USSR: a Marxist critique. Lexington, Mass., [1977]. pp. 149. *bibliog.*

COMMUNISM AND RELIGION.

REKUTS (IVAN FEODOS'EVICH) Filosofskie problemy kritiki religii v ateisticheskom nasledii A.V. Lunacharskogo. Minsk, 1976. pp. 174. *bibliog.*

— Dictionaries and encyclopedias.

KARMANNYI slovar' ateista. Moskva, 1975. pp. 287.

COMMUNISM AND THE ARTS.

ROTE FAHNE, DIE: Zentralorgan der Kommunistischen Partei Deutschlands (Sektion der Kommunistischen Internationale). Die Rote Fahne: Kritik, Theorie, Feuilleton, 1918-1933; ([edited by] Manfred Brauneck). München, [1973]. pp. 513.

DYMSHITS (ALEKSANDR L'VOVICH) Nishcheta sovetologii i revizionizma: [sbornik statei]. Moskva, 1975. pp. 350.

ISKUSSTVO i ideologicheskaia rabota partii. Moskva, 1976. pp. 351.

POSADAS (J.) Art, social relations and human fraternity; selection of articles. London, 1976. pp. 27. *(European Marxist Review. Publications)*

HANKE (HELMUT) and ROSSOW (GERD) Sozialistische Kulturrevolution. Berlin, 1977. pp. 272.

COMMUNISM AND ZIONISM.

MAIATSKII (FEODOSII SEMENOVICH) Dvazhdy obmanutye. Kishinev, 1971. pp. 112. *bibliog.*

SZAJKOWSKI (ZOSA) Jews, wars and communism. New York, 1972-74. 2 vols. *bibliogs.*

COMMUNIST AESTHETICS.

RESZLER (ANDRÉ) Le marxisme devant la culture. [Paris, 1975]. pp. 146. *bibliog.*

CASTRIS (ARCANGELO LEONE DE) Estetica e marxismo. Roma, 1976. pp. 229.

COMMUNIST COUNTRIES

— Bibliography.

SHAFFER (HARRY GEORGE) compiler. Periodicals on the socialist countries and on marxism; a new annotated index of English-language publications. [rev. ed.] New York, 1977. pp. 134, *Edition of 1971 published under title: English language periodic publications on communism.*

— Economic conditions.

BRUS (WŁODZIMIERZ) and others, eds. Ekonomia polityczna socjalizmu; praca zbiorowa...dla studentów uniwersytetów, etc. 3rd ed. Warszawa, 1967. pp. 376.

ZHAMIN (VITALII ALEKSEEVICH) ed. Strukturnye sdvigi v narodnom khoziaistve sotsialisticheskikh stran. Moskva, 1976. pp. 333. *bibliog.*

— — Mathematical models.

BULGARSKA AKADEMIIA NA NAUKITE. Ikonomicheski Institut. Mezhdunarodno Suveshtanie, 1974. Modelirovanie sotsialisticheskogo narodnogo khoziaistva: materialy mezhdunarodnogo soveshchaniia, Sofiia, 11-15 iiunia 1974 g. Sofiia, 1976. pp. 203.

— Economic integration.

KORMNOV (IURII FILIPPOVICH) and LEZNIK (A.D.) Soglasheniia o spetsializatsii i kooperatsii v proizvodstve mezhdu stranami-chlenami SEV: osnovnye elementy; obzor. Moskva, 1973. pp. 33. *bibliog.*

EKONOMICHESKOE SOTRUDNICHESTVO STRAN-CHLENOV SEV; ([pd. by] Sovet Ekonomicheskoi Vzaimopomoshchi Sekretariat [Council for Mutual Economic Assistance Secretariat]). irreg., 1975(1)- Moskva.

GORIZONTOV (BORIS BORISOVICH) Sotsialisticheskaia ekonomicheskaia integratsiia i transport. Moskva, 1975. pp. 199.

KARTSEV (VIKTOR IVANOVICH) and KOMISSAROV (ANATOLII VIKTOROVICH) SEV: sotrudnichestvo razvivaetsia. Moskva, 1975. pp. 135.

REGIONAL'NYE problemy ekonomicheskoi integratsii SSSR v sisteme stran SEV. Moskva, 1975. pp. 271.

VOPROSY razvitiia i sotrudnichestva sotsialisticheskikh stran. Moskva, 1975. pp. 194.

VOPROSY sotsial'no-ekonomicheskogo i politicheskogo razvitiia stran sotsializma. Moskva, 1975. pp. 190.

AGRARNO-promyshlennaia integratsiia stran SEV. Moskva, 1976. pp. 286.

DEGTIAR' (LIUDMILA SERAFIMOVNA) Problemy ratsional'noi zaniatosti pri sotsializme. Moskva, 1976. pp. 141.

DUDINSKII (IL'IA VLADIMIROVICH) Sotsialisticheskoe sodruzhestvo: osnovnye tendentsii razvitiia. Moskva, 1976. pp. 327.

HARKE (HELLMUT) and DISCHEREIT (MARTIN) Geographische Aspekte der sozialistischen ökonomischen Integration. Gotha, 1976. pp. 110.

KOVALEVA (M.F.) and SHEVIAKOV (F.N.) eds. Sotsialisticheskaia integratsiia: protsessrazvitii i sovershenstvovaniia. Moskva, 1976. pp. 334.

PETUSHKOV (IVAN GRIGOR'EVICH) and SHEININ (EDUARD IAKOVLEVICH) Ekonomika Kuby v sisteme mezhdunarodnogo sotsialisticheskogo razdeleniia truda. Moskva, 1976. pp. 167.

PROBLEMY teorii i praktiki razmeshcheniia proizvoditel'nykh sil SSSR. Moskva, 1976. pp. 326. *(Akademiia Nauk SSSR. Sovet po Izucheniiu Proizvoditel'nykh Sil. Problemy Sovetskoi Ekonomiki)*

SOTSIALISTICHESKAIA ekonomicheskaia integratsiia: kritika burzhuaznykh i revizionistskikh teorii. Moskva, 1976. pp. 215.

SOTSIALISTICHESKAIA ekonomicheskaia integratsiia i sotrudnichestvo s razvivaiushchimisia stranami. Moskva, 1976. pp. 233. *bibliog.*

TOKAREVA (PRASKOV'IA ALEKSEEVNA) Uchrezhdenie mezhgosudarstvennykh ekonomicheskikh organizatsii stran- chlenov SEV: pravovye voprosy. Moskva, 1976. pp. 182.

TOKAREVA (PRASKOV'IA ALEKSEEVNA) ed. Mnogostoronnee ekonomicheskoe sotrudnichestvo sotsialisticheskikh gosudarstv: dokumenty za 1972-1975 gg. Moskva, 1976. pp. 408.

VAIS (TIBERII ABRAGAMOVICH) Problemy sotrudnichestva stran SEV v ispol'zovanii trudovykh resursov. Moskva, 1976. pp. 85.

VARZIN (NIKOLAI PROKHOROVICH) Integratsiia i rost proizvoditel'nosti truda v stranakh SEV. Moskva, 1976. pp. 175.

ZHAMIN (VITALII ALEKSEEVICH) ed. Strukturnye sdvigi v narodnom khoziaistve sotsialisticheskikh stran. Moskva, 1976. pp. 333. *bibliog.*

SOZIALISTISCHE ökonomische Integration: Grundlagen und Aufgaben; (Autorenkollektiv: Hans-Georg Haupt [and others]). Berlin, 1977. pp. 292.

— Economic policy.

SOROKIN (GENNADII MIKHAILOVICH) Problemy vosproizvodstva i planirovaniia sotsialisticheskoi ekonomiki; (stat'i, napisannye v techenie 1960-1975 gg.). Moskva, 1976. pp. 559. *(Akademiia Nauk SSSR. Problemy Sovetskoi Ekonomiki)*

WILCZYNSKI (JOZEF) The economics of socialism: principles governing the operation of the centrally planned economies in the USSR and Eastern Europe under the new system. 3rd ed. London, [1977]. pp. 235. *bibliog.*

— Foreign economic relations.

PIONTEK (EUGENIUSZ) Udzial państw socjalistycznych w GATT. Warszawa, 1975. pp. 214. *bibliog.*

— — Treaties.

TOKAREVA (PRASKOV'IA ALEKSEEVNA) ed. Mnogostoronnee ekonomicheskoe sotrudnichestvo sotsialisticheskikh gosudarstv: dokumenty za 1972-1975 gg. Moskva, 1976. pp. 408.

— Foreign relations.

LABETSKII (O.B.) ed. Sotsialisticheskie mezhdunarodnye otnosheniia i ikh kritiki. Moskva, 1975. pp. 205.

MARTIN (ALEXANDER) of the Institut für Internationale Politik und Wirtschaft, ed. Sicherheit und friedliche Zusammenarbeit in Europa: Dokumente 1972-1975. Berlin, 1976. pp. 614.

LOEWENTHAL (RICHARD) Model or ally?: the communist powers and the developing countries. New York, 1977. pp. 400.

— — United States.

BELL (CORAL) The diplomacy of detente: the Kissinger era. London, 1977. pp. 278. *bibliog.*

— — Yugoslavia.

O neistinitim i nepravednim optužbama protiv KPJ: izabrani materijali. Beograd, 1948. pp. 371. *In Cyrillic.*

— Industries.

BUTAKOV (DANIIL DMITRIEVICH) Kredit i intensifikatsiia proizvodstva v stranakh SEV. Moskva, 1976. pp. 207.

— Politics and government.

MARKOVIĆ (MIHAILO) On the legal institutions of socialist democracy. Nottingham, [1976]. pp. 23. *(Spokesman, The. Pamphlets. No. 55)*

POSADAS (J.) The process of partial regeneration in the workers' states; selection of articles 1975. [London], 1976. pp. 20. *(European Marxist Review. Publications)*

POLITICAL culture and political change in communist states; edited by Archie Brown and Jack Gray. London, 1977. pp. 286. *Papers presented at a conference held in St. Antony's College, Oxford, 1975.*

— Social conditions.

MIKUL'SKII (KONSTANTIN IVANOVICH) ed. Sotsializm i narodnoe blagosostoianie. Moskva, 1976. pp. 446.

SOCIAL consequences of modernization in communist societies; edited by Mark G. Field. Baltimore, [1976]. pp. 277. *Papers presented at a symposium in Salzburg in September 1972, sponsored by the American Council of Learned Societies, under the general auspices of its Planning Group on Comparative Communist Studies.*

TODD (EMMANUEL) La chute finale: essai sur la décomposition de la sphère soviétique. Paris, 1976. pp. 324.

COMMUNIST EDUCATION.

SEROVA (IRINA IVANOVNA) Sila, splachivaiushchaia voedino: internatsional'noe vospitanie trudiashchikhsia v razvitom sotsialisticheskom obshchestve. Minsk, 1975. pp. 262. *bibliog.*

AKADEMIIA OBSHCHESTVENNYKH NAUK. Kafedra Teorii i Metodov Ideologicheskoi Raboty. Voprosy Teorii i Metodov Ideologicheskoi Raboty. vyp.6. Partiinoe rukovodstvo ideologicheskoi rabotoi. Moskva, 1976. pp. 311.

— Czechoslovakia.

COMITE CENTRAL DE LA JEUNESSE SLOVAQUE A L'ETRANGER. Demande du Comité...concernant les actes de violence dans l'éducation de la jeunesse slovaque en Tchéco-Slovaquie adressée à l'Organisation Educative, Scientifique et Culturelle des Nations-Unies. Buenos Aires, 1951. pp. (4).

— Romania.

CONGRESUL EDUCAȚIEI POLITICE ȘI AL CULTURII SOCIALISTE, BUCHAREST, 1976. Congresul educației politice și al culturii socialiste, 2-4 iunie 1976. București, 1976. pp. 445.

CONGRESUL EDUCAȚIEI POLITICE ȘI AL CULTURII SOCIALISTE, BUCHAREST, 1976. Der Kongress der Politischen Erziehung und Sozialistischen Kultur, 2.-4. Juni 1976. Bukarest, 1976. pp. 476.

— Russia.

OPYT i metodika perepodgotovki partiinykh i sovetskikh kadrov. Moskva, 1975. pp. 206. *bibliog.*

POZDNIAKOV (PETR VLADIMIROVICH) and others. Effektivnost' ideino-vospitatel'noi raboty: usloviia, faktory, kriterii. Moskva, 1975. pp. 215.

REPA (FEDOR PROKOF'EVICH) Formirovanie moral'no-politicheskikh idealov molodezhi na obraze V.I. Lenina. Dushanbe, 1975. pp. 254.

SUVENIROV (OLEG FEDOTOVICH) Kommunisticheskaia partiia - organizator politicheskogo vospitaniia Krasnoi Armii i Flota, 1921-1928. Moskva, 1976. pp. 291. *bibliog.*

— — Uzbekistan.

ESIN (ANATOLII FEDOROVICH) Radio i televidenie Uzbekistana: rost, dostizheniia, problemy. Tashkent, 1975. pp. 160.

— — White Russia.

LUKASHEV (SERGEI AFANAS'EVICH) Massovo-politicheskaia rabota partiinykh organizatsii sredi trudiashchikhsia Belorussii, 1946-1958 gg.; redaktor...I.E. Marchenko. Minsk, 1976. pp. 182. *bibliog.*

COMMUNIST ETHICS.

SCHLETTE (HEINZ ROBERT) Sowjethumanismus: Prämissen und Maximen kommunistischer Pädagogik. München, [1960]. pp. 136.

REPA (FEDOR PROKOF'EVICH) Formirovanie moral'no-politicheskikh idealov molodezhi na obraze V.I. Lenina. Dushanbe, 1975. pp. 254.

MORAL' razvitogo sotsializma: aktual'nye problemy teorii. Moskva, 1976. pp. 287.

COMMUNIST PARTIES.

BERLINGUER (ENRICO) and others. La via europea al socialismo; con contributi di N. Ceausescu [and others]; a cura di Ignazio Delogu. Roma, 1976. pp. 266.

RATLIFF (WILLIAM E.) Castroism and communism in Latin America, 1959-1976: the varieties of Marxist-Leninist experience. Stanford, Calif., 1976. pp. 240. *(American Enterprise Institute for Public Policy Research and Stanford University. Hoover Institution on War, Revolution and Peace. AEI-Hoover Policy Studies. 19)*

— Congresses.

ZAKARIADZE (NODAR EZHIFANESOVICH) Razvitie leninskoi strategii i taktiki v dokumentakh i materialakh Soveshchaniia kommunisticheskikh i rabochikh partii 1969 goda. Tbilisi, 1975. pp. 144.

COMMUNIST PARTY

— Algeria.

SIVAN (EMMANUEL) Communisme et nationalisme en Algérie, 1920-1962. [Paris, 1976]. pp. 262. *(Fondation Nationale des Sciences Politiques. Travaux et Recherches de Science Politique. 41)*

— Argentine Republic.

PARTIDO COMUNISTA DE LA ARGENTINA. Comite Central. Resoluciones y declaraciones del CC del Partido Comunista de la Argentina, 1973. Buenos Aires, 1974. pp. 179.

— Austria.

PROGRAMME der österreichischen revolutionären Arbeiterparteien, 1888-1946. Wien, 1976. pp. 61. *bibliog.*

— Bulgaria — Congresses.

BULGARSKA KOMUNISTICHESKA PARTIIA. Kongres, 11-i, 1976. Edinadeseti kongres na Bulgarskata komunisticheska partiia, 29 mart - 2 april 1976 g.: stenografski protokol. Sofiia, 1976. pp. 844.

— Canada.

KASHTAN (WILLIAM) Toward socialism:...selected writings, 1966-1976. Toronto, 1976. pp. 372.

— China.

KUL'PIN (EDUARD SAL'MANOVICH) Tekhniko-ekonomicheskaia politika rukovodstva KNR i rabochii klass Kitaia. Moskva, 1975. pp. 199. *bibliog.*

DOMES (JUERGEN) China after the Cultural Revolution: politics between two party congresses; with a contribution by Marie-Luise Näth; translated from the German by Annette Berg and David Goodman. London, [1976]. pp. 283.

GUILLERMAZ (JACQUES) The Chinese Communist Party in power, 1949-1976;... translated by Anne Destenay. Boulder, Colo., 1976. pp. 614. *bibliog.*

— — Bibliography.

STARR (JOHN BRYAN) and DYER (NANCY ANNE) compilers. Post-liberation works of Mao Zedong: a bibliography and index. Berkeley, Calif., [1976]. pp. 222.

— Czechoslovakia.

INSTITUT FÜR MARXISMUS-LENINISMUS (BERLIN). Schon damals kämpften wir gemeinsam: Erinnerungen deutscher und tschechoslowakischer Antifaschisten an ihre illegale Grenzarbeit, 1933 bis 1938; (zusammengestellt und bearbeitet von Ernst Krüger und Gertrud Glondajewski). Berlin, 1961. pp. 136.

— Denmark.

EMANUEL (POUL) DKP: organisation og rolle. [Copenhagen], 1974. pp. 84.

— France.

PARTI COMMUNISTE FRANÇAIS. Comité Central. Statuts du Parti Communiste Français: proposition de modifications. [Paris, 193-]. pp. 18.

PARTI COMMUNISTE FRANÇAIS. Commerçants, artisans: les affaires ne vont pas: comment en sortir? Paris, [1951]. pp. 22.

SERVIN (MARCEL) Le Parti Communiste et la lutte des femmes de France pour la paix, l'indépendance nationale et le progrès social: rapport aux journées nationales des 2 et 3 février 1957 à Montreuil. Paris, 1957. pp. 31.

PARTI COMMUNISTE FRANÇAIS. Pour la paix et la sécurité européenne: documents de la conférence des partis communistes et ouvriers d'Europe, Karlovy-Vary, 24-26 avril, 1967. [Paris, 1967]. pp. 40.

MANDEL (ERNEST) The lessons of May 1968: [and] The commune lives. London, [1971]. pp. 29.

FAJON (ETIENNE) L'union est un combat: textes et documents de M. Thorez, W. Rochet, G. Marchais. Paris, [1975]. pp. 127.

Les PRINCIPES de la politique du Parti communiste français. Paris, [1975]. pp. 127.

BADIE (BERTRAND) Stratégie de la grève. Paris, [1976]. pp. 263. *bibliog. (Fondation Nationale des Sciences Politiques. Travaux et Recherches de Science Politique. 40)*

FAJON (ETIENNE) Ma vie s'appelle liberté. Paris, [1976]. pp. 299.

ROCHET (WALDECK) Ecrits politiques, 1956-1969. Paris, [1976]. pp. 303.

VALIER (JACQUES) Le Parti communiste français et le capitalisme monopoliste d'état. Paris, 1976. pp. 233.

— — Congresses.

PARTI COMMUNISTE FRANÇAIS. Congrès, 22e, 1976. Le socialisme pour la France. Paris, 1976. pp. 221. *Contains the report of the Central Committee and the document adopted by the 22nd congress.*

— Germany.

LENZ (JOSEPH) Was wollen die Kommunisten? Berlin, 1927. pp. 61.

KOMMUNISTISCHE PARTEI DEUTSCHLANDS. Bezirk Grossthüringen. Bauer, wo steht dein Feind?. [Jena?, 1928?]. pp. 24.

KOMMUNISTISCHE PARTEI DEUTSCHLANDS. Zentralkomitee. Richtlinien der KPD zur Wehrfrage. [Berlin?], 1929. pp. 14.

KOMMUNISTISCHE PARTEI DEUTSCHLANDS. Delegierten-Konferenz, Solingen, 1949. Unser Kampf um die nationale Unabhängigkeit: Delegierten-Konferenz...Solingen, 5./6. März 1949. [Frankfurt/Main?, 1949]. pp. 32.

REIMANN (MAX) Die deutsche Nation duldet kein System der Knechtschaft: Erklärung des 1. Vorsitzenden der Kommunistischen Partei Deutschlands...am 26.11.1951, etc. n.p., [1951?]. pp. 8.

KOMMUNISTISCHE PARTEI DEUTSCHLANDS. Zentralkomitee. Das Schandurteil von Karlsruhe: ein Entscheid gegen Frieden, Freiheit, Einheit und Recht; Erwiderung auf die Begründung des Verbots der KPD durch das Bundesverfassungsgericht vom 17. August 1956. Berlin, 1957. pp. 120.

INSTITUT FÜR MARXISMUS-LENINISMUS (BERLIN). Schon damals kämpften wir gemeinsam: Erinnerungen deutscher und tschechoslowakischer Antifaschisten an ihre illegale Grenzarbeit, 1933 bis 1938; (zusammengestellt und bearbeitet von Ernst Krüger und Gertrud Glondajewski). Berlin, 1961. pp. 136.

BARTEL (NORBERT) and WALENDY (UDO) Selbstmord einer Demokratie: Identität von KPD und DKP. Preussisch Oldendorf, [1974]. pp. 119. *bibliog.*

THAELMANN (ERNST) Geschichte und Politik: Artikel und Reden, 1925 bis 1933. Frankfurt am Main, 1974. pp. 238.

INSTITUT FÜR MARXISTISCHE STUDIEN UND FORSCHUNGEN. Zur Aktionseinheitspolitik der KPD, 1919-1946: Dokumente. Frankfurt am Main, 1976. pp. 160. *(Neudrucke zur Sozialistischen Theorie und Gewerkschaftspraxis. Band 8)*

DAHLEM (FRANZ) Am Vorabend des zweiten Weltkrieges:...Erinnerungen. Berlin, 1977 in progress.

IM Kampf bewährt: Erinnerungen deutscher Genossen an den antifaschistischen Widerstand von 1933 bis 1945; eingeleitet und zusammengestellt von Heinz Vosske. 2nd ed. Berlin, 1977. pp. 616.

LEVINE (ROSA) Inside German communism: memoirs of party life in the Weimar Republic; edited and introduced by David Zane Mairowitz. London, 1977. pp. 222.

DEUTSCHE KOMMUNISTISCHE PARTEI. Parteitag. Protokoll. bien., 1969- v.p.

KOMMUNISTISCHE PARTEI DEUTSCHLANDS. Parteikonferenz, Kuntsevo, 1935. Die Brüsseler Konferenz der KPD, 3.-15. Oktober 1935; [held at Kuntsevo near Moscow, called Brüsseler Konferenz for security reasons]; herausgegeben und eingeleitet von Klaus Mammach. Berlin, 1975. pp. 621.

See also KOMMUNISTISCHE ARBEITER-PARTEI DEUTSCHLANDS.

— Germany, Eastern.

HORN (WERNER) Der Kampf der SED um den Aufbau der Grundlagen des Sozialismus in der DDR und um die Herstellung der Einheit Deutschlands als friedliebender, demokratischer Staat, 1952 bis 1955. Berlin, 1960. pp. 110. (Berlin. Parteihochschule Karl Marx. Lektionen)

Die PARTEI vertraut der Jugend: zur Verwirklichung des Kommuniqués des Politbüros des ZK der SED zu Problemen der Jugend; [by Kurt Bürger and others], etc. Berlin, 1962. pp. 92. bibliog. (Sozialistische Einheitspartei Deutschlands. Der Parteiarbeiter. Heft 10)

INSTITUT FÜR MARXISMUS-LENINISMUS (BERLIN). 20 Jahre SED: Zeittafel wichtiger Beratungen und Dokumente; (Redaktion: W. Otto, G. Rossmann). Berlin, 1966. pp. 173. bibliog.

NEUMANN (ALFRED) of the Ministerrat der DDR. Vertrauen in die Kraft der Arbeiterklasse: ausgewählte Reden. Berlin, 1975. pp. 462.

SCHWARZENBACH (RUDOLF) Die Kaderpolitik der SED in der Staatsverwaltung: ein Beitrag zur Entwicklung der Verhältnisses von Partei und Staat in der DDR, 1945-1975. Köln, [1976]. pp. 245. bibliog.

Die VEREINIGUNG von KPD und SPD zur Sozialistischen Einheitspartei Deutschlands in Bildern und Dokumenten; (Herausgeberkollektiv: Günter Benser, Leiter; Kapitelautoren: Günter Benser [and others]). Berlin, 1976. pp. 320.

HONECKER (ERICH) Zur Jugendpolitik der SED: Reden und Aufsätze von 1945 bis zur Gegenwart. Berlin, [1977]. pp. 644.

MUECKENBERGER (ERICH) Im festen Bündnis mit der Partei und dem Lande Lenins: ausgewälte Reden. Berlin, 1977. pp. 477.

— India.

GRAFF (VIOLETTE) Les partis communistes indiens. [Paris, 1974]. pp. 334. (Fondation Nationale des Sciences Politiques. Travaux et Recherches de Science Politique. 30)

— Italy.

CORVISIERI (SILVERIO) Resistenza e democrazia. Milano, [1976]. pp. 170.

MAMMARELLA (GIUSEPPE) Il Partito Communista Italiano, 1945/1975: dalla Liberazione al compromesso storico. 2nd ed. Firenze, [1976]. pp. 286.

NAPOLITANO (GIORGIO) La politique du Parti communiste italien: entretien avec Eric J. Hobsbawm; traduit de l'italien par Claudine Ewenczyk et Jean Rony. Paris, [1976]. pp. 155.

PADOVANI (MARCELLE) La longue marche: le Parti communiste italien. [Paris, 1976]. pp. 270.

— Mexico.

PARTIDO COMUNISTA MEXICANO. Partido Comunista Mexicano, 1967-1972. Mexico, 1973. pp. 523.

— Poland.

KRZEMIEŃ (LESZEK) Przeciwko ideologicznemu rozbrajaniu partii: o niektórych problemach rewizjonizmu na tle pewnych publikacji prasowych w Polsce w latach 1956-57. 2nd ed. Warszawa, 1959. pp. 139.

CZAJKA (STANISŁAW) ed. Nauki społeczne po XVI Plenum KC PZPR. Warszawa, 1976. pp. 272.

RATYŃSKI (WŁADYSŁAW) Partia i związki zawodowe w Polsce Ludowej. Warszawa, 1977. pp. 410.

— — Congresses.

POLSKA ZJEDNOCZONA PARTIA ROBOTNICZA. Zjazd, 4., 1964. IV Zjazd Polskiej Zjednoczonej Partii Robotniczej: stenogram; Warszawa, 15-20. VI. 1964 r. Warszawa, 1964. pp. 989.

POLSKA ZJEDNOCZONA PARTIA ROBOTNICZA. Zjazd, 5., 1968. V Zjazd Polskiej Zjednoczonej Partii Robotniczej: stenogram; Warszawa 11-16. XI. 1968 r. Warszawa, 1969. pp. 1015.

— Portugal.

CUNHAL (ALVARO) Portugal: l'aube de la liberté; textes choisis, présentés et traduits sous la direction de Pierre Gilhodes. Paris, [1975]. pp. 249.

— Russia.

BARYSHNIKOV (NIKOLAI NIKOLAEVICH) and MARTYNOV (BORIS MAKAROVICH) Osnovnye napravleniia ekonomicheskoi politiki partii. Moskva, 1972. pp. 126.

PROBLEMY istoriografii i istochnikovedeniia istorii KPSS. vyp.2. Leningrad, 1973. pp. 204.

ROMANOV (LEONID MIKHAILOVICH) Murmanskaia oblastnaia partiinaia organizatsiia v period perestroiki narodnogo khoziaistva v 1941-1942 gg. Murmansk, 1973. pp. 46.

AKADEMIIA OBSHCHESTVENNYKH NAUK. Kafedra Partiinogo Stroitel'stva. Voprosy Teorii i Praktiki Partiinogo Stroitel'stva. [vyp.1] Partiinoe rukovodstvo ekonomikoi. Moskva, 1974. pp. 287.

MASLOV (NIKOLAI NIKOLAEVICH) and STEPANOV (ZAKHARII VASIL'EVICH) Ocherki istochnikovedeniia i istoriografii istorii KPSS. Leningrad, 1974. pp. 166. bibliog.

NIKIFOROV (IURII NIKIFOROVICH) Shagi neftekhimii respubliki: istoriko-partiinyi ocherk. Ufa, 1974. pp. 215.

GOR'KOVSKAIA partiinaia organizatsiia v gody Velikoi Otechestvennoi voiny, 1941-1945: sbornik dokumentov i materialov. Gor'kii, 1975. pp. 359.

GORNO-Altaiskaia oblastnaia organizatsiia KPSS v tsifrakh. Gorno-Altaisk, 1975. pp. 118.

ISTORICHESKII opyt bor'by KPSS protiv trotskizma. Moskva, 1975. pp. 622. Based upon BOR'BA partii bol'shevikov protiv trotskizma, 1903 - fevral' 1917 g.(1968) and BOR'BA partii bol'shevikov protiv trotskizma v posleoktiabr'skii period (1969).

IVANIDZE (KOBA MELKHISEDEKOVICH) Slavnye stranitsy bor'by i pobed: istoriia deiatel'nosti Kavkazskogo kraevogo komiteta RKP(b), 1917-1920 gody. Tbilisi, 1975. pp. 351.

KRYTYKA burzhuazno-natsionalistychnykh ta revizionists'kykh perekruchen' istorii KPRS. Kyïv, 1975. pp. 351. bibliog.

KURGANSKAIA partiinaia organizatsiia v Velikoi Otechestvennoi voine, 1941-1945: dokumenty i materialy. Cheliabinsk, 1975. pp. 355.

LEONOV (PAVEL ARTEMOVICH) Ocherk istorii Sakhalinskoi organizatsii KPSS. Iuzhno-Sakhalinsk, 1975. pp. 311. bibliog.

OCHERKI istorii Tuvinskoi organizatsii KPSS. Kyzyl, 1975. pp. 405.

PRUSANOV (IVAN PETROVICH) Razvitie partii v protsesse stroitel'stva kommunizma, etc. Moskva, 1975. pp. 208.

ROGOV (ANATOLII IL'ICH) Rukovodstvo KPSS ekonomikoi zrelogo sotsializma. Moskva, 1975. pp. 384.

UCHENYE ZAPISKI KAFEDR OBSHCHESTVENNYKH NAUK VUZOV LENINGRADA. Istoriia KPSS. vyp.15. Ispytannyi avangard mass. Leningrad, 1975. pp. 199.

VSESOIUZNAIA NAUCHNO-TEORETICHESKAIA KONFERENTSIIA, POSVIASHCHENNAIA 10-LETIIU MARTOVSKOGO PLENUMA TSK KPSS, 1975. Problemy agrarnoi politiki KPSS na sovremennom etape: materialy Vsesoiuznoi nauchno-teoreticheskoi konferentsii, posviashchennoi 10- letiiu martovskogo Plenuma TsK KPSS, 24-26 marta 1975 g. Moskva, 1975. 2 vols.

AGRARNAIA politika KPSS v usloviiakh razvitogo sotsializma. Moskva, 1976. pp. 336.

ANIKEEV (VASILII VASIL'EVICH) Deiatel'nost' TsK RKP(b) v 1918-1919 godakh: khronika sobytii; 1918 god, noiabr', dekabr', 1919 god, ianvar'... iiul'. Moskva, 1976. pp. 582.

DMITRENKO (SERGEI LEONIDOVICH) Bor'ba KPSS za edinstvo svoikh riadov, oktiabr' 1917-1937. Moskva, 1976. pp. 320.

The DYNAMICS of Soviet politics. Cambridge, Mass., 1976. pp. 427. (Harvard University. Russian Research Center. Studies. 76)

ISTORIIA Kommunisticheskoi partii Sovetskogo Soiuza: atlas. Moskva, 1976. pp. 128.

METODOLOGICHESKIE problemy istoriko-partiinoi nauki. Kiev, 1976. pp. 255.

MEZHDUNARODNAIA politika KPSS i vneshnie funktsii Sovetskogo gosudarstva. Moskva, 1976. pp. 160.

NA puti k razvitomu sotsializmu: KPSS v bor'be za uprochenie i razvitie sotsializma v Srednei Azii i Kazakhstane, 1938-1958. Tashkent, 1976. pp. 367. bibliog.

RABINOWITCH (ALEXANDER) The Bolsheviks come to power: the revolution of 1917 in Petrograd. New York, [1976]. pp. 393. bibliog.

RABOCHII klass - vedushchaia sila Oktiabr'skoi sotsialisticheskoi revoliutsii: sbornik statei. Moskva, 1976. pp. 414.

— — Congresses.

KOMMUNISTICHESKAIA PARTIIA SOVETSKOGO SOIUZA. S"ezd, 25-yi, 1976. XXV s"ezd Kommunisticheskoi partii Sovetskogo Soiuza, 24 fevralia - 5 marta 1976 goda: stenograficheskii otchet. Moskva, 1976. 3 vols.

KOMMUNISTICHESKAIA PARTIIA SOVETSKOGO SOIUZA. S"ezd, 25-yi, 1976. Our friends speak: greetings to the 25th CPSU Congress. Moscow, 1976. pp. 368.

— — Party work.

POLITICHESKAIA informatsiia: nauchnye osnovy i metody politicheskoi informatsii naseleniia v sovremennykh usloviiakh. Sverdlovsk, 1968. pp. 172.

LOSEV (ALEKSANDR VISSARIONOVICH) and BURAKOV (MITROFAN EGOROVICH) Sovershenstvovanie form i metodov partiinoi raboty na sele. Voronezh, 1975. pp. 212.

OPYT i metodika perepodgotovki partiinykh i sovetskikh kadrov. Moskva, 1975. pp. 206. bibliog.

POZDNIAKOV (PETR VLADIMIROVICH) and others. Effektivnost' ideino-vospitatel'noi raboty: usloviia, faktory, kriterii. Moskva, 1975. pp. 215.

SHILKO (KIRILL PAVLOVICH) Ideologicheskaia rabota Kommunisticheskoi partii v pervye gody Sovetskoi vlasti, oktiabr' 1917 - mart 1919 g. Minsk, 1975. pp. 200.

AKADEMIIA OBSHCHESTVENNYKH NAUK. Kafedra Teorii i Metodov Ideologicheskoi Raboty. Voprosy Teorii i Metodov Ideologicheskoi Raboty. vyp.6. Partiinoe rukovodstvo ideologicheskoi rabotoi. Moskva, 1976. pp. 311.

ISKUSSTVO i ideologicheskaia rabota partii. Moskva, 1976. pp. 351.

NOVOE v partiinoi rabote. [vyp.6]. Moskva, 1976. pp. 331.

SUVENIROV (OLEG FEDOTOVICH) Kommunisticheskaia partiia - organizator politicheskogo vospitaniia Krasnoi Armii i Flota, 1921-1928. Moskva, 1976. pp. 291. bibliog.

VOPROSY raboty KPSS s kadrami na sovremennom etape. Moskva, 1976. pp. 340.

— — Azerbaijan — Congresses.

ALIEV (GEIDER ALIRZA) Otchetnyi doklad Tsentral'nogo Komiteta Kompartii Azerbaidzhana XXIX s"ezdu Kommunisticheskoi partii Azerbaidzhana, 28 ianvaria 1976 goda. Baku, 1976. pp. 101.

— — Georgia — Congresses.

KOMMUNISTICHESKAIA PARTIIA GRUZII. Kommunisticheskaia partiia Gruzii v rezoliutsiiakh i resheniiakh s"ezdov, konferentsii i plenumov TsK, 1920-1976. Tbilisi, 1976 in progress.

— — — Party work.

GUKASIAN (A.R.) Deiatel'nost' Kompartii Gruzii po podgotovke rukovodiashchikh kadrov, 1921-1932 gg. Tbilisi, 1975. pp. 197.

— — Latvia.

BERKOVICH (BORIS TSODIKOVICH) V bor'be s "levoi" frazoi: iz opyta bor'by KPL protiv "levogo" sektantstva i doktrinerstva, 1930-1940. Riga, 1976. pp. 171. bibliog.

— — Lithuania — Congresses.

KOMMUNISTICHESKAIA PARTIIA LITVY. S"ezd, 17-yi, 1976. Materialy XVII s"ezda Kommunisticheskoi partii Litvy. Vil'nius, 1976. pp. 196.

— — Moldavian Republic.

BIBILEISHVILI (N.K.) and others, eds. Rost i organizatsionnoe ukreplenie Kommunisticheskoi partii Moldavii, 1924-1974: sbornik dokumentov i materialov. Kishinev, 1976. pp. 360.

— — — Bibliography.

TODRINA (T.) and others, compilers. 50 let MSSR i Kompartii Moldavii: metodicheskie i bibliograficheskie materialy v pomoshch' bibliotekam. Kishinev, 1974. pp. 58. In Russian and Moldavian.

— — Tajikistan.

ABDUNAZAROV (ABDUALIM) Partiinoe rukovodstvo Sovetami: (iz opyta partiinoi organizatsii Tadzhikistana po povysheniiu roli Sovetov v usloviiakh razvitogo sotsializma). Dushanbe, 1975. pp. 150.

MIRONOV (NIKOLAI IVANOVICH) Bor'ba kompartii Tadzhikistana za melioratsiiu i mekhanizatsiiu v khlopkovodstve, 1945-1965 gg. Dushanbe, 1975. pp. 228.

— — Turkestan.

NURULLIN (RUSTAM ABDURAKHIMOVICH) Bor'ba Kompartii Turkestana za osushchestvlenie politiki "voennogo kommunizma". Tashkent, 1975. pp. 143.

— — Ukraine.

KOMMUNISTICHESKAIA PARTIIA UKRAINY. Komunistychna partiia Ukraïny - boiovyi zahin KPRS. Kyïv, 1976. pp. 143.

PARTIINE kerivnytstvo rozvytkom promyslovosti Ukraïny, 1917- 1975. Kyïv, 1976. pp. 343.

— — — Congresses.

KOMMUNISTICHESKAIA PARTIIA UKRAINY. S"ezd, 25-yi, 1971. Materialy XXV z"izdu Komunistychnoï partiï Ukraïny. Kyïv, 1976. pp. 132.

— — Ukraine, Western.

RADZIEJOWSKI (JANUSZ) Komunistyczna Partia Zachodniej Ukrainy, 1919-1929: węzłowe problemy ideologiczne. Kraków, 1976. pp. 267. bibliog.

— — Uzbekistan.

GENTSHKE (LEV VLADIMIROVICH) Kompartiia i rabochii klass Uzbekistana v bor'be za sotsializm, 1926-1932 gg. Tashkent, 1973. pp. 230.

— — White Russia.

VOPROSY istorii KPSS: nekotorye voprosy organizatorskoi i ideologicheskoi deiatel'nosti KPSS; mezhvedomstvennyi sbornik 7. Minsk, 1976. pp. 264.

— — — Party work.

LUKASHEV (SERGEI AFANAS'EVICH) Massovo-politicheskaia rabota partiinykh organizatsii sredi trudiashchikhsia Belorussii, 1946-1958 gg.; redaktor...I.E. Marchenko. Minsk, 1976. pp. 182. bibliog.

— Spain.

CARRILLO (SANTIAGO) Hacia el post-franquismo; [informe del Comite Ejecutivo al Pleno ampliado del Comite Central del Partido Comunista de España]. Paris, [1974 repr. 1975]. pp. 115.

DIAZ (JOSE) Tres años de lucha: por el Frente Popular; por la libertad; por la independencia de España. Paris, 1970 [or rather 1974]. pp. 631. Reprint of a book of articles and speeches, originally written 1935-1938, with addition of a prologue by Santiago Carrillo.

CARRILLO (SANTIAGO) Mañana España. Paris, [1975]. pp. 269. Cover sub-title: Conversaciones con Régis Debray y Max Gallo.

RUIZ AYUCAR (ANGEL) El Partido Comunista: treinta y siete años de clandestinidad. Madrid, [1976]. pp. 477. bibliog.

— Sweden.

JOSEPHSON (ERLAND F.) SKP och Komintern, 1921-1924: motsättningarna inom Sveriges Kommunistiska Parti och des relationer till den Kommunistiska Internationalen. Uppsala, 1976. pp. 362. bibliog. (Uppsala. Universitet. Historiska Institutionen. Studia Historica Upsaliensia. 84) With English summary.

— United Kingdom.

WOODHOUSE (MICHAEL) and PEARCE (BRIAN LEONARD) Essays on the history of communism in Britain. London, [1975]. pp. 248. Includes articles originally published in Fourth International and Labour Review.

BAIKOVA (ANNA NIKOLAEVNA) Britanskie profsoiuzy i klassovaia bor'ba, vtoraia polovina 60-kh - nachalo 70-kh godov. Moskva, 1976. pp. 375.

HERRMANN (PAUL WOLFGANG) Die Communist Party of Great Britain: Untersuchungen zur geschichtlichen Entwicklung, Organisation, Ideologie und Politik der CPGB von 1920-1970. Meisenheim am Glan, 1976. pp. 448. bibliog.

REID (JIMMY) Reflections of a Clyde-built man. London, 1976. pp. 166.

REVOLUTIONARY COMMUNIST GROUP. Ireland: British labour and British imperialism. London, [1976]. pp. 33. bibliog.

— Yugoslavia.

DOLANC (STANE) Der Bund Kommunisten Jugoslawiens im Selbstverwaltungssystem ([translated from the Serbo-Croat by] Anica Perić- Günther [and others]). Beograd, [1975]. pp. 304.

DOLANC (STANE) Savez komunista Jugoslavije i socijalističko samoupravljanje: [collected speeches, articles, etc.]. Beograd, 1975. pp. 369.

HABERL (OTHMAR NIKOLA) Parteiorganisation und nationale Frage in Jugoslavien. Berlin, 1976. pp. 242. bibliog. (Berlin. Freie Universität. Osteuropa-Institut. Philosophische und Soziologische Veröffentlichungen. Band 13)

COMMUNIST PARTY OF INDIA (MARXIST).

NAMBOODIRIPAD (E.M.S.) Anti-communist gang-up in Kerala: betrayers of U[nited] F[ront] set up anti-people govt. Calcutta, 1970. pp. 75.

COMMUNIST REVISIONISM.

KRZEMIEŃ (LESZEK) Przeciwko ideologicznemu rozbrajaniu partii: o niektórych problemach rewizjonizmu na tle pewnych publikacji prasowych w Polsce w latach 1956-57. 2nd ed. Warszawa, 1959. pp. 139.

DYMSHITS (ALEKSANDR L'VOVICH) Nishcheta sovetologii i revizionizma: [sbornik statei]. Moskva, 1975. pp. 350.

KRYTYKA burzhuazno-natsionalistychnykh ta revizionists'kykh perekruchen' istoriï KPRS. Kyïv, 1975. pp. 351. bibliog.

MILHAU (JACQUES) Lenin und der Revisionismus in der Philosophie; [and] Zeitgemässe Bemerkungen zu Lenins Feststellung, dass der Neukantianismus die philosophische Grundlage des Revisionismus sei; ([by] Robert Steigerwald). Frankfurt/Main, 1975. pp. 98.

ZAGARI (EUGENIO) Marxismo e revisionismo: Bernstein, Sorel, Graziadei, Leone. Napoli, [1975]. pp. 357.

KHAMEI (ANVAR) Le révisionnisme de Marx à Mao-Tsé-Toung. Paris, 1976. pp. 428. bibliog.

MAZUR (VILEN NIKITOVICH) Ekonomicheskii revizionizm: kritika revizionistskoi vul'garizatsii politicheskoi ekonomii sotsializma. Kiev, 1976. pp. 247.

COMMUNIST SELF-CRITICISM.

WHYTE (MARTIN KING) Small groups and political rituals in China. Berkeley, Calif., [1975]. pp. 271. (Michigan University. Center for Chinese Studies. Michigan Studies on China) First published in 1974.

COMMUNIST STATE.

INTERNATSIONAL'NOE i natsional'noe v sotsialisticheskom obshchestve. Kiev, 1976. pp. 331.

MAMUT (LEONID SOLOMONOVICH) Problemy teorii gosudarstva v sovremennoi ideologicheskoi bor'be: protiv burzhuaznoi kritiki vzgliadov K. Marksa na gosudarstvo. Moskva, 1976. pp. 192.

POLITICHESKAIA organizatsiia razvitogo sotsialisticheskogo obshchestva: pravovye problemy. Kiev, 1976. pp. 516.

SOTSIALISTICHESKOE gosudarstvo: sushchnost', funktsii i formy. Moskva, 1976. pp. 167.

COMMUNISTIC SETTLEMENTS.

LOCKLEY (ANDREW) Christian communes. London, 1976. pp. 119.

— Germany.

DEMERIN (PATRICK) Communautés pour le socialisme: pratique de la vie collective chez les étudiants de Berlin-Ouest: origines, développement, perspectives. Paris, 1975. pp. 209. bibliog.

— Israel.

BARKAI (HAIM) Growth patterns of the kibbutz economy. Amsterdam, 1977. pp. 298. bibliog.

COMMUNISTIC SETTLEMENTS.(Cont.)

— Netherlands.

USSEL (JOS VAN) Leven in communes: verslag van een empirisch onderzoek naar communes in Nederland; met medewerking van Harrie Jansen [and others]. Deventer, [1977]. pp. 168. *bibliog.*

— United States.

KEPHART (WILLIAM M.) Extraordinary groups: the sociology of unconventional life-styles. New York, [1976]. pp. 311. *bibliogs.*

COMMUNISTS

— Germany.

IM Kampf bewährt: Erinnerungen deutscher Genossen an den antifaschistischen Widerstand von 1933 bis 1945; eingeleitet und zusammengestellt von Heinz Vosske. 2nd ed. Berlin, 1977. pp. 616.

— Poland.

KASPRZAKOWA (JANINA) Maria Koszutska. Warszawa, 1976. pp. 70. *bibliog.*

PRZYGOŃSKI (ANTONI) Alfred Lampe. Warszawa, 1976. pp. 91. *bibliog.*

— United States.

WEISBORD (VERA BUCH) A radical life. Bloomington, Ind., [1977]. pp. 330.

COMMUNITY.

EDWARDS (ALLAN D.) and JONES (DOROTHY G.) Community and community development. The Hague, [1976]. pp. 326. *bibliogs.*

COMMUNITY AND SCHOOL.

BOYD (WILLIAM L.) Community status and conflict in suburban school politics. Beverly Hills, [1976]. pp. 41. *bibliog.*

COMMUNITY CENTRES

— United Kingdom.

NEWMAN (MICHAEL) Adult education and community action. London, [1973] repr. 1975. pp. 31.

BUTCHER (HUGH) and others. Information and action services for rural areas: a case study in west Cumbria. [York, 1976]. pp. 79. *(Papers in Community Studies. No. 4)*

COMMUNITY DEVELOPMENT.

EDWARDS (ALLAN D.) and JONES (DOROTHY G.) Community and community development. The Hague, [1976]. pp. 326. *bibliogs.*

STRATEGIES for human settlements: habitat and environment; edited by Gwen Bell. Honolulu, [1976]. pp. 172.

LONG (NORMAN) An introduction to the sociology of rural development. London, 1977. pp. 221. *bibliog.*

— Australia.

JAKUBOWICZ (ANDREW) Community development and community development training. [Canberra?], 1974 reprinted 1975. pp. 15. *bibliog. (Australia. Social Welfare Commission. Discussion Papers)*

RAYSMITH (HAYDEN) and EINFELD (STEVE) Community development: the process and the people; a report to the Australian Government Social Welfare Commission. [Canberra?], 1975. pp. 51. *(Australia. Social Welfare Commission. Discussion Papers)*

— Canada.

CANADIAN COUNCIL ON SOCIAL DEVELOPMENT. Integration of physical and social planning with special reference to neighbourhood services and citizen participation; report number two. Ottawa, [1968]. pp. 73. *bibliog. Report of a seminar held 28-29 March 1968 under the joint sponsorship of Special Project on Low-Income Housing and Community Funds and Councils Division of the Canadian Welfare Council.*

— Hong Kong.

RICHES (GRAHAM C.P.) Community development in Hong Kong: Sau Mau Ping, a case study. Hong Kong, 1973. pp. 77. *(Hong Kong. University. Centre of Asian Studies. Occasional Papers and Monographs. No. 15)*

— United Kingdom.

SOCIAL development in new communities; proceedings of a seminar organized by the Centre for Urban and Regional Studies and held in the University of Birmingham, March 28, 1972. Birmingham, 1972. pp. 66. *(Birmingham. University. Centre for Urban and Regional Studies. Research Memoranda. No. 12)*

BIRMINGHAM COMMUNITY DEVELOPMENT PROJECT. First report about the Saltley project area. [Birmingham], 1973. pp. 71. *Photocopy.*

BIRMINGHAM COMMUNITY DEVELOPMENT PROJECT. Second report: strategy. [Birmingham], 1973. pp. 18. *Photocopy.*

CUMBRIA COMMUNITY DEVELOPMENT PROJECT. Initial study of the two parishes Cleator Moor, Arlecdon and Frizington. Cleator Moor, 1973. pp. 54.

NORTH TYNESIDE COMMUNITY DEVELOPMENT PROJECT. A report on the project's work during 1974. [North Shields], 1975. fo. 20

BARTLES-SMITH (DOUGLAS) and GERRARD (DAVID) Urban ghetto. Guildford, 1976. pp. 115.

DARVILL (GILES) Encouraging the community: some findings on the social services departments' contribution. Berkhamsted, 1976. pp. 11.

LANSLEY (JOHN) Voluntary organisations facing change: the report of a project to help Councils for Voluntary Service respond to local government reorganisation. London, 1976. pp. 96. *bibliog.*

SHENTON (NEIL) 'Deneside': a council estate. [York, 1976]. pp. 40. *(Papers in Community Studies. No. 8)*

BARR (ALAN) The practice of neighbourhood community work: experience from Oldham C[ommunity] D[evelopment] P[roject]. [York], 1977. pp. 25. *(Papers in Community Studies. No. 12)*

BENWELL IDEAS GROUP. Four BIG years: the history of Benwell's independent funding organisation, 1973-1977. [Newcastle-upon-Tyne, Benwell Community Development Project, 1977]. pp. 19.

COMMUNITY DEVELOPMENT PROJECT. Gilding the ghetto: the state and the poverty experiments. [London, 1977]. pp. 64.

CORINA (LEWIS) Oldham C[ommunity] D[evelopment] P[roject]: an assessment of its impact and influence on the local authority. [York], 1977. pp. 134. *(Papers in Community Studies. No. 9)*

HATCH (STEPHEN) and others. Research and reform: the case of the Southwark Community Development Project, 1969-1972. London, Home Office, Urban Deprivation Unit, 1977. pp. 292.

TOPPING (PHILIP R.) and SMITH (GEORGE ANTONY NOEL) Government against poverty?: Liverpool Community Development Project, 1970-75. Oxford, 1977. pp. 123. *bibliog.*

— — Wales.

GLAMORGAN-GLYNCORRWG COMMUNITY DEVELOPMENT PROJECT. Director's report to the management committee. [Port Talbot], 1972. fo. (125).

GLAMORGAN-GLYNCORRWG COMMUNITY DEVELOPMENT PROJECT. State of the community report: community health and welfare. [Port Talbot], 1972. pp. 27.

GLAMORGAN-GLYNCORRWG COMMUNITY DEVELOPMENT PROJECT. House improvement, occupational training and job creation: a review of work undertaken by the Upper Afan C[ommunity] D[evelopment] P[roject]. [Port Talbot], 1974. fo. 18.

— United States.

COMMUNITIES left behind: alternatives for development; [edited by] Larry R. Whiting. Ames, Iowa, 1974. pp. 151. *bibliogs. Papers presented at a symposium at South Dakota State University, 1973, sponsored by the North Central Regional Center for Rural Development and the University.*

PERRY (RONALD W.) and others. Social movements and the local community. Beverly Hills, [1976]. pp. 66. *bibliog.*

TWEETEN (LUTHER G.) and BRINKMAN (GEORGE LORIS) Micropolitan development: theory and practice of greater-rural economic development. Ames, Iowa, 1976. pp. 456. *bibliogs.*

COMMUNITY HEALTH SERVICES.

BRADEN (CARRIE JO) and HERBAN (NANCY L.) Community health: a systems approach. New York, [1976]. pp. 178. *bibliogs.*

— United Kingdom.

HALLAS (JACK) C[ommunity] H[ealth] C[ouncil]s in action: a review. London, 1976. pp. 83.

HICKS (DONALD) Primary health care; a review. London, H.M.S.O., 1976. pp. 629. *bibliog.*

LEWIS (JANET) ed. Community health councils: four case studies. London, [1976]. fo.98. *(Centre for Studies in Social Policy. Working Papers)*

— — Citizen participation.

KLEIN (RUDOLF EWALD) and LEWIS (JANET) The politics of consumer representation: a study of community health councils. London, 1976. pp. 205.

COMMUNITY HEALTH SERVICES FOR THE AGED

— Economic aspects — United States.

HEINTZ (KATHERINE McMILLAN) Retirement communities, for adults only. New Brunswick, [1976]. pp. 239.

COMMUNITY LEADERSHIP.

NAYACAKALOU (RUSIATE RAIBOSA) Leadership in Fiji. Melbourne, 1975. pp. 170. *bibliog.*

COMMUNITY LIFE.

MISZTAL (BRONISŁAW) Zagadnienia społecznego uczestnictwa i współdziałania: analiza w świetle teorii i badań socjologicznych. Wrocław, 1977. pp. 276. *bibliog. (Polska Akademia Nauk. Instytut Filozofii i Socjologii. Zespół Badania Struktur Społecznych. Publikacje. [19]) With English, French and German summaries.*

SENNETT (RICHARD) The fall of public man. Cambridge, 1977. pp. 386.

COMMUNITY ORGANIZATION.

SCOTTISH COUNCIL OF SOCIAL SERVICE. Topics. 2. Community councils. 2nd ed. Edinburgh, [1974]. pp. 22,6.

HALL (DEREK) Local participation and neighbourhood councils in Portsmouth. Portsmouth, [1976]. pp. 16. *(Social Services Research and Intelligence Unit [Portsmouth]. Information Sheets. No. 28)*

LOCAL government and the public; edited by Roy Darke and Ray Walker. London, 1977. pp. 255. *bibliogs.*

O'MALLEY (JAN) The politics of community action: a decade of struggle in Notting Hill. Nottingham, 1977. pp. 180.

WOMEN in the community; edited by Marjorie Mayo. London, 1977. pp. 141. *bibliogs.*

COMMUNITY POWER.

KURODA (YASUMASA) Reed Town, Japan: a study in community power structure and political change. Honolulu, [1974]. pp. 283. *bibliog.*

LEDER (ARNOLD) Catalysts of change: Marxist versus Muslim in a Turkish community. Austin, Texas, [1976]. pp. 56. *bibliog. (Texas University. Center for Middle Eastern Studies. Middle East Monographs. No. 1)*

POWER, paradigms, and community research; edited by Roland J. Liebert and Allen W. Imershein. London, [1977]. pp. 339. *bibliogs. Papers prepared for a meeting of the International Sociological Association, Montreal, 1974.*

COMMUTING

— Austria.

EXELI (WALTER) Pendelwanderung der Arbeitnehmer in Tirol, 1964-1974. Innsbruck, [1975]. pp. 299.

— United Kingdom.

HEPBURN (D.R.C.) Analysis of changes in rail commuting to central London, 1966-71. Crowthorne, 1977. pp. 12. *bibliog. (U.K. Transport and Road Research Laboratory. Supplementary Reports. 268)*

COMO (CITY)

— Economic history.

SEVERIN (DANTE) San Gottardo, Spluga e interessi di Como: studio sulla economia dei tracciati ferroviari, 1836-1973. Como, 1974. pp. 187. *bibliog.*

COMPAGNONNAGES.

COORNAERT (EMILE) Les compagnonnages en France du Moyen Age à nos jours. 3rd ed. [Paris, 1976]. pp. 448. *bibliog.*

COMPARATIVE ECONOMICS.

See ECONOMICS, COMPARATIVE.

COMPENSATION (LAW)

— New Zealand.

NEW ZEALAND. Property Law and Equity Reform Committee. 1975. Reform of the Land Transfer Act, 1952. [Wellington, 1975]. fo. 10. *(Working Papers. No. 3)*

COMPETITION.

BROZEN (YALE) ed. The competitive economy: selected readings. Morristown, N.J., [1975]. pp. 481.

BOEHNKE (ROLF) Diversifizierte Unternehmen: eine Untersuchung über wettbewerbliche Wirkungen, Ursachen und Ausmass der Diversifizierung. Berlin, [1976]. pp. 277. *bibliog. With English summary.*

CASE studies in the competitive process; by Peter J. Barker [and others]. London, 1976. pp. 86. *(Economics Association. Case Studies in Economic Analysis. 4)*

GERMANY (BUNDESREPUBLIK). Monopolkommission. 1977. Mehr Wettbewerb ist möglich: (Hauptgutachten 1973/75). 2nd ed. Baden-Baden, 1977. pp. 751. *(Hauptgutachten. 1)*

SOUTH AFRICA. Commission of Inquiry into the Regulation of Monopolistic Conditions Act, 1955. 1977. Report (R.P. 64/1977). in SOUTH AFRICA. Parliament. House of Assembly. Votes and proceedings; (with Printed annexures).

COMPETITION, INTERNATIONAL.

HENKNER (KLAUS) Wettbewerbsrelationen im Aussenhandel westlicher Industrieländer, 1959 bis 1973:...unter besonderer Berücksichtigung der Bundesrepublik Deutschland. Berlin, 1976. pp. 199. *(Deutsches Institut für Wirtschaftsforschung. Beiträge zur Strukturforschung. Heft 39) With English summary.*

COMPUTER-ASSISTED INSTRUCTION.

TURNBULL (JOHN JAMES) The computer in the learning environment. Manchester, [1974]. pp. 97.

DAVISSON (WILLIAM I.) and BONELLO (FRANK J.) Computer-assisted instruction in economic education: a case study. Notre Dame, Ia., [1976]. pp. 269.

COMPUTER GRAPHICS.

MARGERISON (T.A.) Computers and the renaissance of cartography. London, Natural Environment Research Council, [1976]. pp. 20. *bibliog.*

COMPUTER INDUSTRY

— United States.

DATA processing in 1980-1985: a study of potential limitations to progress; [by] T.A. Dolotta [and others]. New York, [1976]. pp. 191. *bibliogs.*

COMPUTER INPUT-OUTPUT EQUIPMENT.

HEBDITCH (DAVID L.) Data communications: an introductory guide. London, 1975. pp. 223.

COMPUTER NETWORKS.

DAVIES (DONALD WATTS) and BARBER (DEREK LESLIE ARTHUR) Communication networks for computers. London, [1973] repr. 1976. pp. 575.

SCHWARTZ (MISCHA) Computer-communication network: design and analysis. Englewood Cliffs, [1977]. pp. 372. *bibliog.*

COMPUTER PROGRAMMING MANAGEMENT.

JOHANNSEN (HANO) and BIRCH (STEPHANIE) Achieving computer profitability: a survey of current practice in 102 companies. London, [1971]. pp. 43. *(British Institute of Management. Management Survey Reports. No. 1)*

BRINCH HANSEN (PER) Operating system principles. Englewood Cliffs, [1973]. pp. 366. *bibliog.*

COMPUTER PROGRAMS

— Evaluation.

GILB (TOM) Software metrics. Cambridge, Mass, [1977]. pp. 282. *bibliog.*

— Reliability.

MYERS (GLENFORD J.) Software reliability: principles and practices. New York, [1976]. pp. 360.

COMPUTERS.

CARDENAS (ALFONSO F.) and others, eds. Computer science. New York, [1972]. pp. 522. *bibliogs.*

NATIONAL COMPUTER CONFERENCE, 1973. National Computer Conference and exposition, June 4-8, 1973, New York. Montvale, N.J., 1973. pp. 816, M01-97. *bibliogs. (American Federation of Information Processing Societies. Conference Proceedings. vol.42)*

NATIONAL COMPUTER CONFERENCE, 1974. National Computer Conference and exposition, May 6-10, 1974, Chicago, Illinois. Montvale, N.J., 1974. pp. 1069. *(American Federation of Information Processing Societies. Conference Proceedings. vol. 43)*

NATIONAL COMPUTER CONFERENCE, 1975. National Computer Conference, May 19-22, 1975, Anaheim, California. Montvale, N.J., 1975. pp. 990. *(American Federation of Information Processing Societies. Conference Proceedings. vol. 44)*

COMPUTER BOARD FOR UNIVERSITIES AND RESEARCH COUNCILS [U.K.]. Computers in higher education and research: the next decade; a statement of future policy...for discussion with universities, research councils, and other interested bodies. London, H.M.S.O., 1976. pp. 24.

GREENBERGER (MARTIN) and others. Models in the policy process: public decision making in the computer era. New York, [1976]. pp. 355.

— Access control.

MAIR (WILLIAM C.) Computer control and audit. 2nd ed. Altamonte Springs, Fla., 1976. pp. 489. *bibliog. Table in end pocket.*

— Social aspects.

LONDON (KEITH R.) The people side of systems: the human aspects of computer systems. London, [1976]. pp. 281. *bibliog.*

COMPUTER privacy: where to and why; compiled and edited by Alan Simpson. Purley, [1977]. pp. 67. *bibliog.*

— Study and teaching.

COMPUTER education: time for change; compiled and edited by Alan Simpson. Purley, [1977]. pp. 101. *bibliogs.*

CONCENTRATION CAMPS

— Russia.

URWICH (JOHANN) Fără paşaport prin URSS. Munchen, 1976 in progress.

— South West Africa.

ERINNERUNGEN an die Internierungszeit, 1939-1946, und zeitgeschichtliche Ergänzungen: Berichte, Erzählungen, Fotos und Zeichnungen...; bearbeitet und herausgegeben von Rudolf Kock. 2nd ed. Windhoek, 1975. pp. 221.

— United Kingdom — Ireland.

KEARNEY (PEADAR) My dear Eva: letters from Ballykinlar internment camp 1921. Dublin, 1976. pp. 46.

CONCORDAT OF 1929 (ITALY).

SPADOLINI (GIOVANNI) La questione del Concordato: con i documenti inediti della Commissione Gonella. Firenze, 1976. pp. 560.

CONCRETE BOATS.

SUTHERLAND (W.M.) Boats from ferro-cement. (ID/85). New York, United Nations, 1972. pp. 123. *bibliog. (United Nations Industrial Development Organization. Utilization of Shipbuilding and Repair Facilities Series. No. 1.)*

CONDOTO

— Economic conditions.

ESCALANTE (AQUILES) La mineria del hambre: Condoto y la Choco Pacifico. [Medellin, 196-?]. pp. 160. *bibliog.*

— Social conditions.

ESCALANTE (AQUILES) La mineria del hambre: Condoto y la Choco Pacifico. [Medellin, 196-?]. pp. 160. *bibliog.*

CONDUCT OF COURT PROCEEDINGS

— United Kingdom.

HARRIS (BRIAN) The courts, the press and the public. Chichester, 1976. pp. 96.

CONDUCT OF LIFE.

[PIC (JEAN)] Le songe d'Alcibiade; traduit du Grec [or rather written by Jean Pic, and edited by the Prince de Grimberghen]. Paris, chez Didot, 1735. pp. 117. *Bound with BOULANGER (NICOLAS ANTOINE) Dissertations sur Elie et Enoch, etc.*

MORAL annals of the poor, and middle ranks of society, in various situations of good and bad conduct. Durham, Pennington, 1793. pp. xv, 44.

JEFFERSON (JOSEPH) Industry, and a pious submission, charity, and a strict economy...; a sermon preached in the parish church of St. Anne, Westminster, on Sunday, the 14th, day of December, 1800, being the day on which His Majesty's proclamation on the scarcity of grain was directed to be read; ([with] An appendix containing the resolutions...for carrying into effect His Majesty's proclamation, etc.) 2nd ed. London, Robson, 1800. pp. 28,6.

CONFESSION

— Catholic Church.

VALENTINI (NORBERTO) La politica in confessionale. Milano, [1974]. pp. 286.

CONFIDENTIAL COMMUNICATIONS

— Banking — Switzerland.

BUECHENBACHER (CHRISTOPH) Tatsachen über das schweizerische Bankgeheimnis. Zürich, [1977]. pp. 336. *bibliog.*

— United Kingdom.

CORNISH (WILLIAM RODOLPH) Protection of confidential information in English law. Weinheim/Bergstr., [1975]. pp. 43-59. *(Reprinted from International Review of Industrial Property and Copyright Law, 1975)*

CONFLICT OF GENERATIONS.

COMMUNITY RELATIONS COMMISSION. Between two cultures: a study of relationships between generations in the Asian community in Britain. London, 1976. pp. 73.

POLITICAL generations and political development; edited by Richard J. Samuels. Lexington, Mass., [1977]. pp. 141. *Based on the 1975-1976 Harvard-MIT Joint Seminar on Political Development.*

CONNOLLY (JAMES).

CORK WORKERS' CLUB. Historical Reprints. No. 15. The Connolly-DeLeon controversy: on wages, marriage and the church. Cork, [1976]. pp. 45.

O'NEIL (DANIEL J.) Three perennial themes of anti-colonialism: the Irish case. Denver, Colo., [1976]. pp. 131. *(Denver. University. Social Science Foundation and Graduate School of International Studies. Monograph Series in World Affairs. vol. 14, no. 1)*

CONRAD (JOHANNES).

KRAWEHL (OTTO ERNST) Die "Jahrbücher für Nationalökonomie und Statistik" unter den Herausgebern Bruno Hildebrand und Johannes Conrad, 1863 bis 1915. München, 1977. pp. 127. *bibliog.*

CONSCIENTIOUS OBJECTORS.

INTERNATIONAL PEACE BUREAU. The right to refuse to kill: a new guide to conscientious objection and service refusal. Geneva, 1971. pp. 35.

— United States.

FOOTE (CALEB) Prison and court manual for conscientious objectors facing prosecution and imprisonment. Philadelphia, [1949]. pp. 38. *bibliog.*

CONSCIOUSNESS.

EVOLUTION and consciousness: human systems in transition; edited by Erich Jantsch and Conrad Waddington. Reading, Mass., 1976. pp. 259. *bibliogs.*

CONSERVATION OF NATURAL RESOURCES.

SCORER (RICHARD SEGAR) A radical approach to pollution, population and resources. London, [1973]. pp. 32. *(Liberal Party. Strategy 2,000. 1st Series. No.1)*

— Mathematical models.

KHALATBARI (FIRAUZEH) Planning, uncertainties and exhaustible resources. 1976 [or rather 1977]. fo.252. *bibliog. Typescript. Ph.D. (London) thesis: unpublished. This thesis is the property of London University and may not be removed from the Library.*

— Study and teaching.

CONNECT: Unesco-UNEP environmental education newsletter; (pd. by) Unesco. irreg., Current issues only. Paris.

— United Kingdom.

CONSERVATION SOCIETY. Resources/Environment Committee. Economics Working Party. The economics of conservation: an outline plan for the United Kingdom. Chertsey, 1973. pp. 24.

MAUDE (BARBARA) The turning tide: towards the post-surplus society. London, 1975. pp. 185. *bibliog.*

DIGEST OF ENVIRONMENTAL STATISTICS: environmental protection and conservation; [pd. by] Department of the Environment. a., 1976 (1st)- London.

— United States.

DITTON (ROBERT B.) and others. Coastal resources management: beyond bureaucracy and the market. Lexington, Mass., [1977]. pp. 196.

PAGE (TALBOT) Conservation and economic efficiency: an approach to materials policy. Baltimore, [1977]. pp. 266.

CONSERVATISM.

JARAMILLO ECHEVERRI (MARINO) Liberales y conservadores en la historia: itinerario de las ideas y del poder. Bogota, 1972. pp. 297.

O'SULLIVAN (NOËL KERRY) Conservatism. London, 1976. pp. 173. *bibliog.*

— Europe.

WEISS (JOHN) Conservatism in Europe, 1770-1945: traditionalism, reaction and counter-revolution. London, [1977]. pp. 180. *bibliog.*

— United Kingdom.

BLAKE (ROBERT NORMAN WILLIAM) Baron Blake. Conservatism in an age of revolution...; paper presented to the Conservative philosophy group. London, 1976. pp. 24.

PARLETT (R.J.) Conservatism: the standpoint of a rank and file Tory. Cobham, [1976]. pp. 16.

GILMOUR (IAN) Inside right: a study of conservatism. London, 1977. pp. 294. *bibliog.*

— United States.

CLECAK (PETER) Crooked paths: reflections on socialism, conservatism and the welfare state. New York, [1977]. pp. 206.

CONSERVATIVE PARTY (CANADA).

PROGRESSIVE CONSERVATIVE PARTY [CANADA]. Summary of leadership conventions, 1927-1967. [Ottawa, c.1970]. pp. 24.

PERLIN (GEORGE CROSBIE) The problem of intra-party conflict in the leadership succession of John Diefenbaker in the Progressive Conservative Party of Canada: a case study. [1977]. fo. 411. *bibliog. Typescript. Ph.D. (London) thesis: unpublished. This thesis is the property of London University and may not be removed from the Library.*

CONSERVATIVE PARTY (UNITED KINGDOM).

CAPEL (PETER JAMES) Gladstone's attitude towards Disraeli's Conservative Party. London, [1975]. fo. 21. *(London. University. London School of Economics and Political Science. Gladstone Memorial Trust Prize Essays. 1975) Typescript.*

BLAKE (ROBERT NORMAN WILLIAM) Baron Blake. Conservatism in an age of revolution...; paper presented to the Conservative philosophy group. London, 1976. pp. 24.

JOSEPH (Sir KEITH SINJOHN) Stranded on the middle ground?: reflections on circumstances and policies. London, 1976. pp. 80.

BEHRENS (ROBERT) The Conservative Party in opposition, 1974-1977: a critical analysis. Coventry, [1977]. pp. 31.

BELLAIRS (CHARLES E.) Conservative social and industrial reform: a record of Conservative legislation between 1800 and 1974; with a foreword by Margaret Thatcher. rev. ed. London, 1977. pp. 128.

The BRITISH right: Conservative and right wing politics in Britain; edited by Neill Nugent [and] Roger King. Farnborough, [1977]. pp. 230. *bibliog.*

The CONSERVATIVES: a history from their origins to 1965; by Norman Gash [and others]; edited with an introduction and epilogue by Lord Butler. London, 1977. pp. 492.

FISHER (Sir NIGEL THOMAS LOVERIDGE) The Tory leaders: their struggle for power. London, [1977]. pp. 209.

GORBIK (VIACHESLAV ALEKSANDROVICH) Konservativnaia i liberal'naia partii v politicheskoi sisteme poslevoennoi Anglii. Kiev, 1977. pp. 222.

GRIFFITHS (ELDON) Fighting for the life of freedom. London, 1977. pp. 23. *(Conservative Political Centre. [Publications]. No. 601)*

WALKER (PETER) M.P. The ascent of Britain. London, 1977. pp. 224.

CONSOLIDATION AND MERGER OF CORPORATIONS

— Liberia.

PORTE (ALBERT) Liberianization or gobbling business?. [Crozierville], 1974. fo. 33.

— United Kingdom.

CHIPLIN (BRIAN) and LEES (DENNIS SAMUEL) Acquisitions and mergers: government policy in Europe. London, [1976]. pp. 104. *(Economists Advisory Group. Business Research Studies)*

MEEKS (GEOFFREY) Disappointing marriage: a study of the gains from merger. Cambridge, 1977. pp. 109. *bibliog. (Cambridge. University. Department of Applied Economics. Occasional Papers. 51)*

CONSTABLE (JOHN).

CONSTABLE (JOHN) Further documents and correspondence;...edited by Leslie Parris [and others]. London, 1975. pp. 371. *(Suffolk Records Society. [Publications]. vol. 18)*

CONSTITUTIONAL COURTS

— Germany.

WEISS (HANS ADALBERT) Die Vollstreckung von Entscheidungen des Bundesverfassungsgerichts. Augsburg, 1976. pp. 208. *bibliog.*

CONSTITUTIONAL LAW.

PRADELSKI (JOE D.) Das verfassungsrechtliche Selbstverständnis von Staaten: eine rechtsvergleichende Untersuchung von Verfassungspräambeln. Augsburg, 1975. pp. 243. *bibliog.*

CONSTRUCTION INDUSTRY

— Canada — Quebec.

QUEBEC (PROVINCE). Commission of Inquiry on the Exercise of Union Freedom in the Construction Industry. 1976. Report; [Robert Cliche, chairman]. [Quebec, 1976]. pp. 603.

— France — Statistics.

FRANCE. Direction du Bâtiment et des Travaux Publics et de la Conjoncture. Service des Statistiques et des Etudes Economiques. 1972- . Annuaire statistique de l'équipement. Paris, [1972 in progress].

— Germany.

FREESE (HEINRICH) Die Bauverhältnisse in Grossberlin vor und nach dem Kriege. Jena, 1915. pp. 43.

— — Statistics.

GERMANY (BUNDESREPUBLIK). Statistisches Bundesamt. Beschäftigung, Umsatz und Investitionen der Unternehmen im Baugewerbe. a., 1975- Wiesbaden. *(Produzierendes Gewerbe. Reihe 5.2) Supersedes GERMANY (BUNDESREPUBLIK). Statistisches Bundesamt. Unternehmen: Beschäftigte und Umsatz, Investitionen.*

GERMANY (BUNDESREPUBLIK). Statistisches Bundesamt. Beschäftigung, Umsatz und Gerätebestand der Betriebe im Baugewerbe (ohne Ausbaugewerbe). a., 1976- Wiesbaden. *(Produzierendes Gewerbe. Reihe 5.1) Supersedes GERMANY (BUNDESREPUBLIK). Statistisches Bundesamt. Betriebe: Beschäftigung und Umsatz, Gerätebestand.*

— Netherlands.

NETHERLANDS. Ministerie van Volkshuisvesting en Ruimtelijke Ordening. Current trends and policies in housing and building (formerly Current trends in housing, building and physical planning). a., 1974- 's-Gravenhage.

NETHERLANDS. Directie Bouwnijverheid. Jaarverslag. a., 1975- 's-Gravenhage. *Supersedes in part NETHERLANDS. Centrale Directie van de Volkshuisvestingen de Bouwnijverheid. Jaarverslag.*

— Poland.

HAJDUK (HENRYK) and SCHMAL (MICHAŁ) Efektywność ekonomiczna budownictwa uprzemysłowionego. Warszawa, 1963. pp. 115. *bibliog.*

— United Kingdom.

BATHER (NICHOLAS JOHN) The speculative residential developer and urban growth: the location decision in a planned environment. Reading, 1976. pp. 44. *bibliog. (Reading. University. Department of Geography. Reading Geographical Papers. No. 47)*

— United States — Statistics.

FREEDMAN (BERNARD N.) Private housing completions: a new dimension in construction statistics. [Washington, 1972]. pp. 20. *(United States. Board of Governors of the Federal Reserve System. Staff Economic Studies. No. 66)*

CONSUMER CREDIT

— Law and legislation — United Kingdom.

U.K. Department of Prices and Consumer Protection. 1977. Counting the cost of credit: the Consumer Credit, Total Charge for Credit, Regulations, 1977. [London], 1977. pp. 17.

CONSUMER EDUCATION.

ANNUAL REPORTS ON CONSUMER POLICY IN OECD MEMBER COUNTRIES; [pd. by] Committee on Consumer Policy, Organisation for Economic Co-operation and Development. a., 1976- Paris.

MAYNES (EDWIN SCOTT) Decision-making for consumers: an introduction to consumer economics. New York, [1976]. pp. 364.

ORGANISATION FOR ECONOMIC CO-OPERATION AND DEVELOPMENT. Committee on Consumer Policy. 1976. The energy label a means of energy conservation: report, etc. Paris, 1976. pp. 47.

— United Kingdom.

A CONSUMER'S guide to local government; edited by Martin Minogue for the National Consumer Council. London, 1977. pp. 196.

— United States.

CREIGHTON (LUCY BLACK) Pretenders to the throne: the consumer movement in the United States. Lexington, Mass., [1976]. pp. 142. *bibliog.*

CONSUMER PROTECTION.

ANNUAL REPORTS ON CONSUMER POLICY IN OECD MEMBER COUNTRIES; [pd. by] Committee on Consumer Policy, Organisation for Economic Co-operation and Development. a., 1976- Paris.

— Law and legislation — European Economic Community countries.

EUROPEAN COMMUNITIES. Commission. 1976. Proposal for a Council directive relating to the approximation of the laws, regulations and administrative provisions of the member states concerning liability for defective products: presented...to the Council on 9 September, 1976. [Brussels], 1976. pp. 20. *bibliog. (Bulletin of the European Communities. Supplements. [1976/11])*

— — United Kingdom — Scotland.

CLARKE (MATTHEW) Consumer law in Scotland; a discussion document. [Glasgow], Scottish Consumer Council, 1976. pp. 18,2.

— European Economic Community countries.

HERMANN (A.H.) and JONES (COLIN) Political writer. Fair trading in Europe. London, 1977. pp. 443. *bibliog.*

— Philippine Islands.

PHILIPPINE ISLANDS. Department of Trade. Semi-annual report. s-a., Jl/D 1975- Quezon City.

— United Kingdom.

REEVES (PETER) Electricity and gas consumers' guide: a summary of the practice of supply authorities and the law applicable to domestic gas and electricity consumers. Oxford, [1975]. pp. 23.

CONFEDERATION OF BRITISH INDUSTRY. Fair trading: guidance for industry and commerce. London, 1976. pp. 27. *bibliog.*

WRAITH (RONALD EDWARD) The consumer cause: a short account of its organization, power and importance. London, 1976. pp. 80. *bibliog. (Royal Institute of Public Administration. RIPA Research Booklets)*

— United States.

CREIGHTON (LUCY BLACK) Pretenders to the throne: the consumer movement in the United States. Lexington, Mass., [1976]. pp. 142. *bibliog.*

REGULATORY reform: highlights of a conference on government regulation...Washington...1975; edited by W.S. Moore. Washington, 1976. pp. 65. *(American Enterprise Institute for Public Policy Research. Domestic Affairs Studies. 45)*

CONSUMERS.

GROSS (HERBERT) Die Wirtschaft sind wir: von der Schlüsselstellung des Verbrauchers. Stuttgart, [1955]. pp. 101. *bibliog.*

BOUDET (CLAUDE) La société concentrationnaire: analyse de la société de consommation. [Paris, 1975]. pp. 200. *bibliog.*

MAYNES (EDWIN SCOTT) Decision-making for consumers: an introduction to consumer economics. New York, [1976]. pp. 364.

PORTER (MICHAEL E.) Interbrand choice, strategy, and bilateral market power. Cambridge, Mass., 1976. pp. 264. *bibliog. (Harvard University. Harvard Economic Studies. vol. 146)*

— Bibliography.

SAMUEL (SUSAN) compiler. Consumer bibliography. [London], Office of Fair Trading, 1976. pp. 43.

— Mathematical models.

RELEVANCE and precision: from quantitative analysis to economic policy; essays in honour of Pieter de Wolff; editors J.S. Cramer [and others]. Alphen aan den Rijn, 1976. pp. 318. *bibliogs.*

— Netherlands.

ECONOMISCH INSTITUUT VOOR HET MIDDEN- EN KLEINBEDRIJF. Bedrijfs- en Sociaaleconomische Publikaties. Wie kopen levensmiddelen bij verbruikersmarkten?; enkele aspecten betreffende de aard van de bezoekers. 's-Gravenhage, 1970. pp. 24.

— Spain.

ORIZO (FRANCISCO ANDRES) Las bases sociales del consumo y del ahorro en España. Madrid, [1977]. pp. 493. *(Confederacion Española de Cajas de Ahorros. Fondo para la Investigacion Economica y Social. Publicaciones. 75)*

CONSUMERS' PREFERENCES

— Mathematical models.

HUDSON (R.) Environmental images, spatial choice and consumer behaviour: a conceptual model and an empirical investigation. Durham, 1976. pp. 19. *bibliog. (Durham. University. Department of Geography. Occasional Publications (New Series). No. 9)*

CONSUMPTION (ECONOMICS).

GROSS (HERBERT) Die Wirtschaft sind wir: von der Schlüsselstellung des Verbrauchers. Stuttgart, [1955]. pp. 101. *bibliog.*

ROBERTS (ALAN) "Consumerism" and the ecological crisis. Nottingham, [1974?]. pp. 22. *(Spokesman, The. Pamphlets. No. 43)*

BLEANEY (MICHAEL F.) Under-consumption theories: a history and critical analysis. London, 1976. pp. 262. *bibliog.*

GREEN (H.A. JOHN) Consumer theory. rev. ed. London, 1976. pp. 344.

PRIVATE and enlarged consumption: essays in methodology and empirical analysis; edited by L. Solari [and] J.N. Du Pasquier. Amsterdam, 1976. pp. 301. *bibliogs. (European Scientific Association of Applied Economics. [Publications]. vol. 5) In English or French.*

The CONSUMER society; edited by I.R.C. Hirst and W. Duncan Reekie. London, 1977. pp. 198. *bibliogs. Papers of a seminar organised by the Faculty of Social Sciences, Edinburgh University, 1973.*

— Mathematical models.

OOMENS (W.J.) The demand for consumer durables. Tilburg, 1976. pp. 263. *bibliog. (Tilburg. Katholieke Hogeschool. Tilburg Institute of Economics. Tilburg Studies on Economics. 15)*

SVENSSON (LARS E.O.) On competitive markets and intertemporal resource allocation. Stockholm, 1976. 1 vol. (various pagings). *bibliogs.*

— Brazil.

CAMBRIDGE. University. Centre of Latin American Studies. Working Papers. No.24. Underconsumption, market size and expenditure patterns in Brazil; by J.R. Wells. Cambridge, 1976. pp. 57.

— Dutch Guiana.

DUTCH GUIANA. Stichting Planbureau Suriname. 1969. Basic budget of household consumption expenditure in Paramaribo and surroundings, 1968-1969. [Paramaribo, 1969?]. pp. 22. *In Dutch and English.*

CONSUMPTION (ECONOMICS).(Cont.)

— Russia.

VALIEV (ENVER ADRAKHMANOVICH) Neobkhodimyi i pribavochnyi produkt v SSSR. Moskva, 1973. pp. 104.

VAL'TUKH (KONSTANTIN KURTOVICH) Udovletvorenie potrebnostei obshchestva i modelirovanie narodnogo khoziaistva; otvetstvennyi redaktor...I.P. Suslov. Novosibirsk, 1973. pp. 378. *(Akademiia Nauk SSSR. Sibirskoe Otdelenie. Institut Ekonomiki i Organizatsii Promyshlennogo Proizvodstva. Problemy Narodnokhoziaistvennogo Optimuma. [vyp.2])*

TIKHONOV (NIKOLAI MAKAROVICH) Neobkhodimyi produkt v usloviiakh razvitogo sotsializma: voprosy teorii. Leningrad, 1974. pp. 239. *bibliog.*

AVANESOV (IURII ARKAD'EVICH) Prognozirovanie sprosa v roznichnoi torgovle. Moskva, 1975. pp. 103. *bibliog.*

EVSTIGNEEVA (LIUDMILA PETROVNA) Formirovanie potrebnostei v razvitom sotsialisticheskom obshchestve. Moskva, 1975. pp. 254.

LEVIN (ALEKSANDR IV'ANOVICH) and IARKIN (ANATOLII PAVLOVICH) Platezhesposobnyi spros naseleniia. Moskva, 1976. pp. 360. *(Akademiia Nauk SSSR. Tsentral'nyi Ekonomiko- Matematicheskii Institut. Problemy Sovetskoi Ekonomiki)*

— Sweden.

MARKOWSKI (ALEKSANDER) and PALMER (EDWARD E.) Fluctuations in the consumption ratio in Sweden: a study of the period 1965-1974. Stockholm, 1977. pp. 194. *(Stockholm. Konjunkturinstitut. Occasional Papers. 10)*

— Underdeveloped areas.

See UNDERDEVELOPED AREAS — Consumption (economics).

CONTINENTAL SHELF

— Economic aspects — Pacific Ocean.

SULLIVAN (JEREMIAH J.) Pacific basin enterprise and the changing law of the sea. Lexington, Mass., [1977]. pp. 218. *bibliog.*

CONTRABAND OF WAR.

POHL (HEINRICH) Englands Konterbandepolitik auf der Zweiten Internationalen Friedenskonferenz. Breslau, 1931. pp. 29. *(Sonder-Abdruck aus der Festgabe der rechts- und staatswissenschaftlichen Fakultät in Breslau für Paul Heilborn zum 70. Geburtstag)*

CONTRACTS

— China.

HSIAO (GENE T.) The role of economic contracts in communist China. Berkeley, Calif., [1965]. pp. 1029-1060. *(California University. Center for Chinese Studies. Reprints. No. 187). Reprinted from California Law Review, vol. 53, no. 4).*

HSIAO (GENE T.) Communist China's foreign trade contracts and means of settling disputes. Berkeley, Calif., [1969]. pp. 503-529. *(California University. Center for Chinese Studies. China Series Reprints. No. C-11) (Reprinted from Vanderbilt Law Review, 1969)*

— United Kingdom.

TREITEL (GUENTER HEINZ) An outline of the law of contract. London, 1975. pp. 384.

DAVIES (FRANCIS RONALD) Contract. 3rd ed. London, 1977. pp. 233.

SMITH (JOHN CYRIL) and THOMAS (JOSEPH ANTHONY CHARLES) A casebook on contract. 6th ed. London, 1977. pp. 588.

U.K. Law Commission. Working Papers. No. 71. Law of contract: implied terms in contracts for the supply of goods. London, 1977. pp. 60.

CONTRACTS, MARITIME.

SCHLAYER (KARL FRIEDRICH VON) Entwurf einer neuen internationalen Konvention für die Güterbeförderung zur See: Bericht über die Ergebnisse der UNCITRAL-Arbeitsgruppe für Schiffahrtsrecht; Vortrag. Hamburg, 1975. pp. 15. *(Deutscher Verein für Internationales Seerecht. Schriften. Reihe A: Berichte und Vorträge. Heft 23)*

CONTROL (PSYCHOLOGY).

KIPNIS (DAVID) The powerholders. Chicago, 1976. pp. 230. *bibliog.*

CONTROL THEORY.

ZAUBERMAN (ALFRED) Note on assimilation of optimal control theory and ramifications in economic planning theory. Bielefeld, 1976. fo. 53. *(Universität Bielefeld. Institut für Mathematische Wirtschaftsforschung. Arbeiten. Nr. 50)*

CARNEGIE-ROCHESTER CONFERENCE ON PUBLIC POLICY. 1976, November Conference. Optimal policies, control theory and technology experts; editors Karl Brunner and Allan H. Meltzer. Amsterdam, 1977. pp. 238. *bibliogs. (Journal of Monetary Economics. Carnegie-Rochester Conference Series on Public Policy. vol. 7)*

CONVENTION ACP-EEC OF LOMÉ.

See LOMÉ, CONVENTION OF.

CONVENTION OF LOMÉ.

See LOMÉ, CONVENTION OF.

CONVEYANCING

— United Kingdom.

WEETCH (KENNETH THOMAS) and PRESTIGE (COLIN) Debate: who does conveyancing on your house?. London, [1976]. pp. 12.

CONVICT LABOUR

— Russia — Kirghizia.

KIRGHIZIA. Statutes, etc. 1971. Ispravitel'no-trudovoi kodeks Kirgizskoi SSR. Frunze, 1970. pp. 243. *In Kirghiz and Russian.*

COOPERATION.

DESROCHES (HENRI CHARLES) Le projet coopératif: son utopie et sa pratique, ses appareils et ses réseaux, ses espérances et ses déconvenues. Paris, [1976]. pp. 461. *bibliog.*

LOESCH (ACHIM VON) Die gemeinwirtschaftliche Unternehmung: vom antikapitalistischen Ordnungsprinzip zum marktwirtschaftlichen Regulativ. Köln, [1977]. pp. 256.

— America, Latin.

FALS BORDA (ORLANDO) El reformismo por dentro en America Latina. Mexico, 1972. pp. 211.

— Chile.

BENECKE (DIETER W.) El movimiento cooperativo en Chile: sus caracteristicas y su desarrollo. Santiago de Chile, 1972. pp. 65. *(Instituto Latinoamericano de Investigaciones Sociales. Estudios y Documentos. 13)*

— Fiji.

WALTER (MICHAEL A.H.B.) Co-operation in East Fiji: a new traditionalism?. Singapore, 1974. pp. 30. *(University of Singapore. Department of Sociology. Working Papers. No. 30)*

— Finland.

KUJALA (MATTI) The cooperative movement in Finland. Tampere, 1975. pp. 55.

— Guyana.

GUYANA. Prime Minister. 1969. The small man a real man in the co-operative republic, Guyana: speeches by the Prime Minister, Mr Forbes Burnham, in the National Assembly on the republic motion. [Georgetown, 1969]. pp. 12.

GUYANA. Ministry of Information. 1970. The co-operative republic. 1. The philosophy of a co-operative socialist society unites the people in a common effort. [Georgetown, 1970]. pp. 15.

— India.

INDIA. Ministry of Industry and Civil Supplies. Report. a., 1975/76- New Delhi.

— — Mysore.

MYSORE. Department of Co-operation. Statistics Branch. 1967. Co-operative movement in Mysore: trend of progress; a brief narration. Bangalore, [1967?]. pp. 40.

— Ireland (Republic).

BOLGER (PATRICK) The Irish co-operative movement: its history and development. Dublin, [1977]. pp. 434.

— Poland.

KOWALAK (TADEUSZ) The cooperative movement in Poland. Warsaw, 1972. pp. 78. *(Instytut Gospodarki Krajów Rozwijajacych Sie. Teaching Papers: Advanced Course in National Economic Planning. vol. 11)*

JANCZYK (TADEUSZ) Spółdzielczość polska: geneza, rozwój, perspektywy. Warszawa, 1976. pp. 154.

— Sudan.

DAWOOD (MOHAMED AHMED) An introduction to the role of the cooperative movement in developing countries. Ljubljana, International Center for Public Enterprises, 1974. fo. 8. *(International Seminar 1974. National Papers)*

— United Kingdom.

CO-OPERATORS' EDUCATIONAL FELLOWSHIP. South Suburban Branch. A conspectus of the British co-operative movement. [London?], 1938 repr. 1939. pp. 35.

HEEB (FRIEDRICH) Von den Maschinenstürmern zu den Redlichen Pionieren: zur Jahrhundertfeier der Genossenschaftsgründung von Rochdale, 1844-1944. [Zürich, 1944]. pp. 72. *bibliog.*

— — Ireland.

BOLGER (PATRICK) The Irish co-operative movement: its history and development. Dublin, [1977]. pp. 434.

COOPERATIVE COMMONWEALTH FEDERATION (CANADA).

COOPERATIVE COMMONWEALTH FEDERATION (CANADA) and NEW DEMOCRATIC PARTY (CANADA). The decline and fall of a good idea: CCF-NDP manifestoes, 1932 to 1969; with an introduction by Michael S. Cross. Toronto, 1974. pp. 47.

COOPERATIVE MARKETING OF FARM PRODUCE

— United Kingdom — Wales.

LE VAY (CLARE) Farmers' attitudes to cooperation: the views of non-members. Aberystwyth, [1976]. pp. 83. *bibliog.*

COOPERATIVE SOCIETIES

— Law.

BURNS (CAMPBELL BLAIN) Co-operative law: a comparative study of the law relating to co- operatives in the United Kingdom, France and Hungary. Loughborough, 1977. pp. 93. *(Loughborough. Co-operative College. Co-operative College Papers. No. 17).*

— **Africa.**

APTHORPE (RAYMOND J.) Rural co-operatives and planned change in Africa: an analytical overview. (UNRISD Reports. No.72.4). Geneva, United Nations Research Institute for Social Development, 1972. pp. 114. *(Rural Institutions and Planned Change. Vol.5)*

— **America, Latin.**

ESTUDIOS de la realidad campesina: cooperacion y cambio: informes y materiales de campo recogidos en Venezuela, Ecuador y Colombia; por R. Pugh [and others]. Ginebra, Instituto de Investigaciones de las Naciones Unidas para el Desarrollo Social, 1970. pp. 421. *(Rural Institutions and Planned Change. Vol.2) Summaries in French and English.*

— **Asia.**

INAYATULLAH. Co-operatives and development in Asia: a study of co-operatives in fourteen rural communities of Iran, Pakistan and Ceylon. (UNRISD Reports. No.72.7). Geneva, United Nations Research Institute for Social Development, 1972. pp. 272. *(Rural Institutions and Planned Change. Vol.7)*

— **Papua New Guinea.**

PAPUA NEW GUINEA. Registry of Co-operative Societies. Annual report. a., 1970/71- Port Moresby.

— **South Africa.**

SOUTH AFRICA. Committee of Inquiry into the Activities of Buy- Aid Associations. 1976. Report (R.P. 85/1976). in SOUTH AFRICA. Parliament. House of Assembly. Votes and proceedings; (with Printed annexures).

— **Spain.**

GORROÑO AREITIO-AURTENA (JOSEBA IÑAKI) Experiencia cooperativa en el Pais Vasco. Durango, [1975]. pp. 181. *bibliog.*

— **Underdeveloped areas.**

See UNDERDEVELOPED AREAS — Cooperative societies.

— **United Kingdom.**

PEARCE (JOHN) An industrial co-operative experiment in Cumbria. [York], 1977. pp. 88. *bibliog. (Papers in Community Studies. No. 13)*

RICHARDSON (Sir WILLIAM ROBERT) The CWS in war and peace, 1938-1976:...the Co-operative Wholesale Society Limited in the Second World War and post-war years. Manchester, 1977. pp. 399.

COOPERS AND COOPERAGE

— **Russia — White Russia.**

TITOV (VIKTOR STEPANOVICH) Narodnye derevoobrabatyvaiushchie promysly Belorussii, 1917-1941 gg.: etnograficheskie ocherki bondarnogo promysla i izgotovleniia transportnykh sredstv; redaktor... V.K. Bondarchik. Minsk, 1976. pp. 135.

COPENHAGEN

— **Social conditions.**

PLOVSING (JAN) Beboere under sanering, etc. København, 1976. pp. 353. *bibliog. (Socialforskningsinstituttet. Publikationer. 71) With English summary.*

— **Social policy.**

KÜHL (POUL HEINRICH) Enghave-Centret: en rapport om et integreringsforsøg. København, 1975. pp. 54. *bibliog. (Socialforskningsinstituttet. Meddelelser. 11)*

COPERNICUS (NICOLAUS).

BRUNO (GIORDANO) The Ash Wednesday supper: La cena de le Ceneri; translated with an introduction and notes by Stanley L. Jaki. The Hague, [1975]. pp. 174.

COPPER MINES AND MINING

— **United Kingdom — Cornwall.**

BURROW (J.C.) and THOMAS (WILLIAM) Instructor at the Camborne School of Mines. 'Mongst mines and miners: being underground scenes by flash-light illustrating and explaining the methods of working in Cornish mines about 1895[sic]. Truro, 1965. pp. 39. *First published in 1893.*

COPYRIGHT

— **Cuba.**

CASTRO RUZ (FIDEL) Speech delivered...at the farewell ceremony for scholarship students who have completed various projects in the Guane-Mantua region and the inauguration of various projects at Guane, Pinar del Rio, sports stadium, April 29, 1967. London, Cuban Embassy, 1967. pp. 15. *(Cuba Information Bulletins. 1967. No. 5)*

— **European Economic Community countries.**

JOHANNES (HARTMUT) Industrial property and copyright in European Community law; (translated by Frank Dorman). Leyden, 1976. pp. 315. *(Council of Europe. European Aspects. Series E: Law. No.17)*

COQUIMBO

— **Population.**

ZUÑIGA IDE (JORGE) La emigracion rural en la provincia de Coquimbo, Chile: informe preliminar. Santiago de Chile, 1972. pp. 95. *bibliog. (Instituto Latinoamericano de Investigaciones Sociales. Estudios y Documentos. 16)*

CORN LAWS

— **United Kingdom.**

An EXPOSITION of the real causes and effective remedies of the agricultural distress; by an impartial looker-on. London, Sherwood, 1822. pp. 42.

CROSBY (TRAVIS L.) English farmers and the politics of protection, 1815-1852. Hassocks, 1977. pp. 224. *bibliog.*

CORPORATE PLANNING.

PORTER (MICHAEL E.) Interbrand choice, strategy, and bilateral market power. Cambridge, Mass., 1976. pp. 264. *bibliog. (Harvard University. Harvard Economic Studies. vol. 146)*

CORPORATE strategy and planning; edited by Bernard Taylor and John R. Sparkes. London, 1977. pp. 402.

— **Algeria.**

BRACHEMI (KACIM) Planning in public enterprises in developing countries; (translated by Meri Radosević). Ljubljana, International Center for Public Enterprises, 1974. fo. 19. *(International Seminar 1974. National Papers)*

— **Bangladesh.**

AHMAD (MUZAFFER) Planning and public sector enterprises in Bangladesh. Ljubljana, International Center for Public Enterprises, 1974. pp. 36. *(International Seminar 1974. National Papers)*

— **Sudan.**

ABDEL MONEIM (ABDEL SALAM) Public industries in the Sudan Industrial Production Corporation. Ljubljana, International Center for Public Enterprises, 1974. fo. 15. *(International Seminar 1974. National Papers)*

— **Tanzania.**

KOROMO (FRANCIS A.) Planning in public enterprises in developing countries. Ljubljana, International Center for Public Enterprises, 1974. fo. 19. *(International Seminar 1974. National Papers)*

— **Yugoslavia.**

ROZMAN (RUDI) and FRANC (VIKTOR) Planning in economic organisations in Yugoslavia; (translated by Meri Radosević). Ljubljana, International Center for Public Enterprises, 1974. fo. (28). *(International Seminar 1974. National Papers)*

CORPORATE STATE.

WILENSKY (HAROLD L.) The "new corporatism", centralization and the welfare state. Beverly Hills, [1976]. pp. 73. *bibliog.*

— **America, Latin.**

AUTHORITARIANISM and corporatism in Latin America; James M. Malloy, editor. Pittsburgh, [1977]. pp. 549. *bibliog. Papers of a conference held at the University of Pittsburgh in April 1974, and sponsored by its Center for International Studies.*

— **Portugal.**

WIARDA (HOWARD J.) Corporation and development: the Portuguese experience. Amherst, 1977. pp. 447. *bibliog.*

CORPORATION LAW.

ROTONDI (MARIO) ed. Inchieste di diritto comparato. 4. Enquête comparative sur les sociétés par actions...: The company limited by shares: an inquiry of comparative law. [Deventer], 1974. 3 vols. *In various languages.*

— **Australia.**

STANDING COMMITTEE OF STATE AND COMMONWEALTH ATTORNEYS-GENERAL [AUSTRALIA]. Company Law Advisory Committee. Fifth interim report, October 1970, on the control of fund raising, share capital and debentures. in AUSTRALIA. Parliament. Parliamentary papers, 1971, vol.2.

— **Europe.**

FROMMEL (S.N.) and THOMPSON (JAMES HERBERT) eds. Company law in Europe. Deventer, 1975. pp. 669. *bibliog.*

— **European Economic Community countries.**

BRANCHES and subsidiaries in the European Common Market: legal and tax aspects; second edition...prepared by members of the European Association for Legal and Fiscal Studies. London, 1976. pp. 322. *bibliogs.*

EUROPEAN COMMUNITIES. Commission. 1976. Proposal for a seventh directive pursuant to Article 54(3)(g) of the EEC Treaty concerning group accounts: submitted to the Council...on 4 May 1976. [Brussels], 1976. pp. 32. *(Bulletin of the European Communities. Supplements. [1976/9])*

— **Germany.**

LUTZ (ELMAR) Die rechtliche Struktur süddeutscher Handelsgesellschaften in der Zeit der Fugger. Tübingen, 1976. 2 vols. *bibliog. (Kommission für Bayerische Landesgeschichte. Schwäbische Forschungsgemeinschaft. Studien zur Fuggergeschichte. Band 25)*

— **Netherlands.**

SANDERS (PIETER) Dutch company law. London, 1977. pp. 277.

— **United Kingdom.**

SMITH (KENNETH) Barrister-at-Law, and KEENAN (DENIS J.) Company law; third edition by Denis J. Keenan. London, 1976. pp. 510.

CHARLESWORTH (JOHN) LL.D., and CAIN (THOMAS EWAN) Company law: eleventh edition by T.E. Cain [and others]. London, 1977. pp. 682.

CHESTERMAN (MICHAEL) Small businesses. London, 1977. pp. 267.

HADDEN (TOM) Company law and capitalism. 2nd ed. London, 1977. pp. 522.

HAHLO (HERMAN ROBERT) Casebook on company law; second edition by H.R. Hahlo and M.J. Trebilcock. London, 1977. pp. 712.

— United States — States.

The CORPORATION manual: statutory provisions relating to the organization, regulation and taxation of domestic business corporations, etc. 75th ed. New York, 1975. 2 vols.

CORPORATION REPORTS.

INSTITUTE OF CHARTERED ACCOUNTANTS IN ENGLAND AND WALES. Accounting Standards Committee. The corporate report: a discussion paper published for comment. London, [1975]. pp. 103.

CORPORATIONS.

KEMPNER (THOMAS) The corporation in modern society: models for participation. Henley-on-Thames, [1976]. pp. 13.

— Taxation.

FROMMEL (S.N.) Taxation of branches and subsidiaries in Western Europe, Canada and the U.S.A. Deventer, [1975]. pp. 121. *Based on a report prepared for the Committee on Taxes of the Section on Business Law of the International Bar Association.*

SAHNI (BALIBIR S.) and MATHEW (T.) The shifting and incidence of the corporation income tax. Rotterdam, 1976. pp. 202. *bibliog.*

— Canada — Taxation.

CANADIAN TAX FOUNDATION. Corporate Management Tax Conference, 1975. Tax aspects of measuring business profits: [proceedings of the conference]. Toronto, [1975]. pp. 148.

— — Quebec (Province).

FOURNIER (PIERRE) The Québec establishment: the ruling class and the state. Montréal, [1976]. pp. 228. *bibliog.*

— European Economic Community countries — Accounting.

EUROPEAN COMMUNITIES. Commission. 1976. Proposal for a seventh directive pursuant to Article 54(3)(g) of the EEC Treaty concerning group accounts: submitted to the Council...on 4 May 1976. [Brussels], 1976. pp. 32. *(Bulletin of the European Communities. Supplements. [1976/9])*

— Italy — Finance.

PELÙ (PAOLO) Priorità della mercatura lucchese in alcune forme collettive di investimento aziendale nel XIV e XV secolo. Lucca, 1974. pp. 27.

— Portugal.

PORTUGAL. Instituto Nacional de Estatistica. Serviços Centrais. Estatisticas das sociedades: continente et ilhas adjacentes: Statistiques des sociétés: continent et îles adjacentes. a., 1970- [Lisboa]. *[in Portuguese and French].*

— Sweden.

PRATTEN (CLIFFORD FREDERICK) A comparison of the performance of Swedish and U.K. companies. Cambridge, 1976. pp. 154. *(Cambridge. University. Department of Applied Economics. Occasional Papers. 47)*

— Switzerland — Finance.

KASPER (PAUL B.) Der Bankkredit als Finanzierungsmittel des schweizerischen Gewerbes: eine betriebswirtschaftliche Untersuchung. [Zuerich, 1975]. pp. 233. *bibliog.*

— United Kingdom.

NORTH TYNESIDE TRADES COUNCIL. A report on companies in North Tyneside: an analysis of ownership, control and profits. [North Shields], North Tyneside Community Development Project. 1975. pp. 73.

PRATTEN (CLIFFORD FREDERICK) A comparison of the performance of Swedish and U.K. companies. Cambridge, 1976. pp. 154. *(Cambridge. University. Department of Applied Economics. Occasional Papers. 47)*

LAWTON (TOM) Financial aspects of corporate planning. London, 1975. pp. 95. *bibliog.*

— — Taxation.

U.K. Board of Inland Revenue. 1973. Income tax and corporation tax: capital allowances on machinery or plant; new system. [London], 1973. pp. 26.

— United States.

LINOWES (DAVID F.) The corporate conscience. New York, [1974]. pp. 239.

BLAKE (DAVID H.) and others. Social auditing: evaluating the impact of corporate programs. New York, 1976. pp. 168. *bibliog.*

NADEL (MARK V.) Corporations and political accountability. Lexington, Mass., [1976]. pp. 265.

— — Accounting.

DYCKMAN (THOMAS R.) and others. Efficient capital markets and accounting: a critical analysis. Englewood Cliffs, [1975]. pp. 130. *bibliog.*

— — Finance.

DYCKMAN (THOMAS R.) and others. Efficient capital markets and accounting: a critical analysis. Englewood Cliffs, [1975]. pp. 130. *bibliog.*

— — Indian Territory.

MINER (H. CRAIG) The corporation and the Indian: tribal sovereignty and industrial civilization in Indian territory, 1865-1907. Columbia, Mo., 1976. pp. 236. *bibliog.*

CORPORATIONS, AMERICAN.

BASCHE (JAMES R.) and DUERR (MICHAEL G.) Experience with foreign production work forces. New York, [1975]. pp. 33. *(National Industrial Conference Board. Conference Board Reports. No. 661)*

HYMER (STEPHEN HERBERT) The international operations of national firms: a study of direct foreign investment. Cambridge, Mass., [1976]. pp. 253. *bibliog.*

— Africa, Subsaharan.

ROGERS (BARBARA) White wealth and black poverty: American investments in southern Africa. Westport, Conn., 1976. pp. 331. *(Denver. University. Center on International Race Relations. Studies in Human Rights. No. 2) "Based on work done for a joint study, with Jennifer Davis, commissioned by the Council for Christian Social Action of the United Church of Christ".*

— America, Latin.

McCANN (THOMAS P.) An American company: the tragedy of United Fruit;...edited by Henry Scammell. New York, [1976]. pp. 244.

— Caribbean Area.

MATTHEWS (HARRY G.) Multinational corporations and black power. Cambridge, Mass., [1976]. pp. 124.

— South Africa.

MYERS (DESAIX) Labor practices of U.S. corporations in South Africa. New York, 1977. pp. 123.

— Underdeveloped areas.

See UNDERDEVELOPED AREAS —
   Corporations, American.

— United Kingdom.

YOUNG (STEPHEN) and HOOD (NEIL) Chrysler U.K.: a corporation in transition. New York, 1977. pp. 342.

CORPORATIONS, BRITISH

— Peru.

ALBERT (BILL) An essay on the Peruvian sugar industry, 1880-1922 and the letters of Ronald Gordon, administrator of the British Sugar Company in the Canete Valley, 1914-1919. Norwich, [1976]. 1 vol.(various pagings).

— South Africa.

CORPORATE responsibility and the institutional investor: report of a seminar held [by Christian Concern for Southern Africa] at the London Graduate School of Business Studies...1973. London, [1974]. pp. 21.

STARES (RODNEY) Consolidated Gold Fields Limited: a review of activities and issues. London, [1975]. pp. 31. *bibliog.*

STARES (RODNEY) The General Electric Company Limited: a review of the company's relationship with South Africa. London, [1976]. fo. 31.

STARES (RODNEY) ICI (Imperial Chemical Industries Limited) in South Africa. London, [1977]. pp. 37. *bibliog.*

— South West Africa.

JEPSON (TREVOR B.) Rio Tinto-Zinc in Namibia. London, [1975]. fo. 18. *bibliog.*

CORPORATIONS, FOREIGN.

ROBINSON (RICHARD D.) National control of foreign business entry: a survey of fifteen countries. New York, 1976. pp. 508. *bibliogs.*

— European Economic Community countries.

BRANCHES and subsidiaries in the European Common Market: legal and tax aspects; second edition...prepared by members of the European Association for Legal and Fiscal Studies. London, 1976. pp. 322. *bibliogs.*

— France.

GORGE (JEAN PIERRE) and MESSECA (ELIE) Etude économique des entreprises et secteurs à forte pénétration étrangère. Paris, [1976]. pp. 73. *(France. Ministère de l'Industrie et de la Recherche. Service du Traitement de l'Information et des Statistiques Industrielles. Traits Fondamentaux du Système Industriel Français. 1)*

— Liberia.

CARLSSON (JERKER) Transnational companies in Liberia: the role of transnational companies in the economic development of Liberia. Uppsala, 1977. pp. 51. *bibliog. (Nordiska Afrikainstitutet. Research Reports. No. 37)*

CORPORATIONS, INTERNATIONAL.

FLIGLER (CARLOS) Multinational public enterprises. [Washington], International Bank for Reconstruction and Development, 1967. pp. 136.

CORPORATIONS, JAPANESE.

TSURUMI (YOSHIHIRO) The Japanese are coming: a multinational interaction of firms and politics. Cambridge, Mass., [1976]. pp. 333.

YOSHINO (MICHAEL Y.) Japan's multinational enterprises. Cambridge, Mass., 1976. pp. 191.

CORPORATIONS, PUBLIC.

ROELOFS (J.M.) Politics, policy and effective planning. Ljubljana, International Center for Public Enterprises, [1974]. fo. 6. *(International Seminar 1974. [Working Papers])*

— Bangladesh.

AHMAD (MUZAFFER) Planning and public sector enterprises in Bangladesh. Ljubljana, International Center for Public Enterprises, 1974. pp. 36. *(International Seminar 1974. National Papers)*

— Brazil.

FRANCO SOBRINHO (MANOEL DE OLIVEIRA) Empresas publicas no Brasil: ação internacional. São Paulo, 1975. pp. 215. *bibliog.*

— Egypt.

KAMEL (ISMAIL KAMEL AHMED) The system of planning, its application and evaluation, and follow- ups of plans in economic units of the general sector. Ljubljana, International Center for Public Enterprises, 1974. fo. 17. *(International Seminar 1974. National Papers)*

— Europe.

GARNER (MAURICE RICHARD) A study of UK nationalised industries: background paper 2: relationships of government and public enterprises in France, West Germany and Sweden; a report to N[ational] E[conomic] D[evelopment] O[ffice]. London, National Economic Development Office, 1976. pp. 76.

— India.

FERNANDES (PRAXY) Public enterprise in India: a perspective view. Ljubljana, International Center for Public Enterprises, 1974. fo. 39,6. *(International Seminar 1974. National Papers)*

— — Finance.

INDIA. Committee of Enquiry into the Expenses of the Life Insurance Corporation. 1969. Report; [R.R. Morarka, chairman]. [Delhi], 1969. 2 pts. (in 1 vol.).

— Iraq.

ALI (ABDULJAWAD N.) Public sector and planning in public enterprises in Iraq. Ljubljana, International Center for Public Enterprises, 1974. fo. 15. *(International Seminar 1974. National Papers)*

— Mali (Republic) — Finance.

MALI. Direction Nationale du Plan et de la Statistique. 1974. Financement des sociétés et entreprises d'état au Mali. [Ljubljana, International Center for Public Enterprises, 1974]. fo. 17. *([International Seminar 1974. Working Papers])*

— Mexico.

MEXICO. Direccion General de Estadistica. Censo Industrial, 1971. IX censo industrial, 1971; datos de 1970: empresas de participacion estatal y organismos descentralizados. Mexico, 1974. pp. 94.

— Nigeria.

ANUMUDU (T.A.) Planning in public enterprises: the Nigerian experience. Ljubljana, International Center for Public Enterprises, 1974. fo. (18). *bibliog. (International Seminar 1974. National Papers)*

NOTTIDGE (DORIS E.) Public enterprises in Nigeria: some problems of planning. Ljubljana, International Center for Public Enterprises, 1974. fo. 18. *(International Seminar 1974. Working Papers)*

— Sri Lanka.

SRI LANKA. 1974. Planning in relation to public sector enterprises: Sri Lanka. [Ljubljana, International Center for Public Enterprises, 1974]. pp. (17). *([International Seminar 1974. Working Papers])*

— Sudan.

ABDEL MONEIM (ABDEL SALAM) Public industries in the Sudan Industrial Production Corporation. Ljubljana, International Center for Public Enterprises, 1974. fo. 15. *(International Seminar 1974. National Papers)*

— Tanzania.

KOROMO (FRANCIS A.) Planning in public enterprises in developing countries. Ljubljana, International Center for Public Enterprises, 1974. fo. 19. *(International Seminar 1974. National Papers)*

— Underdeveloped areas.

See UNDERDEVELOPED AREAS — Corporations, public.

— United Kingdom.

BRITISH NATIONAL OIL CORPORATION. Report and accounts. a., 1976(1st)- London.

GARNER (MAURICE RICHARD) A study of UK nationalised industries: background paper 2: relationships of government and public enterprises in France, West Germany and Sweden; a report to N[ational] E[conomic] D[evelopment] O[ffice]. London, National Economic Development Office, 1976. pp. 76.

NATIONAL ECONOMIC DEVELOPMENT OFFICE. Background paper 3: output, investment and productivity. London, 1976. pp. 108.

NATIONAL ECONOMIC DEVELOPMENT OFFICE. A study of UK nationalised industries: background paper 5: price behaviour. London, 1977. pp. 52.

NATIONAL ECONOMIC DEVELOPMENT OFFICE. A study of UK nationalised industries: background paper 6: relationships with other sectors of the economy: the evidence of input-output analysis. London, 1977. pp. 51.

NATIONAL ECONOMIC DEVELOPMENT OFFICE. A study of UK nationalised industries: background paper 7: exports and imports. London, 1977. pp. 27.

VAUGHAN (G.DOUGLAS) and others. From private to public: an analysis of the choices, problems and performance of newly floated public companies, 1966-74. Cambridge, 1977. pp. 144.

— — Employees.

NATIONAL ECONOMIC DEVELOPMENT OFFICE. A study of U.K. nationalised industries: background paper 4: manpower and pay trends. London, 1977. pp. 170.

— — Finance.

NATIONAL ECONOMIC DEVELOPMENT OFFICE. A study of UK nationalised industries: background paper 1: financial analysis. London, 1976. pp. 121.

CORPULENCE.

SCHMIDT (GERT) and others. Vaegtforhold og funktionsevne blandt aeldre i Odense. København, 1975. pp. 80. *bibliog. (Socialforskningsinstituttet. Meddelelser. 10)*

CORRELATION (STATISTICS).

SIS'KOV (VLADIMIR IVANOVICH) Korreliatsionnyi analiz v ekonomicheskikh issledovaniiakh. Moskva, 1975. pp. 168. *bibliog.*

CORRUPTION (IN POLITICS)

— Canada.

GIBBONS (KENNETH M.) and ROWAT (DONALD CAMERON) eds. Political corruption in Canada: cases, causes and cures. Toronto, [1976]. pp. 307. *bibliog. (Carleton University. Institute of Canadian Studies. Carleton Library. No. 95)*

— Ghana.

GHANA. Committee of Enquiry into the affairs of the Distribution Division of the Ghana Publishing Corporation. 1967. Report; [K.S. Essah, chairman]. Accra, [1968]. pp. 64. *Bound with White Paper on the report.*

GHANA. 1969. White Paper on the report of the Committee of Enquiry into the affairs of the Distribution Division of the erstwhile State Publishing Corporation. [Accra, 1969]. pp. 8. *(W[hite] P[apers]. 1969. No. 1) Bound with the report.*

GHANA. Commission of Enquiry into the State Fishing Corporation. 1969. Interim and final reports; [S.A. Wiredu, chairman]. [Accra, 1969]. pp. 213. *Bound with the White Paper on the report.*

GHANA. 1973. White Paper on the report of the Commission of Enquiry into the management and manner of operation of the State Fishing Corporation. [Accra], 1973. pp. 13. *(W[hite] P[apers]. 1973. No. 4)*

GHANA. Taylor Assets Committee. 1976. Report of the...Committee to enquire into the assets of scheduled persons; [J.N.K. Taylor, chairman]. Accra, [1976 in progress]. *Library has vol. 1, part 1.*

GHANA. 1976. White Paper on [volume 1, part 1 of] the report of the Taylor Assets Committee. Accra, 1976. pp. 24. *(W[hite] P[apers] 1976. No. 1)*

— India.

BHARGAVA (G.S.) India's Watergate: a study of political corruption in India. New Delhi, 1974. pp. 226.

— Ireland (Republic).

EIRE. Dail Eireann. Committee on Procedure and Privileges. 1975. Report...on the report of the tribunal appointed on the 4th July, 1975, to inquire into the allegations made by two members against the Minister for Local Government in the Dail. Dublin, 1975. pp. (8). *In English and Irish.*

REPORT of the tribunal appointed by the Taoiseach on the 4th day of July, 1975, pursuant to resolution passed on the 3rd day of July, 1975, by Dail Eireann and on the 4th day of July, 1975, by Seanad Eireann. Dublin, Stationery Office, [1975]. pp. 16.

— Mexico.

CACIQUISMO y poder politico en el Mexico rural; por Roger Bartra [and others]. Mexico, 1975. pp. 203.

— Russia.

ZEMTSOV (IL'IA GRIGOR'EVICH) Partiia ili mafiia?: razvorovannaia respublika. Paris, 1976. pp. 125.

— United Kingdom.

MILNE (EDWARD JAMES) No shining armour. London, 1976. pp. 263.

CORSICA

— History.

ROCHET (WALDECK) and COSSONEAU (EMILE) L'épopée de la Corse: comment les patriotes du maquis ont libéré l'Ile de Beauté. London, [1943]. pp. 16.

COST.

ALCHIAN (ARMEN ALBERT) Economic forces at work. Indianapolis, [1977]. pp. 523. *bibliogs.*

COST ACCOUNTING.

U.K. Central Statistical Office. 1977. Current cost accounting: guide to price indices for overseas countries. London, 1977. pp. 36.

COST AND STANDARD OF LIVING

— Austria.

KAMMER FÜR ARBEITER UND ANGESTELLTE FÜR OBERÖSTERREICH. Die Lebenshaltung von Arbeitern und Angestellten in Linz, 1974. [Linz], 1976. fo.67. *(Statistik. Heft 48) 120 tables appended.*

— Communist countries.

MIKUL'SKII (KONSTANTIN IVANOVICH) ed. Sotsializm i narodnoe blagosostoianie. Moskva, 1976. pp. 446.

— Finland.

FINLAND. Tilastokeskus. 1976-77. Kotitaloustiedustelu 1971, etc. Helsinki, 1976-77. 3 vols.(in 1). *(Tilastollisia Tiedonantoja. 55) In Finnish and Swedish, with English summaries.*

— New Zealand.

NEW ZEALAND. Department of Statistics. Household sample survey. a., 1973/74 (1st)- Wellington.

— Norway.

NORWAY. Statistiske Centralbyrå. 1976. Forbruk blant skoleungdom og studenter, 1973-1974, etc. Oslo, 1976. pp. 54. *(Statistiske Analyser. 25) With English summary.*

NORWAY. Statistiske Centralbyrå. 1976. Private husholdningers forbruk, 1973, etc. Oslo, 1976. pp. 97. *(Statistiske Analyser. 24) With English summary.*

— Russia.

VALIEV (ENVER ADRAKHMANOVICH) Neobkhodimyi i pribavochnyi produkt v SSSR. Moskva, 1973. pp. 104.

TIKHONOV (NIKOLAI MAKAROVICH) Neobkhodimyi produkt v usloviiakh razvitogo sotsializma: voprosy teorii. Leningrad, 1974. pp. 239. *bibliog.*

KUPRIENKO (LIDIIA PETROVNA) Vliianie urovnia zhizni na raspredelenie trudovykh resursov. Moskva, 1976. pp. 120. *(Akademiia Nauk SSSR. Problemy Sovetskoi Ekonomiki)*

— — Uzbekistan.

ZAKONOMERNOSTI rosta urovnia zhizni naseleniia v usloviiakh nekapitalisticheskogo razvitiia. Tashkent, 1976. pp. 192.

— Sweden.

DAHLIN (LARS) Levnadsniva och hälsotillstånd: utnyttjande av social och medicinsk service i tre Malmödistrikt: (Level of living, health and utilization of social and health services...in Malmö). Malmö, 1975. pp. 141. *bibliog. In Swedish, with English summary.*

— Underdeveloped areas.

See UNDERDEVELOPED AREAS — Cost and standard of living.

— United Kingdom.

EAST ANGLIA ECONOMIC PLANNING COUNCIL. Earnings, other incomes and household expenditure in East Anglia. [London, 1977]. pp. 17.

EDWARDS (A.C.) The account books of Benjamin Mildmay, Earl Fitzwalter. London, [1977]. pp. 224.

FIEGEHEN (GUY) and others. Poverty and progress in Britain, 1953-73: a statistical study of low income households: their numbers, types and expenditure patterns. Cambridge, 1977. pp. 173. *(National Institute of Economic and Social Research. Occasional Papers. 29)*

U.K. Central Statistical Office. 1977. Estimates of household expenditure in the United Kingdom at current prices, 1970-1975: comparison between the family expenditure survey and the national accounts. [London, 1977]. pp. (31).

— United States.

MOON (MARILYN) The measurement of economic welfare: its application to the aged poor. New York, [1977]. pp. 146. *bibliog. (Wisconsin University, Madison. Institute for Research on Poverty. Monograph Series)*

COST EFFECTIVENESS.

LITTLE (F.M.) and STANNARD (ROBERT B.) The King's Reach cost-benefit study: a case study of central London redevelopment. [London], Greater London Council, 1967. fo. (22).

PAPANDREOU (ANDREAS GEORGE) and ZOHAR (URI) The impact approach to project selection: national planning and socioeconomic priorities: a two volume series, (volume 2). New York, 1974. pp. 187.

LESOURNE (JACQUES F.) Cost-benefit analysis and economic theory; translation by Mrs. A. Silvey. Amsterdam, 1975. pp. 521. *bibliog.*

SCOTT (MAURICE FITZGERALD) and others. Project appraisal in practice: the Little-Mirrlees method applied in Kenya. London, 1976. pp. 548. *bibliog.*

USING shadow prices; edited by I.M.D. Little and M. FG. Scott. London, 1976. pp. 254. *bibliogs.*

See also subdivision Cost effectiveness under subjects.

COSTS, INDUSTRIAL

— United States.

ENVIRONMENTAL controls: the impact on industry; edited by Robert A. Leone. Lexington, Mass., [1976]. pp. 129.

COTTAGE INDUSTRIES

— Ethiopia.

ETHIOPIA. Central Statistical Office. Business and Industry Division. 1975. Advance report on the 1972-73 rural survey of cottage and handicraft industries. Addis Ababa, 1975. pp. 82.

— Russia — Uzbekistan.

MUKMINOVA (ROZIIA GALIEVNA) Ocherki po istorii remesla v Samarkande i Bukhare v XVI veke. Tashkent, 1976. pp. 234.

COTTON

— India.

BULLETIN ON COTTON STATISTICS IN INDIA (DISTRICT-WISE); [pd. by] Directorate of Economics and Statistics, Ministry of Agriculture and Irrigation. a., 1975 (1st)- New Delhi.

— Zaire.

MUTOMBO (PIERRE SYLVAIN) Les fibres de coton en République Démocratique du Congo et l'industrie textile. Kinshasa, Office National de la Recherche et du Développement, [1970]. pp. 109. *bibliog.*

COTTON GROWING

— Russia — Tajikistan.

MIRONOV (NIKOLAI IVANOVICH) Bor'ba kompartii Tadzhikistana za melioratsiiu i mekhanizatsiiu v khlopkovodstve, 1945-1965 gg. Dushanbe, 1975. pp. 228.

KADYROV (DZHABAR) Osnovnye ekonomicheskie problemy razvitiia i povysheniia effektivnosti khlopkovodstva v usloviiakh tekhnicheskogo progressa. Dushanbe, 1976. pp. 416. *bibliog.*

COTTON MANUFACTURE

— Poland.

KULCZYKOWSKI (MARIUSZ) Chłopskie tkactwo bawełniane w ośrodku andrychowskim w XIX wieku. Wrocław, 1976. pp. 171. *(Polska Akademia Nauk. Oddział w Krakowie. Komisja Nauk Historycznych. Prace. nr.38) With French summary.*

— United Kingdom.

CLAY (Sir HENRY) Report on the position of the English cotton industry. n.p., 1931. fo. 97.

FITTON (ROBERT SUCKSMITH) Family earnings at the mills of W.G. and J. Strutt of Belper and Milford, Derbyshire, 1801-5. [195-?]. 8 folio sheets. (in 1 vol.). *Manuscript and typescript.*

LANCASHIRE COTTON CORPORATION. The mills and organisation of the Lancashire Cotton Corporation Limited, (1929-1950). [Manchester?, 1951?]. pp. 57.

COTTON TRADE

— European Economic Community countries.

TÜRKIYE SINAÎ KALKINMA BANKASI. Research Department. Sector Research Publications. No. 5. Cotton textile industries in Turkey and in the Common Market countries. Istanbul, 1976. pp. 75, (172). *bibliog.*

— Turkey.

TÜRKIYE SINAÎ KALKINMA BANKASI. Research Department. Sector Research Publications. No. 5. Cotton textile industries in Turkey and in the Common Market countries. Istanbul, 1976. pp. 75, (172). *bibliog.*

— Uganda.

UGANDA. Committee of Inquiry into the Cotton Industry. 1966. Report; [L.M.A. Nyakaana, chairman]. Entebbe, 1966. pp. 78.

— United Kingdom.

CLAY (Sir HENRY) Report on the position of the English cotton industry. n.p., 1931. fo. 97.

— United States.

BOEHM (RICHARD G.) Exporting cotton in Texas: relationships of ports and inland supply points. Austin, [1975]. pp. 78. *bibliog. (Texas University. Bureau of Business Research. Urban and Regional Studies. No. 2)*

COUDENHOVE-KALERGI (RICHARD NICOLAUS) Count.

KAJIMA INSTITUTE OF INTERNATIONAL PEACE. The record of the first Kajima Peace Award, recipient: Count Coudenhove Kalergi. Tokyo, 1968. pp. 143.

COUNCIL FOR MUTUAL ECONOMIC ASSISTANCE.

ASKANAS (BENEDIKT) and others. Structural developments in CMEA foreign trade over the last fifteen years (1960-1974). [Vienna], 1975. pp. 57. *bibliog. (Wiener Institut für Internationale Wirtschaftsvergleiche. Forschungsberichte. Nr. 23)*

DUBROWSKY (HANS JOACHIM) Die Zusammenarbeit der RGW-Länder auf dem Gebiet des Transportwesens. Berlin, [1975]. pp. 71. *bibliog.*

KARTSEV (VIKTOR IVANOVICH) and KOMISSAROV (ANATOLII VIKTOROVICH) SEV: sotrudnichestvo razvivaetsia. Moskva, 1975. pp. 135.

FRANCE. Direction de la Documentation. La Documentation Française. Notes et Etudes Documentaires. Nos. 4,268 - 4, 269 - 4,270. L'intégration économique à l'Est: le C[onseil d'] A[ide] E[conomique] M[utuelle], Comecon; par Catherine Seranne et Françoise Lemoine. Paris, 1976. pp. 115. *bibliog.*

LEBAHN (AXEL) Sozialistische Wirtschaftsintegration und Ost-West-Handel im sowjetischen internationalen Recht: Theorie und Praxis des Offenheitsprinzips, etc. Berlin, [1976]. pp. 495. *bibliog.*

TOKAREVA (PRASKOV'IA ALEKSEEVNA) ed. Mnogostoronnee ekonomicheskoe sotrudnichestvo sotsialisticheskikh gosudarstv: dokumenty za 1972-1975 gg. Moskva, 1976. pp. 408.

GARLAND (JOHN S.) Financing foreign trade in Eastern Europe: problems of bilateralism and currency inconvertibility. New York, 1977. pp. 168. *bibliog.*

KRAFT (GERHARD) Die Zusammenarbeit der Mitliedsländer des RGW auf dem Gebiet der Investitionen. Berlin, 1977. pp. 116.

COUNCIL OF ARAB ECONOMIC UNITY.

COUNCIL OF ARAB ECONOMIC UNITY. 1976. Council of Arab Economic Unity: what is it? What is it for? What did it?. Cairo, 1976. pp. 27.

COUNSELLING.

CHEETHAM (JULIET) Unwanted pregnancy and counselling. London, 1977. pp. 234. *bibliog.*

SWAINSON (MARY) The spirit of counsel: the story of a pioneer in student counselling. London, 1977. pp. 256. *bibliogs.*

COUNTY COURTS

— United Kingdom.

The MATRIMONIAL jurisdiction of registrars: the exercise of the matrimonial jurisdiction by registrars in England and Wales; by W. Barrington Baker [and others]. Oxford, [1977]. pp. 112. *(Oxford. University. Wolfson College. Centre for Socio- Legal Studies. Family Law Studies. No. 2)*

COUPS D'ÉTAT.

COLLIN (RICHARD) The de Lorenzo gambit: the Italian coup manqué of 1964. Beverly Hills, [1976]. pp. 65.

COURT OF JUSTICE OF THE EUROPEAN COMMUNITIES.

COMPENDIUM OF CASE LAW RELATING TO THE EUROPEAN COMMUNITIES. a., 1973- Amsterdam.

SCHERMERS (HENRY G.) Judicial protection in the European Communities. Deventer, 1976. pp. 406. *bibliog.*

COURT RULES

— United Kingdom — Scotland.

SCOTLAND. Court of Session. 1965. Rules of the Court of Session, enacted by Act of Sederunt of the Lords of Council and Session dated 10th November 1964. London, 1965. pp. 262.

COURTS

— Africa, Subsaharan.

NWABUEZE (BENJAMIN OBI) Judicialism in Commonwealth Africa: the role of the courts in government. London, [1977]. pp. 324.

— United States.

FUNSTON (RICHARD Y.) Constitutional counterrevolution?: the Warren court and the Burger court: judicial policy making in modern America. New York, [1977]. pp. 399. *bibliog.*

COURTS-MARTIAL AND COURTS OF INQUIRY

— United Kingdom — Ireland.

WOOLAGHAN (HUGH) defendant. The genuine trial of Hugh Woolaghan, yeoman, by a general court-martial, held in the barracks of Dublin, on Saturday, October 13, 1798, for the murder of Thomas Dogherty to which is added His Excellency Lord Cornwallis's order for the court-martial to be dissolved. 2nd ed. Dublin, printed for J. Milliken, 1798. pp. 27.

CRACOW

— Politics and government.

ZAWISTOWSKI (JERZY) ed. Rewolucyjne wystąpienia proletariatu krakowskiego w 1936 roku. Kraków, 1976. pp. 259.

CREDIT.

CONFERENCE ON BANK CREDIT, MONEY AND INFLATION IN OPEN ECONOMIES, LEUVEN, 1974. Bank credit, money and inflation in open economies; edited by Michele Fratianni [and] Karel Tavernier. Berlin, [1976]. pp. 624. *bibliogs. (Kredit und Kapital. Beihefte. 3) The proceedings of a conference held at the Katholieke Universiteit te Leuven on September 12-13, 1974, organised by the Centrum voor Economische Studien.*

KIRKMAN (PATRICK R.A.) Modern credit management: a study of the management of trade credit under inflationary conditions. London, 1977. pp. 311.

SAVAGE (DONALD T.) Money and banking. Santa Barbara, Calif., [1977]. pp. 491. *bibliogs.*

— Mathematical models.

PETERSSOHN (ERLING) Kreditgivning mellan företag: en mikroekonometrisk studie av företagens finansiella beteende. Stockholm, 1976. pp. 511. *bibliog. With English summary, table of contents, etc.*

— America, Latin.

GALL (PIRIE M.) and others. Municipal development programs in Latin America: an intercounty evaluation. New York, 1976. pp. 124. *bibliog.*

— Communist countries.

BUTAKOV (DANIIL DMITRIEVICH) Kredit i intensifikatsiia proizvodstva v stranakh SEV. Moskva, 1976. pp. 207.

— European Economic Community countries.

PREISIG (KARL W.) Roll-over-Eurokredit: Analyse der Elemente, Darstellung der Technik und der Probleme eines neuen Bankgeschäftes. Bern, 1976. pp. 258. *bibliog.*

— Poland.

CHOLIŃSKI (TADEUSZ) Przedsiębiorstwo a bank. Warszawa, 1972. pp. 146.

— Russia.

KUZ'MIN (VLADIMIR FEDOROVICH) Kreditnye i raschetnye pravootnosheniia v promyshlennosti. Moskva, 1975. pp. 200.

ALLAKHVERDIAN (DERENIK AKOPOVICH) Finansovo-kreditnyi mekhanizm razvitogo sotsializma. Moskva, 1976. pp. 238.

— South Africa — Law.

SOUTH AFRICA. Parliament. House of Assembly. Select Committee on the Credit Agreements Bill. 1977. Report...; proceedings (S.C. 11-1977). in SOUTH AFRICA. Parliament. House of Assembly. Select Committee reports.

— Switzerland.

KASPER (PAUL B.) Der Bankkredit als Finanzierungsmittel des schweizerischen Gewerbes: eine betriebswirtschaftliche Untersuchung. [Zuerich, 1975]. pp. 233. *bibliog.*

— United States.

FRIEDMAN (BENJAMIN M.) Credit rationing: a review. [Washington, 1972]. pp. 27. *bibliog. (United States. Board of Governors of the Federal Reserve System. Staff Economic Studies. No. 72)*

FRIEDMAN (BENJAMIN M.) Regulation Q and the commercial loan market in the 1960's. [Washington, 1972]. pp. 38. *bibliog. (United States. Board of Governors of the Federal Reserve System. Staff Economic Studies. No. 73)*

CREOLES (SIERRA LEONE).

SPITZER (LEO) The Creoles of Sierra Leone: responses to colonialism, 1870- 1945. Madison, Wis., 1974. pp. 260. *bibliog.*

CRIME AND CRIMINALS.

GORI (PIETRO) Sociologia criminale. Spezia, 1911. pp. 223. *(Opere. vol. 6)*

SZABO (DENIS) ed. Déviance et criminalité; textes réunis. Paris, [1970]. pp. 378.

NETTLER (GWYNN) Explaining crime. New York, [1974]. pp. 301. *bibliog.*

ERICSON (RICHARD V.) Criminal reactions: the labelling perspective. Farnborough, [1975]. pp. 169. *bibliog.*

GURR (THEODORE ROBERT) and others. Rogues, rebels, and reformers: a political history of urban crime and conflict. Beverly Hills, Calif., [1976]. pp. 192.

UNITED NATIONS SOCIAL DEFENCE RESEARCH INSTITUTE. 1976. Economic crises and crime: correlations between the state of the economy, deviance and the control of deviance. Rome, 1976. pp. 248. *(Publications. No.15)*

FELDMAN (MAURICE PHILIP) Criminal behaviour: a psychological analysis. London, [1977]. pp. 330. *bibliog.*

GURR (THEODORE ROBERT) and others. The politics of crime and conflict: a comparative history of four cities; with contributions by David Peirce [and others]. Beverly Hills, [1977]. pp. 792.

RADZINOWICZ (Sir LEON) and KING (JOAN FAYE SENDALL) The growth of crime: the international experience. London, 1977. pp. 342.

— Bibliography.

RADZINOWICZ (Sir LEON) and HOOD (ROGER GRAHAME) Criminology and the administration of criminal justice: a bibliography. London, 1976. pp. 400.

— France.

ZEHR (HOWARD) Crime and the development of modern society: patterns of criminality in nineteenth century Germany and France. Totowa, N.J., 1976. pp. 188. *bibliog.*

— Germany.

ZEHR (HOWARD) Crime and the development of modern society: patterns of criminality in nineteenth century Germany and France. Totowa, N.J., 1976. pp. 188. *bibliog.*

— Italy.

POLI (ENZO) Violenza politica e criminalità comune: indagine sull'ordine pubblico in Italia. [Rome, 1976]. pp. 264.

— Russia.

LICHNOST' prestupnika. Moskva, 1975. pp. 270.

NOI (IOSIF SOLOMONOVICH) Metodologicheskie problemy sovetskoi kriminologii. Saratov, 1975. pp. 222.

VOLKOV (BORIS STEPANOVICH) Deterministicheskaia priroda prestupnogo povedeniia. Kazan', 1975. pp. 110.

JUVILER (PETER HENRY) Revolutionary law and order: politics and social change in the USSR. New York, [1976]. pp. 274. *bibliog.*

KUDRIAVTSEV (VLADIMIR NIKOLAEVICH) Prichiny pravonarushenii. Moskva, 1976. pp. 286.

CHALIDZE (VALERII N.) Criminal Russia: essays on crime in the Soviet Union; translated...by P.S. Falla. New York, [1977]. pp. 240. *bibliog.*

— South Africa.

BLOCH (CHEREE) Crime on the Cape Flats: a descriptive study of the living conditions and an assessment of their implications for criminality. [Cape Town, National Institute for Crime Prevention and Rehabilitation of Offenders, 1975]. 1 vol. (various foliations). *bibliog.*

— Spain.

HERRERA PUGA (PEDRO) Sociedad y delincuencia en el Siglo de Oro: aspectos de la vida sevillana en los siglos XVI y XVII. Granada, 1971. pp. 481. *bibliog.*

— Switzerland.

HUGGER (PAUL) Sozialrebellen und Rechtsbrecher in der Schweiz: eine historisch-volkskundliche Studie. Zürich, [1976]. pp. 143. *bibliog.*

— United Kingdom.

The SOCIOLOGY of crime and delinquency in Britain. vol.2. The new criminologies; edited by Paul Wiles. London, 1976. pp. 237. *bibliogs.*

CRIME in England, 1550-1800; edited by J.S. Cockburn. London, [1977]. pp. 364. *bibliog.*

CRIME AND CRIMINALS.(Cont.)

— United States — Ohio.

MONKKONEN (ERIC H.) The dangerous class: crime and poverty in Columbus, Ohio, 1860- 1885. Cambridge, Mass., 1975. pp. 186.

CRIME PREVENTION.

GURR (THEODORE ROBERT) and others. Rogues, rebels, and reformers: a political history of urban crime and conflict. Beverly Hills, Calif., [1976]. pp. 192.

— Russia.

VOPROSY izucheniia prestupnosti i bor'by s neiu: sbornik materialov III Vsesoiuznogo nauchnogo seminara po problemam kriminologii. Moskva, 1975. pp. 227.

ZAKALIUK (ANATOLII PETROVICH) Obshchestvennoe vozdeistvie i preduprezhdenie pravonarushenii. Kiev, 1975. pp. 263.

POTERUZHA (IVAN IVANOVICH) Vospitatel'no-predupreditel'noe znachenie sudebnogo razbiratel'stva ugolovnykh del. Minsk, 1976. pp. 207.

— United States.

MORRIS (NORVAL RAMSDEN) and HAWKINS (GORDON J.) Letter to the President on crime control. Chicago, [1977]. pp. 96. *bibliog.*

CRIMINAL JUSTICE, ADMINISTRATION OF.

EVALUATION research in criminal justice: materials and proceedings of a research conference convened in the context of the Fifth United Nations Congress on the Prevention of Crime and Treatment of Offenders. Rome, United Nations Social Defence Research Institute, 1976. pp. 321. *bibliogs. (Publications. No. 11)*

GURR (THEODORE ROBERT) and others. Rogues, rebels, and reformers: a political history of urban crime and conflict. Beverly Hills, Calif., [1976]. pp. 192.

GOLDSTEIN (HERMAN) Policing a free society. Cambridge, Mass., [1977]. pp. 371. *bibliog.*

GURR (THEODORE ROBERT) and others. The politics of crime and conflict: a comparative history of four cities; with contributions by David Peirce [and others]. Beverly Hills, [1977]. pp. 792.

RADZINOWICZ (Sir LEON) and KING (JOAN FAYE SENDALL) The growth of crime: the international experience. London, 1977. pp. 342.

— Bibliography.

RADZINOWICZ (Sir LEON) and HOOD (ROGER GRAHAME) Criminology and the administration of criminal justice: a bibliography. London, 1976. pp. 400.

— Denmark.

MOXON (BETTY) and others. The administration of criminal justice in Denmark and Sweden; report of a visit to Denmark and Sweden...27 April-8 May 1975. [London, Home Office, 1976]. fo. 37. *bibliog. Photocopy.*

— Russia.

JUVILER (PETER HENRY) Revolutionary law and order: politics and social change in the USSR. New York, [1976]. pp. 274. *bibliog.*

— Sweden.

MOXON (BETTY) and others. The administration of criminal justice in Denmark and Sweden; report of a visit to Denmark and Sweden...27 April-8 May 1975. [London, Home Office, 1976]. fo. 37. *bibliog. Photocopy.*

— Uganda.

UNITED NATIONS SOCIAL DEFENCE RESEARCH INSTITUTE. 1971. Social defence in Uganda: a survey for research. Rome, 1971. pp. 129. *(Publications. No. 3)*

— United States.

MORRIS (NORVAL RAMSDEN) and HAWKINS (GORDON J.) Letter to the President on crime control. Chicago, [1977]. pp. 96. *bibliog.*

CRIMINAL LAW

— Germany.

HEINEMANN (HUGO) Neue Fesseln für das Proletariat durch die Strafgesetzgebung. Berlin, 1912. pp. 15.

PRUSSIA. Justizministerium. 1933. Nationalsozialistisches Strafrecht; Denkschrift des preussischen Justizministers. Berlin, [1933]. pp. 143.

— Italy.

CAVANNA (ADRIANO) La codificazione penale in Italia: le origini lombarde. Milano, 1975. pp. 317. *(Milan. Università. Istituto di Storia del Diritto Italiano. Pubblicazioni. 5)*

— Poland.

PAWELA (STANISŁAW) Wykonanie orzeczeń w sprawach karnych: komentarz; stan na dzień 1 stycznia 1965. Warszawa, 1965. pp. 335.

— Russia.

LAPENNA (IVO) The contemporary crisis of legality in the Soviet Union substantive criminal law. Leyden, 1975. pp. 73-95. *(Offprint from Review of Socialist Law, 1975)*

KUDRIAVTSEV (P.I.) ed. Voprosy ugolovnogo prava i protsessa v praktike prokurorskogo nadzora za sobliudeniem zakonnosti pri rassmotrenii sudami ugolovnykh del. Moskva, 1976. pp. 495.

POTERUZHA (IVAN IVANOVICH) Vospitatel'no-predupreditel'noe znachenie sudebnogo razbiratel'stva ugolovnykh del. Minsk, 1976. pp. 207.

— — Azerbaijan.

BABAEV (ADIL' SALMANOVICH) Sozdanie osnov sovetskogo ugolovnogo i ugolovno-protsessual'nogo prava v Azerbaidzhane. Baku, 1973. pp. 222.

— — Kazakstan.

KAZAKSTAN. Statutes, etc. 1975. Ugolovnyi kodeks Kazakhskoi SSR: ofitsial'nyi tekst s izmeneniiami i dopolneniiami na 1 sentiabria 1975 goda. Alma-Ata, 1976. pp. 200.

— — Ukraine.

UKRAINE. Statutes, etc. 1975. Ugolovnyi kodeks Ukrainskoi SSR: ofitsial'nyi tekst s izmeneniiami i dopolneniiami na 1 ianvaria 1975 goda i postateinymi materialami. Kiev, 1975. pp. 368.

— United Kingdom.

MORIARTY (CECIL CHARLES HUDSON) Police law: an arrangement of law and regulations for the use of police officers; twenty-third edition by William J. Williams. London, 1976. pp. 793.

CRIMINAL LIABILITY (INTERNATIONAL LAW).

VASILENKO (VLADIMIR ANDREEVICH) Otvetstvennost' gosudarstva za mezhdunarodnye pravonarusheniia. Kiev, 1976. pp. 267. *bibliog.*

CRIMINAL PROCEDURE

— Russia.

MARTINOVICH (IZABELLA IVANOVNA) Glasnost' v sovetskom ugolovnom sudoproizvodstve. Minsk, 1968. pp. 74. *bibliog.*

SHPILEV (VENIAMIN NIKOLAEVICH) Uchastniki ugolovnogo protsessa. Minsk, 1970. pp. 176.

BOLDYREV (EVGENII VLADIMIROVICH) and PERGAMENT (ALEKSANDRA IOSIFOVNA) eds. Nauchnyi kommentarii sudebnoi praktiki za 1972 god. Moskva, 1973. pp. 206.

KUDRIAVTSEV (P.I.) ed. Voprosy ugolovnogo prava i protsessa v praktike prokurorskogo nadzora za sobliudeniem zakonnosti pri rassmotrenii sudami ugolovnykh del. Moskva, 1976. pp. 495.

— — Azerbaijan.

AZERBAIJAN. Statutes, etc. 1971. Ugolovno-protsessual'nyi kodeks Azerbaidzhanskoi SSR: s izmeneniiami i dobavleniiami na 1 ianvaria 1970 goda. Baku, 1971. pp. 387.

BABAEV (ADIL' SALMANOVICH) Sozdanie osnov sovetskogo ugolovnogo i ugolovno-protsessual'nogo prava v Azerbaidzhane. Baku, 1973. pp. 222.

— Tasmania.

TASMANIA. Law Reform Commission. 1975. Report and recommendations...on the Criminal Process, Bodily Descriptions, Bill 1974. in TASMANIA. Parliament. Journals and Printed Papers. 1975, no.45.

— United Kingdom.

MORIARTY (CECIL CHARLES HUDSON) Police law: an arrangement of law and regulations for the use of police officers; twenty-third edition by William J. Williams. London, 1976. pp. 793.

HAMPTON (CELIA) Criminal procedure. 2nd ed. London, 1977. pp. 421.

— United States.

WEINREB (LLOYD L.) Denial of justice: criminal process in the United States. New York, [1977]. pp. 177.

CRIMINAL PSYCHOLOGY.

LICHNOST' prestupnika. Moskva, 1975. pp. 270.

VOLKOV (BORIS STEPANOVICH) Deterministicheskaia priroda prestupnogo povedeniia. Kazan', 1975. pp. 110.

EYSENCK (HANS JÜRGEN) Crime and personality. 3rd ed. London, 1977. pp. 222.

FELDMAN (MAURICE PHILIP) Criminal behaviour: a psychological analysis. London, [1977]. pp. 330. *bibliog.*

CRIMINAL STATISTICS

— Norway.

NORWAY. Statistiske Centralbyrå. 1975. Kriminalstatistikk: oversikt, 1960-1972, etc. Oslo, 1975. pp. 119. *bibliog. (Statistiske Analyser. Nr. 17) With English summary.*

CRISES.

[GEL'FAND (ALEKSANDR LAZAREVICH)] Die Handelskrisis und die Gewerkschaften; nebst Anhang: Gesetzentwurf über den achtstündigen Normalarbeitstag; von Parvus [pseud.]. München, 1901. pp. 64.

NAPHTALI (FRITZ) Wirtschaftskrise und Arbeitslosigkeit, volkstümlich dargestellt. Berlin, 1930. pp. 32.

HOBSBAWM (ERIC JOHN ERNEST) The crisis and the outlook. London, [1975]. pp. 16. *Taken from a lecture given to Birkbeck College Socialist Society.*

MANDEL (ERNEST) The generalized recession of the international capitalist economy. Brussels, 1975. pp. 24.

ČUBRILOVIĆ (VASA) and others, eds. Svetska ekonomska kriza, 1929-1934 godine i njen odraz u zemljama jugoistočne Evrope; Crise économique mondiale, 1929-1934 et ses reflets dans les pays du Sud-Est européen. Beograd, 1976. pp. 424. *(Srpska Akademija Nauka i Umetnosti. Balkanološki Institut. Posebna Izdanja. knj.5) Articles in English or French with Serbo-Croat summaries, or in Serbo-Croat with French summaries.*

GOLDBERG (JOERG) and JUNG (HEINZ) Die Wirtschaftskrise 1974-1976 in der Bundesrepublik Deutschland: Ursachen, Auswirkungen, Argumente. Frankfurt am Main, 1976. pp. 92.

HABERLER (GOTTFRIED VON) The world economy, money, and the Great Depression, 1919-1939. Washington, D.C., 1976. pp. 44. (American Enterprise Institute for Public Policy Research. Foreign Affairs Studies. 30)

INOZEMTSEV (NIKOLAI NIKOLAEVICH) and others, eds. Uglublenie obshchego krizisa kapitalizma. Moskva, 1976. pp. 358.

KEDAR (BENJAMIN Z.) Merchants in crisis: Genoese and Venetian men of affairs and the fourteenth-century depression. New Haven, 1976. pp. 260. bibliog.

STAJNER (RIKARD) Kriza: anatomija suvremenih kriza i (jedna) teorija kriza u neoimperijalističkoj fazi razvoja kapitalizma. Beograd, 1976. pp. 174. bibliog. With English and Russian summaries.

SWEET (COLIN) World economic crisis: an analysis of economic, political and military factors. London, [1976]. pp. 40.

HOWSON (SUSAN) and WINCH (DONALD NORMAN) The Economic Advisory Council, 1930-1939: a study in economic advice during depression and recovery. Cambridge, 1977. pp. 424. bibliog.

OLSON (JAMES STUART) Herbert Hoover and the Reconstruction Finance Corporation, 1931-1933. Ames, 1977. pp. 155. bibliog.

SEMAINE DE BRUGES, 1976. The European economy beyond the crisis: from stabilisation to structural change...: l'économie européenne au-delà de la crise: de la stabilisation à la mutation structurelle; (edited by G.R. Denton and J.J.N. Cooper). Bruges, 1977. pp. 409. (College of Europe. Cahiers de Bruges. Nouvelle Série. 35) In English and French.

CRISTERO REBELLION, 1926-1929.

MEYER (JEAN A.) La cristiada. Mexico, 1973-74 repr. 1974-76. 3 vols. bibliog.

CRITICISM

— United States.

WEAPONS of criticism: marxism in America and the literary tradition; edited by Norman Rudich. Palo Alto, [1976]. pp. 389.

CROATIA

— Constitutional history.

LANOVIĆ (MIHAJLO) Zapadno-evropski feudalizam i ugarsko-hrvatski donacionalni sustav. Zagreb, 1928. pp. 106. bibliog.

— History.

OMRČANIN (MARGARET STEWART) Norway, Sweden, Croatia: a comparative study of state secession and formation. Philadelphia, [1976]. pp. 138.

— Nationalism.

OMRČANIN (MARGARET STEWART) Norway, Sweden, Croatia: a comparative study of state secession and formation. Philadelphia, [1976]. pp. 138.

CROCE (BENEDETTO).

POLVERINI (GIORGIO) Benedetto Croce e il comunismo. Como, 1975. pp. 209.

CROWDING STRESS.

BOOTH (ALAN) Urban crowding and its consequences. New York, 1976. pp. 139. bibliog.

CRUELTY TO CHILDREN

— United Kingdom.

SOMERSET. Area Review Committee for Non-accidental Injury to Children. Review Panel. Wayne Brewer; report of the review panel; [by] John Clark [and others]. Taunton, 1977. pp. 51.

CRYING.

DUNN (JUDY) Distress and comfort. London, 1977. pp. 126. bibliog.

CUBA

— Economic conditions.

PETUSHKOV (IVAN GRIGOR'EVICH) and SHEININ (EDUARD IAKOVLEVICH) Ekonomika Kuby v sisteme mezhdunarodnogo sotsialisticheskogo razdeleniia truda. Moskva, 1976. pp. 167.

— Economic history.

MARRERO (LEVI) Cuba: economia y sociedad. Rio Piedras, 1972 in progress. bibliogs.

— Foreign relations — America, Latin.

MARQUEZ STERLING (MANUEL) La diplomacia en nuestra historia. La Habana, 1967. pp. 214. First published in 1909.

— — Russia.

LEVESQUE (JACQUES) L'URSS et la révolution cubaine. Paris, [1976]. pp. 221. bibliog. (Fondation Nationale des Sciences Politiques. Travaux et Recherches de Science Politique. 42)

— — United States.

CASTRO RUZ (RAUL) Speech given by Major Raul Castro Ruz, second secretary of the central committee of the Communist Party of Cuba, in the graduation ceremony for the third course of the General Maximo Gomez Basic School, July 22, 1967. London, Cuban Embassy, 1967. pp. 15. (Cuba Information Bulletins. 1967. No. 9)

CUBA. 1972. (Complete text of the declaration made by the Cuban revolutionary government regarding the hijacking of aircraft, issued on the 15th of November, 1972). [London, Cuban Embassy], 1972. fo. 5. (Press Releases)

— — Venezuela.

PARTIDO COMUNISTA DE CUBA. Comite Central. Statement...on the new threat of imperialist aggression, Havana, May 17, 1967. London, Cuban Embassy, 1967. pp. 6. (Cuba Information Bulletins. 1967. No. 7)

— History — Bibliography.

PEREZ (LOUIS A.) The Cuban revolutionary war, 1953-1958: a bibliography. Metuchen, N.J., 1976. pp. 225.

— — 1933-1959.

MATTHEWS (HERBERT LIONEL) Revolution in Cuba: an essay in understanding. New York, [1975]. pp. 468. bibliog.

— — 1933, Revolution.

RABY (D.L.) The Cuban pre-revolution of 1933: an analysis. Glasgow, 1975. pp. 28. (Glasgow. University. Institute of Latin American Studies. Occasional Papers. No. 18)

— — 1959- .

BAMBIRRA (VANIA) La revolucion cubana: una reinterpretacion. Mexico, 1974. pp. 172. bibliog.

MATTHEWS (HERBERT LIONEL) Revolution in Cuba: an essay in understanding. New York, [1975]. pp. 468. bibliog.

LEVESQUE (JACQUES) L'URSS et la révolution cubaine. Paris, [1976]. pp. 221. bibliog. (Fondation Nationale des Sciences Politiques. Travaux et Recherches de Science Politique. 42)

— Politics and government.

ALMEIDA (JUAN) Speech delivered by Major Juan Almeida, member of the political bureau of the central committee of the Communist Party of Cuba, in commemoration of May 1, international workers' day: Plaza de la Revolucion, May 1, 1967, year of heroic Viet Nam. London, Cuban Embassy, 1967. pp. 15. (Cuba Information Bulletins. 1967. No.6)

FERNANDEZ COSIO (FRANCISCO L.) Cuba en tinieblas. Mexico, 1973. pp. 266.

FARBER (SAMUEL) Revolution and reaction in Cuba, 1933-1960: a political sociology from Machado to Castro. Middletown, Conn., [1976]. pp. 283. bibliog.

FRANQUI (CARLOS) Diario de la revolucion cubana. [Paris, 1976]. pp. 754.

— Relations (general) with Russia.

ROSSIISKO-kubinskie i sovetsko-kubinskie sviazi XVIII-XX vekov. Moskva, 1975. pp. 351.

— Social history.

MARRERO (LEVI) Cuba: economia y sociedad. Rio Piedras, 1972 in progress. bibliogs.

CUDLIPP (HUGH) Baron Cudlipp.

CUDLIPP (HUGH) Baron Cudlipp. Walking on the water. London, 1976. pp. 428.

CUGNET (FRANÇOIS ETIENNE).

NISH (CAMERON) François-Etienne Cugnet, 1719-1751: entrepreneur et entreprises en Nouvelle-France. Montréal, [1975]. pp. 185. bibliog. (Centre de Recherche en Histoire Economique du Canada Français. Histoire Economique et Sociale du Canada Français)

CULLEN (WILLIAM).

DONOVAN (ARTHUR L.) Philosophical chemistry in the Scottish Enlightenment: the doctrines and discoveries of William Cullen and Joseph Black. Edinburgh, [1975]. pp. 343. bibliog.

CULTURAL PROPERTY, PROTECTION OF

— Taxation — United Kingdom.

U.K. Treasury. 1977. Capital taxation and the national heritage. [London], 1977. pp. 19.

— India.

UNITED NATIONS SOCIAL DEFENCE RESEARCH INSTITUTE. 1976. The protection of the artistic and archaeological heritage: a view from Italy and India. Rome, 1976. pp. 259. (Publications. No. 13).

— Italy.

UNITED NATIONS SOCIAL DEFENCE RESEARCH INSTITUTE. 1976. The protection of the artistic and archaeological heritage: a view from Italy and India. Rome, 1976. pp. 259. (Publications. No. 13).

CULTURAL RELATIONS.

DEIBEL (TERRY L.) and ROBERTS (WALTER R.) Culture and information: two foreign policy functions. Beverly Hills, [1976]. pp. 62. bibliog. (Georgetown University. Center for Strategic and International Studies. Washington Papers. vol. 4/40)

CULTURE.

CASCUDO (LUIS DA CAMARA) Civilização e cultura: pesquisas e notas de etnografia geral. Rio, 1973. 2 vols. bibliog.

CULTURE.(Cont.)

ROSENBERG (HAROLD) Discovering the present: three decades in art, culture, and politics. Chicago, 1973. pp. 336.

MAZRUI (ALI AL'AMIN) A world federation of cultures: an African perspective. New York, [1976]. pp. 508.

SCHWARTZ (THEODORE) ed. Socialization as cultural communication: development of a theme in the work of Margaret Mead. Berkeley, Calif., [1976]. pp. 251. *bibliogs. (Reprinted from Ethos, vol.3,no.2, 1975)*

BOURDIEU (PIERRE) and PASSERON (JEAN CLAUDE) Reproduction in education, society and culture; translated from the French by Richard Nice. London, [1977]. pp. 255. *bibliog.*

POLITICAL culture and political change in communist states; edited by Archie Brown and Jack Gray. London, 1977. pp. 286. *Papers presented at a conference held in St. Antony's College, Oxford, 1975.*

CULTUS.

REGIONAL cults; edited by R.P. Werbner. London, 1977. pp. 257. *(Association of Social Anthropologists of the Commonwealth. A.S.A. Monographs. 16) Essays derived mainly from papers presented at the 1976 A.S.A. Conference in Manchester.*

CUMBERLAND

— Economic conditions.

CUMBRIA COMMUNITY DEVELOPMENT PROJECT. Initial study of the two parishes Cleator Moor, Arlecdon and Frizington. Cleator Moor, 1973. pp. 54.

— Social conditions.

CUMBRIA COMMUNITY DEVELOPMENT PROJECT. Initial study of the two parishes Cleator Moor, Arlecdon and Frizington. Cleator Moor, 1973. pp. 54.

CUSTOMS ADMINISTRATION

— Botswana.

BOTSWANA. Department of Customs and Excise. Report. a., 1975/77[2nd]- Gaborone.

CUSTOMS UNIONS.

BUELOW-CUMMEROW (ERNST GOTTFRIED GEORG VON) Der Zollverein, sein System und dessen Gegner. Berlin, Veit, 1844. pp. 123.

CUZCO (DEPARTMENT)

— Social conditions.

VAN DEN BERGHE (PIERRE LOUIS) and PRIMOV (GEORGE P.) Inequality in the Peruvian Andes: class and ethnicity in Cuzco. Columbia, Mo., [1977]. pp. 324. *bibliog.*

CYPRUS

— Constitution.

TORNARITES (KRITON G.) Constitutional and legal problems in the republic of Cyprus. Nicosia, [Public Information Office], 1968. pp. 64.

POLYVIOU (POLYVIOS G.) The problem of Cyprus: constitutional and political aspects. Nicosia, 1974. fo. 77.

— Economic conditions.

CYPRUS. Ministry of Finance. 1972. Address before the House of Representatives on the 1972 budget, the achievements of the second and the targets and objectives of the third five-year plan; by the Minister of Finance Andreas Patsalides. Nicosia, 1972. pp. 39.

— Economic policy.

CYPRUS. Ministry of Finance. 1972. Address before the House of Representatives on the 1972 budget, the achievements of the second and the targets and objectives of the third five-year plan; by the Minister of Finance Andreas Patsalides. Nicosia, 1972. pp. 39.

— Emigration and immigration.

CYPRUS. Statistics and Research Department. Tourism, migration and travel statistics: annual report. a., 1976- [Nicosia]. *[in English and Greek].*

CYPRUS. Statistics and Research Department. Tourism, migration and travel statistics: monthly bulletin. m., Jl 1976- [Nicosia]. *[in Greek and English].*

— Foreign relations — United States.

CYPRUS reviewed: the result of a seminar on the Cyprus problem held in June 3-6, 1976, by the Jus Cypri Association and the Coordinating Committee of Scientific and Cultural Organisations; edited by Michael A. Attalides. Nicosia, 1977. pp. 275.

— History.

VANEZIS (PROCOPIOS NICHOLA) Cyprus: the unfinished agony. London, 1977. pp. 141. *bibliog.*

— — Cyprus crisis, 1974- .

CYPRUS. 1975. Turks usurp Cyprus produce. [Nicosia?, 1975]. pp. 10.

DEVECI (HASAN A.) Cyprus yesterday: today, what next? London, 1976. pp. 60. *(Cyprus Turkish Association. Turkish Cases in English Series. 2)*

— Industries.

CYPRUS. Statistics and Research Department. 1976. Census of industrial production, 1972. [Nicosia, 1976]. 2 vols.(in 1).

— Nationalism.

CYPRUS reviewed: the result of a seminar on the Cyprus problem held in June 3-6, 1976, by the Jus Cypri Association and the Coordinating Committee of Scientific and Cultural Organisations; edited by Michael A. Attalides. Nicosia, 1977. pp. 275.

— Politics and government.

CYPRUS. Public Information Office. 1968. Cyprus: the problem in perspective. rev. ed. Nicosia, 1968. pp. 63.

TORNARITES (KRITON G.) Constitutional and legal problems in the republic of Cyprus. Nicosia, [Public Information Office], 1968. pp. 64.

CYPRUS. Public Information Office. 1969. The Cyprus question: a brief analysis. Nicosia, 1969. pp. 20.

POLYVIOU (POLYVIOS G.) The problem of Cyprus: constitutional and political aspects. Nicosia, 1974. fo. 77.

DEVECI (HASAN A.) Cyprus yesterday: today, what next? London, 1976. pp. 60. *(Cyprus Turkish Association. Turkish Cases in English Series. 2)*

CYPRUS reviewed: the result of a seminar on the Cyprus problem held in June 3-6, 1976, by the Jus Cypri Association and the Coordinating Committee of Scientific and Cultural Organisations; edited by Michael A. Attalides. Nicosia, 1977. pp. 275.

VANEZIS (PROCOPIOS NICHOLA) Cyprus: the unfinished agony. London, 1977. pp. 141. *bibliog.*

— Public works.

CYPRUS. Department of Electrical and Mechanical Service. Annual report. a., 1975(1st)- [Nicosia].

— Race question.

VANEZIS (PROCOPIOS NICHOLA) Cyprus: the unfinished agony. London, 1977. pp. 141. *bibliog.*

— Social policy.

TRISELIOTIS (JOHN P.) Social welfare in Cyprus. London, 1977. pp. 179. *bibliog.*

CZECHOSLOVAKIA

— Antiquities.

SMRŽ (ZDENĚK) Enkláva lužického osídlení v oblasti Boskovské brázdy. Praha, 1975. pp. 70. *bibliog. (Československá Akademie Věd. Archeologický Ústav v Brně. Studie. ročník 3/1974, sv.3) With German summary.*

— Bibliography.

HEJZLAR (ZDENĚK) and KUSIN (VLADIMIR V.) Czechoslovakia, 1968-1969: chronology, bibliography, annotation. New York, 1975. pp. 316.

— Commerce.

ČESKOSLOVENSKÁ OBCHODNÍ KOMORA. Facts on Czechoslovak foreign trade, [1965 ed.]. [Prague], 1965. pp. 256.

— Economic conditions.

RENNER (KARL) Das nationale und das ökonomische Problem der Tschechoslowakei. Prag, 1926. pp. 20.

BARVÍK (JAROMÍR) and KOMÁREK (VALTR) Problémy intenzívního typu rozvoje socialistické ekonomiky. Praha, 1976. pp. 318.

— Economic history.

RUDOLPH (RICHARD L.) Banking and industrialization in Austria-Hungary: the role of banks in the industrialization of the Czech Crownlands, 1873-1914. Cambridge, 1976. pp. 291. *bibliog.*

— Economic policy.

TOLKACHEV (ALEKSANDR SERGEEVICH) ed. Problemy metodologii planirovaniia i izmereniia effektivnosti proizvodstva; (v osnovu knigi polozheny materialy Mezhdunarodnogo seminara...v Marianske Lazne v 1974 g.). Moskva, 1975. pp. 215.

ADAMÍČEK (JOSEF) Entwicklung des gesellschaftlichen Konsums in der ČSSR. Berlin, [1977]. pp. 181. *bibliog. (Osteuropa-Institut, München. Veröffentlichungen. Reihe: Wirtschaft und Gesellschaft. Heft 17)*

— Foreign relations — Poland.

KOWALCZYK (JÓZEF) Za kulisami wydarzeń politycznych z lat 1936-1938 w świetle raportów posła Czechosłowacji w Warszawie i innych archiwaliów: [szkice i dokumenty]. Warszawa, 1976. pp. 149.

— History.

KORBEL (JOSEF) Twentieth-century Czechoslovakia: the meanings of its history. New York, 1977. pp. 346. *bibliog.*

WALLACE (WILLIAM V.) Czechoslovakia. London, 1977. pp. 374. *bibliog.*

— — Sources.

KAVAN (JAN) and DANIEL (JAN) pseud., eds. Sotsialisticheskaia oppozitsiia v Chekhoslovakii, 1973-75: podborka dokumentov; perevod [s cheshskogo] Iriny Khenkinoi. London, 1976. pp. 342. *bibliog.*

— — 1525-1618.

DILLON (KENNETH J.) King and estates in the Bohemian lands, 1526-1564. Bruxelles, 1976. pp. 206. *bibliog. (International Commission for the History of Representative and Parliamentary Institutions. Studies. 57)*

— — 1848, Revolution.

BENEŠ (KAREL JOSEF) ed. 1848 v projevech současníků; s úvodní studií a poznámkami, etc. [Praha], 1932. pp. 179.

— — 1938-1945.

STROEBINGER (RUDOLF) Das Attentat von Prag. Landshut, 1976. pp. 270. *bibliog.*

— — **1948, Coup d'état.**

FEJTÖ (FRANÇOIS) Le coup de Prague, 1948. Paris, [1976]. pp. 283. *bibliog.*

— — **1968- , Intervention.**

HEJZLAR (ZDENĚK) and KUSIN (VLADIMIR V.) Czechoslovakia, 1968-1969: chronology, bibliography, annotation. New York, 1975. pp. 316.

SKILLING (HAROLD GORDON) Czechoslovakia's interrupted revolution. Princeton, N.J. [1976]. pp. 924. *bibliog.*

— **Intellectual life.**

VYŠNÝ (PAUL) Neo-Slavism and the Czechs, 1898-1914. Cambridge, 1977. pp. 287. *bibliog.*

— **Languages.**

POZORNY (REINHARD) Deutsche Schutzarbeit im Sudetenland: die Tätigkeit des Deutschen Kulturverbandes, 1918-1938. Wien, 1974. pp. 51.

— **Learned institutions and societies.**

DESET let Výzkumného ústavu sociálně ekonomických informací: sborník. Praha, 1975. pp. 151.

— **Nationalism.**

ČESKÝ národ ve světové válce a vídeňská vláda: dotaz poslanců Františka Staňka...Zdeňka Tobolky a soudruhů na... ministerského předsedu v příčině chování se vládních kruhů k českému národu za války. Pardubice, 1917. pp. 129.

— **Politics and government.**

HUSÁK (GUSTÁV) Projevy a stati, duben 1969 - leden 1970. Praha, 1970. pp. 403.

HUSÁK (GUSTÁV) Vybrané projevy, květen 1970 - prosinec 1971. Praha, 1972. pp. 511.

KAVAN (JAN) and DANIEL (JAN) pseud., eds. Sotsialisticheskaia oppozitsiia v Chekhoslovakii, 1973-75: podborka dokumentov; perevod [s cheshskogo] Iriny Khenkinoi. London, 1976. pp. 342. *bibliog.*

SKILLING (HAROLD GORDON) Czechoslovakia's interrupted revolution. Princeton, N.J. [1976]. pp. 924. *bibliog.*

JOSTEN (JOSEF) Czechoslovakia: from 1968 to Charter 77: a record of passive resistance. London, 1977. pp. 22. *(Institute for the Study of Conflict. Conflict Studies. No. 86)*

WALLACE (WILLIAM V.) Czechoslovakia. London, 1977. pp. 374. *bibliog.*

— — **Bibliography.**

HEJZLAR (ZDENĚK) and KUSIN (VLADIMIR V.) Czechoslovakia, 1968-1969: chronology, bibliography, annotation. New York, 1975. pp. 316.

— **Population.**

HARMSEN (HANS) ed. Demographische Entwicklungsprobleme der CSSR von 1945 bis 2000 unter Berücksichtigung des 1958 in Kraft getretenen Gesetzes über die künstliche Unterbrechung der Schwangerschaft. Hamburg, 1973. pp. 47.

— **Social conditions.**

ADAMÍČEK (JOSEF) Entwicklung des gesellschaftlichen Konsums in der ČSSR. Berlin, [1977]. pp. 181. *bibliog. (Osteuropa-Institut, München. Veröffentlichungen. Reihe: Wirtschaft und Gesellschaft. Heft 17)*

— **Statistics.**

VÝZKUMNÝ ÚSTAV SOCIÁLNĚ EKONOMICKÝCH INFORMACÍ. 30. let ČSSR: dlouhodobé časové řady; zpracoval jako závazek k 30. výročí osvobozani kolektiv pracovníků VÚSEI. Praha, 1975. pp. 162. *bibliog.*

CZECHS IN AUSTRIA-HUNGARY.

ČESKÝ národ ve světové válce a vídeňská vláda: dotaz poslanců Františka Staňka...Zdeňka Tobolky a soudruhů na... ministerského předsedu v příčině chování se vládních kruhů k českému národu za války. Pardubice, 1917. pp. 129.

DACCA

— **Social conditions.**

FAROUK (A.) and others. The vagrants of Dacca City: a socio-economic survey, 1975. Dacca, 1976. pp. 130.

DAGHESTAN

— **History — 1917-1921, Revolution.**

KASHKAEV (BADRUTDIN OMARIEVICH) Grazhdanskaia voina v Dagestane, 1918-1920 gg. Moskva, 1976. pp. 294. *bibliog.*

— **Statistics.**

DAGHESTAN. Statisticheskoe Upravlenie. 1972. Narodnoe khoziaistvo Dagestanskoi ASSR k 50-letiiu obrazovaniia SSSR: (statisticheskii sbornik). Makhachkala, 1972. pp. 222.

DAHLEM (FRANZ).

DAHLEM (FRANZ) Am Vorabend des zweiten Weltkrieges:...Erinnerungen. Berlin, 1977 in progress.

DAHLSTRÖM (HANS).

EUROPEAN COURT OF HUMAN RIGHTS. Publications. Series B: Pleadings, Oral Arguments and Documents. [B19]. "Schmidt and Dahlström" case, (1974-1975). Strasbourg, Council of Europe, 1977. pp. 199bis. *In English and French.*

DAIRY PRODUCTS

— **Information services.**

UNITED NATIONS INDUSTRIAL DEVELOPMENT ORGANIZATION. Guides to Information Sources. No. 23. Information sources on the dairy product manufacturing industry. (ID/177) (UNIDO/LIB/SER.D/23). New York, United Nations, 1976. pp. 88. *bibliog.*

— **Marketing.**

ECONOMISCH INSTITUUT VOOR HET MIDDEN- EN KLEINBEDRIJF. Bedrijfseconomische Publikaties. De ambulante detailhandel in melk en melkprodukten 1971-1973, 1974, 1975. 's-Gravenhage, 1976. pp. 50.

— **Switzerland.**

HAEGI (HANS RUDOLF) Die schweizerische Milchwirtschaft: Produktion, Verwertung, Aussenhandel, Gesetzgebung, Verwertungsorganisationen. [Bern, 1976]. pp. 39. *bibliog.*

DAIRYING

— **European Economic Community countries.**

EEC DAIRY FACTS AND FIGURES; [pd. by Economics Division, Milk Marketing Board [U.K.]. a., 1973- Thames Ditton.

— **Tanzania.**

WANGWE (S.M.) The problem of underutilization of capacity in industry: a case study of the Mara dairy industry. Dar es Salaam, 1975. pp. 37. *(Dar es Salaam. University. Economic Research Bureau. ERB Papers. 75.4)*

— **United Kingdom — Costs.**

U.K. Ministry of Agriculture, Fisheries and Food. 1976. Costs and efficiency in milk production, 1972/1973. London, 1976. pp. 82.

DAKAR UNIVERSITY.

DAKAR. Université. Faculté des Lettres et Sciences Humaines. Enseignement et recherches africanistes propres à la Faculté, etc. [Dakar, 1963]. fo.15.

DALBERG-ACTON (JOHN EMERICH EDWARD) 1st Baron Acton.

CHADWICK (WILLIAM OWEN) Acton and Gladstone. London, 1976. pp. 56. *(London. University. Creighton Lectures. 1975)*

SCHUETTINGER (ROBERT L.) Lord Acton, historian of liberty. La Salle, Ill., 1976. pp. 251. *bibliog.*

DALMATIA

— **Economic policy.**

PETRIĆ (IVO) Planning at the level of the region and the commune with special reference to planning in the enterprise: Split and Dalmatia; (translated by Meri Radosević). Ljubljana, International Center for Public Enterprises, 1974. fo. 27. *bibliog. (International Seminar 1974. [National Papers])*

DANGEROUS GOODS

— **Transportation.**

UNITED NATIONS. Committee of Experts on the Transport of Dangerous Goods. 1976. Transport of dangerous goods: recommendations. (ST/SG/AC.10/1). New York, 1976. pp. 337.

DANUBE VALLEY

— **History.**

RECKER (MARIE LUISE) England und der Donauraum, 1919-1929: Probleme einer europäischen Nachkriegsordnung. Stuttgart, 1976. pp. 324. *bibliog. (Deutsches Historisches Institut in London. Veröffentlichungen. Band 3)*

DARTINGTON HALL SCHOOL.

PUNCH (MAURICE) Progressive retreat: a sociological study of Dartington Hall School, 1926-1957, and some of its former pupils. Cambridge, 1977. pp. 185. *bibliog. Originally presented as Ph.D. thesis, University of Essex.*

DARTMOOR NATIONAL PARK.

SHARP (EVELYN) Baroness Sharp. Dartmoor: a report...to the Secretary of State for the Environment and the Secretary of State for Defence of a public local inquiry held in December, 1975 and May, 1976 into the continued use of Dartmoor by the Ministry of Defence for training purposes. London, H.M.S.O., 1977. pp. 121.

DARWIN

— **Population.**

AUSTRALIA. Commonwealth Bureau of Census and Statistics. 1975. Population estimates and the effect of cyclone Tracy, Darwin, January 1975. Canberra, 1975. single sheet.

DASANETCH (AFRICAN PEOPLE).

CARR (CLAUDIA J.) Pastoralism in crisis: the Dasanetch and their Ethiopian lands. Chicago, 1977. pp. 319. *bibliog. (Chicago. University. Department of Geography. Research Papers. No.180)*

DATA BASE MANAGEMENT.

CURTICE (ROBERT M.) Access mechanisms and data structure support in data base management systems. Wellesley, Mass., [1975]. pp. 60. *bibliog.*

SUNDGREN (BO) Theory of data bases. New York, 1975. pp. 244. *bibliog.*

COHEN (LEO J.) and others. Data base management systems. Wellesley, Mass., [1976]. 1 vol. (various pagings).

CURTICE (ROBERT M.) Planning for data base systems. Wellesley, Mass., [1976]. pp. 44. *bibliog.*

JONES (PAUL E.) Data base design methodology: a logical framework. Wellesley, Mass., [1976]. pp. 90. *bibliog.*

DATA BASE MANAGEMENT.(Cont.)

LANGEFORS (NILS BÖRJE) and SAMUELSON (KJELL) Information and data in systems. New York, 1976. pp. 124. *bibliog.*

PROTHRO (VIVIAN C.) Information management systems: data base primer. New York, 1976. pp. 109.

GHOSH (SAKTI P.) Data base organization for data management. New York, 1977. pp. 376. *bibliogs.*

TSICHRITZIS (DIONYSIOS C.) and LOCHOVSKY (FREDERICK H.) Data base management systems. New York, [1977]. pp. 388. *bibliog.*

DATA STRUCTURES (COMPUTER SCIENCE).

ELSON (MARK) Data structures. Chicago, [1975]. pp. 307. *bibliog.*

FLORES (IVAN) Data structure and management. 2nd ed. Englewood Cliffs, [1977]. pp. 390.

DATA TRANSMISSION SYSTEMS.

INTERNATIONAL CONFERENCE ON COMPUTER COMMUNICATION, 3RD, TORONTO, 1976. Advancement through resource sharing; edited by Pramode K. Verma. [Washington, D.C.], 1976. pp. 655. *Sponsored by the International Council for Computer Communication.*

SCHWARTZ (MISCHA) Computer-communication network: design and analysis. Englewood Cliffs, [1977]. pp. 372. *bibliog.*

DAY NURSERIES

— United Kingdom.

FINER JOINT ACTION COMMITTEE. Parents, children and day care facilities. [London, 1976]. pp. 12,2.

DAYAN (MOSHE).

DAYAN (MOSHE) Story of my life. London, [1976]. pp. 530.

DEAN (JOHN WESLEY).

DEAN (JOHN WESLEY) Blind ambition: the White House years. New York, [1976]. pp. 415.

DEATH

— Causes.

U.K. Office of Population Censuses and Surveys. Mortality statistics: accidents and violence: review of the Registrar General on deaths attributed to accidental and violent causes in England and Wales. a., 1974 (1st)- London. *Supersedes in part Registrar General's statistical review of England and Wales.*

— Psychology.

WILLANS (JOAN H.) Death and bereavement. London, [1974]. pp. 12. *bibliog. (Age Concern England. Manifesto Series. No. 17)*

DEBTS, EXTERNAL

— Brazil.

CAMBRIDGE. University. Centre of Latin American Studies. Working Papers. No. 13. Euro-dollars, foreign debt and the Brazilian boom; by John Wells. Cambridge, 1973. pp. 35.

DEBTS, PUBLIC

— Mexico.

MEXICO. Statutes, etc. 1883-1957. Legislacion sobre deuda publica. Mexico, 1958. 3 vols.

— Sweden.

LINDGREN (TORGNY) Banko- och riksgäldsrevisionerna, 1782-1807: "de redliga män, som bewakade Ständers rätt". Uppsala, 1975. pp. 198. *bibliog. (Uppsala. Universitet. Historiska Institutionen. Studia Historica Upsaliensia. 72) With summaries in English and Finnish.*

DEBUGGING IN COMPUTER SCIENCE.

BOAR (B.H.) Abend debugging for COBOL programmers. New York, [1976]. pp. 321. *bibliog.*

DECEMBRISTS.

CHERNOV (GEORGII IVANOVICH) Geroi 14 dekabria: zapiski o dekabristakh-vladimirtsakh. Iaroslavl', 1973. pp. 135. *bibliog.*

DEKABRISTY i russkaia kul'tura; Dbcembristes et culture russe. Leningrad, 1975. pp. 355. *With French table of contents.*

DEKABRISTY o Buriatii: stat'i, ocherki, pis'ma. Ulan-Ude, 1975. pp. 232.

IOVVA (IVAN FILIMONOVICH) Dekabristy v Moldavii. Kishinev, 1975. pp. 231. *bibliog.*

KOROLEVA (NINA VALERIANOVNA) Dekabristy i teatr. Leningrad, 1975. pp. 263.

NIKANDROV (PETR FEDOTOVICH) Revoliutsionnaia ideologiia dekabristov. Leningrad, 1976. pp. 191.

PAVLIUCHENKO (ELEONORA ALEKSANDROVNA) V dobrovol'nom izgnanii: o zhenakh i sestrakh dekabristov. Moskva, 1976. pp. 159. *bibliog.*

PROBLEMY istorii obshchestvennoi mysli i istoriografii: k 75- letiiu akademika N.V. Nechkinoi. Moskva, 1976. pp. 387. *bibliog.*

DEKABRISTY i Sibir'. Novosibirsk, 1977. pp. 260.

DECENTRALIZATION IN GOVERNMENT

— Brazil.

BASTOS (AURELIANO CANDIDO TAVARES) A provincia: estudo sobre a descentralização no Brasil; 3a edição feita sobre a 1a edição de 1870. São Paulo, 1975. pp. 254. *Text of first edition of 1870, with an added introduction.*

— France.

DECENTRALISER les responsabilités: pourquoi? comment?; rapports d'enquêtes de Michel Crozier [and others]; présentés par Alain Peyrefitte. Paris, La Documentation Française, 1976. pp. 56, 134.

— Niger.

HENTGEN (E.F.) L'organisation régionale et locale de la République du Niger. Niamey, Ecole Nationale d'Administration de Niamey, 1973. fo.130. *bibliog.*

— United Kingdom.

DALYELL (TAM) Devolution: the end of Britain? London, 1977. pp. 321.

STUTCHBURY (OLIVER PIERS) Too much government?: a political Aeneid. Ipswich, [1977]. pp. 128.

DECIMAL SYSTEM.

DECIMAL CURRENCY BOARD [EIRE]. Bulletins. No. 3. Learning decimal currency: a primer for retailer and customer. [Dublin], Stationery Office, [1969]. pp. 23.

DECISION-MAKING.

UNITED NATIONS. Conference on Trade and Development. 1972. The decision-making process in respect of imports in selected socialist countries of Eastern Europe. (TD/B/341/Rev.1). New York, 1972. pp. 22.

RODRIGUEZ MARIÑO (TOMAS) El proceso de las decisiones publicas. Bogota, 1973. pp. 152. *bibliog.*

BATHER (NICHOLAS JOHN) The speculative residential developer and urban growth: the location decision in a planned environment. Reading, 1976. pp. 44. *bibliog. (Reading. University. Department of Geography. Reading Geographical Papers. No. 47)*

MAYNES (EDWIN SCOTT) Decision-making for consumers: an introduction to consumer economics. New York, [1976]. pp. 364.

PLANNING in a Dutch and a Yugoslav steelworks: a comparative study; by H.C. Dekker [and others]. [Amsterdam], 1976. pp. 177.

CONFERENCE ON COGNITIVE PROCESS MODELS OF FOREIGN POLICY, 1973, LONDON. Thought and action in foreign policy: proceedings of the London Conference...March 1973; (G. Matthew Bonham, Michael J. Shapiro, editors). Basel, 1977. pp. 355. *bibliogs. Published under the auspices of the Center for Advanced Study in the Behavioral Sciences, Stanford, California.*

HAMBURG (MORRIS) Statistical analysis for decision making. 2nd ed. New York, [1977]. pp. 801. *bibliog.*

KAUFMAN (GORDON M.) and THOMAS (HOWARD) eds. Modern decision analysis: selected readings. Harmondsworth, 1977. pp. 507. *bibliogs.*

— Handbooks, manuals, etc.

ADAIR (JOHN) Training for decisions : a tutor's manual: a course in decision making, problem solving and creative thinking. London, 1976. pp. 119. *bibliog.*

— Mathematical models.

BJURULF (BO) A dynamic analysis of Scandinavian roll-call behavior: a test of a prediction model on ten minority situations in three countries. [Lund, 1974]. pp. 70. *bibliog.*

HOWARD (K.) and others. The scope for computer based systems to aid corporate decision- making in the short and medium term in the reorganised local authorities: a feasibility study. Peterlee, 1975. pp. 40. *bibliog. (IBM United Kingdom Limited. UK Scientific Centre. [Technical Reports]. 0074)*

BUEHRING (W.A.) and others. Energy/environment management: application of decision analysis. Laxenburg, 1976. pp. 27. *bibliog. (International Institute for Applied Systems Analysis. Research Memoranda. RM-76-14)*

HOWELL (DAVID ANTONY) The introduction of the Bachelor of Education degree: a case study in British university decision-making, 1963-70. 1976. fo. 438. *bibliog. Typescript. Ph.D. (London) thesis unpublished. This thesis is the property of London University and may not be removed from the Library.*

TELL (BERTIL) A comparative study of some multiple-criteria methods. Stockholm, 1976. pp. 203. *bibliog.*

HARSANYI (JOHN CHARLES) Rational behavior and bargaining equilibrium in games and social situations. Cambridge, 1977. pp. 314. *bibliog.*

DECISION-MAKING, GROUP.

BATTY (MICHAEL) A political theory of planning and design, incorporating concepts of collective decision-making and social power. Reading, 1976. pp. 64. *bibliog. (Reading. University. Department of Geography. Reading Geographical Papers. No. 45)*

D'EICHTHAL (GUSTAVE).

See EICHTHAL (GUSTAVE D').

DELEGATED LEGISLATION

— United States.

AMERICAN ENTERPRISE INSTITUTE FOR PUBLIC POLICY RESEARCH. Legislative Analyses. 94th Congress. No. 16. Regulatory reform: a survey of proposals in the 94th Congress. Washington, D.C., 1976. pp. 60. *bibliog.*

DE LEON (DANIEL).

CORK WORKERS' CLUB. Historical Reprints. No. 15. The Connolly-DeLeon controversy: on wages, marriage and the church. Cork, [1976]. pp. 45.

DELHI (UNION TERRITORY)

— **Industries.**

DELHI (UNION TERRITORY). Bureau of Economics and Statistics. Report on index of industrial production (base 1970 equals 100). a., 1971-72/1975-76- Delhi.

DELHI (UNION TERRITORY). Bureau of Economics and Statistics. Report on annual survey of industries (factory sector). a., 1973/74(2nd)- Delhi.

— **Statistics.**

DELHI (UNION TERRITORY). Bureau of Economics and Statistics. Economic progress in figures. a., 1976- Delhi.

DELHI QUARTERLY DIGEST OF ECONOMICS AND STATISTICS; [pd. by] Bureau of Economics and Statistics [Delhi (Union Territory)]. q., Mr/Je 1976 (v.24, nos. 1/2)- Delhi.

DELHI STATISTICAL HANDBOOK; [pd. by] Bureau of Economics and Statistics [Delhi (Union Territory)]. a., 1976(6th)- Delhi. *[in English and Hindi].*

— **Statistics, Vital.**

DELHI (UNION TERRITORY). Bureau of Economics and Statistics. Registration of Births and Deaths Act. Annual report. a., 1975(5th)- Delhi.

DELINQUENT WOMEN.

SMART (CAROL) Women, crime and criminology: a feminist critique. London, 1977. pp. 208. *bibliog.*

DE LORENZO (GIOVANNI).

See LORENZO (GIOVANNI DE).

DEMOCRACY.

CHAMBERLAIN (HOUSTON STEWART) Demokratie und Freiheit. München, 1917. pp. 83.

DAHMEN (HANS) Wie ist Demokratie heute möglich? Grundlagenprobleme der Nachkriegsdemokratie. Stuttgart, [1955]. pp. 73. *bibliog.*

DEMOKRATIIA razvitogo sotsialisticheskogo obshchestva. Moskva, 1975. pp. 296.

DENISOV (ANDREI IVANOVICH) Obshchaia sistema sotsialisticheskoi demokratii. Moskva, 1975. pp. 247.

SKARD (ØYVIND) Democracy and the individual: some reflections on the process of democratization in working life. [Oslo, 1975?]. pp. 35.

PROSPECTS for constitutional democracy: essays in honor of R. Taylor Cole; edited by John H. Hallowell. Durham, N.C., 1976. pp. 197. *bibliog.*

SCHUMPETER (JOSEPH ALOIS) Capitalism, socialism and democracy. 5th ed. London, 1952 repr. 1976. pp. 437. *Reprint contains a new introduction by Tom Bottomore.*

SNELL (JOHN LESLIE) The democratic movement in Germany, 1789-1914;...edited and completed by Hans A. Schmitt. Chapel Hill, N.C., [1976]. pp. 501. *bibliog. (North Carolina University. James Sprunt Studies in History and Political Science. vol. 55)*

AMUNDSEN (KIRSTEN) A new look at the silenced majority: women and American democracy. new ed. Englewood Cliffs, N.J., [1977]. pp. 172. *1971 edition published under the title The silenced majority.*

COXALL (WILLIAM NORMAN) Two Victorian theorists of democracy: a comparative study of Sir Henry Maine and Matthew Arnold. 1977. fo. 347. *bibliog. Typescript. Ph.D. (London) thesis: unpublished. This thesis is the property of London University and may not be removed from the Library.*

RUBIN (BERNARD) Media, politics, and democracy. New York, 1977. pp. 192.

SILVERT (KALMAN HIRSCH) The reason for democracy. New York, 1977. pp. 136.

DEMOCRATIC PARTY (UNITED STATES).

REEVES (RICHARD) Convention. London, 1977. pp. 246.

DEMOGRAPHY.

COX (PETER R.) Demography. 5th ed. Cambridge, 1976. pp. 393. *bibliogs.*

KAZAKOV (ALEKSEI TIMOFEEVICH) and URLANIS (BORIS TSEZAREVICH) Problemy narodonaseleniia v russkoi marksistskoi mysli. Moskva, 1976. pp. 196. *bibliog.*

PIROZHKOV (SERGEI IVANOVICH) Demograficheskie protsessy i vozrastnaia struktura naseleniia. Moskva, 1976. pp. 136.

VISHNEVSKII (ANATOLII GRIGOR'EVICH) Demograficheskaia revoliutsiia. Moskva, 1976. pp. 240.

— **Mathematical models.**

HENRY (LOUIS) Population: analysis and models; translated by Etienne van de Walle and Elise F. Jones. London, 1976. pp. 301.

DEMOGRAPHIC, economic, and social interaction; edited by Åke E. Andersson [and] Ingvar Holmberg. Cambridge, Mass., [1977]. pp. 352. *bibliogs. Based on the proceedings of a one-day seminar at the University of Gothenburg in 1972, and of a symposium held in October 1974 by the Swedish Council for Social Science Research.*

REES (P.H.) and WILSON (ALAN GEOFFREY) Spatial population analysis. London, 1977. pp. 356.

— **Methodology.**

HENRY (LOUIS) Population: analysis and models; translated by Etienne van de Walle and Elise F. Jones. London, 1976. pp. 301.

— **Research.**

DARSKII (LEONID EVSEEVICH) ed. Rozhdaemost': problemy izucheniia. Moskva, 1976. pp. 142.

DENAZIFICATION.

LANGE (IRMGARD) compiler. Entnazifizierung in Nordrhein-Westfalen: Richtlinien, Anweisungen, Organisation. Siegburg, 1976. pp. 584. *(Veröffentlichungen der Staatlichen Archive des Landes Nordrhein-Westfalen. Reihe C. Quellen und Forschungen. Band 2)*

FAULK (HENRY) Group captives: the re-education of German prisoners of war in Britain, 1945-1948. London, 1977. pp. 233.

DENE INDIANS.

See TINNE INDIANS.

DENMARK

— **Commerce.**

DENMARK. Udenrigsministeriet. Erhvervstjenesten. 1976. Danmarks samhandel med OPEC-landene. København, [1976]. pp. 137.

DENMARK. Udenrigsministeriet. Handelsafdelingen. 1976. Danmarks eksportmarkeder: økonomiske indikatorer 1970-74, samhandelstal 1970-75. København, 1976. pp. 122.

— **Defences.**

HAAGERUP (NIELS JØRGEN) A brief introduction to Danish foreign policy and defence. Copenhagen, The Information and Welfare Service of the Danish Defence, 1975. pp. 39. *bibliog.*

— **Economic conditions — Statistics.**

KJERKEGAARD (ELSE MARIE) ed. Levevilkår: Danmark: statistisk oversigt, 1976, etc. København, Danmarks Statistik and Socialforskningsinstituttet, 1976. pp. 303. *With headings in English.*

— **Economic policy.**

ULIGHED mellem regioner: arbejdspapirer om den danske regionale udvikling; redaktion: Jens Larsen, Søren Villadsen. Esbjerg, 1975. pp. 293. *(Sydjysk Universitetscenter. Regionalforskning. 2)*

— **Foreign relations.**

HAAGERUP (NIELS JØRGEN) A brief introduction to Danish foreign policy and defence. Copenhagen, The Information and Welfare Service of the Danish Defence, 1975. pp. 39. *bibliog.*

— — **Sources.**

DENMARK. Rigsarkivet. 1973. Danish Department of Foreign Affairs until 1770; by Arthur G. Hassø and Erik Kroman; translated by Mogens Møller. Copenhagen, 1973. pp. 196. *(Vejledende Arkivregistraturer. 16)*

— — **Germany — Sources.**

DENMARK. Rigsarkivet. 1973. Danish Department of Foreign Affairs until 1770; by Arthur G. Hassø and Erik Kroman; translated by Mogens Møller. Copenhagen, 1973. pp. 196. *(Vejledende Arkivregistraturer. 16)*

— **Politics and government.**

PEDERSEN (MOGENS N.) Political development and elite transformation in Denmark. Odense, 1974. pp. 82. *bibliog. (Odense Universitet. Institut for Historie og Samfundsvidenskab. Skrifter. [No. 12])*

SECHER (KNUD) De borgerliges borgerkrig: situationer og personer i dansk politik fra 1945 til 1976. København, 1976. pp. 115.

— **Population.**

MATTHIESSEN (POUL CHR.) Population of Denmark: trends and prospects; [published in connection with the World Population Conference, 1974]. Copenhagen, Ministry of Foreign Affairs, [1974]. pp. 23.

JOHANSEN (HANS CHR.) Befolkningsudvikling og familiestruktur i det 18. årdundrede. Odense, 1975. pp. 209. *(Odense Universitet. Studies in History and Social Sciences. vol. 22)*

JOHANSEN (HANS CHR.) ed. Studier i dansk befolkningshistorie, 1750-1890. Odense, 1976. pp. 212. *(Odense Universitet. Studies in History and Social Sciences. vol. 32)*

— **Social conditions — Statistics.**

KJERKEGAARD (ELSE MARIE) ed. Levevilkår: Danmark: statistisk oversigt, 1976, etc. København, Danmarks Statistik and Socialforskningsinstituttet, 1976. pp. 303. *With headings in English.*

— **Social history.**

JOHANSEN (HANS CHR.) ed. Studier i dansk befolkningshistorie, 1750-1890. Odense, 1976. pp. 212. *(Odense Universitet. Studies in History and Social Sciences. vol. 32)*

DEPRESSION, MENTAL.

MITCHELL (ROSS) Depression. Harmondsworth, 1975. pp. 112. *bibliog.*

DOMINIAN (JACK) Depression. London, 1976. pp. 224.

DERBYSHIRE

— **Economic conditions.**

DERBYSHIRE. County Planning Department. Derbyshire structure plan: report of survey. Matlock, 1975-6. 16 vols. (in 1).

— **Economic policy.**

DERBYSHIRE. County Planning Department. Derbyshire structure plan: alternative development options. Matlock, 1975. pp. 115.

DERBYSHIRE. County Planning Department. Derbyshire structure plan: draft for consultation. [Matlock, 1976]. pp. 400. *3 maps in end pocket.*

— **Social conditions.**

DERBYSHIRE. County Planning Department. Derbyshire structure plan: report of survey. Matlock, 1975-6. 16 vols. (in 1).

— **Social policy.**

DERBYSHIRE. County Planning Department. Derbyshire structure plan: alternative development options. Matlock, 1975. pp. 115.

DERBYSHIRE. County Planning Department. Derbyshire structure plan: draft for consultation. [Matlock, 1976]. pp. 400. *3 maps in end pocket.*

DESERTS

— **Russia.**

BABAEV (AGADZHAN GEL'DYEVICH) and FREIKIN (ZAKHAR GRIGOR'EVICH) Pustyni SSSR vchera, segodnia, zavtra. Moskva, 1977. pp. 351. *bibliog.*

DESJARDINS (ALPHONSE).

ROBY (YVES) Les caisses populaires: Alphonse Desjardins, 1900-1920. Québec, 1975. pp. 113. *bibliog.*

DESPAZE (JOSEPH).

PETITE lettre sur une grande satire littéraire, morale et politique de Joseph Despaze. Paris, chez Madame Déjour, [1801]. pp. 20.

DESPOTISM.

HOBSBAWM (ERIC JOHN ERNEST) and BOURN (DOUGLAS) Feudalism, capitalism and the absolute state; [2] reviews of Perry Anderson. London, 1976. pp. 18. *(Communist Party of Great Britain. History Group. Our History. No.66)*

DETENTE.

BALLINGER (RONALD B.) and OLIVIER (GERRIT) Détente in Southern Africa: two views. Braamfontein, 1976. pp. 29. *bibliog.*

BOWN (COLIN) and MOONEY (PETER J.) Cold war to détente. London, 1976. pp. 198. *bibliog.*

CALDWELL (LAWRENCE T.) Soviet-American relations: one half decade of detente problems and issues. Paris, [1976]. pp. 63. *(Atlantic Institute. Atlantic Papers. 1975.5)*

CASSIERS (JUAN) The hazards of peace: a European view of detente. Cambridge, Mass., [1976]. pp. 85. *(Harvard University. Center for International Affairs. Harvard Studies in International Affairs. No. 34)*

DOUGLAS-HOME (ALEXANDER FREDERICK) Baron Home, and others. Diplomacy, détente and the democracies;... edited...by D.K. Adams. Keele, [1976]. pp. 48. *(Keele. University. David Bruce Centre for American Studies. Lectures. 1976)*

GEYSER (OCKERT) Détente in Southern Africa. Bloemfontein, 1976. pp. 59. *bibliog. (Universiteit van die Oranje-Vrystaat. Institute for Contemporary History. Focus on Politics. 2)*

INTER-system detente in Germany and Korea: proceedings of a German-Korean conference in Tutzing and Munich, June 1975; edited by Gottfried-Karl Kindermann. München, [1976]. pp. 288.

PRANGER (ROBERT JOHN) ed. Detente and defense: a reader. Washington, D.C., 1976. pp. 445. *(American Enterprise Institute for Public Policy Research. Foreign Affairs Studies. 40)*

RUMMEL (RUDOLPH JOSEPH) Peace endangered: the reality of détente. Beverly Hills, [1976]. pp. 189.

WEIZSAECKER (CARL FRIEDRICH VON) Freiherr. Wege in der Gefahr: eine Studie über Wirtschaft, Gesellschaft und Kriegsverhütung. München, [1976 repr. 1977]. pp. 265.

BARBER (RICHARD) Conservative, and STAFFORD (IAN) Detente or defence: the bogus dilemma. London, [1977]. pp. 16.

FRIEDLICHE Koexistenz in Europa: Entwicklungstendenzen der Auseinandersetzung zwischen Sozialismus und Imperialismus; (Gesamtredaktion: Peter Klein, Stefan Doernberg). Berlin, 1977. pp. 330.

WETTIG (GERHARD) Broadcasting and détente: eastern policies and their implication for east-west relations. London, [1977]. pp. 110.

DETERRENCE (STRATEGY).

MORGAN (PATRICK M.) Deterrence: a conceptual analysis. Beverly Hills, Calif., [1977]. pp. 215. *bibliogs.*

DEUTSCHE FORTSCHRITTSPARTEI.

FESSER (GERD) Linksliberalismus und Arbeiterbewegung: die Stellung der Deutschen Fortschrittspartei zur Arbeiterbewegung, 1861-1866. Berlin, 1976. pp. 207. *bibliog. (Akademie der Wissenschaften der DDR. Zentralinstitut für Geschichte. Schriften. Band 48)*

DEVELOPMENT BANKS.

BRITISH OVERSEAS TRADE BOARD. The international lending agencies: a guide for manufacturers and consultants. London, 1976. pp. 31.

— **Africa.**

AFRICAN DEVELOPMENT FUND. Board of Directors. Report. a., 1974 (2nd)- Abidjan.

— **Mohammedan countries.**

ISLAMIC DEVELOPMENT BANK. Annual report. a., 1975/76(1st)- [Jeddah].

— **Somali Republic.**

SOMALI DEVELOPMENT BANK. Annual report and statement of accounts. a., 1975 (7th)- Mogadiscio.

— **Sri Lanka.**

SRI LANKA. Bank of Ceylon Commission. 1968. Report...Vol.1; [L.B. de Silva, chairman]. Colombo, 1968. pp. 191. *(Sri Lanka. Parliament. Sessional Papers. 1968. No. 27)*

DEVELOPMENT CREDIT CORPORATIONS

— **Australia.**

AUSTRALIA. Office of Aboriginal Affairs. Commonwealth Capital Fund for Aboriginal Enterprises. Annual report. a., 1968/69 (1st)- Canberra. *Included in AUSTRALIA. Parliament. [Parliamentary papers].*

— **South Africa.**

XHOSA DEVELOPMENT CORPORATION LIMITED. Annual report. a., 1975 (10th)- East London. *[in English and Afrikaans].*

DEVELOPMENTAL PSYCHOLOGY.

LERNER (RICHARD M.) Concepts and theories of human development. Reading, Mass., [1976]. pp. 324. *bibliog.*

INTERNATIONAL SOCIETY FOR THE STUDY OF BEHAVIOURAL DEVELOPMENT. Biennial Conference, 3rd, Guildford, 1975. Ecological factors in human development: [papers from the conference]; edited by Harry McGurk. Amsterdam, 1977. pp. 295. *bibliogs.*

PIAGET and knowing: studies in genetic epistemology; edited by Beryl A. Geber. London, 1977. pp. 258. *bibliogs.*

DEVSIS (DEVELOPMENT SCIENCE INFORMATION SYSTEM).

DEVSIS STUDY TEAM. 1976. DEVSIS: the preliminary design of an international information system for the development sciences. Ottawa, International Development Research Centre [Canada], [1976]. pp. 247. *bibliog.*

D'IACHENKO (VASILII PETROVICH).

D'IACHENKO (VASILII PETROVICH) Tovarno-denezhnye otnosheniia i finansy pri sotsializme; (raboty... , opublikovannye v 1946-1970 gg.). Moskva, 1974. pp. 495. *bibliog.*

DIALECTICAL MATERIALISM.

See MARXISM.

DICKENS (CHARLES).

BROWN (JAMES MELVILLE) A sociological analysis of the novels of Charles Dickens. 1977. fo. 340. *bibliog. Typescript. Ph.D. (London) thesis: unpublished. This thesis is the property of London University and may not be removed from the Library.*

DICTATORS.

VERONESI (UGO) Riflessioni sulla dittatura. 3rd ed. [Mantua, 1975]. pp. 85. *(Partito Liberale Italiano. Atti e Documenti. 9)*

DIEFENBAKER (JOHN GEORGE).

STURSBERG (PETER) Diefenbaker: leadership lost, 1962-67. Toronto, [1976]. pp. 212. *Based on recorded interviews and discussions.*

PERLIN (GEORGE CROSBIE) The problem of intra-party conflict in the leadership succession of John Diefenbaker in the Progressive Conservative Party of Canada: a case study. [1977]. fo. 411. *bibliog. Typescript. Ph.D. (London) thesis: unpublished. This thesis is the property of London University and may not be removed from the Library.*

DIET

— **United Kingdom.**

JOHNSTON (JAMES P.) A hundred years eating: food, drink and the daily diet in Britain since the late nineteenth century. Dublin, 1977. pp. 148. *bibliog.*

— **Yugoslavia.**

YUGOSLAVIA. Savezni Zavod za Statistiku. Studije, Analize i Prikazi. 79. Kvalitativne razlike u ishrani stanovništva Jugoslavije zavisno od socio-ekonomske pripadnosti domaćinstava s posebnim osvrtom na teritorijalne razlike; [by] Milan Č. Petrović. Beograd, 1976. pp. 226. *bibliog. With English and Russian summaries.*

DIETZGEN (JOSEPH).

FINGER (OTTO) Joseph Dietzgen: Beitrag zu den philosophischen Leistungen des deutschen Arbeiterphilosophen. Berlin, 1977. pp. 272.

DIFFERENTIAL GAMES.

ZAUBERMAN (ALFRED) Differential games and other game-theoretic topics in Soviet literature: a survey. New York, 1975. pp. 227.

DIFFUSION OF INNOVATIONS.

DOWNS (GEORGE W.) Bureaucracy, innovation, and public policy. Lexington, Mass., [1976]. pp. 150. *bibliog.*

DIJON

— **Religion.**

LUCHINI (A.M.) La pratique religieuse dominicale dans l'agglomération dijonnaise en 1958: étude de la consultation paroissiale du 19 octobre 1958. Dijon, 1959. pp. 44.

DIMITROV (GEORGI).

FISCHER (ERNST) of the Austrian Communist Party. Das Fanal: der Kampf Dimitroffs gegen die Kriegsbrandstifter. Wien, [1946]. pp. 298.

DOBREV (KRUSTIU ZHELIAZKOV) Problemi na stroitelstvoto na sotsializma v NR Bulgariia: izbrani proizvedeniia; [with an introductory essay by Ivan Stefanov]. Sofiia, 1975. pp. 267. *bibliog.*

DIPLOMACY.

ERICKSON (BONNIE H.) International networks: the structured webs of diplomacy and trade. Beverly Hills, [1975]. pp. 56. *bibliog.*

WILLIAMS (PHIL) Crisis management: confrontation and diplomacy in the nuclear age. London, 1976. pp. 230.

DIPLOMATS

— Bolivia — Correspondence, reminiscences, etc.

ANDRADE (VICTOR) My missions for revolutionary Bolivia, 1944-1962;...edited and with an introduction by Cole Blasier. Pittsburgh, Pa., [1976]. pp. 200.

— China.

SAMELSON (LOUIS J.) Soviet and Chinese negotiating behavior: the Western view. Beverly Hills, [1976]. pp. 62. *bibliog.*

— Poland.

RACZYŃSKI (EDWARD) Count. Od Narcyza Kulikowskiego do Winstona Churchilla. Londyn, 1976. pp. 145.

— Russia.

SAMELSON (LOUIS J.) Soviet and Chinese negotiating behavior: the Western view. Beverly Hills, [1976]. pp. 62. *bibliog.*

— — Correspondence, reminiscences, etc.

NOVIKOV (NIKOLAI VASIL'EVICH) Puti i pereput'ia diplomata: zapiski o 1943-1944 gg. Moskva, 1976. pp. 256.

— — White Russia — Correspondence, reminiscences, etc.

KISELEV (KUZ'MA VENEDIKTOVICH) Zapiski sovetskogo diplomata. Moskva, 1974. pp. 527.

— Spain — Correspondence, reminiscences, etc.

AZCARATE Y FLOREZ (PABLO DE) Mi embajada en Londres durante la guerra civil española. Barcelona, 1976. pp. 403.

DIRECT ACTION.

GALLACHER (WILLIAM) and CAMPBELL (JOHN ROSS) Direct action: an outline of workshop and social organization:... first published 1919, reprinted, with a new introduction by Alastair Hatchett. London, 1972. pp. 32. *(International Socialists. History Group. Reprints in Labour History. No. 3)*

DIRECTORS OF CORPORATIONS

— United Kingdom.

GIBSON (P.B.R.) Boards of directors in small/medium sized private companies: a survey of the composition of boards of directors in 289 private companies. London, [1970]. pp. 21. *bibliog. (British Institute of Management. Information Summaries. No. 149)*

DISARMAMENT.

COMITE POUR L'EXTINCTION DES GUERRES POUR LE DESARMEMENT UNILATERAL DE NOTRE PROPRE NATION. La nation face à l'armée. [Paris], [1967?]. pp. 12.

DINGMAN (ROGER) Power in the Pacific: the origins of naval arms limitation, 1914- 1922. Chicago, [1976]. pp. 318. *bibliog.*

MYRDAL (ALVA) The game of disarmament: how the United States and Russia run the arms race. New York, [1976]. pp. 397.

SCHAFFER (GORDON) Don't let them con you!: we can win peace: your questions answered. London, 1976. pp. 10.

STOCKHOLM INTERNATIONAL PEACE RESEARCH INSTITUTE. Strategic disarmament, verification and national security. London, 1977. pp. 174.

— International cooperation.

COFFEY (JOSEPH IRVING) Arms control and European security: a guide to East-West negotiations. London, 1977. pp. 271. *bibliog. (International Institute for Strategic Studies. Studies in International Security. 19)*

DISASTER RELIEF.

KRIMGOLD (FREDERICK) The role of international aid for pre-disaster planning in developing countries. Stockholm, 1974. pp. 134. *bibliog.*

GREEN (STEPHEN) of the United Nations Association of the United States of America. International disaster relief: towards a responsive system. New York, [1977]. pp. 101. *bibliog. (Council on Foreign Relations. 1980s Project Studies)*

UNDRO NEWSLETTER; [pd. by] the Office of the United Nations Disaster Relief Coordinator. irreg., current issues only. Geneva. *[articles in English and French].*

— United Kingdom.

NATIONAL COUNCIL OF SOCIAL SERVICE. Devil's Bridge coach crash:...the first seventy-two hours; a report on the Yorkshire Dales coach crash, its effect on the community of Thornaby and the implications for statutory and voluntary organisations. London, 1975. pp. 8.

NATIONAL COUNCIL OF SOCIAL SERVICE. How do we know who's involved in a disaster...?; a report on the social consequences of disaster and sudden death and the implications for statutory and voluntary organisations. London, 1975. pp. 8.

DISCIPLINARY POWER

— Russia.

SOTSIALISTICHESKAIA zakonnost' i gosudarstvennaia distsiplina. Moskva, 1975. pp. 222.

DISCLOSURE IN ACCOUNTING.

BENSTON (GEORGE J.) Corporate financial disclosure in the UK and the USA. Farnborough, Hants., [1976]. pp. 206. *bibliog.*

FOLEY (BERNARD J.) and MAUNDERS (KEITH T.) Accounting information disclosure and collective bargaining. London, 1977. pp. 210.

DISCOUNT

— United Kingdom.

FLETCHER (G.A.) The discount houses in London: principles, operations and change. London, 1976. pp. 298.

DISCRIMINATION

— United States.

AFFIRMATIVE action: the answer to discrimination?; (an AEI Round Table held on May 28, 1975...[in] Washington...); Ralph K. Winter, Jr., moderator, etc. Washington, [1976]. pp. 40. *(American Enterprise Institute for Public Policy Research. Round Tables)*

DISCRIMINATION IN EDUCATION

— Economic aspects — United States.

FITZPATRICK (BLANCHE E.) Women's inferior education: an economic analysis. New York, 1976. pp. 189. *bibliog.*

— United States.

DAVIS (ARTHUR) Racial crisis in public education: a quest for social order. New York, [1975]. pp. 250.

HOWARD UNIVERSITY. Institute for the Study of Educational Policy. Equal educational opportunity for blacks in U.S. higher education: an assessment [of the academic year 1973-74]. Washington, D.C., 1976. pp. 330. *bibliog.*

SEDLACEK (WILLIAM E.) and BROOKS (GLENWOOD C.) Racism in American education: a model for change. Chicago, [1976]. pp. 226. *bibliog.*

WEINBERG (MEYER) A chance to learn: the history of race and education in the United States. Cambridge, 1977. pp. 471. *bibliog.*

DISCRIMINATION IN EMPLOYMENT

— Law and legislation — United Kingdom.

U.K. Commission for Racial Equality. 1977. A guide to the new Race Relations Act 1976: employment. [London, 1977]. pp. 8.

U.K. Commission for Racial Equality. 1977. Your rights to equal treatment under the new Race Relations Act 1976: employment. [London, 1977]. pp. 12.

— South Africa.

SOUTH AFRICAN CONGRESS OF TRADE UNIONS. Workers in chains. London, 1976. pp. 19.

MYERS (DESAIX) Labor practices of U.S. corporations in South Africa. New York, 1977. pp. 123.

— United Kingdom.

RUNNYMEDE TRUST. Race relations and employment: written memorandum from the Runnymede Trust to the House of Commons Select Committee on Race Relations and Immigration, submitted on 12 July 1974. London, [1974]. 1 pamphlet (unpaged).

COMMUNITY RELATIONS COMMISSION. Black employees: job levels and discrimination. [London, 1976?]. pp. 4. *(Fact Sheets. No.3. Employment)*

The NEW race law and employment. London, 1976. pp. 93. *(Incomes Data Services Ltd. IDS Handbook Series. No. 4)*

SMITH (DAVID J.) Racial disadvantage in Britain: the PEP report. Harmondsworth, 1977. pp. 349.

— United States.

JOB bias; edited by Lester A. Sobel. New York, [1976]. pp. 190. *Based on records compiled by Facts on File.*

PARLIN (BRADLEY W.) Immigrant professionals in the United States: discrimination in the scientific labor market. New York, 1976. pp. 97. *bibliog.*

GOULD (WILLIAM B.) Black workers in white unions: job discrimination in the United States. Ithaca, N.Y., 1977. pp. 506.

WOMEN, minorities and employment discrimination; edited by Phyllis A. Wallace and Annette M. LaMond. Lexington, Mass., [1977]. pp. 203. *bibliogs. Based on papers and proceedings of a conference held by the Industrial Relations Section of the Alfred P. Sloan School of Management, Massachusetts Institute of Technology, in 1974.*

DISCRIMINATION IN EMPLOYMENT, SEX.

See SEX DISCRIMINATION IN EMPLOYMENT.

DISCRIMINATION IN HOUSING

— United Kingdom.

PARKER (JOHN) Writer on housing, and DUGMORE (KEITH) Colour and the allocation of GLC housing: the report of the GLC lettings survey, 1974-75. [London], 1976. 1 vol. (various pagings). *bibliog.* (*London. Greater London Council. Research Reports. No. 21*)

McKAY (DAVID H.) Housing and race in industrial society: civil rights and urban policy in Britain and the United States. London, [1977]. pp. 193.

SMITH (DAVID J.) Racial disadvantage in Britain: the PEP report. Harmondsworth, 1977. pp. 349.

— United States.

DANIELSON (MICHAEL NILS) The politics of exclusion. New York, 1976. pp. 443.

LISTOKIN (DAVID) Fair share housing allocation. New Brunswick, [1976]. pp. 253.

MANN (MARY SULLIVAN) The right to housing: constitutional issues and remedies in exclusionary zoning. New York, 1976. pp. 191. *bibliog.*

MARANTZ (JANET K.) and others. Discrimination in rural housing: economic and social analysis of six selected markets. Lexington, Mass., [1976]. pp. 213. *bibliog.*

SMOOKLER (HELENE V.) Economic integration in new communities: an evaluation of factors affecting policies and implementation. Cambridge, Mass., [1976]. pp. 236. *bibliog.* (*North Carolina University. Center for Urban and Regional Studies. New Communities Research Series*)

McCOURT (KATHLEEN) Working-class women and grass-roots politics. Bloomington, Ind., [1977]. pp. 256. *bibliog.*

McKAY (DAVID H.) Housing and race in industrial society: civil rights and urban policy in Britain and the United States. London, [1977]. pp. 193.

— — California.

RABINOVITZ (FRANCINE F.) and SIEMBIEDA (WILLIAM J.) Minorities in suburbs: the Los Angeles experience. Lexington, Mass., [1977]. pp. 100. *bibliog.*

DISMEMBERMENT OF NATIONS.

The POLITICS of division, partition, and unification; edited by Ray Edward Johnston. New York, 1976. pp. 98. *bibliog.*

DISRAELI (BENJAMIN) 1st Earl of Beaconsfield.

CAPEL (PETER JAMES) Gladstone's attitude towards Disraeli's Conservative Party. London, [1975]. fo. 21. (*London. University. London School of Economics and Political Science. Gladstone Memorial Trust Prize Essays. 1975*) *Typescript.*

DISSENTERS

— Czechoslovakia.

KAVAN (JAN) and DANIEL (JAN) pseud., eds. Sotsialisticheskaia oppozitsiia v Chekhoslovakii, 1973-75: podborka dokumentov; perevod [s cheshskogo] Iriny Khenkinoi. London, 1976. pp. 342. *bibliog.*

—· Poland.

NA LEWO. zeszyt nr.1. Kłamstwo, fałsz, prawda: 'nowy styl' polskiej biurokracji. n.p., [1976?]. pp. 21. *Reproduced from typescript.*

— Russia.

MEEUS (ANTHONY DE) White book on the internment of dissenters in Soviet mental hospitals. Brussels, [1975?]. pp. 139. *Translated from the French original.*

BARGHOORN (FREDERICK CHARLES) Détente and the democratic movement in the USSR. New York, [1976]. pp. 229.

DISSENTERS, RELIGIOUS

— Europe, Eastern.

KIRÁLY (BÉLA K.) ed. Tolerance and movements of religious dissent in eastern Europe. New York, 1975. pp. 221. (*East European Quarterly. East European Monographs. 13*)

— United Kingdom.

VESTIGIA veritatis: or, The controversy relating to the Act of the thirty fifth of Elizabeth, entituled, An Act to retain the Queens Majesties subjects in their due obedience...with the acts of the 16th and 22nd of his present Majesty against conventicles, etc. London, Janeway, 1681. pp. 15.

BINFIELD (CLYDE) So down to prayers: studies in English nonconformity, 1780-1920. London, 1977. pp. 296. *bibliog.*

SELLERS (IAN) Nineteenth-century nonconformity. London, 1977. pp. 102. *bibliog.*

DISSERTATIONS, ACADEMIC

— Bibliography.

DOSSICK (JESSE JOHN) Doctoral research on Russia and the Soviet Union 1960-1975: a classified list of 3,150 American, Canadian and British dissertations, with some critical and statistical analysis. New York, 1976. pp. 345. *bibliog.*

— United Kingdom — Bibliography.

SOCIOLOGY THESES REGISTER; [pd. by] Social Science Research Council. a., 1976 (1st ed.)- London.

JACOBS (PHYLLIS MAY) compiler. History theses, 1901-70: historical research for higher degrees in the universities of the United Kingdom. London, 1976. pp. 456.

VEAL (A.J.) and DUESBURY (W.K.) compilers. A first list of U.K. students theses and dissertations on planning and urban and regional studies. Birmingham, 1976. pp. 245. (*Birmingham. University. Centre for Urban and Regional Studies. Research Memoranda. No. 55*)

DISTRIBUTION (ECONOMIC THEORY).

ERICSSON (LARS O.) Justice in the distribution of economic resources: a critical and normative study. Stockholm, [1976]. pp. 150. *bibliog.* (*Stockholms Universitet. Acta Universitatis Stockholmiensis. Stockholm Studies in Philosophy. 6*)

DIVERSIFICATION IN INDUSTRY.

BOEHNKE (ROLF) Diversifizierte Unternehmen: eine Untersuchung über wettbewerbliche Wirkungen, Ursachen und Ausmass der Diversifizierung. Berlin, [1976]. pp. 277. *bibliog. With English summary.*

DIVISION OF LABOUR.

BRITISH SOCIOLOGICAL ASSOCIATION. Annual Conference, 1976. Health and the division of labour; [papers presented at the conference]; edited by Margaret Stacey [and others]. London, [1977]. pp. 237. *bibliogs.* (*British Sociological Association. Explorations in Sociology. 10*)

DIVORCE

— Europe.

GROUPE INTERNATIONAL DE RECHERCHE SUR LE DIVORCE. Le divorce en Europe occidentale: données statistiques et juridiques. Paris, 1975. pp. 191. (*France. Ministère de la Justice. Collection Ministère de la Justice*) *With introduction and headings in English.*

— New Zealand.

PATTERSON (SUE M.) Divorce in New Zealand: a statistical study. [Wellington], Research Section, Department of Justice, 1976. pp. 38. *bibliog.*

— Russia — Ukraine.

CHUIKO (LIUBOV' VASIL'EVNA) Braki i razvody: demograficheskoe issledovanie na primere Ukrainskoi SSR. Moskva, 1975. pp. 175.

— Uganda.

UGANDA. Commission on Marriage, Divorce and the Status of Women. 1965. Report; [W.W. Kalema, chairman]. Entebbe, 1965. pp. 133.

— United Kingdom — Ireland, Northern.

IRELAND, NORTHERN. Standing Advisory Commission on Human Rights. 1977. Report on the law in Northern Ireland relating to divorce and homosexuality. London, [1977]. pp. 20.

DMOWSKI (ROMAN).

WASIUTYŃSKI (WOJCIECH) Źródła niepodległości. Londyn, 1977. pp. 178.

DOBREV (KRUSTIU ZHELIAZKOV).

DOBREV (KRUSTIU ZHELIAZKOV) Problemi na stroitelstvoto na sotsializma v NR Bulgariia: izbrani proizvedeniia; [with an introductory essay by Ivan Stefanov]. Sofiia, 1975. pp. 267. *bibliog.*

DOBROLIUBOV (NIKOLAI ALEKSANDROVICH).

KRUZHKOV (VLADIMIR SEMENOVICH) N.A. Dobroliubov: zhizn', deiatel'nost', mirovozzrenie. Moskva, 1976. pp. 432. *bibliog. Incorporates a revised version of his Mirovozzrenie N. A. Dobroliubova (1950).*

DOCK WORKERS

— Safety measures.

INTERNATIONAL LABOUR OFFICE. 1977. Safety and health in dock work. rev. ed. Geneva, 1977. pp. 221. (*Codes of Practice*)

— Denmark.

CHRISTENSEN (ERIK) Historian. Havnearbejderstrejken i Esbjerg i 1893: traek af arbejdsmaendenes fagforenings første år i Esbjerg. København, [1975]. pp. 113. *bibliog.* (*Selskabet til Forskning i Arbejderbevaegelsens Historie. Publikationer. 2*)

— Nigeria.

NIGERIA. Federal Ministry of Economic Development. 1969. Report on the reorganisation of the dock labour industry in Nigerian ports; by A.A. Ayida. Lagos, 1969. pp. 35.

DOLANC (STANE).

DOLANC (STANE) Der Bund Kommunisten Jugoslawiens im Selbstverwaltungssystem ([translated from the Serbo-Croat by] Anica Perić-Günther [and others]). Beograd, [1975]. pp. 304.

DOLANC (STANE) Savez komunista Jugoslavije i socijalističko samoupravljanje: [collected speeches, articles, etc.]. Beograd, 1975. pp. 369.

DOMESDAY BOOK.

DARBY (HENRY CLIFFORD) Domesday England. Cambridge, 1977. pp. 416.

DOMESTIC ECONOMY

— Brazil — Accounting.

CAMBRIDGE. University. Centre of Latin American Studies. Working Papers. No.24. Underconsumption, market size and expenditure patterns in Brazil; by J.R. Wells. Cambridge, 1976. pp. 57.

— United Kingdom — Accounting.

FINER JOINT ACTION COMMITTEE. The income needs of one parent families. [London, 1976]. pp. 14.

EDWARDS (A.C.) The account books of Benjamin Mildmay, Earl Fitzwalter. London, [1977]. pp. 224.

— Zaire — Accounting.

SAULNIERS (ALFRED H.) The economics of prestation systems: a consumer analysis of extended family obligations with application to Zaire. Ann Arbor, 1976. pp. 27. *bibliog. (Michigan University. Center for Research on Economic Development. Discussion Papers. No.54)*

SAULNIERS (ALFRED H.) Unit equivalent scales for specific food commodities, Kinshasa, Zaire. Ann Arbor, 1976. pp. 23. *bibliog. (Michigan University. Center for Research on Economic Development. Discussion Papers. No.53)*

DOMESTIC RELATIONS.

INTERNATIONAL SOCIETY ON FAMILY LAW. Newsletter. No. 3. n.p., 1977. pp. 140.

— Denmark.

KOCH-NIELSEN (INGER) and others. Familie 1975: lov og tal. København, 1976. pp. 55. *bibliog. (Socialforskningsinstituttet. Meddelelser. 19)*

— Germany.

DOELLE (HANS) Familienrecht: Darstellung des deutschen Familienrechts mit rechtsvergleichenden Hinweisen. Karlsruhe, 1964-65. 2 vols. *bibliog.*

BEITZKE (GUENTHER) Familienrecht: ein Studienbuch. 13th ed. München, 1966. pp. 268.

LEHMANN (HEINRICH) Professor at the University of Cologne. Deutsches Familienrecht;... vierte, neubearbeitete Auflage von Dieter Henrich. Berlin, 1967. pp. 335.

— Italy.

La FAMIGLIA oggi tra referendum e riforma del diritto; scritti di Emanuele Ranci Ortigosa [and others]. Milano, 1974. pp. 72. *(Relazioni Sociali. Quaderni. n.7/8)*

— Russia.

VEBERS (IANIS ROBERTOVICH) Pravosub"ektivnost' grazhdan v sovetskom grazhdanskom i semeinom prave. Riga, 1976. pp. 231. *bibliog.*

— — Russia (RSFSR).

RUSSIA (RSFSR). Statutes, etc. 1975. Kodeks o brake i sem'e RSFSR; s prilozheniem postateino-sistematizirovannykh materialov po sostoianiiu na 20 fevralia 1975 goda. Moskva, 1975. pp. 168.

— United Kingdom.

GRANT (HUBERT BRIAN) Family law...; third edition by Jennifer Levin. London, 1977. pp. 183.

STONE (OLIVE MARJORIE) Family law: an account of the law of domestic relations in England and Wales in the last quarter of the twentieth century, with some comparisons. London, 1977. pp. 277. *bibliog.*

— United States.

FOOTE (CALEB) and others. Cases and materials on family law. 2nd ed. Boston, Mass., 1976. pp. 1167.

DOMESTIC RELATIONS COURTS

— United Kingdom.

FINER JOINT ACTION COMMITTEE. One-parent families and family courts. London, [1976]. pp. 13,2.

DOMINICAN REPUBLIC

— History — To 1844.

MOYA PONS (FRANK) Historia colonial de Santo Domingo. Santiago, D.R., 1976. pp. 490. *bibliog. (Universidad Catolica Madre y Maestra. Coleccion Estudios)*

DOMINICANS

— Missions.

REA (WILLIAM FRANCIS) The economics of the Zambezi missions, 1580-1759. Roma, 1976. pp. 189. *bibliog. (Institutum Historicum S.I. Bibliotheca. vol. 39)*

DOMINICANS IN FRANCE.

LUCHINI (A.M.) La pratique religieuse dominicale dans l'agglomération dijonnaise en 1958: étude de la consultation paroissiale du 19 octobre 1958. Dijon, 1959. pp. 44.

DONAUWOERTH

— Charities.

CASSIANEUM. Festschrift hundert Jahre Cassianeum, Verlag und Druckerei Ludwig Auer, Donauwörth: 1875-1975. Donauwörth, [1975]. pp. 120.

DONEGAL

— Politics and government.

SACKS (PAUL MARTIN) The Donegal Mafia: an Irish political machine. New Haven, Conn., 1976. pp. 241.

DOPF (CARL).

BOTZ (GERHARD) and others. Im Schatten der Arbeiterbewegung: zur Geschichte des Anarchismus in Österreich und Deutschland. Wien, [1977]. pp. 190. *(Ludwig Boltzmann Institut für Geschichte der Arbeiterbewegung. Schriftenreihe. 6)*

DORSET

— Statistics.

ABSTRACT OF STATISTICS FOR DORSET, AN; [pd. by] Dorset County Council. a., 1975- Dorchester.

DOSTOEVSKII (FEDOR MIKHAILOVICH).

KARLOVA (TAMARA SERGEEVNA) Dostoevskii i russkii sud. Kazan', 1975. pp. 165.

DOUALA

— Census.

TEIXEIRA (PERY) Analyse des principaux résultats du recensement de Douala, 1964- 1965. [Paris, Ministère de la Coopération, 1975?]. pp. 131.

DOUGLAS-HOME (ALEXANDER FREDERICK) Baron Home.

DOUGLAS-HOME (ALEXANDER FREDERICK) Baron Home. The way the wind blows: an autobiography. London, 1976. pp. 320.

DRAVIDA MUNNETRA KAZHAGAM.

BARNETT (MARGUERITE ROSS) The politics of cultural nationalism in South India. Princeton, N.J., [1976]. pp. 368. *bibliog.*

DREES (WILLEM).

DUYNSTEE (FRANS JOZEPH FERDINAND MARIE) and BOSMANS (J.) Het kabinet Schermerhorn-Drees, 24 juni 1945-3 juli 1946. Assen, 1977. pp. 756. *bibliog. (Katholieke Universiteit Nijmegen. Centrum voor Parlementaire Geschiedenis. Parlementaire Geschiedenis van Nederland na 1945. 1)*

DREIER (FREDERIK).

NYMARK (JOHS.) Frederik Dreiers politisk-ideologiske virksomhed. [Grenå?, 1975]. pp. 184. *bibliog. (Selskabet til Forskning i Arbejderbevaegelsens Historie. Skriftserie. Nr. 2)*

DRIBERG (THOMAS EDWARD NEIL) Baron Bradwell.

DRIBERG (THOMAS EDWARD NEIL) Baron Bradwell. Ruling passions. London, 1977. pp. 271.

DRINKING AND ROAD ACCIDENTS

— Tasmania.

TASMANIA. Law Reform Commission. 1975. Report and recommendations on the Road Safety, Alcohol and Drugs, Act 1970, together with a draft Bill and notes thereon. in TASMANIA. Parliament. Journals and Printed Papers. 1975, no.43.

DRINKING CUSTOMS.

LIMA (OSWALDO GONÇALVES DE) Pulque, balchê e pajauaru na etnobiologia das bebidas e dos alimentos fermentados. Recife, 1975. pp. 405. *bibliog.*

STIVERS (RICHARD) A hair of the dog: Irish drinking and American stereotype. University Park, Penn., [1976!. PP. 197.

DROUGHTS

— Ethiopia.

ETHIOPIA. Relief and Rehabilitation Commission. 1975. Current situation in the drought affected areas. [Addis Ababa], 1975. fo. 7.

REHAB: drought and famine in Ethiopia; editor Abdul Mejid Hussein. London, [1976]. pp. 121. *bibliogs. (International African Institute and Environment Training Programme. African Environment Special Reports. 2)*

DROZ (JULES HUMBERT-).

See HUMBERT-DROZ (JULES).

DRUG ABUSE.

MOORE (JAMES J.) Investigating drug abuse: a multi-national programme of pilot studies into the non-medical use of drugs. Rome, United Nations Social Defence Research Institute, 1976. pp. 192. *(Publications. No.16)*

— Australia.

AUSTRALIA. Parliament. Senate. Select Committee on Drug Trafficking and Drug Abuse. 1971. Report...Part 1. Report; [J.E. Marriott, chairman]. in AUSTRALIA. Parliament. Parliamentary papers, 1971, vol.8.

— United States.

ROCK (PAUL ELLIOTT) ed. Drugs and politics. New Brunswick, N.J., 1977. pp. 331. *bibliogs.*

DRUG ABUSE AND CRIME

— United Kingdom.

EALAND (C.P.H.) Diving off the deep end: a Release report on the sentencing of cannabis offenders in England and Wales. London, [1976]. pp. 17.

DRUG TRADE.

LEVINSON (CHARLES) The multinational pharmaceutical industry. [Geneva, 1973]. pp. 121.

JAMES (BARRIE G.) The future of the multinational pharmaceutical industry to 1990. London, 1977. pp. 283. *bibliogs.*

— Argentine Republic.

KATZ (JORGE M.) Oligopolio, firmas nacionales y empresas multinacionales: la industria farmaceutica argentina. Buenos Aires, 1974. pp. 148.

— Germany.

MOEBIUS (KLAUS) and others. Die pharmazeutische Industrie in der Bundesrepublik Deutschland: Struktur und Wettbewerb. Tübingen, [1976]. pp. 139. *bibliog. (Kiel. Universität. Institut für Weltwirtschaft. Kieler Studien. 140)*

— United Kingdom.

REEKIE (W. DUNCAN) Pricing new pharmaceutical products. London, [1977]. pp. 34.

SLATTER (STUART ST. P.) Competition and marketing strategies in the pharmaceutical industry. London, [1977]. pp. 150. *bibliog.*

— **United States.**

CLARKSON (KENNETH W.) Intangible capital and rates of return: effects of research and promotion on profitability. Washington, [1977]. pp. 77. *(American Enterprise Institute for Public Policy Research. AEI Studies. No. 138)*

DRUGS

— **Labelling — America, Latin.**

SILVERMAN (MILTON) The drugging of the Americas: how multinational drug companies say one thing about their products to physicians in the United States, and another thing to physicians in Latin America. Berkeley, Calif., [1976]. pp. 147.

— — **United States.**

SILVERMAN (MILTON) The drugging of the Americas: how multinational drug companies say one thing about their products to physicians in the United States, and another thing to physicians in Latin America. Berkeley, Calif., [1976]. pp. 147.

— **Laws and legislation — United States.**

AMERICAN ENTERPRISE INSTITUTE FOR PUBLIC POLICY RESEARCH. Legislative Analyses. 94th Congress. No. 13. New drugs: pending legislation. Washington, D.C., 1976. pp. 59.

CAMPBELL (RITA RICARDO) Drug lag: federal government decision making. Stanford, Calif., 1976. pp. 62. *(Stanford University. Hoover Institution on War, Revolution and Peace. Hoover Institution Studies. 55)*

GRABOWSKI (HENRY G.) Drug regulation and innovation: empirical evidence and policy options. Washington, D.C., [1976]. pp. 82. *(American Enterprise Institute for Public Policy Research. Evaluative Studies. 28) This study is part of the research programme of the American Enterprise Institute's Center for Health Policy Research.*

DRUGS AND AUTOMOBILE DRIVERS

— **Tasmania.**

TASMANIA. Law Reform Commission. 1975. Report and recommendations on the Road Safety, Alcohol and Drugs, Act 1970, together with a draft Bill and notes thereon. in TASMANIA. Parliament. Journals and Printed Papers. 1975, no.43.

DRUGS AND MASS MEDIA.

OSTMAN (RONALD ELROY) ed. Communication research and drug education. Beverly Hills, [1976]. pp. 325. *bibliogs.*

DRUGS AND YOUTH.

OSTMAN (RONALD ELROY) ed. Communication research and drug education. Beverly Hills, [1976]. pp. 325. *bibliogs.*

DRUSES.

OPPENHEIMER (JONATHAN WILFRED STRATTON) The social organisation of a Druze village in Israel. 1976. fo. 506. *bibliog. Typescript. Ph.D. (London) thesis: unpublished. This thesis is the property of London University and may not be removed from the Library.*

DUBINSKY (DAVID).

DUBINSKY (DAVID) and RASKIN (ABRAHAM HENRY) David Dubinsky: a life with labor. New York, [1977]. pp. 351.

DUBLIN

— **Cemeteries.**

EIRE. Oireachtas. Joint Committee on the Dublin Cemeteries Committee Bill, 1969. 1970. Report...together with the proceedings. Dublin, 1970. pp. 15. *In English and Irish.*

DUE PROCESS OF LAW

— **United States.**

DUE process; edited by J. Roland Pennock and John W. Chapman. New York, 1977. pp. 362. *(American Society for Political and Legal Philosophy. Nomos. 18)*

DUERO

— **Power utilization.**

GARCIA ZARZA (EUGENIO) El aprovechamiento hidroelectrico Salmantino-Zamorano. Salamanca, 1973. pp. 69. *bibliog.*

DUESSELDORF

— **Poor.**

BALKENHOL (BERND) Armut und Arbeitslosigkeit in der Industrialisierung: dargestellt am Beispiel Düsseldorfs, 1850-1900. Düsseldorf, 1976. pp. 143. *bibliog. (Düsseldorfer Geschichtsverein. Studien zur Düsseldorfer Wirtschaftsgeschichte. Heft 3)*

DUISBURG.

See also HAMBORN.

DUMAY (JEAN BAPTISTE).

DUMAY (JEAN BAPTISTE) Mémoires d'un militant ouvrier du Creusot, 1841-1905; introduction et notes par Pierre Ponsot. Grenoble, 1976. pp. 431. *(Centre d'Histoire du Syndicalisme. Collection)*

DUMONT (GABRIEL).

WOODCOCK (GEORGE) 1912- . Gabriel Dumont: the Métis chief and his lost world. Edmonton, [1975]. pp. 256. *bibliog.*

DUNLOP (ANNIE ISABELLA).

SCOTTISH HISTORY SOCIETY. [Publications]. 4th Series. vol. 12. Calendar of papal letters to Scotland of Clement VII of Avignon, 1378-1394; edited by Charles Burns; [with] Annie I. Dunlop, 1897-1973: a memoir; by Ian B. Cowan. Edinburgh, 1976. pp. 240.

DUNNING (THOMAS).

TESTAMENTS of radicalism: memoirs of working class politicians, 1790-1885; edited and introduced by David Vincent. London, [1977]. pp. 246. *bibliogs.*

DUPLESSIS (MAURICE LENOBLET).

BLACK (CONRAD) Duplessis. Toronto, [1977]. pp. 743. *bibliog.*

DURHAM (CITY)

— **Politics and government.**

ELECTION papers, addresses, poll books, etc., for the city and county of Durham, from 1813 to 1847 inclusive. Durham, Walker, [1847?]. 13 pts. (in 1 vol.). *Lacking Proceedings and poll for 1843.*

The PROCEEDINGS and poll at the Durham City election, on the 7th, 8th, and 9th of July, 1852, with the speeches, etc., on the day of nomination and at the close of the poll. Durham, Walker, 1852. pp. 25.

The PROCEEDINGS and poll at the Durham City election on the 1st, 2nd, and 3rd of December, 1852, with the speeches, etc. on the day of nomination and at the close of poll. Durham, Walker, 1852. pp. 21.

DURHAM (COUNTY)

— **Politics and government.**

ELECTION papers, addresses, poll books, etc., for the city and county of Durham, from 1813 to 1847 inclusive. Durham, Walker, [1847?]. 13 pts. (in 1 vol.). *Lacking Proceedings and poll for 1843.*

DURRUTI (BUENAVENTURA).

ENZENSBERGER (HANS MAGNUS) El corto verano de la anarquia: vida y muerte de Buenaventura Durruti; traduccion de Julio Forcat y Ulrike Hartmann. [Mexico, 1975]. pp. 334. *bibliog.*

DUTCH EAST INDIA COMPANY.

MEILINK-ROELOFSZ (M. ANTOINETTE P.) and others. De V[erenigde] O[ost-Indische] C[ompagnie] in Azië. [Bussum, 1976]. pp. 243. *bibliogs.*

DUTCH GUIANA.

DUTCH GUIANA. Stichting Planbureau Suriname. 1964. Suriname: beknopte beschrijving van het land, de bevolking, de staatkundige-, sociale- en economische struktuur. [Paramaribo], 1964. fo. 101.

— **Boundaries — Guyana.**

GUYANA. [Ministry of Information]. 1968. Guyana-Suriname boundary. [Georgetown], 1968. pp. 16, (3 maps).

— **Economic policy.**

DUTCH GUIANA. Ministerie van Opbouw. 1963. Opbouw 1958-1963: de nationale visie: verslag van departementale werkzaamheden 1958-1963. Paramaribo, 1963. pp. 226.

— **History.**

PRICE (RICHARD) Anthropologist. The Guiana ᵒmaroons: a historical and bibliographical introduction. Baltimore, [1976]. pp. 184. *bibliog.*

— **Relations (general) with Guyana.**

GUYANA. Ministry of External Affairs. 1970. A search for understanding: patterns of conflict resolution: statements and papers relating to recent developments, Guyana-Venezuela relations and Guyana-Surinam relations. Georgetown, 1970. pp. 34.

— **Statistics.**

GERMANY (BUNDESREPUBLIK). Statistisches Bundesamt. Länderkurzberichte: Surinam. a., 1976- Wiesbaden.

DUTCH NEWSPAPERS

— **Circulation.**

CUILENBURG (JAN J. VAN) Lezer, krant en politiek: een empirische studie naar nederlandse dagbladen en hun lezers. Amsterdam, [1977]. pp. 325. *bibliog. With summary in English.*

DUTSCHKE (RUDI).

STEIGERWALD (ROBERT REINHOLD) Der "wahre" oder konterrevolutionäre "Sozialismus": was wollen Havemann, Dutschke, Biermann?. Frankfurt am Main, 1977. pp. 145.

DWELLINGS

— **France — Maintenance and repair.**

NORA (SIMON) and EVENO (BERTRAND) Rapport sur l'amélioration de l'habitat ancien. Paris, La Documentation Française, 1975. pp. 200.

— **Liberia.**

ZETTERSTROM (KJELL) House and settlement in Liberia. Robertsport, Liberia, 1970. fo. 37. *bibliog.*

— United Kingdom — Maintenance and repair.

TRIANGLE ACTION GROUP [NORTH SHIELDS]. The Triangle: which way now?. [North Shields, North Tyneside Community Development Project, 1976]. fo.10.

COMMUNITY DEVELOPMENT PROJECT. Political Economy Collective. The poverty of the improvement programme. rev. ed. Newcastle-upon-Tyne, 1977. pp. 28.

ROBINSON (HILARY) Do council tenants get a fair deal on repairs?: interim report on some survey results. [London], National Consumer Council, [1977]. pp. 28.

— — Wales — Maintenance and repair.

GLAMORGAN-GLYNCORRWG COMMUNITY DEVELOPMENT PROJECT. House improvement, occupational training and job creation: a review of work undertaken by the Upper Afan C[ommunity] D[evelopment] P[roject]. [Port Talbot], 1974. fo. 18.

DYNAMIC PROGRAMMING.

BELLMAN (RICHARD ERNEST) and others. Algorithms, graphs and computers. New York, 1970. pp. 246. *bibliogs.*

EARTHQUAKES

— Peru.

PERU. Comision de Reconstruccion y Rehabilitacion de la Zona Afectada por el Terremoto del 31 de Mayo de 1970. 1971. Plan de rehabilitacion y desarrollo de la zona afectada por el terremoto. Chiclayo, 1971. 3 vols. *bibliog.*

EAST (FAR EAST)

— Economic conditions.

INFLATION and growth: proceedings of a symposium; editor, V.V. Bhanoji Rao. Singapore, 1974. pp. 256. *Organised by the Economic Society of Singapore.*

— Foreign economic relations — United States.

ANDERSON (IRVINE H.) The Standard-Vacuum Oil Company and United States East Asian policy, 1933-1941. Princeton, [1975]. pp. 261. *bibliog.*

— Foreign relations.

MEZHDUNARODNYE otnosheniia na Dal'nem Vostoke; redaktsionnaia kollegiia...E.M. Zhukov,...M.I. Sladkovskii,...A. M. Dubinskii. Moskva, 1973. 2 vols.

HEINZIG (DIETER) Disputed islands in the South China Sea: Paracels, Spratlys, Pratas, Macclesfield Bank. Wiesbaden, 1976. pp. 58.

— — United Kingdom.

KLIMENKO (NIKOLAI PROKOP'EVICH) Kolonial'naia politika Anglii na Dal'nem Vostoke v seredine XIX veka. Moskva, 1976. pp. 309. *bibliog.*

SHAI (ARON) Origins of the war in the east: Britain, China and Japan, 1937- 39. London, [1976]. pp. 267. *bibliog.*

LOWE (PETER) Lecturer in History at Manchester University. Great Britain and the origins of the Pacific war: a study of British policy in East Asia, 1937-1941. Oxford, 1977. pp. 318. *bibliog.*

— — United States.

UTLEY (FREDA) The China story. Chicago, 1951 repr. 1962. pp. 274.

DORWART (JEFFERY M.) The Pigtail War: American involvement in the Sino-Japanese War of 1894-1895. Amherst, Mass., 1975. pp. 168. *bibliog.*

INTERNATIONAL INSTITUTE FOR STRATEGIC STUDIES. Adelphi Papers. No. 132. American security policy in Asia; by Leslie H. Brown. London, 1977. pp. 36.

— History.

UTLEY (FREDA) The China story. Chicago, 1951 repr. 1962. pp. 274.

CAMERON (NIGEL) From bondage to liberation: East Asia, 1860-1952. Hong Kong, 1975. pp. 371. *bibliog.*

— Politics and government.

BARNDS (WILLIAM J.) ed. The two Koreas in East Asian affairs. New York, 1976. pp. 216.

EAST (NEAR EAST)

— Commerce.

WILSON (RODNEY) Trade and investment in the Middle East. London, 1977. pp. 152.

— Economic conditions.

STRANY Blizhnego i Srednego Vostoka: istoriia, ekonomika. Moskva, 1972. pp. 505.

ASKARI (HOSSEIN) and CUMMINGS (JOHN THOMAS) Middle East economies in the 1970s: a comparative approach. New York, 1976. pp. 581. *bibliog.*

The MIDDLE East: oil, conflict and hope; edited by A.L. Udovitch. Lexington, Mass., [1976]. pp. 557. *(Commission on Critical Choices for Americans. Critical Choices for Americans. vol. 10)*

WILSON (RODNEY) Trade and investment in the Middle East. London, 1977. pp. 152.

— Economic policy.

BEN-SHAHAR (HAIM) Oil: prices and capital. Lexington, Mass., [1976]. pp. 124. *bibliog.*

— Foreign relations.

ABIR (MORDECHAI) Persian Gulf oil in Middle East and international conflicts. Jerusalem, 1976. pp. 35. *(Hebrew University. Leonard Davis Institute for International Relations. Jerusalem Papers on Peace Problems. 20)*

INTERNATIONAL INSTITUTE FOR STRATEGIC STUDIES. Adelphi Papers. No. 128. The Arab-Israeli dispute: great power behaviour; by Lawrence L. Whetten. London, 1976. pp. 45.

The MIDDLE East: oil, conflict and hope; edited by A.L. Udovitch. Lexington, Mass., [1976]. pp. 557. *(Commission on Critical Choices for Americans. Critical Choices for Americans. vol. 10)*

PELCOVITS (NATHAN ALBERT) Security guarantees in a Middle East settlement. Beverly Hills, [1976]. pp. 69. *(Foreign Policy Research Institute. Foreign Policy Papers. Vol. 2/5)*

— — Bibliography.

SCHULZ (ANN T.) compiler. International and regional politics in the Middle East and North Africa: a guide to information sources. Detroit, [1977]. pp. 244. *(Gale Research Company. Gale Information Guide Library. International Relations Information Guide Series. 6)*

— — Russia.

INTERNATIONAL INSTITUTE FOR STRATEGIC STUDIES. Adelphi Papers. No. 131. The Soviet Union and the P.L.O.; by Galia Golan. London, 1976. pp. 34.

NOVIKOV (NIKOLAI VASIL'EVICH) Puti i pereput'ia diplomata: zapiski o 1943-1944 gg. Moskva, 1976. pp. 256.

GOLAN (GALIA) Yom Kippur and after: the Soviet Union and the Middle East crisis. Cambridge, 1977. pp. 350. *bibliog. (National Association for Soviet and East European Studies. Soviet and East European Studies)*

— — United Kingdom.

BUSCH (BRITON COOPER) Mudros to Lausanne: Britain's frontier in West Asia, 1918- 1923. Albany, N.Y., 1976. pp. 430. *bibliog.*

— — United States.

TRICE (ROBERT H.) Interest groups and the foreign policy process: U.S. policy in the Middle East. Beverly Hills, [1976]. pp. 80.

BRYSON (THOMAS A.) American diplomatic relations with the Middle East, 1784-1975: survey. Metuchen, N.J., [1977]. pp. 431. *bibliog.*

LATTER (RICHARD) The making of American foreign policy in the Middle East, 1945- 48. 1976 [or rather 1977]. fo. 463. *bibliog. Typescript. Ph.D. (London) thesis: unpublished. This thesis is the property of London University and may not be removed from the Library.*

— History.

STRANY Blizhnego i Srednego Vostoka: istoriia, ekonomika. Moskva, 1972. pp. 505.

BUSCH (BRITON COOPER) Mudros to Lausanne: Britain's frontier in West Asia, 1918- 1923. Albany, N.Y., 1976. pp. 430. *bibliog.*

— Politics and government.

MIDDLE EAST INSTITUTE. 25th Annual Conference, 1971. People, power and political systems: prospects in the Middle East; a summary record. Washington, D.C., 1971. pp. 55.

The MIDDLE East: oil, conflict and hope; edited by A.L. Udovitch. Lexington, Mass., [1976]. pp. 557. *(Commission on Critical Choices for Americans. Critical Choices for Americans. vol. 10)*

KLUG (TONY) Middle East impasse: the only way out. London, 1977. pp. 38. *(Fabian Society. Research Series. [No.] 330)*

— — Bibliography.

DRABEK (ANNE GORDON) and KNAPP (WILFRID FRANCIS) compilers. The politics of African and Middle Eastern states: an annotated bibliography. Oxford, 1976. pp. 192.

— Relations (general) with Russia.

ATAMAMEDOV (N.V.) and GOLOVIN (IULII MIKHAILOVICH) eds. Lenin v sud'bakh narodov Vostoka. Ashkhabad, 1975. pp. 143.

— Social conditions.

COSTELLO (VINCENT FRANCIS) Urbanization in the Middle East. Cambridge, 1977. pp. 121. *bibliog.*

EAST AND WEST.

CAMERON (NIGEL) From bondage to liberation: East Asia, 1860-1952. Hong Kong, 1975. pp. 371. *bibliog.*

DODGE (ERNEST S.) Islands and empires: western impact on the Pacific and East Asia. Minneapolis, Minn., 1976. pp. 364. *bibliog.*

EAST INDIANS IN FOREIGN COUNTRIES.

TINKER (HUGH) The banyan tree: overseas emigrants from India, Pakistan and Bangladesh. Oxford, 1977. pp. 204.

EAST INDIANS IN SOUTH AFRICA.

SOUTH AFRICA. Bureau of Statistics. Education: schools for Coloureds and Asians. a., 1971(5th)- Pretoria. *[in English and Afrikaans].*

PILLAY (BALA) British Indians in the Transvaal: trade, politics and imperial relations, 1885-1906. London, 1976. pp. 259. *bibliog.*

EAST INDIANS IN THE UNITED KINGDOM.

U.K. Parliament. House of Commons. Library. Research Division. Reference Sheets. 76/17. East African Asians: their immigration and citizenship position. [London], 1976. pp. 19. *bibliog.*

EAST INDIANS IN UGANDA.

MELADY (THOMAS PATRICK) and MELADY (MARGARET BADUM) Uganda: the Asian exiles. Maryknoll, N.Y., [1976]. pp. 86. *bibliog.*

EAST LONDON

— Industries.

RENDERS (VERA) and PHILLIPS (BRUCE DALTON) Industrial change in the East London/King William's Town and Port Elizabeth/Uitenhage metropolitan regions, 1960-1970. Port Elizabeth, 1976. fo. 56. *(University of Port Elizabeth. Institute for Planning Research. Information Bulletins. No. 10)*

EAST SUSSEX

— History.

BELL (CHRISTOPHER RICHARD VINCENT) A history of East Sussex County Council, 1889-1974. London, 1975. pp. 119.

— Politics and government.

BELL (CHRISTOPHER RICHARD VINCENT) A history of East Sussex County Council, 1889-1974. London, 1975. pp. 119.

EAST-WEST TRADE (1945-).

KROK-PASZKOWSKI (JAN) Między Brukselą a Moskwą: procesy integracyjne w Europie. London, 1975. pp. 159. *bibliog.*

U.S. financing of East-West trade: the political economy of government credits and the national interest; edited by Paul Marer. Bloomington, Ind., [1975]. pp. 442. *bibliog. (Indiana University. International Development Research Center. Studies in East European and Soviet Planning, Development and Trade. No. 22) Includes papers delivered at a panel discussion on "The political economy of subsidized credits in East-West trade", San Francisco, 1974.*

BOLZ (KLAUS) and others. Die Wirtschaftsbeziehungen zwischen der Bundesrepublik Deutschland und der Sowjetunion: Entwicklung, Bestimmungsfaktoren und Perspektive. Hamburg, 1976. pp. 639. *(Hamburg. Hamburgisches Welt-Wirtschafts-Archiv. Veröffentlichungen) 8 graphs in end pocket.*

EKONOMICHESKIE sviazi Vostok-Zapad: problemy i vozmozhnosti. Moskva, 1976. pp. 324.

FRIESEN (CONNIE M.) The political economy of East-West trade. New York, 1976. pp. 203. *bibliog.*

KLUEMPER (BERNHARD) Finanzierungsprobleme in Ost-West-Handel und -Kooperation. Hamburg, 1976. pp. 260. *bibliog. (Hamburg. Hansische Universität. Institut für Aussenhandel und Überseewirtschaft. Forschungsberichte. Nr. 8) Inaugural-Dissertation zur Erlangung des akademischen Grades eines Doktors der Wirtschaftswissenschaft der Universität Hamburg.*

LEBAHN (AXEL) Sozialistische Wirtschaftsintegration und Ost-West-Handel im sowjetischen internationalen Recht: Theorie und Praxis des Offenheitsprinzips, etc. Berlin, [1976]. pp. 495. *bibliog.*

BLAKER (PETER) and others. Coping with the Soviet Union: a new Tory view. London, 1977. pp. 28. *(Conservative Political Centre. [Publications]. No. 605)*

EASTERN QUESTION.

GILLARD (DAVID R.) The struggle for Asia, 1828-1914: a study in British and Russian imperialism. London, 1977. pp. 214. *bibliog.*

EASTERN QUESTION (BALKAN).

ANDERSON (MATTHEW SMITH) The eastern question, 1774-1923: a study in international relations. London, 1966. pp. 436. *bibliog.*

EASTERN QUESTION (FAR EAST).

MEZHDUNARODNYE otnosheniia na Dal'nem Vostoke; redaktsionnaia kollegiia...E.M. Zhukov,...M.I. Sladkovskii,...A. M. Dubinskii. Moskva, 1973. 2 vols.

EASTERN QUESTION (NEAR EAST).

SHEREMET (VITALII IVANOVICH) Turtsiia i Adrianopol'skii mir 1829 g.: iz istorii Vostochnogo voprosa. Moskva, 1975. pp. 226.

ECOLOGY.

GUDOZHNIK (GRIGORII SERGEEVICH) Nauchno-tekhnicheskaia revoliutsiia i ekologicheskii krizis. Moskva, 1975. pp. 232.

PROBLEMA okruzhaiushchei sredy v mirovoi ekonomike i mezhdunarodnykh otnosheniiakh. Moskva, 1976. pp. 359.

HARVEY (BRIAN W.) and HALLETT (JOHN D.) Environment and society: an introductory analysis. London, 1977. pp. 163. *bibliog.*

OPHULS (WILLIAM) Ecology and the politics of scarcity: prologue to a political theory of the steady state. San Francisco, [1977]. pp. 303. *bibliog.*

— Canada — Ontario.

HILLS (GEORGE ANGUS) and others. Developing a better environment: ecological land-use planning in Ontario: a study of methodology in the development of regional plans. [Toronto], Ontario Economic Council, [1970] repr. 1973. pp. 182. *bibliog.*

— Pacific, The.

SUBSISTENCE and survival: rural ecology in the Pacific; edited by Timothy P. Bayliss-Smith and Richard G. Feachem. London, 1977. pp. 428. *bibliogs.*

— Tanzania.

KJEKSHUS (HELGE) Ecology control and economic development in East African history: the case of Tanganyika 1850-1950. Berkeley, Calif., 1977. pp. 215. *bibliog.*

ECONOMIC ASSISTANCE.

SCHMITT (MATTHIAS) Partnerschaft mit Entwicklungsländern. Stuttgart-Degerloch, [1960]. pp. 112.

LEWIS (Sir WILLIAM ARTHUR) The evolution of foreign aid. Cardiff, [1971]. pp. 18. *(Wales. University of Wales. University College, Cardiff. David Owen Memorial Lectures. No. 1)*

NORTH LONDON HASLEMERE GROUP. The Haslemere declaration: a radical analysis of the relationships between the rich world and the poor world. 6th ed. London, 1972. pp. 28. *bibliog.*

OIKONOMIDES (CHRISTOPHES) Earned international reserve units: the catalyst of two complementary world problems: the monetary and development. Oxford, 1973 repr. 1976. pp. 24.

LIFEBOAT ethics: the moral dilemmas of world hunger; edited by George R. Lucas and Thomas W. Ogletree. New York, [1976]. pp. 162. *bibliog. Originally published in the Spring and Summer 1976 issues of Soundings.*

The POLITICS of aid, trade and investment; edited by Satish Raichur [and] Craig Liske. New York, [1976]. pp. 218. *bibliogs.*

ECONOMIC ASSISTANCE, AMERICAN.

HANSEN (ROGER D.) The U.S. and world development: agenda for action, 1976. New York, 1976. pp. 222.

— Brazil.

BLACK (JAN KNIPPERS) United States penetration of Brazil. [Philadelphia], 1977. pp. 313. *bibliog.*

— China.

HAWES (GRACE M.) The Marshall Plan for China: Economic Co-operation Administration, 1948-1949. Cambridge, Mass., [1977]. pp. 138. *bibliogs.*

— Germany.

WINZER (OTTO) Der Marschallplan: was er bringt und was er nimmt. Berlin, [1948]. pp. 31.

ECONOMIC ASSISTANCE, BRITISH

— Africa, Subsaharan.

JONES (DAVID) of the Overseas Development Institute. Aid and development in southern Africa: British aid to Botswana, Lesotho and Swaziland. London, [1977]. pp. 313.

— Bangladesh.

SCOTT (GUTHRIE MICHAEL) and HUQ (FAZLUL) Britain: Bangladesh: traffic in charity. London, [1976]. pp. 105. *Includes extracts from newspapers.*

— Kenya.

HOLTHAM (GERALD) and HAZLEWOOD (ARTHUR DENNIS) Aid and inequality in Kenya: British development assistance to Kenya. London, 1976. pp. 265.

ECONOMIC ASSISTANCE, CHINESE.

COPPER (JOHN FRANKLIN) China's foreign aid: an instrument of Peking's foreign policy. Lexington, Mass., [1976]. pp. 197. *bibliog.*

ECONOMIC ASSISTANCE, COMMUNIST.

STREPETOVA (MARGARITA PETROVNA) Sotrudnichestvo stran SEV s razvivaiushchimisia gosudarstvami: obrazovanie i podgotovka kadrov. Moskva, 1973. pp. 111. *bibliog.*

SOTSIALISTICHESKAIA ekonomicheskaia integratsiia i sotrudnichestvo s razvivaiushchimisia stranami. Moskva, 1976. pp. 233. *bibliog.*

ECONOMIC ASSISTANCE, DANISH.

DENMARK'S DEVELOPMENT ASSISTANCE: annual report; ([pd. by] Danish International Development Agency. a., 1973- Copenhagen.

ECONOMIC ASSISTANCE, DOMESTIC

— United States.

LAPATRA (JACK W.) Public welfare systems. Springfield, Ill., [1975]. pp. 221.

LEVITAN (SAR A.) Programs in aid of the poor. 3rd ed. Baltimore, Md., [1976]. pp. 146. *bibliogs.*

LEVITAN (SAR A.) and ZICKLER (JOYCE K.) Too little but not too late: federal aid to lagging areas. Lexington, Mass., [1976]. pp. 172.

PERLMAN (RICHARD) The economics of poverty. New York, [1976]. pp. 240.

FRANK (CHARLES R.) Foreign trade and domestic aid. Washington, D.C., [1977]. pp. 180.

RURAL poverty and the policy crisis; coedited by Robert O. Coppedge and Carlton G. Davis. Ames, Iowa, 1977. pp. 220. *bibliog. Based on papers presented at a conference held in February 1975, at Gainesville, Florida, sponsored by the University of Florida.*

ECONOMIC ASSISTANCE, DUTCH.

NETHERLANDS' DEVELOPMENT POLICY; [pd. by] Voorlichtingsdienst Ontwikkelingssamenwerking, Ministerie van Buitenlandse Zaken. a., 1975- The Hague.

ECONOMIC ASSISTANCE, EUROPEAN.

COURIER, THE: European Community-Africa-Caribbean-Pacific (formerly Association news); [pd. by the Commission of the European Communities]. bi-m., Ja/F 1973 (no.17)- Brussels.

— America, Latin.

MARQUEZ (JAVIER) Instrumentos para intensificar la contribucion financiera de Europa a America Latina. Mexico, 1970. pp. 78. *(Centro de Estudios Monetarios Latinoamericanos. Ensayos. 24)*

ECONOMIC ASSISTANCE, FRENCH.

FRANCE. Ministère de la Coopération. 1975. Rapport sur la politique française de coopération, etc. Paris, 1975. pp. 78.

ECONOMIC ASSISTANCE, KUWAITI

— Arab countries.

DEMIR (SOLIMAN) The Kuwait Fund and the political economy of Arab regional development. New York, 1976. pp. 138. *bibliog.*

ECONOMIC ASSISTANCE, RUSSIAN.

ALESKEROV (MURMUZ N.) Ravnopravnoe sotrudnichestvo: sotrudnichestvo SSSR s molodymi nezavisimymi gosudarstvami. Baku, 1975. pp. 216.

— Vietnam.

SSSR - DRV: vospominaniia i stat'i. Moskva, 1975. pp. 285.

ECONOMIC ASSISTANCE IN AFRICA.

AFRICAN DEVELOPMENT FUND. Board of Directors. Report. a., 1974 (2nd)- Abidjan.

ECONOMIC ASSISTANCE IN LATIN AMERICA.

LOEHR (WILLIAM) and others. A comparison of U.S. and multilateral aid recipients in Latin America, 1957-1971. Beverly Hills, [1976]. pp. 45. *bibliog.*

ECONOMIC ASSISTANCE IN MALAWI.

GORDENKER (LEON) International aid and national decisions: development programs in Malawi, Tanzania and Zambia. Princeton, N.J., [1976]. pp. 190.

ECONOMIC ASSISTANCE IN NEPAL.

NEPAL and the Colombo plan: (a review) on the occasion of the 20th anniversary of the Colombo plan. [Kathmandu], National Planning Commission Secretariat, 1971. pp. 35.

ECONOMIC ASSISTANCE IN RUSSIA.

MAKARENKO (OLEKSANDR ANDRIIOVYCH) Moguchaia sila proletarskoi solidarnosti: podderzhka zarubezhnym proletariatom Sovetskoi strany v 1921-1925 gg. Moskva, 1976. pp. 319.

ECONOMIC ASSISTANCE IN TANZANIA.

GORDENKER (LEON) International aid and national decisions: development programs in Malawi, Tanzania and Zambia. Princeton, N.J., [1976]. pp. 190.

ECONOMIC ASSISTANCE IN ZAMBIA.

GORDENKER (LEON) International aid and national decisions: development programs in Malawi, Tanzania and Zambia. Princeton, N.J., [1976]. pp. 190.

ECONOMIC CONDITIONS.

ECONOMIC IMPACT: a q. review of world economics; [pd. by] United States Information Agency. q., 1973 (no.2)- , with gaps (1973, nos. 4, 5; 1975, no.11; 1976, no. 15). Washington.

BLOCK (HERBERT) Economist. Political arithmetic of the world economies. Beverly Hills, [1974]. pp. 90. *bibliog. (Georgetown University. Center for Strategic and International Studies. Washington Papers. vol. 2/15)*

FRANCE. Sénat. Commission des Finances. Rapporteur Général. Note de conjoncture. s-a., Oc 1975(no.1)- Paris.

SOREVNOVANIE dvukh sistem: ekonomika sotsializma i vsemirnoe khoziaistvo. Moskva, 1975. pp. 462. *With German and English tables of contents.*

INOZEMTSEV (NIKOLAI NIKOLAEVICH) and others, eds. Uglublenie obshchego krizisa kapitalizma. Moskva, 1976. pp. 358.

NATIONAL ECONOMIC DEVELOPMENT OFFICE. Recent developments in the U.K. and world economy. [London], 1976. pp. 57.

THEORETICAL problems, current structural changes in the world economy; edited by József Nyilas. Leyden, 1976. pp. 335. *Based on vol.1, 2nd ed. of Korunk világgazdasága (The world economy of our age).*

UNITED NATIONS SOCIAL DEFENCE RESEARCH INSTITUTE. 1976. Economic crises and crime: correlations between the state of the economy, deviance and the control of deviance. Rome, 1976. pp. 248. *(Publications. No.15)*

SIMAI (MIHÁLY) and others. Main tendencies in the world economy 1976-1990; elaborated by a research team directed by Professor M. Simai. Budapest, 1977. pp. 50. *(Hungarian Scientific Council for World Economy. [Publications]. Trends in World Economy. No. 20)*

HAGUE. Institute of Social Studies. Occasional Papers. No. 50- . The Hague. *Last two years only kept.*

ECONOMIC DEVELOPMENT.

WEY (S.O.) Socio-economic problems in political regimes. Lagos, Federal Ministry of Information, 1971. fo. 104, 3.

DEVELOPMENT and environment: report and working papers of a panel of experts convened by the Secretary-General of the United Nations Conference on the Human Environment, Founex, Switzerland, June 4-12, 1971. Paris, 1972. pp. 225. *(Environment and Social Sciences. 1)*

ENSAIOS econômicos: ([in honour of] Octavio Gouvêa de Bulhões); [edited by Mircea Buescu]. Rio de Janeiro, [1972 repr.] 1974. pp. 549.

CAMBRIDGE. University. Centre of Latin American Studies. Working Papers. No. 17. Underdevelopment and dependence: the fundamental connection; by Celso Furtado. Cambridge, 1973. pp. 18.

INTERNATIONAL SYMPOSIUM ON GROWTH AND WORLD EQUILIBRIUM, ELSINORE, 1973. A report [of the symposium]. [Copenhagen, 1973]. pp. 85. *Jointly organised by Danchurchaid and Oxfam of Great Britain.*

LEE (HYUN-JAE) A study of the structural change of expenditures on gross national product in the process of economic growth, with special reference to the Korean economy, as a case of a developing country in comparison with developed countries. Pittsburgh, 1973. pp. 40.

CAMBRIDGE. University. Centre of Latin American Studies. Working Papers. No. 16. The myth of economic development and the future of the third world; by Celso Furtado. Cambridge, 1974. fo. 22. *Photocopy.*

CONGDON (BOB) and OSBORN (PAUL) Directory of ideas, contacts and support for academics working for international development. London, 1974. pp. 40. *(Voluntary Committee on Overseas Aid and Development. Academics against Poverty Project. Higher Education Action for Development. 4)*

WILLIAMS (EDWARD J.) Latin American political thought: a developmental perspective. Tucson, Arizona, [1974]. pp. 69. *bibliog. (Arizona University. Institute of Government Research. Comparative Government Studies. No. 6)*

BRITISH ASSOCIATION FOR THE ADVANCEMENT OF SCIENCE. Section F. Meeting, 1974. The political economy of change: papers presented to Section F. ...; edited by K. J. W. Alexander. Oxford, 1975. pp. 189.

CONGDON (BOB) and OSBORN (PAUL) Evaluation of the contribution of British universities to development. London, [1975]. pp. 16. *(Voluntary Committee on Overseas Aid and Development. Academics against Poverty Project. Higher Education Action for Development. 3)*

DAS GUPTA (AMIYA KUMAR) The economics of austerity. Delhi, 1975. pp. 38. *(Benares Hindu University. Shastri Memorial Lectures. 1974)*

FOXLEY RIOSECO (ALEJANDRO) Estrategia de desarrollo y modelos de planificacion. Mexico, 1975. pp. 180.

FURTADO (CELSO) El desarrollo economico: un mito. Mexico, 1975 repr. 1976. pp. 141.

SEMINAR ON SOCIAL SCIENCE RESEARCH WITH SPECIAL REFERENCE TO POPULATION AND DEVELOPMENT, MONROVIA, LIBERIA, 1975. Seminar...; organized at the University of Liberia...by Liberia College,...University of Liberia and Population Dynamics Programme, University of Ghana, Legon. Monrovia, Liberia, 1975. fo. 75. *bibliogs.*

AKHMEDOVA (MATBUA AMIRSAIDOVNA) Nekapitalisticheskii put': nekotorye problemy teorii i praktiki. Tashkent, 1976. pp. 223.

AMIN (SAMIR) Unequal development: an essay on the social formations of peripheral capitalism: translated [from the French] by Brian Pearce. Hassocks, [1976]. pp. 440. *bibliog.*

BAUER (PETER TAMAS) Dissent on development. rev. ed. Cambridge, Mass., 1976. pp. 320. *bibliog.*

CLARK (CAL) and JOHNSON (KARL F.) Development's influence on Yugoslav political values. Beverly Hills, [1976]. pp. 69. *bibliog.*

The COMMONWEALTH and development: the report of the conference sponsored by O[verseas] D[evelopment] I[nstitute] and St. Catharine's-Cumberland Lodge, at Cumberland Lodge, 13-15 February 1976. London, [1976]. pp. 59.

DIXIT (AVINASH K.) The theory of equilibrium growth. London, 1976. pp. 204. *bibliog.*

GARAUDY (ROGER) Le projet espérance. Paris, [1976]. pp. 218.

GRIFFIN (KEITH) Land concentration and rural poverty. London, 1976. pp. 303.

HAQ (MAHBUS UL) The poverty curtain: choices for the third world. New York, 1976. pp. 247. *bibliog.*

INTERNATIONAL BANK FOR RECONSTRUCTION AND DEVELOPMENT. 1976. World tables 1976: from the data files of the World Bank. Baltimore, 1976. pp. 552.

LACOSTE (YVES) Géographie du sous-développement: géopolitique d'une crise. 3rd ed. [Paris], 1976. pp. 292. *bibliog.*

MONEY and finance in economic growth and development: essays in honour of Edward S. Shaw;...edited by Ronald I. McKinnon. New York, [1976]. pp. 339. *bibliogs. Proceedings of the conference held at Stanford University in April 1974, under the auspices of the Center for Research in Economic Growth.*

PARTANT (FRANÇOIS) La guérilla économique: les conditions du développement. Paris, [1976]. pp. 220. *bibliog.*

RESHAPING the international order: a report to the Club of Rome; Jan Tinbergen, coordinator, Antony J. Dolman, editor, Jan van Ettinger, director. New York, [1976]. pp. 325. *This publication was realised in cooperation with the Foundation Reshaping the International Order (RIO).*

ROSENBERG (NATHAN) Perspectives on technology. Cambridge, 1976. pp. 353. *bibliogs.*

SMYSHLIAEVA (LIUDMILA MATVEEVNA) Ekonomicheskii rost i proportsii kapital'nykh vlozhenii. Moskva, 1976. pp. 191.

The SOCIAL sciences and problems of development: (papers presented at an International Conference in Persepolis Iran, June 1-4, 1974); Khodadad Farmanfarmaian, editor. Princeton, [1976]. pp. 332. *bibliogs. (Princeton University. Program in Near Eastern Studies. Princeton Studies on the Near East) Conference sponsored by the Plan and Budget Organization of Iran, Tehran University, Princeton University.*

SOROKIN (GENNADII MIKHAILOVICH) Problemy vosproizvodstva i planirovaniia sotsialisticheskoi ekonomiki; (stat'i, napisannye v techenie 1960-1975 gg.). Moskva, 1976. pp. 559. (Akademiia Nauk SSSR. Problemy Sovetskoi Ekonomiki)

UNILEVER LIMITED. Unilever and economic development in the third world; (speech delivered in London by Mr. D. A. Orr, ..., and in Rotterdam by Mr. H.F. van den Hoven,...12th May, 1976). London, [1976]. pp. 9.

VALUES and development: appraising Asian experience; edited by Harold Lasswell [and others]. Cambridge, Mass., [1976]. pp. 291. (Massachusetts Institute of Technology. Studies in Comparative Politics) Papers from the 1971-1972 meetings of a continuing seminar sponsored by the South East Asia Development Advisory Group.

ZAKONOMERNOSTI rosta urovnia zhizni naseleniia v usloviiakh nekapitalisticheskogo razvitiia. Tashkent, 1976. pp. 192.

ECONOMIC progress, private values and public policy: essays in honor of William Fellner; edited by Bela Balassa and Richard Nelson. Amsterdam, 1977. pp. 339. bibliogs.

ESSAYS on economic development and cultural change, in honor of Bert F. Hoselitz: Manning Nash, editor. [Chicago, 1977]. pp. 460. bibliog.

LA GRANDVILLE (OLIVIER DE) Théorie de la croissance économique. Paris, 1977. pp. 686. bibliog.

MAIER (HARRY) Gibt es Grenzen des ökonomischen Wachstums? Berlin, 1977. pp. 82.

MISHAN (EDWARD JOSHUA) The economic growth debate: an assessment. London, 1977. pp. 277. bibliog.

NICK (HARRY) Sozialismus und Wirtschaftswachstum. Berlin, 1977. pp. 80.

PARK (SUNG SANG) Growth and development: a physical output and employment strategy. London, 1977. pp. 145.

PECCEI (AURELIO) The human quality. Oxford, 1977. pp. 214.

SACHS (IGNACY) Pour une économie politique du développement: études de planification. [Paris, 1977]. pp. 307. bibliog.

SEMAINE DE BRUGES, 1976. The European economy beyond the crisis: from stabilisation to structural change.... l'économie européenne au-delà de la crise: de la stabilisation à la mutation structurelle; (edited by G.R. Denton and J.J.N. Cooper). Bruges, 1977. pp. 409. (College of Europe. Cahiers de Bruges. Nouvelle Série. 35) In English and French.

SIJBEN (JAC. J.) Money and economic growth. Leiden, 1977. pp. 216. bibliog. (Tilburg. Katholieke Hogeschool. Tilburg Institute of Economics. Tilburg Studies on Economics. 17)

SINGER (HANS WOLFGANG) and ANSARI (JAVED A.) Rich and poor countries. London, 1977. pp. 228.

TODARO (MICHAEL P.) Economic development in the third world: an introduction to problems and policies in a global perspective. London, 1977. pp. 445. bibliogs.

UNITED NATIONS. Department of Economic and Social Affairs. 1977. The future of the world economy: a study on the impact of prospective economic issues and policies on the international development strategy. New York, 1977. pp. 110.

ZOLOTAS (XENOPHON) International monetary issues and development policies: selected essays and statements. Athens, 1977. pp. 503. bibliog.

HAGUE. Institute of Social Studies. Occasional Papers. No. 50- . The Hague. Last two years only kept.

— Congresses.

UNITED NATIONS. Conference on Trade and Development, 2nd, New Delhi, 1968. Rules of procedure. (TD/63/Rev.1). New York, 1968. pp. 23.

— Information services.

DEVSIS STUDY TEAM. 1976. DEVSIS: the preliminary design of an international information system for the development sciences. Ottawa, International Development Research Centre [Canada], [1976]. pp. 247. bibliog.

— Mathematical models.

JAFAR (MAJEED R.) Under-underdevelopment: a regional case study of the Kurdish area in Turkey. Helsinki, 1976. pp. 153. bibliog. (Finnish Social Policy Association. Studies. No. 24)

LOWE (ADOLPH) and PULRANG (STANFORD) The path of economic growth;...with an appendix by Edward J. Nell. Cambridge, 1976. pp. 336.

— Social aspects.

GALBRAITH (JOHN KENNETH) Wirtschaftswachstum und soziale Aktivität; (aus dem Amerikanischen übertragen von Friedrich Scheu; [with an introduction by Bruno Kreisky]). Wien, [1971]. pp. 18.

DELINQUANCE juvénile et développement socio-économique; par Yves Chirol [and others]. La Haye, [1975]. pp. 317. bibliog. (European Coordination Centre for Research and Documentation in Social Sciences. Publications. 6)

HIRSCH (FRED) Social limits to growth. Cambridge, Mass., 1976. pp. 208. bibliog.

KOHR (LEOPOLD) The overdeveloped nations: the diseconomies of scale. Swansea, [1976]. pp. 185. bibliog.

PITT (DAVID C.) The social dynamics of development. Oxford, 1976. pp. 162. bibliog.

SHIMPO (MITSURU) Three decades in Shiwa: economic development and social change in a Japanese farming community. Vancouver, [1976]. pp. 141. bibliog.

ECONOMIC FORECASTING.

UNITAR CONFERENCE ON THE FUTURE, MOSCOW, 1974. The United Nations and the future: proceedings of UNITAR Conference...held in Moscow from June 10 to 14, 1974. Moscow, 1976. pp. 463. In English and French.

GRANGER (CLIVE W.J.) and NEWBOLD (PAUL) Forecasting economic time series. New York, 1977. pp. 333. bibliog.

RAMSEY (JAMES B.) Economic forecasting: models or markets?: an introduction to the role of econometrics in economic policy...with A sceptical view of forecasting in Britain by Ralph Harris. London, 1977. pp. 101. bibliog. (Institute of Economic Affairs. Hobart Papers. 74)

— Mathematical models.

ARCHER (BRIAN H.) Demand forecasting in tourism. Bangor, 1976. pp. 114. bibliog. (Wales. University. University College of North Wales. Bangor Occasional Papers in Economics. No. 9)

U.K. Treasury. Macroeconomic model: technical manual. a., 1977 (3rd)- London.

— Netherlands.

NETHERLANDS. Centraal Planbureau. 1976. De Nederlandse economie in 1980. 's-Gravenhage, 1976. pp. 385.

— Russia.

AVANESOV (IURII ARKAD'EVICH) Prognozirovanie sprosa v roznichnoi torgovle. Moskva, 1975. pp. 103. bibliog.

KARLIUK (IPPOLIT IAKOVLEVICH) and SLOBODIN (V.M.) eds. Prognozirovanie razvitiia sel'skokhoziaistvennogo proizvodstva: nauchnye trudy. Moskva, (no.)1975. pp. 232. (Nauchno-Issledovatel'skii Ekonomicheskii Institut. Nauchnye Trudy)

— Tanzania.

GREEN (REGINALD HERBOLD) Toward socialism and self reliance: Tanzania's striving for sustained transition projected. Uppsala, 1977. pp. 57. (Nordiska Afrikainstitutet. Research Reports. No. 38)

— United Kingdom.

McLEAN (ALAN) Macroeconomic forecasting in the U.K. London, [1976]. pp. 14. (Economics Association. Occasional Papers. No.3)

— United States.

NATIONAL INDUSTRIAL CONFERENCE BOARD. Conference Board Economic Forum, New York, 1973. Boom, inflation, and policy: a mid-year review of the economic outlook: proceedings of the...forum. New York, 1973. pp. 72. (National Industrial Conference Board. Conference Board Reports)

The ECONOMY in transition; edited by Robert C. Blattberg. New York, 1976. pp. 137. (International Telephone and Telegraph Corporation. Key Issues Lecture Series) Essays originally commissioned in 1974 as a series of lectures entitled The economy in disarray.

O'TOOLE (JAMES) Energy and social change. Cambridge, Mass., [1976]. pp. 185. bibliog. Based on research by the Center for Futures Research at the University of Southern California.

ECONOMIC HISTORY.

LENZ (FRIEDRICH BERNHARD HERMANN) Weltwirtschaft im Umbruch: eine kritische Analyse der internationalen Politik und Wirtschaft unserer Gegenwart. Velbert, [1964]. pp. 382.

HABERLER (GOTTFRIED VON) The world economy, money, and the Great Depression, 1919-1939. Washington, D.C., 1976. pp. 44. (American Enterprise Institute for Public Policy Research. Foreign Affairs Studies. 30)

ALDCROFT (DEREK H.) From Versailles to Wall Street, 1919-1929. London, 1977. pp. 372. bibliog.

BRAUDEL (FERNAND) Afterthoughts on material civilization and capitalism;... translated by Patricia M. Ranum. Baltimore, [1977]. pp. 120. (Johns Hopkins University. Department of History. Johns Hopkins Symposia in Comparative History)

ECONOMIC foreign policies of industrial states, edited by Wilfrid L. Kohl. Lexington, Mass., [1977]. pp. 246.

The END of the Keynesian era: essays on the disintegration of the Keynesian political economy; edited by Robert Skidelsky. London, 1977. pp. 114.

FATTI e idee di storia economica nei secoli XII-XX: studi dedicati a Franco Borlandi; (redazione: Bruno Dini [and others]). Bologna, [1977]. pp. 916. With contributions in English, French and German.

— Methodology.

LEE (CLIVE H.) The quantitative approach to economic history. London, 1977. pp. 117. bibliog.

ECONOMIC INDICATORS

— Australia — New South Wales.

NEW SOUTH WALES. Commonwealth Bureau of Census and Statistics. New South Wales Office. Major economic indicators, N.S.W. m., current issues only. Sydney.

— Bangladesh.

ECONOMIC INDICATORS OF BANGLADESH; pd. by Bureau of Statistics. m., Ja 1976(v.3, no.1)- Dacca.

— France.

FRANCE. Commissariat Général du Plan. Indicateurs du 7e Plan: revue trimestrielle. q., Ap 1977(no.1)- Paris. Supersedes FRANCE. Commissariat Général du Plan. Indicateurs associés au 6e Plan.

— New Hebrides.

NEW HEBRIDES. Condominium Bureau of Statistics. Statistical bulletin: Economic indicators. q., S 1976 (3rd)- Vila. *[in English and French].*

— Panama.

PANAMA. Direccion de Estadistica y Censo. Estadistica panameña. Indicadores economicos y sociales. a., 1974/1975- Panama. *Supersedes PANAMA. Direccion de Estadistica y Censo. Estadistica panameña. Serie P. Indicadores economicos.*

— Papua New Guinea.

PAPUA NEW GUINEA. Department of Finance. Quarterly summary of economic conditions. q., My 1976- Port Moresby.

— Singapore.

SINGAPORE ANNUAL KEY INDICATORS; [pd. by] Statistics Department. a., 1968/76- Singapore.

— Yugoslavia.

TURČIĆ (IVAN) Indikatori o efikasnosti jugoslavenske industrije po općinama. Zagreb, 1975. pp. 364. *With English summary.*

ECONOMIC LEGISLATION.

COHEN (MORRIS L.) and others. Law and development classification plan. Medford, Mass., [1976]. pp. 14. *(Tufts University. Fletcher School of Law and Diplomacy. Law and Population Monograph Series. No. 38)*

— European Economic Community countries.

BOERNER (BODO) Studien zum deutschen und europäischen Wirtschaftsrecht. Köln, 1973-77. 2 vols. *(Cologne. Universität. Institut für das Recht der Europäischen Gemeinschaften. Kölner Schriften zum Europarecht. Bände 17,26)*

KAPTEYN (PAUL J.G.) ed. The economic law of the member States in an economic and monetary union. Leyden, 1976. pp. 131. *(Council of Europe. European Aspects. Series E: Law. No.18) Reprinted from Common Market Law Review, 1976.*

— France.

LAUBADERE (ANDRE DE) Droit public économique. 2nd ed. Paris, 1976. pp. 541.

— Germany.

BOERNER (BODO) Studien zum deutschen und europäischen Wirtschaftsrecht. Köln, 1973-77. 2 vols. *(Cologne. Universität. Institut für das Recht der Europäischen Gemeinschaften. Kölner Schriften zum Europarecht. Bände 17,26)*

Die WIRTSCHAFTSVERFASSUNG der Bundesrepublik Deutschland; [by] G. Gutmann [and others]. Stuttgart, 1976. pp. 281. *bibliog.*

— Russia.

LYSOV (MIKHAIL DANILOVICH) Otvetstvennost' za chastnopredprinimatel'skuiu deiatel'nost' po sovetskomu ugolovnomu pravu. Kazan', 1969. pp. 138.

PRAVOVYE voprosy khoziaistvennoi reformy. Vladivostok, 1971. 2 pts (in 1). *(Dal'nevostochnyi Gosudarstvennyi Universitet. Uchenye Zapiski. t.56, ch.1,2)*

KUTAFIN (OLEG EMEL'IANOVICH) Mestnye Sovety i narodnokhoziaistvennoe planirovanie. Moskva, 1976. pp. 142.

— United Kingdom.

UNITED KINGDOM. Statutes, etc. 1662-1783. [A collection of 277 separately published Acts of Parliament relating to banking, bread, coinage, commerce, corn, labour, poor law, settlement, textile and other trades, and taxation]. London, 1662-1783. 277 pts. (in 6 vols.).

BELLAIRS (CHARLES E.) Conservative social and industrial reform: a record of Conservative legislation between 1800 and 1974; with a foreword by Margaret Thatcher. rev. ed. London, 1977. pp. 128.

— Zaire.

BONGOY (MPEKESA) Investissements mixtes au Zaire: (joint ventures pour la période de transition). Kinshasa, 1974. pp. 523. *bibliog.*

ECONOMIC POLICY.

KULMEN (AD.) Die Lösung der sozialen Frage. Leipzig, [1925]. pp. 20. *Originally circulated as manuscript to 30 prominent public figures in 1917.*

LOEWENTHAL (RICHARD) Jenseits des Kapitalismus: ein Beitrag zur sozialistischen Neuorientierung; mit einer ausführlichen Einführung: nach 30 Jahren. Berlin, [1977]. pp. 268. *Reprint of work originally published at Lauf nr. Nuremberg in 1947 under the pseudonym Paul Sering.*

LENZ (FRIEDRICH BERNHARD HERMANN) Weltwirtschaft im Umbruch: eine kritische Analyse der internationalen Politik und Wirtschaft unserer Gegenwart. Velbert, [1964]. pp. 382.

GALBRAITH (JOHN KENNETH) Wirtschaftswachstum und soziale Aktivität; (aus dem Amerikanischen übertragen von Friedrich Scheu; [with an introduction by Bruno Kreisky]). Wien, [1971]. pp. 18.

INTERNATIONAL UNION OF LOCAL AUTHORITIES. [Publications]. 98. Local government as promotor of economic and social development. The Hague, 1971. pp. 100.

PAPANDREOU (ANDREAS GEORGE) and ZOHAR (URI) The impact approach to project selection: national planning and socioeconomic priorities: a two volume series, (volume 2). New York, 1974. pp. 187.

BRITISH ASSOCIATION FOR THE ADVANCEMENT OF SCIENCE. Section F. Meeting, 1974. The political economy of change: papers presented to Section F. ...; edited by K. J. W. Alexander. Oxford, 1975. pp. 189.

SHPIL'KO (GALINA ANTONOVNA) Teorii i metody regulirovaniia kapitalisticheskoi ekonomiki. Moskva, 1975. pp. 191.

SMITH (MARGARET LAWS) Towards the creation of a sustainable economy. Chertsey, 1975. pp. 13.

BAUER (PETER TAMAS) Dissent on development. rev. ed. Cambridge, Mass., 1976. pp. 320. *bibliog.*

CONTROVERSIES and decisions: the social sciences and public policy; Charles Frankel, editor: a study prepared under the auspices of the American Academy of Arts and Sciences. New York, [1976]. pp. 299.

ECONOMIC calculation under inflation; introduction by Helen E. Schultz. Indianapolis, [1976]. pp. 340. *bibliog. Papers delivered at a seminar sponsored by the Liberty Fund, in February 1975.*

LORENZI (JEAN HERVE) Le marché dans la planification. Paris, [1975]. pp. 372. *bibliog.*

MOSS (ALFRED GEORGE) and WINTON (HARRY NATHANIEL MCQUILLIAN) compilers. A new international economic order: selected documents 1945-1975. New York, United Nations Institute for Training and Research, [1976?]. 2 vols. (in 1). *(UNITAR Document Service. No. 1.)*

RELEVANCE and precision: from quantitative analysis to economic policy; essays in honour of Pieter de Wolff; editors J.S. Cramer [and others]. Alphen aan den Rijn, 1976. pp. 318. *bibliogs.*

RESOURCE allocation and economic policy; edited by Michael Allingham and M.L. Burstein. London, 1976. pp. 251. *bibliogs. Proceedings of a conference sponsored by the University College at Buckingham and the Institute of Economic Affairs, held in London in June 1975.*

SIMAI (MIHÁLY) World problems, global projections and social conflicts of our globe. Budapest, 1976. pp. 24. *(Hungarian Scientific Council for World Economy. [Publications]. Trends in World Economy. No. 18)*

SWEET (COLIN) World economic crisis: an analysis of economic, political and military factors. London, [1976]. pp. 40.

WALTERS (ALAN A.) The politicization of economic decisions; [with an] introduction by Harry G. Johnson. Los Angeles, 1976. pp. 12. *(International Institute for Economic Research. Reprint Papers. No. 1)*

BRITISH ASSOCIATION FOR THE ADVANCEMENT OF SCIENCE. Section F. Meeting, 1976. Structure, system and economic policy; proceedings...held at the University of Lancaster 1-8 September 1976; edited by Wassily Leontief. Cambridge, 1977. pp. 223. *bibliogs.*

CARNEGIE-ROCHESTER CONFERENCE ON PUBLIC POLICY. 1976, November Conference. Optimal policies, control theory and technology experts; editors Karl Brunner and Allan H. Meltzer. Amsterdam, 1977. pp. 238. *bibliogs. (Journal of Monetary Economics. Carnegie-Rochester Conference Series on Public Policy. vol. 7)*

CORREA (HECTOR) Integrated economic accounting: theory and applications to national, real, and financial economic planning. Lexington, Mass., [1977]. pp. 222.

DINKEL (REINER) Der Zusammenhang zwischen der ökonomischen und politischen Entwicklung in einer Demokratie: eine Untersuchung mit Hilfe der ökonomischen Theorie der Politik. Berlin, [1977]. pp. 259. *bibliog.*

ECONOMIC progress, private values and public policy: essays in honor of William Fellner; edited by Bela Balassa and Richard Nelson. Amsterdam, 1977. pp. 339. *bibliogs.*

GALBRAITH (JOHN KENNETH) The affluent society. 3rd ed. London, 1977. pp. 287.

JOHANSEN (LEIF) Lectures on macroeconomic planning. Part I. General aspects. Amsterdam, 1977. pp. 355. *bibliogs.*

KEBSCHULL (DIETRICH) and others, eds. Die neue Weltwirtschaftsordnung: Beiträge zu ausgewählten Forderungen der Entwicklungsländer. Hamburg, 1977. pp. 287. *bibliog. (Hamburg. Hamburgisches Welt-Wirtschafts-Archiv. Veröffentlichungen)*

LOESCH (ACHIM VON) Die gemeinwirtschaftliche Unternehmung: vom antikapitalistischen Ordnungsprinzip zum marktwirtschaftlichen Regulativ. Köln, [1977]. pp. 256.

NÊME (JACQUES) and NÊME (COLETTE) Politiques économiques comparées. Paris, [1977]. pp. 428. *bibliogs.*

SHANKS (MICHAEL) Planning and politics: the British experience 1960-1976. London, 1977. pp. 142. *bibliog. Jointly sponsored by the National Economic Development Office and Political and Economic Planning.*

TURNER (R. KERRY) and COLLIS (CLIVE) The economics of planning. London, 1977. pp. 103. *bibliog.*

VEREIN FÜR SOZIALPOLITIK. Schriften. Neue Folge. Band 92. Soziale Probleme der modernen Industriegesellschaft: (Verhandlungen auf der Arbeitstagung...in Augsburg vom 13.-15. September 1976; herausgegeben von Bernhard Külp und Heinz-Dieter Haas). Berlin, [1977]. 2 vols. *bibliogs.*

ZAKER-SHAHRAK (ALI AKBAR) The rationale and scope for state planning in capitalist economies. 1977. fo. 271. *bibliog. Typescript. pp. 262-271 in end pocket. Ph.D. (London) thesis: unpublished. This thesis is the property of London University and may not be removed from the Library.*

— Bibliography.

U.K. Department of Industry. Statistics and Market Intelligence Library. 1976. Development plans available in the Statistics and Market Intelligence Library: (bibliography prepared by Margaret Aitchison). London, 1976. 1 pamphlet (unpaged). *(Sources of Statistics and Market Information. 6).*

ECONOMIC POLICY.(Cont.)

— Dictionaries and encyclopedias.

ZAHN (HANS E.) Wörterbuch zur Politik und Wirtschaftspolitik. Band I: deutsch-englisch-französisch:...Dictionary of politics and economic policy...: Dictionnaire politique et de politique économique, etc. Frankfurt am Main, [1975]. pp. 382. bibliog.

— Mathematical models.

GIANNOLA (ADRIANO) Schemi alternativi di pianificazione in una economia dualistica aperta. [Portici, 1974]. pp. 22. (Naples. Università. Centro di Specializzazione e Ricerche Economico-Agrarie per il Mezzogiorno. Estratti. N. 140) (Estratto dai Quaderni dell' Economia Sarda, Anno 4, N. 2-3, 1974)

WIEDEMANN (PAUL PAT) A consideration of the nature of the objective function in national economic planning, with specific reference to the mathematical modelling of medium-term planning in the Soviet Union and Eastern Europe. 1974. fo. 353. bibliog. Typescript. Ph.D. (London) thesis: unpublished. This thesis is the property of London University and may not be removed from the Library.

ECONOMIC models in regional planning...; proceedings of a seminar sponsored by the Northern Region Strategy Team and the IBM United Kingdom Scientific Centre, Peterlee, County Durham, 20-21 November 1975; [edited by K. Telford]. Peterlee, 1976. pp. 63. bibliog. (IBM United Kingdom Limited. UK Scientific Centre. [Technical Reports]. 0082)

SELECTED topics on planning; ([by] Ludwik Biliński [and others]). Warsaw, 1976. pp. 109. bibliog. (Instytut Gospodarki Krajów Rozwijających Się. Teaching Papers. Advanced Course in National Economic Planning. vol. 22)

ECONOMIC RESEARCH.

NAFPLION COLLOQUIUM ON RESEARCH PROGRAMMES IN PHYSICS AND ECONOMICS, NAFPLION, 1974. Method and appraisal in economics: [essays from the Economics Sessions of the Colloquium]; edited by Spiro J. Latsis. Cambridge, 1976. pp. 230. bibliogs.

— Ireland (Republic).

KENNEDY (KIERAN A.) The ESRI research plan 1976-80 and background analysis. Dublin, 1976. pp. 72.

— Tanzania.

DAR ES SALAAM. University. Economic Research Bureau. Annual report, 1973/74. Dar es Salaam, [1974]. pp. 24.

ECONOMIC STABILIZATION.

CARNEGIE-ROCHESTER CONFERENCE ON PUBLIC POLICY. 1976, November Conference. Optimal policies, control theory and technology experts; editors Karl Brunner and Allan H. Meltzer. Amsterdam, 1977. pp. 238. bibliogs. (Journal of Monetary Economics. Carnegie-Rochester Conference Series on Public Policy. vol. 7)

STABILIZATION of the domestic and international economy; editors, Karl Brunner [and] Allan H. Meltzer. Amsterdam, 1977. pp. 318. bibliogs. (Journal of Monetary Economics. Carnegie-Rochester Conference Series on Public Policy. vol. 5)

TURNOVSKY (STEPHEN J.) Macroeconomic analysis and stabilization policies. Cambridge, 1977. pp. 271. bibliog.

ECONOMIC SURVEYS

— Canada.

CANADA. Statistics Canada. Special Surveys Coordination Division. New surveys: notes on statistical survey activity within the federal government. q., current issues only. Ottawa. [in English and French].

ECONOMIC ZONING

— Russia.

PAVLENKO (VIKTOR FEDOROVICH) Territorial'noe planirovanie v SSSR. Moskva, 1975. pp. 279.

SHELEST (VASILII ANDREEVICH) Regional'nye energoekonomicheskie problemy SSSR. Moskva, 1975. pp. 312. (Akademiia Nauk SSSR. Komissiia po Izucheniiu Proizvodnykh Sil i Prirodnykh Resursov. Problemy Sovetskoi Ekonomiki)

GRANBERG (ALEKSANDR GRIGOR'EVICH) ed. Territorial'nye narodnokhoziaistvennye modeli. Novosibirsk, 1976. pp. 219. (Akademiia Nauk SSSR. Sibirskoe Otdelenie. Institut Ekonomiki i Organizatsii Promyshlennogo Proizvodstva. Optimizatsiia Territorial'nykh Sistem)

PROBLEMY teorii i praktiki razmeshcheniia proizvoditel'nykh sil SSSR. Moskva, 1976. pp. 326. (Akademiia Nauk SSSR. Sovet po Izucheniiu Proizvoditel'nykh Sil. Problemy Sovetskoi Ekonomiki)

NOVYE territorial'nye kompleksy SSSR. Moskva, 1977. pp. 269.

— — Mathematical models.

BANDMAN (MARK KONSTANTINOVICH) ed. Modelirovanie formirovaniia territorial'no-proizvodstvennykh kompleksov; Modelling of territorial-production complexes formation. Novosibirsk, 1976. pp. 338. With brief English summary and table of contents.

— — Estonia.

TARMISTO (VELLO IULIUSOVICH) Vnutriraionnaia territorial'naia organizatsiia proizvodstva: na materiale Estonskoi SSR. Tallin, 1975. pp. 279. With English summary.

— — Siberia.

BELORUSOV (DMITRII VASIL'EVICH) and others. Problemy razvitiia i razmeshcheniia proizvoditel'nykh sil Zapadnoi Sibiri. Moskva, 1976. pp. 269.

— — — Mathematical models.

BANDMAN (MARK KONSTANTINOVICH) ed. Formirovanie territorial'no-proizvodstvennykh kompleksov Angaro-Eniseiskogo regiona: opyt ispol'zovaniia ekonomiko-matematicheskikh modelei v predplanovykh issledovaniiakh. Novosibirsk, 1975. pp. 175. (Akademiia Nauk SSSR. Sibirskoe Otdelenie. Institut Ekonomiki i Organizatsii Promyshlennogo Proizvodstva. Optimizatsiia Territorial'nykh Sistem) With English summary.

— — Ukraine.

PALAMARCHUK (MAKSIM MARTYNOVICH) and others. Problemy razvitiia i razmeshcheniia proizvoditel'nykh sil Iugo-Zapadnogo raiona. Moskva, 1976. pp. 262. bibliog.

SUKHOPARA (FEDOR NIKOLAEVICH) and UDOD (VLADIMIR IVANOVICH) Problemy razvitiia i razmeshcheniia proizvoditel'nykh sil Donetsko-Pridneprovskogo raiona. Moskva, 1976. pp. 256. bibliog.

ECONOMICS.

ECONOMICS and sociology: towards an integration; edited by T. Huppes; contributors, N.J. Smelser [and others]. Leiden, 1976. pp. 178. First written as discussion papers for a symposium organised by the Department of Economics, Groningen University, in September 1975.

ROLL (Sir ERIC) Economics, government and business. London, 1976. pp. 27. (London. University. Stamp Memorial Lectures. 1976)

GALBRAITH (JOHN KENNETH) The age of uncertainty. London, 1977. pp. 366. Published by the BBC simultaneously with the release of the television series of the same name.

LINDER (MARC) The anti-Samuelson. New York, [1977]. 2 vols. bibliog.

PEACOCK (ALAN TURNER) The credibility of liberal economics. London, 1977. pp. 32. (Institute of Economic Affairs. Occasional Papers. 50)

SOCIOLOGICAL theories of the economy; edited by Barry Hindess. London, 1977. pp. 199. bibliog. This book contains revised versions of papers originally prepared for a seminar held in Liverpool in 1975.

The SUBTLE anatomy of capitalism; edited by Jesse Schwartz. Santa Monica, Calif., [1977]. pp. 503. bibliogs.

— Bibliography.

CARPENTER (KENNETH E.) The economic bestsellers before 1850; a catalogue of an exhibition prepared for the History of Economics Society meeting, May 21-24, 1975 at Baker Library. [Cambridge, Mass., 1975]. pp. 29.

INTERNATIONAL MONETARY FUND and INTERNATIONAL BANK FOR RECONSTRUCTION AND DEVELOPMENT. Joint Library. List of recent additions. m. [Washington]. Current issues only kept.

INTERNATIONAL MONETARY FUND and INTERNATIONAL BANK FOR RECONSTRUCTION AND DEVELOPMENT. Joint Library. List of recent periodical articles. m. [Washington]. Current issues only kept.

— Dictionaries and encyclopedias.

RITTERSHAUSEN (HEINRICH) Wirtschaft. Frankfurt am Main, 1958 repr.1960. pp. 363. (Das Fischer Lexikon. 8)

LEXIKON der Wirtschaft: Versicherung; (Herausgeber: Heinrich Bader [and others]). Berlin, [1976]. pp. 696.

TSAGOLOVA (R.S.) ed. Anglo-russkii ekonomicheskii slovar': uchebnyi; English-Russian learner's dictionary of economic terminology. Moskva, 1976. pp. 334.

— History.

MINI (PIERO V.) Philosophy and economics: the origins and development of economic theory. Gainesville, Fla., 1974. pp. 305. bibliog.

CARTELIER (JEAN) Surproduit et reproduction: la formation de l'économie politique classique. Grenoble, 1976. pp. 263.

FRADIN (JACQUES) Les fondements logiques de la théorie néoclassique de l'échange: le postulat du numéraire; introduction à la critique de l'économie politique contemporaine. Grenoble, 1976. pp. 243. bibliog.

MORGENSTERN (OSKAR) Selected economic writings...; edited by Andrew Schotter. New York, 1976. pp. 539. bibliogs.

BUCHANAN (JAMES McGILL) and WAGNER (RICHARD E.) Democracy in deficit: the political legacy of Lord Keynes. New York, [1977]. pp. 195.

DUMONT (LOUIS) From Mandeville to Marx: the genesis and triumph of economic ideology. Chicago, 1977. pp. 236. bibliog. Based on six lectures delivered at Princeton University, 1973.

GALBRAITH (JOHN KENNETH) The age of uncertainty. London, 1977. pp. 366. Published by the BBC simultaneously with the release of the television series of the same name.

HARRIS (RALPH) and SELDON (ARTHUR) Not from benevolence...: 20 years of economic dissent. London, 1977. pp. 159. (Institute of Economic Affairs. Hobart Paperbacks. 10)

HICKS (Sir JOHN RICHARD) Economic perspectives: further essays on money and growth. Oxford, 1977. pp. 199.

LA GRANDVILLE (OLIVIER DE) Théorie de la croissance économique. Paris, 1977. pp. 686. bibliog.

LEVINE (DAVID P.) Economic studies: contributions to the critique of economic theory. London, 1977. pp. 318.

MACHLUP (FRITZ) A history of thought on economic integration. London, 1977. pp. 323. bibliog.

SKAMBRAKS (HANNES) "Das Kapital" von Marx: Waffe im Klassenkampf: Aufnahme und Anwendung der Lehren des Hauptwerkes von Karl Marx durch die deutsche Arbeiterbewegung, 1867 bis 1878. Berlin, 1977. pp. 328. *bibliog.*

— — **Brazil.**

LIMA (HEITOR FERREIRA) Historia do pensamento econômico no Brasil. São Paulo, 1976. pp. 198.

— — **Germany.**

MEISSNER (HERBERT) ed. Bürgerliche Ökonomie ohne Perspektive. Berlin, 1976. pp. 716.

KRAWEHL (OTTO ERNST) Die "Jahrbücher für Nationalökonomie und Statistik" unter den Herausgebern Bruno Hildebrand und Johannes Conrad, 1863 bis 1915. München, 1977. pp. 127. *bibliog.*

— — **Poland.**

LIPIŃSKI (EDWARD) Historia polskiej myśli społeczno-ekonomicznej do końca XVIII wieku. Wrocław, 1975. pp. 464. *With English and Russian afterwords.*

— — **Russia.**

BAKANOV (MIKHAIL IVANOVICH) and others. Ekonomicheskii analiz: teoriia, istoriia, sovremennoe sostoianie, perspektivy. Moskva, 1976. pp. 363. *bibliog.*

STANOVLENIE i razvitie ekonomicheskoi nauki v SSSR: sbornik, posviashchennyi pamiati akademika K.V. Ostrovitianova. Moskva, 1976. pp. 168.

— — — **Latvia.**

KIRTOVSKII (IMANT KHRISTIANOVICH) Ocherki istorii latyshskoi ekonomicheskoi mysli, 1890-1920 gg. Riga, 1976. pp. 184. *bibliog.*

— — **United Kingdom.**

GORDON (BARRY J.) Political economy in Parliament, 1819-1823. London, 1976. pp. 246.

— — **United States.**

LINDBÄCK (ASSAR) The political economy of the new left: an outsider's view. 2nd ed. New York, [1977]. pp. 239.

— — **Yugoslavia — Serbia.**

BLAGOJEVIĆ (OBREN) Ekonomska misao Svetozara Markovića: primljeno na VII skupu Odeljenja društvenih nauka, 28.V 1974; urednik... Dušan Nedeljković; Pensée économique de Svetozar Marković, etc. Beograd, 1975. pp. 306. *bibliog. (Srpska Akademija Nauka i Umetnosti. Posebna Izdanja. knj.479. [being also] Odeljenje Društvenih Nauka. no.76) With French summary. In Cyrillic.*

— **Information services.**

INTERNATIONAL ECONOMIC ASSOCIATION. Conference, 1975, Kiel. The organization and retrieval of economic knowledge: proceedings. ...; edited by Mark Perlman. London, 1977. pp. 520.

— — **Czechoslovakia.**

DESET let Výzkumného ústavu sociálně ekonomických informací: sborník. Praha, 1975. pp. 151.

— **Methodology.**

MINI (PIERO V.) Philosophy and economics: the origins and development of economic theory. Gainesville, Fla., 1974. pp. 305. *bibliog.*

BACHARACH (MICHAEL) Economics and the theory of games. London, 1976. pp. 163. *bibliog.*

MONTIAS (JOHN MICHAEL) The structure of economic systems. New Haven, 1976. pp. 323.

NAFPLION COLLOQUIUM ON RESEARCH PROGRAMMES IN PHYSICS AND ECONOMICS, NAFPLION, 1974. Method and appraisal in economics: [essays from the Economics Sessions of the Colloquium]; edited by Spiro J. Latsis. Cambridge, 1976. pp. 230. *bibliogs.*

HARRIS (RALPH) and SELDON (ARTHUR) Not from benevolence...: 20 years of economic dissent. London, 1977. pp. 159. *(Institute of Economic Affairs. Hobart Paperbacks. 10)*

TESCHNER (MANFRED) Konflikt- contra Gleichgewichtstheorie: zum Einfluss unterschiedlicher Denkansätze auf Wirtschaftstheorie und-politik. Berlin, [1977]. pp. 57.

— **Periodicals.**

LIST ECON: Förteckning över periodica inom ekonomi, handel, ekonomisk geografi och internationell statistik i nordiska bibliotek: List of periodicals in the fields of economics, trade, economic geography and international statistics in Nordic libraries; [pd. by] Biblioteket, Handelshögskolan, Stockholm. irreg., 1976- Stockholm.

— **Philosophy.**

ROSENBERG (ALEXANDER) Microeconomic laws: a philosophical analysis. Pittsburgh, [1976]. pp. 236. *bibliog.*

— **Psychological aspects.**

LESOURNE (JACQUES F.) A theory of the individual for economic analysis. Amsterdam, 1977. pp. 408. *bibliogs.*

— **Societies — Bibliography.**

DEMERSON (PAULA DE) and others, compilers. Las sociedades economicas de amigos del pais en el siglo XVIII: guia del investigador. San Sebastian, 1974. pp. 410.

— **Study and teaching.**

DAVISSON (WILLIAM I.) and BONELLO (FRANK J.) Computer-assisted instruction in economic education: a case study. Notre Dame, Ia., [1976]. pp. 269.

— — **United Kingdom.**

EXTENDING economics within the curriculum; edited by Keith Robinson and Robert Wilson on behalf of the Economics Association. London, 1977. pp. 201. *bibliogs. Papers of the second curriculum development seminar sponsored by the Economics Association, Worcester, 1975.*

— **1776-1876.**

SMITH (THOMAS SHARPE) On the economy of nations. London, Carpenter, 1842. pp. 130.

MARX (KARL) Selected writings; edited by David McLellan. Oxford, 1977. pp. 625. *bibliogs.*

— **1876-1976.**

SAUTAREL (JACQUES) Quand égorgerons-nous enfin?: lueurs économiques. [Montdidier, imprint, 189-?]. pp. 70.

HAHN (LUCIEN ALBERT) Wirtschaftswissenschaft des gesunden Menschenverstandes. 2nd ed. Frankfurt am Main, [1955]. pp. 295.

KRAUS (OTTO JOSEPH) Produktion und Verbrauch: eine Einführung. Berlin, 1957. pp. 186.

AL'TER (LEV BENITSIANOVICH) Izbrannye proizvedeniia. Moskva, 1971-72. 2 vols.

ENSAIOS econômicos: ([in honour of] Octavio Gouvêa de Bulhões); [edited by Mircea Buescu]. Rio de Janeiro, [1972 repr.] 1974. pp. 549.

POSNER (RICHARD A.) Economic analysis of law. Boston, [Mass.], 1973. pp. 415.

GOSSLING (WILLIAM FRANK) Some productive consequences of Engels' law. [London], 1974. pp. 20. *bibliog. (Input-Output Research Association. Occasional Papers. No. 2)*

POLITICHESKAIA ekonomiia sovremennogo monopolisticheskogo kapitalizma. 2nd ed. Moskva, 1975. 2 vols.

SAWYER (JOHN A.) Macroeconomics: theory and policy in the Canadian economy. Toronto, [1975]. pp. 406. *bibliogs.*

BAUMOL (WILLIAM JACK) Selected economic writings...; edited by Elizabeth E. Bailey. New York, 1976. pp. 655. *bibliog.*

EVOLUTION, welfare, and time in economics: essays in honor of Nicholas Georgescu-Roegen. Lexington, Mass., [1976]. pp. 183. *bibliogs.*

FELLNER (WILLIAM JOHN) Towards a reconstruction of macroeconomics: problems of theory and policy. Washington, D.C., [1976]. pp. 150. *bibliog.*

FRANK (ANDRE GUNDER) Economic genocide in Chile: monetarist theory versus humanity; two open letters to Arnold Harberger and Milton Friedman. Nottingham, 1976. pp. 87.

HEILBRONER (ROBERT LOUIS) and FORD (ARTHUR M.) eds. Economic relevance: a second look. 2nd ed. Pacific Palisades, Calif., [1976]. pp. 320.

LEKACHMAN (ROBERT) Economists at bay: why the experts will never solve your problems. New York, [1976]. pp. 311.

MACHLUP (FRITZ) Selected economic writings...; edited by George Bitros. New York, 1976. pp. 603. *bibliog.*

MORGENSTERN (OSKAR) Selected economic writings...; edited by Andrew Schotter. New York, 1976. pp. 539. *bibliogs.*

MORISHIMA (MICHIO) The economic theory of modern society; translated by D.W. Anthony. Cambridge, 1976. pp. 347.

RELEVANCE and precision: from quantitative analysis to economic policy; essays in honour of Pieter de Wolff; editors J.S. Cramer [and others]. Alphen aan den Rijn, 1976. pp. 318. *bibliogs.*

REYNOLDS (LLOYD GEORGE) Macroeconomics: analysis and policy. rev. ed. Homewood, Ill., 1976. pp. 415.

SAMUELS (WARREN J.) ed. The Chicago school of political economy. [East Lansing], 1976. pp. 525. *bibliog. (Michigan State University. MSU Business Studies) Comprising mainly articles and reviews from the December 1975 and March 1976 issues of Journal of Economic Issues.*

SURREY (M.J.C.) ed. Macroeconomic themes: edited readings in macroeconomics with commentaries. Oxford, 1976. pp. 524.

HICKS (Sir JOHN RICHARD) Economic perspectives: further essays on money and growth. Oxford, 1977. pp. 199.

INTERNATIONAL ECONOMIC ASSOCIATION. Conference, [1975], S'Agaro, Spain. The microeconomic foundations of macroeconomics: proceedings...; edited by G.C. Harcourt. London, 1977. pp. 401.

KURZ (HEINZ DIETER) Zur neoricardianischen Theorie des Allgemeinen Gleichgewichts der Produktion und Zirkulation: Wert und Verteilung in Piero Sraffas "Production of commodities by means of commodities". Berlin, [1977]. pp. 276. *bibliog.*

— **1976- .**

BECKER (GARY STANLEY) The economic approach to human behavior. Chicago, 1976. pp. 314. *bibliog.*

CULTURE ET LIBERTE. Les travailleurs face au capitalisme: initiation à l'économie. [Paris, 1976]. pp. 256. *bibliog.*

EICHNER (ALFRED S.) The megacorp and oligopoly: micro foundations of macro dynamics. Cambridge, 1976. pp. 365. *bibliog.*

ECONOMICS.(Cont.)

GEORGESCU-ROEGEN (NICHOLAS) Energy and economic myths: institutional and analytical economic essays. New York, [1976]. pp. 380. *bibliogs.*

MUSSA (MICHAEL) A study in macroeconomics. Amsterdam, 1976. pp. 316. *bibliog.*

RESOURCE allocation and economic policy; edited by Michael Allingham and M.L. Burstein. London, 1976. pp. 251. *bibliogs. Proceedings of a conference sponsored by the University College at Buckingham and the Institute of Economic Affairs, held in London in June 1975.*

SOLMON (LEWIS C.) Macroeconomics. Reading, Mass., 1976 repr. 1977. pp. 537. *bibliog.*

SOLMON (LEWIS C.) Microeconomics. Reading, Mass., 1976 repr. 1977. pp. 497. *bibliog.*

ALCHIAN (ARMEN ALBERT) Economic forces at work. Indianapolis, [1977]. pp. 523. *bibliogs.*

ARMEY (RICHARD K.) Price theory: a policy-welfare approach. Englewood Cliffs, [1977]. pp. 367. *bibliogs.*

ASSOCIATION OF UNIVERSITY TEACHERS OF ECONOMICS. Annual Conference, 1976. Studies in modern economic analysis...; edited by M.J. Artis [and] A.R. Nobay. Oxford, [1977]. pp. 350. *bibliogs.*

BACH (GEORGE LELAND) Microeconomics: analysis and applications. Englewood Cliffs, [1977]. pp. 439. *Originally published in his "Economics", 9th ed., 1977.*

BARKLEY (PAUL W.) Economics: the way we choose. New York, [1977]. pp. 652.

BRITISH ASSOCIATION FOR THE ADVANCEMENT OF SCIENCE. Section F. Meeting, 1976. Structure, system and economic policy; proceedings...held at the University of Lancaster 1-8 September 1976; edited by Wassily Leontief. Cambridge, 1977. pp. 223. *bibliogs.*

BROOMAN (FREDERICK SPENCER) Macroeconomics. 6th ed. London, 1977. pp. 384.

DINKEL (REINER) Der Zusammenhang zwischen der ökonomischen und politischen Entwicklung in einer Demokratie: eine Untersuchung mit Hilfe der ökonomischen Theorie der Politik. Berlin, [1977]. pp. 259. *bibliog.*

ECONOMIC progress, private values and public policy: essays in honor of William Fellner; edited by Bela Balassa and Richard Nelson. Amsterdam, 1977. pp. 339. *bibliogs.*

GALBRAITH (JOHN KENNETH) The affluent society. 3rd ed. London, 1977. pp. 287.

GLAHE (FRED R.) Macroeconomics: theory and policy. 2nd ed. New York, [1977]. pp. 404.

HANSON (JOHN LLOYD) A textbook of economics. 7th ed. Plymouth, 1977. pp. 604. *bibliogs.*

HUTCHISON (TERENCE WILMOT) Knowledge and ignorance in economics. Oxford, [1977]. pp. 186.

INTRODUCING economics; [by] B.J. McCormick [and others]. 2nd ed. Harmondsworth, 1977. pp. 826. *bibliog.*

KOHLER (HEINZ) Scarcity and freedom: an introduction to economics. Lexington, Mass., [1977]. pp. 549. *bibliogs.*

LESOURNE (JACQUES F.) A theory of the individual for economic analysis. Amsterdam, 1977. pp. 408. *bibliogs.*

LEVINE (DAVID P.) Economic studies: contributions to the critique of economic theory. London, 1977. pp. 318.

LINDBÄCK (ASSAR) The political economy of the new left: an outsider's view. 2nd ed. New York, [1977]. pp. 239.

LIVESEY (FRANK) A modern approach to economics. London, 1977. pp. 271. *bibliogs. Published on behalf of the Institute of Marketing.*

NORRIS (KEITH) and VAIZEY (JOHN ERNEST) Baron Vaizey. Economics for everyone. London, 1977. pp. 202. *bibliogs.*

SANDFORD (CEDRIC T.) Social economics. London, 1977. pp. 286. *bibliog.*

VENIERIS (YIANNIS P.) and SEBOLD (FREDERICK D.) Macroeconomics: models and policy. Santa Barbara, [1977]. pp. 655. *bibliogs. Half title and cover title read: Macroeconomic models and policy.*

WESTAWAY (ANTHONY JOHN) and WEYMAN-JONES (T.G.) Macroeconomics: theory, evidence and policy. London, 1977. pp. 333. *bibliog.*

ECONOMICS, COMPARATIVE.

DEUTSCHES INSTITUT FÜR WIRTSCHAFTSFORSCHUNG. Sonderhefte. [Neue Folge]. 115. Das Sozialprodukt der Deutschen Demokratischen Republik im Vergleich mit dem der Bundesrepublik Deutschland; ([by] Herbert Wilkens). Berlin, 1976. pp. 188. *bibliog. With English summary.*

DROLLAS (LEONIDAS) The foreign trade sector in disequilibrium: a comparative study of sixteen developed countries. 1976. fo.330. *Typescript. Ph.D. (London) thesis: unpublished. This thesis is the property of London University and may not be removed from the Library.*

TSAGA (VIKTORIIA FRANTSEVNA) Antikommunismus heute: zu bürgerlichen ökonomischen Theorien; (ins Deutsche übertragen von Leon Nebenzahl). Berlin, [1976]. pp. 159.

HOLESOVSKY (VACLAV) Economic systems: analysis and comparison. New York, [1977]. pp. 495. *bibliogs.*

NÊME (JACQUES) and NÊME (COLETTE) Politiques économiques comparées. Paris, [1977]. pp. 428. *bibliogs.*

WILES (PETER JOHN DE LA FOSSE) Economic institutions compared. Oxford, [1977]. pp. 608.

ECONOMICS, MATHEMATICAL.

MUELLER (MAX GERHARD) ed. Readings in macroeconomics. 2nd ed. Hinsdale, Ill., [1971]. pp. 475. *bibliogs.*

FLECK (FLORIAN H.) Die ökonomische Theorie des technischen Fortschritts und seine Identifikation. Meisenheim am Glan, 1973. pp. 255. *bibliog.*

LESOURNE (JACQUES F.) Cost-benefit analysis and economic theory; translation by Mrs. A. Silvey. Amsterdam, 1975. pp. 521. *bibliog.*

SAWYER (JOHN A.) Macroeconomics: theory and policy in the Canadian economy. Toronto, [1975]. pp. 406. *bibliogs.*

BAKANOV (MIKHAIL IVANOVICH) and others. Ekonomicheskii analiz: teoriia, istoriia, sovremennoe sostoianie, perspektivy. Moskva, 1976. pp. 363. *bibliog.*

COMMON (MICHAEL S.) Basic econometrics. London, 1976. pp. 517.

FRADIN (JACQUES) Les fondements logiques de la théorie néoclassique de l'échange: le postulat du numéraire; introduction à la critique de l'économie politique contemporaine. Grenoble, 1976. pp. 243. *bibliog.*

KYLE (JOHN F.) The balance of payments in a monetary economy. Princeton, N.J., [1976]. pp. 192. *bibliog. (Omicron Delta Epsilon. Irving Fisher Award Series)*

MORGENSTERN (OSKAR) Selected economic writings...; edited by Andrew Schotter. New York, 1976. pp. 539. *bibliogs.*

TSORIS (NICHOLAS D.) Econometric studies of Greece. Athens, 1976. pp. 399. *bibliog.*

ZAUBERMAN (ALFRED) Note on assimilation of optimal control theory and ramifications in economic planning theory. Bielefeld, 1976. fo. 53. *(Universität Bielefeld. Institut für Mathematische Wirtschaftsforschung. Arbeiten. Nr. 50)*

ARCHIBALD (GEORGE CHRISTOPHER) and LIPSEY (RICHARD GEORGE) An introduction to a mathematical treatment of economics. 3rd ed. London, 1977. pp. 523.

ASSOCIATION OF UNIVERSITY TEACHERS OF ECONOMICS. Annual Conference, 1976. Studies in modern economic analysis...; edited by M.J. Artis [and] A.R. Nobay. Oxford, [1977]. pp. 350. *bibliogs.*

PESARAN (BAHRAM) Estimation of dynamic economic models when variables are subject to measurement errors. 1977. fo. 143. *bibliog. Typescript. Ph.D. (London) thesis: unpublished. This thesis is the property of London University and may not be removed from the Library.*

TURNOVSKY (STEPHEN J.) Macroeconomic analysis and stabilization policies. Cambridge, 1977. pp. 271. *bibliog.*

VENIERIS (YIANNIS P.) and SEBOLD (FREDERICK D.) Macroeconomics: models and policy. Santa Barbara, [1977]. pp. 655. *bibliogs. Half title and cover title read: Macroeconomic models and policy.*

ECONOMICS, PRIMITIVE.

CUISENIER (JEAN) Economie et parenté: leurs affinités de structure dans le domaine turc et dans le domaine arabe. Paris, [1975]. pp. 569. *bibliog. (Paris. Ecole Pratique des Hautes Etudes. Section des Sciences Economiques et Sociales. Le Monde d'Outre-Mer Passé et Présent. 1e Série. Etudes. 60)*

L'ANTHROPOLOGIE économique: courants et problèmes; par Lucien Démonio [and others]; sous la direction de François Pouillon. Paris, 1976. pp. 159. *bibliog. (Paris. Ecole des Hautes Etudes en Sciences Sociales. Centre d'Etudes Africaines. Dossiers Africains)*

FOX (JAMES J.) Harvest of the palm: ecological change in eastern Indonesia. Cambridge, Mass., 1977. pp. 290. *bibliog.*

GODELIER (MAURICE) Perspectives in marxist anthropology; translated by Robert Brain. Cambridge, 1977. pp. 243.

ECONOMISTS.

LEKACHMAN (ROBERT) Economists at bay: why the experts will never solve your problems. New York, [1976]. pp. 311.

MACHLUP (FRITZ) A history of thought on economic integration. London, 1977. pp. 323. *bibliog.*

PUTTASWAMAIAH (K.) Nobel economists. Bangalore, 1977. pp. 182. *bibliogs.*

— Russia.

AKTUAL'NYE problemy ekonomicheskoi nauki v trudakh S.G. Strumilina: k 100-letiiu so dnia rozhdeniia. Moskva, 1977. pp. 439.

— United States.

SILK (LEONARD SOLOMON) The economists. New York, [1976]. pp. 294.

ECUADOR

— Appropriations and expenditures.

ECUADOR. Oficina Nacional de Presupuesto. Fondo nacional de participaciones: anexo justificativo de ingresos. a., 1976- [Quito].

ECUADOR. Oficina Nacional de Presupuesto. Presupuesto general del estado: anexo justificativo de ingresos corrientes y transferencias. a., 1976- [Quito].

— Bibliography.

ECUADOR. Junta Nacional de Planificacion y Coordinacion Economica. 1973. Bibliografia social, economica y politica del Ecuador. Quito, [1973?]. 2 vols.

— Census.

ECUADOR. Oficina de los Censos Nacionales. 1975. Compendio de informacion socio-economica de las provincias del Ecuador: Pichincha. Quito, 1975. 2 vols. (in 1). *(Provincias del Ecuador. 3)*

ECUADOR. Census, 1974. III censo de poblacion 1974: resultados definitivos. Quito, 1976 in progress.

— **Economic conditions.**

ECHEVERRIA (ROBERTO) and others. Current economic position and prospects of Ecuador: this report is based on the findings of an economic mission which visited Ecuador during...1972, etc. Washington, International Bank for Reconstruction and Development, 1973. 1 vol.(various pagings). *(Country Economic Reports)*

ECUADOR. President, 1972- (Rodriguez Lara). 1975. Informe a la nacion. [Quito, 1975]. pp. 221.

— — **Bibliography.**

U.K. Department of Industry. Statistics and Market Intelligence Library. 1976. Ecuador. London, 1976. pp. 13. *(Sources of Statistics and Market Information. 5)*

— **Economic policy.**

ECHEVERRIA (ROBERTO) and others. Current economic position and prospects of Ecuador: this report is based on the findings of an economic mission which visited Ecuador during...1972, etc. Washington, International Bank for Reconstruction and Development, 1973. 1 vol.(various pagings). *(Country Economic Reports)*

BROMLEY (R.J.) Development and planning in Ecuador. London, 1977. pp. 116. *bibliog.*

— **Executive departments.**

ECUADOR. Junta Nacional de Planificacion y Coordinacion Economica. 1973. Guia institucional del sector publico ecuatoriano; (version preliminar). [Quito], 1973. pp. 410.

— **Politics and government.**

ECUADOR. President, 1972- (Rodriguez Lara). 1975. Informe a la nacion. [Quito, 1975]. pp. 221.

— **Social conditions.**

ECUADOR. President, 1972- (Rodriguez Lara). 1975. Informe a la nacion. [Quito, 1975]. pp. 221.

— **Social policy.**

BROMLEY (R.J.) Development and planning in Ecuador. London, 1977. pp. 116. *bibliog.*

— **Statistics.**

ECHEVERRIA (ROBERTO) and others. Current economic position and prospects of Ecuador: this report is based on the findings of an economic mission which visited Ecuador during...1972, etc. Washington, International Bank for Reconstruction and Development, 1973. 1 vol.(various pagings). *(Country Economic Reports)*

U.K. Department of Industry. Statistics and Market Intelligence Library. 1976. Ecuador. London, 1976. pp. 13. *(Sources of Statistics and Market Information. 5)*

EDINBURGH

— **City planning.**

The UNMAKING of Edinburgh: the decay, depopulation and destruction of central Edinburgh: an argument for city centre living and a call for action; edited by Helen Peacock. Edinburgh, [1976]. pp. 77.

EDMONTON GIRLS CHARITY SCHOOL.

HOARE (EDDIE) Edmonton Girls Charity School, 1778-1904. Edmonton, [1968?]. pp. 11. *(Edmonton. Edmonton Hundred Historical Society. Occasional Papers. New Series. No. 19)*

EDUCATION.

VAIZEY (JOHN ERNEST) Baron Vaizey, and CLARKE (CHARLES FREDERICK ORME) Education: the state of the debate in America, Britain and Canada. London, 1976. pp. 184. *This book arose from a series of six conferences at Ditchley Park and includes conference papers by various hands.*

— **Aims and objectives.**

ILLICH (IVAN D.) and VERNE (ETIENNE) Imprisoned in the global classroom; [also including Political inversion by Ivan Illich]. London, 1976. pp. 63.

— **Curricula.**

ELVIN (HERBERT LIONEL) The place of commonsense in educational thought. London, 1977. pp. 165.

— **Decision making.**

JENNINGS (ROBERT E.) Education and politics: policy-making in local education authorities. London, 1977. pp. 214. *bibliog.*

— **Economic aspects.**

AHMED (MANZOOR) The economics of nonformal education: resources, costs and benefits. New York, 1975. pp. 122. *bibliog.*

RITZEN (JOZEF MARIA MATHIAS) Education, economic growth and income distribution. Amsterdam, 1977. pp. 271. *bibliog. Proefschrift (doctor in de economische wetenschappen)- Erasmus Universiteit Rotterdam.*

— — **Germany.**

WEISSHUHN (GERNOT) Sozioökonomische Analyse von Bildungs- und Ausbildungsaktivitäten. Berlin, [1977]. pp. 291. *bibliog.*

— — **Russia.**

TURCHENKO (VLADIMIR NIKOLAEVICH) and others, eds. Sotsiologicheskie i ekonomicheskie problemy obrazovaniia. Novosibirsk, 1969. pp. 436.

— **Philosophy.**

ELVIN (HERBERT LIONEL) The place of commonsense in educational thought. London, 1977. pp. 165.

— **America, Latin — Social aspects.**

LA BELLE (THOMAS J.) Nonformal education and social change in Latin America. Los Angeles, 1976. pp. 219. *bibliogs. (California University. Latin American Center. Latin American Studies. vol. 35)*

— **Australia — Queensland.**

HOLTHOUSE (HECTOR) Looking back: the first 150 years of Queensland schools. [Brisbane], Department of Education, 1975. pp. 211.

— **Bangladesh.**

NURUZZAMAN (MOHAMED) Education and educated manpower in Bangladesh: a study of development after the 1947 partition. 1976. fo. 335. *bibliog. Typescript. Ph.D. (London) thesis: unpublished. This thesis is the property of London University and may not be removed from the Library.*

— **Canada — Nova Scotia.**

NOVA SCOTIA. Royal Commission on Education, Public Services and Provincial-Municipal Relations. 1974. Report. vol.1. Summary and recommendations; [John F. Graham, chairman]. Halifax, 1974. pp. 301. *Map in end pocket.*

— **Cyprus.**

CYPRUS TODAY. Vol. 8. No. 3-4. [Special issue on education in Cyprus]. Nicosia, 1970. pp. 88.

— **Czechoslovakia.**

COMITE CENTRAL DE LA JEUNESSE SLOVAQUE A L'ETRANGER. Demande du Comité...concernant les actes de violence dans l'éducation de la jeunesse slovaque en Tchéco-Slovaquie adressée à l'Organisation Educative, Scientifique et Culturelle des Nations-Unies. Buenos Aires, 1951. pp. (4).

— **Denmark.**

NØRREGAARD (CARL) and HANSEN (ERIK JØRGEN) Nogle beregninger over befolkningens skoleuddannelse omkring 1990. København, 1973. fo.36. *bibliog. (Socialforskningsinstituttet. Meddelelser.4)*

— **European Economic Community countries.**

EUROPEAN COMMUNITIES. Economic and Social Committee. 1976. Systems of education and vocational training in the member countries of the European Community. Brussels, 1976. pp. 114. *(Studies)*

— **Finland — History.**

FAL'BORK (GENRIKH ADOL'FOVICH) and CHARNOLUSKII (VLADIMIR IVANOVICH) Narodnoe obrazovanie v Rossii; s prilozheniem stat'i: narodnoe obrazovanie v Finliandii V. Skalona. S.-Peterburg, [1899?]. pp. 264. *bibliog.*

— **Germany.**

Die BILDUNGSREFORM: eine Bilanz; ([by] Hellmut Becker [and others]). Stuttgart, 1976. pp. 78. *(Articles reprinted from Zeit, January and February 1976)*

— — **Finance.**

GRUENDGER (FRITZ) Zum Problem der Bedarfsermittlung bei Investitionen im Bildungs- und Gesundheitswesen: eine vergleichende Untersuchung unter besonderer Berücksichtigung des Schul- und Krankenhaussektors. Berlin, [1977]. pp. 291. *bibliog.*

— **Israel.**

ISRAEL INFORMATION CENTRE. Information Briefings. 4. Education. Jerusalem, [1973]. pp. 8.

— **Ivory Coast.**

MONSON (TERRY D.) A note on measuring educational returns in LDCs. Ann Arbor, 1977. pp. 13. *bibliog. (Michigan University. Center for Research on Economic Development. Discussion Papers. No. 63)*

— **Japan.**

JAPAN. Ministry of Education. Research Bureau. Research Section. 1967. Education in Japan: a graphic presentation. rev. ed. [Tokyo], 1967. pp. 130. *bibliog.*

— **Malaya — History.**

STEVENSON (REX) Cultivators and administrators: British educational policy towards the Malays, 1875-1906. Kuala Lumpur, 1975. pp. 240. *bibliog.*

— **New Spain (Viceroyalty).**

KOBAYASHI (JOSE MARIA) La educacion como conquista: empresa franciscana en Mexico. Mexico, 1974. pp. 423. *bibliog. (Mexico City. Colegio de Mexico. Centro de Estudios Historicos. Nueva Serie. 19)*

— **Nigeria.**

OGUNSOLA (ALBERT F.) Legislation and education in Northern Nigeria. Ibadan, 1974. pp. 111. *bibliog.*

— **Norway — Statistics.**

NORWAY. Statistiske Centralbyrå. Utdanningsstatistikk: oversikt: Educational statistics survey. a., 1974- (1st)- Oslo.

— **Poland — Lódz (Province).**

NOWAKOWSKA (BARBARA) WÝKSZTAŁcenie mieszkańców Łodzi. Warszawa, 1974. pp. 183. *bibliog. (Instytut Polityki Naukowej i Szkolnictwa Wyższego. Monografie i Studia) With Russian and English summaries.*

— **Rhodesia.**

O'CALLAGHAN (MARION) Southern Rhodesia: the effects of a conquest society on education, culture and information;...with a contribution by Reginald Austin. Paris, Unesco, 1977. pp. 293.

EDUCATION.(Cont.)

— Russia — History.

FAL'BORK (GENRIKH ADOL'FOVICH) and CHARNOLUSKII (VLADIMIR IVANOVICH) Narodnoe obrazovanie v Rossii; s prilozheniem stat'i: narodnoe obrazovanie v Finliandii V. Skalona. S.-Peterburg, [1899?]. pp. 264. *bibliog.*

— — Social aspects.

VASIL'EVA (EVELINA KARLOVNA) The young people of Leningrad: school and work options and attitudes. White Plains, N.Y., [1976]. pp. 177.

— South Africa.

STIMIE (CHRISTIAAN MATTHYS) The education of whites in the Republic of South Africa. Pretoria, 1975. pp. 77. *bibliog. (Human Sciences Research Council [South Africa] . Institute for Information and Special Services. Reports. No. IN-24)*

BOZZOLI (G.R.) Education is the key to change in South Africa. [Johannesburg], 1977. pp. 14. *(South African Institute of Race Relations. Hoernlé Memorial Lectures. 1977)*

— Spain.

GINER DE LOS RIOS (FRANCISCO) Ensayos y cartas: edicion de homenaje en el cincuentenario de su muerte. Mexico, [1965]. pp. 188.

— Taiwan — History.

TSURUMI (E. PATRICIA) Japanese colonial education in Taiwan, 1895-1945. Cambridge, Mass., 1977. pp. 334. *bibliog. (Harvard University. East Asian Research Centre. Harvard East Asian Series. 88)*

— Underdeveloped areas.

See UNDERDEVELOPED AREAS — Education.

— United Kingdom.

HINTS to philanthropists; or, A collective view of practical means of improving the condition of the poor, and labouring classes of society. Dublin, Graisberry, 1825. pp. 22. *(Extracted from the Edinburgh Review)*

[ELLIS (WILLIAM) Author of "Outlines of Social Economy"] A few questions on secular education, what it is, and what it ought to be; with an attempt to answer them; preceded by an appeal to Richard Cobden...and the members of the late Anti-Corn-Law League. London, 1848. pp. 23.

EDUCATION AND COMMUNITY RELATIONS; ([pd. by] Community Relations Commission). irreg., M 1971- , with gaps. London.

NATIONAL FRONT. Education for national survival. Teddington, [1976]. pp. 13. *bibliog.*

BELL (ROBERT E.) and GRANT (NIGEL) Patterns of education in the British Isles. London, 1977. pp. 223. *bibliog.*

COX (CHARLES BRIAN) and BOYSON (RHODES) eds. Black paper 1977. London, 1977. pp. 128. *bibliog.*

JENNINGS (ROBERT E.) Education and politics: policy-making in local education authorities. London, 1977. pp. 214. *bibliog.*

U.K. Central Office of Information. Reference Division. Reference Pamphlets. 7. Education in Britain. 7th ed. London, 1977. pp. 30. *bibliog.*

U.K. Department of Education and Science. 1977. Educating our children: four subjects for debate: a background paper for the regional conferences February and March, 1977, etc. London, [1977]. pp. 14.

— — History.

GOSDEN (PETER HENRY JOHN HEATHER) Education in the Second World War: a study in policy and administration. London, 1976. pp. 527. *bibliog.*

POPULAR education and socialization in the nineteenth century; edited by Phillip McCann. London, 1977. pp. 276.

— — Ireland, Northern — Finance.

IRELAND, NORTHERN. Department of Education. Summary of Education and Library Boards' accounts...together with the report of the Comptroller and Auditor General. a., 1973/74 [1st]- Belfast.

— — London.

ILEA CONTACT; [pd. by] Inner London Education Authority. w. London. *Current issues only kept.*

— — Scotland.

BELL (ROBERT E.) and GRANT (NIGEL) Patterns of education in the British Isles. London, 1977. pp. 223. *bibliog.*

— — Wales — Statistics.

STATISTICS OF EDUCATION IN WALES; [pd. by] Welsh Office. a., 1976 (no.1)- Cardiff. *[in English and Welsh].*

EDUCATION, COMPARATIVE.

BELL (ROBERT E.) and GRANT (NIGEL) Patterns of education in the British Isles. London, 1977. pp. 223. *bibliog.*

EDUCATION, ELEMENTARY

— Netherlands.

MEIJSEN (J.H.) compiler. Lager onderwijs in de spiegel der geschiedenis: 175 jaar nationale wetgeving op het lager onderwijs in Nederland, 1801-1976. 's-Gravenhage, Staatsuitgeverij, 1976. pp. 303. *bibliog.*

— United Kingdom.

SHARP (RACHEL) and others. Education and social control: a study in progressive primary education. London, 1975. pp. 256. *bibliog.*

— — History.

ROPER (HENRY) Administering the Elementary Education Acts 1870-1885. Leeds, 1976. pp. 50. *(Leeds. University. Museum of the History of Education. Educational Administration and History: Monographs. No. 5)*

POPULAR education and socialization in the nineteenth century; edited by Phillip McCann. London, 1977. pp. 276.

EDUCATION, HIGHER.

DONGERKERY (SUDIDERRAO RAMRAO) Universities and national life. Bombay, 1950. pp. 115.

— Australia.

AUSTRALIA. Commonwealth Bureau of Census and Statistics. 1976. School leavers, 1970 to 1974: their employment status and education experience in May 1975. Canberra, 1976. pp. 12.

— Canada.

HARRIS (ROBIN S.) A history of higher education in Canada, 1663-1960. Toronto, [1976]. pp. 715. *bibliog.*

— — New Brunswick.

NEW BRUNSWICK. Committee on Higher Education in the French Sector of New Brunswick. 1975. Report; [Louis LeBel, chairman]. [Fredericton], 1975. fo. 84.

— — Nova Scotia.

NOVA SCOTIA. Department of Development. Economics and Statistics Division. 1974. Labour resources in Nova Scotia. [Halifax], 1974. fo. 8.

— Europe.

NEAVE (GUY R.) Patterns of equality: the influence of new structures in European higher education upon the equality of educational opportunity. Windsor, Berks, 1976. pp. 150.

— India.

JOURNAL OF HIGHER EDUCATION; (pd.by) University Grants Commission, India. 3 a yr., autumn 1975 (v.1, no.2)- New Delhi.

— Poland.

GORYŃSKI (JULIUSZ) Problemy infrastruktury szkolnictwa wy'zszego w Polsce. Warszawa, 1977. pp. 95. *(Polska Akademia Nauk. Komitet Przestrzennego Zagospodarowania Kraju. Studia. t.57) With Russian and English summaries.*

— United Kingdom.

McCREATH (M.D.) Report on the surveys of full-time A level students (home) in colleges of further education. [Colchester], 1970. pp. 114. *Part of the Project on Factors Influencing Choice of Higher Education carried out by the University of Essex with the Royal Statistical Society*

ELLWOOD (CAROLINE) Adult learning today: a new role for the universities? London, [1976]. pp. 265. *bibliog.*

BURGESS (TYRRELL) Education after school. Harmondsworth, 1977. pp. 256. *bibliog.*

— — Research.

BEARD (RUTH M.) On the growth of research into higher education. [Bradford, 1976?]. pp. 26. *bibliog.*

— — Ireland, Northern — Finance.

ULSTER COLLEGE. Board of Governors. Accounts...together with the report of the Comptroller and Auditor-General thereon. a., 1973/74 [4th]- Belfast. *1970/71-1972/73 (1st-3rd) included in IRELAND, NORTHERN. Parliament. House of Commons. [Papers].*

— United States.

The MONDAY morning imagination: report from the Boyer Workshop on State University Systems: edited by Martin Kaplan. New York, 1977. pp. 158. *bibliogs. Sponsored by the Aspen Institute for Humanistic Studies.*

— — Ohio.

MILLETT (JOHN DAVID) Politics and higher education. University, Ala., [1974]. pp. 147. *(Southern Regional Training Program in Public Administration. Annual Lecture Series)*

— Zambia.

HIGHER education and the labour market in Zambia: expectations and performance; [by] Bikas C. Sanyal and others; (a research project...at the International Institute for Educational Planning). Paris, Unesco, 1976. pp. 373. *bibliog.*

EDUCATION, PRESCHOOL

— United Kingdom.

TIZARD (JACK) and others. All our children: pre-school services in a changing society. London, 1976. pp. 252. *bibliog.*

EDUCATION, RURAL

— Germany.

BOMMERT (WILFRIED) and BUETTNER (EVA) Bildungsverhalten der Landfrauen: Ergebnisse einer repräsentativen Befragung landwirtschaftlich tätiger Frauen in der Bundesrepublik Deutschland, 1976. Bonn, 1977. pp. 234. *bibliog. (Forschungsgesellschaft für Agrarpolitik und Agrarsoziologie. [Publications]. 244)*

EDUCATION, SECONDARY

— Economic aspects — United Kingdom.

CAMPAIGN FOR COMPREHENSIVE EDUCATION. The expenditure of public money on buying places in independent schools. [London], 1976. pp. 10.

— France — History.

DURKHEIM (EMILE) The evolution of educational thought: lectures on the formation and development of secondary education in France; translated by Peter Collins. London, 1977. pp. 354.

— United Kingdom.

BELLABY (PAUL) The sociology of comprehensive schooling. London, 1977. pp. 127. *bibliog.*

U.K. Department of Education and Science. HM Inspectorate of Schools (England). 1977. Ten good schools: a secondary school enquiry; a discussion paper by some members of HM Inspectorate of Schools. London, 1977. pp. 36. *(Matters for Discussion. 1)*

— — Ireland, Northern.

IRELAND, NORTHERN. Department of Education. 1976. Reorganisation of secondary education in Northern Ireland: a consultative document. Belfast, 1976. pp. 95.

— — Scotland.

MACKENZIE (R.F.) The unbowed head: events at Summerhill Academy 1968-74. Edinburgh, [1977]. pp. 115.

EDUCATION, URBAN

— United Kingdom.

EDUCATION and the urban crisis; edited by Frank Field. London, 1977. pp. 149. *Based on two Gulbenkian conferences on education and the urban crisis.*

EDUCATION AND STATE

— Australia.

AUSTRALIA. Australian Advisory Committee on Research and Development in Education. Annual report. a., 1970/71 (1st)- Canberra. *Included in AUSTRALIA. Parliament. [Parliamentary papers].*

AUSTRALIA. Department of Education. Migrant education programme. Report. a., 1970/71 [1st]- Canberra. *Included in AUSTRALIA. Parliament. [Parliamentary papers].*

— Brazil.

HAAR (JERRY) The politics of higher education in Brazil. New York, 1977. pp. 222. *bibliog.*

— Gambia.

JONES (S.H.M.) Education in the Gambia. Bathurst, Department of Education, 1970. pp. 28.

— India.

RAO (P.V.) and KOHLI (SHANTA) Educational and recreational activities of urban local bodies. New Delhi, [1970]. pp. 86. *bibliog. (Indian Institute of Public Administration. Centre for Training and Research in Municipal Administration. Our Towns. vol. 2)*

INDIA. Ministry of Education, Social Welfare and Culture. Annual report. a., 1973/74- New Delhi.

— Norway.

BALDERSHEIM (HAROLD) Patterns of central control over local service provision in Norway. 1977. fo. 367. *bibliog. Typescript. Ph.D. (London) thesis: unpublished. This thesis is the property of London University and may not be removed from the Library.*

— Russia.

BRUCE (JAMES B.) The politics of Soviet policy formation: Khrushchev's innovative policies in education and agriculture. Denver, Colo., [1976]. pp. 138. *(Denver. University. Social Science Foundation and Graduate School of International Studies. Monograph Series in World Affairs. vol. 13, no. 4)*

— United Kingdom.

CAMPAIGN FOR COMPREHENSIVE EDUCATION. The expenditure of public money on buying places in independent schools. [London], 1976. pp. 10.

REGAN (DAVID EDWARD) Local government and education. London, 1977. pp. 265. *bibliog.*

EDUCATION OF ADULTS.

LENGRAND (PAUL) An introduction to lifelong education. Paris, United Nations Educational, Scientific and Cultural Organization, 1975. pp. 156.

ADULT learning: psychological research and applications; edited by Michael J.A. Howe. London, [1977]. pp. 291. *bibliogs.*

— America, Latin.

LA BELLE (THOMAS J.) Nonformal education and social change in Latin America. Los Angeles, 1976. pp. 219. *bibliogs. (California University. Latin American Center. Latin American Studies. vol. 35)*

— Canada.

CANADA. Statistics Canada. Continuing education: community colleges. a., 1973/74 (1st)- Ottawa. *In English and French.*

CANADA. Statistics Canada. Continuing education: participation in programs of educational institutions. a., 1973/74 (1st)- Ottawa. *[in English and French].*

— India.

REGIONAL CONFERENCE ON CONTINUING EDUCATION, HYDERABAD, 1975. Report of the regional conference…held at Osmania University, Hyderabad, on October 16-19, 1975. New Delhi, University Grants Commission, 1976. pp. 76.

SEMINAR ON CONTINUING EDUCATION, POONA, 1976. Report of the seminar…, University of Poona, February 7, 8 and 9, 1976. New Delhi, University Grants Commission, 1976. pp. 47.

— Kenya.

KENYA. Board of Adult Education. 1972. Adult education in Kenya: a historical perspective: decadal report, 1960-1970. Nairobi, 1972. pp. 34. *bibliog.*

— Nigeria.

NIGERIAN NATIONAL COUNCIL FOR ADULT EDUCATION. Annual Conference, 1st, 1972. Adult education in Nigeria: the next ten years; report… edited by Lalage Bown. [Zaria, 1972]. pp. 182.

— United Kingdom.

NEWMAN (MICHAEL) Adult education and community action. London, [1973] repr. 1975. pp. 31.

RICHARDS (ELFYN JOHN) Adult education : a challenge to all. Cardiff, [1975]. pp. 18.

ELLWOOD (CAROLINE) Adult learning today: a new role for the universities? London, [1976]. pp. 265. *bibliog.*

JENNINGS (BERNARD) New lamps for old?: university adult education in retrospect and prospect. Hull, 1976. pp. 26. *An inaugural lecture delivered in the University of Hull on 4th November, 1975.*

ROGERS (JENNIFER) and GROOMBRIDGE (BRIAN) Right to learn: the case for adult equality. London, 1976. pp. 202.

WILSON (HUGH) AND WOMERSLEY (LEWIS) Firm. Inner area study: Liverpool: adult education. [London], Department of the Environment, [1977]. pp. 29.

EDUCATION OF WOMEN

— Economic aspects — United States.

FITZPATRICK (BLANCHE E.) Women's inferior education: an economic analysis. New York, 1976. pp. 189. *bibliog.*

— Germany.

ZEPLER (WALLY) Welchen Wert hat die Bildung für die Arbeiterin?: ein Vortrag. Berlin, 1907. pp. 15.

BOMMERT (WILFRIED) and BUETTNER (EVA) Bildungsverhalten der Landfrauen: Ergebnisse einer repräsentativen Befragung landwirtschaftlich tätiger Frauen in der Bundesrepublik Deutschland, 1976. Bonn, 1977. pp. 234. *bibliog. (Forschungsgesellschaft für Agrarpolitik und Agrarsoziologie. [Publications]. 244)*

— New Zealand.

EDUCATION and the equality of the sexes: conference on women and education sponsored by the Committee on Women and the Department of Education, 23-27 November 1975, Victoria University of Wellington. Wellington, Department of Education, 1976. pp. 72. *bibliogs.*

EDUCATIONAL ASSISTANCE.

GRUNDERZIEHUNG: Hilfe für Entwicklungsländer: Berichte im Auftrag der Deutschen UNESCO-Kommission; herausgegeben von Heinz Kloss. Stuttgart, 1960. pp. 135. *bibliog.*

EDUCATIONAL ASSOCIATIONS

— Czechoslovakia.

POZORNY (REINHARD) Deutsche Schutzarbeit im Sudetenland: die Tätigkeit des Deutschen Kulturverbandes, 1918-1938. Wien, 1974. pp. 51.

— Switzerland.

BRAUN (JAKOB) Zum 50-jährigen Jubiläum der Gründung des Grütlivereins Chur, 1848-1898; im Auftrage der Festkommission verfasst. Zürich, 1898. pp. 56.

EDUCATIONAL EQUALIZATION.

TYLER (WILLIAM) The sociology of educational inequality. London, 1977. pp. 143. *bibliog.*

— United Kingdom.

MACMILLAN (KEITH) Education welfare: strategy and structure. London, 1977. pp. 165. *bibliog.*

— United States.

EDUCATION, inequality, and national policy; edited by Nelson F. Ashline [and others]. Lexington, Mass., [1976]. pp. 199. *Based on an invitational conference held in Newport, R.I., in June 1975.*

MORGAN (EDWARD P.) Inequality in classroom learning: schooling and democratic citizenship. New York, 1977. pp. 224. *bibliog.*

EDUCATIONAL INNOVATIONS.

DORE (RONALD PHILIP) The diploma disease: education, qualification and development. London, 1976. pp. 214. *bibliog.*

EDUCATIONAL LAW AND LEGISLATION

— Netherlands.

MEIJSEN (J.H.) compiler. Lager onderwijs in de spiegel der geschiedenis: 175 jaar nationale wetgeving op het lager onderwijs in Nederland, 1801-1976. 's-Gravenhage, Staatsuitgeverij, 1976. pp. 303. *bibliog.*

— Nigeria.

OGUNSOLA (ALBERT F.) Legislation and education in Northern Nigeria. Ibadan, 1974. pp. 111. *bibliog.*

— United Kingdom.

ROPER (HENRY) Administering the Elementary Education Acts 1870-1885. Leeds, 1976. pp. 50. *(Leeds. University. Museum of the History of Education. Educational Administration and History: Monographs. No. 5)*

EDUCATIONAL PLANNING.

IIEP BULLETIN; pd. q. [by] International Institute for Educational Planning. q., current issues only. Paris.

— Ecuador.

ECUADOR. Departamento de Planeamiento Integral de la Educacion. 1967. Sintesis del plan ecuatoriano de educacion. Quito, 1967. pp. 49.

— United Kingdom.

ASHTON (D.N.) and FIELD (DAVID) Young workers. London, 1976. pp. 192. *bibliog.*

EDUCATIONAL PSYCHOLOGY.

NORD-LARSEN (MOGENS) and VEDEL-PETERSEN (JACOB) Tabere i skolen: de 9-12 åriges skoletilpasning, etc. København, 1976. pp. 363. *(Socialforskningsinstituttet. Publikationer. 69) With English summary.*

EDUCATIONAL PUBLISHING

— United Kingdom.

EDUCATIONAL PUBLISHERS COUNCIL. Publishing for schools: a short guide to educational publishing. London, 1977. pp. 56.

EDUCATIONAL RESEARCH.

The ORGANISATION and impact of social research: six original case studies in education and behavioural science; edited by Marten Shipman. London, 1976. pp. 155. *bibliogs.*

— Australia.

AUSTRALIA. Australian Advisory Committee on Research and Development in Education. Annual report. a., 1970/71 (1st)- Canberra. *Included in AUSTRALIA. Parliament. [Parliamentary papers].*

EDUCATIONAL SOCIOLOGY.

TURCHENKO (VLADIMIR NIKOLAEVICH) and others, eds. Sotsiologicheskie i ekonomicheskie problemy obrazovaniia. Novosibirsk, 1969. pp. 436.

DORE (RONALD PHILIP) The diploma disease: education, qualification and development. London, 1976. pp. 214. *bibliog.*

ILLICH (IVAN D.) and VERNE (ETIENNE) Imprisoned in the global classroom; [also including Political inversion by Ivan Illich]. London, 1976. pp. 63.

The PROCESS of schooling: a sociological reader; edited by Martyn Hammersley and Peter Woods for the Schooling and Society Course at the Open University. London, 1976. pp. 232. *bibliogs.*

BELLABY (PAUL) The sociology of comprehensive schooling. London, 1977. pp. 127. *bibliog.*

BERNBAUM (GERALD) Knowledge and ideology in the sociology of education. London, 1977. pp. 78. *bibliog. (British Sociological Association. Studies in Sociology)*

BOURDIEU (PIERRE) and PASSERON (JEAN CLAUDE) Reproduction in education, society and culture; translated from the French by Richard Nice. London, [1977]. pp. 255. *bibliog.*

TYLER (WILLIAM) The sociology of educational inequality. London, 1977. pp. 143. *bibliog.*

WOODS (PETER) and HAMMERSLEY (MARTYN) eds. School experience: explorations in the sociology of education. London, 1977. pp. 297. *bibliogs.*

— United Kingdom.

SHARP (RACHEL) and others. Education and social control: a study in progressive primary education. London, 1975. pp. 256. *bibliog.*

EDUCATIONAL TECHNOLOGY

— United Kingdom.

COMPUTER BOARD FOR UNIVERSITIES AND RESEARCH COUNCILS [U.K.]. Computers in higher education and research: the next decade; a statement of future policy...for discussion with universities, research councils, and other interested bodies. London, H.M.S.O., 1976. pp. 24.

EDUCATIONAL VOUCHERS

— United Kingdom.

CREW (MICHAEL A.) and YOUNG (ALISTAIR) Paying by degrees: a study of the financing of higher education students by grants, loans and vouchers. London, 1977. pp. 66. *bibliog. (Institute of Economic Affairs. Hobart Papers. 75)*

EDUCATORS

— Spain.

GINER DE LOS RIOS (FRANCISCO) Ensayos y cartas: edicion de homenaje en el cincuentenario de su muerte. Mexico, [1965]. pp. 188.

EFFICIENCY, INDUSTRIAL.

HILF (HUBERT HUGO) Arbeitswissenschaft: Grundlagen der Leistungsforschung und Arbeitsgestaltung. München, 1957. pp. 341. *bibliog.*

TOLKACHEV (ALEKSANDR SERGEEVICH) ed. Problemy metodologii planirovaniia i izmereniia effektivnosti proizvodstva; (v osnovu knigi polozheny materialy Mezhdunarodnogo seminara...v Marianske Lazne v 1974 g.). Moskva, 1975. pp. 215.

VAVILOV (ANATOLII PAVLOVICH) Effektivnost' sotsialisticheskogo proizvodstva i kachestvo produktsii. Moskva, 1975. pp. 175.

ASHIMBAEV (TUIMEBAI ASHIMBAEVICH) Effektivnost' promyshlennogo proizvodstva: metodologiia, analiz i problemy na materialakh Kazakhstana. Alma-Ata, 1976. pp. 359.

OSNOVNYE napravleniia povysheniia effektivnosti promyshlennosti, stroitel'stva i transporta: materialy respublikanskoi nauchno- prakticheskoi konferentsii. Dushanbe, 1976. pp. 184.

PLYSHEVSKII (BORIS PAVLOVICH) ed. Effektivnost' obshchestvennogo proizvodstva: kriterii, metody rascheta, pokazateli. Moskva, 1976. pp. 215.

— Mathematical models.

CHEW (SOON BENG) A study of efficiency in the manufacturing sector: inter-industry and inter-firm comparisons. [Singapore], National Productivity Board, 1973. fo. 40. *bibliog.*

EGERTON (THOMAS) 1st Viscount Brackley.

KNAFLA (LOUIS A.) Law and politics in Jacobean England: the tracts of Lord Chancellor Ellesmere. Cambridge, 1977. pp. 355.

EGYPT

— Economic policy.

KAMEL (ISMAIL KAMEL AHMED) The system of planning, its application and evaluation, and follow-ups of plans in economic units of the general sector. Ljubljana, International Center for Public Enterprises, 1974. fo. 17. *(International Seminar 1974. National Papers)*

— Foreign relations — Russia.

RUBINSTEIN (ALVIN ZACHARY) Red star on the Nile: the Soviet-Egyptian influence relationship since the June War. Princeton, N.J., [1977]. pp. 383. *bibliog.*

— — United Kingdom.

COTTAM (RICHARD W.) Foreign policy motivation: a general theory and a case study. Pittsburgh, [1977]. pp. 374. *bibliog.*

— History — 1798- .

RICHMOND (J.C.B.) Egypt, 1798-1952: her advance towards a modern identity. London, 1977. pp. 243. *bibliog.*

— — 1882-1936, British occupation.

PARTI NATIONAL EGYPTIEN. Mémoires présentés par le Parti National Egyptien à la Conférence de la paix à Paris et au Congrès socialiste à Berne. Genève, 1919. pp. 32.

— Social conditions.

LEGRAIN (GEORGES ALBERT) Fellah de Karnak, Haute-Egypte: journalier dans le système des engagements momentanés; d'après les renseignements recueillis sur les lieux de 1895 à 1900. Paris, 1902. pp. 289-336. *(Société d'Economie et de Science Sociales. Les Ouvriers de Deux Mondes. 3e Série. 5e fasc.)*

— Social history.

CARLTON (ERIC JAMES) Ideology and social order. London, 1977. pp. 320. *bibliog.*

EICHTHAL (GUSTAVE D').

EICHTHAL (GUSTAVE D') A French sociologist looks at Britain: Gustave d'Eichthal and British society in 1828; translated and edited by Barrie M. Ratcliffe and W.H. Chaloner. Manchester, [1977]. pp. 169. *(Manchester. University. Faculty of Arts. Publications. No. 22)*

EIGHT HOUR MOVEMENT.

[GEL'FAND (ALEKSANDR LAZAREVICH)] Die Handelskrisis und die Gewerkschaften; nebst Anhang: Gesetzentwurf über den achtstündigen Normalarbeitstag; von Parvus [pseud.]. München, 1901. pp. 64.

EILAT

— Harbour.

ISRAEL. Ports Authority. 1967. Port of Eilat. [Jerusalem, 1967?]. pp. [17].

EL SADAT (ANWAR).

ISRAEL INFORMATION CENTRE. Information Briefings. 2. Does Sadat really want peace with Israele? rev. ed. Jerusalem, [1973]. pp. 14.

ELASTICITY (ECONOMICS).

U.K. Working Group on Energy Elasticities. 1977. Report; [T.A. Kennedy, chairman]. London, 1977. pp. 55. *bibliog. (U.K. Department of Energy. Energy Papers. No. 17)*

ELECTION LAW

— Ghana.

GHANA. Commission of Enquiry into Electoral and Local Government Reform. 1967. Parts 1 and 2 of the report; [J.B. Siriboe, chairman]. Accra, 1967. pp. 128, 1 map.

GHANA. 1968. White Paper on parts 1 and 2 of the report of the Commission of Enquiry into Electoral and Local Government Reforms. [Accra], 1968. pp. 4. *(W[hite] P[apers]. 1968. No. 1)*

— Italy — Trentino-Alto Adige.

TRENTINO-ALTO ADIGE. Servizi Elettorali. 1957. Istruzioni per gli uffici elettorali in applicazione della l.r. 6 aprile 1956 n.5, sulla elezione dei consigli comunali nella regione. Trento, [1957?]. pp. 31. *(Pubblicazioni. N.3)*

TRENTINO-ALTO ADIGE. Servizi Elettorali. 1957. Istruzioni per gli uffici elettorali in applicazione della l.r. 6 aprile 1956 n.5. sulla elezione dei consigli communali nella regione: vade mecum per i componenti gli uffici. Trento, [1957?]. pp. 27,4. *(Pubblicazioni. N.2)*

TRENTINO-ALTO ADIGE. Statutes, etc. 1956. Composizione ed elezione degli organi delle amministrazioni communali: legge regionale 6 aprile 1956, N.5. Trento, [1957?]. pp. 62. *(Trentino-Alto Adige. Servizi Elettorali. Pubblicazioni. N.1)*

ELECTIONS.

FAVRE (PIERRE) La décision de majorité. [Paris, 1976]. pp. 326. *bibliogs. (Fondation Nationale des Sciences Politiques. Cahiers. 205)*

MAISEL (LOUIS) ed. Changing campaign techniques: elections and values in contemporary democracies. Beverly Hills, [1976]. pp. 272. *bibliogs.*

— Argentine Republic.

DANA MONTAÑO (SALVADOR M.) Contribucion al estudio del cambio del regimen representativo argentino: legislacion electoral y de los partidos politicos. Buenos Aires, 1972. pp. 102.

— Brazil.

CARDOSO (FERNANDO HENRIQUE) and LAMOUNIER (BOLIVAR) eds. Os partidos e as eleições no Brasil. Rio de Janeiro, 1975. pp. 262.

— Colombia — Cundinamarca.

CUNDINAMARCA. Delegacion Departamental del Estado Civil. 1968. Estadistica electoral, marzo 17 de 1968. [Bogota, 1968?]. pp. 81.

CUNDINAMARCA. Delegacion Departamental del Estado Civil. 1970. Estadistica electoral, abril 19 de 1970. [Bogota, 1970?]. pp. 87.

— Czechoslovakia.

HRONEK (JIŘÍ) Ein Land, dessen Volk sich selbst regiert: Nationalausschusswahlen in der Tschechoslowakei. Praha, 1954. pp. 24.

— France.

PARTI SOCIALISTE. L'élu socialiste au service de tous. Paris, [1965]. pp. 78. *Cover title: Elections municipales 1965.*

— Germany.

WINZER (OTTO) Die grosse Lüge von den "freien Wahlen" in Westdeutschland: ein dokumentarischer Nachweis aus offiziellen Veröffentlichungen des Bonner Parteivorstandes der Sozialdemokratischen Partei Deutschlands. Berlin, 1954. pp. 23.

— — Bibliography.

WAHLSTATISTIK in Deutschland: Bibliographie der deutschen Wahlstatistik, 1848-1975; bearbeitet von Nils Diederich [and others]. München, 1976. pp. 206. *(Berlin. Freie Universität. Zentralinstitut für Sozialwissenschaftliche Forschung. Berichte und Materialien. Band 4)*

— India.

INDIA. Election Commission. 1975. Report on the general elections to the legislative assemblies of Manipur, Nagaland, Orissa, Uttar Pradesh and Pondicherry, 1974: statistical. [Delhi], 1974 [or rather 1975]. pp. 248.

— Italy.

BARNES (SAMUEL HENRY) Representation in Italy: institutionalized tradition and electoral choice. Chicago, 1977. pp. 187.

— Pakistan.

GOPINATH (MEENAKSHI) Pakistan in transition: political development and rise to power of Pakistan People's Party. Delhi, 1975. pp. 162. *bibliog.*

— Russia — Russia (RSFSR).

RUSSIA (RSFSR). Verkhovnyi Sovet. Prezidium. Otdel po Voprosam Raboty Sovetov. 1975. Itogi vyborov i sostav deputatov mestnykh Sovetov deputatov trudiashchikhsia RSFSR 1975 g.: statisticheskii sbornik. Moskva, 1975. pp. 271.

— Spain.

TUSELL GOMEZ (JAVIER) Oligarquia y caciquismo en Andalucia, 1890-1923. Barcelona, 1976. pp. 589.

— Sweden.

SWEDEN. Statistiska Centralbyrån. 1977- . Allmänna valen 1976, etc. Stockholm, 1977 in progress. *(Sveriges Officiella Statistik) With English summaries.*

— United Kingdom — London.

KNOTT (SIMON) The electoral crucible: the politics of London, 1900-1914. [London, 1977]. pp. 194. *bibliog.*

— United States.

GOSNELL (HAROLD FOOTE) and SMOLKA (RICHARD G.) American parties and elections. Columbus, Ohio, [1976]. pp. 288.

MILLER (WARREN EDWARD) and LEVITIN (TERESA E.) Leadership and change: the new politics and the American electorate. Cambridge, Mass., [1976]. pp. 267.

— — Campaign funds.

ALEXANDER (HERBERT E.) and others. Financing the 1972 election. Lexington, Mass., [1976]. pp. 771.

CAMPAIGN money: reform and reality in the States; edited by Herbert E. Alexander. New York, [1976]. pp. 337.

ELECTRIC ENGINEERING

— Cyprus.

CYPRUS. Department of Electrical and Mechanical Service. Annual report. a., 1975(1st)- [Nicosia].

— United States.

HAMMOND (JOHN WINTHROP) Men and volts: the story of General Electric. Philadelphia, [1941]. pp. 436.

ELECTRIC INDUSTRIES

— Netherlands.

PHILIPS (FRITS) 45 jaar met Philips; tekstverzorging Leo Ott. Rotterdam, 1976. pp. 382.

ELECTRIC INDUSTRY WORKERS

— Ireland (Republic).

EIRE. Committee on Industrial Relations in the Electricity Supply Board. 1968. Interim report; [Michael P. Fogarty, chairman]. Dublin, 1968. pp. 36.

ELECTRIC POWER DISTRIBUTION

— Mexico.

MEXICO. Direccion General de Estadistica. Censo Industrial, 1971. IX censo industrial, 1971; datos de 1970: industrias de extraccion y refinacion de petroleo, y petroquimica basica e industria de generacion, transmision y distribucion de energia electrica para servicio publico. Mexico, 1974. pp. 131.

ELECTRIC POWER PLANTS

— United Kingdom.

U.K. Central Policy Review Staff. 1976. The future of the United Kingdom power plant manufacturing industry; report. London, [1976]. pp. 102.

ELECTRICITY SUPPLY

— Costs.

TURVEY (RALPH) and ANDERSON (DENNIS) Electricity economics: essays and case studies. Baltimore, International Bank for Reconstruction and Development, [1977]. pp. 364.

— Law and legislation — United Kingdom.

REEVES (PETER) Electricity and gas consumers' guide: a summary of the practice of supply authorities and the law applicable to domestic gas and electricity consumers. Oxford, [1975]. pp. 23.

— Rates.

TURVEY (RALPH) and ANDERSON (DENNIS) Electricity economics: essays and case studies. Baltimore, International Bank for Reconstruction and Development, [1977]. pp. 364.

— Australia — Queensland.

STATE ELECTRICITY COMMISSION OF QUEENSLAND. The economics of electricity generation in Queensland and the potential employment of nuclear reactors. Sydney, 1958. pp. 265-272. *bibliog. Reprinted from Australian Atomic Energy Symposium 1958.*

— France.

FRANCE. Direction de la Documentation. La Documentation Française. Notes et Etudes Documentaires. Nos. 4,329-4, 330-4,331. Electricité de France: entreprise nationale, industrielle et commerciale. Paris, 1976. pp. 99.

— Ghana.

ELECTRICITY CORPORATION OF GHANA. Annual report and accounts. a., 1969(2nd)- Accra.

— Russia.

VILENSKII (MATVEI ABRAMOVICH) Ekonomicheskie problemy elektrifikatsii SSSR. Moskva, 1975. pp. 200. *(Akademiia Nauk SSSR. Institut Ekonomiki. Problemy Sovetskoi Ekonomiki)*

ENERGETIKA SSSR v 1976-1980 godakh. Moskva, 1977. pp. 287.

— — Buryat Republic.

TUISK (ALEKSANDR GANSOVICH) Toplivnaia promyshlennost' i elektroenergetika Buriatskoi ASSR. Ulan-Ude, 1969. pp. 102.

— — Siberia.

ALEKSEEV (VENIAMIN VASIL'EVICH) Elektrifikatsiia Sibiri: istoricheskoe issledovanie, 1885- (1970 gg.); The electrification of Siberia: a historical essay. Novosibirsk, 1973-76. 2 vols.

— — Tajikistan.

IUNUSOV (BORIS VEN'IAMINOVICH) Elektroenergetika Tadzhikistana: etapy rosta, sovremennoe sostoianie, perspektivy razvitiia. Dushanbe, 1975. pp. 240.

— — Ukraine.

DNEPROVSKIE ogni: kak iz ruin i pepla byl podniat posle voiny Zaporozhskii industrial'nyi kompleks. Kiev, 1976. pp. 190.

— Switzerland.

LIENHARD (HANS) Die schweizerische Elektrizitätswirtschaft: eine Analyse gegenwärtiger und zukünftiger Probleme. Bern, 1976. pp. 212.

— Underdeveloped areas.

See UNDERDEVELOPED AREAS — Electricity supply.

ELECTRICITY SUPPLY(Cont.)

— United Kingdom.

EDWARDS (Sir RONALD STANLEY) Financing electricity supply. London, [1967]. pp. 17.

BRITISH ASSOCIATION OF SETTLEMENTS AND SOCIAL ACTION CENTRES. Energy Research Group. A right to fuel: a...report concerning the disconnection of domestic electricity supplies. London, 1975. pp. 17.

HAWKINS (Sir ARTHUR) Electricity's balancing act. [London], Central Electricity Generating Board, [1976]. pp. 16.

— — Rates.

BRITISH ASSOCIATION OF SETTLEMENTS AND SOCIAL ACTION CENTRES. Energy Research Group. A right to fuel: a...report concerning the disconnection of domestic electricity supplies. London, 1975. pp. 17.

— United States.

MITCHELL (EDWARD J.) and CHAFFETZ (PETER R.) Toward economy in electric power. Washington, 1975. pp. 32. (American Enterprise Institute for Public Policy Research. National Energy Studies. 9)

— — Costs.

CICCHETTI (CHARLES J.) and others. The marginal cost and pricing of electricity: an applied approach. Cambridge, Mass., [1977]. pp. 291. A report to the U.S. National Science Foundation on behalf of the Planning and Conservation Foundation, Sacramento, California.

— — Rates.

CICCHETTI (CHARLES J.) and others. The marginal cost and pricing of electricity: an applied approach. Cambridge, Mass., [1977]. pp. 291. A report to the U.S. National Science Foundation on behalf of the Planning and Conservation Foundation, Sacramento, California.

— Zaire.

MALU (FELIX) Le système énergétique de la République Démocratique du Congo. Kinshasa, Office National de la Recherche et du Développement, 1970. pp. 24. bibliog.

MUTOMBO (A.) and MALU (FELIX) Caractéristiques de la demande d'énergie électrique en R[épublique] D[émocratique du] C[ongo]: indices de consommation d'énergie électrique. 1. Kinshasa, Office National de la Recherche et du Développement, 1970. pp. 30. bibliog.

ZAKRZEWSKI (JANUSZ) and others. Etude de l'extension du centre électro-énergétique de Mbandaka. Kinshasa, Office National de la Recherche et du Développement, 1969 [or rather 1970]. pp. 49.

ELECTRONIC DATA PROCESSING.

KATZAN (HARRY) Computer data security. New York, [1973]. pp. 223. bibliog.

McFARLAN (F. WARREN) and others. Information systems administration. New York, [1973]. pp. 596.

NATIONAL COMPUTER CONFERENCE, 1973. National Computer Conference and exposition, June 4-8, 1973, New York. Montvale, N.J., 1973. pp. 816,M01-97. bibliogs. (American Federation of Information Processing Societies. Conference Proceedings. vol.42)

NATIONAL COMPUTER CONFERENCE, 1974. National Computer Conference and exposition, May 6-10, 1974, Chicago, Illinois. Montvale, N.J., 1974. pp. 1069. (American Federation of Information Processing Societies. Conference Proceedings. vol. 43)

HOWARD (K.) and others. The scope for computer based systems to aid corporate decision-making in the short and medium term in the reorganised local authorities: a feasibility study. Peterlee, 1975. pp. 40. bibliog. (IBM United Kingdom Limited. UK Scientific Centre. [Technical Reports]. 0074)

KATZAN (HARRY) Introduction to computer science. New York, 1975. pp. 500. bibliogs.

LANGEFORS (NILS BÖRJE) and SUNDGREN (BO) Information systems architecture. New York, 1975. pp. 366. bibliog.

NATIONAL COMPUTER CONFERENCE, 1975. National Computer Conference, May 19-22, 1975, Anaheim, California. Montvale, N.J., 1975. pp. 990. (American Federation of Information Processing Societies. Conference Proceedings. vol. 44)

SEMINAR ON GEOGRAPHIC DATA PROCESSING, PETERLEE, 1974. Proceedings of the...seminar...; edited by B.K. Aldred. Peterlee, 1975. pp. 104. (IBM United Kingdom Limited. UK Scientific Centre. [Technical Reports]. 0073)

TREMBLAY (JEAN PAUL) and MANOHAR (RAM P.) Discrete mathematical structures with applications to computer science. New York, [1975]. pp. 606.

BENWELL (NICHOLAS J.) ed. Data preparation techniques. [London, 1976]. pp. 284.

JENKINS (CLIVE) and SHERMAN (BARRIE) Computers and the unions. London, 1977. pp. 135.

See also subdivision Data processing under subjects.

ELECTRONIC DATA PROCESSING DEPARTMENTS.

McFARLAN (F. WARREN) and others. Information systems administration. New York, [1973]. pp. 596.

— Security measures.

KATZAN (HARRY) Computer data security. New York, [1973]. pp. 223. bibliog.

ELECTRONIC DATA PROCESSING IN VOCATIONAL GUIDANCE.

BUTLER (A.M.) and DOWSEY (M.W.) Interactive careers guidance system: final report of the IBM/Cheshire project. Peterlee, 1975. pp. 49. bibliog. (IBM United Kingdom Limited. UK Scientific Centre. [Technical Reports]. 0063)

DOWSEY (M.W.) and BUTLER (A.M.) Interactive careers guidance system: management summary. Peterlee, 1975. pp. 32. bibliog. (IBM United Kingdom Limited. UK Scientific Centre. [Technical Reports]. 0061)

ELECTRONIC DATA PROCESSING PERSONNEL

— Netherlands.

COMMISSIE OVERLEG INZAKE DE PERSONEELSPROBLEEM. Webkgroep Kwantificering. Raming van de behoefte aan computerfunctionarissen in 1975: rapport van de Werkgroep, etc. Alphen aan den Rijn, 1971. pp. 42.

— United Kingdom.

STAMPER (RONALD) Underpinning experience: education for the experienced analyst. [London, 1976]. fo. 5.

ELECTRONIC DIGITAL COMPUTERS.

CHAPIN (NED) Computers: a systems approach. New York, [1971]. pp. 686. bibliogs.

KATZAN (HARRY) Introduction to computer science. New York, 1975. pp. 500. bibliogs.

RANDELL (BRIAN) 1936- , ed. The origins of digital computers: selected papers. 2nd ed. Berlin, 1975. pp. 464. bibliog.

— Education.

HELLERMAN (HERBERT) and CONROY (THOMAS F.) Computer system performance. New York, [1975]. pp. 380. bibliogs.

— Evaluation.

GLASS (ROBERT L.) The universal elixir and other computing projects which failed. Newton, Mass., [1976]. pp. 79.

ELECTRONIC INDUSTRIES

— France.

ZYSMAN (JOHN) Political strategies for industrial order: state, market and industry in France. Berkeley, Calif., [1977]. pp. 230.

— United Kingdom.

U.K. Central Office of Information. Reference Division. Reference Pamphlets. 145. British industry today: electronics. London, 1976. pp. 71. bibliog.

ELISABETHVILLE.

See LUBUMBASHI.

ELITE.

HICKOX (MICHAEL STEPHEN HINDMARSH) The ideology of intellectual elites and its implications for the sociology of knowledge. 1976. fo. 431. bibliog. Typescript. Ph. D. (London) thesis: unpublished. This thesis is the property of London University and may not be removed from the Library.

ROBINS (ROBERT S.) Political institutionalization and the integration of elites. Beverly Hills, [1976]. pp. 220. bibliog.

— Africa.

MARKOVITZ (IRVING LEONARD) Power and class in Africa: an introduction to change and conflict in African politics. Englewood Cliffs, N.J., [1977]. pp. 398. bibliog.

— Africa, Subsaharan.

EDIAFRIC-SERVICE Les élites africaines. 3rd ed. Paris, [1974]. pp. 490. (Bulletin de l'Afrique Noire. Numéro Spécial)

MANGHEZI (ALPHEUS) Class, elite and community in African development. Uppsala, 1976. pp. 118. bibliog.

— China.

WONG (PAUL) China's higher leadership in the socialist tradition. New York, [1976]. pp. 310. bibliog.

— Denmark.

PEDERSEN (MOGENS N.) Political development and elite transformation in Denmark. Odense, 1974. pp. 82. bibliog. (Odense Universitet. Institut for Historie og Samfundsvidenskab. Skrifter. [No. 12])

— European Economic Community countries.

FELD (WERNER J.) and WILDGEN (JOHN K.) Domestic political realities and European unification: a study of mass publics and elites in the European Community countries. Boulder, Col., 1976. pp. 177,11.

— Germany.

BOLZ (WOLFGANG EBERHARD) Elitenselektion in Verbänden. Hamburg, 1976. pp. 331. bibliog. Dissertation zur Erlangung des Grades eines Doktors der Wirtschafts- und Sozialwissenschaften der Universität Hamburg.

BUEDINGER TAGUNG, 1973-1975. Führende Kräfte und Gruppen in der deutschen Arbeiterbewegung: Büdinger Vorträge, 1973-1975; herausgegeben von Hanns Hubert Hofmann. Limburg/Lahn, 1976. pp. 226. (Ranke-Gesellschaft. Deutsche Führungsschichten in der Neuzeit. Gesamtreihe. Band 9)

GEIGER (ELLYNOR) Die soziale Elite der Hansestadt Lemgo und die Entstehung eines Exportgewerbes auf dem Lande in der Zeit von 1450 bis 1650. Detmold, 1976. pp. 278. bibliog. (Naturwissenschaftlicher und Historischer Verein für das Land Lippe. Sonderveröffentlichungen. Band 25)

ROTH (DIETER) Zum Demokratieverständnis von Eliten in der Bundesrepublik Deutschland. Bern, 1976. pp. 187. *bibliog.*

WITJES (CLAUS WINFRIED) Gewerkschaftliche Führungsgruppen: eine empirische Untersuchung zum Sozialprofil...westdeutscher Gewerkschaftsführungen. Berlin, [1976]. pp. 422. *bibliog.*

— **Germany, Eastern.**

RADDE (JUERGEN) Die aussenpolitische Führungselite der DDR: Veränderungen der sozialen Struktur aussenpolitischer Führungsgruppen. Köln, [1976]. pp. 240. *bibliog.*

— **Mexico.**

STANSFIELD (DAVID E.) The Mexican cabinet: an indicator of political change. Glasgow, 1973. pp. 20. *(Glasgow. University. Institute of Latin American Studies. Occasional Papers. No. 8)*

— **Morocco.**

LEVEAU (REMY) Le fellah marocain, défenseur du trône. [Paris, 1976]. pp. 281. *bibliog. (Fondation Nationale des Sciences Politiques. Cahiers. 203)*

— **Pakistan.**

LAPORTE (ROBERT) Power and privilege: influence and decision-making in Pakistan. Berkeley, Calif., [1975]. pp. 225. *bibliog.*

— **Paraguay.**

INSTITUTO DE DESARROLLO INTEGRAL Y ARMONICO. Actitudes y opiniones de los lideres paraguayos acerca de las politicas poblacionales y familiares. [Asuncion, 1972?]. pp. 148. *(Desarrollo y Demografia. 2)* Cover title: *Encuesta a lideres.*

— **Peru.**

BONILLA (HERACLIO) Guano y burguesia en el Peru. Lima, 1974. pp. 186. *bibliog. (Instituto de Estudios Peruanos. Peru Problema. 11)*

— **Russia.**

HILL (RONALD J.) Soviet political elites: the case of Tiraspol. London, 1977. pp. 226. *bibliog.*

— **Singapore.**

KASSIM (ISMAIL) Problems of elite cohesion: a perspective from a minority community. Singapore, [1974]. pp. 146. *bibliog.*

CHEN (PETER S.J.) Elites and nation development in Singapore. Singapore, 1975. pp. 15. *bibliog. (University of Singapore. Department of Sociology. Working Papers. No. 46)*

— **United Kingdom.**

HICKOX (MICHAEL STEPHEN HINDMARSH) The ideology of intellectual elites and its implications for the sociology of knowledge. 1976. fo. 431. *bibliog. Typescript. Ph. D. (London) thesis: unpublished. This thesis is the property of London University and may not be removed from the Library.*

FOSTER (FRANK FREEMAN) The politics of stability: a portrait of the rulers in Elizabethan London. London, 1977. pp. 209. *(Royal Historical Society. Studies in History)*

ELLERMAN FAMILY.

TAYLOR (JAMES ARNOLD) Ellermans: a wealth of shipping. London, 1976. pp. 320.

EMBEZZLEMENT

— **Russia.**

PINAEV (ANATOLII ALEKSEEVICH) Ugolovno-pravovaia bor'ba s khishcheniiami. Khar'kov, 1975. pp. 188. *bibliog.*

EMIGRANT REMITTANCES

— **Western Samoa.**

SHANKMAN (PAUL) Migration and underdevelopment: the case of Western Samoa. Boulder, Col., 1976. pp. 129. *bibliog.*

EMIGRATION AND IMMIGRATION.

GEORGE (PIERRE) Les migrations internationales. [Paris], 1976. pp. 230. *bibliog.*

NEW approaches to the study of migration; David Guillet and Douglas Uzzell, editors. Houston, Texas, 1976. pp. 181. *bibliogs. (Rice University. Rice University Studies. vol. 62, no.3)*

EMIGRATION AND IMMIGRATION LAW

— **Israel.**

KRAINES (OSCAR) The impossible dilemma: who is a Jew in the state of Israel?. New York, [1976]. pp. 156. *bibliog.*

— **United Kingdom.**

IMMIGRATION APPEALS: selected determinations of the Immigration Appeal Tribunal and of Immigration Appeal Adjudicators on appeals under the Immigration Appeals Act 1969 and the Aliens (Appeals) Order 1970 [U.K.]. a., 1970/71 (v.1)- London. *Not pd. 1972/3, 1973/4.*

RUNNYMEDE TRUST. Briefing Papers. 1974, No. 3. Illegal immigration and the law. rev. ed. London, 1974. fo. 5.

U.K. Central Office of Information. Reference Division. 1974. Immigration into Britain. London, 1974. pp. 13. *bibliog.*

EVANS (JOHN M.) Immigration law. London, 1976. pp. 152.

U.K. Parliament. House of Commons. Library. Research Division. Reference Sheets. 76/17. East African Asians: their immigration and citizenship position. [London], 1976. pp. 19. *bibliog.*

EMINENT DOMAIN

— **Germany.**

REICHS-BAUERNBUND. Wie wehrt sich der Bauer gegen Zwangsenteignung?. Berlin, [1931]. pp. 16.

AUSSCHUSS FÜR DEUTSCHE EINHEIT. Schwarzbuch über das Bauernlegen in Westdeutschland. Berlin, 1960. pp. 94.

— **Mexico.**

CORONA (GUSTAVO) Lazaro Cardenas y la expropiacion de la industria petrolera en Mexico. Mexico, 1975. pp. 350.

— **United Kingdom.**

NORTON (ALAN LEWIS) and LONG (JOYCE R.) The community land legislation and its implementation: an analysis of the provisions of the 1975 Community Land Bill and government intentions for its implementation. Birmingham, 1975. pp. 38.

U.K. Department of the Environment. 1975. Scope of the community land scheme. [London], 1975. fo. 7.

RANDALL (SIMON JAMES CRAWFORD) Your land or theirs?: aspects of the Community Land Act 1975 and the Development Land Tax Bill. [Bromley?], 1976. pp. 31.

EMOTIONS.

BUCK (ROSS) Human motivation and emotion. New York, [1976]. pp. 529. *bibliog.*

EMPLOYEE-MANAGEMENT RELATIONS IN GOVERNMENT

— **Canada — Manitoba.**

MANITOBA. Labour Management Review Committee. 1974. Report...on public sector employee-employer relations in Manitoba; [H.D. Woods, chairman]. [Winnipeg], 1974. 1 vol (various pagings).

— **United Kingdom.**

WILLIAMS (Sir LESLIE) Industrial relations in the Civil Service; (transcript of lecture given on 14 May 1974). [London], Civil Service College, [1974]. pp. 18. *(Lectures on Some Management Problems in the Civil Service. No.3)*

McCARTHY (WILLIAM EDWARD JOHN) Baron McCarthy. Making Whitley work: a review of the operation of the National Health Service Whitley Council system. [London, Department of Health and Social Security], 1976. pp. 144.

— **United States.**

POPS (GERALD M.) Emergence of the public sector arbitrator. Lexington, Mass., [1976]. pp. 136.

— — **Maryland.**

PUBLIC SECTOR LABOR RELATIONS CONFERENCE BOARD. Annual Conference, 1st, University of Maryland, 1971. Public sector labor relations in Maryland: issues and prospects; editor, Donald W. O'Connell; contributors, Willoughby Abner [and others]. College Park, Md., 1972. pp. 84. *(Public Sector Labor Relations Conference Board. Publications. No. 1)*

EMPLOYEE MORALE.

LUPTON (THOMAS) Problems of morale and staff relations in large organisations; (transcript of lecture given on 21 May 1974). [London], Civil Service College, [1974]. pp. 10. *(Lectures on Some Management Problems in the Civil Service. No. 4)*

EMPLOYEE OWNERSHIP.

SPEISER (STUART M.) A piece of the action: a plan to provide every family with a [dollar]100,000 stake in the economy. New York, [1977]. pp. 390. *bibliog.*

— **Sweden.**

MEYERSON (PER-MARTIN) Company profits: sources of investment finance: wage earners' investment funds in Sweden: proposals, debate, analysis. Stockholm, 1976. pp. 31. *bibliog.*

— **United Kingdom.**

BURDON (STEPHEN WILLIAM ROGER) Share incentive schemes for executives: a survey of current practice. London, [1971]. pp. 40. *bibliog. (British Institute of Management. Management Survey Reports. No. 6)*

EMPLOYEES, DISMISSAL OF

— **Sudan.**

ALI TAHA (ABDEL RAHMAN E.) and EL JACK (AHMED H.) The regulation of termination of employment in the Sudanese private sector: a study of the law and its application. Khartoum, 1973. pp. 39.

— **United Kingdom.**

CONSUMERS' ASSOCIATION. Dismissal, redundancy and job hunting. London, [1976]. pp. 137.

MESHER (JOHN) Compensation for unemployment. London, 1976. pp. 138. *bibliog.*

RAWLINGS (HUGH FENTON) The problem of redundancy in collective bargaining and the law. 1976. fo. 259. *bibliog. Typescript. Ph.D. (London) thesis: unpublished. This thesis is the property of London University and may not be removed from the Library.*

GREENWOOD (JOHN A.) Worker sit-ins and job protection: case studies of union intervention. Farnborough, Hants, [1977]. pp. 120. *bibliog.*

EMPLOYEES, TRAINING OF

— Cost effectiveness.

OATEY (MICHAEL JOHN) The cost-effectiveness of different media of instruction with special reference to industrial training. 1976. fo. 353. *bibliog. Typescript. Ph.D.(London) thesis: unpublished. This thesis is the property of London University and may not be removed from the Library.*

— United Kingdom.

KILLCROSS (M.C.) and BATES (W.T.G.) Selecting the younger trainee. London, H.M.S.O., 1975. pp. 28. *bibliog. (Training Information Papers. 8)*

PAPER AND PAPER PRODUCTS INDUSTRY TRAINING BOARD [U.K.]. About the Board. Potters Bar, [1977]. pp. 8.

PEARN (M.A.) Selecting and training coloured workers. London, H.M.S.O., 1977. pp. 46. *bibliog. (Training Information Papers. 9)*

EMPLOYEES' REPRESENTATION IN MANAGEMENT.

KARSTENS (DIRK) Die gesetzlichen Grundlagen und die arbeitswissenschaftlichen Aspekte für die Mitwirkung und Mitbestimmung an Massnahmen des Arbeitsstudiums im Industriebetrieb auf Grund des BetrVG 1972. Hamburg, 1976. pp. 223. *bibliog.*

AMERICAN ACADEMY OF POLITICAL AND SOCIAL SCIENCE. Annals. vol.431. Industrial democracy in international perspective; special editor of this volume John P. Windmuller. Philadelphia, [1977]. pp. 195.

CALVERT (JOHN ROBERT) Authority and democracy in industry: the relevance of theories of industrial democracy to contemporary industrial organizations. 1976[or rather 1977]. fo.456. *bibliog. Typescript. Ph.D.(London) thesis: unpublished. This thesis is the property of London University and may not be removed from the Library.*

VANEK (JAROSLAV) The labor-managed economy: essays. Ithaca, N.Y., 1977. pp. 287. *bibliogs.*

— Algeria.

INSTITUTE FOR WORKERS' CONTROL. International Studies in Industrial Democracy. No. 6. Self-management in Algeria: documents on the first phase. Nottingham, [1972?]. pp. 56.

— European Economic Community countries.

CARBY-HALL (JOSEPH ROGER) Worker participation in Europe. London, 1977. pp. 271.

— Germany.

GERMANY (BUNDESREPUBLIK).
Sachverständigenkommission zur Auswertung der bisherigen Erfahrungen bei der Mitbestimmung. 1976. The Biedenkopf report: co-determination in the company; report of the Commission of Experts set up to evaluate the experience to date of co-determination (Co-determination Commission), Bochum 1970; [Kurt H. Biedenkopf, chairman]; translated from the...German...by Duncan O'Neill. Belfast, [1976]. pp. 198.

MITBESTIMMUNG, Wirtschaftsordnung, Grundgesetz: Protokoll der Wissenschaftlichen Konferenz des Deutschen Gewerkschaftsbundes vom 1. bis 3. Oktober 1975 in Frankfurt am Main; Herausgeber: Heinz Oskar Vetter. Frankfurt am Main, 1976. pp. 408.

— Norway.

SKARD (ØYVIND) Democracy and the individual: some reflections on the process of democratization in working life. [Oslo, 1975?]. pp. 35.

EMERY (FREDERICK E.) and THORSRUD (EINAR) Democracy at work: the report of the Norwegian industrial democracy program. Leiden, 1976. pp. 179. *bibliog.*

— Poland.

MODLIŃSKI (EUGENIUSZ) Aspects juridiques de la représentation ouvrière dans les entreprises en Pologne. Warszawa, [1963]. pp. 19. *(Polska Akademia Nauk. Centre Scientifique à Paris. Conférences. Fascicule 33)*

— Portugal.

WORKERS' control in Portugal: a report by the British members of the second Russell Commission of Enquiry organized by the Russell Committee for Portugal. Nottingham, [1976]. pp. 15. *(Institute for Workers' Control. Pamphlet Series. No. 52)*

— Russia.

EHRHARDT (MANFRED) Mitsprache und Interessenvertretung der Belegschaft in den Industriebetrieben der Sowjetunion, etc. Hamburg, 1975. pp. 202. *bibliog. Inaugural-Dissertation zur Erlangung des Doktorgrades des Fachbereichs Wirtschaftswissenschaften der Universität Hamburg.*

COSTELLO (MICK) Workers' participation in the Soviet Union. Moscow, 1977. pp. 167.

— United Kingdom.

ANAGNOSTELIS (JOHN) The Scott Bader Commonwealth: practices, problems and possibilities;...paper presented at the international Seminar on Workers' Participation in Management held...at...Bologna... 1969. [1970?]. pp. 14. *bibliog. Unpublished: photocopy of typescript.*

GRAHAM (ALISTAIR) The workers' next step: the shop-floor struggle and workers' control. London, [1973]. pp. 20. *(Independent Labour Party. Square One Pamphlets. 8)*

AIMS OF INDUSTRY. Guide to industrial participation: essential steps: essential research. London, [1974?]. pp. 12.

BROWN (MICHAEL BARRATT) and COATES (KEN) Accountability and industrial democracy. Nottingham, [1975?]. pp. 13. *(Institute for Workers' Control. Pamphlet Series. No. 50)*

WARREN (BILL) and PRIOR (MIKE) Advanced capitalism and backward socialism. Nottingham, [1975]. pp. 27. *(Spokesman, The. Pamphlets. No. 46)*

LABOUR RESEARCH DEPARTMENT. Industrial democracy: a trade unionist's guide. London, 1976. pp. 39. *bibliog.*

SHARP (ELIZABETH B.) Democracy in industry. London, 1976. pp. 38. *bibliog.*

CAN workers manage?: post-Bullock essays in the economics of the inter-relationships between ownership, control and risk-taking in industry, with special reference to participation by employees; [by] Brian Chiplin [and others]. London, 1977. pp. 109. *bibliog. (Institute of Economic Affairs. Hobart Papers. 77)*

CITY COMPANY LAW COMMITTEE. A reply to Bullock. [London, 1977]. pp. 31.

DENTON (GEOFFREY) Beyond Bullock: economic implications of worker participation in control and ownership of industry. London, [1977]. pp. 25. *(Federal Trust for Education and Research. Federal Trust Reports)*

ELLIOTT (DAVID) The Lucas Aerospace workers' campaign. London, 1977. pp. 20. *(Young Fabian Pamphlets. 46)*

FATCHETT (DEREK J.) Industrial democracy: prospects after Bullock. [Leeds, 1977]. pp. 38. *bibliog. (Leeds. University and Nottingham. University. Occasional Papers in Industrial Relations. 2)*

GENERAL AND MUNICIPAL WORKERS' UNION. Industrial democracy in the light of Bullock. [London], 1977. fo. 10.

LONDON. Greater London Council. Members' Working Party on Industrial Democracy. Industrial democracy in local government: papers considered by a working party of GLC/ILEA members: together with the working party's final report. [London, 1977]. pp. 44.

NATIONAL AND LOCAL GOVERNMENT OFFICERS ASSOCIATION. Industrial democracy. [London], 1977. pp. 29.

NORTH LONDON WORKERS CONTROL GROUP. Bullock A-Z: a guide to the report of the Committee of Inquiry on Industrial Democracy. London, 1977. pp. 46.

SMITH (CYRIL) b.1928. Industrial participation. London, [1977]. pp. 174.

TRADES UNION CONGRESS. Industrial democracy: a statement of policy endorsed by the 1974 Trades Union Congress, together with the supplementary note of evidence submitted by the TUC to the Bullock Committee of Inquiry on Industrial Democracy endorsed by the 1976 Trades Union Congress. London, 1977. pp. 49.

TRADES UNION CONGRESS. TUC guide to the Bullock Report on Industrial Democracy. London, 1977. pp. 26.

WORKER directors speak; by the British Steel Corporation employee directors with John Bank and Ken Jones. Farnborough, Hants., [1977]. pp. 114.

— — Bibliography.

U.K. Parliament. House of Commons. Library. Research Division. Reference Sheets. 77/1. Evidence to the Bullock Committee on Industrial Democracy: [38 references] [London], 1977. pp. 4.

— — Scotland.

SCOTTISH COUNCIL (DEVELOPMENT AND INDUSTRY). Committee on Industrial and Social Conditions. Towards industrial democracy; a report on employee participation in Scotland. [Edinburgh], 1976. pp. 37.

— Yugoslavia.

INSTITUTE FOR WORKERS' CONTROL. International Studies in Industrial Democracy. No. 7. Self-management in Yugoslavia; [by] Bogdan Denitch. Nottingham, [1973?]. pp. 16.

VANEK (JAROSLAV) The labor-managed economy: essays. Ithaca, N.Y., 1977. pp. 287. *bibliogs.*

EMPLOYERS' ASSOCIATIONS

— Germany.

ECKARDT (GUENTHER) Industrie und Politik in Bayern, 1900-1919: der Bayerische Industriellen-Verband als Modell des Einflusses von Wirtschaftsverbänden. Berlin, [1976]. pp. 201. *bibliog. (Munich. Universität. Institut für Bayerische Geschichte. Beiträge zu einer Historischen Strukturanalyse Bayerns im Industriezeitalter. Band 15)*

ULLMANN (HANS PETER) Der Bund der Industriellen: Organisation, Einfluss und Politik klein- und mittelbetrieblicher Industrieller im Deutschen Kaiserreich, 1895-1914. Göttingen, 1976. pp. 464. bibliog.

— United Kingdom.

GRANT (WYN P.) and MARSH (DAVID) The Confederation of British Industry. London, 1977. pp. 226.

EMPLOYMENT (ECONOMIC THEORY).

INTERNATIONAL LABOUR OFFICE. World Employment Programme. 1974. World Employment Programme: a progress report on its research- oriented activities. Geneva, 1974. pp. 132.

INTERNATIONAL LABOUR OFFICE. World Employment Programme. 1976. World Employment Programme: research in retrospect and prospect. Geneva, 1976. pp. 278. *bibliog.*

— Mathematical models.

ROSE (PETER S.) and HUNT (LACY H.) Policy variables, unemployment and price level changes. [Washington, 1972]. pp. 11. *(United States. Board of Governors of the Federal Reserve System. Staff Economic Studies. No. 67) (Reprinted from The Southern Journal of Business, Vol. 6, No. 3, 1971)*

EMPLOYMENT FORECASTING

— Papua New Guinea.

PAPUA NEW GUINEA. Manpower Planning Unit. 1971. The demand for professional manpower in Papua and New Guinea, 1971-80. Port Moresby, 1971. fo.46.. (*Manpower Studies. No. 1*)

— United States.

WOOL (HAROLD) The labor supply for lower-level occupations:...assisted by Bruce Dana Phillips. New York, 1976. pp. 382. *bibliog.*

EMPLOYMENT MANAGEMENT.

THOMPSON (VICTOR A.) Without sympathy or enthusiasm: the problem of administrative compassion. University, Ala., [1975]. pp. 137. *bibliog.*

WEDER (WALTER) Die Einstellung des Mitarbeiters zum Führungsstil der Unternehmung. [Bern, 1976]. pp. 256. *bibliog. Dissertation der Universität Zürich zur Erlangung der Würde eines Doktors der Wirtschaftswissenschaft.*

ENCOMIENDAS (LATIN AMERICA).

RUIZ RIVERA (JULIAN BAUTISTA) Encomienda y mita en Nueva Granada en el siglo XVII. Sevilla, 1975. pp. 454. *(Consejo Superior de Investigaciones Científicas. Escuela de Estudios Hispanoamericanos de Sevilla. Publicaciones. 228)*

KEITH (ROBERT G.) Conquest and agrarian change: the emergence of the hacienda system on the Peruvian coast. Cambridge, Mass., 1976. pp. 176. *bibliog. (Harvard University. Harvard Historical Studies. vol. 93)*

ENDOWMENTS

— Germany.

WATSON (ALAN J.) The political foundations in West Germany. London, [1976?]. pp. 22.

ENERGY CONSERVATION.

HAYES (DENIS) Environmentalist. Energy: the case for conservation. [Washington, D.C.], 1976. pp. 77. *(Worldwatch Institute. Worldwatch Papers. No. 4)*

ORGANISATION FOR ECONOMIC CO-OPERATION AND DEVELOPMENT. Committee on Consumer Policy. 1976. The energy label a means of energy conservation: report, etc. Paris, 1976. pp. 47.

— United Kingdom.

ROBINSON (COLIN) and MORGAN (JON) Economic consequence of controlling the depletion of North Sea oil and gas. London, [1976]. pp. 31. *(Trade Policy Research Centre. Guest Papers. No. 3)*

— United States.

MITCHELL (EDWARD J.) and CHAFFETZ (PETER R.) Toward economy in electric power. Washington, 1975. pp. 32. *(American Enterprise Institute for Public Policy Research. National Energy Studies. 9)*

OSTHEIMER (JOHN M.) and RITT (LEONARD G.) Environment, energy, and black Americans. Beverly Hills, [1976]. pp. 38. *bibliog.*

ENERGY CONSUMPTION.

SOUTH AFRICA. Department of Planning and the Environment. 1975. Energy trends in the world with special reference to South Africa: a report for a subsidiary committee of the Prime Minister's Planning Advisory Council. [Pretoria, 1975]. pp. 121. *bibliog.*

— United Kingdom.

U.K. Working Group on Energy Elasticities. 1977. Report; [T.A. Kennedy, chairman]. London, 1977. pp. 55. *bibliog. (U.K. Department of Energy. Energy Papers. No. 17)*

ENERGY POLICY.

ENERGY policies of the world; edited by Gerard J. Mangone. New York, [1976 in progress]. *bibliog. Organized and edited at the Center for the Study of Marine Policy in the graduate College of Marine Studies of the University of Delaware.*

ATLANTIC COUNCIL OF THE UNITED STATES. Nuclear Fuels Policy Working Group. Nuclear fuels policy. Boulder, Col., 1976. pp. 136.

BUEHRING (W.A.) and others. Energy/environment management: application of decision analysis. Laxenburg, 1976. pp. 27. *bibliog. (International Institute for Applied Systems Analysis. Research Memoranda. RM-76-14)*

HANSEN (ROGER D.) The U.S. and world development: agenda for action, 1976. New York, 1976. pp. 222.

CONFERENCE ON ENERGY POLICIES AND THE INTERNATIONAL SYSTEM, CENTER FOR THE STUDY OF DEMOCRATIC INSTITUTIONS, 1973. Energy technology and global policy: a selection of contributing papers...; [edited by] Stephen Arthur Saltzman. Santa Barbara, Calif., [1977]. pp. 276. *bibliogs.*

GOALS for mankind: a report to the Club of Rome; [edited by] Ervin Laszlo. London, 1977. pp. 434. *bibliog. Fifth report to the Club of Rome.*

ORGANISATION FOR ECONOMIC CO-OPERATION AND DEVELOPMENT. 1977. World energy outlook: a reassessment of long term energy developments and related policies; a report by the Secretary- General. Paris, 1977. pp. 106.

— Environmental aspects.

ORGANISATION FOR ECONOMIC CO-OPERATION AND DEVELOPMENT. 1977. Energy production and environment. Paris, 1977. pp. 107. *bibliog.*

— Europe.

ODELL (PETER R.) The western European energy economy: challenges and opportunities. London, 1975. pp. 40. *(London. University. Stamp Memorial Lectures. 1975)*

CARMOY (GUY DE) Energy for Europe: economic and political implications. Washington, D.C., [1977]. pp. 120. *bibliogs. (American Enterprise Institute for Public Policy Research. AEI Studies. 146)*

— European Economic Community countries.

LUCAS (NIGEL J.D.) Energy and the European Communities. London, [1977]. pp. 175. *Published for the David Davies Memorial Institute of International Studies.*

— Germany.

HORN (MANFRED) Die Energiepolitik der Bundesregierung von 1958 bis 1972: zur Bedeutung der Penetration ausländischer Ölkonzerne in die Energiewirtschaft der BRD, etc. Berlin, [1977]. pp. 320. *bibliog.*

— Russia — Soviet Central Asia.

KIM (K.M.) Sovershenstvovanie struktury toplivno-energeticheskogo balansa Srednei Azii. Tashkent, 1973. pp. 220. *bibliog.*

— Underdeveloped areas.

See UNDERDEVELOPED AREAS — Energy policy.

— United Kingdom.

COUNTER INFORMATION SERVICES. Anti-Reports. No. 8. The oil fix: an investigation into the control and costs of energy. London, [1974]. pp. 49. *bibliog.*

LUBBOCK (ERIC REGINALD) 4th Baron Avebury. The energy crisis: growth, stability or collapse?. Walton-on-Thames, 1974. pp. 12. *(Conservation Society. Presidential Addresses. 1973)*

FABIAN SOCIETY. Fabian Tracts. [No.] 447. A policy for warmth; [by] M. Gray [and others]. London, 1977. pp. 23.

— United States.

BUCKNELL (HOWARD) Energy policy and naval strategy. Beverly Hills, [1975]. pp. 68. *bibliog.*

COMMONER (BARRY) The poverty of power: energy and the economic crisis. New York, 1976. pp. 314.

COPP (EMMANUEL ANTHONY) Regulating competition in oil: government intervention in the U.S. refinery industry, 1948-1975. College Station, Tex., [1976]. pp. 280. *bibliog. (Texas A and M University. Texas A and M University Economics Series. 1)*

CURRENT issues in social; policy edited by W. Boyd Littrell [and] Gideon Sjoberg. Beverly Hills, Calif., [1976]. pp. 248. *bibliogs. Papers prepared for an interdisciplinary conference held in 1975, at the University of Texas.*

ECONOMETRIC dimensions of energy demand and supply; edited by A. Bradley Askin and John Kraft. Lexington, Mass., [1976]. pp. 127. *bibliogs.*

ENERGY policy: a new war between the states?; (an AEI Round Table held on October 2, 1975...); Melvin R. Laird, moderator, etc. Washington, [1976]. pp. 35. *(American Enterprise Institute for Public Policy Research. Round Tables)*

ENERGY supply and government policy; edited by Robert J. Kalter and William A. Vogely. Ithaca, N.Y., 1976. pp. 356.

McFARLAND (ANDREW S.) Public interest lobbies: decision making on energy. Washington, D.C., [1976]. pp. 141. *(American Enterprise Institute for Public Policy Research. National Energy Studies. 14)*

O'TOOLE (JAMES) Energy and social change. Cambridge, Mass., [1976]. pp. 185. *bibliog. Based on research by the Center for Futures Research at the University of Southern California.*

OUR energy future: the role of research, development and demonstration in reaching a national consensus on energy supply; [by] Don E. Kash [and others]. Norman, Okla., 1976. pp. 489. *bibliogs. Based on a study of U.S. energy supply by a research team of the Science and Public Policy Program at the University of Oklahoma.*

TELLER (EDWARD) and others. Power and security. Lexington, Mass., [1976]. pp. 204. *(Commission on Critical Choices for Americans. Critical Choices for Americans. vol. 4)*

WEIDENBAUM (MURRAY L.) and others. Government credit subsidies for energy development. Washington, [1976]. pp. 55. *(American Enterprise Institute for Public Policy Research. AEI Studies. No. 137)*

ENGLER (ROBERT) The brotherhood of oil: energy policy and the public interest. Chicago, 1977. pp. 337.

— — Congresses.

ENERGY: regional goals and the national interest; edited by Edward J. Mitchell. Washington, D.C., [1976]. pp. 101. *A conference sponsored by the National Energy Project of the American Enterprise Institute for Public Policy Research.*

ENGELS (FRIEDRICH).

KARL Marx und Friedrich Engels: die Begründer des wissenschaftlichen Sozialismus; die Bedeutung des "Manifests der Kommunistischen Partei". Berlin, 1953. pp. 72. *bibliog. (Sozialistische Einheitspartei Deutschlands. Zentralkomitee. Abteilung Propaganda. Lehrmaterial für das Parteilehrjahr)*

BARTEL (HORST) Friedrich Engels' Kampf für die Schaffung einer marxistischen Arbeiterpartei in Deutschland: Engels-Konferenz, Berlin, 1955. Berlin, 1956. pp. 96.

ENGELS (FRIEDRICH).(Cont.)

SELSAM (HOWARD) and others, eds. Dynamics of social change: a reader in Marxist social science from the writings of Marx, Engels and Lenin; selected and edited with introduction and notes. New York, [1970]. pp. 416. *bibliog.*

IOVCHUK (MIKHAIL TRIFONOVICH) and others, eds. F. Engel's i sovremennye problemy filosofii marksizma. Moskva, 1971. pp. 567.

SOCIETY and revolution: essays in honour of Engels. New Delhi, 1971. pp. 236.

GOSSLING (WILLIAM FRANK) Some productive consequences of Engels' law. [London], 1974. pp. 20. *bibliog. (Input-Output Research Association. Occasional Papers. No. 2)*

GUREVICH (SEMEN MOISEEVICH) Razoblachenie lzhivoi legendy: K. Marks i F. Engel's o burzhuaznoi pechati. Moskva, 1975. pp. 255.

Der KAMPF von Karl Marx und Friedrich Engels um die revolutionäre Partei der deutschen Arbeiterklasse. Berlin, 1977. pp. 256. *bibliog. (Berlin. Parteihochschule Karl Marx. Lehrstuhl Geschichte der SED. Vorlesungen)*

WESSEL (HARALD) Marginalien zur MEGA [Marx-Engels-Gesamtausgabe] nebst Randglossen über alte und neue "Marxologen". Berlin, 1977. pp. 114.

— Portraits, caricatures, etc.

KARL Marks, Fridrikh Engel's: sobranie fotografii; [Karl Marx, Friedrich Engels: a collection of photographs] . Moskva, 1976. pp. 285. *In Russian, German, English and French.*

ENGINEERING

— Germany.

LUDWIG (KARL HEINZ) Technik und Ingenieure im Dritten Reich. Düsseldorf, [1974]. pp. 544. *bibliog.*

— United Kingdom — Scotland.

MOSS (MICHAEL S.) and HUME (JOHN R.) Workshop of the British Empire: engineering and shipbuilding in the west of Scotland. London, 1977. pp. 192. *bibliog.*

ENGINEERING AS A PROFESSION.

OPPELT (CLAUS) Ingenieure im Beruf: eine empirische Analyse zertifikatsspezifischer Unterschiede im beruflichen Einsatz technischer Arbeitskräfte. Berlin, 1976. pp. 223. *bibliog. (Max-Planck-Institut für Bildungsforschung. Studien und Berichte. 37) With English summary.*

ENGINEERS

— Germany.

OPPELT (CLAUS) Ingenieure im Beruf: eine empirische Analyse zertifikatsspezifischer Unterschiede im beruflichen Einsatz technischer Arbeitskräfte. Berlin, 1976. pp. 223. *bibliog. (Max-Planck-Institut für Bildungsforschung. Studien und Berichte. 37) With English summary.*

— Ireland (Republic).

EIRE. Central Statistics Office. 1968. Engineering manpower survey, 1968. Dublin, 1968. pp. 23.

— United Kingdom.

COMMITTEE ON THE SUPPLY AND UTILISATION OF SKILLED ENGINEERING MANPOWER [U.K.]. Engineering craftsmen: shortages and related problems; a report; [Sir Ronald McIntosh, chairman]. London, National Economic Development Office, 1977. pp. 51.

ENGLISH LANGUAGE

— Dictionaries.

6,000 words: a supplement to Webster's third new international dictionary. Springfield, Mass., [1976]. pp. 220.

FOWLER (HENRY WATSON) and FOWLER (FRANCIS GEORGE) The concise Oxford dictionary of current English; based on the Oxford English dictionary and its supplements...; sixth edition edited by J.B. Sykes. 6th ed. London, 1976. pp. 1368.

— — Italian.

CENTRO LESSICOGRAFICO SANSONI. Dizionario delle lingue italiana e inglese;...realizzato... sotto la direzione di Vladimiro Macchi. Firenze, 1970-76. 4 vols.

— — Polyglot.

ZAHN (HANS E.) Wörterbuch zur Politik und Wirtschaftspolitik. Band I: deutsch-englisch-französisch:...Dictionary of politics and economic policy...: Dictionnaire politique et de politique économique, etc. Frankfurt am Main, [1975]. pp. 382. *bibliog.*

— — Russian.

TSAGOLOVA (R.S.) ed. Anglo-russkii ekonomicheskii slovar': uchebnyi; English- Russian learner's dictionary of economic terminology. Moskva, 1976. pp. 334.

— Grammar.

MONTAGUE grammar; edited by Barbara H. Partee. New York, [1976]. pp. 370. *bibliogs.*

— Study and teaching.

MOBBS (MICHAEL C.) Meeting their needs: an account of language tuition schemes for ethnic minority women. London, Community Relations Commission, 1977. pp. 64. *bibliog.*

ENGLISH LITERATURE

— History and criticism.

KELLY (GARY) The English Jacobin novel, 1780-1805. Oxford, 1976. pp. 291. *bibliog.*

BRANTLINGER (PATRICK) The spirit of reform: British literature and politics, 1832-1867. Cambridge, Mass., 1977. pp. 293.

BROWN (JAMES MELVILLE) A sociological analysis of the novels of Charles Dickens. 1977. fo. 340. *bibliog. Typescript. Ph.D. (London) thesis: unpublished. This thesis is the property of London University and may not be removed from the Library.*

HALPERIN (JOHN) Trollope and politics: a study of the Pallisers and others. London, 1977. pp. 318. *bibliog.*

ENGLISH NEWSPAPERS.

LONDON PRESS EXCHANGE. A survey of reader interest in the national morning and London evening press. London, 1934. 3 vols.

BASNETT (DAVID) and GOODMAN (GEOFFREY) Royal Commission on the Press: minority report. London, 1977. pp. 18.

BOYD-BARRETT (OLIVER) and others. Studies on the press. London, 1977. pp. 397. *(U.K. Royal Commission on the Press, 1974. Working Papers. No.3)*

ENGLISH PERIODICALS.

SPIERS (JOHN) compiler. The underground and alternative press in Britain: a bibliographical guide with historical notes. Hassocks, 1974. pp. 77.

— Bibliography.

HARRISON (ROYDEN JOHN) and others, compilers. The Warwick guide to British labour periodicals, 1790-1970: a check list. Hassocks, 1977. pp. 685.

ENLIGHTENMENT.

Les LUMIÈRES et la formation de la conscience nationale chez les peuples du Sud-Est européen: actes du Colloque international organisé par la Commission de l'AIESEE pour l'histoire des idées...Paris, 11-12 avril 1968. Bucarest, 1970. pp. 129.

DONOVAN (ARTHUR L.) Philosophical chemistry in the Scottish Enlightenment: the doctrines and discoveries of William Cullen and Joseph Black. Edinburgh, [1975]. pp. 343. *bibliog.*

REILL (PETER HANNS) The German Enlightenment and the rise of historicism. Berkeley, Calif., 1975. pp. 308. *bibliog.*

CHITNIS (ANAND C.) The Scottish Enlightenment: a social history. London, 1976. pp. 279. *bibliog.*

ENTREPRENEUR.

NAFZIGER (E. WAYNE) African capitalism: a case study in Nigerian entrepreneurship. Stanford, Calif., 1977. pp. 293. *bibliog. (Stanford University. Hoover Institution on War, Revolution and Peace. Hoover Institution Publications. 169)*

ENVIRONMENTAL IMPACT STATEMENTS.

CATLOW (JOHN) and THIRLWALL (C. GEOFFREY) Environmental impact analysis; a study prepared for the Secretaries of State for the Environment, Scotland and Wales. [London, 1976]. pp. 116. *bibliog. (U.K. Department of the Environment. Research Reports. 11)*

ENVIRONMENTAL impact assessment; edited by T. O'Riordan, R.D. Hey. Westmead, Farnborough, [1976]. pp. 232. *Contains papers and discussion of a seminar sponsored by the Ford Foundation.*

RODGERS (JOSEPH LEE) Environmental impact assessment, growth management, and the comprehensive plan. Cambridge, Mass., [1976]. pp. 185. *bibliog.*

ENVIRONMENTAL LAW.

HALLMAN (ROBERT MARSHALL) Towards an environmentally sound law of the sea. [Washington, D.C., 1974]. pp. 83. *A report of the International Institute for Environment and Development.*

— United States.

ANDREWS (RICHARD N.L.) Environmental policy and administrative change: implementation of the National Environmental Policy Act of 1969. Lexington, Mass., [1976]. pp. 230.

DIMENTO (JOSEPH F.) Managing environmental change: a legal and behavioral perspective. New York, 1976. pp. 218. *bibliog.*

ENVIRONMENTAL POLICY.

DEVELOPMENT and environment: report and working papers of a panel of experts convened by the Secretary-General of the United Nations Conference on the Human Environment, Founex, Switzerland, June 4-12, 1971. Paris, 1972. pp. 225. *(Environment and Social Sciences. 1)*

UNEP:... annual review; by the Executive Director, (United Nations Environment Programme). a., 1975 (1st)- Nairobi.

BUEHRING (W.A.) and others. Energy/environment management: application of decision analysis. Laxenburg, 1976. pp. 27. *bibliog. (International Institute for Applied Systems Analysis. Research Memoranda. RM-76-14)*

HABITAT: UNITED NATIONS CONFERENCE ON HUMAN SETTLEMENTS, VANCOUVER, 1976. Global review of human settlements: a support paper for Habitat: United Nations Conference on Human Settlements; (with Statistical annex) (A/CONF.70/A/1 and A/CONF.70/A/1 Add.1). Oxford, 1976. 2 vols.

HABITAT: UNITED NATIONS CONFERENCE ON HUMAN SETTLEMENTS, VANCOUVER, 1976. Report of Habitat:...Vancouver, 31 May - 11 June 1976. (A/CONF.70/15). New York, 1976. pp. 183.

PROBLEMA okruzhaiushchei sredy v mirovoi ekonomike i mezhdunarodnykh otnosheniiakh. Moskva, 1976. pp. 359.

RESOURCES and the environment: a socialist perspective; edited by Michael Barratt Brown [and others]. Nottingham, 1976. pp. 157. *Papers based on the materials prepared for a 1975 Spokesman conference on the environment.*

STRATEGIES for human settlements: habitat and environment; edited by Gwen Bell. Honolulu, [1976]. pp. 172.

VEREIN FÜR SOZIALPOLITIK. Schriften. Neue Folge. Band 91. Ökonomische Probleme der Umweltschutzpolitik; von Karl-Heinrich Hansmeyer [and others]; herausgegeben von Otmar Issing. Berlin, [1976]. pp. 161. *bibliogs.*

HARVEY (BRIAN W.) and HALLETT (JOHN D.) Environment and society: an introductory analysis. London, 1977. pp. 163. *bibliog.*

HJALTE (KRISTER) and others. Environmental policy and welfare economics;... translated by Curt Wells. Cambridge, 1977. pp. 111. *bibliog.*

OPHULS (WILLIAM) Ecology and the politics of scarcity: prologue to a political theory of the steady state. San Francisco, [1977]. pp. 303. *bibliog.*

— Canada.

CANADIAN ENVIRONMENTAL ADVISORY COUNCIL. Annual review. a., 1973/1974- Ottawa. *[In English and French].*

— Europe.

EUROPEAN NATIONAL STUDENT ORGANISATIONS. European Meeting, 10th, Helsinki, 1972. Environmental pollution: an all-European problem. Prague, [1972]. pp. 31.

— European Economic Community countries.

EUROPEAN COMMUNITIES. Commission. 1976. (European Community action programme on the environment 1977- 1981): continuation and implementation of a European Community policy and action programme on the environment; draft resolution of the Council, presented...on 24 March 1976. [Brussels], 1976. pp. 51. *(Bulletin of the European Communities. Supplements. [1976/6])*

STATE OF THE ENVIRONMENT; (pd. by) Commission of the European Communities. irreg., 1977(1st)- Brussels.

— France.

FRANCE. Commission Agriculture-Environnement. 1975. Agriculture, environnement: éléments pour une évaluation de l'espace rural. Paris, La Documentation Française, 1975. pp. 191. *(Environnement. 43)*

— Sweden.

ORGANISATION FOR ECONOMIC CO-OPERATION AND DEVELOPMENT. 1977. Environmental policy in Sweden. Paris, 1977. pp. 144.

— United Kingdom.

CIVIC TRUST. The local amenity movement; [including chapters by Anthony Barker]. London, 1976. pp. 36.

ENVIRONMENTAL impact assessment; edited by T. O'Riordan, R.D. Hey. Westmead, Farnborough, [1976]. pp. 232. *Contains papers and discussion of a seminar sponsored by the Ford Foundation.*

ENVIRONMENTAL BOARD [U.K.]. First progress report to the Secretary of State for the Environment. London, H.M.S.O., 1977. pp. 10.

HOUSE (JOHN WILLIAM) ed. The U.K. space: resources, environment and the future. 2nd ed. London, 1977. pp. 528. *bibliogs.*

— — Bibliography.

LAMBERT (CLAIRE M.) compiler. The Department of the Environment: organisation and functions. rev. ed. [London, 1976]. pp. 71. *(U.K. Department of the Environment. Library. Bibliographies. No. 158[a])*

— — Ireland, Northern.

ULSTER COMMENTARY. Special Issues. Northern Ireland: development signposts to a better future. [Belfast, 1972]. pp. 16.

IRELAND, NORTHERN. Department of the Environment. Annual report. a., 1974/75 [1st]- Belfast.

— — Wales.

WELSH DEVELOPMENT AGENCY. Welsh Development Agency: a statement of policies and programmes. Pontypridd, 1977. pp. 12.

— United States.

ENVIRONMENTAL BULLETIN: reports from the UK Scientific Mission; issued by the Overseas Technical Information Unit (Department of Trade and Industry) [U.K.]. irreg. London. *Current issues only kept.*

DIMENTO (JOSEPH F.) Managing environmental change: a legal and behavioral perspective. New York, 1976. pp. 218. *bibliog.*

ENVIRONMENTAL controls: the impact on industry; edited by Robert A. Leone. Lexington, Mass., [1976]. pp. 129.

JONES (CHARLES OSCAR) and THOMAS (ROBERT D.) eds. Public policy making in a federal system. Beverly Hills, Calif., [1976]. pp. 284. *bibliogs.*

RODGERS (JOSEPH LEE) Environmental impact assessment, growth management, and the comprehensive plan. Cambridge, Mass., [1976]. pp. 185. *bibliog.*

WHEN values conflict: essays on environmental analysis, discourse and decision; edited by Laurence H. Tribe [and others]. Cambridge, Mass., [1976]. pp. 178. *Essays arising from a research project carried out by the American Academy of Arts and Sciences.*

WHITAKER (JOHN C.) Striking a balance: environment and natural resources policy in the Nixon-Ford years. Washington, D.C., [1976]. pp. 344. *(American Enterprise Institute for Public Policy Research and Stanford University. Hoover Institution on War, Revolution and Peace. AEI-Hoover Policy Studies. 21)*

— — Citizen participation.

CALDWELL (LYNTON KEITH) and others. Citizens and the environment: case studies in popular action. Bloomington , Ind., [1976]. pp. 449. *bibliog.*

ENVIRONMENTAL POLICY RESEARCH

— United Kingdom.

EVERSLEY (DAVID EDWARD CHARLES) and MOODY (MARY) The growth of planning research since the early 1960s: report to the S[ocial] S[cience] R[esearch] C[ouncil] Planning Committee. London, Social Science Research Council, [1976]. pp. 87. *bibliog.*

ENVIRONMENTAL PROTECTION.

PROBLEMA okruzhaiushchei sredy v mirovoi ekonomike i mezhdunarodnykh otnosheniiakh. Moskva, 1976. pp. 359.

ECONOMICS in institutional perspective: memorial essays in honor of K. William Kapp; edited by Rolf Steppacher [and others]. Lexington, Mass., [1977]. pp. 226. *bibliog.*

ORGANISATION FOR ECONOMIC CO-OPERATION AND DEVELOPMENT. 1977. Energy production and environment. Paris, 1977. pp. 107. *bibliog.*

— Cost effectiveness.

MARQUAND (JUDITH) Economic information for environmental, anti-pollution, policy. London, H.M.S.O., 1977. pp. 47. *bibliog. (Government Economic Service Occasional Papers. 13)*

— Mathematical models.

LIPNOWSKI (IRWIN FRANK) Environmental aspects of a steady state economy. 1976. fo. 187. *bibliog. Typescript. Ph.D.(London) thesis: unpublished. This thesis is the property of London University and may not be removed from the Library.*

— Bering Sea region.

YOUNG (ORAN R.) Resource management at the international level: the case of the north Pacific. London, 1977. pp. 252.

— Canada.

CANADA. Department of the Environment. 1972. Canada and the human environment; (a contribution by the government of Canada to the United Nations Conference on the Human Environment, Stockholm, 1972). Ottawa, 1972. pp. 92.

CANADIAN ENVIRONMENTAL ADVISORY COUNCIL. Annual review. a., 1973/1974- Ottawa. *[In English and French].*

— European Economic Community countries.

STATE OF THE ENVIRONMENT; (pd. by) Commission of the European Communities. irreg., 1977(1st)- Brussels.

— Russia.

KOLBASOV (OLEG STEPANOVICH) Ekologiia: politika - pravo: pravovaia okhrana prirody v SSSR; (Ecology: policy - law: legal protection of the environment in the USSR). Moskva, 1976. pp. 230. *With English table of contents.*

— United Kingdom.

DIGEST OF ENVIRONMENTAL STATISTICS: environmental protection and conservation; [pd. by] Department of the Environment. a., 1976 (1st)- London.

ENVIRONMENTAL standards: a description of United Kingdom practice; the report of an inter-departmental working party. London, H.M.S.O., 1977. pp. 30. *(Pollution Papers. No. 11)*

— United States.

OSTHEIMER (JOHN M.) and RITT (LEONARD G.) Environment, energy, and black Americans. Beverly Hills, [1976]. pp. 38. *bibliog.*

ENVIRONMENTAL BULLETIN: reports from the UK Scientific Mission; issued by the Overseas Technical Information Unit (Department of Trade and Industry) [U.K.]. irreg. London. *Current issues only kept.*

EPIDEMICS.

McNEILL (WILLIAM HARDY) Plagues and peoples. Oxford, 1977. pp. 369.

EQUAL PAY FOR EQUAL WORK

— United Kingdom.

COUSSINS (JEAN) The equality report: one year of the Equal Pay Act, the Sex Discrimination Act, the Equal Opportunities Commission. London, [1976]. pp. 123.

EQUALITY.

ROUSSEAU (JEAN JACQUES) The first and second discourses; edited, with introduction and notes, by Roger D. Masters; translated by Roger D. and Judith R. Masters. New York, [1964]. pp. 248.

BERTHOUD (RICHARD) The disadvantages of inequality: a study of social deprivation; a PEP report. London, 1976. pp. 207.

DAHRENDORF (RALF) Inequality, hope, and progress. Liverpool, 1976. pp. 17. *(Eleanor Rathbone Memorial Trust. Eleanor Rathbone Memorial Lectures. 22)*

ERICSSON (LARS O.) Justice in the distribution of economic resources: a critical and normative study. Stockholm, [1976]. pp. 150. *bibliog. (Stockholms Universitet. Acta Universitatis Stockholmiensis. Stockholm Studies in Philosophy. 6)*

NEAVE (GUY R.) Patterns of equality: the influence of new structures in European higher education upon the equality of educational opportunity. Windsor, Berks, 1976. pp. 150.

OFFE (CLAUS) Industry and inequality: the achievement principle in work and social status;...translated by James Wickham. London, 1976. pp. 158. *bibliog.*

SIMMONS (D.A.) Economic power. Northolt, Middx., 1976. pp. 192. *bibliog.*

TRANSPORT AND GENERAL WORKERS' UNION. Inequality: the evidence...to the Royal Commission on the Distribution of Income and Wealth. Nottingham, 1976. pp. 183.

BETEILLE (ANDRE) Inequality among men. Oxford, [1977]. pp. 178.

BOWIE (NORMAN E.) and SIMON (ROBERT L.) The individual and political order: an introduction to social and political philosophy. Englewood Cliffs, [1977]. pp. 280. *bibliogs.*

COATES (BRYAN ELLIS) and others. Geography and inequality. Oxford, 1977. pp. 292. *bibliog.*

CURTIS (RICHARD FARNSWORTH) and JACKSON (ELTON F.) Inequality in American communities. New York, [1977]. pp. 354. *bibliog.*

ROBBINS (LIONEL CHARLES) Baron Robbins. Liberty and equality. London, 1977. pp. 24. *bibliog. (Institute of Economic Affairs. Occasional Papers. 52)*

VAN DEN BERGHE (PIERRE LOUIS) and PRIMOV (GEORGE P.) Inequality in the Peruvian Andes: class and ethnicity in Cuzco. Columbia, Mo., [1977]. pp. 324. *bibliog.*

EQUALITY BEFORE THE LAW

— United States.

WARE (GILBERT) From the black bar: voices for equal justice. New York, [1976]. pp. 341.

EQUALITY OF STATES.

MANUKIAN (KAMO ADIBEKOVICH) Printsip ravnopraviia gosudarstv v mezhdunarodnom prave. Erevan, 1975. pp. 201. *bibliog.*

EQUATORIAL GUINEA

— Politics and government.

CRONJÉ (SUZANNE) Equatorial Guinea: the forgotten dictatorship: forced labour and political murder in Central Africa. London, [1976]. pp. 43. *(Anti-Slavery Society. Research Reports. No. 2)*

EQUILIBRIUM (ECONOMICS).

FITOUSSI (JEAN PAUL) Inflation, équilibre et chômage. Paris, [1973]. pp. 294,(95). *bibliog.*

DIXIT (AVINASH K.) The theory of equilibrium growth. London, 1976. pp. 204. *bibliog.*

MUSSA (MICHAEL) A study in macroeconomics. Amsterdam, 1976. pp. 316. *bibliog.*

— Mathematical models.

LIPNOWSKI (IRWIN FRANK) Environmental aspects of a steady state economy. 1976. fo. 187. *bibliog. Typescript. Ph.D.(London) thesis: unpublished. This thesis is the property of London University and may not be removed from the Library.*

SVENSSON (LARS E.O.) On competitive markets and intertemporal resource allocation. Stockholm, 1976. 1 vol. (various pagings). *bibliogs.*

EREMEEV (KONSTANTIN STEPANOVICH).

BULATSKII (GRIGORII VASIL'EVICH) K.S. Eremeev - revoliutsioner, publitsist. Minsk, 1976. pp. 215.

ERLER (FRITZ).

ERLER (HANS) Fritz Erler contra Willy Brandt: Demokratie oder Volksfront in Europa. Stuttgart, 1976. pp. 208.

ERZBERGER (MATTHIAS).

RUGE (WOLFGANG) Matthias Erzberger: eine politische Biographie. Berlin, [1976]. pp. 143.

ESCOFET I ALSINA (FREDERIC).

ESCOFET I ALSINA (FREDERIC) Al servei de Catalunya i de la Republica. Paris, 1973. 2 vols.(in 1).

ESPIONAGE, GERMAN

— South Africa.

VISSER (GEORGE CLOETE) OB: traitors or patriots?. Johannesburg, 1976. pp. 216.

ESSEX

— Social conditions.

WAKEFIELD (EDWARD) 1774-1854. A letter to the land owners and other contributors to the poor's rates, in the Hundred of Dangye, in Essex. London, Johnson, [1802]. pp. 67.

ESTABLET (ROGER).

SNYDERS (GEORGES) Ecole, classe et lutte des classes: une relecture critique de Baudelot-Establet, Bourdieu-Passeron et Illich. Paris, [1976]. pp. 379.

ESTATE PLANNING

— United Kingdom.

RAY (RALPH P.) and others. Practical capital transfer tax planning. London, 1977. pp. 274.

ESTIMATION THEORY.

PESARAN (BAHRAM) Estimation of dynamic economic models when variables are subject to measurement errors. 1977. fo. 143. *bibliog. Typescript. Ph.D. (London) thesis: unpublished. This thesis is the property of London University and may not be removed from the Library.*

ESTONIA

— Constitutional history.

VARMA (ALEKSANDER) Die historischen, politischen und rechtlichen Grundlagen des Freistaates Estland; (aus dem Estnischen von Erik Thomson). Stockholm, 1960. pp. 32.

— Economic conditions.

LIIV (OTTO) Die wirtschaftliche Lage des estnischen Gebietes am Ausgang des XVII. Jahrhunderts. vol. I. Allgemeiner Überblick, Getreideproduktion und Getreidehandel. Tartu, 1935. pp. 336. *bibliog. (Õpetatud Eesti Selts. Toimetised. 27)*

— History.

PRUUDEN (SALME) Panslavism and Russian communism. London, 1976. pp. 59.

— Industries.

TARMISTO (VELLO IULIUSOVICH) Vnutriraionnaia territorial'naia organizatsiia proizvodstva: na materiale Estonskoi SSR. Tallin, 1975. pp. 279. *With English summary.*

— Politics and government.

PARMING (TÖNU) The collapse of liberal democracy and the rise of authoritarianism in Estonia. London, [1975]. pp. 74. *bibliog.*

ETHICS.

POPPER-LYNKEUS (JOSEF) Das Individuum und die Bewertung menschlicher Existenzen. Dresden, 1910. pp. 223.

MILL (JOHN STUART) (Collected works of John Stuart Mill. vol. 10). Essays on ethics, religion and society; editor of the text, J.M. Robson; introduction, F.E.L. Priestley; essays on Mill's Utilitarianism, D.P. Dryer. Toronto, [1969]. pp. 578. *bibliog.*

BRISTOL CONFERENCE ON CRITICAL PHILOSOPHY, 1ST, UNIVERSITY OF BRISTOL, [1973?] Practical reason:; (proceedings of the...conference) edited by Stephan Körner. Oxford, [1974]. pp. 264. *Held under the auspices of The Society for the Furtherance of Critical Philosophy and the University of Bristol.*

BENSON (GEORGE CHARLES SUMNER) and ENGEMAN (THOMAS S.) Amoral America. Stanford, Calif., 1975. pp. 294. *bibliog. (Stanford University. Hoover Institution on War, Revolution and Peace. Hoover Institution Publications. 150)*

KAPLAN (MORTON A.) Justice, human nature, and political obligation. New York, [1976]. pp. 283.

IRWIN (TERENCE) Plato's moral theory: the early and middle dialogues. Oxford, 1977. pp. 376. *bibliog.*

— History — Russia.

OCHERKI istorii russkoi eticheskoi mysli. Moskva, 1976. pp. 400.

ETHIOPIA

— Boundaries — Sudan.

ALI TAHA (FAISAL ABDEL RAHMAN) The settlement of the Sudan-Ethiopia boundary dispute. Khartoum, 1975. pp. 34.

— Economic conditions.

REHAB: drought and famine in Ethiopia; editor Abdul Mejid Hussein. London, [1976]. pp. 121. *bibliogs. (International African Institute and Environment Training Programme. African Environment Special Reports. 2)*

— Economic policy.

ETHIOPIA. Ministry of Planning and Development. 1967. Forms and explanations for the detailed guidance of the planning committees and units in the ministries and agencies: capital project inventory. Addis Ababa, 1967. 1 pamphlet (various foliations).

ETHIOPIA. Ministry of Planning and Development. 1967. Memorandum on the establishment of appropriate machinery at the central government level for preparation of the third five-year development plan. Addis Ababa, 1967. fo. 19.

GYENGE (ZOLTÁN) Ethiopia on the road of non-capitalist development. Budapest, 1976. pp. 48. *(Magyar Tudományos Akadémia. Világgazdasági Kutató Intézet. Studies on Developing Countries. No. 90)*

— Famines.

The UNKNOWN famine. London, 1973. fo. 6. *(Thames Television. This Week) Transcript of a report on the famine in Ethiopia transmitted on 18 October 1973.*

LUNDSTRÖM (KARL JOHAN) North-eastern Ethiopia: society in famine: a study of three social institutions in a period of severe strain. Uppsala, 1976. pp. 80. *bibliog. (Nordiska Afrikainstitutet. Research Reports. No. 34)*

REHAB: drought and famine in Ethiopia; editor Abdul Mejid Hussein. London, [1976]. pp. 121. *bibliogs. (International African Institute and Environment Training Programme. African Environment Special Reports. 2)*

— Foreign relations.

RUBENSON (SVEN) The survival of Ethiopian independence. London, 1976. pp. 437. *bibliog. (Lund. Universitet. Historiska Institutionen. Lund Studies in International History. [No]. 7)*

— History.

RUBENSON (SVEN) The survival of Ethiopian independence. London, 1976. pp. 437. *bibliog. (Lund. Universitet. Historiska Institutionen. Lund Studies in International History. [No]. 7)*

— Politics and government.

GYENGE (ZOLTÁN) Ethiopia on the road of non-capitalist development. Budapest, 1976. pp. 48. *(Magyar Tudományos Akadémia. Világgazdasági Kutató Intézet. Studies on Developing Countries. No. 90)*

LUNDSTRÖM (KARL JOHAN) North-eastern Ethiopia: society in famine: a study of three social institutions in a period of severe strain. Uppsala, 1976. pp. 80. *bibliog. (Nordiska Afrikainstitutet. Research Reports. No. 34)*

HAMILTON (DAVID) Writer on Ethiopia. Ethiopia's embattled revolutionaries. London, 1977. pp. 20. *(Institute for the Study of Conflict. Conflict Studies. No. 82)*

— Population.

ETHIOPIA. Central Statistical Office. 1974-1975. Results of the national sample survey, second round. Vols. 1,3-5. Addis Ababa, 1974-1975. 4 vols. *(Statistical Bulletins. 10)*

ETHIOPIA. Central Statistical Office. 1975. Results of urban survey, second round: tables of demographic data for ninety new towns. Addis Ababa, 1975. 3 pts. (in 1 vol.) *(Statistical Bulletins. 12)*

HAILE (DANIEL) and YIMER (ERKU) Law and population growth in Ethiopia. Medford, Mass., 1976. pp. 52. *(Tufts University. Fletcher School of Law and Diplomacy. Law and Population Monograph Series. No. 35)*

— Social policy.

ETHIOPIA. Ministry of Planning and Development. 1967. Memorandum on the establishment of appropriate machinery at the central government level for preparation of the third five-year development plan. Addis Ababa, 1967. fo. 19.

ETHNIC ATTITUDES.

STYMEIST (DAVID H.) Ethnics and Indians: social relations in a northwestern Ontario town. Toronto, [1975]. pp. 98. *bibliog.*

MERTON (ROBERT KING) Sociological ambivalence and other essays. New York, [1976]. pp. 287.

ALATAS (SYED HUSSEIN) The myth of the lazy native: a study of the image of the Malays, Filipinos and Javanese from the 16th to the 20th century and its function in the ideology of colonial capitalism. London, 1977. pp. 267. *bibliog.*

AMERICAN ACADEMY OF POLITICAL AND SOCIAL SCIENCE. Annals. vol. 433. Ethnic conflict in the world today; special editor of this volume, Martin O. Heisler. Philadelphia, 1977. pp. 220.

ETHNICITY.

POLL (SOLOMON) and KRAUSZ (ERNEST) eds. On ethnic and religious diversity in Israel. Ramat-Gan, 1975. pp. 124. *bibliog.*

ETHNICITY in an international context; edited by Abdul Said and Luiz R. Simmons. New Brunswick, N.J., [1976]. pp. 241. *bibliog.*

PLURALISM in a democratic society; edited by Melvin M. Tumin and Walter Plotch. New York, 1977. pp. 248. *bibliogs. Based on a conference convened by the Anti-Defamation League of B'nai B'rith, held in April 1975 in New York.*

VAN DEN BERGHE (PIERRE LOUIS) and PRIMOV (GEORGE P.) Inequality in the Peruvian Andes: class and ethnicity in Cuzco. Columbia, Mo., [1977]. pp. 324. *bibliog.*

ETHNOLOGY.

CASCUDO (LUIS DA CAMARA) Civilização e cultura: pesquisas e notas de etnografia geral. Rio, 1973. 2 vols. *bibliog.*

GODELIER (MAURICE) Perspectives in marxist anthropology; translated by Robert Brain. Cambridge, 1977. pp. 243.

RADCLIFFE-BROWN (ALFRED REGINALD) The social anthropology of Radcliffe-Brown; edited by Adam Kuper. London, 1977. pp. 296. *bibliog.*

— Afghanistan.

BLANC (JEAN CHARLES) L'Afghanistan et ses populations. [Paris, 1976]. pp. 166. *bibliog.*

— Africa.

VAN DEN BERGHE (PIERRE LOUIS) ed. Race and ethnicity in Africa. Nairobi, 1975. pp. 357. *bibliog.*

— Africa, Subsaharan.

BOZEMAN (ADDA BRUEMMER) Conflict in Africa: concepts and realities. Princeton, N.J., 1976. pp. 429. *bibliog.*

MAIR (LUCY PHILIP) African kingdoms. Oxford, 1977. pp. 151. *bibliog.*

— Asia.

AKADEMIIA NAUK SSSR. Institut Etnografii. Trudy. Novaia Seriia. tom 39. Peredneaziatskii etnograficheskii sbornik. 1. Moskva, 1958. pp. 337.

— Brazil.

DIEGUES (MANUEL) Etnias e culturas no Brasil. Rio de Janeiro, 1976. pp. 208. *bibliog.*

— Canada — Ontario.

HERITAGE ONTARIO CONGRESS, TORONTO, 1972. Heritage Ontario Congress, June 2,3,4, 1972: report. [Toronto], 1973. pp. 57,61. *In English and French.*

— India.

FUCHS (STEFAN) The aboriginal tribes of India. London, 1977. pp. 308. *First published in India in 1973.*

— Indonesia — Sunda Islands.

FOX (JAMES J.) Harvest of the palm: ecological change in eastern Indonesia. Cambridge, Mass., 1977. pp. 290. *bibliog.*

— Mediterranean.

DAVIS (JOHN HORSLEY RUSSELL) People of the Mediterranean: an essay in comparative social anthropology. London, 1977. pp. 288. *bibliog.*

PITT-RIVERS (JULIAN ALFRED LANE-FOX) The fate of Shechem; or, The politics of sex: essays in the anthropology of the Mediterranean. Cambridge, 1977. pp. 193.

— Spain.

REUNION DE ANTROPOLOGOS ESPAÑOLES, 1a, Sevilla, 1973. Primera reunion de antropologos españoles: actas, comunicaciones, documentacion; edicion preparada por Alfredo Jimenez. Sevilla, [1975]. pp. 401. *bibliog.*

TEMAS de antropologia española; ([by] Maria Catedra Tomas [and others]). Madrid, [1976]. pp. 347. *Papers presented at a symposium held in Puertomarin (Lugo), 3-9 November, 1974. Map in end pocket.*

— — Andalusia.

PITT-RIVERS (JULIAN ALFRED LANE-FOX) The fate of Shechem; or, The politics of sex: essays in the anthropology of the Mediterranean. Cambridge, 1977. pp. 193.

— Thailand.

HOÀNG (MICHEL) La Thailande et ses populations. [Paris, 1976]. pp. 252. *bibliog.*

— Tunisia.

LOUIS (ANDRE) Tunisie du sud: ksars et villages de crêtes. Paris, 1975. pp. 370. *bibliog. (Centre de Recherches et d'Etudes sur les Sociétés Méditerranéennes. Etudes Tunisiennes)*

EUGENICS.

SEARLE (G.R.) Eugenics and politics in Britain, 1900-1914. Leyden, 1976. pp. 147.

EURIPIDES.

RANKIN (H.D.) Pentheus and Plato: a study in social disintegration; an inaugural lecture delivered at the University [of Southampton] 20 November 1975. Southampton, 1975. pp. 32.

EURODOLLAR MARKET.

MILLS (RODNEY H.) Explaining changes in euro-dollar positions: a study of banks in four European countries. [Washington, 1972]. pp. 34. *(United States. Board of Governors of the Federal Reserve System. Staff Economic Studies. No. 71)*

CAMBRIDGE. University. Centre of Latin American Studies. Working Papers. No. 13. Euro-dollars, foreign debt and the Brazilian boom; by John Wells. Cambridge, 1973. pp. 35.

FRANCE. Direction de la Documentation. La Documentation Française. Notes et Etudes Documentaires. Nos. 4,224-4, 225. Le marché des Euro-dollars et des Euro-obligations; par Joël Métais. Paris, 1975. pp. 55.

LAVERNY (PATRICK) L'Euro-dollar et ses problèmes. Paris, 1975. pp. 88. *bibliog. (Paris. Université de Paris II. Travaux et Recherches. Série Sciences Economiques. 1).*

LITTLE (JANE SNEDDON) Euro-dollars: the money-market gypsies. New York, [1975]. pp. 301. *bibliog.*

EUROCURRENCIES and the international monetary system; edited by Carl H. Stem [and others]. Washington, D.C., [1976]. pp. 413. *bibliog. Papers from four conference sessions sponsored by the American Enterprise Institute for Public Policy Research and the U.S. Treasury.*

PREISIG (KARL W.) Roll-over-Eurokredit: Analyse der Elemente, Darstellung der Technik und der Probleme eines neuen Bankgeschäftes. Bern, 1976. pp. 258. *bibliog.*

PRESLEY (JOHN R.) and DENNIS (GEOFFREY EDWIN JAMES) Currency areas. London, 1976. pp. 114.

ZUMPFORT (WOLF DIETER) Untersuchungen zum Wachstum des Eurodollarmarktes. Tübingen, [1977]. pp. 175. *bibliog. (Kiel. Universität. Institut für Weltwirtschaft. Kieler Studien. 142)*

EUROPE

— Civilization.

DUERRENMATT (PETER) Europa will leben: ein Bekenntnis zur europäischen Wirklichkeit. Bern, [1960]. pp. 198.

ARON (RAYMOND) Plaidoyer pour l'Europe décadente. Paris, 1977. pp. 511.

— Commerce.

BALL (J.N.) Merchants and merchandise: the expansion of trade in Europe 1500-1630. London, [1977]. pp. 226. *bibliog.*

FATTI e idee di storia economica nei secoli XII-XX: studi dedicati a Franco Borlandi; (redazione: Bruno Dini [and others]). Bologna, [1977]. pp. 916. *With contributions in English, French and German.*

— — Africa, West.

WAPPAEUS (J.E.) Untersuchungen über die Negerländer der Araber und über den Seehandel der Italiener, Spanier und Portugiesen im Mittelalter. Amsterdam, 1966. pp. 365. *Reprint of work originally published in Göttingen in 1842.*

— — Arab countries.

WAPPAEUS (J.E.) Untersuchungen über die Negerländer der Araber und über den Seehandel der Italiener, Spanier und Portugiesen im Mittelalter. Amsterdam, 1966. pp. 365. *Reprint of work originally published in Göttingen in 1842.*

EUROPE(Cont.)

— — Asia.

FURBER (HOLDEN) Rival empires of trade in the Orient, 1600-1800. Minneapolis, 1976. pp. 408. *bibliog.*

— Defences.

CONFERENCE ON AMERICAN FOREIGN POLICY AND THE NEW EUROPE, BLACKSBURG, 1974. America and European security; edited by Louis J. Mensonides and James A. Kuhlman. Leyden, 1976. pp. 170. *bibliog. (East-West Foundation. East-West Perspectives. 2)*

FRANCE. Direction de la Documentation. La Documentation Française. Notes et Etudes Documentaires. Nos. 4,271 - 4, 272. La Conférence sur la sécurité et la coopération en Europe; par Aleth Manin. Paris, 1976. pp. 80.

INTERNATIONAL INSTITUTE FOR STRATEGIC STUDIES. Adelphi Papers, No. 129. The alliance and Europe: part VI: the European programme group; by D.C.R. Heyhoe. London, 1976. pp. 27.

ROSE (FRANÇOIS DE) La France et la défense de l'Europe. Paris, [1976]. pp. 123.

— Economic conditions.

LIEBERMAN (SIMA) The growth of European mixed economies, 1945-1970: a concise study of the economic evolution of six countries. New York, [1977]. pp. 347. *bibliog.*

UNIVERSITY ASSOCIATION FOR CONTEMPORARY EUROPEAN STUDIES. Annual Conference, 7th, University of Sussex, 1977. Government, business and labour in European capitalism; papers presented at the...Conference...; edited by Richard T. Griffiths. London, 1977. pp. 229.

— Economic history.

MISKIMIN (HARRY ALVIN) The economy of early renaissance Europe, 1300-1460. Cambridge, 1969 repr. 1975. pp. 188. *bibliog.*

DE VRIES (JAN) Economy of Europe in an age of crisis, 1600-1750. Cambridge, 1976. pp. 284.

INDUSTRIALISIERUNG und "europäische Wirtschaft" im 19. Jahrhundert: ein Tagungsbericht; bearbeitet und herausgegeben von Otto Büsch [and others]; mit Beiträgen von François Crouzet [and others]. Berlin, 1976. pp. 148. *(Historische Kommission zu Berlin. Veröffentlichungen. Band 46) Papers of a symposium held in Berlin in 1973; in German or English.*

— Economic integration.

KROK-PASZKOWSKI (JAN) Między Brukselą a Moskwą: procesy integracyjne w Europie. London, 1975. pp. 159. *bibliog.*

SCHULZ (EBERHARD) Moskau und die europäische Integration. München, 1975. pp. 267. *bibliog. (Deutsche Gesellschaft für Auswärtige Politik. Forschungsinstitut. Schriften. Band 38)*

VAUGHAN (RICHARD) Professor of Medieval History, University of Hull. Post-war integration in Europe. London, 1976. pp. 211. *bibliog.*

COFFEY (PETER) Economist. Europe and money. London, 1977. pp. 95.

TSOUKALIS (LOUKAS) The politics and economics of European monetary integration. London, 1977. pp. 192.

— Economic policy.

EUROPE 2000; edited by Peter Hall. London, 1977. pp. 274. *bibliog. Final report of the European Cultural Foundation Plan Europe 2000 Integration Committee.*

UNIVERSITY ASSOCIATION FOR CONTEMPORARY EUROPEAN STUDIES. Annual Conference, 7th, University of Sussex, 1977. Government, business and labour in European capitalism; papers presented at the...Conference...; edited by Richard T. Griffiths. London, 1977. pp. 229.

— Emigration and immigration.

RUNNYMEDE TRUST. Briefing Papers. 1974, No. 1. Immigration policy: the European dimension. London, 1974. fo.18.

SALT (JOHN) Geographer, and CLOUT (HUGH DONALD) eds. Migration in post-war Europe: geographical essays. London, 1976. pp. 228. *bibliogs.*

— Foreign economic relations — Europe, Eastern.

DEUTSCHES INSTITUT FÜR WIRTSCHAFTSFORSCHUNG. Sonderhefte. [Neue Folge]. 114. Perspektiven und Probleme wirtschaftlicher Zusammenarbeit zwischen Ost- und Westeuropa; ([edited by] Doris Cornelsen [and others]). Berlin, [1976]. pp. 204. *Papers of a symposium held in West Berlin in 1975; in various languages.*

— — United States.

URI (PIERRE) Europe et Amérique: relations économiques, problèmes politiques. Nancy, 1966. pp. 28. *(Nancy. Université. Centre Européen Universitaire. Collection des Conférences Européennes. No. 2)*

The EURO-American system: economic and political relations between North America and Western Europe; edited by Ernst-Otto Czempiel and Dankwart A. Rustow. Frankfurt, 1976. pp. 233. *Proceedings of a conference held in Arnoldshain, Germany, 1975.*

— Foreign relations.

BEYOND détente: prospects for East-West co-operation and security in Europe; edited by Nils Andrén and Karl E. Birnbaum. Leyden, 1976. pp. 199. *(East-West Foundation. East-West Perspectives. 3) Papers of a conference held at the Bellagio Center, November 11-16, 1974.*

CASSIERS (JUAN) The hazards of peace: a European view of detente. Cambridge, Mass., [1976]. pp. 85. *(Harvard University. Center for International Affairs. Harvard Studies in International Affairs. No. 34)*

EVROPEISKAIA bezopasnost' i sotrudnichestvo: predposylki, problemy, perspektivy. Moskva, 1976. pp. 302.

INNEN- und Aussenpolitik unter nationalsozialistischer Bedrohung: Determinanten internationaler Beziehungen in historischen Fallstudien; ([edited by] Erhard Forndran [and others]). Opladen, [1977]. pp. 361.

— — France.

SIVERY (GERARD) Mirages méditerranéens ou réalités atlantiques?: XIIIe-XVe siècles. [Paris], 1976. pp. 285. *bibliog.*

— — Russia.

The FUTURE of Soviet military power; edited by Lawrence L. Whetten. New York, [1976]. pp. 190. *Papers of a conference held at Ebenhausen, West Germany, 1975, under the aegis of the Stiftung für Wissenschaft und Politik and the University of Southern California.*

— — Spain.

The HOLY Alliance versus Spain; containing the several notes and declarations of the allied powers, with the firm, spirited, and dignified replies of the Spanish Cortes, accompanied by a few brief prefatory remarks thereon; by a constitutionalist. London, J. Ridgway, 1823. pp. viii, 30.

— — United Kingdom.

RECKER (MARIE LUISE) England und der Donauraum, 1919-1929: Probleme einer europäischen Nachkriegsordnung. Stuttgart, 1976. pp. 324. *bibliog. (Deutsches Historisches Institut in London. Veröffentlichungen. Band 3)*

— — United States.

CONFERENCE ON AMERICAN FOREIGN POLICY AND THE NEW EUROPE, BLACKSBURG, 1974. America and European security; edited by Louis J. Mensonides and James A. Kuhlman. Leyden, 1976. pp. 170. *bibliog. (East-West Foundation. East-West Perspectives. 2)*

The EURO-American system: economic and political relations between North America and Western Europe; edited by Ernst-Otto Czempiel and Dankwart A. Rustow. Frankfurt, 1976. pp. 233. *Proceedings of a conference held in Arnoldshain, Germany, 1975.*

GODSON (ROY) American labor and European politics: the AFL as a transnational force. New York, [1976]. pp. 230. *bibliog.*

MALLY (GERHARD) Interdependence: the European-American connection in the global context. Lexington, Mass., [1976]. pp. 229.

— History.

WEISS (JOHN) Conservatism in Europe, 1770-1945: traditionalism, reaction and counter-revolution. London, [1977]. pp. 180. *bibliog.*

— — To 476.

TODD (MALCOLM) The northern barbarians, 100 B.C. - A.D. 300. London, 1975. pp. 232. *bibliog.*

— — 476-1492.

SIVERY (GERARD) Mirages méditerranéens ou réalités atlantiques?: XIIIe-XVe siècles. [Paris], 1976. pp. 285. *bibliog.*

— — 1517-1648.

ELLIOTT (JOHN HUXTABLE) Europe divided 1559-1598. Glasgow, 1968, repr. 1975. pp. 432. *bibliog.*

— — 1700-1799.

ANDERSON (MATTHEW SMITH) Europe in the eighteenth century, 1713-1783. 2nd ed. London, 1976. pp. 447. *bibliog.*

— — 1800-1899.

ESSAYS on modern European revolutionary history; by Stanley H Palmer [and others];...edited by Bede K. Lackner and Kenneth Roy Philp. Austin, [1977]. pp. 132. *(Texas University. Walter Prescott Webb Memorial Lectures.11)*

— — 1848-1871.

HOBSBAWM (ERIC JOHN ERNEST) The age of capital, 1848-1875. London, [1975]. pp. 354. *bibliog.*

GRENVILLE (JOHN ASHLEY SOAMES) Europe reshaped, 1848-1878. Hassocks, Sussex, 1976. pp. 412. *bibliog.*

— — 1848-1849.

BENEŠ (KAREL JOSEF) ed. 1848 v projevech současníků; s úvodní studií a poznámkami, etc. [Praha], 1932. pp. 179.

— — 1900- .

ROBERTS (MARTIN) A portrait of Europe 1900-1973: the new barbarism? London, 1975. pp. 360. *bibliog.*

ESSAYS on modern European revolutionary history; by Stanley H Palmer [and others];...edited by Bede K. Lackner and Kenneth Roy Philp. Austin, [1977]. pp. 132. *(Texas University. Walter Prescott Webb Memorial Lectures.11)*

— — 1918-1945.

WRYNN (J.F.) The Socialist International and the politics of European reconstruction, 1919-1930. Uithoorn, 1976. pp. 242. *bibliog.*

ADAMTHWAITE (ANTHONY P.) The making of the Second World War. London, 1977. pp. 235. *bibliog. With a selection of documents.*

— 1945- .

BEYOND détente: prospects for East-West co-operation and security in Europe; edited by Nils Andrén and Karl E. Birnbaum. Leyden, 1976. pp. 199. *(East-West Foundation. East-West Perspectives. 3) Papers of a conference held at the Bellagio Center, November 11-16, 1974.*

— Politics and government.

DEUTSCHES Bürgerbuch für 1846, zweiter Jahrgang; herausgegeben von H. Püttmann. Glashütten im Taunus, 1975. pp. 346. *Reprint of work originally published in Mannheim in 1846.*

DUERRENMATT (PETER) Europa will leben: ein Bekenntnis zur europäischen Wirklichkeit. Bern, [1960]. pp. 198.

BAGDASARIAN (NICHOLAS DER) The Austro-German rapprochement, 1870-1879: from the Battle of Sedan to the Dual Alliance. Rutherford, N.J., [1976]. pp. 334. *bibliog.*

BARZEL (RAINER) Es ist noch nicht zu spät. München, 1977. pp. 191.

— Population.

MAGGS (PETER B.) and LEE (LUKE TSUNG-CHOU) North African migrants under western European law. Medford, Mass., 1976. pp. 225-250. *(Tufts University. Fletcher School of Law and Diplomacy. Law and Population Monograph Series. No. 37) (Reprinted from Texas International Law Journal, vol. 11, no. 2)*

SALT (JOHN) Geographer, and CLOUT (HUGH DONALD) eds. Migration in post-war Europe: geographical essays. London, 1976. pp. 228. *bibliogs.*

— Relations (general) with Asia.

DODGE (ERNEST S.) Islands and empires: western impact on the Pacific and East Asia. Minneapolis, Minn., 1976. pp. 364. *bibliog.*

— Relations (general) with Eastern Europe.

WETTIG (GERHARD) Broadcasting and détente: eastern policies and their implication for east-west relations. London, [1977]. pp. 110.

— Relations (general) with the Pacific.

DODGE (ERNEST S.) Islands and empires: western impact on the Pacific and East Asia. Minneapolis, Minn., 1976. pp. 364. *bibliog.*

— Social policy.

EUROPE 2000; edited by Peter Hall. London, 1977. pp. 274. *bibliog. Final report of the European Cultural Foundation Plan Europe 2000 Integration Committee.*

EUROPE, EASTERN

— Church history.

KIRÁLY (BÉLA K.) ed. Tolerance and movements of religious dissent in eastern Europe. New York, 1975. pp. 221. *(East European Quarterly. East European Monographs. 13)*

— Civilization.

AKADEMIIA NAUK SSSR. Institut Slavianovedeniia i Balkanistiki. Balkanskie Issledovaniia. [vyp.2]. Problemy istorii i kul'tury: (stat'i sovetskikh uchenykh - uchastnikov III Mezhdunarodnogo kongressa po izucheniiu Iugo-Vostochnoi Evropy). Moskva, 1976. pp. 352. *bibliog.*

— Commerce.

EUROPEAN COMMUNITIES. Statistical Office. Bloc oriental. [in German and French]. irreg., 1970-[Luxembourg]. *Not pd. 1972-1973.*

— — Africa.

OROSZ (ÁRPÁD) Trade of African developing countries up to 1970 and prognosis to 1980. Budapest, 1975. pp. 91. *bibliog. (Magyar Tudományos Akadémia. Világgazdasági Kutató Intézet. Studies on Developing Countries. No. 70)*

— — America, Latin.

OROSZ (ÁRPÁD) The foreign trade turnover of Latin America till 1970, and its prospective development up to 1980. Budapest, 1976. pp. 121. *bibliog. (Magyar Tudományos Akadémia. Világgazdasági Kutató Intézet. Studies on Developing Countries. No. 81)*

— Commercial policy.

GARLAND (JOHN S.) Financing foreign trade in Eastern Europe: problems of bilateralism and currency inconvertibility. New York, 1977. pp. 168. *bibliog.*

— Economic policy — Mathematical models.

WIEDEMANN (PAUL PAT) A consideration of the nature of the objective function in national economic planning, with specific reference to the mathematical modelling of medium-term planning in the Soviet Union and Eastern Europe. 1974. fo. 353. *bibliog. Typescript. Ph.D. (London) thesis: unpublished. This thesis is the property of London University and may not be removed from the Library.*

— Foreign economic relations — Europe.

DEUTSCHES INSTITUT FÜR WIRTSCHAFTSFORSCHUNG. Sonderhefte. [Neue Folge]. 114. Perspektiven und Probleme wirtschaftlicher Zusammenarbeit zwischen Ost- und Westeuropa; ([edited by] Doris Cornelsen [and others]). Berlin, [1976]. pp. 204. *Papers of a symposium held in West Berlin in 1975; in various languages.*

— Foreign relations — Germany.

MOROZ (PIOTR) Polityka wschodnia FDP w latach 1961-1970. Wrocław, 1976. pp. 207. *bibliog.*

— — Russia.

TARNOFF (CURTIS LEE) Evolving structures of great power blocs: the U.S.A. and Latin America, 1901-1975: the USSR and Eastern Europe, 1945-1975. 1976. fo. 529. *bibliog. Typescript. Ph.D. (London) thesis: unpublished. This thesis is the property of London University and may not be removed from the Library.*

— History.

AKADEMIIA NAUK SSSR. Institut Slavianovedeniia i Balkanistiki. Balkanskie Issledovaniia. [vyp.]. Problemy istorii i kul'tury: (stat'i sovetskikh uchenykh - uchastnikov III Mezhdunarodnogo kongressa po izucheniiu Iugo-Vostochnoi Evropy). Moskva, 1976. pp. 352. *bibliog.*

— Politics and government.

SETON-WATSON (GEORGE HUGH NICHOLAS) The "sick heart" of modern Europe: the problem of the Danubian lands. Seattle, [1975]. pp. 76. *(Seattle. University of Washington. Walker-Ames Lectures. 1973)*

SSSR v bor'be protiv fashistskoi agressii, 1933-1945. Moskva, 1976. pp. 327.

TODD (EMMANUEL) La chute finale: essai sur la décomposition de la sphère soviétique. Paris, 1976. pp. 324.

STAAR (RICHARD FELIX) Communist regimes in Eastern Europe. 3rd ed. Stanford, Calif., 1977. pp. 302. *bibliog. (Stanford University. Hoover Institution on War, Revolution and Peace. Hoover Institution Publications. No. 171)*

— Population.

INTERNATIONAL SLAVIC CONFERENCE, 1ST, BANFF, ALBERTA, 1974. Demographic developments in Eastern Europe; edited by Leszek A. Kosinski. New York, 1977. pp. 343.

— Relations (general) with Europe.

WETTIG (GERHARD) Broadcasting and détente: eastern policies and their implication for east-west relations. London, [1977]. pp. 110.

— Religion.

KIRÁLY (BÉLA K.) ed. Tolerance and movements of religious dissent in eastern Europe. New York, 1975. pp. 221. *(East European Quarterly. East European Monographs. 13)*

— Social conditions.

POLITICAL socialization in eastern Europe: a comparative framework: [based on a panel held during the Annual Meeting of the American Political Science Association in Washington, 1972]; (edited by Ivan Volgyes). New York, 1975. pp. 199.

EUROPEAN COMMUNITIES.

EUROPEAN COMMUNITIES. Economic and Social Committee. 1970. Enlarging the Community. [Luxembourg, 1970]. pp. 12.

EUROPEAN COMMUNITIES. Economic and Social Committee. Annual report. a., 1973(1st)- Brussels.

EUROPEAN PARLIAMENT. Directorate General for Research and Documentation. 1975- . Europe today: state of European integration. [Luxembourg], 1975 in progress. *Loose-leaf binder.*

EUROPEAN COMMUNITIES. [Economic and Social Committee]. 1975. The Economic and Social Committee. Brussels, [1975]. pp. 16.

EUROPEAN COMMUNITIES. Economic and Social Committee. Bulletin. m., Ja 1976 (no.1)- Brussels.

VALE (PETER C.J.) The European Economic Community: a guide to the game of marbles. Braamfontein, 1976. pp. 16.

EUROPEAN COMMUNITIES. Commission. Programme of the Commission. a., 1977- Brussels. *Published in conjunction with the EUROPEAN COMMUNITIES. Commission. General report on the activities of the Communities.*

POLICY-making in the European Communities; edited by Helen Wallace [and others]. London, [1977]. pp. 341. *bibliogs.*

COMMUNITY REPORT: bulletin pd. by the Dublin Office of the European Communities. m. current issues only kept. Dublin.

EUROPEAN COMMUNITIES. Welsh Office. Community news. irreg., current issues only. Cardiff.

— Bibliography.

EUROPEAN COMMUNITIES. Commission. 1977. The European Community: a brief reading list. London, 1977. pp. 34.

— Information services.

KUJATH (K.) The economic libraries of the European Communities;... translation of a paper given at the I[nternational] F[ederation of] L[ibrary] A[ssociations] conference at Budapest, September 1972. London, Department of Trade and Industry, 1973. pp. 21.

— Officials and employees.

EUROPEAN COMMUNITIES. Economic and Social Committee. Year- book. a., 1974/78- Brussels. *[in Community languages].*

EUROPEAN COMMUNITIES. Economic and Social Committee. Directory. irreg., current issues only. Brussels.

— Germany.

INFORMATIONEN ZUR POLITISCHEN BILDUNG. Bonn, Bundeszentrale für Politische Bildung, 1974 in progress.

EUROPEAN COMMUNITIES.(Cont.)

— Ireland (Republic).

COMMUNITY REPORT: bulletin pd. by the Dublin Office of the European Communities. m. current issues only kept. Dublin.

EUROPEAN CONVENTION ON HUMAN RIGHTS.

Il GIUDICE italiano di Fronte alla Convenzione europea dei diritti dell'uomo: atti della Tavola Rotonda tenuta in Roma il 13 dicembre 1972. Padova, 1975. pp. 54.

ROBERTSON (ARTHUR HENRY) Human rights in Europe: being an account of the European Convention for the Protection of Human Rights and Fundamental Freedoms, etc. 2nd ed. Manchester, 1977. pp. 329.

EUROPEAN COOPERATION.

VAUGHAN (RICHARD) Professor of Medieval History, University of Hull. Post-war integration in Europe. London, 1976. pp. 211. *bibliog.*

— Congresses.

FRANCE. Direction de la Documentation. La Documentation Française. Notes et Etudes Documentaires. Nos. 4,271 - 4, 272. La Conférence sur la sécurité et la coopération en Europe; par Aleth Manin. Paris, 1976. pp. 80.

EUROPEAN DEFENCE COMMUNITY.

SCHMIDT-WITTMACK (KARL FRANZ) So geht es nicht weiter. [Berlin, 1954]. pp. 39.

EUROPEAN ECONOMIC COMMUNITY.

ALLEN (POLLY REYNOLDS) Organization and administration of a monetary union. Princeton, 1976. pp. 85. *bibliog. (Princeton University. Department of Economics and Sociology. International Finance Section. Princeton Studies in International Finance. No. 38)*

McCALL (LOUIS A.) Regional integration: a comparison of European and Central American dynamics. Beverly Hills, [1976]. pp. 77. *bibliog.*

ROYAL INSTITUTE OF INTERNATIONAL AFFAIRS and POLITICAL AND ECONOMIC PLANNING. European Series. No. 27. From summit to council: evolution in the EEC; [by] Annette Morgan. London, 1976. pp. 75.

U.K. EEC Information Unit. 1976. EEC: your questions answered: a businessman's guide. London, [1976]. pp. 129. *bibliog.*

VAUGHAN (RICHARD) Professor of Medieval History, University of Hull. Post-war integration in Europe. London, 1976. pp. 211. *bibliog.*

DONAT (MARCELL VON) Brüsseler Machenschaften: dem Euro-Clan auf der Spur. 3rd ed. Baden-Baden, 1977. pp. 205.

MANLEY (ROY) and HASTINGS (HELEN) Influencing Europe: a guide for pressure groups. London, 1977. pp. 19. *bibliog. (Fabian Society. Research Series. [No.] 332)*

MATTHEWS (JACQUELINE D.) Association system of the European Community. New York, 1977. pp. 167. *bibliog.*

SHANKS (MICHAEL) European social policy, today and tomorrow. Oxford, 1977. pp. 105.

— Dictionaries and encyclopedias.

PAXTON (JOHN) A dictionary of the European Economic Community. London, 1977. pp. 287. *bibliog.*

— Africa.

DJAMSON (ERIC C.) The dynamics of Euro-African co-operation: being an analysis and exposition of institutional, legal and socio-economic aspects of association/co-operation with the European Economic Community. The Hague, 1976. pp. 370. *bibliog.*

MATTHEWS (JACQUELINE D.) Association system of the European Community. New York, 1977. pp. 167. *bibliog.*

— Africa, Subsaharan.

BOETTCHER (DETLEV) Entwicklung durch Integration: das Verhältnis der Europäischen Gemeinschaft zu Schwarzafrika. Berlin, 1976. pp. 282. *bibliog. Inaugural-Dissertation zur Erlangung des Grades eines Doktors der Wirtschaftswissenschaften der Freien Universität Berlin.*

— Australia.

MILLER (JOHN DONALD BRUCE) The EEC and Australia. Melbourne, 1976. pp. 137.

— Fiji.

BILLERBECK (KLAUS) Problems and approaches for solution of an association between Fiji, Tonga, Western Samoa and the European community. Berlin, 1974. pp. 71. *(Deutsches Institut für Entwicklungspolitik. Occasional Papers. No. 21)*

— Greece.

EUROPEAN COMMUNITIES. Commission. 1976. Opinion on Greek application for membership: transmitted to the Council by the Commission on 29 January, 1976. [Brussels], 1976. pp. 42. *(Bulletin of the European Communities. Supplements. [1976/2])*

HARRIS (GEOFF) A wider Europe. London, 1976. pp. 20. *(Young Fabian Group. Young Fabian Pamphlets. 45)*

ZOLOTAS (XENOPHON) Greece in the European Community. Athens, 1976. pp. 53. *(Bank of Greece. Papers and Lectures. 33)*

— Mediterranean.

MEDITERRANEAN Europe and the Common Market: studies of economic growth and integration; edited by Eric N. Baklanoff. Alabama, [1976]. pp. 244. *(American Universities Field Staff. Center for Mediterranean Studies. Mediterranean Europe Series. 2)*

— Portugal.

HARRIS (GEOFF) A wider Europe. London, 1976. pp. 20. *(Young Fabian Group. Young Fabian Pamphlets. 45)*

— Russia.

SCHULZ (EBERHARD) Moskau und die europäische Integration. München, 1975. pp. 267. *bibliog. (Deutsche Gesellschaft für Auswärtige Politik. Forschungsinstitut. Schriften. Band 38)*

— Samoa.

BILLERBECK (KLAUS) Problems and approaches for solution of an association between Fiji, Tonga, Western Samoa and the European community. Berlin, 1974. pp. 71. *(Deutsches Institut für Entwicklungspolitik. Occasional Papers. No. 21)*

— Scandinavia.

MILJAN (TOIVO) The reluctant Europeans: the attitudes of the Nordic countries towards European integration. London, [1977]. pp. 325. *bibliog.*

— Spain.

NADAL CAPARA (JOAQUIM DE) Catalunya i el Mercat Comu. Barcelona, 1975. pp. 304.

HARRIS (GEOFF) A wider Europe. London, 1976. pp. 20. *(Young Fabian Group. Young Fabian Pamphlets. 45)*

GRANELL TRIAS (FRANCISCO) The Common Market and the economic future of Spain. [Barcelona, 1977]. pp. 19. *bibliog.*

— Switzerland.

EUROPA-UNION. Europa-Woche, Zürich, 1959. Europa: was wir sind, wo wir stehen, wohin wir gehen; ([by] Carlo Schmid [and others])...; herausgegeben von Thomas Raeber. Zürich, [1960]. pp. 130.

WEBER (MAX) of the Schweizerischer Gewerkschaftsbund. Die Schweiz und die Integration: Referat, etc. Bern, 1963. pp. 18. *(Schweizerischer Metall- und Uhrenarbeiter-Verband. Schriftenreihe. Nr.17)*

— Tonga.

BILLERBECK (KLAUS) Problems and approaches for solution of an association between Fiji, Tonga, Western Samoa and the European community. Berlin, 1974. pp. 71. *(Deutsches Institut für Entwicklungspolitik. Occasional Papers. No. 21)*

— Turkey.

HARRIS (GEOFF) A wider Europe. London, 1976. pp. 20. *(Young Fabian Group. Young Fabian Pamphlets. 45)*

— United Kingdom.

AIMS OF INDUSTRY. Economic Arguments. Now we are in Europe. London, [1973]. pp. 4.

JOWELL (ROGER) and SPENCE (JAMES D.) The grudging Europeans: a study of British attitudes towards the EEC. London, 1975. pp. 44,19.

HEATH (EDWARD RICHARD GEORGE) A British approach to European foreign policy. Leeds, 1976. pp. 14. *(Leeds. University. Montague Burton Lectures on International Relations. No.33)*

THOMSON (GEORGE MORGAN) Britain in Europe: the first four years and the future. London, [1976]. pp. 8. *(David Davies Memorial Institute of International Studies. Annual Memorial Lectures. 1976)*

The BRITISH people: their voice in Europe; report of an independent working party, sponsored by the Hansard Society, on the effects of membership of the European Community on British representative institutions. Farnborough, Hants., [1977]. pp. 207.

KING (ANTHONY) Britain says yes: the 1975 referendum on the Common Market. Washington, D.C., [1977]. pp. 153. *(American Enterprise Institute for Public Policy Research. AEI Studies. 160)*

— United States.

SCHAETZEL (J. ROBERT) The unhinged alliance: America and the European Community. New York, [1975]. pp. 184. *(Council on Foreign Relations. Policy Books)*

EUROPEAN ECONOMIC COMMUNITY ASSOCIATED COUNTRIES.

BOETTCHER (DETLEV) Entwicklung durch Integration: das Verhältnis der Europäischen Gemeinschaft zu Schwarzafrika. Berlin, 1976. pp. 282. *bibliog. Inaugural-Dissertation zur Erlangung des Grades eines Doktors der Wirtschaftswissenschaften der Freien Universität Berlin.*

BOURRINET (JACQUES) La coopération économique eurafricaine. [Paris, 1976]. pp. 191. *bibliog.*

DJAMSON (ERIC C.) The dynamics of Euro-African co-operation: being an analysis and exposition of institutional, legal and socio-economic aspects of association/co-operation with the European Economic Community. The Hague, 1976. pp. 370. *bibliog.*

WALL (DAVID) The European Community's Lomé Convention: "STABEX" and the third world's aspirations. London, [1976]. fo. 22. *(Trade Policy Research Centre. Guest Papers. No. 4)*

EUROPEAN ECONOMIC COMMUNITY COUNTRIES

— Commerce.

EUROPEAN COMMUNTIES. Statistical Office. Foreign trade: standard country nomenclature. [in French, English, German, Italian, Dutch and Danish]. a., 1963- Luxembourg. *Not pd. 1967.*

— Commercial policy.

McINTYRE (ALISTER) The effects of reverse preferences on trade among developing countries. (TD/B/435). New York, United Nations, 1974. pp. 105. *(Conference on Trade and Development. Current Problems on Economic Integration)*

— Economic conditions.

CLOUT (HUGH DONALD) The regional problem in Western Europe. Cambridge, 1976. pp. 59. *bibliog.*

LEE (ROGER) and OGDEN (P.E.) eds. Economy and society in the EEC: spatial perspectives. Farnborough, Hants., [1976]. pp. 294. *bibliogs.*

SEMAINE DE BRUGES, 1976. The European economy beyond the crisis: from stabilisation to structural change...: l'économie européenne au-delà de la crise: de la stabilisation à la mutation structurelle; (edited by G.R. Denton and J.J.N. Cooper). Bruges, 1977. pp. 409. *(College of Europe. Cahiers de Bruges. Nouvelle Série. 35) In English and French.*

— Economic policy.

EUROPEAN COMMUNITIES. Economic and Social Committee. Annual report. a., 1973(1st)- Brussels.

EUROPEAN COMMUNITIES. Economic and Social Committee. Bulletin. m., Ja 1976 (no.1)- Brussels.

EUROPEAN COMMUNITIES. Commission. 1976. The European Regional Development Fund 1975: (first annual report) presented...to the European Parliament and to the Council. [Brussels], 1976. pp. 38. *(Bulletin of the European Communities. Supplements. [1976/7])*

SEMAINE DE BRUGES, 1976. The European economy beyond the crisis: from stabilisation to structural change...: l'économie européenne au-delà de la crise: de la stabilisation à la mutation structurelle; (edited by G.R. Denton and J.J.N. Cooper). Bruges, 1977. pp. 409. *(College of Europe. Cahiers de Bruges. Nouvelle Série. 35) In English and French.*

— Foreign economic relations.

COURIER, THE: European Community-Africa-Caribbean-Pacific (formerly Association news); [pd. by the Commission of the European Communities]. bi-m., Ja/F 1973 (no.17)- Brussels.

WALL (DAVID) The European Community's Lomé Convention: "STABEX" and the third world's aspirations. London, [1976]. fo. 22. *(Trade Policy Research Centre. Guest Papers. No. 4)*

— Foreign relations.

HEATH (EDWARD RICHARD GEORGE) A British approach to European foreign policy. Leeds, 1976. pp. 14. *(Leeds. University. Montague Burton Lectures on International Relations. No.33)*

— Industries.

EUROPEAN COMMUNITIES. Statistical Office. Annual investments in fixed assets in the industrial enterprises of the member countries of the European Communities. a., 1972/74- Luxembourg. *[in Community languages].*

— Relations (general) with the United States.

SCHAETZEL (J. ROBERT) The unhinged alliance: America and the European Community. New York, [1975]. pp. 184. *(Council on Foreign Relations. Policy Books)*

— Social conditions.

LEE (ROGER) and OGDEN (P.E.) eds. Economy and society in the EEC: spatial perspectives. Farnborough, Hants., [1976]. pp. 294. *bibliogs.*

— Social policy.

EUROPEAN COMMUNITIES. Economic and Social Committee. Annual report. a., 1973(1st)- Brussels.

EUROPEAN COMMUNITIES. Economic and Social Committee. Bulletin. m., Ja 1976 (no.1)- Brussels.

EUROPEAN COMMUNITIES. Commission. 1976. Action programme in favour of migrant workers and their families. [Brussels], 1976. pp. 22. *(Bulletin of the European Communities. Supplements. [1976/3])*

EUROPEAN FEDERATION.

EUROPA-UNION. Europa-Woche, Zürich, 1959. Europa: was wir sind, wo wir stehen, wohin wir gehen; ([by] Carlo Schmid [and others])...; herausgegeben von Thomas Raeber. Zürich, [1960]. pp. 130.

UNION EUROPEENNE. Le fédéralisme dans l'Europe à venir. Bâle, 1964. pp. 16.

INTEGRATION: Vierteljahreshefte zur Europaforschung; ([pd. by] Kommission der Europäischen Gemeinschaften). 4 a yr., 1/1969- Brüssel.

ROLO (PAUL JACQUES VICTOR) Britain and the Briand plan: the common market that never was: an inaugural lecture...given in the University of Keele, 1972. Keele, 1973. pp. 23.

CHAPMAN (DONALD) Baron Northfield. The road to European union: proposals to the EEC institutions and governments. Brighton, 1975. pp. 65. *(Brighton. University of Sussex. Centre for Contemporary European Studies. Sussex European Papers. No. 1)*

EUROPEAN COMMUNITIES. Economic and Social Committee. 1975. European union. Brussels, 1975. pp. 33. *(Opinions)*

FELD (WERNER J.) and WILDGEN (JOHN K.) Domestic political realities and European unification: a study of mass publics and elites in the European Community countries. Boulder, Col., 1976. pp. 177,11.

LUTZ (CHRISTIAN) The road to European union: a plea for a constitutional revolution. Paris, 1976. pp. 60. *(Atlantic Institute. Atlantic Papers. 1976.2)*

MONNET (JEAN) Mémoires. [Paris, 1976]. pp. 642.

BLACKSELL (ANDREW MARK YATES) Post-war Europe: a political geography. Folkestone, 1977. pp. 205. *bibliog.*

DECISION making in the European Community; [by] Christoph Sasse [and others]. New York, 1977. pp. 352. *bibliogs.*

EUROPEAN FREE TRADE ASSOCIATION

— Switzerland.

WEBER (MAX) of the Schweizerischer Gewerkschaftsbund. Die Schweiz und die Integration: Referat, etc. Bern, 1963. pp. 18. *(Schweizerischer Metall- und Uhrenarbeiter-Verband. Schriftenreihe. Nr.17)*

EUROPEAN FREE TRADE ASSOCIATION COUNTRIES

— Economic policy.

EUROPEAN FREE TRADE ASSOCIATION. 1973. Regional policy in EFTA: national settlement strategies; a framework for regional development. Geneva, 1973. pp. 241. *bibliog.*

EUROPEAN PARLIAMENT.

EUROPEAN PARLIAMENT. Information digest. irreg., Ja 1971 [1st issue]- Luxembourg.

EUROPEAN PARLIAMENT. Information series: the sittings. irreg. Luxembourg. *Current issues only kept.*

— Elections.

ASHFORD (NIGEL) Direct elections to the European Parliament. [Coventry], 1976. pp. 41. *(University of Warwick. Department of Politics. Working Papers. No. 9)*

EUROPEAN PARLIAMENT. European elections: briefing. irreg., Ja 1977 (no.1)- London.

FABIAN SOCIETY. Fabian Tracts. [No.] 449. Electing Europe's first parliament; [by] Rod Northawl [and] Richard Corbett. London, 1977. pp. 28. *bibliog.*

EUROPEAN REGIONAL DEVELOPMENT FUND.

EUROPEAN COMMUNITIES. Commission. 1976. The European Regional Development Fund 1975: (first annual report) presented...to the European Parliament and to the Council. [Brussels], 1976. pp. 38. *(Bulletin of the European Communities. Supplements. [1976/7])*

EUROPEAN STUDIES.

POSTGRADUATE DEGREES IN EUROPEAN INTEGRATION; ([pd. by] University Information [Service], European Communities). irreg., current issue only. Brussels. *[in English and French].*

EUROPEAN WAR, 1914-1918

— Causes.

HERWIG (HOLGER H.) Politics of frustration: the United States in German naval planning, 1889-1941. Boston, Mass., [1976]. pp. 323. *bibliog.*

NOMIKOS (EUGENIA V.) and NORTH (ROBERT CARVER) International crisis: the outbreak of World War I. Montreal, 1976. pp. 339. *bibliog.*

— Diplomatic history.

LUCIRI (PIERRE) Le prix de la neutralité: la diplomatie secrète de la Suisse en 1914-1915 avec des documents d'archives inédits. Genève, 1976. pp. 336. *bibliog.*

NOMIKOS (EUGENIA V.) and NORTH (ROBERT CARVER) International crisis: the outbreak of World War I. Montreal, 1976. pp. 339. *bibliog.*

BRITISH foreign policy under Sir Edward Grey; edited by F. H. Hinsley. Cambridge, 1977. pp. 702. *bibliog.*

DOSS (KURT) Das deutsche Auswärtige Amt im Übergang vom Kaiserreich zur Weimarer Republik: die Schülersche Reform. Düsseldorf, [1977]. pp. 328. *bibliog.*

— Economic aspects.

GEL'FAND (ALEKSANDR LAZAREVICH) Die soziale Bilanz des Krieges; von Parvus [pseud.]. Berlin, 1917. pp. 30. *Also in his Aufbau und Wiedergutmachung.*

ALDCROFT (DEREK H.) From Versailles to Wall Street, 1919-1929. London, 1977. pp. 372. *bibliog.*

HARDACH (GERD H.) The First World War, 1914-1918. London, 1977. pp. 328. *bibliog.*

— — Austria.

MEJZLIK (HEINRICH) Die Eisenbewirtschaftung im Ersten Weltkrieg: die Planwirtschaft des k. u. k. Kriegsministeriums. Wien, [1977]. pp. 781. *bibliog.*

— — United States.

WARNE (FRANK JULIAN) The workers at war. New York, 1920; New York, 1976. pp. 250.

— Influence and results.

WALWORTH (ARTHUR CLARENCE) America's moment, 1918: American diplomacy at the end of World War I. New York, [1977]. pp. 309. *bibliog.*

— Law and legislation — United Kingdom.

U.K. Statutes, etc. 1915-1918. Defence of the realm acts and regulations passed and made...July 31st, 1915 (consolidated and revised to July 31st, 1918); edited by Alexander Pulling. London, 1915-18. 8 pts. (in 1 vol.).

U.K. Statutes, etc. 1916-1919. Manuals of emergency legislation: defence of the realm manual; edited by Alexander Pulling (and Sir Charles Cook). 2nd - 7th eds. London, 1916-19. 6 vols.

— Peace.

GEL'FAND (ALEKSANDR LAZAREVICH) Die soziale Bilanz des Krieges; von Parvus [pseud.]. Berlin, 1917. pp. 30. *Also in his Aufbau und Wiedergutmachung.*

TROUGHTON (ERNEST R.) It's happening again. London, 1944. pp. 111. *bibliog.*

HAUPTS (LEO) Deutsche Friedenspolitik, 1918-19: eine Alternative zur Machtpolitik des Ersten Weltkrieges. Düsseldorf, [1976]. pp. 489. *bibliog.*

ROBBINS (KEITH GILBERT) The abolition of war: the 'peace movement' in Britain, 1914-1919. Cardiff, 1976. pp. 255. *bibliog.*

STILLIG (JUERGEN) Die Russische Februarrevolution 1917 und die sozialistische Friedenspolitik. Köln, 1977. pp. 331. *bibliog.*

— Reparations.

REMMELE (HERMANN) Sowjetstern oder Hakenkreuz: die Rettung Deutschlands aus der Youngsklaverei und Kapitalsknechtschaft. [Berlin, 1930]. pp. 24.

THAELMANN (ERNST) Im Kampf gegen den deutschen und den amerikanischen Imperialismus: drei Reichstagsreden. Berlin, 1954. pp. 99. *(Institut für Marxismus-Leninismus (Berlin). Beiträge zur Geschichte und Theorie der Arbeiterbewegung. Heft 1) Speeches made in 1924, 1925 and 1930.*

SCHUKER (STEPHEN A.) The end of French predominance in Europe: the financial crisis of 1924 and the adoption of the Dawes plan. Chapel Hill, [1976]. pp. 444. *bibliog.*

— Territorial questions — Romania.

BESSARABIA. Delegation to the Paris Peace Conference. 1919. The Roumanians before the Peace Conference: the question of Bessarabia. Paris, 1919. pp. 27.

— Women's work.

ZIETZ (LUISE) Zur Frage der Frauenerwerbsarbeit während des Krieges und nachher. Berlin, 1916. pp. 47. *(Sozialdemokratische Partei Deutschlands. Vorstand. Sozialdemokratische Frauen-Bibliothek. 9)*

— China.

JONES (ARTHUR PHILIP) Britain's search for Chinese cooperation in the First World War. 1976 [or rather 1977]. fo. 304. *bibliog. Typescript. Ph.D. (London) thesis: unpublished. This thesis is the property of London University and may not be removed from the Library.*

— Czechoslovakia.

ČESKÝ národ ve světové válce a vídeňská vláda: dotaz poslanců Františka Staňka...Zdeňka Tobolky a soudruhů na... ministerského předsedu v příčině chování se vládních kruhů k českému národu za války. Pardubice, 1917. pp. 129.

— Germany.

UNITED STATES. Committee on Public Information. 1919. Die deutsch-bolschewistische Verschwörung: 70 Dokumente über die Beziehungen der Bolschewiki zur deutschen Heeresleitung, Grossindustrie und Finanz, nebst einer Anzahl photographischer Reproduktionen. Bern, 1919. pp. 123. *German translation of the Committee's War Information Series. No.20.*

SCHEIDEMANN (PHILIPP) Wollen wir einen Kriegs-Reichstag?: Abrechnung mit Helfferich und Ludendorff; (nach dem stenographischen Bericht der Reichstagssitzung vom 11. März 1924). [Berlin, 1924]. pp. 32.

BATHE (ROLF) Der Zusammenbruch: ein Wort gegen Dolchstosslüge und Kriegshetzer. [Berlin, 1931]. pp. 40.

HAUPTS (LEO) Deutsche Friedenspolitik, 1918-19: eine Alternative zur Machtpolitik des Ersten Weltkrieges. Düsseldorf, [1976]. pp. 489. *bibliog.*

KITCHEN (MARTIN) The silent dictatorship: the politics of the German High Command under Hindenburg and Ludendorff, 1916-1918. London, [1976]. pp. 301. *bibliog.*

— Greece.

LEON (GEORGE B.) The Greek socialist movement and the First World War: the road to unity. Boulder, Col., 1976. pp. 204. *bibliog. (East European Quarterly. East European Monographs. 18)*

— Russia.

UNITED STATES. Committee on Public Information. 1919. Die deutsch-bolschewistische Verschwörung: 70 Dokumente über die Beziehungen der Bolschewiki zur deutschen Heeresleitung, Grossindustrie und Finanz, nebst einer Anzahl photographischer Reproduktionen. Bern, 1919. pp. 123. *German translation of the Committee's War Information Series. No.20.*

— United Kingdom.

ROBBINS (KEITH GILBERT) The abolition of war: the 'peace movement' in Britain, 1914-1919. Cardiff, 1976. pp. 255. *bibliog.*

JONES (ARTHUR PHILIP) Britain's search for Chinese cooperation in the First World War. 1976 [or rather 1977]. fo. 304. *bibliog. Typescript. Ph.D. (London) thesis: unpublished. This thesis is the property of London University and may not be removed from the Library.*

— United States.

ROCHESTER (STUART I.) American liberal disillusionment in the wake of World War I. University Park, Pa., [1977]. pp. 172.

EVALUATION RESEARCH (SOCIAL ACTION PROGRAMMES).

BERNSTEIN (ILENE N.) ed. Validity issues in evaluative research. Beverly Hills, 1976. pp. 134. *bibliogs. Originally published as vol. 4, no. 1 of Sociological Methods and Research.*

— United States.

EVALUATING the labor-market effects of social programs; edited by Orley Ashenfelter and James Blum. Princeton, 1976. pp. 238. *bibliogs. (Princeton University. Department of Economics and Sociology. Industrial Relations Section. Research Report Series. No.120) Papers presented at a conference held at Princeton University in May 1974, jointly sponsored by the Industrial Relations Section and the Office of the Assistant Secretary for Policy, Evaluation and Research of the U.S. Department of Labor.*

EVANGELICALISM.

BRADLEY (IAN) The call to seriousness: the Evangelical impact on the Victorians. London, 1976. pp. 224. *bibliog.*

MAGNUSON (NORRIS ALDEN) Salvation in the slums: evangelical social work, 1865-1920. Metuchen, N.J., 1977. pp. 299. *bibliog. (American Theological Library Association. ATLA Monograph Series. No. 10)*

EVENING AND CONTINUATION SCHOOLS

— Germany.

GERMANY (BUNDESREPUBLIK). Statistisches Bundesamt. Schulen der allgemeinen Fortbildung. a., 1973/75- Wiesbaden. *(Bildung und Kultur. Reihe 1.2)*

EVOLUTION.

EVOLUTION and consciousness: human systems in transition; edited by Erich Jantsch and Conrad Waddington. Reading, Mass., 1976. pp. 259. *bibliogs.*

EXAMINATIONS

— Africa, West.

WEST AFRICAN EXAMINATIONS COUNCIL. Annual report for the year ended March 31, 1974. [Accra, 1974]. pp. 61.

— India.

INDIA. University Grants Commission. 1976. Examination reform: a plan of action and the recommendations of the zonal workshops. [New Delhi], 1976. pp. 44.

— Sri Lanka.

SRI LANKA. Committee to Inquire into and Report on Public Examinations at Secondary School Level. 1972. Interim report. Colombo, 1972. pp. 57. *(Parliament. Sessional Papers. 1972. No. 5)*

— United Kingdom.

WILLMOTT (ALAN STEWART) CSE and GCE grading standards: the 1973 comparability study. Basingstoke, 1977. pp. 208. *bibliog. (U.K. Department of Education and Science. Schools Council. Research Studies) A report to the Schools Council from the Examinations and Tests Research Unit of the National Foundation for Educational Research in England and Wales.*

EXCAVATIONS (ARCHAEOLOGY)

— United Kingdom.

SYMPOSIUM ON ANGLO-SAXON ARCHAEOLOGY, 2ND, OXFORD, 1973. Anglo-Saxon settlement and landscape: papers presented to a symposium, Oxford 1973; edited by Trevor Rowley. Oxford, 1974. pp. 138. *(British Archaeological Reports. 6)*

The 'SMALL towns' of Roman Britain: papers presented to a conference, Oxford 1975; edited by Warwick Rodwell and Trevor Rowley. Oxford, 1975. pp. 236. *bibliogs. (British Archaeological Reports. 15)*

— United States.

The CRISIS in North American archaeology; edited by Allen G. Pastron [and others]. Berkeley, Calif., 1973. pp. 163. *bibliog. (Kroeber Anthropological Society. Special Publications. No. 3) Papers derived from two symposia held in 1972.*

EXCHANGE.

FRADIN (JACQUES) Les fondements logiques de la théorie néoclassique de l'échange: le postulat du numéraire; introduction à la critique de l'économie politique contemporaine. Grenoble, 1976. pp. 243. *bibliog.*

UCHENYE ZAPISKI KAFEDR OBSHCHESTVENNYKH NAUK VUZOV LENINGRADA. Politicheskaia Ekonomiia. vyp.17. Obmen pri sotsializme. Leningrad, 1976. pp. 199.

MITRA (ASHOK) Terms of trade and class relations: an essay in political economy. London, 1977. pp. 193.

EXECUTIONS (LAW)

— Poland.

WENGEREK (EDMUND) Postępowanie egzekucyjne w sprawach cywilnych. Warszawa, 1961. pp. 335.

PAWELA (STANISŁAW) Wykonanie orzeczeń w sprawach karnych: komentarz; stan na dzień 1 stycznia 1965. Warszawa, 1965. pp. 335.

EXECUTIVE ADVISORY BODIES

— Canada.

CANADIAN ENVIRONMENTAL ADVISORY COUNCIL. Annual review. a., 1973/1974- Ottawa. *[In English and French].*

— United Kingdom.

PERSONAL SOCIAL SERVICES COUNCIL [U.K.]. Report. a., 1975(1st)- London.

— United States.

CAMPBELL (RITA RICARDO) Drug lag: federal government decision making. Stanford, Calif., 1976. pp. 62. *(Stanford University. Hoover Institution on War, Revolution and Peace. Hoover Institution Studies. 55)*

EXECUTIVE POWER

— United States.

NEUSTADT (RICHARD ELLIOT) Presidential power: the politics of leadership with reflections on Johnson and Nixon. 2nd ed. New York, [1976]. pp. 324.

EXECUTIVES

— Salaries, pensions, etc.

MURTHY (K.R. SRINIVASA) Corporate strategy and top executive compensation. Cambridge, Mass., 1977. pp. 138.

— United Kingdom.

BIRCH (STEPHANIE) and MACMILLAN (BRENDA) Managers on the move: a study of British managerial mobility. London, [1971]. pp. 20. (British Institute of Management. Management Survey Reports. No. 7)

BURDON (STEPHEN WILLIAM ROGER) Share incentive schemes for executives: a survey of current practice. London, [1971]. pp. 40. bibliog. (British Institute of Management. Management Survey Reports. No. 6)

ROOK (A.) Contracts of service for senior staff: a survey of current practice in 102 companies. London, [1971]. pp. 53. (British Institute of Management. Management Survey Reports. No.2)

BIRCH (STEPHANIE) Management holidays: a survey of current practice in 200 companies. London, [1972]. pp. 19. (British Institute of Management. Management Survey Reports. No. 11)

U.K. Department of Industry. 1977. Industry, education and management: a discussion paper. [London], 1977. 1 vol. (various pagings). bibliog.

— — Health programmes.

KINGSTON (N.) Executive health care: a survey of current practice in 193 companies. London, [1971]. pp. 20. (British Institute of Management. Management Survey Reports. No. 9)

EXECUTIVES, TRAINING OF

— United Kingdom.

ROAD TRANSPORT INDUSTRY TRAINING BOARD [U.K.]. Introductory notes on management development in transportation. [Wembley, 1971?]. pp. 48.

EXECUTORS AND ADMINISTRATORS

— United Kingdom.

MELLOWS (ANTHONY ROGER) Taxation for executors and trustees. 4th ed. London, 1976. pp. 306.

PARRY (Sir DAVID HUGHES) and CLARK (JOHN BRYAN) The law of succession; seventh edition by J.B. Clark. London, 1977. pp. 487.

EXISTENTIALISM.

DOUGLAS (JACK D.) and JOHNSON (JOHN M.) eds. Existential sociology. Cambridge, 1977. pp. 327. bibliog.

EXPECTATION (PSYCHOLOGY).

STATUS characteristics and social interaction: an expectation-states approach; [by] Joseph Berger [and others]. New York, [1977]. pp. 196. bibliog.

EXPENDITURES, PUBLIC.

ROEDER (PHILLIP W.) Stability and change in the determinants of state expenditures. Beverly Hills, [1976]. pp. 34. bibliog.

The ECONOMICS of public services: proceedings of a conference held by the International Economic Association at Turin, Italy; edited by Martin S. Feldstein [and] Robert P. Inman. London, 1977. pp. 529.

EXPERIENCE.

KÖRNER (STEPHAN) Experience and conduct: a philosophical enquiry into practical thinking. Cambridge, 1976. pp. 268. bibliog.

EXPERIMENTAL DESIGN.

HUCK (SCHUYLER W.) and others. Reading statistics and research. New York, [1974]. pp. 387. bibliogs.

MARTIN (RICHARD JOHN) Spatial models with applications in sampling and experimental design. 1977. fo.201. bibliog. Typescript. Ph.D. (London) thesis: unpublished. This thesis is the property of London University and may not be removed from the Library.

EXPLOSIVES.

LUNDSTRÖM (RAGNHILD) Alfred Nobel som internationell företagare: den nobelska sprängämnesindustrin, 1864-1886. Uppsala, 1974. pp. 272. bibliog. (Uppsala. Universitet. Ekonomisk-Historiska Institution. Ekonomisk-Historiska Studier. 10) Doktorsavhandling vid Uppsala universitet, 1974; with English summary.

EXPORT CREDIT.

KLUEMPER (BERNHARD) Finanzierungsprobleme in Ost-West-Handel und -Kooperation. Hamburg, 1976. pp. 260. bibliog. (Hamburg. Hansische Universität. Institut für Aussenhandel und Überseewirtschaft. Forschungsberichte. Nr. 8) Inaugural-Dissertation zur Erlangung des akademischen Grades eines Doktors der Wirtschaftswissenschaft der Universität Hamburg.

— United States.

U.S. financing of East-West trade: the political economy of government credits and the national interest; edited by Paul Marer. Bloomington, Ind., [1975]. pp. 442. bibliog. (Indiana University. International Development Research Center. Studies in East European and Soviet Planning, Development and Trade. No. 22) Includes papers delivered at a panel discussion on "The political economy of subsidized credits in East-West trade", San Francisco, 1974.

EXPORT-IMPORT BANK OF THE UNITED STATES.

ADAMS (FREDERICK C.) Economic diplomacy: the Export-Import Bank and American foreign policy, 1934-1939. Columbia, Mo., 1976. pp. 289. bibliog.

EXSERVICEMEN

— Employment — United Kingdom.

U.K. [Ministry of Defence]. 1976. Report of the servicemen's resettlement survey, 1974; third survey. [London, 1976]. pp. (120).

— Germany — Societies.

WOLF (HEINRICH) of the Jungdeutscher Orden. Die Entstehung des Jungdeutschen Ordens und seine frühen Jahre, 1918-1922. München, 1970. pp. 47. bibliog. (Jungdeutsches Archiv. Beiträge zur Geschichte des Jungdeutschen Ordens. Heft 1)

WOLF (HEINRICH) of the Jungdeutscher Orden. Der Jungdeutsche Orden in seinen mittleren Jahren, 1922-1925. München, 1972. pp. 71. bibliog. (Jungdeutsches Archiv. Beiträge zur Geschichte des Jungdeutschen Ordens. Heft 2)

EXTERNALITIES (ECONOMICS).

THEORY and measurement of economic externalities; edited by Steven A.Y. Lin. New York, [1976]. pp. 265. bibliogs. "This volume is the direct result of a conference on externalities held at Southern Illinois University at Edwardsville, April 19-20, 1974."

— Mathematical models.

LONDON. University. London School of Economics and Political Science. Graduate School of Geography. Discussion Papers. No. 60. Some thoughts on a model for the location of public facilities; [by] Mark Rosenberg. London, 1977. pp. 25. bibliog.

EYSKENS (GASTON).

TINDEMANS (LEO) Dagboek van de Werkgroep-Eyskens. Lier, [1973]. pp. 216.

FABIAN SOCIETY.

MOCHALOV (LEONID VASIL'EVICH) Marksistsko-leninskaia otsenka fabianskogo sotsializma. Moskva, 1976. pp. 88.

MACKENZIE (NORMAN IAN) and MACKENZIE (JEANNE) The first Fabians. London, [1977]. pp. 446.

FABRE (EDOUARD RAYMOND).

ROY (JEAN LOUIS) Edouard-Raymond Fabre, libraire et patriote canadien, 1799-1854: contre l'isolement et la sujétion. Montréal, 1974. pp. 220. bibliog.

FACTOR ANALYSIS.

KRUEGER (ANNE O.) Growth, distortions, and patterns of trade among many countries. Princeton, 1977. pp. 45. bibliog. (Princeton University. Department of Economics and Sociology. International Finance Section. Princeton Studies in International Finance. No. 40)

SCHILDERINCK (J.H.F.) Regression and factor analysis applied in econometrics. Leiden, 1977. pp. 239. bibliog. (Tilburg. Katholieke Hogeschool. Tilburg Institute of Economics. Tilburg Studies in Econometrics. vol. 1)

FACTORY INSPECTION

— United Kingdom.

U.K. Health and Safety Executive. Industrial air pollution. a., 1975(1st)- London. Supersedes U.K. Department of the Environment. Annual report on alkali, etc., works.

U.K. Health and Safety Executive. Industry and services: a report of the work of H.M. Factory Inspectorate incorporating the annual reports of H.M. Inspector of Railways and H.M. Inspector of Explosives. a., 1975(1st)- London.

— — Ireland, Northern.

IRELAND, NORTHERN. Factory Inspectorate. Report. a., 1974- Belfast. 1950-1973 included in IRELAND, NORTHERN. Parliament. House of Commons. [Papers].

FACTORY LAWS AND LEGISLATION

— United Kingdom.

REDGRAVE (ALEXANDER) Health and safety in factories: replacing Redgrave's Factories Acts 22nd edition; [edited] by Ian Fife and E. Antony Machin. London, 1976. pp. 1949.

— — Ireland, Northern.

IRELAND, NORTHERN. Factory Inspectorate. Report. a., 1974- Belfast. 1950-1973 included in IRELAND, NORTHERN. Parliament. House of Commons. [Papers].

FACTORY SYSTEM

— Japan.

ABEGGLEN (JAMES C.) Management and worker: the Japanese solution. Tokyo, [1973 repr. 1975]. pp. 200.

— United Kingdom.

The MANUFACTURERS, their system, and their operatives: a letter to W. Busfeild Ferrand, Esq., M.P., confirming the statements he made in his recent speeches in the House of Commons; by a factory operative of twenty-five years experience. London, J. Ollivier, 1842. pp. 16.

FAJON (ETIENNE).

FAJON (ETIENNE) Ma vie s'appelle liberté. Paris, [1976]. pp. 299.

FALKLAND ISLANDS.

FITTE (ERNESTO J.) Cronicas del Atlantico sur: Patagonia, Malvinas y Antartida. Buenos Aires, 1974. pp. 469. bibliog.

— Politics and government.

FABIAN SOCIETY. Fabian Tracts. [No.] 450. What future for the Falklands?; [by] Colin Phipps. London, 1977. pp. 16.

FAMILY.

The VALUE of children: a cross-national study;...[by] Fred Arnold [and others]. Honolulu, 1975 in progress.

BALBO (LAURA) Stato di famiglia: bisogni privato collettivo. Milano, 1976. pp. 159.

GOODY (JOHN RANKINE) Production and reproduction: a comparative study of the domestic domain. Cambridge, 1976. pp. 157. *bibliog.*

SCANZONI (LETHA) and SCANZONI (JOHN H.) Men, women and change: a sociology of marriage and family. New York, [1976]. pp. 504. *bibliog.*

— History.

LASLETT (PETER) Family life and illicit love in earlier generations: essays in historical sociology. Cambridge, 1977. pp. 270. *bibliog.*

— Canada.

KOHL (SEENA B.) Working together: women and family in southwestern Saskatchewan. Toronto, [1976]. pp. 139. *bibliog.*

— Denmark.

JOHANSEN (HANS CHR.) Befolkningsudvikling og familiestruktur i det 18. årdundrede. Odense, 1975. pp. 209. *(Odense Universitet. Studies in History and Social Sciences. vol. 22)*

KOCH-NIELSEN (INGER) and others. Familie 1975: lov og tal. København, 1976. pp. 55. *bibliog. (Socialforskningsinstituttet. Meddelelser. 19)*

OLSEN (HENNING) and others. Familiekontakter i den tidlige alderdom: rapport nr. 1 fra forløbsundersøgelsen af de aeldre, etc. København, 1976. pp. 252. *(Socialforskningsinstituttet. Publikationer. 74) With English summary.*

— Egypt.

LEGRAIN (GEORGES ALBERT) Fellah de Karnak, Haute-Egypte: journalier dans le système des engagements momentanés; d'après les renseignements recueillis sur les lieux de 1895 à 1900. Paris, 1902. pp. 289-336. *(Société d'Economie et de Science Sociales. Les Ouvriers de Deux Mondes. 3e Série. 5e fasc.)*

— France.

ROUSSEL (LOUIS) Demographer. La famille après le mariage des enfants: étude des relations entre générations. [Paris], 1976. pp. 262. *(France. Institut National d'Etudes Démographiques. Travaux et Documents. Cahiers. No. 78)*

— Germany.

PFEIL (ELISABETH) Die Familie im Gefüge der Grossstadt: zur Sozialtopographie der Stadt. Hamburg, [1965]. pp. 81. *(Gesellschaft für Wohnungs- und Siedlungswesen, Hamburg. Schriftenreihe)*

— India.

RAMU (G.N.) Family and caste in urban India: a case study. New Delhi, [1977]. pp. 224. *bibliog.*

— Italy.

La FAMIGLIA oggi tra referendum e riforma del diritto; scritti di Emanuele Ranci Ortigosa [and others]. Milano, 1974. pp. 72. *(Relazioni Sociali. Quaderni. n.7/8)*

BALBO (LAURA) Stato di famiglia: bisogni privato collettivo. Milano, 1976. pp. 159.

KENT (FRANCIS WILLIAM) Household and lineage in Renaissance Florence: the family life of the Capponi, Ginori, and Rucellai. Princeton, N.J., [1977]. pp. 325.

— Mexico.

ESSAYS on Mexican kinship; Hugo G. Nutini [and others], editors. Pittsburgh, [1976]. pp. 256. *bibliog. Papers of a symposium held at the 1969 annual meeting of the American Anthropological Association in New Orleans.*

— Russia.

VASIL'EVA (EVELINA KARLOVNA) Sem'ia i ee funktsii: demografo-statisticheskii analiz. Moskva, 1975. pp. 181.

— Tunisia.

DEMEERSEMAN (ANDRE) La famille tunisienne et les temps nouveaux: essai de psychologie sociale. 2nd ed. [Tunis, 1972]. pp. 437.

— Underdeveloped areas.

See UNDERDEVELOPED AREAS — Family.

— United Kingdom.

MORONEY (ROBERT M.) The family and the state: considerations for social policy. London, 1976. pp. 142.

STONE (LAWRENCE) The family, sex and marriage in England, 1500-1800. London, [1977]. pp. 800. *bibliog.*

— United States.

HEISS (JEROLD) The case of the black family: a sociological inquiry. New York, 1975. pp. 246. *bibliog.*

ROLE structure and analysis of the family; [by] F. Ivan Nye [and others]. Beverly Hills, [1976]. pp. 214. *bibliog.*

FAMILY ALLOWANCES

— Canada.

KITCHEN (BRIGITTE) Canadian controversy over family income support policies, 1928-1976. 1977. fo. 511. *bibliog. Typescript. Ph.D. (London) thesis: unpublished. This thesis is the property of London University and may not be removed from the Library.*

FAMILY CORPORATIONS

— Liberia.

PORTE (ALBERT) Liberianization or gobbling business?. [Crozierville], 1974. fo. 33.

— United Kingdom — Taxation.

CONFEDERATION OF BRITISH INDUSTRY. Capital transfer tax: consequences for limited private companies. London, 1975. pp. 9.

FAMILY RESEARCH

— United States.

ROLE structure and analysis of the family; [by] F. Ivan Nye [and others]. Beverly Hills, [1976]. pp. 214. *bibliog.*

FAMILY SIZE

— America, Latin.

CARVAJAL (MANUEL J.) and GEITHMAN (DAVID T.) Family planning and family size determination: the evidence from seven Latin American cities. Gainesville, Fla., 1976. pp. 96. *bibliog. (Florida University. School of Inter-American Studies. Latin American Monographs. 2nd Series. 18)*

— United Kingdom.

BUSFIELD (JOAN) and PADDON (MICHAEL) Thinking about children: sociology and fertility in post-war England. Cambridge, 1977. pp. 312. *bibliog.*

FAMILY SOCIAL WORK

— Canada — Quebec.

QUEBEC (PROVINCE). Conseil des Affaires Sociales et de la Famille. Rapport annuel. a., 1975/76- Québec.

— Underdeveloped areas.

See UNDERDEVELOPED AREAS — Family social work.

— United Kingdom.

JENNENS (ROGER) Casework with a family at risk. London, 1976. pp. 29.

— United States — Arizona.

COMPREHENSIVE services to rural poor families: an evaluation of the Arizona Job Colleges program; [by] Keith Baker [and others]. New York, 1976. pp. 191. *bibliog.*

FAMINES.

LIFEBOAT ethics: the moral dilemmas of world hunger; edited by George R. Lucas and Thomas W. Ogletree. New York, [1976]. pp. 162. *bibliog. Originally published in the Spring and Summer 1976 issues of Soundings.*

FANFANI (AMINTORE)

— Anecdotes.

FO (DARIO) Il Fanfani rapito. Verona, [1975]. pp. 175. *(Comune, La. Testi. Nuova Serie. 4)*

FANON (FRANTZ).

LUCAS (PHILIPPE) Sociologie de Frantz Fanon: contribution à une anthropologie de la libération. [Alger, 1971]. pp. 222. *bibliog.*

FRANTZ Fanon. London, [1975]. pp. 200.

HANSEN (EMMANUEL) Frantz Fanon: social and political thought. Ohio, [1977]. pp. 232. *bibliog.*

FARM MANAGEMENT.

QUEENSLAND. Department of Primary Industries. Economics Research Branch. 1966. Farm management handbook. 2nd ed. Brisbane, 1966. pp. 110.

MANCHESTER. University. Department of Agricultural Economics. Bulletins. [No.] 145. Farm management survey, 1970-71, 1971-72: financial results. Manchester, 1973. pp. 75.

INDIA. Ministry of Agriculture and Irrigation. Directorate of Economics and Statistics. 1976. Studies in economics of farm management in I.A.D.P. region of Surat and Bulsar, Gujarat: combined report for the years 1966- 67 to 1968-69. Delhi, 1976. pp. 464.

— India — Gujarat.

ADHVARYU (J.H.) and PARIKH (GOKUL O.) Studies in the economics of farm management in Surat and Bulsar districts, Gujarat: report for the year 1967-68. [Delhi, Controller of Publications], 1975. 2 vols. (in 1).

FARM OWNERSHIP

— Canada — Ontario.

ONTARIO. Ministry of Agriculture and Food. Economics Branch. 1972. Farm mortgages in Ontario; (by Henry F. Noble). [Toronto], 1972. pp. 13.

FARM PRODUCE

— Marketing.

HARRISON (KELLY) and SHWEDEL (KENNETH) Marketing problems associated with small farm agriculture; report on an ADC/RTN seminar held at Michigan State University, June 7-8, 1974. New York, 1974. pp. 8. *(Research and Training Network. Seminar Reports. No. 5)*

— India — Marketing.

INDIA. Ministry of Food, Agriculture, Community Development and Cooperation. Directorate of Marketing and Inspection. Marketing Series. No. 175. Working of regulated markets in India. Regulated markets. Vol. 2. [Delhi, 1971]. pp. 346. *Vol. 1 issued as Marketing Series No. 91.*

— Nigeria — Marketing.

ADALEMO (ISAAC AYINDE) The marketing of major cash crops in the Kainji Lake basin. [Ibadan, 1972]. pp. 73. *(Nigerian Institute of Social and Economic Research. N.I. S.E.R. Monograph Series. No. 1)*

— Russia.

KARCHIKIAŃ (OGANES KHACHATUROVICH) Proizvodstvo i potreblenie sel'skokhoziaistvennykh produktov: regional'nye razlichiia i puti vyravnivaniia urovnia potrebleniia. Erevan, 1977. pp. 212.

— — Marketing.

BUZULUKOV (N.S.) ed. Ekonomika i organizatsiia gosudarstvennykh zagotovok produktov sel'skogo khoziaistva. 2nd ed. Moskva, 1976. pp. 336.

— South Africa — Marketing.

SOUTH AFRICA. Commission of Inquiry into the Marketing Act, Act No.59 of 1968. 1976. Report (R.P.39/1976). in SOUTH AFRICA. Parliament. House of Assembly. Votes and proceedings; (with Printed annexures).

— United Kingdom — Marketing.

ADVISORY COUNCIL FOR AGRICULTURE AND HORTICULTURE IN ENGLAND AND WALES. Report of an inquiry into agricultural exports. [London], 1976. pp. 61.

— Yugoslavia.

YUGOSLAVIA. Savezni Zavod za Statistiku. Studije, Analize i Prikazi. 77. Razvoj turističke potrošnje važnijih poljoprivredno- prehrambenih proizvoda u Jugoslaviji od 1951. do 1970; Development of tourist consumption of selected agricultural-food products in Yugoslavia, 1951-1970;[by] Zlatinka Leković. Beograd, 1975. pp. 151. *bibliog. With English summary.*

FARM TENANCY

— Hawaiian Islands.

MIKLIUS (W.) and SHANG (YUNG-CHENG) Land management policy: leasing of state-owned agricultural lands. Honolulu, 1971. pp. 46.

FARMERS

— Pensions — Finland.

FARMERS' PENSIONS INSTITUTE (FINLAND). The significance of farm closure pensions and farmers' pension knowledge. Espoo, 1976. fo. 10.

— Argentine Republic — Santa Fe.

GALLO (EZEQUIEL) Farmers in revolt: the revolutions of 1893 in the province of Santa Fe, Argentina. London, 1976. pp. 97. *bibliog. (London. University. Institute of Latin American Studies. Monographs. 7)*

— Australia — New South Wales.

PAUL (PHILLIP B.) Characteristics and adjustment problems of former farm operators: a survey of New South Wales farmers who left the land during the 1968-72 rural recession. Sydney, 1976. pp. 250. *bibliog. (Sydney. University. Department of Agricultural Economics. Mimeographed Reports. No. 6)*

— Canada — Ontario.

PURVIS (JAMES M.) and NOBLE (HENRY F.) A socio-economic study of new farm operators in eastern Ontario. Toronto, Ontario Ministry of Agriculture and Food, 1973. pp. 43.

HANN (RUSSELL G.) Farmers confront industrialism: some historical perspectives on Ontario agrarian movements. 3rd ed. Toronto, 1975. pp. 28.

— France.

RATTIN (SOLANGE) Problèmes relatifs au remplacement des chefs d'exploitations agricoles: analyse de la situation existant lors du recensement général de l'agriculture de 1970. Paris, Service Central des Enquêtes et Etudes Statistiques, 1975. pp. 74.

— United Kingdom.

CROSBY (TRAVIS L.) English farmers and the politics of protection, 1815-1852. Hassocks, 1977. pp. 224. *bibliog.*

ECONOMIC DEVELOPMENT COMMITTEE FOR THE AGRICULTURAL INDUSTRY. Agriculture into the 1980s: manpower. London, National Economic Development Office, 1977. pp. 30.

— United States.

HOLLEY (DONALD) Uncle Sam's farmers: the New Deal communities in the lower Mississippi valley. Urbana, Ill., [1975]. pp. 312. *bibliog.*

— — Political activity.

SCHWARTZ (MICHAEL) Radical protest and social structure: the Southern Farmers' Alliance and cotton tenancy, 1880-1890. New York, [1976]. pp. 302.

FARMS

— Canada — Manitoba.

MANITOBA. Department of Agriculture. 1974. In search of land policy for Manitoba; a working paper. [Winnipeg, 1974?]. 1 vol. (various pagings)

— — Ontario.

PURVIS (JAMES M.) and NOBLE (HENRY F.) A socio-economic study of new farm operators in eastern Ontario. Toronto, Ontario Ministry of Agriculture and Food, 1973. pp. 43.

— Malawi.

MALAWI. Agro-Economic Survey. 1971. Agro-economic survey: 4th report: Mbawa: a sample farm management survey of agricultural households near Mbawa in Mzimba district. Zomba, 1971. fo. 29.

MALAWI. Agro-Economic Survey. 1971. Agro-economic survey: 5th report: Masambanjati: a sample farm management survey of agricultural households near Masambanjati in Thyolo district. Zomba, 1971. fo. 27.

MALAWI. Agro-Economic Survey. 1972. Agro-economic survey: 6th report: Nkhota-Kota: a sample farm management survey of agricultural households near Nkhota- Kota. Zomba, 1972. fo. 27.

— Swaziland.

SWAZILAND. Central Statistical Office. Annual census of individual tenure farms. a., 1972/73 (6th)- Mbabane.

— United Kingdom.

AGRICULTURAL DEVELOPMENT AND ADVISORY SERVICE [U.K.]. An enquiry into the expenses of agricultural land ownership, England and Wales, 1973-74. [Pinner], 1976. pp. 69. *bibliog. (Technical Reports. 25/1)*

— — Accounting.

MANCHESTER. University. Department of Agricultural Economics. Bulletins. [No.] 145. Farm management survey, 1970-71, 1971-72: financial results. Manchester, 1973. pp. 75.

FARMS, COLLECTIVE.

GROUP FARMING CONFERENCE, MADISON, WISCONSIN, 1975. Cooperative and commune: group farming in the economic development of agriculture; edited by Peter Dorner. Madison, Wis., 1977. pp. 392. *Papers of the conference sponsored by the Research and Training Network of the Agricultural Development Council and the Land Tenure Center of Wisconsin-Madison University.*

— Russia.

GRUENBERG (KARL) 1891- . Was geht im kollektivierten Sowjet-Dorf vor? Berlin, [1931]. pp. 16.

DENISOV (IURII PAVLOVICH) Razvitie kolkhoznoi demokratii, 1946-1970 gody. Rostov-na-Donu, 1975. pp. 183.

MINBAEV (BARKY) and TOKTOBAEV (AZIZ) Proizvodstvo i raspredelenie kolkhoznogo pribavochnogo produkta. Tashkent, 1975. pp. 125.

IAKIMOV (VITALII NIKOLAEVICH) Tekhnicheskii progress i vosproizvodstvo rabochei sily v kolkhozakh. Moskva, 1976. pp. 151.

MASLOVS'KYI (MYKOLA ANDRIIOVYCH) Interesy kolhospnoho selianstva: ïkh formuvannia i zadovolennia. Kyïv, 1976. pp. 164. *bibliog.*

TAREL'NIK (BORIS IVANOVICH) Kolkhoznaia demokratiia razvitogo sotsialisticheskogo obshchestva. L'vov, 1976. pp. 154. *bibliog.*

— — Law and legislation.

BRAGA (IVAN GEORGIEVICH) Material'naia otvetstvennost' chlenov kolkhoza: pravovye voprosy. Moskva, 1976. pp. 176.

FARMS; SIZE OF.

HARRISON (KELLY) and SHWEDEL (KENNETH) Marketing problems associated with small farm agriculture; report on an ADC/RTN seminar held at Michigan State University, June 7-8, 1974. New York, 1974. pp. 8. *(Research and Training Network. Seminar Reports. No. 5)*

— Sri Lanka.

SELVANAYAGAM (SOMASUNDARAM) The problem of economic holdings in the peasant agriculture of the dry zone of Ceylon. 1971. fo. 361. *bibliog. Typescript. Ph.D.(London) thesis: unpublished. 3 pamphlets in end pocket.*

FAROE ISLANDS

— Census.

FAROE ISLANDS. Census, 1970. Faerøerne: folke- og boligtaellingen, 16. november 1970; [with] bilag: aegteskaber, fødte og døde 1966-70. København, 1975. pp. 150. *(Denmark. Danmarks Statistik. Statistisk Tabelvaerk. 1975. 1)*

— Statistics, Vital.

FAROE ISLANDS. Census, 1970. Faerøerne: folke- og boligtaellingen, 16. november 1970; [with] bilag: aegteskaber, fødte og døde 1966-70. København, 1975. pp. 150. *(Denmark. Danmarks Statistik. Statistisk Tabelvaerk. 1975. 1)*

FASCISM.

IL FASCISMO nell'analisi sociologica: testi di Gianfranco Bettin [and others]; a cura di Luciano Cavalli. Bologna, [1975]. pp. 215.

LACLAU (ERNESTO) Politics and ideology in marxist theory: capitalism, fascism, populism. London, 1977. pp. 203.

MICHEL (HENRI) Les fascismes. [Paris, 1977]. pp. 127. *bibliog.*

— Austria.

HOVORKA (NIKOLAUS) Der Kampf um die geistige Wiedergeburt Österreichs: Vortrag, gehalten...am 26. Jänner 1946. Wien, 1946. pp. 30. *(Kommunistische Partei Österreichs. Zentralstelle für Volksbildung. Vortragsreihe "Probleme der Zeit". Heft 3)*

CARSTEN (FRANCIS LUDWIG) Fascist movements in Austria: from Schönerer to Hitler. London, [1977]. pp. 356. *bibliog.*

— Germany.

NELHIEBEL (KURT) Die Henleins gestern und heute: Hintergründe und Ziele des Witikobundes. Frankfurt/Main, 1962. pp. 88.

VEREINIGUNG DER VERFOLGTEN DES NAZIREGIMES. Vom Häftlingskomitee zum Bund der Antifaschisten: der Weg der VVN; (Redaktion: Max Oppenheimer). Frankfurt/Main, [1972]. pp. 172.

— Italy.

FASHIZM v Italii: sbornik. Moskva, 1923. pp. 100.

MONTANARA (DINO) Illegal durch Italien; (autorisierte Übersetzung aus dem Italienischen von Lisa Dome). Berlin, [1932]. pp. 47.

SILONE (IGNAZIO) pseud. [i.e. Secondo TRANQUILLI] Die Schule der Diktatoren; autorisierte Übersetzung aus dem Italienischen von Jakob Huber. Zürich, [1938]. pp. 326.

CANNISTRARO (PHILIP V.) La fabbrica del consenso: fascismo e mass media; (traduzione dal nordamericano di Giovanni Ferrara). Roma, 1975. pp. 498.

FRANCESCOTTI (RENZO) Antifascismo e Resistenza nel Trentino, 1920-1945. Roma, 1975. pp. 126. *bibliog.*

LI PERA (LUCIA) ed. Il fascismo dalla polemica alla storiografia;...un saggio introduttivo con i confronti antologici da A. Gramsci [and others]. Messina, 1975. pp. 191. *bibliog.*

CORVISIERI (SILVERIO) Resistenza e democrazia. Milano, [1976]. pp. 170.

RISALITI (RENATO) Antifascismo e resistenza nel Pistoiese. Pistoia, [1976]. pp. 270.

SCHIEDER (WOLFGANG) ed. Faschismus als soziale Bewegung: Deutschland und Italien im Vergleich. Hamburg, 1976. pp. 212. *With English summary.*

SITTI (RENATO) and PREVIATI (LUCILLA) Ferrara: il regime fascista. Milano, [1976]. pp. 283.

VOLPE (GIOACCHINO) Scritti sul fascismo, 1919-1938. Roma, [1976]. 2 vols. (in 1).

MOLONY (JOHN NEYLON) The emergence of political catholicism in Italy: Partito Popolare 1919-1926. London, 1977. pp. 225. *bibliog.*

— Romania.

LEBEDEV (NIKOLAI IVANOVICH) Krakh fashizma v Rumynii. Moskva, 1976. pp. 632. *bibliog.*

— South Africa.

VISSER (GEORGE CLOETE) OB: traitors or patriots?. Johannesburg, 1976. pp. 216.

— Spain.

PASTOR (MANUEL) Los origenes del fascismo en España. Madrid, [1975]. pp. 134.

REDONDO ORTEGA (ONESIMO) Onesimo Redondo: textos politicos. Madrid, 1975. pp. 329.

ZAFRA VALVERDE (JOSE) Alma y cuerpo del Movimiento Nacional. Pamplona, 1975. pp. 212. *(Universidad de Navarra. Facultad de Derecho. Coleccion Juridica. 65)*

— Switzerland.

JOSEPH (ROGER) L'Union nationale, 1932-1939: un fascisme en Suisse romande. Neuchâtel, 1975. pp. 438. *bibliog.*

— United Kingdom.

The BRITISH right: Conservative and right wing politics in Britain; edited by Neill Nugent [and] Roger King. Farnborough, [1977]. pp. 230. *bibliog.*

FECUNDITY.

See FERTILITY, HUMAN.

FEDERAL AID TO EDUCATION

— United States.

EDUCATION, inequality, and national policy; edited by Nelson F. Ashline [and others]. Lexington, Mass., [1976]. pp. 199. *Based on an invitational conference held in Newport, R.I., in June 1975.*

FEDERAL AID TO LIBRARIES

— United States.

MOLZ (REDMOND KATHLEEN) Federal policy and library support. Cambridge, Mass., [1976]. pp. 118. *bibliogs.*

FEDERAL GOVERNMENT.

WATTS (RONALD LAMPMAN) Multi-cultural societies and federalism; report presented to the Royal Commission on Bilingualism and Biculturalism. [Ottawa], 1966. 2 vols.(in 1). *Includes 'Appendix 1'.*

VOYENNE (BERNARD) Histoire de l'idée fédéraliste. [Paris, 1973 in progress]. *bibliog. (Centre International de Formation Européenne. Réalités du Présent. Cahiers. Nos. 9, etc.)*

MAKING federalism work: towards a more efficient, equitable and responsive federal system; edited by Russell Mathews. Canberra, 1976. pp. 219. *Papers of a conference organised in August 1975 by the Australian National University's Centre for Research on Federal Financial Relations.*

SAWER (GEOFFREY) Modern federalism. 2nd ed. Carlton, Vic., 1976. pp. 170.

— Australia.

TASMANIA. Committee appointed to inquire into Tasmanian Disabilities under Federation. 1925. Report;...[N.E. Lewis, chairman]. Hobart, 1925. pp. 45.

SPROULE-JONES (M.H.) Public choice and federalism in Australia and Canada. Canberra, 1975. pp. 103. *bibliog. (Australian National University. Centre for Research on Federal Financial Relations. Research Monographs. No. 11)*

— Canada.

MORIN (ROSAIRE) Le statut particulier: une illusion; faut-it confier aux autres l'avenir des canadiens-français? n.p., [1967?]. pp. 37.

SPROULE-JONES (M.H.) Public choice and federalism in Australia and Canada. Canberra, 1975. pp. 103. *bibliog. (Australian National University. Centre for Research on Federal Financial Relations. Research Monographs. No. 11)*

MORIN (CLAUDE) Quebec versus Ottawa: the struggle for self-government, 1960-72; translated from Le pouvoir québécois...en négociation and from Le combat québécois by Richard Howard. Toronto, [1976]. pp. 164.

CARELESS (ANTHONY G.S.) Initiative and response: the adaptation of Canadian federalism to regional economic development. Montreal, 1977. pp. 244. *(Institute of Public Administration of Canada. Canadian Public Administration Series)*

— Germany.

PRUSSIA, plaintiff. Preussen contra Reich vor dem Staatsgerichtshof: (Stenogrammbericht der Verhandlungen...vom 10. bis 14. und vom 17. Oktober 1932); mit einem Vorwort von [Arnold] Brecht. Glashütten im Taunus, 1976. pp. 520. *Reprint of work originally published in Berlin in 1933.*

— Nigeria.

ELEAZU (UMA O.) Federalism and nation-building: the Nigerian experience, 1954- 1964. Ilfracombe, 1977. pp. 280.

— Spain.

JUTGLAR (ANTONI) Pi y Margall y el federalismo español. Madrid, 1975-76. 2 vols. *bibliog.*

LOPEZ-CORDON CORTEZO (MARIA VICTORIA) El pensamiento politico-internacional del federalismo español, 1868-1874. Barcelona, [1975]. pp. 470.

— Switzerland.

FREY (RENE L.) Zwischen Föderalismus und Zentralismus: ein volkswirtschaftliches Konzept des schweizerischen Bundesstaates. Bern, 1977. pp. 134. *bibliog. (Forschungsinstitut für Föderalismus und Regionalstrukturen. Schriften. Nr.1)*

— United States.

SEIDMAN (HAROLD) Politics, position and power: the dynamics of federal organization. 2nd ed. New York, 1975. pp. 354. *bibliog.*

JONES (CHARLES OSCAR) and THOMAS (ROBERT D.) eds. Public policy making in a federal system. Beverly Hills, Calif., [1976]. pp. 284. *bibliogs.*

RIPLEY (RANDALL B.) and FRANKLIN (GRACE A.) Congress, the bureaucracy and public policy. Homewood, Ill., 1976. pp. 193. *bibliog.*

DANIELSON (MICHAEL NILS) and others. One nation, so many governments. Lexington, Mass., [1977]. pp. 141.

— West Indies.

BARBADOS. Regional Council of Ministers. 1964. Draft federal scheme as amended at ninth meeting of the...Council. ..October 1964. [Bridgetown], 1964. pp. 45.

— Yugoslavia.

HABERL (OTHMAR NIKOLA) Parteiorganisation und nationale Frage in Jugoslavien. Berlin, 1976. pp. 242. *bibliog. (Berlin. Freie Universität. Osteuropa-Institut. Philosophische und Soziologischen Veröffentlichungen. Band 13)*

FEEDS

— European Economic Community countries.

EUROPEAN COMMUNITIES. Statistical Office. Feed balance sheet: resources. a., 1976 (1st)- Luxembourg. *[in Community languages].*

FELDSPAR

— Zambia.

CVETKOVIC (D.) Sources of feldspar in the Serenje and Mita Hills areas. Lusaka, 1973. pp. 15. *(Zambia. Geological Survey Department. Economic Reports. No. 32)* 6 maps in end pocket.

FELLNER (WILLIAM JOHN).

ECONOMIC progress, private values and public policy: essays in honor of William Fellner; edited by Bela Balassa and Richard Nelson. Amsterdam, 1977. pp. 339. *bibliogs.*

FEMINISM.

EVANS (RICHARD JOHN) The feminists: women's emancipation movements in Europe, America and Australasia, 1840-1920. London, [1977]. pp. 266. *bibliog.*

FOREMAN (ANN) Femininity as alienation: women and the family in marxism and psychoanalysis. London, 1977. pp. 168. *bibliog.*

ROWBOTHAM (SHEILA) A new world for women: Stella Browne: socialist feminist. London, 1977. pp. 128.

WOMEN and men: changing roles, relationships and perceptions; [edited by] Libby A. Cater [and others]. New York, [1977]. pp. 277. *bibliogs. Consists of transcriptions of discussions and essays written for a workshop held in Aspen, Colo., August 3-10, 1975, under the auspices of the Aspen Institute for Humanistic Studies.*

— France.

VINCENT (MADELEINE) Femmes: quelle libération? Paris, [1976]. pp. 167.

— United Kingdom — Ireland.

ROSE (CATHERINE) The female experience: the story of the woman movement in Ireland. Galway, [1975]. pp. 110. *bibliog.*

FERRARA

— History.

SITTI (RENATO) and PREVIATI (LUCILLA) Ferrara: il regime fascista. Milano, [1976]. pp. 283.

FERRY, pseud.

See URWICH (JOHANN).

FERTILITY, HUMAN.

GLASS (DAVID VICTOR) Review lecture: recent and prospective trends in fertility in developed countries. London, [1976]. pp. 52. (*London. Royal Society of London. Philosophical Transactions. Series B. vol. 274*)

RIDKER (RONALD GENE) ed. Population and development: the search for selective interventions. Baltimore, [1976]. pp. 465. *bibliog.*

CUTRIGHT (PHILLIPS) and JAFFE (FREDERICK S.) Impact of family planning programs on fertility: the U.S. experience. New York, 1977. pp. 150.

— Mathematical models.

CARVAJAL (MANUEL J.) and GEITHMAN (DAVID T.) Family planning and family size determination: the evidence from seven Latin American cities. Gainesville, Fla., 1976. pp. 96. *bibliog.* (*Florida University. School of Inter-American Studies. Latin American Monographs. 2nd Series. 18*)

HELLER (PETER S.) Interactions of childhood mortality and fertility in W. Malaysia, 1947-1970. Ann Arbor, 1976. pp. 33. *bibliog.* (*Michigan University. Center for Research on Economic Development. Discussion Papers. No.57*)

— Bangladesh.

U.K. Ministry of Overseas Development. Population Bureau. 1977. Report on the 1974 Bangladesh retrospective survey of fertility and mortality. London, 1977. pp. 173.

— Denmark.

MØRKEBERG (HENRIK) Fødslers placering i familiens livsforløb, etc. København, 1976. pp. 158. *bibliog.(Socialforskningsinstituttet. Publikationer. 68) With English summary.*

— Finland.

MYRSKYLÄ (PEKKA) Syntyvyys...: syntyvyyden kehitys ja alueelliset erot Suomessa, etc. Helsinki, 1976. pp. 112. (*Finland. Tilastokeskus. Tutkimuksia. 36 With Swedish and English summaries and table headings.*)

— France.

TUGAULT (YVES) Fécondité et urbanisation. [Paris], 1975. pp. 137. *bibliog.* (*France. Institut National d'Etudes Démographiques. Travaux et Documents. Cahiers. No.74*)

NATALITE et politique démographique, etc. [Paris], 1976. pp. 162. *bibliog.* (*France. Institut National d'Etudes Démographiques. Travaux et Documents. Cahiers. No. 76*)

— Underdeveloped areas.

See UNDERDEVELOPED AREAS — Fertility, Human.

— United Kingdom.

LANGFORD (C.M.) Birth control practice and marital fertility in Great Britain: a report on a survey carried out in 1967-68. London, 1976. pp. 141.

BUSFIELD (JOAN) and PADDON (MICHAEL) Thinking about children: sociology and fertility in post-war England. Cambridge, 1977. pp. 312. *bibliog.*

— — Ireland, Northern.

IRELAND, NORTHERN. Census, 1971. Census of population, 1971: fertility tables. Belfast, 1976. pp. 89.

— United States.

RINDFUSS (RONALD R.) and SWEET (JAMES A.) Postwar fertility trends and differentials in the United States. New York, [1977]. pp. 225. *bibliog.*

WESTOFF (CHARLES F.) and RYDER (NORMAN B.) The contraceptive revolution. Princeton, [1977]. pp. 388. *Published for the Office of Population Research, Princeton University.*

— Yugoslavia.

YUGOSLAVIA. Savezni Zavod za Statistiku. 1975. Fertilitet ženskog stanovništva, 1968-1972: rezultati po republikama i pokrajinama. Beograd, 1975. pp. 271.

FERTILIZER INDUSTRY.

INTERREGIONAL FERTILIZER SYMPOSIUM, 2ND, KIEV AND DELHI, 1971. Recent developments in the fertilizer industry: report, etc. (ID/94) (ID/WG.99/113). New York, United Nations, 1972. pp. 118.

— Information services.

UNITED NATIONS INDUSTRIAL DEVELOPMENT ORGANIZATION. Guides to Information Sources. No. 21. Information sources on the fertilizer industry. (ID/164) (UNIDO/LIB/SER.D/21). New York, United Nations, 1976. pp. 96. *bibliog.*

— India.

LONDON (PAUL A.) Merchants as promoters of rural development: an Indian case study. New York,1975. pp. 159. *bibliog.*

— Ireland (Republic).

EIRE. Fertilisers Prices Advisory Body. 1976. Report of enquiry into the fertiliser industry. Dublin, [1976]. pp. 120.

FEUDALISM.

WHIMSTER (MICHAEL STEPHEN) Patrimonialism: its meaning for nineteenth century German historians with special reference to Max Weber's adoption and use of the term in his Herrschaftssoziologie. 1976. fo.172. *bibliog. Typescript. Ph.D. (London) thesis: unpublished. This thesis is the property of London University and may not be removed from the Library.*

— Europe.

HOBSBAWM (ERIC JOHN ERNEST) and BOURN (DOUGLAS) Feudalism, capitalism and the absolute state; [2] reviews of Perry Anderson. London, 1976. pp. 18. (*Communist Party of Great Britain. History Group. Our History. No.66*)

— France.

EVERGATES (THEODORE) Feudal society in the baillage of Troyes under the counts of Champagne, 1152-1284. Baltimore, [1975]. pp. 273. *bibliog.*

BOIS (GUY) Crise du féodalisme: (économie rurale et démographie en Normandie orientale du début du 14e siècle au milieu du 16e siècle). [Paris, 1976]. pp. 412. *bibliog. (Fondation Nationale des Sciences Politiques. Cahiers. 202)*

— Hungary.

LANOVIĆ (MIHAJLO) Zapadno-evropski feudalizam i ugarsko-hrvatski donacionalni sustav. Zagreb, 1928. pp. 106. *bibliog.*

— Russia — White Russia.

KOZLOVSKII (PAVEL GRIGOR'EVICH) Magnatskoe khoziaistvo Belorussii vo vtoroi polovine XVIII v.: tsentral'naia i zapadnaia zony. Minsk, 1974. pp. 182. *bibliog.*

— United Kingdom.

MILSOM (STROUD FRANCIS CHARLES) The legal framework of English feudalism. Cambridge, 1976. pp. 201. (*Cambridge. University. Maitland Memorial Lectures. 1972*)

— Yugoslavia — Croatia.

LANOVIĆ (MIHAJLO) Zapadno-evropski feudalizam i ugarsko-hrvatski donacionalni sustav. Zagreb, 1928. pp. 106. *bibliog.*

FIANNA FAIL.

SACKS (PAUL MARTIN) The Donegal Mafia: an Irish political machine. New Haven, Conn., 1976. pp. 241.

FICHTE (JOHANN GOTTLIEB).

VORLAENDER (KARL) Kant, Fichte, Hegel und der Sozialismus. Berlin, 1920. pp. 105.

FIELD CROPS

— Mathematical models.

ADAMS (FRANCIS GERARD) and BEHRMAN (JERE R.) Econometric models of world agricultural commodity markets: cocoa, coffee, tea, wool, cotton, sugar, wheat, rice. Cambridge, Mass., [1976]. pp. 160. *bibliog.*

FIELD THEORY (PHYSICS).

SACHS (MENDEL) The field concept in contemporary science. Springfield, Ill., [1973]. pp. 120.

FIJI ISLANDS

— Foreign relations.

See also EUROPEAN ECONOMIC COMMUNITY — Fiji.

— Industries.

FIJI. Bureau of Statistics. 1975. Census of industries, 1973; incorporating 1974 constant price data. Suva, 1975. fo. 31.

— Politics and government.

NAYACAKALOU (RUSIATE RAIBOSA) Leadership in Fiji. Melbourne, 1975. pp. 170. *bibliog.*

FILE ORGANIZATION (COMPUTER SCIENCE).

GHOSH (SAKTI P.) Data base organization for data management. New York, 1977. pp. 376. *bibliogs.*

FILIPINOS IN THE UNITED KINGDOM.

MAW (LEILA) and others. Immigrants and employment in the clothing industry. London, 1974. fo.26. (*Runnymede Trust. Industrial Publications*)

FINANCE.

MATHEWS (RUSSELL LLOYD) and JAY (W.R.C.) Measures of fiscal effort and fiscal capacity in relation to Australian state road finance. Canberra, 1974. pp. 79. (*Australian National University. Centre for Research on Federal Financial Relations. Research Monographs. No. 5*)

CATHELINEAU (JEAN) Finances publiques: politique budgétaire et droit financier. Paris, 1975. pp. 235. *bibliog.*

DUVERGER (MAURICE) Finances publiques. 8th ed. Paris, [1975]. pp. 419. *bibliog.*

FRANCE. Direction de la Documentation. La Documentation Française. Notes et Etudes Documentaires. Nos. 4,226-4, 227-4,228. Le financement du commerce international; per Jacques Blanc. Paris, 1975. pp. 53. *bibliog.*

BECKWITH (BURNHAM PUTNAM) Free goods: the theory of free or communist distribution. Palo Alto, Calif., [1976]. pp. 216. *bibliog.*

MUSGRAVE (RICHARD ABEL) and MUSGRAVE (PEGGY B.) Public finance in theory and practice. 2nd ed. New York, [1976]. pp. 778. *bibliogs.*

PUBLIC and urban economics: essays in honor of William S. Vickrey; edited by Ronald E. Grieson. Lexington, Mass., [1976]. pp. 417. *bibliogs.*

The ECONOMICS of public services: proceedings of a conference held by the International Economic Association at Turin, Italy; edited by Martin S. Feldstein [and] Robert P. Inman. London, 1977. pp. 529.

FINANCIAL crises: institutions and markets in a fragile environment; edited by Edward I. Altman and Arnold W. Sametz. New York, [1977]. pp. 288. *bibliogs. Papers of a conference on financial crises, organized by the Salomon Brothers Center for the Study of Financial Institutions, in New York in 1976.*

SAVAGE (DONALD T.) Money and banking. Santa Barbara, Calif., [1977]. pp. 491. *bibliogs.*

— Accounting — Data processing.

UNION DOUANIERE ET ECONOMIQUE DE L'AFRIQUE CENTRALE. Département des Statistiques. 1970. Informatique et gestion de l'état. Brazzaville, 1970. 2 pts. *(Etudes Statistiques. Nos. 16, 18)*

— Law.

CATHELINEAU (JEAN) Finances publiques: politique budgétaire et droit financier. Paris, 1975. pp. 235. *bibliog.*

— Mathematical models.

MONEY and finance in economic growth and development: essays in honour of Edward S. Shaw;...edited by Ronald I. McKinnon. New York, [1976]. pp. 339. *bibliogs. Proceedings of the conference held at Stanford University in April 1974, under the auspices of the Center for Research in Economic Growth.*

— Angola.

INSTITUTO DE CREDITO DE ANGOLA. Conselho de Administração. Relatorio balanço e contas do Conselho de Administração e parecer do Conselho Fiscal. a., 1970-1972. [Luanda].

— Asia, Southeast.

KOOMSUP (PRAIPHOL) Reserve pooling in the Asean region. Bangkok, 1976. pp. 21. *bibliog. (Bangkok. Thammasat University. Faculty of Economics. Discussion Paper Series. No. 51)*

— Australia.

TASMANIA. Office of the Government Statistician. 1897. Federal finance: observations on the difficulties of the problem; with an enquiry into their underlying causes; by R.M. Johnston; with an introduction and appendix by A. Inglis Clark. Hobart, 1897. pp. 42.

— Austria.

HOLL (BRIGITTE) Hofkammerpräsident Gundaker Thomas Graf Starhemberg und die österreichische Finanzpolitik der Barockzeit, 1703-1715. Wien, 1976. pp. 453. *bibliog. (Archiv für Österreichische Geschichte. Band 132)*

— Barbados.

CENTRAL BANK OF BARBADOS. Quarterly report. a., Je 1977 (v.4, no.2)- Bridgetown.

— Brazil.

BRAZIL. Ministerio da Fazenda. 1972. Ministros da Fazenda, 1822-1972. Rio de Janeiro, 1972. pp. 238.

— Ecuador.

ECUADOR. Ministerio de Finanzas. Informe de labores. a., 1972/73- [Quito].

ECHEVERRIA (ROBERTO) and others. Current economic position and prospects of Ecuador: this report is based on the findings of an economic mission which visited Ecuador during...1972, etc. Washington, International Bank for Reconstruction and Development, 1973. 1 vol.(various pagings). *(Country Economic Reports)*

— Europe.

STRASSER (DANIEL) Les finances de l'Europe. [Paris, 1975]. pp. 312.

— Europe, Eastern.

GARLAND (JOHN S.) Financing foreign trade in Eastern Europe: problems of bilateralism and currency inconvertibility. New York, 1977. pp. 168. *bibliog.*

— European Economic Community countries — Accounting.

EUROPEAN COMMUNITIES. Statistical Office. Regional accounts: economic aggregates. a., 1970 (1st)- Luxembourg. *[in Community languages].*

— France.

Les ELANS d'un patriote: ou, Nouvelles bases politiques. 2nd ed. Paris, chez les Marchands de Nouveautés, 1785. pp. (iv), 59.

RUEFF (JACQUES) Combats pour l'ordre financier: mémoires et documents pour servir à l'histoire du dernier demi-siècle. [Paris, 1972]. pp. 480.

DUVERGER (MAURICE) Finances publiques. 8th ed. Paris, [1975]. pp. 419. *bibliog.*

FRANCE. Comité du Financement. 1976. Rapport...: préparation du 7e Plan; (with Annexes). Paris, 1976. 2 parts.

GREVET (PATRICE) Besoins populaires et financement public. [Paris, 1976]. pp. 543.

SCHUKER (STEPHEN A.) The end of French predominance in Europe: the financial crisis of 1924 and the adoption of the Dawes plan. Chapel Hill, [1976]. pp. 444. *bibliog.*

— Germany.

MUNZEL (DIETER) Die Funktionsfähigkeit von Planungs- und Kontrollsystemen auf der Ebene von Bundesregierung und Bundesverwaltung. Hamburg, 1976. pp. 205. *bibliog. Dissertation zur Erlangung des Grades eines Doktors der Wirtschafts- und Sozialwissenschaften der Universität Hamburg.*

PILZ (FRANK) Regierungsaufgaben und Finanzpolitik: das Aufgaben- und Finanz-, das Finanzplanungs- und Aufgabenplanungssystem der Bundesregierung. Köln, [1976]. pp. 244. *bibliog.*

SCHWANEWEDE (GERD) Finanzmärkte in der Bundesrepublik Deutschland...: ein Beitrag zur Analyse von Finanzierungsrechnungen der Deutschen Bundesbank. Berlin, [1976]. pp. 264. *bibliog. (Bonn. Universität. Institut für das Spar-, Giro- und Kreditwesen. Untersuchungen über das Spar-, Giro- und Kreditwesen. Band 83) With summaries in English and French.*

HERRING (RICHARD J.) and MARSTON (RICHARD C.) National monetary policies and international financial markets. Amsterdam, 1977. pp. 302. *bibliogs.*

VEREIN FÜR SOZIALPOLITIK. Schriften. Neue Folge. Band 75/V. Öffentliche Finanzwirtschaft und Verteilung, V; von Willi Albers [and others]; herausgegeben von Wilhelmine Dreissig. Berlin, [1977]. pp. 202. *With summaries and table of contents in English.*

— — Hamburg.

BETRACHTUNGEN über das Hamburgische Finanzwesen. Hamburg, 1857. pp. 63.

TESCH (HELMUT) Öffentliche Finanzwirtschaft in Ballungsräumen, dargestellt am Ballungsraum Hamburg. Hamburg, 1976. pp. 268. *bibliog. (Hamburg. Hamburgisches Welt-Wirtschafts-Archiv. Veröffentlichungen)*

— Honduras.

BANCO CENTRAL DE HONDURAS. Departamento de Estudios Economicos. Informe economico. a., 1975- Tegucigalpa, D.C.

— India — Andhra Pradesh.

ANDHRA PRADESH. Finance Department. 1973. Memorandum submitted to the sixth Finance Commission. Hyderabad, 1973. 2 vols. (in 1).

— Ireland (Republic) — Accounting.

EIRE. Department of Finance. 1976. An outline of Irish financial procedures. Dublin, [1976]. pp. 33, v.

— Italy.

FANTOZZI (AUGUSTO) Guida fiscale italiana: imposte indirette. Torino, [1976]. 2 vols. *bibliogs.*

— Mexico.

SIERRA BRABATA (CARLOS J.) Historia de la administracion hacendaria en Mexico, 1911-1970. Vol. II. Mexico, Secretaria de Hacienda y Credito Publico, 1971. pp. 45. *(Boletin Bibliografico. Publicaciones)*

— Morocco.

LOZE (MARC) Les finances de l'état. Rabat, Secrétariat d'Etat aux Finances, [1971]. pp. 662.

— Peru.

BARGHOLTZ (PERCY) and others. Current economic position and prospects of Peru: this report is based on the findings of an economic mission which visited Peru in.. .1972 and...1973, etc. Washington, International Bank for Reconstruction and Development, 1973. pp. 219. *(Country Economic Reports)*

— Poland.

FINANSE Polski Ludowej w latach 1944-1960. Warszawa, 1964. pp. 488.

CHOLIŃSKI (TADEUSZ) Przedsiębiorstwo a bank. Warszawa, 1972. pp. 146.

WIT (ZBIGNIEW) Inwestycje, finansowanie i efektywność. Warszawa, 1976. pp. 116. *bibliog.*

— Russia.

VOZNESENSKII (ERNEST ALEKSANDROVICH) Diskussionnye voprosy teorii sotsialisticheskikh finansov. Leningrad, 1969. pp. 158.

D'IACHENKO (VASILII PETROVICH) Tovarno-denezhnye otnosheniia i finansy pri sotsializme; (raboty... , opublikovannye v 1946-1970 gg.). Moskva, 1974. pp. 495. *bibliog.*

BIRMAN (ALEKSANDR MIKHAILOVICH) Ocherki teorii sovetskikh finansov. vyp.3. Moskva, 1975. pp. 255. *bibliog.*

ALLAKHVERDIAN (DERENIK AKOPOVICH) Finansovo-kreditnyi mekhanizm razvitogo sotsializma. Moskva, 1976. pp. 238.

— — Estonia — Tallin.

TALLIN. Stadtkämmerei. Kämmereibuch der Stadt Reval, 1432-1463; bearbeitet von Reinhard Vogelsang. Köln, 1976. 2 vols. (in 1). *bibliog. (Hansischer Geschichtsverein. Quellen und Darstellungen zur Hansischen Geschichte. Neue Folge. Band 22)*

— Sierra Leone.

BANK OF SIERRA LEONE. Economic review. s-a., Ja/Je 1975 (v.9, no. 1/2)- [Freetown].

— Somali Republic.

SOMALI DEVELOPMENT BANK. Annual report and statement of accounts. a., 1975 (7th)- Mogadiscio.

— South Africa — Accounting.

SOUTH AFRICA. Department of the Auditor General. Report...on the accounts of the Central Orange Free State Area Bantu Affairs Administration Board. a., 1972/74(1st)- Pretoria. *[in English and Afrikaans]. Included in SOUTH AFRICA. Parliament. House of Assembly. Votes and proceedings (with Printed annexures).*

SOUTH AFRICA. Department of the Auditor General. Report...on the accounts of the Vaal Triangle Area Bantu Affairs Administration Board. a., 1972/74 (1st)- Pretoria. *[in English and Afrikaans] Included in SOUTH AFRICA. Parliament. House of Assembly. Votes and proceedings (with Printed annexures).*

SOUTH AFRICA. Department of the Auditor General. Report...on the accounts of the Western Transvaal Area Bantu Affairs Administration Board. a., 1972/74- Pretoria. *[in English and Afrikaans]. Included in SOUTH AFRICA. Parliament. House of Assembly. Votes and proceedings (with Printed annexures).*

SOUTH AFRICA. Department of the Auditor-General. Report...on the accounts of the Central Transvaal Area Bantu Affairs Administration Board. a., 1973/75 (1st)- Pretoria. *[in English and Afrikaans] Included in SOUTH AFRICA. Parliament. House of Assembly. Votes and proceedings (with Printed annexures).*

SOUTH AFRICA. Department of the Auditor-General. Report...on the accounts of the Diamond Field Area Bantu Affairs Administration Board. a., 1973/75 (1st)- Pretoria. *[in English and Afrikaans]. Included in South Africa. Parliament. House of Assembly. Votes and proceedings (with Printed annexures).*

SOUTH AFRICA. Department of the Auditor General. Report...on the accounts of the Drakensberg Area Bantu Affairs Administration Board. a., 1973/75 (1st)- Pretoria. *[in English and Afrikaans]. Included in SOUTH AFRICA. Parliament. House of Assembly. Votes and proceedings (with Printed annexures).*

SOUTH AFRICA. Department of the Auditor-General. Report...on the accounts of the East Rand Area Bantu Affairs Administration Board. a., 1973/75 (1st)- Pretoria. *[in English and Afrikaans]. Included in SOUTH AFRICA. Parliament. House of Assembly. Votes and proceedings (with Printed annexures).*

SOUTH AFRICA. Department of the Auditor General. Report...on the accounts of the Eastern Cape Area Bantu Affairs Administration Board. a., 1973/75(1st)- Pretoria. *[in English and Afrikaans]. Included in SOUTH AFRICA. Parliament. House of Assembly. Votes and proceedings (with Printed annexures).*

SOUTH AFRICA. Department of the Auditor General. Report...on the accounts of the Eastern Transvaal Area Bantu Affairs Administration Board. a., 1973/75 (1st)- Pretoria. *[in English and Afrikaans]. Included in SOUTH AFRICA. Parliament. House of Assembly. Votes and proceedings (with Printed annexures)*

SOUTH AFRICA. Department of the Auditor General. Report...on the accounts of the Highveld Area Bantu Affairs Administration Board. a., 1973/75 (1st)- Pretoria. *[in English and Afrikaans]. Included in SOUTH AFRICA. Parliament. House of Assembly. Votes and proceedings (with Printed annexures).*

SOUTH AFRICA. Department of the Auditor General. Report...on the accounts of the Karoo Area Bantu Affairs Administration Board. a., 1973/75 (1st)- Pretoria. *[in English and Afrikaans]. Included in SOUTH AFRICA. Parliament. House of Assembly. Votes and proceedings (with Printed annexures).*

SOUTH AFRICA. Department of the Auditor General. Report...on the accounts of the Midlands Area Bantu Affairs Administration Board. a., 1973/75 (1st)- Pretoria. *[in English and Afrikaans]. Included in SOUTH AFRICA. Parliament. House of Assembly. Votes and proceedings (with Printed annexures).*

SOUTH AFRICA. Department of the Auditor-General. Report...on the accounts of the Northern Natal Area Bantu Affairs Administration Board. a., 1973/75 (1st)- Pretoria. *[in English and Afrikaans] Included in SOUTH AFRICA. Parliament. House of Assembly. Votes and proceedings (with Printed annexures).*

SOUTH AFRICA. Department of the Auditor-General. Report...on the accounts of the Northern Transvaal Area Bantu Affairs Administration Board. a., 1973/75 to date. Pretoria. *[in English and Afrikaans]. Included in SOUTH AFRICA. Parliament. House of Assembly. Votes and proceedings (with Printed annexures).*

SOUTH AFRICA. Department of the Auditor General. Report...on the accounts of the Peninsula Area Bantu Affairs Administration Board. a., 1973/75 (1st)- Pretoria. *[in English and Afrikaans] Included in SOUTH AFRICA. Parliament. House of Assembly. Votes and proceedings (with Printed annexures).*

SOUTH AFRICA. Department of the Auditor-General. Report...on the accounts of the Port Natal Area Bantu Affairs Administration Board. a., 1973/75 (1st)- Pretoria. *[in English and Afrikaans]. Included in SOUTH AFRICA. Parliament. House of Assembly. Votes and proceedings (with Printed annexures)*

SOUTH AFRICA. Department of the Auditor-General. Report...on the accounts of the Southern Transvaal Area Bantu Affairs Administration Board. a., 1973/75 (1st)- Pretoria. *[in English and Afrikaans]. Included in SOUTH AFRICA. Parliament. House of Assembly. Votes and proceedings.*

SOUTH AFRICA. Department of the Auditor-General. Report...on the accounts of the West Rand Area Bantu Affairs Administration Board. a., 1973/75 (1st)- Pretoria. *[in English and Afrikaans].Included in SOUTH AFRICA. Parliament. House of Assembly. Votes and proceedings (with Printed annexures).*

SOUTH AFRICA. Department of the Auditor General. Report...on the accounts of the Northern Orange Free State Area Bantu Affairs Administration Board. a., 1974/75- Pretoria. *[in English and Afrikaans]. Included in SOUTH AFRICA. Parliament. House of Assembly. Votes and proceedings (with Printed annexures).*

— Spain.

LADERO QUESADA (MIGUEL ANGEL) La Hacienda real de Castilla en el siglo XV. La Laguna, Tenerife, 1973. pp. 384. *bibliog. (La Laguna. Universidad. Estudios de Historia. No. 1)*

— Switzerland.

GIOVANOLI (FRIEDRICH) Unter der Herrschaft des Finanzkapitals. [Zurich?, 1934]. pp. 71.

— Underdeveloped areas.

See UNDERDEVELOPED AREAS — Finance.

— United Kingdom.

REMARKS upon some wrong computations and conclusions, contained in a late tract, entitled, Discourses on the publick revenues, and on the trade of England; in a letter to Mr. D.S. London, W. Keblewhite, 1698. pp. 47.

PALGRAVE (Sir ROBERT HARRY INGLIS) Articles in the Quarterly Review...1878-1899. [Great Yarmouth], 1899. 1 vol. (various pagings). *Collected and bound for the author's library.*

JOHNSON (CHRISTOPHER) 1931- . Anatomy of U.K. finance, 1970-75. London, 1976. pp. 275. *bibliog.*

U.K. Committee to Review the Functioning of Financial Institutions. 1977- . Evidence on the financing of industry and trade; (Sir Harold Wilson, chairman). London, 1977 in progress.

CITY CAPITAL MARKETS COMMITTEE. Evidence to the Wilson Committee. [London, 1977]. pp. 40.

MEMORANDUM of evidence to the Committee to review the Functioning of Financial Institutions;...prepared...by Professor M.J. Artis [and others]. London, 1977. pp. 21. *(National Institute of Economic and Social Research. Discussion Papers. No. 3)*

— — Bibliography.

SMITH (GERRY M.) compiler. The financial activities of the City of London; a select bibliography. London, 1976. pp. 27. *(City University. Business School. Business School Bibliographies. No. 1)*

— — Ireland, Northern.

IRELAND, NORTHERN. Trading and other accounts together with the reports of the Comptroller and Auditor-General on them and on other accounts printed separately. a., 1971/72. Belfast. *1951/52-1970/71 included in IRELAND, NORTHERN. Parliament. House of Commons. [Papers]. 1972/73 onwards included in British Parliamentary Papers.*

— — Liverpool.

FINANCES OF THE CITY OF LIVERPOOL, THE; [pd. by Liverpool Corporation]. a., 1929/30 [1st]- 1935/36. Liverpool.

— United States.

The CRISIS met: a reply to Junius. [New York, 1840]. pp. 16.

O'CONNOR (JAMES) The fiscal crisis of the state. New York, [1973]. pp. 276. *bibliog.*

MUSGRAVE (RICHARD ABEL) and MUSGRAVE (PEGGY B.) Public finance in theory and practice. 2nd ed. New York, [1976]. pp. 778. *bibliogs.*

BUCHANAN (JAMES McGILL) and WAGNER (RICHARD E.) Democracy in deficit: the political legacy of Lord Keynes. New York, [1977]. pp. 195.

FINANCIAL crises: institutions and markets in a fragile environment; edited by Edward I. Altman and Arnold W. Sametz. New York, [1977]. pp. 288. *bibliogs. Papers of a conference on financial crises, organized by the Salomon Brothers Center for the Study of Financial Institutions, in New York in 1976.*

MAXWELL (JAMES ACKLEY) and ARONSON (JAY RICHARD) Financing state and local governments. 3rd ed. Washington, D.C., [1977]. pp. 290. *bibliog. (Brookings Institution. Studies of Government Finance)*

— — New Haven.

LOCAL public finance and the fiscal squeeze: a case study; edited by John R. Meyer and John M. Quigley. Cambridge, Mass., [1977]. pp. 201. *Papers from a seminar sponsored by the Institution for Social and Policy Studies at Yale University and the Yale Law School, 1971-73.*

— Yugoslavia.

JAŠIĆ (ZORAN) Financiranje zajedničkih potreba u specifičnim oblastima društvene reprodukcije. Zagreb, 1976. pp. 53. *bibliog.*

— Zaire.

BANQUE DU ZAIRE. Bulletin mensuel de la statistique. m., Ap 1975 (no.3)- [Kinshasa].

FINANCIAL INSTITUTIONS

— Belgium.

CURRENT problems of financial intermediaries; edited by P. Frantzen; contributors: W. Eizenga [and others]. Rotterdam, 1975. pp. 170. *bibliogs. (Vrije Universiteit Brussel. Faculty of Economic, Social and Political Sciences. Yearbook. 1974)*

— Brazil.

BRAZIL. Departamento de Censos. 1975. Censo comercial [1970]: Brasil; inqueritos especiais: comercio e administração de imoveis, bancos comerciais, finanseiras, seguros. [Rio de Janeiro, 1975]. pp. 142.

— United Kingdom.

CITY CAPITAL MARKETS COMMITTEE. Evidence to the Wilson Committee. [London, 1977]. pp. 40.

— United States.

FINANCIAL crises: institutions and markets in a fragile environment; edited by Edward I. Altman and Arnold W. Sametz. New York, [1977]. pp. 288. *bibliogs. Papers of a conference on financial crises, organized by the Salomon Brothers Center for the Study of Financial Institutions, in New York in 1976.*

FINANCIAL STATEMENTS

— United States.

DYCKMAN (THOMAS R.) and others. Efficient capital markets and accounting: a critical analysis. Englewood Cliffs, [1975]. pp. 130. *bibliog.*

FINLAND

— Commercial policy.

NUMERS (BJÖRN VON) Finlands handelspolitik i internationellt perspektiv. [Helsinki, 1975]. pp. 121. *(Ekonomiska Samfundet i Finland. Populärekonomiska Skrifter. Nr. 8)*

— Economic conditions.

LANDER (PATRICIA SLADE) In the shadow of the factory: social change in a Finnish community. New York, [1976]. pp. 191. *bibliog.*

MUSTONEN (MAIJA) and others. Imeväiskuolleisuuteen vaikuttavat sosiaaliset ja taloudelliset tekijät Suomessa 1910-1971, etc. Helsinki, 1976. pp. 148. *bibliog.* *(Finland. Suomen Virallinen Tilasto. Finlands Officiella Statistik. 32. Sosiaalisia Erikoistutkimuksia. 46) With English summary.*

— Foreign relations.

NEVAKIVI (JUKKA TANELI) The appeal that was never made: the Allies, Scandinavia and the Finnish Winter War, 1939-1940. London, [1976]. pp. 225. *bibliog.*

— History.

LANDER (PATRICIA SLADE) In the shadow of the factory: social change in a Finnish community. New York, [1976]. pp. 191. *bibliog.*

— Industries.

FINLAND. Tilastokeskus. Liikevaihtoverotus: Omsättningsbeskattningen. a., 1972- Helsinki. *[in Finnish and Swedish]. File includes Lopetetut liikevaihtoverovelvolliset yritykset.*

SUOMEN teollisuus ja teollinen käsityö, 1900-1965: (Industry and industrial handicraft in Finland, 1900-1965). Helsinki, 1976. pp. 220. *bibliog.* *(Suomen Pankki. Taloustieteellinen Tutkimuslaitos. Julkaisuja. 7) With English summary and table of contents.*

— Social conditions.

LANDER (PATRICIA SLADE) In the shadow of the factory: social change in a Finnish community. New York, [1976]. pp. 191. *bibliog.*

MUSTONEN (MAIJA) and others. Imeväiskuolleisuuteen vaikuttavat sosiaaliset ja taloudelliset tekijät Suomessa 1910-1971, etc. Helsinki, 1976. pp. 148. *bibliog.* *(Finland. Suomen Virallinen Tilasto. Finlands Officiella Statistik. 32. Sosiaalisia Erikoistutkimuksia. 46) With English summary.*

— Statistics, Vital.

MUSTONEN (MAIJA) and others. Imeväiskuolleisuuteen vaikuttavat sosiaaliset ja taloudelliset tekijät Suomessa 1910-1971, etc. Helsinki, 1976. pp. 148. *bibliog.* *(Finland. Suomen Virallinen Tilasto. Finlands Officiella Statistik. 32. Sosiaalisia Erikoistutkimuksia. 46) With English summary.*

FIREARMS.

KENNETT (LEE B.) and ANDERSON (JAMES LAVERNE) The gun in America: the origins of a national dilemma. Westport, Conn., 1975. pp. 339. *bibliog.*

— Laws and regulations — United States.

KENNETT (LEE B.) and ANDERSON (JAMES LAVERNE) The gun in America: the origins of a national dilemma. Westport, Conn., 1975. pp. 339. *bibliog.*

FIREARMS INDUSTRY AND TRADE

— United States.

KENNETT (LEE B.) and ANDERSON (JAMES LAVERNE) The gun in America: the origins of a national dilemma. Westport, Conn., 1975. pp. 339. *bibliog.*

SMITH (MERRITT ROE) Harpers Ferry armory and the new technology: the challenge of change. Ithaca, N.Y., 1977. pp. 363. *bibliog.*

FIREBRACE (Sir HENRY).

FIREBRACE (CORDELL WILLIAM) Honest Harry: being the biography of Sir Henry Firebrace, Knight, 1619-1691. London, 1932. pp. 392. *bibliog.*

FIRMS

— History — Czechoslovakia.

PASOLD (ERIC W.) Ladybird, Ladybird: a story of private enterprise. Manchester, [1977]. pp. 668.

— — Germany.

EIKENBERG (WILTRUD) Das Handelshaus der Runtinger zu Regensburg: ein Spiegel süddeutschen Rechts-, Handels- und Wirtschaftslebens im ausgehenden 14. Jahrhundert, etc. Göttingen, 1976. pp. 336. *bibliog.* *(Max-Planck-Institut für Geschichte. Veröffentlichungen. 43)*

PRAGER (HANS GEORG) Blohm and Voss: ships and machinery for the world; translated by Frederick A. Bishop. Herford, [1977]. pp. 271. *bibliog.*

— — Netherlands.

KAMP (A.F.) De standvastige tinnen soldaat: N.V. Billiton Maatschappij 's- Gravenhage (1860-1960). [The Hague, 1960]. pp. 296. *With English summary and English captions to illustrations.*

PHILIPS (FRITS) 45 jaar met Philips; tekstverzorging Leo Ott. Rotterdam, 1976. pp. 382.

— — Russia — Buryat Republic.

BAZHEEV (DANIIL GAVRILOVICH) Ocherki istorii Timliuiskikh tsementnogo i shifernogo zavodov. Ulan-Ude, 1973. pp. 88.

— — — Siberia.

V tysiachi adresov: istoriia Berdskogo radiozavoda. Novosibirsk, 1976. pp. 261.

— — — Ukraine.

DNEPROVSKIE ogni: kak iz ruin i pepla byl podniat posle voiny Zaporozhskii industrial'nyi kompleks. Kiev, 1976. pp. 190.

— — United Kingdom.

LANCASHIRE COTTON CORPORATION. The mills and organisation of the Lancashire Cotton Corporation Limited, (1929-1950). [Manchester?, 1951?]. pp. 57.

PRESSED STEEL COMPANY. Pressed Steel Company Limited. [London?, 1959?]. pp. 69.

GRACE (DAVID ROBERT) and PHILLIPS (DAVID COLIN) Ransomes of Ipswich: a history of the firm and guide to its records. Reading, Berks, 1975. pp. 64. *bibliog.*

NOCKOLDS (HAROLD) Lucas: the first hundred years. Newton Abbot, [1976 in progress]. *bibliog.*

ALBERT (BILL) An essay on the Peruvian sugar industry, 1880-1922 and the letters of Ronald Gordon, administrator of the British Sugar Company in the Canete Valley, 1914-1919. Norwich, [1976]. 1 vol.(various pagings).

FILBY (PETER) TVR: success against the odds. London, 1976. pp. 224.

GARDINER (LESLIE) Bartholomew: 150 years. Edinburgh, [1976]. pp. 111.

GOODEY (CHARLES) The first hundred years: the story of Richards shipbuilders. Ipswich, 1976. pp. 111.

BARKER (THEODORE CARDWELL) The glassmakers: Pilkington: the rise of an international company, 1826-1976. London, [1977]. pp. 557. *A revised and extended version of the author's Pilkington Brothers and the glass industry.*

PASOLD (ERIC W.) Ladybird, Ladybird: a story of private enterprise. Manchester, [1977]. pp. 668.

RAISTRICK (ARTHUR) Two centuries of industrial welfare: the London (Quaker) Lead Company, 1692-1905: the social policy and work of the "Governor and company for smelting down lead with pit coal and sea coal", mainly in Alston Moor and the Pennines. 2nd ed. Buxton, 1977. pp. 168. *bibliogs.*

— — United States.

HAMMOND (JOHN WINTHROP) Men and volts: the story of General Electric. Philadelphia, [1941]. pp. 436.

[EARLE (WALTER KEESE) and PARLIN (CHARLES COOLIDGE)] Shearman and Sterling, 1873-1973. [New York, 1973]. pp. 549.

BUSH (GEORGE) The wide world of Wickes: an unusual story of an unusual growth company. New York, [1976]. pp. 486.

KUNIANSKY (HARRY RICHARD) A business history of Atlantic Steel Company, 1901-1968. [New York], 1976. pp. 395. *bibliog. Originally presented as the author's thesis, Georgia State University, 1970.*

McCANN (THOMAS P.) An American company: the tragedy of United Fruit;...edited by Henry Scammell. New York, [1976]. pp. 244.

FISH TRADE

— Argentine Republic.

MALARET (ANTONIO EMILIO) El mercado americano y las exportaciones pesqueras argentinas. [Buenos Aires], 1969. pp. 72. *bibliog.*

— United States.

MALARET (ANTONIO EMILIO) El mercado americano y las exportaciones pesqueras argentinas. [Buenos Aires], 1969. pp. 72. *bibliog.*

FISHERIES

— Economic aspects.

ANDERSON (LEE G.) The economics of fisheries management. Baltimore, [1977]. pp. 214. *bibliogs.*

— Canada — British Columbia.

BRITISH COLUMBIA. Bureau of Provincial Information. 1910. The fisheries of British Columbia. 2nd ed. Victoria, 1910. pp. 64. *(Bulletins. No. 20)*

— — Nova Scotia.

NOVA SCOTIA. Department of Development. Economics and Statistics Division. 1973. Fisheries industry profile and impact study. [Halifax], 1973. fo.77.

— European Economic Community countries.

EUROPEAN COMMUNITIES. Commission. Information on Agriculture. [Brussels], 1976 in progress. *[In various Community languages].*

— Ghana.

GHANA. Commission of Enquiry into the State Fishing Corporation. 1969. Interim and final reports; [S.A. Wiredu, chairman]. [Accra, 1969]. pp. 213. *Bound with the White Paper on the report.*

GHANA. 1973. White Paper on the report of the Commission of Enquiry into the management and manner of operation of the State Fishing Corporation. [Accra], 1973. pp. 13. *(W[hite] P[apers]. 1973. No. 4)*

— **United Kingdom.**

CARGILL (GAVIN) Blockade '75: the story of the fishermen's blockade of the ports. Glasgow, 1976. pp. 52.

— — **Scotland.**

CZERKAWSKA (CATHERINE LUCY) Fisher-folk of Carrick: a history of the fishing industry in South Ayrshire. Glasgow, 1975. pp. 59. *bibliog.*

— **Zambia.**

ZAMBIA. Department of Fisheries. Annual report. a., 1974- Lusaka.

FISHERMEN

— **Norway.**

NORWAY. Statistiske Centralbyrå. 1976. Fiskere, 1960-1971: alder, bosetting, inntekt, etc. Oslo, 1976. pp. 72. (*Statistiske Analyser. 23*) With English summary.

FISHERY MANAGEMENT.

ANDERSON (LEE G.) The economics of fisheries management. Baltimore, [1977]. pp. 214. *bibliogs.*

FISHING VILLAGES

— **United Kingdom — Scotland.**

CZERKAWSKA (CATHERINE LUCY) Fisher-folk of Carrick: a history of the fishing industry in South Ayrshire. Glasgow, 1975. pp. 59. *bibliog.*

FITZPATRICK (Sir JAMES PERCY).

FITZPATRICK (Sir JAMES PERCY) Fitzpatrick: South African politician: selected papers, 1888- 1906. Johannesburg, [1976]. pp. 562. *bibliog.*

FITZWILLIAM FAMILY.

MEE (GRAHAM) Aristocratic enterprise: the Fitzwilliam industrial undertakings, 1795-1857. Glasgow, 1975. pp. 222.

FLEMISH MOVEMENT.

WANDT (HEINRICH) Das Justizverbrechen des Reichsgerichts an dem Verfasser der "Etappe Gent". Berlin, 1926. pp. 28.

VOS-GEVERS (LOUIS) and VOS-GEVERS (LIEVE) Dat volk moet herleven: het studententijdschrift De Vlaamsche Vlagge, 1875-1933. Leuven, [1976]. pp. 319. *bibliog.*

WILS (LODE) Honderd jaar Vlaamse beweging. Leuven, [1977 in progress]. *bibliog.*

FLORENCE

— **Social life and customs.**

KENT (FRANCIS WILLIAM) Household and lineage in Renaissance Florence: the family life of the Capponi, Ginori, and Rucellai. Princeton, N.J., [1977]. pp. 325.

FLORISTS

— **Netherlands.**

ECONOMISCH INSTITUUT VOOR HET MIDDEN- EN KLEINBEDRIJF. Bedrijfseconomische Publikaties. De bloemist-speciaalzaak in 1973, 1974 en 1975: bedrijfsgegevens voor de bloemist-speciaalzaak over 1973 en de geraamde uitkomsten over 1974 en 1975. 's-Gravenhage, 1976. pp. 89.

FLOW CHARTS.

BRITISH STANDARDS INSTITUTION. Specification for data processing flow chart symbols, rules and conventions; BS 4058:1973. rev. ed. London, 1973. pp. 26.

FLOW OF FUNDS

— **Japan.**

BANK OF JAPAN. Economic Research Department. Special Papers. No. 61. Recent changes in the flow of funds of the Japanese economy. Tokyo, 1976. pp. 15.

BANK OF JAPAN. Economic Research Department. Special Papers. No. 69. Flow of funds of the Japanese economy in 1976. Tokyo, 1977. pp. 18.

— **United States.**

KENT (CALVIN A.) and JOHNSON (JERRY) Flows of funds on the Yankton Sioux Indian Reservation;... prepared...in cooperation with the Yankton Sioux Tribal Council...and United Sioux Tribes Development Corporation. Minneapolis, [1976]. pp. 24. *bibliog.* (*Federal Reserve Bank of Minneapolis. Ninth District Economic Information Series*)

FOLK LORE

— **America, Latin.**

ROTH (WALTER EDMUND) An inquiry into the animism and folk-lore of the Guiana Indians. New York, 1970. pp. 350. *bibliog. First published in 1915 as one of two papers accompanying the thirtieth annual report of the U.S. Bureau of American Ethnology to the Secretary of the Smithsonian Institution 1908-09.*

CARVALHO-NETO (PAULO DE) El folklore de las luchas sociales: un ensayo de folklore y marxismo. [Mexico], 1973. pp. 217. *bibliog.*

FOOD.

ERNAEHRUNG und Ernährungslehre im 19. Jahrhundert: Vorträge eines Symposiums am 5. und 6. Januar 1973 in Frankfurt am Main; mit Beiträgen von Walter Artelt [and others]; herausgegeben von Edith Heischkel-Artelt. Göttingen, 1976. pp. 409. *bibliogs. (Fritz Thyssen Stiftung. Neunzehntes Jahrhundert. Studien zur Medizingeschichte im Neunzehnten Jahrhundert. Band 6) In German or English.*

— **Composition.**

DEGROOTE (V.A.) Tables de composition alimentaire pour la République Démocratique du Congo. [Kinshasa, Office National de la Recherche et du Développement, 1969?]. pp. 32. *bibliog.*

FOOD AND AGRICULTURE ORGANIZATION.

BASIC TEXTS OF THE FOOD AND AGRICULTURE ORGANIZATION OF THE UNITED NATIONS; ([pd.by] Food and Agriculture Organization). irreg., current issue only. [Rome].

FOOD CONSUMPTION

— **Russia — Armenia.**

KARCHIKIAN (OGANES KHACHATUROVICH) Proizvodstvo i potreblenie sel'skokhoziaistvennykh produktov: regional'nye razlichiia i puti vyravnivaniia urovnia potrebleniia. Erevan, 1977. pp. 212.

— **Zaire — Mathematical models.**

SAULNIERS (ALFRED H.) Unit equivalent scales for specific food commodities, Kinshasa, Zaire. Ann Arbor, 1976. pp. 23. *bibliog. (Michigan University. Center for Research on Economic Development. Discussion Papers. No.53)*

FOOD HABITS.

ERNAEHRUNG und Ernährungslehre im 19. Jahrhundert: Vorträge eines Symposiums am 5. und 6. Januar 1973 in Frankfurt am Main; mit Beiträgen von Walter Artelt [and others]; herausgegeben von Edith Heischkel-Artelt. Göttingen, 1976. pp. 409. *bibliogs. (Fritz Thyssen Stiftung. Neunzehntes Jahrhundert. Studien zur Medizingeschichte im Neunzehnten Jahrhundert. Band 6) In German or English.*

— **China.**

CHANG (KWANG-CHIH) ed. Food in Chinese culture: anthropological and historical perspectives. New Haven, 1977. pp. 429. *bibliog.*

FOOD INDUSTRY AND TRADE

— **Water supply — United Kingdom.**

U.K. Central Water Planning Unit. 1976. Regional distribution of water demand by the food industry. Reading, 1976. pp. 17. (*Technical Notes. No.15*)

— **Germany.**

DICKE (HUGO) Die Wirkungen strukturpolitischer Massnahmen in der Ernährungsindustrie: Analyse und Prognose. Tübingen, [1977]. pp. 230. *bibliog. (Kiel. Universität. Institut für Weltwirtschaft. Kieler Studien. 144)*

— **Underdeveloped areas.**

See UNDERDEVELOPED AREAS — **Food industry and trade.**

— **United Kingdom.**

JOHNSTON (JAMES P.) A hundred years eating: food, drink and the daily diet in Britain since the late nineteenth century. Dublin, 1977. pp. 148. *bibliog.*

FOOD SUPPLY.

BAADE (FRITZ) Welternährungswirtschaft. Hamburg, 1956. pp. 174. *bibliog.*

BOERMA (ADDEKE H.) The world food situation and its implications. Washington, 1972. pp. 11.

CARSON (GUY) and others. Nutrition and underdevelopment. [Toronto, 1974]. pp. 69. *bibliog.*

FOOD: politics, economics, nutrition and research; edited by Philip H. Abelson. Washington, D.C., [1975]. pp. 202. *bibliog. The contents originally appeared in Science, weekly journal of the American Association for the Advancement of Science from January 1972 to March 1975.*

The MAN/food equation: proceedings of a symposium held at the Royal Institution London, September, 1973; edited by F. Steele and A. Bourne. London, 1975. pp. 289. *bibliogs.*

PRITCHARD (COLIN) Half the loaf!: a study on the world food crisis. Edinburgh, 1975. pp. 41. *bibliog.*

HANSEN (ROGER D.) The U.S. and world development: agenda for action, 1976. New York, 1976. pp. 222.

JONES (DAVID) of the Overseas Development Institute. Food and interdependence: the effect of food and agricultural policies of developed countries on the food problems of developing countries. London, [1976]. pp. 51.

LAND for the people; compiled by Herbert Girardet. London, [1976]. pp. 144. *bibliog.*

MAREI (SAYED) The world food crisis. London, 1976. pp. 126.

ROBBINS (CHRISTOPHER) and ANSARI (JAVED A.) The profits of doom: a War on Want investigation into the 'world food crisis'. London, 1976. pp. 26. *bibliog.*

VALLIANATOS (E.G.) Fear in the countryside: the control of agricultural resources in the poor countries by nonpeasant elites. Cambridge, Mass., [1976]. pp. 180.

WALSTON (HENRY DAVID LEONARD GEORGE) Baron Walston. Dealing with hunger. London, 1976. pp. 152.

TUDGE (COLIN) The famine business. London, 1977. pp. 141.

WORLD food prospects and agricultural potential; [by] Marylin Chou [and others]. New York, 1977. pp. 316. *Second of a series under the Hudson Institute's Prospects for Mankind program.*

— **Arab countries.**

MAREI (SAYED) The world food crisis. London, 1976. pp. 126.

FOOD SUPPLY.(Cont.)

— Cambodia.

HILDEBRAND (GEORGE C.) and PORTER (GARETH) Cambodia: starvation and revolution. New York, [1976]. pp. 124.

— European Economic Community countries.

EUROPEAN COMMUNITIES. Statistical Office. Supply balance sheets. a., 1976- Luxembourg. *[in Community languages]*.

— India.

MUKERJEE (RADHAKAMAL) Food planning for four hundred millions. London, 1938. pp. 267.

— Russia.

KNIAZEVA (RAISA SEMENOVNA) Pribyl' i rentabel'nost' predpriiatii obshchestvennogo pitaniia. Moskva, 1973. pp. 56.

— Underdeveloped areas.

See UNDERDEVELOPED AREAS — Food supply.

— United Kingdom.

HESLOP (LUKE) A comparative statement of the food produced from arable and grass land, and the returns arising from each; with observations on the late inclosures, and the probable effect of a general act for inclosing commons or wastes, heaths, etc.; together with other matters; addressed to John Fane, Esq. M.P. London, Reynolds, 1801. pp. iv, 18.

— United States.

HALCROW (HAROLD GRAHAM) Food policy for America. New York, [1977]. pp. 564.

FORD (GERALD RUDOLPH) President of the United States.

MOLLENHOFF (CLARK R.) The man who pardoned Nixon. New York, [1976]. pp. 312.

SOBEL (LESTER A.) ed. Ford and the economy. New York, [1976]. pp. 248. *Revised version of the weekly reports compiled by Facts on File.*

FORECASTING.

CORPORATE strategy and planning; edited by Bernard Taylor and John R. Sparkes. London, 1977. pp. 402.

FOREIGN EXCHANGE.

JOHNSON (HARRY GORDON) The problems of central bankers in a world of floating rates. [Elmont, N.Y.], 1973. fo. 3. *Reprinted from Euromoney, July 1973.*

JOHNSON (HARRY GORDON) Why devaluations often appear to fail. 1974. 1 pamphlet (unpaged). *Photocopy of typescript: unpublished.*

BRENNER (MICHAEL J.) The politics of international monetary reform: the exchange crisis. Cambridge, Mass., [1976]. pp. 144.

BROWN (WEIR M.) World afloat: national policies ruling the waves. Princeton, [1976]. pp. 33. *bibliog. (Princeton University. Department of Economics and Sociology. International Finance Section. Essays in International Finance. No. 116)*

CARNEGIE-ROCHESTER CONFERENCE ON PUBLIC POLICY. 1974, November Conference. Institutional arrangements and the inflation problem: [papers and discussions from the conference]; editors Karl Brunner [and] Allan H. Meltzer. Amsterdam, 1976. pp. 248. *bibliogs. (Journal of Monetary Economics. Carnegie-Rochester Conference Series on Public Policy. vol. 3)*

DANIELS (JOHN D.) and others. International business: environments and operations. Reading, Mass., [1976]. pp. 554. *bibliogs.*

EUROCURRENCIES and the international monetary system; edited by Carl H. Stem [and others]. Washington, D.C., [1976]. pp. 413. *bibliog. Papers from four conference sessions sponsored by the American Enterprise Institute for Public Policy Research and the U.S. Treasury.*

MACHLUP (FRITZ) International payments, debts and gold; collected essays. 2nd ed. New York, 1976. pp. 514.

TOWER (EDWARD) and WILLETT (THOMAS D.) The theory of optimum currency areas and exchange-rate flexibility. Princeton, N.J., 1976. pp. 98. *bibliog. (Princeton University. Department of Economics and Sociology. International Finance Section. Special Papers in International Economics. No. 11)*

CROCKETT (ANDREW) International money: issues and analyses. Sunbury-on-Thames, 1977. pp. 250. *bibliogs.*

HALM (GEORGE NIKOLAUS) Jamaica and the par-value system. Princeton, 1977. pp. 21. *bibliog. (Princeton University. Department of Economics and Sociology. International Finance Section. Essays in International Finance. No. 120)*

WILLIAMSON (JOHN) Economist. The failure of world monetary reform, 1971-74. Sunbury-on-Thames, 1977. pp. 221. *bibliog.*

— Law.

LAZAR (LEONARD) Transnational economic and monetary law, transactions and contracts. Dobbs Ferry, N.Y., 1977 in progress. *Loose leaf.*

— — Indonesia.

INDONESIA. 1970. Regulations of the government of the republic of Indonesia concerning improvements and reforms in trade, monetary and fiscal policies as from April 17, 1970. [Djakarta], 1970. pp. 79.

— Mathematical models.

BLACK (STANLEY W.) International money markets and flexible exchange rates. [Washington, 1972]. pp. 72, 2. *(United States. Board of Governors of the Federal Reserve System. Staff Economic Studies. No. 70)*

— Sweden.

ROSENGREN (BJÖRN) Valutareglering och nationell ekonomisk politik: en studie med anknytning till svenska erfarenheter åren 1959-1973. Göteborg, 1975. fo. 311. *bibliog. (Göteborgs Universitet. Nationalekonomiska Institutionen. Memoranda. Nr. 46) With English summary.*

— Underdeveloped areas.

See UNDERDEVELOPED AREAS — Foreign exchange.

— United Kingdom.

CASE studies in international economics; edited by Peter Maunder; [by] Peter Barker [and others]. London, 1977. pp. 87. *bibliogs. (Economics Association. Case Studies in Economic Analysis. 6)*

FOREIGN EXCHANGE PROBLEM

— United Kingdom.

NATIONAL ECONOMIC DEVELOPMENT OFFICE. International price competitiveness, non-price factors and export performance. London, 1977. pp. 45. *bibliog.*

FOREIGN NEWS.

CULBERT (DAVID HOLBROOK) News for everyman: radio and foreign affairs in thirties America. Westport, Conn., 1976. pp. 238. *bibliog.*

FOREIGN TRADE PROMOTION

— Asia.

VITTAL (NAGARAJAN) ed. Export processing zones in Asia: some dimensions. Tokyo, Asian Productivity Organization, [1977]. pp. 122.

— Philippine Islands.

STAELIN (CHARLES P.) The impact of export incentives and export-related policies on the firms of the less developed countries: a case study of the Philippines. Ann Arbor, 1976. pp. 29. *(Michigan University. Center for Research on Economic Development. Discussion Papers. No. 59)*

— Underdeveloped areas.

See UNDERDEVELOPED AREAS — Foreign trade promotion.

— United Kingdom.

ADVISORY COUNCIL FOR AGRICULTURE AND HORTICULTURE IN ENGLAND AND WALES. Report of an inquiry into agricultural exports. [London], 1976. pp. 61.

FOREIGN TRADE REGULATION.

SCHMITTHOFF (CLIVE MACMILLAN) and SIMMONDS (KENNETH R.) eds. International economic and trade law: universal and regional integration. Leyden, 1976. pp. 252.

LAZAR (LEONARD) Transnational economic and monetary law, transactions and contracts. Dobbs Ferry, N.Y., 1977 in progress. *Loose leaf.*

KOUL (AUTAR KRISHAN) The legal framework of UNCTAD in world trade. Leyden, 1977. pp. 255. *bibliog.*

— Bibliography.

STERN (ROBERT M.) and others, compilers. Price elasticities in international trade: an annotated bibliography. London, 1976. pp. 363. *bibliog.*

— China.

GINSBURGS (GEORGE) The legal framework of trade between the USSR and the People's Republic of China. The Hague, 1976. pp. 117. *bibliog.*

LAW and politics in China's foreign trade; edited by Victor H. Li. Seattle, [1977]. pp. 467. *(Washington University. School of Law. Asian Law Series. No. 4) Papers of a conference jointly sponsored by the Subcommittee on Chinese Law of the Joint Committee on Contemporary China of the Social Science Research Council and the American Council of Learned Societies and by the University of Illinois, and held in London in 1971.*

— Russia.

GINSBURGS (GEORGE) The legal framework of trade between the USSR and the People's Republic of China. The Hague, 1976. pp. 117. *bibliog.*

POZDNIAKOV (VLADIMIR SERGEEVICH) Sovetskoe gosudarstvo i vneshniaia torgovlia: pravovye voprosy. Moskva, 1976. pp. 175.

FOREMEN

— Denmark.

MØLLER (IVER HORNEMANN) The effectiveness of shop stewards and supervisors. København, 1976 in progress. *bibliog. (Socialforskningsinstituttet. Studier. Nr. 33)*

FOREST POLICY.

DIGBY (MARGARET) and EDWARDSON (T.E.) The organisation of forestry co-operatives. [Oxford, 1976]. pp. 250. *(Horace Plunkett Foundation. Occasional Papers. No. 41)*

FOREST PRODUCTS

— Australia.

AUSTRALIA. Forestry and Timber Bureau. Forest resources. 1975 (1st)- Canberra. *Supersedes AUSTRALIA. Forestry and Timber Bureau. Annual report.*

— Europe.

ANNUAL FOREST PRODUCTS MARKET REVIEW; [pd. by] Economic Commission for Europe, United Nations. a., 1966/67- , with gaps (1966/67, pt.1; 1970/71, pt.2). Geneva. *1966/67- 1971/72 pd. in 3 pts. Supplement of the TIMBER BULLETIN FOR EUROPE.*

FOREST PRODUCTS MARKET TRENDS...AND PROSPECTS (formerly Review of European Forest Products Markets); [pd.by] Economic Commission for Europe, United Nations. a.(formerly s-a.), 1966/67- Geneva. *[in English and French from 1966/67-1968]. Supplement of the TIMBER BULLETIN FOR EUROPE.*

FORESTS AND FORESTRY

— Australia.

AUSTRALIA. Forestry and Timber Bureau. Forest resources. 1975 (1st)- Canberra. *Supersedes AUSTRALIA. Forestry and Timber Bureau. Annual report.*

— Canada — British Columbia.

TAYLOR (GEOFFREY W.) Timber: history of the forest industry in B.C. Vancouver, 1975. pp. 208.

— — New Brunswick.

NEW BRUNSWICK. Office of the Economic Advisor. 1971. Forestry in New Brunswick, 1961-1969. [Fredericton], 1971. pp. 69.

— Papua New Guinea.

PAPUA NEW GUINEA. Department of Forests. 1973. New horizons: forestry in Papua New Guinea. Brisbane, 1973. pp. 76. *bibliog.*

— United Kingdom.

RACKHAM (OLIVER) Trees and woodland in the British landscape. London, 1976. pp. 204. *bibliog.*

FORESTS AND FORESTRY, COOPERATIVE.

DIGBY (MARGARET) and EDWARDSON (T.E.) The organisation of forestry co-operatives. [Oxford, 1976]. pp. 250. *(Horace Plunkett Foundation. Occasional Papers. No. 41)*

FORGERY

— Russia.

PINKHASOV (BORIS IL'ICH) Zashchita dokumentov po sovetskomu pravu. Tashkent, 1976. pp. 198.

FORWARD EXCHANGE.

GOSS (BARRY ANDREW) and YAMEY (BASIL SELIG) eds. The economics of futures trading: readings. New York, 1976. pp. 236. *bibliog.*

FOSTER HOME CARE

— United Kingdom.

SOCIAL SERVICES RESEARCH AND INTELLIGENCE UNIT [PORTSMOUTH]. Information Sheets. No. 26. Fostering of disturbed adolescents. Portsmouth, [1976]. pp. 3.

FOUNDLINGS

— Belgium.

LETTRE d'un patriote bruxellois, à un patriote gantois, sur la mendicité, les enfans trouvés, et un monument à élever à la gloire des auteurs de la révolution pour la liberté des Pays-Bas. Bruxelles, the Author, 1790 pp. 7.

FOX (HENRY RICHARD VASSALL) 3rd Baron Holland.

FOX (HENRY RICHARD VASSALL) 3rd Baron Holland. The Holland House diaries, 1831-1840: the diary of Henry Richard Vassall Fox, third Lord Holland, with extracts from the diary of Dr. John Allen; edited with an introductory essay and notes by Abraham D. Kriegel. London, 1977. pp. 513.

FOX-HUNTING

— United Kingdom.

ITZKOWITZ (DAVID C.) Peculiar privilege: a social history of English foxhunting, 1753- 1885. Hassocks, Sussex, 1977. pp. 248. *bibliog.*

FRANCE.

DANDELOT (MARC) and FROMENT-MEURICE (FRANÇOIS) France. Paris, La Documentation Française, 1975. pp. 320.

— Administrative and political divisions.

FRANCE. Direction de la Documentation. La Documentation Française. Notes et Etudes Documentaires. Nos. 4,249-4, 250. L'administration territoriale: le département; par Marcel Piquemal avec la collaboration de Dominique Bernard. Paris, 1975. pp. 52.

— Air force — History.

FRIDENSON (PATRICK) and LECUIR (JEAN) La France et la Grande-Bretagne face aux problèmes aériens, 1935-mai 1940. Vincennes, Service Historique de l'Armée de l'Air, 1976. pp. 208.

— Appropriations and expenditures.

FRANCE. Projet de loi de finances: coût et rendement des services publics. a., 1963-1964. Paris.

FRANCE. Comité Central d'Enquête sur le Coût et le Rendement des Services Publics. 1976. Rapport général, années 1971 à 1975. Paris, [1976]. pp. 260.

— Army.

GALLOIS (PIERRE MARIE) L'adieu aux armées. [Paris, 1976]. pp. 364.

— Census.

FRANCE. Census, 1968. Recensement général de la population de 1968; résultats du sondage au 1/4: population, ménages, logements, immeubles; fascicules régionaux ([including] Récapitulation pour la France entière). Paris, 1972. 23 pts. (in 2 vols.)

— Church history.

REMOND (RENE) L'anti-cléricalisme en France de 1815 à nos jours. Paris, [1976]. pp. 374. *bibliog.*

— Colonies.

BOUVIER (JEAN) and GIRAULT (RENE) eds. L'impérialisme français d'avant 1914: recueil de textes. Paris, [1976]. pp. 335. *bibliogs. (Paris. Ecole des Hautes Etudes en Sciences Sociales. Le Savoir Historique. 10)*

GUILLEBAUD (JEAN CLAUDE) Les confettis de l'empire: Martinique, Guadeloupe, Guyane Française, etc. Paris, [1976]. pp. 318. *bibliog.*

— Commerce.

SCHEMA général d'aménagement de la France: la façade atlantique; ouverture sur le monde. Paris, 1975. pp. 111. *(France. Délégation à l'Aménagement du Territoire et à l'Action Régionale. Travaux et Recherches de Prospective. 51)*

— Constitutional law.

MACHELON (JEAN PIERRE) La République contre les libertés?...: les restrictions aux libertés publiques de 1879 à 1914. Paris, [1976]. pp. xvii, 462. *(Fondation Nationale des Sciences Politiques. Cahiers. 206)*

FABRE (MICHEL HENRY) Principes républicains de droit constitutionnel. 3rd ed. Paris, 1977. pp. 515.

— Defences.

COMITE POUR L'EXTINCTION DES GUERRES POUR LE DESARMEMENT UNILATERAL DE NOTRE PROPRE NATION. La nation face à l'armée. [Paris], [1967?]. pp. 12.

ROSE (FRANÇOIS DE) La France et la défense de l'Europe. Paris, [1976]. pp. 123.

RUEHL (LOTHAR) La politique militaire de la cinquième république. [Paris, 1976]. pp. 430. *(Fondation Nationale des Sciences Politiques. Cahiers. 193)*

— Economic conditions.

FRANCE. Sénat. Commission des Finances. Rapporteur Général. Note de conjoncture. s-a., Oc 1975(no.1)- Paris.

PROFIL économique de la France: (structures et tendances); sous la direction de Jean-Pierre Pagé, etc. Paris, La Documentation Française, 1975. pp. 347.

BOSQUET (MICHEL) Capitalism in crisis and everyday life; translated from the French by John Howe. Hassocks, Sussex, 1977. pp. 199.

MARCEAU (JANE) Class and status in France: economic change and social immobility 1945-1975. Oxford, 1977. pp. 217. *bibliog.*

— Economic history.

KAPLAN (STEVEN L.) Bread, politics and political economy in the reign of Louis XV. The Hague, 1976. 2 vols. *bibliog.*

— Economic policy.

PARTI COMMUNISTE FRANÇAIS. Commerçants, artisans: les affaires ne vont pas: comment en sortir? Paris, [1951]. pp. 22.

RUEFF (JACQUES) Combats pour l'ordre financier: mémoires et documents pour servir à l'histoire du dernier demi-siècle. [Paris, 1972]. pp. 480.

FRANCE. [Commissariat Général du Plan.] 1976. VIIe Plan de développement économique et social, 1976-1980. Paris, La Documentation Française, [1976]. pp. 158.

— Executive departments.

FRANCE. Direction de la Documentation. La Documentation Française. Notes et Etudes Documentaires. Nos. 4,254-4, 255-4,256. Domaine et instruments de la politique étrangère de la France; par Jean du Boisberranger. Paris, 1976. pp. 90.

— Foreign relations.

FRANCE. Embassy. (U.K.). Press and Information Service. Speeches and statements. irreg., 1976(no.11)- London.

AUFFRAY (BERNARD) Pierre de Margerie, 1861-1942, et la vie diplomatique de son temps. Paris, [1976]. pp. 528. *bibliog.*

FRANCE. Direction de la Documentation. La Documentation Française. Notes et Etudes Documentaires. Nos. 4,254-4, 255-4,256. Domaine et instruments de la politique étrangère de la France; par Jean du Boisberranger. Paris, 1976. pp. 90.

— — Balkan States.

DAMIANOV (SIMEON) Frenskata politika na Balkanite, 1829-1853; La politique française aux Balkans, 1829-1853. Sofiia, 1977. pp. 324. *bibliog. With Russian and French summaries.*

— — China.

ZARETSKAIA (SOF'IA IL'INICHNA) Vneshniaia politika Kitaia v 1856-1860 godakh: otnosheniia s Angliei i Frantsiei. Moskva, 1976. pp. 221. *bibliog.*

FRANCE.(Cont.)

— — Europe.

SIVERY (GERARD) Mirages méditerranéens ou réalités atlantiques?: XIIIe- XVe siècles. [Paris], 1976. pp. 285. *bibliog.*

— — Germany.

RAULFF (HEINER) Zwischen Machtpolitik und Imperialismus: die deutsche Frankreichpolitik, 1904/06. Düsseldorf, [1976]. pp. 215. *bibliog.*

— — Morocco.

DUNN (ROSS E.) Resistance in the desert: Moroccan responses to French imperialism, 1881-1912. London, [1977]. pp. 291. *bibliog.*

— — Russia.

SHNEERSON (LEV MIKHAILOVICH) Franko-prusskaia voina i Rossiia: iz istorii russko-prusskikh i russko-frantsuzskikh otnoshenii v 1867-1871 gg. Minsk, 1976. pp. 304.

— — United Kingdom.

ROLO (PAUL JACQUES VICTOR) Britain and the Briand plan: the common market that never was: an inaugural lecture...given in the University of Keele, 1972. Keele, 1973. pp. 23.

— History.

DROIT privé et institutions régionales: études historiques offertes à Jean Yver. Paris, [1976]. pp. 713. *bibliog.* *(Rouen. Université. Publications. 31) In various languages.*

— — Sources.

TURGOT (ANNE ROBERT JACQUES) Baron de l'Aulne. Lettres de Turgot à la duchesse d'Enville, 1764-74 et 1777-80: édition critique préparée...sous la direction de Joseph Ruwet [and others]. Louvain, 1976. pp. 215. *bibliog.* *(Louvain. Université. Faculté de Philosophie et Lettres. Travaux. 16)*

— — 1589-1789, Bourbons.

BRIGGS (ROBIN) Early modern France, 1560-1715. Oxford, 1977. pp. 242. *bibliog.*

FRANCE in crisis, 1620-1675; selected, translated and introduced by P.J. Coveney. London, 1977. pp. 273. *bibliog.*

— — 1789-1799, Revolution.

CENSER (JACK RICHARD) Prelude to power: the Parisian radical press, 1789-1791. Baltimore, Md., [1976]. pp. 186. *bibliog.*

SOBOUL (ALBERT) Problèmes paysans de la révolution, 1789-1848: études d'histoire révolutionnaire. Paris, 1976. pp. 442.

— — 1848, February Revolution.

AGULHON (MAURICE) Les Quarante-huitards. [Paris], 1975. pp. 253. *bibliog.*

SOBOUL (ALBERT) Problèmes paysans de la révolution, 1789-1848: études d'histoire révolutionnaire. Paris, 1976. pp. 442.

— — 1940-1945, German occupation.

AMOUROUX (HENRI) La grande histoire des Français sous l'occupation. Paris, [1976 in progress]. *bibliog.*

La LIBERATION de la France: actes du colloque international tenu à Paris du 28 au 31 octobre 1974. Paris, Comité d'Histoire de la Deuxième Guerre Mondiale, 1976. pp. 1054.

— — 1945- .

FONVIEILLE-ALQUIER (FRANÇOIS) Plaidoyer pour la IVe République. Paris, [1976]. pp. 372.

— Industries.

FRANCE. Ministère de l'Industrie et de la Recherche. 1975-76. L'industrie française. Paris, 1975-76. 2 vols.

BERTIN (GILLES Y.) L'industrie française face aux multinationales. Paris, 1975. pp. 143. *(France. Commissariat Général du Plan. Economie et Planification)*

SCHEMA général d'aménagement de la France: la façade atlantique; ouverture sur le monde. Paris, 1975. pp. 111. *(France. Délégation à l'Aménagement du Territoire et à l'Action Régionale. Travaux et Recherches de Prospective. 51)*

FRANCE. Commission de l'Industrie. 1976. Rapport...: préparation du 7e Plan. Paris, 1976. pp. 243.

FRANCE. Ministère de l'Industrie et de la Recherche. 1976. Préparation du 7e Plan: perspectives sectorielles pour l'industrie; synthèses des travaux des groupes sectoriels d'analyse et de prévision, etc. Paris, 1976. pp. 99. *(Etudes de Politique Industrielle. 11)*

FRANÇOIS (JEAN PAUL) Les entreprises moyennes dans l'économie industrielle;...avec la collaboration de R. Stutzman et J.F. Minder. Paris, [1976]. pp. 228. *(France. Ministère de l'Industrie et de la Recherche. Service du Traitement de l'Information et des Statistiques Industrielles. Traits Fondamentaux du Système Industriel Français. 2)*

— Military policy.

GALLOIS (PIERRE MARIE) L'adieu aux armées. [Paris], 1976]. pp. 364.

RAWLINSON (ROGER) The Battle of Larzac. New Malden, [1976]. pp. 59. *bibliog.*

RUEHL (LOTHAR) La politique militaire de la cinquième république. [Paris, 1976]. pp. 430. *(Fondation Nationale des Sciences Politiques. Cahiers. 193)*

— Parliament — Assemblée Nationale — Rules and practice.

PARSONAGE (CLARISSA) The development of the French National Assembly 1962-1965. 1976 [or rather 1977]. fo.389. *bibliog. Typescript. Ph.D. (London) thesis: unpublished. This thesis is the property of London University and may not be removed from the Library.*

— — Chambre des Députés.

La CHAMBRE des Députés en 1837-1839: composition, activité, vocabulaire; [by] Louis Girard [and others]. Paris, 1976. pp. 243. *(Paris. Université de Paris I (Panthéon-Sorbonne) and others. Publications de la Sorbonne. Série Etudes. tome 11)*

— — — Voting.

WARWICK (PAUL) The French Popular Front: a legislative analysis. Chicago, 1977. pp. 211. *bibliog.*

— Politics and government.

FRANCE. Embassy. (U.K.). Press and Information Service. Speeches and statements. irreg., 1976(no.11)- London.

BAECQUE (FRANCIS DE) Qui gouverne la France?: essai sur la répartition du pouvoir entre le chef de l'état et le chef du gouvernement. Paris, [1976]. pp. 208. *bibliog.*

PACTET (PIERRE) Les institutions françaises. [Paris], 1976. pp. 128. *bibliog.*

— — 1589-1789.

KAPLAN (STEVEN L.) Bread, politics and political economy in the reign of Louis XV. The Hague, 1976. 2 vols. *bibliog.*

— — 1789-1900.

RUGE (ARNOLD) Politician. Zwei Jahre in Paris: Studien und Erinnerungen. Leipzig, Jurany, 1846; Leipzig, 1975. 2 vols. *Facsimile reprint.*

NADAUD (MARTIN) Léonard, maçon de la Creuse. Paris, 1976. pp. 399. *bibliog.*

— — 1870-1940.

DOTY (CHARLES STEWART) From cultural rebellion to counterrevolution: the politics of Maurice Barrès. Athens, Ohio, [1976]. pp. 294. *bibliog.*

JEANNENEY (JEAN NOËL) François de Wendel en république: l'argent et le pouvoir, 1914-1940. Paris, [1976]. pp. 670.

ANDERSON (ROBERT D.) France, 1870-1914: politics and society. London, 1977. pp. 215. *bibliog.*

DERFLER (LESLIE) Alexandre Millerand: the socialist years. The Hague, [1977]. pp. 326. *bibliog.*

WARWICK (PAUL) The French Popular Front: a legislative analysis. Chicago, 1977. pp. 211. *bibliog.*

— — 1900- .

AS they are: French Political portraits; by ***; translated from the French by Winifred Katzin. London, 1924. pp. 217.

HISTOIRE du réformisme en France depuis 1920. Paris, [1976]. 2 vols. (in 1).

MOCH (JULES) Une si longue vie. Paris, [1976]. pp. 653.

TIXIER-VIGNANCOUR (JEAN LOUIS) Des Républiques, des justices et des hommes. [Paris, 1976]. pp. 413.

— — 1940-1945.

FOULON (CHARLES LOUIS) Le pouvoir en province à la Libération: les commissaires de la République, 1943-1946. [Paris, 1975]. pp. 301. *(Fondation Nationale des Sciences Politiques. Travaux et Recherches de Science Politique. 32)*

SWEETS (JOHN F.) The politics of resistance in France, 1940-1944: a history of the Mouvements Unis de la Résistance. DeKalb, Ill., [1976]. pp. 260. *bibliog.*

— — 1945- .

ESTIER (CLAUDE) Ce qu'est la Convention. 2nd ed. [Paris], 1967]. pp. 61. *(Convention des Institutions Républicaines. Cahiers. 8)*

MANDEL (ERNEST) The lessons of May 1968: [and] The commune lives. London, [1971]. pp. 29.

PONIATOWSKI (MICHEL CASIMIR) Prince. Cartes sur table. [Paris, 1972]. pp. 250.

MARTINET (GILLES) Le système Pompidou. Paris, [1973]. pp. 188.

AVRIL (PIERRE) Le régime politique de la Ve République. 3rd ed. Paris, 1975. pp. 449. *bibliog.*

FRANCE. Président, 1974- . (Valéry Giscard d'Estaing). 1976- . Discours et déclarations de Valéry Giscard d'Estaing, Président de la République Française. Paris, 1976 in progress.

ANTONI (PASCALE) and ANTONI (JEAN DOMINIQUE) Les ministres de la Ve République. Paris, 1976. pp. 95. *bibliog. (Paris. Université de Paris II. Travaux et Recherches. Série Science Politique. 8)*

FAJON (ETIENNE) Ma vie s'appelle liberté. Paris, [1976]. pp. 299.

FONVIEILLE-ALQUIER (FRANÇOIS) Plaidoyer pour la IVe République. Paris, [1976]. pp. 372.

GISCARD D'ESTAING (VALERY) Démocratie française. Paris, 1976. pp. 175.

NOEL (LEON) De Gaulle et les débuts de la Ve République. [Paris, 1976]. pp. 310.

ROCHET (WALDECK) Ecrits politiques, 1956-1969. Paris, [1976]. pp. 303.

DEFFERRE (GASTON) Si demain la gauche...: réponses à Pierre Desgraupes. Paris, [1977]. pp. 286.

GIESBERT (FRANZ OLIVIER) François Mitterand; ou, La tentation de l'histoire. Paris, [1977]. pp. 334.

GISCARD D'ESTAING (VALERY) Towards a new democracy; translated by Vincent Cronin. London, 1977. pp. 150.

PARSONAGE (CLARISSA) The development of the French National Assembly 1962-1965. 1976 [or rather 1977]. fo.389. *bibliog. Typescript. Ph.D. (London) thesis: unpublished. This thesis is the property of London University and may not be removed from the Library.*

— **Population policy.**

NATALITE et politique démographique, etc. [Paris], 1976. pp. 162. *bibliog. (France. Institut National d'Etudes Démographiques. Travaux et Documents. Cahiers. No. 76)*

— **Presidents.**

BAECQUE (FRANCIS DE) Qui gouverne la France?: essai sur la répartition du pouvoir entre le chef de l'état et le chef du gouvernement. Paris, [1976]. pp. 208. *bibliog.*

— **Relations (general) with Germany.**

ARNDT (ERNST MORITZ) Noch ein Wort über die Franzosen und über uns. [Leipzig], 1814. pp. 44,4. *With Vorschlag eines Fremdengesetzes vom Österreich. Hauptmann von M...r.*

— **Rural conditions.**

FRANCE. Commission Agriculture-Environnement. 1975. Agriculture, environnement: éléments pour une évaluation de l'espace rural. Paris, La Documentation Française, 1975. pp. 191. *(Environnement. 43)*

WEBER (EUGEN) Peasants into Frenchmen: the modernization of rural France, 1870-1914. Stanford, Calif., 1976. pp. 615. *bibliog.*

— **Social conditions.**

RAPPORT sur l'aménagement du temps; [prepared by a study group; Bertrand Labrusse, coordinator]. Paris, La Documentation Française, 1976. pp. 79. *(Environnement. 47)*

GISCARD D'ESTAING (VALERY) Towards a new democracy; translated by Vincent Cronin. London, 1977. pp. 150.

— **Social policy.**

FRANCE. Comité Central d'Enquête sur le Coût et le Rendement des Services Publics. 1976. L'aménagement des services publics dans les zones à faible densité de population: rapport présenté par M. Duchene-Marullaz [and] M. Zwickert [and] conclusions du Comité, etc. Paris, [1976]. pp. 99. *Cover title reads: L'amélioration des services publics, etc.*

FRANCE. Comité Central d'Enquête sur le Coût et le Rendement des Services Publics. 1976. Rapport général, années 1971 à 1975. Paris, [1976]. pp. 260.

FRANCE. [Commissariat Général du Plan.] 1976. VIIe Plan de développement économique et social, 1976-1980. Paris, La Documentation Française, [1976]. pp. 158.

— **Statistics, Vital.**

CHESNAIS (JEAN CLAUDE) Les morts violentes en France depuis 1826: comparaisons internationales. [Paris], 1976. pp. 346. *bibliog. (France. Institut National d'Etudes Démographiques. Travaux et Documents. Cahiers. No. 75)*

— **Territories and possessions — Economic policy.**

FRANCE. Commission des Départements d'Outre-Mer. 1976. Rapport...: préparation du 7e Plan. Paris, 1976. pp. 87.

— — **Social policy.**

FRANCE. Commission des Départements d'Outre-Mer. 1976. Rapport...: préparation du 7e Plan. Paris, 1976. pp. 87.

FRANCISCANS IN MEXICO.

MOTOLINIA (TORIBIO) Historia de los indios de la Nueva España: relacion de los ritos antiguos, idolatrias y sacrificios de los indios de la Nueva España, y de la maravillosa conversion que Dios en ellos ha obrado; estudio critico, apendices, notas e indice de Edmundo O'Gorman. Mexico, 1969 repr. 1973. pp. 256. *bibliog. First published in Mexico in 1858.*

FRANCISCANS IN NEW SPAIN (VICEROYALTY).

KOBAYASHI (JOSE MARIA) La educacion como conquista: empresa franciscana en Mexico. Mexico, 1974. pp. 423. *bibliog. (Mexico City. Colegio de Mexico. Centro de Estudios Historicos. Nueva Serie. 19)*

FRANCO BAHAMONDE (FRANCISCO).

ARRARAS (JOAQUIN) Franco. Burgos, 1938. pp. 315.

FRANCO-GERMAN WAR, 1870-1871.

AUER (IGNAZ) Sedanfeier und Sozialdemokratie: eine Rede. [Berlin, 1895?]. pp. 15. *Wanting title-page.*

SHNEERSON (LEV MIKHAILOVICH) Franko-prusskaia voina i Rossiia: iz istorii russko-prusskikh i russko-frantsuzskikh otnoshenii v 1867-1871 gg. Minsk, 1976. pp. 304.

FRANKFURT AM MAIN

— **History.**

MAUSBACH-BROMBERGER (BARBARA) Arbeiterwiderstand in Frankfurt am Main gegen den Faschismus, 1933-1945. Frankfurt am Main, [1976]. pp. 312. *bibliog.*

FRANKFURTER (FELIX).

FRANKFURTER (FELIX) From the diaries of Felix Frankfurter; with a biographical essay and notes by Joseph P. Lash. New York, [1975]. pp. 336.

FRANKLIN (BENJAMIN).

SEEGER (RAYMOND JOHN) Benjamin Franklin: new world physicist; [with selected readings]. Oxford, 1973. pp. 190. *bibliog.*

FRANQUI (CARLOS).

FRANQUI (CARLOS) Diario de la revolucion cubana. [Paris, 1976]. pp. 754.

FRASER (HUGH CHARLES PATRICK JOSEPH).

FRASER (HUGH CHARLES PATRICK JOSEPH) A rebel for the right reasons; a selection of speeches and writings. Stafford, 1975. pp. 99.

FRAUD

— **United Kingdom.**

SCOTT (GUTHRIE MICHAEL) and HUQ (FAZLUL) Britain: Bangladesh: traffic in charity. London, [1976]. pp. 105. *Includes extracts from newspapers.*

FREDERICK II, called the Great, King of Prussia.

[GUIBERT (JACQUES ANTOINE HIPPOLYTE DE) Comte] Observations on the military establishment and discipline of his Majesty the King of Prussia; with an account of the private life of that...monarch; and occasional anecdotes of the principal persons of his court...etc.; translated from the French by J. Johnson. London, Fielding and Walker, 1780. pp. iv, 101.

FREE CHOICE OF EMPLOYMENT

— **Germany.**

ROHRSCHEIDT (KURT VON) Vom Zunftzwange zur Gewerbefreiheit: (eine Studie nach den Quellen). Glashütten im Taunus, 1976. pp. 668. *bibliog. Reprint of work originally published in Berlin in 1898.*

Die ZERSTOERUNG der Demokratie in der BRD durch Berufsverbote; herausgegeben von Horst Bethge [and others] . Köln, [1976]. pp. 396.

FREE TRADE AND PROTECTION.

[HALL (GEORGE WEBB)] The origin and proceedings of the agricultural associations in Great Britain, in which their claims to protection against foreign produce, duty-free, are fully and ably set forth, etc. London, Sherwood, Neely, and Jones, [1819]. pp. 39.

RUDALL (EDWARD) Protection to native industry; or, The effect on the labouring classes of the withdrawal of the protecting duties; examined in a lecture, read to the members of the Launceston Institution. Launceston, Cater and Maddox, 1841. pp. 30.

YEAGER (LELAND BENNETT) and TUERCK (DAVID G.) Foreign trade and U.S. policy: the case for free international trade. New York, 1976. pp. 295. *A revision of Trade policy and the price system.*

VITTAL (NAGARAJAN) ed. Export processing zones in Asia: some dimensions. Tokyo, Asian Productivity Organization, [1977]. pp. 122.

FREEDMEN IN JAMAICA.

CAMPBELL (MAVIS CHRISTINE) The dynamics of change in a slave society: a sociopolitical history of the free coloreds of Jamaica, 1800-1865. Cranbury, N.J., [1976]. pp. 393. *bibliog.*

FREEDMEN IN THE UNITED STATES.

BELZ (HERMAN) A new birth of freedom: the Republican Party and freedmen's rights, 1861-1866. Westport, Conn., 1976. pp. 199. *bibliogs.*

MAGDOL (EDWARD) A right to the land: essays on the freedmen's community. Westport, Conn., 1977. pp. 290. *bibliog.*

FREEDOM OF ASSOCIATION

— **Germany.**

GERMANY. Reichstag. 1898. Graf Posadowsky und die Koalitionsfreiheit vor dem Reichstag: Verhandlungen des Deutschen Reichstags über den Erlass des Staatssekretärs des Innern vom 11.Dezember 1897, etc. Berlin, 1898. pp. 112.

SCHIPPEL (MAX) Gewerkschaften und Koalitionsrecht der Arbeiter. Berlin, 1899. pp. 48.

— **Spain.**

ALARCON CARACUEL (MANUEL RAMON) El derecho de asociacion obrera en España, 1839-1900. Madrid, [1975]. pp. 507.

FREEDOM OF INFORMATION

— **Bibliography.**

MACCAFFERTY (MAXINE) compiler. The right to know. London, [1976]. pp. 81. *(Association of Special Libraries and Information Bureaux. Aslib Bibliographies. 1)*

— **Denmark.**

MORTENSEN (FRANDS) ed. Ytringsfrihed og offentlighed: de hemmelige dokumenter fra Danmarks Radios afskedigelse af Erik Thygesen, kommenteret af Erik Thygesen og Frands Mortensen. Århus, 1975 repr. 1976. pp. 430. *bibliog.*

— **Europe.**

DAKE (ANTONIE C. A.) Impediments to the free flow of information between East and West; a study carried out...for the Information Working Group of the Atlantic Treaty Association. Paris, [1973]. pp. 32.

— **Europe, Eastern.**

ABSHIRE (DAVID M.) International broadcasting: a new dimension of Western diplomacy. Beverly Hills, [1976]. pp. 90. *bibliog. (Georgetown University. Center for Strategic and International Studies. Washington Papers. vol. 4/35)*

FREEDOM OF INFORMATION(Cont.)

— United Kingdom.

WRAITH (RONALD EDWARD) Open government: the British interpretation. London, 1977. pp. 74. *(Royal Institute of Public Administration. RIPA Research Booklets)*

— United States.

PORTER (WILLIAM E.) Assault on the media: the Nixon years. Ann Arbor, [1976]. pp. 320.

FREEDOM OF MOVEMENT

— Europe.

DAKE (ANTONIE C. A.) Impediments to the free flow of information between East and West; a study carried out...for the Information Working Group of the Atlantic Treaty Association. Paris, [1973]. pp. 32.

FREEMASONS

— Spain.

ZAVALA (IRIS M.) Masones, comuneros y carbonarios. Madrid, 1971. pp. 363.

FREIE DEMOKRATISCHE PARTEI.

MOROZ (PIOTR) Polityka wschodnia FDP w latach 1961-1970. Wrocław, 1976. pp. 207. *bibliog.*

FREIGHT AND FREIGHTAGE.

UNITED NATIONS. Conference on Trade and Development. 1970. Route study: the liner trades between France (Bayonne- Dunkirk range of ports) and Morocco; report, etc. (TD/B/C. 4/61/Rev.1). New York, 1970. pp. 49.

SCHLAYER (KARL FRIEDRICH VON) Entwurf einer neuen internationalen Konvention für die Güterbeförderung zur See: Bericht über die Ergebnisse der UNCITRAL-Arbeitsgruppe für Schiffahrtsrecht; Vortrag. Hamburg, 1975. pp. 15. *(Deutscher Verein für Internationales Seerecht. Schriften. Reihe A: Berichte und Vorträge. Heft 23)*

— Senegal.

SENEGAL. Direction des Transports. Bureau d'Etudes. 1971. Les flux et les moyens de transport de marchandises au Sénégal. Dakar, 1971. fo.155.

— Sweden.

RYDÉN (INGER) Transportkostnader och regional utveckling: modeller för analys av regionalpolitiskt stöd av godstransporter. Stockholm, [1976]. pp. 208. *bibliog. With English summary.*

FREISOZIALE UNION.

FREISOZIALE UNION. Gegenwartsprogramm, etc. [Hamburg, 1971]. pp. 11.

FREITAS (MICHAEL DE).

See MALIK (MICHAEL ABDUL).

FRENCH CANADIANS.

FALARDEAU (JEAN CHARLES) The rise of social sciences in French Canada. Quebec, Department of Cultural Affairs, 1967. pp. 67. *bibliog. (Series on the Arts, Humanities and Sciences in French Canada. 6)*

CHARBONNEAU (HUBERT) Vie et mort de nos ancêtres: étude démographique. Montréal, 1975. pp. 267.

NEW BRUNSWICK. Committee on Higher Education in the French Sector of New Brunswick. 1975. Report; [Louis LeBel, chairman]. [Fredericton], 1975. fo. 84.

SWEENY (ALASTAIR) George-Etienne Cartier: a biography. Toronto, [1976]. pp. 352. *bibliog.*

FRENCH IN RUSSIA.

ZAK (LIUDMILA MARKOVNA) Des Français dans la Révolution d'Octobre: contribution à l'histoire du Groupe communiste français près le P.C. (b)R., 1918-1920. Paris, [1976]. pp. 274.

FRENCH LANGUAGE.

QUESTIONS à la sociologie française;...textes réunis et préparés par Yvonne Roux. [Paris, 1976]. pp. 279. *(Association Internationale des Sociologues de Langue Française. Cahiers Internationaux de Sociologie) Papers of a round table sponsored by the Association in 1974.*

— Dictionaries — Polyglot.

ZAHN (HANS E.) Wörterbuch zur Politik und Wirtschaftspolitik. Band I: deutsch-englisch-französisch:...Dictionary of politics and economic policy...: Dictionnaire politique et de politique économique, etc. Frankfurt am Main, [1975]. pp. 382. *bibliog.*

FRENCH LANGUAGE IN CANADA.

QUEBEC (PROVINCE). Commission of Inquiry on the Position of the French Language and on Language Rights in Québec. 1972. Report; [Jean-Denis Gendron, Chairman.]. Québec, 1972. 3 vols. (in l).

FRENCH LITERATURE

— History and criticism.

MUÑOZ (MARYSE BERTRAND DE) La guerre civile espagnole et la littérature française. [Montreal], 1972. pp. xvi,355. *bibliog.*

FRENCH NEWSPAPERS.

MAILLARD (FIRMIN) Histoire des journaux publiés à Paris pendant le Siège et sous la Commune, 4 septembre 1870 au 28 mai 1871. Amsterdam, 1971. pp. 267. *Reprint of Paris edition of 1871.*

FRENCH PERIODICALS.

WAGNER (JACQUES) Marmontel, journaliste, et la Mercure de France, 1725-1761. Grenoble, 1975. pp. 338. *bibliog. (Clermont-Ferrand. Université. Faculté des Lettres et Sciences Humaines. Ouvrages. No. 34)*

FREUD (SIGMUND).

PRIBRAM (KARL H.) and GILL (MERTON MAX) Freud's Project reassessed. London, 1976. pp. 192. *bibliog.*

JAHODA (MARIE) Freud and the dilemmas of psychology. London, 1977. pp. 186.

FRIEDMAN (MILTON).

MILTON Friedman in Australia, 1975; [proceedings of a seminar organized by the Graduate Business School Club in 1975 in Sydney and of a dinner meeting organized by Constable and Bain in 1975 in Sydney]. Darlinghurst, [1975]. pp. 80.

FRIENDLY SOCIETIES

— United Kingdom.

FRIENDLY SOCIETY OF SAILORS, &c., AT SOUTHWOLD. Articles made and agreed to by a Friendly Society of Sailors, c, at Southwold, in Suffolk, on the 8th day of January, 1805. Halesworth, printed by J.T. Allcock, [1805]. pp. 15. *With ms. amendments.*

FRIENDLY SOCIETY OF SAILORS, &c., AT SOUTHWOLD. Articles made and agreed to by a Friendly Society of Sailors, c, at Southwold, in Suffolk, on the 8th day of January, 1805; revised and altered March 5th, 1834. Southwold, Bye, printer, [1834]. pp. 14. *Cover bears signature Willm. Swain, one of the Society's members.*

LANCASHIRE AND CHESHIRE MINER'S PERMANENT RELIEF SOCIETY, THE. Report of proceedings at the...annual and special general meetings. a., 1873/87, 1905. Wigan.

— — Wales.

NORTH WALES PERMANENT RELIEF SOCIETY, THE. Report of proceedings at the...general annual meeting. a., 1889/1903. Wrexham.

FRIENDS, SOCIETY OF.

BROOKS (LEONARD S.) World citizenship: rejection of political nationality: an appeal and a challenge to the Quaker conscience in Western Europe, North America, Southern Africa and Australasia. Eastbourne, [1975]. pp. 12.

— United Kingdom.

SOCIETY OF FRIENDS. Social Responsibility Council. The national economic situation: a Quaker view. [London, 1974]. pp. 14.

RAISTRICK (ARTHUR) Two centuries of industrial welfare: the London (Quaker) Lead Company, 1692-1905: the social policy and work of the "Governor and company for smelting down lead with pit coal and sea coal", mainly in Alston Moor and the Pennines. 2nd ed. Buxton, 1977. pp. 168. *bibliogs.*

FRONT DE LIBERATION NATIONALE.

JACKSON (HENRY F.) The FLN in Algeria: party development in a revolutionary society. Westport, Conn., 1977. pp. 255. *bibliog.*

FRONTIER AND PIONEER LIFE

— United States.

SAVAGE (WILLIAM SHERMAN) Blacks in the West. Westport, 1976. pp. 230. *bibliog.*

FRUIT

— European Economic Community countries.

EUROPEAN COMMUNITIES. Statistical Office. Production of vegetables and fruit. a., 1976 [covering 1972/1974]- Luxembourg.

FUCÍK (JULIUS).

FUČÍK (JULIUS) Reportage, unter dem Strang geschrieben; (aus dem Tschechischen übersetzt von Franz Peter Künzel). Frankfurt am Main, [1976]. pp. 126.

FUEL

— Russia — Buryat Republic.

TUISK (ALEKSANDR GANSOVICH) Toplivnaia promyshlennost' i elektroenergetika Buriatskoi ASSR. Ulan-Ude, 1969. pp. 102.

— United Kingdom.

CHAPMAN (PETER) and others. Future transport fuels. Crowthorne, 1976. pp. 210. *bibliogs. (U.K. Transport and Road Research Laboratory. Supplementary Reports. 251)*

— — Costs.

NATIONAL CONSUMER COUNCIL. Paying for fuel: interim report to the Secretary of State for Prices and Consumer Protection. London, 1976. pp. 30.

— — Prices.

FABIAN SOCIETY. Fabian Tracts. [No.] 447. A policy for warmth; [by] M. Gray [and others]. London, 1977. pp. 23.

FIELD (JULIA) and HEDGES (BARRY M.) National fuel and heating survey;...prepared for the National Consumer Council. London, 1977. 1 vol. (various pagings).

U.K. Working Group on Energy Elasticities. 1977. Report; [T.A. Kennedy, chairman]. London, 1977. pp. 55. *bibliog. (U.K. Department of Energy. Energy Papers. No. 17)*

FULAH EMPIRE.

SMALDONE (JOSEPH P.) Warfare in the Sokoto caliphate: historical and sociological perspectives. Cambridge, 1977. pp. 228. *bibliog. (Cambridge. University. African Studies Centre. African Studies Series. 19)*

FULAHS.

AZARYA (VICTOR) Dominance and change in North Cameroon: the Fulbe aristocracy. Beverly Hills, [1976]. pp. 71. *bibliog.*

FULL EMPLOYMENT POLICIES.

INTERNATIONAL LABOUR OFFICE. World Employment Programme. 1974. World Employment Programme: a progress report on its research- oriented activities. Geneva, 1974. pp. 132.

INTERNATIONAL LABOUR OFFICE. World Employment Programme. 1976. World Employment Programme: research in retrospect and prospect. Geneva, 1976. pp. 278. *bibliog.*

— Underdeveloped areas.

See UNDERDEVELOPED AREAS — Full employment policies.

FUNCTIONAL LOAD (LINGUISTICS).

CHICAGO LINGUISTIC SOCIETY. [Regional Meeting, 11th, 1975]. Papers from the parasession on functionalism, April 17th, 1975; edited by Robin E. Grossman [and others]. Chicago, 1975. pp. 609. *bibliogs.*

FUNCTIONS OF REAL VARIABLES.

HEWITT (EDWIN) and STROMBERG (KARL) Real and abstract analysis: a modern treatment of the theory of functions of a real variable. Berlin, 1965. pp. 476.

GABON

— Economic conditions.

FRANCE. Ministère de la Coopération. Direction des Affaires Economiques et Financières. 1962. République de Gabon: comptes économiques, année 1960; [by] René Condomines [and others]. [Paris], 1962. pp. 111, xix.

FRANCE. Ministère de la Coopération. Service des Etudes Economiques et des Questions Internationales.6. Gabon: données statistiques sur les activités économiques, culturelles et sociales. Paris, 1976. pp. 241.

— Social conditions.

FRANCE. Ministère de la Coopération. Service des Etudes Economiques et des Questions Internationales.6. Gabon: données statistiques sur les activités économiques, culturelles et sociales. Paris, 1976. pp. 241.

— Statistics.

FRANCE. Ministère de la Coopération. Service des Etudes Economiques et des Questions Internationales.6. Gabon: données statistiques sur les activités économiques, culturelles et sociales. Paris, 1976. pp. 241.

GALANSKOV (IURII TIMOFEEVICH).

GINZBURG (ALEKSANDR IL'CH) and GALANSKOV (IURII TIMOFEEVICH) defendants. L'affaire Guinzbourg Galanskov: (les nouveaux procès de Moscou); dossier réuni et présenté par J.J. Marie et Carol Head; traduit du russe par Jean Jacques et Nadine Marie. Paris, [1969]. pp. 203.

GALAPAGOS (PROVINCE)

— Economic policy.

ECUADOR. Junta Nacional de Planificacion y Coordinacion Economica. 1975. Plan de conservacion y desarrollo selectivo para la provincia de Galapagos. Quito, 1975. pp. 275.

GALBRAITH (JOHN KENNETH).

FRIEDMAN (MILTON) From Galbraith to economic freedom. London, 1977. pp. 64. *bibliog. (Institute of Economic Affairs. Occasional Papers. 49)*

McFADZEAN (Sir FRANK S.) The economics of John Kenneth Galbraith: a study in fantasy. London, 1977. pp. 51.

GALICIA (SPAIN)

— Economic conditions.

PAZ-ANDRADE (VALENTIN) La marginacion de Galicia. Madrid, 1970. pp. 359.

— History.

BARREIRO FERNANDEZ (JOSE RAMON) El carlismo gallego. Santiago de Compostela, 1976. pp. 359. *bibliog.*

— Politics and government.

ALFONSO BOZZO (ALFONSO) Los partidos politicos y la autonomia en Galicia, 1931-1936. Madrid, [1976]. pp. 392. *bibliog.*

— Social conditions.

PAZ-ANDRADE (VALENTIN) La marginacion de Galicia. Madrid, 1970. pp. 359.

GAMBIA

— Economic conditions.

GAMBIA. Ministry of Finance and Trade. 1971. Budget speech by S.M. Dibba, Minister of Finance and Trade, 25th June, 1971 in the House of Representatives. Bathurst, 1971. pp. 20. *(Gambia. Sessional Papers. 1971. No. 3)*

— Politics and government.

GAMBIA. Governor-General. 1967. Speech by His Excellency the acting Governor-General at the opening of the budget session of the House of Representatives, 22nd June, 1967. Bathurst, 1967. pp. 8. *(Sessional Papers. 1967. No. 5)*

GAMBIA. Governor-General. 1968. Speech by His Excellency the Governor-General at the opening session of the House of Representatives, 20th June, 1968. [Bathurst], 1968. pp. 9. *(Sessional Papers. 1968. No. 5)*

GAMBIA. Governor-General. 1969. Speech by His Excellency the Governor-General at the opening session of the House of Representatives, 16th June, 1969. Bathurst, 1969. pp. 11. *(Sessional Papers. 1969. No. 2)*

GAMBIA. President, 1970- . (Jawara). Speech by His Excellency the President of the Republic at the state opening of Parliament, 30th June, 1970. Bathurst, 1970. pp. 12. *(Sessional Papers. 1970. No. 4)*

— Relations (general) with Senegal.

REPORT on the alternatives for association between the Gambia and Senegal; by Hubertus J. van Mook [and others], appointed under the United Nations Programme of Technical Assistance. [Bathurst], 1964. pp. 97. *(Gambia. Sessional Papers. 1964. No. 13)*

GAMES, THEORY OF.

PRETECEILLE (EDMOND) Jeux, modèles et simulations: critique des jeux urbains. Paris, [1974]. pp. 208. *bibliog.*

ZAUBERMAN (ALFRED) Differential games and other game-theoretic topics in Soviet literature: a survey. New York, 1975. pp. 227.

BACHARACH (MICHAEL) Economics and the theory of games. London, 1976. pp. 163. *bibliog.*

HARSANYI (JOHN CHARLES) Rational behavior and bargaining equilibrium in games and social situations. Cambridge, 1977. pp. 314. *bibliog.*

GANDHI (INDIRA).

GHOSE (SANKAR) Indira Gandhi, the resurgent Congress and socialism. New Delhi, 1975. pp. 58.

INDIRA Gandhi's India: a political system reappraised; edited by Henry C. Hart. Boulder, Col., 1976. pp. 313.

GANDHI (MOHANDAS KARAMCHAND).

PRASAD (RAJENDRA) Mahatma Gandhi and Bihar: some reminiscences. Bombay, 1949. pp. 132.

LAHIRY (ASHUTOSH) Gandhi in Indian politics: a critical review. Calcutta, 1976. pp. 221.

BROWN (JUDITH M.) Gandhi and civil disobedience: the Mahatma in Indian politics, 1928-34. Cambridge, 1977. pp. 414. *bibliog.*

GAPON (GEORGII APOLLONOVICH).

SABLINSKY (WALTER) The road to Bloody Sunday: Father Gapon and the St. Petersburg massacre of 1905. Princeton, N.J., [1976]. pp. 414. *bibliog. (Columbia University. Russian Institute. Studies)*

GARNET (HENRY HIGHLAND).

SCHOR (JOEL A.) Henry Highland Garnet: a voice of black radicalism in the nineteenth century. Westport, Conn., 1977. pp. 250. *bibliog.*

GARVEY (MARCUS).

MARTIN (TONY) Race first: the ideological and organizational struggles of Marcus Garvey and the Universal Negro Improvement Association. Westport, Conn., 1976. pp. 421. *bibliog.*

GAS

— Law and legislation — United Kingdom.

REEVES (PETER) Electricity and gas consumers' guide: a summary of the practice of supply authorities and the law applicable to domestic gas and electricity consumers. Oxford, [1975]. pp. 23.

GAS, NATURAL

— Canada.

GOULD (ED) Oil: the history of Canada's oil and gas industry. [Victoria, B.C., 1976]. pp. 288. *bibliog.*

— — Pipe lines.

CANADIAN LABOUR CONGRESS. Submission to the Mackenzie Valley pipeline inquiry. Yellowknife, 1976. fo.23.

— Europe.

CHAPMAN (KEITH P.) North Sea oil and gas: a geographical perspective. Newton Abbot, [1976]. pp. 240.

— United Kingdom.

U.K. Offshore Supplies Office. Offshore: an analysis of orders placed (formerly Offshore oil and gas: a summary of orders placed by operators of oil and gas fields on the U.K. Continental Shelf. a., 1974- London.

KING (P.J.) BSc, PhD, CEng, MIChem E, and others. Report of the inquiry into serious gas explosions. London, H.M.S.O., 1977. pp. 104.

GAS, NATURAL, IN SUBMERGED LANDS

— North Sea.

ROBINSON (COLIN) and MORGAN (JON) Economic consequence of controlling the depletion of North Sea oil and gas. London, [1976]. pp. 31. *(Trade Policy Research Centre. Guest Papers. No. 3)*

GAS INDUSTRY

— Russia.

CAMPBELL (ROBERT WELLINGTON) Trends in the Soviet oil and gas industry. Baltimore, Md., [1976]. pp. 125. *bibliog.*

GASES, ASPHYXIATING AND POISONOUS

— War use.

HABER (LUDWIG FRITZ) Gas warfare, 1915-1945: the legend and the facts. [London], 1976. pp. 18. *(London. University. Bedford College. Stevenson Lectures. 1975)*

GATES (FREDERICK TAYLOR).

GATES (FREDERICK TAYLOR) Chapters in my life;...with the Frederick Taylor Gates Lectures by Robert Swain Morison. New York, [1977]. pp. 305.

GAULLE (CHARLES DE).

NOEL (LEON) De Gaulle et les débuts de la Ve République. [Paris, 1976]. pp. 310.

GAXIOLA OCHOA (FRANCISCO JAVIER).

GAXIOLA OCHOA (FRANCISCO JAVIER) Memorias. Mexico, 1975. pp. 356.

GAZANKULU

— Economic conditions.

SOUTH AFRICA. Bureau for Economic Research re Bantu Development. 1976. Gazankulu:...economic revue [sic], etc. Pretoria, [1976]. pp. 72. *bibliog. In English and Afrikaans.*

GEDDES (Sir PATRICK).

STEVENSON (W.I.) Patrick Geddes and geography: biobibliographical study. London, 1975. 1 pamphlet (unpaged). *(London. University. University College. Department of Geography. Occasional Papers. No. 27)*

— Bibliography.

STEVENSON (W.I.) Patrick Geddes and geography: biobibliographical study. London, 1975. 1 pamphlet (unpaged). *(London. University. University College. Department of Geography. Occasional Papers. No. 27)*

GEM (COMPUTER PROGRAM).

SLATER (LUCY JOAN) Gem: a general econometric matrix program. Cambridge, 1976. pp. 86. *(Cambridge. University. Department of Applied Economics. Occasional Papers. 46)*

GENERAL AGREEMENT ON TARIFFS AND TRADE.

HUDEC (ROBERT E.) The GATT legal system and world trade diplomacy. New York, [1975]. pp. 399.

PIONTEK (EUGENIUSZ) Udzial państw socjalistycznych w GATT. Warszawa, 1975. pp. 214. *bibliog.*

GENERAL STRIKE.

COMITE DE PROPAGANDE DE LA GREVE GENERALE. La grève générale. Paris, 1901. pp. 16.

GENERAL STRIKE, SOUTH AFRICA, 1913.

KATZ (ELAINE N.) A trade union aristocracy: a history of white workers in the Transvaal and the general strike of 1913. Johannesburg, 1976. pp. 601. *bibliog. (Johannesburg. University of the Witwatersrand. African Studies Institute. ASI Communications. No. 3)*

GENERAL STRIKE, UNITED KINGDOM, 1926.

TROTSKII (LEV DAVYDOVICH) Collected writings and speeches on Britain: in three volumes...; edited by R. Chappell and Alan Clinton. London, [1974] 3 vols.

TRORY (ERNIE) Soviet trade unions and the general strike. Brighton, 1975. pp. 48. *bibliog.*

DAVIES (TREVOR) Bolton, May 1926: a review of the general strike as it affected Bolton and district. [Bolton, 1976]. pp. 19.

McLEAN (JOHN) Historian. The 1926 general strike in north Lanarkshire. London, 1976. pp. 25. *bibliog. (Communist Party of Great Britain. History Group. Our History. No. 65)*

MORRIS (MARGARET) The general strike. Harmondsworth, 1976. pp. 479.

The NINE days in Birmingham: the general strike 4-12 May, 1926; [written by a working party of the Workers' Educational Association, the Birmingham Trades Council and the Social Sciences Department of the Reference Library]. Birmingham, 1976. pp. 43.

TROTSKII (LEV DAVYDOVICH) and others. General strike, 1926: articles. London, [1976]. pp. 59.

KIBBLEWHITE (LIZ) and RIGBY (ANDREW) Aberdeen in the general strike. Aberdeen, 1977. pp. 32. *bibliog.*

GENERAL STRIKE, URUGUAY, 1973.

LUSTEMBERG (HUGO) Uruguay: imperialismo y estrategia de liberacion; las enseñanzas de la huelga general. Buenos Aires, [1975]. pp. 223.

GENERALS

— Germany.

BRETT-SMITH (RICHARD) Hitler's generals. London, 1976. pp. 306. *bibliog.*

GENERATIVE GRAMMAR.

HUDSON (RICHARD ANTHONY) Arguments for a non-transformational grammar. Chicago, 1976. pp. 214. *bibliog.*

MONTAGUE grammar; edited by Barbara H. Partee. New York, [1976]. pp. 370. *bibliogs.*

STOCKWELL (ROBERT PAUL) Foundations of syntactic theory. Englewood Cliffs, [1977]. pp. 217. *bibliog.*

GENETIC COUNSELLING.

U.K. Central Health Services Council. Standing Medical Advisory Committee. 1972. Human genetics. London, 1972. pp. 20. *bibliog.*

GENETICS.

DAWKINS (RICHARD) The selfish gene. Oxford, 1976. pp. 224. *bibliog.*

GENETICS, HUMAN.

See HUMAN GENETICS.

GENEVA CONVENTIONS.

DROIT humanitaire et conflits armés:...colloque des 28, 29 et 30 janvier 1970. Bruxelles, [1976]. pp. 302. *(Brussels. Université Libre. Institut de Sociologie. Centre de Droit International. [Publications]. 7) In French or English.*

DELESSERT (CHRISTIANE SHIELDS) Release and repatriation of prisoners of war at the end of active hostilities: a study of Article 118, Paragraph 1, of the Third Geneva Convention relative to the Treatment of Prisoners of War. Zürich, [1977]. pp. 225. *bibliog. (Schweizerische Vereinigung für Internationales Recht. Schweizer Studien zum Internationalen Recht. Band 5)*

GENOA

— Commerce.

KEDAR (BENJAMIN Z.) Merchants in crisis: Genoese and Venetian men of affairs and the fourteenth-century depression. New Haven, 1976. pp. 260. *bibliog.*

GENOCIDE.

HOROWITZ (IRVING LOUIS) Genocide: state power and mass murder. New Brunswick. N.J., [1976]. pp. 80. *bibliog.*

KUPER (LEO) The pity of it all: polarisation of racial and ethnic relations. London, 1977. pp. 302: *bibliog.*

GEOGRAPHICAL PERCEPTION.

EYLES (JOHN D.) Environmental satisfaction and London's docklands: problems and policies in the Isle of Dogs. London, 1976. pp. 31. *bibliog. (London. University. Queen Mary College. Department of Geography. Occasional Papers. No. 5)*

PICHE (DENISE) The geographical understanding of children aged 5 to 8 years. 1977. fo. 348. *bibliog. Typescript. Ph. D. (London) thesis: unpublished. This thesis is the property of London University and may not be removed from the Library.*

— Bibliography.

VEAL (A.J.) compiler. Environmental perception and recreation: a review and annotated bibliography. Birmingham, 1974. pp. 201. *bibliog. (Birmingham. University. Centre for Urban and Regional Studies. Research Memoranda. No. 39)*

— Mathematical models.

HUDSON (R.) Environmental images, spatial choice and consumer behaviour: a conceptual model and an empirical investigation. Durham, 1976. pp. 19. *bibliog. (Durham. University. Department of Geography. Occasional Publications (New Series). No. 9)*

GEOGRAPHY.

BURGESS (ROD) Marxism and geography. London, 1976. pp. 42. *(London. University. University College. Department of Geography. Occasional Papers. No. 30)*

POLSKA AKADEMIA NAUK. Instytut Geografii. Geographia Polonica. 36. (The collection of studies presented to Professor Stanislaw Leszczycki in commemoration of the 50th anniversary of his scientific activity; edited by Jerzy Kostrowicki). Warsaw, 1977. pp. 237. *bibliog.*

— Computer programs.

MACDOUGALL (E. BRUCE) Computer programming for spatial problems. London, 1976. pp. 160. *bibliog.*

— Statistical methods.

HAGGETT (PETER) and others. Locational analysis in human geography. 2nd ed. London, 1977. pp. 605. *bibliog.*

GEOGRAPHY, ECONOMIC.

SPATIAL dimensions of public policy; edited by John Terence Coppock and W.R. Derrick Sewell. Oxford, 1976. pp. 271. *bibliogs. Based on papers presented at the annual meeting of the Institute of British Geographers, University of East Anglia, 1974.*

HAGGETT (PETER) and others. Locational analysis in human geography. 2nd ed. London, 1977. pp. 605. *bibliog.*

SMITH (DAVID MARSHALL) Human geography: a welfare approach. London, 1977. pp. 402. *bibliog.*

— Periodicals.

LIST ECON: Förteckning över periodica inom ekonomi, handel, ekonomisk geografi och internationell statistik i nordiska bibliotek: List of periodicals in the fields of economics, trade, economic geography and international statistics in Nordic libraries; [pd. by] Biblioteket, Handelshögskolan, Stockholm. irreg., 1976- Stockholm.

GEOGRAPHY, MATHEMATICAL.

SEMINAR ON GEOGRAPHIC DATA PROCESSING, PETERLEE, 1974. Proceedings of the...seminar...; edited by B.K. Aldred. Peterlee, 1975. pp. 104. *(IBM United Kingdom Limited. UK Scientific Centre. [Technical Reports]. 0073)*

RODRIGUEZ-BACHILLER (AGUSTIN) Gravity models in a dynamic framework. Reading, 1976. pp. 54. *bibliog. (Reading. University. Department of Geography. Reading Geographical Papers. No. 40)*

SILK (JOHN) A comparison of regression lines using dummy variable analysis: models and examples for the bivariate case. Reading, 1976. pp. 39. *bibliog. (Reading. University, Department of Geography. Reading Geographical Papers. No. 44)*

TAYLOR (PETER JOHN) Quantitative methods in geography: an introduction to spatial analysis. Atlanta, [1977]. pp. 386. *bibliog.*

GEOLOGY

— Zambia.

VRANA (S.) The geology of the area south of the Lukanga swamp: explanation of degree sheet 1427, SE. quarter. Lusaka, 1974. pp. 29. *bibliog. (Zambia. Geological Survey Department. Reports. No.28)* 2 maps in end pocket.

GEOMORPHOLOGY.

POLSKA AKADEMIA NAUK. Instytut Geografii. Geographia Polonica. 34. Approaches to the study of man-environment interactions: proceedings of the Anglo-Polish Geographical Seminar, Toruń, September 1974; edited by Eric H. Brown and Rajmund Galon. Warszawa, 1976. pp. 290. *bibliogs.* Map in end pocket.

GEOPOLITICS.

PINOCHET UGARTE (AUGUSTO) Geopolitica. Santiago, Chile, 1968 repr. 1974. pp. 252. *bibliog.*

GEORGE (DAVID LLOYD) 1st Earl Lloyd George.

GEORGE (WILLIAM RICHARD PHILIP) The making of Lloyd George. London, 1976. pp. 184.

CAMPBELL (JOHN) Ph.D. Lloyd George: the goat in the wilderness 1922-1931. London, 1977. pp. 383. *bibliog.*

GEORGESCU-ROEGEN (NICHOLAS).

EVOLUTION, welfare, and time in economics: essays in honor of Nicholas Georgescu-Roegen. Lexington, Mass., [1976]. pp. 183. *bibliogs.*

GEORGIA

— Economic policy.

MELKADZE (VALERIAN IRAKLISOVICH) Kompleksnaia programma uskorennogo rosta ekonomiki Sovetskoi Gruzii. Tbilisi, 1975. pp. 73.

— History.

GEGECHKORI (EVGENII) L'avenir de la Géorgie;...publié par le Comité international pour la Géorgie. Genève, 1927. pp. 13.

MAKHARADZE (N.B.) and others, eds. Revoliutsiia 1905-1907 gg. v Gruzii: sbornik statei, etc. Tbilisi, 1975. pp. 165. *Articles in Russian or Georgian.*

BAGRATIONI (VAKHUSHTI) Istoriia tsarstva gruzinskogo; perevel [s gruzinskogo], snabdil predisloviem, slovariami i ukazatelem N.T. Nakashidze. Tbilisi, 1976. pp. 339. *Date of composition of original circa 1750.*

— — 1917-1921, Revolution.

ROOBOL (W.H.) Tsereteli - a democrat in the Russian revolution: a political biography; translated from the Dutch by Philip Hyams and Lynne Richards. The Hague, 1976. pp. 273. *bibliog. (International Institute of Social History. Studies in Social History. No.1)*

— Nationalism.

GEGECHKORI (EVGENII) L'avenir de la Géorgie;...publié par le Comité international pour la Géorgie. Genève, 1927. pp. 13.

GEORGIA (UNITED STATES)

— Politics and government.

CARTER (JAMES EARL) President of the United States. A government as good as its people. New York, [1977]. pp. 262.

GERMAN AMERICANS.

CONZEN (KATHLEEN NEILS) Immigrant Milwaukee, 1836-1860: accommodation and community in a frontier city. Cambridge, Mass., 1976. pp. 300.

See also PENNSYLVANIA GERMANS.

GERMAN CONFEDERATION, 1815-1866.

WERNER (GEORGE S.) Bavaria in the German Confederation, 1820-1848. Rutherford, N.J., [1977]. pp. 270. *bibliog.*

GERMAN LANGUAGE

— Dictionaries — Polyglot.

ZAHN (HANS E.) Wörterbuch zur Politik und Wirtschaftspolitik. Band I: deutsch-englisch-französisch:...Dictionary of politics and economic policy...: Dictionnaire politique et de politique économique, etc. Frankfurt am Main, [1975]. pp. 382. *bibliog.*

GERMAN NEWSPAPERS.

ROTE FAHNE, DIE: Zentralorgan der Kommunistischen Partei Deutschlands (Sektion der Kommunistischen Internationale). Die Rote Fahne: Kritik, Theorie, Feuilleton, 1918-1933; ([edited by] Manfred Brauneck). München, [1973]. pp. 513.

Die KOENIGSBERGER Allgemeine Zeitung: Festschrift zum 100. Gründungstag...; [by the] Arbeitsgemeinschaft ehemaliger KAZ-Mitarbeiter. [Hamburg, 1975]. pp. 178.

GERMAN PERIODICALS.

FRITZSCHE (KLAUS) Politische Romantik und Gegenrevolution: Fluchtwege in der Krise der bürgerlichen Gesellschaft: das Beispiel des "Tat" Kreises. Frankfurt am Main, 1976. pp. 437. *bibliog.*

KRAWEHL (OTTO ERNST) Die "Jahrbücher für Nationalökonomie und Statistik" unter den Herausgebern Bruno Hildebrand und Johannes Conrad, 1863 bis 1915. München, 1977. pp. 127. *bibliog.*

GERMAN REUNIFICATION QUESTION (1949-).

DEUTSCHER VOLKSKONGRESS, 1., BERLIN, 1947. Protokoll...am 6. und 7. Dezember 1947 in der Deutschen Staatsoper, Berlin. Berlin, [1948]. pp. 111. *(Deutscher Volkskongress für Einheit und Gerechten Frieden. Schriftenreihe für Einheit und Gerechten Frieden. Heft 1)*

SCHMIDT-WITTMACK (KARL FRANZ) So geht es nicht weiter. [Berlin, 1954]. pp. 39.

SCHUETZ (WILHELM WOLFGANG) Wir wollen überleben: Aussenpolitik im Atomzeitalter. Stuttgart, [1956]. pp. 216.

SCHMID (GUENTHER) Politik des Ausverkaufs?: die Deutschlandpolitik der Regierung Brandt/Scheel. München, [1975]. pp. 313. *bibliog.*

INTER-system detente in Germany and Korea: proceedings of a German-Korean conference in Tutzing and Munich, June 1975; edited by Gottfried-Karl Kindermann. München, [1976]. pp. 288.

WETTIG (GERHARD) Die Sowjetunion, die DDR und die Deutschland-Frage, 1965-1976: Einvernehmen und Konflikt im sozialistischen Lager. Stuttgart, 1976 repr. 1977. pp. 232. *bibliog.*

GERMANIC TRIBES.

TODD (MALCOLM) The northern barbarians, 100 B.C. - A.D. 300. London, 1975. pp. 232. *bibliog.*

GERMANS IN CHILE.

YOUNG (GEORGE F.W.) The Germans in Chile: immigration and colonization, 1849-1914. New York, [1974]. pp. 234. *bibliog.*

GERMANS IN CZECHOSLOVAKIA.

RENNER (KARL) Das nationale und das ökonomische Problem der Tschechoslowakei. Prag, 1926. pp. 20.

NELHIEBEL (KURT) Die Henleins gestern und heute: Hintergründe und Ziele des Witikobundes. Frankfurt/Main, 1962. pp. 88.

POZORNY (REINHARD) Deutsche Schutzarbeit im Sudetenland: die Tätigkeit des Deutschen Kulturverbandes, 1918-1938. Wien, 1974. pp. 51.

GERMANS IN EASTERN EUROPE.

DE ZAYAS (ALFRED M.) Nemesis at Potsdam: the Anglo-Americans and the expulsion of the Germans: background, execution, consequences. London, 1977. pp. 268. *bibliog.*

GERMANS IN LITHUANIA.

MIKULICZ (SERGIUSZ) Kłajpeda w polityce europejskiej, 1918-1939. Warszawa, 1976. pp. 352. *bibliog.*

GERMANS IN POLAND.

PARADOWSKA (MARIA) Bambrzy: mieszkańcy dawnych wsi miasta Poznania. Warszawa, 1975. pp. 177. *(Poznań. Urząd Miasta. Wydział Kultury. Biblioteka Kroniki Miasta Poznania)*

SOŁOMA (ANTONI) Za każdą cenę: niemiecki kler katolicki wobec ludności polskiej na Warmii, Mazurach i Powiślu w latach 1919-1939. Warszawa, 1976. pp. 394. *bibliog.*

GERMANS IN SILESIA.

JANAS (EUGENIUSZ) Działalność pohitlerowskiego zbrojnego podziemia na Śląsku odzyskanym w latach 1945-1947. Opole, 1975. pp. 100. *bibliog.*

BENISZ (ADAM) W burzy życia; do druku przygotował Mieczysław Wrzosek. Opole, 1976. pp. 200.

GERMANS IN SWITZERLAND.

URNER (KLAUS) Die Deutschen in der Schweiz: von den Anfängen der Kolonienbildung bis zum Ausbruch des Ersten Weltkrieges. Frauenfeld, [1976]. pp. 848. *bibliog.*

GERMANS IN THE UNITED STATES.

See GERMAN AMERICANS.

GERMANY

— Air force.

HOMZE (EDWARD L.) Arming the Luftwaffe: the Reich Air Ministry and the German aircraft industry, 1919-39. Lincoln, Neb., [1976]. pp. 296. *bibliog.*

— Armed forces.

NUSS (KARL) Militär und Wiederaufrüstung in der Weimarer Republik: zur politischen Rolle und Entwicklung der Reichswehr. Berlin, 1977. pp. 372. *bibliog. (Militärgeschichtliches Institut der Deutschen Demokratischen Republik. Schriften)*

VOGL (FRIEDRICH) Widerstand im Waffenrock: österreichische Freiheitskämpfer in der Deutschen Wehrmacht, 1938-1945. Wien, 1977. pp. 258. *bibliog. (Ludwig Boltzmann Institut für Geschichte der Arbeiterbewegung. Materialien zur Arbeiterbewegung. Nr. 7)*

— — Political activity.

PORTNER (DIETER) Bundeswehr und Linksextremismus. München, [1976]. pp. 210. *bibliog.*

— Army — Biography.

BRETT-SMITH (RICHARD) Hitler's generals. London, 1976. pp. 306. *bibliog.*

— — History.

KITCHEN (MARTIN) The silent dictatorship: the politics of the German High Command under Hindenburg and Ludendorff, 1916-1918. London, [1976]. pp. 301. *bibliog.*

— Bundesrat.

FROMME (FRIEDRICH KARL) Gesetzgebung im Widerstreit: wer beherrscht den Bundesrat?: die Kontroverse, 1969-1976. Stuttgart, 1976. pp. 226. *bibliog.*

— Bundestag.

GERMANY (BUNDESREPUBLIK). Deutscher Bundestag. Wissenschaftliche Dienste. 1976. Die Wissenschaftlichen Dienste des Deutschen Bundestages. Bonn, 1976. pp. 19. *(Materialien. 47)*

KUERSCHNERS Volkshandbuch Deutscher Bundestag: 8. Wahlperiode, 1976, etc. Rheinbreitbach, [1977]. pp. 224. *(Sonderdruck des Presse- und Informationszentrums des Deutschen Bundestages, Öffentlichkeitsarbeit)*

LUNZE (ARNULF) ed. Berlin: Initiativen im Deutschen Bundestag in der 7. Wahlperiode. Bonn, 1977. pp. 72. *(Germany (Bundesrepublik). Deutscher Bundestag. Wissenschaftliche Dienste. Materialien. 48)*

— — Committees.

KREMER (KLEMENS) Unterrichtungsrecht der Parlamentsausschüsse über Verordnungsentwürfe. Bonn, 1976. pp. 14. *(Germany (Bundesrepublik) . Deutscher Bundestag. Wissenschaftliche Dienste. Materialien. 44)*

— — Elections.

INTER NATIONES E.V. The Federal Republic of Germany goes to the polls on 3rd October 1976. Bonn, [1976]. pp. 116. *bibliog.*

WEISS (HANS JUERGEN) Wahlkampf im Fernsehen: Untersuchungen zur Rolle der grossen Fernsehdebatten im Bundestagswahlkampf, 1972. Berlin, 1976. pp. 292. *bibliog. (Arbeitsgemeinschaft für Kommunikationsforschung. AfK Studien. Band 5)*

— — Rules and practice.

KREMER (KLEMENS) Unterrichtungsrecht der Parlamentsausschüsse über Verordnungsentwürfe. Bonn, 1976. pp. 14. *(Germany (Bundesrepublik) . Deutscher Bundestag. Wissenschaftliche Dienste. Materialien. 44)*

— Census.

GERMANY (BUNDESREPUBLIK). Statistisches Bundesamt. 1972. Amtliches Gemeindeverzeichnis für die Bundesrepublik Deutschland: Ausgabe 1971, Bevölkerungsstand: 27.5.1970, Gebietsstand: 1.1.1971. Wiesbaden, 1972. pp. 772.

— Civilization.

SCHEEL (WALTER) Vom Recht des anderen: Gedanken zur Freiheit. Düsseldorf, 1977. pp. 188. *Speeches by the Federal German President, 1974-76.*

— Colonies.

MY, pseud. Flottenkoller und Weltmachtspolitik. Dresden, 1900. pp. 30.

Die DEUTSCHE Kolonialpolitik. [Berlin, 1907]. pp. 16. *Wanting title-page.*

— Commerce.

HENKNER (KLAUS) Wettbewerbsrelationen im Aussenhandel westlicher Industrieländer, 1959 bis 1973:...unter besonderer Berücksichtigung der Bundesrepublik Deutschland. Berlin, 1976. pp. 199. *(Deutsches Institut für Wirtschaftsforschung. Beiträge zur Strukturforschung. Heft 39) With English summary.*

— — Iran.

SOHRAB (SIAWUSCH) Die deutsch-persischen Wirtschaftsbeziehungen vor dem Ersten Weltkrieg. Frankfurt/M., 1976. pp. 514. *bibliog.*

— Commercial policy.

BUELOW-CUMMEROW (ERNST GOTTFRIED GEORG VON) Der Zollverein, sein System und dessen Gegner. Berlin, Veit, 1844. pp. 123.

REUSS (INGO) Ökonomie des Aussenhandels: Sicherheit durch Beteiligung am Welthandel und Weltverkehr. Baden-Baden, [1956]. pp. 204.

AUSSENHANDEL, Direktinvestitionen und Industriestruktur der deutschen Wirtschaft: eine Untersuchung ihrer Entwicklung unter Berücksichtigung der Wechselkursänderungen von Hans Baumann [and others]. Berlin, [1977]. pp. 242. *bibliog.*

WEITOWITZ (ROLF GUNTER) German trade policies and politics under the chancellorship of Count Leo von Caprivi, 1890-1894. 1977. fo.366. *bibliog. Typescript. Ph.D. (London) thesis: unpublished. This thesis is the property of London University and may not be removed from the Library.*

— Constitution.

MITBESTIMMUNG, Wirtschaftsordnung, Grundgesetz: Protokoll der Wissenschaftlichen Konferenz des Deutschen Gewerkschaftsbundes vom 1. bis 3. Oktober 1975 in Frankfurt am Main; Herausgeber: Heinz Oskar Vetter. Frankfurt am Main, 1976. pp. 408.

— Constitutional history.

JUNG (OTMAR) Zum Kulturstaatsbegriff: Johann Gottlieb Fichte; Verfassung des Freistaates Bayern; Godesberger Grundsatzprogramm der SPD. Meisenheim am Glan, 1976. pp. 255. *bibliog.*

RITTER (GERHARD A.) Arbeiterbewegung, Parteien und Parlamentarismus: Aufsätze zur deutschen Sozial- und Verfassungsgeschichte des 19. und 20. Jahrhunderts. Göttingen, 1976. pp. 412.

WEDEL (HENNING VON) Das Verfahren der demokratischen Verfassunggebung, dargestellt am Beispiel Deutschlands 1848/49, 1919, 1948/49. Berlin, 1976. pp. 298. *bibliog.*

— Constitutional law.

SEYDEL (MAX VON) Staatsrechtliche und politische Abhandlungen;...Neue Folge... herausgegeben von Karl Krazeisen. Tübingen, 1902. pp. 343.

WEBER (WERNER) Dr. jur. Neue Aspekte der Freiheit von Forschung und Lehre: die verfassungsrechtlichen Grenzen der Mitbestimmung im akademischen Bereich. Göttingen, 1969. pp. 36.

HAMMER (ECKEHARD) Möglichkeiten einer Wiedereingliederung verfassungsfeindlicher Parteien. Berlin, [1976]. pp. 253. *bibliog.*

KIRCHHEIMER (OTTO) Von der Weimarer Republik zum Faschismus: die Auflösung der demokratischen Rechtsordnung; herausgegeben von Wolfgang Luthardt. Frankfurt am Main, 1976. pp. 255. *bibliog.*

WEDEL (HENNING VON) Das Verfahren der demokratischen Verfassunggebung, dargestellt am Beispiel Deutschlands 1848/49, 1919, 1948/49. Berlin, 1976. pp. 298. *bibliog.*

— — Cases.

PRUSSIA, plaintiff. Preussen contra Reich vor dem Staatsgerichtshof: (Stenogrammbericht der Verhandlungen...vom 10. bis 14. und vom 17. Oktober 1932); mit einem Vorwort von [Arnold] Brecht. Glashütten im Taunus, 1976. pp. 520. *Reprint of work originally published in Berlin in 1933.*

— Defences.

KOMMUNISTISCHE PARTEI DEUTSCHLANDS. Zentralkomitee. Richtlinien der KPD zur Wehrfrage. [Berlin?], 1929. pp. 14.

SCHMIDT-WITTMACK (KARL FRANZ) So geht es nicht weiter. [Berlin, 1954]. pp. 39.

SCHLOTTER (PETER) Rüstungspolitik in der Bundesrepublik Deutschland: die Beispiele Starfighter und Phantom. Frankfurt, [1975]. pp. 210.

BONIN (BOGISLAW VON) Opposition gegen Adenauers Sicherheitspolitik: eine Dokumentation; zusammengestellt von Heinz Brill. Hamburg, [1976]. pp. 187. *bibliog.*

KNORR (LORENZ) Sicherheit und Sicherheitspolitik in der BRD. Frankfurt am Main, 1976. pp. 46.

LEICHTHAMMER (JOERG) Die Wahl des Wehrsystems als wirtschaftliches Problem. Frankfurt am Main, 1976. pp. 284. *bibliog. Inaugural-Dissertation zur Erlangung des akademischen Grades eines Doktors der Wirtschafts- und Sozialwissenschaften der Friedrich-Alexander-Universität Erlangen-Nürnberg.*

— Diplomatic and consular service.

CECIL (LAMAR J.R.) The German diplomatic service, 1871-1914. Princeton, N.J., [1976]. pp. 352. *bibliog.*

— Economic conditions.

REINERS (LUDWIG) Die wirkliche Wirtschaft. München, [1932-33]. 2 vols. *bibliog. vol.1 is of the 4th edition.*

INDUSTRIEGEWERKSCHAFT METALL FÜR DIE BUNDESREPUBLIK DEUTSCHLAND. Tagung "Krise und Reform in der Industriegesellschaft", 1976. Protokoll ([and] Materialien)...; Redaktion: Hans- Adam Pfromm. Frankfurt am Main, [1976]. 2 vols.

EINFLUSS multinationaler Unternehmen auf Aussenwirtschaft und Branchenstruktur der Bundesrepublik Deutschland; [by] Rolf Jungnickel [and others]. Hamburg, 1977. pp. 431. *bibliog. (Hamburg. Hamburgisches Welt-Wirtschafts-Archiv. Veröffentlichungen)*

— — Mathematical models.

REHM (HELMUT) Aufbau eines ökonometrischen Modells für die deutsche Volkswirtschaft, 1960-1974, nach der Methode der erweiterten schriftweisen Regression. [Erlangen-Nürnberg, 1976]. pp. 158. *bibliog. Inaugural-Dissertation zur Erlangung des akademischen Grades eines Doktors der Wirtschafts- und Sozialwissenschaften der Friedrich-Alexander-Universität Erlangen-Nürnberg.*

— — Statistics.

ECONOMIC SITUATION IN THE FEDERAL REPUBLIC OF GERMANY, THE: monthly review; [pd. by] Bundesministerium für Wirtschaft. m., Oc 1976 (no.10)-Bonn.

— Economic history.

KUCZYNSKI (JUERGEN) Die Kolonialisierung und Remilitarisierung Westdeutschlands. 2nd ed. Berlin, 1951. pp. 80.

FREMDLING (RAINER) Eisenbahnen und deutsches Wirtschaftswachstum, 1840-1879: ein Beitrag zur Entwicklungstheorie und zur Theorie der Infrastruktur. Dortmund, 1975. pp. 217. *bibliog. (Gesellschaft für Westfälische Wirtschaftsgeschichte. Untersuchungen zur Wirtschafts-, Sozial- und Technikgeschichte. Band 2) With English summary.*

GOLDBERG (JOERG) and JUNG (HEINZ) Die Wirtschaftskrise 1974-1976 in der Bundesrepublik Deutschland: Ursachen, Auswirkungen, Argumente. Frankfurt am Main, 1976. pp. 92.

HARDACH (KARL W.) Wirtschaftsgeschichte Deutschlands im 20. Jahrhundert. Göttingen, [1976]. pp. 271. *bibliog.*

TIPTON (FRANK B.) Regional variations in the economic development of Germany during the nineteenth century. Middletown, Conn., [1976]. pp. 270. *bibliog.*

GLASTETTER (WERNER) Die wirtschaftliche Entwicklung der Bundesrepublik Deutschland im Zeitraum 1950 bis 1975: Befunde und Aspekte. Berlin, 1977. pp. 261.

KEHR (ECKART) Economic interest, militarism, and foreign policy: essays on German history; edited...by Gordon A. Craig; translated by Grete Heinz. Berkeley, [1977]. pp. 209.

PETZINA (DIETMAR) Die deutsche Wirtschaft in der Zwischenkriegszeit. Wiesbaden, 1977. pp. 205. *bibliog.*

SPREE (REINHARD) Die Wachstumszyklen der deutschen Wirtschaft von 1840 bis 1880; mit einem konjunkturstatistischen Anhang. Berlin, [1977]. pp. 577.

— — Bibliography.

WEHLER (HANS ULRICH) compiler. Bibliographie zur modernen deutschen Wirtschaftsgeschichte, 18.- 20. Jahrhundert. Göttingen, [1976]. pp. 242.

— Economic policy.

BASSERMANN (ERNST) Reichstagsabg. Bassermann über die innere und äussere Politik Deutschlands: Rede gehalten in Magdeburg am 15. April 1907. Berlin, [1907]. pp. 28. (Nationalliberale Partei Deutschlands. Nationalliberale Schriften. Nr. 6)

WISSELL (RUDOLF) and STRIEMER (ALFRED) Ohne Planwirtschaft kein Aufbau: eine Aufklärungsschrift. Stuttgart, 1921. pp. 80.

SACK (RUDOLF) Muss Arbeitslosigkeit Dauerzustand für Deutschland bleiben?: Wege zu neuer Wirtschaftsgestaltung. Frankfurt am Main, 1931. pp. 12.

KOMMUNISTISCHE PARTEI DEUTSCHLANDS. Ausschuss für Wirtschaftsfragen. Referat und Diskussion über die Richtlinien der KPD zur Wirtschaftspolitik: (Neuaufbau der deutschen Wirtschaft). Berlin, 1946. pp. 119.

VERNER (PAUL) Die Legende vom Wirtschaftswunder: zur Lage der Arbeiterklasse in Westdeutschland und in Westberlin. Berlin, 1956. pp. 40.

WIRTSCHAFTSTAG, 1971. Soziale Marktwirtschaft: Gebot der Vernunft, Motor des Fortschritts; Protokoll; (herausgegeben vom Wirtschaftsrat der CDU). Bonn, 1971. pp. 179.

GULDIMANN (TIM) Die Grenzen des Wohlfahrtsstaates: am Beispiel Schwedens und der Bundesrepublik. München, [1976]. pp. 181.

HEIDERMANN (HORST) ed. Wirtschaftsstruktur und Beschäftigung. Bonn-Bad Godesberg, [1976]. pp. 198.

INDUSTRIEGEWERKSCHAFT METALL FÜR DIE BUNDESREPUBLIK DEUTSCHLAND. Tagung "Krise und Reform in der Industriegesellschaft", 1976. Protokoll ([and] Materialien)...; Redaktion: Hans-Adam Pfromm. Frankfurt am Main, [1976]. 2 vols.

MUNZEL (DIETER) Die Funktionsfähigkeit von Planungs- und Kontrollsystemen auf der Ebene von Bundesregierung und Bundesverwaltung. Hamburg, 1976. pp. 205. bibliog. Dissertation zur Erlangung des Grades eines Doktors der Wirtschafts- und Sozialwissenschaften der Universität Hamburg.

ZWEIG (KONRAD) Germany through inflation and recession: an object lesson in economic management 1973-1976. London, 1976. pp. 52. bibliog.

BARKAI (AVRAHAM) Das Wirtschaftssystem des Nationalsozialismus: der historische und ideologische Hintergrund, 1933-1936. Köln, [1977]. pp. 215. bibliog.

— Emigration and immigration.

YOUNG (GEORGE F.W.) The Germans in Chile: immigration and colonization, 1849-1914. New York, [1974]. pp. 234. bibliog.

DOMINGUEZ (JAVIER) El hombre como mercancia: españoles en Alemania. Bilbao, [1976]. pp. 234. bibliog.

GESELLSCHAFT FÜR WOHNUNGS- UND SIEDLUNGSWESEN, HAMBURG. Spätaussiedler: Struktur, Situation und Eingliederungsprobleme: Bestandsaufnahme und Empfehlungen;... Projektleitung: A.Schildmeier, etc. Hamburg, 1976. pp. 125. bibliog. (Schriftenreihe. Neue Folge. 18)

— Executive departments.

CECIL (LAMAR J.R.) The German diplomatic service, 1871-1914. Princeton, N.J., [1976]. pp. 352. bibliog.

DOSS (KURT) Das deutsche Auswärtige Amt im Übergang vom Kaiserreich zur Weimarer Republik: die Schülersche Reform. Düsseldorf, [1977]. pp. 328. bibliog.

— Foreign economic relations — Netherlands.

BLAESING (JOACHIM F.E.) Das goldene Delta und sein eisernes Hinterland, 1815-1851: von niederländisch-preussischen zu deutsch-niederländischen Wirtschaftsbeziehungen. Leiden, 1973. pp. 275. bibliog.

— — Poland.

STAATSANGEHOERIGKEIT, soziale Grundrechte, wirtschaftliche Zusammenarbeit nach dem Recht der Bundesrepublik Deutschland und der Volksrepublik Polen: Referate des Rechtscolloquiums 1974; herausgegeben von Józef Kokot und Krzysztof Skubiszewski. Berlin, 1976. pp. 293.

— — Russia.

BOLZ (KLAUS) and others. Die Wirtschaftsbeziehungen zwischen der Bundesrepublik Deutschland und der Sowjetunion: Entwicklung, Bestimmungsfaktoren und Perspektive. Hamburg, 1976. pp. 639. (Hamburg. Hamburgisches Welt-Wirtschafts-Archiv. Veröffentlichungen) 8 graphs in end pocket.

MUELLER-LINK (HORST) Industrialisierung und Aussenpolitik: Preussen-Deutschland und das Zarenreich von 1860 bis 1890. Göttingen, 1977. pp. 506. bibliog.

— Foreign opinion.

RADIO FREE EUROPE. Audience and Public Opinion Research Department. The images of Polish, American, Russian, German and Chinese youth as seen by Poles. [Munich?], 1973. fo. 55.

— Foreign relations.

BASSERMANN (ERNST) Reichstagsabg. Bassermann über die innere und äussere Politik Deutschlands: Rede gehalten in Magdeburg am 15. April 1907. Berlin, [1907]. pp. 28. (Nationalliberale Partei Deutschlands. Nationalliberale Schriften. Nr. 6)

Die MAROKKOKRISE vor dem Reichstag. Berlin, 1911. pp. 32.

THAELMANN (ERNST) Im Kampf gegen den deutschen und den amerikanischen Imperialismus: drei Reichstagsreden. Berlin, 1954. pp. 99. (Institut für Marxismus-Leninismus (Berlin). Beiträge zur Geschichte und Theorie der Arbeiterbewegung. Heft 1) Speeches made in 1924, 1925 and 1930.

SCHUETZ (WILHELM WOLFGANG) Wir wollen überleben: Aussenpolitik im Atomzeitalter. Stuttgart, [1956]. pp. 216.

ART (ROBERT J.) The influence of foreign policy on seapower: new weapons and Weltpolitik in Wilhelminian Germany. Beverly Hills, [1973]. pp. 49. bibliog.

INFORMATIONEN ZUR POLITISCHEN BILDUNG. Bonn, Bundeszentrale für Politische Bildung, 1974 in progress.

CECIL (LAMAR J.R.) The German diplomatic service, 1871-1914. Princeton, N.J., [1976]. pp. 352. bibliog.

FUNKE (MANFRED) ed. Hitler, Deutschland und die Mächte: Materialien zur Aussenpolitik des Dritten Reiches. Düsseldorf, 1976 repr.1977. pp. 848. (Bonn. Universität. Seminar für Politische Wissenschaft. Bonner Schriften zur Politik und Zeitgeschichte. 12)

KLEIN (FRITZ) ed. Studien zum deutschen Imperialismus vor 1914. Berlin, 1976. pp. 291. (Akademie der Wissenschaften der DDR. Zentralinstitut für Geschichte. Schriften. Band 47)

DOSS (KURT) Das deutsche Auswärtige Amt im Übergang vom Kaiserreich zur Weimarer Republik: die Schülersche Reform. Düsseldorf, [1977]. pp. 328. bibliog.

EMMERSON (JAMES THOMAS) The Rhineland crisis, 7 March 1936: a study in multilateral diplomacy. London, 1977. pp. 383. bibliog.

INNEN- und Aussenpolitik unter nationalsozialistischer Bedrohung: Determinanten internationaler Beziehungen in historischen Fallstudien; ([edited by] Erhard Forndran [and others]). Opladen, [1977]. pp. 361.

SCHEEL (WALTER) Vom Recht des anderen: Gedanken zur Freiheit. Düsseldorf, 1977. pp. 188. Speeches by the Federal German President, 1974-76.

WINZEN (PETER) Bülows Weltmachtkonzept: Untersuchung zur Frühphase seiner Aussenpolitik, 1897-1901. Boppard am Rhein, [1977]. pp. 462. bibliog. (Germany (Bundesrepublik). Bundesarchiv. Schriften. 22)

— — Treaties.

SCHRAMM (THEODOR) Das Verhältnis der Bundesrepublik Deutschland zur DDR nach dem Grundvertrag: eine Einführung in die staats- und völkerrechtlichen Problembereiche mit Dokumentensammlung. 2nd ed. Köln, 1975. pp. 275. bibliog.

— — America, Latin.

POMMERIN (REINER) Das Dritte Reich und Lateinamerika: die deutsche Politik gegenüber Süd- und Mittelamerika, 1939-1942. Düsseldorf, [1977]. pp. 377. bibliog.

— — Arab countries.

ABEDISEID (MOHAMMAD) Die deutsch-arabischen Beziehungen: Probleme und Krisen. Stuttgart Degerloch, [1976]. pp. 303. bibliog.

— — Austria.

BAGDASARIAN (NICHOLAS DER) The Austro-German rapprochement, 1870-1879: from the Battle of Sedan to the Dual Alliance. Rutherford, N.J., [1976]. pp. 334. bibliog.

— — Denmark — Sources.

DENMARK. Rigsarkivet. 1973. Danish Department of Foreign Affairs until 1770; by Arthur G. Hassø and Erik Kroman; translated by Mogens Møller. Copenhagen, 1973. pp. 196. (Vejledende Arkivregistraturer. 16)

— — Europe, Eastern.

MOROZ (PIOTR) Polityka wschodnia FDP w latach 1961-1970. Wrocław, 1976. pp. 207. bibliog.

— — France.

RAULFF (HEINER) Zwischen Machtpolitik und Imperialismus: die deutsche Frankreichpolitik, 1904/06. Düsseldorf, [1976]. pp. 215. bibliog.

— — Germany, Eastern.

SCHMID (GUENTHER) Politik des Ausverkaufs?: die Deutschlandpolitik der Regierung Brandt/Scheel. München, [1975]. pp. 313. bibliog.

SCHRAMM (THEODOR) Das Verhältnis der Bundesrepublik Deutschland zur DDR nach dem Grundvertrag: eine Einführung in die staats- und völkerrechtlichen Problembereiche mit Dokumentensammlung. 2nd ed. Köln, 1975. pp. 275. bibliog.

— — India.

BAROOAH (NIRODE KUMAR) India and the official Germany, 1886-1914. Frankfurt, 1977. pp. 254. bibliog.

— — Israel.

WALICHNOWSKI (TADEUSZ) The Tel Aviv-Bonn axis and Poland. Warsaw, 1968. pp. 88. bibliog.

— — Mexico.

VOLLAND (KLAUS) Das Dritte Reich und Mexiko: Studien zur Entwicklung der deutsch-mexikanischen Verhältnisses, 1933-1942, unter besonderer Berücksichtigung der Ölpolitik. Frankfurt/M., 1976. pp. 364. bibliog.

— — Poland.

JACOBSEN (HANS ADOLF) Fünf Jahre Warschauer Vertrag: Versuch einer Bilanz der Beziehungen zwischen der Bundesrepublik Deutschland und der Volksrepublik Polen, 1970-1975. Berlin, [1976]. pp. 96. (Einzelausgabe aus der Zeitschrift Die Friedenswarte, Band 58, Heft 3,4)

— — Russia.

WINZER (OTTO) Der Rapallo-Vertrag und seine nationale Bedeutung für Deutschland. Berlin, 1952. pp. 42.

KOCH (GERDA) Die deutsche Arbeiterklasse und der Rapallo-Vertrag, März bis Juni 1922. [Berlin, 1957]. pp. 60.

SHNEERSON (LEV MIKHAILOVICH) Franko-prusskaia voina i Rossiia: iz istorii russko-prusskikh i russko-frantsuzskikh otnoshenii v 1867-1871 gg. Minsk, 1976. pp. 304.

MUELLER-LINK (HORST) Industrialisierung und Aussenpolitik: Preussen-Deutschland und das Zarenreich von 1860 bis 1890. Göttingen, 1977. pp. 506. *bibliog.*

— — Switzerland.

CAWIL (H.) Der Fall Jacob. Zürich, [1935]. pp. 38.

— — United Kingdom.

GERMANY. Reichstag. 1908. Das persönliche Regiment vor dem Deutschen Reichstage: die Verhandlungen...vom 10. und 11. November 1908. Berlin, 1908. pp. 128.

— — United States.

HERWIG (HOLGER H.) Politics of frustration: the United States in German naval planning, 1889-1941. Boston, Mass., [1976]. pp. 323. *bibliog.*

— History — Sources.

KONGRESS DER ARBEITER-, BAUERN- UND SOLDATENRÄTE DEUTSCHLANDS, 2., BERLIN, 1919. II. Kongress...8. bis 14. April 1919 im Herrenhaus zu Berlin: stenographisches Protokoll; Anhang: Vom I. Rätekongress zur Nationalversammlung: die Tätigkeit des Zentralrates der sozialistischen Republik Deutschlands. Glashütten im Taunus, 1975. pp. 278, 47. *Reprint of works originally published in Berlin in 1919.*

ENGELBERG (ERNST) ed. Im Widerstreit um die Reichsgründung: eine Quellensammlung zur Klassenauseinandersetzung in der deutschen Geschichte von 1849 bis 1871;...bearbeitet von Rolf Weber. Berlin, 1970. pp. 507.

GERMANY (BUNDESREPUBLIK). Bundesarchiv. 1976-. Akten zur Vorgeschichte der Bundesrepublik Deutschland, 1945- 1949. München, 1976 in progress.

GERMANY. Reichskanzlei. 1925-1926. Die Kabinette Luther I und II: 15. Januar 1925 bis 20. Januar 1926, 20. Januar 1926 bis 17. Mai 1926; bearbeitet von Karl-Heinz Minuth. Boppard am Rhein, 1977. 2 vols. *bibliog. (Akten der Reichskanzlei, Weimarer Republik)*

— — 1848-1870.

ENGELBERG (ERNST) ed. Im Widerstreit um die Reichsgründung: eine Quellensammlung zur Klassenauseinandersetzung in der deutschen Geschichte von 1849 bis 1871;...bearbeitet von Rolf Weber. Berlin, 1970. pp. 507.

STERN (FRITZ RICHARD) Gold and iron: Bismarck, Bleichröder, and the building of the German Empire. London, 1977. pp. 620.

— — 1871-1918.

BISMARCKS Sturz: zur Rolle der Klassen in der Endphase des preussisch-deutschen Bonapartismus 1884/85 bis 1890...; wissenschaftliche Redaktion: Gustav Seeber, Heinz Wolter; Autoren: Konrad Canis [and others]. Berlin, 1977. pp. 422. *bibliog. (Akademie der Wissenschaften der DDR. Zentralinstitut für Geschichte. Schriften. Band 52)*

STERN (FRITZ RICHARD) Gold and iron: Bismarck, Bleichröder, and the building of the German Empire. London, 1977. pp. 620.

— — 1918-1929, Allied occupation.

LOEFFLER (HEINRICH) Das Proletariat und die Besetzung des Ruhrgebiets;...Referat, gehalten vor den Funktionären der Vereinigten Sozialdemokratischen Partei, Bezirksverband Berlin. Berlin, [1923]. pp. 13.

— — 1918-1919, Revolution.

KONGRESS DER ARBEITER-, BAUERN- UND SOLDATENRÄTE DEUTSCHLANDS, 2., BERLIN, 1919. II. Kongress...8. bis 14. April 1919 im Herrenhaus zu Berlin: stenographisches Protokoll; Anhang: Vom I. Rätekongress zur Nationalversammlung: die Tätigkeit des Zentralrates der sozialistischen Republik Deutschlands. Glashütten im Taunus, 1975. pp. 278, 47. *Reprint of works originally published in Berlin in 1919.*

KONGRESS DER ARBEITER-, BAUERN- UND SOLDATENRÄTE, MÜNCHEN, 1919. Stenographischer Bericht über die Verhandlungen...vom 25. Februar bis 8. März 1919 in München; eingeleitet von Gisela Kissel und Hiltrud Witt. Glashütten im Taunus, 1974. pp. 200. *Reprint of work originally published in Munich in 1919.*

LAUFENBERG (HEINRICH) and WOLFFHEIM (FRITZ) Moskau und die deutsche Revolution: eine kritische Erledigung der bolschewistischen Methoden. Hamburg, [1920]. pp. 48.

PETZOLD (JOACHIM) Der 9. November 1918 in Berlin: Berliner Arbeiterveteranen berichten über die Vorbereitung der Novemberrevolution und ihren Ausbruch am 9. November 1918 in Berlin. Berlin, 1958. pp. 47. *(Sozialistische Einheitspartei Deutschlands. Bezirksleitung Gross-Berlin. Kommission zur Erforschung der Geschichte der Berliner Arbeiterbewegung. Die Novemberrevolution 1918/1919 in Berlin)*

Die ROTE Fahne über Leipzig: ein Beitrag zur Geschichte der November-Revolution 1918 in Leipzig;...Autoren-Kollektiv: Horst Beutel [and others]. Leipzig, [1958]. pp. 128.

WROBEL (KURT) Der Sieg der Arbeiter und Matrosen im Dezember 1918 in Berlin: Berliner Arbeiterveteranen berichten über ihren Kampf in der Novemberrevolution. Berlin, 1958. pp. 64. *(Sozialistische Einheitspartei Deutschlands. Bezirksleitung Gross-Berlin. Kommission zur Erforschung der Geschichte der Berliner Arbeiterbewegung. Die Novemberrevolution 1918/1919 in Berlin)*

KLEIN (ULRICH) and SCHERER (KLAUS JUERGEN) Bürgerräte gegen die Arbeiterbewegung: Untersuchungen und Dokumente am Beispiel Elberfeld-Barmen, 1918-1922. Wentorf/Hamburg, 1976. pp. 124. *bibliog.*

— — 1933-1945.

STEINER (JOHN M.) Power politics and social change in National Socialist Germany: a process of escalation into mass destruction. The Hague, 1976. pp. 466. *bibliog.*

EMMERSON (JAMES THOMAS) The Rhineland crisis, 7 March 1936: a study in multilateral diplomacy. London, 1977. pp. 383. *bibliog.*

— — 1945-1955, Allied occupation.

GERMANY (BUNDESREPUBLIK). Bundesarchiv. 1976-. Akten zur Vorgeschichte der Bundesrepublik Deutschland, 1945- 1949. München, 1976 in progress.

KIMBALL (WARREN F.) Swords or ploughshares?: the Morgenthau plan for defeated Nazi Germany, 1943-1946. Philadelphia, [1976]. pp. 172. *bibliog.*

NIETHAMMER (LUTZ) and others, eds. Arbeiterinitiative 1945: antifaschistische Ausschüsse und Reorganisation der Arbeiterbewegung in Deutschland; Autoren: Ulrich Borsdorf [and others]. Wuppertal, [1976]. pp. 782. *bibliog.*

— History, Naval.

HERWIG (HOLGER H.) Politics of frustration: the United States in German naval planning, 1889-1941. Boston, Mass., [1976]. pp. 323. *bibliog.*

— Industries.

BANNOCK (GRAHAM) The smaller business in Britain and Germany. London, 1976. pp. 152. *bibliog.*

— Intellectual life.

ARNDT (ERNST MORITZ) Entwurf einer teutschen Gesellschaft. Frankfurt am Main, Eichenberg, 1814. pp. 40.

DICKENS (ARTHUR GEOFFREY) The German nation and Martin Luther. Glasgow, 1976. pp. 254. *bibliog. First published in London, 1974.*

REILL (PETER HANNS) The German Enlightenment and the rise of historicism. Berkeley, Calif., 1975. pp. 308. *bibliog.*

— Learned institutions and societies — Directories.

HANDBUCH der deutschen wissenschaftlichen Akademien und Gesellschaften...; herausgegeben von Friedrich Domay. 2nd ed. Wiesbaden, 1977. pp. 1209.

— Nationalism.

ARNDT (ERNST MORITZ) Entwurf einer teutschen Gesellschaft. Frankfurt am Main, Eichenberg, 1814. pp. 40.

ARNDT (ERNST MORITZ) Noch ein Wort über die Franzosen und über uns. [Leipzig], 1814. pp. 44,4. *With Vorschlag eines Fremdengesetzes vom Österreich. Hauptmann von M...r.*

WOLF (HEINRICH) of the Jungdeutscher Orden. Die Entstehung des Jungdeutschen Ordens und seine frühen Jahre, 1918-1922. München, 1970. pp. 47. *bibliog. (Jungdeutsches Archiv. Beiträge zur Geschichte des Jungdeutschen Ordens. Heft 1)*

WOLF (HEINRICH) of the Jungdeutscher Orden. Der Jungdeutsche Orden in seinen mittleren Jahren, 1922-1925. München, 1972. pp. 71. *bibliog. (Jungdeutsches Archiv. Beiträge zur Geschichte des Jungdeutschen Ordens. Heft 2)*

ASHKENASI (ABRAHAM) Modern German nationalism. New York, [1976]. pp. 222.

— Navy.

MY, pseud. Flottenkoller und Weltmachtspolitik. Dresden, 1900. pp. 30.

— — History.

ART (ROBERT J.) The influence of foreign policy on seapower: new weapons and Weltpolitik in Wilhelminian Germany. Beverly Hills, [1973]. pp. 49. *bibliog.*

DEIST (WILHELM) Flottenpolitik und Flottenpropaganda: das Nachrichtenbureau des Reichsmarineamtes, 1897-1914. Stuttgart, 1976. pp. 344. *bibliog. (Militärgeschichtliches Forschungsamt. Beiträge zur Militär- und Kriegsgeschichte. Band 17)*

— Occupations.

GERMANY. Statistisches Reichsamt. Statistik des Deutschen Reichs. Neue Folge. Bände 102-119. Berufs- und Gewerbezählung vom 14. Juni 1895. Osnabrück, 1975. 18 vols. *Photographic reprint of 1897-99 ed. originally published in Berlin.*

— Officials and employees.

FISCHER (EDMUND) Sozialismus und Beamtenschaft. [Berlin, 1919]. pp. 23.

ARMANSKI (GERHARD) and others. Lohnarbeit im öffentlichen Dienst der BRD: Staatstreue oder Klassenkampf?. Berlin, [1976]. pp. 357. *bibliog.*

— Politics and government.

INFORMATIONEN ZUR POLITISCHEN BILDUNG. Bonn, Bundeszentrale für Politische Bildung, 1974 in progress.

— — 1789-1900.

DEUTSCHES Bürgerbuch für 1846, zweiter Jahrgang; herausgegeben von H. Püttmann. Glashütten im Taunus, 1975. pp. 346. *Reprint of work originally published in Mannheim in 1846.*

RUGE (ARNOLD) Politiker. Zwei Jahre in Paris: Studien und Erinnerungen. Leipzig, Jurany, 1846; Leipzig, 1975. 2 vols. *Facsimile reprint.*

SNELL (JOHN LESLIE) The democratic movement in Germany, 1789-1914;...edited and completed by Hans A. Schmitt. Chapel Hill, N.C., [1976]. pp. 501. bibliog. (North Carolina University. James Sprunt Studies in History and Political Science. vol. 55)

— — 1871- .

RITTER (GERHARD A.) Arbeiterbewegung, Parteien und Parlamentarismus: Aufsätze zur deutschen Sozial- und Verfassungsgeschichte des 19. und 20. Jahrhunderts. Göttingen, 1976. pp. 412.

— — 1871-1918.

SEYDEL (MAX VON) Staatsrechtliche und politische Abhandlungen;...Neue Folge... herausgegeben von Karl Krazeisen. Tübingen, 1902. pp. 343.

BASSERMANN (ERNST) Reichstagsabg. Bassermann über die innere und äussere Politik Deutschlands: Rede gehalten in Magdeburg am 15. April 1907. Berlin, [1907]. pp. 28. (Nationalliberale Partei Deutschlands. Nationalliberale Schriften. Nr. 6)

KLEIN (FRITZ) ed. Studien zum deutschen Imperialismus vor 1914. Berlin, 1976. pp. 291. (Akademie der Wissenschaften der DDR. Zentralinstitut für Geschichte. Schriften. Band 47)

SNELL (JOHN LESLIE) The democratic movement in Germany, 1789-1914;...edited and completed by Hans A. Schmitt. Chapel Hill, N.C., [1976]. pp. 501. bibliog. (North Carolina University. James Sprunt Studies in History and Political Science. vol. 55)

WILKE (EKKEHARD-TEJA P.W.) Political decadence in imperial Germany: personnel-political aspects of the German government crisis, 1894-97. Urbana, Ill., [1976]. pp. 311. bibliog. (Illinois University. Illinois Studies in the Social Sciences. 59)

WEITOWITZ (ROLF GUNTER) German trade policies and politics under the chancellorship of Count Leo von Caprivi, 1890-1894. 1977. fo.366. bibliog. Typescript. Ph.D. (London) thesis: unpublished. This thesis is the property of London University and may not be removed from the Library.

— — 1900- .

SCHOLDER (KLAUS) Die Problematik der politischen Verantwortung in unserer jüngsten Geschichte. Wiesbaden, 1959. pp. 42. (Institut für Europäische Geschichte. Vorträge. Nr. 27)

— — 1918-1945.

RATHENAU (WALTHER) Die neue Gesellschaft. Berlin, 1923. pp. 102. Originally published in 1919.

LOEFFLER (HEINRICH) Das Proletariat und die Besetzung des Ruhrgebiets;...Referat, gehalten vor den Funktionären der Vereinigten Sozialdemokratischen Partei, Bezirksverband Berlin. Berlin, [1923]. pp. 13.

PRUSSIA, plaintiff. Preussen contra Reich vor dem Staatsgerichtshof: (Stenogrammbericht der Verhandlungen...vom 10. bis 14. und vom 17. Oktober 1932); mit einem Vorwort von [Arnold] Brecht. Glashütten im Taunus, 1976. pp. 520. Reprint of work originally published in Berlin in 1933.

CASSINELLI (CHARLES WILLIAM) Total revolution: a comparative study of Germany under Hitler, the Soviet Union under Stalin and China under Mao. Santa Barbara, Calif., [1976]. pp. 252.

FRITZSCHE (KLAUS) Politische Romantik und Gegenrevolution: Fluchtwege in der Krise der bürgerlichen Gesellschaft: das Beispiel des "Tat" Kreises. Frankfurt am Main, 1976. pp. 437. bibliog.

STEINER (JOHN M.) Power politics and social change in National Socialist Germany: a process of escalation into mass destruction. The Hague, 1976. pp. 466. bibliog.

REISSNER (LARISSA) Hamburg at the barricades, and other writings on Weimar Germany; translated from the Russian and edited by Richard Chappell. London, 1977. pp. 209.

— — 1945- .

STEIN (GUSTAV) ed. Unternehmer in der Politik;...verfasst von Herbert Gross [and others]. Düsseldorf, [1954]. pp. 330.

WINZER (OTTO) Die grosse Lüge von den "freien Wahlen" in Westdeutschland: ein dokumentarischer Nachweis aus offiziellen Veröffentlichungen des Bonner Parteivorstandes der Sozialdemokratischen Partei Deutschlands. Berlin, 1954. pp. 23.

VEREINIGUNG DER VERFOLGTEN DES NAZIREGIMES. Vom Häftlingskomitee zum Bund der Antifaschisten: der Weg der VVN; (Redaktion: Max Oppenheimer). Frankfurt/Main, [1972]. pp. 172.

ASHKENASI (ABRAHAM) Modern German nationalism. New York, [1976]. pp. 222.

BRAUSWETTER (HARTMUT H.) Kanzlerprinzip, Ressortprinzip und Kabinettsprinzip in der ersten Regierung Brandt, 1969-1972. Bonn, [1976]. pp. 208. bibliog. (Institut für Begabtenförderung . Beiträge zu Wissenschaft und Politik. Band 14)

FROMME (FRIEDRICH KARL) Gesetzgebung im Widerstreit: wer beherrscht den Bundesrat?: die Kontroverse, 1969-1976. Stuttgart, 1976. pp. 226. bibliog.

GRAF (WILLIAM DAVID) The German left since 1945: socialism and social democracy in the German Federal Republic. Cambridge, [1976]. pp. 318. bibliog.

LEHMBRUCH (GERHARD) Parteienwettbewerb im Bundesstaat. Stuttgart, [1976]. pp. 187. bibliog.

NEGT (OSKAR) Keine Demokratie ohne Sozialismus: über den Zusammenhang von Politik, Geschichte und Moral. Frankfurt am Main, 1976. pp. 496. bibliog. Collection of essays and speeches.

NIETHAMMER (LUTZ) and others, eds. Arbeiterinitiative 1945: antifaschistische Ausschüsse und Reorganisation der Arbeiterbewegung in Deutschland; Autoren: Ulrich Borsdorf [and others]. Wuppertal, [1976]. pp. 782. bibliog.

SCHUMANN (HANS GERD) ed. Die Rolle der Opposition in der Bundesrepublik Deutschland. Darmstadt, 1976. pp. 530. bibliog.

WATSON (ALAN J.) The political foundations in West Germany. London, [1976?]. pp. 22.

AUF dem Weg zum Einparteienstaat; herausgegeben von Wolf-Dieter Narr; mit Beiträgen von Johannes Agnoli [and others]. Opladen, [1977]. pp. 249. bibliogs. Essays offered to Wolfgang Abendroth on his 70th birthday.

LATHAM (HUGH) The West German face of McCarthyism. London, [1977]. pp. 18.

SCHEEL (WALTER) Vom Recht des anderen: Gedanken zur Freiheit. Düsseldorf, 1977. pp. 188. Speeches by the Federal German President, 1974-76.

— Relations (general) with Eastern Germany.

SANKELMARK-ARBEITSTAGUNG, 1976. Gesundheitspolitische Gegenwartsfrage in der DDR; herausgegeben von Hans Harmsen. Hamburg, 1976. pp. 209.

— Relations (general) with France.

ARNDT (ERNST MORITZ) Noch ein Wort über die Franzosen und über uns. [Leipzig], 1814. pp. 44,4. With Vorschlag eines Fremdengesetzes vom Österreich. Hauptmann von M...r.

— Relations (general) with Poland.

GERMAN Polish dialogue: letters of the Polish and German bishops and international statements. Bonn, 1966. pp. 127.

— Rural conditions.

MEYHOEFFER (WOLF ECKART) Struktureller Wandel und gesellschaftliches Bewusstsein in zehn ehemals kleinbäuerlichen Dörfern der Bundesrepublik Deutschland. Bonn, 1976. pp. 254. bibliog. (Forschungsgesellschaft für Agrarpolitik und Agrarsoziologie. [Publications]. 238)

BUROSE (HANS) Analyse der agrarstrukturellen Entwicklung ehemals kleinbaulicher Dörfer unter besonderer Berücksichtigung exemplarischer Tragfähigkeitsberechnungen. Bonn, 1977. pp. 349. bibliog. (Forschungsgesellschaft für Agrarpolitik und Agrarsoziologie. [Publications]. 236)

WALTER (WULF) Die Entwicklung der Agrarstruktur zehn ehemaliger Kleinbauerndörfer und daraus abgeleitete Konsequenzen für Planungen im ländlichen Raum. Bonn, 1977. pp. 167. bibliog. (Forschungsgesellschaft für Agrarpolitik und Agrarsoziologie. [Publications]. 237)

— Social conditions.

RATHENAU (WALTHER) Die neue Gesellschaft. Berlin, 1923. pp. 102. Originally published in 1919.

EHRENBERG (RICHARD) Klassenkampf und Sozialfrieden: weitere sozialphysikalische Klärung. Jena, 1922. pp. 35. (Sonderabdruck aus Archiv für exakte Wirtschaftsforschung, Bd.IX, Heft 4)

REISSNER (LARISSA) Hamburg at the barricades, and other writings on Weimar Germany; translated from the Russian and edited by Richard Chappell. London, 1977. pp. 209.

— Social history.

DICKENS (ARTHUR GEOFFREY) The German nation and Martin Luther. Glasgow, 1976. pp. 254. bibliog. First published in London, 1974.

STEINBACH (LOTHAR) Didaktik der Sozialgeschichte: eine Fallstudie zum Thema: Arbeiter, Schule und Sozialdemokratie im Wilhelminischen Deutschland. Stuttgart, [1976]. pp. 301. bibliogs.

KEHR (ECKART) Economic interest, militarism, and foreign policy: essays on German history; edited...by Gordon A. Craig; translated by Grete Heinz. Berkeley, [1977]. pp. 209.

— Social policy.

BUDISCHIN (HANS JOERG) Die Formung der staatlichen Sozialpolitik in der Bundesrepublik Deutschland. Berlin, [1976]. pp. 183. bibliog.

GULDIMANN (TIM) Die Grenzen des Wohlfahrtsstaates: am Beispiel Schwedens und der Bundesrepublik. München, [1976]. pp. 181.

INDUSTRIEGEWERKSCHAFT METALL FÜR DIE BUNDESREPUBLIK DEUTSCHLAND. Tagung "Krise und Reform in der Industriegesellschaft", 1976. Protokoll ([and] Materialien)...; Redaktion: Hans-Adam Pfromm Frankfurt am Main, [1976]. 2 vols.

MASON (TIMOTHY W.) Sozialpolitik im Dritten Reich: Arbeiterklasse und Volksgemeinschaft. Opladen, [1977]. pp. 374. bibliog.

SOZIALPOLITIK nach 1945: Geschichte und Analysen; ([edited by] Reinhart Bartholomäi [and others]; Ernst Schellenberg zum 70. Geburtstag). Bonn-Bad Godesberg, [1977]. pp. 592.

GERMANY, EASTERN

— Civilization.

KOCH (HANS) of the Institut für Gesellschaftswissenschaften. Kulturpolitik in der Deutschen Demokratischen Republik. Berlin, 1976. pp. 111.

HANKE (HELMUT) and ROSSOW (GERD) Sozialistische Kulturrevolution. Berlin, 1977. pp. 272.

— Diplomatic and consular service.

RADDE (JUERGEN) Die aussenpolitische Führungselite der DDR: Veränderungen in der sozialen Struktur aussenpolitischer Führungsgruppen. Köln, [1976]. pp. 240. bibliog.

— Economic conditions — Mathematical models.

WOELFLING (MANFRED) Ein ökonometrisches Modell der Volkswirtschaft der DDR. Berlin, 1977. pp. 151. *bibliog. (Akademie der Wissenschaften der DDR. ·Zentralinstitut für Wirtschaftswissenschaften. Forschungsberichte. Nr.21)*

— — Statistics.

GERMANY (BUNDESREPUBLIK). Bundesministerium für Gesamtdeutsche Fragen. 1964. Wirtschaftszahlen aus der SBZ: eine Zusammenstellung statistischer Daten zur wirtschaftlichen Entwicklung in der sowjetischen Besatzungszone und in Ost Berlin, teilweise im Vergleich zur Bundesrepublik; bearbeitet von Hellmuth Kalns. 4th ed. Bonn, 1964. pp. 194.

— Economic history.

HARDACH (KARL W.) Wirtschaftsgeschichte Deutschlands im 20. Jahrhundert. Göttingen, [1976]. pp. 271. *bibliog.*

— Economic policy.

LUFT (HANS) and others. Ökonomische Gesetze und sozialistische Planwirtschaft. Berlin, 1975. pp. 102.

HOFMANN (HANS) and LOOSE (WOLFGANG) Ökonomie, Politik, Ideologie. Berlin, 1976. pp. 196. *bibliog.*

LEITUNG der sozialistischen Wirtschaft: Einführung; herausgegeben von Gerd Friedrich [and others]. Berlin, [1976]. pp. 348.

KRUBKE (ERWIN) Wirtschaftspolitik zwischen gestern und morgen: die Stellungnahme der CDU zur Herausbildung der sozialistischen Planwirtschaft in der DDR, etc. [Berlin], 1977. pp. 136. *bibliog. (Christlich-Demokratische Union [D.D.R.]. Beiträge zur Geschichte)*

LEENEN (WOLF RAINER) Zur Frage der Wachstumsorientierung der marxistisch- leninistischen Sozialpolitik in der DDR. Berlin, [1977]. pp. 225. *bibliog.*

SOEDER (GUENTER) Ökonomie, Politik, Wirtschaftspolitik: weltanschaulich- philosophische Aspekte des Verhältnisses von Politik und Wirtschaft im Sozialismus. Berlin, 1977. pp. 117.

ZU Problemen der Entwicklungstendenzen der sozialistischen Produktionsverhältnisse in der DDR; (Autoren: Ottomar Kratsch [and others]). Berlin, [1977]. pp. 141. *(Akademie der Wissenschaften der DDR. Zentralinstitut für Wirtschaftswissenschaften. Forschungsberichte. Nr.24)*

— Foreign relations — Germany.

SCHMID (GUENTHER) Politik des Ausverkaufs?: die Deutschlandpolitik der Regierung Brandt/Scheel. München, [1975]. pp. 313. *bibliog.*

SCHRAMM (THEODOR) Das Verhältnis der Bundesrepublik Deutschland zur DDR nach dem Grundvertrag: eine Einführung in die staats- und völkerrechtlichen Problembereiche mit Dokumentensammlung. 2nd ed. Köln, 1975. pp. 275. *bibliog.*

— — Russia.

CROAN (MELVIN) East Germany: the Soviet connection. Beverly Hills, [1976]. pp. 71. *bibliog. (Georgetown University. Center for Strategic and International Studies. Washington Papers. vol. 4/36)*

WETTIG (GERHARD) Die Sowjetunion, die DDR und die Deutschland-Frage, 1965- 1976: Einvernehmen und Konflikt im sozialistischen Lager. Stuttgart, 1976 repr. 1977. pp. 232. *bibliog.*

MUECKENBERGER (ERICH) Im festen Bündnis mit der Partei und dem Lande Lenins: ausgewälte Reden. Berlin, 1977. pp. 477.

— History.

LUDZ (PETER CHRISTIAN) Die DDR zwischen Ost und West: politische Analysen 1961 bis 1976. München, [1977]. pp. 367.

— — Chronology.

INSTITUT FÜR MARXISMUS-LENINISMUS (BERLIN). 20 Jahre SED: Zeittafel wichtiger Beratungen und Dokumente; (Redaktion: W. Otto, G. Rossmann). Berlin, 1966. pp. 173. *bibliog.*

— Politics and government.

JENDRETZKY (HANS) Sie hetzen, wir bauen auf: für die Einheit Berlins, gegen die Spalterwahlen. Berlin, [1948]. pp. 31.

GROTEWOHL (OTTO) Wer handelt im Interesse der Nation?: (aus dem Referat...vor dem 3. Deutschen Volkskongress in Berlin am 30. Mai 1949). Berlin, [1949]. pp. 15.

NEUMANN (ALFRED) of the Ministerrat der DDR. Vertrauen in die Kraft der Arbeiterklasse: ausgewählte Reden. Berlin, 1975. pp. 462.

HAVEMANN (ROBERT) Berliner Schriften; herausgegeben von Andreas W. Mytze. 3rd ed. Berlin, 1977. pp. 152.

STEELE (JONATHAN) Socialism with a German face: the state that came in from the cold. London, 1977. pp. 256.

— Relations (general) with Germany.

SANKELMARK-ARBEITSTAGUNG, 1976. Gesundheitspolitische Gegenwartsfrage in der DDR; herausgegeben von Hans Harmsen. Hamburg, 1976. pp. 209.

— Social conditions.

SOZIALSTRUKTUR und Sozialplanung in der DDR: achte Tagung zum Stand der DDR-Forschung in der Bundesrepublik, 20. bis 23. Mai 1975. [Cologne], 1975. pp. 176. *(Deutschland Archiv. Sonderhefte. 1975)*

STEELE (JONATHAN) Socialism with a German face: the state that came in from the cold. London, 1977. pp. 256.

— Social policy.

SOZIALSTRUKTUR und Sozialplanung in der DDR: achte Tagung zum Stand der DDR-Forschung in der Bundesrepublik, 20. bis 23. Mai 1975. [Cologne], 1975. pp. 176. *(Deutschland Archiv. Sonderhefte. 1975)*

LEENEN (WOLF RAINER) Zur Frage der Wachstumsorientierung der marxistisch-leninistischen Sozialpolitik in der DDR. Berlin, [1977]. pp. 225. *bibliog.*

GERRYMANDER.

MUSGROVE (PHILIP) The general theory of gerrymandering. Beverly Hills, [1977]. pp. 78. *bibliog.*

GERTSEN (ALEKSANDR IVANOVICH).

AZANOV (VLADIMIR IVANOVICH) Pamflety Gertsena v "Kolokole"; pod redaktsiei...E.I. Pokusaeva. Saratov, 1974. pp. 50.

ROOT (ANDREI ALEKSANDROVICH) Tipologiia peredovykh statei Gertsena v "Kolokole": lektsii po spetskursu dlia studentov-zhurnalistov. Kazan', 1974. pp. 102. *bibliog.*

HERZEN, Ogarev, Bakounine: lettres inédites; introduction, traductions et notes par Michel Mervaud. Paris, 1975. pp. 158. *With French translations of letters in German and Russian. Includes in addition eight letters from Victor Hugo to Herzen.*

GESTURE.

JOUSSE (MARCEL) La manducation de la parole. [Paris, 1975]. pp. 287. *(L'anthropologie du geste.2)*

GEYER (CURT).

GEYER (CURT) Die revolutionäre Illusion: zur Geschichte des linken Flügels der USPD: Erinnerungen...; herausgegeben von Wolfgang Benz und Hermann Graml. Stuttgart, [1976]. pp. 304. *bibliog. (Vierteljahrshefte für Zeitgeschichte. Schriftenreihe. Nr.33)*

GHANA

— Administrative and political divisions.

GHANA. 1975. White Paper on the report of the Commission of Enquiry into the Duffor Traditional Area. Accra, 1975. pp. 3. *(W[hite] P[apers]. 1975. No. 2) Bound with the Report.*

GHANA. Commission of Inquiry into Duffor Traditional Area. 1975. Report; [F.K. Apaloo, chairman]. Accra, [1975]. pp. 51. *Bound with White Paper on the Report.*

— Armed forces — Political activity.

PINKNEY (ROBERT) The politics of military rule in Ghana, 1966-69. 1976 [or rather 1977]. fo.373. *bibliog. Typescript. Ph.D.(London) thesis: unpublished. This thesis is the property of London University and may not be removed from the Library.*

— Economic conditions.

GHANA. Speeches and interviews by Commissioners. s-a., Ja/Je 1973 (v.1)- Accra.

— Economic policy.

GHANA. 1975. Guidelines for the five-year development plan, 1975-1980. [Accra], 1975. pp. 51.

— Foreign relations — Africa, Subsaharan.

GHANA. Ministry of Information. 1966. Nkrumah's subversion in Africa: documentary evidence of Nkrumah's interference in the affairs of other African States. [Accra, 1966]. pp. 91.

GHANA. Information Services Department. 1967. Nkrumah's deception of Africa. [Accra, 1967]. pp. 95.

— History.

JAMES (CYRIL LIONEL ROBERT) Nkrumah and the Ghana revolution. London, 1977. pp. 227.

— Politics and government.

NKRUMAH (KWAME) Dark days in Ghana. London, 1968. pp. 227.

GHANA. Speeches and interviews by Commissioners. s-a., Ja/Je 1973 (v.1)- Accra.

NKRUMAH (KWAME) The struggle continues. London, [1973]. pp. 83.

JAMES (CYRIL LIONEL ROBERT) Nkrumah and the Ghana revolution. London, 1977. pp. 227.

PINKNEY (ROBERT) The politics of military rule in Ghana, 1966-69. 1976 [or rather 1977]. fo.373. *bibliog. Typescript. Ph.D.(London) thesis: unpublished. This thesis is the property of London University and may not be removed from the Library.*

— Relations (general) with Ivory Coast.

GHANA. Ministry of Information. 1970. Ghana-Ivory Coast fraternity:...a record of the official visit of the Prime Minister of Ghana, the Rt. Hon. Dr. K. A. Busia, to the Ivory Coast from April 29, to May 9, 1970. [Accra, 1970]. pp. 69 bis. *In English and French.*

— Social conditions.

GHANA. Speeches and interviews by Commissioners. s-a., Ja/Je 1973 (v.1)- Accra.

— Social policy.

GHANA. 1975. Guidelines for the five-year development plan, 1975-1980. [Accra], 1975. pp. 51.

GIBRALTAR

— Politics and government.

GRANADOS AGUIRRE (MARIANO) Los republicanos españoles y Gibraltar. [Mexico, 1970]. pp. 281.

GIBSON (A.H.)

FASE (M.M.G.) and NIEUWKERK (MARIUS VAN) Anticipated inflation and interest rates in an open economy: a study of the Gibson paradox for the Netherlands. Amsterdam, [1975?]. pp. 24. *bibliog.* *(Nederlandsche Bank. Reprints. No. 17)*

GIEREK (EDWARD).

GIEREK (EDWARD) O wojsku i obronności: [extracts from speeches, 1971-73]. Warszawa, 1974. pp. 118. *Illustrated.*

GIETRZWALD

— History.

ZIENTARA-MALEWSKA (MARIA) Gietrzwałd - dzieje polskości; opracował Tadeusz Swat. Warszawa, 1976. pp. 104.

GIFTS

— Zaire — Mathematical models.

SAULNIERS (ALFRED H.) The economics of prestation systems: a consumer analysis of extended family obligations with application to Zaire. Ann Arbor, 1976. pp. 27. *bibliog. (Michigan University. Center for Research on Economic Development. Discussion Papers. No.54)*

GILBERT AND ELLICE ISLANDS COLONY

— Census.

GILBERT AND ELLICE ISLANDS COLONY. Census, 1973. Report on the 1973 census of population. Tarawa, 1975 in progress.

— Commerce.

GILBERT AND ELLICE ISLANDS COLONY. Statistical Unit. Trade. a., 1973- Tarawa.

— Statistics.

GILBERT AND ELLICE ISLANDS COLONY. Statistical Unit. Quarterly digest of statistics. q., Ja/D 1975- Tarawa.

GILDS

— Germany.

ROHRSCHEIDT (KURT VON) Vom Zunftswange zur Gewerbefreiheit: (eine Studie nach den Quellen). Glashütten im Taunus, 1976. pp. 668. *bibliog. Reprint of work originally published in Berlin in 1898.*

GOETTMANN (FRANK) Die Frankfurter Bäckerzunft im späten Mittelalter: Aufbau und Aufgaben städtischer Handwerkergenossenschaften. Frankfurt am Main, 1975. pp. 128. *bibliog. (Frankfurter Verein für Geschichte und Landeskunde. Studien zur Frankfurter Geschichte. Heft 10)*

FROEHLICH (SIGRID) Die soziale Sicherung bei Zünften und Gesellenverbänden: Darstellung, Analyse, Vergleich. Berlin, [1976]. pp. 294. *bibliog.*

GINZBURG (ALEKSANDR IL'ICH).

GINZBURG (ALEKSANDR IL'CH) and GALANSKOV (IURII TIMOFEEVICH) defendants. L'affaire Guinzbourg Galanskov: (les nouveaux procès de Moscou); dossier réuni et présenté par J.J. Marie et Carol Head; traduit du russe par Jean Jacques et Nadine Marie. Paris, [1969]. pp. 203.

GIPSIES

— United Kingdom.

CRIPPS (JOHN) Accommodation for gypsies: a report on the working of the Caravan Sites Act 1968. London, H.M.S.O., 1977. pp. 50.

GIRONDE

— Economic conditions.

DELAUNAY (GABRIEL) Essai sur une doctrine économique du Sud-Ouest Atlantique et, plus particulièrement, du Département de la Gironde. [Paris, 1960]. pp. 24.

— Economic policy.

DELAUNAY (GABRIEL) Essai sur une doctrine économique du Sud-Ouest Atlantique et, plus particulièrement, du Département de la Gironde. [Paris, 1960]. pp. 24.

GISCARD D'ESTAING (VALERY).

FRANCE. Président, 1974- . (Valéry Giscard d'Estaing). 1976- . Discours et déclarations de Valéry Giscard d'Estaing, Président de la République Française. Paris, 1976 in progress.

GLACIAL LANDFORMS

— Spain.

THORNES (JOHN B.) Glacial and periglacial features in the Urbión Mountains, Spain. [Madrid], 1968. pp. 9. *bibliog. (Repr. from Estudios Geologicos, vol. 24, Dec. 1968*

GLADSTONE (WILLIAM EWART).

CAPEL (PETER JAMES) Gladstone's attitude towards Disraeli's Conservative Party. London, [1975]. fo. 21. *(London. University. London School of Economics and Political Science. Gladstone Memorial Trust Prize Essays. 1975) Typescript.*

CHADWICK (WILLIAM OWEN) Acton and Gladstone. London, 1976. pp. 56. *(London. University. Creighton Lectures. 1975)*

GLASGOW

— Economic history.

DAICHES (DAVID) Glasgow. London, 1977. pp. 243. *bibliog.*

— History.

CHECKLAND (SIDNEY GEORGE) The upas tree: Glasgow, 1875-1975: a study in growth and contraction. Glasgow, 1976. pp. 124. *bibliog.*

DAICHES (DAVID) Glasgow. London, 1977. pp. 243. *bibliog.*

— Social life and customs.

DAICHES (DAVID) Glasgow. London, 1977. pp. 243. *bibliog.*

GLASS INDUSTRY AND TRADE

— United Kingdom.

BARKER (THEODORE CARDWELL) The glassmakers: Pilkington: the rise of an international company, 1826-1976. London, [1977]. pp. 557. *A revised and extended version of the author's Pilkington Brothers and the glass industry.*

GLENDAIRY PRISON, BARBADOS.

BARBADOS. 1863. Rules and regulations for the Glendairy Prison; approved and confirmed by the Governor in Council, the 2nd day of June, 1863. [Bridgetown?, 1863?]. pp. 30.

BARBADOS. 1870. Rules and regulations for the Female Department, Glendairy Prison; approved and confirmed by the Governor and Council, on the 11th day of January, 1870. [Bridgetown?, 1870?]. pp. 6.

BARBADOS. 1877. Additional rules and regulations for the Glendairy Prison, Barbados, approved and confirmed by the Lieutenant Governor in Council, 13th July 1877. [Bridgetown, 1877.] *Photocopy.*

GLOUCESTERSHIRE

— History — Sources.

The GOODS and chattels of our forefathers: Frampton Cotterell and district probate inventories, 1539-1804; edited by John S. Moore. London, 1976. pp. 364. *(Frampton Cotterell and District Local History Group. Frampton Cotterell and District Historical Studies. 1)*

— Social conditions.

FIELD (JULIA) Gloucestershire: a survey of attitudes among elected representatives. London, 1975. 1 vol. (various pagings).

GLUCKMAN (HERMAN MAX).

FREEDOM and constraint: a memorial tribute to Max Gluckman; edited by Myron J. Aronoff. Assen, 1976. pp. 179. *bibliogs.*

GOA, DAMAN AND DIU

— Relations (general) with Portugal.

D'SOUZA (BENTO GRACIANO) Goan society in transition: a study in social change. Bombay, 1975. pp. 364. *bibliog.*

— Social conditions.

D'SOUZA (BENTO GRACIANO) Goan society in transition: a study in social change. Bombay, 1975. pp. 364. *bibliog.*

— Social history.

D'SOUZA (BENTO GRACIANO) Goan society in transition: a study in social change. Bombay, 1975. pp. 364. *bibliog.*

GODWIN (MARY).

TIMS (MARGARET) Mary Wollstonecraft: a social pioneer. London, 1976. pp. 374. *bibliog.*

GODWIN (WILLIAM).

GODWIN (WILLIAM) Enquiry concerning political justice and its influence on modern morals and happiness; [edited by Isaac Kramnick]. Harmondsworth, 1976. pp. 825. *bibliog.*

GOEPPINGEN

— Officials and employees.

BUEHLER (HEINZ) Das beamtete Bürgertum in Göppingen und sein soziales Verhalten, 1815-1848. Göppingen, [1976]. pp. 215. *bibliog. (Göppingen. Stadtarchiv. Veröffentlichungen. Band 12)*

GOERING (HERMANN WILHELM).

MOSLEY (LEONARD OSWALD) The Reich Marshal: a biography of Hermann Goering. London, 1977. pp. 476.

GOGOLEV (ZAKHAR VASIL'EVICH).

BASHARIN (GEORGII PROKOP'EVICH) Sotsial'no-ekonomicheskie otnosheniia v Iakutii vtoroi poloviny XIX - nachala XX veka: po povodu knigi Z.V. Gogoleva "Iakutiia na rubezhe XIX-XX vv.". Iakutsk, 1974. pp. 216. *bibliog.*

GOKHALE (GOPAL KRISHNA).

DEOGIRIKAR (TRIMBAK RAGHUNATH) Gopal Krishna Gokhale. 2nd ed. New Delhi, 1969. pp. 219. *(Builders of Modern India)*

GOLD.

MACHLUP (FRITZ) International payments, debts and gold; collected essays. 2nd ed. New York, 1976. pp. 514.

VIÑAS MARTIN (ANGEL) El oro español en la guerra civil. [Madrid], Instituto de Estudios Fiscales, [1976]. pp. 618. *bibliog.*

GOLD MINERS

— New Zealand.

HOLLAND (HENRY EDMUND) and others. The tragic story of the Waihi strike. Wellington, N.Z., 1913; Dunedin, 1975. pp. 202. *Facsimile reprint.*

— South Africa.

STARES (RODNEY) Consolidated Gold Fields Limited: a review of activities and issues. London, [1975]. pp. 31. *bibliog.*

GOLD MINES AND MINING

— Papua New Guinea.

NELSON (HANK) Black, white and gold: goldmining in Papua New Guinea, 1878- 1930. Canberra, 1976. pp. 298. *bibliog.*

GOLD STANDARD.

HARDACH (GERD H.) Weltmarktorientierung und relative Stagnation: Währungspolitik in Deutschland, 1924-1931. Berlin, [1976]. pp. 182. *bibliog.*

GOLENDORF (PIERRE).

GOLENDORF (PIERRE) 7 ans à Cuba: 38 mois dans les prisons de Fidel Castro. Paris, [1976]. pp. 319.

GOMEL' (OBLAST')

— History — 1917-1921, Revolution.

DIRENOK (EFIM DMITRIEVICH) Bol'sheviki Gomel'shchiny v period Oktiabr'skoi revoliutsii i grazhdanskoi voiny. Minsk, 1976. pp. 192.

GOMPERS (SAMUEL).

REED (JOHN) Labor's grand old man. London, 1976. pp. 43. *Written in 1917, published for the first time in 1976.*

GÖPPINGEN.

See GOEPPINGEN.

GOR'KII (OBLAST')

— History — Sources.

GOR'KOVSKAIA partiinaia organizatsiia v gody Velikoi Otechestvennoi voiny, 1941-1945: sbornik dokumentov i materialov. Gor'kii, 1975. pp. 359.

GORNO-ALTAISK (OBLAST')

— Politics and government.

GORNO-Altaiskaia oblastnaia organizatsiia KPSS v tsifrakh. Gorno-Altaisk, 1975. pp. 118.

GOSSIP.

PEEL (LYNDA MAY) Village gossip: a study of the evaluation system employed in a Hebridean village. 1976 [or rather 1977]. fo.301. *bibliog. Typescript. Ph.D.(London) thesis: unpublished. This thesis is the property of London University and may not be removed from the Library.*

GOTHENBURG

— Economic conditions.

PERSSON (KENT) Sysselsättningen i centrum: sysselsättningsförändringar i stadscentrum, deras orsaker och verkan, med exempel från Göteborg. Göteborg, 1977. pp. 282. *bibliog. (Göteborgs Universitet. Geografiska Institutioner. Meddelanden. Ser.B. Nr.60) With English summary.*

— Occupations.

PERSSON (KENT) Sysselsättningen i centrum: sysselsättningsförändringar i stadscentrum, deras orsaker och verkan, med exempel från Göteborg. Göteborg, 1977. pp. 282. *bibliog. (Göteborgs Universitet. Geografiska Institutioner. Meddelanden. Ser.B. Nr.60) With English summary.*

GOVERNMENT, COMPARATIVE.

BONNOT DE MABLY (GABRIEL) Sur la théorie du pouvoir politique; introduction et notes par Peter Friedmann. Paris, [1975]. pp. 288.

BALL (ALAN R.) Modern politics and government. 2nd ed. London, 1977. pp. 276. *bibliog.*

— Methodology.

CZUDNOWSKI (MOSHE M.) Comparing political behavior. Beverly Hills, [1976]. pp. 178. *bibliog.*

GOVERNMENT BUSINESS ENTERPRISES

— Bangladesh.

AHMAD (MUZAFFER) Planning and public sector enterprises in Bangladesh. Ljubljana, International Center for Public Enterprises, 1974. pp. 36. *(International Seminar 1974. National Papers)*

— Egypt.

KAMEL (ISMAIL KAMEL AHMED) The system of planning, its application and evaluation, and follow- ups of plans in economic units of the general sector. Ljubljana, International Center for Public Enterprises, 1974. fo. 17. *(International Seminar 1974. National Papers)*

— Ghana.

GHANA. Commission of Enquiry into the State Fishing Corporation. 1969. Interim and final reports; [S.A. Wiredu, chairman]. [Accra, 1969]. pp. 213. *Bound with the White Paper on the report.*

GHANA. 1973. White Paper on the report of the Commission of Enquiry into the management and manner of operation of the State Fishing Corporation. [Accra], 1973. pp. 13. *(W[hite] P[apers]. 1973. No. 4)*

— India.

INDIA. Bureau of Public Enterprises. Information and Research Division. 1970. A handbook of information on public enterprises: comprehensive volume, 1969. [Delhi, 1970]. pp. 124.

INDIA. Bureau of Public Enterprises. Annual report on the working of industrial and commercial undertakings of the central government. a., 1974/75- New Delhi. *In 3 v.; v.1, Text; v. 2, Sectoral analyses; v.3, Analysis of accounts.*

FERNANDES (PRAXY) Public enterprise in India: a perspective view. Ljubljana, International Center for Public Enterprises, 1974. fo. 39,6. *(International Seminar 1974. National Papers)*

— Iraq.

ALI (ABDULJAWAD N.) Public sector and planning in public enterprises in Iraq. Ljubljana, International Center for Public Enterprises, 1974. fo. 15. *(International Seminar 1974. National Papers)*

— Italy.

MORTARA (ALBERTO) ed. Il settore pubblico dell'economia: dati e notizie, 1970-1974. Milano, [1976]. pp. 1456. *bibliog. (Centro Italiano di Ricerche e d'Informazione sull'Economia delle Imprese Pubbliche e di Pubblico Interesse. Studi e Documenti sul Settore Pubblico dell'Economia. 18)*

— Korea.

JONES (LEROY P.) Public enterprise and economic development: the Korean case. Seoul, 1975. pp. 293. *bibliog. (Korean Development Institute. KDI Studies in Economics)*

— Mali (Republic) — Finance.

MALI. Direction Nationale du Plan et de la Statistique. 1974. Financement des sociétés et entreprises d'état au Mali. [Ljubljana, International Center for Public Enterprises, 1974]. fo. 17. *([International Seminar 1974. Working Papers])*

— Poland — Finance.

WERALSKI (MARIAN) Le développement du système financier des entreprises d'état en Pologne; (conférence faite à l'Ecole des Hautes Etudes, VIe section, à Paris...le 9 janvier 1963). Warszawa, [1963]. pp. 15. *(Polska Akademia Nauk. Centre Scientifique à Paris. Conférences. Fascicule 43)*

— Russia.

KHRUSTALEV (BORIS FEDOROVICH) Gosudarstvennoe predpriiatie - sub"ekt trudovogo prava. Moskva, 1976. pp. 159.

— Sri Lanka.

SRI LANKA. 1974. Planning in relation to public sector enterprises: Sri Lanka. [Ljubljana, International Center for Public Enterprises, 1974]. pp. (17). *([International Seminar 1974. Working Papers])*

— Sudan.

ABDEL MONEIM (ABDEL SALAM) Public industries in the Sudan Industrial Production Corporation. Ljubljana, International Center for Public Enterprises, 1974. fo. 15. *(International Seminar 1974. National Papers)*

— Sweden.

STATSFÖRETAG AB. The Statsföretag group of Sweden. [Ljubljana, International Center for Public Enterprises, 1974]. fo. 5. *([International Seminar 1974. Working Papers])*

— Tanzania.

KOROMO (FRANCIS A.) Planning in public enterprises in developing countries. Ljubljana, International Center for Public Enterprises, 1974. fo. 19. *(International Seminar 1974. National Papers)*

GOVERNMENT CONSULTANTS.

LERNER (ALLAN W.) The politics of decision-making: strategy, cooperation and conflict. Beverly Hills, [1976]. pp. 213. *bibliog.*

— Nigeria.

DAVIS (MORRIS) Interpreters for Nigeria: the Third World and international public relations. Urbana, Ill., [1977]. pp. 197. *bibliog.*

GOVERNMENT EXECUTIVES

— Africa, Subsaharan.

BAUM (EDWARD) and GAGLIANO (FELIX V.) Chief executives in Black Africa and Southeast Asia: a descriptive analysis of social background characteristics. Athens, Ohio, [1976]. pp. 35. *(Ohio University. Center for International Studies. Papers in International Studies. Africa Series. No. 29)*

— Asia, Southeast.

BAUM (EDWARD) and GAGLIANO (FELIX V.) Chief executives in Black Africa and Southeast Asia: a descriptive analysis of social background characteristics. Athens, Ohio, [1976]. pp. 35. *(Ohio University. Center for International Studies. Papers in International Studies. Africa Series. No. 29)*

GOVERNMENT INFORMATION

— Germany, Eastern.

PICAPER (JEAN PAUL) Kommunikation und Propaganda in der DDR. Stuttgart, [1976]. pp. 222. *bibliog.*

GOVERNMENT LENDING

— United Kingdom.

KARN (VALERIE A.) Priorities for local authority mortgage lending: a case study of Birmingham. Birmingham, 1976. pp. 45. *(Birmingham. University. Centre for Urban and Regional Studies. Research Memoranda. No. 52)*

GOVERNMENT OWNERSHIP

— Chile.

BRUNN (REINHARD VON) Chile: con leyes tradicionales hacia una nueva economia?; (traductor: Leonardo Halpern). Santiago de Chile, 1972. pp. 154. *(Instituto Latinoamericano de Investigaciones Sociales. Estudios y Documentos. 18)*

— France.

BRACHET (PHILIPPE) and GALLUS (JACQUES) Les nationalisations: quand la droite se sert de la gauche. Paris, 1973. pp. 94.

— Germany.

BARTH (EMIL) Sozialisierung: ihre Notwendigkeit, ihre Möglichkeit. Neukölln, 1920. pp. 37.

— Iraq.

ALI (ABDULJAWAD N.) Public sector and planning in public enterprises in Iraq. Ljubljana, International Center for Public Enterprises, 1974. fo. 15. *(International Seminar 1974. National Papers)*

— Russia — Tatar Republic.

NAZIPOVA (KLARA ABDULKHAKOVNA) Natsionalizatsiia promyshlennosti v Tatarii, 1917-1921 gg. Moskva, 1976. pp. 312. *bibliog.*

— Underdeveloped areas.

See UNDERDEVELOPED AREAS — Government ownership.

— United Kingdom.

AIMS OF INDUSTRY. Economic Arguments. Socialists on the board: the case against the National Enterprise Board. London, [1974]. pp. 4.

HARLOW (CHRIS) Innovation and productivity under nationalisation: the first thirty years. London, 1977. pp. 256.

U.K. Department of Industry. 1977. The National Enterprise Board: guidelines. London, 1977. pp. 12.

GOVERNMENT PUBLICATIONS

— Bibliography.

PALIC (VLADIMIR M.) compiler. Government publications: a guide to bibliographic tools; incorporating Government organization manuals: a bibliography. Oxford, [1977]. pp. 553.

GOVERNMENT PUBLICITY.

DEIBEL (TERRY L.) and ROBERTS (WALTER R.) Culture and information: two foreign policy functions. Beverly Hills, [1976]. pp. 62. *bibliog. (Georgetown University. Center for Strategic and International Studies. Washington Papers. vol. 4/40)*

— Nigeria.

DAVIS (MORRIS) Interpreters for Nigeria: the Third World and international public relations. Urbana, Ill., [1977]. pp. 197. *bibliog.*

— Singapore.

SEAH CHEE MEOW Public relations in the Singapore bureaucracy: a neglected aspect in administration. Singapore, 1973. fo. 27. *(University of Singapore. Department of Political Science. Occasional Papers. No. 4)*

— United Kingdom.

BRADSHAW (JONATHAN) and others. Batley welfare benefits project. [York, 1976]. pp. 33. *(Papers in Community Studies. No. 5)*

GOVERNMENT PURCHASING

— Russia.

BUZULUKOV (N.S.) ed. Ekonomika i organizatsiia gosudarstvennykh zagotovok produktov sel'skogo khoziaistva. 2nd ed. Moskva, 1976. pp. 336.

— United Kingdom.

CONFEDERATION OF BRITISH INDUSTRY. A guide to government contracts for stores and services: a survey of procedures and practices of government purchasing departments. London, 1975. pp. 57.

GOVERNMENT SPENDING POLICY

— United Kingdom.

COUNTER INFORMATION SERVICES and others. Cutting the welfare state: who profits?. London, [1976]. pp. 39. *(Counter Information Services. Anti-Reports. No. 13)*

GOVERNMENTAL INVESTIGATIONS

— France.

FRANCE. Direction de la Documentation. La Documentation Française. Notes et Etudes Documentaires. Nos. 4,262 - 4, 263 - 4,264. Les commissions parlementaires d'enquête ou de contrôle en droit français; par Jacques Desandre. Paris, 1976. pp. 100. *bibliog.*

— United States.

LIPSKY (MICHAEL) and OLSON (DAVID J.) Commission politics: the processing of racial crisis in America. New Brunswick, N.J., [1977]. pp. 476.

GRADING AND MARKING (STUDENTS).

WILLMOTT (ALAN STEWART) CSE and GCE grading standards: the 1973 comparability study. Basingstoke, 1977. pp. 208. *bibliog. (U.K. Department of Education and Science. Schools Council. Research Studies) A report to the Schools Council from the Examinations and Tests Research Unit of the National Foundation for Educational Research in England and Wales.*

GRADUATES

— United Kingdom.

BRITISH INSTITUTE OF MANAGEMENT. Information Summaries. No. 132. The employment of graduates. London, 1968 [repr. 1971]. pp. 52. *bibliog.*

KINGSTON (N.) and WOLFE (PETER DEREK) Graduates in industry...; in conjunction with the Cambridge University Management Group. London, [1972]. pp. 25. *bibliog. (British Institute of Management. Management Survey Reports. No. 14)*

JOHNSON (RICHARD) of the University of Birmingham. Trade unionism and the academics: Swansea, 1974. London, [1974]. pp. 30. *(Council for Academic Freedom and Democracy. Reports)*

GRAIN

— Storage.

MARCHAL (MAURICE) Le nouveau silo portuaire de Strasbourg: sa place dans la politique céréalière française. Strasbourg, 1964. pp. 8.

TREZISE (PHILIP H.) Rebuilding grain reserves: toward an international system. Washington, [1976]. pp. 66.

— Canada.

CANADIAN GRAIN COMMISSION. Economics and Statistics Division. Visible grain supplies and disposition. a., 1975/76- Winnipeg.

— Russia.

GROSSKOPF (SIGRID) L'alliance ouvrière et paysanne en U.R.S.S., 1921-1928: le problème du blé. Paris, 1976. pp. 459. *bibliog.*

— Tunisia.

HAURI (IRENE) Le projet céréalier en Tunisie: études aux niveaux national et local. Genève, Institut de Recherche des Nations Unies pour le Développement Social, 1974. pp. 100. *(United Nations Research Institute for Social Development. UNRISD Reports. No. 74. 4)*

GRAIN TRADE

— Management.

TREZISE (PHILIP H.) Rebuilding grain reserves: toward an international system. Washington, [1976]. pp. 66.

— Belgium — Prices.

TITS-DIEUAIDE (MARIE JEANNE) La formation des prix céréaliers en Brabant et en Flandre au XVe siècle. Bruxelles, [1975]. pp. 406. *bibliog.*

— Ethiopia.

HOLMBERG (JOHAN) Grain marketing and land reform in Ethiopia: an analysis of the marketing and pricing of food grains in 1976 after the land reform. Uppsala, 1977. pp. 34. *(Nordiska Afrikainstitutet. Research Reports. No. 41)*

— France.

KAPLAN (STEVEN L.) Bread, politics and political economy in the reign of Louis XV. The Hague, 1976. 2 vols. *bibliog.*

— Russia — Estonia.

LIIV (OTTO) Die wirtschaftliche Lage des estnischen Gebietes am Ausgang des XVII. Jahrhunderts. vol. I. Allgemeiner Überblick, Getreideproduktion und Getreidehandel. Tartu, 1935. pp. 336. *bibliog. (Õpetatud Eesti Selts. Toimetised. 27)*

GRAMMAR, COMPARATIVE AND GENERAL.

CHICAGO LINGUISTIC SOCIETY. [Regional Meeting, 11th, 1975]. Papers from the parasession on functionalism, April 17th, 1975; edited by Robin E. Grossman [and others]. Chicago, 1975. pp. 609. *bibliogs.*

The APPLICATION and ordering of grammatical rules; edited by Andreas Koutsoudas. The Hague, 1976. pp. 360. *bibliog. Based on papers and discussions from a conference held at Indiana University, 1973.*

HUDSON (RICHARD ANTHONY) Arguments for a non-transformational grammar. Chicago, 1976. pp. 214. *bibliog.*

LYONS (JOHN) Semantics. Cambridge, 1977. 2 vols. *bibliogs.*

— Phonology.

CHICAGO LINGUISTIC SOCIETY. [Regional Meeting, 10th, 1974]. Papers from the parasession on natural phonology, April 18, 1974; edited by Anthony Bruck [and others]. Chicago, 1974. pp. 395. *bibliogs.*

KENSTOWICZ (MICHAEL J.) and KISSEBERTH (CHARLES W.) Topics in phonological theory. New York, [1977]. pp. 242. *bibliog.*

— Syntax.

CHICAGO LINGUISTIC SOCIETY. [Regional Meeting, 12th, 1976]. Papers from the parasession on diachronic syntax, April 22, 1976; edited by Sanford B. Steever [and others]. Chicago, 1976. pp. 364. *bibliogs.*

MONTAGUE grammar; edited by Barbara H. Partee. New York, [1976]. pp. 370. *bibliogs.*

STOCKWELL (ROBERT PAUL) Foundations of syntactic theory. Englewood Cliffs, [1977]. pp. 217. *bibliog.*

GRAMSCI (ANTONIO).

GRAMSCI (ANTONIO) Selections from political writings, 1910-1920; with additional texts by Bordiga and Tasca; selected and edited by Quintin Hoare; translated by John Mathews. London, 1977 in progress.

GRAMSCI (ANTONIO).(Cont.)

CLARK (MARTIN) Antonio Gramsci and the revolution that failed. New Haven, 1977. pp. 255. *bibliog.*

DAVIDSON (ALASTAIR) Antonio Gramsci: towards an intellectual biography. London, 1977. pp. 337. *bibliog.*

JOLL (JAMES) Gramsci. Glasgow, 1977. pp. 128. *bibliog.*

GRANTS-IN-AID

— United States.

HARBERT (ANITA S.) Federal grants-in-aid: maximizing benefits to the states. New York, 1976. pp. 173. *bibliog.*

HOPE (JOHN) 1909- . Minority access to Federal grants-in-aid: the gap between policy and performance. New York, 1976. pp. 267. *bibliog.*

GRAPH THEORY.

BELLMAN (RICHARD ERNEST) and others. Algorithms, graphs and computers. New York, 1970. pp. 246. *bibliogs.*

GRAZIADEI (ANTONIO).

ZAGARI (EUGENIO) Marxismo e revisionismo: Bernstein, Sorel, Graziadei, Leone. Napoli, [1975]. pp. 357.

GREAT WESTERN RAILWAY.

POLE (Sir FELIX JOHN CLEWETT) Felix J.C. Pole: his book. Bracknell, Berks, 1968. pp. 233. *Printed for private circulation only, Christmas, 1954.*

GREECE

— Economic conditions.

DAMALAS (BASILE V.) Plaidoyer pour la Grèce martyre. Athènes, 1962. pp. 28.

ZOLOTAS (XENOPHON) Summary of the statement...at the annual meeting of shareholders, 29 April 1976. Athens, 1976. pp. 29.

— — Mathematical models.

TSORIS (NICHOLAS D.) Econometric studies of Greece. Athens, 1976. pp. 399. *bibliog.*

— Economic policy — Mathematical models.

BALTAS (N.) and KANBUR (M.G.) An econometric study of capital formation and growth in Greek economy, 1954-1972. Birmingham, 1976. pp. 22. *bibliog. (Birmingham. University. Faculty of Commerce and Social Science. Discussion Papers. Series A. No. 163)*

— Foreign relations.

See also EUROPEAN ECONOMIC COMMUNITY — Greece.

— History.

WOODHOUSE (CHRISTOPHER MONTAGUE) Modern Greece: a short history. London, 1968. pp. 332. *bibliog.*

— Politics and government.

NATIONAL UNION OF GREEK STUDENTS. Greece 1963-1970. London, [1973?]. pp. 61.

POULANTZAS (NICOS) The crisis of the dictatorships: Portugal, Greece, Spain; translated by David Fernbach. London, 1976. pp. 166.

THEODORACOPULOS (TAKI) The Greek upheaval: kings, demagogues and bayonets. London, 1976. pp. 262.

GREECE, ANCIENT

— Economic history.

AUSTIN (M.M.) and VIDAL-NAQUET (PIERRE) Economic and social history of ancient Greece: an introduction; translated and revised by M.M. Austin. London, 1977. pp. 397. *bibliogs.*

— History.

SEALEY (RAPHAEL) A history of the Greek city states ca. 700-338 B.C. Berkeley, Calif., [1976]. pp. 516.

— Social history.

AUSTIN (M.M.) and VIDAL-NAQUET (PIERRE) Economic and social history of ancient Greece: an introduction; translated and revised by M.M. Austin. London, 1977. pp. 397. *bibliogs.*

GREEKS IN AUSTRALIA.

ISAACS (EVA) Greek children in Sydney. Canberra, 1976. pp. 128. *(Academy of the Social Sciences in Australia. Immigrants in Australia. 6)*

GREENE, LOWER SAXONY.

— Social conditions.

LEHMANN (ALBRECHT) Das Leben in einem Arbeiterdorf: eine empirische Untersuchung über die Lebensverhältnisse von Arbeitern. Stuttgart, 1976. pp. 192. *bibliog.*

GREENLAND

— Census.

GREENLAND. Census, 1970. Grønland: folke- og boligtaellingen, 31. december 1970; [with] bilag: aegteskaber, fødte og døde 1966-70. København, 1974. pp. 224. *(Denmark. Danmarks Statistik. Statistisk Tabelvaerk. 1974. 6)*

— Economic conditions.

FROM (ANDERS) Kalâtdlit-nunâne ingerdlausek kanok-ípa?...; Grønlandsk oversaettelse af Ole Brandt. København, 1976. pp. 112. *(Socialforskningsinstituttet. Pjecer. 5) In Greenlandic and Norwegian.*

— Social conditions.

FROM (ANDERS) Kalâtdlit-nunâne ingerdlausek kanok-ípa?...; Grønlandsk oversaettelse af Ole Brandt. København, 1976. pp. 112. *(Socialforskningsinstituttet. Pjecer. 5) In Greenlandic and Norwegian.*

— Statistics, Vital.

GREENLAND. Census, 1970. Grønland: folke- og boligtaellingen, 31. december 1970; [with] bilag: aegteskaber, fødte og døde 1966-70. København, 1974. pp. 224. *(Denmark. Danmarks Statistik. Statistisk Tabelvaerk. 1974. 6)*

GREENWICH

— Social policy.

DALE (ANGELA MARGARET) Homeless families in a London borough: a case study of policy and practice from 1965-1972. 1977. fo.173. *bibliog. Typescript. M. Phil. (London) thesis: unpublished. This thesis is the property of London University and may not be removed from the Library.*

GRENADA

— Executive departments.

GRENADA. Annual administration reports of the colony...for the year 1901. Saint George, 1903. pp. 141.

— Statistics.

GRENADA. Annual administration reports of the colony...for the year 1901. Saint George, 1903. pp. 141.

GREY (EDWARD) 1st Viscount Grey of Fallodon.

BRITISH foreign policy under Sir Edward Grey; edited by F. H. Hinsley. Cambridge, 1977. pp. 702. *bibliog.*

GRIBOEDOV (ALEKSANDR SERGEEVICH).

NECHKINA (MILITSA VASIL'EVNA) A.S. Griboedov i dekabristy. Moskva, 1947. pp. 599.

GRIEVANCE PROCEDURES.

INTERNATIONAL CONFEDERATION OF FREE TRADE UNIONS. Labour Relations Series. Grievance handling. Brussels, 1975. pp. 23.

GRIFFITH (ARTHUR).

DAVIS (RICHARD P.) Arthur Griffith. Dundalk, 1976. pp. 48. *bibliog. (Dublin Historical Association. Irish History Series. No. 10)*

O'NEIL (DANIEL J.) Three perennial themes of anti-colonialism: the Irish case. Denver, Colo., [1976]. pp. 131. *(Denver. University. Social Science Foundation and Graduate School of International Studies. Monograph Series in World Affairs. vol. 14, no. 1)*

GRIQUAS.

ROSS (ROBERT) Adam Kok's Griquas: a study in the development of stratification in South Africa. Cambridge, 1976. pp. 194. *bibliog.*

GROCERY TRADE

— Ireland (Republic).

EIRE. Restrictive Practices Commission. 1976. Report of special review by means of public enquiry of the operation of Articles 2 and 3 of the Restrictive Practices, Groceries, Order, 1973, as amended by the Restrictive Practices, Groceries, Amendment Order, 1973. Dublin, [1976]. pp. 58.

GROSS DOMESTIC PRODUCT

— Finland.

SUOMEN teollisuus ja teollinen käsityö, 1900-1965: (Industry and industrial handicraft in Finland, 1900-1965). Helsinki, 1976. ˙pp. 220. *bibliog. (Suomen Pankki. Taloustieteellinen Tutkimuslaitos. Julkaisuja. Kasvututkimuksia. 7) With English summary and table of contents.*

GROSS NATIONAL PRODUCT.

BARLOW (ROBIN) A test of alternative methods of making international product comparisons. Ann Arbor, 1976. pp. 15. *bibliog. (Michigan University. Center for Research on Economic Development. Discussion Papers. No. 56)*

— Germany, Eastern.

DEUTSCHES INSTITUT FÜR WIRTSCHAFTSFORSCHUNG. Sonderhefte. [Neue Folge]. 115. Das Sozialprodukt der Deutschen Demokratischen Republik im Vergleich mit dem der Bundesrepublik Deutschland; ([by] Herbert Wilkens). Berlin, 1976. pp. 188. *bibliog. With English summary.*

— Underdeveloped areas.

See UNDERDEVELOPED AREAS — Gross national product.

GROUP LEGAL SERVICES.
See PREPAID LEGAL SERVICES.

GRUBER (KARL).

GRUBER (KARL) Ein politisches Leben: Österreichs Weg zwischen den Diktaturen. Wien, [1976]. pp. 300.

GUADELOUPE, NUESTRA SEÑORA DE.

LAFAYE (JACQUES) Quetzalcóatl and Guadalupe: the formation of Mexican national consciousness, 1531-1813; foreword by Octavio Paz; translated by Benjamin Keen. Chicago, 1976. pp. 336.

GUANO.

BONILLA (HERACLIO) Guano y burguesia en el Peru. Lima, 1974. pp. 186. *bibliog. (Instituto de Estudios Peruanos. Peru Problema. 11)*

GUARDIA (FIORELLO HENRY LA).

See LA GUARDIA (FIORELLO HENRY).

HAGUE

— International Court of Justice.

HAGUE. International Court of Justice. [Series D]. Acts and Documents Concerning the Organization of the Court. No. 2. Rules of Court adopted on 6 May 1946, as amended on 10 May 1972. [Leyden], 1972. pp. 31 [bis]. *In English and French.*

DUGARD (JOHN) and GROSSKOPF (E.M.) South West Africa and the International Court: two viewpoints on the 1971 advisory opinion. Johannesburg, [1975]. pp. 31.

PROTT (LYNDEL VON) Der internationale Richter im Spannungsfeld der Rechtskulturen: eine rechtssoziologische Studie über die Elemente des Selbstverständnisses des Internationalen Gerichtshofs. Berlin, [1975]. pp. 257. *bibliog.*

HAGUE. International Court of Justice. [Series D.] Acts and Documents concerning the Organization of the Court. No.3. Charter of the United Nations, statute and rules of Court and other documents. [3rd ed.] [The Hague], 1977. pp. 242. *In English and French.*

HAGUE PEACE CONFERENCES.

DAVIS (CALVIN DEARMOND) The United States and the second Hague Peace Conference: American diplomacy and international organization, 1899-1914. Durham, N.C., 1975. pp. 398. *bibliog.*

HAIN (PETER).

HAIN (PETER) Mistaken identity: the wrong face of the law. London, 1976. pp. 184.

HAINAUT

— Economic conditions.

BELGIUM. Ministère des Affaires Etrangères et du Commerce Extérieur. 1970. Some aspects of the regeneration of the province of Hainault. [Brussels], 1970. pp. 68. *(Memo from Belgium. No.131) Articles taken from the supplement of the "Agence économique et financière" of October 18th, 1970.*

Le HAINAUT franco-belge. [Valenciennes, 1971]. pp. 106. *Papers of a study conference held 18th May 1971 and organised by the Institut d'Etudes et d'Action Démographiques des Régions Nord et Picardie.*

— Industries.

BELGIUM. Ministère des Affaires Etrangères et du Commerce Extérieur. 1970. Some aspects of the regeneration of the province of Hainault. [Brussels], 1970. pp. 68. *(Memo from Belgium. No.131) Articles taken from the supplement of the "Agence économique et financière" of October 18th, 1970.*

HAITI

— Economic history.

WORKING papers in Haitian society and culture; Sidney W. Mintz, editor. New Haven, Conn., [1975]. pp. 290. *(Yale University. Antilles Research Program. Occasional Papers. 4)*

— Social history.

WORKING papers in Haitian society and culture; Sidney W. Mintz, editor. New Haven, Conn., [1975]. pp. 290. *(Yale University. Antilles Research Program. Occasional Papers. 4)*

HALFWAY HOUSES

— United States.

HUGHES (PATRICK H.) Behind the wall of respect: community experiments in heroin addiction control. Chicago, 1977. pp. 162.

HALLUCINOGENIC DRUGS.

REICHEL-DOLMATOFF (GERARDO) The shaman and the jaguar: a study of narcotic drugs among the Indians of Colombia. Philadelphia, 1975. pp. 280. *bibliog.*

HAMBORN

— Social history.

LUCAS (ERHARD) Zwei Formen von Radikalismus in der deutschen Arbeiterbewegung. Frankfurt am Main, [1976]. pp. 334. *bibliog.*

HAMBURG

— Civic improvement.

GRUETTNER (MICHAEL) Wem die Stadt gehört: Stadtplanung und Stadtentwicklung in Hamburg, 1965-1975. Hamburg, 1976. pp. 266. *bibliog.*

— Commerce.

MEYER's Contor-Handbuch, 1827-1829: Faksimile-Ausgabe der Beiträge Altona, Bremen, Hamburg. Hamburg, 1977. 1 vol. (various pagings). *(Wirtschaftsgeschichtliche Forschungsstelle. Veröffentlichungen. Band 40) With postscripts by Maria Möring and Heinz Sarkowski.*

— Economic history.

BAUM (HANS PETER) Hochkonjunktur und Wirtschaftskrise im spätmittelalterlichen Hamburg: Hamburger Rentengeschäfte, 1371-1410. Hamburg, 1976. pp. 235. *bibliog. (Verein für Hamburgische Geschichte. Beiträge zur Geschichte Hamburgs. Band 11)*

— Economic policy.

TESCH (HELMUT) Öffentliche Finanzwirtschaft in Ballungsräumen, dargestellt am Ballungsraum Hamburg. Hamburg, 1976. pp. 268. *bibliog. (Hamburg. Hamburgisches Welt-Wirtschafts-Archiv. Veröffentlichungen)*

— History.

REISSNER (LARISSA) Hamburg at the barricades, and other writings on Weimar Germany; translated from the Russian and edited by Richard Chappell. London, 1977. pp. 209.

— Social conditions.

PFEIL (ELISABETH) Die Familie im Gefüge der Grosstadt: zur Sozialtopographie der Stadt. Hamburg, [1965]. pp. 81. *(Gesellschaft für Wohnungs- und Siedlungswesen, Hamburg. Schriftenreihe)*

HAMPSHIRE

— Rural conditions.

UNITED KINGDOM. Parliament. House of Commons. Select Committee on Andover Union. 1846. Report. The north-west Hampshire agricultural labourer, 1846 (or "the new poor law"); edited by J.E.H. Spaul; and The north-west Hampshire agricultural labourer, 1867-1875; by George E. Brickell. Andover, 1975. pp. 30.

— Social history.

UNITED KINGDOM. Parliament. House of Commons. Select Committee on Andover Union. 1846. Report. The north-west Hampshire agricultural labourer, 1846 (or "the new poor law"); edited by J.E.H. Spaul; and The north-west Hampshire agricultural labourer, 1867-1875; by George E. Brickell. Andover, 1975. pp. 30.

YATES (EDWARD MARSHALL) Tudor Greatham, a social geography of a Hampshire village. London, 1977. pp. 60. *(London. University. King's College. Geography Department. Occasional Papers. No. 4)*

HANDICAPPED

— Employment — Germany, Eastern.

ORGANISATION der geschützten Arbeit in der DDR. Berlin, 1975. pp. 103.

— — United States.

LEVITAN (SAR A.) and TAGGART (ROBERT) Jobs for the disabled. Baltimore, [1977]. pp. 129.

— Australia.

AUSTRALIA. Parliament. Senate. Standing Committee on Health and Welfare. 1971. Report on mentally and physically handicapped persons in Australia; [Ivy Wedgwood, chairman]. in AUSTRALIA. Parliament. Parliamentary papers, 1971, vol.8.

AUSTRALIA. Commonwealth Bureau of Census and Statistics. 1976. Chronic illnesses, injuries and impairments, May 1974. Canberra, [1976]. pp. 32.

— United Kingdom.

BLAXTER (MILDRED) The meaning of disability: a sociological study of impairment. London, 1976. pp. 259.

MORONEY (ROBERT M.) The family and the state: considerations for social policy. London, 1976. pp. 142.

— United States.

BERKOWITZ (MONROE) and others. Public policy toward disability. New York, 1976. pp. 150. *bibliogs.*

HANDICAPPED CHILDREN

— Education — Germany — North Rhine-Westphalia.

NORTH RHINE-WESTPHALIA. Landesamt für Datenverarbeitung und Statistik. Beiträge zur Statistik des Landes Nordrhein- Westfalen. Heft 374. Die Sonderschulen in Nordrhein-Westfalen, 1965 bis 1975. Düsseldorf, 1977. pp. 61.

HANDICRAFT

— Ethiopia.

ETHIOPIA. Central Statistical Office. Business and Industry Division. 1975. Advance report on the 1972-73 rural survey of cottage and handicraft industries. Addis Ababa, 1975. pp. 82.

— Poland.

KWAPIEŃ (MARIA) and others. Studia nad produkcją rzemieślniczą w Polsce, XIV-XVIII w. Wrocław, 1976. pp. 244. *(Polska Akademia Nauk. Instytut Historii Kultury Materialnej. Studia i Materiały z Historii Kultury Materialnej. tom 51) With English summaries.*

HANDLOOM INDUSTRY

— India.

INDIA. High Powered Study Team on the Problems of Handloom Industry. 1975. Report; [B. Sivaraman, chairman]. [Delhi, 1975]. pp. 105.

HANDYSIDE (RICHARD).

EUROPEAN COURT OF HUMAN RIGHTS. Publications. Series A: Judgments and Decisions. [A24]. ...Handyside case: 1. Decision of 29 April 1976; 2. Judgment of 7 December 1976. Strasbourg, Council of Europe, 1976. pp. 37 [bis]. *In English and French.*

HANSA TOWNS.

SCHEPER (BURCHARD) Frühe bürgerliche Institutionen norddeutscher Hansestädte: Beiträge zu einer vergleichenden Verfassungsgeschichte Lübecks, Bremens, Lüneburgs und Hamburgs im Mittelalter. Köln, 1975. pp. 223. *bibliog. (Hansischer Geschichtsverein. Quellen und Darstellungen zur Hansischen Geschichte. Neue Folge. Band 20)*

FRITZE (KONRAD) Bürger und Bauern zur Hansezeit: Studien zu den Stadt- Land-Beziehungen an der südwestlichen Ostseeküste vom 13. bis zum 16. Jahrhundert. Weimar, 1976. pp. 118. *bibliog. (Historiker-Gesellschaft der Deutschen Demokratischen Republik. Hansische Arbeitsgemeinschaft. Abhandlungen zur Handels- und Sozialgeschichte. Band 16)*

HANSEATIC LEAGUE.

HANSISCHES SYMPOSION, 1974. Frühformen englisch-deutscher Handelspartnerschaft: Referate und Diskussionen des Hansischen Symposions...in London vom 9. bis 11. September 1974;...bearbeitet von Klaus Friedland. Köln, 1976. pp. 120. *(Hansischer Geschichtsverein. Quellen und Darstellungen zur Hansischen Geschichte. Neue Folge. Band 23) In German or English.*

HAPPINESS.

BOULANGER (NICOLAS ANTOINE) Dissertations sur Elie et Enoch, sur Esope fabuliste, et Traité mathématique sur le bonheur (par Irenée Krantzovius [pseud., i.e. Benjamin Stillingfleet]). n.p. [17--]. pp. xvi, 284. *Half-title: each part has special title page. Bound with [PIC] Le songe d'Alcibiade, published 1735. From internal evidence this copy known to have been published after 1740.*

HARBOURS

— Statistics.

UNITED NATIONS. Conference on Trade and Development. 1971. Port statistics: selection, collection and presentation of port information and statistics; manual prepared by the UNCTAD secretariat. (TD/B/C.4/79/Rev. 1). New York, 1971. pp. 40.

— Israel.

ISRAEL. Ports Authority. 1976. Israel Ports Authority. [Tel Aviv, 1976]. pp. 80.

— United Kingdom.

PORTEOUS (JOHN DOUGLAS) Canal ports: the urban achievement of the canal age. London, 1977. pp. 249.

HARDING (Mrs. STAN).

HARDING (Mrs. STAN) The underworld of state;...with an introduction by Bertrand Russell. London, 1925. pp. 256.

HARDING (WARREN GAMALIEL) President of the United States.

GRIEB (KENNETH J.) The Latin American policy of Warren G. Harding. Fort Worth, Texas, [1976]. pp. 223. *bibliog.*

HARDY (THOMAS) Political writer.

TESTAMENTS of radicalism: memoirs of working class politicians, 1790-1885; edited and introduced by David Vincent. London, [1977]. pp. 246. *bibliogs.*

HARPERS FERRY, WEST VIRGINIA

— Armouries.

SMITH (MERRITT ROE) Harpers Ferry armory and the new technology: the challenge of change. Ithaca, N.Y., 1977. pp. 363. *bibliog.*

HARRISON (MARGUERITE ELTON).

HARDING (Mrs. STAN) The underworld of state;...with an introduction by Bertrand Russell. London, 1925. pp. 256.

HARRISON (THOMAS).

SIMPKINSON (CHARLES HARE) Thomas Harrison: regicide and Major-General. London, 1905. pp. 304.

HARTSOP VALLEY.

RURAL PLANNING SERVICES. A study of the Hartsop valley; a report to the Countryside Commission and the Lake District Special Planning Board; prepared during 1975 by... M.J. Feist [and others]. [Cheltenham, Countryside Commission], 1976. pp. 146. *bibliog.*

HARYANA

— Social conditions.

AGGARWAL (PARTAP C.) and ASHRAF (MOHD. SIDDIQ) Equality through privilege: a study of special privileges of scheduled castes in Haryana. New Delhi, [1976]. pp. 206. *bibliog.*

HASSAN II, King of Morocco.

HASSAN II, King of Morocco. Le défi. Paris, [1976]. pp. 284.

HAVEMANN (ROBERT).

STEIGERWALD (ROBERT REINHOLD) Der "wahre" oder konterrevolutionäre "Sozialismus": was wollen Havemann, Dutschke, Biermann?. Frankfurt am Main, 1977. pp. 145.

HAWAIIAN ISLANDS

— Public lands.

MIKLIUS (W.) and SHANG (YUNG-CHENG) Land management policy: leasing of state-owned agricultural lands. Honolulu, 1971. pp. 46.

HAZARDOUS SUBSTANCES

— Bibliography.

U.K. Parliament. House of Commons. Library. Research Division. Reference Sheets. 77/8. Industrial hazards, chemical and metallurgical: [75 references]; (compiled by B.L. Miller). [London], 1977. fo. 7.

HEALTH EDUCATION.

LEVIN (LOWELL S.) and others. Self-care: lay initiatives in health. London, 1977. pp. 133. *bibliog. "This book is the direct outgrowth of the International Symposium on the Role of the Individual in Primary Health Care, held in Copenhagen...1975".*

HEALTH SERVICES ADMINISTRATION

— United Kingdom.

LEWIS (JANET) ed. Community health councils: four case studies. London, [1976]. fo.98. *(Centre for Studies in Social Policy. Working Papers)*

BARNARD (KEITH) and LEE (KENNETH) eds. Conflicts in the National Health Service. London, [1977]. pp. 252. *bibliog.*

— — Ireland, Northern.

IRELAND, NORTHERN. Department of Health and Social Services. Central Services Agency. Annual report. a., Oc/D 1973 (1st)- Belfast. *1st issue contains statistics of the work of the General Health Services Board covering Ap/S 1973.*

HEALTH SURVEYS

— United States.

ANDERSEN (RONALD) and others. Two decades of health services: social survey trends in use and expenditure. Cambridge, Mass., [1976]. pp. 387. *bibliog.*

— — Rhode Island.

MONTEIRO (LOIS A.) Monitoring health status and medical care. Cambridge, Mass., [1976]. pp. 221. *bibliog.*

HEARST (PATRICIA CAMPBELL).

McLELLAN (VIN) and AVERY (PAUL) The voices of guns: the definitive and dramatic story of the twenty-two-month career of the Symbionese Liberation Army - one of the most bizarre chapters in the history of the American left. New York, [1977]. pp. 544.

HEBRIDES

— Social conditions.

PEEL (LYNDA MAY) Village gossip: a study of the evaluation system employed in a Hebridean village. 1976 [or rather 1977]. fo.301. *bibliog. Typescript. Ph.D.(London) thesis: unpublished. This thesis is the property of London University and may not be removed from the Library.*

HECKERT (FRITZ).

FRITZ Heckert, ein revolutionärer Führer des Proletariats: eine biographische Skizze; (Text: Willi Glier [and others]). [Karl-Marx-Stadt, 1968]. pp. 79.

HEGEL (GEORG WILHELM FRIEDRICH).

VORLAENDER (KARL) Kant, Fichte, Hegel und der Sozialismus. Berlin, 1920. pp. 105.

HARRIS (HENRY S.) Hegel's development. Oxford, 1972 in progress. *bibliog.*

NORMAN (RICHARD) Hegel's Phenomenology: a philosophical introduction. London, 1976. pp. 139. *bibliog.*

HEINEMANN (GUSTAV WALTER)

— Bibliography.

LOTZ (MARTIN) compiler. Gustav W. Heinemann Bibliographie. Bonn-Bad Godesberg, [1976]. pp. 114.

HENNING (ERNST).

KOMMUNISTISCHE PARTEI DEUTSCHLANDS. Bezirk Wasserkante. Mord über Deutschland. [Hamburg?, 1931?]. pp. 24.

HENRIQUES (Sir BASIL LUCAS QUIXANO).

LOEWE (L.L.) Basil Henriques: a portrait based on his diaries, letters and speeches as collated by his widow, Rose Henriques. London, 1976. pp. 181.

HEROIN.

HUNT (LEON GIBSON) and CHAMBERS (CARL D.) The heroin epidemics: a study of heroin use in the United States, 1965-75. New York, [1976]. pp. 145.

HUGHES (PATRICK H.) Behind the wall of respect: community experiments in heroin addiction control. Chicago, 1977. pp. 162.

HERWEGH (GEORG).

VOLKART (OTTO) Georg Herwegh: Rede...zum 100. Geburtstag des sozialistischen Republikaners, 1917. Zürich, 1917. pp. 30.

HEYDRICH (REINHARD).

STROEBINGER (RUDOLF) Das Attentat von Prag. Landshut, 1976. pp. 270. *bibliog.*

HIDEYOSHI TOYOTOMI.

See TOYOTOMI (HIDEYOSHI).

HIGHWAY PLANNING.

See ROAD PLANNING.

HIJACKING OF AIRCRAFT.

CUBA. 1972. (Complete text of the declaration made by the Cuban revolutionary government regarding the hijacking of aircraft, issued on the 15th of November, 1972. [London, Cuban Embassy], 1972. fo. 5. *(Press Releases)*

HILDEBRAND (BRUNO).

KRAWEHL (OTTO ERNST) Die "Jahrbücher für Nationalökonomie und Statistik" unter den Herausgebern Bruno Hildebrand und Johannes Conrad, 1863 bis 1915. München, 1977. pp. 127. *bibliog.*

HILL (DAVID JAYNE).

PARKMAN (AUBREY) David Jayne Hill and the problem of world peace. Lewisburg, [1975]. pp. 293. *bibliogs.*

HILL FARMING

— Switzerland.

BERTHOUD (GERALD) Changements économiques et sociaux de la montagne: Vernamiège en Valais. Berne, [1967]. pp. 237. *bibliog. (Société Suisse des Sciences Humaines. Travaux.8)*

— United Kingdom.

RURAL PLANNING SERVICES. A study of the Hartsop valley; a report to the Countryside Commission and the Lake District Special Planning Board; prepared during 1975 by... M.J. Feist [and others]. [Cheltenham, Countryside Commission], 1976. pp. 146. *bibliog.*

HINDENBURG (PAUL LUDWIG HANS ANTON VON).

KITCHEN (MARTIN) The silent dictatorship: the politics of the German High Command under Hindenburg and Ludendorff, 1916-1918. London, [1976]. pp. 301. *bibliog.*

RUGE (WOLFGANG) Hindenburg: Porträt eines Militaristen. Berlin, 1977. pp. 488. *bibliog.*

HINDUISM

— India.

PEGGS (JAMES) India's cries to British humanity, relative to infanticide, British connection with idolatry, Ghaut murders, suttee, slavery, and colonization in India; to which are added, humane hints for the melioration of the state of society in British India. London, 1832. pp. 500.

HIPO TECHNIQUE.

KATZAN (HARRY) Systems design and documentation: an introduction to the HIPO method. New York, [1976]. pp. 157. *bibliogs.*

HISTORIANS

— Denmark.

ØSTERGAARD (UFFE) ed. Den materialistiske historieopfattelse i Danmark før 1945. I. En antologi med eksempler på forholdet mellem teori og praksis. Århus, 1973. pp. 351. *No more published.*

— Germany.

GILBERT (FELIX) History: choice and commitment. Cambridge, Mass., 1977. pp. 549. *bibliog. Selected essays.*

HISTORICAL LINGUISTICS.

INTERNATIONAL CONFERENCE ON HISTORICAL LINGUISTICS, 2ND, TUCSON, 1976. Current progress in historical linguistics: proceedings of the... Conference...; editor William M. Christie. Amsterdam, 1976. pp. 409. *bibliogs.*

HISTORICAL RESEARCH

— Bibliography.

JACOBS (PHYLLIS MAY) compiler. History theses, 1901-70: historical research for higher degrees in the universities of the United Kingdom. London, 1976. pp. 456.

HISTORIOGRAPHY.

SCHULIN (ERNST) Weltgeschichte und europäische Geschichte in der Auffassung des 20. Jahrhunderts. Oulu, 1969. pp. 33. *(Oulu. Yliopisto. Department of History. Collected Papers of the Guest Lecturers. Nr.4)*

PROBLEMY istorii mezhdunarodnykh otnoshenii i ideologicheskaia bor'ba: sbornik statei. Moskva, 1976. pp. 295.

PROBLEMY istorii obshchestvennoi mysli i istoriografii: k 75- letiiu akademika N.V. Nechkinoi. Moskva, 1976. pp. 387. *bibliog.*

HISTORY

— Congresses.

INTERNATIONAL CONGRESS OF HISTORICAL SCIENCES, 14TH, SAN FRANCISCO, 1975. Proceedings. New York, 1976. pp. 233.

— Methodology.

TUÑON DE LARA (MANUEL) Metodologia de la historia social de España. Madrid, 1973 repr. 1974. pp. 201.

TOPOLSKI (JERZY) Methodology of history; translated from the Polish by Olgierd Wojtasiewicz. Warszawa, 1976. pp. 690.

— Philosophy.

BRADLEY (FRANCIS HERBERT) The presuppositions of critical history; edited with introduction and commentary by Lionel Rubinoff. Chicago, [1968]. pp. 147. *bibliog.*

DUJOVNE (LEON) La concepcion de la historia en la obra de Ortega y Gasset. Buenos Aires, [1968]. pp. 218.

ADLER (HANS GUENTHER) Die Freiheit des Menschen: Aufsätze zur Sociologie und Geschichte. Tübingen, 1976. pp. 358. *Some of the essays were originally published in the author's Die Erfahrung der Ohnmacht in 1964.*

ROTENSTREICH (NATHAN) Philosophy, history and politics: studies in contemporary English philosophy of history. The Hague, 1976. pp. 158. *bibliog.*

— Study and teaching — Ireland (Republic).

HARKNESS (D.W.) History and the Irish. Belfast, [1976]. pp. 15. *(Belfast. Queen's University. Lectures. New Series. No.93)*

— — United Kingdom — Ireland, Northern.

HARKNESS (D.W.) History and the Irish. Belfast, [1976]. pp. 15. *(Belfast. Queen's University. Lectures. New Series. No.93)*

HISTORY, ANCIENT.

JARAMILLO ECHEVERRI (MARINO) Liberales y conservadores en la historia: itinerario de las ideas y del poder. Bogota, 1972. pp. 297.

HISTORY, UNIVERSAL.

WELLS (HERBERT GEORGE) The outline of history: being a plain history of life and mankind; ...(revised and brought up to date by Raymond Postgate and G. P. Wells, with maps and plans by J.F. Horrabin). London, 1972. pp. 1103. *This revised ed. originally published Garden City, N.Y., 1971. Previous ed. 1961.*

QUESTER (GEORGE H.) Offense and defense in the international system. New York, [1977]. pp. 219.

HITLER (ADOLF).

WAITE (ROBERT GEORGE LEESON) The psychopathic god: Adolf Hitler. New York, [1977]. pp. 482.

HLINKA (ANDREJ).

JELINEK (YESHAYAHU) The parish republic: Hlinka's Slovak People's Party, 1939-1945. New York, 1976. pp. 204. *bibliog. (East European Quarterly. East European Monographs. 14)*

HOARE (SAMUEL JOHN GURNEY) 1st Viscount Templewood.

CROSS (JOHN ARTHUR) Sir Samuel Hoare: a political biography. London, 1977. pp. 414. *bibliog.*

HOBBES (THOMAS).

COLEMAN (FRANK M.) Hobbes and America: exploring the constitutional foundations. Toronto, [1977]. pp. 159.

RAPHAEL (DAVID DAICHES) Hobbes: morals and politics. London, 1977. pp. 104.

HOBHOUSE (Sir CHARLES EDWARD HENRY).

HOBHOUSE (Sir CHARLES EDWARD HENRY) Inside Asquith's Cabinet: from the diaries of Charles Hobhouse; edited by Edward David. London, [1977]. pp. 295.

HOELZ (MAX).

MUEHSAM (ERICH) Gerechtigkeit für Max Hoelz! 3rd ed. Berlin, 1976. pp. 77. *Reprint of work originally published in Berlin in 1926.*

HOHENLOHE-SCHILLINGSFUERST (CHLODWIG KARL VIKTOR) Prince.

WILKE (EKKEHARD-TEJA P.W.) Political decadence in imperial Germany: personnel-political aspects of the German government crisis, 1894-97. Urbana, Ill., [1976]. pp. 311. *bibliog. (Illinois University. Illinois Studies in the Social Sciences. 59)*

HOLDING COMPANIES

— Accounting.

BOGIE (DAVID JAMES) On group accounts; third edition edited by John C. Shaw. Bristol, 1973. pp. 428.

HOLIDAYS

— Australia.

AUSTRALIA. Commonwealth Bureau of Census and Statistics. Annual leave. a., 1974- Canberra.

— United Kingdom.

BIRCH (STEPHANIE) Management holidays: a survey of current practice in 200 companies. London, [1972]. pp. 19. *(British Institute of Management. Management Survey Reports. No. 11)*

HOLINESS CHURCHES

— United States.

JONES (CHARLES EDWIN) Perfectionist persuasion: the holiness movement and American Methodism, 1867-1936. Metuchen, N.J., 1974. pp. 242. *(American Theological Library Association. ATLA Monograph Series. No.5)*

HOLISM.

PHILLIPS (D.C.) Holistic thought in social science. Stanford, 1976. pp. 149. *bibliog.*

HOLY ALLIANCE.

The HOLY Alliance versus Spain; containing the several notes and declarations of the allied powers, with the firm, spirited, and dignified replies of the Spanish Cortes, accompanied by a few brief prefatory remarks thereon; by a constitutionalist. London, J. Ridgway, 1823. pp. viii, 30.

HOMANS (GEORGE CASPAR).

BEHAVIORAL theory in sociology: essays in honor of George C. Homans; edited by Robert L. Hamblin and John H. Kunkel. New Brunswick, N.J., [1977]. pp. 546. *bibliogs.*

HOME AND SCHOOL.

LOCAL government, schools and parents. [Billericay, 1971]. 1 pamphlet (various pagings). *(Confederation for the Advancement of State Education. Caseviews. 4) Incorporates 2 issues of Parents and Schools, vol. 5 no.2 and vol. 6 no.4.*

HOME RULE

— Ireland.

O'DAY (ALAN) The English face of Irish nationalism: Parnellite involvement in British politics, 1880-86. Dublin, 1977. pp. 210. *bibliog.*

— Scotland.

U.K. 1976. Devolution: the new assemblies for Scotland and Wales; [main points of the White Paper]. [London, 1976]. pp. 15.

U.K. Office of the Lord President of the Council. 1976. Devolution: the English dimension: a consultative document. London, 1976. pp. 22.

U.K. Parliament. House of Commons. Library. Research Division. Background Papers. No.57. The devolution debate: regional statistics. [London, 1977]. pp. 18.

— Wales.

U.K. 1976. Devolution: the new assemblies for Scotland and Wales; [main points of the White Paper]. [London, 1976]. pp. 15.

U.K. Office of the Lord President of the Council. 1976. Devolution: the English dimension: a consultative document. London, 1976. pp. 22.

U.K. Parliament. House of Commons. Library. Research Division. Background Papers. No.57. The devolution debate: regional statistics. [London, 1977]. pp. 18.

HOMELESSNESS

— Germany.

GRAF (PEDRO) and others. Sozialarbeit im Obdachlosenbereich: Gemeinwesenarbeit zwischen Betroffenen und Institutionen. Westberlin, [1976]. pp. 207.

— United Kingdom.

KARN (VALERIE A.) and others. No place that's home: a report on accommodation for homeless young single people in Birmingham. Birmingham, 1974. pp. 99. *bibliog. (Birmingham. University. Centre for Urban and Regional Studies. Research Memoranda. No. 32)*

HELP for the other travellers: social provision in relation to London travel termini; report of an inter-agency working party. London, [1976]. pp. 8.

SHELTER. Shelter 1976: ten years on; a progress report. London, [1976]. pp. 24.

DALE (ANGELA MARGARET) Homeless families in a London borough: a case study of policy and practice from 1965-1972. 1977. fo.173. *bibliog. Typescript. M. Phil. (London) thesis: unpublished. This thesis is the property of London University and may not be removed from the Library.*

WILSON (HUGH) AND WOMERSLEY (LEWIS) Firm. Inner area study: Liverpool: single and homeless: (an account of four action projects on special housing need). [London], Department of the Environment, [1977]. pp. 73.

HOMOSEXUALITY.

WEST (DONALD JAMES) Homosexuality re-examined. 4th ed. London, 1977. pp. 359. *bibliog. Previous editions published as Homosexuality.*

— Bibliography.

LIBRARIANS FOR SOCIAL CHANGE COLLECTIVE. Sexual politics: a basic reading list. London, [1975]. pp. 23.

— United Kingdom.

FRIEND. [LONDON GROUP]. Introducing Friend in London. [London, 1977?]. pp. 11.

WEEKS (JEFFREY) Coming out: homosexual politics in Britain, from the nineteenth century to the present. London, 1977. pp. 278. *bibliog.*

— — Ireland, Northern.

IRELAND, NORTHERN. Standing Advisory Commission on Human Rights. 1977. Report on the law in Northern Ireland relating to divorce and homosexuality. London, [1977]. pp. 20.

HOMOSEXUALITY AND EMPLOYMENT

— United Kingdom.

FERRIS (DAVE) Homosexuality and the social services: the report of an NCCL survey of local authority social services committees. London, [1977]. pp. 89.

HOMOSEXUALITY AND LITERATURE

— Bibliography.

LIBRARIANS FOR SOCIAL CHANGE COLLECTIVE. Sexual politics: a basic reading list. London, [1975]. pp. 23.

HONDURAS

— Census.

HONDURAS. Census, 1974. Censo nacional de poblacion (marzo 74). Tegucigalpa, 1976 in progress.

HONE (WILLIAM) Bookseller.

[SLOP, Dr., pseud.] Slop's shave at a broken Hone. London, Wright, 1820. pp. 42. *Satires in verse on W. Hone anticipating his "Slap at Slop".*

HONECKER (ERICH).

ERICH Honecker: Skizze seines politischen Lebens; ([edited by the] Institut für Marxismus-Leninismus beim ZK der SED). Berlin, 1977. pp. 223.

HONG KONG

— Census.

HONG KONG. Census, 1966. The census and you, 1966; by K.M.A. Barnett. Hong Kong, 1967. pp. 21.

— Economic conditions.

HONG KONG. The...budget: economic background. a., 1977/78- Hong Kong.

— Population — Bibliography.

SAW (SWEE-HOCK) and CHENG (SIOK-HWA) compilers. A bibliography of the demography of Hong Kong. Singapore, 1976. pp. 112.

HONOUR.

PITT-RIVERS (JULIAN ALFRED LANE-FOX) The fate of Shechem; or, The politics of sex: essays in the anthropology of the Mediterranean. Cambridge, 1977. pp. 193.

HOOVER (HERBERT CLARK) President of the United States.

ROBINSON (EDGAR EUGENE) and BORNET (VAUGHN DAVIS) Herbert Hoover: president of the United States. Stanford, 1975. pp. 398. *bibliog. (Stanford University. Hoover Institution on War, Revolution and Peace. Hoover Institution Publications. 149)*

OLSON (JAMES STUART) Herbert Hoover and the Reconstruction Finance Corporation, 1931-1933. Ames, 1977. pp. 155. *bibliog.*

ROSEN (ELLIOT A.) Hoover, Roosevelt, and the Brains Trust: from Depression to New Deal. New York, 1977. pp. 446.

HORKHEIMER (MAX).

TAR (ZOLTÁN) The Frankfurt School: the critical theories of Max Horkheimer and Theodor W. Adorno. New York, [1977]. pp. 243. *bibliog.*

HOSPITAL CARE

— United Kingdom.

ELLIOTT (JAMES R.) Living in hospital: the social needs of people in long-term care. London, 1975. pp. 84. *bibliog.*

HOSPITALITY

— Mathematical models.

SAULNIERS (ALFRED H.) The economics of prestation systems: a consumer analysis of extended family obligations with application to Zaire. Ann Arbor, 1976. pp. 27. *bibliog. (Michigan University. Center for Research on Economic Development. Discussion Papers. No.54)*

HOSPITALS

— Bahamas.

HUGHES (HUGH LLEWELYN GLYN) The Bahamas: a survey of the medical services, November, 1960. [Nassau], 1960. pp. 77.

— Canada.

NURSING IN CANADA: Canadian nursing statistics; (pd. by) Statistics Canada. a., 1975 (1st)- Ottawa. *[in English and French].*

— United Kingdom — Cost of operation.

HURST (J.W.) Saving hospital expenditure by reducing in-patient stay. London, H.M.S.O., 1977. pp. 14. *bibliog. (Government Economic Service Occasional Papers. 14)*

— United States — New York.

ROTHENBERG (ELEANORE) Regulation and expansion of health facilities: the certificate of need experience in New York State. New York, 1976. pp. 128. *bibliog.*

HOTELS, TAVERNS, ETC.

— Poland.

SZCZEPANIAK (MARIAN) Karczma, wieś, dwór: rola propinacji na wsi wielkopolskiej od połowy XVII do schyłku XVIII wieku. Warszawa, 1977. pp. 186. *With Russian and German summaries.*

— United Kingdom — Finance.

ENGLISH TOURIST BOARD. The hotel development incentives scheme in England; (an appraisal by Philip Clarke). London, [1976]. pp. 40.

HOUGHTON (DESMOND HOBART).

TRUU (M.L.) ed. Public policy and the South African economy: essays in memory of Desmond Hobart Houghton. Cape Town, 1976. pp. 206. *bibliog.*

HOURS OF LABOUR.

RUSTANT (MAURICE) Vers la semaine de 30 heures: étude sur la réduction de la durée du travail. Paris, [1975]. pp. 134. *bibliog.*

— France.

RUSTANT (MAURICE) Vers la semaine de 30 heures: étude sur la réduction de la durée du travail. Paris, [1975]. pp. 134. *bibliog.*

— Germany.

GERMANY. Statutes, etc. 1923. Die Verordnung über die Arbeitszeit, mit Erläuterungen; im Auftrage des Allgemeinen Deutschen Gewerkschafts-Bundes herausgegeben von Th. Leipart. Berlin, 1924. pp. 32.

— New Zealand.

NEW ZEALAND. Department of Labour. Research and Planning Division. 1975. An experiment with flexi-time. Wellington, 1975. pp. 76.

— Russia.

ZBARSKII (MOISEI ISAAKOVICH) Sotsial'no-ekonomicheskie problemy rabochego dnia pri sotsializme. Moskva, 1976. pp. 222.

HOUSE BUYING.

WILLIAMS (C.V.) Company housing policy: a survey of house purchase schemes and assistance with removal expenses. London, 1969. pp. 29. *bibliog. (British Institute of Management. Information Summaries. No. 141)*

HOUSEWIVES.

BRITISH SOCIOLOGICAL ASSOCIATION. Annual Conference, 1974. Dependence and exploitation in work and marriage: [papers presented at the conference; edited] by Diana Leonard Barker and Sheila Allen. London, 1976. pp. 265. *bibliog. (British Sociological Association. Explorations in Sociology. 7)*

COX (NICOLE) and FEDERICI (SILVIA)
Counter-planning from the kitchen: wages for housework: a
perspective on capital and the left. 2nd ed. New York,
1976. pp. 23.

HOUSING.

WOLF (JULIUS) Die Wohnungsfrage als Gegenstand der
Sozialpolitik: Vortrag gehalten im Rathaus zu Zürich am 5.
Dezember 1895. Jena, 1896. pp. 38.

HOEHMANN (PETER) Wie Obdachlosigkeit gemacht
wird: die Entstehung und Entwicklung eines sozialen
Problems. Neuwied, [1976]. pp. 128. *bibliog.*

BURNS (LELAND S.) and GREBLER (LEO) The housing
of nations: analysis and policy in a comparative
framework. London, 1977. pp. 255.

INTERREGIONAL SEMINAR ON THE SOCIAL
ASPECTS OF HOUSING, HOLTE, 1975. The social
impact of housing: goals, standards, social indicators and
popular participation: report of an Interregional Seminar...
14-27 September, 1975. (ESA/OTC/SEM/77/2). New York,
United Nations, 1977. pp. 93. *bibliogs.*

— Environmental aspects.

MICHELSON (WILLIAM) Environmental choice, human
behavior, and residential satisfaction. New York, 1977. pp.
403. *bibliog.*

— Finance.

UNITED NATIONS. [Centre for Housing, Building and
Planning]. 1972. Proposals for action on finance for
housing, building and planning. (E/C.6/106/Rev.1)
(ST/ECA/168). New York, 1972. pp. 89. *bibliog.*

— Mathematical models.

PRAKASH (VED) and SPILLANE (JAMES J.) An
economic framework for investment planning in housing
and urban infrastructure. (ST/ECA/186). New York,
United Nations, 1973. pp. 47.

ROMANOS (MICHAEL C.) Residential spatial structure.
Lexington, Mass., [1976]. pp. 197. *bibliog.*

— Algeria — Statistics.

ALGERIA. Census, 1966. Recensement général de la
population et de l'habitat, 1966, etc. Oran, 1970 in
progress.

— Australia — Queensland.

STATE ADVANCES CORPORATION [QUEENSLAND].
Workers' homes: the Workers' Homes Acts, 1919 to 1922.
4th ed. [Brisbane], 1924. pp. 27.

— Austria — Vienna.

VIENNA. Magistrat. Abteilung für Landes- und
Stadtplanung. Wohnen in Wien: Ergebnisse und
Folgerungen aus einer Untersuchung von Wiener
Wohnverhältnissen, Wohnwünschen und städtischer
Umwelt; Mitarbeiter: Gustav Krall [and others]. Wien,
1956. pp. 108. *(Aufbau, Der. Monographien. 8)*

FELDBAUER (PETER) Stadtwachstum und
Wohnungsnot: Determinanten unzureichender
Wohnungsversorgung in Wien, 1848 bis 1914. Wien, 1977.
pp. 340. *bibliog. (Vienna. Universität. Institut für
Wirtschafts- und Sozialgeschichte. Sozial- und
Wirtschaftshistorische Studien. Band 9)*

— Brazil.

BRAZIL. Departamento de Censos. 1974. Censo predial
[1970]: Brasil [whole country]. [Rio de Janeiro, 1974]. pp.
74.

— Canada.

RENT control: a popular paradox: evidence on the
economic effects of rent control; by F.A. Hayek [and
others]. Vancouver, 1975. pp. 212.

— — Toronto.

TORONTO. Social Planning Council. The rent race: a
study of housing quality, shelter costs and family budgets
for social assistance recipients in metropolitan Toronto.
Toronto, 1974. 1 vol. (various pagings). *Study
commissioned by the Municipality of Metropolitan Toronto
Social Services and Housing Committee.*

MICHELSON (WILLIAM) Environmental choice, human
behavior, and residential satisfaction. New York, 1977. pp.
403. *bibliog.*

— Chile.

COLEGIO DE ARQUITECTOS DE CHILE. Plan nacional
de desarrollo urbano, rural y de vivienda: planteamientos
basicos, diagnosticos, estrategias. Santiago de Chile, 1973.
pp. 255. *bibliog.*

— Europe.

UNITED NATIONS. Economic Commission for Europe.
Committee on Housing, Building and Planning. 1973.
Housing requirements and demand: current methods of
assessment and problems of estimation. (ST/ECE/HBP/46).
Geneva, 1973. pp. 87. *bibliogs.*

— Europe, Eastern — Public opinion.

RADIO FREE EUROPE. Audience and Public Opinion
Research Department. The East European housing problem
in a global frame of reference. [Munich?], 1977. fo. 3.

— France.

ARDITTI (S.) and others, eds. Etude sur l'habitat
insalubre: le logement des travailleurs immigrés. [Paris],
Service des Affaires Economiques et Internationales, 1974.
pp. 146.

NORA (SIMON) and EVENO (BERTRAND) Rapport sur
l'amélioration de l'habitat ancien. Paris, La Documentation
Française, 1975. pp. 200.

— — Finance.

FRANCE. Commission d'Etude d'une Réforme du
Financement du Logement. 1976. Rapport de la
Commission...; présidée par Raymond Barre. Paris, 1975
[or rather 1976]. pp. 166.

— — Statistics.

FRANCE. Direction du Bâtiment et des Travaux Publics et
de la Conjoncture. Service des Statistiques et des Etudes
Economiques. 1972- . Annuaire statistique de
l'équipement. Paris, [1972 in progress].

FRANCE. Census, 1968. Recensement général de la
population de 1968; résultats du sondage au 1/4:
population, ménages, logements, immeubles; fascicules
régionaux ([including] Récapitulation pour la France
entière). Paris, 1972. 23 pts. (in 2 vols.)

— Germany.

FRANZ (PETER) Die Auswirkungen des
Wohnungswechsels kinderreicher und obdachloser
Familien: empirische Untersuchung eines Wohnprojekts.
[Erlangen, 1976]. pp. 194. *bibliog. Inaugural-Dissertation
zur Erlangung des akademischen Grades eines Doktors der
Wirtschafts- und Sozialwissenschaften der
Friedrich-Alexander-Universität Erlangen-Nürnberg.*

GESELLSCHAFT FÜR WOHNUNGS- UND
SIEDLUNGSWESEN, HAMBURG. Obdachlosigkeit in
der Bundesrepublik Deutschland;... Projektleitung: A.
Kögler, etc. Hamburg, 1976. pp. 278. *bibliog.
(Schriftenreihe. Neue Folge. 19)*

JENKIS (HELMUT WALTER) Wohnungswirtschaft und
Wohnungspolitik in beiden deutschen Staaten: Versuch
eines Vergleichs. 2nd ed. Hamburg, [1976]. pp. 224.

— — North Rhine-Westphalia — Statistics.

NORTH RHINE-WESTPHALIA. Landesamt für
Datenverarbeitung und Statistik. Beiträge zur Statistik des
Landes Nordrhein-Westfalen. Heft 355. Wohnungsbestand
in den Gemeinden Nordrhein-Westfalens, 1968 bis 1974:
Gebietsstand 1.1. 1975. Düsseldorf, 1976. pp. 71.

— Germany, Eastern.

JENKIS (HELMUT WALTER) Wohnungswirtschaft und
Wohnungspolitik in beiden deutschen Staaten: Versuch
eines Vergleichs. 2nd ed. Hamburg, [1976]. pp. 224.

— Honduras — Statistics.

HONDURAS. Direccion General de Estadistica y Censos.
1976. Censo nacional de vivienda, [1974]. Tegucigalpa, 1976
in progress.

— Iceland — Statistics.

ICELAND. Hagstofa. 1968. Húsnaedisskýrslur, 1.
desember 1960; Housing statistics, 1960. Reykjavík, 1968.
pp. 78. *(Hagskýrslur Islands. 2. [Series]. 43) With English
translations of table headings.*

— Japan — Statistics.

JAPAN. Census of Housing, 1973. 1973 housing survey of
Japan. Vol. 1. Results for whole Japan. [Tokyo, 1975]. pp.
667,(8). *In English and Japanese.*

— Netherlands.

NETHERLANDS. Ministerie van Volkshuisvesting en
Ruimtelijke Ordening. Current trends and policies in
housing and building (formerly Current trends in housing,
building and physical planning). a., 1974- 's-Gravenhage.

NETHERLANDS. Centrale Directie van de
Volkshuisvesting. Jaarverslag. a., 1975- 's-Gravenhage.
*Supersedes in part NETHERLANDS. Centrale Directie van
de Volkshuisvesting en de Bouwnijverheid. Jaarverslag.*

— Paraguay — Statistics.

PARAGUAY. Census, 1972. Censo nacional de poblacion
y viviendas, 1972. [Asuncion], 1975. pp. 561.

— Peru — Statistics.

PERU. Census, 1972. Censos nacionales VII de poblacion
II de vivienda, 4 de junio de 1972: resultados definitivos;
nivel nacional. Lima, 1974. 2 vols.

PERU. Census, 1972. Censos nacionales VII de poblacion
II de vivienda, 4 de junio de 1972: [departmental results].
Lima, 1974 [or rather 1975] in progress.

— South Africa.

HORRELL (MURIEL) Housing schemes for urban
Africans in municipal areas and the homelands; [paper
given at the 42nd annual council meeting of the South
African Institute of Race Relations, held in Durban in
1972]. Durban, 1972. pp. 36.

— Sweden — Statistics.

SWEDEN. Census, 1975. Folk- och bostadsräkningen.
1975. Stockholm, 1976 in progress.

— Tunisia — Statistics.

TUNIS. Census, 1966. Recensement général de la
population et des logements du 3 mai 1966. Tunis, [1973]. 4
vols. (in 1). *Map in end pocket.*

— Underdeveloped areas.

**See UNDERDEVELOPED AREAS —
Housing.**

— United Kingdom.

CONSTABLE (MOIRA) Shelter report on tied
accommodation. London, [1974]. pp. 32. *(Shelter. Action
Series. No. 2)*

RAPER (MARTIN) Housing for single young people: (a
study related to the demand for existing housing stock).
York, 1974. pp. 127. *(York. University. Institute of
Advanced Architectural Studies. Research Papers. 7)*

U.K. Department of the Environment. Homeless
households reported by local authorities in England. s-a.,
1975 [1st]- London.

BRITISH PROPERTY FEDERATION. Policy for housing. London, 1975. pp. 20.

NATIONAL FEDERATION OF HOUSING ASSOCIATIONS. Housing associations. London, 1975. pp. 8.

AMBROSE (PETER JOHN) The land market and the housing system. Brighton, 1976. fo. 37. *bibliog. (Brighton. University of Sussex. Sussex Working Papers in Urban and Regional Studies. 3)*

DUNCAN (S.S.) The housing crisis and the structure of the housing market. Brighton, 1976. fo.41. *(Brighton. University of Sussex. Sussex Working Papers in Urban and Regional Studies. 2)*

FINER JOINT ACTION COMMITTEE. Housing difficulties of one parent families. London, [1976]. fo. 18.

HADJIMATHEOU (GEORGE G.) Housing and mortgage markets: the UK experience. Farnborough, Hants., [1976]. pp. 178. *bibliog.*

NORTHERN REGION STRATEGY TEAM. Housing in the northern region. Newcastle upon Tyne, 1976. 2 vols. (in 1). *(Technical Reports. No.15)*

ROBERTS (J. TREVOR) General Improvement Areas. Farnborough, Hants., [1976]. pp. 188.

U.K. Department of the Environment. Housing Improvement Group. 1976. Housing action areas: a detailed examination of declaration reports. London, 1976. pp. 89. *(Improvement Research Notes. 76-2)*

U.K. Parliament. House of Commons. Library. Research Division. Background Papers. No. 52. Homelessness: the role of local authorities. [London, 1976]. pp. 7.

U.K. Working Group on Homeless Young People. 1976. Report. [London], 1976. pp. 81.

U.K. Department of the Environment. 1977- . Housing policy: technical volume. London, 1977 in progress. *Main report published as British Parliamentary Paper Cmnd. 6851, Session 1976-77.*

MIDDLE class housing in Britain; edited by M.A. Simpson and T.H. Lloyd. Newton Abbot, 1977. pp. 217.

SAUNDERS (P.R.) Housing tenure and class interests. Brighton, 1977. fo.22. *(Brighton. University of Sussex. Sussex Working Papers in Urban and Regional Studies. 6)*

WILLIAMSON (R.L.) A review of the economics and finance of housing. London, [1977]. pp. 66. *(London. Greater London Council. Research Memoranda. 517)*

— — Bibliography.

DERRICK (E.F.) compiler. House and area improvement in Britain; [a bibliography and abstracts]. Birmingham, 1976. pp. 120. *(Birmingham University. Centre for Urban and Regional Studies. Research Memoranda. No.54)*

— — Finance.

COMMUNITY DEVELOPMENT PROJECT. Profits against houses: (an alternative guide to housing finance). London, 1976. pp. 56.

WILLIAMSON (R.L.) A review of the economics and finance of housing. London, [1977]. pp. 66. *(London. Greater London Council. Research Memoranda. 517)*

— — Birmingham.

FORREST (RAY) and MURIE (ALAN S.) Social segregation, housing need and the sale of council houses. Birmingham, 1976. pp. 50. *(Birmingham. University. Centre for Urban and Regional Studies. Research Memoranda. No. 53)*

LLEWELYN-DAVIES WEEKS [AND PARTNERS]. Inner area study: Birmingham: housing policies for the inner city. [London], Department of the Environment, [1976]. pp. 159. *bibliog.*

— — Brighton.

AMBROSE (PETER JOHN) Who plans Brighton's housing crisis? London, [1976]. pp. 19. *(Shelter. Local Reports. 1)*

— — Cheltenham.

BIRMINGHAM. University. Centre for Urban and Regional Studies. The Cheltenham housing study. Birmingham, 1975. pp. 145. *(Research Memoranda. No. 48)*

— — Huddersfield.

DUNCAN (S.S.) The housing crisis and the structure of the housing market. Brighton, 1976. fo.41. *(Brighton. University of Sussex. Sussex Working Papers in Urban and Regional Studies. 2)*

— — Ireland, Northern.

NORTHERN IRELAND HOUSING EXECUTIVE. Accounts...together with the report of the Comptroller and Auditor-General thereon. a., 1971/72- Belfast. *1945/46 - 1970/71 included in IRELAND, NORTHERN. Parliament. House of Commons. [Papers]. File includes the last accounts for the period Ap 1 to Oc 3 1971 of the IRELAND, NORTHERN. Housing Trust.*

NORTHERN IRELAND HOUSING EXECUTIVE. Corporate Planning Department. Housing condition survey, 1974, Northern Ireland: final report. Belfast, [1975]. pp. 59.

NORTHERN IRELAND HOUSING EXECUTIVE. Corporate Planning Department. Northern Ireland household survey, 1975. [Belfast, 1976]. pp. 178.

— — London.

POLLARD (JOHN) Dr. Squat; a report written in conjunction with the squatters, West Kentish Town, Sept., 1972. London, 1972. fo. 7. *bibliog.*

HOMELESS IN HAMMERSMITH. Reports. No. 1. London, [1975]. pp. 17. *bibliog.*

WATES (NICHOLAS HERON) The battle for Tolmers Square. London, 1976. pp. 232. *bibliog.*

LEE (TREVOR ROSS) Race and residence: the concentration and dispersal of immigrants in London. Oxford, 1977. pp. 193. *bibliog.*

O'DELL (ALAN) and PARKER (JAMES) M.A., Writer on Housing. The use of census data to identify and describe housing stress. Watford, [1977]. pp. 33. *(Building Research Establishment [U.K.]. Current Papers. 77/6)*

O'MALLEY (JAN) The politics of community action: a decade of struggle in Notting Hill. Nottingham, 1977. pp. 180.

PITT (JAMES) Gentrification in Islington: the return of the middle classes to an inner London borough and the subsequent effects on housing. London, [1977]. fo. 36.

ROBSON (PAUL) London borough of Newham: public health and housing. London, Canning Town Community Development Project and the Public Health Advisory Service, 1977. pp. 61, vii.

WOHL (ANTHONY STEPHEN) The eternal slum: housing and social policy in Victorian London. London, 1977. pp. 386. *bibliog.*

WORKING PARTY ON THE PROVISION OF ACCOMMODATION FOR SINGLE PEOPLE. Final report; [S. Woolf, chairman]. [London], 1977. pp. 45.

— — North Shields.

NORTH TYNESIDE COMMUNITY DEVELOPMENT PROJECT. Some housing and town planning issues in North Tyneside: an overview. [North Shields, 1976]. pp. 163.

TRIANGLE ACTION GROUP [NORTH SHIELDS]. The Triangle: which way now?. [North Shields, North Tyneside Community Development Project, 1976]. fo.10.

— — Northumberland.

SHELTER. Blyth Valley Group. Blyth Valley housing report, 1975. Newcastle, [1975]. fo. 33.

— — Portsmouth.

SOCIAL SERVICES RESEARCH AND INTELLIGENCE UNIT [PORTSMOUTH]. Occasional Papers. No. 2. Households: Portsmouth and neighbouring areas. Portsmouth, 1973. fo. 27. *bibliog.*

— — Wales — Abercregan.

GLAMORGAN-GLYNCORRWG COMMUNITY DEVELOPMENT PROJECT. Abercregan housing study: an assessment of the use of existing legislation in solving the housing problems of a small, peripheral settlement. [Port Talbot], 1973. pp. (47). *bibliog.*

— — Wolverhampton.

BARNSBY (GEORGE) A history of housing in Wolverhampton 1750 to 1975. Wolverhampton, [1976]. pp. 69.

— United States.

LISTOKIN (DAVID) Fair share housing allocation. New Brunswick, [1976]. pp. 253.

STEGMAN (MICHAEL A.) and SUMKA (HOWARD J.) Nonmetropolitan urban housing: an economic analysis of problems and policies. Cambridge, Mass., [1976]. pp. 304. *bibliog.*

— — Statistics.

FREEDMAN (BERNARD N.) Private housing completions: a new dimension in construction statistics. [Washington, 1972]. pp. 20. *(United States. Board of Governors of the Federal Reserve System. Staff Economic Studies. No. 66)*

— — Massachusetts.

GOETZE (ROLF) Building neighborhood confidence: a humanistic strategy for urban housing. Cambridge, Mass., [1976]. pp. 176.

— — New York (City).

JACKSON (ANTHONY) A place called home: a history of low-cost housing in Manhattan. Cambridge, Mass., [1976]. pp. 359. *bibliog.*

STERNLIEB (GEORGE S.) and HUGHES (JAMES W.) Housing and economic reality: New York City, 1976. New Brunswick, [1976]. pp. 255.

— — New York (State).

SANDS (GARY) and BOWER (LEWIS L.) Housing turnover and housing policy: case studies of vacancy chains in New York State. New York, 1976. pp. 169. *bibliog.*

— Venezuela — Caracas.

ACEDO MENDOZA (CARLOS) La vivienda en el area metropolitana de Caracas. [Caracas, 1967]. pp. 209. *bibliog. (Comision Nacional del Cuatricentenario de la Fundacion de Caracas. Ediciones del Cuatricentenario de Caracas. Serie de Obras Economicas)*

HOUSING, RURAL

— United Kingdom.

IRVING (BARRIE L.) and HILGENDORF (LINDEN) Tied cottages in British agriculture: working paper no.1: basic statistics. London, 1975. pp. 104.

WIDDOWSON (BOB) Agricultural tied cottages: Shelter's reply to the government consultative document on the abolition of agricultural tied cottages. London, [1975]. fo.10.

— United States.

MARANTZ (JANET K.) and others. Discrimination in rural housing: economic and social analysis of six selected markets. Lexington, Mass., [1976]. pp. 213. *bibliog.*

HOUSING AND HEALTH

— United Kingdom.

ROBSON (PAUL) London borough of Newham: public health and housing. London, Canning Town Community Development Project and the Public Health Advisory Service, 1977. pp. 61, vii.

HOUSING MANAGEMENT.

[BIRMINGHAM COMMUNITY DEVELOPMENT PROJECT]. Municipal housing allocation in Birmingham. [Birmingham, 1974]. 1 pamphlet (various pagings).

NATIONAL CONSUMER COUNCIL. Tenancy agreements between councils and their tenants. London, 1976. pp. 44. (Discussion Papers. 2)

PARKER (JOHN) Writer on housing, and DUGMORE (KEITH) Colour and the allocation of GLC housing: the report of the GLC lettings survey, 1974-75. [London], 1976. 1 vol. (various pagings). bibliog. (London. Greater London Council. Research Reports. No. 21)

U.K. Department of the Environment. 1976. Consultation paper: records and information relating to the housing of members of ethnic groups. [London, 1976]. fo.8.

WELSH CONSUMER COUNCIL. Council housing: a survey of allocation policies in Wales. [Cardiff], 1976. pp. 47.

LONDON HOUSING RESEARCH GROUP. Working Party on Race and Housing. Race and local authority housing: information on ethnic groups; a report; [Rob Hammond, chairman]. London, Community Relations Commission, 1977. pp. 16.

SHANKLAND-COX PARTNERSHIP and INSTITUTE OF COMMUNITY STUDIES. Inner area study: Lambeth: housing management and design. [London], Department of the Environment, [1977]. pp. 99.

U.K. Race Relations Board. 1977. Comments on the government's consultation paper on records and information relating to the housing of members of ethnic groups. [London, 1977]. fo.4.

WILSON (HUGH) AND WOMERSLEY (LEWIS) Firm. Inner area study: Liverpool: housing management. [London], Department of the Environment, [1977]. pp. 27, 1 map.

HOUSING POLICY.

BURNS (LELAND S.) and GREBLER (LEO) The housing of nations: analysis and policy in a comparative framework. London, 1977. pp. 255.

— Australia.

AUSTRALIAN INSTITUTE OF URBAN STUDIES. Task Force. Housing for Australia: philosophy and policies. Canberra, 1975. pp. 86. (Australian Institute of Urban Studies. Publications. No. 58)

— Brazil.

BRAZIL DEVELOPMENT SERIES. No.3. São Paulo, 1972. 2 vols. Vol. 2 entitled The National Housing Plan.

— Germany.

HALLETT (GRAHAM) Housing and land policies in West Germany and Britain. London, 1977. pp. 161.

— United Kingdom.

HOUSING strategy in the seventies; (a report of the seminar for local authority chief officers held at the Centre for Extension Studies, Loughborough University of Technology, 27-29 January 1975;...compiled by the Housing Improvement Group/H6 of the Department of the Environment). [Loughborough, 1975]. pp. 67.

FORREST (RAY) and MURIE (ALAN S.) Social segregation, housing need and the sale of council houses. Birmingham, 1976. pp. 50. (Birmingham. University. Centre for Urban and Regional Studies. Research Memoranda. No. 53)

NORTHERN REGION STRATEGY TEAM. Housing in the northern region. Newcastle upon Tyne, 1976. 2 vols. (in 1). (Technical Reports. No.15)

U.K. Department of the Environment. 1977- . Housing policy: technical volume. London, 1977 in progress. Main report published as British Parliamentary Paper Cmnd. 6851, Session 1976-77.

HALLETT (GRAHAM) Housing and land policies in West Germany and Britain. London, 1977. pp. 161.

McKAY (DAVID H.) Housing and race in industrial society: civil rights and urban policy in Britain and the United States. London, [1977]. pp. 193.

— — Birmingham.

LLEWELYN-DAVIES WEEKS [AND PARTNERS]. Inner area study: Birmingham: housing policies for the inner city. [London], Department of the Environment, [1976]. pp. 159. bibliog.

— — London.

CANNING TOWN COMMUNITY DEVELOPMENT PROJECT. Canning Town inside out: housing cuts. [London], 1975. pp. 14.

— — North Tyneside.

NORTH TYNESIDE COMMUNITY DEVELOPMENT PROJECT. The politics of housing in North Tyneside; an action report. [North Shields], 1975. pp. 11.

— — Scotland.

SCOTLAND. Scottish Development Department. 1976. Housing plans. Edinburgh, 1976. pp. 2. (SDD Circulars. 1976/76)

SCOTLAND. Working Party on Housing Plans. 1976. Interim report; [P.C. Rendle, chairman]. [Edinburgh, 1976]. fo.15,2.

SCOTLAND. Scottish Development Department. 1977. Preparation of housing plans, 1977. [Edinburgh], 1977. pp. 5. (SDD Circulars. 1977/6)

SCOTLAND. Working Party on Housing Plans. 1977. Final report; [P.C. Rendle, chairman]. [Edinburgh, 1977]. 1 pamphlet (various pagings).

— United States.

DANIELSON (MICHAEL NILS) The politics of exclusion. New York, 1976. pp. 443.

STEGMAN (MICHAEL A.) and SUMKA (HOWARD J.) Nonmetropolitan urban housing: an economic analysis of problems and policies. Cambridge, Mass., [1976]. pp. 304. bibliog.

McKAY (DAVID H.) Housing and race in industrial society: civil rights and urban policy in Britain and the United States. London, [1977]. pp. 193.

HOUSING RESEARCH.

UNITED NATIONS. Ad Hoc Group of Experts on Social Programming of Housing in Urban Areas. 1971. Social programming of housing in urban areas: report of the Ad Hoc Group of Experts on (its meetings, held) New York, 17- 28 August 1970. (ST/SOA/109). New York, 1971. pp. 81.

UNITED NATIONS. Ad Hoc Group of Experts on Social Indicators for Housing and Urban Development. 1973. Social indicators for housing and urban development: report of the Ad Hoc Group of Experts, Dublin, Ireland, 4-8 October 1971. (ST/ECA/173). New York, 1973. pp. 31.

HOUSING SUBSIDIES

— Ireland (Republic).

NATIONAL ECONOMIC AND SOCIAL COUNCIL [EIRE]. Report on housing subsidies. Dublin, Stationery Office, [1976]. pp. 95. ([Reports]. No. 23)

HOUSING SURVEYS.

NORTHERN IRELAND HOUSING EXECUTIVE. Corporate Planning Department. Housing condition survey, 1974, Northern Ireland: final report. Belfast, [1975]. pp. 59.

HUDDERSFIELD

— Foreign population.

DUNCAN (S.S.) Housing disadvantage and residential mobility: immigrants and institutions in a northern town. Brighton, 1977. fo.28. (Brighton. University of Sussex. Sussex Working Papers in Urban and Regional Studies. 5)

HUGO (VICTOR MARIE) Vicomte.

HERZEN, Ogarev, Bakounine: lettres inédites; introduction, traductions et notes par Michel Mervaud. Paris, 1975. pp. 158. With French translations of letters in German and Russian. Includes in addition eight letters from Victor Hugo to Herzen.

HUK REBELLION.

KERKVLIET (BENEDICT J.) The Huk rebellion: a study of peasant revolt in the Philippines. Berkeley, Calif., [1977]. pp. 305. bibliog.

HUMAN BEHAVIOUR.

BENNETT (SPENCER) and BOWERS (DAVID) An introduction to multivariate techniques for social and behavioural sciences. London, 1976. pp. 156. bibliog.

DISCOURS biologique et ordre social; ([by] Pierre Achard [and others]). Paris, [1977]. pp. 286.

GAULD (ALAN) and SHOTTER (JOHN) Human action and its psychological investigation. London, 1977. pp. 237. bibliog.

HUMAN nature in politics; edited by J. Roland Pennock and John W. Chapman. New York, 1977. pp. 348. bibliog. (American Society for Political and Legal Philosophy. Nomos. 17)

PORTEOUS (JOHN DOUGLAS) Environment and behavior: planning and everyday urban life. Reading, Mass., [1977]. pp. 446. bibliog.

HUMAN CAPITAL

— Brazil.

URBANIZACION y recursos humanos: el caso de San Pablo; Paul Singer, coordinador. Buenos Aires, 1973. pp. 285.

— Germany.

WEISSHUHN (GERNOT) Sozioökonomische Analyse von Bildungs- und Ausbildungsaktivitäten. Berlin, [1977]. pp. 291. bibliog.

— Singapore.

GOH (ROSALIND S.L.) Human resources and productivity in Singapore. [Singapore], National Productivity Board, 1973. fo. 28. bibliog.

— Zambia.

HIGHER education and the labour market in Zambia: expectations and performance; [by] Bikas C. Sanyal and others; (a research project...at the International Institute for Educational Planning). Paris, Unesco, 1976. pp. 373. bibliog.

HUMAN ECOLOGY.

ASHBY (ERIC) Baron Ashby. Reflections on doom. Cardiff, [1974]. pp. 17. (Wales. University of Wales. University College, Cardiff. David Owen Memorial Lectures. No. 3)

HARDY (SHIRLEY-ANNE) Ecologists and the land: a look at the special land issue of Resurgence, Sept.-Oct. 1974. Kingston, Surrey, [1974?]. pp. 22.

ROBERTS (ALAN) "Consumerism" and the ecological crisis. Nottingham, [1974?]. pp. 22. (Spokesman, The. Pamphlets. No. 43)

BECHT (J. EDWIN) and BELZUNG (L.D.) World resource management: key to civilizations and social achievement. Englewood Cliffs, [1975]. pp. 339. *bibliog.*

COLLIER (GEORGE ALLEN) Fields of the Tzotzil: the ecological bases of tradition in highland Chiapas. Austin, Texas, [1975]. pp. 255. *bibliog.*

SMITH (MARGARET LAWS) Towards the creation of a sustainable economy. Chertsey, 1975. pp. 13.

WALTERS (ALAN A.) The outer limits and beyond. London, [1975?]. pp. 12. *(Foundation for Business Responsibilities. Discussion Papers. No.12)*

MAN in urban environments; edited by G.A. Harrison and J.B. Gibson. Oxford, 1976. pp. 367. *bibliogs. Based on a series of meetings held by the Royal Society Study Group on Human Biology in Urban Environments.*

POLSKA AKADEMIA NAUK. Instytut Geografii. Geographia Polonica. 34. Approaches to the study of man-environment interactions: proceedings of the Anglo-Polish Geographical Seminar, Toruń, September 1974; edited by Eric H. Brown and Rajmund Galon. Warszawa, 1976. pp. 290. *bibliogs. Map in end pocket.*

SIMAI (MIHÁLY) World problems, global projections and social conflicts of our globe. Budapest, 1976. pp. 24. *(Hungarian Scientific Council for World Economy. [Publications]. Trends in World Economy. No. 18)*

SMOLE (WILLIAM J.) The Yanoama Indians: a cultural geography. Austin, Tex., [1976]. pp. 272. *bibliog.*

GOODWIN (GARY C.) Cherokees in transition: a study of changing culture and environment prior to 1775. Chicago, 1977. pp. 207. *bibliog. (Chicago. University. Department of Geography. Research Papers. No. 181)*

INTERNATIONAL SOCIETY FOR THE STUDY OF BEHAVIOURAL DEVELOPMENT. Biennial Conference, 3rd, Guildford, 1975. Ecological factors in human development: [papers from the conference]; edited by Harry McGurk. Amsterdam, 1977. pp. 295. *bibliogs.*

PORTEOUS (JOHN DOUGLAS) Environment and behavior: planning and everyday urban life. Reading, Mass., [1977]. pp. 446. *bibliog.*

SCORER (RICHARD SEGAR) The clever moron. London, 1977. pp. 171.

SUBSISTENCE and survival: rural ecology in the Pacific; edited by Timothy P. Bayliss-Smith and Richard G. Feachem. London, 1977. pp. 428. *bibliogs.*

— Bibliography.

STAPP (WILLIAM B.) and LISTON (MARY DAWN) Environmental education: a guide to information sources. Detroit, 1975. pp. 225.

— Directories.

STAPP (WILLIAM B.) and LISTON (MARY DAWN) Environmental education: a guide to information sources. Detroit, 1975. pp. 225.

— Study and teaching — United States.

STAPP (WILLIAM B.) and LISTON (MARY DAWN) Environmental education: a guide to information sources. Detroit, 1975. pp. 225.

HUMAN ENGINEERING.

CONFERENCE ON THE HUMAN OPERATOR IN COMPLEX SYSTEMS, BIRMINGHAM, 1966. Proceedings...; edited by W.T. Singleton [and others] on behalf of the University of Aston in Birmingham and the Industrial Section of the Ergonomics Research Society. London, 1967 repr. 1971. pp. 198. *bibliog.*

HUMAN EVOLUTION.

BLAGA (LUCIAN) Aspecte antropologice; ediţie îngrijită şi prefaţă de Ion Maxim, postfaţă de Al. Tănase. [n.p.], 1976. pp. 203.

HUMAN diversity: its causes and social significance...; edited by Bernard D. Davis and Patricia Flaherty. Cambridge, Mass., [1976]. pp. 248. *bibliog. The proceedings of a series of seminars sponsored by the Committee on Human Diversity of the American Academy of Arts and Sciences 1973-1974.*

STEWARD (JULIAN HAYNES) Evolution and ecology: essays on social transformation; edited by Jane C. Steward and Robert F. Murphy. Urbana, Ill., [1977]. pp. 406. *bibliogs.*

HUMAN GENETICS.

U.K. Central Health Services Council. Standing Medical Advisory Committee. 1972. Human genetics. London, 1972. pp. 20. *bibliog.*

EUGENICS SOCIETY. Annual Symposium, 12th, 1975. Equalities and inequalities in health: proceedings...; edited by C.O. Carter and John Peel. London, 1976. pp. 170. *bibliogs.*

HUMAN diversity: its causes and social significance...; edited by Bernard D. Davis and Patricia Flaherty. Cambridge, Mass., [1976]. pp. 248. *bibliog. The proceedings of a series of seminars sponsored by the Committee on Human Diversity of the American Academy of Arts and Sciences 1973-1974.*

HUMANISM

— 20th century.

RYNER (HAN) pseud. [i.e. Jacques Elie Henri Ambroise Mathieu Ernest NER] Les artisans de l'avenir: conférence prononcée le 27 février à Paris, Salle Procope, pour la première matinée de la ghilde "Les Artisans de l'Avenir". Anvers, 1921. pp. 42.

SCHLETTE (HEINZ ROBERT) Sowjethumanismus: Prämissen und Maximen kommunistischer Pädagogik. München, [1960]. pp. 136.

HUMANITIES

— Methodology.

BROWN (RICHARD HARVEY) A poetic for sociology: toward a logic of discovery for the human sciences. Cambridge, 1977. pp. 302. *bibliog.*

HUMBERSIDE

— Economic conditions.

HUMBERSIDE. County Council. Planning Department. Humberside structure plan: background studies: consultation draft, June 1976. [Beverley] 1976. pp. 177.

— Economic policy.

HUMBERSIDE. County Council. Planning Department. Humberside structure plan: policies: consultation draft, June 1976. [Beverley], 1976. pp. 92.

U.K. Department of the Environment. 1977. Government response to the Yorkshire and Humberside regional strategy review 1975: the next ten years. [London], 1977. pp. 19.

— Maps.

U.K. Department of the Environment. Yorkshire and Humberside Regional Office. 1975- . Yorkshire and Humberside regional atlas. [2nd ed.] [Leeds, 1975 in progress]. 1 vol.(loose-leaf).

— Social conditions.

HUMBERSIDE. County Council. Planning Department. Humberside structure plan: background studies: consultation draft, June 1976. [Beverley], 1976. pp. 177.

— Social policy.

HUMBERSIDE. County Council. Planning Department. Humberside structure plan: policies: consultation draft, June 1976. [Beverley], 1976. pp. 92.

HUMBERT-DROZ (JULES).

HUMBERT-DROZ (JENNY) Une pensée, une conscience, un combat : la carrière politique de Jules Humdert-Droz retracée par sa femme. Neuchâtel, [1976]. pp. 227.

HUME (DAVID)

— Bibliography.

HALL (ROLAND) compiler. A Hume bibliography from 1930. York, 1971. pp. 80.

HUMPHREY (HUBERT HORATIO).

HUMPHREY (HUBERT HORATIO) The education of a public man;...edited by Norman Sherman. Garden City, N.Y., 1976. pp. 513.

HUNAN, CHINA (PROVINCE)

— Politics and government.

LEWIS (CHARLTON M.) Prologue to the Chinese revolution: the transformation of ideas and institutions in Hunan Province, 1891-1907. London, 1976. pp. 317. *bibliog. (Harvard University. East Asian Research Center. Harvard East Asian Monographs. 70)*

HUNGARIAN PERIODICALS

— Bibliography.

MILDSCHUETZ (KOLOMAN) compiler. Bibliographie der ungarischen Exilpresse, 1945-1975; ergänzt und zum Druck vorbereitet von Béla Grolshammer. München, 1977. pp. 149. *(Ungarisches Institut München. Studia Hungarica. 12)*

HUNGARY

— Economic conditions.

RURAL transformation in Hungary; edited by Gy. Enyedi. Budapest, 1976. pp. 116. *bibliogs. (Magyar Tudományos Akadémia. Geographical Research Institute. Studies in Geography in Hungary. 13)*

— Economic history.

GOTTAS (FRIEDRICH) Ungarn im Zeitalter des Hochliberalismus: Studien zur Tisza-Ära, 1875-1890. Wien, 1976. pp. 257. *bibliog. (Österreichische Akademie der Wissenschaften. Kommission für die Geschichte der Österreichisch-Ungarischen Monarchie, 1848-1918. Studien zur Geschichte der Österreichisch-Ungarischen Monarchie. Band 16)*

— Economic policy.

TIMÁR (MÁTYÁS) Reflections on the economic development of Hungary 1967-1973; (translated by Gy. Hajdu). Leyden, 1975. pp. 219. *bibliog.*

GADÓ (OTTÓ) The economic mechanism in Hungary: how it works in 1976. Leyden, 1976. pp. 203. *A revised and enlarged version of the Hungarian Közgazdasági szabályozó rendszerünk 1976-ban.*

— Foreign relations.

PASTOR (PETER) Hungary between Wilson and Lenin: the Hungarian Revolution of 1918-1919 and the big three. New York, 1976. pp. 191. *bibliog. (East European Quarterly. East European Monographs. 20)*

— History — 1848-1849, Uprising of.

DEME (LASZLO) The radical left in the Hungarian revolution of 1848. New York, [1976]. pp. 162. *bibliog. (East European Quarterly. East European Monographs. 19)*

— — 1849-1853.

HIDAS (PETER I.) The metamorphosis of a social class in Hungary during the reign of young Franz Joseph. New York, 1977. pp. 140. *bibliog. (East European Quarterly. East European Monographs. 26)*

HUNGARY(Cont.)

— — 1867-1918.

GOTTAS (FRIEDRICH) Ungarn im Zeitalter des Hochliberalismus: Studien zur Tisza- Ära, 1875-1890. Wien, 1976. pp. 257. *bibliog. (Österreichische Akademie der Wissenschaften. Kommission für die Geschichte der Österreichisch-Ungarischen Monarchie, 1848-1918. Studien zur Geschichte der Österreichisch-Ungarischen Monarchie. Band 16)*

— — 1918-1919, Revolution.

PASTOR (PETER) Hungary between Wilson and Lenin: the Hungarian Revolution of 1918-1919 and the big three. New York, 1976. pp. 191. *bibliog. (East European Quarterly. East European Monographs. 20)*

— — 1956, Revolution.

INTERNATIONAL CONFEDERATION OF FREE TRADE UNIONS. Four days of freedom: the uprising in Hungary and the free trade unions of the world; (translated by Edward Fitzgerald). Brussels, 1957. pp. 215.

— Politics and government.

TOMA (PETER A.) and VÖLGYES (IVÁN) Politics in Hungary. San Francisco, [1977]. pp. 188. *bibliog.*

— Rural conditions.

RURAL transformation in Hungary; edited by Gy. Enyedi. Budapest, 1976. pp. 116. *bibliogs. (Magyar Tudományos Akadémia. Geographical Research Institute. Studies in Geography in Hungary. 13)*

— Social history.

HIDAS (PETER I.) The metamorphosis of a social class in Hungary during the reign of young Franz Joseph. New York, 1977. pp. 140. *bibliog. (East European Quarterly. East European Monographs. 26)*

HUNTER (Sir WILLIAM WILSON).

SKRINE (FRANCIS HENRY) Life of Sir William Wilson Hunter, K.C.S.I., M.A., LL.D. , a vice-president of the Royal Asiatic Society, etc. London, 1901. pp. 496.

HUSÁK (GUSTÁV).

HUSÁK (GUSTÁV) Projevy a stati, duben 1969 - leden 1970. Praha, 1970. pp. 403.

HUSÁK (GUSTÁV) Vybrané projevy, květen 1970 - prosinec 1971. Praha, 1972. pp. 511.

HYDRAULIC ENGINEERING

— Spain.

GARCIA ZARZA (EUGENIO) El aprovechamiento hidroelectrico Salmantino-Zamorano. Salamanca, 1973. pp. 69. *bibliog.*

HYDROGRAPHY

— United Kingdom.

FRIENDLY (ALFRED) Beaufort of the Admiralty: the life of Sir Francis Beaufort, 1774-1857. London, 1977. pp. 362. *bibliog.*

HYGIENE, PUBLIC.

INCONTRO INTERNAZIONALE DI STUDIO SUL RUOLO DELLA REGIONE NELLA ORGANIZZAZIONE DEI SERVIZI SANITARI, BOLZANO, 1967. Atti...Bolzano, 7-8 dicembre 1967; a cura dell'Assessorato Previdenza Sociale e Sanità. Trento, 1968. pp. 192. *(Trentino-Alto Adige. Ufficio Studi Statistica e Programmazione. Quaderni. 11)*

— Bahamas.

HUGHES (HUGH LLEWELYN GLYN) The Bahamas: a survey of the medical services, November, 1960. [Nassau], 1960. pp. 77.

— Canada — British Columbia.

BRITISH COLUMBIA. Department of Health. Annual report. a., 1975(1st)- Victoria. *Supersedes BRITISH COLUMBIA. Health Branch. Annual report of the public health services of British Columbia and BRITISH COLUMBIA. Hospital Insurance Service. Annual report.*

— Ecuador.

ECUADOR. Instituto Nacional de Estadistica. Encuesta anual de recursos y actividades de salud. a., 1973- Quito.

— France.

PROBLEMES de santé dans une agglomération urbaine en mutation: Boulogne-Billancourt; [by] D. Minvielle [and others]. Le Vésinet, Division de la Recherche Médico-Sociale, 1975. pp. 161. *bibliog. With English summary.*

— — Limousin.

INSTITUT NATIONAL DE LA SANTE ET DE LA RECHERCHE MEDICALE [FRANCE]. Division de la Recherche Médico-Sociale. Section Information en Santé Publique. Etudes régionales: le Limousin; recensement de données sanitaires. Le Vésinet, 1972. pp. 66. *bibliog.*

— Germany — Finance.

GRUENDGER (FRITZ) Zum Problem der Bedarfsermittlung bei Investitionen im Bildungs- und Gesundheitswesen: eine vergleichende Untersuchung unter besonderer Berücksichtigung des Schul- und Krankenhaussektors. Berlin, [1977]. pp. 291. *bibliog.*

— Germany, Eastern.

BAER (ADOLAR HEINER) and others, eds. Ausgewählte Probleme der Ökonomie und Planung des Gesundheitswesens der DDR. Jena, 1975. pp. 133. *(Zeitschrift für Ärztliche Fortbildung. Beihefte. 4)*

SANKELMARK-ARBEITSTAGUNG, 1976. Gesundheitspolitische Gegenwartsfrage in der DDR; herausgegeben von Hans Harmsen. Hamburg, 1976. pp. 209.

— Israel.

ISRAEL INFORMATION CENTRE. Information Briefings. 16. Health in Israel. Jerusalem, [1974]. pp. 15.

— Russia.

POPOV (GEORGII ALEKSEEVICH) Ekonomika i planirovanie zdravookhraneniia. Moskva, 1976. pp. 376.

— Tunisia.

CHANGE in Tunisia: studies in the social sciences; edited by Russell A. Stone and John Simmons. Albany, N.Y., 1976. pp. 333. *bibliogs.*

— Underdeveloped areas.

See UNDERDEVELOPED AREAS — Hygiene, Public.

— United Kingdom.

MORRIS (R.J.) Cholera, 1832: the social response to an epidemic. London, [1976]. pp. 235. *bibliog.*

NORTHERN REGION STRATEGY TEAM. Health in the northern region. Newcastle upon Tyne, 1976. 1 vol. (various pagings). *(Technical Reports. No. 13)*

OWEN (DAVID) In sickness and in health: the politics of medicine. London, 1976. pp. 178.

— — Abstracts.

STUDIES ON COMMUNITY HEALTH AND PERSONAL SOCIAL SERVICES: a classified selection of periodical articles and books which appeared in the monthly "Current Literature on Community Health and Personal Social Services"; [pd. by] Department of Health and Social Security Library. a., 1972. London.

— — Bibliography.

U.K. Department of Health and Social Security. Library. Annual list of publications. a., 1975- London.

— — Wales.

GLAMORGAN-GLYNCORRWG COMMUNITY DEVELOPMENT PROJECT. State of the community report: community health and welfare. [Port Talbot], 1972. pp. 27.

— United States — Rhode Island.

MONTEIRO (LOIS A.) Monitoring health status and medical care. Cambridge, Mass., [1976]. pp. 221. *bibliog.*

IAROSLAVL'.

See YAROSLAVL.

IATROGENIC DISEASES.

ILLICH (IVAN D.) Limits to medicine: medical nemesis: the expropriation of health. Harmondsworth, 1977. pp. 296. *First published in 1976. "Definitive version of Medical nemesis - the expropriation of health".*

IBM 370 (COMPUTER).

BURIAN (BARBARA J.) A simplified approach to S/370 assembly language programming. Englewood Cliffs, [1977]. pp. 558.

IBSEN (HENRIK).

EWBANK (INGA-STINA) Shakespeare, Ibsen and the unspeakable. [London], 1976. pp. 27.

ICELAND

— Presidents — Election.

ICELAND. Hagstofa. 1968. Forsetakjör, 30 júní 1968; Presidential election, 1968. Reykjavík, 1968. pp. 15. *(Hagskýrslur Islands. 2. [Series]. 45) With English translations of table headings.*

— Statistics.

ICELAND. Hagstofa. 1976. Tölfraedihandbók, 1974, etc. Reykjavík, 1976. pp. 253. *(Hagskýrslur Islands. 2. [Series]. 63) With English table headings.*

IDEALISM.

ROZENTAL' (MARK MOISEEVICH) Materialistische und idealistische Weltanschauung; [translated from the Russian by Gerhard Harig]. Berlin, [1947]. pp. 47.

IDENTIFICATION.

HAIN (PETER) Mistaken identity: the wrong face of the law. London, 1976. pp. 184.

IDENTITY.

KAPLAN (MORTON A.) Alienation and identification. New York, [1976]. pp. 206.

IDEOLOGY.

CHAMPION DE CRESPIGNY (ANTHONY RICHARD) and CRONIN (JEREMY) eds. Ideologies of politics. Cape Town, 1975. pp. 160.

POST (HEINZ R.) Against ideologies. London, [1975?]. pp. 18. *Inaugural lecture given at Chelsea College in 1974.*

MITIN (MARK BORISOVICH) Problemy sovremennoi ideologicheskoi bor'by: kritika sotsiologicheskikh i sotsial'no-politicheskikh kontseptsii. Moskva, 1976. pp. 319.

ROSE (HILARY) and ROSE (STEVEN) eds. The political economy of science: ideology of/in the natural sciences. London, 1976. pp. 218.

CARLTON (ERIC JAMES) Ideology and social order. London, 1977. pp. 320. *bibliog.*

CULTURE and its creators: essays in honor of Edward Shils; edited by Joseph Ben-David and Terry Nichols Clark. Chicago, 1977. pp. 325.

FRANZ (PETER) and JANKOW (MITRJU) Information contra Materialismus?: zum Missbrauch der Informationswissenschaften in der gegenwärtigen bürgerlichen Ideologie. Berlin, 1977. pp. 124.

LACLAU (ERNESTO) Politics and ideology in marxist theory: capitalism, fascism, populism. London, 1977. pp. 203.

LOYE (DAVID) The leadership passion: (a psychology of ideology). San Francisco, 1977. pp. 249. bibliog.

SELIGER (MARTIN) The marxist conception of ideology: a critical essay. Cambridge, 1977. pp. 229. bibliog.

IDOLS AND IMAGES

— Worship.

PEGGS (JAMES) India's cries to British humanity, relative to infanticide, British connection with idolatry, Ghaut murders, suttee, slavery, and colonization in India; to which are added, humane hints for the melioration of the state of society in British India. London, 1832. pp. 500.

IGLESIAS POSSE (PABLO).

IGLESIAS POSSE (PABLO) Escritos 1: reformismo social y lucha de clases y otros textos; edicion a cargo de Santiago Castillo y Manuel Perez Ledesma. Madrid, 1975. pp. 330.

LOSADA (JUAN) Ideario politico de Pablo Iglesias. Barcelona, 1976. pp. 243. bibliog.

ILCHESTER PRISON.

VISITS to a prison: a peep at the prisoners: and a description of the interior of Ilchester gaol: in letters to a friend. Guernsey, 1976. pp. 17. Photocopy reprint of work published at Ilminster in 1821.

ILLEGITIMACY

— United Kingdom.

LASLETT (PETER) Family life and illicit love in earlier generations: essays in historical sociology. Cambridge, 1977. pp. 270. bibliog.

ILLICH (IVAN D.).

SNYDERS (GEORGES) Ecole, classe et lutte des classes: une relecture critique de Baudelot-Establet, Bourdieu-Passeron et Illich. Paris, [1976]. pp. 379.

ILLINOIS STATE UNIVERSITY.

KOCH (JAMES V.) and CHIZMAR (JOHN F.) The economics of affirmative action. Lexington, Mass., [1976]. pp. 158. bibliog.

ILLITERACY

— Ethiopia.

SJÖSTRÖM (MARGARETA) and SJÖSTRÖM (ROLF) Literacy schools in a rural society: a study of Yemissrach Dimts literacy campaign in Ethiopia. Uppsala, 1977. pp. 130. bibliog. (Nordiska Afrikainstitutet. Research Reports. No. 39)

— India.

NATARAJAN (D.) Extracts from the all India census reports on literacy. [Delhi, 1972]. pp. 118. (India. Census, 1971. Census Centenary Monographs. No.9)

IMPERIAL PREFERENCE.

McINTYRE (ALISTER) The effects of reverse preferences on trade among developing countries. (TD/B/435). New York, United Nations, 1974. pp. 105. (Conference on Trade and Development. Current Problems on Economic Integration)

IMPERIALISM.

BRITISH AND IRISH COMMUNIST ORGANISATION. Policy Statements. No. 8. Imperialism. Belfast, 1975. pp. 63.

VALIER (JACQUES) Sur l'impérialisme. Paris, 1975. pp. 166.

BOUVIER (JEAN) and GIRAULT (RENE) eds. L'impérialisme français d'avant 1914: recueil de textes. Paris, [1976]. pp. 335. bibliogs. (Paris. Ecole des Hautes Etudes en Sciences Sociales. Le Savoir Historique. 10)

KLEIN (FRITZ) ed. Studien zum deutschen Imperialismus vor 1914. Berlin, 1976. pp. 291. (Akademie der Wissenschaften der DDR. Zentralinstitut für Geschichte. Schriften. Band 47)

O'NEIL (DANIEL J.) Three perennial themes of anti-colonialism: the Irish case. Denver, Colo., [1976]. pp. 131. (Denver. University. Social Science Foundation and Graduate School of International Studies. Monograph Series in World Affairs. vol. 14, no. 1)

GILLARD (DAVID R.) The struggle for Asia, 1828-1914: a study in British and Russian imperialism. London, 1977. pp. 214. bibliog.

IMPORT QUOTAS

— Europe, Eastern.

UNITED NATIONS. Conference on Trade and Development. 1972. The decision-making process in respect of imports in selected socialist countries of Eastern Europe. (TD/B/341/Rev.1). New York, 1972. pp. 22.

— India.

INDIA. Ministry of Foreign Trade and Supply. 1969. Import trade control policy for the year April 1969-March 1970. [Delhi, 1969]. 2 vols. (in 1).

— United Kingdom.

CABLE (VINCENT) Import controls: the case against. London, 1977. pp. 32. (Fabian Society. Research Series. [No.] 335)

— United States.

BARZEL (YORAM) and HALL (CHRISTOPHER D.) The political economy of the oil import quota. Stanford, [1977]. pp. 96. bibliog. (Stanford University. Hoover Institution on War, Revolution and Peace. Hoover Institution Publications. 172)

IMPRISONMENT

— United Kingdom.

LEVENSON (HOWARD) Children in prison. London, 1976. pp. 21. (National Council for Civil Liberties. Reports. No.15)

INCAS.

MURRA (JOHN VICTOR) Formaciones economicas y politicas del mundo andino. Lima, 1975. pp. 339. bibliog. (Instituto de Estudios Peruanos. Historia Andina. 3)

INCENTIVES IN INDUSTRY.

LOKTEV (VLADIMIR PETROVICH) Ekonomicheskie rychagi upravleniia v usloviiakh razvitogo sotsializma. Minsk, 1976. pp. 95.

— America, North.

VOLPE (JOHN) Industrial incentive policies and programs in the Canadian-American context. [Washington], 1976. pp. 53.

— Thailand — Mathematical models.

AKRASANEE (NARONGCHAI) and WIBOONCHUTIKUL (PAITOON) Incentives and factor intensity in the manufacturing sector in Thailand. Bangkok, 1976. pp. 39. bibliog. (Bangkok. Thammasat University. Faculty of Economics. Discussion Paper Series. No. 52)

INCLOSURES.

HESLOP (LUKE) A comparative statement of the food produced from arable and grass land, and the returns arising from each; with observations on the late inclosures, and the probable effect of a general act for inclosing commons or wastes, heaths, etc.; together with other matters; addressed to John Fane, Esq. M.P. London, Reynolds, 1801. pp. iv, 18.

TURNER (M.E.) Land shortage as a prelude to Parliamentary enclosure: the example of Buckinghamshire. Sheffield, 1975. pp. 22. (Sheffield. University. Department of Economic and Social History. Studies in Economic and Social History. 1)

INCOME

— Argentine Republic.

RUBINSTEIN (JUAN CARLOS) Urbanizacion, estructura de ingresos y movilidad social en Argentina, 1960-1970. Santiago de Chile, 1972. pp. 46. (Instituto Latinoamericano de Investigaciones Sociales. Estudios y Documentos. 14)

— Peru.

WEBB (RICHARD CHARLES) Government policy and the distribution of income in Peru, 1963- 1973. Cambridge, Mass., 1977. pp. 239. (Harvard University. Harvard Economic Studies. vol. 147)

— Sweden.

SWEDEN. Statistiska Centralbyrån. Folkpensionärernas inkomstförhållanden: Incomes for national basic pensioners. a., 1974- Stockholm. [in Swedish with summary and table headings in English].

— United Kingdom.

KRISHNA-MURTY (R.) Earnings and incomes data for Greater London. rev. ed. London, 1977. pp. 68. (London. Greater London Council. Research Memoranda. 504)

INCOME DISTRIBUTION.

MERA (KOICHI) Income distribution and regional development. Tokyo, 1975. pp. 242. bibliog.

GRANTS and exchange; editor Martin Pfaff. Amsterdam, 1976. pp. 485. Based on papers from a series of international conferences held in 1972 and sponsored by the Association for the Study of the Grants Economy and the Committee on Comparative Urban Economics.

HIRSCH (FRED) Social limits to growth. Cambridge, Mass., 1976. pp. 208. bibliog.

BROWN (Sir ERNEST HENRY PHELPS) The inequality of pay. Oxford, 1977. pp. 360. bibliog.

RITZEN (JOZEF MARIA MATHIAS) Education, economic growth and income distribution. Amsterdam, 1977. pp. 271. bibliog. Proefschrift (doctor in de economische wetenschappen)- Erasmus Universiteit Rotterdam.

— Mathematical models.

MIYAZAWA (KEN'ICHI) Input-output analysis and the structure of income distribution. Berlin, 1976. pp. 135. bibliog.

RELEVANCE and precision: from quantitative analysis to economic policy; essays in honour of Pieter de Wolff; editors J.S. Cramer [and others]. Alphen aan den Rijn, 1976. pp. 318. bibliogs.

— Bangladesh.

ISLAM (RIZWANUL) Factor intensity and labour absorption in manufacturing industries: the case of Bangladesh. 1976. fo. 471. bibliog. Typescript. Ph.D. (London) thesis: unpublished. This thesis is the property of London University and may not be removed from the Library.

INCOME DISTRIBUTION.(Cont.)

— Brazil.

CAMBRIDGE. University. Centre of Latin American Studies. Working Papers. No. 11. Distribution of earnings, growth and structure of demand in Brazil, 1959-1971; [by John Wells]. Cambridge, [1973]. fo. 39. *bibliog. Photocopy.*

— Canada.

JOHNSON (LEO A.) Poverty in wealth: the capitalist labour market and income distribution in Canada. rev. ed. Toronto, 1974. pp. 35.

KITCHEN (BRIGITTE) Canadian controversy over family income support policies, 1928-1976. 1977. fo. 511. *bibliog. Typescript. Ph.D. (London) thesis: unpublished. This thesis is the property of London University and may not be removed from the Library.*

— Finland.

FINLAND. Tilastokeskus. 1976. Finnish survey on relative income differences, (1971); supervised by Jorma Linnaila. Helsinki, 1976. pp. 79. *(Tutkimuksia. 35)*

FINLAND. Tilastokeskus. 1976. Tulonjako: kotitalouksien ja yksityisten tulonsaajien tulonjako ja sen kehitys vuosina 1966-1974. Helsinki, 1976. pp. 52. *(Tutkimuksia. 37)*

— Germany.

ADAM (HERMANN) Die Einkommensverteilung in der Bundesrepublik Deutschland. Köln, [1976]. pp. 56.

HEILMANN (MARTIN) Die Umverteilung der Einkommen durch den Staat in der Bundesrepublik Deutschland, 1960-1972. Göttingen, [1976]. pp. 138. *bibliog. (Kommission für Wirtschaftlichen und Sozialen Wandel. Schriften. 71)*

VEREIN FÜR SOZIALPOLITIK. Schriften. Neue Folge. Band 75/V. Öffentliche Finanzwirtschaft und Verteilung, V; von Willi Albers [and others]; herausgegeben von Wilhelmine Dreissig. Berlin, [1977]. pp. 202. *With summaries and table of contents in English.*

— India.

LOPEZ (MICHAEL) The determinants of income and its distribution in four villages in India. Ann Arbor, 1977. pp. 31,45. *(Michigan University. Center for Research on Economic Development. Discussion Papers. No. 64)*

— Malaysia.

THILLAINATHAN (RAMASAMY) An analysis of the effects of policies for the redistribution of income and wealth in West Malaysia, 1957-1975. 1976. fo. 300. *bibliog. Typescript. Ph.D. (London) thesis: unpublished. This thesis is the property of London University and may not be removed from the Library.*

— Netherlands.

NETHERLANDS. Centraal Bureau voor de Statistiek. Inkomensverdeling: regionale gegevens [and] Aanvullende gegevens: Distribution of personal income: regional data [and] Additional data. irreg., 1958- 's-Gravenhage.

MASSIZZO (A.I.V.) De personele inkomensverdeling, 1952-1967. 's-Gravenhage, Staatsuitgeverij, 1975. pp. 178. *bibliog. (Netherlands. Centraal Planbureau. Monografieën. No. 19)*

— Peru.

WEBB (RICHARD CHARLES) and FIGUEROA (ADOLFO) Distribucion del ingreso en el Peru. Lima, 1975. pp. 167. *(Instituto de Estudios Peruanos. Peru Problema. 14)*

WEBB (RICHARD CHARLES) Government policy and the distribution of income in Peru, 1963- 1973. Cambridge, Mass., 1977. pp. 239. *(Harvard University. Harvard Economic Studies. vol. 147)*

— Sweden.

SWEDEN. Statistiska Centralbyrån. Inkomstfördelningsstudien. a., 1972 (1st)- Stockholm.

SWEDEN. Statistiska Centralbyrån. Inkomstfördelningen inom regioner: Income distribution in various regions. a., 1975- Stockholm. *[in Swedish and English].*

SWEDEN. Statistiska Centralbyrån. Inkomst- och förmögenhetsfördelningen: Income and wealth distribution. a., current issue only. Stockholm. *[in Swedish and English].*

— United Kingdom.

BROWN (CHARLES VICTOR) The impact of tax changes on income distribution. London, 1973. pp. 31. *(Institute for Fiscal Studies. Publications. No. 4)*

CITY CAPITAL MARKETS COMMITTEE. Written evidence to the Royal Commission on the Distribution of Income and Wealth. [London], 1975. fo. 12.

COMMUNITY RELATIONS COMMISSION. CRC evidence to the Royal Commission on the Distribution of Income and Wealth to aid their inquiry into incomes at the lower levels. London, 1976. pp. 17. *bibliog.*

TRADES UNION CONGRESS. The distribution of income and wealth: a TUC digest of the first four reports of the Royal Commission on the Distribution of Income and Wealth. London, 1976. pp. 31.

TRANSPORT AND GENERAL WORKERS' UNION. Inequality: the evidence...to the Royal Commission on the Distribution of Income and Wealth. Nottingham, 1976. pp. 183.

— United States.

KEINTZ (RITA M.) National health insurance and income distribution. Lexington, Mass., [1976]. pp. 218. *bibliog.*

INCOME redistribution; edited by Colin D. Campbell. Washington, D.C., [1977]. pp. 267. *bibliog. Papers presented at a conference jointly sponsored by the American Enterprise Institute for Public Policy Research and the Hoover Institution on War, Revolution and Peace, in Washington, May 20-21 1976.*

JUBILEE for our times: a practical program for income equality; edited by Alvin L. Schorr. New York, 1977. pp. 320.

REYNOLDS (MORGAN) and SMOLENSKY (EUGENE) Public expenditures, taxes, and the distribution of income: the United States, 1950, 1961, 1970. New York, [1977]. pp. 145. *bibliogs. (Wisconsin University, Madison. Institute for Research on Poverty. Monograph Series)*

RURAL poverty and the policy crisis; coedited by Robert O. Coppedge and Carlton G. Davis. Ames, Iowa, 1977. pp. 220. *bibliog. Based on papers presented at a conference held in February 1975, at Gainesville, Florida, sponsored by the University of Florida.*

INCOME MAINTENANCE PROGRAMMES.

GRANTS and exchange; editor Martin Pfaff. Amsterdam, 1976. pp. 485. *Based on papers from a series of international conferences held in 1972 and sponsored by the Association for the Study of the Grants Economy and the Committee on Comparative Urban Economics.*

INCOME TAX.

BARR (NICHOLAS A.) and others. Self-assessment for income tax. London, 1977. pp. 218.

— Australia.

COLLINS (DAVID J.) The Australian personal income tax reforms, 1975-76. London, [1977]. pp. 30. *(Institute for Fiscal Studies. Lecture Series. No. 8)*

— Brazil.

SILVA (FERNANDO ANTONIO REZENDE DA) O imposto sobre a renda e a justiça fiscal. Rio de Janeiro, 1974. pp. 114. *bibliog. (Brazil. Instituto de Planejamento Econômico e Social. Instituto de Pesquisas. Monografias. No. 14)*

— Germany.

HERTZ (PAUL) and RINNER (ERICH) Wie ermässigt man die Lohnsteuer? Berlin, 1927. pp. 64.

— — Law.

DAIBER (HANS JOACHIM) Einkommensteuerliche Folgen der Wohnsitzverlegung ins niedrigbesteuernde Ausland. Nürnberg, 1976. pp. 203,xxxvi. *bibliog.*

— Mexico.

MEXICO. Direccion General del Impuesto sobre la Renta. 1959. Jurisprudencia de la Suprema Corte de Justicia de la Nacion y del Tribunal Fiscal de la Federacion en materia de la ley del impuesto sobre la renta y su reglamento, 1929-1957. Tomo 2. Mexico, 1959. pp. 866.

— — Law.

MEXICO. Statutes, etc. 1953-1974. Ley del impuesto sobre la renta y su reglamento. Mexico, 1963-75. 1 vol. (looseleaf).

MEXICO. Statutes, etc. 1964-1975. Ley del impuesto sobre la renta: confrontada 1974-1975. Mexico, [1975]. pp. 344.

— New Zealand — Law.

RODGERS (J.) Income tax: practice notes. Wellington, N.Z., 1976. Loose-leaf.

— Papua New Guinea.

PAPUA NEW GUINEA. Taxation Office. Annual report. a., 1974/75(16th)- Port Moresby.

— Switzerland.

RICHENBERGER (HANS) Die Besteuerung des Einkommens in der Schweiz: ein Beitrag zur Steuerharmonisierung aus wirtschaftlicher Sicht. Bern, 1976. pp. 163. *bibliog.*

— United Kingdom.

U.K. Board of Inland Revenue. 1973. Income tax and corporation tax: capital allowances on machinery or plant; new system. [London], 1973. pp. 26.

BARR (NICHOLAS A.) and others. Self-assessment for income tax. London, 1977. pp. 218.

— United States.

INFLATION and the income tax; Henry J. Aaron, editor. Washington, D.C., [1976]. pp. 340. *(Brookings Institution. Studies of Government Finance) A report of a conference sponsored by the Fund for Public Policy Research and the Brookings Institution.*

INDEPENDENT REGULATORY COMMISSIONS

— United States.

HOOGENBOOM (ARI ARTHUR) and HOOGENBOOM (OLIVE) A history of the ICC: from panacea to palliative. New York, [1976]. pp. 207. *bibliog.*

INDEX NUMBERS (ECONOMICS).

PLYSHEVSKII (BORIS PAVLOVICH) ed. Effektivnost' obshchestvennogo proizvodstva: kriterii, metody rascheta, pokazateli. Moskva, 1976. pp. 215.

INDEXATION (ECONOMICS).

CAMPBELL (COLIN D.) Over-indexed benefits: the decoupling proposals for social security. Washington, D.C., 1976. pp. 23. *(American Enterprise Institute for Public Policy Research. Domestic Affairs Studies. 46)*

STABILIZATION of the domestic and international economy; editors, Karl Brunner [and] Allan H. Meltzer. Amsterdam, 1977. pp. 318. *bibliogs. (Journal of Monetary Economics. Carnegie- Rochester Conference Series on Public Policy. vol. 5)*

INDIA.

DUNDAS (LAWRENCE JOHN LUMLEY) 2nd Marquess of Zetland. India: a bird's-eye view. London, 1924. pp. 314.

— Census.

INDIA. Census. Papers. 1969. No. 1. General population tables and primary census abstracts of reorganized states of Punjab and Haryana and Union Territories of Chandigarh and Himachal Pradesh. 1961 census. [Delhi, 1972]. pp. 173.

— — Bibliography.

JADHAV (C.G.) compiler. Bibliography of census publications in India...; edited by B.K. Roy Burman. [Delhi, 1972]. pp. 520. *bibliog. (India. Census, 1971. Census Centenary [Monographs].No. 5)*

— Civilization.

INDIA. Ministry of Education, Social Welfare and Culture. Annual report. a., 1973/74- New Delhi.

— Colonization.

PEGGS (JAMES) India's cries to British humanity, relative to infanticide, British connection with idolatry, Ghaut murders, suttee, slavery, and colonization in India; to which are added, humane hints for the melioration of the state of society in British India. London, 1832. pp. 500.

— Commerce.

NAYYAR (DEEPAK) India's exports and export policies in the 1960s. Cambridge, 1976. pp. 392. *bibliog. (Cambridge. University. Centre of South Asian Studies. Cambridge South Asian Studies. No. 19)*

— Commercial policy.

NAYYAR (DEEPAK) India's exports and export policies in the 1960s. Cambridge, 1976. pp. 392. *bibliog. (Cambridge. University. Centre of South Asian Studies. Cambridge South Asian Studies. No. 19)*

SCHUBERT (JOACHIM) Aussenhandel und Unterentwicklung, dargestellt am Beispiel Indiens. Berlin, 1976. pp. 375. *bibliog. Inaugural-Dissertation zur Erlangung des Grades eines Doktors der Wirtschaftswissenschaften der Freien Universität Berlin.*

— Constitution.

SINH (RAGHUBIR) Indian states and the new regime. Calcutta, [imprint], 1937. pp. 469. *Printed for private circulation.*

— Constitutional law.

SEERVAI (H.M.) Constitutional law of India: a critical commentary. 2nd ed. Bombay, 1975-76. 2 vols.

— Defences.

COMBINED INTER-SERVICES HISTORICAL SECTION, INDIA AND PAKISTAN. Official history of the Indian armed forces in the second World War, 1939-45. Defence of India: policy and plans; (by Bisheshwar Prasad). [New Delhi], 1963. pp. 278.

— Description and travel.

[SHERER (JOSEPH MOYLE)] Sketches of India: written by an officer for fire-side travellers at-home. 2nd ed. London, 1824. pp. 358.

ORLICH (LEOPOLD VON) Travels in India, including Sinde and the Punjab;... translated from the German by H. Evans Lloyd. vol. 1. London, 1845. pp. 278. *Letters addressed to Alexander von Humboldt and Carl Ritter, 1842-43.*

SKRINE (FRANCIS HENRY) Life of Sir William Wilson Hunter, K.C.S.I., M.A., LL.D. , a vice-president of the Royal Asiatic Society, etc. London, 1901. pp. 496.

— Economic conditions.

RECORD OF ECONOMIC CONDITIONS IN INDIA, A; [pd by] Office of the Economic Adviser. m., Je/Jl-S 1944 (nos. 58-60). New Delhi.

ISSUES in the Indian economy: papers and proceedings relating to the first conference of the Association of Indian Economics Studies, Albany, New York, August 29-30, 1975; edited by Romesh Diwan. [Troy, N.Y.], 1976. pp. 133.

— Economic history — Sources.

CRAWFURD (JOHN) F.R.S. Letters from British settlers in the interior of India, descriptive of their own condition and that of the native inhabitants under the government of the East India Company. London, Ridgway, 1831. pp. vii,98.

— Economic policy.

MITRA (ASHOK) Growth and diseconomies. Poona, [1975]. pp. 17. *(Gokhale Institute of Politics and Economics. R.R. Kale Memorial Lectures. 1975)*

NIGAM (RAJ KUMAR) Social justice through public sector. New Delhi, [1976]. pp. 64.

ECONOMIC revolution in India; foreword by Indira Gandhi; [edited by] Dr. S.D. Punekar [and others]. Bombay, 1977. pp. 587.

— Emigration and immigration.

TINKER (HUGH) The banyan tree: overseas emigrants from India, Pakistan and Bangladesh. Oxford, 1977. pp. 204.

— Executive departments.

INDIA. Ministry of Education, Social Welfare and Culture. Annual report. a., 1973/74- New Delhi.

INDIA. Ministry of Industry and Civil Supplies. Report. a., 1975/76- New Delhi.

— Foreign economic relations — Poland.

FIKUS (DARIUSZ) Polska-Indie: gospodarka, stosunki ekonomiczne. Warszawa, 1976. pp. 196.

— Foreign relations.

INDIA. Ministry of External Affairs. Report. a., 1969/70- New Delhi.

INDIA. Ministry of External Affairs. 1971. U.N. Assembly session: address by Sardar Swaran Singh, Minister of External Affairs, September 27, 1971. [New Delhi, 1971]. pp. 22.

DUNBAR (WILLIAM) pseud. India in transition. Beverly Hills, [1976]. pp. 80. *bibliog. (Georgetown University. Center for Strategic and International Studies. Washington Papers. vol. 3/31)*

— — Bangladesh.

INDIA. Ministry of External Affairs. 1971. Bangla Desh needs political solution: Foreign Minister Sardar Swaran Singh's address to the National Press Club, Washington, June 17, 1971. [New Delhi, 1971]. pp. 8.

INDIA. Prime Minister. 1971. India recognises Bangla Desh: Prime Minister's statement in Parliament and some important communications from Bangla Desh leaders. [Delhi, 1971]. pp. 17.

— — Germany.

BAROOAH (NIRODE KUMAR) India and the official Germany, 1886-1914. Frankfurt, 1977. pp. 254. *bibliog.*

— Full employment policies.

SIVASWAMY (NADIMINTI RAMA) Employment potential of the Indian industrial sector. Hydrabad, 1976. pp. 200. *bibliog.*

— Historical geography.

SATIN (LOWELL ROBERT) Towards a spatial strategy for Indian development. 1976. pp. 378. *Typescript. Ph.D. (London) thesis: unpublished. This thesis is the property of London University and may not be removed from the Library.*

— History — 1800-1899.

INDIAN society and the beginnings of modernisation, c. 1830-1850; edited by C.H. Philips and Mary Doreen Wainwright. London, 1976. pp. 243. *Discussion papers of a study group which met at the School of Oriental and African Studies, London University, on 15 and 16 December 1975.*

— Industries.

INDIA. Ministry of Industry and Civil Supplies. Report. a., 1975/76- New Delhi.

— Politics and government.

KUMAR (SATISH) ed. India: democracy defied; [selected speeches and statements]. London, [1976]. pp. 19.

— — 1900- .

ROBB (P.G.) The government of India and reform: policies towards politics and the constitution, 1916-1921. Oxford, 1976. pp. 379. *bibliog. (London. University. School of Oriental and African Studies. London Oriental Series. vol. 32)*

— — 1919-1947.

SINH (RAGHUBIR) Indian states and the new regime. Calcutta, [imprint], 1937. pp. 469. *Printed for private circulation.*

LAHIRY (ASHUTOSH) Gandhi in Indian politics: a critical review. Calcutta, 1976. pp. 221.

TOMLINSON (B.R.) The Indian National Congress and the Raj, 1929-1942: the penultimate phase. London, 1976. pp. 208. *bibliog.*

BROWN (JUDITH M.) Gandhi and civil disobedience: the Mahatma in Indian politics, 1928-34. Cambridge, 1977. pp. 414. *bibliog.*

— — 1947- .

GHOSE (SANKAR) Indira Gandhi, the resurgent Congress and socialism. New Delhi, 1975. pp. 58.

HARDGRAVE (ROBERT L.) India: government and politics in a developing nation. 2nd ed. New York, [1975]. pp. 250. *bibliogs.*

COMMITTEE FOR FREEDOM IN INDIA. India: democracy or dictatorship?: a handbook of facts, documents, analysis. Chicago, [1976?]. pp. 79.

DUNBAR (WILLIAM) pseud. India in transition. Beverly Hills, [1976]. pp. 80. *bibliog. (Georgetown University. Center for Strategic and International Studies. Washington Papers. vol. 3/31)*

INDIRA Gandhi's India: a political system reappraised; edited by Henry C. Hart. Boulder, Col., 1976. pp. 313.

NAYAR (KULDIP) The judgement: inside story of the emergency in India. New Delhi, 1977. pp. 228.

— Population.

SATIN (LOWELL ROBERT) Towards a spatial strategy for Indian development. 1976. pp. 378. *Typescript. Ph.D. (London) thesis: unpublished. This thesis is the property of London University and may not be removed from the Library.*

— Rural conditions.

SEN GUPTA (BADAL) Sozialer Wandel im ländlichen Indien: fördernde und hemmende Faktoren der Ergebnisse der Diffusion und Adoption der Innovationen "lokale Selbstverwaltung", etc. [Nürnberg, 1972]. pp. 332. *bibliog. Inaugural-Dissertation zur Erlangung des Grades eines Doktors der Wirtschafts- und Sozialwissenschaften der Friedrich-Alexander-Universität Erlangen-Nürnberg.*

INDIA.(Cont.)

LONDON (PAUL A.) Merchants as promoters of rural development: an Indian case study. New York,1975. pp. 159. *bibliog.*

— Scheduled tribes.

MOSER (RUPERT R.) The situation of the Adivasis of Chotanagpur and Santal Parganas, Bihar, India. Copenhagen, 1972. pp. 11. *(International Work Group for Indigenous Affairs. Documents. 4)*

— Social conditions.

PEGGS (JAMES) India's cries to British humanity, relative to infanticide, British connection with idolatry, Ghaut murders, suttee, slavery, and colonization in India; to which are added, humane hints for the melioration of the state of society in British India. London, 1832. pp. 500.

MAIN currents in Indian sociology. 1. Contemporary India: some sociological perspectives; edited by Giri Raj Gupta. Durham, North Carolina, [1976]. pp. 328. *bibliogs.*

— Social history.

INDIAN society and the beginnings of modernisation, c. 1830-1850; edited by C.H. Philips and Mary Doreen Wainwright. London, 1976. pp. 243. *Discussion papers of a study group which met at the School of Oriental and African Studies, London University, on 15 and 16 December 1975.*

— Social policy.

ECONOMIC revolution in India; foreword by Indira Gandhi; [edited by] Dr. S.D. Punekar [and others]. Bombay, 1977. pp. 587.

INDIAN NATIONAL CONGRESS.

TOMLINSON (B.R.) The Indian National Congress and the Raj, 1929-1942: the penultimate phase. London, 1976. pp. 208. *bibliog.*

INDIAN OCEAN REGION

— Foreign relations.

AUSTRALIA. Parliament. Joint Committee on Foreign Affairs. 1971. Report...on the Indian Ocean region; [J.P. Sim, chairman]. in AUSTRALIA. Parliament. Parliamentary papers, 1971, vol.8.

ADIE (WILLIAM ANDREW CHARLES) Oil, politics and seapower: the Indian Ocean vortex. New York, [1975]. pp. 95. *bibliog. (National Strategy Information Center. Strategy Papers. No. 24)*

— Politics and government.

VÁLI (FERENC ALBERT) Politics of the Indian Ocean region: the balances of power. New York, [1976]. pp. 272. *bibliogs.*

— Relations (general) with Australia.

AUSTRALIA. Parliament. Joint Committee on Foreign Affairs. 1971. Report...on the Indian Ocean region; [J.P. Sim, chairman]. in AUSTRALIA. Parliament. Parliamentary papers, 1971, vol.8.

INDIAN TERRITORY

— History.

MINER (H. CRAIG) The corporation and the Indian: tribal sovereignty and industrial civilization in Indian territory, 1865-1907. Columbia, Mo., 1976. pp. 236. *bibliog.*

INDIANS.

COMAS CAMPS (JUAN) Antropologia de los pueblos iberoamericanos. Barcelona, 1974. pp. 223. *bibliog.*

STEWARD (JULIAN HAYNES) Evolution and ecology: essays on social transformation; edited by Jane C. Steward and Robert F. Murphy. Urbana, Ill., [1977]. pp. 406. *bibliogs.*

— Food.

LIMA (OSWALDO GONÇALVES DE) Pulque, balchê e pajauaru na etnobiologia das bebidas e dos alimentos fermentados. Recife, 1975. pp. 405. *bibliog.*

— Social life and customs.

LIMA (OSWALDO GONÇALVES DE) Pulque, balchê e pajauaru na etnobiologia das bebidas e dos alimentos fermentados. Recife, 1975. pp. 405. *bibliog.*

INDIANS, TREATMENT OF

— Canada.

FUMOLEAU (RENE) As long as this land shall last: a history of Treaty 8 and Treaty 11, 1870-1939. Toronto, [1973?]. pp. 415. *bibliog.*

INDIANS OF CENTRAL AMERICA.

HANDBOOK of middle American Indians. vol. 6. Social anthropology; Manning Nash, volume editor. Austin, Texas, [1967] repr. 1975. pp. 597. *bibliog. Edited at Middle American Research Institute, Tulane University, under the sponsorship of the National Research Council Committee on Latin American Anthropology.*

— Antiquities.

The EARLY Mesoamerican village; edited by Kent V. Flannery. New York, [1976]. pp. 377. *bibliogs.*

INDIANS OF MEXICO.

HANDBOOK of middle American Indians. vol. 6. Social anthropology; Manning Nash, volume editor. Austin, Texas, [1967] repr. 1975. pp. 597. *bibliog. Edited at Middle American Research Institute, Tulane University, under the sponsorship of the National Research Council Committee on Latin American Anthropology.*

MOTOLINIA (TORIBIO) Historia de los indios de la Nueva España: relacion de los ritos antiguos, idolatrias y sacrificios de los indios de la Nueva España, y de la maravillosa conversion que Dios en ellos ha obrado; estudio critico, apendices, notas e indice de Edmundo O'Gorman. Mexico, 1969 repr. 1973. pp. 256. *bibliog. First published in Mexico in 1858.*

ESSAYS on Mexican kinship; Hugo G. Nutini [and others], editors. Pittsburgh, [1976]. pp. 256. *bibliog. Papers of a symposium held at the 1969 annual meeting of the American Anthropological Association in New Orleans.*

KEMPER (ROBERT V.) Migration and adaptation: Tzintzuntzan peasants in Mexico City. Beverly Hills, [1977]. pp. 223. *bibliog.*

— Agriculture.

COLLIER (GEORGE ALLEN) Fields of the Tzotzil: the ecological bases of tradition in highland Chiapas. Austin, Texas, [1975]. pp. 255. *bibliog.*

— Antiquities.

The EARLY Mesoamerican village; edited by Kent V. Flannery. New York, [1976]. pp. 377. *bibliogs.*

— Education.

KOBAYASHI (JOSE MARIA) La educacion como conquista: empresa franciscana en Mexico. Mexico, 1974. pp. 423. *bibliog. (Mexico City. Colegio de Mexico. Centro de Estudios Historicos. Nueva Serie. 19)*

INDIANS OF NORTH AMERICA

— Children.

BEUF (ANN H.) Red children in white America. [Philadelphia], 1977. pp. 155. *bibliog.*

— Employment.

KIRKPATRICK (THOMAS A.) and WINSOR (THOMAS S.) Indian employment and retention in the Upper-Midwest: employment practices in North Dakota, South Dakota, and Montana. Helena, [1975]. pp. 120.

— Race identity.

SIMON (RITA JAMES) and ALTSTEIN (HOWARD) Transracial adoption. New York, [1977]. pp. 197.

— Canada — Government relations.

DENE nation: the colony within; edited by Mel Watkins for the University League for Social Reform. Toronto, [1977]. pp. 187. *bibliogs. Based on material presented at the Mackenzie Valley Pipeline Inquiry (Berger Inquiry).*

— — Ontario.

STYMEIST (DAVID H.) Ethnics and Indians: social relations in a northwestern Ontario town. Toronto, [1975]. pp. 98. *bibliog.*

— United States.

THREE perspectives on ethnicity: Blacks, Chicanos and native Americans; [edited] by Carlos E. Cortés [and others]. New York, [1976]. pp. 429.

— — Indian Territory.

MINER (H. CRAIG) The corporation and the Indian: tribal sovereignty and industrial civilization in Indian territory, 1865-1907. Columbia, Mo., 1976. pp. 236. *bibliog.*

INDIANS OF SOUTH AMERICA.

SYMPOSIUM ON INTER-ETHNIC CONFLICT IN SOUTH AMERICA, BRIDGETOWN, BARBADOS. 1971. Declaration of Barbados; (for the liberation of the Indians); [declaration by members of a symposium sponsored jointly by the Programme to Combat Racism and the Churches Commission on International Affairs of the World Council of Churches, and the Ethnology Department of the University of Berne]. Copenhagen, 1971. pp. 8. *(International Work Group for Indigenous Affairs. Documents. 1)*

— Religion and mythology.

ROTH (WALTER EDMUND) An inquiry into the animism and folk-lore of the Guiana Indians. New York, 1970. pp. 350. *bibliog. First published in 1915 as one of two papers accompanying the thirtieth annual report of the U.S. Bureau of American Ethnology to the Secretary of the Smithsonian Institution 1908-09.*

— Bolivia.

TORRICO PRADO (BENJAMIN) Indigenas en el corazon de America: vid y costumbres de los indigenas de Bolivia. La Paz, 1971. pp. 292.

— Colombia.

REICHEL-DOLMATOFF (GERARDO) The shaman and the jaguar: a study of narcotic drugs among the Indians of Colombia. Philadelphia, 1975. pp. 280. *bibliog.*

— Ecuador.

WHITTEN (NORMAN E.) Ecuadorian ethnocide and indigenous ethnogenesis: Amazonian resurgence amidst Andean colonialism. Copenhagen, 1976. pp. 39. *bibliog. (International Work Group for Indigenous Affairs. Documents. 23)*

— — Government relations.

WHITTEN (NORMAN E.) and others. Sacha Runa: ethnicity and adaptation of Ecuadorian Jungle Quichua. Urbana, Ill., [1976]. pp. 348. *bibliog.*

— Guyana.

MENEZES (MARY NOEL) British policy towards the Amerindians in British Guiana, 1803- 1873. Oxford, 1977. pp. 326. *bibliog.*

— — Government relations.

GUYANA. Ministry of Information and Culture. 1970. A brief outline of the progress of integration in Guyana. [Georgetown], 1970. pp. 64. *bibliog. Cover title: Amerindian integration.*

— New Granada (Viceroyalty).

GONZALEZ (MARGARITA) El Resguardo en el Nuevo Reino de Granada. Bogota, 1970. pp. 197.

— Paraguay.

SUSNIK (BRANISLAVA) El indio colonial del Paraguay ([vol.] 3, [part] 1): el chaqueño. Asuncion, 1971. pp. 195. *bibliog. Vols. 1 and 2 are out of print.*

— Peru.

FARABEE (WILLIAM CURTIS) Indian tribes of eastern Peru. New York, 1971. pp. 194. *bibliog. (Harvard University. Peabody Museum. Papers. vol. 10) Facsimile reprint of the work first published in Cambridge, Mass., 1922.*

INDICTMENTS

— Russia.

MARTYNCHIK (EVGENII GRIGOR'EVICH) Garantii prav obviniaemogo v sude pervoi instantsii; pod redaktsiei...P.S. Nikitiuka. Kishinev, 1975. pp. 219.

INDIVIDUALISM.

POPPER-LYNKEUS (JOSEF) Das Individuum und die Bewertung menschlicher Existenzen. Dresden, 1910. pp. 223.

INDIVIDUALIZED INSTRUCTION.

JAY (PEGGY) No one to laugh at you. London, 1973. pp. 15. *(Fabian Society. Fabian Occasional Papers. 7)*

INDOCHINA

— Politics and government.

CAMERON (ALLAN W.) Indochina: prospects after the end. Washington, 1976. pp. 37. *(American Enterprise Institute for Public Policy Research. Foreign Affairs Studies. 35)*

INDONESIA

— Commerce.

INDONESIA. Biro Pusat Statistik. Buletin statistik perdagangan: ekspor: Trade statistical bulletin: exports. m. (formerly irreg.), Ja/Mr 1975 (no.1)- Jakarta. *[in Indonesian and English].*

INDONESIA. Biro Pusat Statistik. Buletin statistik perdagangan: impor: Trade statistical bulletin: imports. m. (formerly irreg.) F/Mr 1975- Jakarta. *[in Indonesian and English].*

— Commercial policy.

INDONESIA. 1970. Regulations of the government of the republic of Indonesia concerning improvements and reforms in trade, monetary and fiscal policies as from April 17, 1970. [Djakarta], 1970. pp. 79.

— Economic conditions — Bibliography.

CWIK (HANS JUERGEN) and others, compilers. Entwicklungswirtschaftlich relevante Ressourcen in den A[ssociation of] S[outh]-E[ast] A[sian] N[ations]-Ländern, Auswahlbibliographie: A select bibliography, etc. Hamburg, 1974. pp. 133. *(Hamburg. Institut für Asienkunde. Dokumentations- Leitstelle Asien. Dokumentationsdienst Asien. Reihe A. 5)*

— Economic history.

BURGER (DIONIJS HUIBERT) Sociologisch-economische geschiedenis van Indonesia; (met een historiografische introductie door J.S. Wigboldus). The Hague, 1975. 2 vols. *bibliogs.*

— Economic policy.

INDONESIA. Department of Information. 1973. Indonesia develops: repelita 2: second five year development plan, 1974/75-1978/79. [Djakarta, 1973]. pp. 30.

— Foreign economic relations — Japan.

NISHIHARA (MASASHI) The Japanese and Sukarno's Indonesia: Tokyo-Jakarta relations, 1951-1966. Honolulu, [1976]. pp. 244. *bibliog. (Kyoto. University. Center for Southeast Asian Studies. Monographs: English Series. 8)*

— Foreign relations.

SUHARTO (T.N.J.) Statement...to the summit meeting of the third Conference of Non- Aligned Countries, Lusaka, September 8-10, 1970. [Djakarta], Department of Information, [1970]. pp. 17.

WEINSTEIN (FRANKLIN B.) Indonesian foreign policy and the dilemma of dependence: from Sukarno to Soeharto. Ithaca, 1976. pp. 384.

— — Japan.

VAN vriend tot vijand: de betrekkingen tusschen Nederlandsch-Indië en Japan; samengesteld onder toezicht van A.C.D. de Graeff door M. Boerstra [and others]. Amsterdam, 1945. pp. 382.

TEKTJENG (LIE) An Indonesian perspective: Japanese-Indonesian relations in the seventies. Djakarta, 1971. pp. 19. *(Lembaga Ilmu Pengetahuan Indonesia. Lembaga Research Kebudajaan Nasional. Terbitan Tak Berkala. No. 2/5)*

NISHIHARA (MASASHI) The Japanese and Sukarno's Indonesia: Tokyo-Jakarta relations, 1951-1966. Honolulu, [1976]. pp. 244. *bibliog. (Kyoto. University. Center for Southeast Asian Studies. Monographs: English Series. 8)*

— — Russia.

SHOLMOV (IURII ALEKSEEVICH) Sovetskii Soiuz - Indoneziia, 1945-1954. Moskva, 1976. pp. 165. *bibliog.*

— Historiography.

BURGER (DIONIJS HUIBERT) Sociologisch-economische geschiedenis van Indonesia; (met een historiografische introductie door J.S. Wigboldus). The Hague, 1975. 2 vols. *bibliogs.*

— History.

JONKMAN (JAN ANNE) Nederland en Indonesië beide vrij, gezien vanuit het Nederlands Parlement: memoires. Assen, 1977. pp. 298.

— Politics and government.

INDONESIA. President, 1968- (Suharto). Address of state by the President of the republic of Indonesia before the House of Representatives on the eve of the 25th independence day; Djakarta, August 16, 1970. [Djakarta, 1970]. pp. 52.

— Population.

NAIM (MOCHTAR) Voluntary migration in Indonesia. Singapore, 1974. pp. 41. *(University of Singapore. Department of Sociology. Working Papers. No.26)*

— Race question.

MACKIE (J.A.C) ed. The Chinese in Indonesia: five essays. Melbourne, 1976. pp. 282. *bibliog.*

— Relations (general) with the United States.

SUHARTO (T.N.J.) Address[es] by the President of the republic of Indonesia [on a visit to the United States, 1970]. [Djakarta, 1970]. 5 pts.

— Social history.

BURGER (DIONIJS HUIBERT) Sociologisch-economische geschiedenis van Indonesia; (met een historiografische introductie door J.S. Wigboldus). The Hague, 1975. 2 vols. *bibliogs.*

— Social policy.

INDONESIA. Department of Information. 1973. Indonesia develops: repelita 2: second five year development plan, 1974/75-1978/79. [Djakarta, 1973]. pp. 30.

INDUSTRIAL ACCIDENTS

— France.

FRANCE. Direction de la Documentation. La Documentation Française. Notes et Etudes Documentaires. Nos. 4,257-4, 258-4,259. Les accidents du travail en France; par Odile Godard. Paris, 1976. pp. 104. *bibliog.*

— Israel.

ISRAEL. National Insurance Institute. Bureau of Research and Planning. 1976. Beneficiaries of workmen's compensation benefits in the years 1970-1972; by Yosi Mutsafi and Rivka Prior. Jerusalem, 1976. pp. 401. *(Surveys. No.19) In English and Hebrew.*

— Italy.

ITALY. Istituto Nazionale per l'Assicurazione contro gli Infortuni sul Lavoro. Centro di Informazione e di Documentazione Infortunistica. Statistiche per la prevenzione. s-a., My/D 1974- Roma. *File in two parts; Serie Monografica and Serie Dati globali.*

— United Kingdom.

LEE (G.L.) and WRENCH (K. J.) Accidents are colour-blind: industrial accidents and the immigrant worker; a pilot study; published...for the Birmingham Community Relations Council. [London], Community Relations Commission, 1977. pp. 24. *bibliog.*

— — Ireland, Northern.

IRELAND, NORTHERN. Factory Inspectorate. Report. a., 1974- Belfast. *1950-1973 included in IRELAND, NORTHERN. Parliament. House of Commons. [Papers].*

INDUSTRIAL CAPACITY

— Canada.

CANADA. Statistics Canada. Capacity utilization rates in Canadian manufacturing. q., 1976 (3rd)- Ottawa. *[in English and French].*

— Tanzania.

WANGWE (S.M.) The problem of underutilization of capacity in industry: a case study of the Mara dairy industry. Dar es Salaam, 1975. pp. 37. *(Dar es Salaam. University. Economic Research Bureau. ERB Papers. 75.4)*

INDUSTRIAL CONCENTRATION.

ORNSTEIN (STANLEY I.) Industrial concentration and advertising intensity. Los Angeles, [1977]. pp. 85. *(American Enterprise Institute for Public Policy Research. AEI Studies. 152)*

— Colombia.

MISAS A. (GABRIEL) Contribucion al estudio del grado de concentracion en la industria colombiana. Santiago de Chile, 1973. pp. 111. *bibliog. (Instituto Latinoamericano de Investigaciones Sociales. Estudios y Documentos. 26)*

— Germany.

GERMANY (BUNDESREPUBLIK). Monopolkommission. 1977. Mehr Wettbewerb ist möglich: (Hauptgutachten 1973/75). 2nd ed. Baden-Baden, 1977. pp. 751. *(Hauptgutachten. 1)*

— South Africa.

SOUTH AFRICA. Commission of Inquiry into the Regulation of Monopolistic Conditions Act, 1955. 1977. Report (R.P. 64/1977). in SOUTH AFRICA. Parliament. House of Assembly. Votes and proceedings; (with Printed annexures).

— Switzerland.

HOEPFLINGER (FRANÇOIS) Das unheimliche Imperium: Wirtschaftsverflechtung in der Schweiz. Zürich, [1977]. pp. 251.

INDUSTRIAL CONCENTRATION.(Cont.)

— United Kingdom.

GEORGE (KENNETH DESMOND) Big business, competition and the state; an inaugural lecture given on 13 November 1974 at University College, Cardiff. Cardiff, [1974]. pp. 17.

PRAIS (SIGBERT JON) The evolution of giant firms in Britain: a study of the growth of concentration in manufacturing industry in Britain, 1909-70. Cambridge, 1976. pp. 321. *bibliog. (National Institute of Economic and Social Research. Economic and Social Studies. 30)*

HANNAH (LESLIE) and KAY (JOHN ANDERSON) Concentration in modern industry: theory, measurement and the U.K. experience. London, 1977. pp. 144. *bibliog.*

JEWKES (JOHN) Delusions of dominance: a critique of the theory of large-scale industrial dominance and of the pretence of government to "restructure" British industry. London, 1977. pp. 62. *bibliog. (Institute of Economic Affairs. Hobart Papers. 76)*

— United States.

CONFERENCE ON INDUSTRIAL CONCENTRATION, AIRLIE HOUSE, VIRGINIA, 1974. Industrial concentration: the new learning; edited by Harvey J. Goldschmid [and others]. Boston, Mass., 1974. pp. 470. *bibliogs. Papers of the conference sponsored by Columbia University School of Law.*

INDUSTRIAL DEVELOPMENT BONDS

— United States.

HELLMAN (DARYL A.) and others. State financial incentives to industry. Lexington, [1976]. pp. 146. *bibliog.*

INDUSTRIAL DISTRICTS

— Russia.

NOVYE industrial'nye goroda: opyt proektirovaniia. Leningrad, 1975. pp. 94.

INDUSTRIAL HYGIENE.

CIBA FOUNDATION. Symposia. New Series. 32. Health and industrial growth; [editors Katherine Elliott and Julie Knight]. Amsterdam, 1975. pp. 267. *bibliogs.*

— European Economic Community countries.

EUROPEAN COAL AND STEEL COMMUNITY. 1969. Répertoire des centres de recherche des Communautés européennes: médecine du travail. Luxembourg, 1969. pp. 209. *(Collection d'Hygiène et de Médecine du Travail. Numéro hors série)*

— Russia.

HARMSEN (HANS) ed. Gesundheitspolitisch relevante Probleme der neuen Gesetzgebung in der DDR wie auch in Ungarn und der UdSSR. Hamburg, 1977. pp. 136. *(Akademie für Staatsmedizin in Hamburg. Zur Entwicklung und Organisation des Gesundheitswesens in der DDR unter Berücksichtigung der UdSSR und Osteuropäischer Volksdemokratien. Band 74)*

— United Kingdom — Laws and legislation.

REDGRAVE (ALEXANDER) Health and safety in factories: replacing Redgrave's Factories Acts 22nd edition; [edited] by Ian Fife and E. Antony Machin. London, 1976. pp. 1949.

— United States.

BUREAU OF NATIONAL AFFAIRS. O[ccupational] S[afety and] H[ealth] A[ct] and the unions: bargaining on job safety and health. Washington, [1973]. pp. 56.

— — Law and legislation.

SMITH (ROBERT STEWART) The Occupational Health and Safety Act: its goals and its achievements. Washington, 1976. pp. 104. *(American Enterprise Institute for Public Policy Research. Evaluative Studies. 25)*

INDUSTRIAL LAWS AND LEGISLATION

— Russia.

ABOVA (TAMARA EVGEN'EVNA) Okhrana khoziaistvennykh prav predpriiatii. Moskva, 1975. pp. 215.

KUZ'MIN (VLADIMIR FEDOROVICH) Kreditnye i raschetnye pravootnosheniia v promyshlennosti. Moskva, 1975. pp. 200.

— United Kingdom.

POLITICAL ECONOMY COLLECTIVE. Workers and the industry bill: time for a rank and file response. London, 1975. pp. 32.

INDUSTRIAL MANAGEMENT.

MANAGEMENT RESEARCH GROUPS. General Series. No. 1. Management Research Groups: what they are and how they work. London, 1927. pp. 16.

BROWN (GEOFF) Sabotage: a study in industrial conflict. Nottingham, 1977. pp. 396.

CALVERT (JOHN ROBERT) Authority and democracy in industry: the relevance of theories of industrial democracy to contemporary industrial organizations. 1976[or rather 1977]. fo.456. *bibliog. Typescript. Ph.D.(London) thesis: unpublished. This thesis is the property of London University and may not be removed from the Library.*

VANEK (JAROSLAV) The labor-managed economy: essays. Ithaca, N.Y., 1977. pp. 287. *bibliogs.*

— Germany, Eastern.

SOZIALISTISCHE Betriebswirtschaft...: Lehrbuch, ([edited by] Hans Arnold [and others]). 3rd ed. Berlin, [1975]. pp. 792. *bibliog.*

— Poland.

CHOLIŃSKI (TADEUSZ) Przedsiębiorstwo a bank. Warszawa, 1972. pp. 146.

— Russia.

LAVRIKOV (IURII ALEKSANDROVICH) and others. Integratsiia sotsialisticheskogo proizvodstva i upravlenie. Moskva, 1976. pp. 278. *bibliog.*

PROBLEMY sovershenstvovaniia upravleniia sotsialisticheskoi ekonomikoi. Moskva, 1976. pp. 272.

— United Kingdom.

NORTH west regional symposium: manufacturing management and the industrial technologies: symposium papers. [London], Department of Industry, Industrial Technologies Secretariat, 1976. pp. 73.

TURNER (HERBERT ARTHUR) and others. Management characteristics and labour conflict: a study of managerial organisation, attitudes and industrial relations. Cambridge, 1977. pp. 80. *(Cambridge. University. Department of Applied Economics. Papers in Industrial Relations and Labour. 3)*

INDUSTRIAL ORGANIZATION.

LUPTON (THOMAS) Problems of morale and staff relations in large organisations; (transcript of lecture given on 21 May 1974). [London], Civil Service College, [1974]. pp. 10. *(Lectures on Some Management Problems in the Civil Service. No. 4)*

HARVEY (EDWARD B.) Industrial society: structures, roles, and relations. Homewood, Ill., 1975. pp. 417. *bibliog.*

BELOUSOV (REM ALEKSANDROVICH) Plan, Interessen und Aktivität der Werktätigen; (Übersetzer [from the Russian]: Günter Wermusch). Berlin, 1976. pp. 223. *bibliog.*

HERBST (PHILIP G.) Alternatives to hierarchies. Leiden, 1976. pp. 111. *bibliog.*

PORTER (MICHAEL E.) Interbrand choice, strategy, and bilateral market power. Cambridge, Mass., 1976. pp. 264. *bibliog. (Harvard University. Harvard Economic Studies. vol. 146)*

SIMMONS (D.A.) Economic power. Northolt, Middx., 1976. pp. 192. *bibliog.*

SUSMAN (GERALD I.) Autonomy at work: a sociotechnical analysis of participative management. New York, 1976. pp. 230. *bibliog.*

KANTER (ROSABETH MOSS) Men and women of the corporation. New York, [1977]. pp. 348. *bibliog.*

— China.

ANDORS (STEPHEN) China's industrial revolution: politics, planning and management, 1949 to the present. London, [1977]. pp. 344. *bibliog.*

— France.

DYAS (GARETH P.) and THANHEISER (HEINZ T.) The emerging European enterprise: strategy and structure in French and German industry. London, 1976. pp. 337. *bibliog.*

— Germany.

DYAS (GARETH P.) and THANHEISER (HEINZ T.) The emerging European enterprise: strategy and structure in French and German industry. London, 1976. pp. 337. *bibliog.*

— Germany, Eastern.

LEITUNG der sozialistischen Wirtschaft: Einführung; herausgegeben von Gerd Friedrich [and others]. Berlin, [1976]. pp. 348.

WISSENSCHAFT und Produktion im Sozialismus: zur organischen Verbindung der Errungenschaften der wissenschaftlich-technischen Revolution...; (Autorenkollektiv: Hans-Joachim Beyer [and others]). Berlin, 1976. pp. 367.

ZU Problemen der Entwicklungstendenzen der sozialistischen Produktionsverhältnisse in der DDR; (Autoren: Ottomar Kratsch [and others]). Berlin, [1977]. pp. 141. *(Akademie der Wissenschaften der DDR. Zentralinstitut für Wirtschaftswissenschaften. Forschungsberichte. Nr.24)*

— Nigeria.

NAFZIGER (E. WAYNE) African capitalism: a case study in Nigerian entrepreneurship. Stanford, Calif., 1977. pp. 293. *bibliog. (Stanford University. Hoover Institution on War, Revolution and Peace. Hoover Institution Publications. 169)*

— Norway.

SKARD (ØYVIND) Democracy and the individual: some reflections on the process of democratization in working life. [Oslo, 1975?]. pp. 35.

EMERY (FREDERICK E.) and THORSRUD (EINAR) Democracy at work: the report of the Norwegian industrial democracy program. Leiden, 1976. pp. 179. *bibliog.*

— Russia.

BERLINER (JOSEPH SCHOLOM) The innovation decision in Soviet industry. Cambridge, Mass., [1976]. pp. 561. *bibliog.*

LAVRIKOV (IURII ALEKSANDROVICH) and others. Integratsiia sotsialisticheskogo proizvodstva i upravlenie. Moskva, 1976. pp. 278. *bibliog.*

MAKHNOVA (VERA IVANOVNA) Proizvodstvennye sviazi sotsialisticheskikh predpriiatii: (politiko-ekonomicheskii analiz). Moskva, 1976. pp. 205.

SUBOTSKII (IURII VENIAMINOVICH) Razvitie ob"edinenii v promyshlennosti: voprosy teorii i metodologii. Moskva, 1977. pp. 229. *(Akademiia Nauk SSSR. Problemy Sovetskoi Ekonomiki)*

INDUSTRIAL PROCUREMENT.

UNITED NATIONS INDUSTRIAL DEVELOPMENT ORGANIZATION. 1972. A guide to industrial purchasing. (ID/82). New York, 1972. pp. 45. *bibliog.*

INDUSTRIAL PROMOTION

— Australia.

AUSTRALIAN INDUSTRY DEVELOPMENT CORPORATION. Annual report. a., 1970/71 (1st)- Canberra. *Included in AUSTRALIA. Parliament. [Parliamentary papers].*

— India.

INDIA. Ministry of Industry and Civil Supplies. Report. a., 1975/76- New Delhi.

— Ireland (Republic).

KILLEEN (MICHAEL J.) Industrial development and full employment;...paper given...to Symposium on Increasing Employment in Ireland, held under the auspices of the Statistical and Social Inquiry Society of Ireland on 20th November, 1975. Dublin, Industrial Development Authority, 1976. pp. 18. *(Publication Series. Paper 3)*

— Pakistan.

PAKISTAN INDUSTRIAL DEVELOPMENT CORPORATION. Annual report and statement of accounts. a., 1954/55- Karachi.

— United Kingdom — Wales.

WELSH DEVELOPMENT AGENCY. Welsh Development Agency: a statement of policies and programmes. Pontypridd, 1977. pp. 12.

— United States.

HELLMAN (DARYL A.) and others. State financial incentives to industry. Lexington, [1976]. pp. 146. *bibliog.*

INDUSTRIAL PROPERTY.

INDUSTRIAL PROPERTY: m. review of the World Intellectual Property Organization. m., 1962 (1st.)- Geneva. *Continuation of file of French ed., La Propriété industrielle (1885-1961).*

— European Economic Community countries.

JOHANNES (HARTMUT) Industrial property and copyright in European Community law; (translated by Frank Dorman). Leyden, 1976. pp. 315. *(Council of Europe. European Aspects. Series E: Law. No.17)*

INDUSTRIAL PSYCHIATRY.

BRODSKY (CARROLL M.) The harassed worker. Lexington, Mass., [1976]. pp. 174. *bibliog.*

INDUSTRIAL RELATIONS.

LUPTON (THOMAS) Problems of morale and staff relations in large organisations; (transcript of lecture given on 21 May 1974). [London], Civil Service College, [1974]. pp. 10. *(Lectures on Some Management Problems in the Civil Service. No. 4)*

AMERICAN ACADEMY OF POLITICAL AND SOCIAL SCIENCE. Annals. vol.431. Industrial democracy in international perspective; special editor of this volume John P. Windmuller. Philadelphia, [1977]. pp. 195.

— Cameroun.

KENDRICK (ROBIN) A survey of labor relations in Cameroon. Ann Arbor, 1976. pp. 39. *bibliog. (Michigan University. Center for Research on Economic Development. Discussion Papers. No. 50)*

— Canada.

BROWN (LORNE) Breaking down myths of peace and harmony in Canadian labour history. Winnipeg, [1974]. 1 pamphlet (unpaged).

— France.

NEUSCHWANDER (CLAUDE MAURICE RAYMOND JEAN) Patron, mais...: entretiens avec Bernard Guetta. Paris, [1975]. pp. 189.

SCHEMA général d'aménagement de la France: décentralisation industrielle et relations de travail. Paris, 1976. pp. 117. *(France. Délégation à l'Aménagement du Territoire et à l'Action Régionale. Travaux et Recherches de Prospective. 61)*

— Germany.

BOMERS (G.B.J.) Multinational corporations and industrial relations: a comparative study of West Germany and the Netherlands. Assen, 1976. pp. 226. *bibliog.*

NIEDENHOFF (HORST UDO) Jetzt muss etwas getan werden: die Basisarbeit Linksextremer Gruppen im Betrieb. Köln, [1976]. pp. 183. *bibliog.*

BAROTH (HANS DIETER) In unseren Betrieben: ein Schwarzbuch über deutsche Betriebe. Köln, [1977]. pp. 168.

— Ireland (Republic).

EIRE. Committee on Industrial Relations in the Electricity Supply Board. 1968. Interim report; [Michael P. Fogarty, chairman]. Dublin, 1968. pp. 36.

— Japan.

ABEGGLEN (JAMES C.) Management and worker: the Japanese solution. Tokyo, [1973 repr. 1975]. pp. 200.

— Netherlands.

BOMERS (G.B.J.) Multinational corporations and industrial relations: a comparative study of West Germany and the Netherlands. Assen, 1976. pp. 226. *bibliog.*

— Norway.

SKARD (ØYVIND) Democracy and the individual: some reflections on the process of democratization in working life. [Oslo, 1975?]. pp. 35.

BOLWEG (JOEP F.) Job design and industrial democracy: the case of Norway. Leiden, 1976. pp. 139. *bibliog.*

— Russia.

EHRHARDT (MANFRED) Mitsprache und Interessenvertretung der Belegschaft in den Industriebetrieben der Sowjetunion, etc. Hamburg, 1975. pp. 202. *bibliog. Inaugural-Dissertation zur Erlangung des Doktorgrades der Fachbereichs Wirtschaftswissenschaften der Universität Hamburg.*

— Singapore.

PANG (ENG FONG) and KAY (THELMA) Change and continuity in Singapore's industrial relations system. Singapore, 1974. pp. 27. *(University of Singapore. Department of Sociology. Working Papers. No. 35)*

— South Africa.

COETZEE (J.A. GREY) Industrial relations in South Africa: an event-structure of labour; with the co-operation of some leading South African trade unionists. Cape Town, [1976]. pp. 238. *bibliog.*

— Sweden.

FORSEBÄCK (LENNART) Industrial relations and employment in Sweden. [Stockholm], 1976. pp. 138. *bibliog.*

— Switzerland.

GALLATI (RENATUS) Der Arbeitsfriede in der Schweiz und seine wohlstandspolitische Bedeutung im Vergleich mit der Entwicklung in einigen anderen Staaten. Bern, 1976. pp. 312. *bibliog.*

— United Kingdom.

THOMASON (GEORGE F.) The management of industrial relations; an inaugural lecture given on 15 January 1971 at University College, Cardiff. Cardiff, [1971]. pp. 23.

TAYLOR (NANCY) The search for the industrial relations panacea. London, [1974]. pp. 10.

HENDERSON (JOAN) A guide to the Employment Protection Act, 1975. London, 1975 [repr. 1976]. pp. 39.

HYMAN (RICHARD) Industrial relations: a Marxist introduction. London, 1975. pp. 220. *bibliog.*

ALDRIDGE (ALAN) Power, authority and restrictive practices: a sociological essay on industrial relations. Oxford, [1976]. pp. 135. *bibliog.*

CHAPPLE (FRANK) The responsibility of trade unions and managers. London, [1976]. pp. 5. *(Foundation for Business Responsibilities. Seminar Papers)*

CLEGG (HUGH ARMSTRONG) The system of industrial relations in Great Britain. 3rd ed. Oxford, 1976. pp. 522. *([Warwick Studies in Industrial Relations])*

COOPER (BRUCE MICHAEL) and BARTLETT (A.F.) Industrial relations: a study in conflict. London, 1976. pp. 310.

HUISKAMP (M.J.) Shop stewards en arbeiderszeggenschap: een onderzoek naar arbeidsverhoudingen in de Britse metaalverwerkende industrie 1830-1975. Alphen aan den Rijn, 1976. pp. 234. *bibliog. With English summary.*

The INDUSTRIAL Relations Act and the fight for a general strike; [articles from Workers' Fight]. London, [1976]. 1 pamphlet (unpaged). *(Workers' Fight. Phoenix Pamphlets. No. 4)*

LABOUR RESEARCH DEPARTMENT. LRD guide to the Employment Protection Act, 1975, and to the Trade Union and Labour Relations Act, 1974. London, 1976. pp. 48.

CROUCH (COLIN) Class conflict and the industrial relations crisis: compromise and corporatism in the policies of the British state. London, 1977. pp. 302. *bibliog.*

GRANT (WYN P.) and MARSH (DAVID) The Confederation of British Industry. London, 1977. pp. 226.

GREENWOOD (JOHN A.) Worker sit-ins and job protection: case studies of union intervention. Farnborough, Hants, [1977]. pp. 120. *bibliog.*

JACKSON (MICHAEL P.) Industrial relations: a textbook. London, [1977]. pp. 281. *bibliog.*

JENKINS (CLIVE) and SHERMAN (BARRIE) Computers and the unions. London, 1977. pp. 135.

MORAN (MICHAEL) The politics of industrial relations: the origins, life and death of the 1971 Industrial Relations Act. London, 1977. pp. 195.

TURNER (HERBERT ARTHUR) and others. Management characteristics and labour conflict: a study of managerial organisation, attitudes and industrial relations. Cambridge, 1977. pp. 80. *(Cambridge. University. Department of Applied Economics. Papers in Industrial Relations and Labour. 3)*

U.K. Central Office of Information. Reference Division. Reference Pamphlets. 148. Manpower and employment in Britain: industrial relations. London, 1977. pp. 37. *bibliog.*

— — Bibliography.

MACCAFFERTY (MAXINE) compiler. Employment relations in the U.K. London, [1976]. pp. 48. *(Association of Special Libraries and Information Bureaux. Aslib Bibliographies. 2)*

— United States.

CHAUHAN (D.S.) and ROUNSAVALL (MARK) Public labor relations: a comparative state study. Beverly Hills, [1976]. pp. 70. *bibliog.*

WERTHER (WILLIAM B.) and LOCKHART (CAROL ANN) Labor relations in the health professions: the basis of power, the means of change. Boston, Mass, [1976]. pp. 255. *bibliogs.*

INDUSTRIAL SAFETY

— Standards.

UNITED STATES. OSHA Task Force. 1977. OSHA safety regulation: report;...edited by Paul W. MacAvoy. Washington, D.C., [1977]. pp. 104. *(American Enterprise Institute for Public Policy Research. AEI Studies. 151)*

— Russia — Law and legislation.

SEMENKOV (VIKTOR IVANOVICH) Okhrana truda v SSSR: pravovye problemy. 2nd ed. Minsk, 1976. pp. 287.

— United Kingdom.

U.K. Health and Safety Executive. Industry and services: a report of the work of H.M. Factory Inspectorate incorporating the annual reports of H.M. Inspector of Railways and H.M. Inspector of Explosives. a., 1975(1st)- London.

— — Laws and legislation.

REDGRAVE (ALEXANDER) Health and safety in factories: replacing Redgrave's Factories Acts 22nd edition; [edited] by Ian Fife and E. Antony Machin. London, 1976. pp. 1949.

— United States.

BUREAU OF NATIONAL AFFAIRS. O[ccupational] S[afety and] H[ealth] A[ct] and the unions: bargaining on job safety and health. Washington, [1973]. pp. 56.

UNITED STATES. OSHA Task Force. 1977. OSHA safety regulation: report;...edited by Paul W. MacAvoy. Washington, D.C., [1977]. pp. 104. *(American Enterprise Institute for Public Policy Research. AEI Studies. 151)*

— — Law and legislation.

SMITH (ROBERT STEWART) The Occupational Health and Safety Act: its goals and its achievements. Washington, 1976. pp. 104. *(American Enterprise Institute for Public Policy Research. Evaluative Studies. 25)*

INDUSTRIAL SOCIOLOGY.

HARVEY (EDWARD B.) Industrial society: structures, roles, and relations. Homewood, Ill., 1975. pp. 417. *bibliog.*

LINDHOLM (ROLF) and NORSTEDT (JAN-PEDER) The Volvo report;...translated by David Jenkins. [Stockholm, 1975]. pp. 92.

NUGAEV (MAGDII ALIMZHANOVICH) Trudovaia aktivnost' rabochego klassa razvitogo sotsialisticheskogo obshchestva: teoretiko-metodologicheskii aspekt. Kazan', 1975. pp. 293.

ZURHORST (GUENTER) Gewerkschaftspolitik und technischer Fortschritt: zum Problem einer basisorientierten Mitbestimmung. Berlin, [1975]. pp. 163. *bibliog.*

KLEIN (LISL KAROLINE) A social scientist in industry. Epping, 1976. pp. 257.

TASK and organization; edited by Eric J. Miller. London, [1976]. pp. 379. *bibliogs. Includes a list of publications by A.K. Rice.*

The SOCIOLOGY of industry; [by] S.R. Parker [and others] . 3rd ed. London, 1977. pp. 208. *bibliogs.*

— India.

HOLMSTRÖM (MARK N.) South Indian factory workers: their life and their world. Cambridge, 1976. pp. 158. *bibliog. (Cambridge. University. Centre of South Asian Studies. Cambridge South Asian Studies. 20)*

— Poland.

JĘDRZYCKI (WIESŁAW) Socjolog w zakładzie pracy. Wrocław, 1971. pp. 271. *bibliog. With English and Russian summaries.*

— Romania.

BĂDINA (OVIDIU) ed. Tineret industrial: acţiune şi integrare socială; cercetare sociologică condusă de Ovidiu Bădina. Bucureşti, 1972. pp. 170. *(Centrul de Cercetări pentru Problemele Tineretului. Tineretul şi Lumea de Mîine) With French, English, Russian and German tables of contents.*

— Russia.

KAPELIAN (EFIM KHAIMOVICH) Proizvoditel'nye sily: struktura, funktsii, tipologiia; voprosy metodologii i teorii. Minsk, 1976. pp. 191.

— United Kingdom.

NICHOLS (THEO) and BEYNON (HUW) Living with capitalism: class relations and the modern factory. London, 1977. pp. 204.

— United States.

MONTAGNA (PAUL D.) Occupations and society: toward a sociology of the labor market. New York, [1977]. pp. 456.

INDUSTRIAL STATISTICS.

RYBAKOV (IURII IAKOVLEVICH) Promyshlennaia statiska Rossii XIX v.: istochnikovedcheskoe issledovanie. Moskva, 1976. pp. 277.

INDUSTRIALIZATION.

MUNS ALBUIXECH (JOAQUIN) Industrializacion y crecimiento de los paises en desarrollo. Barcelona, [1972]. pp. 312. *bibliog. (Barcelona. Universidad. Facultad de Ciencias Economicas. Departamento de Teoria Economica. Publicaciones)*

CIBA FOUNDATION. Symposia. New Series. 32. Health and industrial growth; [editors Katherine Elliott and Julie Knight]. Amsterdam, 1975. pp. 267. *bibliogs.*

— Abstracts.

INDUSTRIAL DEVELOPMENT ABSTRACTS; ([pd. by] United Nations Industrial Development Organization). irreg., 1971 (nos.1/2)- New York.

— Mathematical models.

LOWE (ADOLPH) and PULRANG (STANFORD) The path of economic growth;...with an appendix by Edward J. Nell. Cambridge, 1976. pp. 336.

INDUSTRIES, LOCATION OF.

INDUSTRIAL location: alternative frameworks; edited by Doreen Massey [and] W.I. Morrison. London, [1975?]. pp. 136. *bibliogs. (Centre for Environmental Studies. Conference Papers. 15) Proceedings of a workshop held at CES in December 1974.*

AFANAS'EVSKII (EVGENII ALEKSANDROVICH) Legkaia promyshlennost': ekonomicheskie problemy razmeshcheniia. Moskva, 1976. pp. 263. *bibliog.*

MILLER (EUGENE WILLARD) Manufacturing: a study of industrial location. Pennsylvania, [1977]. pp. 286.

— Mathematical models.

MODELI razmeshcheniia proizvodstva. Moskva, 1975. pp. 216. *(Akademiia Nauk SSSR. Problemy Sovetskoi Ekonomiki)*

— France.

SCHEMA général d'aménagement de la France: décentralisation industrielle et relations de travail. Paris, 1976. pp. 117. *(France. Délégation à l'Aménagement du Territoire et à l'Action Régionale. Travaux et Recherches de Prospective. 61)*

— Russia.

METODICHESKIE voprosy razmeshcheniia promyshlennosti: sbornik statei. Moskva, 1975. pp. 179.

PROBLEMY teorii i praktiki razmeshcheniia proizvoditel'nykh sil SSSR. Moskva, 1976. pp. 326. *(Akademiia Nauk SSSR. Sovet po Izucheniiu Proizvoditel'nykh Sil. Problemy Sovetskoi Ekonomiki)*

— United Kingdom.

KEEBLE (DAVID ETHERTON) Industrial location and planning in the United Kingdom. London, 1976. pp. 317. *bibliog.*

— United States.

MILLER (EUGENE WILLARD) Manufacturing: a study of industrial location. Pennsylvania, [1977]. pp. 286.

INDUSTRY.

FRANCE. Groupe de Réflexion sur les Stratégies Industrielles. 1976. La division internationale du travail. Paris, 1976. 2 vols. (in 1). *(France. Ministère de l'Industrie et de la Recherche. Etudes de Politique Industrielle. 9)*

— Environmental aspects — Mathematical models.

LIPNOWSKI (IRWIN FRANK) Environmental aspects of a steady state economy. 1976. fo. 187. *bibliog. Typescript. Ph.D.(London) thesis: unpublished. This thesis is the property of London University and may not be removed from the Library.*

— Social aspects.

CIBA FOUNDATION. Symposia. New Series. 32. Health and industrial growth; [editors Katherine Elliott and Julie Knight]. Amsterdam, 1975. pp. 267. *bibliogs.*

PLESSER (ERNST H.) Changing conflicts in industry: short and long-term solutions. London, 1976. pp. 7. *(Foundation for Business Responsibilities. Seminar Papers)*

The SOCIOLOGY of industry; [by] S.R. Parker [and others] . 3rd ed. London, 1977. pp. 208. *bibliogs.*

— — Japan.

CONFERENCE ON JAPANESE INDUSTRIALIZATION AND ITS SOCIAL CONSEQUENCES, UNIVERSITY OF WASHINGTON, 1973. Japanese industrialization and its social consequences; edited by Hugh Patrick, with the assistance of Larry Meissner. Berkeley, Calif., [1976]. pp. 505. *bibliogs. Proceedings of a conference sponsored by the Joint Committee on Japanese Studies of the American Council of Learned Societies and the Social Science Research Council.*

— — United Kingdom.

YOUNG LIBERAL MOVEMENT. Economics and Industry Commission. Industry and the community: a Young Liberal approach to industry, economics and the community. Loughborough, [1976]. pp. 39. *bibliog.*

ELLIOTT (DAVID) The Lucas Aerospace workers' campaign. London, 1977. pp. 20. *(Young Fabian Pamphlets. 46)*

— — United States.

LINOWES (DAVID F.) The corporate conscience. New York, [1974]. pp. 239.

BLAKE (DAVID H.) and others. Social auditing: evaluating the impact of corporate programs. New York, 1976. pp. 168. *bibliog.*

NOBLE (DAVID F.) America by design: science, technology, and the rise of corporate capitalism. New York, 1977. pp. 384.

SETHI (S. PRAKASH) Advocacy advertising and large corporations: social conflict, big business image, the news media and public policy. Lexington, Mass., [1977]. pp. 355. *bibliog.*

INDUSTRY AND EDUCATION.

ABRAHAM (KARL) Der Betrieb als Erziehungsfaktor: die funktionale Erziehung durch den modernen wirtschaftlichen Betrieb. 2nd ed. Freiburg im Breisgau, 1957. pp. 182. *bibliog.*

— United Kingdom.

WATSON (WILLIAM FERGUSON) University research and the needs of industry. Bradford, [1974]. pp. 14. *(University of Bradford. Professor Moore Memorial Lectures. 1974)*

EDUCATION and training for the industrial technologies: papers for a series of regional symposia. [London], Department of Industry, Industrial Technologies Education and Training Secretariat, [1977]. 1 vol. (various pagings).

U.K. Department of Industry. 1977. Industry, education and management: a discussion paper. [London], 1977. 1 vol. (various pagings). *bibliog.*

INDUSTRY AND STATE.

BERTHOIN (GEORGES) Industry and government. London, [1972]. pp. 17. *(Foundation for Business Responsibilities. Sir George Earle Memorial Lectures. 1972)*

ROBINSON (RICHARD D.) National control of foreign business entry: a survey of fifteen countries. New York, 1976. pp. 508. *bibliogs.*

ROLL (Sir ERIC) Economics, government and business. London, 1976. pp. 27. *(London. University. Stamp Memorial Lectures. 1976)*

— Mathematical models.

SKOURAS (ATHANASSIOS S.) Government activity and private profits. London, 1975. pp. 20. *(Thames Polytechnic. School of Social Sciences. Thames Papers in Political Economy)*

— America, Latin.

The STATE and economic development in Latin America; proceedings of a conference held at Cambridge in December 1976; edited by E.V.K. Fitzgerald [and others]. Cambridge, 1977. pp. 342. *(Cambridge. University. Centre of Latin American Studies. Occasional Papers. 1) In English or Spanish.*

— Canada — Quebec (Province).

FOURNIER (PIERRE) The Québec establishment: the ruling class and the state. Montréal, [1976]. pp. 228. *bibliog.*

— France.

ZYSMAN (JOHN) Political strategies for industrial order: state, market and industry in France. Berkeley, Calif., [1977]. pp. 230.

— Germany.

ROHRSCHEIDT (KURT VON) Vom Zunftzwange zur Gewerbefreiheit: (eine Studie nach den Quellen). Glashütten im Taunus, 1976. pp. 668. *bibliog. Reprint of work originally published in Berlin in 1898.*

ULLMANN (HANS PETER) Der Bund der Industriellen: Organisation, Einfluss und Politik klein- und mittelbetrieblicher Industrieller im Deutschen Kaiserreich, 1895-1914. Göttingen, 1976. pp. 464. bibliog.

FELDMAN (GERALD D.) Iron and steel in the German inflation, 1916-1923. Princeton, [1977]. pp. 518. *bibliog.*

JAECKERING (WERNER) Die politischen Auseinandersetzungen um die Novellierung des Gesetzes gegen Wettbewerbsbeschränkungen (GWB). Berlin, [1977]. pp. 287. *bibliog.*

— Ghana.

GHANA. 1968. Government policy on the promotion of Ghanaian business enterprises. [Accra], 1968. pp. 8.

— India.

INDIA. Bureau of Public Enterprises. Annual report on the working of industrial and commercial undertakings of the central government. a., 1974/75- New Delhi. *In 3 v.; v.1, Text; v. 2, Sectoral analyses; v.3, Analysis of accounts.*

— Liberia.

PORTE (ALBERT) Liberianization or gobbling business?. [Crozierville], 1974. fo. 33.

— Nigeria.

GOVERNMENT role in the Nigerian oil industry. [Lagos?, 1972?]. pp. 19.

— Underdeveloped areas.

See UNDERDEVELOPED AREAS — Industry and state.

— United Kingdom.

AIMS OF INDUSTRY. Economic Arguments. The Industry Act: should industry help the executioner?. London, [1974]. pp. 4.

GEORGE (KENNETH DESMOND) Big business, competition and the state; an inaugural lecture given on 13 November 1974 at University College, Cardiff. Cardiff, [1974]. pp. 17.

ROBERTSON (DAVID) 1943- , and HENDERSON (JOAN) A guide to the Industry Act 1975. London, 1975. pp. 21.

BROADWAY (FRANK) Upper Clyde Shipbuilders: a study of government intervention in industry; the way the money goes. London, 1976. pp. 58.

CHIPLIN (BRIAN) and LEES (DENNIS SAMUEL) Acquisitions and mergers: government policy in Europe. London, [1976]. pp. 104. *(Economists Advisory Group. Business Research Studies)*

GOVERNMENT and industry relationships; edited by David Lethbridge. Oxford, 1976. pp. 194. *(Oxford. University. Maurice Lubbock Memorial Lectures. 1974-1975)*

NATIONAL ECONOMIC DEVELOPMENT COUNCIL. N[ational] E[conomic] D[evelopment] C[ouncil] industrial strategy: [reports of Economic Development Committees and sector working parties]. [London, National Economic Development Office, 1976]. 22 pts.

U.K. Treasury. 1976. Industrial strategy: the first stage; memorandum by the Chancellor of the Exchequer and the Secretary of State for Industry; (with Industrial strategy: analysis of sector reports; memorandum by the chairman of the Industrial Strategy Staff Group; (with Annexes)). [London, 1976]. 2 pts.

JEWKES (JOHN) Delusions of dominance: a critique of the theory of large-scale industrial dominance and of the pretence of government to "restructure" British industry. London, 1977. pp. 62. *bibliog. (Institute of Economic Affairs. Hobart Papers. 76)*

JONES (COLIN) Political writer. The £200,000 job!: a study of government intervention in aluminium smelting: the way the money goes. London, 1977. pp. 34.

U.K. Department of Industry. 1977. The National Enterprise Board: guidelines. London, 1977. pp. 12.

WAINE (PETER) Withering heights: a contribution to the debate on Britain's industrial ills. London, [1977]. pp. 12.

— — Ireland, Northern.

IRELAND, NORTHERN. 1976. Economic and industrial strategy for Northern Ireland: report by review team, 1976; [W.G.H. Quigley, chairman]. Belfast, 1976. pp. 106. *bibliog.*

— United States.

AGAPOS (A.M.) Government-industry and defense: economics and administration. University, Alabama, [1975]. pp. 184. *bibliog.*

BLOUGH (ROGER M.) The Washington embrace of business. New York, [1975]. pp. 162. *(Carnegie-Mellon University. Benjamin F. Fairless Memorial Lectures. 1974). Also contains his President Kennedy and steel prices.*

COPP (EMMANUEL ANTHONY) Regulating competition in oil: government intervention in the U.S. refinery industry, 1948-1975. College Station, Tex., [1976]. pp. 280. *bibliog. (Texas A and M University. Texas A and M University Economics Series. 1)*

DAWSON (FRANK G.) Nuclear power: development and management of a technology. Seattle, [1976]. pp. 320. *bibliog.*

REGULATORY reform: highlights of a conference on government regulation...Washington...1975; edited by W.S. Moore. Washington, 1976. pp. 65. *(American Enterprise Institute for Public Policy Research. Domestic Affairs Studies. 45)*

WALKER (WILLIAM N.) International limits to government intervention in the market-place: focus on subsidies to the private sector. London, 1976. pp. 5. *(Trade Policy and Research Centre. Lectures in Commercial Diplomacy. No. 1)*

WALLIS (WILSON ALLEN) An overgoverned society. New York, [1976]. pp. 292.

WEIDENBAUM (MURRAY L.) The new wave of government regulation of business. Washington, 1976. pp. 9. *(American Enterprise Institute for Public Policy Research. Reprints. No. 39) (Reprinted from Business and Society Review, 1975)*

UNITED STATES. Task Force on Reform of Federal Energy Administration. 1977. Federal Energy Administration regulation: report of the Presidential Task Force; edited by Paul W. MacAvoy. Washington, D.C., [1977]. pp. 195. *(American Enterprise Institute for Public Policy Research. AEI Studies. 150)*

WEIDENBAUM (MURRAY L.) Business, government and the public. Englewood Cliffs, N.J., [1977]. pp. 336. *bibliog.*

INFANTICIDE.

PEGGS (JAMES) India's cries to British humanity, relative to infanticide, British connection with idolatry, Ghaut murders, suttee, slavery, and colonization in India; to which are added, humane hints for the melioration of the state of society in British India. London, 1832. pp. 500.

INFANTS

— Care and hygiene.

DUNN (JUDY) Distress and comfort. London, 1977. pp. 126. *bibliog.*

— Mortality.

U.K. Office of Population Censuses and Surveys. Mortality statistics: childhood: review of the Registrar General on deaths in England and Wales. a., 1974 (1st)- London. *Supersedes in part Registrar-General's statistical review of England and Wales.*

MUSTONEN (MAIJA) and others. Imeväiskuolleisuuteen vaikuttavat sosiaaliset ja taloudelliset tekijät Suomessa 1910-1971, etc. Helsinki, 1976. pp. 148. *bibliog. (Finland. Suomen Virallinen Tilasto. Finlands Officiella Statistik. 32. Sosiaalisia Erikoistutkimuksia. 46) With English summary.*

TABUTIN (DOMINIQUE) Mortalité infantile et juvénile en Algérie. [Paris], 1976. pp. 275. *bibliog. (France. Institut National d'Etudes Démographiques. Travaux et Documents., Cahiers. No. 77)*

INFLATION (FINANCE).

FITOUSSI (JEAN PAUL) Inflation, équilibre et chômage. Paris, [1973]. pp. 294,(95). *bibliog.*

INFLATION and growth: proceedings of a symposium; editor, V.V. Bhanoji Rao. Singapore, 1974. pp. 256. *Organised by the Economic Society of Singapore.*

ANSWERS to inflation and recession: economic policies for a modern society; edited by Albert T. Sommers; a colloquium held April 8-9, 1975 at the Mayflower Hotel, Washington, D. C. [New York], [1975]. pp. 154. *(National Industrial Conference Board. Conference Board Reports. No. 666)*

MILTON Friedman in Australia, 1975; [proceedings of a seminar organized by the Graduate Business School Club in 1975 in Sydney and of a dinner meeting organized by Constable and Bain in 1975 in Sydney]. Darlinghurst, [1975]. pp. 80.

CARNEGIE-ROCHESTER CONFERENCE ON PUBLIC POLICY. 1974, November Conference. Institutional arrangements and the inflation problem: [papers and discussions from the conference]; editors Karl Brunner [and] Allan H. Meltzer. Amsterdam, 1976. pp. 248. *bibliogs. (Journal of Monetary Economics. Carnegie-Rochester Conference Series on Public Policy. vol. 3)*

CONFERENCE ON BANK CREDIT, MONEY AND INFLATION IN OPEN ECONOMIES, LEUVEN, 1974. Bank credit, money and inflation in open economies; edited by Michele Fratianni [and] Karel Tavernier. Berlin, [1976]. pp. 624. *bibliogs. (Kredit und Kapital. Beihefte. 3) The proceedings of a conference held at the Katholieke Universiteit te Leuven on September 12-13, 1974, organised by the Centrum voor Economische Studien.*

ECONOMIC calculation under inflation; introduction by Helen E. Schultz. Indianapolis, [1976]. pp. 340. *bibliog. Papers delivered at a seminar sponsored by the Liberty Fund, in February 1975.*

INFLATION in open economies; (edited by Michael Parkin and George Zis). Manchester, 1976. pp. 298. *bibliogs.*

TRADE, inflation and ethics. Lexington, Mass., [1976]. pp. 303. *bibliog. (Commission on Critical Choices for Americans. Critical Choices for Americans. vol.5) Prepared under the auspices of the Commission on Critical Choices for Americans.*

ALCHIAN (ARMEN ALBERT) Economic forces at work. Indianapolis, [1977]. pp. 523. *bibliogs.*

BURG (HELMUT) Inflation und Klassenkampf: Ursachen, Widersprüche und Konsequenzen der Inflation im Imperialismus. Berlin, 1977. pp. 174.

HAGGER (ALFRED JAMES) Inflation: theory and policy. London, 1977. pp. 290.

INFLATION; [by] Michael Jefferson [and others]. London, 1977. pp. 192.

INTERNATIONAL ECONOMIC ASSOCIATION. Conference, 1975, Saltsjöbaden. Inflation theory and anti-inflation policy: proceedings of a conference held by the International Economic Association at Saltsjöbaden, Sweden; edited by Erik Lundberg. London, 1977. pp. 545.

THOMAS (JEAN GABRIEL) Inflation et nouvel ordre monétaire. Paris, [1977]. pp. 304.

TREVITHICK (JAMES ANTHONY) Inflation: a guide to the crisis in economics. Harmondsworth, 1977. pp. 132. *bibliog.*

WORLDWIDE inflation: theory and recent experience; [by] Odd Aukrust [and others]; (Lawrence B. Krause and Walter S. Salant, editors). Washington, D.C., [1977]. pp. 686. *Based on a conference organized by the Brooking's Institution in November 1974.*

— Mathematical models.

FRIEDMAN (MILTON) Inflation and unemployment: the new dimension of politics. London, 1977. pp. 35. *bibliog. (Institute of Economic Affairs. Occasional Papers. 51)*

— America, Latin.

PAZOS (FELIPE) Chronic inflation in Latin America; translated by Ernesto Cuesta in collaboration with the author. New York, 1972. pp. 186.

— Canada.

CANADA. Anti-Inflation Board. Report. a., 1976 (1st)-Ottawa. *[In English and French].*

COURCHENE (THOMAS J.) Money, inflation and the Bank of Canada: an analysis of Canadian monetary policy from 1970 to early 1975. Montreal, [1976]. pp. 283. *bibliogs. (Howe (C.D.) Research Institute. Special Studies)*

— Germany.

ZWEIG (KONRAD) Germany through inflation and recession: an object lesson in economic management 1973-1976. London, 1976. pp. 52. *bibliog.*

FELDMAN (GERALD D.) Iron and steel in the German inflation, 1916-1923. Princeton, [1977]. pp. 518. *bibliog.*

— Netherlands — Mathematical models.

FASE (M.M.G.) and NIEUWKERK (MARIUS VAN) Anticipated inflation and interest rates in an open economy: a study of the Gibson paradox for the Netherlands. Amsterdam, [1975?]. pp. 24. *bibliog. (Nederlandsche Bank. Reprints. No. 17)*

— Panama.

LOONEY (ROBERT E.) The economic development of Panama: the impact of world inflation on an open economy. New York, 1976. pp. 248. *bibliog.*

— United Kingdom.

HARDWICK (PHILIP) Inflation and the sinking pound. London, [1976]. pp. 14. *(Economics Association. Occasional Papers. No.2)*

MORGAN (DAVID RAYMOND) Over-taxation by inflation: a study of the effects of inflation on taxation and government expenditure, and of its correction by indexing. London, 1977. pp. 94. *bibliog. (Institute of Economic Affairs. Hobart Papers. 72). Including post-budget edition supplement.*

— United States.

NATIONAL INDUSTRIAL CONFERENCE BOARD. Conference Board Economic Forum, New York, 1973. Boom, inflation, and policy: a mid-year review of the economic outlook: proceedings of the...forum. New York, 1973. pp. 72. *(National Industrial Conference Board. Conference Board Reports)*

NATIONAL INDUSTRIAL CONFERENCE BOARD. Conference Board Economic Forum, New York, 1974. Inflation in the United States: causes and consequences; proceedings [of] the...forum. New York, [1974]. pp. 102. *(National Industrial Conference Board. Conference Board Reports. No. 630)*

WEISSBROD (RICHARD) Diffusion of relative wage inflation in Southeast Pennsylvania. Evanston, Ill., 1976. pp. 166. *bibliog. (Northwestern University. Studies in Geography. No. 23).*

— — Mathematical models.

ROSE (PETER S.) and HUNT (LACY H.) Policy variables, unemployment and price level changes. [Washington, 1972]. pp. 11. *(United States. Board of Governors of the Federal Reserve System. Staff Economic Studies. No. 67) (Reprinted from The Southern Journal of Business, Vol. 6, No. 3, 1971)*

INFLATION (FINANCE) AND ACCOUNTING.

DAVIDSON (SIDNEY) and others. Inflation accounting: a guide for the accountant and the financial analyst. New York, [1976]. pp. 242. *bibliog.*

KIRKMAN (PATRICK R.A.) Modern credit management: a study of the management of trade credit under inflationary conditions. London, 1977. pp. 311.

INFLATION (FINANCE) AND TAXATION

— United States.

INFLATION and the income tax; Henry J. Aaron, editor. Washington, D.C., [1976]. pp. 340. *(Brookings Institution. Studies of Government Finance) A report of a conference sponsored by the Fund for Public Policy Research and the Brookings Institution.*

INFLUENCE (PSYCHOLOGY).

KING (STEPHEN W.) Communication and social influence. Reading, Mass., [1975]. pp. 169. *bibliog.*

MOSCOVICI (SERGE) Social influence and social change. London, 1976. pp. 239. *bibliog. (European Association of Experimental Social Psychology. European Monographs in Social Psychology. 10)*

INFORMATION MEASUREMENT

— Mathematical models.

BATTY (MICHAEL) and MARCH (LIONEL) Dynamic urban models based on information-minimising. Reading, 1976. pp. 41. *bibliog. (Reading. University. Department of Geography. Reading Geographical Papers. No. 48)*

INFORMATION SCIENCE.

ACCELERATING innovation; papers given at a symposium held at the University of Nottingham, March 1969, arranged by Aslib in collaboration with the Ministry of Technology and the Research Associations. London, [1970]. pp. 64. *bibliogs.*

— Study and teaching.

STAMPER (RONALD) A philosophy for the IFIP systems curriculum appropriate for a university; [paper presented at the 2nd World Conference on Computers and Education, Marseilles, 1975]. London, [1975]. fo. 5. *bibliog.*

INFORMATION SERVICES

— Australia.

CILES REPORT; [pd.by] Central Information, Library and Editorial Section, Commonwealth Scientific and Industrial Research Organization, Australia. a., current issue only. Melbourne.

— Czechoslovakia.

INFORMAČNÍ soustava organizací: sborník. Praha, 1975. pp. 299. *bibliog. With English table of contents.*

— Germany.

GERMANY (BUNDESREPUBLIK). Deutscher Bundestag. Wissenschaftliche Dienste. 1976. Die Wissenschaftlichen Dienste des Deutschen Bundestages. Bonn, 1976. pp. 19. *(Materialien. 47)*

— Underdeveloped areas.

See UNDERDEVELOPED AREAS — Information services.

— United Kingdom.

BUTCHER (HUGH) and others. Information and action services for rural areas: a case study in west Cumbria. [York, 1976]. pp. 79. *(Papers in Community Studies. No. 4)*

COMMUNITY DEVELOPMENT PROJECT. Limits of the law. London, 1977. pp. 54. *bibliog.*

NATIONAL CONSUMER COUNCIL. The fourth right of citizenship: a review of local advice services. London, 1977. pp. 80. *bibliog. (Discussion Papers. 4)*

— United States.

PORAT (MARC URI) The information economy. Ann Arbor, Mich., [1976]. 2 vols. *Ph.D. dissertation, Stanford University.*

INFORMATION STORAGE AND RETRIEVAL SYSTEMS.

COMPUTER AND INFORMATION SCIENCES SYMPOSIUM, 4TH, MIAMI BEACH, FLA., 1972. Information systems: COINS IV; edited by Julius T. Tou. New York, [1974]. pp. 506.

KOCHEN (MANFRED) Principles of information retrieval. Los Angeles, [1974]. pp. 203. *bibliog.*

LANGEFORS (NILS BÖRJE) and SUNDGREN (BO) Information systems architecture. New York, 1975. pp. 366. *bibliog.*

SYSTEMEERING 75; ([edited by] Mats Lundeberg and Janis Bubenko). Lund, 1975. pp. 323. *bibliogs. Festschrift in honour of Börje Langefors.*

CONFERENCE ON NATIONAL PLANNING FOR INFORMATICS IN DEVELOPING COUNTRIES, BAGHDAD, 1975. National planning for informatics in developing countries: proceedings of the IBI International Symposium, Baghdad, 2-6 November 1975; organized by National Computers Centre of Iraq-NCC; edited by G. Russell Pipe and A.A.M. Veenhuis. Amsterdam, 1976. pp. 531.

DATAFAIR '75 CONFERENCE, LONDON, 1975. Progress in information systems: the Datafair papers; edited by D. Simpson. [London, 1976]. pp. 224. *Conference organised by the British Computer Society.*

LANGEFORS (NILS BÖRJE) and SAMUELSON (KJELL) Information and data in systems. New York, 1976. pp. 124. *bibliog.*

McKEAG (R.M.) and WILSON (R.) M.Sc. Studies in operating systems;...edited by D.H.R. Huxtable. London, [1976]. pp. 263. *bibliogs. (Automatic Programming Information Centre. Studies in Data Processing. No.13)*

— Administration.

ADLER (MICHAEL) Lecturer in Social Administration, and DU FEU (D.) A computer based welfare benefits information system: the Inverclyde project; a joint project between the University of Edinburgh, Inverclyde District Council [and] IBM United Kingdom. Peterlee, 1975. pp. 56. *(IBM United Kingdom Limited. UK Scientific Centre. [Technical Reports]. 0078)*

— Automation.

LOCAL AUTHORITIES MANAGEMENT SERVICES AND COMPUTER COMMITTEE. Computer Panel. Computers in local authorities. London, 1970. pp. 23.

LOCAL AUTHORITIES MANAGEMENT SERVICES AND COMPUTER COMMITTEE. Computer Panel. Computer installations in local government and river authorities. London, 1972. pp. 14.

— Economics.

INTERNATIONAL ECONOMIC ASSOCIATION. Conference, 1975, Kiel. The organization and retrieval of economic knowledge: proceedings. ..; edited by Mark Perlman. London, 1977. pp. 520.

— Engineering.

STAMPER (RONALD) Information systems and community water systems; paper prepared for the meeting of public health chief engineers, Bombay, December 1975. [1976?]. fo. 3. *Unpublished: photocopy of typescript.*

— Evaluation.

LONDON (KEITH R.) The people side of systems: the human aspects of computer systems. London, [1976]. pp. 281. *bibliog.*

— Law.

GERMANY (BUNDESREPUBLIK). Bundesministerium der Justiz. 1972. The judicial information system: analysis, planning, regulations; resumé of the report of the study group BMJ/GMD/C-E-I-R. Karlsruhe, 1972. fo. 55.

GERMANY (BUNDESREPUBLIK). Bundesministerium der Justiz. 1972. Das juristische Informationssystem: Analyse, Planung, Vorschläge. Karlsruhe, [1972]. pp. 487. *bibliog.*

— — Germany.

GERMANY (BUNDESREPUBLIK). Bundesministerium der Justiz. 1972. The judicial information system: analysis, planning, regulations; resumé of the report of the study group BMJ/GMD/C-E-I-R. Karlsruhe, 1972. fo. 55.

GERMANY (BUNDESREPUBLIK). Bundesministerium der Justiz. 1972. Das juristische Informationssystem: Analyse, Planung, Vorschläge. Karlsruhe, [1972]. pp. 487. *bibliog.*

— Social sciences.

SCONUL EXCHANGE OF EXPERIENCE SEMINAR IN THE SOCIAL SCIENCES, YORK, 1975. Proceedings of the Exchange of Experience Seminar in the Social Sciences organized by the Information Services Group of SCONUL. [London, 1976]. pp. 23. *bibliog.*

SOCIAL SCIENCE RESEARCH COUNCIL SURVEY ARCHIVE. Bulletin. q., current issue only. Colchester.

— Water-supply.

STAMPER (RONALD) Information systems and community water systems; paper prepared for the meeting of public health chief engineers, Bombay, December 1975. [1976?]. fo. 3. *Unpublished: photocopy of typescript.*

INHERITANCE AND SUCCESSION

— Germany.

BARTHOLOMEYCZIK (HORST) Erbrecht: ein Studienbuch. 7th ed. München, 1965. pp. 408.

— United Kingdom.

PARRY (Sir DAVID HUGHES) and CLARK (JOHN BRYAN) The law of succession; seventh edition by J.B. Clark. London, 1977. pp. 487.

— United States.

BRITTAIN (JOHN A.) The inheritance of economic status. Washington, D.C., [1977]. pp. 185. *(Brookings Institution. Studies in Social Economics)*

INHERITANCE AND TRANSFER TAX.

SAVAGE (JOHN K.) and BULCKE (D. VAN DEN) Transfer taxes: their effect on productivity and control of our economy. Toronto, Ontario Economic Council, 1968. pp. 98. *bibliogs.*

— Canada.

SAVAGE (JOHN K.) and BULCKE (D. VAN DEN) Transfer taxes: their effect on productivity and control of our economy. Toronto, Ontario Economic Council, 1968. pp. 98. *bibliogs.*

— United Kingdom.

U.K. Statutes, etc. Taxes acts: the capital transfer tax enactments in force...with other legislation and statutory regulations etc. affecting the application of the tax, and an index. irreg., 1974/76- London.

CHOWN (JOHN F.) A guide to capital transfer tax. London, 1975. pp. 214.

CONFEDERATION OF BRITISH INDUSTRY. Capital transfer tax: consequences for limited private companies. London, 1975. pp. 9.

RAY (RALPH P.) and others. Practical capital transfer tax planning. London, 1977. pp. 274.

— United States.

WAGNER (RICHARD E.) Inheritance and the state: tax principles for a free and prosperous commonwealth. Washington, D.C. [1977]. pp. 95. *(American Enterprise Institute for Public Policy Research. AEI Studies. 154)*

INJUNCTIONS

— New Zealand.

SZAKATS (ALEXANDER) Law and trade unions: the use of injunctions. Wellington, 1975. pp. 33. *(Victoria University of Wellington. Industrial Relations Centre. Occasional Papers in Industrial Relations. No. 12)*

INLAND NAVIGATION

— France — Laws and regulations.

HERTSLET (MICHAEL) Die Binnenwasserstrassen und ihre Verwaltung in Frankreich. [Mannheim?, 1976?]. pp. 200. *bibliog. Inaugural-Dissertation der Fakultät für Rechtswissenschaft der Universität Mannheim.*

— United Kingdom.

U.K. British Transport Commission. 1977. British Transport Commission historical records: canal, dock, harbour, navigation and steamship records: RAIL 800-887: class list. London, 1977. pp. 380. *(List and Index Society. [Publications]. vol.142)*

INLAND WATER TRANSPORTATION

— France.

FRANCE. Département des Statistiques des Transports. Enquête annuelle d'entreprise: transports fluviaux de marchandises pour compte d'autrui. a., 1974- Paris.

INPUT DESIGN, COMPUTER.

GILB (TOM) and WEINBERG (GERALD M.) Humanized input: techniques for reliable keyed input. Cambridge, Mass., [1977]. pp. 283. *bibliog.*

INQUISITION

— Spain.

MARTI GILABERT (FRANCISCO) La abolicion de la inquisicion en España. Pamplona, 1975. pp. 358.

INSIDER TRADING IN SECURITIES

— United Kingdom.

JUSTICE (BRITISH SECTION OF THE INTERNATIONAL COMMISSION OF JURISTS) Insider trading: (a report); Chairman of committee William Goodhart. London, 1972. pp. 11.

INSTITUTIONAL ECONOMICS.

SCIENCE and ceremony: the institutional economics of C.E. Ayres; edited by William Breit and William Patton Culbertson; foreword by John Kenneth Galbraith. Austin, Texas, [1976]. pp. 210. *bibliog.*

ECONOMICS in institutional perspective: memorial essays in honor of K. William Kapp; edited by Rolf Steppacher [and others]. Lexington, Mass., [1977]. pp. 226. *bibliog.*

INSURANCE.

THOMEREAU (ALFRED) Pourquoi l'assurance ne doit jamais être obligatoire. Paris, [1897]. pp. 29. *(Extrait du Moniteur des Assurances du 15 mars 1897)*

— Dictionaries and encyclopedias.

LEXIKON der Wirtschaft: Versicherung; (Herausgeber: Heinrich Bader [and others]). Berlin, [1976]. pp. 696.

— Directories — United Kingdom.

INSURANCE DIRECTORY AND YEAR BOOK, THE (POST MAGAZINE ALMANACK); containing statistics and facts of ordinary life, industrial life, motor, property, liability, personal accident, pecuniary loss and marine, etc., insurance. a., 1977(136th)- Brentford.

— Rates and tables.

DOHERTY (NEIL) Insurance pricing and loss prevention. Farnborough, Hants., [1976]. pp. 134.

INSTITUTE OF ACTUARIES and FACULTY OF ACTUARIES [IN SCOTLAND]. Continuous Mortality Investigation Committee. Continuous mortality investigation reports. No. 2. [London, 1976]. pp. 103.

— Germany — State supervision.

SCHMITT-LERMANN (HANS) Hundert Jahre Bayerische Versicherungskammer. München, 1975. pp. 548. *bibliog.*

— Italy.

ITALY. Istituto Nazionale delle Assicurazioni. [1976]. Relazione sull'andamento della gestione nel quinquennio 1967-1971. [Roma, 1976?]. pp. 341.

INSURANCE.(Cont.)

— United Kingdom.

CARTER (ROBERT LEWIS) Economics and insurance: an introduction to the economic aspects of insurance. Stockport, [1972]. pp. 157. *bibliog.*

— United States — State supervision.

UNITED STATES. Department of Justice. Antitrust Division. 1977. Federal-state regulation of the pricing and marketing of insurance; ...edited by Paul W. MacAvoy. Washington, D.C., [1977]. pp. 103. *(American Enterprise Institute for Public Policy Research. AEI Studies. 155)*

INSURANCE, ACCIDENT

— United Kingdom.

WILLIAMS (C.V.) Insurance policies: survey of personal accident and sickness cover. London, 1969 (repr.1971). pp. 16. *(British Institute of Management. Information Summaries. No.142)*

INSURANCE, AGRICULTURAL

— Russia — Tajikistan.

IULDASHEV (IASHIN NIIAZOVICH) Voprosy gosudarstvennogo strakhovaniia sel'skokhoziaistvennogo proizvodstva: na primere kolkhozov Tadzhikskoi SSR. Dushanbe, 1976. pp. 190.

INSURANCE, AUTOMOBILE

— South Africa.

SOUTH AFRICA. Commission of Inquiry into Certain Aspects of Compulsory Motor Vehicle Insurance, 1974. 1976. Report (R.P. 52/1976). in SOUTH AFRICA. Parliament. House of Assembly. Votes and proceedings; (with Printed annexures).

INSURANCE, DISABILITY

— United States.

BERKOWITZ (MONROE) and others. Public policy toward disability. New York, 1976. pp. 150. *bibliogs.*

INSURANCE, EXPORT CREDIT

— United Kingdom.

U.K. Export Credits Gurarantee Department. Trading results. a., 1974/75- London.

U.K. Export Credits Guarantee Department. 1976. Insurance facilities of the British government's Export Credits Guarantee Department. [rev. ed.] [London, 1976]. pp. 58.

INSURANCE, GOVERNMENT

— Australia.

POWER (FRANCIS RENTON) The fight for "life", 1975. Sandringham, Victoria, [1977]. pp. 63.

INSURANCE, HEALTH

— Australia.

AUSTRALIA. Commonwealth Bureau of Census and Statistics. 1974. Persons covered by hospital and medical expenditure assistance schemes, August 1972. Canberra, [1974]. pp. 12.

— Germany.

BUHL (BARBARA) Die Selbstbeteiligung in der gesetzlichen Krankenversicherung. Bonn, 1976. pp. 38. *bibliog. (Germany (Bundesrepublik). Deutscher Bundestag. Wissenschaftliche Dienste. Materialien. 46)*

HEINZE (HELMUT) Zum Beitragszuschuss: rechtliche Gestaltung und Problematik einer Sozialleistung für Rentner an der Grenze zwischen gesetzlicher und privater Krankenversicherung. Köln, 1976. pp. 76. *bibliog. (Verband der Privaten Krankenversicherung. Dokumentationen. 5)*

— United Kingdom.

WILLIAMS (C.V.) Insurance policies: survey of personal accident and sickness cover. London, 1969 (repr.1971). pp. 16. *(British Institute of Management. Information Summaries. No.142)*

— United States.

ANDERSEN (RONALD) and others. Two decades of health services: social survey trends in use and expenditure. Cambridge, Mass., [1976]. pp. 387. *bibliog.*

KEINTZ (RITA M.) National health insurance and income distribution. Lexington, Mass., [1976]. pp. 218. *bibliog.*

INSURANCE, INDUSTRIAL

— United Kingdom.

GENERAL BENEFIT INSURANCE COMPANY. Proposals for the insurance of weekly allowance, medical attendance and medicine, during sickness; sums of money at death, burial expences, etc., annuities in old age, and other important provisions; established July 1820, etc. 19th ed. London, 1822. pp. 20.

INSURANCE, INVESTMENT GUARANTY.

MERON (THEODOR) Investment insurance in international law. Dobbs Ferry, N.Y., 1976. pp. 935.

INSURANCE, LIFE

— Australia.

AUSTRALIA. Commonwealth Bureau of Census and Statistics. 1975. Foreign ownership and control of life insurance business, 1973. Canberra, 1975. pp. 37.

— India.

INDIA. Committee of Enquiry into the Expenses of the Life Insurance Corporation. 1969. Report; [R.R. Morarka, chairman]. [Delhi], 1969. 2 pts. (in 1 vol.).

INSURANCE, MARINE

— Belgium.

GROOTE (HENRY L.V. DE) De zeeassurantie te Antwerpen en te Brugge in de zestiende eeuw. Antwerpen, 1975. pp. 181. *bibliog.*

INSURANCE, MATERNITY

— United Kingdom.

COUSSINS (JEAN) Maternity rights for working women. [London, 1976]. pp. 24.

INSURANCE, SOCIAL.

DOLE (GEORGES) Les ecclésiastiques et la sécurité sociale en droit comparé: intégration des clercs dans la cité. Paris, 1976. pp. 554. *bibliog.*

— Accounting.

INTERNATIONAL LABOUR OFFICE. 1976. The cost of social security: eighth international inquiry, 1967- 1971; with a supplement on the cost of non-statutory schemes. Geneva, 1976. pp. 189. *In various languages.*

— Belgium.

VERTONGEN-GOENS (ALBERT) Avant projet de loi sur l'assurance contre la maladie, les accidents, l'invalidité et la vieillesse, présenté à Mr. le Ministre de l'Industrie et du Travail. Termonde, 1897. pp. 26.

— Bolivia.

TEORIA Y PRACTICA DE LA SEGURIDAD SOCIAL; [pd. by] Instituto Boliviano de Seguridad Social. s-a., J1/D 1975 (no. 5)- La Paz.

— Canada.

CANADA. Statistics Canada. Social security: national programs. a., 1976(1st) [covering 1946-1975]- Ottawa. *[in English and French].*

— — Finance.

BIRD (RICHARD MILLER) Charging for public services: a new look at an old idea. Toronto, 1976. pp. 269. *bibliog. (Canadian Tax Foundation. Canadian Tax Papers. No. 59)*

— France.

FRANCE. Direction de la Sécurité Sociale. 1975. La sécurité sociale en France. Paris, 1975. pp. 104.

GREVET (PATRICE) Besoins populaires et financement public. [Paris, 1976]. pp. 543.

— Germany.

URBAN (OTTO) Das Wahlrecht der weiblichen Angestellten in der Reichsversicherungsordnung, im Versicherungsgesetz für Angestellte und bei den Kaufmannsgerichten. Berlin, 1912. pp. 24. *(Zentralverband der Handlungsgehilfen und -Gehilfinnen Deutschlands. Schriften. 25)*

— Israel.

ISRAEL. National Insurance Institute. 1958. Social insurance in Israel; an extract of an article written by G. Lotan. Jerusalem, [1958]. pp. 24.

— Nicaragua.

NICARAGUA. Junta Nacional de Asistencia y Previsión Social. Memoria. a., 1957/58-1958/59. Managua.

— Russia.

SOTSIAL'NOE strakhovanie v SSSR: sbornik ofitsial'nykh materialov. 2nd ed. Moskva, 1976. pp. 255.

NAVARRO (VICENTE) Social security and medicine in the USSR: a Marxist critique. Lexington, Mass., [1977]. pp. 149. *bibliog.*

— Sweden.

ENGLUND (KARL) Arbetarförsäkringsfrågan i svensk politik, 1884-1901. Uppsala, 1976. pp. 205. *bibliog. (Uppsala. Universitet. Historiska Institutionen. Studia Historica Upsaliensia. 82) With summary and list of tables in English.*

— Switzerland.

ENTSCHEIDUNGEN DES SCHWEIZERISCHEN BUNDESGERICHTES...: amtliche Sammlung. 5. Teil: Sozialversicherungsrecht. [in German or French]. 20-30 issues a yr., 1970 (96.Bd.)- Lausanne. *Continues Entscheidungen des eidgenössischen Versicherungsgerichtes (1926-1942, 1944-1969)*

— United Kingdom.

LISTER (RUTH) As man and wife?: a study of the cohabitation rule. London, [1973]. pp. 56. *(Child Poverty Action Group. Poverty Research Series. 2)*

ADLER (MICHAEL) Lecturer in Social Administration, and DU FEU (D.) A computer based welfare benefits information system: the Inverclyde project; a joint project between the University of Edinburgh, Inverclyde District Council [and] IBM United Kingdom. Peterlee, 1975. pp. 56. *(IBM United Kingdom Limited. UK Scientific Centre. [Technical Reports]. 0078)*

LAWRIE (PETER) pseud. On the dole: your guide to unemployment benefit plus other things you need to know. London, 1976. pp. 96.

LEWIS (PAUL) Child interim benefit: an interim guide. 2nd ed. London, 1976. pp. 20.

LISTER (RUTH) ed. National welfare benefits handbook. 6th ed. London, 1976. pp. 88. *(Child Poverty Action Group. Poverty Pamphlets. 13)*

POND (CHRIS) The attack on inflation: who pays?; a reply to the White Paper on the pay policy. London, 1976. fo.16. *(Low Pay Unit. Low Pay Papers. No. 11)*

TITMUSS (RICHARD MORRIS) Essays on 'The welfare state'; introduction by Brian Abel-Smith. 3rd ed. London, 1976. pp. 262.

CLARK (COLIN GRANT) Poverty before politics: a proposal for a reverse income tax. London, 1977. pp. 69. *bibliog. (Institute of Economic Affairs. Hobart Papers. 73)*

DRABBLE (RICHARD) Contributory benefits: unemployment, sickness and death, maternity, pensions, child benefits. London, 1977. pp. 62. *(Child Poverty Action Group. CPAG Rights Guide. No. 3)*

TAYLOR-GOOBY (PETER) and LAKEMAN (SUSAN) Welfare benefits advocacy (in Batley): official discretion and claimants' rights. [York], 1977. pp. 45. *bibliog. (Papers in Community Studies. No. 11)*

U.K. Central Office of Information. Reference Division. Reference Pamphlets. 90. Social security in Britain. 4th ed. London, 1977. pp. 44. *bibliog.*

— — **Bibliography.**

U.K. Department of Health and Social Security. Library. Annual list of publications. a., 1975- London.

— — **Research.**

SOCIAL security research: papers presented at a D[epartment of] H[ealth and] S[ocial] S[ecurity] seminar on 7 - 9 April 1976. London, H.M.S.O., 1977. pp. 217.

— — **Ireland, Northern.**

IRELAND, NORTHERN. National Insurance Fund, National Insurance (Reserve) Fund, Industrial Injuries Fund. Accounts...together with the report of the Comptroller and Auditor-General thereon. a., 1971/72- Belfast. *1948/49 - 1970/71 included in IRELAND, NORTHERN. Parliament. House of Commons. [Papers].*

— **United States.**

BRINKER (PAUL A.) and KLOS (JOSEPH J.) Poverty, manpower, and social security. [2nd ed.]. Austin, Tex., [1976]. pp. 560. *bibliogs.*

CAMPBELL (COLIN D.) Over-indexed benefits: the decoupling proposals for social security. Washington, D.C., 1976. pp. 23. *(American Enterprise Institute for Public Policy Research. Domestic Affairs Studies. 46)*

KAPLAN (ROBERT S.) Financial crisis in the social security system. Washington, D.C. [1976]. pp. 18. *(American Enterprise Institute for Public Policy Research. Domestic Affairs Studies. 47)*

VAN GORKOM (J.W.) Social security: the long-term deficit. Washington, [1976]. pp. 28. *(American Enterprise Institute for Public Policy Research. AEI Studies. No. 135)*

CAMPBELL (RITA RICARDO) Social security: promise and reality. Stanford, Calif., [1977]. pp. 351. *bibliog. (Stanford University. Hoover Institution on War, Revolution and Peace. Hoover Institution Publications. 179)*

MUNNELL (ALICIA HAYDOCK) The future of social security. Washington, D.C., [1977]. pp. 190. *(Brookings Institution. Studies in Social Economics)*

INSURANCE, UNEMPLOYMENT

— **Australia — Queensland.**

QUEENSLAND. Statutes, etc. 1922. An act to make provision for the insurance of unemployed workers, and for other ancillary purposes. [Brisbane, 1922]. pp. 15.

QUEENSLAND. 1924. Regulations, rules and orders in council under the Unemployed Workers Insurance Act of 1922. Brisbane, 1924. pp. 20.

— **Sweden.**

EDEBALK (PER GUNNAR) Arbetslöshetsförsäkringsdebatten: en studie i svensk socialpolitik, 1892-1934. Lund, 1975. pp. 327. *bibliog. (Lund. Ekonomisk-Historiska Föreningen. Skrifter vol. 17) Akademisk avhandling för avläggande av filosofie doktorsexamen, Lunds Universitet; with English summary.*

— **Switzerland.**

ILG (KONRAD) Sozialversicherung oder "politisches Geschäft"?: zur Debatte über die Sanierung der Arbeitslosen-Versicherung in der Nationalratssession vom Dezember 1936. Bern, 1937. pp. 39.

— **United Kingdom.**

DEACON (ALAN) In search of the scrounger: the administration of unemployment insurance in Britain, 1920-1931. London, 1976. pp. 110. *(Social Administration Research Trust. Occasional Papers on Social Administration. No. 60)*

LAWRIE (PETER) pseud. On the dole: your guide to unemployment benefit plus other things you need to know. London, 1976. pp. 96.

MESHER (JOHN) Compensation for unemployment. London, 1976. pp. 138. *bibliog.*

U.K. Parliament. House of Commons. Library. Research Division. Background Papers. No. 51. Unemployment benefit for occupational pensioners. [London, 1976]. pp. 7.

— **United States.**

HAMERMESH (DANIEL S.) Jobless pay and the economy. Baltimore, [1977]. pp. 114. *bibliog.*

INSURANCE COMPANIES

— **Australia.**

AUSTRALIA. Commonwealth Bureau of Census and Statistics. 1975. Foreign ownership and control of general insurance business, 1972-73 Canberra, 1975. pp. 39.

— **India.**

INDIA. Committee of Enquiry into the Expenses of the Life Insurance Corporation. 1969. Report; [R.R. Morarka, chairman]. [Delhi], 1969. 2 pts. (in 1 vol.).

— **Mexico.**

MEXICO. Statutes, etc. 1892-1956. Legislacion sobre seguros. Mexico, 1958. 2 vols. (in 1)

INSURANCE LAW

— **Mexico.**

MEXICO. Statutes, etc. 1892-1956. Legislacion sobre seguros. Mexico, 1958. 2 vols. (in 1)

INSURANCE LAW, INTERNATIONAL.

MERON (THEODOR) Investment insurance in international law. Dobbs Ferry, N.Y., 1976. pp. 935.

INSURGENCY

— **Kenya.**

CLAYTON (ANTHONY) Counter-insurgency in Kenya: a study of military operations against Mau Mau. Nairobi, 1976. pp. 63.

INTANGIBLE PROPERTY.

CLARKSON (KENNETH W.) Intangible capital and rates of return: effects of research and promotion on profitability. Washington, [1977]. pp. 77. *(American Enterprise Institute for Public Policy Research. AEI Studies. No. 138)*

INTELLECT.

WELFORD (ALAN TRAVISS) Skilled performance: perceptual and motor skills. Glenview, Ill., [1976]. pp. 200. *bibliog.*

INTELLECTUAL LIFE.

EISENSTADT (SHMUEL N.) and CURELARU (M.) The form of sociology: paradigms and crises. New York, [1976]. pp. 386.

CULTURE and its creators: essays in honor of Edward Shils; edited by Joseph Ben-David and Terry Nichols Clark. Chicago, 1977. pp. 325.

HIRSCHMAN (ALBERT O.) The passions and the interests: political arguments for capitalism before its triumph. Princeton, N.J., [1977]. pp. 153.

INTELLECTUALS.

HICKOX (MICHAEL STEPHEN HINDMARSH) The ideology of intellectual elites and its implications for the sociology of knowledge. 1976. fo. 431. *bibliog. Typescript. Ph. D. (London) thesis: unpublished. This thesis is the property of London University and may not be removed from the Library.*

The INTELLIGENTSIA and the intellectuals: theory, method and case study; edited by Aleksander Gella. London, [1976]. pp. 231. *bibliogs. Based on a round table discussion organised for the 8th World Congress of Sociology, Toronto, 1974.*

— **Argentine Republic — Political activity.**

MARSAL (JUAN FRANCISCO) La sombra del poder: (intelectuales y politica en España, Argentina y Mexico). Madrid, 1975. pp. 282.

— **Mexico — Political activity.**

MARSAL (JUAN FRANCISCO) La sombra del poder: (intelectuales y politica en España, Argentina y Mexico). Madrid, 1975. pp. 282.

— **Russia.**

USHAKOV (ANATOLII VASIL'EVICH) Revoliutsionnoe dvizhenie demokraticheskoi intelligentsii v Rossii, 1895-1904. Moskva, 1976. pp. 240.

— — **Ukraine.**

KURNOSOV (IURII OLEKSIIOVYCH) Intelihentsiia Ukraïns'koï RSR i naukovo-tekhnichnyi prohres, 1959-1970. Kyïv, 1975. pp. 208. *bibliog.*

— **Spain — Political activity.**

MARSAL (JUAN FRANCISCO) La sombra del poder: (intelectuales y politica en España, Argentina y Mexico). Madrid, 1975. pp. 282.

— **Underdeveloped areas.**

See UNDERDEVELOPED AREAS — Intellectuals.

— **United Kingdom.**

HICKOX (MICHAEL STEPHEN HINDMARSH) The ideology of intellectual elites and its implications for the sociology of knowledge. 1976. fo. 431. *bibliog. Typescript. Ph. D. (London) thesis: unpublished. This thesis is the property of London University and may not be removed from the Library.*

— **Venezuela — Political activity.**

VENEZUELA: crecimiento sin desarrollo; [by] D.F. Maza Zavala [and others]. Mexico, 1974. pp. 441.

INTELLIGENCE LEVELS.

KAMIN (LEON J.) The science and politics of I.Q. Harmondsworth, 1977. pp. 252.

INTELLIGENCE SERVICE

— **Russia.**

MIAGKOV (ALEKSEI) Inside the KGB: an exposé by an officer of the Third Directorate. Richmond, Surrey, 1976. pp. 131.

— **United States.**

The LAWLESS state: the crimes of the U.S. intelligence agencies; by Morton H. Halperin [and others]. Harmondsworth, 1976. pp. 328. *bibliog.*

WISE (DAVID) The American police state: the government against the people. New York, [1976]. pp. 437.

UNITED STATES. House of Representatives. Select Committee on Intelligence. 1977. CIA: the Pike report; with an introduction by Philip Agee. Nottingham, 1977. pp. 284.

INTER-AMERICAN DEVELOPMENT BANK.

ORTIZ MENA (ANTONIO) Development in Latin America: a view from the IDB; addresses and documents, 1971-75. [Washington, Inter-American Development Bank, 1976?]. pp. 515.

IDB NEWS; [pd. by] Inter-American Development Bank. m. Washington. *Current issues only kept.*

INTERCONTINENTAL BALLISTIC MISSILES.

BEARD (EDMUND) Developing the ICBM: a study in bureaucratic politics. New York, 1976. pp. 273. *bibliog. (Columbia University. Institute of War and Peace Studies)*

INTERCULTURAL COMMUNICATION.

OSGOOD (CHARLES EGERTON) and others. Cross-cultural universals of affective meaning. Urbana, [1975]. pp. 486. *bibliog.*

READ (WILLIAM H.) America's mass media merchants. Baltimore, [1976]. pp. 209.

VARIATIONS in black and white perceptions of the social environment; edited by Harry C. Triandis. Urbana, [1976]. pp. 202. *bibliog. Tables on microfiche (3 cards).*

INTERCULTURAL EDUCATION.

SIKKEMA (MILDRED) and NIYEKAWA-HOWARD (AGNES M.) Cross-cultural learning and self-growth: getting to know ourselves and others. New York, [1977]. pp. 121. *bibliog.*

INTEREST AND USURY

— Netherlands — Mathematical models.

FASE (M.M.G.) and NIEUWKERK (MARIUS VAN) Anticipated inflation and interest rates in an open economy: a study of the Gibson paradox for the Netherlands. Amsterdam, [1975?]. pp. 24. *bibliog. (Nederlandsche Bank. Reprints. No. 17)*

INTERGOVERNMENTAL FISCAL RELATIONS

— Australia.

TASMANIA. Treasury. 1975. Grants to Tasmania. in TASMANIA. Parliament. Journals and Printed Papers. 1975, no.33.

— United States.

JONES (CHARLES OSCAR) and THOMAS (ROBERT D.) eds. Public policy making in a federal system. Beverly Hills, Calif., [1976]. pp. 284. *bibliogs.*

MAXWELL (JAMES ACKLEY) and ARONSON (JAY RICHARD) Financing state and local governments. 3rd ed. Washington, D.C., [1977]. pp. 290. *bibliog. (Brookings Institution. Studies of Government Finance)*

INTERGOVERNMENTAL TAX RELATIONS

— Canada.

VICTORIA CONFERENCE ON NATURAL RESOURCE REVENUES, 1975. Natural resource revenues: a test of federalism; edited by Anthony Scott. Vancouver, [1976]. pp. 261. *bibliog. (British Columbia Institute for Economic Policy Analysis. Analysis Series)*

INTERINDUSTRY ECONOMICS.

CHEW (SOON BENG) A study of efficiency in the manufacturing sector: inter-industry and inter-firm comparisons. [Singapore], National Productivity Board, 1973. fo. 40. *bibliog.*

GOH (ROSALIND S.L.) and CHEW (SOON BENG) A study of the productivity performance of manufacturing industries under different capital ownership, 1968-1970. [Singapore], National Productivity Board, 1973. fo. 43.

DIEKMANN (ACHIM) Die Automobilnachfrage als Konjunktur und Wachstumsfaktor: eine Input-Output-Studie. Tübingen, [1975]. pp. 489. *bibliog. (Tübingen. Institut für Angewandte Wirtschaftsforschung. Schriftenreihe. Band 29)*

ISRAEL. Central Bureau of Statistics. 1975. Input-output tables, 1968/69; by David Chen. Jerusalem, 1975. pp. 255. *(Special Series. No.471) In English and Hebrew.*

ENERGY and the environment: a structural analysis; edited by Anne P. Carter. Hanover, N.H.,1976. pp. 262. *bibliogs. Based on work carried out by a research team from Harvard and Brandeis universities.*

McNICOLL (IAIN H.) The Shetland economy: an empirical study in regional input-output analysis. Glasgow, [1976]. pp. 56. *bibliog. (Glasgow. University of Strathclyde. Fraser of Allander Institute. Research Monographs. No. 2)*

MIYAZAWA (KEN'ICHI) Input-output analysis and the structure of income distribution. Berlin, 1976. pp. 135. *bibliog.*

BRITISH ASSOCIATION FOR THE ADVANCEMENT OF SCIENCE. Section F. Meeting, 1976. Structure, system and economic policy; proceedings...held at the University of Lancaster 1-8 September 1976; edited by Wassily Leontief. Cambridge, 1977. pp. 223. *bibliogs.*

NATIONAL ECONOMIC DEVELOPMENT OFFICE. A study of UK nationalised industries: background paper 6: relationships with other sectors of the economy: the evidence of input-output analysis. London, 1977. pp. 51.

INTERNAL SECURITY

— United States.

PURIFOY (LEWIS McCARROLL) Harry Truman's China policy: McCarthyism and the diplomacy of hysteria, 1947-1951. New York, 1976. pp. 316.

INTERNATIONAL, THE.

RAKOVSKII (KHRISTIAN GEORGIEVICH) Das Wiedererwachen der Internationale: Rede gehalten am internationalen Massenmeeting vom 8. Februar 1916 im Volkshaus in Bern. Bern, [1916]. pp. 16.

BAUMANN (WILHELM) Krieg und Proletariat. Wien, 1924. pp. 156.

COMMUNIST INTERNATIONAL. Projet de programme de l'Internationale Communiste adopté par la Commission du programme du C.E. de l'I.C., le 25 mai 1928. Paris, 1928. pp. 39. *(Cahiers du Communisme. Suppléments)*

KLOTZ (HENRY) La Russie des Soviets: faits et documents: qu'y a-t-il de vrai dans la formule: le communisme, voilà l'ennemi. Paris, 1928. pp. 189. *bibliog.*

INTERNATIONAL MARXIST GROUP. The struggle in Bengal and the Fourth International. [London, 1971]. pp. 14.

BRONSON (HAROLD E.) The renegade revolutionaries. Vancouver, [1975]. pp. 157. *bibliog.*

DUIKER (WILLIAM J.) The Comintern and Vietnamese communism. Athens, Ohio, 1975. pp. 42. *(Ohio University. Center for International Studies. Papers in International Studies. Southeast Asia Series. No. 37)*

LEWIN (ERWIN) and SCHUMACHER (HORST) Einheit im Kampf gegen Faschismus und Krieg!: der VII. Kongress der Kommunistischen Internationale, 1935. Berlin, 1975. pp. 141. *bibliog.*

GRAHAM (MARCUS) Marxism and a free society: an anarchist reply to Isaac Deutscher's address On socialist man with particular reference to the minutes of the First International and the sabotaging of the Hague Congress by the Marx clique. London, 1976. pp. 16.

INTERNATIONAL WORKING MEN'S ASSOCIATION. Congress, [5th], The Hague, 1872. The Hague congress of the First International, September 2- 7, 1872: minutes and documents; (translated by Richard Dixon and Alex Miller). Moscow, [1976]. pp. 758. *(Institut Marksizma-Leninizma. Documents of the First International)*

JOSEPHSON (ERLAND F.) SKP och Komintern, 1921-1924: motsättningarna inom Sveriges Kommunistiska Parti och des relationer till den Kommunistiska Internationalen. Uppsala, 1976. pp. 362. *bibliog. (Uppsala. Universitet. Historiska Institutionen. Studia Historica Upsaliensia. 84) With English summary.*

KOMMUNISTICHESKOE dvizhenie v avangarde bor'by za mir, natsional'noe i sotsial'noe osvobozhdenie: k 40-letiiu VII kongressa Kommunisticheskogo Internatsionala. Moskva, 1976. pp. 366.

KRIVOGUZ (IGOR' MIKHAILOVICH) Osnovnye periody i zakonomernosti mezhdunarodnogo rabochego dvizheniia do Oktiabria 1917 g. Moskva, 1976. pp. 364.

MIKHAILOV (MIKHAIL IVANOVICH) Bor'ba protiv bakunizma v I Internatsionale. Moskva, 1976. pp. 351.

VILENSKA (ESTHER) Confrontation and unity within the labor movement, 1889-1923. New York, [1976]. pp. 98. *bibliog.*

WRYNN (J.F.) The Socialist International and the politics of European reconstruction, 1919-1930. Uithoorn, 1976. pp. 242. *bibliog.*

DAHLEM (FRANZ) Am Vorabend des zweiten Weltkrieges:...Erinnerungen. Berlin, 1977 in progress.

BARTSCH (GUENTER) Trotzkismus als eigentlicher Sowjetkommunismus?: die IV. Internationale und ihre Konkurrenzverbände. Berlin, [1977]. pp. 194.

COMMUNIST INTERNATIONAL. World Congress, 2nd, 1920. Second congress of the Communist International: minutes of the proceedings; [translated by R.A. Archer]. London, [1977]. 2 vols. *bibliog.*

KOMINTERN, KIM i molodezhnoe dvizhenie, 1919-1943: sbornik dokumentov. Moskva, 1977. 2 vols.

— Bibliography.

LIBRA. Libra Antiquaria Catalogues. N.1. Socialisme; Troisième Internationale. Milan, 1958. pp. 30.

INTERNATIONAL AGENCIES.

MOELLER (HANS) of Munich. Internationale Wirtschaftsorganisationen. Wiesbaden, [1961]. pp. 171. *bibliog.*

TOKAREVA (PRASKOV'IA ALEKSEEVNA) Uchrezhdenie mezhgosudarstvennykh ekonomicheskikh organizatsii stran-chlenov SEV: pravovye voprosy. Moskva, 1976. pp. 182.

LUARD (DAVID EVAN TRANT) International agencies: the emerging framework of interdependence. London, 1977. pp. 338.

— Information services.

DEVSIS STUDY TEAM. 1976. DEVSIS: the preliminary design of an international information system for the development sciences. Ottawa, International Development Research Centre [Canada], [1976]. pp. 247. *bibliog.*

— Law and legislation.

TOKAREVA (PRASKOV'IA ALEKSEEVNA) ed. Mnogostoronnee ekonomicheskoe sotrudnichestvo sotsialisticheskikh gosudarstv: dokumenty za 1972-1975 gg. Moskva, 1976. pp. 408.

INTERNATIONAL AGRICULTURAL COOPERATION.

AGRARNO-promyshlennaia integratsiia stran SEV. Moskva, 1976. pp. 286.

INTERNATIONAL AND MUNICIPAL LAW

— Italy.

Il GIUDICE italiano di Fronte alla Convenzione europea dei diritti dell'uomo: atti della Tavola Rotonda tenuta in Roma il 13 dicembre 1972. Padova, 1975. pp. 54.

INTERNATIONAL ATOMIC ENERGY AGENCY.

INTERNATIONAL ATOMIC ENERGY AGENCY. Annual report. a., 1960/61(4th)- [Vienna]. *1957/58-1959/60 (1st-3rd) included in INTERNATIONAL ATOMIC ENERGY AGENCY. General Conference. [Documents]. 2nd Session, 1958-1961.*

INTERNATIONAL ATOMIC ENERGY AGENCY. The Agency's budget (formerly Program and budget). a., 1962- [Vienna]. *From 1965-1968 in 2 pts; The Agency's programme and The Agency's budget. From 1969- every alternate issue of the Agency's budget included the Agency's programme.*

INTERNATIONAL ATOMIC ENERGY AGENCY. General Conference. Press release[s]. irreg., current issues only. Vienna.

— Finance.

INTERNATIONAL ATOMIC ENERGY AGENCY. The Agency's accounts. a., 1960- [Vienna].

INTERNATIONAL ATOMIC ENERGY AGENCY. The Agency's budget (formerly Program and budget). a., 1962- [Vienna]. *From 1965-1968 in 2 pts; The Agency's programme and The Agency's budget. From 1969- every alternate issue of the Agency's budget included the Agency's programme.*

— Technical assistance.

INTERNATIONAL ATOMIC ENERGY AGENCY. Director General. The provision of technical assistance by the Agency. a., 1968- [Vienna].

INTERNATIONAL BROADCASTING.

ABSHIRE (DAVID M.) International broadcasting: a new dimension of Western diplomacy. Beverly Hills, [1976]. pp. 90. *bibliog. (Georgetown University. Center for Strategic and International Studies. Washington Papers. vol. 4/35)*

INTERNATIONAL BUSINESS ENTERPRISES.

UFERMANN (PAUL) Die Internationale der Unternehmer: überstaatliche Verbindungen der Industrie, des Handels und des Verkehrs: ein erweiterter Vortrag. Lübeck, [1926]. pp. 42.

FLIGLER (CARLOS) Multinational public enterprises. [Washington], International Bank for Reconstruction and Development, 1967. pp. 136.

LEVINSON (CHARLES) The multinational pharmaceutical industry. [Geneva, 1973]. pp. 121.

COUNTER INFORMATION SERVICES. Anti-Reports. No. 8. The oil fix: an investigation into the control and costs of energy. London, [1974]. pp. 49. *bibliog.*

LUNDSTRÖM (RAGNHILD) Alfred Nobel som internationell företagare: den nobelska sprängämnesindustrin, 1864-1886. Uppsala, 1974. pp. 272. *bibliog. (Uppsala. Universitet. Ekonomisk-Historiska Institution. Ekonomisk-Historiska Studier. 10) Doktorsavhandling vid Uppsala universitet, 1974; with English summary.*

BERTIN (GILLES Y.) L'industrie française face aux multinationales. Paris, 1975. pp. 143. *(France. Commissariat Général du Plan. Economie et Planification)*

The ECONOMIC effects of multinational corporations: lectures given at Western Michigan University under the sponsorship of the Department of Economics, academic year 1974-75; Werner Sichel, editor. Ann Arbor, [1975]. pp. 87. *(Michigan University. Bureau of Business Research. Michigan Business Papers. No. 61)*

The FUTURE of the multinational corporation; edited by Michael T. Skully. Darlinghurst, N.S.W., 1975. fo. 55.

GENERAL FEDERATION OF TRADE UNIONS. Courtaulds: the anatomy of a multinational. London, [1975]. pp. 112.

HJELMVIK (SIGVARD) Gränslösa affärer: om export och utlandsinvesteringar. [Stockholm, 1975]. pp. 222. *bibliog.*

RADICE (HUGO) ed. International firms and modern imperialism: selected readings. Harmondsworth, 1975. pp. 264. *bibliog.*

BOEHNKE (ROLF) Diversifizierte Unternehmen: eine Untersuchung über wettbewerbliche Wirkungen, Ursachen und Ausmass der Diversifizierung. Berlin, [1976]. pp. 277. *bibliog. With English summary.*

BOMERS (G.B.J.) Multinational corporations and industrial relations: a comparative study of West Germany and the Netherlands. Assen, 1976. pp. 226. *bibliog.*

CRONJÉ (SUZANNE) and others. Lonrho: portrait of a multinational. Harmondsworth, 1976. pp. 316.

HELLINGER (DOUGLAS A.) and HELLINGER (STEPHEN H.) Unemployment and the multinationals: a strategy for technological change in Latin America. Port Washington, N.Y., 1976. pp. 158. *bibliog.*

HYMER (STEPHEN HERBERT) The international operations of national firms: a study of direct foreign investment. Cambridge, Mass., [1976]. pp. 253. *bibliog.*

JAINARAIN (ISERDEO) Trade and underdevelopment: a study of the small Caribbean countries and large multinational corporations. Guyana, 1976. pp. 390. *bibliog.*

KOLDE (ENDEL JAKOB) The Pacific quest: the concept and scope of an oceanic community. Lexington, Mass., [1976]. pp. 161.

MATTHEWS (HARRY G.) Multinational corporations and black power. Cambridge, Mass., [1976]. pp. 124.

ROBINSON (RICHARD D.) National control of foreign business entry: a survey of fifteen countries. New York, 1976. pp. 508. *bibliogs.*

SANIO (ERHARD) and others. Internationale Konzerne und Arbeiterklasse. Frankfurt am Main, 1976. pp. 200. *(Institut für Marxistische Studien und Forschungen. Klassenkämpfe im Kapitalistischen Europa. Band 7)*

SAUVANT (KARL P.) and LAVIPOUR (FARID G.) eds. Controlling multinational enterprises: problems, strategies, counterstrategies. London, 1976. pp. 335. *bibliog.*

STOBAUGH (ROBERT B.) and others. Nine investments abroad and their impact at home: case studies on multinational enterprises and the U.S. economy. Boston, [Mass.], 1976. pp. 222.

TSURUMI (YOSHIHIRO) The Japanese are coming: a multinational interaction of firms and politics. Cambridge, Mass., [1976]. pp. 333.

UNILEVER LIMITED. Unilever and economic development in the third world; (speech delivered in London by Mr. D. A. Orr, ..., and in Rotterdam by Mr. H.F. van den Hoven,...12th May, 1976). London, [1976]. pp. 9.

YOSHINO (MICHAEL Y.) Japan's multinational enterprises. Cambridge, Mass., 1976. pp. 191.

The CASE for the multinational corporation; [by] J. Fred Weston [and others]; edited by Carl H. Madden. New York, 1977. pp. 212. *Papers of the National Chamber Foundation national conference in Washington, D.C., November 25-26, 1975.*

EINFLUSS multinationaler Unternehmen auf Aussenwirtschaft und Branchenstruktur der Bundesrepublik Deutschland; [by] Rolf Jungnickel [and others]. Hamburg, 1977. pp. 431. *bibliog. (Hamburg. Hamburgisches Welt-Wirtschafts-Archiv. Veröffentlichungen)*

JAMES (BARRIE G.) The future of the multinational pharmaceutical industry to 1990. London, 1977. pp. 283. *bibliogs.*

JENKINS (RHYS OWEN) Dependent industrialization in Latin America: the automotive industry in Argentina, Chile, and Mexico. New York, 1977. pp. 298.

MATTHIES (KLAUS) Transnationale Unternehmen in Mexiko. Hamburg, 1977. pp. 185. *bibliog. (Hamburg. Hamburgisches Welt-Wirtschafts-Archiv. Veröffentlichungen)*

The MULTINATIONAL enterprise in a hostile world: proceedings of a conference held in Geneva under the auspices of the Graduate Institute of International Studies [and others]; edited by Gerard Curzon and Victoria Curzon, etc. London, 1977. pp. 147.

MULTINATIONALS from small countries; edited by Tamir Agmon and Charles P. Kindleberger. Cambridge, Mass., [1977]. pp. 224. *Based on a colloquium held by the M.I.T. Center for International Studies and the Sloan School of Management in 1976.*

VERNON (RAYMOND) Storm over the multinationals: the real issues. Cambridge, Mass., 1977. pp. 260.

WILMS-WRIGHT (CARL) Transnational corporations: a stategy for control. London, 1977. pp. 36. *(Fabian Society. Research Series. [No.] 334)*

YOUNG (STEPHEN) and HOOD (NEIL) Chrysler U.K.: a corporation in transition. New York, 1977. pp. 342.

— Accounting.

BURNS (JOSEPH M.) Accounting standards and international finance; with special reference to multinationals. Washington, D.C., 1976. pp. 59. *(American Enterprise Institute for Public Policy Research. Domestic Affairs Studies. 49)*

— Bibliography.

BROOKE (MICHAEL Z.) and others, compilers. International business bibliography. London, 1977. pp. 480.

— Finance.

POMPER (CLAUDE L.) International investment planning: an integrated approach. Amsterdam, 1976. pp. 204.

— Mathematical models.

POMPER (CLAUDE L.) International investment planning: an integrated approach. Amsterdam, 1976. pp. 204.

— Taxation.

ADAMS (J.D.R.) and WHALLEY (JOHN) The international taxation of multinational enterprises in developed countries. London, 1977. pp. 178.

— Netherlands.

NETHERLANDS. Commissie van Drie. 1976. Rapport...: onderzoek naar de juistheid van verklaringen over betalingen door een Amerikaanse vliegtuigfabriek. 's-Gravenhage, 1976. pp. 240.

— Underdeveloped areas.

See UNDERDEVELOPED AREAS — International business enterprises.

INTERNATIONAL CENTRE FOR SETTLEMENT OF INVESTMENT DISPUTES.

INTERNATIONAL CENTRE FOR SETTLEMENT OF INVESTMENT DISPUTES. Administrative Council. Annual meeting: summary proceedings. a., 1972(6th), 1974(8th)- Washington.

INTERNATIONAL CHILDREN'S CENTRE.

FRANCE. Direction de la Documentation. La Documentation Française. Notes et Etudes Documentaires. No. 4,240. Le Centre international de l'enfance. Paris, 1975. pp. 31.

INTERNATIONAL COOPERATION.

INTERNATIONAL COOPERATION.

EVROPEISKAIA bezopasnost' i sotrudnichestvo: predposylki, problemy, perspektivy. Moskva, 1976. pp. 302.

FREYMOND (JACQUES) International co-operation in a changing world order. [Lagos, 1976]. pp. 33. *(Nigerian Institute of International Affairs. Lecture Series. No. 5)*

NORTH-South: developing a new relationship; edited by Pierre Uri. Paris, [1976]. pp. 58. *(Atlantic Institute. Atlantic Papers. 1975.6)*

SIMAI (MIHÁLY) World problems, global projections and social conflicts of our globe. Budapest, 1976. pp. 24. *(Hungarian Scientific Council for World Economy. [Publications]. Trends in World Economy. No. 18)*

TREZISE (PHILIP H.) Rebuilding grain reserves: toward an international system. Washington, [1976]. pp. 66.

GOALS for mankind: a report to the Club of Rome; [edited by] Ervin Laszlo. London, 1977. pp. 434. *bibliog. Fifth report to the Club of Rome.*

INTERNATIONAL ECONOMIC INTEGRATION.

CONFERENCE OF FOREIGN MINISTERS OF NON-ALIGNED COUNTRIES, GEORGETOWN, 1972. The Georgetown declaration, the action programme for economic co-operation and related documents. [Georgetown, Ministry of Foreign Affairs, 1973?]. pp. 61.

ALLEN (POLLY REYNOLDS) Organization and administration of a monetary union. Princeton, 1976. pp. 85. *bibliog. (Princeton University. Department of Economics and Sociology. International Finance Section. Princeton Studies in International Finance. No. 38)*

INTERNATIONAL ECONOMIC ASSOCIATION. Congress, 4th, Budapest, 1974. Economic integration: worldwide, regional, sectoral: proceedings of the Fourth Congress...; edited by Fritz Machlup. London, 1976. pp. 375. *bibliog.*

SCHMITTHOFF (CLIVE MACMILLAN) and SIMMONDS (KENNETH R.) eds. International economic and trade law: universal and regional integration. Leyden, 1976. pp. 252.

BHUTTO (ZULFIKAR ALI) The third world: new directions. London, 1977. pp. 144.

MACHLUP (FRITZ) A history of thought on economic integration. London, 1977. pp. 323. *bibliog.*

MILJAN (TOIVO) The reluctant Europeans: the attitudes of the Nordic countries towards European integration. London, [1977]. pp. 325. *bibliog.*

INTERNATIONAL ECONOMIC RELATIONS.

KOBATSCH (RUDOLF) Internationale Wirtschaftspolitik: ein Versuch ihrer wissenschaftlichen Erklärung auf entwicklungsgeschichtlicher Grundlage. Wien, 1907. pp. 473.

MOELLER (HANS) of Munich. Internationale Wirtschaftsorganisationen. Wiesbaden, [1961]. pp. 171. *bibliog.*

NORTH LONDON HASLEMERE GROUP. The Haslemere declaration: a radical analysis of the relationships between the rich world and the poor world. 6th ed. London, 1972. pp. 28. *bibliog.*

UNITED NATIONS. Conference on Trade and Development. 1972. The international monetary situation: impact on world trade and development; report. (TD/140/Rev.1). New York, 1972. pp. 70.

INTERNATIONAL SYMPOSIUM ON GROWTH AND WORLD EQUILIBRIUM, ELSINORE, 1973. A report [of the symposium]. [Copenhagen, 1973]. pp. 85. *Jointly organised by Danchurchaid and Oxfam of Great Britain.*

[WORKING papers prepared for the Commonwealth Group of Experts drawing up practical measures for closing the gap between rich and poor countries]. [London, Commonwealth Secretariat, 1975-77]. 56 pts. (in 1 vol.)

BOGNÁR (JÓZSEF) New forces and currents in the international economy. Budapest, 1975. pp. 23. *(Magyar Tudományos Akadémia. Világgazdasági Kutató Intézet. Studies on Developing Countries. No. 83)*

CORBET (HUGH) Raw materials: beyond the rhetoric of commodity power. London, 1975. pp. 41. *(Trade Policy Research Centre. International Issues. No. 1)*

HJELMVIK (SIGVARD) Gränslösa affärer: om export och utlandsinvesteringar. [Stockholm, 1975]. pp. 222. *bibliog.*

SALVATORE (DOMINICK) Schaum's outline of theory and problems of international economics. New York, [1975]. pp. 191.

The WORLD economy in transition; a tripartite report by seventeen economists from the European Community...Japan...and North America...[based on a conference held at Kiel in 1975] . Washington, [1975]. pp. 45. *(Brookings Institution and others. Tripartite Reports)*

AMIN (SAMIR) Unequal development: an essay on the social formations of peripheral capitalism: translated [from the French] by Brian Pearce. Hassocks, [1976]. pp. 440. *bibliog.*

BALANCE of power or hegemony: the interwar monetary system; Benjamin M. Rowland, editor, [and others]. New York, 1976. pp. 266. *Essays originally presented as working papers at the Lehrman Institute's International Monetary Seminar, 1973-1974.*

The COMMONWEALTH and development: the report of the conference sponsored by O[verseas] D[evelopment] I[nstitute] and St. Catharine's-Cumberland Lodge, at Cumberland Lodge, 13-15 February 1976. London, [1976]. pp. 59.

DEUTSCHES INSTITUT FÜR WIRTSCHAFTSFORSCHUNG. Sonderhefte. [Neue Folge]. 114. Perspektiven und Probleme wirtschaftlicher Zusammenarbeit zwischen Ost- und Westeuropa; ([edited by] Doris Cornelsen [and others]). Berlin, [1976]. pp. 204. *Papers of a symposium held in West Berlin in 1975; in various languages.*

FRANCE. Groupe de Réflexion sur les Stratégies Industrielles. 1976. La division mondiale du travail. Paris, 1976. 2 vols. (in 1). *(France. Ministère de l'Industrie et de la Recherche. Etudes de Politique Industrielle. 9)*

INTEGRATION in the world economy: East-West and inter-state relations; edited by József Nyilas; English translation by József Illés and István Véges. Leyden, 1976. pp. 275. *Based on Korunk világgazdasága. vol. 1, under the auspices of the Department of World Economy, Karl Marx University of Economic Sciences, Budapest.*

INTERNATIONAL ECONOMIC STUDIES INSTITUTE. Raw materials and foreign policy. Washington, D.C., [1976]. pp. 416.

KEMPER (RIA) Nationale Verfügung über natürliche Ressourcen und die neue Weltwirtschaftsordnung der Vereinten Nationen. Berlin, [1976]. pp. 155. *bibliog.*

MALLY (GERHARD) Interdependence: the European-American connection in the global context. Lexington, Mass., [1976]. pp. 229.

NORTH-South: developing a new relationship; edited by Pierre Uri. Paris, [1976]. pp. 58. *(Atlantic Institute. Atlantic Papers. 1975.6)*

OBMINSKIJ (ERNEST EVGEN'EVICH) The mechanism of exploiting developing countries. Budapest, 1976. pp. 33. *(Magyar Tudományos Akadémia. Világgazdasági Kutató Intézet. Studies on Developing Countries. No. 77)*

PARTANT (FRANÇOIS) La guérilla économique: les conditions du développement. Paris, [1976]. pp. 220. *bibliog.*

The POLITICS of aid, trade and investment; edited by Satish Raichur [and] Craig Liske. New York, [1976]. pp. 218. *bibliogs.*

RESHAPING the international order: a report to the Club of Rome; Jan Tinbergen, coordinator, Antony J. Dolman, editor, Jan van Ettinger, director. New York, [1976]. pp. 325. *This publication was realised in cooperation with the Foundation Reshaping the International Order (RIO).*

SCHNEIDER (WILLIAM) Food, foreign policy and raw materials cartels. New York, [1976]. pp. 119. *(National Strategy Information Center. Strategy Papers. No. 28)*

SHARP (ROBIN) Whose right to work?: international aspects of employment in Britain and the developing countries and their implications for UK policy. London, [1976]. pp. 49. *bibliog. (Oxfam. Public Affairs Unit. Oxfam Public Affairs Reports. 2)*

SIMAI (MIHÁLY) World problems, global projections and social conflicts of our globe. Budapest, 1976. pp. 24. *(Hungarian Scientific Council for World Economy. [Publications]. Trends in World Economy. No. 18)*

STREETEN (PAUL PATRICK) The dynamics of the new poor power. Oxford, [1976]. pp. 13. *(Oxford. University. Institute of Commonwealth Studies. Reprint Series. No. 84 E)*

TRADE, inflation and ethics. Lexington, Mass., [1976]. pp. 303. *bibliog. (Commission on Critical Choices for Americans. Critical Choices for Americans. vol.5) Prepared under the auspices of the Commission on Critical Choices for Americans.*

LAZAR (LEONARD) Transnational economic and monetary law, transactions and contracts. Dobbs Ferry, N.Y., 1977 in progress. *Loose leaf.*

CORDEN (WARNER MAX) Inflation, exchange rates and the world economy: lectures on international monetary economics. Oxford, 1977. pp. 160. *bibliogs.*

ECONOMIC foreign policies of industrial states, edited by Wilfrid L. Kohl. Lexington, Mass., [1977]. pp. 246.

FAWCETT (JAMES EDMUND SANDFORD) International economic conflicts: prevention and resolution. London, [1977]. pp. 127.

GOALS for mankind: a report to the Club of Rome; [edited by] Ervin Laszlo. London, 1977. pp. 434. *bibliog. Fifth report to the Club of Rome.*

HIRSCH (FRED) and others. Alternatives to monetary disorder. New York, [1977]. pp. 153. *bibliog. (Council on Foreign Relations. 1980s Project Studies)*

KOJIMA (KIYOSHI) Japan and a new world economic order. London, [1977]. pp. 190. *A revision of previously published essays.*

The LOMÉ Convention and a new international economic order; edited by Frans A.M. Alting von Geusau. Leyden, 1977. pp. 249. *(John F. Kennedy Institute. Center for International Studies. Publications. Nr. 11) Based on papers from an international colloqium held by the Institute in 1975.*

SINGER (HANS WOLFGANG) and ANSARI (JAVED A.) Rich and poor countries. London, 1977. pp. 228.

TOWARDS a new international economic order: a final report by a Commonwealth Experts' Group; [Alister McIntyre, chairman] . London, Commonwealth Secretariat, [1977]. pp. 104.

— Mathematical models.

QUANTITATIVE studies of international economic relations; editor Herbert Glejser. Amsterdam, 1976. pp. 281. *bibliogs. Papers of an international meeting held at the Facultés Universitaires Notre Dame de la Paix of Namur in 1974.*

INTERNATIONAL FINANCE.

OIKONOMIDES (CHRISTOPHES) Earned international reserve units: the catalyst of two complementary world problems: the monetary and development. Oxford, 1973 repr. 1976. pp. 24.

HODGMAN (DONALD RENWICK) National monetary policies and international monetary cooperation. Boston, Mass., [1974]. pp. 266.

SANDERSON (FRED H.) and CLEVELAND (HAROLD VAN BUREN) Strains in international finance and trade. Beverly Hills, [1974]. pp. 71. *bibliogs. (Georgetown University. Center for Strategic and International Studies. Washington Papers. vol. 2/14)*

ASCHHEIM (JOSEPH) and PARK (YOON S.) Artificial currency units: the formation of functional currency areas. Princeton, 1976. pp. 29. *bibliog. (Princeton University. Department of Economics and Sociology. International Finance Section. Essays in International Finance. No.114)*

BRENNER (MICHAEL J.) The politics of international monetary reform: the exchange crisis. Cambridge, Mass., [1976]. pp. 144.

BROWN (WEIR M.) World afloat: national policies ruling the waves. Princeton, [1976]. pp. 33. *bibliog. (Princeton University. Department of Economics and Sociology. International Finance Section. Essays in International Finance. No. 116)*

BURNS (JOSEPH M.) Accounting standards and international finance; with special reference to multinationals. Washington, D.C., 1976. pp. 59. *(American Enterprise Institute for Public Policy Research. Domestic Affairs Studies. 49)*

CARBAUGH (ROBERT J.) and FAN (LIANG-SHING) The international monetary system: history, institutions, analyses. Lawrence, Kan., [1976]. pp. 168. *bibliog.*

EMMINGER (OTMAR) On the way to a new international monetary order. Washington, D.C., [1976]. pp. 21. *(American Enterprise Institute for Public Policy Research. Foreign Affairs Studies. 39)*

EUROCURRENCIES and the international monetary system; edited by Carl H. Stem [and others]. Washington, D.C., [1976]. pp. 413. *bibliog. Papers from four conference sessions sponsored by the American Enterprise Institute for Public Policy Research and the U.S. Treasury.*

INTERNATIONAL CENTER FOR MONETARY AND BANKING STUDIES. Conference, 2nd, Geneva, 1973. Capital movements and their control: proceedings of the second conference...; edited by Alexander K. Swoboda. Leiden, 1976. pp. 240. *bibliogs. (Geneva. Graduate Institute of International Studies. International Economics Series. 3)*

KENEN (PETER BAIN) Capital mobility and financial integration: a survey. Princeton, 1976. pp. 78. *bibliog. (Princeton University. Department of Economics and Sociology. International Finance Section. Princeton Studies in International Finance. No. 39)*

MOSCHETTO (BRUNO) and PLAGNOL (ANDRE) Les activités bancaires internationales. [Paris], 1976. pp. 125. *bibliog.*

PARIS-DAUPHINE CONFERENCE ON MONEY AND INTERNATIONAL MONETARY PROBLEMS, 3RD, 1974. Recent issues in international monetary economics: [proceedings of the conference]; edited by E. Claassen and P. Salin. Amsterdam, 1976. pp. 428. *bibliogs.*

POULLAIN (LUDWIG) Entwicklungstendenzen an den internationalen Finanzmärkten. Tübingen, 1976. pp. 15. *(Kiel. Universität. Institut für Weltwirtschaft. Kieler Vorträge. Neue Folge. 82)*

REFLECTIONS on Jamaica; [by] Edward M. Bernstein [and others]. Princeton, 1976. pp. 59. *(Princeton University. Department of Economics and Sociology. International Finance Section. Essays in International Finance. No.115)*

ANDERSEN (UWE) Das internationale Währungssystem zwischen nationaler Souveränität und supranationaler Integration: Entwicklungstendenzen seit Bretton Woods im Spannungsfeld der Interessen. Berlin, [1977]. pp. 464. *bibliog.*

BLOCK (FRED L.) The origins of international economic disorder: a study of United States international monetary policy from World War II to the present. Berkeley, Calif., [1977]. pp. 282. *bibliog.*

CHANNON (DEREK F.) British banking strategy and the international challenge. London, 1977. pp. 207.

GRUBEL (HERBERT G.) The international monetary system: efficiency and practical alternatives. 3rd ed. Harmondsworth, 1977. pp. 237. *bibliog.*

HIRSCH (FRED) and others. Alternatives to monetary disorder. New York, [1977]. pp. 153. *bibliog. (Council on Foreign Relations. 1980s Project Studies)*

POEHL (KARL OTTO) Probleme der internationalen Währungs- und Wirtschaftspolitik. Tübingen, 1977. pp. 20. *(Kiel. Universität. Institut für Weltwirtschaft. Kieler Vorträge. Neue Folge. 84)*

The POLITICAL economy of monetary reform; edited by Robert Z. Aliber. London, 1977. pp. 270. *Papers of a conference held at Racine, Wisconsin in 1974, sponsored by the Chicago University Graduate School of Business.*

SAVAGE (DONALD T.) Money and banking. Santa Barbara, Calif., [1977]. pp. 491. *bibliogs.*

TEW (JOHN HEDLEY BRIAN) The evolution of the international monetary system, 1945-77. London, 1977. pp. 254. *bibliog.*

WAGNER (ANTONIN) Verwaltete Währung: Krise und Reform des internationalen Währungssystems unter besonderer Berücksichtigung der Entwicklungsländer. Bern, [1977]. pp. 262. *bibliogs. (Zürich. Universität. Institut für Schweizerisches Bankwesen. Bankwirtschaftliche Forschungen. Band 39)*

WILLIAMSON (JOHN) Economist. The failure of world monetary reform, 1971-74. Sunbury-on-Thames, 1977. pp. 221. *bibliog.*

ZOLOTAS (XENOPHON) International monetary issues and development policies: selected essays and statements. Athens, 1977. pp. 503. *bibliog.*

— Bibliography.

INTERNATIONAL MONETARY FUND and INTERNATIONAL BANK FOR RECONSTRUCTION AND DEVELOPMENT. Joint Library. List of recent additions. m. [Washington]. *Current issues only kept.*

INTERNATIONAL MONETARY FUND and INTERNATIONAL BANK FOR RECONSTRUCTION AND DEVELOPMENT. Joint Library. List of recent periodical articles. m. [Washington]. *Current issues only kept.*

— History.

WISELEY (WILLIAM) A tool of power: the political history of money. New York, [1977]. pp. 401. *bibliog.*

— Mathematical models.

PETERSSOHN (ERLING) Kreditgivning mellan företag: en mikroekonometrisk studie av företagens finansiella beteende. Stockholm, 1976. pp. 511. *bibliog. With English summary, table of contents, etc.*

HERRING (RICHARD J.) and MARSTON (RICHARD C.) National monetary policies and international financial markets. Amsterdam, 1977. pp. 302. *bibliogs.*

INTERNATIONAL LABOUR ORGANISATION.

WALINE (PIERRE) Un patron au Bureau international du Travail, 1922-1974. Paris, [1976]. pp. 301.

— Kenya.

KENYA. Sessional Papers. 1963/65. No. 15. International Labour Conference: proposed action by the government of Kenya on certain instruments adopted by the International Labour Conference. [Nairobi, 1965]. pp. 6.

INTERNATIONAL LAW.

DAVIES (ITHEL) and JOYCE (JAMES AVERY) World law: a manifesto on the reconstruction of international law. London, 1948. pp. 12. *(World Citizenship Movement. World Unity Pamphlets. No. 3)*

UDECHUKU (EMMANUEL CHUKWUKELO) African unity and international law. London, [1974]. pp. 228.

ALESKEROV (MURMUZ N.) Ravnopravnoe sotrudnichestvo: sotrudnichestvo SSSR s molodymi nezavisimymi gosudarstvami. Baku, 1975. pp. 216.

MINASIAN (NIKOLAI MIKHAILOVICH) Sotsializm i mezhdunarodnoe pravo. Saratov, 1975. pp. 287. *With brief English summary.*

ZHUKOV (GENNADII PETROVICH) and CHERNICHENKO (STANISLAV VALENTINOVICH) Sovetskaia Programma mira i mezhdunarodnoe pravo. Moskva, 1975. pp. 111.

LEVI (WERNER) Law and politics in the international society. Beverly Hills, [1976]. pp. 189. *bibliog.*

AKEHURST (MICHAEL BARTON) A modern introduction to international law. 3rd ed. London, 1977. pp. 283.

STARKE (JOSEPH GABRIEL) An introduction to international law. 8th ed. London, 1977. pp. 711, 45. *bibliog.*

— Bibliography.

FEL'DMAN (DAVID ISAAKOVICH) ed. Mezhdunarodnoe pravo: bibliografiia 1917-1972 gg. Moskva, 1976. pp. 598.

— Cases.

MUELLER (JOERG PAUL) and WILDHABER (LUZIUS) Praxis des Völkerrechts. Bern, 1977. pp. 551.

— Codification.

RAMCHARAN (B.G.) The International Law Commission: its approach to the codification and progressive development of international law. The Hague, 1977. pp. 227. *bibliog.*

— Digests.

WHITEMAN (MARJORIE MILLACE) Digest of international law. Washington, 1963-73. 15 vols. *(U.S. Department of State. Publications. 7403, etc.)*

— History — Russia.

LEBAHN (AXEL) Sozialistische Wirtschaftsintegration und Ost-West-Handel im sowjetischen internationalen Recht: Theorie und Praxis des Offenheitsprinzips, etc. Berlin, [1976]. pp. 495. *bibliog.*

— — Switzerland.

REPERTOIRE suisse de droit international public: documentation concernant la pratique de la Confédération en matière de droit international public, 1914-1939; présenté par ordre du Conseil fédéral suisse par Paul Guggenheim [and others]. Bâle, [1975 in progress].

INTERNATIONAL LAW, PRIVATE.

KAHN-FREUND (Sir OTTO) General problems of private international law. Leyden, [1976]. pp. 336. *bibliog.*

— Capacity and disability.

LEQUETTE (YVES) Recherches sur les modes de protection des incapables en droit international privé. Paris, 1976. pp. 335.

— Italy.

VITTA (EDOARDO) Corso di diritto internazionale privato e processuale. Torino, [1976]. pp. 316. *bibliogs.*

— Russia.

MAKAROV (ALEKSANDR NIKOLAEVICH) Précis de droit international privé d'après la législation et la doctrine russes;...traduit par E. Nolde et P. Pereverzeff. Paris, 1932. pp. 471.

INTERNATIONAL LAW COMMISSION.

RAMCHARAN (B.G.) The International Law Commission: its approach to the codification and progressive development of international law. The Hague, 1977. pp. 227. *bibliog.*

INTERNATIONAL LIQUIDITY.

CARBAUGH (ROBERT J.) and FAN (LIANG-SHING) The international monetary system: history, institutions, analyses. Lawrence, Kan., [1976]. pp. 168. *bibliog.*

HALM (GEORGE NIKOLAUS) Jamaica and the par-value system. Princeton, 1977. pp. 21. *bibliog. (Princeton University. Department of Economics and Sociology. International Finance Section. Essays in International Finance. No. 120)*

INTERNATIONAL MONETARY FUND.

COURIEL (ALBERTO) and LICHTENSZTEJN (SAMUEL) El F.M.I. y la crisis economica nacional. Montevideo, 1967 [repr. 1971]. pp. 201. *Reprint of 1st ed. (1967) with a new prologue.*

IMF SURVEY; (pd. by the International Monetary Fund). s-m., Ag 14 1972 [v.1, no.1]- Washington.

DE VRIES (MARGARET GARRITSEN) The International Monetary Fund, 1966-1971: the system under stress. Washington, International Monetary Fund, 1976. 2 vols. *bibliogs.*

EMMINGER (OTMAR) On the way to a new international monetary order. Washington, D.C., [1976]. pp. 21. *(American Enterprise Institute for Public Policy Research. Foreign Affairs Studies. 39)*

KAFKA (ALEXANDRE) The International Monetary Fund: reform without reconstruction? Princeton, 1976. pp. 33. *(Princeton University. Department of Economics and Sociology. International Finance Section. Essays in International Finance. No.118)*

REFLECTIONS on Jamaica; [by] Edward M. Bernstein [and others]. Princeton, 1976. pp. 59. *(Princeton University. Department of Economics and Sociology. International Finance Section. Essays in International Finance. No.115)*

INTERNATIONAL ORGANIZATION.

GARNETT (JAMES CLERK MAXWELL) World loyalty: a study of the spiritual pilgrimage towards world order. London, 1928. pp. 122. *(Beckly Social Service Lectures. 1928)*

ENDRUCKS (BERNHARD) Das Ende aller Kriege: ein Appell an die Menschheit. Krailling bei München, [1959]. pp. 152.

JUENGER (ERNST) Der Weltstaat: Organismus und Organisation. Stuttgart, [1960]. pp. 75.

PARKMAN (AUBREY) David Jayne Hill and the problem of world peace. Lewisburg, [1975]. pp. 293. *bibliogs.*

LUARD (DAVID EVAN TRANT) Types of international society. New York, [1976]. pp. 389.

MALLY (GERHARD) Interdependence: the European-American connection in the global context. Lexington, Mass., [1976]. pp. 229.

MAZRUI (ALI AL'AMIN) A world federation of cultures: an African perspective. New York, [1976]. pp. 508.

RESHAPING the international order: a report to the Club of Rome; Jan Tinbergen, coordinator, Antony J. Dolman, editor, Jan van Ettinger, director. New York, [1976]. pp. 325. *This publication was realised in cooperation with the Foundation Reshaping the International Order (RIO).*

BULL (HEDLEY) The anarchical society: a study of order in world politics. London, 1977. pp. 335.

— Bibliography.

PALIC (VLADIMIR M.) compiler. Government publications: a guide to bibliographic tools; incorporating Government organization manuals: a bibliography. Oxford, [1977]. pp. 553.

INTERNATIONAL RELATIONS.

SCHUETZ (WILHELM WOLFGANG) Organische Aussenpolitik: vom Einzelstaat zum Überstaat. Stuttgart, 1951. pp. 216.

INTERNATIONAL PERSPECTIVES: a jl. of the Department of External Affairs [Canada]. bi-m., Ja/F 1972 (1)- Ottawa. *Supersedes its External affairs.*

INTERNATIONAL events and the comparative analysis of foreign policy; edited by Charles W. Kegley [and others]. Columbia, S.C., 1975. pp. 317. *bibliog. (South Carolina University. Institute of International Studies. International Relations Series. No. 4)*

WALL (G.R.) The dynamics of polarization: an inquiry into the processes of bipolarization in the international system and its regions, 1946-1970. Stockholm, 1975. pp. 138. *bibliog. (Stockholms Universitet. Statsvetenskapliga Institutionen. Stockholm Studies in Politics. 8)*

BEYOND détente: prospects for East-West co-operation and security in Europe; edited by Nils Andrén and Karl E. Birnbaum. Leyden, 1976. pp. 199. *(East-West Foundation. East-West Perspectives. 3) Papers of a conference held at the Bellagio Center, November 11-16, 1974.*

DEIBEL (TERRY L.) and ROBERTS (WALTER R.) Culture and information: two foreign policy functions. Beverly Hills, [1976]. pp. 62. *bibliog. (Georgetown University. Center for Strategic and International Studies. Washington Papers. vol. 4/40)*

LARIN (V.) Mezhdunarodnye otnosheniia i ideologicheskaia bor'ba, 60-70-e gody. Moskva, 1976. pp. 247. *bibliog.*

LEVI (WERNER) Law and politics in the international society. Beverly Hills, [1976]. pp. 189. *bibliog.*

LUARD (DAVID EVAN TRANT) Types of international society. New York, [1976]. pp. 389.

MAZRUI (ALI AL'AMIN) A world federation of cultures: an African perspective. New York, [1976]. pp. 508.

PROBLEMY istorii mezhdunarodnykh otnoshenii i ideologicheskaia bor'ba: sbornik statei. Moskva, 1976. pp. 295.

SULLIVAN (MICHAEL P.) International relations: theories and evidence. Englewood Cliffs, [1976]. pp. 385.

BASIUK (VICTOR) Technology, world politics, and American policy. New York, 1977. pp. 409. *bibliog.*

BOOTH (KEN) Navies and foreign policy. London, [1977]. pp. 294.

WENDZEL (ROBERT L.) International relations: a policymaker focus. New York, [1977]. pp. 286. *bibliog.*

— Bibliography.

ELOVAINIO (MAURI K.) and LEHTINEN (RAUNO) compilers. A bibliography on international relations: literature published in Denmark, Finland, Norway and Sweden, 1945-1960. Stockholm, [197-]. pp. 200.

LABARR (DOROTHY F.) and SINGER (JOEL DAVID) compilers. The study of international politics: a guide to the sources for the student, teacher, and researcher. Santa Barbara, Calif., [1976]. pp. 211. *bibliog.*

— Research.

HARLE (VILHO) International tension: an application of cohesion theory and event analysis to East-West relations during the post-war years. Tampere, 1975. pp. 270. *bibliog. (Tampere. Yliopisto. Institute of Political Science. Research Reports. No. 39)*

VORONTSOV (GENNADII ANATOL'EVICH) Burzhuaznaia nauka na sluzhbe politiki: novye tendentsii v razrabotke vneshnei politiki burzhuaznogo gosudarstva. Moskva, 1975. pp. 183. *bibliog.*

IN search of global patterns; edited by James N. Rosenau. New York, [1976]. pp. 389. *bibliogs.*

JERVIS (ROBERT) Perception and misperception in international politics. Princeton, N.J., [1976]. pp. 445. *bibliog.*

ZINNES (DINA A.) Contemporary research in international relations: a perspective and a critical appraisal. New York, [1976]. pp. 477. *bibliog.*

CONFERENCE ON COGNITIVE PROCESS MODELS OF FOREIGN POLICY, 1973, LONDON. Thought and action in foreign policy: proceedings of the London Conference...March 1973; (G. Matthew Bonham, Michael J. Shapiro, editors). Basel, 1977. pp. 355. *bibliogs. Published under the auspices of the Center for Advanced Study in the Behavioral Sciences, Stanford, California.*

COTTAM (RICHARD W.) Foreign policy motivation: a general theory and a case study. Pittsburgh, [1977]. pp. 374. *bibliog.*

NONSTATE nations in international politics: comparative system analyses; edited by Judy S. Bertelsen. New York, 1977. pp. 263. *bibliogs.*

— Study and teaching.

LABARR (DOROTHY F.) and SINGER (JOEL DAVID) compilers. The study of international politics: a guide to the sources for the student, teacher, and researcher. Santa Barbara, Calif., [1976]. pp. 211. *bibliog.*

— — Europe.

INTERNATIONAL studies in six European countries: United Kingdom, France, Federal Republic of Germany, the Ntherlands, Sweden, Italy. [New York, 1976]. pp. 312. *A report to the Ford Foundation.*

— Yearbooks.

SAGE INTERNATIONAL YEARBOOK OF FOREIGN POLICY STUDIES. a., 1973 (v.1)- London.

INTERNATIONAL RELIEF.

KRIMGOLD (FREDERICK) The role of international aid for pre-disaster planning in developing countries. Stockholm, 1974. pp. 134. *bibliog.*

— Sudan.

BETTS (TRISTRAM) The Southern Sudan: the ceasefire and after; report prepared for the Africa Publications Trust. London, 1974. pp. 155.

INTERNATIONALISM.

MATVEEVA (TAMARA STEPANOVNA) Internatsional'nyi dolg i sovremennost': na materialakh Turkmenskoi SSR. Ashkhabad, 1970. pp. 141.

SEROVA (IRINA IVANOVNA) Sila, splachivaiushchaia voedino: internatsional'noe vospitanie trudiashchikhsia v razvitom sotsialisticheskom obshchestve. Minsk, 1975. pp. 262. *bibliog.*

INTERNATSIONAL'NOE i natsional'noe v sotsialisticheskom obshchestve. Kiev, 1976. pp. 331.

MAKARENKO (OLEKSANDR ANDRIIOVYCH) Moguchaia sila proletarskoi solidarnosti: podderzhka zarubezhnym proletariatom Sovetskoi strany v 1921-1925 gg. Moskva, 1976. pp. 319.

INTER-PARLIAMENTARY UNION.

DOUGLAS (JAMES) Assistant Secretary General of the Inter-Parliamentary Union. Parliaments across frontiers: a short history of the Inter-Parliamentary Union. London. H.M.S.O., 1975. pp. 104. *bibliog.*

DOUGLAS (JAMES) Assistant Secretary General of the Inter-Parliamentary Union. Parliaments across frontiers: a short history of the Inter-Parliamentary Union. 2nd ed. London, H.M.S.O., 1976. pp. 108. *bibliog.*

INTERPERSONAL RELATIONS.

FRIEDMANN (JOHN REMBERT PETER) Retracking America: the theory of transactive planning. Garden City, N.Y., 1973. pp. 289. *bibliog.*

SWENSEN (CLIFFORD H.) Introduction to interpersonal relations. Glenview, Ill., [1973]. pp. 474. *bibliogs.*

DUCK (STEVEN W.) The study of acquaintance. Westmead, [1977]. pp. 236. *bibliog.*

WOMEN and men: changing roles, relationships and perceptions; [edited by] Libby A. Cater [and others]. New York, [1977]. pp. 277. *bibliogs. Consists of transcriptions of discussions and essays written for a workshop held in Aspen, Colo., August 3-10, 1975, under the auspices of the Aspen Institute for Humanistic Studies.*

INTERRACIAL ADOPTION

— United Kingdom.

JACKSON (BARBARA) Family experiences of inter-racial adoption. London, [1976]. pp. 32. *bibliog.*

JACKSON (BARBARA) Family experiences of inter-racial adoption: adopting a black child. London, [1976]. pp. 14. *bibliog.*

— United States.

SIMON (RITA JAMES) and ALTSTEIN (HOWARD) Transracial adoption. New York, [1977]. pp. 197.

INTERRACIAL MARRIAGE

— Singapore.

HASSAN (RIAZ) and BENJAMIN (GEOFFREY) Ethnic outmarriage rates in Singapore: the influence of traditional socio-cultural organization. Singapore, 1972. pp. 30. *bibliog. (University of Singapore. Department of Sociology. Working Papers. No. 1)*

KUO (EDDIE C.Y.) and HASSAN (RIAZ) Some social concomitants of interethnic marriage in Singapore. Singapore, 1974. pp. 28. *bibliog. (University of Singapore. Department of Sociology. Working Papers. No. 32)*

INTERSTATE COMMERCE

— Canada.

MELVIN (JAMES R.) The effects of energy price changes on commodity prices, interprovincial trade, and employment. Toronto, [1976]. pp. 106. *bibliog. (Ontario. Economic Council. Research Studies. No. 3)*

INVESTMENT ANALYSIS.

BROCKINGTON (RAYMOND BERNARD) Information, intuition and the investor. 1976. fo. 128. *bibliog. Typescript. M.Sc.(London) thesis: unpublished. This thesis is the property of London University and may not be removed from the Library.*

INVESTMENT OF PUBLIC FUNDS.

KIPPER (HEINZ) Entscheidungen in öffentlichen Organisationen: zur Problematik öffentlicher Investitionsentscheidungen und Beschaffungsprozesse. [Mannheim], 1975. pp. 355,xxxvi. *bibliog. Dissertation - Universität Mannheim.*

INVESTMENT TRUSTS

— European Economic Community countries.

CORNER (DESMOND CARTERET) and STAFFORD (D.C.) Open-ended investment funds in the EEC and Switzerland. London, 1977. pp. 254. *bibliog.*

— Switzerland.

CORNER (DESMOND CARTERET) and STAFFORD (D.C.) Open-ended investment funds in the EEC and Switzerland. London, 1977. pp. 254. *bibliog.*

INVESTMENTS.

The POLITICS of aid, trade and investment; edited by Satish Raichur [and] Craig Liske. New York, [1976]. pp. 218. *bibliogs.*

RISK and return in finance; edited by Irwin Friend [and] James L. Bicksler. Cambridge, Mass., [1977]. 2 vols. *bibliogs. Thirteen of the seventeen papers in these two volumes were originally presented at a Conference on Risk and the Rate of Return, sponsored by the American Telephone and Telegraph Company and held in Vail, Colorado, during August 5-10, 1973.*

— Communist countries.

KRAFT (GERHARD) Die Zusammenarbeit der Mitliedsländer des RGW auf dem Gebiet der Investitionen. Berlin, 1977. pp. 116.

INVESTMENTS, AMERICAN.

HYMER (STEPHEN HERBERT) The international operations of national firms: a study of direct foreign investment. Cambridge, Mass., [1976]. pp. 253. *bibliog.*

STOBAUGH (ROBERT B.) and others. Nine investments abroad and their impact at home: case studies on multinational enterprises and the U.S. economy. Boston, [Mass.], 1976. pp. 222.

— Africa, Subsaharan.

ROGERS (BARBARA) White wealth and black poverty: American investments in southern Africa. Westport, Conn., 1976. pp. 331. *(Denver. University. Center on International Race Relations. Studies in Human Rights. No. 2) "Based on work done for a joint study, with Jennifer Davis, commissioned by the Council for Christian Social Action of the United Church of Christ".*

— Colombia.

BEJARANO (JESUS A.) El capital monopolista y las inversiones privadas norteamericanas en Colombia. Bogota, [1972]. pp. 116.

— Germany.

SUTTON (ANTONY C.) Wall Street and the rise of Hitler. Seal Beach, Calif., [1976]. pp. 220. *bibliog.*

— South Africa.

HORNER (DUDLEY B.) United States corporate investment and social change in South Africa. Johannesburg, [1971?]. 1 pamphlet (various pagings).

INVESTMENTS, BRITISH

— Canada.

PATERSON (DONALD G.) British direct investment in Canada, 1890-1914. Toronto, [1976]. pp. 147. *bibliog.*

— Mexico.

CAMBRIDGE. University. Centre of Latin American Studies. Working Papers. No. 21. British capital and the Mexican silver mining industry, 1820-50; by T.J. Cassidy. Cambridge. [1974]. pp. 24, vii.

— South Africa.

CORPORATE responsibility and the institutional investor: report of a seminar held [by Christian Concern for Southern Africa] at the London Graduate School of Business Studies...1973. London, [1974]. pp. 21.

BAILEY (MARTIN DAWSON) Barclays and South Africa. [Birmingham, 1975]. pp. 12.

END LOANS TO SOUTHERN AFRICA. Letters and papers from Midland. [London, 1976]. pp. 12.

GOOD (DORCAS) and WILLIAMS (MICHAEL) South Africa: the crisis in Britain and the apartheid economy. London, 1976. pp. 23. *bibliog. (Anti-Apartheid Movement. Foreign Investment in South Africa: a Discussion Series. No. 1)*

INVESTMENT in South Africa: the options; report of a seminar [held by Christian Concern for Southern Africa] at the Methodist Missionary Society, London, 24 February 1976. London, [1976]. pp. 59.

STARES (RODNEY) The General Electric Company Limited: a review of the company's relationship with South Africa. London, [1976]. fo. 31.

STARES (RODNEY) ICI (Imperial Chemical Industries Limited) in South Africa. London, [1977]. pp. 37. *bibliog.*

— Underdeveloped areas.

See UNDERDEVELOPED AREAS — Investments, British.

INVESTMENTS, FOREIGN.

DANIELS (JOHN D.) and others. International business: environments and operations. Reading, Mass., [1976]. pp. 554. *bibliogs.*

HYMER (STEPHEN HERBERT) The international operations of national firms: a study of direct foreign investment. Cambridge, Mass., [1976]. pp. 253. *bibliog.*

ROBINSON (RICHARD D.) National control of foreign business entry: a survey of fifteen countries. New York, 1976. pp. 508. *bibliogs.*

— Bibliography.

BROOKE (MICHAEL Z.) and others, compilers. International business bibliography. London, 1977. pp. 480.

— Law and legislation — Brazil.

BANCO CENTRAL DO BRASIL. Departamento de Fiscalização e Registro de Capitais Estrangeiros. Foreign investments in Brazil: legislation. [Rio de Janeiro], 1977. pp. 269.

— America, Latin.

OUDIETTE (JACQUES) Problèmes d'épargne et d'investissement en Amérique Latine. Paris, [1962]. pp. 20.

— — Bibliography.

STANZICK (KARL HEINZ) and MEDINA A. (MARIA TERESA) compilers. La inversion privada extranjera en America Latina: bibliografia selecta. Santiago de Chile, 1971. pp. 147. *(Instituto Latinoamericano de Investigaciones Sociales. Estudios y Documentos. 8)*

— Australia.

AUSTRALIA. Commonwealth Bureau of Census and Statistics. 1974. Foreign ownership and control of the mining industry, 1971-72. Canberra, 1974. pp. 33.

AUSTRALIA. Commonwealth Bureau of Census and Statistics. 1975. Foreign ownership and control of finance companies, 1973. Canberra, 1975. pp. 40.

AUSTRALIA. Commonwealth Bureau of Census and Statistics. 1975. Foreign ownership and control of general insurance business, 1972-73 Canberra, 1975. pp. 39.

AUSTRALIA. Commonwealth Bureau of Census and Statistics. 1975. Foreign ownership and control of life insurance business, 1973. Canberra, 1975. pp. 37.

— Colombia.

BOYCE (JAMES E.) and LOMBARD (FRANÇOIS J.) Colombia's treatment of foreign banks: a precedent setting case?. Washington, D.C., 1976. pp. 56. *(American Enterprise Institute for Public Policy Research. Foreign Affairs Studies. 36)*

— Ecuador.

GALARZA ZAVALA (JAIME) El festin del petroleo. Quito, 1974. pp. 462. *bibliog.*

— France.

BANQUE NATIONALE POUR LE COMMERCE ET L'INDUSTRIE. New regulations governing foreign investments in France. Paris, 1965. pp. 3. *With appendix.*

BERTIN (GILLES Y.) L'industrie française face aux multinationales. Paris, 1975. pp. 143. *(France. Commissariat Général du Plan. Economie et Planification)*

FARHI (ANDRE) and MICHON-SAVARIT (CATHERINE) Schéma général d'aménagement de la France: prospectives des investissements étrangers en France. Paris, 1976. pp. 101. *(France. Délégation à l'Aménagement du Territoire et à l'Action Régionale. Travaux et Recherches de Prospective. 62)*

INVESTMENTS, FOREIGN.(Cont.)

— Germany.

EINFLUSS multinationaler Unternehmen auf Aussenwirtschaft und Branchenstruktur der Bundesrepublik Deutschland; [by] Rolf Jungnickel [and others]. Hamburg, 1977. pp. 431. *bibliog. (Hamburg. Hamburgisches Welt-Wirtschafts-Archiv. Veröffentlichungen)*

— Korea.

KOREA (REPUBLIC). Foreign Investment Bureau. 1962. A golden opportunity for investment in Korea. [Seoul], 1962. pp. 79.

— Mexico.

MAY (HERBERT K.) and FERNANDEZ ARENA (JOSE ANTONIO) Impact of foreign investment in Mexico. Washington, [1972?]. pp. 92.

SEPULVEDA AMOR (BERNARDO) and others. Las empresas transnacionales en Mexico. Mexico, 1974. pp. 167. *(Mexico City. Colegio de Mexico. Centro de Estudios Internacionales. Coleccion. 12)*

MATTHIES (KLAUS) Transnationale Unternehmen in Mexiko. Hamburg, 1977. pp. 185. *bibliog. (Hamburg. Hamburgisches Welt-Wirtschafts-Archiv. Veröffentlichungen)*

— Philippine Islands.

PHILIPPINE INDUSTRY AND INVESTMENT; pd. by Board of Investments. q., 1976 (1st)- Manila. *Supersedes PHILIPPINE PROGRESS: business and economic information.*

— South Africa.

WAESBERGE (ROBERT VAN) Do we participate in apartheid?; reflections by black South Africans on themselves, us and our investments; translated [from the Dutch] by Esau du Plessis. Geneva, [1975]. pp. 56.

— Spain.

GRANELL TRIAS (FRANCISCO) El decreto 2.495-1973 y el control de las inversiones extranjeras en España. [Barcelona, 1974]. pp. 145-162. *Publicado en la Revista Jurídica de Cataluña, Num.1, 1974.*

— Underdeveloped areas.

See UNDERDEVELOPED AREAS — Investments, Foreign.

— United Kingdom — Wales.

DAVIES (GLYN) and THOMAS (IAN) Overseas investment in Wales: the welcome invasion. Swansea, 1976. pp. 221.

— United States.

NATIONAL INDUSTRIAL CONFERENCE BOARD. International Division. Foreign investment in the United States: policy, problems and obstacles; [by a team supervised by G. Clark Thompson]. New York, [1974]. pp. 40. *(National Industrial Conference Board. Conference Board Reports. No. 625)*

— Yugoslavia.

ORGANISATION FOR ECONOMIC CO-OPERATION AND DEVELOPMENT. Committee for Invisible Transactions. 1974. Foreign investment in Yugoslavia, 1974. Paris, 1974. pp. 58.

— Zaire.

BONGOY (MPEKESA) Investissements mixtes au Zaire: (joint ventures pour la période de transition). Kinshasa, 1974. pp. 523. *bibliog.*

INVESTMENTS, GERMAN.

AUSSENHANDEL, Direktinvestitionen und Industriestruktur der deutschen Wirtschaft: eine Untersuchung ihrer Entwicklung unter Berücksichtigung der Wechselkursänderungen von Hans Baumann [and others]. Berlin, [1977]. pp. 242. *bibliog.*

INVESTMENTS, JAPANESE.

TSURUMI (YOSHIHIRO) The Japanese are coming: a multinational interaction of firms and politics. Cambridge, Mass., [1976]. pp. 333.

INVESTMENTS, SWEDISH.

— South Africa.

MAGNUSSON (ÅKE) Sverige - Sydafrika: en studie av en ekonomisk relation. Uppsala, 1974. pp. 174.

INVESTMENTS, SWISS

— Underdeveloped areas.

See UNDERDEVELOPED AREAS — Investments, Swiss.

IRAN

— Commerce — Statistics.

IRAN. Bureau of Statistics. 1967. Trends in industrial and commercial statistics. [Tehran, 1967]. pp. 53.

— — Germany.

SOHRAB (SIAWUSCH) Die deutsch-persischen Wirtschaftsbeziehungen vor dem Ersten Weltkrieg. Frankfurt/M., 1976. pp. 514. *bibliog.*

— Economic conditions.

The SOCIAL sciences and problems of development: (papers presented at an International Conference in Persepolis Iran, June 1-4, 1974); Khodadad Farmanfarmaian, editor. Princeton, [1976]. pp. 332. *bibliogs. (Princeton University. Program in Near Eastern Studies. Princeton Studies on the Near East) Conference sponsored by the Plan and Budget Organization of Iran, Tehran University, Princeton University.*

LOONEY (ROBERT E.) Iran at the end of the century: a Hegelian forecast. Lexington, Mass., [1977]. pp. 155. *bibliog.*

— Economic policy.

The SOCIAL sciences and problems of development: (papers presented at an International Conference in Persepolis Iran, June 1-4, 1974); Khodadad Farmanfarmaian, editor. Princeton, [1976]. pp. 332. *bibliogs. (Princeton University. Program in Near Eastern Studies. Princeton Studies on the Near East) Conference sponsored by the Plan and Budget Organization of Iran, Tehran University, Princeton University.*

— Foreign relations.

ORLOV (EVGENII ALEKSANDROVICH) Vneshniaia politika Irana posle vtoroi mirovoi voiny. Moskva, 1975. pp. 224. *bibliog.*

— — United Kingdom.

AHMAD (ISHTIAQ) Anglo-Iranian relations, 1905-1919. Bombay, [1974]. pp. 389. *bibliog.*

— Industries.

IRAN. Bureau of Statistics. 1967. Trends in industrial and commercial statistics. [Tehran, 1967]. pp. 53.

RESEARCH CENTER FOR INDUSTRIAL AND TRADE DEVELOPMENT [IRAN]. Industrial development in Iran: present and future prospects. Tehran, Ministry of Economy, 1971. fo. 21.

— Social conditions.

The SOCIAL sciences and problems of development: (papers presented at an International Conference in Persepolis Iran, June 1-4, 1974); Khodadad Farmanfarmaian, editor. Princeton, [1976]. pp. 332. *bibliogs. (Princeton University. Program in Near Eastern Studies. Princeton Studies on the Near East) Conference sponsored by the Plan and Budget Organization of Iran, Tehran University, Princeton University.*

— Social policy.

The SOCIAL sciences and problems of development: (papers presented at an International Conference in Persepolis Iran, June 1-4, 1974); Khodadad Farmanfarmaian, editor. Princeton, [1976]. pp. 332. *bibliogs. (Princeton University. Program in Near Eastern Studies. Princeton Studies on the Near East) Conference sponsored by the Plan and Budget Organization of Iran, Tehran University, Princeton University.*

IRAQ

— Economic conditions.

IRAQ. Ministry of Planning. Progress under planning. a., 1971 (1st)- Baghdad.

— Foreign relations — United Kingdom.

COHEN (STUART A.) British policy in Mesopotamia, 1903-1914. London, 1976. pp. 361. *bibliog. (Oxford. University. St. Antony's College. Middle East Centre. St. Antony's Middle East Monographs. No.5)*

SLUGLETT (PETER) Britain in Iraq, 1914-1932. London, 1976. pp. 360. *bibliog. (Oxford. University. St. Antony's College. Middle East Centre. St. Antony's Middle East Monographs. No.4)*

— Politics and government.

COHEN (STUART A.) British policy in Mesopotamia, 1903-1914. London, 1976. pp. 361. *bibliog. (Oxford. University. St. Antony's College. Middle East Centre. St. Antony's Middle East Monographs. No.5)*

SLUGLETT (PETER) Britain in Iraq, 1914-1932. London, 1976. pp. 360. *bibliog. (Oxford. University. St. Antony's College. Middle East Centre. St. Antony's Middle East Monographs. No.4)*

HUSSEIN (SADDAM) Saddam Hussein on current events in Iraq; translated by Khalid Kishtainy. London, 1977. pp. 91.

— Social conditions.

IRAQ. Ministry of Planning. Progress under planning. a., 1971 (1st)- Baghdad.

IRELAND

— Description and travel.

ORME (A.R.) Ireland. London, 1970 repr. 1976. pp. 276. *bibliog.*

— Economic conditions.

CURSORY observations on Ireland; by a member of the Dublin Society. Dublin, Faulkner, 1779. pp. 63. *Ms. note in copy at Royal Irish Academy, Dublin, attributes this work to Sir John Hasler.*

— Economic history.

ORME (A.R.) Ireland. London, 1970 repr. 1976. pp. 276. *bibliog.*

COMPARATIVE aspects of Scottish and Irish economic and social history 1600-1900; edited by L.M. Cullen and T.C. Smout. Edinburgh, [1977?]. pp. 252. *Based mainly on papers presented at a seminar at Trinity College, Dublin in 1976.*

— Emigration and immigration.

HORTON (Sir ROBERT JOHN WILMOT) An inquiry into the causes and remedies of pauperism: third series: containing letters to Sir Francis Burdett, Bart, M. P. upon pauperism in Ireland. 2nd ed. London, Lloyd, 1831. pp. iv, 86.

— History.

BECKETT (JAMES CAMLIN) The Anglo-Irish tradition. London, 1976. pp. 159.

LEBOW (RICHARD NED) White Britain and black Ireland: the influence of stereotypes on colonial policy. Philadelphia, Pa., [1976]. pp. 152. *bibliog.*

O'NEIL (DANIEL J.) Three perennial themes of anti-colonialism: the Irish case. Denver, Colo., [1976]. pp. 131. *(Denver. University. Social Science Foundation and Graduate School of International Studies. Monograph Series in World Affairs. vol. 14, no. 1)*

MACDONAGH (OLIVER) Ireland: the Union and its aftermath. rev. ed. London, 1977. pp. 176. *bibliog.*

— — 1760-1820.

REFLECTIONS on the Irish conspiracy; and on the necessity of an armed association in Great Britain; to which are added observations on the debates and resolutions of the Whig Club, on the sixth of June, 1797. London, J. Sewell, 1797. pp. 156.

— — 1798, Rebellion of.

CONSIDERATIONS on the situation to which Ireland is reduced by the government of Lord Camden; the sixth edition, improved and corrected, to which is added a copy of the state paper!!! Dublin, 1798. pp. 34.

WOOLAGHAN (HUGH) defendant. The genuine trial of Hugh Woolaghan, yeoman, by a general court-martial, held in the barracks of Dublin, on Saturday, October 13, 1798, for the murder of Thomas Dogherty to which is added His Excellency Lord Cornwallis's order for the court-martial to be dissolved. 2nd ed. Dublin, printed for J. Milliken, 1798. pp. 27.

— — 1900- .

KOLPAKOV (ARTEMII DMITRIEVICH) Irlandiia na puti k revoliutsii, 1900-1918 gg. Moskva, 1976. pp. 280. *bibliog.*

— — 1910-1921.

KEARNEY (PEADAR) My dear Eva: letters from Ballykinlar internment camp 1921. Dublin, 1976. pp. 46.

DANGERFIELD (GEORGE) The damnable question: a study in Anglo-Irish relations. London, 1977. pp. 400. *bibliog.*

— Maps — Bibliography.

EIRE. Ordnance Survey. 1968. Catalogue of small scale maps and charts. Dublin, 1968. pp. 11, fo. (3).

— Nationalism.

BRITISH AND IRISH COMMUNIST ORGANISATION. Aspects of nationalism. Belfast, 1972. pp. 51.

O'DAY (ALAN) The English face of Irish nationalism: Parnellite involvement in British politics, 1880-86. Dublin, 1977. pp. 210. *bibliog.*

— Parliament — House of Commons.

MASON (JOHN MONCK) and LANGRISHE (Sir HERCULES) Parliamentary reform; the speeches...on Saturday, 20th of March, 1784, when Mr. Flood moved that the bill for a parliamentary reform should be committed. Dublin, printed by N. Kelly, 1797. pp. 22.

— Politics and government.

REFLECTIONS on the Irish conspiracy; and on the necessity of an armed association in Great Britain; to which are added observations on the debates and resolutions of the Whig Club, on the sixth of June, 1797. London, J. Sewell, 1797. pp. 156.

BECKETT (JAMES CAMLIN) The Anglo-Irish tradition. London, 1976. pp. 159.

— Rural conditions.

TUKE (JAMES HACK) A visit to Connaught in the autumn of 1847: a letter addressed to the Central Relief Committee of the Society of Friends, Dublin;...second edition with notes of a subsequent visit to Erris. London, Gilpin, 1848. pp. 71.

— Social conditions.

CURSORY observations on Ireland; by a member of the Dublin Society. Dublin, Faulkner, 1779. pp. 63. *Ms. note in copy at Royal Irish Academy, Dublin, attributes this work to Sir John Hasler.*

— Social history.

ORME (A.R.) Ireland. London, 1970 repr. 1976. pp. 276. *bibliog.*

COMPARATIVE aspects of Scottish and Irish economic and social history 1600-1900; edited by L.M. Cullen and T.C. Smout. Edinburgh, [1977?]. pp. 252. *Based mainly on papers presented at a seminar at Trinity College, Dublin in 1976.*

IRELAND (REPUBLIC)

— Economic conditions.

EIRE. 1976. Economic and social development, 1976-1980. Dublin, [1976]. pp. 39.

NATIONAL ECONOMIC AND SOCIAL COUNCIL [EIRE]. Prelude to planning. Dublin, Stationery Office, [1976]. pp. 75. ([Reports]. No. 26)

ECONOMIC activity in Ireland: a study of two open economies; editors: Norman J. Gibson and John E. Spencer; contributors: W. Black [and others]. Dublin, 1977. pp. 272. *bibliogs.*

NATIONAL ECONOMIC AND SOCIAL COUNCIL [EIRE]. Comments on Economic and social development 1976-1980. Dublin, Stationery Office, [1977]. pp. 37. ([Reports]. No. 33)

— Economic policy.

EIRE. 1976. Economic and social development, 1976-1980. Dublin, [1976]. pp. 39.

NATIONAL ECONOMIC AND SOCIAL COUNCIL [EIRE]. Institutional arrangements for regional economic development. Dublin, Stationery Office, [1976]. pp. 54. ([Reports]. No. 22)

NATIONAL ECONOMIC AND SOCIAL COUNCIL [EIRE]. Prelude to planning. Dublin, Stationery Office, [1976]. pp. 75. ([Reports]. No. 26)

NATIONAL ECONOMIC AND SOCIAL COUNCIL [EIRE]. Comments on Economic and social development 1976-1980. Dublin, Stationery Office, [1977]. pp. 37. ([Reports]. No. 33)

NATIONAL ECONOMIC AND SOCIAL COUNCIL [EIRE]. Service-type employment and regional development; (by Michael J. Bannon [and others]). Dublin, Stationery Office, [1977]. pp. 142. *bibliog.* ([Reports]. No. 28)

— Foreign relations — United States.

DWYER (T. RYLE) Irish neutrality and the USA 1939-47. Dublin, 1977. pp. 241.

— Full employment policies.

KILLEEN (MICHAEL J.) Industrial development and full employment;...paper given...to Symposium on Increasing Employment in Ireland, held under the auspices of the Statistical and Social Inquiry Society of Ireland on 20th November, 1975. Dublin, Industrial Development Authority, 1976. pp. 18. *(Publication Series. Paper 3)*

— History.

MACDONAGH (OLIVER) Ireland: the Union and its aftermath. rev. ed. London, 1977. pp. 176. *bibliog.*

— Nationalism.

RUMPF (ERHARD) and HEPBURN (ANTHONY C.) Nationalism and socialism in twentieth-century Ireland. Liverpool, 1977. pp. 275. *bibliog.*

— Neutrality.

DWYER (T. RYLE) Irish neutrality and the USA 1939-47. Dublin, 1977. pp. 241.

— Oireachtas — Privileges and immunities.

EIRE. Dail Eireann. Committee on Procedure and Privileges. 1970. Report...on a magazine item containing criticism of the Ceann Comhairle. Dublin, 1970. pp. (14). *In English and Irish.*

— Politics and government.

BAX (MART) Harpstrings and confessions: machine-style politics in the Irish Republic. Assen, 1976. pp. 224. *bibliog.*

O'MAHANONY (T.P.) The politics of dishonour: Ireland, 1916-1977. Dublin, 1977. pp. 151. *bibliog.*

RUMPF (ERHARD) and HEPBURN (ANTHONY C.) Nationalism and socialism in twentieth-century Ireland. Liverpool, 1977. pp. 275. *bibliog.*

— Rural conditions.

NATIONAL ECONOMIC AND SOCIAL COUNCIL [EIRE]. Rural areas: social planning problems. Dublin, Stationery Office, [1976]. pp. 93. ([Reports]. No. 19)

— Social conditions.

SOCIOLOGICAL ASSOCIATION OF IRELAND. Annual Conference, 2nd, Dublin, 1975. Proceedings of the...conference...; edited by A.E.C.W. Spencer and P.A. O'Dwyer. Belfast, 1976. pp. 137. *bibliogs.*

MAC GRÉIL (MÍCHEÁL) Prejudice and tolerance in Ireland: based on a survey of intergroup attitudes of Dublin adults and other sources. Dublin, 1977. pp. 634. *bibliog.*

— — Statistics.

NATIONAL ECONOMIC AND SOCIAL COUNCIL [EIRE]. Statistics for social policy. Dublin, Stationery Office, [1976]. pp. 79. ([Reports]. No. 17)

NATIONAL ECONOMIC AND SOCIAL COUNCIL [EIRE]. Towards a social report. Dublin, Stationery Office, [1976]. pp. 200. *bibliogs.* ([Reports]. No. 25)

McGILVRAY (JAMES) Social statistics in Ireland: a guide to their sources and uses. Dublin, 1977. pp. 204. *bibliogs.*

— Social history.

O'MAHANONY (T.P.) The politics of dishonour: Ireland, 1916-1977. Dublin, 1977. pp. 151. *bibliog.*

— Social policy.

CATHOLIC CHURCH OF IRELAND. Council for Social Welfare. Planning for social development: what needs to be done. Dublin, 1976. fo. 28.

NATIONAL ECONOMIC AND SOCIAL COUNCIL [EIRE]. Rural areas: social planning problems. Dublin, Stationery Office, [1976]. pp. 93. ([Reports]. No. 19)

— Statistics.

McGILVRAY (JAMES) Social statistics in Ireland: a guide to their sources and uses. Dublin, 1977. pp. 204. *bibliogs.*

— Statistics, Medical.

EIRE. Department of Health. Planning Unit. Statistical information relevant to the health services. a., 1976- Dublin.

— Statistics, Vital.

EIRE. Department of Health. Planning Unit. Statistical information relevant to the health services. a., 1976- Dublin.

IRELAND, NORTHERN

— Administrative and political divisions.

IRELAND, NORTHERN. Census, 1971. Census of population, 1971: supplement to the 1961 topographical index. Belfast, 1976. pp.179.

— Appropriations and expenditures.

IRELAND, NORTHERN. Department of Finance. Statement of excess: a statement of the sum required to be voted in order to make good an excess. irreg., 1971/72- Belfast. *Previously included in IRELAND, NORTHERN. Parliament. House of Commons. [Papers].*

IRELAND, NORTHERN. Department of Finance, Vote on account: an estimate showing the several services for which a vote on account is required. a., 1974/75- Belfast. *1921/22 - 1972/73 included in IRELAND, NORTHERN. Parliament. House of Commons. [Papers].*

— Assembly — Privileges and immunities.

IRELAND, NORTHERN. Northern Ireland Assembly. Committee of Privileges. 1974. Second report...together with the proceedings of the Committee and appendices: member's complaint that he was prevented in the corridors from approaching Mr. Speaker's room. Belfast, 1974. pp. 16. *(Northern Ireland Assembly. [Reports and Papers]. 19)*

— — Rules and practice.

IRELAND, NORTHERN. Northern Ireland Assembly. 1973-74. Standing orders: public business, 1973; (with Additional standing order made on 23 January 1974). Belfast, 1973[-74]. pp. 22, (2). *([Reports and Papers]. 2)*

IRELAND, NORTHERN. Northern Ireland Assembly. Presiding Officer's Committee on Standing Orders, Etc. 1973. Report...together with the proceedings of the Committee and appendices; (with Minutes of evidence). Belfast, 1973. 2 pts. *(Northern Ireland Assembly. [Reports and Papers]. 1)*

— Census.

IRELAND, NORTHERN. Census, 1971. Census of population, 1971: fertility tables. Belfast, 1976. pp. 89.

IRELAND, NORTHERN. Census, 1971. Census of population, 1971: economic activity tables. Belfast, 1977. pp. 303.

— Convention.

McALLISTER (IAN) The 1975 Northern Ireland Convention election. Glasgow, 1975. pp. 73. *(Glasgow. University of Strathclyde. Survey Research Centre. Occasional Papers. No. 14)*

IRELAND, NORTHERN. Northern Ireland Convention. 1975. Rules of procedure. Belfast, 1975. pp. 18. *([Papers]. N.I.C. 2)*

— Economic conditions.

ECONOMIC activity in Ireland: a study of two open economies; editors: Norman J. Gibson and John E. Spencer; contributors: W. Black [and others]. Dublin, 1977. pp. 272. *bibliogs.*

— Economic policy.

IRELAND, NORTHERN. 1976. Economic and industrial strategy for Northern Ireland: report by review team, 1976; [W.G.H. Quigley, chairman]. Belfast, 1976. pp. 106. *bibliog.*

— Executive departments.

IRELAND, NORTHERN. Department of Health and Social Services. Central Services Agency. Annual report. a., Oc/D 1973 (1st)- Belfast. *1st issue contains statistics of the work of the General Health Services Board covering Ap/S 1973.*

— History.

MACDONAGH (OLIVER) Ireland: the Union and its aftermath. rev. ed. London, 1977. pp. 176. *bibliog.*

STEWART (ANTHONY TERENCE QUINCEY) The narrow ground: aspects of Ulster 1609-1969. London, 1977. pp. 208. *bibliog.*

— Industries.

IRELAND, NORTHERN. 1976. Economic and industrial strategy for Northern Ireland: report by review team, 1976; [W.G.H. Quigley, chairman]. Belfast, 1976. pp. 106. *bibliog.*

— Nationalism.

BRITISH AND IRISH COMMUNIST ORGANISATION. Against Ulster nationalism: a review of the development of the Catholic and Protestant communities and their interaction with each other and with Britain in reply to Tom Nairn of "New Left Review" and others. Belfast, [1975?]. pp. 97.

NAIRN (TOM) The break-up of Britain: crisis and neo-nationalism. London, [1977]. pp. 368.

RUMPF (ERHARD) and HEPBURN (ANTHONY C.) Nationalism and socialism in twentieth-century Ireland. Liverpool, 1977. pp. 275. *bibliog.*

— Politics and government.

MYANT (CHRIS) and WARREN (JENNIFER) Ireland: no peace in the White Paper. London, [1973]. pp. 23. *bibliog.*

BURTON (FRANK PATRICK) The social meanings of Catholicism in Northern Ireland. 1976. fo. 311. *bibliog. Typescript. Ph.D. (London) thesis: unpublished. This thesis is the property of London University and may not be removed from the Library.*

McKEOWN (CIARAN) The price of peace. Belfast, [1976]. pp. 34.

YOU and Northern Ireland; [papers of a conference arranged by the Peace Pledge Union in 1975]. London, 1976. 1 pamphlet (various pagings).

RUMPF (ERHARD) and HEPBURN (ANTHONY C.) Nationalism and socialism in twentieth-century Ireland. Liverpool, 1977. pp. 275. *bibliog.*

— Population.

NORTHERN IRELAND HOUSING EXECUTIVE. Corporate Planning Department. Northern Ireland household survey, 1975. [Belfast, 1976]. pp. 178.

— Social conditions.

BURTON (FRANK PATRICK) The social meanings of Catholicism in Northern Ireland. 1976. fo. 311. *bibliog. Typescript. Ph.D. (London) thesis: unpublished. This thesis is the property of London University and may not be removed from the Library.*

IRIAN BARAT

— International status.

INDONESIA. Department of Foreign Affairs. 1969. Implementation of the Indonesia-Netherlands Agreement on West Irian: report of the Indonesian government to the Secretary-General of the U.N., concerning the conduct and the results of the 'act of free choice' in West Irian, pursuant to article 21 of the New York agreement 1962. [Djakarta], 1969. pp. 78.

IRISH AMERICANS.

CONZEN (KATHLEEN NEILS) Immigrant Milwaukee, 1836-1860: accommodation and community in a frontier city. Cambridge, Mass., 1976. pp. 300.

IRISH IN THE UNITED STATES.

See IRISH AMERICANS.

IRISH LANGUAGE.

EIRE. 1969. White Paper on the restoration of the Irish language: progress report for the period ended 31 March, 1968. Dublin, 1969. pp. 45. *In English and Irish.*

IRISH QUESTION.

MYANT (CHRIS) and WARREN (JENNIFER) Ireland: no peace in the White Paper. London, [1973]. pp. 23. *bibliog.*

COUGHLAN (ANTHONY) The way to peace in Ireland: the necessity for a British commitment to end the Union. [Dublin, 1974]. pp. 16.

BRITISH AND IRISH COMMUNIST ORGANISATION. Against Ulster nationalism: a review of the development of the Catholic and Protestant communities and their interaction with each other and with Britain in reply to Tom Nairn of "New Left Review" and others. Belfast, [1975?]. pp. 97.

DOWDEN (RICHARD) Northern Ireland and the Catholic Church in Britain; published...for the Commission for International Justice and Peace of England and Wales as a contribution to public debate. Abbots Langley, [1975]. pp. 27.

HARKNESS (D.W.) History and the Irish. Belfast, [1976]. pp. 15. *(Belfast. Queen's University. Lectures. New Series. No.93)*

LEBOW (RICHARD NED) White Britain and black Ireland: the influence of stereotypes on colonial policy. Philadelphia, Pa., [1976]. pp. 152. *bibliog.*

REVOLUTIONARY COMMUNIST GROUP. Ireland: British labour and British imperialism. London, [1976]. pp. 33. *bibliog.*

DANGERFIELD (GEORGE) The damnable question: a study in Anglo-Irish relations. London, 1977. pp. 400. *bibliog.*

O'DAY (ALAN) The English face of Irish nationalism: Parnellite involvement in British politics, 1880-86. Dublin, 1977. pp. 210. *bibliog.*

IRISH REPUBLICAN ARMY.

BURTON (FRANK PATRICK) The social meanings of Catholicism in Northern Ireland. 1976. fo. 311. *bibliog. Typescript. Ph.D. (London) thesis: unpublished. This thesis is the property of London University and may not be removed from the Library.*

GIBSON (BRIAN) The Birmingham bombs;...with additional research by Stephanie Silk and the help of the entire B.B.C. T.V. 'Day and Night' team, etc. Chichester, [1976]. pp. 164.

IRON AND STEEL WORKERS

— Canada — Nova Scotia.

MACEWAN (PAUL) Miners and steelworkers: labour in Cape Breton. Toronto, 1976. pp. 400. *bibliog.*

— Poland.

HUTA im. Lenina i jej zaloga. Kraków, 1976. pp. 130. *(Cracow. Uniwersytet Jagielloński. Zeszyty Naukowe. 447 [being also] Prace Socjologiczne. z.3) With English and Russian summaries.*

— United States.

SWEENEY (VINCENT D.) The United Steelworkers of America: twenty years later, 1936-1956. n.p., [1956]. pp. 239. *Without title page. Caption title.*

IRON INDUSTRY AND TRADE

— Austria.

MEJZLIK (HEINRICH) Die Eisenbewirtschaftung im Ersten Weltkrieg: die Planwirtschaft des k. u. k. Kriegsministeriums. Wien, [1977]. pp. 781. *bibliog.*

— Canada — Quebec.

NISH (CAMERON) François-Etienne Cugnet, 1719-1751: entrepreneur et entreprises en Nouvelle-France. Montréal. [1975]. pp. 185. *bibliog. (Centre de Recherche en Histoire Economique du Canada Français. Histoire Economique et Sociale du Canada Français)*

— France.

DUMAY (JEAN BAPTISTE) Mémoires d'un militant ouvrier du Creusot, 1841-1905; introduction et notes par Pierre Ponsot. Grenoble, 1976. pp. 431. *(Centre d'Histoire du Syndicalisme. Collection)*

FRANCE. Groupe sectoriel d'Analyse et de Prévision: Mines de Fer, Sidérurgie, Première Transformation de l'Acier. 1976. Rapport...: préparation du 7e Plan. Paris, 1976. pp. 100.

— Germany.

FELDMAN (GERALD D.) Iron and steel in the German inflation, 1916-1923. Princeton, [1977]. pp. 518. *bibliog.*

— Italy.

FRUMENTO (ARMANDO) Miniere ferrose e altoforni lombardi del 1848 e del 1849 in un censimento inedito della I.R. Luogotenenza. Milano, 1975. pp. 31. *(Estratto da Archivio Storico Lombardo, 1974, Anno C)*

— Russia — Georgia.

KANDELAKI (EVGRAF IAKENT'EVICH) Ekonomicheskie problemy chernoi metallurgii Gruzinskoi SSR. t.1. Tbilisi, 1968. pp. 343. *bibliog.*

— — Ukraine.

DNEPROVSKIE ogni: kak iz ruin i pepla byl podniat posle voiny Zaporozhskii industrial'nyi kompleks. Kiev, 1976. pp. 190.

— Turkey.

TURKIYE SINAÎ KALKINMA BANKASI. Sector Research Publications. No. 6. Study on the casting industry...; research by Aykut Civelek. Istanbul, 1976. pp. 101.

— United Kingdom.

HYDE (CHARLES K.) Technological change and the British iron industry, 1700-1870. Princeton, [1977]. pp. 283. *bibliog.*

— — Wales.

DAVIES (EDWARD JOHN) Sometime Chairman, Blaenavon Urban District Council. The Blaenavon story. 2nd ed. [Pontypool], Torfaen Borough Council, 1975. pp. 125.

IRON MINES AND MINING

— Italy.

FRUMENTO (ARMANDO) Miniere ferrose e altoforni lombardi del 1848 e del 1849 in un censimento inedito della I.R. Luogotenenza. Milano, 1975. pp. 31. *(Estratto da Archivio Storico Lombardo, 1974, Anno C)*

IRON-WORKS

— United Kingdom.

MEE (GRAHAM) Aristocratic enterprise: the Fitzwilliam industrial undertakings, 1795-1857. Glasgow, 1975. pp. 222.

IRRIGATION

— Environmental aspects.

ARID land irrigation in developing countries: environmental problems and effects; based on the international symposium, 16-21 February 1976, Alexandria, Egypt; editor E. Barton Worthington. Oxford, [1977]. pp. 463.

— Botswana.

MITCHELL (A.J.B.) The irrigation potential of soils along the main rivers of eastern Botswana: a reconnaissance assessment. Tolworth, 1976. pp. 216, 7 maps, 4 sheets of photomosaics. *bibliog. (U.K. Ministry of Overseas Development. Land Resources Division. Land Resource Studies. 7)*

— Ethiopia.

PROSPECTS for irrigation development around Lake Zwai, Ethiopia: [by] M.J. Makin [and others]. Tolworth, 1976. pp. 312 and 7 maps boxed separately. *bibliog.(U.K. Ministry of Overseas Development. Land Resources Division. Land Resource Studies. 26)*

— India.

JOSHI (NARHAR SADASHIV) and DHEKNEY (B.R.) Irrigation and agriculture in the first five year plan: an appraisal. Poona, 1954. 2 vols.

— South Africa.

SOUTH AFRICA. Parliament. House of Assembly. Select Committee on Irrigation Matters. 1977. Report...; proceedings (S.C. 10-1977). in SOUTH AFRICA. Parliament. House of Assembly. Select Committee reports.

— Underdeveloped areas.

See UNDERDEVELOPED AREAS — Irrigation.

ISLE OF MAN

— Census.

ISLE OF MAN. Census, 1976. Isle of Man census, 1976: report. [Douglas], 1976. pp. 17.

ISLINGTON

— Social conditions.

PITT (JAMES) Gentrification in Islington: the return of the middle classes to an inner London borough and the subsequent effects on housing. London, [1977]. fo. 36.

— Transit systems.

CARTER (PETER) Transport in Islington. London, [1976]. pp. 20.

ISRAEL

— Boundaries.

KISHTAINY (KHALID) Whither Israel?: a study of Zionist expansionism. Beirut, 1970. pp. 138. *bibliog. (Palestine Research Center. Palestine Books. No. 29)*

— Civilization.

POLL (SOLOMON) and KRAUSZ (ERNEST) eds. On ethnic and religious diversity in Israel. Ramat-Gan, 1975. pp. 124. *bibliog.*

— Commerce.

POMFRET (RICHARD W.T.) Trade policies and industrialization in a small country: the case of Israel. Tübingen, 1976. pp. 204. *bibliog. (Kiel. Universität. Institut für Weltwirtschaft. Kieler Studien. 141)*

— Commercial policy.

POMFRET (RICHARD W.T.) Trade policies and industrialization in a small country: the case of Israel. Tübingen, 1976. pp. 204. *bibliog. (Kiel. Universität. Institut für Weltwirtschaft. Kieler Studien. 141)*

— Defences.

PRANGER (ROBERT JOHN) and TAHTINEN (DALE R.) Implications of the 1976 Arab-Israeli military status. Washington, 1976. pp. 49. *(American Enterprise Institute for Public Policy Research. Foreign Affairs Studies. 34)*

HARKAVY (ROBERT E.) Spectre of a middle eastern holocaust: the strategic and diplomatic implications of the Israeli nuclear weapons program. Denver, [1977]. pp. 126. *(Denver. University. Social Science Foundation and Graduate School of International Studies. Monograph Series in World Affairs. vol. 14, no. 4)*

— Economic conditions.

ISRAEL. Economic Planning Authority. 1972. The Israel economy, 1970-1971. Report no. 3. Jerusalem, 1972. fo. 33.

BANK OF ISRAEL. Research Department. Recent economic developments. Jerusalem, 1976. pp. 74.

— Economic policy.

ISRAEL. Economic Plannng Authority. 1972. Economic development plan, 1972-1976: summary. Jerusalem, 1972. fo. 37.

ISRAEL. Economic Planning Authority. 1976. National economic plan, 1976-1980: proposal. Jerusalem, 1976. fo. (48). *Cover title: National economic plan, 1976-1980: summary.*

— Emigration and immigration.

ISRAEL. Ministry of Immigrant Absorption. Division of Research and Planning. Immigrant absorption: summary and conclusions. a., 1972- [Jerusalem]. *Reprint from the Ministry's annual report.*

ISRAEL INFORMATION CENTRE. Information Briefings. 3. Aliyah. Jerusalem, [1973]. pp. 12. *bibliog.*

FEASEY (R.A.) Israel: planning and immigration in relation to spatial development. Durham, 1976. pp. 75. *bibliog. (Durham. University. Department of Geography. Occasional Publications (New Series). No.8)*

— Foreign economic relations — Arab countries.

CHILL (DAN S.) The Arab boycott of Israel: economic aggression and world reaction. New York, 1976. pp. 121. *bibliog.*

— Foreign opinion, Arab.

HARKABI (YEHOSHAFAT) Arab strategies and Israel's response. New York, [1977]. pp. 194.

— Foreign relations.

BRECHER (MICHAEL) Decisions in Israel's foreign policy. London, 1974. pp. 639. *bibliog.*

— — Arab countries.

AL-ABID (IBRAHIM) Israel and negotiations. Beirut, 1970. pp. 29. *(Palestine Research Center. Palestine Essays. No. 20)*

— — Germany.

WALICHNOWSKI (TADEUSZ) The Tel Aviv-Bonn axis and Poland. Warsaw, 1968. pp. 88. *bibliog.*

— — Syria.

ISRAEL INFORMATION CENTRE. Information Briefings. 25. Israel-Syria disengagement agreement, 31 May 1974: documents and statements. Jerusalem, [1974]. pp. 17.

— History.

SACHAR (HOWARD MORLEY) A history of Israel: from the rise of Zionism to our time. Oxford, 1977. pp. 883, xlix. *bibliog.*

— Industries.

ISRAEL. Central Bureau of Statistics. 1975. Input-output tables, 1968/69; by David Chen. Jerusalem, 1975. pp. 255. *(Special Series. No.471) In English and Hebrew.*

— Politics and government.

ISRAEL INFORMATION CENTRE. Information Briefings. 24. Basic principles of the government's programme; submitted for approval by the Knesset upon presentation of the new government on 10 March 1974. Jerusalem, [1974]. pp. 19.

HAZAN (BARUCH A.) Soviet propaganda: a case study of the Middle East conflict. New Brunswick, N.J., [1976]. pp. 293.

LIEBMAN (CHARLES S.) Pressure without sanctions: the influence of American Jewry on Israeli policy. Cranbury, N.J., [1977]. pp. 304. *bibliog.*

SCHIFF (GARY S.) Tradition and politics: the religious parties of Israel. Detroit, 1977. pp. 267. *bibliog. (Columbia University. Middle East Institute. Modern Middle East Series. vol.9)*

WEIDENFELD (ARTHUR GEORGE) Baron Weidenfeld. The seven deadly cliches;... address to the Anglo-Israel Association annual general meeting on Tuesday, 14 December 1976. London, 1977. pp. 14.

— Population.

ISRAEL. Central Bureau of Statistics. 1976. Society in Israel: selected statistics; edited by V.O. Schmelz. 2nd ed. Jerusalem, 1976. pp. 172. *In English and Hebrew.*

— Religion.

POLL (SOLOMON) and KRAUSZ (ERNEST) eds. On ethnic and religious diversity in Israel. Ramat-Gan, 1975. pp. 124. *bibliog.*

SCHNEIDER (KARLHEINZ) Religion in Israel: eine Studie zum Verhältnis Person, Religion, Gesellschaft. Meisenheim am Glan, [1976]. pp. 267. *bibliog.*

— Social conditions.

MARX (EMANUEL) The social context of violent behaviour: a social anthropological study in an Israeli immigrant town. London, 1976. pp. 130. *bibliog.*

— — Statistics.

ISRAEL. Central Bureau of Statistics. 1976. Society in Israel: selected statistics; edited by V.O. Schmelz. 2nd ed. Jerusalem, 1976. pp. 172. *In English and Hebrew.*

— Social policy.

ISRAEL. Economic Planning Authority. 1976. National economic plan, 1976-1980: proposal. Jerusalem, 1976. fo. (48). *Cover title: National economic plan, 1976-1980: summary.*

ISRAEL AND THE DIASPORA.

LIEBMAN (CHARLES S.) Pressure without sanctions: the influence of world Jewry on Israeli policy. Cranbury, N.J., [1977]. pp. 304. *bibliog.*

ISRAEL-ARAB CONFLICT, 1948- .

ISRAEL INFORMATION CENTRE. Information Briefings. 2. Does Sadat really want peace with Israele? rev. ed. Jerusalem, [1973]. pp. 14.

PRANGER (ROBERT JOHN) and TAHTINEN (DALE R.) Implications of the 1976 Arab-Israeli military status. Washington, 1976. pp. 49. *(American Enterprise Institute for Public Policy Research. Foreign Affairs Studies. 34)*

SID-AHMED (MOHAMED) After the guns fall silent: peace or Armageddon in the Middle- East. London, 1976. pp. 144.

— Foreign public opinion, American.

ESSAYS on the American public opinion and the Palestine problem. Beirut, 1969. pp. 192. *bibliog. (Palestine Research Center. Palestine Monographs. 53)*

ISRAEL-ARAB WAR, 1967

— Atrocities.

INSTITUTE FOR PALESTINE STUDIES. Israel and the Geneva Conventions; [collected articles]. Beirut, 1968. pp. 63. *(Institute for Palestine Studies. Anthology Series. No. 3)*

— Occupied territories.

INSTITUTE FOR PALESTINE STUDIES. Israel and the Geneva Conventions; [collected articles]. Beirut, 1968. pp. 63. *(Institute for Palestine Studies. Anthology Series. No. 3)*

AL-ABID (IBRAHIM) Israel and human rights. Beirut, 1969. pp. 172. *(Palestine Research Center. Palestine Books. No. 24)*

AL-ABID (IBRAHIM) Human rights in the occupied territories. Beirut, 1970. pp. 171. *(Palestine Research Center. Palestine Monographs. 73)*

ISRAEL. Coordinator of Government Operations in the Administered Territories. 1972. The administered territories, 1971/72: data on civilian activities in Judaea and Samaria, the Gaza strip and northern Sinai. [Tel Aviv, 1972?]. pp. 292.

ISRAEL INFORMATION CENTRE. Information Briefings. 6. Israeli settlements in the administered areas. Jerusalem, [1973]. pp. 3.

ISRAEL INFORMATION CENTRE. Information Briefings. 10. The administered areas: aspects of Israeli policy. Jerusalem, [1974]. pp. 28.

ISRAEL INFORMATION CENTRE. Information Briefings. 18. Administration of justice in the areas administered by Israel. rev. ed. Jerusalem, [1974]. pp. 12.

BULL (VIVIAN A.) The West Bank: is it viable?. Lexington, Mass., [1975]. pp. 170. *bibliog.*

ISRAEL-ARAB WAR, 1973.

GOLAN (GALIA) Yom Kippur and after: the Soviet Union and the Middle East crisis. Cambridge, 1977. pp. 350. *bibliog. (National Association for Soviet and East European Studies. Soviet and East European Studies)*

ISRAELI NEWSPAPERS

— Directories.

ISRAEL. Government Press Office. 1967. Newspapers and periodicals appearing in Israel. [Jerusalem], 1967. pp. 37.

ISRAELI PERIODICALS

— Directories.

ISRAEL. Government Press Office. 1967. Newspapers and periodicals appearing in Israel. [Jerusalem], 1967. pp. 37.

ITALIAN AMERICANS.

KESSNER (THOMAS) The golden door: Italian and Jewish immigrant mobility in New York City, 1880-1915. New York, 1977. pp. 224. *bibliog.*

ITALIAN LANGUAGE

— Dictionaries — English.

CENTRO LESSICOGRAFICO SANSONI. Dizionario delle lingue italiana e inglese;...realizzato... sotto la direzione di Vladimiro Macchi. Firenze, 1970-76. 4 vols.

ITALIAN NEWSPAPERS.

LICATA (GLAUCO) Storia del Corriere della Sera. Milano, [1976]. pp. 677.

ITALIANS IN AFRICA.

BOCA (ANGELO DEL) Gli italiani in Africa Orientale: dall'Unità alla marcia su Roma. Roma, 1976. pp. 909.

ITALIANS IN BRAZIL.

DURHAM (EUNICE RIBEIRO) Assimilação e mobilidade: a historia do imigrante italiano num municipio paulista. São Paulo, 1966. pp. 67. *bibliog. (São Paulo. Universidade. Instituto de Estudos Brasileiros. Publicações. 3)*

FAE (WALTER JOSE) Italianos no Rio Grande do Sul, 1875-1975. São Paulo, [1975]. pp. 228. *bibliog.*

ITALIANS IN THE UNITED STATES.

See ITALIAN AMERICANS.

ITALO-ETHIOPIAN WAR, 1935-1936.

BAER (GEORGE WEBSTER) Test case: Italy, Ethiopia, and the League of Nations. Stanford, Calif., [1976]. pp. 367. *bibliog. (Stanford University. Hoover Institution on War, Revolution and Peace. Hoover Institution Publications. 159)*

ITALY

— Army — History.

WHITTAM (JOHN) The politics of the Italian army, 1861-1918. London, 1977. pp. 216. *bibliog.*

— Colonies — History.

BOCA (ANGELO DEL) Gli italiani in Africa Orientale: dall'Unità alla marcia su Roma. Roma, 1976. pp. 909.

— Commerce — Sicily.

ABULAFIA (DAVID) The two Italies: economic relations between the Norman kingdom of Sicily and the northern communes. Cambridge, 1977. pp. 310. *bibliog.*

— Economic conditions.

CRISI e ristrutturazione nell'economia italiana: diciotto interventi a cura di Augusto Graziani. Torino, [1975]. pp. 559. *Papers of a conference held in the Centro di Specializzazione e Ricerche Economico-Agrarie per il Mezzogiorno of the Università di Napoli in 1974.*

MORTARA (ALBERTO) ed. Il settore pubblico dell'economia: dati e notizie, 1970-1974. Milano, [1976]. pp. 1456. *bibliog. (Centro Italiano di Ricerche e d'Informazione sull'Economia delle Imprese Pubbliche e di Pubblico Interesse. Studi e Documenti sul Settore Pubblico dell'Economia. 18)*

— Economic history.

AVAGLIANO (LUCIO) Studi di storia del Mezzogiorno.1. Problemi dello sviluppo economico. [Salerno, 1975]. pp. 81.

L'ECONOMIA italiana nel periodo fascista; a cura di Pierluigi Ciocca e Gianni Toniolo. Bologna, [1976]. pp. 448. *bibliog.*

EVANS (ROBERT H.) Life and politics in a Venetian community. Notre Dame, Ind., [1976]. pp. 228. *bibliog. (Notre Dame. University. Committee on International Relations. International Studies)*

FATTI e idee di storia economica nei secoli XII-XX: studi dedicati a Franco Borlandi; (redazione: Bruno Dini [and others]). Bologna, [1977]. pp. 916. *With contributions in English, French and German.*

— Economic policy.

CAGLIOZZI (ROBERTO) Infrastrutture di trasporto e sviluppo del Mezzogiorno. Milano, 1975. pp. 80. *(Associazione per lo Sviluppo dell'Industria nel Mezzogiorno. Centro per gli Studi sullo Sviluppo Economico. Collana di Monografie)*

CHAPMAN (GRAHAM) Development and underdevelopment in Southern Italy. Reading, 1976. pp. 32. *bibliog. (Reading. University. Department of Geography. Reading Geographical Papers. No. 41)*

— Historiography.

LI PERA (LUCIA) ed. Il fascismo dalla polemica alla storiografia;...un saggio introduttivo con i confronti antologici da A. Gramsci [and others]. Messina, 1975. pp. 191. *bibliog.*

GILBERT (FELIX) History: choice and commitment. Cambridge, Mass., 1977. pp. 549. *bibliog. Selected essays.*

— History — 1815-1870.

WHITTAM (JOHN) The politics of the Italian army, 1861-1918. London, 1977. pp. 216. *bibliog.*

— — 1870- .

STORIA dell'Italia contemporanea; diretta da Renzo De Felice. Napoli, [1976 in progress]. *bibliogs.*

— — 1870-1915.

WHITTAM (JOHN) The politics of the Italian army, 1861-1918. London, 1977. pp. 216. *bibliog.*

— — 1914-1945.

QUAZZA (GUIDO) Resistenza e storia d'Italia: problemi e ipotesi di ricerca. Milano, 1976. pp. 468.

CLARK (MARTIN) Antonio Gramsci and the revolution that failed. New Haven, 1977. pp. 255. *bibliog.*

— Industries.

ISTITUTO DI STUDI PER LA PROGRAMMAZIONE ECONOMICA [ITALY]. Centro di Studi e Piani Economici. Le prospettive di sviluppo industriale al 1975 e 1980 in Italia e nelle sue regioni. [Rome, 1973-74]. 2 vols. *(Istituto di Studi per la Programmazione Economica [Italy] Collana di Studi e Ricerche)*

— Officials and employees — Discipline.

LI VECCHI (ROSARIO) I delitti dei pubblici ufficiali contro la pubblica amministrazione: rassegna di dottrina e raccolta di giurisprudenza. Catania, 1975. pp. 571. *bibliog.*

— Parliament.

ITALY. Camera dei Deputati. 1948. Manuale parlamentare. Roma, 1948. pp. 613.

ITALY. Senato. 1964. Manuale parlamentare: legislatura IV. Roma, 1964. pp. 1057.

ITALY. Senato. 1969. Manuale parlamentare: legislatura V. Roma, 1969. pp. 1107.

— — Rules and practice.

PALMA (GIUSEPPE DI) Surviving without governing: the Italian parties in Parliament. Berkeley, Calif., [1977]. pp. 299.

— Politics and government.

ZUCKERMAN (ALAN) Political clienteles in power: party factions and cabinet coalitions in Italy. Beverly Hills, [1975]. pp. 51. *bibliog.*

GILBERT (FELIX) History: choice and commitment. Cambridge, Mass., 1977. pp. 549. *bibliog. Selected essays.*

— — 1900- .

GRAMSCI (ANTONIO) La rivoluzione italiana; introduzione e cura di Dino Ferreri. Roma, 1976. pp. 260.

— — 1914-1945.

MOLONY (JOHN NEYLON) The emergence of political catholicism in Italy: Partito Popolare 1919-1926. London, 1977. pp. 225. *bibliog.*

— — 1922-1945.

CAPRIOLI (MAURA PICCIALUTI) ed. Radio Londra, 1940-1945: inventario delle trasmissioni per l'Italia. Roma, 1976. 2 vols. *(Italy. Direzione Generale degli Archivi di Stato. Pubblicazioni degli Archivi di Stato. 89, 90)*

— — 1945- .

BIBES (GENEVIEVE) Il sistema politico italiano;...traduzione e bibliografia a cura di Neri Gori. Rimini, [1975]. pp. 201. *bibliog.*

COLLIN (RICHARD) The de Lorenzo gambit: the Italian coup manqué of 1964. Beverly Hills, [1976]. pp. 65.

NAPOLITANO (GIORGIO) La politique du Parti communiste italien: entretien avec Eric J. Hobsbawm; traduit de l'italien par Claudine Ewenczyk et Jean Rony. Paris, [1976]. pp. 155.

BARNES (SAMUEL HENRY) Representation in Italy: institutionalized tradition and electoral choice. Chicago, 1977. pp. 187.

— Social history.

EVANS (ROBERT H.) Life and politics in a Venetian community. Notre Dame, Ind., [1976]. pp. 228. *bibliog. (Notre Dame. University. Committee on International Relations. International Studies)*

— Social policy.

CHAPMAN (GRAHAM) Development and underdevelopment in Southern Italy. Reading, 1976. pp. 32. *bibliog. (Reading. University. Department of Geography. Reading Geographical Papers. No. 41)*

IVORY COAST

— Commerce.

IVORY COAST. Service de la Statistique et de la Mécanographie. 1955. Commerce extérieur de la Côte d'Ivoire et de la Haute- Volta de 1931 à 1954. [Abidjan], 1955. pp. 118. *(Ivory Coast. Direction de la Statistique et des Etudes Economiques et Démographiques. Bulletin mensuel de statistique. Annexes)*

— Economic conditions.

DUTHEIL DE LA ROCHÈRE (JACQUELINE) L'état et le développement économique de la Côte d'Ivoire. Paris, [1976]. pp. 420. *(Bordeaux. Université. Centre d'Etude d'Afrique Noire. Bibliothèque. Série Afrique Noire. 6)*

FRANCE. Ministère de la Coopération. Sous-Direction des Etudes Economiques et de la Planification. 1976. Côte d'Ivoire: données statistiques sur les activités économiques, culturelles et sociales. Paris, 1976. pp. 228.

— Economic policy.

[AUTORITE POUR L'AMENAGEMENT DE LA REGION DU SUD-OUEST [IVORY COAST]]. San Pédro: pôle de développement du sud-ouest ivoirien. [Abidjan?, 1973?]. pp. 110.

DUTHEIL DE LA ROCHÈRE (JACQUELINE) L'état et le développement économique de la Côte d'Ivoire. Paris, [1976]. pp. 420. *(Bordeaux. Université. Centre d'Etude d'Afrique Noire. Bibliothèque. Série Afrique Noire. 6)*

— Foreign relations — Nigeria.

HOUPHOUËT-BOIGNY (FELIX) Biafra: press conference given by the President of the Republic of Ivory Coast, just a few hours before leaving for Abidjan on May 9. [Paris, Centre d'Information et de Documentation Ivoirien, 1968]. fo.(4). *Supplement to Réalités Ivoiriennes, No.75, May 1968.*

— Industries.

IVORY COAST. Direction du Développement Industriel. 1972. La situation de l'industrie ivoirienne à fin 1970. [Abidjan, 1972]. pp. 32.

— Relations (general) with Ghana.

GHANA. Ministry of Information. 1970. Ghana-Ivory Coast fraternity:...a record of the official visit of the Prime Minister of Ghana, the Rt. Hon. Dr. K. A. Busia, to the Ivory Coast from April 29, to May 9, 1970. [Accra, 1970]. pp. 69 bis. *In English and French.*

— Social conditions.

FRANCE. Ministère de la Coopération. Sous-Direction des Etudes Economiques et de la Planification. 1976. Côte d'Ivoire: données statistiques sur les activités économiques, culturelles et sociales. Paris, 1976. pp. 228.

— Statistics.

FRANCE. Ministère de la Coopération. Sous-Direction des Etudes Economiques et de la Planification. 1976. Côte d'Ivoire: données statistiques sur les activités économiques, culturelles et sociales. Paris, 1976. pp. 228.

JABHAT AL-TAHRIR AL-QAWMI.

See FRONT DE LIBERATION NATIONALE.

JACOB (BERTHOLD).

CAWIL (H.) Der Fall Jacob. Zürich, [1935]. pp. 38.

JACOBINS.

MARKOV (WALTER) Die Jakobinerfrage heute. Oulu, 1967. pp. 24. *(Oulu. Yliopisto. Department of History. Collected Papers of the Guest Lecturers. Nr. 1)*

JACQUIN DE MARGERIE (PIERRE).

See MARGERIE (PIERRE DE).

JAMAICA

— Constitutional law.

BARNETT (LLOYD G.) The constitutional law of Jamaica. Oxford, 1977. pp. 468.

— House of Assembly.

BINNS ( ) Dr. An appeal to the good sense of the British nation, against the monstrous charges of Daniel O'Connell, Esq., and other members of the Anti-Slavery Convention, touching the Jamaica House of Assembly. London, Effingham Wilson, 1840. pp. 18.

— Politics and government.

LACEY (TERRY) Violence and politics in Jamaica, 1960-70: internal security in a developing country. Manchester, [1977]. pp. 184.

— Race question.

CAMPBELL (MAVIS CHRISTINE) The dynamics of change in a slave society: a sociopolitical history of the free coloreds of Jamaica, 1800-1865. Cranbury, N.J., [1976]. pp. 393. *bibliog.*

— Social history.

CAMPBELL (MAVIS CHRISTINE) The dynamics of change in a slave society: a sociopolitical history of the free coloreds of Jamaica, 1800-1865. Cranbury, N.J., [1976]. pp. 393. *bibliog.*

JANSENISTS.

TOMSICH (MARIA GIOVANNA) El jansenismo en España: estudio sobre ideas religiosas en la segunda mitad del siglo XVIII. Madrid, 1972. pp. 207. *bibliog.*

JAPAN.

REISCHAUER (EDWIN OLDFATHER) The Japanese. Cambridge, Mass., [1977]. pp. 443. *bibliog.*

— Census.

JAPAN. Census, 1970. Population of Japan. [Tokyo, 1972]. pp. 142. *(Abridged Report Series. No.1) In English and Japanese.*

JAPAN. Census, 1970. Population of Japan: summary of the results of 1970 population census of Japan. [Tokyo, 1975]. pp. 818. *In English and Japanese.*

JAPAN. Census, 1975. 1975 population census of Japan: preliminary count of population. [Tokyo, 1975]. pp. 105. *In English and Japanese.*

JAPAN. Census, 1975. 1975 population census of Japan: prompt report of the basic findings: result for one-percent tabulation. [Tokyo, 1976]. pp. 651. *In English and Japanese.*

— Commerce.

MOULDER (FRANCES V.) Japan, China and the modern world economy: toward a reinterpretation of East Asian development ca. 1600 to ca. 1918. Cambridge, 1977. pp. 255. *bibliog.*

— Economic conditions.

KOSAKA (MASATAKA) 100 million Japanese: the postwar experience. Tokyo, 1972. pp. 282.

WHITE paper on Japanese economy 1973. Tokyo, [1973]. pp. 119. *Based on the White paper on Japanese economy prepared by the Economic Planning Agency.*

BANK OF JAPAN. Economic Research Department. Special Papers. No. 65. The Japanese economy in 1975. Tokyo, 1976. pp. 36.

HAITANI (KANJI) The Japanese economic system: an institutional overview. Lexington, Mass., [1976]. pp. 190.

KOJIMA (KIYOSHI) Japan and a new world economic order. London, [1977]. pp. 190. *A revision of previously published essays.*

— — Mathematical models.

MIYAZAWA (KEN'ICHI) Input-output analysis and the structure of income distribution. Berlin, 1976. pp. 135. *bibliog.*

ECONOMIC studies of Japan; edited by Richard Kosobud and Ryoshin Minami. Urbana, [1977]. pp. 512.

JAPAN.(Cont.)

— — Statistics.

ESTIMATES of long-term economic statistics of Japan since 1868; edited by Kazushi Ohkawa [and others]. Tokyo, 1965 in progress. *bibliogs. With summaries and headings to statistical tables in English.*

— Economic history.

LIVINGSTON (JON) and others, eds. The Japan reader. Harmondsworth, 1976. 2 vols. *bibliogs.*

MOULDER (FRANCES V.) Japan, China and the modern world economy: toward a reinterpretation of East Asian development ca. 1600 to ca. 1918. Cambridge, 1977. pp. 255. *bibliog.*

— Foreign economic relations.

The FOREIGN policy of modern Japan; edited by Robert A. Scalapino. Berkeley, Calif., [1977]. pp. 426. *Proceedings of a conference sponsored by the Joint Committee on Japanese Studies of the American Council of Learned Societies and the Social Science Research Council.*

KOJIMA (KIYOSHI) Japan and a new world economic order. London, [1977]. pp. 190. *A revision of previously published essays.*

— — Asia, Southeast.

MANGLAPUS (RAUL S.) Japan in Southeast Asia: collision course. New York, [1976]. pp. 151. *bibliog.*

— — China.

LEE (CHAE-JIN) Japan faces China: political and economic relations in the postwar era. Baltimore, [1976]. pp. 242.

— — Indonesia.

NISHIHARA (MASASHI) The Japanese and Sukarno's Indonesia: Tokyo-Jakarta relations, 1951-1966. Honolulu, [1976]. pp. 244. *bibliog. (Kyoto. University. Center for Southeast Asian Studies. Monographs: English Series. 8)*

— — Netherlands.

VAN vriend tot vijand: de betrekkingen tusschen Nederlandsch-Indië en Japan; samengesteld onder toezicht van A.C.D. de Graeff door M. Boerstra [and others]. Amsterdam, 1945. pp. 382.

— Foreign relations.

DEVA (JAYA) Japan's kampf. London, 1942. pp. 192.

KAJIMA (MORINOSUKE) The diplomacy of Japan, 1894-1922. Tokyo, 1976 in progress. *bibliog.*

The FOREIGN policy of modern Japan; edited by Robert A. Scalapino. Berkeley, Calif., [1977]. pp. 426. *Proceedings of a conference sponsored by the Joint Committee on Japanese Studies of the American Council of Learned Societies and the Social Science Research Council.*

NISH (IAN HILL) Japanese foreign policy, 1869-1942: Kasumigaseki to Miyakezaka. London, 1977. pp. 346. *bibliog.*

— — China.

LEE (CHAE-JIN) Japan faces China: political and economic relations in the postwar era. Baltimore, [1976]. pp. 242.

— — Indonesia.

VAN vriend tot vijand: de betrekkingen tusschen Nederlandsch-Indië en Japan; samengesteld onder toezicht van A.C.D. de Graeff door M. Boerstra [and others]. Amsterdam, 1945. pp. 382.

TEKTJENG (LIE) An Indonesian perspective: Japanese-Indonesian relations in the seventies. Djakarta, 1971. pp. 19. *(Lembaga Ilmu Pengetahuan Indonesia. Lembaga Research Kebudajaan Nasional. Terbitan Tak Berkala. No. 2/5)*

NISHIHARA (MASASHI) The Japanese and Sukarno's Indonesia: Tokyo-Jakarta relations, 1951-1966. Honolulu, [1976]. pp. 244. *bibliog. (Kyoto. University. Center for Southeast Asian Studies. Monographs: English Series. 8)*

— — United States.

JAPANESE-American relations; (an AEI Round Table held on 17 December 1974...); Donald C. Hellman, moderator, etc. Washington, [1975]. pp. 27. *(American Enterprise Institute for Public Policy Research. Round Tables)*

PFALTZGRAFF (ROBERT L.) and DAVIS (JACQUELYN K.) Japanese-American relations in a changing security environment. Beverly Hills, [1975]. pp. 49.

CHINA and Japan: a new balance of power; edited by Donald C. Hellmann. Lexington, Mass., [1976]. pp. 305. *(Commission on Critical Choices for Americans. Critical Choices for Americans. vol.12)*

MANAGING an alliance: the politics of U.S.-Japanese relations; ([by]) I.M. Destler [and others]. Washington, D.C., [1976]. pp. 209. *bibliog.*

— History.

LIVINGSTON (JON) and others, eds. The Japan reader. Harmondsworth, 1976. 2 vols. *bibliogs.*

— — 1568-1603.

TOYOTOMI (HIDEYOSHI) 101 letters of Hideyoshi: the private correspondence of Toyotomi Hideyoshi; edited and translated by Adriana Boscaro. Tokyo, [1975]. pp. 114. *bibliog. (Sophia University. Monumenta Nipponica. Monographs. 54)*

— Industries.

JAPAN. Establishment Census, 1975. 1975 establishment census of Japan. [Tokyo, 1976 in progress]. *In English and Japanese.*

CONFERENCE ON JAPANESE INDUSTRIALIZATION AND ITS SOCIAL CONSEQUENCES, UNIVERSITY OF WASHINGTON, 1973. Japanese industrialization and its social consequences; edited by Hugh Patrick, with the assistance of Larry Meissner. Berkeley, Calif., [1976]. pp. 505. *bibliogs. Proceedings of a conference sponsored by the Joint Committee on Japanese Studies of the American Council of Learned Societies and the Social Science Research Council.*

— National Diet — Elections.

JAPAN at the polls: the House of Councillors election of 1974; edited by Michael K. Blaker. Washington, D.C., 1976. pp. 157. *(American Enterprise Institute for Public Policy Research. Foreign Affairs Studies. 37)*

— Navy — History.

DINGMAN (ROGER) Power in the Pacific: the origins of naval arms limitation, 1914- 1922. Chicago, [1976]. pp. 318. *bibliog.*

— Politics and government.

KOBAYASHI (TAKIJI) Der 15. März 1928: eine japanische Arbeiter-Erzählung; (autorisierte Übersetzung aus dem Japanischen). Berlin, [1931]. pp. 47.

DEVA (JAYA) Japan's kampf. London, 1942. pp. 192.

KOSAKA (MASATAKA) 100 million Japanese: the postwar experience. Tokyo, 1972. pp. 282.

KURODA (YASUMASA) Reed Town, Japan: a study in community power structure and political change. Honolulu, [1974]. pp. 283. *bibliog.*

JAPAN at the polls: the House of Councillors election of 1974; edited by Michael K. Blaker. Washington, D.C., 1976. pp. 157. *(American Enterprise Institute for Public Policy Research. Foreign Affairs Studies. 37)*

— Social conditions.

KOSAKA (MASATAKA) 100 million Japanese: the postwar experience. Tokyo, 1972. pp. 282.

CONFERENCE ON JAPANESE INDUSTRIALIZATION AND ITS SOCIAL CONSEQUENCES, UNIVERSITY OF WASHINGTON, 1973. Japanese industrialization and its social consequences; edited by Hugh Patrick, with the assistance of Larry Meissner. Berkeley, Calif., [1976]. pp. 505. *bibliogs. Proceedings of a conference sponsored by the Joint Committee on Japanese Studies of the American Council of Learned Societies and the Social Science Research Council.*

LIVINGSTON (JON) and others, eds. The Japan reader. Harmondsworth, 1976. 2 vols. *bibliogs.*

SOCIAL change and community politics in urban Japan; edited by James W. White and Frank Munger. Chapel Hill, N.C., 1976. pp. 132. *bibliogs. (North Carolina University. Center for Urban and Regional Studies. Comparative Urban Studies. Monographs. No.4)*

JAPANESE AMERICANS.

CONNOR (JOHN W.) Tradition and change in three generations of Japanese Americans. Chicago, [1977]. pp. 356. *bibliog.*

JAPANESE IN CANADA.

ADACHI (KEN) The enemy that never was: a history of the Japanese Canadians. Toronto, [1976]. pp. 456. *bibliog.*

JAPANESE IN SOUTHEAST ASIA.

MANGLAPUS (RAUL S.) Japan in Southeast Asia: collision course. New York, [1976]. pp. 151. *bibliog.*

JAPANESE IN THE UNITED STATES.

See JAPANESE AMERICANS.

JAPANESE LANGUAGE

— Social aspects.

MILLER (ROY ANDREW) The Japanese language in contemporary Japan: some sociolinguistic observations. Washington, D.C., [1977]. pp. 105. *bibliog. (American Enterprise Institute for Public Policy Research, and Stanford University. Hoover Institution on War, Revolution and Peace. AEI-Hoover Policy Studies. 22)*

JAURÈS (JEAN).

WOJNAR-SUJECKA (JANINA) Myśl, działanie, rzeczywistość: studium o światopoglądzie socjalistycznym Jean Jaurèsa. Warszawa, 1976. pp. 287.

JAVA

— Population.

INDONESIA. Biro Pusat Statistik. Penduduk Mar Jawa: hasil registrasi penduduk: Population of outer Java: results of population registration. a., 1972-1973. Jakarta. *[in Indonesian and English].*

JEHOVAH'S WITNESSES

— Canada.

PENTON (M. JAMES) Jehovah's Witnesses in Canada: champions of freedom of speech and worship. Toronto, [1976]. pp. 388. *bibliog.*

JERUSALEM

— History.

ISRAEL INFORMATION CENTRE. Information Briefings. 27. Jerusalem: issues and perspectives. rev. ed. Jerusalem, [1973]. pp. 32. *bibliog.*

— International status.

ISRAEL INFORMATION CENTRE. Information Briefings. 27. Jerusalem: issues and perspectives. rev. ed. Jerusalem, [1973]. pp. 32. *bibliog.*

JESUITS

— Missions.

REA (WILLIAM FRANCIS) The economics of the Zambezi missions, 1580-1759. Roma, 1976. pp. 189. *bibliog. (Institutum Historicum S.I. Bibliotheca. vol. 39)*

JEWELLERY TRADE

— Ireland (Republic).

EIRE. Fair Trade Commission. 1968. Report of enquiry into the conditions which obtain in regard to the supply and distribution to retailers of jewellery, watches and clocks. Dublin, [1968]. pp. 27.

JEWISH AMERICANS.

SZAJKOWSKI (ZOSA) Jews, wars and communism. New York, 1972-74. 2 vols. *bibliogs.*

COHEN (NAOMI WEINER) American Jews and the Zionist idea. [New York, 1975]. pp. 172. *bibliog.*

BLAU (JOSEPH LEON) Judaism in America: from curiosity to third faith. Chicago, 1976. pp. 156.

HOWE (IRVING) and LIBO (KENNETH) World of our fathers. New York, [1976]. pp. 714. *bibliog.*

KARP (ABRAHAM J.) Jewish perceptions of America: from melting pot to mosaic. [Syracuse, N.Y.], 1976. pp. 20. *(Syracuse University. B.G. Rudolph Lectures in Judaic Studies. 1976)*

DOLGIN (JANET L.) Jewish identity and the JDL. Princeton, [1977]. pp. 189. *bibliog. Based on Ph.D. thesis, Princeton University, 1974.*

KESSNER (THOMAS) The golden door: Italian and Jewish immigrant mobility in New York City, 1880-1915. New York, 1977. pp. 224. *bibliog.*

LIEBMAN (CHARLES S.) Pressure without sanctions: the influence of world Jewry on Israeli policy. Cranbury, N.J., [1977]. pp. 304. *bibliog.*

JEWISH-ARAB RELATIONS.

FOOT (HUGH MACKINTOSH) Baron Caradon of St. Cleer. A plan for peace. n.p., [1970?] pp. 19. *(Repr. from 3 issues of the Sunday Times, of July 5, 12, and 19, 1970)*

JABBOUR (GEORGE) Settler colonialism in Southern Africa and the Middle East. Beirut, 1970. pp. 216. *(Palestine Research Center. Palestine Books. No. 30)*

KISHTAINY (KHALID) Whither Israel?: a study of Zionist expansionism. Beirut, 1970. pp. 138. *bibliog. (Palestine Research Center. Palestine Books. No. 29)*

RAZZOUK (ASS'AD) Greater Israel: a study in Zionist expansionist thought. Beirut, 1970. pp. 326. *bibliog. (Palestine Research Center. Palestine Books. No. 13)*

AL-ABID (IBRAHIM) A handbook to the Palestine question: questions and answers. 2nd ed. Beirut, 1971. pp. 198. *bibliog. (Palestine Research Center. Palestine Books. No. 17)*

KISHTAINY (KHALID) Palestine in perspective: on the image and reality of Palestine throughout the ages. Beirut, 1971. pp. 126. *bibliog. (Palestine Research Center. Palestine Books. No. 34)*

ISRAEL INFORMATION CENTRE. Information Briefings. 22. Towards peace: a documentary record of Israel's statements on peace and regional cooperation and proposals for their attainment, from 1947 to the present day. Jerusalem, [1974]. pp. 47.

ALI (RUSTUM) Sheikh. Saudi Arabia and oil diplomacy. New York, 1976. pp. 197. *bibliog.*

CATTAN (HENRY) Palestine and international law: the legal aspects of the Arab- Israeli conflict. 2nd ed. London, 1976. pp. 362.

CHILL (DAN S.) The Arab boycott of Israel: economic aggression and world reaction. New York, 1976. pp. 121. *bibliog.*

HAZAN (BARUCH A.) Soviet propaganda: a case study of the Middle East conflict. New Brunswick, N.J., [1976]. pp. 293.

INTERNATIONAL INSTITUTE FOR STRATEGIC STUDIES. Adelphi Papers. No. 128. The Arab-Israeli dispute: great power behaviour; by Lawrence L. Whetten. London, 1976. pp. 45.

MANDEL (NEVILLE J.) The Arabs and Zionism before World War I. Berkeley, Calif., [1976]. pp. 258. *bibliog.*

SID-AHMED (MOHAMED) After the guns fall silent: peace or Armageddon in the Middle- East. London, 1976. pp. 144.

HARKABI (YEHOSHAFAT) Arab strategies and Israel's response. New York, [1977]. pp. 194.

PORATH (YEHOSHUA) The Palestinian Arab national movement: from riots to rebellion;...1929-1939. London, 1977. pp. 414. *bibliog. Vol.2 of his The emergence of the Palestinian-Arab national movement, 1918-1929.*

WEIDENFELD (ARTHUR GEORGE) Baron Weidenfeld. The seven deadly cliches;... address to the Anglo-Israel Association annual general meeting on Tuesday, 14 December 1976. London, 1977. pp. 14.

— Bibliography.

DEVORE (RONALD M.) compiler. The Arab-Israeli conflict: a historical, political, social, and military bibliography. Santa Barbara, Calif., [1976]. pp. 273.

JEWISH BOARD OF GUARDIANS.

See JEWISH WELFARE BOARD.

JEWISH DEFENSE LEAGUE.

DOLGIN (JANET L.) Jewish identity and the JDL. Princeton, [1977]. pp. 189. *bibliog. Based on Ph.D. thesis, Princeton University, 1974.*

JEWISH QUESTION.

ZUKERMAN (WILLIAM) The Jew in revolt: the modern Jew in the world crisis. London, 1937. pp. 255.

JEWISH WELFARE BOARD.

MAGNUS (LAURIE) The Jewish Board of Guardians and the men who made it, 1859- 1909: an illustrated record. London, [1909]. pp. 152.

JEWS

— History — Maps.

GILBERT (MARTIN) Jewish history atlas; cartography by Arthur Banks and T.A. Bicknell. 2nd ed. London, 1976. pp. 126. *bibliog.*

— Legal status, laws etc. — Israel.

KRAINES (OSCAR) The impossible dilemma: who is a Jew in the state of Israel?. New York, [1976]. pp. 156. *bibliog.*

— Political and social conditions.

SZAJKOWSKI (ZOSA) Jews, wars and communism. New York, 1972-74. 2 vols. *bibliogs.*

— Public opinion.

SZAJKOWSKI (ZOSA) Jews, wars and communism. New York, 1972-74. 2 vols. *bibliogs.*

— Restoration.

KISHTAINY (KHALID) Whither Israel?: a study of Zionist expansionism. Beirut, 1970. pp. 138. *bibliog. (Palestine Research Center. Palestine Books. No. 29)*

RAZZOUK (ASS'AD) Greater Israel: a study in Zionist expansionist thought. Beirut, 1970. pp. 326. *bibliog. (Palestine Research Center. Palestine Books. No. 13)*

MAIATSKII (FEODOSII SEMENOVICH) Dvazhdy obmanutye. Kishinev, 1971. pp. 112. *bibliog.*

COHEN (NAOMI WEINER) American Jews and the Zionist idea. [New York, 1975]. pp. 172. *bibliog.*

BLAU (JOSEPH LEON) Judaism in America: from curiosity to third faith. Chicago, 1976. pp. 156.

SACHAR (HOWARD MORLEY) A history of Israel: from the rise of Zionism to our time. Oxford, 1977. pp. 883, xlix. *bibliog.*

SCHIFF (GARY S.) Tradition and politics: the religious parties of Israel. Detroit, 1977. pp. 267. *bibliog. (Columbia University. Middle East Institute. Modern Middle East Series. vol.9)*

JEWS IN ARAB COUNTRIES.

GILBERT (MARTIN) The Jews of Arab lands: their history in maps. Oxford, 1976. pp. 32.

JEWS IN BRAZIL.

NICOLAIEWSKY (EVA) Israelitas no Rio Grande do Sul. Porto Alegre, 1975. pp. 108,(70). *bibliog. Second part consists of photographs.*

JEWS IN GERMANY.

LUFT (GERDA) Heimkehr ins Unbekannte: eine Darstellung der Einwanderung von Juden aus Deutschland nach Palästina...1933-1939. Wuppertal, [1977]. pp. 142.

JEWS IN GIBRALTAR.

HASSAN (Sir JOSHUA ABRAHAM) The Treaty of Utrecht, 1713, and the Jews of Gibraltar; lecture delivered to the Jewish Historical Society of England in London 15 May 1963. London, 1970. pp. 16.

JEWS IN PALESTINE.

LOWDERMILK (WALTER CLAY) Palestine: land of promise. London, 1946. pp. 167.

LUFT (GERDA) Heimkehr ins Unbekannte: eine Darstellung der Einwanderung von Juden aus Deutschland nach Palästina...1933-1939. Wuppertal, [1977]. pp. 142.

JEWS IN POLAND.

HELLER (CELIA STOPNICKA) On the edge of destruction: Jews of Poland between the two world wars. New York, 1977. pp. 369.

— Persecutions.

[TENENBAUM (JOSEF)] Der Lemberger Judenpogrom, November 1918-Jänner 1919; von Joseph Bendow [pseud.]. Wien, 1919. pp. 167.

JEWS IN RUSSIA.

ISRAEL INFORMATION CENTRE. Information Briefings. 26. Jews in the Soviet Union. Jerusalem, [1974]. pp. 14.

BARON (SALO WITTMAYER) The Russian Jew under tsars and Soviets. 2nd ed. New York, [1976]. pp. 468.

JEWS IN THE UNITED KINGDOM.

FISHER (SAMUEL) Baron Fisher of Camden. Brodetsky: leader of the Anglo-Jewish community. Leeds, 1976. pp. 29. *(Leeds. University. Selig Brodetsky Memorial Lectures. No. 17)*

STEEL city Jews: a study of ethnicity and social mobility in the Jewish population of the city of Sheffield, South Yorkshire; by Barry A. Kosmin [and others]. London, 1976. pp. 28.

JEWS IN THE UNITED STATES.

See JEWISH AMERICANS.

JEWS IN VENEZUELA.

EMMANUEL (ISAAC S.) The Jews of Coro, Venezuela. Cincinnati, 1973. pp. 63. *(American Jewish Archives. Monographs. No. 8)*

JIHAD.

SMALDONE (JOSEPH P.) Warfare in the Sokoto caliphate: historical and sociological perspectives. Cambridge, 1977. pp. 228. *bibliog. (Cambridge. University. African Studies Centre. African Studies Series. 19)*

JOB ANALYSIS.

HILF (HUBERT HUGO) Arbeitswissenschaft: Grundlagen der Leistungsforschung und Arbeitsgestaltung. München, 1957. pp. 341. *bibliog.*

JOB EVALUATION.

ADVISORY, CONCILIATION AND ARBITRATION SERVICE [U.K.]. Job evaluation. London, [1975]. pp. 12. *bibliog. (Guides. No.1)*

THAKUR (MANAB) and GILL (DEIRDRE ROCKINGHAM) Job evaluation in practice: a survey of 213 organizations in the UK. London, 1976. pp. 97. *bibliog. (Institute of Personnel Management. Information Reports. New Series. 21)*

JOB SATISFACTION.

WEIR (MARY) ed. Job satisfaction: challenge and response in modern Britain; [readings]. Glasgow, 1976. pp. 288. *bibliogs.*

DICKSON (PAUL W.) Work revolution. London, 1977. pp. 378. *Originally published in USA as "The future of the workplace".*

HUMANISING the workplace: new proposals and perspectives; edited by Richard N. Ottaway. London, [1977]. pp. 175. *bibliogs.*

— United States.

WIDICK (B.J.) ed. Auto work and its discontents. Baltimore, [1976]. pp. 112. *bibliog.*

JOB VACANCIES

— Canada.

CANADA. Statistics Canada. Annual report on job vacancies. a., 1976(1st)- Ottawa. *[in English and French]*

JOHNSON (LYNDON BAINES) President of the United States.

SCHANDLER (HERBERT Y.) The unmaking of a president: Lyndon Johnson and Vietnam. Princeton, [1977]. pp. 419. *bibliog.*

JOINT ADVENTURES

— America, Latin.

INSTITUTE FOR LATIN AMERICAN INTEGRATION. 1974. Asociacion internacional de empresas en America Latina: aspectos juridicos. Buenos Aires, 1974. pp. 524. *3 sheets of tables in end pocket.*

— Zaire.

BONGOY (MPEKESA) Investissements mixtes au Zaire: (joint ventures pour la période de transition). Kinshasa, 1974. pp. 523. *bibliog.*

JONKMAN (JAN ANNE).

JONKMAN (JAN ANNE) Nederland en Indonesië beide vrij, gezien vanuit het Nederlands Parlement: memoires. Assen, 1977. pp. 298.

JORDAN

— Commerce.

JORDAN. Department of Statistics. External trade statistics. a., 1965, 1966, 1969- Amman.

JOSEPH II, Emperor of Germany.

[BRISSOT (JACQUES PIERRE) called Brissot de Warville] Un avvocato del popolo all'imperatore, Giuseppe II. sopra il suo regolamento concernente l'emigrazione, sue diverse riforme, etc. ; traduzione dal Francese. Dublino, 1785. pp. 61.

JOURNALISM

— Objectivity.

ALTHEIDE (DAVID L.) Creating reality: how TV news distorts events. Beverly Hills, [1976]. pp. 220. *bibliog.*

— Political aspects.

ALTHEIDE (DAVID L.) Creating reality: how TV news distorts events. Beverly Hills, [1976]. pp. 220. *bibliog.*

— France.

WAGNER (JACQUES) Marmontel, journaliste, et la Mercure de France, 1725-1761. Grenoble, 1975. pp. 338. *bibliog. (Clermont-Ferrand. Université. Faculté des Lettres et Sciences Humaines. Ouvrages. No. 34)*

— Germany — Political aspects.

MUELLER-SORGE (MARIA M.) Journalismus: Offenheit und Konformität; die politische Tagespresse in der Bundesrepublik. Bern, 1975. pp. 193. *bibliog.*

SOESEMANN (BERND) Das Ende der Weimarer Republik in der Kritik demokratischer Publizisten: Theodor Wolff, Ernst Feder, Julius Elbau, Leopold Schwarzschild. Berlin, 1976. pp. 251. *bibliog. (Berlin. Freie Universität. Institut für Publizistik. Abhandlungen und Materialien zur Publizistik. Band 9)*

— Russia.

BEREZINA (VALENTINA GRIGOR'EVNA) Belinskii i voprosy istorii russkoi zhurnalistiki. Leningrad, 1973. pp. 144.

MEL'NIKOV (ALEKSANDR IVANOVICH) Sergei Mironovich Kirov. Moskva, 1973. pp. 110. *bibliog. (Kommunisticheskaia Partiia Sovetskogo Soiuza. Tsentral'nyi Komitet. Vysshaia Partiinaia Shkola. Kafedra Zhurnalistiki. Partiinye Publitsisty)*

MOSTIEV (BORIS MUKHARBEKOVICH) Revoliutsionnaia publitsistika S.M. Kirova, 1909-1917 gg. Ordzhonikidze, 1973. pp. 475.

ROOT (ANDREI ALEKSANDROVICH) Tipologiia peredovykh statei Gertsena v "Kolokole": lektsii po spetskursu dlia studentov-zhurnalistov. Kazan', 1974. pp. 102. *bibliog.*

BARSEGIAN (KHIKAR AKOPOVICH) Stepan Georgievich Shaumian. Moskva, 1975. pp. 102. *bibliog. (Kommunisticheskaia Partiia Sovetskogo Soiuza. Tsentral'nyi Komitet. Vysshaia Partiinaia Shkola. Kafedra Zhurnalistiki. Partiinye Publitsisty)*

BULATSKII (GRIGORII VASIL'EVICH) K.S. Eremeev - revoliutsioner, publitsist. Minsk, 1976. pp. 215.

— United Kingdom.

NATIONAL UNION OF JOURNALISTS. Equality Working Party. Images of women: guidelines for promoting equality through journalism. London, [1975]. pp. 10.

BELOFF (NORA) Freedom under Foot: the battle over the closed shop in British journalism. London, 1976. pp. 143.

JOURNALISM, SOCIALIST

— Germany.

LORECK (JOCHEN) Wie man früher Sozialdemokrat wurde: das Kommunikationsverhalten in der deutschen Arbeiterbewegung und die Konzeption der sozialistischen Parteipublizistik durch August Bebel. Bonn-Bad Godesberg, [1977]. pp. 290. *(Friedrich-Ebert-Stiftung. Forschungsinstitut. Schriftenreihe. Band 130)*

JOURNALISTS

— Germany.

MUELLER-SORGE (MARIA M.) Journalismus: Offenheit und Konformität; die politische Tagespresse in der Bundesrepublik. Bern, 1975. pp. 193. *bibliog.*

SOESEMANN (BERND) Das Ende der Weimarer Republik in der Kritik demokratischer Publizisten: Theodor Wolff, Ernst Feder, Julius Elbau, Leopold Schwarzschild. Berlin, 1976. pp. 251. *bibliog. (Berlin. Freie Universität. Institut für Publizistik. Abhandlungen und Materialien zur Publizistik. Band 9)*

— United Kingdom.

CHRISTIAN (HAROLD) The development of trade unionism and professionalism among British journalists: a sociological inquiry. 1976. fo.379. *bibliogs. Typescript. Ph.D.(London) thesis: unpublished. This thesis is the property of London University and may not be removed from the Library.*

— United States.

CULBERT (DAVID HOLBROOK) News for everyman: radio and foreign affairs in thirties America. Westport, Conn., 1976. pp. 238. *bibliog.*

JUDAISM.

MAIATSKII (FEODOSII SEMENOVICH) Dvazhdy obmanutye. Kishinev, 1971. pp. 112. *bibliog.*

BLAU (JOSEPH LEON) Judaism in America: from curiosity to third faith. Chicago, 1976. pp. 156.

JUDAISM AND SOCIAL PROBLEMS.

SCHNEIDER (KARLHEINZ) Religion in Israel: eine Studie zum Verhältnis Person, Religion, Gesellschaft. Meisenheim am Glan, [1976]. pp. 267. *bibliog.*

JUDGES.

PROTT (LYNDEL VON) Der internationale Richter im Spannungsfeld der Rechtskulturen: eine rechtssoziologische Studie über die Elemente des Selbstverständnisses des Internationalen Gerichtshofs. Berlin, [1975]. pp. 257. *bibliog.*

— Education — United Kingdom.

U.K. Working Party on Judicial Training and Information. 1976. Consultative working paper; [Lord Justice Bridge, chairman]. London, 1976. pp. 26.

— Africa, Subsaharan.

NWABUEZE (BENJAMIN OBI) Judicialism in Commonwealth Africa: the role of the courts in government. London, [1977]. pp. 324.

— United Kingdom.

DENNING (ALFRED THOMPSON) Baron Denning. The independence of the judges. Birmingham, [1950]. pp. 15. *(Birmingham. University. Holdsworth Club. Presidential Addresses. 1950)*

DUMAN (DANIEL) The judges of England, 1780-1875: a social, economic, and institutional history. Baltimore, 1975. fo. 388.

GRIFFITH (JOHN ANEURIN GREY) The politics of the judiciary. [London, 1977]. pp. 224.

JUDGMENTS

— Mathematical models.

KORT (FRED) A special and a general multivariate theory of judicial decisions. Beverly Hills, [1977]. pp. 42. *bibliog.*

JUDICIAL ERROR

— Germany.

WANDT (HEINRICH) Das Justizverbrechen des Reichsgerichts an dem Verfasser der "Etappe Gent". Berlin, 1926. pp. 28.

JUDICIAL PROCESS

— United States.

HOROWITZ (DONALD L.) The courts and social policy. Washington, D.C., [1977]. pp. 309.

JUDICIAL REVIEW

— Russia.

MELKUMOV (VLADIMIR GAVRILOVICH) Sovetskaia prokuratura i problemy obshchego nadzora. Dushanbe, 1970. pp. 243.

KUDRIAVTSEV (P.I.) ed. Voprosy ugolovnogo prava i protsessa v praktike prokurorskogo nadzora za sobliudeniem zakonnosti pri rassmotrenii sudami ugolovnykh del. Moskva, 1976. pp. 495.

— — Bibliography.

POPOVA (SVETLANA IVANOVNA) and SAFONOV (ALEKSANDR PETROVICH) compilers. Prokurorskii nadzor v SSSR: bibliografiia, 1965-1970 gg. Moskva, 1974. pp. 168.

JUDICIAL REVIEW OF ADMINISTRATIVE ACTS

— Australia.

AUSTRALIA. Commonwealth Administrative Review Committee. 1971. Report; [J.R. Kerr, chairman]. in AUSTRALIA. Parliament. Parliamentary papers, 1971, vol.1.

— Poland.

LITWIN (JOZEF) Les conflits d'attributions entre les organes administratifs et les tribunaux de droit commun d'après un projet de loi polonais de 1962. Warszawa, [1962]. pp. 24. (Polska Akademia Nauk. Centre Scientifique à Paris. Conférences. Fascicule 28)

JUNG (CHARLES GUSTAVE).

ODAJNYK (VOLODYMYR WALTER) Jung and politics: the political and social ideas of C. G. Jung. New York, 1976. pp. 190.

JURISPRUDENCE.

TWINING (WILLIAM) and MIERS (DAVID) How to do things with rules: a primer of interpretation. London, [1976]. pp. 270. bibliog.

FARRAR (JOHN HYNES) Introduction to legal method. London, 1977. pp. 258. bibliog.

LAW, morality and society: essays in honour of H.L.A. Hart; edited by P.M.S. Hacker and J. Raz. Oxford, 1977. pp. 312. bibliog.

RECHT und Sprache: Vorträge auf der Tagung der Deutschen Sektion der Internationalen Vereinigung für Rechts- und Sozialphilosophie (IVR) in der Bundesrepublik Deutschland, Mainz, 3.X. - 5.X.1974: herausgegeben...von Theodor Viehweg und Frank Rotter. Wiesbaden, 1977. pp. 134. (Archiv für Rechts- und Sozialphilosophie. Beihefte. Neue Folge. Nr. 9)

WATSON (ALAN) The nature of law. Edinburgh, [1977]. pp. 148.

JURISTIC PERSONS

— Russia.

VEBERS (IANIS ROBERTOVICH) Pravosub"ektivnost' grazhdan v sovetskom grazhdanskom i semeinom prave. Riga, 1976. pp. 231. bibliog.

JUSTICE.

KAPLAN (MORTON A.) Alienation and identification. New York, [1976]. pp. 206.

KAPLAN (MORTON A.) Justice, human nature, and political obligation. New York, [1976]. pp. 283.

BOWIE (NORMAN E.) and SIMON (ROBERT L.) The individual and political order: an introduction to social and political philosophy. Englewood Cliffs, [1977]. pp. 280. bibliogs.

WOLFF (ROBERT PAUL) Understanding Rawls: a reconstruction and critique of A theory of justice. Princeton, N.J., [1977]. pp. 224. bibliog.

JUSTICE, ADMINISTRATION OF

— Cyprus.

CYPRUS TODAY. Vol. 9. No. 1-2. [Special issue on law and justice in Cyprus]. Nicosia, 1971. pp. 68.

— France.

CHARVIN (ROBERT) and QUIOT (GERARD) La justice en France: mutations de l'appareil judiciaire et lutte de classes. Paris, [1976]. pp. 142.

— Germany, Eastern.

PLENIKOWSKI (ANTON) Die Aufgaben der Parteiorganisationen in der Justiz: Rede... am 19. Januar 1952. Berlin, 1952. pp. 51. (Sozialistische Einheitspartei Deutschlands. Schriftenreihe für den Parteiarbeiter. Heft 8)

RIEMANN (TORD) and others. Law and justice in a socialist society: the legal system of the German Democratic Republic. Berlin, 1976. pp. 64.

— Israel.

ISRAEL INFORMATION CENTRE. Information Briefings. 18. Administration of justice in the areas administered by Israel. rev. ed. Jerusalem, [1974]. pp. 12.

— Liberia.

PORTE (ALBERT) Speaking out. [Crozierville, Liberia?], 1975. fo. 10.

— Nepal.

GYAWALI (S.P.) Towards rule of law. 2nd ed. Kathmandu, Department of Information, 1970. pp. 83.

— United Kingdom.

EDDEY (KEITH JAMES) The English legal system. 2nd ed. London, 1977. pp. 179. bibliog.

— — Scotland.

WALKER (DAVID MAXWELL) The Scottish legal system: an introduction to the study of Scots law. 4th ed. Edinburgh, 1976. pp. 536.

JUSTICES OF THE PEACE

— United Kingdom.

KING (MICHAEL) The effects of a duty solicitor scheme: an assessment of the impact upon a magistrates court. London, 1976. pp. 52. bibliog.

JUTE INDUSTRY

— Bangladesh.

AHMAD (QAZI KHOLIQUZZOMAN) The jute manufacturing industry of Bangladesh, 1947-74. 1976 [or rather 1977]. fo. 173. bibliog. Typescript. Ph.D. (London) thesis: unpublished. This thesis is the property of London University and may not be removed from the Library.

JUVENILE COURTS.

UNITED NATIONS SOCIAL DEFENCE RESEARCH INSTITUTE. 1976. Juvenile justice: an international survey; country reports, related materials and suggestions for future research. Rome, 1976. pp. 251, xxviii. (Publications. No. 12).

JUVENILE DELINQUENCY.

DELINQUANCE juvénile et développement socio-économique; par Yves Chirol [and others]. La Haye, [1975]. pp. 317. bibliog. (European Coordination Centre for Research and Documentation in Social Sciences. Publications. 6)

DELINQUENCY, crime and society; edited by James F. Short. Chicago, [1976]. pp. 325. bibliogs. Mainly papers originally presented at the Symposium on Juvenile Delinquency, University of Chicago, 1972, held to honour Henry Donald McKay.

UNITED NATIONS SOCIAL DEFENCE RESEARCH INSTITUTE. 1976. Juvenile justice: an international survey; country reports, related materials and suggestions for future research. Rome, 1976. pp. 251, xxviii. (Publications. No. 12).

— Research.

MALEWSKA (HANNA) and PEYRE (VINCENT) Juvenile delinquency and development: a cross-national study. Beverly Hills, [1976]. pp. 40. bibliog.

— United Kingdom.

U.K. Home Office. 1975. Juvenile offenders and juveniles in need of care or control, England and Wales. [London], 1975. pp. 22.

LEVENSON (HOWARD) Children in prison. London, 1976. pp. 21. (National Council for Civil Liberties. Reports. No.15)

CHILD guidance and delinquency in a London borough. Oxford, 1977. pp. 190. bibliog. (Bethlem Royal Hospital and Maudsley Hospital. Institute of Psychiatry. Maudsley Monographs. No. 24) Reports the findings of a survey into the relationship between child guidance rates, delinquency rates, and the social environment of the child population.

INTERMEDIATE TREATMENT STUDY GROUP [U.K.]. A future for intermediate treatment; report; [Mia Kellmer Pringle, chairman]. [London], Personal Social Services Council, 1977. pp. 109. bibliog.

LAYCOCK (GLORIA K.) Absconding from borstals; a Home Office Research Unit report. London, 1977. pp. 77. bibliog. (U.K. Home Office. Home Office Research Studies. No. 41)

McGURK (B.J.) and others. A study of the variables relating to recidivism in delinquent boys. London, 1977. pp. 7. bibliog. (U.K. Prison Department. Directorate of Psychological Services. DPS Reports. Series 1. No. 9)

PRIESTLEY (PHILIP) and others. Justice for juveniles: the 1969 Children and Young Persons Act: a case for reform? London, 1977. pp. 120. bibliog.

WADSWORTH (MICHAEL EDWIN JOHN) Home life and later delinquency: a longitudinal study of a national cohort during the first 21 years of life. 1976 [or rather 1977]. fo.192. bibliog. Reprint in end pocket. Typescript. Ph.D. (London) thesis: unpublished. This thesis is the property of London University and may not be removed from the Library.

WEST (DONALD JAMES) and FARRINGTON (DAVID P.) The delinquent way of life: third report of the Cambridge study in delinquent development;...with the assistance of Gwen Gundry [and others]. London, 1977. pp. 209. bibliog. (Cambridge. University. Institute of Criminology. Cambridge Studies in Criminology. vol. 35).

— United States.

FINESTONE (HAROLD) Victims of change: juvenile delinquents in American society. Westport, Conn., 1976. pp. 235. bibliog.

KABARDINO-BALKARIAN REPUBLIC

— Economic history.

MASAEV (SHAKHIMGERI IAKH'IAEVICH) Profsoiuzy Kabardino-Balkarii v period bor'by za pobedu sotsializma v SSSR, 1920-1937 gg. Nal'chik, 1975. pp. 208. bibliog.

KABIRO (NGUGI).

KABIRO (NGUGI) Man in the middle: the story of Ngugi Kabiro; taped and edited by Don Barnett. Richmond, B.C., [1973]. pp. 76. (Liberation Support Movement. Information Center. Life Histories from the Revolution. Kenya, Mau-Mau. 2)

KABYLES.

BOURDIEU (PIERRE) Outline of theory of practice; translated by Richard Nice. Cambridge, 1977. pp. 248.

KALEDIN (ALEKSEI MAKSIMOVICH).

KIRIENKO (IURII KONSTANTINOVICH) Krakh kaledinshchiny. Moskva, 1976. pp. 246. *bibliog.*

KALININ (MIKHAIL IVANOVICH).

KALININ (MIKHAIL IVANOVICH) Stat'i i rechi, 1941-1946 gg. Moskva, 1975. pp. 672.

MIKHAIL Ivanovich Kalinin: kratkaia biografiia. Moskva, 1975. pp. 288.

KALMYK REPUBLIC

— Constitutional history.

KALMYK REPUBLIC. Obshchekalmytskii S"ezd Sovetov, 1-yi, 1920. Pervyi Obshchekalmytskii s"ezd Sovetov, 2-9 iiulia 1920 goda: protokoly; pod redaktsiei…D.A. Chugaeva. Elista, 1971. pp. 220.

— Statistics, Vital.

KASPAROV (E.L.) Dinamika rozhdaemosti i brachnosti v Kalmytskoi ASSR. Elista, 1974. pp. 139.

KANT (IMMANUEL).

VORLAENDER (KARL) Kant, Fichte, Hegel und der Sozialismus. Berlin, 1920. pp. 105.

SHASHKOV (N.I.) Kant i "eticheskii sotsializm": lektsii po spetskursu dlia studentov filosofskogo fakul'teta. Sverdlovsk, 1975. pp. 147.

KANTEMIR (DMITRII KONSTANTINOVICH).

KORBU (KH.) and CHOBANU (L.) eds. Nasledie Dmitriia Kantemira i sovremennost'. Kishinev, 1976. pp. 230.

KAPP (KARL WILHELM).

ECONOMICS in institutional perspective: memorial essays in honor of K. William Kapp; edited by Rolf Steppacher [and others]. Lexington, Mass., [1977]. pp. 226. *bibliog.*

KARACHAI-CHERKESS AUTONOMOUS OBLAST'

— Industries.

TEBUEV (RAMAZAN SAGITOVICH) Zarozhdenie promyshlennosti v Karachaevo-Cherkesii, 40-e gody XIX v. - 1917 g. Cherkessk, 1975. pp. 167. *bibliog.*

KARAMZIN (NIKOLAI MIKHAILOVICH).

KISLIAGINA (LOIA GEORGIEVNA) Formirovanie obshchestvenno-politicheskikh vzgliadov N.M. Karamzina, 1785-1803 gg.; pod redaktsiei… I.A. Fedosova. Moskva, 1976. pp. 199.

KARELIA

— International status.

STRUPP (KARL) La question carélienne et le droit des gens: avis consultatif. Helsinki, 1924. pp. 38.

KAWAKAMI (HAJIME).

BERNSTEIN (GAIL LEE) Japanese marxist: a portrait of Kawakami Hajime, 1879-1946. Cambridge, Mass., 1976. pp. 221. *bibliog. (Harvard University. East Asian Research Center. Harvard East Asian Series. 86)*

KAZAKSTAN

— Industries.

ASHIMBAEV (TUIMEBAI ASHIMBAEVICH) Effektivnost' promyshlennogo proizvodstva: metodologiia, analiz i problemy na materialakh Kazakhstana. Alma-Ata, 1976. pp. 359.

— Maps.

GLAVNOE UPRAVLENIE GEODEZII I KARTOGRAFII. Atlas avtomobil'nykh dorog: Kazakhstan i Sredniaia Aziia. Moskva, 1975. pp. 30.

— Politics and government.

NA puti k razvitomu sotsializmu: KPSS v bor'be za uprochenie i razvitie sotsializma v Srednei Azii i Kazakhstane, 1938-1958. Tashkent, 1976. pp. 367. *bibliog.*

KAZAN' UNIVERSITY.

MAZITOVA (NAZIFA ARIFOVNA) Izuchenie Blizhnego i Srednego Vostoka v Kazanskom universitete, pervaia polovina XIX veka. Kazan', 1972. pp. 225.

KEARNEY (PEADAR).

KEARNEY (PEADAR) My dear Eva: letters from Ballykinlar internment camp 1921. Dublin, 1976. pp. 46.

KEKCHI INDIANS.

HOWARD (MICHAEL C.) Anthropologist. Ethnicity in southern Belize: the Kekchi and the Mopan. Colombia, Mo., 1975. pp. 19. *bibliog. (Missouri University. Museum of Anthropology. Museum Briefs. No. 21)*

KELSO (LOUIS O.).

SPEISER (STUART M.) A piece of the action: a plan to provide every family with a [dollar]100,000 stake in the economy. New York, [1977]. pp. 390. *bibliog.*

KENNEDY (JOHN FITZGERALD) President of the United States.

BLOUGH (ROGER M.) The Washington embrace of business. New York, [1975]. pp. 162. *(Carnegie-Mellon University. Benjamin F. Fairless Memorial Lectures. 1974). Also contains his President Kennedy and steel prices.*

BRADLEE (BENJAMIN C.) Conversations with Kennedy. London, 1976. pp. 251. *First published in New York in 1975.*

PAKENHAM (FRANCIS AUNGIER) 7th Earl of Longford. Kennedy. London, [1976]. pp. 223. *bibliog.*

BRAUER (CARL M.) John F. Kennedy and the second reconstruction. New York, 1977. pp. 396. *bibliog.*

KENT

— Economic conditions.

KENT. Planning Department. Kent county structure plan: [reports]: nos. 1B-14B [with] supplement [to no.] 4B. Maidstone, [1974-5]. 15 pts. (in 1 vol.).

— Social conditions.

KENT. Planning Department. Kent county structure plan: [reports]: nos. 1B-14B [with] supplement [to no.] 4B. Maidstone, [1974-5]. 15 pts. (in 1 vol.).

— Social history.

CLARK (PETER) English provincial society from the reformation to the revolution: religion, politics and society in Kent, 1500-1640. Hassocks, Sussex, [1977]. pp. 504.

KENTUCKY

— Economic conditions.

CAUDILL (HARRY M.) The watches of the night. Boston, [Mass.], [1976]. pp. 275.

— Politics and government.

LANDY (MARC KARNIS) The politics of environmental reform: controlling Kentucky strip mining. Washington, D.C., 1976. pp. 400. *bibliog. (Resources for the Future, Inc. Working Papers. PD-2)*

— Social conditions.

CAUDILL (HARRY M.) The watches of the night. Boston, [Mass.], [1976]. pp. 275.

KENYA

— Economic conditions.

AGRICULTURAL development in Kenya: an economic assessment; editors Judith Heyer [and others]. Nairobi, 1976. pp. 372.

— Economic policy.

KENYA. Town Planning Department. 1971. Coast Province regional physical development plan. [Nairobi], 1971. fo.153.

— Forest policy.

KENYA. Sessional Papers. 1968. No.1. A forest policy for Kenya. Nairobi, 1968. pp. 9.

— Nationalism.

KABIRO (NGUGI) Man in the middle: the story of Ngugi Kabiro; taped and edited by Don Barnett. Richmond, B.C., [1973]. pp. 76. *(Liberation Support Movement. Information Center. Life Histories from the Revolution. Kenya, Mau-Mau. 2)*

— Native races.

CLAYTON (ANTHONY) Counter-insurgency in Kenya: a study of military operations against Mau Mau. Nairobi, 1976. pp. 63.

— Politics and government.

KENYA. Sessional Papers. 1963. No. 2. Kenya: preparations for independence. [Nairobi], 1963. single sheet.

LEYS (NORMAN MACLEAN) and OLDHAM (JOSEPH HOULDSWORTH) By Kenya possessed: the correspondence of Norman Leys and J. H. Oldham, 1918-1926; edited and with an introduction by John W. Cell. Chicago, 1976. pp. 382.

ROELKER (JACK R.) Mathu of Kenya: a political study. Stanford, Calif., [1976]. pp. 202. *bibliog. (Stanford University. Hoover Institution on War, Revolution and Peace. Hoover Institution Publications. 157)*

WASSERMAN (GARY) Politics of decolonization: Kenya Europeans and the land issue, 1960-1965. Cambridge, 1976. pp. 225. *bibliog. (Cambridge. University. African Studies Centre. African Studies Series. 17)*

— Population.

INTERNATIONAL PLANNED PARENTHOOD FEDERATION. The people of Kenya. Nairobi, 1971. pp. 22. *bibliog.*

KERALA

— Politics and government.

NAMBOODIRIPAD (E.M.S.) Anti-communist gang-up in Kerala: betrayers of U[nited] F[ront] set up anti-people govt. Calcutta, 1970. pp. 75.

KETT'S REBELLION, 1549.

CORNWALL (JULIAN) Revolt of the peasantry, 1549. London, 1977. pp. 254. *bibliog.*

KEYNES (JOHN MAYNARD) 1st Baron Keynes.

BUCHANAN (JAMES McGILL) and WAGNER (RICHARD E.) Democracy in deficit: the political legacy of Lord Keynes. New York, [1977]. pp. 195.

The END of the Keynesian era: essays on the disintegration of the Keynesian political economy; edited by Robert Skidelsky. London, 1977. pp. 114.

KHERSON (OBLAST')

— History — Sources.

KHERSONSKAIA oblast' v gody Velikoi Otechestvennoi voiny, 1941-1945: sbornik dokumentov i materialov. Simferopol', 1975. pp. 320. *bibliog.*

KHOREZM PEOPLE'S SOVIET REPUBLIC

— History — Sources.

ISTORIIA Khorezmskoi Narodnoi Sovetskoi Respubliki, 1920-1924 gg.: sbornik dokumentov. Tashkent, 1976. pp. 374.

KHRUSHCHEV (NIKITA SERGEEVICH).

BRUCE (JAMES B.) The politics of Soviet policy formation: Khrushchev's innovative policies in education and agriculture. Denver, Colo., [1976]. pp. 138. (Denver. University. Social Science Foundation and Graduate School of International Studies. Monograph Series in World Affairs. vol. 13, no. 4)

LAZITCH (BRANKO) Le Rapport Khrouchtchev et son histoire. [Paris, 1976]. pp. 191.

MEDVEDEV (ROI ALEKSANDROVICH) and MEDVEDEV (ZHORES ALEKSANDROVICH) Khrushchev: the years in power;...translated by Andrew R. Durkin. London, 1977. pp. 198.

KHVOSTOV (VLADIMIR MIKHAILOVICH).

VOPROSY istorii vneshnei politiki SSSR i mezhdunarodnykh otnoshenii: sbornik statei pamiati akademika Vladimira Mikhailovicha Khvostova. Moskva, 1976. pp. 399.

KIDNAPPING

— Switzerland.

CAWIL (H.) Der Fall Jacob. Zürich, [1935]. pp. 38.

KING (MARTIN LUTHER).

POWER (JONATHAN) Martin Luther King: a reassessment. London, [1976]. pp. 20. bibliog.

KING'S LYNN

— Almshouses and workhouses.

KING'S LYNN. St. James's Workhouse. Rules and regulations, for the management of the poor. [King's Lynn], printed by W. Whittingham, 1829. pp. 18.

KINGS AND RULERS

— Duties.

CAMDEN SOCIETY. [Publications]. 4th Series. vol. 18. Four English political tracts of the Later Middle Ages; edited...by Jean-Philippe Genet. London, 1977. pp. 229.

KINGSTON, ONTARIO

— History.

TO preserve and defend: essays on Kingston in the nineteenth century; edited by Gerald Tulchinsky. Montreal, 1976. pp. 402.

KINSHIP.

GOODY (JOHN RANKINE) Production and reproduction: a comparative study of the domestic domain. Cambridge, 1976. pp. 157. bibliog.

— Arab countries.

CUISENIER (JEAN) Economie et parenté: leurs affinités de structure dans le domaine turc et dans le domaine arabe. Paris, [1975]. pp. 569. bibliog. (Paris. Ecole Pratique des Hautes Etudes. Section des Sciences Economiques et Sociales. Le Monde d'Outre-Mer Passé et Présent. 1e Série. Etudes. 60)

— India.

DUBE (LEELA) Sociology of kinship: an analytical survey of literature. Bombay, 1974. pp. 154. bibliog.

— — Kerala.

FULLER (CHRISTOPHER J.) The Nayars today. Cambridge, 1976. pp. 173. bibliog. Based, in part, on the author's Ph.D. thesis, University of Manchester, 1974.

— Mexico.

ESSAYS on Mexican kinship; Hugo G. Nutini [and others], editors. Pittsburgh, [1976]. pp. 256. bibliog. Papers of a symposium held at the 1969 annual meeting of the American Anthropological Association in New Orleans.

— Turkey.

CUISENIER (JEAN) Economie et parenté: leurs affinités de structure dans le domaine turc et dans le domaine arabe. Paris, [1975]. pp. 569. bibliog. (Paris. Ecole Pratique des Hautes Etudes. Section des Sciences Economiques et Sociales. Le Monde d'Outre-Mer Passé et Présent. 1e Série. Etudes. 60)

KIRCHNER (JOHANNA).

OPPENHEIMER (MAX) Das kämpferische Leben der Johanna Kirchner: Porträt einer antifaschistischen Widerstandskämpferin. Frankfurt am Main, [1974]. pp. 48. bibliog.

KIRGHIZIA

— Languages.

KANIMETOV (ABDULDA KANIMETOVICH) Iazyk bratskogo edinstva. Frunze, 1976. pp. 199. bibliog.

KIROV (SERGEI MIRONOVICH).

TROTSKII (LEV DAVYDOVICH) La bureaucratie stalinienne et l'assassinat de Kirov. Paris, [1935]. pp. 44.

MEL'NIKOV (ALEKSANDR IVANOVICH) Sergei Mironovich Kirov. Moskva, 1973. pp. 110. bibliog. (Kommunisticheskaia Partiia Sovetskogo Soiuza. Tsentral'nyi Komitet. Vysshaia Partiinaia Shkola. Kafedra Zhurnalistiki. Partiinye Publitsisty)

MOSTIEV (BORIS MUKHARBEKOVICH) Revoliutsionnaia publitsistika S.M. Kirova, 1909-1917 gg. Ordzhonikidze, 1973. pp. 475.

KISELEV (KUZ'MA VENEDIKTOVICH).

KISELEV (KUZ'MA VENEDIKTOVICH) Zapiski sovetskogo diplomata. Moskva, 1974. pp. 527.

KISSINGER (HENRY ALFRED).

FALK (RICHARD A.) What's wrong with Henry Kissinger's foreign policy? Princeton, 1974. pp. 36. (Princeton University. Center of International Studies. Policy Memoranda. No. 39)

MAZLISH (BRUCE) Kissinger: the European mind in American policy. New York, [1976]. pp. 330.

STOESSINGER (JOHN GEORGE) Henry Kissinger: the anguish of power. New York, [1976]. pp. 234.

BELL (CORAL) The diplomacy of detente: the Kissinger era. London, 1977. pp. 278. bibliog.

MORRIS (ROGER) Uncertain greatness: Henry Kissinger and American foreign policy. New York, [1977]. pp. 312.

KISTIAKOWSKY (GEORGE BOGDAN).

KISTIAKOWSKY (GEORGE BOGDAN) A scientist at the White House: the private diary of President Eisenhower's special assistant for science and technology. Cambridge, Mass., 1976. pp. 448.

KITALE

— Social conditions.

MULLER (MARIA S.) Actions and interactions: social relationships in a low-income housing estate in Kitale, Kenya. [Leiden, 1975]. pp. 149, 12. bibliog.

KITCHENER (HORATIO HERBERT) Earl of Khartoum.

SPIES (S. BURRIDGE) Methods of barbarism?: Roberts and Kitchener and civilians in the Boer republics, January 1900-May 1902. Cape Town, 1977. pp. 416. bibliog.

KJELDSEN (VIKING and ANNEMARIE).

EUROPEAN COURT OF HUMAN RIGHTS. Publications. Series A: Judgments and Decisions. [A 23]. ...Case of Kjeldsen, Busk Madsen and Pedersen: judgment of 7 December 1976. Strasbourg, Council of Europe, 1976. pp. 33 [bis]. In English and French.

KLAIPEDA

— History.

MIKULICZ (SERGIUSZ) Kłajpeda w polityce europejskiej, 1918-1939. Warszawa, 1976. pp. 352. bibliog.

KNOWLEDGE, SOCIOLOGY OF.

HICKOX (MICHAEL STEPHEN HINDMARSH) The ideology of intellectual elites and its implications for the sociology of knowledge. 1976. fo. 431. bibliog. Typescript. Ph. D. (London) thesis: unpublished. This thesis is the property of London University and may not be removed from the Library.

KATZ (FRED E.) Structuralism in sociology: an approach to knowledge. Albany, N.Y., 1976. pp. 218.

The NEW social sciences; edited by Baidya Nath Varma. Westport, Conn., 1976. pp. 276. bibliogs. Papers based on the Columbia University faculty seminar entitled "Content and Methods of the Social Sciences".

BARNES (BARRY) Interests and the growth of knowledge. London, 1977. pp. 109. bibliog.

PHILLIPS (DEREK L.) Wittgenstein and scientific knowledge: a sociological perspective. London, 1977. pp. 248.

UNDERSTANDING and social inquiry; edited by Fred R. Dallmayr and Thomas A. McCarthy. Notre Dame, Ind., [1977]. pp. 365. bibliogs.

KNOWLEDGE, THEORY OF.

HAMLYN (DAVID WALTER) The theory of knowledge. London, 1971. pp. 308. bibliog.

HAMPSHIRE (STUART NEWTON) Knowledge and the future. Southampton, 1976. pp. 17. (Southampton. University. Fawley Foundation. Lectures. 22)

GELWICK (RICHARD) The way of discovery: an introduction to the thought of Michael Polanyi. Oxford, [1977]. pp. 181.

LOCKE on human understanding: selected essays; edited by I.C. Tipton. Oxford, [1977]. pp. 170. bibliog.

PIAGET and knowing: studies in genetic epistemology; edited by Beryl A. Geber. London, 1977. pp. 258. bibliogs.

STEUSSLOFF (HANS) Erkenntnis und Praxis, Wahrheit und Parteilichkeit. Berlin, 1977. pp. 204.

KNOX (WILLIAM).

BELLOT (LELAND J.) William Knox: the life and thought of an eighteenth-century imperialist. Austin, Tex., [1977]. pp. 264. bibliog.

KOENIG (HEINRICH).

WAGNER (JOHANNES VOLKER) Nur Mut, sei Kämpfer!: Heinrich König, ein Leben für die Freiheit: Bochumer politische Lebensbilder aus der Zeit der Weimarer Republik und des Nationalsozialismus. Bochum, 1976. pp. 231. bibliog. (Bochum. Stadtarchiv. Veröffentlichungen)

KOHLBERG (LAURENCE).

DUSKA (RONALD) and WHELAN (MARIELLEN) Moral development: a guide to Piaget and Kohlberg. Dublin, 1977. pp. 128. bibliog.

KOK (ADAM).

ROSS (ROBERT) Adam Kok's Griquas: a study in the development of stratification in South Africa. Cambridge, 1976. pp. 194. bibliog.

KOMMUNISTISCHE ARBEITER-PARTEI DEUTSCHLANDS.

MUELLER (HANS HARALD) Intellektueller Linksradikalismus in der Weimarer Republik: seine Entstehung, Geschichte und Literatur, dargestellt am Beispiel der Berliner Gründergruppe der Kommunistischen Arbeiter-Partei Deutschlands. Kronberg/Is., 1977. pp. 173. *bibliog.*

KÖNIG.

See KOENIG.

KOO (VI KYUIN WELLINGTON).

TUNG (WILLIAM L.) V.K. Wellington Koo and China's wartime diplomacy. New York, [1977]. pp. 179. *bibliog. (New York (City). St. John's University. Center of Asian Studies. Asia in the Modern World. No. 17)*

KOREA

— Commerce.

SUK (TAI SUH) Import substitution and economic development in Korea. [Seoul], 1975. pp. 345. *bibliog. (Korea Development Institute. Working Papers. 7519)*

— Economic conditions.

KOREA (REPUBLIC). Foreign Investment Bureau. 1962. A golden opportunity for investment in Korea. [Seoul], 1962. pp. 79.

KOREA (REPUBLIC). Ministry of Public Information. 1966. New aspects of Korea: achievements of the first five year economic development plan [1962-1966 and] prospect of the second...plan [1967-1971]. [Seoul, 1966]. pp. 147.

LEE (HYUN-JAE) A study of the structural change of expenditures on gross national product in the process of economic growth, with special reference to the Korean economy, as a case of a developing country in comparison with developed countries. Pittsburgh, 1973. pp. 40.

JONES (LEROY P.) Public enterprise and economic development: the Korean case. Seoul, 1975. pp. 293. *bibliog. (Korean Development Institute. KDI Studies in Economics)*

KONOVALOV (EVGENII ALEKSANDROVICH) and others, eds. Koreiskaia Narodno-Demokraticheskaia Respublika. Moskva, 1975. pp. 156. *(Akademiia Nauk SSSR. Institut Ekonomiki Mirovoi Sotsialisticheskoi Sistemy. Ekonomika i Politika Zarubezhnykh Stran Sotsializma)*

BRUN (ELLEN) and HERSH (JACQUES) Socialist Korea: a case study in the strategy of economic development. New York, [1976]. pp. 432.

HASAN (PARVEZ) Korea: problems and issues in a rapidly growing economy. Washington, International Bank for Reconstruction and Development, [1976]. pp. 277. *([Country Economic Reports])*

CRISIS in Korea; edited by Gavan McCormack and John Gittings. Nottingham, 1977. pp. 190. *bibliog. Produced by the Korea Committee, London and the Transnational Institute, Amsterdam.*

KUZNETS (PAUL W.) Economic growth and structure in the Republic of Korea. New Haven, [1977]. pp. 238. *bibliog. Part of a series published by Yale University, Economic Growth Center.*

— Economic history.

SUK (TAI SUH) Import substitution and economic development in Korea. [Seoul], 1975. pp. 345. *bibliog. (Korea Development Institute. Working Papers. 7519)*

— Economic policy.

KOREA (REPUBLIC). Ministry of Public Information. 1966. New aspects of Korea: achievements of the first five year economic development plan [1962-1966] and prospect of the second...plan [1967-1971]. [Seoul, 1966]. pp. 147.

JONES (LEROY P.) Public enterprise and economic development: the Korean case. Seoul, 1975. pp. 293. *bibliog. (Korean Development Institute. KDI Studies in Economics)*

BRUN (ELLEN) and HERSH (JACQUES) Socialist Korea: a case study in the strategy of economic development. New York, [1976]. pp. 432.

HASAN (PARVEZ) Korea: problems and issues in a rapidly growing economy. Washington, International Bank for Reconstruction and Development, [1976]. pp. 277. *([Country Economic Reports])*

KUZNETS (PAUL W.) Economic growth and structure in the Republic of Korea. New Haven, [1977]. pp. 238. *bibliog. Part of a series published by Yale University, Economic Growth Center.*

— Foreign opinion.

NORTH Korea seen from abroad. Seoul, 1976. pp. 153.

— Foreign relations.

BARNDS (WILLIAM J.) ed. The two Koreas in East Asian affairs. New York, 1976. pp. 216.

INSTITUTE FOR EAST ASIAN STUDIES. North Korea's policy toward the United Nations. Seoul, Korea, [1976?]. pp. 84.

KIYOSAKI (WAYNE S.) North Korea's foreign relations: the politics of accommodation, 1945-75. New York, 1976. pp. 133. *bibliog.*

CRISIS in Korea; edited by Gavan McCormack and John Gittings. Nottingham, 1977. pp. 190. *bibliog. Produced by the Korea Committee, London and the Transnational Institute, Amsterdam.*

See also UNITED NATIONS — Korea.

— History.

OSVOBOZHDENIE Korei: vospominaniia i stat'i. Moskva, 1976. pp. 336.

— Politics and government.

KONOVALOV (EVGENII ALEKSANDROVICH) and others, eds. Koreiskaia Narodno-Demokraticheskaia Respublika. Moskva, 1975. pp. 156. *(Akademiia Nauk SSSR. Institut Ekonomiki Mirovoi Sotsialisticheskoi Sistemy. Ekonomika i Politika Zarubezhnykh Stran Sotsializma)*

POLITICAL leadership in Korea; edited by Dae-Sook Suh and Chae-Jin Lee. Seattle, [1976]. pp. 272. *(Washington State University. Institute for Comparative and Foreign Area Studies. Publications on Asia. No. 27) Selected papers presented at two symposia held in Seoul during the summers of 1971 and 1972 under the auspices of the University of Washington, Seattle.*

CRISIS in Korea; edited by Gavan McCormack and John Gittings. Nottingham, 1977. pp. 190. *bibliog. Produced by the Korea Committee, London and the Transnational Institute, Amsterdam.*

KOREAN REUNIFICATION QUESTION (1945-).

BARNDS (WILLIAM J.) ed. The two Koreas in East Asian affairs. New York, 1976. pp. 216.

INTER-system detente in Germany and Korea: proceedings of a German-Korean conference in Tutzing and Munich, June 1975; edited by Gottfried-Karl Kindermann. München, [1976]. pp. 288.

KOSZUTSKA (MARIA).

See KOSZUTSKA (MARIANNA KAROLINA SABINA).

KOSZUTSKA (MARIANNA KAROLINA SABINA).

KASPRZAKOWA (JANINA) Maria Koszutska. Warszawa, 1976. pp. 70. *bibliog.*

KRASNOYARSK (KRAI)

— Economic history.

MAKIEVSKII (GRIGORII MOISEEVICH) Sozidateli novoi Sibiri: iz istorii rabochikh Krasnoiarskogo kraia, 1945-1975 gg. Krasnoiarsk, 1976. pp. 222.

KRAUS (KARL).

PFABIGAN (ALFRED) Karl Kraus und der Sozialismus: eine politische Biographie. Wien, [1976]. pp. 364.

KREISKY (BRUNO).

AMERONGEN (MARTIN VAN) Kreisky und seine unbewältigte Gegenwart; (ins Deutsche übertragen [from the Dutch] von Gerhard Hartmann). Graz, 1977. pp. 128.

KROPOTKIN (PETR ALEKSEEVICH) Prince.

LEBEDEV (NIKOLAI KONSTANTINOVICH) Muzei P.A. Kropotkina, Moskva, ul. Kropotkina, per. Kropotkina, 26; (Peter Kropotkin's Museum: guide-book). Leningrad, 1928. pp. 80. *In Russian.*

KRZYWICKI (LUDWIK).

KOWALIK (TADEUSZ) and HOŁDA-RÓZIEWICZ (HENRYKA) Ludwik Krzywicki. Warszawa, 1976. pp. 175. *bibliog.*

KUCZYNSKI (JUERGEN)

— Bibliography.

KUCZYNSKI (JUERGEN) Die Muse und der Historiker: Studien über Jacob Burckhardt, Hyppolite[sic] Taine, Henry Adams; und eine Bibliographie sämtlicher Schriften von Jürgen Kuczynski, zusammengestellt von Erika Behm. Berlin, 1974. pp. 247. *bibliog. (Jahrbuch für Wirtschaftsgeschichte. Sonderbände)*

KUNG (AFRICAN PEOPLE).

See BUSHMEN.

KURDS IN SYRIA.

VANLY (ISMET CHERIFF) Le problème kurde en Syrie: plans pour le génocide d'une minorité nationale. [Lausanne?], Comité pour la Défense des Droits du Peuple Kurde, 1968. pp. 40.

KURGAN (OBLAST')

— History — Sources.

KURGANSKAIA partiinaia organizatsiia v Velikoi Otechestvennoi voine, 1941-1945: dokumenty i materialy. Cheliabinsk, 1975. pp. 355.

KWAZULU

— Economic conditions.

SOUTH AFRICA. Bureau for Economic Research re Bantu Development. 1975. KwaZulu:...economic revue [sic], 1975...compiled...at the request of the kwaZulu government. Pretoria, 1975. pp. 78. *bibliog. In English and Afrikaans.*

LABOUR AND LABOURING CLASSES.

ROBERTSON (FREDERICK WILLIAM) Lectures and addresses on literary and social topics. London, 1858. pp. 308.

BENAS (BARON LOUIS) The philosophy of the labour question: inaugural address read before the Literary and Philosophical Society of Liverpool at the opening of the eightieth session 1890-91. Liverpool, Marples, 1890. pp. 45.

LEWIS (AUSTIN) Proletarian and petit-bourgeois. Chicago, [1911]. pp. 48.

BASCHE (JAMES R.) and DUERR (MICHAEL G.) Experience with foreign production work forces. New York, [1975]. pp. 33. *(National Industrial Conference Board. Conference Board Reports. No. 661)*

GLABERMAN (MARTIN) The working class and social change: four essays on the working class. Toronto, 1975. pp. 41.

MOVIMIENTO obrero y accion politica; [by] Lucio Magri [and others; edited by Victor Flores Olea]. Mexico, 1975. pp. 233.

LABOUR AND SOCIETY: q. jl. of the International Institute for Labour Studies. q., Ja 1976 (v.1, no.1)- Geneva.

MEZHDUNARODNOE rabochee dvizhenie: voprosy istorii i teorii. Moskva, 1976 in progress.

KRIVOGUZ (IGOR' MIKHAILOVICH) Osnovnye periody i zakonomernosti mezhdunarodnogo rabochego dvizheniia do Oktiabria 1917 g. Moskva, 1976. pp. 364.

TECHNOLOGY, the labor process, and the working class: essays; by Rosalyn Baxandall [and others]. New York, [1976]. pp. 124.

COATES (KEN) Beyond wage slavery. Nottingham, 1977. pp. 170.

— Congresses.

INTERNATIONAL WORKING MEN'S ASSOCIATION. Congress, [5th], The Hague, 1872. The Hague congress of the First International, September 2- 7, 1872: minutes and documents; (translated by Richard Dixon and Alex Miller). Moscow, [1976]. pp. 758. *(Institut Marksizma-Leninizma. Documents of the First International)*

— Education.

In previous volumes of the Bibliography similar material relating to a particular country will be found under the heading LABOUR AND LABOURING CLASSES— [country] — Education.

— — Germany.

FISCHER (HILDEGARD) Der politische Sinn der Arbeiterbildung; mit einem Vorwort von Lutz v. Werder. Westberlin, [1975]. pp. 190. *bibliog. Reprint, with new introduction, of work originally published in Langensalza in 1933.*

— — Israel.

SHACHAR (BEZALEL) Workers' education in Israel. [Tel Aviv], 1962. pp. 46.

— — Russia — White Russia.

LUKASHEV (SERGEI AFANAS'EVICH) Massovo-politicheskaia rabota partiinykh organizatsii sredi trudiashchikhsia Belorussii, 1946-1958 gg.; redaktor...I.E. Marchenko. Minsk, 1976. pp. 182. *bibliog.*

— — Switzerland.

BRAUN (JAKOB) Zum 50-jährigen Jubiläum der Gründung des Grütlivereins Chur, 1848-1898; im Auftrage der Festkommission verfasst. Zürich, 1898. pp. 56.

— Periodicals — Bibliography.

FONDAZIONE GIANGIACOMO FELTRINELLI. Catalogo dei periodici della biblioteca. Nendeln, 1977. 3 vols.

— Africa, Subsaharan.

LE BRIS (EMILE) and others. Capitalisme négrier: la marche des paysans vers le prolétariat. Paris, 1976. pp. 211.

— Argentine Republic.

LOPEZ (ALFREDO) Argentinian trade union leader. Historia del movimiento social y la clase obrera argentina. Buenos Aires, [1971]. pp. 436.

— Australia.

AUSTRALIA. Commonwealth Bureau of Census and Statistics. Labour statistics. a., 1975(1st)- Canberra. *Supersedes AUSTRALIA. Commonwealth Bureau of Census and Statistics. Labour report.*

— Brazil.

DEAN (WARREN) Rio Clara: a Brazilian plantation system, 1820-1920. Stanford, Calif., 1976. pp. 234.

MARTINS (JOSÉ DE SOUZA) Agriculture and industry in Brazil: two studies. Cambridge, 1977. pp. 32. *(Cambridge. University. Centre of Latin American Studies. Working Papers. No. 27)*

— Canada.

KEALEY (GREGORY S.) Hogtown: working class Toronto at the turn of the century. Toronto, 1974. pp. 30.

LANGDON (STEVEN) The emergence of the Canadian working class movement, 1845-1875. Toronto, 1975. pp. 31.

SEYMOUR (EDWARD E.) An illustrated history of Canadian labour, 1800-1974. Ottawa, [1976]. pp. 91. *bibliog.*

— — Newfoundland.

NEWFOUNDLAND AND LABRADOR FEDERATION OF LABOUR. Submission...to the government of Newfoundland. St. John's, 1971. fo. 13.

— — Nova Scotia.

NOVA SCOTIA. Department of Labour. 1967. The Nova Scotia Department of Labour. [Halifax, 1967?]. 1 pamphlet (unpaged).

— China.

KUL'PIN (EDUARD SAL'MANOVICH) Tekhniko-ekonomicheskaia politika rukovodstva KNR i rabochii klass Kitaia. Moskva, 1975. pp. 199. *bibliog.*

— Egypt.

LEGRAIN (GEORGES ALBERT) Fellah de Karnak, Haute-Egypte: journalier dans le système des engagements momentanés; d'après les renseignements recueillis sur les lieux de 1895 à 1900. Paris, 1902. pp. 289-336. *(Société d'Economie et de Science Sociales. Les Ouvriers de Deux Mondes. 3e Série. 5e fasc.)*

— Finland.

GEBHARD (HANNES) Jordbruksbefolkningen: dess förhållande till andra yrkesgrupper och dess sociala sammansättning i Finlands landskommuner år 1901. Helsingfors, 1913. pp. 151, 127. *(Finland. Subkomitén för den Obesuttna Befolkningen. Statistisk undersökning af socialekonomiska förhållenden i Finlands landskommuner år 1901. 1)*

— France.

DUMAY (JEAN BAPTISTE) Mémoires d'un militant ouvrier du Creusot, 1841-1905; introduction et notes par Pierre Ponsot. Grenoble, 1976. pp. 431. *(Centre d'Histoire du Syndicalisme. Collection)*

FRANCE. Comité de l'Emploi et du Travail. 1976. Rapport...: préparation du 7e Plan. Paris, 1976. pp. 400.

GUIN (YANNICK) Le mouvement ouvrier nantais: essai sur le syndicalisme d'action directe à Nantes et à Saint-Nazaire. Paris, 1976. pp. 413.

MONATTE (PIERRE) La lutte syndicale; présentation de Colette Chambelland. Paris, 1976. pp. 318.

NADAUD (MARTIN) Léonard, maçon de la Creuse. Paris, 1976. pp. 399. *bibliog.*

— Germany.

KUCZYNSKI (JUERGEN) Die Kolonialisierung und Remilitarisierung Westdeutschlands. 2nd ed. Berlin, 1951. pp. 80.

VERNER (PAUL) Die Legende vom Wirtschaftswunder: zur Lage der Arbeiterklasse in Westdeutschland und in Westberlin. Berlin, 1956. pp. 40.

INSTITUT FÜR MARXISTISCHE STUDIEN UND FORSCHUNGEN. Aus der Geschichte der deutschen Arbeiterjugendbewegung, 1904- 1945: (Dokumente und Materialien). Frankfurt/Main, 1975. pp. 169. *(Institut für Marxistische Studien und Forschungen. Neudrucke zur Sozialistischen Theorie und Gewerkschaftspraxis. Band 7)*

LEHMANN (ALBRECHT) Das Leben in einem Arbeiterdorf: eine empirische Untersuchung über die Lebensverhältnisse von Arbeitern. Stuttgart, 1976. pp. 192. *bibliog.*

LUCAS (ERHARD) Zwei Formen von Radikalismus in der deutschen Arbeiterbewegung. Frankfurt am Main, [1976]. pp. 334. *bibliog.*

WAGNER (WOLF) Verelendungstheorie: die hilflose Kapitalismuskritik. Frankfurt am Main, 1976. pp. 253. *bibliog.*

MASON (TIMOTHY W.) Sozialpolitik im Dritten Reich: Arbeiterklasse und Volksgemeinschaft. Opladen, [1977]. pp. 374. *bibliog.*

— — Statistics.

GERMANY. Statistisches Reichsamt. Statistik des Deutschen Reichs. Neue Folge. Bände 102-119. Berufs- und Gewerbezählung vom 14. Juni 1895. Osnabrück, 1975. 18 vols. *Photographic reprint of 1897-99 ed. originally published in Berlin.*

— India.

INDIA. Labour Bureau, 1975. Rural labour enquiry, 1963-65: final report. [Delhi, 1975]. pp. 688.

HOLMSTRÖM (MARK N.) South Indian factory workers: their life and their world. Cambridge, 1976. pp. 158. *bibliog. (Cambridge. University. Centre of South Asian Studies. Cambridge South Asian Studies. 20)*

— Israel.

ISRAEL INFORMATION CENTRE. Information Briefings. 15. Labour in Israel. Jerusalem, [1973]. pp. 11. *bibliog.*

— Italy.

GRAMEGNA (GIUSEPPE) Braccianti e popolo in Puglia, 1944-1971: cronache di un protagonista. Bari, [1976]. pp. 343.

GRISONI (DOMINIQUE) and PORTELLI (HUGUES) Les luttes ouvrières en Italie, 1960-1976. Paris, [1976]. pp. 268. *bibliog.*

— Japan.

ABEGGLEN (JAMES C.) Management and worker: the Japanese solution. Tokyo, [1973 repr. 1975]. pp. 200.

— Mexico.

DIAZ RAMIREZ (MANUEL) Apuntes sobre el movimiento obrero y campesino de Mexico, 1844- 1880. Mexico, [1974]. pp. 143.

ANGUIANO (ARTURO) El Estado y la politica obrera del cardenismo. Mexico, 1975. pp. 187. *bibliog.*

— Poland.

ZAWISTOWSKI (JERZY) ed. Rewolucyjne wystąpienia proletariatu krakowskiego w 1936 roku. Kraków, 1976. pp. 259.

— Puerto Rico.

QUINTERO RIVERA (ANGEL GUILLERMO) The working class and Puerto Rican politics in the process of change from a traditional to a capitalist agricultural economy. 1976. fo. 464. *bibliog. Typescript. Ph.D.(London) thesis: unpublished. This thesis is the property of London University and may not be removed from the Library.*

— Romania.

BĂDINA (OVIDIU) ed. Tineret industrial: acţiune şi integrare socială; cercetare sociologică condusă de Ovidiu Bădina. Bucureşti, 1972. pp. 170. *(Centrul de Cercetări pentru Problemele Tineretului. Tineretul şi Lumea de Mîine) With French, English, Russian and German tables of contents.*

— Russia.

AKTUAL'NYE problemy istorii sovetskogo rabochego klassa. Moskva, 1975. pp. 221.

NUGAEV (MAGDII ALIMZHANOVICH) Trudovaia aktivnost' rabochego klassa razvitogo sotsialisticheskogo obshchestva: teoretiko-metodologicheskii aspekt. Kazan', 1975. pp. 293.

NUGAEV (RASHID ALIMZHANOVICH) Sovokupnaia rabochaia sila i zakonomernosti ee razvitiia. Kazan', 1975. pp. 246.

RABOCHII klass SSSR i ego vedushchaia rol' v stroitel'stve kommunizma. Moskva, 1975. pp. 568.

GROSSKOPF (SIGRID) L'alliance ouvrière et paysanne en U.R.S.S., 1921-1928: le problème du blé. Paris, 1976. pp. 459. *bibliog.*

KAPELIAN (EFIM KHAIMOVICH) Proizvoditel'nye sily: struktura, funktsii, tipologiia; voprosy metodologii i teorii. Minsk, 1976. pp. 191.

KEEP (JOHN LESLIE HOWARD) The Russian revolution: a study in mass mobilization. London, [1976]. pp. 614. *bibliog.*

KRUZE (EL'ZA EDUARDOVNA) Polozhenie rabochego klassa Rossii v 1900-1914 gg. Leningrad, 1976. pp. 299.

LINHART (ROBERT) Lénine, les paysans, Taylor: essai d'analyse matérialiste historique de la naissance du système productif soviétique. Paris, [1976]. pp. 173.

MOISEEV (LEONID ALEKSEEVICH) Zakon peremeny truda v sotsialisticheskom proizvodstve. Moskva, 1976. pp. 88.

RABOCHII klass - vedushchaia sila Oktiabr'skoi sotsialisticheskoi revoliutsii: sbornik statei. Moskva, 1976. pp. 414.

SABLINSKY (WALTER) The road to Bloody Sunday: Father Gapon and the St. Petersburg massacre of 1905. Princeton, N.J., [1976]. pp. 414. *bibliog. (Columbia University. Russian Institute. Studies)*

VDOVIN (ALEKSANDR IVANOVICH) and DROBIZHEV (VLADIMIR ZINOV'EVICH) Rost rabochego klassa SSSR, 1917-1940 gg. Moskva, 1976. pp. 264.

— — Kazakstan.

ASYLBEKOV (MALIK KHANTEMIRULY) and others. Rost industrial'nykh kadrov rabochego klassa v Kazakhstane, 1946-1965 gg. Alma-Ata, 1976. pp. 272.

— — Russia (RSFSR).

KAZANTSEV (BORIS NIKOLAEVICH) Rabochie Moskvy i Moskovskoi gubernii v seredine XIX veka, 40-50-e gody. Moskva, 1976. pp. 182.

— — Siberia.

MAKIEVSKII (GRIGORII MOISEEVICH) Sozidateli novoi Sibiri: iz istorii rabochikh Krasnoiarskogo kraia, 1945-1975 gg. Krasnoiarsk, 1976. pp. 222.

— — Turkestan.

BABAKHANOV (MANSUR) Predposylki revoliutsionnogo soiuza trudiashchikhsia Turkestanskogo kraia s rossiiskim proletariatom. Dushanbe, 1975. pp. 312.

— — Turkmenistan.

ISTORIIA rabochego klassa Sovetskogo Turkmenistana, 1917-1965 gg. Ashkhabad, 1969. pp. 495.

— — Uzbekistan.

GENTSHKE (LEV VLADIMIROVICH) Kompartiia i rabochii klass Uzbekistana v bor'be za sotsializm, 1926-1932 gg. Tashkent, 1973. pp. 230.

— — White Russia.

MARCHENKO (IVAN EGOROVICH) Trudovoi podvig rabochego klassa Belorusskoi SSR, 1943-1950 gg. Minsk, 1977. pp. 247.

— Scandinavia.

PETERSEN (CARL HEINRICH) Fra klassekampens slagmark i Norden. [Århus], 1973. pp. 252. *bibliog. Selection of broadcasts, articles and essays.*

— South Africa.

GOOD (DORCAS) and WILLIAMS (MICHAEL) South Africa: the crisis in Britain and the apartheid economy. London, 1976. pp. 23. *bibliog. (Anti-Apartheid Movement. Foreign Investment in South Africa: a Discussion Series. No. 1)*

SOUTH AFRICAN CONGRESS OF TRADE UNIONS. Workers in chains. London, 1976. pp. 19.

— Spain.

ALARCON CARACUEL (MANUEL RAMON) El derecho de asociacion obrera en España, 1839-1900. Madrid, [1975]. pp. 507.

CALERO AMOR (ANTONIO MARIA) Movimientos sociales en Andalucia, 1820-1936. Madrid, 1976. pp. 178. *bibliog.*

SAGARDOY BENGOECHEA (JUAN ANTONIO) La realidad laboral española: algunas reflexiones. Madrid, 1976. pp. 317.

TEORIA y practica del movimiento obrero en España, 1900-1936; (edicion a cargo de Albert Balcells). Valencia, [1977]. pp. 335.

— Sweden.

SCASE (RICHARD) Social democracy in capitalist society: working class politics in Britain and Sweden. London, [1977]. pp. 184. *bibliog. Revision of author's thesis (Ph.D.), University of Kent, 1974.*

— Switzerland.

CONTRO i movimenti xenofobi, per l'unità della classe operaia. Lugano-Breganzona, 1974. pp. 48.

— United Kingdom.

RUDALL (EDWARD) Protection to native industry; or, The effect on the labouring classes of the withdrawal of the protecting duties; examined in a lecture, read to the members of the Launceston Institution. Launceston, Cater and Maddox, 1841. pp. 30.

EMANCIPATION of industry. [London, imprint]. 1844. pp. 8. *Without title-page. Caption title. Signed M.M.*

SLANEY (ROBERT AGLIONBY) A plea to power and parliament for the working classes. London, Longman, 1847. pp. viii, 158.

MARX (ELEANOR) Die Arbeiterclassen-Bewegung in England;...übersetzt von Gertrud Liebknecht; mit einem Vorwort von W. Liebknecht. Nürnberg, 1895. pp. 24. *(Separat-Abdruck aus Band II des Volks-Lexikon, herausgegeben von E. Wurm)*

GRAHAM (ALISTAIR) The workers' next step: the shop-floor struggle and workers' control. London, [1973]. pp. 20. *(Independent Labour Party. Square One Pamphlets. 8)*

NEWTON (ARTHUR) b. 1902. Years of change: autobiography of a Hackney shoemaker. London, [1974, repr. 1975]. pp. 68. *(Workers' Educational Association. Hackney Branch. A People's Autobiography of Hackney)*

TROTSKII (LEV DAVYDOVICH) Collected writings and speeches on Britain: in three volumes...; edited by R. Chappell and Alan Clinton. London, [1974]. 3 vols.

POLITICAL ECONOMY COLLECTIVE. Workers and the industry bill: time for a rank and file response. London, 1975. pp. 32.

WORKING lives...: a people's autobiography of Hackney. London, [1976 in progress]. *Accounts tape-recorded or written for a local history project based on a W.E.A. evening class.*

BAIKOVA (ANNA NIKOLAEVNA) Britanskie profsoiuzy i klassovaia bor'ba, vtoraia polovina 60-kh - nachalo 70-kh godov. Moskva, 1976. pp. 375.

THOLFSEN (TRYGVE R.) Working class radicalism in mid-Victorian England. London, 1976. pp. 332.

ZWEIG (FERDYNAND) The new acquisitive society. Chichester, 1976. pp. 144.

BARNSBY (GEORGE) The working class movement in the Black Country, 1750 to 1867. Wolverhampton, 1977. pp. 233. *bibliog.*

ESSAYS in labour history, [vol. 3], 1918-1939; edited by Asa Briggs [and] John Saville. London, [1977]. pp. 292.

SCASE (RICHARD) Social democracy in capitalist society: working class politics in Britain and Sweden. London, [1977]. pp. 184. *bibliog. Revision of author's thesis (Ph.D.), University of Kent, 1974.*

WILLIS (PAUL E.) Learning to labour: how working class kids get working class jobs. Farnborough, [1977]. pp. 204.

— — Bibliography.

LABOUR history of Manchester and Salford: a bibliography; compiled by Eddie Conway [and others]. Manchester, [1977?]. pp. 34. *(Manchester Centre for Marxist Education. Pamphlets)*

— — Periodicals—Bibliography.

HARRISON (ROYDEN JOHN) and others, compilers. Th Warwick guide to British labour periodicals, 1790-1970: a check list. Hassocks, 1977. pp. 685.

— United States.

WARNE (FRANK JULIAN) The workers at war. New York, 1920; New York, 1976. pp. 250.

SENNETT (RICHARD) and COBB (JONATHAN) The hidden injuries of class. Cambridge, 1977. pp. 275. *bibliog. First published in the United States in 1972.*

CLEAVER (KATHLEEN) On the vanguard role of the black urban lumpenproletariat. London, [1975]. pp. 26.

PARKER (JOHN J.) The rape of the American worker. Hicksville, N.Y., [1976]. pp. 385.

TECHNOLOGY, the labor process, and the working class: essays; by Rosalyn Baxandall [and others]. New York, [1976]. pp. 124.

HOWE (LOUISE KAPP) Pink collar workers: inside the world of women's work. New York, [1977]. pp. 301. *bibliog.*

McCOURT (KATHLEEN) Working-class women and grass-roots politics. Bloomington, Ind., [1977]. pp. 256. *bibliog.*

MONTAGNA (PAUL D.) Occupations and society: toward a sociology of the labor market. New York, [1977]. pp. 456.

PETERSEN (GENE B.) and others. Southern newcomers to northern cities: work and social adjustment in Cleveland. New York, 1977. pp. 269.

YELLOWITZ (IRWIN) Industrialization and the American labor movement, 1850-1900. Port Washington, N.Y., 1977. pp. 183. *bibliog.*

UNITED STATES. Embassy (U.K.) Labour bulletin: current developments in U.S. industrial relations and social affairs. irreg., current issues only. London.

— — Political activity.

FONER (PHILIP SHELDON) Labor and the American revolution. Westport, Conn., [1976]. pp. 256. *bibliog.*

FONER (PHILIP SHELDON) ed. We, the other people: alternative declarations of independence by labor groups, farmers, woman's rights advocates, socialists, and blacks, 1829-1975. Urbana, Ill., [1976]. pp. 205.

LABOUR CONTRACT

— Spain.

SPAIN. Consejo Economico Nacional (Organizacion Sindical). Informacion mensual de convenios colectivos sindicales. m., Ja 1967 - D 1967 (nos.1-12). [Madrid].

— United Kingdom.

DIX (DOROTHY KNIGHT) Contracts of employment; fifth edition [by] D.W. Crump. London, 1976. pp. 528.

LABOUR COSTS

— Canada.

CANADA. Statistics Canada. Labour costs in Canada: services to business management. a., 1975- Ottawa. *[in English and French].*

— Germany — North Rhine-Westphalia.

NORTH RHINE-WESTPHALIA. Landesamt für Datenverarbeitung und Statistik. Beiträge zur Statistik des Landes Nordrhein-West falen. Heft 364. Die Arbeitskosten im Handel sowie im Bank- und Versicherungsgewerbe, 1974. Düsseldorf, 1976. pp. 107.

LABOUR DISPUTES

— France.

JAVILLIER (JEAN CLAUDE) Les conflits du travail. [Paris], 1976. pp. 126. *bibliog.*

— Germany.

NIEDENHOFF (HORST UDO) Jetzt muss etwas getan werden: die Basisarbeit Linksextremer Gruppen im Betrieb. Köln, [1976]. pp. 183. *bibliog.*

ARBEITSKAMPF im Krisenalltag: wie man sich wehrt und warum; [edited by] Rainer Duhm, Ulrich Mückenberger. Berlin, [1977]. pp. 158.

— Italy.

GRISONI (DOMINIQUE) and PORTELLI (HUGUES) Les luttes ouvrières en Italie, 1960-1976. Paris, [1976]. pp. 268. *bibliog.*

— Spain.

INSTITUTO DE ESTUDIOS LABORALES. El conflicto obrero en España, 1960-1970. Barcelona, 1972. 2 vols.(fo. 631).

— United Kingdom.

TRADES UNION CONGRESS. TUC disputes: principles and procedures. London, [1976]. pp. 26.

LABOUR ECONOMICS.

NUGAEV (RASHID ALIMZHANOVICH) Sovokupnaia rabochaia sila i zakonomernosti ee razvitiia. Kazan', 1975. pp. 246.

The LABOUR process and class strategies. London, [1976]. pp. 129. *(Conference of Socialist Economists. Pamphlets. No. 1)*

MARSHALL (F. RAY) and others. Labor economics: wages, employment, and trade unionism. 3rd ed. Homewood, Ill., 1976. pp. 633. *bibliogs.*

PISSARIDES (CHRISTOFOROS ANTONIOU) Labour market adjustment: microeconomic foundations of short-run neoclassical and Keynesian dynamics. Cambridge, 1976. pp. 258. *bibliog.*

RESTRUCTURING employment opportunities in Australia; G.J.R. Linge, ed. Canberra, 1976. pp. 215. *bibliogs. (Australian National University. Research School of Pacific Studies. Department of Human Geography. Publications. HG/11) Papers presented at an urbanization seminar, Australian National University, 1975.*

LABOUR LAWS AND LEGISLATION

— Austria.

LEICHTER (KAETHE) Frauenarbeit und Arbeiterinnenschutz in Österreich. Wien, 1927. pp. 238.

— Germany.

KARSTENS (DIRK) Die gesetzlichen Grundlagen und die arbeitswissenschaftlichen Aspekte für die Mitwirkung und Mitbestimmung an Massnahmen des Arbeitsstudiums im Industriebetrieb auf Grund des BetrVG 1972. Hamburg, 1976. pp. 223. *bibliog.*

— Mexico.

MEXICO. Statutes, etc. 1970-1975. Nueva ley federal del trabajo reformada: comentarios, jurisprudencia y bibliografia prontuario de la ley; ([edited by] Alberto Trueba Urbina [and] Jorge Trueba Barrera). 27th ed. Mexico, 1975. pp. 828. *bibliog.*

— Peru.

ZAVALETA CRUZADO (ROGER E.) El procedimiento laboral en el Peru. 2nd ed. Trujillo, Peru, 1975. pp. 407.

— Poland.

SZUBERT (WACŁAW) Zarys prawa pracy. Warszawa, 1976. pp. 410.

— Russia.

KHRUSTALEV (BORIS FEDOROVICH) Gosudarstvennoe predpriiatie - sub"ekt trudovogo prava. Moskva, 1976. pp. 159.

ZENIN (VLADIMIR PETROVICH) Rabochii klass i kolkhoznoe krest'ianstvo: sblizhenie ikh pravovykh statusov. Kiev, 1976. pp. 155. *bibliog.*

— — Russia (RSFSR).

RUSSIA (RSFSR). Statutes, etc. 1975. Kodeks zakonov o trude RSFSR: s izmeneniiami i dopolneniiami na 1 sentiabria 1975 g. s prilozheniem postateino-sistematizirovannykh materialov. Moskva, 1976. pp. 199.

— — Ukraine.

UKRAINE. Statutes, etc. 1975. Kodeks zakoniv pro pratsiu Ukraïns'koï RSR: ofitsiinyi tekst iz zminamy i dopovnenniamy stanom na 1 lystopada 1975 roku. Kyïv, 1976. pp. 112.

— São Tomé e Principe.

SÃO TOMÉ E PRINCIPE. Statutes, etc. 1957-1959. Direito do trabalho...1. Nota explicativa. 2. Legislação. [2nd ed.] S. Tomé, 1959. pp. 135.

— Spain.

RIERA MARRA (JUAN) Los derechos del trabajador: guia legal practica laboral sobre contratos y conflictos de trabajo, convenios, Seguridad Social, etc. Barcelona, [1975]. pp. 318. *bibliog.*

— Sweden.

SCHMIDT (FOLKE FREDRIK) Law and industrial relations in Sweden. Stockholm, 1977. pp. 255.

— United Kingdom.

FIELD (FRANK) 1942- . The rights of lower paid workers: a reply to the Employment Protection Bill: consultative document. London, 1974. fo.13. *(Low Pay Unit. Low Pay Papers. No. 1)*

CARBY-HALL (J.R.) Labour relations and the law. Bradford, [1975]. pp. 40. *(Reprinted from Managerial Law, vol. 18, 1975)*

HENDERSON (JOAN) A guide to the Employment Protection Act, 1975. London, 1975 [repr. 1976]. pp. 39.

RUBENSTEIN (MICHAEL) A practical guide to the Employment Protection Bill. London, 1975. pp. 40.

CARBY-HALL (J.R.) ed. Studies in labour law. Bradford, [1976]. pp. 283.

CLEMITSON (IVOR) A worker's guide to the Employment Protection Act. Nottingham, 1976. pp. 60.

COUSSINS (JEAN) Maternity rights for working women. [London, 1976]. pp. 24.

HEPPLE (BOB ALEXANDER) and O'HIGGINS (PAUL) Employment law: being the second edition of Individual employment law. London, 1976. pp. 337. *bibliog.*

The INDUSTRIAL Relations Act and the fight for a general strike; [articles from Workers' Fight]. London, [1976]. 1 pamphlet (unpaged). *(Workers' Fight. Phoenix Pamphlets. No. 4)*

INDUSTRIAL SOCIETY. Legal problems of employment. 6th ed. London, 1976. pp. 95.

LABOUR RESEARCH DEPARTMENT. LRD guide to the Employment Protection Act, 1975, and to the Trade Union and Labour Relations Act, 1974. London, 1976. pp. 48.

RAWLINGS (HUGH FENTON) The problem of redundancy in collective bargaining and the law. 1976. fo. 259. *bibliog. Typescript. Ph.D. (London) thesis: unpublished. This thesis is the property of London University and may not be removed from the Library.*

TRADES UNION CONGRESS. New laws to protect you in your job: a short guide to the Labour government's new legislation on workers at work. London, [1976?]. pp. 8.

TRADES UNION CONGRESS. TUC Guides to the Employment Protection Act. No. 1. Recognition. London, 1976. pp. 11.

TRADES UNION CONGRESS. TUC Guides to the Employment Protection Act. No. 2. Redundancy. London, 1976. pp. 16.

GILL (TESS) Protective laws: evidence to the Equal Opportunities Commission. London, 1977. pp. 18. *(National Council for Civil Liberties. Reports. No. 17)*

KITCHEN (JONATHAN) Labour law and off-shore oil. London, [1977]. pp. 266.

— United States.

BUREAU OF NATIONAL AFFAIRS. O[ccupational] S[afety and] H[ealth] A[ct] and the unions: bargaining on job safety and health. Washington, [1973]. pp. 56.

LABOUR MOBILITY.

GAUDEMAR (JEAN PAUL DE) Mobilité du travail et accumulation du capital. Paris, 1976. pp. 272. *bibliog.*

— India.

PAPOLA (TRILOK SINGH) and SUBRAHMANIAN (K.K.) Wage structure and labour mobility in a local labour market: a study in Ahmedabad. Ahmedabad, 1975. pp. 214. *(Sardar Patel Institute of Economic and Social Research. Monograph Series. 4)*

— Russia.

PANIUKOV (VLADIMIR SEMENOVICH) Ustoichivost' kadrov v promyshlennosti: teoriia i metody sotsial'nogo upravleniia. Kiev, 1976. pp. 267. *bibliog.*

— United Kingdom.

BIRCH (STEPHANIE) and MACMILLAN (BRENDA) Managers on the move: a study of British managerial mobility. London, [1971]. pp. 20. *(British Institute of Management. Management Survey Reports. No. 7)*

— — Wales.

NEWPORT AND MONMOUTHSHIRE COLLEGE OF TECHNOLOGY. Department of Business and Management Studies. Labour mobility in Monmouthshire. Newport, Mon., 1967. pp. 152, 10.

LABOUR PARTY

— Australia.

LABOUR and the constitution, 1972-1975: essays and commentaries on the constitutional controversies of the Whitlam years in Australian government; edited by Gareth Evans. Melbourne, 1977. pp. 383. *Proceedings of a seminar sponsored by the Faculty of Law of the University of Melbourne in 1976 to commemorate the 75th Anniversary of the Australian Federation.*

— Israel.

ARONOFF (MYRON J.) Power and ritual in the Israel Labor Party: a study in political anthropology. Assen, 1977. pp. 184. *bibliog.*

— United Kingdom.

TROTSKII (LEV DAVYDOVICH) Collected writings and speeches on Britain: in three volumes...; edited by R. Chappell and Alan Clinton. London, [1974]. 3 vols.

LEAGUE FOR SOCIALIST ACTION. The Labour Party: which way?. London, [1975?]. pp. 31.

PEREGUDOV (SERGEI PETROVICH) Leiboristskaia partiia v sotsial'no-politicheskoi sisteme Velikobritanii. Moskva, 1975. pp. 413.

YOUNG SOCIALISTS. Labour's youth fights for socialism. London, [1975]. pp. 32.

BENN (ANTHONY NEIL WEDGWOOD) A new course for Labour. Nottingham, [1976]. pp. 20. *(Institute for Workers' Control. Pamphlet Series. No. 51)*

COATES (KEN) Socialists and the Labour Party; [reprint of an article published in The Socialist Register in 1973]. Nottingham, [1976?]. pp. 24. *(Spokesman, The. Pamphlets. No. 52)*

DEFENCE cuts and Labour's industrial strategy; (based on the proceedings of a delegate conference...called by the Labour Committee of the Campaign for Nuclear Disarmament...London.. .1976). London, [1976]. pp. 33. *bibliog.*

MILNE (EDWARD JAMES) No shining armour. London, 1976. pp. 263.

POSADAS (J.) The tasks for the left in the Labour Party. London, [1976]. pp. 18. *(European Marxist Review. Publications)*

ROSE (HAROLD BERTRAM) Banking and finance; a reply to the Labour Party National Executive Committee's statement presented to the Labour Party annual conference, September 1976. [London, 1976]. pp. 25.

RYZHIKOV (VLADIMIR ALEKSANDROVICH) "Sozialismus" auf Labour-Art: Mythen und Wirklichkeit; (deutsch von I. Markow). Moskau, [1976]. pp. 300.

SUDEIKIN (ALEKSANDR GRIGOR'EVICH) Kolonial'naia politika leiboristskoi partii Anglii mezhdu mirovymi voinami. Moskva, 1976. pp. 268. *bibliog.*

THWAITES (PETER JAMES) The Independent Labour Party, 1938-1950. 1976. fo. 273. *bibliog. Typescript. Ph.D.(London) thesis: unpublished. This thesis is the property of London University and may not be removed from the Library.*

WINKLER (HENRY RALPH) ed. Twentieth-century Britain: national power and social welfare. New York, 1976. pp. 272. *bibliog.*

COATES (KEN) Beyond wage slavery. Nottingham, 1977. pp. 170.

FABIAN SOCIETY. Fabian Tracts. [No.] 446. Labour and local politics; [by] John Gyford [and] Richard Baker. London, 1977. pp. 19. *(Fabian Society. Initiatives in Local Government. 4)*

FABIAN SOCIETY. Fabian Tracts. [No.] 451. The Labour Party: crisis and prospects; [by] Dianne Hayter. London, 1977. pp. 31.

LABOUR PARTY. A is for achievement. London, 1977. 1 pamphlet (unpaged).

PIMLOTT (BEN) Labour and the Left in the 1930s. Cambridge, 1977. pp. 259. *bibliog.*

STUTCHBURY (OLIVER PIERS) Too much government?: a political Aeneid. Ipswich, [1977]. pp. 128.

WOMEN in the labour movement: the British experience; edited by Lucy Middleton. London, 1977. pp. 221. *bibliog.*

— — Bibliography.

WOOLVEN (GILLIAN B.) compiler. Publications of the Independent Labour Party, 1893-1932. Coventry, 1977. pp. 38. *(Society for the Study of Labour History. Aids to Research. No. 2)*

LABOUR POLICY

— Germany.

HEIDERMANN (HORST) ed. Wirtschaftsstruktur und Beschäftigung. Bonn-Bad Godesberg, [1976]. pp. 198.

— United Kingdom.

CROUCH (COLIN) Class conflict and the industrial relations crisis: compromise and corporatism in the policies of the British state. London, 1977. pp. 302. *bibliog.*

— United States.

WARNE (FRANK JULIAN) The workers at war. New York, 1920; New York, 1976. pp. 250.

LABOUR SERVICE

— Switzerland.

WALDVOGEL (T.) Der Arbeitsdienst der Schweizer-Jugend: seine Gönner und die bisher durchgeführten Versuche auf freiwilligem Wege. Zürich, 1928. pp. 54.

LABOUR SUPPLY.

SOCIAL SCIENCE RESEARCH COUNCIL. Committee on Manpower, Population and Economic Change. Inventory of data for comparative international studies of labor force growth and structure. n.p. 1966. pp. 236. *bibliog.*

FRANCE. Groupe de Réflexion sur les Stratégies Industrielles. 1976. La division internationale du travail. Paris, 1976. 2 vols. (in 1). *(France. Ministère de l'Industrie et de la Recherche. Etudes de Politique Industrielle. 9)*

MARSHALL (F. RAY) and others. Labor economics: wages, employment, and trade unionism. 3rd ed. Homewood, Ill., 1976. pp. 633. *bibliogs.*

MALINVAUD (EDMOND) The theory of unemployment reconsidered. Oxford, [1977]. pp. 128. *(Yrjö Jahnssonin Säätio. Yrjö Jahnsson Lectures. 1977)*

— Bibliography.

CONNELL (JOHN) 1946- , compiler. Labour utilization: an annotated bibliography of village studies; ...prepared for the International Labour Office within the framework of the World Employment Programme. [Brighton], University of Sussex, Institute of Development Studies, 1975. pp. 305.

— Mathematical models.

PISSARIDES (CHRISTOFOROS ANTONIOU) Labour market adjustment: microeconomic foundations of short-run neoclassical and Keynesian dynamics. Cambridge, 1976. pp. 258. *bibliog.*

ZABALZA-MARTI (ANTONIO) Occupational choice and labour market adjustments: the case of teachers in England and Wales, 1960-1970. 1976. fo. 308. *bibliog. Typescript. Ph.D. (London) thesis: unpublished. This thesis is the property of London University and may not be removed from the Library.*

FRIEDMAN (MILTON) Inflation and unemployment: the new dimension of politics. London, 1977. pp. 35. *bibliog. (Institute of Economic Affairs. Occasional Papers. 51)*

— Research.

INTERNATIONAL LABOUR OFFICE. World Employment Programme. 1974. World Employment Programme: a progress report on its research- oriented activities. Geneva, 1974. pp. 132.

INTERNATIONAL LABOUR OFFICE. World Employment Programme. 1976. World Employment Programme: research in retrospect and prospect. Geneva, 1976. pp. 278. *bibliog.*

— Asia.

MEHTA (MADHAVA MAL) Industrialization and employment; with special reference to Asia and the Far East. Bombay, 1976. pp. 128.

— Australia.

AUSTRALIA. Commonwealth Bureau of Census and Statistics. Labour force experience. bien., 1972- Canberra.

RESTRUCTURING employment opportunities in Australia; G.J.R. Linge, ed. Canberra, 1976. pp. 215. *bibliogs. (Australian National University. Research School of Pacific Studies. Department of Human Geography. Publications. HG/11) Papers presented at an urbanization seminar, Australian National University, 1975.*

— Austria.

AUSTRIA. Statistisches Zentralamt. 1976- . Arbeitsstättenzählung, 1973, etc. Wien, 1976 in progress. *(Beiträge zur Österreichischen Statistik. Heft 433)*

— Bangladesh.

ISLAM (RIZWANUL) Factor intensity and labour absorption in manufacturing industries: the case of Bangladesh. 1976. fo. 471. *bibliog. Typescript. Ph.D. (London) thesis: unpublished. This thesis is the property of London University and may not be removed from the Library.*

— Belgium.

FAERMAN (M.) and SCHYNS (J.) Essai sur la structure spatiale de l'emploi tertiaire en Belgique. [Brussels, Institut Economique et Social des Classes Moyennes, 1971]. pp. 319.

— British Virgin Islands.

EMPLOYMENT IN THE BRITISH VIRGIN ISLANDS; [pd. by Statistics Office]. a., 1974- Tortola.

— Canada.

JOHNSON (LEO A.) Poverty in wealth: the capitalist labour market and income distribution in Canada. rev. ed. Toronto, 1974. pp. 35.

HOLLAND (JOHN W.) and SKOLNIK (MICHAEL L.) Public policy and manpower development. Toronto, [1975]. pp. 152. *bibliog.*

— — Nova Scotia.

NOVA SCOTIA. Department of Development. Economics and Statistics Division. 1974. Labour resources in Nova Scotia. [Halifax], 1974. fo. 8.

— Communist countries.

APER'IAN (VLADIMIR EREMEEVICH) Vosproizvodstvo i trudovye resursy v sotsialisticheskikh stranakh. Moskva, 1976. pp. 328.

VAIS (TIBERII ABRAGAMOVICH) Problemy sotrudnichestva stran SEV v ispol'zovanii trudovykh resursov. Moskva, 1976. pp. 85.

— Cuba.

MESA LAGO (CARMELO) The labor force, employment, unemployment and underemployment in Cuba, 1899-1970. Beverly Hills, [1972]. pp. 71. *bibliog.*

— France — Lorraine.

GRAU (C.) Evolution de l'emploi industriel salarié en Lorraine de 1965 à 1972. Nancy, Echelon Régional de l'Emploi de Nancy, 1975. fo. 201.

— — Région Centre.

HONNORAT (P.) Evolution de l'emploi salarié industriel dans la Région Centre, 1965-1972. Orléans, Echelon Régional de l'Emploi d'Orléans, 1975. pp. 193.

— Hong Kong.

HONG KONG. Census and Statistics Department. Report on... labour force survey. s-a., Oc 75/Mr 76 (2nd)- Hong Kong.

— India.

SIVASWAMY (NADIMINTI RAMA) Employment potential of the Indian industrial sector. Hydrabad, 1976. pp. 200. *bibliog.*

— — Bombay.

JOSHI (HEATHER) and JOSHI (VIJAY CHANDRA) Surplus labour and the city: a study of Bombay. Delhi, 1976. pp. 189.

— Ireland (Republic).

EIRE. Central Statistics Office. 1977. Labour force survey, 1975: first results. Dublin, 1977. pp. 19.

NATIONAL ECONOMIC AND SOCIAL COUNCIL [EIRE]. Service-type employment and regional development; (by Michael J. Bannon [and others]). Dublin, Stationery Office, [1977]. pp. 142. *bibliog.* ([Reports]. No. 28)

— Israel.

ISRAEL. Ministry of Labour. Manpower Planning Authority. 1973. Israel's manpower: past trends and future developments. [Jerusalem, 1973]. pp. 47.

— Mauritius.

MAURITIUS. Ministry of Employment. Report. a., 1972- Port Louis.

— Morocco.

EMPLOYMENT problems and policies in developing countries: the case of Morocco; edited by Willy van Rijckeghem. Rotterdam, 1976. pp. 211. *Papers of a conference held March 28th-30th, 1974, in the Free University of Brussels.*

— New Zealand.

NEW ZEALAND. Department of Labour. Research and Planning Division. 1975. Employment distribution and potential in Otago. Wellington, 1975. pp. 43. *bibliog.*

NEW ZEALAND. Department of Labour. Research and Planning Division. 1976. Employment distribution and potential in Gisborne. Wellington, 1976. pp. 21.

— Papua New Guinea.

PAPUA NEW GUINEA. Bureau of Statistics. 1967. Census of employers, July, 1967: preliminary bulletin. Konedobu, 1967. pp. 7.

PAPUA NEW GUINEA. Manpower Planning Unit. 1971. The demand for professional manpower in Papua and New Guinea, 1971-80. Port Moresby, 1971. fo.46.. (*Manpower Studies. No. 1*)

PAPUA NEW GUINEA. Manpower Planning Unit. 1974. Monetary sector workforce, 30th June, 1971, classified by a) industry by occupation group by manpower class and b) occupation group by industry by manpower class. Port Moresby, 1974. pp. 127. (*Manpower Studies. No.9*)

— Philippine Islands.

PHILIPPINE ISLANDS. Overseas Employment Development Board. Annual report. a., 1975/76 [1st]- Manila.

— Poland.

SOBCZAK (LECH) Rynek pracy w Polsce Ludowej. Warszawa, 1971. pp. 288. *bibliog.*

— Russia.

TOPILIN (ANATOLII VASIL'EVICH) Territorial'noe pereraspredelenie trudovykh resursov v SSSR. Moskva, 1975. pp. 159. *bibliog.*

KUPRIENKO (LIDIIA PETROVNA) Vliianie urovnia zhizni na raspredelenie trudovykh resursov. Moskva, 1976. pp. 120. (*Akademiia Nauk SSSR. Problemy Sovetskoi Ekonomiki*)

MASLOVA (INGA SERGEEVNA) Ekonomicheskie voprosy pereraspredeleniia rabochei sily pri sotsializme. Moskva, 1976. pp. 231. *bibliog.* (*Akademiia Nauk SSSR. Problemy Sovetskoi Ekonomiki*)

PROBLEMY teorii i praktiki razmeshcheniia proizvoditel'nykh sil SSSR. Moskva, 1976. pp. 326. (*Akademiia Nauk SSSR. Sovet po Izucheniiu Proizvoditel'nykh Sil. Problemy Sovetskoi Ekonomiki*)

USTENKO (ALEKSANDR ANDREEVICH) Trudovye resursy neproizvodstvennoi sfery. L'vov, 1976. pp. 171. *bibliog.*

— — Uzbekistan.

REGIONAL'NYE problemy vosproizvodstva rabochei sily v Uzbekistane. Tashkent, 1976. pp. 182.

— South Africa.

SOUTH AFRICA. Census, 1970. Population census, 1970: industry. [Pretoria, 1976]. pp. 552. (*Bureau of Statistics. Reports. No. 02-05-09*) *In English and Afrikaans.*

SOUTH AFRICA. Census, 1970. Population census, 1970: occupations: age, level of education, marital status, citizenship, birth-place, national unit. [Pretoria, 1976]. pp. 302. (*Bureau of Statistics. Reports. No. 02-05-11*) *In English and Afrikaans.*

— Sweden.

BERGLIND (HANS) and RUNDBLAD (BENGT G.) Arbetsmarknaden i Sverige: ett sociologiskt perspektiv. Stockholm, [1975]. pp. 142. *bibliog.*

FORSEBÄCK (LENNART) Industrial relations and employment in Sweden. [Stockholm], 1976. pp. 138. *bibliog.*

— Tanzania.

SABOT (R.H.) Open unemployment and the employed compound of urban surplus labour. Dar es Salaam, [1974]. pp. 93. (*Dar es Salaam. University. Economic Research Bureau. ERB Papers. 74.4*)

— Thailand.

THAILAND. Census, 1970. 1970 population and housing census: economic characteristics. [Bangkok], 1975. pp. 31,77. (*Subject Reports. No. 1*)

— Underdeveloped areas.

See UNDERDEVELOPED AREAS — Labour supply.

— United Kingdom.

The MANNING of public services in London; a study by a joint group of officials of the Department of the Environment, the Department of Employment, the Greater London Council, and the London Boroughs Association; [T.H. Shearer, chairman]. London, Department of the Environment, 1975. pp. 120.

GREENWOOD (DAVID E.) The employment consequences of reduced defence spending. Aberdeen, 1976. pp. 34. (*Aberdeen. University. Department of Political Economy. Aberdeen Studies in Defence Economics. No. 8*)

LLEWELYN-DAVIES WEEKS [AND PARTNERS]. Inner area study: Birmingham: industrial employment and property availability. [London], Department of the Environment, [1976]. pp. 85. *bibliog.*

SHARP (ROBIN) Whose right to work?: international aspects of employment in Britain and the developing countries and their implications for UK policy. London, [1976]. pp. 49. *bibliog.* (*Oxfam. Public Affairs Unit. Oxfam Public Affairs Reports. 2*)

BUXTON (NEIL KEITH) and MACKAY (DONALD IAIN) British employment statistics: a guide to sources and methods;... assisted by C.L. Wood. Oxford, [1977]. pp. 197. *bibliogs.* (*Warwick Studies in Industrial Relations*)

KNIGHT (D.R.W.) and others. The structure of employment in Greater London, 1961-81. London, [1977]. pp. 53. (*London. Greater London Council. Research Memoranda. 501*)

SHANKLAND-COX PARTNERSHIP and INSTITUTE OF COMMUNITY STUDIES. Inner area study: Lambeth: local employers' study. [London], Department of the Environment, [1977]. pp. 88.

U.K. Department of Employment. Unit for Manpower Studies. 1977. The role of immigrants in the labour market; project report. London, [1977]. pp. 230. *bibliog.*

— — Bibliography.

COCKETT (IEN) compiler. Statistics concerning employment in London. London, 1977. 1 pamphlet (various pagings). (*London. Greater London Council. Research Library. Research Bibliographies. No. 85*)

— — Ireland, Northern.

IRELAND, NORTHERN. Census, 1971. Census of population, 1971: economic activity tables. Belfast, 1977. pp. 303.

— — Wales.

ALDEN (JEREMY D.) State of the community report: job getting and holding capacities. [Port Talbot], Glamorgan-Glyncorrwg Community Development Project, 1972. fo. 58.

— United States.

The URBAN labor market: institutions, information, linkages; [by] David Lewin [and others]. New York, 1974. pp. 155. (*Columbia University. Graduate School of Business. Conservation of Human Resources Project. Conservation of Human Resources Studies*)

BRINKER (PAUL A.) and KLOS (JOSEPH J.) Poverty, manpower, and social security. [2nd ed.]. Austin, Tex., [1976]. pp. 560. *bibliogs.*

MITCHELL (DANIEL J.B.) Labor issues of American international trade and investment. Baltimore, [1976]. pp. 112.

WOOL (HAROLD) The labor supply for lower-level occupations:...assisted by Bruce Dana Phillips. New York, 1976. pp. 382. *bibliog.*

MONTAGNA (PAUL D.) Occupations and society: toward a sociology of the labor market. New York, [1977]. pp. 456.

— — Mathematical models.

EVALUATING the labor-market effects of social programs; edited by Orley Ashenfelter and James Blum. Princeton, 1976. pp. 238. *bibliogs.* (*Princeton University. Department of Economics and Sociology. Industrial Relations Section. Research Report Series. No.120) Papers presented at a conference held at Princeton University in May 1974, jointly sponsored by the Industrial Relations Section and the Office of the Assistant Secretary for Policy, Evaluation and Research of the U.S. Department of Labor.*

LABRADOR

— Social history.

ZIMMERLY (DAVID WILLIAM) Cain's land revisited: culture change in central Labrador, 1775-1972. St. John's, Newfoundland, 1975. pp. 346. *bibliogs. (St. John's. Memorial University of Newfoundland. Institute of Social and Economic Research. Newfoundland Social and Economic Studies. No. 16) Ph.D. thesis (1973), University of Colorado.*

LACORTE (MANUEL TAGÜEÑA).

See TAGÜEÑA LACORTE (MANUEL).

LA GUARDIA (FIORELLO HENRY).

MANNERS (WILLIAM) Patience and fortitude: Fiorello La Guardia, a biography. New York, [1976]. pp. 290. *bibliog.*

LAISSEZ-FAIRE.

BRAY (RONALD) A return to free enterprise. London, [1973]. pp. 9. *(Aims of Industry. Economic Arguments)*

CONFERENCE ON INDIVIDUAL LIBERTY AND GOVERNMENTAL POLICIES IN THE 1970'S, OHIO UNIVERSITY, 1975. Governmental controls and the free market: the U.S. economy in the 1970's: (papers presented at the conference); edited by Svetozar Pejovich. College Station, Tex., [1976]. pp. 225. *Conference held under the auspices of the Department of Economics, Ohio University.*

HABERLER (GOTTFRIED VON) The challenge to the free market economy; translated from the German by Eric Schiff. Washington, 1976. pp. 19. *(American Enterprise Institute for Public Policy Research. Reprints. No. 38) A revised and enlarged version of a speech delivered in German at the International Management Symposium, Saint Gall, 1975.*

FRIEDMAN (MILTON) From Galbraith to economic freedom. London, 1977. pp. 64. *bibliog. (Institute of Economic Affairs. Occasional Papers. 49)*

LAKATOS (IMRE).

ESSAYS in memory of Imre Lakatos; edited by R.S. Cohen [and others]. Dordrecht, [1976]. pp. 767. *bibliog. (Boston Colloquium for the Philosophy of Science. Boston Studies in the Philosophy of Science. vol. 39)*

LAMB (WILLIAM) 2nd Viscount Melbourne.

ZIEGLER (PHILIP) Melbourne: a biography of William Lamb, 2nd Viscount Melbourne. London, 1976. pp. 412.

LAMBETH

— Politics and government.

SHANKLAND-COX PARTNERSHIP and INSTITUTE OF COMMUNITY STUDIES. Inner area study: Lambeth: multi-service project. [London], Department of the Environment, [1976]. pp. 30.

— Poor.

SHANKLAND-COX PARTNERSHIP and INSTITUTE OF COMMUNITY STUDIES. Inner area study: Lambeth: second report on multiple deprivation. [London], Department of the Environment, [1977]. pp. 70.

— Social conditions.

SHANKLAND-COX PARTNERSHIP and INSTITUTE OF COMMUNITY STUDIES. Inner London: policies for dispersal and balance: final report of the Lambeth inner area study. London, H.M.SO., 1977. pp. 243. *bibliog.*

LAMPE (ALFRED).

PRZYGOŃSKI (ANTONI) Alfred Lampe. Warszawa, 1976. pp. 91. *bibliog.*

LANARKSHIRE

— Economic history.

McLEAN (JOHN) Historian. The 1926 general strike in north Lanarkshire. London, 1976. pp. 25. *bibliog. (Communist Party of Great Britain. History Group. Our History. No. 65)*

LAND.

HARDY (SHIRLEY-ANNE) Ecologists and the land: a look at the special land issue of Resurgence, Sept.-Oct. 1974. Kingston, Surrey, [1974?]. pp. 6.

DAVIS (KENNETH PICKETT) Land use. New York, [1976]. pp. 324. *bibliogs.*

CLARK (COLIN GRANT) Population growth and land use. 2nd ed. London, 1977. pp. 415.

The GOVERNMENT land developers: studies of public land- ownership policy in seven countries; edited by Neal Alison Roberts. Lexington, Mass., [1977]. pp. 249.

HARRISON (ANTHONY J.) Economics and land use planning. London, [1977]. pp. 256. *bibliog.*

— Cost effectiveness.

SIMPSON (BARRY JOHN) The theoretical development and application of threshold analysis to assess land development costs. 1976 [or rather 1977]. fo. 342. *bibliog. Typescript. Ph.D. (London) thesis: unpublished. This thesis is the property of London University and may not be removed from the Library.*

— Mathematical models.

ROMANOS (MICHAEL C.) Residential spatial structure. Lexington, Mass., [1976]. pp. 197. *bibliog.*

— Taxation — United Kingdom.

KNIGHT, FRANK AND RUTLEY. The land question. II. London, 1923. pp. 24.

RANDALL (SIMON JAMES CRAWFORD) Your land or theirs?: aspects of the Community Land Act 1975 and the Development Land Tax Bill. [Bromley?], 1976. pp. 31.

— Africa, Subsaharan.

The DEVELOPMENT of land resources in East, Central and Southern Africa: the role of surveying and land economy; report of the proceedings of a seminar held at the Mulungushi Hall, Lusaka, Zambia on 6-9 April 1976. London, 1976. pp. 134.

— Asia.

INTERNATIONAL SEMINAR ON URBAN LAND USE POLICY, TAXATION AND ECONOMIC DEVELOPMENT, SINGAPORE, 1974. The cities of Asia: a study of urban solutions and urban finance; papers...edited by John Wong. Singapore, [1976]. pp. 450.

— Australia.

AUSTRALIA. Commonwealth Bureau of Census and Statistics. Rural land use, improvements, agricultural machinery and labour. a., 1971/72 [1st]- Canberra. *Formerly included in AUSTRALIA. Commonwealth Bureau of Census and Statistics. Rural land use and crop production.*

ARCHER (R.W.) Urban development and land prices: part I: planning and managing metropolitan development and land supply: rationalising the government roles in metropolitan development and land use. Melbourne, 1976. pp. 74. *(Committee for Economic Development of Australia. P Series. No. 19)*

— Bahamas.

LAND resources of the Bahamas: a summary; [by] B.G. Little [and others]. Tolworth, 1977. pp. 130. *bibliog. (U.K. Ministry of Overseas Development. Land Resources Division. Land Resource Studies. 27) 2 maps in end pocket.*

— Belize.

The AGRICULTURAL development potential of the Belize Valley; [by] R.N. Jenkin [and others]. Tolworth, 1976. pp. 344. *bibliog. (U.K. Ministry of Overseas Development. Land Resources Division. Land Resource Studies. 24) 8 maps in end pocket.*

— Brazil — Para.

PENTEADO (ANTONIO ROCHA) O uso da terra na região Bragantina-Para. São Paulo, 1967. pp. 111. *bibliog. (São Paulo. Universidade. Instituto de Estudos Brasileiros. Publicações. 8)*

— Canada — Manitoba.

MANITOBA. Department of Agriculture. 1974. In search of land policy for Manitoba; a working paper. [Winnipeg, 1974?]. 1 vol. (various pagings)

MANITOBA. Municipal Planning Branch. 1975. Land division in Manitoba: study of selected towns and rural municipalities. [Winnipeg], 1975. fo. 145.

— — Ontario.

ONTARIO. Economic Council. 1966. People and land in transition: opportunities for resource development on rural Ontario's marginal and abandoned acres. Toronto, 1966. pp. 36.

HILLS (GEORGE ANGUS) and others. Developing a better environment: ecological land-use planning in Ontario: a study of methodology in the development of regional plans. [Toronto], Ontario Economic Council, [1970] repr. 1973. pp. 182. *bibliog.*

— European Economic Community countries.

EUROPEAN COMMUNITIES. Statistical Office. Land use and production. a., 1976- Luxembourg. *[in Community languages] Earlier information included in various issues of EUROPEAN COMMUNITIES. Statistical Office. Agricultural statistics.*

— France.

RAWLINSON (ROGER) The Battle of Larzac. New Malden, [1976]. pp. 59. *bibliog.*

— New Zealand.

NEW ZEALAND INSTITUTE OF PUBLIC ADMINISTRATION. [Annual Convention, 27th, 1975]. Land use policies: (papers presented at the...Convention); edited by W.R. Dale. Wellington, N.Z., 1976. pp. 185. *(New Zealand Institute of Public Administration. Studies in Public Administration. No. 21)*

— Poland.

POLSKA AKADEMIA NAUK. Instytut Geografii. Geographia Polonica. 34. Approaches to the study of man-environment interactions: proceedings of the Anglo-Polish Geographical Seminar, Toruń, September 1974; edited by Eric H. Brown and Rajmund Galon. Warszawa, 1976. pp. 290. *bibliogs. Map in end pocket.*

— Russia.

DANILOV (VIKTOR PETROVICH) Sovetskaia dokolkhoznaia derevnia: naselenie, zemlepol'zovanie, khoziaistvo. Moskva, 1977. pp. 319.

KARNAUKHOVA (EVFRAZIIA STEPANOVNA) Differentsial'naia renta i ekonomicheskaia otsenka zemli: voprosy metodologii i opyt issledovaniia. Moskva, 1977. pp. 256.

— — Kazakstan.

ABISHEV (AITPAI) Zemli Kazakhstana i ikh ispol'zovanie. Alma-Ata, 1969. pp. 113.

— Sabah — Classification.

THOMAS (P.) and others. The land capability classification of Sabah. Tolworth, 1976. 4 vols. (in 1), 10 maps. *bibliogs. (U.K. Ministry of Overseas Development. Land Resources Division. Land Resource Studies. 25)*

— Seychelles.

SEYCHELLES. Lands Department. Annual report. a., 1973 [1st]- [Mahé]. *Supersedes in part SEYCHELLES. Lands and Surveys Department. Annual report.*

— Singapore.

FONSECA (RORY) Planning and land-use in Singapore. Singapore, 1975. pp. 26. *(University of Singapore. Department of Sociology. Working Papers. No. 48)*

— United Kingdom.

TURNER (M.E.) Land shortage as a prelude to Parliamentary enclosure: the example of Buckinghamshire. Sheffield, 1975. pp. 22. *(Sheffield. University. Department of Economic and Social History. Studies in Economic and Social History. 1)*

AGRICULTURAL DEVELOPMENT AND ADVISORY SERVICE [U.K.]. An enquiry into the expenses of agricultural land ownership, England and Wales, 1973-74. [Pinner], 1976. pp. 69. *bibliog. (Technical Reports. 25/1)*

AMBROSE (PETER JOHN) The land market and the housing system. Brighton, 1976. fo. 37. *bibliog. (Brighton. University of Sussex. Sussex Working Papers in Urban and Regional Studies. 3)*

BRITISH PROPERTY FEDERATION. Policy for land. London, 1976. pp. 16.

POLSKA AKADEMIA NAUK. Instytut Geografii. Geographia Polonica. 34. Approaches to the study of man-environment interactions: proceedings of the Anglo-Polish Geographical Seminar, Toruń, September 1974; edited by Eric H. Brown and Rajmund Galon. Warszawa, 1976. pp. 290. *bibliogs. Map in end pocket.*

RATCLIFFE (JOHN) Land policy: an exploration of the nature of land in society. London, 1976. pp. 128.

READING. University. Centre for Agricultural Strategy. CAS Reports. 1. Land for agriculture. Reading, 1976. pp. 100. *bibliogs.*

BALCHIN (PAUL N.) and KIEVE (JEFFREY LAWRENCE) Urban land economics. London, 1977. pp. 278. *bibliog.*

DAVIDSON (JOAN) and WIBBERLEY (GERALD PERCY) Planning and the rural environment. Oxford, 1977. pp. 225.

ECONOMIC DEVELOPMENT COMMITTEE FOR THE AGRICULTURAL INDUSTRY. Agriculture into the 1980s: land use. London, National Economic Development Office, 1977. pp. 32.

GREEN (DANIEL) To colonize Eden: land and Jeffersonian democracy. London, [1977]. pp. 200. *bibliog.*

AGRICULTURAL DEVELOPMENT AND ADVISORY SERVICE [U.K.]. Agricultural land classification of England and Wales: the definition and identification of sub-grades within grade 3. [London], 1976. pp. 10. *(Technical Reports. 11/1)*

LAND, NATIONALIZATION OF.

LAND for the people; compiled by Herbert Girardet. London, [1976]. pp. 144. *bibliog.*

— United Kingdom.

U.K. Department of the Environment. 1975. Scope of the community land scheme. [London], 1975. fo. 7.

U.K. Department of the Environment. 1976. The community land scheme. (Booklet) 3. Disposal notification areas. [London, 1976]. pp. 7.

LAND REFORM.

LAND for the people; compiled by Herbert Girardet. London, [1976]. pp. 144. *bibliog.*

MARTINEZ-ALIER (JUAN) Haciendas, plantations and collective farms: agrarian class societies, Cuba and Peru. London, 1977. pp. 185. *bibliog.*

— America, Latin.

ARECES (NIDIA R.) Campesinado y reforma agraria en America Latina. Buenos Aires, [1972]. pp. 143.

FALS BORDA (ORLANDO) El reformismo por dentro en America Latina. Mexico, 1972. pp. 211.

CAMBRIDGE. University. Centre of Latin American Studies. Working Papers. No. 25. A theory of agrarian structure: typology and paths of transformation in Latin America; [by] David Iehmann. Cambridge, [1976]. pp. 104.

— China.

BANDYOPADHYAYA (KALYANI) Agricultural development in China and India: a comparative study. New Delhi, [1976]. pp. 204. *bibliog.*

— Colombia.

ESCOBAR SIERRA (HUGO) Las invasiones en Colombia. Bogota, 1972. pp. 125.

— Denmark.

HOLM (PETER EDVARD) Kampen om Landboreformerne i Danmark i Slutningen af 18. Aarhundrede, 1773-1791. Kjøbenhavn, 1888; København, 1974. pp. 255. *bibliog. Facsimile reprint.*

— Ethiopia.

HOLMBERG (JOHAN) Grain marketing and land reform in Ethiopia: an analysis of the marketing and pricing of food grains in 1976 after the land reform. Uppsala, 1977. pp. 34. *(Nordiska Afrikainstitutet. Research Reports. No. 41)*

STÅHL (MICHAEL) New seeds in old soil: a study of the land reform process in Western Wollega, Ethiopia, 1975-76. Uppsala, 1977. pp. 90. *bibliog. (Nordiska Afrikainstitutet. Research Reports. No. 40)*

— India.

BANDYOPADHYAYA (KALYANI) Agricultural development in China and India: a comparative study. New Delhi, [1976]. pp. 204. *bibliog.*

SATIN (LOWELL ROBERT) Towards a spatial strategy for Indian development. 1976. pp. 378. *Typescript. Ph.D. (London) thesis: unpublished. This thesis is the property of London University and may not be removed from the Library.*

SIDHU (BALDEV SINGH) Land reform, welfare and economic growth. Bombay, 1976. pp. 271. *bibliog.*

— — Maharashtra.

MAHARASHTRA. Committee...for Evaluation of Land Reforms. 1974. Report; [M.P. Pande, chairman]. Nagpur, 1974. pp. 407.

— Iran.

BERGMANN (HERBERT) and KHADEMADAM (NASSER) The impacts of large-scale farms on development in Iran: a case study of certain aspects of the Iranian agrarian reform. Saarbrücken, 1975. pp. 204. *bibliog. (Research Centre for International Agrarian Development. Publications. 4)*

— Nepal.

REGMI (MAHESH CHANDRA) Landownership in Nepal. Berkeley, Calif., [1976]. pp. 252. *bibliog.*

— Peru.

CAMBRIDGE. University. Centre of Latin American Studies. Working Papers. No. 15. Agrarian reform and agrarian struggles in Peru; [by Colin Harding]. Cambridge, 1974. fo. 26. *Photocopy.*

ZUTTER (PIERRE DE) Campesinado y revolucion. Lima, 1975. pp. 312.

— Poland.

GÓRA (WŁADYSŁAW) Reforma rolna PKWN. Warszawa, 1969. pp. 276. *bibliog.*

— Spain.

BERNAL (ANTONIO MIGUEL) La propiedad de la tierra y las luchas agrarias andaluzas. Barcelona, [1974]. pp. 189.

LAND SETTLEMENT

— Argentine Republic.

DIAZ (BENITO) Inmigracion y agricultura en la epoca de Rosas. Buenos Aires, [1975]. pp. 79.

— Liberia.

ZETTERSTROM (KJELL) House and settlement in Liberia. Robertsport, Liberia, 1970. fo. 37. *bibliog.*

— Underdeveloped areas.
See UNDERDEVELOPED AREAS — Land settlement.

— United States.

HOLLEY (DONALD) Uncle Sam's farmers: the New Deal communities in the lower Mississippi valley. Urbana, Ill., [1975]. pp. 312. *bibliog.*

LAND TENURE.

DICK (ROBERT) M.D. On the evils, impolicy, and anomaly of individuals being landlords, and nations tenants; together with twelve propositions on labour, wages, etc. London, Chapman, 1856. pp. 32.

— Australia.

PITTOCK (A. BARRIE) Aboriginal land rights. Copenhagen, 1973. pp. 24. *(International Work Group for Indigenous Affairs. Documents. 3)*

— Brazil.

GUIMARÃES (ALBERTO PASSOS) Quatro seculos de latifundio. 3rd ed. Rio de Janeiro, [1974]. pp. 255.

— Canada — North West Territories.

CUMMING (PETER A.) Canada: native land rights and northern development. Copenhagen, 1977. pp. 64. *(International Work Group for Indigenous Affairs. Documents. 26)*

— — Yukon.

CUMMING (PETER A.) Canada: native land rights and northern development. Copenhagen, 1977. pp. 64. *(International Work Group for Indigenous Affairs. Documents. 26)*

— Ethiopia.

LUNDSTRÖM (KARL JOHAN) North-eastern Ethiopia: society in famine: a study of three social institutions in a period of severe strain. Uppsala, 1976. pp. 80. *bibliog. (Nordiska Afrikainstitutet. Research Reports. No. 34)*

— France.

DUCLOS (JACQUES) La défense des petits propriétaires: discours prononcé à Montreuil le 11 avril 1937;...au cours d'une réunion de la Fédération Nationale des Petits Propriétaires de France, etc. Paris, 1937. pp. 31.

— India — Bengal, West.

MITTER (SWASTI) Peasant movements in West Bengal: their impact on agrarian class relations since 1967. Cambridge, 1977. pp. 85. *bibliog. (Cambridge. University. Department of Land Economy. Occasional Papers. No. 8)*

— Kenya.

WASSERMAN (GARY) Politics of decolonization: Kenya Europeans and the land issue, 1960-1965. Cambridge, 1976. pp. 225. *bibliog. (Cambridge. University. African Studies Centre. African Studies Series. 17)*

LAND TENURE.(Cont.)

— Mexico.

BARTRA (ROGER) Estructura agraria y clases sociales en Mexico. Mexico, 1974. pp. 182. *bibliog.*

— — Law.

LUNA ARROYO (ANTONIO) Derecho agrario mexicano. Mexico, 1975. pp. 827.

— Nepal.

REGMI (MAHESH CHANDRA) Landownership in Nepal. Berkeley, Calif., [1976]. pp. 252. *bibliog.*

— New Granada (Viceroyalty).

GONZALEZ (MARGARITA) El Resguardo en el Nuevo Reino de Granada. Bogota, 1970. pp. 197.

— New Zealand.

KAWHARU (IAN HUGH) Maori land tenure: studies of a changing institution. Oxford, 1977. pp. 363. *bibliog.*

— Philippine Islands.

ROTH (DENNIS MORROW) The friar estates of the Philippines. Albuquerque, [1977]. pp. 197. *bibliog.*

— Poland.

SZEMBERG (ANNA) Przemiany w układzie przestrzennym struktury agrarnej w Polsce. Warszawa, 1976. pp. 99. *(Polska Akademia Nauk. Komitet Przestrzennego Zagospodarowania Kraju. Studia. t.55) With Russian and English summaries.*

— Rhodesia.

PALMER (ROBIN) Land and racial domination in Rhodesia. Berkeley, 1977. pp. 307. *bibliog.*

— Russia.

FIELD (DANIEL) The end of serfdom: nobility and bureaucracy in Russia, 1855- 1861. Cambridge, Mass., 1976. pp. 472. *bibliog. (Harvard University. Russian Research Center. Studies. 75)*

— — Russia (RSFSR) — Law.

RUSSIA (RSFSR). Statutes, etc. 1970. Zemel'nyi kodeks RSFSR: ofitsial'nyi tekst. Moskva, 1974. pp. 64.

— — White Russia.

KOZLOVSKII (PAVEL GRIGOR'EVICH) Magnatskoe khoziaistvo Belorussii vo vtoroi polovine XVIII v.: tsentral'naia i zapadnaia zony. Minsk, 1974. pp. 182. *bibliog.*

— Spain.

BERNAL (ANTONIO MIGUEL) La propiedad de la tierra y las luchas agrarias andaluzas. Barcelona, [1974]. pp. 189.

— Sumatra.

EVERS (HANS DIETER) Changing pattern of Minangkabau urban landownership. Singapore, 1974. pp. 45. *bibliog. (University of Singapore. Department of Sociology. Working Papers. No.22)*

— Underdeveloped areas.

See UNDERDEVELOPED AREAS — Land tenure.

— United Kingdom.

PEACE (J.W. GRAHAM) The great robbery. London, 1933. pp. 128.

RATCLIFFE (JOHN) Land policy: an exploration of the nature of land in society. London, 1976. pp. 128.

GREEN (DANIEL) To colonize Eden: land and Jeffersonian democracy. London, [1977]. pp. 200. *bibliog.*

RABAN (SANDRA) The estates of Thorney and Crowland: a study in medieval monastic tenure. Cambridge, 1977. pp. 106. *bibliog. (Cambridge. University. Department of Land Economy. Occasional Papers. No.7)*

— — Law.

MILSOM (STROUD FRANCIS CHARLES) The legal framework of English feudalism. Cambridge, 1976. pp. 201. *(Cambridge. University. Maitland Memorial Lectures. 1972)*

HARWOOD (MICHAEL) Cases and materials on English land law. Abingdon, 1977. pp. 488.

— — Scotland.

McEWEN (JOHN) 1887- . Who owns Scotland?: a study in land ownership. Edinburgh, [1977]. pp. 136.

LAND TENURE (MAORI LAW).

KAWHARU (IAN HUGH) Maori land tenure: studies of a changing institution. Oxford, 1977. pp. 363. *bibliog.*

LAND TITLES

— Registration and transfer — New Zealand.

NEW ZEALAND. Property Law and Equity Reform Committee. 1975. Reform of the Land Transfer Act, 1952. [Wellington, 1975]. fo. 10. *(Working Papers. No. 3)*

— — South Africa.

SOUTH AFRICA. Commission of Inquiry into the Seats of and Areas served by Certain Deeds Registries. 1976. Report (R.P. 104/1976). in SOUTH AFRICA. Parliament. House of Assembly. Votes and proceedings; (with Printed annexures).

— — United Kingdom.

HAYTON (DAVID J.) Registered land. 2nd ed. London, 1977. pp. 214.

LANDAUER (GUSTAV).

HYMAN (RUTH LINK-SALINGER) Gustav Landauer: philosopher of Utopia. Indianapolis, [1977]. pp. 171. *bibliogs.*

LANDLORD AND TENANT

— United Kingdom.

NATIONAL CONSUMER COUNCIL. Tenancy agreements between councils and their tenants. London, 1976. pp. 44. *(Discussion Papers. 2)*

NATIONAL CONSUMER COUNCIL. Reforming the rent acts: evidence to the Department of the Environment's review of the rent acts. [London], 1977. pp. 122.

U.K. Department of the Environment. 1977. The review of the rent acts: a consultation paper. [London, 1977]. 1 pamphlet (various pagings).

LANDSCAPE.

ETUDE des paysages de la Vallée du Lot; [by] Yves Le Bars [and others]. [Cahors?], Ministère de l'Agriculture et du Développement Rural, 1973. pp. 147. *bibliog. Transparent map in end pocket.*

SYMPOSIUM ON ANGLO-SAXON ARCHAEOLOGY, 2ND, OXFORD, 1973. Anglo-Saxon settlement and landscape: papers presented to a symposium, Oxford 1973; edited by Trevor Rowley. Oxford, 1974. pp. 138. *(British Archaeological Reports. 6)*

ADAMS (IAN HUGH) Agrarian landscape terms: a glossary for historical geography. London, 1976. pp. 314. *bibliog. (Institute of British Geographers. Special Publications. No.9)*

LANDSCAPE PROTECTION

— United Kingdom.

RURAL PLANNING SERVICES. A study of the Hartsop valley; a report to the Countryside Commission and the Lake District Special Planning Board; prepared during 1975 by... M.J. Feist [and others]. [Cheltenham, Countryside Commission], 1976. pp. 146. *bibliog.*

LANGUAGE AND LANGUAGES.

EWBANK (INGA-STINA) Shakespeare, Ibsen and the unspeakable. [London], 1976. pp. 27.

LANGUAGES

— Political aspects.

PICAPER (JEAN PAUL) Kommunikation und Propaganda in der DDR. Stuttgart, [1976]. pp. 222. *bibliog.*

LAPPS IN FINLAND.

INGOLD (TIM) The Skolt Lapps today. Cambridge, [1976]. pp. 276. *bibliog.*

LARCENY

— United Kingdom.

DITTON (JASON) Part-time crime: an ethnography of fiddling and pilferage. London, 1977. pp. 195. *bibliog.*

SMITH (JOHN CYRIL) The law of theft. 3rd ed. London, 1977. pp. 255.

LATIN AMERICAN FEDERATION.

PACHECO QUINTERO (JORGE) El Congreso Anfictionico de Panama y la politica internacional de los Estados Unidos. Bogota, 1971. pp. 170. *(Academia Colombiana de Historia. Coleccion de Bolsilibros. 18)*

LATIN AMERICAN STUDIES.

STATISTICAL ABSTRACT OF LATIN AMERICA. Supplement Series. 6. Quantitative Latin American studies: methods and findings...; edited by James W. Wilkie [and] Kenneth Ruddle. Los Angeles, 1977. pp. 91. *bibliogs.*

LATVIA

— Economic policy — Mathematical models.

AKADEMIIA NAUK LATVIISKOI SSR. Institut Ekonomiki. Matematicheskie Metody v Ekonomike. vyp.12. Voprosy sozdaniia territorial'nykh avtomatizirovannykh sistem upravleniia. Riga, 1974. pp. 120. *bibliog.*

— Foreign relations — United Kingdom.

VARSLAVAN (AL'BERT IANOVICH) Angliiskii imperializm i burzhuaznaia Latviia: politiko-diplomaticheskie vzaimootnosheniia, 1924-1929 gg. Riga, 1975. pp. 287. *bibliog.*

— Politics and government.

BERKOVICH (BORIS TSODIKOVICH) V bor'be s "levoi" frazoi: iz opyta bor'by KPL protiv "levogo" sektantstva i doktrinerstva, 1930-1940. Riga, 1976. pp. 171. *bibliog.*

— Social conditions.

ZILE (LIUBOV' IAKOVLEVNA) Periody i etapy stroitel'stva sotsializma i izmenenie sotsial'noi struktury obshchestva: na materialakh Latviiskoi SSR. Riga, 1975. pp. 198.

BALANS vremeni naseleniia Latviiskoi SSR. Riga, 1976. pp. 256. *bibliog.*

LAUSITZ CULTURE.

SMRŽ (ZDENĚK) Enkláva lužického osídlení v oblasti Boskovské brázdy. Praha, 1975. pp. 70. *bibliog. (Československá Akademie Věd. Archeologický Ústav v Brně. Studie. ročník 3/1974, sv.3) With German summary.*

LAW.

POSNER (RICHARD A.) Economic analysis of law. Boston, [Mass.], 1973. pp. 415.

— **Language.**

RECHT und Sprache: Vorträge auf der Tagung der Deutschen Sektion der Internationalen Vereinigung für Rechts- und Sozialphilosophie (IVR) in der Bundesrepublik Deutschland, Mainz, 3.X. - 5.X.1974: herausgegeben...von Theodor Viehweg und Frank Rotter. Wiesbaden, 1977. pp. 134. (*Archiv für Rechts- und Sozialphilosophie. Beihefte. Neue Folge. Nr. 9*)

— **Mathematical models.**

NAGEL (STUART S.) and NEEF (MARIAN) Operations research methods as applied to political science and the legal process. Beverly Hills, [1976]. pp. 76. *bibliog.*

— **Methodology.**

FEL'DMAN (DAVID ISAAKOVICH) and others. Teoreticheskie problemy metodologii issledovaniia gosudarstva i prava. Kazan', 1975. pp. 118.

— **Philosophy.**

IAVICH (LEV SAMOILOVICH) Obshchaia teoriia prava. Leningrad, 1976. pp. 287.

DWORKIN (RONALD M.) ed. The philosophy of law. Oxford, 1977. pp. 177. *bibliog.*

DWORKIN (RONALD) Taking rights seriously. London, 1977. pp. 293.

— **Study and teaching — Russia.**

RIABKO (IVAN FEDOROVICH) Pravosoznanie i pravovoe vospitanie mass v sovetskom obshchestve. Rostov, 1969. pp. 191.

RIABKO (IVAN FEDOROVICH) Pravosoznanie i pravovoe vospitanie mass v sovetskom obshchestve. Rostov, 1969. pp. 191.

KERIMOV (DZHANGIR ALI-ABASOVICH) and SPIRIDONOV (LEV IVANOVICH) eds. Voprosy teorii i praktiki pravovoi propagandy. Leningrad, 1973. pp. 109.

— **Africa.**

BRYDE (BRUN OTTO) The politics and sociology of African legal development. Frankfurt am Main, 1976. pp. 290. *bibliog.* (*Hamburg. Hansische Universität. Institut für Internationale Angelegenheiten. Veröffentlichungen. Band 2*)

— **Algeria.**

BEDJAOUI (MOHAMMED) Law and the Algerian revolution. Brussels, 1961. pp. 260.

— **Communist countries — Bibliography.**

AKADEMIE FÜR STAATS- UND RECHTSWISSENSCHAFT DER DDR. Informationszentrum Staat und Recht. Spezialbibliographien zu Fragen des Staates und des Rechts. Heft 16. Katalog iuridicheskikh dokumentatsionnykh istochnikov sotsialisticheskikh stran: Register of legal documentation of socialist states, etc. Potsdam, 1976. 3 vols. (in 1). *In various languages.*

— **Cyprus.**

CYPRUS TODAY. Vol. 9. No. 1-2. [Special issue on law and justice in Cyprus]. Nicosia, 1971. pp. 68.

— **Ethiopia.**

HAILE (DANIEL) and YIMER (ERKU) Law and population growth in Ethiopia. Medford, Mass., 1976. pp. 52. (*Tufts University. Fletcher School of Law and Diplomacy. Law and Population Monograph Series. No. 35*)

— **European Economic Community countries.**

COMPENDIUM OF CASE LAW RELATING TO THE EUROPEAN COMMUNITIES. a., 1973- Amsterdam.

BLECKMANN (ALBERT) Europarecht: das Recht der Europäischen Wirtschaftsgemeinschaft. Köln, 1976. pp. 404.

EUROPEAN law and the individual; edited by F.G. Jacobs. Amsterdam, 1976. pp. 211. *Papers of a workshop held in 1975 by the Institute of Advanced Legal Studies, University of London.*

Les INSTRUMENTS du rapprochement des législations dans la Communauté Economique Européenne; par D. De Ripainsel-Landy [and others]. Bruxelles, 1976. pp. 189. (*Brussels. Université Libre. Institut d'Etudes Européennes. Thèses et Travaux Juridiques*)

LECOURT (ROBERT) L'Europe des juges. Bruxelles, 1976. pp. 321. *bibliog.*

SCHERMERS (HENRY G.) Judicial protection in the European Communities. Deventer, 1976. pp. 406. *bibliog.*

SMIT (HANS) and HERZOG (PETER E.) eds. The law of the European Economic Community: a commentary on the EEC treaty. New York, [1976]. 5 vols. *bibliog. Loose-leaf.*

STEIN (ERIC) and others. European Community law and institutions in perspective: text, cases and readings...: a successor to Law and institutions in the Atlantic area, 1967. Indianapolis, [1976]. pp. 1132. *Volume of documents not held by the Library.*

BUENTEN (WILFRIED) Staatsgewalt und Gemeinschaftshoheit bei der innerstaatlichen Durchführung des Rechts der Europäischen Gemeinschaften durch die Mitgliedstaaten. Berlin, 1977. pp. 217. *bibliog.*

MACKENZIE STUART (ALEXANDER JOHN) Lord. The European Communities and the rule of law. London, 1977. pp. 125. (*Hamlyn Lectures. 29th Series*)

— **France — History and criticism.**

DROIT privé et institutions régionales: études historiques offertes à Jean Yver. Paris, [1976]. pp. 713. *bibliog.* (*Rouen. Université. Publications. 31) In various languages.*

— **Germany.**

KIRCHHEIMER (OTTO) Von der Weimarer Republik zum Faschismus: die Auflösung der demokratischen Rechtsordnung; herausgegeben von Wolfgang Luthardt. Frankfurt am Main, 1976. pp. 255. *bibliog.*

— **Germany, Eastern.**

RIEMANN (TORD) and others. Law and justice in a socialist society: the legal system of the German Democratic Republic. Berlin, 1976. pp. 64.

— **Nigeria.**

NIGERIAN ASSOCIATION OF LAW TEACHERS. Annual Conference, 1977. [Papers]. [Lagos, 1977]. 7 pts. (in 1 vol.).

— **Russia.**

LABRY (RAOUL) ed. Une législation communiste: recueil des lois, décrets, arrétés principaux du gouvernement bolchéviste. Paris, 1920. pp. 590.

RUSSIA (R.S.F.S.R.). Statutes, etc. 1917-1918. Die Gesetzgebung der Bolschewiki; übersetzt und bearbeitet von H. Klibanski. Leipzig, 1920. pp. 193. (*Osteuropa-Institut in Breslau. Quellen und Studien. Abteilung: Recht und Wirtschaft. 2.Heft*)

FREYTAGH-LORINGHOVEN (AXEL VON) Freiherr. Die Entwicklung des Bolschewismus in seiner Gesetzgebung. Halle, 1921. pp. 110.

DAVID (RENE) and HAZARD (JOHN NEWBOLD) Le droit soviétique. Paris, 1954. 2 vols. (*Paris. Université. Institut de Droit Comparé. Les Systèmes de Droit Contemporains. 7-8*)

RUSSIA (USSR). Statutes, etc. 1938-1975. Sbornik zakonov SSSR i ukazov Prezidiuma Verkhovnogo Soveta SSSR. Moskva, 1975-76. 4 vols.

FEL'DMAN (DAVID ISAAKOVICH) and others. Teoreticheskie problemy metodologii issledovaniia gosudarstva i prava. Kazan', 1975. pp. 118.

IAVICH (LEV SAMOILOVICH) Obshchaia teoriia prava. Leningrad, 1976. pp. 287.

NAZAROV (BORIS LAZAREVICH) Sotsialisticheskoe pravo v sisteme sotsial'nykh sviazei: razvitie vzgliadov na osnovnye vnutrennie i vneshnie sviazi sotsialisticheskogo prava. Moskva, 1976. pp. 311.

SOROKIN (VALENTIN DMITRIEVICH) Metod pravovogo regulirovaniia: teoreticheskie problemy. Moskva, 1976. pp. 142.

— — **Interpretation and construction.**

BOLDYREV (EVGENII VLADIMIROVICH) and PERGAMENT (ALEKSANDRA IOSIFOVNA) eds. Nauchnyi kommentarii sudebnoi praktiki za 1972 god. Moskva, 1973. pp. 206.

— — **Russia (RSFSR).**

RUSSIA (RSFSR). Statutes, etc. 1920. Dekrety Sovetskoi vlasti. t.8. aprel'-mai 1920 g. Moskva, 1976. pp. 444.

— — **Tuva.**

TUVA. Statutes, etc. 1974. Sbornik zakonov Tuvinskoi ASSR, ukazov Prezidiuma Verkhovnogo Soveta Tuvinskoi ASSR i postanovlenii Soveta Ministrov Tuvinskoi ASSR. Kyzyl, 1974. pp. 260.

— — **Ukraine — History and criticism.**

ISTORIIA gosudarstva i prava Ukrainskoi SSR. Kiev, 1976. pp. 759.

— — **White Russia.**

ISTORIIA gosudarstva i prava Belorusskoi SSR, 1917-1975 gg. Minsk, 1970-76. 2 vols.

— **United Kingdom.**

U.K. Statutes, etc. 1101-1713. The statutes of the realm; printed by command of His Majesty King George the Third in pursuance of an address of the House of Commons of Great Britain; from original records and authentic manuscripts. [London], 1810-28. 10 vols.

ENGLISH law and social policy: a symposium based on Sir Leslie Scarman's 1974 Hamlyn Lectures. London, [1975]. pp. 46. *The report of a seminar held by the Centre for Studies in Social Policy on November 15th 1975.*

COMMUNITY DEVELOPMENT PROJECT. Limits of the law. London, 1977. pp. 54. *bibliog.*

FARRAR (JOHN HYNES) Introduction to legal method. London, 1977. pp. 258. *bibliog.*

HOWE (Sir GEOFFREY) Too much law?: the effects of legislation on economic growth. London, 1977. pp. 16.

RAISBECK (BERTRAM L.) Law and the social worker. London, 1977. pp. 153.

ROLPH (C.H.) pseud. [i.e. Cecil Rolph HEWITT]. Mr Prone: a week in the life of an ignorant man. Oxford, 1977. pp. 166.

ZANDER (MICHAEL) Social workers, their clients and the law. 2nd ed. London, 1977. pp. 140.

— — **History and criticism.**

KNAFLA (LOUIS A.) Law and politics in Jacobean England: the tracts of Lord Chancellor Ellesmere. Cambridge, 1977. pp. 355.

— — **Scotland.**

INDEPENDENCE and devolution: the legal implications for Scotland; editor John P. Grant. Edinburgh, 1976. pp. 233.

WALKER (DAVID MAXWELL) The Scottish legal system: an introduction to the study of Scots law. 4th ed. Edinburgh, 1976. pp. 536.

— **United States — History and criticism.**

HURST (JAMES WILLARD) Law and social order in the United States. Ithaca, N.Y., 1977. pp. 318.

LAW, COMPARATIVE.

SZABÓ (IMRE) and PÉTERI (ZOLTÁN) eds. A socialist approach to comparative law. Leyden, 1977. pp. 235.

LAW AND ETHICS.

DUTHOIT (EUGENE) Aux confins de la morale et du droit public. Paris, 1919. pp. 295.

STANKIEWICZ (WLADYSLAW JOZEF) Sovereign authority and the function of law in a democratic society. Madrid, 1973. pp. (7). *(Reprinted from Anuario de Filosofia del Derecho, vol.17, 1973-74)*

SCARMAN (Sir LESLIE) Common law and ethical principle. London, [1976]. pp. 19. *(South Place Ethical Society. Conway Memorial Lectures. 1976)*

LAW AND SOCIALISM.

NAZAROV (BORIS LAZAREVICH) Sotsialisticheskoe pravo v sisteme sotsial'nykh sviazei: razvitie vzgliadov na osnovnye vnutrennie i vneshnie sviazi sotsialisticheskogo prava. Moskva, 1976. pp. 311.

LAW ENFORCEMENT

— Italy.

SICUREZZA democratica e lotta alla criminalità: la difesa dell'ordine costituzionale e della sicurezza dei cittadini...: atti del Convegno organizzato dal Centro di Studi e Iniziative per la Riforma dello Stato, Roma 25-26 febbraio 1975. Roma, 1975. pp.468. *(Centro di Studi e Iniziative per la Riforma dello Stato. Quaderni)*

POLI (ENZO) Violenza politica e criminalità comune: indagine sull'ordine pubblico in Italia. [Rome, 1976]. pp. 264.

— United States.

POTHOLM (CHRISTIAN P.) and MORGAN (RICHARD E.) eds. Focus on police: police in American society. New York, [1976]. pp. 412.

WEINREB (LLOYD L.) Denial of justice: criminal process in the United States. New York, [1977]. pp. 177.

LAW LIBRARIES

— United Kingdom — Directories.

MANGLES (BARBARA) ed. Directory of law libraries in the British Isles. [Sheffield], 1976. pp. 150.

LAW REFORM

— United Kingdom.

U.K. Law Commission. Working Papers. No. 71. Law of contract: implied terms in contracts for the supply of goods. London, 1977. pp. 60.

U.K. Law Commission. Working Papers. No. 72. Second programme, Item XVIII. Codification of the Criminal Law: treason, sedition and allied offences. London, 1977. pp. 64.

LAW REPORTS, DIGESTS, ETC.

— Israel.

ISRAEL. Supreme Court. 1948- . Selected judgments of the Supreme Court of Israel; edited by E. David Goitein [and others]. Jerusalem, 1962 in progress.

LAWYERS

— Russia.

RECHI sovetskikh advokatov po grazhdanskim delam. Moskva, 1976. pp. 246.

— United Kingdom.

KING (MICHAEL) The effects of a duty solicitor scheme: an assessment of the impact upon a magistrates court. London, 1976. pp. 52. *bibliog.*

ZANDER (MICHAEL) Royal Commission on Legal Services: evidence. [London], 1976. pp. 194.

— United States.

[EARLE (WALTER KEESE) and PARLIN (CHARLES COOLIDGE)] Shearman and Sterling, 1873-1973. [New York, 1973]. pp. 549.

NADER (RALPH) and GREEN (MARK J.) eds. Verdicts on lawyers. New York, 1976. pp. 341.

LAZO (SERGEI GEORGIEVICH)

— Bibliography.

KOZHUKHAR' (P.M.) and ROTAR' (P.D.) compilers. Sergei Georgievich Lazo, 1894-1920: biobibliograficheskii ukazatel'; pod redaktsiei...I.I. Nemirova. Kishinev, 1973. pp. 51. *In Moldavian and Russian.*

LEAD INDUSTRY AND TRADE

— United Kingdom.

RAISTRICK (ARTHUR) Two centuries of industrial welfare: the London (Quaker) Lead Company, 1692-1905: the social policy and work of the "Governor and company for smelting down lead with pit coal and sea coal", mainly in Alston Moor and the Pennines. 2nd ed. Buxton, 1977. pp. 168. *bibliogs.*

LEAD MINES AND MINING

— United Kingdom.

RAISTRICK (ARTHUR) Two centuries of industrial welfare: the London (Quaker) Lead Company, 1692-1905: the social policy and work of the "Governor and company for smelting down lead with pit coal and sea coal", mainly in Alston Moor and the Pennines. 2nd ed. Buxton, 1977. pp. 168. *bibliogs.*

LEADERSHIP.

INSTITUTO DE DESARROLLO INTEGRAL Y ARMONICO. Actitudes y opiniones de los lideres paraguayos acerca de las politicas poblacionales y familiares. [Asuncion, 1972?]. pp. 148. *(Desarrollo y Demografia. 2) Cover title: Encuesta a lideres.*

KURODA (YASUMASA) Reed Town, Japan: a study in community power structure and political change. Honolulu, [1974]. pp. 283. *bibliog.*

BAILEY (CONNER) Broker, mediator, patron, and kinsman: an historical analysis of key leadership roles in a rural Malaysian district. Athens, Ohio, [1976]. pp. 79. *bibliog. (Ohio University. Center for International Studies. Papers in International Studies. Southeast Asia Series. No. 38)*

BUEDINGER TAGUNG, 1973-1975. Führende Kräfte und Gruppen in der deutschen Arbeiterbewegung: Büdinger Vorträge, 1973-1975; herausgegeben von Hanns Hubert Hofmann. Limburg/Lahn, 1976. pp. 226. *(Ranke-Gesellschaft. Deutsche Führungsschichten in der Neuzeit. Gesamtreihe. Band 9)*

POLITICAL leadership in Korea; edited by Dae-Sook Suh and Chae-Jin Lee. Seattle, [1976]. pp. 272. *(Washington State University. Institute for Comparative and Foreign Area Studies. Publications on Asia. No. 27) Selected papers presented at two symposia held in Seoul during the summers of 1971 and 1972 under the auspices of the University of Washington, Seattle.*

WEDER (WALTER) Die Einstellung des Mitarbeiters zum Führungsstil des Unternehmung. [Bern, 1976]. pp. 256. *bibliog. Dissertation der Universität Zürich zur Erlangung der Würde eines Doktors der Wirtschaftswissenschaft.*

KIECHL (ROLF) Zur Autorität in der Unternehmensführung: normative Überlegungen über die Autoritätsformen im kooperativen Führungsstil. [Zurich], 1977. pp. 221. *bibliog. Dissertation der Universität Zürich zur Erlangung der Würde eines Doktors der Wirtschaftswissenschaft.*

LOYE (DAVID) The leadership passion: (a psychology of ideology). San Francisco, 1977. pp. 249. *bibliog.*

A PSYCHOLOGICAL examination of political leaders; edited by Margaret G. Hermann with Thomas W. Milburn. New York, [1977]. pp. 516. *bibliog.*

LEAGUE OF NATIONS.

BAER (GEORGE WEBSTER) Test case: Italy, Ethiopia, and the League of Nations. Stanford, Calif., [1976]. pp. 367. *bibliog. (Stanford University. Hoover Institution on War, Revolution and Peace. Hoover Institution Publications. 159)*

RASCHHOFER (HERMANN) Völkerbund und Münchener Abkommen: die Staatengesellschaft von 1938. München, [1976]. pp. 239. *(Hanns-Seidel-Stiftung. Berichte und Studien. Band 9)*

— Germany.

KIMMICH (CHRISTOPH M.) Germany and the League of Nations. Chicago, [1976]. pp. 266. *bibliog.*

LEARNING, PSYCHOLOGY OF.

CROWDER (ROBERT G.) Principles of learning and memory. Hillsdale, N.J., 1976. pp. 523. *bibliog.*

ADULT learning: psychological research and applications; edited by Michael J.A. Howe. London, [1977]. pp. 291. *bibliogs.*

LEATHER INDUSTRY AND TRADE.

VILLA (J.A.) The interrelationship between parameters of the leather industry. (ID/99) (ID/WG.79/6/Rev.1). New York, United Nations, 1973. pp. 35.

— France.

FRANCE. Groupe sectoriel d'Analyse et de Prévision Industries du Cuir. 1976. Rapport...: préparation du 7e Plan. Paris, 1976. pp. 73.

— Turkey.

ÇAGLAR (METIN) Leather and leather products industry: I: raw hide and skin, leather processing and leather garments. Istanbul, 1976. pp. 92. *bibliog. (Turkiye Sinaî Kalkinma Bankasi. Sector Research Publications. No. 3)*

— Underdeveloped areas.

See UNDERDEVELOPED AREAS — Leather industry and trade.

LEAVE OF ABSENCE

— United States.

MINER (MARY GREEN) Paid leave and leave of absence policies. Washington, 1975. pp. 46. *(Bureau of National Affairs. Personnel Policies Forum. Surveys. No. 111)*

LEBANON

— Constitutional history.

KOURY (ENVER M.) The crisis in the Lebanese system: confessionalism and chaos. Washington, D.C., 1976. pp. 92. *(American Enterprise Institute for Public Policy Research. Foreign Affairs Studies. 38)*

— Economic conditions.

SAYEGH (YOUSSEF ABDALLAH) and ATALLAH (MOHAMMED) Second regard sur l'économie libanaise. Damas, 1967. pp. 38.

— History.

SALIBI (KAMAL SULEIMAN) Crossroads to civil war: Lebanon, 1958-1976. London, 1976. pp. 178.

— — 1975- , Civil War.

BARAKAT (HALIM ISBER) Lebanon in strife: student preludes to the civil war. Austin, [1977]. pp. 242. *bibliog. (Texas University. Center for Middle Eastern Studies. Modern Middle Eastern Series. No.2)*

— Parliament.

BAAKLINI (ABDO I.) Legislative and political development: Lebanon, 1842-1972. Durham, N.C., 1976. pp. 316. *bibliog. (Consortium for Comparative Legislative Studies. Publications. 2)*

— Politics and government.

BAAKLINI (ABDO I.) Legislative and political development: Lebanon, 1842-1972. Durham, N.C., 1976. pp. 316. *bibliog. (Consortium for Comparative Legislative Studies. Publications. 2)*

KOURY (ENVER M.) The crisis in the Lebanese system: confessionalism and chaos. Washington, D.C., 1976. pp. 92. *(American Enterprise Institute for Public Policy Research. Foreign Affairs Studies. 38)*

SALIBI (KAMAL SULEIMAN) Crossroads to civil war: Lebanon, 1958-1976. London, 1976. pp. 178.

BARAKAT (HALIM ISBER) Lebanon in strife: student preludes to the civil war. Austin, [1977]. pp. 242. *bibliog. (Texas University. Center for Middle Eastern Studies. Modern Middle Eastern Series. No.2)*

— Population.

DIB (GEORGE MOUSSA) Law and population in Lebanon. Medford, Mass., 1975. pp. 47. *(Tufts University. Fletcher School of Law and Diplomacy. Law and Population Monograph Series. No. 29)*

— Social conditions.

DUBAR (CLAUDE) and NASR (SALIM) Les classes sociales au Liban. [Paris, 1976]. pp. 365. *(Fondation Nationale des Sciences Politiques. Cahiers. 204.)*

BARAKAT (HALIM ISBER) Lebanon in strife: student preludes to the civil war. Austin, [1977]. pp. 242. *bibliog. (Texas University. Center for Middle Eastern Studies. Modern Middle Eastern Series. No.2)*

LEBOWA

— Economic conditions.

SOUTH AFRICA. Bureau for Economic Research re Bantu Development. 1976. Lebowa:...economic revue [sic], 1976, etc. Pretoria, 1976. pp. 59. *bibliog. In English and Afrikaans.*

LEEDS

— Politics and government.

HOWARD (JONATHAN) Voting trends in the Leeds city-region. 1976. fo. 44. *Typescript: unpublished.*

LEFEBVRE (RAYMOND).

GINSBURG (SHAUL) Raymond Lefebvre et les origines du communisme français. Paris, 1975. pp. 261. *bibliog.*

LEGA MARXISTA RIVOLUZIONARIA.

LEGA MARXISTA RIVOLUZIONARIA. Contro l'offensiva padronale: la risposta dei marxisti rivoluzionari; elementi per un programma d'azione. [Lugano, 1974]. pp. 16.

LEGAL AID

— Germany.

SCHROEDER-HOHENWARTH (HANS HINRICH) Das Armenrecht in der Bundesrepublik und seine Reform unter besonderer Berücksichtigung wirtschaftlicher und rechtsvergleichender Aspekte. Frankfurt/M., 1976. pp. 320. *bibliog.*

— United Kingdom.

NEWHAM RIGHTS CENTRE. Report and analysis of a community law centre, 1974-1975. [London, 1975]. pp. 102. *bibliog.*

ZANDER (MICHAEL) Royal Commission on Legal Services: evidence. [London], 1976. pp. 194.

— — Ireland, Northern.

INCORPORATED LAW SOCIETY OF NORTHERN IRELAND. Report...on the Aid Scheme...[and the comments made by the Advisory Committee]. a., 1968/69 (4th)- Belfast. *1965/66-1967/68 (1st-3rd) included in IRELAND, NORTHERN. Parliament. House of Commons. [Papers].*

— United States.

CHAMPAGNE (ANTHONY) Legal services: an exploratory study of effectiveness. Beverly Hills, [1976]. pp. 44. *bibliog.*

LEGAL RESEARCH

— Canada.

INDEX TO CURRENT LEGAL RESEARCH IN CANADA; compiled in the Department of Justice. a., current issue only. Ottawa. *[in English and French].*

LEGISLATION

— Czechoslovakia.

KIESEWETTER (ZBYŇEK) and others. Socialistické zákonodárství ČSSR a jeho další zdokonalování. Praha, 1977. pp. 134. *With Russian summary.*

— Ireland (Republic).

EIRE. Seanad Eireann. Select Committee on Statutory Instruments. 1970. First report of the Select Committee on Statutory Instruments appointed 10th December, 1969. Dublin, 1970. pp. 31. *In English and Irish.*

— South Africa.

SOUTH AFRICA. Parliament. House of Assembly. Committee on Standing Rules and Orders. 1977. Report (S.C. 12-1977). in SOUTH AFRICA. Parliament. House of Assembly. Select Committee reports.

— United Kingdom.

HOWE (Sir GEOFFREY) Too much law?: the effects of legislation on economic growth. London, 1977. pp. 16.

LEGISLATIVE AUDITING

— United States — States.

CRANE (EDGAR G.) Legislative review of government programs: tools for accountability. New York, [1977]. pp. 289. *bibliog.*

LEGISLATIVE BODIES

— Brazil.

BAAKLINI (ABDO I.) and HEAPHEY (JAMES J.) Legislative institution building in Brazil, Costa Rica and Lebanon. Beverly Hills, [1976]. pp. 57. *bibliog.*

— Costa Rica.

BAAKLINI (ABDO I.) and HEAPHEY (JAMES J.) Legislative institution building in Brazil, Costa Rica and Lebanon. Beverly Hills, [1976]. pp. 57. *bibliog.*

— Lebanon.

BAAKLINI (ABDO I.) and HEAPHEY (JAMES J.) Legislative institution building in Brazil, Costa Rica and Lebanon. Beverly Hills, [1976]. pp. 57. *bibliog.*

— Russia.

KARIMOV (AZAL' MIRGALIMOVICH) Kompetentsiia vysshikh organov vlasti avtonomnoi respubliki: po materialam Tatarskoi ASSR. Kazan', 1975. pp. 144.

KHACHATRIAN (GENRIK MKRTYCHEVICH) Verkhovnyi Sovet soiuznoi respubliki. Moskva, 1975. pp. 167.

— Scandinavia — Voting — Mathematical models.

BJURULF (BO) A dynamic analysis of Scandinavian roll-call behavior: a test of a prediction model on ten minority situations in three countries. [Lund, 1974]. pp. 70. *bibliog.*

— United States.

NORWICK (KENNETH P.) Lobbying for freedom: censorship: a citizen's guide to state legislatures and how to make them respond on vital issues involving individual freedom. [New York, 1974]. pp. 72.

BALUTIS (ALAN P.) and BUTLER (DARON K.) eds. The political pursestrings: the role of the legislature in the budgetary process. New York, [1975]. pp. 221.

— — States.

LEGISLATIVE reform and public policy; edited by Susan Welch and John G. Peters. New York, 1977. pp. 222. *bibliogs. Based on a symposium sponsored by the Department of Political Science at the University of Nebraska, 1976.*

USLANER (ERIC M.) and WEBER (RONALD E.) Patterns of decision making in state legislatures. New York, 1977. pp. 210. *bibliog.*

LEGISLATORS

— Brazil.

BRAZIL. Congresso. Câmara dos Deputados. Centro de Documentação e Informação. 1976. Deputados brasileiros: repertorio biografico dos membros da Câmara dos Deputados, Oitava Legislatura, 1975-1979. 2nd ed. Brasilia, 1976. pp. 454.

— Canada.

KORNBERG (ALLAN) and MISHLER (WILLIAM T.E.) Influence in parliament: Canada. Durham, N.C., 1976. pp. 403. *(Consortium for Comparative Legislative Studies. Publications)*

— Germany.

BADURA (BERNHARD) and REESE (JUERGEN) Jungparlamentarier in Bonn: ihre Sozialisation im Deutschen Bundestag. Stuttgart-Bad Cannstatt, [1976]. pp. 177. *With English summary.*

KUERSCHNERS Volkshandbuch Deutscher Bundestag: 8. Wahlperiode, 1976, etc. Rheinbreitbach, [1977]. pp. 224. *(Sonderdruck des Presse- und Informationszentrums des Deutschen Bundestages, Öffentlichkeitsarbeit)*

— Tasmania.

TASMANIA. Parliament. House of Assembly. 1961. The Parliament of Tasmania, 1856-1960: being a record of the services of members and officers of the Legislative-Council and the House of Assembly since the introduction of responsible government; and containing, also, a brief history of the Parliament, and keys to the photographic records of members; compiled by L.A. Thompson. [Hobart, 1961]. pp. 38.

— United Kingdom.

CAMBRIDGE (RICHARD OWEN) A dialogue between a member of Parliament and his servant in imitation of the seventh satire of the second book of Horace. London, Dodsley, 1752. pp. 25. *The text of the seventh satire in Latin and that of the imitation in English are given on opposite pages.*

The CRITIC in Parliament and in public since 1835. London, Bell, 1841. pp. 188.

— United States.

PEABODY (ROBERT LEE) Leadership in Congress: stability, succession and change. Boston, [Mass., 1976]. pp. 522.

DIAMOND (IRENE) Sex roles in the state house. New Haven, 1977. pp. 214.

FIORINA (MORRIS P.) Congress: keystone of the Washington establishment. New Haven, 1977. pp. 105.

— — States.

USLANER (ERIC M.) and WEBER (RONALD E.) Patterns of decision making in state legislatures. New York, 1977. pp. 210. *bibliog.*

LEGOL (COMPUTER PROGRAM LANGUAGE).

STAMPER (RONALD) The automation of legal reasoning: problems and prospects. [1976?]. pp. 18. *bibliog. Unpublished: photocopy of typescript.*

STAMPER (RONALD) The LEGOL project: a survey. Peterlee, 1976. pp. 36. *(IBM United Kingdom Limited. UK Scientific Centre. [Technical Reports]. 0081)*

LEIGH

— Poor.

WILSON (M.D.) The paupers of Leigh: their persecution and poor relief 1660-1860. Leigh, 1976. pp. 32. *bibliog.* *(Leigh. Local History Society. Publications. No. 4)*

LEINER (NORBERT).

ONTARIO. Royal Commission of Inquiry respecting the Arrest and Detention of Rabbi Norbert Leiner by the Metropolitan Toronto Police Force, 1962. Report...; Dalton C. Wells, commissioner. [Toronto, 1962?]. pp. 99.

LEIPZIG

— History.

Die ROTE Fahne über Leipzig: ein Beitrag zur Geschichte der November-Revolution 1918 in Leipzig;...Autoren-Kollektiv: Horst Beutel [and others]. Leipzig, [1958]. pp. 128.

LEISURE.

INTERNATIONAL UNION OF LOCAL AUTHORITIES. [Publications]. 102. The age of leisure. The Hague, 1973. pp. 58.

CHEEK (NEIL H.) and BURCH (WILLIAM R.) The social organization of leisure in human society. New York, [1976]. pp. 283. *bibliog.*

— Denmark.

KÜHL (POUL HEINRICH) and KOCH-NIELSEN (INGER) Fritid, 1975. København, 1976. pp. 97. *(Socialforskningsinstituttet. Meddelelser. 14)*

— Poland.

POLAND. Główny Urząd Statystyczny. Statystyka Polski: Materiały Statystyczne. zeszyt 77(199). Bud'zet czasu rodzin pracowniczych, 1969. Warszawa, 1970. pp. 231.

— Russia.

PISHCHULIN (NIKOLAI PETROVICH) Proizvodstvennyi kollektiv, chelovek i svobodnoe vremia. Moskva, 1976. pp. 200.

— United Kingdom.

RECREATION planning and management in the new local authorities: seminar proceedings; edited by A.J. Veal. Birmingham, 1975. pp. 81. *bibliog. (Birmingham. University. Centre for Urban and Regional Studies. Seminar Papers) Papers collected from 2 seminars organized by the Centre for Urban and Regional Studies and the Institute of Local Government Studies at the University of Birmingham in 1974.*

INSTITUTE OF FAMILY AND ENVIRONMENTAL RESEARCH and DARTINGTON AMENITY RESEARCH TRUST. Leisure provision and human need: stage I report; prepared for the Department of the Environment. [Totnes?], 1976. 1 vol. (unpaged). *bibliogs.*

LEMGO

— Economic history.

GEIGER (ELLYNOR) Die soziale Elite der Hansestadt Lemgo und die Entstehung eines Exportgewerbes auf dem Lande in der Zeit von 1450 bis 1650. Detmold, 1976. pp. 278. *bibliog. (Naturwissenschaftlicher und Historischer Verein für das Land Lippe. Sonderveröffentlichungen. Band 25)*

— Social history.

GEIGER (ELLYNOR) Die soziale Elite der Hansestadt Lemgo und die Entstehung eines Exportgewerbes auf dem Lande in der Zeit von 1450 bis 1650. Detmold, 1976. pp. 278. *bibliog. (Naturwissenschaftlicher und Historischer Verein für das Land Lippe. Sonderveröffentlichungen. Band 25)*

LENIN (VLADIMIR IL'ICH).

SHAPOVALOV (ALEKSANDR SIDOROVICH) Mit Lenin in Sibirien; (autorisierte Übersetzung aus dem Russischen von Maria Einstein). Berlin, [1931]. pp. 47.

WINTERNITZ (JOSEPH) Lenin und die Agrarfrage in Deutschland. Berlin, [1949]. pp. 48.

SELSAM (HOWARD) and others, eds. Dynamics of social change: a reader in Marxist social science from the writings of Marx, Engels and Lenin; selected and edited with introduction and notes. New York, [1970]. pp. 416. *bibliog.*

FEJTÖ (FRANÇOIS) L'héritage de Lénine: introduction à l'histoire du communisme mondial. [Paris, 1973]. pp. 397.

BAKALO (IVAN A.) Natsional'na polityka Lenina; Lenin's nationality policy. Miunkhen, 1974. pp. 211. *bibliog.*

ATAMAMEDOV (N.V.) and GOLOVIN (IULII MIKHAILOVICH) eds. Lenin v sud'bakh narodov Vostoka. Ashkhabad, 1975. pp. 143.

IVANSKII (ANATOLII IVANOVICH) compiler. Lenin: sibirskaia ssylka; po vospominaniiam sovremennikov i dokumentam. Moskva, 1975. pp. 319. *bibliog.*

KSENOFONTOV (VALENTIN IVANOVICH) Leninskie idei v sovetskoi filosofskoi nauke 20-kh godov: diskussiia "dialektikov" s mekhanistami. Leningrad, 1975. pp. 100.

MILHAU (JACQUES) Lenin und der Revisionismus in der Philosophie; [and] Zeitgemässe Bemerkungen zu Lenins Feststellung, dass der Neukantianismus die philosophische Grundlage des Revisionismus sei; ([by] Robert Steigerwald). Frankfurt/Main, 1975. pp. 98.

REPA (FEDOR PROKOF'EVICH) Formirovanie moral'no-politicheskikh idealov molodezhi na obraze V.I. Lenina. Dushanbe, 1975. pp. 254.

AGAIAN (TSATUR PAVLOVICH) V.I. Lenin i sozdanie zakavkazskikh sovetskikh respublik. Erevan, 1976. pp. 263.

CHAMBRE (HENRI) De Karl Marx à Lénine et Mao Tsé-toung. Paris, [1976]. pp. 413.

KAZAKOV (ALEKSEI TIMOFEEVICH) and URLANIS (BORIS TSEZAREVICH) Problemy narodonaseleniia v russkoi marksistskoi mysli. Moskva, 1976. pp. 196. *bibliog.*

LENIN i kul'tura: khronika sobytii, dooktiabr'skii period. Moskva, 1976. pp. 463.

LINHART (ROBERT) Lénine, les paysans, Taylor: essai d'analyse matérialiste historique de la naissance du système productif soviétique. Paris, [1976]. pp. 173.

RABINOWITCH (ALEXANDER) The Bolsheviks come to power: the revolution of 1917 in Petrograd. New York, [1976]. pp. 393. *bibliog.*

SHARAPOV (IURII PAVLOVICH) Lenin kak chitatel'. Moskva, 1976. pp. 208.

— Bibliography.

LENINIANA: bibliografiia proizvedenii V.I. Lenina i literatury o nem, 1956-1967 gg. Moskva, 1971-76. 3 vols. (in 4).

TVORY V.I. Lenina na Ukraïni, 1894 - liutyi 1917 r.: pokazhchyk arkhivnykh dokumentiv. Kyïv, 1977. pp. 255.

LENINGRAD

— History.

BONDAREVSKAIA (TAISIIA PAVLOVNA) Peterburgskii komitet RSDRP v revoliutsii 1905-1907 gg. Leningrad, 1975. pp. 327.

RABINOWITCH (ALEXANDER) The Bolsheviks come to power: the revolution of 1917 in Petrograd. New York, [1976]. pp. 393. *bibliog.*

SABLINSKY (WALTER) The road to Bloody Sunday: Father Gapon and the St. Petersburg massacre of 1905. Princeton, N.J., [1976]. pp. 414. *bibliog. (Columbia University. Russian Institute. Studies)*

TOKAREV (IURII SERGEEVICH) Petrogradskii Sovet rabochikh i soldatskikh deputatov v marte - aprele 1917 g. Leningrad, 1976. pp. 205.

— Intellectual life.

STEPANOV (ZAKHARII VASIL'EVICH) Kul'turnaia zhizn' Leningrada 20-kh - nachala 30-kh godov. Leningrad, 1976. pp. 288.

— Politics and government.

ALEKSEEV (BORIS KONSTANTINOVICH) and PERFIL'EV (MARAT NIKOLAEVICH) Printsipy i tendentsii razvitiia predstavitel'nogo sostava mestnykh Sovetov: sotsiologicheskoe issledovanie. Leningrad, 1976. pp. 303.

LEON (PAOLO).

GOSSLING (WILLIAM FRANK) Some productive consequences of Engels' law. [London], 1974. pp. 20. *bibliog. (Input-Output Research Association. Occasional Papers. No. 2)*

LEONE (ENRICO).

ZAGARI (EUGENIO) Marxismo e revisionismo: Bernstein, Sorel, Graziadei, Leone. Napoli, [1975]. pp. 357.

LESSNER (FRIEDRICH).

TETZLAFF (KARL ULRICH) Friedrich Lessner: ein Kampfgefährte von Karl Marx und Friedrich Engels; aus Anlass seines 150. Geburtstages. Weimar, [1975]. pp. 31. *bibliog. (Stadtmuseum Weimar. Weimarer Schriften zur Heimatgeschichte und Naturkunde. Heft 27)*

LEVELLERS.

BENN (ANTHONY NEIL WEDGWOOD) The Levellers and the English democratic tradition: text of a speech delivered in Burford on Saturday May 15 1976. Nottingham, [1976]. pp. 15. *(Spokesman, The. Pamphlets. No. 54)*

LEVI-STRAUSS (CLAUDE)

— Bibliography.

LAPOINTE (FRANÇOIS H.) and LAPOINTE (CLAIRE C.) Claude Lévi-Strauss and his critics: an international bibliography of criticism (1950-1976) followed by a bibliography of the writings of Claude Lévi-Strauss. New York, 1977. pp. 219. *bibliog.*

LEVINE (ROSA).

LEVINE (ROSA) Inside German communism: memoirs of party life in the Weimar Republic; edited and introduced by David Zane Mairowitz. London, 1977. pp. 222.

LEYS (NORMAN MACLEAN).

LEYS (NORMAN MACLEAN) and OLDHAM (JOSEPH HOULDSWORTH) By Kenya possessed: the correspondence of Norman Leys and J. H. Oldham, 1918-1926; edited and with an introduction by John W. Cell. Chicago, 1976. pp. 382.

LIABILITY (LAW)

— United Kingdom.

GREENOAK (FRANCESCA) and others. What right have you got?: your rights and responsibilities as a citizen. London, 1976-77. 2 pts.(in 1 vol.). *bibliog. Part 2 edited by John Thomas.*

LIBERAL PARTY

— Belgium.

DECHESNE (MICHEL) Le Parti Liberal à Liège, 1848-1899. Leuven, 1974. pp. 126. *(Centre Interuniversitaire d'Histoire Contemporaine. Cahiers. 76)*

— Canada.

MACKINNON (WAYNE E.) The life of the Party: a history of the Liberal Party in Prince Edward Island. Summerside, P.E.I., 1973. pp. 153.

SCHULL (JOHN JOSEPH) Edward Blake: leader and exile, 1881-1912. Toronto, [1976]. pp. 266. *bibliog.*

— Germany.

THIEL (JUERGEN) Die Grossblockpolitik der Nationalliberalen Partei Badens, 1905 bis 1914: ein Beitrag zur Zusammenarbeit von Liberalismus und Sozialdemokratie in der Spätphase des Wilhelminischen Deutschlands. Stuttgart, 1976. pp. 283. *bibliog. (Kommission für Geschichtliche Landeskunde in Baden-Württemberg. Veröffentlichungen. Reihe B: Forschungen. 86. Band)*

See also DEUTSCHE FORTSCHRITTSPARTEI.

— United Kingdom.

STEEL (DAVID) 1938- . A new political agenda. London, 1976. pp. 21. *Address...at the Llandudno assembly 1976.*

VINCENT (JOHN RUSSELL) The formation of the British Liberal Party, 1857-1868. 2nd ed. Hassocks, Sussex, 1976. pp. 300. *bibliog.*

BENTLEY (MICHAEL) The liberal mind, 1924-1929. Cambridge, 1977. pp. 279. *bibliog.*

CYR (ARTHUR) Liberal Party politics in Britain. London, 1977. pp. 318. *bibliog.*

GORBIK (VIACHESLAV ALEKSANDROVICH) Konservativnaia i liberal'naia partii v politicheskoi sisteme poslevoennoi Anglii. Kiev, 1977. pp. 222.

HAMER (DAVID ALLAN) The politics of electoral pressure: a study in the history of Victorian reform agitations. Hassocks, 1977. pp. 386.

LIBERALISM.

JARAMILLO ECHEVERRI (MARINO) Liberales y conservadores en la historia: itinerario de las ideas y del poder. Bogota, 1972. pp. 297.

ČAVOŠKI (KOSTA) Filozofija otvorenog društva: politički liberalizam Karla Poppera. Beograd, 1975. pp. 315. *bibliog. (Filozofsko Društvo Srbije. Filozofske Studije. Biblioteka. 6) With English summary.*

DAHRENDORF (RALF) Liberalismus: Sonderbeitrag. Mannheim, [1975]. pp. 47-51. *(Sonderdruck aus Meyers Enzyklopädischem Lexikon)*

MANNING (DAVID JOHN) Liberalism. London, 1976. pp. 174. *bibliog.*

GOLDSTENE (PAUL N.) The collapse of liberal empire: science and revolution in the twentieth century. New Haven, 1977. pp. 139.

NOTT (KATHLEEN) The good want power: an essay in the psychological possibilities of liberalism. London, 1977. pp. 319. *bibliog.*

— Canada — Bibliography — Union lists.

KEHDE (NED) compiler. The American left, 1955-1970: a National Union Catalog of pamphlets published in the United States and Canada. Westport, Conn., 1976. pp. 515. *bibliog.*

— Hungary.

GOTTAS (FRIEDRICH) Ungarn im Zeitalter des Hochliberalismus: Studien zur Tisza-Ära, 1875-1890. Wien, 1976. pp. 257. *bibliog. (Österreichische Akademie der Wissenschaften. Kommission für die Geschichte der Österreichisch- Ungarischen Monarchie, 1848-1918. Studien zur Geschichte der Österreichisch-Ungarischen Monarchie. Band 16)*

SLONIMSKII (ANATOLII GRIGOR'EVICH) Katastrofa russkogo liberalizma: progressivnyi blok nakanune i vo vremia Fevral'skoi revoliutsii 1917 goda. Dushanbe, 1975. pp. 320.

— Spain.

GINER DE LOS RIOS (FRANCISCO) Ensayos y cartas: edicion de homenaje en el cincuentenario de su muerte. Mexico, [1965]. pp. 188.

LAPORTA SAN MIGUEL (FRANCISCO J.) Adolfo Posada: politica y sociologia en la crisis del liberalismo español. Madrid, 1974. pp. 355. *bibliog.*

— United Kingdom.

HARVIE (CHRISTOPHER) The lights of Liberalism: university Liberals and the challenge of democracy, 1860-86. London, 1976. pp. 343.

BENTLEY (MICHAEL) The liberal mind, 1924-1929. Cambridge, 1977. pp. 279. *bibliog.*

— United States.

CLECAK (PETER) Crooked paths: reflections on socialism, conservatism and the welfare state. New York, [1977]. pp. 206.

COLEMAN (FRANK M.) Hobbes and America: exploring the constitutional foundations. Toronto, [1977]. pp. 159.

GOLDSTENE (PAUL N.) The collapse of liberal empire: science and revolution in the twentieth century. New Haven, 1977. pp. 139.

KARIEL (HENRY S.) Beyond liberalism, where relations grow. San Francisco, [1977]. pp. 137.

ROCHESTER (STUART I.) American liberal disillusionment in the wake of World War I. University Park, Pa., [1977]. pp. 172.

SOSNA (MORTON) In search of the silent south: (southern liberals and the race issue). New York, 1977. pp. 275. *bibliog.*

— — Bibliography — Union lists.

KEHDE (NED) compiler. The American left, 1955-1970: a National Union Catalog of pamphlets published in the United States and Canada. Westport, Conn., 1976. pp. 515. *bibliog.*

LIBERIA

— Economic policy.

BENJAMIN (GEORGE J.) Manifesto for a new Liberia: an analysis and interpretation of the 1974 annual message. [Monrovia, 1974]. fo.52.

INTERNATIONAL LABOUR OFFICE. [World Employment Programme]. 1974. Total involvement: a strategy for development in Liberia; a report prepared by an inter-agency team...and financed by the United Nations Development Programme. Geneva, 1974. pp. 138.

— Politics and government.

BENJAMIN (GEORGE J.) Manifesto for a new Liberia: an analysis and interpretation of the 1974 annual message. [Monrovia, 1974]. fo.52.

— Social policy.

BENJAMIN (GEORGE J.) Manifesto for a new Liberia: an analysis and interpretation of the 1974 annual message. [Monrovia, 1974]. fo.52.

INTERNATIONAL LABOUR OFFICE. [World Employment Programme]. 1974. Total involvement: a strategy for development in Liberia; a report prepared by an inter-agency team...and financed by the United Nations Development Programme. Geneva, 1974. pp. 138.

LIBERTY.

JENKINS (DAVID) One of the Judges for South Wales. The works of the eminent and learned Judge Jenkins upon divers statutes concerning the King's prerogative and the liberty of the subject; now reprinted from the original authentick copy, written and published by himself, when prisoner in Newgate. London, Heyrick, [1681]. pp. (xiv), 94.

CHAMBERLAIN (HOUSTON STEWART) Demokratie und Freiheit. München, 1917. pp. 83.

PARTI COMMUNISTE FRANÇAIS. Pour la victoire de la liberté. Paris, [195-?]. pp. 14.

DOMINATION: (essays edited by Alkis Kontos for the University League for Social Reform). Toronto, [1975]. pp. 228.

ADLER (HANS GUENTHER) Die Freiheit des Menschen: Aufsätze zur Sociologie und Geschichte. Tübingen, 1976. pp. 358. *Some of the essays were originally published in the author's Die Erfahrung der Ohnmacht in 1964.*

GIBBS (BENJAMIN) Freedom and liberation. London, 1976. pp. 144. *"This book is the substance of lectures given at Sussex University in 1973 and 1974" (preface)*

BOWIE (NORMAN E.) and SIMON (ROBERT L.) The individual and political order: an introduction to social and political philosophy. Englewood Cliffs, [1977]. pp. 280. *bibliogs.*

GRIFFITHS (ELDON) Fighting for the life of freedom. London, 1977. pp. 23. *(Conservative Political Centre. [Publications]. No. 601)*

MILL (JOHN STUART) (Collected works of John Stuart Mill. vols. 18-19). Essays on politics and society;...editor of the text, J.M. Robson; introduction by Alexander Brody. Toronto, [1977]. 2 vols. *bibliog.*

ROBBINS (LIONEL CHARLES) Baron Robbins. Liberty and equality. London, 1977. pp. 24. *bibliog. (Institute of Economic Affairs. Occasional Papers. 52)*

LIBERTY OF SPEECH

— Italy.

BARILE (PAOLO) Libertà di manifestazione del pensiero. Milano, 1975. pp. 151. *bibliog. (Reprinted from Enciclopedia del diritto, vol. 24)*

LIBERTY OF THE PRESS

— France.

LE POITTEVIN (GUSTAVE) La liberté de la presse depuis la révolution, 1789-1815. Genève, 1975. pp. 330. *Reprint of Paris edition of 1901.*

— United States.

FREEDOM of the press; (an AEI Round Table held on July 29 and 30, 1975...) William Ruckelshaus and Elie Abel, moderators, etc. Washington, D.C., [1976]. pp. 101. *(American Enterprise Institute for Public Policy Research. Round Tables)*

LIBRARIANS.

WIEGAND (DIETMAR) Professioneller Status und Kontrolle über ein (symbolisches) soziales Objekt am Beispiel des wissenschaftlichen Bibliothekars, etc. Bern, 1976. pp. 193. *bibliog.*

LIBRARIES

— Canada — Directories.

DIRECTORY OF CANADIAN URBAN INFORMATION SOURCES; [pd. by] Ministry of State for Urban Affairs. a., current issue only. Ottawa.

— Poland — Directories.

LEWANSKI (RICHARD CASIMIR) compiler. Guide to Polish libraries and archives. New York, 1974. pp. 209. *bibliog. (East European Quarterly. East European Monograp 6)*

— Scandinavia — Directories.

RUOKONEN (KYLLIKKI) Directory of economic libraries in Scandinavia. Helsinki, 1976. pp. 105. *(Helsinki. Kauppakorkeakoulu. Julkaisuja. Sarja D-12)*

LIBRARIES(Cont.)

— United Kingdom.

PEMBERTON (JOHN EDWARD) Politics and public libraries in England and Wales, 1850-1970. London, 1977. pp. 149. *bibliog.*

— — Directories.

LEVINE (HERBERT M.) and OWEN (DOLORES B.) An American guide to British social science resources. Metuchen, N.J., 1976. pp. 281.

LIBRARY ASSOCIATION. Libraries in the United Kingdom and the Republic of Ireland: a complete list of public library services and a select list of academic and other library addresses. 7th ed. London, 1977. pp. 166.

— — Statistics.

MOORE (NICK) Statistical series relevant to libraries. London, 1976. pp. 34. *(British Library. Research and Development Department. Reports. 5300)*

— United States — Special collections.

STANFORD UNIVERSITY. Hoover Institution on War, Revolution and Peace. Archival and manuscript materials...; a checklist of major collections. Stanford, [1975]. pp. 22.

— Yugoslavia — Directories.

JOVANOVIĆ (SLOBODAN) and ROJNIĆ (MATKO) compilers. A guide to Yugoslav libraries and archives;...translation of a paper given at the I[nternational] F[ederation of] L[ibrary] A[ssociations] conference at Budapest, September 1972. London, Department of Trade and Industry, 1973. pp. 21.

LIBRARIES, GOVERNMENTAL, ADMINISTRATIVE, ETC.

— Australia.

CILES REPORT; [pd.by] Central Information, Library and Editorial Section, Commonwealth Scientific and Industrial Research Organization, Australia. a., current issue only. Melbourne.

— Europe.

KUJATH (K.) The economic libraries of the European Communities;... a paper given at the I[nternational] F[ederation of] L[ibrary] A[ssociations] conference at Budapest, September 1972. London, Department of Trade and Industry, 1973. pp. 21.

LIBRARIES, NATIONAL

— Singapore.

SINGAPORE. National Library. Report. a., current issue only. Singapore.

LIBRARIES, UNIVERSITY AND COLLEGE

— Bibliography.

MANN (MARGARET GWENDOLINE) compiler. The role of books in higher education: a select annotated bibliography. Sheffield, 1974. pp. 86.

— United States.

CHEN (CHING-CHIH) Applications of operations research models to libraries: a case study of the use of monographs in the Francis A. Countway Library of Medicine, Harvard University. Cambridge, Mass., [1976]. pp. 212. *bibliog.*

LIBRARIES AND EDUCATION

— Bibliography.

MANN (MARGARET GWENDOLINE) compiler. The role of books in higher education: a select annotated bibliography. Sheffield, 1974. pp. 86.

LIBRARY FINANCE

— United Kingdom — Ireland, Northern.

IRELAND, NORTHERN. Department of Education. Summary of Education and Library Boards' accounts...together with the report of the Comptroller and Auditor General. a., 1973/74 [1st]- Belfast.

LIBRARY LEGISLATION

— United Kingdom.

MORRIS (ROGER JOHN BOWRING) Parliament and the public libraries: a survey of legislative activity promoting the municipal library service in England and Wales, 1850-1976. London, 1977. pp. 477. *bibliog.*

PEMBERTON (JOHN EDWARD) Politics and public libraries in England and Wales, 1850-1970. London, 1977. pp. 149. *bibliog.*

LIBRARY USE STUDIES

— United States.

CHEN (CHING-CHIH) Applications of operations research models to libraries: a case study of the use of monographs in the Francis A. Countway Library of Medicine, Harvard University. Cambridge, Mass., [1976]. pp. 212. *bibliog.*

LIBYA

— History.

GUENERON (HERVE) La Libye. [Paris], 1976. pp. 127. *bibliog.*

LICENCE SYSTEM

— United Kingdom.

TWO reports made by a committee of magistrates of the county of Surrey, to whom it had been referred to take into consideration the great increase of the number of shops for the sale of gin and other spirituous liquors, in the Borough of Southwark and East Half- Hundred of Brixton...; by a Magistrate. London, Hatchard, 1830. pp. 19.

LIEBHARDT (JOHANN).

BEZBORODOV (SERGEI KONSTANTINOVICH) Johann Liebhardt und Thomas Monger: zwei ausländische Helden des Fünfjahrplans. Moskau, 1932. pp. 46.

LIEBKNECHT (KARL).

SWIENTY (WILHELM) Karl Liebknecht. Berlin, [1931]. pp. 48.

BARTEL (WALTER) Karl Liebknecht. Dortmund, [1974]. pp. 96. *bibliog.*

LIEBKNECHT (SOPHIE).

LUXEMBURG (ROSA) Lettere dal carcere; traduzione italiana di Amalia Sacerdote. Milano, 1922. pp. 16. *Letters to Sophie Liebknecht only; with a preface by Gustavo Sacerdote.*

LIEGE (PROVINCE)

— Politics and government.

DECHESNE (MICHEL) Le Parti Liberal à Liège, 1848-1899. Leuven, 1974. pp. 126. *(Centre Interuniversitaire d'Histoire Contemporaine. Cahiers. 76)*

LIFE EXPECTANCY.

SAW (SWEE HOCK) Construction of Malayan abridged life tables 1956-1958. Hong Kong, 1970. pp. 18. *bibliog.*

LILLE.

FRANCE. Direction de la Documentation. La Documentation Française. Notes et Etudes Documentaires. Nos. 4,297-4, 298-4,299. Les villes françaises: Lille et sa communauté urbaine; par Pierre Bruyelle avec la collaboration de A. Adam. Paris, 1976. pp. 132. *bibliog.*

— Politics and government.

SEYNAVE (RENÉ) La communauté urbaine de Lille: naissance d'une nouvelle personne morale de droit public. Lille, 1970. 2 vols.(in 1).

LIMBURG (PROVINCE)

— Economic conditions.

BELGIUM. Ministère des Affaires Etrangères, du Commerce Extérieur et de la Coopération au Développement. 1972. Limburg: province in expansion. [Brussels], 1972. pp. 42. *(Memo from Belgium. No.148)*

— Industries.

BELGIUM. Ministère des Affaires Etrangères, du Commerce Extérieur et de la Coopération au Développement. 1972. Limburg: province in expansion. [Brussels], 1972. pp. 42. *(Memo from Belgium. No.148)*

LIMESTONE

— Canada — Ontario.

HEWITT (D.F.) and VOS (M.A.) The limestone industries of Ontario. rev. ed. Toronto, .1972. pp. 79. *bibliog. (Ontario. Division of Mines. Industrial Mineral Reports. No. 39) Map in end pocket.*

LIMOUSIN

— Economic conditions.

LIMOUSIN. Préfecture. 1976. Le Limousin et ses institutions régionales. Limoges, 1976. pp. 67.

— Executive departments.

LIMOUSIN. Préfecture. 1976. Le Limousin et ses institutions régionales. Limoges, 1976. pp. 67.

— Social conditions.

LIMOUSIN. Préfecture. 1976. Le Limousin et ses institutions régionales. Limoges, 1976. pp. 67.

— Statistics, Vital.

INSTITUT NATIONAL DE LA SANTE ET DE LA RECHERCHE MEDICALE [FRANCE]. Division de la Recherche Médico-Sociale. Section Information en Santé Publique. Etudes régionales: le Limousin; recensement de données sanitaires. Le Vésinet, 1972. pp. 66. *bibliog.*

LIN (PIAO).

GINNEKEN (JAAP VAN) The rise and fall of Lin Piao; translated by Danielle Adkinson. Harmondsworth, 1976. pp. 348. *bibliog.*

LINCOLN (ABRAHAM) President of the United States.

THUROW (GLEN E.) Abraham Lincoln and American political religion. Albany, N.Y., 1976. pp. 133. *bibliog.*

LINEAR PROGRAMMING.

NAGEL (STUART S.) and NEEF (MARIAN) The application of mixed strategies: civil rights and other multiple-activity policies. Beverly Hills, [1976]. pp. 60.

KANTOROVICH (LEONID VITAL'EVICH) Essays in optimal planning; selected with an introduction by Leon Smolinski. Oxford, 1977. pp. 251. *bibliog.*

POWELL (SUSAN ELLEN) A product form of the reduced basis simplex algorithm for linear programming. 1976 [or rather 1977]. fo. 145. *bibliog. Typescript. Ph.D. (London) thesis: unpublished. This thesis is the property of London University and may not be removed from the Library.*

LINEN

— United Kingdom — Ireland.

PRIOR (THOMAS) of Rathdowney. An essay to encourage and extend the linen-manufacture in Ireland, by praemiums and other means. Dublin, printed by G. Faulkner, 1749. pp. 56.

LINGUISTIC CHANGE.

SOCIOCULTURAL dimensions of language change; edited by Ben G. Blount [and] Mary Sanches. New York, [1977]. pp. 293. *bibliogs.*

LINGUISTICS.

CHICAGO LINGUISTIC SOCIETY. Regional Meeting, 11th, 1975. Papers...; edited by Robin E. Grossman [and others]. Chicago, 1975. pp. 686. *bibliogs.*

CHICAGO LINGUISTIC SOCIETY. Regional Meeting, 12th, 1976. Papers...; edited by Salikoko S. Mufwene [and others]. Chicago, 1976. pp. 697. *bibliogs.*

An INTEGRATED theory of linguistic ability; [by] Thomas G. Bever [and others]. New York, [1976]. pp. 432. *bibliogs.*

ALLWOOD (JENS) and others. Logic in linguistics. Cambridge, 1977. pp. 185. *bibliog. Original Swedish edition entitled Logik för lingvister.*

LINOTYPE.

KRETSCHMER (BRUNO) 25 Jahre Zentralkommission der Maschinensetzer Deutschlands, VDDB, 1903-1928: ein Rückblick. [Berlin, 1928]. pp. 95.

LINZ

— Economic conditions.

KAMMER FÜR ARBEITER UND ANGESTELLTE FÜR OBERÖSTERREICH. Die Lebenshaltung von Arbeitern und Angestellten in Linz, 1974. [Linz], 1976. fo.67. *(Statistik. Heft 48) 120 tables appended.*

LIPINSKI (EDWARD).

LIPIŃSKI (EDWARD) Historia polskiej myśli społeczno-ekonomicznej do końca XVIII wieku. Wrocław, 1975. pp. 464. *With English and Russian afterwords.*

LIPPE

— Economic history.

STEINBACH (PETER) Der Eintritt Lippes in das Industriezeitalter: Sozialstruktur und Industrialisierung des Fürstentums Lippe im 19. Jahrhundert. Lemgo, [1976]. pp. 556. *bibliog. (Landesverband Lippe in Detmold. Lippische Studien. Band 3)*

— Landtag — Elections.

CIOLEK-KUEMPER (JUTTA) Wahlkampf in Lippe: die Wahlkampfpropaganda der NSDAP zur Januar 1933. München, 1976. pp. 406. *bibliog.*

— Politics and government.

SENGOTTA (HANS JUERGEN) Der Reichsstatthalter in Lippe 1933 bis 1939: reichsrechtliche Bestimmungen und politische Praxis. Detmold, 1976. pp. 422. *bibliog. (Naturwissenschaftlicher und Historischer Verein für das Land Lippe. Sonderveröffentlichungen. Band 26)*

— Social history.

STEINBACH (PETER) Der Eintritt Lippes in das Industriezeitalter: Sozialstruktur und Industrialisierung des Fürstentums Lippe im 19. Jahrhundert. Lemgo, [1976]. pp. 556. *bibliog. (Landesverband Lippe in Detmold. Lippische Studien. Band 3)*

LIQUEFIED PETROLEUM GAS INDUSTRY

— Australia.

AUSTRALIA. Parliament. Senate. Standing Committee on Primary and Secondary Industry and Trade. 1971. Report on availability of liquefied petroleum gas; [E.W. Prowse, chairman]. in AUSTRALIA. Parliament. Parliamentary papers, 1971, vol.11.

LIQUIDATION

— United Kingdom.

SALES (CHARLES ALLISON) The law relating to bankruptcy, liquidations and receiverships; sixth edition by J.H. Thompson. Plymouth, 1977. pp. 332.

LIQUOR PROBLEM

— Africa, Subsaharan.

PAN (LYNN) Alcohol in colonial Africa. Helsinki, [1975]. pp. 121. *bibliog. (Väkijuomakysymyksen Tutkimuussäätiö. [Publications. No.] 22)*

— Switzerland.

LEU (ROBERT) and LUTZ (PETER) Ökonomische Aspekte des Alkoholkonsums in der Schweiz. Zürich, 1977. pp. 638. *bibliog. Basler Dissertation.*

— United Kingdom.

TWO reports made by a committee of magistrates of the county of Surrey, to whom it had been referred to take into consideration the great increase of the number of shops for the sale of gin and other spirituous liquors, in the Borough of Southwark and East Half-Hundred of Brixton...; by a Magistrate. London, Hatchard, 1830. pp. 19.

CARVANA (S.) and others. Social aspects of alcohol and alcoholism. London, [1976]. pp. 55. *bibliog.*

— — Ireland.

STIVERS (RICHARD) A hair of the dog: Irish drinking and American stereotype. University Park, Penn., [1976!. PP. 197.

— United States.

STIVERS (RICHARD) A hair of the dog: Irish drinking and American stereotype. University Park, Penn., [1976!. PP. 197.

LIQUOR TRAFFIC

— Africa, Subsaharan.

PAN (LYNN) Alcohol in colonial Africa. Helsinki, [1975]. pp. 121. *bibliog. (Väkijuomakysymyksen Tutkimuussäätiö. [Publications. No.] 22)*

— Poland.

SZCZEPANIAK (MARIAN) Karczma, wieś, dwór: rola propinacji na wsi wielkopolskiej od połowy XVII do schyłku XVIII wieku. Warszawa, 1977. pp. 186. *With Russian and German summaries.*

— United Kingdom — Taxation.

[HEATH (BENJAMIN)] The case of the county of Devon, with respect to the consequences of the new excise duty on cyder and perry: published by the direction of the committee appointed at a general meeting of that county to superintend the application for the repeal of that duty. London, Johnston, 1763. pp. 32.

LITERATURE.

WILSON (EDMUND) American writer. Letters on literature and politics 1912-1972; edited by Elena Wilson. London, 1977. pp. 768.

— History and criticism.

PRAWER (SIEGBERT S.) Karl Marx and world literature. Oxford, 1976. pp. 446. *bibliog.*

WEAPONS of criticism: marxism in America and the literary tradition; edited by Norman Rudich. Palo Alto, [1976]. pp. 389.

LITERATURE AND MORALS.

TURCO (ALFRED) Shaw's moral vision: the self and salvation. Ithaca, 1976. pp. 297. *bibliog.*

LITERATURE AND SOCIETY.

SERGE (VICTOR) pseud. [i.e. Viktor L'vovich KIBAL'CHICH] Littérature et révolution; suivi de Littérature prolétarienne?, et Une littérature prolétarienne est-elle possible?. Paris, 1976. pp. 122.

BROWN (JAMES MELVILLE) A sociological analysis of the novels of Charles Dickens. 1977. fo. 340. *bibliog. Typescript. Ph.D. (London) thesis: unpublished. This thesis is the property of London University and may not be removed from the Library.*

CLOWERS (MYLES L.) and MORI (STEVEN H.) Understanding sociology through fiction. New York, [1977]. pp. 223. *bibliog.*

MILNER (ANDREW JOHN) John Milton and the English revolution: a study in the sociology of literature. [1977]. fo. 334. *bibliog. Typescript. Ph.D. (London) thesis: unpublished. This thesis is the property of London University and may not be removed from the Library.*

LITHUANIA

— Economic conditions.

MANIUSHIS (IOSIF ANTONOVICH) Ekonomika i kul'tura Sovetskoi Litvy. Vil'nius, 1973. pp. 135.

— Foreign relations.

MIKULICZ (SERGIUSZ) Kłajpeda w polityce europejskiej, 1918-1939. Warszawa, 1976. pp. 352. *bibliog.*

— History.

BIENHOLD (MARIANNE) Die Entstehung des litauischen Staates in den Jahren 1918-1919 im Spiegel deutscher Akten. Bochum, 1976. 1 vol.(various pagings). *bibliog. Inauguraldissertation.*

— Social conditions.

MANIUSHIS (IOSIF ANTONOVICH) Ekonomika i kul'tura Sovetskoi Litvy. Vil'nius, 1973. pp. 135.

LITTLE LAUREL

— Social life and customs.

HICKS (GEORGE LEON) Appalachian Valley. New York, [1976]. pp. 112. *bibliog.*

LIVERPOOL

— City planning.

WILSON (HUGH) AND WOMERSLEY (LEWIS) Firm, and others. Inner area study: Liverpool: fourth study review. [London], Department of the Environment, [1976]. pp. 32.

WILSON (HUGH) AND WOMERSLEY (LEWIS) Firm, and JAMIESON MACKAY AND PARTNERS. Inner area study: Liverpool: environmental care project. [London], Department of the Environment, [1977]. pp. 60.

WILSON (HUGH) AND WOMERSLEY (LEWIS) Firm, and others. Change or decay: final report of the Liverpool inner area study. London, H.M.S.O., 1977. pp. 240.

— Economic conditions.

WILSON (HUGH) AND WOMERSLEY (LEWIS) Firm, and TYM (ROGER) AND ASSOCIATES. Inner area study: Liverpool: getting a job. [London], Department of the Environment, [1977]. pp. 45.

WILSON (HUGH) AND WOMERSLEY (LEWIS) Firm, and TYM (ROGER) AND ASSOCIATES. Inner area study: Liverpool: economic development of the inner area. [London], Department of the Environment, [1977]. pp. 129.

— Economic policy.

WILSON (HUGH) AND WOMERSLEY (LEWIS) Firm, and TYM (ROGER) AND ASSOCIATES. Inner area study: Liverpool: economic development of the inner area. [London], Department of the Environment, [1977]. pp. 129.

— Playgrounds.

WILSON (HUGH) AND WOMERSLEY (LEWIS) Firm. Inner area study: Liverpool: inner area play; (report of action projects on adventure playgrounds and play on wheels). [London], Department of the Environment, [1977]. pp. 67, 6 maps.

— Social conditions.

JONES (PAULINE) and others. All their future: a study of the problems of a group of school leavers in a disadvantaged area of Liverpool. Oxford, 1975. pp. 57.

WILSON (HUGH) AND WOMERSLEY (LEWIS) Firm, and others. Inner area study: Liverpool: fourth study review. [London], Department of the Environment, [1976]. pp. 32.

WILSON (HUGH) AND WOMERSLEY (LEWIS) Firm. Inner area study: Liverpool: community care of the elderly. [London], Department of the Environment, [1977]. pp. 61, 1 map.

WILSON (HUGH) AND WOMERSLEY (LEWIS) Firm. Inner area study: Liverpool: single parent families. [London], Department of the Environment, [1977]. pp. 31.

WILSON (HUGH) AND WOMERSLEY (LEWIS) Firm, and others. Change or decay: final report of the Liverpool inner area study. London, H.M.S.O., 1977. pp. 240.

— Social policy.

TOPPING (PHILIP R.) and SMITH (GEORGE ANTONY NOEL) Government against poverty?: Liverpool Community Development Project, 1970-75. Oxford, 1977. pp. 123. *bibliog.*

WILSON (HUGH) AND WOMERSLEY (LEWIS) Firm, and others. Change or decay: final report of the Liverpool inner area study. London, H.M.S.O., 1977. pp. 240.

LIVINGSTONE (DAVID).

KRIZSÁN (LÁSZLÓ) "Homo regius" in Africa: in commemoration of the centenary of David Livingstone's death. Budapest, 1975. pp. 38. *(Magyar Tudományos Akadémia. Világgazdasági Kutató Intézet. Studies on Developing Countries. No. 78)*

LOBBYING.

NORWICK (KENNETH P.) Lobbying for freedom: censorship: a citizen's guide to state legislatures and how to make them respond on vital issues involving individual freedom. [New York, 1974]. pp. 72.

WALTERS (ALAN A.) The politicization of economic decisions; [with an] introduction by Harry G. Johnson. Los Angeles, 1976. pp. 12. *(International Institute for Economic Research. Reprint Papers. No. 1)*

LOCAL ELECTIONS

— Brazil.

LEAL (VICTOR NUNES) Coronelismo: the municipality and representative government in Brazil;...translated by June Henfrey. Cambridge, 1977. pp. 237. *bibliog. Translation of Coronelismo, enxada e voto.*

LOCAL FINANCE

— Australia.

AUSTRALIA. Commonwealth Bureau of Census and Statistics. Public authority finance: public authority estimates. a., 1974/75- Canberra.

— Europe.

COUNCIL OF EUROPE. Division of Local Authorities. Information bulletin: municipal and regional matters. s-a., 1974 (no. 6)- Strasbourg.

— Iceland.

ICELAND. Hagstofa. 1970. Sveitarsjódareikningar 1966-68; Communal finance 1966-68. Reykjavík, 1970. pp. 93. *(Hagskýrslur Íslands. 2. [Series]. 48) With English translations of table headings.*

ICELAND. Hagstofa. 1974. Sveitarsj ódareikningar 1969-71; Communal finance 1969-71. Reykjavík, 1974. pp. 95. *(Hagskýrslur Íslands. 2. [Series]. 56)*

— Ireland (Republic).

EIRE. Interdepartmental Committee on Local Finance and Taxation. 1968. Report on rates and other sources of revenue for local authorities. Dublin, [1968]. pp. 59.

— — Accounting.

GOLDEN (T.P.) Local authority accounting in Ireland. Dublin, [1977]. pp. 276.

— Netherlands.

VERENIGING VAN NEDERLANDSE GEMEENTEN. Municipal finance in the Netherlands. [The Hague?, 1966?]. pp. 8.

— United Kingdom.

CRIPPS (FRANCIS) and GODLEY (WYNNE) Local government finance and its reform: a critique of the Layfield committee's report. [Cambridge], 1976. pp. 58.

HARRIS (RALPH) and SELDON (ARTHUR) Pricing or taxing?: evidence on charging for local government services invited by the Layfield Committee and a critique of its report. London, 1976. pp. 103. *bibliog. (Institute of Economic Affairs. Hobart Papers. 71)*

U.K. Committee of Inquiry into Local Government Finance. 1976. Local government finance: appendix 10 to the report of the committee of inquiry under the chairmanship of Frank Layfield. London, 1976. Microfiche [22 cards].

— — Ireland, Northern.

IRELAND, NORTHERN. Department of the Environment. District councils' summary of statement of accounts. a., Oc 1973/Mr 1974 (1st)- Belfast.

IRELAND, NORTHERN. Department of the Environment. Local authority financial returns. s-a. (formerly a.), Mr/S 1973- Belfast. *1922/23-1938/39, 1945/46-1972/73 included in IRELAND, NORTHERN. Parliament. [Command Papers]. Suspended publication. 1939/40-1944/45.*

— United States.

ROEDER (PHILLIP W.) Stability and change in the determinants of state expenditures. Beverly Hills, [1976]. pp. 34. *bibliog.*

MAXWELL (JAMES ACKLEY) and ARONSON (JAY RICHARD) Financing state and local governments. 3rd ed. Washington, D.C., [1977]. pp. 290. *bibliog. (Brookings Institution. Studies of Government Finance)*

LOCAL GOVERNMENT.

INTERNATIONAL UNION OF LOCAL AUTHORITIES. [Publications]. 98. Local government as promotor of economic and social development. The Hague, 1971. pp. 100.

ASHFORD (DOUGLAS ELLIOTT) Democracy, decentralization and decisions in subnational politics. Beverly Hills, [1976]. pp. 59. *bibliog.*

— Economic aspects — United Kingdom.

BARRAS (R.) Local authority resource allocation: analysis and modelling. London, 1976. pp. 78. *bibliog. (Planning Research Applications Group. PRAG Technical Papers. TP 17)*

— Chile.

VALENZUELA (ARTURO) Political brokers in Chile: local government in a centralized polity. Durham, N.C., 1977. pp. 272. *bibliog.*

— Czechoslovakia.

HRONEK (JIŘÍ) Ein Land, dessen Volk sich selbst regiert: Nationalausschusswahlen in der Tschechoslowakei. Praha, 1954. pp. 24.

— Europe.

COUNCIL OF EUROPE. Division of Local Authorities. Information bulletin: municipal and regional matters. s-a., 1974 (no. 6)- Strasbourg.

— France.

BECQUART-LECLERCQ (JEANNE) Paradoxes du pouvoir local. Paris, [1976]. pp. 233. *(Fondation Nationale des Sciences Politiques. Travaux et Recherches de Science Politique. 38).*

FRANCE. Commission de Développement des Responsabilités Locales. 1976. Vivre ensemble: rapport ([and] annexes) [Olivier Guichard, chairman]. Paris, 1976. 2 vols. (in 1).

MACHIN (HOWARD) The prefect in French public administration. London, [1977]. pp. 210.

TARROW (SIDNEY G.) Between center and periphery: grassroots politicians in Italy and France. New Haven, 1977. pp. 272.

— Germany.

FREY (RAINER) ed. Kommunale Demokratie: Beiträge für die Praxis der kommunalen Selbstverwaltung. Bonn-Bad Godesberg, [1976]. pp. 304.

— Guyana.

MENEZES (MARY NOEL) British policy towards the Amerindians in British Guiana, 1803-1873. Oxford, 1977. pp. 326. *bibliog.*

— India.

CRAWFURD (JOHN) F.R.S. Letters from British settlers in the interior of India, descriptive of their own condition and that of the native inhabitants under the government of the East India Company. London, Ridgway, 1831. pp. vii,98.

— Ireland (Republic).

BAX (MART) Harpstrings and confessions: machine-style politics in the Irish Republic. Assen, 1976. pp. 224. *bibliog.*

— Italy.

TARROW (SIDNEY G.) Between center and periphery: grassroots politicians in Italy and France. New Haven, 1977. pp. 272.

— Mexico.

CACIQUISMO y poder politico en el Mexico rural; por Roger Bartra [and others]. Mexico, 1975. pp. 203.

— Niger.

HENTGEN (E.F.) L'organisation régionale et locale de la République du Niger. Niamey, Ecole Nationale d'Administration de Niamey, 1973. fo.130. *bibliog.*

— Norway.

BALDERSHEIM (HAROLD) Patterns of central control over local service provision in Norway. 1977. fo. 367. *bibliog. Typescript. Ph.D. (London) thesis: unpublished. This thesis is the property of London University and may not be removed from the Library.*

— Russia.

CHEKHARIN (IVAN MIKHAILOVICH) Postoiannye komissii mestnykh Sovetov. Moskva, 1975. pp. 176.

KARLOV (ALEKSANDR ALEKSANDROVICH) Mestnye Sovety deputatov trudiashchikhsia: voprosy organizatsii i deiatel'nosti. Moskva, 1975. pp. 184.

VASIL'EV (RUSLAN FEDOROVICH) Pravovye akty mestnykh Sovetov: ocherki o iuridicheskoi prirode. Moskva, 1975. pp. 152.

BARANCHIKOV (VLADIMIR ALEKSANDROVICH) Oblastnoi Sovet deputatov trudiashchikhsia. Moskva, 1976. pp. 160.

ELEONSKII (VLADIMIR ALEKSANDROVICH) Nabliudatel'nye komissii ispolkomov mestnykh Sovetov. Moskva, 1976. pp. 128.

KUTAFIN (OLEG EMEL'IANOVICH) Mestnye Sovety i narodnokhoziaistvennoe planirovanie. Moskva, 1976. pp. 142.

— — Moldavia.

HILL (RONALD J.) Soviet political elites: the case of Tiraspol. London, 1977. pp. 226. *bibliog.*

— — Russia (RSFSR).

RUSSIA (RSFSR). Verkhovnyi Sovet. Prezidium. Otdel po Voprosam Raboty Sovetov. 1975. Itogi vyborov i sostav deputatov mestnykh Sovetov deputatov trudiashchikhsia RSFSR 1975 g.: statisticheskii sbornik. Moskva, 1975. pp. 271.

ALEKSEEV (BORIS KONSTANTINOVICH) and PERFIL'EV (MARAT NIKOLAEVICH) Printsipy i tendentsii razvitiia predstavitel'nogo sostava mestnykh Sovetov: sotsiologicheskoe issledovanie. Leningrad, 1976. pp. 303.

ALESHCHENKO (NIKOLAI MIKHAILOVICH) Moskovskii Sovet v 1917-1941 gg. Moskva, 1976. pp. 591.

— Sweden.

BIRGERSSON (BENGT OWE) Kommunen som serviceproducent: kommunal service och serviceattityder i 36 svenska kommuner. [Stockholm, 1975]. pp. 195. *bibliog. (Stockholms Universitet. Statsvetenskapliga Institutionen. Stockholm Studies in Politics. 7) With English summary.* ·

— United Kingdom.

SANDERS (WILLIAM) Englische lokale Selbstverwaltung und ihre Erfolge. Berlin, 1908. pp. 42.

SCOTT (Sir LESLIE FREDERIC) Local government. Liverpool, 1949. pp. 31. *(Literary and Philosophical Society of Liverpool. Roscoe Lectures. 1949)*

LOCAL AUTHORITIES MANAGEMENT SERVICES AND COMPUTER COMMITTEE. Computer Panel. Computers in local authorities. London, 1970. pp. 23.

LOCAL AUTHORITIES MANAGEMENT SERVICES AND COMPUTER COMMITTEE. Computer Panel. Computer installations in local government and river authorities. London, 1972. pp. 14.

U.K. Commission for Local Administration in England. Report. a., 1975/76 [1st]- London.

CORINA (LEWIS) Local government decision making: some influences on elected members' role playing. [York, 1975]. pp. 39. *(Papers in Community Studies. No. 2)*

NORTON (ALAN LEWIS) and LONG (JOYCE R.) The community land legislation and its implementation: an analysis of the provisions of the 1975 Community Land Bill and government intentions for its implementation. Birmingham, 1975. pp. 38.

BENINGTON (JOHN) Local government becomes big business. 2nd. ed. London, 1976. pp. 28. *bibliog.*

GYFORD (JOHN) Local politics in Britain. London, [1976]. pp. 193. *bibliog.*

STANYER (JEFFREY) Understanding local government. Glasgow, 1976. pp. 320. *bibliog.*

WOOD (BRUCE) The process of local government reform, 1966-74. London, 1976. pp. 205.

COMMUNITY RELATIONS COMMISSION. The multi-racial community: a guide for local councillors. London, 1977. pp. 34. *bibliog.*

A CONSUMER'S guide to local government; edited by Martin Minogue for the National Consumer Council. London, 1977. pp. 196.

FABIAN SOCIETY. Fabian Tracts. [No.] 446. Labour and local politics; [by] John Gyford [and] Richard Baker. London, 1977. pp. 19. *(Fabian Society. Initiatives in Local Government. 4)*

KEITH-LUCAS (BRYAN) English local government in the nineteenth and twentieth centuries. London, [1977]. pp. 42. *bibliog. (Historical Association. General Series. G.90)*

LABOUR PARTY. Regional authorities and local government reform: a consultation document for the labour movement. London, 1977. pp. 28.

LOCAL government and the public; edited by Roy Darke and Ray Walker. London, 1977. pp. 255. *bibliogs.*

MINOGUE (MARTIN) ed. Documents on contemporary British government. Cambridge, 1977. 2 vols. *bibliogs.*

REGAN (DAVID EDWARD) Local government and education. London, 1977. pp. 265. *bibliog.*

U.K. Central Policy Review Staff. 1977. Relations between central government and local authorities; report. London, 1977. pp. 60.

— — Ireland, Northern.

IRELAND, NORTHERN. Commissioner for Complaints. Annual report. a., 1973 (6th) Belfast. *1968-1971 (1st-4th) included in IRELAND, NORTHERN. Parliament. House of Commons. [Papers]. 1972 (5th) included in British Parliamentary Papers session 1972/3, vol. 27 (H.C. Paper 158). 1974 onwards included in British Parliamentary Papers.*

— United States.

HAWKINS (ROBERT B.) Self government by district: myth and reality. Stanford, Calif., 1976. pp. 149. *bibliog. (Stanford University. Hoover Institution on War, Revolution and Peace. Hoover Institution Publications. 162)*

STATE and local government: the political economy of reform; edited by Alan K. Campbell and Roy W. Bahl. New York, [1976]. pp. 211. *Based on papers presented to a conference sponsored by the Metropolitan Studies Program of the Maxwell School of Citizenship and Public Affairs of Syracuse University.*

DANIELSON (MICHAEL NILS) and others. One nation, so many governments. Lexington, Mass., [1977]. pp. 141.

YIN (ROBERT K.) and others. Tinkering with the system: technological innovations in state and local services. Lexington, Mass., [1977]. pp. 275. *bibliog.*

— — Bibliography.

HUTCHESON (JOHN D.) and SHEVIN (JANN) compilers. Citizen groups in local politics: a bibliographic review. Santa Barbara, [1976]. pp. 275. *bibliogs.*

LOCAL GOVERNMENT OFFICIALS AND EMPLOYEES

— United Kingdom.

MALLABY (Sir HOWARD GEORGE CHARLES) Local government councillors: their motives and manners. Chichester, [1976]. pp. 20.

U.K. Local Government Staff Commission for England. 1977. The report of the...Commission; [Lord Greenwood of Rossendale, chairman]. London, 1977. pp. 160.

LOCAL TAXATION

In earlier volumes of the Bibliography similar material will be found under the heading LOCAL FINANCE.

— France.

FRANCE. Direction de la Documentation. La Documentation Française. Notes et Etudes Documentaires. Nos. 4,277-4,278. La modernisation de la fiscalité directe locale, 1959-1975; par Alain Delorme. Paris, 1976. pp. 45. *bibliog.*

LOCAL TRANSIT

— United Kingdom — Wales.

WRAGG (RICHARD) and REES (GRAHAM L.) A study of the passenger transport needs of urban Wales; prepared for the Welsh Council. [Cardiff, Welsh Council, 1977]. pp. 283.

LOCKE (JOHN).

MACKIE (JOHN LESLIE) Problems from Locke. Oxford, 1976. pp. 237. *bibliog.*

LOCKE on human understanding: selected essays; edited by I.C. Tipton. Oxford, [1977]. pp. 170. *bibliog.*

LODGE (HENRY CABOT).

LODGE (HENRY CABOT) 1902- . As it was: an inside view of politics and power in the '50s and '60s. New York, [1976]. pp. 224.

LÓDZ

— Social conditions.

NOWAKOWSKA (BARBARA) Wyksztalcenie mieszkańców Łodzi. Warszawa, 1974. pp. 183. *bibliog. (Instytut Polityki Naukowej i Szkolnictwa Wy'zszego. Monografie i Studia) With Russian and English summaries.*

LOGIC.

HENRY (DESMOND PAUL) Medieval logic and metaphysics: a modern introduction. London, 1972. pp. 133. *bibliog.*

EXPLANATION: papers and discussions by Peter Achinstein [and others]; edited by Stephan Körner. Oxford, [1975]. pp. 219. *Proceedings of a conference.*

ALLWOOD (JENS) and others. Logic in linguistics. Cambridge, 1977. pp. 185. *bibliog. Original Swedish edition entitled Logik för lingvister.*

LOGIC, SYMBOLIC AND MATHEMATICAL.

ESSAYS in memory of Imre Lakatos; edited by R.S. Cohen [and others]. Dordrecht, [1976]. pp. 767. *bibliog. (Boston Colloquium for the Philosophy of Science. Boston Studies in the Philosophy of Science. vol. 39)*

LOMBARDY

— Economic history.

FRUMENTO (ARMANDO) Miniere ferrose e altoforni lombardi del 1848 e del 1849 in un censimento inedito della I.R. Luogotenenza. Milano, 1975. pp. 31. *(Estratto da Archivio Storico Lombardo, 1974, Anno C)*

— History.

CAVANNA (ADRIANO) La codificazione penale in Italia: le origini lombarde. Milano, 1975. pp. 317. *(Milan. Università. Istituto di Storia del Diritto Italiano. Pubblicazioni. 5)*

LOMÉ, CONVENTION OF.

WALL (DAVID) The European Community's Lomé Convention: "STABEX" and the third world's aspirations. London, [1976]. fo. 22. *(Trade Policy Research Centre. Guest Papers. No. 4)*

EUROPEAN ECONOMIC COMMUNITY. Treaties. 1975- . Convention ACP-EEC of Lomé: collected acts. [Brussels, 1977 in progress]. 1 vol. (looseleaf).

The LOMÉ Convention and a new international economic order; edited by Frans A.M. Alting von Geusau. Leyden, 1977. pp. 249. *(John F. Kennedy Institute. Center for International Studies. Publications. Nr. 11) Based on papers from an international colloquium held by the Institute in 1975.*

LOMONOSOV (MIKHAIL VASIL'EVICH).

LYSTSOV (VIKENTII PAVLOVICH) M.V. Lomonosov o sotsial'no-ekonomicheskom razvitii Rossii. Voronezh, 1969. pp. 262. *bibliog.*

LONDON (JACK).

BARLTROP (ROBERT) Jack London: the man, the writer, the rebel. London, 1976. pp. 206.

LONDON

— Benevolent and moral institutions and societies.

STRANGERS' FRIEND SOCIETY. Committee. Report...(for the year 1818); with an account of some of the cases visited in the year 1817, etc. London, Butterworth, 1818. pp. 112.

— Bridges — Hammersmith Bridge.

DESCRIPTIVE particulars of the suspension bridge, Hammersmith; a list of tolls; with remarks on local objects and scenery: and a table, showing the distance of the towns, bridges, etc., from London to Windsor by water. 2nd ed. Hammersmith, Page, 1828. pp. 12.

— Census.

COLE (B.) Social and economic indices for London constituencies, 1971 census. London, [1976]. pp. 46. *(London. Greater London Council. Research Memoranda. 502)*

MORREY (C.R.) 1971 census: demographic, social and economic indices for wards in Greater London. London, [1976]. 2 vols. (in 1). *bibliog. (London. Greater London Council. Research Reports. 20)*

— Charities, Medical.

ROYAL STATISTICAL SOCIETY. Committee on Beneficent Institutions. First report...1. The medical charities of the metropolis. London, Parker, 1857. pp. 68.

— Church history — Sources.

LONDON. London Record Society. Publications. vol. 13. The church in London, 1375-1392; [edited by] A.K. McHardy. London, 1977. pp. 126.

— City planning.

LITTLE (F.M.) and STANNARD (ROBERT B.) The King's Reach cost-benefit study: a case study of central London redevelopment. [London], Greater London Council, 1967. fo. (22).

LONDON. Greater London Council. Planned growth outside London; report. [London], 1975. pp. (31).

DOCKLANDS JOINT COMMITTEE. London docklands strategic plan. London, [1976]. pp. 115.

EYLES (JOHN D.) Environmental satisfaction and London's docklands: problems and policies in the Isle of Dogs. London, 1976. pp. 31. *bibliog. (London. University. Queen Mary College. Department of Geography. Occasional Papers. No. 5)*

LONDON. Greater London Council. Planned growth outside London: consultations; report. [London], 1976. 1 vol. (various pagings).

LONDON looks forward: [conference held in London, 1977]; conference background papers, nos. 1-7. [London, 1977]. 7 pts. (in 1 vol.). *bibliogs.*

SHANKLAND-COX PARTNERSHIP and INSTITUTE OF COMMUNITY STUDIES. Inner London: policies for dispersal and balance: final report of the Lambeth inner area study. London, H.M.S.O., 1977. pp. 243. *bibliog.*

— Commerce.

WILSON (JOHN STUART GLADSTONE) The London money markets. Tilburg, 1976. pp. 70. *(Société Universitaire Européenne de Recherches Financières. Série SUERF. 17A)*

— — Bibliography.

SMITH (GERRY M.) compiler. The financial activities of the City of London: a select bibliography. London, 1976. pp. 27. *(City University. Business School. Business School Bibliographies. No. 1)*

— Docks.

DOCKLANDS JOINT COMMITTEE. London docklands strategic plan. London, [1976]. pp. 115.

EYLES (JOHN D.) Environmental satisfaction and London's docklands: problems and policies in the Isle of Dogs. London, 1976. pp. 31. *bibliog. (London. University. Queen Mary College. Department of Geography. Occasional Papers. No. 5)*

— Economic conditions.

LONDON looks forward: [conference held in London, 1977]; conference background papers, nos. 1-7. [London, 1977]. 7 pts. (in 1 vol.). *bibliogs.*

— Exhibitions.

A TONIC to the nation: the Festival of Britain, 1951; (edited by Mary Banham and Bevis Hillier); with a prologue by Roy Strong. London, [1976]. pp. 200.

— Foreign population.

LEE (TREVOR ROSS) Race and residence: the concentration and dispersal of immigrants in London. Oxford, 1977. pp. 193. *bibliog.*

— Gilds — Butchers' Company.

JONES (PHILIP EDMUND) The butchers of London: a history of the Worshipful Company of Butchers of the City of London. London, 1976. pp. 246.

— Growth.

OLSEN (DONALD JAMES) The growth of Victorian London. London, 1976. pp. 384.

— History.

MYERS (ALEC REGINALD) London in the age of Chaucer. Norman, Okla., 1972 repr. 1974. pp. 239. *bibliog.*

OLSEN (DONALD JAMES) The growth of Victorian London. London, 1976. pp. 384.

LONDON in the age of reform; edited by John Stevenson. Oxford, [1977]. pp. 214. *bibliog.*

— Industries.

KNIGHT (D.R.W.) and others. The structure of employment in Greater London, 1961-81. London, [1977]. pp. 53. *(London. Greater London Council. Research Memoranda. 501)*

SHANKLAND-COX PARTNERSHIP and INSTITUTE OF COMMUNITY STUDIES. Inner area study: Lambeth: local employers' study. [London], Department of the Environment, [1977]. pp. 88.

— — Bibliography.

COCKETT (IEN) compiler. Statistics concerning employment in London. London, 1977. 1 pamphlet (various pagings). *(London. Greater London Council. Research Library. Research Bibliographies. No. 85)*

— Lodging houses.

CHESTERTON (ADA ELIZABETH) In darkest London. London, 1926. pp. 255.

— Officials and employees.

The MANNING of public services in London; a study by a joint group of officials of the Department of the Environment, the Department of Employment, the Greater London Council, and the London Boroughs Association; [T.H. Shearer, chairman]. London, Department of the Environment, 1975. pp. 120.

LONDON. Greater London Council. Members' Working Party on Industrial Democracy. Industrial democracy in local government: papers considered by a working party of GLC/ILEA members: together with the working party's final report. [London, 1977]. pp. 44.

— Parks.

POULSEN (CHARLES) Victoria Park: a study in the history of east London. London, 1976. pp. 117. *bibliog.*

— Police.

MILLER (WILBUR R.) Cops and bobbies: police authority in New York and London, 1830-1870. Chicago, 1977. pp. 233. *bibliog.*

— Politics and government.

FOSTER (FRANK FREEMAN) The politics of stability: a portrait of the rulers in Elizabethan London. London, 1977. pp. 209. *(Royal Historical Society. Studies in History)*

KNOTT (SIMON) The electoral crucible: the politics of London, 1900-1914. [London, 1977]. pp. 194. *bibliog.*

LONDON in the age of reform; edited by John Stevenson. Oxford, [1977]. pp. 214. *bibliog.*

WILCOX (DAVID) and RICHARDS (DAVID) London: the heartless city. London, 1977. pp. 172. *bibliogs.*

— Poor.

CHESTERTON (ADA ELIZABETH) In darkest London. London, 1926. pp. 255.

— Population — Mathematical models.

BONNAR (DESMOND M.) Stochastic models for migration analysis: applications to Greater London. Reading, 1976. pp. 44. *bibliog. (Reading. University. Department of Geography. Reading Geographical Papers. No. 51)*

— Race question.

PARKER (JOHN) Writer on housing, and DUGMORE (KEITH) Colour and the allocation of GLC housing: the report of the GLC lettings survey, 1974-75. [London], 1976. 1 vol. (various pagings). *bibliog. (London. Greater London Council. Research Reports. No. 21)*

LONDON HOUSING RESEARCH GROUP. Working Party on Race and Housing. Race and local authority housing: information on ethnic groups; a report; [Rob Hammond, chairman]. London, Community Relations Commission, 1977. pp. 16.

— Social conditions.

CHESTERTON (ADA ELIZABETH) In darkest London. London, 1926. pp. 255.

LONDON looks forward: [conference held in London, 1977]; conference background papers, nos. 1-7. [London, 1977]. 7 pts. (in 1 vol.). *bibliogs.*

O'MALLEY (JAN) The politics of community action: a decade of struggle in Notting Hill. Nottingham, 1977. pp. 180.

WILCOX (DAVID) and RICHARDS (DAVID) London: the heartless city. London, 1977. pp. 172. *bibliogs.*

— Social history.

WOHL (ANTHONY STEPHEN) The eternal slum: housing and social policy in Victorian London. London, 1977. pp. 386. *bibliog.*

— Social policy.

PINCH (STEVEN PAUL) The geography of local authority housing, health and welfare, resource allocation in London, 1965-1973. 1976. fo. 632. *bibliog. Typescript. Ph.D. (London) thesis: unpublished. This thesis is the property of London University and may not be removed from the Library.*

— Stock Exchange.

LONDON. Stock Exchange. Financial Information Services. Second one-day transaction study, 8th October, 1975. [London, 1976]. pp. 22.

— **Transit systems.**

LONDON. Greater London Council. Transport policy consultation document: Greater London Council's comments. London, 1976. pp. 7.

LONDON TRANSPORT EXECUTIVE. Comments on Transport policy: a consultation document. London, 1976. pp. (14), 3.

SOUTH east London bus study; report of the steering group; members of the steering group: officers of the Greater London Council and London Transport Executive; [D.A. Quarmby, chairman]. [London, Greater London Council], 1976. pp. 61, fo. 39.

LONDON UNIVERSITY

— **London School of Economics and Political Science.**

MY LSE; [by] Chaim Bermant [and others]; edited and introduced by Joan Abse. London, 1977. pp. 223.

LONG-TERM CARE OF THE SICK.

ELLIOTT (JAMES R.) Living in hospital: the social needs of people in long-term care. London, 1975. pp. 84. *bibliog.*

LONGEVITY.

[SINCLAIR (Sir JOHN)] Hints on longevity: (drawn up with the view of being inserted in the Analysis of the statistical account of Scotland, etc.). [London], printed by W. Bulmer, [1802]. pp. 12.

LONGFIELD (MOUNTIFORT).

MOSS (LAURENCE S.) Mountifort Longfield: Ireland's first professor of political economy. Ottawa, Ill., 1976. pp. 249. *bibliog.*

LOPEZ (JUAN).

LOPEZ (JUAN) Una mision sin importancia: memorias de un sindicalista. Madrid, [1972]. pp. 269.

LORENZO (GIOVANNI DE).

COLLIN (RICHARD) The de Lorenzo gambit: the Italian coup manqué of 1964. Beverly Hills, [1976]. pp. 65.

LORRAINE

— **Economic conditions.**

BURTENSHAW (DAVID) Saar-Lorraine. London, 1976. pp. 48. *bibliog.*

— **Industries.**

GRAU (C.) Evolution de l'emploi industriel salarié en Lorraine de 1965 à 1972. Nancy, Echelon Régional de l'Emploi de Nancy, 1975. fo. 201.

— **Social conditions.**

BURTENSHAW (DAVID) Saar-Lorraine. London, 1976. pp. 48. *bibliog.*

LOS ANGELES

— **Race question.**

RABINOVITZ (FRANCINE F.) and SIEMBIEDA (WILLIAM J.) Minorities in suburbs: the Los Angeles experience. Lexington, Mass., [1977]. pp. 100. *bibliog.*

— **Suburbs and environs.**

RABINOVITZ (FRANCINE F.) and SIEMBIEDA (WILLIAM J.) Minorities in suburbs: the Los Angeles experience. Lexington, Mass., [1977]. pp. 100. *bibliog.*

LOT VALLEY.

ETUDE des paysages de la Vallée du Lot; [by] Yves Le Bars [and others]. [Cahors?], Ministère de l'Agriculture et du Développement Rural, 1973. pp. 147. *bibliog. Transparent map in end pocket.*

LOUISIANA

— **History.**

TAYLOR (JOE GRAY) Louisiana reconstructed, 1863-1877. Baton Rouge, La., [1974]. pp. 552. *bibliog.*

LOVE STORIES.

MANN (PETER HENRY) A new survey: the facts about romantic fiction;...in collaboration with Mills and Boon Ltd. London, [1974]. pp. 24.

LUANDA

— **Social conditions.**

VALENTE (ANTUNES) and OLIVEIRA (J. CASIMIRO F. D') Alguns aspectos socio-economicos da Ilha do Cabo, Luanda. [Luanda, Instituto de Investigação Cientifica de Angola], 1966. pp. 263-286. *(Offprint from the Boletim do Instituto de Investigação Cientifica de Angola, 3(2), 1966) With abstracts in English and French.*

LUBLIN

— **History.**

SZCZYGIEŁ (RYSZARD) Konflikty społeczne w Lublinie w pierwszej połowie XVI wieku. Warszawa, 1977. pp. 197. *bibliog. (Lubelskie Towarzystwo Naukowe. Wydział Humanistyczny. Prace. Monografie. t.6)*

LUBUMBASHI

— **History.**

FETTER (BRUCE) The creation of Elisabethville, 1910-1940. Stanford, [1976]. pp. 211. *(Stanford University. Hoover Institution on War, Revolution and Peace. Hoover Institution Publications. 154)*

LUCCA

— **Economic history.**

PELÙ (PAOLO) Priorità della mercatura lucchese in alcune forme collettive di investimento aziendale nel XIV e XV secolo. Lucca, 1974. pp. 27.

LUDENDORFF (ERICH FRIEDRICH WILHELM).

KITCHEN (MARTIN) The silent dictatorship: the politics of the German High Command under Hindenburg and Ludendorff, 1916-1918. London, [1976]. pp. 301. *bibliog.*

LUDWIGSBURG

— **History.**

HEINEN-TENRICH (JUERGEN) Die Entwicklung Ludwigsburgs zur multifunktionalen Mittelstadt, 1860-1914: ein Beitrag zur Untersuchung des Wandels der Stadt im 19. Jahrhundert. Stuttgart, 1976. pp. 102. *bibliog. (Kommission für Geschichtliche Landeskunde in Baden-Württemberg. Veröffentlichungen. Reihe B: Forschungen. 79. Band) 21 tables appended.*

LUKÁCS (GEORG).

GRUNENBERG (ANTONIA) Bürger und Revolutionär: Georg Lukács, 1918-1928. Köln, [1976]. pp. 301. *bibliog.*

LOWY (MICHAEL) Pour une sociologie des intellectuels révolutionnaires: l'évolution politique de Lukacs, 1909-1929. Paris, [1976]. pp. 319. *bibliog.*

LUMUMBA (PATRICE).

PATRICE Lumumba. London, [1973]. pp. 215.

LUNACHARSKII (ANATOLII VASIL'EVICH).

O Lunacharskom: issledovaniia, vospominaniia. Moskva, 1976. pp. 192. *bibliog.*

PATSURIIA (LARISA B.) A.V. Lunacharskii i intelligentsiia Zakavkaz'ia. Tbilisi, 1976. pp. 144.

REKUTS (IVAN FEODOS'EVICH) Filosofskie problemy kritiki religii v ateisticheskom nasledii A.V. Lunacharskogo. Minsk, 1976. pp. 174. *bibliog.*

LUND

— **Social history.**

EK (SVEN B.) 14 augusti 1894: en bok om arbetarna i bokbinderi och emballageindustri i Lund. Lund, 1974. pp. 135. *bibliog. (Etnologiska Sällskapet i Lund. Skrifter. 5) With English summary.*

LUSATIA

— **Social history.**

SCHOENE (BERND) Kultur und Lebensweise Lausitzer Bandweber, 1750-1850. Berlin, 1977. pp. 197. *bibliog. (Akademie der Wissenschaften der DDR. Zentralinstitut für Geschichte. Veröffentlichungen zur Volkskunde und Kulturgeschichte. Band 64)*

LUTHER (HANS).

GERMANY. Reichskanzlei. 1925-1926. Die Kabinette Luther I und II: 15. Januar 1925 bis 20. Januar 1926, 20. Januar 1926 bis 17. Mai 1926; bearbeitet von Karl-Heinz Minuth. Boppard am Rhein, 1977. 2 vols. *bibliog. (Akten der Reichskanzlei, Weimarer Republik)*

LUTHER (MARTIN).

DICKENS (ARTHUR GEOFFREY) The German nation and Martin Luther. Glasgow, 1976. pp. 254. *bibliog. First published in London, 1974.*

LUXEMBOURG

— **Economic history.**

HOUTTE (JAN A. VAN) An economic history of the Low Countries, 800-1800. London, [1977]. pp. 342. *bibliog.*

— **History.**

KOCH-KENT (HENRI) and others. Hitlertum in Luxemburg, 1933-1944: Beiträge zur Zeitgeschichte. [Luxembourg, 1972]. pp. 47. *3 papers presented at the congress of the Association des Enrôlés de Force, Victimes du Nazisme, held in Walferdingen in 1972.*

LUXEMBURG (ROSA).

LUXEMBURG (ROSA) Lettere dal carcere; traduzione italiana di Amalia Sacerdote. Milano, 1922. pp. 16. *Letters to Sophie Liebknecht only; with a preface by Gustavo Sacerdote.*

LUXEMBURG (ROSA) The national question: selected writings; edited and with an introduction by Horace B. Davis. New York, [1976]. pp. 320. *Articles from Przegląd socjaldemokratyczny, 1908-1909, in English translation.*

LUXURY.

MEMOIRE sur la question proposée en 1779, par la Société de bienfaisance et d'encouragement établie à Basle: savoir, jusqu'à quel point il est à propos de régler la dépense des citoyens dans une république, dont la prospérité est fondée sur le commerce. Basle, chez Jean-Jacques Flick, 1781. pp. 40.

L'VOV

— **Massacre.**

[TENENBAUM (JOSEF)] Der Lemberger Judenpogrom, November 1918-Jänner 1919; von Joseph Bendow [pseud.]. Wien, 1919. pp. 167.

LYTHE (SAMUEL GEORGE EDGAR).

SCOTTISH themes: essays in honour of Professor S.G.E. Lythe; edited by John Butt and J.T. Ward. Edinburgh, 1976. pp. 189. *bibliog.*

MACAULAY (HERBERT).

TAMUNO (TEKENA NITONYE) Herbert Macaulay, Nigerian patriot. London, 1975. pp. 48.

MACAULAY (THOMAS BABINGTON) Baron Macaulay.

HAMBURGER (JOSEPH) Macaulay and the Whig tradition. Chicago, 1976. pp. 274.

MACCHIAVELLI (NICCOLÒ).

MARCHAND (JEAN JACQUES) Niccolò Machiavelli: I primi scritti politici, 1499-1512; nascita di un pensiero e di uno stile. Padova, 1975. pp. 542. *bibliog.*

GILBERT (FELIX) History: choice and commitment. Cambridge, Mass., 1977. pp. 549. *bibliog. Selected essays.*

MACDONALD (JAMES RAMSAY).

MARQUAND (DAVID) Ramsay MacDonald. London, 1977. pp. 903.

MACDONALD (Sir JOHN ALEXANDER).

WAITE (PETER BUSBY) Macdonald: his life and world. Toronto, [1975]. pp. 224. *bibliog.*

MACEDONIAN QUESTION.

BOBCHEV (STEFAN SAVOV) Pis'ma o Makedonii i makedonskom voprose. [rev.ed.]. S.-Peterburg, 1889. pp. 84. *Earlier versions published in Varshavskii dnevnik and Slavianskie izvestiia.*

MACHINE THEORY.

TREMBLAY (JEAN PAUL) and MANOHAR (RAM P.) Discrete mathematical structures with applications to computer science. New York, [1975]. pp. 606.

MACHINE-TOOLS

— Trade and manufacture — Information services.

UNITED NATIONS INDUSTRIAL DEVELOPMENT ORGANIZATION. Guides to Information Sources. No. 22. Information sources on the machine tool industry. (ID/168) (UNIDO/LIB/SER.D/22). New York, United Nations, 1976. pp. 71. *bibliog.*

— — France.

L'INDUSTRIE française de la machine-outil: perspectives d'évolution: (rapport des six groupes de travail spécialisés et de la commission administrative constitués au Ministère de l'Industrie et de la Recherche). Paris, [1976]. pp. 80. *(France. Ministère de l'Industrie et de la Recherche. Etudes de Politique Industrielle. 13) Alternative title reads: Perspectives d'évolution à moyen terme du secteur de la machine-outil.*

— — United Kingdom.

FLOUD (RODERICK) The British machine tool industry, 1850-1914. Cambridge, 1976. pp. 217. *bibliog.*

NATIONAL ECONOMIC DEVELOPMENT OFFICE. Manpower and Industrial Relations Division. Machine tools: the employees' view of the industry;...study... carried out for the Machine Tools E[conomic] D[evelopment] C[ommittee]. London, 1977. pp. 47.

MACHINERY IN INDUSTRY.

McCUTCHEON (ALAN) Wheel and spindle: aspects of Irish industrial history. Belfast, [1977]. pp. 84. *bibliog.*

YELLOWITZ (IRWIN) Industrialization and the American labor movement, 1850-1900. Port Washington, N.Y., 1977, pp. 183. *bibliog.*

McKAY (HENRY DONALD).

DELINQUENCY, crime and society; edited by James F. Short. Chicago, [1976]. pp. 325. *bibliogs. Mainly papers originally presented at the Symposium on Juvenile Delinquency, University of Chicago, 1972, held to honour Henry Donald McKay.*

MACKINDER (Sir HALFORD JOHN)

— Bibliography.

GAINSBOROUGH. Public Library. Local History Handbooks. No. 7. Halford J. Mackinder, 1861-1947: [biographical notes and bibliography]. Gainsborough, 1974. pp. 5.

MADAGASCAR

— Economic conditions — Statistics.

MADAGASCAR. Institut National de la Statistique et de la Recherche Economique. 1969. Inventaire socio-économique, (1964-1968). [Tananarive], 1969. 2 vols. (in 1).

— Economic policy.

MADAGASCAR. Ministère du Plan. 1974. Plan de développement national, 1974-1977; traduit par la Direction du Plan. Tananarive, 1974. pp. 201.

— History.

RALAIMIHOATRA (EDOUARD) Histoire de Madagascar. 2nd ed. Tananarive, [1969]. pp. 325. *bibliog.*

— Social conditions — Statistics.

MADAGASCAR. Institut National de la Statistique et de la Recherche Economique. 1969. Inventaire socio-économique, (1964-1968). [Tananarive], 1969. 2 vols. (in 1).

— Social policy.

MADAGASCAR. Ministère du Plan. 1974. Plan de développement national, 1974-1977; traduit par la Direction du Plan. Tananarive, 1974. pp. 201.

MADEIRA

— Statistics.

MADEIRA. Delegação do Instituto Nacional de Estatistica do Funchal. Boletim trimestral de estatistica, arquipelago de Madeira. q., 1972 (año 1, no.1)- Funchal.

MADERO (FRANCISCO INDALECIO).

CAMBRIDGE. University. Centre of Latin American Studies. Working Papers. No.12. Some aspects of economic change and the origins of the Mexican revolution, 1876-1910; [by Dudley Ankerson]. Cambridge, [1973]. fo.40. *Photocopy.*

MADHYA BHARAT

— Statistics.

STATISTICS OF MADHYA BHARAT; [pd. by] Central Economic and Statistical Organisation. a., 1951/52. Gwalior.

MADOX (RICHARD).

MADOX (RICHARD) An Elizabethan in 1582: the diary of Richard Madox, Fellow of All Souls; [edited] by Elizabeth Story Donno. London, 1976. pp. 365. *(Hakluyt Society. Works. 2nd Series. No. 147)*

MADRAS

— Nationalism.

BARNETT (MARGUERITE ROSS) The politics of cultural nationalism in South India. Princeton, N.J., [1976]. pp. 368. *bibliog.*

— Politics and government.

BARNETT (MARGUERITE ROSS) The politics of cultural nationalism in South India. Princeton, N.J., [1976]. pp. 368. *bibliog.*

WASHBROOK (D.A.) The emergence of provincial politics: the Madras Presidency, 1870-1920. Cambridge, 1976. pp. 358. *bibliog. (Cambridge. University. Centre of South Asian Studies. Cambridge South Asian Studies. No. 18)*

MADRID

— History.

HILLS (GEORGE) The battle for Madrid. London, 1976. pp. 192. *bibliog.*

MADSEN (ARNE and INGER BUSK).

EUROPEAN COURT OF HUMAN RIGHTS. Publications. Series A: Judgments and Decisions. [A 23]. ...Case of Kjeldsen, Busk Madsen and Pedersen: judgment of 7 December 1976. Strasbourg, Council of Europe, 1976. pp. 33 [bis]. *In English and French.*

MAGIC.

BRUNO (GIORDANO) The Ash Wednesday supper: La cena de le Ceneri; translated with an introduction and notes by Stanley L. Jaki. The Hague, [1975]. pp. 174.

MAHARASHTRA

— Economic policy.

MAHARASHTRA. Planning Department. Annual plan. a., 1972/73 (pt.2), 1973/74 (pt.2), 1974/75- Bombay.

— Social policy.

MAHARASHTRA. Planning Department. Annual plan. a., 1972/73 (pt.2), 1973/74 (pt.2), 1974/75- Bombay.

MAINE (Sir HENRY SUMNER).

COXALL (WILLIAM NORMAN) Two Victorian theorists of democracy: a comparative study of Sir Henry Maine and Matthew Arnold. 1977. fo. 347. *bibliog. Typescript. Ph.D. (London) thesis: unpublished. This thesis is the property of London University and may not be removed from the Library.*

MAITLAND (FREDERIC WILLIAM).

MAITLAND (FREDERIC WILLIAM) Letters to George Neilson; edited by E.L.G. Stones. Glasgow, 1976. pp. 56. *bibliog.*

MAIZE

— Panama.

PANAMA. Direccion de Estadistica y Censo. Estadistica panameña. Superficie sembrada y cosecha de arroz, maiz y frijol de bejuco. a., 1975/76- Panama. *Supersedes in part PANAMA. Direccion de Estadistica y Censo. Estadistica panameña. Serie H. Informacion agropecuaria.*

— Tanzania.

MOHELE (A.T.) The Ismani maize credit programme. Dar es Salaam, 1975. pp. 51. *(Dar es Salaam. University. Economic Research Bureau. ERB Papers. 75.2)*

MAJORCA

— History.

MELIA (JOSEP) Los mallorquines; (traduccion y notas de Gabriel Cisneros). Madrid, 1968. pp. 257. *bibliog.*

— Politics and government.

LLULL (ANSELM) El mallorquinisme politic, 1840-1936: del regionalisme al nacionalisme. Paris, 1975. 2 vols. *bibliog.*

— Social life and customs.

MELIA (JOSEP) Los mallorquines; (traduccion y notas de Gabriel Cisneros). Madrid, 1968. pp. 257. *bibliog.*

MAJORITIES.

FAVRE (PIERRE) La décision de majorité. [Paris, 1976]. pp. 326. *bibliogs. (Fondation Nationale des Sciences Politiques. Cahiers. 205)*

MALAWI

— Foreign relations.

BANDA (HASTINGS KAMUZU) [Various speeches, press conferences and broadcasts, 1966 to 1970]. Blantyre, Department of Information, 1966-1970. 25 pts. (in 1 vol.)

— History.

FROM Nyasaland to Malawi: studies in colonial history; edited by Roderick J. Macdonald. Nairobi, 1975. pp. 316.

— Politics and government.

BANDA (HASTINGS KAMUZU) [Various speeches, press conferences and broadcasts, 1966 to 1970]. Blantyre, Department of Information, 1966-1970. 25 pts. (in 1 vol.)

McCRACKEN (K. JOHN) Politics and Christianity in Malawi 1875-1940: the impact of the Livingstonia Mission in the Northern Province. Cambridge, 1977. pp. 324. bibliog.

MALAYA

— Legislative Council — Rules and practice.

FEDERATION OF MALAYA. Legislative Council. 1948. Standing rules and orders of the Legislative Council. Kuala Lumpur, 1948. fo. 29.

MALAYANS IN SINGAPORE.

KASSIM (ISMAIL) Problems of elite cohesion: a perspective from a minority community. Singapore, [1974]. pp. 146. bibliog.

MALAYSIA

— Appropriations and expenditures.

FEDERATION OF MALAYSIA. Treasury. Expenditure budget of the federal government (formerly Budget summary of federal government expenditure). a., 1969-1975. Kuala Lumpur.

— Biography.

WHO'S who in Malaysia, 1975-1976 and guide to Singapore; edited and published by J. Victor Morais. Kuala Lumpur, [1976]. 1 vol. (various pagings).

— Commerce.

THOBURN (JOHN T.) Primary commodity exports and economic development: theory, evidence and a study of Malaysia. London, [1977]. pp. 310. bibliog.

— Constitutional history.

THIO (EUNICE) British policy in the Malay peninsula, 1880-1910. Kuala Lumpur, 1969 in progress. bibliog.

SADKA (EMILY) The protected Malay states, 1874-1895. Singapore, 1968. pp. 464. bibliog.

— Defences.

CHIN (KIN WAH) The Anglo-Malayan (Malaysian) defence agreement: a study in alliance transformation. 1977. fo. 448. bibliog. Typescript. Ph.D. (London) thesis: unpublished. This thesis is the property of London University and may not be removed from the Library. With printed article in end pocket.

— Economic conditions.

THOBURN (JOHN T.) Primary commodity exports and economic development: theory, evidence and a study of Malaysia. London, [1977]. pp. 310. bibliog.

— Economic policy.

FEDERATION OF MALAYSIA. Ministry of National and Rural Development. 1966. First Malaysia plan: full text of speech by Deputy Prime Minister and Minister for National and Rural Development, Tun Abdul Razak bin Hussein, in moving the adoption of the first Malaysia plan 1966-70 at the House of Representatives on 15th December 1965. [Kuala Lumpur, 1966?]. pp. 22.

RAZAK BIN HUSSEIN (TUN ABDUL) Highlights of the second Malaysia plan, 1971-1975: statement by the Prime Minister...at the press conference at the National Operations Room, Kuala Lumpur, on May 27, 1971. [Kuala Lumpur, 1971]. pp. 15.

RUDNER (MARTIN) Nationalism, planning, and economic modernization in Malaysia: the politics of beginning development. Beverly Hills, [1975]. pp. 85. bibliog.

— History.

THIO (EUNICE) British policy in the Malay peninsula, 1880-1910. Kuala Lumpur, 1969 in progress. bibliog.

SADKA (EMILY) The protected Malay states, 1874-1895. Singapore, 1968. pp. 464. bibliog.

RYAN (NEIL JOSEPH) A history of Malaysia and Singapore. Kuala Lumpur, 1976. pp. 322. bibliog. A revised edition of the 4th edition of the author's The making of modern Malaysia.

— Politics and government.

FEDERATION OF MALAYSIA. National Operations Council. 1969. The May 13 tragedy; a report. Kuala Lumpur, 1969. pp. 96.

RUDNER (MARTIN) Nationalism, planning, and economic modernization in Malaysia: the politics of beginning development. Beverly Hills, [1975]. pp. 85. bibliog.

SHAW (WILLIAM) Author of Tun Razak. Tun Razak: his life and times. London, 1976. pp. 267. bibliog.

— Population.

NATIONAL SEMINAR ON GENERAL CONSEQUENCES OF POPULATION GROWTH, 2ND, KUALA LUMPUR, 1970. Proceedings of the...Seminar, etc. Kuala Lumpur, National Family Planning Board, [1970?]. pp. 189.

— — Bibliography.

SAW (SWEE-HOCK) and CHENG (SIOK-HWA) compilers. A bibliography of the demography of Malaysia and Brunei. Singapore, 1975. pp. 103.

— Race question.

FEDERATION OF MALAYSIA. National Operations Council. 1969. The May 13 tragedy; a report. Kuala Lumpur, 1969. pp. 96.

— Relations (military) with the United Kingdom.

CHIN (KIN WAH) The Anglo-Malayan (Malaysian) defence agreement: a study in alliance transformation. 1977. fo. 448. bibliog. Typescript. Ph.D. (London) thesis: unpublished. This thesis is the property of London University and may not be removed from the Library. With printed article in end pocket.

— Rural conditions.

BAILEY (CONNER) Broker, mediator, patron, and kinsman: an historical analysis of key leadership roles in a rural Malaysian district. Athens, Ohio, [1976]. pp. 79. bibliog. (Ohio University. Center for International Studies. Papers in International Studies. Southeast Asia Series. No. 38)

— Social policy.

RAZAK BIN HUSSEIN (TUN ABDUL) Highlights of the second Malaysia plan, 1971-1975: statement by the Prime Minister...at the press conference at the National Operations Room, Kuala Lumpur, on May 27, 1971. [Kuala Lumpur, 1971]. pp. 15.

MALCOLM X, pseud.

BREITMAN (GEORGE) and others. The assassination of Malcolm X; edited with an introduction by Malik Miah. New York, [1976]. pp.190. Articles reprinted from various sources.

MALI (REPUBLIC)

— Economic policy.

JONES (WILLIAM I.) Planning and economic policy: socialist Mali and her neighbors. Washington, D.C., 1976. pp. 422. bibliog.

— Rural conditions.

ERNST (KLAUS) Tradition and progress in the African village: the non- capitalist transformation of rural communities in Mali; (translated from the German). London, 1976. pp. 262. bibliog.

MALIK (MICHAEL ABDUL).

HUMPHRY (DEREK) and TINDALL (DAVID) False messiah: the story of Michael X. London, 1977. pp. 221.

MALINDI

— History.

MARTIN (ESMOND BRADLEY) The history of Malindi: a geographical analysis of an East African coastal town from the Portuguese period to the present. Nairobi, 1973. pp. 301. bibliog.

MALMÖ

— Social conditions.

DAHLIN (LARS) Levnadsniva och hälsotillstånd: utnyttjande av social och medicinsk service i tre Malmödistrikt: (Level of living, health and utilization of social and health services...in Malmö). Malmö, 1975. pp. 141. bibliog. In Swedish, with English summary.

MALNUTRITION.

CARSON (GUY) and others. Nutrition and underdevelopment. [Toronto, 1974]. pp. 69. bibliog.

ECKHOLM (ERIK P.) and RECORD (FRANK) The two faces of malnutrition. Washington, 1976. pp. 63. (Worldwatch Institute. Worldwatch Papers. No. 9)

MALRAUX (CLARA).

MALRAUX (CLARA) La fin et le commencement. Paris, [1976]. pp. 230. (Le bruit de nos pas. 5)

MALTA

— Constitution.

MALTA. Constitution. 1964-74. Constitution of the republic of Malta. [Valletta], 1975. pp. 102.

— Economic conditions.

MALTA. Economic Division. Economic survey. a., 1973, 1975- [Valletta].

METWALLY (MOKHTAR M.) Structure and performance of the Maltese economy. [Valletta , 1977]. pp. 169.

— Economic policy.

MALTA. Prime Minister's Office. 1974. Development plan for Malta, 1973-1980. [Valletta], 1974. pp. 206.

— Social policy.

MALTA. Prime Minister's Office. 1974. Development plan for Malta, 1973-1980. [Valletta], 1974. pp. 206.

MALTHUSIANISM.

MIREAUX (EMILE) Actualité de Malthus. Paris, [1965]. pp. 16. Address at the Séance Publique Annuelle for 1965 of the Académie des Sciences Morales et Politiques.

MÁLYUSZ (ELEMÉR).

ALBUM Elemér Mályusz. Bruxelles, 1976. pp. 404. bibliogs. (International Commission for the History of Representative and Parliamentary Institutions. Studies. 56) In English, French, German and Spanish.

MAN.

LENGRAND (PAUL) An introduction to lifelong education. Paris, United Nations Educational, Scientific and Cultural Organization, 1975. pp. 156.

EVOLUTION and consciousness: human systems in transition; edited by Erich Jantsch and Conrad Waddington. Reading, Mass., 1976. pp. 259. *bibliogs.*

HOLLIS (MARTIN) Models of man: philosophical thoughts on social action. Cambridge, 1977. pp. 198. *bibliog.*

— Animal nature.

LEACH (Sir EDMUND RONALD) Humanity and animality. London, [1972]. pp. 20. *(South Place Ethical Society. Conway Memorial Lectures. 1972)*

MAN-MACHINE SYSTEMS.

CONFERENCE ON THE HUMAN OPERATOR IN COMPLEX SYSTEMS, BIRMINGHAM, 1966. Proceedings...; edited by W.T. Singleton [and others] on behalf of the University of Aston in Birmingham and the Industrial Section of the Ergonomics Research Society. London, 1967 repr. 1971. pp. 198. *bibliog.*

MANAGEMENT.

MORRIS (B.R.) Statistical information for recruitment policy and management: a report of a review of statistical work in the Civil Service Commission. [London], 1969. pp. 49. *(U.K. Civil Service Department. Statistics Division. [Statistical Review Series]. R-02)*

UNITED NATIONS INDUSTRIAL DEVELOPMENT ORGANIZATION. 1972. The development of management consultancy in Latin America: report of UNIDO meeting held in Santiago, Chile 5-9 July 1971. (ID/89). New York, United Nations, 1972. pp. 27.

UNITED NATIONS INDUSTRIAL DEVELOPMENT ORGANIZATION. 1973. The development of management consultancy, with special reference to Latin America: a digest of papers presented to the UNIDO meeting held at Santiago, Chile, July 1971. (ID/95). New York, United Nations, 1973. pp. 132.

CUCKNEY (JOHN GRAHAM) The commercial approach to government operations; (transcript of lecture given on 13 June 1974). [London], Civil Service College, [1974]. pp. 17, 3. *(Lectures on Some Management Problems in the Civil Service. No. 6)*

NEWSTROM (JOHN W.) and others, eds. A contingency approach to management: readings. New York, [1975]. pp. 570.

SOUTH EAST THAMES REGIONAL HEALTH AUTHORITY. Management Services Division. A planning system for the National Health Service. [Croydon], 1975. 1 vol. (various pagings).

CHAPPLE (FRANK) The responsibility of trade unions and managers. London, [1976]. pp. 5. *(Foundation for Business Responsibilities. Seminar Papers)*

ELIASSON (GUNNAR) Business economic planning: theory, practice and comparison. Stockholm, 1976. pp. 324. *bibliog.*

WEST MIDLANDS HEALTH AUTHORITIES MANAGEMENT REVIEW TEAM. Report on management functions. [Birmingham?], 1976. pp. 38.

RICHARDSON (REED COTT) Collective bargaining by objectives: positive approach. Englewood Cliffs, N.J., [1977]. pp. 387. *bibliogs.*

WEINSHALL (THEODORE D.) ed. Culture and management: selected readings. Harmondsworth, 1977. pp. 447. *bibliogs.*

— Dictionaries and encyclopedias.

FRENCH (DEREK) and SAWARD (HEATHER) Dictionary of management. London, 1977. pp. 447. *First published in 1975.*

— Mathematical models.

SCHODERBEK (PETER P.) and others. Management systems: conceptual considerations. Dallas, Texas, 1975. pp. 370. *bibliog.*

— Study and teaching — United Kingdom.

MORE than management development: action learning at GEC; edited by David Casey and David Pearce. Farnborough, Hants., [1977]. pp. 146.

TRAINING SERVICES AGENCY [U.K.]. A discussion document on management development. [London, 1977]. pp. 25.

MANAGEMENT INFORMATION SYSTEMS.

LLEWELLYN (ROBERT W.) Information systems. Englewood Cliffs, N.J., [1976]. pp. 347.

MANAGERIAL ACCOUNTING.

U.K. Civil Service Department. Management Services. 1976. Management accounting in the civil service. [London], 1976. pp. 76. *bibliog. (Handbooks)*

MANAGERIAL ECONOMICS.

ELIASSON (GUNNAR) Business economic planning: theory, practice and comparison. Stockholm, 1976. pp. 324. *bibliog.*

MANCHESTER

— Economic history.

FROW (EDMUND) and FROW (RUTH) To make that future - now!: a history of the Manchester and Salford Trades Council. Manchester, 1976. pp. 181.

— Politics and government.

SPIERS (MAURICE) Victoria Park, Manchester: a nineteenth-century suburb in its social and administrative context. Manchester, 1976. pp. 104. *bibliog. (Chetham Society. Remains, Historical and Literary, connected with the Palatine Counties of Lancaster and Chester. 3rd series. vol. 23)*

— Poor.

ROBERTS (ROBERT) of the Prison Department. A ragged schooling: growing up in the classic slum. Manchester, [1976]. pp. 224.

— Social history — Bibliography.

LABOUR history of Manchester and Salford: a bibliography; compiled by Eddie Conway [and others]. Manchester, [1977?]. pp. 34. *(Manchester Centre for Marxist Education. Pamphlets)*

— Social life and customs.

ROBERTS (ROBERT) of the Prison Department. A ragged schooling: growing up in the classic slum. Manchester, [1976]. pp. 224.

— Suburbs and environs.

SPIERS (MAURICE) Victoria Park, Manchester: a nineteenth-century suburb in its social and administrative context. Manchester, 1976. pp. 104. *bibliog. (Chetham Society. Remains, Historical and Literary, connected with the Palatine Counties of Lancaster and Chester. 3rd series. vol. 23)*

MANIEMA.

SYMETAIN. Maniema: le pays de l'étain. Bruxelles, 1953. pp. 391. *bibliog.*

MANNERHEIM (CARL GUSTAF EMIL).

JÄGERSKIÖLD (STIG) Mannerheim mellan världskrigen. [Helsinki, 1972]. pp. 326. *bibliog.*

MANPOWER POLICY.

VULIĆ-ŠMALC (ELVIRA) Utjecaj tehnoloških transformacija na zapošljavanje kadrova. Zagreb, 1975. pp. 82. *bibliog. With brief English summary.*

KEYSER (WILLIAM) and SHARP (TIM) A case for active social marketing: manpower policy and individuals: the management of change. Oxford, 1976. pp. 210.

— Bangladesh.

NURUZZAMAN (MOHAMED) Education and educated manpower in Bangladesh: a study of development after the 1947 partition. 1976. fo. 335. *bibliog. Typescript. Ph.D. (London) thesis: unpublished. This thesis is the property of London University and may not be removed from the Library.*

— Cameroun.

CLIGNET (REMI) The Africanization of the labor market: educational and occupational segmentation in the Cameroun. Berkeley, Calif., [1976]. pp. 230.

— Canada.

HOLLAND (JOHN W.) and SKOLNIK (MICHAEL L.) Public policy and manpower development. Toronto, [1975]. pp. 152. *bibliog.*

— Communist countries.

DEGTIAR' (LIUDMILA SERAFIMOVNA) Problemy ratsional'noi zaniatosti pri sotsializme. Moskva, 1976. pp. 141.

— Israel.

GINZBERG (ELI) Fourth report on manpower in Israel. [Jerusalem, 1964]. fo. 16. *(Israel. Ministry of Labour. Manpower Planning Authority. Manpower Surveys)*

— Kenya.

KENYA. Sessional Papers. 1973. No. 10. Employment. [Nairobi], 1973. pp. 73.

— United Kingdom.

OWEN (TREVOR) The place of manpower planning in management; (transcript of lecture given on 4 June 1974). [London], Civil Service College, [1974]. pp. 25. *(Lectures on Some Management Problems in the Civil Service. No. 5)*

KEYSER (WILLIAM) and SHARP (TIM) A case for active social marketing: manpower policy and individuals: the management of change. Oxford, 1976. pp. 210.

MANPOWER SERVICES COMMISSION [U.K.]. Towards a comprehensive manpower policy. London, [1976]. pp. 43.

SHOWLER (BRIAN) The public employment service. London, 1976. pp. 101.

SMITH (ANTHONY ROBERT) ed. Manpower planning in the civil service; [by] A.R. Smith [and others]. London, 1976. pp. 292. *bibliog. (U.K. Civil Service Department. Civil Service Studies. No. 3)*

ROAD TRANSPORT INDUSTRY TRAINING BOARD [U.K.]. Local manpower studies, 1976-1977: six micro-economic studies in manpower planning in the road transport industry. Wembley, 1977. pp. 121.

— United States.

The URBAN labor market: institutions, information, linkages; [by] David Lewin [and others]. New York, 1974. pp. 155. *(Columbia University. Graduate School of Business. Conservation of Human Resources Project. Conservation of Human Resources Studies)*

CLAGUE (EWAN) and KRAMER (LEO) Manpower policies and programs: a review, 1935-75. Kalamazoo, Mich., 1976. pp. 93. *(W.E. Upjohn Institute for Employment Research. Studies in Employment and Unemployment)*

MANUSCRIPTS

— United Kingdom — Catalogues.

SOTHEBY AND COMPANY. Bibliotheca Phillippica...new series, eleventh part: catalogue of manuscripts on papyrus, vellum and paper from the celebrated collection formed by Sir Thomas Phillipps, Bt., 1792-1872, etc. London, [1976]. pp. 94.

BRITISH LIBRARY. Department of Manuscripts. 'Rough register' of acquisitions of the Department of Manuscripts, British Library, 1971-1975. London, 1977. pp. 246. *(List and Index Society. Special Series. Vol. 10)*

MAO (TSE-TUNG).

MAO (TSE-TUNG) and LIN (PIAO) Post-revolutionary writings; edited by K. Fan. Garden City, 1972. pp. 536.

VELIKODERZHAVNAIA politika maoistov v natsional'nykh raionakh KNR. Moskva, 1975. pp. 126.

BURLATSKII (FEDOR MIKHAILOVICH) Mao Tsze-dun: "nash koronnyi nomer - eto voina, diktatura". Moskva, 1976. pp. 391.

CARTER (PETER) Mao. London, 1976. pp. 164. *bibliog.*

CHAMBRE (HENRI) De Karl Marx à Lénine et Mao Tsé-toung. Paris, [1976]. pp. 413.

FITZGERALD (CHARLES PATRICK) Mao Tsetung and China. New York, 1976. pp. 166. *bibliog.*

GURLEY (JOHN G.) China's economy and the Maoist strategy. New York, [1976]. pp. 325.

MARMOR (FRANÇOIS) Le maoïsme: philosophie et politique. [Paris, 1976]. pp. 127. *bibliog.*

PYE (LUCIAN WILMOT) Mao Tse-tung: the man in the leader. New York, [1976]. pp. 346.

RAMANENKO (O.M.) Antisotsialisticheskaia sushchnost' maoizma. Moskva, 1976. pp. 127.

— Bibliography.

STARR (JOHN BRYAN) and DYER (NANCY ANNE) compilers. Post-liberation works of Mao Zedong: a bibliography and index. Berkeley, Calif., [1976]. pp. 222.

MAP INDUSTRY AND TRADE

— United Kingdom — Scotland.

GARDINER (LESLIE) Bartholomew: 150 years. Edinburgh, [1976]. pp. 111.

MARCUSE (LUDWIG).

FISCHER (KLAUS UWE) Ludwig Marcuses schriftstellerische Tätigkeiten im französischen Exil, 1933-1939. Kronberg/Ts., 1976. pp. 164. *bibliog.*

MARGERIE (PIERRE DE).

AUFFRAY (BERNARD) Pierre de Margerie, 1861-1942, et la vie diplomatique de son temps. Paris, [1976]. pp. 528. *bibliog.*

MARI REPUBLIC

— Economic history.

PO planu partii. Ioshkar-Ola, 1976. pp. 298.

MARIATEGUI (JOSE CARLOS).

MESEGUER ILLAN (DIEGO) Jose Carlos Mariategui y su pensamiento revolucionario. Lima, 1974. pp. 265. *bibliog. (Instituto de Estudios Peruanos. Ideologia y Politica. 1)*

MARINE POLLUTION

— Law and legislation.

ABECASSIS (D.W.) Marine oil pollution: the international legal regime relating to the prevention of marine-based oil pollution. Cambridge, 1976. pp. 123. *bibliog. (Cambridge. University. Department of Land Economy. Occasional Papers. No. 6)*

MARINE RESOURCES

— Pacific Ocean.

KOLDE (ENDEL JAKOB) The Pacific quest: the concept and scope of an oceanic community. Lexington, Mass., [1976]. pp. 161.

— United Kingdom.

OCEANIC management: conflicting uses of the Celtic Sea and other western U.K. waters: report of a conference held at University College of Swansea, 19-22 September 1975; edited by M.M. Sibthorp, assisted by M. Unwin. London, [1977]. pp. 220. *Conference organised by the David Davies Memorial Institute of International Studies.*

MARINE RESOURCES AND STATE.

BUZAN (BARRY GORDON) Seabed politics. New York, 1976. pp. 311.

GAMBLE (JOHN KING) Marine policy: a comparative approach. Lexington, Mass., [1977]. pp. 146. *bibliog.*

MARITIME LAW.

BIERZANEK (REMIGIUSZ) Morze otwarte ze stanowiska prawa międzynarodowego. Warszawa, 1960. pp. 354. *bibliog. With English and Russian summaries.*

HALLMAN (ROBERT MARSHALL) Towards an environmentally sound law of the sea. [Washington, D.C., 1974]. pp. 83. *A report of the International Institute for Environment and Development.*

BURKE (WILLIAM THOMAS) and others. National and international law enforcement in the ocean. Seattle, [1975]. pp. 244.

IVANCHENKO (NIKOLAI SEMENOVICH) Ratsional'noe ispol'zovanie zhivykh resursov moria: mezhdunarodno-pravovye voprosy. Moskva, 1975. pp. 156. *bibliog.*

JANIS (MARK W.) Sea power and the law of the sea. [Lexington, Mass., 1976]. pp. 99.

— Bibliography.

SYBESMA-KNOL (NERI) and REGOUT (ALFREDA) compilers. Bibliografie van het nieuwe zeerecht: een keuze uit boeken en U.N.O.-Dokumenten: Bibliography of the new law of the sea: a selective list of books and U.N. documents. Brussel, 1976-77. 2 vols.

YOUNG (MARION) compiler. The law of the sea: a bibliography;... revised and enlarged by Dawn Adie. Aberdeen, Marine Laboratory Library, 1976. fo.26.

MARKETING.

DAVIES (ROSSER LLEWELYN) Marketing geography: with special reference to retailing. Corbridge, [1976]. pp. 300.

DOYLE (PETER) Marketing and the responsive university: an inaugural lecture delivered at the University of Bradford on 13 January 1976. Bradford, [1976]. pp. 26.

PORTER (MICHAEL E.) Interbrand choice, strategy, and bilateral market power. Cambridge, Mass., 1976. pp. 264. *bibliog. (Harvard University. Harvard Economic Studies. vol. 146)*

— United Kingdom.

SLATTER (STUART ST. P.) Competition and marketing strategies in the pharmaceutical industry. London, [1977]. pp. 150. *bibliog.*

MARKETING MANAGEMENT.

HAYHURST (ROY) Marketing organisation in British industry: a survey of current practice in 550 companies. London, 1970. pp. 26. *(British Institute of Management. Information Summaries. No.148)*

MARKETING RESEARCH.

MASNATA (ALBERT) L'étude du marché à l'exportation: principes et applications pratiques. Lausanne, 1956. pp. 22. *(Office Suisse d'Expansion Commerciale. Rapports Spéciaux. Série B. No. 50) (Tirage à part des Informations Economiques Nos. 14 et 15 des 11 et 18 avril 1956)*

MARKETS

— Ethiopia.

BIRKE (LAKEW) A survey of the marketing methods and facilities in Alemaya district. Dire Dawa, Ethiopia, 1974. fo. 34.

MARKOVIC (SVETOZAR).

BLAGOJEVIĆ (OBREN) Ekonomska misao Svetozara Markovića: primljeno na VII skupu Odeljenja društvenih nauka, 28.V 1974; urednik... Dušan Nedeljković; Pensée économique de Svetozar Marković, etc. Beograd, 1975. pp. 306. *bibliog. (Srpska Akademija Nauka i Umetnosti. Posebna Izdanja. knj.479. [being also] Odeljenje Društvenih Nauka. no.76) With French summary. In Cyrillic.*

MARMONTEL (JEAN FRANÇOIS).

WAGNER (JACQUES) Marmontel, journaliste, et la Mercure de France, 1725-1761. Grenoble, 1975. pp. 338. *bibliog. (Clermont-Ferrand. Université. Faculté des Lettres et Sciences Humaines. Ouvrages. No. 34)*

MAROONS.

PRICE (RICHARD) Anthropologist. Saramaka social structure: analysis of a Maroon society in Surinam. Rio Piedras, 1975. pp. 177. *bibliog. (Puerto Rico University. Institute of Caribbean Studies. Caribbean Monograph Series. No. 12)*

PRICE (RICHARD) Anthropologist. The Guiana maroons: a historical and bibliographical introduction. Baltimore, [1976]. pp. 184. *bibliog.*

MARR (WILHELM).

MARR (WILHELM) Das junge Deutschland in der Schweiz: (ein Beitrag zur Geschichte der geheimen Verbindungen unserer Tage); Anhang: Anarchie oder Autorität?. Glashütten im Taunus, 1976. pp. 364,132. *Reprint of the works originally published in Leipzig in 1846 and in Hamburg in 1852.*

MARRIAGE.

CORK WORKERS' CLUB. Historical Reprints. No. 15. The Connolly-DeLeon controversy: on wages, marriage and the church. Cork, [1976]. pp. 45.

SCANZONI (LETHA) and SCANZONI (JOHN H.) Men, women and change: a sociology of marriage and family. New York, [1976]. pp. 504. *bibliog.*

— Denmark.

KOCH-NIELSEN (INGER) Aegteskabets fremtid. København, 1977. pp. 35. *bibliog. (Socialforskningsinstituttet. Pjecer. 7)*

— France.

ROUSSEL (LOUIS) Demographer. Le mariage dans la société française: faits de population, données d'opinion; préface d'Alain Girard. [Paris], 1975. pp. 407. *bibliog. (France. Institut National d'Etudes Démographiques. Travaux et Documents. Cahiers. No.73)*

ROUSSEL (LOUIS) Demographer. La famille après le mariage des enfants: étude des relations entre générations. [Paris], 1976. pp. 262. *(France. Institut National d'Etudes Démographiques. Travaux et Documents. Cahiers. No. 78)*

MARRIAGE.(Cont.)

— Russia.

CHECHOT (DMITRII MIKHAILOVICH) Molodezh' i brak: zametki iurista. Leningrad, 1976. pp. 104.

— — Ukraine.

CHUIKO (LIUBOV' VASIL'EVNA) Braki i razvody: demograficheskoe issledovanie na primere Ukrainskoi SSR. Moskva, 1975. pp. 175.

— Sierra Leone.

HARRELL-BOND (BARBARA E.) Modern marriage in Sierra Leone: a study of the professional group. The Hague, [1975]. pp. 369. *bibliog. (Afrika-Studiecentrum. Change and Continuity in Africa)*

— United Kingdom.

BUSFIELD (JOAN) and PADDON (MICHAEL) Thinking about children: sociology and fertility in post-war England. Cambridge, 1977. pp. 312. *bibliog.*

STONE (LAWRENCE) The family, sex and marriage in England, 1500-1800. London, [1977]. pp. 800. *bibliog.*

— United States.

LANTZ (HERMAN R.) Marital incompatibility and social change in early America. Beverly Hills, [1976]. pp. 48. *bibliog.*

MARRIAGE CUSTOMS AND RITES

— Nepal.

NEPAL. Department of Information. 1970. Hindu marriage in Nepal. Kathmandu, 1970. pp. 10.

MARRIAGE CUSTOMS AND RITES, HINDU.

NEPAL. Department of Information. 1970. Hindu marriage in Nepal. Kathmandu, 1970. pp. 10.

MARRIAGE LAW

— Germany.

MUELLER-FREIENFELS (WOLFRAM) Ehe und Recht. Tübingen, 1962. pp. 362.

— Uganda.

UGANDA. Commission on Marriage, Divorce and the Status of Women. 1965. Report; [W.W. Kalema, chairman]. Entebbe, 1965. pp. 133.

— United Kingdom.

GIESEN (DIETER) Grundlagen und Entwicklung des englischen Eherechts in der Neuzeit bis zum Beginn des 19. Jahrhunderts. Bielefeld, 1973. pp. 836. *bibliog.*

MARSHALL (JOHN) Chief Justice of the United States of America.

MARSHALL (JOHN) Chief Justice of the United States of America. The papers of John Marshall;...[edited by] Herbert Alan Johnson [and others]. Chapel Hill, N.C., [1974 in progress].

MARX (KARL).

DAVE (VICTOR) Michel Bakounine et Karl Marx. [Bordeaux, 1970?]. pp. 55. *Originally published in Paris in 1900.*

KARL Marx und Friedrich Engels: die Begründer des wissenschaftlichen Sozialismus; die Bedeutung des "Manifests der Kommunistischen Partei". Berlin, 1953. pp. 72. *bibliog. (Sozialistische Einheitspartei Deutschlands. Zentralkomitee. Abteilung Propaganda. Lehrmaterial für das Parteilehrjahr)*

MULLER (PHILIPPE) Philosophie et économie politique chez le jeune Marx. Basel, [1965]. pp. 126-135. *(Studia Philosophica. Separata. vol. 25)*

SELSAM (HOWARD) and others, eds. Dynamics of social change: a reader in Marxist social science from the writings of Marx, Engels and Lenin; selected and edited with introduction and notes. New York, [1970]. pp. 416. *bibliog.*

FONER (PHILIP SHELDON) ed. When Karl Marx died: comments in 1883. New York, 1973. pp. 272.

GUREVICH (SEMEN MOISEEVICH) Razoblachenie lzhivoi legendy: K. Marks i F. Engel's o burzhuaznoi pechati. Moskva, 1975. pp. 255.

AKTUELLE Bedeutung der Marxschen Randglossen zum Gothaer Programm; (Autoren: Wolfgang Heinrichs [and others]). Berlin, 1976. pp. 140. *(Akademie der Wissenschaften der DDR. Zentralinstitut für Wirtschaftswissenschaften. Forschungsberichte. Nr.18)*

CHAMBRE (HENRI) De Karl Marx à Lénine et Mao Tsé-toung. Paris, [1976]. pp. 413.

GRAHAM (MARCUS) Marxism and a free society: an anarchist reply to Isaac Deutscher's address On socialist man with particular reference to the minutes of the First International and the sabotaging of the Hague Congress by the Marx clique. London, 1976. pp. 16.

HANISCH (ERNST) Karl Marx und die Berichte der österreichischen Geheimpolizei. Trier, [1976]. pp. 30. *(Karl-Marx-Haus. Schriften. 16)*

KUZ'MIN (VSEVOLOD PETROVICH) Printsip sistemnosti v teorii i metodologii K. Marksa. Moskva, 1976. pp. 247.

LAPIN (NIKOLAI IVANOVICH) Molodoi Marks. 2nd ed. Moskva, 1976. pp. 415. *bibliog.*

LEVY (FRANÇOISE P.) Karl Marx: histoire d'un bourgeois allemand. Paris, [1976]. pp. 431.

MAMUT (LEONID SOLOMONOVICH) Problemy teorii gosudarstva v sovremennoi ideologicheskoi bor'be: protiv burzhuaznoi kritiki vzgliadov K. Marksa na gosudarstvo. Moskva, 1976. pp. 192.

OIZERMAN (TEODOR IL'ICH) Der "junge" Marx im ideologischen Kampf der Gegenwart. Frankfurt/Main, 1976. pp. l47.

OLLMAN (BERTELL) Alienation: Marx's conception of man in capitalist society. 2nd ed. Cambridge, 1976. pp. 338. *bibliog.*

PRAWER (SIEGBERT S.) Karl Marx and world literature. Oxford, 1976. pp. 446. *bibliog.*

DRAPER (HAL) Karl Marx's theory of revolution. New York, [1977] in progress. *bibliogs.*

Der KAMPF von Karl Marx und Friedrich Engels um die revolutionäre Partei der deutschen Arbeiterklasse. Berlin, 1977. pp. 256. *bibliog. (Berlin. Parteihochschule Karl Marx. Lehrstuhl Geschichte der SED. Vorlesungen)*

McBRIDE (WILLIAM LEON) The philosophy of Marx. London, 1977. pp. 175. *bibliog.*

ROSEN (ZVI) Bruno Bauer and Karl Marx: the influence of Bruno Bauer on Marx's thought. The Hague, 1977. pp. 254. *bibliog. (International Institute of Social History. Studies in Social History. [No.]2)*

SKAMBRAKS (HANNES) "Das Kapital" von Marx: Waffe im Klassenkampf: Aufnahme und Anwendung der Lehren des Hauptwerkes von Karl Marx durch die deutsche Arbeiterbewegung, 1867 bis 1878. Berlin, 1977. pp. 328. *bibliog.*

WESSEL (HARALD) Marginalien zur MEGA [Marx-Engels-Gesamtausgabe] nebst Randglossen über alte und neue "Marxologen". Berlin, 1977. pp. 114.

— Bibliography.

DRAHN (ERNST) compiler. Marx-Bibliographie: ein Lebensbild Karl Marx' in biographisch-bibliographischen Daten;...1. Heft. Karl Marx' Leben und Schriften. 2nd ed. London, 1975. pp. 30. *Reprint of work originally published in Berlin in 1923.*

— Portraits, caricatures, etc.

KARL Marks, Fridrikh Engel's: sobranie fotografii; [Karl Marx, Friedrich Engels: a collection of photographs] . Moskva, 1976. pp. 285. *In Russian, German, English and French.*

MARXIAN ECONOMICS.

BRUS (WŁODZIMIERZ) and others, eds. Ekonomia polityczna socjalizmu; praca zbiorowa...dla studentów uniwersytetów, etc. 3rd ed. Warszawa, 1967. pp. 376.

ECONOMICHESKIE NAUKI; ([pd. by] Ministerstvo Vysshego i Srednego Spetsial'nogo Obrazovaniia SSSR). m., [Je] 1970 (god 13, [no.] 6)- Moskva.

VALIEV (ENVER ADRAKHMANOVICH) Neobkhodimyi i pribavochnyi produkt v SSSR. Moskva, 1973. pp. 104.

ANDERSON (CHARLES HOYT) The political economy of social class. Englewood Cliffs, [1974]. pp. 340.

TIKHONOV (NIKOLAI MAKAROVICH) Neobkhodimyi produkt v usloviiakh razvitogo sotsializma: voprosy teorii. Leningrad, 1974. pp. 239. *bibliog.*

DOBREV (KRUSTIU ZHELIAZKOV) Problemi na stroitelstvoto na sotsializma v NR Bulgariia: izbrani proizvedeniia; [with an introductory essay by Ivan Stefanov]. Sofiia, 1975. pp. 267. *bibliog.*

EKONOMICHESKIE problemy nauchno-tekhnicheskoi revoliutsii pri sotsializme. Moskva, 1975. pp. 263.

EVSTIGNEEVA (LIUDMILA PETROVNA) Formirovanie potrebnostei v razvitom sotsialisticheskom obshchestve. Moskva, 1975. pp. 254.

FAL'TSMAN (VLADIMIR KONSTANTINOVICH) Potrebnost' v sredstvakh proizvodstva. Moskva, 1975. pp. 238.

HYMAN (RICHARD) Industrial relations: a Marxist introduction. London, 1975. pp. 220. *bibliog.*

KASHIN (VALENTIN NIKOLAEVICH) Poznanie i ispol'zovanie ekonomicheskikh zakonov pri sotsializme. Moskva, 1975. pp. 196.

LUFT (HANS) and others. Ökonomische Gesetze und sozialistische Planwirtschaft. Berlin, 1975. pp. 102.

MALAFEEV (ALEKSEI NIKOLAEVICH) Proshloe i nastoiashchee teorii tovarnogo proizvodstva pri sotsializme. Moskva, 1975. pp. 191.

NUGAEV (RASHID ALIMZHANOVICH) Sovokupnaia rabochaia sila i zakonomernosti ee razvitiia. Kazan', 1975. pp. 246.

ZAGAINOV (LEONID IVANOVICH) Sotsialisticheskoe gosudarstvo i zakony ekonomiki. Moskva, 1975. pp. 318.

AKHMEDOVA (MATBUA AMIRSAIDOVNA) Nekapitalisticheskii put': nekotorye problemy teorii i praktiki. Tashkent, 1976. pp. 223.

BAKANOV (MIKHAIL IVANOVICH) and others. Ekonomicheskii analiz: teoriia, istoriia, sovremennoe sostoianie, perspektivy. Moskva, 1976. pp. 363. *bibliog.*

BARVÍK (JAROMÍR) and KOMÁREK (VALTR) Problémy intenzívního typu rozvoje socialistické ekonomiky. Praha, 1976. pp. 318.

DOKUKIN (VLADIMIR IGNAT'EVICH) and KONDRAT'EV (L.F.) eds. Effektivnost' ekonomiki razvitogo sotsializma. Moskva, 1976. pp. 312. *bibliog.*

DUNAEVA (VERA SERGEEVNA) Ekonomicheskie zakony sotsializma i problemy narodnokhoziaistvennogo optimuma. Moskva, 1976. pp. 264.

FEDOSEEV (PETR NIKOLAEVICH) ed. Sootnoshenie dvukh podrazdelenii obshchestvennogo proizvodstva. Moskva, 1976. pp. 240.

HAUSTEIN (HEINZ DIETER) and MANZ (GUENTER) Bedürfnisse, Bedarf, Planung. Berlin, [1976]. pp. 168. *bibliog.*

HOFMANN (HANS) and LOOSE (WOLFGANG) Ökonomie, Politik, Ideologie. Berlin, 1976. pp. 196. *bibliog.*

KAPELIAN (EFIM KHAIMOVICH) Proizvoditel'nye sily: struktura, funktsii, tipologiia; voprosy metodologii i teorii. Minsk, 1976. pp. 191.

KUEHNE (KARL) Geschichtskonzept und Profitrate im Marxismus. Neuwied, [1976]. pp. 267.

LEVIN (ALEKSANDR IVANOVICH) and IARKIN (ANATOLII PAVLOVICH) Platezhesposobnyi spros naseleniia. Moskva, 1976. pp. 360. *(Akademiia Nauk SSSR. Tsentral'nyi Ekonomiko- Matematicheskii Institut. Problemy Sovetskoi Ekonomiki)*

LUTOKHINA (E.A.) ed. Formy neobkhodimogo produkta pri sotsializme. Minsk, 1976. pp. 270.

MAL'TSEV (NIKOLAI ALEKSANDROVICH) Problemy raspredeleniia v razvitom sotsialisticheskom obshchestve. Moskva, 1976. pp. 198.

MARX (KARL) Value: studies by Karl Marx; translated and edited by Albert Dragstedt. London, [1976]. pp. 229. *"Of the four independent texts of Marx presented here, three appear for the first time in English".*

MAZUR (VILEN NIKITOVICH) Ekonomicheskii revizionizm: kritika revizionistskoi vul'garizatsii politicheskoi ekonomii sotsializma. Kiev, 1976. pp. 247.

MEDVEDEV (VADIM ANDREEVICH) Sotsialisticheskoe proizvodstvo: politiko-ekonomicheskoe issledovanie. Moskva, 1976. pp. 326.

NATIONALEINKOMMEN im Sozialismus: Produktion, Verteilung...; ([by an] Autorenkollektiv aus der VRB, der DDR und der UdSSR; Leiter...: D. Porjasow). Berlin, 1976. pp. 503.

NOTKIN (ALEKSANDR IL'ICH) ed. Proportsii vosproizvodstva v period razvitogo sotsializma. Moskva, 1976. pp. 431. *(Akademiia Nauk SSSR. Institut Ekonomiki. Problemy Sovetskoi Ekonomiki)*

SIK (OTA) The third way: Marxist-Leninist theory and modern industrial society;...translated by Marian Sling. London, 1976. pp. 431. *bibliog.*

TECHNOLOGY, the labor process, and the working class: essays; by Rosalyn Baxandall [and others]. New York, [1976]. pp. 124.

TSAGA (VIKTORIIA FRANTSEVNA) Antikommunizm heute: zu bürgerlichen ökonomischen Theorien; (ins Deutsche übertragen von Leon Nebenzahl). Berlin, [1976]. pp. 159.

TUSHUNOV (ANATOLII VASIL'EVICH) Voprosy agrarnoi teorii. Moskva, 1976. pp. 318.

UCHENYE ZAPISKI KAFEDR OBSHCHESTVENNYKH NAUK VUZOV LENINGRADA. Politicheskaia Ekonomiia. vyp.17. Obmen pri sotsializme. Leningrad, 1976. pp. 199.

VALIER (JACQUES) Le Parti communiste français et le capitalisme monopoliste d'état. Paris, 1976. pp. 233.

WAGENER (HANS JUERGEN) Marx's economics as a theory of economic systems. Leiden, 1976. pp. 19. *bibliog.*

AKTUAL'NYE problemy ekonomicheskoi nauki v trudakh S.G. Strumilina: k 100-letiiu so dnia rozhdeniia. Moskva, 1977. pp. 209.

CHERKOVETS (VIKTOR NIKITICH) ed. Problemy razvitogo sotsializma v politicheskoi ekonomii, etc. Moskva, 1977. pp. 335. *(Akademiia Nauk SSSR. Problemy Sovetskoi Ekonomiki)*

EKONOMICHESKIE problemy razvitogo sotsialisticheskogo obshchestva. Kiev, 1977. pp. 283.

GREENBERG (EDWARD S.) The American political system: a radical approach. Cambridge, Mass., [1977]. pp. 501. *bibliogs.*

GRUNDFRAGEN der sozialistischen Preistheorie; (Herausgeber: Kurt Ambrée [and others]; Autoren: Kurt Ambrée [and others]). Berlin, 1977. pp. 303.

HINDESS (BARRY) and HIRST (PAUL QUENTIN) Mode of production and social formation: an auto-critique of Pre-capitalist modes of production. London, 1977. pp. 82. *bibliog.*

MARX (KARL) Selected writings; edited by David McLellan. Oxford, 1977. pp. 625. *bibliogs.*

NICK (HARRY) Sozialismus und Wirtschaftswachstum. Berlin, 1977. pp. 80.

SOEDER (GUENTER) Ökonomie, Politik, Wirtschaftspolitik: weltanschaulich-philosophische Aspekte des Verhältnisses von Politik und Wirtschaft im Sozialismus. Berlin, 1977. pp. 117.

The SUBTLE anatomy of capitalism; edited by Jesse Schwartz. Santa Monica, Calif., [1977]. pp. 503. *bibliogs.*

TELFORD (SHIRLEY) Economic and political peace, volume II. Portland, Or., [1977]. pp. 154. *Appears to be intended to be used with any edition of the author's earlier work with the same title.*

— Methodology.

GUZNIAEV (ANATOLII GRIGOR'EVICH) Problemy predmeta politicheskoi ekonomii sotsializma: teoriia, istoriia, metodologiia. Kazan', 1976. pp. 222.

METODOLOGICHESKIE problemy issledovaniia ekonomiki razvitogo sotsializma. Moskva, 1976. pp. 248.

— Study and teaching.

ABALKIN (LEONID IVANOVICH) ed. Metodologicheskie problemy politicheskoi ekonomii sotsializma. Leningrad, 1976. pp. 136.

MARXISM.

JORDI (HUGO) Sozialistische Entwicklungslinien: neue Betrachtungen über den klassischen Marxismus. Bern, 1947. pp. 40. *Originally published as a series of articles in "Volksrecht".*

POLAK (KARL) Marxismus und Staatslehre. Berlin, [1947]. pp. 40. *(Einheit: Zeitschrift für Theorie und Praxis des wissenschaftlichen Sozialismus. Schriftenreihe: Erkenntnis und Wille. Heft 1)*

RACKWITZ (ARTHUR) Der Marxismus im Lichte des Evangeliums: Untersuchungen über das Kommunistische Manifest. Berlin, 1948. pp. 23.

KARL Marx und Friedrich Engels: die Begründer des wissenschaftlichen Sozialismus; die Bedeutung des "Manifests der Kommunistischen Partei". Berlin, 1953. pp. 72. *bibliog. (Sozialistische Einheitspartei Deutschlands. Zentralkomitee. Abteilung Propaganda. Lehrmaterial für das Parteilehrjahr)*

KOCH (HANS) 1894-1959, ed. Theorie, Taktik, Technik des Weltkommunismus: eine Zitatensammlung von Marx bis Chruschtschow;...bearbeitet von Eugen Wieber. Pfaffenhofen/Ilm, 1959. pp. 504. *bibliog.*

KUUSINEN (OTTO VILHELM) Die Frage der wissenschaftlichen Voraussicht in der Theorie des Marxismus-Leninismus und einige Perspektiven der Demokratie und des Sozialismus. Berlin, 1960. pp. 46. *Referat auf der Theoretischen Konferenz des ZK der SED am 29./30. Januar 1960 in Berlin.*

SCHLETTE (HEINZ ROBERT) Sowjethumanismus: Prämissen und Maximen kommunistischer Pädagogik. München, [1960]. pp. 136.

FREYDORF (KARL) ed. Neuer Roter Katechismus, etc. München, 1968. pp. 266.

SELSAM (HOWARD) and others, eds. Dynamics of social change: a reader in Marxist social science from the writings of Marx, Engels and Lenin; selected and edited with introduction and notes. New York, [1970]. pp. 416. *bibliog.*

HARNECKER (MARTA) Los conceptos elementales del materialismo historico. 2nd ed. [Paris, 1971?]. pp. 341. *bibliog.*

IOVCHUK (MIKHAIL TRIFONOVICH) and others, eds. F. Engel's i sovremennye problemy filosofii marksizma. Moskva, 1971. pp. 567.

ØSTERGAARD (UFFE) ed. Den materialistiske historieopfattelse i Danmark før 1945. I. En antologi med eksempler på forholdet mellem teori og praksis. Århus, 1973. pp. 351. *No more published.*

RAMOS (JORGE ABELARDO) Marxismo para latinoamericanos. Buenos Aires, [1973]. pp. 341.

ANDERSON (CHARLES HOYT) The political economy of social class. Englewood Cliffs, [1974]. pp. 340.

ARNAU (ROGER) ed. Marxisme catala i questio nacional catalana, 1930-1936. Paris, 1974. 2 vols. (in 1).

ALBRECHT (RICHARD) Marxismus, bürgerliche Ideologie, Linksradikalismus: zur Ideologie und Sozialgeschichte des westeuropäischen Linksradikalismus. Frankfurt/Main, 1975. pp. 169.

CHAGIN (BORIS ALEKSANDROVICH) and KLUSHIN (VLADIMIR IVANOVICH) Bor'ba za istoricheskii materializm v SSSR v 20-e gody. Leningrad, 1975. pp. 411.

CLEAVER (KATHLEEN) On the vanguard role of the black urban lumpenproletariat. London, [1975]. pp. 26.

FEDOSEEV (PETR NIKOLAEVICH) Dialektika sovremennoi epokhi. 2nd ed. Moskva, 1975. pp. 576.

IRALA (DOMINGO) pseud. [i.e. Domingo BLANCO FERNANDEZ] Las relaciones de produccion socialistas: criterios de la transicion. Valencia, [1975]. pp. 99.

JULIER (ELMAR) Marx-Engels-Verfälschung und Krise der bürgerlichen Ideologie. Frankfurt/Main, 1975. pp. 106.

KSENOFONTOV (VALENTIN IVANOVICH) Leninskie idei v sovetskoi filosofskoi nauke 20-kh godov: diskussiia "dialektikov" s mekhanistami. Leningrad, 1975. pp. 100.

MANDEL (ERNEST) De la desigualdad social a la sociedad sin clases. [Lausanne, 1975]. pp. 102. *bibliog.*

MILHAU (JACQUES) Le marxisme en mouvement. [Paris, 1975]. pp. 182.

SCHLEIFSTEIN (JOSEF) Zur Geschichte und Strategie der Arbeiterbewegung: ausgewählte Beiträge. Frankfurt am Main, 1975. pp. 290.

TADZHIKSKII GOSUDARSTVENNYI UNIVERSITET. Problemy istoricheskogo materializma. sb.4. Dushanbe, 1975. pp. 147.

ZAGARI (EUGENIO) Marxismo e revisionismo: Bernstein, Sorel, Graziadei, Leone. Napoli, [1975]. pp. 357.

MEZHDUNARODNOE rabochee dvizhenie: voprosy istorii i teorii. Moskva, 1976 in progress.

ALTHUSSER (LOUIS) Positions, 1964-1975. Paris, [1976]. pp. 173.

ANDERSON (PERRY) Considerations on western Marxism. London, 1976. pp. 125.

BAUMEISTER (REINER) Die Konzeption der Zukunftsgesellschaft bei Karl Marx, Friedrich Engels und bei neueren westeuropäischen Marxisten: eine ordnungspolitische Analyse. Köln, 1976. pp. 191. *bibliog. (Cologne. Universität. Institut für Wirtschaftspolitik. Untersuchungen. 34)*

BUHR (MANFRED) and IRRLITZ (GERD) Der Anspruch der Vernunft: die klassische bürgerliche deutsche Philosophie als theoretische Quelle des Marxismus, etc. Köln, 1976. pp. 280. *With summaries in various languages.*

BURGESS (ROD) Marxism and geography. London, 1976. pp. 42. *(London. University. University College. Department of Geography. Occasional Papers. No. 30)*

CAMERON (KENNETH NEILL) Marx and Engels today: a modern dialogue on philosophy and history. Hicksville, N.Y., [1976]. pp. 89.

CASTRIS (ARCANGELO LEONE DE) Estetica e marxismo. Roma, 1976. pp. 229.

CHAMBRE (HENRI) De Karl Marx à Lénine et Mao Tsé-toung. Paris, [1976]. pp. 413.

EAGLETON (TERRY) Criticism and ideology: a study in Marxist literary theory. London, [1976]. pp. 191.

FINGER (OTTO) Der Materialismus der "kritischen Theorie". Berlin, 1976. pp. 62.

GERNS (WILLI) Krise der bürgerlichen Ideologie und ideologischen Kampf in der BRD. Frankfurt/Main, 1976. pp. 268.

GRAHAM (MARCUS) Marxism and a free society: an anarchist reply to Isaac Deutscher's address On socialist man with particular reference to the minutes of the First International and the sabotaging of the Hague Congress by the Marx clique. London, 1976. pp. 16.

HANAK (TIBOR) Die marxistische Philosophie und Soziologie in Ungarn. Stuttgart, 1976. pp. 231.

HEGEDÜS (ANDRÁS) Socialism and bureaucracy. London, 1976. pp. 193.

HEROD (CHARLES C.) The nation in the history of marxian thought: the concept of nations with history and nations without history. The Hague, 1976. pp. 138. *bibliog.*

The HUMANISATION of socialism: writings of the Budapest school; [by] Andras Hegedus [and others]. London, 1976. pp. 177. *Articles translated from various Hungarian journals published during the period 1967-1972.*

JAEGGI (URS) Theoretische Praxis: Probleme eines strukturalen Marxismus. Frankfurt am Main, 1976. pp. 213.

JANICKI (JANUSZ) and MUSZYŃSKI (JERZY) eds. Ideologia i polityka współczesnego lewactwa. Warszawá, 1976. pp. 387.

KAZAKOV (ALEKSEI TIMOFEEVICH) and URLANIS (BORIS TSEZAREVICH) Problemy narodonaseleniia v russkoi marksistskoi mysli. Moskva, 1976. pp. 196. *bibliog.*

KRITIKA súčasných buržoáznych sociálno-ekonomických teórií. Bratislava, 1976. pp. 399.

MARKOVIĆ (MIHAILO) On the legal institutions of socialist democracy. Nottingham, [1976]. pp. 23. *(Spokesman, The. Pamphlets. No. 55)*

PERLMAN (SELIG) Selig Perlman's lectures on capitalism and socialism; [edited by] A.L. Riesch Owen. Madison, 1976. pp. 183. *bibliog.*

RATLIFF (WILLIAM E.) Castroism and communism in Latin America, 1959-1976: the varieties of Marxist-Leninist experience. Stanford, Calif., 1976. pp. 240. *(American Enterprise Institute for Public Policy Research and Stanford University. Hoover Institution on War, Revolution and Peace. AEI-Hoover Policy Studies. 19)*

RODRIGUEZ DE YURRE (GREGORIO) El marxismo: exposicion y critica. Madrid, 1976. 2 vols.

UTOPIE - marxisme selon Ernst Bloch: un système de l'inconstructible; hommages à Ernst Bloch pour son 90e anniversaire publiés sous la direction de Gérard Raulet. Paris, 1976. pp. 334. *bibliog.*

WAGNER (WOLF) Verelendungstheorie: die hilflose Kapitalismuskritik. Frankfurt am Main, 1976. pp. 253. *bibliog.*

WEAPONS of criticism: marxism in America and the literary tradition; edited by Norman Rudich. Palo Alto, [1976]. pp. 389.

ZOLL (RAINER) Der Doppelcharakter der Gewerkschaften: zur Aktualität der Marxschen Gewerkschaftstheorie. Frankfurt am Main, 1976. pp. 199.

GRAMSCI (ANTONIO) Selections from political writings, 1910-1920; with additional texts by Bordiga and Tasca; selected and edited by Quintin Hoare; translated by John Mathews. London, 1977 in progress.

ARON (RAYMOND) Plaidoyer pour l'Europe décadente. Paris, 1977. pp. 511.

ASH (WILLIAM FRANKLIN) Morals and politics: the ethics of revolution. London, 1977. pp. 170. *bibliog.*

FRANZ (PETER) and JANKOW (MITRJU) Information contra Materialismus?: zum Missbrauch der Informationswissenschaften in der gegenwärtigen bürgerlichen Ideologie. Berlin, 1977. pp. 124.

GODELIER (MAURICE) Perspectives in marxist anthropology; translated by Robert Brain. Cambridge, 1977. pp. 243.

HOWARD (DICK) The Marxian legacy. London, 1977. pp. 340.

Der KAMPF von Karl Marx und Friedrich Engels um die revolutionäre Partei der deutschen Arbeiterklasse. Berlin, 1977. pp. 256. *bibliog. (Berlin. Parteihochschule Karl Marx. Lehrstuhl Geschichte der SED. Vorlesungen)*

LACLAU (ERNESTO) Politics and ideology in marxist theory: capitalism, fascism, populism. London, 1977. pp. 203.

McBRIDE (WILLIAM LEON) The philosophy of Marx. London, 1977. pp. 175. *bibliog.*

MELOTTI (UMBERTO) Marx and the third world;...translated by Pat Ransford; edited with a foreword by Malcolm Caldwell. London, 1977. pp. 222. *bibliog.*

MILIBAND (RALPH) Marxism and politics. Oxford, 1977. pp. 199. *bibliog.*

ROSEN (ZVI) Bruno Bauer and Karl Marx: the influence of Bruno Bauer on Marx's thought. The Hague, 1977. pp. 254. *bibliog. (International Institute of Social History. Studies in Social History. [No.]2)*

SCHNEIDER (WOLFGANG) Zur Geschichte der Theorie des wissenschaftlichen Kommunismus: Marx, Engels und Lenin über das Wesen und die Phasen der kommunistischen Gesellschaft. Berlin, 1977. pp. 296. *bibliog.*

SELIGER (MARTIN) The marxist conception of ideology: a critical essay. Cambridge, 1977. pp. 229. *bibliog.*

SLATER (PHILIP E.) Origin and significance of the Frankfurt School: a marxist perspective. London, 1977. pp. 185. *bibliog.*

SOCIETY FOR THE PHILOSOPHICAL STUDY OF DIALECTICAL MATERIALISM. Marxism, revolution and peace: from the proceedings of the society. ..; edited by Howard L. Parsons and John Somerville. Amsterdam, 1977. pp. 241.

STEUSSLOFF (HANS) Erkenntnis und Praxis, Wahrheit und Parteilichkeit. Berlin, 1977. pp. 204.

STIEHLER (GOTTFRIED) Widerspruchsdialektik und Gesellschaftsanalyse. Berlin, 1977. pp. 168.

SWINGEWOOD (ALAN WILLIAM) The myth of mass culture. London, 1977. pp. 146. *bibliog.*

TORRANCE (JOHN) Estrangement, alienation and exploitation: a sociological approach to historical materialism. London, 1977. pp. 374.

WESSEL (HARALD) Marginalien zur MEGA [Marx-Engels-Gesamtausgabe] nebst Randglossen über alte und neue "Marxologen". Berlin, 1977. pp. 114.

WESTERN Marxism: a critical reader; [by] Gareth Stedman Jones [and others]. London, [1977]. pp. 354. *(Essays reprinted from New Left Review)*

WILHELM (DONALD) Creative alternatives to communism: guidelines for tomorrow's world. London, 1977. pp. 173.

MARY, Virgin

— Cultus — United States.

GRIMES (RONALD L.) Symbol and conquest: public ritual and drama in Santa Fe, New Mexico. Ithaca, 1976. pp. 281. *bibliog.*

MARYLAND

— Politics and government.

BAKER (JEAN H.) Ambivalent Americans: the Know-Nothing party in Maryland. Baltimore, [1977]. pp. 206. *bibliog.*

MASS MEDIA.

BRETZ (RUDOLPH) A taxonomy of communication media. Englewood Cliffs, N.J., [1971] repr. 1974. pp. 165.

TUNSTALL (JEREMY) The media are American: Anglo-American media in the world. London, 1977. pp. 352. *bibliog.*

— Political aspects.

KRAUS (SIDNEY) and DAVIS (DENNIS) The effects of mass communication on political behavior. University Park, Pa., [1976]. pp. 308.

COMMUNICATIONS policy for national development: a comparative perspective; edited by Majid Teheranian, [and others]. London, 1977. pp. 286. *Studies arising out of the Prospective Planning Project of National Iranian Radio and Television.*

— — Italy.

CANNISTRARO (PHILIP V.) La fabbrica del consenso: fascismo e mass media; (traduzione dal nordamericano di Giovanni Ferrara). Roma, 1975. pp. 498.

— — United Kingdom.

EMERSON (TONY) Mass communication, or mass deception. Leeds, 1976. pp. 18.

— — United States.

AMERICAN ACADEMY OF POLITICAL AND SOCIAL SCIENCE. Annals. vol. 427. Role of the mass media in American politics; special editor of this volume L. John Martin. Philadelphia, 1976. pp. 193.

RUBIN (BERNARD) Media, politics, and democracy. New York, 1977. pp. 192.

— Africa, Subsaharan.

WILCOX (DENNIS L.) Mass media in black Africa: philosophy and control. New York, 1975. pp. 170. *bibliog.*

— Caribbean Area.

COMMUNICATIONS and information for development purposes in the Caribbean area; [report of a seminar held at] Georgetown, Guyana, 1-8 December, 1974 [organized by the International Broadcast Institute in co-operation with the Friedrich Naumann Stiftung and the Ministry of Information and Culture Guyana]. London, [1975]. pp.

— Europe, Eastern.

POLITICAL socialization in eastern Europe: a comparative framework: [based on a panel held during the Annual Meeting of the American Political Science Association in Washington, 1972]; (edited by Ivan Volgyes). New York, 1975. pp. 199.

— Underdeveloped areas.

See UNDERDEVELOPED AREAS — Mass media.

— United States.

READ (WILLIAM H.) America's mass media merchants. Baltimore, [1976]. pp. 209.

— Yugoslavia.

ROBINSON (GERTRUDE JOCH) Tito's maverick media: the politics of mass communications in Yugoslavia. Urbana, Ill., [1977]. pp. 263. *bibliog.*

MASS MEDIA AND RACE PROBLEMS

— United Kingdom.

CAMPAIGN AGAINST RACISM IN THE MEDIA. In black and white: racist reporting and how to fight it. London, [1976]. pp. 40.

MASS MEDIA AND TRADE UNIONS

— United Kingdom.

TRADE unions and the media; edited by Peter Beharrell and Greg Philo. London, 1977. pp. 150. *bibliog.*

MASS SOCIETY.

BENNETT (GORDON A.) Yundong: mass campaigns in Chinese communist leadership. Berkeley, [1976]. pp. 133. *bibliog. (California University. Center for Chinese Studies. China Research Monographs. No. 12)*

HALEBSKY (SANDOR) Mass society and political conflict: toward a reconstruction of theory. Cambridge, 1976. pp. 309.

MASSACRES.

KUPER (LEO) The pity of it all: polarization of racial and ethnic relations. London, 1977. pp. 302. *bibliog.*

MATACO INDIANS

— Religion and mythology.

ARANCIBIA (UBEN GERARDO) Vida y mitos del mundo mataco. Buenos Aires, 1973. pp. 107. *bibliog. (Universidad del Salvador. Facultad de Psicopedagogia. Instituto de Investigaciones. Series Conducta y Comunicacion. 4)*

MATANZIMA (KAIZER DALIWONGA).

MATANZIMA (KAIZER DALIWONGA) Independence my way. Pretoria, [1976]. pp. 138.

MATERIALISM.

ROZENTAL' (MARK MOISEEVICH) Materialistische und idealistische Weltanschauung; [translated from the Russian by Gerhard Harig]. Berlin, [1947]. pp. 47.

POLTEN (ERIC P.) Critique of the psycho-physical identity theory: a refutation of scientific materialism and an establishment of mind-matter dualism by means of philosophy and scientific method. The Hague, [1973]. pp. 290. *bibliog.*

MATHEMATICAL MODELS.

GREENBERGER (MARTIN) and others. Models in the policy process: public decision making in the computer era. New York, [1976]. pp. 355.

MARTIN (RICHARD JOHN) Spatial models with applications in sampling and experimental design. 1977. fo.201. *bibliog. Typescript. Ph.D. (London) thesis: unpublished. This thesis is the property of London University and may not be removed from the Library.*

MATHEMATICAL OPTIMIZATION.

FEDORENKO (NIKOLAI PROKOF'EVICH) ed. Sistema modelei optimal'nogo planirovaniia. Moskva, 1975. pp. 376. *bibliog. (Akademiia Nauk SSSR. Tsentral'nyi Ekonomiko-Matematicheskii Institut. Problemy Sovetskoi Ekonomiki)*

PUGACHEV (VSEVOLOD FEDOROVICH) Problemy mnogostupenchatoi optimizatsii narodnokhoziaistvennogo planirovaniia. Moskva, 1975. pp. 79. *bibliog.*

BATTY (MICHAEL) and MARCH (LIONEL) Dynamic urban models based on information-minimising. Reading, 1976. pp. 41. *bibliog. (Reading. University. Department of Geography. Reading Geographical Papers. No. 48)*

KANTOROVICH (LEONID VITAL'EVICH) Essays in optimal planning; selected with an introduction by Leon Smolinski. Oxford, 1977. pp. 251. *bibliog.*

MATHEMATICS.

TREMBLAY (JEAN PAUL) and MANOHAR (RAM P.) Discrete mathematical structures with applications to computer science. New York, [1975]. pp. 606.

— Dictionaries and encyclopedias.

SKRAPEK (WAYNE A.) and others. Mathematical dictionary for economics and business administration. Boston, Mass., [1976]. pp. 369.

— Philosophy.

ARISTOTLE. Metaphysics: books M and N; translated with introduction and notes by Julia Annas. London, 1976. pp. 227. *bibliog.*

— Tables, etc.

MATHEMATICAL functions and their approximations. New York, 1975. pp. 568. *bibliog. An updated version of part of Handbook of mathematical functions with formulas, graphs and mathematical tables, edited by M. Abramowitz and A. Stegun.*

MATHU (ELIUD WAMBU).

ROELKER (JACK R.) Mathu of Kenya: a political study. Stanford, Calif., [1976]. pp. 202. *bibliog. (Stanford University. Hoover Institution on War, Revolution and Peace. Hoover Institution Publications. 157)*

MATO GROSSO

— Economic conditions.

RONDON (J. LUCIDIO N.) Recursos econômicos de Mato Grosso: terras, minerais, aguas, potenciais e usinas hidreletricas, etc. Cuiaba, 1972. pp. 236.

— Economic policy.

SILVESTRE FILHO (DEMOSTHENES S.) and ROMEU (NILTON) Caracteristicas e potencialidades do patanal matogrossense. Brasilia, 1974. pp. 218. *bibliog. (Brazil. Instituto de Planejamento Econômico e Social. Instituto de Planejamento. Estudos para o Planejamento. No. 10)*

MATRIMONIAL ACTIONS

— United Kingdom.

The MATRIMONIAL jurisdiction of registrars: the exercise of the matrimonial jurisdiction by registrars in England and Wales; by W. Barrington Baker [and others]. Oxford, [1977]. pp. 112. *(Oxford. University. Wolfson College. Centre for Socio- Legal Studies. Family Law Studies. No. 2)*

MAURITANIA

— Economic policy.

WESTEBBE (RICHARD M.) Mauritania: guidelines for a four-year development program; report of a mission organized by the International Bank for Reconstruction and Development at the request of the Islamic Republic of Mauritania. [Washington], International Bank for Reconstruction and Development, 1968. pp. 146.

— Social policy.

WESTEBBE (RICHARD M.) Mauritania: guidelines for a four-year development program; report of a mission organized by the International Bank for Reconstruction and Development at the request of the Islamic Republic of Mauritania. [Washington], International Bank for Reconstruction and Development, 1968. pp. 146.

MAURITIUS

— Economic conditions.

MAURITIUS ECONOMIC REVIEW (formerly Mauritius economic survey); [pd. by] Ministry of Economic Planning and Development. irreg., 1972/74- [Port Louis].

— Executive departments.

MAURITIUS. Ministry of Employment. Report. a., 1972- Port Louis.

— Social conditions.

MAURITIUS ECONOMIC REVIEW (formerly Mauritius economic survey); [pd. by] Ministry of Economic Planning and Development. irreg., 1972/74- [Port Louis].

MAY DAY (LABOUR HOLIDAY).

STOCKER (WERNER) 50 Jahre Kampf um die Freiheit: ein Gedenkwort zur fünfzigsten Maifeier. Zürich, 1939. pp. 32.

MAYAS.

PRESS (IRWIN) Tradition and adaptation: life in a modern Yucatan Maya village. Westport, Conn., 1975. pp. 224.

MAYORS

— France.

TARROW (SIDNEY G.) Between center and periphery: grassroots politicians in Italy and France. New Haven, 1977. pp. 272.

— Italy.

TARROW (SIDNEY G.) Between center and periphery: grassroots politicians in Italy and France. New Haven, 1977. pp. 272.

MBAGUTA.

KARUGIRE (SAMWIRI RUBARAZA) Nuwa Mbaguta. Nairobi, 1973. pp. 89.

MEAD (MARGARET).

SCHWARTZ (THEODORE) ed. Socialization as cultural communication: development of a theme in the work of Margaret Mead. Berkeley, Calif., [1976]. pp. 251. *bibliogs. (Reprinted from Ethos, vol.3,no.2, 1975)*

— Bibliography.

MEAD (MARGARET) Margaret Mead: the complete bibliography, 1925-1975; edited by Joan Gordan. The Hague, 1976. pp. 202. *bibliog. Introduction in English, French and Spanish.*

MEAT

— European Economic Community countries.

EUROPEAN COMMUNITIES. Statistical Office. Monthly statistics of meat. m., 1976 (no.3)- Luxembourg. *[in Community languages].*

MEAT INDUSTRY AND TRADE

— Information services.

UNITED NATIONS INDUSTRIAL DEVELOPMENT ORGANIZATION. Guides to Information Sources. No.1/Rev.1. Information sources on the meat-processing industry. (ID/163) (UNIDO/LIB/SER.D/1/Rev.1). New York, United Nations, 1976. pp. 88. *bibliog.*

MECHANICAL ENGINEERING

— Cyprus.

CYPRUS. Department of Electrical and Mechanical Service. Annual report. a., 1975(1st)- [Nicosia].

MEDIATION, INTERNATIONAL.

GUERRERO YOACHAM (CRISTIAN) Las conferencias del Niagara Falls: la mediacion de Argentina, Brasil y Chile en el conflicto entre Estados Unidos y Mexico en 1914. Santiago de Chile, 1966. pp. 189. *bibliog.*

MEDICAL ANTHROPOLOGY.

SOCIAL anthropology and medicine; edited by J.B. Loudon. London, 1976. pp. 600. *bibliogs. (Association of Social Anthropologists of the Commonwealth. A.S.A. Monographs. 13) Revised papers of the annual conference of the Association of Social Anthropologists, held in 1972 at the University of Kent.*

MEDICAL CARE.

EUGENICS SOCIETY. Annual Symposium, 12th, 1975. Equalities and inequalities in health: proceedings...; edited by C.O. Carter and John Peel. London, 1976. pp. 170. *bibliogs.*

ILLICH (IVAN D.) Limits to medicine: medical nemesis: the expropriation of health. Harmondsworth, 1977. pp. 296. *First published in 1976. "Definitive version of Medical nemesis - the expropriation of health".*

INTERNATIONAL aspects of the provision of medical care; edited by P.W. Kent. Stocksfield, Northumberland, 1976. pp. 216. *bibliogs. Papers of a symposium held at Christ Church, Oxford, in September 1974, under the auspices of the Board of Management of the Foster Wills Scholarships at Oxford University and of the German Academic Exchange Service.*

LEVIN (LOWELL S.) and others. Self-care: lay initiatives in health. London, 1977. pp. 133. *bibliog. "This book is the direct outgrowth of the International Symposium on the Role of the Individual in Primary Health Care, held in Copenhagen...1975".*

— America, Latin.

NAVARRO (VICENTE) Medicine under capitalism. New York, [1976]. pp. 230. *bibliogs.*

— Europe, Eastern.

KASER (MICHAEL CHARLES) Health care in the Soviet Union and Eastern Europe. London, 1976. pp. 278.

— France.

PROBLEMES de santé dans une agglomération urbaine en mutation: Boulogne-Billancourt; [by] D. Minvielle [and others]. Le Vésinet, Division de la Recherche Médico-Sociale, 1975. pp. 161. *bibliog. With English summary.*

— Gambia.

JONES (C.R.) Report on the medical and health services of the Gambia. Bathurst, 1970. pp. 12. *(Gambia. Sessional Papers. 1970. No. 3)*

— Ireland (Republic).

NATIONAL ECONOMIC AND SOCIAL COUNCIL [EIRE] Some major issues in health policy; (by A.J.Culyer and A.K. Maynard). Dublin, Stationery Office, [1977]. pp. 94. *bibliog. ([Reports]. No. 29)*

— Kenya.

CARMAN (JOHN A.) A medical history of the colony and protectorate of Kenya: a personal memoir. London, 1976. pp. 110.

— Malaysia — Mathematical models.

HELLER (PETER S.) A model of the demand for medical and health services in West Malaysia. Ann Arbor, 1976. pp. 52. *bibliog. (Michigan University. Center for Research on Economic Development. Discussion Papers. No. 62)*

— Russia.

KASER (MICHAEL CHARLES) Health care in the Soviet Union and Eastern Europe. London, 1976. pp. 278.

POPOV (GEORGII ALEKSEEVICH) Ekonomika i planirovanie zdravookhraneniia. Moskva, 1976. pp. 376.

— United Kingdom.

CIBA FOUNDATION. Symposia. New Series. 43. Health care in a changing setting: the U.K. experience; (editors Ruth Porter and David W. Fitzsimons). Amsterdam, 1976. pp. 188. *bibliogs.*

GODBER (Sir GEORGE EDWARD) Attainable goals in health. Glasgow, 1976. pp. 24. *(Glasgow. University. Maurice Bloch Lectures. 16)*

A QUESTION of quality?: roads to assurance in medical care; contributors: Sir George Godber [and others]; edited by Gordon McLachlan. London, [1976]. pp. 297. *bibliogs. Based on the proceedings of a working group for the evaluation of the quality of care, convened by the Nuffield Provincial Hospitals Trust.*

— United States.

NAVARRO (VICENTE) Medicine under capitalism. New York, [1976]. pp. 230. *bibliogs.*

PRIMARY care in a specialized world: [by] Philip R. Lee [and others]. Cambridge, Mass., [1976]. pp. 224.

WEAVER (JERRY L.) National health policy and the underserved: ethnic minorities, women, and the elderly. Saint Louis, 1976. pp. 161.

MEDICAL CARE, COST OF

— Germany.

GERMANY (BUNDESREPUBLIK). Statistisches Bundesamt. Kostenstruktur bei Ärzten, Zahnärzten, Tierärzten. irreg., 1975- Wiesbaden. *(Unternehmen und Arbeitsstätten. Reihe 1.6.1.)*

— United States.

ANDERSEN (RONALD) and others. Two decades of health services: social survey trends in use and expenditure. Cambridge, Mass., [1976]. pp. 387. *bibliog.*

MEDICAL ECONOMICS.

NAVARRO (VICENTE) Medicine under capitalism. New York, [1976]. pp. 230. *bibliogs.*

— Bibliography.

CULYER (ANTHONY J.) and others. An annotated bibliography of health economics: (English language sources). London, 1977. pp. 361.

— Canada.

SYMPOSIUM ON HEALTH CARE ECONOMICS, 1ST, QUEEN'S UNIVERSITY, KINGSTON, ONTARIO, 1974. Health economics symposium: proceedings of the first Canadian conference, September...1974; R.D. Fraser, editor. Kingston, Ont., 1976. pp. 209. *Conference sponsored by the Institute for Economic Research, Queen's University at Kingston.*

— Germany.

GRUENDGER (FRITZ) Zum Problem der Bedarfsermittlung bei Investitionen im Bildungs- und Gesundheitswesen: eine vergleichende Untersuchung unter besonderer Berücksichtigung des Schul- und Krankenhaussektors. Berlin, [1977]. pp. 291. *bibliog.*

— Russia.

POPOV (GEORGII ALEKSEEVICH) Ekonomika i planirovanie zdravookhraneniia. Moskva, 1976. pp. 376.

— Underdeveloped areas.

See UNDERDEVELOPED AREAS — Medical economics.

MEDICAL ETHICS.

[TWEEDALE (JOHN)] A short history of the cabal; in a letter addressed to Mr. Thomas Ingle, surgeon, Lynn. Lynn, Wade, printer, 1826. pp. 12.

MEDICAL LAWS AND LEGISLATION.

PAXMAN (JOHN M.) and others. Expanded roles for non-physicians in fertility regulation: legal perspectives. Medford, Mass., 1976. pp. 117. *(Tufts University. Fletcher School of Law and Diplomacy. Law and Population Monograph Series. No. 41)*

MEDICAL PERSONNEL.

PAXMAN (JOHN M.) and others. Expanded roles for non-physicians in fertility regulation: legal perspectives. Medford, Mass., 1976. pp. 117. *(Tufts University. Fletcher School of Law and Diplomacy. Law and Population Monograph Series. No. 41)*

BRITISH SOCIOLOGICAL ASSOCIATION. Annual Conference, 1976. Health and the division of labour; [papers presented at the conference]; edited by Margaret Stacey [and others]. London, [1977]. pp. 237. *bibliogs. (British Sociological Association. Explorations in Sociology. 10)*

— Russia — Salaries, pensions, etc.

RIABININ (ANATOLII IAKOVLEVICH) Oplata truda rabotnikov zdravookhraneniia. Moskva, 1969. pp. 86.

— United Kingdom.

McCARTHY (WILLIAM EDWARD JOHN) Baron McCarthy. Making Whitley work: a review of the operation of the National Health Service Whitley Council system. [London, Department of Health and Social Security], 1976. pp. 144.

— — Salaries, pensions, etc.

U.K. Department of Health and Social Security. [Circulars]: H.C. (P.C.). [Pay and conditions of service]. irreg., Jl 1976 (no.15)- London.

— United States.

PRIMARY care in a specialized world: [by] Philip R. Lee [and others]. Cambridge, Mass., [1976]. pp. 224.

WERTHER (WILLIAM B.) and LOCKHART (CAROL ANN) Labor relations in the health professions: the basis of power, the means of change. Boston, Mass, [1976]. pp. 255. *bibliogs.*

MEDICAL POLICY

— United States.

CURRENT issues in social; policy edited by W. Boyd Littrell [and] Gideon Sjoberg. Beverly Hills, Calif., [1976]. pp. 248. *bibliogs. Papers prepared for an interdisciplinary conference held in 1975, at the University of Texas.*

PRIMARY care in a specialized world: [by] Philip R. Lee [and others]. Cambridge, Mass., [1976]. pp. 224.

MEDICAL RESEARCH

— United Kingdom.

U.K. Advisory Panel on Health and Health Policy. 1977. Health and health policy: priorities for research;...report... to the Research Initiatives Board; [M. Kogan, chairman]. [London, 1977]. 1 vol. (various pagings). *bibliog.*

MEDICAL SOCIAL WORK

— United Kingdom.

DINGWALL (ROBERT) The social organisation of health visitor training. London, [1977]. pp. 249. *bibliog.*

MEDICINE

— Bibliography.

REICHE-JUHR (HANNELORE) compiler. Das Gesundheitswesen in der Bundesrepublik Deutschland und in anderen Ländern, 1970-1975: Auswahlbibliographie. Bonn, 1976. pp. 111. *(Germany (Bundesrepublik). Deutscher Bundestag. Wissenschaftliche Dienste. Bibliographien. 47)*

— Germany — Bibliography.

REICHE-JUHR (HANNELORE) compiler. Das Gesundheitswesen in der Bundesrepublik Deutschland und in anderen Ländern, 1970-1975: Auswahlbibliographie. Bonn, 1976. pp. 111. *(Germany (Bundesrepublik). Deutscher Bundestag. Wissenschaftliche Dienste. Bibliographien. 47)*

— **Ireland (Republic) — Formulae, receipts, prescriptions.**

EIRE. Working Party on Prescribing and Dispensing in the General Medical Service. 1976. Report. Dublin, [1976]. pp. 56. *bibliog.*

— **Kenya.**

CARMAN (JOHN A.) A medical history of the colony and protectorate of Kenya: a personal memoir. London, 1976. pp. 110.

— **United Kingdom — History.**

CARTWRIGHT (FREDERICK FOX) A social history of medicine. London, 1977. pp. 209. *bibliog.*

MEDICINE, STATE

— **Canada — British Columbia.**

BRITISH COLUMBIA. Department of Health. Annual report. a., 1975(1st)- Victoria. *Supersedes BRITISH COLUMBIA. Health Branch. Annual report of the public health services of British Columbia and BRITISH COLUMBIA. Hospital Insurance Service. Annual report.*

— **Ireland (Republic).**

McMANUS (JOHN) Health care: the case for socialist medical care. Dublin, [1977]. pp. 14.

— **Russia.**

NAVARRO (VICENTE) Social security and medicine in the USSR: a Marxist critique. Lexington, Mass., [1977]. pp. 149. *bibliog.*

— **United Kingdom.**

BROWN (RUPERT GEOFFREY STUART) The changing National Health Service. London, 1973. pp. 118. *bibliog.*

SOUTH EAST THAMES REGIONAL HEALTH AUTHORITY. Management Services Division. A planning system for the National Health Service. [Croydon], 1975. 1 vol. (various pagings).

CIBA FOUNDATION. Symposia. New Series. 43. Health care in a changing setting: the U.K. experience; (editors Ruth Porter and David W. Fitzsimons). Amsterdam, 1976. pp. 188. *bibliogs.*

POWELL (JOHN ENOCH) Medicine and politics: 1975 and after. Tunbridge Wells, 1976. pp. 83.

RADICAL STATISTICS HEALTH GROUP. Pamphlets. No. 1. Whose priorities? London, [1976]. pp. 36.

WEST MIDLANDS HEALTH AUTHORITIES MANAGEMENT REVIEW TEAM. Report on management functions. [Birmingham?], 1976. pp. 38.

WEST MIDLANDS REGIONAL HEALTH AUTHORITY. Priorities for health, 1976: a commentary upon the Department of Health and Social Security consultative document Priorities for health and personal social services in England, with regional guidelines for development of health services. Birmingham, 1976. pp. 35.

BARNARD (KEITH) and LEE (KENNETH) eds. Conflicts in the National Health Service. London, [1977]. pp. 252. *bibliog.*

COMMUNITY RELATIONS COMMISSION. Evidence to the Royal Commission on the National Health Service. London, 1977. pp. 20.

LABOUR PARTY. The right to health: the Labour Party's evidence to the Royal Commission on the National Health Service. London, 1977. pp. 59.

The ROLE of psychologists in the health services; report of the Sub-Committee; chairman: W.H. Trethowan. London, H.M.S.O., 1977. pp. 33.

U.K. Department of Health and Social Security. 1977. Priorities in the health and social services: the way forward: further discusssion of the Government's strategy based on the consultative document Priorities for health and personal social services in England. London, 1977. pp. 52. *bibliog.*

— — **Bibliography.**

U.K. Department of Health and Social Security. Library. Annual list of publications. a., 1975- London.

— — **Wales.**

U.K. Welsh Office. 1976. Proposed all-Wales policies and priorities for the planning and provision of health and personal social services from 1976/77 to 1979/80: consultative document. [Cardiff], 1976. fo. 34.

U.K. Welsh Office. Health and Social Work Department. 1976. A guide to health and social services statistics. Cardiff, 1976. pp. 73.

— **United States.**

REGULATORY reform: highlights of a conference on government regulation...Washington...1975; edited by W.S. Moore. Washington, 1976. pp. 65. *(American Enterprise Institute for Public Policy Research. Domestic Affairs Studies. 45)*

MEDITERRANEAN

— **Defences.**

LEWIS (JESSE W.) The strategic balance in the Mediterranean. Washington, D.C., 1976. pp. 169. *(American Enterprise Institute for Public Policy Research. Foreign Affairs Studies. 29)*

— **Economic conditions.**

MEDITERRANEAN Europe and the Common Market: studies of economic growth and integration; edited by Eric N. Baklanoff. Alabama, [1976]. pp. 244. *(American Universities Field Staff. Center for Mediterranean Studies. Mediterranean Europe Series. 2)*

DAVIS (JOHN HORSLEY RUSSELL) People of the Mediterranean: an essay in comparative social anthropology. London, 1977. pp. 288. *bibliog.*

— **Foreign relations.**

For a related heading see EUROPEAN ECONOMIC COMMUNITY— Mediterranean.

— **Politics and government.**

PATRONS and clients in Mediterranean societies; edited by Ernest Gellner and John Waterbury. London, 1977. pp. 348. *bibliogs. Based mostly on papers presented at a conference held under the patronage of the Center for Mediterranean Studies of the American Universities Field Staff in Rome.*

— **Relations (military) with other countries.**

LEWIS (JESSE W.) The strategic balance in the Mediterranean. Washington, D.C., 1976. pp. 169. *(American Enterprise Institute for Public Policy Research. Foreign Affairs Studies. 29)*

— **Social life and customs.**

DAVIS (JOHN HORSLEY RUSSELL) People of the Mediterranean: an essay in comparative social anthropology. London, 1977. pp. 288. *bibliog.*

MEETINGS.

SHACKLETON (FRANK) The law and practice of meetings; sixth edition by A. Harding Boulton. London, 1977. pp. 369.

MEINHOF (ULRIKE).

BRUECKNER (PETER) Ulrike Marie Meinhof und die deutschen Verhältnisse. Berlin, [1976]. pp. 192. *Includes extracts from the writings of Ulrike Meinhof.*

MEMORY.

CROWDER (ROBERT G.) Principles of learning and memory. Hillsdale, N.J., 1976. pp. 523. *bibliog.*

MENANGKABAU (INDONESIAN PEOPLE).

EVERS (HANS DIETER) Changing pattern of Minangkabau urban landownership. Singapore, 1974. pp. 45. *bibliog. (University of Singapore. Department of Sociology. Working Papers. No.22)*

MENTAL HEALTH LAWS

— **United Kingdom.**

JACOB (JOSEPH M.) The Mental Health Act explained;...edited by Denise Winn. [London 1975]. pp. 35.

HOGGETT (BRENDA MARJORIE) Mental health. London, 1976. pp. 246.

— **United States — California.**

BARDACH (EUGENE) The implementation game: what happens after a bill becomes law. Cambridge, Mass., 1977. pp. 323. *bibliogs. (Massachusetts Institute of Technology. MIT Studies in American Politics and Public Policy. 1)*

MENTAL HYGIENE.

COAN (RICHARD W.) Hero, artist, sage or saint?: a survey of views on what is variously called mental health, normality, maturity, self- actualization and human fulfillment. New York, 1977. pp. 322.

MENTAL ILLNESS.

FOULDS (G.A.) The hierarchical nature of personal illness. London, 1976. pp. 158. *bibliog.*

ORFORD (JIM) The social psychology of mental disorder. Harmondsworth, 1976. pp. 266. *bibliog.*

— **United Kingdom.**

COMMUNITY RELATIONS COMMISSION. Aspects of mental health in a multi-cultural society: notes for the guidance of doctors and social workers; (with Summary). London, 1976. 2 pts. *bibliog.*

MENTALLY HANDICAPPED

— **Care and treatment.**

MARAIS (ELIZABETH) and MARAIS (MICHAEL) Lives worth living: the right of all the handicapped. London, 1976. pp. 282. *bibliog.*

— **Institutional care — United States.**

BIRENBAUM (ARNOLD) and SEIFFER (SAMUEL) Resettling retarded adults in a managed community. New York, 1976. pp. 143. *bibliogs.*

— **Rehabilitation.**

BROLIN (DONN E.) Vocational preparation of retarded citizens. Columbus, Ohio, [1976]. pp. 312. *bibliog.*

— — **United States.**

BIRENBAUM (ARNOLD) and SEIFFER (SAMUEL) Resettling retarded adults in a managed community. New York, 1976. pp. 143. *bibliogs.*

— **United Kingdom — Ireland, Northern.**

IRELAND, NORTHERN. Department of Health and Social Services. 1976. Consultative document on services for the mentally handicapped. Belfast, 1976. pp. 54.

MENTALLY HANDICAPPED CHILDREN

— **United Kingdom.**

NATIONAL SOCIETY FOR MENTALLY HANDICAPPED CHILDREN. Parents' Information Bulletin. No. 13. Mental handicap: A-Z: your questions answered. London, [1972]. pp. 16.

CAMPAIGN FOR THE MENTALLY HANDICAPPED. Whose children?. London, [1975]. pp. 14.

MERCHANT MARINE.

ADVANCES in maritime economics; edited by R.O. Goss. Cambridge, 1977. pp. 294.

MERCHANTS, BRITISH.

MARSHALL (PETER JAMES) East Indian fortunes: the British in Bengal in the eighteenth century. London, 1976. pp. 284. *bibliog.*

MERCHANTS, ITALIAN.

KEDAR (BENJAMIN Z.) Merchants in crisis: Genoese and Venetian men of affairs and the fourteenth-century depression. New Haven, 1976. pp. 260. *bibliog.*

MERCURY

— Toxicology.

LUNDQVIST (LENNART J.) The case of mercury pollution in Sweden: scientific information and public response. Stockholm, 1974. pp. 55. *bibliog. (Sweden. Forskningsekonomiska Kommittén. Rapporter. 4)*

MERLEAU-PONTY (MAURICE).

KRUKS (SONIA RUTH) A study of the political philosophy of Merleau-Ponty. 1977. fo. 387. *bibliog. Typescript. Ph.D. (London) thesis: unpublished. This thesis is the property of London University and may not be removed from the Library.*

MERTON (ROBERT KING).

COSER (LEWIS ALFRED) ed. The idea of social structure: papers in honor of Robert K. Merton. New York, [1975]. pp. 547. *bibliog.*

METAL TRADE

— United Kingdom.

BRACKENBURY (M.C.) AND COMPANY. Dealing on the London Metal Exchange and commodity markets. London, [1975?]. pp. 117. *Lacks title page. Title from cover.*

GIBSON-JARVIE (ROBERT) The London Metal Exchange: a commodity market. Cambridge, 1976. pp. 191.

METAL WORK.

VIETORISZ (THOMAS) and LISSAK (RICHARD) Planning and programming of the metalworking industries with a special view to exports. (ID/23 vol. II) (ID/WG.10/13/Add. 1). New York, United Nations, 1972. pp. 240. *bibliog.*

METAL WORKERS

— Germany.

SCHARMANN (THEODOR) Der Industriebürger: gesellschaftliche Orientierung und berufliche Einstellung junger Arbeiter und Angestellter. Bern, [1976]. pp. 203. *bibliog.*

— Switzerland.

SCHARMANN (THEODOR) Der Industriebürger: gesellschaftliche Orientierung und berufliche Einstellung junger Arbeiter und Angestellter. Bern, [1976]. pp. 203. *bibliog.*

— United Kingdom.

HUISKAMP (M.J.) Shop stewards en arbeiderszeggenschap: een onderzoek naar arbeidsverhoudingen in de Britse metaalverwerkende industrie 1830-1975. Alphen aan den Rijn, 1976. pp. 234. *bibliog. With English summary.*

METAPHYSICS.

HENRY (DESMOND PAUL) Medieval logic and metaphysics: a modern introduction. London, 1972. pp. 133. *bibliog.*

HEGEL (GEORG WILHELM FRIEDRICH) Phenomenology of spirit; translated by A.V. Miller with analysis of the text and foreword by J.N. Findlay. Oxford, [1977]. pp. 595. *This translation has been made from the fifth edition, edited by J. Hoffmeister, 1952.*

METHODISM.

TRUTH and reform against the world; or, Letters to W. Cooke in reply to his attack on Mr. Joseph Barker. [Newcastle-upon-Tyne, J. Barker, c. 1845]. 7 pts. (in 1 vol.). *Signed, A. Christian.*

METHODIST CHURCH IN THE UNITED STATES.

JONES (CHARLES EDWIN) Perfectionist persuasion: the holiness movement and American Methodism, 1867-1936. Metuchen, N.J., 1974. pp. 242. *(American Theological Library Association. ATLA Monograph Series. No.5)*

METHODOLOGY.

DESCARTES (RENÉ) Discourse on method; translated with an introduction, by Laurence J. Lafleur. Indianapolis, [1950(repr. 1976)]. pp. 50.

METRIC SYSTEM.

— Australia.

METRIC CONVERSION BOARD [AUSTRALIA]. Annual report. a., 1970/71 (1st)- Canberra. *Included in AUSTRALIA. Parliament. [Parliamentary papers].*

— United Kingdom.

METRICATION BOARD [U.K.]. Metrication and elderly people: a report based on research by the Tavistock Institute of Human Relations and by National Opinion Polls Limited. London, [1976]. pp. 64.

METROPOLITAN AREAS

— Australia.

ARCHER (R.W.) Urban development and land prices: part I: planning and managing metropolitan development and land supply: rationalising the government roles in metropolitan development and land use. Melbourne, 1976. pp. 74. *(Committee for Economic Development of Australia. P Series. No. 19)*

— France.

PROBLEMES de santé dans une agglomération urbaine en mutation: Boulogne-Billancourt; [by] D. Minvielle [and others]. Le Vésinet, Division de la Recherche Médico-Sociale, 1975. pp. 161. *bibliog. With English summary.*

— Germany.

STADTREGIONEN in der Bundesrepublik Deutschland, 1970. Hannover, 1975. pp. 134. *(Akademie für Raumforschung und Landesplanung. Forschungs- und Sitzungsberichte. Band 103) Map in end pocket.*

— United States.

DANIELSON (MICHAEL NILS) The politics of exclusion. New York, 1976. pp. 443.

ECONOMIC issues in metropolitan growth; edited by Paul R. Portney; papers presented at a forum conducted by Resources for the Future, May 28-29, 1975, in Washington, D.C. Baltimore, [1976]. pp. 143.

METROPOLITAN FINANCE

— United States.

ECONOMIC issues in metropolitan growth; edited by Paul R. Portney; papers presented at a forum conducted by Resources for the Future, May 28-29, 1975, in Washington, D.C. Baltimore, [1976]. pp. 143.

The FINANCIAL crises of our cities; (a Round Table held on December 10, 1975...); Melvin R. Laird, moderator, etc. Washington, [1976]. pp. 41. *(American Enterprise Institute for Public Policy Research. Round Tables)*

METROPOLITAN GOVERNMENT

— United States.

METROPOLITANIZATION and public services;...papers by John G. Wofford [and others]. Washington, [1972]. pp. 69. *(Resources for the Future, Inc. The Governance of Metropolitan Regions. No. 3)*

ROSENBAUM (WALTER A.) and KAMMERER (GLADYS MARIE) Against long odds: the theory and practice of successful governmental consolidation. Beverly Hills, [1974]. pp. 84.

HARRIGAN (JOHN J.) Political change in the metropolis. Boston, Mass., [1976]. pp. 450.

MEXICAN AMERICANS.

REISLER (MARK) By the sweat of their brow: Mexican immigrant labor in the United States, 1900-1940. Westport, Conn., 1976. pp. 298. *bibliog.*

THREE perspectives on ethnicity: Blacks, Chicanos and native Americans; [edited by] Carlos E. Cortés [and others]. New York, [1976]. pp. 429.

BRIGGS (VERNON M.) and others. The Chicano worker. Austin, Tex., [1977]. pp. 129. *bibliog.*

SAMORA (JULIAN) and SIMON (PATRICIA VANDEL) A history of the Mexican-American people. Notre Dame, Ind., [1977]. pp. 238. *bibliogs.*

MEXICO

— Antiquities.

The EARLY Mesoamerican village; edited by Kent V. Flannery. New York, [1976]. pp. 377. *bibliogs.*

— Civilization.

LAFAYE (JACQUES) Quetzalcóatl and Guadalupe: the formation of Mexican national consciousness, 1531-1813; foreword by Octavio Paz; translated by Benjamin Keen. Chicago, 1976. pp. 336.

— Commerce — Statistics.

MEXICO. Direccion General de Estadistica. Censo Comercial, 1971. VI censo comercial, 1971; datos de 1970: resumen general. Mexico, 1975. pp. 678.

— Economic conditions.

AGUILAR MONTEVERDE (ALONSO) Hacia un cambio radical: ensayos. Mexico, 1975. pp. 235.

CRUZ CASTELLANOS (FEDERICO) Capitalismo subdesarrollado en Mexico: critica de la economia. Mexico, [1975]. pp. 239. *bibliog.*

INTERNATIONAL CONGRESS OF MEXICAN HISTORY, 4TH, SANTA MONICA, CALIF., 1973. Contemporary Mexico: papers of the...Congress...; edited by James W. Wilkie [and others]. Berkeley, Calif., [1976]. pp. 858. *(California University. Latin American Center. Latin American Studies. vol. 29)*

FERNANDEZ (RAUL A.) The United States-Mexico border: a politico-economic profile. Notre Dame, Ind., [1977]. pp. 174.

MATTHIES (KLAUS) Transnationale Unternehmen in Mexiko. Hamburg, 1977. pp. 185. *bibliog. (Hamburg. Hamburgisches Welt-Wirtschafts-Archiv. Veröffentlichungen)*

— Economic history.

CAMBRIDGE. University. Centre of Latin American Studies. Working Papers. No.12. Some aspects of economic change and the origins of the Mexican revolution, 1876-1910; [by Dudley Ankerson]. Cambridge, [1973]. fo.40. *Photocopy.*

— — Sources.

El BANCO de Avio y el fomento de la industria nacional. Mexico, 1966. pp. 350. *(Banco Nacional de Comercio Exterior. Coleccion de Documentos para la Historia del Comercio Exterior de Mexico. 2a Serie. 3)*

— Economic policy.

MEXICO. Secretaria de Hacienda y Credito Publico. Direccion General de Prensa, Memoria, Bibliotecas y Publicaciones. 1958. Discursos pronunciados por los CC. Secretarios de Hacienda y Credito Publico en las Convenciones Bancarias celebradas del año 1934 a 1958. Mexico, [1958?]. pp. 291.

ORTIZ MENA (ANTONIO) Discursos y declaraciones, 1964-1970. [Mexico, 1970]. pp. 649.

MEXICO. Secretaria de Hacienda y Credito Publico. Direccion General de Prensa, Memorias, Bibliothecas y Publicaciones. Documentos economicos de la administracion publica. irreg., Je 1971-Ap 1973 (nos. 5-21), with gaps (nos. 6, 12- 15). [Mexico City]. *Speeches, etc. of Hugo B. Margáin.*

SEPULVEDA AMOR (BERNARDO) and others. Las empresas transnacionales en Mexico. Mexico, 1974. pp. 167. *(Mexico City. Colegio de Mexico. Centro de Estudios Internacionales. Coleccion. 12)*

AGUILAR MONTEVERDE (ALONSO) Hacia un cambio radical: ensayos. Mexico, 1975. pp. 235.

CRUZ CASTELLANOS (FEDERICO) Capitalismo subdesarrollado en Mexico: critica de la economia. Mexico, [1975]. pp. 239. *bibliog.*

La POLITICA presidencial. [Mexico, 1975]. pp. 166. *(Partido Revolucionario Institucional. Instituto de Estudios Politicos, Economicos y Sociales. Archivos del IEPES. Temas Nacionales. 8) Commentaries on Presidential Messages, 1971-1974, presented at meetings organized by the Institute and the Executive Committee of the P.R.I.*

GRINDLE (MERILEE SERRILL) Bureaucrats, politicians, and peasants in Mexico. Berkeley, [1977]. pp. 220. *bibliog.*

— Foreign relations.

TORRE VILLAR (ERNESTO DE LA) Mexico y su politica interamericana: la mision de Don Tadeo Ortiz de Ayala. Guadalajara, Mexico, 1973. pp. 214.

[ECHEVERRIA (LUIS)] La politica exterior de Mexico, 1970-1974; seleccion y prologo de Manuel Tello. Mexico, 1975. pp. 239.

— — America, Latin.

MEXICO y America Latina: la nueva politica exterior; [edited by Mario Ojeda Gomez]. Mexico, 1974. pp. 201. *(Mexico City. Colegio de Mexico. Centro e Estudios Internacionales. Coleccion. 11)*

— — Germany.

VOLLAND (KLAUS) Das Dritte Reich und Mexiko: Studien zur Entwicklung des deutsch-mexikanischen Verhältnisses, 1933-1942, unter besonderer Berücksichtigung der Ölpolitik. Frankfurt/M., 1976. pp. 364. *bibliog.*

— — United States.

GUERRERO YOACHAM (CRISTIAN) Las conferencias del Niagara Falls: la mediacion de Argentina, Brasil y Chile en el conflicto entre Estados Unidos y Mexico en 1914. Santiago de Chile, 1966. pp. 189. *bibliog.*

MEYER (LORENZO) Mexico and the United States in the oil controversy, 1917-1942. Austin, [Tex., 1972]. pp. 367. *bibliog.*

— History.

INTERNATIONAL CONGRESS OF MEXICAN HISTORY, 4TH, SANTA MONICA, CALIF., 1973. Contemporary Mexico: papers of the...Congress...; edited by James W. Wilkie [and others]. Berkeley, Calif., [1976]. pp. 858. *(California University. Latin American Center. Latin American Studies. vol. 29)*

— — Sources.

ZAVALA (LORENZO DE) Obras: el historiador y el representante popular; Ensayo critico [sic] de las revoluciones de Mexico desde 1808 hasta 1830; prologo, ordenacion y notas de Manuel Gonzalez Ramirez. Mexico, 1969. pp. 969. *Also contains other writings and speeches for years 1820-1834.*

— — 1810- .

ZAVALA (LORENZO DE) Obras: el historiador y el representante popular; Ensayo critico [sic] de las revoluciones de Mexico desde 1808 hasta 1830; prologo, ordenacion y notas de Manuel Gonzalez Ramirez. Mexico, 1969. pp. 969. *Also contains other writings and speeches for years 1820-1834.*

ESTUDIOS de historia moderna y contemporanea de Mexico: publicacion eventual del Instituto de Investigaciones Historicas de la Universidad Nacional Autonoma. vol. 3. Mexico, 1970. pp. 161. *Editor of this volume, J. Valero Silva. Volumes 1 and 2 are out of print.*

BAZANT (JAN) A concise history of Mexico from Hidalgo to Cárdenas, 1805- 1940. Cambridge, 1977. pp. 222.

— — 1821-1861.

COSTELOE (MICHAEL P.) La primera Republica Federal de Mexico, 1824-1835: un estudio de los partidos politicos en el Mexico independiente; traduccion de Manuel Fernadez Gasalla. Mexico, 1975. pp. 492. *bibliog.*

— — 1867-1910.

CAMBRIDGE. University. Centre of Latin American Studies. Working Papers. No.12. Some aspects of economic change and the origins of the Mexican revolution, 1876-1910; [by Dudley Ankerson]. Cambridge, [1973]. fo.40. *Photocopy.*

— — 1910-1929, Revolution.

GILLY (ADOLFO) La revolucion interrumpida: Mexico, 1910-1920; una guerra campesina por la tierra y el poder. Mexico, [1971 repr. 1975]. pp. 397.

— Industries.

WIONCZEK (MIGUEL S.) and others. La transferencia internacional de tecnologia. Mexico, 1974. pp. 230. *bibliog.*

— Maps.

GARCIA DE MIRANDA (ENRIQUETA) and FALCON DE GYVES (ZAIDA) Atlas: nuevo atlas Porrua de la Republica Mexicana. 2nd ed. Mexico, 1974. pp. 197.

— Nobility.

LADD (DORIS M.) The Mexican nobility at independence, 1780-1826. Austin, Texas, [1976]. pp. 316. *bibliog. (Texas University. Institute of Latin American Studies. Latin American Monographs. No. 40)*

— Politics and government.

CORDOVA (ARNALDO) La formacion del poder politico en Mexico. Mexico, 1972 repr. 1975. pp. 99.

PARTIDO ACCION NACIONAL. Respuestas. Mexico, 1973. pp. 335.

GAXIOLA OCHOA (FRANCISCO JAVIER) Memorias. Mexico, 1975. pp. 356.

COLEMAN (KENNETH M.) Diffuse support in Mexico: the potential for crisis. Beverly Hills, [1976]. pp. 51. *bibliog.*

INTERNATIONAL CONGRESS OF MEXICAN HISTORY, 4TH, SANTA MONICA, CALIF., 1973. Contemporary Mexico: papers of the...Congress...; edited by James W. Wilkie [and others]. Berkeley, Calif., [1976]. pp. 858. *(California University. Latin American Center. Latin American Studies. vol. 29)*

GRINDLE (MERILEE SERRILL) Bureaucrats, politicians, and peasants in Mexico. Berkeley, [1977]. pp. 220. *bibliog.*

— Population.

LAW and population in Mexico; [by] Gerardo Cornejo [and others]. Medford, Mass., 1975. pp. 78. *(Tufts University. Fletcher School of Law and Diplomacy. Law and Population Monograph Series. No. 23)*

— Presidents.

COSIO VILLEGAS (DANIEL) La sucesion presidencial. Mexico, 1975. pp. 151.

— Relations (general) with the United States.

FOX (ANNETTE BAKER) The politics of attraction: four middle powers and the United States. New York, 1977. pp. 371.

— Religion.

LAFAYE (JACQUES) Quetzalcóatl and Guadalupe: the formation of Mexican national consciousness, 1531-1813; foreword by Octavio Paz; translated by Benjamin Keen. Chicago, 1976. pp. 336.

— Rural conditions.

CACIQUISMO y poder politico en el Mexico rural; por Roger Bartra [and others]. Mexico, 1975. pp. 203.

DURAND (PIERRE) Nanacatlan: société paysanne et lutte des classes au Mexique. Montréal, 1975. pp. 257. *bibliog.*

— Social conditions.

INTERNATIONAL CONGRESS OF MEXICAN HISTORY, 4TH, SANTA MONICA, CALIF., 1973. Contemporary Mexico: papers of the...Congress...; edited by James W. Wilkie [and others]. Berkeley, Calif., [1976]. pp. 858. *(California University. Latin American Center. Latin American Studies. vol. 29)*

— Social history.

LADD (DORIS M.) The Mexican nobility at independence, 1780-1826. Austin, Texas, [1976]. pp. 316. *bibliog. (Texas University. Institute of Latin American Studies. Latin American Monographs. No. 40)*

— Social policy.

La POLITICA presidencial. [Mexico, 1975]. pp. 166. *(Partido Revolucionario Institucional. Instituto de Estudios Politicos, Economicos y Sociales. Archivos del IEPES. Temas Nacionales. 8) Commentaries on Presidential Messages, 1971-1974, presented at meetings organized by the Institute and the Executive Committee of the P.R.I.*

GRINDLE (MERILEE SERRILL) Bureaucrats, politicians, and peasants in Mexico. Berkeley, [1977]. pp. 220. *bibliog.*

MEXICO CITY

— Social conditions.

KEMPER (ROBERT V.) Migration and adaptation: Tzintzuntzan peasants in Mexico City. Beverly Hills, [1977]. pp. 223. *bibliog.*

MICHAEL X, pseud.

See MALIK (MICHAEL ABDUL).

MICROCLIMATOLOGY

— Zaire.

CRABBE (MARCEL) L'écoclimat de Yangambi, 0 49'N, 24 29'E, 470 m, de 1960 à 1965. Kinshasa, Office National de la Recherche et du Développement, [1970]. pp. 95.

MICROCOMPUTERS.

SIPPL (CHARLES J.) Microcomputer handbook. New York, 1977. pp. 454.

MIDDLE AGES

— History.

CHURCH and government in the Middle Ages: essays presented to C.R. Cheney on his 70th birthday;...edited by C.N.L. Brooke [and others]. Cambridge, 1976. pp. 312. *bibliog.*

MIDDLE CLASSES.

LEWIS (AUSTIN) Proletarian and petit-bourgeois. Chicago, [1911]. pp. 48.

— Germany.

KLEIN (ULRICH) and SCHERER (KLAUS JUERGEN) Bürgerräte gegen die Arbeiterbewegung: Untersuchungen und Dokumente am Beispiel Elberfeld-Barmen, 1918-1922. Wentorf/Hamburg, 1976. pp. 124. *bibliog.*

WEILER (HEINRICH) Gewinnsteuerreform und gewerblicher Mittelstand. Göttingen, 1976. pp. 313. *bibliog. (Institut für Mittelstandsforschung. Schriften zur Mittelstandsforschung. Nr.71)*

— United Kingdom.

CROSSICK (GEOFFREY) ed. The lower middle class in Britain 1870-1914. London, [1977]. pp. 213.

MIDDLE class housing in Britain; edited by M.A. Simpson and T.H. Lloyd. Newton Abbot, 1977. pp. 217.

PITT (JAMES) Gentrification in Islington: the return of the middle classes to an inner London borough and the subsequent effects on housing. London, [1977]. fo. 36.

MIGRANT LABOUR.

GEORGE (PIERRE) Les migrations internationales. [Paris], 1976. pp. 230. *bibliog.*

NEW approaches to the study of migration; David Guillet and Douglas Uzzell, editors. Houston, Texas, 1976. pp. 181. *bibliogs. (Rice University. Rice University Studies. vol. 62, no.3)*

— Africa.

MIGRANTS and strangers in Africa; guest editor: Niara Sudarkasa. East Lansing, [1975]. pp. 124. *bibliogs. (Michigan State University. African Studies Center. African Urban Notes. Series B, No. 1)*

— Africa, Subsaharan.

LE BRIS (EMILE) and others. Capitalisme négrier: la marche des paysans vers le prolétariat. Paris, 1976. pp. 211.

— European Economic Community countries.

EUROPEAN COMMUNITIES. Commission. 1976. Action programme in favour of migrant workers and their families. [Brussels], 1976. pp. 22. *(Bulletin of the European Communities. Supplements. [1976/3])*

— France.

ARDITTI (S.) and others, eds. Etude sur l'habitat insalubre: le logement des travailleurs immigrés. [Paris], Service des Affaires Economiques et Internationales, 1974. pp. 146.

MILDMAY (BENJAMIN) Earl Fitzwalter.

EDWARDS (A.C.) The account books of Benjamin Mildmay, Earl Fitzwalter. London, [1977]. pp. 224.

MILITARISM.

CORTESE (CHARLES F.) Modernization, threat and the power of the military. Beverly Hills, [1976]. pp. 64. *bibliog.*

— Germany.

KEHR (ECKART) Economic interest, militarism, and foreign policy: essays on German history; edited...by Gordon A. Craig; translated by Grete Heinz. Berkeley, [1977]. pp. 209.

NUSS (KARL) Militär und Wiederaufrüstung in der Weimarer Republik: zur politischen Rolle und Entwicklung der Reichswehr. Berlin, 1977. pp. 372. *bibliog. (Militärgeschichtliches Institut der Deutschen Demokratischen Republik. Schriften)*

MILITARY ART AND SCIENCE.

CLAUSEWITZ (CARL VON) On war; edited and translated by Michael Howard and Peter Paret...with a commentary by Bernard Brodie. Princeton, N.J., [1976]. pp. 711.

— Dictionaries and encyclopedias.

SOVETSKAIA voennaia entsiklopediia. Moskva, 1976 in progress.

— History.

SMALDONE (JOSEPH P.) Warfare in the Sokoto caliphate: historical and sociological perspectives. Cambridge, 1977. pp. 228. *bibliog. (Cambridge. University. African Studies Centre. African Studies Series. 19)*

MILITARY ASSISTANCE, AMERICAN.

LOBE (THOMAS) United States national security policy and aid to the Thailand police. Denver, Col., [1977]. pp. 161. *(Denver. University. Social Science Foundation and Graduate School of International Studies. Monograph Series in World Affairs. vol. 14, no. 2)*

MILITARY BASES, AMERICAN

— Spain.

CHAMORRO (EDUARDO) and FONTES (IGNACIO) Las bases norteamericanas en España. Barcelona, 1976. pp. 328.

MILITARY EDUCATION

— Asia, Southeast.

LEBRA (JOYCE CHAPMAN) Japanese-trained armies in southeast Asia: independence and volunteer forces in World War II. New York, 1977. pp. 226. *bibliog.*

MILITARY LAW

— Italy.

ITALY. Statutes, etc. 1941-1974. Codici penali militari di pace e di guerra annotati con la giurisprudenza; a cura di Saverio Malizia. 4th ed. Milano, 1975. pp. 568.

— Poland.

POLAND. Najwy'zszy Sąd Wojskowy. 1960. Orzecznictwo Najwy'zszego Sądu Wojskowego: [za lata 1954-1959]. Warszawa, 1960. pp. 440.

MILITARY OCCUPATION.

GILMORE (WILLIAM C.) Belligerent occupation, public property and war crimes in Namibia: a new role for international law. Ottawa, 1976. pp. 24. *(Carleton University. Norman Paterson School of International Affairs. Current Comment. 11)*

MILITARY POSTS

— Russia.

GESSEN (SERGEI IAKOVLEVICH) Arakcheevskaia barshchina: istoricheskie zarisovki iz epokhi voennykh poselenii. Moskva, 1932. pp. 119.

MILITARY SERVICE, COMPULSORY

— United Kingdom.

LAMONT (ARCHIE) How Scots opposed the peacetime call-up. Carlops by Penicuik, [1976]. pp. 31.

MILITARY SERVICE AS A PROFESSION.

The SOCIAL psychology of military service; edited by Nancy L. Goldman and David R. Segal. Beverly Hills, 1976. pp. 299. *bibliog. Papers of a conference held at the Center for Continuing Education, University of Chicago, 1975.*

MILITARY TRAINING CAMPS

— United Kingdom.

SHARP (EVELYN) Baroness Sharp. Dartmoor: a report...to the Secretary of State for the Environment and the Secretary of State for Defence of a public local inquiry held in December, 1975 and May, 1976 into the continued use of Dartmoor by the Ministry of Defence for training purposes. London, H.M.S.O., 1977. pp. 121.

MILK

— European Economic Community countries.

EUROPEAN COMMUNITIES. Statistical Office. Monthly statistics of milk. m., 1976 (no.4)- Luxembourg. *[in Community languages],.*

MILK SUPPLY

— European Economic Community countries.

EUROPEAN COMMUNITIES. Commission. 1976. Action programme, 1977-80, for the progressive achievement of balance in the milk market: presented...to the Council on 9 July 1976. [Brussels], 1976. pp. 18. *(Bulletin of the European Communities. Supplements. [1976/10])*

MILK TRADE

— European Economic Community countries.

EUROPEAN COMMUNITIES. Commission. 1976. Action programme, 1977-80, for the progressive achievement of balance in the milk market: presented...to the Council on 9 July 1976. [Brussels], 1976. pp. 18. *(Bulletin of the European Communities. Supplements. [1976/10])*

— Netherlands.

ECONOMISCH INSTITUUT VOOR HET MIDDEN- EN KLEINBEDRIJF. Bedrijfseconomische Publikaties. De ambulante detailhandel in melk en melkprodukten 1971-1973, 1974, 1975. 's-Gravenhage, 1976. pp. 50.

— Switzerland.

HAEGI (HANS RUDOLF) Die schweizerische Milchwirtschaft: Produktion, Verwertung, Aussenhandel, Gesetzgebung, Verwertungsorganisationen. [Bern, 1976]. pp. 39. *bibliog.*

MILL (JAMES).

JAMES and John Stuart Mill: papers of the centenary conference; edited by John M. Robson and Michael Laine. Toronto, [1976]. pp. 160. *Conference held in Toronto, 1973, to celebrate the bicentenary of James Mill's birth and the centenary of John Stuart Mill's death.*

MILL (JOHN STUART).

JAMES and John Stuart Mill: papers of the centenary conference; edited by John M. Robson and Michael Laine. Toronto, [1976]. pp. 160. *Conference held in Toronto, 1973, to celebrate the bicentenary of James Mill's birth and the centenary of John Stuart Mill's death.*

THOMPSON (DENNIS FRANK) John Stuart Mill and representative government. Princeton, N.J., [1976]. pp. 241.

MILLENNIUM.

NAQUIN (SUSAN) Millenarian rebellion in China: the Eight Trigams uprising of 1813. New Haven, Conn., 1976. pp. 384. *bibliog. (Yale University. Yale Historical Publications. Miscellany. 108)*

JANSMA (LAMMERT GOSSE) Melchiorieten, Munstersen en Batenburgers: een sociologische analyse van een millennistische beweging uit de 16e eeuw. 1977. pp. 348. *bibliog. Proefschrift (doctor) - Erasmus Universiteit Rotterdam.*

— History of doctrines.

DAVIDSON (JAMES WEST) The logic of millennial thought: eighteenth-century New England. New Haven, 1977. pp. 308. *bibliog. (Yale University. Yale Historical Publications. Miscellany. 112)*

MILLERAND (ALEXANDRE).

DERFLER (LESLIE) Alexandre Millerand: the socialist years. The Hague, [1977]. pp. 326. *bibliog.*

MILLETT (JOHN DAVID).

MILLETT (JOHN DAVID) Politics and higher education. University, Ala., [1974]. pp. 147. *(Southern Regional Training Program in Public Administration. Annual Lecture Series)*

MILLS (CHARLES WRIGHT).

SCIMECCA (JOSEPH) The sociological theory of C. Wright Mills. Port Washington, N.Y., 1977. pp. 148. *bibliog.*

MILTON (JOHN).

MILNER (ANDREW JOHN) John Milton and the English revolution: a study in the sociology of literature. [1977]. fo. 334. *bibliog. Typescript. Ph.D. (London) thesis: unpublished. This thesis is the property of London University and may not be removed from the Library.*

MILTON KEYNES

— Growth.

READING. University. Department of Agricultural Economics and Management. Miscellaneous Studies. No. 57. Milton Keynes 1973: case studies in a dwindling agriculture. Reading, 1974. pp. 25.

MILWAUKEE

— Economic history.

McSHANE (CLAY) Technology and reform: street railways and the growth of Milwaukee, 1887-1900. Madison, Wisconsin, [1974]. pp. 187. *bibliog. Author's thesis (M.A.), University of Wisconsin.*

— Emigration and immigration.

CONZEN (KATHLEEN NEILS) Immigrant Milwaukee, 1836-1860: accommodation and community in a frontier city. Cambridge, Mass., 1976. pp. 300.

— Social history.

CONZEN (KATHLEEN NEILS) Immigrant Milwaukee, 1836-1860: accommodation and community in a frontier city. Cambridge, Mass., 1976. pp. 300.

MINANGKABAU (INDONESIAN PEOPLE).

See MENANGKABAU (INDONESIAN PEOPLE).

MINAS GERAIS

— Rural conditions.

MERCADANTE (PAULO) Os sertões do leste: estudo de uma região, a Mata Mineira. Rio de Janeiro, 1973. pp. 135.

— Social life and customs.

MERCADANTE (PAULO) Os sertões do leste: estudo de uma região, a Mata Mineira. Rio de Janeiro, 1973. pp. 135.

MIND AND BODY.

POLTEN (ERIC P.) Critique of the psycho-physical identity theory: a refutation of scientific materialism and an establishment of mind-matter dualism by means of philosophy and scientific method. The Hague, [1973]. pp. 290. *bibliog.*

MINERAL INDUSTRIES

— Bolivia.

CORPORACION MINERA DE BOLIVIA. Memoria. a., 1973- La Paz.

— China.

WANG (KUNG-PING) Mineral resources and basic industries in the People's Republic of China. Boulder, 1977. pp. 211.

— Greece.

GREECE. Ethnike Statistike Hyperesia. Etesia statistike ereuna oruxeion (metalleion - latomeion - alukon): Annual statistical survey on mines, quarries and salterns. a., 1974- Athenai.

— Iran.

RESEARCH CENTER FOR INDUSTRIAL AND TRADE DEVELOPMENT [IRAN]. The development of mining in Iran. Tehran, Ministry of Economy, 1971. fo. 10.

— Mexico.

MEXICO. Direccion General de Estadistica. Estadistica minerometalurgica: produccion y exportacion. a., 1968/69-1971. [Mexico City].

— Underdeveloped areas.

See UNDERDEVELOPED AREAS —
  Mineral industries.

— United States.

POLITICS, minerals, and survival; edited by Ralph W. Marsden. Madison, 1975. pp. 86. *Proceedings of a symposium sponsored by the Society of Economic Geologists and the Mining and Exploration Division, Society of Mining Engineers, American Institute of Mining, Metallurgical and Petroleum Engineers.*

MINERAL RESOURCES IN SUBMERGED LANDS.

LEIPZIGER (DANNY M.) and MUDGE (JAMES L.) Seabed mineral resources and the economic interests of developing countries. Cambridge, Mass., [1976]. pp. 240. *bibliog.*

MINERAL WATERS

— Zambia.

LEGG (C.A.) A reconnaissance survey of the hot and mineralised springs of Zambia. Lusaka, 1974. pp. 60. *bibliog. (Zambia. Geological Survey Department. Economic Reports. No. 50) 9 maps in end pocket.*

MINERS

— Colombia.

ESCALANTE (AQUILES) La mineria del hambre: Condoto y la Choco Pacifico. [Medellin, 196-?]. pp. 160. *bibliog.*

— Peru.

BONILLA MAYTA (HERACLIO) El minero de los Andes: una aproximacion a su estudio. Lima, 1974. pp. 89. *(Instituto de Estudios Peruanos. Coleccion Minima. 4)*

— United Kingdom.

LANCASHIRE AND CHESHIRE MINER'S PERMANENT RELIEF SOCIETY, THE. Report of proceedings at the...annual and special general meetings. a., 1873/87, 1905. Wigan.

SAMUEL (RAPHAEL) ed. Miners, quarrymen and saltworkers. London, 1977. pp. 363. *(History Workshop. History Workshop Series)*

— — Wales.

NORTH WALES PERMANENT RELIEF SOCIETY, THE. Report of proceedings at the...general annual meeting. a., 1889/1903. Wrexham.

MINES AND MINERAL RESOURCES

— Canada — Ontario.

HEWITT (D.F.) and YUNDT (S.E.) Mineral resources of the Toronto-centred region. Toronto, 1971. pp. 34. *bibliog. (Ontario. Department of Mines and Northern Affairs. Industrial Mineral Reports. No.38) Map sheet in end pocket.*

— China.

WANG (KUNG-PING) Mineral resources and basic industries in the People's Republic of China. Boulder, 1977. pp. 211.

— India — Goa, Daman and Diu.

GOA, DAMAN AND DIU. Centro de Informação e Turismo. 1960. Goa's mining industry: a survey. [Panjim, 1960]. pp. 6.

— South Africa.

SOUTH AFRICA. Geological Survey. 1976. Mineral resources of the republic of South Africa;...edited by C.B. Coetzee. 5th ed. Pretoria, 1976. pp. 462. *bibliogs. (Handbooks. 7) 2 maps and a chart in end pocket.*

— Tasmania.

TASMANIA. Commonwealth Bureau of Census and Statistics. Tasmanian Office. Mining industry. a., 1974/75- Hobart.

MINES AND MINING

— United Kingdom.

MEE (GRAHAM) Aristocratic enterprise: the Fitzwilliam industrial undertakings, 1795-1857. Glasgow, 1975. pp. 222.

MINIATURE COMPUTERS.

IFIP TC-2 CONFERENCE ON SOFTWARE FOR MINICOMPUTERS, KESZTHELY, HUNGARY, 1975. Minicomputer software: proceedings of the...conference; edited by James R. Bell and C. Gordon Bell. Amsterdam, 1976. pp. 333.

MINING CORPORATIONS

— Australia.

AUSTRALIA. Commonwealth Bureau of Census and Statistics. 1974. Foreign ownership and control of the mining industry, 1971-72. Canberra, 1974. pp. 33.

— Colombia.

ESCALANTE (AQUILES) La mineria del hambre: Condoto y la Choco Pacifico. [Medellin, 196-?]. pp. 160. *bibliog.*

— South Africa.

STARES (RODNEY) Consolidated Gold Fields Limited: a review of activities and issues. London, [1975]. pp. 31. *bibliog.*

— South West Africa.

JEPSON (TREVOR B.) Rio Tinto-Zinc in Namibia. London, [1975]. fo. 18. *bibliog.*

MINING INDUSTRY AND FINANCE

— United Kingdom.

U.K. Department of Industry. 1975. Mineral Exploration and Investment Grants Act 1972: financial assistance for mineral exploration in Great Britain: a guide for industry. [rev.ed.] London, 1975. pp. 13.

MINORITIES.

NONSTATE nations in international politics: comparative system analyses; edited by Judy S. Bertelsen. New York, 1977. pp. 263. *bibliogs.*

MINORITIES.(Cont.)

— Economic conditions — United Kingdom.

COMMUNITY RELATIONS COMMISSION. CRC evidence to the Royal Commission on the Distribution of Income and Wealth to aid their inquiry into incomes at the lower levels. London, 1976. pp. 17. *bibliog.*

— Education — United States.

WOLLENBERG (CHARLES M.) All deliberate speed: segregation and exclusion in California schools, 1855-1975. Berkeley, Calif., [1976]. pp. 201.

WEINBERG (MEYER) A chance to learn: the history of race and education in the United States. Cambridge, 1977. pp. 471. *bibliog.*

— Education (Higher) — United States.

BROWN (FRANK) and STENT (MADELON DELANY) Minorities in U.S. institutions of higher education. New York, 1977. pp. 178. *bibliog.*

— Employment — United Kingdom.

LEE (G.L.) and WRENCH (K. J.) Accidents are colour-blind: industrial accidents and the immigrant worker; a pilot study; published…for the Birmingham Community Relations Council. [London], Community Relations Commission, 1977. pp. 24. *bibliog.*

PEARN (M.A.) Selecting and training coloured workers. London, H.M.S.O., 1977. pp. 46. *bibliog. (Training Information Papers. 9)*

U.K. Department of Employment. Unit for Manpower Studies. 1977. The role of immigrants in the labour market; project report. London, [1977]. pp. 230. *bibliog.*

— Health and hygiene — United Kingdom.

COMMUNITY RELATIONS COMMISSION. Evidence to the Royal Commission on the National Health Service. London, 1977. pp. 20.

— Housing — United Kingdom.

U.K. Department of the Environment. 1976. Consultation paper: records and information relating to the housing of members of ethnic groups. [London, 1976]. fo.8.

COMMUNITY RELATIONS COMMISSION. Housing choice and ethnic concentration: an attitude study. London, 1977. pp. 69.

DUNCAN (S.S.) Housing disadvantage and residential mobility: immigrants and institutions in a northern town. Brighton, 1977. fo.28. *(Brighton. University of Sussex. Sussex Working Papers in Urban and Regional Studies. 5)*

LONDON HOUSING RESEARCH GROUP. Working Party on Race and Housing. Race and local authority housing: information on ethnic groups; a report; [Rob Hammond, chairman]. London, Community Relations Commission, 1977. pp. 16.

U.K. Race Relations Board. 1977. Comments on the government's consultation paper on records and information relating to the housing of members of ethnic groups. [London, 1977]. fo.4.

— Australia.

PITTOCK (A. BARRIE) Beyond white Australia: a short history of race relations in Australia. Surry Hills, N.S.W., 1975. pp. 51.

— Austria.

KALT (HANS) Minderheiten in Österreich: worum geht es eigentlich? [Vienna, 1976]. pp. 30.

— China.

VELIKODERZHAVNAIA politika maoistov v natsional'nykh raionakh KNR. Moskva, 1975. pp. 126.

DREYER (JUNE TEUFEL) China's forty millions: minority nationalities and national integration in the People's Republic of China. Cambridge, Mass., 1976. pp. 333. *bibliog. (Harvard University. East Asian Research Center. Harvard East Asian Series. 87)*

— Finland — Bibliography.

SCHWARZ (DAVID) compiler. Invandrar- och minoritetsfrågor: nordisk bibliografi. Stockholm, [1976]. pp. 105. *With table of contents in English.*

— Russia.

LEWIS (ROBERT ALDEN) and others. Nationality and population change in Russia and the USSR: an evaluation of census data, 1897-1970. New York, 1976. pp. 456. *bibliog. (Population Change in Russia and the USSR, 1897-1970. vol. 1)*

PRUUDEN (SALME) Panslavism and Russian communism. London, 1976. pp. 59.

TASHKENTSKII protsess: sud nad desiat'iu predstaviteliami krymskotatarskogo naroda, 1 iiulia - 5 avgusta 1969 g.: sbornik dokumentov s illiustratsiiami. Amsterdam, 1976. pp. 854. *(Alexander Herzen Foundation. Seriia "Biblioteka Samizdata". No.7)*

— Scandinavia — Bibliography.

SCHWARZ (DAVID) compiler. Invandrar- och minoritetsfrågor: nordisk bibliografi. Stockholm, [1976]. pp. 105. *With table of contents in English.*

— South Africa.

BROWETT (J.G.) and HART (T.) White minority population groups in Johannesburg. Johannesburg, 1976. pp. 30. *bibliog. (Johannesburg. University of the Witwatersrand. Urban and Regional Research Unit. Occasional Papers. No. 14)*

— Sweden.

ARNSTBERG (KARL OLOV) and EHN (BILLY) Etniska minoriteter i Sverige förr och nu. Lund, [1976]. pp. 141. *bibliog.*

— United Kingdom.

AIREY (COLIN) and others. A technical report on a survey of racial minorities. London, 1976. pp. 99.

BRITISH COUNCIL OF CHURCHES. Community and Race Relations Unit and RUNNYMEDE TRUST. Ethnic minorities in society: a reference guide. [London], 1976. pp. 55. *bibliog.*

— United States.

RYAN (JOHN PAUL) Cultural diversity and the American experience: political participation among blacks, Appalachians, and Indians. Beverly Hills, [1975]. pp. 64. *bibliog.*

GREELEY (ANDREW M.) Ethnicity, denomination and inequality. Beverly Hills, [1976]. pp. 85. *bibliog.*

HAHN (HARLAN) and HOLLAND (ROLAND WILLIAM) American government: minority rights versus majority rule. New York, [1976]. pp. 203.

HOPE (JOHN) 1909- . Minority access to Federal grants-in-aid: the gap between policy and performance. New York, 1976. pp. 267. *bibliog.*

WEAVER (JERRY L.) National health policy and the underserved: ethnic minorities, women, and the elderly. Saint Louis, 1976. pp. 161.

MINORITY BUSINESS ENTERPRISES

— United Kingdom.

ALDRICH (HOWARD) and FEIT (STEPHANIE) Black entrepreneurs in England: a summary of the literature and some suggestions for further research. 1975. fo. 40. *bibliog. Typescript: unpublished.*

— United States.

EMERGING issues in black economic development; edited by Benjamin F. Bobo and Alfred E. Osborne. Lexington, Mass., [1976]. pp. 239. *Based on a conference sponsored by The Joint Center for Community Studies, 1975.*

MIRBEAU (OCTAVE).

CARR (REG) Anarchism in France: the case of Octave Mirbeau. Manchester, 1977. pp. 190. *bibliog.*

MIRONOV (PHILLIPP KUZ'MICH).

MEDVEDEV (ROI ALEKSANDROVICH) La révolution d'octobre était-elle inéluctable?: suivi d'une lettre à Lénine par Philippe Mironov; traduit du russe par Jean Chantal. Paris, [1976]. pp. 188.

MISCEGENATION

— America, Latin.

COMAS CAMPS (JUAN) Antropologia de los pueblos iberoamericanos. Barcelona, 1974. pp. 223. *bibliog.*

MISCONDUCT IN OFFICE

— Italy.

LI VECCHI (ROSARIO) I delitti dei pubblici ufficiali contro la pubblica amministrazione: rassegna di dottrina e raccolta di giurisprudenza. Catania, 1975. pp. 571. *bibliog.*

MISSIONS

— Africa, Subsaharan.

REA (WILLIAM FRANCIS) The economics of the Zambezi missions, 1580-1759. Roma, 1976. pp. 189. *bibliog. (Institutum Historicum S.I. Bibliotheca. vol. 39)*

— China.

WEST (PHILIP) Yenching University and Sino-Western relations, 1916-1952. Cambridge, Mass., 1976. pp. 327. *bibliog. (Harvard University. East Asian Research Center. Harvard East Asian Series. 85)*

— Malawi.

McCRACKEN (K. JOHN) Politics and Christianity in Malawi 1875-1940: the impact of the Livingstonia Mission in the Northern Province. Cambridge, 1977. pp. 324. *bibliog.*

— Rwanda.

LINDEN (IAN) Church and revolution in Rwanda. Manchester, [1977]. pp. 304. *bibliog.*

MISSISSIPPI VALLEY

— Rural conditions.

HOLLEY (DONALD) Uncle Sam's farmers: the New Deal communities in the lower Mississippi valley. Urbana, Ill., [1975]. pp. 312. *bibliog.*

MITTERAND (FRANÇOIS).

GIESBERT (FRANZ OLIVIER) François Mitterand; ou, La tentation de l'histoire. Paris, [1977]. pp. 334.

MLYNARSKI (FELIKS JOHN).

MŁYNARSKI (FELIKS JOHN) Wspomnienia. Warszawa, 1971. pp. 563.

MNONG (INDOCHINESE TRIBE).

CONDOMINAS (GEORGES) We have eaten the forest: the story of a Montagnard village in the central highlands of Vietnam; translated from the French by Adrienne Foulke. London, 1977. pp. 423. *bibliog.*

MOCH (JULES).

MOCH (JULES) Une si longue vie. Paris, [1976]. pp. 653.

MODERNISM

— Catholic Church.

POULAT (EMILE) Catholicisme, démocratie et socialisme: le mouvement catholique et Mgr. Benigni de la naissance du socialisme à la victoire du fascisme. [Paris, 1977]. pp. 562. *bibliog.*

MOHAMMEDAN EMPIRE

— Economic history.

DOLS (MICHAEL WALTERS) The Black Death in the Middle East. Princeton, N.J., [1977]. pp. 390. *bibliog.*

— Social history.

DOLS (MICHAEL WALTERS) The Black Death in the Middle East. Princeton, N.J., [1977]. pp. 390. *bibliog.*

MOHAMMEDANS IN RUSSIA.

ASHIROV (NUGMAN) Islam i natsii. Moskva, 1975. pp. 144.

MOLDAVIA

— Census.

SOVETOV (P.V.) ed. Moldaviia v epokhu feodalizma. t. 7, ch.1. Perepisi naseleniia Moldavii 1772-1773 i 1774 gg.; sostavlenie, vstupitel'naia stat'ia i kommentarii P.G. Dmitrieva. Kishinev, 1975. pp. 606.

— History.

IOVVA (IVAN FILIMONOVICH) Dekabristy v Moldavii. Kishinev, 1975. pp. 231. *bibliog.*

MOLDAVIAN REPUBLIC

— History — Bibliography.

TODRINA (T.) and others, compilers. 50 let MSSR i Kompartii Moldavii: metodicheskie i bibliograficheskie materialy v pomoshch' bibliotekam. Kishinev, 1974. pp. 58. *In Russian and Moldavian.*

— — Sources.

MOLDAVSKAIA SSR v Velikoi Otechestvennoi voine Sovetskogo Soiuza, 1941-1945: sbornik dokumentov i materialov v dvukh tomakh. Kishinev, 1975-76. 2 vols.

— Intellectual life.

KUL'TURA Moldavii za gody Sovetskoi vlasti: sbornik dokumentov v 4-kh tomakh. Kishinev, 1975 in progress.

MONARCHY.

IOFFE (GENRIKH ZINOV'EVICH) Krakh rossiiskoi monarkhicheskoi kontrrevoliutsii. Moskva, 1977. pp. 320.

MONASTERIES

— Russia.

BULYGIN (IL'IA ANDREEVICH) Monastyrskie krest'iane Rossii v pervoi chetverti XVIII veka. Moskva, 1977. pp. 327.

— United Kingdom.

RABAN (SANDRA) The estates of Thorney and Crowland: a study in medieval monastic tenure. Cambridge, 1977. pp. 106. *bibliog. (Cambridge. University. Department of Land Economy. Occasional Papers. No.7)*

MONATTE (PIERRE).

MONATTE (PIERRE) La lutte syndicale; présentation de Colette Chambelland. Paris, 1976. pp. 318.

MONDLANE (EDUARDO).

EDUARDO Mondlane. London, [1972]. pp. 174.

MONETARY POLICY.

MUNDELL (ROBERT ALEXANDER) Monetary theory: inflation, interest, and growth in the world economy. Pacific Palisades, [1971]. pp. 189.

CONFERENCE ON BANK CREDIT, MONEY AND INFLATION IN OPEN ECONOMIES, LEUVEN, 1974. Bank credit, money and inflation in open economies; edited by Michele Fratianni [and] Karel Tavernier. Berlin, [1976]. pp. 624. *bibliogs. (Kredit und Kapital. Beihefte. 3) The proceedings of a conference held at the Katholieke Universiteit te Leuven on September 12-13, 1974, organised by the Centrum voor Economische Studien.*

KENEN (PETER BAIN) Capital mobility and financial integration: a survey. Princeton, 1976. pp. 78. *bibliog. (Princeton University. Department of Economics and Sociology. International Finance Section. Princeton Studies in International Finance. No. 39)*

LUCKETT (DUDLEY G.) Money and banking. New York, [1976]. pp. 585.

The POLITICAL economy of monetary reform; edited by Robert Z. Aliber. London, 1977. pp. 270. *Papers of a conference held at Racine, Wisconsin in 1974, sponsored by the Chicago University Graduate School of Business.*

— History.

BALANCE of power or hegemony: the interwar monetary system; Benjamin M. Rowland, editor, [and others]. New York, 1976. pp. 266. *Essays originally presented as working papers at the Lehrman Institute's International Monetary Seminar, 1973-1974.*

— Mathematical models.

BLACK (STANLEY W.) International money markets and flexible exchange rates. [Washington, 1972]. pp. 72, 2. *(United States. Board of Governors of the Federal Reserve System. Staff Economic Studies. No. 70)*

ROUZIER (PHILIPPE) The evaluation of optimal monetary and fiscal policies with a macroeconomic model for Belgium. Louvain, 1975. pp. 156. *(Louvain. Université. Faculté des Sciences Économiques, Sociales et Politiques. [Publications]. Nouvelle Série. No.123)*

HERRING (RICHARD J.) and MARSTON (RICHARD C.) National monetary policies and international financial markets. Amsterdam, 1977. pp. 302. *bibliogs.*

— Canada.

COURCHENE (THOMAS J.) Money, inflation and the Bank of Canada: an analysis of Canadian monetary policy from 1970 to early 1975. Montreal, [1976]. pp. 283. *bibliogs. (Howe (C.D.) Research Institute. Special Studies)*

— European Economic Community countries.

HODGMAN (DONALD RENWICK) National monetary policies and international monetary cooperation. Boston, Mass., [1974]. pp. 266.

WERNER (PIERRE) L'Europe monétaire reconsidérée. Lausanne, 1977. pp. 74. *(Lausanne. Université. Centre de Recherches Européennes. Publications. 2. Le Processus d'Union de l'Europe)*

— France.

BOUVIER (GEORGES YVES) and GAUBERT (PHILIPPE) Offre de monnaie, politique monétaire: analyse du cas français depuis 1965. Paris, [1976]. pp. 137. *bibliog. (Paris. Université de Paris II. Travaux et Recherches. Série Sciences Economiques. 2)*

— United States.

LOMBRA (RAYMOND E.) and TORTO (RAYMOND G.) Federal Reserve defensive behavior and the reverse causation argument. [Washington, 1972]. pp. 15,3. *bibliog. (United States. Board of Governors of the Federal Reserve System. Staff Economic Studies. No. 75)*

RUGINA (ANGHEL N.) American capitalism at a crossroadse': where do we go from here?: a chronicle of how three U.S. presidents missed sound economic advice to resolve the problems of inflation, unemployment, poverty and deficits in the balance of payments. Hicksville, [1976]. pp. 269.

BLOCK (FRED L.) The origins of international economic disorder: a study of United States international monetary policy from World War II to the present. Berkeley, Calif., [1977]. pp. 282. *bibliog.*

— — Mathematical models.

HERRING (RICHARD J.) and MARSTON (RICHARD C.) National monetary policies and international financial markets. Amsterdam, 1977. pp. 302. *bibliogs.*

MONETARY UNIONS.

ALLEN (POLLY REYNOLDS) Organization and administration of a monetary union. Princeton, 1976. pp. 85. *bibliog. (Princeton University. Department of Economics and Sociology. International Finance Section. Princeton Studies in International Finance. No. 38)*

ASCHHEIM (JOSEPH) and PARK (YOON S.) Artificial currency units: the formation of functional currency areas. Princeton, 1976. pp. 29. *bibliog. (Princeton University. Department of Economics and Sociology. International Finance Section. Essays in International Finance. No.114)*

PRESLEY (JOHN R.) and DENNIS (GEOFFREY EDWIN JAMES) Currency areas. London, 1976. pp. 114.

TOWER (EDWARD) and WILLETT (THOMAS D.) The theory of optimum currency areas and exchange-rate flexibility. Princeton, N.J., 1976. pp. 98. *(Princeton University. Department of Economics and Sociology. International Finance Section. Special Papers in International Economics. No. 11)*

MONEY.

JOHNSON (HARRY GORDON) Macroeconomics and monetary theory: [lecture notes for the M.Sc. course at the London School of Economics, transcribed during the 1969-70 session and revised for publication]. London, 1971. pp. 214. *bibliog.*

MUNDELL (ROBERT ALEXANDER) Monetary theory: inflation, interest, and growth in the world economy. Pacific Palisades, [1971]. pp. 189.

UNITED NATIONS. Conference on Trade and Development. 1972. The international monetary situation: impact on world trade and development; report. (TD/140/Rev.1). New York, 1972. pp. 70.

JOHNSON (HARRY GORDON) I motivi dell'inefficacia delle svalutazioni. Siena, 1974. pp. 18. *(Estratto da Note Economiche, n.1.) With English and French summaries.*

ANIKIN (ANDREI VLADIMIROVICH) Valiutnyi krizis na Zapade. Moskva, 1975. pp. 199. *bibliog.*

RIZZO (BRUNO) Monnaie et richesse. Paris, 1975. pp. 142. *bibliog.*

BAIN (ANDREW DAVID) The control of the money supply. 2nd ed. Harmondsworth, 1976. pp. 176. *bibliog.*

CARBAUGH (ROBERT J.) and FAN (LIANG-SHING) The international monetary system: history, institutions, analyses. Lawrence, Kan., [1976]. pp. 168. *bibliog.*

CONFERENCE ON BANK CREDIT, MONEY AND INFLATION IN OPEN ECONOMIES, LEUVEN, 1974. Bank credit, money and inflation in open economies; edited by Michele Fratianni [and] Karel Tavernier. Berlin, [1976]. pp. 624. *bibliogs. (Kredit und Kapital. Beihefte. 3) The proceedings of a conference held at the Katholieke Universiteit te Leuven on September 12-13, 1974, organised by the Centrum voor Economische Studien.*

FRANK (ANDRE GUNDER) Economic genocide in Chile: monetarist theory versus humanity; two open letters to Arnold Harberger and Milton Friedman. Nottingham, 1976. pp. 87.

HAID (ALFRED) Zur Theorie der Geldnachfrage: ein theoretischer und empirischer Beitrag. [Erlangen, 1976]. pp. 370. *bibliog. Inaugural-Dissertation zur Erlangung des akademischen Grades eines Doktors der Wirtschafts- und Sozialwissenschaften der Friedrich-Alexander-Universität Erlangen-Nürnberg.*

USOSKIN (VALENTIN MARKOVICH) Teorii deneg. Moskva, 1976. pp. 228.

ANDERSEN (UWE) Das internationale Währungssystem zwischen nationaler Souveränität und supranationaler Integration: Entwicklungstendenzen seit Bretton Woods im Spannungsfeld der Interessen. Berlin, [1977]. pp. 464. *bibliog.*

MONEY.(Cont.)

POEHL (KARL OTTO) Probleme der internationalen Währungs- und Wirtschaftspolitik. Tübingen, 1977. pp. 20. *(Kiel. Universität. Institut für Weltwirtschaft. Kieler Vorträge. Neue Folge. 84)*

RANLETT (JOHN GRANT) Money and banking: an introduction to analysis and policy. 3rd ed. Santa Barbara, [1977]. pp. 614. *bibliogs.*

REES-MOGG (WILLIAM) Democracy and the value of money: the theory of money from Locke to Keynes. London, 1977. pp. 32. *(Institute of Economic Affairs. Occasional Papers. 53)*

SAVAGE (DONALD T.) Money and banking. Santa Barbara, Calif., [1977]. pp. 491. *bibliogs.*

SIJBEN (JAC. J.) Money and economic growth. Leiden, 1977. pp. 216. *bibliog. (Tilburg. Katholieke Hogeschool. Tilburg Institute of Economics. Tilburg Studies on Economics. 17)*

TEW (JOHN HEDLEY BRIAN) The evolution of the international monetary system, 1945-77. London, 1977. pp. 254. *bibliog.*

THOMAS (JEAN GABRIEL) Inflation et nouvel ordre monétaire. Paris, [1977]. pp. 304.

WAGNER (ANTONIN) Verwaltete Währung: Krise und Reform des internationalen Währungssystems unter besonderer Berücksichtigung der Entwicklungsländer. Bern, [1977]. pp. 262. *bibliogs. (Zürich. Universität. Institut für Schweizerisches Bankwesen. Bankwirtschaftliche Forschungen. Band 39)*

ZOLOTAS (XENOPHON) International monetary issues and development policies: selected essays and statements. Athens, 1977. pp. 503. *bibliog.*

— History.

GRIERSON (PHILIP) The origins of money. London, 1977. pp. 44. *(London. University. Creighton Lectures. 1970)*

WISELEY (WILLIAM) A tool of power: the political history of money. New York, [1977]. pp. 401. *bibliog.*

— Mathematical models.

MONEY and finance in economic growth and development: essays in honour of Edward S. Shaw;...edited by Ronald I. McKinnon. New York, [1976]. pp. 339. *bibliogs. Proceedings of the conference held at Stanford University in April 1974, under the auspices of the Center for Research in Economic Growth.*

INTERNATIONAL MONETARY FUND. 1977. The monetary approach to the balance of payments: a collection of research papers by members of the staff of the International Monetary Fund. Washington, 1977. pp. 290. *bibliogs.*

— Tables, etc.

AMERICAN INTERNATIONAL INVESTMENT CORPORATION. World currency charts. 8th ed. San Francisco, 1977. fo. 82.

— Brazil.

NEUHAUS (PAULO) Historia monetaria do Brasil, 1900-45. Rio de Janeiro, 1975. pp. 198. *bibliog.*

— Canada — Mathematical models.

WHITE (WILLIAM R.) The demand for money in Canada and the control of monetary aggregates: evidence from the monthly data. [Ottawa], 1976. pp. 157. *bibliog. (Bank of Canada. Staff Research Studies. No. 12)*

— Cayman Islands.

CAYMAN ISLANDS. Currency Board. Report. a., 1975- Grand Cayman.

— Colombia.

ALVIAR RAMIREZ (OSCAR) Instrumentos de direccion monetaria en Colombia. 3rd ed. Bogota, 1974. pp. 258.

— Europe.

COFFEY (PETER) Economist. Europe and money. London, 1977. pp. 95.

— European Economic Community countries.

NORMAN D'AUDENHOVE (PHILIPPE DE) Intégration économique et monétaire européenne. Bruxelles, 1972. pp. 48.

FRANCE. Direction de la Documentation. La Documentation Française. Notes et Etudes Documentaires. Nos. 4,224-4,225. Le marché des Euro-dollars et des Euro-obligations; par Joël Métais. Paris, 1975. pp. 55.

CORDEN (WARNER MAX) Monetary union: main issues facing the European Community. London, 1976. pp. 20. *(Trade Policy Research Centre. International Issues. No. 2)*

TSOUKALIS (LOUKAS) The politics and economics of European monetary integration. London, 1977. pp. 192.

WERNER (PIERRE) L'Europe monétaire reconsidérée. Lausanne, 1977. pp. 74. *(Lausanne. Université. Centre de Recherches Européennes. Publications. 2. Le Processus d'Union de l'Europe)*

— France.

BOUVIER (GEORGES YVES) and GAUBERT (PHILIPPE) Offre de monnaie, politique monétaire: analyse du cas français depuis 1965. Paris, [1976]. pp. 137. *bibliog. (Paris. Université de Paris II. Travaux et Recherches. Série Sciences Economiques. 2)*

SCHUKER (STEPHEN A.) The end of French predominance in Europe: the financial crisis of 1924 and the adoption of the Dawes plan. Chapel Hill, [1976]. pp. 444. *bibliog.*

— Germany.

HARDACH (GERD H.) Weltmarktorientierung und relative Stagnation: Währungspolitik in Deutschland, 1924-1931. Berlin, [1976]. pp. 182. *bibliog.*

TRAPP (PETER) Geldmenge, Ausgaben und Preisanstieg in der Bundesrepublik Deutschland. Tübingen, 1976. pp. 229. *bibliog. (Kiel. Universität. Institut für Weltwirtschaft. Kieler Studien. 138)*

— Germany, Eastern.

EHLERT (WILLI) and others, eds. Geldzirkulation und Kredit in der sozialistischen Planwirtschaft. Berlin, 1976. pp. 408.

— India — Mathematical models.

KHETAN (CHANDRA PRAKASH) and others. The monetary structure of the Indian economy: a quarterly econometric model. Delhi, 1976. pp. 120. *bibliog.*

— Mexico.

MEXICO. Statutes, etc. 1903-1918. Legislacion monetaria. Tomo 1. Mexico, 1959. pp. 733.

— Netherlands — Mathematical models.

NIEUWKERK (MARIUS VAN) Trade credit and monetary policy in the Netherlands: an empirical investigation into the determinants of domestic trade credit under a system of direct credit control. Amsterdam, [1976?]. pp. 17. *bibliog. (Nederlandsche Bank. Reprints. No. 18)*

— Nigeria.

FALEGAN (S.B.) Management of Nigeria's external reserves. [Lagos, 1976]. pp. 20. *(Nigerian Institute of International Affairs. Lecture Series. No. 6)*

— Norway.

ISACHSEN (ARNE JON) The demand for money in Norway. Oslo, 1975. pp. 48. *bibliog. (Norges Bank. Skriftserie. No. 3)*

— Russia.

D'IACHENKO (VASILII PETROVICH) Tovarno-denezhnye otnosheniia i finansy pri sotsializme; (raboty... , opublikovannye v 1946-1970 gg.). Moskva, 1974. pp. 495. *bibliog.*

GORODETSKII (EVGENII SERGEEVICH) ed. Problemy ispol'zovaniia tovarno-denezhnykh otnoshenii v usloviiakh razvitogo sotsializma. Moskva, 1975. pp. 121.

— South Africa.

GOEDHUYS (D.W.) Money and banking. Johannesburg, [1975] repr. 1976. pp. 231. *bibliogs.*

— Switzerland.

GROSSMANN (EUGEN) Das Irrlicht der Währungsabwertung. Zürich, 1935. pp. 101.

— Underdeveloped areas.

See UNDERDEVELOPED AREAS — Money.

— United Kingdom.

PAGET (THOMAS) 1778-1862. A letter addressed to David Ricardo, Esq. M.P. on the true principle of estimating the extent of the late depreciation in the currency, etc. London, Richardson, 1822. pp. 47. *Also contains his The price of gold an imperfect index of the depreciation in the currency: a letter addressed to Sir Francis Burdett, Bart., etc.*

BAIN (ANDREW DAVID) The control of the money supply. 2nd ed. Harmondsworth, 1976. pp. 176. *bibliog.*

HOLLOWAY (EDWARD) Honest money: the case for a currency commission. London, [1976]. pp. 12. *bibliog.*

WILSON (JOHN STUART GLADSTONE) The London money markets. Tilburg, 1976. pp. 70. *(Société Universitaire Européenne de Recherches Financières. Série SUERF. 17A)*

— United States.

RANLETT (JOHN GRANT) Money and banking: an introduction to analysis and policy. 3rd ed. Santa Barbara, [1977]. pp. 614. *bibliogs.*

MONEY SUPPLY

— United States.

LOMBRA (RAYMOND E.) and TORTO (RAYMOND G.) Federal Reserve defensive behavior and the reverse causation argument. [Washington, 1972]. pp. 15,3. *bibliog. (United States. Board of Governors of the Federal Reserve System. Staff Economic Studies. No. 75)*

— — Seasonal variations.

KAUFMAN (HERBERT M.) and LOMBRA (RAYMOND E.) Shortrun variations in the money stock: seasonal or cyclical? [Washington, 1974]. pp. 24,3. *bibliog. (United States. Board of Governors of the Federal Reserve System. Staff Economic Studies. No.82)*

MONGER (THOMAS).

BEZBORODOV (SERGEI KONSTANTINOVICH) Johann Liebhardt und Thomas Monger: zwei ausländische Helden des Fünfjahrplans. Moskau, 1932. pp. 46.

MONGOLIA

— Foreign relations — Russia.

SOVETSKO-mongol'skie otnosheniia, 1921-1974: dokumenty i materialy. Moskva, 1975 in progress.

— History.

NATSOKDORZHI (SH.) Iz istorii aratskogo dvizheniia vo Vneshnei Mongolii. Moskva, 1958. pp. 123. *With facsimiles of Mongolian documents.*

HISTORY of the Mongolian People's Republic; translated from the Mongolian and annotated by William A. Brown and Urgunge Onon. Cambridge, Mass., 1976. pp. 910. *bibliog.* (*Harvard University. East Asian Research Center. Harvard East Asian Monographs. 65*)

NAMSARAI (TSOGTYN) Sotsialisticheskaia nadstroika v stranakh, minovavshikh kapitalizm: na opyte MNR. Moskva, 1976. pp. 246. *bibliog.*

MONMOUTHSHIRE

— Economic conditions.

NEWPORT AND MONMOUTHSHIRE COLLEGE OF TECHNOLOGY. Department of Business and Management Studies. Labour mobility in Monmouthshire. Newport, Mon., 1967. pp. 152, 10.

MONNET (JEAN).

MONNET (JEAN) Mémoires. [Paris, 1976]. pp. 642.

MONOPOLIES.

POLITICHESKAIA ekonomiia sovremennogo monopolisticheskogo kapitalizma. 2nd ed. Moskva, 1975. 2 vols.

INSTITUT FÜR MARXISTISCHE STUDIEN UND FORSCHUNGEN. Kolloquium, 1976. Das Monopol: ökonomischer Kern des heutigen Kapitalismus: theoretische und aktuelle Gesichtspunkte der marxistisch-leninistischen Monopoltheorie: Referate...Frankfurt am Main vom 26./27. Juni 1976. Frankfurt am Main, 1976. pp. 322.

CLARKSON (KENNETH W.) Intangible capital and rates of return: effects of research and promotion on profitability. Washington, [1977]. pp. 77. (*American Enterprise Institute for Public Policy Research. AEI Studies. No. 138*)

MONTAGUE (RICHARD).

MONTAGUE grammar; edited by Barbara H. Partee. New York, [1976]. pp. 370. *bibliogs.*

MONTAGUT (LLUIS).

MONTAGUT (LLUIS) J'étais deuxième classe dans l'armée républicaine espagnole, 1936-1945. Paris, 1976. pp. 385.

MONTAILLOU

— Social history.

LE ROY LADURIE (EMMANUEL) Montaillou, village occitan de 1294 à 1324. [Paris, 1976]. pp. 642. *bibliog.*

MONTGELAS DE GARNERIN (MAXIMILIAN JOSEPH) Graf.

HAUSMANN (FRIEDERIKE) Die Agrarpolitik der Regierung Montgelas: Untersuchungen zum gesellschaftlichen Strukturwandel Bayerns um die Wende vom 18. zum 19. Jahrhundert. Bern, 1975. pp. 288. *bibliog.*

MONTREAL

— Industries.

TULCHINSKY (GERALD J. J.) The river barons: Montreal businessmen and the growth of industry and transportation, 1837-53. Toronto, [1977]. pp. 310. *bibliog.*

MOONEY (THOMAS J.).

MAL'KOV (VIKTOR LEONIDOVICH) Tom Muni [i.e. Mooney]: uznik San-Kventina. Moskva, 1976. pp. 168.

MOPAN INDIANS.

HOWARD (MICHAEL C.) Anthropologist. Ethnicity in southern Belize: the Kekchi and the Mopan. Colombia, Mo., 1975. pp. 19. *bibliog.* (*Missouri University. Museum of Anthropology. Museum Briefs. No. 21*)

MORAL EDUCATION.

BENSON (GEORGE CHARLES SUMNER) and ENGEMAN (THOMAS S.) Amoral America. Stanford, Calif., 1975. pp. 294. *bibliog.* (*Stanford University. Hoover Institution on War, Revolution and Peace. Hoover Institution Publications. 150*)

DUSKA (RONALD) and WHELAN (MARIELLEN) Moral development: a guide to Piaget and Kohlberg. Dublin, 1977. pp. 128. *bibliog.*

MORGAN (Sir CHARLES).

FROST (JOHN) of Newport. A second letter to Sir Charles Morgan of Tredegar, in the county of Monmouth, Baronet, M.P.;...also a letter to the farmers. Newport, the Author, 1822. pp. 39.

MORISCOS.

For a related heading see MUDEJARES.

MORMONS AND MORMONISM.

DAVIES (JOSEPH KENNETH) Deseret's sons of toil: a history of the worker movements of territorial Utah, 1852-1896. Salt Lake City, [1977]. pp. 264. *bibliogs.*

MOROCCAN CRISIS, 1904-1906.

EISNER (KURT) Der Sultan des Weltkrieges: ein marokkanisches Sittenbild deutscher Diplomaten-Politik. Dresden, 1906. pp. 72.

MOROCCAN CRISIS, 1911.

ALLAIN (JEAN CLAUDE) Agadir 1911: une crise impérialiste en Europe pour la conquête du Maroc. Paris, 1976. pp. 471. *bibliog.* (*Paris. Université de Paris I (Panthéon- Sorbonne). Publications. Série Internationale. 7*)

MOROCCANS IN ISRAEL.

MARX (EMANUEL) The social context of violent behaviour: a social anthropological study in an Israeli immigrant town. London, 1976. pp. 130. *bibliog.*

MOROCCO

— Commerce.

MOROCCO. Ministère des Finances. Office des Changes. Statistiques du commerce extérieur. a., 1974- [Rabat].

— Foreign relations — France.

DUNN (ROSS E.) Resistance in the desert: Moroccan responses to French imperialism, 1881-1912. London, [1977]. pp. 291. *bibliog.*

— — Spain.

REZETTE (ROBERT) The Spanish enclaves in Morocco. Paris. [1976]. pp. 188. *bibliog.*

— History.

BURKE (EDMUND) 1940- . Prelude to protectorate in Morocco: precolonial protest and resistance, 1860-1912. Chicago, 1976. pp. 306. *bibliog.*

HASSAN II, King of Morocco. Le défi. Paris, [1976]. pp. 284.

DUNN (ROSS E.) Resistance in the desert: Moroccan responses to French imperialism, 1881-1912. London, [1977]. pp. 291. *bibliog.*

— — 1900- .

ABD el-Krim et la République du Rif: actes du colloque international d'études historiques et sociologiques, 18-20 janvier 1973. Paris, 1976. pp. 536.

ALLAIN (JEAN CLAUDE) Agadir 1911: une crise impérialiste en Europe pour la conquête du Maroc. Paris, 1976. pp. 471. *bibliog.* (*Paris. Université de Paris I (Panthéon-Sorbonne). Publications. Série Internationale. 7*)

— Politics and government.

HASSAN II, King of Morocco. Le défi. Paris, [1976]. pp. 284.

LEVEAU (REMY) Le fellah marocain, défenseur du trône. [Paris, 1976]. pp. 281. *bibliog.* (*Fondation Nationale des Sciences Politiques. Cahiers. 203*)

MORRIS (WILLIAM).

MORRIS (WILLIAM) Selected writings and designs; edited with an introduction by Asa Briggs; with a supplement by Graeme Shankland on William Morris, designer, illustrated by twenty-four plates. Harmondsworth, 1962. repr. 1977. pp. 309. *bibliog.*

MORRIS (WILLIAM RICHARD) 1st Viscount Nuffield.

OVERY (R.J.) William Morris, Viscount Nuffield. London, [1976]. pp. 151. *bibliog.*

MORRISON (JAMES).

GATTY (RICHARD) Portrait of a merchant prince: James Morrison, 1789-1857. Northallerton, [1977?]. pp. 326. *bibliog.*

MORTALITY.

PRESTON (SAMUEL H.) Mortality patterns in national populations: with special reference to recorded causes of death. New York, [1976]. pp. 201. *bibliog.*

— Tables.

KŐRÖSI (JÓZSEF) Welche Unterlagen hat die Statistik zu beschaffen um richtige Mortalitäts-Tabellen zu gewinnen?: Denkschrift im Auftrage der Internationalen Statistischen Commission. Berlin, Verlag des Königlichen Statistischen Bureau's, 1874. pp. 83.

SAW (SWEE HOCK) Construction of Malayan abridged life tables 1956-1958. Hong Kong, 1970. pp. 18. *bibliog.*

U.K. Office of Population Censuses and Surveys. Mortality statistics: area: review of the Registrar General on deaths by area of usual residence, in England and Wales. a., 1974 (1st)- London. *Supersedes in part Registrar General's statistical review of England and Wales.*

U.K. Office of Population Censuses and Surveys. Mortality statistics: cause: review of the Registrar General on deaths by cause, sex and age, in England and Wales. a., 1974 (1st)- London. *Supersedes in part Registrar General's statistical review of England and Wales.*

U.K. Office of Population Censuses and Surveys. Mortality statistics: childhood: review of the Registrar General on deaths in England and Wales. a., 1974 (1st)- London. *Supersedes in part Registrar-General's statistical review of England and Wales.*

U.K. Office of Population Censuses and Surveys. Mortality statistics: review of the Registrar General on deaths in England and Wales. a., 1974(1st)- London. *Supersedes in part Registrar General's statistical review of England and Wales.*

INSTITUTE OF ACTUARIES and FACULTY OF ACTUARIES [IN SCOTLAND]. Continuous Mortality Investigation Committee. Continuous mortality investigation reports. No. 2. [London, 1976]. pp. 103.

SWITZERLAND. Bureau Fédéral de Statistique. 1976. Schweizerische Sterbetafel..., 1968-1973: Sterblichkeit nach Todesursachen...; Ausscheide- und Ueberlebensordnungen nach Zivilstand, etc. Bern, 1976. pp. 93. (*Statistiques de la Suisse. 577e fasc.*) *In German and French.*

U.K. Ministry of Overseas Development. Population Bureau. 1977. Report on the 1974 Bangladesh retrospective survey of fertility and mortality. London, 1977. pp. 173.

MORTGAGE LOANS

— United Kingdom.

KARN (VALERIE A.) Priorities for local authority mortgage lending: a case study of Birmingham. Birmingham, 1976. pp. 45. *(Birmingham. University. Centre for Urban and Regional Studies. Research Memoranda. No. 52)*

MORTGAGES

— Canada.

HATCH (JAMES E.) The Canadian mortgage market. [Toronto], Ministry of Treasury, Economics and Intergovernmental Affairs, 1975. pp. 273. *bibliog.*

— — Ontario.

ONTARIO. Ministry of Agriculture and Food. Economics Branch. 1972. Farm mortgages in Ontario; (by Henry F. Noble). [Toronto], 1972. pp. 13.

— United Kingdom.

DUNCAN (S.S.) The housing crisis and the structure of the housing market. Brighton, 1976. fo.41. *(Brighton. University of Sussex. Sussex Working Papers in Urban and Regional Studies. 2)*

HADJIMATHEOU (GEORGE G.) Housing and mortgage markets: the UK experience. Farnborough, Hants., [1976]. pp. 178. *bibliog.*

MOSCOW

— History

GRUNT (ALEKSANDR IANOVICH) Moskva 1917-i: revoliutsiia i kontrrevoliutsiia. Moskva, 1976. pp. 387.

— — Sources.

VOSSTANIE v Moskve 1682 goda: sbornik dokumentov. Moskva, 1976. pp. 347.

— Politics and government.

ALESHCHENKO (NIKOLAI MIKHAILOVICH) Moskovskii Sovet v 1917-1941 gg. Moskva, 1976. pp. 591.

— Statistics.

MOSCOW. Statisticheskoe Upravlenie. Moskva v tsifrakh, 1971-1975 gg.: kratkii statisticheskii sbornik. Moskva, 1976. pp. 223.

MOSCOW (OBLAST')

— Social history.

KAZANTSEV (BORIS NIKOLAEVICH) Rabochie Moskvy i Moskovskoi gubernii v seredine XIX veka, 40-50-e gody. Moskva, 1976. pp. 182.

MOSCOW TRIALS, 1936-1937.

SEDOV (LEV) Livre rouge sur le procès de Moscou: documents recueillis et rédigés. Paris, [1936]. pp. 125. *With pencil annotations.*

MOTHER AND CHILD.

MACFARLANE (AIDAN) The psychology of childbirth. London, 1977. pp. 128. *bibliog.*

SCHAFFER (RUDOLPH) Mothering. London, 1977. pp. 127. *bibliog.*

TALKING to children: language input and acquisition: papers from a conference sponsored by the Committee on Sociolinguistics of the Social Science Research Council (USA); edited by Catherine E. Snow and Charles A. Ferguson. Cambridge, 1977. pp. 369. *bibliog.*

MOTHERS.

MOTHERS IN ACTION. Educational arrangements for schoolage mothers: a survey of provisions made by schools and l[ocal] e[ducation] a[uthoritie]s. London, [1974]. pp. 5. *(Mothers in Action. Study Pamphlets. No. 5)*

— Employment — United Kingdom.

TIZARD (JACK) and others. All our children: pre-school services in a changing society. London, 1976. pp. 252. *bibliog.*

— Mortality.

BARROS (SILVIO OLIVEIRA DE) Mortalidade materna em S. Paulo. São Paulo, 1945. pp. 59-66. *(Separata Arquivos de Higiene e Saude Publica, vol. X, 1945. no. 25)*

MOTIVATION (PSYCHOLOGY).

BUCK (ROSS) Human motivation and emotion. New York, [1976]. pp. 529. *bibliog.*

LOYE (DAVID) The leadership passion: (a psychology of ideology). San Francisco, 1977. pp. 249. *bibliog.*

MOTOR BUS LINES

— Barbados.

BARBADOS. Committee appointed...to Inquire into Public Transport Services of the Island. 1964. Report; [E.R.L. Ward, chairman]. [Bridgetown, 1964]. pp. 12.

— United Kingdom.

MITCHELL (C.G.B.) Some social aspects of public passenger transport;...a paper presented at the Symposium on Unconventional Bus Services held at the Transport and Road Research Laboratory in October 1976. Crowthorne, 1977. pp. 29. *bibliog. (U.K. Transport and Road Research Laboratory. Supplementary Reports. 278)*

— — Employees.

FAIR (PENNY) On the buses. London, 1976. pp. 18. *(Solidarity: [for workers' power]. Pamphlets. [No.] 53*

— — London.

SOUTH east London bus study; report of the steering group; members of the steering group: officers of the Greater London Council and London Transport Executive; [D.A. Quarmby, chairman]. [London, Greater London Council], 1976. pp. 61, fo. 39.

MOTOR BUSES

— Australia.

AUSTRALIA. Bureau of Transport Economics. 1976. Consumer preferences in urban buses and bus services: results of a survey conducted in Perth in conjunction with the Metropolitan (Perth) Transport Trust during August and September, 1974. Canberra, 1976. 3 parts.

MOTOR TRUCKS

— Environmental aspects — United Kingdom.

LORRIES AND THE ENVIRONMENT COMMITTEE [U.K.]. Report on transhipment; [Sir Daniel Pettit, chairman]. London, [1976]. pp. 41.

MOTOR VEHICLES

— United Kingdom — Fuel.

CHAPMAN (PETER) and others. Future transport fuels. Crowthorne, 1976. pp. 210. *bibliogs. (U.K. Transport and Road Research Laboratory. Supplementary Reports. 251)*

MOUNTAIN LIFE

— Tunisia.

LOUIS (ANDRE) Tunisie du sud: ksars et villages de crêtes. Paris, 1975. pp. 370. *bibliog. (Centre de Recherches et d'Etudes sur les Sociétés Méditerranéennes. Etudes Tunisiennes)*

MOUNTAINS

— France.

BROCARD (JEAN) L'aménagement du territoire en montagne: pour que la montagne vive; rapport au gouvernement. Paris, La Documentation Française, 1975. pp. 229.

MOUVEMENT POPULAIRE DE LA REVOLUTION.

MOUVEMENT POPULAIRE DE LA REVOLUTION. Bureau Politique. Histoire du Mouvement Populaire de la Révolution. Kinshasa, [1976?]. pp. 118.

MOUVEMENTS UNIS DE LA RESISTANCE.

SWEETS (JOHN F.) The politics of resistance in France, 1940-1944: a history of the Mouvements Unis de la Résistance. DeKalb, Ill., [1976]. pp. 260. *bibliog.*

MOVIMENTO DAS FÔRÇAS ARMADAS.

CLARET SERRA (ANDREU) Hablan los capitanes: Portugal: genesis, ideologia y practica politica del Movimiento de las Fuerzas Armadas. Barcelona, 1975. pp. 237. *bibliog.*

MOVIMENTO POPULAR DE LIBERTAÇAO DE ANGOLA.

LEGUM (COLIN) and HODGES (TONY) After Angola: the war over southern Africa. London, 1976. pp. 85.

MOVIMIENTO DE IZQUIERDA REVOLUCIONARIA (VENEZUELA).

MOLEIRO (MOISES) El MIR. La Habana, 1967. pp. 241.

MOVING PICTURE INDUSTRY

— United Kingdom.

CHANAN (MICHAEL) Labour power in the British film industry. London, 1976. pp. 57.

MOVING PICTURES

— Argentine Republic.

La CULTURA popular del Peronismo; [by] Norman Briski [and others]. [Buenos Aires], 1973. pp. 155.

— Russia.

TAYLOR (RICHARD TRUEMAN) The politics of the Soviet cinema, 1917-1929. 1977. fo. 324. *bibliog. Typescript. Ph.D. (London) thesis: unpublished. This thesis is the property of London University and may not be removed from the Library.*

MOVING PICTURES IN PROPAGANDA.

TAYLOR (RICHARD TRUEMAN) The politics of the Soviet cinema, 1917-1929. 1977. fo. 324. *bibliog. Typescript. Ph.D. (London) thesis: unpublished. This thesis is the property of London University and may not be removed from the Library.*

MOYNIHAN (DANIEL PATRICK).

BALLINGER (RONALD B.) Dr. Moynihan and the Amalekites: the United States and the United Nations. Braamfontein, 1976. pp. 17.

MOZAMBIQUE

— History.

ISAACMAN (ALLEN F.) The tradition of resistance in Mozambique: the Zambesi Valley 1850-1921. Berkeley, Calif., 1976. pp. 232. *bibliog.*

— Politics and government.

ISAACMAN (ALLEN F.) The tradition of resistance in Mozambique: the Zambesi Valley 1850-1921. Berkeley, Calif., 1976. pp. 232. *bibliog.*

MUDEJARES.

Here are entered works on Muslims living in Spain under Christian protection before 1492 who did not convert to Christianity. In earlier volumes of the Bibliography such works have been entered under MORISCOS.

BURNS (ROBERT IGNATIUS) Medieval colonialism: postcrusade exploitation of Islamic Valencia. Princeton, N.J., [1975]. pp. 394. *bibliog.*

MUENSTER

— Economic history.

NOLL (ADOLF) Sozio-ökonomischer Strukturwandel des Handwerks in der zweiten Phase der Industrialisierung: unter besonderer Berücksichtigung der Regierungsbezirke Arnsberg und Münster. Göttingen, 1975. pp. 386. *bibliog. (Fritz Thyssen Stiftung. Neunzehntes Jahrhundert. Studien zum Wandel von Gesellschaft und Bildung im Neunzehnten Jahrhundert. Band 10)*

MULTIPLIER (ECONOMICS).

HANNA (MAX) Tourism multipliers in Britain: a guide to economic multipliers in theory and practice. London, English Tourist Board, 1976. fo. 23.

MULTIVARIATE ANALYSIS.

BENNETT (SPENCER) and BOWERS (DAVID) An introduction to multivariate techniques for social and behavioural sciences. London, 1976. pp. 156. *bibliog.*

The ANALYSIS of survey data; edited by Colm A. O'Muircheartaigh and Clive Payne. London, [1977]. 2 vols. *bibliogs.*

MUNICH FOUR POWER AGREEMENT, 1938.

KOWALCZYK (JÓZEF) Za kulisami wydarzeń politycznych z lat 1936-1938 w świetle raportów posła Czechosłowacji w Warszawie i innych archiwaliów: [szkice i dokumenty]. Warszawa, 1976. pp. 149.

RASCHHOFER (HERMANN) Völkerbund und Münchener Abkommen: die Staatengesellschaft von 1938. München, [1976]. pp. 239. *(Hanns-Seidel-Stiftung. Berichte und Studien. Band 9)*

MUNICIPAL CORPORATIONS

— Germany.

SCHEPER (BURCHARD) Frühe bürgerliche Institutionen norddeutscher Hansestädte: Beiträge zu einer vergleichenden Verfassungsgeschichte Lübecks, Bremens, Lüneburgs und Hamburgs im Mittelalter. Köln, 1975. pp. 223. *bibliog. (Hansischer Geschichtsverein. Quellen und Darstellungen zur Hansischen Geschichte. Neue Folge. Band 20)*

MUNICIPAL FINANCE

— Switzerland.

PFLUEGER (PAUL) and HUEPPY (JOHANN) Handbuch des schweizerischen Gemeindesozialismus. Zürich, 1910. pp. 267.

MUNICIPAL GOVERNMENT.

INTERNATIONAL UNION OF LOCAL AUTHORITIES. [Publications]. 102. The age of leisure. The Hague, 1973. pp. 58.

— Brazil.

LEAL (VICTOR NUNES) Coronelismo: the municipality and representative government in Brazil;...translated by June Henfrey. Cambridge, 1977. pp. 237. *bibliog. Translation of Coronelismo, enxada e voto.*

— Canada — Nova Scotia.

BECK (J. MURRAY) The evolution of municipal government in Nova Scotia, 1749-1973: a study prepared for the Nova Scotia Royal Commission on Education, Public Services and Provincial-Municipal Relations. [Halifax], 1973. pp. 60. *bibliog.*

NOVA SCOTIA. Royal Commission on Education, Public Services and Provincial-Municipal Relations. 1974. Report. vol.1. Summary and recommendations; [John F. Graham, chairman]. Halifax, 1974. pp. 301. *Map in end pocket.*

— France.

SERUSCLAT (FRANCK) Elections municipales, élections politiques. Paris, [1977]. pp. 190.

— India.

RAO (P.V.) and KOHLI (SHANTA) Educational and recreational activities of urban local bodies. New Delhi, [1970]. pp. 86. *bibliog. (Indian Institute of Public Administration. Centre for Training and Research in Municipal Administration. Our Towns. vol. 2)*

— Japan.

KURODA (YASUMASA) Reed Town, Japan: a study in community power structure and political change. Honolulu, [1974]. pp. 283. *bibliog.*

— Switzerland.

PFLUEGER (PAUL) and HUEPPY (JOHANN) Handbuch des schweizerischen Gemeindesozialismus. Zürich, 1910. pp. 267.

— United Kingdom.

STEWART (JOHN DAVID) and others. Local government: approaches to urban deprivation. [London, 1976]. pp. 62. *(U.K. Home Office. Urban Deprivation Unit. Occasional Papers. No. 1)*

— United States.

MURPHY (THOMAS P.) and REHFUSS (JOHN) Urban politics in the suburban era. Homewood, Ill., 1976. pp. 285.

THEORETICAL perspectives on urban politics; [by] Willis D. Hawley and others. Englewood Clifs, N.J., [1976]. pp. 229.

URBAN governance and minorities; edited by Herrington J. Bryce. New York, 1976. pp. 220. *Based on a one-day Public Policy Forum on Urban Governance held in Washington in 1975 and sponsored by the Joint Center for Political Studies.*

CARALEY (DEMETRIOS) City governments and urban problems: a new introduction to urban politics. Englewood Cliffs, [1977]. pp. 448.

SCHIESL (MARTIN J.) The politics of efficiency: municipal administration and reform in America 1800-1920. Berkeley, Calif., [1977]. pp. 259. *bibliog.*

MUNICIPAL RESEARCH

— Canada — Directories.

DIRECTORY OF CANADIAN URBAN INFORMATION SOURCES; [pd. by] Ministry of State for Urban Affairs. a., current issue only. Ottawa.

— United Kingdom.

U.K. Department of the Environment. Library. 1977. Urban and regional research in the United Kingdom, 1976-1977; prepared...for the United Nations Economic Commission for Europe, Committee for Housing, Building and Planning, Group of Experts on Urban and Regional Research. [London], 1977. pp. 289. *(Information Series)*

MUNICIPAL SERVICES.

BECKWITH (BURNHAM PUTNAM) Free goods: the theory of free or communist distribution. Palo Alto, Calif., [1976]. pp. 216. *bibliog.*

— Canada.

BIRD (RICHARD MILLER) Charging for public services: a new look at an old idea. Toronto, 1976. pp. 269. *bibliog. (Canadian Tax Foundation. Canadian Tax Papers. No. 59)*

— United States.

COWING (THOMAS G.) and HOLTMANN (ALPHONSE G.) The economics of public service consolidation. Lexington, Mass., [1976]. pp, 166. *bibliog.*

STATE and local government: the political economy of reform; edited by Alan K. Campbell and Roy W. Bahl. New York, [1976]. pp. 211. *Based on papers presented to a conference sponsored by the Metropolitan Studies Program of the Maxwell School of Citizenship and Public Affairs of Syracuse University.*

LINEBERRY (ROBERT L.) Equality and urban policy: the distribution of municipal public services. Beverly Hills, [1977]. pp. 205. *bibliog.*

— — Connecticut — New Haven.

LOCAL public finance and the fiscal squeeze: a case study; edited by John R. Meyer and John M. Quigley. Cambridge, Mass., [1977]. pp. 201. *Papers from a seminar sponsored by the Institution for Social and Policy Studies at Yale University and the Yale Law School, 1971-73.*

MUNITIONS.

STOCKHOLM INTERNATIONAL PEACE RESEARCH INSTITUTE. Armaments and disarmament in the nuclear age: a handbook; [edited by...Marek Thee]. Atlantic Highlands, N.J., [1976]. pp. 306. *bibliog.*

STOCKHOLM INTERNATIONAL PEACE RESEARCH INSTITUTE. World armaments: the nuclear threat. Stockholm, [1977]. pp. 39.

— International cooperation — Europe.

INTERNATIONAL INSTITUTE FOR STRATEGIC STUDIES. Adelphi Papers, No. 129. The alliance and Europe: part V1: the European programme group; by D.C.R. Heyhoe. London, 1976. pp. 27.

— Trade and manufacture.

CATHOLIC CHURCH IN ENGLAND AND WALES. Bishops' Conference. Commission for International Justice and Peace. Christians and the arms trade. [Abbots Langley, 1976?]. pp. 19. *bibliog.*

TUCKER (GARDINER) and BASAGNI (FABIO) Towards rationalizing allied weapons production. Paris, [1976]. pp. 54. *(Atlantic Institute. Atlantic Papers. 1976.1)*

SAMPSON (ANTHONY) The arms bazaar: the companies, the dealers, the bribes: from Vickers to Lockheed. London, [1977]. pp. 352.

— — Austria.

KARNER (STEFAN) Kärntens Wirtschaft, 1938-1945, unter besonderer Berücksichtigung der Rüstungsindustrie. Klagenfurt, 1976. pp. 384. *bibliog. (Klagenfurt. Magistrat. Wissenschaftliche Veröffentlichungen der Landeshauptstadt Klagenfurt. Band 2)*

MURDER

— United Kingdom.

NATIONAL CAMPAIGN FOR THE ABOLITION OF CAPITAL PUNISHMENT and HOWARD LEAGUE FOR PENAL REFORM. Murder and capital punishment in England and Wales. London, 1974. pp. 17.

MURDOCH (KEITH RUPERT).

REGAN (SIMON) Rupert Murdoch: a business biography. London, 1976. pp. 246.

MURDOCH (RUPERT).

See MURDOCH (KEITH RUPERT).

MURMANSK (OBLAST')

— Politics and government.

ROMANOV (LEONID MIKHAILOVICH) Murmanskaia oblastnaia partiinaia organizatsiia v period perestroiki narodnogo khoziaistva v 1941-1942 gg. Murmansk, 1973. pp. 46.

MUSHROOMS, EDIBLE

— United Kingdom.

THOMPSON (PETER) Writer on agriculture. National mushroom study 1975: a survey of economic aspects. Manchester, 1977. pp. 49. *(Agricultural Enterprise Studies in England and Wales. Economic Reports. No. 55)*

MUSIC

— Economic aspects.

SALEM (MAHMOUD) Organisational survival in the performing arts: the making of the Seattle Opera. New York, 1976. pp. 210. *bibliog.*

— Austria.

KOTLAN-WERNER (HENRIETTE) Kunst und Volk: David Josef Bach, 1874-1947. Wien, 1977. pp. 174. *(Ludwig-Boltzmann-Institut für Geschichte der Arbeiterbewegung. Materialien zur Arbeiterbewegung. Nr. 6)*

MUSSOLINI (BENITO).

VALERA (PAOLO) Mussolini;...a cura di Enrico Ghidetti. Milano, [1975]. pp. 204. *bibliog.*

MYSORE

— Economic policy.

MYSORE. Planning Department. Annual plan. a., 1974/75- Bangalore.

— Population.

INDIA. Census, 1971. Series 14. Mysore: portrait of population; [by] P. Padmanabha. [Delhi, 1974]. pp. 214.

— Social policy.

MYSORE. Planning Department. Annual plan. a., 1974/75- Bangalore.

NADAUD (MARTIN).

NADAUD (MARTIN) Léonard, maçon de la Creuse. Paris, 1976. pp. 399. *bibliog.*

NAGAS.

SCOTT (GUTHRIE MICHAEL) A void of law: (Britain and Bangladesh). London, [1975]. pp. 98.

NAILS AND SPIKES.

LEUNINGER (ALOIS) Die Nagelschmiede von Mengerskirchen: zur Geschichte eines ausgestorbenen Gewerbes. [Weilburg, 1972?]. pp. 24. *(Sonderdruck aus "Land und Leute im Oberlahnkreis", Heimatkundliche Beilage des "Weilburger Tageblatt")*

NAIROBI

— Growth.

HAKE (ANDREW) African metropolis: Nairobi's self-help city. London, 1977. pp. 284.

— History.

HAKE (ANDREW) African metropolis: Nairobi's self-help city. London, 1977. pp. 284.

— Social conditions.

HAKE (ANDREW) African metropolis: Nairobi's self-help city. London, 1977. pp. 284.

NAIRS

— Social life and customs.

FULLER (CHRISTOPHER J.) The Nayars today. Cambridge, 1976. pp. 173. *bibliog. Based, in part, on the author's Ph.D. thesis, University of Manchester, 1974.*

NAMES, GEOGRAPHICAL.

EUROPEAN COMMUNTIES. Statistical Office. Foreign trade: standard country nomenclature. [in French, English, German, Italian, Dutch and Danish]. a., 1963- Luxembourg. *Not pd. 1967.*

UNITED NATIONS. Conference on the Standardization of Geographical Names, 1st, Geneva, 1967. United Nations Conference on the Standardization of Geographical Names, Geneva, 4-22 September, 1967. Report... (and Proceedings...and technical papers) (E/CONF. 53/3, E/CONF. 53/4). New York, 1968-69. 2 vols. *bibliog.*

UNITED NATIONS. Conference on the Standardization of Geographical Names, 2nd, London, 1972. Second...Conference...London, 10-31 May 1972. Report... (and Technical papers) (E/CONF. 61/4, E/CONF. 61/4/Add.1) . New York, 1974. 2 vols. *bibliog.*

— Canada.

CANADA. Statistics Canada. Changes to municipal boundaries, status and names. a., 1975- Ottawa. *[in English and French].*

NAMIBIA.

See SOUTH WEST AFRICA.

NANACATLAN, MEXICO

— Rural conditions.

DURAND (PIERRE) Nanacatlan: société paysanne et lutte des classes au Mexique. Montréal, 1975. pp. 257. *bibliog.*

NANTES

— Economic history.

GUIN (YANNICK) Le mouvement ouvrier nantais: essai sur le syndicalisme d'action directe à Nantes et à Saint-Nazaire. Paris, 1976. pp. 413.

NARCOTIC HABIT

— Treatment — United States.

HUGHES (PATRICK H.) Behind the wall of respect: community experiments in heroin addiction control. Chicago, 1977. pp. 162.

— United States.

HUNT (LEON GIBSON) and CHAMBERS (CARL D.) The heroin epidemics: a study of heroin use in the United States, 1965-75. New York, [1976]. pp. 145.

NARCOTIC LAWS

— United Kingdom.

LYDIATE (PETER WILLIAM H.) The law relating to the misuse of drugs. London, 1977. pp. 152.

NARCOTICS, CONTROL OF

— Australia.

AUSTRALIA. Parliament. Senate. Select Committee on Drug Trafficking and Drug Abuse. 1971. Report...Part 1. Report; [J.E. Marriott, chairman]. in AUSTRALIA. Parliament. Parliamentary papers, 1971, vol.8.

— Hong Kong.

HONG KONG NARCOTICS REPORT; [pd. by] Action Committee Against Narcotics. [Hong Kong]. a., 1975/76- Hong Kong.

— United Kingdom.

EALAND (C.P.H.) Diving off the deep end: a Release report on the sentencing of cannabis offenders in England and Wales. London, [1976]. pp. 17.

— United States.

ROCK (PAUL ELLIOTT) ed. Drugs and politics. New Brunswick, N.J., 1977. pp. 331. *bibliogs.*

NARCOTICS AND YOUTH

— Denmark.

BEHRENDT (FINN BENNIKE) Narkotikaepidemien i Danmark, 1965-70. [Copenhagen, 1971]. pp. 25.

NASH (Sir WALTER).

SINCLAIR (KEITH) Walter Nash. Auckland, 1976. pp. 439. *bibliog.*

NATIONAL CHARACTERISTICS, CATALONIAN.

HANSEN (EDWARD C.) Rural Catalonia under the Franco regime: the fate of regional culture since the Spanish Civil War. Cambridge, 1977. pp. 182. *bibliog.*

NATIONAL CHARACTERISTICS, FILIPINO.

ALATAS (SYED HUSSEIN) The myth of the lazy native: a study of the image of the Malays, Filipinos and Javanese from the 16th to the 20th century and its function in the ideology of colonial capitalism. London, 1977. pp. 267. *bibliog.*

NATIONAL CHARACTERISTICS, JAVANESE.

ALATAS (SYED HUSSEIN) The myth of the lazy native: a study of the image of the Malays, Filipinos and Javanese from the 16th to the 20th century and its function in the ideology of colonial capitalism. London, 1977. pp. 267. *bibliog.*

NATIONAL CHARACTERISTICS, MALAY.

ALATAS (SYED HUSSEIN) The myth of the lazy native: a study of the image of the Malays, Filipinos and Javanese from the 16th to the 20th century and its function in the ideology of colonial capitalism. London, 1977. pp. 267. *bibliog.*

NATIONAL FRONT.

SOCIALIST WORKER. Pamphlets. The fight against the racists: the Nazional Front and how to smash it. London, [1976]. pp. 15.

WALKER (MARTIN) The National Front. Glasgow, 1977. pp. 224.

NATIONAL INCOME.

NATIONALEINKOMMEN im Sozialismus: Produktion, Verteilung...; ([by an] Autorenkollektiv aus der VRB, der DDR und der UdSSR; Leiter...: D. Porjasow). Berlin, 1976. pp. 503.

STONE (Sir JOHN RICHARD NICHOLAS) and STONE (GIOVANNA) National income and expenditure. 10th ed. London, 1977. pp. 175. *bibliog.*

— Accounting.

CORREA (HECTOR) Integrated economic accounting: theory and applications to national, real, and financial economic planning. Lexington, Mass., [1977]. pp. 222.

— Canada — Quebec — Accounting.

QUEBEC (PROVINCE). Service des Etudes en Développement Economique. 1968. Tableaux types des comptes économiques du Québec, 1946-1968. [Quebec?, 1968?]. pp. 63. *bibliog.*

— Central African Republic — Accounting.

FRANCE. Secrétariat d'Etat aux Affaires Etrangères. 1970. Comptes économiques, 1967: (République Centrafricaine). Paris, 1970. pp. 132.

— Germany, Eastern — Accounting.

DEUTSCHES INSTITUT FÜR WIRTSCHAFTSFORSCHUNG. Sonderhefte. [Neue Folge]. 115. Das Sozialprodukt der Deutschen Demokratischen Republik im Vergleich mit dem der Bundesrepublik Deutschland; ([by] Herbert Wilkens). Berlin, 1976. pp. 188. *bibliog. With English summary.*

— India — Accounting.

INDIA. Committee on Regional Accounts. 1976. Final report; [M. Mukherjee, chairman]. [Delhi], 1976. pp. 79.

— — Delhi (Union Territory) — Accounting.

ESTIMATES OF STATE INCOME OF DELHI; [pd. by] Bureau of Economics and Statistics [Delhi (Union Territory)]. a., 1960-61/1974-75(5th)- Delhi. *[in English and Hindi].*

— Malawi — Accounting.

MALAWI. National Statistical Office. National accounts report. a., 1964/68- Zomba.

— Malaysia — Accounting.

NATIONAL ACCOUNTS OF PENINSULAR MALAYSIA; [pd. by] Department of Statistics, Malaysia. irreg., 1960/71- Kuala Lumpur. *[in English and Malay].*

— Pakistan — Accounting.

PAKISTAN. Statistical Division. National accounts. a., 1969-70/1971-72- Karachi.

— Panama — Accounting.

PANAMA. Direccion de Estadistica y Censo. Estadistica panameña. Cuentas nacionales. a., 1973/1975- Panama. *Supersedes PANAMA. Direccion de Estadistica y Censo. Estadistica panameña. Serie C. Ingreso nacional.*

— Papua New Guinea — Accounting.

PAPUA NEW GUINEA. Bureau of Statistics. 1974. National accounts statistics: principal economic accounts and supporting tables, 1960/61-1973/74. Port Moresby, 1974. pp. 219.

— Singapore — Accounting.

SINGAPORE. Statistics Department. 1975. Singapore national accounts, 1960-1973. Singapore, 1975. pp. 51.

— Yugoslavia — Accounting.

YUGOSLAVIA. Savezni Zavod za Statistiku. Studije, Analize i Prikazi. 78. Privredni bilansi Jugoslavije, 1974; Economic balances of Yugoslavia, 1974; Balansy narodnogo khoziaistva Iugoslavii, 1974. Beograd, 1976. pp. 183. *With English and Russian summaries.*

NATIONAL PARKS AND RESERVES

— Ecuador — Galapagos (Province).

ECUADOR. Junta Nacional de Planificacion y Coordinacion Economica. 1975. Plan de conservacion y desarrollo selectivo para la provincia de Galapagos. Quito, 1975. pp. 275.

— United Kingdom.

DAVIES (E.T.) The Dartmoor and Exmoor National Parks: changes in farming structure 1952-1972. Exeter, 1976. pp. 33. *(Exeter. University. Agricultural Economics Unit. Reports. No. 197)*

— — Administration.

DETAILS of administrative arrangements in national parks. [London, Countryside Commission, 1971]. pp. 24.

NATIONAL SOCIALISM.

HOEGNER (WILHELM) Der Volksbetrug der Nationalsozialisten: Rede (in der Reichstagssitzung vom 18. Oktober 1930). Berlin, 1930. pp. 16.

REMMELE (HERMANN) Sowjetstern oder Hakenkreuz: die Rettung Deutschlands aus der Youngsklaverei und Kapitalsknechtschaft. [Berlin, 1930]. pp. 24.

OTTWALT (ERNST) Deutschland erwache!: Geschichte des Nationalsozialismus. Berlin, 1975. pp. 390. *bibliog. Reprint of work originally published in Vienna in 1932.*

STRASSER (OTTO) Sozialistische Revolution oder faschistischer Krieg? [Prague, 1934]. pp. 15.

CAWIL (H.) Der Fall Jacob. Zürich, [1935]. pp. 38.

SILONE (IGNAZIO) pseud. [i.e. Secondo TRANQUILLI] Die Schule der Diktatoren; autorisierte Übersetzung aus dem Italienischen von Jakob Huber. Zürich, [1938]. pp. 326.

FISCHER (ERNST) of the Austrian Communist Party. Das Fanal: der Kampf Dimitroffs gegen die Kriegsbrandstifter. Wien, [1946]. pp. 298.

WERNER (KURT) and BIERNAT (KARL HEINZ) Die Köpenicker Blutwoche, Juni 1933. Berlin, 1958. pp. 49.

NELHIEBEL (KURT) Die Henleins gestern und heute: Hintergründe und Ziele des Witikobundes. Frankfurt/Main, 1962. pp. 88.

KOCH-KENT (HENRI) and others. Hitlertum in Luxemburg, 1933-1944: Beiträge zur Zeitgeschichte. [Luxembourg, 1972]. pp. 47. *3 papers presented at the congress of the Association des Enrôlés de Force, Victimes du Nazisme, held in Walferdingen in 1972.*

LUDWIG (KARL HEINZ) Technik und Ingenieure im Dritten Reich. Düsseldorf, [1974]. pp. 544. *bibliog.*

MERKL (PETER HANS) Political violence under the Swastika: 581 early Nazis. Princeton, 1975. pp. 735. *bibliog.*

CIOLEK-KUEMPER (JUTTA) Wahlkampf in Lippe: die Wahlkampfpropaganda der NSDAP zur Januar 1933. München, 1976. pp. 406. *bibliog.*

FARQUHARSON (JOHN E.) The plough and the swastika: the NSDAP and agriculture in Germany, 1928-45. London, [1976]. pp. 312. *bibliog.*

FUNKE (MANFRED) ed. Hitler, Deutschland und die Mächte: Materialien zur Aussenpolitik des Dritten Reiches. Düsseldorf, 1976 repr.1977. pp. 848. *(Bonn. Universität. Seminar für Politische Wissenschaft. Bonner Schriften zur Politik und Zeitgeschichte. 12)*

HAMBRECHT (RAINER) Der Aufstieg der NSDAP in Mittel- und Oberfranken, 1925-1933. Nürnberg, 1976. pp. 612. *bibliog. (Nuremberg. Stadtarchiv. Nürnberger Werkstücke zur Stadt- und Landesgeschichte. Band 17) Würzburger Phil. Dissertation 1975.*

HUMBEL (KURT) Nationalsozialistische Propaganda in der Schweiz, 1931-1939, etc. Bern, [1976]. pp. 295. *bibliog.*

JOCH (WINFRIED) Politische Leibeserziehung und ihre Theorie im nationalsozialistischen Deutschland: Voraussetzungen, Begründungszusammenhang, Dokumentation. Bern, 1976. pp. 249. *bibliog.*

KADRITZKE (NIELS) Faschismus und Krise: zum Verhältnis von Politik und Ökonomie im Nationalsozialismus. Frankfurt, [1976]. pp. 216. *bibliog.*

SCHIEDER (WOLFGANG) ed. Faschismus als soziale Bewegung: Deutschland und Italien im Vergleich. Hamburg, 1976. pp. 212. *With English summary.*

SENGOTTA (HANS JUERGEN) Der Reichsstatthalter in Lippe 1933 bis 1939: reichsrechtliche Bestimmungen und politische Praxis. Detmold, 1976. pp. 422. *bibliog. (Naturwissenschaftlicher und Historischer Verein für das Land Lippe. Sonderveröffentlichungen. Band 26)*

SSSR v bor'be protiv fashistskoi agressii, 1933-1945. Moskva, 1976. pp. 327.

STEINER (JOHN M.) Power politics and social change in National Socialist Germany: a process of escalation into mass destruction. The Hague, 1976. pp. 466. *bibliog.*

SUTTON (ANTONY C.) Wall Street and the rise of Hitler. Seal Beach, Calif., [1976]. pp. 220. *bibliog.*

WAGNER (JOHANNES VOLKER) Nur Mut, sei Kämpfer!: Heinrich König, ein Leben für die Freiheit: Bochumer politische Lebensbilder aus der Zeit der Weimarer Republik und des Nationalsozialismus. Bochum, 1976. pp. 231. *bibliog. (Bochum. Stadtarchiv. Veröffentlichungen)*

BARKAI (AVRAHAM) Das Wirtschaftssystem des Nationalsozialismus: der historische und ideologische Hintergrund, 1933-1936. Köln, [1977]. pp. 215. *bibliog.*

INNEN- und Aussenpolitik unter nationalsozialistischer Bedrohung: Determinanten internationaler Beziehungen in historischen Fallstudien; ([edited by] Erhard Forndran [and others]). Opladen, [1977]. pp. 361.

KONZEPT für die "Neuordnung" der Welt: die Kriegsziele des faschistischen deutschen Imperialismus im zweiten Weltkrieg; von einem Autorenkollektiv unter Leitung von Wolfgang Schumann. Berlin, 1977. pp. 141.

MASON (TIMOTHY W.) Sozialpolitik im Dritten Reich: Arbeiterklasse und Volksgemeinschaft. Opladen, [1977]. pp. 374. *bibliog.*

POMMERIN (REINER) Das Dritte Reich und Lateinamerika: die deutsche Politik gegenüber Süd- und Mittelamerika, 1939-1942. Düsseldorf, [1977]. pp. 377. *bibliog.*

RINGLER (RALF ROLAND) Illusion einer Jugend: Lieder, Fahnen und das bittere Ende; Hitler-Jugend in Österreich: ein Erlebnisbericht. St. Pölten, 1977. pp. 223.

NATIONALISM.

VIBRAYE (REGIS DE) Où mène le nationalisme? Paris, [1929]. pp. 188.

NATIONALISM: the nature and evolution of an idea; editor Eugene Kamenka. London, 1976. pp. 135. *bibliog. Originally published in Canberra in 1973.*

BONANNO (ALFREDO M.) Anarchism and the national liberation struggle. Port Glasgow, [1976]. pp. 16. *(Bratach Dubh Collective. Anarchist Pamphlets. No. 1)*

HEROD (CHARLES C.) The nation in the history of marxian thought: the concept of nations with history and nations without history. The Hague, 1976. pp. 138. *bibliog.*

INTERNATSIONAL'NOE i natsional'noe v sotsialisticheskom obshchestve. Kiev, 1976. pp. 331.

SNYDER (LOUIS LEO) Varieties of nationalism: a comparative study. Hinsdale, Ill., [1976]. pp. 326. *bibliog.*

MODZELEWSKI (WOJCIECH) Naród i postęp: problematyka narodowa w ideologii i myśli społecznej pozytywistów warszawskich. Warszawa, 1977. pp. 243.

NATIONALISM AND RELIGION

— Russia.

ASHIROV (NUGMAN) Islam i natsii. Moskva, 1975. pp. 144.

— — Ukraine.

DOBRETSOVA (VIOLLI VIACHESLAVIVNA) Natsionalizm i relihiia na sluzhbi antykomunizmu: pro kontrrevoliutsiinu diial'nist' burzhuazno-natsionalistychnykh i klerykal'nykh orhanizatsii na zakhidnoukraïns'kykh zemliakh u 20-30-kh rokakh ta borot'bu proty nykh prohresyvnykh syl. L'viv, 1976. pp. 204.

NATIONALITIES, PRINCIPLE OF.

NONSTATE nations in international politics: comparative system analyses; edited by Judy S. Bertelsen. New York, 1977. pp. 263. *bibliogs.*

NATURAL LAW.

ROUSSEAU (JEAN JACQUES) The first and second discourses; edited, with introduction and notes, by Roger D. Masters; translated by Roger D. and Judith R. Masters. New York, [1964]. pp. 248.

KAPLAN (MORTON A.) Justice, human nature, and political obligation. New York, [1976]. pp. 283.

NATURAL RESOURCES.

GUTTMANN (HENRY) Die Weltwirtschaft und ihre Rohstoffe. Berlin, [1956]. pp. 532. *bibliog.*

BECHT (J. EDWIN) and BELZUNG (L.D.) World resource management: key to civilizations and social achievement. Englewood Cliffs, [1975]. pp. 339. *bibliog.*

GUDOZHNIK (GRIGORII SERGEEVICH) Nauchno-tekhnicheskaia revoliutsiia i ekologicheskii krizis. Moskva, 1975. pp. 232.

KEMPER (RIA) Nationale Verfügung über natürliche Ressourcen und die neue Weltwirtschaftsordnung der Vereinten Nationen. Berlin, [1976]. pp. 155. *bibliog.*

RESOURCES and the environment: a socialist perspective; edited by Michael Barratt Brown [and others]. Nottingham, 1976. pp. 157. *Papers based on the materials prepared for a 1975 Spokesman conference on the environment.*

SCHACHTER (OSCAR) Sharing the world's resources. New York, 1977. pp. 172.

— Taxation — Canada.

VICTORIA CONFERENCE ON NATURAL RESOURCE REVENUES, 1975. Natural resource revenues: a test of federalism; edited by Anthony Scott. Vancouver, [1976]. pp. 261. *bibliog. (British Columbia Institute for Economic Policy Analysis. Analysis Series)*

— Bering Sea region.

YOUNG (ORAN R.) Resource management at the international level: the case of the north Pacific. London, 1977. pp. 252.

— Brazil — Mato Grosso.

RONDON (J. LUCIDIO N.) Recursos econômicos de Mato Grosso: terras, minerais, aguas, potenciais e usinas hidreletricas, etc. Cuiaba, 1972. pp. 236.

— Canada — British Columbia.

CARMICHAEL (HERBERT) Alberni district, British Columbia. Victoria, 1908. pp. 25. *(British Columbia. Bureau of Provincial Information. Bulletins. No. 24) Map in end pocket.*

BRITISH COLUMBIA. Bureau of Provincial Information. 1911. Columbia-Kootenay valley and its resources and capabilities. Victoria, 1911. pp. 97. *(Bulletins. No. 26) Map in end pocket.*

— — Ontario.

NELLES (HENRY VIVIAN) The politics of development: forests, mines and hydro-electric power in Ontario, 1849-1941. Toronto, [1974]. pp. 514.

— Dutch Guiana.

DUTCH GUIANA. Ministerie van Opbouw. 1963. Opbouw 1958-1963: de nationale visie: verslag van departementale werkzaamheden 1958-1963. Paramaribo, 1963. pp. 226.

— Peru.

PERU. Oficina Nacional de Evaluacion de Recursos Naturales. Direccion de Planificacion. Memoria de la ejecucion del plan bienal. bien., 1971/1972- Lima.

— Russia — Siberia.

EXPLOITATION of Siberia's natural resources: main findings of round table held 30th January - 1st February, 1974 in Brussels; editor and chairman of round table Yves Laulan, etc. [Brussels?], NATO Directorate of Economic Affairs, [1974]. pp. 199. *In English and French.*

SHABAD (THEODORE) and MOTE (VICTOR L.) Gateway to Siberian resources: the BAM. New York, 1977. pp. 189. *bibliogs.*

— Sabah.

THOMAS (P.) and others. The land capability classification of Sabah. Tolworth, 1976. 4 vols. (in 1), 10 maps. *bibliogs. (U.K. Ministry of Overseas Development. Land Resources Division. Land Resource Studies. 25)*

NATURE AND NURTURE.

HUMAN diversity: its causes and social significance...; edited by Bernard D. Davis and Patricia Flaherty. Cambridge, Mass., [1976]. pp. 248. *bibliog. The proceedings of a series of seminars sponsored by the Committee on Human Diversity of the American Academy of Arts and Sciences 1973-1974.*

NATURE CONSERVATION

— Sweden.

WAHLSTRÖM (LAGE) Naturvården i regional och lokal planering : geografiska studier med exempel fram Göteborgsregionen...: Nature conservancy in regional and local planning, etc. Kungälv, 1977. pp. 285. *bibliog. (Göteborgs Universitet. Geografiska Institutioner. Meddelanden. Ser. B. Nr. 59) In Swedish, with English summary.*

NAVAL OFFENCES

— United States.

PERRY (RONALD W.) Racial discrimination and military justice. New York, 1977. pp. 101. *bibliog.*

NAYARS.

See NAIRS.

NECHKINA (MILITSA VASIL'EVNA).

PROBLEMY istorii obshchestvennoi mysli i istoriografii: k 75- letiiu akademika N.V. Nechkinoi. Moskva, 1976. pp. 387. *bibliog.*

NEGATIVE INCOME TAX

— United Kingdom.

CLARK (COLIN GRANT) Poverty before politics: a proposal for a reverse income tax. London, 1977. pp. 69. *bibliog. (Institute of Economic Affairs. Hobart Papers. 73)*

NEGLIGENCE

— United Kingdom.

PRICHARD (M.J.) Scott v. Shepherd, 1773, and the emergence of the tort of negligence. London, 1976. pp. 43. *(Selden Society. Annual Lectures. 1973)*

NEGOTIATION.

SAMELSON (LOUIS J.) Soviet and Chinese negotiating behavior: the Western view. Beverly Hills, [1976]. pp. 62. *bibliog.*

NEGRO CHILDREN.

ABRAMSON (PAUL R.) The political socialization of black Americans: a critical evaluation of research on efficacy and trust. New York, [1977]. pp. 195. *bibliog.*

— United Kingdom.

NATIONAL CATHOLIC COMMISSION FOR RACIAL JUSTICE. Where creed and colour matter: a survey on black children and Catholic schools. London, [1975]. pp. 47.

NEGRO-ENGLISH DIALECTS.

BLACK English: a seminar; edited by Deborah Sears Harrison [and] Tom Trabasso. Hillsdale, N.J., 1976. pp. 301. *bibliogs.*

NEGRO-JEWISH RELATIONS.

DINER (HASIA R.) In the almost promised land: American Jews and blacks, 1915-1935. Westport, Conn., 1977. pp. 271. *bibliog.*

NEGRO RACE.

WHITTEN (NORMAN E.) and SZWED (JOHN F.) eds. Afro-American anthropology: contemporary perspectives. New York, [1970]. pp. 468. *bibliog.*

KILSON (MARTIN LUTHER) and ROTBERG (ROBERT IRWIN) eds. The African diaspora: interpretive essays. Cambridge, Mass., 1976. pp. 510.

[GARVEY (MARCUS)] More philosophy and opinions of Marcus Garvey; selected and edited from previously unpublished material by E.U. Essien-Udom and Amy Jacques Garvey. London, 1977. pp. 248. *This is volume 3 of Philosophy and opinions of Marcus Garvey.*

— History — Sources.

IRWIN (GRAHAM W.) ed. Africans abroad: a documentary history of the black diaspora in Asia, Latin America, and the Caribbean during the age of slavery. New York, 1977. pp. 408. *bibliog.*

NEGROES.

CLEAVER (KATHLEEN) On the vanguard role of the black urban lumpenproletariat. London, [1975]. pp. 26.

HEISS (JEROLD) The case of the black family: a sociological inquiry. New York, 1975. pp. 246. *bibliog.*

OSTHEIMER (JOHN M.) and RITT (LEONARD G.) Environment, energy, and black Americans. Beverly Hills, [1976]. pp. 38. *bibliog.*

THREE perspectives on ethnicity: Blacks, Chicanos and native Americans; [edited] by Carlos E. Cortés [and others]. New York, [1976]. pp. 429.

— Civil rights.

BELZ (HERMAN) A new birth of freedom: the Republican Party and freedmen's rights, 1861-1866. Westport, Conn., 1976. pp. 199. *bibliogs.*

FRANKLIN (JOHN HOPE) Racial equality in America. Chicago, 1976. pp. 113. *bibliog. (National Endowment for the Humanities. Jefferson Lectures in the Humanities. 1976)*

MEIER (AUGUST) and RUDWICK (ELLIOTT M.) Along the color line: explorations in the black experience. Urbana, Ill., [1976]. pp. 404.

VAUGHAN (PHILIP H.) The Truman administration's legacy for black America. Reseda, Calif., [1976]. pp. 116. *bibliog.*

BRAUER (CARL M.) John F. Kennedy and the second reconstruction. New York, 1977. pp. 396. *bibliog.*

KLUGER (RICHARD) Simple justice: the history of Brown v. Board of Education and black America's struggle for equality. London, 1977. pp. 823,xxiii. *bibliog.*

— Economic conditions.

CASH (WILLIAM L.) and OLIVER (LUCY R.) eds. Black economic development: analysis and implications: an anthology. Ann Arbor, Mich., [1975]. pp. 426. *bibliogs.*

EMERGING issues in black economic development; edited by Benjamin F. Bobo and Alfred E. Osborne. Lexington, Mass., [1976]. pp. 239. *Based on a conference sponsored by The Joint Center for Community Studies, 1975.*

NATIONAL SYMPOSIUM ON THE STATE OF THE BLACK ECONOMY, 5TH, 1975. Survival in the face of crises: selected proceedings of the fifth National Symposium...; sponsored by the Chicago Economic Development Corporation; edited by Gerald F. Whittaker. [Ann Arbor, 1976]. pp. 147.

HIGGS (ROBERT) Competition and coercion: blacks in the American economy, 1865-1914. Cambridge, England, 1977. pp. 208. *bibliog. (Stanford University. Hoover Institution on War, Revolution and Peace. Hoover Institution Publications. 163)*

— Education.

DAVIS (ARTHUR) Racial crisis in public education: a quest for social order. New York, [1975]. pp. 250.

— Education, Higher.

HOWARD UNIVERSITY. Institute for the Study of Educational Policy. Equal educational opportunity for blacks in U.S. higher education: an assessment [of the academic year 1973-74]. Washington, D.C., 1976. pp. 330. *bibliog.*

— Employment.

CADITZ (JUDITH) White liberals in transition: current dilemmas of ethnic integration. New York, [1976]. pp. 187. *bibliog.*

EMERGING issues in black economic development; edited by Benjamin F. Bobo and Alfred E. Osborne. Lexington, Mass., [1976]. pp. 239. *Based on a conference sponsored by The Joint Center for Community Studies, 1975.*

NATIONAL SYMPOSIUM ON THE STATE OF THE BLACK ECONOMY, 5TH, 1975. Survival in the face of crises: selected proceedings of the fifth National Symposium...; sponsored by the Chicago Economic Development Corporation; edited by Gerald F. Whittaker. [Ann Arbor, 1976]. pp. 147.

RITTENOURE (R. LYNN) Black employment in the South: the case of the federal government. Austin, Texas, 1976. pp. 190. *bibliog. (Texas University. Bureau of Business Research. Studies in Human Resource Development. No. 4)*

— History.

PEERY (NELSON) The Negro national colonial question. 2nd ed. Chicago, [1975]. pp. 190. *First ed. (1972) prepared by the Communist League of America.*

CAMEJO (PETER) Racism, revolution, reaction, 1861-1877: the rise and fall of radical reconstruction. New York, [1976]. pp. 269. *bibliog.*

FRANKLIN (JOHN HOPE) Racial equality in America. Chicago, 1976. pp. 113. *bibliog. (National Endowment for the Humanities. Jefferson Lectures in the Humanities. 1976)*

KLINGMAN (PETER D.) Josiah Walls: Florida's black congressman of reconstruction. Gainesville, 1976. pp. 157. *bibliog.*

MEIER (AUGUST) and RUDWICK (ELLIOTT M.) Along the color line: explorations in the black experience. Urbana, Ill., [1976]. pp. 404.

RECKONING with slavery: a critical study in the quantitative history of American Negro slavery; by Paul A. David [and others]; with an introduction by Kenneth M. Stampp. New York, 1976. pp. 398. *bibliog.*

SAVAGE (WILLIAM SHERMAN) Blacks in the West. Westport, 1976. pp. 230. *bibliog.*

— — Sources.

MULLIN (MICHAEL) ed. American negro slavery: a documentary history. New York, 1976. pp. 283.

— Housing.

ROSE (HAROLD M.) Black suburbanization: access to improved quality of life or maintenance of th status quo? Cambridge, Mass., [1976]. pp. 288. *bibliog.*

— — United States — California.

RABINOVITZ (FRANCINE F.) and SIEMBIEDA (WILLIAM J.) Minorities in suburbs: the Los Angeles experience. Lexington, Mass., [1977]. pp. 100. *bibliog.*

— Legal status, laws, etc.

WARE (GILBERT) From the black bar: voices for equal justice. New York, [1976]. pp. 341.

KLUGER (RICHARD) Simple justice: the history of Brown v. Board of Education and black America's struggle for equality. London, 1977. pp. 823,xxiii. *bibliog.*

— Politics and suffrage.

BASS (JACK) and DE VRIES (WALTER) The transformation of southern politics: social change and political consequence since 1945. New York, [1976]. pp. 527. *bibliog.*

KLINGMAN (PETER D.) Josiah Walls: Florida's black congressman of reconstruction. Gainesville, 1976. pp. 157. *bibliog.*

LAWSON (STEVEN F.) Black ballots: voting rights in the South, 1944-1969. New York, 1976. pp. 474. *bibliog.*

URBAN governance and minorities; edited by Herrington J. Bryce. New York, 1976. pp. 220. *Based on a one-day Public Policy Forum on Urban Governance held in Washington in 1975 and sponsored by the Joint Center for Political Studies.*

[GARVEY (MARCUS)] More philosophy and opinions of Marcus Garvey; selected and edited from previously unpublished material by E.U. Essien-Udom and Amy Jacques Garvey. London, 1977. pp. 248. *This is volume 3 of Philosophy and opinions of Marcus Garvey.*

— Psychology.

VARIATIONS in black and white perceptions of the social environment; edited by Harry C. Triandis. Urbana, [1976]. pp. 202. *bibliog. Tables on microfiche (3 cards).*

ABRAMSON (PAUL R.) The political socialization of black Americans: a critical evaluation of research on efficacy and trust. New York, [1977]. pp. 195. *bibliog.*

— Race identity.

SIMON (RITA JAMES) and ALTSTEIN (HOWARD) Transracial adoption. New York, [1977]. pp. 197.

— Segregation.

CADITZ (JUDITH) White liberals in transition: current dilemmas of ethnic integration. New York, [1976]. pp. 187. *bibliog.*

— Social conditions.

LEY (DAVID) The black inner city as frontier outpost: images and behavior of a Philadelphia neighbourhood. Washington, D.C., [1974]. pp. 282. *bibliog. (Association of American Geographers. Monograph Series. No. 7)*

PERKINS (EUGENE) Home is a dirty street: the social oppression of black children. Chicago, [1975]. pp. 193.

WARREN (DONALD I.) Black neighbourhoods: an assessment of community power. Ann Arbor, [1975]. pp. 194.

SOLOMON (BARBARA) Black empowerment: social work in oppressed communities. New York, 1976. pp. 438.

— Alabama.

WIGGINS (SARAH WOOLFOLK) The scalawag in Alabama politics, 1865-1881. University, Ala., [1977]. pp. 220. *bibliog.*

— Boston.

DIFFERENT strokes: pathways to maturity in the Boston ghetto; a report to the Ford Foundation; ([by] Robert Rosenthal [and others]). Boulder, Colo., 1976. pp. 358. *bibliog.*

— Chicago.

PERKINS (EUGENE) Home is a dirty street: the social oppression of black children. Chicago, [1975]. pp. 193.

— Detroit.

WARREN (DONALD I.) Black neighbourhoods: an assessment of community power. Ann Arbor, [1975]. pp. 194.

— Ohio.

GERBER (DAVID A.) Black Ohio and the color line, 1860-1915. Urbana, Ill., [1976]. pp. 500. *bibliog.*

— Philadelphia.

LEY (DAVID) The black inner city as frontier outpost: images and behavior of a Philadelphia neighbourhood. Washington, D.C., [1974]. pp. 282. *bibliog. (Association of American Geographers. Monograph Series. No. 7)*

NEGROES AS BUSINESSMEN.

NATIONAL SYMPOSIUM ON THE STATE OF THE BLACK ECONOMY, 5TH, 1975. Survival in the face of crises: selected proceedings of the fifth National Symposium...; sponsored by the Chicago Economic Development Corporation; edited by Gerald F. Whittaker. [Ann Arbor, 1976]. pp. 147.

NEGROES AS CONSUMERS.

EMERGING issues in black economic development; edited by Benjamin F. Bobo and Alfred E. Osborne. Lexington, Mass., [1976]. pp. 239. *Based on a conference sponsored by The Joint Center for Community Studies, 1975.*

NEGROES IN AFRICA

— Ethnicity.

VAN DEN BERGHE (PIERRE LOUIS) ed. Race and ethnicity in Africa. Nairobi, 1975. pp. 357. *bibliog.*

NEGROES IN LATIN AMERICA.

PESCATELLO (ANN M.) ed. The African in Latin America; edited with an introduction. New York, [1975]. pp. 270. *bibliog.*

ROUT (LESLIE B.) The African experience in Spanish America: 1502 to the present day. Cambridge, 1976. pp. 404. *bibliog.*

NEGROES IN SOUTH AFRICA.

HORRELL (MURIEL) Housing schemes for urban Africans in municipal areas and the homelands; [paper given at the 42nd annual council meeting of the South African Institute of Race Relations, held in Durban in 1972]. Durban, 1972. pp. 36.

SOUTH AFRICA. Parliament. House of Assembly. Select Committee on Bantu Affairs. 1977. First, second, third and fourth reports...; proceedings (S.C. 7- 1977). in SOUTH AFRICA. Parliament. House of Assembly. Select Committee reports.

SUEDAFRIKA: Revolution oder Evolution: Studien zur Lebenslage der Schwarzen; herausgegeben von Heinz-Dietrich Ortlieb, Arnt Spandau. Hamburg, 1977. pp. 324. *(Hamburg. Hamburgisches Welt-Wirtschaftsarchiv. Veröffentlichungen)*

— Employment.

MYERS (DESAIX) Labor practices of U.S. corporations in South Africa. New York, 1977. pp. 123.

NEGROES IN THE UNITED KINGDOM.

SHYLLON (FOLARIN OLAWALE) Black people in Britain, 1555-1833. London, 1977. pp. 290. *bibliog.*

NEILSON (GEORGE).

MAITLAND (FREDERIC WILLIAM) Letters to George Neilson; edited by E.L.G. Stones. Glasgow, 1976. pp. 56. *bibliog.*

NEPAL

— Politics and government.

SHRESTHA (MANGAL KRISHNA) Trends in public administration in Nepal. Kathmandu, Department of Information, 1969. pp. 119. *bibliog.*

NETHERLANDS

— Commercial policy — Mathematical models.

NIEUWKERK (MARIUS VAN) Trade credit and monetary policy in the Netherlands: an empirical investigation into the determinants of domestic trade credit under a system of direct credit control. Amsterdam, [1976?]. pp. 17. *bibliog.* (*Nederlandsche Bank. Reprints. No. 18*)

— Economic conditions.

NETHERLANDS. Centraal Planbureau. 1976. De Nederlandse economie in 1980. 's-Gravenhage, 1976. pp. 385.

— — Mathematical models.

SCHILDERINCK (J.H.F.) Regression and factor analysis applied in econometrics. Leiden, 1977. pp. 239. *bibliog.* (*Tilburg. Katholieke Hogeschool. Tilburg Institute of Economics. Tilburg Studies in Econometrics. vol. 1*)

— Economic history.

MOKYR (JOEL) Industrialization in the Low Countries, 1795-1850. New Haven, 1976. pp. 295. *bibliog.*

De ECONOMISCHE geschiedenis van Nederland: uitgegeven ter gelegenheid van het tweehonderdjarig bestaan van de Nederlandsche Maatschappij voor Nijverheid en Handel; onder redactie van J. H. van Stuijvenberg. Groningen, 1977. pp. 398. *bibliogs.*

HOUTTE (JAN A. VAN) An economic history of the Low Countries, 800-1800. London, [1977]. pp. 342. *bibliog.*

— Foreign economic relations — Germany.

BLAESING (JOACHIM F.E.) Das goldene Delta und sein eisernes Hinterland, 1815-1851: von niederländisch-preussischen zu deutsch-niederländischen Wirtschaftsbeziehungen. Leiden, 1973. pp. 275. *bibliog.*

— — Japan.

VAN vriend tot vijand: de betrekkingen tusschen Nederlandsch-Indië en Japan; samengesteld onder toezicht van A.C.D. de Graeff door M. Boerstra [and others]. Amsterdam, 1945. pp. 382.

— — Prussia.

BLAESING (JOACHIM F.E.) Das goldene Delta und sein eisernes Hinterland, 1815-1851: von niederländisch-preussischen zu deutsch-niederländischen Wirtschaftsbeziehungen. Leiden, 1973. pp. 275. *bibliog.*

— Foreign relations.

LEEUW (ALEXANDER SALOMON DE) Nederland in de wereldpolitiek van 1900 tot heden. Nijmegen, 1975. pp. 259. *Facsimile reprint of the work originally published in Zeist, 1936, with the addition of the foreword to the 2nd edition, Amsterdam, 1939, and an index.*

GRENZEN en mogelijkheden van de Nederlandse buitenlandse politiek: een discussie; (met bijdragen van Huub A.J. Coppens [and others]). Baarn, [1976]. pp. 102. *Papers and discussions from a colloquium held in the Hague, 1976, by the Nederlands Genootschap voor Internationale Zaken and other organisations.*

JONKMAN (JAN ANNE) Nederland en Indonesië beide vrij, gezien vanuit het Nederlands Parlement: memoires. Assen, 1977. pp. 298.

— History.

KOSSMANN (ERNST HEINRICH) De Lage Landen 1780-1940: anderhalve eeuw Nederland en België. Amsterdam, 1976. pp. 618. *bibliog.*

— — 1556-1648, Wars of Independence.

PARKER (NOEL GEOFFREY) The Dutch revolt. London, 1977. pp. 327. *bibliog.*

— — 1795-1815.

SCHAMA (SIMON) Patriots and liberators: revolution in the Netherlands, 1780-1813. London, 1977. pp. 745.

— Industries.

MOKYR (JOEL) Industrialization in the Low Countries, 1795-1850. New Haven, 1976. pp. 295. *bibliog.*

— Parliament — History.

DUYNSTEE (FRANS JOZEPH FERDINAND MARIE) and BOSMANS (J.) Het kabinet Schermerhorn-Drees, 24 juni 1945-3 juli 1946. Assen, 1977. pp. 756. *bibliog.* (*Katholieke Universiteit Nijmegen. Centrum voor Parlementaire Geschiedenis. Parlementaire Geschiedenis van Nederland na 1945. 1*)

— Politics and government.

DUYNSTEE (FRANS JOZEPH FERDINAND MARIE) and BOSMANS (J.) Het kabinet Schermerhorn-Drees, 24 juni 1945-3 juli 1946. Assen, 1977. pp. 756. *bibliog.* (*Katholieke Universiteit Nijmegen. Centrum voor Parlementaire Geschiedenis. Parlementaire Geschiedenis van Nederland na 1945. 1*)

JONKMAN (JAN ANNE) Nederland en Indonesië beide vrij, gezien vanuit het Nederlands Parlement: memoires. Assen, 1977. pp. 298.

— Statistics.

NETHERLANDS. Centraal Bureau voor de Statistiek. 1975. 75 jaar statistiek van Nederland. 's-Gravenhage, 1975. 1 vol. (various pagings)

NEUBURG

— Economic history.

TAUSENDPFUND (ALFRED) Die Manufaktur im Fürstentum Neuburg: Studien zur Sozial- und Wirtschaftsgeschichte unter besonderer Berücksichtigung der grossbetrieblichen Entwicklung im Zeitalter des Merkantilismus. Nürnberg, 1975. pp. 430. *bibliog.* (*Nuremberg. Stadtarchiv. Nürnberger Werkstücke zur Stadt- und Landesgeschichte. Band 16) Erlanger Phil. Dissertation 1975.*

NEUCHÂTEL (CANTON)

— Economic policy.

OSTORERO (J.L.) Vers une nouvelle politique économique de la république et canton de Neuchâtel, etc. [Neuchâtel], Commission Consultative pour les Questions d'Ordre Economique, 1976. fo. 214. *bibliog.*

NEUROPSYCHOLOGY.

BLAKEMORE (COLIN) Mechanics of the mind. Cambridge, 1977. pp. 208. *bibliog.* (*British Broadcasting Corporation. Reith Lectures. 1976*)

NEUTRALITY.

SUHARTO (T.N.J.) Statement...to the summit meeting of the third Conference of Non- Aligned Countries, Lusaka, September 8-10, 1970. [Djakarta], Department of Information, [1970]. pp. 17.

The ORIGIN and growth of non-alignment. Lusaka, 1971. pp. 15.

GUYANA. Ministry of External Affairs. 1972. The thrust of non-alignment: the origin and development of the movement. Georgetown, 1972. pp. 28.

CONFERENCE OF FOREIGN MINISTERS OF NON-ALIGNED COUNTRIES, GEORGETOWN, 1972. The Georgetown declaration, the action programme for economic co- operation and related documents. [Georgetown, Ministry of Foreign Affairs, 1973?]. pp. 61.

TUZMUKHAMEDOV (RAIS ABDULKHAKOVICH) Neprisoedinenie i razriadka mezhdunarodnoi napriazhennosti. Moskva, 1976. pp. 120.

NEW BRUNSWICK

— Legislative Assembly — Rules and practice.

NEW BRUNSWICK. Legislative Assembly. 1963. Standing rules of the Legislative Assembly, adopted June 19, 1963; to which is added an appendix containing notes on the general procedure of the House and other information of use to members. Fredericton, 1963. pp. 68.

— Politics and government.

ATLANTIC PROVINCES ECONOMIC COUNCIL. Submission to the maritime union study. Halifax, Nova Scotia, 1969. pp. 35.

— Social policy.

NEW BRUNSWICK. 1970. White Paper on social development and social welfare. [Fredericton, 1970]. fo. 44.

NEW CALEDONIA

— Statistics.

NOUVELLE CALEDONIE EN CHIFFRES, LA; [pd. by] Service de la Statistique [New Caledonia]. a., current issue only. [Noumea].

NEW DEMOCRATIC PARTY (CANADA).

COOPERATIVE COMMONWEALTH FEDERATION (CANADA) and NEW DEMOCRATIC PARTY (CANADA). The decline and fall of a good idea: CCF-NDP manifestoes, 1932 to 1969; with an introduction by Michael S. Cross. Toronto, 1974. pp. 47.

WAFFLE MOVEMENT. The Waffle manifesto; (including resolutions prepared by the movement for the Federal Convention of the New Democratic Party). Vancouver, [1974]. pp. 60. *bibliog.*

NEW GRANADA (VICEROYALTY)

— Race question.

GONZALEZ (MARGARITA) El Resguardo en el Nuevo Reino de Granada. Bogota, 1970. pp. 197.

— Social history.

RUIZ RIVERA (JULIAN BAUTISTA) Encomienda y mita en Nueva Granada en el siglo XVII. Sevilla, 1975. pp. 454. (*Consejo Superior de Investigaciones Científicas. Escuela de Estudios Hispanoamericanos de Sevilla. Publicaciones. 228*)

NEW GUINEA

— Politics and government.

VAN DER KROEF (JUSTUS MARIA) Patterns of conflict in Eastern Indonesia. London, 1977. pp. 16. (*Institute for the Study of Conflict. Conflict Studies. No. 79*)

NEW PRODUCTS.

MIDGLEY (DAVID F.) Innovation and new product marketing. London, [1977]. pp. 296. *bibliog.*

NEW SOUTH WALES

— Legislative Assembly — Elections.

HUGHES (COLIN ANFIELD) and GRAHAM (BRUCE DESMOND) Voting for the New South Wales Legislative Assembly. Canberra, 1975. pp. 518. *Supplement to the same authors' A handbook of Australian government and politics 1890-1964.*

NEW TOWNS.

GOLANY (GIDEON) ed. Innovations for future cities. New York, 1976. pp. 264. *bibliogs.*

— France.

FRANCE. Direction de la Documentation. La Documentation Française. Notes et Etudes Documentaires. Nos. 4.286-4, 287-4,288. Les villes nouvelles francaises; par Pierre Merlin. Paris, 1976. pp. 110. *bibliog.*

— United States.

KAISER (EDWARD JOHN) Residential mobility in new communities: an analysis of recent in- movers and prospective out-movers. Cambridge, Mass., [1976]. pp. 188. *bibliog. (North Carolina University. Center for Urban and Regional Studies. New Communities Research Series)*

SMOOKLER (HELENE V.) Economic integration in new communities: an evaluation of factors affecting policies and implementation. Cambridge, Mass., [1976]. pp. 236. *bibliog. (North Carolina University. Center for Urban and Regional Studies. New Communities Research Series)*

NEW YORK (CITY)

— Economic conditions.

NEWFIELD (JACK) and DU BRUL (PAUL A.) The abuse of power: the permanent government and the fall of New York. New York, 1977. pp. 368.

— Foreign population.

KESSNER (THOMAS) The golden door: Italian and Jewish immigrant mobility in New York City, 1880-1915. New York, 1977. pp. 224. *bibliog.*

— Intellectual life.

HOWE (IRVING) and LIBO (KENNETH) World of our fathers. New York, [1976]. pp. 714. *bibliog.*

— Police.

MILLER (WILBUR R.) Cops and bobbies: police authority in New York and London, 1830-1870. Chicago, 1977. pp. 233. *bibliog.*

— Politics and government.

NEWFIELD (JACK) and DU BRUL (PAUL A.) The abuse of power: the permanent government and the fall of New York. New York, 1977. pp. 368.

— Social conditions.

HOWE (IRVING) and LIBO (KENNETH) World of our fathers. New York, [1976]. pp. 714. *bibliog.*

NEWFIELD (JACK) and DU BRUL (PAUL A.) The abuse of power: the permanent government and the fall of New York. New York, 1977. pp. 368.

NEW YORK (STATE)

— Government publications — Bibliography.

DICTIONARY CATALOG OF OFFICIAL PUBLICATIONS OF THE STATE OF NEW YORK; catalogued by the New York State Library. irreg., D 1973/S 1976 (1st)- Albany.

NEW ZEALAND

— Administrative and political divisions.

NEW ZEALAND. Local Government Commission. 1973. Regions and districts of New Zealand: areas adopted to date for various administrative and research purposes. [Wellington], [1973] repr. 1976. pp. 87.

— Economic conditions — Mathematical models.

HAYWOOD (E.) and CAMPBELL (COLIN) M.A. (Oxford) The New Zealand economy: measurement of economic fluctuations and indicators of economic activity, 1947-74. Wellington, 1976. pp. 32. *(Reserve Bank of New Zealand. Research Papers. No. 19)*

— Emigration and immigration — Bibliography.

NEW ZEALAND. Department of Labour. Research and Planning Division. 1975. Immigration and immigrants - a bibliography: a bibliography of the historical, demographic, social and economic aspects of immigration to and immigrants in New Zealand. Wellington, 1975. pp. 69.

— History.

The FEEL of truth: essays in New Zealand and Pacific history presented to F.L.W. Wood and J.C. Beaglehole on the occasion of their retirement; edited by Peter Munz. Wellington, N.Z., 1969. pp. 274.

— Politics and government.

SINCLAIR (KEITH) Walter Nash. Auckland, 1976. pp. 439. *bibliog.*

— Population.

NEW ZEALAND. Department of Statistics. 1976. New Zealand sub-national population projections 1976-1991. Report[s] no.1-[20]. [Wellington, 1976]. 20 pts. (in 1 vol.)

— Public works.

NOONAN (ROSSLYN JOY) By design: a brief history of the Public Works Department, Ministry of Works, 1870-1970. [Wellington, Ministry of Works and Development], 1975. pp. 330.

— Social policy.

SOCIAL science research applications in the public sector: a trend report; editor M.T.V. Reidy; published by the Department of Justice on behalf of the Wellington branch of the Royal Society of New Zealand. [Wellington], 1975. fo. 52.

NEWCASTLE-UPON-TYNE

— Economic conditions — Statistics.

URBAN TRENDS: a report on the Newcastle upon Tyne household survey; [pd. by] Newcastle upon Tyne City Council. a., 1975 [1st]- Newcastle upon Tyne.

— Social conditions — Statistics.

URBAN TRENDS: a report on the Newcastle upon Tyne household survey; [pd. by] Newcastle upon Tyne City Council. a., 1975 [1st]- Newcastle upon Tyne.

— Social history.

BARKE (MIKE) Social change in Benwell; written...in conjunction with Benwell Community Project. Newcastle-upon-Tyne, Benwell Community Development Project, [1977]. pp. 49.

— Social policy.

BENWELL IDEAS GROUP. Four BIG years: the history of Benwell's independent funding organisation, 1973-1977. [Newcastle-upon-Tyne, Benwell Community Development Project, 1977]. pp. 19.

NEWFOUNDLAND

— Constitutional history.

HILLER (JAMES K.) ed. The confederation issue in Newfoundland, 1864-1869: selected documents. [St. John's], 1974. pp. 113. *bibliog.*

— Politics and government.

ATLANTIC PROVINCES ECONOMIC COUNCIL. Submission to the maritime union study. Halifax, Nova Scotia, 1969. pp. 35.

HILLER (JAMES K.) ed. The confederation issue in Newfoundland, 1864-1869: selected documents. [St. John's], 1974. pp. 113. *bibliog.*

NEWFOUNDLAND AND LABRADOR

— Statistics.

NEWFOUNDLAND. Department of Finance. Economics and Statistics Division. 1970-74. Historical statistics of Newfoundland and Labrador; (with Supplement). St. John's, 1970-74. 2 vols. (in 1).

NEWS AGENCIES

— France.

FRANCE. Direction de la Documentation. La Documentation Française. Notes et Etudes Documentaires. Nos. 4,336-4,337. L'Agence France-Presse (A.F.P.). Paris, 1976. pp. 65. *bibliog.*

— Russia.

BRYLIAKOV (NIKOLAI ANDREEVICH) Rossiiskoe telegrafnoe.... Moskva, 1976. pp. 117.

NEWSPAPER COURT REPORTING

— United Kingdom.

HARRIS (BRIAN) The courts, the press and the public. Chichester, 1976. pp. 96.

NEWSPAPER PUBLISHING

— United Kingdom.

THOMSON (ROY) Baron Thomson. After I was sixty: a chapter of autobiography. London, 1975. pp. 224.

NEWSPAPERS

— Bibliography — Union lists.

WEBBER (ROSEMARY) compiler. World list of national newspapers: a union list of national newspapers in libraries in the British Isles. London, 1976. pp. 95. *bibliog.*

— Biography.

REGAN (SIMON) Rupert Murdoch: a business biography. London, 1976. pp. 246.

NEWTON (ARTHUR).

NEWTON (ARTHUR) b. 1902. Years of change: autobiography of a Hackney shoemaker. London, [1974, repr. 1975]. pp. 68. *(Workers' Educational Association. Hackney Branch. A People's Autobiography of Hackney)*

NEWTON (HUEY PIERCE).

HEATH (G. LOUIS) ed. The Black Panther leaders speak: Huey P. Newton, Bobby Seale, Eldridge Cleaver and company speak out through the Black Panther Party's official newspaper. Metuchen, N.J., 1976. pp. 165. *bibliog.*

NEXØ (MARTIN ANDERSEN).

See ANDERSEN NEXØ (MARTIN).

NICARAGUA

— Economic conditions.

UNITED NATIONS. II.G. Reports of the Economic Commission for Latin America. 1967. 2. El desarrollo economico de Nicaragua. (E/CN.12/742/Rev. 1). Nueva York, 1966. pp. 220. *(Analyses and Projections of Economic Development. 9)*

NIGER VALLEY.

GUILLAUME ( ) Agronomist. Rapport d'une mission d'études des aménagements hydroagricoles dans la vallée du Niger et de leurs possibilités d'extension. [Paris? 1959?]. 2 vols.

NIGERIA

— Appropriations and expenditures.

NIGERIA (NORTH-CENTRAL STATE). Recurrent estimates of the Government of North-Central State of Nigeria. a., 1969/70. Kaduna.

HARE (ALEXANDER PAUL) and BLUMBERG (HERBERT H.) eds. Liberation without violence: a third-party approach. London, 1977. pp. 368. *bibliog. Reprinted from various sources.*

NORD (DEPARTMENT)

— Population.

PROBLÈMES de peuplement de la métropole Nord. [Lille, 1969]. pp. 68. *Papers of a study conference held 26 February 1969 and organised by the Institut d'Etudes et d'Action Démographiques des Régions Nord et Picardie.*

NORDISK RÅD.

SOLEM (ERIK TORALF) The Nordic Council and Scandinavian integration. New York, 1977. pp. 197. *bibliog.*

NORFOLK

— Economic conditions.

NORFOLK. County Council. Norfolk structure plan: report of survey and studies.

— Economic policy.

NORFOLK. County Council. Norfolk structure plan: report of survey and studies.

— Social conditions.

NORFOLK. County Council. Norfolk structure plan: report of survey and studies.

— Social policy.

NORFOLK. County Council. Norfolk structure plan: report of survey and studies.

NORMANDY

— Economic history.

BOIS (GUY) Crise du féodalisme: (économie rurale et démographie en Normandie orientale du début du 14e siècle au milieu du 16e siècle). [Paris, 1976]. pp. 412. *bibliog.* (Fondation Nationale des Sciences Politiques. *Cahiers. 202*)

NORRLAND

— Economic policy.

RYDÉN (INGER) Transportkostnader och regional utveckling: modeller för analys av regionalpolitiskt stöd av godstransporter. Stockholm, [1976]. pp. 208. *bibliog. With English summary.*

NORTH ATLANTIC TREATY ORGANIZATION.

NORTH ATLANTIC TREATY ORGANIZATION. Committee on Non-Military Co-operation. 1957. Non-military co-operation in NATO: text of the report of the Committee of Three. Paris, 1957. pp. 15. (*NATO Letter. Special Supplements. vol. 5, no. 1*)

NORTH ATLANTIC TREATY ORGANIZATION. Information Service. 1957. The trade unions and NATO; with a preface by George Meany. Paris, 1957. pp. 41.

NORTH ATLANTIC TREATY ORGANIZATION. Secretary General. 1957. April 1952 to April 1957: text of Lord Ismay's report to the Ministerial Meeting of the North Atlantic Council at Bonn, May 1957. Paris, 1957. pp. 19. (*NATO Letter. Special Supplements. vol. 5, no. 6*)

NORTH ATLANTIC TREATY ORGANIZATION. 1959. Ten years of Atlantic co-operation, 1949-1959. Paris, 1959. pp. 39. (*NATO Letter. Special Issues*)

SLOSS (LEON) NATO reform: prospects and priorities. Beverly Hills, [1975]. pp. 66.

INTERNATIONAL INSTITUTE FOR STRATEGIC STUDIES. Adelphi Papers, No. 129. The alliance and Europe: part VI: the European programme group; by D.C.R. Heyhoe. London, 1976. pp. 27.

ROSE (FRANÇOIS DE) La France et la défense de l'Europe. Paris, [1976]. pp. 123.

NORTH CAROLINA

— Economic conditions.

HAYES (CHARLES R.) The dispersed city: the case of Piedmont, North Carolina. Chicago, 1976. pp. 157. *bibliog.* (Chicago. University. Department of Geography. Research Papers. No. 173)

NORTH OSSETIAN REPUBLIC

— Statistics.

NORTH OSSETIAN REPUBLIC. Statisticheskoe Upravlenie. 1974. Severnaia Osetiia za 50 let: statisticheskii sbornik. Ordzhonikidze, 1974. pp. 168.

NORTH RHINE-WESTPHALIA

— Economic conditions — Statistics.

NORTH RHINE-WESTPHALIA. Landesamt für Datenverarbeitung und Statistik. Beiträge zur Statistik des Landes Nordrhein-Westfalen. Heft 368. Volkswirtschaftliche Gesamtrechnung und ergänzende Daten bis 1974. Düsseldorf, 1977. pp. 77.

NORTH SHIELDS

— City planning.

NORTH TYNESIDE COMMUNITY DEVELOPMENT PROJECT. Some housing and town planning issues in North Tyneside: an overview. [North Shields, 1976]. pp. 163.

NORTH WEST TERRITORIES

— Native races.

CUMMING (PETER A.) Canada: native land rights and northern development. Copenhagen, 1977. pp. 64. (International Work Group for Indigenous Affairs. Documents. 26)

NORTHAMPTONSHIRE

— Economic conditions.

NORTHAMPTONSHIRE. County Planning Department. Northamptonshire county structure plan: report of survey: consultation draft. [Northampton], 1976. 1 vol (unpaged].

— Economic policy.

NORTHAMPTONSHIRE. County Planning Department. Northamptonshire county structure plan: the alternatives. [Northampton], 1976. pp. 17. *Bound with Northamptonshire county structure plan: draft written statement.*

NORTHAMPTONSHIRE. County Planning Department. Northamptonshire county structure plan: draft written statement. [Northampton], 1977. 1 vol. (unpaged).

— Social conditions.

NORTHAMPTONSHIRE. County Planning Department. Northamptonshire county structure plan: report of survey: consultation draft. [Northampton], 1976. 1 vol (unpaged).

— Social policy.

NORTHAMPTONSHIRE. County Planning Department. Northamptonshire county structure plan: the alternatives. [Northampton], 1976. pp. 17. *Bound with Northamptonshire county structure plan: draft written statement.*

NORTHAMPTONSHIRE. County Planning Department. Northamptonshire county structure plan: draft written statement. [Northampton], 1977. 1 vol. (unpaged).

NORTHERN TERRITORY

— Statistics.

NORTHERN TERRITORY STATISTICAL SUMMARY; [pd. by Northern Territory Office], Commonwealth Bureau of Census and Statistics [Australia]. a., 1975/1976 (16th)- [Darwin].

NORWAY

— Constitutional history.

HEIBERG (PETER ANDREAS) Nogle Betragtninger over National-Repraesentationen under en konstitutionel monarkisk Regjering, fornemmelig med Hensyn til Kongeriget Norge. Christiansand, Moe, 1817. pp. viii, 88.

— Executive departments.

BALDERSHEIM (HAROLD) Patterns of central control over local service provision in Norway. 1977. fo. 367. *bibliog. Typescript. Ph.D. (London) thesis: unpublished. This thesis is the property of London University and may not be removed from the Library.*

— History — 1905, Separation from Sweden.

OMRČANIN (MARGARET STEWART) Norway, Sweden, Croatia: a comparative study of state secession and formation. Philadelphia, [1976]. pp. 138.

— Politics and government.

KLINGMAN (DAVID) Social change, political change, and public policy: Norway and Sweden, 1875-1965. London, [1976]. pp. 54. *bibliog.*

— Population.

DYRVIK (STÅLE) and others. The demographic crises in Norway in the 17th and 18th centuries: some data and interpretations. Bergen, [1976]. pp. 48.

— Social conditions.

MARTINUSSEN (WILLY) The distant democracy: social inequality, political resources and political influence in Norway. London, [1977]. pp. 246. *bibliog. Based on the author's Fjerndemokratiet.*

— Social history.

KLINGMAN (DAVID) Social change, political change, and public policy: Norway and Sweden, 1875-1965. London, [1976]. pp. 54. *bibliog.*

— Social policy.

MARTINUSSEN (WILLY) The distant democracy: social inequality, political resources and political influence in Norway. London, [1977]. pp. 246. *bibliog. Based on the author's Fjerndemokratiet.*

NOTTINGHAMSHIRE

— Economic conditions.

NOTTINGHAMSHIRE. Department of Planning and Transportation. Nottinghamshire structure plan: draft report of survey. [Nottingham, 1976]. pp. 200. *bibliog.*

— Economic policy.

NOTTINGHAMSHIRE. Department of Planning and Transportation. Nottinghamshire structure plan: draft written statement. Nottingham, [1976]. pp. 245, iv..

— Social conditions.

NOTTINGHAMSHIRE. Department of Planning and Transportation. Nottinghamshire structure plan: draft report of survey. [Nottingham, 1976]. pp. 200. *bibliog.*

— Social policy.

NOTTINGHAMSHIRE. Department of Planning and Transportation. Nottinghamshire structure plan: draft written statement. Nottingham, [1976]. pp. 245, iv..

NOVA SCOTIA

— Executive departments.

NOVA SCOTIA. Department of Labour. 1967. The Nova Scotia Department of Labour. [Halifax, 1967?]. 1 pamphlet (unpaged).

— Politics and government.

ATLANTIC PROVINCES ECONOMIC COUNCIL. Submission to the maritime union study. Halifax, Nova Scotia, 1969. pp. 35.

NUCLEAR FUELS.

ATLANTIC COUNCIL OF THE UNITED STATES. Nuclear Fuels Policy Working Group. Nuclear fuels policy. Boulder, Col., 1976. pp. 136.

NUREMBERG

— History.

BEER (HELMUT) Widerstand gegen den Nationalsozialismus in Nürnberg, 1933-1945. Nürnberg, [1976]. pp. 398. *bibliog. (Nuremberg. Stadtarchiv. Nürnberger Werkstücke zur Stadt- und Landesgeschichte. Band 20) Erlanger Phil. Dissertation 1976.*

NURSES AND NURSING.

CONGALTON (ATHOL ALEXANDER) The individual in society: an introduction to sociology for nurses. Sydney, [1976]. pp. 259. *bibliogs.*

— Canada.

NURSING IN CANADA: Canadian nursing statistics; (pd. by) Statistics Canada. a., 1975 (1st)- Ottawa. *[in English and French].*

— United Kingdom.

CLARK (JILL) Time out?: a study of absenteeism among nurses. London, [1975]. pp. 68. *bibliog. (Royal College of Nursing and National Council of Nurses of the United Kingdom. Research Series)*

NUTRITION.

FOOD: politics, economics, nutrition and research; edited by Philip H. Abelson. Washington, D.C., [1975]. pp. 202. *bibliog. The contents originally appeared in Science, weekly journal of the American Association for the Advancement of Science from January 1972 to March 1975.*

The MAN/food equation: proceedings of a symposium held at the Royal Institution London, September, 1973; edited by F. Steele and A. Bourne. London, 1975. pp. 289. *bibliogs.*

— Underdeveloped areas.

See UNDERDEVELOPED AREAS — Nutrition.

OAXACA

— Social conditions.

YOUNG (CATHERINE MARY) The social setting of migration: factors affecting migration from a Sierra Zapotec village in Oaxaca, Mexico. 1976. fo. 318. *bibliog. Typescript. Ph.D. (London) thesis: unpublished. This thesis is the property of London University and may not be removed from the Library.*

OBLIGATIONS (LAW).

SMITH (JOSEPH C.) Legal obligation. London, 1976. pp. 256.

OBSCENITY (LAW)

— United Kingdom.

EUROPEAN COURT OF HUMAN RIGHTS. Publications. Series A: Judgments and Decisions. [A24]. ...Handyside case: 1. Decision of 29 April 1976; 2. Judgment of 7 December 1976. Strasbourg, Council of Europe, 1976. pp. 37 [bis]. *In English and French.*

OCCUPATIONAL DISEASES.

MILLER (ARNOLD RAY) The wages of neglect: death and disease in the American workplace. San Francisco, 1975. pp. 8. *(National Conference on Social Welfare. 102nd Annual Forum, San Francisco, 1975)*

OCCUPATIONAL MOBILITY

— United States.

MONTAGNA (PAUL D.) Occupations and society: toward a sociology of the labor market. New York, [1977]. pp. 456.

OCCUPATIONAL PRESTIGE.

TREIMAN (DONALD J.) Occupational prestige in comparative perspective. New York, [1977]. pp. 514. *bibliog.*

OCCUPATIONAL TRAINING

— Denmark.

PLATZ (MERETE) and others. Ansøgere til de erhvervsfaglige grunduddannelser. København, 1975. pp. 144. *bibliog. (Socialforskningsinstituttet. Meddelelser.8)*

— Finland.

LÄHTEINEN (MARTTI) Eri ikäisten teollisuuden työntekijäin koulutus, etc. Helsinki, 1977. pp. 123. *bibliog. (Finland. Suomen Virallinen Tilasto. Finlands Officiella Statistik. 32. Sosiaalisia Erikoistutkimuksia. 50) With English summary.*

— Germany.

STELZL (HANS JOACHIM) Die Diskussion um das Berufsbildungs- und das Ausbildungsplatzförderungsgesetz. Bonn, 1976. pp. 132. *(Germany (Bundesrepublik). Deutscher Bundestag. Wissenschaftliche Dienste. Materialien. 45)*

— United Kingdom.

ROAD TRANSPORT INDUSTRY TRAINING BOARD [U.K.]. Transport and distribution: meeting the manpower needs. Wembley, [1975?]. pp. 23.

ROAD TRANSPORT INDUSTRY TRAINING BOARD [U.K.]. Local manpower studies, 1976-1977: six micro-economic studies in manpower planning in the road transport industry. Wembley, 1977. pp. 121.

— — Wales.

GLAMORGAN-GLYNCORRWG COMMUNITY DEVELOPMENT PROJECT. House improvement, occupational training and job creation: a review of work undertaken by the Upper Afan C[ommunity] D[evelopment] P[roject]. [Port Talbot], 1974. fo. 18.

OCEAN BOTTOM (MARITIME LAW).

BUZAN (BARRY GORDON) Seabed politics. New York, 1976. pp. 311.

SULLIVAN (JEREMIAH J.) Pacific basin enterprise and the changing law of the sea. Lexington, Mass., [1977]. pp. 218. *bibliog.*

O'CONNELL (DANIEL).

BINNS ( ) Dr. An appeal to the good sense of the British nation, against the monstrous charges of Daniel O'Connell, Esq., and other members of the Anti-Slavery Convention, touching the Jamaica House of Assembly. London, Effingham Wilson, 1840. pp. 18.

O'CONNELL (DANIEL PETER).

ROBINSON (FRANK S.) Machine politics: a study of Albany's O'Connells. New Brunswick, N.J., [1977]. pp. 262.

ODER RIVER.

ODRA i Nadodrze. Warszawa, 1976. pp. 371.

OFFENCES AGAINST PROPERTY

— Canada.

AVIO (KENNETH L.) and CLARK (CECIL SCOTT) Property crime in Canada: an econometric study. Toronto, 1976. pp. 86. *bibliog. (Ontario. Economic Council. Research Studies. No. 2)*

OFFENCES AGAINST THE PERSON

— Russia — Ukraine.

STASHIS (VLADIMIR VLADIMIROVICH) and BAZHANOV (MARK IGOREVICH) Ugolovno-pravovaia okhrana lichnosti: nauchno-prakticheskii kommentarii deistvuiushchego ugolovnogo zakonodatel'stva USSR. Khar'kov, 1976. pp. 220.

OFFICES

— Cleaning.

SULLIVAN (JILL) The brush off: a study of the contract cleaning industry. London, 1977. pp. 32. *(Low Pay Unit. Low Pay Pamphlets. No. 5)*

— Location — Ireland (Republic).

NATIONAL ECONOMIC AND SOCIAL COUNCIL [EIRE]. Service-type employment and regional development; (by Michael J. Bannon [and others]). Dublin, Stationery Office, [1977]. pp. 142. *bibliog. ([Reports]. No. 28)*

OGAREV (NIKOLAI PLATONOVICH).

HERZEN, Ogarev, Bakounine: lettres inédites; introduction, traductions et notes par Michel Mervaud. Paris, 1975. pp. 158. *With French translations of letters in German and Russian. Includes in addition eight letters from Victor Hugo to Herzen.*

OHIO

— Race question.

GERBER (DAVID A.) Black Ohio and the color line, 1860-1915. Urbana, Ill., [1976]. pp. 500. *bibliog.*

OKLAHOMA

— Politics and government.

BURBANK (GARIN) When farmers voted red: the gospel of socialism in the Oklahoma countryside, 1910-1924. Westport, Conn., 1976. pp. 224. *bibliog.*

OLD AGE

— Austria.

MAJCE (GERHARD) and HOERL (JOSEF) Formen der Altenhilfe: Aufgaben und Probleme der offenen und geschlossenen Altenbetreuung. Wien, [1974]. pp. 119. *bibliog. (Institut für Stadtforschung. Publikationen. 19)*

OESTERREICHISCHES KOMITEE FÜR SOZIALARBEIT and OESTERREICHISCHER STÄDTEBUND. Arbeitskreis Altenbetreuung. Altenhilfe in Österreich: eine Dokumentation. Wien, [1974?]. pp. 208. *(Institut für Stadtforschung. Publikationen. 18)*

— Denmark.

SCHMIDT (GERT) and others. Vaegtforhold og funktionsevne blandt aeldre i Odense. København, 1975. pp. 80. *bibliog. (Socialforskningsinstituttet. Meddelelser. 10)*

OLSEN (HENNING) and others. Familiekontakter i den tidlige alderdom: rapport nr. 1 fra forløbsundersøgelsen af de aeldre, etc. København, 1976. pp. 252. *(Socialforskningsinstituttet. Publikationer. 74) With English summary.*

— France.

STEARNS (PETER N.) Old age in European society: the case of France. London, [1977]. pp. 163.

— Germany.

Die LEBENSLAGE älterer Menschen in der Bundesrepublik Deutschland: Analyse der Mängel und Vorschläge zur Verbesserung; Projektleitung und wissenschaftliche Koordination: Gisela Kiesau; Mitarbeiter: Maria Balassa [and others]. pp. 462. *bibliog.* *(Deutscher Gewerkschaftsbund. Wirtschafts- und Sozialwissenschaftliches Institut. WSI-Studien zur Wirtschafts- und Sozialforschung. Nr. 31)*

— United Kingdom.

METRICATION BOARD [U.K.]. Metrication and elderly people: a report based on research by the Tavistock Institute of Human Relations and by National Opinion Polls Limited. London, [1976]. pp. 64.

— — Care and hygiene.

BAILEY (ROGER) Environmental safety and the elderly. London, [1974]. pp. 12. *bibliog. (Age Concern England. Manifesto Series. No. 22)*

WILLANS (JOAN H.) Death and bereavement. London, [1974]. pp. 12. *bibliog. (Age Concern England. Manifesto Series. No. 17)*

AGE CONCERN ENGLAND. Age Concern at work. London, [1976]. pp. 28.

— — Dwellings.

SOCIAL SERVICES RESEARCH AND INTELLIGENCE UNIT [PORTSMOUTH]. Occasional Papers. No. 2. Households: Portsmouth and neighbouring areas. Portsmouth, 1973. fo. 27. *bibliog.*

BAILEY (ROGER) Environmental safety and the elderly. London, [1974]. pp. 12. *bibliog. (Age Concern England. Manifesto Series. No. 22)*

The ROLE of sheltered housing in the care of the elderly: a reappraisal; a report on a seminar held at the University of Nottingham, 9th to 11th April, 1975. Stafford, [1975]. pp. 31.

AGE CONCERN ENGLAND. Home truths on housing for the elderly. [London, 1976]. pp. 19.

— — Institutional care.

BROCKLEHURST (JOHN CHARLES) Old people in institutions: their rights. London, 1974. pp. 10. *bibliog. (Age Concern England. Manifesto Series. No. 10)*

— United States.

HEINTZ (KATHERINE McMILLAN) Retirement communities, for adults only. New Brunswick, [1976]. pp. 239.

HESS (BETH B.) ed. Growing old in America. New Brunswick, N.J., [1976]. pp. 498. *bibliogs.*

LAWTON (MORTIMER POWELL) and others, eds. Community planning for an aging society: designing services and facilities. Stroudsburg, Penn., [1976]. pp. 340.

PRATT (HENRY J.) The gray lobby. Chicago, 1976. pp. 250. *bibliog.*

FISCHER (DAVID HACKETT) Growing old in America. New York, 1977. pp. 242. *The Bland-Lee lectures delivered at Clark University.*

MOON (MARILYN) The measurement of economic welfare: its application to the aged poor. New York, [1977]. pp. 146. *bibliog. (Wisconsin University, Madison. Institute for Research on Poverty. Monograph Series)*

— — Care and hygiene.

WEAVER (JERRY L.) National health policy and the underserved: ethnic minorities, women, and the elderly. Saint Louis, 1976. pp. 161.

— — Dwellings.

LAWTON (MORTIMER POWELL) and others, eds. Community planning for an aging society: designing services and facilities. Stroudsburg, Penn., [1976]. pp. 340.

OLD AGE ASSISTANCE

— United Kingdom.

U.K. Department of Health and Social Security. Statistics and Research Division. 1976. The elderly and the personal social services; a report...based on The needs of old people in Glamorgan; by Margaret Watson and Martin Albrow. [London, 1976]. pp. 111.

PLANK (DAVID) Caring for the elderly: report of a study of various means of caring for dependent elderly people in eight London boroughs. London, [1977]. pp. 235. *(London. Greater London Council. Research Memoranda. 512)*

U.K. Central Office of Information. Reference Division. Reference Pamphlets. 121. Care of the elderly in Britain. 2nd ed. London, 1977. pp. 36. *bibliog.*

— — Ireland, Northern.

IRELAND, NORTHERN. Department of Health and Social Services. 1976. Development of health and personal social services for the elderly in Northern Ireland. [Belfast], 1976. pp. 29.

— — Scotland.

STANLEY (GILLIAN) and LUTZ (W.) Meals services for the elderly in Scotland. [Edinburgh], Scottish Home and Health Department, 1976. pp. 266. *bibliog. (Scottish Health Service Studies. No. 35)*

— United States.

LAWTON (MORTIMER POWELL) and others, eds. Community planning for an aging society: designing services and facilities. Stroudsburg, Penn., [1976]. pp. 340.

MOON (MARILYN) The measurement of economic welfare: its application to the aged poor. New York, [1977]. pp. 146. *bibliog. (Wisconsin University, Madison. Institute for Research on Poverty. Monograph Series)*

OLD AGE HOMES.

TOBIN (SHELDON S.) and LIEBERMAN (MORTON A.) Last home for the aged: (critical implications of institutionalization). San Francisco, 1976. pp. 304. *bibliog.*

— Austria.

MAJCE (GERHARD) and HOERL (JOSEF) Formen der Altenhilfe: Aufgaben und Probleme der offenen und geschlossenen Altenbetreuung. Wien, [1974]. pp. 119. *bibliog. (Institut für Stadtforschung. Publikationen. 19)*

OESTERREICHISCHES KOMITEE FÜR SOZIALARBEIT and OESTERREICHISCHER STÄDTEBUND. Arbeitskreis Altenbetreuung. Altenhilfe in Österreich: eine Dokumentation. Wien, [1974?]. pp. 208. *(Institut für Stadtforschung. Publikationen. 18)*

— United Kingdom.

BREARLEY (CHRISTOPHER PAUL) Residential work with the elderly. London, 1977. pp. 197. *bibliog.*

OLD AGE PENSIONS.

ORGANISATION FOR ECONOMIC CO-OPERATION AND DEVELOPMENT. 1977. Old age pension schemes. Paris, 1977. pp. 206. *bibliog.*

— Barbados.

BARBADOS. Committee appointed to Consider and Report on the Question of Introducing a Scheme of Old Age Pensions in Barbados. 1936. Report; [E.K. Walcott, chairman]. [Bridgetown, 1936]. pp. 12.

— France.

FRANCE. Direction de la Documentation. La Documentation Française. Notes et Etudes Documentaires. Nos. 4,260-4,261. Le système des retraites en France; par Jean-François Chadelat et Daniel Hossard. Paris, 1976. pp. 78. *bibliog.*

— United Kingdom.

FOGARTY (MICHAEL PATRICK) Pensions - where next?. [London, 1976]. pp. 162.

— United States.

GREENOUGH (WILLIAM CROAN) and KING (FRANCIS PAUL) Pension plans and public policy. New York, 1976. pp. 311.

OLDHAM (JOSEPH HOULDSWORTH).

LEYS (NORMAN MACLEAN) and OLDHAM (JOSEPH HOULDSWORTH) By Kenya possessed: the correspondence of Norman Leys and J. H. Oldham, 1918-1926; edited and with an introduction by John W. Cell. Chicago, 1976. pp. 382.

OLDHAM

— Politics and government.

CORINA (LEWIS) Oldham C[ommunity] D[evelopment] P[roject]: an assessment of its impact and influence on the local authority. [York], 1977. pp. 134. *(Papers in Community Studies. No. 9)*

OLIGARCHY.

TUSELL GOMEZ (JAVIER) Oligarquia y caciquismo en Andalucia, 1890-1923. Barcelona, 1976. pp. 589.

OLIGOPOLIES.

EICHNER (ALFRED S.) The megacorp and oligopoly: micro foundations of macro dynamics. Cambridge, 1976. pp. 365. *bibliog.*

O'MAHONY (LIAM).

DEATH of Liam O'Mahony: report of the tribunal appointed by the Minister for Justice on July 19th, 1967, pursuant to a resolution passed on July 18th, 1967, by Dail Eireann and on July 19th, 1967, by Seanad Eireann. Dublin, Stationery Office, [1968]. pp. 48.

OMAN

— Economic conditions.

TOWNSEND (JOHN) Oman: the making of a modern state. London, [1977]. pp. 212. *bibliog.*

— Nationalism.

GULF COMMITTEE. 9th June Studies. Documents of the national struggle in Oman and the Arabian Gulf. London, 1974. pp. 106.

— Politics and government.

TOWNSEND (JOHN) Oman: the making of a modern state. London, [1977]. pp. 212. *bibliog.*

OMBUDSMAN

— Canada — Newfoundland.

NEWFOUNDLAND. Office of the Parliamentary Commissioner (Ombudsman). Annual report (formerly Report). a., Ag/D 1975(1st)- St. John's.

— France.

FRANCE. Médiateur. Rapport...au Président de la République et au Parlement (formerly Rapport annuel). a., 1973(1st)- , with gap(1975). Paris.

— Israel.

ISRAEL. Commissioner for Complaints from the Public. Annual report. a., 1972/73 (2nd). Jerusalem. *Not subsequently translated into English.*

CAIDEN (GERALD ELLIOT) To right wrong: the Ombudsman experience in Israel. Haifa, 1975. fo. 277.

— New Zealand.

HILL (LARRY B.) The model Ombudsman: institutionalizing New Zealand's democratic experiment. Princeton, N.J., [1976]. pp. 411. *bibliog.*

— United Kingdom.

U.K. Commission for Local Administration in England. Report. a., 1975/76 [1st]- London.

— Ireland, Northern.

IRELAND, NORTHERN. Commissioner for Complaints. Annual report. a., 1973 (6th) Belfast. *1968-1971 (1st-4th) included in IRELAND, NORTHERN. Parliament. House of Commons. [Papers]. 1972 (5th) included in British Parliamentary Papers session 1972/3, vol. 27 (H.C. Paper 158). 1974 onwards included in British Parliamentary Papers.*

IRELAND, NORTHERN. Parliamentary Commissioner for Administration. Annual report. a., 1973(5th) Belfast. *Jl/S 1969-1971 (1st-3rd) included in IRELAND, NORTHERN. Parliament. House of Commons. [Papers]. 1972 (4th) included in the file of British Parliamentary Papers, session 1972/73, vol. 27 (H.C. Paper 159). 1974 onwards included in British Parliamentary Papers.*

ON-LINE DATA PROCESSING.

YOURDON (EDWARD) Design of on-line computer systems. Englewood Cliffs, [1972]. pp. 608.

PRITCHARD (J.A.T.) Introduction to on-line systems. Newton Abbot, [1973]. pp. 100. *bibliog.*

ONTARIO

— Commerce.

WILLIAMS (JAMES RALLA) Resources, tariffs, and trade: Ontario's stake. Toronto, 1976. pp. 117. *bibliog. (Ontario. Economic Council. Research Studies. No. 6)*

— Economic conditions.

WILLIAMS (JAMES RALLA) Resources, tariffs, and trade: Ontario's stake. Toronto, 1976. pp. 117. *bibliog. (Ontario. Economic Council. Research Studies. No. 6)*

— Economic history.

NELLES (HENRY VIVIAN) The politics of development: forests, mines and hydro-electric power in Ontario, 1849-1941. Toronto, [1974]. pp. 514.

— Economic policy.

ONTARIO. Department of Treasury and Economics. 1971. Design for development: a policy statement on the northwestern Ontario region. [Toronto], 1971. fo. 7.

— Forest policy.

ONTARIO. Economic Council. 1970. A forest policy for Ontario. Toronto, 1970. pp. 38.

— Social policy.

HERITAGE ONTARIO CONGRESS, TORONTO, 1972. Heritage Ontario Congress, June 2,3,4, 1972: report. [Toronto], 1973. pp. 57,61. *In English and French.*

OPEN AND CLOSED SHOP

— United Kingdom.

BELOFF (NORA) Freedom under Foot: the battle over the closed shop in British journalism. London, 1976. pp. 143.

OPEN PRISONS

— United Kingdom.

JONES (HOWARD) and CORNES (PAUL) Open prisons. London, 1977. pp. 275.

OPERATION OVERLORD.

STOLER (MARK A.) The politics of the second front: American military planning and diplomacy in coalition warfare, 1941-1943. Westport, Conn., 1977. pp. 244. *bibliogs.*

OPERATIONS RESEARCH.

CHEN (CHING-CHIH) Applications of operations research models to libraries: a case study of the use of monographs in the Francis A. Countway Library of Medicine, Harvard University. Cambridge, Mass., [1976]. pp. 212. *bibliog.*

NAGEL (STUART S.) and NEEF (MARIAN) Operations research methods as applied to political science and the legal process. Beverly Hills, [1976]. pp. 76. *bibliog.*

NATIONAL RESEARCH COUNCIL. Commission on International Relations. Board on Science and Technology for International Development. Systems analysis and operations research: a tool for policy and program planning for developing countries: report of an ad hoc panel. Washington, D.C., 1976. pp. 98. *bibliog. With summaries in Spanish and French.*

OPPOSITION (POLITICAL SCIENCE).

PONTON (GEOFFREY) Political opposition. London, [1976]. pp. 34. *bibliog. (Politics Association. Occasional Publications. 4)*

SCHUMANN (HANS GERD) ed. Die Rolle der Opposition in der Bundesrepublik Deutschland. Darmstadt, 1976. pp. 530. *bibliog.*

OPUS DEI.

SOTO (FRANCISCO) Fascismo y Opus Dei en Chile: estudios de literatura e ideologia. Barcelona, 1976. pp. 261.

ORANGEMEN.

[GIFFARD (JOHN)] Orange: a political rhapsody in three cantos. 9th ed. Dublin, printed for J. Milliken, 1798. pp. 22, 23, 24. *Also attributed to G. Faulkner the Younger.*

The ORANGE institution: a slight sketch; with an appendix containing the rules and regulations of the Orange societies of the United Kingdom. London, Stockdale, 1813. pp. 27.

ORGANIZATION.

FRIEDMANN (JOHN REMBERT PETER) Retracking America: the theory of transactive planning. Garden City, N.Y., 1973. pp. 289. *bibliog.*

ANNA (HENRY J.) Task groups and linkages in complex organizations: a case study of NASA. Beverly Hills, Calif., [1976]. pp. 64. *bibliog.*

BOWEY (ANGELA M.) The sociology of organisations. London, 1976. pp. 228. *bibliog.*

EVAN (WILLIAM M.) Organization theory: structures, systems and environments. New York, [1976]. pp. 312. *bibliogs.*

SWINGLE (PAUL G.) The management of power. Hillsdale, N.J., 1976. pp. 178. *bibliog.*

TASK and organization; edited by Eric J. Miller. London, [1976]. pp. 379. *bibliogs. Includes a list of publications by A.K. Rice.*

THUNG (MADY A.) The precarious organisation: sociological explorations of the church's mission and structure. The Hague, [1976]. pp. 348. *bibliog.*

CLEGG (STEWART) and DUNKERLEY (DAVID) eds. Critical issues in organizations. London, 1977. pp. 109. *bibliog.*

ORGANIZATION OF AFRICAN UNITY.

UDECHUKU (EMMANUEL CHUKWUKELO) African unity and international law. London, [1974]. pp. 228.

ORGANIZATION OF AMERICAN STATES

— Finance.

ORGANIZATION OF AMERICAN STATES. 1969. Consolidated proposed programs and budgets of the General Secretariat; biennium 1970/72 with projections of activities and expenditures for 1972/76. (Official Records. OEA/Series D/II. 1). [Washington, 1969]. 3 vols.

ORGANIZATION OF THE PETROLEUM EXPORTING COUNTRIES.

VALLENILLA (LUIS) Oil: the making of a new economic order: Venezuelan oil and OPEC. New York, [1975]. pp. 302.

OPEC REVIEW: a digest of energy reports; [pd.by] Information Department, Organization of the Petroleum Exporting Countries. irreg., Oc 1976 (v.1, no.1)- Vienna.

DENMARK. Udenrigsministeriet. Erhvervstjenesten. 1976. Danmarks samhandel med OPEC-landene. København, [1976]. pp. 137.

RUSTOW (DANKWART ALEXANDER) and MUGNO (JOHN F.) OPEC: success and prospects. New York, 1976. pp. 179.

GHADAR (FARIBORZ) The evolution of OPEC strategy. Lexington, Mass., [1977]. pp. 196. *bibliog.*

ORGANIZATIONAL BEHAVIOUR.

KANTER (ROSABETH MOSS) Men and women of the corporation. New York, [1977]. pp. 348. *bibliog.*

ORGANIZATIONAL CHANGE.

GRAVES (DESMOND JAMES TURNER) Organisational change in a port operating authority. London, National Ports Council, 1976. fo. 88.

ORIENTAL STUDIES

— Australia.

THOMAS (WILLIAM L.) Paths to Asia: Asian studies at universities in Australia;. ..a report on the findings of a study-trip...1974 to Australian universities...with summary, conclusions and recommendations. Nedlands, 1974. pp. 91. *(Western Australia, University of. Centre for Asian Studies. Working Papers in Asian Studies. No. 6)*

— Russia.

MAZITOVA (NAZIFA ARIFOVNA) Izuchenie Blizhnego i Srednego Vostoka v Kazanskom universitete, pervaia polovina XIX veka. Kazan', 1972. pp. 225.

ORISSA

— Economic conditions.

FREEMAN (JAMES M.) Scarcity and opportunity in an Indian village. Menlo Park, Calif., [1977]. pp. 177. *bibliog.*

— Rural conditions.

FREEMAN (JAMES M.) Scarcity and opportunity in an Indian village. Menlo Park, Calif., [1977]. pp. 177. *bibliog.*

ORPHANS AND ORPHAN ASYLUMS

— United Kingdom.

LASLETT (PETER) Family life and illicit love in earlier generations: essays in historical sociology. Cambridge, 1977. pp. 270. *bibliog.*

ORTEGA Y GASSET (JOSE).

DUJOVNE (LEON) La concepcion de la historia en la obra de Ortega y Gasset. Buenos Aires, [1968]. pp. 218.

ORTIZ DE AYALA (TADEO).

TORRE VILLAR (ERNESTO DE LA) Mexico y su politica interamericana: la mision de Don Tadeo Ortiz de Ayala. Guadalajara, Mexico, 1973. pp. 214.

OSTROVITIANOV (KONSTANTIN VASIL'EVICH).

STANOVLENIE i razvitie ekonomicheskoi nauki v SSSR: sbornik, posviashchennyi pamiati akademika K.V. Ostrovitianova. Moskva, 1976. pp. 168.

OTTO, Archduke of Austria.

MOMMSEN-REINDL (MARGARETA) Die österreichische Proporzdemokratie und der Fall Habsburg. Wien, 1976. pp. 264. *bibliog.*

OUTDOOR RECREATION

— Bibliography.

VEAL (A.J.) compiler. Environmental perception and recreation: a review and annotated bibliography. Birmingham, 1974. pp. 201. *(Birmingham. University. Centre for Urban and Regional Studies. Research Memoranda. No. 39)*

— United Kingdom.

U.K. Countryside Commission. 1976. Digest of countryside recreation statistics: published...on behalf of the Countryside Recreation Research Advisory Group. [3rd ed.] [London], 1976. 1 vol. (loose-leaf). *bibliog.*

HOCKIN (RICHARD) and others. The site requirements and planning of outdoor recreation activities. Reading, 1977. pp. 52. *bibliog. (Reading. University. Department of Geography. Reading Geographical Papers. No. 54)*

OXFORD

— Bibliography.

OXFORD. Oxford Historical Society. [Publications]. New Series. vol. 25. A bibliography of printed works relating to the city of Oxford; by E.H. Cordeaux and D.H. Merry. Oxford, 1976. pp. 377.

— City planning.

LONDON. University. London School of Economics and Political Science. Graduate School of Geography. Discussion Papers. No. 57. Social justice and planning: the use of the accessibility matrix; [by] Tisha Loodmer. London, 1976. pp. 16. *bibliog.*

PACIFIC, THE

— Economic conditions.

KOLDE (ENDEL JAKOB) The Pacific quest: the concept and scope of an oceanic community. Lexington, Mass., [1976]. pp. 161.

— History.

The FEEL of truth: essays in New Zealand and Pacific history presented to F.L.W. Wood and J.C. Beaglehole on the occasion of their retirement; edited by Peter Munz. Wellington, N.Z., 1969. pp. 274.

— Relations (general) with Europe.

DODGE (ERNEST S.) Islands and empires: western impact on the Pacific and East Asia. Minneapolis, Minn., 1976. pp. 364. *bibliog.*

— Social conditions.

SUBSISTENCE and survival: rural ecology in the Pacific; edited by Timothy P. Bayliss-Smith and Richard G. Feachem. London, 1977. pp. 428. *bibliogs.*

PACIFIC SETTLEMENT OF INTERNATIONAL DISPUTES.

BOZEMAN (ADDA BRUEMMER) Conflict in Africa: concepts and realities. Princeton, N.J., 1976. pp. 429. *bibliog.*

PACIFISM.

HERVE (GUSTAVE) Das Vaterland der Reichen; [translated from the French]. Zürich, [190-?]. pp. 259.

MURRY (JOHN MIDDLETON) The necessity of pacifism. London, 1937. pp. 132.

CLARK (ROBERT EDWARD DAVID) Does the Bible teach pacifism?. [London, 1976]. pp. 70.

PACKAGING.

HOCHART (BERNARD) Wood as a packaging material in the developing countries. (ID/72). New York, United Nations, 1972. pp. 111. *bibliog.*

PAINE (THOMAS).

FONER (ERIC) Tom Paine and revolutionary America. New York, 1976. pp. 326.

PAINE (THOMAS) Common sense; edited with an introduction by Isaac Kramnick. Harmondsworth, 1976. pp. 128. *bibliog.*

PAKISTAN

— Census.

PAKISTAN. Census, 1972. Census Bulletins. No. 1. Provisional tables. Islamabad, 1973. pp. 4.

PAKISTAN. Census, 1972. Census Bulletins. No. 2. Population by geographical levels. Islamabad, 1974-75. 5 vols.

— Description and travel.

TOYNBEE (ARNOLD JOSEPH) Between Oxus and Jumna. London, 1961. pp. 211.

— Emigration and immigration.

TINKER (HUGH) The banyan tree: overseas emigrants from India, Pakistan and Bangladesh. Oxford, 1977. pp. 204.

— Foreign relations.

BHUTTO (ZULFIKAR ALI) Speeches and statements. [Karachi, Department of Films and Publications, 1972 in progress].

BHUTTO (ZULFIKAR ALI) The third world: new directions. London, 1977. pp. 144.

— Politics and government.

BHUTTO (ZULFIKAR ALI) Speeches and statements. [Karachi, Department of Films and Publications, 1972 in progress].

GOPINATH (MEENAKSHI) Pakistan in transition: political development and rise to power of Pakistan People's Party. Delhi, 1975. pp. 162. *bibliog.*

LAPORTE (ROBERT) Power and privilege: influence and decision-making in Pakistan. Berkeley, Calif., [1975]. pp. 225. *bibliog.*

PAKISTAN. Attorney-General. 1975. Attorney General Yahya Bakhtiar's opening address in the Supreme Court of Pakistan in the reference by the Islamic Republic of Pakistan on dissolution of National Awami Party, Rawalpindi, June 19, 20 and 23, 1975. [Islamabad, 1975?]. pp. 95.

PAKISTAN. Supreme Court. 1975. Supreme Court judgement on dissolution of N[ational] A[wami] P[arty], Rawalpindi, October 30, 1975. [Islamabad, 1975?]. pp. 226.

PAKISTAN. Attorney-General. 1976. Concluding address in Supreme Court by Yahya Bakhtiar...in government's reference on N[ational] A[wami] P[arty]'s dissolution, Rawalpindi, September 8-17, 1975. [Islamabad, 1976]. pp. 251.

PAKISTAN PEOPLE'S PARTY.

GOPINATH (MEENAKSHI) Pakistan in transition: political development and rise to power of Pakistan People's Party. Delhi, 1975. pp. 162. *bibliog.*

PAKISTANIS IN FOREIGN COUNTRIES.

TINKER (HUGH) The banyan tree: overseas emigrants from India, Pakistan and Bangladesh. Oxford, 1977. pp. 204.

PAKISTANIS IN THE UNITED KINGDOM.

RUNNYMEDE TRUST. Briefing Papers. 1974, No. 2. The crisis of the Pakistani dependants. London, 1974. fo. 10.

PALESTINE

— Economic conditions.

LOWDERMILK (WALTER CLAY) Palestine: land of promise. London, 1946. pp. 167.

— Economic policy.

LOWDERMILK (WALTER CLAY) Palestine: land of promise. London, 1946. pp. 167.

— Emigration and immigration.

LUFT (GERDA) Heimkehr ins Unbekannte: eine Darstellung der Einwanderung von Juden aus Deutschland nach Palästina...1933-1939. Wuppertal, [1977]. pp. 142.

— Foreign relations — United States.

JANSEN (MICHAEL E.) The three basic American decisions on Palestine. Beirut, 1971. pp. 46. *(Palestine Research Center. Palestine Essays. No. 25)*

— History.

KISHTAINY (KHALID) Palestine in perspective: on the image and reality of Palestine throughout the ages. Beirut, 1971. pp. 126. *bibliog. (Palestine Research Center. Palestine Books. No. 34)*

PORATH (YEHOSHUA) The Palestinian Arab national movement: from riots to rebellion;...1929-1939. London, 1977. pp. 414. *bibliog. Vol.2 of his The emergence of the Palestinian-Arab national movement, 1918-1929.*

— International status.

YAHIA (F.) The Palestine question and international law. Beirut, 1970. pp. 220. *(Palestine Research Center. Palestine Books. No. 28)*

CATTAN (HENRY) Palestine and international law: the legal aspects of the Arab- Israeli conflict. 2nd ed. London, 1976. pp. 362.

— Politics and government.

ISRAEL INFORMATION CENTRE. Information Briefings. 29. Aspects of the Palestinian problem. rev. ed. Jerusalem, [1975]. pp. 39.

PALESTINE LIBERATION ORGANIZATION.

HUSSAIN (MEHMOOD) The Palestine Liberation Organisation: a study in ideology, strategy and tactics. Delhi, [1975]. pp. 156. *bibliog.*

INTERNATIONAL INSTITUTE FOR STRATEGIC STUDIES. Adelphi Papers. No. 131. The Soviet Union and the P.L.O.; by Galia Golan. London, 1976. pp. 34.

PALESTINIAN ARABS.

SAYEGH (ANIS) Palestine and Arab nationalism. Beirut, 1970. pp. 86. *(Palestine Research Center. Palestine Essays. No. 3)*

SIRHAN (BASSEM) Palestinian children: the generation of liberation: a sociological study. Beirut, 1970. pp. 55. *(Palestine Research Center. Palestine Essays. No. 23)*

MA'OZ (MOSHE) ed. Palestinian Arab politics. Jerusalem, 1975. pp. 144. *(Hebrew University. Harry S. Truman Research Institute. Truman Institute Studies. Middle East [Series])*

STEBBING (JOHN) The making of a Palestinian Arab state: an outline of a possible structure of a new state supported by a U.N. world district in eastern Sinai. [London], 1976. pp. 56.

— Israel.

KISHTAINY (KHALID) Whither Israel?: a study of Zionist expansionism. Beirut, 1970. pp. 138. *bibliog. (Palestine Research Center. Palestine Books. No. 29)*

LEBANESE ASSOCIATION FOR INFORMATION ON PALESTINE. Palestinian political prisoners and repression in Israel and the occupied territories. n.p. 1975. pp. 12.

PALMS

— Indonesia — Sunda Islands.

FOX (JAMES J.) Harvest of the palm: ecological change in eastern Indonesia. Cambridge, Mass., 1977. pp. 290. *bibliog.*

PAMIR

— Native races.

MUKHIDDINOV (IKROMIDDIN) Zemledelie pamirskikh tadzhikov Vakhana i Ishkashima v XIX - nachale XX v.: istoriko-etnograficheskii ocherk. Moskva, 1975. pp. 127. *bibliog.*

PAMPHLETS.

AZANOV (VLADIMIR IVANOVICH) Pamflety Gertsena v "Kolokole"; pod redaktsiei...E.I. Pokusaeva. Saratov, 1974. pp. 50.

PANAFRICANISM.

NGUYEN VAN CHIEN. Les politiques d'unité africaine. Lubumbashi, 1975. pp. 401. *bibliog. Thèse (Doctorat d'Etat es-Lettres et Sciences Humaines) - Université de Paris V.*

PANAMA

— Economic conditions.

LOONEY (ROBERT E.) The economic development of Panama: the impact of world inflation on an open economy. New York, 1976. pp. 248. *bibliog.*

— Industries.

PANAMA. Direccion de Estadistica y Censo. Estadistica panameña. Industria. a., 1975- Panama. *Supersedes PANAMA. Direccion de Estadistica y Censo. Estadistica panameña. Serie F. Industrias.*

PANAMA. Direccion de Estadistica y Censo. Estadistica panameña. Industria. q., 1976(no.1)- Panama. *Supersedes PANAMA. Direccion de Estadistica y Censo. Estadistica panameña. Serie F. Industrias.*

— Maps.

PANAMA. Comision del Atlas de Panama. 1975. Atlas nacional de Panama, 1975. [Panama, 1975]. 1 vol. (unpaged) *bibliogs.*

PANARE INDIANS.

DUMONT (JEAN PAUL) Under the rainbow: nature and supernature among the Panare Indians. Austin, Texas, [1976]. pp. 178. *bibliog. Revision of the author's thesis, University of Pittsburgh, 1972.*

PANSLAVISM.

PRUUDEN (SALME) Panslavism and Russian communism. London, 1976. pp. 59.

VYŠNÝ (PAUL) Neo-Slavism and the Czechs, 1898-1914. Cambridge, 1977. pp. 287. *bibliog.*

PAPEN (FRANZ VON).

BACH (JUERGEN A.) Franz von Papen in der Weimarer Republik: Aktivitäten in Politik und Presse, 1918-1932. Düsseldorf, [1977]. pp. 354. *bibliog.*

PAPER INDUSTRY WORKERS

— United Kingdom.

PAPER AND PAPER PRODUCTS INDUSTRY TRAINING BOARD [U.K.]. About the Board. Potters Bar, [1977]. pp. 8.

PAPER MAKING AND TRADE

— Canada.

JEGR (K.M.) and THOMPSON (K.M.) The Canadian pulp and paper industry: threats and opportunities, 1980-1990. [Pointe Claire, 1975]. 2 vols. (in 1). *Part 2, the appendix, also in form of 4 microfiche cards in end pocket.*

PAPER MONEY

— Brazil.

TRIGUEIROS (F. DOS SANTOS) Dinheiro no Brasil. Rio de Janeiro, 1966. pp. 245. *bibliog.*

PAPUA NEW GUINEA

— Economic conditions.

PAPUA NEW GUINEA. Department of Finance. Quarterly summary of economic conditions. q., My 1976- Port Moresby.

— Economic policy.

PAPUA NEW GUINEA. Office of the Economic Adviser. 1969. Chimbu district draft economic development programme. [Port Moresby?], 1969. fo. 24.

PAPUA NEW GUINEA. Office of the Economic Adviser. 1970. East Sepik district draft economic development programme. [Port Moresby?], 1970. pp. 47.

PAPUA NEW GUINEA. Office of the Economic Adviser. 1970. Gulf district draft economic development programme. [Port Moresby?], 1970. pp. 48.

PAPUA NEW GUINEA. Office of the Economic Adviser. 1970. Western district draft economic development programme. [Port Moresby?], 1970. pp. 40.

PAPUA NEW GUINEA. Office of Programming and Co-ordination. 1972. First Papua New Guinea development programme: review of progress 1971-72. Port Moresby, 1972. pp. 58.

— History.

WOOLFORD (DONALD MARK) Papua New Guinea: initiation and independence. [Brisbane, 1976]. pp. 268. *bibliog.*

— House of Assembly — Elections.

PAPUA NEW GUINEA. Chief Electoral Officer. 1973. Report...on the 1972 House of Assembly general election. Port Moresby, 1973. pp. 91.

— Politics and government.

PAPUA NEW GUINEA. National Parliament. Debates. sess., S 16 1975 (v.1, no.1)- [Port Moresby]. *Supersedes PAPUA NEW GUINEA. House of Assembly. Debates.*

HASLUCK (Sir PAUL MEERNAA CAEDWALLA) A time for building: Australian administration in Papua and New Guinea 1951-1963. Melbourne, 1976. pp. 452.

PRELUDE to self-government; editor, David Stone. Canberra, 1976. pp. 547. *bibliog. Cover sub-title: Electoral politics in Papua New Guinea, 1972.*

WOOLFORD (DONALD MARK) Papua New Guinea: initiation and independence. [Brisbane, 1976]. pp. 268. *bibliog.*

— Relations (general) with Australia.

HASLUCK (Sir PAUL MEERNAA CAEDWALLA) A time for building: Australian administration in Papua and New Guinea 1951-1963. Melbourne, 1976. pp. 452.

— Social policy.

PAPUA NEW GUINEA. Office of the Economic Adviser. 1969. Chimbu district draft economic development programme. [Port Moresby?], 1969. fo. 24.

PAPUA NEW GUINEA. Office of the Economic Adviser. 1970. East Sepik district draft economic development programme. [Port Moresby?], 1970. pp. 47.

PAPUA NEW GUINEA. Office of the Economic Adviser. 1970. Gulf district draft economic development programme. [Port Moresby?], 1970. pp. 48.

PAPUA NEW GUINEA. Office of the Economic Adviser. 1970. Western district draft economic development programme. [Port Moresby?], 1970. pp. 40.

PAPUA NEW GUINEA. Office of Programming and Co-ordination. 1972. First Papua New Guinea development programme: review of progress 1971-72. Port Moresby, 1972. pp. 58.

PARACEL ISLANDS

— International status.

HEINZIG (DIETER) Disputed islands in the South China Sea: Paracels, Spratlys, Pratas, Macclesfield Bank. Wiesbaden, 1976. pp. 58.

PARADOX.

BRAMS (STEVEN J.) Paradoxes in politics: an introduction to the nonobvious in political science. New York, [1976]. pp. 231.

PARAGUAY

— Boundaries — Brazil.

CARDOZO (EFRAIM) 20 preguntas sin respuesta sobre los Saltos del Guaira: recopilacion de articulos publicados en "El Radical". Asuncion, 1971. pp. 122.

— Census.

PARAGUAY. Census, 1972. Censo nacional de poblacion y viviendas, 1972. [Asuncion], 1975. pp. 561.

— Economic history.

PLA (JOSEFINA) The British in Paraguay, 1850-1870; translated from the Spanish by Brian Charles MacDermot. Richmond, Surrey, [1976]. pp. 277. *bibliog.*

— Politics and government.

MARTINEZ ARBOLEYA (JOAQUIN) Charlas con el General Stroessner. Montevideo, 1973. pp. 123.

— Population.

INSTITUTO DE DESARROLLO INTEGRAL Y ARMONICO. Actitudes y opiniones de los lideres paraguayos acerca de las politicas poblacionales y familiares. [Asuncion, 1972?]. pp. 148. *(Desarrollo y Demografia. 2) Cover title: Encuesta a lideres.*

— Social conditions.

INSTITUTO DE DESARROLLO INTEGRAL Y ARMONICO. Actitudes y opiniones de los lideres paraguayos acerca de las politicas poblacionales y familiares. [Asuncion, 1972?]. pp. 148. *(Desarrollo y Demografia. 2) Cover title: Encuesta a lideres.*

PARAPROFESSIONALS IN SOCIAL SERVICE

— United States.

COHEN (ROBERT) 1941- . 'New careers' grows older: a perspective on the paraprofessional experience, 1965-1975. Baltimore, [1976]. pp. 132. *bibliog.*

PARENT AND CHILD.

PEINE (HERMANN A.) and HOWARTH (ROY) Children and parents: everyday problems of behaviour. Harmondsworth, 1975. pp. 133.

RAPOPORT (RHONA) and others. Fathers, mothers and others: towards new alliances. London, 1977. pp. 421. *bibliog.*

PARENT AND CHILD (LAW)

— Russia.

CHERVIAKOV (KONSTANTIN KUZ'MICH) Ustanovlenie i prekrashchenie roditel'skikh prav i obiazannostei. Moskva, 1975. pp. 104.

— United Kingdom.

HOGGETT (BRENDA MARJORIE) Parents and children. London, 1977. pp. 275. *bibliog.*

PARIS

— History — 1871, Commune.

MAILLARD (FIRMIN) Histoire des journaux publiés à Paris pendant le Siège et sous la Commune, 4 septembre 1870 au 28 mai 1871. Amsterdam, 1971. pp. 267. *Reprint of Paris edition of 1871.*

— Libraries.

HARTMANN (PETER CLAUS) Pariser Archive, Bibliotheken und Dokumentationszentren zur Geschichte des 19. und 20. Jahrhunderts: eine Einführung, etc. München, 1976. pp. 131. *(Deutsches Historisches Institut, Paris. Dokumentation Westeuropa. Band 1)*

— Politics and government.

FRANCE. Direction de la Documentation. La Documentation Française. Notes et Etudes Documentaires. Nos. 4,332-4,333. Le nouveau statut de Paris: loi du 31 décembre 1975; par Jean-Louis Pezant. Paris, 1976. pp. 60. *bibliog.*

PARISHES

— United Kingdom.

HOARE (EDDIE) The work of the Edmonton vestry 1739-48 and 1782-98. London, 1968. pp. 42. *(Edmonton. Edmonton Hundred Historical Society. Occasional Papers. New Series. No. 16)*

PARK (ROBERT EZRA).

MATTHEWS (FRED H.) Quest for an American sociology: Robert E. Park and the Chicago School. Montreal, 1977. pp. 278. *bibliog.*

PARKES (JAMES WILLIAM).

RAZZOUK (ASSAD) The partisan views of Reverend James Parkes. Beirut, 1970. pp. 56. *(Palestine Research Center. Palestine Essays. No. 22)*

PARLIAMENTARY PRACTICE

— Australia.

CONFERENCE OF PRESIDING OFFICERS AND CLERKS OF THE PARLIAMENT OF AUSTRALIA, COOK ISLANDS, FIJI, NAURU, PAPUA NEW GUINEA AND WESTERN SAMOA, 4th, SUVA, 1971. [Report]. in AUSTRALIA. Parliament. Parliamentary papers, 1971, vol.7.

PARNELL (CHARLES STEWART).

O'DAY (ALAN) The English face of Irish nationalism: Parnellite involvement in British politics, 1880-86. Dublin, 1977. pp. 210. *bibliog.*

PAROLE

— United Kingdom.

PAROLE in England and Wales; [by] C.P. Nuttall [and others]; a Home Office Research Unit report. London, 1977. pp. 87. *bibliog. (U.K. Home Office. Home Office Research Studies. No. 38)*

— United States.

CARNEY (LOUIS P.) Probation and parole: legal and social dimensions. New York, [1977]. pp. 346.

PARSONS (TALCOTT).

MENZIES (KENNETH) Talcott Parsons and the social image of man. London, 1976 [or rather 1977]. pp. 197. *bibliog.*

PART-TIME EMPLOYMENT

— Netherlands.

ECONOMISCH INSTITUUT VOOR HET MIDDEN- EN KLEINBEDRIJF. Sociaal-Economische Publikaties. Part-time arbeid in de detailhandel: een onderzoek bij vestigingen waar part-timers werkzaam zijn. 's-Gravenhage, 1975. pp. 160.

PARTIDO ACCION NACIONAL.

PARTIDO ACCION NACIONAL. Respuestas. Mexico, 1973. pp. 335.

PARTIDO AFRICANO DA INDEPENDENCIA DE GUINE E CABO VERDE.

FISAS ARMENGOL (VICENÇ) Amilcar Cabral y la independencia de Guinea-Bissau; [with two articles by Amilcar Cabral included as appendices]. Barcelona, 1974. pp. 132.

PARTIDO REPUBLICANO RADICAL.

RUIZ MANJON-CABEZA (OCTAVIO) El Partido Republicano Radical, 1908-1936. Madrid, [1976]. pp. 711. *bibliog.*

PARTIES TO ACTIONS

— France.

BARAQUIN (YVES) Les Français et la justice civile: enquête psycho-sociologique auprès des justiciables. Paris, 1975. pp. 275. *bibliog. (France. Ministère de la Justice. Collection Ministère de la Justice)*

PARTITO POPOLARE ITALIANO.

MOLONY (JOHN NEYLON) The emergence of political catholicism in Italy: Partito Popolare 1919-1926. London, 1977. pp. 225. *bibliog.*

PARTNERSHIP

— United Kingdom.

CHESTERMAN (MICHAEL) Small businesses. London, 1977. pp. 267.

DRAKE (CHARLES DOMINIC) Law of partnership. 2nd ed. London, 1977. pp. 266.

PARTY AFFILIATION

— United States.

CONVERSE (PHILIP E.) The dynamics of party support: cohort-analyzing party identification. Beverly Hills, [1976]. pp. 174. *bibliog.*

KNOKE (DAVID) Change and continuity in American politics: the social bases of political parties. Baltimore, [1976]. pp. 192. *bibliog.*

MILLER (WARREN EDWARD) and LEVITIN (TERESA E.) Leadership and change: the new politics and the American electorate. Cambridge, Mass., [1976]. pp. 267.

TRILLING (RICHARD J.) Party image and electoral behavior. New York, [1976]. pp. 234.

STRONG (DONALD S.) Issue voting and party realignment. University, Ala., [1977]. pp. 110.

PASOLD (ERIC W.).

PASOLD (ERIC W.) Ladybird, Ladybird: a story of private enterprise. Manchester, [1977]. pp. 668.

PASQUALINI (JEAN).

PASQUALINI (JEAN) and CHELMINSKI (RUDOLPH) Prisoner of Mao. Harmondsworth, 1973. pp. 326.

PASSERON (JEAN CLAUDE).

SNYDERS (GEORGES) Ecole, classe et lutte des classes: une relecture critique de Baudelot-Establet, Bourdieu-Passeron et Illich. Paris, [1976]. pp. 379.

PASSIVE RESISTANCE

— India.

BROWN (JUDITH M.) Gandhi and civil disobedience: the Mahatma in Indian politics, 1928-34. Cambridge, 1977. pp. 414. *bibliog.*

PATAGONIA

— Emigration and immigration.

OWEN (GERAINT DYFNALLT) Crisis in Chubut: a chapter in the history of the Welsh colony in Patagonia. Swansea, 1977. pp. 161. *bibliog.*

PATENT LICENCES.

JOHNSON (HARRY GORDON) Aspects of patents and licenses as stimuli to innovation. Kiel, 1976. pp. 36. *(Kiel. Universität. Institut für Weltwirtschaft. Bernhard-Harms-Vorlesungen. 7)*

PATENT SEARCHING.

RIMMER (BRENDA MAY) Patent Cooperation Treaty: minimum documentation: a guide to the patent documents and journals currently proposed for inclusion. London, British Library, Science Reference Library, [1975]. pp. 24. bibliog. *(Occasional Publications)*

PATENTS.

JOHNSON (HARRY GORDON) Aspects of patents and licenses as stimuli to innovation. Kiel, 1976. pp. 36. *(Kiel. Universität. Institut für Weltwirtschaft. Bernhard-Harms-Vorlesungen. 7)*

— Bibliography.

RIMMER (BRENDA MAY) Patent Cooperation Treaty: minimum documentation: a guide to the patent documents and journals currently proposed for inclusion. London, British Library, Science Reference Library, [1975]. pp. 24. bibliog. *(Occasional Publications)*

— Russia — Tajikistan.

RASULI (MARAT) Razvitie izobretatel'skoi i patentnoi deiatel'nosti v Tadzhikskoi SSR: obzor. Dushanbe, 1975. pp. 44. *bibliog.*

PATRIOTISM

— France.

HERVE (GUSTAVE) Das Vaterland der Reichen; [translated from the French]. Zürich, [190-?]. pp. 259.

PATRONAGE, POLITICAL

— Canada — Quebec.

LEMIEUX (VINCENT) and HUDON (RAYMOND) Patronage et politique au Québec, 1944-1972. Québec, 1975. pp. 187.

— Mediterranean.

PATRONS and clients in Mediterranean societies; edited by Ernest Gellner and John Waterbury. London, 1977. pp. 348. *bibliogs. Based mostly on papers presented at a conference held under the patronage of the Center for Mediterranean Studies of the American Universities Field Staff in Rome.*

— United States.

HECLO (HUGH) A government of strangers: executive politics in Washington. Washington, D.C., [1977]. pp. 272.

PAYMENT

— Switzerland.

MARBACHER (JOSEF) Das Zahlungsverkehrs-System der Schweiz: eine Analyse der Geschichte...des nationalen monetären Transfer-Systems. Bern, 1976. pp. 383. *bibliog. Dissertation der Universität Zürich zur Erlangung der Würde eines Doktors der Wirtschaftswissenschaft.*

PEACE.

ENDRUCKS (BERNHARD) Das Ende aller Kriege: ein Appell an die Menschheit. Krailling bei München, [1959]. pp. 152.

RUSSELL (BERTRAND ARTHUR WILLIAM) 3rd Earl Russell. Bertrand Russell speaks his mind. Darmstadt, 1976. pp. 175. *Transcript of a television series of 13 interviews with Bertrand Russell, by Woodrow Wyatt. Originally published in 1960 by the World Publishing Company, Cleveland.*

KAJIMA INSTITUTE OF INTERNATIONAL PEACE. The record of the first Kajima Peace Award, recipient: Count Coudenhove Kalergi. Tokyo, 1968. pp. 143.

ZHUKOV (GENNADII PETROVICH) and CHERNICHENKO (STANISLAV VALENTINOVICH) Sovetskaia Programma mira i mezhdunarodnoe pravo. Moskva, 1975. pp. 111.

FAHEY (JOSEPH J.) Peace, war and the Christian conscience. New York, [1976]. pp. 20.

GRAY (TONY) Champions of peace: (the story of Alfred Nobel, the Peace Prize and the laureates). [London, 1976]. pp. 320. *bibliog.*

McKEOWN (CIARAN) The price of peace. Belfast, [1976]. pp. 34.

PEACE PLEDGE UNION. "Mummy I want a ploughshare for Christmas". London, [1976]. pp. 31.

— Research.

DEDRING (JUERGEN) Recent advances in peace and conflict research: a critical survey. Beverly Hills, [1976]. pp. 249. *bibliog. (United Nations Institute for Training and Research. UNITAR Studies)*

WEHR (PAUL) and WASHBURN (MICHAEL) Peace and world order systems: teaching and research. Beverly Hills, Calif., [1976]. pp. 254. *bibliog.*

— Study and teaching.

WEHR (PAUL) and WASHBURN (MICHAEL) Peace and world order systems: teaching and research. Beverly Hills, Calif., [1976]. pp. 254. *bibliog.*

PEACE SOCIETIES.

ROBBINS (KEITH GILBERT) The abolition of war: the 'peace movement' in Britain, 1914-1919. Cardiff, 1976. pp. 255. *bibliog.*

PEARSE (PATRICK).

O'NEIL (DANIEL J.) Three perennial themes of anti-colonialism: the Irish case. Denver, Colo., [1976]. pp. 131. *(Denver. University. Social Science Foundation and Graduate School of International Studies. Monograph Series in World Affairs. vol. 14, no. 1)*

EDWARDS (RUTH DUDLEY) Patrick Pearse: the triumph of failure. London, 1977. pp. 384. *bibliog.*

PEASANT UPRISINGS

— India — Bengal, West.

MITTER (SWASTI) Peasant movements in West Bengal: their impact on agrarian class relations since 1967. Cambridge, 1977. pp. 85. *bibliog. (Cambridge. University. Department of Land Economy. Occasional Papers. No. 8)*

— Russia.

KLIBANOV (ALEKSANDR IL'ICH) Narodnaia sotsial'naia utopiia v Rossii: period feodalizma. Moskva, 1977. pp. 335.

— United Kingdom.

CORNWALL (JULIAN) Revolt of the peasantry, 1549. London, 1977. pp. 254. *bibliog.*

PEASANTRY.

MENDRAS (HENRI) Sociétés paysannes: éléments pour une théorie de la paysannerie. Paris, [1976]. pp. 238. *bibliog.*

MARTINEZ-ALIER (JUAN) Haciendas, plantations and collective farms: agrarian class societies, Cuba and Peru. London, 1977. pp. 185. *bibliog.*

— Religious life.

POTTER (JACK M.) Wind, water, bones and souls: the religious world of the Cantonese peasant. Berkeley, [1970]. pp. 14. *(California University. Center for Chinese Studies. China Reprint Series. No. C-18) (Reprinted from Journal of Oriental Studies, vol. 3, no. 1, 1970)*

— Africa, Subsaharan.

LE BRIS (EMILE) and others. Capitalisme négrier: la marche des paysans vers le prolétariat. Paris, 1976. pp. 211.

— Chile.

GALJART (BENNO F.) Peasant mobilization and solidarity. Assen, 1976. pp. 132. *bibliog. (Centrum voor Landbouwpublikaties en Landbouwdocumentatie. Studies of Developing Countries. [No.] 19)*

— China.

POTTER (JACK M.) Wind, water, bones and souls: the religious world of the Cantonese peasant. Berkeley, [1970]. pp. 14. *(California University. Center for Chinese Studies. China Reprint Series. No. C-18) (Reprinted from Journal of Oriental Studies, vol. 3, no. 1, 1970)*

— Colombia.

ESCOBAR SIERRA (HUGO) Las invasiones en Colombia. Bogota, 1972. pp. 125.

— France.

RAWLINSON (ROGER) The Battle of Larzac. New Malden, [1976]. pp. 59. *bibliog.*

SOBOUL (ALBERT) Problèmes paysans de la révolution, 1789-1848: études d'histoire révolutionnaire. Paris, 1976. pp. 442.

WEBER (EUGEN) Peasants into Frenchmen: the modernization of rural France, 1870-1914. Stanford, Calif., 1976. pp. 615. *bibliog.*

— Germany.

KOMMUNISTISCHE PARTEI DEUTSCHLANDS. Bezirk Grossthüringen. Bauer, wo steht dein Feind?. [Jena?, 1928?]. pp. 24.

REICHS-BAUERNBUND. Wie wehrt sich der Bauer gegen Zwangsenteignung?. Berlin, [1931]. pp. 16.

AUSSCHUSS FÜR DEUTSCHE EINHEIT. Schwarzbuch über das Bauernlegen in Westdeutschland. Berlin, 1960. pp. 94.

— Italy.

BERNARDI (ULDERICO) Una cultura in estinzione: ricerche sull'identità contadina fra Piave e Livenza. Venezia, 1975. pp. 195.

— Kenya.

LEONARD (DAVID KING) Reaching the peasant farmer: organization theory and practice in Kenya. Chicago, 1977. pp. 297.

— Mexico.

WARMAN (ARTURO) Los campesinos: hijos predilectos del regimen. Mexico, 1972 repr. 1974. pp. 138. *bibliog.*

DIAZ RAMIREZ (MANUEL) Apuntes sobre el movimiento obrero y campesino de Mexico, 1844- 1880. Mexico, [1974]. pp. 143.

DURAND (PIERRE) Nanacatlan: société paysanne et lutte des classes au Mexique. Montréal, 1975. pp. 257. *bibliog.*

— Morocco.

LEVEAU (REMY) Le fellah marocain, défenseur du trône. [Paris, 1976]. pp. 281. *bibliog. (Fondation Nationale des Sciences Politiques. Cahiers. 203)*

— Peru.

ZUTTER (PIERRE DE) Campesinado y revolucion. Lima, 1975. pp. 312.

WHYTE (WILLIAM FOOTE) and ALBERTI (GIORGIO) Power, politics and progress: social change in rural Peru. New York, [1976]. pp. 307. *bibliog.*

— Poland.

OBREBSKI (JOSEPH) The changing peasantry of Eastern Europe; edited by Barbara and Joel Halpern. Cambridge, Mass., [1976]. pp. 102. *bibliog. Lectures given at Oxford University in 1946.*

RURAL social change in Poland; editors: Jan Turowski [and] Lili Maria Szwengrub. Wrocław, 1976. pp. 334. *bibliogs. Edited on the occasion of the Fourth World Congress for Rural Sociology, Toruń, Poland, 1976, and Ninth Congress of the European Society for Rural Sociology.*

— Russia.

GROSSKOPF (SIGRID) L'alliance ouvrière et paysanne en U.R.S.S., 1921-1928: le problème du blé. Paris, 1976. pp. 459. *bibliog.*

KEEP (JOHN LESLIE HOWARD) The Russian revolution: a study in mass mobilization. London, [1976]. pp. 614. *bibliog.*

MASLOVS'KYI (MYKOLA ANDRIIOVYCH) Interesy kolhospnoho selianstva: ïkh formuvannia i zadovolennia. Kyïv, 1976. pp. 164. *bibliog.*

ZENIN (VLADIMIR PETROVICH) Rabochii klass i kolkhoznoe krest'ianstvo: sblizhenie ikh pravovykh statusov. Kiev, 1976. pp. 155. *bibliog.*

BULYGIN (IL'IA ANDREEVICH) Monastyrskie krest'iane Rossii v pervoi chetverti XVIII veka. Moskva, 1977. pp. 327.

DANILOV (VIKTOR PETROVICH) Sovetskaia dokolkhoznaia derevnia: naselenie, zemlepol'zovanie, khoziaistvo. Moskva, 1977. pp. 319.

SMITH (ROBERT ERNEST FREDERICK) Peasant farming in Muscovy. Cambridge, 1977. pp. 289. *bibliog.*

SMITH (ROBERT ERNEST FREDERICK) ed. The Russian peasant: 1920 and 1984. London, 1977. pp. 120. *bibliog. (Reprinted from The Journal of Peasant Studies, vol.4, no.1)*

— — Estonia.

KAHK (JUHAN) and others. Beiträge zur marxistischen Agrargeschichte Estlands der Feudalzeit: neue Ergebnisse, neue Probleme, neue Methoden; [translated from the Russian]. Tallinn, 1974. pp. 152.

— — Lithuania.

NEUPOKOEV (VALENTIN IVANOVICH) Krest'ianskii vopros v Litve vo vtoroi treti XIX veka. Moskva, 1976. pp. 309.

— — Moldavian Republic.

SYTNIK (MIKHAIL KONDRAT'EVICH) Kollektivizatsiia sel'skogo khoziaistva i formirovanie klassa kolkhoznogo krest'ianstva v Moldavii. Kishinev, 1976. pp. 355. *bibliog.*

— — Siberia.

ISTORIOGRAFIIA krest'ianstva sovetskoi Sibiri. Novosibirsk, 1976. pp. 477.

— — Ukraine.

LOS' (FEDIR IEVDOKYMOVYCH) and MYKHAILIUK (OLEKSII HRYHOROVYCH) Klasova borot'ba v ukraïns'komu seli, 1907-1914. Kyïv, 1976. pp. 283. *bibliog.*

— Sri Lanka.

SELVANAYAGAM (SOMASUNDARAM) The problem of economic holdings in the peasant agriculture of the dry zone of Ceylon. 1971. fo. 361. *bibliog. Typescript. Ph.D.(London) thesis: unpublished. 3 pamphlets in end pocket.*

— Switzerland.

MUEHLESTEIN (HANS) Arbeiter und Bauer: Vortrag gehalten...in Winterthur am 15. August 1944. [Zürich], 1945. pp. 24. *(Partei der Arbeit der Schweiz. Schriftenreihe. Nr.2)*

PEDERSEN (HANS and ELLEN).

EUROPEAN COURT OF HUMAN RIGHTS. Publications. Series A: Judgments and Decisions. [A 23]. ...Case of Kjeldsen, Busk Madsen and Pedersen: judgment of 7 December 1976. Strasbourg, Council of Europe, 1976. pp. 33 [bis]. *In English and French.*

PEDLARS AND PEDDLING

— Ireland (Republic).

EIRE. Restrictive Practices Commission. 1976. Report of study of roadside and street trading and sales from temporary retail outlets. Dublin, [1976]. pp. 70.

PEEL (Sir ROBERT).

CROSBY (TRAVIS L.) Sir Robert Peel's administration, 1841-1846. Newton Abbot, 1976. pp. 190. *bibliog.*

PENNSYLVANIA

— Economic conditions.

WEISSBROD (RICHARD) Diffusion of relative wage inflation in Southeast Pennsylvania. Evanston, Ill., 1976. pp. 166. *bibliog. (Northwestern University. Studies in Geography. No. 23).*

PENNSYLVANIA GERMANS.

PARSONS (WILLIAM T.) The Pennsylvania Dutch: a persistent minority. Boston, Mass., [1976]. pp. 316. *bibliog.*

PENOLOGY

— United States.

CARNEY (LOUIS P.) Probation and parole: legal and social dimensions. New York, [1977]. pp. 346.

PENSION TRUSTS

— United Kingdom.

HOSKING (GORDON ALBERT) Pension schemes and retirement benefits; fourth edition by K. Muir McKelvey [and others]. London, 1977. pp. 372.

— — Investments.

ARTHUR (TERRY) Pension fund investment...by whom?. London, [1976]. pp. 19.

— United States.

TURE (NORMAN B.) and FIELDS (BARBARA) The future of private pension plans. Washington, D.C., [1976]. pp. 128. *(American Enterprise Institute for Public Policy Research. Social Security and Retirement Policy Studies. 1)*

PENSIONS

— Denmark.

SOCIALFORSKNINGSINSTITUTTET. Invalidepensionistundersøgelserne, etc. København, 1976. 2 pts. *bibliog. (Meddelelser. 16,17)*

— Ireland (Republic).

EIRE. Department of Social Welfare. 1976. A national income-related pension scheme; a discussion paper. Dublin, [1976]. pp. 195.

— Mexico.

MEXICO. Statutes, etc. 1930-1956. Legislacion sobre pensiones. Mexico, 1958. pp. 212.

— South Africa.

SOUTH AFRICA. Parliament. House of Assembly. Select Committee on Pensions. 1977. First and second reports (S.C. 6-1977). in SOUTH AFRICA. Parliament. House of Assembly. Select Committee reports.

— Sweden.

SWEDEN. Statistiska Centralbyrån. Folkpensionärernas inkomstförhållanden: Incomes for national basic pensioners. a., 1974- Stockholm. *[in Swedish with summary and table headings in English].*

— United Kingdom.

U.K. Department of Health and Social Security. 1976. Pension age: memorandum of evidence to the Equal Opportunities Commission. [London], 1976. pp. 18.

U.K. Parliament. House of Commons. Library. Research Division. Background Papers. No. 51. Unemployment benefit for occupational pensioners. [London, 1976]. pp. 7.

PENSIONS, MILITARY

— United Kingdom.

PENSIONS APPEAL TRIBUNALS [U.K.]. Assessment appeals: notes for the guidance of appellants. 7th ed. London, H.M.S.O., 1976. pp. 11.

PEOPLE'S ACTION PARTY.

CHAN (HENG CHEE) The dynamics of one party dominance: the PAP at the grass-roots. Singapore, [1976]. pp. 272. *bibliog.*

PERCEPTION.

CORCORAN (D.W.J.) Pattern recognition. Harmondsworth, 1971. pp. 223. *bibliog.*

BOWER (THOMAS GILLIE RUSSELL) The perceptual world of the child. London, 1977. pp. 93. *bibliog.*

PERCEPTUAL-MOTOR LEARNING.

WELFORD (ALAN TRAVISS) Skilled performance: perceptual and motor skills. Glenview, Ill., [1976]. pp. 200. *bibliog.*

PERFORMANCE.

SHERIF (FOUAD) Planning for improved performance of public enterprise in developing countries: some lessons of international experience. Ljubljana, International Center for Public Enterprises, 1974. fo. 19 *(International Seminar 1974. Background Papers)*

PERFORMING ARTS

— Law and legislation — United Kingdom.

COTTERELL (LESLIE E.) Performance. Eastbourne, 1977. pp. 368.

PERJURY

— Russia.

KHABIBULLIN (MINNULA KHALIULLOVICH) Otvetstvennost' za zavedomo lozhnyi donos i zavedomo lozhnoe pokazanie po sovetskomu ugolovnomu pravu. Kazan', 1975. pp. 160.

PERONISM.

MANUAL de doctrina nacional. Buenos Aires, 1953 repr. 1974. pp. 185. *Reprinted with a new prologue.*

GAMBINI (HUGO) El Peronismo y la iglesia. Buenos Aires, [1971]. pp. 116.

COOKE (JOHN WILLIAM) Apuntes para la militancia: Peronismo critico. [Buenos Aires, 1973]. pp. 117.

La CULTURA popular del Peronismo; [by] Norman Briski [and others]. [Buenos Aires], 1973. pp. 155.

BEARN (GEORGES) ed. La décade péroniste. [Paris, 1975]. pp. 253. *bibliog.*

MERCIER VEGA (LUIS) Autopsia de Peron: balance del peronismo; [translated from the French by] Menene Gras. Barcelona, [1975]. pp. 270.

MONZALVO (LUIS) Testigo de la primera hora del peronismo: [memorias de un ferroviario]. Buenos Aires, [1975]. pp. 272.

HODGES (DONALD CLARK) Argentina, 1943-1976: the national revolution and resistance. Albuquerque, [1976]. pp. 207. *bibliog.*

VILLAR ARAUJO (CARLOS) Argentina: de Peron al golpe militar. Madrid, 1976. pp. 220. *bibliog.*

PERPIGNAN.

FRANCE. Direction de la Documentation. La Documentation Française. Notes et Etudes Documentaires. Nos. 4,308-4,309-4,310. Les villes francaises: Perpignan; par Michel Vigouroux et Robert Ferras. Paris, 1976. pp. 97. *bibliog.*

PERRY.

[HEATH (BENJAMIN)] The case of the county of Devon, with respect to the consequences of the new excise duty on cyder and perry: published by the direction of the committee appointed at a general meeting of that county to superintend the application for the repeal of that duty. London, Johnston, 1763. pp. 32.

PERSECUTION

— Psychological aspects.

BRODSKY (CARROLL M.) The harassed worker. Lexington, Mass., [1976]. pp. 174. *bibliog.*

PERSIAN GULF

— Foreign economic relations — Russia.

YODFAT (ARYEH) and ABIR (MORDECHAI) In the direction of the Persian Gulf: the Soviet Union and the Persian Gulf. London, 1977. pp. 167. *bibliog.*

— Foreign relations — Russia.

YODFAT (ARYEH) and ABIR (MORDECHAI) In the direction of the Persian Gulf: the Soviet Union and the Persian Gulf. London, 1977. pp. 167. *bibliog.*

— Nationalism.

GULF COMMITTEE. 9th June Studies. Documents of the national struggle in Oman and the Arabian Gulf. London, 1974. pp. 106.

— Social conditions.

OSBORNE (CHRISTINE) The Gulf States and Oman. London, [1977]. pp. 208. *bibliog.*

PERSONAL PROPERTY

— Russia.

EREMEEV (DMITRII FEDOROVICH) Okhrana imushchestvennykh prav sovetskikh grazhdan. Minsk, 1970. pp. 78.

PERSONAL RAPID TRANSIT

— United Kingdom — Cost effectiveness.

LANGDON (M.G.) A comparative cost benefit assessment of Minitram and other urban transport systems. Crowthorne, 1977. pp. 31. *bibliog. (U.K. Transport and Road Research Laboratory. Reports. LR 747)*

PERSONALITY.

LUNDBERG (MARGARET J.) The incomplete adult: social class constraints on personality development. Westport, Conn., [1974]. pp. 245. *bibliog.*

EYSENCK (HANS JÜRGEN) Crime and personality. 3rd ed. London, 1977. pp. 222.

HOLLAND (RAY) Self and social context. London, 1977. pp. 303. *bibliog.*

PERSONALITY, DISORDERS OF.

FOULDS (G.A.) The hierarchical nature of personal illness. London, 1976. pp. 158. *bibliog.*

PERSONNEL SERVICE IN EDUCATION

— United Kingdom.

MACMILLAN (KEITH) Education welfare: strategy and structure. London, 1977. pp. 165. *bibliog.*

PERTH, WESTERN AUSTRALIA

— Economic conditions.

ALEXANDER (IAN C.) The city centre: patterns and problems. Nedlands, W.A., 1974. pp. 216. *bibliog.*

— Social conditions.

ALEXANDER (IAN C.) The city centre: patterns and problems. Nedlands, W.A., 1974. pp. 216. *bibliog.*

PERU

— Armed forces — Political activity.

TRIAS (VIVIAN) Peru: fuerzas armadas y revolucion. Montevideo, [1971]. pp. 175.

— Census.

PERU. Census, 1972. Censos nacionales VII de poblacion II de vivienda, 4 de junio de 1972: resultados definitivos; nivel nacional. Lima, 1974. 2 vols.

PERU. Census, 1972. Censos nacionales VII de poblacion II de vivienda, 4 de junio de 1972: [departmental results]. Lima, 1974 [or rather 1975] in progress.

— Economic conditions.

BARGHOLTZ (PERCY) and others. Current economic position and prospects of Peru: this report is based on the findings of an economic mission which visited Peru in.. .1972 and...1973, etc. Washington, International Bank for Reconstruction and Development, 1973. pp. 219. *(Country Economic Reports)*

BANCO CENTRAL DE RESERVA DEL PERU. El desarrollo economico y financiero del Peru, 1968-1973. [Lima, 1974?]. pp. 296.

KUCZYNSKI (PEDRO PABLO) Peruvian democracy under economic stress: an account of the Belaúnde administration, 1963-1968. Princeton, N.J., [1977]. pp. 308. *bibliog.*

— Economic history.

TRIAS (VIVIAN) Peru: fuerzas armadas y revolucion. Montevideo, [1971]. pp. 175.

BONILLA MAYTA (HERACLIO) Guano y burguesia en el Peru. Lima, 1974. pp. 186. *bibliog. (Instituto de Estudios Peruanos. Peru Problema. 11)*

SOCIAL and economic change in modern Peru; edited by Rory Miller [and others]. [Liverpool, 1976]. pp. 197. *bibliog. (Liverpool. University. Centre for Latin American Studies. Monograph Series. No. 6) Papers originally presented at a conference at the Centre for Latin American Studies, Liverpool University, 1974.*

— Economic policy.

PERU. Comision de Reconstruccion y Rehabilitacion de la Zona Afectada por el Terremoto del 31 de Mayo 1970. 1971. Plan de rehabilitacion y desarrollo de la zona afectada por el terremoto. Chiclayo, 1971. 3 vols. *bibliog.*

BARGHOLTZ (PERCY) and others. Current economic position and prospects of Peru: this report is based on the findings of an economic mission which visited Peru in.. .1972 and...1973, etc. Washington, International Bank for Reconstruction and Development, 1973. pp. 219. *(Country Economic Reports)*

KUCZYNSKI (PEDRO PABLO) Peruvian democracy under economic stress: an account of the Belaúnde administration, 1963-1968. Princeton, N.J., [1977]. pp. 308. *bibliog.*

WEBB (RICHARD CHARLES) Government policy and the distribution of income in Peru, 1963- 1973. Cambridge, Mass., 1977. pp. 239. *(Harvard University. Harvard Economic Studies. vol. 147)*

— Executive departments.

PERU. Oficina Nacional de Evaluacion de Recursos Naturales. Direccion de Planificacion. Memoria de la ejecucion del plan bienal. bien., 1971/1972- Lima.

— History — Chronology.

PEASE GARCIA (HENRY) and VERME INSUA (OLGA) Peru, 1968-1973: cronologia politica. Lima, 1974. 2 vols.

— — To 1548.

MURRA (JOHN VICTOR) Formaciones economicas y politicas del mundo andino. Lima, 1975. pp. 339. *bibliog. (Instituto de Estudios Peruanos. Historia Andina. 3)*

— Politics and government.

TRIAS (VIVIAN) Peru: fuerzas armadas y revolucion. Montevideo, [1971]. pp. 175.

MOREIRA (NEIVA) Modelo peruano. Buenos Aires, [1974]. pp. 349.

PEASE GARCIA (HENRY) and VERME INSUA (OLGA) Peru, 1968-1973: cronologia politica. Lima, 1974. 2 vols.

ALISKY (MARVIN) Peruvian political perspective. 2nd ed. Tempe, 1975. pp. 44.

KUCZYNSKI (PEDRO PABLO) Peruvian democracy under economic stress: an account of the Belaúnde administration, 1963-1968. Princeton, N.J., [1977]. pp. 308. *bibliog.*

— Rural conditions.

CAMBRIDGE. University. Centre of Latin American Studies. Working Papers. No. 15. Agrarian reform and agrarian struggles in Peru; [by Colin Harding]. Cambridge, 1974. fo. 26. *Photocopy.*

WHYTE (WILLIAM FOOTE) and ALBERTI (GIORGIO) Power, politics and progress: social change in rural Peru. New York, [1976]. pp. 307. *bibliog.*

— Social conditions.

KEITH (ROBERT G.) Conquest and agrarian change: the emergence of the hacienda system on the Peruvian coast. Cambridge, Mass., 1976. pp. 176. *bibliog. (Harvard University. Harvard Historical Studies. vol. 93)*

— Social history.

SOCIAL and economic change in modern Peru; edited by Rory Miller [and others]. [Liverpool, 1976]. pp. 197. *bibliog. (Liverpool. University. Centre for Latin American Studies. Monograph Series. No. 6) Papers originally presented at a conference at the Centre for Latin American Studies, Liverpool University, 1974.*

— Social policy.

PERU. Comision de Reconstruccion y Rehabilitacion de la Zona Afectada por el Terremoto del 31 de Mayo 1970. 1971. Plan de rehabilitacion y desarrollo de la zona afectada por el terremoto. Chiclayo, 1971. 3 vols. *bibliog.*

— Statistics.

BARGHOLTZ (PERCY) and others. Current economic· position and prospects of Peru: this report is based on the findings of an economic mission which visited Peru in.. .1972 and...1973, etc. Washington, International Bank for Reconstruction and Development, 1973. pp. 219. *(Country Economic Reports)*

PERU. Oficina Nacional de Estadistica y Censos. 1975. Indicadores demograficos, sociales, economicos y geograficos del Peru. vol. 2. 2nd ed. Lima, 1975. pp. 354.

PETROL.

EIRE. Fair Trade Commission. 1971. Report of enquiry into the conditions which obtain in regard to the supply and distribution of motor spirit in so far as they effect the nature and growth in numbers of motor spirit retail outlets. Dublin, [1971]. pp. 83.

PETROLEUM

— Taxation — United Kingdom.

KEMP (ALEXANDER G.) Taxation and the profitability of North Sea oil. [Glasgow, 1976]. pp. 35. *bibliog. (Glasgow. University of Strathclyde. Fraser of Allander Institute. Research Monographs. No. 4)*

The TAXATION of North Sea oil; papers and summary of discussion of a conference...[organized by the Institute for Fiscal Studies]. [London], 1976. pp. 78.

PETROLEUM CHEMICALS INDUSTRY

— Brazil.

SILVA FILHO (AMILCAR PEREIRA DA) and RIBEIRO (ANTONIO CARLOS DA MOTTA) Perspectivas da industria petroquimica no Brasil. Brasilia, 1974. pp. 149. *(Brazil. Instituto de Planejamento Econômico e Social. Instituto de Planejamento. Estudos para o Planejamento. No. 9)*

— Iran.

RESEARCH CENTER FOR INDUSTRIAL AND TRADE DEVELOPMENT [IRAN]. Chemical and petrochemical industries in Iran. Tehran, Ministry of Economy, 1971. fo.9.

— Russia — Bashkir Republic.

NIKIFOROV (IURII NIKIFOROVICH) Shagi neftekhimii respubliki: istoriko-partiinyi ocherk. Ufa, 1974. pp. 215.

PETROLEUM IN SUBMERGED LANDS.

OFFSHORE oil: costs and benefits; (an AEI round table held on March 21, 1975); Tom Bradley, moderator, etc. Washington, [1976]. pp. 47. *(American Enterprise Institute for Public Policy Research. Round Tables)*

— Australia.

AUSTRALIA. Parliament. Senate. Select Committee on Off- shore Petroleum Resources. 1971. Report...Vol.1. Report; [H.W. Young, chairman]. in AUSTRALIA. Parliament. Parliamentary papers, 1971, vol.8.

— North Sea.

REED (LAURANCE) The political consequences of North Sea oil discoveries. Edinburgh, 1973. 1 pamphlet (unpaged).

DAM (KENNETH W.) Oil resources: who gets what how?. Chicago, 1976. pp. 193.

KEMP (ALEXANDER G.) Taxation and the profitability of North Sea oil. [Glasgow, 1976]. pp. 35. *bibliog. (Glasgow. University of Strathclyde. Fraser of Allander Institute. Research Monographs. No. 4)*

ODELL (PETER R.) and ROSING (KENNETH E.) Optimal development of the North Sea's oil fields: a study in divergent government and company interests and their reconciliation. London, 1976. pp. 189.

ROBINSON (COLIN) and MORGAN (JON) Economic consequence of controlling the depletion of North Sea oil and gas. London, [1976]. pp. 31. *(Trade Policy Research Centre. Guest Papers. No. 3)*

The TAXATION of North Sea oil; papers and summary of discussion of a conference...[organized by the Institute for Fiscal Studies]. [London], 1976. pp. 78.

GASKIN (MAXWELL) North Sea oil and Scotland: the changing prospect. Edinburgh, 1977. pp. 22.

INTERNATIONAL REGISTER OF RESEARCH ON THE SOCIAL IMPACT OF OFFSHORE OIL DEVELOPMENT; [pd.by] North Sea Oil Panel, Social Science Research Council. irreg., current issues only. Aberdeen.

— — Bibliography.

MACAULAY (ALEXANDER JOHN) compiler. North Sea oil, January-June, 1974; select list [of] periodical and newspaper articles. Edinburgh, [1976]. pp. 72.

MACLEAN (IAN) compiler. North Sea oil information sources: a source guide, bibliography and media data summary. London, 1976]. fo. 77

— — Societies, etc.

MACLEAN (IAN) compiler. North Sea oil information sources: a source guide, bibliography and media data summary. London, 1976]. fo. 77

— United Kingdom.

U.K. Offshore Supplies Office. Offshore: an analysis of orders placed (formerly Offshore oil and gas: a summary of orders placed by operators of oil and gas fields on the U.K. Continental Shelf). a., 1974- London.

— United States.

The QUESTION of offshore oil; edited by Edward J. Mitchell. Washington, D.C., [1976]. pp. 159. *A conference sponsored by the American Enterprise Institute's National Energy Project in March 1975.*

PETROLEUM INDUSTRY AND TRADE.

REINHARD (ERNST) Petrole': ein Beispiel imperialistischer Politik. Bern, 1925. pp. 99 . *bibliog.*

COUNTER INFORMATION SERVICES. Anti-Reports. No. 8. The oil fix: an investigation into the control and costs of energy. London, [1974]. pp. 49. *bibliog.*

OPEC REVIEW: a digest of energy reports; [pd.by] Information Department, Organization of the Petroleum Exporting Countries. irreg., Oc 1976 (v.1, no.1)- Vienna.

COLLOQUE INTERNATIONAL D'ECONOMIE PETROLIERE, 2E, 1975. Le nouvel ordre pétrolier de la firme transnationale aux rapports entre États; The new petroleum order from the transnational company to relations between governments; Colloque...tenu à l'université Laval...1975; publié sous la direction de Antoine Ayoub. Quebec, 1976. pp. 234. *In English or French.*

ECKBO (PAUL LEO) The future of world oil. Cambridge, Mass., [1976]. pp. 142.

BLAIR (JOHN M.) The control of oil. London, 1977. pp. 442.

INTERNATIONAL INSTITUTE FOR STRATEGIC STUDIES. Adelphi Papers. No. 136. Oil and security: problems and prospects of importing countries; by Edward N. Krapels. London, 1977. pp. 34.

— Government ownership.

DAM (KENNETH W.) Oil resources: who gets what how?. Chicago, 1976. pp. 193.

GHADAR (FARIBORZ) The evolution of OPEC strategy. Lexington, Mass., [1977]. pp. 196. *bibliog.*

— Licenses — Norway.

DAM (KENNETH W.) Oil resources: who gets what how?. Chicago, 1976. pp. 193.

— — United Kingdom.

DAM (KENNETH W.) Oil resources: who gets what how?. Chicago, 1976. pp. 193.

— Algeria.

MAHIOUT (RABAH) Le pétrole algérien. Alger, [1974]. pp. 243.

— Arab countries.

ORGANIZATION OF ARAB PETROLEUM EXPORTING COUNTRIES. General Secretary. Annual report presented to the...ordinary meeting of the Council of Ministers. a., 1974 (1st)- Kuwait.

— Brazil.

SMITH (PETER SEABORN) Oil and politics in modern Brazil. Toronto, [1976]. pp. 289. *bibliog.*

— Canada.

DOSMAN (EDGAR J.) The national interest: the politics of Northern development, 1968-75. Toronto, [1975]. pp. 224.

GOULD (ED) Oil: the history of Canada's oil and gas industry. [Victoria, B.C., 1976]. pp. 288. *bibliog.*

— — Ontario.

MELVIN (JAMES R.) The effects of energy price changes on commodity prices, interprovincial trade, and employment. Toronto, [1976]. pp. 106. *bibliog. (Ontario. Economic Council. Research Studies. No. 3)*

— China.

BARTKE (WOLFGANG) Oil in the People's Republic of China: industry structure, production, exports; (translated by Waldtraut Jarke). London, [1977]. pp. 125.

— East (Near East).

SHAMSEDIN (EZZEDIN M.) Arab oil and the United States: an admixture of politics and economics. [Columbia], 1974. pp. 54. *(South Carolina University. Bureau of Business and Economic Research. Essays in Economics. No. 29)*

BEN-SHAHAR (HAIM) Oil: prices and capital. Lexington, Mass., [1976]. pp. 124. *bibliog.*

LENCZOWSKI (GEORGE) Middle East oil in a revolutionary age. Washington, 1976. pp. 36. *(American Enterprise Institute for Public Policy Research. National Energy Studies. 10)*

SHWADRAN (BENJAMIN) Middle East oil: issues and problems. Cambridge, Mass., [1977]. pp. 122. *bibliog.*

— Ecuador.

GALARZA ZAVALA (JAIME) El festin del petroleo. Quito, 1974. pp. 462. *bibliog.*

— Europe.

ODELL (PETER R.) The western European energy economy: challenges and opportunities. London, 1975. pp. 40. *(London. University. Stamp Memorial Lectures. 1975)*

CHAPMAN (KEITH P.) North Sea oil and gas: a geographical perspective. Newton Abbot, [1976]. pp. 240.

— France.

STRASBOURG, port pétrolier. [Strasbourg, imprint, 1961]. pp. 53.

FRANCE. Direction de la Documentation. La Documentation Française. Notes et Etudes Documentaires. No. 4,279. Le problème pétrolier français; par Jean Choffel. Paris, 1976. pp. 32.

— Germany.

HORN (MANFRED) Die Energiepolitik der Bundesregierung von 1958 bis 1972: zur Bedeutung der Penetration ausländischer Ölkonzerne in die Energiewirtschaft der BRD, etc. Berlin, [1977]. pp. 320. *bibliog.*

— Indian Ocean region.

ADIE (WILLIAM ANDREW CHARLES) Oil, politics and seapower: the Indian Ocean vortex. New York, [1975]. pp. 95. *bibliog. (National Strategy Information Center. Strategy Papers. No. 24)*

— Mexico.

MEYER (LORENZO) Mexico and the United States in the oil controversy, 1917-1942. Austin, [Tex., 1972]. pp. 367. *bibliog.*

MEXICO. Direccion General de Estadistica. Censo Industrial, 1971. IX censo industrial, 1971; datos de 1970: industrias de extraccion y refinacion de petroleo, y petroquimica basica e industria de generacion, transmision y distribucion de energia electrica para servicio publico. Mexico, 1974. pp. 131.

SEPULVEDA AMOR (BERNARDO) and others. Las empresas transnacionales en Mexico. Mexico, 1974. pp. 167. *(Mexico City. Colegio de Mexico. Centro de Estudios Internacionales. Coleccion. 12)*

CORONA (GUSTAVO) Lazaro Cardenas y la expropiacion de la industria petrolera en Mexico. Mexico, 1975. pp. 350.

— Nigeria.

GOVERNMENT role in the Nigerian oil industry. [Lagos?, 1972?]. pp. 19.

— Persian Gulf.

ABIR (MORDECHAI) Persian Gulf oil in Middle East and international conflicts. Jerusalem, 1976. pp. 35. *(Hebrew University. Leonard Davis Institute for International Relations. Jerusalem Papers on Peace Problems. 20)*

OSBORNE (CHRISTINE) The Gulf States and Oman. London, [1977]. pp. 208. *bibliog.*

— Russia.

CAMPBELL (ROBERT WELLINGTON) Trends in the Soviet oil and gas industry. Baltimore, Md., [1976]. pp. 125. *bibliog.*

TOLF (ROBERT W.) The Russian Rockefellers: the saga of the Nobel family and the Russian oil industry. Stanford, Calif., [1976]. pp. 269. *bibliog. (Stanford University. Hoover Institution on War, Revolution and Peace. Hoover Institution Publications. 158)*

KLINGHOFFER (ARTHUR JAY) The Soviet Union and international oil politics. New York, 1977. pp. 389. *bibliog.*

— — Siberia.

KARIAGIN (IVAN DMITRIEVICH) Ekonomicheskie problemy razvitiia neftianoi promyshlennosti Zapadnoi Sibiri. Moskva, 1975. pp. 143.

— Saudi Arabia.

ALI (RUSTUM) Sheikh. Saudi Arabia and oil diplomacy. New York, 1976. pp. 197. *bibliog.*

— United Kingdom.

REED (LAURANCE) The political consequences of North Sea oil discoveries. Edinburgh, 1973. 1 pamphlet (unpaged).

COUNTER INFORMATION SERVICES. Anti-Reports. No. 8. The oil fix: an investigation into the control and costs of energy. London, [1974]. pp. 49. *bibliog.*

BRITISH NATIONAL OIL CORPORATION. Report and accounts. a., 1976(1st)- London.

KEMP (ALEXANDER G.) Taxation and the profitability of North Sea oil. [Glasgow, 1976]. pp. 35. *bibliog.* (*Glasgow. University of Strathclyde. Fraser of Allander Institute. Research Monographs. No. 4*)

ROBINSON (COLIN) and MORGAN (JON) Effects of North Sea oil on the United Kingdom's balance of payments. London, [1976]. fo. 39. (*University of Surrey. Department of Economics. Guest Papers. No. 5*)

— — **Bibliography.**

MACLEAN (IAN) compiler. North Sea oil information sources: a source guide, bibliography and media data summary. London, 1976]. fo. 77

— — **Societies, etc.**

MACLEAN (IAN) compiler. North Sea oil information sources: a source guide, bibliography and media data summary. London, 1976]. fo. 77

— — **Scotland.**

The SHETLAND way of oil: reactions of a small community to big business; edited by John Button. Sandwick, Shetland, 1976. pp. 134. *bibliog.*

GASKIN (MAXWELL) North Sea oil and Scotland: the changing prospect. Edinburgh, 1977. pp. 22.

— **United States.**

ANDERSON (IRVINE H.) The Standard-Vacuum Oil Company and United States East Asian policy, 1933-1941. Princeton, [1975]. pp. 261. *bibliog.*

COPP (EMMANUEL ANTHONY) Regulating competition in oil: government intervention in the U.S. refinery industry, 1948-1975. College Station, Tex., [1976]. pp. 280. *bibliog.* (*Texas A and M University. Texas A and M University Economics Series. 1*)

TEECE (DAVID J.) Vertical integration and vertical divestiture in the U.S. oil industry: economic analysis and policy implications. Stanford, Calif., 1976. pp. 141. *bibliog.*

BARZEL (YORAM) and HALL (CHRISTOPHER D.) The political economy of the oil import quota. Stanford, [1977]. pp. 96. *bibliog.* (*Stanford University. Hoover Institution on War, Revolution and Peace. Hoover Institution Publications. 172*)

BLAIR (JOHN M.) The control of oil. London, 1977. pp. 442.

ENGLER (ROBERT) The brotherhood of oil: energy policy and the public interest. Chicago, 1977. pp. 337.

UNITED STATES. Task Force on Reform of Federal Energy Administration. 1977. Federal Energy Administration regulation: report of the Presidential Task Force; edited by Paul W. MacAvoy. Washington, D.C., [1977]. pp. 195. (*American Enterprise Institute for Public Policy Research. AEI Studies. 150*)

— **Venezuela.**

MOMMER (DOROTHEA) El Estado Venezolano y la industria petrolera. Santiago de Chile, 1971. pp. 83. *bibliog.* (*Instituto Latinoamericano de Investigaciones Sociales. Estudios y Documentos. 11*)

MEJIA ALARCON (PEDRO ESTEBAN) La industria del petroleo en Venezuela. [Caracas, 1972]. pp. 388. *bibliog.*

VALLENILLA (LUIS) Oil: the making of a new economic order: Venezuelan oil and OPEC. New York, [1975]. pp. 302.

SALAZAR-CARRILLO (JORGE) Oil in the economic development of Venezuela. New York, 1976. pp. 215.

PETROLEUM LAW AND LEGISLATION

— **Australia.**

AUSTRALIA. Parliament. Senate. Select Committee on Off-shore Petroleum Resources. 1971. Report...Vol.1. Report; [H.W. Young, chairman]. in AUSTRALIA. Parliament. Parliamentary papers, 1971, vol.8.

— **Ecuador.**

ECUADOR. Junta Nacional de Planificacion y Coordinacion Economica. 1975. Legislacion petrolera ecuatoriana. Quito, [1975?]. 4 vols. (in 7)

— **Venezuela.**

NACIONALIZACION del petroleo en Venezuela: tesis y documentos fundamentales. Caracas, 1975. pp. 310.

VENEZUELA. Oficina Central de Informacion. 1975. Nationalization of the oil industry: (towards a great Venezuela). Caracas, 1975. pp. 63.

PETROLEUM PRODUCTS

— **Prices.**

BEN-SHAHAR (HAIM) Oil: prices and capital. Lexington, Mass., [1976]. pp. 124. *bibliog.*

ECKBO (PAUL LEO) The future of world oil. Cambridge, Mass., [1976]. pp. 142.

HOUTHAKKER (HENDRIK SAMUEL) The world price of oil: a medium-term analysis. Washington, 1976. pp. 37. (*American Enterprise Institute for Public Policy Research. National Energy Studies. 13*)

BLAIR (JOHN M.) The control of oil. London, 1977. pp. 442.

— — **Canada.**

MELVIN (JAMES R.) The effects of energy price changes on commodity prices, interprovincial trade, and employment. Toronto, [1976]. pp. 106. *bibliog.* (*Ontario. Economic Council. Research Studies. No. 3*)

PETROLEUM REFINERIES

— **United States.**

COPP (EMMANUEL ANTHONY) Regulating competition in oil: government intervention in the U.S. refinery industry, 1948-1975. College Station, Tex., [1976]. pp. 280. *bibliog.* (*Texas A and M University. Texas A and M University Economics Series. 1*)

PETROLEUM WASTE

— **United Kingdom.**

WASTE MANAGEMENT ADVISORY COUNCIL [U.K.]. An economic case study of waste oil and its wider significance. London, H.M.S.O., 1976. pp. 28. (*Papers. No.3*)

PETROLEUM WORKERS

— **United Kingdom.**

KITCHEN (JONATHAN) Labour law and off-shore oil. London, [1977]. pp. 266.

PHARMACY

— **Russia — Uzbekistan.**

DZHURAEV (I.N.) and RISHAL' (L.D.) Razvitie aptechnogo dela v Uzbekistane za gody Sovetskoi vlasti. Tashkent, 1967. pp. 16. *Cover title: 50 let zdravookhraneniia Uzbekistana.*

PHENOMENOLOGY.

NORMAN (RICHARD) Hegel's Phenomenology: a philosophical introduction. London, 1976. pp. 139. *bibliog.*

PHILADELPHIA

— **Politics and government.**

FONER (ERIC) Tom Paine and revolutionary America. New York, 1976. pp. 326.

— **Social conditions.**

LEY (DAVID) The black inner city as frontier outpost: images and behavior of a Philadelphia neighbourhood. Washington, D.C., [1974]. pp. 282. *bibliog.* (*Association of American Geographers. Monograph Series. No. 7*)

PHILANTHROPISTS

— **United States.**

GATES (FREDERICK TAYLOR) Chapters in my life;...with the Frederick Taylor Gates Lectures by Robert Swain Morison. New York, [1977]. pp. 305.

PHILIPPINE ISLANDS

— **Commerce.**

PHILIPPINE ISLANDS. Department of Trade. Semi-annual report. s-a., Jl/D 1975- Quezon City.

STAELIN (CHARLES P.) The impact of export incentives and export-related policies on the firms of the less developed countries: a case study of the Philippines. Ann Arbor, 1976. pp. 29. (*Michigan University. Center for Research on Economic Development. Discussion Papers. No. 59*)

— **Congress.**

STAUFFER (ROBERT BURTON) The Philippine Congress: causes of structural change. Beverly Hills, [1975]. pp. 64. *bibliog.*

— **Economic conditions.**

CHEETHAM (RUSSELL J.) and HAWKINS (EDWARD KENNETH) The Philippines: priorities and prospects for development; report of a mission sent to the Philippines by the World Bank. Washington, International Bank for Reconstruction and Development, 1976. pp. 573. (*Country Economic Reports*).

— — **Bibliography.**

CWIK (HANS JUERGEN) and others, compilers. Entwicklungswirtschaftlich relevante Ressourcen in den A[ssociation of] S[outh]-E[ast] A[sian] N[ations]- Ländern, Auswahlbibliographie: A select bibliography, etc. Hamburg, 1974. pp. 133. (*Hamburg. Institut für Asienkunde. Dokumentations- Leitstelle Asien. Dokumentationsdienst Asien. Reihe A. 5*)

— **Economic policy.**

CHEETHAM (RUSSELL J.) and HAWKINS (EDWARD KENNETH) The Philippines: priorities and prospects for development; report of a mission sent to the Philippines by the World Bank. Washington, International Bank for Reconstruction and Development, 1976. pp. 573. (*Country Economic Reports*).

— **Emigration and immigration.**

PHILIPPINE ISLANDS. Overseas Employment Development Board. Annual report. a., 1975/76 [1st]- Manila.

— **Foreign relations — China.**

HSIAO (SHI-CHING) Chinese-Philippine diplomatic relations, 1946-1975. Quezon City, 1975. pp. 317.

— **History.**

CONSTANTINO (RENATO) A history of the Philippines: from the Spanish colonization to the Second World War; with the collaboration of Letizia R. Constantino. New York, [1975]. pp. 459.

— — **1945- .**

KERKVLIET (BENEDICT J.) The Huk rebellion: a study of peasant revolt in the Philippines. Berkeley, Calif., [1977]. pp. 305. *bibliog.*

— **Industries.**

PHILIPPINE INDUSTRY AND INVESTMENT; pd. by Board of Investments. q., 1976 (1st)- Manila. *Supersedes PHILIPPINE PROGRESS: business and economic information.*

— **Native races.**

RAZON (FELIX) and HENSMAN (RICHARD) The oppression of the indigenous peoples of the Philippines. Copenhagen, 1976. pp. 58. (*International Work Group for Indigenous Affairs. Documents. 25*)

— Politics and government.

ARANETA (SALVADOR) Bayanikasan: the effective democracy for all. Manila, [1976]. pp. 349. *bibliog.*

KERKVLIET (BENEDICT J.) The Huk rebellion: a study of peasant revolt in the Philippines. Berkeley, Calif., [1977]. pp. 305. *bibliog.*

— Population.

QUEZON CITY. University of the Philippines. Population Institute. Philippine population: profiles, prospects, problems. Quezon City, 1969. pp. 82. *bibliog.*

— Rural conditions.

KERKVLIET (BENEDICT J.) The Huk rebellion: a study of peasant revolt in the Philippines. Berkeley, Calif., [1977]. pp. 305. *bibliog.*

PHILIPS (FRITS).

PHILIPS (FRITS) 45 jaar met Philips; tekstverzorging Leo Ott. Rotterdam, 1976. pp. 382.

PHILOSOPHICAL ANTHROPOLOGY.

UTKINA (NINA FEDOROVNA) Pozitivizm, antropologicheskii materializm i nauka v Rossii: vtoraia polovina XIX veka. Moskva, 1975. pp. 319.

PHILOSOPHY

— History.

MINI (PIERO V.) Philosophy and economics: the origins and development of economic theory. Gainesville, Fla., 1974. pp. 305. *bibliog.*

PHILOSOPHY, AMERICAN.

KARIMSKII (ANIUR MUSEEVICH) Revoliutsiia 1776 goda i stanovlenie amerikanskoi filosofii. Moskva, 1976. pp. 296. *bibliog.*

PHILOSOPHY, BRITISH.

SCHNEEWIND (JEROME B.) Sidgwick's ethics and Victorian moral philosophy. Oxford, 1977. pp. 465. *bibliog.*

PHILOSOPHY, GERMAN.

RUGE (ARNOLD) Politician. Zwei Jahre in Paris: Studien und Erinnerungen. Leipzig, Jurany, 1846; Leipzig, 1975. 2 vols. *Facsimile reprint.*

BUHR (MANFRED) and IRRLITZ (GERD) Der Anspruch der Vernunft: die klassische bürgerliche deutsche Philosophie als theoretische Quelle des Marxismus, etc. Köln, 1976. pp. 280. *With summaries in various languages.*

ROSEN (ZVI) Bruno Bauer and Karl Marx: the influence of Bruno Bauer on Marx's thought. The Hague, 1977. pp. 254. *bibliog. (International Institute of Social History. Studies in Social History. [No.]2)*

PHILOSOPHY, HUNGARIAN.

HANAK (TIBOR) Die marxistische Philosophie und Soziologie in Ungarn. Stuttgart, 1976. pp. 231.

PHILOSOPHY, MEDIEVAL.

HENRY (DESMOND PAUL) Medieval logic and metaphysics: a modern introduction. London, 1972. pp. 133. *bibliog.*

PHILOSOPHY, MODERN.

RUSSELL (BERTRAND ARTHUR WILLIAM) 3rd Earl Russell. Bertrand Russell speaks his mind. Darmstadt, 1976. pp. 175. *Transcript of a television series of 13 interviews with Bertrand Russell, by Woodrow Wyatt. Originally published in 1960 by the World Publishing Company, Cleveland.*

REFLEXIVE water: the basic concerns of mankind: [a series of television debates; byz] A.J. Ayer [and others; edited by] Fons Elders. London, 1974. pp. 307.

FEDOSEEV (PETR NIKOLAEVICH) Dialektika sovremennoi epokhi. 2nd ed. Moskva, 1975. pp. 576.

ALTHUSSER (LOUIS) Positions, 1964-1975. Paris, [1976]. pp. 173.

HAWTHORN (GEOFFREY) Enlightenment and despair: a history of sociology. Cambridge, 1976. pp. 295. *bibliog.*

POPPER (Sir KARL RAIMUND) Unended quest: an intellectual autobiography. rev.ed. Glasgow, 1976. pp. 255. *bibliog.*

HEGEL (GEORG WILHELM FRIEDRICH) Phenomenology of spirit; translated by A.V. Miller with analysis of the text and foreword by J.N. Findlay. Oxford, [1977]. pp. 595. *This translation has been made from the fifth edition, edited by J. Hoffmeister, 1952.*

KENNEDY (ELLEN LEE) 'Freedom' and 'the open society': Henri Bergson's contribution to political philosophy. 1977. fo. 278. *bibliog. Typescript. Ph.D. (London) thesis: unpublished. This thesis is the property of London University and may not be removed from the Library.*

LOCKE (JOHN) the Philosopher. The Locke reader: selections from the works of John Locke with a general introduction and commentary [by] John W. Yolton. Cambridge, 1977. pp. 335. *bibliog.*

— History.

BENTON (TED) Philosophical foundations of the three sociologies. London, 1977. pp. 225.

PHILOSOPHY, PERSIAN.

AGAKHI (ABDULKHUSEIN M.) Iz istorii obshchestvennoi i filosofskoi mysli v Irane, vtoraia polovina XVII - pervaia chetvert' XIX vv. Baku, 1971. pp. 216.

PHILOSOPHY, POLISH.

MODZELEWSKI (WOJCIECH) Naród i postęp: problematyka narodowa w ideologii i myśli społecznej pozytywistów warszawskich. Warszawa, 1977. pp. 243.

PHILOSOPHY, RUSSIAN.

CHAGIN (BORIS ALEKSANDROVICH) and KLUSHIN (VLADIMIR IVANOVICH) Bor'ba za istoricheskii materializm v SSSR v 20-e gody. Leningrad, 1975. pp. 411.

KSENOFONTOV (VALENTIN IVANOVICH) Leninskie idei v sovetskoi filosofskoi nauke 20-kh godov: diskussiia "dialektikov" s mekhanistami. Leningrad, 1975. pp. 100.

UTKINA (NINA FEDOROVNA) Pozitivizm, antropologicheskii materializm i nauka v Rossii: vtoraia polovina XIX veka. Moskva, 1975. pp. 319.

PHILOSOPHY, SCOTTISH.

OLSON (RICHARD) Scottish philosophy and British physics, 1750-1880: a study in the foundations of the Victorian scientific style. Princeton, N.J., [1975]. pp. 349.

CHITNIS (ANAND C.) The Scottish Enlightenment: a social history. London, 1976. pp. 279. *bibliog.*

PHILOSOPHY, WHITE RUSSIAN.

MOKHNACH (NINEL' NIKOLAEVNA) Ot Prosveshcheniia k revoliutsionnomu demokratizmu: obshchestvenno-politicheskaia i filosofskaia mysl' Belorussii kontsa 10-kh — nachala 50-kh godov XIX v. Minsk, 1976. pp. 184.

PHOSPHATE INDUSTRY.

REYSSET (BERNARD) Le marché mondial des phosphates et des engrais phosphatés. [Paris], Caisse Centrale de Coopération Economique, 1975. fo. 68.

— Solomon Islands.

MONBERG (TORBEN) The reactions of people of Bellona Island towards a mining project. Copenhagen, 1976. pp. 61. *bibliog. (International Work Group for Indigenous Affairs. Documents. 24)*

PHOSPHATIC FERTILIZERS

— Australia.

AUSTRALIA. Bureau of Agricultural Economics. 1976. Phosphatic fertilisers: submission to the Industries Assistance Commission Inquiry. Canberra, 1976. pp. 155. *bibliog. (Industry Economics Monographs. No. 15)*

PHYSICAL EDUCATION AND TRAINING

— Germany.

JOCH (WINFRIED) Politische Leibeserziehung und ihre Theorie im nationalsozialistischen Deutschland: Voraussetzungen, Begründungszusammenhang, Dokumentation. Bern, 1976. pp. 249. *bibliog.*

PHYSICAL GEOGRAPHY

— Mathematical models.

LONDON. University. London School of Economics and Political Science. Graduate School of Geography. Discussion Papers. No. 61. Stochastic-dynamic models for some environmental systems: transfer-function approach; [by] Pong-wai Lai. London, 1977. pp. 25. *bibliog.*

— Russia — Siberia.

MIKHAILOV (NIKOLA IVANOVICH) Priroda Sibiri: geograficheskie problemy. Moskva, 1976. pp. 158. *bibliog.*

PHYSICALLY HANDICAPPED

— United Kingdom.

HYMAN (MAVIS) The extra costs of disabled living: a case history study. [London], 1977. pp. 196.

PHYSICIANS

— United Kingdom — Ireland, Northern.

NORTHERN IRELAND MEDICAL MANPOWER ADVISORY COMMITTEE. General Medical Practitioner and GP Training Grades Sub-Committee. Report...on medical staffing in general practice. [Belfast], 1975. fo.(31). *Photocopy.*

PHYSICS

— History.

JACOB (MARGARET C.) The Newtonians and the English Revolution, 1689-1720. Ithaca, N.Y., 1976. pp. 288. *bibliog.*

— — United Kingdom.

OLSON (RICHARD) Scottish philosophy and British physics, 1750-1880: a study in the foundations of the Victorian scientific style. Princeton, N.J., [1975]. pp. 349.

— Philosophy.

OLSON (RICHARD) Scottish philosophy and British physics, 1750-1880: a study in the foundations of the Victorian scientific style. Princeton, N.J., [1975]. pp. 349.

PIAGET (JEAN).

DUSKA (RONALD) and WHELAN (MARIELLEN) Moral development: a guide to Piaget and Kohlberg, Dublin, 1977. pp. 128. *bibliog.*

PIAGET and knowing: studies in genetic epistemology; edited by Beryl A. Geber. London, 1977. pp. 258. *bibliogs.*

PICHINCHA

— Maps.

ECUADOR. Oficina de los Censos Nacionales. 1975. Compendio de informacion socio-economica de las provincias del Ecuador: Pichincha. Quito, 1975. 2 vols. (in 1). *(Provincias del Ecuador. 3)*

PICKETING

— United Kingdom.

LABOUR RESEARCH DEPARTMENT. Picketing: a trade unionists' guide. London, 1976. pp. 9.

RALPH (CHRIS) The picket and the law. London, 1977. pp. 22. *(Fabian Society. Research Series. [No.] 331)*

PIECK (WILHELM).

GELOEBNIS zur Einheit: Kundgebungen für die antifaschistisch- demokratische Einheit anlässlich des 70. Geburtstages von Wilhelm Pieck. Berlin, 1946. pp. 79.

BRANDT (EDITH) Wilhelm Pieck, 1876-1976: Festansprache zum 100. Geburtstag... am 6. Januar 1976. Halle (Saale), 1976. pp. 15. *(Halle. Universität. Wissenschaftliche Beiträge. 1976/7 (A 29))*

PILBARA

— Industries.

AUSTRALIA. Department of Northern Development. 1974. The Pilbara study: report on the industrial development of the Pilbara. Canberra, 1974. 1 vol.(various pagings).

PIPE LINES

— Canada — Northwest Territories.

DENE nation: the colony within; edited by Mel Watkins for the University League for Social Reform. Toronto, [1977]. pp. 187. *bibliogs. Based on material presented at the Mackenzie Valley Pipeline Inquiry (Berger Inquiry).*

PISTOIA (PROVINCE)

— History.

RISALITI (RENATO) Antifascismo e resistenza nel Pistoiese. Pistoia, [1976]. pp. 270.

PI SUNYER (CARLES).

PI SUNYER (CARLES) La Republica y la Guerra: memorias de un politico catalan; traducido del catalan por el autor. Mexico, 1975. pp. 654.

PITT (WILLIAM) Earl of Chatham.

A REPLY to the Vindication of Mr. Pitt, by an English officer in the Prussian service. London, Cooper, 1758. pp. 45.

PI Y MARGALL (FRANCISCO).

JUTGLAR (ANTONI) Pi y Margall y el federalismo español. Madrid, 1975-76. 2 vols. *bibliog.*

PLANNING.

FRIEDMANN (JOHN REMBERT PETER) Retracking America: the theory of transactive planning. Garden City, N.Y., 1973. pp. 289. *bibliog.*

FOXLEY RIOSECO (ALEJANDRO) Estrategia de desarrollo y modelos de planificacion. Mexico, 1975. pp. 180.

BATHER (NICHOLAS JOHN) and others. Strategic choice in practice: the West Berkshire structure plan experience. Reading, 1976. pp. 62. *(Reading. University. Department of Geography. Reading Geographical Papers. No. 50)*

BATTY (MICHAEL) A political theory of planning and design, incorporating concepts of collective decision-making and social power. Reading, 1976. pp. 64. *bibliog. (Reading. University. Department of Geography. Reading Geographical Papers. No. 45)*

ROTHSCHILD (NATHANIEL MEYER VICTOR) 3rd Baron Rothschild. The best laid plans...: what is planning: what is not planning: what is a planner. n.p., 1976. pp. 24. *(Israel Sieff Memorial Lectures. 1976)*

KANTOROVICH (LEONID VITAL'EVICH) Essays in optimal planning; selected with an introduction by Leon Smolinski. Oxford, 1977. pp. 251. *bibliog.*

TURNER (R. KERRY) and COLLIS (CLIVE) The economics of planning. London, 1977. pp. 103. *bibliog.*

— Bibliography.

VEAL (A.J.) and DUESBURY (W.K.) compilers. A first list of U.K. students theses and dissertations on planning and urban and regional studies. Birmingham, 1976. pp. 245. *(Birmingham. University. Centre for Urban and Regional Studies. Research Memoranda. No. 55).*

— Mathematical models.

FRIEDMANN (JOHN REMBERT PETER) Innovation, flexible response and social learning: a problem in the theory of meta-planning. Reading, 1976. pp. 18. *bibliog. (Reading. University. Department of Geography. Reading Geographical Papers. No. 49)*

LONDON. University. London School of Economics and Political Science. Graduate School of Geography. Discussion Papers. No. 57. Social justice and planning: the use of the accessibility matrix; [by] Tisha Loodmer. London, 1976. pp. 16. *bibliog.*

— Study and teaching.

CHERRY (GORDON E.) Urban and regional planning: promise and potential in the West Midlands; an inaugural lecture delivered in the University of Birmingham on 4th November 1976. Birmingham, 1976. pp. 22. *bibliog.*

PLANTATION LIFE

— Africa, East.

COOPER (FREDERICK) Plantation slavery on the East coast of Africa. New Haven, 1977. pp. 314. *bibliog. (Yale University. Yale Historical Publications. Miscellany. 113)*

PLANTATIONS

— Brazil.

DEAN (WARREN) Rio Clara: a Brazilian plantation system, 1820-1920. Stanford, Calif., 1976. pp. 234.

— Colombia.

KNIGHT (ROLF) Sugar plantations and labor patterns in the Cauca Valley, Colombia. Toronto, 1972. pp. 209. *bibliog. (Toronto. University. Department of Anthropology. Anthropological Series. No.12)*

— Cuba.

MARTINEZ-ALIER (JUAN) Haciendas, plantations and collective farms: agrarian class societies, Cuba and Peru. London, 1977. pp. 185. *bibliog.*

PLATO.

RANKIN (H.D.) Pentheus and Plato: a study in social disintegration; an inaugural lecture delivered at the University [of Southampton] 20 November 1975. Southampton, 1975. pp. 32.

IRWIN (TERENCE) Plato's moral theory: the early and middle dialogues. Oxford, 1977. pp. 376. *bibliog.*

PLAY.

GARVEY (CATHERINE) Play. London, 1977. pp. 128. *bibliog.*

PLAY THERAPY.

HALL (DAVID J.) Social relations and innovation: changing the state of play in hospitals. London, 1977. pp. 222. *bibliog.*

PLEAS (CRIMINAL PROCEDURE).

BALDWIN (JOHN) Ph.D. and McCONVILLE (MICHAEL) Negotiated justice: pressures to plead guilty. London, 1977. pp. 128.

PLEKHANOV (GEORGII VALENTINOVICH).

KAZAKOV (ALEKSEI TIMOFEEVICH) and URLANIS (BORIS TSEZAREVICH) Problemy narodonaseleniia v russkoi marksistskoi mysli. Moskva, 1976. pp. 196. *bibliog.*

PLIUSHCH (LEONID IVANOVICH).

ISTORIIA bolezni Leonida Pliushcha; sostavlenie i kommentarii Tat'iany Khodorovich. Amsterdam, 1974. pp. 208.

PLURALISM (SOCIAL SCIENCES).

HOLBERT (ROBERT LEE) Tax law and political access: the bias of pluralism revisited. Beverly Hills, [1975]. pp. 72. *bibliog.*

GREELEY (ANDREW M.) Ethnicity, denomination and inequality. Beverly Hills, [1976]. pp. 85. *bibliog.*

HALEBSKY (SANDOR) Mass society and political conflict: toward a reconstruction of theory. Cambridge, 1976. pp. 309.

BERGER (PETER L.) and NEUHAUS (RICHARD JOHN) To empower people: the role of mediating structures in public policy. Washington, [1977]. pp. 45. *(American Enterprise Institute for Public Policy Research. AEI Studies. 139)*

PLURALISM in a democratic society; edited by Melvin M. Tumin and Walter Plotch. New York, 1977. pp. 248. *bibliogs. Based on a conference convened by the Anti-Defamation League of B'nai B'rith, held in April 1975 in New York.*

WINTER (HERBERT R.) and BELLOWS (THOMAS J.) People and politics: an introduction to political science. New York, [1977]. pp. 514. *bibliogs.*

POETRY.

ROBERTSON (FREDERICK WILLIAM) Lectures and addresses on literary and social topics. London, 1858. pp. 308.

POLAND

— Appropriations and expenditures.

KRZY'ZANOWSKI (KAZIMIERZ) Wydatki wojskowe Polski w latach 1918-1939. Warszawa, 1976. pp. 207. *bibliog.*

— Constitution.

POLAND. Constitution. 1921. Constitution de la république de Pologne du 17 mars 1921 contenant le texte du projet de la Commission constitutionnelle de la Diète, du 8 juillet 1920, et les amendements de la minorité; préface, introduction historique et traduction par Michel Potulicki. Varsovie, [1921]. pp. 83.

ASSOCIATION OF POLISH STUDENTS AND GRADUATES IN EXILE. The changing of the constitution of the Polish People's Republic. [London, 1976]. pp. 14.

— Defences.

KRZY'ZANOWSKI (KAZIMIERZ) Wydatki wojskowe Polski w latach 1918-1939. Warszawa, 1976. pp. 207. *bibliog.*

— Economic conditions.

LESZCZYCKI (STANISŁAW) ed. Zarys geografii ekonomicznej Polski: praca zbiorowa, etc. 2nd ed. Warszawa, 1971. pp. 260. *bibliog.*

ODRA i Nadodrze. Warszawa, 1976. pp. 371.

— Economic history.

LIPIŃSKI (EDWARD) Historia polskiej myśli społeczno-ekonomicznej do końca XVIII wieku. Wrocław, 1975. pp. 464. *With English and Russian afterwords.*

BUJAK (FRANCISZEK) Wybór pism; przedmowa, komentarze, przypisy i ogólna redakcja naukowa Helena Madurowicz-Urbańska. Warszawa, 1976. 2 vols. *bibliog.*

LANDAU (ZBIGNIEW) and TOMASZEWSKI (JERZY) Druga Rzeczpospolita, gospodarka - społeczeństwo - miejsce w świecie: sporne problemy badań; (zebrane szkice). Warszawa, 1977. pp. 429.

— Economic policy.

POLITYKA gospodarcza a polityka społeczna. Warszawa, 1971. pp. 243.

— Foreign economic relations — Germany.

STAATSANGEHOERIGKEIT, soziale Grundrechte, wirtschaftliche Zusammenarbeit nach dem Recht der Bundesrepublik Deutschland und der Volksrepublik Polen: Referate des Rechtscolloquiums 1974; herausgegeben von Józef Kokot und Krzysztof Skubiszewski. Berlin, 1976. pp. 293.

— — India.

FIKUS (DARIUSZ) Polska-Indie: gospodarka, stosunki ekonomiczne. Warszawa, 1976. pp. 196.

— — Russia.

WILK (MARIAN) Pomoc i współpraca: polsko-radzieckie stosunki gospodarcze w latach 1944-1945. Warszawa, 1976. pp. 259. *bibliog.*

— Foreign relations — Czechoslovakia.

KOWALCZYK (JÓZEF) Za kulisami wydarzeń politycznych z lat 1936-1938 w świetle raportów posła Czechosłowacji w Warszawie i innych archiwaliów: [szkice i dokumenty]. Warszawa, 1976. pp. 149.

— — Germany.

JACOBSEN (HANS ADOLF) Fünf Jahre Warschauer Vertrag: Versuch einer Bilanz der Beziehungen zwischen der Bundesrepublik Deutschland und der Volksrepublik Polen, 1970-1975. Berlin, [1976]. pp. 96. *(Einzelausgabe aus der Zeitschrift Die Friedenswarte, Band 58, Heft 3,4)*

— — Russia.

LECZYK (MARIAN) Polityka II Rzeczypospolitej wobec ZSRR w latach 1925-1934: studium z historii dyplomacji. Warszawa, 1976. pp. 380. *bibliog.*

MIKHUTINA (IRINA VASIL'EVNA) Sovetsko-pol'skie otnosheniia, 1931-1935. Moskva, 1977. pp. 287. *bibliog.*

— Gentry.

KAMLER (MARCIN) Folwark szlachecki w Wielkopolsce w latach 1580-1655. Warszawa, 1976. pp. 175. *With French summary.*

— History.

KIENIEWICZ (STEFAN) Historia Polski, 1795-1918. [2nd ed.]. Warszawa, 1969. pp. 611. *bibliog.*

KIENIEWICZ (STEFAN) Historia Polski, 1795-1918. [4th ed.]. Warszawa, 1975. pp. 604. *bibliog.*

BUJAK (FRANCISZEK) Wybór pism; przedmowa, komentarze, przypisy i ogólna redakcja naukowa Helena Madurowicz-Urbańska. Warszawa, 1976. 2 vols. *bibliog.*

WASIUTYŃSKI (WOJCIECH) Źródła niepodległości. Londyn, 1977. pp. 178.

— — 1863-1864, Revolution.

KIENIEWICZ (STEFAN) Powstanie styczniowe. Warszawa, 1972. pp. 801.

MOROZOVA (OL'GA PAVLOVNA) Pol'skii revoliutsioner-demokrat Bronislav Shvartse. Moskva, 1975. pp. 288.

— — 1900- .

DZIEWANOWSKI (M.K.) Poland in the twentieth century. New York, 1977. pp. 309.

— — 1918-1945.

PERNOT (MAURICE) L'épreuve de la Pologne. Paris, [1921]. pp. 311.

HELLER (CELIA STOPNICKA) On the edge of destruction: Jews of Poland between the two world wars. New York, 1977. pp. 369.

— — 1939-1945, Occupation.

OSTROWSKI (KAROL) Hitlerowska polityka podatkowa w Generalnym Gubernatorstwie. Warszawa, 1977. pp. 159. *(Zeszyty Naukowe Uniwersytetu Jagiellońskiego. Prace Prawnicze. zeszyt 29) With Russian and German summaries.*

UMBREIT (HANS) Deutsche Militärverwaltungen, 1938/39: die militärische Besetzung der Tschechoslowakei und Polens. Stuttgart, 1977. pp. 296. *bibliog. (Militärgeschichtliches Forschungsamt. Beiträge zur Militär- und Kriegsgeschichte. Band 18)*

— — 1945- .

WALICHNOWSKI (TADEUSZ) The Tel Aviv-Bonn axis and Poland. Warsaw, 1968. pp. 88. *bibliog.*

— Industries.

FIERLA (IRENA) Migracje ludności w Polsce a uprzemysłowienie. Warszawa, 1976. pp. 150. *bibliog. (Polska Akademia Nauk. Komitet i Zakład Badań Rejonów Uprzemysławianych. Problemy Rejonów Uprzemysławianych) With brief Russian and English summaries.*

— Military policy.

GIEREK (EDWARD) O wojsku i obronności: [extracts from speeches, 1971-73]. Warszawa, 1974. pp. 118. *Illustrated.*

KRZYŻANOWSKI (KAZIMIERZ) Wydatki wojskowe Polski w latach 1918-1939. Warszawa, 1976. pp. 207. *bibliog.*

— Nationalism.

LUXEMBURG (ROSA) The national question: selected writings; edited and with an introduction by Horace B. Davis. New York, [1976]. pp. 320. *Articles from Przegląd socjaldemokratyczny, 1908-1909, in English translation.*

GOĆKOWSKI (JANUSZ) and WALICKI (ANDRZEJ) eds. Idee i koncepcje narodu w polskiej myśli politycznej czasów porozbiorowych. Warszawa, 1977. pp. 339. *(Powszechny Zjazd Historyków Polskich, 11-y, 1974. Prace. 7)*

MROCZKO (MARIAN) Związek Obrony Kresów Zachodnich, 1921-1934: powstanie i działalność. Gdańsk, 1977. pp. 264. *bibliog.*

— Politics and government.

KRZEMIEŃ (LESZEK) Przeciwko ideologicznemu rozbrajaniu partii: o niektórych problemach rewizjonizmu na tle pewnych publikacji prasowych w Polsce w latach 1956-57. 2nd ed. Warszawa, 1959. pp. 139.

MŁYNARSKI (FELIKS JOHN) Wspomnienia. Warszawa, 1971. pp. 563.

LAMMICH (SIEGFRIED) Regierung und Verwaltung in Polen. Köln, [1975]. pp. 347. *bibliog. (Cologne. Universität. Institut für Ostrecht, and others. Dokumente zum Ostrecht. Band 8)*

ASSOCIATION OF POLISH STUDENTS AND GRADUATES IN EXILE. The changing of the constitution of the Polish People's Republic. [London, 1976]. pp. 14.

IAZHBOROVSKAIA (INESSA SERGEEVNA) and BUKHARIN (N.I.) U istokov pol'skogo sotsialisticheskogo dvizheniia. Moskva, 1976. pp. 412.

NA LEWO. zeszyt nr.1. Kłamstwo, fałsz, prawda: 'nowy styl' polskiej biurokracji. n.p., [1976?]. pp. 21. *Reproduced from typescript.*

ŻALIŃSKI (HENRYK) Kształt polityczny Polski w ideologii Towarzystwa Demokratycznego Polskiego, 1832-1846. Wrocław, 1976. pp. 167. *(Polska Akademia Nauk. Oddział w Krakowie. Komisja Nauk Historycznych. Prace. Nr.36) With French summary.*

— Population.

MIROWSKI (WŁODZIMIERZ) Przemiany społeczne w małym mieście a procesy migracyjne: studium monograficzne wychodźstwa ludności. Wrocław, 1976. pp. 260. *bibliog. With English and Russian summaries.*

ROZMIESZCZENIE i migracje ludności a system osadniczy Polski Ludowej; Distribution, migrations of population and settlement system of Poland. Wrocław, 1977. pp. 343. *bibliog. (Polska Akademia Nauk. Instytut Geografii. Prace Geograficzne. Nr.117) With Russian and English summaries.*

— Relations (general) with Germany.

GERMAN Polish dialogue: letters of the Polish and German bishops and international statements. Bonn, 1966. pp. 127.

— Rural conditions.

RURAL social change in Poland; editors: Jan Turowski [and] Lili Maria Szwengrub. Wrocław, 1976. pp. 334. *bibliogs. Edited on the occasion of the Fourth World Congress for Rural Sociology, Toruń, Poland, 1976, and Ninth Congress of the European Society for Rural Sociology.*

JASIEWICZ (ZBIGNIEW) Rodzina wiejska na Ziemi Lubuskiej: studium przeobra'zeń rodziny na podstawie badań etnograficznych w wybranych waiach. Warszawa, 1977. pp. 119. *bibliog. With English summary.*

— Sejm.

ROZMARYN (STEFAN) Le Parlement et les conseils locaux en Pologne; (conférence tenue...le 11 mai 1962). Wrocław, 1963. pp. 21. *(Accademia Polacca di Scienze e Lettere. Biblioteca de Roma. Conference. fasc. 19)*

— Social conditions.

VESELOVSKII (V.) and RUTKEVICH (MIKHAIL NIKOLAEVICH) eds. Problemy razvitiia sotsial'noi struktury obshchestva v Sovetskom Soiuze i Pol'she. Moskva, 1976. pp. 231.

— Social history.

ZIELIŃSKI (HENRYK) ed. Drogi integracji społeczeństwa w Polsce XIX-XX w. Wrocław, 1976. pp. 216. *(Powszechny Zjazd Historyków Polskich. 11-y, 1974. Prace. 10)*

— Social policy.

POLITYKA gospodarcza a polityka społeczna. Warszawa, 1971. pp. 243.

ŻUK (DOBROSŁAW) Związki zawodowe a polityka socjalna w PRL. Warszawa, 1971. pp. 183.

POLANYI (MICHAEL).

GELWICK (RICHARD) The way of discovery: an introduction to the thought of Michael Polanyi. Oxford, [1977]. pp. 181.

POLE (Sir FELIX JOHN CLEWETT).

POLE (Sir FELIX JOHN CLEWETT) Felix J.C. Pole: his book. Bracknell, Berks, 1968. pp. 233. *Printed for private circulation only, Christmas, 1954.*

POLES IN CANADA.

PAST and present: selected topics on the Polish group in Canada; edited by Benedykt Heydenkorn. Toronto, 1974. pp. 224. *bibliogs. (Canadian-Polish Research Institute. Studies. 8)*

FROM prairies to cities; papers on the Poles in Canada at the 8th World Congress of Sociology; edited by Benedykt Heydenkorn. Toronto, 1975. pp. 80. *bibliog. (Canadian-Polish Research Institute. Studies. 9)*

POLES IN LATIN AMERICA.

PARADOWSKA (MARIA) Polacy w Ameryce Południowej. Wrocław, 1977. pp. 316. *bibliog.*

POLES IN THE UNITED STATES.

GRZELOŃSKI (BOGDAN) Polacy w Stanach Zjednoczonych Ameryki, 1776-1865. [Warszawa], 1976. pp. 235. *bibliog.*

POLESIE

— Rural conditions.

OBREBSKI (JOSEPH) The changing peasantry of Eastern Europe; edited by Barbara and Joel Halpern. Cambridge, Mass., [1976]. pp. 102. *bibliog. Lectures given at Oxford University in 1946.*

POLICE.

TOCH (HANS H.) Peacekeeping: police, prisons, and violence. Lexington, Mass., [1976]. pp. 137. *bibliog.*

GOLDSTEIN (HERMAN) Policing a free society. Cambridge, Mass., [1977]. pp. 371. *bibliog.*

MUIR (WILLIAM KER) Police: streetcorner politicians. Chicago, 1977. pp. 306. *bibliog.*

— Bibliography.

FERRACUTI (FRANCO) and GIANNINI (MARIA CRISTINA) compilers. Manpower and training in the field of social defence: a commentary and bibliography. Rome, United Nations Social Defence Research Institute, 1970. pp. 111. *bibliog. (Publications. No. 2)*

— Belgium.

EUROPEAN COURT OF HUMAN RIGHTS. Publications. Series B: Pleadings, Oral Arguments and Documents. [B17]. National Union of Belgian Police case, (1974-1975). Strasbourg, Council of Europe, 1976. pp. 269bis, 271-337. *In English and French.*

— France.

PANZANI (ALEX) Une prison clandestine de la police française: Arenc. Paris, 1975. pp. 105.

— Israel.

ISRAEL. Israel Police. Annual report. a., 1975- Jerusalem.

— Italy.

SICUREZZA democratica e lotta alla criminalità: la difesa dell'ordine costituzionale e della sicurezza dei cittadini...: atti del Convegno organizzato dal Centro di Studi e Iniziative per la Riforma dello Stato, Roma 25-26 febbraio 1975. Roma, 1975. pp.468. *(Centro di Studi e Iniziative per la Riforma dello Stato. Quaderni)*

— Thailand.

LOBE (THOMAS) United States national security policy and aid to the Thailand police. Denver, Col., [1977]. pp. 161. *(Denver. University. Social Science Foundation and Graduate School of International Studies. Monograph Series in World Affairs. vol. 14, no. 2)*

— United Kingdom.

LEWIS (ROY) A force for the future: the role of the police in the next ten years. London, 1976. pp. 316.

MARK (Sir ROBERT) Policing a perplexed society. London, 1977. pp. 132.

— United States.

POTHOLM (CHRISTIAN P.) and MORGAN (RICHARD E.) eds. Focus on police: police in American society. New York, [1976]. pp. 412.

LEVI (MARGARET) Bureaucratic insurgency: the case of police unions. Lexington, Mass., [1977]. pp. 165.

POLICE, POLITICAL AND SECRET

— Russia.

HARDING (Mrs. STAN) The underworld of state;...with an introduction by Bertrand Russell. London, 1925. pp. 256.

GERSON (LENNARD D.) The secret police in Lenin's Russia. Philadelphia, 1976. pp. 332. *bibliog.*

MIAGKOV (ALEKSEI) Inside the KGB: an exposé by an officer of the Third Directorate. Richmond, Surrey, 1976. pp. 131.

VEREEKEN (GEORGES) The GPU in the Trotskyist movement; [translated from the French]. London, [1976]. pp. 390.

POLICY SCIENCES.

REPORT of the Inter-American Policy Research Group (Grupo para investigaciones de sistemas político-administrativos interamericanos). Austin, 1973. pp. 50. *bibliog. (American Society for Public Administration. Latin American Development Administration Committee and Texas University. Institute of Latin American Studies. LADAC Occasional Papers. Series 2. No. 8) Report of a workshop held in Rio de Janeiro in 1973.*

AMACHER (RYAN C.) and others, eds. The economic approach to public policy: selected readings. Ithaca, N.Y., 1976. pp. 528.

BASU (KAUSHIK) Revealed preference of government: concepts, analysis and evaluation. 1976. fo. 179. *bibliog. Typescript. Ph. D. (London) thesis: unpublished. This thesis is the property of London University and may not be removed from the Library.*

DYE (THOMAS R.) Policy analysis: what governments do, why they do it, and what difference it makes. Alabama, [1976]. pp. 122.

GREENBERGER (MARTIN) and others. Models in the policy process: public decision making in the computer era. New York, [1976]. pp. 355.

WALT (AUDREY GILLIAN) Policy making in Britain: a comparative study of fluoridation and family planning, 1960-1974. 1976. fo. 273. *bibliog. Typescript. Ph.D. (London) thesis: unpublished. This thesis is the property of London University and may not be removed from the Library.*

WASBY (STEPHEN L.) ed. Civil liberties: policy and policy making. Lexington, Mass., [1976]. pp. 235. *bibliogs.*

BARDACH (EUGENE) The implementation game: what happens after a bill becomes law. Cambridge, Mass., 1977. pp. 323. *bibliogs. (Massachusetts Institute of Technology. MIT Studies in American Politics and Public Policy. 1)*

FAIRLEY (WILLIAM B.) and MOSTELLER (CHARLES FREDERICK) eds. Statistics and public policy. Reading, Mass., [1977]. pp. 397.

SHULL (STEVEN A.) Interrelated concepts in policy research. Beverly Hills, [1977]. pp. 76. *bibliog.*

USING social research in public policy making; edited by Carol H. Weiss. Lexington, [1977]. pp. 256. *(Policy Studies Organization. Policy Studies Organization Series. 11)*

— Mathematical models.

MODELS for indicator development: a framework for policy analysis; [by] Harvey A. Garn [and others]. Washington, 1976. pp. 61.

POLISH PERIODICALS.

SMOŁKA (LEONARD) Prasa polska na Śląsku Opolskim, 1922-1939. Warszawa, 1976. pp. 200. *(Wrocław. Uniwersytet. Acta Universitatis Wratislaviensis. No.327. Nauki Polityczne. 8) With German summary.*

POLITICAL BALLADS AND SONGS, ARGENTINIAN.

PINEDO (JORGE) Consignas y lucha popular en el proceso revolucionario argentino, 1955-1973. Buenos Aires, [1974]. pp. 143. *bibliog.*

POLITICAL BALLADS AND SONGS, IRISH.

[GIFFARD (JOHN)] Orange: a political rhapsody in three cantos. 9th ed. Dublin, printed for J. Milliken, 1798. pp. 22, 23, 24. *Also attributed to G. Faulkner the Younger.*

POLITICAL CLUBS.

ESTIER (CLAUDE) Ce qu'est la Convention. 2nd ed. [Paris, 1967]. pp. 61. *(Convention des Institutions Républicaines. Cahiers. 8)*

— Germany.

NELHIEBEL (KURT) Die Henleins gestern und heute: Hintergründe und Ziele des Witikobundes. Frankfurt/Main, 1962. pp. 88.

POLITICAL CONVENTIONS.

KIRKPATRICK (JEANE J.) The new presidential elite: men and women in national politics. New York, [1976]. pp. 605.

POLITICAL CRIMES AND OFFENCES

— China.

GRIFFIN (PATRICIA E.) The Chinese communist treatment of counter-revolutionaries, 1924- 1949. Princeton, N.J., [1976]. pp. 256. *bibliog. (Harvard University. Harvard Studies in East Asian Law)*

— Italy.

POLI (ENZO) Violenza politica e criminalità comune: indagine sull'ordine pubblico in Italia. [Rome, 1976]. pp. 264.

— Russia.

TROTSKII (LEV DAVYDOVICH) La bureaucratie stalinienne et l'assassinat de Kirov. Paris, [1935]. pp. 44.

POLITICAL ETHICS.

ASH (WILLIAM FRANKLIN) Morals and politics: the ethics of revolution. London, 1977. pp. 170. *bibliog.*

POLITICAL PARTICIPATION.

SCAFF (LAWRENCE A.) Participation in the Western political tradition: a study of theory and practice. Tucson, [1975]. pp. 100. *bibliog. (Arizona University. Institute of Government Research. Political Theory Studies. No. 2)*

— Argentine Republic — Santa Fe.

GALLO (EZEQUIEL) Farmers in revolt: the revolutions of 1893 in the province of Santa Fe, Argentina. London, 1976. pp. 97. *bibliog. (London. University. Institute of Latin American Studies. Monographs. 7)*

— Asia.

ASPECTS of political mobilization in South Asia; Robert I. Crane, editor; contributors, Agehananda Bharati [and others] . Syracuse, N.Y., 1976. pp. 159. *(Syracuse University. Maxwell Graduate School of Citizenship and Public Affairs. Foreign and Comparative Studies. South Asian Series. No. 1) Papers of a symposium held at the Maxwell School in 1973.*

— Europe.

WERNICKE (IMMO H.) Die Bedingungen politischer Partizipation: eine international vergleichende Kontext- und Aggregatdatenanalyse für Grossbritannien, Norwegen, Deutschland (BRD) und Frankreich. Meisenheim am Glan, 1976. pp. 309. *bibliog.*

— European Economic Community countries.

INGLEHART (RONALD) The silent revolution: changing values and political styles among western publics. Princeton, [1977]. pp. 482. *bibliog.*

— Germany.

SCHOLDER (KLAUS) Die Problematik der politischen Verantwortung in unserer jüngsten Geschichte. Wiesbaden, 1959. pp. 42. (Institut für Europäische Geschichte. Vorträge. Nr. 27)

— Ireland (Republic).

POLITICAL culture in Ireland: the views of two generations; [by] John Raven [and others]; with an introduction by John H. Whyte. Dublin, [1976]. pp. 206.

— Norway.

MARTINUSSEN (WILLY) The distant democracy: social inequality, political resources and political influence in Norway. London, [1977]. pp. 246. bibliog. Based on the author's Fjerndemokratiet.

— Russia.

GRUPPENINTERESSEN und Entscheidungsprozess in der Sowjetunion; herausgegeben von Boris Meissner und Georg Brunner. Köln, [1975]. pp. 264. Papers based on the proceedings of a conference held in 1973.

— Turkey.

LEDER (ARNOLD) Catalysts of change: Marxist versus Muslim in a Turkish community. Austin, Texas, [1976]. pp. 56. bibliog. (Texas University. Center for Middle Eastern Studies. Middle East Monographs. No. 1)

ÖZBUDUN (ERGUN) Social change and political participation in Turkey. Princeton, N.J., [1976]. pp. 254. bibliog.

— United Kingdom.

HAIN (PETER) Radical regeneration. London, [1975]. pp. 181.

HALL (DEREK) Local participation and neighbourhood councils in Portsmouth. Portsmouth, [1976]. pp. 16. (Social Services Research and Intelligence Unit [Portsmouth]. Information Sheets. No. 28)

HILL (MICHAEL J.) The state, administration and the individual. London, 1976. pp. 256. bibliog.

— United States.

HOLBERT (ROBERT LEE) Tax law and political access: the bias of pluralism revisited. Beverly Hills, [1975]. pp. 72. bibliog.

RYAN (JOHN PAUL) Cultural diversity and the American experience: political participation among blacks, Appalachians, and Indians. Beverly Hills, [1975]. pp. 64. bibliog.

KIRKPATRICK (JEANE J.) The new presidential elite: men and women in national politics. New York, [1976]. pp. 605.

McKENNA (GEORGE) American politics: ideals and realities. New York, [1976]. pp. 345.

URBAN governance and minorities; edited by Herrington J. Bryce. New York, 1976. pp. 220. Based on a one-day Public Policy Forum on Urban Governance held in Washington in 1975 and sponsored by the Joint Center for Political Studies.

BERGER (PETER L.) and NEUHAUS (RICHARD JOHN) To empower people: the role of mediating structures in public policy. Washington, [1977]. pp. 45. (American Enterprise Institute for Public Policy Research. AEI Studies. 139)

INGLEHART (RONALD) The silent revolution: changing values and political styles among western publics. Princeton, [1977]. pp. 482. bibliog.

— — Bibliography.

HUTCHESON (JOHN D.) and SHEVIN (JANN) compilers. Citizen groups in local politics: a bibliographic review. Santa Barbara, [1976]. pp. 275. bibliogs.

POLITICAL PARTIES.

RIVANERA CARLES (FEDERICO) Los partidos politicos: representantes del pueblo o de la burguesia?. Buenos Aires, [1973]. pp. 137. bibliog.

LAWSON (KAY) The comparative study of political parties. New York, [1976]. pp. 261. bibliog.

BUDGE (IAN) and FARLIE (DENNIS) Voting and party competition: a theoretical critique and synthesis applied to surveys from ten democracies. London, [1977]. pp. 555.

— Africa, Subsaharan.

SILVEIRA (ONESIMO) Africa south of the Sahara: party systems and ideologies of socialism. Uppsala, [1976]. pp. 212. bibliog. (Uppsala, Statsvetenskapliga Föreningen. Skrifter. 71) Doctoral thesis, Uppsala University, 1976.

— America, Latin.

RATLIFF (WILLIAM E.) Castroism and communism in Latin America, 1959-1976: the varieties of Marxist-Leninist experience. Stanford, Calif., 1976. pp. 240. (American Enterprise Institute for Public Policy Research and Stanford University. Hoover Institution on War, Revolution and Peace. AEI-Hoover Policy Studies. 19)

— Argentine Republic.

DANA MONTAÑO (SALVADOR M.) Contribucion al estudio del cambio del regimen representativo argentino: legislacion electoral y de los partidos politicos. Buenos Aires, 1972. pp. 102.

ANDINO (RAMON) and PAREDES (EDUARDO J.) Breve historia de los partidos politicos argentinos. Buenos Aires, [1974]. pp. 259. bibliog.

— Australia.

AITKIN (DONALD ALEXANDER) Stability and change in Australian politics. Canberra, 1977. pp. 301.

— Brazil.

CARDOSO (FERNANDO HENRIQUE) and LAMOUNIER (BOLIVAR) eds. Os partidos e as eleições no Brasil. Rio de Janeiro, 1975. pp. 262.

— Canada.

MEISEL (JOHN) Working papers on Canadian politics. 2nd ed. Montreal, 1973. pp. 257.

— France.

MITTERRAND (FRANÇOIS) Un plan pour la Fédération. Paris, [1966]. pp. 38. (Convention des Institutions Républicaines. Cahiers. 1) (Supplément à Combat Républicain, no. 14, mars 1966)

TOUCHARD (JEAN) La gauche en France depuis 1900. Paris, [1977]. pp. 383. bibliog.

— Germany.

AUTHIER (DENIS) and BARROT (JEAN) La gauche communiste en Allemagne, 1918-1921; avec des textes de H. Laufenberg, F. Wolffheim, H. Gorter, H. Roland-Holst, A. Pannekoek; traduits par Denis Authier. Paris, 1976. pp. 390.

GRAF (WILLIAM DAVID) The German left since 1945: socialism and social democracy in the German Federal Republic. Cambridge, [1976]. pp. 318. bibliog.

GRUBE (FRANK) and others. Politische Planung in Parteien und Parlamentsfraktionen. Göttingen, [1976]. pp. 244. bibliog. (Kommission für Wirtschaftlichen und Sozialen Wandel. Schriften. 122)

HAMMER (ECKEHARD) Möglichkeiten einer Wiedereingliederung verfassungsfeindlicher Parteien. Berlin, [1976]. pp. 253. bibliog.

LEHMBRUCH (GERHARD) Parteienwettbewerb im Bundesstaat. Stuttgart, [1976]. pp. 187. bibliog.

Das STAATSVERSTAENDNIS der Parteien in der Bundesrepublik Deutschland; mit Beiträgen von Christian H. Hoffmann [and others];...Redaktion Holger Christian Asmussen. Bonn, [1976]. pp. 109. bibliog. (Politische Akademie Eichholz. Untersuchungen und Beiträge zu Politik und Zeitgeschehen. Band 22)

AUF dem Weg zum Einparteienstaat; herausgegeben von Wolf- Dieter Narr; mit Beiträgen von Johannes Agnoli [and others]. Opladen, [1977]. pp. 249. bibliogs. Essays offered to Wolfgang Abendroth on his 70th birthday.

GREVEN (MICHAEL TH.) Parteien und politische Herrschaft: zur Interdependenz von innerparteilicher Ordnung und Demokratie in der BRD. Meisenheim am Glan, 1977. pp. 414. bibliog.

See also FREISOZIALE UNION; KOMMUNISTISCHE ARBEITER-PARTEI DEUTSCHLANDS.

— India.

FICKETT (LEWIS P.) The major socialist parties of India: a study in leftist fragmentation. Syracuse, N.Y., 1976. pp. 185. (Syracuse University. Maxwell Graduate School of Citizenship and Public Affairs. Foreign and Comparative Studies. South Asian Series. No. 2)

— Ireland (Republic).

GALLAGHER (MICHAEL) Electoral support for Irish political parties 1927-1973. London, [1976]. pp. 75. bibliog.

— Israel.

SCHIFF (GARY S.) Tradition and politics: the religious parties of Israel. Detroit, 1977. pp. 267. bibliog. (Columbia University. Middle East Institute. Modern Middle East Series. vol.9)

— Italy.

PALMA (GIUSEPPE DI) Surviving without governing: the Italian parties in Parliament. Berkeley, Calif., [1977]. pp. 299.

— Mexico.

COSTELOE (MICHAEL P.) La primera Republica Federal de Mexico, 1824-1835: un estudio de los partidos politicos en el Mexico independiente; traduccion de Manuel Fernandez Gasalla. Mexico, 1975. pp. 492. bibliog.

Los PARTIDOS politicos de Mexico; ([by] Jose Angel Conchello [and others]). Mexico, 1975. pp. 476.

— Pakistan.

PAKISTAN. Attorney-General. 1975. Attorney General Yahya Bakhtiar's opening address in the Supreme Court of Pakistan in the reference by the Islamic Republic of Pakistan on dissolution of National Awami Party, Rawalpindi, June 19, 20 and 23, 1975. [Islamabad, 1975?]. pp. 95.

PAKISTAN. Supreme Court. 1975. Supreme Court judgement on dissolution of N[ational] A[wami] P[arty], Rawalpindi, October 30, 1975. [Islamabad, 1975?]. pp. 226.

PAKISTAN. Attorney-General. 1976. Concluding address in Supreme Court by Yahya Bakhtiar...in government's reference on N[ational] A[wami] P[arty]'s dissolution, Rawalpindi, September 8-17, 1975. [Islamabad, 1976]. pp. 251.

— Papua New Guinea.

STEPHEN (DAVID) A history of political parties in Papua New Guinea. Melbourne, 1972. pp. 188. bibliog.

— Puerto Rico.

QUINTERO RIVERA (ANGEL GUILLERMO) The working class and Puerto Rican politics in the process of change from a traditional to a capitalist agricultural economy. 1976. fo. 464. bibliog. Typescript. Ph.D.(London) thesis: unpublished. This thesis is the property of London University and may not be removed from the Library.

POLITICAL PARTIES.(Cont.)

— Spain.

ARTOLA GALLEGO (MIGUEL) Partidos y programas politicos, 1808-1936. Madrid, 1975-77. 2 vols. *bibliog.*

ALFONSO BOZZO (ALFONSO) Los partidos politicos y la autonomia en Galicia, 1931-1936. Madrid, [1976]. pp. 392. *bibliog.*

— United Kingdom.

WHITE PANTHER PARTY U.K. Our programme: July 1971. London, [1971]. pp. 3.

— United States.

GOSNELL (HAROLD FOOTE) and SMOLKA (RICHARD G.) American parties and elections. Columbus, Ohio, [1976]. pp. 288.

TRILLING (RICHARD J.) Party image and electoral behavior. New York, [1976]. pp. 234.

ZVESPER (JOHN) Political philosophy and rhetoric: a study of the origins of American party politics. Cambridge, 1977. pp. 237.

— — States.

HUCKSHORN (ROBERT JACK) Party leadership in the states. [Amherst, Mass.], 1976. pp. 300.

POLITICAL PLAYS

— South Africa.

INTERNATIONAL DEFENCE AND AID FUND. Fact Papers on Southern Africa. No. 2. Black theatre in South Africa. London, 1976. pp. 11.

POLITICAL POETRY, ENGLISH.

[WOLCOT (JOHN)] Choice cabinet pictures; with a few portraits done to the life: by Peter Pindar, Esq. [pseud.]. London, S.W. Fores, 1817. pp. 40.

ASMODEUS (JUAN) pseud. A political lecture on heads, alias blockheads!!: a characteristic poem, containing the heads of Derry Down Triangle...and the Grand Lama of the Kremlin; drawn from craniological inspection, after the manner of doctors Gall and Spurzheim, of Vienna. 3rd ed. London, J. Fairburn, [1820]. pp. 35.

The ASSES' skin memorandum book, lost in St. Paul's; to which is added, a condolence with the ultras, etc. etc. etc.; (Old Tom, editor). London, Wright, 1820. pp. 15. *Verse satire on Alderman Matthew Wood, friend and adviser to Queen Caroline.*

[SLOP, Dr., pseud.] Slop's shave at a broken Hone. London, Wright, 1820. pp. 42. *Satires in verse on W. Hone anticipating his "Slap at Slop".*

[TOM, Old, of Oxford, pseud.] The new Christmas budget, etc. London, Wright, 1820. pp. 15. *Satires in verse on the Queen and her supporters.*

TOM, Old, of Oxford, pseud. Types of the times. London, Wright, 1820. pp. 32.

POLITICAL PRISONERS.

MORAND (BERNADETTE) Les écrits des prisonniers politiques. [Paris], 1976. pp. 267. *bibliog.*

MORRIS (COLIN) Christian writer. The captive conscience. [London], 1977. pp. 26.

— Argentine Republic.

AMNESTY INTERNATIONAL. Report of an Amnesty International mission to Argentina, 6-15 November 1976. London, 1977. pp. 92.

— Chile.

CAYUELA (JOSE) ed. Chile: la masacre de un pueblo: testimonios de nueve venezolanos victimas del golpe militar chileno. Caracas, [1973]. pp. 109.

— — Personal narratives.

VALDES (HERNAN) Diary of a Chilean concentration camp;...translated [from the Spanish] by Jo Labanyi. London, 1975. pp. 160.

— China.

PASQUALINI (JEAN) and CHELMINSKI (RUDOLPH) Prisoner of Mao. Harmondsworth, 1973. pp. 326.

— Cuba.

GOLENDORF (PIERRE) 7 ans à Cuba: 38 mois dans les prisons de Fidel Castro. Paris, [1976]. pp. 319.

— Czechoslovakia.

AMNESTY INTERNATIONAL. Briefing Papers. No. 9. Czechoslovakia. London, 1977. pp. 16.

— France — Personal narratives.

TALEB (AHMED) Lettres de prison, (1957-1961). Alger, 1966. pp. 189.

— Guatemala.

AMNESTY INTERNATIONAL. Briefing Papers. No. 8. Guatemala. London, 1976. pp. 17.

— Indonesia.

TAPOL (BRITISH CAMPAIGN FOR THE RELEASE OF INDONESIAN POLITICAL PRISONERS) Indonesia: unions behind bars. London, 1976. pp. 20. *(Tapol Background and Information Series. No. 2)*

— Israel.

LEBANESE ASSOCIATION FOR INFORMATION ON PALESTINE. Palestinian political prisoners and repression in Israel and the occupied territories. n.p. 1975. pp. 12.

— Malawi.

AMNESTY INTERNATIONAL. Briefing Papers. No. 5. Malawi. London, 1976. pp. 9.

— Paraguay.

AMNESTY INTERNATIONAL. Briefing Papers. No. 4. Paraguay. London, 1976. pp. 13.

— Philippine Islands.

AMNESTY INTERNATIONAL. Report of...mission to the Republic of the Philippines, 22 November-5 December 1975. London, [1976]. pp. 60.

— Rhodesia.

AMNESTY INTERNATIONAL. Briefing Papers. No. 2. Rhodesia/Zimbabwe. London, 1976. pp. 13.

— Russia.

ISTORIIA bolezni Leonida Pliushcha; sostavlenie i kommentarii Tat'iany Khodorovich. Amsterdam, 1974. pp. 208.

MEEUS (ANTHONY DE) White book on the internment of dissenters in Soviet mental hospitals. Brussels, [1975?]. pp. 139. *Translated from the French original.*

— Singapore.

AMNESTY INTERNATIONAL. Briefing Papers. No. 1. The Republic of Singapore. London, 1976. pp. 9.

— Spain.

FERNANDEZ (ALBERTO) Procès à Madrid: des fées, des hommes et des bourreaux; récit. Paris, [1973]. pp. 202.

LIBRO blanco sobre las carceles franquistas, 1939-1976; (by Angel Suarez [pseud. and] Colectivo 36). [Paris, 1976]. pp. 312. *bibliog.*

— Taiwan.

AMNESTY INTERNATIONAL. Briefing Papers. No. 6. Taiwan (Republic of China). London, 1976. pp. 11.

— Yemen, Southern.

AMNESTY INTERNATIONAL. Briefing Papers. No. 3. People's Democratic Republic of Yemen. London, 1976. pp. 12.

POLITICAL PSYCHOLOGY.

ELMS (ALAN C.) Personality in politics. New York, [1976]. pp. 200. *bibliog.*

ENZENSBERGER (HANS MAGNUS) Raids and reconstructions: essays on politics, crime and culture; translations by Michael Roloff [and others]. London, 1976. pp. 312.

ODAJNYK (VOLODYMYR WALTER) Jung and politics: the political and social ideas of C. G. Jung. New York, 1976. pp. 190.

SEGAL (MARSHALL H.) Human behavior and public policy: a political psychology. New York, [1976]. pp. 321. *bibliog.*

HUMAN nature in politics; edited by J. Roland Pennock and John W. Chapman. New York, 1977. pp. 348. *bibliog. (American Society for Political and Legal Philosophy. Nomos. 17)*

A PSYCHOLOGICAL examination of political leaders; edited by Margaret G. Hermann with Thomas W. Milburn. New York, [1977]. pp. 516. *bibliog.*

POLITICAL QUESTIONS AND JUDICIAL POWER

— Israel.

ZEMACH (YAACOV S.) Political questions in the courts: a judicial function in democracies; Israel and the United States. Detroit, 1976. pp. 296. *bibliog.*

— United States.

ZEMACH (YAACOV S.) Political questions in the courts: a judicial function in democracies; Israel and the United States. Detroit, 1976. pp. 296. *bibliog.*

POLITICAL SCIENCE.

KAMIENNA (ADA) Diktatur der Arbeit: der wahre Sinn der kommenden Ordnung; von einer im Weltkrieg erwachten "Bürgerlichen". Zürich, 1920. pp. 8.

HASS (ERNST) Die Chance: Politik als angewandte Wissenschaft vom Menschen. München, [1962]. pp. 253. *bibliog.*

ROUSSEAU (JEAN JACQUES) The first and second discourses; edited, with introduction and notes, by Roger D. Masters; translated by Roger D. and Judith R. Masters. New York, [1964]. pp. 248.

FRAGA IRIBARNE (MANUEL) El desarrollo politico. Madrid, 1971 repr. 1975. pp. 317.

JAGUARIBE (HELIO) Sociedad, cambio y sistema politico: desarrollo politico; una investigacion en teoria social y politica y un estudio del caso latinoamericano. Buenos Aires, 1972. pp. 226. *bibliog.*

KONRAD, von Megenberg. Werke. Ökonomik. Buch I; herausgegeben von Sabine Krüger. Stuttgart, 1973. pp. 390. *bibliog. (Monumenta Germaniae Historica. Staatsschriften des Späteren Mittelalters. 3.Band. Die Werke des Konrad von Megenberg. 5. Stück. Yconomica) In Latin.*

CONDE (FRANCISCO JAVIER) Escritos y fragmentos politicos. Madrid, 1974. 2 vols.

BONNOT DE MABLY (GABRIEL) Sur la théorie du pouvoir politique; introduction et notes par Peter Friedmann. Paris, [1975]. pp. 288.

CHAMPION DE CRESPIGNY (ANTHONY RICHARD) and CRONIN (JEREMY) eds. Ideologies of politics. Cape Town, 1975. pp. 160.

BERNSTEIN (RICHARD J.) The restructuring of social and political theory. New York, [1976]. pp. 286. *bibliog.*

BRAMS (STEVEN J.) Paradoxes in politics: an introduction to the nonobvious in political science. New York, [1976]. pp. 231.

GODWIN (WILLIAM) Enquiry concerning political justice and its influence on modern morals and happiness; [edited by Isaac Kramnick]. Harmondsworth, 1976. pp. 825. *bibliog.*

MEADOWS (MARTIN) The discipline sans histories: the curious case of political science. [1976]. fo. 17. *Typescript: unpublished. Paper presented at the Political Studies Association Conference, Nottingham, 1976.*

BALL (ALAN R.) Modern politics and government. 2nd ed. London, 1977. pp. 276. *bibliog.*

CROPSEY (JOSEPH) Political philosophy and the issues of politics. Chicago, 1977. pp. 329.

HANSEN (EMMANUEL) Frantz Fanon: social and political thought. Ohio, [1977]. pp. 232. *bibliog.*

HARRINGTON (JAMES) Author of "Oceana". The political works of James Harrington; edited with an introduction by J.G.A. Pocock. Cambridge, 1977. pp. 878.

HUMAN nature in politics; edited by J. Roland Pennock and John W. Chapman. New York, 1977. pp. 348. *bibliog. (American Society for Political and Legal Philosophy. Nomos. 17)*

KENNEDY (ELLEN LEE) 'Freedom' and 'the open society': Henri Bergson's contribution to political philosophy. 1977. fo. 278. *bibliog. Typescript. Ph.D. (London) thesis: unpublished. This thesis is the property of London University and may not be removed from the Library.*

LUKES (STEVEN) Essays in social theory. London, 1977. pp. 227.

MARX (KARL) Selected writings; edited by David McLellan. Oxford, 1977. pp. 625. *bibliogs.*

MILL (JOHN STUART) (Collected works of John Stuart Mill. vols. 18-19). Essays on politics and society;...editor of the text, J.M. Robson; introduction by Alexander Brody. Toronto, [1977]. 2 vols. *bibliog.*

MORRALL (JOHN BRIMYARD) Aristotle. London, 1977. pp. 120. *bibliog.*

SECONDAT (CHARLES LOUIS DE) Baron de Montesquieu. The political theory of Montesquieu; [edited by] Melvin Richter. Cambridge, 1977. pp. 355.

VAN DALEN (HENDRIK) and ZEIGLER (LUTHER HARMON) Introduction to political science: people, politics, and perception. Englewood Cliffs, [1977]. pp. 275. *bibliogs.*

WINTER (HERBERT R.) and BELLOWS (THOMAS J.) People and politics: an introduction to political science. New York, [1977]. pp. 514. *bibliogs.*

— Bibliography.

BIBLIOGRAFIIA obshchestvenno-politicheskoi literatury, etc. 2nd ed. Moskva, 1968-76. 2 vols.

— Congresses.

POLITICAL STUDIES ASSOCIATION OF THE UNITED KINGDOM. Annual Conference, 1970. [Papers presented to the Conference]. 1970. 10 pts.(in 1 vol.)

POLITICAL STUDIES ASSOCIATION OF THE UNITED KINGDOM. Annual Conference, 1977. [Papers presented to the Conference]. 1977. 13 pts.(in 1 vol.)

— Decision making.

BRECHER (MICHAEL) Decisions in Israel's foreign policy. London, 1974. pp. 639. *bibliog.*

SHAFFER (WILLIAM R.) and WEBER (RONALD E.) Policy responsiveness in the American states. Beverly Hills, [1974]. pp. 64. *bibliog.*

HORELICK (ARNOLD LAWRENCE) and others. The study of Soviet foreign policy: decision-theory-related approaches. Beverly Hills, [1975]. pp. 79. *bibliog.*

WHAT government does; Matthew Holden and Dennis L. Dresang, editors. Beverly Hills, [1975]. pp. 320. *bibliogs.*

ASHFORD (DOUGLAS ELLIOTT) Democracy, decentralization and decisions in subnational politics. Beverly Hills, [1976]. pp. 59. *bibliog.*

BATTY (MICHAEL) A political theory of planning and design, incorporating concepts of collective decision-making and social power. Reading, 1976. pp. 64. *bibliog. (Reading. University. Department of Geography. Reading Geographical Papers. No. 45)*

The DYNAMICS of Soviet politics. Cambridge, Mass., 1976. pp. 427. *(Harvard University. Russian Research Center. Studies. 76)*

ANDERSON (CHARLES WILLIAM) Statecraft: an introduction to political choice and judgment. New York, [1977]. pp. 318. *bibliogs.*

GRINDLE (MERILEE SERRILL) Bureaucrats, politicians, and peasants in Mexico. Berkeley, [1977]. pp. 220. *bibliog.*

— — Mathematical models.

YOUNG (H.P.) Power, prices, and incomes in voting systems. Laxenburg, 1977. pp. 28. *bibliog. (International Institute for Applied Systems Analysis. Research Memoranda. RM-77-5)*

— Dictionaries and encyclopedias.

ZAHN (HANS E.) Wörterbuch zur Politik und Wirtschaftspolitik. Band I: deutsch-englisch-französisch:...Dictionary of politics and economic policy...: Dictionnaire politique et de politique économique, etc. Frankfurt am Main, [1975]. pp. 382. *bibliog.*

DIZIONARIO di politica; diretto da Norberto Bobbio e Nicola Matteucci; redattore Gianfranco Pasquino. Torino, [1976]. pp. 1097.

— History.

POLITICHESKIE ucheniia: istoriia i sovremennost'. Moskva, 1976 in progress.

CONTEMPORARY political philosophers; edited by Anthony de Crespigny and Kenneth Minogue. London, 1976. pp. 296. *bibliog.*

— — America, Latin.

WILLIAMS (EDWARD J.) Latin American political thought: a developmental perspective. Tucson, Arizona, [1974]. pp. 69. *bibliog. (Arizona University. Institute of Government Research. Comparative Government Studies. No. 6)*

— — Europe.

SCHELLHASE (KENNETH C.) Tacitus in renaissance political thought. Chicago, 1976. pp. 270. *bibliog.*

— — Germany.

JUNG (OTMAR) Zum Kulturstaatsbegriff: Johann Gottlieb Fichte; Verfassung des Freistaates Bayern; Godesberger Grundsatzprogramm der SPD. Meisenheim am Glan, 1976. pp. 255. *bibliog.*

BRUECKNER (JUTTA) Staatswissenschaften, Kameralismus und Naturrecht: ein Beitrag zur Geschichte der Politischen Wissenschaft im Deutschland des späten 17. und frühen 18. Jahrhunderts. München, [1977]. pp. 323. *bibliog. (Munich. University. Geschwister-Scholl- Institut für Politische Wissenschaft. Münchener Studien zur Politik. 27. Band)*

— — Russia.

MAVRODIN (VLADIMIR VASIL'EVICH) Klassovaia bor'ba i obshchestvenno-politicheskaia mysl' v Rossii v XVIII veke, 1773-1790 gg.: kurs lektsii. Leningrad, 1975. pp. 214. *bibliog.*

— — — White Russia.

MOKHNACH (NINEL' NIKOLAEVNA) Ot Prosveshcheniia k revoliutsionnomu demokratizmu: obshchestvenno-politicheskaia i filosofskaia mysl' Belorussii kontsa 10-kh - nachala 50-kh godov XIX v. Minsk, 1976. pp. 184.

SAMBUK (SUSANNA MIKHAILOVNA) Obshchestvenno-politicheskaia mysl' Belorussii vo vtoroi polovine XIX veka: po materialam periodicheskoi pechati. Minsk, 1976. pp. 183.

— — Spain.

FERNÁNDEZ-SANTAMARIA (J.A.) The state, war and peace: Spanish political thought in the renaissance, 1516-1559. Cambridge, 1977. pp. 316. *bibliog.*

— — United Kingdom.

HARVIE (CHRISTOPHER) The lights of Liberalism: university Liberals and the challenge of democracy, 1860-86. London, 1976. pp. 343.

CAMDEN SOCIETY. [Publications]. 4th Series. vol. 18. Four English political tracts of the Later Middle Ages; edited...by Jean-Philippe Genet. London, 1977. pp. 229.

— — United States.

COLEMAN (FRANK M.) Hobbes and America: exploring the constitutional foundations. Toronto, [1977]. pp. 159.

KARIEL (HENRY S.) Beyond liberalism, where relations grow. San Francisco, [1977]. pp. 137.

— Mathematical models.

NAGEL (STUART S.) and NEEF (MARIAN) Operations research methods as applied to political science and the legal process. Beverly Hills, [1976]. pp. 76. *bibliog.*

— Methodology.

CZUDNOWSKI (MOSHE M.) Comparing political behavior. Beverly Hills, [1976]. pp. 178. *bibliog.*

GARSON (G. DAVID) Political science methods. Boston, Mass., [1976]. pp. 540.

DINKEL (REINER) Der Zusammenhang zwischen der ökonomischen und politischen Entwicklung in einer Demokratie: eine Untersuchung mit Hilfe der ökonomischen Theorie der Politik. Berlin, [1977]. pp. 259. *bibliog.*

POLITICAL SOCIALIZATION.

DEMUNTER (PAUL) Luttes politiques au Zaïre: le processus de politisation des masses rurales du Bas-Zaïre. Paris, [1975]. pp. 333. *bibliog.*

POLITICAL socialization in eastern Europe: a comparative framework: [based on a panel held during the Annual Meeting of the American Political Science Association in Washington, 1972]; (edited by Ivan Volgyes). New York, 1975. pp. 199.

KRAUS (SIDNEY) and DAVIS (DENNIS) The effects of mass communication on political behavior. University Park, Pa., [1976]. pp. 308.

MERELMAN (RICHARD M.) Political reasoning in adolescence: some bridging themes. Beverly Hills, [1976]. pp. 37. *bibliog.*

PAMMETT (JON H.) and WHITTINGTON (MICHAEL S.) eds. Foundations of political culture: political socialization in Canada. Toronto, [1976]. pp. 318.

POLITICAL culture in Ireland: the views of two generations; [by] John Raven [and others]; with an introduction by John H. Whyte. Dublin, [1976]. pp. 206.

ABRAMSON (PAUL R.) The political socialization of black Americans: a critical evaluation of research on efficacy and trust. New York, [1977]. pp. 195. *bibliog.*

STRADLING (ROBERT) The political awareness of the school leaver. London, [1977]. pp. 81. *(Hansard Society for Parliamentary Government and Politics Association. Programme For Political Education)*

POLITICAL SOCIOLOGY.

ENZENSBERGER (HANS MAGNUS) Raids and reconstructions: essays on politics, crime and culture; translations by Michael Roloff [and others]. London, 1976. pp. 312.

HALEBSKY (SANDOR) Mass society and political conflict: toward a reconstruction of theory. Cambridge, 1976. pp. 309.

KRADER (LAWRENCE) Dialectic of civil society. Assen, 1976. pp. 279.

ROBINS (ROBERT S.) Political institutionalization and the integration of elites. Beverly Hills, [1976]. pp. 220. bibliog.

ROSE (RICHARD) ed. Studies in British politics: a reader in political sociology. 3rd ed. London, 1976. pp. 547. bibliog.

GIDDENS (ANTHONY) Studies in social and political theory. London, 1977. pp. 416.

MARTIN (RODERICK) The sociology of power. London, 1977. pp. 203.

POLITICAL generations and political development; edited by Richard J. Samuels. Lexington, Mass., [1977]. pp. 141. Based on the 1975-1976 Harvard-MIT Joint Seminar on Political Development.

WINTER (HERBERT R.) and BELLOWS (THOMAS J.) People and politics: an introduction to political science. New York, [1977]. pp. 514. bibliogs.

POLITICS, PRACTICAL.

BULLITT (STIMSON) To be a politician. rev.ed. New Haven, 1977. pp. 294.

POLITICS AND EDUCATION.

JENNINGS (ROBERT E.) Education and politics: policy-making in local education authorities. London, 1977. pp. 214. bibliog.

POLITICS IN LITERATURE.

KELLY (GARY) The English Jacobin novel, 1780-1805. Oxford, 1976. pp. 291. bibliog.

BRANTLINGER (PATRICK) The spirit of reform: British literature and politics, 1832-1867. Cambridge, Mass., 1977. pp. 293.

HALPERIN (JOHN) Trollope and politics: a study of the Pallisers and others. London, 1977. pp. 318. bibliog.

WATSON (GEORGE) Politics and literature in modern Britain. London, 1977. pp. 190.

POLITICS IN MOVING PICTURES.

MACBEAN (JAMES ROY) Film and revolution. Bloomington, Ind., [1975]. pp. 339.

POLLUTION.

SCORER (RICHARD SEGAR) A radical approach to pollution, population and resources. London, [1973]. pp. 32. (Liberal Party. Strategy 2,000. 1st Series. No.1)

CIBA FOUNDATION. Symposia. New Series. 32. Health and industrial growth; [editors Katherine Elliott and Julie Knight]. Amsterdam, 1975. pp. 267. bibliogs.

The CONSUMER society; edited by I.R.C. Hirst and W. Duncan Reekie. London, 1977. pp. 198. bibliogs. Papers of a seminar organised by the Faculty of Social Sciences, Edinburgh University, 1973.

— Economic aspects.

ATKINS (M.H.) and LOWE (J.F.) Pollution control costs in industry: an economic study. Oxford, 1977. pp. 166.

KNEESE (ALLEN V.) Economics and the environment. Harmondsworth, 1977. pp. 286.

— — Netherlands.

NETHERLANDS. Centraal Planbureau. 1975. Economische gevolgen van bestrijding van milieuverontreiniging. 's-Gravenhage, 1975. pp. 104. (Monografieën. No. 20)

— — United States.

ENERGY and the environment: a structural analysis; edited by Anne P. Carter. Hanover, N.H.,1976. pp. 262. bibliogs. Based on work carried out by a research team from Harvard and Brandeis universities.

— Europe.

EUROPEAN NATIONAL STUDENT ORGANISATIONS. European Meeting, 10th, Helsinki, 1972. Environmental pollution: an all-European problem. Prague, [1972]. pp. 31.

— Ireland (Republic).

EIRE. Industrial Development Authority. 1976. A survey of pollution in Ireland. Dublin, 1976. pp. 31. (Publication Series. Paper 2)

— Sweden.

LUNDQVIST (LENNART J.) The case of mercury pollution in Sweden: scientific information and public response. Stockholm, 1974. pp. 55. bibliog. (Sweden. Forskningsekonomiska Kommittén. Rapporter. 4)

— United Kingdom.

DIGEST OF ENVIRONMENTAL STATISTICS: environmental protection and conservation; [pd. by] Department of the Environment. a., 1976 (1st)- London.

OCEANIC management: conflicting uses of the Celtic Sea and other western U.K. waters: report of a conference held at University College of Swansea, 19-22 September 1975; edited by M.M. Sibthorp, assisted by M. Unwin. London, [1977]. pp. 220. Conference organised by the David Davies Memorial Institute of International Studies.

POLSKI ZWIAZEK ZACHODNI.

MROCZKO (MARIAN) Związek Obrony Kresów Zachodnich, 1921-1934: powstanie i działalność. Gdańsk, 1977. pp. 264. bibliog.

POLYNESIA

— Politics and government.

PANOFF (MICHEL) Aspects méconnus de la vie politique en Polynésie française. Paris, 1964. fo. 8. (Paris. Ecole Pratique des Hautes Etudes. Centre Documentaire pour l'Océanie. Rapports et Documents. 4)

POMPIDOU (GEORGES).

MARTINET (GILLES) Le système Pompidou. Paris, [1973]. pp. 188.

PONIATOWSKI (MICHEL CASIMIR) Prince.

PONIATOWSKI (MICHEL CASIMIR) Prince. Cartes sur table. [Paris, 1972]. pp. 250.

POOR.

SURINGAR (WILLEM HENDRIK DOMINICUS) Rede über das Bedürfniss einer zwechmässigern Armenpflege und der Errichtung eines Patronats sowie über das bei seiner Ausübung zu beobachtende Verfahren; gehalten zu Amsterdam am 22. Januar 1842, etc. Kitzingen, Dürr, [1842]. pp. 29.

— Information services — United Kingdom.

BRADSHAW (JONATHAN) and others. Batley welfare benefits project. [York, 1976]. pp. 33. (Papers in Community Studies. No. 5)

NORTH TYNESIDE COMMUNITY DEVELOPMENT PROJECT. Welfare rights: the North Shields campaign, summer 1975. North Shields, [1976?]. pp. 84.

TAYLOR-GOOBY (PETER) and LAKEMAN (SUSAN) Welfare benefits advocacy (in Batley): official discretion and claimants' rights. [York], 1977. pp. 45. bibliog. (Papers in Community Studies. No. 11)

— Belgium.

LETTRE d'un patriote bruxellois, à un patriote gantois, sur la mendicité, les enfans trouvés, et un monument à élever à la gloire des auteurs de la révolution pour la liberté des Pays- Bas. Bruxelles, the Author, 1790. pp. 7.

— Canada.

JOHNSON (LEO A.) Poverty in wealth: the capitalist labour market and income distribution in Canada. rev. ed. Toronto, 1974. pp. 35.

— Germany.

VASKOVICS (LASZLO A.) Segregierte Armut: Randgruppenbildung in Notunterkünften. Frankfurt/Main, [1976]. pp. 216. bibliog.

— Portugal.

CARVALHO (MANOEL PEDRO HENRIQUES DE) Noticia historica sobre a origem da pobresa e da mendicidade, das suas causas mais influentes, dos seus espantosos progresos, finalmente dos meios que tem tentado em algumas nações para reprimir uma, e anniquillar a outra. Lisboa, Nery, 1835. pp. 46.

— Rhodesia.

RIDDELL (ROGER C.) and HARRIS (PETER S.) The poverty datum line as a wage fixing standard: an application to Rhodesia. Gwelo, 1975. pp. 96.

— South Africa.

POTGIETER (J.F.) The household subsistence level in the major urban centres of the Republic of South Africa, October, 1976. Port Elizabeth, 1976. pp. 56. (University of Port Elizabeth. Institute for Planning Research. Fact Papers. No.18)

— Switzerland — Vaud (Canton).

BRIOD (ALICE) L'assistance des pauvres au moyen âge dans le Pays de Vaud. Lausanne, [1976]. pp. 120. First published in 1926 under the title, L'assistance des pauvres dans le Pays de Vaud du commencement du moyen âge à la fin du XVIe siècle.

— Underdeveloped areas.

See UNDERDEVELOPED AREAS — Poor.

— United Kingdom.

ALCOCK (THOMAS) Observations on the defects of the poor laws, and on the causes and consequences of the great increase and burden of the poor, with a proposal for redressing these grievances, in a letter to a member of Parliament. London, printed for R. Baldwin, etc., 1752. pp. 76.

MORAL annals of the poor, and middle ranks of society, in various situations of good and bad conduct. Durham, Pennington, 1793. pp. xv, 44.

HILL (JOHN) M.R.C.S. The means of reforming the morals of the poor, by the prevention of poverty; and a plan for meliorating the condition of parish paupers, and diminishing the enormous expence of maintaining them. London, Hatchard, 1801. pp. iii-xx, 5-157.

HORTON (Sir ROBERT JOHN WILMOT) The causes and remedies of pauperism in the United Kingdom considered: introductory series: being a defence of the principles and conduct of the Emigration Committee against the charges of Mr. Sadler. London, Lloyd, 1830. pp. viii, 150.

HORTON (Sir ROBERT JOHN WILMOT) Causes and remedies of pauperism: fourth series: explanation of Mr. Wilmot Horton's Bill in a letter and queries addressed to N.W.Senior...with his answers, etc. London, Lloyd, 1830. pp. vi, 3-112, xxiv.

HORTON (Sir ROBERT JOHN WILMOT) An inquiry into the causes and remedies of pauperism: first series: containing correspondence with C. Poulett Thomson, Esq., M.P., upon the conditions under which colonization would be justifiable as a national measure. 2nd ed. London, Lloyd, 1831. pp. 38.

HORTON (Sir ROBERT JOHN WILMOT) An inquiry into the causes and remedies of pauperism: second series: containing correspondence with M. Duchatel...; with an explanatory preface. 2nd ed. London, Lloyd, 1831. pp. 46.

LISTER (RUTH) ed. National welfare benefits handbook. 6th ed. London, 1976. pp. 88. *(Child Poverty Action Group. Poverty Pamphlets. 13)*

NATIONAL CONSUMER COUNCIL. Paying for fuel: interim report to the Secretary of State for Prices and Consumer Protection. London, 1976. pp. 30.

COMMUNITY DEVELOPMENT PROJECT. Gilding the ghetto: the state and the poverty experiments. [London, 1977]. pp. 64.

EDUCATION and the urban crisis; edited by Frank Field. London, 1977. pp. 149. *Based on two Gulbenkian conferences on education and the urban crisis.*

FIEGEHEN (GUY) and others. Poverty and progress in Britain, 1953-73: a statistical study of low income households: their numbers, types and expenditure patterns. Cambridge, 1977. pp. 173. *(National Institute of Economic and Social Research. Occasional Papers. 29)*

FIELD (FRANK) and others. To him who hath: a study of poverty and taxation. Harmondsworth, 1977. pp. 254.

— — Ireland.

HORTON (Sir ROBERT JOHN WILMOT) An inquiry into the causes and remedies of pauperism: third series: containing letters to Sir Francis Burdett, Bart, M. P. upon pauperism in Ireland. 2nd ed. London, Lloyd, 1831. pp. iv, 86.

— — Scotland.

LOCH (Sir CHARLES STEWART) Poor relief in Scotland: its statistics and development, 1791- 1891. New York, 1976. pp. 271-370. *Facsimile reprint of a paper read before the Royal Statistical Society in 1898.*

— — Wales.

WILDING (PAUL) Poverty: the facts in Wales. London, 1977. pp. 61. *(Child Poverty Action Group. Poverty Pamphlets. 29)*

— United States.

PLOTNICK (ROBERT D.) and SKIDMORE (FELICITY) Progress against poverty: a review of the 1964-1974 decade. New York, [1975]. pp. 247. *(Wisconsin University, Madison. Institute for Research on Poverty. Poverty Policy Analysis)*

BRINKER (PAUL A.) and KLOS (JOSEPH J.) Poverty, manpower, and social security. [2nd ed.]. Austin, Tex., [1976]. pp. 560. *bibliogs.*

LEVITAN (SAR A.) Programs in aid of the poor. 3rd ed. Baltimore, Md., [1976]. pp. 146. *bibliogs.*

PERLMAN (RICHARD) The economics of poverty. New York, [1976]. pp. 240.

MAGNUSON (NORRIS ALDEN) Salvation in the slums: evangelical social work, 1865-1920. Metuchen, N.J., 1977. pp. 299. *bibliog. (American Theological Library Association. ATLA Monograph Series. No. 10)*

WELFARE and the poor; edited by Lester A. Sobel. New York, [1977]. pp. 198. *Based on records compiled by Facts on File.*

POOR AS CONSUMERS

— United Kingdom.

NATIONAL CONSUMER COUNCIL. Means tested benefits. London, 1976. pp. 111. *(Discussion Papers. 3)*

FABIAN SOCIETY. Fabian Tracts. [No.] 447. A policy for warmth; [by] M. Gray [and others]. London, 1977. pp. 23.

WILLIAMS (FRANCES) ed. Why the poor pay more; edited...for the National Consumer Council. London, 1977. pp. 240.

POOR LAWS

— United Kingdom.

[BRUCE (Sir ALEXANDER)] Proposals for improving able beggars to the best advantage. [Edinburgh?, c. 1680]. pp. 3.

ALCOCK (THOMAS) Observations on the defects of the poor laws, and on the causes and consequences of the great increase and burden of the poor, with a proposal for redressing these grievances, in a letter to a member of Parliament. London, printed for R. Baldwin, etc., 1752. pp. 76.

HILL (JOHN) M.R.C.S. The means of reforming the morals of the poor, by the prevention of poverty; and a plan for meliorating the condition of parish paupers, and diminishing the enormous expence of maintaining them. London, Hatchard, 1801. pp. iii-xx, 5-157.

WAKEFIELD (EDWARD) 1774-1854. A letter to the land owners and other contributors to the poor's rates, in the Hundred of Dangye, in Essex. London, Johnson, [1802]. pp. 67.

BOLTON (ANDREW) Thoughts on the Poor Laws, in a letter to a friend, attempting to shew the causes of the increase of the poor rates, as well as pointing out who are benefited, or who suffer by such increase. London, Kirby, 1818. pp. 27.

HALCOMB (JOHN) A practical measure of relief from the present system of the poor-laws; submitted to the consideration of Parliament and the country, etc. London, J. Murray, 1826. pp. 32.

O'BRIEN (WILLIAM SMITH) Plan for the relief of the poor in Ireland; with observations on the English and Scotch Poor Laws; addressed to the landed proprietors of Ireland. London, Richardson, 1830. pp. 59.

WILSON (M.D.) The paupers of Leigh: their persecution and poor relief 1660-1860. Leigh, 1976. pp. 32. *bibliog. (Leigh. Local History Society. Publications. No. 4)*

— — Ireland.

STOPFORD (EDWARD ADDERLEY) The rate-screw for Ireland, considered in reference to the Public Works Act, the Relief Act, and the new Poor Law; in a letter to the most noble the Marquis of Lansdowne, etc. Dublin, Grant and Bolton, 1847. pp. 39.

— — Scotland.

LOCH (Sir CHARLES STEWART) Poor relief in Scotland: its statistics and development, 1791-1891. New York, 1976. pp. 271-370. *Facsimile reprint of a paper read before the Royal Statistical Society in 1898.*

POPPER (Sir KARL RAIMUND).

ČAVOŠKI (KOSTA) Filozofija otvorenog društva: politički liberalizam Karla Poppera. Beograd, 1975. pp. 315. *bibliog. (Filozofsko Društvo Srbije. Filozofske Studije. Biblioteka. 6) With English summary.*

ACKERMANN (ROBERT JOHN) The philosophy of Karl Popper. Amherst, 1976. pp. 212. *bibliog.*

POPPER (Sir KARL RAIMUND) Unended quest: an intellectual autobiography. rev.ed. Glasgow, 1976. pp. 255. *bibliog.*

ROTENSTREICH (NATHAN) Philosophy, history and politics: studies in contemporary English philosophy of history. The Hague, 1976. pp. 158. *bibliog.*

POPULAR CULTURE.

MARTINET (MARCEL) Culture prolétarienne. Paris, 1976. pp. 165. *First published in 1935.*

SWINGEWOOD (ALAN WILLIAM) The myth of mass culture. London, 1977. pp. 146. *bibliog.*

POPULAR FRONTS.

INSTITUT FÜR MARXISTISCHE STUDIEN UND FORSCHUNGEN. Zur Aktionseinheitspolitik der KPD, 1919-1946: Dokumente. Frankfurt am Main, 1976. pp. 160. *(Neudrucke zur Sozialistischen Theorie und Gewerkschaftspraxis. Band 8)*

POPULATION.

SYMPOSIUM ON LAW AND POPULATION, TUNIS, 1974. The symposium on law and population: (proceedings, background papers and recommendations); sponsored by the United Nations Fund for Population Activities and the United Nations [and others]. [New York, United Nations Fund for Population Activities, 1975]. pp. 309. *bibliog.*

BROWN (LESTER RUSSELL) and others. Twenty-two dimensions of the population problem. [Washington, D.C.], 1976. pp. 83. *bibliog. (Worldwatch Institute. Worldwatch Papers. No. 5)*

POPULATION REFERENCE BUREAU. World population growth and response: 1965-1975: a decade of global action. Washington, D.C., 1976. pp. 271.

VIEL VICUNA (BENJAMIN) The demographic explosion: the Latin American experience;... translated from the Spanish and updated by James Walls. New York, [1976]. pp. 249. *bibliog.*

CLARK (COLIN GRANT) Population growth and land use. 2nd ed. London, 1977. pp. 415.

LORAINE (JOHN A.) Syndromes of the seventies: population, sex and social change. London, 1977. pp. 217. *bibliog.*

PARSONS (JACK) Population fallacies. London, 1977. pp. 286. *bibliog.*

— Bibliography.

BUSSINK (TINE) and others, compilers. Sourcebook on population, 1970-1976. Washington, 1976. pp. 72. *Continues Bibliography on population and Source book on population which were issued in Population Bulletin, the former in 1966 as a supplement to vol. 22, no. 3, and the latter in 1969 as vol. 25, no. 5.*

UNITED STATES. Bureau of the Census. Library. 1976. Catalogs of the Bureau of the Census Library, Washington, D.C. Boston, 1976. 20 vols.

VALENTEI (DMITRII IGNAT'EVICH) and BURNASHEV (E.IU.) eds. Bibliografiia po problemam narodonaseleniia, 1972-1975 gg. Moskva, 1977. pp. 232.

— Congresses.

CARILLO-FLORES (ANTONIO) The World Population Conference 1974. Cardiff, [1975]. pp. 11. *(Wales. University of Wales. University College, Cardiff. David Owen Memorial Lectures. No. 4)*

— Statistics.

HABITAT: UNITED NATIONS CONFERENCE ON HUMAN SETTLEMENTS, VANCOUVER, 1976. Global review of human settlements: a support paper for Habitat: United Nations Conference on Human Settlements; (with Statistical annex) (A/CONF.70/A/1 and A/CONF.70/A/1 Add.1). Oxford, 1976. 2 vols.

POPULATION FORECASTING.

ANGELONI (ROLANDO) Previsioni demografiche per le provincie di Trento e Bolzano. Trento, 1964. pp. 41. *(Trentino-Alto Adige. Ufficio Studi Statistica e Programmazione. Quaderni. 5)*

— Germany — North Rhine-Westphalia.

NORTH RHINE-WESTPHALIA. Landesamt für Datenverarbeitung und Statistik. Beiträge zur Statistik des Landes Nordrhein-Westfalen. Heft 373. Vorausberechnung der Wohnbevölkerung in den kreisfreien Städten und Kreisen Nordrhein-Westfalens: Regionalprognose 1976 bis 1990. Düsseldorf, 1977. pp. 122.

POPULATION FORECASTING.(Cont.)

— New Zealand.

NEW ZEALAND. Department of Statistics. 1976. New Zealand sub-national population projections 1976-1991. Report[s] no.1-[20]. [Wellington, 1976]. 20 pts. (in 1 vol.)

— United Kingdom.

U.K. Office of Population Censuses and Surveys. Population projections: area: population projections by sex and age for standard regions, counties and metropolitan districts of England. a., 1974/1991 (1st)- London.

U.K. Central Policy Review Staff. 1977. Population and the social services; report. London, 1977. pp. 106.

— — Scotland.

SCOTLAND. Scottish Development Department. 1975. Demographic analysis for planning purposes: a manual on sources and techniques: regional reports advice. [Edinburgh], 1975. pp. 55. *bibliog. (Planning Advice Notes. No.8)*

POPULATION POLICY.

NATIONAL SEMINAR ON GENERAL CONSEQUENCES OF POPULATION GROWTH, 2ND, KUALA LUMPUR, 1970. Proceedings of the...Seminar, etc. Kuala Lumpur, National Family Planning Board, [1970?]. pp. 189.

SCORER (RICHARD SEGAR) A radical approach to pollution, population and resources. London, [1973]. pp. 32. *(Liberal Party. Strategy 2,000. 1st Series. No.1)*

ANNUAL REVIEW OF POPULATION LAW; [pd. by] Fletcher School of Law and Diplomacy, Tufts University. a., 1974- Medford, Mass.

BERELSON (BERNARD) The great debate on population policy: an instructive entertainment. New York, [1975]. pp. 32. *(Population Council. Occasional Papers)*

NATALITE et politique démographique, etc. [Paris], 1976. pp. 162. *bibliog. (France. Institut National d'Etudes Démographiques. Travaux et Documents. Cahiers. No. 76)*

RIDKER (RONALD GENE) ed. Population and development: the search for selective interventions. Baltimore, [1976]. pp. 465. *bibliog.*

POPULATION RESEARCH.

SEMINAR ON SOCIAL SCIENCE RESEARCH WITH SPECIAL REFERENCE TO POPULATION AND DEVELOPMENT, MONROVIA, LIBERIA, 1975. Seminar...; organized at the University of Liberia...by Liberia College,...University of Liberia and Population Dynamics Programme, University of Ghana, Legon. Monrovia, Liberia, 1975. fo. 75. *bibliogs.*

— Nigeria.

McWILLIAM (JOHN) and UCHE (CHUKWUDUM) Nigeria: selected studies: social science research for population and family planning policies and programme. London, 1976. pp. 50. *bibliog. (International Planned Parenthood Federation. Research for Action. No. 1)*

POPULATION TRANSFERS

— Germans.

DE ZAYAS (ALFRED M.) Nemesis at Potsdam: the Anglo-Americans and the expulsion of the Germans: background, execution, consequences. London, 1977. pp. 268. *bibliog.*

POPULISM.

LACLAU (ERNESTO) Politics and ideology in marxist theory: capitalism, fascism, populism. London, 1977. pp. 203.

— Colombia.

POPULISMO; ([by] Alvaro Gomez Hurtado [and others]). Bogota, 1970. pp. 117.

PALACIOS (MARCO) El populismo en Colombia. Bogota, 1971. pp. 130.

— Poland.

BROCK (PETER) Polish revolutionary populism: a study in agrarian socialist thought from the 1830s to the 1850s. Toronto, [1977]. pp. 125. *bibliog.*

— Russia.

TKACHEV (PETR NIKITICH) Sochineniia v dvukh tomakh; (obshchaia redaktsiia A.A. Galaktionova [and others]). Moskva, 1975-76. 2 vols. *bibliog. (Akademiia Nauk SSSR. Institut Filosofii. Filosofskoe Nasledie)*

MAEVSKAIA (TAT'IANA PETROVNA) Idei i obrazy russkogo narodnicheskogo romana, 70-80-e gody XIX v. Kiev, 1975. pp. 207. *bibliog.*

— United States.

GOODWYN (LAWRENCE) Democratic promise: the Populist Movement in America. New York, 1976. pp. 718.

PORK INDUSTRY AND TRADE

— India.

INDIA. Ministry of Food, Agriculture, Community Development and Cooperation. Directorate of Marketing and Inspection. Marketing Series. No. 174. Marketing of pork and pork products in India. [Delhi, 1971]. pp. 41.

PORT ELIZABETH

— Industries.

RENDERS (VERA) and PHILLIPS (BRUCE DALTON) Industrial change in the East London/King William's Town and Port Elizabeth/Uitenhage metropolitan regions, 1960-1970. Port Elizabeth, 1976. fo. 56. *(University of Port Elizabeth. Institute for Planning Research. Information Bulletins. No. 10)*

PORT MORESBY

— History.

ORAM (NIGEL DENIS) Colonial town to Melanesian city: Port Moresby, 1884-1974. Canberra, 1976. pp. 289. *bibliog.*

— Social conditions.

ORAM (NIGEL DENIS) Colonial town to Melanesian city: Port Moresby, 1884-1974. Canberra, 1976. pp. 289. *bibliog.*

PORT OF LONDON AUTHORITY.

GRAVES (DESMOND JAMES TURNER) Organisational change in a port operating authority. London, National Ports Council, 1976. fo. 88.

PORTLAND CEMENT.

INTERREGIONAL SEMINAR ON THE MANUFACTURE AND UTILIZATION OF PORTLAND CEMENT, HOLTE, 1972. The manufacture and utilization of Portland cement: report of the Interregional Seminar held at Holte, Denmark, 7-20 May 1972, including a summary of lectures presented to the seminar. (ID/97) (ID/WG.125/8/Rev.1). New York, United Nations, 1972. pp. 26.

PORTO MARGHERA

— Economic history.

CHINELLO (CESCO) Forze politiche e sviluppo capitalistico: Porto Marghera e Venezia, 1951-1973. Roma, 1975. pp. 293.

PORTSMOUTH

— Social conditions.

SOCIAL SERVICES RESEARCH AND INTELLIGENCE UNIT [PORTSMOUTH]. Occasional Papers. No. 2. Households: Portsmouth and neighbouring areas. Portsmouth, 1973. fo. 27. *bibliog.*

PORTUGAL.

PORTUGAL. Secretariado Nacional da Informação, Cultura Popular e Turismo. 1965. Portugal, 1965: any more questions, please? [Lisbon, 1965]. pp. 91.

PORTUGAL. Secretaria de Estado da Informação e Turismo. Direcção-Geral de Informação. 1971. Portugal: any more questions, please? [rev. ed.] [Lisbon], 1971. pp. 135.

PORTUGAL INFORMATION; (pd. by) Director-Geral da Divulgação, Ministério da Communicação Social. m., Ja 1976 (no.1)- Lisbon. *Supersedes PORTUGAL: (an informative review).*

— Colonies — Administration.

ISAACMAN (ALLEN F.) The tradition of resistance in Mozambique: the Zambesi Valley 1850-1921. Berkeley, Calif., 1976. pp. 232. *bibliog.*

— — Politics and government.

GRAHAM (LAWRENCE S.) Portugal: the bureaucracy of empire. Austin, 1973. pp. 50, viii. *(American Society for Public Administration. Latin American Development Administration Committee and Texas University. Institute of Latin American Studies. LADAC Occasional Papers. Series 2. No. 9)*

— Commerce.

WAPPAEUS (J.E.) Untersuchungen über die Negerländer der Araber und über den Seehandel der Italiener, Spanier und Portugiesen im Mittelalter. Amsterdam, 1966. pp. 365. *Reprint of work originally published in Göttingen in 1842.*

— — Africa, West.

KUNSTMANN (FRIEDRICH) Die Handelsverbindungen der Portugiesen mit Timbuktu im XV. Jahrhunderte. [Munich, 1850]. pp. 171-235. *(Bayerische Akademie der Wissenschaften. 3. Classe. Abhandlungen. 6. Band, 1. Abth.)*

— Commercial policy.

[RIBEIRO DE SÁ (SEBASTIÃO JOSÉ)] As fabricas nacionaes são uma historiaê': pamphleto economico pelo redactor da Revista Universal. Lisboa, [imprint], 1850. pp. 28.

— Economic history.

COSTA (RAMIRO DA) O desenvolvimento do capitalismo em Portugal. Lisboa, 1975 repr. 1976. pp. 219. *bibliog.*

— Economic policy.

PORTUGAL: Industrie und Industriepolitik vor dem Beitritt zur Europäischen Gemeinschaft; ([by] Klaus Esser [and others]). Berlin, 1977. pp. 316. *bibliog. (Deutsches Institut für Entwicklungspolitik. Schriften. Band 47)*

— Foreign relations.

For a related heading see EUROPEAN ECONOMIC COMMUNITY — Portugal.

— History.

LIVERMORE (HAROLD VICTOR) A new history of Portugal. 2nd. ed. Cambridge, 1976. pp. 408.

— — 1974, Revolution.

BOROVIK (GENRIKH AVIEZEROVICH) Mai v Lissabone: ocherk. Moskva, 1975. pp. 200.

FOUBERT (CHARLES) Portugal, 1974-1975: les années de l'espoir. Paris, [1975]. pp. 127. *bibliog.*

PORTUGAL: the revolution in the labyrinth; edited by Jean Pierre Faye from the papers of the Russell Committee for Portugal. Nottingham, 1976. pp. 231.

PORTUGUESE revolution 1974-76; edited by Lester A. Sobel. New York, [1976]. pp. 151. *Based on records compiled by Facts on File.*

MAILER (PHIL) Portugal: the impossible revolution?. London, 1977. pp. 399.

— Industries.

PORTUGAL: Industrie und Industriepolitik vor dem Beitritt zur Europäischen Gemeinschaft; ([by] Klaus Esser [and others]). Berlin, 1977. pp. 316. *bibliog. (Deutsches Institut für Entwicklungspolitik. Schriften. Band 47)*

— Nationalism.

ALMEIDA (JOÃO DE) O Estado Novo. Lisboa, 1932. pp. 371.

— Politics and government.

[BORGES CARNEIRO (MANOEL)] Portugal regenerado em 1820. Lisboa, Typografia Lacerdina, 1820. pp. 47. *This work consists of a "Discurso" and "Addicionamento" each signed D.C.N. Publicola.*

ALMEIDA (JOÃO DE) O Estado Novo. Lisboa, 1932. pp. 371.

GRAHAM (LAWRENCE S.) Portugal: the bureaucracy of empire. Austin, 1973. pp. 50, viii. *(American Society for Public Administration. Latin American Development Administration Committee and Texas University. Institute of Latin American Studies. LADAC Occasional Papers. Series 2. No. 9)*

CAETANO (MARCELLO) Testimonio. Madrid, 1975. pp. 226. *bibliog.*

CLARET SERRA (ANDREU) Hablan los capitanes: Portugal: genesis, ideologia y practica politica del Movimiento de las Fuerzas Armadas. Barcelona, 1975. pp. 237. *bibliog.*

CUNHAL (ALVARO) Portugal: l'aube de la liberté; textes choisis, présentés et traduits sous la direction de Pierre Gilhodes. Paris, [1975]. pp. 249.

FOUBERT (CHARLES) Portugal, 1974-1975: les années de l'espoir. Paris, [1975]. pp. 127. *bibliog.*

GRAHAM (LAWRENCE S.) Portugal: the decline and collapse of an authoritarian order. Beverly Hills, [1975]. pp. 67. *bibliog.*

LEWIS (ROGER) Some impressions of Portugal. [London, 1975]. fo. 6.

OLIVEIRA (CESAR) MFA y revolucion socialista; (traduccion: Jose Luis Rodriguez). Barcelona, [1975]. pp. 158.

SCHMITTER (PHILIPPE C.) Corporatism and public policy in authoritarian Portugal. London, [1975]. pp. 72.

BENSAÏD (DANIEL) and others. Lecciones de abril: analisis politico de la experiencia portuguesa. Barcelona, [1976]. pp. 281.

HARSGOR (MIKHAËL) Portugal in revolution. Beverly Hills, [1976]. pp. 90. *bibliog. (Georgetown University. Center for Strategic and International Studies. Washington Papers. vol. 3/32)*

PORTUGAL: the revolution in the labyrinth; edited by Jean Pierre Faye from the papers of the Russell Committee for Portugal. Nottingham, 1976. pp. 231.

PORTUGAL and Spain: transition politics; [report of an international conference held in London in 1975]. London, 1976. pp. 24. *(Institute for the Study of Conflict. Special Reports)*

PORTUGUESE revolution 1974-76; edited by Lester A. Sobel. New York, [1976]. pp. 151. *Based on records compiled by Facts on File.*

POULANTZAS (NICOS) The crisis of the dictatorships: Portugal, Greece, Spain; translated by David Fernbach. London, 1976. pp. 166.

WIARDA (HOWARD J.) Corporation and development: the Portuguese experience. Amherst, 1977. pp. 447. *bibliog.*

— — 1974- .

NAVILLE (PIERRE) Pouvoir militaire et socialisme au Portugal. Paris, [1975]. pp. 192.

SOARES (MARIO) Portugal: quelle révolution?; entretiens avec Dominique Pouchin. [Paris, 1976]. pp. 255.

— Relations (general) with Goa, Daman and Diu.

D'SOUZA (BENTO GRACIANO) Goan society in transition: a study in social change. Bombay, 1975. pp. 364. *bibliog.*

PORTUGUESE GUINEA

— Politics and government.

FISAS ARMENGOL (VICENÇ) Amilcar Cabral y la independencia de Guinea-Bissau; [with two articles by Amilcar Cabral included as appendices]. Barcelona, 1974. pp. 132.

PORTUGUESE IN BELGIUM.

POHL (HANS) Die Portugiesen in Antwerpen, 1567-1648: zur Geschichte einer Minderheit. Wiesbaden, 1977. pp. 439. *bibliog. (Vierteljahrschrift für Sozial- und Wirtschaftsgeschichte. Beihefte. Nr. 63) 1 map in end pocket.*

POSADA (ADOLFO).

LAPORTA SAN MIGUEL (FRANCISCO J.) Adolfo Posada: politica y sociologia en la crisis del liberalismo español. Madrid, 1974. pp. 355. *bibliog.*

POSADOWSKY-WEHNER (ARTHUR) Graf.

GERMANY. Reichstag. 1898. Graf Posadowsky und die Koalitionsfreiheit vor dem Reichstag: Verhandlungen des Deutschen Reichstags über den Erlass des Staatssekretärs des Innern vom 11.Dezember 1897, etc. Berlin, 1898. pp. 112.

POSITIVISM.

UTKINA (NINA FEDOROVNA) Pozitivizm, antropologicheskii materializm i nauka v Rossii: vtoraia polovina XIX veka. Moskva, 1975. pp. 319.

MODZELEWSKI (WOJCIECH) Naród i postęp: problematyka narodowa w ideologii i myśli społecznej pozytywistów warszawskich. Warszawa, 1977. pp. 243.

POSTAL SAVINGS BANKS

— Uganda.

UGANDA. Post Office Savings Bank Reorganization Committee of Inquiry. 1968. The report; [A.J.P.M. Ssentongo, chairman]. [Entebbe, 1968]. pp. 41.

POSTAL SERVICE

— South Africa — Accounting.

SOUTH AFRICA. Parliament. House of Assembly. Select Committee on Posts and Telecommunications. 1976. Report (with Proceedings and Minutes of evidence) (S.C.3- 1976). in SOUTH AFRICA. Parliament. House of Assembly. Select Committee reports.

— Taiwan.

STATISTICAL ABSTRACT OF TRANSPORTATION AND COMMUNICATIONS: REPUBLIC OF CHINA; [pd. by] Ministry of Communications. a., 1975- [Taipei]. *[in English and Chinese].*

— United Kingdom — Employees.

BEALEY (FRANK) The Post Office Engineering Union: the history of the Post Office engineers, 1870-1970. London, 1976. pp. 432.

POTATOES

— Law and legislation — Canada — New Brunswick.

NEW BRUNSWICK. Department of Agriculture. Potato Branch. 1963. History of potato legislation in the province of New Brunswick: 50 years of progress, 1914-1963. [Fredericton, 1963]. pp. 14; 16. *In English and French.*

— Prices — United Kingdom.

U.K. Price Commission. 1977. Price Commission report on prices and margins of potatoes and other fresh vegetables: December 1976. London, 1977. fo. (8).

— Venezuela.

DUBUC PICON (ROBERTO) and UGALDE (LUIS) Evolucion historica del sector agropecuario y su crisis actual. Caracas, 1973 [or rather 1974]. pp. 139. *bibliog.*

POULTRY INDUSTRY

— South Africa.

SOUTH AFRICA. Commission of Inquiry regarding the Import of Poultry Breeding Material. 1976. Report (R.P. 89/1976). in SOUTH AFRICA. Parliament. House of Assembly. Votes and proceedings; (with Printed annexures).

POUND, BRITISH.

FABIAN SOCIETY. Fabian Tracts. [No.] 452. A competitive pound; [by] Bryan Gould [and others]. London, 1977. pp. 32.

— Devaluation.

HARDWICK (PHILIP) Inflation and the sinking pound. London, [1976]. pp. 14. *(Economics Association. Occasional Papers. No.2)*

POVERTY.

LEONARD (PETER TERRANCE) Poverty, consciousness and action. Birmingham, [1975]. pp. 10. *(British Association of Social Workers. Publications)*

BERTHOUD (RICHARD) The disadvantages of inequality: a study of social deprivation; a PEP report. London, 1976. pp. 207.

HAQ (MAHBUS UL) The poverty curtain: choices for the third world. New York, 1976. pp. 247. *bibliog.*

LIPTON (MICHAEL) Why poor people stay poor: a study of urban bias in world development. London, 1977. pp. 467. *bibliog.*

POWELL (JOHN ENOCH).

BERKELEY (HUMPHRY) The odyssey of Enoch: a political memoir. London, 1977. pp. 146.

SCHOEN (DOUGLAS E.) Enoch Powell and the Powellites. London, 1977. pp. 317. *bibliog.*

POWER (MECHANICS).

KENWARD (MICHAEL) Potential energy: an analysis of world energy technology. Cambridge, 1976. pp. 227. *bibliog.*

CONFERENCE ON ENERGY POLICIES AND THE INTERNATIONAL SYSTEM, CENTER FOR THE STUDY OF DEMOCRATIC INSTITUTIONS, 1973. Energy technology and global policy: a selection of contributing papers...; [edited by] Stephen Arthur Saltzman. Santa Barbara, Calif., [1977]. pp. 276. *bibliogs.*

POWER (SOCIAL SCIENCES).

RADCLIFFE (CYRIL JOHN) Viscount Radcliffe. The problem of power. London, 1952. pp. 110. *(British Broadcasting Corporation. Reith Lectures. 1951)*

DOMINATION: (essays edited by Alkis Kontos for the University League for Social Reform). Toronto, [1975]. pp. 228.

DUKE (JAMES T.) Conflict and power in social life. Provo, Utah, [1976]. pp. 287.

The DYNAMICS of Soviet politics. Cambridge, Mass., 1976. pp. 427. *(Harvard University. Russian Research Center. Studies. 76)*

POWER and control: social structures and their transformation; edited by Tom R. Burns and Walter Buckley. London, [1976]. pp. 290. *bibliogs.*

SWINGLE (PAUL G.) The management of power. Hillsdale, N.J., 1976. pp. 178. *bibliog.*

CONNELL (ROBERT WILLIAM) Ruling class, ruling culture: studies of conflict, power and hegemony in Australian life. Cambridge, 1977. pp. 250.

INTERNATIONAL INSTITUTE FOR STRATEGIC STUDIES. Adelphi Papers. No. 134. The diffusion of power: II: conflict and its control; papers presented...at the eighteenth annual conference of the IISS at Baden bei Wien, Austria, in September 1976. London, 1977. pp. 36.

LEVI (MARGARET) Bureaucratic insurgency: the case of police unions. Lexington, Mass., [1977]. pp. 165.

MARTIN (RODERICK) The sociology of power. London, 1977. pp. 203.

MUIR (WILLIAM KER) Police: streetcorner politicians. Chicago, 1977. pp. 306. *bibliog.*

MULDER (MAUK) The daily power game. Leiden, 1977. pp. 96. *bibliog.*

POWER OF ATTORNEY

— United Kingdom.

CAPLIN (CHARLES) and WEXLER (ARNOLD) Powers of attorney: fourth edition by J.F. Josling. London, 1976. pp. 103. *bibliog.*

POWER RESOURCES.

COUNTER INFORMATION SERVICES. Anti-Reports. No. 8. The oil fix: an investigation into the control and costs of energy. London, [1974]. pp. 49. *bibliog.*

BECHT (J. EDWIN) and BELZUNG (L.D.) World resource management: key to civilizations and social achievement. Englewood Cliffs, [1975]. pp. 339. *bibliog.*

SOUTH AFRICA. Department of Planning and the Environment. 1975. Energy trends in the world with special reference to South Africa: a report for a subsidiary committee of the Prime Minister's Planning Advisory Council. [Pretoria, 1975]. pp. 121. *bibliog.*

ENERGY policies of the world; edited by Gerard J. Mangone. New York, [1976 in progress]. *bibliog. Organized and edited at the Center for the Study of Marine Policy in the graduate College of Marine Studies of the University of Delaware.*

OPEC REVIEW: a digest of energy reports; [pd.by] Information Department, Organization of the Petroleum Exporting Countries. irreg., Oc 1976 (v.1, no.1)- Vienna.

KENWARD (MICHAEL) Potential energy: an analysis of world energy technology. Cambridge, 1976. pp. 227. *bibliog.*

LORAINE (JOHN A.) Syndromes of the seventies: population, sex and social change. London, 1977. pp. 217. *bibliog.*

— Research — United Kingdom.

COMMITTEE ON ENERGY RESEARCH [U.K.]. Energy research: the research councils' contribution. [London, Advisory Board for the Research Councils, 1974]. pp. 34.

— — United States.

OUR energy future: the role of research, development and demonstration in reaching a national consensus on energy supply; [by] Don E. Kash [and others]. Norman, Okla., 1976. pp. 489. *bibliogs. Based on a study of U.S. energy supply by a research team of the Science and Public Policy Program at the University of Oklahoma.*

— Statistics.

ENERGY BALANCES OF OECD COUNTRIES; [pd. by] Organisation for Economic Co-operation and Development. irreg., 1960/74- Paris. *[in English and French].*

— Europe.

CARMOY (GUY DE) Energy for Europe: economic and political implications. Washington, D.C., [1977]. pp. 120. *bibliogs. (American Enterprise Institute for Public Policy Research. AEI Studies. 146)*

— Germany.

HORN (MANFRED) Die Energiepolitik der Bundesregierung von 1958 bis 1972: zur Bedeutung der Penetration ausländischer Ölkonzerne in die Energiewirtschaft der BRD, etc. Berlin, [1977]. pp. 320. *bibliog.*

— Russia.

SHELEST (VASILII ANDREEVICH) Regional'nye energoekonomicheskie problemy SSSR. Moskva, 1975. pp. 312. *(Akademiia Nauk SSSR. Komissiia po Izucheniiu Proizvoditel'nykh Sil i Prirodnykh Resursov. Problemy Sovetskoi Ekonomiki)*

— — Siberia.

EXPLOITATION of Siberia's natural resources: main findings of round table held 30th January - 1st February, 1974 in Brussels; editor and chairman of round table Yves Laulan, etc. [Brussels?], NATO Directorate of Economic Affairs, [1974] . pp. 199. *In English and French.*

— United Kingdom.

COUNTER INFORMATION SERVICES. Anti-Reports. No. 8. The oil fix: an investigation into the control and costs of energy. London, [1974]. pp. 49. *bibliog.*

U.K. Central Office of Information. Reference Division. Reference Pamphlets. 124. British industry today: energy. 3rd ed. London, 1977. pp. 31. *bibliog.*

— — Wales.

WELSH COUNCIL. Energy resources in Wales. [Cardiff], 1977. pp. 51. *Map in end pocket.*

— United States.

COMMONER (BARRY) The poverty of power: energy and the economic crisis. New York, 1976. pp. 314.

ECONOMETRIC dimensions of energy demand and supply; edited by A. Bradley Askin and John Kraft. Lexington, Mass., [1976]. pp. 127. *bibliogs.*

ENERGY supply and government policy; edited by Robert J. Kalter and William A. Vogely. Ithaca, N.Y., 1976. pp. 356.

NUCLEAR ENERGY POLICY STUDY GROUP. Nuclear power issues and choices; foreword by McGeorge Bundy ...Spurgeon M. Keeny, chairman. Cambridge, Mass., [1977]. pp. 418.

— — Environmental aspects.

ENERGY and the environment: a structural analysis; edited by Anne P. Carter. Hanover, N.H.,1976. pp. 262. *bibliogs. Based on work carried out by a research team from Harvard and Brandeis universities.*

— Zaire.

MALU (FELIX) Le système énergétique de la République Démocratique du Congo. Kinshasa, Office National de la Recherche et du Développement, 1970. pp. 24. *bibliog.*

POZNAN

— Social history.

PARADOWSKA (MARIA) Bambrzy: mieszkańcy dawnych wsi miasta Poznania. Warszawa, 1975. pp. 177. *(Poznań. Urząd Miasta. Wydział Kultury. Biblioteka Kroniki Miasta Poznania)*

PRACTICE (PHILOSOPHY).

KÖRNER (STEPHAN) Experience and conduct: a philosophical enquiry into practical thinking. Cambridge, 1976. pp. 268. *bibliog.*

PRAGMATICS.

BATES (ELIZABETH) Language and context: the acquisition of pragmatics. New York, [1976]. pp. 375. *bibliog.*

PRASLIN (CHARLES LAURE HUGUES THEOBALD DE) Duc.

See CHOISEUL-PRASLIN (CHARLES LAURE HUGUES THEOBALD DE) Duc.

PRASLIN (FANNY DE) Duchesse.

See CHOISEUL-PRASLIN (FANNY DE) Duchesse.

PRATAS ISLANDS

— International status.

HEINZIG (DIETER) Disputed islands in the South China Sea: Paracels, Spratlys, Pratas, Macclesfield Bank. Wiesbaden, 1976. pp. 58.

PREDICTION THEORY.

HILDEBRAND (DAVID KENT) and others. Prediction analysis of cross classifications. New York, [1977]. pp. 311. *bibliog.*

PREFECTS (FRENCH GOVERNMENT).

MACHIN (HOWARD) The prefect in French public administration. London, [1977]. pp. 210.

PREGNANCY.

CHEETHAM (JULIET) Unwanted pregnancy and counselling. London, 1977. pp. 234. *bibliog.*

PREGNANT SCHOOLGIRLS

— United Kingdom.

MOTHERS IN ACTION. Educational arrangements for schoolage mothers: a survey of provisions made by schools and l[ocal] e[ducation] a[uthoritie]s. London, [1974]. pp. 5. *(Mothers in Action. Study Pamphlets. No. 5)*

— United States.

FURSTENBERG (FRANK F.) Unplanned parenthood: the social consequences of teenage childbearing. New York, [1976]. pp. 293. *bibliog.*

PRELIMINARY EXAMINATIONS (CRIMINAL PROCEDURE)

— Poland.

BAFIA (JERZY) Zwrot sprawy przez sąd do uzupełnienia śledztwa lub dochodzenia. Warszawa, 1961. pp. 142. *bibliog.*

— Russia.

BEKESHKO (SERGEI PETROVICH) and MATVIENKO (EVGENII ALEKSANDROVICH) Podozrevaemyi v sovetskom ugolovnom protsesse. Minsk, 1969. pp. 128.

PREPAID LEGAL SERVICES

— United States.

MACKENZIE (SUSAN T.) Group legal services. Ithaca, 1975. pp. 68. *bibliog. (Cornell University. New York State School of Industrial and Labor Relations. Key Issue Series. No. 18)*

PREROGATIVE, ROYAL.

JENKINS (DAVID) One of the Judges for South Wales. The works of the eminent and learned Judge Jenkins upon divers statutes concerning the King's prerogative and the liberty of the subject; now reprinted from the original authentick copy, written and published by himself, when prisoner in Newgate. London, Heyrick, [1681]. pp. (xiv), 94.

— United Kingdom.

SELDEN SOCIETY. Publications. Vol. 92. Sir Matthew Hale's The prerogatives of the King; edited...by D.E.C. Yale. London, 1976. pp. 353.

PRESCRIPTION PRICING

— United Kingdom.

U.K. Prescription Pricing Authority. Advanced statistical data relating to prescriptions dispensed by: (a) chemists including drug stores (b) appliance contractors. irreg., D 9 1975- Newcastle upon Tyne. *Supersedes U.K. Ministry of Health. Pharmaceutical Section. National Health Service: Expenditure on drugs and appliances supplied by chemists in England.*

TRICKER (R. IAN) Report of the inquiry into the Prescription Pricing Authority. [London, Department of Health and Social Security, 1977]. pp. 116.

— — Wales.

U.K. Welsh Health Technical Services Organisation. Welsh Pricing Committee. Advanced statistical data relating to prescriptions dispensed by: (a) chemists including drug stores (b) appliance contractors. irreg., F 18 1976- Cardiff.

PRESS

— Canada — Quebec.

LAGRAVE (JEAN PAUL DE) Les origines de la presse au Québec, 1760-1791. Montréal, [1975]. pp. 159.

— France.

PARTI COMMUNISTE FRANCAIS. Un journale' ça compte, dans la vie.... Paris, 1953. pp. 16.

CENSER (JACK RICHARD) Prelude to power: the Parisian radical press, 1789-1791. Baltimore, Md., [1976]. pp. 186. *bibliog.*

— India.

PRESS IN INDIA:...report of the Registrar of Newspapers for India under the Press and Registration of Books Act; [pd. by] Ministry of Information and Broadcasting. a., 1975(19th). New Delhi.

— Mexico.

RUIZ CASTAÑEDA (MARIA DEL CARMEN) and others. El periodismo en Mexico: 450 años de historia. Mexico, 1974. pp. 380.

— Poland — Silesia.

SMOŁKA (LEONARD) Prasa polska na Śląsku Opolskim, 1922-1939. Warszawa, 1976. pp. 200. *(Wrocław. Uniwersytet. Acta Universitatis Wratislaviensis. No.327. Nauki Polityczne. 8) With German summary.*

— Russia — Russia (RSFSR).

ANTIUKHIN (GEORGII VLADIMIROVICH) Ocherki istorii partiino-sovetskoi pechati Voronezhskoi oblasti, 1917-1945. Voronezh, 1976. pp. 238.

— — Tatar Republic.

NASYROV (TALGAT MIRZASALIKHOVICH) Oktiabr' i pechat' Tatarii, 1917-1920 gg. Kazan', 1975. pp. 211. *bibliog.*

— — Turkestan.

ERNAZAROV (TUGAN E.) and AKBAROV (ADKHAM IBRAGIMOVICH) Istoriia pechati Turkestana, 1870-1925 gg. Tashkent, 1976. pp. 287. *bibliog.*

— Switzerland.

BOLLINGER (ERNST) La presse suisse: structure et diversité. Frankfurt/M., 1976. pp. 327. *bibliog.*

MEURANT (JACQUES) La presse et l'opinion de la Suisse romande face à l'Europe en guerre, 1939-1941. Neuchâtel, [1976]. pp. 765. *bibliog.*

— United Kingdom.

CUDLIPP (HUGH) Baron Cudlipp. Walking on the water. London, 1976. pp. 428.

LEE (ALAN JOHN FRANK) The origins of the popular press in England, 1855-1914. London, 1976. pp. 310. *bibliog.*

PRESS, COMMUNIST

— France.

PARTI COMMUNISTE FRANCAIS. Un journal! ca compte, dans la vie.... Paris, 1953. pp. 16.

— Germany.

ROTE FAHNE, DIE: Zentralorgan der Kommunistischen Partei Deutschlands (Sektion der Kommunistischen Internationale). Die Rote Fahne: Kritik, Theorie, Feuilleton, 1918-1933; ([edited by] Manfred Brauneck). München, [1973]. pp. 513.

— United Kingdom.

RAMAZANOVA (NELLI KAIUMOVNA) Ezhednevnaia kommunisticheskaia pechat' Anglii v gody vtoroi mirovoi voiny i v poslevoennyi period, 1939-1972 gg.: "Deili uorker" - "Morning star". Moskva, 1974. pp. 72. *bibliog.*

PRESS AND POLITICS.

GUREVICH (SEMEN MOISEEVICH) Razoblachenie lzhivoi legendy: K. Marks i F. Engel's o burzhuaznoi pechati. Moskva, 1975. pp. 255.

— Germany.

FRITZSCHE (KLAUS) Politische Romantik und Gegenrevolution: Fluchtwege in der Krise der bürgerlichen Gesellschaft: das Beispiel des "Tat" Kreises. Frankfurt am Main, 1976. pp. 437. *bibliog.*

SOESEMANN (BERND) Das Ende der Weimarer Republik in der Kritik demokratischer Publizisten: Theodor Wolff, Ernst Feder, Julius Elbau, Leopold Schwarzschild. Berlin, 1976. pp. 251. *bibliog. (Berlin. Freie Universität. Institut für Publizistik. Abhandlungen und Materialien zur Publizistik. Band 9)*

LORECK (JOCHEN) Wie man früher Sozialdemokrat wurde: das Kommunikationsverhalten in der deutschen Arbeiterbewegung und die Konzeption der sozialistischen Parteipublizistik durch August Bebel. Bonn-Bad Godesberg, [1977]. pp. 290. *(Friedrich-Ebert-Stiftung. Forschungsinstitut. Schriftenreihe. Band 130)*

— Netherlands.

CUILENBURG (JAN J. VAN) Lezer, krant en politiek: een empirische studie naar nederlandse dagbladen en hun lezers. Amsterdam, [1977]. pp. 325. *bibliog. With summary in English.*

PRESS LAW

— Canada.

KESTERTON (WILFRED H.) The law and the press in Canada. Toronto, 1976. pp. 242. *bibliog.*

— Yugoslavia.

YUGOSLAVIA. Statutes, etc. 1965. Zbirka zakona o štampi, novinskim i izdavačkim preduzećima i ustanovama, radio-saobraćaju i radio-difuznim ustanovama i autorskom pravu. Beograd, 1965. pp. 131. *(Zbirka Saveznih Propisa. br.31)*

PRESSURE GROUPS

— Germany.

GESSNER (DIETER) Agrarverbände in der Weimarer Republik: wirtschaftliche und soziale Voraussetzungen agrarkonservativer Politik vor 1933. Düsseldorf, [1976]. pp. 304. *bibliog.*

WEBER (JUERGEN) Die Interessengruppen im politischen System der Bundesrepublik Deutschland. Stuttgart, [1977]. pp. 392. *bibliog.*

— United Kingdom.

AIMS FOR FREEDOM AND ENTERPRISE. Freedom or socialism?: campaign 1976. London, [1976]. pp. 10.

HAMER (DAVID ALLAN) The politics of electoral pressure: a study in the history of Victorian reform agitations. Hassocks, 1977. pp. 386.

MANLEY (ROY) and HASTINGS (HELEN) Influencing Europe: a guide for pressure groups. London, 1977. pp. 19. *bibliog. (Fabian Society. Research Series. [No.] 332)*

WILSON (GRAHAM K.) Special interests and policymaking: agricultural policies and politics in Britain and the United States of America, 1956-70. London, [1977]. pp. 205. *bibliog.*

— United States.

BACHRACK (STANLEY D.) The Committee of One Million: "China Lobby" politics, 1953-1971. New York, 1976. pp. 371. *bibliog.*

CALDWELL (LYNTON KEITH) and others. Citizens and the environment: case studies in popular action. Bloomington , Ind., [1976]. pp. 449. *bibliog.*

McFARLAND (ANDREW S.) Public interest lobbies: decision making on energy. Washington, D.C., [1976]. pp. 141. *(American Enterprise Institute for Public Policy Research. National Energy Studies. 14)*

TRICE (ROBERT H.) Interest groups and the foreign policy process: U.S. policy in the Middle East. Beverly Hills, [1976]. pp. 80.

PINCUS (JONATHAN J.) Pressure groups and politics in antebellum tariffs. New York, 1977. pp. 237. *bibliog.*

WILSON (GRAHAM K.) Special interests and policymaking: agricultural policies and politics in Britain and the United States of America, 1956-70. London, [1977]. pp. 205. *bibliog.*

PRESTIGE, OCCUPATIONAL.

See OCCUPATIONAL PRESTIGE.

PRICE (RICHARD).

THOMAS (DAVID OSWALD) The honest mind: the thought and work of Richard Price. Oxford, 1977. pp. 366. *bibliog.*

PRICE DISCRIMINATION.

EVERTON (ANN R.) Price discrimination: a comparative study in legal control. Bradford, 1976. pp. 58. *(Reprinted from Managerial Law, vol. 19, 1976)*

PRICE INDEXES.

U.K. Central Statistical Office. 1977. Current cost accounting: guide to price indices for overseas countries. London, 1977. pp. 36.

— Mathematical models.

EICHHORN (WOLFGANG) and VOELLER (JOACHIM) Theory of the price index: Fisher's test approach and generalizations. Berlin, 1976. pp. 95. *bibliog. Takes as its starting point Irving Fisher's contributions to the theory of the price index.*

— Bahamas.

BAHAMAS. Department of Statistics. Retail price index. m., Ja 1975- Nassau.

— Bolivia — La Paz.

BOLIVIA. Instituto Nacional de Estadistica. Indice de precios al consumidor: ciudad de La Paz. a., 1974 (1st)- La Paz.

— Canada.

CANADA. Statistics Canada. Industry price indexes. m., 1971/1975 (1st)- Ottawa. *[in English and French]. Supersedes in part CANADA. Statistics Canada. Prices and price indexes.*

— Finland.

TUOMINEN (PENTTI) and PUUSTINEN (TIMO) Consumer price index: methods and practice; consumer price indices (1972:100) by regions and population groups and consumer price statistics by regions. Helsinki, 1977. 1 vol. (various pagings). *(Finland. Tilastokeskus. Tutkimuksia. 38)*

— India.

INDIA. Labour Bureau. 1972. Working class consumer price index numbers in India: a monograph. vol.1. [Delhi, 1972]. 1 vol. (various pagings).

— New Hebrides.

NEW HEBRIDES. Condominium Bureau of Statistics. Statistical bulletin: Consumer price indexes. q., Je 1976- Vila. *[in English and French]*.

— Panama.

PANAMA. Direccion de Estadistica y Censo. Estadistica panameña. Indice de precios al por mayor y al consumidor. q., 1975(4th)- Panama. *Supersedes PANAMA Direccion de Estadistica y Censo. Estadistica panameña. Serie G. Precios y costo de la vida.*

— Singapore.

SINGAPORE. Statistics Department. 1974. The consumer price index, Singapore, based on household expenditure survey 1972/73. Singapore, 1974. pp. 19.

PRICE MAINTENANCE.

GROSS (HERBERT) Die Preisbindung im Handel: neue Eindrücke aus Nordamerika und Westeuropa. Düsseldorf, [1957]. pp. 147.

PRICE POLICY.

EICHNER (ALFRED S.) The megacorp and oligopoly: micro foundations of macro dynamics. Cambridge, 1976. pp. 365. *bibliog.*

PRICE REGULATION

— Communist countries.

The SOCIALIST price mechanism; edited by Alan Abouchar. Durham, N.C., 1977. pp. 298. *bibliogs. Based on papers presented at a symposium at the University of Toronto in 1974.*

— United Kingdom.

U.K. Department of Prices and Consumer Protection. 1977. Consultative document: a new prices policy. [London, 1977]. pp. 5.

— United States.

POSNER (RICHARD A.) The Robinson-Patman Act: federal regulation of price differences. Washington, [1976]. pp. 53. *(American Enterprise Institute for Public Policy Research. AEI Studies. No. 131)*

PRICES.

TASMANIA. Office of the Government Statistician. 1913. Results of a special investigation of the primary causes which determine the production and distribution of consumable wealth, together with an enquiry regarding the dominant influences which determine prices, and the purchasing power of labour over commodities; by R.M. Johnston. Hobart, 1913. pp. 10.

AKTUAL'NYE voprosy planovogo tsenoobrazovaniia. Leningrad, 1973. pp. 130.

FRIEDMAN (MILTON) Price theory. Chicago, 1976. pp. 357. *bibliog.*

STEINER (ROBERT L.) Does advertising lower consumer prices?. Washington, 1976. pp. 18. *(American Enterprise Institute for Public Policy Research. Reprints. No. 37) (Reprinted from Journal of Marketing, vol. 37, no. 4, October 1973)*

USING shadow prices; edited by I.M.D. Little and M. FG. Scott. London, 1976. pp. 254. *bibliogs.*

ARMEY (RICHARD K.) Price theory: a policy-welfare approach. Englewood Cliffs, [1977]. pp. 367. *bibliogs.*

GABOR (ANDRE) Pricing: principles and practices;...with an analytical appendix by C.W.J. Granger. London, 1977. pp. 276. *bibliogs.*

GRUNDFRAGEN der sozialistischen Preistheorie; (Herausgeber: Kurt Ambrée [and others]; Autoren: Kurt Ambrée [and others]). Berlin, 1977. pp. 303.

RYAN (WILLIAM JAMES LOUDEN) Price theory;...revised by D.W. Pearce. rev. ed. London, 1977. pp. 399.

The SOCIALIST price mechanism; edited by Alan Abouchar. Durham, N.C., 1977. pp. 298. *bibliogs. Based on papers presented at a symposium at the University of Toronto in 1974.*

U.K. Ministry of Overseas Development. Statistics Division. Commodity price charts. irreg., Current issue only. London.

— Bibliography.

STERN (ROBERT M.) and others, compilers. Price elasticities in international trade: an annotated bibliography. London, 1976. pp. 363. *bibliog.*

— Mathematical models.

PRIMARY commodity prices: analysis and forecasting; edited by W. Driehuis. Rotterdam, [1976]. pp. 346. *bibliogs. Selected papers of the Working Group on Primary Commodities of the Association of European Conjuncture-Institutes.*

— Balkan States.

BEROV (LIUBEN) Dvizhenieto na tsenite na Balkanite prez XVI-XIX v. i Evropeiskata revoliutsiia na tsenite; Prices in the Balkans during the 16th-19th centuries and the European revolution of prices. Sofiia, 1976. pp. 323. *bibliog. With Russian and English summaries.*

— Communist countries.

The SOCIALIST price mechanism; edited by Alan Abouchar. Durham, N.C., 1977. pp. 298. *bibliogs. Based on papers presented at a symposium at the University of Toronto in 1974.*

— Germany.

TRAPP (PETER) Geldmenge, Ausgaben und Preisanstieg in der Bundesrepublik Deutschland. Tübingen, 1976. pp. 229. *bibliog. (Kiel. Universität. Institut für Weltwirtschaft. Kieler Studien. 138)*

— India.

CHAKRABARTI (SANTIKUMAR) The behaviour of prices in India, 1952-70: an empirical study. Delhi, 1977. pp. 202. *bibliog.*

— Japan.

JAPAN. Bureau of Statistics. 1975. 1974 national survey of prices. Vols. 1 and 2. [Tokyo, 1975]. 2 vols. (in 1). *In English and Japanese.*

— Kuwait.

KUWAIT. Central Office of Statistics. Yearly bulletin of price statistics: retail, wholesale. a., 1974- Kuwait.

— Pakistan.

PAKISTAN. Statistical Division. Consumer prices in urban centres. a., 1969/70 (1st)- Karachi.

— Russia.

AKTUAL'NYE voprosy planovogo tsenoobrazovaniia. Leningrad, 1973. pp. 130.

GORODETSKII (EVGENII SERGEEVICH) ed. Problemy ispol'zovaniia tovarno-denezhnykh otnoshenii v usloviiakh razvitogo sotsializma. Moskva, 1975. pp. 121.

MANEVICH (VITALII EFIMOVICH) Razvitie teorii planovogo tsenoobrazovaniia v sovetskoi ekonomicheskoi literature. Moskva, 1975. pp. 184. *(Akademiia Nauk SSSR. Institut Ekonomiki. Problemy Sovetskoi Ekonomiki)*

KANTOR (LAZAR' MOISEEVICH) ed. Teoriia i metodologiia planovogo tsenoobrazovaniia. Moskva, 1976. pp. 336.

— Sweden.

AHLSTRÖM (GÖRAN) Studier i svensk ekonomisk politik och prisutveckling, 1776-1802. Lund, 1974. pp. 159. *bibliog. (Lund. Ekonomisk-Historiska Föreningen. Skrifter. vol. 14) Akademisk avhandling för avläggande av filosofie doktorsexamen, Lunds Universitet; with English summary.*

— United Kingdom.

NATIONAL ECONOMIC DEVELOPMENT OFFICE. A study of UK nationalised industries: background paper 5: price behaviour. London, 1977. pp. 52.

NATIONAL ECONOMIC DEVELOPMENT OFFICE. International price competitiveness, non-price factors and export performance. London, 1977. pp. 45. *bibliog.*

— United States — Mathematical models.

ROSE (PETER S.) and HUNT (LACY H.) Policy variables, unemployment and price level changes. [Washington, 1972]. pp. 11. *(United States. Board of Governors of the Federal Reserve System. Staff Economic Studies. No. 67) (Reprinted from The Southern Journal of Business, Vol. 6, No. 3, 1971)*

— Yugoslavia.

KOROŠIĆ (MARIJAN) Cijene i strukturne promjene u privredi. Zagreb, 1976. pp. 243. *bibliog.*

PRIETO (INDALECIO).

PRIETO (INDALECIO) De mi vida: recuerdos, estampas, siluetas, sombras. Mexico, 1968-70. 2 vols. *Vol.1 is a 1975 reprint of the 2nd ed.; vol.2 is the 1st ed.*

PRIME MINISTERS.

ZILEMENOS (CONSTANTIN) Naissance et évolution de la fonction de premier ministre dans le régime parlementaire. Paris, 1976. pp. 293. *bibliog.*

— Australia.

HUGHES (COLIN ANFIELD) Mr. Prime Minister: Australia's Prime Ministers, 1901- 1972. Melbourne, 1976. pp. 208. *bibliogs.*

— Canada.

BENJAMIN (JACQUES) Comment on fabrique un premier ministre québécois: de 1960 à nos jours. Montréal, [1975]. pp. 190.

MATHESON (WILLIAM A.) The Prime Minister and the cabinet. Toronto, [1976]. pp. 246.

— France.

BAECQUE (FRANCIS DE) Qui gouverne la France?: essai sur la répartition du pouvoir entre le chef de l'état et le chef du gouvernement. Paris, [1976]. pp. 208. *bibliog.*

— Japan.

ISHIDA (TAKESHI) Content analysis of public speeches given by prime ministers. [Tokyo], 1971. pp. 84. *In Japanese and English.*

— United Kingdom.

WILSON (Sir HAROLD) The governance of Britain. London, 1976. pp. 219.

PRINCE EDWARD ISLAND

— Politics and government.

ATLANTIC PROVINCES ECONOMIC COUNCIL. Submission to the maritime union study. Halifax, Nova Scotia, 1969. pp. 35.

PRINTERS

— Austria.

VERBAND DER VEREINE DER BUCHDRUCKER UND SCHRIFTGIESSER UND VERWANDTER BERUFE ÖSTERREICHS. Vorstand. Statistik über die Arbeits- und Lohnverhältnisse der in den Buchdruckereien und Schriftgiessereien Österreichs beschäftigten Berufsangehörigen...im Jahre 1909, etc. Wien, 1911. pp. 90.

— Germany.

HARTMANN (PETER) Mobilmachung: der Arbeitskampf in der Druckindustrie, 1976. Mainz, [1977]. pp. 212.

PRINTING

— History — Venezuela.

FEBRES CORDERO (JULIO) Historia de la imprenta y del periodismo en Venezuela, 1800-1830. Caracas, 1974. pp. 262. *bibliog. (Banco Central de Venezuela. Coleccion Cuatricentenario de Caracas. 11)*

— Germany — Societies.

KRETSCHMER (BRUNO) 25 Jahre Zentralkommission der Maschinensetzer Deutschlands, VDDB, 1903-1928: ein Rückblick. [Berlin, 1928]. pp. 95.

PRINTING, PUBLIC

— Kuwait.

KUWAIT. Ministry of Guidance and Information. 1963. Kuwait government press. Kuwait, 1963. pp. 56.

PRINTING INDUSTRY

— Switzerland.

BERUFSGEMEINSCHAFT IM SCHWEIZERISCHEN BUCHDRUCKERGEWERBE. Verhandlungs-Bericht über die Abänderungs-Anträge zum schweizerischen Buchdrucker-Tarif und über die Beratung der Berufs-Ordnung...August-Dezember 1917. Basel, 1918. pp. 238.

BERUFSORDNUNG für das Schweizerische Buchdruckgewerbe, 1918- 1922. [Einsiedeln, 1923?]. pp. 130.

PRISON RIOTS

— United Kingdom.

PROP (PRESERVATION OF THE RIGHTS OF PRISONERS). Hull '76. London, [1976]. pp. 16.

PRISON SENTENCES

— United Kingdom.

ADVISORY COUNCIL ON THE PENAL SYSTEM. The length of prison sentences; interim report; [Baroness Serota, chairman]. London, H.M.S.O., 1977. pp. 6.

PRISONERS

— Personal narratives.

SOBELL (MORTON) On doing time. Toronto, 1976. pp. 436. *Originally published in New York, 1974.*

— United Kingdom.

FITZGERALD (MIKE) Prisoners in revolt. Harmondsworth, 1977. pp. 278. *bibliog.*

PRISONERS' FAMILIES.

TOMLINSON (P.) Report on the work of the Prisoners' Wives' Service;...under the direction of Pauline Morris. [London, 1971]. pp. 23.

PRISONERS OF WAR.

DELESSERT (CHRISTIANE SHIELDS) Release and repatriation of prisoners of war at the end of active hostilities: a study of Article 118, Paragraph 1, of the Third Geneva Convention relative to the Treatment of Prisoners of War. Zürich, [1977]. pp. 225. *bibliog. (Schweizerische Vereinigung für Internationales Recht. Schweizer Studien zum Internationalen Recht. Band 5)*

PRISONERS OF WAR, GERMAN.

ERINNERUNGEN an die Internierungszeit, 1939-1946, und zeitgeschichtliche Ergänzungen: Berichte, Erzählungen, Fotos und Zeichnungen...; bearbeitet und herausgegeben von Rudolf Kock. 2nd ed. Windhoek, 1975. pp. 221.

PRISONERS' WRITINGS.

MORAND (BERNADETTE) Les écrits des prisonniers politiques. [Paris], 1976. pp. 267. *bibliog.*

PRISONS.

TOCH (HANS H.) Peacekeeping: police, prisons, and violence. Lexington, Mass., [1976]. pp. 137. *bibliog.*

— Employees — Bibliography.

FERRACUTI (FRANCO) and GIANNINI (MARIA CRISTINA) compilers. Manpower and training in the field of social defence: a commentary and bibliography. Rome, United Nations Social Defence Research Institute, 1970. pp. 111. *bibliog. (Publications. No. 2)*

— Barbados — Laws and regulations.

BARBADOS. 1870. Rules and regulations for the common gaol, and district houses of correction, of Barbados; approved and confirmed by the Governor-in-Council, on the 11th day of January, 1870. [Bridgetown?, 1870?]. pp. 28.

— Canada.

CANADA. Parliament. House of Commons. Standing Committee on Justice and Legal Affairs. Sub-Committee on the Penitentiary system in Canada. Minutes of proceedings and evidence. irreg., Oc 26 1976 (no.1)- Ottawa. *[in English and French].*

— France.

PANZANI (ALEX) Une prison clandestine de la police française: Arenc. Paris, 1975. pp. 105.

— India.

TYLER (MARY) My years in an Indian prison;...with illustrations by Dilip Ray. London, 1977. pp. 191.

— Russia.

HARDING (Mrs. STAN) The underworld of state;...with an introduction by Bertrand Russell. London, 1925. pp. 256.

— Spain.

LIBRO blanco sobre las carceles franquistas, 1939-1976; (by Angel Suarez [pseud. and] Colectivo 36). [Paris, 1976]. pp. 312. *bibliog.*

— United Kingdom.

The PROPER use of prisons; a Conservative study group report. London, 1977. pp. 28. *(Conservative Political Centre. [Publications]. No. 609)*

PRIVACY, RIGHT OF

— United States.

WAR on privacy; edited by Lester A. Sobel. New York, [1976]. pp. 247. *Based on records compiled by Facts on File.*

PRIVATE COMPANIES

— United Kingdom.

VAUGHAN (G.DOUGLAS) and others. From private to public: an analysis of the choices, problems and performance of newly floated public companies, 1966-74. Cambridge, 1977. pp. 144.

PRIVATE SCHOOLS

— United Kingdom.

CAMPAIGN FOR COMPREHENSIVE EDUCATION. The expenditure of public money on buying places in independent schools. [London], 1976. pp. 10.

PROBABILITIES.

FINETTI (BRUNO DE) Theory of probability: a critical introductory treatment;... translated by Antonio Machi and Adrian Smith. London, [1974-75]. 2 vols.

PROBATE RECORDS

— United Kingdom.

The GOODS and chattels of our forefathers: Frampton Cotterell and district probate inventories, 1539-1804; edited by John S. Moore. London, 1976. pp. 364. *(Frampton Cotterell and District Local History Group. Frampton Cotterell and District Historical Studies. 1)*

PROBATION

— Poland.

LEONIENI (MIKOŁAJ) Warunkowe zawieszenie wykonania kary: podstawy stosowania. Warszawa, 1961. pp. 188. *bibliog.*

— United Kingdom.

BOCHEL (DOROTHY) Probation and after-care: its development in England and Wales. Edinburgh, 1976. pp. 289. *bibliog.*

HICKS (JOHN) Probation officer. Probation and sentencing. Thornton Heath, Surrey, 1976. pp. 8. *(National Association of Probation Officers. Committee on the Role and Structure of the Probation Service. [Papers]. No. 1)*

LLOYD (MIKE) Probation and intervention. Thornton Heath, Surrey, 1977. pp. 8. *(National Association of Probation Officers. Committee on the Role and Structure of the Probation Service. [Papers]. No. 3)*

— United States.

CARNEY (LOUIS P.) Probation and parole: legal and social dimensions. New York, [1977]. pp. 346.

PROBATION OFFICERS

— Bibliography.

FERRACUTI (FRANCO) and GIANNINI (MARIA CRISTINA) compilers. Manpower and training in the field of social defence: a commentary and bibliography. Rome, United Nations Social Defence Research Institute, 1970. pp. 111. *bibliog. (Publications. No. 2)*

— United Kingdom.

U.K. Home Office. 1976. The probation and after-care service in a changing society. [London, 1976]. pp. 30. *bibliog.*

PROBLEM CHILDREN

— Denmark.

NORD-LARSEN (MOGENS) and VEDEL-PETERSEN (JACOB) Tabere i skolen: de 9-12 åriges skoletilpasning, etc. København, 1976. pp. 363. *(Socialforskningsinstituttet. Publikationer. 69) With English summary.*

— United Kingdom.

SOCIAL SERVICES RESEARCH AND INTELLIGENCE UNIT [PORTSMOUTH]. Information Sheets. No. 26. Fostering of disturbed adolescents. Portsmouth, [1976]. pp. 3.

PRODUCE TRADE

— Mathematical models.

ADAMS (FRANCIS GERARD) and BEHRMAN (JERE R.) Econometric models of world agricultural commodity markets: cocoa, coffee, tea, wool, cotton, sugar, wheat, rice. Cambridge, Mass., [1976]. pp. 160. *bibliog.*

— European Economic Community countries.

VENZI (LORENZO) La politica commerciale della CEE, con particolare riferimento ai prodotti agricoli. Napoli, 1973. pp. 9. *bibliog.* (*Naples. Università. Centro di Specializzazione e Ricerche Economico-Agrarie per il Mezzogiorno. Estratti. n. 130*)

PRODUCT MANAGEMENT.

BRODIN (BENGT) Produktutvecklingsprocesser: en studie ur marknadsföringssynvinkel av produktutveckling i svenska företag. Stockholm, 1976. 2 vols. (in 1). *bibliog.* *With English summary.*

PRODUCTION (ECONOMIC THEORY).

PAELINCK (JEAN H.P.) and MEESTER (J.C. DE) Fonction de production néo-classique dérivée de fonctions technologiques: la fonction C.E.S. non homogène. Namur, 1968. pp. 203-242. *bibliog.* (*Namur. Facultés Universitaires Notre-Dame de la Paix. Collection Economie Mathématique et Econométrie. No.2*)

IRALA (DOMINGO) pseud. [i.e. Domingo BLANCO FERNANDEZ] Las relaciones de produccion socialistas: criterios de la transicion. Valencia, [1975]. pp. 99.

GEORGESCU-ROEGEN (NICHOLAS) Energy and economic myths: institutional and analytical economic essays. New York, [1976]. pp. 380. *bibliogs.*

HEERTJE (ARNOLD) Economics and technical change. London, [1977]. pp. 334.

HINDESS (BARRY) and HIRST (PAUL QUENTIN) Mode of production and social formation: an auto-critique of Pre-capitalist modes of production. London, 1977. pp. 82. *bibliog.*

NOBLE (DAVID F.) America by design: science, technology, and the rise of corporate capitalism. New York, 1977. pp. 384.

— Mathematical models.

SVENSSON (LARS E.O.) On competitive markets and intertemporal resource allocation. Stockholm, 1976. 1 vol. (various pagings). *bibliogs.*

PRODUCTION FUNCTIONS (ECONOMIC THEORY).

TENCH (ANDREW B.) Socio-economic factors influencing agricultural output, with special reference to Zambia. Saarbrücken, 1975. pp. 309. *bibliog.*

PRODUCTION PLANNING.

STONE (MERLIN) Product planning: an integrated approach. London, 1976. pp. 142. *bibliog.*

ELLIOTT (DAVID) The Lucas Aerospace workers' campaign. London, 1977. pp. 20. (*Young Fabian Pamphlets. 46*)

PRODUCTIVITY.

BASCHE (JAMES R.) and DUERR (MICHAEL G.) Experience with foreign production work forces. New York, [1975]. pp. 33. (*National Industrial Conference Board. Conference Board Reports. No. 661*)

MUNDEL (MARVIN E.) Measuring and enhancing the productivity of service and government organizations. Tokyo, Asian Productivity Organization, [1975]. pp. 296.

— Papua New Guinea.

DIXON (R.) Economist. Productivity growth in secondary industry in Papua New Guinea, over the period 1960-1973. Port Moresby, Central Planning Office, [1974?]. pp. 32.

— Russia.

DOKUKIN (VLADIMIR IGNAT'EVICH) and KONDRAT'EV (L.F.) eds. Effektivnost' ekonomiki razvitogo sotsializma. Moskva, 1976. pp. 312. *bibliog.*

PLYSHEVSKII (BORIS PAVLOVICH) ed. Effektivnost' obshchestvennogo proizvodstva: kriterii, metody rascheta, pokazateli. Moskva, 1976. pp. 215.

PROIZVODITEL'NOST' truda v usloviiakh razvitogo sotsializma. Moskva, 1976. pp. 344. (*Akademiia Nauk SSSR. Problemy Sovetskoi Ekonomiki*)

— — Estonia.

TARMISTO (VELLO IULIUSOVICH) Vnutriraionnaia territorial'naia organizatsiia proizvodstva: na materiale Estonskoi SSR. Tallin, 1975. pp. 279. *With English summary.*

— Singapore.

GOH (ROSALIND S.L.) Human resources and productivity in Singapore. [Singapore], National Productivity Board, 1973. fo. 28. *bibliog.*

GOH (ROSALIND S.L.) and CHEW (SOON BENG) A study of the productivity performance of manufacturing industries under different capital ownership, 1968-1970. [Singapore], National Productivity Board, 1973. fo. 43.

LIM (ROBIN ENG SWEE) Factors affecting productivity: an empirical study on the manufacturing sector, Singapore. [Singapore], National Productivity Board, 1973. fo. 33. *bibliog.*

OW (CHIN HOCK) and TING (GRACE) Productivity in Singapore. [Singapore], National Productivity Board, 1973. 1 vol. (various foliations). *bibliog.*

— — Mathematical models.

CHEW (SOON BENG) A study of efficiency in the manufacturing sector: inter-industry and inter-firm comparisons. [Singapore], National Productivity Board, 1973. fo. 40. *bibliog.*

— Thailand — Mathematical models.

AKRASANEE (NARONGCHAI) and WIBOONCHUTIKUL (PAITOON) Incentives and factor intensity in the manufacturing sector in Thailand. Bangkok, 1976. pp. 39. *bibliog.* (*Bangkok. Thammasat University. Faculty of Economics. Discussion Paper Series. No. 52*)

— United Kingdom.

NATIONAL ECONOMIC DEVELOPMENT OFFICE. a STUDY OF uk NATIONALISED INDUSTRIES: background paper 3: output, investment and productivity. London, 1976. pp. 108.

HARLOW (CHRIS) Innovation and productivity under nationalisation: the first thirty years. London, 1977. pp. 256.

PROFESSIONS

— Papua New Guinea.

PAPUA NEW GUINEA. Manpower Planning Unit. 1971. The demand for professional manpower in Papua and New Guinea, 1971-80. Port Moresby, 1971. fo.46.. (*Manpower Studies. No. 1*)

— Switzerland.

GSELL-TRUEMPI (FRIEDA) Die Frau in höhern Berufen: Ergebnisse einer Rundfrage. Glarus, 1937. pp. 75.

— United States.

GERSTL (JOEL EMERY) and JACOBS (GLENN) eds. Professions for the people: the politics of skill. New York, [1976], pp. 230. *bibliogs.*

PARLIN (BRADLEY W.) Immigrant professionals in the United States: discrimination in the scientific labor market. New York, 1976. pp. 97. *bibliog.*

PROFIT.

STAERCKE (ROGER DE) Le salaire de l'entreprise. Bruxelles, [1966]. pp. 12.

KUEHNE (KARL) Geschichtskonzept und Profitrate im Marxismus. Neuwied, [1976]. pp. 267.

— Accounting.

CLARKSON (KENNETH W.) Intangible capital and rates of return: effects of research and promotion on profitability. Washington, [1977]. pp. 77. (*American Enterprise Institute for Public Policy Research. AEI Studies. No. 138*)

— Mathematical models.

SKOURAS (ATHANASSIOS S.) Government activity and private profits. London, 1975. pp. 20. (*Thames Polytechnic. School of Social Sciences. Thames Papers in Political Economy*)

— Russia.

KNIAZEVA (RAISA SEMENOVNA) Pribyl' i rentabel'nost' predpriiatii obshchestvennogo pitaniia. Moskva, 1973. pp. 56.

ZHEVTIAK (PETR NAUMOVICH) and KOLESNIKOV (VIKTOR IVANOVICH) Pribyl' v sotsialisticheskom rasshirennom vosproizvodstve. Moskva, 1976. pp. 272.

— United Kingdom.

NORTH TYNESIDE TRADES COUNCIL. A report on companies in North Tyneside: an analysis of ownership, control and profits. [North Shields], North Tyneside Community Development Project. 1975. pp. 73.

— — Accounting.

REVIEW BOARD FOR GOVERNMENT CONTRACTS. Report on the second general review of the profit formula for non- competitive government contracts; [Sir William Slimmings, chairman]. London, H.M.S.O., 1977. pp. 56.

PROFIT SHARING.

FISSENEWERT (HORST) Die betrieblich-investive Erfolgsbeteiligung der Arbeitnehmer: eine problemtheoretische Analyse. [Mannheim], 1974. pp. 277. *bibliog. Inaugural-Dissertation zur Erlangung der Würde eines Doktors der Wirtschaftswissenschaften der Universität Mannheim.*

PROFITS TAX

— Canada.

CANADIAN TAX FOUNDATION. Corporate Management Tax Conference, 1975. Tax aspects of measuring business profits: [proceedings of the conference]. Toronto, [1975]. pp. 148.

— Germany.

WEILER (HEINRICH) Gewinnsteuerreform und gewerblicher Mittelstand. Göttingen, 1976. pp. 313. *bibliog.* (*Institut für Mittelstandsforschung. Schriften zur Mittelstandsforschung. Nr.71*)

PROGRAMME BUDGETING

— Germany.

PILZ (FRANK) Regierungsaufgaben und Finanzpolitik: das Aufgaben- und Finanz-, das Finanzplanungs- und Aufgabenplanungssystem der Bundesregierung. Köln, [1976]. pp. 244. *bibliog.*

PROGRAMMING, STRUCTURED.

See STRUCTURED PROGRAMMING.

PROGRAMMING (ELECTRONIC COMPUTERS).

ADVANCED COURSE ON SOFTWARE ENGINEERING, MUNICH, 1972. Software engineering: an advanced course; edited by F.L. Bauer. Berlin, 1975. pp. 545. *bibliogs. First published in 1973 under the title: Advanced course on software engineering. Course organised by the Mathematical Institute of the Technical University of Munich and the Leibnitz Computing Centre of the Bavarian Academy of Sciences.*

COMPUTER AND INFORMATION SCIENCES SYMPOSIUM, 4TH, MIAMI BEACH, FLA., 1972. Information systems: COINS IV; edited by Julius T. Tou. New York, [1974]. pp. 506.

ELSON (MARK) Data structures. Chicago, [1975]. pp. 307. *bibliog.*

GRAHAM (ROBERT M.) Principles of systems programming. New York, [1975]. pp. 422.

JACKSON (M.A.) Principles of program design. London, 1975. pp. 299. *bibliog. (Automatic Programming Information Centre. Studies in Data Processing. No. 12)*

STRUCTURED programming: tutorial; [edited by] Victor R. Basili [and] Terry Baker. Washington, D.C., 1975. pp. 241. *Lectures given at a tutorial held on the day before the 11th COMPCON Conference, Fall, 1975.*

DIJKSTRA (EDSGER WYBE) A discipline of programming. Englewood Cliffs, N.J., [1976]. pp. 217.

GLASS (ROBERT L.) The universal elixir and other computing projects which failed. Newton, Mass., [1976]. pp. 79.

MACDOUGALL (E. BRUCE) Computer programming for spatial problems. London, 1976. pp. 160. *bibliog.*

McKEAG (R.M.) and WILSON (R.) M.Sc. Studies in operating systems;...edited by D.H.R. Huxtable. London, [1976]. pp. 263. *bibliogs. (Automatic Programming Information Centre. Studies in Data Processing. No.13)*

STRUCTURED programming: Infotech state of the art report; [D. Bates, editor]. Maidenhead, Berks., [1976]. pp. 495. *bibliog.*

ULLMAN (JEFFREY D.) Fundamental concepts of programming systems. Reading, Mass., [1976]. pp. 328. *bibliog.*

WARNIER (JEAN DOMINIQUE) Logical construction of programs. 3rd ed. New York, [1976]. pp. 230.

GILB (TOM) Software metrics. Cambridge, Mass, [1977]. pp. 282. *bibliog.*

— Law and legislation.

SOFTWARE protection: the legal protection of computer programs: two day conference...13th and 14th November, 1969: report of proceedings. [London?, 1970]. pp. 55. *bibliog. Conference sponsored by the British Computer Society.*

PROGRAMMING LANGUAGES (ELECTRONIC COMPUTERS).

ADVANCED COURSE ON SOFTWARE ENGINEERING, MUNICH, 1972. Software engineering: an advanced course; edited by F.L. Bauer. Berlin, 1975. pp. 545. *bibliogs. First published in 1973 under the title: Advanced course on software engineering. Course organised by the Mathematical Institute of the Technical University of Munich and the Leibnitz Computing Centre of the Bavarian Academy of Sciences.*

STRACHEY (CHRISTOPHER) The varieties of programming language. Oxford, 1973. pp. 20. *bibliog. (Oxford. University. Computing Laboratory. Programming Research Group. Technical Monographs. PRG 10)*

IFIP TC-2 CONFERENCE ON SOFTWARE FOR MINICOMPUTERS, KESZTHELY, HUNGARY, 1975. Minicomputer software: proceedings of the...conference; edited by James R. Bell and C. Gordon Bell. Amsterdam, 1976. pp. 333.

PROGRESS.

LAUDAN (LARRY) Progress and its problems: toward a theory of scientific growth. Berkeley, Calif., [1977]. pp. 257. *bibliog.*

PROGRESSIVISM (U.S. POLITICS).

BATES (JAMES LEONARD) The United States, 1898-1928: progressivism and a society in transition. New York, [1976]. pp. 339. *bibliogs.*

PROKSCH (ANTON).

PROKSCH (ANTON) Anton Proksch und seine Zeit; herausgegeben und kommentiert von Bettina Hirsch. Wien, [1977]. pp. 188.

PROLETARIAT.

LEWIS (AUSTIN) Proletarian and petit-bourgeois. Chicago, [1911]. pp. 48.

KRIVOGUZ (IGOR' MIKHAILOVICH) Osnovnye periody i zakonomernosti mezhdunarodnogo rabochego dvizheniia do Oktiabria 1917 g. Moskva, 1976. pp. 364.

MARTINET (MARCEL) Culture prolétarienne. Paris, 1976. pp. 165. *First published in 1935.*

PROPAGANDA.

RAUZE (MARIANNE) La propagande socialiste. Paris, 1919. pp. 23.

FABREGAT CUNEO (ROBERTO) Propaganda y sociedad. Mexico, 1961. pp. 313. *(Mexico City. Universidad Nacional Autonoma de Mexico. Instituto de Investigaciones Sociales. Cuadernos de Sociologia)*

PROPAGANDA, CHILEAN.

SOTO (FRANCISCO) Fascismo y Opus Dei en Chile: estudios de literatura e ideologia. Barcelona, 1976. pp. 261.

PROPAGANDA, COMMUNIST.

PARTI COMMUNISTE FRANÇAIS. Ce que veulent les communistes. Paris, [1946?]. pp. 16.

POLITICHESKAIA informatsiia: nauchnye osnovy i metody politicheskoi informatsii naseleniia v sovremennykh usloviiakh. Sverdlovsk, 1968. pp. 172.

NAUCHNYE osnovy kommunisticheskoi propagandy: materialy mezhdunarodnogo simpoziuma, Moskva, 11-13 fevralia 1975 goda. Moskva, 1975. pp. 463.

AKADEMIIA OBSHCHESTVENNYKH NAUK. Kafedra Teorii i Metodov Ideologicheskoi Raboty. Voprosy Teorii i Metodov Ideologicheskoi Raboty. vyp.6. Partiinoe rukovodstvo ideologicheskoi rabotoi. Moskva, 1976. pp. 311.

— Germany, Eastern.

PICAPER (JEAN PAUL) Kommunikation und Propaganda in der DDR. Stuttgart, [1976]. pp. 222. *bibliog.*

PROPAGANDA, GERMAN.

DEIST (WILHELM) Flottenpolitik und Flottenpropaganda: das Nachrichtenbureau des Reichsmarineamtes, 1897-1914. Stuttgart, 1976. pp. 344. *bibliog. (Militärgeschichtliches Forschungsamt. Beiträge zur Militär- und Kriegsgeschichte. Band 17)*

— Switzerland.

HUMBEL (KURT) Nationalsozialistische Propaganda in der Schweiz, 1931-1939, etc. Bern, [1976]. pp. 295. *bibliog.*

PROPAGANDA, RUSSIAN.

HAZAN (BARUCH A.) Soviet propaganda: a case study of the Middle East conflict. New Brunswick, N.J., [1976]. pp. 293.

PROPAGANDA, SOUTH AFRICAN.

MAGNUSSON (ÅKE) The Voice of South Africa. Uppsala, 1976. pp. 55. *bibliog. (Nordiska Afrikainstitutet. Research Reports. No. 35)*

The GREAT white hoax: South Africa's international propaganda machine; a report by Julian Burgess [and others]. London, [1977]. pp. 119. *bibliog.*

PROPERTY.

PROPERTY in a humane economy: a selection of essays compiled by the Institute for Humane Studies; edited by Samuel L. Blumenfeld. Lasalle, Ill., 1974. pp. 278.

ALCHIAN (ARMEN ALBERT) Economic forces at work. Indianapolis, [1977]. pp. 523. *bibliogs.*

— Netherlands.

NETHERLANDS. Centraal Bureau voor de Statistiek. Vermogensverdeling: regionale gegevens [and] Aanvullende gegevens: Distribution of personal property: regional data [and] Additional data. irreg., 1961- 's-Gravenhage.

— Poland.

TOPIŃSKI (JAN) ed. Zarząd mieniem ogólnonarodowym. Warszawa, 1956. pp. 278.

— Russia.

MASLIAEV (ALEKSEI IVANOVICH) Pravo sobstvennosti profsoiuzov SSSR. Moskva, 1975. pp. 222.

RAKHMANKULOV (KHADZHI-AKBAR) Pravovye formy regulirovaniia imushchestvennykh otnoshenii sotsialisticheskikh khoziaistvennykh organizatsii. Tashkent, 1976. pp. 279.

PROPERTY, RIGHT OF.

See RIGHT OF PROPERTY.

PROPERTY TAX.

RATHS (ERNST) Bedeutung und Rechtfertigung der Vermögensteuer in historischer und heutiger Sicht. Zürich, 1977. pp. 287. *bibliog.*

— Germany — North Rhine-Westphalia.

NORTH RHINE-WESTPHALIA. Landesamt für Datenverarbeitung und Statistik. Beiträge zur Statistik des Landes Nordrhein-Westfalen. Heft 369. Das steuerpflichtige Vermögen in Nordrhein-Westfalen, 1972. Düsseldorf, 1977. pp. 87.

PROTESTANTISM AND CAPITALISM.

WEBER (MAX) The Protestant ethic and the spirit of capitalism; translated by Talcott Parsons; introduction by Anthony Giddens. 2nd ed. London, 1976. pp. 292.

PROUDHON (PIERRE JOSEPH).

BOUGLE (CELESTIN CHARLES ALFRED) Proudhon. Paris, 1930. pp. 156.

VOYENNE (BERNARD) Histoire de l'idée fédéraliste. [Paris, 1973 in progress]. *bibliog. (Centre International de Formation Européenne. Réalités du Présent. Cahiers. Nos. 9, etc.)*

PRUSSIA

— Foreign economic relations — Netherlands.

BLAESING (JOACHIM F.E.) Das goldene Delta und sein eisernes Hinterland, 1815-1851: von niederländisch-preussischen zu deutsch-niederländischen Wirtschaftsbeziehungen. Leiden, 1973. pp. 275. *bibliog.*

PSYCHIATRIC HOSPITALS

— Russia.

MEEUS (ANTHONY DE) White book on the internment of dissenters in Soviet mental hospitals. Brussels, [1975?]. pp. 139. *Translated from the French original.*

PSYCHIATRIC HOSPITALS(Cont.)

— United Kingdom — Statistics.

U.K. Department of Health and Social Security. 1976. The facilities and services of mental illness and mental handicap hospitals in England, 1974. London, 1976. pp. 125. *(Statistical and Research Report Series. No.15)*

U.K. Department of Health and Social Security. 1977. In-patient statistics from the mental health enquiry for England, 1974. London, 1977. pp. 124. *(Statistical and Research Report Series. No.17)*

PSYCHIATRY.

ALEXANDER (FRANZ) and SELESNICK (SHELDON T.) The history of psychiatry: an evaluation of psychiatric thought and practice from prehistoric times to the present. New York, [1966], repr. 1968. pp. 573. *bibliog. Reprint of a hardcover edition published by Harper and Row.*

ZAX (MELVIN) and COWEN (EMORY LELAND) Abnormal psychology: changing conceptions. 2nd ed. New York, [1976]. pp. 643. *bibliog.*

— Scandinavia.

NORDISKA PSYKIATRISKA SAMARBETSKOMMITÉN. Symposium, Stockholm, 1970. Psykiatrisk vårdplanering. [Stockholm, 1971]. pp. 83. *(Sjukvårdens och Socialvårdens Planerings- och Rationaliseringsinstitut. Rapporter. 1971.17)*

PSYCHICAL RESEARCH.

GREELEY (ANDREW M.) The sociology of the paranormal: a reconnaissance. Beverly Hills, [1975]. pp. 88. *bibliog.*

GREEN (CELIA) The decline and fall of science. London, 1976. pp. 184. *bibliog.*

PSYCHOLINGUISTICS.

GEORGETOWN UNIVERSITY ROUND TABLE ON LANGUAGES AND LINGUISTICS, 1975. Developmental psycholinguistics: theory and applications; Daniel P. Dato, editor. Washington, D.C., [1975]. pp. 297. *bibliogs.*

OSGOOD (CHARLES EGERTON) and others. Cross-cultural universals of affective meaning. Urbana, [1975]. pp. 486. *bibliog.*

AITCHISON (JEAN) The articulate mammal: an introduction to psycholinguistics. London, 1976. pp. 256. *bibliog.*

BATES (ELIZABETH) Language and context: the acquisition of pragmatics. New York, [1976]. pp. 375. *bibliog.*

MILLER (GEORGE ARMITAGE) and JOHNSON-LAIRD (PHILIP N.) Language and perception. Cambridge, [1976]. pp. 760. *bibliog.*

NEW approaches to language mechanisms: a collection of psycholinguistic studies; editors R.J. Wales and Edward Walker. Amsterdam, 1976. pp. 296. *bibliogs.*

CLARK (HERBERT H.) and CLARK (EVE V.) Psychology and language: an introduction to psycholinguistics. New York, [1977]. pp. 608. *bibliog.*

PSYCHOLINGUISTICS series. 1. Developmental and pathological; [by] Eve V. Clark [and others]. London, 1977. pp. 160. *bibliogs.*

TALKING to children: language input and acquisition: papers from a conference sponsored by the Committee on Sociolinguistics of the Social Science Research Council (USA); edited by Catherine E. Snow and Charles A. Ferguson. Cambridge, 1977. pp. 369. *bibliog.*

PSYCHOLOGY.

BINDRA (DALBIR) A theory of intelligent behavior. New York, [1976]. pp. 447. *bibliog.*

ODAJNYK (VOLODYMYR WALTER) Jung and politics: the political and social ideas of C. G. Jung. New York, 1976. pp. 190.

PSYCHOLOGY, INDUSTRIAL.

HILF (HUBERT HUGO) Arbeitswissenschaft: Grundlagen der Leistungsforschung und Arbeitsgestaltung. München, 1957. pp. 341. *bibliog.*

McCORMICK (ERNEST J.) and TIFFIN (JOSEPH) Industrial psychology. 6th ed. London, 1975. pp. 625.

SUSMAN (GERALD I.) Autonomy at work: a sociotechnical analysis of participative management. New York, 1976. pp. 230. *bibliog.*

PSYCHOLOGY, MILITARY.

The SOCIAL psychology of military service; edited by Nancy L. Goldman and David R. Segal. Beverly Hills, 1976. pp. 299. *bibliog. Papers of a conference held at the Center for Continuing Education, University of Chicago, 1975.*

PSYCHOLOGY, PATHOLOGICAL.

ZAX (MELVIN) and COWEN (EMORY LELAND) Abnormal psychology: changing conceptions. 2nd ed. New York, [1976]. pp. 643. *bibliog.*

PSYCHOLOGY, PHYSIOLOGICAL.

FISHER (SEYMOUR) Body consciousness. Glasgow, 1976. pp. 221. *bibliog. First published in 1973.*

BLAKEMORE (COLIN) Mechanics of the mind. Cambridge, 1977. pp. 208. *bibliog. (British Broadcasting Corporation. Reith Lectures. 1976)*

PUBLIC CONTRACTS

— United Kingdom — Accounting.

REVIEW BOARD FOR GOVERNMENT CONTRACTS. Report on the second general review of the profit formula for non-competitive government contracts; [Sir William Slimmings, chairman]. London, H.M.S.O., 1977. pp. 56.

PUBLIC HEALTH ADMINISTRATION

— United Kingdom.

REGIONAL chairmen's enquiry into the working of the D[epartment of] H[ealth and] S[ocial] S[ecurity] in relation to regional health authorities; a report by the chairmen of the regional health authorities of the National Health Service. [London], Department of Health and Social Security, 1976. pp. 102.

PUBLIC HEALTH LAWS

— Germany, Eastern.

HARMSEN (HANS) ed. Gesundheitspolitisch relevante Probleme der neuen Gesetzgebung in der DDR wie auch in Ungarn und der UdSSR. Hamburg, 1977. pp. 136. *(Akademie für Staatsmedizin in Hamburg. Zur Entwicklung und Organisation des Gesundheitswesens in der DDR unter Berücksichtigung der UdSSR und Osteuropäischer Volksdemokratien. Band 74)*

— Hungary.

HARMSEN (HANS) ed. Gesundheitspolitisch relevante Probleme der neuen Gesetzgebung in der DDR wie auch in Ungarn und der UdSSR. Hamburg, 1977. pp. 136. *(Akademie für Staatsmedizin in Hamburg. Zur Entwicklung und Organisation des Gesundheitswesens in der DDR unter Berücksichtigung der UdSSR und Osteuropäischer Volksdemokratien. Band 74)*

— South Africa.

SOUTH AFRICA. Commission of Inquiry into the Health Bill. 1976. Report (R.P. 94/1976). in SOUTH AFRICA. Parliament. House of Assembly. Votes and proceedings; (with Printed annexures).

PUBLIC HOUSING

— Singapore.

SINGAPORE. Housing and Development Board. 1970. First decade in public housing, 1960-69. Singapore, 1970. pp. 91.

HASSAN (RIAZ) Families in flats: a study of low income families in public housing. Singapore, [1977]. pp. 249. *bibliog.*

— United Kingdom.

ANDREWS (C. LESLEY) Where we live. [London], Department of the Environment, Housing Development Directorate, Social Research Division, [1976] . pp. 20.

FORREST (RAY) and MURIE (ALAN S.) Social segregation, housing need and the sale of council houses. Birmingham, 1976. pp. 50. *(Birmingham. University. Centre for Urban and Regional Studies. Research Memoranda. No. 53)*

NATIONAL CONSUMER COUNCIL. Tenancy agreements between councils and their tenants. London, 1976. pp. 44. *(Discussion Papers. 2)*

DALE (JENNIFER ANN) Public housing, England and Wales, 1919-1969. 1977. fo. 467. *bibliog. Typescript. Ph. D. (London) thesis: unpublished. This thesis is the property of London University and may not be removed from the Library.*

ORBACH (LAURENCE F.) Homes for heroes: a study of the evolution of British public housing, 1915-1921. London, 1977. pp. 171. *bibliog.*

ROBINSON (HILARY) Do council tenants get a fair deal on repairs?: interim report on some survey results. [London], National Consumer Council, [1977]. pp. 28.

U.K. Race Relations Board. 1977. Comments on the government's consultation paper on records and information relating to the housing of members of ethnic groups. [London, 1977]. fo.4.

— — Rent.

NATIONAL CONSUMER COUNCIL. Behind with the rent: a study of council tenants in rent arrears. London, 1976. pp. 44. *(Discussion Papers. [1])*

— — Birmingham.

[BIRMINGHAM COMMUNITY DEVELOPMENT PROJECT]. Municipal housing allocation in Birmingham. [Birmingham, 1974]. 1 pamphlet (various pagings).

— — Liverpool.

WILSON (HUGH) AND WOMERSLEY (LEWIS) Firm. Inner area study: Liverpool: housing management. [London], Department of the Environment, [1977]. pp. 27, 1 map.

— — London.

PARKER (JOHN) Writer on housing, and DUGMORE (KEITH) Colour and the allocation of GLC housing: the report of the GLC lettings survey, 1974-75. [London], 1976. 1 vol. (various pagings). *bibliog. (London. Greater London Council. Research Reports. No. 21)*

PINCH (STEVEN PAUL) The geography of local authority housing, health and welfare, resource allocation in London, 1965-1973. 1976. fo. 632. *bibliog. Typescript. Ph.D. (London) thesis: unpublished. This thesis is the property of London University and may not be removed from the Library.*

LONDON HOUSING RESEARCH GROUP. Working Party on Race and Housing. Race and local authority housing: information on ethnic groups; a report; [Rob Hammond, chairman]. London, Community Relations Commission, 1977. pp. 16.

SHANKLAND-COX PARTNERSHIP and INSTITUTE OF COMMUNITY STUDIES. Inner area study: Lambeth: housing management and design. [London], Department of the Environment, [1977]. pp. 99.

— — — Finance.

NEWHAM ACTION COMMITTEE. The cost of housing, Newham 1976. [London, 1976]. pp. 26.

— — — Oldham.

SHENTON (NEIL) 'Deneside': a council estate. [York, 1976]. pp. 40. *(Papers in Community Studies. No. 8) ·*

— — **Wales.**

WELSH CONSUMER COUNCIL. Council housing: a survey of allocation policies in Wales. [Cardiff], 1976. pp. 47.

PUBLIC INTEREST.

SCHICK (RICHARD P.) and COUTURIER (JEAN J.) The public interest in government labor relations. Cambridge, Mass., [1977]. pp. 264. *bibliog.*

PUBLIC LANDS.

PUBLIC LAND OWNERSHIP CONFERENCE, YORK UNIVERSITY, TORONTO, 1976. Public land ownership: frameworks for evaluation: a record of idea and debate; edited by Dalton Kehoe [and others]. Lexington, Mass., [1976]. pp. 211.

The GOVERNMENT land developers: studies of public land-ownership policy in seven countries; edited by Neal Alison Roberts. Lexington, Mass., [1977]. pp. 249.

PUBLIC LAW

— France.

DUTHOIT (EUGENE) Aux confins de la morale et du droit public. Paris, 1919. pp. 295.

PUBLIC LIBRARIES

— United Kingdom.

MORRIS (ROGER JOHN BOWRING) Parliament and the public libraries: a survey of legislative activity promoting the municipal library service in England and Wales, 1850-1976. London, 1977. pp. 477. *bibliog.*

PUBLIC OPINION.

KLINE (STEPHEN CHARLES) Audio and visual characteristics of television news broadcasting: their effects on opinion change. 1977. fo. 360. *bibliog. Typescript. Ph.D. (London) thesis: unpublished. This thesis is the property of London University and may not be removed from the Library.*

— Australia.

SPROULE-JONES (M.H.) Public choice and federalism in Australia and Canada. Canberra, 1975. pp. 103. *bibliog. (Australian National University. Centre for Research on Federal Financial Relations. Research Monographs. No. 11)*

— Canada.

CANADIAN INSTITUTE OF INTERNATIONAL AFFAIRS and others. Public consultation on population questions: a report to the government of Canada. Toronto, 1974. pp. 69.

SPROULE-JONES (M.H.) Public choice and federalism in Australia and Canada. Canberra, 1975. pp. 103. *bibliog. (Australian National University. Centre for Research on Federal Financial Relations. Research Monographs. No. 11)*

— Europe, Eastern.

RADIO FREE EUROPE. Audience and Public Opinion Research Department. The best government as seen by East European respondents. [Munich?, 1975?]. fo. 33.

— European Economic Community countries.

FELD (WERNER J.) and WILDGEN (JOHN K.) Domestic political realities and European unification: a study of mass publics and elites in the European Community countries. Boulder, Col., 1976. pp. 177,11.

— Germany.

DEIST (WILHELM) Flottenpolitik und Flottenpropaganda: das Nachrichtenbureau des Reichsmarineamtes, 1897-1914. Stuttgart, 1976. pp. 344. *bibliog. (Militärgeschichtliches Forschungsamt. Beiträge zur Militär- und Kriegsgeschichte. Band 17)*

ROTH (DIETER) Zum Demokratieverständnis von Eliten in der Bundesrepublik Deutschland. Bern, 1976. pp. 187. *bibliog.*

— Nigeria.

AGUDA (OLUWADARE) The Nigerian approach to politics. Khartoum, [c.1970]. fo.40. *(Khartoum. University. Faculty of Arts. Sudan Research Unit. African Studies Seminar Papers. No. 2)*

OLORUNSOLA (VICTOR A.) Soldiers and power: the development performance of the Nigerian military regime. Stanford, 1977. pp. 168. *bibliog. (Stanford University. Hoover Institution on War, Revolution and Peace. Hoover Institution Publications. 168)*

— Poland.

RADIO FREE EUROPE. Audience and Public Opinion Research Department. The images of Polish, American, Russian, German and Chinese youth as seen by Poles. [Munich?], 1973. fo. 55.

— Russia.

SOTSIOLOGICHESKIE problemy obshchestvennogo mneniia i sredstv massovoi informatsii. Moskva, 1975. pp. 202.

GIBERT (STEPHEN P.) and others. Soviet images of America. London, [1977]. pp. 167. *bibliog.*

— Solomon Islands.

MONBERG (TORBEN) The reactions of people of Bellona Island towards a mining project. Copenhagen, 1976. pp. 61. *bibliog. (International Work Group for Indigenous Affairs. Documents. 24)*

— United Kingdom.

DOUGHERTY (JAMES E.) British perspectives on a changing global balance. Beverly Hills, [1975]. pp. 108.

FIELD (JULIA) Gloucestershire: a survey of attitudes among elected representatives. London, 1975. 1 vol. (various pagings).

HEDGES (BARRY M.) Methodological report on the 1975 referendum survey. London, 1975. pp. 15.

JOWELL (ROGER) and SPENCE (JAMES D.) The grudging Europeans: a study of British attitudes towards the EEC. London, 1975. pp. 44,19.

RUSH (MICHAEL) Parliament and the public. London, 1976. pp. 140. *bibliog.*

— United States.

ESSAYS on the American public opinion and the Palestine problem. Beirut, 1969. pp. 192. *bibliog. (Palestine Research Center. Palestine Monographs. 53)*

SZAJKOWSKI (ZOSA) Jews, wars and communism. New York, 1972-74. 2 vols. *bibliogs.*

ANDREWS (BRUCE) Public constraint and American policy in Vietnam. Beverly Hills, [1976]. pp. 64. *bibliog.*

LEIGH (MICHAEL) Mobilizing consent: public opinion and American foreign policy, 1937-1947. Westport, Conn., 1976. pp. 187. *bibliog.*

OSTHEIMER (JOHN M.) and RITT (LEONARD G.) Environment, energy, and black Americans. Beverly Hills, [1976]. pp. 38. *bibliog.*

SCHNEIDER (ANNE L.) Opinions and policies in the American states: the role of political characteristics. Beverly Hills, [1976]. pp. 47. *bibliog.*

TRILLING (RICHARD J.) Party image and electoral behavior. New York, [1976]. pp. 234.

— — Mathematical models.

WISE (CHARLES R.) Clients evaluate authority: the view from the other side. Beverly Hills, [1976]. pp. 91. *bibliog.*

— Yugoslavia.

CLARK (CAL) and JOHNSON (KARL F.) Development's influence on Yugoslav political values. Beverly Hills, [1976]. pp. 69. *bibliog.*

PUBLIC OPINION POLLS.

N.O.P. MARKET RESEARCH. A guide to the working of an NOP poll. London, [1973]. pp. 10.

HEDGES (BARRY M.) Community preference surveys in structure planning. London, [1975]. pp. 74.

PUBLIC RECORDS

— Russia — Ukraine.

MITIUKOV (OLEKSANDR HEORHIIOVYCH) Radians'ke arkhivne budivnytstvo na Ukraïni, 1917-1973. Kyïv, 1975. pp. 271. *With Russian, English and French summaries.*

PUBLIC RELATIONS

— Corporations.

SETHI (S. PRAKASH) Advocacy advertising and large corporations: social conflict, big business image, the news media and public policy. Lexington, Mass., [1977]. pp. 355. *bibliog.*

— Police.

POPE (DAVID) Community relations: the police response. London, 1976. pp. 65.

— United Kingdom.

U.K. Central Office of Information. Reference Division. Reference Pamphlets. 146. Advertising and public relations in Britain. London, 1976. pp. 30. *bibliog.*

PUBLIC SERVICE.

STEWART (MARY ELIZABETH HENDERSON) Baroness Stewart. Public service for the community. London, 1969. pp. 11. *(Fabian Society. Fabian Occasional Papers. 5)*

PUBLIC UTILITIES

— Finance.

NEW dimensions in public utility pricing; edited by Harry M. Trebing. East Lansing, Mich., 1976. pp. 619. *bibliogs. (Michigan State University. Institute of Public Utilities. MSU Public Utilities Studies) Includes papers from the 1975 conference of the Institute of Public Utilities, Graduate School of Business Administration, Michigan State University.*

— United Kingdom.

SELDON (ARTHUR) Charge. London, 1977. pp. 224. *bibliog.*

— United States — Finance.

NEW dimensions in public utility pricing; edited by Harry M. Trebing. East Lansing, Mich., 1976. pp. 619. *bibliogs. (Michigan State University. Institute of Public Utilities. MSU Public Utilities Studies) Includes papers from the 1975 conference of the Institute of Public Utilities, Graduate School of Business Administration, Michigan State University.*

PUBLICITY (LAW)

— United Kingdom.

HARRIS (BRIAN) The courts, the press and the public. Chichester, 1976. pp. 96.

PUBLISHERS AND PUBLISHING

— Directories.

CLARKE (TIMOTHY) International academic and specialist publishers' directory. New York, [1975]. pp. 555.

PUBLISHERS AND PUBLISHING(Cont.)

— France.

SPIRE (ANTOINE) and VIALA (JEAN PIERRE) La bataille du livre. Paris, [1976]. pp. 302.

— Germany.

[A COLLECTION of documents relating to book censorship and the book trade in Germany during the years immediately following World War II]. 1945-48. pp. various..

CASSIANEUM. Festschrift hundert Jahre Cassianeum, Verlag und Druckerei Ludwig Auer, Donauwörth: 1875-1975. Donauwörth, [1975]. pp. 120.

— India.

ALTBACH (PHILIP G.) Publishing in India: an analysis. Delhi, 1975. pp. 115. *bibliog.*

— Russia.

BELOV (SERGEI VLADIMIROVICH) and TOLSTIAKOV (ARTUR PAVLOVICH) Russkie izdateli kontsa XIX - nachala XX veka. Leningrad, 1976. pp. 170. *(Akademiia Nauk SSSR. Seriia "Istoriia Nashei Rodiny")*

— Underdeveloped areas.

See UNDERDEVELOPED AREAS — Publishers and publishing.

— United Kingdom.

UNWIN (Sir STANLEY) The truth about publishing;...eighth edition revised and partly re- written by Philip Unwin. London, 1976. pp. 256. *bibliog.*

PUERTO RICO

— Constitutional history.

SMITH (CARLOS J.) Estructuras politicas de Puerto Rico. 2nd ed. Rio Piedras, 1972. pp. 145.

— Economic history.

QUINTERO RIVERA (ANGEL GUILLERMO) The working class and Puerto Rican politics in the process of change from a traditional to a capitalist agricultural economy. 1976. fo. 464. *bibliog. Typescript. Ph.D.(London) thesis: unpublished. This thesis is the property of London University and may not be removed from the Library.*

— Politics and government.

SMITH (CARLOS J.) Estructuras politicas de Puerto Rico. 2nd ed. Rio Piedras, 1972. pp. 145.

PULQUE

— Mexico.

CAMBRIDGE. University. Centre of Latin American Studies. Working Papers. No. 9. Plata y pulque en el siglo XVIII mexicano; by Alvaro Jara. Cambridge, 1973. pp. 45.

PUNISHMENT

— China.

GRIFFIN (PATRICIA E.) The Chinese communist treatment of counter-revolutionaries, 1924-1949. Princeton, N.J., [1976]. pp. 256. *bibliog. (Harvard University. Harvard Studies in East Asian Law)*

— South Africa.

SOUTH AFRICA. Commission of Inquiry into the Penal System. 1976. Report (R.P. 78/1976). in SOUTH AFRICA. Parliament. House of Assembly. Votes and proceedings; (with Printed annexures).

PUNJAB (PAKISTAN)

— Economic conditions.

PUNJAB DEVELOPMENT REVIEW AND PROSPECTS; [pd. by] Planning and Development Department [Punjab (Pakistan)]. a., 1971 (1st)- Lahore.

— Social conditions.

PUNJAB DEVELOPMENT REVIEW AND PROSPECTS; [pd. by] Planning and Development Department [Punjab (Pakistan)]. a., 1971 (1st)- Lahore.

PURITANS.

CARROLL (JOHN) Puritan, paranoid, remissive: a sociology of modern culture. London, 1977. pp. 148. *bibliog.*

PUSTUNICH, MEXICO

— Social life and customs.

PRESS (IRWIN) Tradition and adaptation: life in a modern Yucatan Maya village. Westport, Conn., 1975. pp. 224.

QATAR.

QATAR. Ministry of Information. Press and Publication Department. 1976. Qatar today. [Dohar, 1976]. pp. 103.

QUALITY CONTROL.

VAVILOV (ANATOLII PAVLOVICH) Effektivnost' sotsialisticheskogo proizvodstva i kachestvo produktsii. Moskva, 1975. pp. 175.

EUROPEAN COMMUNITIES. Commission. 1976. Proposal for a Council directive relating to the approximation of the laws, regulations and administrative provisions of the member states concerning liability for defective products: presented...to the Council on 9 September, 1976. [Brussels], 1976. pp. 20. *bibliog. (Bulletin of the European Communities. Supplements. [1976/11])*

QUARRIES AND QUARRYING

— United Kingdom.

SAMUEL (RAPHAEL) ed. Miners, quarrymen and saltworkers. London, 1977. pp. 363. *(History Workshop. History Workshop Series)*

QUEBEC (PROVINCE)

— Economic conditions.

FRECHETTE (PIERRE) and others. L'économie du Québec. Quebec, [1975]. pp. 436.

TREMBLAY (RODRIGUE) ed. L'économie québécoise: histoire, développement, politiques. Montréal, 1976. pp. 493.

— Economic history.

NISH (CAMERON) François-Etienne Cugnet, 1719-1751: entrepreneur et entreprises en Nouvelle-France. Montréal, [1975]. pp. 185. *bibliog. (Centre de Recherche en Histoire Economique du Canada Français. Histoire Economique et Sociale du Canada Français)*

— Economic policy.

FRECHETTE (PIERRE) and others. L'économie du Québec. Quebec, [1975]. pp. 436.

FOURNIER (PIERRE) The Québec establishment: the ruling class and the state. Montréal, [1976]. pp. 228. *bibliog.*

TREMBLAY (RODRIGUE) ed. L'économie québécoise: histoire, développement, politiques. Montréal, 1976. pp. 493.

— History.

McROBERTS (KENNETH) and POSGATE (DALE) Quebec: social change and political crisis. Toronto, [1976]. pp. 216.

— Languages.

QUEBEC (PROVINCE). Commission of Inquiry on the Position of the French Language and on Language Rights in Québec. 1972. Report; [Jean-Denis Gendron, Chairman.]. Québec, 1972. 3 vols. (in l).

— Legislative Assembly — Elections.

BENJAMIN (JACQUES) Comment on fabrique un premier ministre québécois: de 1960 à nos jours. Montréal, [1975]. pp. 190.

— Nationalism.

LAURIN (CAMILLE) Témoignage de Camille Laurin: pourquoi je suis souverainiste. Montreal, [1973?]. pp. 60.

DION (LEON) Nationalismes et politiques au Québec. Montréal, [1975]. pp. 177.

ROBERT (JEAN CLAUDE) Du Canada français au Québec libre: histoire d'un mouvement indépendantiste. Ottawa, [1975]. pp. 324. *bibliog.*

— — Bibliography.

LAMBERT (RONALD D.) compiler. Nationalism and national ideologies in Canada and Quebec: a bibliography. rev. ed. Waterloo, Ont., 1975. fo. 144.

— Politics and government.

LAURIN (CAMILLE) Témoignage de Camille Laurin: pourquoi je suis souverainiste. Montreal, [1973?]. pp. 60.

QUEBEC society and politics: views from the inside; (Dale C. Thomson, editor). Toronto, [1973]. pp. 272. *A revision of lectures delivered in autumn 1971 at the Johns Hopkins University's Center of Canadian Studies, with additional essays.*

LEMIEUX (VINCENT) and HUDON (RAYMOND) Patronage et politique au Québec, 1944-1972. Québec, 1975. pp. 187.

BROSSARD (JACQUES) Professor of Law, University of Montreal. L'accession à la souveraineté et le cas du Québec: conditions et modalités politico-juridiques. Montréal, 1976. pp. 799. *bibliog.*

McROBERTS (KENNETH) and POSGATE (DALE) Quebec: social change and political crisis. Toronto, [1976]. pp. 216.

MORIN (CLAUDE) Quebec versus Ottawa: the struggle for self-government, 1960-72; translated from Le pouvoir québécois...en négociation and from Le combat québécois by Richard Howard. Toronto, [1976]. pp. 164.

BLACK (CONRAD) Duplessis. Toronto, [1977]. pp. 743. *bibliog.*

— Population.

CALDWELL (GARY) A demographic profile of the English-speaking population of Quebec, 1921-1971. Quebec, 1974. pp. 175. *bibliog. (International Center for Research on Bilingualism. Publications. B-51)*

— Social conditions.

QUEBEC society and politics: views from the inside; (Dale C. Thomson, editor). Toronto, [1973]. pp. 272. *A revision of lectures delivered in autumn 1971 at the Johns Hopkins University's Center of Canadian Studies, with additional essays.*

QUEENSLAND.

QUEENSLAND. State Public Relations Bureau. 1963. Queensland: land of the sun. [Brisbane, 1963]. pp. 48.

— Economic conditions.

QUEENSLAND. Intelligence and Tourist Bureau. 1923. Queensland, the rich but sparsely peopled country, a paradise for willing workers. [new ed.] Brisbane, [1923]. pp. 64.

— Economic policy.

FOLEY (THOMAS ANDREW) Post-war planning in Queensland. Brisbane, [1944]. pp. 25. *Reprinted from Rydge's Journal, April, 1943.*

QUEENSLAND. Department of Development and Mines. 1960. Pioneering a new era of development in Queensland:...by Ernest Evans,...Minister for Development, Mines and Main Roads. [Brisbane], 1960. pp. 24.

QUEENSLAND. Department of Development and Mines. 1963. Queensland unlimited: a progress report; by E. Evans, Minister for Development, Mines, Main Roads, and Electricity. [Brisbane], 1963. pp. 20.

QUETZALCÓATL.

LAFAYE (JACQUES) Quetzalcóatl and Guadalupe: the formation of Mexican national consciousness, 1531-1813; foreword by Octavio Paz; translated by Benjamin Keen. Chicago, 1976. pp. 336.

QUEUEING THEORY.

KLEINROCK (LEONARD) Queueing systems. New York, [1975-6]. 2 vols. bibliogs.

COHEN (JACOB WILLEM) On regenerative processes in queueing theory. Berlin, 1976. pp. 93.

RABIES.

OFFICE OF HEALTH ECONOMICS. [Studies in Current Health Problems]. No. 56. Rabies. London, [1976]. pp. 27. bibliog.

U.K. Department of Health and Social Security. 1977. Memorandum on rabies. London, [1977]. pp. 37. bibliog.

RABIN (YITZHAK).

SLATER (ROBERT) Journalist. Rabin of Israel: a biography. London, [1977]. pp. 304.

RACE.

HUMAN diversity: its causes and social significance...; edited by Bernard D. Davis and Patricia Flaherty. Cambridge, Mass., [1976]. pp. 248. bibliog. The proceedings of a series of seminars sponsored by the Committee on Human Diversity of the American Academy of Arts and Sciences 1973-1974.

BANTON (MICHAEL PARKER) The idea of race. London, 1977. pp. 190. bibliog.

RACE AWARENESS.

ROSENBERG (MORRIS) and SIMMONS (ROBERTA G.) Black and white self-esteem: the urban school child. Washington, D.C., [1971?]. pp. 160. bibliog. (American Sociological Association. Arnold and Caroline Rose Monograph Series in Sociology)

NORBURN (VERONICA) and PUSHKIN (I.) Ethnic awareness in young children: a follow-up study into early adolescence. London, 1973. pp. 70, 66. bibliog.

MILNER (DAVID) Children and race. Harmondsworth, 1975. pp. 281. bibliog.

AMERICAN ACADEMY OF POLITICAL AND SOCIAL SCIENCE. Annals. vol. 433. Ethnic conflict in the world today; special editor of this volume, Martin O. Heisler. Philadelphia, 1977. pp. 220.

BEUF (ANN H.) Red children in white America. [Philadelphia], 1977. pp. 155. bibliog.

RACE DISCRIMINATION.

BREITMAN (GEORGE) Race prejudice: how it began; when it will end. New York, 1971. pp. 15.

— Law and legislation — United Kingdom.

U.K. Commission for Racial Equality. 1977. Your rights to equal treatment under the new Race Relations Act 1976: a general guide. [London, 1977]. pp. (8).

U.K. Commission for Racial Equality. 1977. Your rights to equal treatment under the new Race Relations Act 1976: housing, education and services. [London, 1977]. pp. 12.

U.K. Home Office. 1977. Racial Discrimination: a guide to the Race Relations Act 1976. [London, 1977]. pp. 53.

— America, Latin.

COMAS CAMPS (JUAN) Antropologia de los pueblos iberoamericanos. Barcelona, 1974. pp. 223. bibliog.

— Botswana.

BOTSWANA. Legislative Council. Select Committee on Racial Discrimination. 1963. Report; [A.C.A. Adams, chairman]. [Gaborone, 1963?] 1 vol.(various pagings).

— Syria.

VANLY (ISMET CHERIFF) Le problème kurde en Syrie: plans pour le génocide d'une minorité nationale. [Lausanne?], Comité pour la Défense des Droits du Peuple Kurde, 1968. pp. 40.

— United Kingdom.

RUNNYMEDE TRUST. Briefing Papers. 1977, No. 2. A summary [of] The facts of racial disadvantage: a national survey. London, 1977. fo. 20.

— United States.

PERRY (RONALD W.) Racial discrimination and military justice. New York, 1977. pp. 101. bibliog.

WELLMAN (DAVID T.) Portraits of white racism. Cambridge, 1977. pp. 254. bibliog.

RACE PROBLEMS.

BANTON (MICHAEL PARKER) The idea of race. London, 1977. pp. 190. bibliog.

RACE PROBLEMS AND THE PRESS

— United Kingdom.

EVANS (PETER C.C.) Publish and be damned? London, 1976. pp. 37.

COMMUNITY RELATIONS COMMISSION. Reporting on race: the role and responsibility of the press in reporting on race relations; a memorandum. [London], 1977. pp. 36.

RACE PROBLEMS IN LITERATURE.

PROCTOR (CHRIS) Racist textbooks. London, [1975]. pp. 41.

RACZYNSKI (EDWARD) Count.

RACZYŃSKI (EDWARD) Count. Od Narcyza Kulikowskiego do Winstona Churchilla. Londyn, 1976. pp. 145.

RADEK (KARL).

MOELLER (DIETRICH) ed. Revolutionär, Intrigant, Diplomat: Karl Radek in Deutschland. Köln, [1976]. pp. 303. bibliog.

STEFFEN (JOCHEN) and WIEMERS (ADALBERT) Auf zum letzten Verhör: Erkenntnisse des verantwortlichen Hofnarren der Revolution Karl Radek. München, [1977]. pp. 369. bibliog.

RADICALISM.

FREYDORF (KARL) ed. Neuer Roter Katechismus, etc. München, 1968. pp. 266.

HALEBSKY (SANDOR) Mass society and political conflict: toward a reconstruction of theory. Cambridge, 1976. pp. 309.

JANICKI (JANUSZ) and MUSZYŃSKI (JERZY) eds. Ideologia i polityka współczesnego lewactwa. Warszawa, 1976. pp. 287.

LINDBÄCK (ASSAR) The political economy of the new left: an outsider's view. 2nd ed. New York, [1977]. pp. 239.

YOUNG (NIGEL) An infantile disorder?: the crisis and decline of the New Left. London, 1977. pp. 490. bibliog.

— Canada — Bibliography — Union lists.

KEHDE (NED) compiler. The American left, 1955-1970: a National Union Catalog of pamphlets published in the United States and Canada. Westport, Conn., 1976. pp. 515. bibliog.

— France.

TOUCHARD (JEAN) La gauche en France depuis 1900. Paris, [1977]. pp. 383. bibliog.

— Germany.

ALBRECHT (RICHARD) Marxismus, bürgerliche Ideologie, Linksradikalismus: zur Ideologie und Sozialgeschichte des westeuropäischen Linksradikalismus. Frankfurt/Main, 1975. pp. 169.

LANGGUTH (GERD) Die Protestbewegung in der Bundesrepublik Deutschland, 1968-1976. Köln, [1976]. pp. 364. bibliog.

LUCAS (ERHARD) Zwei Formen von Radikalismus in der deutschen Arbeiterbewegung. Frankfurt am Main, [1976]. pp. 334. bibliog.

PORTNER (DIETER) Bundeswehr und Linksextremismus. München, [1976]. pp. 210. bibliog.

ENGELMANN (BERNT) Trotz alledem: deutsche Radikale, 1777-1977. München, [1977]. pp. 415.

— Hungary.

DEME (LASZLO) The radical left in the Hungarian revolution of 1848. New York, [1976]. pp. 162. bibliog. (East European Quarterly. East European Monographs. 19)

— Russia.

GERTSEN (ALEKSANDR IVANOVICH) and OGAREV (NIKOLAI PLATONOVICH) Golosa iz Rossii: sborniki, (kommentarii i ukazateli; rukovodstvo izdaniem...M.V. Nechkinoi). Moskva, 1974-76. 10 vols. (in 4). Facsimile of original ed. of 1856-60.

AZANOV (VLADIMIR IVANOVICH) Pamflety Gertsena v "Kolokole"; pod redaktsiei...E.I. Pokusaeva. Saratov, 1974. pp. 50.

TKACHEV (PETR NIKITICH) Sochineniia v dvukh tomakh; (obshchaia redaktsiia A.A. Galaktionova [and others]). Moskva, 1975-76. 2 vols. bibliog. (Akademiia Nauk SSSR. Institut Filosofii. Filosofskoe Nasledie)

USHAKOV (ANATOLII VASIL'EVICH) Revoliutsionnoe dvizhenie demokraticheskoi intelligentsii v Rossii, 1895-1904. Moskva, 1976. pp. 240.

BORCKE (ASTRID VON) Die Ursprünge des Bolschewismus: die jakobinische Tradition in Russland und die Theorie der revolutionären Diktatur. München, [1977]. pp. 646. bibliog.

— Switzerland.

JOST (HANS ULRICH) Die Altkommunisten: Linksradikalismus und Sozialismus in der Schweiz, 1919 bis 1921. Frauenfeld, [1977]. pp. 232. bibliog.

— United Kingdom.

A REVIEW of the principles of radical reformers, and the measures which they have proposed for reform in Parliament. Edinburgh, Bayne, 1820. pp. 34.

HAIN (PETER) Radical regeneration. London, [1975]. pp. 181.

ROYLE (EDWARD) ed. The infidel tradition from Paine to Bradlaugh. London, 1976. pp. 228. bibliog.

THOLFSEN (TRYGVE R.) Working class radicalism in mid-Victorian England. London, 1976. pp. 332.

TESTAMENTS of radicalism: memoirs of working class politicians, 1790-1885; edited and introduced by David Vincent. London, [1977]. pp. 246. bibliogs.

RADICALISM.(Cont.)

— United States.

The BURDEN of the Berrigans. Worcester, Mass., 1971. pp. 80. *(Holy Cross Quarterly. vol.4. no.1)*

WOOD (JAMES L.) New left ideology: its dimensions and development. Beverly Hills, [1975]. pp. 70. *bibliog.*

FONER (PHILIP SHELDON) ed. We, the other people: alternative declarations of independence by labor groups, farmers, woman's rights advocates, socialists, and blacks, 1829-1975. Urbana, Ill., [1976]. pp. 205.

LINDBÄCK (ASSAR) The political economy of the new left: an outsider's view. 2nd ed. New York, [1977]. pp. 239.

— — Bibliography — Union lists.

KEHDE (NED) compiler. The American left, 1955-1970: a National Union Catalog of pamphlets published in the United States and Canada. Westport, Conn., 1976. pp. 515. *bibliog.*

RADIO BROADCASTING.

SCHLOSSER (HERBERT S.) Broadcasters in a free society: common problems, common purpose. London, 1976. pp. 16. *(British Broadcasting Corporation. B.B.C. Lunch-time Lectures. 10th Series. 5)*

— Canada.

HALLMAN (EUGENE S.) and HINDLEY (H.) Broadcasting in Canada. London, 1977. pp. 90.

— Denmark.

FRANCE. Direction de la Documentation. La Documentation Française. Notes et Etudes Documentaires. Nos. 4,232-4,233. La radiodiffusion-télévision au Danemark; par René Albrecht. Paris, 1975. pp. 33. *bibliog.*

MORTENSEN (FRANDS) ed. Ytringsfrihed og offentlighed: de hemmelige dokumenter fra Danmarks Radios afskedigelse af Erik Thygesen, kommenteret af Erik Thygesen og Frands Mortensen. Århus, 1975 repr. 1976. pp. 430. *bibliog.*

— France.

KUHN (RAYMOND) Government and broadcasting in France, 1969-1975. [Coventry], 1975. pp. 46. *(University of Warwick. Department of Politics. Working Papers. No. 8)*

— Italy.

FRANCE. Direction de la Documentation. La Documentation Française. Notes et Etudes Documentaires. Nos. 4,251-4,252-4,253. La radio et la télévision en Italie; par Adrien Popovici. Paris, 1976. pp. 101. *bibliog.*

— Malaysia.

ADHIKARYA (RONNY) and others. Broadcasting in peninsular Malaysia. London, 1977. pp. 102. *bibliog.*

— Russia.

GUREVICH (PAVEL SEMENOVICH) and RUZHNIKOV (VSEVOLOD NIKOLAEVICH) Sovetskoe radioveshchanie: stranitsy istorii. Moskva, 1976. pp. 382. *bibliog.*

— — Uzbekistan.

ESIN (ANATOLII FEDOROVICH) Radio i televidenie Uzbekistana: rost, dostizheniia, problemy. Tashkent, 1975. pp. 160.

— Sweden.

PLOMAN (EDWARD W.) Broadcasting in Sweden. London, 1976. pp. 65.

— United Kingdom.

STANDING CONFERENCE ON BROADCASTING. Evidence to the Committee on the Future of Broadcasting from the Standing Conference on Broadcasting. London, 1976. pp. 156. *Cover title: The SCOB papers: broadcasting in the UK.*

RADIO IN POLITICS

— France.

KUHN (RAYMOND) Government and broadcasting in France, 1969-1975. [Coventry], 1975. pp. 46. *(University of Warwick. Department of Politics. Working Papers. No. 8)*

RADIO IN PROPAGANDA.

HALE (JULIAN) Radio power: propaganda and international broadcasting. London, 1975. pp. 196. *bibliog.*

CAPRIOLI (MAURA PICCIALUTI) ed. Radio Londra, 1940-1945: inventario delle trasmissioni per l'Italia. Roma, 1976. 2 vols. *(Italy. Direzione Generale degli Archivi di Stato. Pubblicazioni degli Archivi di Stato. 89, 90)*

MAGNUSSON (ÅKE) The Voice of South Africa. Uppsala, 1976. pp. 55. *bibliog. (Nordiska Afrikainstitutet. Research Reports. No. 35)*

WETTIG (GERHARD) Broadcasting and détente: eastern policies and their implication for east-west relations. London, [1977]. pp. 110.

RADIO INDUSTRY AND TRADE

— Russia — Siberia.

V tysiachi adresov: istoriia Berdskogo radiozavoda. Novosibirsk, 1976. pp. 261.

RADIO JOURNALISM

— United States.

CULBERT (DAVID HOLBROOK) News for everyman: radio and foreign affairs in thirties America. Westport, Conn., 1976. pp. 238. *bibliog.*

RADIOACTIVE POLLUTION.

DREYER (GUENTHER) and VINKE (HANS) Absolute Sicherheit oder verbrannte Erde: der Kampf gegen das Atommüll-Zentrum im Emsland. Hamburg, 1977. pp. 125.

RAILWAYS

— Rates.

[ACWORTH (Sir WILLIAM MITCHELL)] State control of railway rates abroad. [1894?]. fo. 78. *Typescript.*

— Safety measures — United Kingdom.

U.K. Health and Safety Executive. Industry and services: a report of the work of H.M. Factory Inspectorate incorporating the annual reports of H.M. Inspector of Railways and H.M. Inspector of Explosives. a., 1975(1st)- London.

— Train load.

STARR (JOHN T.) The evolution of the unit train, 1960-1969. Chicago, 1976. pp. 233. *bibliog. (Chicago. University. Department of Geography. Research Papers. No. 158)*

— Argentine Republic — Employees.

MONZALVO (LUIS) Testigo de la primera hora del peronismo: [memorias de un ferroviario]. Buenos Aires, [1975]. pp. 272.

— Bangladesh.

BANGLADESH. Provincial Statistical Board and Bureau of Commercial and Industrial Intelligence. Trade supplement: an account relating to the foreign trade, coastal trade, navigation, East Bengal Railway. Statistics and balance of trade of East Pakistan. m., Je 1958. Dacca.

— Brazil — São Paulo — History.

MATOS (ODILON NOGUEIRA DE) Cafe e ferrovias: a evolução ferroviaria de São Paulo e o desenvolvimento da cultura cafeeira. São Paulo, 1974. pp. 135. *bibliog.*

— Canada — History.

TULCHINSKY (GERALD J. J.) The river barons: Montreal businessmen and the growth of industry and transportation, 1837-53. Toronto, [1977]. pp. 310. *bibliog.*

— China.

LEE (EN-HAN) China's quest for railway autonomy, 1904-1911: a study of the Chinese railway-rights recovery movement. Singapore, [1977]. pp. 316. *bibliog.*

— France.

SNCF, LA; ([pd. by] Société Nationale des Chemins de Fer Français). a., 1975- Paris.

— — Employees.

FRUIT (ELIE) Les syndicats dans les chemins de fer en France, 1890-1910. Paris, [1976]. pp. 216. *bibliog.*

— Germany — Finance.

FISCHER (HANS) Writer on railway finance. Finanzielle Leistungen, insbesondere Abgeltungsleistungen, des Bundes an die Deutsche Bundesbahn (DB). Berlin, 1974. pp. 450. *bibliog. Lacking pp. 449-50. Dissertation - Freie Universität Berlin.*

— — History.

FREMDLING (RAINER) Eisenbahnen und deutsches Wirtschaftswachstum, 1840-1879: ein Beitrag zur Entwicklungstheorie und zur Theorie der Infrastruktur. Dortmund, 1975. pp. 217. *bibliog. (Gesellschaft für Westfälische Wirtschaftsgeschichte. Untersuchungen zur Wirtschafts-, Sozial- und Technikgeschichte. Band 2) With English summary.*

— Italy — History.

SEVERIN (DANTE) San Gottardo, Spluga e interessi di Como: studio sulla economia dei tracciati ferroviari, 1836-1973. Como, 1974. pp. 187. *bibliog.*

— Russia.

KUMANEV (GEORGII ALEKSANDROVICH) Na sluzhbe fronta i tyla: zheleznodorozhnyi transport SSSR nakanune i v gody Velikoi Otechestvennoi voiny, 1938-1945. Moskva, 1976. pp. 455.

— — History.

SOLOV'EVA (AIDA MIKHAILOVNA) Zheleznodorozhnyi transport Rossii vo vtoroi polovine XIX v. Moskva, 1975. pp. 315.

— — Caucasus — Employees.

TEVZADZE (GEORGII GEORGIEVICH) Bor'ba zheleznodorozhnikov Zakavkaz'ia za ustanovlenie i uprochenie Sovetskoi vlasti. Tbilisi, 1975. pp. 126.

— Sweden — Employees.

EUROPEAN COURT OF HUMAN RIGHTS. Publications. Series B: Pleadings, Oral Arugments and Documents. [B18]. ...Swedish engine drivers' union case. Strasbourg, Council of Europe, 1977. pp. 216[bis], 217-260. *In English and French.*

— Switzerland — History.

SEVERIN (DANTE) San Gottardo, Spluga e interessi di Como: studio sulla economia dei tracciati ferroviari, 1836-1973. Como, 1974. pp. 187. *bibliog.*

— United Kingdom — Commuting traffic.

HEPBURN (D.R.C.) Analysis of changes in rail commuting to central London, 1966-71. Crowthorne, 1977. pp. 12. *bibliog. (U.K. Transport and Road Research Laboratory. Supplementary Reports. 268)*

— — Electrification.

TRANSPORT 2000. An electrifying case. London, [1976]. pp. 8.

— — History.

PERKIN (HAROLD J.) The age of the railway. Newton Abbot, 1970 repr. 1971. pp. 351. *bibliogs.*

MITCHELL (WILLIAM REGINALD) and MUSSETT (N.J.) Seven years hard: building the Settle-Carlisle railway. Clapham, North Yorks., 1976. pp. 65. *bibliog.*

— — Passenger traffic.

RESEARCH PROJECTS LIMITED. Final report: conclusions and recommendations, London-Norwich interval service project; for Eastern Region headquarters, British Railways; (with Reports 1-8 and associated correspondence and papers 1963-65). London, 1963. 9 vols., 1 folder.

— United States — Freight.

STARR (JOHN T.) The evolution of the unit train, 1960-1969. Chicago, 1976. pp. 233. *bibliog. (Chicago. University. Department of Geography. Research Papers. No. 158)*

— — History.

GILBERT (HEATHER) The end of the road: the life of Lord Mount Stephen, vol. II, 1891-1921. Aberdeen, 1977. pp. 442.

— — Alaska.

INDIANA STATE UNIVERSITY. Department of Geography and Geology. Professional Papers. No. 7. [Selected articles]. Terre Haute, Ind., 1975. pp. 56.

— Zaire — Electrification.

LUMBILA (D.) and MALU (FELIX) A propos de l'électrification de la voie ferrée Bas-Congo-Katanga. Kinshasa, Office National de la Recherche et du Développement, 1970. pp. 8, 1 map. *bibliog.*

RAILWAYS AND STATE.

[ACWORTH (Sir WILLIAM MITCHELL)] State control of railway rates abroad. [1894?]. fo. 78. *Typescript.*

— United States.

HOOGENBOOM (ARI ARTHUR) and HOOGENBOOM (OLIVE) A history of the ICC: from panacea to palliative. New York, [1976]. pp. 207. *bibliog.*

RAMIREZ SANCHEZ (ILICH).

DOBSON (CHRISTOPHER) and PAYNE (RONALD) The Carlos complex: a study in terror. New York, 1977. pp. 254.

RAMOS (JORGE ABELARDO).

PEÑA (MILCIADES) Industria, burguesia industrial y liberacion nacional. Buenos Aires, 1974. pp. 195.

RAMSAY (JAMES) Vicar of Teston.

SHYLLON (FOLARIN OLAWALE) James Ramsay: the unknown abolitionist. Edinburgh, 1977. pp. 144. *bibliog.*

RANKIN (HARRY).

RANKIN (HARRY) A socialist perspective for Vancouver. Toronto, [1974?]. pp. 83.

RAPALLO, TREATY OF, 1922.

WINZER (OTTO) Der Rapallo-Vertrag und seine nationale Bedeutung für Deutschland. Berlin, 1952. pp. 42.

KOCH (GERDA) Die deutsche Arbeiterklasse und der Rapallo-Vertrag, März bis Juni 1922. [Berlin, 1957]. pp. 60.

RAPE

— United Kingdom.

COOTE (ANNA) and GILL (TESS) The rape controversy: the law, the myths, the facts: changes that are needed: and what to do if it happens to you. London, [1975]. pp. 39.

RATIONALISM.

BOULANGER (NICOLAS ANTOINE) Dissertations sur Elie et Enoch, sur Esope fabuliste, et Traité mathématique sur le bonheur (par Irenée Krantzovius [pseud., i.e. Benjamin Stillingfleet]). n.p. [17--]. pp. xvi, 284. *Half-title: each part has special title page. Bound with [PIC] Le songe d'Alcibiade, published 1735. From internal evidence this copy known to have been published after 1740.*

RAW MATERIALS.

PAHL (WALTHER) Rohstoffe: der Kampf um die Güter der Erde. München, [1952]. pp. 397.

GUTTMANN (HENRY) Die Weltwirtschaft und ihre Rohstoffe. Berlin, [1956]. pp. 532. *bibliog.*

CORBET (HUGH) Raw materials: beyond the rhetoric of commodity power. London, 1975. pp. 41. *(Trade Policy Research Centre. International Issues. No. 1)*

INTERNATIONAL ECONOMIC STUDIES INSTITUTE. Raw materials and foreign policy. Washington, D.C., [1976]. pp. 416.

KONJUNKTURPOLITIK: Zeitschrift für angewandte Konjunkturforschung. Beihefte. Heft 23. Die Versorgung der Weltwirtschaft mit Rohstoffen: Bericht über den wissenschaftlichen Teil der 39. Mitgliederversammlung der Arbeitsgemeinschaft deutscher wirtschaftswissenschaftlicher Forschungsinstitute...1976. Berlin, [1976]. pp. 132. *In German or English.*

SCHNEIDER (WILLIAM) Food, foreign policy and raw materials cartels. New York, [1976]. pp. 119. *(National Strategy Information Center. Strategy Papers. No. 28)*

— Germany.

KEBSCHULL (DIETRICH) and others. Das integrierte Rohstoffprogramm: Prüfung entwicklungspolitischer Ansätze im Rohstoffvorschlag der UNCTAD. Hamburg, 1977. pp. 401. *bibliog. (Hamburg. Hamburgisches Welt-Wirtschafts-Archiv. Veröffentlichungen)*

— Underdeveloped areas.

See UNDERDEVELOPED AREAS — Raw materials.

— United States.

INTERNATIONAL ECONOMIC STUDIES INSTITUTE. Raw materials and foreign policy. Washington, D.C., [1976]. pp. 416.

PAGE (TALBOT) Conservation and economic efficiency: an approach to materials policy. Baltimore, [1977]. pp. 266.

RAWLS (JOHN).

WOLFF (ROBERT PAUL) Understanding Rawls: a reconstruction and critique of A theory of justice. Princeton, N.J., [1977]. pp. 224. *bibliog.*

RAZAK BIN HUSSEIN (ABDUL).

See ABDUL RAZAK BIN HUSSEIN.

REACTOR FUEL REPROCESSING.

DREYER (GUENTHER) and VINKE (HANS) Absolute Sicherheit oder verbrannte Erde: der Kampf gegen das Atommüll-Zentrum im Emsland. Hamburg, 1977. pp. 125.

READERSHIP SURVEYS

— United Kingdom.

LONDON PRESS EXCHANGE. A survey of reader interest in the national morning and London evening press. London, 1934. 3 vols.

MANN (PETER HENRY) A new survey: the facts about romantic fiction;...in collaboration with Mills and Boon Ltd. London, [1974]. pp. 24.

READING

— City planning — Mathematical models.

BATTY (MICHAEL) and MARCH (LIONEL) Dynamic urban models based on information-minimising. Reading, 1976. pp. 41. *bibliog. (Reading. University. Department of Geography. Reading Geographical Papers. No. 48)*

REAL ESTATE BUSINESS

— Law and legislation — South Africa.

SOUTH AFRICA. Parliament. House of Assembly. Select Committee on the Development Schemes Bill. 1977. Report...proceedings and evidence (S.C. 13-1977). in SOUTH AFRICA. Parliament. House of Assembly. Select Committee reports.

— Brazil.

BRAZIL. Departamento de Censos. 1975. Censo comercial [1970]: Brasil; inqueritos especiais: comercio e administração de imoveis, bancos comerciais, finanseiras, seguros. [Rio de Janeiro, 1975]. pp. 142.

— United Kingdom.

TURVEY (RALPH) The property market in London. [195-?]. fo. (198). *Typescript.*

WATES (NICHOLAS HERON) The battle for Tolmers Square. London, 1976. pp. 232. *bibliog.*

REAL ESTATE INVESTMENT

— United States.

HENRY (RENE A.) How to profitably buy and sell land. New York, [1977]. pp. 203.

REAL PROPERTY

— New Zealand.

REAL ESTATE MARKET IN NEW ZEALAND, THE; [pd. by] Valuation Department. a., 1975- Wellington. *Supersedes RURAL REAL ESTATE IN NEW ZEALAND and URBAN REAL ESTATE IN NEW ZEALAND.*

— South Africa — Valuation.

BOADEN (B.G.) and HART (T.) Residential land values in the PWV region, 1966 to 1975. Johannesburg, 1977. pp. 65. *bibliog. (Johannesburg. University of the Witwatersrand. Urban and Regional Research Unit. Occasional Papers. No. 15)*

— United Kingdom.

U.K. Department of the Environment. 1976. The community land scheme. (Booklet) 3. Disposal notification areas. [London, 1976]. pp. 7.

U.K. Department of the Environment. Directorate of Statistics. 1976. Commercial and industrial property 1975: facts and figures. London, [1976]. pp. 63.

HARWOOD (MICHAEL) Cases and materials on English land law. Abingdon, 1977. pp. 488.

REAL PROPERTY TAX

— United Kingdom.

KNIGHT, FRANK AND RUTLEY. The land question. II. London, 1923. pp. 24.

REASON.

BRISTOL CONFERENCE ON CRITICAL PHILOSOPHY, 1ST, UNIVERSITY OF BRISTOL, [1973?] Practical reason:; (proceedings of the...conference) edited by Stephan Körner. Oxford, [1974]. pp. 264. *Held under the auspices of The Society for the Furtherance of Critical Philosophy and the University of Bristol.*

RECEIVERS

— United Kingdom.

SALES (CHARLES ALLISON) The law relating to bankruptcy, liquidations and receiverships; sixth edition by J.H. Thompson. Plymouth, 1977. pp. 332.

RECIDIVISTS

— United Kingdom.

McGURK (B.J.) and others. A study of the variables relating to recidivism in delinquent boys. London, 1977. pp. 7. *bibliog. (U.K. Prison Department. Directorate of Psychological Services. DPS Reports. Series 1. No. 9)*

RECOGNITION (INTERNATIONAL LAW).

BEDJAOUI (MOHAMMED) Law and the Algerian revolution. Brussels, 1961. pp. 260.

RECONSTRUCTION (1914-1939)

— Germany.

RATHENAU (WALTHER) Die neue Gesellschaft. Berlin, 1923. pp. 102. *Originally published in 1919.*

RECONSTRUCTION (1939-1951)

— Australia — Queensland.

FOLEY (THOMAS ANDREW) Post-war planning in Queensland. Brisbane, [1944]. pp. 25. *Reprinted from Rydge's Journal, April, 1943.*

— Austria.

AUSCH (KARL) Die neue Wirtschaft im neuen Österreich;...mit einem Vorwort von Stefan Wirlandner. 2nd ed. Wien, [1947]. pp. 24.

— Germany.

KOMMUNISTISCHE PARTEI DEUTSCHLANDS. Ausschuss für Wirtschaftsfragen. Referat und Diskussion über die Richtlinien der KPD zur Wirtschaftspolitik: (Neuaufbau der deutschen Wirtschaft). Berlin, 1946. pp. 119.

KIMBALL (WARREN F.) Swords or ploughshares?: the Morgenthau plan for defeated Nazi Germany, 1943-1946. Philadelphia, [1976]. pp. 172. *bibliog.*

WOLLASCH (HANS JOSEF) ed. Humanitäre Auslandshilfe für Deutschland nach dem Zweiten Weltkrieg: Darstellung und Dokumentation kirchlicher und nichtkirchlicher Hilfen. Freiburg im Breisgau, 1976. pp. 390. *bibliog.*

RECONSTRUCTION (UNITED STATES).

TAYLOR (JOE GRAY) Louisiana reconstructed, 1863-1877. Baton Rouge, La., [1974]. pp. 552. *bibliog.*

CAMEJO (PETER) Racism, revolution, reaction, 1861-1877: the rise and fall of radical reconstruction. New York, [1976]. pp. 269. *bibliog.*

KLINGMAN (PETER D.) Josiah Walls: Florida's black congressman of reconstruction. Gainesville, 1976. pp. 157. *bibliog.*

MAGDOL (EDWARD) A right to the land: essays on the freedmen's community. Westport, Conn., 1977. pp. 290. *bibliog.*

WIGGINS (SARAH WOOLFOLK) The scalawag in Alabama politics, 1865-1881. University, Ala., [1977]. pp. 220. *bibliog.*

RECONSTRUCTION FINANCE CORPORATION.

OLSON (JAMES STUART) Herbert Hoover and the Reconstruction Finance Corporation, 1931-1933. Ames, 1977. pp. 155. *bibliog.*

RECREATION.

CHEEK (NEIL H.) and BURCH (WILLIAM R.) The social organization of leisure in human society. New York, [1976]. pp. 283. *bibliog.*

— United Kingdom.

VEAL (A.J.) Recreation planning in new communities: a review of British experience. Birmingham, 1975. pp. 106. *bibliog. (Birmingham. University. Centre for Urban and Regional Studies. Research Memoranda. No. 46)*

RECREATION AND STATE

— India.

RAO (P.V.) and KOHLI (SHANTA) Educational and recreational activities of urban local bodies. New Delhi, [1970]. pp. 86. *bibliog. (Indian Institute of Public Administration. Centre for Training and Research in Municipal Administration. Our Towns. vol. 2)*

RECRUITING OF EMPLOYEES

— United Kingdom.

KILLCROSS (M.C.) and BATES (W.T.G.) Selecting the younger trainee. London, H.M.S.O., 1975. pp. 28. *bibliog. (Training Information Papers. 8)*

PEARN (M.A.) Selecting and training coloured workers. London, H.M.S.O., 1977. pp. 46. *bibliog. (Training Information Papers. 9)*

RECYCLING (WASTE, ETC.).

THOMAS (CHRISTINE) Material gains: reclamation, recycling and re-use. London, [1974]. pp. 91.

— United States — New Jersey.

GREENBERG (MICHAEL R.) and others. Solid waste planning in metropolitan regions. New Brunswick, N.J., [1976]. pp. 218.

RED CROSS.

FREYMOND (JACQUES) Guerres, révolutions, Croix-Rouge: réflexions sur le rôle du Comité international de la Croix-Rouge. Genève, 1976. pp. 222.

REED (JOHN).

STARTSEV (ABEL' ISAAKOVICH) Russkie bloknoty Dzhona Rida; [i.e. John Reed]. 2nd ed. Moskva, 1977. pp. 286.

REFERENDUM

— Switzerland.

Die SCHWEIZ hält durch: Buch der Volksumfrage unter dem Patronat der Neuen Helvetischen Gesellschaft. Zürich, 1948. pp. 180.

— United Kingdom.

HEDGES (BARRY M.) Methodological report on the 1975 referendum survey. London, 1975. pp. 15.

KING (ANTHONY) Britain says yes: the 1975 referendum on the Common Market. Washington, D.C., [1977]. pp. 153. *(American Enterprise Institute for Public Policy Research. AEI Studies. 160)*

REFORMATION

— Germany.

DICKENS (ARTHUR GEOFFREY) The German nation and Martin Luther. Glasgow, 1976. pp. 254. *bibliog. First published in London, 1974.*

REFORMATORIES

— United Kingdom.

ERICSON (RICHARD V.) Young offenders and their social work. Farnborough, Hants., [1975]. pp. 225. *bibliog.*

CLARKSON (FELICITY) Offences against discipline at HM Borstal, Feltham. London, 1976. pp. 19. *(U.K. Prison Department. Directorate of Psychological Services. DPS Reports. Series 1. No. 8)*

LAYCOCK (GLORIA K.) Absconding from borstals; a Home Office Research Unit report. London, 1977. pp. 77. *bibliog. (U.K. Home Office. Home Office Research Studies. No. 41)*

REFUGEES, DANISH.

GRUNDT LARSEN (JØRGEN) Modstandsbevaegelsens Kontaktudvalg i Stockholm, 1944-45. Odense, 1976. pp. 181. *bibliog. (Odense Universitet. Studies in History and Social Sciences. vol. 31)*

REFUGEES, GERMAN.

MARR (WILHELM) Das junge Deutschland in der Schweiz: (ein Beitrag zur Geschichte der geheimen Verbindungen unserer Tage); Anhang: Anarchie oder Autorität?. Glashütten im Taunus, 1976. pp. 364,132. *Reprint of the works originally published in Leipzig in 1846 and in Hamburg in 1852.*

EBNETH (RUDOLF) Die österreichische Wochenschrift "Der Christliche Ständestaat": deutsche Emigration in Österreich, 1933- 1938. Mainz, [1976]. pp. 271. *bibliog. (Kommission für Zeitgeschichte. Veröffentlichungen. Reihe B: Forschungen. Band 19)*

REFUGEES, HUNGARIAN

— Periodicals — Bibliography.

MILDSCHUETZ (KOLOMAN) compiler. Bibliographie der ungarischen Exilpresse, 1945-1975; ergänzt und zum Druck vorbereitet von Béla Grolshammer. München, 1977. pp. 149. *(Ungarisches Institut München. Studia Hungarica. 12)*

REFUGEES, RUSSIAN.

BROOK-SHEPHERD (GORDON) The storm petrels: the first Soviet defectors, 1928-1938. London, 1977. pp. 257.

REFUGEES, SPANISH.

TAGÜEÑA LACORTE (MANUEL) Testimonio de dos guerras. Mexico, 1973. pp. 672.

REFUGEES IN AUSTRIA.

MACHUNZE (ERWIN) Vom Rechtlosen zum Gleichberechtigten: die Flüchtlings- und Vertriebenenfrage im Wiener Parlament. Salzburg, 1974-76. 2 vols.(in 1).

EBNETH (RUDOLF) Die österreichische Wochenschrift "Der Christliche Ständestaat": deutsche Emigration in Österreich, 1933- 1938. Mainz, [1976]. pp. 271. *bibliog. (Kommission für Zeitgeschichte. Veröffentlichungen. Reihe B: Forschungen. Band 19)*

REFUGEES IN FRANCE.

ROCHCAU (GEORGES) and others. Ces étrangers parmi nous. Paris, [1975]. pp. 128. *bibliog.*

REFUGEES IN GERMANY.

DE ZAYAS (ALFRED M.) Nemesis at Potsdam: the Anglo-Americans and the expulsion of the Germans: background, execution, consequences. London, 1977. pp. 268. *bibliog.*

REFUGEES IN INDIA.

CANADA. Parliamentary Delegation to India. 1971. Press conference by the Canadian parliamentary delegation. [New Delhi, Ministry of External Affairs, 1971]. pp. 14.

INDIA. Prime Minister. 1971. Refugees are international responsibility: statement of Prime Minister Shrimati Indira Gandhi in Rajya Sabha on June 15, 1971. [New Delhi, 1971]. pp. 7.

REFUGEES IN SWEDEN.

GRUNDT LARSEN (JØRGEN) Modstandsbevaegelsens Kontaktudvalg i Stockholm, 1944-45. Odense, 1976. pp. 181. *bibliog. (Odense Universitet. Studies in History and Social Sciences. vol. 31)*

REFUGEES IN SWITZERLAND.

MARR (WILHELM) Das junge Deutschland in der Schweiz: (ein Beitrag zur Geschichte der geheimen Verbindungen unserer Tage); Anhang: Anarchie oder Autorität?. Glashütten im Taunus, 1976. pp. 364,132. *Reprint of the works originally published in Leipzig in 1846 and in Hamburg in 1852.*

REFUSE AND REFUSE DISPOSAL

— United Kingdom.

U.K. Department of the Environment. Local authority waste disposal statistics: annual analysis of returns from English waste disposal authorities. a., 1974/75 (1st)- London.

— United States — New Jersey.

GREENBERG (MICHAEL R.) and others. Solid waste planning in metropolitan regions. New Brunswick, N.J., [1976]. pp. 218.

REGENSBURG

— Commerce.

EIKENBERG (WILTRUD) Das Handelshaus der Runtinger zu Regensburg: ein Spiegel süddeutschen Rechts-, Handels- und Wirtschaftslebens im ausgehenden 14. Jahrhundert, etc. Göttingen, 1976. pp. 336. *bibliog. (Max-Planck-Institut für Geschichte. Veröffentlichungen. 43)*

REGION CENTRE

— Industries.

HONNORAT (P.) Evolution de l'emploi salarié industriel dans la Région Centre, 1965-1972. Orléans, Echelon Régional de l'Emploi d'Orléans, 1975. pp. 193.

REGIONAL DEVELOPMENT

— United Kingdom — Bibliography.

DERRICK (E.F.) compiler. House and area improvement in Britain: [a bibliography and abstracts]. Birmingham, 1976. pp. 120. *(Birmingham. University. Centre for Urban and Regional Studies. Research Memoranda. No.54)*

REGIONAL ECONOMICS.

MERA (KOICHI) Income distribution and regional development. Tokyo, 1975. pp. 242. *bibliog.*

ULIGHED mellem regioner: arbejdspapirer om den danske regionale udvikling; redaktion: Jens Larsen, Søren Villadsen. Esbjerg, 1975. pp. 293. *(Sydjysk Universitetscenter. Regionalforskning. 2)*

BUTTON (K.J.) and GILLINGWATER (DAVID) Case studies in regional economics. London, 1976. pp. 88. *(Economics Association. Case Studies in Economic Analysis. 3)*

BROWN (ARTHUR JOSEPH) Professor of Economics in the University of Leeds, and BURROWS (E. MICHAEL) Regional economic problems: comparative experiences of some market economies. London, 1977. pp. 209. *bibliog.*

— Mathematical models.

HEWINGS (GEOFFREY J.D.) Regional industrial analysis and development. London, 1977. pp. 180. *bibliog.*

REGIONAL PLANNING.

KRIESIS (PAUL) Physical planning ad absurdum. Athens, 1976. pp. 55.

REGIONAL and rural development: essays in theory and practice; edited by P.J. Drudy. Chalfont St. Giles, [1976]. pp. 116. *Based on a conference on 'Regional development in practice' held under the auspices of the Regional Studies Association.*

SPATIAL dimensions of public policy; edited by John Terence Coppock and W.R. Derrick Sewell. Oxford, 1976. pp. 271. *bibliogs. Based on papers presented at the annual meeting of the Institute of British Geographers, University of East Anglia, 1974.*

HARRISON (ANTHONY J.) Economics and land use planning. London, [1977]. pp. 256. *bibliog.*

— Bibliography.

VEAL (A.J.) and DUESBURY (W.K.) compilers. A first list of U.K. students theses and dissertations on planning and urban and regional studies. Birmingham, 1976. pp. 245. *(Birmingham. University. Centre for Urban and Regional Studies. Research Memoranda. No. 55).*

— Citizen participation.

FAGENCE (MICHAEL) Citizen participation in planning. Oxford, 1977. pp. 378.

PUBLIC participation in planning; edited by W.R. Derrick Sewell and J.T. Coppock. London, 1977. pp. 217. *Based on a joint seminar organized by the University of Edinburgh School of the Built Environment and Centre for Human Ecology, held in 1973.*

— Cost effectiveness.

SIMPSON (BARRY JOHN) The theoretical development and application of threshold analysis to assess land development costs. 1976 [or rather 1977]. fo. 342. *bibliog. Typescript. Ph.D. (London) thesis: unpublished. This thesis is the property of London University and may not be removed from the Library.*

— Mathematical models.

ECONOMIC models in regional planning...; proceedings of a seminar sponsored by the Northern Region Strategy Team and the IBM United Kingdom Scientific Centre, Peterlee, County Durham, 20-21 November 1975; [edited by K. Telford]. Peterlee, 1976. pp. 63. *bibliog. (IBM United Kingdom Limited. UK Scientific Centre. [Technical Reports]. 0082)*

— Research — United Kingdom.

U.K. Department of the Environment. Library. 1977. Urban and regional research in the United Kingdom, 1976-1977; prepared...for the United Nations Economic Commission for Europe, Committee for Housing, Building and Planning, Group of Experts on Urban and Regional Research. [London], 1977. pp. 289. *(Information Series)*

— Brazil.

KOCH-WESER (CAIO K.) La SUDENE: doce años de planificacion para el desarrollo en el nordeste brasileño; analisis de una politica de reformas neutralizada. Santiago de Chile, 1973. pp. 91. *(Instituto Latinoamericano de Investigaciones Sociales. Estudios y Documentos. 22)*

— Canada.

CARELESS (ANTHONY G.S.) Initiative and response: the adaptation of Canadian federalism to regional economic development. Montreal, 1977. pp. 244. *(Institute of Public Administration of Canada. Canadian Public Administration Series)*

— — Newfoundland.

NEWFOUNDLAND. Commission of Enquiry into the St. John's Urban Region Study. 1974-76. The first ([and] second) interim report[s] ([and] third and final report); [Alec G. Henley, chairman]. [St. John's], 1974-76. 4 vols.(in 2).

— — Ontario.

HILLS (GEORGE ANGUS) and others. Developing a better environment: ecological land-use planning in Ontario: a study of methodology in the development of regional plans. [Toronto], Ontario Economic Council, [1970] repr. 1973. pp. 182. *bibliog.*

ONTARIO. Department of Treasury and Economics. 1971. Design for development: a policy statement on the northwestern Ontario region. [Toronto], 1971. fo. 7.

ONTARIO. Regional Development Branch. 1972. Design for development: prospects for the eastern Ontario region. [Toronto], 1972. pp. 20.

ONTARIO. Regional Development Branch. 1972. Design for development: prospects for the Georgian Bay region. [Toronto], 1972. pp. 24.

ONTARIO. Regional Development Branch. 1972. Design for development: prospects for the Lake Erie region. [Toronto], 1972. pp. 23.

ONTARIO. Regional Development Branch. 1972. Design for development: prospects for the Lake Ontario region. [Toronto], 1972. pp. 20.

ONTARIO. Regional Development Branch. 1972. Design for development: prospects for the St. Clair region. [Toronto], 1972. pp. 23.

— — Prince Edward Island — Citizen participation.

McNIVEN (J.D.) Evaluation of the public participation programme embodied in the Prince Edward Island development plan. Halifax, N.S., 1974 repr. 1976. pp. 252. *bibliog. (Dalhousie University. Institute of Public Affairs. [Current Publications]. No. 103)*

— Europe.

COUNCIL OF EUROPE. Division of Local Authorities. Information bulletin: municipal and regional matters. s-a., 1974 (no. 6)- Strasbourg.

— European Free Trade Association countries.

EUROPEAN FREE TRADE ASSOCIATION. 1973. Regional policy in EFTA: national settlement strategies; a framework for regional development. Geneva, 1973. pp. 241. *bibliog.*

— France.

ETUDE des paysages de la Vallée du Lot; [by] Yves Le Bars [and others]. [Cahors?], Ministère de l'Agriculture et du Développement Rural, 1973. pp. 147. *bibliog. Transparent map in end pocket.*

MONOD (JEROME) Transformation d'un pays: pour une géographie de la liberté. [Paris, 1974]. pp. 187.

SCHEMA général d'aménagement de la France: la façade atlantique; ouverture sur le monde. Paris, 1975. pp. 111. *(France. Délégation à l'Aménagement du Territoire et à l'Action Régionale. Travaux et Recherches de Prospective. 51)*

FRANCE. Commission de l'Aménagement du Territoire et du Cadre de Vie. 1976. Rapport...: préparation du 7e Plan. Paris, 1976. pp. 176.

PASSERON (HERVE) Deux scénarios de développement régional à moyen terme. Paris, Institut National de la Statistique et des Etudes Economiques, 1976. pp. 108.

— Germany.

STADTREGIONEN in der Bundesrepublik Deutschland, 1970. Hannover, 1975. pp. 134. *(Akademie für Raumforschung und Landesplanung. Forschungs- und Sitzungsberichte. Band 103) Map in end pocket.*

GRUETTNER (MICHAEL) Wem die Stadt gehört: Stadtplanung und Stadtentwicklung in Hamburg, 1965-1975. Hamburg, 1976. pp. 266. *bibliog.*

— Ireland (Republic).

NATIONAL ECONOMIC AND SOCIAL COUNCIL [EIRE]. Institutional arrangements for regional economic development. Dublin, Stationery Office, [1976]. pp. 54. *([Reports]. No. 22)*

— Israel.

BRUTZKUS (ELIEZER) Regional policy in Israel. Jerusalem, Government Printer, 1970. pp. 79. *bibliog.*

FEASEY (R.A.) Israel: planning and immigration in relation to spatial development. Durham, 1976. pp. 75. *bibliog.* (*Durham. University. Department of Geography. Occasional Publications (New Series). No.8*)

— Kenya.

KENYA. Town Planning Department. 1971. Coast Province regional physical development plan. [Nairobi], 1971. fo.153.

OBUDHO (ROBERT) and WALLER (PETER P.) Periodic markets, urbanization, and regional planning: a case study from western Kenya. Westport, Conn., 1976. pp. 289. *bibliog.*

— Nigeria.

BARBOUR (KENNETH MICHAEL) ed. Planning for Nigeria: a geographical approach. Ibadan, 1972. pp. 228. *bibliogs. A collection of essays on the nature and significance of regional planning by members of the Department of Geography of the University of Ibadan.*

— Poland.

POLSKA AKADEMIA NAUK. Instytut Geografii. Geographia Polonica. 32. (Selected reports on research into physical development of Poland; edited by Kazimierz Dziewónski). Warszawa, 1975. pp. 145.

ODRA i Nadodrze. Warszawa, 1976. pp. 371.

— Russia.

GRANBERG (ALEKSANDR GRIGOR'EVICH) ed. Territorial'nye narodnokhoziaistvennye modeli. Novosibirsk, 1976. pp. 219. (*Akademiia Nauk SSSR. Sibirskoe Otdelenie. Institut Ekonomiki i Organizatsii Promyshlennogo Proizvodstva. Optimizatsiia Territorial'nykh Sistem)*

NOVYE territorial'nye kompleksy SSSR. Moskva, 1977. pp. 269.

— — Ukraine.

EMEL'IANOV (ALEKSANDR SERGEEVICH) ed. Sovershenstvovanie territorial'nogo planirovaniia v soiuznoi respublike: na primere USSR. Moskva, 1976. pp. 200. *bibliog.*

— Turkey.

PLANNING IN TURKEY; [pd. by] Devlet Plânlama Teşkilâti. a., 1964 (no.2). Ankara.

— Underdeveloped areas.

**See UNDERDEVELOPED AREAS —
    Regional planning.**

— United Kingdom.

MIDLANDS TOMORROW; issued by West Midlands Economic Planning Council. irreg., 1968 (no.1)- Birmingham.

REGIONAL development in Britain; [by] Gerald Manners [and others]. London, [1972]. pp. 448. *bibliogs.*

KENT. Planning Department. Kent county structure plan: [reports]: nos. 1B-14B [with] supplement [to no.] 4B. Maidstone, [1974-5]. 15 pts. (in 1 vol.).

SURREY. Planning Department. Structure plan: (background papers). Kingston upon Thames, 1974-75. 12 vols. (in 1).

DERBYSHIRE. County Planning Department. Derbyshire structure plan: report of survey. Matlock, 1975-6. 16 vols. (in 1).

BERKSHIRE. Planning Department. West Berkshire structure plan: report of survey. [Reading, Berks.], 1975. pp. 223.

DERBYSHIRE. County Planning Department. Derbyshire structure plan: alternative development options. Matlock, 1975. pp. 115.

LONDON. Greater London Council. Planned growth outside London; report. [London], 1975. pp. (31).

AVON. County Council. Planning Department. Avon County structure plan: situation reports. Bristol, 1976. 10 parts (in 1 vol.)

BATHER (NICHOLAS JOHN) and others. Strategic choice in practice: the West Berkshire structure plan experience. Reading, 1976. pp. 62. (*Reading. University. Department of Geography. Reading Geographical Papers. No. 50)*

BERKSHIRE. Planning Department. East Berkshire structure plan: report of survey. [Reading, Berks.], 1976. pp. 282.

CENTRE FOR ENVIRONMENTAL STUDIES. Structure Planning Conference, University of Birmingham, 1975. Papers. London, 1976. pp. 201. *bibliogs.* (*Centre for Environmental Studies. Conference Papers. 16)*

CHERRY (GORDON E.) Urban and regional planning: promise and potential in the West Midlands; an inaugural lecture delivered in the University of Birmingham on 4th November 1976. Birmingham, 1976. pp. 22. *bibliog.*

CHERRY (GORDON E.) ed. Rural planning problems;...contributors Gordon E. Cherry [and others]. London, 1976. pp. 286. *bibliogs.*

DERBYSHIRE. County Planning Department. Derbyshire structure plan: draft for consultation. [Matlock, 1976]. pp. 400. *3 maps in end pocket.*

EAST MIDLANDS ECONOMIC PLANNING COUNCIL. East midlands: a forward economic look. [Nottingham, 1976]. pp. 85.

HUMBERSIDE. County Council. Planning Department. Humberside structure plan: background studies: consultation draft, June 1976. [Beverley], 1976. pp. 177.

HUMBERSIDE. County Council. Planning Department. Humberside structure plan: policies: consultation draft, June 1976. [Beverley], 1976. pp. 92.

LONDON. Greater London Council. Planned growth outside London: consultations; report. [London], 1976. 1 vol. (various pagings).

NORTHAMPTONSHIRE. County Planning Department. Northamptonshire county structure plan: report of survey: consultation draft. [Northampton], 1976. 1 vol (unpaged].

NORTHAMPTONSHIRE. County Planning Department. Northamptonshire county structure plan: the alternatives. [Northampton], 1976. pp. 17. *Bound with Northamptonshire county structure plan: draft written statement.*

NOTTINGHAMSHIRE. Department of Planning and Transportation. Nottinghamshire structure plan: draft report of survey. [Nottingham, 1976]. pp. 200. *bibliog.*

NOTTINGHAMSHIRE. Department of Planning and Transportation. Nottinghamshire structure plan: draft written statement. Nottingham, [1976]. pp. 245, iv..

SOUTH EAST JOINT PLANNING TEAM. Strategy for the South East: 1976 review; report with recommendations; (with Reports of study groups). London, H.M.S.O., 1976. 8 pts. (in 2 vols.).

DAVIDSON (JOAN) and WIBBERLEY (GERALD PERCY) Planning and the rural environment. Oxford, 1977. pp. 225.

HOUSE (JOHN WILLIAM) ed. The U.K. space: resources, environment and the future. 2nd ed. London, 1977. pp. 528. *bibliogs.*

NORTHAMPTONSHIRE. County Planning Department. Northamptonshire county structure plan: draft written statement. [Northampton], 1977. 1 vol. (unpaged).

— — Bibliography.

JOHNSTONE (PAMELA) and LAMBERT (CLAIRE M.) compilers. Structure plans: list B: the literature and debate on structure plans and structure planning. [London, 1976]. pp. 33. (*U.K. Department of the Environment. Library. Bibliographies. No. 152B) Bound with Structure plans: list A: structure plan documents.*

LAMBERT (CLAIRE M.) compiler. Structure plans: list A: structure plan documents. London, 1976. pp. 63. (*U.K. Department of the Environment. Library. Bibliographies. No. 152A) Bound with Structure plans: list B: the literature and debate on structure plans and structure planning.*

McIVER (GLENYS) compiler. Planning: list A: basic list for the general library; list B: extended list of publications; list C: list for local authority planning departments; edited by Claire M. Lambert. [rev. ed.]. London, 1976. 3 pts. (in 1 vol.). (*U.K. Department of the Environment. Library. Bibliographies. No. 160A, B and C).*

NAUGHTON (M.R.) compiler. Regional studies and reports of the economic planning councils. [London], 1976. pp. 10. (*U.K. Department of the Environment. Library. Bibliographies. No. 195)*

— — Citizen participation.

HEDGES (BARRY M.) Community preference surveys in structure planning. London, [1975]. pp. 74.

JOWELL (ROGER) A review of public involvement in planning. London, 1975. pp. 35. (*Social and Community Planning Research. Occasional Papers)*

— — — Bibliography.

COCKETT (IEN) compiler. Public participation in planning: the British experience. 2nd ed. London, 1976. pp. 42. (*London. Greater London Council. Research Library. Research Bibliographies. No. 55)*

— — Mathematical models.

BARRAS (R.) Local authority resource allocation: analysis and modelling. London, 1976. pp. 78. *bibliog.* (*Planning Research Applications Group. PRAG Technical Papers. TP 17)*

— — Ireland, Northern.

ARMAGH area plan public inquiry; report on public inquiry by H.A. Patton. [Belfast, H.M.S.O., 1975]. pp. 57.

IRELAND, NORTHERN. Department of the Environment. 1976. West Tyrone area plan: statement by Department, etc. Belfast, [1976]. pp. 25.

IRELAND, NORTHERN. Department of the Environment. 1977. East Antrim area plan. Belfast, 1977. pp. 51. *3 maps in each pocket.*

IRELAND, NOTHERN. Department of the Environment. 1977. Northern Ireland: regional physical development strategy, 1975- 95. Belfast, 1977. pp. 95.

— — Scotland.

SCOTLAND. Scottish Development Department. 1975. Demographic analysis for planning purposes: a manual on sources and techniques: regional reports advice. [Edinburgh], 1975. pp. 55. *bibliog.* (*Planning Advice Notes. No.8)*

BRYDEN (JOHN M.) and HOUSTON (GEORGE F.B.) Agrarian change in the Scottish Highlands: the role of the Highlands and Islands Development Board in the agricultural economy of the crofting counties. London, 1976. pp. 152. *bibliog.* (*Glasgow. University. Social and Economic Research Studies. 4.) Published in association with the Highlands and Islands Development Board.*

— United States.

TWEETEN (LUTHER G.) and BRINKMAN (GEORGE LORIS) Micropolitan development: theory and practice of greater-rural economic development. Ames, Iowa, 1976. pp. 456. *bibliogs.*

— — New York (State).

GOTTDIENER (MARK) Planned sprawl: private and public interests in suburbia. Beverly Hills, [1977]. pp. 188. *bibliog.*

REGIONALISM.

DUNFORD (M.F.) Regional policy and the restructuring of capital. Brighton, 1977. fo. 46. *bibliog. (Brighton. University of Sussex. Sussex Working Papers in Urban and Regional Studies. 4)*

— Australia.

AUSTRALIA. Task Force on a Regional Basis for Australian Government Administration. 1975. A regional basis for Australian government administration: Task Force report: report to the Royal Commission on Australian Government Administration by a Task Force appointed...to design a flexible basis for administration at regional and local levels. [Canberra], 1975. 2 vols. (in 1.). *bibliog.*

— China.

SOLINGER (DOROTHY J.) Regional government and political integration in Southwest China, 1949-1954: a case study. Berkeley, Calif., [1977]. pp. 291. *bibliog.*

— Europe.

COUNCIL OF EUROPE. Division of Local Authorities. Information bulletin: municipal and regional matters. s-a., 1974 (no. 6)- Strasbourg.

— European Economic Community countries.

CLOUT (HUGH DONALD) The regional problem in Western Europe. Cambridge, 1976. pp. 59. *bibliog.*

EUROPEAN COMMUNITIES. Economic and Social Committee. 1976. Regional development problems of the Community during the period 1975/1977 and establishment of a common regional policy. Brussels, 1976. pp. 11. *(Opinions)*

— Italy.

DUNFORD (M.F.) Regional policy and the restructuring of capital. Brighton, 1977. fo. 46. *bibliog. (Brighton. University of Sussex. Sussex Working Papers in Urban and Regional Studies. 4)*

— United Kingdom.

KITAMURA (KIMIHIKO) Regionalism in England. n.p. [1974?]. fo. 69. *Photocopy of typescript.*

LABOUR PARTY. Regional authorities and local government reform: a consultation document for the labour movement. London, 1977. pp. 28.

U.K. Parliament. House of Commons. Library. Research Division. Background Papers. No.57. The devolution debate: regional statistics. [London, 1977]. pp. 18.

REGIONALISM (INTERNATIONAL ORGANIZATION).

KOLDE (ENDEL JAKOB) The Pacific quest: the concept and scope of an oceanic community. Lexington, Mass., [1976]. pp. 161.

REGISTERS OF BIRTHS, ETC.

— United Kingdom.

[RENNIE (JOHN) Vicar of Long Itchington] A proposed plan of a national register of marriages, baptisms, and burials. [London, 1811]. pp. 7. *Authorship ascribed in a ms. note on p. 7: "A copy also was transmitted on 25 Feby last to The Right Honble George Rose, by the writer, the Rev.d John Rennie, Vicar of Long Itchington, Warwickshire".*

REGRESSION ANALYSIS.

FULLER (WAYNE A.) Introduction to statistical time series. New York, [1976]. pp. 470. *bibliog.*

REHM (HELMUT) Aufbau eines ökonometrischen Modells für die deutsche Volkswirtschaft, 1960-1974, nach der Methode der erweiterten schriftweisen Regression. [Erlangen-Nürnberg, 1976]. pp. 158. *bibliog. Inaugural-Dissertation zur Erlangung des akademischen Grades eines Doktors der Wirtschafts- und Sozialwissenschaften der Friedrich-Alexander-Universität Erlangen-Nürnberg.*

SILK (JOHN) A comparison of regression lines using dummy variable analysis: models and examples for the bivariate case. Reading, 1976. pp. 39. *bibliog. (Reading. University. Department of Geography. Reading Geographical Papers. No. 44)*

SCHILDERINCK (J.H.F.) Regression and factor analysis applied in econometrics. Leiden, 1977. pp. 239. *bibliog. (Tilburg. Katholieke Hogeschool. Tilburg Institute of Economics. Tilburg Studies in Econometrics. vol. 1)*

REHABILITATION.

GLANVILLE (H.J.) What is rehabilitation?. Southampton, 1976. pp. 26. *Inaugural lecture at the University of Southampton 1976.*

— Canada — Ontario.

INTERNATIONAL SEMINAR ON REHABILITATION PROGRAMS IN WORKMEN'S COMPENSATION AND RELATED FIELDS, TORONTO, 1969. Selected papers. [Toronto, Workmen's Compensation Board of Ontario, 1969] . pp. 38. *(Rehabilitation in Canada. Supplements. No.2)*

REHABILITATION, RURAL

— Greece.

WEINTRAUB (DOV) and SHAPIRA (M.) Rural reconstruction in Greece: differential social prerequisites and achievements during the development process. Beverly Hills, [1975]. pp. 80. *bibliog.*

— Tanzania.

SENDER (JOHN) Some preliminary notes on the political economy of rural development in Tanzania based on a case-study in the western Usambaras. Dar es Salaam, 1974. pp. 59. *(Dar es Salaam. University. Economic Research Bureau. ERB Papers. 74.5)*

— United Kingdom.

NORTHERN REGION STRATEGY TEAM. Rural development in the northern region. Newcastle upon Tyne, 1976. pp. (152). *(Technical Reports. No. 16)*

— — Scotland.

BROWNRIGG (MARK) and GREIG (MICHAEL A.) Tourism and regional development. Glasgow, [1976]. pp. 14. *bibliog. (Glasgow. University of Strathclyde. Fraser of Allander Institute. Speculative Papers. No. 5)*

REHABILITATION OF CRIMINALS

— United Kingdom.

U.K. Home Office. 1976. The probation and after-care service in a changing society. [London, 1976]. pp. 30. *bibliog.*

REHABILITATION OF JUVENILE DELINQUENTS.

ERICSON (RICHARD V.) Young offenders and their social work. Farnborough, Hants., [1975]. pp. 225. *bibliog.*

— United States.

DOWNS (GEORGE W.) Bureaucracy, innovation, and public policy. Lexington, Mass., [1976]. pp. 150. *bibliog.*

REICHSBANK.

PALGRAVE (Sir ROBERT HARRY INGLIS) translator. Reports and transactions of the Bank of France and the Bank of Germany from 1876 to (1897). [Great Yarmouth, n.d.]. 2 vols. *Collected and bound for the author's library.*

PALGRAVE (Sir ROBERT HARRY INGLIS) Reports and transactions of the Bank of France, Germany, and Belgium, 1898-(1905). [Great Yarmouth, n.d.]. 3 vols. *(Reprinted from the Bankers' Magazine) Collected and bound for the author's library. Covering title-page lacking: title taken from the spine.*

PALGRAVE (Sir ROBERT HARRY INGLIS) translator. Reports and transactions of the Banks of France, Germany, Belgium and the Netherlands, 1909-(1917). Great Yarmouth, 1912-17. 5 vols. *(Reprinted from the Bankers' Magazine) Collected and bound for the author's library.*

REID (JIMMY).

REID (JIMMY) Reflections of a Clyde-built man. London, 1976. pp. 166.

REISSNER (LARISSA).

REISSNER (LARISSA) Hamburg at the barricades, and other writings on Weimar Germany; translated from the Russian and edited by Richard Chappell. London, 1977. pp. 209.

RELIGION.

DAWSON (CHRISTOPHER HENRY) Enquiries into religion and culture. London, [1933]. pp. 347. *Consists mainly of reprinted essays.*

MILL (JOHN STUART) (Collected works of John Stuart Mill. vol. 10). Essays on ethics, religion and society; editor of the text, J.M. Robson; introduction, F.E.L. Priestley; essays on Mill's Utilitarianism, D.P. Dryer. Toronto, [1969]. pp. 578. *bibliog.*

— History.

KRYVELEV (IOSIF ARONOVI. Istoriia religii: ocherki v dvukh tomakh. Moskva, 1975 in progress.

— Philosophy.

REKUTS (IVAN FEODOS'EVICH) Filosofskie problemy kritiki religii v ateisticheskom nasledii A.V. Lunacharskogo. Minsk, 1976. pp. 174. *bibliog.*

RELIGION AND LAW.

GOL'ST (GEORGII ROBERTOVICH) Religiia i zakon. Moskva, 1975. pp. 110.

RELIGION AND SCIENCE.

JACOB (MARGARET C.) The Newtonians and the English Revolution, 1689-1720, Ithaca, N.Y., 1976. pp. 288. *bibliog.*

RELIGION AND SOCIOLOGY.

WALLIS (ROY) The road to total freedom: a sociological analysis of scientology. London, 1976. pp. 282. *bibliog.*

CARROLL (JOHN) Puritan, paranoid, remissive: a sociology of modern culture. London, 1977. pp. 148. *bibliog.*

RELIGION AND STATE

— Israel.

LIEBMAN (CHARLES S.) Pressure without sanctions: the influence of world Jewry on Israeli policy. Cranbury, N.J., [1977]. pp. 304. *bibliog.*

SCHIFF (GARY S.) Tradition and politics: the religious parties of Israel. Detroit, 1977. pp. 267. *bibliog. (Columbia University. Middle East Institute. Modern Middle East Series. vol.9)*

— Lebanon.

KOURY (ENVER M.) The crisis in the Lebanese system: confessionalism and chaos. Washington, D.C., 1976. pp. 92. *(American Enterprise Institute for Public Policy Research. Foreign Affairs Studies. 38)*

RELIGIOUS LAW AND LEGISLATION

— Russia.

LUCHTERHANDT (OTTO) Der Sowjetstaat und die Russisch-Orthodoxe Kirche: eine rechtshistorische und rechtssystematische Untersuchung. Köln, [1976]. pp. 319. *bibliog. (Bundesinstitut für Ostwissenschaftliche und Internationale Studien. Abhandlungen. Band 30)*

RELIGIOUS LIBERTY

— Canada.

PENTON (M. JAMES) Jehovah's Witnesses in Canada: champions of freedom of speech and worship. Toronto, [1976]. pp. 388. *bibliog.*

RELIGIOUS THOUGHT

— United States.

DAVIDSON (JAMES WEST) The logic of millennial thought: eighteenth-century New England. New Haven, 1977. pp. 308. *bibliog. (Yale University. Yale Historical Publications. Miscellany. 112)*

REMIRO (JOE).

BRYAN (JOHN) 1934- . This soldier still at war. London, 1976. pp. 341.

REMOTE SENSING SYSTEMS.

LEGAL implications of remote sensing from outer space; edited by Nicolas Mateesco Matte and Hamilton DeSaussure. Leyden, 1976. pp. 197. *Papers of a symposium organised by the Institute of Air and Space Law, McGill University.*

REMSCHEID

— Social history.

LUCAS (ERHARD) Zwei Formen von Radikalismus in der deutschen Arbeiterbewegung. Frankfurt am Main, [1976]. pp. 334. *bibliog.*

RENAISSANCE.

SCHELLHASE (KENNETH C.) Tacitus in renaissance political thought. Chicago, 1976. pp. 270. *bibliog.*

RENT

— Russia.

KARNAUKHOVA (EVFRAZIIA STEPANOVNA) Differentsial'naia renta i ekonomicheskaia otsenka zemli: voprosy metodologii i opyt issledovaniia. Moskva, 1977. pp. 256.

— United Kingdom.

SOCIAL SERVICES RESEARCH AND INTELLIGENCE UNIT [PORTSMOUTH]. Information Sheets. No.14. The rent supervision scheme in Portsmouth. Portsmouth, 1973. fo.10.

RENT CONTROL.

RENT control: a popular paradox: evidence on the economic effects of rent control; by F.A. Hayek [and others]. Vancouver, 1975. pp. 212.

— Kenya.

KENYA. Working Party on Rent Control. 1965. Report made to the Minister for Commerce and Industry; [S.N. Waruhiu, chairman]. [Nairobi, 1965]. pp. 17.

— United Kingdom.

BEIRNE (PIERS) Fair rent and legal fiction: housing rent legislation in a capitalist society. London, 1977. pp. 240. *bibliog.*

— United States.

LETT (MONICA R.) Rent control: concepts, realities and mechanisms. New Brunswick, N.J., [1976]. pp. 294.

RENT SUBSIDIES

— United Kingdom.

LEGG (CHARLES) and BRION (MARION) The administration of the rent rebate and rent allowance schemes. [London], Department of the Environment, [1976]. pp. 198. *bibliogs.*

— United Kingdom.

ADVISORY COMMITTEE ON RENT REBATES AND RENT ALLOWANCES [U.K.]. Report No. 2. July 1974 to December 1976. London, H.M.S.O., 1977. pp. 42.

REPATRIATION.

DELESSERT (CHRISTIANE SHIELDS) Release and repatriation of prisoners of war at the end of active hostilities: a study of Article 118, Paragraph 1, of the Third Geneva Convention relative to the Treatment of Prisoners of War. Zürich, [1977]. pp. 225. *bibliog. (Schweizerische Vereinigung für Internationales Recht. Schweizer Studien zum Internationalen Recht. Band 5)*

REPRESENTATION IN ADMINISTRATIVE PROCEEDINGS

— United Kingdom.

FROST (ANNE) and HOWARD (CORAL) Representation and administrative tribunals. London, 1977. pp. 94. *bibliog.*

REPRESENTATIVE GOVERNMENT AND REPRESENTATION.

HEIBERG (PETER ANDREAS) Nogle Betragtninger over National-Repraesentationen under en konstitutionel monarkisk Regjering, fornemmelig med Hensyn til Kongeriget Norge. Christiansand, Moe, 1817. pp. viii, 88.

ALBUM Elemér Mályusz. Bruxelles, 1976. pp. 404. *bibliogs. (International Commission for the History of Representative and Parliamentary Institutions. Studies. 56) In English, French, German and Spanish.*

THOMPSON (DENNIS FRANK) John Stuart Mill and representative government. Princeton, N.J., [1976]. pp. 241.

MILL (JOHN STUART) (Collected works of John Stuart Mill. vols. 18-19). Essays on politics and society;...editor of the text, J.M. Robson; introduction by Alexander Brody. Toronto, [1977]. 2 vols. *bibliog.*

— Italy.

BARNES (SAMUEL HENRY) Representation in Italy: institutionalized tradition and electoral choice. Chicago, 1977. pp. 187.

REPUBLICAN PARTY (UNITED STATES).

BELZ (HERMAN) A new birth of freedom: the Republican Party and freedmen's rights, 1861-1866. Westport, Conn., 1976. pp. 199. *bibliogs.*

DARILEK (RICHARD E.) A loyal opposition in time of war: the Republican Party and the politics of foreign policy from Pearl Harbour to Yalta. Westport, Conn., 1976. pp. 239. *bibliog.*

WIGGINS (SARAH WOOLFOLK) The scalawag in Alabama politics, 1865-1881. University, Ala., [1977]. pp. 220. *bibliog.*

REPUBLICANISM IN SPAIN.

SEMPRUN GURREA (JOSE MARIA DE) Una republica para España. New York, 1961. pp. 626.

RESEARCH.

HUCK (SCHUYLER W.) and others. Reading statistics and research. New York, [1974]. pp. 387. *bibliogs.*

ORGANISATION FOR ECONOMIC CO-OPERATION AND DEVELOPMENT. Directorate for Scientific Affairs. 1976. The measurement of scientific and technical activities: proposed standard practice for surveys of research and experimental development; Frascati manual. Paris, 1976. pp. 139. *bibliog.*

— Management.

HIGGINS (TOM) Research planning and innovation: a study of success and failure in innovation and the implications for R and D management and choice; (study...supported by An Foras Taluntais...and the National Science Council). Dublin, Stationery Office, 1977. pp. 283. *bibliog.*

— Psychological aspects.

NORDBECK (BERTIL) Critical factors in research work: factors influencing the individual's research process with special reference to biological research work. Stockholm, 1976. pp. 72. *bibliog. (Sweden. Forskningsekonomiska Kommittén. Rapporter. 7)*

— Canada.

CANADA. Ministry of State for Science and Technology. Federal science programs. a., 1977/78(1st)- [Ottawa]. *[in English and French].*

— European Economic Community countries.

EUROPEAN COMMUNITIES. Commission. 1976. Objectives, priorities and resources for a common research and development policy: communication of the Commission to the Council, transmitted on 3 November, 1975. [Brussels], 1976. pp. 19. *(Bulletin of the European Communities. Supplements. [1976/4])*

EUROPEAN COMMUNITIES. Economic and Social Committee. 1976. Objectives and priorities for a common research and development policy. Brussels, 1976. pp. 37. *(Studies)*

— France.

FRANCE. Commission de la Recherche. 1976. Rapport...: préparation du 7e Plan. Paris, 1976. pp. 345.

— Germany, Eastern.

DEUTSCHES INSTITUT FÜR WIRTSCHAFTSFORSCHUNG. Sonderhefte. [Neue Folge]. 116. Zur Planung, Organisation und Lenkung von Forschung und Entwicklung in der DDR: Aspekte des wissenschaftlich-technischen Fortschritts; ([by] Angela Scherzinger). Berlin, 1977. pp. 214. *bibliog. With English summary.*

— Portugal.

CARAMONA (MARIA HELENA) Inquerito sobre os meios nacionais de investigação e desenvolvimento. [Lisbon, 1972]. pp. 108. *(Portugal. Instituto Nacional de Estatistica. Estudos. No.43) With summaries in English and French.*

— Russia.

PLEKHANOV (NIKOLAI NIKOLAEVICH) Dialektika prevrashcheniia nauki v proizvoditel'nuiu silu. Kishinev, 1975. pp. 141. *bibliog.*

— United Kingdom.

WATSON (WILLIAM FERGUSON) University research and the needs of industry. Bradford, [1974]. pp. 14. *(University of Bradford. Professor Moore Memorial Lectures. 1974)*

U.K. Cabinet Office. Government research and development: a guide to sources of information. a., 1975 [2nd]- London.

BRIGHTON. University of Sussex. Science Policy Research Unit. Annual report 1975 and ten year review 1966-1976. Brighton, [1976]. pp. 103. *bibliog.*

U.K. Central Statistical Office. 1976. Research and development: expenditure and employment. London, 1976. pp. 54. *(Studies in Official Statistics. No. 27)*

ROTHSCHILD (NATHANIEL MEYER VICTOR) 3rd Baron Rothschild. Meditations of a broomstick. London, 1977. pp. 187. *bibliog.*

— Zaire — Directories.

MPEKESA (BONGOY) and others. Répertoire des institutions de recherche scientifique au Zaire; (Repertory of scientific research institutions in Zaire). Kinshasa, Centre de Coordination des Recherches et de la Documentation en Sciences Sociales pour l'Afrique Sub-Saharienne, 1975. fo. 72. *In English and French.*

RESEARCH, INDUSTRIAL.

DEFAY (JACQUES) La science facteur de production: recherche sur l'intégration d la recherche-développement dans la fonction de production. Bruxelles, Services de Programmation de la Politique Scientifique, 1973. pp. 268. *(Recherche et Croissance Economique. 3)*

— Portugal.

CARAMONA (MARIA HELENA) Inquerito sobre os meios nacionais de investigação e desenvolvimento. [Lisbon, 1972]. pp. 108. *(Portugal. Instituto Nacional de Estatistica. Estudos. No.43) With summaries in English and French.*

— United Kingdom.

U.K. Central Statistical Office. 1976. Research and development: expenditure and employment. London, 1976. pp. 54. *(Studies in Official Statistics. No. 27)*

— — Evaluation.

PROGRAMMES ANALYSIS UNIT. The Programmes Analysis Unit: 'the second five years', 1971-1976. Chilton, 1976. pp. 80.

RESEARCH AND DEVELOPMENT CONTRACTS.

ORGANISATION FOR ECONOMIC CO-OPERATION AND DEVELOPMENT. Directorate for Scientific Affairs. 1976. The measurement of scientific and technical activities: proposed standard practice for surveys of research and experimental development; Frascati manual. Paris, 1976. pp. 139. *bibliog.*

— Underdeveloped areas.

See UNDERDEVELOPED AREAS —
Research and development contracts.

RESIDENTIAL MOBILITY

— United Kingdom.

WILLIAMS (ALLAN MORGAN) Social change and residential differentiation: a case study of nineteenth century Cardiff. 1976. fo. 525. *bibliog. Ph.D. (London) thesis: unpublished. This thesis is the property of London University and may not be removed from the Library. Two transparencies in end pocket.*

DUNCAN (S.S.) Housing disadvantage and residential mobility: immigrants and institutions in a northern town. Brighton, 1977. fo.28. *(Brighton. University of Sussex. Sussex Working Papers in Urban and Regional Studies. 5)*

— — Mathematical models.

BONNAR (DESMOND M.) Stochastic models for migration analysis: applications to Greater London. Reading, 1976. pp. 44. *bibliog. (Reading. University. Department of Geography. Reading Geographical Papers. No. 51)*

— United States.

KAISER (EDWARD JOHN) Residential mobility in new communities: an analysis of recent in-movers and prospective out-movers. Cambridge, Mass., [1976]. pp. 188. *bibliog. (North Carolina University. Center for Urban and Regional Studies. New Communities Research Series)*

ROSE (HAROLD M.) Black suburbanization: access to improved quality of life or maintenance of th status quo? Cambridge, Mass., [1976]. pp. 288. *bibliog.*

— — New York (State).

SANDS (GARY) and BOWER (LEWIS L.) Housing turnover and housing policy: case studies of vacancy chains in New York State. New York, 1976. pp. 169. *bibliog.*

RESPONSIBILITY, LEGAL

— Russia.

BRATUS' (SERGEI NIKITICH) Iuridicheskaia otvetstvennost' i zakonnost': ocherk teorii. Moskva, 1976. pp. 213.

RESTAURANT MANAGEMENT.

BOWEY (ANGELA M.) The sociology of organisations. London, 1976. pp. 228. *bibliog.*

RESTRAINT OF TRADE

— Germany.

WENDLER (DIETRICH) Die wirtschaftliche Bedeutung der Bereichsausnahme für die Landwirtschaft im GWB. Berlin, [1977]. pp. 266. *bibliog.*

— Ireland (Republic).

EIRE. Fair Trade Commission. 1968. Report of enquiry into the conditions which obtain in regard to the supply and distribution to retailers of jewellery, watches and clocks. Dublin, [1968]. pp. 27.

EIRE. Fair Trade Commission. 1971. Report of enquiry into the conditions which obtain in regard to the supply and distribution of motor spirit in so far as they effect the nature and growth in numbers of motor spirit retail outlets. Dublin, [1971]. pp. 83.

EIRE. Restrictive Practices Commission. 1976. Report of special review by means of public enquiry of the operation of Articles 2 and 3 of the Restrictive Practices, Groceries, Order, 1973, as amended by the Restrictive Practices, Groceries, Amendment Order, 1973. Dublin, [1976]. pp. 58.

— South Africa.

SOUTH AFRICA. Commission of Inquiry into the Regulation of Monopolistic Conditions Act, 1955. 1977. Report (R.P. 64/1977). in SOUTH AFRICA. Parliament. House of Assembly. Votes and proceedings; (with Printed annexures).

RETAIL TRADE.

DAVIES (ROSSER LLEWELYN) Marketing geography: with special reference to retailing. Corbridge, [1976]. pp. 300.

— Brazil.

BRAZIL. Departamento de Censos. 1975. Censo comercial [1970]: Brasil [whole country]. [Rio de Janeiro, 1975]. pp. 157.

— Canada — Alberta.

ALBERTA. Bureau of Statistics. Retail and service trade statistics. a., 1975(4th)- Edmonton.

— Germany.

GERMANY (BUNDESREPUBLIK). Statistisches Bundesamt. Wareneinkauf, Lagerbestand und Rohertrag im Einzelhandel. a., 1974- Wiesbaden. *(Handel, Gastgewerbe, Reiseverkehr. Reihe 3.2)*

BECKERMANN (THEO) and RAU (RAINER) Der Einzelhandel, 1959-1985. Berlin, [1977]. pp. 95. *bibliog. (Rheinisch-Westfälisches Institut fur Wirtschaftsforschung, Essen. Schriftenreihe. Neue Folge. 39)*

— Ireland (Republic).

EIRE. Restrictive Practices Commission. 1976. Report of study of roadside and street trading and sales from temporary retail outlets. Dublin, [1976]. pp. 70.

EIRE. Central Statistics Office. 1977. Census of distribution, 1971: detailed results. Dublin, 1977. 3 pts. (in 1 vol.).

— Netherlands.

ECONOMISCH INSTITUUT VOOR HET MIDDEN- EN KLEINBEDRIJF. Gegevens over de Omzet in het Midden-en Kleinbedrijf. No. 37. Het weekpatroon van de geldomzetten. 3. 's-Gravenhage, 1965. pp. 9.

ECONOMISCH INSTITUUT VOOR HET MIDDEN- EN KLEINBEDRIJF. Gegevens over de Omzet in het Midden-en Kleinbedrijf. No. 39. De omzetontwikkeling in het jaar 1965. 's-Gravenhage, 1966. pp. 17.

ECONOMISCH INSTITUUT VOOR HET MIDDEN- EN KLEINBEDRIJF. Gegevens over de Omzet in het Midden-en Kleinbedrijf. No. 42. De omzetontwikkeling in het eerste tot en met het derde kwartaal 1966. 's-Gravenhage, 1966. pp. 10.

ECONOMISCH INSTITUUT VOOR HET MIDDEN- EN KLEINBEDRIJF. Gegevens over de Omzet in het Midden-en Kleinbedrijf. No. 45. Het weekpatroon van de geldomzetten. 4. 's-Gravenhage, 1967. pp. 10.

ECONOMISCH INSTITUUT VOOR HET MIDDEN- EN KLEINBEDRIJF. Gegevens over de Omzet in het Midden-en Kleinbedrijf. No. 50. Het weekpatroon van de geldomzetten. 5. 's-Gravenhage, 1968. pp. 12.

ECONOMISCH INSTITUUT VOOR HET MIDDEN- EN KLEINBEDRIJF. Sociaal-Economische Publikaties. Part-time arbeid in de detailhandel: een onderzoek bij vestigingen waar part-timers werkzaam zijn. 's-Gravenhage, 1975. pp. 160.

— Russia.

AVANESOV (IURII ARKAD'EVICH) Prognozirovanie sprosa v roznichnoi torgovle. Moskva, 1975. pp. 103. *bibliog.*

— Underdeveloped areas.

See UNDERDEVELOPED AREAS — Retail trade.

— United Kingdom.

WILLSON (JOAN) Note on the 1971 census of distribution for London and the south east:...some pointers to changes in the pattern of retail trade in London and the south-east region. London, [1975]. pp. 14, 5 maps. *(London. Greater London Council. Research Memoranda. 486)*

RETIREMENT

SPIERS (PETER) and SPIERS (BARBARA) Transition in retirement: an account of some conversations with recently retired manual workers. London, 1975. pp. 22.

U.K. Equal Opportunities Commission. 1977. Sex equality and the pension age: a choice of routes. [Manchester, 1977?]. pp. 22.

RETIREMENT, PLACES OF

— Economic aspects — United States.

HEINTZ (KATHERINE McMILLAN) Retirement communities, for adults only. New Brunswick, [1976]. pp. 239.

— United Kingdom.

KARN (VALERIE A.) Retiring to the seaside. London, 1977. pp. 388. *bibliog.*

RETRAINING, OCCUPATIONAL

— United Kingdom.

SEEAR (BEATRICE NANCY) Baroness Seear. Training: the fulcrum of change. London, 1976. pp. 8. *(British Association for Commercial and Industrial Education. Annual Willis Jackson Lectures. 1976)*

REVENUE SHARING

— United States.

DOMMEL (PAUL R.) The politics of revenue sharing. Bloomington, Ind., [1974]. pp. 211. *bibliog.*

REVENUE SHARING(Cont.)

HARBERT (ANITA S.) Federal grants-in-aid: maximizing benefits to the states. New York, 1976. pp. 173. *bibliog.*

REVENUE sharing: methodological approaches and problems; edited by David A. Caputo and Richard L. Cole. Lexington, Mass., [1976]. pp. 185.

TERRELL (PAUL) and WEISNER (STANLEY) The social impact of revenue sharing: planning, participation and the purchase of service. New York, 1976. pp. 114. *bibliog.*

NATHAN (RICHARD P.) and ADAMS (CHARLES F.) Revenue sharing: the second round. Washington, D.C., [1977]. pp. 268. *bibliog.*

REVERSE INCOME TAX.

See NEGATIVE INCOME TAX.

REVOLUTIONISTS.

BLACKEY (ROBERT) and PAYNTON (CLIFFORD) Revolution and the revolutionary ideal. Cambridge, Mass., [1976]. pp. 295. *bibliog.*

JANICKI (JANUSZ) and MUSZYŃSKI (JERZY) eds. Ideologia i polityka współczesnego lewactwa. Warszawa, 1976. pp. 387.

— Europe.

ESSAYS on modern European revolutionary history; by Stanley H Palmer [and others];...edited by Bede K. Lackner and Kenneth Roy Philp. Austin, [1977]. pp. 132. *(Texas University. Walter Prescott Webb Memorial Lectures.11)*

— Oman.

GULF COMMITTEE and OMAN SOLIDARITY COMMITTEE. Women and the revolution in Oman. London, [1975]. pp. 43.

— Russia.

SERGE (VICTOR) pseud. [i.e. Viktor L'vovich KIBAL'CHICH] Vie des révolutionnaires. Paris, [1929]. pp. 30.

DUNLOP (JOHN B.) The new Russian revolutionaries. Belmont, Mass., 1976. pp. 344. *bibliog.*

HARVARD UNIVERSITY. Library. Houghton Library. Russian revolutionary literature collection. New Haven, Conn., 1976. Microfilm: 47 reels.

— — Bibliography.

HARVARD UNIVERSITY. Library. Houghton Library. Russian revolutionary literature collection, Houghton Library, Harvard University: a descriptive guide and key to the collection on microfilm; [compiled by Kenneth E. Carpenter]. New Haven, Conn., 1976. pp. x, 220.

— Underdeveloped areas.

See UNDERDEVELOPED AREAS — Revolutionists.

REVOLUTIONS.

[ASCHER (SAUL)] Ideen zur natürlichen Geschichte der Revolutionen. Kronberg/Is., 1975. pp. 231. *Reprint of work originally published in Leipzig in 1802.*

LANGER (ALFRED) Der Weg zum Sieg: die Kunst des bewaffneten Aufstandes. [Zürich, 1931]. pp. 55.

CORNEJO CHAVEZ (HECTOR) Democracia Cristiana y revolucion. [Lima, 1967]. pp. 38.

GALTUNG (JOHAN) A structural theory of revolutions; [based on a paper presented at the International Working Conference on Violence and Non- violent Action in Industrialized Societies]. Rotterdam, 1974. pp. 78. *(Vrije Universiteit Brussel. Polemological Centre. Publications. vol.5)*

BELL (J. BOWYER) On revolt: strategies of national liberation. Cambridge, Mass., 1976. pp. 272. *bibliog.*

BLACKEY (ROBERT) and PAYNTON (CLIFFORD) Revolution and the revolutionary ideal. Cambridge, Mass., [1976]. pp. 295. *bibliog.*

CASSINELLI (CHARLES WILLIAM) Total revolution: a comparative study of Germany under Hitler, the Soviet Union under Stalin and China under Mao. Santa Barbara, Calif., [1976]. pp. 252.

LASKY (MELVIN J.) Utopia and revolution: on the origins of a metaphor; or, Some illustrations of the problem of political temperament and intellectual climate and how ideas, ideals, and ideologies have been historically related. Chicago, 1976. pp. 726.

ROLLE und Formen der Volksbewegung im bürgerlichen Revolutionszyklus; herausgegeben von Manfred Kossok. Glashütten/Taunus, 1976. pp. 351. *Revised papers of an international symposium held in 1974.*

SALERT (BARBARA) Revolutions and revolutionaries: four theories. New York, [1976]. pp. 161. *bibliog.*

DEBRAY (REGIS) A critique of arms...; translated by Rosemary Sheed. Harmondsworth, 1977 in progress.

DRAPER (HAL) Karl Marx's theory of revolution. New York, [1977] in progress. *bibliogs.*

SHIPLEY (PETER) Trotskyism: "entryism" and permanent revolution. London, 1977. pp. 20. *(Institute for the Study of Conflict. Conflict Studies. No. 81)*

— Europe.

ESSAYS on modern European revolutionary history; by Stanley H Palmer [and others];...edited by Bede K. Lackner and Kenneth Roy Philp. Austin, [1977]. pp. 132. *(Texas University. Walter Prescott Webb Memorial Lectures.11)*

— Mexico.

KAUTSKY (JOHN HANS) Patterns of modernizing revolutions: Mexico and the Soviet Union. Beverly Hills, [1975]. pp. 59. *bibliog.*

— Russia.

KAUTSKY (JOHN HANS) Patterns of modernizing revolutions: Mexico and the Soviet Union. Beverly Hills, [1975]. pp. 59. *bibliog.*

RHINELAND-PALATINATE

— Beratende Landesversammlung.

See RHINELAND-PALATINATE — Landtag.

— Landtag.

JUNG (HORST WILHELM) Rheinland-Pfalz zwischen Antifaschismus und Antikommunismus: zur Geschichte des Landesparlaments, 1946-1948. Meisenheim am Glan, 1976. pp. 136.

— Politics and government.

JUNG (HORST WILHELM) Rheinland-Pfalz zwischen Antifaschismus und Antikommunismus: zur Geschichte des Landesparlaments, 1946-1948. Meisenheim am Glan, 1976. pp. 136.

RHODE ISLAND

— Statistics, Medical.

MONTEIRO (LOIS A.) Monitoring health status and medical care. Cambridge, Mass., [1976]. pp. 221. *bibliog.*

RHODES (CECIL JOHN).

FLINT (JOHN E.) Cecil Rhodes. London, 1976. pp. 268. *bibliog.*

RHODESIA

— Biography.

CARY (ROBERT) and MITCHELL (DIANA) African nationalist leaders in Rhodesia: who's who. Bulawayo, 1977. pp. 310. *bibliog.*

— Economic conditions.

HANDFORD (JOHN) Portrait of an economy: Rhodesia under sanctions. Salisbury, Rhodesia, 1976. pp. 204. *bibliog.*

— Economic history.

PALMER (ROBIN) Land and racial domination in Rhodesia. Berkeley, 1977. pp. 307. *bibliog.*

— Foreign economic relations.

PORTER (RICHARD C.) Economic sanctions: the theory and evidence from Rhodesia. Ann Arbor, 1977. pp. 19. *bibliog. (Michigan University. Center for Research on Economic Development. Discussion Papers. No. 68)*

— — United States.

LAKE (ANTHONY) The "tar baby" option: American policy toward Southern Rhodesia. New York, 1976. pp. 316. *bibliog.*

— Foreign relations.

NKRUMAH (KWAME) Rhodesia file. London, [1976]. pp. 168.

— — United States.

LAKE (ANTHONY) The "tar baby" option: American policy toward Southern Rhodesia. New York, 1976. pp. 316. *bibliog.*

— Nationalism.

CARY (ROBERT) and MITCHELL (DIANA) African nationalist leaders in Rhodesia: who's who. Bulawayo, 1977. pp. 310. *bibliog.*

— Politics and government.

WAINWRIGHT (ANDREW) Letters from Zimbabwe. Leeds, [1975?]. pp. 70.

NKRUMAH (KWAME) Rhodesia file. London, [1976]. pp. 168.

VENTER (DENIS) The Rhodesian constitutional dispute: black majority rule or meritocracy? Braamfontein, 1976. pp. 28.

PALMER (ROBIN) Land and racial domination in Rhodesia. Berkeley, 1977. pp. 307. *bibliog.*

— Race question.

JABBOUR (GEORGE) Settler colonialism in Southern Africa and the Middle East. Beirut, 1970. pp. 216. *(Palestine Research Center. Palestine Books. No. 30)*

O'CALLAGHAN (MARION) Southern Rhodesia: the effects of a conquest society on education, culture and information;...with a contribution by Reginald Austin. Paris, Unesco, 1977. pp. 293.

PALMER (ROBIN) Land and racial domination in Rhodesia. Berkeley, 1977. pp. 307. *bibliog.*

— Social conditions.

O'CALLAGHAN (MARION) Southern Rhodesia: the effects of a conquest society on education, culture and information;...with a contribution by Reginald Austin. Paris, Unesco, 1977. pp. 293.

RHÔNE-ALPES

— Industries.

RHÔNE-ALPES. Mission Régionale. Les structures industrielles de la région Rhône-Alpes. [Lyons], 1974. pp. 254.

RICARDO (DAVID).

GORDON (BARRY J.) Political economy in Parliament, 1819-1823. London, 1976. pp. 246.

WEATHERALL (DAVID) David Ricardo: a biography. The Hague, 1976. pp. 201. *bibliog.*

RICE.

VERON (JEAN BERNARD) Le riz dans le monde et en Afrique Noire. [Paris], Caisse Centrale de Coopération Economique, 1975. fo. 30.

— Africa.

VERON (JEAN BERNARD) Le riz dans le monde et en Afrique Noire. [Paris], Caisse Centrale de Coopération Economique, 1975. fo. 30.

— Asia.

PALMER (INGRID) The new rice in Asia: conclusions from four country studies. (UNRISD Reports. No. 76.6). Geneva, United Nations Research Institute for Social Development, 1976. pp. 146. *([Studies on the Green Revolution. No.12])*

— India.

INDIA. Ministry of Agriculture. Directorate of Economics and Statistics. 1974. Rice economy of India. 2nd ed. [Delhi], 1973 [or rather 1974]. pp. 227.

— — Madras.

GREEN revolution?: technology and change in rice-growing areas of Tamil Nadu and Sri Lanka; edited by B.H. Farmer. London, 1977. pp. 429. *bibliogs.*

— Panama.

PANAMA. Direccion de Estadistica y Censo. Estadistica panameña. Superficie sembrada y cosecha de arroz, maiz y frijol de bejuco. a., 1975/76- Panama. *Supersedes in part PANAMA. Direccion de Estadistica y Censo. Estadistica panameña. Serie H. Informacion agropecuaria.*

— Sierra Leone.

PILGRIM (JOHN W.) Review of research into social and economic aspects of rice farming in Sierra Leone. Njala, Sierra Leone, [1968?]. pp. 42. *bibliog. (Njala University College. School of Development Studies. Development Studies. No. 1)*

— Sri Lanka.

GREEN revolution?: technology and change in rice-growing areas of Tamil Nadu and Sri Lanka; edited by B.H. Farmer. London, 1977. pp. 429. *bibliogs.*

RICE revolution in Sri Lanka; [by] N. D. Abdul Hameed [and others]. (UNRISD Reports. No. 76.7). Geneva, United Nations Research Institute for Social Development, 1977. pp. 282. *([Studies on the Green Revolution. No. 13])*

— Thailand.

CHAIPRAVAT (OLARN) Aggregate structures of production and domestic demand for rice in Thailand: a time series analysis, 1951-1973. Bangkok, 1975. pp. 36. *(Bank of Thailand. Papers, No. 4)*

RIGHT AND LEFT (POLITICAL SCIENCE).

ETZKOWITZ (HENRY) and SCHWAB (PETER) eds. Is America necessary? Conservative, Liberal and Socialist perspectives of United States political institutions. St. Paul, [1976]. pp. 658. *bibliog.*

GRAF (WILLIAM DAVID) The German left since 1945: socialism and social democracy in the German Federal Republic. Cambridge, [1976]. pp. 318. *bibliog.*

The BRITISH right: Conservative and right wing politics in Britain; edited by Neill Nugent [and] Roger King. Farnborough, [1977]. pp. 230. *bibliog.*

TOUCHARD (JEAN) La gauche en France depuis 1900. Paris, [1977]. pp. 383. *bibliog.*

RIGHT OF PROPERTY.

BECKER (LAWRENCE CARLYLE) Property rights: philosophic foundations. London, 1977. pp. 135.

RIGHT TO LABOUR.

FANTETTI (ANTONIO) Il lavoro come diritto: alcuni profili giuridici. Milano, 1975 in progress.

RINGLER (RALF ROLAND).

RINGLER (RALF ROLAND) Illusion einer Jugend: Lieder, Fahnen und das bittere Ende; Hitler-Jugend in Österreich: ein Erlebnisbericht. St. Pölten, 1977. pp. 223.

RIOT CONTROL.

VERWEY (WIL D.) Riot control agents and herbicides in war: their humanitarian, toxicological, ecological, military, polemological, and legal aspects. Leyden, 1977. pp. 377. *bibliog.*

RIOTS

— Barbados.

BARBADOS. Commission appointed to Enquire into the Disturbances which took place in Barbados on the 27th July 1937 and subsequent days. 1937. Report; [G.C. Deane, chairman]. [Bridgetown, 1937]. pp. 41.

— Malaysia.

FEDERATION OF MALAYSIA. National Operations Council. 1969. The May 13 tragedy; a report. Kuala Lumpur, 1969. pp. 96.

— United States.

LIPSKY (MICHAEL) and OLSON (DAVID J.) Commission politics: the processing of racial crisis in America. New Brunswick, N.J., [1977]. pp. 476.

RISK.

RISK and return in finance; edited by Irwin Friend [and] James L. Bicksler. Cambridge, Mass., [1977]. 2 vols. *bibliogs. Thirteen of the seventeen papers in these two volumes were originally presented at a Conference on Risk and the Rate of Return, sponsored by the American Telephone and Telegraph Company and held in Vail, Colorado, during August 5-10, 1973.*

RISK (INSURANCE).

DOHERTY (NEIL) Insurance pricing and loss prevention. Farnborough, Hants., [1976]. pp. 134.

RITES AND CEREMONIES.

VIZEDOM (MONIKA BASCH) Rites and relationships: rites of passage and contemporary anthropology. Beverly Hills, [1976]. pp. 63. *bibliog.*

RIVERS

— United Kingdom.

WISDOM (ALLEN SIDNEY) The law of rivers and watercourses. 3rd ed. London, 1975. pp. 397.

ROAD ACCIDENTS

— United Kingdom.

NATIONAL COUNCIL OF SOCIAL SERVICE. Devil's Bridge coach crash:...the first seventy-two hours; a report on the Yorkshire Dales coach crash, its effect on the community of Thornaby and the implications for statutory and voluntary organisations. London, 1975. pp. 8.

SCOTT (P.P.) and BARTON (A.J.) The effects on road accident rates of the fuel shortage of November 1973 and consequent legislation. Crowthorne, 1976. pp. 33. *bibliog. (U.K. Transport and Road Research Laboratory. Supplementary Reports. 236)*

ROAD CONSTRUCTION

— United States — Florida.

SIMMONS (ADINA) The effects of public primary investment on private development of rural-scenic areas: a case study of the impact of highway improvements in north central Florida, 1950-1970. 1976. fo. 428. *bibliog. Typescript. Ph.D. (London) thesis: unpublished. This thesis is the property of London University and may not be removed from the Library.*

ROAD PLANNING

— United Kingdom — Citizen participation.

PRESCOTT-CLARKE (PATRICIA) Public consultation and participation in road planning. London, 1975. pp. 178,18. *Maps in end-pocket.*

ROAD TRANSPORT WORKERS

— United Kingdom.

ROAD TRANSPORT INDUSTRY TRAINING BOARD [U.K.]. Introductory notes on management development in transportation. [Wembley, 1971?]. pp. 48.

ROAD TRANSPORT INDUSTRY TRAINING BOARD [U.K.]. Transport and distribution: meeting the manpower needs. Wembley, [1975?]. pp. 23.

ROAD TRANSPORT INDUSTRY TRAINING BOARD [U.K.]. Local manpower studies, 1976-1977: six micro-economic studies in manpower planning in the road transport industry. Wembley, 1977. pp. 121.

ROADS

— Economic aspects — United States — Florida.

SIMMONS (ADINA) The effects of public primary investment on private development of rural-scenic areas: a case study of the impact of highway improvements in north central Florida, 1950-1970. 1976. fo. 428. *bibliog. Typescript. Ph.D. (London) thesis: unpublished. This thesis is the property of London University and may not be removed from the Library.*

— Environmental aspects — United Kingdom.

PROFESSIONAL INSTITUTIONS COUNCIL FOR CONSERVATION. The urban road in relation to the conservation and renewal of the environment; [report by a PICC working party; edited by J.T. Williams]. London, [1974]. pp. 21.

— — United States — Florida.

SIMMONS (ADINA) The effects of public primary investment on private development of rural-scenic areas: a case study of the impact of highway improvements in north central Florida, 1950-1970. 1976. fo. 428. *bibliog. Typescript. Ph.D. (London) thesis: unpublished. This thesis is the property of London University and may not be removed from the Library.*

— Africa, East.

ETHIOPIA. Imperial Highway Authority. 1966. The development of international routes in Ethiopia and their place in the eastern African and trans-African highway systems; presented at the fifth world meeting of International Road Federation, London, September 18-24, 1966. [Addis Ababa?, 1966?]. pp. 18.

— Australia — Finance.

MATHEWS (RUSSELL LLOYD) and JAY (W.R.C.) Measures of fiscal effort and fiscal capacity in relation to Australian state road finance. Canberra, 1974. pp. 79. *(Australian National University. Centre for Research on Federal Financial Relations. Research Monographs. No. 5)*

ROADS(Cont.)

— Ethiopia.

ETHIOPIA. Imperial Highway Authority. 1966. The development of international routes in Ethiopia and their place in the eastern African and trans-African highway systems; presented at the fifth world meeting of International Road Federation, London, September 18-24, 1966. [Addis Ababa?, 1966?]. pp. 18.

— Mexico.

MEXICO. Secretaria de Obras Publicas. 1975. Censo nacional de caminos: resumen general abreviado. Mexico, 1975. pp. 567.

— Norway.

BALDERSHEIM (HAROLD) Patterns of central control over local service provision in Norway. 1977. fo. 367. *bibliog. Typescript. Ph.D. (London) thesis: unpublished. This thesis is the property of London University and may not be removed from the Library.*

— United Kingdom — Ireland, Northern — Finance.

IRELAND, NORTHERN. Road Fund. Account...together with the report of the Comptroller and Auditor-General thereon. a., 1971/72- Belfast. *1921/22-1970/71 included in IRELAND, NORTHERN. Parliament. House of Commons. [Papers].*

— — London.

LONDON. Greater London Council. Priorities for highway investment in Greater London; report. [London], 1976. 1 pamphlet (various pagings).

ROADSIDE MARKETING.

EIRE. Restrictive Practices Commission. 1976. Report of study of roadside and street trading and sales from temporary retail outlets. Dublin, [1976]. pp. 70.

ROBERTS (FREDERICK SLEIGH) 1st Earl Roberts.

SPIES (S. BURRIDGE) Methods of barbarism?: Roberts and Kitchener and civilians in the Boer republics, January 1900-May 1902. Cape Town, 1977. pp. 416. *bibliog.*

ROBERTS (ROBERT).

ROBERTS (ROBERT) of the Prison Department. A ragged schooling: growing up in the classic slum. Manchester, [1976]. pp. 224.

ROCKEFELLER FAMILY.

ALLEN (GARY) The Rockefeller file. Seal Beach, Calif., 1976. pp. 195.

ROLE CONFLICT.

STANFORTH (JOHN) Role conflict and attitude change: a study of the effects of teaching practice on third year students at a college of education. 1977. fo. 244. *bibliog. Typescript. Ph.D. (London) thesis: unpublished. This thesis is the property of London University and may not be removed from the Library.*

ROLE PLAYING.

CORINA (LEWIS) Local government decision making: some influences on elected members' role playing. [York, 1975]. pp. 39. *(Papers in Community Studies. No. 2)*

ROMANCE LANGUAGES

— Phonology.

HALL (ROBERT ANDERSON) Comparative romance grammar. vol. 1. Proto-romance phonology. New York, [1976]. pp. 297. *bibliog.*

ROMANIA

— Foreign relations.

BOICU (LEONID) Geneza "chestiunii române" ca problemă internaţională. Iaşi, 1975. pp. 149. *With French summary.*

BRAUN (AUREL) Romanian foreign policy under Nicolae Ceausescu, 1965-1972: the political and military limits of autonomy. 1976. fo. 318. *bibliog. Typescript. Ph.D. (London) thesis: unpublished. This thesis is the property of London University and may not be removed from the Library.*

PROBLEME internaţionale: agendă. Bucureşti, 1976. pp. 589.

ROMANIA and the non-aligned states. Bucharest, 1976. 3 vols. (in 1).

BOTORAN (CONSTANTIN) and UNC (GHEORGHE) Tradiţii de solidaritate ale mişcării muncitoreşti şi democratice din România cu lupta de emancipare naţională şi socială a popoarelor din Asia, Africa şi America Latină. Bucureşti, 1977. pp. 255. *With English, French, German, Russian and Spanish tables of contents.*

— — Treaties.

IONAŞCU (ION) and others, eds. Tratatele internaţionale ale României, 1354-1920; texte rezumate, adnotări, bibliografie. Bucureşti, 1975. pp. 528.

— History.

LEBEDEV (NIKOLAI IVANOVICH) Krakh fashizma v Rumynii. Moskva, 1976. pp. 632. *bibliog.*

— — Chronology.

HISTOIRE chronologique de la Roumanie; par Horia C. Matei [and others]; sous la rédaction de Constantin C. Giurescu. Bucarest, 1976. pp. 549.

— — Sources.

MEHMED (MUSTAFA A.) ed. Documente turceşti privind istoria României. Bucureşti, 1976 in progress. *(Academia de Ştiinţe Sociale şi Politice a Republicii Socialiste România. Institutul de Studii Sud-Est Europene. Izvoare Orientale privind Istoria României. 3)*

— Rural conditions.

BĂDINA (OVIDIU) and others. Buciumi: un sat din Ţara de Sub Munte, etc. Bucureşti, 1970. pp. 410. *(Centrul de Cercetări pentru Problemele Tineretului. Tineretul şi Lumea de Mîine) With English, French, German, Russian and Spanish tables of contents.*

ROMANTICISM

— United States.

KARIEL (HENRY S.) Beyond liberalism, where relations grow. San Francisco, [1977]. pp. 137.

ROME, ANCIENT

— Civilization.

CAMERON (ALAN) Circus factions: Blues and Greens at Rome and Byzantium. Oxford, 1976. pp. 364. *bibliog.*

— Politics and government.

CAMERON (ALAN) Circus factions: Blues and Greens at Rome and Byzantium. Oxford, 1976. pp. 364. *bibliog.*

GRIFFIN (MIRIAM TAMARA) Seneca: a philosopher in politics. Oxford, 1976. pp. xii, 504. *bibliog.*

ROOSEVELT (ANNA ELEANOR).

ROOSEVELT (JAMES) My parents: a differing view;...with Bill Libby. London, 1977. pp. 369.

ROOSEVELT (FRANKLIN DELANO) President of the United States.

ADAMIC (LOUIS) Dinner at the White House. New York, [1946]. pp. 276.

LASH (JOSEPH P.) Roosevelt and Churchill, 1939-1941: the partnership that saved the West. New York, [1976]. pp. 528.

ROOSEVELT (JAMES) My parents: a differing view;...with Bill Libby. London, 1977. pp. 369.

ROSEN (ELLIOT A.) Hoover, Roosevelt, and the Brains Trust: from Depression to New Deal. New York, 1977. pp. 446.

TUGWELL (REXFORD GUY) Roosevelt's revolution: the first year; a personal perspective. New York, [1977]. pp. 327.

ROOSEVELT (THEODORE) President of the United States.

McKEE (DELBER L.) Chinese exclusion versus the open door policy, 1900-1906: clashes over China policy in the Roosevelt era. Detroit, 1977. pp. 292. *bibliog.*

ROOSEVELT FAMILY.

ROOSEVELT (JAMES) My parents: a differing view;...with Bill Libby. London, 1977. pp. 369.

ROSENBERG (ETHEL and JULIUS).

SOBELL (MORTON) On doing time. Toronto, 1976. pp. 436. *Originally published in New York, 1974.*

ROSTOV (OBLAST')

— History — 1917-1921, Revolution.

KIRIENKO (IURII KONSTANTINOVICH) Krakh kaledinshchiny. Moskva, 1976. pp. 246. *bibliog.*

ROTHSCHILD (NATHANIEL MEYER VICTOR) 3rd Baron Rothschild.

ROTHSCHILD (NATHANIEL MEYER VICTOR) 3rd Baron Rothschild. Meditations of a broomstick. London, 1977. pp. 187. *bibliog.*

ROTTERDAM

— Economic history.

DIJK (HENDRIK VAN) Rotterdam 1810-1880: aspecten van een stedelijke samenleving. [Rotterdam, 1976]. pp. 472. *bibliog. Proefschrift (Doctor in de sociale wetenschappen) - Erasmus Universiteit Rotterdam.*

— Social history.

DIJK (HENDRIK VAN) Rotterdam 1810-1880: aspecten van een stedelijke samenleving. [Rotterdam, 1976]. pp. 472. *bibliog. Proefschrift (Doctor in de sociale wetenschappen) - Erasmus Universiteit Rotterdam.*

ROUSIERS FAMILY.

ROUSIERS (PAUL DE) Une famille de hobereaux pendant six siècles. [Paris, 1934]. pp. 276.

ROUSSEAU (JEAN JACQUES).

LEVINE (ANDREW) The politics of autonomy: a Kantian reading of Rousseau's Social contract. Amherst, Mass., 1976. pp. 211. *bibliog.*

ROYAL BANK OF SCOTLAND.

In earlier volumes of the Bibliography similar material is entered under BANK OF SCOTLAND.

The ROYAL Bank of Scotland, 1727-1977. [Edinburgh, 1977]. 1 vol. (unpaged).

ROYAL DESCENT, FAMILIES OF.

BURKE'S guide to the royal family. London, 1973. pp. 358.

ROYAL SUPREMACY (CHURCH OF ENGLAND).

IMPERIAL PROTESTANT FEDERATION. House of Lords; statement presented on Tuesday, June 25th, 1901, to the Select Committee on the King's declaration against transubstantiation: [signed T. Myles Sandys]. London, [1901]. pp. 26.

IMPERIAL PROTESTANT FEDERATION. The King's declaration against transubstantiation; (with Addendum). London, 1904. 2 pts.

KNOX CLUB. Memorial...to the members of the Houses of Parliament against alteration of the Royal declaration; [signed by Thomas Burns and F.J.Robertson]. [Edinburgh, 1910]. pp. (4).

RUBBER INDUSTRY AND TRADE

— Brazil.

BRAZIL. Superintendência da Borracha. Relatorio de atividades. a., 1972- [Rio de Janeiro].

RUEFF (JACQUES).

RUEFF (JACQUES) Combats pour l'ordre financier: mémoires et documents pour servir à l'histoire du dernier demi-siècle. [Paris, 1972]. pp. 480.

RUFA'A AL-HOI.

ABD-AL GHAFFAR (MUHAMMAD AHMAD) Shaykhs and followers: political struggle in the Rufa'a al- Hoi Nazirate in the Sudan. Khartoum, 1974. pp. 170. *bibliog.*

RUGE (ARNOLD).

RUGE (ARNOLD) Politician. Zwei Jahre in Paris: Studien und Erinnerungen. Leipzig, Jurany, 1846; Leipzig, 1975. 2 vols. *Facsimile reprint.*

RUHR

— Economic history.

KONZE (HEINZ) Entwicklung des Steinkohlenbergbaus im Ruhrgebiet, 1957-1974: Grundlagen und Strukturdaten für die Stadt- und Regionalplanung. Essen, 1975. pp. 64. *bibliog. (Siedlungsverband Ruhrkohlenbezirk. Schriftenreihe. Nr. 56) Includes supplement containing 18 maps.*

— History.

PEUKERT (DETLEV) Ruhrarbeiter gegen den Faschismus: Dokumentation über den Widerstand im Ruhrgebiet, 1933-1945. Frankfurt/Main, [1976]. pp. 412. *bibliog.*

— Politics and government.

LOEFFLER (HEINRICH) Das Proletariat und die Besetzung des Ruhrgebiets;...Referat, gehalten vor den Funktionären der Vereinigten Sozialdemokratischen Partei, Bezirksverband Berlin. Berlin, [1923]. pp. 13.

RULE OF LAW

— Russia.

LAPENNA (IVO) The contemporary crisis of legality in the Soviet Union substantive criminal law. Leyden, 1975. pp. 73-95. *(Offprint from Review of Socialist Law, 1975)*

SOTSIALISTICHESKAIA zakonnost' i gosudarstvennaia distsiplina. Moskva, 1975. pp. 222.

RUMOUR.

ROUQUETTE (MICHEL LOUIS) Les rumeurs. [Paris, 1975]. pp. 127. *bibliog.*

RURAL DEVELOPMENT.

REGIONAL and rural development: essays in theory and practice; edited by P.J. Drudy. Chalfont St. Giles, [1976]. pp. 116. *Based on a conference on 'Regional development in practice' held under the auspices of the Regional Studies Association.*

STRATEGIES for small farmer development: an empirical study of rural development projects in the Gambia, Ghana, Kenya, Lesotho, Nigeria, Bolivia, Colombia, Mexico, Paraguay and Peru; [by] Elliott R. Morss [and others]. Boulder, Co., 1976. 2 vols. *A study prepared for the Office of Development Administration, Agency for International Development.*

DIAZ BORDENAVE (JUAN E.) Communication and rural development. Paris, Unesco, 1977. pp. 109. *bibliog.*

LONG (NORMAN) An introduction to the sociology of rural development. London, 1977. pp. 221. *bibliog.*

— Botswana.

VENGROFF (RICHARD) Botswana: rural development in the shadow of apartheid. Rutherford, N.J., [1977]. pp. 205. *bibliog.*

RURAL FAMILIES

— Germany.

BOMMERT (WILFRIED) and BUETTNER (EVA) Bildungsverhalten der Landfrauen: Ergebnisse einer repräsentativen Befragung landwirtschaftlich tätiger Frauen in der Bundesrepublik Deutschland, 1976. Bonn, 1977. pp. 234. *bibliog. (Forschungsgesellschaft für Agrarpolitik und Agrarsoziologie. [Publications]. 244)*

— Poland.

KOCIK (LUCJAN) Przeobra'zenia funkcji współczesnej rodziny wiejskiej. Wrocław, 1976. pp. 130. *(Polska Akademia Nauk. Oddział w Krakowie. Komisja Socjologiczna. Prace. nr. 39) With Russian and English summaries.*

JASIEWICZ (ZBIGNIEW) Rodzina wiejska na Ziemi Lubuskiej: studium przeobra'zeń rodziny na podstawie badań etnograficznych w wybranych waiach. Warszawa, 1977. pp. 119. *bibliog. With English summary.*

— Sweden.

WINBERG (CHRISTER) Folkökning och proletarisering: kring den sociala strukturomvandlingen på Sveriges landsbygd under den agrara revolutionen. 2nd ed. [Lund, 1977]. pp. 344. *bibliog. With English summary.*

RURAL GEOGRAPHY.

ROBERTS (BRIAN K.) Rural settlement in Britain. Folkestone, 1977. pp. 221. *bibliog.*

RURAL HEALTH SERVICES

— Malaysia.

JAYESURIA (L.W.) A review of the rural health services in west Malaysia. Kuala Lumpur, Ministry of Health, 1967. pp. 33.

RURAL POOR

— United States.

RURAL poverty and the policy crisis; coedited by Robert O. Coppedge and Carlton G. Davis. Ames, Iowa, 1977. pp. 220. *bibliog. Based on papers presented at a conference held in February 1975, at Gainesville, Florida, sponsored by the University of Florida.*

RURAL-URBAN MIGRATION

— Argentine Republic.

RUBINSTEIN (JUAN CARLOS) Urbanizacion, estructura de ingresos y movilidad social en Argentina, 1960-1970. Santiago de Chile, 1972. pp. 46. *(Instituto Latinoamericano de Investigaciones Sociales. Estudios y Documentos. 14)*

— Australia — New South Wales.

PAUL (PHILLIP B.) Characteristics and adjustment problems of former farm operators: a survey of New South Wales farmers who left the land during the 1968-72 rural recession. Sydney, 1976. pp. 250. *bibliog. (Sydney. University. Department of Agricultural Economics. Mimeographed Reports. No. 6)*

— Canada.

FROM prairies to cities; papers on the Poles in Canada at the 8th World Congress of Sociology; edited by Benedykt Heydenkorn. Toronto, 1975. pp. 80. *bibliog. (Canadian-Polish Research Institute. Studies. 9)*

— Chile.

ZUÑIGA IDE (JORGE) La emigracion rural en la provincia de Coquimbo, Chile: informe preliminar. Santiago de Chile, 1972. pp. 95. *bibliog. (Instituto Latinoamericano de Investigaciones Sociales. Estudios y Documentos. 16)*

— Colombia.

FORNAGUERA (MIGUEL) and GUHL (ERNESTO) Colombia: ordenacion del territorio en base del epicentrismo regional. Bogota, 1969. pp. 175,(19).

— Europe.

BEIJER (G.) and HENDRIKS (GRADUS) Rural migration...: report for the fifth meeting of the ad hoc working party on rural sociological problems in 1964. The Hague, Ministry of Cultural Affairs, Recreation and Social Welfare, 1964. pp. 11.

— France.

TUGAULT (YVES) Fécondité et urbanisation. [Paris], 1975. pp. 137. *bibliog. (France. Institut National d'Etudes Démographiques. Travaux et Documents. Cahiers. No.74)*

— Germany.

FRITZE (KONRAD) Bürger und Bauern zur Hansezeit: Studien zu den Stadt-Land-Beziehungen an der südwestlichen Ostseeküste vom 13. bis zum 16. Jahrhundert. Weimar, 1976. pp. 118. *bibliog. (Historiker-Gesellschaft der Deutschen Demokratischen Republik. Hansische Arbeitsgemeinschaft. Abhandlungen zur Handels- und Sozialgeschichte. Band 16)*

— Poland.

FIERLA (IRENA) Migracje ludności w Polsce a uprzemysłowienie. Warszawa, 1976. pp. 150. *bibliog. (Polska Akademia Nauk. Komitet i Zakład Badań Rejonów Uprzemysławianych. Problemy Rejonów Uprzemysławianych) With brief Russian and English summaries.*

MIROWSKI (WŁODZIMIERZ) Przemiany społeczne w małym mieście a procesy migracyjne: studium monograficzne wychodźstwa ludności. Wrocław, 1976. pp. 260. *bibliog. With English and Russian summaries.*

PROBLEMY urbanizatsii i rasseleniia: II sovetsko-pol'skii seminar po urbanizatsii. Moskva, 1976. pp. 269. *With Polish and English tables of contents.*

ROZMIESZCZENIE i migracje ludności a system osadniczy Polski Ludowej; Distribution, migrations of population and settlement system of Poland. Wrocław, 1977. pp. 343. *bibliog. (Polska Akademia Nauk. Instytut Geografii. Prace Geograficzne. Nr.117) With Russian and English summaries.*

— Russia.

STAROVEROV (VLADIMIR IVANOVICH) Sotsial'no-demograficheskie problemy derevni: metodologiia, metodika, opyt analiza migratsii sel'skogo naseleniia. Moskva, 1975. pp. 287. *bibliog. With English table of contents.*

KHOREV (BORIS SERGEEVICH) and MOISEENKO (VALENTINA MIKHAILOVNA) Sdvigi v razmeshchenii naseleniia SSSR. Moskva, 1976. pp. 102.

PROBLEMY urbanizatsii i rasseleniia: II sovetsko-pol'skii seminar po urbanizatsii. Moskva, 1976. pp. 269. *With Polish and English tables of contents.*

— Turkey.

KARPAT (KEMAL H.) The gecekondu: rural migration and urbanization. Cambridge, 1976. pp. 291. *bibliog.*

— Underdeveloped areas.

See UNDERDEVELOPED AREAS —
Rural-urban migration.

RURAL-URBAN MIGRATION(Cont.)

— United Kingdom.

RURAL depopulation: report by an interdepartmental group, (1972- 73); (with Appendices). [London], H.M. Treasury, [1976]. 2 pts.

— United States.

PETERSEN (GENE B.) and others. Southern newcomers to northern cities: work and social adjustment in Cleveland. New York, 1977. pp. 269.

— Zambia.

BATES (ROBERT H.) Rural responses to industrialization: a study of village Zambia. New Haven, 1976. pp. 380. *bibliog.*

RURAL YOUTH

— Romania.

TINERETUL rural '68...: anchetă sociologică, etc. Bucureşti, 1970. pp. 263. *(Centrul de Cercetări pentru Problemele Tineretului. Tineretul şi Lumea de Mîine. Seria A: Sociologia Tineretului. 1) With English and Russian summaries and tables of contents.*

— Russia.

SOTSIAL'NYI oblik kolkhoznoi molodezhi: po materialam sotsiologicheskikh obsledovanii 1938 i 1969 gg. Moskva, 1976. pp. 294.

RUSSELL (BERTRAND ARTHUR WILLIAM) 3rd Earl Russell.

RUSSELL (BERTRAND ARTHUR WILLIAM) 3rd Earl Russell. Bertrand Russell speaks his mind. Darmstadt, 1976. pp. 175. *Transcript of a television series of 13 interviews with Bertrand Russell, by Woodrow Wyatt. Originally published in 1960 by the World Publishing Company, Cleveland.*

RUSSIA

— Armed forces.

The POLITICAL implications of Soviet military power; edited by Lawrence L. Whetten. London, [1977]. pp. 183. *Papers presented at an international conference convened at Ebenhausen, West Germany in May 1975 under the auspices of the Stiftung für Wissenschaft und Politik and the University of Southern California.*

— — Political activity.

ANDREEV (ANATOLII MIKHAILOVICH) Soldatskie massy garnizonov russkoi armii v Oktiabr'skoi revoliutsii. Moskva, 1975. pp. 343.

SUVENIROV (OLEG FEDOTOVICH) Kommunisticheskaia partiia - organizator politicheskogo vospitaniia Krasnoi Armii i Flota, 1921-1928. Moskva, 1976. pp. 291. *bibliog.*

— Army.

ZAITSOV (A.A.) Die Rote Armee. Berlin-Spandau, [1934]. pp. 119.

— — History.

VERKHOS' (VLADIMIR PAVLOVICH) Krasnaia gvardiia v Oktiabr'skoi revoliutsii. Moskva, 1976. pp. 264.

BOR'BA partii bol'shevikov za armiiu v sotsialisticheskoi revoliutsii: sbornik dokumentov. Moskva, 1977. pp. 520.

— Bibliography.

BIBLIOGRAFIIA obshchestvenno-politicheskoi literatury, etc. 2nd ed. Moskva, 1968-76. 2 vols.

DOSSICK (JESSE JOHN) Doctoral research on Russia and the Soviet Union 1960-1975: a classified list of 3,150 American, Canadian and British dissertations, with some critical and statistical analysis. New York, 1976. pp. 345. *bibliog.*

— Boundaries — China.

PROKHOROV (A.) K voprosu o sovetsko-kitaiskoi granitse. Moskva, 1975. pp. 288.

— Civilization.

POZNANSKII (VIKTOR VLADIMIROVICH) Ocherk formirovaniia russkoi natsional'noi kul'tury, pervaia polovina XIX veka. Moskva, 1975. pp. 223. *bibliog.*

VOSPRIIATIE russkoi kul'tury na Zapade: ocherki. Leningrad, 1975. pp. 279. *bibliog.*

— Commerce.

MARPERGER (PAUL JACOB) P.J. Marpergers Moscowitischer Kauffmann, das ist: Ausführliche Beschreibung der Commercien, welche in Moscau.. .getrieben werden, etc. Lübeck, Böckmann, 1705; Leipzig, 1976. pp. 168. *Facsimile reprint.*

GORODETSKII (EVGENII SERGEEVICH) ed. Problemy ispol'zovaniia tovarno-denezhnykh otnoshenii v usloviiakh razvitogo sotsializma. Moskva, 1975. pp. 121.

MAWRIZKI (SERGE) Aussenhandel der Sowjetunion gestern und heute: Grundlagen, Entwicklung und der Westhandel nach dem Zweiten Weltkrieg. Bern, 1976. pp. 238. *bibliog. (Mainz. Universität. Fachbereich Angewandte Sprachwissenschaft. Publikationen. Reihe A: Abhandlungen und Sammelbände. 4)*

— — United States.

FRIESEN (CONNIE M.) The political economy of East-West trade. New York, 1976. pp. 203. *bibliog.*

— Commercial policy.

POZDNIAKOV (VLADIMIR SERGEEVICH) Sovetskoe gosudarstvo i vneshniaia torgovlia: pravovye voprosy. Moskva, 1976. pp. 175.

— Constitution.

HAZARD (JOHN NEWBOLD) Fifty years of the Soviet Federation. [Princeton, 1973?]. pp. 23.

SZEFTEL (MARC) The Russian constitution of April 23, 1906: political institutions of the Duma monarchy. Bruxelles, 1976. pp. 517. *bibliog. (International Commission for the History of Representative and Parliamentary Institutions. Studies. 61)*

RUSSIA (USSR). Constitution. 1977. Konstitutsiia (Osnovnoi Zakon) Soiuza Sovetskikh Sotsialisticheskikh Respublik. Moskva, 1977. pp. 62.

— Constitutional history.

SOVETY deputatov trudiashchikhsia i razvitie sotsialisticheskoi demokratii. Moskva, 1976. pp. 431.

— Constitutional law.

FEL'DMAN (DAVID ISAAKOVICH) and others. Teoreticheskie problemy metodologii issledovaniia gosudarstva i prava. Kazan', 1975. pp. 118.

SOVETSKOE gosudarstvennoe pravo. 2nd ed. Moskva, 1975. pp. 574.

POLITICHESKAIA organizatsiia razvitogo sotsialisticheskogo obshchestva: pravovye problemy. Kiev, 1976. pp. 516.

— Defences.

MYRDAL (ALVA) The game of disarmament: how the United States and Russia run the arms race. New York, [1976]. pp. 397.

WHO's first in defense: the U.S. or the U.S.S.R.?; (an AEI round table held on June 3, 1976...); John Charles Daly, moderator, etc. Washington, [1976]. pp. 39. *(American Enterprise Institute for Public Policy Research. Round Tables)*

— Description and travel.

HOYLAND (JOHN SOMERVELL) The new Russia. London, 1933. pp. 94. *bibliog.*

POTTS (J.H.) Through the Soviet Union in war-time: the impressions of a British trade union leader during a three months' war-time tour of the U.S.S.R. [London, 1942?]. pp. 15.

— Duma.

CHERMENSKII (EVGENII DMITRIEVICH) IV Gosudarstvennaia duma i sverzhenie tsarizma v Rossii. Moskva, 1976. pp. 316.

— Economic conditions.

BEZBORODOV (SERGEI KONSTANTINOVICH) Johann Liebhardt und Thomas Monger: zwei ausländische Helden des Fünfjahrplans. Moskau, 1932. pp. 46.

ECONOMICHESKIE NAUKI; ([pd. by] Ministerstvo Vysshego i Srednego Spetsial'nogo Obrazovaniia SSSR). m., [Je] 1970 (god 13, [no.] 6)- Moskva.

DOKUKIN (VLADIMIR IGNAT'EVICH) and KONDRAT'EV (L.F.) eds. Effektivnost' ekonomiki razvitogo sotsializma. Moskva, 1976. pp. 312. *bibliog.*

KAPELIAN (EFIM KHAIMOVICH) Proizvoditel'nye sily: struktura, funktsii, tipologiia; voprosy metodologii i teorii. Minsk, 1976. pp. 191.

MAL'TSEV (NIKOLAI ALEKSANDROVICH) Problemy raspredeleniia v razvitom sotsialisticheskom obshchestve. Moskva, 1976. pp. 198.

MEDVEDEV (VADIM ANDREEVICH) Sotsialisticheskoe proizvodstvo: politiko-ekonomicheskoe issledovanie. Moskva, 1976. pp. 326.

NOTKIN (ALEKSANDR IL'ICH) ed. Proportsii vosproizvodstva v period razvitogo sotsializma. Moskva, 1976. pp. 431. *(Akademiia Nauk SSSR. Institut Ekonomiki. Problemy Sovetskoi Ekonomiki)*

PAKHOMOV (IURII NIKOLAEVICH) Proizvodstvennye otnosheniia razvitogo sotsializma. Kiev, 1976. pp. 338.

SOTSIAL'NO-ekonomicheskie problemy istorii razvitogo sotsializma v SSSR. Moskva, 1976. pp. 487. *bibliog.*

ZAGORODNII (VASILII IVANOVICH) and others. Zakonomirnosti rozvytku narodno-hospodars'koho kompleksu Soiuzu RSR. Kyїv, 1976. pp. 303.

AURTHUR (JONATHAN) Socialism in the Soviet Union. Chicago, 1977. pp. 174. *bibliog.*

CHERKOVETS (VIKTOR NIKITICH) ed. Problemy razvitogo sotsializma v politicheskoi ekonomii, etc. Moskva, 1977. pp. 335. *(Akademiia Nauk SSSR. Problemy Sovetskoi Ekonomiki)*

NOVE (ALEXANDER) The Soviet economic system. London, 1977. pp. 399. *bibliog.*

— — Mathematical models.

MARTINKEVICH (FELIKS STANISLAVOVICH) and others, eds. Voprosy teorii i otsenki ekonomicheskoi effektivnosti narodnogo khoziaistva. Minsk, 1976. pp. 303.

MIRKIN (BORIS GRIGOR'EVICH) and VAL'TUKH (KONSTANTIN KURTOVICH) eds. Ukrupnennye i mezhotraslevye modeli narodnogo khoziaistva. Novosibirsk, 1976. pp. 254. *(Akademiia Nauk SSSR. Sibirskoe Otdelenie. Institut Ekonomiki i Organizatsii Promyshlennogo Proizvodstva. Problemy Postroeniia i Ispol'zovaniia Narodnokhoziaistvennykh Modelei)*

— — Research.

METODOLOGICHESKIE problemy issledovaniia ekonomiki razvitogo sotsializma. Moskva, 1976. pp. 248.

— Economic history.

LIASHENKU (PETR IVANOVICH) History of the national economy of Russia to the 1917 revolution; ...translated by L.M. Herman. New York, 1970. pp. 880. *bibliog. A reprint of the translation first published in 1949 by the American Council of Learned Societies.*

ISTORIIA sotsialisticheskoi ekonomiki SSSR v semi tomakh. Moskva, 1976 in progress.

GROSSKOPF (SIGRID) L'alliance ouvrière et paysanne en U.R.S.S., 1921-1928: le problème du blé. Paris, 1976. pp. 459. bibliog.

SOROKIN (GENNADII MIKHAILOVICH) Problemy vosproizvodstva i planirovaniia sotsialisticheskoi ekonomiki; (stat'i, napisannye v techenie 1960-1975 gg.). Moskva, 1976. pp. 559. (Akademiia Nauk SSSR. Problemy Sovetskoi Ekonomiki)

— — Sources.

PROBLEMY istoriografii i istochnikovedeniia istorii KPSS. vyp.2. Leningrad, 1973. pp. 204.

RYBAKOV (IURII IAKOVLEVICH) Promyshlennaia statistika Rossii XIX v.: istochnikovedcheskoe issledovanie. Moskva, 1976. pp. 277.

— Economic policy.

UNSERE Stellung zu Sowjet-Russland: Lehren und Perspektiven der russischen Revolution; Verfasser: Theodor Hartwig [and others]. Berlin-Tempelhof, [1931]. pp. 190. (Marxistische Büchergemeinde. Rote Bücher. 3. Buch)

BARYSHNIKOV (NIKOLAI NIKOLAEVICH) and MARTYNOV (BORIS MAKAROVICH) Osnovnye napravleniia ekonomicheskoi politiki partii. Moskva, 1972. pp. 126.

AKADEMIIA OBSHCHESTVENNYKH NAUK. Kafedra Partiinogo Stroitel'stva. Voprosy Teorii i Praktiki Partiinogo Stroitel'stva. [vyp.1] Partiinoe rukovodstvo ekonomikoi. Moskva, 1974. pp. 287.

GORODETSKII (EVGENII SERGEEVICH) ed. Problemy ispol'zovaniia tovarno-denezhnykh otnoshenii v usloviiakh razvitogo sotsializma. Moskva, 1975. pp. 121.

KASHIN (VALENTIN NIKOLAEVICH) Poznanie i ispol'zovanie ekonomicheskikh zakonov pri sotsializme. Moskva, 1975. pp. 196.

PAVLENKO (VIKTOR FEDOROVICH) Territorial'noe planirovanie v SSSR. Moskva, 1975. pp. 279.

ROGOV (ANATOLII IL'ICH) Rukovodstvo KPSS ekonomikoi zrelogo sotsializma. Moskva, 1975. pp. 384.

TOLKACHEV (ALEKSANDR SERGEEVICH) ed. Problemy metodologii planirovaniia i izmereniia effektivnosti proizvodstva; (v osnovu knigi polozheny materialy Mezhdunarodnogo seminara...v Marianske Lazne v 1974 g.). Moskva, 1975. pp. 215.

ZAGAINOV (LEONID IVANOVICH) Sotsialisticheskoe gosudarstvo i zakony ekonomiki. Moskva, 1975. pp. 318.

BREZHNEV (LEONID IL'ICH) Voprosy upravleniia ekonomikoi razvitogo sotsialisticheskogo obshchestva: rechi, doklady, vystupleniia. Moskva, 1976. pp. 600.

KUTAFIN (OLEG EMEL'IANOVICH) Mestnye Sovety i narodnokhoziaistvennoe planirovanie. Moskva, 1976. pp. 142.

McCAULEY (MARTIN) Khrushchev and the development of Soviet agriculture: the Virgin Land Programme, 1953-1964. London, 1976. pp. 232. bibliog. (London. University. School of Slavonic and East European Studies. Studies in Russian and East European History)

PROBLEMY sovershenstvovaniia upravleniia sotsialisticheskoi ekonomikoi. Moskva, 1976. pp. 272.

PROBLEMY teorii i praktiki razmeshcheniia proizvoditel'nykh sil SSSR. Moskva, 1976. pp. 326. (Akademiia Nauk SSSR. Sovet po Izucheniiu Proizvoditel'nykh Sil. Problemy Sovetskoi Ekonomiki)

ZAKONOMERNOSTI sozdaniia material'no-tekhnicheskoi bazy kommunizma. Moskva, 1976. pp. 367.

EKONOMICHESKIE problemy razvitogo sotsialisticheskogo obshchestva. Kiev, 1977. pp. 283.

EKONOMICHESKIE problemy razvitogo sotsializma i ego pererastaniia v kommunizm. Moskva, 1977. pp. 311.

The FUTURE of agriculture in the Soviet Union and Eastern Europe: the 1976-80 five year plans; edited by Roy D. Laird [and others]. Boulder, Colo., 1977. pp. 242. Papers of two panels of the autumn 1976 meeting of the American Association for the Advancement of Slavic Studies.

PROBLEMY razvitiia material'no-tekhnicheskoi bazy sotsializma. Moskva, 1977. pp. 271.

— — Mathematical models.

VAL'TUKH (KONSTANTIN KURTOVICH) Udovletvorenie potrebnostei obshchestva i modelirovanie narodnogo khoziaistva; otvetstvennyi redaktor...I.P. Suslov. Novosibirsk, 1973. pp. 378. (Akademiia Nauk SSSR. Sibirskoe Otdelenie. Institut Ekonomiki i Organizatsii Promyshlennogo Proizvodstva. Problemy Narodnokhoziaistvennogo Optimuma. [vyp.2])

KRAVCHENKO (TAT'IANA KONSTANTINOVNA) Protsess priniatiia planovykh reshenii: informatsionnye modeli. Moskva, 1974. pp. 183. bibliog.

WIEDEMANN (PAUL PAT) A consideration of the nature of the objective function in national economic planning, with specific reference to the mathematical modelling of medium-term planning in the Soviet Union and Eastern Europe. 1974. fo. 353. bibliog. Typescript. Ph.D. (London) thesis: unpublished. This thesis is the property of London University and may not be removed from the Library.

FEDORENKO (NIKOLAI PROKOF'EVICH) ed. Sistema modelei optimal'nogo planirovaniia. Moskva, 1975. pp. 376. bibliog. (Akademiia Nauk SSSR. Tsentral'nyi Ekonomiko-Matematicheskii Institut. Problemy Sovetskoi Ekonomiki)

GAVRILOV (EVGENII IVANOVICH) Ekonomika i effektivnost' nauchno-tekhnicheskogo progressa; pod nauchnoi redaktsiei i s predisloviem E.N. Bliokova. Minsk, 1975. pp. 318. bibliog.

MODELI razmeshcheniia proizvodstva. Moskva, 1975. pp. 216. (Akademiia Nauk SSSR. Problemy Sovetskoi Ekonomiki)

PUGACHEV (VSEVOLOD FEDOROVICH) Problemy mnogostupenchatoi optimizatsii narodnokhoziaistvennogo planirovaniia. Moskva, 1975. pp. 79. bibliog.

DUNAEVA (VERA SERGEEVNA) Ekonomicheskie zakony sotsializma i problemy narodnokhoziaistvennogo optimuma. Moskva, 1976. pp. 264.

MINTS (LEV EFIMOVICH) Statisticheskie balansy i ekonomiko-matematicheskie modeli v planirovanii. Moskva, 1976. pp. 287.

RAJECKAS (RAIMUNDAS) Sistema modelei planirovaniia i prognozirovaniia. Moskva, 1976. pp. 286. bibliog. With English summary.

SMEKHOV (BORIS MOISEEVICH) and URINSON (IAKOV MOISEEVICH) Metody optimizatsii narodnokhoziaistvennogo plana. Moskva, 1976. pp. 198.

SUSLOV (IVAN PETROVICH) ed. Nauchno-tekhnicheskii progress; Modelirovanie narodnogo khoziaistva. Novosibirsk, 1976. pp. 349. (Akademiia Nauk SSSR. Sibirskoe Otdelenie. Institut Ekonomiki i Organizatsii Promyshlennogo Proizvodstva. Problemy Narodnokhoziaistvennogo Optimuma. [vyp.4])

TOLPEKIN (S.Z.) Ekonomicheskie problemy kompleksnogo ispol'zovaniia osnovnykh sredstv proizvodstva: voprosy teorii, metodologii i metodov analiza. Moskva, 1976. pp. 536.

VOPROSY ekonomicheskogo rosta SSSR, etc. Moskva, 1976. pp. 215.

— Famines.

MAKARENKO (OLEKSANDR ANDRIIOVYCH) Moguchaia sila proletarskoi solidarnosti: podderzhka zarubezhnym proletariatom Sovetskoi strany v 1921-1925 gg. Moskva, 1976. pp. 319.

— Foreign economic relations.

BLAKER (PETER) and others. Coping with the Soviet Union: a new Tory view. London, 1977. pp. 28. (Conservative Political Centre. [Publications]. No. 605)

KLINGHOFFER (ARTHUR JAY) The Soviet Union and international oil politics. New York, 1977. pp. 389. bibliog.

— — Germany.

BOLZ (KLAUS) and others. Die Wirtschaftsbeziehungen zwischen der Bundesrepublik Deutschland und der Sowjetunion: Entwicklung, Bestimmungsfaktoren und Perspektive. Hamburg, 1976. pp. 639. (Hamburg. Hamburgisches Welt-Wirtschafts-Archiv. Veröffentlichungen) 8 graphs in end pocket.

MUELLER-LINK (HORST) Industrialisierung und Aussenpolitik: Preussen-Deutschland und das Zarenreich von 1860 bis 1890. Göttingen, 1977. pp. 506. bibliog.

— — Persian Gulf.

YODFAT (ARYEH) and ABIR (MORDECHAI) In the direction of the Persian Gulf: the Soviet Union and the Persian Gulf. London, 1977. pp. 167. bibliog.

— — Poland.

WILK (MARIAN) Pomoc i współpraca: polsko-radzieckie stosunki gospodarcze w latach 1944-1945. Warszawa, 1976. pp. 259. bibliog.

— — United States.

SSSR - SShA: ekonomicheskie otnosheniia: problemy i vozmozhnosti. Moskva, 1976. pp. 416.

— Foreign opinion.

RADIO FREE EUROPE. Audience and Public Opinion Research Department. The images of Polish, American, Russian, German and Chinese youth as seen by Poles. [Munich?], 1973. fo. 55.

VOSPRIIATIE russkoi kul'tury na Zapade: ocherki. Leningrad, 1975. pp. 279. bibliog.

— Foreign opinion, American.

LEVERING (RALPH B.) American opinion and the Russian alliance, 1939-1945. Chapel Hill, N.C., [1976]. pp. 262. bibliog.

— Foreign relations.

SANAKOEV (SHALVA PARSADANOVICH) ed. Vneshniaia politika Sovetskogo Soiuza: aktual'nye problemy. Moskva, 1973. pp. 199.

KISELEV (KUZ'MA VENEDIKTOVICH) Zapiski sovetskogo diplomata. Moskva, 1974. pp. 527.

HORELICK (ARNOLD LAWRENCE) and others. The study of Soviet foreign policy: decision-theory-related approaches. Beverly Hills, [1975]. pp. 79. bibliog.

MINASIAN (NIKOLAI MIKHAILOVICH) Sotsializm i mezhdunarodnoe pravo. Saratov, 1975. pp. 287. With brief English summary.

SAKHAROV (ANDREI DMITRIEVICH) My country and the world;...translated by Guy V. Daniels. New York, 1975. pp. 109.

ZHUKOV (GENNADII PETROVICH) and CHERNICHENKO (STANISLAV VALENTINOVICH) Sovetskaia Programma mira i mezhdunarodnoe pravo. Moskva, 1975. pp. 111.

BARGHOORN (FREDERICK CHARLES) Détente and the democratic movement in the USSR. New York, [1976]. pp. 229.

LARIN (V.) Mezhdunarodnye otnosheniia i ideologicheskaia bor'ba, 60-70-e gody. Moskva, 1976. pp. 247. bibliog.

McEWAN (CHRISTOPHER B.) The Soviet Union and the conventional threat to South Africa: a strategic analysis. Braamfontein, 1976. pp. 28.

MENZHINSKII (VIKTOR IVANOVICH) Neprimenenie sily v mezhdunarodnykh otnosheniiakh. Moskva, 1976. pp. 295.

MEZHDUNARODNAIA politika KPSS i vneshnie funktsii Sovetskogo gosudarstva. Moskva, 1976. pp. 160.

PROBLEMY istorii mezhdunarodnykh otnoshenii i ideologicheskaia bor'ba: sbornik statei. Moskva, 1976. pp. 295.

PRUUDEN (SALME) Panslavism and Russian communism. London, 1976. pp. 59.

SECOND WORLD DEFENCE. Pamphlets. No. 1. The superpowers, the threat of war and the British working class. London, 1976. pp. 23.

SOLZHENITSYN (ALEKSANDR ISAEVICH) Détente: prospects for democracy and dictatorship;...with commentary by Alex Simirenko [and others]. New Brunswick, [1976]. pp. 112. *Based on addresses given in Washington, D.C. and New York in 1975.*

The SOVIET empire: expansion and détente; edited by William E. Griffith. Lexington, Mass., [1976]. pp. 417. *(Commission on Critical Choices for Americans. Critical Choices for Americans. vol.9)*

SSSR v bor'be protiv fashistskoi agressii, 1933-1945. Moskva, 1976. pp. 327.

VOPROSY istorii vneshnei politiki SSSR i mezhdunarodnykh otnoshenii: sbornik statei pamiati akademika Vladimira Mikhailovicha Khvostova. Moskva, 1976. pp. 399.

BLAKER (PETER) and others. Coping with the Soviet Union: a new Tory view. London, 1977. pp. 28. *(Conservative Political Centre. [Publications]. No. 605)*

The POLITICAL implications of Soviet military power; edited by Lawrence L. Whetten. London, [1977]. pp. 183. *Papers presented at an international conference convened at Ebenhausen, West Germany in May 1975 under the auspices of the Stiftung für Wissenschaft und Politik and the University of Southern California.*

ROFFMAN (HOWARD) Understanding the cold war: a study of the cold war in the interwar period. Cranbury, N.J., [1977]. pp. 198. *bibliog.*

SOVIET naval influence: domestic and foreign dimensions; edited by Michael MccGwire and John McDonnell. New York, 1977. pp. 657. *Deriving from a seminar held at Dalhousie University, Halifax, Nova Scotia, in 1974.*

STOLER (MARK A.) The politics of the second front: American military planning and diplomacy in coalition warfare, 1941-1943. Westport, Conn., 1977. pp. 244. *bibliogs.*

See also EUROPEAN ECONOMIC
COMMUNITY — Russia.

— — Asia.

KOVALENKO (IVAN IVANOVICH) Sovetskii Soiuz v bor'be za mir i kollektivnuiu bezopasnost' v Azii. Moskva, 1976. pp. 431. *bibliog.*

— — Balkan States.

NOVIKOV (NIKOLAI VASIL'EVICH) Puti i pereput'ia diplomata: zapiski o 1943-1944 gg. Moskva, 1976. pp. 256.

— — Bulgaria.

SOVETSKO-bolgarskie otnosheniia i sviazi: dokumenty i materialy. Moskva, 1976 in progress. *bibliog.*

— — China.

SCOTT (JACK) Two roads: the origin of the Sino-Soviet dispute. Vancouver, 1974. pp. 63.

BORISOV (OLEG BORISOVICH) Sovetskii Soiuz i Man'chzhurskaia revoliutsionnaia baza, 1945- 1949: k 30-letiiu razgroma militaristskoi Iaponii. Moskva, 1975. pp. 220.

LEONG (SOW-THENG) Sino-Soviet diplomatic relations, 1917-1926. Canberra, 1976. pp. 361. *bibliog.*

LOW (ALFRED D.) The Sino-Soviet dispute: an analysis of the polemics. Cranbury, N.J., [1976]. pp. 364. *bibliog.*

— — Cuba.

LEVESQUE (JACQUES) L'URSS et la révolution cubaine. Paris, [1976]. pp. 221. *bibliog. (Fondation Nationale des Sciences Politiques. Travaux et Recherches de Science Politique. 42)*

— — East (Near East).

INTERNATIONAL INSTITUTE FOR STRATEGIC STUDIES. Adelphi Papers. No. 131. The Soviet Union and the P.L.O.; by Galia Golan. London, 1976. pp. 34.

NOVIKOV (NIKOLAI VASIL'EVICH) Puti i pereput'ia diplomata: zapiski o 1943-1944 gg. Moskva, 1976. pp. 256.

GOLAN (GALIA) Yom Kippur and after: the Soviet Union and the Middle East crisis. Cambridge, 1977. pp. 350. *bibliog. (National Association for Soviet and East European Studies. Soviet and East European Studies)*

— — Egypt.

RUBINSTEIN (ALVIN ZACHARY) Red star on the Nile: the Soviet-Egyptian influence relationship since the June War. Princeton, N.J., [1977]. pp. 383. *bibliog.*

— — Europe.

The FUTURE of Soviet military power; edited by Lawrence L. Whetten. New York, [1976]. pp. 190. *Papers of a conference held at Ebenhausen, West Germany, 1975, under the aegis of the Stiftung für Wissenschaft und Politik and the University of Southern California.*

— — Europe, Eastern.

TARNOFF (CURTIS LEE) Evolving structures of great power blocs: the U.S.A. and Latin America, 1901-1975: the USSR and Eastern Europe, 1945-1975. 1976. fo. 529. *bibliog. Typescript. Ph.D. (London) thesis: unpublished. This thesis is the property of London University and may not be removed from the Library.*

— — France.

SHNEERSON (LEV MIKHAILOVICH) Franko-prusskaia voina i Rossiia: iz istorii russko-prusskikh i russko-frantsuzskikh otnoshenii v 1867-1871 gg. Minsk, 1976. pp. 304.

— — Germany.

WINZER (OTTO) Der Rapallo-Vertrag und seine nationale Bedeutung für Deutschland. Berlin, 1952. pp. 42.

KOCH (GERDA) Die deutsche Arbeiterklasse und der Rapallo-Vertrag, März bis Juni 1922. [Berlin, 1957]. pp. 60.

SHNEERSON (LEV MIKHAILOVICH) Franko-prusskaia voina i Rossiia: iz istorii russko-prusskikh i russko-frantsuzskikh otnoshenii v 1867-1871 gg. Minsk, 1976. pp. 304.

MUELLER-LINK (HORST) Industrialisierung und Aussenpolitik: Preussen-Deutschland und das Zarenreich von 1860 bis 1890. Göttingen, 1977. pp. 506. *bibliog.*

— — Germany, Eastern.

CROAN (MELVIN) East Germany: the Soviet connection. Beverly Hills, [1976]. pp. 71. *bibliog. (Georgetown University. Center for Strategic and International Studies. Washington Papers. vol. 4/36)*

WETTIG (GERHARD) Die Sowjetunion, die DDR und die Deutschland-Frage, 1965-1976: Einvernehmen und Konflikt im sozialistischen Lager. Stuttgart, 1976 repr. 1977. pp. 232. *bibliog.*

MUECKENBERGER (ERICH) Im festen Bündnis mit der Partei und dem Lande Lenins: ausgewälte Reden. Berlin, 1977. pp. 477.

— — Indonesia.

SHOLMOV (IURII ALEKSEEVICH) Sovetskii Soiuz - Indoneziia, 1945-1954. Moskva, 1976. pp. 165. *bibliog.*

— — Mongolia.

SOVETSKO-mongol'skie otnosheniia, 1921-1974: dokumenty i materialy. Moskva, 1975 in progress.

— — Persian Gulf.

YODFAT (ARYEH) and ABIR (MORDECHAI) In the direction of the Persian Gulf: the Soviet Union and the Persian Gulf. London, 1977. pp. 167. *bibliog.*

— — Poland.

LECZYK (MARIAN) Polityka II Rzeczypospolitej wobec ZSRR w latach 1925-1934: studium z historii dyplomacji. Warszawa, 1976. pp. 380. *bibliog.*

MIKHUTINA (IRINA VASIL'EVNA) Sovetsko-pol'skie otnosheniia, 1931-1935. Moskva, 1977. pp. 287. *bibliog.*

— — Turkey.

CHERNIKOV (IHOR FEDIROVYCH) V interesakh mira i dobrososedstva: o sovetsko-turetskikh otnosheniiakh v 1935-1970 gg. Kiev, 1977. pp. 198. *bibliog.*

— — United Kingdom.

GILLARD (DAVID R.) The struggle for Asia, 1828-1914: a study in British and Russian imperialism. London, 1977. pp. 214. *bibliog.*

GORODETSKY (GABRIEL) The precarious truce: Anglo-Soviet relations, 1924-27. Cambridge, 1977. pp. 289. *bibliog.*

— — United States.

KHRUSHCHEV (NIKITA SERGEEVICH) Comment la conférence au sommet a été torpillée. Paris, [imprint], 1960. pp. 27. *"Texte intégral de la conférence de presse de N. Khrouchtchev". (p.7)*

STEIBEL (GERALD L.) Detente: promises and pitfalls. New York, [1975]. pp. 85. *(National Strategy Information Center. Strategy Papers. No. 25)*

BOLKHOVITINOV (NIKOLAI NIKOLAEVICH) Rossiia i voina SShA za nezavisimost', 1775-1783. Moskva, 1976. pp. 272. *bibliog.*

CALDWELL (LAWRENCE T.) Soviet-American relations: one half decade of detente problems and issues. Paris, [1976]. pp. 63. *(Atlantic Institute. Atlantic Papers. 1975.5)*

The FUTURE of Soviet military power; edited by Lawrence L. Whetten. New York, [1976]. pp. 190. *Papers of a conference held at Ebenhausen, West Germany, 1975, under the aegis of the Stiftung für Wissenschaft und Politik and the University of Southern California.*

LEVERING (RALPH B.) American opinion and the Russian alliance, 1939-1945. Chapel Hill, N.C., [1976]. pp. 262. *bibliog.*

PRANGER (ROBERT JOHN) ed. Detente and defense: a reader. Washington, D.C., 1976. pp. 445. *(American Enterprise Institute for Public Policy Research. Foreign Affairs Studies. 40)*

RUMMEL (RUDOLPH JOSEPH) Peace endangered: the reality of détente. Beverly Hills, [1976]. pp. 189.

The SOVIET empire: expansion and détente; edited by William E. Griffith. Lexington, Mass., [1976]. pp. 417. *(Commission on Critical Choices for Americans. Critical Choices for Americans. vol.9)*

YERGIN (DANIEL) Shattered peace: the origins of the cold war and the national security state. Boston, Mass., 1977. pp. 526. *bibliog.*

— — Yugoslavia.

GIRENKO (IURII STEPANOVICH) Sovetskii Soiuz - Iugoslaviia: traditsionnaia druzhba, vsestoronnee sotrudnichestvo. Moskva, 1975. pp. 87.

RADONJIĆ (RADOVAN) Sukob KPJ sa Kominformom i društveni razvoj Jugoslavije, 1948-1950. 2nd ed. Zagreb, 1976. pp. 276. *bibliog. (Zagreb. Narodno Sveučilište. Centar za Aktualni Politički Studij. Političke Teme: Biblioteka Suvremene Političke Misli)*

— — — **Bibliography.**

HUNTER (BRIAN READ) Soviet-Yugoslav relations, 1948-1972: a bibliography of Soviet, western and Yugoslav comment and analysis. New York, 1976. pp. 223.

— **Historical geography.**

ISTORICHESKAIA geografiia Rossii, XII - nachalo xx v.: sbornik statei k 70-letiiu professora Liubomira Grigor'evicha Beskrovnogo. Moskva, 1975. pp. 347. *bibliog.*

— **Historiography.**

LYSTSOV (VIKENTII PAVLOVICH) M.V. Lomonosov o sotsial'no-ekonomicheskom razvitii Rossii. Voronezh, 1969. pp. 262. *bibliog.*

KAS'IANENKO (VASILII IGNAT'EVICH) Razvitoi sotsializm: istoriografiia i metodologiia problemy. Moskva, 1976. pp. 270. *bibliog.*

PROBLEMY istorii obshchestvennoi mysli i istoriografii: k 75- letiiu akademika N.V. Nechkinoi. Moskva, 1976. pp. 387. *bibliog.*

ZYRIANOV (PAVEL NIKOLAEVICH) and SHELOKHAEV (VALENTIN VALENTINOVICH) Pervaia russkaia revoliutsiia v amerikanskoi i angliiskoi istoriografii. Moskva, 1976. pp. 184.

— **History.**

ISTORIIA SSSR s drevneishikh vremen do nashikh dnei, v dvukh seriiakh, v dvenadtsati tomakh. Moskva, 1966-73. 12 vols. (in 10). *bibliog.*

KLIBANOV (ALEKSANDR IL'ICH) Narodnaia sotsial'naia utopiia v Rossii: period feodalizma. Moskva, 1977. pp. 335.

RIASANOVSKY (NICHOLAS VALENTINE) A history of Russia. 3rd ed. New York, 1977. pp. 762. *bibliog.*

— — **Pictorial works.**

REVE (K. VAN HET) Rusland hoe het was: een merkwaardige verzameling foto's van 80 jaar Rusland (1852-1932) met verklarende tekst. Amsterdam, [1976]. pp. 160.

— — **Sources.**

ISTORIIA dorevoliutsionnoi Rossii v dnevnikakh i vospominaniiakh: annotirovannyi ukazatel' knig i publikatsii v zhurnalakh. Moskva, 1976 in progress.

— — **1533-1613.**

SKRYNNIKOV (RUSLAN GRIGOR'EVICH) Rossiia posle oprichniny: ocherki politicheskoi i sotsial'noi istorii. Leningrad, 1975. pp. 223.

— — **1800-1899.**

RIASANOVSKY (NICHOLAS VALENTINE) A parting of ways: government and the educated public in Russia, 1801-1855. Oxford, 1976. pp. 323. *bibliog.*

— — **1825, Conspiracy of December.**

NECHKINA (MILITSA VASIL'EVNA) A.S. Griboedov i dekabristy. Moskva, 1947. pp. 599.

NECHKINA (MILITSA VASIL'EVNA) Dekabristy. Moskva, 1975. pp. 183. *(Akademiia Nauk SSSR. Seriia "Istoriia Nashei Rodiny")*

NECHKINA (MILITSA VASIL'EVNA) Den' 14 dekabria 1825 goda. 2nd ed. Moskva, 1975. pp. 398.

— — **1894-1917.**

ASCHER (ABRAHAM) ed. The Mensheviks in the Russian Revolution. Ithaca, N.Y., 1976. pp. 147. *bibliog. A selection of important documents.*

CHERMENSKII (EVGENII DMITRIEVICH) IV Gosudarstvennaia duma i sverzhenie tsarizma v Rossii. Moskva, 1976. pp. 316.

— — **1905, Revolution of.**

LENIN (VLADIMIR IL'ICH) Rede über die Revolution von 1905. Wien, [1925]. pp. 48. *Lecture given in Zurich on 22nd January, 1917; Russian version originally published in Pravda, No.18, on 22nd January, 1925.*

LENIN (VLADIMIR IL'ICH) The revolution of 1905. London, [1931]. pp. 55.

BONDAREVSKAIA (TAISIIA PAVLOVNA) Peterburgskii komitet RSDRP v revoliutsii 1905-1907 gg. Leningrad, 1975. pp. 327.

LENIN (VLADIMIR IL'ICH) Ein Vortrag über die Revolution von 1905; (Vorbemerkung: Renate Hertzfeldt). Berlin, 1975. pp. 48. *Lecture given in January 1917 in Zurich; Russian version originally published in Pravda, No.18, on 22nd January, 1925.*

LISOVSKII (NIKOLAI KUZ'MICH) Doloi samoderzhavie.: 1905 god na Iuzhnom Urale. Cheliabinsk, 1975. pp. 237. *Colophon has sub-title: iz istorii revoliutsii 1905-1907 gg. na Iuzhnom Urale.*

MAKHARADZE (N.B.) and others, eds. Revoliutsiia 1905-1907 gg. v Gruzii: sbornik statei, etc. Tbilisi, 1975. pp. 165. *Articles in Russian or Georgian.*

MODESTOV (VLADIMIR VASIL'EVICH) and others. Pervaia groza: istoricheskii ocherk o vooruzhennykh vosstaniiakh na iuge Rossii v 1905 godu. Rostov, 1975. pp. 176.

PERVAIA russkaia...: sbornik vospominanii aktivnykh uchastnikov revoliutsii, 1905-1907 gg. Moskva, 1975. pp. 304.

REVOLIUTSIIA 1905-1907 godov v Rossii. Moskva, 1975. pp. 431. *bibliog.*

KIRILLOV (VIKTOR SERGEEVICH) Bol'sheviki vo glave massovykh politicheskikh stachek v pervoi russkoi revoliutsii, 1905-1907. Moskva, 1976. pp. 368.

PERVAIA russkaia revoliutsiia, 1905-1907 gg.: problemy i sovremennost'. Leningrad, 1976. pp. 247.

SABLINSKY (WALTER) The road to Bloody Sunday: Father Gapon and the St. Petersburg massacre of 1905. Princeton, N.J., [1976]. pp. 414. *bibliog. (Columbia University. Russian Institute. Studies)*

TSENTRAL'NAIA bol'shevistskaia pechat' ob Azerbaidzhane, 1905- 1907 gg.: sbornik materialov. Baku, 1976. pp. 200.

ZYRIANOV (PAVEL NIKOLAEVICH) and SHELOKHAEV (VALENTIN VALENTINOVICH) Pervaia russkaia revoliutsiia v amerikanskoi i angliiskoi istoriografii. Moskva, 1976. pp. 184.

— — **1917, February Revolution.**

ADAMOV (VLADIMIR VASIL'EVICH) Fevral'skaia revoliutsiia na Urale. Sverdlovsk, 1967. pp. 64.

SLONIMSKII (ANATOLII GRIGOR'EVICH) Katastrofa russkogo liberalizma: progressivnyi blok nakanune i vo vremia Fevral'skoi revoliutsii 1917 goda. Dushanbe, 1975. pp. 320.

TOKAREV (IURII SERGEEVICH) Petrogradskii Sovet rabochikh i soldatskikh deputatov v marte - aprele 1917 g. Leningrad, 1976. pp. 205.

STILLIG (JUERGEN) Die Russische Februarrevolution 1917 und die sozialistische Friedenspolitik. Köln, 1977. pp. 331. *bibliog.*

— — **1917- .**

ULAM (ADAM BRUNO) A history of Soviet Russia. New York, 1976. pp. 312.

— — **1917-1921, Revolution.**

La REVOLTE de la Mer noire: ses enseignements: pour la commémoration de son Xe anniversaire, avril 1929. Paris, [1929]. pp. 32. *At head of title: Pour la lutte contre la guerre impérialiste, pour la défense de l'U.R.S.S.*

ANDREEV (ANATOLII MIKHAILOVICH) Soldatskie massy garnizonov russkoi armii v Oktiabr'skoi revoliutsii. Moskva, 1975. pp. 343.

[EIKHENBAUM (VSEVOLOD MIKHAILOVICH)] The unknown revolution, 1917-1921; ([by] Voline [pseud.]); foreword by Rudolf Rocker. New York, [1975]. pp. 717.

ASCHER (ABRAHAM) ed. The Mensheviks in the Russian Revolution. Ithaca, N.Y., 1976. pp. 147. *bibliog. A selection of important documents.*

BERKMAN (ALEXANDER) The Russian tragedy: comprising The Russian tragedy; The Russian revolution and the Communist Party; The Kronstadt rebellion;...compiled and introduced by William G. Nowlin. Sanday, Orkney, 1976. pp. 108.

KEEP (JOHN LESLIE HOWARD) The Russian revolution: a study in mass mobilization. London, [1976]. pp. 614. *bibliog.*

LINHART (ROBERT) Lénine, les paysans, Taylor: essai d'analyse matérialiste historique de la naissance du système productif soviétique. Paris, [1976]. pp. 173.

MEDVEDEV (ROI ALEKSANDROVICH) La révolution d'octobre était-elle inéluctable?: suivi d'une lettre à Lénine par Philippe Mironov; traduit du russe par Jean Chantal. Paris, [1976]. pp. 188.

POLIKARPOV (VASILII DMITRIEVICH) Prolog grazhdanskoi voiny v Rossii, oktiabr' 1917 - fevral' 1918. Moskva, 1976. pp. 415.

RABINOWITCH (ALEXANDER) The Bolsheviks come to power: the revolution of 1917 in Petrograd. New York, [1976]. pp. 393. *bibliog.*

RABOCHII klass - vedushchaia sila Oktiabr'skoi sotsialisticheskoi revoliutsii: sbornik statei. Moskva, 1976. pp. 414.

ROOBOL (W.H.) Tsereteli - a democrat in the Russian revolution: a political biography; translated from the Dutch by Philip Hyams and Lynne Richards. The Hague, 1976. pp. 273. *bibliog. (International Institute of Social History. Studies in Social History. No.1)*

IOFFE (GENRIKH ZINOV'EVICH) Krakh rossiiskoi monarkhicheskoi kontrrevoliutsii. Moskva, 1977. pp. 320.

— — — **Campaigns.**

WOJNA (ROMUALD) W ogniu rosyjskiej wojny wewnętrznej, 1918-1920. Warszawa, 1975. pp. 326. *bibliog.*

VERKHOS' (VLADIMIR PAVLOVICH) Krasnaia gvardiia v Oktiabr'skoi revoliutsii. Moskva, 1976. pp. 264.

— — — **Foreign participation, French.**

ZAK (LIUDMILA MARKOVNA) Des Français dans la Révolution d'Octobre: contribution à l'histoire du Groupe communiste français près le P.C. (b)R., 1918-1920. Paris, [1976]. pp. 274.

— — — **Personal narratives.**

HARDING (Mrs. STAN) The underworld of state;...with an introduction by Bertrand Russell. London, 1925. pp. 256.

STARTSEV (ABEL' ISAAKOVICH) Russkie bloknoty Dzhona Rida; [i.e. John Reed]. 2nd ed. Moskva, 1977. pp. 286.

— — — **Sources.**

ANIKEEV (VASILII VASIL'EVICH) Dokumenty Velikogo Oktiabria. Moskva, 1977. pp. 238.

BOR'BA partii bol'shevikov za armiiu v sotsialisticheskoi revoliutsii: sbornik dokumentov. Moskva, 1977. pp. 520.

— — **1918-1920, Allied intervention.**

La REVOLTE de la Mer noire: ses enseignements: pour la commémoration de son Xe anniversaire, avril 1929. Paris, [1929]. pp. 32. *At head of title: Pour la lutte contre la guerre impérialiste, pour la défense de l'U.R.S.S.*

— History, Military — Dictionaries and encyclopedias.

SOVETSKAIA voennaia entsiklopediia. Moskva, 1976 in progress.

— Industries.

VAVILOV (ANATOLII PAVLOVICH) Effektivnost' sotsialisticheskogo proizvodstva i kachestvo produktsii. Moskva, 1975. pp. 175.

AFANAS'EVSKII (EVGENII ALEKSANDROVICH) Legkaia promyshlennost': ekonomicheskie problemy razmeshcheniia. Moskva, 1976. pp. 263. *bibliog.*

KLOCHKO (VASILII STEPANOVICH) Vosproizvodstvo osnovnykh fondov promyshlennosti SSSR. Khar'kov, 1976. pp. 139. *bibliog.*

LOKTEV (VLADIMIR PETROVICH) Ekonomicheskie rychagi upravleniia v usloviiakh razvitogo sotsializma. Minsk, 1976. pp. 95.

RYBAKOV (IURII IAKOVLEVICH) Promyshlennaia statistika Rossii XIX v.: istochnikovedcheskoe issledovanie. Moskva, 1976. pp. 277.

SUBOTSKII (IURII VENIAMINOVICH) Razvitie ob"edinenii v promyshlennosti: voprosy teorii i metodologii. Moskva, 1977. pp. 229. *(Akademiia Nauk SSSR. Problemy Sovetskoi Ekonomiki)*

— Intellectual life.

DEKABRISTY i russkaia kul'tura; Dbcembristes et culture russe. Leningrad, 1975. pp. 355. *With French table of contents.*

LENIN i kul'tura: khronika sobytii, dooktiabr'skii period. Moskva, 1976. pp. 463.

RIASANOVSKY (NICHOLAS VALENTINE) A parting of ways: government and the educated public in Russia, 1801-1855. Oxford, 1976. pp. 323. *bibliog.*

— Languages.

VERYHA (WASYL) Communication media and Soviet nationality policy: status of national languages in Soviet T.V. broadcasting. New York, 1972. pp. 59. *bibliog. (Revised and enlarged reprint from The Ukrainian Quarterly, vol. 17, nos. 2 and 3, 1971)*

DESHERIEV (IUNUS DESHERIEVICH) Razvitie obshchestvennykh funktsii literaturnykh iazykov. Moskva, 1976. pp. 431. *(Akademiia Nauk SSSR. Institut Iazykoznaniia. Nauchnyi Sovet po Kompleksnoi Probleme "Zakonomernosti Razvitiia Natsional'nykh Iazykov v Sviazi s Razvitiem Sotsialisticheskikh Natsii". Zakonomernosti Razvitiia Literaturnykh Iazykov Narodov SSSR v Sovetskuiu Epokhu)*

KANIMETOV (ABDULDA KANIMETOVICH) Iazyk bratskogo edinstva. Frunze, 1976. pp. 199. *bibliog.*

RAZVITIE natsional'no-russkogo dvuiazychiia. Moskva, 1976. pp. 368.

— Maps.

ISTORIIA Kommunisticheskoi partii Sovetskogo Soiuza: atlas. Moskva, 1976. pp. 128.

— Military policy.

INTERNATIONAL INSTITUTE FOR STRATEGIC STUDIES. Adelphi Papers. No. 76. Technology, management and the Soviet military establishment; by David Holloway. London, 1971. pp. 44. *bibliog.*

STEIBEL (GERALD L.) Detente: promises and pitfalls. New York, [1975]. pp. 85. *(National Strategy Information Center. Strategy Papers. No. 25)*

The FUTURE of Soviet military power; edited by Lawrence L. Whetten. New York, [1976]. pp. 190. *Papers of a conference held at Ebenhausen, West Germany, 1975, under the aegis of the Stiftung für Wissenschaft und Politik and the University of Southern California.*

McEWAN (CHRISTOPHER B.) The Soviet Union and the conventional threat to South Africa: a strategic analysis. Braamfontein, 1976. pp. 32.

PRUUDEN (SALME) Panslavism and Russian communism. London, 1976. pp. 59.

RUMMEL (RUDOLPH JOSEPH) Peace endangered: the reality of détente. Beverly Hills, [1976]. pp. 189.

SECOND WORLD DEFENCE. Pamphlets. No. 1. The superpowers, the threat of war and the British working class. London, 1976. pp. 23.

SOVIET naval influence: domestic and foreign dimensions; edited by Michael MccGwire and John McDonnell. New York, 1977. pp. 657. *Deriving from a seminar held at Dalhousie University, Halifax, Nova Scotia, in 1974.*

— — Dictionaries and encyclopedias.

SOVETSKAIA voennaia entsiklopediia. Moskva, 1976 in progress.

— Militia.

VERKHOS' (VLADIMIR PAVLOVICH) Krasnaia gvardiia v Oktiabr'skoi revoliutsii. Moskva, 1976. pp. 264.

— Moral conditions.

MORAL' razvitogo sotsializma: aktual'nye problemy teorii. Moskva, 1976. pp. 287.

— Nationalism.

BAKALO (IVAN A.) Natsional'na polityka Lenina; Lenin's nationality policy. Miunkhen, 1974. pp. 211. *bibliog.*

INTERNATSIONAL'NOE i natsional'noe v sotsialisticheskom obshchestve. Kiev, 1976. pp. 331.

— Navy.

REES (DAVID) Soviet sea power: the covert support fleet. London, [1977]. pp. 13. *(Institute for the Study of Conflict. Conflict Studies. No. 84)*

SOVIET naval influence: domestic and foreign dimensions; edited by Michael MccGwire and John McDonnell. New York, 1977. pp. 657. *Deriving from a seminar held at Dalhousie University, Halifax, Nova Scotia, in 1974.*

— Non-Russian territories.

AKHMEDOVA (MATBUA AMIRSAIDOVNA) Nekapitalisticheskii put': nekotorye problemy teorii i praktiki. Tashkent, 1976. pp. 223.

— — Verkhovnyi Sovet.

KHACHATRIAN (GENRIK MKRTYCHEVICH) Verkhovnyi Sovet soiuznoi respubliki. Moskva, 1975. pp. 167.

— Politics and government.

MALEVSKII-MALEVICH (PETR NIKOLAEVICH) A new party in Russia. London, 1928. pp. 119.

TROTSKII (LEV DAVYDOVICH) La bureaucratie stalinienne et l'assassinat de Kirov. Paris, [1935]. pp. 44.

CHEKHARIN (EVGENII MIKHAILOVICH) Sovetskaia politicheskaia sistema v usloviiakh razvitogo sotsializma. Moskva, 1975. pp. 351.

DEMOKRATIIA razvitogo sotsialisticheskogo obshchestva. Moskva, 1975. pp. 296.

DENISOV (ANDREI IVANOVICH) Obshchaia sistema sotsialisticheskoi demokratii. Moskva, 1975. pp. 247.

RABOCHII klass SSSR i ego vedushchaia rol' v stroitel'stve kommunizma. Moskva, 1975. pp. 568.

POLITICHESKAIA organizatsiia razvitogo sotsialisticheskogo obshchestva: pravovye problemy. Kiev, 1976. pp. 516.

SAKHAROV (ANDREI DMITRIEVICH) O strane i mire: sbornik proizvedenii. N'iu-Iork, 1976. pp. xxiv,183.

— — 1689-1800.

MAVRODIN (VLADIMIR VASIL'EVICH) Klassovaia bor'ba i obshchestvenno-politicheskaia mysl' v Rossii v XVIII veke, 1773-1790 gg.: kurs lektsii. Leningrad, 1975. pp. 214. *bibliog.*

— — 1800-1899.

GERTSEN (ALEKSANDR IVANOVICH) and OGAREV (NIKOLAI PLATONOVICH) Golosa iz Rossii: sborniki, (kommentarii i ukazateli; rukovodstvo izdaniem...M.V. Nechkinoi). Moskva, 1974-76. 10 vols. (in 4). *Facsimile of original ed. of 1856-60.*

TKACHEV (PETR NIKITICH) Sochineniia v dvukh tomakh; (obshchaia redaktsiia A.A. Galaktionova [and others]). Moskva, 1975-76. 2 vols. *bibliog. (Akademiia Nauk SSSR. Institut Filosofii. Filosofskoe Nasledie)*

FIELD (DANIEL) The end of serfdom: nobility and bureaucracy in Russia, 1855-1861. Cambridge, Mass., 1976. pp. 472. *bibliog. (Harvard University. Russian Research Center. Studies. 75)*

HARVARD UNIVERSITY. Library. Houghton Library. Russian revolutionary literature collection. New Haven, Conn., 1976. Microfilm: 47 reels.

PROBLEMY istorii obshchestvennoi mysli i istoriografii: k 75- letiiu akademika N.V. Nechkinoi. Moskva, 1976. pp. 387. *bibliog.*

RIASANOVSKY (NICHOLAS VALENTINE) A parting of ways: government and the educated public in Russia, 1801-1855. Oxford, 1976. pp. 323. *bibliog.*

— — — Bibliography.

HARVARD UNIVERSITY. Library. Houghton Library. Russian revolutionary literature collection, Houghton Library, Harvard University: a descriptive guide and key to the collection on microfilm; [compiled by Kenneth E. Carpenter]. New Haven, Conn., 1976. pp. x, 220.

— — 1894-1936.

SVERDLOV (IAKOV MIKHAILOVICH) Izbrannye proizvedeniia: stat'i, rechi, pis'ma; (sostaviteli M.M. Vasser i L.V. Ivanova). Moskva, 1976. pp. 367.

— — 1894-1917.

CONROY (MARY SCHAEFFER) Peter Arkad'evich Stolypin: practical politics in late Tsarist Russia. Boulder, Col., 1976. pp. 235. *bibliog.*

HARVARD UNIVERSITY. Library. Houghton Library. Russian revolutionary literature collection. New Haven, Conn., 1976. Microfilm: 47 reels.

USHAKOV (ANATOLII VASIL'EVICH) Revoliutsionnoe dvizhenie demokraticheskoi intelligentsii v Rossii, 1895-1904. Moskva, 1976. pp. 240.

— — — Bibliography.

HARVARD UNIVERSITY. Library. Houghton Library. Russian revolutionary literature collection, Houghton Library, Harvard University: a descriptive guide and key to the collection on microfilm; [compiled by Kenneth E. Carpenter]. New Haven, Conn., 1976. pp. x, 220.

— — 1917- .

HAZARD (JOHN NEWBOLD) Fifty years of the Soviet Federation. [Princeton, 1973?]. pp. 23.

GRUPPENINTERESSEN und Entscheidungsprozess in der Sowjetunion; herausgegeben von Boris Meissner und Georg Brunner. Köln, [1975]. pp. 264. *Papers based on the proceedings of a conference held in 1973.*

MOTE (MAX E.) Would a communication model add to Soviet lore? Edmonton, 1976. fo. 42. *(Alberta University. Division of East European Studies. Occasional Papers. No.1)*

TODD (EMMANUEL) La chute finale: essai sur la décomposition de la sphère soviétique. Paris, 1976. pp. 324.

McAULEY (MARY) Politics and the Soviet Union. Harmondsworth, 1977. pp. 352. *bibliog.*

— — 1917-1936.

UNITED STATES. Committee on Public Information. 1919. Die deutsch-bolschewistische Verschwörung: 70 Dokumente über die Beziehungen der Bolschewiki zur deutschen Heeresleitung, Grossindustrie und Finanz, nebst einer Anzahl photographischer Reproduktionen. Bern, 1919. pp. 123. *German translation of the Committee's War Information Series. No.20.*

KLOTZ (HENRY) La Russie des Soviets: faits et documents: qu'y a-t-il de vrai dans la formule: le communisme, voilà l'ennemi. Paris, 1928. pp. 189. *bibliog.*

UNSERE Stellung zu Sowjet-Russland: Lehren und Perspektiven der russischen Revolution; Verfasser: Theodor Hartwig [and others]. Berlin-Tempelhof, [1931]. pp. 190. *(Marxistische Büchergemeinde. Rote Bücher. 3. Buch)*

SHILKO (KIRILL PAVLOVICH) Ideologicheskaia rabota Kommunisticheskoi partii v pervye gody Sovetskoi vlasti, oktiabr' 1917 - mart 1919 g. Minsk, 1975. pp. 200.

ELLEINSTEIN (JEAN) The Stalin phenomenon. London, 1976. pp. 221.

TROTSKII (LEV DAVYDOVICH) Trotsky's diary in exile, 1935; translated from the Russian by Elena Zarudnaya; with a foreword by Jean van Heijenoort. Cambridge, Mass., 1976. pp. 218.

— — 1936-1953.

KALININ (MIKHAIL IVANOVICH) Stat'i i rechi, 1941-1946 gg. Moskva, 1975. pp. 672.

CASSINELLI (CHARLES WILLIAM) Total revolution: a comparative study of Germany under Hitler, the Soviet Union under Stalin and China under Mao. Santa Barbara, Calif., [1976]. pp. 252.

— — 1953- .

BARGHOORN (FREDERICK CHARLES) Détente and the democratic movement in the USSR. New York, [1976]. pp. 229.

BRUCE (JAMES B.) The politics of Soviet policy formation: Khrushchev's innovative policies in education and agriculture. Denver, Colo., [1976]. pp. 138. *(Denver. University. Social Science Foundation and Graduate School of International Studies. Monograph Series in World Affairs. vol. 13, no. 4)*

The DYNAMICS of Soviet politics. Cambridge, Mass., 1976. pp. 427. *(Harvard University. Russian Research Center. Studies. 76)*

KHRUSHCHEV (NIKITA SERGEEVICH) The 'secret' speech delivered to the closed session of the Twentieth Congress of the Communist Party of the Soviet Union;...with an introduction by Zhores A. Medvedev and Roy A. Medvedev. Nottingham, 1976. pp. 134.

LAZITCH (BRANKO) Le Rapport Khrouchtchev et son histoire. [Paris, 1976]. pp. 191.

SOLZHENITSYN (ALEKSANDR ISAEVICH) Détente: prospects for democracy and dictatorship;...with commentary by Alex Simirenko [and others]. New Brunswick, [1976]. pp. 112. *Based on addresses given in Washington, D.C. and New York in 1975.*

The SOVIET empire: expansion and détente; edited by William E. Griffith. Lexington, Mass., [1976]. pp. 417. *(Commission on Critical Choices for Americans. Critical Choices for Americans. vol.9)*

MEDVEDEV (ROI ALEKSANDROVICH) and MEDVEDEV (ZHORES ALEKSANDROVICH) Khrushchev: the years in power;...translated by Andrew R. Durkin. London, 1977. pp. 198.

— Population.

KAZAKOV (ALEKSEI TIMOFEEVICH) and URLANIS (BORIS TSEZAREVICH) Problemy narodonaseleniia v russkoi marksistskoi mysli. Moskva, 1976. pp. 196. *bibliog.*

KHOREV (BORIS SERGEEVICH) and MOISEENKO (VALENTINA MIKHAILOVNA) Sdvigi v razmeshchenii naseleniia SSSR. Moskva, 1976. pp. 102.

KURMAN (MIKHAIL VENIAMINOVICH) Aktual'nye voprosy demografii: demograficheskie protsessy v SSSR v poslevoennyi period. Moskva, 1976. pp. 219.

LEWIS (ROBERT ALDEN) and others. Nationality and population change in Russia and the USSR: an evaluation of census data, 1897-1970. New York, 1976. pp. 456. *bibliog. (Population Change in Russia and the USSR, 1897-1970. vol. 1)*

VISHNEVSKII (ANATOLII GRIGOR'EVICH) Demograficheskaia revoliutsiia. Moskva, 1976. pp. 240.

INTERNATIONAL SLAVIC CONFERENCE, 1ST, BANFF, ALBERTA, 1974. Demographic developments in Eastern Europe; edited by Leszek A. Kosinski. New York, 1977. pp. 343.

VODARSKII (IAROSLAV EVGEN'EVICH) Naselenie Rossii v kontse XVII - nachale XVIII veka: chislennost', soslovno-klassovyi sostav, razmeshchenie. Moskva, 1977. pp. 265.

— — Bibliography.

VALENTEI (DMITRII IGNAT'EVICH) and BURNASHEV (E.IU.) eds. Bibliografiia po problemam narodonaseleniia, 1972-1975 gg. Moskva, 1977. pp. 232.

— Population policy.

RUBIN (IAKOV IZRAILEVICH) Problema narodonaseleniia kak ob"ekt ideino-politicheskoi bor'by. Minsk, 1976. pp. 256.

— Relations (general) with Asia.

ATAMAMEDOV (N.V.) and GOLOVIN (IULII MIKHAILOVICH) eds. Lenin v sud'bakh narodov Vostoka. Ashkhabad, 1975. pp. 143.

— Relations (general) with Cuba.

ROSSIISKO-kubinskie i sovetsko-kubinskie sviazi XVIII-XX vekov. Moskva, 1975. pp. 351.

— Relations (general) with other countries.

ALESKEROV (MURMUZ N.) Ravnopravnoe sotrudnichestvo: sotrudnichestvo SSSR s molodymi nezavisimymi gosudarstvami. Baku, 1975. pp. 216.

VOROBTSOVA (IULIIA IVANOVNA) Internatsional'naia deiatel'nost' bol'shevistskoi partii v period podgotovki Oktiabria, fevral'-oktiabr' 1917 g. Leningrad, 1975. pp. 127.

MAKARENKO (OLEKSANDR ANDRIIOVYCH) Moguchaia sila proletarskoi solidarnosti: podderzhka zarubezhnym proletariatom Sovetskoi strany v 1921-1925 gg. Moskva, 1976. pp. 319.

— Relations (general) with the Near East.

ATAMAMEDOV (N.V.) and GOLOVIN (IULII MIKHAILOVICH) eds. Lenin v sud'bakh narodov Vostoka. Ashkhabad, 1975. pp. 143.

— Relations (general) with Vietnam.

SSSR - DRV: vospominaniia i stat'i. Moskva, 1975. pp. 285.

— Relations (military) with Subsaharan Africa.

REES (DAVID) Soviet strategic penetration of Africa. London, 1976. pp. 20. *(Institute for the Study of Conflict. Conflict Studies. No. 77).*

— Relations (military) with the Mediterranean.

LEWIS (JESSE W.) The strategic balance in the Mediterranean. Washington, D.C., 1976. pp. 169. *(American Enterprise Institute for Public Policy Research. Foreign Affairs Studies. 29)*

— Religion.

GOL'ST (GEORGII ROBERTOVICH) Religiia i zakon. Moskva, 1975. pp. 110.

— Rural conditions.

BAKHTIN (NIKOLAI IVANOVICH) Gorod i derevnia: ekonomicheskie aspekty. Minsk, 1974. pp. 191.

STAROVEROV (VLADIMIR IVANOVICH) Sotsial'no-demograficheskie problemy derevni: metodologiia, metodika, opyt analiza migratsii sel'skogo naseleniia. Moskva, 1975. pp. 287. *bibliog. With English table of contents.*

MEDVEDEV (NIKOLAI ANDREEVICH) Razvitie obshchestvennykh otnoshenii v sovetskoi derevne na sovremennom etape. Moskva, 1976. pp. 188.

DANILOV (VIKTOR PETROVICH) Sovetskaia dokolkhoznaia derevnia: naselenie, zemlepol'zovanie, khoziaistvo. Moskva, 1977. pp. 319.

SMITH (ROBERT ERNEST FREDERICK) Peasant farming in Muscovy. Cambridge, 1977. pp. 289. *bibliog.*

— Social conditions.

HOYLAND (JOHN SOMERVELL) The new Russia. London, 1933. pp. 94. *bibliog.*

SAKHAROV (ANDREI DMITRIEVICH) My country and the world;...translated by Guy V. Daniels. New York, 1975. pp. 109.

SOTSIALISTICHESKOE obshchestvo: sotsial'no-filosofskie problemy sovremennogo sovetskogo obshchestva. Moskva, 1975. pp. 343. *With English, Spanish, German and French summaries.*

SOTSIALISTICHESKII obraz zhizni i sovremennaia ideologicheskaia bor'ba. Moskva, 1976. pp. 350.

SOTSIAL'NAIA struktura sotsialisticheskogo obshchestva v SSSR. Moskva, 1976. pp. 224.

SOTSIAL'NO-ekonomicheskie problemy istorii razvitogo sotsializma v SSSR. Moskva, 1976. pp. 487. *bibliog.*

VESELOVSKII (V.) and RUTKEVICH (MIKHAIL NIKOLAEVICH) eds. Problemy razvitiia sotsial'noi struktury obshchestva v Sovetskom Soiuze i Pol'she. Moskva, 1976. pp. 231.

PROBLEMY sotsialisticheskogo obrza zhizni. Moskva, 1977. pp. 288.

— Social history.

IZMENENIIA sotsial'noi struktury sovetskogo obshchestva, oktiabr' 1917-1920. Moskva, 1976. pp. 343.

KLIBANOV (ALEKSANDR IL'ICH) Narodnaia sotsial'naia utopiia v Rossii: period feodalizma. Moskva, 1977. pp. 335.

— — Pictorial works.

REVE (K. VAN HET) Rusland hoe het was: een merkwaardige verzameling foto's van 80 jaar Rusland (1852-1932) met verklarende tekst. Amsterdam, [1976]. pp. 160.

— Statistics, Vital.

DARSKII (LEONID EVSEEVICH) ed. Rozhdaemost': problemy izucheniia. Moskva, 1976. pp. 142.

RUSSIA (RSFSR)

— Economic conditions.

CANADA. Department of Indian and Northern Affairs. Summary of development in the Soviet North based on extracts from the Soviet press. a., 1974/75- Ottawa.

— Population.

RYBAKOVSKII (LEONID LEONIDOVICH) ed. Territorial'nye osobennosti narodonaseleniia RSFSR. Moskva, 1976. pp. 232.

— Rural conditions.

SELEZNEV (VALERII ALEKSANDROVICH) and GUTAROV (ALEKSANDR NIKOLAEVICH) Sovetskaia derevnia v predvoennye gody, 1938-1941: iz istorii kolkhoznogo stroitel'stva v osnovnykh raionakh Severo-Zapada RSFSR, Leningradskaia oblast'; kratkii istoricheskii ocherk. Leningrad, 1976. pp. 112.

RUSSIAN-AMERICAN COMPANY.

DOCUMENTS on the history of the Russian-American Company; translated by Marina Ramsay; edited by Richard A. Pierce. Kingston, Ont., [1976]. pp. 220.

RUSSIAN DIARIES.

ISTORIIA dorevoliutsionnoi Rossii v dnevnikakh i vospominaniiakh: annotirovannyi ukazatel' knig i publikatsii v zhurnalakh. Moskva, 1976 in progress.

RUSSIAN LANGUAGE IN KIRGHIZIA.

KANIMETOV (ABDULDA KANIMETOVICH) Iazyk bratskogo edinstva. Frunze, 1976. pp. 199. *bibliog.*

RUSSIAN LITERATURE.

ZINOV'EV (ALEKSANDR ALEKSANDROVICH) Ziiaiushchie vysoty. [Lausanne, 1976]. pp. 563.

— History and criticism.

MAEVSKAIA (TAT'IANA PETROVNA) Idei i obrazy russkogo narodnicheskogo romana, 70-80-e gody XIX v. Kiev, 1975. pp. 207. *bibliog.*

VOSPRIIATIE russkoi kul'tury na Zapade: ocherki. Leningrad, 1975. pp. 279. *bibliog.*

MEDVEDEV (ROI ALEKSANDROVICH) Problems in the literary biography of Mikhail Sholokhov. Cambridge, 1977. pp. 227.

RUSSIAN NEWSPAPERS

— Bibliography.

SAZONOV (IVAN SERGEEVICH) compiler. K 50-letiiu leninskoi gazety "Pravda": kratkii spisok literatury o "Pravde", 1912-1914 i 1917 gg. Leningrad, 1962. pp. 24.

RUSSIANS IN ALASKA.

DOCUMENTS on the history of the Russian-American Company; translated by Marina Ramsay; edited by Richard A. Pierce. Kingston, Ont., [1976]. pp. 220.

RUSSIANS IN CHINA.

CHEREPANOV (ALEKSANDR IVANOVICH) Zapiski voennogo sovetnika v Kitae, [1925-1939]. [3rd ed., erroneously designated 2nd ed.]. Moskva, 1976. pp. 648.

NA kitaiskoi zemle: vospominaniia sovetskikh dobrovol'tsev, 1925-1945. 2nd ed. Moskva, 1977. pp. 445.

RUSSIANS IN FOREIGN COUNTRIES.

BROOK-SHEPHERD (GORDON) The storm petrels: the first Soviet defectors, 1928-1938. London, 1977. pp. 257.

RUSSIANS IN FRANCE.

DELEHELLE (JEAN) La situation juridique des Russes en France. Lille, 1926. pp. 244. *bibliog.*

RUSSIANS IN KOREA.

OSVOBOZHDENIE Korei: vospominaniia i stat'i. Moskva, 1976. pp. 336.

RUSSIANS IN SIBERIA.

KOLESNIKOV (ALEKSANDR DMITRIEVICH) Russkoe naselenie Zapadnoi Sibiri v XVIII - nachale XIX vv. Omsk, 1973. pp. 439.

RUSSIANS IN VIETNAM.

SSSR - DRV: vospominaniia i stat'i. Moskva, 1975. pp. 285.

RUSSO-FINNISH WAR, 1939-1940.

NEVAKIVI (JUKKA TANELI) The appeal that was never made: the Allies, Scandinavia and the Finnish Winter War, 1939-1940. London, [1976]. pp. 225. *bibliog.*

RUSSO-TURKISH WAR, 1828-1829.

SHEREMET (VITALII IVANOVICH) Turtsiia i Adrianopol'skii mir 1829 g.: iz istorii Vostochnogo voprosa. Moskva, 1975. pp. 226.

RUTHENIA

— Population.

KOPCHAK (VALENTINA PAVLOVNA) and KOPCHAK (STEPAN IVANOVYCH) Naselenie Zakarpat'ia za 100 let: statistiko-demograficheskoe issledovanie. L'vov, 1977. pp. 199. *bibliog.*

RWANDA

— Politics and government.

LINDEN (IAN) Church and revolution in Rwanda. Manchester, [1977]. pp. 304. *bibliog.*

— Race question.

KUPER (LEO) The pity of it all: polarisation of racial and ethnic relations. London, 1977. pp. 302. *bibliog.*

SAARLAND

— Economic conditions.

BURTENSHAW (DAVID) Saar-Lorraine. London, 1976. pp. 48. *bibliog.*

— Social conditions.

BURTENSHAW (DAVID) Saar-Lorraine. London, 1976. pp. 48. *bibliog.*

SABAH

— Economic conditions.

FEDERATION OF MALAYSIA. Department of Information, Sabah. 1969. Sabah since Malaysia: progress and achievements in development 1963-1968. rev.ed. [Kota Kinabalu], 1969. pp. 157.

FEDERATION OF MALAYSIA. Department of Information, Sabah. 1971. Sabah's revolution for progress: a review of progress and achievements during the first Malaysia plan, 1966-1970; [edited by John J. Padasian and others]. [Kota Kinabalu, 1971]. pp. 251.

THOMAS (P.) and others. The land capability classification of Sabah. Tolworth, 1976. 4 vols. (in 1), 10 maps. *bibliogs. (U.K. Ministry of Overseas Development. Land Resources Division. Land Resource Studies. 25)*

— Executive departments.

FEDERATION OF MALAYSIA. Department of Information, Sabah. 1969. Sabah since Malaysia: progress and achievements in development 1963-1968. rev.ed. [Kota Kinabalu], 1969. pp. 157.

FEDERATION OF MALAYSIA. Department of Information, Sabah. 1971. Sabah's revolution for progress: a review of progress and achievements during the first Malaysia plan, 1966-1970; [edited by John J. Padasian and others]. [Kota Kinabalu, 1971]. pp. 251.

— History.

LEE (EDWIN) The towkays of Sabah: Chinese leadership and indigenous challenge in the last phase of British rule. Singapore, [1976]. pp. 271. *bibliog.*

— International status.

FEDERATION OF MALAYSIA. Delegation to the Malaysia/Philippines Official Talks on the Philippine Claim to Sabah. 1968. Malaysia's stand on Sabah: statement by Tan Sri M. Ghazali bin Shafie, leader of the...delegation. [Kuala Lumpur, 1968]. pp. 22.

FEDERATION OF MALAYSIA. Department of Information. 1968. Sabah "claim" through some Filipino eyes. [Kuala Lumpur, 1968?]. pp. 26.

— Legislative Assembly — Elections.

FEDERATION OF MALAYSIA. Election Commission. 1967. Report on the Sabah State Legislative Assembly general election, 1967. Kuala Lumpur, 1967. pp. 42, 1 map.

— Social conditions.

FEDERATION OF MALAYSIA. Department of Information, Sabah. 1969. Sabah since Malaysia: progress and achievements in development 1963-1968. rev.ed. [Kota Kinabalu], 1969. pp. 157.

FEDERATION OF MALAYSIA. Department of Information, Sabah. 1971. Sabah's revolution for progress: a review of progress and achievements during the first Malaysia plan, 1966-1970; [edited by John J. Padasian and others]. [Kota Kinabalu, 1971]. pp. 251.

SABOTAGE.

BROWN (GEOFF) Sabotage: a study in industrial conflict. Nottingham, 1977. pp. 396.

SACRAMENTO

— Social conditions.

CONNOR (JOHN W.) Tradition and change in three generations of Japanese Americans. Chicago, [1977]. pp. 356. *bibliog.*

SAIGON

— History.

TERZANI (TIZIANO) Giai Phong!: the fall and liberation of Saigon; translated from the Italian by John Shepley. London, 1976. pp. 317.

ST. JOHN'S

— City planning.

NEWFOUNDLAND. Commission of Enquiry into the St. John's Urban Region Study. 1974-76. The first ([and] second) interim report[s] ([and] third and final report); [Alec G. Henley, chairman]. [St. John's], 1974-76. 4 vols.(in 2).

SAINT-NAZAIRE

— Economic history.

GUIN (YANNICK) Le mouvement ouvrier nantais: essai sur le syndicalisme d'action directe à Nantes et à Saint-Nazaire. Paris, 1976. pp. 413.

ST. VINCENT'S COMMUNITY HOME.

APPROVED school to community home: report of an exercise held in conjunction with Liverpool Catholic Children's and Social Services at St Vincent's, Formby, Lancashire; (edited by Barbara Kahan). London, H.M.S.O., 1976. pp. 73.

SAKHALIN

— Politics and government.

LEONOV (PAVEL ARTEMOVICH) Ocherk istorii Sakhalinskoi organizatsii KPSS. Iuzhno-Sakhalinsk, 1975. pp. 311. *bibliog.*

SAKHAROV (ANDREI DMITRIEVICH).

SAKHAROV (ANDREI DMITRIEVICH) O strane i mire: sbornik proizvedenii. N'iu-Iork, 1976. pp. xxiv,183.

SALARIED EMPLOYEES

— Germany.

SPEIER (HANS) Die Angestellten vor dem Nationalsozialismus: ein Beitrag zum Verständnis der deutschen Sozialstruktur, 1918-1933. Göttingen, 1977. pp. 202. *bibliog. Revised version of work originally prepared for publication in 1932/3 and suppressed for political reasons.*

SALES PERSONNEL

— United Kingdom — Salaries, commissions, etc.

ROOK (A.) Methods of remunerating salesmen: a survey of 197 companies. London, 1970. pp. 16. *bibliog. (British Institute of Management. Information Summaries. No.146)*

SALFORD

— Social history — Bibliography.

LABOUR history of Manchester and Salford: a bibliography; compiled by Eddie Conway [and others]. Manchester, [1977?]. pp. 34. *(Manchester Centre for Marxist Education. Pamphlets)*

SALISBURY, RHODESIA

— Description.

SALISBURY: a geographical survey of the capital of Rhodesia; edited by George Kay and Michael Smout. London, 1977. pp. 119.

SALT (HENRY STEPHENS).

HENDRICK (GEORGE) Henry Salt: humanitarian reformer and man of letters. Urbana, [1977]. pp. 228.

SALT (Sir TITUS).

SUDDARDS (ROGER W.) ed. Titus of Salts. Bradford, [1976]. pp. 64. *bibliog.*

SALT WORKERS

— United Kingdom.

SAMUEL (RAPHAEL) ed. Miners, quarrymen and saltworkers. London, 1977. pp. 363. *(History Workshop. History Workshop Series)*

SALTYKOV-SHCHEDRIN (MIKHAIL EVGRAFOVICH).

BUSHMIN (ALEKSEI SERGEEVICH) Saltykov-Shchedrin: iskusstvo satiry. Moskva, 1976. pp. 253.

SAMARKAND

— Economic history.

MUKMINOVA (ROZIIA GALIEVNA) Ocherki po istorii remesla v Samarkande i Bukhare v XVI veke. Tashkent, 1976. pp. 234.

SAMOA

— Census.

WESTERN SAMOA. Census, 1966. Population census, 1966. Apia, 1968. 2 vols.(in 1)

— Foreign relations.

For a related heading see EUROPEAN ECONOMIC COMMUNITY — Samoa.

SAMPLING (STATISTICS).

STUART (ALAN) Sampling in television research. London, 1960. pp. 16. *(Associated Television. ATV Research Library. No. 6)*

SUDMAN (SEYMOUR) Applied sampling. New York, [1976]. pp. 249. *bibliog.*

MARTIN (RICHARD JOHN) Spatial models with applications in sampling and experimental design. 1977. fo.201. *bibliog.* Typescript. Ph.D. (London) thesis: unpublished. *This thesis is the property of London University and may not be removed from the Library.*

SAMUELSON (PAUL ANTHONY).

LINDER (MARC) The anti-Samuelson. New York, [1977]. 2 vols. *bibliog.*

SAN FRANCISCO

— Politics and government.

KREFETZ (SHARON PERLMAN) Welfare policy making and city politics. New York, 1976. pp. 218.

SAN PEDRO (IVORY COAST)

— Growth.

[AUTORITE POUR L'AMENAGEMENT DE LA REGION DU SUD-OUEST [IVORY COAST]]. San Pédro: pôle de développement du sud-ouest ivoirien. [Abidjan?, 1973?]. pp. 110.

SANCTIONS (INTERNATIONAL LAW).

BROWN-JOHN (C. LLOYD) Multilateral sanctions in international law: a comparative analysis. New York, 1975. pp. 426. *bibliog.*

PORTER (RICHARD C.) Economic sanctions: the theory and evidence from Rhodesia. Ann Arbor, 1977. pp. 19. *bibliog. (Michigan University. Center for Research on Economic Development. Discussion Papers. No. 68)*

SANTA BARBARA, CALIFORNIA

— Growth.

The EFFECTS of urban growth: a population impact analysis; [by] Richard P. Appelbaum [and others]. New York, 1976. pp. 330. *bibliog.*

— Population.

The EFFECTS of urban growth: a population impact analysis; [by] Richard P. Appelbaum [and others]. New York, 1976. pp. 330. *bibliog.*

SANTA FE, ARGENTINA (PROVINCE)

— History.

GALLO (EZEQUIEL) Farmers in revolt: the revolutions of 1893 in the province of Santa Fe, Argentina. London, 1976. pp. 97. *bibliog. (London. University. Institute of Latin American Studies. Monographs. 7)*

SANTA FE, NEW MEXICO

— Social life and customs.

GRIMES (RONALD L.) Symbol and conquest: public ritual and drama in Santa Fe, New Mexico. Ithaca, 1976. pp. 281. *bibliog.*

SÃO PAULO (CITY)

— Population.

URBANIZACION y recursos humanos: el caso de San Pablo; Paul Singer, coordinador. Buenos Aires, 1973. pp. 285.

— Social policy.

URBANIZACION y recursos humanos: el caso de San Pablo; Paul Singer, coordinador. Buenos Aires, 1973. pp. 285.

SÃO TOME E PRINCIPE

— Commerce.

SÃO TOME E PRINCIPE. Repartição Provincial dos Serviços de Estatística. Estatísticas do comercio externo: comercio por mercadorias, paises e territorios estatisticos: Statistiques du commerce extérieur: commerce par marchandises, pays et territoires statistiques. a., 1970 (ano 32)- [São Tomé]. *[In Portuguese and French].*

— Statistics.

SÃO TOME E PRINCIPE. Repartição Provincial dos Serviços de Estatística. Boletim trimestral de estatística. q., 1971 (ano 1, no.1)- São Tomé.

SAR LUK, VIETNAM

— Social life and customs.

CONDOMINAS (GEORGES) We have eaten the forest: the story of a Montagnard village in the central highlands of Vietnam; translated from the French by Adrienne Foulke. London, 1977. pp. 423. *bibliog.*

SASKATCHEWAN

— Rural conditions.

KOHL (SEENA B.) Working together: women and family in southwestern Saskatchewan. Toronto, [1976]. pp. 139. *bibliog.*

SATIRE, ENGLISH.

The ASSES' skin memorandum book, lost in St. Paul's; to which is added, a condolence with the ultras, etc. etc. etc.; (Old Tom, editor). London, Wright, 1820. pp. 15. *Verse satire on Alderman Matthew Wood, friend and adviser to Queen Caroline.*

[SLOP, Dr., pseud.] Slop's shave at a broken Hone. London, Wright, 1820. pp. 42. *Satires in verse on W. Hone anticipating his "Slap at Slop".*

[TOM, Old, of Oxford, pseud.] The new Christmas budget, etc. London, Wright, 1820. pp. 15. *Satires in verse on the Queen and her supporters.*

TOM, Old, of Oxford, pseud. Types of the times. London, Wright, 1820. pp. 32.

SATIRE, FRENCH.

PETITE lettre sur une grande satire littéraire, morale et politique de Joseph Despaze. Paris, chez Madame Déjour, [1801]. pp. 20.

SATIRE, ITALIAN.

SILONE (IGNAZIO) pseud. [i.e. Secondo TRANQUILLI] Die Schule der Diktatoren; autorisierte Übersetzung aus dem Italienischen von Jakob Huber. Zürich, [1938]. pp. 326.

SATIRE, RUSSIAN.

BUSHMIN (ALEKSEI SERGEEVICH) Saltykov-Shchedrin: iskusstvo satiry. Moskva, 1976. pp. 253.

ZINOV'EV (ALEKSANDR ALEKSANDROVICH) Ziiaiushchie vysoty. [Lausanne, 1976]. pp. 563.

SATISFACTION.

QUALITY of life survey: urban Britain: 1973: (users' manual); [by] John Hall [and others]. [London, Social Science Research Council Survey Unit, 1976 in progress].

ABRAMS (MARK ALEXANDER) A review of work on subjective social indicators 1971 to 1975. London, Social Science Research Council Survey Unit, [1976]. pp. 54. *(Occasional Papers in Survey Research. 8)*

O'MUIRCHEARTAIGH (COLM A.) and WHELAN (BRENDAN J.) Statistical aspects of subjective measures of quality of life. London, Social Science Research Council Survey Unit, [1976]. pp. 75. *(Occasional Papers in Survey Research. 4)*

SAUDI ARABIA

— Economic conditions.

LONG (DAVID E.) Saudi Arabia. Beverly Hills, [1976]. pp. 71. *bibliog. (Georgetown University. Center for Strategic and International Studies. Washington Papers. vol. 4/39)*

— — Mathematical models.

AL-BASHIR (FAISAL SAFOOQ) A structural econometric model of the Saudi Arabian economy, 1960-1970. New York, [1977]. pp. 134. *bibliog.*

SAUDI ARABIA(Cont.)

— Economic policy.

SAUDI ARABIA. Central Planning Organization. 1975. Development plan 1395-1400 [i.e.] 1975-1980. [Riyadh], 1975. pp. 663. *Photocopy.*

WELLS (DONALD A.) Saudi Arabian development strategy. Washington, D.C., 1976. pp. 80. *(American Enterprise Institute for Public Policy Research. National Energy Studies. 12)*

— Foreign relations — United States.

ALI (RUSTUM) Sheikh. Saudi Arabia and oil diplomacy. New York, 1976. pp. 197. *bibliog.*

— Politics and government.

LONG (DAVID E.) Saudi Arabia. Beverly Hills, [1976]. pp. 71. *bibliog. (Georgetown University. Center for Strategic and International Studies. Washington Papers. vol. 4/39)*

— Social policy.

SAUDI ARABIA. Central Planning Organization. 1975. Development plan 1395-1400 [i.e.] 1975-1980. [Riyadh], 1975. pp. 663. *Photocopy.*

WELLS (DONALD A.) Saudi Arabian development strategy. Washington, D.C., 1976. pp. 80. *(American Enterprise Institute for Public Policy Research. National Energy Studies. 12)*

SAURASHTRA, INDIA (STATE)

— Economic conditions.

SPODEK (HOWARD) Urban-rural integration in regional development: a case study of Saurashtra, India, 1800-1960. Chicago, 1976. pp. 144. *bibliog. (Chicago. University. Department of Geography. Research Papers. No. 171)*

SAVING AND INVESTMENT

— Greece — Mathematical models.

BALTAS (N.) and KANBUR (M.G.) An econometric study of capital formation and growth in Greek economy, 1954-1972. Birmingham, 1976. pp. 22. *bibliog. (Birmingham. University. Faculty of Commerce and Social Science. Discussion Papers. Series A. No. 163)*

— Spain.

ORIZO (FRANCISCO ANDRES) Las bases sociales del consumo y del ahorro en España. Madrid, [1977]. pp. 493. *(Confederacion Española de Cajas de Ahorros. Fondo para la Investigacion Economica y Social. Publicaciones. 75)*

— United Kingdom.

U.K. Department for National Savings. Annual report. a., 1973/74- London.

NATIONAL ECONOMIC DEVELOPMENT OFFICE. Background paper 3: output, investment and productivity. London, 1976. pp. 108.

SAWYER (CHARLES).

MARCUS (MAEVA) Truman and the steel seizure case: the limits of presidential power. New York, 1977. pp. 390. *bibliog.*

SCALING (SOCIAL SCIENCES).

GORDEN (RAYMOND L.) Unidimensional scaling of social variables: concepts and procedures. New York, [1977]. pp. 175. *bibliog.*

SCANDINAVIA.

SCOTT (FRANKLIN DANIEL) Scandinavia. rev. ed. Cambridge, Mass., 1975. pp. 330. *bibliog.*

— Commerce.

INTERSKANDINAVISK Handelsomsaetning i Aarene 1900-1906; paa Grundlag af de tre nordiske Landes officielle Handelsstatistik. København, 1909. pp. 58,214.

— Economic integration.

SOLEM (ERIK TORALF) The Nordic Council and Scandinavian integration. New York, 1977. pp. 197. *bibliog.*

— Foreign economic relations.

MILJAN (TOIVO) The reluctant Europeans: the attitudes of the Nordic countries towards European integration. London, [1977]. pp. 325. *bibliog.*

See also EUROPEAN ECONOMIC COMMUNITY — Scandinavia.

— Foreign relations.

HASKEL (BARBARA G.) The Scandinavian option: opportunities and opportunity costs in postwar Scandinavian foreign policies. Oslo, [1976]. pp. 266. *bibliog.*

See also EUROPEAN ECONOMIC COMMUNITY — Scandinavia.

— Politics and government.

SOLEM (ERIK TORALF) The Nordic Council and Scandinavian integration. New York, 1977. pp. 197. *bibliog.*

— Relations (general) with the United States.

SCOTT (FRANKLIN DANIEL) Scandinavia. rev. ed. Cambridge, Mass., 1975. pp. 330. *bibliog.*

SCANDINAVIANISM.

SOLEM (ERIK TORALF) The Nordic Council and Scandinavian integration. New York, 1977. pp. 197. *bibliog.*

SCHACHT (HORACE GREELEY HJALMAR).

SCHACHT (HORACE GREELEY HJALMAR) My first seventy-six years: the autobiography of Hjalmar Schacht; translated by Diana Pyke. London, 1955. pp. 552.

SCHERMERHORN (WILLEM).

DUYNSTEE (FRANS JOZEPH FERDINAND MARIE) and BOSMANS (J.) Het kabinet Schermerhorn-Drees, 24 juni 1945-3 juli 1946. Assen, 1977. pp. 756. *bibliog. (Katholieke Universiteit Nijmegen. Centrum voor Parlementaire Geschiedenis. Parlementaire Geschiedenis van Nederland na 1945. 1)*

SCHIZOPHRENIA.

LIDZ (THEODORE) The origin and treatment of schizophrenic disorders. London, 1975. pp. 145. *bibliog.*

WING (JOHN KENNETH) ed. Schizophrenia from within. London, [1975]. pp. 65. *bibliog.*

NATIONAL SCHIZOPHRENIA FELLOWSHIP. Living with schizophrenia: by the relatives. London, [1976]. pp. 54.

SCHIZOPHRENICS

— Family relationships.

HIRSCH (STEVEN R.) and LEFF (JULIAN P.) Abnormalities in parents of schizophrenics: a review of the literature and an investigation of communication defects and deviances. London, 1975. pp. 200. *bibliog. (Bethlem Royal Hospital and Maudsley Hospital. Institute of Psychiatry. Maudsley Monographs. No. 22)*

SCHLESWIG-HOLSTEIN

— Landtag.

ASMUS (RUDOLF) and MALETZKE (ERICH) Das Haus an der Förde: 25 Jahre Schleswig- Holsteinischer Landtag, 1947-1972. Kiel, Präsident des Schleswig-Holsteinischen Landtages, [1972?]. pp. 284. *bibliog.*

— Population.

SCHLESWIG-HOLSTEIN. Statistisches Landesamt, 1972. Die Bevölkerung der Gemeinden in Schleswig-Holstein, 1867- 1970: historisches Gemeindeverzeichnis. Kiel, 1972. pp. 291,fo. 10.

— Social history.

KOESTLIN (KONRAD) Gilden in Schleswig-Holstein: die Bestimmung des Standes durch "Kultur". Göttingen, [1976]. pp. 320. *bibliog.*

SCHMIDT (FOLKE).

EUROPEAN COURT OF HUMAN RIGHTS. Publications. Series B: Pleadings, Oral Arguments and Documents. [B19]. "Schmidt and Dahlström" case, (1974-1975). Strasbourg, Council of Europe, 1977. pp. 199bis. *In English and French.*

SCHOLARLY PUBLISHING

— United Kingdom.

TRENDS in scholarly publishing. London, 1976. pp. 86. *bibliog. (British Library. Research and Development Department. Reports. 5299 HC)*

SCHOLARSHIPS

— Directories.

The GRANTS register, 1977-1979; editor Roland Turner. London, 1977. pp. 764.

SCHOOL CHILDREN

— Transportation — United States.

BUSING: constructive or divisive?; (a Round Table held on March 18, 1976...[in] Washington...); Virginia Trotter, moderator, etc. Washington, [1976]. pp. 45. *(American Enterprise Institute for Public Policy Research. Round Tables)*

— United Kingdom.

WILLIS (PAUL E.) Learning to labour: how working class kids get working class jobs. Farnborough, [1977]. pp. 204.

SCHOOL INTEGRATION

— United States.

The COURTS, social science, and school desegregation; edited by Betsy Levin and Willis D. Hawley. New Brunswick, N.J., [1975]. pp. 432.

CADITZ (JUDITH) White liberals in transition: current dilemmas of ethnic integration. New York, [1976]. pp. 187. *bibliog.*

— — Massachusetts.

HILLSON (JON) The battle of Boston. New York, [1977]. pp. 286.

LUPO (ALAN) Liberty's chosen home: the politics of violence in Boston. Boston, [Mass.], 1977. pp. 334.

SCHOOL MANAGEMENT AND ORGANIZATION

— Brazil.

HAAR (JERRY) The politics of higher education in Brazil. New York, 1977. pp. 222. *bibliog.*

— United Kingdom.

A NEW partnership for our schools; report of the Committee of Enquiry appointed jointly by the Secretary of State for Education and Science and the Secretary of State for Wales under the chairmanship of Tom Taylor. London, H.M.S.O., 1977. pp. 228.

WILLIAMS (PAUL) The lessons of Tyndale: an examination of the William Tyndale school affair. London, 1977. pp. 16. *(Conservative Political Centre. [Publications]. No.599)*

SCHOOL SOCIAL WORK

— United Kingdom.

MACMILLAN (KEITH) Education welfare: strategy and structure. London, 1977. pp. 165. *bibliog.*

SCHOOLS

— South Africa.

SOUTH AFRICA. Bureau of Statistics. Education: schools for Coloureds and Asians. a., 1971(5th)- Pretoria. *[in English and Afrikaans].*

— United Kingdom.

U.K. Department of Education and Science. HM Inspectorate of Schools (England). 1977. Ten good schools: a secondary school enquiry; a discussion paper by some members of HM Inspectorate of Schools. London, 1977. pp. 36. *(Matters for Discussion. 1)*

— United States.

BOYD (WILLIAM L.) Community status and conflict in suburban school politics. Beverly Hills, [1976]. pp. 41. *bibliog.*

SCHUELER (EDMUND).

DOSS (KURT) Das deutsche Auswärtige Amt im Übergang vom Kaiserreich zur Weimarer Republik: die Schülersche Reform. Düsseldorf, [1977]. pp. 328. *bibliog.*

SCHUTZ (ALFRED).

GORMAN (ROBERT A.) The dual vision: Alfred Schutz and the myth of phenomenological social science. London, 1977. pp. 234. *bibliog.*

SCHUYLKILL COUNTY

— Politics and government.

GUDELUNAS (WILLIAM A.) and SHADE (WILLIAM G.) Before the Molly Maguires: the emergence of the ethno-religious factor in the politics of the lower anthracite region, 1844-1872. New York, 1976. pp. 165. *bibliog.*

SCIENCE.

GREEN (CELIA) The decline and fall of science. London, 1976. pp. 184. *bibliog.*

— History — Baltic States.

IZ istorii estestvoznaniia i tekhniki Pribaltiki. t.5. Riga, 1976. pp. 342. *With English table of contents.*

— — Russia — Tajikistan.

SHAGALOV (EFIM SOLOMONOVICH) Nauka v Tadzhikistane v period sotsialisticheskogo stroitel'stva, 1917-1958 gg. Dushanbe, 1975. pp. 240.

— Information services.

CILES REPORT; [pd.by] Central Information, Library and Editorial Section, Commonwealth Scientific and Industrial Research Organization, Australia. a., current issue only. Melbourne.

— Methodology.

PHILLIPS (DEREK L.) Wittgenstein and scientific knowledge: a sociological perspective. London, 1977. pp. 248.

— Philosophy.

The STRUCTURE of scientific theories; edited with a critical introduction by Frederick Suppe. Urbana, Ill., [1974]. pp. 682. *bibliog. Proceedings of a symposium held at the University of Illinois, 1969.*

POST (HEINZ R.) Against ideologies. London, [1975?]. pp. 18. *Inaugural lecture given at Chelsea College in 1974.*

UTKINA (NINA FEDOROVNA) Pozitivizm, antropologicheskii materializm i nauka v Rossii: vtoraia polovina XIX veka. Moskva, 1975. pp. 319.

ESSAYS in memory of Imre Lakatos; edited by R.S. Cohen [and others]. Dordrecht, [1976]. pp. 767. *bibliog. (Boston Colloquium for the Philosophy of Science. Boston Studies in the Philosophy of Science. vol. 39)*

ROSE (HILARY) and ROSE (STEVEN) eds. The political economy of science: ideology of/in the natural sciences. London, 1976. pp. 218.

LAUDAN (LARRY) Progress and its problems: toward a theory of scientific growth. Berkeley, Calif., [1977]. pp. 257. *bibliog.*

— Social aspects.

KUITENBROUWER (JOOST B.W.) Science and technology: for or against the people. The Hague, 1975. pp. 30. *(The Hague. Institute of Social Studies. Occasional Papers. No. 49)*

MEREDITH MEMORIAL LECTURES. 1975. Science in the community in the seventies. Bundoora, Victoria, 1976. 4 pts.

ROSE (HILARY) and ROSE (STEVEN) eds. The political economy of science: ideology of/in the natural sciences. London, 1976. pp. 218.

ROSE (HILARY) and ROSE (STEVEN) eds. The radicalisation of science: ideology of/in the natural sciences. London, 1976. pp. 205.

IVANOVA (NINEL' IAKOVLEVNA) Sotsial'no-kul'turnye funktsii estestvennykh nauk: gumanisticheskii aspekt. Kiev,1977. pp. 167. *bibliog.*

PERSPECTIVES in the sociology of science; edited by Stuart S. Blume. Chichester, [1977]. pp. 237. *bibliogs.*

SCIENCE, technology and society: a cross-disciplinary perspective; edited by Ina Spiegel-Rösing and Derek de Solla Price. London, [1977]. pp. 602. *bibliogs.*

— America, Latin.

SAGASTI (FRANCISCO R.) and GUERRERO C. (MAURICIO) El desarrollo cientifico y tecnologico de America Latina: diagnostico, bases para la accion y estructuras de cooperacion. Buenos Aires, Instituto para la Integracion de America Latina, [1974]. pp. 203.

KRATOCHWIL (GERMÁN) Wissenschaftlich-technologische Entwicklung und internationale Zusammenarbeit in Lateinamerika. Tübingen, [1976]. pp. 175. *(Institut für Iberoamerika-Kunde. Schriftenreihe. Band 24) With Spanish summary.*

— — Statistics.

THEBAUD (SCHILLER) Statistics on science and technology in Latin America: experience with Unesco pilot projects 1972-1974. Paris, United Nations Educational, Scientific and Cultural Organization, 1976. pp. 76. *(Statistical Reports and Studies. [No. 20])*

— Russia — Tajikistan — Bibliography.

LEIVI (DALILA SEMENOVNA) and SHCHERBAKOVA (NATAL'IA GLEBOVNA) compilers. Nauka v Sovetskom Tadzhikistane: bibliograficheskii ukazatel', 1961-1975. Dushanbe, 1976. pp. 478.

SCIENCE AND STATE.

PARLIAMENTARY AND SCIENTIFIC CONFERENCE, 4TH, FLORENCE, 1975. The sciences and democratic government: highlights of the... Conference; compiled and presented by André Boulloche [and others]. London, 1976. pp. 149.

PERSPECTIVES in the sociology of science; edited by Stuart S. Blume. Chichester, [1977]. pp. 237. *bibliogs.*

— Canada.

CANADA. Ministry of State for Science and Technology. Federal science programs. a., 1977/78(1st)- [Ottawa]. *[in English and French].*

— China.

RIDLEY (CHARLES PRICE) China's scientific policies: implications for international cooperation. Washington, D.C., 1976. pp. 92. *bibliog. (American Enterprise Institute for Public Policy Research and Stanford University. Hoover Institution on War, Revolution and Peace. AEI-Hoover Policy Studies. 20)*

— Russia.

PLEKHANOV (NIKOLAI NIKOLAEVICH) Dialektika prevrashcheniia nauki v proizvoditel'nuiu silu. Kishinev, 1975. pp. 141. *bibliog.*

RIGBY (THOMAS HENRY RICHARD) and MILLER (ROBERT F.) Political and administrative aspects of the scientific and technical revolution in the USSR. Canberra, 1976. pp. 115. *(Australian National University. Research School of Social Sciences. Department of Political Science. Occasional Papers. No. 11)*

— United Kingdom.

U.K. Central Office of Information. Reference Division. 1975. The promotion of the sciences in Britain. rev. ed. London, 1975. pp. 33. *bibliog.*

ZUCKERMAN (SOLLY) Baron Zuckerman. Advice and responsibility. Oxford, 1975. pp. 40. *bibliog. (Oxford. University. Romanes Lectures. 1975)*

ROTHSCHILD (NATHANIEL MEYER VICTOR) 3rd Baron Rothschild. Meditations of a broomstick. London, 1977. pp. 187. *bibliog.*

— United States.

KISTIAKOWSKY (GEORGE BOGDAN) A scientist at the White House: the private diary of President Eisenhower's special assistant for science and technology. Cambridge, Mass., 1976. pp. 448.

SCIENTOLOGY.

WALLIS (ROY) The road to total freedom: a sociological analysis of scientology. London, 1976. pp. 282. *bibliog.*

SCOTLAND

— Economic conditions.

LOCH (DAVID) Essay on the trade, commerce, and manufactures of Scotland. Edinburgh, printed for the Author, 1775. pp. 92. *Copy presented by the Author to Dr. Thomas Young.*

The FUTURE of Scotland; edited by Robert Underwood. London, [1977]. pp. 181.

GASKIN (MAXWELL) North Sea oil and Scotland: the changing prospect. Edinburgh, 1977. pp. 22.

— Economic history.

COMPARATIVE aspects of Scottish and Irish economic and social history 1600-1900; edited by L.M. Cullen and T.C. Smout. Edinburgh, [1977?]. pp. 252. *Based mainly on papers presented at a seminar at Trinity College, Dublin in 1976.*

— Economic policy.

BRITISH ASSOCIATION FOR THE ADVANCEMENT OF SCIENCE. Section F. Meeting, 1974. The political economy of change: papers presented to Section F. ...; edited by K. J. W. Alexander. Oxford, 1975. pp. 189.

BRUCE-GARDYNE (JOCK) Scotland to 1980. London, [1975]. pp. 106.

SCOTTISH COUNCIL (DEVELOPMENT AND INDUSTRY). International Forum, 5th, Aviemore, 1974. Investing in Scotland; (compiled by Jack McGill). Glasgow, [1975]. pp. 224. *bibliog.*

BRYDEN (JOHN M.) and HOUSTON (GEORGE F.B.) Agrarian change in the Scottish Highlands: the role of the Highlands and Islands Development Board in the agricultural economy of the crofting counties. London, 1976. pp. 152. *bibliog. (Glasgow. University. Social and Economic Research Studies. 4.) Published in association with the Highlands and Islands Development Board.*

SPECIAL regional assistance in Scotland; [by] H.M. Begg [and others]. Glasgow, [1976]. pp. 22. *(Glasgow. University of Strathclyde. Fraser of Allander Institute. Regional Monographs. No. 3)*

SCOTLAND 1980: the economics of self-government; edited by Donald Mackay. Edinburgh, 1977. pp. 211. *bibliogs.*

— History.

SCOTTISH themes: essays in honour of Professor S.G.E. Lythe; edited by John Butt and J.T. Ward. Edinburgh, 1976. pp. 189. *bibliog.*

HARVIE (CHRISTOPHER) Scotland and nationalism: Scottish society and politics, 1707- 1977. London, 1977. pp. 318. *bibliog.*

— — 1707, The Union.

DAICHES (DAVID) Scotland and the Union. London, [1977]. pp. 212. *bibliog.*

— Industries.

MOSS (MICHAEL S.) and HUME (JOHN R.) Workshop of the British Empire: engineering and shipbuilding in the west of Scotland. London, 1977. pp. 192. *bibliog.*

— Intellectual life.

DONOVAN (ARTHUR L.) Philosophical chemistry in the Scottish Enlightenment: the doctrines and discoveries of William Cullen and Joseph Black. Edinburgh, [1975]. pp. 343. *bibliog.*

OLSON (RICHARD) Scottish philosophy and British physics, 1750-1880: a study in the foundations of the Victorian scientific style. Princeton, N.J., [1975]. pp. 349.

CHITNIS (ANAND C.) The Scottish Enlightenment: a social history. London, 1976. pp. 279. *bibliog.*

HARVIE (CHRISTOPHER) Scotland and nationalism: Scottish society and politics, 1707-1977. London, 1977. pp. 318. *bibliog.*

— Moral conditions.

FREE CHURCH OF SCOTLAND. Home Mission. Report on agricultural labourers. [Edinburgh, 1879]. pp. 15.

— Nationalism.

The RADICAL approach: papers on an independent Scotland; [edited by Gavin Kennedy]. Edinburgh, [1976]. pp. 109.

HARVIE (CHRISTOPHER) Scotland and nationalism: Scottish society and politics, 1707-1977. London, 1977. pp. 318. *bibliog.*

NAIRN (TOM) The break-up of Britain: crisis and neo-nationalism. London, [1977]. pp. 368.

WEBB (KEITH) The growth of nationalism in Scotland. Glasgow, 1977. pp. 147. *bibliog.*

— Politics and government.

MORRISON (Sir NICHOLAS) The Scottish Office: an example of administrative devolution; (transcript of lecture given on 22 April 1974). [London], Civil Service College, [1974]. pp. 11. *(Lectures on Some Management Problems in the Civil Service. No. 1)*

BRUCE-GARDYNE (JOCK) Scotland to 1980. London, [1975]. pp. 106.

ROSE (RICHARD) The future of Scottish politics: a dynamic analysis. Glasgow, [1975]. pp. 27. *(Glasgow. University of Strathclyde. Fraser of Allander Institute. Speculative Papers. No. 3)*

INDEPENDENCE and devolution: the legal implications for Scotland; editor John P. Grant. Edinburgh, 1976. pp. 233.

TRADES UNION CONGRESS. TUC policy on devolution. London, 1976. pp. 8.

U.K. 1976. Devolution: the new assemblies for Scotland and Wales; [main points of the White Paper]. [London, 1976]. pp. 15.

DALYELL (TAM) Devolution: the end of Britain? London, 1977. pp. 321.

HARVIE (CHRISTOPHER) Scotland and nationalism: Scottish society and politics, 1707- 1977. London, 1977. pp. 318. *bibliog.*

U.K. Parliament. House of Commons. Library. Research Division. Background Papers. No.57. The devolution debate: regional statistics. [London, 1977]. pp. 18.

— Population.

SCOTLAND. Scottish Development Department. 1975. Demographic analysis for planning purposes: a manual on sources and techniques: regional reports advice. [Edinburgh], 1975. pp. 55. *bibliog. (Planning Advice Notes. No.8)*

— Social conditions.

The FUTURE of Scotland; edited by Robert Underwood. London, [1977]. pp. 181.

— Social history.

FORBES (DAVID) ed. The Sutherland clearances, 1806-1820: a documentary survey. Ayr, [1976]. pp. 53. *bibliog.*

COMPARATIVE aspects of Scottish and Irish economic and social history 1600-1900; edited by L.M. Cullen and T.C. Smout. Edinburgh, [1977?]. pp. 252. *Based mainly on papers presented at a seminar at Trinity College, Dublin in 1976.*

SCOTTISH LABOUR PARTY.

ARMSTRONG (ALLAN) Nationalism or socialism?: the SNP and SLP exposed. London, [1976]. pp. 8. *(Socialist Worker. Pamphlets)*

SCOTTISH NATIONAL PARTY.

WOLFE (BILLY) Scotland lives. Edinburgh, [1973]. pp. 167.

ARMSTRONG (ALLAN) Nationalism or socialism?: the SNP and SLP exposed. London, [1976]. pp. 8. *(Socialist Worker. Pamphlets)*

LAMONT (ARCHIE) How Scots opposed the peacetime call-up. Carlops by Penicuik, [1976]. pp. 31.

The RADICAL approach: papers on an independent Scotland; [edited by Gavin Kennedy]. Edinburgh, [1976]. pp. 109.

SCOTTISH NEWSPAPERS.

McKAY (RON) and BARR (BRIAN) The story of the Scottish Daily News. Edinburgh, 1976. pp. 170.

SCULLIN (JAMES HENRY).

ROBERTSON (JOHN) Historian. J.H. Scullin: a political biography. Nedlands, W.A. 1974. pp. 495. *bibliog.*

SEA POWER.

ADIE (WILLIAM ANDREW CHARLES) Oil, politics and seapower: the Indian Ocean vortex. New York, [1975]. pp. 95. *bibliog. (National Strategy Information Center. Strategy Papers. No. 24)*

JANIS (MARK W.) Sea power and the law of the sea. [Lexington, Mass., 1976]. pp. 99.

BOOTH (KEN) Navies and foreign policy. London, [1977]. pp. 294.

SEALE (BOBBY).

HEATH (G. LOUIS) ed. The Black Panther leaders speak: Huey P. Newton, Bobby Seale, Eldridge Cleaver and company speak out through the Black Panther Party's official newspaper. Metuchen, N.J., 1976. pp. 165. *bibliog.*

SEAMEN

— United Kingdom.

FRIENDLY SOCIETY OF SAILORS, &c., AT SOUTHWOLD. Articles made and agreed to by a Friendly Society of Sailors, c, at Southwold, in Suffolk, on the 8th day of January, 1805. Halesworth, printed by J.T. Allcock, [1805]. pp. 15. *With ms. amendments.*

FRIENDLY SOCIETY OF SAILORS, &c., AT SOUTHWOLD. Articles made and agreed to by a Friendly Society of Sailors, c, at Southwold, in Suffolk, on the 8th day of January, 1805; revised and altered March 5th, 1834. Southwold, Bye, printer, [1834]. pp. 14. *Cover bears signature Willm. Swain, one of the Society's members.*

PRESS (JONATHAN) The merchant seamen of Bristol, 1747-1789. Bristol, 1976. pp. 23. *bibliog. (Historical Association. Bristol Branch. Local History Pamphlets. No. 38)*

SEASIDE RESORTS

— United Kingdom.

KARN (VALERIE A.) Retiring to the seaside. London, 1977. pp. 388. *bibliog.*

SECESSION.

LONDON. University. Institute of Commonwealth Studies. Collected seminar papers on the politics of separatism, October 1974-June 1975; ...papers...presented at the Comparative Politics Seminar held at the Institute of Commonwealth Studies between October 1974 and June 1975. London, 1976. pp. 99. *(London. University. Institute of Commonwealth Studies. Collected Seminar Papers. No. 19)*

OMRČANIN (MARGARET STEWART) Norway, Sweden, Croatia: a comparative study of state secession and formation. Philadelphia, [1976]. pp. 138.

SECKER (THOMAS) Archbishop of Canterbury.

PORTEUS (BEILBY) successively Bishop of Chester and of London. A review of the life and character of the Right Rev. Dr. Thomas Secker, late Lord Archbishop of Canterbury. 5th ed. London, Rivington, 1797. pp. vi, 118.

SECONDAT (CHARLES LOUIS DE) Baron de Montesquieu.

SECONDAT (CHARLES LOUIS DE) Baron de Montesquieu. The political theory of Montesquieu; [edited by] Melvin Richter. Cambridge, 1977. pp. 355.

SECRET SOCIETIES

— China.

DAVIS (FEI-LING) Primitive revolutionaries of China: a study of secret societies in the late nineteenth century. London, 1977. pp. 254. *bibliog.*

— Malaysia.

MAK (LAU-FONG) Chinese secret societies in Ipoh town, 1945-1969. Singapore, 1975. pp. 17. *bibliog. (University of Singapore. Department of Sociology. Working Papers. No. 42)*

— Spain.

ZAVALA (IRIS M.) Masones, comuneros y carbonarios. Madrid, 1971. pp. 363.

SECTS

— China.

NAQUIN (SUSAN) Millenarian rebellion in China: the Eight Trigams uprising of 1813. New Haven, Conn., 1976. pp. 384. *bibliog. (Yale University. Yale Historical Publications. Miscellany. 108)*

— Russia.

USHINSKII (A.D.) O prichinakh poiavleniia ratsionalisticheskikh uchenii shtundy i nekotorykh drugikh podobnykh sekt v sel'skom pravoslavnom naselenii i o merakh protiv rasprostraneniia ucheniia etikh sekt. Kiev, 1884. pp. 80.

SECURITIES

— Mexico.

MEXICO. Statutes, etc. 1895-1957. Legislacion sobre fianzas. Mexico, 1958. pp. 275.

SECURITY, INTERNATIONAL.

ARMS, defense policy and arms control; essays by Franklin A. Long [and others]; edited by Franklin A. Long and George W. Rathjens. New York, [1976]. pp. 222.

CROZIER (BRIAN) Security and the myth of peace: surviving the Third World War. London, [1976]. pp. 24. *(Institute for the Study of Conflict. Conflict Studies. No. 76)*

EVROPEISKAIA bezopasnost' i sotrudnichestvo: predposylki, problemy, perspektivy. Moskva, 1976. pp. 302.

FOR peace, security, cooperation and social progress in Europe: document adopted by the conference of 29 Communist and workers' parties of Europe, Berlin, 29/30 June 1976. London, 1976. 1 pamphlet (unpaged).

INTERNATIONAL INSTITUTE FOR STRATEGIC STUDIES. Adelphi Papers. No. 127. Defending the central front: the balance of forces; by Robert Lucas Fischer. London, 1976. pp. 45.

MARTIN (ALEXANDER) of the Institut für Internationale Politik und Wirtschaft, ed. Sicherheit und friedliche Zusammenarbeit in Europa: Dokumente 1972-1975. Berlin, 1976. pp. 614.

PELCOVITS (NATHAN ALBERT) Security guarantees in a Middle East settlement. Beverly Hills, [1976]. pp. 69. *(Foreign Policy Research Institute. Foreign Policy Papers. Vol. 2/5)*

SECOND WORLD DEFENCE. Pamphlets. No. 1. The superpowers, the threat of war and the British working class. London, 1976. pp. 23.

WEIZSAECKER (CARL FRIEDRICH VON) Freiherr. Wege in der Gefahr: eine Studie über Wirtschaft, Gesellschaft und Kriegsverhütung. München, [1976 repr. 1977]. pp. 265.

WHITSON (WILLIAM W.) ed. Foreign policy and U.S. national security: major postelection issues. New York, 1976. pp. 368. *bibliog.*

BARBER (RICHARD) Conservative, and STAFFORD (IAN) Detente or defence: the bogus dilemma. London, [1977]. pp. 16.

BEYOND nuclear deterrence: new aims, new arms; edited by Johan J. Holst [and] Uwe Nerlich. New York, [1977]. pp. 314. *bibliog.*

BLAKER (PETER) and others. Coping with the Soviet Union: a new Tory view. London, 1977. pp. 28. *(Conservative Political Centre. [Publications]. No. 605)*

INTERNATIONAL INSTITUTE FOR STRATEGIC STUDIES. Adelphi Papers. No. 133. The diffusion of power: I. Proliferation of force; [papers presented at the 18th annual conference of the IISS at Baden bei Wien, 1976]. London, 1977. pp. 41.

INTERNATIONAL INSTITUTE FOR STRATEGIC STUDIES. Adelphi Papers. No. 134. The diffusion of power: II: conflict and its control; papers presented...at the eighteenth annual conference of the IISS at Baden bei Wien, Austria, in September 1976. London, 1977. pp. 36.

— Congresses.

PARTI COMMUNISTE FRANÇAIS. Pour la paix et la sécurité européenne: documents de la conférence des partis communistes et ouvriers d'Europe, Karlovy- Vary, 24-26 avril, 1967. [Paris, 1967]. pp. 40.

SEDITION

— United Kingdom.

U.K. Law Commission. Working Papers. No. 72. Second programme, Item XVIII. Codification of the Criminal Law: treason, sedition and allied offences. London, 1977. pp. 64.

SEGREGATION IN EDUCATION

— Law and legislation — United States.

The COURTS, social science, and school desegregation; edited by Betsy Levin and Willis D. Hawley. New Brunswick, N.J., [1975]. pp. 432.

KLUGER (RICHARD) Simple justice: the history of Brown v. Board of Education and black America's struggle for equality. London, 1977. pp. 823,xxiii. *bibliog.*

— United States.

WOLLENBERG (CHARLES M.) All deliberate speed: segregation and exclusion in California schools, 1855-1975. Berkeley, Calif., [1976]. pp. 201.

SEGREGATION IN SPORTS

— South Africa.

LAPCHICK (RICHARD EDWARD) The politics of race and international sport: the case of South Africa. Westport, 1975. pp. 268. *bibliog. (Denver. University. Center on International Race Relations. Studies in Human Rights. No. 1)*

SEIDEL (ROBERT).

ERNST (HEINRICH) Zum 80. Geburtstage von Robert Seidel: Feierrede...zu Seidels 70. Geburtstag, 1920, gehalten in der Kirche St. Jakob in Zürich, etc. Zürich, 1930. pp. 22.

SELF.

ZILLER (ROBERT C.) The social self. New York, [1973]. pp. 205. *bibliog.*

KREILKAMP (THOMAS A.) The corrosion of the self: society's effects on people. New York, 1976. pp. 235. *bibliog.*

SELF-ESTEEM.

ROSENBERG (MORRIS) and SIMMONS (ROBERTA G.) Black and white self-esteem: the urban school child. Washington, D.C., [1971?]. pp. 160. *bibliog. (American Sociological Association. Arnold and Caroline Rose Monograph Series in Sociology)*

SELF-EVALUATION.

ROSENBERG (MORRIS) and SIMMONS (ROBERTA G.) Black and white self-esteem: the urban school child. Washington, D.C., [1971?]. pp. 160. *bibliog. (American Sociological Association. Arnold and Caroline Rose Monograph Series in Sociology)*

SELF-MEDICATION.

LEVIN (LOWELL S.) and others. Self-care: lay initiatives in health. London, 1977. pp. 133. *bibliog. "This book is the direct outgrowth of the International Symposium on the Role of the Individual in Primary Health Care, held in Copenhagen...1975".*

SEMANTICS.

OSGOOD (CHARLES EGERTON) and others. Cross-cultural universals of affective meaning. Urbana, [1975]. pp. 486. *bibliog.*

MONTAGUE grammar; edited by Barbara H. Partee. New York, [1976]. pp. 370. *bibliogs.*

LYONS (JOHN) Semantics. Cambridge, 1977. 2 vols. *bibliogs.*

SEMANTICS (PHILOSOPHY).

FRANZ (PETER) and JANKOW (MITRJU) Information contra Materialismus?: zum Missbrauch der Informationswissenschaften in der gegenwärtigen bürgerlichen Ideologie. Berlin, 1977. pp. 124.

SEMANTICS, COMPARATIVE.

CAMBRIDGE COLLOQUIUM ON FORMAL SEMANTICS OF NATURAL LANGUAGE, 1973. Formal semantics of natural language: papers from [the] colloquium sponsored by the King's College Research Centre, Cambridge; edited by Edward L. Keenan. Cambridge, 1975. pp. 475. *bibliogs.*

SEMIOLOGY.

STAMPER (RONALD) A philosophy for the IFIP systems curriculum appropriate for a university; [paper presented at the 2nd World Conference on Computers and Education, Marseilles, 1975]. London, [1975]. fo. 5. *bibliog.*

COWARD (ROSALIND) and ELLIS (JOHN) Writer on language. Language and materialism: developments in semiology and the theory of the subject. London, 1977. pp. 165. *bibliog.*

SENECA (LUCIUS ANNAEUS).

GRIFFIN (MIRIAM TAMARA) Seneca: a philosopher in politics. Oxford, 1976. pp. xii, 504. *bibliog.*

SENEGAL

— Economic policy — Bibliography.

SENEGAL. Archives du Sénégal. Centre de Documentation. Bibliographie: la planification au Sénégal, IIIème et IVème plans; (with Mise à jour). [Dakar, 1973-75]. 2 pts.

— History.

GELLAR (SHELDON) Structural changes and colonial dependency: Senegal 1885-1945. Beverly Hills, [1976]. pp. 80. *bibliog.*

— — Sources.

BA (OUMAR) ed. La pénétration française au Cayor du règne de Birima N'Goné Latyr à l'intronisation de Madiodo Dèguène Codou:...documents, etc. Dakar, 1976 in progress.

— Relations (general) with Gambia.

REPORT on the alternatives for association between the Gambia and Senegal; by Hubertus J. van Mook [and others], appointed under the United Nations Programme of Technical Assistance. [Bathurst], 1964. pp. 97. *(Gambia. Sessional Papers. 1964. No. 13)*

— Social policy — Bibliography.

SENEGAL. Archives du Sénégal. Centre de Documentation. Bibliographie: la planification au Sénégal, IIIème et IVème plans; (with Mise à jour). [Dakar, 1973-75]. 2 pts.

SENSES AND SENSATION.

MACH (ERNST) The analysis of sensations and the relation of the physical to the psychical; with a new introduction by Thomas S.Szasz; translated from the first German edition by C.M. Williams; revised and supplemented from the fifth German edition by Sydney Waterlow. New York, [1959]. pp. 380. *bibliog.*

SENTENCES (CRIMINAL PROCEDURE)

— United Kingdom.

HICKS (JOHN) Probation officer. Probation and sentencing. Thornton Heath, Surrey, 1976. pp. 8. *(National Association of Probation Officers. Committee on the Role and Structure of the Probation Service. [Papers]. No. 1)*

U.K. Working Party on Judicial Training and Information. 1976. Consultative working paper; [Lord Justice Bridge, chairman]. London, 1976. pp. 26.

SEPARATION OF POWERS

— United States.

SOFAER (ABRAHAM D.) War, foreign affairs and constitutional power: the origins. Cambridge, Mass., [1976]. pp. 533. *bibliog.*

SERBIA

— History.

PETROVICH (MICHAEL BORO) A history of modern Serbia, 1804-1918. New York, [1976]. 2 vols. *bibliog.*

SERBIAN LITERATURE

— History and criticism.

STAJIĆ (MIODRAG) Ideje i ljudi; predgovor Slobodan Jovanović. London, 1972. pp. 96. *In Cyrillic.*

SERBS IN HUNGARY.

HASELSTEINER (HORST) Die Serben und der Ausgleich: zur politischen und staatsrechtlichen Stellung der Serben Südungarns in den Jahren 1860-1867. Wien, 1976. pp. 125. *bibliog. (Vienna. Universität. Institut für Osteuropäische Geschichte und Südostforschung. Wiener Archiv für Geschichte des Slawentums und Osteuropas. Band 9)*

SERBS IN THE UNITED STATES

— Bibliography.

GAKOVICH (ROBERT P.) and RADOVICH (MILAN M.) compilers. Serbs in the United States and Canada: a comprehensive bibliography;...edited by Joseph D. Dwyer. [Minneapolis], 1976. pp. 129. *(Minnesota University. Immigration History Research Center. IHRC Ethnic Bibliographies. No. 1)*

SERFDOM

— Russia.

SKRYNNIKOV (RUSLAN GRIGOR'EVICH) Rossiia posle oprichniny: ocherki politicheskoi i sotsial'noi istorii. Leningrad, 1975. pp. 223.

FIELD (DANIEL) The end of serfdom: nobility and bureaucracy in Russia, 1855-1861. Cambridge, Mass., 1976. pp. 472. *bibliog. (Harvard University. Russian Research Center. Studies. 75)*

— — Lithuania.

MATERIALY nauchnoi sessii po teme "Razlozhenie krepostnicheskoi sistemy i protsess formirovaniia kapitalisticheskogo uklada v sel'skom khoziaistve Belorussii i Litvy". Vil'nius, 1975. pp. 131.

— — White Russia.

MATERIALY nauchnoi sessii po teme "Razlozhenie krepostnicheskoi sistemy i protsess formirovaniia kapitalisticheskogo uklada v sel'skom khoziaistve Belorussii i Litvy". Vil'nius, 1975. pp. 131.

SERGEEV (FEDOR ANDREEVICH).

TOVARISHCH Artem: vospominaniia o Fedore Andreeviche Sergeeve, Arteme. Khar'kov, 1975. pp. 288.

SERMONS, ENGLISH.

JEFFERSON (JOSEPH) Industry, and a pious submission, charity, and a strict economy...; a sermon preached in the parish church of St. Anne, Westminster, on Sunday, the 14th, day of December, 1800, being the day on which His Majesty's proclamation on the scarcity of grain was directed to be read; ([with] An appendix containing the resolutions...for carrying into effect His Majesty's proclamation, etc.) 2nd ed. London, Robson, 1800. pp. 28,6.

SERVANTS

— Canada.

BARBADOS. 196-. Advice to West Indian women recruited for work in Canada as household helps. [Bridgetown, 196-?]. 1 pamphlet (unpaged).

— Finland.

KARJALAINEN (PIRKKO) Kotiapulaiset ja heidän työnantajansa, etc. Helsinki, 1976. pp. 238. *bibliog. (Finland. Suomen Virallinen Tilasto. Finlands Officiella Statistik. 32. Sosiaalisia Erikoistutkimuksia. 45)* With English summary.

— United Kingdom.

EBERY (MARK) and PRESTON (BRIAN) Domestic service in late Victorian and Edwardian England, 1871-1914. Reading, 1976. pp. 117. *(Reading. University. Department of Geography. Reading Geographical Papers. No. 42)*

SERVICE, COMPULSORY NON-MILITARY

— China.

PASQUALINI (JEAN) and CHELMINSKI (RUDOLPH) Prisoner of Mao. Harmondsworth, 1973. pp. 326.

— Switzerland.

ASSOCIATION SUISSE POUR LE SERVICE CIVIL INTERNATIONAL. Proposition pour la création d'un service civil en Suisse. La Chaux-de-Fonds, 1974. pp. 64.

SERVICE INDUSTRIES

— Australia.

The ECONOMICS of the Australian service sector; edited by K. A. Tucker. London, [1977]. pp. 443. *bibliogs.*

— Belgium.

FAERMAN (M.) and SCHYNS (J.) Essai sur la structure spatiale de l'emploi tertiaire en Belgique. [Brussels, Institut Economique et Social des Classes Moyennes, 1971]. pp. 319.

— Brazil.

BRAZIL. Departamento de Censos. 1975. Censo dos serviços [1970]: Brasil [whole country]. [Rio de Janeiro, 1975]. pp. 71.

— Canada — Alberta.

ALBERTA. Bureau of Statistics. Retail and service trade statistics. a., 1975(4th)- Edmonton.

— Ireland (Republic).

EIRE. Central Statistics Office. 1977. Census of distribution, 1971: detailed results. Dublin, 1977. 3 pts. (in 1 vol.).

NATIONAL ECONOMIC AND SOCIAL COUNCIL [EIRE]. Service-type employment and regional development; (by Michael J. Bannon [and others]). Dublin, Stationery Office, [1977]. pp. 142. *bibliog. ([Reports]. No. 28)*

— Russia.

RUTGAIZER (VALERII MAKSOVICH) Resursy razvitiia neproizvodstvennoi sfery. Moskva, 1975. pp. 229.

USTENKO (ALEKSANDR ANDREEVICH) Trudovye resursy neproizvodstvennoi sfery. L'vov, 1976. pp. 171. *bibliog.*

ABRAMOV (MAKSIM ABRAMOVICH) Proizvodstvo i sfera obsluzhivaniia: razmeshchenie, vzaimosviaz', kompleksnoe razvitie; (nauchnyi redaktor i avtor predisloviia...I. V. Nikol'skii). Moskva, 1977. pp. 239. *bibliog.*

— Singapore.

SINGAPORE. Statistics Department. 1974. Report on the census of services, 1972. Singapore, 1974. pp. 60.

SEVEN YEARS' WAR, 1756-1763.

PARALLELE de la conduite du roi avec celle du roi d'Angleterre, electeur d'Hanovre, relativement aux affaires de l'Empire et nommément à la rupture de la capitulation de Closter-Seven par les Hanovriens. Amsterdam, Rey, 1758. pp. (iv), 192.

SEVILLE

— Prisons and reformatories.

HERRERA PUGA (PEDRO) Sociedad y delincuencia en el Siglo de Oro: aspectos de la vida sevillana en los siglos XVI y XVII. Granada, 1971. pp. 481. *bibliog.*

— Social history.

HERRERA PUGA (PEDRO) Sociedad y delincuencia en el Siglo de Oro: aspectos de la vida sevillana en los siglos XVI y XVII. Granada, 1971. pp. 481. *bibliog.*

SEWING MACHINE INDUSTRY

— United States.

BRANDON (RUTH) Singer and the sewing machine: a capitalist romance. London, 1977. pp. 244. *bibliog.*

SEX CUSTOMS

— Mediterranean.

PITT-RIVERS (JULIAN ALFRED LANE-FOX) The fate of Shechem; or, The politics of sex: essays in the anthropology of the Mediterranean. Cambridge, 1977. pp. 193.

— United Kingdom.

STONE (LAWRENCE) The family, sex and marriage in England, 1500-1800. London, [1977]. pp. 800. *bibliog.*

SEX DIFFERENCES.

GOLDBERG (STEVEN) The inevitability of patriarchy. London, 1977. pp. 224.

SEX DISCRIMINATION

— Law and legislation — United Kingdom.

The SEX Discrimination Act and the struggle for women's rights. London, [1976?]. pp. 22. *(Socialist Woman. Fight for Women's Rights Pamphlet Series. No. 1)*

SEX DISCRIMINATION AGAINST WOMEN.

WOMEN and the workplace: the implications of occupational segregation; edited by Martha Blaxall and Barbara Reagan. Chicago, 1976. pp. 326. *(Reprinted from a supplement to Signs, vol. 1, no. 3, pt. 2). Papers of a conference, May 1975, sponsored jointly by the American Economic Association Committee on the Status of Women in the Economics Profession and the Center for Research on Women in Higher Education...at Wellesley College.*

— United Kingdom.

ASSOCIATION OF CINEMATOGRAPH AND TELEVISION TECHNICIANS. Patterns of discrimination against women in film and television industries. London, 1975. pp. 62.

— United States.

KOCH (JAMES V.) and CHIZMAR (JOHN F.) The economics of affirmative action. Lexington, Mass., [1976]. pp. 158. *bibliog.*

SEX DISCRIMINATION IN EDUCATION

— New Zealand.

EDUCATION and the equality of the sexes: conference on women and education sponsored by the Committee on Women and the Department of Education, 23-27 November 1975, Victoria University of Wellington. Wellington, Department of Education, 1976. pp. 72. *bibliogs.*

— United States.

FITZPATRICK (BLANCHE E.) Women's inferior education: an economic analysis. New York, 1976. pp. 189. *bibliog.*

SEX DISCRIMINATION IN EMPLOYMENT.

WOMEN and the workplace: the implications of occupational segregation; edited by Martha Blaxall and Barbara Reagan. Chicago, 1976. pp. 326. *(Reprinted from a supplement to Signs, vol. 1, no. 3, pt. 2). Papers of a conference, May 1975, sponsored jointly by the American Economic Association Committee on the Status of Women in the Economics Profession and the Center for Research on Women in Higher Education...at Wellesley College.*

— Law and legislation — United Kingdom.

NATIONAL COUNCIL FOR CIVIL LIBERTIES. A model bill to prevent discrimination on grounds of sex, together with an explanatory memorandum. London, 1974. pp. 25.

DYER (BARBARA) a guide to the Sex Discrimination Bill. London, 1975. pp. 10.

The SEX Discrimination Act and the struggle for women's rights. London, [1976?]. pp. 22. *(Socialist Woman. Fight for Women's Rights Pamphlet Series. No. 1)*

— United Kingdom.

ASSOCIATION OF CINEMATOGRAPH AND TELEVISION TECHNICIANS. Patterns of discrimination against women in film and television industries. London, 1975. pp. 62.

U.K. Department of Health and Social Security. 1976. Pension age: memorandum of evidence to the Equal Opportunities Commission. [London], 1976. pp. 18.

U.K. Equal Opportunities Commission. 1977. Sex equality and the pension age: a choice of routes. [Manchester, 1977?]. pp. 22.

— United States — Illinois.

KOCH (JAMES V.) and CHIZMAR (JOHN F.) The economics of affirmative action. Lexington, Mass., [1976]. pp. 158. *bibliog.*

SEX INSTRUCTION.

EUROPEAN COURT OF HUMAN RIGHTS. Publications. Series A: Judgments and Decisions. [A 23]. ...Case of Kjeldsen, Busk Madsen and Pedersen: judgment of 7 December 1976. Strasbourg, Council of Europe, 1976. pp. 33 [bis]. *In English and French.*

SEX ROLE.

BRITISH SOCIOLOGICAL ASSOCIATION. Annual Conference, 1974. Dependence and exploitation in work and marriage: [papers presented at the conference; edited] by Diana Leonard Barker and Sheila Allen. London, 1976. pp. 265. *bibliog. (British Sociological Association. Explorations in Sociology. 7)*

SCANZONI (LETHA) and SCANZONI (JOHN H.) Men, women and change: a sociology of marriage and family. New York, [1976]. pp. 504. *bibliog.*

DIAMOND (IRENE) Sex roles in the state house. New Haven, 1977. pp. 214.

WOMEN and men: changing roles, relationships and perceptions; [edited by] Libby A. Cater [and others]. New York, [1977]. pp. 277. *bibliogs. Consists of transcriptions of discussions and essays written for a workshop held in Aspen, Colo., August 3-10, 1975, under the auspices of the Aspen Institute for Humanistic Studies.*

SEYCHELLES

— Executive departments.

SEYCHELLES. Lands Department. Annual report. a., 1973 [1st]- [Mahé]. *Supersedes in part SEYCHELLES. Lands and Surveys Department. Annual report.*

SEYCHELLES. Survey Department. Annual report. a., 1973 [1st]- [Mahé]. *Supersedes in part SEYCHELLES. Lands and Survey Department. Annual report.*

— Surveys.

SEYCHELLES. Survey Department. Annual report. a., 1973 [1st]- [Mahé]. *Supersedes in part SEYCHELLES. Lands and Survey Department. Annual report.*

SEYDEWITZ (MAX).

SEYDEWITZ (MAX) Es hat sich gelohnt zu leben: Lebenserinnerungen eines alten Arbeiterfunktionärs. Berlin, 1976. pp. 485.

SHAKESPEARE (WILLIAM).

EWBANK (INGA-STINA) Shakespeare, Ibsen and the unspeakable. [London], 1976. pp. 27.

SHAMANISM

— Colombia.

REICHEL-DOLMATOFF (GERARDO) The shaman and the jaguar: a study of narcotic drugs among the Indians of Colombia. Philadelphia, 1975. pp. 280. *bibliog.*

SHAPOVALOV (ALEKSANDR SIDOROVICH).

SHAPOVALOV (ALEKSANDR SIDOROVICH) Mit Lenin in Sibirien; (autorisierte Übersetzung aus dem Russischen von Maria Einstein). Berlin, [1931]. pp. 47.

SHAUMIAN (STEPAN GEORGIEVICH).

BARSEGIAN (KHIKAR AKOPOVICH) Stepan Georgievich Shaumian. Moskva, 1975. pp. 102. *bibliog. (Kommunisticheskaia Partiia Sovetskogo Soiuza. Tsentral'nyi Komitet. Vysshaia Partiinaia Shkola. Kafedra Zhurnalistiki. Partiinye Publitsisty)*

SHAW (CLIFFORD ROBE).

DELINQUENCY, crime and society; edited by James F. Short. Chicago, [1976]. pp. 325. *bibliogs. Mainly papers originally presented at the Symposium on Juvenile Delinquency, University of Chicago, 1972, held to honour Henry Donald McKay.*

SHAW (GEORGE BERNARD).

TURCO (ALFRED) Shaw's moral vision: the self and salvation. Ithaca, 1976. pp. 297. *bibliog.*

SHEEP

— Australia.

AUSTRALIAN GRAZING INDUSTRY SURVEY, THE: incorporating former sheep industry survey; [pd. by] Bureau of Agricultural Economics. a., 1973/74(1st)- Canberra.

— — Victoria.

AUSTRALIA. Bureau of Agricultural Economics. 1975. Prime lamb production in Victoria: an economic survey. Canberra, 1975. pp. 103. *(Lamb Research Reports. No. 3)*

— United Kingdom.

HOWE (K.S.) The cost of mortality in sheep production in the U.K. 1971-74. Exeter, 1976. pp. 30. *(Exeter. University. Agricultural Economics Unit. Reports. No. 198)*

SHEFFIELD

— Foreign population.

STEEL city Jews: a study of ethnicity and social mobility in the Jewish population of the city of Sheffield, South Yorkshire; by Barry A. Kosmin [and others]. London, 1976. pp. 28.

— Industries.

BARRACLOUGH (K.C.) Sheffield steel. Buxton, [1976]. pp. 112. *bibliog.*

SHETLAND ISLANDS

— Economic conditions.

McNICOLL (IAIN H.) The Shetland economy: an empirical study in regional input-output analysis. Glasgow, [1976]. pp. 56. *bibliog. (Glasgow. University of Strathclyde. Fraser of Allander Institute. Research Monographs. No. 2)*

The SHETLAND way of oil: reactions of a small community to big business; edited by John Button. Sandwick, Shetland, 1976. pp. 134. *bibliog.*

— Social conditions.

The SHETLAND way of oil: reactions of a small community to big business; edited by John Button. Sandwick, Shetland, 1976. pp. 134. *bibliog.*

SHIPBUILDING

— Germany.

PRAGER (HANS GEORG) Blohm and Voss: ships and machinery for the world; translated by Frederick A. Bishop. Herford, [1977]. pp. 271. *bibliog.*

— Sweden.

SWEDEN. Varvskommittén. 1970. De svenska storvarvens problem: betänkande avgivet...den 2 februari 1970. [Stockholm], 1970. fo. 64,53. *(Sweden. I[ndustridepartementet]. Stencil. 1970. 1)*

— United Kingdom.

GOODEY (CHARLES) The first hundred years: the story of Richards shipbuilders. Ipswich, 1976. pp. 111.

— — Scotland.

BROADWAY (FRANK) Upper Clyde Shipbuilders: a study of government intervention in industry; the way the money goes. London, 1976. pp. 58.

MOSS (MICHAEL S.) and HUME (JOHN R.) Workshop of the British Empire: engineering and shipbuilding in the west of Scotland. London, 1977. pp. 192. *bibliog.*

SHIPPING.

SEMINAR ON SHIPPING ECONOMICS, GENEVA, 1966. Shipping and the world economy: report of a seminar...(held in Geneva from 1-12 August, 1966). (TD/14) (TD/B/C.4/17/Rev.1). New York, United Nations, 1966. pp. 36.

UNITED NATIONS. Conference on Trade and Development. 1972. Multinational shipping enterprises: report, etc. (TD/108/Supp. 1/Rev.1). New York, 1972. pp. 24.

UNITED NATIONS. Conference on Trade and Development. 1972. Shipping in the seventies: report. (TD/177). New York, 1972. pp. 42.

ADVANCES in maritime economics; edited by R.O. Goss. Cambridge, 1977. pp. 294.

— Australia — Rates.

AUSTRALIA. Parliament. Senate. Standing Committee on Primary and Secondary Industry and Trade. 1971. Report...on freight rates on Australian National Line shipping services to and from Tasmania; [T.L. Bull, chairman]. in AUSTRALIA. Parliament. Parliamentary papers, 1971, vol.11.

SHIPPING.(Cont.)

— Bangladesh.

BANGLADESH. Provincial Statistical Board and Bureau of Commercial and Industrial Intelligence. Trade supplement: an account relating to the foreign trade, coastal trade, navigation, East Bengal Railway. Statistics and balance of trade of East Pakistan. m., Je 1958. Dacca.

— Canada.

TULCHINSKY (GERALD J. J.) The river barons: Montreal businessmen and the growth of industry and transportation, 1837-53. Toronto, [1977]. pp. 310. *bibliog.*

— Rhine.

STRASBOURG. Port Autonome. Trafics des ports rhénans fran

SHIPPING BOUNTIES AND SUBSIDIES.

HINNEBERG (JOHN WALTER) Seeschiffahrtssubventionen: staatliche Hilfen an einen besonderen Wirtschaftszweig und deren Problematik. Zürich, 1976. pp. 189. *bibliog. Dissertation der Universität Zürich zur Erlangung der Würde eines Doktors der Wirtschaftswissenschaft.*

SHIPPING CONFERENCES.

UNITED NATIONS. Conference on Trade and Development. 1970. The liner conference system: report, etc. (TD/B/C.4/62/Rev.1) . New York, 1970. pp. 100.

UNITED NATIONS. Conference on Trade and Development. 1972. The regulation of liner conferences: a code of conduct for the liner conference system; report, etc. (TD/104/Rev. 1). New York, 1972. pp. 33.

SHIWA

— Rural conditions.

SHIMPO (MITSURU) Three decades in Shiwa: economic development and social change in a Japanese farming community. Vancouver, [1976]. pp. 141. *bibliog.*

SHOEMAKERS

— United Kingdom.

NEWTON (ARTHUR) b. 1902. Years of change: autobiography of a Hackney shoemaker. London, [1974, repr. 1975]. pp. 68. *(Workers' Educational Association. Hackney Branch. A People's Autobiography of Hackney)*

— United States — Massachusetts.

DAWLEY (ALAN) Class and community: the industrial revolution in Lynn. Cambridge, Mass., 1976. pp. 301. *bibliog. (Harvard University. Harvard Studies in Urban History)*

SHOLOKHOV (MIKHAIL ALEKSANDROVICH).

MEDVEDEV (ROI ALEKSANDROVICH) Problems in the literary biography of Mikhail Sholokhov. Cambridge, 1977. pp. 227.

SHOP ASSISTANTS

— Switzerland.

FURRER (MILLY) and WALTER (HEDY) Die wirtschaftliche Lage und die Unterstützungsleistungen von Bürolistinnen und Verkäuferinnen der Stadt Zürich: Ergebnisse einer Umfrage, etc. Zürich, 1939. pp. 32.

SHOP STEWARDS

— Denmark.

MØLLER (IVER HORNEMANN) The effectiveness of shop stewards and supervisors. København, 1976 in progress. *bibliog. (Socialforskningsinstituttet. Studier. Nr. 33)*

MØLLER (IVER HORNEMANN) Tillidsmandens roller. København, 1976. pp. 33. *(Socialforskningsinstituttet. Pjecer. 6)*

— United Kingdom.

HUISKAMP (M.J.) Shop stewards en arbeiderszeggenschap: een onderzoek naar arbeidsverhoudingen in de Britse metaalverwerkende industrie 1830-1975. Alphen aan den Rijn, 1976. pp. 234. *bibliog. With English summary.*

SHAFTO (THOMAS ANTHONY CHESHIRE) An enquiry into the work and problems of shop stewards in selected establishments of the West Midlands; with special reference to differing expectations on their roles and to the development and implications of shop steward factory organisation. 1976. fo. 446. *bibliog. Typescript. Ph.D.(London) thesis: unpublished. This thesis is the property of London University and may not be removed from the Library.*

BATSTONE (ERIC) and others. Shop stewards in action: the organization of workplace conflict and accommodation. Oxford, [1977]. pp. 316. *bibliog. (Warwick Studies in Industrial Relations)*

SHOPPING

— Netherlands.

ECONOMISCH INSTITUUT VOOR HET MIDDEN- EN KLEINBEDRIJF. Bedrijfs- en Sociaaleconomische Publikaties. Wie kopen levensmiddelen bij verbruikersmarkten?; enkele aspecten betreffende de aard van de bezoekers. 's-Gravenhage, 1970. pp. 24.

— Sweden.

HALLOFF (ULF) Inköpsresor i ett rumsligt system: metodstudier på grundval av empiriskt material från några stadsdelar i Göteborg. Stockholm, 1977. pp. 167,11. *bibliog. (Göteborgs Universitet. Geografiska Institutioner. Meddelanden Ser. B. Nr. 57)*

SHROPSHIRE

— Politics and government.

PHILANTHUS, pseud. The Pelham gazette: Pelham and Childe; or, The candidates for Shropshire. Shrewsbury, Howell, 1822. pp. 16.

SIBERIA

— Economic conditions.

BELORUSOV (DMITRII VASIL'EVICH) and others. Problemy razvitiia i razmeshcheniia proizvoditel'nykh sil Zapadnoi Sibiri. Moskva, 1976. pp. 269.

MIKHAILOV (NIKOLA IVANOVICH) Priroda Sibiri: geograficheskie problemy. Moskva, 1976. pp. 158. *bibliog.*

SHABAD (THEODORE) and MOTE (VICTOR L.) Gateway to Siberian resources: the BAM. New York, 1977. pp. 189. *bibliogs.*

— Economic history.

APOLLOVA (NATAL'IA GENNADIEVNA) Khoziaistvennoe osvoenie Priirtysh'ia v kontse XVI - pervoi polovine XIX v. Moskva, 1976. pp. 371.

— Economic policy — Mathematical models.

BANDMAN (MARK KONSTANTINOVICH) ed. Formirovanie territorial'no-proizvodstvennykh kompleksov Angaro- Eniseiskogo regiona: opyt ispol'zovaniia ekonomiko- matematicheskikh modelei v predplanovykh issledovaniiakh. Novosibirsk, 1975. pp. 175. *(Akademiia Nauk SSSR. Sibirskoe Otdelenie. Institut Ekonomiki i Organizatsii Promyshlennogo Proizvodstva. Optimizatsiia Territorial'nykh Sistem) With English summary.*

— Historiography.

ISTORIOGRAFIIA krest'ianstva sovetskoi Sibiri. Novosibirsk, 1976. pp. 477.

— History.

DEKABRISTY i Sibir'. Novosibirsk, 1977. pp. 260.

— Population.

KOLESNIKOV (ALEKSANDR DMITRIEVICH) Russkoe naselenie Zapadnoi Sibiri v XVIII - nachale XIX vv. Omsk, 1973. pp. 439.

— Rural conditions — Research.

SOSKINA (ANNA NOEVNA) Istoriia sotsial'nykh obsledovanii sibirskoi derevni v 20-e gody. Novosibirsk, 1976. pp. 286.

SICILY

— Commerce — Italy.

ABULAFIA (DAVID) The two Italies: economic relations between the Norman kingdom of Sicily and the northern communes. Cambridge, 1977. pp. 310. *bibliog.*

SICK

— Denmark.

SOCIALFORSKNINGSINSTITUTTET. Invalidepensionistundersøgelserne, etc. København, 1976. 2 pts. *bibliog. (Meddelelser. 16,17)*

SIDGWICK (HENRY).

SCHNEEWIND (JEROME B.) Sidgwick's ethics and Victorian moral philosophy. Oxford, 1977. pp. 465. *bibliog.*

SIERRA LEONE

— Description and travel.

MADOX (RICHARD) An Elizabethan in 1582: the diary of Richard Madox, Fellow of All Souls; [edited] by Elizabeth Story Donno. London, 1976. pp. 365. *(Hakluyt Society. Works. 2nd Series. No. 147)*

— Economic conditions.

BANK OF SIERRA LEONE. Economic review. s-a., Ja/Je 1975 (v.9, no. 1/2)- [Freetown].

BANK OF SIERRA LEONE. Economic trends. q., Oc/D 1975- [Freetown].

BANK OF SIERRA LEONE. Research Department. Charts on the economy of Sierra Leone. [Freetown], 1975. 1 pamphlet (unpaged).

SIKORSKI (WLADYSLAW).

KOWALCZYK (JÓZEF) Za kulisami wydarzeń politycznych z lat 1936-1938 w świetle raportów posła Czechosłowacji w Warszawie i innych archiwaliów: [szkice i dokumenty]. Warszawa, 1976. pp. 149.

SILESIA

— Economic conditions.

BARTECZEK (ANDRZEJ) Integracyjna funkcja infrastruktury gospodarczej w świetle badań nad Górnośląskim Okręgiem Przemysłowym. Warszawa, 1977. pp. 139. *bibliog. (Polska Akademia Nauk. Komitet Przestrzennego Zagospodarowania Kraju. Studia. t.59) With Russian and English summaries.*

— History.

BAHR (ERNST) and others. Oberschlesien nach dem Zweiten Weltkrieg: Verwaltung, Bevölkerung, Wirtschaft;...herausgegeben von Richard Breyer. Marburg/Lahn, 1975. pp. 342. *bibliogs. 5 maps in end pocket.*

JANAS (EUGENIUSZ) Działalność pohitlerowskiego zbrojnego podziemia na Śląsku odzyskanym w latach 1945-1947. Opole, 1975. pp. 100. *bibliog.*

— Politics and government.

BENISZ (ADAM) W burzy 'zycia; do druku przygotował Mieczysław Wrzosek. Opole, 1976. pp. 200.

— Population.

BALARYN (JERZY) Sytuacja demograficzna Opolszczyzny po II wojnie swiatowej: studium demograficzne. Opole, 1975. pp. 407. *bibliog.*

SILESIAN PERIODICALS.

SMOŁKA (LEONARD) Prasa polska na Śląsku Opolskim, 1922-1939. Warszawa, 1976. pp. 200. *(Wrocław. Uniwersytet. Acta Universitatis Wratislaviensis. I lo.327. Nauki Polityczne. 8) With German summary.*

SILOS

— France.

MARCHAL (MAURICE) Le nouveau silo portuaire de Strasbourg: sa place dans la politique céréalière française. Strasbourg, 1964. pp. 8.

SILVER MINES AND MINING

— Mexico.

CAMBRIDGE. University. Centre of Latin American Studies. Working Papers. No. 21. British capital and the Mexican silver mining industry, 1820-50; by T.J. Cassidy. Cambridge. [1974]. pp. 24, vii.

SIMMEL (GEORG).

LAWRENCE (PETER A.) Georg Simmel: sociologist and European. Sunbury-on-Thames, 1976. pp. 275.

SIMULATION METHODS.

PRETECEILLE (EDMOND) Jeux, modèles et simulations: critique des jeux urbains. Paris, [1974]. pp. 208. *bibliog.*

SINGAPORE

— Biography.

WHO'S who in Malaysia, 1975-1976 and guide to Singapore; edited and published by J. Victor Morais. Kuala Lumpur, [1976]. 1 vol. (various pagings).

— City planning.

SINGAPORE. Housing and Development Board. 1970. First decade in public housing, 1960-69. Singapore, 1970. pp. 91.

FONSECA (RORY) Planning and land-use in Singapore. Singapore, 1975. pp. 26. *(University of Singapore. Department of Sociology. Working Papers. No. 48)*

— Commerce.

SINGAPORE. Statistics Department. 1974. Memorandum on unit value and volume indices of Singapore external trade: base year 1972 [equals] 100. Singapore, 1974. fo. (12).

SINGAPORE HALF-YEARLY TRADE STATISTICS: imports and exports; [pd. by] Statistics Department. s-a., Ja/Je 1975 (v.1, no.1)- Singapore.

— Economic conditions.

NAIR (C.V. DEVAN) ed. Socialism that works: the Singapore way. Singapore, [1976]. pp. 267.

— History.

RYAN (NEIL JOSEPH) A history of Malaysia and Singapore. Kuala Lumpur, 1976. pp. 322. *bibliog. A revised edition of the 4th edition of the author's The making of modern Malaysia.*

— Nationalism.

CHEN (PETER S.J.) Elites and nation development in Singapore. Singapore, 1975. pp. 15. *bibliog. (University of Singapore. Department of Sociology. Working Papers. No. 46)*

— Politics and government.

KASSIM (ISMAIL) Problems of elite cohesion: a perspective from a minority community. Singapore, [1974]. pp. 146. *bibliog.*

POLITICAL and social change in Singapore; edited by Wu Teh- yao. Singapore, 1975. pp. 202. *(Institute of Southeast Asian Studies. Southeast Asian Perspectives. No. 3)*

CHAN (HENG CHEE) The dynamics of one party dominance: the PAP at the grass-roots. Singapore, [1976]. pp. 272. *bibliog.*

— Population — Bibliography.

SAW (SWEE-HOCK) and CHENG (SIOK-HWA) compilers. A bibliography of the demography of Singapore. Singapore, 1975. pp. 120.

— Social conditions.

HASSAN (RIAZ) Families in flats: a study of low income families in public housing. Singapore, [1977]. pp. 249. *bibliog.*

— Social policy.

POLITICAL and social change in Singapore; edited by Wu Teh- yao. Singapore, 1975. pp. 202. *(Institute of Southeast Asian Studies. Southeast Asian Perspectives. No. 3)*

SINGAPORE STUDENTS IN IRELAND (REPUBLIC).

NG (KWEE CHOO) Singapore students in the United Kingdom and Eire. Singapore, Economics Section, Economic Development Division, 1970. pp. 38.

SINGAPORE STUDENTS IN THE UNITED KINGDOM.

NG (KWEE CHOO) Singapore students in the United Kingdom and Eire. Singapore, Economics Section, Economic Development Division, 1970. pp. 38.

SINGER (ISAAC MERRITT).

BRANDON (RUTH) Singer and the sewing machine: a capitalist romance. London, 1977. pp. 244. *bibliog.*

SINGLE PARENT FAMILY

— United Kingdom.

The FINER report: recommendations and responses; proceedings of a conference held on 20th and 21st February 1975 [by the National Council for One Parent Families]. London, [1975]. pp. 30.

FINER JOINT ACTION COMMITTEE. Housing difficulties of one parent families. London, [1976]. fo. 18.

FINER JOINT ACTION COMMITTEE. The income needs of one parent families. [London, 1976]. pp. 14.

FINER JOINT ACTION COMMITTEE. One-parent families and family courts. London, [1976]. pp. 13,2.

FINER JOINT ACTION COMMITTEE. Parents, children and day care facilities. [London, 1976]. pp. 12,2.

HOPKINSON (ANGELA) Single mothers: the first year: a Scottish study of mothers bringing up their children on their own. Edinburgh, 1976. pp. 256. *bibliog.*

LEWIS (PAUL) Child interim benefit: an interim guide. 2nd ed. London, 1976. pp. 20.

WILSON (HUGH) AND WOMERSLEY (LEWIS) Firm. Inner area study: Liverpool: single parent families. [London], Department of the Environment, [1977]. pp. 31.

SINGLE PEOPLE.

ADAMS (MARGARET) Single blessedness: observations on the single status in married society. London, 1976. pp. 264.

— Dwellings — United Kingdom.

KARN (VALERIE A.) and others. No place that's home: a report on accommodation for homeless young single people in Birmingham. Birmingham, 1974. pp. 99. *bibliog. (Birmingham. University. Centre for Urban and Regional Studies. Research Memoranda. No. 32)*

RAPER (MARTIN) Housing for single young people: (a study related to the demand for existing housing stock). York, 1974. pp. 127. *(York. University. Institute of Advanced Architectural Studies. Research Papers. 7)*

WILSON (HUGH) AND WOMERSLEY (LEWIS) Firm. Inner area study: Liverpool: single and homeless: (an account of four action projects on special housing need). [London], Department of the Environment, [1977]. pp. 73.

WORKING PARTY ON THE PROVISION OF ACCOMMODATION FOR SINGLE PEOPLE. Final report; [S. Woolf, chairman]. [London], 1977. pp. 45.

SISTERS OF CHARITY.

JAMESON (ANNA BROWNELL) Sisters of charity, Catholic and Protestant; and, The communion of labor. [2nd ed.] Boston, [Mass.], 1857; Westport, Conn., 1976. pp. 302. *Facsimile reprint.*

SIT DOWN STRIKES

— United Kingdom.

GRAHAM (ALISTAIR) The workers' next step: the shop-floor struggle and workers' control. London, [1973]. pp. 20. *(Independent Labour Party. Square One Pamphlets. 8)*

GREENWOOD (JOHN A.) Worker sit-ins and job protection: case studies of union intervention. Farnborough, Hants, [1977]. pp. 120. *bibliog.*

SKILLED LABOUR

— Europe.

AUSTRALIA. Tripartite Mission to Study Methods of Training Skilled Workers in Europe. 1970. The training of skilled workers in Europe; report...1968-69. in AUSTRALIA. Parliament. Parliamentary papers, 1970, vol.10.

— Russia.

KLOCHKOV (IVAN DANILOVICH) Sovershenstvovanie podgotovki kvalifitsirovannykh rabochikh. Moskva, 1975. pp. 215. *bibliog.*

— — Turkmenistan.

UMAROVA (AIDZHAN ATAKHANOVNA) Kul'tura, tekhnika, trud. Ashkhabad, 1969. pp. 102.

SLATE

— Russia — Buryat Republic.

BAZHEEV (DANIIL GAVRILOVICH) Ocherki istorii Timliuiskikh tsementnogo i shifernogo zavodov. Ulan-Ude, 1973. pp. 88.

SLAVE TRADE.

PESCATELLO (ANN M.) ed. The African in Latin America; edited with an introduction. New York, [1975]. pp. 270. *bibliog.*

KILSON (MARTIN LUTHER) and ROTBERG (ROBERT IRWIN) eds. The African diaspora: interpretive essays. Cambridge, Mass., 1976. pp. 510.

— Africa.

LIEBER (ERNST) and others. Christenthum und Sklavenfrage: aus den Reden der Abgeordneten Lieber, Schall und A. Bebel in der Reichstagssitzung vom 20. Februar 1894. [Berlin, 1894]. pp. 16.

— Africa, West.

ANSTEY (ROGER T.) and HAIR (PAUL EDWARD HEDLEY) eds. Liverpool, the African slave trade, and abolition: essays to illustrate current knowledge and research. [Liverpool], 1976. pp. 244. *(Historic Society of Lancashire and Cheshire. Occasional Series. vol. 2)*

SLAVE TRADE.(Cont.)

— United Kingdom.

ANSTEY (ROGER T.) and HAIR (PAUL EDWARD HEDLEY) eds. Liverpool, the African slave trade, and abolition: essays to illustrate current knowledge and research. [Liverpool], 1976. pp. 244. *(Historic Society of Lancashire and Cheshire. Occasional Series. vol. 2)*

SLAVERY

— Emancipation.

ANSTEY (ROGER T.) and HAIR (PAUL EDWARD HEDLEY) eds. Liverpool, the African slave trade, and abolition: essays to illustrate current knowledge and research. [Liverpool], 1976. pp. 244. *(Historic Society of Lancashire and Cheshire. Occasional Series. vol. 2)*

— History — Sources.

IRWIN (GRAHAM W.) ed. Africans abroad: a documentary history of the black diaspora in Asia, Latin America, and the Caribbean during the age of slavery. New York, 1977. pp. 408. *bibliog.*

SLAVERY IN BRAZIL.

GOULART (MAURICIO) Escravidão africana no Brasil: das origens a extinção do trafico. São Paulo, 1975. pp. 300. *bibliog.*

DEAN (WARREN) Rio Clara: a Brazilian plantation system, 1820-1920. Stanford, Calif., 1976. pp. 234.

SLAVERY IN CHILE

— Emancipation.

FELIU CRUZ (GUILLERMO) La abolicion de la esclavitud en Chile: estudio historico y social. 2nd ed. Santiago de Chile, [1973]. pp. 185. *bibliog. First published in 1942.*

SLAVERY IN EAST AFRICA.

COOPER (FREDERICK) Plantation slavery on the East coast of Africa. New Haven, 1977. pp. 314. *bibliog. (Yale University. Yale Historical Publications. Miscellany. 113)*

SLAVERY IN INDIA.

PEGGS (JAMES) India's cries to British humanity, relative to infanticide, British connection with idolatry, Ghaut murders, suttee, slavery, and colonization in India; to which are added, humane hints for the melioration of the state of society in British India. London, 1832. pp. 500.

SLAVERY IN JAMAICA.

CAMPBELL (MAVIS CHRISTINE) The dynamics of change in a slave society: a sociopolitical history of the free coloreds of Jamaica, 1800-1865. Cranbury, N.J., [1976]. pp. 393. *bibliog.*

HIGMAN (B.W.) Slave population and economy in Jamaica, 1807-1834. Cambridge, 1976. pp. 327. *bibliog.*

SLAVERY IN LATIN AMERICA.

PESCATELLO (ANN M.) ed. The African in Latin America; edited with an introduction. New York, [1975]. pp. 270. *bibliog.*

ROUT (LESLIE B.) The African experience in Spanish America: 1502 to the present day. Cambridge, 1976. pp. 404. *bibliog.*

CLEMENTI (HEBE) La abolicion de la esclavitud en America Latina. Buenos Aires, [1974]. pp. 219. *bibliog.*

SLAVERY IN NORTH AFRICA.

CLISSOLD (STEPHEN) The Barbary slaves. London, 1977. pp. 181.

SLAVERY IN THE UNITED KINGDOM

— Antislavery movements.

MARSHALL (PETER D.) Bristol and the abolition of slavery: the politics of emancipation. Bristol, 1975. pp. 28,iv. *bibliog. (Historical Association. Bristol Branch. Local History Pamphlets. No. 37)*

SLAVERY IN THE UNITED STATES.

MULLIN (MICHAEL) ed. American negro slavery: a documentary history. New York, 1976. pp. 283.

RECKONING with slavery: a critical study in the quantitative history of American Negro slavery; by Paul A. David [and others]; with an introduction by Kenneth M. Stampp. New York, 1976. pp. 398. *bibliog.*

LASLETT (PETER) Family life and illicit love in earlier generations: essays in historical sociology. Cambridge, 1977. pp. 270. *bibliog.*

— Antislavery movements.

SEWELL (RICHARD HERBERT) Ballots for freedom: antislavery politics in the United States, 1837-1860. New York, 1976. pp. 379.

WALTERS (RONALD G.) The antislavery appeal: American abolitionism after 1830. Baltimore, [1976]. pp. 196. *bibliog.*

SCHOR (JOEL A.) Henry Highland Garnet: a voice of black radicalism in the nineteenth century. Westport, Conn., 1977. pp. 250. *bibliog.*

— Emancipation.

SCHOR (JOEL A.) Henry Highland Garnet: a voice of black radicalism in the nineteenth century. Westport, Conn., 1977. pp. 250. *bibliog.*

SLAVERY IN THE WEST INDIES.

SYNNOTT (ANTHONY JASPER NICHOLAS) Slave revolts in the Caribbean. 1976. pp. 454. *bibliog. Typescript. Ph.D.(London) thesis: unpublished. This thesis is the property of London University and may not be removed from the Library.*

SLOVAKIA

— History.

ŠTÚDIE o Slovenskom národnom povstaní; (venované 30. výročiu Slovenského národneho povstania a oslobodenia Československa Sovietskou armádou). Bratislava, 1975. pp. 229. *With Russian and English summaries.*

BROCK (PETER) The Slovak national awakening: an essay in the intellectual history of east central Europe. Toronto, [1976]. pp. 104. *bibliog.*

— Nationalism.

BROCK (PETER) The Slovak national awakening: an essay in the intellectual history of east central Europe. Toronto, [1976]. pp. 104. *bibliog.*

— Social conditions.

SOCIÁLNE premeny Slovenska. Bratislava, 1975. pp. 197.

SLOVENES IN CARINTHIA.

KALT (HANS) Minderheiten in Österreich: worum geht es eigentlich? [Vienna, 1976]. pp. 30.

SLOVENSKÁ L'UDOVA STRANA.

JELINEK (YESHAYAHU) The parish republic: Hlinka's Slovak People's Party, 1939-1945. New York, 1976. pp. 204. *bibliog. (East European Quarterly. East European Monographs. 14)*

SLUMS

— Denmark — Copenhagen.

PLOVSING (JAN) Beboere under sanering, etc. København, 1976. pp. 353. *bibliog. (Socialforskningsinstituttet. Publikationer. 71) With English summary.*

— United Kingdom.

ENGLISH (JOHN) and others. Slum clearance: the social and administrative context in England and Wales. London, 1976. pp. 223.

— — North Shields.

WESTERN AREA ACTION GROUP [NORTH SHIELDS]. A report on the findings of the survey of the western area carried out during April 1974 by members of the action group with the assistance of the North Tyneside Community Development Project. [North Shields, North Tyneside Community Development Project], 1974. fo. 29.

SOUTH MEADOWELL ACTION COMMITTEE and BARMOUTH WAY ACTION GROUP. The forgotten slums; a joint report. [North Shields, North Tyneside Community Development Project], 1975. fo. 11.

PERCY MAIN PUSHERS CLEARANCE GROUP. We want action!: report on the Percy Main clearance area. [North Shields, North Tyneside Community Development Project], 1976. fo.11.

SMALL BUSINESS

— Management.

PRODUCTIVITY through consultancy in small industrial enterprises. Tokyo, Asian Productivity Organization, [1974]. pp. 504.

— Australia.

AUSTRALIA. Office of Aboriginal Affairs. Commonwealth Capital Fund for Aboriginal Enterprises. Annual report. a., 1968/69 (1st)- Canberra. *Included in AUSTRALIA. Parliament. [Parliamentary papers].*

— Brazil.

WIPPLINGER (GUENTER) Kleine und mittlere Industrieunternehmen in Brasilien: Strukturen, Probleme, Förderung. Tübingen, [1976]. pp. 170. *bibliog. (Institut für Iberoamerika-Kunde. Schriftenreihe. Band 27)*

— European Economic Community countries.

EUROPEAN COMMUNITIES. Economic and Social Committee. 1975. The situation of small and medium-sized undertakings in the European Community. Brussels, 1975. pp. 66. *(Studies)*

— France.

FRANÇOIS (JEAN PAUL) Les entreprises moyennes dans l'économie industrielle;...avec la collaboration de R. Stutzman et J.F. Minder. Paris, [1976]. pp. 228. *(France. Ministère de l'Industrie et de la Recherche. Service du Traitement de l'Information et des Statistiques Industrielles. Traits Fondamentaux du Système Industriel Français. 2)*

— Germany.

NOLL (ADOLF) Sozio-ökonomischer Strukturwandel des Handwerks in der zweiten Phase der Industrialisierung: unter besonderer Berücksichtigung der Regierungsbezirke Arnsberg und Münster. Göttingen, 1975. pp. 386. *bibliog. (Fritz Thyssen Stiftung. Neunzehntes Jahrhundert. Studien zum Wandel von Gesellschaft und Bildung im Neunzehnten Jahrhundert. Band 10)*

BANNOCK (GRAHAM) The smaller business in Britain and Germany. London, 1976. pp. 152. *bibliog.*

— Kenya.

SMALL scale enterprise; proceedings of a conference organized by the Institute for Development Studies, University of Nairobi, and held at Masai Lodge, Nairobi, 26 and 27 February, 1973...; edited by Frank C. Child and Mary E. Kempe. Nairobi, 1973. pp. 157. *bibliogs. (University of Nairobi. Institute for Development Studies. Occasional Papers. No. 6)*

— Nigeria.

LEWIS (A. OLUFEMI) and OGUNTUASE (E.K.) Small-scale industries: North-Eastern State of Nigeria;...assisted by E.K. Oguntuase. Ile-Ife, Nigeria, 1974. pp. 150.

— Peru.

MINKNER (MECHTHILD) Kleinindustrie in Peru: Entwicklungsprobleme und -perspektiven. Tübingen, [1976]. 1 vol.(various pagings). *bibliog. (Institut für Iberoamerika-Kunde. Schriftenreihe. Band 26)*

— United Kingdom.

GIBSON (P.B.R.) Boards of directors in small/medium sized private companies: a survey of the composition of boards of directors in 289 private companies. London, [1970]. pp. 21. *bibliog. (British Institute of Management. Information Summaries. No. 149)*

ALDRICH (HOWARD) and FEIT (STEPHANIE) Black entrepreneurs in England: a summary of the literature and some suggestions for further research. 1975. fo. 40. *bibliog. Typescript: unpublished.*

BANNOCK (GRAHAM) The smaller business in Britain and Germany. London, 1976. pp. 152. *bibliog.*

MINTER (MICHAEL) Death by taxation: the threat to the smaller firm. London, [1976?]. pp. 11.

SMALL GROUPS.

WHYTE (MARTIN KING) Small groups and political rituals in China. Berkeley, Calif., [1975]. pp. 271. *(Michigan University. Center for Chinese Studies. Michigan Studies on China) First published in 1974.*

SMALL HOLDINGS

— Malawi.

MALAWI. Department of Census and Statistics. 1968. A sample survey of agricultural small holdings in the lower Shire Valley, Malawi, September-October, 1967. Zomba, [1968?]. pp. 96.

SMITH (ADAM).

FOLEY (VERNARD) The social physics of Adam Smith. West Lafayette, Ind., 1976. pp. 265. *bibliog.*

The MARKET and the state: essays in honour of Adam Smith. Oxford, 1976. pp. 359. *Papers presented at a conference at the University of Glasgow, April 1976, to mark the bicentenary of the publication of the Wealth of nations.*

WEST (EDWIN GEORGE) Adam Smith: (the man and his works). Indianapolis, [1976]. pp. 254. *bibliog.*

SMITH (ADAM) LL.D., F.R.S. The correspondence of Adam Smith; edited by Ernest Campbell Mossner and Ian Simpson Ross. Oxford, 1977. pp. 441. *bibliog. (Glasgow. University. Glasgow Edition of the Works and Correspondence of Adam Smith)*

SMOKING

— Statistics.

LEE (P.N.) ed. Tobacco consumption in various countries. 4th ed. London, 1975. pp. 85. *(Tobacco Research Council. Research Papers. [No.] 6)*

TOBACCO RESEARCH COUNCIL. Statistics of smoking in the United Kingdom; edited by P.N. Lee; compiled by M.J. Wilson. 7th ed. London, 1976. pp. 119. *(Tobacco Research Council. Research Papers. 1)*

SMUGGLING

— United Kingdom.

[GRAY (JEFFERY)] A proposal fully to prevent the smugling of wool, which...also adds more than ten millions yearly to the trade of the British nation, etc. London, printed for the Author, and sold by W. Meadows, 1732. pp. 32. *Signed Philo-Britannicus.*

SNEEVLIET (HENDRICUS JOSEPHUS FRANCISCUS MARIE).

PERTHUS (MAX) pseud. [i.e. Pieter Pleunis van 't HART] Henk Sneevliet, revolutionair-socialist in Europa en Azië. Nijmegen, [1976]. pp. 512. *bibliog.*

SOBELL (MORTON).

SOBELL (MORTON) On doing time. Toronto, 1976. pp. 436. *Originally published in New York, 1974.*

SOCIAL ACTION.

HOLLIS (MARTIN) Models of man: philosophical thoughts on social action. Cambridge, 1977. pp. 198. *bibliog.*

SOCIAL CASE WORK.

PINCUS (ALLEN) and MINAHAN (ANNE) Social work practice: model and method. Itasca, Ill., [1973] repr. 1975. pp. 355. *bibliog.*

NURSTEN (JEAN PATRICIA) Process of casework. London, 1974. pp. 234. *bibliog.*

RAGG (NICHOLAS M.) People not cases: a philosophical approach to social work. London, 1977. pp. 159. *bibliog.*

SMALE (GERALD G.) Prophecy, behaviour and change: an examination of self-fulfilling prophecies in helping relationships. London, 1977. pp. 103. *bibliog.*

TIMMS (NOEL) and TIMMS (RITA) Perspectives in social work. London, 1977. pp. 233. *bibliog.*

SOCIAL CHANGE.

RUSSELL (BERTRAND ARTHUR WILLIAM) 3rd Earl Russell. Bertrand Russell speaks his mind. Darmstadt, 1976. pp. 175. *Transcript of a television series of 13 interviews with Bertrand Russell, by Woodrow Wyatt. Originally published in 1960 by the World Publishing Company, Cleveland.*

KINDERMANN (GOTTFRIED KARL) ed. Kulturen im Umbruch: Studien zur Problematik und Analyse des Kulturwandels in Entwicklungsländern. Freiburg im Breisgau, [1962]. pp. 422. *bibliogs.*

SELSAM (HOWARD) and others, eds. Dynamics of social change: a reader in Marxist social science from the writings of Marx, Engels and Lenin; selected and edited with introduction and notes. New York, [1970]. pp. 416. *bibliog.*

SEN GUPTA (BADAL) Sozialer Wandel im ländlichen Indien: fördernde und hemmende Faktoren der Ergebnisse der Diffusion und Adoption der Innovationen "lokale Selbstverwaltung", etc. [Nürnberg, 1972]. pp. 332. *bibliog. Inaugural-Dissertation zur Erlangung des Grades eines Doktors der Wirtschafts- und Sozialwissenschaften der Friedrich-Alexander-Universität Erlangen-Nürnberg.*

WHITELOCK (NOREEN BLYTH) The choice is yours. Weybridge, [1973]. pp. 138.

FALLERS (LLOYD A.) The social anthropology of the nation-state. Chicago, 1974. pp. 171. *bibliog. (Rochester, N.Y. University. Lewis Henry Morgan Lectures. 1971)*

CAPLOW (THEODORE) Toward social hope. New York, [1975]. pp. 229.

GLABERMAN (MARTIN) The working class and social change; four essays on the working class. Toronto, 1975. pp. 41.

KAUTSKY (JOHN HANS) Patterns of modernizing revolutions: Mexico and the Soviet Union. Beverly Hills, [1975]. pp. 59. *bibliog.*

RANKIN (H.D.) Pentheus and Plato: a study in social disintegration; an inaugural lecture delivered at the University [of Southampton] 20 November 1975. Southampton, 1975. pp. 32.

GARAUDY (ROGER) Le projet espérance. Paris, [1976]. pp. 218.

HIRST (PAUL QUENTIN) Social evolution and sociological categories. London, 1976. pp. 135. *bibliog.*

LANTZ (HERMAN R.) Marital incompatibility and social change in early America. Beverly Hills, [1976]. pp. 48. *bibliog.*

MAIN currents in Indian sociology. 1. Contemporary India: some sociological perspectives; edited by Giri Raj Gupta. Durham, North Carolina, [1976]. pp. 328. *bibliogs.*

MOSCOVICI (SERGE) Social influence and social change. London, 1976. pp. 239. *bibliog. (European Association of Experimental Social Psychology. European Monographs in Social Psychology. 10)*

RURAL social change in Poland; editors: Jan Turowski [and] Lili Maria Szwengrub. Wrocław, 1976. pp. 334. *bibliogs. Edited on the occasion of the Fourth World Congress for Rural Sociology, Toruń, Poland, 1976, and Ninth Congress of the European Society for Rural Sociology.*

WHYTE (WILLIAM FOOTE) and ALBERTI (GIORGIO) Power, politics and progress: social change in rural Peru. New York, [1976]. pp. 307. *bibliog.*

ESSAYS on economic development and cultural change, in honor of Bert F. Hoselitz: Manning Nash, editor. [Chicago, 1977]. pp. 460. *bibliog.*

HARE (ALEXANDER PAUL) and BLUMBERG (HERBERT H.) eds. Liberation without violence: a third-party approach. London, 1977. pp. 368. *bibliog. Reprinted from various sources.*

LORAINE (JOHN A.) Syndromes of the seventies: population, sex and social change. London, 1977. pp. 217. *bibliog.*

STEWARD (JULIAN HAYNES) Evolution and ecology: essays on social transformation; edited by Jane C. Steward and Robert F. Murphy. Urbana, Ill., [1977]. pp. 406. *bibliogs.*

WILHELM (DONALD) Creative alternatives to communism: guidelines for tomorrow's world. London, 1977. pp. 173.

SOCIAL CLASSES.

ANDERSON (CHARLES HOYT) The political economy of social class. Englewood Cliffs, [1974]. pp. 340.

LUNDBERG (MARGARET J.) The incomplete adult: social class constraints on personality development. Westport, Conn., [1974]. pp. 245. *bibliog.*

ADLAM (DIANA S.) Code in context. London, 1977. pp. 253. *bibliog.*

BRITISH SOCIOLOGICAL ASSOCIATION. Annual Conference, 1975. Industrial society: class, cleavage and control; edited by Richard Scase. London, 1977. pp. 221. *bibliog. (British Sociological Association. Explorations in Sociology. 8)*

MITRA (ASHOK) Terms of trade and class relations: an essay in political economy. London, 1977. pp. 193.

— Africa.

MARKOVITZ (IRVING LEONARD) Power and class in Africa: an introduction to change and conflict in African politics. Englewood Cliffs, N.J., [1977]. pp. 398. *bibliog.*

— Africa, Subsaharan.

MANGHEZI (ALPHEUS) Class, elite and community in African development. Uppsala, 1976. pp. 118. *bibliog.*

SILVEIRA (ONESIMO) Africa south of the Sahara: party systems and ideologies of socialism. Uppsala, [1976]. pp. 212. *bibliog. (Uppsala, Statsvetenskapliga Föreningen. Skrifter. 71) Doctoral thesis, Uppsala University, 1976.*

— Argentine Republic.

PEÑA (MILCIADES) Industria, burguesia industrial y liberacion nacional. Buenos Aires, 1974. pp. 195.

GASTIAZORO (EUGENIO) Argentina hoy: latifundio, dependencia y estructura de clases. 3rd ed. Buenos Aires, 1975. pp. 236.

— Australia.

CONNELL (ROBERT WILLIAM) Ruling class, ruling culture: studies of conflict, power and hegemony in Australian life. Cambridge, 1977. pp. 250.

— Brazil.

MARTINS (JOSÉ DE SOUZA) Agriculture and industry in Brazil: two studies. Cambridge, 1977. pp. 32. *(Cambridge. University. Centre of Latin American Studies. Working Papers. No. 27)*

— Canada.

FORCESE (DENNIS P.) The Canadian class structure. Toronto, [1975]. pp. 148. *bibliog.*

— Chile.

REVOLUCION y contrarrevolucion en Chile; [by] Volker Lühr y otros; (traducido de la edicion alemana por Francisco Zanutigh Nuñez). Buenos Aires, [1974]. pp. 195.

CASTELLS (MANUEL) La lucha de clases en Chile. [Buenos Aires], 1974 [or rather 1975]. pp. 435.

— France.

QUIN (CLAUDE) Classes sociales et union du peuple de France. Paris, [1976]. pp. 221. *bibliog.*

MARCEAU (JANE) Class and status in France: economic change and social immobility 1945-1975. Oxford, 1977. pp. 217. *bibliog.*

— Germany.

MATERIALIEN zur Klassenstruktur der BRD. 2. Teil. Grundriss der Klassenverhältnisse, 1950-1970; ([by] Projekt Klassenanalyse). Westberlin, [1974]. pp. 591. *First part out of print.*

— Guatemala.

MENDEZ DOMINGUEZ (ALFREDO) Zaragoza: la estratificacion social de una comunidad ladina guatemalteca. Guatemala, 1967. pp. 264. *bibliog. (Guatemala. Seminario de Integracion Social Guatemalteca. Publicaciones. No. 21)*

GUZMAN-BÖCKLER (CARLOS) and HERBERT (JEAN LOUP) Guatemala: una interpretacion historico-social. Mexico, 1970 repr. 1975. pp. 205. *bibliog.*

— India.

BHATT (ANIL) Caste, class and politics: an empirical profile of social stratification in modern India. Delhi, 1975. pp. 224. *bibliog.*

— Italy.

BARBANO (FILIPPO) Classi e struttura sociale in Italia: studi e ricerche, 1955- 1975. Torino, 1976. pp. 397. *bibliog.*

— Lebanon.

DUBAR (CLAUDE) and NASR (SALIM) Les classes sociales au Liban. [Paris, 1976]. pp. 365. *(Fondation Nationale des Sciences Politiques. Cahiers. 204.)*

— Mexico.

BARTRA (ROGER) Estructura agraria y clases sociales en Mexico. Mexico, 1974. pp. 182. *bibliog.*

— Peru.

VAN DEN BERGHE (PIERRE LOUIS) and PRIMOV (GEORGE P.) Inequality in the Peruvian Andes: class and ethnicity in Cuzco. Columbia, Mo., [1977]. pp. 324. *bibliog.*

— Portugal.

COSTA (RAMIRO DA) O desenvolvimento do capitalismo em Portugal. Lisboa, 1975 repr. 1976. pp. 219. *bibliog.*

— Puerto Rico.

QUINTERO RIVERA (ANGEL GUILLERMO) The working class and Puerto Rican politics in the process of change from a traditional to a capitalist agricultural economy. 1976. fo. 464. *bibliog. Ph.D.(London) thesis: unpublished. This thesis is the property of London University and may not be removed from the Library.*

— Russia.

IZMENENIIA sotsial'noi struktury sovetskogo obshchestva, oktiabr' 1917-1920. Moskva, 1976. pp. 343.

— — Latvia.

ZILE (LIUBOV' IAKOVLEVNA) Periody i etapy stroitel'stva sotsializma i izmenenie sotsial'noi struktury obshchestva: na materialakh Latviiskoi SSR. Riga, 1975. pp. 198.

— Rwanda.

LINDEN (IAN) Church and revolution in Rwanda. Manchester, [1977]. pp. 304. *bibliog.*

— Sweden.

SCASE (RICHARD) Social democracy in capitalist society: working class politics in Britain and Sweden. London, [1977]. pp. 184. *bibliog. Revision of author's thesis (Ph.D.), University of Kent, 1974.*

— Underdeveloped areas.

See UNDERDEVELOPED AREAS — Social classes.

— United Kingdom.

ZWEIG (FERDYNAND) The new acquisitive society. Chichester, 1976. pp. 144.

The FRAGMENTARY class structure; [by] K. Roberts [and others]. London, 1977. pp. 200. *bibliog.*

HAWKINS (PETER R.) Social class, the nominal group and verbal strategies. London, 1977. pp. 242. *bibliog.*

LABOUR RESEARCH DEPARTMENT. Inequality in Britain today. London, 1977. pp. 31.

REID (IVAN) Social class differences in Britain: a sourcebook. London, 1977. pp. 266. *bibliog.*

SAUNDERS (P.R.) Housing tenure and class interests. Brighton, 1977. fo.22. *(Brighton. University of Sussex. Sussex Working Papers in Urban and Regional Studies. 6)*

SCASE (RICHARD) Social democracy in capitalist society: working class politics in Britain and Sweden. London, [1977]. pp. 184. *bibliog. Revision of author's thesis (Ph.D.), University of Kent, 1974.*

— United States.

SENNETT (RICHARD) and COBB (JONATHAN) The hidden injuries of class. Cambridge, 1977. pp. 275. *bibliog. First published in the United States in 1972.*

GREELEY (ANDREW M.) Ethnicity, denomination and inequality. Beverly Hills, [1976]. pp. 85. *bibliog.*

CURTIS (RICHARD FARNSWORTH) and JACKSON (ELTON F.) Inequality in American communities. New York, [1977]. pp. 354. *bibliog.*

— — Massachusetts.

DAWLEY (ALAN) Class and community: the industrial revolution in Lynn. Cambridge, Mass., 1976. pp. 301. *bibliog. (Harvard University. Harvard Studies in Urban History)*

SOCIAL CONDITIONS.

GALBRAITH (JOHN KENNETH) The age of uncertainty. London, 1977. pp. 366. *Published by the BBC simultaneously with the release of the television series of the same name.*

SOCIAL CONFLICT.

EHRENBERG (RICHARD) Klassenkampf und Sozialfrieden: weitere sozialphysikalische Klärung. Jena, 1922. pp. 35. *(Sonderabdruck aus Archiv für exakte Wirtschaftsforschung, Bd.IX, Heft 4)*

DUKE (JAMES T.) Conflict and power in social life. Provo, Utah, [1976]. pp. 287.

FREEDOM and constraint: a memorial tribute to Max Gluckman; edited by Myron J. Aronoff. Assen, 1976. pp. 179. *bibliogs.*

BINNS (DAVID) Beyond the sociology of conflict. London, 1977. pp. 257. *bibliog.*

— Africa, Subsaharan.

BOZEMAN (ADDA BRUEMMER) Conflict in Africa: concepts and realities. Princeton, N.J., 1976. pp. 429. *bibliog.*

— America, Latin.

CARVALHO-NETO (PAULO DE) El folklore de las luchas sociales: un ensayo de folklore y marxismo. [Mexico], 1973. pp. 217. *bibliog.*

— Australia.

CONNELL (ROBERT WILLIAM) Ruling class, ruling culture: studies of conflict, power and hegemony in Australian life. Cambridge, 1977. pp. 250.

— Chile.

CASTELLS (MANUEL) La lucha de clases en Chile. [Buenos Aires], 1974 [or rather 1975]. pp. 435.

— China.

LUBMAN (STANLEY) Mao and mediation: politics and dispute resolution in communist China. Berkeley, Calif., [1968]. pp. 1284-1359. *(California University. Centre for Chinese Studies. China Series Reprints. No. C-3) (Reprinted from California Law Review, 1967, vol. 55, no. 5)*

— Mexico.

DURAND (PIERRE) Nanacatlan: société paysanne et lutte des classes au Mexique. Montréal, 1975. pp. 257. *bibliog.*

— Poland.

SZCZYGIEŁ (RYSZARD) Konflikty społeczne w Lublinie w pierwszej połowie XVI wieku. Warszawa, 1977. pp. 197. *bibliog. (Lubelskie Towarzystwo Naukowe. Wydział Humanistyczny. Prace. Monografie. t.6)*

— Scandinavia.

PETERSEN (CARL HEINRICH) Fra klassekampens slagmark i Norden. [Århus], 1973. pp. 252. *bibliog. Selection of broadcasts, articles and essays.*

— Spain.

BERNAL (ANTONIO MIGUEL) La propiedad de la tierra y las luchas agrarias andaluzas. Barcelona, [1974]. pp. 189.

— Underdeveloped areas.

See UNDERDEVELOPED AREAS — Social conflict.

SOCIAL CONTROL.

BRITISH SOCIOLOGICAL ASSOCIATION. Annual Conference, 1975. Industrial society: class, cleavage and control; edited by Richard Scase. London, 1977. pp. 221. *bibliog. (British Sociological Association. Explorations in Sociology. 8)*

CARLTON (ERIC JAMES) Ideology and social order. London, 1977. pp. 320. *bibliog.*

LOBE (THOMAS) United States national security policy and aid to the Thailand police. Denver, Col., [1977]. pp. 161. *(Denver. University. Social Science Foundation and Graduate School of International Studies. Monograph Series in World Affairs. vol. 14, no. 2)*

SOCIAL DEMOCRATIC AND LABOUR PARTY.

McALLISTER (IAN) The Northern Ireland Social Democratic and Labour Party: political opposition in a divided society. London, 1977. pp. 200. *bibliog.*

SOCIAL DEMOCRATIC PARTY (GERMANY).

BLUM (HANS GEORG MAXIMILIAN) Die Lügen unserer Sozialdemokratie: eine historische Dokumentation; (herausgegeben von Bernhard C. Wintzek). Asendorf, 1977. pp. xiv, 422. *Reprint, with new introduction, of work originally published in Wismar in 1891.*

FALK (KURT) Die Bestrebungen der Socialdemokratie, beleuchtet vom Irrsinn Eugen Richters. Nürnberg, 1891. pp. 70.

AUER (IGNAZ) Sedanfeier und Sozialdemokratie: eine Rede. [Berlin, 1895?]. pp. 15. *Wanting title-page.*

HACKMACK (HANS) Die sozialistische Jugendbewegung. Berlin, [1918]. pp. 39.

SOZIALDEMOKRATISCHE PARTEI DEUTSCHLANDS. Unser Programm in Wort und Bild. [Berlin, 1931]. pp. 73.

FECHNER (MAX) Wege und Ziele der Sozialdemokratie: Rede...am 13. Oktober 1945 in der Sozialistischen Tribüne. Berlin, [1945]. pp. 15.

SCHUMACHER (KURT) 1895-1952. Das Referat im Berliner Poststadion; im Anhang: Die Kundgebung der Sozialdemokratischen Partei, angenommen auf dem Parteitag in Hannover. [Berlin-Wilmersdorf, 1946]. pp. 16.

SOZIALDEMOKRATISCHE PARTEI DEUTSCHLANDS. Das Heidelberger Programm, beschlossen auf dem Parteitag...in Heidelberg am 18. September 1925. Offenbach a.M., 1947. pp. 116.

BARTEL (HORST) Friedrich Engels' Kampf für die Schaffung einer marxistischen Arbeiterpartei in Deutschland: Engels-Konferenz, Berlin, 1955. Berlin, 1956. pp. 96.

SOZIALDEMOKRATISCHE PARTEI DEUTSCHLANDS. Langzeitprogramm 1: (Entwurf eines ökonomisch-politischen Orientierungsrahmens für die Jahre 1973-1985): Texte. Bonn-Bad Godesberg, [1972]. pp. 216.

PROGRAMMATISCHE Dokumente der deutschen Sozialdemokratie; herausgegeben und eingeleitet von Dieter Dowe und Kurt Klotzbach. Berlin, [1973]. pp. 387. *bibliog.*

SOZIALDEMOKRATISCHE PARTEI DEUTSCHLANDS. Langzeitprogramm 5: Beiträge zu Einzelproblemen des "Entwurfs eines ökonomisch-politischen Orientierungsrahmens für die Jahre 1973-1985" herausgegeben von Helmut Schmidt und Hans-Jochen Vogel. Bonn-Bad Godesberg, [1973]. pp. 130.

INSTITUT FÜR MARXISTISCHE STUDIEN UND FORSCHUNGEN. Aus der Geschichte der deutschen Arbeiterjugendbewegung, 1904- 1945: (Dokumente und Materialien). Frankfurt/Main, 1975. pp. 169. *(Institut für Marxistische Studien und Forschungen. Neudrucke zur Sozialistischen Theorie und Gewerkschaftspraxis. Band 7)*

KRAUSE (WOLFGANG) and others. Zwischen Anpassung und sozialistischer Politik: zur Geschichte der Jungsozialisten seit 1945. Berlin, 1975. pp. 146.

AKTUELLE Bedeutung der Marxschen Randglossen zum Gothaer Programm; (Autoren: Wolfgang Heinrichs [and others]). Berlin, 1976. pp. 140. *(Akademie der Wissenschaften der DDR. Zentralinstitut für Wirtschaftswissenschaften. Forschungsberichte. Nr.18)*

BUEDINGER TAGUNG, 1973-1975. Führende Kräfte und Gruppen in der deutschen Arbeiterbewegung, 1904-1975; herausgegeben von Hanns Hubert Hofmann. Limburg/Lahn, 1976. pp. 226. *(Ranke-Gesellschaft. Deutsche Führungsschichten in der Neuzeit. Gesamtreihe. Band 9)*

ERLER (HANS) Fritz Erler contra Willy Brandt: Demokratie oder Volksfront in Europa. Stuttgart, 1976. pp. 208.

FRICKE (DIETER) Die deutsche Arbeiterbewegung, 1869 bis 1914: ein Handbuch über ihre Organisation und Tätigkeit im Klassenkampf. Westberlin, [1976]. pp. 976. *bibliog.*

GRASMANN (PETER) Sozialdemokraten gegen Hitler, 1933-1945. München, [1976]. pp. 163. *bibliog.*

HUBER (WOLFGANG) and SCHWERDTFEGER (JOHANNES) eds. Frieden, Gewalt, Sozialismus: Studien zur Geschichte der sozialistischen Arbeiterbewegung. Stuttgart, [1976]. pp. 850. *bibliogs. (Evangelische Studiengemeinschaft. Forschungen und Berichte. Band 32)*

LIEBKNECHT (WILHELM PHILIPP MARTIN CHRISTIAN LUDWIG) Kleine politische Schriften; (herausgegeben von Wolfgang Schröder). Leipzig, 1976. pp. 413.

LODGE (JULIET) The European policy of the SPD. Beverly Hills, [1976]. pp. 95. *bibliog.*

NA'AMAN (SHLOMO) ed. Von der Arbeiterbewegung zur Arbeiterpartei: der Fünfte Vereinstag der Deutschen Arbeitervereine zu Nürnberg im Jahre 1868; eine Dokumentation. Berlin, 1976. pp. 186. *bibliog. (IWK: internationale wissenschaftliche Korrespondenz zur Geschichte der deutschen Arbeiterbewegung. Beihefte. 4)*

SCHACHT (KURT) Bilanz sozialdemokratischer Reformpolitik. Frankfurt am Main, 1976. pp. 114.

SCHARRER (MANFRED) Arbeiterbewegung im Obrigkeitsstaat: SPD und Gewerkschaft nach dem Sozialistengesetz. Berlin, [1976]. pp. 127. *bibliog.*

SCHULZ (URSULA) ed. Die deutsche Arbeiterbewegung, 1848-1919, in Augenzeugenberichten. München, 1976. pp. 437. *bibliog.*

STRUTYNSKI (PETER) Die Auseinandersetzungen zwischen Marxisten und Revisionisten in der deutschen Arbeiterbewegung um die Jahrhundertwende. Köln, [1976]. pp. 344. *bibliog.*

THIEL (JUERGEN) Die Grossblockpolitik der Nationalliberalen Partei Badens, 1905 bis 1914: ein Beitrag zur Zusammenarbeit von Liberalismus und Sozialdemokratie in der Spätphase des Wilhelminischen Deutschlands. Stuttgart, 1976. pp. 283. *bibliog. (Kommission für Geschichtliche Landeskunde in Baden-Württemberg. Veröffentlichungen. Reihe B: Forschungen. 86. Band)*

IM Kampf um den revolutionären Charakter der proletarischen Partei: Briefe führender deutscher Arbeiterfunktionäre, Dezember 1884 bis Juli 1885; (Redaktion: Ursula Herrmann [and others]). Berlin, [1977]. pp. 431. *bibliog.*

Der KAMPF von Karl Marx und Friedrich Engels um die revolutionäre Partei der deutschen Arbeiterklasse. Berlin, 1977. pp. 256. *bibliog. (Berlin. Parteihochschule Karl Marx. Lehrstuhl Geschichte der SED. Vorlesungen)*

LORECK (JOCHEN) Wie man früher Sozialdemokrat wurde: das Kommunikationsverhalten in der deutschen Arbeiterbewegung und die Konzeption der sozialistischen Parteipublizistik durch August Bebel. Bonn-Bad Godesberg, [1977]. pp. 290. *(Friedrich-Ebert-Stiftung. Forschungsinstitut. Schriftenreihe. Band 130)*

VOLLMAR (GEORG VON) Reden und Schriften zur Reformpolitik; ausgewählt und eingeleitet von Willy Albrecht. Berlin, [1977]. pp. 254. *bibliog.*

See also UNABHAENGIGE SOZIALDEMOKRATISCHE PARTEI DEUTSCHLANDS.

SOCIAL DEMOCRATIC PARTY (RUSSIA).

LINDAU (RUDOLF) Zwei Parteien, zwei Wege, zwei Welten: zum 40. Jahrestag der Formierung der Bolschewiki zu einer selbstständigen Partei. Berlin, 1952. pp. 23. *(Haus der Kultur der Sowjetunion, Berlin. Vorträge)*

BONDAREVSKAIA (TAISIIA PAVLOVNA) Peterburgskii komitet RSDRP v revoliutsii 1905-1907 gg. Leningrad, 1975. pp. 327.

BOR'BA protiv opportunizma za sozdanie i ukreplenie partiinykh organizatsii Urala, 1894-1917 gg. Perm', 1975. pp. 395. *bibliog.*

ISTORICHESKII opyt bor'by KPSS protiv trotskizma. Moskva, 1975. pp. 622. *Based upon BOR'BA partii bol'shevikov protiv trotskizma, 1903 - fevral' 1917 g.(1968) and BOR'BA partii bol'shevikov protiv trotskizma v posleoktiabr'skii period (1969).*

NAKROKHIN (EFIM ALEKSANDROVICH) Inogo ne bylo puti. Voronezh, 1975. pp. 133.

PLAMENNOE bol'shevistskoe slovo: podpol'naia literatura v Iaroslavskoi gubernii, 1902-1917 gg. Iaroslavl', 1975. pp. 303.

VOROBTSOVA (IULIIA IVANOVNA) Internatsional'naia deiatel'nost' bol'shevistskoi partii v period podgotovki Oktiabria, fevral'-oktiabr' 1917 g. Leningrad, 1975. pp. 127.

BIL'SHOVYTS'KI orhanizatsiï Ukraïny v borot'bi za hehemoniiu proletariatu v tr'okh rosiis'kykh revoliutsiiakh. Kyïv, 1976. pp. 176.

DIRENOK (EFIM DMITRIEVICH) Bol'sheviki Gomel'shchiny v period Oktiabr'skoi revoliutsii i grazhdanskoi voiny. Minsk, 1976. pp. 192.

KIRILLOV (VIKTOR SERGEEVICH) Bol'sheviki vo glave massovykh politicheskikh stachek v pervoi russkoi revoliutsii, 1905-1907. Moskva, 1976. pp. 368.

MUSIIENKO (VOLODYMYR VASYL'OVYCH) Bil'shovyky Ukraïny v Zhovtnevii revoliutsiï, berezen' 1917 r. - berezen' 1918 r.: do istoriohrafiï problemy. Kyïv, 1976. pp. 195.

BOR'BA partii bol'shevikov za armiiu v sotsialisticheskoi revoliutsii: sbornik dokumentov. Moskva, 1977. pp. 520.

— Periodicals.

TSENTRAL'NAIA bol'shevistskaia pechat' ob Azerbaidzhane, 1905- 1907 gg.: sbornik materialov. Baku, 1976. pp. 200.

SOCIAL DEMOCRATIC PARTY (RUSSIA) (MENSHEVIKS).

PODBOLOTOV (PAVEL ALEKSEEVICH) Krakh esero-men'shevistskoi kontrrevoliutsii. Leningrad, 1975. pp. 120.

ASCHER (ABRAHAM) ed. The Mensheviks in the Russian Revolution. Ithaca, N.Y., 1976. pp. 147. *bibliog. A selection of important documents.*

ROOBOL (W.H.) Tsereteli - a democrat in the Russian revolution: a political biography; translated from the Dutch by Philip Hyams and Lynne Richards. The Hague, 1976. pp. 273. *bibliog. (International Institute of Social History. Studies in Social History. No.1)*

SOCIAL DEMOCRATIC PARTY (SWEDEN).

PETERSON (CARL GUNNAR) Ungdom och politik: en studie av Sveriges Socialdemokratiska Ungdomsförbund. Stockholm, [1975]. pp. 282. *bibliog. With English summary.*

ANNERS (ERIK) Den socialdemokratiska maktapparaten. [Stockholm, 1976]. pp. 272.

SOCIAL DEMOCRATIC PARTY (SWITZERLAND).

GRIMM (ROBERT) Die Arbeiterschaft in der Kriegszeit;...eine Rede vor dem Parteitag der bernischen Sozialdemokratie vom 18. Februar 1940. [Bern?, 1940]. pp. 32.

OPRECHT (HANS) Der zweite Weltkrieg und die schweizerische Arbeiterschaft. [Zürich, 1941]. pp. 31. *(Sozialdemokratische Partei der Schweiz. Kultur und Arbeit)*

WEBER (MAX) of the Schweizerischer Gewerkschaftsbund. Für eine soziale Schweiz. [Zürich], 1955. pp. 23.

SOCIAL ETHICS.

POPPER-LYNKEUS (JOSEF) Das Individuum und die Bewertung menschlicher Existenzen. Dresden, 1910. pp. 223.

ERICSSON (LARS O.) Justice in the distribution of economic resources: a critical and normative study. Stockholm, [1976]. pp. 150. *bibliog. (Stockholms Universitet. Acta Universitatis Stockholmiensis. Stockholm Studies in Philosophy. 6)*

SOCIAL ETHICS.(Cont.)

LIFEBOAT ethics: the moral dilemmas of world hunger; edited by George R. Lucas and Thomas W. Ogletree. New York, [1976]. pp. 162. *bibliog. Originally published in the Spring and Summer 1976 issues of Soundings.*

MAPPES (THOMAS A.) and ZEMBATY (JANE S.) Social ethics: morality and social policy. New York, [1977]. pp. 375. *bibliogs.*

SOCIAL GROUP WORK.

ROBERTS (ROBERT W.) and NORTHEN (HELEN) eds. Theories of social work with groups. New York, 1976. pp. 401. *bibliogs.*

SOCIAL GROUPS.

KEPHART (WILLIAM M.) Extraordinary groups: the sociology of unconventional life-styles. New York, [1976]. pp. 311. *bibliogs.*

— Mathematical models.

MAYER (THOMAS F.) Mathematical models of group structure. Indianapolis, [1975]. pp. 77. *bibliog.*

MACKENZIE (KENNETH D.) A theory of group structures. New York, [1976]. 2 vols. *bibliogs.*

SOCIAL HISTORY.

HASS (ERNST) Die Chance: Politik als angewandte Wissenschaft vom Menschen. München, [1962]. pp. 253. *bibliog.*

CAPLOW (THEODORE) Toward social hope. New York, [1975]. pp. 229.

INTERNATIONAL BANK FOR RECONSTRUCTION AND DEVELOPMENT. 1976. World tables 1976: from the data files of the World Bank. Baltimore, 1976. pp. 552.

STEINBACH (LOTHAR) Didaktik der Sozialgeschichte: eine Fallstudie zum Thema: Arbeiter, Schule und Sozialdemokratie im Wilhelminischen Deutschland. Stuttgart, [1976]. pp. 301. *bibliogs.*

ZEHR (HOWARD) Crime and the development of modern society: patterns of criminality in nineteenth century Germany and France. Totowa, N.J., 1976. pp. 188. *bibliog.*

SENNETT (RICHARD) The fall of public man. Cambridge, 1977. pp. 386.

SOCIAL INDICATORS.

UNITED NATIONS. Ad Hoc Group of Experts on Social Indicators for Housing and Urban Development. 1973. Social indicators for housing and urban development: report of the Ad Hoc Group of Experts, Dublin, Ireland, 4-8 October 1971. (ST/ECA/173). New York, 1973. pp. 31.

ABRAMS (MARK ALEXANDER) A review of work on subjective social indicators 1971 to 1975. London, Social Science Research Council Survey Unit, [1976]. pp. 54. *(Occasional Papers in Survey Research. 8)*

— Ireland (Republic).

NATIONAL ECONOMIC AND SOCIAL COUNCIL [EIRE]. Towards a social report. Dublin, Stationery Office, [1976]. pp. 200. *bibliogs. ([Reports]. No. 25)*

— Israel.

ISRAEL. Central Bureau of Statistics. 1976. Society in Israel: selected statistics; edited by V.O. Schmelz. 2nd ed. Jerusalem, 1976. pp. 172. *In English and Hebrew.*

— Panama.

PANAMA. Direccion de Estadistica y Censo. Estadistica panameña. Indicadores economicos y sociales. a., 1974/1975- Panama. *Supersedes PANAMA. Direccion de Estadistica y Censo. Estadistica panameña. Serie P. Indicadores economicos.*

— Singapore.

SINGAPORE ANNUAL KEY INDICATORS; [pd. by] Statistics Department. a., 1968/76- Singapore.

— United Kingdom.

QUALITY of life survey: urban Britain: 1973: (users' manual); [by] John Hall [and others]. [London, Social Science Research Council Survey Unit, 1976 in progress].

O'MUIRCHEARTAIGH (COLM A.) and WHELAN (BRENDAN J.) Statistical aspects of subjective measures of quality of life. London, Social Science Research Council Survey Unit, [1976]. pp. 75. *(Occasional Papers in Survey Research. 4)*

IMBER (VALERIE) A classification of the English personal social services authorities. London, 1977. pp. 57. *(U.K. Department of Health and Social Security. Statistical and Research Report Series. No.16)*

SOCIAL INSTITUTIONS.

KREILKAMP (THOMAS A.) The corrosion of the self: society's effects on people. New York, 1976. pp. 235. *bibliog.*

ROBINS (ROBERT S.) Political institutionalization and the integration of elites. Beverly Hills, [1976]. pp. 220. *bibliog.*

ROWBOTTOM (RALPH W.) Social analysis: a collaborative method of gaining usable scientific knowledge of social institutions. London, 1977. pp. 178. *bibliog.*

— Japan.

HAITANI (KANJI) The Japanese economic system: an institutional overview. Lexington, Mass., [1976]. pp. 190.

SOCIAL INTERACTION.

MULLER (MARIA S.) Actions and interactions: social relationships in a low-income housing estate in Kitale, Kenya. [Leiden, 1975]. pp. 149, 12. *bibliog.*

WELFORD (ALAN TRAVISS) Skilled performance: perceptual and motor skills. Glenview, Ill., [1976]. pp. 200. *bibliog.*

LEINHARDT (SAMUEL) ed. Social networks: a developing paradigm. New York, 1977. pp. 465. *bibliogs.*

MORRIS (MONICA B.) An excursion into creative sociology. Oxford, 1977. pp. 212. *bibliog.*

PEEL (LYNDA MAY) Village gossip: a study of the evaluation system employed in a Hebridean village. 1976 [or after 1977]. fo.301. *bibliog. Typescript. Ph.D.(London) thesis: unpublished. This thesis is the property of London University and may not be removed from the Library.*

SENNETT (RICHARD) The fall of public man. Cambridge, 1977. pp. 386.

WOODS (PETER) and HAMMERSLEY (MARTYN) eds. School experience: explorations in the sociology of education. London, 1977. pp. 297. *bibliogs.*

— Mathematical models.

HARSANYI (JOHN CHARLES) Rational behavior and bargaining equilibrium in games and social situations. Cambridge, 1977. pp. 314. *bibliog.*

SOCIAL JUSTICE.

STAATSANGEHOERIGKEIT, soziale Grundrechte, wirtschaftliche Zusammenarbeit nach dem Recht der Bundesrepublik Deutschland und der Volksrepublik Polen: Referate des Rechtscolloquiums 1974; herausgegeben von Józef Kokot und Krzysztof Skubiszewski. Berlin, 1976. pp. 293.

SCHACHTER (OSCAR) Sharing the world's resources. New York, 1977. pp. 172.

SOCIAL LEGISLATION

— European Economic Community countries.

EUROPEAN law and the individual; edited by F.G. Jacobs. Amsterdam, 1976. pp. 211. *Papers of a workshop held in 1975 by the Institute of Advanced Legal Studies, University of London.*

— United Kingdom.

BELLAIRS (CHARLES E.) Conservative social and industrial reform: a record of Conservative legislation between 1800 and 1974; with a foreword by Margaret Thatcher. rev. ed. London, 1977. pp. 128.

SOCIAL LIFE AND CUSTOMS.

SENNETT (RICHARD) The fall of public man. Cambridge, 1977. pp. 386.

SOCIAL MEDICINE.

STUDIES in everyday medical life; edited by Michael Wadsworth and David Robinson. London, 1976. pp. 218. *bibliog. Essays prepared for a seminar at the London School of Economics.*

BRITISH SOCIOLOGICAL ASSOCIATION. Annual Conference, 1976. Health and the division of labour; [papers presented at the conference]; edited by Margaret Stacey [and others]. London, [1977]. pp. 237. *bibliogs. (British Sociological Association. Explorations in Sociology. 10)*

— United Kingdom.

CARTWRIGHT (FREDERICK FOX) A social history of medicine. London, 1977. pp. 209. *bibliog.*

HEALTH care and popular medicine in nineteenth century England: essays in the social history of medicine; edited by John Woodward and David Richards. London, [1977]. pp. 195.

SOCIAL MOBILITY

— Argentine Republic.

RUBINSTEIN (JUAN CARLOS) Urbanizacion, estructura de ingresos y movilidad social en Argentina, 1960-1970. Santiago de Chile, 1972. pp. 46. *(Instituto Latinoamericano de Investigaciones Sociales. Estudios y Documentos. 14)*

— Canada.

TEPPERMAN (LORNE) Social mobility in Canada. Toronto, [1975]. pp. 220. *bibliog.*

— United States.

KESSNER (THOMAS) The golden door: Italian and Jewish immigrant mobility in New York City, 1880-1915. New York, 1977. pp. 224. *bibliog.*

SOCIAL MOVEMENTS.

PERRY (RONALD W.) and others. Social movements and the local community. Beverly Hills, [1976]. pp. 66. *bibliog.*

SOCIAL PARTICIPATION.

HEDEBRO (GÖRAN) Information och engagemang: individuella och miljömässiga förutsättningar för deltagande i det lokala samhällslivet: exempel skola. Stockholm, 1976. pp. 237. *bibliog. With English summary.*

MISZTAL (BRONISŁAW) Zagadnienia społecznego uczestnictwa i współdziałania: analiza w świetle teorii i badań socjologicznych. Wrocław, 1977. pp. 276. *bibliog. (Polska Akademia Nauk. Instytut Filozofii i Socjologii. Zespół Badania Struktur Społecznych. Publikacje. [19]) With English, French and German summaries.*

SOCIAL PERCEPTION.

VARIATIONS in black and white perceptions of the social environment; edited by Harry C. Triandis. Urbana, [1976]. pp. 202. *bibliog. Tables on microfiche (3 cards).*

SOCIAL POLICY.

INTERNATIONAL UNION OF LOCAL AUTHORITIES. [Publications]. 98. Local government as promotor of economic and social development. The Hague, 1971. pp. 100.

SYMPOSIUM ON LAW AND POPULATION, TUNIS, 1974. The symposium on law and population: (proceedings, background papers and recommendations); sponsored by the United Nations Fund for Population Activities and the United Nations [and others]. [New York, United Nations Fund for Population Activities, 1975]. pp. 309. *bibliog.*

The USE and abuse of social science: behavioral research and policy making; edited by Irving Louis Horowitz. 2nd ed. New Brunswick, [1975]. pp. 509. *Selected papers from a conference held in 1969 at Rutgers University, together with eleven new papers.*

CONTROVERSIES and decisions: the social sciences and public policy; Charles Frankel, editor: a study prepared under the auspices of the American Academy of Arts and Sciences. New York, [1976]. pp. 299.

ETZIONI (AMITAI) Social problems. Englewood Cliffs, N.J., [1976]. pp. 182.

GIL (DAVID G.) The challenge of social equality: essays on social policy, social development and political practice. Cambridge, Mass., [1976]. pp. 225.

GULDIMANN (TIM) Die Grenzen des Wohlfahrtsstaates: am Beispiel Schwedens und der Bundesrepublik. München, [1976]. pp. 181.

REIN (MARTIN) Social science and public policy. Harmondsworth, 1976. pp. 272.

TALKING about welfare: readings in philosophy and social policy; edited by Noel Timms and David Watson. London, 1976. pp. 306. *bibliog.*

KOELNER ZEITSCHRIFT FÜR SOZIOLOGIE UND SOZIALPSYCHOLOGIE. Sonderhefte. 19. Soziologie und Sozialpolitik; herausgegeben von Christian von Ferber und Franz-Xaver Kaufmann. Opladen, 1977. pp. 649. *bibliogs. Mainly consisting of revised versions of papers presented at the 18. Deutscher Soziologentag, 1976.*

MAPPES (THOMAS A.) and ZEMBATY (JANE S.) Social ethics: morality and social policy. New York, [1977]. pp. 375. *bibliogs.*

PECCEI (AURELIO) The human quality. Oxford, 1977. pp. 214.

VEREIN FÜR SOZIALPOLITIK. Schriften. Neue Folge. Band 92. Soziale Probleme der modernen Industriegesellschaft: (Verhandlungen auf der Arbeitstagung...in Augsburg vom 13.-15. September 1976; herausgegeben von Bernhard Külp und Heinz-Dieter Haas). Berlin, [1977]. 2 vols. *bibliogs.*

— **Bibliography.**

U.K. Department of Industry. Statistics and Market Intelligence Library. 1976. Development plans available in the Statistics and Market Intelligence Library: (bibliography prepared by Margaret Aitchison). London, 1976. 1 pamphlet (unpaged). *(Sources of Statistics and Market Information. 6).*

— **Economic aspects.**

SANDFORD (CEDRIC T.) Social economics. London, 1977. pp. 286. *bibliog.*

SOCIAL PROBLEMS.

WHITELOCK (NOREEN BLYTH) The choice is yours. Weybridge, [1973]. pp. 138.

ALIENATION in contemporary society: a multidisciplinary examination; edited by Roy S. Bryce-Laporte, Claudewell S. Thomas. New York, 1976. pp. 394.

ETZIONI (AMITAI) Social problems. Englewood Cliffs, N.J., [1976]. pp. 182.

GIL (DAVID G.) The challenge of social equality: essays on social policy, social development and political practice. Cambridge, Mass., [1976]. pp. 225.

HABITAT: UNITED NATIONS CONFERENCE ON HUMAN SETTLEMENTS, VANCOUVER, 1976. Report of Habitat:...Vancouver, 31 May - 11 June 1976. (A/CONF.70/15). New York, 1976. pp. 183.

LE GRAND (JULIAN) and ROBINSON (RAY) The economics of social problems. London, 1976. pp. 245. *bibliog.*

TURNER (JONATHAN H.) Social problems in America. New York, [1977]. pp. 555. *bibliog.*

VEREIN FÜR SOZIALPOLITIK. Schriften. Neue Folge. Band 92. Soziale Probleme der modernen Industriegesellschaft: (Verhandlungen auf der Arbeitstagung...in Augsburg vom 13.-15. September 1976; herausgegeben von Bernhard Külp und Heinz-Dieter Haas). Berlin, [1977]. 2 vols. *bibliogs.*

SOCIAL PSYCHOLOGY.

GRISEZ (JEAN) Méthodes de la psychologie sociale. [Paris, 1975]. pp. 191. *bibliog.*

ARONSON (ELLIOT) The social animal. 2nd ed. San Francisco, [1976]. pp. 336.

KREILKAMP (THOMAS A.) The corrosion of the self: society's effects on people. New York, 1976. pp. 235. *bibliog.*

MOSCOVICI (SERGE) Social influence and social change. London, 1976. pp. 239. *bibliog. (European Association of Experimental Social Psychology. European Monographs in Social Psychology. 10)*

ORFORD (JIM) The social psychology of mental disorder. Harmondsworth, 1976. pp. 266. *bibliog.*

PROBLEMY sotsial'noi psikhologii; (nekotorye raboty uchastnikov Vtorogo mezhdunarodnogo kollokviuma po sotsial'noi psikhologii). Tbilisi, 1976. pp. 307.

THIBAUT (JOHN WALTER) and others, eds. Contemporary topics in social psychology. Morristown, N.J., [1976]. pp. 477. *bibliogs.*

BEHAVIORAL theory in sociology: essays in honor of George C. Homans; edited by Robert L. Hamblin and John H. Kunkel. New Brunswick, N.J., [1977]. pp. 546. *bibliogs.*

MORLEY (IAN E.) and STEPHENSON (GEOFFREY M.) The social psychology of bargaining. London, 1977. pp. 317. *bibliog.*

SOCIAL ROLE.

ROLE structure and analysis of the family; [by] F. Ivan Nye [and others]. Beverly Hills, [1976]. pp. 214. *bibliog.*

SOCIAL SCIENCE LITERATURE.

ROBERTS (NORMAN) ed. Use of social sciences literature. London, 1977. pp. 326. *bibliogs.*

SOCIAL SCIENCE RESEARCH.

SEMINAR ON SOCIAL SCIENCE RESEARCH WITH SPECIAL REFERENCE TO POPULATION AND DEVELOPMENT, MONROVIA, LIBERIA, 1975. Seminar...; organized at the University of Liberia...by Liberia College,...University of Liberia and Population Dynamics Programme, University of Ghana, Legon. Monrovia, Liberia, 1975. fo. 75. *bibliogs.*

DOUGLAS (JACK D.) Investigative social research: individual and team field research. Beverly Hills, [1976]. pp. 229. *bibliog.*

KLEIN (LISL KAROLINE) A social scientist in industry. Epping, 1976. pp. 257.

NACHMIAS (DAVID) and NACHMIAS (CHAVA) Research methods in the social sciences. London, 1976. pp. 335. *bibliogs.*

The NEW social sciences; edited by Baidya Nath Varma. Westport, Conn., 1976. pp. 276. *bibliogs. Papers based on the Columbia University faculty seminar entitled "Content and Methods of the Social Sciences".*

The ORGANISATION and impact of social research: six original case studies in education and behavioural science; edited by Marten Shipman. London, 1976. pp. 155. *bibliogs.*

REIN (MARTIN) Social science and public policy. Harmondsworth, 1976. pp. 272.

BULMER (MARTIN) ed. Sociological research methods: an introduction. London, 1977. pp. 363. *bibliog.*

DEMOGRAPHIC, economic, and social interaction; edited by Åke E. Andersson [and] Ingvar Holmberg. Cambridge, Mass., [1977]. pp. 352. *bibliogs. Based on the proceedings of a one-day seminar at the University of Gothenburg in 1972, and of a symposium held in October 1974 by the Swedish Council for Social Science Research.*

POWER, paradigms, and community research; edited by Roland J. Liebert and Allen W. Imershein. London, [1977]. pp. 339. *bibliogs. Papers prepared for a meeting of the International Sociological Association, Montreal, 1974.*

INTERNATIONAL REGISTER OF RESEARCH ON THE SOCIAL IMPACT OF OFFSHORE OIL DEVELOPMENT; [pd.by] North Sea Oil Panel, Social Science Research Council. irreg., current issues only. Aberdeen.

— **America, Latin.**

STAVENHAGEN (RODOLFO) Sociologia y subdesarrollo. Mexico, 1971 repr. 1974. pp. 236. *bibliog.*

— **Ireland (Republic).**

KENNEDY (KIERAN A.) The ESRI research plan 1976-80 and background analysis. Dublin, 1976. pp. 72.

— **Malaysia.**

CONFERENCE ON THE ROLE AND ORIENTATION OF SOCIAL SCIENCE AND SOCIAL SCIENTISTS IN MALAYSIA, 1974. [Papers delivered or circulated at the Conference organised by the Department of Anthropology and Sociology, National University of Malaysia, Kuala Lumpur]. 1974. 8 pts. (in 1 vol.)

— **New Zealand.**

SOCIAL science research applications in the public sector: a trend report; editor M.T.V. Reidy; published by the Department of Justice on behalf of the Wellington branch of the Royal Society of New Zealand. [Wellington], 1975. fo. 52.

— **Nigeria.**

McWILLIAM (JOHN) and UCHE (CHUKWUDUM) Nigeria: selected studies: social science research for population and family planning policies and programme. London, 1976. pp. 50. *bibliog. (International Planned Parenthood Federation. Research for Action. No. 1)*

— **United Kingdom.**

LEVINE (HERBERT M.) and OWEN (DOLORES B.) An American guide to British social science resources. Metuchen, N.J., 1976. pp. 281.

SOCIAL SCIENCE RESEARCH COUNCIL SURVEY ARCHIVE. Bulletin. q., current issue only. Colchester.

— **United States.**

USING social research in public policy making; edited by Carol H. Weiss. Lexington, [1977]. pp. 256. *(Policy Studies Organization. Policy Studies Organization Series. 11)*

SOCIAL SCIENCES.

RILEY (GRESHAM) ed. Values, objectivity, and the social sciences. Reading, Mass., [1974]. pp. 152. *bibliog.*

The USE and abuse of social science: behavioral research and policy making; edited by Irving Louis Horowitz. 2nd ed. New Brunswick, [1975]. pp. 509. *Selected papers from a conference held in 1969 at Rutgers University, together with eleven new papers.*

BECKER (GARY STANLEY) The economic approach to human behavior. Chicago, 1976. pp. 314. *bibliog.*

BERNSTEIN (RICHARD J.) The restructuring of social and political theory. New York, [1976]. pp. 286. *bibliog.*

CONTROVERSIES and decisions: the social sciences and public policy; Charles Frankel, editor: a study prepared under the auspices of the American Academy of Arts and Sciences. New York, [1976]. pp. 299.

The NEW social sciences; edited by Baidya Nath Varma. Westport, Conn., 1976. pp. 276. *bibliogs. Papers based on the Columbia University faculty seminar entitled "Content and Methods of the Social Sciences".*

REIN (MARTIN) Social science and public policy. Harmondsworth, 1976. pp. 272.

— Bibliography.

BIBLIOGRAFIIA obshchestvenno-politicheskoi literatury, etc. 2nd ed. Moskva, 1968-76. 2 vols.

SCONUL EXCHANGE OF EXPERIENCE SEMINAR IN THE SOCIAL SCIENCES, YORK, 1975. Proceedings of the Exchange of Experience Seminar in the Social Sciences organized by the Information Services Group of SCONUL. [London, 1976]. pp. 23. *bibliog.*

— Directories.

LEVINE (HERBERT M.) and OWEN (DOLORES B.) An American guide to British social science resources. Metuchen, N.J., 1976. pp. 281.

— Field work.

DOUGLAS (JACK D.) Investigative social research: individual and team field research. Beverly Hills, [1976]. pp. 229. *bibliog.*

— History — Canada — Quebec.

FALARDEAU (JEAN CHARLES) The rise of social sciences in French Canada. Quebec, Department of Cultural Affairs, 1967. pp. 67. *bibliog. (Series on the Arts, Humanities and Sciences in French Canada. 6)*

— Information services.

SCONUL EXCHANGE OF EXPERIENCE SEMINAR IN THE SOCIAL SCIENCES, YORK, 1975. Proceedings of the Exchange of Experience Seminar in the Social Sciences organized by the Information Services Group of SCONUL. [London, 1976]. pp. 23. *bibliog.*

ROBERTS (NORMAN) ed. Use of social sciences literature. London, 1977. pp. 326. *bibliogs.*

— Methodology.

BENNETT (SPENCER) and BOWERS (DAVID) An introduction to multivariate techniques for social and behavioural sciences. London, 1976. pp. 156. *bibliog.*

NACHMIAS (DAVID) and NACHMIAS (CHAVA) Research methods in the social sciences. London, 1976. pp. 335. *bibliogs.*

NOWAK (STEFAN) Understanding and prediction: essays in the methodology of social and behavioral theories. Dordrecht, [1976]. pp. 482. *bibliogs.*

SYSTEMS theory in the social sciences: stochastic and control systems, pattern recognition, fuzzy analysis, simulation, behavioral models; (Hartmut Bossel [and others, eds.]). Basel, 1976. pp. 552. *bibliogs. Based on an interdisciplinary workshop sponsored by the Zentrum für interdisziplinäre Forschung of the University of Bielefeld.*

BROWN (RICHARD HARVEY) A poetic for sociology: toward a logic of discovery for the human sciences. Cambridge, 1977. pp. 302. *bibliog.*

HINDESS (BARRY) Philosophy and methodology in the social sciences. Hassocks, 1977. pp. 258. *bibliog.*

ROWBOTTOM (RALPH W.) Social analysis: a collaborative method of gaining usable scientific knowledge of social institutions. London, 1977. pp. 178. *bibliog.*

— Philosophy.

KRITIKA súčasných buržoáznych sociálno-ekonomických teórií. Bratislava, 1976. pp. 399.

PHILLIPS (D.C.) Holistic thought in social science. Stanford, 1976. pp. 149. *bibliog.*

— Statistical methods.

NOWAK (STEFAN) Understanding and prediction: essays in the methodology of social and behavioral theories. Dordrecht, [1976]. pp. 482. *bibliogs.*

— Study and teaching — America, Latin.

GRACIARENA (JORGE) Formacion de postgrado en ciencias sociales en America Latina. Buenos Aires, [1974]. pp. 160.

— — Poland.

CZAJKA (STANISŁAW) ed. Nauki społeczne po XVI Plenum KC PZPR. Warszawa, 1976. pp. 272.

SOCIAL SCIENCES AND STATE

— United States.

USING social research in public policy making; edited by Carol H. Weiss. Lexington, [1977]. pp. 256. *(Policy Studies Organization. Policy Studies Organization Series. 11)*

SOCIAL SCIENTISTS

— Malaysia.

CONFERENCE ON THE ROLE AND ORIENTATION OF SOCIAL SCIENCE AND SOCIAL SCIENTISTS IN MALAYSIA, 1974. [Papers delivered or circulated at the Conference organised by the Department of Anthropology and Sociology, National University of Malaysia, Kuala Lumpur]. 1974. 8 pts. (in 1 vol).

SOCIAL SERVICE.

LEONARD (PETER TERRANCE) Poverty, consciousness and action. Birmingham, [1975]. pp. 10. *(British Association of Social Workers. Publications)*

THURSZ (DANIEL) and VIGILANTE (JOSEPH L.) eds. Meeting human needs: an overview of nine countries. Beverly Hills, Calif., [1975]. pp. 288. *bibliogs.*

BECKWITH (BURNHAM PUTNAM) Free goods: the theory of free or communist distribution. Palo Alto, Calif., [1976]. pp. 216. *bibliog.*

BUTRYM (ZOFIA T.) The nature of social work. London, 1976. pp. 167.

LEVIN (GILBERT) and ROBERTS (EDWARD BAER) The dynamics of human service delivery. Cambridge, Mass., [1976]. pp. 257.

MEYER (CAROL H.) Social work practice. 2nd ed. New York, [1976]. pp. 268. *bibliog.*

TALKING about welfare: readings in philosophy and social policy; edited by Noel Timms and David Watson. London, 1976. pp. 306. *bibliog.*

WORKING PARTY ON THE TEACHING OF THE VALUE BASES OF SOCIAL WORK [U.K.]. Social work curriculum study: values in social work; a discussion paper; [R.S. Downie, chairman]. London, Central Council for Education and Training in Social Work, 1976. pp. 86. *bibliogs. (Papers. 13)*

FURNISS (NORMAN) and TILTON (TIMOTHY ALAN) The case for the welfare state: from social security to social equality. Bloomington, [1977]. pp. 249. *bibliog.*

LOEWENBERG (FRANK M.) Fundamentals of social intervention: core concepts and skills for social work practice. New York, 1977. pp. 374. *bibliog.*

— Finance.

PETERSEN (JØRN HENRIK) Co-ordination of the use of financial resources at and between central and local levels within the public sector. Odense, [1975?]. 1 vol. (various pagings). *(Odense Universitet. Institut for Historie og Samfundsvidenskab. Skrifter. No. 20) Paper presented at United Nations Seminar on Problems of Policy, Administration and Coordination in the Financing of the Social Services, Killarney, Ireland, 1975.*

— Information services — United Kingdom.

ADLER (MICHAEL) Lecturer in Social Administration, and DU FEU (D.) A computer based welfare benefits information system: the Inverclyde project; a joint project between the University of Edinburgh, Inverclyde District Council [and] IBM United Kingdom. Peterlee, 1975. pp. 56. *(IBM United Kingdom Limited. UK Scientific Centre. [Technical Reports]. 0078)*

BRADSHAW (JONATHAN) and others. Batley welfare benefits project. [York, 1976]. pp. 33. *(Papers in Community Studies. No. 5)*

NORTH TYNESIDE COMMUNITY DEVELOPMENT PROJECT. Welfare rights: the North Shields campaign, summer 1975. North Shields, [1976?]. pp. 84.

— Research — United Kingdom.

SOCIAL SERVICES RESEARCH AND INTELLIGENCE UNIT [PORTSMOUTH]. Information Sheets. No. 25. Social services research in 1975. Portsmouth, 1976. pp. 9.

— Angola.

INSTITUTO DE ASSISTENCIA SOCIAL DE ANGOLA. Relatorio anual. a., 1972- [Luanda].

— Australia.

AUSTRALIA. Social Welfare Commission. 1976. An idea before its time. [Canberra?], 1976. 1 vol. (various pagings) *bibliog. (Reference Papers)*

SOCIAL work in Australia: responses to a changing context; edited by Phillip J. Boas and Jim Crawley. Melbourne, 1976. pp. 271. *bibliogs. Based mainly on papers prepared for the 14th National Conference of the Australian Association of Social Workers held in Melbourne, 1975.*

— Bolivia.

TEORIA Y PRACTICA DE LA SEGURIDAD SOCIAL; [pd. by] Instituto Boliviano de Seguridad Social. s-a., J1/D 1975 (no. 5)- La Paz.

— Canada — British Columbia.

BRITISH COLUMBIA. Department of Human Resources. Statistical reports and tables: annual report. a., 1972/73- Victoria.

— — New Brunswick.

NEW BRUNSWICK. 1970. White Paper on social development and social welfare. [Fredericton, 1970]. fo. 44.

— — Quebec.

QUEBEC (PROVINCE). Conseil des Affaires Sociales et de la Famille. Rapport annuel. a., 1975/76- Québec.

— Cyprus.

TRISELIOTIS (JOHN P.) Social welfare in Cyprus. London, 1977. pp. 179. *bibliog.*

— Denmark.

KÜHL (POUL HEINRICH) Enghave-Centret: en rapport om et integreringsforsøg. København, 1975. pp. 54. *bibliog. (Socialforskningsinstituttet. Meddelelser. 11)*

— Finland — Finance.

ELLALA (ESA) and KOTIRANTA (MAIJA LIISA) Sosiaalimenot vuonna 1974 sekä ennakkotiedot vuodelle 1975, etc. Helsinki, 1976. pp. 119. *(Finland. Suomen Virallinen Tilasto. Finlands Officiella Statistik. 32. Sosiaalisia Erikoistutkimuksia. 49) In Finnish, Swedish and English.*

— France.

FRANCE. Comité Central d'Enquête sur le Coût et le Rendement des Services Publics. 1976. L'aménagement des services publics dans les zones à faible densité de population: rapport présenté par M. Duchene-Marullaz [and] M. Zwickert [and] conclusions du Comité, etc. Paris, [1976]. pp. 99. *Cover title reads: L'amélioration des services publics, etc.*

— Germany.

GRAF (PEDRO) and others. Sozialarbeit im Obdachlosenbereich: Gemeinwesenarbeit zwischen Betroffenen und Institutionen. Westberlin, [1976]. pp. 207.

— Ireland (Republic).

EIRE. Department of Health. Planning Unit. Statistical information relevant to the health services. a., 1976- Dublin.

— Israel.

ISRAEL. Ministry of Social Welfare. Department of Research and Planning. Biennial report on family, child and youth welfare. bien., 1951/1952 [1st]. Jerusalem. *No more pd?*

— Netherlands.

NETHERLANDS. Ministerie van Cultuur, Recreatie en Maatschappelijk Werk. 1966. Some findings of social welfare research sponsored by the Ministry of Cultural Affairs, Recreation and Social Welfare. Rijswijk, [1966?]. pp. 101.

— Underdeveloped areas.

See UNDERDEVELOPED AREAS — Social service.

— United Kingdom.

SOCIAL development in new communities; proceedings of a seminar organized by the Centre for Urban and Regional Studies and held in the University of Birmingham, March 28, 1972. Birmingham, 1972. pp. 66. *(Birmingham. University. Centre for Urban and Regional Studies. Research Memoranda. No. 12)*

PERSONAL SOCIAL SERVICES COUNCIL [U.K.]. Report. a., 1975(1st)- London.

U.K. Department of Health and Social Security. [Circulars]: L.A.C. [Local Authority]. irreg., N 12 1975 (no.16)- , with gaps. London.

U.K. Department of Health and Social Security. [Letters]: L.A.S.S.L. [Local Authority Social Services]. irreg., F 1975 (no.2)- , with gaps. London.

COMMUNITY RELATIONS COMMISSION. Working in multi-racial areas: a training handbook for social services departments. London, 1976. pp. 21. *bibliogs.*

COUNTER INFORMATION SERVICES and others. Cutting the welfare state: who profits?. London, [1976]. pp. 39. *(Counter Information Services. Anti-Reports. No. 13)*

DARVILL (GILES) Encouraging the community: some findings on the social services departments' contribution. Berkhamsted, 1976. pp. 11.

HALL (PHOEBE) Reforming the welfare: the politics of change in the personal social services. London, 1976. pp. 162.

HELP for the other travellers: social provision in relation to London travel termini; report of an inter-agency working party. London, [1976]. pp. 8.

MORONEY (ROBERT M.) The family and the state: considerations for social policy. London, 1976. pp. 142.

RADICAL STATISTICS HEALTH GROUP. Pamphlets. No. 1. Whose priorities? London, [1976]. pp. 36.

SOCIAL SERVICES RESEARCH AND INTELLIGENCE UNIT [PORTSMOUTH]. Information Sheets. No. 27. Planning alternatives: social services thinks ahead. Portsmouth, [1976]. pp. 8.

U.K. Department of Health and Social Security. Statistics and Research Division. 1976. The elderly and the personal social services; a report...based on The needs of old people in Glamorgan; by Margaret Watson and Martin Albrow. [London, 1976]. pp. 111.

The WELFARE society: a guide for discussion groups; edited by Joan Eyden. London, [1976]. pp. 47. *bibliog.*

FERRIS (DAVE) Homosexuality and the social services: the report of an NCCL survey of local authority social services committees. London, [1977]. pp. 89.

FOUNDATIONS of social administration; edited by Helmuth Heisler. London, 1977. pp. 251.

IMBER (VALERIE) A classification of the English personal social services authorities. London, 1977. pp. 57. *(U.K. Department of Health and Social Security. Statistical and Research Report Series. No.16)*

INTEGRATING social work methods; with Catherine Briscoe, Nano McCaughan and Chris Payne; edited by Harry Specht and Anne Vickery. London, 1977. pp. 260. *(National Institute for Social Work Training. National Institute Social Services Library. No. 31)*

PLANK (DAVID) Caring for the elderly: report of a study of various means of caring for dependent elderly people in eight London boroughs. London, [1977]. pp. 235. *(London. Greater London Council. Research Memoranda. 512)*

RIDLEY (NICHOLAS) Social service sense. London, [1977]. pp. 12.

SAINSBURY (ERIC E.) The personal social services. London, 1977. pp. 265. *bibliog.*

U.K. Department of Health and Social Security. 1977. Priorities in the health and social services: the way forward: further discusssion of the Government's strategy based on the consultative document Priorities for health and personal social services in England. London, 1977. pp. 52. *bibliog.*

WARHAM (JOYCE) An open case: the organisational context of social work. London, 1977. pp. 161. *bibliog.*

— — Abstracts.

STUDIES ON COMMUNITY HEALTH AND PERSONAL SOCIAL SERVICES: a classified selection of periodical articles and books which appeared in the monthly "Current Literature on Community Health and Personal Social Services"; [pd. by] Department of Health and Social Security Library. a., 1972. London.

SOCIAL SERVICE ABSTRACTS: monthly summaries of selected journal articles, reports, books and pamphlets received in the Department of Health and Social Security Library. m., Ja 1977 (no.1)- London.

— — Directories.

BAREFOOT (PATIENCE) and CUNNINGHAM (P. JEAN) Community services: the health worker's A-Z. London, 1977. pp. 284.

— — Societies, etc.

TOMLINSON (P.) Report on the work of the Prisoners' Wives' Service;...under the direction of Pauline Morris. [London, 1971]. pp. 23.

PIVOT: the report of a working party on the National Association of Voluntary Help Organisers (NAVHO): chairman, Geraldine M. Aves. Berkhamsted, 1976. pp. 30.

— — Ireland, Northern.

IRELAND, NORTHERN. Department of Health and Social Services. 1976. Development of health and personal social services for the elderly in Northern Ireland. [Belfast], 1976. pp. 29.

— — Wales.

GLAMORGAN-GLYNCORRWG COMMUNITY DEVELOPMENT PROJECT. State of the community report: community health and welfare. [Port Talbot], 1972. pp. 27.

U.K. Welsh Office. 1976. Proposed all-Wales policies and priorities for the planning and provision of health and personal social services from 1976/77 to 1979/80: consultative document. [Cardiff], 1976. fo. 34.

— — — Statistics.

U.K. Welsh Office. Health and Social Work Department. 1976. A guide to health and social services statistics. Cardiff, 1976. pp. 73.

— United States.

LAPATRA (JACK W.) Public welfare systems. Springfield, Ill., [1975]. pp. 221.

KAMERMAN (SHEILA B.) and KAHN (ALFRED J.) Social services in the United States: policies and programs. Philadelphia, 1976. pp. 561.

SCHNEIDER (ANNE L.) Opinions and policies in the American states: the role of political characteristics. Beverly Hills, [1976]. pp. 47. *bibliog.*

WELFARE reform: why?; (a Round Table held on May 20, 1976 under the joint sponsorship of the American Enterprise Institute...and the Hoover Institution...); Robert H. Bork, moderator, etc. Washington, [1976]. pp. 41. *(American Enterprise Institute for Public Policy Research. Round Tables)*

GRØNBJERG (KIRSTEN A.) Mass society and the extension of welfare, 1960-1970. Chicago, 1977. pp. 266. *bibliog.*

WELFARE and the poor; edited by Lester A. Sobel. New York, [1977]. pp. 198. *Based on records compiled by Facts on File.*

— — Arizona.

COMPREHENSIVE services to rural poor families: an evaluation of the Arizona Job Colleges program; [by] Keith Baker [and others]. New York, 1976. pp. 191. *bibliog.*

— — California.

KREFETZ (SHARON PERLMAN) Welfare policy making and city politics. New York, 1976. pp. 218.

— — Maryland.

KREFETZ (SHARON PERLMAN) Welfare policy making and city politics. New York, 1976. pp. 218.

— Uruguay.

FERRARI (FRANCISCO DE) La seguridad social en el Uruguay: bases para su planificacion. Montevideo, 1967. pp. 48.

SOCIAL SETTLEMENTS

— Germany.

GERTH (FRANZ JAKOB) Bahnbrechendes Modell einer neuen Gesellschaft: die Soziale Arbeitsgemeinschaft Berlin-Ost, 1911-1940. Hamburg, 1975. pp. 118. *bibliog.*

SOCIAL STATUS.

KOESTLIN (KONRAD) Gilden in Schleswig-Holstein: die Bestimmung des Standes durch "Kultur". Göttingen, [1976]. pp. 320. *bibliog.*

BRITTAIN (JOHN A.) The inheritance of economic status. Washington, D.C., [1977]. pp. 185. *(Brookings Institution. Studies in Social Economics)*

CURTIS (RICHARD FARNSWORTH) and JACKSON (ELTON F.) Inequality in American communities. New York, [1977]. pp. 354. *bibliog.*

STATUS characteristics and social interaction: an expectation- states approach; [by] Joseph Berger [and others]. New York, [1977]. pp. 196. *bibliog.*

SOCIAL STRUCTURE.

SOCIAL STRUCTURE.

AMERICAN SOCIOLOGICAL ASSOCIATION. Annual Meeting, 69th, 1974. Approaches to the study of social structure; edited by Peter M. Blau. New York, [1975]. pp. 294. *bibliog. Revised versions of the thematic presentations made at the plenary sessions of the meeting.*

COSER (LEWIS ALFRED) ed. The idea of social structure: papers in honor of Robert K. Merton. New York, [1975]. pp. 547. *bibliog.*

BROWN (D.E.) Principles of social structure: Southeast Asia. London, 1976. pp. 248. *bibliog.*

MERTON (ROBERT KING) Sociological ambivalence and other essays. New York, [1976]. pp. 287.

POWER and control: social structures and their transformation; edited by Tom R. Burns and Walter Buckley. London, [1976]. pp. 290. *bibliogs.*

BRITISH SOCIOLOGICAL ASSOCIATION. Annual Conference, 1975. Industrial society: class, cleavage and control; edited by Richard Scase. London, 1977. pp. 221. *bibliog. (British Sociological Association. Explorations in Sociology. 8)*

MARCEAU (JANE) Class and status in France: economic change and social immobility 1945-1975. Oxford, 1977. pp. 217. *bibliog.*

SOCIAL SURVEYS.

SUDMAN (SEYMOUR) Applied sampling. New York, [1976]. pp. 249. *bibliog.*

The ANALYSIS of survey data; edited by Colm A. O'Muircheartaigh and Clive Payne. London, [1977]. 2 vols. *bibliogs.*

NOWAK (STEFAN) Methodology of sociological research: general problems; translated from the Polish by Maria Olga Lepa. Dordrecht, [1977]. pp. 504.

— Canada.

CANADA. Statistics Canada. Special Surveys Coordination Division. New surveys: notes on statistical survey activity within the federal government. q., current issues only. Ottawa. *[in English and French].*

— United Kingdom.

HEDGES (BARRY M.) Methodological report on the 1975 referendum survey. London, 1975. pp. 15.

WILKS (H.C.) Report of survey of [the] Isle of Dogs [carried out by pupils of George Green's School], 1974-5. London, 1975. pp. 54.

QUALITY of life survey: urban Britain: 1973: (users' manual); [by] John Hall [and others]. [London, Social Science Research Council Survey Unit, 1976 in progress].

AIREY (COLIN) and others. A technical report on a survey of racial minorities. London, 1976. pp. 99.

SOCIAL SCIENCE RESEARCH COUNCIL SURVEY ARCHIVE. Bulletin. q., current issue only. Colchester.

SOCIAL SYSTEMS.

EVOLUTION and consciousness: human systems in transition; edited by Erich Jantsch and Conrad Waddington. Reading, Mass., 1976. pp. 259. *bibliogs.*

LOOMIS (CHARLES PRICE) and DYER (EVERETT D.) Social systems: the study of sociology. Cambridge, Mass., [1976]. pp. 458.

SOCIAL VALUES.

WHEN values conflict: essays on environmental analysis, discourse and decision; edited by Laurence H. Tribe [and others]. Cambridge, Mass., [1976]. pp. 178. *Essays arising from a research project carried out by the American Academy of Arts and Sciences.*

INGLEHART (RONALD) The silent revolution: changing values and political styles among western publics. Princeton, [1977]. pp. 482. *bibliog.*

MOONEY (GAVIN H.) The valuation of human life. London, 1977. pp. 165. *bibliogs.*

SOCIAL WORK ADMINISTRATION.

NEW frontiers: public lecture series, spring 1973; edited by A.P. Williamson; papers read at a series of public lectures at the New University of Ulster, arranged under the auspices of Social Administration. Coleraine, [1973]. 1 vol. (various pagings). *(New University of Ulster. Priorities: Occasional Papers in Social Administration)*

— United Kingdom.

SAINSBURY (ERIC E.) The personal social services. London, 1977. pp. 265. *bibliog.*

— — Ireland, Northern.

NEW frontiers: public lecture series, spring 1973; edited by A.P. Williamson; papers read at a series of public lectures at the New University of Ulster, arranged under the auspices of Social Administration. Coleraine, [1973]. 1 vol. (various pagings). *(New University of Ulster. Priorities: Occasional Papers in Social Administration)*

SOCIAL WORK AS A PROFESSION.

BRITISH ASSOCIATION OF SOCIAL WORKERS. The social work task; a BASW working party report. Birmingham, 1977. pp. 75.

COMMUNITY work: learning and supervision; edited by Catherine Briscoe and David N. Thomas. London, 1977. pp. 190. *(National Institute for Social Work Training. National Institute Social Services Library. No. 32)*

INTEGRATING social work methods; with Catherine Briscoe, Nano McCaughan and Chris Payne; edited by Harry Specht and Anne Vickery. London, 1977. pp. 260. *(National Institute for Social Work Training. National Institute Social Services Library. No. 31)*

TIMMS (NOEL) and TIMMS (RITA) Perspectives in social work. London, 1977. pp. 233. *bibliog.*

WARHAM (JOYCE) An open case: the organisational context of social work. London, 1977. pp. 161. *bibliog.*

SOCIAL WORK EDUCATION.

WORKING PARTY ON THE TEACHING OF THE VALUE BASES OF SOCIAL WORK [U.K.]. Social work curriculum study: values in social work; a discussion paper; [R.S. Downie, chairman]. London, Central Council for Education and Training in Social Work, 1976. pp. 86. *bibliogs. (Papers. 13)*

COMMUNITY work: learning and supervision; edited by Catherine Briscoe and David N. Thomas. London, 1977. pp. 190. *(National Institute for Social Work Training. National Institute Social Services Library. No. 32)*

— Kenya.

WEISNER (STANLEY) Professional social work in Kenya: training and performance. Lower Kabete, 1972. pp. 71. *(Kenya Institute of Administration. K.I.A. Occasional Papers. No. 4)*

— United Kingdom.

CENTRAL COUNCIL FOR EDUCATION AND TRAINING IN SOCIAL WORK [U.K.]. Information Service. Professional training for social work: the certificate of qualification in social work, CQSW. [London], 1975. pp. 46. *(Leaflets. 2:1)*

DINGWALL (ROBERT) The social organisation of health visitor training. London, [1977]. pp. 249. *bibliog.*

SOCIAL WORK WITH CHILDREN

— United Kingdom.

WORKING together for children and their families; report of a project undertaken with South Glamorgan County Council by Social Work Service Development Group; (edited by Barbara Kahan). London, H.M.S.O., 1977. pp. 207. *bibliog.*

SOCIAL WORK WITH NEGROES.

SOLOMON (BARBARA) Black empowerment: social work in oppressed communities. New York, 1976. pp. 438.

SOCIAL WORK WITH THE AGED

— United Kingdom.

WILSON (HUGH) AND WOMERSLEY (LEWIS) Firm. Inner area study: Liverpool: community care of the elderly. [London], Department of the Environment, [1977]. pp. 61, 1 map.

SOCIAL WORK WITH YOUTH

— United Kingdom.

EGGLESTON (S. JOHN) Adolescence and community: the youth service in Britain;... with the assistance of Patricia Allatt. London, 1976. pp. 253. *bibliog.*

COMMUNITY RELATIONS COMMISSION. Youth and Community Section. Seen but not served: black youth and the youth service; report of a series of six seminars held in 1975/76 to examine statutory provision for young people from racial minorities. London, 1977. pp. 42.

SOCIAL WORKERS.

LOEWENBERG (FRANK M.) Fundamentals of social intervention: core concepts and skills for social work practice. New York, 1977. pp. 374. *bibliog.*

— In-service training — United Kingdom.

COMMUNITY RELATIONS COMMISSION. Working in multi-racial areas: a training handbook for social services departments. London, 1976. pp. 21. *bibliogs.*

— Australia.

AUSTRALIA. Social Welfare Commission. 1975. Progress report on social welfare manpower. [Canberra?], 1975. pp. 76.

— United Kingdom.

COMMUNITY RELATIONS COMMISSION. The views of social workers in multi-racial areas. London, 1977. pp. 15.

RAISBECK (BERTRAM L.) Law and the social worker. London, 1977. pp. 153.

ZANDER (MICHAEL) Social workers, their clients and the law. 2nd ed. London, 1977. pp. 140.

— United States — Salaries, pensions, etc.

SMITH (MICHAEL J.) Salary study, 1972: a report of administrative and professional salaries in voluntary CWLA member agencies, January 1, 1972. New York, 1972. pp. 32.

SOCIALISM.

PROUDHON (PIERRE JOSEPH) Theoretischer und praktischer Beweis des Sozialismus; oder, Revolution durch dem Credit (Proudhon's neueste Schrift); herausgegeben von Theodor Opitz. Leipzig, Fernau, 1849. pp. 84.

SCHAEFFLE (ALBERT EBERHARD FRIEDRICH) Die Quintessenz des Sozialismus. 13th ed. Gotha, 1891. pp. 65.

WILLAEY ( ) Parti de la Justice Sociale: par le droit et le devoir naturels adoptés comme base de la société; parti d'union socialiste: projet de programme. Paris, 1896. pp. 64.

CATHREIN (VICTOR) Socialism: its theoretical basis and practical application;... authorized translation of the 8th German edition, with special reference to the condition of socialism in the United States; revised and enlarged by Victor F. Gettelmann. 3rd ed. New York, 1904. pp. 424.

HERZBERG (WILHELM) Sozialdemokratie und Anarchismus. Ludwigshafen am Rhein, 1906. pp. 32.

FULLERTON (R.) Socialism and the workingman. Dublin, 1911. pp. 234.

MARCHIONINI (KARL) Was ist Sozialismus?: ein Blick in die sozialistische Republik. Leipzig, 1919. pp. 32.

ZEPLER (WALLY) Der Weg zum Sozialismus. Berlin, [1919?]. pp. 31.

MURRY (JOHN MIDDLETON) The necessity of pacifism. London, 1937. pp. 132.

UNIVERSITY LABOUR FEDERATION. Pamphlets. No. 15. Why socialism? 2nd ed. Cambridge, 1944. pp. 32. *bibliog.*

JORDI (HUGO) Sozialistische Entwicklungslinien: neue Betrachtungen über den klassischen Marxismus. Bern, 1947. pp. 40. *Originally published as a series of articles in "Volksrecht".*

LOEWENTHAL (RICHARD) Jenseits des Kapitalismus: ein Beitrag zur sozialistischen Neuorientierung; mit einer ausführlichen Einführung: nach 30 Jahren. Berlin, [1977]. pp. 268. *Reprint of work originally published at Lauf nr. Nuremberg in 1947 under the pseudonym Paul Sering.*

MARWITZ (W.G.) Freiheit und Sozialismus: Gedanken eines deutschen Sozialisten. Frankfurt am Main, [1953]. pp. 52.

MORRIS (WILLIAM) Selected writings and designs; edited with an introduction by Asa Briggs; with a supplement by Graeme Shankland on William Morris, designer, illustrated by twenty-four plates. Harmondsworth, 1962, repr. 1977. pp. 309. *bibliog.*

KUENZLI (ARNOLD) Tradition und Revolution: zur Theorie eines nachmarxistischen Sozialismus. Basel, [1975]. pp. 197.

SHASHKOV (N.I.) Kant i "eticheskii sotsializm": lektsii po spetskursu dlia studentov filosofskogo fakul'teta. Sverdlovsk, 1975. pp. 147.

MEZHDUNARODNOE rabochee dvizhenie: voprosy istorii i teorii. Moskva, 1976 in progress.

BECKWITH (BURNHAM PUTNAM) The case for liberal socialism. 3rd ed. Hicksville, N.Y., [1976]. pp. 181. *bibliog. Originally published as The modern case for socialism under the pseudonym John Putnam.*

EATON (JOHN) Towards socialism. Nottingham, [1976]. pp. 36. *(Spokesman, The. Pamphlets. No. 48)*

HEGEDÜS (ANDRÁS) Socialism and bureaucracy. London, 1976. pp. 193.

JANICKI (JANUSZ) and MUSZYŃSKI (JERZY) eds. Ideologia i polityka współczesnego lewactwa. Warszawa, 1976. pp. 387.

The LABOUR process and class strategies. London, [1976]. pp. 129. *(Conference of Socialist Economists. Pamphlets. No. 1)*

MAYER (DANIEL) Socialisme: le droit de l'homme au bonheur. [Paris, 1976]. pp. 171.

RESOURCES and the environment: a socialist perspective; edited by Michael Barratt Brown [and others]. Nottingham, 1976. pp. 157. *Papers based on the materials prepared for a 1975 Spokesman conference on the environment.*

SCHUMPETER (JOSEPH ALOIS) Capitalism, socialism and democracy. 5th ed. London, 1952 repr. 1976. pp. 437. *Reprint contains a new introduction by Tom Bottomore.*

SIK (OTA) The third way: Marxist-Leninist theory and modern industrial society;...translated by Marian Sling. London, 1976. pp. 431. *bibliog.*

VILENSKA (ESTHER) Confrontation and unity within the labor movement, 1889-1923. New York, [1976]. pp. 98. *bibliog.*

COATES (KEN) Beyond wage slavery. Nottingham, 1977. pp. 170.

The JUST society; edited by Ken Coates and Fred Singleton. Nottingham, 1977. pp. 183. *A selection of papers submitted to the Bradford Seminar, The Just Society, sponsored by Bradford University and the Bertrand Russell Peace Foundation in Sept. 1976.*

TILLICH (PAUL JOHANNES OSKAR) The socialist decision; translated by Franklin Sherman. New York, [1977]. pp. 185.

— **Congresses.**

INTERNATIONAL WORKING MEN'S ASSOCIATION. Congress, [5th], The Hague, 1872. The Hague congress of the First International, September 2- 7, 1872: minutes and documents; (translated by Richard Dixon and Alex Miller). Moscow, [1976]. pp. 758. *(Institut Marksizma-Leninizma. Documents of the First International)*

— **Historiography.**

ØSTERGAARD (UFFE) ed. Den materialistiske historieopfattelse i Danmark før 1945. I. En antologi med eksempler på forholdet mellem teori og praksis. Århus, 1973. pp. 351. *No more published.*

— **History.**

KRIVOGUZ (IGOR' MIKHAILOVICH) Osnovnye periody i zakonomernosti mezhdunarodnogo rabochego dvizheniia do Oktiabria 1917 g. Moskva, 1976. pp. 364.

VOLGIN (VIACHESLAV PETROVICH) Ocherki istorii sotsialisticheskikh idei: pervaia polovina XIX v. Moskva, 1976. pp. 419.

— **Periodicals — Bibliography.**

FONDAZIONE GIANGIACOMO FELTRINELLI. Catalogo dei periodici della biblioteca. Nendeln, 1977. 3 vols.

SOCIALISM, CHRISTIAN.

EAGLESON (JOHN) ed. Christians and socialism: documentation of the Christians for Socialism movement in Latin America; translated by John Durry. Maryknoll, N.Y., [1975]. pp. 246.

SOCIALISM AND CATHOLIC CHURCH.

EAGLESON (JOHN) ed. Christians and socialism: documentation of the Christians for Socialism movement in Latin America; translated by John Durry. Maryknoll, N.Y., [1975]. pp. 246.

CHAPUIS (ROBERT) Les Chrétiens et le socialisme: témoignage et bilan. [Paris, 1976]. pp. 270.

CORK WORKERS' CLUB. Historical Reprints. No. 15. The Connolly-DeLeon controversy: on wages, marriage and the church. Cork, [1976]. pp. 45.

POULAT (EMILE) Catholicisme, démocratie et socialisme: le mouvement catholique et Mgr. Benigni de la naissance du socialisme à la victoire du fascisme. [Paris, 1977]. pp. 562. *bibliog.*

SOCIALISM AND EDUCATION.

WINTER (MAX) Das Kind und der Sozialismus: eine Betrachtung. Berlin, 1924. pp. 135.

FISCHER (HILDEGARD) Der politische Sinn der Arbeiterbildung; mit einem Vorwort von Lutz v. Werder. Westberlin, [1975]. pp. 190. *bibliog. Reprint, with new introduction, of work originally published in Langensalza in 1933.*

SOCIALISM AND RELIGION.

FELIX (CELESTIN JOSEPH) Christianisme et socialisme. Paris, [1892]. pp. 36.

POUJOL (PIERRE) Socialistes et chrétiens avant 1848. Paris, [1956]. pp. 60.

POUJOL (PIERRE) Socialistes et chrétiens depuis 1924. Paris, [1957]. pp. 64.

SOCIALISM AND THE ARTS.

SIEMSEN (ANNA) Politische Kunst und Kunstpolitik. Berlin, 1927. pp. 48. *(Reichsleitung der Jungsozialisten. Jungsozialistische Schriftenreihe)*

SOCIALISM AND YOUTH.

HACKMACK (HANS) Die sozialistische Jugendbewegung. Berlin, [1918]. pp. 39.

DORIOT (JACQUES) La jeunesse communiste;...conférence faite à la première Ecole nationale du propagandiste de la jeunesse sur le but et le rôle de la jeunesse. Paris, [192-?]. pp. 39.

Die PARTEI vertraut der Jugend: zur Verwirklichung des Kommuniqués des Politbüros des ZK der SED zu Problemen der Jugend; [by Kurt Bürger and others], etc. Berlin, 1962. pp. 92. *bibliog. (Sozialistische Einheitspartei Deutschlands. Der Parteiarbeiter. Heft 10)*

INSTITUT FÜR MARXISTISCHE STUDIEN UND FORSCHUNGEN. Aus der Geschichte der deutschen Arbeiterjugendbewegung, 1904-1945: (Dokumente und Materialien). Frankfurt/Main, 1975. pp. 169. *(Institut für Marxistische Studien und Forschungen. Neudrucke zur Sozialistischen Theorie und Gewerkschaftspraxis. Band 7)*

KRAUSE (WOLFGANG) and others. Zwischen Anpassung und sozialistischer Politik: zur Geschichte der Jungsozialisten seit 1945. Berlin, 1975. pp. 146.

PETERSON (CARL GUNNAR) Ungdom och politik: en studie av Sveriges Socialdemokratiska Ungdomsförbund. Stockholm, [1975]. pp. 282. *bibliog. With English summary.*

HONECKER (ERICH) Zur Jugendpolitik der SED: Reden und Aufsätze von 1945 bis zur Gegenwart. Berlin, [1977]. pp. 644.

SOCIALISM IN AFRICA.

GOSUDARSTVO sotsialisticheskoi orientatsii. Moskva, 1975. pp. 376. *bibliog. (Akademiia Nauk SSSR. Institut Gosudarstva i Prava. Gosudarstvo i Pravo Stran, Osvobodivshikhsia ot Kolonial'noi Zavisimosti. [5])*

SOCIALISM IN ASIA.

GOSUDARSTVO sotsialisticheskoi orientatsii. Moskva, 1975. pp. 376. *bibliog. (Akademiia Nauk SSSR. Institut Gosudarstva i Prava. Gosudarstvo i Pravo Stran, Osvobodivshikhsia ot Kolonial'noi Zavisimosti. [5])*

SOCIALISM IN AUSTRIA.

WINTER (MAX) Das Kind und der Sozialismus: eine Betrachtung. Berlin, 1924. pp. 135.

DEUTSCH (JULIUS) Was wollen die Sozialisten?; mit einem Vorwort von Adolf Schärf. Wien, [1949]. pp. 192.

KLENNER (FRITZ) Denkanstösse zum Überleben: Diskussionsbeitrag zu einem neuen SPÖ-Programm. Wien, [1976]. pp. 174. *bibliog.*

SOCIALISM IN CANADA.

RANKIN (HARRY) A socialist perspective for Vancouver. Toronto, [1974?]. pp. 83.

WAFFLE MOVEMENT. The Waffle manifesto; (including resolutions prepared by the movement for the Federal Convention of the New Democratic Party). Vancouver, [1974]. pp. 60. *bibliog.*

SOCIALISM IN CHILE.

ROXBOROUGH (IAN) and others. Chile: the state and revolution. London, 1977. pp. 304. *bibliog.*

SOCIALISM IN CHINA.

CELL (CHARLES PRESTON) Revolution at work: mobilization campaigns in China. New York, [1977]. pp. 221. *bibliog.*

SOCIALISM IN CZECHOSLOVAKIA.

KAVAN (JAN) and DANIEL (JAN) pseud., eds. Sotsialisticheskaia oppozitsiia v Chekhoslovakii, 1973-75: podborka dokumentov; perevod [s cheshskogo] Iriny Khenkinoi. London, 1976. pp. 342. *bibliog.*

SOCIALISM IN EUROPE.

SOCIALISM IN EUROPE.

DEUTSCHES Bürgerbuch für 1846, zweiter Jahrgang; herausgegeben von H. Püttmann. Glashütten im Taunus, 1975. pp. 346. *Reprint of work originally published in Mannheim in 1846.*

NENNING (GUENTHER) Realisten oder Verräter?: die Zukunft der Sozialdemokratie. München, [1976]. pp. 255.

ARON (RAYMOND) Plaidoyer pour l'Europe décadente. Paris, 1977. pp. 511.

The JUST society; edited by Ken Coates and Fred Singleton. Nottingham, 1977. pp. 183. *A selection of papers submitted to the Bradford Seminar, The Just Society, sponsored by Bradford University and the Bertrand Russell Peace Foundation in Sept. 1976.*

SOCIALISM IN FRANCE.

RUGE (ARNOLD) Politician. Zwei Jahre in Paris: Studien und Erinnerungen. Leipzig, Jurany, 1846; Leipzig, 1975. 2 vols. *Facsimile reprint.*

HERVE (GUSTAVE) Das Vaterland der Reichen; [translated from the French]. Zürich, [190-?]. pp. 259.

SAUMONEAU (LOUISE) Etudes et critiques. [Paris, 192-?]. 5 pts.(in 1 vol.). *(Femme Socialiste, La. Publications)*

VAILLANT (EDOUARD) Opportunistes, radicaux et socialistes et autres articles. Paris, 1930. pp. 23. *(Femme Socialiste, La. Publications)*

VERECQUE (CHARLES) Misères et guerre: articles et poèmes. Paris, 1934. pp. 23. *(Femme Socialiste, La. Publications)*

DUMAY (JEAN BAPTISTE) Mémoires d'un militant ouvrier du Creusot, 1841-1905; introduction et notes par Pierre Ponsot. Grenoble, 1976. pp. 431. *(Centre d'Histoire du Syndicalisme. Collection)*

HISTOIRE du réformisme en France depuis 1920. Paris, [1976]. 2 vols. (in 1).

DEFFERRE (GASTON) Si demain la gauche...: réponses à Pierre Desgraupes. Paris, [1977]. pp. 286.

TOUCHARD (JEAN) La gauche en France depuis 1900. Paris, [1977]. pp. 383. *bibliog.*

— Congresses.

PARTI COMMUNISTE FRANÇAIS. Congrès, 22e, 1976. Le socialisme pour la France. Paris, 1976. pp. 221. *Contains the report of the Central Committee and the document adopted by the 22nd congress.*

SOCIALISM IN GERMANY.

DEUTSCHES Bürgerbuch für 1846, zweiter Jahrgang; herausgegeben von H. Püttmann. Glashütten im Taunus, 1975. pp. 346. *Reprint of work originally published in Mannheim in 1846.*

STEIN (LORENZ VON) Schriften zum Sozialismus, 1848, 1852, 1854; mit einem Vorwort zum Nachdruck von Eckart Pankoke. Darmstadt, 1974. pp. 101. *Contains reprints of 3 articles which were originally published in "Die Gegenwart".*

FALK (KURT) Die Bestrebungen der Socialdemokratie, beleuchtet vom Irrsinn Eugen Richters. Nürnberg, 1891. pp. 70.

FISCHER (EDMUND) Sozialismus und Beamtenschaft. [Berlin, 1919]. pp. 23.

MINCK (FRIEDRICH M.) Wirtschafts-Sozialismus. Berlin, [1919]. pp. 23.

OPPENHEIMER (FRANZ) Die soziale Forderung der Stunde: Gedanken und Vorschläge. Leipzig, 1919. pp. 39.

ZEPLER (WALLY) Der Weg zum Sozialismus. Berlin, [1919?]. pp. 31.

BARTH (EMIL) Sozialisierung: ihre Notwendigkeit, ihre Möglichkeit. Neukölln, 1920. pp. 37.

VORLAENDER (KARL) Kant, Fichte, Hegel und der Sozialismus. Berlin, 1920. pp. 105.

FECHNER (MAX) Wege und Ziele der Sozialdemokratie: Rede...am 13. Oktober 1945 in der Sozialistischen Tribüne. Berlin, [1945]. pp. 15.

SCHUMACHER (KURT) 1895-1952. Das Referat im Berliner Poststadion; im Anhang: Die Kundgebung der Sozialdemokratischen Partei, angenommen auf dem Parteitag in Hannover. [Berlin-Wilmersdorf, 1946]. pp. 16.

Die FRUEHSOZIALISTISCHEN Bünde in der Geschichte der deutschen Arbeiterbewegung: vom "Bund der Gerechten" zum "Bund der Kommunisten", 1836-1847: ein Tagungsbericht; bearbeitet und herausgegeben von Otto Büsch, Hans Herzfeld. ..; mit Beiträgen von Frolinde Balser [and others]. Berlin, 1975. pp. 209. *(IWK: internationale wissenschaftliche Korrespondenz zur Geschichte der deutschen Arbeiterbewegung. Beihefte. 2)*

SCHLEIFSTEIN (JOSEF) Zur Geschichte und Strategie der Arbeiterbewegung: ausgewählte Beiträge. Frankfurt am Main, 1975. pp. 290.

TETZLAFF (KARL ULRICH) Friedrich Lessner: ein Kampfgefährte von Karl Marx und Friedrich Engels; aus Anlass seines 150. Geburtstages. Weimar, [1975]. pp. 31. *bibliog. (Stadtmuseum Weimar. Weimarer Schriften zur Heimatgeschichte und Naturkunde. Heft 27)*

AKTUELLE Bedeutung der Marxschen Randglossen zum Gothaer Programm; (Autoren: Wolfgang Heinrichs [and others]). Berlin, 1976. pp. 140. *(Akademie der Wissenschaften der DDR. Zentralinstitut für Wirtschaftswissenschaften. Forschungsberichte. Nr.18)*

FRICKE (DIETER) Die deutsche Arbeiterbewegung, 1869 bis 1914: ein Handbuch über ihre Organisation und Tätigkeit im Klassenkampf. Westberlin, [1976]. pp. 976. *bibliog.*

GERNS (WILLI) Krise der bürgerlichen Ideologie und ideologischer Kampf in der BRD. Frankfurt/Main, 1976. pp. 268.

GRAF (WILLIAM DAVID) The German left since 1945: socialism and social democracy in the German Federal Republic. Cambridge, [1976]. pp. 318. *bibliog.*

LIEBKNECHT (WILHELM PHILIPP MARTIN CHRISTIAN LUDWIG) Kleine politische Schriften; (herausgegeben von Wolfgang Schröder). Leipzig, 1976. pp. 413.

NA'AMAN (SHLOMO) ed. Von der Arbeiterbewegung zur Arbeiterpartei: der Fünfte Vereinstag der Deutschen Arbeitervereine zu Nürnberg im Jahre 1868; eine Dokumentation. Berlin, 1976. pp. 186. *bibliog. (IWK: internationale wissenschaftliche Korrespondenz zur Geschichte der deutschen Arbeiterbewegung. Beihefte. 4)*

NEGT (OSKAR) Keine Demokratie ohne Sozialismus: über den Zusammenhang von Politik, Geschichte und Moral. Frankfurt am Main, 1976. pp. 496. *bibliog. Collection of essays and speeches.*

RITTER (GERHARD A.) Arbeiterbewegung, Parteien und Parlamentarismus: Aufsätze zur deutschen Sozial- und Verfassungsgeschichte des 19. und 20. Jahrhunderts. Göttingen, 1976. pp. 412.

SCHULZ (URSULA) ed. Die deutsche Arbeiterbewegung, 1848-1919, in Augenzeugenberichten. München, 1976. pp. 437. *bibliog.*

SKAMBRAKS (HANNES)"Das Kapital" von Marx: Waffe im Klassenkampf: Aufnahme und Anwendung der Lehren des Hauptwerkes von Karl Marx durch die deutsche Arbeiterbewegung, 1867 bis 1878. Berlin, 1977. pp. 328. *bibliog.*

VOLLMAR (GEORG VON) Reden und Schriften zur Reformpolitik; ausgewählt und eingeleitet von Willy Albrecht. Berlin, [1977]. pp. 254. *bibliog.*

— Bibliography.

LIBRA. Libra Antiquaria Catalogues. N.1. Socialisme; Troisième Internationale. Milan, 1958. pp. 30.

SOCIALISM IN GREECE.

LEON (GEORGE B.) The Greek socialist movement and the First World War: the road to unity. Boulder, Col., 1976. pp. 204. *bibliog. (East European Quarterly. East European Monographs. 18)*

SOCIALISM IN GUYANA.

JAGAN (CHEDDI BERRETT) Towards understanding...; the text of an address to the National Press Club, Washington, D.C., U.S.A., October, 1961. [Georgetown, 1961]. pp. 7.

GUYANA. Ministry of Information. 1970. The co-operative republic. 1. The philosophy of a co-operative socialist society unites the people in a common effort. [Georgetown, 1970]. pp. 15.

SOCIALISM IN INDIA.

GHOSE (SANKAR) Indira Gandhi, the resurgent Congress and socialism. New Delhi, 1975. pp. 58.

FICKETT (LEWIS P.) The major socialist parties of India: a study in leftist fragmentation. Syracuse, N.Y., 1976. pp. 185. *(Syracuse University. Maxwell Graduate School of Citizenship and Public Affairs. Foreign and Comparative Studies. South Asian Series. No. 2)*

SOCIALISM IN IRELAND.

RUMPF (ERHARD) and HEPBURN (ANTHONY C.) Nationalism and socialism in twentieth-century Ireland. Liverpool, 1977. pp. 275. *bibliog.*

SOCIALISM IN KOREA.

BRUN (ELLEN) and HERSH (JACQUES) Socialist Korea: a case study in the strategy of economic development. New York, [1976]. pp. 432.

SOCIALISM IN LITERATURE.

MORRIS (WILLIAM) Selected writings and designs; edited with an introduction by Asa Briggs; with a supplement by Graeme Shankland on William Morris, designer, illustrated by twenty-four plates. Harmondsworth, 1962, repr. 1977. pp. 309. *bibliog.*

ESSAYS in B.C. political economy; edited by Paul Knox and Philip Resnick. Vancouver, [1974]. pp. 81. *Essays mainly from the first conference of the British Columbia Committee on Socialist Studies, held at the University of British Columbia in January, 1973.*

SOCIALISM IN MALI (REPUBLIC).

ERNST (KLAUS) Tradition and progress in the African village: the non-capitalist transformation of rural communities in Mali; (translated from the German). London, 1976. pp. 262. *bibliog.*

SOCIALISM IN POLAND.

IAZHBOROVSKAIA (INESSA SERGEEVNA) and BUKHARIN (N.I.) U istokov pol'skogo sotsialisticheskogo dvizheniia. Moskva, 1976. pp. 412.

BROCK (PETER) Polish revolutionary populism: a study in agrarian socialist thought from the 1830s to the 1850s. Toronto, [1977]. pp. 125. *bibliog.*

SOCIALISM IN PORTUGAL.

OLIVEIRA (CESAR) MFA y revolucion socialista; (traduccion: Jose Luis Rodriguez). Barcelona, [1975]. pp. 158.

SOCIALISM IN RUSSIA.

AURTHUR (JONATHAN) Socialism in the Soviet Union. Chicago, 1977. pp. 174. *bibliog.*

BORCKE (ASTRID VON) Die Ursprünge des Bolschewismus: die jakobinische Tradition in Russland und die Theorie der revolutionären Diktatur. München, [1977]. pp. 646. *bibliog.*

SOCIALISM IN SCANDINAVIA.

PETERSEN (CARL HEINRICH) Fra klassekampens slagmark i Norden. [Århus], 1973. pp. 252. *bibliog. Selection of broadcasts, articles and essays.*

SOCIALISM IN SINGAPORE.

NAIR (C.V. DEVAN) ed. Socialism that works: the Singapore way. Singapore, [1976]. pp. 267.

SOCIALISM IN SPAIN.

PRIETO (INDALECIO) De mi vida: recuerdos, estampas, siluetas, sombras. Mexico, 1968-70. 2 vols. *Vol.1 is a 1975 reprint of the 2nd ed.; vol.2 is the 1st ed.*

PRIETO (INDALECIO) Palabras al viento. Mexico, 1969. pp. 366. *First published in 1942.*

BALCELLS (ALBERT) Trabajo industrial y organizacion obrera en la Cataluña contemporanea, 1900-1936. Barcelona, 1974. pp. 324.

IGLESIAS POSSE (PABLO) Escritos 1: reformismo social y lucha de clases y otros textos; edicion a cargo de Santiago Castillo y Manuel Perez Ledesma. Madrid, 1975. pp. 330.

IGLESIAS POSSE (PABLO) Escritos 2: el socialismo en España; escritos en la prensa socialista y liberal, 1870-1925; seleccion y estudio preliminar de Luis Arranz [and others]. Madrid, 1975. pp. 464.

LOSADA (JUAN) Ideario politico de Pablo Iglesias. Barcelona, 1976. pp. 243. *bibliog.*

TEORIA y practica del movimiento obrero en España, 1900-1936; (edicion a cargo de Albert Balcells). Valencia, [1977]. pp. 335.

SOCIALISM IN SUBSAHARAN AFRICA.

SILVEIRA (ONESIMO) Africa south of the Sahara: party systems and ideologies of socialism. Uppsala, [1976]. pp. 212. *bibliog. (Uppsala, Statsvetenskapliga Föreningen. Skrifter. 71) Doctoral thesis, Uppsala University, 1976.*

SOCIALISM IN SWEDEN.

DAHLKVIST (MATS) Staten, socialdemokratin och socialismen: en inledande analys. [Stockholm, 1975]. pp. 236. *bibliog.*

SVENSSON (JÖRN) Du skall ta ledningen och makten: om socialismens uppbyggnad i Sverige. 3rd ed. Stockholm, 1975. pp. 323.

SCASE (RICHARD) Social democracy in capitalist society: working class politics in Britain and Sweden. London, [1977]. pp. 184. *bibliog. Revision of author's thesis (Ph.D.), University of Kent, 1974.*

SOCIALISM IN SWITZERLAND.

PFLUEGER (PAUL) and HUEPPY (JOHANN) Handbuch des schweizerischen Gemeindesozialismus. Zürich, 1910. pp. 267.

ENDERLI (HANS) Herunter mit der Maskee' Kampf den Schweizer Bolschewistene': ein Wort der Aufklärung und Mahnung an die schweizerische Arbeiterschaft. Zürich, 1918. pp. 31. *(Separat-Abdruck aus dem "Grütlianer")*

STOCKER (WERNER) 50 Jahre Kampf um die Freiheit: ein Gedenkwort zur fünfzigsten Maifeier. Zürich, 1939. pp. 32.

GRIMM (ROBERT) Die Arbeiterschaft in der Kriegszeit;...eine Rede vor dem Parteitag der bernischen Sozialdemokratie vom 18. Februar 1940. [Bern?, 1940]. pp. 32.

OPRECHT (HANS) Der zweite Weltkrieg und die schweizerische Arbeiterschaft. [Zürich, 1941]. pp. 31. *(Sozialdemokratische Partei der Schweiz. Kultur und Arbeit)*

WEBER (MAX) of the Schweizerischer Gewerkschaftsbund. Für eine soziale Schweiz. [Zürich], 1955. pp. 23.

SOCIALISM IN TANZANIA.

MSAMBICHAKA (L.A.) and MABELE (ROBERT B.) Agricultural credit and the development of Ujamaa villages in Tanzania. Dar es Salaam, [1974]. pp. 40. *bibliog. (Dar es Salaam. University. Economic Research Bureau. ERB Papers. 74.10)*

HYDEN (GORAN) "We must run while others walk": policy making for socialist development in the Tanzania-type of polities. Dar-es-Salaam, 1975. pp. 48. *bibliog. (Dar es Salaam. University. Economic Research Bureau. ERB Papers. 75.1)*

NYERERE (JULIUS KAMBARAGE) We must run while they walk; [two speeches]. Dar es Salaam, 1975. pp. 19. *(Reprinted from Mbioni: the journal of Kivukoni College, vol. 7, no. 8, 1975)*

URFER (SYLVAIN) Socialisme et église en Tanzanie; suivi d'une étude de Jacques Van Nieuwenhove sur présence chrétienne en société socialiste. Paris, [1975]. pp. 168. *bibliog.*

URFER (SYLVAIN) Une Afrique socialiste, la Tanzanie. Paris, [1976]. pp. 239. *bibliog.*

GREEN (REGINALD HERBOLD) Toward socialism and self reliance: Tanzania's striving for sustained transition projected. Uppsala, 1977. pp. 57. *(Nordiska Afrikainstitutet. Research Reports. No. 38)*

SOCIALISM IN THE NETHERLANDS.

VOS (HARMEN DE) Geschiedenis van het socialisme in Nederland in het kader van zijn tijd. Baarn, [1976]. 2 vols.

SOCIALISM IN THE UNITED KINGDOM.

PHILLPOTTS (HENRY) Bishop of Exeter. Socialism; speech of the Right Reverend the Lord Bishop of Exeter on socialism. London, Walter, 1840. pp. 16.

MARX (ELEANOR) Die Arbeiterclassen-Bewegung in England;...übersetzt von Gertrud Liebknecht; mit einem Vorwort von W. Liebknecht. Nürnberg, 1895. pp. 24. *(Separat-Abdruck aus Band II des Volks-Lexikon, herausgegeben von E. Wurm)*

MURRY (JOHN MIDDLETON) The necessity of pacifism. London, 1937. pp. 132.

COATES (KEN) Socialists and the Labour Party; [reprint of an article published in The Socialist Register in 1973]. Nottingham, [1976?]. pp. 24. *(Spokesman, The. Pamphlets. No. 52)*

MOCHALOV (LEONID VASIL'EVICH) Marksistsko-leninskaia otsenka fabianskogo sotsializma. Moskva, 1976. pp. 88.

RYZHIKOV (VLADIMIR ALEKSANDROVICH) "Sozialismus" auf Labour-Art: Mythen und Wirklichkeit; (deutsch von I. Markow). Moskau, [1976]. pp. 300.

CHALLINOR (RAYMOND) The origins of British bolshevism. London, 1977. pp. 291. *bibliogs.*

COMMUNIST PARTY OF GREAT BRITAIN. The British road to socialism; draft of the programme...prepared. ..for discussion...in the period up to the 35th national congress... 1977. London, [1977?]. 1 pamphlet (unpaged).

ESSAYS in labour history, [vol. 3], 1918-1939; edited by Asa Briggs [and] John Saville. London, [1977]. pp. 292.

FOOT (PAUL) Why you should be a socialist: the case for a new socialist party; ...cartoons by Phil Evans. London, 1977. pp. 93.

PIMLOTT (BEN) Labour and the Left in the 1930s. Cambridge, 1977. pp. 259. *bibliog.*

SCASE (RICHARD) Social democracy in capitalist society: working class politics in Britain and Sweden. London, [1977]. pp. 184. *bibliog. Revision of author's thesis (Ph.D.), University of Kent, 1974.*

TYRRELL (R. EMMETT) ed. The future that doesn't work: social democracy's failures in Britain; by Samuel Brittan [and others]. Garden City, N.Y., 1977. pp. 208.

SOCIALISM IN THE UNITED STATES.

FAILURE of a dream?: essays in the history of American socialism; edited by John H.M. Laslett and Seymour Martin Lipset. Garden City, N.Y., 1974. pp. 754.

BURBANK (GARIN) When farmers voted red: the gospel of socialism in the Oklahoma countryside, 1910-1924. Westport, Conn., 1976. pp. 224. *bibliog.*

CLECAK (PETER) Crooked paths: reflections on socialism, conservatism and the welfare state. New York, [1977]. pp. 206.

MYERS (CONSTANCE ASHTON) The prophet's army: Trotskyists in America, 1928-1941. Westport, Conn., 1977. pp. 281. *bibliog.*

SOCIALISM IN YUGOSLAVIA.

SOCIALISM in Yugoslav theory and practice: collection of conferences; [organized by the International Center for Social Sciences, University of Belgrade]. Beograd, 1976. pp. 179. *(Belgrade. Univerzitet. Medjunarodni Univerzitetski Centar za Društvene Nauke. [Publications]. 8) In English or French.*

SOCIALISM IN ZAMBIA.

KAUNDA (KENNETH DAVID) Humanism in Zambia and a guide to its implementation. Lusaka, 1968-74. 2 pts. (in 1 vol.).

SOCIALIST COMPETITION.

ESDERTS (HANS JOACHIM) Der sozialistische Wettbewerb: Darstellung und Problematik. Berlin, 1976. pp. 244,xxxii. *bibliog. Inaugural-Dissertation zur Erlangung des Grades eines Doktors der Wirtschaftswissenschaft an der Freien Universität Berlin.*

SOCIALIST PARTIES.

PROGRAMMI e statuti socialisti, 1890-1903; presentazione di Franco Andreucci. Firenze, 1974. pp. 49.

FICKETT (LEWIS P.) The major socialist parties of India: a study in leftist fragmentation. Syracuse, N.Y., 1976. pp. 185. *(Syracuse University. Maxwell Graduate School of Citizenship and Public Affairs. Foreign and Comparative Studies. South Asian Series. No. 2)*

SOCIALIST PARTY (ARGENTINE REPUBLIC).

PARTIDO SOCIALISTA DE LA ARGENTINA. Causes qui motivèrent le conflit interne du Parti Socialiste de la République Argentine: rapport présenté au camarade Emile Vandervelde par le Comité exécutif national. Buenos Aires, 1928. pp. 62.

SOCIALIST PARTY (AUSTRIA).

DEUTSCH (JULIUS) Was wollen die Sozialisten?; mit einem Vorwort von Adolf Schärf. Wien, [1949]. pp. 192.

KLUB DER SOZIALISTISCHEN ABGEORDNETEN UND BUNDESRÄTE. Die Bundesregierung informiert: verwirklicht und gehalten; ein Leistungsbericht der Regierung Kreisky. 2nd ed. Wien, 1971. pp. 104.

KREISKY (BRUNO) Vom Heute ins Morgen: Rede vor dem Villacher Parteitag 1972 der SPÖ. Wien, [1972]. pp. 36.

Das JAHR 1934: 12. Februar; Protokoll des Symposiums in Wien am 5. Februar 1974; (herausgegeben von Ludwig Jedlicka und Rudolf Neck). Wien, 1975. pp. 163. *bibliog. (Theodor-Körner-Stiftungsfonds and Leopold-Kunschak-Preis. Wissenschaftliche Kommission zur Erforschung der Österreichischen Geschichte der Jahre 1927 bis 1938. Veröffentlichungen. Band 2)*

KLENNER (FRITZ) Denkanstösse zum Überleben: Diskussionsbeitrag zu einem neuen SPÖ-Programm. Wien, [1976]. pp. 174. *bibliog.*

KONECNY (ALBRECHT K.) Sozialismus: von der Utopie zur Realität: Anmerkungen zu einem sozialistischen Programm. Wien, [1976]. pp. 104.

PROGRAMME der österreichischen revolutionären Arbeiterparteien, 1888-1946. Wien, 1976. pp. 61. *bibliog.*

SOCIALIST PARTY (AUSTRIA).(Cont.)

WEBER (FRIEDRICH) Historian. Die linken Sozialisten, 1945-1948: Parteiopposition im beginnenden Kalten Krieg. Salzburg, 1977. 2 vols. *bibliog. Dissertation zur Erlangung des Doktorgrades an der Philosophischen Fakultät der Universität Salzburg.*

SOCIALIST PARTY (FRANCE).

RAUZE (MARIANNE) La propagande socialiste. Paris, 1919. pp. 23.

PARTI SOCIALISTE. L'élu socialiste au service de tous. Paris, [1965]. pp. 78. *Cover title: Elections municipales 1965.*

HISTOIRE du réformisme en France depuis 1920. Paris, [1976]. 2 vols. (in 1).

JUDT (TONY) La reconstruction du Parti socialiste, 1921-1926. Paris, [1976]. pp. 232. *bibliog. (Fondation Nationale des Sciences Politiques. Travaux et Recherches de Science Politique. 39)*

SOCIALIST PARTY (ITALY).

LEZIONI di storia del Partito Socialista Italiano, 1892-1975; [by] G. Arfè [and others]. Firenze, 1976. pp. 268. *bibliog.*

SOCIALIST PARTY (UNITED STATES).

BURBANK (GARIN) When farmers voted red: the gospel of socialism in the Oklahoma countryside, 1910-1924. Westport, Conn., 1976. pp. 224. *bibliog.*

SOCIALIST-REVOLUTIONARY PARTY (RUSSIA).

KAPTSUGOVICH (IGOR' SEVAST'IANOVICH) Istoriia politicheskoi gibeli eserov na Urale. Perm', 1975. pp. 191.

PODBOLOTOV (PAVEL ALEKSEEVICH) Krakh esero-men'shevistskoi kontrrevoliutsii. Leningrad, 1975. pp. 120.

PERRIE (MAUREEN) The agrarian policy of the Russian Socialist-Revolutionary Party from its origins through the revolution of 1905-1907. Cambridge, 1976. pp. 216. *bibliog. (National Association for Soviet and East European Studies. Soviet and East European Studies)*

SOCIALIST WORKERS PARTY (UNITED STATES).

MYERS (CONSTANCE ASHTON) The prophet's army: Trotskyists in America, 1928-1941. Westport, Conn., 1977. pp. 281. *bibliog.*

SOCIALISTS.

POUJOL (PIERRE) Socialistes et chrétiens avant 1848. Paris, [1956]. pp. 60.

POUJOL (PIERRE) Socialistes et chrétiens depuis 1924. Paris, [1957]. pp. 64.

— Germany.

HIRSCH (HELMUT) Freiheitsliebende Rheinländer: neue Beiträge zur deutschen Sozialgeschichte: Friedrich Engels, Robert Blum, Carl Heinrich Marx, August Bebel, Karl Marx, Ferdinand Lassalle, etc. Düsseldorf, 1977. pp. 272.

SOCIALIZATION.

SOCIALISATION in Australia; edited by F.J. Hunt. Sydney, 1972. pp. 317.

LUNDBERG (MARGARET J.) The incomplete adult: social class constraints on personality development. Westport, Conn., [1974]. pp. 245. *bibliog.*

SCANZONI (LETHA) and SCANZONI (JOHN H.) Men, women and change: a sociology of marriage and family. New York, [1976]. pp. 504. *bibliog.*

SCHWARTZ (THEODORE) ed. Socialization as cultural communication: development of a theme in the work of Margaret Mead. Berkeley, Calif., [1976]. pp. 251. *bibliogs. (Reprinted from Ethos, vol.3,no.2, 1975)*

TELEVISION and socialization processes in the family: a documentation of the Prix Jeunesse Seminar, 1975. München, [1976]. pp. 192. *Special English issue of Fernsehen und Bildung, vol. 9, 2/3.*

LACEY (COLIN) The socialization of teachers. London, 1977. pp. 160. *bibliog.*

PLURALISM in a democratic society; edited by Melvin M. Tumin and Walter Plotch. New York, 1977. pp. 248. *bibliogs. Based on a conference convened by the Anti-Defamation League of B'nai B'rith, held in April 1975 in New York.*

POPULAR education and socialization in the nineteenth century; edited by Phillip McCann. London, 1977. pp. 276.

SOCIALLY HANDICAPPED

— United Kingdom.

U.K. Department of the Environment. 1975. Study of the inner areas of conurbations: supplement: analysis of 1971 census indicators. [London], 1975. pp. 72.

McGRATH (MORAG) Batley East and West: a C[ommunty] D[evelopment] P[roject] survey. [York, 1976]. pp. 62. *(Papers in Community Studies. No. 6)*

STEWART (JOHN DAVID) and others. Local government: approaches to urban deprivation. [London, 1976]. pp. 62. *(U.K. Home Office. Urban Deprivation Unit. Occasional Papers. No. 1)*

COMMUNITY DEVELOPMENT PROJECT. Gilding the ghetto: the state and the poverty experiments. [London, 1977]. pp. 64.

COMMUNITY DEVELOPMENT PROJECT. Limits of the law. London, 1977. pp. 54. *bibliog.*

COMMUNITY RELATIONS COMMISSION. Urban deprivation, racial inequality and social policy; a report. London, H.M.S.O., 1977. pp. 100.

LLEWELYN-DAVIES WEEKS [AND PARTNERS]. Unequal city: final report of the Birmingham inner area study. London, H.M.S.O., 1977. pp. 339. *bibliog.*

SHANKLAND-COX PARTNERSHIP and INSTITUTE OF COMMUNITY STUDIES. Inner area study: Lambeth: second report on multiple deprivation. [London], Department of the Environment, [1977]. pp. 70.

SHANKLAND-COX PARTNERSHIP and INSTITUTE OF COMMUNITY STUDIES. Inner London: policies for dispersal and balance: final report of the Lambeth inner area study. London, H.M.S.O., 1977. pp. 243. *bibliog.*

U.K. Department of the Environment. 1977. Inner area studies: Liverpool, Birmingham and Lambeth: summaries of consultants' final reports. London, 1977. pp. 49.

WILSON (HUGH) AND WOMERSLEY (LEWIS) Firm, and others. Change or decay: final report of the Liverpool inner area study. London, H.M.S.O., 1977. pp. 240.

— — Research.

RUTTER (MICHAEL LLEWELLYN) and MADGE (NICOLA) Cycles of disadvantage: a review of research. London, 1976. pp. 413. *bibliog.*

— United States — Research.

RUTTER (MICHAEL LLEWELLYN) and MADGE (NICOLA) Cycles of disadvantage: a review of research. London, 1976. pp. 413. *bibliog.*

SOCIALLY HANDICAPPED CHILDREN

— Education — United States.

TORBERT (WILLIAM R.) Creating a community of inquiry: conflict, collaboration, transformation. London, [1976]. pp. 184. *bibliog.*

— United Kingdom.

DAVIE (RONALD) Children and families with special needs; an inaugural lecture given on 22 January 1975 at University College, Cardiff. Cardiff, [1975]. pp. 17. *bibliog.*

BELL (LORNA) Underprivileged underfives. London, 1976. pp. 121. *bibliogs.*

SOCIALLY HANDICAPPED YOUTH

— United Kingdom.

JONES (PAULINE) and others. All their future: a study of the problems of a group of school leavers in a disadvantaged area of Liverpool. Oxford, 1975. pp. 57.

SOCIOLINGUISTICS.

QUESTIONS à la sociologie française;...textes réunis et préparés par Yvonne Roux. [Paris, 1976]. pp. 279. *(Association Internationale des Sociologues de Langue Française. Cahiers Internationaux de Sociologie) Papers of a round table sponsored by the Association in 1974.*

ADLAM (DIANA S.) Code in context. London, 1977. pp. 253. *bibliog.*

HAWKINS (PETER R.) Social class, the nominal group and verbal strategies. London, 1977. pp. 242. *bibliog.*

SOCIOCULTURAL dimensions of language change; edited by Ben G. Blount [and] Mary Sanches. New York, [1977]. pp. 293. *bibliogs.*

TALKING to children: language input and acquisition: papers from a conference sponsored by the Committee on Sociolinguistics of the Social Science Research Council (USA); edited by Catherine E. Snow and Charles A. Ferguson. Cambridge, 1977. pp. 369. *bibliog.*

SOCIOLOGICAL JURISPRUDENCE.

BANKOWSKI (ZENON) and MUNGHAM (GEOFF) Images of law. London, 1976. pp. 178. *bibliog.*

BRYDE (BRUN OTTO) The politics and sociology of African legal development. Frankfurt am Main, 1976. pp. 290. *bibliog. (Hamburg. Hansische Universität. Institut für Internationale Angelegenheiten. Veröffentlichungen. Band 2)*

NAZAROV (BORIS LAZAREVICH) Sotsialisticheskoe pravo v sisteme sotsial'nykh sviazei: razvitie vzgliadov na osnovnye vnutrennie i vneshnie sviazi sotsialisticheskogo prava. Moskva, 1976. pp. 311.

SOCIOLOGICAL REVIEW, THE; [published by] the University of Keele. Monographs. No. 23. The sociology of law; issue editor, Pat Carlen. Keele, 1976. pp. 250. *bibliogs.*

BEIRNE (PIERS) Fair rent and legal fiction: housing rent legislation in a capitalist society. London, 1977. pp. 240. *bibliog.*

HOROWITZ (DONALD L.) The courts and social policy. Washington, D.C., [1977]. pp. 309.

HURST (JAMES WILLARD) Law and social order in the United States. Ithaca, N.Y., 1977. pp. 318.

SOCIAL anthropology and law; edited by Ian Hamnett. London, 1977. pp. 234. *(Association of Social Anthropologists of the Commonwealth. A.S.A. Monographs. 14) Papers of a conference held at the University of Keele in March 1974.*

WATSON (ALAN) Society and legal change. Edinburgh, [1977]. pp. 148.

SOCIOLOGICAL RESEARCH.

COMMUNICATION and communication barriers in sociology; [by] Gunnar Boalt [and others]. Stockholm, [1976]. pp. 63. *bibliogs.*

EISENSTADT (SHMUEL N.) and CURELARU (M.) The form of sociology: paradigms and crises. New York, [1976]. pp. 386.

— History.

FREIDHEIM (ELIZABETH A.) Sociological theory in research practice. Cambridge, Mass., 1976. pp. 325. *bibliogs.*

SOCIOLOGISTS.

COMMUNICATION and communication barriers in sociology; [by] Gunnar Boalt [and others]. Stockholm, [1976]. pp. 63. *bibliogs.*

SOCIOLOGY.

BERGER (PETER L.) Invitation to sociology: a humanistic perspective. Harmondsworth, 1963. pp. 219. *bibliog.*

SCHNEIDER (LOUIS) The sociological way of looking at the world. New York, [1975]. pp. 343. *bibliog.*

AMERICAN SOCIOLOGICAL ASSOCIATION. Annual Meeting, 70th, 1975. The uses of controversy in sociology; edited by Lewis A. Coser and Otto N. Larsen. New York, [1976]. pp. 398. *bibliogs. Papers originally written for presentation at the 1975 annual meeting.*

CONGALTON (ATHOL ALEXANDER) The individual in society: an introduction to sociology for nurses. Sydney, [1976]. pp. 259. *bibliogs.*

CONGALTON (ATHOL ALEXANDER) and DANIEL (ANN E.) The individual in the making: an introduction to sociology. Sydney, [1976]. pp. 285. *bibliogs.*

ECONOMICS and sociology: towards an integration; edited by T. Huppes; contributors, N.J. Smelser [and others]. Leiden, 1976. pp. 178. *First written as discussion papers for a symposium organised by the Department of Economics, Groningen University, in September 1975.*

EISENSTADT (SHMUEL N.) and CURELARU (M.) The form of sociology: paradigms and crises. New York, [1976]. pp. 386.

LAWRENCE (PETER A.) Georg Simmel: sociologist and European. Sunbury-on-Thames, 1976. pp. 275.

MERTON (ROBERT KING) Sociological ambivalence and other essays. New York, [1976]. pp. 287.

The NEW social sciences; edited by Baidya Nath Varma. Westport, Conn., 1976. pp. 276. *bibliogs. Papers based on the Columbia University faculty seminar entitled "Content and Methods of the Social Sciences".*

OFFE (CLAUS) Industry and inequality: the achievement principle in work and social status;...translated by James Wickham. London, 1976. pp. 158. *bibliog.*

SOCIOLOGICAL ASSOCIATION OF IRELAND. Annual Conference, 2nd, Dublin, 1975. Proceedings of the...conference...; edited by A.E.C.W. Spencer and P.A. O'Dwyer. Belfast, 1976. pp. 137. *bibliogs.*

BINNS (DAVID) Beyond the sociology of conflict. London, 1977. pp. 257. *bibliog.*

CLOWERS (MYLES L.) and MORI (STEVEN H.) Understanding sociology through fiction. New York, [1977]. pp. 223. *bibliog.*

CULTURE and its creators: essays in honor of Edward Shils; edited by Joseph Ben-David and Terry Nichols Clark. Chicago, 1977. pp. 325.

DOUGLAS (JACK D.) and JOHNSON (JOHN M.) eds. Existential sociology. Cambridge, 1977. pp. 327. *bibliog.*

GIDDENS (ANTHONY) Studies in social and political theory. London, 1977. pp. 416.

GOUDSBLOM (JOHAN) Sociology in the balance: a critical essay. Oxford, [1977]. pp. 232. *bibliog.*

INTERESSE und Gesellschaft: Definitionen, Kontroversen, Perspektiven; herausgegeben von Peter Massing, Peter Reichel. München, [1977]. pp. 290. *bibliog.*

KINLOCH (GRAHAM CHARLES) Sociological theory: its development and major paradigms. New York, [1977]. pp. 319. *bibliogs.*

KOELNER ZEITSCHRIFT FÜR SOZIOLOGIE UND SOZIALPSYCHOLOGIE. Sonderhefte. 19. Soziologie und Sozialpolitik; herausgegeben von Christian von Ferber und Franz-Xaver Kaufmann. Opladen, 1977. pp. 649. *bibliogs. Mainly consisting of revised versions of papers presented at the 18. Deutscher Soziologentag, 1976.*

LUKES (STEVEN) Essays in social theory. London, 1977. pp. 227.

MORRIS (MONICA B.) An excursion into creative sociology. Oxford, 1977. pp. 212. *bibliog.*

SCIMECCA (JOSEPH) The sociological theory of C. Wright Mills. Port Washington, N.Y., 1977. pp. 148. *bibliog.*

SOCIOLOGICAL theories of the economy; edited by Barry Hindess. London, 1977. pp. 199. *bibliog. This book contains revised versions of papers originally prepared for a seminar held in Liverpool in 1975.*

— Bibliography.

SOCIOLOGY THESES REGISTER; [pd. by] Social Science Research Council. a., 1976 (1st ed.)- London.

— History.

DE COPPENS (PETER ROCHE) Ideal man in classical sociology: the views of Comte, Durkheim, Pareto, and Weber. University Park, Pa., [1976]. pp. 174. *bibliog.*

FREIDHEIM (ELIZABETH A.) Sociological theory in research practice. Cambridge, Mass., 1976. pp. 325. *bibliogs.*

HAWTHORN (GEOFFREY) Enlightenment and despair: a history of sociology. Cambridge, 1976. pp. 295. *bibliog.*

HIRST (PAUL QUENTIN) Social evolution and sociological categories. London, 1976. pp. 135. *bibliog.*

WRONG (DENNIS HUME) Skeptical sociology. New York, 1976. pp. 322.

BENTON (TED) Philosophical foundations of the three sociologies. London, 1977. pp. 225.

— — Germany.

WHIMSTER (MICHAEL STEPHEN) Patrimonialism: its meaning for nineteenth century German historians with special reference to Max Weber's adoption and use of the term in his Herrschaftssoziologie. 1976. fo.172. *Typescript. Ph.D. (London) thesis: unpublished. This thesis is the property of London University and may not be removed from the Library.*

SLATER (PHILIP E.) Origin and significance of the Frankfurt School: a marxist perspective. London, 1977. pp. 185. *bibliog.*

TAR (ZOLTÁN) The Frankfurt School: the critical theories of Max Horkheimer and Theodor W. Adorno. New York, [1977]. pp. 243. *bibliog.*

— — Hungary.

HANAK (TIBOR) Die marxistische Philosophie und Soziologie in Ungarn. Stuttgart, 1976. pp. 231.

— — Spain.

LAPORTA SAN MIGUEL (FRANCISCO J.) Adolfo Posada: política y sociología en la crisis del liberalismo español. Madrid, 1974. pp. 355. *bibliog.*

— — United States.

MATTHEWS (FRED H.) Quest for an American sociology: Robert E. Park and the Chicago School. Montreal, 1977. pp. 278. *bibliog.*

— Mathematical models.

SOCIOLOGICAL REVIEW, THE; [published by] University of Keele. Monographs. [No.] 24. Mathematical models of sociology; issue editor, P. Krishnan. Keele, 1977. pp. 229. *bibliog.*

— Methodology.

AMERICAN SOCIOLOGICAL ASSOCIATION. Annual Meeting, 69th, 1974. Approaches to the study of social structure; edited by Peter M. Blau. New York, [1975]. pp. 294. *bibliog. Revised versions of the thematic presentations made at the plenary sessions of the meeting.*

BALDAMUS (WILHELM) The structure of sociological inference. London, 1976. pp. 238. *bibliog.*

DE COPPENS (PETER ROCHE) Ideal man in classical sociology: the views of Comte, Durkheim, Pareto, and Weber. University Park, Pa., [1976]. pp. 174. *bibliog.*

NOWAK (STEFAN) Understanding and prediction: essays in the methodology of social and behavioral theories. Dordrecht, [1976]. pp. 482. *bibliogs.*

SMELSER (NEIL JOSEPH) Comparative methods in the social sciences. Englewood Cliffs, [1976]. pp. 253.

BULMER (MARTIN) ed. Sociological research methods: an introduction. London, 1977. pp. 363. *bibliog.*

BUSFIELD (JOAN) and PADDON (MICHAEL) Thinking about children: sociology and fertility in post-war England. Cambridge, 1977. pp. 312. *bibliog.*

GORMAN (ROBERT A.) The dual vision: Alfred Schutz and the myth of phenomenological social science. London, 1977. pp. 234. *bibliog.*

NOWAK (STEFAN) Methodology of sociological research: general problems; translated from the Polish by Maria Olga Lepa. Dordrecht, [1977]. pp. 504.

UNDERSTANDING and social inquiry; edited by Fred R. Dallmayr and Thomas A. McCarthy. Notre Dame, Ind., [1977]. pp. 365. *bibliogs.*

— Philosophy.

ADLER (HANS GUENTHER) Die Freiheit des Menschen: Aufsätze zur Sociologie und Geschichte. Tübingen, 1976. pp. 358. *Some of the essays were originally published in the author's Die Erfahrung der Ohnmacht in 1964.*

CONNERTON (PAUL) ed. Critical sociology: selected readings. Harmondsworth, 1976. pp. 520. *bibliogs.*

PIASER (ANTONIO) Pour une sociologie scientifique: épistémologie comparée de l'analyse conceptuelle. Paris, [1976]. pp. 303.

— Study and teaching.

COMMUNICATION and communication barriers in sociology; [by] Gunnar Boalt [and others]. Stockholm, [1976]. pp. 63. *bibliogs.*

— — America, Latin.

FALS-BORDA (ORLANDO) Ciencia propia y colonialismo intelectual. Bogota, 1971. pp. 138. *Reprint of 1st ed. published in Mexico in 1970.*

SOCIOLOGY, CHRISTIAN.

RECKITT (MAURICE BENINGTON) Faith and society: a study of the structures, outlook and opportunity of the Christian social movement in Great Britain and the United States of America. London, 1932. pp. 467.

MARTY (MARTIN EMIL) A nation of behavers. Chicago, 1976. pp. 239.

SOCIOLOGY, MILITARY.

HARRIES-JENKINS (GWYN) The army in Victorian society. London, 1977. pp. 320.

PERLMUTTER (AMOS) The military and politics in modern times: on professionals, praetorians and revolutionary soldiers. New Haven, 1977. pp. 335. *Written under the auspices of the Center for International Affairs, Harvard University.*

WORLD perspectives in the sociology of the military; edited by George A. Kourvetaris and Betty A. Dobratz. New Brunswick, N.J., [1977]. pp. 294. *bibliogs.*

SOCIOLOGY, RURAL.

COMMUNITIES left behind: alternatives for development; [edited by] Larry R. Whiting. Ames, Iowa, 1974. pp. 151. *bibliogs. Papers presented at a symposium at South Dakota State University, 1973, sponsored by the North Central Regional Center for Rural Development and the University.*

SOCIOLOGY, URBAN.

PFEIL (ELISABETH) Die Familie im Gefüge der Grossstadt: zur Sozialtopographie der Stadt. Hamburg, [1965]. pp. 81. *(Gesellschaft für Wohnungs- und Siedlungswesen, Hamburg. Schriftenreihe)*

EUROPEAN FREE TRADE ASSOCIATION. 1973. Regional policy in EFTA: national settlement strategies; a framework for regional development. Geneva, 1973. pp. 241. *bibliog.*

BOOTH (ALAN) Urban crowding and its consequences. New York, 1976. pp. 139. *bibliog.*

MAN in urban environments; edited by G.A. Harrison and J.B. Gibson. Oxford, 1976. pp. 367. *bibliogs. Based on a series of meetings held by the Royal Society Study Group on Human Biology in Urban Environments.*

PICKVANCE (CHRISTOPHER GEOFFREY) ed. Urban sociology: critical essays. London, 1976. pp. 223. *bibliogs.*

BERRY (BRIAN JOE LOBLEY) and KASARDA (JOHN D.) Contemporary urban ecology. New York, [1977]. pp. 497. *bibliog.*

CAPTIVE cities: studies in the political economy of cities and regions; edited by Michael Harloe. London, [1977]. pp. 218. *Sponsored by the International Sociological Association Research Committee on the Sociology of Regional and Urban Development.*

MELLOR (J.R.) Urban sociology in an urbanized society. London, 1977. pp. 309.

SOIL MOISTURE

— Mathematical models.

LONDON. University. London School of Economics and Political Science. Graduate School of Geography. Discussion Papers. No. 58. Empirical evaluation of soil tension with emphasis on variations during a drying period; [by] Pong-wai Lai. London, 1976. pp. 29. *bibliog.*

SOIL SURVEYS

— Botswana.

MITCHELL (A.J.B.) The irrigation potential of soils along the main rivers of eastern Botswana: a reconnaissance assessment. Tolworth, 1976. pp. 216, 7 maps, 4 sheets of photomosaics. *bibliog. (U.K. Ministry of Overseas Development. Land Resources Division. Land Resource Studies. 7)*

— Nigeria.

SOILS of the Western State savanna in Nigeria; [by] G. Murdoch [and others]. Tolworth, 1976. 3 vols. and maps. *bibliog. (U.K. Ministry of Overseas Development. Land Resources Division. Land Resource Studies. 23)*

SOLOMON ISLANDS

— Constitution.

SOLOMON ISLANDS. Governing Council. Special Select Committee on Constitutional Development. 1972. Report; [T. Russell, chairman]. Honiara, 1972. 1 vol. (various pagings). *(Governing Council. Papers. 1972. No.89)*

— Economic policy.

SOLOMON ISLANDS. Office of the Chief Minister. 1975. National development plan, 1975-1979. Honiara, 1975. 3 vols.

— Social policy.

SOLOMON ISLANDS. Office of the Chief Minister. 1975. National development plan, 1975-1979. Honiara, 1975. 3 vols.

SOLZHENITSYN (ALEKSANDR ISAEVICH).

CARTER (STEPHEN) The politics of Solzhenitsyn. New York, 1977. pp. 162. *bibliog.*

SOMALI REPUBLIC

— Economic conditions.

SOMALI DEVELOPMENT BANK. Annual report and statement of accounts. a., 1975 (7th)- Mogadiscio.

— Economic policy.

SOMALI REPUBLIC. Ministry of Planning and Coordination. 1971. Development programme, 1971-1973. Mogadishu, 1971. pp. 232.

SOMALI REPUBLIC. Ministry of Planning and Coordination. 1974. Five year development programme, 1974-1978. Mogadishu, 1974. pp. 298.

— Social policy.

SOMALI REPUBLIC. Ministry of Planning and Coordination. 1971. Development programme, 1971-1973. Mogadishu, 1971. pp. 232.

SOMALI REPUBLIC. Ministry of Planning and Coordination. 1974. Five year development programme, 1974-1978. Mogadishu, 1974. pp. 298.

SOREL (GEORGES).

ZAGARI (EUGENIO) Marxismo e revisionismo: Bernstein, Sorel, Graziadei, Leone. Napoli, [1975]. pp. 357.

SOUL.

PELLETIER (MADELEINE) L'âme existe-t-elle? Paris, 1924. pp. 12. *(Brochure Mensuelle, La. No.24A)*

SOUTH AFRICA

— Census.

SOUTH AFRICA. Census, 1970. Population census, 1970: industry. [Pretoria, 1976]. pp. 552. *(Bureau of Statistics. Reports. No. 02-05-09) In English and Afrikaans.*

SOUTH AFRICA. Census, 1970. Population census, 1970: occupations: age, level of education, marital status, citizenship, birth-place, national unit. [Pretoria, 1976]. pp. 302. *(Bureau of Statistics. Reports. No. 02-05-11) In English and Afrikaans.*

— Civil defence.

SOUTH AFRICA. Parliament. House of Assembly. Select Committee on the Civil Protection Bill. 1977. First and second reports...; proceedings (S.C.4-1977). in SOUTH AFRICA. Parliament. House of Assembly. Select Committee reports.

— Defences.

McEWAN (CHRISTOPHER B.) The Soviet Union and the conventional threat to South Africa: a strategic analysis. Braamfontein, 1976. pp. 32.

— Description and travel.

SCHREINER (OLIVE) Thoughts on South Africa. Johannesburg, 1976. pp. 398. *Reprint of the 1923 edition with new foreword and illustrations.*

— Economic conditions.

MALAN (T.) and HATTINGH (P.S.) Black homelands in South Africa. Pretoria, 1976. pp. 254. *bibliog.*

TRUU (M.L.) ed. Public policy and the South African economy: essays in memory of Desmond Hobart Houghton. Cape Town, 1976. pp. 206. *bibliog.*

SOUTH AFRICA. Office of the Economic Adviser to the Prime Minister. 1977. Economic development programme for the republic of South Africa: summary and policy implications. [Pretoria, 1977]. pp. 29.

— — Mathematical models.

PORTER (RICHARD C.) A model of a South-African-type economy. Ann Arbor, 1976. pp. 42. *bibliog. (Michigan University. Center for Research on Economic Development. Discussion Papers. No.60)*

— Economic history.

BROWETT (J.G.) The evolution of the South African space economy: a summary and synthesis. Johannesburg, 1976. pp. 53. *bibliog. (Johannesburg. University of the Witwatersrand. Urban and Regional Research Unit. Occasional Papers. No. 10)*

— Economic policy.

TRUU (M.L.) ed. Public policy and the South African economy: essays in memory of Desmond Hobart Houghton. Cape Town, 1976. pp. 206. *bibliog.*

SOUTH AFRICA. Office of the Economic Adviser to the Prime Minister. 1977. Economic development programme for the republic of South Africa: summary and policy implications. [Pretoria, 1977]. pp. 29.

— Emigration and immigration.

WILSON (FRANCIS) Economist. International migration in southern Africa. Cape Town, 1976. pp. 42. *(Southern Africa Labour and Development Research Unit. SALDRU Working Papers. No. 1)*

— Foreign economic relations — Sweden.

MAGNUSSON (ÅKE) Sverige - Sydafrika: en studie av en ekonomisk relation. Uppsala, 1974. pp. 174.

— Foreign relations.

GEYSER (OCKERT) Détente in Southern Africa. Bloemfontein, 1976. pp. 59. *bibliog. (Universiteit van die Oranje-Vrystaat. Institute for Contemporary History. Focus on Politics. 2)*

LEGUM (COLIN) Vorster's gamble for Africa: how the search for peace failed. London, 1976. pp. 127.

JOHNSON (RICHARD WILLIAM) How long will South Africa survive? London, 1977. pp. 327.

— — Africa, Subsaharan.

METROWICH (F.R.) ed. Towards dialogue and détente. Sandton, S.A., 1975. pp. 139.

— — United States.

CARTER (GWENDOLEN MARGARET) American policy and the search for justice and reconciliation in South Africa; originally prepared for the Wingspread Symposium on South Africa: Policy Alternatives for the United States, convened April 1975 [at] Wingspread, Racine, Wisconsin, revised by the author in September 1976. Racine, Wisc., [1976]. pp. 52.

SOUTH Africa - the vital link; edited by Robert L. Schuettinger. Washington, D.C., 1976. pp. 120. *Essays from a seminar on United States-South African relations in Washington, D.C., on July 20, 1976, sponsored by the Council on American Affairs.*

— Historiography.

WRIGHT (HARRISON MORRIS) The burden of the present: liberal-radical controversy over Southern African history. Cape Town, 1977. pp. 137. *bibliog.*

— History.

DAVENPORT (THOMAS RODNEY HOPE) South Africa: a modern history. London, 1977. pp. 432. *bibliog.*

— — Sources.

FITZPATRICK (Sir JAMES PERCY) Fitzpatrick: South African politician: selected papers, 1888- 1906. Johannesburg, [1976]. pp. 562. *bibliog.*

— Industries.

SOUTH AFRICA. Census, 1970. Population census, 1970: industry. [Pretoria, 1976]. pp. 552. *(Bureau of Statistics. Reports. No. 02-05-09) In English and Afrikaans.*

— Learned institutions and societies.

EGELAND (LEIF) Report...[to the] meeting of the national executive council [of the South African Institute of International Affairs, Cape Town], 23 February, 1976. Braamfontein, [1976]. pp. 11.

— Native races.

SOUTH AFRICA. Department of the Auditor General. Report...on the accounts of the Central Orange Free State Area Bantu Affairs Administration Board. a., 1972/74(1st)- Pretoria. *[in English and Afrikaans]. Included in SOUTH AFRICA. Parliament. House of Assembly. Votes and proceedings (with Printed annexures).*

SOUTH AFRICA. Department of the Auditor General. Report...on the accounts of the Vaal Triangle Area Bantu Affairs Administration Board. a., 1972/74 (1st)- Pretoria. *[in English and Afrikaans] Included in SOUTH AFRICA. Parliament. House of Assembly. Votes and proceedings (with Printed annexures).*

SOUTH AFRICA. Department of the Auditor-General. Report...on the accounts of the Western Transvaal Area Bantu Affairs Administration Board. a., 1972/74- Pretoria. *[in English and Afrikaans]. Included in SOUTH AFRICA. Parliament. House of Assembly. Votes and proceedings (with Printed annexures).*

SOUTH AFRICA. Department of the Auditor-General. Report...on the accounts of the Central Transvaal Area Bantu Affairs Administration Board. a., 1973/75 (1st)- Pretoria. *[in English and Afrikaans] Included in SOUTH AFRICA. Parliament. House of Assembly. Votes and proceedings (with Printed annexures).*

SOUTH AFRICA. Department of the Auditor-General. Report...on the accounts of the Diamond Field Area Bantu Affairs Administration Board. a., 1973/75 (1st)- Pretoria. *[in English and Afrikaans]. Included in South Africa. Parliament. House of Assembly. Votes and proceedings (with Printed annexures).*

SOUTH AFRICA. Department of the Auditor-General. Report...on the accounts of the Drakensberg Area Bantu Affairs Administration Board. a., 1973/75 (1st)- Pretoria. *[in English and Afrikaans]. Included in SOUTH AFRICA. Parliament. House of Assembly. Votes and proceedings (with Printed annexures).*

SOUTH AFRICA. Department of the Auditor-General. Report...on the accounts of the East Rand Area Bantu Affairs Administration Board. a., 1973/75 (1st)- Pretoria. *[in English and Afrikaans]. Included in SOUTH AFRICA. Parliament. House of Assembly. Votes and proceedings (with Printed annexures).*

SOUTH AFRICA. Department of the Auditor General. Report...on the accounts of the Eastern Cape Area Bantu Affairs Administration Board. a., 1973/75(1st)- Pretoria. *[in English and Afrikaans]. Included in SOUTH AFRICA. Parliament. House of Assembly. Votes and proceedings (with Printed annexures).*

SOUTH AFRICA. Department of the Auditor General. Report...on the accounts of the Eastern Transvaal Area Bantu Affairs Administration Board. a., 1973/75 (1st)- Pretoria. *[in English and Afrikaans]. Included in SOUTH AFRICA. Parliament. House of Assembly. Votes and proceedings (with Printed annexures)*

SOUTH AFRICA. Department of the Auditor General. Report...on the accounts of the Highveld Area Bantu Affairs Administration Board. a., 1973/75 (1st)- Pretoria. *[in English and Afrikaans]. Included in SOUTH AFRICA. Parliament. House of Assembly. Votes and proceedings (with Printed annexures).*

SOUTH AFRICA. Department of the Auditor General. Report...on the accounts of the Karoo Area Bantu Affairs Administration Board. a., 1973/75 (1st)- Pretoria. *[in English and Afrikaans]. Included in SOUTH AFRICA. Parliament. House of Assembly. Votes and proceedings (with Printed annexures).*

SOUTH AFRICA. Department of the Auditor General. Report...on the accounts of the Midlands Area Bantu Affairs Administration Board. a., 1973/75 (1st)- Pretoria. *[in English and Afrikaans]. Included in SOUTH AFRICA. Parliament. House of Assembly. Votes and proceedings (with Printed annexures).*

SOUTH AFRICA. Department of the Auditor General. Report...on the accounts of the Northern Natal Area Bantu Affairs Administration Board. a., 1973/75 (1st)- Pretoria. *[in English and Afrikaans] Included in SOUTH AFRICA. Parliament. House of Assembly. Votes and proceedings (with Printed annexures).*

SOUTH AFRICA. Department of the Auditor-General. Report...on the accounts of the Northern Transvaal Area Bantu Affairs Administration Board. a., 1973/75 to date. Pretoria. *[in English and Afrikaans]. Included in SOUTH AFRICA. Parliament. House of Assembly. Votes and proceedings (with Printed annexures).*

SOUTH AFRICA. Department of the Auditor General. Report...on the accounts of the Peninsula Area Bantu Affairs Administration Board. a., 1973/75 (1st)- Pretoria. *[in English and Afrikaans] Included in SOUTH AFRICA. Parliament. House of Assembly. Votes and proceedings (with Printed annexures).*

SOUTH AFRICA. Department of the Auditor-General. Report...on the accounts of the Port Natal Area Bantu Affairs Administration Board. a., 1973/75 (1st)- Pretoria. *[in English and Afrikaans]. Included in SOUTH AFRICA. Parliament. House of Assembly. Votes and proceedings (with Printed annexures)*

SOUTH AFRICA. Department of the Auditor-General. Report...on the accounts of the Southern Transvaal Area Bantu Affairs Administration Board. a., 1973/75 (1st)- Pretoria. *[in English and Afrikaans]. Included in SOUTH AFRICA. Parliament. House of Assembly. Votes and proceedings.*

SOUTH AFRICA. Department of the Auditor-General. Report...on the accounts of the West Rand Area Bantu Affairs Administration Board. a., 1973/75 (1st)- Pretoria. *[in English and Afrikaans].Included in SOUTH AFRICA. Parliament. House of Assembly. Votes and proceedings (with Printed annexures).*

SOUTH AFRICA. Department of the Auditor General. Report...on the accounts of the Northern Orange Free State Area Bantu Affairs Administration Board. a., 1974/75- Pretoria. *[in English and Afrikaans]. Included in SOUTH AFRICA. Parliament. House of Assembly. Votes and proceedings (with Printed annexures).*

MALAN (T.) and HATTINGH (P.S.) Black homelands in South Africa. Pretoria, 1976. pp. 254. *bibliog.*

OCCUPATIONAL and social change among coloured people in South Africa: proceedings of a workshop of the Centre for Intergroup Studies at the University of Cape Town; edited by Hendrik W. van der Merwe and C.J. Groenewald. Cape Town, 1976. pp. 278. *bibliog.*

SOUTH AFRICA. Commission of Enquiry into Matters Relating to the Coloured Population Group. 1976. The Theron Commission report: a summary of the findings and recommendations of the Commission...; edited by S.T. van der Horst. Johannesburg, 1976. pp. 124.

SOUTH AFRICA. Parliament. House of Assembly. Select Committee on Bantu Affairs. 1977. First, second, third and fourth reports...; proceedings (S.C. 7- 1977). in SOUTH AFRICA. Parliament. House of Assembly. Select Committee reports.

— Politics and government.

SOUTH AFRICA. Coloured Persons Representative Council. Debates and proceedings. sess., My/S 1975-(2nd council, 1st and 2nd sess.)- Pretoria. *[In English and Afrikaans].*

MITCHELL (M.L.) The Christian Institute: the United Party view. Johannesburg, [1975]. fo. 5. *In English and Afrikaans.*

VORSTER (BALTHAZAR JOHANNES) Geredigeerde toesprake van die sewende eerste minister van Suid-Afrika;...onder redaksie van O. Geyser. Bloemfontein, [1976 in progress]. *bibliog.*

LEGUM (COLIN) Vorster's gamble for Africa: how the search for peace failed. London, 1976. pp. 127.

MALAN (T.) and HATTINGH (P.S.) Black homelands in South Africa. Pretoria, 1976. pp. 254. *bibliog.*

BROTZ (HOWARD MERVIN) The politics of South Africa: democracy and racial diversity. Oxford, 1977. pp. 164.

JOHNSON (RICHARD WILLIAM) How long will South Africa survive? London, 1977. pp. 327.

MAHABANE (E.E.) The urgent need for fundamental change in South Africa. Johannesburg, [1977]. pp. 11. *(South African Institute of Race Relations. Presidential Addresses. 1977)*

— Population.

BROWETT (J.G.) and FAIR (T.J.D.) South Africa: population potentials, 1867 to 1970. Johannesburg, 1972. fo. 20. *bibliogs.*

— Public lands.

SOUTH AFRICA. Parliament. House of Assembly. Select Committee on State-owned land. 1977. Report...; proceedings (S.C. 8-1977). in SOUTH AFRICA. Parliament. House of Assembly. Select Committee reports.

— Race question.

SCHREINER (OLIVE) Thoughts on South Africa. Johannesburg, 1976. pp. 398. *Reprint of the 1923 edition with new foreword and illustrations.*

SIEGFRIED (ANDRÉ) Les problèmes ethniques de l'Afrique du Sud; conférence faite à la tribune de l'Université Coloniale de Belgique à Anvers le 21 février 1949. [Anvers?, 1949?]. pp. 13. *(Supplément au Bulletin de l'Association des Anciens Etudiants de l'Université Coloniale de Belgique)*

SOUTH AFRICA. Supreme Court. Special Criminal Court, Pretoria. 1961. In the matter of the application of Farrid Adams and 29 others and the Crown: reasons for judgment [Mr. Justice Rumpff]. [Johannesburg?, 1961]. fo. 11.

JABBOUR (GEORGE) Settler colonialism in Southern Africa and the Middle East. Beirut, 1970. pp. 216. *(Palestine Research Center. Palestine Books. No. 30)*

NKONDO (G.M.) ed. Turfloop testimony: the dilemma of a black university in South Africa; [a memorandum by the Black Academic Staff Association of the University of the North to a Commission of Inquiry Concerning Certain Matters Relating to the University]. Johannesburg, 1976. pp. 93.

NTSHONA (V.K. SCRAPE) Soweto, June 1976: the call to arms. London, [1976]. pp. 20.

SEPARATION in South Africa: [no.]1: People and policies; edited by David M. Smith. London, 1976. pp. 76. *bibliogs. (London. University. Queen Mary College. Department of Geography. Occasional Papers. No.6)*

SEPARATION in South Africa: [no.] 2: Homelands and cities; edited by David M. Smith. London, 1976. pp. 97. *bibliogs. (London. University. Queen Mary College. Department of Geography. Occasional Papers. No. 7)*

SOUTH AFRICA. Commission of Enquiry into Matters Relating to the Coloured Population Group. 1976. The Theron Commission report: a summary of the findings and recommendations of the Commission...; edited by S.T. van der Horst. Johannesburg, 1976. pp. 124.

SOUTH AFRICAN CONGRESS OF TRADE UNIONS. Workers in chains. London, 1976. pp. 19.

TRUU (M.L.) ed. Public policy and the South African economy: essays in memory of Desmond Hobart Houghton. Cape Town, 1976. pp. 206. *bibliog.*

BOZZOLI (G.R.) Education is the key to change in South Africa. [Johannesburg], 1977. pp. 14. *(South African Institute of Race Relations. Hoernlé Memorial Lectures. 1977)*

MAHABANE (E.E.) The urgent need for fundamental change in South Africa. Johannesburg, [1977]. pp. 11. *(South African Institute of Race Relations. Presidential Addresses. 1977)*

SOUTH AFRICA(Cont.)

— Social conditions.

MALAN (T.) and HATTINGH (P.S.) Black homelands in South Africa. Pretoria, 1976. pp. 254. *bibliog.*

SOUTH AFRICAN WAR, 1899-1902.

SPIES (S. BURRIDGE) Methods of barbarism?: Roberts and Kitchener and civilians in the Boer republics, January 1900-May 1902. Cape Town, 1977. pp. 416. *bibliog.*

SOUTH AUSTRALIA

— Parliament — Elections.

HUGHES (COLIN ANFIELD) and GRAHAM (BRUCE DESMOND) Voting for the South Australian, Western Australian and Tasmanian Lower Houses, 1890-1964. Canberra, 1976. pp. 639. *Fifth and final supplement to the same authors' A handbook of Australian government and politics, 1890-1964, to which it also contains corrigenda.*

SOUTH SEA COMPANY.

[TRENCHARD (JOHN) Political writer, and GORDON (THOMAS) of Kirkcudbright]. A collection of all the political letters in the London Journal to December 17, inclusive, 1720. London, printed for J. Roberts, 1721. pp. ii, 60.

SOUTH WEST AFRICA.

SOUTH AFRICA. Department of Foreign Affairs. 1975. South West Africa survey, 1974. Pretoria, 1975. pp. (120).

— Constitution.

INTERNATIONAL DEFENCE AND AID FUND. Fact Papers on Southern Africa. No. 3. All options and none: the constitutional talks in Namibia. London, 1976. pp. 16.

— International status.

DUGARD (JOHN) and GROSSKOPF (E.M.) South West Africa and the International Court: two viewpoints on the 1971 advisory opinion. Johannesburg, [1975]. pp. 31.

DUGARD (JOHN) Namibia and human rights: a report on the Dakar conference and its implications for the South West Africa issue and détente. Braamfontein, 1976. pp. 19.

GILMORE (WILLIAM C.) Belligerent occupation, public property and war crimes in Namibia: a new role for international law. Ottawa, 1976. pp. 24. *(Carleton University. Norman Paterson School of International Affairs. Current Comment. 11)*

— Politics and government.

FRAENKEL (PETER) The Namibians of South West Africa. London, 1974. pp. 48. *bibliog. (Minority Rights Group. Reports. No. 19)*

INTERNATIONAL DEFENCE AND AID FUND. Fact Papers on Southern Africa. No. 3. All options and none: the constitutional talks in Namibia. London, 1976. pp. 16.

SERFONTEIN (J.H.P.) Namibia? Randburg, 1976. pp. 433.

WINTER (COLIN O'BRIEN) Bishop of Damaraland. Namibia. Guildford, 1977. pp. 234.

— Social conditions.

WINTER (COLIN O'BRIEN) Bishop of Damaraland. Namibia. Guildford, 1977. pp. 234.

SOUTH YORKSHIRE

— Statistics.

SOUTH YORKSHIRE STATISTICS; [pd. by] South Yorkshire County Council. a., 1975 (1st)- Barnsley.

SOUTHERN RAILWAY.

KLAPPER (CHARLES FREDERICK) Sir Herbert Walker's Southern Railway. London, 1973. pp. 295.

SOUTHWARK

— Politics and government.

HATCH (STEPHEN) and others. Research and reform: the case of the Southwark Community Development Project, 1969-1972. London, Home Office, Urban Deprivation Unit, 1977. pp. 292.

SOVEREIGNTY.

BEREZOWSKI (CEZARY) Zagadnienia zwierzchnictwa terytorialnego: z teorii prawa międzynarodowego. Warszawa, 1957. pp. 199. *With Russian and English summaries.*

STANKIEWICZ (WLADYSLAW JOZEF) Sovereign authority and the function of law in a democratic society. Madrid, 1973. pp. (7). *(Reprinted from Anuario de Filosofia del Derecho, vol.17, 1973-74)*

SOVIET CENTRAL ASIA

— Maps.

GLAVNOE UPRAVLENIE GEODEZII I KARTOGRAFII. Atlas avtomobil'nykh dorog: Kazakhstan i Sredniaia Aziia. Moskva, 1975. pp. 30.

— Politics and government.

NA puti k razvitomu sotsializmu: KPSS v bor'be za uprochenie i razvitie sotsializma v Srednei Azii i Kazakhstane, 1938-1958. Tashkent, 1976. pp. 367. *bibliog.*

SOVIETS

— Germany.

KONGRESS DER ARBEITER-, BAUERN- UND SOLDATENRÄTE DEUTSCHLANDS, 2., BERLIN, 1919. II. Kongress...8. bis 14. April 1919 im Herrenhaus zu Berlin: stenographisches Protokoll; Anhang: Vom I. Rätekongress zur Nationalversammlung: die Tätigkeit des Zentralrates der sozialistischen Republik Deutschlands. Glashütten im Taunus, 1975. pp. 278, 47. *Reprint of works originally published in Berlin in 1919.*

KONGRESS DER ARBEITER-, BAUERN- UND SOLDATENRÄTE, MÜNCHEN, 1919. Stenographischer Bericht über die Verhandlungen...vom 25. Februar bis 8. März 1919 in München; eingeleitet von Gisela Kissel und Hiltrud Witt. Glashütten im Taunus, 1974. pp. 200. *Reprint of work originally published in Munich in 1919.*

MINCK (FRIEDRICH M.) Wirtschafts-Sozialismus. Berlin, [1919]. pp. 23.

— Russia.

ALESHCHENKO (NIKOLAI MIKHAILOVICH) Moskovskii Sovet v 1917-1941 gg. Moskva, 1976. pp. 591.

SOVETY deputatov trudiashchikhsia i razvitie sotsialisticheskoi demokratii. Moskva, 1976. pp. 431.

TOKAREV (IURII SERGEEVICH) Petrogradskii Sovet rabochikh i soldatskikh deputatov v marte - aprele 1917 g. Leningrad, 1976. pp. 205.

— — Kalmyk Republic.

KALMYK REPUBLIC. Obshchekalmytskii S"ezd Sovetov, 1-yi, 1920. Pervyi Obshchekalmytskii s"ezd Sovetov, 2-9 iiulia 1920 goda: protokoly; pod redaktsiei...D.A. Chugaeva. Elista, 1971. pp. 220.

— — Russia (RSFSR).

ALEKSEEV (BORIS KONSTANTINOVICH) and PERFIL'EV (MARAT NIKOLAEVICH) Printsipy i tendentsii razvitiia predstavitel'nogo sostava mestnykh Sovetov: sotsiologicheskoe issledovanie. Leningrad, 1976. pp. 303.

SOWETO

— Riots.

NTSHONA (V.K. SCRAPE) Soweto, June 1976: the call to arms. London, [1976]. pp. 20.

SPAAK (PAUL HENRI).

WILLEQUET (JACQUES) Paul-Henri Spaak: un homme, des combats. [Bruxelles, 1975]. pp. 283.

SPACE AND TIME.

ČAPEK (MILIČ) ed. The concepts of space and time: their structure and their development. Dordrecht, [1976]. pp. 570. *(Boston Colloquium for the Philosophy of Science. Boston Studies in the Philosophy of Science. vol. 22).*

SPACE FRAME STRUCTURES.

MAKOWSKI (Z.S.) Trends and developments in space structures. Guildford, [1975]. pp. 32.

SPACE IN ECONOMICS.

BROWETT (J.G.) and FAIR (T.J.D.) South Africa: population potentials, 1867 to 1970. Johannesburg, 1972. fo. 20. *bibliogs.*

HUDSON (R.) Environmental images, spatial choice and consumer behaviour: a conceptual model and an empirical investigation. Durham, 1976. pp. 19. *bibliog. (Durham. University. Department of Geography. Occasional Publications (New Series). No. 9)*

— Mathematical models.

BROWETT (J.G.) The evolution of the South African space economy: a summary and synthesis. Johannesburg, 1976. pp. 53. *bibliog. (Johannesburg. University of the Witwatersrand. Urban and Regional Research Unit. Occasional Papers. No. 10)*

LONDON. University. London School of Economics and Political Science. Graduate School of Geography. Discussion Papers. No. 60. Some thoughts on a model for the location of public facilities; [by] Mark Rosenberg. London, 1977. pp. 25. *bibliog.*

SPACE LAW.

SZTUCKI (JERZY) Problemy prawne kosmosu. Warsawa, 1965. pp. 176. *With English and Russian summaries.*

OGUNBANWO (OGUNSOLA O.) International law and outer space activities. The Hague, 1975. pp. 272. *bibliog.*

LEGAL implications of remote sensing from outer space; edited by Nicolas Mateesco Matte and Hamilton DeSaussure. Leyden, 1976. pp. 197. *Papers of a symposium organised by the Institute of Air and Space Law, McGill University.*

SPAIN

— Administrative and political divisions.

INSTITUTO DE ESTUDIOS DE ADMINISTRACION LOCAL. Seminario de Investigacion, 11o, 1970. La comarca en la reestructuracion del territorio; (ponentes, D. Luis Amat Escandell [and others]). Madrid, 1972. pp. 384.

— Army — History.

ROMERO-MAURA (JOAQUIN) The Spanish army and Catalonia: the Cu-Cut incident and the Law of Jurisdictions, 1905-1906. Beverly Hills, [1976]. pp. 31.

— Colonies.

PRIETO (INDALECIO) Con el rey o contra el rey. Mexico, 1972. pp. 310.

— — Administration.

GONZALEZ (MARGARITA) El Resguardo en el Nuevo Reino de Granada. Bogota, 1970. pp. 197.

BOZA (GUILLERMO) Estructura y cambio en Venezuela colonial. [Caracas, 1973]. pp. 153. *bibliog.*

— — Economic history.

CAMBRIDGE. University. Centre of Latin American Studies. Working Papers. No. 9. Plata y pulque en el siglo XVIII mexicano; by Alvaro Jara. Cambridge, 1973. pp. 45.

ARTOLA GALLEGO (MIGUEL) Partidos y programas politicos, 1808-1936. Madrid, 1975-77. 2 vols. *bibliog.*

CARRILLO (SANTIAGO) Mañana España. Paris, [1975]. pp. 269. *Cover sub-title: Conversaciones con Régis Debray y Max Gallo.*

GONZALEZ CASANOVA (JOSE ANTONIO) La lucha por la democracia en España. Barcelona, 1975. pp. 244.

ONETO (JOSE) Arias entre dos crisis, 1973-1975. [Madrid, 1975]. pp. 299.

REDONDO ORTEGA (ONESIMO) Onesimo Redondo: textos politicos. Madrid, 1975. pp. 329.

TAMAMES GOMEZ (RAMON) Un proyecto de democracia para el futuro de España. Madrid, 1975. pp. 153.

ZAFRA VALVERDE (JOSE) Alma y cuerpo del Movimiento Nacional. Pamplona, 1975. pp. 212. *(Universidad de Navarra. Facultad de Derecho. Coleccion Juridica. 65)*

FRAGA IRIBARNE (MANUEL) Un objetivo nacional. Barcelona, 1976. pp. 263.

GREATER MANCHESTER TRADE UNION SPANISH SOLIDARITY COMMITTEE. Spain today: trade union solidarity with the Spanish people. Manchester, [1976]. 1 pamphlet (unpaged).

POLITICS and society in twentieth-century Spain; edited with an introduction by Stanley G. Payne. New York, 1976. pp. 244. *bibliog.*

PORTUGAL and Spain: transition politics; [report of an international conference held in London in 1975]. London, 1976. pp. 24. *(Institute for the Study of Conflict. Special Reports)*

POULANTZAS (NICOS) The crisis of the dictatorships: Portugal, Greece, Spain; translated by David Fernbach. London, 1976. pp. 166.

AMODIA (JOSÉ) Franco's political legacy: from dictatorship to facade democracy. London, 1977. pp. 348. *bibliog.*

FERNÁNDEZ-SANTAMARIA (J.A.) The state, war and peace: Spanish political thought in the renaissance, 1516-1559. Cambridge, 1977. pp. 316. *bibliog.*

HANSEN (EDWARD C.) Rural Catalonia under the Franco regime: the fate of regional culture since the Spanish Civil War. Cambridge, 1977. pp. 182. *bibliog.*

TUSELL GOMEZ (JAVIER) La oposicion democratica al franquismo, 1939-1962. Barcelona, [1977]. pp. 452. *bibliog.*

— Population policy.

CAMPO URBANO (SALUSTIANO DEL) Politica demografica de España. Madrid, 1974. pp. 238.

— Religion.

TOMSICH (MARIA GIOVANNA) El jansenismo en España: estudio sobre ideas religiosas en la segunda mitad del siglo XVIII. Madrid, 1972. pp. 207. *bibliog.*

— Social conditions — Bibliography.

SPAIN. Servicio Nacional de Consejos Economico-Sociales Sindicales. 1976. Publicaciones...: catalogo 1940-1975. Madrid, 1976. pp. 240.

— Social history.

TUÑON DE LARA (MANUEL) Metodologia de la historia social de España. Madrid, 1973 repr. 1974. pp. 201.

SANCHEZ-ALBORNOZ (NICOLAS) Jalones en la modernizacion de España. Barcelona, 1975. pp. 181.

— Social life and customs.

PRIETO (INDALECIO) Palabras al viento. Mexico, 1969. pp. 366. *First published in 1942.*

— Territories and possessions.

REZETTE (ROBERT) The Spanish enclaves in Morocco. Paris. [1976]. pp. 188. *bibliog.*

SPANIARDS IN GERMANY.

DOMINGUEZ (JAVIER) El hombre como mercancia: españoles en Alemania. Bilbao, [1976]. pp. 234. *bibliog.*

SPANISH SAHARA

— Politics and government.

GRETTON (JOHN) Western Sahara: the fight for self-determination. London, [1976]. pp. 53. *(Anti-Slavery Society. Committee for Indigenous Peoples. Research Reports. No. 1)*

SPATIAL ANALYSIS (STATISTICS).

BARTLETT (MAURICE STEVENSON) The statistical analysis of spatial pattern. London, 1975. pp. 90. *bibliog.*

SPECIAL ASSESSMENTS

— United Kingdom.

GOY (DAVID) Development land tax...; with accountancy examples by Nick Kelsey. London, 1976. pp. 199.

SPEECHES, ADDRESSES, ETC.

ISHIDA (TAKESHI) Content analysis of public speeches given by prime ministers. [Tokyo], 1971. pp. 84. *In Japanese and English.*

SPEED LIMITS

— Ireland (Republic).

HALL (P.A.) and others. The 60m.p.h. general speed limit in Ireland. Dublin, National Institute for Physical Planning and Construction Research, 1970. pp. 73. *bibliog. ([Reports]. RS 62)*

— United Kingdom.

SCOTT (P.P.) and BARTON (A.J.) The effects on road accident rates of the fuel shortage of November 1973 and consequent legislation. Crowthorne, 1976. pp. 33. *bibliog. (U.K. Transport and Road Research Laboratory. Supplementary Reports. 236)*

SPEER (ALBERT).

SPEER (ALBERT) Spandau: the secret diaries;...translated from the German by Richard and Clara Winston. London, 1976. pp. 465.

SPHERES OF INFLUENCE.

DORAN (CHARLES F.) Domestic conflict in state relations: the American sphere of influence. Beverly Hills, [1976]. pp. 58. *bibliog.*

SPLIT

— Economic policy.

PETRIĆ (IVO) Planning at the level of the region and the commune with special reference to planning in the enterprise: Split and Dalmatia; (translated by Meri Radosević). Ljubljana, International Center for Public Enterprises, 1974. fo. 27. *bibliog. (International Seminar 1974. [National Papers])*

SPORTS

— Germany.

25 Jahre Deutscher Sportbund; [by] Willy Weyer [and others]. [Frankfurt/Main. 1975]. pp. 16.

— South Africa.

LAPCHICK (RICHARD EDWARD) The politics of race and international sport: the case of South Africa. Westport, 1975. pp. 268. *bibliog. (Denver. University. Center on International Race Relations. Studies in Human Rights. No. 1)*

— United Kingdom.

KNAPP (BARBARA) and others. A long-term study of the influence of Rugby sports centre on the sporting life of the town: report on phase 3: sports centre survey 23-29 March 1974. Birmingham, 1976. pp. 113, 22. *(Birmingham. University. Centre for Urban and Regional Studies. Research Memoranda. No.51)*

SPRATLY ISLANDS

— International status.

HEINZIG (DIETER) Disputed islands in the South China Sea: Paracels, Spratlys, Pratas, Macclesfield Bank. Wiesbaden, 1976. pp. 58.

SPRINGS

— Zambia.

LEGG (C.A.) A reconnaissance survey of the hot and mineralised springs of Zambia. Lusaka, 1974. pp. 60. *bibliog. (Zambia. Geological Survey Department. Economic Reports. No. 50) 9 maps in end pocket.*

SQUATTERS

— Colombia.

ESCOBAR SIERRA (HUGO) Las invasiones en Colombia. Bogota, 1972. pp. 125.

— Turkey.

KARPAT (KEMAL H.) The gecekondu; rural migration and urbanization. Cambridge, 1976. pp. 291. *bibliog.*

— United Kingdom.

POLLARD (JOHN) Dr. Squat; a report written in conjunction with the squatters, West Kentish Town, Sept., 1972. London, 1972. fo. 7. *bibliog.*

NATIONAL COUNCIL FOR CIVIL LIBERTIES. Squatting, trespass and civil liberties. London, 1976. pp. 58.

SQUATTERS' ACTION COUNCIL. Dossier of anti-squatting lies; for discussion by trade unionists, students and the housing movement with a view to the setting-up of a labour movement inquiry into anti-squatting stories in the media. London, [1976]. pp. 5.

SQUATTERS' ACTION COUNCIL. Squatting: what's it all about?. London, [1976]. pp. 12.

SQUATTERS' ACTION COUNCIL. The truth about the anti-squatting lies [and] The squatting charter. London, [1976]. pp. 9.

WOLMAR (CHRISTIAN) Homes or jails?: squatters and the law. London, [1976]. pp. 16.

SRAFFA (PIERO).

KURZ (HEINZ DIETER) Zur neoricardianischen Theorie des Allgemeinen Gleichgewichts der Produktion und Zirkulation: Wert und Verteilung in Piero Sraffas "Production of commodities by means of commodities". Berlin, [1977]. pp. 276. *bibliog.*

SRI LANKA.

SRI Lanka: a survey; (K.M. de Silva, editor). London, [1977]. pp. 496.

— Economic policy.

GUNATILLEKE (GODFREY) Welfare and growth: a case study of Sri Lanka prepared for the UNRISD project "The Unified Approach to Development Planning and Analysis". Colombo, 1974. pp. 130. *(Marga Institute. Marga Research Studies. 2)*

SRI LANKA. 1974. Planning in relation to public sector enterprises: Sri Lanka. [Ljubljana, International Center for Public Enterprises, 1974]. pp. (17). *([International Seminar 1974. Working Papers])*

— Politics and government.

PHADNIS (URMILA) Religion and politics in Sri Lanka. London, 1976. pp. 376. *bibliog.*

— Population.

JAYASURIYA (D.C.) Law and population in Sri Lanka. Medford, Mass., 1976. pp. 42. *bibliog. (Tufts University. Fletcher School of Law and Diplomacy. Law and Population Monograph Series. No. 40).*

— Religion.

PHADNIS (URMILA) Religion and politics in Sri Lanka. London, 1976. pp. 376. *bibliog.*

— Rural conditions.

ÖHRLING (STAFFAN) Rural change and spatial reorganization in Sri Lanka: barriers against development of traditional Sinhalese local communities. London, 1977. pp. 289. *bibliog. (Scandinavian Institute of Asian Studies. Monograph Series. No. 34).*

— Social policy.

GUNATILLEKE (GODFREY) Welfare and growth: a case study of Sri Lanka prepared for the UNRISD project "The Unified Approach to Development Planning and Analysis". Colombo, 1974. pp. 130. *(Marga Institute. Marga Research Studies. 2)*

STAJIC (MIODRAG).

STAJIĆ (MIODRAG) Ideje i ljudi; predgovor Slobodan Jovanović. London, 1972. pp. 96. *In Cyrillic.*

STALIN (IOSIF VISSARIONOVICH).

TROTSKII (LEV DAVYDOVICH) Bolchévisme et stalinisme: ([with] Le régime communiste aux U.S.A.); avant-propos de G. Bloch. [Paris, La Vérité, 1956]. pp. 28. *First published in 1937 and 1935 respectively.*

ELLEINSTEIN (JEAN) The Stalin phenomenon. London, 1976. pp. 221.

KHRUSHCHEV (NIKITA SERGEEVICH) The 'secret' speech delivered to the closed session of the Twentieth Congress of the Communist Party of the Soviet Union;...with an introduction by Zhores A. Medvedev and Roy A. Medvedev. Nottingham, 1976. pp. 134.

STAMP DUTIES

— Mexico.

MEXICO. Statutes, etc. 1821-1953. El papel sellado y la ley del timbre, 1821, 1871, 1971: relacion documental. Mexico, 1972. pp. 826.

— United Kingdom.

MONROE (JOHN GEORGE) and NOCK (R.S.) The law of stamp duties. 5th ed. London, 1976. pp. 281.

STANDARDIZED TERMS OF CONTRACT

— United States.

DEUTCH (SINAI) Unfair contracts: the doctrine of unconscionability. Lexington, Mass., [1977]. pp. 314. *bibliog.*

STARHEMBERG (GUNDAKER THOMAS) Graf.

HOLL (BRIGITTE) Hofkammerpräsident Gundaker Thomas Graf Starhemberg und die österreichische Finanzpolitik der Barockzeit, 1703-1715. Wien, 1976. pp. 453. *bibliog. (Archiv für Österreichische Geschichte. Band 132)*

STARZYNSKI (STEFAN).

DROZDOWSKI (MARIAN MAREK) Stefan Starzyński, prezydent Warszawy. Warszawa, 1976. pp. 384. *(Towarzystwo Miłośników Historii w Warszawie. Biblioteka Wiedzy o Warszawie)*

STATE, THE.

JUENGER (ERNST) Der Weltstaat: Organismus und Organisation. Stuttgart, [1960]. pp. 75.

PINOCHET UGARTE (AUGUSTO) Geopolitica. Santiago, Chile, 1968 repr. 1974. pp. 252. *bibliog.*

FALLERS (LLOYD A.) The social anthropology of the nation-state. Chicago, 1974. pp. 171. *bibliog. (Rochester, N.Y. University. Lewis Henry Morgan Lectures. 1971)*

PRADELSKI (JOE D.) Das verfassungsrechtliche Selbstverständnis von Staaten: eine rechtsvergleichende Untersuchung von Verfassungspräambeln. Augsburg, 1975. pp. 243. *bibliog.*

JUNG (OTMAR) Zum Kulturstaatsbegriff: Johann Gottlieb Fichte; Verfassung des Freistaates Bayern; Godesberger Grundsatzprogramm der SPD. Meisenheim am Glan, 1976. pp. 255. *bibliog.*

MAMUT (LEONID SOLOMONOVICH) Problemy teorii gosudarstva v sovremennoi ideologicheskoi bor'be: protiv burzhuaznoi kritiki vzgliadov K. Marksa na gosudarstvo. Moskva, 1976. pp. 192.

MOREAU DE BELLAING (LOUIS) L'état et son autorité: idéologie paternaliste. Paris, [1976]. pp. 414. *bibliog.*

PAINE (THOMAS) Common sense; edited with an introduction by Isaac Kramnick. Harmondsworth, 1976. pp. 128. *bibliog.*

CARRILLO (SANTIAGO) Eurocomunismo y estado. Barcelona, [1977]. pp. 219.

SECONDAT (CHARLES LOUIS DE) Baron de Montesquieu. The political theory of Montesquieu; [edited by] Melvin Richter. Cambridge, 1977. pp. 355.

WIGHT (MARTIN) Systems of states;...edited with an introduction by Hedley Bull. Leicester, 1977. pp. 232. *bibliog.*

STATE AID TO PRIVATE SCHOOLS

— United States.

ROBISON (JOSEPH B.) The case against parochiaid. New York, 1972. pp. 16.

STATE ENCOURAGEMENT OF SCIENCE, LITERATURE AND ART

— France.

FRANCE. Direction de la Documentation. La Documentation Française. Notes et Etudes Documentaires. Nos. 4,273-4,274. Les aides publiques à la création artistique en France. Paris, 1976. pp. 45.

STATE FARMS

— Hungary.

HOLÁCS (IBOLYA) Some results of sociological research in co-operative and state farms. Keszthely, 1975. pp. 74. *bibliog. (Keszthelyi Agrártudományi Egyetem. Studies. 6) .*

VÁGI (FERENC) Die betriebliche Interessiertheit und der Mechanismus ihrer Durchsetzung in den Staatsgütern; (aus dem Ungarischen übersetzt von Kornelia Ferenczy). Budapest, 1977. pp. 151. *bibliog.*

— Russia — Soviet Far East.

PANKRAT'EV (MAKSIM NIKIFOROVICH) Voprosy povysheniia effektivnosti proizvodstva v sovkhozakh Dal'nego Vostoka. Khabarovsk, 1975. pp. 174.

STATE GOVERNMENTS

— United States.

SHAFFER (WILLIAM R.) and WEBER (RONALD E.) Policy responsiveness in the American states. Beverly Hills, [1974]. pp. 64. *bibliog.*

STATE and local government: the political economy of reform; edited by Alan K. Campbell and Roy W. Bahl. New York, [1976]. pp. 211. *Based on papers presented to a conference sponsored by the Metropolitan Studies Program of the Maxwell School of Citizenship and Public Affairs of Syracuse University.*

DANIELSON (MICHAEL NILS) and others. One nation, so many governments. Lexington, Mass., [1977]. pp. 141.

YIN (ROBERT K.) and others. Tinkering with the system: technological innovations in state and local services. Lexington, Mass., [1977]. pp. 275. *bibliog.*

STATE SUCCESSION.

BROSSARD (JACQUES) Professor of Law, University of Montreal. L'accession à la souveraineté et le cas du Québec: conditions et modalités politico-juridiques. Montréal, 1976. pp. 799. *bibliog.*

STATESMEN

— Africa.

The MAKING of politicians: studies from Africa and Asia; edited by W.H. Morris-Jones. London, 1976. pp. 249. *(London. University. Institute of Commonwealth Studies. Commonwealth Papers. 20) Papers presented during 1972-74 to a seminar on comparative politics at the Institute.*

— Africa, Subsaharan.

VENTER (ALBERTUS JOHANNES) Black leaders of southern Africa. Randburg, [1976]. pp. 208.

— Asia.

The MAKING of politicians: studies from Africa and Asia; edited by W.H. Morris-Jones. London, 1976. pp. 249. *(London. University. Institute of Commonwealth Studies. Commonwealth Papers. 20) Papers presented during 1972-74 to a seminar on comparative politics at the Institute.*

— France.

AS they are: French political portraits; by***; translated from the French by Winifred Katzin. London, 1924. pp. 217.

ANTONI (PASCALE) and ANTONI (JEAN DOMINIQUE) Les ministres de la Ve République. Paris, 1976. pp. 95. *bibliog. (Paris. Université de Paris II. Travaux et Recherches. Série Science Politique. 8)*

— United Kingdom.

SHLAIM (AVI) and others. British foreign secretaries since 1945. Newton Abbot, [1977]. pp. 267.

STATISTICS.

HUCK (SCHUYLER W.) and others. Reading statistics and research. New York, [1974]. pp. 387. *bibliogs.*

MOSER (Sir CLAUS ADOLF) Statistics and economic policy. [Reading, 1974]. pp. 31. *(Reading. University. Mercantile Credit Lectures. 1973)*

CHETVERIKOV (NIKOLAI SERGEEVICH) Statisticheskie issledovaniia: teoriia i praktika. Moskva, 1975. pp. 388.

HAUSER (PHILIP MORRIS) Social statistics in use. New York, [1975]. pp. 385. *bibliogs.*

WORLD STATISTICS IN BRIEF; (pd. by) Statistical Office, United Nations. a., 1976 [1st]- New York.

INTERNATIONAL BANK FOR RECONSTRUCTION AND DEVELOPMENT. 1976. World tables 1976: from the data files of the World Bank. Baltimore, 1976. pp. 552.

— History — Germany.

KRAWEHL (OTTO ERNST) Die "Jahrbücher für Nationalökonomie und Statistik" unter den Herausgebern Bruno Hildebrand und Johannes Conrad, 1863 bis 1915. München, 1977. pp. 127. *bibliog.*

STATISTICS.(Cont.)

— Periodicals.

LIST ECON: Förteckning över periodica inom ekonomi, handel, ekonomisk geografi och internationell statistik i nordiska bibliotek: List of periodicals in the fields of economics, trade, economic geography and international statistics in Nordic libraries; [pd. by] Biblioteket, Handelshögskolan, Stockholm. irreg., 1976- Stockholm.

— Theory, methods, etc.

KORÖSI (JÓZSEF) Welche Unterlagen hat die Statistik zu beschaffen um richtige Mortalitäts-Tabellen zu gewinnen?: Denkschrift im Auftrage der Internationalen Statistischen Commission. Berlin, Verlag des Königlichen Statistischen Bureau's, 1874. pp. 83.

COX (DAVID ROXBEE) and HINKLEY (DAVID VICTOR) Theoretical statistics. London, 1974. pp. 511. bibliog.

BRAIN drain statistics: empirical evidence and guidelines; (report on an international expert meeting in Stockholm 1973 and guidelines for future studies); editor, Göran Friborg. Stockholm, 1975. pp. 283. (Sweden. Forskningsekonomiska Kommittén. Rapporter. 6)

BERGSTROM (ALBERT REX) ed. Statistical inference in continuous time economic models. Amsterdam, 1976. pp. 333. bibliogs.

FAIRLEY (WILLIAM B.) and MOSTELLER (CHARLES FREDERICK) eds. Statistics and public policy. Reading, Mass., [1977]. pp. 397.

HAMBURG (MORRIS) Statistical analysis for decision making. 2nd ed. New York, [1977]. pp. 801. bibliog.

WONNACOTT (THOMAS HERBERT) and WONNACOTT (RONALD JOHNSTON) Introductory statistics for business and economics. 2nd ed. Santa Barbara, [1977]. pp. 753.

STEAM ENGINES.

ROGERS (KENNETH H.) The Newcomen engine in the West of England. Bradford-on-Avon, Wilts, 1976. pp. 63.

STEAMBOAT LINES

— United Kingdom.

TAYLOR (JAMES ARNOLD) Ellermans: a wealth of shipping. London, 1976. pp. 320.

— Yugoslavia.

FIJO (OLIVER) Parobrodarstvo Dalmacije, 1878.-1918. Zadar, 1962. pp. 212, [x]. (Jugoslavenska Akademija Znanosti i Umjetnosti. Institut u Zadru. Djela. knj.2) With English summary.

STEEL

— Prices — United States.

BLOUGH (ROGER M.) The Washington embrace of business. New York, [1975]. pp. 162. (Carnegie-Mellon University. Benjamin F. Fairless Memorial Lectures. 1974). Also contains his President Kennedy and steel prices.

STEEL INDUSTRY AND TRADE

— France.

FRANCE. Groupe sectoriel d'Analyse et de Prévision Mines de Fer, Sidérurgie, Première Transformation de l'Acier. 1976. Rapport...: préparation du 7e Plan. Paris, 1976. pp. 100.

— Netherlands — Management.

PLANNING in a Dutch and a Yugoslav steelworks: a comparative study; by H.C. Dekker [and others]. [Amsterdam], 1976. pp. 177.

— Switzerland.

IMPERATORI (ALDO) Der schweizerische Stahlmarkt: Marktbeobachtung und Marktanalyse. Winterthur, 1956. pp. 204. bibliog. Zürcher Dissertation.

— Turkey.

TURKIYE SINAÎ KALKINMA BANKASI. Sector Research Publications. No. 6. Study on the casting industry...; research by Aykut Civelek. Istanbul, 1976. pp. 101.

— United Kingdom.

PRESSED STEEL COMPANY. Pressed Steel Company Limited. [London?, 1959?]. pp. 69.

BARRACLOUGH (K.C.) Sheffield steel. Buxton, [1976]. pp. 112. bibliog.

— United States.

ABEL (I.W.) Collective bargaining: labor relations in steel, then and now. New York, [1976]. pp. 62. (Carnegie-Mellon University. Benjamin F. Fairless Memorial Lectures. 1975)

KUNIANSKY (HARRY RICHARD) A business history of Atlantic Steel Company, 1901-1968. [New York], 1976. pp. 395. bibliog. Originally presented as the author's thesis, Georgia State University, 1970.

MARCUS (MAEVA) Truman and the steel seizure case: the limits of presidential power. New York, 1977. pp. 390. bibliog.

— Yugoslavia — Management.

PLANNING in a Dutch and a Yugoslav steelworks: a comparative study; by H.C. Dekker [and others]. [Amsterdam], 1976. pp. 177.

STENTON (DORIS MARY) Lady.

PIPE ROLL SOCIETY. Publications. New Series. vol. 41. Liber memorialis Doris Mary Stenton, Honorary Secretary to the Pipe Roll Society, 1923-1961. London, 1976. pp. 220.

STEPHEN (GEORGE) 1st Baron Mount Stephen.

GILBERT (HEATHER) The end of the road: the life of Lord Mount Stephen, vol. II, 1891-1921. Aberdeen, 1977. pp. 442.

STERILIZATION (BIRTH CONTROL).

MADGE (NIC) Sterilization of minors; NCCL's comments on the DHSS discussion paper. London, 1976. pp. 13. (National Council for Civil Liberties. Reports. No. 14)

STEWARD (JULIAN HAYNES).

STEWARD (JULIAN HAYNES) Evolution and ecology: essays on social transformation; edited by Jane C. Steward and Robert F. Murphy. Urbana, Ill., [1977]. pp. 406. bibliogs.

STEWART (FRANCES).

ELLIOTT (JAMES A.M.) Will raising wages in the high-wage sector increase total employment?: a critique of the Stewart-Weeks view on the relationship between wage changes and unemployment in LDCs. Ann Arbor, 1976. pp. 18, 13, 6. (Michigan University. Center for Research on Economic Development. Discussion Papers. No.55)

STOCHASTIC DIFFERENTIAL EQUATIONS.

BERGSTROM (ALBERT REX) ed. Statistical inference in continuous time economic models. Amsterdam, 1976. pp. 333. bibliogs.

STOCHASTIC PROCESSES.

BARTLETT (MAURICE STEVENSON) Stochastic population models in ecology and epidemiology. London, 1960 repr. 1970. pp. 90. bibliog.

STOCK AND STOCK BREEDING

— Colombia.

COLOMBIA. Departamento Administrativo Nacional de Estadistica. 1975. Memoria del sector agropecuario 1954-1974. [Bogota, 1975]. pp. 448.

— France.

FRANCE. Direction de la Documentation. La Documentation Française. Notes et Etudes Documentaires. Nos. 4,341-4,342. L'élevage en France; par Francois Spindler. Paris, 1976. pp. 51.

— New Zealand.

NEW ZEALAND. Ministry of Agriculture and Fisheries. 1976. State of the livestock industry. [Wellington], 1976. pp. 50.

STOCK EXCHANGE

— Argentine Republic.

BERARDI (JORGE ENRIQUE) La crisis del mercado de valores argentino en la capitalizacion empresaria. Buenos Aires, [1974]. pp. 230. bibliog.

— United Kingdom.

[TRENCHARD (JOHN) Political writer, and GORDON (THOMAS) of Kirkcudbright]. A collection of all the political letters in the London Journal to December 17, inclusive, 1720. London, printed for J. Roberts, 1721. pp. ii, 60.

STOCKTON AND DARLINGTON RAILWAY.

RAIL 150: the Stockton and Darlington Railway and what followed; by Ken Hoole [and others]. London, 1975. pp. 198. bibliog.

STOLYPIN (PETR ARKAD'EVICH).

CONROY (MARY SCHAEFFER) Peter Arkad'evich Stolypin: practical politics in late Tsarist Russia. Boulder, Col., 1976. pp. 235. bibliog.

STOPES (MARIE CARMICHAEL)

— Bibliography.

EATON (PETER) and WARNICK (MARILYN) compilers. Marie Stopes: a checklist of her writings. London, [1977]. pp. 59.

STORE LOCATION

— United Kingdom.

GUY (CLIFFORD) The location of shops in the Reading area. Reading, 1976. pp. 54. bibliog. (Reading. University. Department of Geography. Reading Geographical Papers. No. 46)

STRASBOURG

— Harbour.

STRASBOURG, port pétrolier. [Strasbourg, imprint, 1961]. pp. 53.

STRATHCLYDE

— Transit systems.

SCOTTISH ASSOCIATION FOR PUBLIC TRANSPORT. Memoranda. 75/5. Strathclyde's transport tomorrow: a submission to the Strathclyde region. Glasgow, 1975. pp. 8.

STRIKES AND LOCKOUTS.

STREIK und Aussperrung: Protokoll der wissenschaftlichen Veranstaltung der Industriegewerkschaft Metall vom 13. bis 15. September 1973 in München; herausgegeben von Michael Kittner. Frankfurt am Main, [1973]. pp. 567. (Otto Brenner Stiftung. Schriftenreihe. 3)

— Bibliography.

PETTMAN (BARRIE OWEN) Strikes: a selected bibliography. Bradford, [1976]. pp. 64.

— Denmark.

CHRISTENSEN (ERIK) Historian. Havnearbejderstrejken i Esbjerg i 1893: traek af arbejdsmaendenes fagforenings første år i Esbjerg. København, [1975]. pp. 113. *bibliog. (Selskabet til Forskning i Arbejderbevaegelsens Historie. Publikationer. 2)*

— France.

CAPDEVIELLE (JACQUES) and others. La grève du Joint français: les incidences politiques d'un conflit social. [Paris, 1975]. pp. 166. *(Fondation Nationale des Sciences Politiques. Travaux et Recherches de Science Politique. 34)*

BADIE (BERTRAND) Stratégie de la grève. Paris, [1976]. pp. 263. *bibliog. (Fondation Nationale des Sciences Politiques. Travaux et Recherches de Science Politique. 40)*

— Germany.

KOMMUNISTISCHE PARTEI DEUTSCHLANDS. Der Streik der Berliner Verkehrs-Arbeiter. [Berlin?, 1932?]. pp. 24.

HARTMANN (PETER) Mobilmachung: der Arbeitskampf in der Druckindustrie, 1976. Mainz, [1977]. pp. 212.

— New Zealand.

HOLLAND (HENRY EDMUND) and others. The tragic story of the Waihi strike. Wellington, N.Z., 1913; Dunedin, 1975. pp. 202. *Facsimile reprint.*

— Russia.

KIRILLOV (VIKTOR SERGEEVICH) Bol'sheviki vo glave massovykh politicheskikh stachek v pervoi russkoi revoliutsii, 1905-1907. Moskva, 1976. pp. 368.

— United Kingdom.

EVANS (ERIC WYN) and CREIGH (S. W.) eds. Industrial conflict in Britain. London, 1977. pp. 292. *bibliog.*

— United States.

WEISBORD (ALBERT) Passaic: the story of a struggle against starvation wages and the right to organize. Chicago, 1926; New York, 1976. pp. 64.

STRIP MINING

— Environmental aspects — United States.

LANDY (MARC KARNIS) The politics of environmental reform: controlling Kentucky strip mining. Washington, D.C., 1976. pp. 400. *bibliog. (Resources for the Future, Inc. Working Papers. PD-2)*

STROESSNER (ALFREDO).

MARTINEZ ARBOLEYA (JOAQUIN) Charlas con el General Stroessner. Montevideo, 1973. pp. 123.

STRUCTURAL ANTHROPOLOGY.

DUMONT (JEAN PAUL) Under the rainbow: nature and supernature among the Panare Indians. Austin, Texas, [1976]. pp. 178. *bibliog. Revision of the author's thesis, University of Pittsburgh, 1972.*

LEACH (Sir EDMUND RONALD) Culture and communication, the logic by which symbols are connected: an introduction to the use of structuralist analysis in social anthropology. Cambridge, 1976. pp. 105. *bibliog.*

BOURDIEU (PIERRE) Outline of theory of practice; translated by Richard Nice. Cambridge, 1977. pp. 248.

LEVI-STRAUSS (CLAUDE) Structural anthropology, volume 2; translated from the French by Monique Layton. London, 1977. pp. 383. *bibliog.*

— Bibliography.

LAPOINTE (FRANÇOIS H.) and LAPOINTE (CLAIRE C.) Claude Lévi-Strauss and his critics: an international bibliography of criticism (1950-1976) followed by a bibliography of the writings of Claude Lévi-Strauss. New York, 1977. pp. 219. *bibliog.*

STRUCTURALISM.

KATZ (FRED E.) Structuralism in sociology: an approach to knowledge. Albany, N.Y., 1976. pp. 218.

STRUCTURED PROGRAMMING.

McGOWAN (CLEMENT L.) and KELLY (JOHN R.) Top-down structured programming techniques. New York, 1975. pp. 288. *bibliog.*

HUGHES (JOAN KIRKBY) and MICHTOM (JAY I.) A structured approach to programming. Englewood Cliffs, [1977]. pp. 264. *bibliog.*

STRUMILIN (STANISLAV GUSTAVOVICH).

AKTUAL'NYE problemy ekonomicheskoi nauki v trudakh S.G. Strumilina: k 100-letiiu so dnia rozhdeniia. Moskva, 1977. pp. 439.

STUDENT AID

— Ghana.

GHANA. Committee appointed...to advise Government on the Future Policy for Financial Support for University Students in Ghana. 1970. Report; [M. Dowuona, chairman]. Accra, 1970. pp. 30.

GHANA. 1971. Statement by Government on the students' loans scheme. [Accra, 1971]. pp. 5. *(W[hite] P[apers]. 1971. No. 2)*

— United Kingdom.

CREW (MICHAEL A.) and YOUNG (ALISTAIR) Paying by degrees: a study of the financing of higher education students by grants, loans and vouchers. London, 1977. pp. 66. *bibliog. (Institute of Economic Affairs. Hobart Papers. 75)*

U.K. Parliament. House of Commons. Library. Research Division. Background Papers. No. 58. Student fees and student grants: the current situation. [London, 1977]. pp. 11.

STUDENT COUNSELLORS.

SWAINSON (MARY) The spirit of counsel: the story of a pioneer in student counselling. London, 1977. pp. 256. *bibliogs.*

STUDENT TEACHERS

— United Kingdom.

STANFORTH (JOHN) Role conflict and attitude change: a study of the effects of teaching practice on third year students at a college of education. 1977. fo. 244. *bibliog. Typescript. Ph.D. (London) thesis: unpublished. This thesis is the property of London University and may not be removed from the Library.*

STUDENTS

— Political activity.

ROUND TABLE ON INTERNATIONAL STUDENT UNREST, PARIS, 1968. [Papers of the conference sponsored by the International Social Science Council]. [1968]. 21 pts. (in 1 vol.).

GOLD (ALICE ROSS) and others. Fists and flowers: a social psychological interpretation of student dissent. New York, 1976. pp. 204. *bibliog.*

LEVOE studencheskoe dvizhenie v stranakh kapitala. Moskva, 1976. pp. 311. *bibliog.*

— Australia.

LITTLE (FRANK GRAHAM) Faces on the campus: a psychosocial study. Melbourne, 1975. pp. 307.

— Belgium.

VOS-GEVERS (LOUIS) and VOS-GEVERS (LIEVE) Dat volk moet herleven: het studententijdschrift De Vlaamsche Vlagge, 1875-1933. Leuven, [1976]. pp. 319. *bibliog.*

— Canada.

CANADA. Statistics Canada. Fall enrolment in universities. a., 1972-73/1973-74- Ottawa. *[In English and French].*

— China — Political activity.

WEST (PHILIP) Yenching University and Sino-Western relations, 1916-1952. Cambridge, Mass., 1976. pp. 327. *bibliog. (Harvard University. East Asian Research Center. Harvard East Asian Series. 85)*

— Czechoslovakia.

CZECHOSLOVAKIA. Odbor pro Politické Zpravodajství. Dokumenty Doby: Sbírka Publikací o Utrpení Českého a Slovenského Národa v Boji za Svobodu. řada 1, svazek 2. Persekuce českého studentstva za okupace, etc. Praha, 1946. pp. 157,(19).

— France — Political activity.

SEMENOV (ALEKSANDR LEONIDOVICH) Levoe studencheskoe dvizhenie vo Frantsii, 1956-1968 gg. Moskva, 1975. pp. 231.

— Germany.

DEMERIN (PATRICK) Communautés pour le socialisme: pratique de la vie collective chez les étudiants de Berlin-Ouest: origines, développement, perspectives. Paris, 1975. pp. 209. *bibliog.*

— — Political activity.

AUSSCHUSS FÜR DEUTSCHE EINHEIT. Zur politischen Haltung einiger westdeutscher Studentenorganisationen. Berlin, [1961]. pp. 39.

BRIEM (JUERGEN) Der S[ozialistische] D[eutsche] S[tudentenbund]: die Geschichte des bedeutendsten Studentenverbandes der BRD seit 1945. Frankfurt, [1976]. pp. 483. *bibliog.*

LANGGUTH (GERD) Die Protestbewegung in der Bundesrepublik Deutschland, 1968-1976. Köln, [1976]. pp. 364. *bibliog.*

STUDENTENBEWEGUNG, 1967-69: Protokolle und Materialien; herausgegeben und eingeleitet von Frank Wolff und Eberhard Windaus. Frankfurt am Main, 1977. pp. 253. *bibliog.*

— Lebanon — Political activity.

BARAKAT (HALIM ISBER) Lebanon in strife: student preludes to the civil war. Austin, [1977]. pp. 242. *bibliog. (Texas University. Center for Middle Eastern Studies. Modern Middle Eastern Series. No.2)*

— Mexico — Political activity.

PONIATOWSKA (ELENA) ed. Massacre in Mexico;...translated from the Spanish by Helen R. Lane. New York, 1975. pp. 333.

— Nigeria.

BECKETT (PAUL) Political scientist, and O'CONNELL (JAMES) Social background, political identity and developmental values among Nigerian university students. [Coventry], 1976. pp. 38,8. *(University of Warwick. Department of Politics. Working Papers. No. 10)*

— — Attitudes.

BECKETT (PAUL) Political scientist, and O'CONNELL (JAMES) Social background, political identity and developmental values among Nigerian university students. [Coventry], 1976. pp. 38,8. *(University of Warwick. Department of Politics. Working Papers. No. 10)*

— — Political activity.

BECKETT (PAUL) Political scientist, and O'CONNELL (JAMES) Social background, political identity and developmental values among Nigerian university students. [Coventry], 1976. pp. 38,8. *(University of Warwick. Department of Politics. Working Papers. No. 10)*

— Norway.

NORWAY. Statistiske Centralbyrå. 1976. Forbruk blant skoleungdom og studenter, 1973-1974, etc. Oslo, 1976. pp. 54. *(Statistiske Analyser. 25) With English summary.*

— Portugal.

NAMORADO (RUI) Movimento estudantil e politica educacional. [Coimbra], 1972. pp. 168.

— Switzerland — Attitudes.

STUDENTEN denken anders als manche denken: Generation 85: die Schweiz nach uns. Zürich, [1969]. pp. 42. *Results of a pilot survey carried out on behalf of the Schweizerische Handelszeitung.*

— United Kingdom.

McCREATH (M.D.) Report on the surveys of full-time A level students (home) in colleges of further education. [Colchester], 1970. pp. 114. *Part of the Project on Factors Influencing Choice of Higher Education carried out by the University of Essex with the Royal Statistical Society*

U.K. Department of Education and Science. 1976. Undergraduate income and spending: summary report of a survey;.. .provisionally summarises the main findings of a survey of undergraduate student income and expenditure conducted in the 1974-75 academic year by the Social Survey Division of the Office of Population Censuses and Surveys. London, [1976]. pp. 12.

WHITBURN (JULIA) and others. People in polytechnics: a survey of polytechnic staff and students, 1972-3. Guildford, Surrey, 1976. pp. 212. *bibliog. (Society for Research into Higher Education. Research into Higher Education Monographs. 27)*

AIMS FOR FREEDOM AND ENTERPRISE. Attitudes of students to politics, economics and society. London, [1976]. pp. 3.

— United States.

NOVAK (STEVEN J.) The rights of youth: American colleges and student revolt, 1798- 1815. Cambridge, Mass., 1977. pp. 218. *bibliog.*

— — Political activity.

WOOD (JAMES L.) Political consciousness and student activism. Beverly Hills, [1974]. pp. 55. *bibliog.*

ERICSON (EDWARD E.) Radicals in the university. Stanford, Calif., [1975]. pp. 281. *bibliog. (Stanford University. Hoover Institution on War, Revolution and Peace. Hoover Institution Publications. 144)*

WOOD (JAMES L.) New left ideology: its dimensions and development. Beverly Hills, [1975]. pp. 70. *bibliog.*

GOLD (ALICE ROSS) and others. Fists and flowers: a social psychological interpretation of student dissent. New York, 1976. pp. 204. *bibliog.*

HEATH (G. LOUIS) ed. Vandals in the bomb factory: the history and literature of the Students for a Democratic Society. Metuchen, N.J., 1976. pp. 485. *bibliog.*

STUDENTS, PART-TIME

— United Kingdom.

CONFERENCE ON TECHNICAL EDUCATION AND DAY RELEASE, BRUNEL UNIVERSITY, 1973. Learning and earning: aspects of day-release in further education; [papers presented at the conference]; edited by W. van der Eyken and S.M. Kaneti Barry. Windsor, 1975. pp. 110. *bibliogs.*

UNIVERSITIES' COMMITTEE ON INTEGRATED SANDWICH COURSES. Panel on Assessment. The assessment of undergraduate students during industrial or other professional training or experience; a report by the panel...; edited by V.C. Marshall. Bradford, [1975, repr. 1976]. pp. 18.

STUDENTS, RATING OF

— United Kingdom.

UNIVERSITIES' COMMITTEE ON INTEGRATED SANDWICH COURSES. Panel on Assessment. The assessment of undergraduate students during industrial or other professional training or experience; a report by the panel...; edited by V.C. Marshall. Bradford, [1975, repr. 1976]. pp. 18.

STUDENTS FOR A DEMOCRATIC SOCIETY.

HEATH (G. LOUIS) ed. Vandals in the bomb factory: the history and literature of the Students for a Democratic Society. Metuchen, N.J., 1976. pp. 485. *bibliog.*

STUDENTS' SOCIETIES

— Germany.

AUSSCHUSS FÜR DEUTSCHE EINHEIT. Zur politischen Haltung einiger westdeutscher Studentenorganisationen. Berlin, [1961]. pp. 39.

BRIEM (JUERGEN) Der S[ozialistische] D[eutsche] S[tudentenbund]: die Geschichte des bedeutendsten Studentenverbandes der BRD seit 1945. Frankfurt, [1976]. pp. 483. *bibliog.*

STUDENTENBEWEGUNG, 1967-69: Protokolle und Materialien; herausgegeben und eingeleitet von Frank Wolff und Eberhard Windaus. Frankfurt am Main, 1977. pp. 253. *bibliog.*

STUDENTS' SOCIO-ECONOMIC STATUS

— Australia.

LITTLE (FRANK GRAHAM) Faces on the campus: a psychosocial study. Melbourne, 1975. pp. 307.

STUNDISTS.

USHINSKII (A.D.) O prichinakh poiavleniia ratsionalisticheskikh uchenii shtundy i nekotorykh drugikh podobnykh sekt v sel'skom pravoslavnom naselenii i o merakh protiv rasprostraneniia ucheniia etikh sekt. Kiev, 1884. pp. 80.

STURZO (LUIGI).

MOLONY (JOHN NEYLON) The emergence of political catholicism in Italy: Partito Popolare 1919-1926. London, 1977. pp. 225. *bibliog.*

STUTCHBURY (OLIVER PIERS).

STUTCHBURY (OLIVER PIERS) Too much government?: a political Aeneid. Ipswich, [1977]. pp. 128.

SUAKIN

— Economic history.

RODEN (D.) The twentieth century decline of Suakin. Khartoum, 1970. pp. 22. *(Khartoum. University. Faculty of Arts. Sudan Research Unit. Suakin Project Series. No. 1)*

SUBSIDIES

— Sweden.

RYDÉN (INGER) Transportkostnader och regional utveckling: modeller för analys av regionalpolitiskt stöd av godstransporter. Stockholm, [1976]. pp. 208. *bibliog. With English summary.*

— United Kingdom.

U.K. Department of Industry. 1975. Mineral Exploration and Investment Grants Act 1972: financial assistance for mineral exploration in Great Britain: a guide for industry. [rev.ed.] London, 1975. pp. 13.

ENGLISH TOURIST BOARD. The hotel development incentives scheme in England; (an appraisal by Philip Clarke). London, [1976]. pp. 40.

— United States.

WALKER (WILLIAM N.) International limits to government intervention in the market-place: focus on subsidies to the private sector. London, 1976. pp. 15. *(Trade Policy and Research Centre. Lectures in Commercial Diplomacy. No. 1)*

WEIDENBAUM (MURRAY L.) and others. Government credit subsidies for energy development. Washington, [1976]. pp. 55. *(American Enterprise Institute for Public Policy Research. AEI Studies. No. 137)*

SUBURBAN SCHOOLS.

BOYD (WILLIAM L.) Community status and conflict in suburban school politics. Beverly Hills, [1976]. pp. 41. *bibliog.*

SUBURBS

— United States.

DANIELSON (MICHAEL NILS) The politics of exclusion. New York, 1976. pp. 443.

ECONOMIC issues in metropolitan growth; edited by Paul R. Portney; papers presented at a forum conducted by Resources for the Future, May 28-29, 1975, in Washington, D.C. Baltimore, [1976]. pp. 143.

ROSE (HAROLD M.) Black suburbanization: access to improved quality of life or maintenance of th status quo? Cambridge, Mass., [1976]. pp. 288. *bibliog.*

GOTTDIENER (MARK) Planned sprawl: private and public interests in suburbia. Beverly Hills, [1977]. pp. 188. *bibliog.*

SUBVERSIVE ACTIVITIES.

BURTON (ANTHONY M.) The destruction of loyalty: an examination of the threat of propaganda and subversion against the armed forces of the West. London, [1976]. pp. 63. *bibliog.*

— Germany.

NIEDENHOFF (HORST UDO) Jetzt muss etwas getan werden: die Basisarbeit Linksextremer Gruppen im Betrieb. Köln, [1976]. pp. 183. *bibliog.*

— United Kingdom.

YOUNG (THOM) and KETTLE (MARTIN) Incitement to disaffection: a Cobden Trust Study. London, [1976]. pp. 117.

— United States.

WATSON (FRANK M.) "The Movement": role of the U.S. activists. London, 1977. pp. 16. *(Institute for the Study of Conflict. Conflict Studies. No. 80)*

SUDAN

— Boundaries — Ethiopia.

ALI TAHA (FAISAL ABDEL RAHMAN) The settlement of the Sudan-Ethiopia boundary dispute. Khartoum, 1975. pp. 34.

— Census.

SUDAN. Census, 1955/56. First population census of Sudan, 1955/56: methods report, vol. 2: appendices and charts. Khartoum, 1958. pp. 352. 2 maps.

— Economic conditions.

SUDAN. Central Office of Information. 1963. Progress: 5th anniversary Sudan revolution, 17 November, 1963. Khartoum, [1963]. pp. 180, 1 map.

LEES (FRANCIS A.) and BROOKS (HUGH C.) The economic and political development of the Sudan. London, 1977. pp. 172. *bibliog.*

— Economic policy.

SUDAN. Ministry of Planning. 1970. Five year plan of economic and social development of the Democratic Republic of the Sudan for 1970/71-1974/75 (draft). Vol. 1. Major trends of development. Khartoum, 1970. pp. 116.

BETTS (TRISTRAM) The Southern Sudan: the ceasefire and after; report prepared for the Africa Publications Trust. London, 1974. pp. 155.

LEES (FRANCIS A.) and BROOKS (HUGH C.) The economic and political development of the Sudan. London, 1977. pp. 172. *bibliog.*

— Executive departments.

BETTS (TRISTRAM) The Southern Sudan: the ceasefire and after; report prepared for the Africa Publications Trust. London, 1974. pp. 155.

— Foreign economic relations.

LEES (FRANCIS A.) and BROOKS (HUGH C.) The economic and political development of the Sudan. London, 1977. pp. 172. *bibliog.*

— History.

O'BALLANCE (EDGAR) The secret war in the Sudan: 1955-1972. London, 1977. pp. 174. *bibliog.*

— Officials and employees — Salaries, allowances, etc.

SUDAN. Unclassified Staff Wages Commission. 1951. Report. Khartoum, 1951. 1 vol. (various pagings).

— Politics and government.

ABD-AL GHAFFAR (MUHAMMAD AHMAD) Shaykhs and followers: political struggle in the Rufa'a al- Hoi Nazirate in the Sudan. Khartoum, 1974. pp. 170. *bibliog.*

BECHTOLD (PETER K.) Politics in the Sudan: parliamentary and military rule in an emerging African nation. New York, 1976. pp. 359.

O'BALLANCE (EDGAR) The secret war in the Sudan: 1955-1972. London, 1977. pp. 174. *bibliog.*

— Social conditions.

SUDAN. Central Office of Information. 1963. Progress: 5th anniversary Sudan revolution, 17 November, 1963. Khartoum, [1963]. pp. 180, 1 map.

— Social policy.

SUDAN. Ministry of Planning. 1970. Five year plan of economic and social development of the Democratic Republic of the Sudan for 1970/71-1974/75 (draft). Vol. 1. Major trends of development. Khartoum, 1970. pp. 116.

— Statistics.

SUDAN. Ministry of Culture and Information. 1974. Sudan facts and figures. [Khartoum], 1974. pp. 62.

SUEZ CANAL.

SERVIN (MARCEL) Pour la solution pacifique du problème de Suez; conférence prononcée le 13 septembre 1956, Salle de la Mutualité, à Paris. Paris, [imprint, 1956]. pp. 31.

SUFFOLK

— History — Sources.

MACCULLOCH (DIARMAID) ed. The chorography of Suffolk. Ipswich, 1976. pp. 170. (*Suffolk Records Society. [Publications]. vol. 19*)

— Rural conditions.

NEWBY (HOWARD) The deferential worker: a study of farm workers in East Anglia. London, 1977. pp. 462.

SUFFRAGE.

PARAF-JAVAL (MATHIAS GEORGES) L'absurdité de la politique. new ed. Paris, 1906. pp. 16.

— United Kingdom.

GRAHAM (THOMAS) Printer. An account of the state of the right of election of members of Parliament in the several counties, cities, and boroughs of the United Kingdom: strongly demonstrating the necessity for a reform in the representation of the people in the House of Commons. London, the Author. 1818. pp. 24.

SUGAR

— Manufacture and refining.

HAGELBERG (G.B.) Outline of the world sugar economy. Berlin, 1976. pp. 60. *bibliog.* (*Berlin. Technische Universität Berlin-Charlottenburg. Institut für Zuckerindustrie. Forschungsberichte. 3*)

— — Australia.

SUGAR EXPERIMENT STATIONS BOARD [QUEENSLAND]. The Australian sugar industry: some facts and figures; compiled by Norman J. King. [Brisbane?, 1954]. pp. 35.

— — France.

FIERAIN (JACQUES) Les raffineries de sucre des ports en France, XIXe-début du XXe siecles. Lille, 1976. pp. 738. *bibliog.*

— — Underdeveloped areas.

See UNDERDEVELOPED AREAS — Sugar — Manufacture and refining.

— — United Kingdom.

CANNING TOWN COMMUNITY DEVELOPMENT PROJECT. Canning Town's declining community income: case study: Tate and Lyle. [London, 1976]. pp. 33.

SUGAR CANE

— India.

BULLETIN ON SUGARCANE STATISTICS IN INDIA (DISTRICT-WISE); [pd. by] Directorate of Economics and Statistics, Ministry of Agriculture and Irrigation. a., 1976 (1st)- New Delhi.

— Panama.

PANAMA. Direccion de Estadistica y Censo. Estadistica panameña. Superficie sembrada y cosecha de café, tabaco y caña de azucar. a., 1975/76- Panama. *Supersedes in part PANAMA. Direccion de Estadistica y Censo. Estadistica panameña. Serie H. Informacion agropecuaria.*

SUGAR GROWING.

HAGELBERG (G.B.) Outline of the world sugar economy. Berlin, 1976. pp. 60. *bibliog.* (*Berlin. Technische Universität Berlin-Charlottenburg. Institut für Zuckerindustrie. Forschungsberichte. 3*)

— Australia.

SUGAR EXPERIMENT STATIONS BOARD [QUEENSLAND]. The Australian sugar industry: some facts and figures; compiled by Norman J. King. [Brisbane?, 1954]. pp. 35.

— Colombia.

KNIGHT (ROLF) Sugar plantations and labor patterns in the Cauca Valley, Colombia. Toronto, 1972. pp. 209. *bibliog.* (*Toronto. University. Department of Anthropology. Anthropological Series. No.12*)

— Peru.

ALBERT (BILL) An essay on the Peruvian sugar industry, 1880-1922 and the letters of Ronald Gordon, administrator of the British Sugar Company in the Canete Valley, 1914-1919. Norwich, [1976]. 1 vol.(various pagings).

— Spain.

CAMILLERI LAPEYRE (ARTURO) XXXIII años de politica azucarera en España, 1940-1973. Madrid, [1975]. pp. 590. (*Confederacion Española de Cajas de Ahorros. Fondo para la Investigacion Economica y Social. Publicaciones. 68*)

— Underdeveloped areas.

See UNDERDEVELOPED AREAS — Sugar growing.

— Venezuela.

SEQUERA DE SEGNINI (ISBELIA) and SEQUERA TAMAYO (PEDRO ELIAS) La productividad en la agricultura: un caso especifico. [Caracas, 1968]. pp. 84. *bibliog.* (*Caracas. Concejo Municipal del Distrito Federal. Ediciones del Cuatricentenario de Caracas*)

SUGAR TRADE.

VERON (JEAN BERNARD) Les nouveaux problèmes de l'économie sucrière. [Paris], Caisse Centrale de Coopération Economique, 1974. fo. 39.

— Spain.

CAMILLERI LAPEYRE (ARTURO) XXXIII años de politica azucarera en España, 1940-1973. Madrid, [1975]. pp. 590. (*Confederacion Española de Cajas de Ahorros. Fondo para la Investigacion Economica y Social. Publicaciones. 68*)

— Venezuela.

SEQUERA DE SEGNINI (ISBELIA) and SEQUERA TAMAYO (PEDRO ELIAS) La productividad en la agricultura: un caso especifico. [Caracas, 1968]. pp. 84. *bibliog.* (*Caracas. Concejo Municipal del Distrito Federal. Ediciones del Cuatricentenario de Caracas*)

SUGAR WORKERS

— Colombia.

KNIGHT (ROLF) Sugar plantations and labor patterns in the Cauca Valley, Colombia. Toronto, 1972. pp. 209. *bibliog.* (*Toronto. University. Department of Anthropology. Anthropological Series. No.12*)

SUICIDE.

LESTER (GENE) and LESTER (DAVID) Suicide: the gamble with death. Englewood Cliffs, [1971]. pp. 176. *bibliogs.*

— France.

MORBIDITE et mortalité par suicide; [by] F. Davidson [and others]. Le Vésinet, Division de la Recherche Médico-Sociale, 1975. pp. 97. *bibliog. With English summary.*

LANGLOIS (DENIS) Les dossiers noirs du suicide. Paris, [1976]. pp. 173.

— United Kingdom.

SOCIAL SERVICES RESEARCH AND INTELLIGENCE UNIT [PORTSMOUTH]. Information Sheets. No. 29. Suicide in Portsmouth 1954-1975. Portsmouth, 1976. pp. 13.

SULPHUR.

HORSEMAN (M.N.J.) World sulphur supply and demand, 1960-1980. (ID/76). New York, United Nations, 1973. pp. 165.

SUMMER HOMES

— Netherlands.

ECONOMISCH INSTITUUT VOOR HET MIDDEN- EN KLEINBEDRIJF. Bedrijfseconomische Publikaties. Resultaten van kampeerbedrijven: bedrijfsgegevens en enige ontwikkelingslijnen van campings, bungalowbedrijven en mengvormen van beide. 's-Gravenhage, 1972 repr.1973. pp. 94.

SUMMERHILL ACADEMY, ABERDEEN.

MACKENZIE (R.F.) The unbowed head: events at Summerhill Academy 1968-74. Edinburgh, [1977]. pp. 115.

SUMMERLIN (WILLIAM TALLEY).

HIXSON (JOSEPH R.) The patchwork mouse. Garden City, N.Y., 1976. pp. 228.

SUN (YAT-SEN).

WILBUR (CLARENCE MARTIN) Sun Yat-sen: frustrated patriot. New York, 1976. pp. 410. *bibliog. (Columbia University. East Asian Institute. Studies)*

SUNDA ISLANDS

— Economic history.

FOX (JAMES J.) Harvest of the palm: ecological change in eastern Indonesia. Cambridge, Mass., 1977. pp. 290. *bibliog.*

SUNDAY LEGISLATION

— Australia.

AUSTRALIA. Parliament. Joint Committee on the Australian Capital Territory. 1971. Report on Sunday observance in the Australian Capital Territory; [John E. Marriott, chairman]. in AUSTRALIA. Parliament. Parliamentary papers, 1971, vol.8.

SUPPLY AND DEMAND.

U.K. Empire Marketing Board. Statistics and Intelligence Branch. 1933. Regulation of supply: notes on schemes for regulating production, exports and stocks of certain primary products; prepared for the British commonwealth delegations, (Monetary and Economic Conference). [London], 1933. pp. 94.

EVSTIGNEEVA (LIUDMILA PETROVNA) Formirovanie potrebnostei v razvitom sotsialisticheskom obshchestve. Moskva, 1975. pp. 254.

HAUSTEIN (HEINZ DIETER) and MANZ (GUENTER) Bedürfnisse, Bedarf, Planung. Berlin, [1976]. pp. 168. *bibliog.*

JONES (RICHARD MORRIS) Supply in a market economy. London, 1976. pp. 191.

LEVIN (ALEKSANDR IVANOVICH) and IARKIN (ANATOLII PAVLOVICH) Platezhesposobnyi spros naseleniia. Moskva, 1976. pp. 360. *(Akademiia Nauk SSSR. Tsentral'nyi Ekonomiko- Matematicheskii Institut. Problemy Sovetskoi Ekonomiki)*

PORTER (MICHAEL E.) Interbrand choice, strategy, and bilateral market power. Cambridge, Mass., 1976. pp. 264. *bibliog. (Harvard University. Harvard Economic Studies. vol. 146)*

— Mathematical models.

KATZNER (DONALD W.) Static demand theory. New York, [1970]. pp. 242. *bibliogs.*

CHAIPRAVAT (OLARN) Aggregate structures of production and domestic demand for rice in Thailand: a time series analysis, 1951-1973. Bangkok, 1975. pp. 36. *(Bank of Thailand. Papers, No. 4)*

AFRIAT (S.N.) Combinatorial theory of demand. London, 1976. pp. 26. *(Input-Output Research Association. Occasional Papers. No. 1)*

OOMENS (W.J.) The demand for consumer durables. Tilburg, 1976. pp. 263. *bibliog. (Tilburg. Katholieke Hogeschool. Tilburg Institute of Economics. Tilburg Studies on Economics. 15)*

SUPPORT (DOMESTIC RELATIONS)

— Ireland (Republic).

EIRE. Dail Eireann. Special Committee on the Family Law (Maintenance of Spouses and Children) Bill, 1975. 1975. Report...together with the proceedings. Dublin, 1975. pp. (12). *In English and Irish.*

— Poland.

ANDREJEW (IGOR) Le refus des aliments en droit pénal polonais délit consistant à se soustraire à l'obligation alimentaire. Warszawa, [1962]. pp. 15. *(Polska Akademia Nauk. Centre Scientifique à Paris. Conférences. Fascicule 24)*

SURREY

— Economic conditions.

SURREY. Planning Department. Structure plan: (background papers). Kingston upon Thames, 1974-75. 12 vols. (in 1).

— Social conditions.

SURREY. Planning Department. Structure plan: (background papers). Kingston upon Thames, 1974-75. 12 vols. (in 1).

SURVEYING

— Africa, Subsaharan.

The DEVELOPMENT of land resources in East, Central and Southern Africa: the role of surveying and land economy; report of the proceedings of a seminar held at the Mulungushi Hall, Lusaka, Zambia on 6-9 April 1976. London, 1976. pp. 134.

SURVIVORS' BENEFITS

— Canada — Quebec.

QUEBEC (PROVINCE). Pension Board. Actuarial Branch. 1973. Survivors' benefits of the Quebec pension plan: present values. [Quebec], 1973. pp. 44,44. *In English and French.*

SUTTEE.

PEGGS (JAMES) India's cries to British humanity, relative to infanticide, British connection with idolatry, Ghaut murders, suttee, slavery, and colonization in India; to which are added, humane hints for the melioration of the state of society in British India. London, 1832. pp. 500.

SVERDLOV (IAKOV MIKHAILOVICH).

SVERDLOV (IAKOV MIKHAILOVICH) Izbrannye proizvedeniia: stat'i, rechi, pis'ma; (sostaviteli M.M. Vasser i L.V. Ivanova). Moskva, 1976. pp. 367.

SWAINSON (MARY).

SWAINSON (MARY) The spirit of counsel: the story of a pioneer in student counselling. London, 1977. pp. 256. *bibliogs.*

SWAZILAND

— Appropriations and expenditures.

SWAZILAND. Recurrent budget: estimates for the financial year. a., 1970/71. [Mbabane].

SWEDEN

— Census.

SWEDEN. Census, 1975. Folk- och bostadsräkningen. 1975. Stockholm, 1976 in progress.

— Commerce.

LINDSTRÖM (LENNART) and OLSSON (HANS) Prospects for Swedish exports, 1980. Stockholm, 1976. pp. 138. *(Stockholm. Konjunkturinstitut. Occasional Papers. 9)*

— Economic history.

AHLSTRÖM (GÖRAN) Studier i svensk ekonomisk politik och prisutveckling, 1776-1802. Lund, 1974. pp. 159. *bibliog. (Lund. Ekonomisk-Historiska Föreningen. Skrifter. vol. 14) Akademisk avhandling för avläggande av filosofie doktorsexamen, Lunds Universitet; with English summary.*

— Economic policy.

DAHLKVIST (MATS) Staten, socialdemokratin och socialismen: en inledande analys. [Stockholm, 1975]. pp. 236. *bibliog.*

KVIST (KENNETH) Den krisfria kapitalismen och andra myter: några drag i den svenska ekonomins utveckling. Stockholm, 1975. pp. 181.

ROSENGREN (BJÖRN) Valutareglering och nationell ekonomisk politik: en studie med anknytning till svenska erfarenheter åren 1959-1973. Göteborg, 1975. fo. 311. *bibliog. (Göteborgs Universitet. Nationalekonomiska Institutionen. Memoranda. Nr. 46) With English summary.*

GULDIMANN (TIM) Die Grenzen des Wohlfahrtsstaates: am Beispiel Schwedens und der Bundesrepublik. München, [1976]. pp. 181.

— Foreign economic relations — South Africa.

MAGNUSSON (ÅKE) Sverige - Sydafrika: en studie av en ekonomisk relation. Uppsala, 1974. pp. 174.

— Industries.

DU RIETZ (GUNNAR) Etablering, nedläggning och industriell tillväxt i Sverige, 1954-1970. Stockholm, [1975]. pp. 116. *With contents and summary in English.*

— Politics and government.

DAHLKVIST (MATS) Staten, socialdemokratin och socialismen: en inledande analys. [Stockholm, 1975]. pp. 236. *bibliog.*

LINDROTH (BENGT) Bingo!: en kritisk granskning av folkrörelserna i Sverige, 1850-1975. [Stockholm, 1975]. pp. 225. *bibliog.*

KLINGMAN (DAVID) Social change, political change, and public policy: Norway and Sweden, 1875-1965. London, [1976]. pp. 54. *bibliog.*

— Population.

NORBORG (KNUT) Befolkningens fördelning och flyttningar i Sverige. Lund, [1974]. pp. 141. *bibliog.*

FALK (THOMAS) Urban Sweden: changes in the distribution of population: the 1960s in focus. Stockholm, 1976. pp. 224. *bibliog.*

HOFSTEN (ERLAND ADOLF GERHARD VON) and LUNDSTRÖM (HANS) Swedish population history: main trends from 1750 to 1970. Stockholm, 1976. pp. 186. *bibliog. (Sweden. Statistiska Centralbyrån. Urval. 8)*

WINBERG (CHRISTER) Folkökning och proletarisering: kring den sociala strukturomvandlingen på Sveriges landsbygd under den agrara revolutionen. 2nd ed. [Lund, 1977]. pp. 344. *bibliog. With English summary.*

— — Mathematical models.

DEMOGRAPHIC, economic, and social interaction; edited by Åke E. Andersson [and] Ingvar Holmberg. Cambridge, Mass., [1977]. pp. 352. *bibliogs. Based on the proceedings of a one-day seminar at the University of Gothenburg in 1972, and of a symposium held in October 1974 by the Swedish Council for Social Science Research.*

— Social history.

LINDROTH (BENGT) Bingo!: en kritisk granskning av folkrörelserna i Sverige, 1850-1975. [Stockholm, 1975]. pp. 225. *bibliog.*

KLINGMAN (DAVID) Social change, political change, and public policy: Norway and Sweden, 1875-1965. London, [1976]. pp. 54. *bibliog.*

WINBERG (CHRISTER) Folkökning och proletarisering: kring den sociala strukturomvandlingen på Sveriges landsbygd under den agrara revolutionen. 2nd ed. [Lund, 1977]. pp. 344. *bibliog. With English summary.*

— Social policy.

NASENIUS (JAN) and RITTER (KRISTIN) Delad välfärd: svensk socialpolitik förr och nu. Stockholm, [1974]. pp. 197.

GULDIMANN (TIM) Die Grenzen des Wohlfahrtsstaates: am Beispiel Schwedens und der Bundesrepublik. München, [1976]. pp. 181.

SWINE

— Belgium.

BELGIUM. Institut Economique Agricole. La rentabilité des productions porcines dans les exploitations spécialisées (formerly La rentabilité des productions porcines). a., 1969/74 [2nd]- Brussels.

— United Kingdom.

BURNSIDE (ESTELLE) and others. Pig production in South West England 1975-76. Exeter, 1977. pp. 47. *(Agricultural Enterprise Studies in England and Wales. Economic Reports. No. 52)*

SWISS IN AUSTRALIA.

CHEDA (GIORGIO) L'emigrazione ticinese in Australia. [Locarno], 1976. 2 vols. *bibliog.*

SWITZERLAND

— Bundesversammlung.

STENGEL (KARL) Die Parlamentsdienste im Bund: Entstehung, Arbeitsweise und verfassungsrechtliche Grundlage. Bern, [1977]. pp. 218. *bibliog. Dissertation - Universität Zürich.*

— — Elections.

SWITZERLAND. Bureau Fédéral de Statistique. 1977. Nationalratswahlen..., 1975. Bern, 1977. pp. 161. *(Statistiques de la Suisse. 596e fasc.) In German and French.*

— Climate.

PFISTER (CHRISTIAN) Climatologist. Agrarkonjunktur und Witterungsverlauf im westlichen Schweizer Mittelland zur Zeit der Ökonomischen Patrioten, 1755-1797: ein Beitrag zur Umwelt- und Wirtschaftsgeschichte des 18. Jahrhunderts. Bern, 1975. pp. 279. *bibliog.*

— Commerce — United States.

MEIER (ROLF HANS) Die Aufteilung des Frachttransportes auf Luft- und Oberflächenverkehr. Zürich, 1977. pp. 190. *bibliog. Dissertation der Universität Zürich zur Erlangung der Würde eines Doktors der Wirtschaftswissenschaft.*

— Commercial policy.

REHSCHE (GUNTRAM) Schweizerische Aussenwirtschaftspolitik und Dritte Welt: Ziele und Instrumente; Exportförderung kontra Entwicklungspolitik? Bern, 1977. pp. 73. *bibliog. (Schweizerischer Evangelischer Kirchenbund. Institut für Sozialethik. Entwicklungspolitische Diskussionsbeiträge. 8)*

SPAHNI (WALTER) Der Ausbruch der Schweiz aus der Isolation nach dem Zweiten Weltkrieg: untersucht anhand ihrer Aussenhandelspolitik, 1944- 1947. Frauenfeld, [1977]. pp. 304. *bibliog.*

— Economic conditions.

GIOVANOLI (FRIEDRICH) Unter der Herrschaft des Finanzkapitals. [Zurich?, 1934]. pp. 71.

STEINBERG (JONATHAN) Why Switzerland?. Cambridge, 1976. pp. 214.

— Economic history.

DUPERREX (EMILE) 1869-1969: 100 Jahre Schweizerische Volksbank, Schweizer Wirtschaftsleben; herausgegeben...anlässlich der Hundertjahrfeier ihrer Gründung, etc. Bern, 1969. pp. 192.

— Economic policy.

RUEEGG (HANS) Wirtschaft am Wendepunkt: Folgerungen eines Arbeitgebers. Zürich, 1975. pp. 12. *(Wirtschaftsförderung: Gesellschaft zur Förderung der Schweizerischen Wirtschaft. Stimmen zur Staats- und Wirtschaftspolitik. 59)*

FREY (RENE L.) Zwischen Föderalismus und Zentralismus: ein volkswirtschaftliches Konzept des schweizerischen bundesstaates. Bern, 1977. pp. 134. *bibliog. (Forschungsinstitut für Föderalismus und Regionalstrukturen. Schriften. Nr.1)*

— Emigration and immigration.

KAMMERMANN (JOHANN) Der Familiennachzug der ausländischen Arbeitskräfte: eine Überprüfung auf Verfassungsmässigkeit und Menschenrechte. Zürich, [1976]. pp. 217. *bibliog. (Zuerich. Universität. Rechts- und staatswissenschaftliche Fakultät. Zuercher Beiträge zur Rechtswissenschaft. Neue Folge. Heft 503)*

— Foreign economic relations.

ZIEGLER (JEAN) Une Suisse au-dessus de tout soupçon. Paris, [1976]. pp. 182.

— Foreign relations.

LUCIRI (PIERRE) Le prix de la neutralité: la diplomatie secrète de la Suisse en 1914-1915 avec des documents d'archives inédits. Genève, 1976. pp. 336. *bibliog.*

See also EUROPEAN ECONOMIC COMMUNITY — Switzerland.

— — Germany.

CAWIL (H.) Der Fall Jacob. Zürich, [1935]. pp. 38.

— History.

STEINBERG (JONATHAN) Why Switzerland?. Cambridge, 1976. pp. 214.

— Languages.

STEINBERG (JONATHAN) Why Switzerland?. Cambridge, 1976. pp. 214.

— Neutrality.

LUCIRI (PIERRE) Le prix de la neutralité: la diplomatie secrète de la Suisse en 1914-1915 avec des documents d'archives inédits. Genève, 1976. pp. 336. *bibliog.*

ZIEGLER (JEAN) Une Suisse au-dessus de tout soupçon. Paris, [1976]. pp. 182.

— Officials and employees.

Der VPOD [Verband des Personals Öffentlicher Dienste], (1905-1955), im Spiegel des Zeitgeschehens; [by] Robert Grimm [and others]. Zürich, 1955. 3 vols.(in 1).

STENGEL (KARL) Die Parlamentsdienste im Bund: Entstehung, Arbeitsweise und verfassungsrechtliche Grundlage. Bern, [1977]. pp. 218. *bibliog. Dissertation - Universität Zürich.*

— Politics and government.

Die SCHWEIZ hält durch: Buch der Volksumfrage unter dem Patronat der Neuen Helvetischen Gesellschaft. Zürich, 1948. pp. 180.

FREISINNIG-DEMOKRATISCHE PARTEI DER SCHWEIZ. Frauen stellen kritische Fragen zur Politik. Bern, [1975]. pp. 36. *(Schriften. Nr. 167)*

STEINBERG (JONATHAN) Why Switzerland?. Cambridge, 1976. pp. 214.

— Rural conditions.

WEINBERG (DANIELA) Peasant wisdom: cultural adaptation in a Swiss village. Berkeley, Calif., [1975]. pp. 214. *bibliog.*

— Statistics, Vital.

SWITZERLAND. Bureau Fédéral de Statistique. 1976. Schweizerische Sterbetafel..., 1968-1973: Sterblichkeit nach Todesursachen...; Ausscheide- und Ueberlebensordnungen nach Zivilstand, etc. Bern, 1976. pp. 93. *(Statistiques de la Suisse. 577e fasc.) In German and French.*

SYDNEY

— Social conditions.

ISAACS (EVA) Greek children in Sydney. Canberra, 1976. pp. 128. *(Academy of the Social Sciences in Australia. Immigrants in Australia. 6)*

SYMBIONESE LIBERATION ARMY.

BRYAN (JOHN) 1934- . This soldier still at war. London, 1976. pp. 341.

McLELLAN (VIN) and AVERY (PAUL) The voices of guns: the definitive and dramatic story of the twenty-two-month career of the Symbionese Liberation Army - one of the most bizarre chapters in the history of the American left. New York, [1977]. pp. 544.

SYMBOLISM.

GRIMES (RONALD L.) Symbol and conquest: public ritual and drama in Santa Fe, New Mexico. Ithaca, 1976. pp. 281. *bibliog.*

SYMETAIN.

SYMETAIN. Maniema: le pays de l'étain. Bruxelles, 1953. pp. 391. *bibliog.*

SYNDICALISM

— France.

GUIN (YANNICK) Le mouvement ouvrier nantais: essai sur le syndicalisme d'action directe à Nantes et à Saint-Nazaire. Paris, 1976. pp. 413.

MONATTE (PIERRE) La lutte syndicale; présentation de Colette Chambelland. Paris, 1976. pp. 318.

— Spain.

LOPEZ (JUAN) Una mision sin importancia: memorias de un sindicalista. Madrid, [1972]. pp. 269.

— United Kingdom.

HOLTON (BOB) British syndicalism, 1900-1914: myths and realities. London, 1976. pp. 232.

SYRACUSE (PROVINCE)

— Economic conditions.

HILOWITZ (JANE) Economic development and social change in Sicily. Cambridge, Mass., [1976]. pp. 204. *bibliog.*

— Social conditions.

HILOWITZ (JANE) Economic development and social change in Sicily. Cambridge, Mass., [1976]. pp. 204. *bibliog.*

SYRIA

— Foreign relations — Israel.

ISRAEL INFORMATION CENTRE. Information Briefings. 25. Israel-Syria disengagement agreement, 31 May 1974: documents and statements. Jerusalem, [1974]. pp. 17.

SYSTEM ANALYSIS.

SYSTEMEERING 75; ([edited by] Mats Lundeberg and Janis Bubenko). Lund, 1975. pp. 323. *bibliogs. Festschrift in honour of Börje Langefors.*

BRADEN (CARRIE JO) and HERBAN (NANCY L.) Community health: a systems approach. New York, [1976]. pp. 178. *bibliogs.*

KATZAN (HARRY) Systems design and documentation: an introduction to the HIPO method. New York, [1976]. pp. 157. *bibliogs.*

NATIONAL RESEARCH COUNCIL. Commission on International Relations. Board on Science and Technology for International Development. Systems analysis and operations research: a tool for policy and program planning for developing countries: report of an ad hoc panel. Washington, D.C., 1976. pp. 98. *bibliog. With summaries in Spanish and French.*

SYSTEM ANALYSTS.

CRAWLEY (MARGARET) and MORRIS (JENNIFER) Systems analyst selection; a preliminary study undertaken for the National Computing Centre Limited by Margaret Crawley, and Jennifer Morris of the National Institute of Industrial Psychology. Manchester, [1970]. pp. 52. *bibliog.*

SYSTEM THEORY.

BEER (STAFFORD) Platform for change: a message from Stafford Beer. London, [1975]. pp. 457.

SCHODERBEK (PETER P.) and others. Management systems: conceptual considerations. Dallas, Texas, 1975. pp. 370. *bibliog.*

ANDERSON (BRIAN D.O.) and others. Foundations of system theory: finitary and infinitary conditions. Berlin, 1976. pp. 93. *bibliog.*

EVOLUTION and consciousness: human systems in transition; edited by Erich Jantsch and Conrad Waddington. Reading, Mass., 1976. pp. 259. *bibliogs.*

SYSTEMS theory in the social sciences: stochastic and control systems, pattern recognition, fuzzy analysis, simulation, behavioral models; (Hartmut Bossel [and others, eds.]). Basel, 1976. pp. 552. *bibliogs. Based on an interdisciplinary workshop sponsored by the Zentrum für interdisziplinäre Forschung of the University of Bielefeld.*

SYSTEMS ENGINEERING.

WILSON (IRA GAULBERT) and WILSON (MARTHANN E.) From idea to working model. New York, [1970]. pp. 267. *bibliog.*

SZCZECIN

— Growth.

ZAREMBA (PIOTR) Wspomnienia prezydenta Szczecina, 1945-1950. Poznań, 1977. pp. 862.

SZCZERCÓW

— Social conditions.

MIROWSKI (WŁODZIMIERZ) Przemiany społeczne w małym mieście a procesy migracyjne: studium monograficzne wychodźstwa ludności. Wrocław, 1976. pp. 260. *bibliog. With English and Russian summaries.*

SZWARCE (BRONISLAW).

MOROZOVA (OL'GA PAVLOVNA) Pol'skii revoliutsioner-demokrat Bronislav Shvartse. Moskva, 1975. pp. 288.

TACITUS.

SCHELLHASE (KENNETH C.) Tacitus in renaissance political thought. Chicago, 1976. pp. 270. *bibliog.*

TACNA-ARICA QUESTION.

PALACIOS RODRIGUEZ (RAUL) La chilenizacion de Tacna y Arica, 1883-1929. Lima, [1974]. pp. 317. *bibliog.*

TAGÜEÑA (MANUEL).

See TAGÜEÑA LACORTE (MANUEL).

TAGÜEÑA LACORTE (MANUEL).

TAGÜEÑA LACORTE (MANUEL) Testimonio de dos guerras. Mexico, 1973. pp. 672.

TAINE (HIPPOLYTE ADOLPHE).

KUCZYNSKI (JUERGEN) Die Muse und der Historiker: Studien über Jacob Burckhardt, Hyppolite[sic] Taine, Henry Adams; und eine Bibliographie sämtlicher Schriften von Jürgen Kuczynski, zusammengestellt von Erika Behm. Berlin, 1974. pp. 247. *bibliog. (Jahrbuch für Wirtschaftsgeschichte. Sonderbände)*

TAIWAN

— Economic conditions.

LUMLEY (F.A.) The Republic of China under Chiang Kai-Shek: Taiwan today. London, 1976. pp. 167. *bibliog.*

— History.

LUMLEY (F.A.) The Republic of China under Chiang Kai-Shek: Taiwan today. London, 1976. pp. 167. *bibliog.*

— Social conditions.

LUMLEY (F.A.) The Republic of China under Chiang Kai-Shek: Taiwan today. London, 1976. pp. 167. *bibliog.*

TAJIKISTAN

— Economic policy.

OSNOVNYE napravleniia povysheniia effektivnosti promyshlennosti, stroitel'stva i transporta: materialy respublikanskoi nauchno- prakticheskoi konferentsii. Dushanbe, 1976. pp. 184.

— Industries.

KAIUMOV (NURIDDIN) and PYSHNOGRAI (SVETLANA PAVLOVNA) Oborotnye proizvodstvennye fondy legkoi promyshlennosti Tadzhikistana i ikh ispol'zovanie; pod redaktsiei...L.I. Itina. Dushanbe, 1975. pp. 206.

— Politics and government.

ABDUNAZAROV (ABDUALIM) Partiinoe rukovodstvo Sovetami: (iz opyta partiinoi organizatsii Tadzhikistana po povysheniiu roli Sovetov v usloviiakh razvitogo sotsializma). Dushanbe, 1975. pp. 150.

TAK (PIETER LODEWIJK).

BORRIE (G.W.B.) Pieter Lodewijk Tak, 1848-1907: journalist en politicus. Assen, 1973. pp. 327. *bibliog. (International Institute of Social History. Sociaal-Historische Studiën. 6)*

TALLIN

— Commerce.

ETZOLD (GOTTFRIED) Seehandel und Kaufleute in Reval nach dem Frieden von Nystad bis zur Mitte des 18. Jahrhunderts. Marburg/Lahn, 1975. pp. 245. *bibliog. (Johann-Gottfried-Herder-Institut. Wissenschaftliche Beiträge zur Geschichte und Landeskunde Ostmitteleuropas. Nr.99)*

— History — Sources.

TALLIN. Stadtkämmerei. Kämmereibuch der Stadt Reval, 1432-1463; bearbeitet von Reinhard Vogelsang. Köln, 1976. 2 vols. (in 1). *bibliog. (Hansischer Geschichtsverein. Quellen und Darstellungen zur Hansischen Geschichte. Neue Folge. Band 22)*

TAMBOV (OBLAST')

— History — 1917-1921, Revolution.

NAKROKHIN (EFIM ALEKSANDROVICH) Inogo ne bylo puti. Voronezh, 1975. pp. 133.

— Politics and government.

NAKROKHIN (EFIM ALEKSANDROVICH) Inogo ne bylo puti. Voronezh, 1975. pp. 133.

TAMIL NADU.

See MADRAS.

TAMILS.

BARNETT (MARGUERITE ROSS) The politics of cultural nationalism in South India. Princeton, N.J., [1976]. pp. 368. *bibliog.*

TANNING.

EIRE. Committee on Industrial Progress. 1971. Report on tanning and dressing of leather industry. Dublin, [1971]. pp. 80.

TANZANIA

— Economic history.

KJEKSHUS (HELGE) Ecology control and economic development in East African history: the case of Tanganyika 1850-1950. Berkeley, Calif., 1977. pp. 215. *bibliog.*

— Economic policy.

COULSON (A.C.) A simplified political economy of Tanzania. Dar es Salaam, [1974]. pp. 54. *bibliog. (Dar es Salaam. University. Economic Research Bureau. ERB Papers. 74.9)*

HYDÉN (GÖRAN) "We must run while others walk": policy making for socialist development in the Tanzania-type of polities. Dar-es-Salaam, 1975. pp. 48. *bibliog. (Dar es Salaam. University. Economic Research Bureau. ERB Papers. 75.1)*

GREEN (REGINALD HERBOLD) Toward socialism and self reliance: Tanzania's striving for sustained transition projected. Uppsala, 1977. pp. 57, *(Nordiska Afrikainstitutet. Research Reports. No. 38)*

— Politics and government.

NYERERE (JULIUS KAMBARAGE) We must run while they walk; [two speeches]. Dar es Salaam, 1975. pp. 19. *(Reprinted from Mbioni: the journal of Kivukoni College, vol. 7, no. 8, 1975)*

URFER (SYLVAIN) Une Afrique socialiste, la Tanzanie. Paris, [1976]. pp. 239. *bibliog.*

— — Bibliography.

RWEYEMAMU (ANTHONY H.) compiler. Government and politics in Tanzania: a bibliography. Nairobi, 1972. pp. 39. *(East African Academy. Research Information and Publications Services. Information Circulars. No.6)*

— Rural conditions.

MBILINYI (MARJORIE J.) The transition to capitalism in rural Tanzania. Dar es Salaam, [1974]. pp. 49. *bibliog. (Dar es Salaam. University. Economic Research Bureau. ERB Papers. 74.7)*

TAPIRAPE INDIANS.

WAGLEY (CHARLES) Welcome of tears: the Tapirapé Indians of Central Brazil. New York, 1977. pp. 328. *bibliog.*

TARASCO INDIANS.

KEMPER (ROBERT V.) Migration and adaptation: Tzintzuntzan peasants in Mexico City. Beverly Hills, [1977]. pp. 223. *bibliog.*

TARDY (LOUIS).

FEDERATION NATIONALE DU CREDIT AGRICOLE. Louis Tardy, 1875-1961. [Paris, 1962]. pp. 20.

TARIFFS.

HUDEC (ROBERT E.) The GATT legal system and world trade diplomacy. New York, [1975]. pp. 399.

— Canada.

WILLIAMS (JAMES RALLA) Resources, tariffs, and trade: Ontario's stake. Toronto, 1976. pp. 117. *bibliog. (Ontario. Economic Council. Research Studies. No. 6)*

— Germany.

BUELOW-CUMMEROW (ERNST GOTTFRIED GEORG VON) Der Zollverein, sein System und dessen Gegner. Berlin, Veit, 1844. pp. 123.

— Underdeveloped areas.

See UNDERDEVELOPED AREAS — Tariffs.

— United Kingdom.

[HALL (GEORGE WEBB)] The origin and proceedings of the agricultural associations in Great Britain, in which their claims to protection against foreign produce, duty-free, are fully and ably set forth, etc. London, Sherwood, Neely, and Jones, [1819]. pp. 39.

RUDALL (EDWARD) Protection to native industry; or, The effect on the labouring classes of the withdrawal of the protecting duties; examined in a lecture, read to the members of the Launceston Institution. Launceston, Cater and Maddox, 1841. pp. 30.

SMITH (THOMAS) Editor of the London Mercantile Journal. Import duties considered in reference to the present state of the trade of Great Britain and her possessions, with the tables prepared by order of the Select Committee thereon. London, Hopcraft, 1841. pp. 54.

CABLE (VINCENT) Import controls: the case against. London, 1977. pp. 32. (Fabian Society. Research Series. [No.] 335)

— United States.

PINCUS (JONATHAN J.) Pressure groups and politics in antebellum tariffs. New York, 1977. pp. 237. bibliog.

TASMANIA

— Appropriations and expenditures.

TASMANIA. Treasury. 1975. Grants to Tasmania. in TASMANIA. Parliament. Journals and Printed Papers. 1975, no.33.

— Economic conditions.

TASMANIA. Committee appointed to inquire into Tasmanian Disabilities under Federation. 1925. Report;...[N.E. Lewis, chairman]. Hobart, 1925. pp. 45.

— Parliament — Elections.

HUGHES (COLIN ANFIELD) and GRAHAM (BRUCE DESMOND) Voting for the South Australian, Western Australian and Tasmanian Lower Houses, 1890-1964. Canberra, 1976. pp. 639. Fifth and final supplement to the same authors' A handbook of Australian government and politics, 1890-1964, to which it also contains corrigenda.

— — Officials and employees.

TASMANIA. Parliament. House of Assembly. 1961. The Parliament of Tasmania, 1856-1960: being a record of the services of members and officers of the Legislative-Council and the House of Assembly since the introduction of responsible government; and containing, also, a brief history of the Parliament, and keys to the photographic records of members; compiled by L.A. Thompson. [Hobart, 1961]. pp. 38.

TATAR PERIODICALS.

KARIMULLIN (ABRAR GIBADULLOVICH) U istokov tatarskoi knigi: ot nachala vozniknoveniia do 60-kh godov XIX veka. Kazan', 1971. pp. 223. bibliog.

TATAR REPUBLIC

— History — 1917-1921, Revolution.

NASYROV (TALGAT MIRZASALIKHOVICH) Oktiabr' i pechat' Tatarii, 1917-1920 gg. Kazan', 1975. pp. 211. bibliog.

— Industries.

NAZIPOVA (KLARA ABDULKHAKOVNA) Natsionalizatsiia promyshlennosti v Tatarii, 1917-1921 gg. Moskva, 1976. pp. 312. bibliog.

— Verkhovnyi Sovet.

KARIMOV (AZAL' MIRGALIMOVICH) Kompetentsiia vysshikh organov vlasti avtonomnoi respubliki: po materialam Tatarskoi ASSR. Kazan', 1975. pp. 144.

TATARS.

TASHKENTSKII protsess: sud nad desiat'iu predstaviteliami krymskotatarskogo naroda, 1 iiulia - 5 avgusta 1969 g.: sbornik dokumentov s illiustratsiiami. Amsterdam, 1976. pp. 854. (Alexander Herzen Foundation. Seriia "Biblioteka Samizdata". No.7)

TAX ACCOUNTING.

STITT (IAIN P.A.) Practical aspects of deferred tax accounting: a working guide to SSAP 8 and SSAP 11. London, 1976. pp. 193. bibliog. With appendices attached inside back cover.

TAX DEDUCTIONS

— United Kingdom.

POND (CHRIS) The attack on inflation: who pays?; a reply to the White Paper on the pay policy. London, 1976. fo.16. (Low Pay Unit. Low Pay Papers. No. 11)

TAX PLANNING.

DAIBER (HANS JOACHIM) Einkommensteuerliche Folgen der Wohnsitzverlegung ins niedrigbesteuernde Ausland. Nürnberg, 1976. pp. 203,xxxvi. bibliog.

— United Kingdom.

NELSON-JONES (JOHN A.) and SMITH (BERTRAM) Practical tax saving. London, 1976. pp. 317.

TAXATION.

WAGNER (ADOLPH) Theorie der Besteurung, Gebührenlehre und allgemeine Steuerlehre. 2nd ed. Leipzig, 1890. pp.814.

MATHUR (GAUTAM) Disparity tax in a composite economy. Delhi, 1975. pp. 264.

BRACEWELL-MILNES (JOHN BARRY) The camel's back: an international comparison of tax burdens. London, 1976. pp. 72. bibliog.

— Mathematical models.

BOES (DIETER) and GENSER (BERND) Steuerfunktionen in Prognose- und Entscheidungsmodellen: eine aggregationstheoretische Fundierung. Wien, 1977. pp. 218. bibliog. (Österreichische Akademie der Wissenschaften. Philosophisch-Historische Klasse. Sitzungsberichte. 311. Band)

— Andean Group countries.

FISCAL harmonization in the Andean countries; by Dr. Adolfo Atchabahian [and others]. Amsterdam, 1975. pp. 118. bibliog. (International Bureau of Fiscal Documentation. International Fiscal Harmonization. No.3)

— Barbados.

BARBADOS. 1952. Five year plan of development and taxation. [Bridgetown, 1952?]. pp. 28.

— Brazil.

SILVA (FERNANDO ANTONIO REZENDE DA) O imposto sobre a renda e a justiça fiscal. Rio de Janeiro, 1974. pp. 114. bibliog. (Brazil. Instituto de Planejamento Econômico e Social. Instituto de Pesquisas. Monografias. No. 14)

— Canada.

BIRD (RICHARD MILLER) Charging for public services: a new look at an old idea. Toronto, 1976. pp. 269. bibliog. (Canadian Tax Foundation. Canadian Tax Papers. No. 59)

— Ecuador.

ECUADOR. Direccion General de Recaudaciones. Boletin de estadisticas: recaudaciones efectuadas por jefaturas provinciales. a., 1973 (no.12)- Quito.

— France.

Les ELANS d'un patriote: ou, Nouvelles bases politiques. 2nd ed. Paris, chez les Marchands de Nouveautés, 1785. pp. (iv), 59.

HALPERN (LIONEL) Taxes in France;... adapted from... Les impôts en France, by Claude Gambier. 2nd ed. London, 1976. pp. 250.

RODRIGUE (JEAN) and REDJAH (MICHEL) Pourquoi nous payons trop d'impôts: la fiscalité giscardienne. Paris, [1976]. pp. 158.

— Germany.

SCHEIDEMANN (PHILIPP) Wollen wir einen Kriegs-Reichstag?: Abrechnung mit Helfferich und Ludendorff; (nach dem stenographischen Bericht der Reichstagssitzung vom 11. März 1924). [Berlin, 1924]. pp. 32.

— Italy.

FANTOZZI (AUGUSTO) Guida fiscale italiana: imposte indirette. Torino, [1976]. 2 vols. bibliogs.

— Netherlands — Law.

PETERS (J.) Author of Algemene beginselen van behoorlijk bestuur. Algemene beginselen van behoorlijk bestuur: debater: Prof. Mr. D. Simons: (voordracht gehouden op de Belastingconsulentendag 1971 georganiseerd door de Nederlandse Federatie van Belastingconsulenten). Deventer, 1971. pp. 47. (Nederlandse Federatie van Belastingconsulenten. Serie Belastingconsulentendagen. Nr. 16.)

— New Zealand — Law.

NEW ZEALAND. Statutes, etc. 1946-1976. Statutes and regulations [relating to taxation in New Zealand]; [edited] by F.D. O'Flynn. Wellington, 1976. loose-leaf.

— Poland.

OSTROWSKI (KAROL) Hitlerowska polityka podatkowa w Generalnym Gubernatorstwie. Warszawa, 1977. pp. 159. (Zeszyty Naukowe Uniwersytetu Jagiellońskiego. Prace Prawnicze. zeszyt 29) With Russian and German summaries.

— Spain — History.

BURNS (ROBERT IGNATIUS) Medieval colonialism: postcrusade exploitation of Islamic Valencia. Princeton, N.J., [1975]. pp. 394. bibliog.

— Switzerland — Mathematical models.

HAUSER (GERALD) Das Stabilisierungsvermögen des schweizerischen Steuersystems, 1948-1965. Zürich, 1976. pp. 170. bibliog.

— United Kingdom.

[TORRENS (ROBERT)] The budget: a series of letters on financial, commercial, and colonial policy; by a member of the Political Economy Club. No.6. (On the distinctive effects of taxes upon realized property and of taxes upon industry). London, Smith, Elder, 1842. pp. 141-170.

BROWN (CHARLES VICTOR) The impact of tax changes on income distribution. London, 1973. pp. 31. (Institute for Fiscal Studies. Publications. No. 4)

POND (CHRIS) Taxing the social contract: a memorandum to the Chancellor of the Exchequer from the Low Pay Unit. London, 1975. fo.7. (Low Pay Unit. Low Pay Papers. No. 2)

BRACEWELL-MILNES (JOHN BARRY) The camel's back: an international comparison of tax burdens. London, 1976. pp. 72. bibliog.

MELLOWS (ANTHONY ROGER) Taxation for executors and trustees. 4th ed. London, 1976. pp. 306.

FIELD (FRANK) and others. To him who hath: a study of poverty and taxation. Harmondsworth, 1977. pp. 254.

TAXATION.(Cont.)

MORGAN (DAVID RAYMOND) Over-taxation by inflation: a study of the effects of inflation on taxation and government expenditure, and of its correction by indexing. London, 1977. pp. 94. *bibliog. (Institute of Economic Affairs. Hobart Papers. 72). Including post-budget edition supplement.*

The STATE of taxation: consistency, inflation, incentives, public choice, terms of trade, government expenditure, enforcement, avoidance/evasion, escapes, bureaucracy, 50/60/70 per cent?, impact/incidence; [by] A.R. Prest [and others]. London, 1977. pp. 116. *(Institute of Economic Affairs. Readings. 16)*

U.K. Central Office of Information. Reference Division. Reference Pamphlets. 112. The British system of taxation; (with Supplement: the 1977 budget's main tax proposals). 3rd ed. London, 1977. 2 pts. *bibliog.*

— — Law.

U.K. Statutes, etc. Taxes acts: the capital transfer tax enactments in force...with other legislation and statutory regulations etc. affecting the application of the tax, and an index. irreg., 1974/76- London.

CONFEDERATION OF BRITISH INDUSTRY. Economic Directorate. Taxation Department. The Finance (no.2) Act 1975: an explanatory guide. London, 1975. pp. 26.

PINSON (BARRY) On revenue law: comprising income tax, capital gains tax, development land tax, etc. 11th ed. London, 1977. pp. 620.

— United States.

FORSYTHE (DALL W.) Taxation and political change in the young nation, 1781-1833. New York, 1977. pp. 167. *bibliog.*

PECHMAN (JOSEPH A.) Federal tax policy. 3rd ed. Washington, D.C., [1977]. pp. 401. *bibliog. (Brookings Institution. Studies of Government Finance)*

REYNOLDS (MORGAN) and SMOLENSKY (EUGENE) Public expenditures, taxes, and the distribution of income: the United States, 1950, 1961, 1970. New York, [1977]. pp. 145. *bibliogs. (Wisconsin University, Madison. Institute for Research on Poverty. Monograph Series)*

HOLBERT (ROBERT LEE) Tax law and political access: the bias of pluralism revisited. Beverly Hills, [1975]. pp. 72. *bibliog.*

— — Connecticut — New Haven.

LOCAL public finance and the fiscal squeeze: a case study; edited by John R. Meyer and John M. Quigley. Cambridge, Mass., [1977]. pp. 201. *Papers from a seminar sponsored by the Institution for Social and Policy Studies at Yale University and the Yale Law School, 1971-73.*

TAYLOR (FREDERICK WINSLOW).

LINHART (ROBERT) Lénine, les paysans, Taylor: essai d'analyse matérialiste historique de la naissance du système productif soviétique. Paris, [1976]. pp. 173.

TEA TRADE

— India — Assam.

TAGORE (SAUMYENDRANATH) Teeplantagenkulis: eine indische Erzählung; (autorisierte Übersetzung aus dem Indischen). Berlin, [1932]. pp. 45.

TEACHERS

— Supply and demand — United Kingdom.

ZABALZA-MARTI (ANTONIO) Occupational choice and labour market adjustments: the case of teachers in England and Wales, 1960-1970. 1976. fo. 308. *bibliog. Typescript. Ph.D. (London) thesis: unpublished. This thesis is the property of London University and may not be removed from the Library.*

— Canada — Salaries, pensions etc.

CANADA. Statistics Canada. Teachers in universities: salaries general. a., 1972-73/1974-75- Ottawa. *[in English and French].*

— France.

BAECQUE (FRANCIS DE) La situation des personnels enseignants des universités: éléments de réflexion pour une réforme, etc. Paris, La Documentation Française, 1974. pp. 73.

— United Kingdom.

CONGDON (BOB) and OSBORN (PAUL) Directory of ideas, contacts and support for academics working for international development. London, 1974. pp. 40. *(Voluntary Committee on Overseas Aid and Development. Academics against Poverty Project. Higher Education Action for Development. 4)*

WHITBURN (JULIA) and others. People in polytechnics: a survey of polytechnic staff and students, 1972-3. Guildford, Surrey, 1976. pp. 212. *bibliog. (Society for Research into Higher Education. Research into Higher Education Monographs. 27)*

— — Salaries, pensions, etc.

ALEXANDER (WILLIAM PICKEN) Baron Alexander. The Burnham Further Education Report 1973 and the Burnham Farm Institutes Report 1973: a commentary. London, 1973. pp. 12.

U.K. Department of Education and Science. 1977. Scales of salaries for teachers in primary and secondary schools, England and Wales, 1977; being the document...setting out the scales of salaries and other provisions for determining the remuneration of teachers in primary and secondary schools maintained by local education authorities. London, 1977. pp. 54.

— United States.

ERICSON (EDWARD E.) Radicals in the university. Stanford, Calif., [1975]. pp. 281. *bibliog. (Stanford University. Hoover Institution on War, Revolution and Peace. Hoover Institution Publications. 144)*

TEACHERS, TRAINING OF

— United Kingdom.

LACEY (COLIN) The socialization of teachers. London, 1977. pp. 160. *bibliog.*

TEACHERS' COLLEGES

— United Kingdom.

OSBORNE (RICHARD HORSLEY) and MOLYNEUX (FRANK HENRY) A spatial survey of higher education provision in the East Midlands, with special reference to colleges of education in the University of Nottingham Area Training Organisation. Nottingham, 1974. pp. 16. *bibliog.*

TEACHERS' UNIONS

— United Kingdom.

JOHNSON (RICHARD) of the University of Birmingham. Trade unionism and the academics: Swansea, 1974. London, [1974]. pp. 30. *(Council for Academic Freedom and Democracy. Reports)*

SWABE (ANTHONY IAN) The Association of Teachers in Technical Institutions, 1904-1945: white-collar unionism among professional people. 1977. fo.213. *bibliog. Typescript. M.Phil. (London) thesis: unpublished. This thesis is the property of London University and may not be removed from the Library.*

TEACHING.

WOODS (PETER) and HAMMERSLEY (MARTYN) eds. School experience: explorations in the sociology of education. London, 1977. pp. 297. *bibliogs.*

TEACHING, FREEDOM OF.

HALSEY (ALBERT HENRY) Academic freedom and the idea of a university. Cape Town, 1976. pp. 16. *(Cape Town. University. T.B. Davie Memorial Lectures. 17)*

— Germany.

WEBER (WERNER) Dr. jur. Neue Aspekte der Freiheit von Forschung und Lehre: die verfassungsrechtlichen Grenzen der Mitbestimmung im akademischen Bereich. Göttingen, 1969. pp. 36.

TEAR GAS MUNITIONS.

VERWEY (WIL D.) Riot control agents and herbicides in war: their humanitarian, toxicological, ecological, military, polemological, and legal aspects. Leyden, 1977. pp. 377. *bibliog.*

TECHNICAL ASSISTANCE.

LEWIS (Sir WILLIAM ARTHUR) The evolution of foreign aid. Cardiff, [1971]. pp. 18. *(Wales. University of Wales. University College, Cardiff. David Owen Memorial Lectures. No. 1)*

UNITED NATIONS. Conference on Trade and Development. 1971. Special measures in favour of the least developed among the developing countries: report of the Ad Hoc Group of Experts, etc. (TD/B/349/Rev.1). New York, 1971. pp. 29.

TECHNICAL ASSISTANCE, AMERICAN.

NAU (HENRY R.) and others. Technology transfer and U.S. foreign policy. New York, 1976. pp. 325.

TECHNICAL ASSISTANCE, BRITISH.

TECHNICAL EDUCATION AND TRAINING ORGANISATION FOR OVERSEAS COUNTRIES [U.K.]. Annual report. a., 1973/74 [2nd]- London.

FOREMAN-PECK (JAMES) Overseas development: home truths. London, [1976]. pp. 16.

TECHNICAL ASSISTANCE, GERMAN

— America, Latin.

KRATOCHWIL (GERMÁN) Wissenschaftlich-technologische Entwicklung und internationale Zusammenarbeit in Lateinamerika. Tübingen, [1976]. pp. 175. *(Institut für Iberoamerika-Kunde. Schriftenreihe. Band 24) With Spanish summary.*

TECHNICAL ASSISTANCE IN LATIN AMERICA.

GALL (PIRIE M.) and others. Municipal development programs in Latin America: an intercounty evaluation. New York, 1976. pp. 124. *bibliog.*

TECHNICAL EDUCATION.

ABRAHAM (KARL) Der Betrieb als Erziehungsfaktor: die funktionale Erziehung durch den modernen wirtschaftlichen Betrieb. 2nd ed. Freiburg im Breisgau, 1957. pp. 182. *bibliog.*

TECHNICAL EDUCATION AND TRAINING ORGANISATION FOR OVERSEAS COUNTRIES [U.K.]. Annual report. a., 1973/74 [2nd]- London.

— Asia.

DASGUPTA (R.) A survey of technician training in commonwealth countries of Asia. London, Commonwealth Secretariat, 1976. pp. 104. *(Education in the Commonwealth. No. 12)*

— United Kingdom.

PERRY (PETER J.C.) The evolution of British manpower policy: from the Statute of Artificers 1563 to the Industrial Training Act 1964. London, [1976]. pp. 329.

EDUCATION and training for the industrial technologies: papers for a series of regional symposia. [London], Department of Industry, Industrial Technologies Education and Training Secretariat, [1977]. 1 vol. (various pagings).

— — Commonwealth.

DASGUPTA (R.) A survey of technician training in commonwealth countries of Asia. London, Commonwealth Secretariat, 1976. pp. 104. *(Education in the Commonwealth. No. 12)*

TECHNOCRACY.

AKIN (WILLIAM E.) Technocracy and the American dream: the technocrat movement, 1900-1941. Berkeley, Calif., [1977]. pp. 227. *bibliog.*

WINNER (LANGDON) Autonomous technology: technics-out-of-control as a theme in political thought. Cambridge, Mass., [1977]. pp. 386.

TECHNOLOGICAL FORECASTING.

EKONOMICHESKIE aspekty nauchno-tekhnicheskogo prognozirovaniia; pod redaktsiei...M.A. Vilenskogo. Moskva, 1975. pp. 222.

TECHNOLOGICAL INNOVATIONS.

ACCELERATING innovation; papers given at a symposium held at the University of Nottingham, March 1969, arranged by Aslib in collaboration with the Ministry of Technology and the Research Associations. London, [1970]. pp. 64. *bibliogs.*

FLECK (FLORIAN H.) Die ökonomische Theorie des technischen Fortschritts und seine Identifikation. Meisenheim am Glan, 1973. pp. 255. *bibliog.*

GUDOZHNIK (GRIGORII SERGEEVICH) Nauchno-tekhnicheskaia revoliutsiia i ekologicheskii krizis. Moskva, 1975. pp. 232.

RASMUSSEN (POUL NØRREGAARD) The economics of technological change. Stockholm, 1975. pp. 43. *bibliog. (Wicksell Lecture Society. Wicksell Lectures. 1975)*

ZURHORST (GUENTER) Gewerkschaftspolitik und technischer Fortschritt: zum Problem einer basisorientierten Mitbestimmung. Berlin, [1975]. pp. 163. *bibliog.*

JOHNSON (HARRY GORDON) Aspects of patents and licenses as stimuli to innovation. Kiel, 1976. pp. 36. *(Kiel. Universität. Institut für Weltwirtschaft. Bernhard-Harms-Vorlesungen. 7)*

HEERTJE (ARNOLD) Economics and technical change. London, [1977]. pp. 334.

— Social aspects.

VULIĆ-ŠMALC (ELVIRA) Utjecaj tehnoloških transformacija na zapošljavanje kadrova. Zagreb, 1975. pp. 82. *bibliog. With brief English summary.*

— Communist countries.

EKONOMICHESKIE problemy nauchno-tekhnicheskoi revoliutsii pri sotsializme. Moskva, 1975. pp. 263.

— Germany.

HORN (ERNST JUERGEN) Technologische Neuerungen und internationale Arbeitsteilung: die Bundesrepublik Deutschland im internationalen Vergleich. Tübingen, [1976]. pp. 382. *bibliog. (Kiel. Universität. Institut für Weltwirtschaft. Kieler Studien. 139)*

— Germany, Eastern.

WISSENSCHAFT und Produktion im Sozialismus: zur organischen Verbindung der Errungenschaften der wissenschaftlich-technischen Revolution...; (Autorenkollektiv: Hans-Joachim Beyer [and others]). Berlin, 1976. pp. 367.

DEUTSCHES INSTITUT FÜR WIRTSCHAFTSFORSCHUNG. Sonderhefte. [Neue Folge]. 116. Zur Planung, Organisation und Lenkung von Forschung und Entwicklung in der DDR: Aspekte des wissenschaftlich-technischen Fortschritts; ([by] Angela Scherzinger). Berlin, 1977. pp. 214. *bibliog. With English summary.*

— Russia.

INTERNATIONAL INSTITUTE FOR STRATEGIC STUDIES. Adelphi Papers. No. 76. Technology, management and the Soviet military establishment; by David Holloway. London, 1971. pp. 44. *bibliog.*

GAVRILOV (EVGENII IVANOVICH) Ekonomika i effektivnost' nauchno-tekhnicheskogo progressa; pod nauchnoi redaktsiei i s predisloviem E.N. Bliokova. Minsk, 1975. pp. 318. *bibliog.*

BERLINER (JOSEPH SCHOLOM) The innovation decision in Soviet industry. Cambridge, Mass., [1976]. pp. 561. *bibliog.*

NEVESELÝ (JAROSLAV) Innovationsförderung in der UdSSR nach der Wirtschaftsreform von 1965: eine Untersuchung der Funktionsproblematik des 'Neuen ökonomischen Systems'. [Mannheim, 1976]. pp. 202. *bibliog. Inaugural-Dissertation zur Erlangung der Würde eines Doktors der Wirtschaftswissenschaften der Universität Mannheim.*

— — Social aspects.

KAPELIAN (EFIM KHAIMOVICH) Proizvoditel'nye sily: struktura, funktsii, tipologiia; voprosy metodologii i teorii. Minsk, 1976. pp. 191.

SOTSIAL'NO-ekonomicheskie problemy nauchno-tekhnicheskoi revoliutsii. Moskva, 1976. pp. 368.

— — Ukraine.

KURNOSOV (IURII OLEKSIIOVYCH) Intelihentsiia Ukraïns'koï RSR i naukovo-tekhnichnyi prohres, 1959-1970. Kyïv, 1975. pp. 208. *bibliog.*

— Sweden.

BRODIN (BENGT) Produktutvecklingsprocesser: en studie ur marknadsföringssynvinkel av produktutveckling i svenska företag. Stockholm, 1976. 2 vols. (in 1). *bibliog. With English summary.*

— United Kingdom.

HARLOW (CHRIS) Innovation and productivity under nationalisation: the first thirty years. London, 1977. pp. 256.

— United States.

ROSENBERG (NATHAN) Perspectives on technology. Cambridge, 1976. pp. 353. *bibliogs.*

YIN (ROBERT K.) and others. Tinkering with the system: technological innovations in state and local services. Lexington, Mass., [1977]. pp. 275. *bibliog.*

— Yugoslavia.

VULIĆ-ŠMALC (ELVIRA) Utjecaj tehnoloških transformacija na zapošljavanje kadrova. Zagreb, 1975. pp. 82. *bibliog. With brief English summary.*

TECHNOLOGY

— History — Baltic States.

IZ istorii estestvoznaniia i tekhniki Pribaltiki. t.5. Riga, 1976. pp. 342. *With English table of contents.*

— — Germany.

LUDWIG (KARL HEINZ) Technik und Ingenieure im Dritten Reich. Düsseldorf, [1974]. pp. 544. *bibliog.*

— — Russia.

OCHERKI razvitiia tekhniki v SSSR. Moskva, 1968-76. 5 vols.

— — United Kingdom.

HYDE (CHARLES K.) Technological change and the British iron industry, 1700-1870. Princeton, [1977]. pp. 283. *bibliog.*

— — United States.

MORISON (ELTING ELMORE) From know-how to nowhere: the development of American technology. New York, [1974]. pp. 199. *bibliog.*

— Philosophy.

WINNER (LANGDON) Autonomous technology: technics-out-of-control as a theme in political thought. Cambridge, Mass., [1977]. pp. 386.

— Social aspects.

KUITENBROUWER (JOOST B.W.) Science and technology: for or against the people. The Hague, 1975. pp. 30. *(The Hague. Institute of Social Studies. Occasional Papers. No. 49)*

NEGROTTI (MASSIMO) Sociologia dell'ambiente tecnico: saggio sull'equilibrio futuro del sistema culturatecnica. Milano, [1975]. pp. 118. *(Parma. Università. Istituto di Sociologia. Collana. Sezione "Momenti del Pensiero Sociologico". 3)*

ABOLTIN (V.IA.) ed. Kritika burzhuaznykh kontseptsii nauchno-tekhnicheskoi revoliutsii. Moskva, 1976. pp. 271. *(Akademiia Nauk SSSR. Institut Mirovoi Ekonomiki i Mezhdunarodnykh Otnoshenii. Sovremennyi Kapitalizm i Ideologicheskaia Bor'ba)*

DAVIES (DUNCAN SHEPPEY) and others. The humane technologist. London, 1976. pp. 180.

TECHNOLOGY as a social and political phenomenon; [edited by] Philip L. Bereano. New York, [1976]. pp. 544.

BASIUK (VICTOR) Technology, world politics, and American policy. New York, 1977. pp. 409. *bibliog.*

SCIENCE, technology and society: a cross-disciplinary perspective; edited by Ina Spiegel-Rösing and Derek de Solla Price. London, [1977]. pp. 602. *bibliogs.*

SCORER (RICHARD SEGAR) The clever moron. London, 1977. pp. 171.

WINNER (LANGDON) Autonomous technology: technics-out-of-control as a theme in political thought. Cambridge, Mass., [1977]. pp. 386.

— — United States.

KASSON (JOHN F.) Civilizing the machine: technology and Republican values in America, 1776-1900. New York, 1976. pp. 274.

AKIN (WILLIAM E.) Technocracy and the American dream: the technocrat movement, 1900-1941. Berkeley, Calif., [1977]. pp. 227. *bibliog.*

NOBLE (DAVID F.) America by design: science, technology, and the rise of corporate capitalism. New York, 1977. pp. 384.

— America, Latin.

SAGASTI (FRANCISCO R.) and GUERRERO C. (MAURICIO) El desarrollo cientifico y tecnologico de America Latina: diagnostico, bases para la accion y estructuras de cooperacion. Buenos Aires, Instituto para la Integracion de America Latina, [1974]. pp. 203.

HELLINGER (DOUGLAS A.) and HELLINGER (STEPHEN H.) Unemployment and the multinationals: a strategy for technological change in Latin America. Port Washington, N.Y., 1976. pp. 158. *bibliog.*

KRATOCHWIL (GERMÁN) Wissenschaftlich-technologische Entwicklung und internationale Zusammenarbeit in Lateinamerika. Tübingen, [1976]. pp. 175. *(Institut für Iberoamerika-Kunde. Schriftenreihe. Band 24) With Spanish summary.*

— — Statistics.

THEBAUD (SCHILLER) Statistics on science and technology in Latin America: experience with Unesco pilot projects 1972-1974. Paris, United Nations Educational, Scientific and Cultural Organization, 1976. pp. 76. *(Statistical Reports and Studies. [No. 20])*

— India.

SEMINAR ON APPROPRIATE TECHNOLOGY, NEW DELHI, 1971. Appropriate technology for rapid economic growth: (proceedings of the seminar). Delhi, 1972. pp. 160. *bibliog. (India. Ministry of Industrial Development. Appropriate Technology Cell. Monographs. No. 1)*

TECHNOLOGY(Cont.)

— Underdeveloped areas.

See UNDERDEVELOPED AREAS —
Technology.

— United Kingdom.

NORTH west regional symposium: manufacturing management and the industrial technologies: symposium papers. [London], Department of Industry, Industrial Technologies Secretariat, 1976. pp. 73.

— United States.

TELLER (EDWARD) and others. Power and security. Lexington, Mass., [1976]. pp. 204. *(Commission on Critical Choices for Americans. Critical Choices for Americans. vol. 4)*

TECHNOLOGY AND CIVILIZATION.

MARTIN (JULES) Des machines, conséquences économiques et morales qui résultent de leur puissance productive; conférences faites à Périgueux...le 16 mars et le 25 novembre 1867. Périgueux, Dupont, 1867. pp. 77. *(Extrait du journal L'echo de la Dordogne)*

ROMAN (VALTER) Secolul XX - secolul marilor revoluţii: sinteze şi perspective. [Bucureşti], 1976. pp. 539. *bibliog. With tables of contents in various languages.*

STRATEGIES for human settlements: habitat and environment; edited by Gwen Bell. Honolulu, [1976]. pp. 172.

TECHNOLOGY AND STATE.

BASIUK (VICTOR) Technology, world politics, and American policy. New York, 1977. pp. 409. *bibliog.*

— Mexico.

WIONCZEK (MIGUEL S.) and others. La transferencia internacional de tecnologia. Mexico, 1974. pp. 230. *bibliog.*

— United Kingdom.

ZUCKERMAN (SOLLY) Baron Zuckerman. Advice and responsibility. Oxford, 1975. pp. 40. *bibliog. (Oxford. University. Romanes Lectures. 1975)*

— United States.

KISTIAKOWSKY (GEORGE BOGDAN) A scientist at the White House: the private diary of President Eisenhower's special assistant for science and technology. Cambridge, Mass., 1976. pp. 448.

NAU (HENRY R.) and others. Technology transfer and U.S. foreign policy. New York, 1976. pp. 325.

TECHNOLOGY TRANSFER.

WIONCZEK (MIGUEL S.) and others. La transferencia internacional de tecnologia. Mexico, 1974. pp. 230. *bibliog.*

INTRA-NATIONAL transfer of technology. Tokyo, Asian Productivity Organization, 1976. pp. 161.

NAU (HENRY R.) and others. Technology transfer and U.S. foreign policy. New York, 1976. pp. 325.

CARNEGIE-ROCHESTER CONFERENCE ON PUBLIC POLICY. 1976, November Conference. Optimal policies, control theory and technology experts; editors Karl Brunner and Allan H. Meltzer. Amsterdam, 1977. pp. 238. *bibliogs. (Journal of Monetary Economics. Carnegie-Rochester Conference Series on Public Policy. vol. 7)*

TELECOMMUNICATION.

HEBDITCH (DAVID L.) Data communications: an introductory guide. London, 1975. pp. 223.

MARTIN (JAMES THOMAS) Future developments in telecommunications. 2nd ed. Englewood Cliffs, [1977]. pp. 668.

— Social aspects.

SHORT (JOHN) and others. The social psychology of telecommunications. London, [1976]. pp. 195. *bibliog.*

— Australia.

OVERSEAS TELECOMMUNICATIONS COMMISSION (AUSTRALIA). Annual report. a., 1946/47 (1st)- Canberra. *Included in AUSTRALIA. Parliament. [Parliamentary papers].*

— South Africa — Accounting.

SOUTH AFRICA. Parliament. House of Assembly. Select Committee on Posts and Telecommunications. 1976. Report (with Proceedings and Minutes of evidence) (S.C.3- 1976). in SOUTH AFRICA. Parliament. House of Assembly. Select Committee reports.

— Taiwan.

STATISTICAL ABSTRACT OF TRANSPORTATION AND COMMUNICATIONS: REPUBLIC OF CHINA; [pd. by] Ministry of Communications. a., 1975- [Taipei]. *[in English and Chinese].*

— United Kingdom — Employees.

POST OFFICE ENGINEERING UNION. Discussion Pamphlets. 1. Telecommunications grading and structure. [London, 1975?]. pp. 24.

POST OFFICE ENGINEERING UNION. Discussion Pamphlets. 2. Union organisation. [London, 1976?]. pp. 11.

— United States.

OETTINGER (ANTHONY G.) and others. High and low politics: information resources for the 80s. Cambridge, Mass., [1977]. pp. 260.

TELEPHONE.

The SOCIAL impact of the telephone; Ithiel de Sola Pool, editor. Cambridge, Mass., [1977]. pp. 502. *bibliogs. (Massachusetts Institute of Technology. M.I.T. Bicentennial Studies) The papers in this volume were originally presented at a series of seminars held at MIT in celebration of the centennial of the telephone.*

TELEVISION AND CHILDREN.

TELEVISION and socialization processes in the family: a documentation of the Prix Jeunesse Seminar, 1975. München, [1976]. pp. 192. *Special English issue of Fernsehen und Bildung, vol. 9, 2/3.*

TELEVISION AUDIENCES

— United Kingdom.

STUART (ALAN) Sampling in television research. London, 1960. pp. 16. *(Associated Television. ATV Research Library. No. 6)*

TELEVISION BROADCASTING.

SCHLOSSER (HERBERT S.) Broadcasters in a free society: common problems, common purpose. London, 1976. pp. 16. *(British Broadcasting Corporation. B.B.C. Lunch-time Lectures. 10th Series. 5)*

— Social aspects.

TELEVISION and socialization processes in the family: a documentation of the Prix Jeunesse Seminar, 1975. München, [1976]. pp. 192. *Special English issue of Fernsehen und Bildung, vol. 9, 2/3.*

— Canada.

HALLMAN (EUGENE S.) and HINDLEY (H.) Broadcasting in Canada. London, 1977. pp. 90.

— Denmark.

FRANCE. Direction de la Documentation. La Documentation Française. Notes et Etudes Documentaires. Nos. 4,232-4,233. La radiodiffusion-télévision au Danemark; par René Albrecht. Paris, 1975. pp. 33. *bibliog.*

— France.

KUHN (RAYMOND) Government and broadcasting in France, 1969-1975. [Coventry], 1975. pp. 46. *(University of Warwick. Department of Politics. Working Papers. No. 8)*

— Italy.

FRANCE. Direction de la Documentation. La Documentation Française. Notes et Etudes Documentaires. Nos. 4,251-4,252-4,253. La radio et la télévision en Italie; par Adrien Popovici. Paris, 1976. pp. 101. *bibliog.*

— Malaysia.

ADHIKARYA (RONNY) and others. Broadcasting in peninsular Malaysia. London, 1977. pp. 102. *bibliog.*

— Russia.

VERYHA (WASYL) Communication media and Soviet nationality policy: status of national languages in Soviet T.V. broadcasting. New York, 1972. pp. 59. *bibliog. (Revised and enlarged reprint from The Ukrainian Quarterly, vol. 17, nos. 2 and 3, 1971)*

— — Uzbekistan.

ESIN (ANATOLII FEDOROVICH) Radio i televidenie Uzbekistana: rost, dostizheniia, problemy. Tashkent, 1975. pp. 160.

— Sweden.

PLOMAN (EDWARD W.) Broadcasting in Sweden. London, 1976. pp. 65.

— United Kingdom.

1955-1976: twenty one years of Independent Television. London, 1976. pp. 139. *A supplement to Broadcast.*

STANDING CONFERENCE ON BROADCASTING. Evidence to the Committee on the Future of Broadcasting from the Standing Conference on Broadcasting. London, 1976. pp. 156. *Cover title: The SCOB papers: broadcasting in the UK.*

GOLDIE (GRACE WYNDHAM) Facing the nation: television and politics 1936-1976. London, 1977. pp. 368. *bibliog.*

— United States.

The FUTURE of public broadcasting; [edited by] Douglass Cater and Michael J. Nyhan. New York, 1976. pp. 372. *bibliog.*

TELEVISION BROADCASTING OF NEWS.

KLINE (STEPHEN CHARLES) Audio and visual characteristics of television news broadcasting: their effects on opinion change. 1977. fo. 360. *bibliog. Typescript. Ph.D. (London) thesis: unpublished. This thesis is the property of London University and may not be removed from the Library.*

— United Kingdom.

GLASGOW UNIVERSITY MEDIA GROUP. Bad news. London, 1976 in progress.

— United States.

ALTHEIDE (DAVID L.) Creating reality: how TV news distorts events. Beverly Hills, [1976]. pp. 220. *bibliog.*

HOFSTETTER (C. RICHARD) Bias in the news: network television coverage of the 1972 election campaign. Columbus, Ohio, [1976]. pp. 213.

TELEVISION IN POLITICS.

PATTERSON (THOMAS E.) and McCLURE (ROBERT D.) The unseeing eye: the myth of television power in national politics. New York, [1976]. pp. 218.

— France.

KUHN (RAYMOND) Government and broadcasting in France, 1969-1975. [Coventry], 1975. pp. 46. *(University of Warwick. Department of Politics. Working Papers. No. 8)*

— Germany.

WEISS (HANS JUERGEN) Wahlkampf im Fernsehen: Untersuchungen zur Rolle der grossen Fernsehdebatten im Bundestagswahlkampf, 1972. Berlin, 1976. pp. 292. *bibliog.* (*Arbeitsgemeinschaft für Kommunikationsforschung. AfK Studien. Band 5*)

— United Kingdom.

GOLDIE (GRACE WYNDHAM) Facing the nation: television and politics 1936-1976. London, 1977. pp. 368. *bibliog.*

— United States.

HOFSTETTER (C. RICHARD) Bias in the news: network television coverage of the 1972 election campaign. Columbus, Ohio, [1976]. pp. 213.

TELEVISION PROGRAMMES, PUBLIC SERVICE.

The FUTURE of public broadcasting; [edited by] Douglass Cater and Michael J. Nyhan. New York, 1976. pp. 372. *bibliog.*

TEMPERANCE.

ERISMANN (FRIEDRICH) Das alkoholfreie Volkshaus in Zürich 4: Geschichte, Baubeschreibung, Betrieb. Zürich, 1913. pp. 55.

TERRORISM.

HONDERICH (TED) Political violence. Ithaca, N.Y., 1976. pp. 118.

CLUTTERBUCK (RICHARD LEWIS) Guerrillas and terrorists. London, 1977. pp. 125. *bibliog.*

DOBSON (CHRISTOPHER) and PAYNE (RONALD) The Carlos complex: a study in terror. New York, 1977. pp. 254.

LAQUEUR (WALTER ZE'EV) Terrorism. London, [1977]. pp. 277. *bibliog.*

WILKINSON (PAUL) Terrorism and the liberal state. London, 1977. pp. 257. *bibliog.*

— America, Latin.

HALPERIN (ERNST) Terrorism in Latin America. Beverly Hills, [1976]. pp. 90. *bibliog.* (*Georgetown University. Center for Strategic and International Studies. Washington Papers. vol.4/33*)

— East (Near East).

ISRAEL INFORMATION CENTRE. Information Briefings. 23. The treatment of Arab terrorists. Jerusalem, [1974]. pp. 14.

— France.

ROCKER (RUDOLF) Di geshikhte fun der teroristisher bevegung in Frankraykh. London, "Arbeyter Freynd" Drukerey, [190-?]. 2 vols. (in 1). *In Yiddish with Hebrew characters. Bound with Jean Grave, Di obshtorbende gezelshaft, etc.*

— United Kingdom.

GIBSON (BRIAN) The Birmingham bombs;...with additional research by Stephanie Silk and the help of the entire B.B.C. T.V. 'Day and Night' team, etc. Chichester, [1976]. pp. 164.

SCORER (CATHERINE) The Prevention of Terrorism Acts 1974 and 1976: a report on the operation of the law. London, [1976]. pp. 39.

TEXTBOOKS

— Ghana.

GHANA. Committee of Enquiry into the affairs of the Distribution Division of the Ghana Publishing Corporation. 1967. Report; [K.S. Essah, chairman]. Accra, [1968]. pp. 64. *Bound with White Paper on the report.*

GHANA. 1969. White Paper on the report of the Committee of Enquiry into the affairs of the Distribution Division of the erstwhile State Publishing Corporation. [Accra, 1969]. pp. 8. (*W[hite] P[apers]. 1969. No. 1) Bound with the report.*

— United Kingdom.

PROCTOR (CHRIS) Racist textbooks. London, [1975]. pp. 41.

TEXTILE INDUSTRY AND FABRICS

— Quality control.

CHAIKIN (M.) and COLLINS (J.D.) Quality control in the textile industry. (ID/91) (ID/WG.58/12, Rev.1) (ID/WG.58/18, Rev.1). New York, United Nations, 1972. pp. 57.

— France.

FRANCE. Groupe sectoriel d'Analyse et de Prévision Textile-Habillement. 1976. Rapport...: préparation du 7e Plan. Paris, 1976. pp. 79.

— Netherlands.

ECONOMISCH INSTITUUT VOOR HET MIDDEN- EN KLEINBEDRIJF. Bedrijfseconomische Publikaties. Bedrijfsgegevens voor de textieldetailhandel over 1973 en 1974: gespecialiseerde bedrijven; [with] Tabellen. 's-Gravenhage, 1975. 2 pts.

— Portugal.

[RIBEIRO DE SÁ (SEBASTIÃO JOSÉ)] As fabricas nacionaes são uma historiaê': pamphleto economico pelo redactor da Revista Universal. Lisboa, [imprint], 1850. pp. 28.

— United Kingdom.

GENERAL FEDERATION OF TRADE UNIONS. Courtaulds: the anatomy of a multinational. London, [1975]. pp. 112.

JOINT TEXTILE COMMITTEE [U.K.]. Textile trends 1966-75: an economic profile of the UK textile and clothing industries. London, National Economic Development Office, 1976. pp. 64. *bibliog.*

— Zaire.

MUTOMBO (PIERRE SYLVAIN) Les fibres de coton en République Démocratique du Congo et l'industrie textile. Kinshasa, Office National de la Recherche et du Développement, [1970]. pp. 109. *bibliog.*

TEXTILE WORKERS

— Congresses.

INTERNATIONAL TEXTILE, GARMENT AND LEATHER WORKERS' FEDERATION. World Congress, 1st, Amsterdam, 1972. Reports from affiliated organisations. London, 1972. pp. 220.

— United States.

WEISBORD (ALBERT) Passaic: the story of a struggle against starvation wages and the right to organize. Chicago, 1926; New York, 1976. pp. 64.

THAILAND

— Census.

THAILAND. Census, 1970. 1970 population and housing census: economic characteristics. [Bangkok], 1975. pp. 31,77. (*Subject Reports. No. 1)*

— Politics and government.

SUKSAMRAN (SOMBOON) Political Buddhism in southeast Asia: the role of the Sangha in the modernization of Thailand;...edited with an introduction by Trevor O. Ling. London, [1977]. pp. 154. *bibliog.*

— Population.

HOÀNG (MICHEL) La Thailande et ses populations. [Paris, 1976]. pp. 252. *bibliog.*

THEATRE

— Russia.

KOROLEVA (NINA VALERIANOVNA) Dekabristy i teatr. Leningrad, 1975. pp. 263.

THOMSON (ROY) Baron Thomson.

THOMSON (ROY) Baron Thomson. After I was sixty: a chapter of autobiography. London, 1975. pp. 224.

THOUGHT AND THINKING.

KÖRNER (STEPHAN) Experience and conduct: a philosophical enquiry into practical thinking. Cambridge, 1976. pp. 268. *bibliog.*

THYGESEN (ERIK).

MORTENSEN (FRANDS) ed. Ytringsfrihed og offentlighed: de hemmelige dokumenter fra Danmarks Radios afskedigelse af Erik Thygesen, kommenteret af Erik Thygesen og Frands Mortensen. Århus, 1975 repr. 1976. pp. 430. *bibliog.*

TICINO

— Emigration and immigration.

CHEDA (GIORGIO) L'emigrazione ticinese in Australia. [Locarno], 1976. 2 vols. *bibliog.*

TILES

— United States.

McCOLLAM (C. HAROLD) The brick and tile industry in Stark County, 1809-1976: a history. Canton, Ohio, 1976. pp. 337.

TIMBUKTU

— Commerce.

KUNSTMANN (FRIEDRICH) Die Handelsverbindungen der Portugiesen mit Timbuktu im XV. Jahrhundert. [Munich, 1850]. pp. 171-235. (*Bayerische Akademie der Wissenschaften. 3. Classe. Abhandlungen. 6. Band, 1. Abth.)*

TIME ALLOCATION.

BALANS vremeni naseleniia Latviiskoi SSR. Riga, 1976. pp. 256. *bibliog.*

RAPPORT sur l'aménagement du temps; [prepared by a study group; Bertrand Labrusse, coordinator]. Paris, La Documentation Française, 1976. pp. 79. (*Environnement. 47)*

TIME ALLOCATION SURVEYS

— Denmark.

KÜHL (POUL HEINRICH) and MUNK (JENS KRISTIAN) Døgnrytme: befolkningens tidsanvendelse på ugens dage. København, 1976. pp. 97. (*Socialforskningsinstituttet. Meddelelser. 15)*

— United States.

ROBINSON (JOHN P.) How Americans use time: a social-psychological analysis of everyday behavior. New York, 1977. pp. 209. *bibliog.*

TIME AND ECONOMIC REACTIONS.

EVOLUTION, welfare, and time in economics: essays in honor of Nicholas Georgescu-Roegen. Lexington, Mass., [1976]. pp. 183. *bibliogs.*

TIME AND MOTION STUDY.

SLEPOV (I.A.) and CHERNENKO (G.T.) Die WAO [wissenschaftliche Arbeitsorganisation] heute und die Gewerkschaften; (ins Deutsche übertragen von Karl Hübner). Berlin, [1976]. pp. 205.

TIME SERIES ANALYSIS.

FULLER (WAYNE A.) Introduction to statistical time series. New York, [1976]. pp. 470. *bibliog.*

TIME SERIES ANALYSIS.(Cont.)

GRANGER (CLIVE W.J.) and NEWBOLD (PAUL)
Forecasting economic time series. New York, 1977. pp.
333. *bibliog.*

— Methodology.

BARTELS (CORNELIS P.) and others. The composition
of and associations between regional unemployment series:
an application of some time-series methods. Groningen,
1977. pp. 25. *(Groningen. Rijksuniversiteit. Economisch
Instituut. Onderzoekmemoranda. Nr. 32) Paper presented at
the colloquium on Séries chronologiques: approaches
fréquentielle et temporelle held in Brussels in 1977.*

TIME-SHARING COMPUTER SYSTEMS.

BRINCH HANSEN (PER) Operating system principles.
Englewood Cliffs, [1973]. pp. 366. *bibliog.*

INTERNATIONAL CONFERENCE ON COMPUTER
COMMUNICATION, 3RD, TORONTO, 1976.
Advancement through resource sharing; edited by Pramode
K. Verma. [Washington, D.C.], 1976. pp. 655. *Sponsored
by the International Council for Computer Communication.*

TIMOR

— Politics and government.

VAN DER KROEF (JUSTUS MARIA) Patterns of conflict
in Eastern Indonesia. London, 1977. pp. 16. *(Institute for
the Study of Conflict. Conflict Studies. No. 79)*

TIN INDUSTRY

— Japan.

TAKAHASHI (HISASHI) Tinplate development in Japan.
[Tokyo], 1972. fo. 11.

TIN MINES AND MINING

— Indonesia.

KAMP (A.F.) De standvastige tinnen soldaat: N.V. Billiton
Maatschappij 's- Gravenhage (1860-1960). [The Hague,
1960]. pp. 296. *With English summary and English captions
to illustrations.*

— United Kingdom — Cornwall.

BURROW (J.C.) and THOMAS (WILLIAM) Instructor at
the Camborne School of Mines. 'Mongst mines and miners:
being underground scenes by flash-light illustrating and
explaining the methods of working in Cornish mines about
1895[sic]. Truro, 1965. pp. 39. *First published in 1893.*

— Zaire.

SYMETAIN. Maniema: le pays de l'étain. Bruxelles, 1953.
pp. 391. *bibliog.*

TINKERS

— Ireland (Republic).

GMELCH (GEORGE) The Irish tinkers: the urbanization
of an itinerant people. Menlo Park, Calif., [1977]. pp. 178.
bibliog.

TINNE INDIANS.

DENE nation: the colony within; edited by Mel Watkins
for the University League for Social Reform. Toronto,
[1977]. pp. 187. *bibliogs. Based on material presented at the
Mackenzie Valley Pipeline Inquiry (Berger Inquiry).*

TIRASPOL

— Politics and government.

HILL (RONALD J.) Soviet political elites: the case of
Tiraspol. London, 1977. pp. 226. *bibliog.*

TITO (JOSIP BROZ).

LAZITCH (BRANKO) Titov pokret i režim u Jugoslaviji,
1941-1946. [n.p.], 1946. pp. 219.

TIXIER-VIGNANCOUR (JEAN LOUIS).

TIXIER-VIGNANCOUR (JEAN LOUIS) Des
Républiques, des justices et des hommes. [Paris, 1976]. pp.
413.

TKACHEV (PETR NIKITICH).

TKACHEV (PETR NIKITICH) Sochineniia v dvukh
tomakh; (obshchaia redaktsiia A.A. Galaktionova [and
others]). Moskva, 1975-76. 2 vols. *bibliog. (Akademiia
Nauk SSSR. Institut Filosofii. Filosofskoe Nasledie)*

TOBACCO

— Panama.

PANAMA. Direccion de Estadistica y Censo. Estadistica
panameña. Superficie sembrada y cosecha de café, tabaco
y caña de azucar. a., 1975/76- Panama. *Supersedes in part
PANAMA. Direccion de Estadistica y Censo. Estadistica
panameña. Serie H. Informacion agropecuaria.*

TOGLIATTI (PALMIRO).

RAGIONIERI (ERNESTO) Palmiro Togliatti: per una
biografia politica e intellettuale. Roma, 1976. pp. 786.

TOLL ROADS

— United Kingdom.

PAWSON (ERIC) Transport and economy: the turnpike
roads of eighteenth century Britain. London, 1977. pp. 407.
bibliog.

TONGA

— Foreign relations.

For a related heading see EUROPEAN ECONOMIC COMMUNITY — Tonga.

TORIES, ENGLISH.

[SWIFT (JONATHAN)] The management of the four last
years vindicated: in which Her late Majesty, and her
ministry, are fully cleared from the false aspersions cast on
them in a late pamphlet [by Charles Povey], entituled An
enquiry into the miscarriages of the four last years reign,
etc. [London], Morphew, 1714. pp. 48. *Signed C.B.*

TORONTO

— City planning — Citizen participation.

QUIGLEY (MAUREEN) Citizen participation in
development in the city of Toronto. [Toronto], Ontario
Department of Municipal Affairs, [1971]. fo. 105. *Cover
title: Democracy is us.*

— Foreign population.

HARNEY (ROBERT F.) and TROPER (HAROLD
MARTIN) Immigrants: a portrait of the urban experience,
1890-1930. Toronto, [1975]. pp. 212.

— Police.

ONTARIO. Royal Commission of Inquiry respecting the
Arrest and Detention of Rabbi Norbert Leiner by the
Metropolitan Toronto Police Force, 1962. Report...; Dalton
C. Wells, commissioner. [Toronto, 1962?]. pp. 99.

— Social conditions.

HARNEY (ROBERT F.) and TROPER (HAROLD
MARTIN) Immigrants: a portrait of the urban experience,
1890-1930. Toronto, [1975]. pp. 212.

— Social history.

KEALEY (GREGORY S.) Hogtown: working class
Toronto at the turn of the century. Toronto, 1974. pp. 30.

— Social policy.

TORONTO. Social Planning Council. The rent race: a
study of housing quality, shelter costs and family budgets
for social assistance recipients in metropolitan Toronto.
Toronto, 1974. 1 vol. (various pagings). *Study
commissioned by the Municipality of Metropolitan Toronto
Social Services and Housing Committee.*

TORRIENTE Y BRAU (PABLO FELIX ALEJANDRO SALVADOR DE LA).

TORRIENTE Y BRAU (PABLO FELIX ALEJANDRO
SALVADOR DE LA) En España, peleando con los
milicianos; seleccion y estudio preliminar de Jorge Max
Rojas. Mexico, 1972. pp. 159.

TORTS

— United Kingdom.

BAKER (CHARLES DAVID) Tort. 2nd ed. London, 1976.
pp. 332.

DIAS (REGINALD WALTER MICHAEL) and
MARKESINIS (B.S.) The English law of torts: a
comparative introduction. Brussels, 1976. pp. 287. *bibliog.*

SALMOND (Sir JOHN WILLIAM) The law of torts;
seventeenth edition by R.F.V. Heuston. London, 1977. pp.
629.

TORTURE

— Brazil.

TORTURE in Brazil: testimony given to the Rome session
of the Russell Tribunal. Nottingham, [1976]. pp. 19.
(Spokesman, The. Pamphlets. No. 53)

— Chile.

CAYUELA (JOSE) ed. Chile: la masacre de un pueblo:
testimonios de nueve venezolanos victimas del golpe militar
chileno. Caracas, [1973]. pp. 109.

— Guatemala.

AMNESTY INTERNATIONAL. Briefing Papers. No. 8.
Guatemala. London, 1976. pp. 17.

— Malawi.

AMNESTY INTERNATIONAL. Briefing Papers. No. 5.
Malawi. London, 1976. pp. 9.

— Paraguay.

AMNESTY INTERNATIONAL. Briefing Papers. No. 4.
Paraguay. London, 1976. pp. 13.

— Philippine Islands.

AMNESTY INTERNATIONAL. Report of...mission to
the Republic of the Philippines, 22 November-5 December
1975. London, [1976]. pp. 60.

— Singapore.

AMNESTY INTERNATIONAL. Briefing Papers. No. 1.
The Republic of Singapore. London, 1976. pp. 9.

— Taiwan.

AMNESTY INTERNATIONAL. Briefing Papers. No. 6.
Taiwan (Republic of China). London, 1976. pp. 11.

— Uruguay.

AMNESTY INTERNATIONAL. Tortured to death in
Uruguay: 22 known cases. London, [1976]. pp. 8.

TOTALITARIANISM.

MARWITZ (W.G.) Freiheit und Sozialismus: Gedanken
eines deutschen Sozialisten. Frankfurt am Main, [1953]. pp.
52.

PICKERING (CRAIG ROBERT) The concept of totalitarianism and its use in political philosophy, political science and history. 1976 [or rather 1977]. fo. 404. *bibliog. Typescript. Ph.D. (London) thesis: unpublished. This thesis is the property of London University and may not be removed from the Library.*

TOURIST TRADE

— Mathematical models.

ARCHER (BRIAN H.) Demand forecasting in tourism. Bangor, 1976. pp. 114. *bibliog. (Wales. University. University College of North Wales. Bangor Occasional Papers in Economics. No. 9)*

— Barbados.

BARBADOS. Statistical Service. Digest of tourist statistics. a., 1974 (1st)- , with gap (1975) St. Michael. *Supersedes BARBADOS. Statistical Service. Bednights surveys of hotels and guest houses.*

— Canada — Ontario.

ONTARIO. Economic Council. Tourist Industry Committee. 1965. Ontario's tourist industry: its potentials and its problems; an evaluation. Toronto, 1965. pp. 96.

— Cyprus.

CYPRUS. Statistics and Research Department. Tourism, migration and travel statistics: annual report. a., 1976- [Nicosia]. *[in English and Greek].*

CYPRUS. Statistics and Research Department. Tourism, migration and travel statistics: monthly bulletin. m., Jl 1976- [Nicosia]. *[in Greek and English].*

— Israel.

ISRAEL INFORMATION CENTRE. Information Briefings. 5. Tourism. Jerusalem, [1973]. pp. 7.

— Italy — Trentino-Alto Adige.

CARONE (GIUSEPPE) Conoscere il fenomeno turistico: note preliminari su di un sondaggio a mezzo di questionari. Trento, 1956. pp. 20.

— Singapore.

SINGAPORE. Tourist Promotion Board. Research Department. 1972. Survey of overseas visitor expenditure in Singapore. [Singapore], 1972. pp. 36.

— United Kingdom.

BRITISH TOURIST AUTHORITY. International tourism and strategic planning. [London, 1976]. pp. 18.

BRITISH TOURIST AUTHORITY and others. Tourism in Britain: the broad perspective;...a joint review by the British Tourist Authority, English Tourist Board, Scottish Tourist Board and Wales Tourist Board. [London, 1976]. pp. 24.

HANNA (MAX) Tourism multipliers in Britain: a guide to economic multipliers in theory and practice. London, English Tourist Board, 1976. fo. 23.

RURAL PLANNING SERVICES. A study of the Hartsop valley; a report to the Countryside Commission and the Lake District Special Planning Board; prepared during 1975 by... M.J. Feist [and others]. [Cheltenham, Countryside Commission], 1976. pp. 146. *bibliog.*

ADLEY (ROBERT JAMES) and GREGORY (CONAL) A policy for tourism? London, 1977. pp. 24. *(Conservative Political Centre. [Publications]. No. 607)*

— — Scotland.

BROWNRIGG (MARK) and GREIG (MICHAEL A.) Tourism and regional development. Glasgow, [1976]. pp. 14. *bibliog. (Glasgow. University of Strathclyde. Fraser of Allander Institute. Speculative Papers. No. 5)*

— — Wales.

WALES TOURIST BOARD. Research and Strategic Planning Unit. Tourism in Wales: a plan for the future; a consultative report. [Cardiff], 1976. 1 vol. (unfoliated). *bibliog.*

— Yugoslavia.

YUGOSLAVIA. Savezni Zavod za Statistiku. Studije, Analize i Prikazi. 77. Razvoj turističke potrošnje važnijih poljoprivredno- prehrambenih proizvoda u Jugoslaviji od 1951. do 1970; Development of tourist consumption of selected agricultural-food products in Yugoslavia, 1951-1970;[by] Zlatinka Leković. Beograd, 1975. pp. 151. *bibliog. With English summary.*

TOWARZYSTWO DEMOKRATYCZNE POLSKIE.

ŻALIŃSKI (HENRYK) Kształt polityczny Polski w ideologii Towarzystwa Demokratycznego Polskiego, 1832-1846. Wrocław, 1976. pp. 167. *(Polska Akademia Nauk. Oddział w Krakowie. Komisja Nauk Historycznych. Prace. Nr.36) With French summary.*

TOWER HAMLETS

— Social conditions.

WILKS (H.C.) Report of survey of [the] Isle of Dogs [carried out by pupils of George Green's School], 1974-5. London, 1975. pp. 54.

TOYOTOMI (HIDEYOSHI).

TOYOTOMI (HIDEYOSHI) 101 letters of Hideyoshi: the private correspondence of Toyotomi Hideyoshi; edited and translated by Adriana Boscaro. Tokyo, [1975]. pp. 114. *bibliog. (Sophia University. Monumenta Nipponica. Monographs. 54)*

TRADE AND PROFESSIONAL ASSOCIATIONS

— Switzerland.

BERUFSGEMEINSCHAFT IM SCHWEIZERISCHEN BUCHDRUCKERGEWERBE. Verhandlungs-Bericht über die Abänderungs-Anträge zum schweizerischen Buchdrucker-Tarif und über die Beratung der Berufs-Ordnung...August-Dezember 1917. Basel, 1918. pp. 238.

ROTH (ALFRED G.) Die Gründung der Käseunion GSK/SK, 1914: Referat vor dem Verwaltungsrat zum 60. Jahrestag. Bern, 1975. pp. 60. *bibliog.*

— United Kingdom — Scotland.

FORBES (R.N.) The history of the Institute of Bankers in Scotland, 1875-1975. Edinburgh, [1975]. pp. 52.

TRADE MARKS

— European Economic Community countries.

EUROPEAN COMMUNITIES. Commission. 1976. Memorandum on the creation of an EEC trade mark: adopted...on 6 July 1976. [Brussels], 1976. pp. 37. *(Bulletin of the European Communities. Supplements. [1976/8])*

TRADE ROUTES.

UNITED NATIONS. Conference on Trade and Development. 1970. Route study: the liner trades between France (Bayonne-Dunkirk range of ports) and Morocco; report, etc. (TD/B/C. 4/61/Rev.1). New York, 1970. pp. 49.

TRADE UNIONS.

NORTH ATLANTIC TREATY ORGANIZATION. Information Service. 1957. The trade unions and NATO; with a preface by George Meany. Paris, 1957. pp. 41.

ZURHORST (GUENTER) Gewerkschaftspolitik und technischer Fortschritt: zum Problem einer basisorientierten Mitbestimmung. Berlin, [1975]. pp. 163. *bibliog.*

BAIN (GEORGE SAYERS) and ELSHEIKH (FAROUK) Union growth and the business cycle: an econometric analysis. Oxford, [1976]. pp. 155. *(Warwick Studies in Industrial Relations)*

CLEGG (HUGH ARMSTRONG) Trade unionism under collective bargaining: a theory based on comparisons of six countries. Oxford, [1976]. pp. 121. *(Warwick Studies in Industrial Relations)*

INTERNATIONAL CONFEDERATION OF FREE TRADE UNIONS. World Congress, 11th, Mexico City, 1975. Human and trade union rights; [proceedings of the conference]. Brussels, 1976. pp. 47.

MARSHALL (F. RAY) and others. Labor economics: wages, employment, and trade unionism. 3rd ed. Homewood, Ill., 1976. pp. 633. *bibliogs.*

VILENSKA (ESTHER) Confrontation and unity within the labor movement, 1889-1923. New York, [1976]. pp. 98. *bibliog.*

ZOLL (RAINER) Der Doppelcharakter der Gewerkschaften: zur Aktualität der Marxschen Gewerkschaftstheorie. Frankfurt am Main, 1976. pp. 199.

SEKULES (EVA) The Miners' International Federation, 1945-1967: a case study of international trade unionism. 1977. fo.299. *bibliog. Typescript. M. Phil. (London) thesis: unpublished. This thesis is the property of London University and may not be removed from the Library.*

— Congresses.

INTERNATIONAL TEXTILE, GARMENT AND LEATHER WORKERS' FEDERATION. World Congress, 1st, Amsterdam, 1972. Reports from affiliated organisations. London, 1972. pp. 220.

— America, Latin.

COLOQUIO SOBRE SINDICALISMO EN AMERICA LATINA, BUENOS AIRES, 1972. Movimiento obrero, sindicatos y poder en America Latina; [papers]. Buenos Aires, [1975]. pp. 438. *A conference organized by the Centro de Estudios e Investigaciones Laborales, Universidad Nacional de La Plata.*

— Argentine Republic.

MONZALVO (LUIS) Testigo de la primera hora del peronismo: [memorias de un ferroviario]. Buenos Aires, [1975]. pp. 272.

ARGENTINA SUPPORT MOVEMENT. Argentina: the trade union struggle. London, [1976]. 1 pamphlet (unpaged).

— Austria.

VERBAND DER VEREINE DER BUCHDRUCKER UND SCHRIFTGIESSER UND VERWANDTER BERUFE ÖSTERREICHS. Vorstand. Statistik über die Arbeits- und Lohnverhältnisse der in den Buchdruckereien und Schriftgiessereien Österreichs beschäftigten Berufsangehörigen...im Jahre 1909, etc. Wien, 1911. pp. 90.

PROKSCH (ANTON) Anton Proksch und seine Zeit; herausgegeben und kommentiert von Bettina Hirsch. Wien, [1977]. pp. 188.

— Belgium.

EUROPEAN COURT OF HUMAN RIGHTS. Publications. Series B: Pleadings, Oral Arguments and Documents. [B17]. National Union of Belgian Police case, (1974-1975). Strasbourg, Council of Europe, 1976. pp. 269[bis], 271-337. *In English and French.*

— Canada.

LANGDON (STEVEN) The emergence of the Canadian working class movement, 1845-1875. Toronto, 1975. pp. 31.

WILLIAMS (JACK) The story of unions in Canada. [Don Mills, Ont., 1975]. pp. 252.

SEYMOUR (EDWARD E.) An illustrated history of Canadian labour, 1800-1974. Ottawa, [1976]. pp. 91. *bibliog.*

WATSON (LOUISE) She never was afraid: the biography of Annie Buller. Toronto, 1976. pp. 129.

— — Nova Scotia.

MACEWAN (PAUL) Miners and steelworkers: labour in Cape Breton. Toronto, 1976. pp. 400. *bibliog.*

— — Quebec.

QUEBEC (PROVINCE). Commission of Inquiry on the Exercise of Union Freedom in the Construction Industry. 1976. Report; [Robert Cliche, chairman]. [Quebec, 1976]. pp. 603.

— France.

DUMAY (JEAN BAPTISTE) Mémoires d'un militant ouvrier du Creusot, 1841-1905; introduction et notes par Pierre Ponsot. Grenoble, 1976. pp. 431. *(Centre d'Histoire du Syndicalisme. Collection)*

FRUIT (ELIE) Les syndicats dans les chemins de fer en France, 1890-1910. Paris, [1976]. pp. 216. *bibliog.*

GUIN (YANNICK) Le mouvement ouvrier nantais: essai sur le syndicalisme d'action directe à Nantes et à Saint-Nazaire. Paris, 1976. pp. 413.

MONATTE (PIERRE) La lutte syndicale; présentation de Colette Chambelland. Paris, 1976. pp. 318.

— Germany.

POERSCH (BRUNO) Woran krankt die deutsche Gewerkschaftsbewegung?: ein zeitgemässes Wort mit besonderer Berücksichtigung der Arbeitslosen-Unterstützungsfrage. Berlin, 1897. pp. 31.

GERMANY. Reichstag. 1898. Graf Posadowsky und die Koalitionsfreiheit vor dem Reichstag: Verhandlungen des Deutschen Reichstags über den Erlass des Staatssekretärs des Innern vom 11.Dezember 1897, etc. Berlin, 1898. pp. 112.

SCHIPPEL (MAX) Gewerkschaften und Koalitionsrecht der Arbeiter. Berlin, 1899. pp. 48.

[GEL'FAND (ALEKSANDR LAZAREVICH)] Die Handelskrisis und die Gewerkschaften; nebst Anhang: Gesetzentwurf über den achtstündigen Normalarbeitstag; von Parvus [pseud.]. München, 1901. pp. 64.

KRETSCHMER (BRUNO) 25 Jahre Zentralkommission der Maschinensetzer Deutschlands, VDDB, 1903-1928: ein Rückblick. [Berlin, 1928]. pp. 95.

WARNKE (HERBERT) Überblick über die Geschichte der deutschen Gewerkschaftsbewegung. Kleinmachnow, 1952. pp. 100.

LEPINSKI (FRANZ) Die Gewerkschaftsbewegung in Deutschland. [Düsseldorf, 1962]. pp. 32.

KLEIN (JUERGEN) Bürgerliche Demokraten oder christliche, sozialdemokratische und kommunistische Gewerkschafter: Hand in Hand gegen die Arbeiter. Hamburg, 1974. pp. 436. *bibliog.*

CULLINGFORD (E.C.M.) Trade unions in West Germany. London, 1976. pp. 114. *bibliog.*

FRICKE (DIETER) Die deutsche Arbeiterbewegung, 1869 bis 1914: ein Handbuch über ihre Organisation und Tätigkeit im Klassenkampf. Westberlin, [1976]. pp. 976. *bibliog.*

WITJES (CLAUS WINFRIED) Gewerkschaftliche Führungsgruppen: eine empirische Untersuchung zum Sozialprofil...westdeutscher Gewerkschaftsführungen. Berlin, [1976]. pp. 422. *bibliog.*

— Germany, Eastern.

WARNKE (HERBERT) Gewerkschaften: Sachwalter der Arbeiterinteressen: ausgewählte Reden und Aufsätze, 1971-1975; [edited by Alfred Förster and others]. Berlin, 1977. pp. 560.

— Indonesia.

TAPOL (BRITISH CAMPAIGN FOR THE RELEASE OF INDONESIAN POLITICAL PRISONERS) Indonesia: unions behind bars. London, 1976. pp. 20. *(Tapol Background and Information Series. No. 2)*

— Ireland (Republic).

McCARTHY (CHARLES) Trade unions in Ireland 1894-1960. Dublin, [1977]. pp. 671. *bibliog.*

— Italy.

STRUMENTI e linee di azione della C.I.S.L. in agricoltura: atti della tavola rotonda sul CeNaSCA, Roma, 29-30 gennaio 1969. Roma, 1969. pp. 47. *(Centro Nazionale per lo Sviluppo della Cooperazione Agricola. [Publications]. 2)*

FORBICE (ALDO) and CHIABERGE (RICCARDO) Il sindacato dei consigli. Verona, [1975]. pp. 230.

BONIFAZI (ALBERTO) and SALVARANI (GIANNI) Dalla parte dei lavoratori: storia del movimento sindacale italiano. Milano, [1976]. 4 vols.

GRAMEGNA (GIUSEPPE) Braccianti e popolo in Puglia, 1944-1971: cronache di un protagonista. Bari, [1976]. pp. 343.

— — Political activity.

CLARK (MARTIN) Antonio Gramsci and the revolution that failed. New Haven, 1977. pp. 255. *bibliog.*

— Mexico.

LOMBARDO TOLEDANO (VICENTE) La libertad sindical en Mexico, 1926. [Mexico, 1974]. pp. 320. *bibliog. Text of the first edition published in 1927, with the addition of a prologue.*

— New Zealand.

HOLLAND (HENRY EDMUND) and others. The tragic story of the Waihi strike. Wellington, N.Z., 1913; Dunedin, 1975. pp. 202. *Facsimile reprint.*

— — Law.

SZAKATS (ALEXANDER) Law and trade unions: the use of injunctions. Wellington, 1975. pp. 33. *(Victoria University of Wellington. Industrial Relations Centre. Occasional Papers in Industrial Relations. No. 12)*

— Poland.

'ZUK (DOBROSŁAW) Związki zawodowe a polityka socjalna w PRL. Warszawa, 1971. pp. 183.

RATYŃSKI (WŁADYSŁAW) Partia i związki zawodowe w Polsce Ludowej. Warszawa, 1977. pp. 410.

— Russia.

BELIAVSKII (F.) Ocherki iz istorii professional'nogo dvizheniia v Rossii. Moskva, 1918. pp. 32.

DUNN (ROBERT WILLIAMS) Soviet trade unions. New York, [1928]. pp. 238.

TRORY (ERNIE) Soviet trade unions and the general strike. Brighton, 1975. pp. 48. *bibliog.*

SABLINSKY (WALTER) The road to Bloody Sunday: Father Gapon and the St. Petersburg massacre of 1905. Princeton, N.J., [1976]. pp. 414. *bibliog. (Columbia University. Russian Institute. Studies)*

COSTELLO (MICK) Workers' participation in the Soviet Union. Moscow, 1977. pp. 167.

— — Law.

MASLIAEV (ALEKSEI IVANOVICH) Pravo sobstvennosti profsoiuzov SSSR. Moskva, 1975. pp. 222.

— — Kabardino-Balkarian Republic.

MASAEV (SHAKHIMGERI IAKH'IAEVICH) Profsoiuzy Kabardino-Balkarii v period bor'by za pobedu sotsializma v SSSR, 1920-1937 gg. Nal'chik, 1975. pp. 208. *bibliog.*

— — Moldavian Republic.

PROFSOIUZY Moldavii za 50 let v tsifrakh i faktakh. Kishinev, 1975. pp. 34.

— South Africa.

COETZEE (J.A. GREY) Industrial relations in South Africa: an event-structure of labour; with the co-operation of some leading South African trade unionists. Cape Town, [1976]. pp. 238. *bibliog.*

DU TOIT (M.A.) South African trade unions: history, legislation, policy. Johannesburg, [1976]. pp. 198.

KATZ (ELAINE N.) A trade union aristocracy: a history of white workers in the Transvaal and the general strike of 1913. Johannesburg, 1976. pp. 601. *bibliog. (Johannesburg. University of the Witwatersrand. African Studies Institute. ASI Communications. No. 3)*

— Spain.

BALCELLS (ALBERT) Trabajo industrial y organizacion obrera en la Cataluña contemporanea, 1900-1936. Barcelona, 1974. pp. 324.

CAMACHO (MARCELINO) Ecrits de la prison: le mouvement syndical espagnol et les Commissions ouvrières. Paris. [1976]. pp. 157.

ROSAL DIAZ (AMARO DEL) Historia de la U.G.T. de España, 1901-1939. Barcelona, 1977. 2 vols. *bibliog.*

TEORIA y practica del movimiento obrero en España, 1900-1936; (edicion a cargo de Albert Balcells). Valencia, [1977]. pp. 335.

— — Bibliography.

SPAIN. Servicio Nacional de Consejos Economico-Sociales Sindicales. 1976. Publicaciones...: catalogo 1940-1975. Madrid, 1976. pp. 240.

— — Law.

LOPEZ MEDEL (JESUS) Ciencia social, derecho y sindicalismo. Madrid, 1975. pp. 276.

— Sweden.

EK (SVEN B.) 14 augusti 1894: en bok om arbetarna i bokbinderi och emballageindustri i Lund. Lund, 1974. pp. 135. *bibliog. (Etnologiska Sällskapet i Lund. Skrifter. 5) With English summary.*

EUROPEAN COURT OF HUMAN RIGHTS. Publications. Series B: Pleadings, Oral Arugments and Documents. [B18]. ...Swedish engine drivers' union case. Strasbourg, Council of Europe, 1977. pp. 216bis, 217-260. *In English and French.*

EUROPEAN COURT OF HUMAN RIGHTS. Publications. Series B: Pleadings, Oral Arguments and Documents. [B19]. "Schmidt and Dahlström" case, (1974-1975). Strasbourg, Council of Europe, 1977. pp. 199bis. *In English and French.*

— Switzerland.

SCHWEIZERISCHER GEWERKSCHAFTSBUND. Minimalprogramm...mit Kommentar. Bern, 1926. pp. 39.

MUELLER-TRENKA (J.) Fünfzig Jahre Bäcker und Konditoren, Sektion Zürich, V[erband der] H[andels-,] T[ransport- und] L[ebensmittelarbeiter], 1897-1947, etc. [Zürich, 1947?]. pp. 88.

Der VPOD [Verband des Personals Öffentlicher Dienste], (1905-1955), im Spiegel des Zeitgeschehens; [by] Robert Grimm [and others]. Zürich, 1955. 3 vols.(in 1).

HOEPFLINGER (FRANÇOIS) Industriegewerkschaften in der Schweiz: eine soziologische Untersuchung. Zürich, [1976]. pp. 259. *bibliog.*

— Uganda.

UGANDA. 1969. Government memorandum on the report of the Commission of Inquiry into the Dispute within the Executive Board of the Uganda Labour Congress. Entebbe, [1969]. pp. 5. *Bound with the report.*

UGANDA. Commission of Inquiry into Dispute affecting the Executive Board of the Uganda Labour Congress. 1969. Report; [G.L. Binaisa, commissioner]. Entebbe, [1969?]. pp. 139. *Bound with government memorandum on the report.*

— Underdeveloped areas.

See UNDERDEVELOPED AREAS — Trade unions.

— United Kingdom.

MARX (ELEANOR) Die Arbeiterclassen-Bewegung in England;...übersetzt von Gertrud Liebknecht; mit einem Vorwort von W. Liebknecht. Nürnberg, 1895. pp. 24. *(Separat-Abdruck aus Band II des Volks-Lexikon, herausgegeben von E. Wurm)*

NATIONAL UNION OF DISTRIBUTIVE AND ALLIED WORKERS. Rules...as revised and amended...1928, (1930, 1932, 1934, 1935, 1938, 1939, 1940, 1943, 1945, 1946). Manchester, [1928]-46. 11 pts. (in 1 vol.).

UNION OF SHOP, DISTRIBUTIVE AND ALLIED WORKERS. Rules...1947, (1949, 1951, 1953, 1954, 1956, 1957, 1957/58, 1961). Manchester, 1947-61. 9 pts. (in 1 vol.).

BAIKOVA (ANNA NIKOLAEVNA) Britanskie profsoiuzy i klassovaia bor'ba, vtoraia polovina 60-kh - nachalo 70-kh godov. Moskva, 1976. pp. 375.

BEALEY (FRANK) The Post Office Engineering Union: the history of the Post Office engineers, 1870-1970. London, 1976. pp. 432.

CHANAN (MICHAEL) Labour power in the British film industry. London, 1976. pp. 57.

CHAPPLE (FRANK) The responsibility of trade unions and managers. London, [1976]. pp. 5. *(Foundation for Business Responsibilities. Seminar Papers)*

CHRISTIAN (HAROLD) The development of trade unionism and professionalism among British journalists: a sociological inquiry. 1976. fo.379. *bibliogs. Typescript. Ph.D.(London) thesis: unpublished. This thesis is the property of London University and may not be removed from the Library.*

FROW (EDMUND) and FROW (RUTH) To make that future - now!: a history of the Manchester and Salford Trades Council. Manchester, 1976. pp. 181.

LABOUR RESEARCH DEPARTMENT. The Lords against the unions. London, 1976. pp. 27.

MACDONALD (DONALD FARQUHAR) The state and the trade unions. 2nd ed. London, 1976. pp. 217.

MARTIN (PETER) No foundation: the truth about union power. London, [1976]. pp. 13.

TRADES UNION CONGRESS. Trades councils guide: a handbook for officers and delegates of trades councils and county associations. rev ed. London, 1976. pp. 43.

TRADES UNION CONGRESS. TUC policy on devolution. London, 1976. pp. 8.

ADVISORY, CONCILIATION AND ARBITRATION SERVICE [U.K.]. Applications to ACAS on trade union recognition issues: notes for guidance on applications to ACAS under sections 11 and 13 of the Employment Protection Act 1975, and related matters. [London, 1977?]. pp. 11.

ESSAYS in labour history, [vol. 3], 1918-1939; edited by Asa Briggs [and] John Saville. London, [1977]. pp. 292.

INSTITUTE OF PERSONNEL MANAGEMENT. National Committee on Employee Relations. Trade union recognition. London, 1977. pp. 68.

JENKINS (CLIVE) and SHERMAN (BARRIE) Computers and the unions. London, 1977. pp. 135.

LOVELL (JOHN) British trade unions, 1875-1933. London, 1977. pp. 75. *bibliog. (Economic History Society. Studies in Economic and Social History)*

TRADE unions under capitalism; (edited by Tom Clarke and Laurie Clements). [Glasgow], 1977. pp. 413. *bibliogs.*

— — Officials and employees.

POST OFFICE ENGINEERING UNION. Discussion Pamphlets. 2. Union organisation. [London, 1976?]. pp. 11.

SOCIALIST WORKER. Training Series. 2. The trade union leaders. [London, 1976?]. pp. 23.

— — Political activity.

LABOUR PARTY. Leaflets. No. 61. Trade unionism and political action: a plain talk to trade unionists. London, [1910?]. pp. (4).

GREATER MANCHESTER TRADE UNION SPANISH SOLIDARITY COMMITTEE. Spain today: trade union solidarity with the Spanish people. Manchester, [1976]. 1 pamphlet (unpaged).

MULLER (WILLIAM D.) The 'kept men'?: the first century of trade union representation in the British House of Commons, 1874-1975. Hassocks, Sussex, 1977. pp. 283. *bibliog.*

— United States.

SWEENEY (VINCENT D.) The United Steelworkers of America: twenty years later, 1936- 1956. n.p., [1956]. pp. 239. *Without title page. Caption title.*

GODSON (ROY) American labor and European politics: the AFL as a transnational force. New York, [1976]. pp. 230. *bibliog.*

NEVIN (JACK) and NEVIN (LORNA) AFGE-Federal Union: the story of the American Federation of Government Employees. [Washington, D.C., 1976]. pp. 211.

DUBINSKY (DAVID) and RASKIN (ABRAHAM HENRY) David Dubinsky: a life with labor. New York, [1977]. pp. 351.

LEVI (MARGARET) Bureaucratic insurgency: the case of police unions. Lexington, Mass., [1977]. pp. 165.

LEVY (ELIZABETH) and RICHARDS (TAD) Struggle and lose, struggle and win: the United Mine Workers;...photo essay by Henry E.F. Gordillo. New York, [1977]. pp. 122. *bibliog.*

MEISTER (DICK) and LOFTIS (ANNE) A long time coming: the struggle to unionize America's farm workers. New York, 1977. pp. 241.

TAFT (PHILIP) Rights of union members and the government. Westport, Conn., 1975. pp. 348. *bibliogs.*

YELLOWITZ (IRWIN) Industrialization and the American labor movement, 1850-1900. Port Washington, N.Y., 1977. pp. 183. *bibliog.*

— — Law.

GETMAN (JULIUS G) and others. Union representation elections: law and reality. New York, [1976]. pp. 218.

— — Negro membership.

GOULD (WILLIAM B.) Black workers in white unions: job discrimination in the United States. Ithaca, N.Y., 1977. pp. 506.

— — Utah.

DAVIES (JOSEPH KENNETH) Deseret's sons of toil: a history of the worker movements of territorial Utah, 1852-1896. Salt Lake City, [1977]. pp. 264. *bibliogs.*

TRADE UNIONS, CATHOLIC

— Austria.

OTTE (BERNHARD) Christliche Gewerkschaften und Sozialismus: Rede...auf dem IV. Kongress der christlichen Gewerkschaften Österreichs, 4. -7. September 1921. Wien, [1921?]. pp. 16.

HEMALA (FRANZ) Die Wahrheit über die christl. Gewerkschaften: eine Antwort auf Angriffe und Kritiken. [Vienna, 1928?] . pp. 30.

TRADE UNIONS AND COMMUNISM.

ZOLL (RAINER) Der Doppelcharakter der Gewerkschaften: zur Aktualität der Marxschen Gewerkschaftstheorie. Frankfurt am Main, 1976. pp. 199.

— United States.

WEISBORD (VERA BUCH) A radical life. Bloomington, Ind., [1977]. pp. 330.

TRADE UNIONS AND FOREIGN POLICY

— United States.

GODSON (ROY) American labor and European politics: the AFL as a transnational force. New York, [1976]. pp. 230. *bibliog.*

TRAFFIC ESTIMATION

— Sweden.

HALLOFF (ULF) Inköpsresor i ett rumsligt system: metodstudier på grundval av empiriskt material från några stadsdelar i Göteborg. Stockholm, 1977. pp. 167,11. *bibliog. (Göteborgs Universitet. Geografiska Institutioner. Meddelanden Ser. B. Nr. 57)*

— Underdeveloped areas.

See UNDERDEVELOPED AREAS — Traffic estimation.

— United Kingdom — Mathematical models.

DAVIES (F.) Methods for calculating planning data for use in the national traffic model. [London], 1972. pp. 13. *(U.K. Department of the Environment. Mathematical Advisory Unit. MAU Notes. 253)*

HILL (E.S.) Production and attraction trip rates for the national traffic model. [London], 1974. pp. 37. *(U.K. Department of the Environment. Mathematical Advisory Unit. MAU Notes. 252)*

TRAFFIC SURVEYS

— Switzerland.

SWITZERLAND. Bureau Fédéral de Statistique. 1977. Schweizerische Strassenverkehrszählung..., 1975. Bern, 1977. pp. 61. *(Statistiques de la Suisse. 590e fasc.) In German and French. 3 maps in end pocket.*

— United Kingdom — London.

FRYER (J.A.) and others. Goods vehicle activity in Greater London. London, [1977]. pp. 31. *(London. Greater London Council. Research Memoranda. 491)*

TRAILS

— United Kingdom.

GOODEY (BRIAN) Urban walks and town trails: origins, principles and sources. Birmingham, 1974. 1 vol.(various pagings). *bibliog. (Birmingham. University. Centre for Urban and Regional Studies. Research Memoranda. No.40)*

TRAINS, UNIT.

See RAILWAYS — Train load.

TRAMPS

— Bangladesh.

FAROUK (A.) and others. The vagrants of Dacca City: a socio-economic survey, 1975. Dacca, 1976. pp. 130.

TRAMWAYS

— United States.

McSHANE (CLAY) Technology and reform: street railways and the growth of Milwaukee, 1887-1900. Madison, Wisconsin, [1974]. pp. 187. *bibliog. Author's thesis (M.A.), University of Wisconsin.*

TRANSFER FUNCTIONS.

LONDON. University. London School of Economics and Political Science. Graduate School of Geography. Discussion Papers. No. 61. Stochastic-dynamic models for some environmental systems: transfer-function approach; [by] Pong-wai Lai. London, 1977. pp. 25. *bibliog.*

TRANSFER PRICING.

ROOK (A.) Transfer pricing: a measure of management performance in multi- divisional companies. London, [1971]. pp. 22. *bibliog. (British Institute of Management. Management Survey Reports. No. 8)*

TRANSKEI.

KIRBY (ALEXANDER) South Africa's bantustans: what independence for the Transkei?. Geneva, [1976]. pp. 70. *bibliog.*

— Economic conditions.

SOUTH AFRICA. Bureau for Economic Research re Bantu Development. 1975. Transkei:...economic revue [sic], 1975, etc. Pretoria, 1975. pp. 76. *bibliog. In English and Afrikaans.*

— Economic policy.

XHOSA DEVELOPMENT CORPORATION LIMITED. Annual report. a., 1975 (10th)- East London. *[in English and Afrikaans].*

— Politics and government.

KRAUSE (OTTO) and others. The implications of Transkeian independence. Braamfontein, 1976. pp. 4. *(South African Institute of International Affairs. Transkei Series. No. 1)*

MATANZIMA (KAIZER DALIWONGA) Independence my way. Pretoria, [1976]. pp. 138.

TRANSLITERATION.

PRUSSIA. Ministerium der Geistlichen, Unterrichts- und Medizinal-Angelegenheiten. 1915. Instruktionen für die alphabetischen Kataloge der preuszischen Bibliotheken vom 10. Mai 1899; zweite Ausgabe in der Fassung vom 10.August 1908. Berlin, 1915, repr. 1938. pp. 179.

TRANSPORT WORKERS

— Germany.

KOMMUNISTISCHE PARTEI DEUTSCHLANDS. Der Streik der Berliner Verkehrs-Arbeiter. [Berlin?, 1932?]. pp. 24.

TRANSPORTATION.

INTERNATIONAL CHAMBER OF COMMERCE. General Transport Commission. Politique des investissements en matière d'infrastructure de transport: étude préliminaire. Paris, [1964]. pp. 8.

HUTCHINS (JOHN GREENWOOD BROWN) Transportation and the environment. London, 1977. pp. 106.

— Environmental aspects.

HUTCHINS (JOHN GREENWOOD BROWN) Transportation and the environment. London, 1977. pp. 106.

— — United Kingdom.

HAMER (MICK) Getting nowhere fast. London, [1976]. pp. 90.

SHARP (CLIFFORD H.) and JENNINGS (TONY) Transport and the environment. Leicester, 1976. pp. 229. *bibliog.*

— Finance.

ABOUCHAR (ALAN) Transportation economics and public policy: with urban extensions. New York, [1977]. pp. 326. *bibliogs.*

— Mathematical models.

FITZPATRICK (MICHAEL DESMOND) Varying parameter estimation and trends in the parameters which determine the modal choice associated with long distance international travel. 1976 [or rather 1977]. fo.231. *bibliog. Typescript. Ph.D.(London) thesis: unpublished. This thesis is the property of London University and may not be removed from the Library.*

— Africa, Subsaharan.

BURGESS (JULIAN) Interdependence in southern Africa: trade and transport links in south, central and east Africa. London, 1976. pp. 93. *(Economist Intelligence Unit. EIU Special Reports. No. 32)*

— America, Latin.

INTERNATIONAL BANK FOR RECONSTRUCTION AND DEVELOPMENT. Western Hemisphere Department. 1967. Economic development and prospects of Central America. vol. 6. Transportation. [Washington], 1967. 1 vol. (various pagings). *(Reports. No. WH-170a)*

POLITICAS de transporte en esquemas de integración económica: con especial referencia al transporte vial. Buenos Aires, Instituto para la Integración de América Latina, [1975]. pp. 506.

— Canada — Quebec — Passenger traffic.

QUEBEC (PROVINCE). Comité d'Etude du Transport en Commun de l'Agglomération Québécoise. 1969. Le transport en commun dans l'agglomération Québécoise: sommaire du rapport du comité d'étude; [Raymond L. Lacasse, chairman]. [Québec], 1969. pp. 44.

— Communist countries.

DUBROWSKY (HANS JOACHIM) Die Zusammenarbeit der RGW-Länder auf dem Gebiet des Transportwesens. Berlin, [1975]. pp. 71. *bibliog.*

GORIZONTOV (BORIS BORISOVICH) Sotsialisticheskaia ekonomicheskaia integratsiia i transport. Moskva, 1975. pp. 199.

— Germany — Cost of operation.

GERMANY (BUNDESREPUBLIK). Statistisches Bundesamt. Kostenstruktur der nichtbundeseigenen Eisenbahnen, des öffentlichen Strassenverkehrs, der Reiseveranstaltung und Reisevermittlung (Reisebüros), (formerly Nichtbundeseigene Eisenbahnen, öffentlicher Strassenverkehr, Reiseveranstaltung und Reisevermittlung (Reisebüros). irreg., 1971- Wiesbaden. *(Unternehmen und Arbeitsstätten. Reihe 1.5.1).*

— — Finance.

LANKENAU (EHRFRIED) Verkehrspolitik der Bundesrepublik Deutschland: das Verkehrsfinanzgesetz 1955. Bonn, 1974. pp. 34. *bibliog.*

— — Laws and regulations.

LANKENAU (EHRFRIED) Verkehrspolitik der Bundesrepublik Deutschland: das Verkehrsfinanzgesetz 1955. Bonn, 1974. pp. 34. *bibliog.*

— Hong Kong.

SMITH (WILBUR) AND ASSOCIATES. Hong Kong comprehensive transport study; prepared for the Hong Kong government; ([with] Report in brief). [Hong Kong], 1976. 2 vols. (in 1).

— Italy.

CONFERENZA REGIONALE DEI TRASPORTI, CAGLIARI, 1967. Atti ufficiali, Cagliari, 30 novembre-3 dicembre 1967. [Cagliari, 1969]. pp. 347.

CAGLIOZZI (ROBERTO) Infrastrutture di trasporto e sviluppo del Mezzogiorno. Milano, 1975. pp. 80. *(Associazione per lo Sviluppo dell'Industria nel Mezzogiorno. Centro per gli Studi sullo Sviluppo Economico. Collana di Monografie)*

— — Sardinia.

CONFERENZA REGIONALE DEI TRASPORTI, CAGLIARI, 1967. Atti ufficiali, Cagliari, 30 novembre-3 dicembre 1967. [Cagliari, 1969]. pp. 347.

— Netherlands — Statistics.

NETHERLANDS. Centraal Bureau voor de Statistiek. 1974-76. Transporttelling...1969. 's-Gravenhage, 1974-76. 7 pts. (in 1 vol.).

— Portugal — Statistics.

PORTUGAL. Instituto Nacional de Estatistica. Serviços Centrais. Estatisticas dos transportes: continente e ilhas adjacentes: Statistiques des transports: continent et îles adjacentes. a., 1970- [Lisboa]. *[in Portuguese and French].*

— Russia — Tajikistan.

BRONSHTEIN (IAKOV TEV'EVICH) Perspektivy razvitiia transporta Tadzhikskoi SSR: metody i rezul'taty prognoza; pod redaktsiei...R.K. Rakhimova. Dushanbe, 1973. pp. 221. *bibliog.*

— Sweden — Cost of operation.

RYDÉN (INGER) Transportkostnader och regional utveckling: modeller för analys av regionalpolitiskt stöd av godstransporter. Stockholm, [1976]. pp. 208. *bibliog. With English summary.*

— Taiwan.

STATISTICAL ABSTRACT OF TRANSPORTATION AND COMMUNICATIONS: REPUBLIC OF CHINA; [pd. by] Ministry of Communications. a., 1975- [Taipei]. *[in English and Chinese].*

— United Kingdom.

ESSEX. County Council. Transport policies and programmes. a., 1975/76 [1st]- Chelmsford.

WEST MIDLANDS. County Council. Transportation policies and programme. a., 1975/76 (3rd)- Birmingham. *File includes supplement, 1976.*

U.K. Department of Transport. Circulars. irreg., D 1976 (no. 4/76)- London.

CARTER (PETER) Transport in Islington. London, [1976]. pp. 20.

SUFFOLK. County Council. The...submission of the transport policies and programmes. a., 1977/78- [Ipswich].

A POLICY for transport?: papers presented to a conference [held in 1976] at Nuffield Lodge with an introduction by C.D. Foster. London, 1977. pp. 84.

— — Passenger traffic.

NATIONAL CONSUMER COUNCIL. Priority for passengers: comments...on the government's consultation development [i.e. document] on transport policy. London, [1976]. pp. 18.

U.K. Department of the Environment. 1976. National travel survey, 1972/73: a comparison of 1965 and 1972/73 surveys. London, 1976. pp. 42.

— — Ireland, Northern.

IRELAND, NORTHERN. Department of the Environment. Annual report. a., 1974/75 [1st]- Belfast.

— — Scotland.

SCOTTISH ASSOCIATION FOR PUBLIC TRANSPORT. The review of transport policy: a submission to government. [Glasgow], 1976. pp. 12.

— — Wales.

GLAMORGAN-GLYNCORRWG COMMUNITY DEVELOPMENT PROJECT. Transport and the younger unemployed. [Port Talbot], 1973. pp. 14.

— United States — Illinois.

ILLINOIS. Chicago Area Transportation Study. Annual report. a., 1975- Chicago.

TRANSPORTATION, AUTOMOTIVE.

INTERNATIONAL ROAD TRANSPORT UNION. Road transport: driving force of progress. [Geneva, 1976]. pp. 47.

— Germany — Freight.

GERMANY (BUNDESREPUBLIK). Kraftfahrt-Bundesamt. Grenzüberschreitender Güterkraftverkehr in seiner Bewegung zwischen inlandischen Verkehrsbezirken und Ländern nach Güterhauptgruppen. a., 1975- Bonn.

— Ireland (Republic) — Laws and regulations.

EIRE. Statutes, etc. 1968. Road Traffic Act, 1968: explanatory memorandum. [Dublin, 1969]. pp. 74.

— Switzerland — Freight.

SWITZERLAND. Bureau Fédéral de Statistique. 1976. Erhebung über die Gütertransporte..., 1974. Bern, 1976. pp. 166. *(Statistiques de la Suisse. 588e fasc.) In German and French.*

— — Statistics.

SWITZERLAND. Bureau Fédéral de Statistique. 1976. Schweizerische Strassenrechnung: nach Motorfahrzeugkategorien gegliederte Ergebnisse..., 1970-1974. Bern, 1976. pp. 63. *(Statistiques de la Suisse. 578e fasc.) In German and French.*

— United Kingdom — Costs — Mathematical models.

NICHOLS (A.J.) Standard generalised cost parameters for modelling inter urban traffic and evaluating inter urban road schemes. [London], 1975. pp. 15. *(U.K. Department of the Environment. Mathematical Advisory Unit. MAU Notes. 255)*

— — Freight.

LORRIES AND THE ENVIRONMENT COMMITTEE [U.K.]. Report on transhipment; [Sir Daniel Pettit, chairman]. London, [1976]. pp. 41.

— United States — Freight.

WYCKOFF (D. DARYL) and MAISTER (DAVID H.) The motor-carrier industry. Lexington, Mass., [1977]. pp. 191. *bibliog.*

TRANSPORTATION, MILITARY.

WHITEHURST (CLINTON H.) The defense transportation system: competitor or complement to the private sector?. Washington, D.C., [1976]. pp. 171. *bibliog. (American Enterprise Institute for Public Policy Research. Domestic Affairs Studies. 48)*

TRANSPORTATION AND STATE.

ABOUCHAR (ALAN) Transportation economics and public policy: with urban extensions. New York, [1977]. pp. 326. *bibliogs.*

— Canada.

LANGFORD (JOHN W.) Transport in transition: the reorganization of the federal transport portfolio. Montreal, 1976. pp. 267. *(Institute of Public Administration of Canada. Canadian Public Administration Series)*

— United Kingdom.

NATIONAL CONSUMER COUNCIL. Priority for passengers: comments...on the government's consultation development [i.e. document] on transport policy. London, [1976]. pp. 18.

— — Bibliography.

LAMBERT (CLAIRE M.) compiler. Transport policy consultation document, 1976: responses to the Government's transport policy consultation document: a select list of material. [London, 1977]. pp. 27. *(U.K. Department of the Environment. Library. Bibliographies. No. 17D)*

TRANSPORTATION PLANNING

— Bibliography.

LAMBERT (CLAIRE M.) compiler. Transport policies and planning: a select list of material. [London, 1977]. pp. 82. *(U.K. Department of the Environment. Library. Bibliographies. No. 17A)*

— United Kingdom.

WRAGG (RICHARD) and REES (GRAHAM L.) A study of the passenger transport needs of urban Wales; prepared for the Welsh Council. [Cardiff, Welsh Council, 1977]. pp. 283.

— — Bibliography.

LAMBERT (CLAIRE M.) compiler. Transport policies and planning: a select list of material. [London, 1977]. pp. 82. *(U.K. Department of the Environment. Library. Bibliographies. No. 17A)*

TRANS-SIBERIA RAILWAY.

See also BAIKAL-AMUR RAILWAY.

TRANSUBSTANTIATION.

IMPERIAL PROTESTANT FEDERATION. House of Lords; statement presented on Tuesday, June 25th, 1901, to the Select Committee on the King's declaration against transubstantiation: [signed T. Myles Sandys]. London, [1901]. pp. 26.

IMPERIAL PROTESTANT FEDERATION. The King's declaration against transubstantiation; (with Addendum). London, 1904. 2 pts.

KNOX CLUB. Memorial...to the members of the Houses of Parliament against alteration of the Royal declaration; [signed by Thomas Burns and F.J.Robertson]. [Edinburgh, 1910]. pp. (4).

TRANSVAAL

— Race question.

PILLAY (BALA) British Indians in the Transvaal: trade, politics and imperial relations, 1885-1906. London, 1976. pp. 259. *bibliog.*

TRAVEL AGENTS

— United Kingdom.

AIR TRANSPORT AND TRAVEL INDUSTRY TRAINING BOARD [U.K.]. Manpower in air transport and travel, 1973 to 1976. [Staines, 1974]. pp. 14.

AIR TRANSPORT AND TRAVEL INDUSTRY TRAINING BOARD [U.K.]. Manpower in travel, 1975. [Staines, 1976]. pp. 34.

TREASON

— United Kingdom.

U.K. Law Commission. Working Papers. No. 72. Second programme, Item XVIII. Codification of the Criminal Law: treason, sedition and allied offences. London, 1977. pp. 64.

TREES

— United Kingdom.

RACKHAM (OLIVER) Trees and woodland in the British landscape. London, 1976. pp. 204. *bibliog.*

TRENT AFFAIR, NOV.8, 1861.

FERRIS (NORMAN B.) The Trent affair: a diplomatic crisis. Knoxville, Tenn., [1977]. pp. 280. *bibliog.*

TRENTINO-ALTO ADIGE

— Population.

ANGELONI (ROLANDO) Previsioni demografiche per le provincie di Trento e Bolzano. Trento, 1964. pp. 41. *(Trentino-Alto Adige. Ufficio Studi Statistica e Programmazione. Quaderni. 5)*

— Statistics.

CARONE (GIUSEPPE) Contributi alla ricerca scientifica: cinque anni di attività dell'Ufficio Coordinamento Statistiche e Studi della Regione. Trento, Assessorato Industria, Commercio, Turismo e Trasporti Ufficio Coordinamento Statistiche e Studi, 1956. pp. 30. *bibliog.*

TRENTO (PROVINCE)

— History.

FRANCESCOTTI (RENZO) Antifascismo e Resistenza nel Trentino, 1920-1945. Roma, 1975. pp. 126. *bibliog.*

TRESPASS.

RELEASE. Entering and remaining on property: the evidence of Release to the Law Commission on its proposals for criminal law reform, as contained in Working Paper No. 54. [London, 1975]. pp. 16.

— United Kingdom.

NATIONAL COUNCIL FOR CIVIL LIBERTIES. Squatting, trespass and civil liberties. London, 1976. pp. 58.

CAMPAIGN AGAINST A CRIMINAL TRESPASS LAW. Secret Rent Act 1977: officially known as Part Two of the Criminal Law Bill. London, [1977]. pp. 23.

TREVELYAN (Sir CHARLES PHILIPS).

MORRIS (ANDREW JAMES ANTHONY) C.P. Trevelyan, 1870-1958: portrait of a radical. Belfast, [1977]. pp. 209.

TREVISO

— Rural conditions.

BERNARDI (ULDERICO) Una cultura in estinzione: ricerche sull'identità contadina fra Piave e Livenza. Venezia, 1975. pp. 195.

TRIADS (SECRET SOCIETIES).

ROBERTSON (FRANK) Triangle of death: the inside story of the Triads - the Chinese Mafia. London, 1977. pp. 184. *bibliog.*

TRIALS

— Russia.

RECHI sovetskikh advokatov po grazhdanskim delam. Moskva, 1976. pp. 246.

TRIALS (BLASPHEMY)

— Germany.

RICHTER (AUG.) Vor dem Schwurgericht: Verteidigungsrede...am 30. Mai 1906 im Justizpalast zu München...wegen...Beschimpfung der katholischen Kirche. München, 1906. pp. 15.

TRIALS (ESPIONAGE)

— United States.

SOBELL (MORTON) On doing time. Toronto, 1976. pp. 436. *Originally published in New York, 1974.*

TRIALS (MURDER)

— United Kingdom — Ireland.

WOOLAGHAN (HUGH) defendant. The genuine trial of Hugh Woolaghan, yeoman, by a general court- martial, held in the barracks of Dublin, on Saturday, October 13, 1798, for the murder of Thomas Dogherty to which is added His Excellency Lord Cornwallis's order for the court- martial to be dissolved. 2nd ed. Dublin, printed for J. Milliken, 1798. pp. 27.

TRIALS (POLITICAL CRIMES AND OFFENCES)

— Germany.

KOMMUNISTISCHE PARTEI DEUTSCHLANDS. Zentralkomitee. Das Schandurteil von Karlsruhe: ein Entscheid gegen Frieden, Freiheit, Einheit und Recht; Erwiderung auf die Begründung des Verbots der KPD durch das Bundesverfassungsgericht vom 17. August 1956. Berlin, 1957. pp. 120.

— Russia.

GINZBURG (ALEKSANDR IL'CH) and GALANSKOV (IURII TIMOFEEVICH) defendants. L'affaire Guinzbourg Galanskov: (les nouveaux procès de Moscou); dossier réuni et présenté par J.J. Marie et Carol Head; traduit du russe par Jean Jacques et Nadine Marie. Paris, [1969]. pp. 203.

KARLOVA (TAMARA SERGEEVNA) Dostoevskii i russkii sud. Kazan', 1975. pp. 165.

TASHKENTSKII protsess: sud nad desiat'iu predstaviteliami krymskotatarskogo naroda, 1 iiulia - 5 avgusta 1969 g.: sbornik dokumentov s illiustratsiiami. Amsterdam, 1976. pp. 854. *(Alexander Herzen Foundation. Seriia "Biblioteka Samizdata". No.7)*

TRIALS (TREASON)

— Germany.

WANDT (HEINRICH) Das Justizverbrechen des Reichsgerichts an dem Verfasser der "Etappe Gent". Berlin, 1926. pp. 28.

FISCHER (ERNST) of the Austrian Communist Party. Das Fanal: der Kampf Dimitroffs gegen die Kriegsbrandstifter. Wien, [1946]. pp. 298.

— South Africa.

SOUTH AFRICA. Supreme Court. Special Criminal Court, Pretoria. 1961. In the matter of the application of Farrid Adams and 29 others and the Crown: reasons for judgment [Mr. Justice Rumpff]. [Johannesburg?, 1961]. fo. 11.

TRIBES AND TRIBAL SYSTEM

— Ghana.

GHANA. 1975. White Paper on the report of the Commission of Enquiry into the Duffor Traditional Area. Accra, 1975. pp. 3. *(W[hite] P[apers]. 1975. No. 2) Bound with the Report.*

GHANA. Commission of Inquiry into Duffor Traditional Area. 1975. Report; [F.K. Apaloo, chairman]. Accra, [1975]. pp. 51. *Bound with White Paper on the Report.*

— India.

FUCHS (STEFAN) The aboriginal tribes of India. London, 1977. pp. 308. *First published in India in 1973.*

— Papua New Guinea.

PAPUA NEW GUINEA. Committee investigating Tribal Fighting in the Highlands. 1973. Report; [P.Paney, chairman]. Port Moresby, 1973. pp. 50.

TRIESTE

— Economic history.

WEISS (OTTOCARO) Triest und die Wirtschaftspolitik Österreichs zur Zeit Karls VI.: ein Beitrag zur Geschichte des Merkantilismus. Zürich, 1921. pp. 66. *Inauguraldissertation zur Erlangung der Würde eines Doctor rerum cameralium der Universität Zürich.*

— History.

TAMARO (ATTILIO) Storia di Trieste; saggio introduttivo di G. Cervani: La "Storia di Trieste" di Attilio Tamaro: genesi e motivazioni di una storia. Trieste, 1924 repr. 1976. 2 vols.

TRINIDAD AND TOBAGO

— Nationalism.

MATTHEWS (HARRY G.) Multinational corporations and black power. Cambridge, Mass., [1976]. pp. 124.

— Rural conditions.

FLOYD (BARRY NEIL) Small-scale agriculture in Trinidad: a Caribbean case study in the problems of transforming rural societies in the tropics. [Durham, 1977]. pp. 69. *bibliog. (Durham. University. Department of Geography. Occasional Publications (New Series). No. 10)*

TROLLOPE (ANTHONY).

HALPERIN (JOHN) Trollope and politics: a study of the Pallisers and others. London, 1977. pp. 318. *bibliog.*

TROTSKII (LEV DAVYDOVICH).

BRONSON (HAROLD E.) The renegade revolutionaries. Vancouver, [1975]. pp. 157. *bibliog.*

ISTORICHESKII opyt bor'by KPSS protiv trotskizma. Moskva, 1975. pp. 622. *Based upon BOR'BA partii bol'shevikov protiv trotskizma, 1903 - fevral' 1917 g.(1968) and BOR'BA partii bol'shevikov protiv trotskizma v posleoktiabr'skii period (1969).*

TROTSKII (LEV DAVYDOVICH) Trotsky's diary in exile, 1935; translated from the Russian by Elena Zarudnaya; with a foreword by Jean van Heijenoort. Cambridge, Mass., 1976. pp. 218.

VEREEKEN (GEORGES) The GPU in the Trotskyist movement; [translated from the French]. London, [1976]. pp. 390.

BARTSCH (GUENTER) Trotzkismus als eigentlicher Sowjetkommunismus?: die IV. Internationale und ihre Konkurrenzverbände. Berlin, [1977]. pp. 194.

SHIPLEY (PETER) Trotskyism: "entryism" and permanent revolution. London, 1977. pp. 20. *(Institute for the Study of Conflict. Conflict Studies. No. 81)*

TRUMAN (HARRY S.) President of the United States.

VAUGHAN (PHILIP H.) The Truman administration's legacy for black America. Reseda, Calif., [1976]. pp. 116. *bibliog.*

WALTON (RICHARD J.) Henry Wallace, Harry Truman, and the Cold War. New York, 1976. pp. 388. *bibliog.*

MARCUS (MAEVA) Truman and the steel seizure case: the limits of presidential power. New York, 1977. pp. 390. *bibliog.*

TRUSTS, INDUSTRIAL

— European Economic Community countries — Law.

CROTTI (ALFRED F.) Trading under EEC and US antitrust laws. London, 1977. pp. 361.

HERMANN (A.H.) and JONES (COLIN) Political writer. Fair trading in Europe. London, 1977. pp. 443. *bibliog.*

— Germany.

FELDMAN (GERALD D.) Iron and steel in the German inflation, 1916-1923. Princeton, [1977]. pp. 518. *bibliog.*

— — Law.

JAECKERING (WERNER) Die politischen Auseinandersetzungen um die Novellierung des Gesetzes gegen Wettbewerbsbeschränkungen (GWB). Berlin, [1977]. pp. 287. *bibliog.*

— United States.

CONFERENCE ON ANTITRUST ISSUES IN TODAY'S ECONOMY, 13th, 1974. Antitrust and shifting national controls policies: impact on differently positioned companies...; transcript of conference, March 7, 1974. New York, [1974]. pp. 35. *(National Industrial Conference Board. Conference Board Reports. No. 626)*

— — Law.

NEALE (ALAN D.) The antitrust laws of the United States of America: a study of competition enforced by law. Cambridge, 1960 repr. 1968. pp. 516. *bibliog. (National Institute of Economic and Social Research. Economic and Social Studies. 19)*

VAN CISE (JERROLD G.) The federal antitrust laws. 3rd ed. Washington, D.C., 1975. pp. 88. *(American Enterprise Institute for Public Policy Research. Domestic Affairs Studies. 33)*

ELZINGA (KENNETH G.) and BREIT (WILLIAM) The antitrust penalties: a study in law and economics. New Haven, 1976. pp. 160.

POSNER (RICHARD A.) Antitrust law: an economic perspective. Chicago, 1976. pp. 262.

CROTTI (ALFRED F.) Trading under EEC and US antitrust laws. London, 1977. pp. 361.

TRUSTS AND TRUSTEES

— Ireland (Republic).

KEETON (GEORGE WILLIAMS) and SHERIDAN (LIONEL ASTOR) The comparative law of trusts in the Commonwealth and the Irish Republic. Chichester, 1976. pp. 370.

— United Kingdom — Taxation.

MELLOWS (ANTHONY ROGER) Taxation for executors and trustees. 4th ed. London, 1976. pp. 306.

— — Commonwealth.

KEETON (GEORGE WILLIAMS) and SHERIDAN (LIONEL ASTOR) The comparative law of trusts in the Commonwealth and the Irish Republic. Chichester, 1976. pp. 370.

TSERETELI (IRAKLII GEORGIEVICH).

ROOBOL (W.H.) Tsereteli - a democrat in the Russian revolution: a political biography; translated from the Dutch by Philip Hyams and Lynne Richards. The Hague, 1976. pp. 273. *bibliog. (International Institute of Social History. Studies in Social History. No.1)*

TUN RAZAK.

See ABDUL RAZAK BIN HUSSEIN.

TUNISIA

— Census.

TUNIS. Census, 1966. Recensement général de la population et des logements du 3 mai 1966. Tunis, [1973]. 4 vols. (in 1). *Map in end pocket.*

— Economic conditions.

CHANGE in Tunisia: studies in the social sciences; edited by Russell A. Stone and John Simmons. Albany, N.Y., 1976. pp. 333. *bibliogs.*

SEKLANI (MAHMOUD) Economie et population du sud tunisien. Paris, 1976. pp. 455. *bibliog.*

— — Mathematical models.

HAWRYLYSHYN (OLI) and others. Planning for economic development: the construction and use of a multisectoral model for Tunisia. New York, 1976. pp. 201. *bibliog. A project of the International Institute of Quantitative Economics.*

— Economic policy — Mathematical models.

HAWRYLYSHYN (OLI) and others. Planning for economic development: the construction and use of a multisectoral model for Tunisia. New York, 1976. pp. 201. *bibliog. A project of the International Institute of Quantitative Economics.*

— Politics and government.

BOURGUIBA (HABIB) Discours. Tunis, 1974 in progress.

— Population.

SEKLANI (MAHMOUD) Economie et population du sud tunisien. Paris, 1976. pp. 455. *bibliog.*

— Social conditions.

CHANGE in Tunisia: studies in the social sciences; edited by Russell A. Stone and John Simmons. Albany, N.Y., 1976. pp. 333. *bibliogs.*

— Social life and customs.

LOUIS (ANDRE) Tunisie du sud: ksars et villages de crêtes. Paris, 1975. pp. 370. *bibliog. (Centre de Recherches et d'Etudes sur les Sociétés Méditerranéennes. Etudes Tunisiennes)*

TURGOT (ANNE ROBERT JACQUES) Baron de l'Aulne.

TURGOT (ANNE ROBERT JACQUES) Baron de l'Aulne. Lettres de Turgot à la duchesse d'Enville, 1764-74 et 1777-80: édition critique préparée...sous la direction de Joseph Ruwet [and others]. Louvain, 1976. pp. 215. *bibliog. (Louvain. Université. Faculté de Philosophie et Lettres. Travaux. 16)*

TURKESTAN

— Economic history.

NURULLIN (RUSTAM ABDURAKHIMOVICH) Bor'ba Kompartii Turkestana za osushchestvlenie politiki "voennogo kommunizma". Tashkent, 1975. pp. 143.

— Politics and government.

BABAKHANOV (MANSUR) Predposylki revoliutsionnogo soiuza trudiashchikhsia Turkestanskogo kraia s rossiiskim proletariatom. Dushanbe, 1975. pp. 312.

TURKEY

— Census.

TURKEY. Census, 1975. Population census of Turkey, 26 October 1975: 1 per cent sample results. Ankara, 1976. pp. 49. *(Istatistik Umum Müdürlügü. Yayinlar. No. 771) In English and Turkish.*

TURKEY. Census, 1970. Census of population, (25.10.1970): social and economic characteristics of population. Ankara, 1977. pp. 222. *(Istatistik Umum Müdürlügü. Yayinlar No. 756) In English and Turkish.*

— Economic conditions.

JAFAR (MAJEED R.) Under-underdevelopment: a regional case study of the Kurdish area in Turkey. Helsinki, 1976. pp. 153. *bibliog. (Finnish Social Policy Association. Studies. No. 24)*

— Economic policy.

PLANNING IN TURKEY; [pd. by] Devlet Plânlama Teşkilâti. a., 1964 (no.2). Ankara.

— Foreign relations.

ANDERSON (MATTHEW SMITH) The eastern question, 1774-1923: a study in international relations. London, 1966. pp. 436. *bibliog.*

MANGO (ANDREW J.A.) Turkey: a delicately poised ally. Beverly Hills, [1975]. pp. 73. *bibliog. (Georgetown University. Center for Strategic and International Studies. Washington Papers. vol. 3/28)*

TAMKOC (METIN) The warrior diplomats: guardians of the national security and modernization of Turkey. Salt Lake City, [1976]. pp. 394. *bibliog.*

See also EUROPEAN ECONOMIC COMMUNITY — Turkey.

— — Russia.

CHERNIKOV (IHOR FEDIROVYCH) V interesakh mira i dobrososedstva: o sovetsko-turetskikh otnosheniiakh v 1935-1970 gg. Kiev, 1977. pp. 198. *bibliog.*

— — United Kingdom.

ZHIVKOVA (LUDMILA) Anglo-Turkish relations, 1933-1939. London, 1976. pp. 132. *bibliog.*

— History.

FALLERS (LLOYD A.) The social anthropology of the nation-state. Chicago, 1974. pp. 171. *bibliog. (Rochester, N.Y. University. Lewis Henry Morgan Lectures. 1971)*

SHAW (STANFORD JAY) History of the Ottoman Empire and modern Turkey. Cambridge, 1976 in progress. *bibliog.*

— Nationalism.

KUSHNER (DAVID) The rise of Turkish nationalism, 1876-1908. London, 1977. pp. 126. *bibliog.*

— Politics and government.

MANGO (ANDREW J.A.) Turkey: a delicately poised ally. Beverly Hills, [1975]. pp. 73. *bibliog. (Georgetown University. Center for Strategic and International Studies. Washington Papers. vol. 3/28)*

TAMKOC (METIN) The warrior diplomats: guardians of the national security and modernization of Turkey. Salt Lake City, [1976]. pp. 394. *bibliog.*

AHMAD (FEROZ) The Turkish experiment in democracy, 1950-1975. London, 1977. pp. 474. *bibliog.*

— Presidents.

TAMKOC (METIN) The warrior diplomats: guardians of the national security and modernization of Turkey. Salt Lake City, [1976]. pp. 394. *bibliog.*

— Rural conditions.

LEDER (ARNOLD) Catalysts of change: Marxist versus Muslim in a Turkish community. Austin, Texas, [1976]. pp. 56. *bibliog. (Texas University. Center for Middle Eastern Studies. Middle East Monographs. No. 1)*

— Social conditions.

CUISENIER (JEAN) Economie et parenté: leurs affinités de structure dans le domaine turc et dans le monde arabe. Paris, [1975]. pp. 569. *bibliog. (Paris. Ecole Pratique des Hautes Etudes. Section des Sciences Economiques et Sociales. Le Monde d'Outre-Mer Passé et Présent. 1e Série. Etudes. 60)*

ÖZBUDUN (ERGUN) Social change and political participation in Turkey. Princeton, N.J., [1976]. pp. 254. *bibliog.*

TURKMENISTAN

— Economic history.

ISTORIIA rabochego klassa Sovetskogo Turkmenistana, 1917-1965 gg. Ashkhabad, 1969. pp. 495.

— History.

ISTORIIA Sovetskogo Turkmenistana. Ashkhabad, 1970 in progress.

— Industries.

MEREDOV (KHUDAIBERDY) Po puti razvitiia i sovershenstvovaniia. Ashkhabad, 1969. pp. 182.

— Intellectual life.

ISTORIIA kul'tury Sovetskogo Turkmenistana, 1917-1970. Ashkhabad, 1975. pp. 466.

— Politics and government.

MATVEEVA (TAMARA STEPANOVNA) Internatsional'nyi dolg i sovremennost': na materialakh Turkmenskoi SSR. Ashkhabad, 1970. pp. 141.

TURNHOUT

— Industries.

AUTENBOER (EUGEEN VAN) The Turnhout playing card industry, 1826-1976...: preceded by a History of Belgian playing cards from 1379 to 1826; by Louis Tummers; in collaboration with Jan Bauwens. Brussels, Ministry of Foreign Affairs, External Trade and Cooperation in Development, 1976. pp. 152. *bibliog. (Memo from Belgium. No.174)*

TURNOVER (BUSINESS)

— Netherlands.

ECONOMISCH INSTITUUT VOOR HET MIDDEN- EN KLEINBEDRIJF. Gegevens over de Omzet in het Midden- en Kleinbedrijf. No. 37. Het weekpatroon van de geldomzetten. 3. 's-Gravenhage, 1965. pp. 9.

ECONOMISCH INSTITUUT VOOR HET MIDDEN- EN KLEINBEDRIJF. Gegevens over de Omzet in het Midden- en Kleinbedrijf. No. 39. De omzetontwikkeling in het jaar 1965. 's-Gravenhage, 1966. pp. 17.

ECONOMISCH INSTITUUT VOOR HET MIDDEN- EN KLEINBEDRIJF. Gegevens over de Omzet in het Midden- en Kleinbedrijf. No. 42. De omzetontwikkeling in het eerste tot en met het derde kwartaal 1966. 's-Gravenhage, 1966. pp. 10.

ECONOMISCH INSTITUUT VOOR HET MIDDEN- EN KLEINBEDRIJF. Gegevens over de Omzet in het Midden- en Kleinbedrijf. No. 45. Het weekpatroon van de geldomzetten. 4. 's-Gravenhage, 1967. pp. 10.

ECONOMISCH INSTITUUT VOOR HET MIDDEN- EN KLEINBEDRIJF. Gegevens over de Omzet in het Midden- en Kleinbedrijf. No. 50. Het weekpatroon van de geldomzetten. 5. 's-Gravenhage, 1968. pp. 12.

TURNOVER TAX

— Finland.

FINLAND. Tilastokeskus. Liikevaihtoverotus: Omsättningsbeskattningen. a., 1972- Helsinki. *[in Finnish and Swedish]. File includes Lopetetut liikevaihtoverovelvolliset yritykset.*

TUVA

— Politics and government.

OCHERKI istorii Tuvinskoi organizatsii KPSS. Kyzyl, 1975. pp. 405.

TUVALU

— Politics and government.

TUVALU. House of Assembly. Official report. sess., Oc 28/N 1 1975 (1st session, 1st meeting)- Funafuti.

TWENTIETH CENTURY.

ROMAN (VALTER) Secolul XX - secolul marilor revoluţii: sinteze şi perspective. [Bucureşti], 1976. pp. 539. *bibliog. With tables of contents in various languages.*

TWENTIETH CENTURY.(Cont.)

— Forecasts.

1994: the world of tomorrow. Washington, D.C., [1973]. pp. 192. *Issued by U.S. News and World Report.*

BASIUK (VICTOR) Technology, world politics, and American policy. New York, 1977. pp. 409. *bibliog.*

SIMAI (MIHÁLY) and others. Main tendencies in the world economy 1976-1990; elaborated by a research team directed by Professor M. Simai. Budapest, 1977. pp. 50. *(Hungarian Scientific Council for World Economy. [Publications]. Trends in World Economy. No. 20)*

TWENTY-FIRST CENTURY

— Forecasts.

WALTERS (ALAN A.) The outer limits and beyond. London, [1975?]. pp. 12. *(Foundation for Business Responsibilities. Discussion Papers. No.12)*

SAKHAROV (ANDREI DMITRIEVICH) O strane i mire: sbornik proizvedenii. N'iu-Iork, 1976. pp. xxiv,183.

BASIUK (VICTOR) Technology, world politics, and American policy. New York, 1977. pp. 409. *bibliog.*

TYABJI (BADRUDDIN).

NOORANI (A.G.) Badruddin Tyabji. New Delhi, 1969. pp. 201. *bibliog. (Builders of Modern India)*

TYLER (MARY).

TYLER (MARY) My years in an Indian prison;...with illustrations by Dilip Ray. London, 1977. pp. 191.

TYNE AND WEAR

— Population — Maps.

ATLAS of Tyne and Wear; computer-produced using the Symap program; [by] P.J. Taylor [and others]. Newcastle-upon-Tyne, 1976. fo.30. *(Newcastle-upon-Tyne. University. Department of Geography. Research Series. No.11)*

— Social conditions — Maps.

ATLAS of Tyne and Wear; computer-produced using the Symap program; [by] P.J. Taylor [and others]. Newcastle-upon-Tyne, 1976. fo.30. *(Newcastle-upon-Tyne. University. Department of Geography. Research Series. No.11)*

TYNESIDE

— Social history.

COLLS (ROBERT M.) The collier's rant: song and culture in the industrial village. London, [1977]. pp. 216.

TYRONE

— Economic policy.

IRELAND, NORTHERN. Department of the Environment. 1976. West Tyrone area plan: statement by Department, etc. Belfast, [1976]. pp. 25.

TZINTZUNTZAN.

KEMPER (ROBERT V.) Migration and adaptation: Tzintzuntzan peasants in Mexico City. Beverly Hills, [1977]. pp. 223. *bibliog.*

TZOTZIL INDIANS

— Agriculture.

COLLIER (GEORGE ALLEN) Fields of the Tzotzil: the ecological bases of tradition in highland Chiapas. Austin, Texas, [1975]. pp. 255. *bibliog.*

— Social life and customs.

COLLIER (GEORGE ALLEN) Fields of the Tzotzil: the ecological bases of tradition in highland Chiapas. Austin, Texas, [1975]. pp. 255. *bibliog.*

UDRUZENJE CETNIKA.

ŠEHIĆ (NUSRET) Četništvo u Bosni i Hercegovini, 1918-1941: politička uloga i oblici djelatnosti četničkih udruženja; Le mouvement des tchetniks en Bosnie-Herzegovine, etc.; uredník Hamdija Kapidžić. Sarajevo, 1971. pp. 239. *bibliog. (Akademija Nauka i Umjetnosti Bosne i Hercegovine. Djela. kn.42 [being also] Odjeljenje Društvenih Nauka. kn.27) With German summary.*

UGANDA

— History.

KARUGIRE (SAMWIRI RUBARAZA) Nuwa Mbaguta. Nairobi, 1973. pp. 89.

— Officials and employees — Salaries, allowances, etc.

UGANDA. Board of Inquiry into a Wages Increase Claim in respect of Group Employees in the Uganda Public Service. 1966. Report; A.K. Mayanja, chairman. Entebbe, 1966. pp. 20.

— Politics and government.

CAMPBELL (HORACE) Four essays on neo-colonialism in Uganda: the military dictatorship of Idi Amin. Toronto, [1975]. pp. 56.

MELADY (THOMAS PATRICK) and MELADY (MARGARET BADUM) Uganda: the Asian exiles. Maryknoll, N.Y., [1976]. pp. 86. *bibliog.*

— Population.

KIAPI (ABRAHAM) Law and population in Uganda. Medford, Mass., 1977. pp. 53. *(Tufts University. Fletcher School of Law and Diplomacy. Law and Population Monograph Series. No. 42)*

UGANDA COMMERCIAL BANK.

UGANDA COMMERCIAL BANK. Origins and growth of Uganda Commercial Bank 1950-75. [Kampala, 1976?]. pp. 26.

UKRAINE

— Constitutional history.

ISTORIIA gosudarstva i prava Ukrainskoi SSR. Kiev, 1976. pp. 759.

— Economic conditions.

NAIDENOV (VIKTOR SERGEEVICH) and others. Deviataia piatiletka: dostizheniia ekonomiki razvitogo sotsializma: na materialakh Ukrainskoi SSR. Kiev, 1976. pp. 191.

PALAMARCHUK (MAKSIM MARTYNOVICH) and others. Problemy razvitiia i razmeshcheniia proizvoditel'nykh sil Iugo- Zapadnogo raiona. Moskva, 1976. pp. 262. *bibliog.*

SUKHOPARA (FEDOR NIKOLAEVICH) and UDOD (VLADIMIR IVANOVICH) Problemy razvitiia i razmeshcheniia proizvoditel'nykh sil Donetsko-Pridneprovskogo raiona. Moskva, 1976. pp. 256. *bibliog.*

— Economic policy.

EMEL'IANOV (ALEKSANDR SERGEEVICH) ed. Sovershenstvovanie territorial'nogo planirovaniia v soiuznoi respublike: na primere USSR. Moskva, 1976. pp. 200. *bibliog.*

— History — Sources — Bibliography.

TVORY V.I. Lenina na Ukraïni, 1894 - liutyi 1917 r.: pokazhchyk arkhivnykh dokumentiv. Kyïv, 1977. pp. 255.

— — 1917-1921, Revolution — Historiography.

MUSIIENKO (VOLODYMYR VASYL'OVYCH) Bil'shovyky Ukraïny v Zhovtnevii revoliutsiï, berezen' 1917 r. - berezen' 1918 r.: do istoriohrafiï problemy. Kyïv, 1976. pp. 195.

— Industries.

PARTIINE kerivnytstvo rozvytkom promyslovosti Ukraïny, 1917- 1975. Kyïv, 1976. pp. 343.

— Nationalism.

VARVARTSEV (MYKOLA MYKOLAIOVYCH) Burzhuazne "ukraïnoznavstvo" - znariaddia ideolohichnykh dyversii imperializmu. Kyïv, 1976. pp. 185. *bibliog.*

— Politics and government.

BIL'SHOVYTS'KI orhanizatsiï Ukraïny v borot'bi za hehemoniiu proletariatu v tr'okh rosiis'kykh revoliutsiiakh. Kyïv, 1976. pp. 176.

— Rural conditions.

LOS' (FEDIR IEVDOKYMOVYCH) and MYKHAILIUK (OLEKSII HRYHOROVYCH) Klasova borot'ba v ukraïns'komu seli, 1907-1914. Kyïv, 1976. pp. 283. *bibliog.*

— Statistics.

UKRAINE. Tsentral'noe Statisticheskoe Upravlenie. 1972. Ukraïns'ka RSR u tsyfrakh v 1971 rotsi: korotkyi statystychnyi dovidnyk. Kyïv, 1972. pp. 143.

UKRAINE, WESTERN

— Nationalism.

DOBRETSOVA (VIOLLI VIACHESLAVIVNA) Natsionalizm i relihiia na sluzhbi antykomunizmu: pro kontrrevoliutsiinu diial'nist' burzhuazno-natsionalistychnykh i klerykal'nykh orhanizatsii na zakhidnoukraïns'kykh zemliakh u 20-30-kh rokakh ta borot'bu proty nykh prohresyvnykh syl. L'viv, 1976. pp. 204.

— Rural conditions.

SOTSIAL'NI peretvorennia u radians'komu seli: na prykladi sil zakhidnykh oblastei Ukraïns'koï RSR. Kyïv, 1976. pp. 233.

UKRAINIAN STUDIES.

VARVARTSEV (MYKOLA MYKOLAIOVYCH) Burzhuazne "ukraïnoznavstvo" - znariaddia ideolohichnykh dyversii imperializmu. Kyïv, 1976. pp. 185. *bibliog.*

UNABHAENGIGE SOZIALDEMOKRATISCHE PARTEI DEUTSCHLANDS.

MARCHIONINI (KARL) Was trennt uns Unabhängige von den Rechtssozialisten?. Leipzig, 1919. pp. 31.

CALKINS (KENNETH R.) Hugo Haase: Demokrat und Revolutionär; aus dem Amerikanischen übersetzt von Arthur Mandel. Berlin, [1976]. pp. 245. *bibliog.*

GEYER (CURT) Die revolutionäre Illusion: zur Geschichte des linken Flügels der USPD: Erinnerungen...; herausgegeben von Wolfgang Benz und Hermann Graml. Stuttgart, [1976]. pp. 304. *bibliog. (Vierteljahrshefte für Zeitgeschichte. Schriftenreihe. Nr.33)*

UNDERDEVELOPED AREAS.

KINDERMANN (GOTTFRIED KARL) ed. Kulturen im Umbruch: Studien zur Problematik und Analyse des Kulturwandels in Entwicklungsländern. Freiburg im Breisgau, [1962]. pp. 422. *bibliogs.*

AKHMEDOVA (MATBUA AMIRSAIDOVNA) Nekapitalisticheskii put': nekotorye problemy teorii i praktiki. Tashkent, 1976. pp. 223.

ECONOMICS in institutional perspective: memorial essays in honor of K. William Kapp; edited by Rolf Steppacher [and others]. Lexington, Mass., [1977]. pp. 226. *bibliog.*

TODARO (MICHAEL P.) Economic development in the third world: an introduction to problems and policies in a global perspective. London, 1977. pp. 445. *bibliogs.*

— Agriculture.

A REVIEW of rural co-operation in developing areas: papers on Latin America, Asia and Africa; by T.F. Carroll [and others]. Geneva, United Nations Research Institute for Social Development, 1969. pp. 348. *bibliog. (Rural Institutions and Planned Change. Vol.1)*

CARSON (GUY) and others. Nutrition and underdevelopment. [Toronto, 1974]. pp. 69. *bibliog.*

FEDER (ERNEST) Dr., of the University of Nebraska. The new penetration of the agricultures of the underdeveloped countries by the industrial nations and their multinational concerns. Glasgow, 1975. pp. 26. *(Glasgow. University. Institute of Latin American Studies. Occasional Papers. No. 19)*

TENCH (ANDREW B.) Socio-economic factors influencing agricultural output, with special reference to Zambia. Saarbrücken, 1975. pp. 309. *bibliog.*

GRIFFIN (KEITH) Land concentration and rural poverty. London, 1976. pp. 303.

LUMUMBA (TOLENGA EMERY) Le rôle de l'agriculture dans les pays du Tiers Monde, particulièrement au Zaïre. Budapest, 1976. pp. 24. *(Magyar Tudományos Akadémia. Világgazdasági Kutató Intézet. Studies on Developing Countries. No. 89)*

STIMULATING local development; [edited by Guy Hunter and Janice Jiggins]. London, [1976]. pp. 56. *(Overseas Development Institute. Agricultural Administration Unit. Occasional Papers)*

STRATEGIES for small farmer development: an empirical study of rural development projects in the Gambia, Ghana, Kenya, Lesotho, Nigeria, Bolivia, Colombia, Mexico, Paraguay and Peru; [by] Elliott R. Morss [and others]. Boulder, Co., 1976. 2 vols. *A study prepared for the Office of Development Administration, Agency for International Development.*

VALLIANATOS (E.G.) Fear in the countryside: the control of agricultural resources in the poor countries by nonpeasant elites. Cambridge, Mass., [1976]. pp. 180.

WALSTON (HENRY DAVID LEONARD GEORGE) Baron Walston. Dealing with hunger. London, 1976. pp. 152.

GROWING out of poverty; edited by Elizabeth Stamp. Oxford, 1977. pp. 165.

— Armed forces — Political activity.

FIDEL (KENNETH) ed. Militarism in developing countries. New Brunswick, [1975]. pp. 319.

— Automation — Economic aspects.

ROUND-TABLE DISCUSSION ON THE MANPOWER PROBLEMS ASSOCIATED WITH THE INTRODUCTION OF AUTOMATION AND ADVANCED TECHNOLOGY IN DEVELOPING COUNTRIES, GENEVA, 1970. Automation in developing countries. Geneva, International Labour Office, 1972. pp. 246.

— Banks and banking.

NWANKWO (GREEN ONYEKABA) New dimensions in banking in developing countries: collected essays. Lagos, [1977?]. pp. 304.

— Birth control.

FARLEY (JOHN U.) and TOKARSKI (STEVEN S.) Legal restrictions on the distribution of contraceptives in the developing nations: some suggestions for determining priorities and estimating impact of change. Medford, Mass., 1975. pp. 415-445. *(Tufts University. Fletcher School of Law and Diplomacy. Law and Population Monograph Series. No. 27) (Reprinted from Columbia Human Rights Law Review, vol. 6)*

EDUCATION for family welfare: a component of development; proceedings of a subregional seminar on family welfare as a component of development: new forms for old, held in Accra...1976. New York, [1977]. pp. 128. *Sponsored by the International Association of Schools of Social Work, the International Planned Parenthood Federation and the Department of Sociology of the University of Ghana.*

The FEASIBILITY of fertility planning: micro perspectives: edited by T. Scarlett Epstein and Darrell Jackson. Oxford, 1977. pp. 244. *bibliog. Based on papers of a conference held at the Institute of Development Studies, University of Sussex, 1975.*

SAI (FRED T.) Defining family health needs, standards of care and priorities with particular reference to family planning. London, 1977. pp. 32. *(International Planned Parenthood Federation. Occasional Essays. No. 4)*

— Children — Care and hygiene — Mathematical models.

HELLER (PETER S.) and DRAKE (WILLIAM D.) Malnutrition, child morbidity and the family decision process. Ann Arbor, 1976. pp. 43. *bibliog. (Michigan University. Center for Research on Economic Development. Discussion Papers. No. 58)*

— — Nutrition — Mathematical models.

HELLER (PETER S.) and DRAKE (WILLIAM D.) Malnutrition, child morbidity and the family decision process. Ann Arbor, 1976. pp. 43. *bibliog. (Michigan University. Center for Research on Economic Development. Discussion Papers. No. 58)*

— Cities and towns.

HABITAT: UNITED NATIONS CONFERENCE ON HUMAN SETTLEMENTS, VANCOUVER, 1976. Global review of human settlements: a support paper for Habitat: United Nations Conference on Human Settlements; (with Statistical annex) (A/CONF.70/A/1 and A/CONF.70/A/1 Add.1). Oxford, 1976. 2 vols.

— City planning.

HABITAT: UNITED NATIONS CONFERENCE ON HUMAN SETTLEMENTS, VANCOUVER, 1976. Report of Habitat:...Vancouver, 31 May - 11 June 1976. (A/CONF.70/15). New York, 1976. pp. 183.

— Commerce.

FERRERO (RÓMULO A.) Trade problems of primary producing countries: a position paper prepared...for a panel session at the International Industrial Conference, jointly sponsored by the National Industrial Conference Board and Stanford Research Institute...1965 in San Francisco. Menlo Park, Calif., 1965. fo. 63.

UNITED NATIONS. Conference on Trade and Development. 1966. Trade expansion and economic co-operation among developing countries: report, etc. (TD/B/68/Rev.1). Geneva, 1966. pp. 41.

McINTYRE (ALISTER) The effects of reverse preferences on trade among developing countries. (TD/B/435). New York, United Nations, 1974. pp. 105. *(Conference on Trade and Development. Current Problems on Economic Integration)*

MORRISON (THOMAS K.) Manufactured exports from developing countries. New York, [1976]. pp. 108. *bibliog.*

SCHUBERT (JOACHIM) Aussenhandel und Unterentwicklung, dargestellt am Beispiel Indiens. Berlin, 1976. pp. 375. *bibliog. Inaugural-Dissertation zur Erlangung des Grades eines Doktors der Wirtschaftswissenschaften der Freien Universität Berlin.*

MORTON (KATHRYN) and TULLOCH (PETER) Trade and developing countries. London, [1977]. pp. 376. *bibliog.*

REHSCHE (GUNTRAM) Schweizerische Aussenwirtschaftspolitik und Dritte Welt: Ziele und Instrumente; Exportförderung kontra Entwicklungspolitik? Bern, 1977. pp. 73. *bibliog. (Schweizerischer Evangelischer Kirchenbund. Institut für Sozialethik. Entwicklungspolitische Diskussionsbeiträge. 8)*

— Communication.

COMMUNICATION and change: the last ten years - and the next; edited by Wilbur Schramm [and] Daniel Lerner. Honolulu, [1976]. pp. 372. *bibliog. Papers presented at a conference held at the East- West Center, Honolulu in Jan. 1975.*

— Consumption (economics).

WANDER (HILDE) Bevölkerungswachstum und Konsumstruktur in Entwicklungsländern: Fakten, Zusammenhänge und politische Implikationen. Tübingen, [1977]. pp. 117. *bibliog. (Kiel. Universität. Institut für Weltwirtschaft. Kieler Studien. 149)*

— Cooperative societies.

A REVIEW of rural co-ooperation in developing areas: papers on Latin America, Asia and Africa; by T.F. Carroll [and others]. Geneva, United Nations Research Institute for Social Development, 1969. pp. 348. *bibliog. (Rural Institutions and Planned Change. Vol.1)*

— Corporations, American.

NATIONAL ACADEMY OF SCIENCES. Office of the Foreign Secretary. Board on Science and Technology for International Development. U.S. international firms and R, D and E in developing countries; a report of an ad hoc panel of the board, etc. Washington, 1973. pp. 73.

— Corporations, Public.

SHERIF (FOUAD) Planning for improved performance of public enterprise in developing countries: some lessons of international experience. Ljubljana, International Center for Public Enterprises, 1974. fo. 19 *(International Seminar 1974. Background Papers)*

— Cost and standard of living.

ZAKONOMERNOSTI rosta urovnia zhizni naseleniia v usloviiakh nekapitalisticheskogo razvitiia. Tashkent, 1976. pp. 192.

— Economic conditions.

LEE (HYUN-JAE) A study of the structural change of expenditures on gross national product in the process of economic growth, with special reference to the Korean economy, as a case of a developing country in comparison with developed countries. Pittsburgh, 1973. pp. 40.

LACOSTE (YVES) Géographie du sous-développement: géopolitique d'une crise. 3rd ed. [Paris], 1976. pp. 292. *bibliog.*

BHUTTO (ZULFIKAR ALI) The third world: new directions. London, 1977. pp. 144.

LIPTON (MICHAEL) Why poor people stay poor: a study of urban bias in world development. London, 1977. pp. 467. *bibliog.*

MELOTTI (UMBERTO) Marx and the third world;...translated by Pat Ransford; edited with a foreword by Malcolm Caldwell. London, 1977. pp. 222. *bibliog.*

POLSKA AKADEMIA NAUK. Instytut Geografii. Geographia Polonica. 35. (Proceedings of the Polish-Soviet Seminar on Contemporary Problems of Developing Countries, Warsaw, November 1973; edited by Marcin Rościszewski [and others]). Warszawa, 1977. pp. 148. *bibliogs.*

TODARO (MICHAEL P.) Economics for a developing world: an introduction to principles, problems and policies for development. London, 1977. pp. 444. *bibliogs.*

— Economic integration.

UNITED NATIONS. Conference on Trade and Development. 1966. Trade expansion and economic co-operation among developing countries: report, etc. (TD/B/68/Rev.1). Geneva, 1966. pp. 41.

— Economic policy.

UNITED NATIONS. Conference on Trade and Development. 1971. Special measures in favour of the least developed among the developing countries: report of the Ad Hoc Group of Experts, etc. (TD/B/349/Rev.1). New York, 1971. pp. 29.

MUNS ALBUIXECH (JOAQUIN) Industrializacion y crecimiento de los paises en desarrollo. Barcelona, [1972]. pp. 312. *bibliog. (Barcelona. Universidad. Facultad de Ciencias Economicas. Departamento de Teoria Economica. Publicaciones)*

RAJ (KAKKADAN NANDANATH) The politics and economies of "intermediate regimes". Poona, [1973?]. pp. 22. *(Gokhale Institute of Politics and Economics. R. R. Kale Memorial Lectures. 1973)*

RODRIGUEZ MARIÑO (TOMAS) El proceso de las decisiones publicas. Bogota, 1973. pp. 152. *bibliog.*

COLANOVIĆ (BRANISLAV) and others. Planning to serve development and the foundations of planning in Yugoslavia; (translated by Nina Udovicki). Ljubljana, International Center for Public Enterprises, 1974. fo. 33. *(International Seminar 1974. Background Papers)*

KHAMIS (I.A.) Impediments to economic growth in the developing countries. Dar es Salaam, 1974. pp. 14. *(Dar es Salaam. University. Economic Research Bureau. ERB Papers. 74. 6)*

PAPANDREOU (ANDREAS GEORGE) and ZOHAR (URI) The impact approach to project selection: national planning and socioeconomic priorities: a two volume series, (volume 2). New York, 1974. pp. 187.

SIMAI (MIHÁLY) Planning and plan implementation in the developing countries. Budapest, 1975. pp. 54. *(Magyar Tudományos Akadémia. Világgazdasági Kutató Intézet. Studies on Developing Countries. No. 72)*

KUPRIANOV (ALEXEI B.) Developing countries: internal regional disproportions in growing economies. Budapest, 1976. pp. 63. *(Magyar Tudományos Akadémia. Világgazdasági Kutató Intézet. Studies on Developing Countries. No 85)*

LEIPZIGER (DANNY M.) and MUDGE (JAMES L.) Seabed mineral resources and the economic interests of developing countries. Cambridge, Mass., [1976]. pp. 240. *bibliog.*

NATIONAL RESEARCH COUNCIL. Commission on International Relations. Board on Science and Technology for International Development. Systems analysis and operations research: a tool for policy and program planning for developing countries: report of an ad hoc panel. Washington, D.C., 1976. pp. 98. *bibliog. With summaries in Spanish and French.*

PARTANT (FRANÇOIS) La guérilla économique: les conditions du développement. Paris, [1976]. pp. 220. *bibliog.*

PITT (DAVID C.) The social dynamics of development. Oxford, 1976. pp. 162. *bibliog.*

The ROLE of the state in socio-economic reforms in developing countries; [under the general editorship of V.F. Stanis and others]. Moscow, [1976]. pp. 239.

VEREIN FÜR SOZIALPOLITIK. Schriften. Neue Folge. Band 90. Integration der Entwicklungsländer in eine instabile Wirtschaft: Probleme, Chancen, Gefahren; von Michael Bohnet [and others]; herausgegeben von Winfried von Urff. Berlin, [1976]. pp. 226.

BALASSA (BELA A.) Policy reform in developing countries. Oxford, 1977. pp. 175.

KEBSCHULL (DIETRICH) and others, eds. Die neue Weltwirtschaftsordnung: Beiträge zu ausgewählten Forderungen der Entwicklungsländer. Hamburg, 1977. pp. 287. *bibliog. (Hamburg. Hamburgisches Welt-Wirtschafts-Archiv. Veröffentlichungen)*

LIPTON (MICHAEL) Why poor people stay poor: a study of urban bias in world development. London, 1977. pp. 467. *bibliog.*

SACHS (IGNACY) Pour une économie politique du développement: études de planification. [Paris, 1977]. pp. 307. *bibliog.*

TODARO (MICHAEL P.) Economics for a developing world: an introduction to principles, problems and policies for development. London, 1977. pp. 444. *bibliogs.*

— Education.

AHMED (MANZOOR) The economics of nonformal education: resources, costs and benefits. New York, 1975. pp. 122. *bibliog.*

DORE (RONALD PHILIP) The diploma disease: education, qualification and development. London, 1976. pp. 214. *bibliog.*

MONSON (TERRY D.) A note on measuring educational returns in LDCs. Ann Arbor, 1977. pp. 13. *bibliog. (Michigan University. Center for Research on Economic Development. Discussion Papers. No. 63)*

— Education of adults.

GRUNDERZIEHUNG: Hilfe für Entwicklungsländer: Berichte im Auftrag der Deutschen UNESCO-Kommission; herausgegeben von Heinz Kloss. Stuttgart, 1960. pp. 135. *bibliog.*

— Electricity supply — Finance.

TURVEY (RALPH) and ANDERSON (DENNIS) Electricity economics: essays and case studies. Baltimore, International Bank for Reconstruction and Development, [1977]. pp. 364.

— Energy policy.

CHANGING resource problems of the fourth world; Ronald G. Ridker, editor. Washington, D.C., 1976. pp. 157. *(Resources for the Future, Inc. Working Papers. PD-1)*

— Family — Mathematical models.

HELLER (PETER S.) and DRAKE (WILLIAM D.) Malnutrition, child morbidity and the family decision process. Ann Arbor, 1976. pp. 43. *bibliog. (Michigan University. Center for Research on Economic Development. Discussion Papers. No. 58)*

— Family social work.

EDUCATION for family welfare: a component of development; proceedings of a subregional seminar on family welfare as a component of development: new forms for old, held in Accra...1976. New York, [1977]. pp. 128. *Sponsored by the International Association of Schools of Social Work, the International Planned Parenthood Federation and the Department of Sociology of the University of Ghana.*

— Fertility, Human.

SAI (FRED T.) Food, population and politics. London, 1977. pp. 35. *bibliog. (International Planned Parenthood Federation. Occasional Essays. No. 3)*

— Finance.

UNITED NATIONS. Conference on Trade and Development. 1971. Special measures in favour of the least developed among the developing countries: report of the Ad Hoc Group of Experts, etc. (TD/B/349/Rev.1). New York, 1971. pp. 29.

UNITED NATIONS. Conference on Trade and Development. 1972. The international monetary situation: impact on world trade and development; report. (TD/140/Rev.1). New York, 1972. pp. 70.

MONEY and finance in economic growth and development: essays in honour of Edward S. Shaw;...edited by Ronald I. McKinnon. New York, [1976]. pp. 339. *bibliogs. Proceedings of the conference held at Stanford University in April 1974, under the auspices of the Center for Research in Economic Growth.*

— Food industry and trade.

SAI (FRED T.) Food, population and politics. London, 1977. pp. 35. *bibliog. (International Planned Parenthood Federation. Occasional Essays. No. 3)*

— Food supply.

WALSTON (HENRY DAVID LEONARD GEORGE) Baron Walston. Dealing with hunger. London, 1976. pp. 152.

SAI (FRED T.) Food, population and politics. London, 1977. pp. 35. *bibliog. (International Planned Parenthood Federation. Occasional Essays. No. 3)*

— Foreign economic relations.

COURIER, THE: European Community-Africa-Caribbean-Pacific (formerly Association news); [pd. by the Commission of the European Communities). bi-m., Ja/F 1973 (no.17)- Brussels.

HOWE (JAMES W.) The developing countries in a changing international economic order: a survey of research needs. Washington, D.C. 1973. pp. 71. *(Overseas Development Council. Occasional Papers. No. 7)*

[WORKING papers prepared for the Commonwealth Group of Experts drawing up practical measures for closing the gap between rich and poor countries]. [London, Commonwealth Secretariat, 1975-77). 56 pts. (in 1 vol.)

FEDER (ERNEST) Dr., of the University of Nebraska. The new penetration of the agricultures of the underdeveloped countries by the industrial nations and their multinational concerns. Glasgow, 1975. pp. 26. *(Glasgow. University. Institute of Latin American Studies. Occasional Papers. No. 19)*

NORTH-South: developing a new relationship; edited by Pierre Uri. Paris, [1976]. pp. 58. *(Atlantic Institute. Atlantic Papers. 1975.6)*

OBMINSKIJ (ERNEST EVGEN'EVICH) The mechanism of exploiting developing countries. Budapest, 1976. pp. 33. *(Magyar Tudományos Akadémia. Világgazdasági Kutató Intézet. Studies on Developing Countries. No. 77)*

WALL (DAVID) The European Community's Lomé Convention: "STABEX" and the third world's aspirations. London, [1976]. fo. 22. *(Trade Policy Research Centre. Guest Papers. No. 4)*

TOWARDS a new international economic order: a final report by a Commonwealth Experts' Group; [Alister McIntyre, chairman] . London, Commonwealth Secretariat, [1977]. pp. 104.

WEISSKOPF (THOMAS E.) Dependence as an explanation of underdevelopment: a critique. Ann Arbor, 1977. pp. 32. *bibliog. (Michigan University. Center for Research on Economic Development. Discussion Papers. No.66)*

— Foreign exchange.

BLACK (STANLEY W.) Exchange policies for less developed countries in a world of floating rates. Princeton, 1976. pp. 43. *bibliog. (Princeton University. Department of Economics and Sociology. International Finance Section. Essays in International Finance. No. 119)*

— Foreign relations.

BOTORAN (CONSTANTIN) and UNC (GHEORGHE) Tradiţii de solidaritate ale mişcării muncitoreşti şi democratice din România cu lupta de emancipare naţională şi socială a popoarelor din Asia, Africa şi America Latină. Bucureşti, 1977. pp. 255. *With English, French, German, Russian and Spanish tables of contents.*

LOEWENTHAL (RICHARD) Model or ally?: the communist powers and the developing countries. New York, 1977. pp. 400.

— Foreign trade promotion.

STAELIN (CHARLES P.) The impact of export incentives and export-related policies on the firms of the less developed countries: a case study of the Philippines. Ann Arbor, 1976. pp. 29. *(Michigan University. Center for Research on Economic Development. Discussion Papers. No. 59)*

— Full employment policies.

ROUND-TABLE DISCUSSION ON THE MANPOWER PROBLEMS ASSOCIATED WITH THE INTRODUCTION OF AUTOMATION AND ADVANCED TECHNOLOGY IN DEVELOPING COUNTRIES, GENEVA, 1970. Automation in developing countries. Geneva, International Labour Office, 1972. pp. 246.

— Government ownership.

WORLD FEDERATION OF TRADE UNIONS. Developing countries: the public sector and the role of the trade unions. [Prague, 1976]. pp. 35.

— Gross national product.

LEE (HYUN-JAE) A study of the structural change of expenditures on gross national product in the process of economic growth, with special reference to the Korean economy, as a case of a developing country in comparison with developed countries. Pittsburgh, 1973. pp. 40.

— Housing.

GRIMES (ORVILLE F.) Housing for low-income urban families: economics and policy in the developing world. Baltimore, [1976]. pp. 176. *bibliog. (International Bank for Reconstruction and Development. World Bank Research Publications)*

UNITED NATIONS. Department of Economic and Social Affairs. 1976. Housing policy guidelines for developing countries (ST/ESA/50). New York, 1976. pp. 124.

— — Finance.

UNITED NATIONS. [Centre for Housing, Building and Planning]. 1972. Proposals for action on finance for housing, building and planning. (E/C.6/106/Rev.1) (ST/ECA/168). New York, 1972. pp. 89. *bibliog.*

— — Statistics.

PRAKASH (VED) and SPILLANE (JAMES J.) An economic framework for investment planning in housing and urban infrastructure. (ST/ECA/186). New York, United Nations, 1973. pp. 47.

— Hygiene, Public.

SAI (FRED T.) Defining family health needs, standards of care and priorities with particular reference to family planning. London, 1977. pp. 32. *(International Planned Parenthood Federation. Occasional Essays. No. 4)*

SAI (FRED T.) Health, nutrition and population in human settlements. London, 1977. pp. 31. *bibliog. (International Planned Parenthood Federation. Occasional Essays. No. 5.)*

— Industries.

MUNS ALBUIXECH (JOAQUIN) Industrializacion y crecimiento de los paises en desarrollo. Barcelona, [1972]. pp. 312. *bibliog. (Barcelona. Universidad. Facultad de Ciencias Economicas. Departamento de Teoria Economica. Publicaciones)*

STREETEN (PAUL PATRICK) Industrialization in a unified development strategy. Oxford, 1975. pp. 9. *(Oxford. University. Institute of Commonwealth Studies. Reprint Series. No. 76E) (Repr. from World Development, vol.3, no. 1, 1975)*

— Industry and state.

The ROLE of the state in socio-economic reforms in developing countries; [under the general editorship of V.F. Stanis and others]. Moscow, [1976]. pp. 239.

— Information services.

CONFERENCE ON NATIONAL PLANNING FOR INFORMATICS IN DEVELOPING COUNTRIES, BAGHDAD, 1975. National planning for informatics in developing countries: proceedings of the IBI International Symposium, Baghdad, 2-6 November 1975; organized by National Computers Centre of Iraq-NCC; edited by G. Russell Pipe and A.A.M. Veenhuis. Amsterdam, 1976. pp. 531.

— Intellectuals.

ALATAS (SYED HUSSEIN) Intellectuals in developing societies. London, 1977. pp. 130. *bibliog.*

— International business enterprises.

The MULTINATIONAL corporation and social change; edited by David E. Apter, Louis Wolf Goodman. New York, 1976. pp. 234. *Papers presented at a conference held in 1974 under the auspices of the Institution for Social and Policy Studies, Yale University.*

LALL (SANJAYA) and STREETEN (PAUL PATRICK) Foreign investment, transnationals and developing countries. London, 1977. pp. 280. *bibliog.*

— Investments, British.

U.K. Ministry of Overseas Development. 1976. Official support for pre-investment studies in developing countries. [London], 1976. pp. 8.

— Investments, Foreign.

SCHMITT (MATTHIAS) Partnerschaft mit Entwicklungsländern. Stuttgart-Degerloch, [1960]. pp. 112.

— Investments, Swiss.

ZIEGLER (JEAN) Une Suisse au-dessus de tout soupçon. Paris, [1976]. pp. 182.

— Irrigation.

ARID land irrigation in developing countries: environmental problems and effects; based on the international symposium, 16-21 February 1976, Alexandria, Egypt; editor E. Barton Worthington. Oxford, [1977]. pp. 463.

— Labour supply.

SHARP (ROBIN) Whose right to work?: international aspects of employment in Britain and the developing countries and their implications for UK policy. London, [1976]. pp. 49. *bibliog. (Oxfam. Public Affairs Unit. Oxfam Public Affairs Reports. 2)*

CONNELL (JOHN) 1946- , and LIPTON (MICHAEL) Assessing village labour situations in developing countries;... prepared for the International Labour Office within the framework of the World Employment Programme. Delhi, 1977. pp. 180. *bibliog.*

— — Mathematical models.

ELLIOTT (JAMES A.M.) Will raising wages in the high-wage sector increase total employment?: a critique of the Stewart-Weeks view on the relationship between wage changes and unemployment in LDCs. Ann Arbor, 1976. pp. 18, 13, 6. *(Michigan University. Center for Research on Economic Development. Discussion Papers. No.55)*

— Land settlement.

SAI (FRED T.) Health, nutrition and population in human settlements. London, 1977. pp. 31. *bibliog. (International Planned Parenthood Federation. Occasional Essays. No. 5.)*

— Land tenure.

GRIFFIN (KEITH) Land concentration and rural poverty. London, 1976. pp. 303.

— Leather industry and trade.

NAYUDAMMA (Y.) The growth of the leather industry in developing countries: problems and prospects. (ID/93) (ID/WG. 79/5/Rev. 1). New York, United Nations, 1972. pp. 31.

— Manufactures.

MORRISON (THOMAS K.) Manufactured exports from developing countries. New York, [1976]. pp. 108. *bibliog.*

— Mass media.

SEMINAR ON MOTIVATION, INFORMATION AND COMMUNICATION FOR DEVELOPMENT IN AFRICAN AND ASIAN COUNTRIES, IBADAN, 1974. Seminar on motivation, information and communication for development in African and Asian countries, Ibadan, Nigeria, 1-9 July, 1974; [organized by] the International Broadcast Institute in co-operation with the Friedrich Naumann Stiftung [and] the Nigerian Broadcasting Corporation. London, [1975]. pp. 71.

COMMUNICATIONS policy for national development: a comparative perspective; edited by Majid Teheranian, [and others]. London, 1977. pp. 286. *Studies arising out of the Prospective Planning Project of National Iranian Radio and Television.*

— Medical economics.

SORKIN (ALAN L.) Health economics in developing countries. Lexington, Mass., [1976]. pp. 200.

HELLER (PETER S.) Issues in the allocation of resources in the health sector of developing countries. Ann Arbor, 1977. pp. 34. *bibliog. (Michigan University. Center for Research on Economic Development. Discussion Papers. No. 67)*

— Mineral industries.

LEIPZIGER (DANNY M.) and MUDGE (JAMES L.) Seabed mineral resources and the economic interests of developing countries. Cambridge, Mass., [1976]. pp. 240. *bibliog.*

— Money.

MONEY and finance in economic growth and development: essays in honour of Edward S. Shaw;...edited by Ronald I. McKinnon. New York, [1976]. pp. 339. *bibliogs. Proceedings of the conference held at Stanford University in April 1974, under the auspices of the Center for Research in Economic Growth.*

WAGNER (ANTONIN) Verwaltete Währung: Krise und Reform des internationalen Währungssystems unter besonderer Berücksichtigung der Entwicklungsländer. Bern, [1977]. pp. 262. *bibliogs. (Zürich. Universität. Institut für Schweizerisches Bankwesen. Bankwirtschaftliche Forschungen. Band 39)*

— Nutrition.

SAI (FRED T.) Food, population and politics. London, 1977. pp. 35. *bibliog. (International Planned Parenthood Federation. Occasional Essays. No. 3)*

SAI (FRED T.) Health, nutrition and population in human settlements. London, 1977. pp. 31. *bibliog. (International Planned Parenthood Federation. Occasional Essays. No. 5.)*

— Politics and government.

RAJ (KAKKADAN NANDANATH) The politics and economies of "intermediate regimes". Poona, [1973?]. pp. 22. *(Gokhale Institute of Politics and Economics. R. R. Kale Memorial Lectures. 1973)*

FIDEL (KENNETH) ed. Militarism in developing countries. New Brunswick, [1975]. pp. 319.

CIVILIAN control of the military: theory and cases from developing countries; edited by Claude E. Welch. Albany, 1976. pp. 337. *bibliogs. Based on papers presented at a conference in October 1974.*

FREEDOM and constraint: a memorial tribute to Max Gluckman; edited by Myron J. Aronoff. Assen, 1976. pp. 179. *bibliogs.*

GAMER (ROBERT E.) The developing nations: a comparative perspective. Boston, Mass., [1976]. pp. 393.

BHUTTO (ZULFIKAR ALI) The third world: new directions. London, 1977. pp. 144.

NORDLINGER (ERIC A.) Soldiers in politics: military coups and governments. Englewood Cliffs, [1977]. pp. 224. *bibliog.*

ROY (MAURICE PIERRE) Les régimes politiques du tiers monde. Paris, 1977. pp. 615. *bibliog.*

— Poor.

EPSTEIN (TRUDE SCARLETT) and JACKSON (DARRELL) eds. The paradox of poverty: socio-economic aspects of population growth. Delhi, 1975. pp. 127. *bibliog.*

GRIFFIN (KEITH) Land concentration and rural poverty. London, 1976. pp. 303.

HAQ (MAHBUS UL) The poverty curtain: choices for the third world. New York, 1976. pp. 247. *bibliog.*

LIPTON (MICHAEL) Why poor people stay poor: a study of urban bias in world development. London, 1977. pp. 467. *bibliog.*

— Population.

EPSTEIN (TRUDE SCARLETT) and JACKSON (DARRELL) eds. The paradox of poverty: socio-economic aspects of population growth. Delhi, 1975. pp. 127. *bibliog.*

RIDKER (RONALD GENE) ed. Population and development: the search for selective interventions. Baltimore, [1976]. pp. 465. *bibliog.*

The FEASIBILITY of fertility planning: micro perspectives: edited by T. Scarlett Epstein and Darrell Jackson. Oxford, 1977. pp. 244. *bibliog. Based on papers of a conference held at the Institute of Development Studies, University of Sussex, 1975.*

SAI (FRED T.) Health, nutrition and population in human settlements. London, 1977. pp. 31. *bibliog. (International Planned Parenthood Federation. Occasional Essays. No. 5.)*

SAI (FRED T.) Population and national development: the dilemma of developing countries. London, 1977. pp. 30. *(International Planned Parenthood Federation. Occasional Essays. No. 2)*

WANDER (HILDE) Bevölkerungswachstum und Konsumstruktur in Entwicklungsländern: Fakten, Zusammenhänge und politische Implikationen. Tübingen, [1977]. pp. 117. *bibliog. (Kiel. Universität. Institut für Weltwirtschaft. Kieler Studien. 149)*

— — Statistics.

PRAKASH (VED) and SPILLANE (JAMES J.) An economic framework for investment planning in housing and urban infrastructure. (ST/ECA/186). New York, United Nations, 1973. pp. 47.

— Publishers and publishing.

ALTBACH (PHILIP G.) Publishing in India: an analysis. Delhi, 1975. pp. 115. *bibliog.*

— Raw materials.

CHANGING resource problems of the fourth world; Ronald G. Ridker, editor. Washington, D.C., 1976. pp. 157. *(Resources for the Future, Inc. Working Papers. PD-1)*

KEBSCHULL (DIETRICH) and others. Das integrierte Rohstoffprogramm: Prüfung entwicklungspolitischer Ansätze im Rohstoffvorschlag der UNCTAD. Hamburg, 1977. pp. 401. *bibliog. (Hamburg. Hamburgisches Welt-Wirtschafts-Archiv. Veröffentlichungen)*

— Regional planning.

KUPRIANOV (ALEXEI B.) Developing countries: internal regional disproportions in growing economies. Budapest, 1976. pp. 63. *(Magyar Tudományos Akadémia. Világgazdasági Kutató Intézet. Studies on Developing Countries. No 85)*

— Research and development contracts.

NATIONAL ACADEMY OF SCIENCES. Office of the Foreign Secretary. Board on Science and Technology for International Development. U.S. international firms and R, D and E in developing countries; a report of an ad hoc panel of the board, etc. Washington, 1973. pp. 73.

— Revolutionists.

CHALIAND (GERARD) Revolution in the third world: myths and prospects. Hassocks, 1977. pp. 195.

— Rural conditions.

A REVIEW of rural co-ooperation in developing areas: papers on Latin America, Asia and Africa; by T.F. Carroll [and others]. Geneva, United Nations Research Institute for Social Development, 1969. pp. 348. *bibliog. (Rural Institutions and Planned Change. Vol.1)*

— Rural-urban migration.

MIGRATION from rural areas: the evidence from village studies; by John Connell [and others]; a study prepared for the International Labour Office...at the Institute of Development Studies, University of Sussex, etc. Delhi, 1976. pp. 228. *bibliog.*

— Social classes.

RAJ (KAKKADAN NANDANATH) The politics and economies of "intermediate regimes". Poona, [1973?]. pp. 22. *(Gokhale Institute of Politics and Economics. R. R. Kale Memorial Lectures. 1973)*

— Social conditions.

GOODY (JOHN RANKINE) Production and reproduction: a comparative study of the domestic domain. Cambridge, 1976. pp. 157. *bibliog.*

— Social conflict.

STEWART (FRANCES) A note on social cost-benefit analysis and class conflict in LDCs. Oxford, 1975. pp. 8. *bibliog. (Oxford. University. Institute of Commonwealth Studies. Reprint Series. No. 75E) (Repr. from World Development, vol.3, no.1, January 1975)*

— Social policy.

RODRIGUEZ MARIÑO (TOMAS) El proceso de las decisiones publicas. Bogota, 1973. pp. 152. *bibliog.*

STEWART (FRANCES) A note on social cost-benefit analysis and class conflict in LDCs. Oxford, 1975. pp. 8. *bibliog. (Oxford. University. Institute of Commonwealth Studies. Reprint Series. No. 75E) (Repr. from World Development, vol.3, no.1, January 1975)*

LONG (NORMAN) An introduction to the sociology of rural development. London, 1977. pp. 221. *bibliog.*

— Social service.

DESHMUKH (DURGABAI) Social welfare and economic development; two lectures delivered at the Asian Institute for Economic Development and Planning, Bangkok, on February 26 and 28, 1964. [Bangkok?, 1964?]. 1 vol. (various pagings).

— Sugar — Manufacture and refining.

HAGELBERG (G.B.) Structural and institutional aspects of the sugar industry in developing countries. Berlin, 1976. pp. 69. *bibliog. (Berlin. Technische Universität Berlin-Charlottenburg. Institut für Zuckerindustrie. Forschungsberichte. 5)*

— Sugar growing.

HAGELBERG (G.B.) Structural and institutional aspects of the sugar industry in developing countries. Berlin, 1976. pp. 69. *bibliog. (Berlin. Technische Universität Berlin-Charlottenburg. Institut für Zuckerindustrie. Forschungsberichte. 5)*

— Tariffs.

BALASSA (BELA A.) Policy reform in developing countries. Oxford, 1977. pp. 175.

— Technology.

STEWART (FRANCES) Technology and underdevelopment. London, 1977. pp. 303. *bibliog.*

— Trade unions.

WORLD FEDERATION OF TRADE UNIONS. Developing countries: the public sector and the role of the trade unions. [Prague, 1976]. pp. 35.

— Traffic estimation.

HOWE (J.D.G.F.) and TENNANT (B.S.) Forecasting rural road travel in developing countries from studies of land use. Crowthorne, 1977. pp. 33. *bibliog. (U.K. Transport and Road Research Laboratory. Reports. LR 754)*

— Urbanization.

VALUES and development: appraising Asian experience; edited by Harold Lasswell [and others]. Cambridge, Mass., [1976]. pp. 291. *(Massachusetts Institute of Technology. Studies in Comparative Politics) Papers from the 1971-1972 meetings of a continuing seminar sponsored by the South East Asia Development Advisory Group.*

— Villages.

CONNELL (JOHN) 1946- , and LIPTON (MICHAEL) Assessing village labour situations in developing countries;... prepared for the International Labour Office within the framework of the World Employment Programme. Delhi, 1977. pp. 180. *bibliog.*

— Wages — Mathematical models.

ELLIOTT (JAMES A.M.) Will raising wages in the high-wage sector increase total employment?: a critique of the Stewart-Weeks view on the relationship between wage changes and unemployment in LDCs. Ann Arbor, 1976. pp. 18, 13, 6. *(Michigan University. Center for Research on Economic Development. Discussion Papers. No.55)*

— — Minimun wage.

SEVERIN (JOERG) Mindestlohnregelungen in Entwicklungsländern: das Beispiel Indien. Hamburg, 1975. pp. 383. *bibliog. Dissertation - Universität Hamburg.*

— Water resources development.

SAUNDERS (ROBERT J.) and WARFORD (JEREMY J.) Village water supply: economics and policy in the developing world. Baltimore, 1976. pp. 279. *bibliog. (International Bank for Reconstruction and Development. World Bank Research Publications)*

— Water supply.

SAUNDERS (ROBERT J.) and WARFORD (JEREMY J.) Village water supply: economics and policy in the developing world. Baltimore, 1976. pp. 279. *bibliog. (International Bank for Reconstruction and Development. World Bank Research Publications)*

— Women's employment.

SEMINAR ON WOMEN IN DEVELOPMENT, MEXICO, 1975. Women and world development: with an annotated bibliography; edited by Irene Tinker [and others]. New York, 1976. pp. 382. *Papers of the seminar convened and co-sponsored by the American Association for the Advancement of Science.*

— Wood-using industries.

HOCHART (BERNARD) Wood as a packaging material in the developing countries. (ID/72). New York, United Nations, 1972. pp. 111. *bibliog.*

UNDERGROUND LITERATURE

— Russia.

AL'MANAKH samizdata: nepodtsenzuraia mysl ' v SSSR. No.1. Amsterdam, 1974. pp. 112. *With English table of contents.*

HARVARD UNIVERSITY. Library. Houghton Library. Russian revolutionary literature collection. New Haven, Conn., 1976. Microfilm: 47 reels.

— — Bibliography.

HARVARD UNIVERSITY. Library. Houghton Library. Russian revolutionary literature collection, Houghton Library, Harvard University: a descriptive guide and key to the collection on microfilm; [compiled by Kenneth E. Carpenter]. New Haven, Conn., 1976. pp. x, 220.

— — Russia (RSFSR).

PLAMENNOE bol'shevistskoe slovo: podpol'naia literatura v Iaroslavskoi gubernii, 1902-1917 gg. Iaroslavl', 1975. pp. 303.

— United Kingdom — Bibliography.

SPIERS (JOHN) compiler. The underground and alternative press in Britain: a bibliographical guide with historical notes. Hassocks, 1974. pp. 77.

UNEMPLOYED.

FITOUSSI (JEAN PAUL) Inflation, équilibre et chômage. Paris, [1973]. pp. 294,(95). bibliog.

VULIĆ-ŠMALC (ELVIRA) Utjecaj tehnoloških transformacija na zapošljavanje kadrova. Zagreb, 1975. pp. 82. bibliog. With brief English summary.

MALINVAUD (EDMOND) The theory of unemployment reconsidered. Oxford, [1977]. pp. 128. (Yrjö Jahnssonin Säätio. Yrjö Jahnsson Lectures. 1977)

— Africa, Subsaharan.

MBITHI (PHILIP M.) Youth employment problems: a discussion of policy issues with special reference to the African experience. [London], Commonwealth Secretariat, [1975]. pp. 27. (Commonwealth Youth Programme. Occasional Papers. Employment Series. 2).

— America, Latin.

HELLINGER (DOUGLAS A.) and HELLINGER (STEPHEN H.) Unemployment and the multinationals: a strategy for technological change in Latin America. Port Washington, N.Y., 1976. pp. 158. bibliog.

— France.

CHÔMAGE: la jeunesse accuse; états généraux des comités CGT de jeunes sans emploi, Paris, le 11 mars 1976. Paris, [1976]. pp. 159.

— — Burgundy.

HUMBERT (ANNIE) Le chômage féminin en Bourgogne. Dijon, Echelon Régional de l'Emploi de Dijon, 1976. fo. 22.

— Germany.

HAHN (LUCIEN ALBERT) Ist Arbeitslosigkeit unvermeidlich? Berlin, 1930. pp. 53. (Magazin der Wirtschaft. Schriften. 2)

NAPHTALI (FRITZ) Wirtschaftskrise und Arbeitslosigkeit, volkstümlich dargestellt. Berlin, 1930. pp. 32.

SACK (RUDOLF) Muss Arbeitslosigkeit Dauerzustand für Deutschland bleiben?: Wege zu neuer Wirtschaftsgestaltung. Frankfurt am Main, 1931. pp. 12.

LATURNER (SYBILLE) and SCHOEN (BERNARD) eds. Jugendarbeitslosigkeit: Materialien und Analysen zu einem neuen Problem. Reinbek bei Hamburg, 1975 repr. 1976. pp. 217. bibliog.

BALKENHOL (BERND) Armut und Arbeitslosigkeit in der Industrialisierung: dargestellt am Beispiel Düsseldorfs, 1850-1900. Düsseldorf, 1976. pp. 143. bibliog. (Düsseldorfer Geschichtsverein. Studien zur Düsseldorfer Wirtschaftsgeschichte. Heft 3)

EGLE (FRANZ) and others. Verdeckte Arbeitslosigkeit: Probleme der Messung in der Bundesrepublik. Göttingen, [1976]. pp. 221. bibliog. (Kommission für Wirtschaftlichen und Sozialen Wandel. Schriften. 77)

— India.

INDIA. Committee on Unemployment. 1974. Report; [B. Bhagavati, chairman]. [Delhi, 1974]. pp. 410.

INDIA. Panel on the Assessment of the Extent of Unemployment and Under Employment. 1975. Report...November, 1972; [Ashok Mitra, chairman]. [Delhi, 1975]. pp. 577.

— Morocco.

EMPLOYMENT problems and policies in developing countries: the case of Morocco; edited by Willy van Rijckeghem. Rotterdam, 1976. pp. 211. Papers of a conference held March 28th-30th, 1974, in the Free University of Brussels.

— Netherlands — Mathematical models.

BARTELS (CORNELIS P.) and others. The composition of and associations between regional unemployment series: an application of some time-series methods. Groningen, 1977. pp. 25. (Groningen. Rijksuniversiteit. Economisch Instituut. Onderzoekmemoranda. Nr. 32) Paper presented at the colloquium on Séries chronologiques: approaches fréquentielle et temporelle held in Brussels in 1977.

— United Kingdom.

CONSUMERS' ASSOCIATION. Dismissal, redundancy and job hunting. London, [1976]. pp. 137.

COUNTER INFORMATION SERVICES and TRANSNATIONAL INSTITUTE. Who's next for the chop?: the essential facts on unemployment. London, [1976]. pp. 33. bibliog. (Counter Information Services. Anti-Reports. No. 14)

HILL (MICHAEL J.) and STEVENSON (OLIVE) From the general to the specific. [Oxford, 1976]. pp. 120. bibliog.

YOUNG SOCIALISTS. National Committee. Unemployment and the crisis of capitalism; (for presentation to the 15th annual conference of the Labour Party Young Socialists, Blackpool, April 17th-19th 1976). [London, 1976]. pp. 16.

The CONSCRIPT army: a study of Britain's unemployed; edited by Frank Field. London, 1977. pp. 160. bibliog.

HARVEY (ROBERT) Journalist. Unemployed sheep and goats. London, [1977]. pp. 10.

NORTH TYNESIDE TRADES COUNCIL. Unemployment and young workers in North Tyneside. [North Shields], North Tyneside Community Development Project, 1977. pp. 87.

— — Wales.

GLAMORGAN-GLYNCORRWG COMMUNITY DEVELOPMENT PROJECT. Transport and the younger unemployed. [Port Talbot], 1973. pp. 14.

— United States.

The VOCATIONAL rehabilitation of public assistance recipients: a national survey of clients served and rehabilitation outcomes; [by] John E. Muthard [and others]. Gainesville, Fla., 1976. pp. 277. bibliog.

UNEMPLOYMENT, TECHNOLOGICAL.

ROUND-TABLE DISCUSSION ON THE MANPOWER PROBLEMS ASSOCIATED WITH THE INTRODUCTION OF AUTOMATION AND ADVANCED TECHNOLOGY IN DEVELOPING COUNTRIES, GENEVA, 1970. Automation in developing countries. Geneva, International Labour Office, 1972. pp. 246.

UNFAIR LABOUR PRACTICES

— Germany.

BAROTH (HANS DIETER) In unseren Betrieben: ein Schwarzbuch über deutsche Betriebe. Köln, [1977]. pp. 168.

UNIDAD POPULAR.

MISTRAL (CARLOS) Chile: del triunfo popular al golpe fascista; economia y politica de la Unidad Popular. Mexico, 1974. pp. 167.

CASTELLS (MANUEL) La lucha de clases en Chile. [Buenos Aires], 1974 [or rather 1975]. pp. 435.

ECONOMIA politica en la Unidad Popular: materiales de los Cuadernos de la Realidad Nacional, 1970-1973; presentacion, Manuel Antonio Garreton. Barcelona, 1975. pp. 341.

RODRIGUEZ (FELIPE) Critica de la Unidad Popular. Barcelona, [1975]. pp. 251. bibliog.

CUSACK (DAVID F.) Revolution and reaction: the internal dynamics of conflict and confrontation in Chile. Denver, [1977]. pp. 147. (Denver. University. Social Science Foundation and Graduate School of International Studies. Monograph Series in World Affairs. vol. 14, no. 3)

UNION CIVICA RADICAL.

CAMBRIDGE. University. Centre of Latin American Studies. Working Papers. No. 7. The rise of the Argentine Radical Party (the Union Civica Radical), 1891-1916; [by David Rock]. Cambridge, [1973]. fo. 50. Photocopy.

UNION DES POPULATIONS DU CAMEROUN.

JOSEPH (RICHARD A.) Radical nationalism in Cameroun: social origins of the U.P.C. rebellion. Oxford, 1977. pp. 383. bibliog.

UNIT TRAINS.

See RAILWAYS — Train load.

UNITED ARAB EMIRATES.

TUR (JEAN JACQUES L.) Les émirats du golfe Arabe: le Koweït, Bahreïn, Qatar et les Emirats Arabes Unis. [Paris, 1976]. pp. 127. bibliog.

UNITED KINGDOM.

COLBOURNE (MAURICE DALE) America and Britain: a mutual introduction with special reference to the British Empire. London, 1943. pp. 230.

— Administrative and political divisions.

GRAHAM (THOMAS) Printer. An account of the state of the right of election of members of Parliament in the several counties, cities, and boroughs of the United Kingdom: strongly demonstrating the necessity for a reform in the representation of the people in the House of Commons. London, the Author. 1818. pp. 24.

— Air force.

HYDE (HARFORD MONTGOMERY) British air policy between the wars, 1918-1939. London, [1976]. pp. 539. bibliog.

— — History.

FRIDENSON (PATRICK) and LECUIR (JEAN) La France et la Grande-Bretagne face aux problèmes aériens, 1935-mai 1940. Vincennes, Service Historique de l'Armée de l'Air, 1976. pp. 208.

— Appropriations and expenditures.

NORTHERN REGION STRATEGY TEAM. Public expenditure in the northern region and other British regions, 1969/70-1973/74; (draft). Newcastle upon Tyne, 1976. pp. 229. (Technical Reports. No. 12)

RED WEEKLY. Pamphlets. The socialist challenge to Labour's cuts. London, [1976]. pp. 30.

DU CANN (EDWARD) Parliament and the purse strings: how to bring public expenditure under Parliamentary control. London, 1977. pp. 24. (Conservative Political Centre. [Publications]. No. 604)

— Army — History.

HARRIES-JENKINS (GWYN) The army in Victorian society. London, 1977. pp. 320.

— — Social services.

U.K. Army Welfare Inquiry Committee. 1976. Report...; chairman: J.C. Spencer. London, 1976. pp. 220.

— Census.

O'DELL (ALAN) and PARKER (JAMES) M.A., Writer on Housing. The use of census data to identify and describe housing stress. Watford, [1977]. pp. 33. (Building Research Establishment [U.K.]. Current Papers. 77/6)

U.K. Office of Population Censuses and Surveys. 1977. Guide to census reports, Great Britain, 1801-1966. London, 1977. pp. 279.

— — 1971.

U.K. Census, 1971. Parliamentary constituency tables, as defined by the Representation of the People Act 1948, as amended up to and including June 1970: England: [100 per cent population and households]. Titchfield, 1973. 2 vols.

U.K. Census, 1971. Parliamentary constituency tables, as defined by the Representation of the People Act 1948, as amended up to and including June 1970: Wales: [100 per cent population and households]. Titchfield, 1973. 1 pamphlet (unfoliated).

U.K. Census, 1971. Parliamentary constituency tables, as defined by the Representation of the People Act 1948, as at February 1974: England: [10 per cent sample figures]. Titchfield, 1974. 2 pts.

U.K. Census, 1971. Parliamentary constituency tables, as defined by the Representation of the People Act 1948, as at February 1974: England: [100 per cent population and households]. Titchfield, 1974. 2 pts. (in 1 vol.).

U.K. Census, 1971. Parliamentary constituency tables, as defined by the Representation of the People Act 1948, as at February 1974: Wales: [10 per cent sample figures]. Titchfield, 1974. pp. 72.

U.K. Census, 1971. Parliamentary constituency tables as defined by the Representation of the People Act 1948, as at February 1974: Wales: [100 per cent population and households]. Titchfield, 1974. pp. 36.

U.K. Department of the Environment. 1975. Study of the inner areas of conurbations: supplement: analysis of 1971 census indicators. [London], 1975. pp. 72.

— Civilization.

A TONIC to the nation: the Festival of Britain, 1951; (edited by Mary Banham and Bevis Hillier); with a prologue by Roy Strong. London, [1976]. pp. 200.

— Commerce.

SMITH (THOMAS) Editor of the London Mercantile Journal. Import duties considered in reference to the present state of the trade of Great Britain and her possessions, with the tables prepared by order of the Select Committee thereon. London, Hopcraft, 1841. pp. 54.

ADVISORY COUNCIL FOR AGRICULTURE AND HORTICULTURE IN ENGLAND AND WALES. Report of an inquiry into agricultural exports. [London], 1976. pp. 61.

HANSISCHES SYMPOSION, 1974. Frühformen englisch-deutscher Handelspartnerschaft: Referate und Diskussionen des Hansischen Symposions...in London vom 9. bis 11. September 1974;...bearbeitet von Klaus Friedland. Köln, 1976. pp. 120. (Hansischer Geschichtsverein. Quellen und Darstellungen zur Hansischen Geschichte. Neue Folge. Band 23) In German or English.

POPULATION and marketing: two studies in the history of the south-west; edited by Walter Minchinton. Exeter, 1976. pp. 139. (Exeter University. Department of Economic History. Exeter Papers in Economic History. No. 11). Papers of two seminars held at Dartington.

U.K. Central Office of Information. Reference Division. 1976. Britain's overseas trade and payments. rev. ed. London, 1976. pp. 24. bibliog.

CHARTRES (J.A.) Internal trade in England, 1500-1700. London, 1977. pp. 79. bibliog. (Economic History Society. Studies in Economic and Social History)

CROWHURST (PATRICK) The defence of British trade, 1689-1815. Folkestone, 1977. pp. 281. bibliog.

LLOYD (TERENCE H.) The English wool trade in the middle ages. Cambridge, 1977. pp. 351. bibliog.

NATIONAL ECONOMIC DEVELOPMENT OFFICE. International price competitiveness, non-price factors and export performance. London, 1977. pp. 45. bibliog.

NATIONAL ECONOMIC DEVELOPMENT OFFICE. A study of UK nationalised industries: background paper 7: exports and imports. London, 1977. pp. 27.

— — Statistics.

OVERSEAS TRADE STATISTICS OF THE UNITED KINGDOM; [pd. by] Department of Trade. a., 1976 (1st)- London.

STATISTICS OF TRADE THROUGH UNITED KINGDOM PORTS; [pd. by] Customs and Excise Department. q., 1976 (1st)- London.

STATISTICS OF TRADE THROUGH UNITED KINGDOM PORTS; [pd.by] Customs and Excise Department. a., 1976(1st)- London.

— Commercial policy.

MANLEY (THOMAS) 1628-1690. A discourse shewing that the exportation of wooll is destructive to this kingdom; wherein is also shewed the absolute necessity of promoting our woollen manufacture, and moderating the importation of some commodities, etc. London, Crouch, 1677. pp. (iv), 12.

ON how to cope with Britain's trade position: by Hugh Corbet [and others]. London, 1977. pp. 72. (Trade Policy Research Centre. Thames Essays. No. 8)

— Constitution.

TRENAMAN (NANCY KATHLEEN) Some administrative consequences of the adoption of the Kilbrandon Commission recommendations: a personal view; (transcript of lecture given on 2 July 1974). [London], Civil Service College, [1974]. pp. 22. (Lectures on Some Management Problems in the Civil Service. No. 7)

HOGG (QUINTON McGAREL) Baron Hailsham. Elective dictatorship. London, 1976. pp. 17. (British Broadcasting Corporation. Richard Dimbleby Lectures. 1976)

U.K. Office of the Lord President of the Council. 1976. Devolution: the English dimension: a consultative document. London, 1976. pp. 22.

WILSON (Sir HAROLD) The governance of Britain. London, 1976. pp. 219.

JOHNSON (NEVIL) In search of the constitution: reflections on state and society in Britain. Oxford, 1977. pp. 239.

MINOGUE (MARTIN) ed. Documents on contemporary British government. Cambridge, 1977. 2 vols. bibliogs.

U.K. Central Office of Information. Reference Division. Reference Pamphlets. 40. The central government of Britain. 9th ed. London, 1977. pp. 37. bibliog.

— Constitutional law.

WILSON (GEOFFREY PHILIP) Cases and materials on constitutional and administrative law. 2nd ed. Cambridge, 1976. pp. 803.

DE SMITH (STANLEY ALEXANDER) Constitutional and administrative law; third edition...revised by Harry Street [and others]. Harmondsworth, 1977. pp. 729.

— Defences.

DEFENCE cuts and Labour's industrial strategy; (based on the proceedings of a delegate conference...called by the Labour Committee of the Campaign for Nuclear Disarmament...London.. .1976). London, [1976]. pp. 33. bibliog.

GREENWOOD (DAVID E.) The employment consequences of reduced defence spending. Aberdeen, 1976. pp. 34. (Aberdeen. University. Department of Political Economy. Aberdeen Studies in Defence Economics. No. 8)

SECOND WORLD DEFENCE. Pamphlets. No. 1. The superpowers, the threat of war and the British working class. London, 1976. pp. 23.

BARBER (RICHARD) Conservative, and STAFFORD (IAN) Detente or defence: the bogus dilemma. London, [1977]. pp. 16.

SHAY (ROBERT PAUL) British rearmament in the thirties: politics and profits. Princeton, N.J., [1977]. pp. 315. bibliog.

— Description and travel.

MADOX (RICHARD) An Elizabethan in 1582: the diary of Richard Madox, Fellow of All Souls; [edited] by Elizabeth Story Donno. London, 1976. pp. 365. (Hakluyt Society. Works. 2nd Series. No. 147)

— Diplomatic and consular service.

MOORHOUSE (GEOFFREY) The diplomats: the Foreign Office today. London, 1977. pp. 405. bibliog.

U.K. Central Policy Review Staff. 1977. Review of overseas representation: report. London, 1977. pp. 442.

— Directories — Bibliography.

CURRENT British directories: a guide to the directories published in Great Britain, Ireland, the British Commonwealth and South Africa; edited by I.G. Anderson. 8th ed. Beckenham, 1977. pp. 430.

— Economic conditions.

PHILIPS (ERASMUS) Misellaneous works consisting of essays political and moral. London, printed for Mr. Waller, 1751. pp. 508.

LOWE (JOSEPH) The present state of England in regard to agriculture, trade, and finance; with a comparison of the prospects of England and France. London, printed for Longman, etc. 1822. pp. xxiv, 352, 130.

SOCIETY OF FRIENDS. Social Responsibility Council. The national economic situation: a Quaker view. [London, 1974]. pp. 14.

EAST MIDLANDS ECONOMIC PLANNING COUNCIL. East midlands: a forward economic look. [Nottingham, 1976]. pp. 85.

NATIONAL ECONOMIC DEVELOPMENT OFFICE. Recent developments in the U.K. and world economy. [London], 1976. pp. 57.

NORTH WEST INDUSTRIAL DEVELOPMENT ASSOCIATION. North West England...: the facts. Manchester, [1976?]. pp. 23.

NORTHERN REGION STRATEGY TEAM. Rural development in the northern region. Newcastle upon Tyne, 1976. pp. (152). (Technical Reports. No. 16)

PREST (ALAN RICHMOND) and COPPOCK (DENNIS JOHN) eds. The UK economy: a manual of applied economics. 6th ed. London, 1976. pp. 322. bibliog.

WOOD (PETER A.) The West Midlands;...with contributions on the Potteries, coal and power by A. Moyes. Newton Abbot, [1976]. pp. 263.

ZWEIG (FERDYNAND) The new acquisitive society. Chichester, 1976. pp. 144.

BRITAIN'S crisis in sociological perspective; papers from a one day conference held on 26 June, 1976 under the auspices of the Department of Sociology, University of Reading...; edited by M.B. Hamilton and K.G. Robertson. Reading, [1977?]. pp. 75.

BRITISH ASSOCIATION FOR THE ADVANCEMENT OF SCIENCE. Section F. Meeting, 1976. Structure, system and economic policy; proceedings...held at the University of Lancaster 1-8 September 1976; edited by Wassily Leontief. Cambridge, 1977. pp. 223. *bibliogs.*

CASE studies in macroeconomics; edited by Peter Maunder; [by] John Day [and others]. London, 1977. pp. 86. *bibliogs.* (*Economics Association. Case Studies in Economic Analysis. 5*)

EICHTHAL (GUSTAVE D') A French sociologist looks at Britain: Gustave d'Eichthal and British society in 1828; translated and edited by Barrie M. Ratcliffe and W.H. Chaloner. Manchester, [1977]. pp. 169. (*Manchester. University. Faculty of Arts. Publications. No. 22*)

HOUSE (JOHN WILLIAM) ed. The U.K. space: resources, environment and the future. 2nd ed. London, 1977. pp. 528. *bibliogs.*

PRINGLE (ROBIN) The growth merchants: economic consequences of wishful thinking. London, 1977. pp. 82. *bibliog.*

SANDFORD (CEDRIC T.) Social economics. London, 1977. pp. 286. *bibliog.*

— — Mathematical models.

ECONOMIC structure and policy with applications to the British economy; editor Terence S. Barker. London, 1976. pp. 421. *bibliog.* (*Cambridge. University. Department of Applied Economics. Cambridge Studies in Applied Econometrics. 2*)

A MODEL of output, employment, wages and prices in the U.K.; [by] I.F. Pearce [and others]. Cambridge, 1976. pp. 172. *bibliog.*

U.K. Treasury. Macroeconomic model: technical manual. a., 1977 (3rd)- London.

— — Statistics.

AIMS FOR FREEDOM AND ENTERPRISE. Economic facts for business spokesmen. London, 1976. pp. 24.

— Economic history.

HARVEY (JOHN H.) Mediaeval craftsmen. London, 1975. pp. 231. *bibliog.*

MEE (GRAHAM) Aristocratic enterprise: the Fitzwilliam industrial undertakings, 1795-1857. Glasgow, 1975. pp. 222.

GORDON (BARRY J.) Political economy in Parliament, 1819-1823. London, 1976. pp. 246.

HOLDERNESS (B.A.) Pre-industrial England: economy and society, 1500-1750. London, 1976. pp. 244. *bibliogs.*

HOSKINS (WILLIAM GEORGE) The age of plunder: King Henry's England, 1500-1547. London, 1976. pp. 262. *bibliog.*

KNOX (FRANCIS) Governments and growth. Farnborough, Hants., [1976]. pp. 142.

NORTHERN REGION STRATEGY TEAM. Settlement patterns and policies in the northern region. Newcastle upon Tyne, 1976. pp. 84. (*Technical Reports. No. 14*)

THOMIS (MALCOLM I.) Responses to industrialisation: the British experience, 1780- 1850. Newton Abbot, 1976. pp. 194.

COLEMAN (DONALD CUTHBERT) The economy of England, 1450-1750. London, 1977. pp. 223. *bibliog.*

EDWARDIAN monetary affairs, 1279-1344: a symposium held in Oxford, August 1976; edited by N.J. Mayhew. Oxford, 1977. pp. 186. *bibliog.* (*British Archaeological Reports. 36*)

HOWSON (SUSAN) and WINCH (DONALD NORMAN) The Economic Advisory Council, 1930-1939: a study in economic advice during depression and recovery. Cambridge, 1977. pp. 424. *bibliog.*

JACK (SYBIL M.) Trade and industry in Tudor and Stuart England. London, 1977. pp. 200. *bibliogs. With selected documents.*

PAWSON (ERIC) Transport and economy: the turnpike roads of eighteenth century Britain. London, 1977. pp. 407. *bibliog.*

— Economic policy.

LOWE (JOSEPH) The present state of England in regard to agriculture, trade, and finance; with a comparison of the prospects of England and France. London, printed for Longman, etc. 1822. pp. xxiv, 352, 130.

MIDLANDS TOMORROW; issued by West Midlands Economic Planning Council. irreg., 1968 (no.1)- Birmingham.

CAMBRIDGE POLITICAL ECONOMY GROUP. Britain's economic crisis; by...Michael Ellman [and others]. Nottingham, [1974]. pp. 38. (*Spokesman, The. Pamphlets. No. 44*)

MOSER (Sir CLAUS ADOLF) Statistics and economic policy. [Reading, 1974]. pp. 31. (*Reading. University. Mercantile Credit Lectures. 1973*)

BRUCE-GARDYNE (JOCK) Myths and magic in economic management: an analysis of the evidence given to the House of Commons Expenditure Committee in the summer of 1974 on public expenditure, inflation, and the balance of payments. Chichester, 1976. pp. 48.

BUTTON (K.J.) and GILLINGWATER (DAVID) Case studies in regional economics. London, 1976. pp. 88. (*Economics Association. Case Studies in Economic Analysis. 3*)

CONFEDERATION OF BRITISH INDUSTRY. The road to recovery. London, 1976. pp. 72.

CROSBY (TRAVIS L.) Sir Robert Peel's administration, 1841-1846. Newton Abbot, 1976. pp. 190. *bibliog.*

GORDON (BARRY J.) Political economy in Parliament, 1819-1823. London, 1976. pp. 246.

HARRISON (MARK) The economics of capitalism. London, 1976. pp. 41.

JOSEPH (Sir KEITH SINJOHN) Stranded on the middle ground?: reflections on circumstances and policies. London, 1976. pp. 80.

KNOX (FRANCIS) Governments and growth. Farnborough, Hants., [1976]. pp. 142.

NORTHERN REGION STRATEGY TEAM. Third interim report: main themes of the strategic plan. Newcastle upon Tyne, 1976. pp. 173, (8).

PREST (ALAN RICHMOND) and COPPOCK (DENNIS JOHN) eds. The UK economy: a manual of applied economics. 6th ed. London, 1976. pp. 322. *bibliog.*

TRADES UNION CONGRESS. The social contract 1976-77. London, [1976]. pp. 14.

TRADES UNION CONGRESS. Special Congress, 1976. Report of special trades union congress on the social contract, 1976-77, held in the Central Hall, London, on 16th June 1976. London, [1976]. pp. 48.

YOUNG SOCIALISTS. National Committee. Unemployment and the crisis of capitalism; (for presentation to the 15th annual conference of the Labour Party Young Socialists, Blackpool, April 17th-19th 1976). [London, 1976]. pp. 16.

BOSANQUET (NICHOLAS) Economic strategy: a new social contract. London, 1977. pp. 44. (*Fabian Society. Research Series. [No.] 333*)

BROADBENT (T.A.) Planning and profit in the urban economy. London, 1977. pp. 274. *bibliog.*

CASE studies in macroeconomics; edited by Peter Maunder; [by] John Day [and others]. London, 1977. pp. 86. *bibliogs.* (*Economics Association. Case Studies in Economic Analysis. 5*)

The ECONOMIC system in the U.K.; edited by Derek Morris. Oxford, 1977. pp. 490. *bibliogs. Based on material used at the Oxford University Business Summer School.*

HARRIS (RALPH) and SELDON (ARTHUR) Not from benevolence...: 20 years of economic dissent. London, 1977. pp. 159. (*Institute of Economic Affairs. Hobart Paperbacks. 10*)

HARTLEY (KEITH) Problems of economic policy. London, 1977. pp. 233. *bibliog.*

HOUSE (JOHN WILLIAM) ed. The U.K. space: resources, environment and the future. 2nd ed. London, 1977. pp. 528. *bibliogs.*

HOWSON (SUSAN) and WINCH (DONALD NORMAN) The Economic Advisory Council, 1930-1939: a study in economic advice during depression and recovery. Cambridge, 1977. pp. 424. *bibliog.*

LIVESEY (FRANK) A modern approach to economics. London, 1977. pp. 271. *bibliogs. Published on behalf of the Institute of Marketing.*

PRICE (CATHERINE M.) Welfare economics in theory and practice. London, 1977. pp. 175. *bibliogs.*

PRINGLE (ROBIN) The growth merchants: economic consequences of wishful thinking. London, 1977. pp. 82. *bibliog.*

RAMELSON (BERT) Bury the social contract: the case for an alternative policy. London, [1977]. pp. 36. (*Communist Party of Great Britain. Communist Party Pamphlets*)

SANDFORD (CEDRIC T.) and BRADBURY (M.S.) eds. Economic policy. 2nd ed. London, 1977. pp. 284. *bibliog.*

SHANKS (MICHAEL) Planning and politics: the British experience 1960-1976. London, 1977. pp. 142. *bibliog. Jointly sponsored by the National Economic Development Office and Political and Economic Planning.*

STEWART (MICHAEL JAMES) The Jekyll and Hyde years: politics and economic policy since 1964. London, 1977. pp. 272. *bibliog.*

TRADES UNION CONGRESS and LABOUR PARTY. Liaison Committee. The next three years and into the eighties. London, 1977. pp. 16.

WALKER (PETER) M.P. The ascent of Britain. London, 1977. pp. 224.

— — Bibliography.

NAUGHTON (M.R.) compiler. Regional studies and reports of the economic planning councils. [London], 1976. pp. 10. (*U.K. Department of the Environment. Library. Bibliographies. No. 195*)

— Emigration and immigration.

HORTON (Sir ROBERT JOHN WILMOT) The causes and remedies of pauperism in the United Kingdom considered: introductory series: being a defence of the principles and conduct of the Emigration Committee against the charges of Mr. Sadler. London, Lloyd, 1830. pp. viii, 150.

HORTON (Sir ROBERT JOHN WILMOT) Causes and remedies of pauperism: fourth series: explanation of Mr. Wilmot Horton's Bill in a letter and queries addressed to N.W.Senior...with his answers, etc. London, Lloyd, 1830. pp. vi, 3-112, xxiv.

HORTON (Sir ROBERT JOHN WILMOT) An inquiry into the causes and remedies of pauperism: first series: containing correspondence with C. Poulett Thomson, Esq., M.P., upon the conditions under which colonization would be justifiable as a national measure. 2nd ed. London, Lloyd, 1831. pp. 38.

HORTON (Sir ROBERT JOHN WILMOT) An inquiry into the causes and remedies of pauperism: second series: containing correspondence with M. Duchatel...; with an explanatory preface. 2nd ed. London, Lloyd, 1831. pp. 46.

BARBADOS. 195-. Information booklet for intending emigrants to Britain. [Bridgetown, 195-]. pp. 24.

BARBADOS. 195-. Information booklet for intending emigrants to Britain. [rev.ed.]. [Bridgetown, 195-]. pp. 31.

RUNNYMEDE TRUST. Briefing Papers. 1974, No. 2. The crisis of the Pakistani dependants. London, 1974. fo. 10.

RUNNYMEDE TRUST. Briefing Papers. 1974, No. 3. Illegal immigration and the law. rev. ed. London, 1974. fo. 5.

BIDWELL (SIDNEY) Red, white and black: race relations in Britain. London, [1976]. pp. 213. bibliog.

BRITISH COUNCIL OF CHURCHES. Community and Race Relations Unit and RUNNYMEDE TRUST. Ethnic minorities in society: a reference guide. [London], 1976. pp. 55. bibliog.

U.K. Parliament. House of Commons. Library. Research Division. Background Papers. No.56. Commonwealth immigration into the United Kingdom from the 1950s to 1975: a survey of statistical sources. [London, 1976]. pp. 25. bibliog.

JONES (CATHERINE JOY) Immigration and social policy in Britain. London, 1977. pp. 291. bibliog.

— Executive departments.

REGIONAL chairmen's enquiry into the working of the D[epartment of] H[ealth and] S[ocial] S[ecurity] in relation to regional health authorities; a report by the chairmen of the regional health authorities of the National Health Service. [London], Department of Health and Social Security, 1976. pp. 102.

U.K. Central Policy Review Staff. 1977. Review of overseas representation: report. London, 1977. pp. 442.

U.K. Department of Industry. 1977. The National Enterprise Board: guidelines. London, 1977. pp. 12.

LAMBERT (CLAIRE M.) compiler. The Department of the Environment: organisation and functions. rev. ed. [London, 1976]. pp. 71. (U.K. Department of the Environment. Library. Bibliographies. No. 158[a])

— Foreign economic relations.

HOGAN (MICHAEL J.) Informal entente: the private structure of cooperation in Anglo-American diplomacy, 1918-1928. Columbia, Mo., 1977. pp. 254. bibliog.

U.K. Central Policy Review Staff. 1977. Review of overseas representation: report. London, 1977. pp. 442.

See also EUROPEAN ECONOMIC COMMUNITY — United Kingdom.

— — Africa, Subsaharan.

WODDIS (JACK) Southern Africa: which side is Britain on?. London, [1976]. pp. 12. (Communist Party of Great Britain. Communist Party Pamphlets)

— Foreign population.

COMMUNITY RELATIONS COMMISSION. Aspects of mental health in a multi-cultural society: notes for the guidance of doctors and social workers; (with Summary). London, 1976. 2 pts. bibliog.

COMMUNITY RELATIONS COMMISSION. Working in multi-racial areas: a training handbook for social services departments. London, 1976. pp. 21. bibliogs.

COMMUNITY RELATIONS COMMISSION. Housing choice and ethnic concentration: an attitude study. London, 1977. pp. 69.

PEARN (M.A.) Selecting and training coloured workers. London, H.M.S.O., 1977. pp. 46. bibliog. (Training Information Papers. 9)

U.K. Department of Employment. Unit for Manpower Studies. 1977. The role of immigrants in the labour market; project report. London, [1977]. pp. 230. bibliog.

— Foreign relations.

TROTSKII (LEV DAVYDOVICH) Collected writings and speeches on Britain: in three volumes...; edited by R. Chappell and Alan Clinton. London, [1974]. 3 vols.

DOUGHERTY (JAMES E.) British perspectives on a changing global balance. Beverly Hills, [1975]. pp. 108.

WINKLER (HENRY RALPH) ed. Twentieth-century Britain: national power and social welfare. New York, 1976. pp. 272. bibliog.

BRITISH foreign policy under Sir Edward Grey; edited by F. H. Hinsley. Cambridge, 1977. pp. 702. bibliog.

ROCK (WILLIAM R.) British appeasement in the 1930s. London, 1977. pp. 111. bibliog.

SHAY (ROBERT PAUL) British rearmament in the thirties: politics and profits. Princeton, N.J., [1977]. pp. 315. bibliog.

SHLAIM (AVI) and others. British foreign secretaries since 1945. Newton Abbot, [1977]. pp. 267.

STOLER (MARK A.) The politics of the second front: American military planning and diplomacy in coalition warfare, 1941-1943. Westport, Conn., 1977. pp. 244. bibliogs.

U.K. Central Policy Review Staff. 1977. Review of overseas representation: report. London, 1977. pp. 442.

See also EUROPEAN ECONOMIC COMMUNITY — United Kingdom.

— — Africa, Subsaharan.

WODDIS (JACK) Southern Africa: which side is Britain on?. London, [1976]. pp. 12. (Communist Party of Great Britain. Communist Party Pamphlets)

— — America, Latin.

LABOUR PARTY. National Executive Committee. Argentina, Chile and Brazil; a statement. London, 1977. pp. 7.

— — Argentine Republic.

FELL (BRIAN JOHN) Britain and the Argentine, 1914-1918. 1976. fo.379. bibliog. Typescript. Ph.D.(London) thesis: unpublished. This thesis is the property of London University and may not be removed from the Library.

— — Canada.

WIGLEY (PHILIP G.) Canada and the transition to Commonwealth: British-Canadian relations, 1917-1926. Cambridge, 1977. pp. 294. bibliog.

— — China.

ZARETSKAIA (SOF'IA IL'INICHNA) Vneshniaia politika Kitaia v 1856-1860 godakh: otnosheniia s Angliei i Frantsiei. Moskva, 1976. pp. 221. bibliog.

JAIN (JAGDISH PRASAD) China in world politics: a study of Sino-British relations, 1949-1975. London, 1977. pp. 373. bibliog.

JONES (ARTHUR PHILIP) Britain's search for Chinese cooperation in the First World War. 1976 [or rather 1977]. fo. 304. bibliog. Typescript. Ph.D. (London) thesis: unpublished. This thesis is the property of London University and may not be removed from the Library.

— — East (Far East).

KLIMENKO (NIKOLAI PROKOP'EVICH) Kolonial'naia politika Anglii na Dal'nem Vostoke v seredine XIX veka. Moskva, 1976. pp. 309. bibliog.

SHAI (ARON) Origins of the war in the east: Britain, China and Japan, 1937- 39. London, [1976]. pp. 267. bibliog.

LOWE (PETER) Lecturer in History at Manchester University. Great Britain and the origins of the Pacific war: a study of British policy in East Asia, 1937-1941. Oxford, 1977. pp. 318. bibliog.

— East (Near East).

BUSCH (BRITON COOPER) Mudros to Lausanne: Britain's frontier in West Asia, 1918- 1923. Albany, N.Y., 1976. pp. 430. bibliog.

— Egypt.

COTTAM (RICHARD W.) Foreign policy motivation: a general theory and a case study. Pittsburgh, [1977]. pp. 374. bibliog.

— Europe.

RECKER (MARIE LUISE) England und der Donauraum, 1919-1929: Probleme einer europäischen Nachkriegsordnung. Stuttgart, 1976. pp. 324. bibliog. (Deutsches Historisches Institut in London. Veröffentlichungen. Band 3)

— France.

ROLO (PAUL JACQUES VICTOR) Britain and the Briand plan: the common market that never was: an inaugural lecture...given in the University of Keele, 1972. Keele, 1973. pp. 23.

— Germany.

GERMANY. Reichstag. 1908. Das persönliche Regiment vor dem Deutschen Reichstage: die Verhandlungen...vom 10. und 11. November 1908. Berlin, 1908. pp. 128.

— Iran.

AHMAD (ISHTIAQ) Anglo-Iranian relations, 1905-1919. Bombay, [1974]. pp. 389. bibliog.

— Iraq.

COHEN (STUART A.) British policy in Mesopotamia, 1903-1914. London, 1976. pp. 361. bibliog. (Oxford. University. St. Antony's College. Middle East Centre. St. Antony's Middle East Monographs. No.5)

SLUGLETT (PETER) Britain in Iraq, 1914-1932. London, 1976. pp. 360. bibliog. (Oxford. University. St. Antony's College. Middle East Centre. St. Antony's Middle East Monographs. No.4)

— Russia.

GILLARD (DAVID R.) The struggle for Asia, 1828-1914: a study in British and Russian imperialism. London, 1977. pp. 214. bibliog.

GORODETSKY (GABRIEL) The precarious truce: Anglo-Soviet relations, 1924-27. Cambridge, 1977. pp. 289. bibliog.

— — Latvia.

VARSLAVAN (AL'BERT IANOVICH) Angliiskii imperializm i burzhuaznaia Latviia: politiko-diplomaticheskie vzaimootnosheniia, 1924-1929 gg. Riga, 1975. pp. 287. bibliog.

— — Spain.

AZCARATE Y FLOREZ (PABLO DE) Mi embajada en Londres durante la guerra civil española. Barcelona, 1976. pp. 403.

— — Turkey.

ZHIVKOVA (LUDMILA) Anglo-Turkish relations, 1933-1939. London, 1976. pp. 132. bibliog.

— — United States.

CHRISTIE (IAN RALPH) and LABAREE (BENJAMIN WOODS) Empire or independence, 1760-1776: a British-American dialogue on the coming of the American revolution. Oxford, 1976. pp. 332. bibliog.

REES (MARK STEPHEN) Anglo-American relations, 1953-55: the institutional and operational levels of compromise. [1976]. fo. 249. bibliog. Typescript. M.Phil. (London) thesis: unpublished. This thesis is the property of London University and may not be removed from the Library.

FERRIS (NORMAN B.) The Trent affair: a diplomatic crisis. Knoxville, Tenn., [1977]. pp. 280. *bibliog.*

GRIFFITH (SAMUEL B.) In defense of the public liberty: Britain, America, and the struggle for independence, 1760-81. London, 1977. pp. 725. *bibliog.*

— Gentry.

MINGAY (GORDON EDMUND) The gentry: the rise and fall of a ruling class. London, 1976. pp. 216.

— Government publications.

O'NEILL (THOMAS P.) British Parliamentary Papers: a monograph on blue books. Shannon, 1969. pp. 32.

U.K. Office of Population Censuses and Surveys. 1977. Guide to census reports, Great Britain, 1801-1966. London, 1977. pp. 279.

— — Bibliography.

U.K. Cabinet Office. Government research and development: a guide to sources of information. a., 1975 [2nd]- London.

U.K. Department of Health and Social Security. Library. Annual list of publications. a., 1975- London.

— — Indexes.

BLACKMORE (RUTH MATTESON) compiler. Cumulative index to the annual catalogues of Her Majesty's Stationery Office publications, 1922-1972. Washington, 1976. 2 vols.

FORD (GRACE) compiler. A select list of reports and other papers in journals of the House of Commons, 1688-1800. Nendeln, Liechtenstein, [1976]. pp. 120. *(Southampton. University. Studies in Parliamentary Papers)*

MORGAN (A. MARY) and STEPHEN (LORNA R.) compilers. British government publications: an index to chairmen, 1967-1971. London, [1976]. pp. 40.

— Historic houses, etc.

WIGHT (JANE A.) Brick building in England: from the middle ages to 1550. London, 1972. pp. 439. *bibliog.*

— Historical geography.

DARBY (HENRY CLIFFORD) Domesday England. Cambridge, 1977. pp. 416.

— History.

TROTSKII (LEV DAVYDOVICH) Collected writings and speeches on Britain: in three volumes...; edited by R. Chappell and Alan Clinton. London, [1974]. 3 vols.

— — Bibliography.

GUTH (DELLOYD J.) Late-medieval England, 1377-1485. Cambridge, 1976. pp. 143. *(Conference on British Studies. Bibliographical Handbooks)*

BROWN (LUCY M.) and CHRISTIE (IAN RALPH) eds. Bibliography of British history, 1789-1851; issued under the direction of the American Historical Association and the Royal Historical Society of Great Britain. Oxford, 1977. pp. 759.

— — Sources.

PIPE ROLL SOCIETY. Publications. New Series. vol. 41. Liber memorialis Doris Mary Stenton, Honorary Secretary to the Pipe Roll Society, 1923-1961. London, 1976. pp. 220.

PIPE ROLL SOCIETY. Publications. New Series. vol. 42. The great roll of the pipe for the third year of the reign of King Henry III, Michaelmas, 1219, Pipe Roll 63;...with an introduction by B.E. Harris. London, 1976. pp. 314.

BYERLY (BENJAMIN F.) and BYERLY (CATHERINE RIDDER) eds. Records of the wardrobe and household, 1285-1286. London, H.M.S.O., 1977. pp. 309.

FOX (HENRY RICHARD VASSALL) 3rd Baron Holland. The Holland House diaries, 1831-1840: the diary of Henry Richard Vassall Fox, third Lord Holland, with extracts from the diary of Dr. John Allen; edited with an introductory essay and notes by Abraham D. Kriegel. London, 1977. pp. 513.

— — 55 B.C.-449A.D., Roman period.

The 'SMALL towns' of Roman Britain: papers presented to a conference, Oxford 1975; edited by Warwick Rodwell and Trevor Rowley. Oxford, 1975. pp. 236. *bibliogs.* *(British Archaeological Reports. 15)*

— — 449-1066, Anglo-Saxon period.

SYMPOSIUM ON ANGLO-SAXON ARCHAEOLOGY, 2ND, OXFORD, 1973. Anglo-Saxon settlement and landscape: papers presented to a symposium, Oxford 1973; edited by Trevor Rowley. Oxford, 1974. pp. 138. *(British Archaeological Reports. 6)*

— — 1066-1485, Medieval period.

LLOYD (TERENCE H.) The English wool trade in the middle ages. Cambridge, 1977. pp. 351. *bibliog.*

— — 1485-1603, Tudors.

HOAK (DALE EUGENE) The King's council in the reign of Edward VI. Cambridge, 1976. pp. 374. *bibliog.*

HOSKINS (WILLIAM GEORGE) The age of plunder: King Henry's England, 1500-1547. London, 1976. pp. 262. *bibliog.*

CORNWALL (JULIAN) Revolt of the peasantry, 1549. London, 1977. pp. 254. *bibliog.*

POWELL (KEN) and COOK (CHRISTOPHER PIERS) English historical facts, 1485-1603. London, 1977. pp. 228. *bibliog.*

— — 1603-1649, Early Stuarts.

AIKIN (LUCY) Memoirs of the court of King Charles the First. 2nd ed. London, 1833. 2 vols.

KNAFLA (LOUIS A.) Law and politics in Jacobean England: the tracts of Lord Chancellor Ellesmere. Cambridge, 1977. pp. 355.

— — 1642-1660, Puritan Revolution.

SIMPKINSON (CHARLES HARE) Thomas Harrison: regicide and Major-General. London, 1905. pp. 304.

— — 1688, Revolution of.

JACOB (MARGARET C.) The Newtonians and the English Revolution, 1689-1720. Ithaca, N.Y., 1976. pp. 288. *bibliog.*

— — 1760-1820.

MONEY (JOHN) Experience and identity: Birmingham and the West Midlands, 1760-1800. Manchester, [1977]. pp. 312. *bibliog.*

— History, Local.

POPULATION and marketing: two studies in the history of the south-west; edited by Walter Minchinton. Exeter, 1976. pp. 139. *(Exeter University. Department of Economic History. Exeter Papers in Economic History. No. 11). Papers of two seminars held at Dartington.*

— Industries.

EMANCIPATION of industry. [London, imprint]. 1844. pp. 8. *Without title-page. Caption title. Signed M.M.*

MEE (GRAHAM) Aristocratic enterprise: the Fitzwilliam industrial undertakings, 1795-1857. Glasgow, 1975. pp. 222.

The BANKS and industry; based on the seminar held at... Cambridge, 5-10 September, 1976. London, 1976. pp. 106. *bibliog.*

BANNOCK (GRAHAM) The smaller business in Britain and Germany. London, 1976. pp. 152. *bibliog.*

DEFENCE cuts and Labour's industrial strategy; (based on the proceedings of a delegate conference...called by the Labour Committee of the Campaign for Nuclear Disarmament...London.. .1976). London, [1976]. pp. 33. *bibliog.*

KEEBLE (DAVID ETHERTON) Industrial location and planning in the United Kingdom. London, 1976. pp. 317. *bibliog.*

LORD (ALAN) A stategy for industry. York, [1976]. pp. 20. *(York. University. Sir Ellis Hunter Memorial Lectures. 8)*

NATIONAL ECONOMIC DEVELOPMENT COUNCIL. N[ational] E[conomic] D[evelopment] C[ouncil] industrial strategy: [reports of Economic Development Committees and sector working parties]. [London, National Economic Development Office, 1976]. 22 pts.

PRAIS (SIGBERT JON) The evolution of giant firms in Britain: a study of the growth of concentration in manufacturing industry in Britain, 1909-70. Cambridge, 1976. pp. 321. *bibliog. (National Institute of Economic and Social Research. Economic and Social Studies. 30)*

WOOD (PETER A.) The West Midlands;...with contributions on the Potteries, coal and power by A. Moyes. Newton Abbot, [1976]. pp. 263.

U.K. Central Office of Information. Reference Division. Reference Pamphlets. 126. British industry today: manufacturing industries. 2nd ed. London, 1977. pp. 23. *bibliog.*

U.K. Central Office of Information. Reference Division. Reference Pamphlets. 127. British industry today: organisation and production. 2nd ed. London, 1977. pp. 30. *bibliog.*

— Intellectual life.

CHADWICK (WILLIAM OWEN) Acton and Gladstone. London, 1976. pp. 56. *(London. University. Creighton Lectures. 1975)*

JACOB (MARGARET C.) The Newtonians and the English Revolution, 1689-1720. Ithaca, N.Y., 1976. pp. 288. *bibliog.*

WATSON (GEORGE) Politics and literature in modern Britain. London, 1977. pp. 190.

— Kings and rulers.

PETTY (Sir WILLIAM) M.D., Surveyor-General of Ireland to Charles II. A political essay; or, Summary review of the kings and government of England since the Norman conquest. London, 1698. pp. 195.

BURKE'S guide to the royal family. London, 1973. pp. 358.

U.K. Central Office of Information. Reference Division. Reference Pamphlets. 118. The monarchy in Britain. 3rd ed. London, 1977. pp. 39. *bibliog.*

— Maps.

U.K. Department of the Environment. North West Regional Office. North West regional atlas. [2nd ed.] Manchester, [1974 in progress]. 1 vol.(loose- leaf).

U.K. Department of the Environment. Cartographic Services. 1976- . Atlas of the environment, England and Wales. [London, 1976 in progress].

— Moral conditions.

TREVELYAN (ARTHUR) To the people: the moral lunacy of our class legislators, and of their supporters, demonstrated. London, Watson, 1849. pp. 16.

— Nationalism.

NAIRN (TOM) The break-up of Britain: crisis and neo-nationalism. London, [1977]. pp. 368.

— Navy — History.

DINGMAN (ROGER) Power in the Pacific: the origins of naval arms limitation, 1914- 1922. Chicago, [1976]. pp. 318. *bibliog.*

— — Recruiting, enlistment, etc.

NAVY RECORDS SOCIETY. Publications. vol. 119. The manning of the Royal Navy: selected public pamphlets, 1693-1873; edited by J.S. Bromley. London, 1974. pp. 409.

— — Supplies and stores.

THOMPSON (WILLIAM) Wine Cooper. The Royal Navy-men's advocate wherein from a collection of several original and authentic tracts are fully set forth the corrupt practices of victualling the Royal Navy, to which is prefix'd an account of the author's character and conduct, and subjoined some proposals for a better future conduct. London, Slater, 1757. pp. 3, 59.

— Officials and employees — Appointment, qualifications, tenure, etc.

The FOLLY of appointing men of parts to great offices in a state. London, Coote, 1758. pp. 24.

ANSTEY (EDGAR) Civil service administrators: a long-term follow-up. London, 1976. pp. 23. *bibliog.* (*U.K. Civil Service Department. Behavioural Sciences Research Division. Reports. No. 31*)

— — Salaries, allowances, etc.

A LETTER to the Right Hon. Robert Peel,...on the recommendation of the Finance Committee, that the superannuation tax should be re-enacted; with remarks and statements, shewing the extent to which reductions of salaries in the public offices...have been already made. London, Richards, [1828]. pp. 16,xvii-xxix. *Signed: A clerk.*

— Parliament.

A REVIEW of the principles of radical reformers, and the measures which they have proposed for reform in Parliament. Edinburgh, Bayne, 1820. pp. 34.

RUSH (MICHAEL) Parliament and the public. London, 1976. pp. 140. *bibliog.*

HORWITZ (HENRY) Parliament, policy and politics in the reign of William III. Manchester, [1977]. pp. 385.

— — Elections.

ELECTION papers, addresses, poll books, etc., for the city and county of Durham, from 1813 to 1847 inclusive. Durham, Walker, [1847?]. 13 pts. (in 1 vol.). *Lacking Proceedings and poll for 1843.*

PHILANTHUS, pseud. The Pelham gazette: Pelham and Childe; or, The candidates for Shropshire. Shrewsbury, Howell, 1822. pp. 16.

WELLS (SAMUEL) A letter to the Marquis of Tavistock on the best means of obtaining pure and less expensive elections on the dissolution of Parliament. London, Ridgway, 1825. pp. 59.

The PROCEEDINGS and poll at the Durham City election, on the 7th, 8th, and 9th of July, 1852, with the speeches, etc., on the day of nomination and at the close of the poll. Durham, Walker, 1852. pp. 25.

The PROCEEDINGS and poll at the Durham City election on the 1st, 2nd, and 3rd of December, 1852, with the speeches, etc. on the day of nomination and at the close of poll. Durham, Walker, 1852. pp. 21.

SPENCE (JAMES D.) The British election study of October 1974: methodological report. London, 1975. 1 vol. (various pagings).

CRAIG (FREDERICK WALTER SCOTT) ed. British electoral facts, 1885-1975. 3rd ed. London, 1976. pp. 182. *bibliog. First published under the title British parliamentary election statistics.*

HANSARD SOCIETY FOR PARLIAMENTARY GOVERNMENT. Commission on Electoral Reform. Report...June 1976. [London, 1976]. pp. 54.

CRAIG (FREDERICK WALTER SCOTT) ed. British parliamentary election results, 1832-1885. London, 1977. pp. 692.

CRAIG (FREDERICK WALTER SCOTT) ed. British parliamentary election results, 1918-1949. rev. ed. London, 1977. pp. 785.

— — History.

CAMDEN SOCIETY. [Publications]. 4th Series. vol. 19. Proceedings of the Short Parliament of 1640; edited for the Royal Historical Society by Esther S. Cope in collaboration with Willson H. Coates. London, 1977. pp. 340. *bibliog.*

LEHMBERG (STANFORD E.) The later Parliaments of Henry VIII, 1536-1547. Cambridge, 1977. pp. 379. *bibliog.*

SNOW (VERNON F.) Parliament in Elizabethan England: John Hooker's Order and usage. New Haven, Conn., 1977. pp. 221.

— — House of Commons.

COMMITTEE OF ASSOCIATION OF THE COUNTY OF YORK. An address from the Committee...to the electors of Great Britain: to which are prefixed the resolutions of that committee at their meetings held on the 3rd and 4th of January, 1781, and the instrument of instructions to their deputies. [York], 1781. pp. 18. *Chairman: Rev. Mr. Wyvill.*

GRAHAM (THOMAS) Printer. An account of the state of the right of election of members of Parliament in the several counties, cities, and boroughs of the United Kingdom: strongly demonstrating the necessity for a reform in the representation of the people in the House of Commons. London, the Author. 1818. pp. 24.

FORD (GRACE) compiler. A select list of reports and other papers in journals of the House of Commons, 1688-1800. Nendeln, Liechtenstein, [1976]. pp. 120. (*Southampton. University. Studies in Parliamentary Papers*)

UNITED KINGDOM. Parliament. House of Commons. Debates. 1628. Commons debates, 1628;...edited by Robert C. Johnson [and others]. New Haven, 1977 in progress.

FABIAN SOCIETY. Fabian Tracts. [No.] 448. Reforming the House of Commons: [by] Lisanne Radice. London, 1977. pp. 19.

MULLER (WILLIAM D.) The 'kept men'?: the first century of trade union representation in the British House of Commons, 1874-1975. Hassocks, Sussex, 1977. pp. 283. *bibliog.*

STUDY OF PARLIAMENT GROUP. The Commons in the seventies; edited by S.A. Walkland and Michael Ryle. 2nd ed. [London], 1977. pp. 285.

— — — Speaker.

LLOYD (SELWYN) Baron Selwyn-Lloyd. Mr Speaker, sir. London, 1976. pp. 192.

— — House of Lords.

LABOUR RESEARCH DEPARTMENT. The Lords against the unions. London, 1976. pp. 27.

SAINTY (JOHN CHRISTOPHER) and DEWAR (DAVID) Senior Clerk, House of Lords, compilers. Divisions in the House of Lords: an analytical list, 1685 to 1857. London, 1976. pp. 41. (*U.K. Parliament. House of Lords. Record Office. Occasional Publications. No. 2*) List of divisions on microfiche (8 cards)

— — Rules and practice.

U.K. Parliament. House of Lords. 1976. Brief guide to the procedure and practice of the House of Lords. [London], 1976. pp. 25.

— Peerage.

BURKE'S guide to the royal family. London, 1973. pp. 358.

— Politics and government.

PETTY (Sir WILLIAM) M.D., Surveyor-General of Ireland to Charles II. A political essay; or, Summary review of the kings and government of England since the Norman conquest. London, 1698. pp. 195.

ROSE (RICHARD) ed. Studies in British politics: a reader in political sociology. 3rd ed. London, 1976. pp. 547. *bibliog.*

MACKINTOSH (JOHN PITCAIRN) The government and politics of Britain. 4th ed. London, 1977. pp. 244. *bibliog.*

NAIRN (TOM) The break-up of Britain: crisis and neo-nationalism. London, [1977]. pp. 368.

U.K. Central Policy Review Staff. 1977. Relations between central government and local authorities; report. London, 1977. pp. 60.

— — 1485-1603.

EPSTEIN (JOEL J.) Francis Bacon: a political biography. Athens, Ohio, [1977]. pp. 187.

LEHMBERG (STANFORD E.) The later Parliaments of Henry VIII, 1536-1547. Cambridge, 1977. pp. 379. *bibliog.*

— — 1603-1714.

JENKINS (DAVID) One of the Judges for South Wales. The works of the eminent and learned Judge Jenkins upon divers statutes concerning the King's prerogative and the liberty of the subject; now reprinted from the original authentick copy, written and published by himself, when prisoner in Newgate. London, Heyrick, [1681]. pp. (xiv), 94.

[SWIFT (JONATHAN)] The management of the four last years vindicated: in which Her late Majesty, and her ministry, are fully cleared from the false aspersions cast on them in a late pamphlet [by Charles Povey], entituled An enquiry into the miscarriages of the four last years reign, etc. [London], Morphew, 1714. pp. 48. *Signed C.B.*

UNITED KINGDOM. Parliament. House of Commons. Debates. 1628. Commons debates, 1628;...edited by Robert C. Johnson [and others]. New Haven, 1977 in progress.

CAMDEN SOCIETY. [Publications]. 4th Series. vol. 19. Proceedings of the Short Parliament of 1640; edited for the Royal Historical Society by Esther S. Cope in collaboration with Willson H. Coates. London, 1977. pp. 340. *bibliog.*

EPSTEIN (JOEL J.) Francis Bacon: a political biography. Athens, Ohio, [1977]. pp. 187.

HORWITZ (HENRY) Parliament, policy and politics in the reign of William III. Manchester, [1977]. pp. 385.

— — 1700-1719.

PHILIPS (ERASMUS) Misellaneous works consisting of essays political and moral. London, printed for Mr. Waller, 1751. pp. 508.

— — 1756-1837.

A REPLY to the Vindication of Mr. Pitt, by an English officer in the Prussian service. London, Cooper, 1758. pp. 45.

[RUFFHEAD (OWEN)] Considerations on the present dangerous crisis. 2nd ed. London, Becket, 1763. pp. 47.

[COOPER (Sir GREY)] The merits of the new administration truly stated; in answer to the several pamphlets and papers published against them. London, Williams, 1765. pp. 48.

CANDID truth, in answer to a pamphlet, entitled A letter to us, from one of ourselves. London, Law, 1777. pp. 47.

REFLECTIONS on the Irish conspiracy; and on the necessity of an armed association in Great Britain; to which are added observations on the debates and resolutions of the Whig Club, on the sixth of June, 1797. London, J. Sewell, 1797. pp. 156.

[WOLCOT (JOHN)] Choice cabinet pictures; with a few portraits done to the life: by Peter Pindar, Esq. [pseud.]. London, S.W. Fores, 1817. pp. 48.

ASMODEUS (JUAN) pseud. A political lecture on heads, alias blockheads!!: a characteristic poem, containing the heads of Derry Down Triangle...and the Grand Lama of the Kremlin; drawn from craniological inspection, after the manner of doctors Gall and Spurzheim, of Vienna. 3rd ed. London, J. Fairburn, [1820]. pp. 35.

SUBSTANCE of the debate in the County Hall, Edinburgh, on the motion of Sir John Hope, Bart., for an address to his Majesty on the state of the country, December 22. 1820. Edinburgh, Black, 1820. pp. 36.

[CARPENTER (WILLIAM) Editor of the "Political Letter"]. The rights of nations: a treatise on representative government, despotism, and reform; in which, political institutions are deduced from philosophical principles, and systematized; by the author of "The reformer's catechism," and "The people's charter". London, Brooks, 1832. pp. 454.

The GRAND festival in honour of George Byng, Esq., M.P....: a short hand report of the speeches...; also a jeremiad on the miseries of the "Times" reporter, etc. London, H. Cunningham, 1840. pp. 24.

RITCHESON (CHARLES RAY) Edmund Burke and the American Revolution. Leicester, 1976. pp. 15. *(Sir George Watson Lectures. 1976)*

THOMIS (MALCOLM I.) and HOLT (PETER) Threats of revolution in Britain, 1789-1848. [London], 1977. pp. 147. *bibliog.*

— — 1800-1899.

HAMBURGER (JOSEPH) Macaulay and the Whig tradition. Chicago, 1976. pp. 274.

CROSBY (TRAVIS L.) English farmers and the politics of protection, 1815-1852. Hassocks, 1977. pp. 224. *bibliog.*

FOX (HENRY RICHARD VASSALL) 3rd Baron Holland. The Holland House diaries, 1831-1840: the diary of Henry Richard Vassall Fox, third Lord Holland, with extracts from the diary of Dr. John Allen; edited with an introductory essay and notes by Abraham D. Kriegel. London, 1977. pp. 513.

PREST (JOHN) Politics in the age of Cobden. London, 1977. pp. 165.

— — 1837-1901.

The CRITIC in Parliament and in public since 1835. London, Bell, 1841. pp. 188.

WHITTET (JAMES) Letter to the ministers of the gospel on matters which deeply interest the working millions of Great Britain and Ireland. Perth, printed by G. Baxter, 1842. pp. 16.

TREVELYAN (ARTHUR) To the people: the moral lunacy of our class legislators, and of their supporters, demonstrated. London, Watson, 1849. pp. 16.

CHADWICK (WILLIAM OWEN) Acton and Gladstone. London, 1976. pp. 56. *(London. University. Creighton Lectures. 1975)*

CROSBY (TRAVIS L.) Sir Robert Peel's administration, 1841-1846. Newton Abbot, 1976. pp. 190. *bibliog.*

HARVIE (CHRISTOPHER) The lights of Liberalism: university Liberals and the challenge of democracy, 1860-86. London, 1976. pp. 343.

MACDONAGH (OLIVER) Early Victorian government, 1830-1870. London, [1977]. pp. 242. *bibliog.*

O'DAY (ALAN) The English face of Irish nationalism: Parnellite involvement in British politics, 1880-86. Dublin, 1977. pp. 210. *bibliog.*

THOMIS (MALCOLM I.) and HOLT (PETER) Threats of revolution in Britain, 1789-1848. [London], 1977. pp. 147. *bibliog.*

— — 1900- .

TROTSKII (LEV DAVYDOVICH) Collected writings and speeches on Britain: in three volumes...; edited by R. Chappell and Alan Clinton. London, [1974]. 3 vols.

DOUGLAS-HOME (ALEXANDER FREDERICK) Baron Home. The way the wind blows: an autobiography. London, 1976. pp. 320.

RYZHIKOV (VLADIMIR ALEKSANDROVICH) "Sozialismus" auf Labour-Art: Mythen und Wirklichkeit; (deutsch von I. Markow). Moskau, [1976]. pp. 300.

WINKLER (HENRY RALPH) ed. Twentieth-century Britain: national power and social welfare. New York, 1976. pp. 272. *bibliog.*

BROCKWAY (ARCHIBALD FENNER) Baron Brockway. Towards tomorrow: the autobiography of Fenner Brockway. London, 1977. pp. 280.

MORRIS (ANDREW JAMES ANTHONY) C.P. Trevelyan, 1870-1958: portrait of a radical. Belfast, [1977]. pp. 209.

— — 1901-1945.

BENTLEY (MICHAEL) The liberal mind, 1924-1929. Cambridge, 1977. pp. 279. *bibliog.*

CAMPBELL (JOHN) Ph.D. Lloyd George: the goat in the wilderness 1922-1931. London, 1977. pp. 383. *bibliog.*

— — 1901-1918.

SCOTT (W. STANLEY) "The man in the street": essays. Cockermouth, [imprint], 1910. pp. 187.

SEARLE (G.R.) Eugenics and politics in Britain, 1900-1914. Leyden, 1976. pp. 147.

HOBHOUSE (Sir CHARLES EDWARD HENRY) Inside Asquith's Cabinet: from the diaries of Charles Hobhouse; edited by Edward David. London, [1977]. pp. 295.

— — 1918-1945.

SHAY (ROBERT PAUL) British rearmament in the thirties: politics and profits. Princeton, N.J., [1977]. pp. 315. *bibliog.*

— — 1945- .

CADOGAN (PETER) Direct democracy: an appeal to the professional classes, to the politically disenchanted and to the deprived: the case for an England of sovereign regional republics, extraparliamentary democracy and a new active non-violence of the centre. 2nd ed. London, 1975. pp. 36.

FRASER (HUGH CHARLES PATRICK JOSEPH) A rebel for the right reasons; a selection of speeches and writings. Stafford, 1975. pp. 99.

HAIN (PETER) Radical regeneration. London, [1975]. pp. 181.

HOBSBAWM (ERIC JOHN ERNEST) The crisis and the outlook. London, [1975]. pp. 16. *Taken from a lecture given to Birkbeck College Socialist Society.*

HOGG (QUINTON McGAREL) Baron Hailsham. Elective dictatorship. London, 1976. pp. 17. *(British Broadcasting Corporation. Richard Dimbleby Lectures. 1976)*

RED WEEKLY. Pamphlets. The socialist challenge to Labour's cuts. London, [1976]. pp. 30.

BERKELEY (HUMPHRY) The odyssey of Enoch: a political memoir. London, 1977. pp. 146.

BRITAIN'S crisis in sociological perspective; papers from a one day conference held on 26 June, 1976 under the auspices of the Department of Sociology, University of Reading...; edited by M.B. Hamilton and K.G. Robertson. Reading, [1977?]. pp. 75.

GILMOUR (IAN) Inside right: a study of conservatism. London, 1977. pp. 294. *bibliog.*

HAINES (JOE) The politics of power. London, 1977. pp. 228.

JOHNSON (NEVIL) In search of the constitution: reflections on state and society in Britain. Oxford, 1977. pp. 239.

MINOGUE (MARTIN) ed. Documents on contemporary British government. Cambridge, 1977. 2 vols. *bibliogs.*

NEW trends in British politics: issues for research; edited by Dennis Kavanagh and Richard Rose. London, [1977]. pp. 254. *bibliogs. Based on papers presented to a meeting of the British Politics Group, August 1976.*

PARLIAMENTARY LABOUR PARTY. Manifesto Group. What we must do: (a democratic socialist approach to Britain's crisis). [London], 1977. pp. 36.

STEWART (MICHAEL JAMES) The Jekyll and Hyde years: politics and economic policy since 1964. London, 1977. pp. 272. *bibliog.*

STUTCHBURY (OLIVER PIERS) Too much government?: a political Aeneid. Ipswich, [1977]. pp. 128.

TRADES UNION CONGRESS and LABOUR PARTY. Liaison Committee. The next three years and into the eighties. London, 1977. pp. 16.

WALKER (PETER) M.P. The ascent of Britain. London, 1977. pp. 224.

— Population.

U.K. Office of Population Censuses and Surveys. Population projections: area: population projections by sex and age for standard regions, counties and metropolitan districts of England. a., 1974/1991 (1st)- London.

WEST MIDLANDS JOINT MONITORING STEERING GROUP. Joint Technical Working Group. General population analysis. [London, Department of the Environment], 1974. 1 pamphlet (various foliations). *Photocopy.*

NORTHERN REGION STRATEGY TEAM. Settlement patterns and policies in the northern region. Newcastle upon Tyne, 1976. pp. 84. *(Technical Reports. No. 14)*

POPULATION and marketing: two studies in the history of the south-west; edited by Walter Minchinton. Exeter, 1976. pp. 139. *(Exeter University. Department of Economic History. Exeter Papers in Economic History. No. 11). Papers of two seminars held at Dartington.*

HOUSE (JOHN WILLIAM) ed. The U.K. space: resources, environment and the future. 2nd ed. London, 1977. pp. 528. *bibliogs.*

PARSONS (JACK) Population fallacies. London, 1977. pp. 286. *bibliog.*

— Privy Council.

HOAK (DALE EUGENE) The King's council in the reign of Edward VI. Cambridge, 1976. pp. 374. *bibliog.*

— Race question.

EDUCATION AND COMMUNITY RELATIONS; ([pd. by] Community Relations Commission). irreg., M 1971- , with gaps. London.

LOMAS (GLENYS BARBARA GILLIAN) Census 1971: the coloured population of Great Britain; preliminary report...summarised by K. Campbell-Platt. London, 1974. fo. 23. *(Runnymede Trust. Briefing Papers. No. 4/74)*

RUNNYMEDE TRUST. Race relations and employment: written memorandum from the Runnymede Trust to the House of Commons Select Committee on Race Relations and Immigration, submitted on 12 July 1974. London, [1974]. 1 pamphlet (unpaged).

MILNER (DAVID) Children and race. Harmondsworth, 1975. pp. 281. *bibliog.*

NATIONAL CONFERENCE FOR COMMUNITY RELATIONS COUNCILS. Report. a., 1976(6th)- [London].

BAILEY (DAVE) The socialist challenge to racism. London, [1976]. pp. 32. *bibliog. (Red Weekly. Pamphlets)*

BIDWELL (SIDNEY) Red, white and black: race relations in Britain. London, [1976]. pp. 213. *bibliog.*

BRITISH COUNCIL OF CHURCHES. Community and Race Relations Unit and RUNNYMEDE TRUST. Ethnic minorities in society: a reference guide. [London], 1976. pp. 55. *bibliog.*

COMMUNIST PARTY OF GREAT BRITAIN. One race: the human race: a...broadsheet on the menace of racism. London, [1976]. pp. 4.

COMMUNITY RELATIONS COMMISSION. Black employees: job levels and discrimination. [London, 1976?]. pp. 4. *(Fact Sheets. No.3. Employment)*

COMMUNITY RELATIONS COMMISSION. CRC evidence to the Royal Commission on the Distribution of Income and Wealth to aid their inquiry into incomes at the lower levels. London, 1976. pp. 17. *bibliog.*

COUNTER INFORMATION SERVICES and INSTITUTE OF RACE RELATIONS. Racism: who profits?. London, [1976]. pp. 40. *bibliog. (Counter Information Services. Anti-Reports. No. 16)*

POPE (DAVID) Community relations: the police response. London, 1976. pp. 65.

RUNNYMEDE TRUST. Race Relations Bill Briefing Group. Briefs, nos. 1-10. London, [1976]. 10 pts. (in 1 vol.). *bibliog.*

U.K. Department of the Environment. 1976. Consultation paper: records and information relating to the housing of members of ethnic groups. [London, 1976]. fo.8.

COMMUNITY RELATIONS COMMISSION. Evidence to the Royal Commission on the National Health Service. London, 1977. pp. 20.

COMMUNITY RELATIONS COMMISSION. The multi-racial community: a guide for local councillors. London, 1977. pp. 34. *bibliog.*

COMMUNITY RELATIONS COMMISSION. Urban deprivation, racial inequality and social policy; a report. London, H.M.S.O., 1977. pp. 100.

COMMUNITY RELATIONS COMMISSION. The views of social workers in multi-racial areas. London, 1977. pp. 15.

COMMUNITY RELATIONS COMMISSION. Youth and Community Section. Seen but not served: black youth and the youth service; report of a series of six seminars held in 1975/76 to examine statutory provision for young people from racial minorities. London, 1977. pp. 42.

LEE (G.L.) and WRENCH (K. J.) Accidents are colour-blind: industrial accidents and the immigrant worker; a pilot study; published...for the Birmingham Community Relations Council. [London], Community Relations Commission, 1977. pp. 24. *bibliog.*

SMITH (DAVID J.) Racial disadvantage in Britain: the PEP report. Harmondsworth, 1977. pp. 349.

U.K. Race Relations Board. 1977. Comments on the government's consultation paper on records and information relating to the housing of members of ethnic groups. [London, 1977]. fo.4.

— Relations (general) with Bangladesh.

SCOTT (GUTHRIE MICHAEL) A void of law: (Britain and Bangladesh). London, [1975]. pp. 98.

— Relations (general) with the United States.

COLBOURNE (MAURICE DALE) America and Britain: a mutual introduction with special reference to the British Empire. London, 1943. pp. 230.

— Relations (military) with Malaysia.

CHIN (KIN WAH) The Anglo-Malayan (Malaysian) defence agreement: a study in alliance transformation. 1977. fo. 448. *bibliog. Typescript. Ph.D. (London) thesis: unpublished. This thesis is the property of London University and may not be removed from the Library. With printed article in end pocket.*

— Royal household.

BYERLY (BENJAMIN F.) and BYERLY (CATHERINE RIDDER) eds. Records of the wardrobe and household, 1285-1286. London, H.M.S.O., 1977. pp. 309.

— Rural conditions.

CHERRY (GORDON E.) ed. Rural planning problems;...contributors Gordon E. Cherry [and others]. London, 1976. pp. 286. *bibliogs.*

HORN (PAMELA) Labouring life in the Victorian countryside. Dublin, 1976. pp. 292. *bibliog.*

ITZKOWITZ (DAVID C.) Peculiar privilege: a social history of English foxhunting, 1753- 1885. Hassocks, Sussex, 1977. pp. 248. *bibliog.*

MINGAY (GORDON EDMUND) Rural life in Victorian England. London, 1977. pp. 212. *bibliog.*

— Social conditions.

SLANEY (ROBERT AGLIONBY) A plea to power and parliament for the working classes. London, Longman, 1847. pp. viii, 158.

WARD (COLIN) ed. Vandalism. London, 1973. pp. 327. *bibliog.*

BERTHOUD (RICHARD) The disadvantages of inequality: a study of social deprivation; a PEP report. London, 1976. pp. 207.

LE GRAND (JULIAN) and ROBINSON (RAY) The economics of social problems. London, 1976. pp. 245. *bibliog.*

NORTH WEST INDUSTRIAL DEVELOPMENT ASSOCIATION. North West England...: the facts. Manchester, [1976?]. pp. 23.

ROSE (RICHARD) ed. Studies in British politics: a reader in political sociology. 3rd ed. London, 1976. pp. 547. *bibliog.*

BRITAIN'S crisis in sociological perspective; papers from a one day conference held on 26 June, 1976 under the auspices of the Department of Sociology, University of Reading...; edited by M.B. Hamilton and K.G. Robertson. Reading, [1977?]. pp. 75.

EICHTHAL (GUSTAVE D') A French sociologist looks at Britain: Gustave d'Eichthal and British society in 1828; translated and edited by Barrie M. Ratcliffe and W.H. Chaloner. Manchester, [1977]. pp. 169. *(Manchester. University. Faculty of Arts. Publications. No. 22)*

RYDER (JUDITH) and SILVER (HAROLD) Modern English society. 2nd ed. London, 1977. pp. 390. *bibliogs.*

— Social history.

HOLDERNESS (B.A.) Pre-industrial England: economy and society, 1500-1750. London, 1976. pp. 244. *bibliogs.*

THOMIS (MALCOLM I.) Responses to industrialisation: the British experience, 1780- 1850. Newton Abbot, 1976. pp. 194.

CROSSICK (GEOFFREY) ed. The lower middle class in Britain 1870-1914. London, [1977]. pp. 213.

HEALTH care and popular medicine in nineteenth century England: essays in the social history of medicine; edited by John Woodward and David Richards. London, [1977]. pp. 195.

JOHNSTON (JAMES P.) A hundred years eating: food, drink and the daily diet in Britain since the late nineteenth century. Dublin, 1977. pp. 148. *bibliog.*

RYDER (JUDITH) and SILVER (HAROLD) Modern English society. 2nd ed. London, 1977. pp. 390. *bibliogs.*

STEVENSON (JOHN) Historian. Social conditions in Britain between the wars. Harmondsworth, 1977. pp. 295.

STONE (LAWRENCE) The family, sex and marriage in England, 1500-1800. London, [1977]. pp. 800. *bibliog.*

THOMIS (MALCOLM I.) and HOLT (PETER) Threats of revolution in Britain, 1789-1848. [London], 1977. pp. 147. *bibliog.*

— — Sources.

MADOX (RICHARD) An Elizabethan in 1582: the diary of Richard Madox, Fellow of All Souls; [edited] by Elizabeth Story Donno. London, 1976. pp. 365. *(Hakluyt Society. Works. 2nd Series. No. 147)*

EDWARDS (A.C.) The account books of Benjamin Mildmay, Earl Fitzwalter. London, [1977]. pp. 224.

— Social life and customs.

REYNOLDS (SUSAN) An introduction to the history of English medieval towns. Oxford, 1977. pp. 234. *bibliog.*

— Social policy.

ENGLISH law and social policy: a symposium based on Sir Leslie Scarman's 1974 Hamlyn Lectures. London, [1975]. pp. 46. *The report of a seminar held by the Centre for Studies in Social Policy on November 15th 1975.*

CROSBY (TRAVIS L.) Sir Robert Peel's administration, 1841-1846. Newton Abbot, 1976. pp. 190. *bibliog.*

HILL (MICHAEL J.) The state, administration and the individual. London, 1976. pp. 256. *bibliog.*

MORONEY (ROBERT M.) The family and the state: considerations for social policy. London, 1976. pp. 142.

NORTHERN REGION STRATEGY TEAM. Third interim report: main themes of the strategic plan. Newcastle upon Tyne, 1976. pp. 173, (8).

SOCIAL SERVICES RESEARCH AND INTELLIGENCE UNIT [PORTSMOUTH]. Information Sheets. No. 27. Planning alternatives: social services thinks ahead. Portsmouth, [1976]. pp. 8.

TITMUSS (RICHARD MORRIS) Essays on 'The welfare state'; introduction by Brian Abel-Smith. 3rd ed. London, 1976. pp. 262.

WALT (AUDREY GILLIAN) Policy making in Britain: a comparative study of fluoridation and family planning, 1960-1974. 1976. fo. 273. *bibliog. Typescript. Ph.D. (London) thesis: unpublished. This thesis is the property of London University and may not be removed from the Library.*

The WELFARE society: a guide for discussion groups; edited by Joan Eyden. London, [1976]. pp. 47. *bibliog.*

WINKLER (HENRY RALPH) ed. Twentieth-century Britain: national power and social welfare. New York, 1976. pp. 272. *bibliog.*

COMAN (PETER W.) Catholics and the welfare state. London, 1977. pp. 118. *bibliog.*

COMMUNITY RELATIONS COMMISSION. Urban deprivation, racial inequality and social policy; a report. London, H.M.S.O., 1977. pp. 100.

FOUNDATIONS of social administration; edited by Helmuth Heisler. London, 1977. pp. 251.

JONES (CATHERINE JOY) Immigration and social policy in Britain. London, 1977. pp. 291. *bibliog.*

SANDFORD (CEDRIC T.) Social economics. London, 1977. pp. 286. *bibliog.*

TYRRELL (R. EMMETT) ed. The future that doesn't work: social democracy's failures in Britain; by Samuel Brittan [and others]. Garden City, N.Y., 1977. pp. 208.

U.K. Central Policy Review Staff. 1977. Population and the social services; report. London, 1977. pp. 106.

U.K. Central Policy Review Staff. 1977. Relations between central government and local authorities; report. London, 1977. pp. 60.

— Statistics, Vital.

U.K. Office of Population Censuses and Surveys. Birth statistics: review of the Registrar-General on births and patterns of family building in England and Wales. a., 1974 (1st)- London. *Supersedes in part Registrar-General's statistical review of England and Wales.*

U.K. Office of Population Censuses and Surveys. Local authority vital statistics: vital statistics for administrative and health areas of England and Wales. a., 1974 (1st)- London.

U.K. Office of Population Censuses and Surveys. Mortality statistics: accidents and violence: review of the Registrar General on deaths attributed to accidental and violent causes in England and Wales. a., 1974 (1st)- London. *Supersedes in part Registrar General's statistical review of England and Wales.*

U.K. Office of Population Censuses and Surveys. Mortality statistics: area: review of the Registrar General on deaths by area of usual residence, in England and Wales. a., 1974 (1st)- London. *Supersedes in part Registrar General's statistical review of England and Wales.*

U.K. Office of Population Censuses and Surveys. Mortality statistics: cause: review of the Registrar General on deaths by cause, sex and age, in England and Wales. a., 1974 (1st)- London. *Supersedes in part Registrar General's statistical review of England and Wales.*

U.K. Office of Population Censuses and Surveys. Mortality statistics: childhood: review of the Registrar General on deaths in England and Wales. a., 1974 (1st)- London. *Supersedes in part Registrar-General's statistical review of England and Wales.*

U.K. Office of Population Censuses and Surveys. Mortality statistics: review of the Registrar General on deaths in England and Wales. a., 1974(1st)- London. *Supersedes in part Registrar General's statistical review of England and Wales.*

INSTITUTE OF ACTUARIES and FACULTY OF ACTUARIES [IN SCOTLAND]. Continuous Mortality Investigation Committee. Continuous mortality investigation reports. No. 2. [London, 1976]. pp. 103.

— Commonwealth.

COMMONWEALTH SECRETARIAT. Information Division. The commonwealth today. London, 1973. pp. 33.

NICOL (DAVIDSON) New and modern roles for the Empire and Commonwealth. Cambridge, 1976. pp. 30. *(Cambridge. University. Commonwealth Lectures. 1975)*

INGRAM (DEREK) The imperfect Commonwealth. London, 1977. pp. 165. *bibliog.*

WIGLEY (PHILIP G.) Canada and the transition to Commonwealth: British-Canadian relations, 1917-1926. Cambridge, 1977. pp. 294. *bibliog.*

— — Bibliography.

LONDON. University. Institute of Commonwealth Studies. Theses in progress in Commonwealth studies: a cumulative list. London, 1973. pp. 34.

— — Foreign economic relations.

The COMMONWEALTH and development: the report of the conference sponsored by O[verseas] D[evelopment] I[nstitute] and St. Catharine's-Cumberland Lodge, at Cumberland Lodge, 13-15 February 1976. London, [1976]. pp. 59.

— — History.

HYAM (RONALD) and MARTIN (GED) Reappraisals in British imperial history. Toronto, 1975. pp. 234.

KLIMENKO (NIKOLAI PROKOP'EVICH) Kolonial'naia politika Anglii na Dal'nem Vostoke v seredine XIX veka. Moskva, 1976. pp. 309. *bibliog.*

SUDEIKIN (ALEKSANDR GRIGOR'EVICH) Kolonial'naia politika leiboristskoi partii Anglii mezhdu mirovymi voinami. Moskva, 1976. pp. 268. *bibliog.*

BELLOT (LELAND J.) William Knox: the life and thought of an eighteenth-century imperialist. Austin, Tex., [1977]. pp. 264. *bibliog.*

— — Nationalism.

BELL (J. BOWYER) On revolt: strategies of national liberation. Cambridge, Mass., 1976. pp. 272. *bibliog.*

UNITED NATIONS.

GUYANA. Ministry of External Affairs. 1971. The charter's mandate: fulfilment through internationalism: statements delivered in the general debate of the 26th session of the U.N. General Assembly, September 28, 1971, and in the debate on Namibia in the Security Council, September 27, 1971; by Shridath S. Ramphal, Minister of State for External Affairs. Georgetown, 1971. pp. 25.

BEERITS (HENRY C.) The United Nations and human survival. Philadelphia, 1976. pp. 85.

KEMPER (RIA) Nationale Verfügung über natürliche Ressourcen und die neue Weltwirtschaftsordnung der Vereinten Nationen. Berlin, [1976]. pp. 155. *bibliog.*

REYNOLDS (PHILIP ALAN) and HUGHES (EMMET JOHN) The historian as diplomat: Charles Kingsley Webster and the United Nations, 1939-1946. London, 1976. pp. 198.

SIGNITZER (BENNO) Regulation of direct broadcasting from satellites: the U.N. involvement. New York, 1976. pp. 112. *bibliog.*

UNITAR CONFERENCE ON THE FUTURE, MOSCOW, 1974. The United Nations and the future: proceedings of UNITAR Conference...held in Moscow from June 10 to 14, 1974. Moscow, 1976. pp. 463. *In English and French.*

ATLANTIC COUNCIL OF THE UNITED STATES. Working Group on the United Nations. The future of the UN: a strategy for like-minded nations;... Lincoln P. Bloomfield, rapporteur. Boulder, 1977. pp. 58.

The FUTURE of the United Nations; (a Round Table held on November 16, 1976...[in] Washington); John Charles Daly, moderator, etc. Washington, [1977]. pp. 48. *(American Enterprise Institute for Public Policy Research. Round Tables)*

UNITED NATIONS. Office of Public Information. 1977. The United Nations and decolonization: highlights of thirty years of United Nations efforts on behalf of colonial countries and peoples. New York, 1977. pp. 36.

— Armed Forces.

ZEIDAN (ABDEL-LATIF M.) The United Nations Emergency Force, 1956-1967. Stockholm, [1976]. pp. 267. *bibliog.*

— Charter.

CURRENT problems of international law: essays on U.N. law and on the law of armed conflict; edited by Antonio Cassese. Milano, 1975. pp. 375. *(Pisa. Università. Facoltà di Giurisprudenza. Pubblicazioni. 60) Lectures given in the University of Pisa. In English or French.*

— Economic assistance.

GORDENKER (LEON) International aid and national decisions: development programs in Malawi, Tanzania and Zambia. Princeton, N.J., [1976]. pp. 190.

ACTION UNDP; (pd. by) United Nations Development Programme. bi-m., current issues only. New York.

— Officials and employees.

MERON (THEODOR) The United Nations Secretariat: the rules and the practice. Lexington, Mass., [1977]. pp. 208.

— Sanctions.

HASSE (ROLF) Wirtschaftliche Sanktionen als Mittel der Aussenpolitik: das Rhodesien-Embargo. Berlin, [1977]. pp. 299. *bibliog.*

— Secretariat.

MERON (THEODOR) The United Nations Secretariat: the rules and the practice. Lexington, Mass., [1977]. pp. 208.

— Voting.

HIRSCHMANN (DAVID) Southern African voting patterns in the United Nations General Assembly, 1971 and 1972. Johannesburg, 1973. pp. 13.

— Africa, Subsaharan.

HIRSCHMANN (DAVID) Southern African voting patterns in the United Nations General Assembly, 1971 and 1972. Johannesburg, 1973. pp. 13.

— China.

BACHRACK (STANLEY D.) The Committee of One Million: "China Lobby" politics, 1953-1971. New York, 1976. pp. 371. *bibliog.*

— Korea.

INSTITUTE FOR EAST ASIAN STUDIES. North Korea's policy toward the United Nations. Seoul, Korea, [1976?]. pp. 84.

— Rhodesia.

HASSE (ROLF) Wirtschaftliche Sanktionen als Mittel der Aussenpolitik: das Rhodesien-Embargo. Berlin, [1977]. pp. 299. *bibliog.*

— Russia — White Russia.

KISELEV (KUZ'MA VENEDIKTOVICH) Zapiski sovetskogo diplomata. Moskva, 1974. pp. 527.

— United States.

BALLINGER (RONALD B.) Dr. Moynihan and the Amalekites: the United States and the United Nations. Braamfontein, 1976. pp. 17.

UNITED NATIONS CONFERENCE ON TRADE AND DEVELOPMENT.

UNITED NATIONS. Conference on Trade and Development. 1968. The significance of the second session of the United Nations Conference on Trade and Development: report to the Secretary-General of the United Nations, etc. (TD/96/Rev. 1). New York, 1968. pp. 12.

UNITED NATIONS. Conference on Trade and Development, 2nd, New Delhi, 1968. Rules of procedure. (TD/63/Rev.1). New York, 1968. pp. 23.

MATZKE (OTTO) and STANZICK (KARL HEINZ) Unctad III: perspectivas y resultados. Santiago de Chile, 1972. pp. 207. *(Instituto Latinoamericano de Investigaciones Sociales. Estudios y Documentos. 17).*

UNITED NATIONS. Conference on Trade and Development. 1973. Rules of procedure of the Trade and Development Board. (TD/B/16/Rev. 2). [New York], 1973. pp. 52.

KEBSCHULL (DIETRICH) and others. Das integrierte Rohstoffprogramm: Prüfung entwicklungspolitischer Ansätze im Rohstoffvorschlag der UNCTAD. Hamburg, 1977. pp. 401. *bibliog. (Hamburg. Hamburgisches Welt-Wirtschafts-Archiv. Veröffentlichungen)*

KOUL (AUTAR KRISHAN) The legal framework of UNCTAD in world trade. Leyden, 1977. pp. 255. *bibliog.*

UNITED NATIONS ECONOMIC COMMISSION FOR EUROPE.

UNITED NATIONS. Economic Commission for Europe. Secretariat. 1973. Compendium of resolutions and decisions of the Economic Commission for Europe 1947-1972. (E/ECE/836). [Geneva], 1973. pp. 260.

UNITED NATIONS ECONOMIC COMMISSION FOR LATIN AMERICA.

GUZMAN (GABRIEL) El desarrollo latinoamericano y la CEPAL. Barcelona, 1976. pp. 359. *bibliog.*

UNITED NATIONS EDUCATIONAL, SCIENTIFIC AND CULTURAL ORGANIZATION

— Bibliography.

UNITED NATIONS EDUCATIONAL, SCIENTIFIC AND CULTURAL ORGANIZATION. Publications catalogue. irreg., 1977- Paris.

UNITED NATIONS ENVIRONMENT PROGRAMME.

UNEP:... annual review; by the Executive Director, (United Nations Environment Programme). a., 1975 (1st)-Nairobi.

UNITED SOUTH AFRICAN NATIONAL PARTY.

MITCHELL (M.L.) The Christian Institute: the United Party view. Johannesburg, [1975]. fo. 5. *In English and Afrikaans.*

UNITED STATES.

COLBOURNE (MAURICE DALE) America and Britain: a mutual introduction with special reference to the British Empire. London, 1943. pp. 230.

— Air Force.

BEARD (EDMUND) Developing the ICBM: a study in bureaucratic politics. New York, 1976. pp. 273. *bibliog. (Columbia University. Institute of War and Peace Studies)*

— Antiquities.

The CRISIS in North American archaeology; edited by Allen G. Pastron [and others]. Berkeley, Calif., 1973. pp. 163. *bibliog. (Kroeber Anthropological Society. Special Publications. No. 3) Papers derived from two symposia held in 1972.*

— Appropriations and expenditures.

LAMBRO (DONALD) The federal rathole. New Rochelle, N.Y., [1975]. pp. 207.

ECONOMIC impact of large public programs: the NASA experience; [by] Eli Ginzberg [and others]. Salt Lake City, [1976]. pp. 176. *bibliogs.*

KEMP (JACK) and ASPIN (LES) How much defense spending is enough?. Washington, [1976]. pp. 64. *(American Enterprise Institute for Public Policy Research. Rational Debate Series)*

REYNOLDS (MORGAN) and SMOLENSKY (EUGENE) Public expenditures, taxes, and the distribution of income: the United States, 1950, 1961, 1970. New York, [1977]. pp. 145. *bibliogs. (Wisconsin University, Madison. Institute for Research on Poverty. Monograph Series)*

— Armed forces.

KORB (LAWRENCE J.) The joint chiefs of staff: the first twenty-five years. Bloomington, Ind., [1976]. pp. 210.

SHERRY (MICHAEL S.) Preparing for the next war: American plans for postwar defense, 1941-45. New Haven, 1977. pp. 260. *bibliog.*

— — Women.

BINKIN (MARTIN) and BACH (SHIRLEY J.) Women and the military. Washington, D.C., [1977]. pp. 134. *(Brookings Institution. Studies in Defense Policy)*

— Church history.

HANDY (ROBERT THEODORE) A history of the churches in the United States and Canada. Oxford, 1976. pp. 471. *bibliog.*

— Civilization.

ESCRIVA PELLICER (M.) El desafio yanqui y España. Santander, [1974]. pp. 272.

KASSON (JOHN F.) Civilizing the machine: technology and Republican values in America, 1776-1900. New York, 1976. pp. 274.

QUALITIES of life. Lexington, Mass., [1976]. pp. 475. *(Commission on Critical Choices for Americans. Critical Choices for Americans. vol. 7)*

PLURALISM in a democratic society; edited by Melvin M. Tumin and Walter Plotch. New York, 1977. pp. 248. *bibliogs. Based on a conference convened by the Anti-Defamation League of B'nai B'rith, held in April 1975 in New York.*

— Commerce.

MITCHELL (DANIEL J.B.) Labor issues of American international trade and investment. Baltimore, [1976]. pp. 112.

FRANK (CHARLES R.) Foreign trade and domestic aid. Washington, D.C., [1977]. pp. 180.

— — Russia.

FRIESEN (CONNIE M.) The political economy of East-West trade. New York, 1976. pp. 203. *bibliog.*

— — Switzerland.

MEIER (ROLF HANS) Die Aufteilung des Frachttransportes auf Luft- und Oberflächenverkehr. Zürich, 1977. pp. 190. *bibliog. Dissertation der Universität Zürich zur Erlangung der Würde eines Doktors der Wirtschaftswissenschaft.*

— Commercial policy.

WEIL (GORDON LEE) American trade policy: a new round. New York, 1975. pp. 78.

TRADE, inflation and ethics. Lexington, Mass., [1976]. pp. 303. *bibliog. (Commission on Critical Choices for Americans. Critical Choices for Americans. vol.5) Prepared under the auspices of the Commission on Critical Choices for Americans.*

YEAGER (LELAND BENNETT) and TUERCK (DAVID G.) Foreign trade and U.S. policy: the case for free international trade. New York, 1976. pp. 295. *A revision of Trade policy and the price system.*

— Congress.

FRYE (ALTON) A responsible Congress: the politics of national security. New York, [1975]. pp. 238.

ORFIELD (GARY) Congressional power: Congress and social change. New York, [1975]. pp. 339.

PEABODY (ROBERT LEE) Leadership in Congress: stability, succession and change. Boston, [Mass., 1976]. pp. 522.

RIPLEY (RANDALL B.) and FRANKLIN (GRACE A.) Congress, the bureaucracy and public policy. Homewood, Ill., 1976. pp. 193. *bibliog.*

CONGRESS reconsidered; edited by Lawrence C. Dodd and Bruce I. Oppenheimer. New York, 1977. pp. 315. *bibliog.*

FIORINA (MORRIS P.) Congress: keystone of the Washington establishment. New Haven, 1977. pp. 105.

LEGISLATIVE reform and public policy; edited by Susan Welch and John G. Peters. New York, 1977. pp. 222. *bibliogs. Based on a symposium sponsored by the Department of Political Science at the University of Nebraska, 1976.*

— — Elections.

ALEXANDER (HERBERT E.) and others. Financing the 1972 election. Lexington, Mass., [1976]. pp. 771.

— — House of Representatives — Committees.

DAVIDSON (ROGER H.) and OLESZEK (WALTER J.) Congress against itself. Bloomington, Ind., [1977]. pp. 306. *bibliog.*

— Constitution.

DENENBERG (R.V.) Understanding American politics. [London], 1976 repr. 1977. pp. 218. *bibliog.*

— — 1st-10th Amendments.

BERNS (WALTER) The First amendment and the future of American democracy. New York, [1976]. pp. 266.

SCHWARTZ (BERNARD) The great rights of mankind: a history of the American Bill of Rights. New York, 1977. pp. 279.

— Defences.

AGAPOS (A.M.) Government-industry and defense: economics and administration. University, Alabama, [1975]. pp. 184. *bibliog.*

FRYE (ALTON) A responsible Congress: the politics of national security. New York, [1975]. pp. 238.

ARMS, defense policy and arms control; essays by Franklin A. Long [and others]; edited by Franklin A. Long and George W. Rathjens. New York, [1976]. pp. 222.

BEARD (EDMUND) Developing the ICBM: a study in bureaucratic politics. New York, 1976. pp. 273. *bibliog. (Columbia University. Institute of War and Peace Studies)*

KEMP (JACK) and ASPIN (LES) How much defense spending is enough?. Washington, [1976]. pp. 64. *(American Enterprise Institute for Public Policy Research. Rational Debate Series)*

MYRDAL (ALVA) The game of disarmament: how the United States and Russia run the arms race. New York, [1976]. pp. 397.

RUMMEL (RUDOLPH JOSEPH) Peace endangered: the reality of détente. Beverly Hills, [1976]. pp. 189.

TELLER (EDWARD) and others. Power and security. Lexington, Mass., [1976]. pp. 204. *(Commission on Critical Choices for Americans. Critical Choices for Americans. vol. 4)*

WHITEHURST (CLINTON H.) The defense transportation system: competitor or complement to the private sector?. Washington, D.C., [1976]. pp. 171. *bibliog. (American Enterprise Institute for Public Policy Research. Domestic Affairs Studies. 48)*

WHO's first in defense: the U.S. or the U.S.S.R.?; (an AEI round table held on June 3, 1976...); John Charles Daly, moderator, etc. Washington, [1976]. pp. 39. *(American Enterprise Institute for Public Policy Research. Round Tables)*

— Diplomatic and consular service.

SCHULZINGER (ROBERT D.) The making of the diplomatic mind: the training, outlook, and style of United States Foreign Service officers, 1908-1931. Middletown, Conn., [1975]. pp. 237. *bibliog.*

— Economic conditions.

ECONOMIC IMPACT: a q. review of world economics; [pd. by] United States Information Agency. q., 1973 (no.2)-, with gaps (1973, nos. 4, 5; 1975, no. 11; 1976, no. 15). Washington.

NATIONAL INDUSTRIAL CONFERENCE BOARD. Conference Board Economic Forum, New York, 1973. Boom, inflation, and policy: a mid-year review of the economic outlook: proceedings of the...forum. New York, 1973. pp. 72. *(National Industrial Conference Board. Conference Board Reports)*

AEI studies on contemporary economic problems; William Fellner, editor. Washington, D.C., [1976]. pp. 369.

BACKMAN (JULES) ed. Business and the American economy, 1776-2001. New York, 1976. pp. 196. *(New York (City). University. College of Business and Public Administration. Key Issues Lecture Series. 5)*

The ECONOMY in transition; edited by Robert C. Blattberg. New York, 1976. pp. 137. *(International Telephone and Telegraph Corporation. Key Issues Lecture Series) Essays originally commissioned in 1974 as a series of lectures entitled The economy in disarray.*

ESTALL (ROBERT CHARLES) A modern geography of the United States: aspects of life and economy. 2nd ed. Harmondsworth, 1976. pp. 466. *bibliog.*

HELLER (WALTER W.) The economy: old myths and new realities. New York, [1976]. pp. 224. *bibliog.*

MILES (RUFUS E.) Awakening from the American dream: the social and political limits to growth. New York, 1976. pp. 246.

PARKER (JOHN J.) The rape of the American worker. Hicksville, N.Y., [1976]. pp. 385.

STOBAUGH (ROBERT B.) and others. Nine investments abroad and their impact at home: case studies on multinational enterprises and the U.S. economy. Boston, [Mass.], 1976. pp. 222.

FERNANDEZ (RAUL A.) The United States-Mexico border: a politico-economic profile. Notre Dame, Ind., [1977]. pp. 174.

GALBRAITH (JOHN KENNETH) The affluent society. 3rd ed. London, 1977. pp. 287.

GOLDSTENE (PAUL N.) The collapse of liberal empire: science and revolution in the twentieth century. New Haven, 1977. pp. 139.

GREENBERG (EDWARD S.) The American political system: a radical approach. Cambridge, Mass., [1977]. pp. 501. bibliogs.

SPEISER (STUART M.) A piece of the action: a plan to provide every family with a [dollar]100,000 stake in the economy. New York, [1977]. pp. 390. bibliog.

— — Information services.

PORAT (MARC URI) The information economy. Ann Arbor, Mich., [1976]. 2 vols. Ph.D. dissertation, Stanford University.

— — Mathematical models.

MIRKIN (BORIS GRIGOR'EVICH) and VAL'TUKH (KONSTANTIN KURTOVICH) eds. Ukrupnennye i mezhotraslevye modeli narodnogo khoziaistva. Novosibirsk, 1976. pp. 254. (Akademiia Nauk SSSR. Sibirskoe Otdelenie. Institut Ekonomiki i Organizatsii Promyshlennogo Proizvodstva. Problemy Postroeniia i Ispol'zovaniia Narodnokhoziaistvennykh Modelei)

— Economic history.

HILL (PETER JENSEN) The economic impact of immigration into the United States. New York, 1976. pp. 130. Originally presented as a Ph.D. thesis, University of Chicago, 1970.

BRUCHEY (STUART WEEMS) Growth of the modern American economy. New York, 1975. pp. 154. bibliog.

VATTER (HAROLD G.) The drive to industrial maturity: the U.S. economy, 1860-1914. Westport, Conn., 1975. pp. 368. bibliog.

GUNDERSON (GERALD) A new economic history of America. New York, [1976]. pp. 530. bibliogs.

— Economic policy.

ANSWERS to inflation and recession: economic policies for a modern society; edited by Albert T. Sommers; a colloquium held April 8-9, 1975 at the Mayflower Hotel, Washington, D. C. [New York], [1975]. pp. 154. (National Industrial Conference Board. Conference Board Reports. No. 666)

CASH (WILLIAM L.) and OLIVER (LUCY R.) eds. Black economic development: analysis and implications: an anthology. Ann Arbor, Mich., [1975]. pp. 426. bibliogs.

AEI studies on contemporary economic problems; William Fellner, editor. Washington, D.C., [1976]. pp. 369.

AMACHER (RYAN C.) and others, eds. The economic approach to public policy: selected readings. Ithaca, N.Y., 1976. pp. 528.

COMMONER (BARRY) The poverty of power: energy and the economic crisis. New York, 1976. pp. 314.

CONFERENCE ON INDIVIDUAL LIBERTY AND GOVERNMENTAL POLICIES IN THE 1970'S, OHIO UNIVERSITY, 1975. Governmental controls and the free market: the U.S. economy in the 1970's (papers presented at the conference); edited by Svetozar Pejovich. College Station, Tex., [1976]. pp. 225. Conference held under the auspices of the Department of Economics, Ohio University.

HELLER (WALTER W.) The economy: old myths and new realities. New York, [1976]. pp. 224. bibliog.

LEONTIEF (WASSILY W.) and STEIN (HERBERT) The economic system in an age of discontinuity: long-range planning or market reliance?. New York, 1976. pp. 148. (New York (City). University. College of Business and Public Administration. Charles C. Moskowitz Memorial Lectures. No.17)

MARSHALL (F. RAY) and others. Labor economics: wages, employment, and trade unionism. 3rd ed. Homewood, Ill., 1976. pp. 633. bibliogs.

NATIONAL economic planning: right or wrong for the U.S.?; (an AEI Round Table held on April 1, 1976 [in Washington] ...); John Charles Daly, moderator, etc. Washington, [1976]. pp. 51. (American Enterprise Institute for Public Policy Research. Round Tables)

RUGINA (ANGHEL N.) American capitalism at a crossroadse': where do we go from here?: a chronicle of how three U.S. presidents missed sound economic advice to resolve the problems of inflation, unemployment, poverty and deficits in the balance of payments. Hicksville, [1976]. pp. 269.

SOBEL (LESTER A.) ed. Ford and the economy. New York, [1976]. pp. 248. Revised version of the weekly reports compiled by Facts on File.

WALLIS (WILSON ALLEN) An overgoverned society. New York, [1976]. pp. 292.

BUCHANAN (JAMES McGILL) and WAGNER (RICHARD E.) Democracy in deficit: the political legacy of Lord Keynes. New York, [1977]. pp. 195.

HUGHES (JONATHAN ROBERTS TYSON) The governmental habit: economic controls from colonial times to the present. New York, [1977]. pp. 260.

LEWIS (EUGENE) American politics in a bureaucratic age: citizens, constituents, clients and victims. Cambridge, Mass., [1977]. pp. 182.

TUGWELL (REXFORD GUY) Roosevelt's revolution: the first year; a personal perspective. New York, [1977]. pp. 327.

— Emigration and immigration.

HILL (PETER JENSEN) The economic impact of immigration into the United States. New York, 1976. pp. 130. Originally presented as a Ph.D. thesis, University of Chicago, 1970.

BOGINA (SHIFRA ABRAMOVNA) Immigrantskoe naselenie SShA, 1865-1900 gg. Leningrad, 1976. pp. 274. With English summary.

CURRENT issues in social; policy edited by W. Boyd Littrell [and] Gideon Sjoberg. Beverly Hills, Calif., [1976]. pp. 248. bibliogs. Papers prepared for an interdisciplinary conference held in 1975, at the University of Texas.

REISLER (MARK) By the sweat of their brow: Mexican immigrant labor in the United States, 1900-1940. Westport, Conn., 1976. pp. 298. bibliog.

McKEE (DELBER L.) Chinese exclusion versus the open door policy, 1900-1906: clashes over China policy in the Roosevelt era. Detroit, 1977. pp. 292. bibliog.

— Executive departments.

LAMBRO (DONALD) The federal rathole. New Rochelle, N.Y., [1975]. pp. 207.

CAMPBELL (RITA RICARDO) Drug lag: federal government decision making. Stanford, Calif., 1976. pp. 62. (Stanford University. Hoover Institution on War, Revolution and Peace. Hoover Institution Studies. 55)

AMERICAN ENTERPRISE INSTITUTE FOR PUBLIC POLICY RESEARCH. Legislative Analyses. 95th Congress. No. 2. The Executive Reorganization Act: a survey of proposals for renewal and modification. Washington, 1977. pp. 15.

HAWES (GRACE M.) The Marshall Plan for China: Economic Co-operation Administration, 1948-1949. Cambridge, Mass., [1977]. pp. 138. bibliogs.

HECLO (HUGH) A government of strangers: executive politics in Washington. Washington, D.C., [1977]. pp. 272.

MAGDOL (EDWARD) A right to the land: essays on the freedmen's community. Westport, Conn., 1977. pp. 290. bibliog.

— Foreign economic relations.

BARNET (RICHARD JOSEPH) Roots of war. New York, 1973 repr. 1976. pp. 350.

DECLASSIFIED DOCUMENTS REFERENCE SYSTEM, THE, [retrospective and annual collections]. q., [Retrospective collection and annual collection from] 1975 (1st)- Washington.

ADAMS (FREDERICK C.) Economic diplomacy: the Export-Import Bank and American foreign policy, 1934-1939. Columbia, Mo., 1976. pp. 289. bibliog.

AEI studies on contemporary economic problems; William Fellner, editor. Washington, D.C., [1976]. pp. 369.

INTERNATIONAL ECONOMIC STUDIES INSTITUTE. Raw materials and foreign policy. Washington, D.C., [1976]. pp. 416.

SCHNEIDER (WILLIAM) Food, foreign policy and raw materials cartels. New York, [1976]. pp. 119. (National Strategy Information Center. Strategy Papers. No. 28)

TRADE, inflation and ethics. Lexington, Mass., [1976]. pp. 303. bibliog. (Commission on Critical Choices for Americans. Critical Choices for Americans. vol.5) Prepared under the auspices of the Commission on Critical Choices for Americans.

BLOCK (FRED L.) The origins of international economic disorder: a study of United States international monetary policy from World War II to the present. Berkeley, Calif., [1977]. pp. 282. bibliog.

HOGAN (MICHAEL J.) Informal entente: the private structure of cooperation in Anglo- American diplomacy, 1918-1928. Columbia, Mo., 1977. pp. 254. bibliog.

— — America, Latin.

HANSEN (ROGER D.) U.S.-Latin American economic policy: bilateral, regional, or global? Washington, D.C., 1975. pp. 69. (Overseas Development Council. Development Papers. 18)

BAILY (SAMUEL L.) The United States and the development of South America, 1945- 1975. New York, 1976. pp. 246. bibliog.

SWANSBROUGH (ROBERT H.) The embattled colossus: economic nationalism and United States investors in Latin America. Gainesville, Florida, 1976. pp. 261. bibliog. (Florida University. School of Inter-American Studies. Latin American Monographs. 2nd Series. 16)

UNITED States policy towards Latin America: antecedents and alternatives; Lewis A. Tambs, editor. Tempe, [1976]. pp. 220. A collection of papers presented at a conference held at Arizona State University..., 1975 and sponsored by the Center for Latin American Studies...and the American Graduate School of International Management.

— — Andes Region.

PIKE (FREDERICK BRAUN) The United States and the Andean Republics: Peru, Bolivia, and Ecuador. Cambridge, Mass., 1977. pp. 493. bibliogs.

— — Canada.

DOSMAN (EDGAR J.) The national interest: the politics of Northern development, 1968-75. Toronto, [1975]. pp. 224.

— — East (Far East).

ANDERSON (IRVINE H.) The Standard-Vacuum Oil Company and United States East Asian policy, 1933-1941. Princeton, [1975]. pp. 261. bibliog.

— — Europe.

URI (PIERRE) Europe et Amérique: relations économiques, problèmes politiques. Nancy, 1966. pp. 28. (Nancy. Université. Centre Européen Universitaire. Collection des Conférences Européennes. No. 2)

The EURO-American system: economic and political relations between North America and Western Europe; edited by Ernst-Otto Czempiel and Dankwart A. Rustow. Frankfurt, 1976. pp. 233. *Proceedings of a conference held in Arnoldshain, Germany, 1975.*

— — Rhodesia.

LAKE (ANTHONY) The "tar baby" option: American policy toward Southern Rhodesia. New York, 1976. pp. 316. *bibliog.*

— — Russia.

SSSR - SShA: ekonomicheskie otnosheniia: problemy i vozmozhnosti. Moskva, 1976. pp. 416.

— Foreign opinion.

RADIO FREE EUROPE. Audience and Public Opinion Research Department. The images of Polish, American, Russian, German and Chinese youth as seen by Poles. [Munich?], 1973. fo. 55.

— Foreign opinion, Russian.

GIBERT (STEPHEN P.) and others. Soviet images of America. London, [1977]. pp. 167. *bibliog.*

— Foreign relations.

PARTIDO COMUNISTA DE CUBA. Comite Central. Statement...on the new threat of imperialist aggression, Havana, May 17, 1967. London, Cuban Embassy, 1967. pp. 6. *(Cuba Information Bulletins. 1967. No. 7)*

HILSMAN (ROGER) The politics of policy making in defense and foreign affairs. New York, [1971]. pp. 198.

PARENTI (MICHAEL) ed. Trends and tragedies in American foreign policy. Boston, Mass., [1971]. pp. 228.

BARNET (RICHARD JOSEPH) Roots of war. New York, 1973 repr. 1976. pp. 350.

PATERSON (THOMAS GRAHAM) ed. American imperialism and anti-imperialism. New York, [1973]. pp. 149. *bibliog.*

COPLIN (WILLIAM D.) and others. American foreign policy: an introduction to analysis and evaluation. North Scituate, Mass., [1974]. pp. 272. *bibliog.*

FALK (RICHARD A.) What's wrong with Henry Kissinger's foreign policy? Princeton, 1974. pp. 36. *(Princeton University. Center of International Studies. Policy Memoranda. No. 39)*

DECLASSIFIED DOCUMENTS REFERENCE SYSTEM, THE, [retrospective and annual collections]. q., [Retrospective collection and annual collection from] 1975 (1st)- Washington.

DAVIS (CALVIN DEARMOND) The United States and the second Hague Peace Conference: American diplomacy and international organization, 1899-1914. Durham, N.C., 1975. pp. 398. *bibliog.*

IRISH (MARIAN DORIS) and FRANK (ELKE) U.S. foreign policy: context, conduct, content. New York, [1975]. pp. 562. *bibliog.*

LEVY (REYNOLD) Nearing the crossroads: contending approaches to contemporary American foreign policy. New York, [1975]. pp. 180. *bibliog.*

PARKMAN (AUBREY) David Jayne Hill and the problem of world peace. Lewisburg, [1975]. pp. 293. *bibliogs.*

ADAMS (FREDERICK C.) Economic diplomacy: the Export-Import Bank and American foreign policy, 1934-1939. Columbia, Mo., 1976. pp. 289. *bibliog.*

ALLISON (GRAHAM T.) and SZANTON (PETER L.) Remaking foreign policy: the organizational connection. New York, [1976]. pp. 238.

DARILEK (RICHARD E.) A loyal opposition in time of war: the Republican Party and the politics of foreign policy from Pearl Harbour to Yalta. Westport, Conn., 1976. pp. 239. *bibliog.*

DORAN (CHARLES F.) Domestic conflict in state relations: the American sphere of influence. Beverly Hills, [1976]. pp. 58. *bibliog.*

DOUGLAS-HOME (ALEXANDER FREDERICK) Baron Home, and others. Diplomacy, détente and the democracies;... edited...by D.K. Adams. Keele, [1976]. pp. 48. *(Keele. University. David Bruce Centre for American Studies. Lectures. 1976)*

GARDNER (LLOYD C.) Imperial America: American foreign policy since 1898. New York, [1976]. pp. 301. *bibliogs.*

LEHMAN (JOHN) The Executive, Congress and foreign policy: studies of the Nixon administration. New York, 1976. pp. 247. *bibliog.*

LEIGH (MICHAEL) Mobilizing consent: public opinion and American foreign policy, 1937-1947. Westport, Conn., 1976. pp. 187. *bibliog.*

LODGE (HENRY CABOT) 1902- . As it was: an inside view of politics and power in the '50s and '60s. New York, [1976]. pp. 224.

McLELLAN (DAVID S.) Dean Acheson : the State Department years. New York, [1976]. pp. 466.

MAZLISH (BRUCE) Kissinger: the European mind in American policy. New York, [1976]. pp. 330.

NAU (HENRY R.) and others. Technology transfer and U.S. foreign policy. New York, 1976. pp. 325.

PURIFOY (LEWIS McCARROLL) Harry Truman's China policy: McCarthyism and the diplomacy of hysteria, 1947-1951. New York, 1976. pp. 316.

SOFAER (ABRAHAM D.) War, foreign affairs and constitutional power: the origins. Cambridge, Mass., [1976]. pp. 533. *bibliog.*

SOLZHENITSYN (ALEKSANDR ISAEVICH) Détente: prospects for democracy and dictatorship;...with commentary by Alex Simirenko [and others]. New Brunswick, [1976]. pp. 112. *Based on addresses given in Washington, D.C. and New York in 1975.*

STOESSINGER (JOHN GEORGE) Henry Kissinger: the anguish of power. New York, [1976]. pp. 234.

WALTON (RICHARD J.) Henry Wallace, Harry Truman, and the Cold War. New York, 1976. pp. 388. *bibliog.*

WHITSON (WILLIAM W.) ed. Foreign policy and U.S. national security: major postelection issues. New York, 1976. pp. 368. *bibliog.*

BARNETT (ARTHUR DOAK) China policy: old problems and new challenges. Washington, D.C., [1977]. pp. 131.

BASIUK (VICTOR) Technology, world politics, and American policy. New York, 1977. pp. 409. *bibliog.*

BERKOWITZ (MORTON) and others. The politics of American foreign policy: the social context of decisions. Englewood Cliffs, N.J., [1977]. pp. 310. *bibliogs.*

GIBERT (STEPHEN P.) and others. Soviet images of America. London, [1977]. pp. 167. *bibliog.*

GRAEBNER (NORMAN ARTHUR) Cold war diplomacy: American foreign policy, 1945-1975. New York, [1977]. pp. 248. *bibliog.*

IRIYE (AKIRA) From nationalism to internationalism: U.S. foreign policy to 1914. London, 1977. pp. 368.

MORRIS (ROGER) Uncertain greatness: Henry Kissinger and American foreign policy. New York, [1977]. pp. 312.

SHOUP (LAURENCE H.) and MINTER (WILLIAM) Imperial brain trust: the Council on Foreign Relations and United States foreign policy. New York, [1977]. pp. 334. *bibliog.*

STOLER (MARK A.) The politics of the second front: American military planning and diplomacy in coalition warfare, 1941-1943. Westport, Conn., 1977. pp. 244. *bibliogs.*

WALWORTH (ARTHUR CLARENCE) America's moment, 1918: American diplomacy at the end of World War I. New York, [1977]. pp. 309. *bibliog.*

YERGIN (DANIEL) Shattered peace: the origins of the cold war and the national security state. Boston, Mass., 1977. pp. 526. *bibliog.*

See also EUROPEAN ECONOMIC COMMUNITY — United States; UNITED NATIONS — United States.

— — Treaties.

PACHECO QUINTERO (JORGE) El Congreso Anfictionico de Panama y la politica internacional de los Estados Unidos. Bogota, 1971. pp. 170. *(Academia Colombiana de Historia. Coleccion de Bolsilibros. 18)*

— — America, Latin.

CASTRO RUZ (FIDEL) Speech delivered...at the ceremony held in the Chaplin Theatre, April 19, 1967, commemorating the anniversary of the defeat of Yankee imperialism at Playa Giron. London, Cuban Embassy, 1967. pp. 15. *(Cuba Information Bulletins. 1967. No. 4)*

GRIEB (KENNETH J.) The Latin American policy of Warren G. Harding. Fort Worth, Texas, [1976]. pp. 223. *bibliog.*

TARNOFF (CURTIS LEE) Evolving structures of great power blocs: the U.S.A. and Latin America, 1901-1975: the USSR and Eastern Europe, 1945-1975. 1976. fo. 529. *bibliog. Typescript. Ph.D. (London) thesis: unpublished. This thesis is the property of London University and may not be removed from the Library.*

UNITED States policy towards Latin America: antecedents and alternatives; Lewis A. Tambs, editor. Tempe, [1976]. pp. 220. *A collection of papers presented at a conference held at Arizona State University..., 1975 and sponsored by the Center for Latin American Studies...and the American Graduate School of International Management.*

— — Asia.

ROSE (LISLE ABBOTT) Roots of tragedy: the United States and the struggle for Asia, 1945-1953. Westport, Conn., 1976. pp. 262. *bibliog.*

SOUTHERN Asia: the politics of poverty and peace; edited by Donald C. Hellmann. Lexington, Mass., [1976]. pp. 297. *(Commission on Critical Choices for Americans. Critical Choices for Americans. vol. 13)*

— — Asia, Southeast.

MARTIN (EDWIN W.) Southeast Asia and China: the end of containment. Boulder, Colo., 1977. pp. 114. *Prepared for the Center for Strategic and International Studies, Georgetown University.*

— — Bolivia.

ANDRADE (VICTOR) My missions for revolutionary Bolivia, 1944-1962;...edited and with an introduction by Cole Blasier. Pittsburgh, Pa., [1976]. pp. 200.

— — Brazil.

BLACK (JAN KNIPPERS) United States penetration of Brazil. [Philadelphia], 1977. pp. 313. *bibliog.*

— — Chile.

CHILE: the balanced view: a recopilation of articles about the Allende years and after; (edited by Francisco Orrego Vicuña). [Santiago, 1975]. pp. 298. *(Santiago de Chile. Universidad de Chile. Instituto de Estudios Internacionales. Estudios Internacionales)*

URIBE ARCE (ARMANDO) The black book of American intervention in Chile;...translated from the Spanish by Jonathan Casart. Boston, [Mass], [1975]. pp. 163.

— — China.

AMERICAN FRIENDS SERVICE COMMITTEE. Working Party on China Policy. A new China policy: some Quaker proposals. New Haven, Conn., [1965]. pp. 68. *bibliog.*

BACHRACK (STANLEY D.) The Committee of One Million: "China Lobby" politics, 1953-1971. New York, 1976. pp. 371. *bibliog.*

CHINA and Japan: a new balance of power; edited by Donald C. Hellmann. Lexington, Mass., [1976]. pp. 305. *(Commission on Critical Choices for Americans. Critical Choices for Americans. vol.12)*

HINTON (HAROLD CLENDENIN) Peking-Washington: Chinese foreign policy and the United States. Beverly Hills, [1976]. pp. 96. *bibliog. (Georgetown University. Center for Strategic and International Studies. Washington Papers. vol. 4/34)*

PURIFOY(LEWIS McCARROLL) Harry Truman's China policy: McCarthyism and the diplomacy of hysteria, 1947-1951. New York, 1976. pp. 316.

McKEE (DELBER L.) Chinese exclusion versus the open door policy, 1900-1906: clashes over China policy in the Roosevelt era. Detroit, 1977. pp. 292. *bibliog.*

— — Communist countries.

BELL (CORAL) The diplomacy of detente: the Kissinger era. London, 1977. pp. 278. *bibliog.*

— — Cuba.

CASTRO RUZ (RAUL) Speech given by Major Raul Castro Ruz, second secretary of the central committee of the Communist Party of Cuba, in the graduation ceremony for the third course of the General Maximo Gomez Basic School, July 22, 1967. London, Cuban Embassy, 1967. pp. 15. *(Cuba Information Bulletins. 1967. No. 9)*

CUBA. 1972. (Complete text of the declaration made by the Cuban revolutionary government regarding the hijacking of aircraft, issued on the 15th of November, 1972). [London, Cuban Embassy], 1972. fo. 5. *(Press Releases)*

— — Cyprus.

CYPRUS reviewed: the result of a seminar on the Cyprus problem held in June 3-6, 1976, by the Jus Cypri Association and the Coordinating Committee of Scientific and Cultural Organisations; edited by Michael A. Attalides. Nicosia, 1977. pp. 275.

— — East (Far East).

UTLEY (FREDA) The China story. Chicago, 1951 repr. 1962. pp. 274.

DORWART (JEFFERY M.) The Pigtail War: American involvement in the Sino-Japanese War of 1894-1895. Amherst, Mass., 1975. pp. 168. *bibliog.*

INTERNATIONAL INSTITUTE FOR STRATEGIC STUDIES. Adelphi Papers. No. 132. American security policy in Asia; by Leslie H. Brown. London, 1977. pp. 36.

— — East (Near East).

TRICE (ROBERT H.) Interest groups and the foreign policy process: U.S. policy in the Middle East. Beverly Hills, [1976]. pp. 80.

BRYSON (THOMAS A.) American diplomatic relations with the Middle East, 1784-1975: survey. Metuchen, N.J., [1977]. pp. 431. *bibliog.*

LATTER (RICHARD) The making of American foreign policy in the Middle East, 1945- 48. 1976 [or rather 1977]. fo. 463. *bibliog. Typescript. Ph.D. (London) thesis: unpublished. This thesis is the property of London University and may not be removed from the Library.*

— — Europe.

CONFERENCE ON AMERICAN FOREIGN POLICY AND THE NEW EUROPE, BLACKSBURG, 1974. America and European security; edited by Louis J. Mensonides and James A. Kuhlman. Leyden, 1976. pp. 170. *bibliog. (East-West Foundation. East-West Perspectives. 2)*

The EURO-American system: economic and political relations between North America and Western Europe; edited by Ernst- Otto Czempiel and Dankwart A. Rustow. Frankfurt, 1976. pp. 233. *Proceedings of a conference held in Arnoldshain, Germany, 1975.*

GODSON (ROY) American labor and European politics: the AFL as a transnational force. New York, [1976]. pp. 230. *bibliog.*

MALLY (GERHARD) Interdependence: the European-American connection in the global context. Lexington, Mass., [1976]. pp. 229.

— — Germany.

HERWIG (HOLGER H.) Politics of frustration: the United States in German naval planning, 1889-1941. Boston, Mass., [1976]. pp. 323. *bibliog.*

— — Ireland (Republic).

DWYER (T. RYLE) Irish neutrality and the USA 1939-47. Dublin, 1977. pp. 241.

— — Japan.

JAPANESE-American relations; (an AEI Round Table held on 17 December 1974...); Donald C. Hellman, etc. Washington, [1975]. pp. 27. *(American Enterprise Institute for Public Policy Research. Round Tables)*

PFALTZGRAFF (ROBERT L.) and DAVIS (JACQUELYN K.) Japanese-American relations in a changing security environment. Beverly Hills, [1975]. pp. 49.

CHINA and Japan: a new balance of power; edited by Donald C. Hellmann. Lexington, Mass., [1976]. pp. 305. *(Commission on Critical Choices for Americans. Critical Choices for Americans. vol.12)*

MANAGING an alliance: the politics of U.S.-Japanese relations; ([by]) I.M. Destler [and others]. Washington, D.C., [1976]. pp. 209. *bibliog.*

— — Mexico.

GUERRERO YOACHAM (CRISTIAN) Las conferencias del Niagara Falls: la mediacion de Argentina, Brasil y Chile en el conflicto entre Estados Unidos y Mexico en 1914. Santiago de Chile, 1966. pp. 189. *bibliog.*

MEYER (LORENZO) Mexico and the United States in the oil controversy, 1917-1942. Austin, [Tex., 1972]. pp. 367. *bibliog.*

— — Palestine.

JANSEN (MICHAEL E.) The three basic American decisions on Palestine. Beirut, 1971. pp. 46. *(Palestine Research Center. Palestine Essays. No. 25)*

— — Rhodesia.

LAKE (ANTHONY) The "tar baby" option: American policy toward Southern Rhodesia. New York, 1976. pp. 316. *bibliog.*

— — Russia.

KHRUSHCHEV (NIKITA SERGEEVICH) Comment la conférence au sommet a été torpillée. Paris, [imprint], 1960. pp. 27. *"Texte intégral de la conférence de presse de N. Khrouchtchev". (p.7)*

STEIBEL (GERALD L.) Detente: promises and pitfalls. New York, [1975]. pp. 85. *(National Strategy Information Center. Strategy Papers. No. 25)*

BOLKHOVITINOV (NIKOLAI NIKOLAEVICH) Rossiia i voina SShA za nezavisimost', 1775-1783. Moskva, 1976. pp. 272. *bibliog.*

CALDWELL (LAWRENCE T.) Soviet-American relations: one half decade of detente problems and issues. Paris, [1976]. pp. 63. *(Atlantic Institute. Atlantic Papers. 1975.5)*

The FUTURE of Soviet military power; edited by Lawrence L. Whetten. New York, [1976]. pp. 190. *Papers of a conference held at Ebenhausen, West Germany, 1975, under the aegis of the Stiftung für Wissenschaft und Politik and the University of Southern California.*

LEVERING (RALPH B.) American opinion and the Russian alliance, 1939-1945. Chapel Hill, N.C., [1976]. pp. 262. *bibliog.*

PRANGER (ROBERT JOHN) ed. Detente and defense: a reader. Washington, D.C., 1976. pp. 445. *(American Enterprise Institute for Public Policy Research. Foreign Affairs Studies. 40)*

RUMMEL (RUDOLPH JOSEPH) Peace endangered: the reality of détente. Beverly Hills, [1976]. pp. 189.

The SOVIET empire: expansion and détente; edited by William E. Griffith. Lexington, Mass., [1976]. pp. 417. *(Commission on Critical Choices for Americans. Critical Choices for Americans. vol.9)*

YERGIN (DANIEL) Shattered peace: the origins of the cold war and the national security state. Boston, Mass., 1977. pp. 526. *bibliog.*

— — Saudi Arabia.

ALI (RUSTUM) Sheikh. Saudi Arabia and oil diplomacy. New York, 1976. pp. 197. *bibliog.*

— — South Africa.

CARTER (GWENDOLEN MARGARET) American policy and the search for justice and reconciliation in South Africa; originally prepared for the Wingspread Symposium on South Africa: Policy Alternatives for the United States, convened April 1975 [at] Wingspread, Racine, Wisconsin, revised by the author in September 1976. Racine, Wisc., [1976]. pp. 52.

SOUTH Africa - the vital link; edited by Robert L. Schuettinger. Washington, D.C., 1976. pp. 120. *Essays from a seminar on United States-South African relations in Washington, D.C., on July 20, 1976, sponsored by the Council on American Affairs.*

— — Spain.

CHAMORRO (EDUARDO) and FONTES (IGNACIO) Las bases norteamericanas en España. Barcelona, 1976. pp. 328.

— — United Kingdom.

CHRISTIE (IAN RALPH) and LABAREE (BENJAMIN WOODS) Empire or independence, 1760-1776: a British-American dialogue on the coming of the American revolution. Oxford, 1976. pp. 332. *bibliog.*

REES (MARK STEPHEN) Anglo-American relations, 1953-55: the institutional and operational levels of compromise. [1976]. fo. 249. *bibliog. Typescript. M.Phil. (London) thesis: unpublished. This thesis is the property of London University and may not be removed from the Library.*

FERRIS (NORMAN B.) The Trent affair: a diplomatic crisis. Knoxville, Tenn., [1977]. pp. 280. *bibliog.*

GRIFFITH (SAMUEL B.) In defense of the public liberty: Britain, America, and the struggle for independence, 1760-81. London, 1977. pp. 725. *bibliog.*

— — Vietnam.

ANDREWS (BRUCE) Public constraint and American policy in Vietnam. Beverly Hills, [1976]. pp. 64. *bibliog.*

— Foreign relations administration.

BARNET (RICHARD JOSEPH) Roots of war. New York, 1973 repr. 1976. pp. 350.

SCHULZINGER (ROBERT D.) The making of the diplomatic mind: the training, outlook, and style of United States Foreign Service officers, 1908-1931. Middletown, Conn., [1975]. pp. 237. *bibliog.*

— Government publications.

MOREHEAD (JOE) Introduction to United States public documents. Littleton, Colo., 1975. pp. 289. *bibliogs.*

— — Bibliography.

DECLASSIFIED DOCUMENTS QUARTERLY CATALOG, THE. q., Ja/Mr 1975 (v.1, no. 1)- Washington. *In 2 pts; pt. 1 Abstracts; pt. 2 Cumulative subject index.*

LEIDY (WILLIAM PHILIP) compiler. A popular guide to government publications. 4th ed. New York, 1976. pp. 440.

PALIC (VLADIMIR M.) compiler. Government publications: a guide to bibliographic tools; incorporating Government organization manuals: a bibliography. Oxford, [1977]. pp. 553.

— — Indexes.

DECLASSIFIED DOCUMENTS QUARTERLY CATALOG, THE. q., Ja/Mr 1975 (v.1, no. 1)- Washington. *In 2 pts; pt. 1 Abstracts; pt. 2 Cumulative subject index.*

— History.

WOODWARD (COMER VANN) ed. A comparative approach to American history. Washington, D.C., 1968 repr. 1974. pp. 390. *bibliog. (United States. United States Information Agency. Voice of America. Forum Lectures)*

NOVACK (GEORGE) ed. America's revolutionary heritage: Marxist essays edited with an introduction. New York, [1976]. pp. 414.

— — 1775-1783, Revolution.

BOLKHOVITINOV (NIKOLAI NIKOLAEVICH) Rossiia i voina SShA za nezavisimost', 1775-1783. Moskva, 1976. pp. 272. *bibliog.*

CALHOON (ROBERT M.) Revolutionary America: an interpretive overview. New York, [1976]. pp. 212. *bibliogs.*

FONER (PHILIP SHELDON) Labor and the American revolution. Westport, Conn., [1976]. pp. 256. *bibliog.*

KARIMSKII (ANIUR MUSEEVICH) Revoliutsiia 1776 goda i stanovlenie amerikanskoi filosofii. Moskva, 1976. pp. 296. *bibliog.*

PAINE (THOMAS) Common sense; edited with an introduction by Isaac Kramnick. Harmondsworth, 1976. pp. 128. *bibliog.*

GRIFFITH (SAMUEL B.) In defense of the public liberty: Britain, America, and the struggle for independence, 1760-81. London, 1977. pp. 725. *bibliog.*

— — — Causes.

CHRISTIE (IAN RALPH) and LABAREE (BENJAMIN WOODS) Empire or independence, 1760-1776: a British-American dialogue on the coming of the American revolution. Oxford, 1976. pp. 332. *bibliog.*

— — — Foreign public opinion.

AMERICAN ACADEMY OF POLITICAL AND SOCIAL SCIENCE. Annals. vol. 428. The American Revolution abroad; special editor of this volume: Richard L. Park. Philadelphia, [1976]. pp. 195.

— — — French participation.

GRIFFITH (SAMUEL B.) In defense of the public liberty: Britain, America, and the struggle for independence, 1760-81. London, 1977. pp. 725. *bibliog.*

— — — Influence.

AMERICAN ACADEMY OF POLITICAL AND SOCIAL SCIENCE. Annals. vol. 428. The American Revolution abroad; special editor of this volume: Richard L. Park. Philadelphia, [1976]. pp. 195.

— — 1865-1898.

KELLER (MORTON) Affairs of state: public life in late nineteenth century America. Cambridge, Mass., 1977. pp. 631.

— — 1900- .

PHILLIPS (CABELL B.H.) The 1940s: decade of triumph and trouble. New York, [1975]. pp. 414.

BATES (JAMES LEONARD) The United States, 1898-1928: progressivism and a society in transition. New York, [1976]. pp. 339. *bibliogs.*

— — 1945- .

HODGSON (GODFREY) In our time: America from World War II to Nixon. London, 1977. pp. 564. *First published in the United States of America in 1976*

— History, Naval.

HERWIG (HOLGER H.) Politics of frustration: the United States in German naval planning, 1889-1941. Boston, Mass., [1976]. pp. 323. *bibliog.*

— Industries.

VATTER (HAROLD G.) The drive to industrial maturity: the U.S. economy, 1860-1914. Westport, Conn., 1975. pp. 368. *bibliog.*

MILLER (EUGENE WILLARD) Manufacturing: a study of industrial location. Pennsylvania, [1977]. pp. 286.

— Intellectual life.

ROSENBERG (HAROLD) Discovering the present: three decades in art, culture, and politics. Chicago, 1973. pp. 336.

— Military policy.

KORB (LAWRENCE J.) The joint chiefs of staff: the first twenty-five years. Bloomington, Ind., [1976]. pp. 210.

GIBERT (STEPHEN P.) and others. Soviet images of America. London, [1977]. pp. 167. *bibliog.*

INTERNATIONAL INSTITUTE FOR STRATEGIC STUDIES. Adelphi Papers. No. 132. American security policy in Asia; by Leslie H. Brown. London, 1977. pp. 36.

LENS (SIDNEY) The day before doomsday: an anatomy of the nuclear arms race. New York, 1977. pp. 274.

LEWIS (EUGENE) American politics in a bureaucratic age: citizens, constituents, clients and victims. Cambridge, Mass., [1977]. pp. 182.

SHERRY (MICHAEL S.) Preparing for the next war: American plans for postwar defense, 1941-45. New Haven, 1977. pp. 260. *bibliog.*

— Moral conditions.

BENSON (GEORGE CHARLES SUMNER) and ENGEMAN (THOMAS S.) Amoral America. Stanford, Calif., 1975. pp. 294. *bibliog. (Stanford University. Hoover Institution on War, Revolution and Peace. Hoover Institution Publications. 150)*

— National security.

YERGIN (DANIEL) Shattered peace: the origins of the cold war and the national security state. Boston, Mass., 1977. pp. 526. *bibliog.*

— Navy.

BUCKNELL (HOWARD) Energy policy and naval strategy. Beverly Hills, [1975]. pp. 68. *bibliog.*

PERRY (RONALD W.) Racial discrimination and military justice. New York, 1977. pp. 101. *bibliog.*

— — History.

DINGMAN (ROGER) Power in the Pacific: the origins of naval arms limitation, 1914- 1922. Chicago, [1976]. pp. 318. *bibliog.*

— Occupations.

MONTAGNA (PAUL D.) Occupations and society: toward a sociology of the labor market. New York, [1977]. pp. 456.

— Officials and employees.

CHAUHAN (D.S.) and ROUNSAVALL (MARK) Public labor relations: a comparative state study. Beverly Hills, [1976]. pp. 70. *bibliog.*

NEVIN (JACK) and NEVIN (LORNA) AFGE-Federal Union: the story of the American Federation of Government Employees. [Washington, D.C., 1976]. pp. 211.

RITTENOURE (R. LYNN) Black employment in the South: the case of the federal government. Austin, Texas, 1976. pp. 190. *bibliog. (Texas University. Bureau of Business Research. Studies in Human Resource Development. No. 4)*

HECLO (HUGH) A government of strangers: executive politics in Washington. Washington, D.C., [1977]. pp. 272.

SCHICK (RICHARD P.) and COUTURIER (JEAN J.) The public interest in government labor relations. Cambridge, Mass., [1977]. pp. 264. *bibliog.*

— — Political activity.

BOLTON (JOHN R.) The Hatch Act: a civil libertarian defense. Washington, D.C., 1976. pp. 22. *(American Enterprise Institute for Public Policy Research. Domestic Affairs Studies. 43)*

— Politics and government.

REDFORD (EMMETTE SHELBURN) Ideal and practice in public administration. University, Ala., 1958 repr. 1975. pp. 155. *Presented as lectures in the annual lecture series in public administration at the University of Alabama.*

DECLASSIFIED DOCUMENTS REFERENCE SYSTEM, THE, [retrospective and annual collections]. q., [Retrospective collection and annual collection from] 1975 (1st)- Washington.

DENENBERG (R.V.) Understanding American politics. [London], 1976 repr. 1977. pp. 218. *bibliog.*

ETZKOWITZ (HENRY) and SCHWAB (PETER) eds. Is America necessary? Conservative, Liberal and Socialist perspectives of United States political institutions. St. Paul, [1976]. pp. 658. *bibliog.*

HAHN (HARLAN) and HOLLAND (ROLAND WILLIAM) American government: minority rights versus majority rule. New York, [1976]. pp. 203.

MANLEY (JOHN F.) American government and public policy. New York, [1976]. pp. 515.

RIPLEY (RANDALL B.) and FRANKLIN (GRACE A.) Congress, the bureaucracy and public policy. Homewood, Ill., 1976. pp. 193. *bibliog.*

ROELOFS (H. MARK) Ideology and myth in American politics: a critique of a national political mind. Boston, Mass., [1976]. pp. 262.

BULLITT (STIMSON) To be a politician. rev.ed. New Haven, 1977. pp. 294.

LEWIS (EUGENE) American politics in a bureaucratic age: citizens, constituents, clients and victims. Cambridge, Mass., [1977]. pp. 182.

ZVESPER (JOHN) Political philosophy and rhetoric: a study of the origins of American party politics. Cambridge, 1977. pp. 237.

— — 1607-1783, Colonial period.

FONER (ERIC) Tom Paine and revolutionary America. New York, 1976. pp. 326.

— — 1783-1865.

The CRISIS met: a reply to Junius. [New York, 1840]. pp. 16.

FONER (ERIC) Tom Paine and revolutionary America. New York, 1976. pp. 326.

FORSYTHE (DALL W.) Taxation and political change in the young nation, 1781-1833. New York, 1977. pp. 167. *bibliog.*

— — **1815-1861.**

SEWELL (RICHARD HERBERT) Ballots for freedom: antislavery politics in the United States, 1837-1860. New York, 1976. pp. 379.

— — **1865-1898.**

KELLER (MORTON) Affairs of state: public life in late nineteenth century America. Cambridge, Mass., 1977. pp. 631.

— — **1898-1945.**

ROBINSON (EDGAR EUGENE) and BORNET (VAUGHN DAVIS) Herbert Hoover: president of the United States. Stanford, 1975. pp. 398. *bibliog. (Stanford University. Hoover Institution on War, Revolution and Peace. Hoover Institution Publications. 149)*

DARILEK (RICHARD E.) A loyal opposition in time of war: the Republican Party and the politics of foreign policy from Pearl Harbour to Yalta. Westport, Conn., 1976. pp. 239. *bibliog.*

ROCHESTER (STUART I.) American liberal disillusionment in the wake of World War I. University Park, Pa., [1977]. pp. 172.

ROSEN (ELLIOT A.) Hoover, Roosevelt, and the Brains Trust: from Depression to New Deal. New York, 1977. pp. 446.

TUGWELL (REXFORD GUY) Roosevelt's revolution: the first year; a personal perspective. New York, [1977]. pp. 327.

— — **1900- .**

BARNET (RICHARD JOSEPH) Roots of war. New York, 1973 repr. 1976. pp. 350.

HESS (STEPHEN) Organizing the presidency. Washington, D.C., [1976]. pp. 228.

McKENNA (GEORGE) American politics: ideals and realities. New York, [1976]. pp. 345.

STOHL (MICHAEL) War and domestic political violence: the American capacity for repression and reaction. Beverly Hills, [1976]. pp. 151. *bibliog.*

— — **1945- .**

DOMMEL (PAUL R.) The politics of revenue sharing. Bloomington, Ind., [1974]. pp. 211. *bibliog.*

HALL (GUS) The crisis of U.S. capitalism and the fight-back: report to the 21st Convention of the Communist Party, U.S.A. New York, 1975. pp. 93.

TWO decades of change: the South since the Supreme Court desegregation decision; edited by Ernest M. Lander and Richard J. Calhoun. Columbia, S.C., 1975. pp. 119. *Papers of a symposium sponsored by the College of Liberal Arts at Clemson University in September 1973.*

The AMERICAN commonwealth, 1976; edited by Nathan Glazer and Irving Kristol. New York, [1976]. pp. 224. *Based on a special issue of The Public Interest published in 1975.*

BASS (JACK) and DE VRIES (WALTER) The transformation of southern politics: social change and political consequence since 1945. New York, [1976]. pp. 527. *bibliog.*

BUTLER (PHYLLIS) and GRAY (DOROTHY) Everywoman's guide to political awareness. Millbrae, Calif., 1976. pp. 128. *bibliog.*

DEAN (JOHN WESLEY) Blind ambition: the White House years. New York, [1976]. pp. 415.

HUMPHREY (HUBERT HORATIO) The education of a public man; ...edited by Norman Sherman. Garden City, N.Y., 1976. pp. 513.

KIRKPATRICK (JEANE J.) The new presidential elite: men and women in national politics. New York, [1976]. pp. 605.

KNOKE (DAVID) Change and continuity in American politics: the social bases of political parties. Baltimore, [1976]. pp. 192. *bibliog.*

LODGE (HENRY CABOT) 1902- . As it was: an inside view of politics and power in the '50s and '60s. New York, [1976]. pp. 224.

MILLER (WARREN EDWARD) and LEVITIN (TERESA E.) Leadership and change: the new politics and the American electorate. Cambridge, Mass., [1976]. pp. 267.

MOLLENHOFF (CLARK R.) The man who pardoned Nixon. New York, [1976]. pp. 312.

NEUSTADT (RICHARD ELLIOT) Presidential power: the politics of leadership with reflections on Johnson and Nixon. 2nd ed. New York, [1976]. pp. 324.

TRILLING (RICHARD J.) Party image and electoral behavior. New York, [1976]. pp. 234.

VAUGHAN (PHILIP H.) The Truman administration's legacy for black America. Reseda, Calif., [1976]. pp. 116. *bibliog.*

WHITAKER (JOHN C.) Striking a balance: environment and natural resources policy in the Nixon-Ford years. Washington, D.C., [1976]. pp. 344. *(American Enterprise Institute for Public Policy Research and Stanford University. Hoover Institution on War, Revolution and Peace. AEI-Hoover Policy Studies. 21)*

WISE (DAVID) The American police state: the government against the people. New York, [1976]. pp. 437.

BRAUER (CARL M.) John F. Kennedy and the second reconstruction. New York, 1977. pp. 396. *bibliog.*

CARTER (JAMES EARL) President of the United States. A government as good as its people. New York, [1977]. pp. 262.

GREENBERG (EDWARD S.) The American political system: a radical approach. Cambridge, Mass., [1977]. pp. 501. *bibliogs.*

HOROWITZ (IRVING LOUIS) Ideology and utopia in the United States, 1956-1976. London, 1977. pp. 464. *bibliog.*

SCHANDLER (HERBERT Y.) The unmaking of a president: Lyndon Johnson and Vietnam. Princeton, [1977]. pp. 419. *bibliog.*

— Presidents.

CUNLIFFE (MARCUS) American presidents and the presidency. 2nd ed. New York, [1976]. pp. 467. *bibliog. 1st ed. published under the title The American heritage history of the presidency.*

GRIFFITH (ERNEST STACEY) The American presidency: the dilemmas of shared power and divided government. New York, 1976. pp. 241.

NEUSTADT (RICHARD ELLIOT) Presidential power: the politics of leadership with reflections on Johnson and Nixon. 2nd ed. New York, [1976]. pp. 324.

— — **Election.**

ALEXANDER (HERBERT E.) and others. Financing the 1972 election. Lexington, Mass., [1976]. pp. 771.

HOFSTETTER (C. RICHARD) Bias in the news: network television coverage of the 1972 election campaign. Columbus, Ohio, [1976]. pp. 213.

KIRKPATRICK (SAMUEL A.) ed. American electoral behavior: change and stability. Beverly Hills, Calif., 1976. pp. 143. *bibliogs.*

WALTON (RICHARD J.) Henry Wallace, Harry Truman, and the Cold War. New York, 1976. pp. 388. *bibliog.*

YUNKER (JOHN H.) and LONGLEY (LAWRENCE D.) The electoral college: its biases newly measured for the 1960s and 1970s. Beverly Hills, [1976]. pp. 56. *bibliog.*

REEVES (RICHARD) Convention. London, 1977. pp. 246.

ROSEN (ELLIOT A.) Hoover, Roosevelt, and the Brains Trust: from Depression to New Deal. New York, 1977. pp. 446.

— — **Powers and duties.**

CRONIN (THOMAS E.) The state of the presidency. Boston, Mass., [1975]. pp. 355. *bibliog.*

HART (JOHN) Political Scientist. Presidential power revisited. [1976]. pp. 18. *Typescript: unpublished. Paper presented at Political Studies Association Conference, Nottingham, 1976.*

ROSE (RICHARD) Managing presidential objectives. London, 1977. pp. 180. *bibliog.*

— — **Staff.**

HESS (STEPHEN) Organizing the presidency. Washington, D.C., [1976]. pp. 228.

— — **Succession.**

SINDLER (ALLAN PAUL) Unchosen presidents: the vice-president and other frustrations of presidential succession. Berkeley, Calif., [1976]. pp. 118.

— Race question.

TWO decades of change: the South since the Supreme Court desegregation decision; edited by Ernest M. Lander and Richard J. Calhoun. Columbia, S.C., 1975. pp. 119. *Papers of a symposium sponsored by the College of Liberal Arts at Clemson University in September 1973.*

CADITZ (JUDITH) White liberals in transition: current dilemmas of ethnic integration. New York, [1976]. pp. 187. *bibliog.*

CAMEJO (PETER) Racism, revolution, reaction, 1861-1877: the rise and fall of radical reconstruction. New York, [1976]. pp. 269. *bibliog.*

FRANKLIN (JOHN HOPE) Racial equality in America. Chicago, 1976. pp. 113. *bibliog. (National Endowment for the Humanities. Jefferson Lectures in the Humanities. 1976)*

HAHN (HARLAN) and HOLLAND (ROLAND WILLIAM) American government: minority rights versus majority rule. New York, [1976]. pp. 203.

KLUGER (RICHARD) Simple justice: the history of Brown v. Board of Education and black America's struggle for equality. London, 1977. pp. 823,xxiii. *bibliog.*

LIPSKY (MICHAEL) and OLSON (DAVID J.) Commission politics: the processing of racial crisis in America. New Brunswick, N.J., [1977]. pp. 476.

SOSNA (MORTON) In search of the silent south: (southern liberals and the race issue). New York, 1977. pp. 275. *bibliog.*

WELLMAN (DAVID T.) Portraits of white racism. Cambridge, 1977. pp. 254. *bibliog.*

— Relations (general) with Canada.

MORSE (RANDY) and PRATT (LARRY) Darkness at the end of the tunnel: a radical analysis of Canadian-American relations. Toronto, 1975. pp. 39.

CANADA-United States relations; edited by Harry Edward English. New York, 1976. pp. 180. *Papers of a conference sponsored by the Academy of Political Science and the Center of Canadian Studies, Johns Hopkins University, in Washington, D.C., 1975.*

— Relations (general) with China.

BARNETT (ARTHUR DOAK) China policy: old problems and new challenges. Washington, D.C., [1977]. pp. 131.

CHINA and America: the search for a new relationship; edited by William J. Barnds. New York, 1977. pp. 254. *A Council on Foreign Relations Book.*

— Relations (general) with Indonesia.

SUHARTO (T.N.J.) Address[es] by the President of the republic of Indonesia [on a visit to the United States, 1970]. [Djakarta, 1970]. 5 pts.

— Relations (general) with Latin America.

FALS-BORDA (ORLANDO) Ciencia propia y colonialismo intelectual. Bogota, 1971. pp. 138. *Reprint of 1st ed. published in Mexico in 1970.*

WHITAKER (ARTHUR PRESTON) The United States and the southern cone: Argentina, Chile, and Uruguay. Cambridge, Mass., 1976. pp. 464. *bibliog.*

— Relations (general) with other countries.

FOX (ANNETTE BAKER) The politics of attraction: four middle powers and the United States. New York, 1977. pp. 371.

— Relations (general) with Scandinavia.

SCOTT (FRANKLIN DANIEL) Scandinavia. rev. ed. Cambridge, Mass., 1975. pp. 330. *bibliog.*

— Relations (general) with the United Kingdom.

COLBOURNE (MAURICE DALE) America and Britain: a mutual introduction with special reference to the British Empire. London, 1943. pp. 230.

— Relations (military) with the Mediterranean.

LEWIS (JESSE W.) The strategic balance in the Mediterranean. Washington, D.C., 1976. pp. 169. *(American Enterprise Institute for Public Policy Research. Foreign Affairs Studies. 29)*

— Religion.

GLOCK (CHARLES Y.) and BELLAH (ROBERT NEELLY) eds. The new religious consciousness. Berkeley, Calif., [1976]. pp. 391.

GREELEY (ANDREW M.) Ethnicity, denomination and inequality. Beverly Hills, [1976]. pp. 85. *bibliog.*

MARTY (MARTIN EMIL) A nation of behavers. Chicago, 1976. pp. 239.

— Rural conditions.

COMMUNITIES left behind: alternatives for development; [edited by] Larry R. Whiting. Ames, Iowa, 1974. pp. 151. *bibliogs. Papers presented at a symposium at South Dakota State University, 1973, sponsored by the North Central Regional Center for Rural Development and the University.*

SHOVER (JOHN L.) First majority - last minority: the transforming of rural life in America. DeKalb, Ill., [1976]. pp. 338. *bibliog.*

TWEETEN (LUTHER G.) and BRINKMAN (GEORGE LORIS) Micropolitan development: theory and practice of greater-rural economic development. Ames, Iowa, 1976. pp. 456. *bibliogs.*

AMERICAN ACADEMY OF POLITICAL AND SOCIAL SCIENCE. Annals. vol. 429. The new rural America; special editor of this volume Frank Clemente. Philadelphia, Pa., [1977]. pp. 208.

— Social conditions.

BENSON (GEORGE CHARLES SUMNER) and ENGEMAN (THOMAS S.) Amoral America. Stanford, Calif., 1975. pp. 294. *bibliog. (Stanford University. Hoover Institution on War, Revolution and Peace. Hoover Institution Publications. 150)*

HALL (GUS) The crisis of U.S. capitalism and the fight-back: report to the 21st Convention of the Communist Party, U.S.A. New York, 1975. pp. 93.

BASS (JACK) and DE VRIES (WALTER) The transformation of southern politics: social change and political consequence since 1945. New York, [1976]. pp. 527. *bibliog.*

ETZIONI (AMITAI) Social problems. Englewood Cliffs, N.J., [1976]. pp. 182.

LOOMIS (CHARLES PRICE) and DYER (EVERETT D.) Social systems: the study of sociology. Cambridge, Mass., [1976]. pp. 458.

MILES (RUFUS E.) Awakening from the American dream: the social and political limits to growth. New York, 1976. pp. 246.

O'TOOLE (JAMES) Energy and social change. Cambridge, Mass., [1976]. pp. 185. *bibliog. Based on research by the Center for Futures Research at the University of Southern California.*

QUALITIES of life. Lexington, Mass., [1976]. pp. 475. *(Commission on Critical Choices for Americans. Critical Choices for Americans. vol. 7)*

TURNER (JONATHAN H.) Social problems in America. New York, [1977]. pp. 555. *bibliog.*

WILSON (H. T.) The American ideology: science, technology and organization as modes of rationality in advanced industrial societies. London, 1977. pp. 355. *bibliog.*

— — Statistics.

HAUSER (PHILIP MORRIS) Social statistics in use. New York, [1975]. pp. 385. *bibliogs.*

— Social life and customs.

KEPHART (WILLIAM M.) Extraordinary groups: the sociology of unconventional life-styles. New York, [1976]. pp. 311. *bibliogs.*

— Social policy.

FRIEDMANN (JOHN REMBERT PETER) Retracking America: the theory of transactive planning. Garden City, N.Y., 1973. pp. 289. *bibliog.*

CAPLOW (THEODORE) Toward social hope. New York, [1975]. pp. 229.

AMACHER (RYAN C.) and others, eds. The economic approach to public policy: selected readings. Ithaca, N.Y., 1976. pp. 528.

CURRENT issues in social; policy edited by W. Boyd Littrell [and] Gideon Sjoberg. Beverly Hills, Calif., [1976]. pp. 248. *bibliogs. Papers prepared for an interdisciplinary conference held in 1975, at the University of Texas.*

EVALUATING the labor-market effects of social programs; edited by Orley Ashenfelter and James Blum. Princeton, 1976. pp. 238. *bibliogs. (Princeton University. Department of Economics and Sociology. Industrial Relations Section. Research Report Series. No.120) Papers presented at a conference held at Princeton University in May 1974, jointly sponsored by the Industrial Relations Section and the Office of the Assistant Secretary for Policy, Evaluation and Research of the U.S. Department of Labor.*

JONES (CHARLES OSCAR) and THOMAS (ROBERT D.) eds. Public policy making in a federal system. Beverly Hills, Calif., [1976]. pp. 284. *bibliogs.*

SCHNEIDER (ANNE L.) Opinions and policies in the American states: the role of political characteristics. Beverly Hills, [1976]. pp. 47. *bibliog.*

TERRELL (PAUL) and WEISNER (STANLEY) The social impact of revenue sharing: planning, participation and the purchase of service. New York, 1976. pp. 114. *bibliog.*

BERGER (PETER L.) and NEUHAUS (RICHARD JOHN) To empower people: the role of mediating structures in public policy. Washington, [1977]. pp. 45. *(American Enterprise Institute for Public Policy Research. AEI Studies. 139)*

LEWIS (EUGENE) American politics in a bureaucratic age: citizens, constituents, clients and victims. Cambridge, Mass., [1977]. pp. 182.

— Statistics, Vital.

RINDFUSS (RONALD R.) and SWEET (JAMES A.) Postwar fertility trends and differentials in the United States. New York, [1977]. pp. 225. *bibliog.*

UNITIZED CARGO SYSTEMS.

UNITED NATIONS. Conference on Trade and Development. 1970. Unitization of cargo: report, etc. (TD/B/C.4/75). New York, 1970. pp. 147.

— Bibliography.

RAMM (DOROTHY V.) compiler. Containerization: a bibliography, January-December 1970. Evanston, Ill., 1971. pp. 34.

UNIVERSAL NEGRO IMPROVEMENT ASSOCIATION.

MARTIN (TONY) Race first: the ideological and organizational struggles of Marcus Garvey and the Universal Negro Improvement Association. Westport, Conn., 1976. pp. 421. *bibliog.*

UNIVERSITIES AND COLLEGES.

HALSEY (ALBERT HENRY) Academic freedom and the idea of a university. Cape Town, 1976. pp. 16. *(Cape Town. University. T.B. Davie Memorial Lectures. 17)*

UNIVERSITAET heute: wem dient sie? ; wer steuert sie?; herausgegeben von Andreas Flitner und Ulrich Herrmann. München, [1977]. pp. 270. *bibliogs.*

— European Economic Community countries.

FRANCE. Direction de la Documentation. La Documentation Française. Notes et Etudes Documentaires. Nos. 4,229-4,230-4,231. Université européenne et Europe des universités; par Daniel Thérond. Paris, 1975. pp. 56. *bibliog.*

— France — Finance.

FRANCE. Commission chargée de Proposer une Meilleure Répartition des Crédits de l'Etat aux Universités. 1976. Le financement des universités: rapport, etc. Paris, 1976. pp. 122.

— Germany.

TILFORD (ROGER BERTRAM) The West German university: the problem of social responsibility. Bradford, 1976. pp. 19. *bibliog. An inaugural lecture delivered at the University of Bradford on 16 March 1976.*

UNIVERSITAET heute: wem dient sie? ; wer steuert sie?; herausgegeben von Andreas Flitner und Ulrich Herrmann. München, [1977]. pp. 270. *bibliogs.*

— India.

DONGERKERY (SUDIDERRAO RAMRAO) Universities and national life. Bombay, 1950. pp. 115.

INDIA. University Grants Commission. 1972. India pocket book of university education. [3rd ed.] New Delhi, 1972. pp. 261.

— Papua New Guinea.

PAPUA NEW GUINEA. Committee of Enquiry into University Development. 1974. Report; [Gabriel B. Gris, chairman]. [Konedobu], 1974. pp. 182. *bibliog.*

— Portugal.

NAMORADO (RUI) Movimento estudantil e politica educacional. [Coimbra], 1972. pp. 168.

— Russia.

SHCHETININA (GALINA ISIDOROVNA) Universitety v Rossii i ustav 1884 goda. Moskva, 1976. pp. 231.

— United Kingdom.

GRIFFITHS (RICHARD CERDIN) The prospect for universities: from Robbins to 1984. Cardiff, [1974]. pp. 10. *(Wales. University of Wales. University College, Cardiff. Page Fund Lectures. 1974)*

CONGDON (BOB) and OSBORN (PAUL) Evaluation of the contribution of British universities to development. London, [1975]. pp. 16. (*Voluntary Committee on Overseas Aid and Development. Academics against Poverty Project. Higher Education Action for Development. 3*)

DOYLE (PETER) Marketing and the responsive university: an inaugural lecture delivered at the University of Bradford on 13 January 1976. Bradford, [1976]. pp. 26.

HARVIE (CHRISTOPHER) The lights of Liberalism: university Liberals and the challenge of democracy, 1860-86. London, 1976. pp. 343.

WHITBURN (JULIA) and others. People in polytechnics: a survey of polytechnic staff and students, 1972-3. Guildford, Surrey, 1976. pp. 212. *bibliog.* (*Society for Research into Higher Education. Research into Higher Education Monographs. 27*)

— — **Administration.**

ASHBY (ERIC) Baron Ashby. University hierarchies. London, 1976. pp. 12. (*London. University. Imperial College of Science and Technology. Joan Woodward Memorial Lectures. 1976*)

HOWELL (DAVID ANTONY) The introduction of the Bachelor of Education degree: a case study in British university decision-making, 1963-70. 1976. fo. 438. *bibliog. Typescript. Ph.D. (London) thesis unpublished. This thesis is the property of London University and may not be removed from the Library.*

— — **Finance.**

U.K. Parliament. House of Commons. Library. Research Division. Background Papers. No. 58. Student fees and student grants: the current situation. [London, 1977]. pp. 11.

U.K. University Grants Committee. 1977. Notes on procedure 1977: capital grants. 6th ed. London, 1977. pp. 54.

— **United States.**

TORBERT (WILLIAM R.) Creating a community of inquiry: conflict, collaboration, transformation. London, [1976]. pp. 184. *bibliog.*

ZOGLIN (MARY LOU) Power and politics in the community college. Palm Springs, Calif., 1976. pp. 170.

UNIVERSITY OF THE NORTH.

NKONDO (G.M.) ed. Turfloop testimony: the dilemma of a black university in South Africa; [a memorandum by the Black Academic Staff Association of the University of the North to a Commission of Inquiry Concerning Certain Matters Relating to the University]. Johannesburg, 1976. pp. 93.

UNMARRIED COUPLES

— **Denmark.**

ANDERSEN (DINES) Papirløst samliv blandt de 20-29 årige. København, 1976. pp. 67. *bibliog. (Socialforskningsinstituttet. Meddelelser. 18) With separately printed English summary.*

UNMARRIED MOTHERS

— **Bibliography.**

SÃO PAULO (STATE). Serviço Social. Biblioteca. 1954. Assistência a mãe solteira: bibliografia por ordem alfabetica de autores. [São Paulo], 1954. fo. 13.

— **United Kingdom.**

HOPKINSON (ANGELA) Single mothers: the first year: a Scottish study of mothers bringing up their children on their own. Edinburgh, 1976. pp. 256. *bibliog.*

— **United States.**

FURSTENBERG (FRANK F.) Unplanned parenthood: the social consequences of teenage childbearing. New York, [1976]. pp. 293. *bibliog.*

UNSKILLED LABOUR

— **United States.**

WOOL (HAROLD) The labor supply for lower-level occupations:...assisted by Bruce Dana Phillips. New York, 1976. pp. 382. *bibliog.*

UNTOUCHABLES.

AGGARWAL (PARTAP C.) and ASHRAF (MOHD. SIDDIQ) Equality through privilege: a study of special privileges of scheduled castes in Haryana. New Delhi, [1976]. pp. 206. *bibliog.*

UPPER CLASSES

— **Italy.**

KENT (FRANCIS WILLIAM) Household and lineage in Renaissance Florence: the family life of the Capponi, Ginori, and Rucellai. Princeton, N.J., [1977]. pp. 325.

— **Sweden.**

KULLENBERG (ANNETTE) Överklassen i Sverige. [Stockholm, 1974]. pp. 286. *bibliog.*

UPPER SILESIAN QUESTION.

PRZEWŁOCKI (JAN) Mocarstwa zachodnioeuropejskie wobec problemów Górnego Śląska w latach 1918-1933. Katowice, 1975. pp. 274. *bibliog.*

UPPER VOLTA

— **Commerce.**

IVORY COAST. Service de la Statistique et de la Mécanographie. 1955. Commerce extérieur de la Côte d'Ivoire et de la Haute-Volta de 1931 à 1954. [Abidjan], 1955. pp. 118. (*Ivory Coast. Direction de la Statistique et des Etudes Economiques et Démographiques. Bulletin mensuel de statistique. Annexes*)

URAL REGION

— **Economic policy.**

SERGEEV (M.A.) ed. Nekotorye problemy razvitiia ekonomiki Urala. Sverdlovsk, 1975. pp. 143.

— **History.**

ADAMOV (VLADIMIR VASIL'EVICH) Fevral'skaia revoliutsiia na Urale. Sverdlovsk, 1967. pp. 64.

LISOVSKII (NIKOLAI KUZ'MICH) Doloi samoderzhavie'.: 1905 god na Iuzhnom Urale. Cheliabinsk, 1975. pp. 237. *Colophon has sub-title: iz istorii revoliutsii 1905-1907 gg. na Iuzhnom Urale.*

— **Politics and government.**

BOR'BA protiv opportunizma za sozdanie i ukreplenie partiinykh organizatsii Urala, 1894-1917 gg. Perm', 1975. pp. 395. *bibliog.*

KAPTSUGOVICH (IGOR' SEVAST'IANOVICH) Istoriia politicheskoi gibeli eserov na Urale. Perm', 1975. pp. 191.

URANIUM MINES AND MINING

— **Australia.**

COMMITTEE FOR ECONOMIC DEVELOPMENT OF AUSTRALIA. Research Group. Uranium. Melbourne, 1976. pp. 32. (*Committee for Economic Development of Australia. Energy Project. Position Papers. No. 4*)

— **South West Africa.**

JEPSON (TREVOR B.) Rio Tinto-Zinc in Namibia. London, [1975]. fo. 18. *bibliog.*

URANIUM ORES

— **Zaire.**

MALU (FELIX) Prospection, exploitation et développement des minerais énergétiques dans la R[épublique] D[émocratique du] C[ongo]. Kinshasa, Office National de la Recherche et du Développement, [1970]. pp. 16. *bibliog.*

URBAN ECONOMICS.

MILLS (EDWIN S.) Urban economics. Glenview, Ill., [1972]. pp. 277. *bibliogs.*

BATTY (MICHAEL) and MARCH (LIONEL) Dynamic urban models based on information-minimising. Reading, 1976. pp. 41. *bibliog.* (*Reading. University. Department of Geography. Reading Geographical Papers. No. 48*)

PUBLIC and urban economics: essays in honor of William S. Vickrey; edited by Ronald E. Grieson. Lexington, Mass., [1976]. pp. 417. *bibliogs.*

BALCHIN (PAUL N.) and KIEVE (JEFFREY LAWRENCE) Urban land economics. London, 1977. pp. 278. *bibliog.*

BROADBENT (T.A.) Planning and profit in the urban economy. London, 1977. pp. 274. *bibliog.*

CAPTIVE cities: studies in the political economy of cities and regions; edited by Michael Harloe. London, [1977]. pp. 218. *Sponsored by the International Sociological Association Research Committee on the Sociology of Regional and Urban Development.*

PRED (ALLAN R.) City-systems in advanced economies: past growth, present processes and future development options. London, 1977. pp. 256. *bibliog.*

URBAN RENEWAL.

LOTTMAN (HERBERT R.) How cities are saved. New York, 1976. pp. 255.

— **United Kingdom.**

BARTLES-SMITH (DOUGLAS) and GERRARD (DAVID) Urban ghetto. Guildford, 1976. pp. 115.

ROBERTS (J. TREVOR) General Improvement Areas. Farnborough, Hants., [1976]. pp. 188.

DEMUTH (CLARE) Government initiatives on urban deprivation. London, [1977]. fo. 19. (*Runnymede Trust. Briefing Papers. No. 1/77*)

— — **London.**

WILCOX (DAVID) and RICHARDS (DAVID) London: the heartless city. London, 1977. pp. 172. *bibliogs.*

URBAN TRANSPORTATION.

HENSHER (DAVID A.) ed. Urban transport economics. Cambridge, 1977. pp. 277.

JONES (IAN S.) Urban transport appraisal. London, 1977. pp. 144.

THOMSON (J. MICHAEL) Great cities and their traffic. London, 1977. pp. 344. *bibliog.*

— **United Kingdom.**

JAMIESON MACKAY AND PARTNERS. Transportation study: Bath area: final report. Bristol, 1976. pp. 117.

JAMIESON MACKAY AND PARTNERS. Transportation study: Bath area: report of surveys. Bristol, [1976?]. pp. 85.

BUTTON (K.J.) The economics of urban transport. Farnborough, [1977]. pp. 181. *bibliog.*

MITCHELL (C.G.B.) and TOWN (STEPHEN W.) Accessibility of various social groups to different activities. Crowthorne, 1977. pp. 31. *bibliog.* (*U.K. Transport and Road Research Laboratory. Supplementary Reports. 258*)

URBAN TRANSPORTATION POLICY.

ABOUCHAR (ALAN) Transportation economics and public policy: with urban extensions. New York, [1977]. pp. 326. *bibliogs.*

— United Kingdom.

PROFESSIONAL INSTITUTIONS COUNCIL FOR CONSERVATION. The urban road in relation to the conservation and renewal of the environment; [report by a PICC working party; edited by J.T. Williams]. London, [1974]. pp. 21.

LONDON TRANSPORT EXECUTIVE. Comments on Transport policy: a consultation document. London, 1976. pp. (14), 3.

URBANIZATION.

CARTER (HAROLD) The study of urban geography. 2nd ed. London, 1975. pp. 398. *bibliogs.*

MAN in urban environments; edited by G.A. Harrison and J.B. Gibson. Oxford, 1976. pp. 367. *bibliogs. Based on a series of meetings held by the Royal Society Study Group on Human Biology in Urban Environments.*

— Africa, Subsaharan.

KNIGHT (C. GREGORY) and NEWMAN (JAMES L.) eds. Contemporary Africa: geography and change. Englewood Cliffs, N.J., [1976]. pp. 546. *bibliog.*

— Asia.

ASIA urbanizing: population growth and concentration and the problems thereof; a comparative symposium by Asian and Western experts in search of wise approaches; edited by Social Science Research Institute, International Christian University. Tokyo, [1976]. pp. 178. *Papers of an international symposium convened by the Institute and held May 6-7, 1975 in Tokyo.*

— Brazil.

URBANIZACION y recursos humanos: el caso de San Pablo; Paul Singer, coordinador. Buenos Aires, 1973. pp. 285.

— Czechoslovakia.

KANSKY (KAREL JOSEPH) Urbanization under socialism: the case of Czechoslovakia. New York, 1976. pp. 313. *bibliog.*

— East (Near East).

COSTELLO (VINCENT FRANCIS) Urbanization in the Middle East. Cambridge, 1977. pp. 121. *bibliog.*

— India — Saurashtra.

SPODEK (HOWARD) Urban-rural integration in regional development: a case study of Saurashtra, India, 1800-1960. Chicago, 1976. pp. 144. *bibliog. (Chicago. University. Department of Geography. Research Papers. No. 171)*

— Kenya.

OBUDHO (ROBERT) and WALLER (PETER P.) Periodic markets, urbanization, and regional planning: a case study from western Kenya. Westport, Conn., 1976. pp. 289. *bibliog.*

— Mexico.

UNIKEL (LUIS) and others. El desarrollo urbano de Mexico: diagnostico e implicaciones futuras. Mexico, 1976. pp. 466. *bibliog.*

— Russia.

LEWIS (ROBERT ALDEN) and others. Nationality and population change in Russia and the USSR: an evaluation of census data, 1897-1970. New York, 1976. pp. 456. *bibliog. (Population Change in Russia and the USSR, 1897-1970. vol. 1)*

— Sweden.

FALK (THOMAS) Urban Sweden: changes in the distribution of population: the 1960s in focus. Stockholm, 1976. pp. 224. *bibliog.*

— Turkey.

KARPAT (KEMAL H.) The gecekondu: rural migration and urbanization. Cambridge, 1976. pp. 291. *bibliog.*

— Underdeveloped areas.

See UNDERDEVELOPED AREAS — Urbanization.

— United States.

HARRIGAN (JOHN J.) Political change in the metropolis. Boston, Mass., [1976]. pp. 450.

WHEAT (LEONARD F.) Urban growth in the nonmetropolitan South. Lexington, Mass., [1976]. pp. 171.

MAGNUSON (NORRIS ALDEN) Salvation in the slums: evangelical social work, 1865-1920. Metuchen, N.J., 1977. pp. 299. *bibliog. (American Theological Library Association. ATLA Monograph Series. No. 10)*

— — California.

The EFFECTS of urban growth: a population impact analysis; [by] Richard P. Appelbaum [and others]. New York, 1976. pp. 330. *bibliog.*

— — Milwaukee.

McSHANE (CLAY) Technology and reform: street railways and the growth of Milwaukee, 1887-1900. Madison, Wisconsin, [1974]. pp. 187. *bibliog. Author's thesis (M.A.), University of Wisconsin.*

— — North Carolina.

HAYES (CHARLES R.) The dispersed city: the case of Piedmont, North Carolina. Chicago, 1976. pp. 157. *bibliog. (Chicago. University. Department of Geography. Research Papers. No. 173)*

URUGUAY

— Economic conditions.

ASOCIACION DE BANCOS DEL URUGUAY. Resumen de los principales aspectos de la actividad economica del Uruguay [during 1970]. Montevideo, [1971]. 1 vol. (various pagings).

— Economic history.

COURIEL (ALBERTO) and LICHTENSZTEJN (SAMUEL) El F.M.I. y la crisis economica nacional. Montevideo, 1967 [repr. 1971]. pp. 201. *Reprint of 1st ed. (1967) with a new prologue.*

— Economic policy.

COURIEL (ALBERTO) and LICHTENSZTEJN (SAMUEL) El F.M.I. y la crisis economica nacional. Montevideo, 1967 [repr. 1971]. pp. 201. *Reprint of 1st ed. (1967) with a new prologue.*

— History.

WHITAKER (ARTHUR PRESTON) The United States and the southern cone: Argentina, Chile, and Uruguay. Cambridge, Mass., 1976. pp. 464. *bibliog.*

— Politics and government.

LUSTEMBERG (HUGO) Uruguay: imperialismo y estrategia de liberacion; las enseñanzas de la huelga general. Buenos Aires, [1975]. pp. 223.

URWICH (JOHANN).

URWICH (JOHANN) Fără pașaport prin URSS. Munchen, 1976 in progress.

UTILITARIANISM.

MILL (JOHN STUART) (Collected works of John Stuart Mill. vol. 10). Essays on ethics, religion and society; editor of the text, J.M. Robson; introduction, F.E.L. Priestley; essays on Mill's Utilitarianism, D.P. Dryer. Toronto, [1969]. pp. 578. *bibliog.*

UTILITY THEORY.

TESFATSION (LEIGH) "Bayes' theorem" for utility. Minneapolis, 1976. fo. 33. *bibliog. (Minnesota University. Center for Economic Research. Discussion Papers. No. 65)*

UTOPIAS.

MICHAELIS (RICHARD C.) A sequel to Looking backward; or, "Looking further forward". 4th ed. London, [1891?]. pp. 103. *"This work is a reply to Bellamy's Looking backward"*

LASKY (MELVIN J.) Utopia and revolution: on the origins of a metaphor; or, Some illustrations of the problem of political temperament and intellectual climate and how ideas, ideals, and ideologies have been historically related. Chicago, 1976. pp. 726.

UTOPIE - marxisme selon Ernst Bloch: un système de l'inconstructible; hommages à Ernst Bloch pour son 90e anniversaire publiés sous la direction de Gérard Raulet. Paris, 1976. pp. 334. *bibliog.*

HARRINGTON (JAMES) Author of "Oceana". The political works of James Harrington; edited with an introduction by J.G.A. Pocock. Cambridge, 1977. pp. 878.

KLIBANOV (ALEKSANDR IL'ICH) Narodnaia sotsial'naia utopiia v Rossii: period feodalizma. Moskva. 1977. pp. 335.

SMITH (ROBERT ERNEST FREDERICK) ed. The Russian peasant: 1920 and 1984. London, 1977. pp. 120. *bibliog. (Reprinted from The Journal of Peasant Studies. vol.4, no.1)*

UTRECHT, TREATY OF, 1713.

HASSAN (Sir JOSHUA ABRAHAM) The Treaty of Utrecht, 1713, and the Jews of Gibraltar; lecture delivered to the Jewish Historical Society of England in London 15 May 1963. London, 1970. pp. 16.

UTTAR PRADESH

— Economic policy.

UTTAR PRADESH. Planning Department. 1961. Third five year plan. Vol. 1. Report. [Lucknow], 1961. pp. 202.

— Social policy.

UTTAR PRADESH. Planning Department. 1961. Third five year plan. Vol. 1. Report. [Lucknow], 1961. pp. 202.

UZBEKISTAN

— Economic history.

GENTSHKE (LEV VLADIMIROVICH) Kompartiia i rabochii klass Uzbekistana v bor'be za sotsializm, 1926-1932 gg. Tashkent, 1973. pp. 230.

— Economic policy.

VOPROSY sovershenstvovaniia territorial'nogo planirovaniia. Tashkent, 1975. pp. 173.

— History — 1917-1921, Revolution — Chronology.

KHRONIKA sobytii Velikoi Oktiabr'skoi sotsialisticheskoi revoliutsii v Uzbekistane. Tashkent, 1962 in progress.

— Population.

MULLIADZHANOV (ISKHAK RASHIDOVICH) and others. Naselenie Uzbekskoi SSR. Tashkent, 1973. pp. 138.

— Rural conditions.

NURULLAEV (A.N.) Sel'skokhoziaistvennyi otriad rabochego klassa Uzbekistana v period stroitel'stva sotsializma, 1924-1941 gg. Tashkent, 1975. pp. 195.

VALENCIA, SPAIN (REGION)

— Economic history.

BURNS (ROBERT IGNATIUS) Medieval colonialism: postcrusade exploitation of Islamic Valencia. Princeton, N.J., [1975]. pp. 394. *bibliog.*

VALUE.

MARX (KARL) Value: studies by Karl Marx; translated and edited by Albert Dragstedt. London, [1976]. pp. 229. *"Of the four independent texts of Marx presented here, three appear for the first time in English".*

ASH (WILLIAM FRANKLIN) Morals and politics: the ethics of revolution. London, 1977. pp. 170. *bibliog.*

VANCOUVER

— Economic policy.

RANKIN (HARRY) A socialist perspective for Vancouver. Toronto, [1974?]. pp. 83.

— Social policy.

RANKIN (HARRY) A socialist perspective for Vancouver. Toronto, [1974?]. pp. 83.

VANCOUVER ISLAND

— Economic conditions.

CARMICHAEL (HERBERT) Alberni district, British Columbia. Victoria, 1908. pp. 25. *(British Columbia. Bureau of Provincial Information. Bulletins. No. 24) Map in end pocket.*

VANDALISM.

WARD (COLIN) ed. Vandalism. London, 1973. pp. 327. *bibliog.*

U.K. Standing Committee on Crime Prevention. 1976. Protection against vandalism. [London], 1975 [or rather 1976]. pp. 49.

VASCONCELOS (JOSE).

GARRIDO (LUIS) Jose Vasconcelos. Mexico, 1963. pp. 170. *bibliog.*

VEGETABLES

— Prices — United Kingdom.

U.K. Price Commission. 1977. Price Commission report on prices and margins of potatoes and other fresh vegetables: December 1976. London, 1977. fo. (8).

— European Economic Community countries.

EUROPEAN COMMUNITIES. Statistical Office. Production of vegetables and fruit. a., 1976 [covering 1972/1974]- Luxembourg.

— Russia — Uzbekistan.

KABANOVA (KLAVDIIA ANDREEVNA) Razvitie i razmeshchenie ovoshchevodstva v Uzbekistane. Tashkent, 1976. pp. 173.

VENDA

— Economic conditions.

SOUTH AFRICA. Bureau for Economic Research re Bantu Development. 1977. Venda:...economic revue [sic], etc. Pretoria, [1977]. pp. 72. *bibliog. In English and Afrikaans.*

VENDEAN WAR, 1793-1800.

ROSS (MICHAEL) Banners of the king: the war of the Vendée 1793-4. London, 1975. pp. 336.

VENEZIA EUGANEA

— History.

MOVIMENTO cattolico e sviluppo capitalistico: atti del Convegno su "Movimento...nel Veneto". Venezia, 1974. pp. 189. *Conference held in Padua in June 1973, with contributions by Emilio Franzina, and others.*

DINELLI (UMBERTO) La guerra partigiana nel Veneto. Venezia, 1976. pp. 229. *bibliog.*

VENEZUELA

— Boundaries — Guyana.

GUYANA. Ministry of External Affairs. 1966. Guyana-Venezuela boundary: the Ankoko affair: notes on Guyana's protest. [Georgetown, 1966]. pp. 10,xvii.

— Congress.

NUÑEZ ECARRI (CARLOS) El Congreso de la Republica: origen y funciones del parlamento en Venezuela. Caracas, Congreso de la Republica, 1971. pp. 46.

— Economic conditions.

VENEZUELA: crecimiento sin desarrollo; [by] D.F. Maza Zavala [and others]. Mexico, 1974. pp. 441.

CHAVEZ (CARLOS R.) Hechos y cifras de Venezuela. [Caracas, 1976]. pp. 490.

SALAZAR-CARRILLO (JORGE) Oil in the economic development of Venezuela. New York, 1976. pp. 215.

— Economic history.

VENEZUELA: crecimiento sin desarrollo; [by] D.F. Maza Zavala [and others]. Mexico, 1974. pp. 441.

— Foreign relations — Cuba.

PARTIDO COMUNISTA DE CUBA. Comite Central. Statement...on the new threat of imperialist aggression, Havana, May 17, 1967. London, Cuban Embassy, 1967. pp. 6. *(Cuba Information Bulletins. 1967. No. 7)*

— — Guyana.

GUYANA. Ministry of External Affairs. 1968. Guyana-Venezuela relations. Georgetown, 1968. pp. 83, 1 map.

GUYANA. Ministry of External Affairs. 1970. A search for understanding: patterns of conflict resolution: statements and papers relating to recent developments, Guyana- Venezuela relations and Guyana-Surinam relations. Georgetown, 1970. pp. 34.

— History — To 1810.

BOZA (GUILLERMO) Estructura y cambio en Venezuela colonial. [Caracas, 1973]. pp. 153. *bibliog.*

— Population.

VENEZUELA: crecimiento sin desarrollo; [by] D.F. Maza Zavala [and others]. Mexico, 1974. pp. 441.

LOMBARDI (JOHN V.) People and places in colonial Venezuela;...maps and figures by Cathryn L. Lombardi. Bloomington, Ind., [1976]. pp. 484.

— Rural conditions.

COPPENS (WALTER) The anatomy of a land invasion scheme in Yekuana territory, Venezuela. Copenhagen, 1972. pp. 22. *bibliog. (International Work Group for Indigenous Affairs. Documents. 9)*

— Statistical services.

RODRIGUEZ (MANUEL ALFREDO) La estadistica en la historia de Venezuela. Caracas, Ministerio de Fomento, [1974]. pp. 342. *bibliog.*

VENEZUELAN NEWSPAPERS.

FEBRES CORDERO (JULIO) Historia de la imprenta y del periodismo en Venezuela, 1800-1830. Caracas, 1974. pp. 262. *bibliog. (Banco Central de Venezuela. Coleccion Cuatricentenario de Caracas. 11)*

VENEZUELAN PERIODICALS.

FEBRES CORDERO (JULIO) Historia de la imprenta y del periodismo en Venezuela, 1800-1830. Caracas, 1974. pp. 262. *bibliog. (Banco Central de Venezuela. Coleccion Cuatricentenario de Caracas. 11)*

VENICE

— Commerce.

KEDAR (BENJAMIN Z.) Merchants in crisis: Genoese and Venetian men of affairs and the fourteenth-century depression. New Haven, 1976. pp. 260. *bibliog.*

— Economic history.

CHINELLO (CESCO) Forze politiche e sviluppo capitalistico: Porto Marghera e Venezia, 1951-1973. Roma, 1975. pp. 293.

— Politics and government.

CHINELLO (CESCO) Forze politiche e sviluppo capitalistico: Porto Marghera e Venezia, 1951-1973. Roma, 1975. pp. 293.

— Threat of destruction.

FAY (STEPHEN) and KNIGHTLEY (PHILLIP) The death of Venice. London, 1976. pp. 190.

VEREINSTAG DEUTSCHER ARBEITERVEREINE.

NA'AMAN (SHLOMO) ed. Von der Arbeiterbewegung zur Arbeiterpartei: der Fünfte Vereinstag der Deutschen Arbeitervereine zu Nürnberg im Jahre 1868; eine Dokumentation. Berlin, 1976. pp. 186. *bibliog. (IWK: internationale wissenschaftliche Korrespondenz zur Geschichte der deutschen Arbeiterbewegung. Beihefte. 4)*

VERNAMIEGE EN VALAIS

— Rural conditions.

BERTHOUD (GERALD) Changements économiques et sociaux de la montagne: Vernamiège en Valais. Berne, [1967]. pp. 237. *bibliog. (Société Suisse des Sciences Humaines. Travaux.8)*

VERONESI (ENZO).

VERONESI (UGO) Riflessioni sulla dittatura. 3rd ed. [Mantua, 1975]. pp. 85. *(Partito Liberale Italiano. Atti e Documenti. 9)*

VERSAILLES, TREATY OF, JUNE 28, 1919 (GERMANY).

U.K. Foreign Office. 1920. The treaty of peace between the allied and associated powers and Germany, and other treaty engagements, signed at Versailles, June 28th, 1919; together with the reply of the allied and associated powers to the observations of the German delegation on the conditions of peace. London, 1920. pp. 310. *Copy interleaved in places with additional typescript material.*

VETERINARY MEDICINE

— European Economic Community countries.

EUROPEAN COMMUNITIES. Commission. Information on Agriculture. [Brussels], 1976 in progress. *[In various Community languages].*

VICTIMS OF CRIME.

VICTIMS and society; edited by Emilio C. Viano. Washington, D.C. [1976]. pp. 641. *Mainly papers from the International Study Institute on Victimology, July 1975, in Italy.*

VICTORIA, AUSTRALIA

— Politics and government.

SAFFIN (N.W.) Left and right in Bendigo and Shepparton, 1947-51. Kilmore, Victoria, 1974. pp. 95.

VIENNA

— City planning.

VIENNA. Magistrat. Abteilung für Landes- und Stadtplanung. Wohnen in Wien: Ergebnisse und Folgerungen aus einer Untersuchung von Wiener Wohnverhältnissen, Wohnwünschen und städtischer Umwelt; Mitarbeiter: Gustav Krall [and others]. Wien, 1956. pp. 108. *(Aufbau, Der. Monographien. 8)*

— Growth.

FELDBAUER (PETER) Stadtwachstum und Wohnungsnot: Determinanten unzureichender Wohnungsversorgung in Wien, 1848 bis 1914. Wien, 1977. pp. 340. *bibliog. (Vienna. Universität. Institut für Wirtschafts- und Sozialgeschichte. Sozial- und Wirtschaftshistorische Studien. Band 9)*

VIETNAM

— Constitution.

BUDANOV (ANATOLII GAVRILOVICH) Demokraticheskaia Respublika V'etnam: osnovy gosudarstvennogo stroia. Moskva, 1975. pp. 271.

— Description and travel.

SSSR - DRV: vospominaniia i stat'i. Moskva, 1975. pp. 285.

— Economic conditions.

OGNETOV (I.A.) and others, eds. Demokraticheskaia Respublika V'etnam. Moskva, 1975. pp. 144. *(Akademiia Nauk SSSR. Institut Ekonomiki Mirovoi Sotsialisticheskoi Sistemy. Ekonomika i Politika Zarubezhnykh Stran Sotsializma).*

— Foreign relations — United States.

ANDREWS (BRUCE) Public constraint and American policy in Vietnam. Beverly Hills, [1976]. pp. 64. *bibliog.*

— Politics and government.

OGNETOV (I.A.) and others, eds. Demokraticheskaia Respublika V'etnam. Moskva, 1975. pp. 144. *(Akademiia Nauk SSSR. Institut Ekonomiki Mirovoi Sotsialisticheskoi Sistemy. Ekonomika i Politika Zarubezhnykh Stran Sotsializma).*

— Relations (general) with Russia.

SSSR - DRV: vospominaniia i stat'i. Moskva, 1975. pp. 285.

VIETNAMESE WARS, 1945-1975.

PRINCIPALES victoires des F[orces] A[rmées de] L[ibération] du Sud Vietnam pendant la saison sèche, de novembre 1965 à mars 1966. [Saigon?], 1966. pp. 62.

ASPREY (ROBERT B.) War in the shadows: the guerrilla in history. London, 1976. pp. 1615. *bibliog.*

WASMES (ALAIN) Viêt-nam: la peau du pachyderme. Paris, [1976]. pp. 317.

BURCHETT (WILFRED G.) Grasshoppers and elephants: why Viet Nam fell. New York, [1977]. pp. 265.

BUTTINGER (JOSEPH) Vietnam: the unforgettable tragedy. London, 1977. pp. 191. *bibliog.*

The LESSONS of Vietnam; edited by W. Scott Thompson and Donaldson D. Frizzell. London, [1977]. pp. 288. *Papers and discussions of a colloquium, 1973-74, and a spring conference, 1974 sponsored by the Fletcher School of Law and Diplomacy's International Security Studies Program.*

SCHANDLER (HERBERT Y.) The unmaking of a president: Lyndon Johnson and Vietnam. Princeton, [1977]. pp. 419. *bibliog.*

— Desertions.

KASINSKY (RENÉE GOLDSMITH) Refugees from militarism: draft-age Americans in Canada. New Brunswick, N.J., [1976]. pp. 301.

BASKIR (LAWRENCE M.) and STRAUSS (WILLIAM A.) Reconciliation after Vietnam: a program of relief for Vietnam era draft and military offenders. Notre Dame, Ind., [1977]. pp. 150. *bibliogs. A report of the Vietnam Offender Study Center for Civil Rights, University of Notre Dame.*

— Draft resisters.

KASINSKY (RENÉE GOLDSMITH) Refugees from militarism: draft-age Americans in Canada. New Brunswick, N.J., [1976]. pp. 301.

BASKIR (LAWRENCE M.) and STRAUSS (WILLIAM A.) Reconciliation after Vietnam: a program of relief for Vietnam era draft and military offenders. Notre Dame, Ind., [1977]. pp. 150. *bibliogs. A report of the Vietnam Offender Study Center for Civil Rights, University of Notre Dame.*

— Personal narratives, Italian.

TERZANI (TIZIANO) Giai Phong!: the fall and liberation of Saigon; translated from the Italian by John Shepley. London, 1976. pp. 317.

VILLAGE COMMUNITIES

— France.

LE ROY LADURIE (EMMANUEL) Montaillou, village occitan de 1294 à 1324. [Paris, 1976]. pp. 642. *bibliog.*

— Mali (Republic).

ERNST (KLAUS) Tradition and progress in the African village: the non-capitalist transformation of rural communities in Mali; (translated from the German). London, 1976. pp. 262. *(bibliog.)*

— Mexico.

The EARLY Mesoamerican village; edited by Kent V. Flannery. New York, [1976]. pp. 377. *bibliogs.*

— Switzerland.

WEINBERG (DANIELA) Peasant wisdom: cultural adaptation in a Swiss village. Berkeley, Calif., [1975]. pp. 214. *bibliog.*

— Tanzania.

MSAMBICHAKA (L.A.) and MABELE (ROBERT B.) Agricultural credit and the development of Ujamaa villages in Tanzania. Dar es Salaam, [1974]. pp. 40. *bibliog. (Dar es Salaam. University. Economic Research Bureau. ERB Papers. 74.10)*

SUMRA (SULEMAN) Problems of agricultural production in Ujamaa villages in Handeni districts. Dar es Salaam, 1975. pp. 19. *(Dar es Salaam. University. Economic Research Bureau. ERB Papers. 75.3)*

VILLAGES

— Bibliography.

CONNELL (JOHN) 1946- , compiler. Labour utilization: an annotated bibliography of village studies; ...prepared for the International Labour Office within the framework of the World Employment Programme. [Brighton], University of Sussex, Institute of Development Studies, 1975. pp. 305.

— Hungary.

RURAL transformation in Hungary; edited by Gy. Enyedi. Budapest, 1976. pp. 116. *bibliogs. (Magyar Tudományos Akadémia. Geographical Research Institute. Studies in Geography in Hungary. 13)*

— India.

FREEMAN (JAMES M.) Scarcity and opportunity in an Indian village. Menlo Park, Calif., [1977]. pp. 177. *bibliog.*

— Italy.

EVANS (ROBERT H.) Life and politics in a Venetian community. Notre Dame, Ind., [1976]. pp. 228. *bibliog. (Notre Dame. University. Committee on International Relations. International Studies)*

— Malaysia — Pahang.

WILDER (WILLIAM DEAN) Social structure and t' communications systems in a Malay village in Pahang, Malaya. 1976. fo. 406. *bibliog. 6 offprints in front pocket. Typescript. Ph.D. (London) thesis: unpublished. This thesis is the property of London University and may not be removed from the Library.*

— Nepal.

MESSERSCHMIDT (DONALD A.) The Gurungs of Nepal: conflict and change in a village society. Warminster, Wilts., [1976]. pp. 151. *bibliog.*

— Russia.

MEDVEDEV (NIKOLAI ANDREEVICH) Razvitie obshchestvennykh otnoshenii v sovetskoi derevne na sovremennom etape. Moskva, 1976. pp. 188. ·

— Sri Lanka.

ÖHRLING (STAFFAN) Rural change and spatial reorganization in Sri Lanka: barriers against development of traditional Sinhalese local communities. London, 1977. pp. 289. *bibliog. (Scandinavian Institute of Asian Studies. Monograph Series. No. 34).*

— Tunisia.

LOUIS (ANDRE) Tunisie du sud: ksars et villages de crêtes. Paris, 1975. pp. 370. *bibliog. (Centre de Recherches et d'Etudes sur les Sociétés Méditerranéennes. Etudes Tunisiennes)*

— Underdeveloped areas.

See UNDERDEVELOPED AREAS — Villages.

— United Kingdom.

WOODRUFFE (BRIAN J.) Rural settlement: policies and plans. London, 1976. pp. 64. *bibliog.*

YATES (EDWARD MARSHALL) Tudor Greatham, a social geography of a Hampshire village. London, 1977. pp. 60. *(London. University. King's College. Geography Department. Occasional Papers. No. 4)*

— Western Samoa.

MASTERMAN (SYLVIA) Western Samoa. Wellington, [1966]. pp. 56. *bibliog. (New Zealand. School Publications Branch. Secondary School Bulletins. Vol. 16. No. 7) Cover title: Village life in Western Samoa.*

VIOLENCE.

BELL (J. BOWYER) On revolt: strategies of national liberation. Cambridge, Mass., 1976. pp. 272. *bibliog.*

HONDERICH (TED) Political violence. Ithaca, N.Y., 1976. pp. 118.

HONDERICH (TED) Three essays on political violence. Oxford, [1976]. pp. 118.

MARX (EMANUEL) The social context of violent behaviour: a social anthropological study in an Israeli immigrant town. London, 1976. pp. 130. *bibliog.*

STOHL (MICHAEL) War and domestic political violence: the American capacity for repression and reaction. Beverly Hills, [1976]. pp. 151. *bibliog.*

TOCH (HANS H.) Peacekeeping: police, prisons, and violence. Lexington, Mass., [1976]. pp. 137. *bibliog.*

— Austria.

BOTZ (GERHARD) Gewalt in der Politik: Attentate, Zusammenstösse, Putschversuche, Unruhen in Österreich, 1918 bis 1934. München, 1976. pp. 358. *bibliog.*

— **Jamaica.**

LACEY (TERRY) Violence and politics in Jamaica, 1960-70: internal security in a developing country. Manchester, [1977]. pp. 184.

— **United States.**

STOHL (MICHAEL) War and domestic political violence: the American capacity for repression and reaction. Beverly Hills, [1976]. pp. 151. *bibliog.*

VIOLENT DEATHS

— **France.**

CHESNAIS (JEAN CLAUDE) Les morts violentes en France depuis 1826: comparaisons internationales. [Paris], 1976. pp. 346. *bibliog. (France. Institut National d'Etudes Démographiques. Travaux et Documents. Cahiers. No. 75)*

VITAL STATISTICS.

KORÖSI (JÓZSEF) Welche Unterlagen hat die Statistik zu beschaffen um richtige Mortalitäts-Tabellen zu gewinnen?: Denkschrift im Auftrage der Internationalen Statistischen Commission. Berlin, Verlag des Königlichen Statistischen Bureau's, 1874. pp. 83.

PRESTON (SAMUEL H.) Mortality patterns in national populations: with special reference to recorded causes of death. New York, [1976]. pp. 201. *bibliog.*

VOCATIONAL EDUCATION.

BROLIN (DONN E.) Vocational preparation of retarded citizens. Columbus, Ohio, [1976]. pp. 312. *bibliog.*

— **Europe.**

AUSTRALIA. Tripartite Mission to Study Methods of Training Skilled Workers in Europe. 1970. The training of skilled workers in Europe; report...1968-69. in AUSTRALIA. Parliament. Parliamentary papers, 1970, vol.10.

— **European Economic Community countries.**

EUROPEAN COMMUNITIES. Economic and Social Committee. 1976. Systems of education and vocational training in the member countries of the European Community. Brussels, 1976. pp. 114. *(Studies)*

— **Germany.**

GERMANY (BUNDESREPUBLIK). Statistisches Bundesamt. Schulen der beruflichen Fortbildungen. a., 1973- Wiesbaden. *(Bildung und Kultur. Reihe 2.2)*

GERMANY (BUNDESREPUBLIK). Statistisches Bundesamt. Schulen der beruflichen Ausbildung. a., 1974- Wiesbaden. *(Bildung und Kultur. Reihe 2.1)*

— **Russia.**

KLOCHKOV (IVAN DANILOVICH) Sovershenstvovanie podgotovki kvalifitsirovannykh rabochikh. Moskva, 1975. pp. 215. *bibliog.*

— **United Kingdom.**

U.K. Department of Education and Science. 1976. Unified vocational preparation: a pilot approach; a government statement. [London, 1976]. pp. 16.

VOCATIONAL GUIDANCE.

REUBENS (BEATRICE G.) Bridges to work: international comparisons of transition services. London, 1977. pp. 275. *bibliog.*

— **Russia — Estonia.**

TITMA (MIKK KHARRIEVICH) Vybor professii kak sotsial'naia problema: na materialakh konkretnykh issledovanii v ESSR. Moskva, 1975. pp. 198.

VOCATIONAL REHABILITATION

— **United States.**

The VOCATIONAL rehabilitation of public assistance recipients: a national survey of clients served and rehabilitation outcomes; [by] John E. Muthard [and others]. Gainesville, Fla., 1976. pp. 277. *bibliog.*

LEVITAN (SAR A.) and TAGGART (ROBERT) Jobs for the disabled. Baltimore, [1977]. pp. 129.

VOICE OF SOUTH AFRICA.

MAGNUSSON (ÅKE) The Voice of South Africa. Uppsala, 1976. pp. 55. *bibliog. (Nordiska Afrikainstitutet. Research Reports. No. 35)*

VOLGA BASIN

— **History — 1917-1921, Revolution.**

MEDVEDEV (EFREM IGNAT'EVICH) Grazhdanskaia voina v Srednem Povolzh'e, 1918-1919 gg. Saratov, 1974. pp. 352.

VOLUNTEER WORKERS IN SOCIAL SERVICE

— **United Kingdom.**

CIVIC TRUST. The local amenity movement; [including chapters by Anthony Barker]. London, 1976. pp. 36.

LANSLEY (JOHN) Voluntary organisations facing change: the report of a project to help Councils for Voluntary Service respond to local government reorganisation. London, 1976. pp. 96. *bibliog.*

PIVOT: the report of a working party on the National Association of Voluntary Help Organisers (NAVHO): chairman, Geraldine M. Aves. Berkhamsted, 1976. pp. 30.

WEBB (ADRIAN L.) and others. Voluntary social service manpower resources. [London], Personal Social Services Council, 1976. pp. 49.

MOORE (SHEILA) Working for free: a practical guide for volunteers. London, [1977]. pp. 256.

VORONEZH (OBLAST')

— **History — Sources.**

ANTIUKHIN (GEORGII VLADIMIROVICH) Ocherki istorii partiino-sovetskoi pechati Voronezhskoi oblasti, 1917-1945. Voronezh, 1976. pp. 238.

— — **1917-1921, Revolution.**

NAKROKHIN (EFIM ALEKSANDROVICH) Inogo ne bylo puti. Voronezh, 1975. pp. 133.

— **Politics and government.**

NAKROKHIN (EFIM ALEKSANDROVICH) Inogo ne bylo puti. Voronezh, 1975. pp. 133.

VOTING.

BUDGE (IAN) and FARLIE (DENNIS) Voting and party competition: a theoretical critique and synthesis applied to surveys from ten democracies. London, [1977]. pp. 555.

— **Australia.**

HUGHES (COLIN ANFIELD) and GRAHAM (BRUCE DESMOND) Voting for the New South Wales Legislative Assembly. Canberra, 1975. pp. 518. *Supplement to the same authors' A handbook of Australian government and politics 1890-1964.*

HUGHES (COLIN ANFIELD) and GRAHAM (BRUCE DESMOND) Voting for the South Australian, Western Australian and Tasmanian Lower Houses, 1890-1964. Canberra, 1976. pp. 639. *Fifth and final supplement to the same authors' A handbook of Australian government and politics, 1890-1964, to which it also contains corrigenda.*

— **Ireland (Republic).**

GALLAGHER (MICHAEL) Electoral support for Irish political parties 1927-1973. London, [1976]. pp. 75. *bibliog.*

— **United Kingdom.**

FISHBEIN (MARTIN) and others. Voting behaviour in Britain: an attitudinal analysis. London, Social Science Research Council Survey Unit, [1976]. pp. 69, 19. *bibliog. (Occasional Papers in Survey Research. 7)*

HOWARD (JONATHAN) Voting trends in the Leeds city-region. 1976. fo. 44. *Typescript: unpublished.*

— **United States.**

KIRKPATRICK (SAMUEL A.) ed. American electoral behavior: change and stability. Beverly Hills, Calif., 1976. pp. 143. *bibliogs.*

KNOKE (DAVID) Change and continuity in American politics: the social bases of political parties. Baltimore, [1976]. pp. 192. *bibliog.*

MILLER (WARREN EDWARD) and LEVITIN (TERESA E.) Leadership and change: the new politics and the American electorate. Cambridge, Mass., [1976]. pp. 267.

TRILLING (RICHARD J.) Party image and electoral behavior. New York, [1976]. pp. 234.

STRONG (DONALD S.) Issue voting and party realignment. University, Ala., [977]. pp. 110.

VOTING RESEARCH

— **United States.**

STRONG (DONALD S.) Issue voting and party realignment. University, Ala., [977]. pp. 110.

VOWELL (JOHN) otherwise HOOKER.

SNOW (VERNON F.) Parliament in Elizabethan England: John Hooker's Order and usage. New Haven, Conn., 1977. pp. 221.

VOYAGES AND TRAVELS.

MADOX (RICHARD) An Elizabethan in 1582: the diary of Richard Madox, Fellow of All Souls; [edited by] Elizabeth Story Donno. London, 1976. pp. 365. *(Hakluyt Society. Works. 2nd Series. No. 147)*

VSEROSSIISKII SOTSIAL-KHRISTIANSKII SOIUZ OSVOBOZHDENIIA NARODA.

DUNLOP (JOHN B.) The new Russian revolutionaries. Belmont, Mass., 1976. pp. 344. *bibliog.*

WAGE PAYMENT SYSTEMS

— **Australia.**

AUSTRALIA. Commonwealth Bureau of Census and Statistics. 1975. Frequency of pay, August 1974. Canberra, 1975. pp. 5.

WAGE-PRICE POLICY.

DAS GUPTA (AMIYA KUMAR) A theory of wage policy. Delhi, 1976. pp. 78.

BRITTAN (SAMUEL) and LILLEY (PETER) The delusion of incomes policy. London, 1977. pp. 254. *bibliog.*

— **United Kingdom.**

POND (CHRIS) The attack on inflation: who pays?; a reply to the White Paper on the pay policy. London, 1976. fo.16. *(Low Pay Unit. Low Pay Papers. No. 11)*

— **United States.**

MITCHELL (DANIEL J.B.) and AZEVEDO (ROSS E.) Wage-price controls and labor market distortions. Los Angeles, [1976]. pp. 174. *(California University. Institute of Industrial Relations. Industrial Relations Monographs. No. 16)*

WAGE SURVEYS.

EUROPEAN COMMUNITIES. Statistical Office. Social Statistics. Special Series: Structure of Earnings in Industry, 1972. Luxembourg, 1975 in progress.

WAGES.

CORK WORKERS' CLUB. Historical Reprints. No. 15. The Connolly-DeLeon controversy: on wages, marriage and the church. Cork, [1976]. pp. 45.

COX (NICOLE) and FEDERICI (SILVIA) Counter-planning from the kitchen: wages for housework: a perspective on capital and the left. 2nd ed. New York, 1976. pp. 23.

MARSHALL (F. RAY) and others. Labor economics: wages, employment, and trade unionism. 3rd ed. Homewood, Ill., 1976. pp. 633. *bibliogs.*

— Minimum wage — Canada — Quebec.

QUEBEC (PROVINCE). Department of Labour and Manpower. Research Branch. 1972. Coordination of social aid policies and the minimum wage versus the ability of enterprises to meet wage increase. Quebec, 1972. pp. 63.

— — France.

PICARD (ROGER) Le minimum légal de salaire. Paris, 1913. pp. 63. *(Parti Socialiste. Cahiers du Socialiste. Nos. 16-17)*

— — India.

SEVERIN (JOERG) Mindestlohnregelungen in Entwicklungsländern: das Beispiel Indien. Hamburg, 1975. pp. 383. *bibliog. Dissertation - Universität Hamburg.*

— — Underdeveloped areas.

See UNDERDEVELOPED AREAS — Wages — Minimum wage.

— Africa — Bibliography.

MALAN (T.) compiler. Source material on labour earnings in African countries. Pretoria, 1975. fo. 35. *(Africa Institute. Occasional Papers. No. 39).*

— Canada — Nova Scotia.

NOVA SCOTIA. Department of Labour. Economics and Research Division. 1968. Current and historical trends in average weekly wages and salaries by industry for Nova Scotia, 1961 to 1967. Halifax, [1968]. fo. 28.

NOVA SCOTIA. Department of Labour. Economics and Research Division. 1970. Average weekly wages and salaries in the sixties by industry for Nova Scotia. Halifax, [1970]. fo. 35.

— European Economic Community countries.

EUROPEAN COMMUNITIES. Statistical Office. Social Statistics. Special Series: Structure of Earnings in Industry, 1972. Luxembourg, 1975 in progress.

— France.

STRASBOURG. Chambre de Commerce et d'Industrie. Assemblée Plénière. Réunion du 17 mai 1965. L'évolution comparative des salaires dans le Bas-Rhin et dans le Land Bade-Wurtemberg depuis 1958: les charges sociales, le coût salarial, les salaires nets et les prestations des salaires. Strasbourg, 1965. fo.13.

— Germany.

HESSE. Statistisches Landesamt. Beiträge zur Statistik Hessens. Neue Folge. Nr. 71. Die Struktur der Arbeiter- und Angestelltenverdienste in der gewerblichen Wirtschaft und im Dienstleistungsbereich, 1972: Ergebnisse der Gehalts- und Lohnstrukturerhebung, 1972. Wiesbaden, 1976. pp. 242.

— — Baden-Wuerttemberg.

STRASBOURG. Chambre de Commerce et d'Industrie. Assemblée Plénière. Réunion du 17 mai 1965. L'évolution comparative des salaires dans le Bas-Rhin et dans le Land Bade-Wurtemberg depuis 1958: les charges sociales, le coût salarial, les salaires nets et les prestations des salaires. Strasbourg, 1965. fo.13.

— India.

PALEKAR (SHREEKANT A.) Problems of wage policy for economic development, with special reference to India. London, [1962]. pp. 343.

PAPOLA (TRILOK SINGH) and SUBRAHMANIAN (K.K.) Wage structure and labour mobility in a local labour market: a study in Ahmedabad. Ahmedabad, 1975. pp. 214. *(Sardar Patel Institute of Economic and Social Research. Monograph Series. 4)*

— Papua New Guinea.

PAPUA NEW GUINEA. Bureau of Statistics. 1967. Census of employers, July, 1967: preliminary bulletin. Konedobu, 1967. pp. 7.

— Rhodesia.

RIDDELL (ROGER C.) and HARRIS (PETER S.) The poverty datum line as a wage fixing standard: an application to Rhodesia. Gwelo, 1975. pp. 96.

— Russia.

RIABININ (ANATOLII IAKOVLEVICH) Oplata truda rabotnikov zdravookhraneniia. Moskva, 1969. pp. 86.

— South Africa.

BIESHEUVEL (SIMON) The black-white wage gap: what can be done about it?. Johannesburg, 1972. pp. 19.

— Underdeveloped areas.

See UNDERDEVELOPED AREAS — Wages.

— United Kingdom.

FITTON (ROBERT SUCKSMITH) Family earnings at the mills of W.G. and J. Strutt of Belper and Milford, Derbyshire, 1801-5. [195-?]. 8 folio sheets. (in 1 vol.). *Manuscript and typescript.*

FIELD (FRANK) 1942- . The rights of lower paid workers: a reply to the Employment Protection Bill: consultative document. London, 1974. fo.13. *(Low Pay Unit. Low Pay Papers. No. 1)*

FIELD (FRANK) 1942- , and WINYARD (STEVE) Action not words: a submission to the Royal Commission on the Distribution of Income and Wealth. London, 1975. fo.5. *(Low Pay Unit. Low Pay Papers. No. 3)*

U.K. Office of Wages Councils. [Wages orders]. irreg., 1976- London. *Formerly included in U.K. Statutory instruments.*

LOW PAY UNIT. Low Pay Papers. No. 9. Axing low pay: a call for a trade union plan of action against low pay. London, 1976. fo. 11.

TAYLOR (ERIC) 1934- . The better temper: a commemorative history of the Midland Iron and Steel Wages Board, 1876-1976. London, [1976]. pp. 38.

WINYARD (STEVE) Nine into two equals progress: an examination of the merging of the retail wages councils. London, 1976. fo. 14. *(Low Pay Unit. Low Pay Papers. No. 10)*

ARE low wages inevitable?; edited by Frank Field. Nottingham, [1977?]. pp. 144. *bibliog.*

EAST ANGLIA ECONOMIC PLANNING COUNCIL. Earnings, other incomes and household expenditure in East Anglia. [London, 1977]. pp. 17.

KRISHNA-MURTY (R.) Earnings and incomes data for Greater London. rev. ed. London, 1977. pp. 68. *(London. Greater London Council. Research Memoranda. 504)*

NATIONAL ECONOMIC DEVELOPMENT OFFICE. A study of U.K. nationalised industries: background paper 4: manpower and pay trends. London, 1977. pp. 170.

SULLIVAN (JILL) The brush off: a study of the contract cleaning industry. London, 1977. pp. 32. *(Low Pay Unit. Low Pay Pamphlets. No. 5)*

— United States.

WEISBORD (ALBERT) Passaic: the story of a struggle against starvation wages and the right to organize. Chicago, 1926; New York, 1976. pp. 64.

WOMEN, minorities and employment discrimination; edited by Phyllis A. Wallace and Annette M. LaMond. Lexington, Mass., [1977]. pp. 203. *bibliogs. Based on papers and proceedings of a conference held by the Industrial Relations Section of the Alfred P. Sloan School of Management, Massachusetts Institute of Technology, in 1974.*

— — Mathematical models.

WEISSBROD (RICHARD) Diffusion of relative wage inflation in Southeast Pennsylvania. Evanston, Ill., 1976. pp. 166. *bibliog. (Northwestern University. Studies in Geography. No. 23).*

WAGES AND PRODUCTIVITY

— Russia.

MAL'TSEV (NIKOLAI ALEKSANDROVICH) Problemy raspredeleniia v razvitom sotsialisticheskom obshchestve. Moskva, 1976. pp. 198.

WALES

— Administrative and political divisions.

U.K. Local Government Boundary Commission for Wales. 1975- . Special community review[s]: draft proposals. [Cardiff, 1975 in progress]. *In English and Welsh.*

U.K. Local Government Boundary Commission for Wales. 1977- . Special community review[s]: report[s] and proposals. [Cardiff, 1977 in progress]. *In English and Welsh.*

— Economic conditions.

U.K. Welsh Office. 1974. 10 years of progress. [Cardiff, 1974]. pp. 16. *In English and Welsh.*

— — Bibliography.

BAGGS (TERESA) and others, compilers. The South Wales valleys: a contemporary socio-economic bibliography;...compiled for the Valleys '74 conference held at Glamorgan Polytechnic...2nd November, 1974. Aberfan, [1974]. pp. 122. *bibliog.*

— Economic policy.

WELSH DEVELOPMENT AGENCY. Welsh Development Agency: a statement of policies and programmes. Pontypridd, 1977. pp. 12.

— Industries.

DAVIES (GLYN) and THOMAS (IAN) Overseas investment in Wales: the welcome invasion. Swansea, 1976. pp. 221.

— Nationalism.

BRITISH AND IRISH COMMUNIST ORGANISATION. Is Wales a nation? Belfast, 1972. pp. 24.

HEARNE (DERRICK K.) The joy of freedom. Talybont, 1977. pp. 112.

NAIRN (TOM) The break-up of Britain: crisis and neo-nationalism. London, [1977]. pp. 368.

— Politics and government.

TRADES UNION CONGRESS. TUC policy on devolution. London, 1976. pp. 8.

U.K. 1976. Devolution: the new assemblies for Scotland and Wales; [main points of the White Paper]. [London, 1976]. pp. 15.

U.K. Parliament. House of Commons. Library. Research Division. Background Papers. No.57. The devolution debate: regional statistics. [London, 1977]. pp. 18.

— Population.

U.K. Welsh Office. Planning Services Division. 1975. Wales population change, 1961-1971. [Cardiff], 1975. fo. 23, 7 maps. *(Occasional Papers. No.1)*

— Rural conditions.

COLYER (RICHARD J.) The Welsh cattle drovers: agriculture and the Welsh cattle trade before and during the nineteenth century. Cardiff, 1976. pp. 155. *bibliog.*

— Social conditions.

U.K. Welsh Office. 1974. 10 years of progress. [Cardiff, 1974]. pp. 16. *In English and Welsh.*

— — Bibliography.

BAGGS (TERESA) and others, compilers. The South Wales valleys: a contemporary socio-economic bibliography;...compiled for the Valleys '74 conference held at Glamorgan Polytechnic...2nd November, 1974. Aberfan, [1974]. pp. 122. *bibliog.*

WALKER (Sir HERBERT ASHCOMBE).

KLAPPER (CHARLES FREDERICK) Sir Herbert Walker's Southern Railway. London, 1973. pp. 295.

WALLACE (GEORGE CORLEY).

WALLACE (GEORGE CORLEY) Stand up for America. Garden City, N.Y., 1976. pp. 183.

WALLACE (HENRY AGARD).

WALTON (RICHARD J.) Henry Wallace, Harry Truman, and the Cold War. New York, 1976. pp. 388. *bibliog.*

WALLONIA

— Economic conditions.

CROISSANCE de l'économie de la Wallonie; par L.E. Davin [and others]; actes du Carrefour Scientifique de Namur, décembre 1965. Bruxelles, 1966. pp. 40. *(Liège. Université. Séminaire Interdisciplinaire de Science Economique des Professeurs Harsin et Davin. Documents et Travaux. No.5)*

WALLS (JOSIAH T.)

KLINGMAN (PETER D.) Josiah Walls: Florida's black congressman of reconstruction. Gainesville, 1976. pp. 157. *bibliog.*

WAR.

BEER (FRANCIS A.) How much war in history: definitions, estimates, extrapolations and trends. Beverly Hills, [1974]. pp. 37. *bibliog.*

CLAUSEWITZ (CARL VON) On war; edited and translated by Michael Howard and Peter Paret...with a commentary by Bernard Brodie. Princeton, N.J., [1976]. pp. 711.

— Economic aspects.

MILWARD (ALAN S.) War, economy and society, 1939-1945. Berkeley, Calif., [1977]. pp. 395. *bibliog.*

WAR (INTERNATIONAL LAW).

CURRENT problems of international law: essays on U.N. law and on the law of armed conflict; edited by Antonio Cassese. Milano, 1975. pp. 375. *(Pisa. Università. Facoltà di Giurisprudenza. Pubblicazioni. 60) Lectures given in the University of Pisa. In English or French.*

DROIT humanitaire et conflits armés:...colloque des 28, 29 et 30 janvier 1970. Bruxelles, [1976]. pp. 302. *(Brussels. Université Libre. Institut de Sociologie. Centre de Droit International. [Publications]. 7) In French or English.*

POLTORAK (ARKADII IOSIFOVICH) and SAVINSKII (LEV ISAAKOVICH) Vooruzhennye konflikty i mezhdunarodnoe pravo: osnovnye problemy. Moskva, 1976. pp. 416.

WAR AND EMERGENCY POWERS.

MARCUS (MAEVA) Truman and the steel seizure case: the limits of presidential power. New York, 1977. pp. 390. *bibliog.*

— United States.

SOFAER (ABRAHAM D.) War, foreign affairs and constitutional power: the origins. Cambridge, Mass., [1976]. pp. 533. *bibliog.*

WAR AND RELIGION.

LIECHTENHAN (RUDOLF) Ist Abrüstung Christenpflicht?; im Auftrag der schweizerischen Vereinigung antimilitaristischer Pfarrer verfasst. Bern, 1927. pp. 80.

ALL AFRICA CONFERENCE OF CHURCHES. The hard road to peace: a report to the churches in Africa on their part in the reconciliation in the Sudan and an appeal. Nairobi, [1972]. pp. 28.

CLARK (ROBERT EDWARD DAVID) Does the Bible teach pacifism?. [London, 1976]. pp. 70.

KENT (BRUCE) and others. Christians and nuclear disarmament. London, [1977]. pp. 17. *(Campaign for Nuclear Disarmament. Christian Group. Christian CND Pamphlets)*

WAR AND SOCIALISM.

HERVE (GUSTAVE) Das Vaterland der Reichen; [translated from the French]. Zürich, [190-?]. pp. 259.

SOZIALDEMOKRATISCHE PARTEI DEUTSCHLANDS. Vorstand. Die Greuel des Krieges. [Berlin, 1912]. pp. 16. *(Sozialdemokratische Flugschriften. 14) Wanting title-page.*

SOZIALDEMOKRATISCHE PARTEI DEUTSCHLANDS. Vorstand. Krieg dem Kriege! [Berlin, 1912]. pp. 16. *(Sozialdemokratische Flugschriften. 15) Includes extracts from the minutes of the International Socialist Congress, Basel, 1912. Wanting title-page.*

BAUMANN (WILHELM) Krieg und Proletariat. Wien, 1924. pp. 156.

KOMMUNISTISCHE PARTEI DEUTSCHLANDS. Zentralkomitee. Richtlinien der KPD zur Wehrfrage. [Berlin?], 1929. pp. 14.

HUBER (WOLFGANG) and SCHWERDTFEGER (JOHANNES) eds. Frieden, Gewalt, Sozialismus: Studien zur Geschichte der sozialistischen Arbeiterbewegung. Stuttgart, [1976]. pp. 850. *bibliogs. (Evangelische Studiengemeinschaft. Forschungen und Berichte. Band 32)*

STILLIG (JUERGEN) Die Russische Februarrevolution 1917 und die sozialistische Friedenspolitik. Köln, 1977. pp. 331. *bibliog.*

WARREN (EARL).

WARREN (EARL) The memoirs of Earl Warren. New York, 1977. pp. 394.

WARSAW

— Politics and government.

DROZDOWSKI (MARIAN MAREK) Stefan Starzyński, prezydent Warszawy. Warszawa, 1976. pp. 384. *(Towarzystwo Miłośników Historii w Warszawie. Biblioteka Wiedzy o Warszawie)*

WARWICK UNIVERSITY.

STOREY (RICHARD A.) and DRUKER (JANET) Guide to the Modern Records Centre, University of Warwick Library. Warwick, [1977]. pp. 152. *(University of Warwick. Library. Occasional Publications. No. 2)*

WATER

— Fluoridation.

WALT (AUDREY GILLIAN) Policy making in Britain: a comparative study of fluoridation and family planning, 1960-1974. 1976. fo. 273. *bibliog. Typescript. Ph.D. (London) thesis: unpublished. This thesis is the property of London University and may not be removed from the Library.*

— — United Kingdom.

BRITISH DENTAL ASSOCIATION and others. Fluoridation of water supplies: questions and answers. London, 1976. pp. 87.

— Laws and legislation — South Africa.

SOUTH AFRICA. Parliament. House of Assembly. Select Committee on the Water Amendment Bill. 1977. Report...; proceedings (S.C.5-1977). in SOUTH AFRICA. Parliament. House of Assembly. Select Committee reports.

— — United Kingdom.

WISDOM (ALLEN SIDNEY) The law of rivers and watercourses. 3rd ed. London, 1975. pp. 397.

— Pollution — Europe.

JOHNSON (RALPH WHITNEY) and BROWN (GARDNER MALLARD) Cleaning up Europe's waters: economics, management and policies. New York, 1976. pp. 313.

WATER CONSUMPTION

— United Kingdom.

WATER DATA UNIT [U.K.]. Water demand in England and Wales, 1974. Reading, 1976. pp. 25. *(Technical Memoranda. No. 9)*

WATER DISTRICTS

— United Kingdom.

NORTH WEST WATER AUTHORITY. Annual report. a., 1974/75(1st)- Warrington.

WESSEX WATER AUTHORITY. Annual report and accounts. a., 1974/75(1st)- Bristol.

NORTHUMBRIAN WATER AUTHORITY. Annual report and accounts. a., 1975/76(2nd)- Newcastle-upon-Tyne.

SOUTHERN WATER AUTHORITY. Annual report and accounts. a., 1975/76(2nd)- Worthing.

U.K. Department of the Environment. 1976. Review of the water industry in England and Wales: a consultative document. [London, 1976]. pp. 38.

WATER POWER ELECTRIC PLANTS

— Malaysia.

NATIONAL ELECTRICITY BOARD [FEDERATION OF MALAYSIA]. Batang Padang hydro-electric scheme. [Kuala Lumpur, 1968?]. pp. 57. *In English and Malay.*

— Russia — Ukraine.

MOTORNYI (OLEKSANDR DAVYDOVYCH) Kremhes. Dnipropetrovs'k, 1969. pp. 45.

WATER QUALITY MANAGEMENT

— Europe.

JOHNSON (RALPH WHITNEY) and BROWN (GARDNER MALLARD) Cleaning up Europe's waters: economics, management and policies. New York, 1976. pp. 313.

— France.

FRANCE. Secrétariat d'Etat à l'Environnement. Bilan d'activité des agences financières de bassin. a., 1969/72- Paris.

WELSH IN THE UNITED STATES.

WILLIAMS (GLANMOR) A prospect of paradise?: Wales and the United States, 1776-1914. [London], 1976. pp. 29. *(British Broadcasting Corporation, Wales. Annual Lectures. 1976)*

WELSH LANGUAGE.

BETTS (CLIVE) Culture in crisis: the future of the Welsh language. Upton, Wirral, [1976]. pp. 243.

WENDEL (FRANÇOIS DE).

JEANNENEY (JEAN NOËL) François de Wendel en république: l'argent et le pouvoir, 1914-1940. Paris, [1976]. pp. 670.

WEST INDIANS IN CANADA.

BARBADOS. 196-. Advice to West Indian women recruited for work in Canada as household helps. [Bridgetown, 196-?]. 1 pamphlet (unpaged).

WEST INDIANS IN THE UNITED KINGDOM.

RUNNYMEDE TRUST. The Runnymede Trust's submission to the Parliamentary Select Committee on Race Relations and Immigration: West Indians in Britain. London, 1976. fo. 4.

LEE (TREVOR ROSS) Race and residence: the concentration and dispersal of immigrants in London. Oxford, 1977. pp. 193. *bibliog.*

WEST INDIES

— Constitutional history.

WALLACE (ELISABETH) The British Caribbean: from the decline of colonialism to the end of federation. Toronto, [1977]. pp. 274. *bibliog.*

— Economic conditions.

WALLACE (ELISABETH) The British Caribbean: from the decline of colonialism to the end of federation. Toronto, [1977]. pp. 274. *bibliog.*

— Politics and government.

BARBADOS. Regional Council of Ministers. 1964. Draft federal scheme as amended at ninth meeting of the...Council. ..October 1964. [Bridgetown], 1964. pp. 45.

WALLACE (ELISABETH) The British Caribbean: from the decline of colonialism to the end of federation. Toronto, [1977]. pp. 274. *bibliog.*

WEST MIDLANDS

— Economic conditions.

WEST MIDLANDS. County Council. Annual economic review. a., 1975/76 (no. 1)- [Birmingham].

— Economic policy.

WEST MIDLANDS. County Council. Annual economic review. a., 1975/76 (no. 1)- [Birmingham].

— Statistics.

WEST MIDLANDS. County Council. Central Statistical Information and Research Unit. Annual statistical abstract. a., 1976 (2nd)- Birmingham.

WESTERN AUSTRALIA

— Parliament.

WESTERN AUSTRALIA. Parliament. Digest. a., 1976- [Perth].

— — Elections.

HUGHES (COLIN ANFIELD) and GRAHAM (BRUCE DESMOND) Voting for the South Australian, Western Australian and Tasmanian Lower Houses, 1890-1964. Canberra, 1976. pp. 639. *Fifth and final supplement to the same authors' A handbook of Australian government and politics, 1890-1964, to which it also contains corrigenda.*

WESTERN SAMOA

— Economic conditions.

SHANKMAN (PAUL) Migration and underdevelopment: the case of Western Samoa. Boulder, Col., 1976. pp. 129. *bibliog.*

— Emigration and immigration.

SHANKMAN (PAUL) Migration and underdevelopment: the case of Western Samoa. Boulder, Col., 1976. pp. 129. *bibliog.*

— Social life and customs.

MASTERMAN (SYLVIA) Western Samoa. Wellington, [1966]. pp. 56. *bibliog. (New Zealand. School Publications Branch. Secondary School Bulletins. Vol. 16. No. 7) Cover title: Village life in Western Samoa.*

WHITE COLLAR WORKERS.

KANTER (ROSABETH MOSS) Men and women of the corporation. New York, [1977]. pp. 348. *bibliog.*

WHITE RUSSIA

— Constitutional history.

ISTORIIA gosudarstva i prava Belorusskoi SSR, 1917-1975 gg. Minsk, 1970-76. 2 vols.

— Economic conditions — Mathematical models.

MARTINKEVICH (FELIKS STANISLAVOVICH) and others, eds. Voprosy teorii i otsenki ekonomicheskoi effektivnosti narodnogo khoziaistva. Minsk, 1976. pp. 303.

— Economic history.

KUPREEVA (ANNA PAVLOVNA) Vozrozhdenie narodnogo khoziaistva Belorussii; nauchnyi redaktor. ..P.T. Petrikov. Minsk, 1976. pp. 220. *bibliog.*

MARCHENKO (IVAN EGOROVICH) Trudovoi podvig rabochego klassa Belorusskoi SSR, 1943-1950 gg. Minsk, 1977. pp. 247.

— Foreign relations.

For a related heading see UNITED NATIONS — Russia — White Russia.

— Politics and government.

SAMBUK (SUSANNA MIKHAILOVNA) Obshchestvenno-politicheskaia mysl' Belorussii vo vtoroi polovine XIX veka: po materialam periodicheskoi pechati. Minsk, 1976. pp. 183.

WHITE RUSSIAN PERIODICALS.

SAMBUK (SUSANNA MIKHAILOVNA) Obshchestvenno-politicheskaia mysl' Belorussii vo vtoroi polovine XIX veka: po materialam periodicheskoi pechati. Minsk, 1976. pp. 183.

WHOLESALE TRADE

— Brazil.

BRAZIL. Departamento de Censos. 1975. Censo comercial [1970]: Brasil [whole country]. [Rio de Janeiro, 1975]. pp. 157.

— Canada.

CANADA. Statistics Canada. Merchandising businesses survey: agents and brokers. bien., 1974 (1st)- Ottawa. *[in English and French]*.

— Finland.

FINLAND. Tilastokeskus. Tukkukauppa ja agenturitoiminta: Parti handeln och agenturverksamheten. a., 1972- Helsinki. [in Finnish and Swedish].

— Iran.

IRAN. Bureau of Statistics. 1967. Report on the results of survey of wholesale trade establishments of Tehran and suburbs, 1966, etc. [Tehran, 1967]. pp. (47).

— Ireland (Republic).

EIRE. Central Statistics Office. 1977. Census of distribution, 1971: detailed results. Dublin, 1977. 3 pts. (in 1 vol.).

WIESENTHAL (SIMON).

AMERONGEN (MARTIN VAN) Kreisky und seine unbewältigte Gegenwart; (ins Deutsche übertragen [from the Dutch] von Gerhard Hartmann). Graz, 1977. pp. 128.

WIFE BEATING.

TRACY (DICK) Battered wives. [London, 1974?]. pp. 6.

WILBERFORCE (WILLIAM).

POLLOCK (JOHN) 1923- . Wilberforce. London, 1977. pp. 368. *bibliog.*

WILLIAM II, Emperor of Germany.

GERMANY. Reichstag. 1908. Das persönliche Regiment vor dem Deutschen Reichstage: die Verhandlungen...vom 10. und 11. November 1908. Berlin, 1908. pp. 128.

WILLIAM TYNDALE JUNIOR AND INFANTS SCHOOLS.

WILLIAMS (PAUL) The lessons of Tyndale: an examination of the William Tyndale school affair. London, 1977. pp. 16. *(Conservative Political Centre. [Publications]. No.599)*

WILLS

— United Kingdom.

VALE (M.G.A.) Piety, charity and literacy among the Yorkshire gentry, 1370-1480. York, 1976. pp. 32. *(York. University. Borthwick Institute of Historical Research. Borthwick Papers. No.50)*

WILSON (BENJAMIN) Radical.

TESTAMENTS of radicalism: memoirs of working class politicians, 1790-1885; edited and introduced by David Vincent. London, [1977]. pp. 246. *bibliogs.*

WILSON (EDMUND).

WILSON (EDMUND) American writer. Letters on literature and politics 1912-1972; edited by Elena Wilson. London, 1977. pp. 768.

WILSON (WOODROW) President of the United States.

WALWORTH (ARTHUR CLARENCE) America's moment, 1918: American diplomacy at the end of World War I. New York, [1977]. pp. 309. *bibliog.*

WINE AND WINE MAKING.

OFFICE INTERNATIONAL DU VIN. Textes de l'arrangement international et des règlements relatifs à l'Office International du Vin. Corbeil, [imprint], 1928. pp. 14.

DOUARCHE (LEON) L'Office International du Vin. Paris, [1929]. pp. 43.

— Italy.

BELTRAME (CARLO) Le cantine sociali in provincia di Alessandria: situazione, problemi, linee di azione; relazione introduttiva per un dibattito allargato. Alessandria, 1972. pp. 44. *(Alessandria (Province). Centro Documentazione e Ricerche Economico-Sociali. Quaderni. n.68)*

— South Africa.

ZYL (D.J. VAN) Kaapse wyn en brandewyn, 1795-1860:...die geskiedenis van wynbou en wynhandel in die Kaapkolonie. Kaapstad, 1975. pp. 360. *bibliog.*

WINNIPEG

— General strike, 1919.

McNAUGHT (KENNETH) and BERCUSON (DAVID JAY) The Winnipeg strike, 1919. Don Mills, Ontario, [1974]. pp. 126.

WIT AND HUMOUR

— Psychology.

WILSON (CHRISTOPHER PAUL) Structure and function of the joke: an experimental and theoretical study. 1977. fo. 484. *Typescript. Ph.D. (London) thesis: unpublished. This thesis is the property of London University and may not be removed from the Library.*

WITCHCRAFT

— Spain.

SAINT-MARTIN (KARMELE) Nosotras las brujas vascas. San Sebastian, [1976]. pp. 133.

WITOS (WINCENTY).

ZAKRZEWSKI (ANDRZEJ) Wincenty Witos: chłopski polityk i mąż stanu. Warszawa, 1977. pp. 431. *bibliog.*

WITTGENSTEIN (LUDWIG).

PEARS (DAVID FRANCIS) Ludwig Wittgenstein. Harmondsworth, 1977. pp. 208. *bibliog.*

PHILLIPS (DEREK L.) Wittgenstein and scientific knowledge: a sociological perspective. London, 1977. pp. 248.

WOLFE (BILLY).

WOLFE (BILLY) Scotland lives. Edinburgh, [1973]. pp. 167.

WOMEN.

COBBOLD (RICHARD) The character of woman, in a lecture, delivered at the Hanover Square Rooms, April 13th, 1848, for the benefit of the Governesses Benevolent Institution. London, [1848]. pp. 64. *Presentation copy.*

— Bibliography.

SEMINAR ON WOMEN IN DEVELOPMENT, MEXICO, 1975. Women and world development: with an annotated bibliography; edited by Irene Tinker [and others]. New York, 1976. pp. 382. *Papers of the seminar convened and co-sponsored by the American Association for the Advancement of Science.*

— Congresses.

SEMINAR ON WOMEN IN DEVELOPMENT, MEXICO, 1975. Women and world development: with an annotated bibliography; edited by Irene Tinker [and others]. New York, 1976. pp. 382. *Papers of the seminar convened and co-sponsored by the American Association for the Advancement of Science.*

— Employment.

BRITISH SOCIOLOGICAL ASSOCIATION. Annual Conference, 1974. Dependence and exploitation in work and marriage: [papers presented at the conference; edited] by Diana Leonard Barker and Sheila Allen. London, 1976. pp. 265. *bibliog. (British Sociological Association. Explorations in Sociology. 7)*

WOMEN and the workplace: the implications of occupational segregation; edited by Martha Blaxall and Barbara Reagan. Chicago, 1976. pp. 326. *(Reprinted from a supplement to Signs, vol. 1, no. 3, pt. 2). Papers of a conference, May 1975, sponsored jointly by the American Economic Association Committee on the Status of Women in the Economics Profession and the Center for Research on Women in Higher Education...at Wellesley College.*

WOMEN AT WORK; [pd. by] Office for Women Workers' Questions, International Labour Office. 3 a yr., 1977 (no.1)- Geneva.

See also MOTHERS — Employment.

— — Australia.

RYAN (EDNA) and CONLON (ANNE) Gentle invaders: Australian women at work, 1788-1974. West Melbourne, 1975. pp. 196.

— — Austria.

LEICHTER (KAETHE) Frauenarbeit und Arbeiterinnenschutz in Österreich. Wien, 1927. pp. 238.

— — Denmark.

FOGED (BRITA) Kvindearbejde, 1950-71; efterskrift ved Randi Markussen and Birte Siim, etc. Aarhus, 1975. pp. 153. *bibliogs.*

— — France — Burgundy.

HUMBERT (ANNIE) Le chômage féminin en Bourgogne. Dijon, Echelon Régional de l'Emploi de Dijon, 1976. fo. 22.

— — — Lorraine.

DIDELOT (BERNADETTE) L'emploi féminin en Lorraine dans les activités à main-d'oeuvre masculine prépondérante. Nancy, Echelon Régional de l'Emploi de Nancy, 1976. fo. 77.

— — Germany.

URBAN (OTTO) Das Wahlrecht der weiblichen Angestellten in der Reichsversicherungsordnung, im Versicherungsgesetz für Angestellte und bei den Kaufmannsgerichten. Berlin, 1912. pp. 24. *(Zentralverband der Handlungsgehilfen und -Gehilfinnen Deutschlands. Schriften. 25)*

ZIETZ (LUISE) Zur Frage der Frauenerwerbsarbeit während des Krieges und nachher. Berlin, 1916. pp. 47. *(Sozialdemokratische Partei Deutschlands. Vorstand. Sozialdemokratische Frauen-Bibliothek. 9)*

— — India.

KAPUR (PROMILLA) The changing status of the working woman in India. Delhi, [1974]. pp. 178. *bibliog.*

— — Ivory Coast.

MONTGOMERY (BARBARA) The economic role of the Ivorian women. Ann Arbor, 1977. pp. 50. *bibliog. (Michigan University. Center for Research on Economic Development. Discussion Papers. No. 61)*

— — Poland.

ROGUSZKA-KLUPŚ (MARIA) Przemiany pozycji społecznej kobiety pracującej zawodowo: na przykładzie Wielkopolski. Poznań, 1975. pp. 194.

— — Russia — Russia (RSFSR).

KOTLIAR (ALEKSANDR EMIL'EVICH) and TURCHANINOVA (SVETLANA IAKOVLEVNA) Zaniatost' zhenshchin v proizvodstve: statistiko-sotsiologicheskii ocherk. Moskva, 1975. pp. 143.

— — Spain.

BALCELLS (ALBERT) Trabajo industrial y organizacion obrera en la Cataluña contemporanea, 1900-1936. Barcelona, 1974. pp. 324.

— — Switzerland.

KREBS (HANNA) Die Frau im Gewerbe. Zürich, [1928]. pp. 64. *(Schweizer Ausstellung für Frauenarbeit, Bern, 1928. Schriften zur Saffa)*

GSELL-TRUEMPI (FRIEDA) Die Frau in höhern Berufen: Ergebnisse einer Rundfrage. Glarus, 1937. pp. 75.

FURRER (MILLY) and WALTER (HEDY) Die wirtschaftliche Lage und die Unterstützungsleistungen von Bürolistinnen und Verkäuferinnen der Stadt Zürich: Ergebnisse einer Umfrage, etc. Zürich, 1939. pp. 32.

LAUBER (GISELA) Unfälle berufstätiger Frauen: sozialstatistische Untersuchung anhand von Akten der Schweizerischen Unfallversicherungsanstalt des Jahres 1969. Zürich, 1976. pp. 276. *bibliog. Dissertation der Universität Zürich zur Erlangung der Würde eines Doktors der Wirtschaftswissenschaft.*

— — Underdeveloped areas.

See UNDERDEVELOPED AREAS — Women's employment.

— — United Kingdom.

ENNIS (KATH) Women fight back. [London, 1973?]. pp. 31.

COUNTER INFORMATION SERVICES. Anti-Reports. No. 15. Women under attack. London, [1976]. pp. 33. *bibliog.*

COUSSINS (JEAN) The equality report: one year of the Equal Pay Act, the Sex Discrimination Act, the Equal Opportunities Commission. London, [1976]. pp. 123.

COUSSINS (JEAN) Maternity rights for working women. [London, 1976]. pp. 24.

GILL (TESS) Protective laws: evidence to the Equal Opportunities Commission. London, 1977. pp. 18. *(National Council for Civil Liberties. Reports. No. 17)*

MACKIE (LINDSAY) and PATTULLO (POLLY) Women at work. London, 1977. pp. 192. *bibliog.*

WHEELER-BENNETT (JOAN) Women at the top: achievement and family life;...in collaboration with Beatrice Musgrave and Zoë Hersov. London, 1977. pp. 157.

— — United States.

BINKIN (MARTIN) and BACH (SHIRLEY J.) Women and the military. Washington, D.C., [1977]. pp. 134. *(Brookings Institution. Studies in Defense Policy)*

HOWE (LOUISE KAPP) Pink collar workers: inside the world of women's work. New York, [1977]. pp. 301. *bibliog.*

— Health and hygiene.

WEAVER (JERRY L.) National health policy and the underserved: ethnic minorities, women, and the elderly. Saint Louis, 1976. pp. 161.

— History.

SELIVANOVA (NINA NIKOLAEVNA) Russia's women. New York, 1923; Westport, Conn., 1976. pp. 226. *Facsimile reprint.*

COMMUNIST PARTY OF GREAT BRITAIN. Women: oppression and liberation: part 1: the beginning. London, 1976. pp. 29.

GRIFFITHS (NAOMI E.S.) Penelope's web: some perceptions of women in European and Canadian society. Toronto, 1976. pp. 249. *bibliog.*

WILSON (ELIZABETH) Lecturer at the Polytechnic of North London. Women and the welfare state. London, 1977. pp. 208. *bibliog.*

— Legal status, laws, etc.

MILBURN (JOSEPHINE F.) Women as citizens: a comparative review. London, [1976]. pp. 45. *bibliog.*

— — South Africa.

HORRELL (MURIEL) The rights of African women: some suggested reforms. 2nd ed. Johannesburg, 1975. pp. 18.

— — United Kingdom.

LISTER (RUTH) As man and wife?: a study of the cohabitation rule. London, [1973]. pp. 56. *(Child Poverty Action Group. Poverty Research Series. 2)*

NATIONAL COUNCIL FOR CIVIL LIBERTIES.
Women's rights: the National Council for Civil Liberties:
comments on the government's proposals for an anti-
discrimination law. London, 1973. 1 pamphlet(unpaged).

COUSSINS (JEAN) The equality report: one year of the
Equal Pay Act, the Sex Discrimination Act, the Equal
Opportunities Commission. London, [1976]. pp. 123.

COUSSINS (JEAN) Maternity rights for working women.
[London, 1976]. pp. 24.

— Psychology.

FOREMAN (ANN) Femininity as alienation: women and
the family in marxism and psychoanalysis. London, 1977.
pp. 168. bibliog.

— Social conditions.

RYAN (EDNA) and CONLON (ANNE) Gentle invaders:
Australian women at work, 1788-1974. West Melbourne,
1975. pp. 196.

CONFERENCE OF SOCIALIST ECONOMISTS. Political
Economy of Women Group. On the political economy of
women: stage 1. London, [1976]. pp. 37. (Conference of
Socialist Economists. Pamphlets. No.2)

— Statistics.

HANDBOOK of international data on women; [by] Elise
Boulding [and others]. New York, [1976]. pp. 468. bibliog.

— Study and teaching.

HARTNETT (OONAGH) and RENDEL (MARGHERITA
NANCY) Women's studies in the UK;...edited by Zoe
Fairbairns. London, 1975. pp. 30.

— Suffrage.

WOMEN in rebellion, 1900: two views on class, socialism
and liberation: Working women and the suffrage, by Mrs.
Wibaut: Woman's freedom, by Lily Gair Wilkinson. Leeds,
[1973]. pp. 28. (Independent Labour Party. Square One
Pamphlets. 6)

GOOT (MURRAY) and REID (ELIZABETH) Women and
voting studies: mindless matrons or sexist scientism?.
London, [1975]. pp. 44. bibliog.

— — Spain.

CAPEL MARTINEZ (ROSA MARIA) El sufragio
femenino en la 2a. Republica española. Granada, 1975. pp.
328. bibliog.

— — Switzerland.

SCHWEIZERISCHER KATHOLISCHER
FRAUENBUND. Studientagung, Luzern, 1945.
Referate...über Fragen des politischen Frauenstimm- und
Wahlrechtes...am 12. und 13. Oktober 1945 in Luzern.
[Luzern, 1945?]. pp. 80. bibliogs.

— — United Kingdom — Ireland.

OWENS (ROSEMARY) Votes for women: Irish women's
struggle for the vote. Dublin, [1975]. pp. 27. Prepared for
an exhibition on the Irish Women's Suffrage Movement.

— Austria.

RIGLER (EDITH) Frauenleitbild und Frauenarbeit in
Österreich vom ausgehenden 19. Jahrhundert bis zum
Zweiten Weltkrieg, etc. München, 1976. pp. 186. bibliog.
(Vienna. Universität. Institut für Wirtschafts- und
Sozialgeschichte. Sozial- und Wirtschaftshistorische
Studien. Band 8)

— Canada.

GRIFFITHS (NAOMI E.S.) Penelope's web: some
perceptions of women in European and Canadian society.
Toronto, 1976. pp. 249. bibliog.

KOHL (SEENA B.) Working together: women and family
in southwestern Saskatchewan. Toronto, [1976]. pp. 139.
bibliog.

— China.

BROYELLE (CLAUDIE) Women's liberation in
China;...translated from the French by Michèle Cohen and
Gary Herman. Hassocks, 1977. pp. 174.

— Europe.

GRIFFITHS (NAOMI E.S.) Penelope's web: some
perceptions of women in European and Canadian society.
Toronto, 1976. pp. 249. bibliog.

— France.

SERVIN (MARCEL) Le Parti Communiste et la lutte des
femmes de France pour la paix, l'indépendance nationale et
le progrès social: rapport aux journées nationales des 2 et 3
février 1957 à Montreuil. Paris, 1957. pp. 31.

VINCENT (MADELEINE) Femmes: quelle libération?
Paris, [1976]. pp. 167.

MACLEAN (IAN) 1945- . Woman triumphant: feminism in
French literature, 1610-1652. Oxford, 1977. pp. 314.
bibliog.

— Mozambique.

LIBERATION SUPPORT MOVEMENT. The
Mozambican woman in the revolution. Richmond, B.C.,
[1973?]. pp. 27.

— Poland.

ROGUSZKA-KLUPŚ (MARIA) Przemiany pozycji
społecznej kobiety pracującej zawodowo: na przykładzie
Wielkopolski. Poznań, 1975. pp. 194.

— Russia.

SELIVANOVA (NINA NIKOLAEVNA) Russia's women.
New York, 1923; Westport, Conn., 1976. pp. 226.
Facsimile reprint.

RUSSIA (USSR). Tsentral'noe Statisticheskoe Upravlenie.
1975. Zhenshchiny v SSSR: statisticheskii sbornik.
Moskva, 1975. pp. 135.

— — Latvia — Statistics.

LATVIA. Tsentral'noe Statisticheskoe Upravlenie. 1975.
Zhenshchiny v Latviiskoi SSR: statisticheskii sbornik.
Riga, 1975. pp. 110.

— Serbia.

COPELAND (FANNY S.) The women of Serbia: a
lecture, etc. [London, 1917?]. pp. 16.

— South Africa.

HORRELL (MURIEL) The rights of African women: some
suggested reforms. 2nd ed. Johannesburg, 1975. pp. 18.

— Spain.

ITURBE (LOLA) Mujer en la lucha social y en la guerra
civil de España. Mexico, 1974. pp. 221. bibliog.

BELTRAN (NURIA) Muerte civil de la española?
Barcelona, [1975]. pp. 190.

— Switzerland.

GSELL-TRUEMPI (FRIEDA) Die Frau in höhern
Berufen: Ergebnisse einer Rundfrage. Glarus, 1937. pp. 75.

— Uganda.

UGANDA. Commission on Marriage, Divorce and the
Status of Women. 1965. Report; [W.W. Kalema,
chairman]. Entebbe, 1965. pp. 133.

— United Kingdom.

FAULDER (CAROLYN) and others. The women's
directory. London, 1976. pp. 240. bibliog.

Les FEMMES dans la société britannique; sous la direction
de Monica Charlot. Paris, [1977]. pp. 253. bibliog.

WILSON (ELIZABETH) Lecturer at the Polytechnic of
North London. Women and the welfare state. London,
1977. pp. 208. bibliog.

WOMEN in the community; edited by Marjorie Mayo.
London, 1977. pp. 141. bibliogs.

— United States.

AMUNDSEN (KIRSTEN) A new look at the silenced
majority: women and American democracy. new ed.
Englewood Cliffs, N.J., [1977]. pp. 172. 1971 edition
published under the title The silenced majority.

CHAFE (WILLIAM HENRY) Women and equality:
changing patterns in American culture. New York, 1977.
pp. 207.

WOMEN, NEGRO.

REID (WILLIE MAE) Black women's struggle for
equality. New York, 1976. pp. 15.

WOMEN AND SOCIALISM.

SAUMONEAU (LOUISE) Les femmes socialistes contre
la guerre. [Paris, 192-]. 3 pts. (Femme Socialiste, La.
Publications)

SAUMONEAU (LOUISE) Luttes et souffrances de la
femme. 1. La femme dans son intérieur. [Paris, 192-]. pp.
15. (Femme Socialiste, La. Publications)

SAUMONEAU (LOUISE) Principes et action féministes
socialistes. [Paris, 192-?]. pp. 16. (Femme Socialiste, La.
Publications)

SCOTT (HILDA) Women and socialism: experiences from
Eastern Europe. [2nd ed.] London, 1976. pp. 240.
Originally published in 1974 under the title Does socialism
liberate women?

FOREMAN (ANN) Femininity as alienation: women and
the family in marxism and psychoanalysis. London, 1977.
pp. 168. bibliog.

KNIGHT (AMY WINDLE) The participation of women in
the revolutionary movement in Russia from 1890 to 1914.
1977. fo. 321. bibliog. Typescript. Ph.D. (London) thesis:
unpublished. This thesis is the property of London
University and may not be removed from the Library.

WOMEN in the labour movement: the British experience;
edited by Lucy Middleton. London, 1977. pp. 221. bibliog.

WOMEN IN BUSINESS.

KANTER (ROSABETH MOSS) Men and women of the
corporation. New York, [1977]. pp. 348. bibliog.

WOMEN IN CHRISTIANITY.

STUDENT CHRISTIAN MOVEMENT. Theology and
sexual politics. Bristol, [1976]. pp. 24.

WOMEN IN COMMUNITY
DEVELOPMENT.

WOMEN in the community; edited by Marjorie Mayo.
London, 1977. pp. 141. bibliogs.

— Africa, Subsaharan.

MICKELWAIT (DONALD R.) and others. Women in rural
development: a survey of the roles of women in Ghana,
Lesotho, Kenya, Nigeria, Bolivia, Paraguay and Peru.
Boulder, Col., 1976. pp. 224. bibliog.

— America, Latin.

MICKELWAIT (DONALD R.) and others. Women in rural
development: a survey of the roles of women in Ghana,
Lesotho, Kenya, Nigeria, Bolivia, Paraguay and Peru.
Boulder, Col., 1976. pp. 224. bibliog.

WOMEN IN LITERATURE.

MACLEAN (IAN) 1945- . Woman triumphant: feminism in
French literature, 1610-1652. Oxford, 1977. pp. 314.
bibliog.

OFFE (CLAUS) Industry and inequality: the achievement principle in work and social status;...translated by James Wickham. London, 1976. pp. 158. *bibliog.*

ANTHONY (P.D.) The ideology of work. London, 1977. pp. 340. *bibliog.*

WORK DESIGN.

BOLWEG (JOEP F.) Job design and industrial democracy: the case of Norway. Leiden, 1976. pp. 139. *bibliog.*

SUSMAN (GERALD I.) Autonomy at work: a sociotechnical analysis of participative management. New York, 1976. pp. 230. *bibliog.*

WORK MEASUREMENT.

HILF (HUBERT HUGO) Arbeitswissenschaft: Grundlagen der Leistungsforschung und Arbeitsgestaltung. München, 1957. pp. 341. *bibliog.*

DAELEMANS (J.) Arbeidsorganisatie in de landbouw. Merelbeke, Rijksstation voor Landbouwtechniek, 1972. pp. 315. *bibliogs. Chart in end pocket.*

KARSTENS (DIRK) Die gesetzlichen Grundlagen und die arbeitswissenschaftlichen Aspekte für die Mitwirkung und Mitbestimmung an Massnahmen des Arbeitsstudiums im Industriebetrieb auf Grund des BetrVG 1972. Hamburg, 1976. pp. 223. *bibliog.*

WORKERS' SELF-MANAGEMENT.

See WORKS COUNCILS.

WORKING CAPITAL.

FIRTH (MICHAEL A.) Management of working capital. London, 1976. pp. 148.

WORKMEN'S COMPENSATION

— Canada — Ontario.

INTERNATIONAL SEMINAR ON REHABILITATION PROGRAMS IN WORKMEN'S COMPENSATION AND RELATED FIELDS, TORONTO, 1969. Selected papers. [Toronto, Workmen's Compensation Board of Ontario, 1969] . pp. 38. *(Rehabilitation in Canada. Supplements. No.2)*

— Israel.

ISRAEL. National Insurance Institute. Bureau of Research and Planning. 1976. Beneficiaries of workmen's compensation benefits in the years 1970-1972; by Yosi Mutsafi and Rivka Prior. Jerusalem, 1976. pp. 401. *(Surveys. No.19) In English and Hebrew.*

WORKS COUNCILS

— Algeria.

BRACHEMI (KACIM) Planning in public enterprises in developing countries; (translated by Meri Radosević). Ljubljana, International Center for Public Enterprises, 1974. fo. 19. *(International Seminar 1974. National Papers)*

— European Economic Community countries.

CARBY-HALL (JOSEPH ROGER) Worker participation in Europe. London, 1977. pp. 271.

— Germany.

WARNKE (HERBERT) Das Betriebsrätegesetz und seine Anwendung; herausgegeben vom Bundesvorstand des FDGB. Berlin, 1947. pp. 40.

— Italy.

FORBICE (ALDO) and CHIABERGE (RICCARDO) Il sindacato dei consigli. Verona, [1975]. pp. 230.

— Yugoslavia.

ROZMAN (RUDI) and FRANC (VIKTOR) Planning in economic organisations in Yugoslavia; (translated by Meri Radosević). Ljubljana, International Center for Public Enterprises, 1974. fo. (28). *(International Seminar 1974. National Papers)*

RADONJIĆ (RADOVAN) Sukob KPJ sa Kominformom i društveni razvoj Jugoslavije, 1948-1950. 2nd ed. Zagreb, 1976. pp. 276. *bibliog. (Zagreb. Narodno Sveučilište. Centar za Aktualni Politički Studij. Političke Teme: Biblioteka Suvremene Političke Misli)*

WORLD HEALTH ORGANIZATION

— Finance.

HOOLE (FRANCIS W.) Politics and budgeting in the World Health Organization. Bloomington, Ind., 1976. pp. 226. *bibliog. (Indiana University. International Development Research Center. Studies in Development. No. 11)*

WORLD POLITICS.

DUERRENMATT (PETER) Zerfall und Wiederaufbau der Politik. Bern, [1951]. pp. 240.

SCHUETZ (WILHELM WOLFGANG) Wir wollen überleben: Aussenpolitik im Atomzeitalter. Stuttgart, [1956]. pp. 216.

DUERRENMATT (PETER) Die Welt zwischen Krieg und Frieden. Bern, [1959]. pp. 246.

ENDRUCKS (BERNHARD) Das Ende aller Kriege: ein Appell an die Menschheit. Krailling bei München, [1959]. pp. 152.

ALDERSON (ALBERT WILLIAM) The only way to everlasting peace. London, 1960. pp. 305.

KHRUSHCHEV (NIKITA SERGEEVICH) Comment la conférence au sommet a été torpillée. Paris, [imprint], 1960. pp. 27. *"Texte intégral de la conférence de presse de N. Khrouchtchev". (p.7)*

REISBERG (ARNOLD) Lenins Idee der Koexistenz wird triumphieren. Berlin, 1960. pp. 48.

KAJIMA INSTITUTE OF INTERNATIONAL PEACE. The record of the first Kajima Peace Award, recipient: Count Coudenhove Kalergi. Tokyo, 1968. pp. 143.

BLOCK (HERBERT) Economist. Political arithmetic of the world economies. Beverly Hills, [1974]. pp. 90. *bibliog. (Georgetown University. Center for Strategic and International Studies. Washington Papers. vol. 2/15)*

DECLASSIFIED DOCUMENTS REFERENCE SYSTEM, THE, [retrospective and annual collections]. q., [Retrospective collection and annual collection from] 1975 (1st)- Washington.

DOUGHERTY (JAMES E.) British perspectives on a changing global balance. Beverly Hills, [1975]. pp. 108.

ZHUKOV (GENNADII PETROVICH) and CHERNICHENKO (STANISLAV VALENTINOVICH) Sovetskaia Programma mira i mezhdunarodnoe pravo. Moskva, 1975. pp. 111.

ABIR (MORDECHAI) Persian Gulf oil in Middle East and international conflicts. Jerusalem, 1976. pp. 35. *(Hebrew University. Leonard Davis Institute for International Relations. Jerusalem Papers on Peace Problems. 20)*

AKADEMIIA OBSHCHESTVENNYKH NAUK. Kafedra Teorii i Metodov Ideologicheskoi Raboty. Voprosy Teorii i Metodov Ideologicheskoi Raboty. vyp.5. Mirnoe sosushchestvovanie gosudarstv s razlichnym sotsial'nym stroem i sovremennaia ideologicheskaia bor'ba. Moskva, 1976. pp. 309.

BOWN (COLIN) and MOONEY (PETER J.) Cold war to détente. London, 1976. pp. 198. *bibliog.*

CASSIERS (JUAN) The hazards of peace: a European view of detente. Cambridge, Mass., [1976]. pp. 85. *(Harvard University. Center for International Affairs. Harvard Studies in International Affairs. No. 34)*

ETHNICITY in an international context; edited by Abdul Said and Luiz R. Simmons. New Brunswick, N.J., [1976]. pp. 241. *bibliog.*

GRAEBNER (NORMAN ARTHUR) ed. The cold war: a conflict of ideology and power. 2nd ed. Lexington, Mass., [1976]. pp. 206. *bibliog.*

LARIN (V.) Mezhdunarodnye otnosheniia i ideologicheskaia bor'ba, 60-70-e gody. Moskva, 1976. pp. 247. *bibliog.*

LUTTWAK (EDWARD) Strategic power: military capabilities and political utility. Beverly Hills, [1976]. pp. 70. *bibliog. (Georgetown University. Center for Strategic and International Studies. Washington Papers. vol. 4/38)*

MEZHDUNARODNAIA politika KPSS i vneshnie funktsii Sovetskogo gosudarstva. Moskva, 1976. pp. 160.

MITIN (MARK BORISOVICH) Problemy sovremennoi ideologicheskoi bor'by: kritika sotsiologicheskikh i sotsial'no-politicheskikh kontseptsii. Moskva, 1976. pp. 319.

PRUUDEN (SALME) Panslavism and Russian communism. London, 1976. pp. 59.

REYNOLDS (PHILIP ALAN) and HUGHES (EMMET JOHN) The historian as diplomat: Charles Kingsley Webster and the United Nations, 1939-1946. London, 1976. pp. 198.

SAKHAROV (ANDREI DMITRIEVICH) O strane i mire: sbornik proizvedenii. N'iu-Iork, 1976. pp. xxiv,183.

TARNOFF (CURTIS LEE) Evolving structures of great power blocs: the U.S.A. and Latin America, 1901-1975: the USSR and Eastern Europe, 1945-1975. 1976. fo. 529. *bibliog. Typescript. Ph.D. (London) thesis: unpublished. This thesis is the property of London University and may not be removed from the Library.*

TUZMUKHAMEDOV (RAIS ABDULKHAKOVICH) Neprisoedinenie i razriadka mezhdunarodnoi napriazhennosti. Moskva, 1976. pp. 120.

WILLIAMS (PHIL) Crisis management: confrontation and diplomacy in the nuclear age. London, 1976. pp. 230.

ADAMTHWAITE (ANTHONY P.) The making of the Second World War. London, 1977. pp. 235. *bibliog. With a selection of documents.*

BARZEL (RAINER) Es ist noch nicht zu spät. München, 1977. pp. 191.

BASIUK (VICTOR) Technology, world politics, and American policy. New York, 1977. pp. 409. *bibliog.*

BERKOWITZ (MORTON) and others. The politics of American foreign policy: the social context of decisions. Englewood Cliffs, N.J., [1977]. pp. 310. *bibliogs.*

BEYOND nuclear deterrence: new aims, new arms; edited by Johan J. Holst [and] Uwe Nerlich. New York, [1977]. pp. 314. *bibliog.*

BULL (HEDLEY) The anarchical society: a study of order in world politics. London, 1977. pp. 335.

FRIEDLICHE Koexistenz in Europa: Entwicklungstendenzen der Auseinandersetzung zwischen Sozialismus und Imperialismus; (Gesamtredaktion: Peter Klein, Stefan Doernberg). Berlin, 1977. pp. 330.

GRAEBNER (NORMAN ARTHUR) Cold war diplomacy: American foreign policy, 1945-1975. New York, [1977]. pp. 248. *bibliog.*

KLINGHOFFER (ARTHUR JAY) The Soviet Union and international oil politics. New York, 1977. pp. 389. *bibliog.*

LEWIS (W. RUSSELL) The survival of the capitalist system: challenge to the pluralist societies of the West; report of a study group of the Institute for the Study of Conflict. London, 1977. pp. 56. *(Institute for the Study of Conflict. Special Reports)*

ROCK (WILLIAM R.) British appeasement in the 1930s. London, 1977. pp. 111. *bibliog.*

ROFFMAN (HOWARD) Understanding the cold war: a study of the cold war in the interwar period. Cranbury, N.J., [1977]. pp. 198. *bibliog.*

YERGIN (DANIEL) Shattered peace: the origins of the cold war and the national security state. Boston, Mass., 1977. pp. 526. *bibliog.*

— Congresses.

ATLANTIC CONGRESS, LONDON, 1959. Report. London, [1959]. pp. 95.

WORLD WAR, 1939-1945.

SAMSONOV (ALEKSANDR MIKHAILOVICH) Krakh fashistskoi agressii, 1939-1945: istoricheskii ocherk. Moskva, 1975. pp. 647.

LUKACS (JOHN ADALBERT) The last European war: September 1939/December 1941. London, 1976 [or rather 1977]. pp. 562. *bibliog.*

— Aerial operations, British.

FRIDENSON (PATRICK) and LECUIR (JEAN) La France et la Grande-Bretagne face aux problèmes aériens, 1935-mai 1940. Vincennes, Service Historique de l'Armée de l'Air, 1976. pp. 208.

— Aerial operations, French.

FRIDENSON (PATRICK) and LECUIR (JEAN) La France et la Grande-Bretagne face aux problèmes aériens, 1935-mai 1940. Vincennes, Service Historique de l'Armée de l'Air, 1976. pp. 208.

— Atrocities.

CZECHOSLOVAKIA. Odbor pro Politické Zpravodajství. Dokumenty Doby: Sbírka Publikací o Utrpení Českého a Slovenského Národa v Boji za Svobodu. řada 1, svazek 2. Persekuce českého studentstva za okupace, etc. Praha, 1946. pp. 157,(19).

— Bibliography.

ENSER (A.G.S.) A subject bibliography of the Second World War: books in English, 1939-1974. London, 1977. pp. 592.

— Campaigns.

BALDWIN (HANSON WEIGHTMAN) The crucial years, 1939-1941: the world at war. London, 1976. pp. 499.

— — Eastern.

GOSZTONY (PÉTER) Hitlers fremde Heere: das Schicksal der nichtdeutschen Armeen im Ostfeldzug. Düsseldorf, 1976. pp. 545. *bibliog.*

— — Pacific.

BORISOV (OLEG BORISOVICH) Sovetskii Soiuz i Man'chzhurskaia revoliutsionnaia baza, 1945-1949: k 30-letiiu razgroma militaristskoi Iaponii. Moskva, 1975. pp. 220.

OSVOBOZHDENIE Korei: vospominaniia i stat'i. Moskva, 1976. pp. 336.

— — Russia.

ZHUKOV (GEORGII KONSTANTINOVICH) Vospominaniia i razmyshleniia. 2nd ed. Moskva, 1974. 2 vols.

GRECHKO (ANDREI ANTONOVICH) Gody voiny, 1941-1943. Moskva, 1976. pp. 573.

POGRANICHNYE voiska SSSR v Velikoi Otechestvennoi voine, 1941: sbornik dokumentov i materialov. Moskva, 1976. pp. 944.

— Causes.

HERWIG (HOLGER H.) Politics of frustration: the United States in German naval planning, 1889-1941. Boston, Mass., [1976]. pp. 323. *bibliog.*

SUTTON (ANTONY C.) Wall Street and the rise of Hitler. Seal Beach, Calif., [1976]. pp. 220. *bibliog.*

ADAMTHWAITE (ANTHONY P.) The making of the Second World War. London, 1977. pp. 235. *bibliog. With a selection of documents.*

EMMERSON (JAMES THOMAS) The Rhineland crisis, 7 March 1936: a study in multilateral diplomacy. London, 1977. pp. 383. *bibliog.*

ROCK (WILLIAM R.) British appeasement in the 1930s. London, 1977. pp. 111. *bibliog.*

— Diplomatic history.

ADAMIC (LOUIS) Dinner at the White House. New York, [1946]. pp. 276.

DARILEK (RICHARD E.) A loyal opposition in time of war: the Republican Party and the politics of foreign policy from Pearl Harbour to Yalta. Westport, Conn., 1976. pp. 239. *bibliog.*

LASH (JOSEPH P.) Roosevelt and Churchill, 1939-1941: the partnership that saved the West. New York, [1976]. pp. 528.

REYNOLDS (PHILIP ALAN) and HUGHES (EMMET JOHN) The historian as diplomat: Charles Kingsley Webster and the United Nations, 1939-1946. London, 1976. pp. 198.

DWYER (T. RYLE) Irish neutrality and the USA 1939-47. Dublin, 1977. pp. 241.

STOLER (MARK A.) The politics of the second front: American military planning and diplomacy in coalition warfare, 1941-1943. Westport, Conn., 1977. pp. 244. *bibliogs.*

— Economic aspects.

KRIEGSWIRTSCHAFT und Rüstung, 1939-1945;...herausgegeben von Friedrich Forstmeier [and] Hans-Erich Volkmann. Düsseldorf, [1977]. pp. 420.

MILWARD (ALAN S.) War, economy and society, 1939-1945. Berkeley, Calif., [1977]. pp. 395. *bibliog.*

— — Germany.

KONZEPT für die "Neuordnung" der Welt: die Kriegsziele des faschistischen deutschen Imperialismus im zweiten Weltkrieg; von einem Autorenkollektiv unter Leitung von Wolfgang Schumann. Berlin, 1977. pp. 141.

— — Russia — Russia (RSFSR).

ROMANOV (LEONID MIKHAILOVICH) Murmanskaia oblastnaia partiinaia organizatsiia v period perestroiki narodnogo khoziaistva v 1941-1942 gg. Murmansk, 1973. pp. 46.

— — United Kingdom.

U.K. [Cabinet Office]. History of the Second World War: United Kingdom Civil Series. Coal; by W.H.B. Court. rev. ed. London, 1976. pp. 426,27. *Confidential version with full sources references.*

— Education and the war.

CZECHOSLOVAKIA. Odbor pro Politické Zpravodajství. Dokumenty Doby: Sbírka Publikací o Utrpení Českého a Slovenského Národa v Boji za Svobodu. řada 1, svazek 2. Persekuce českého studentstva za okupace, etc. Praha, 1946. pp. 157,(19).

GOSDEN (PETER HENRY JOHN HEATHER) Education in the Second World War: a study in policy and administration. London, 1976. pp. 527. *bibliog.*

— Historiography.

RZHESHEVSKII (OLEG ALEKSANDROVICH) Voina i istoriia: burzhuaznaia istoriografiia SShA o vtoroi mirovoi voine. Moskva, 1976. pp. 292.

— Peace.

TROUGHTON (ERNEST R.) It's happening again. London, 1944. pp. 111. *bibliog.*

— Personal narratives, British.

COLVILLE (Sir JOHN) Footprints in time. London, 1976. pp. 287.

— Personal narratives, Polish.

BENISZ (ADAM) W burzy 'zycia; do druku przygotował Mieczysław Wrzosek. Opole, 1976. pp. 200.

— Personal narratives, Russian.

ZHUKOV (GEORGII KONSTANTINOVICH) Vospominaniia i razmyshleniia. 2nd ed. Moskva, 1974. 2 vols.

OSVOBOZHDENIE Korei: vospominaniia i stat'i. Moskva, 1976. pp. 336.

— Personal narratives, Spanish.

MONTAGUT (LLUIS) J'étais deuxième classe dans l'armée républicaine espagnole, 1936-1945. Paris, 1976. pp. 385.

— Prisoners and prisons, British.

FAULK (HENRY) Group captives: the re-education of German prisoners of war in Britain, 1945-1948. London, 1977. pp. 233.

— Prisoners and prisons, South West African.

ERINNERUNGEN an die Internierungszeit, 1939-1946, und zeitgeschichtliche Ergänzungen: Berichte, Erzählungen, Fotos und Zeichnungen...; bearbeitet und herausgegeben von Rudolf Kock. 2nd ed. Windhoek, 1975. pp. 221.

— Propaganda.

CAPRIOLI (MAURA PICCIALUTI) ed. Radio Londra, 1940-1945: inventario delle trasmissioni per l'Italia. Roma, 1976. 2 vols. *(Italy. Direzione Generale degli Archivi di Stato. Pubblicazioni degli Archivi di Stato. 89, 90)*

RHODES (ANTHONY RICHARD EWART) Propaganda: the art of persuasion: World War II;...edited by Victor Margolin. New York, [1976]. pp. 319. *bibliog.*

— Public opinion — Switzerland.

MEURANT (JACQUES) La presse et l'opinion de la Suisse romande face à l'Europe en guerre, 1939-1941. Neuchâtel, [1976]. pp. 765. *bibliog.*

— Reparations.

TROUGHTON (ERNEST R.) It's happening again. London, 1944. pp. 111. *bibliog.*

— Sources.

MOLDAVSKAIA SSR v Velikoi Otechestvennoi voine Sovetskogo Soiuza, 1941-1945: sbornik dokumentov i materialov v dvukh tomakh. Kishinev, 1975-76. 2 vols.

BURIATIIA v gody Velikoi Otechestvennoi voiny, 1941-1945 gg.: sbornik dokumentov. Ulan-Ude, 1975. pp. 452.

GOR'KOVSKAIA partiinaia organizatsiia v gody Velikoi Otechestvennoi voiny, 1941-1945: sbornik dokumentov i materialov. Gor'kii, 1975. pp. 359.

KHERSONSKAIA oblast' v gody Velikoi Otechestvennoi voiny, 1941-1945: sbornik dokumentov i materialov. Simferopol', 1975. pp. 320. *bibliog.*

KURGANSKAIA partiinaia organizatsiia v Velikoi Otechestvennoi voine, 1941-1945: dokumenty i materialy. Cheliabinsk, 1975. pp. 355.

POGRANICHNYE voiska SSSR v Velikoi Otechestvennoi voine, 1941: sbornik dokumentov i materialov. Moskva, 1976. pp. 944.

U.K. War Cabinet. 1939-45. Cabinet Office list of War Cabinet memoranda, CAB 66, W.P. and C.P. series, 1939 Sept. - 1945 July. London, 1977. pp. 211. *(List and Index Society. [Publications]. Vol. 136)*

— Supplies.

KARNER (STEFAN) Kärntens Wirtschaft, 1938-1945, unter besonderer Berücksichtigung der Rüstungsindustrie. Klagenfurt, 1976. pp. 384. *bibliog. (Klagenfurt. Magistrat. Wissenschaftliche Veröffentlichungen der Landeshauptstadt Klagenfurt. Band 2)*

KRIEGSWIRTSCHAFT und Rüstung,
1939-1945;...herausgegeben von Friedrich Forstmeier [and]
Hans-Erich Volkmann. Düsseldorf, [1977]. pp. 420.

— Transportation.

KUMANEV (GEORGII ALEKSANDROVICH) Na
sluzhbe fronta i tyla: zheleznodorozhnyi transport SSSR
nakanune i v gody Velikoi Otechestvennoi voiny,
1938-1945. Moskva, 1976. pp. 455.

— Underground movements.

FOOT (MICHAEL RICHARD DAMELL) Resistance: an
analysis of European resistance to Nazism, 1940-1945.
London, 1976. pp. 346. *bibliog.*

— — Austria.

TIDL (MARIE) Die Roten Studenten: Dokumente und
Erinnerungen, 1938-1945. Wien, 1976. pp. 300. *bibliog.*
*(Ludwig-Boltzmann-Institut fur Geschichte der
Arbeiterbewegung. Materialien zur Arbeiterbewegung. Nr. 3)*

VOGL (FRIEDRICH) Widerstand im Waffenrock:
österreichische Freiheitskämpfer in der Deutschen
Wehrmacht, 1938-1945. Wien, 1977. pp. 258. *bibliog.*
*(Ludwig Boltzmann Institut für Geschichte der
Arbeiterbewegung. Materialien zur Arbeiterbewegung. Nr. 7)*

— — Corsica.

ROCHET (WALDECK) and COSSONEAU (EMILE)
L'épopée de la Corse: comment les patriotes du maquis ont
libéré l'Ile de Beauté. London, [1943]. pp. 16.

— — Czechoslovakia.

FUČÍK (JULIUS) Reportage, unter dem Strang
geschrieben; (aus dem Tschechischen übersetzt von Franz
Peter Künzel). Frankfurt am Main, [1976]. pp. 126.

STROEBINGER (RUDOLF) Das Attentat von Prag.
Landshut, 1976. pp. 270. *bibliog.*

— — Denmark.

THOMAS (JOHN ORAM) The giant-killers: the story of
the Danish Resistance Movement, 1940-1945. London,
1976. pp. 347. *First published in 1975.*

CHRISTENSEN (POUL) Af en illegals erindringer;
udgivet i samarbejde med Hans Kirchhoff. [Copenhagen],
1976. pp. 152. *(Selskabet til Forskning i
Arbejderbevaegelsens Historie. Publikationer. 4)*

GRUNDT LARSEN (JØRGEN) Modstandsbevaegelsens
Kontaktudvalg i Stockholm, 1944-45. Odense, 1976. pp.
181. *bibliog. (Odense Universitet. Studies in History and
Social Sciences. vol. 31)*

— — France.

MALRAUX (CLARA) La fin et le commencement. Paris,
[1976]. pp. 230. *(Le bruit de nos pas. 5)*

SWEETS (JOHN F.) The politics of resistance in France,
1940-1944: a history of the Mouvements Unis de la
Résistance. DeKalb, Ill., [1976]. pp. 260. *bibliog.*

— — Italy.

FRANCESCOTTI (RENZO) Antifascismo e Resistenza nel
Trentino, 1920-1945. Roma, 1975. pp. 126. *bibliog.*

RUZZENENTI (MARINO) Il movimento operaio
bresciano nella Resistenza. Roma, 1975. pp. 227.

VERONESI (UGO) Riflessioni sulla dittatura. 3rd ed.
[Mantua, 1975]. pp. 85. *(Partito Liberale Italiano. Atti e
Documenti. 9)*

CORVISIERI (SILVERIO) Resistenza e democrazia.
Milano, [1976]. pp. 170.

DINELLI (UMBERTO) La guerra partigiana nel Veneto.
Venezia, 1976. pp. 229. *bibliog.*

QUAZZA (GUIDO) Resistenza e storia d'Italia: problemi e
ipotesi di ricerca. Milano, 1976. pp. 468.

RISALITI (RENATO) Antifascismo e resistenza nel
Pistoiese. Pistoia, [1976]. pp. 270.

— — Poland.

NEUHAUS (BARBARA) Funksignale vom
Wartabogen:...über den gemeinsamen Kampf deutscher
Kommunisten, sowjetischer und polnischer Partisanen.
Berlin, [1975 repr. 1977]. pp. 604.

STACHIEWICZ (PIOTR) Akcja "Koppe". Warszawa, 1975.
pp. 204.

— — South Africa.

VISSER (GEORGE CLOETE) OB: traitors or patriots?.
Johannesburg, 1976. pp. 216.

— — Yugoslavia.

LAZITCH (BRANKO) Titov pokret i režim u Jugoslaviji,
1941-1946. [n.p.], 1946. pp. 219.

— Atlantic Ocean.

MIDDLEBROOK (MARTIN) Convoy: the battle for
Convoys SC.122 and HX.229. London, 1976. pp. 378.
bibliog.

— Balkan States.

Les GRANDES puissances et les Balkans a la veille et au
début de la Deuxieme Guerre mondiale, 1937-1941;
conférence internationale, Sofia, 21-16 avril, 1971;
(rédaction, Nikolaj Todorov, Christina Mihova). Sofia,
1973. pp. 430. *(Bulgarska Akademiia na Naukite. Institut
za Balkanistika. Studia Balcanica. 7) In various languages.*

— France.

FOULON (CHARLES LOUIS) Le pouvoir en province à
la Libération: les commissaries de la République, 1943-1946.
[Paris, 1975]. pp. 301. *(Fondation Nationale des Sciences
Politiques. Travaux et Recherches de Science Politique. 32)*

AMOUROUX (HENRI) La grande histoire des Français
sous l'occupation. Paris, [1976 in progress]. *bibliog.*

— Germany.

KONZEPT für die "Neuordnung" der Welt: die Kriegsziele
des faschistischen deutschen Imperialismus im zweiten
Weltkrieg; von einem Autorenkollektiv unter Leitung von
Wolfgang Schumann. Berlin, 1977. pp. 141.

— India.

COMBINED INTER-SERVICES HISTORICAL
SECTION, INDIA AND PAKISTAN. Official history of
the Indian armed forces in the second World War, 1939-45.
Defence of India: policy and plans; (by Bisheshwar
Prasad). [New Delhi], 1963. pp. 278.

— Italy.

CAPRIOLI (MAURA PICCIALUTI) ed. Radio Londra,
1940-1945: inventario delle trasmissioni per l'Italia. Roma,
1976. 2 vols. *(Italy. Direzione Generale degli Archivi di
Stato. Pubblicazioni degli Archivi di Stato. 89, 90)*

— Luxembourg.

KOCH-KENT (HENRI) and others. Hitlertum in
Luxemburg, 1933-1944: Beiträge zur Zeitgeschichte.
[Luxembourg, 1972]. pp. 47. *3 papers presented at the
congress of the Association des Enrôlés de Force, Victimes
du Nazisme, held in Walferdingen in 1972.*

— Poland.

UMBREIT (HANS) Deutsche Militärverwaltungen,
1938/39: die militärische Besetzung der Tschechoslowakei
und Polens. Stuttgart, 1977. pp. 296. *bibliog.
(Militärgeschichtliches Forschungsamt. Beiträge zur Militär-
und Kriegsgeschichte. Band 18)*

— Romania.

LEBEDEV (NIKOLAI IVANOVICH) Krakh fashizma v
Rumynii. Moskva, 1976. pp. 632. *bibliog.*

— Russia.

POTTS (J.H.) Through the Soviet Union in war-time: the
impressions of a British trade union leader during a three
months' war-time tour of the U.S.S.R. [London, 1942?].
pp. 15.

NAUCHNAIA KONFERENTSIIA,
POSVIASHCHENNAIA 30-LETIIU POBEDY
SOVETSKOGO NARODA V VELIKOI
OTECHESTVENNOI VOINE 1941-1945 GODOV.
Velikaia pobeda sovetskogo naroda , 1941-1945: materialy
nauchnoi konferentsii, posviashchennoi 30-letiiu pobedy
sovetskogo naroda v Velikoi Otechestvennoi voine
1941-1945 godov. Moskva, 1976. pp. 648.

SSSR v bor'be protiv fashistskoi agressii, 1933-1945.
Moskva, 1976. pp. 327.

— — Buryat Republic.

BURIATIIA v gody Velikoi Otechestvennoi voiny,
1941-1945 gg.: sbornik dokumentov. Ulan-Ude, 1975. pp.
452.

— — Moldavian Republic.

MOLDAVSKAIA SSR v Velikoi Otechestvennoi voine
Sovetskogo Soiuza, 1941-1945: sbornik dokumentov i
materialov v dvukh tomakh. Kishinev, 1975-76. 2 vols.

— — Russia (RSFSR).

GOR'KOVSKAIA partiinaia organizatsiia v gody Velikoi
Otechestvennoi voiny, 1941-1945: sbornik dokumentov i
materialov. Gor'kii, 1975. pp. 359.

KURGANSKAIA partiinaia organizatsiia v Velikoi
Otechestvennoi voine, 1941-1945: dokumenty i materialy.
Cheliabinsk, 1975. pp. 355.

— — Ukraine.

KHERSONSKAIA oblast' v gody Velikoi Otechestvennoi
voiny, 1941-1945: sbornik dokumentov i materialov.
Simferopol', 1975. pp. 320. *bibliog.*

— Switzerland.

OPRECHT (HANS) Der zweite Weltkrieg und die
schweizerische Arbeiterschaft. [Zürich, 1941]. pp. 31.
*(Sozialdemokratische Partei der Schweiz. Kultur und
Arbeit)*

WORTH.

WORKING PARTY ON THE TEACHING OF THE
VALUE BASES OF SOCIAL WORK [U.K.]. Social
work curriculum study: values in social work; a discussion
paper; [R.S. Downie, chairman]. London, Central Council
for Education and Training in Social Work, 1976. pp. 86.
bibliogs. (Papers. 13)

WUPPERTAL

— Economic history.

HOTH (WOLFGANG) Die Industrialisierung einer
rheinischen Gewerbestadt, dargestellt am Beispiel
Wuppertal. Köln, 1975. pp. 280. *bibliog.
(Rheinisch-Westfälisches Wirtschaftsarchiv zu Köln.
Schriften zur Rheinisch-Westfälischen
Wirtschaftsgeschichte. Band 28)*

— History.

KAMIŃSKI (ANDRZEJ JÓZEF) Vom Polizei- zum
Bürgerstaat: zur Geschichte der Demokratie am Beispiel
einer deutschen Stadt [Wuppertal]. Wuppertal, [1976]. pp.
316. *bibliog.*

KLEIN (ULRICH) and SCHERER (KLAUS JUERGEN)
Bürgerräte gegen die Arbeiterbewegung: Untersuchungen
und Dokumente am Beispiel Elberfeld-Barmen, 1918-1922.
Wentorf/Hamburg, 1976. pp. 124. *bibliog.*

YAKUTIA

— Economic history.

BASHARIN (GEORGII PROKOP'EVICH)
Sotsial'no-ekonomicheskie otnosheniia v Iakutii vtoroi
poloviny XIX - nachala XX veka: po povodu knigi Z.V.
Gogoleva "Iakutiia na rubezhe XIX-XX vv.". Iakutsk, 1974.
pp. 216. *bibliog.*

YAMASKA BASIN.

QUEBEC (PROVINCE). Office de Planification et de
Développement. 1973. Bassin de la Yamaska: proposition
d'utilisation des eaux. [Quebec], 1973. pp. 48.

YANKTON INDIANS.

KENT (CALVIN A.) and JOHNSON (JERRY) Flows of
funds on the Yankton Sioux Indian Reservation;...
prepared...in cooperation with the Yankton Sioux Tribal
Council...and United Sioux Tribes Development
Corporation. Minneapolis, [1976]. pp. 24. *bibliog. (Federal
Reserve Bank of Minneapolis. Ninth District Economic
Information Series)*

YANOAMA INDIANS.

SMOLE (WILLIAM J.) The Yanoama Indians: a cultural
geography. Austin, Tex., [1976]. pp. 272. *bibliog.*

YAROSLAVL (OBLAST')

— Politics and government.

PLAMENNOE bol'shevistskoe slovo: podpol'naia
literatura v Iaroslavskoi gubernii, 1902-1917 gg. Iaroslavl',
1975. pp. 303.

YECUANA INDIANS.

COPPENS (WALTER) The anatomy of a land invasion
scheme in Yekuana territory, Venezuela. Copenhagen,
1972. p. 22. *bibliog. (International Work Group for
Indigenous Affairs. Documents. 9)*

YENCHING UNIVERSITY.

WEST (PHILIP) Yenching University and Sino-Western
relations, 1916-1952. Cambridge, Mass., 1976. pp. 327.
*bibliog. (Harvard University. East Asian Research Center.
Harvard East Asian Series. 85)*

YORKSHIRE

— Economic history.

POLLARD (SIDNEY) and HOLMES (COLIN) eds.
Essays in the economic and social history of South
Yorkshire. Sheffield, South Yorkshire County Council,
Recreation, Culture and Health Department, 1976. pp. 308.

— Economic policy.

U.K. Department of the Environment. 1977. Government
response to the Yorkshire and Humberside regional
strategy review 1975: the next ten years. [London], 1977.
pp. 19.

— Gentry.

VALE (M.G.A.) Piety, charity and literacy among the
Yorkshire gentry, 1370-1480. York, 1976. pp. 32. *(York.
University. Borthwick Institute of Historical Research.
Borthwick Papers. No.50)*

— Maps.

U.K. Department of the Environment. Yorkshire and
Humberside Regional Office. 1975- . Yorkshire and
Humberside regional atlas. [2nd ed.] [Leeds, 1975 in
progress]. 1 vol.(loose-leaf).

— Religion.

VALE (M.G.A.) Piety, charity and literacy among the
Yorkshire gentry, 1370-1480. York, 1976. pp. 32. *(York.
University. Borthwick Institute of Historical Research.
Borthwick Papers. No.50)*

— Social history.

HARTLEY (MARIE) and INGILBY (JOAN) Life and
tradition in West Yorkshire. London, 1976. pp. 160.

— Social life and customs.

HARTLEY (MARIE) and INGILBY (JOAN) Life and
tradition in West Yorkshire. London, 1976. pp. 160.

YOUNG CHINA PARTY.

See CHINESE YOUTH PARTY.

YOUNG COMMUNIST INTERNATIONAL.

KOMINTERN, KIM i molodezhnoe dvizhenie, 1919-1943:
sbornik dokumentov. Moskva, 1977. 2 vols.

YOUNG COMMUNIST LEAGUE

— Russia.

VSESOIUZNYI LENINSKII KOMMUNISTICHESKII
SOIUZ MOLODEZHI. Tsentral'nyi Komitet. Dokumenty
TsK VLKSM, 1974. Moskva, 1975. pp. 334.

YOUNG GERMANY.

MARR (WILHELM) Das junge Deutschland in der
Schweiz: (ein Beitrag zur Geschichte der geheimen
Verbindungen unserer Tage); Anhang: Anarchie oder
Autorität?. Glashütten im Taunus, 1976. pp. 364,132.
*Reprint of the works originally published in Leipzig in 1846
and in Hamburg in 1852.*

YOUTH.

FIELD (MICHEL) and BROHM (JEAN MARIE) Jeunesse
et révolution: pour une organisation révolutionnaire de la
jeunesse. Paris, 1975. pp. 171.

— Employment.

REUBENS (BEATRICE G.) Bridges to work: international
comparisons of transition services. London, 1977. pp. 275.
bibliog.

— — Africa, Subsaharan.

MBITHI (PHILIP M.) Youth employment problems: a
discussion of policy issues with special reference to the
African experience. [London], Commonwealth Secretariat,
[1975]. pp. 27. *(Commonwealth Youth Programme.
Occasional Papers. Employment Series. 2).*

— — Australia.

AUSTRALIA. Commonwealth Bureau of Census and
Statistics. 1976. School leavers, 1970 to 1974: their
employment status and education experience in May 1975.
Canberra, 1976. pp. 12.

— — France.

CHÔMAGE: la jeunesse accuse; états généraux des
comités CGT de jeunes sans emploi, Paris, le 11 mars 1976.
Paris, [1976]. pp. 159.

— — Germany.

LATURNER (SYBILLE) and SCHOEN (BERNARD) eds.
Jugendarbeitslosigkeit: Materialien und Analysen zu einem
neuen Problem. Reinbek bei Hamburg, 1975 repr. 1976. pp.
217. *bibliog.*

— — United Kingdom.

ASHTON (D.N.) and FIELD (DAVID) Young workers.
London, 1976. pp. 192. *bibliog.*

NORTH TYNESIDE TRADES COUNCIL.
Unemployment and young workers in North Tyneside.
[North Shields], North Tyneside Community Development
Project, 1977. pp. 87.

WILSON (HUGH) AND WOMERSLEY (LEWIS) Firm,
and TYM (ROGER) AND ASSOCIATES. Inner area
study: Liverpool: getting a job. [London], Department of
the Environment, [1977]. pp. 45.

— Public opinion.

RADIO FREE EUROPE. Audience and Public Opinion
Research Department. The images of Polish, American,
Russian, German and Chinese youth as seen by Poles.
[Munich?], 1973. fo. 55.

— Austria — Political activity.

RINGLER (RALF ROLAND) Illusion einer Jugend:
Lieder, Fahnen und das bittere Ende; Hitler-Jugend in
Österreich: ein Erlebnisbericht. St. Pölten, 1977. pp. 223.

— China.

YOUTH in China; (edited by E. Stuart Kirby). Hong
Kong, [1965]. pp. 251.

— France.

DORIOT (JACQUES) La jeunesse
communiste;...conférence faite à la première Ecole
nationale du propagandiste de la jeunesse sur le but et le
rôle de la jeunesse. Paris, [192-?]. pp. 39.

— Germany.

NIKLES (BRUNO W.) Jugendpolitik in der
Bundesrepublik Deutschland: Entwicklungen, Merkmale,
Orientierungen. Opladen, 1976. pp. 244. *bibliog.*

SCHARMANN (THEODOR) Der Industriebürger:
gesellschaftliche Orientierung und berufliche Einstellung
junger Arbeiter und Angestellter. Bern, [1976]. pp. 203.
bibliog.

VOM Proletarier zum Industriebürger; herausgegeben von
Theodor Scharmann und Erwin Roth. Bern, [1976]. pp.
235. *bibliog.*

— — Political activity.

HACKMACK (HANS) Die sozialistische Jugendbewegung.
Berlin, [1918]. pp. 39.

INSTITUT FÜR MARXISTISCHE STUDIEN UND
FORSCHUNGEN. Aus der Geschichte der deutschen
Arbeiterjugendbewegung, 1904-1945: (Dokumente und
Materialien). Frankfurt/Main, 1975. pp. 169. *(Institut für
Marxistische Studien und Forschungen. Neudrucke zur
Sozialistischen Theorie und Gewerkschaftspraxis. Band 7)*

KRAUSE (WOLFGANG) and others. Zwischen
Anpassung und sozialistischer Politik: zur Geschichte der
Jungsozialisten seit 1945. Berlin, 1975. pp. 146.

LINSE (ULRICH) Die anarchistische und
anarcho-syndikalistische Jugendbewegung, 1919-1933: zur
Geschichte und Ideologie, etc. Frankfurt am Main, 1976.
pp. 330. *bibliog.*

— Germany, Eastern — Political activity.

Die PARTEI vertraut der Jugend: zur Verwirklichung des
Kommuniqués des Politbüros des ZK der SED zu
Problemen der Jugend; [by Kurt Bürger and others], etc.
Berlin, 1962. pp. 92. *bibliog. (Sozialistische Einheitspartei
Deutschlands. Der Parteiarbeiter. Heft 10)*

HONECKER (ERICH) Zur Jugendpolitik der SED: Reden
und Aufsätze von 1945 bis zur Gegenwart. Berlin, [1977].
pp. 644.

— Poland.

ADAMSKI (WŁADYSŁAW) Młodzie'z i społeczeństwo.
Warszawa, 1976. pp. 213.

— Romania.

TINERETUL: obiect de cercetare ştiinţifică. Bucureşti,
1969. pp. xiv,455. *(Centrul de Cercetări pentru Problemele
Tineretului. Colecţia Manifestări Ştiinţifice. nr.1) With
French, English, Russian and German forewords,
afterwords and tables of contents.*

TINERETUL - factor de schimbare, etc. Bucureşti, 1970.
pp. 440. *(Centrul de Cercetări pentru Problemele
Tineretului. Studii şi Sinteze. nr. 2-3) With English,
German, French and Russia summaries and tables of
contents.*

BĂDINA (OVIDIU) ed. Tineret industrial: acţiune şi integrare socială; cercetare sociologică condusă de Ovidiu Bădina. Bucureşti, 1972. pp. 170. *(Centrul de Cercetări pentru Problemele Tineretului. Tineretul şi Lumea de Mîine) With French, English, Russian and German tables of contents.*

— Russia.

REPA (FEDOR PROKOF'EVICH) Formirovanie moral'no-politicheskikh idealov molodezhi na obraze V.I. Lenina. Dushanbe, 1975. pp. 254.

CHECHOT (DMITRII MIKHAILOVICH) Molodezh' i brak: zametki iurista. Leningrad, 1976. pp. 104.

VASIL'EVA (EVELINA KARLOVNA) The young people of Leningrad: school and work options and attitudes. White Plains, N.Y., [1976]. pp. 177.

— Sweden — Political activity.

PETERSON (CARL GUNNAR) Ungdom och politik: en studie av Sveriges Socialdemokratiska Ungdomsförbund. Stockholm, [1975]. pp. 282. *bibliog. With English summary.*

— Switzerland.

WALDVOGEL (T.) Der Arbeitsdienst der Schweizer-Jugend: seine Gönner und die bisher durchgeführten Versuche auf freiwilligem Wege. Zürich, 1928. pp. 54.

SCHARMANN (THEODOR) Der Industriebürger: gesellschaftliche Orientierung und berufliche Einstellung junger Arbeiter und Angestellter. Bern, [1976]. pp. 203. *bibliog.*

VOM Proletarier zum Industriebürger; herausgegeben von Theodor Scharmann und Erwin Roth. Bern, [1976]. pp. 235. *bibliog.*

— United Kingdom.

KARN (VALERIE A.) and others. No place that's home: a report on accommodation for homeless young single people in Birmingham. Birmingham, 1974. pp. 99. *bibliog. (Birmingham. University. Centre for Urban and Regional Studies. Research Memoranda. No. 32)*

U.K. Working Group on Homeless Young People. 1976. Report. [London], 1976. pp. 81.

SPRINGHALL (JOHN) Youth, empire and society: British youth movements, 1883-1940. London, [1977]. pp. 163. *bibliog.*

— — Attitudes.

STRADLING (ROBERT) The political awareness of the school leaver. London, [1977]. pp. 81. *(Hansard Society for Parliamentary Government and Politics Association. Programme For Political Education)*

— — Political activity.

STRADLING (ROBERT) The political awareness of the school leaver. London, [1977]. pp. 81. *(Hansard Society for Parliamentary Government and Politics Association. Programme For Political Education)*

— United States.

GLOCK (CHARLES Y.) and BELLAH (ROBERT NEELLY) eds. The new religious consciousness. Berkeley, Calif., [1976]. pp. 391.

YUGOSLAVIA

— Administrative and political divisions.

YUGOSLAVIA. Savezni Zavod za Statistiku. 1972. Pregled promena političko-teritorijalne podele kod opština, 1961-1971. Beograd, 1972. pp. 151.

— Constitution.

YUGOSLAVIA. Constitution. 1974. The constitution of the Socialist Federal Republic of Yugoslavia; (editor in chief, Dragoljub Durović). Belgrade, 1974. pp. 318.

— Economic history.

ORGANISATION FOR ECONOMIC CO-OPERATION AND DEVELOPMENT. Committee for Invisible Transactions. 1974. Foreign investment in Yugoslavia, 1974. Paris, 1974. pp. 58.

— Economic policy.

COLANOVIĆ (BRANISLAV) and others. Planning to serve development and the foundations of planning in Yugoslavia; (translated by Nina Udovicki). Ljubljana, International Center for Public Enterprises, 1974. fo. 33. *(International Seminar 1974. Background Papers)*

PETRIĆ (IVO) Planning at the level of the region and the commune with special reference to planning in the enterprise: Split and Dalmatia; (translated by Meri Radosević). Ljubljana, International Center for Public Enterprises, 1974. fo. 27. *bibliog. (International Seminar 1974. [National Papers])*

KONTETZKI (HEINZ) Agrarpolitischer Wandel und Modernisierung in Jugoslawien: Zwischenbilanz einer sozialistischen Entwicklungsstrategie. Nürnberg, [1976]. pp. 563. *bibliog. (Südosteuropa-Gesellschaft. Südosteuropa-Studien. 24)*

— — Bibliography.

PERPAR (GABRIJEL) and JEREB (JANEZ) compilers. A selective bibliography of socio-economic planning in Yugoslavia; (translated by Gabrijel Perpar). Ljubljana, International Center for Public Enterprises, 1974. fo. 41. *(International Seminar 1974. [Bibliographies])*

— Foreign relations.

REUTER-HENDRICHS (IRENA) Jugoslawische Aussenpolitik, 1948-1968: aussenpolitische Grundsätze und internationale Ordnungsvorstellungen; eine Untersuchung der überregionalen Tagespresse. Köln, [1976]. pp. 363. *bibliog.*

— — Communist countries.

O neistinitim i nepravednim optužbama protiv KPJ: izabrani materijali. Beograd, 1948. pp. 371. *In Cyrillic.*

— — Russia.

GIRENKO (IURII STEPANOVICH) Sovetskii Soiuz - Iugoslaviia: traditsionnaia druzhba, vsestoronnee sotrudnichestvo. Moskva, 1975. pp. 87.

RADONJIĆ (RADOVAN) Sukob KPJ sa Kominformom i društveni razvoj Jugoslavije, 1948-1950. 2nd ed. Zagreb, 1976. pp. 276. *bibliog. (Zagreb. Narodno Sveučilište. Centar za Aktualni Politički Studij. Političke Teme: Biblioteka Suvremene Političke Misli)*

— — — Bibliography.

HUNTER (BRIAN READ) Soviet-Yugoslav relations, 1948-1972: a bibliography of Soviet, western and Yugoslav comment and analysis. New York, 1976. pp. 223.

— History.

RUSINOW (DENNISON I.) The Yugoslav experiment, 1948-1974. London, 1977. pp. 410. *bibliog.*

— — 1941-1945, Axis occupation.

LAZITCH (BRANKO) Titov pokret i režim u Jugoslaviji, 1941-1946. [n.p.], 1946. pp. 219.

— Industries.

TURČIĆ (IVAN) Indikatori o efikasnosti jugoslavenske industrije po općinama. Zagreb, 1975. pp. 364. *With English summary.*

— Politics and government.

JOHNSON (A. ROSS) Yugoslavia: in the twilight of Tito. Beverly Hills, [1974]. pp. 67. *bibliog. (Georgetown University. Center for Strategic and International Studies. Washington Papers. vol.2/16)*

DOLANC (STANE) Der Bund Kommunisten Jugoslawiens im Selbstverwaltungssystem ([translated from the Serbo-Croat by] Anica Perić- Günther [and others]). Beograd, [1975]. pp. 304.

DOLANC (STANE) Savez komunista Jugoslavije i socijalističko samoupravljanje: [collected speeches, articles, etc.]. Beograd, 1975. pp. 369.

ROBINSON (GERTRUDE JOCH) Tito's maverick media: the politics of mass communications in Yugoslavia. Urbana, Ill., [1977]. pp. 263. *bibliog.*

— Population.

YUGOSLAVIA. Savezni Zavod za Statistiku. 1973. Projekcije stanovništva Jugoslavije 1970-2000. godine po polu i petogodišnjim grupama starosti. Beograd, 1973. 5 pts. (in 1).

— Rural conditions.

KONTETZKI (HEINZ) Agrarpolitischer Wandel und Modernisierung in Jugoslawien: Zwischenbilanz einer sozialistischen Entwicklungsstrategie. Nürnberg, [1976]. pp. 563. *bibliog. (Südosteuropa-Gesellschaft. Südosteuropa-Studien. 24)*

— Social history.

RADONJIĆ (RADOVAN) Sukob KPJ sa Kominformom i društveni razvoj Jugoslavije, 1948-1950. 2nd ed. Zagreb, 1976. pp. 276. *bibliog. (Zagreb. Narodno Sveučilište. Centar za Aktualni Politički Studij. Političke Teme: Biblioteka Suvremene Političke Misli)*

— Social policy.

PETRIĆ (IVO) Planning at the level of the region and the commune with special reference to planning in the enterprise: Split and Dalmatia; (translated by Meri Radosević). Ljubljana, International Center for Public Enterprises, 1974. fo. 27. *bibliog. (International Seminar 1974. [National Papers])*

— — Bibliography.

PERPAR (GABRIJEL) and JEREB (JANEZ) compilers. A selective bibliography of socio-economic planning in Yugoslavia; (translated by Gabrijel Perpar). Ljubljana, International Center for Public Enterprises, 1974. fo. 41. *(International Seminar 1974. [Bibliographies])*

— Statistics, Vital.

YUGOSLAVIA. Savezni Zavod za Statistiku. 1975. Fertilitet ženskog stanovništva, 1968-1972: rezultati po republikama i pokrajinama. Beograd, 1975. pp. 271.

YUKON

— Native races.

CUMMING (PETER A.) Canada: native land rights and northern development. Copenhagen, 1977. pp. 64. *(International Work Group for Indigenous Affairs. Documents. 26)*

ZAIRE

— Economic conditions — Statistics.

BANQUE DU ZAIRE. Bulletin mensuel de la statistique. m., Ap 1975 (no.3)- [Kinshasa].

— Economic policy.

BONGOY (MPEKESA) Investissements mixtes au Zaire: (joint ventures pour la période de transition). Kinshasa, 1974. pp. 523. *bibliog.*

— History.

FARINHA (ANTONIO LOURENÇO) D. Afonso I, rei do Congo. [2nd ed.] Lisboa, Agência Geral do Ultramar, 1969. pp. 109. *(Figuras e Feitos de Alem-Mar. 3)*

— Politics and government.

DEMUNTER (PAUL) Luttes politiques au Zaïre: le processus de politisation des masses rurales du Bas-Zaïre. Paris, [1975]. pp. 333. *bibliog.*

ZAIRE(Cont.)

MOUVEMENT POPULAIRE DE LA REVOLUTION.
Bureau Politique. Histoire du Mouvement Populaire de la
Révolution. Kinshasa, [1976?]. pp. 118.

— Population.

ZAIRE. Bureau du Président. 1972. Perspectives
démographiques provisoires pour la République du Zaïre,
1970-1980; avec la collaboration de l'Institut National de la
Statistique. Kinshasa, 1972. fo.32.

ZAMBIA

— Economic conditions.

ZAMBIA. Office of the Cabinet Minister for the North-
Western Province. Annual report. a., 1973- Lusaka.

ZAMBIA. Office of the Cabinet Minister for the
Copperbelt Province. Annual report. a., 1974- Lusaka.

— Economic history.

BATES (ROBERT H.) Rural responses to industrialization:
a study of village Zambia. New Haven, 1976. pp. 380.
bibliog.

— Economic policy.

KAUNDA (KENNETH DAVID) Humanism in Zambia
and a guide to its implementation. Lusaka, 1968-74. 2 pts.
(in 1 vol.).

— Politics and government.

ZAMBIA. Office of the Cabinet Minister for the North-
Western Province. Annual report. a., 1973- Lusaka.

ZAMBIA. Office of the Cabinet Minister for the
Copperbelt Province. Annual report. a., 1974- Lusaka.

— Rural conditions.

BATES (ROBERT H.) Rural responses to industrialization:
a study of village Zambia. New Haven, 1976. pp. 380.
bibliog.

— Social conditions.

ZAMBIA. Office of the Cabinet Minister for the North-
Western Province. Annual report. a., 1973- Lusaka.

ZAMBIA. Office of the Cabinet Minister for the
Copperbelt Province. Annual report. a., 1974- Lusaka.

— Social policy.

KAUNDA (KENNETH DAVID) Humanism in Zambia
and a guide to its implementation. Lusaka, 1968-74. 2 pts.
(in 1 vol.).

ZANZIBAR

— Race question.

KUPER (LEO) The pity of it all: polarisation of racial and
ethnic relations. London, 1977. pp. 302. *bibliog.*

ZAPOROZH'E (OBLAST')

— Industries.

DNEPROVSKIE ogni: kak iz ruin i pepla byl podniat posle
voiny Zaporozhskii industrial'nyi kompleks. Kiev, 1976.
pp. 190.

ZAPOTEC INDIANS.

YOUNG (CATHERINE MARY) The social setting of
migration: factors affecting migration from a Sierra
Zapotec village in Oaxaca, Mexico. 1976. fo. 318. *bibliog.*
*Typescript. Ph.D. (London) thesis: unpublished. This thesis
is the property of London University and may not be
removed from the Library.*

ZAREMBA (PIOTR).

ZAREMBA (PIOTR) Wspomnienia prezydenta Szczecina,
1945-1950. Poznań, 1977. pp. 862.

ZEHRER (HANS).

FRITZSCHE (KLAUS) Politische Romantik und
Gegenrevolution: Fluchtwege in der Krise der bürgerlichen
Gesellschaft: das Beispiel des "Tat" Kreises. Frankfurt am
Main, 1976. pp. 437. *bibliog.*

ZETKIN (CLARA).

PIECK (WILHELM) Clara Zetkin: Leben und Kampf;
geboren 5. Juli 1857, gestorben 20. Juni 1933. Berlin,
[1948]. pp. 48.

ZHELIABOV (ANDREI IVANOVICH).

ASHESHOV (NIKOLAI PETROVICH) Andrei Ivanovich
Zheliabov: materialy dlia biografii i kharakteristiki.
Petrograd, 1919. pp. 159.

ZHIVKOV (TODOR).

ZHIVKOV (TODOR) Izbrannye stat'i i rechi, 1965-1975;
[perevod s bolgarskogo]. Moskva, 1975. pp. 583.

ZHUKOV (GEORGII KONSTANTINOVICH).

ZHUKOV (GEORGII KONSTANTINOVICH)
Vospominaniia i razmyshleniia. 2nd ed. Moskva, 1974. 2
vols.

ZIEMIA LUBUSKA.

JASIEWICZ (ZBIGNIEW) Rodzina wiejska na Ziemi
Lubuskiej: studium przeobra'zeń rodziny na podstawie
badań etnograficznych w wybranych waiach. Warszawa,
1977. pp. 119. *bibliog. With English summary.*

ZONING

— Mathematical models.

SAMMONS (ROGER) Zoning systems for spatial models.
Reading, 1976. pp. 53. *bibliog. (Reading. University.
Department of Geography. Reading Geographical Papers.
No. 52)*

ZONING LAW

— United States.

MANN (MARY SULLIVAN) The right to housing:
constitutional issues and remedies in exclusionary zoning.
New York, 1976. pp. 191. *bibliog.*

ZUERICH (CITY)

— Politics and government.

PFLUEGER (PAUL) Der Gemeindesozialismus der Stadt
Zürich: Denkschrift zum sozialdemokratischen
Kommunaltag in Zürich vom 23./24. Mai 1908. Zürich,
1908. pp. 40.

— Social conditions.

PFLUEGER (PAUL) Der Gemeindesozialismus der Stadt
Zürich: Denkschrift zum sozialdemokratischen
Kommunaltag in Zürich vom 23./24. Mai 1908. Zürich,
1908. pp. 40.

ZWIAZEK OBRONY KRESÓW ZACHODNICH.

See POLSKI ZWIAZEK ZACHODNI.

ZWINGLI (ULRICH).

POTTER (GEORGE RICHARD) Ulrich Zwingli. London,
[1977]. pp. 46. *bibliog. (Historical Association. General
Series. G.89)*

ZWOLLE

— Economic conditions.

VUUREN (LOUIS VAN) Rapport betreffende een
onderzoek naar de welvaartsbronnen van de gemeente
Zwolle, uitgebracht in opdracht van het gemeentebestuur,
etc. Zwolle, 1939. pp. 331.

— Social conditions.

VUUREN (LOUIS VAN) Rapport betreffende een
onderzoek naar de welvaartsbronnen van de gemeente
Zwolle, uitgebracht in opdracht van het gemeentebestuur,
etc. Zwolle, 1939. pp. 331.

— Statistics.

VUUREN (LOUIS VAN) Rapport betreffende een
onderzoek naar de welvaartsbronnen van de gemeente
Zwolle, uitgebracht in opdracht van het gemeentebestuur,
etc. Zwolle, 1939. pp. 331.

List of subject headings used
in the Bibliography
arranged under topics

TABLE OF SUBJECT SUB-DIVISIONS

SUBJECT SUB-DIVISIONS UNDER NAMES OF CONTINENTS, COUNTRIES, STATES OR TOWNS

Works on the following subjects, if confined to a particular geographical area, are entered not under subject, but under the name of the country, etc., with the subject sub-division.

Administrative and political divisions
Air force
Annexation
Antiquities
Appropriations and expenditures
Armed forces
Army

Bibliography
Bio-bibliography
Biography
Boundaries

Capital
Census
Centennial celebrations, etc.
Charters, grants, privileges
Church history
City planning
Civilization
Claims
Climate
Clubs
Colonies
Colonization
Commerce
Commercial policy
Commercial treaties
Constitution
Constitutional conventions
Constitutional history
Constitutional laws
Courts and courtiers

Defences
Description and travel
Dictionaries and encyclopaedias
Diplomatic and consular service
Directories
Discovery and exploration

Economic conditions
Economic history
Economic integration
Economic policy

Emigration and immigration
Executive departments
Exiles

Fairs
Famines
Foreign economic relations
Foreign opinion
Foreign population
Foreign relations
Foreign relations — Treaties
Foreign relations administration

Gazeteers
Genealogy
Gentry
Government property
Government publications
Government vessels
Governors

Historic houses, etc.
Historical geography
History
History, Local
History, Military
History, Naval

Industries
Intellectual life
International status

Kings and rulers

Languages
Learned institutions and societies

Manufactures
Maps
Military policy
Militia
Moral conditions

Nationalism
Native races

Navy
Neutrality
Nobility

Occupations
Officials and employees

Parliament (Congress, Nationalrat, etc.)
Peerage
Politics and government
Population
Presidents
Public buildings
Public lands
Public works

Race question
Registers
Relations (general) with (country)
Relations (military) with (country)
Religion
Religion and mythology
Rural conditions

Sanitary affairs
Seal
Semi-centennial celebrations, etc.
Social conditions
Social history
Social life and customs
Social policy
Statistics
Statistics, Medical
Statistics, Vital
Surveys

Territorial expansion
Territories and possessions
Tornadoes

Vice-Presidents
Voting registers

Year-books

SUBJECT SUB-DIVISIONS USED ONLY UNDER NAMES OF CITIES OR TOWNS

Works on the following matters, if confined to a particular region or country, are entered under the subject, with local sub-division; if confined to a particular city or town, under the name of the city or town, with subject sub-division.

Almshouses and workhouses
Ambulance service
Amusements

Benevolent and moral institutions
    and societies
Bridges
Buildings

Cemeteries
Charities
Civic improvement
Clubs

Description
Docks

Earthquake
Evening and continuation schools
Exhibitions
Fires and fire prevention

Fortifications

Gilds
Growth

Harbour
Hospitals
Hotels. taverns. etc.

Libraries
Lodging-houses

Markets
Massacre
Music-halls (Variety-theatres.
    cabarets. etc.)

Office buildings

Parks
Police
Poor
Port

Porters
Prisons and reformatories
Public laundries

Rapid transit
Recreation areas
Recreational activities
Riots

Schools
Sewerage
Stock Exchange (Beurs. Bourse. etc.)
Street cleaning
Streets
Suburbs and environs
Synagogues

Theatres
Transit systems

Water-supply

AGRICULTURE (including ANIMAL AND PLANT INDUSTRIES)

General.

AGRICULTURAL ADMINISTRATION
AGRICULTURAL ASSISTANCE.
AGRICULTURAL COLONIES
AGRICULTURAL CREDIT
AGRICULTURAL EXTENSION WORK
AGRICULTURAL INDUSTRIES
AGRICULTURAL INNOVATIONS.
AGRICULTURAL LAWS AND
   LEGISLATION
AGRICULTURAL MACHINERY
AGRICULTURAL PRICE SUPPORTS
AGRICULTURAL PRICES
AGRICULTURAL RESEARCH.
AGRICULTURAL SOCIETIES
AGRICULTURAL SURPLUS
AGRICULTURE.
AGRICULTURE, COOPERATIVE.
AGRICULTURE AND STATE
ANIMAL INDUSTRY
BANANA TRADE
CATTLE TRADE
CATTLE TRAILS.
COOPERATIVE MARKETING OF FARM
   PRODUCE
COTTON GROWING
COTTON TRADE
DAIRY PRODUCTS
DAIRYING
FARM MANAGEMENT.
FARM OWNERSHIP
FARM PRODUCE
FARM TENANCY
FARMS
FARMS, COLLECTIVE.
FARMS, SIZE OF.
FEEDS
FERTILIZER INDUSTRY.
FIELD CROPS
FOOD AND AGRICULTURE
   ORGANIZATION.
FOREST POLICY.
FOREST PRODUCTS
FORESTS AND FORESTRY
FORESTS AND FORESTRY,
   COOPERATIVE.
HACIENDAS
HILL FARMING
INTERNATIONAL AGRICULTURAL
   COOPERATION.
IRRIGATION
LAND REFORM.
MILK SUPPLY
PHOSPHATIC FERTILIZERS
PLANTATIONS
SILOS
SMALL HOLDINGS
SOIL SURVEYS
STATE FARMS
STOCK AND STOCK BREEDING
SUGAR GROWING.
VETERINARY MEDICINE

Particular animals and animal products.

BEEF
BEEF CATTLE
CATTLE
GUANO.
MEAT
MILK
SHEEP
SWINE

Particular crops and plant products.

BEANS
CITRUS FRUITS
COCOA
COFFEE
COTTON
FRUIT
GRAIN
MAIZE
MUSHROOMS, EDIBLE
PALMS
POTATOES
RICE
SUGAR
SUGAR CANE
TOBACCO
TREES
VEGETABLES

Fisheries.

FISH TRADE
FISHERIES
FISHERY MANAGEMENT.
FISHING VILLAGES

BIBLIOGRAPHY AND GENERAL WORKS.

ACQUISITIONS (LIBRARIES).
ARCHIVES
BIBLIOGRAPHICAL SERVICES
BIBLIOGRAPHY
BIBLIOGRAPHY, NATIONAL
BOOKS.
BOOKS AND READING.
BROADSIDES
CATALOGUES, LIBRARY.
CATALOGUES, UNION.
CATALOGUING.
CLASSIFICATION
CLASSIFICATION, LIBRARY OF
   CONGRESS.
DEVSIS (DEVELOPMENT SCIENCE
   INFORMATION SYSTEM).
EDUCATIONAL PUBLISHING
FEDERAL AID TO LIBRARIES
GOVERNMENT PUBLICATIONS
INFORMATION MEASUREMENT
INFORMATION SCIENCE.
INFORMATION SERVICES
INFORMATION STORAGE AND
   RETRIEVAL SYSTEMS
LAW LIBRARIES
LIBRARIES
LIBRARIES, GOVERNMENTAL,
   ADMINISTRATIVE, ETC.
LIBRARIES, NATIONAL
LIBRARIES, UNIVERSITY AND COLLEGE
LIBRARIES AND EDUCATION
LIBRARY FINANCE
LIBRARY LEGISLATION
LIBRARY USE STUDIES
LINOTYPE.
MANUSCRIPTS
PAMPHLETS.
PRINTING
PRINTING, PUBLIC
PRINTING INDUSTRY
PUBLIC LIBRARIES
PUBLIC RECORDS
PUBLISHERS AND PUBLISHING
READERSHIP SURVEYS
SCHOLARLY PUBLISHING
SOCIAL SCIENCE LITERATURE.
TEXTBOOKS

BIOGRAPHY.

ABD EL-KRIM.
ABDUL RAZAK BIN HUSSEIN.
ABENDROTH (WOLFGANG).
ACHESON (DEAN GOODERHAM).
ADAMS (HENRY BROOKS).
ADORNO (THEODOR WIESENGRUND).
AFONSO I, King of the Congo.
ALLENDE (SALVADOR).
AMIN (IDI).
ANDERSEN NEXØ (MARTIN).
ANDERSON (PERRY).
ANDRADE (VICTOR).
ANNE, Queen of Great Britain and Ireland.
ANSO (MARIANO).
ANTONOV-OVSEENKO (VLADIMIR
   ALEKSANDROVICH).
ARAKCHEEV (ALEKSEI ANDREEVICH)
   Graf.
ARISTOTLE.
ARNOLD (MATTHEW).
ASQUITH (HERBERT HENRY) 1st Earl of
   Oxford and Asquith.
AYRES (CLARENCE EDWIN).
AZCARATE Y FLOREZ (PABLO DE).
AZIZBEKOV (MESHADI AZIM-BEK-OGLY).
BACH (DAVID JOSEF).
BACON (FRANCIS) Viscount St. Albans.
BAEUMLER (ALFRED).
BAKUNIN (MIKHAIL ALEKSANDROVICH).
BALDWIN (ROGER NASH).
BARKER (JOSEPH).
BARNARD (Sir JOHN).
BARRÈS (AUGUSTE MAURICE).
BARTHOLOMEW FAMILY.
BARZEL (RAINER).
BAUDELOT (CHRISTIAN).
BAUER (BRUNO).
BEAUFORT (Sir FRANCIS).
BEBEL (AUGUST).
BELINSKII (VISSARION GRIGOR'EVICH).
BELLO (ANDRÉS).
BELZU (MANUEL ISIDORO).
BENEDICT XIII, Antipope, 1399-1419.
BENIGNI (UMBERTO).
BENISZ (ADAM).
BENTHAM (JEREMY).
BERDIAEV (NIKOLAI
   ALEKSANDROVICH).
BERGSON (HENRI LOUIS).
BERLIN (Sir ISAIAH).
BERNAYS (KARL LUDWIG).
BERNHARD, Prince of the Netherlands.
BERNSTEIN (EDUARD).
BERRIGAN (DANIEL).
BERRIGAN (PHILIP F.).
BESKROVNYI (LIUBOMIR
   GRIGOR'EVICH).
BEVERIDGE (WILLIAM HENRY) 1st Baron
   Beveridge.
BEZER (JOHN JAMES).
BIERMANN (WOLF).
BIERUT (BOLESŁAW).
BISMARCK-SCHOENHAUSEN (OTTO
   EDUARD LEOPOLD VON) Prince.
BLACK (JOSEPH).
BLAGA (LUCIAN).
BLAKE (EDWARD).
BLEICHROEDER (GERSON VON).
BLOCH (ERNST).
BONNOT DE MABLY (GABRIEL).
BORDEN (ROBERT LAIRD).
BOURDIEU (PIERRE).
BRADLEY (FRANCIS HERBERT).
BRANDT (WILLY).
BRAUN (OTTO).
BRECHT (BERTOLT).
BREWER (WAYNE).
BREZHNEV (LEONID IL'ICH).
BRIAND (ARISTIDE PIERRE HENRI).

BROCKWAY (ARCHIBALD FENNER) Baron Brockway.
BRODETSKY (SELIG).
BROWNE (FRANCES WORSLEY STELLA).
BRUCE (DAVID KIRKPATRICK ESTE).
BRUCE (THOMAS) 7th Earl of Elgin and 11th Earl of Kincardine.
BRUNO (GIORDANO).
BUELOW (BERNHARD HEINRICH MARTIN KARL) Fürst von.
BUJAK (FRANCISZEK).
BULLER (ANNIE).
BURCKHARDT (JACOB).
BURKE (EDMUND).
BURNS (JOHN).
BUTLER (JOSEPH) successively Bishop of Bristol and of Durham.
CABRAL (AMILCAR).
CAETANO (MARCELLO).
CAMACHO (MARCELINO).
CANARIS (WILHELM).
CANNON (JAMES PATRICK).
CAPRIVI (LEO VON) Graf.
CARDENAS (LAZARO).
CAROLINE AMELIA ELIZABETH, Queen Consort of George IV, King of Great Britain and Ireland.
CARRERO BLANCO (LUIS).
CARTER (JAMES EARL) President of the United States.
CARTIER (Sir GEORGES ETIENNE).
CEAUSESCU (NICOLAE).
CHAMBERLAIN (JOSEPH).
CHARLES I, King of Great Britain and Ireland.
CHEREPANOV (ALEKSANDR IVANOVICH).
CHETVERIKOV (NIKOLAI SERGEEVICH).
CHIANG (CHING).
CHIANG (KAI-SHEK).
CHOISEUL-PRASLIN (CHARLES LAURE HUGUES THEOBALD DE) Duc.
CHOISEUL-PRASLIN (FANNY DE) Duchesse.
CHOU (EN-LAI).
CHRISTENSEN (POUL).
CHURCHILL (Sir WINSTON LEONARD SPENCER).
CLEAVER (ELDRIDGE).
CLEMENT VII, Antipope, 1378-1394.
COLLINGWOOD (ROBIN GEORGE).
COLVILLE (Sir JOHN).
CONNOLLY (JAMES).
CONRAD (JOHANNES).
CONSTABLE (JOHN).
COPERNICUS (NICOLAUS).
COUDENHOVE-KALERGI (RICHARD NICOLAUS) Count.
CROCE (BENEDETTO).
CUDLIPP (HUGH) Baron Cudlipp.
CUGNET (FRANÇOIS ETIENNE).
CULLEN (WILLIAM).
DAHLEM (FRANZ).
DAHLSTRÖM (HANS).
DALBERG-ACTON (JOHN EMERICH EDWARD) 1st Baron Acton.
DAYAN (MOSHE).
DEAN (JOHN WESLEY).
DE LEON (DANIEL).
DESJARDINS (ALPHONSE).
DESPAZE (JOSEPH).
D'IACHENKO (VASILII PETROVICH).
DICKENS (CHARLES).
DIEFENBAKER (JOHN GEORGE).
DIETZGEN (JOSEPH).
DIMITROV (GEORGI).
DISRAELI (BENJAMIN) 1st Earl of Beaconsfield.
DMOWSKI (ROMAN).
DOBREV (KRUSTIU ZHELIAZKOV).
DOBROLIUBOV (NIKOLAI ALEKSANDROVICH).
DOLANC (STANE).

DOPF (CARL).
DOSTOEVSKII (FEDOR MIKHAILOVICH).
DOUGLAS-HOME (ALEXANDER FREDERICK) Baron Home.
DREES (WILLEM).
DREIER (FREDERIK).
DRIBERG (THOMAS EDWARD NEIL) Baron Bradwell.
DUBINSKY (DAVID).
DUMAY (JEAN BAPTISTE).
DUMONT (GABRIEL).
DUNLOP (ANNIE ISABELLA).
DUNNING (THOMAS).
DUPLESSIS (MAURICE LENOBLET).
DURRUTI (BUENAVENTURA).
DUTSCHKE (RUDI).
EGERTON (THOMAS) 1st Viscount Brackley.
EICHTHAL (GUSTAVE D').
EL SADAT (ANWAR).
ELLERMAN FAMILY.
ENGELS (FRIEDRICH).
EREMEEV (KONSTANTIN STEPANOVICH).
ERLER (FRITZ).
ERZBERGER (MATTHIAS).
ESCOFET I ALSINA (FREDERIC).
ESTABLET (ROGER).
EURIPIDES.
EYSKENS (GASTON).
FABRE (EDOUARD RAYMOND).
FAJON (ETIENNE).
FANFANI (AMINTORE)
FANON (FRANTZ).
FELLNER (WILLIAM JOHN).
FICHTE (JOHANN GOTTLIEB).
FIREBRACE (Sir HENRY).
FITZPATRICK (Sir JAMES PERCY).
FITZWILLIAM FAMILY.
FORD (GERALD RUDOLPH) President of the United States.
FOX (HENRY RICHARD VASSALL) 3rd Baron Holland.
FRANCO BAHAMONDE (FRANCISCO).
FRANKFURTER (FELIX).
FRANKLIN (BENJAMIN).
FRANQUI (CARLOS).
FRASER (HUGH CHARLES PATRICK JOSEPH).
FREDERICK II, King of Prussia.
FREUD (SIGMUND).
FRIEDMAN (MILTON).
FUČÍK (JULIUS).
GALANSKOV (IURII TIMOFEEVICH).
GALBRAITH (JOHN KENNETH).
GANDHI (INDIRA).
GANDHI (MOHANDAS KARAMCHAND).
GAPON (GEORGII APOLLONOVICH).
GARNET (HENRY HIGHLAND).
GARVEY (MARCUS).
GATES (FREDERICK TAYLOR).
GAULLE (CHARLES DE).
GAXIOLA OCHOA (FRANCISCO JAVIER).
GEDDES (Sir PATRICK).
GEORGE (DAVID LLOYD) 1st Earl Lloyd George.
GEORGESCU-ROEGEN (NICHOLAS).
GERTSEN (ALEKSANDR IVANOVICH).
GEYER (CURT).
GIBSON (A.H.).
GIEREK (EDWARD).
GINZBURG (ALEKSANDR IL'ICH).
GISCARD D'ESTAING (VALERY).
GLADSTONE (WILLIAM EWART).
GLUCKMAN (HERMAN MAX).
GODWIN (MARY).
GODWIN (WILLIAM).
GOERING (HERMANN WILHELM).
GOGOLEV (ZAKHAR VASIL'EVICH).
GOKHALE (GOPAL KRISHNA).
GOLENDORF (PIERRE).
GOMPERS (SAMUEL).
GRAMSCI (ANTONIO).
GRAZIADEI (ANTONIO).

GREY (EDWARD) 1st Viscount Grey of Fallodon.
GRIBOEDOV (ALEKSANDR SERGEEVICH).
GRIFFITH (ARTHUR).
GRUBER (KARL).
GUEVARA (ERNESTO).
HAASE (HUGO).
HAIN (PETER).
HANDYSIDE (RICHARD).
HARDING (Mrs. STAN).
HARDING (WARREN GAMALIEL) President of the United States.
HARDY (THOMAS) Political writer.
HARRISON (MARGUERITE ELTON).
HARRISON (THOMAS).
HASSAN II, King of Morocco.
HAVEMANN (ROBERT).
HEARST (PATRICIA CAMPBELL).
HECKERT (FRITZ).
HEGEL (GEORG WILHELM FRIEDRICH).
HEINEMANN (GUSTAV WALTER)
HENNING (ERNST).
HENRIQUES (Sir BASIL LUCAS QUIXANO).
HERWEGH (GEORG).
HEYDRICH (REINHARD).
HILDEBRAND (BRUNO).
HILL (DAVID JAYNE).
HINDENBURG (PAUL LUDWIG HANS ANTON VON).
HITLER (ADOLF).
HLINKA (ANDREJ).
HOARE (SAMUEL JOHN GURNEY) 1st Viscount Templewood.
HOBBES (THOMAS).
HOBHOUSE (Sir CHARLES EDWARD HENRY).
HOELZ (MAX).
HOHENLOHE-SCHILLINGSFUERST (CHLODWIG KARL VIKTOR) Prince.
HOMANS (GEORGE CASPAR).
HONE (WILLIAM) Bookseller.
HONECKER (ERICH).
HOOVER (HERBERT CLARK) President of the United States.
HORKHEIMER (MAX).
HOUGHTON (DESMOND HOBART).
HUGO (VICTOR MARIE) Vicomte.
HUMBERT-DROZ (JULES).
HUME (DAVID).
HUMPHREY (HUBERT HORATIO).
HUNTER (Sir WILLIAM WILSON).
HUSÁK (GUSTÁV).
IBSEN (HENRIK).
IGLESIAS POSSE (PABLO).
ILLICH (IVAN D.).
JACOB (BERTHOLD).
JAURÈS (JEAN).
JOHNSON (LYNDON BAINES) President of the United States.
JONKMAN (JAN ANNE).
JOSEPH II, Emperor of Germany.
JUNG (CHARLES GUSTAVE).
KABIRO (NGUGI).
KALEDIN (ALEKSEI MAKSIMOVICH).
KALININ (MIKHAIL IVANOVICH).
KANT (IMMANUEL).
KANTEMIR (DMITRII KONSTANTINOVICH).
KAPP (KARL WILHELM).
KARAMZIN (NIKOLAI MIKHAILOVICH).
KAWAKAMI (HAJIME).
KEARNEY (PEADAR).
KELSO (LOUIS O.).
KENNEDY (JOHN FITZGERALD) President of the United States.
KEYNES (JOHN MAYNARD) 1st Baron Keynes.
KHRUSHCHEV (NIKITA SERGEEVICH).
KHVOSTOV (VLADIMIR MIKHAILOVICH).
KING (MARTIN LUTHER).
KIRCHNER (JOHANNA).
KIROV (SERGEI MIRONOVICH).

KISELEV (KUZ'MA VENEDIKTOVICH).
KISSINGER (HENRY ALFRED).
KISTIAKOWSKY (GEORGE BOGDAN).
KITCHENER (HORATIO HERBERT) Earl of
Khartoum.
KJELDSEN (VIKING and ANNEMARIE).
KNOX (WILLIAM).
KOENIG (HEINRICH).
KOHLBERG (LAURENCE).
KOK (ADAM).
KOO (VI KYUIN WELLINGTON).
KOSZUTSKA (MARIANNA KAROLINA
SABINA).
KRAUS (KARL).
KREISKY (BRUNO).
KROPOTKIN (PETR ALEKSEEVICH) Prince.
KRZYWICKI (LUDWIK).
KUCZYNSKI (JUERGEN)
LA GUARDIA (FIORELLO HENRY).
LAKATOS (IMRE).
LAMB (WILLIAM) 2nd Viscount Melbourne.
LAMPE (ALFRED).
LANDAUER (GUSTAV).
LAZO (SERGEI GEORGIEVICH)
LEFEBVRE (RAYMOND).
LEINER (NORBERT).
LENIN (VLADIMIR IL'ICH).
LEON (PAOLO).
LEONE (ENRICO).
LESSNER (FRIEDRICH).
LEVI-STRAUSS (CLAUDE)
LEVINE (ROSA).
LEYS (NORMAN MACLEAN).
LIEBHARDT (JOHANN).
LIEBKNECHT (KARL).
LIEBKNECHT (SOPHIE).
LIN (PIAO).
LINCOLN (ABRAHAM) President of the
United States.
LIPIŃSKI (EDWARD).
LIVINGSTONE (DAVID).
LOCKE (JOHN).
LODGE (HENRY CABOT).
LOMONOSOV (MIKHAIL VASIL'EVICH).
LONDON (JACK).
LONGFIELD (MOUNTIFORT).
LOPEZ (JUAN).
LORENZO (GIOVANNI DE).
LUDENDORFF (ERICH FRIEDRICH
WILHELM).
LUKÁCS (GEORG).
LUMUMBA (PATRICE).
LUNACHARSKII (ANATOLII
VASIL'EVICH).
LUTHER (HANS).
LUTHER (MARTIN).
LUXEMBURG (ROSA).
LYTHE (SAMUEL GEORGE EDGAR).
MACAULAY (HERBERT).
MACAULAY (THOMAS BABINGTON) Baron
Macaulay.
MACCHIAVELLI (NICCOLÒ).
MACDONALD (JAMES RAMSAY).
MACDONALD (Sir JOHN ALEXANDER).
McKAY (HENRY DONALD).
MACKINDER (Sir HALFORD JOHN)
MADERO (FRANCISCO INDALECIO).
MADOX (RICHARD).
MADSEN (ARNE and INGER BUSK).
MAINE (Sir HENRY SUMNER).
MAITLAND (FREDERIC WILLIAM).
MALCOLM X, pseud.
MALIK (MICHAEL ABDUL).
MALRAUX (CLARA).
MÁLYUSZ (ELEMÉR).
MANNERHEIM (CARL GUSTAF EMIL).
MAO (TSE-TUNG).
MARCUSE (LUDWIG).
MARGERIE (PIERRE DE).
MARIATEGUI (JOSE CARLOS).
MARKOVIĆ (SVETOZAR).
MARMONTEL (JEAN FRANÇOIS).

MARR (WILHELM).
MARSHALL (JOHN) Chief Justice of the
United States.
MARX (KARL).
MATANZIMA (KAIZER DALIWONGA).
MATHU (ELIUD WAMBU).
MEAD (MARGARET).
MEINHOF (ULRIKE).
MERLEAU-PONTY (MAURICE).
MERTON (ROBERT KING).
MILDMAY (BENJAMIN) Earl Fitzwalter.
MILL (JAMES).
MILL (JOHN STUART).
MILLERAND (ALEXANDRE).
MILLETT (JOHN DAVID).
MILLS (CHARLES WRIGHT).
MILTON (JOHN).
MIRBEAU (OCTAVE).
MIRONOV (PHILLIPP KUZ'MICH).
MITTERAND (FRANÇOIS).
MŁYNARSKI (FELIKS JOHN).
MOCH (JULES).
MONATTE (PIERRE).
MONDLANE (EDUARDO).
MONGER (THOMAS).
MONNET (JEAN).
MONTAGUE (RICHARD).
MONTAGUT (LLUIS).
MONTGELAS DE GARNERIN
(MAXIMILIAN JOSEPH) Graf.
MOONEY (THOMAS J.).
MORGAN (Sir CHARLES).
MORRIS (WILLIAM).
MORRIS (WILLIAM RICHARD) 1st Viscount
Nuffield.
MORRISON (JAMES).
MOYNIHAN (DANIEL PATRICK).
MURDOCH (KEITH RUPERT).
MUSSOLINI (BENITO).
NADAUD (MARTIN).
NASH (Sir WALTER).
NECHKINA (MILITSA VASIL'EVNA).
NEILSON (GEORGE).
NEWTON (ARTHUR).
NEWTON (HUEY PIERCE).
NIXON (RICHARD MILHOUS) President of
the United States.
NKRUMAH (KWAME).
NOBEL (ALFRED BERNHARD).
NOBEL FAMILY.
NOBEL PRIZES.
O'CONNELL (DANIEL).
O'CONNELL (DANIEL PETER).
OGAREV (NIKOLAI PLATONOVICH).
OLDHAM (JOSEPH HOULDSWORTH).
O'MAHONY (LIAM).
ORTEGA Y GASSET (JOSE).
ORTIZ DE AYALA (TADEO).
OSTROVITIANOV (KONSTANTIN
VASIL'EVICH).
OTTO, Archduke of Austria.
PAINE (THOMAS).
PAPEN (FRANZ VON).
PARK (ROBERT EZRA).
PARKES (JAMES WILLIAM).
PARNELL (CHARLES STEWART).
PARSONS (TALCOTT).
PASOLD (ERIC W.).
PASQUALINI (JEAN).
PASSERON (JEAN CLAUDE).
PEARSE (PATRICK).
PEDERSEN (HANS and ELLEN).
PEEL (Sir ROBERT).
PHILIPS (FRITS).
PI SUNYER (CARLES).
PI Y MARGALL (FRANCISCO).
PIAGET (JEAN).
PIECK (WILHELM).
PITT (WILLIAM) Earl of Chatham.
PLEKHANOV (GEORGII
VALENTINOVICH).
PLIUSHCH (LEONID IVANOVICH).

POLANYI (MICHAEL).
POLE (Sir FELIX JOHN CLEWETT).
POMPIDOU (GEORGES).
PONIATOWSKI (MICHEL CASIMIR) Prince.
POPPER (Sir KARL RAIMUND).
POSADA (ADOLFO).
POSADOWSKY-WEHNER (ARTHUR) Graf.
POWELL (JOHN ENOCH).
PRICE (RICHARD).
PRIETO (INDALECIO).
PROKSCH (ANTON).
PROUDHON (PIERRE JOSEPH).
RABIN (YITZHAK).
RACZYŃSKI (EDWARD) Count.
RADEK (KARL).
RAMIREZ SANCHEZ (ILICH).
RAMOS (JORGE ABELARDO).
RAMSAY (JAMES) Vicar of Teston.
RANKIN (HARRY).
RAWLS (JOHN).
REED (JOHN).
REID (JIMMY).
REISSNER (LARISSA).
REMIRO (JOE).
RHODES (CECIL JOHN).
RICARDO (DAVID).
RINGLER (RALF ROLAND).
ROBERTS (FREDERICK SLEIGH) 1st Earl
Roberts.
ROBERTS (ROBERT).
ROCKEFELLER FAMILY.
ROOSEVELT (ANNA ELEANOR).
ROOSEVELT (FRANKLIN DELANO)
President of the United States.
ROOSEVELT (THEODORE) President of the
United States.
ROOSEVELT FAMILY.
ROSENBERG (ETHEL and JULIUS).
ROTHSCHILD (NATHANIEL MEYER
VICTOR) 3rd Baron Rothschild.
ROUSIERS FAMILY.
ROUSSEAU (JEAN JACQUES).
ROYAL DESCENT, FAMILIES OF.
RUEFF (JACQUES).
RUGE (ARNOLD).
RUSSELL (BERTRAND ARTHUR WILLIAM)
3rd Earl Russell.
SAKHAROV (ANDREI DMITRIEVICH).
SALT (HENRY STEPHENS).
SALT (Sir TITUS).
SALTYKOV-SHCHEDRIN (MIKHAIL
EVGRAFOVICH).
SAMUELSON (PAUL ANTHONY).
SAWYER (CHARLES).
SCHACHT (HORACE GREELEY HJALMAR).
SCHERMERHORN (WILLEM).
SCHMIDT (FOLKE).
SCHUELER (EDMUND).
SCHUTZ (ALFRED).
SCULLIN (JAMES HENRY).
SEALE (BOBBY).
SECKER (THOMAS) Archbishop of
Canterbury.
SECONDAT (CHARLES LOUIS DE) Baron de
Montesquieu.
SEIDEL (ROBERT).
SENECA (LUCIUS ANNAEUS).
SERGEEV (FEDOR ANDREEVICH).
SEYDEWITZ (MAX).
SHAKESPEARE (WILLIAM).
SHAPOVALOV (ALEKSANDR
SIDOROVICH).
SHAUMIAN (STEPAN GEORGIEVICH).
SHAW (CLIFFORD ROBE).
SHAW (GEORGE BERNARD).
SHOLOKHOV (MIKHAIL
ALEKSANDROVICH).
SIDGWICK (HENRY).
SIKORSKI (WŁADYSŁAW).
SIMMEL (GEORG).
SINGER (ISAAC MERRITT).
SMITH (ADAM).

SNEEVLIET (HENDRICUS JOSEPHUS FRANCISCUS MARIE).
SOBELL (MORTON).
SOLZHENITSYN (ALEKSANDR ISAEVICH).
SOREL (GEORGES).
SPAAK (PAUL HENRI).
SPEER (ALBERT).
SRAFFA (PIERO).
STAJIĆ (MIODRAG).
STALIN (IOSIF VISSARIONOVICH).
STARHEMBERG (GUNDAKER THOMAS) Graf.
STARZYŃSKI (STEFAN).
STENTON (DORIS MARY) Lady.
STEPHEN (GEORGE) 1st Baron Mount Stephen.
STEWARD (JULIAN HAYNES).
STEWART (FRANCES).
STOLYPIN (PETR ARKAD'EVICH).
STOPES (MARIE CARMICHAEL)
STROESSNER (ALFREDO).
STRUMILIN (STANISLAV GUSTAVOVICH).
STURZO (LUIGI).
STUTCHBURY (OLIVER PIERS).
SUMMERLIN (WILLIAM TALLEY).
SUN (YAT-SEN).
SVERDLOV (IAKOV MIKHAILOVICH).
SWAINSON (MARY).
SZWARCE (BRONISLAW)
TACITUS.
TAGÜEÑA LACORTE (MANUEL).
TAINE (HIPPOLYTE ADOLPHE).
TAK (PIETER LODEWIJK).
TARDY (LOUIS).
TAYLOR (FREDERICK WINSLOW).
THOMSON (ROY) Baron Thomson.
THYGESEN (ERIK).
TITO (JOSIP BROZ).
TIXIER-VIGNANCOUR (JEAN LOUIS).
TKACHEV (PETR NIKITICH).
TOGLIATTI (PALMIRO).
TORRIENTE Y BRAU (PABLO FELIX ALEJANDRO SALVADOR DE LA).
TOYOTOMI (HIDEYOSHI).
TREVELYAN (Sir CHARLES PHILIPS).
TROLLOPE (ANTHONY).
TROTSKII (LEV DAVYDOVICH).
TRUMAN (HARRY S.) President of the United States.
TSERETELI (IRAKLII GEORGIEVICH).
TURGOT (ANNE ROBERT JACQUES) Baron de l'Aulne.
TYABJI (BADRUDDIN).
TYLER (MARY).
URWICH (JOHANN).
VASCONCELOS (JOSE).
VERONESI (ENZO).
VOWELL (JOHN) otherwise HOOKER.
WALKER (Sir HERBERT ASHCOMBE).
WALLACE (GEORGE CORLEY).
WALLACE (HENRY AGARD).
WALLS (JOSIAH T.).
WARREN (EARL).
WATSON (JAMES) Radical.
WEBER (MAX).
WEBSTER (Sir CHARLES KINGSLEY).
WEEKS (JOHN).
WEHNER (HERBERT).
WEISBORD (VERA BUCH).
WENDEL (FRANÇOIS DE).
WIESENTHAL (SIMON).
WILBERFORCE (WILLIAM).
WILLIAM II, Emperor of Germany.
WILSON (BENJAMIN) Radical.
WILSON (EDMUND).
WILSON (WOODROW) President of the United States.
WITOS (WINCENTY).
WITTGENSTEIN (LUDWIG).
WOLFE (BILLY).
WOOD (MATTHEW).
ZAREMBA (PIOTR).

ZEHRER (HANS).
ZETKIN (CLARA).
ZHELIABOV (ANDREI IVANOVICH).
ZHIVKOV (TODOR).
ZHUKOV (GEORGII KONSTANTINOVICH).
ZWINGLI (ULRICH).

COMMERCE AND INDUSTRY.

General.

ACCOUNTING.
ACCOUNTING AND PRICE FLUCTUATIONS.
ADVERTISING.
APPLICATIONS FOR POSITIONS.
ARBITRATION, INDUSTRIAL.
AUDITING.
BALANCE OF TRADE
BIG BUSINESS.
BILLS OF LADING.
BUDGET IN BUSINESS.
BUSINESS.
BUSINESS AND POLITICS
BUSINESS CYCLES.
BUSINESS EDUCATION
BUSINESS FORECASTING.
BUSINESS RECORDS
CENTRAL AMERICAN COMMON MARKET.
CENTRAL BUSINESS DISTRICTS.
CHAMBERS OF COMMERCE
COMMERCE.
COMMERCIAL POLICY.
COMMERCIAL PRODUCTS.
COMMODITY CONTROL.
COMMODITY EXCHANGES.
COMMUNICATION IN MANAGEMENT
CONSOLIDATION AND MERGER OF CORPORATIONS
CONSUMER EDUCATION.
CONSUMER PROTECTION.
CONSUMERS.
CONSUMERS' PREFERENCES
CONTRACTS
COOPERATION.
COOPERATIVE MARKETING OF FARM PRODUCE
COOPERATIVE SOCIETIES
CORPORATION REPORTS.
CORPORATIONS.
CORPORATIONS, AMERICAN.
CORPORATIONS, BRITISH
CORPORATIONS, FOREIGN.
CORPORATIONS, INTERNATIONAL.
CORPORATIONS, JAPANESE.
CORPORATIONS, PUBLIC.
DANGEROUS GOODS
DISCLOSURE IN ACCOUNTING.
DIVERSIFICATION IN INDUSTRY.
EAST-WEST TRADE (1945-).
EFFICIENCY, INDUSTRIAL.
ELECTRONIC DATA PROCESSING IN VOCATIONAL GUIDANCE.
EMPLOYEE MORALE.
EMPLOYEE OWNERSHIP.
EMPLOYEES, DISMISSAL OF
EMPLOYEES, TRAINING OF
EMPLOYEES' REPRESENTATION IN MANAGEMENT.
EMPLOYERS' ASSOCIATIONS
EMPLOYMENT FORECASTING
EMPLOYMENT MANAGEMENT.
EUROPEAN ECONOMIC COMMUNITY.
EUROPEAN FREE TRADE ASSOCIATION
EXECUTIVES, TRAINING OF
EXPORT CREDIT.
FACTORY INSPECTION
FACTORY SYSTEM
FAMILY CORPORATIONS
FIRMS
FOREIGN TRADE PROMOTION

FOREIGN TRADE REGULATION.
GOVERNMENT BUSINESS ENTERPRISES
HANDICRAFT
HAZARDOUS SUBSTANCES
HOLDING COMPANIES
IMPERIAL PREFERENCE.
IMPORT QUOTAS
INCENTIVES IN INDUSTRY.
INDUSTRIAL ACCIDENTS
INDUSTRIAL CAPACITY
INDUSTRIAL CONCENTRATION.
INDUSTRIAL DISTRICTS
INDUSTRIAL HYGIENE.
INDUSTRIAL MANAGEMENT.
INDUSTRIAL ORGANIZATION.
INDUSTRIAL PROCUREMENT.
INDUSTRIAL PROMOTION
INDUSTRIAL PROPERTY.
INDUSTRIAL PSYCHIATRY.
INDUSTRIAL RELATIONS.
INDUSTRIAL SAFETY
INDUSTRIAL STATISTICS.
INDUSTRIALIZATION.
INDUSTRIES, LOCATION OF.
INDUSTRY.
INDUSTRY AND EDUCATION.
INDUSTRY AND STATE.
INFLATION (FINANCE) AND ACCOUNTING.
INTERNATIONAL BUSINESS ENTERPRISES.
INTERSTATE COMMERCE
JOINT ADVENTURES
LICENCE SYSTEM
LOMÉ, CONVENTION OF.
MACHINERY IN INDUSTRY.
MANAGEMENT.
MANAGEMENT INFORMATION SYSTEMS.
MANAGERIAL ACCOUNTING.
MANAGERIAL ECONOMICS.
MARKETING.
MARKETING MANAGEMENT.
MARKETING RESEARCH.
MARKETS
MINORITY BUSINESS ENTERPRISES
NEGOTIATION.
NEGROES AS BUSINESSMEN.
NEGROES AS CONSUMERS.
NEW PRODUCTS.
OCCUPATIONAL MOBILITY
OCCUPATIONAL TRAINING
OFFICES
OPERATIONS RESEARCH.
ORGANIZATION OF THE PETROLEUM EXPORTING COUNTRIES.
PACKAGING.
PATENTS.
PEDLARS AND PEDDLING
PERFORMANCE.
PIPE LINES
POOR AS CONSUMERS
POWER (MECHANICS).
POWER RESOURCES.
PRIVATE COMPANIES
PRODUCT MANAGEMENT.
PRODUCTION PLANNING.
PRODUCTIVITY.
PROFESSIONS
PUBLIC CONTRACTS
PUBLIC UTILITIES
QUALITY CONTROL.
RAW MATERIALS.
RECRUITING OF EMPLOYEES
RECYCLING (WASTE, ETC.).
RESEARCH, INDUSTRIAL.
RESEARCH AND DEVELOPMENT CONTRACTS.
RESTAURANT MANAGEMENT.
RETAIL TRADE.
ROADSIDE MARKETING.
SHOPPING
SMALL BUSINESS

STANDARDIZED TERMS OF CONTRACT
STORE LOCATION
TIME ALLOCATION.
TRADE MARKS
TURNOVER (BUSINESS)
UNITED NATIONS CONFERENCE ON
   TRADE AND DEVELOPMENT.
VOCATIONAL GUIDANCE.
VOCATIONAL REHABILITATION
WELFARE WORK IN INDUSTRY
WHOLESALE TRADE
WOOD AS FUEL.
WORK DESIGN.
WORK MEASUREMENT.
WORKMEN'S COMPENSATION

Occupations and professions.

AGRICULTURAL LABOURERS.
ARTISANS
AUTOMOBILE INDUSTRY WORKERS
BAKERY EMPLOYEES
BANK EMPLOYEES
BLACKSMITHS
BOOKBINDERS
BUSINESS CONSULTANTS.
BUSINESSMEN
CAPITALISTS AND FINANCIERS
CARTOGRAPHERS.
CLERGY
CLERKS
CLOTHING WORKERS
COAL MINERS.
COFFEE PLANTATION WORKERS
DIPLOMATS
DIPLOMATS, RUSSIAN
DIRECTORS OF CORPORATIONS
DOCK WORKERS
ELECTRIC INDUSTRY WORKERS
ELECTRONIC DATA PROCESSING
   PERSONNEL
ENGINEERING AS A PROFESSION.
ENGINEERS
EXECUTIVES
FARMERS
FISHERMEN
FLORISTS
FOREMEN
GOLD MINERS
IRON AND STEEL WORKERS
JOURNALISTS
JUDGES.
LAWYERS
LIBRARIANS.
MEDICAL PERSONNEL.
MERCHANTS, BRITISH.
MERCHANTS, ITALIAN.
METAL WORKERS
MILITARY SERVICE AS A PROFESSION.
MINERS
NURSES AND NURSING.
PAPER INDUSTRY WORKERS
PARAPROFESSIONALS IN SOCIAL
   SERVICE
PETROLEUM WORKERS
PHYSICIANS
PRINTERS
ROAD TRANSPORT WORKERS
SALES PERSONNEL
SALT WORKERS
SEAMEN
SERVANTS
SHOEMAKERS
SHOP ASSISTANTS
SOCIAL WORK AS A PROFESSION.
SUGAR WORKERS
SYSTEM ANALYSTS.
TEACHERS
TEXTILE WORKERS
TINKERS
TRANSPORT WORKERS

TRAVEL AGENTS
WEAVERS
WOMEN IN BUSINESS.
WOMEN IN THE MOTION PICTURE
   INDUSTRY.
WOMEN IN THE TELEVISION INDUSTRY.

Particular trades and industries.

AEROPLANE INDUSTRY AND TRADE
AEROSPACE INDUSTRIES
ALCOHOL.
ALUMINIUM INDUSTRY AND TRADE
ATOMIC POWER INDUSTRY
ATOMIC POWER PLANTS
AUTOMOBILE INDUSTRY AND TRADE
BAKERS AND BAKERIES
BANANA TRADE
BICYCLE INDUSTRY
BOOK INDUSTRIES AND TRADE.
BOOKSELLERS AND BOOKSELLING
BOOTS AND SHOES
BRICK TRADE
BUILDING
BUILDING, BRICK.
BUILDING MATERIALS INDUSTRY
BUILDINGS.
CARDS.
CARRIAGE AND WAGON MAKING
CATTLE TRADE
CEMENT INDUSTRIES
CHEESE INDUSTRY
CHEMICAL INDUSTRIES.
CHEMICALS
CIDER.
CLAY INDUSTRIES
CLEANING COMPOUNDS
CLOCKS AND WATCHES
CLOTHING TRADE
COAL
COAL MINES AND MINING
COCOA TRADE.
COMPUTER INDUSTRY
CONSTRUCTION INDUSTRY
COOPERS AND COOPERAGE
COPPER MINES AND MINING
COTTAGE INDUSTRIES
COTTON MANUFACTURE
COTTON TRADE
DRUG TRADE.
ELECTRIC ENGINEERING
ELECTRIC INDUSTRIES
ELECTRIC POWER DISTRIBUTION
ELECTRIC POWER PLANTS
ELECTRICITY SUPPLY
ELECTRONIC DATA PROCESSING.
ELECTRONIC DATA PROCESSING
   DEPARTMENTS.
ELECTRONIC DIGITAL COMPUTERS.
ELECTRONIC INDUSTRIES
ENGINEERING
EXPLOSIVES.
FERTILIZER INDUSTRY.
FIREARMS INDUSTRY AND TRADE
FOOD INDUSTRY AND TRADE
FOOD SUPPLY.
GAS
GAS, NATURAL
GAS, NATURAL, IN SUBMERGED LANDS
GAS INDUSTRY
GLASS INDUSTRY AND TRADE
GOLD MINES AND MINING
GRAIN TRADE
GROCERY TRADE
GUANO.
HANDLOOM INDUSTRY
HOTELS, TAVERNS, ETC.
IRON INDUSTRY AND TRADE
IRON MINES AND MINING
IRON-WORKS
JEWELLERY TRADE

JUTE INDUSTRY
LEAD INDUSTRY AND TRADE
LEAD MINES AND MINING
LEATHER INDUSTRY AND TRADE.
LIMESTONE
LINEN
LIQUEFIED PETROLEUM GAS INDUSTRY
LIQUOR TRAFFIC
MACHINE-TOOLS
MAP INDUSTRY AND TRADE
MEAT INDUSTRY AND TRADE
MECHANICAL ENGINEERING
MERCURY
METAL TRADE
METAL WORK.
MILK SUPPLY
MILK TRADE
MINERAL INDUSTRIES
MINES AND MINERAL RESOURCES
MINES AND MINING
MINING CORPORATIONS
MINING INDUSTRY AND FINANCE
MOVING PICTURE INDUSTRY
MUNITIONS.
NAILS AND SPIKES.
NEWS AGENCIES
NEWSPAPER PUBLISHING
NUCLEAR FUELS.
PAPER MAKING AND TRADE
PERRY.
PETROL.
PETROLEUM
PETROLEUM CHEMICALS INDUSTRY
PETROLEUM IN SUBMERGED LANDS.
PETROLEUM INDUSTRY AND TRADE.
PETROLEUM PRODUCTS
PETROLEUM REFINERIES
PETROLEUM WASTE
PHARMACY
PHOSPHATE INDUSTRY.
PORK INDUSTRY AND TRADE
PORTLAND CEMENT.
POULTRY INDUSTRY
PRINTING INDUSTRY
PRODUCE TRADE
PUBLISHERS AND PUBLISHING
PULQUE
QUARRIES AND QUARRYING
RADIO INDUSTRY AND TRADE
REACTOR FUEL REPROCESSING.
REAL ESTATE BUSINESS
RUBBER INDUSTRY AND TRADE
SERVICE INDUSTRIES
SEWING MACHINE INDUSTRY
SHIPBUILDING
SILVER MINES AND MINING
STEAM ENGINES.
STEEL
STEEL INDUSTRY AND TRADE
STRIP MINING
SUGAR TRADE.
SULPHUR.
TANNING.
TEA TRADE
TEXTILE INDUSTRY AND FABRICS
TILES
TIN INDUSTRY
TIN MINES AND MINING
TOURIST TRADE
URANIUM MINES AND MINING
WATER DISTRICTS
WATER POWER ELECTRIC PLANTS
WINE AND WINE MAKING.
WOOD-USING INDUSTRIES
WOOL TRADE AND INDUSTRY

ECONOMICS.

see also AGRICULTURE; COMMERCE
AND INDUSTRY; FINANCE;
TRANSPORT

ABSENTEEISM (LABOUR)
ACCIDENTS
ADMINISTRATION OF ESTATES
AFFIRMATIVE ACTION PROGRAMMES
AFRICANIZATION
AGE AND EMPLOYMENT
ALIEN LABOUR
ALIEN LABOUR, FILIPINO.
ALIEN LABOUR, MEXICAN
ANDEAN GROUP.
AUSTRIAN SCHOOL OF ECONOMISTS.
BRAIN DRAIN.
BREAD.
CAPITALISM.
CHRISTIANITY AND ECONOMICS.
CHURCH AND LABOUR
COLLECTIVE BARGAINING.
COLLECTIVE LABOUR AGREEMENTS
COMPAGNONNAGES.
COMPETITION.
COMPETITION, INTERNATIONAL.
CONSUMPTION (ECONOMICS).
CONVICT LABOUR
CORPORATE PLANNING.
COST.
COST AND STANDARD OF LIVING
COST EFFECTIVENESS.
COSTS, INDUSTRIAL
COUNCIL FOR MUTUAL ECONOMIC
    ASSISTANCE.
COUNCIL OF ARAB ECONOMIC UNITY.
CRISES.
DISCRIMINATION IN EMPLOYMENT
DISTRIBUTION (ECONOMIC THEORY).
DIVISION OF LABOUR.
DOMESTIC ECONOMY
ECONOMIC ASSISTANCE.
ECONOMIC ASSISTANCE, AMERICAN.
ECONOMIC ASSISTANCE, BRITISH
ECONOMIC ASSISTANCE, CHINESE.
ECONOMIC ASSISTANCE, COMMUNIST.
ECONOMIC ASSISTANCE, DANISH.
ECONOMIC ASSISTANCE, DOMESTIC
ECONOMIC ASSISTANCE, DUTCH.
ECONOMIC ASSISTANCE, EUROPEAN.
ECONOMIC ASSISTANCE, FRENCH.
ECONOMIC ASSISTANCE, KUWAITI
ECONOMIC ASSISTANCE, RUSSIAN.
ECONOMIC ASSISTANCE IN AFRICA.
ECONOMIC ASSISTANCE IN LATIN
    AMERICA.
ECONOMIC ASSISTANCE IN MALAWI.
ECONOMIC ASSISTANCE IN NEPAL.
ECONOMIC ASSISTANCE IN RUSSIA.
ECONOMIC ASSISTANCE IN TANZANIA.
ECONOMIC ASSISTANCE IN ZAMBIA.
ECONOMIC CONDITIONS.
ECONOMIC DEVELOPMENT.
ECONOMIC FORECASTING.
ECONOMIC HISTORY.
ECONOMIC INDICATORS
ECONOMIC LEGISLATION.
ECONOMIC POLICY.
ECONOMIC RESEARCH.
ECONOMIC STABILIZATION.
ECONOMIC SURVEYS
ECONOMIC ZONING
ECONOMICS.
ECONOMICS, COMPARATIVE.
ECONOMICS, MATHEMATICAL.
ECONOMICS, PRIMITIVE.
ECONOMISTS.
EIGHT HOUR MOVEMENT.
ELASTICITY (ECONOMICS).
EMPLOYMENT (ECONOMIC THEORY).
ENERGY CONSUMPTION.

ENERGY POLICY.
ENTREPRENEUR.
ENVIRONMENTAL IMPACT STATEMENTS.
ENVIRONMENTAL POLICY.
ENVIRONMENTAL POLICY RESEARCH
ENVIRONMENTAL PROTECTION.
EQUAL PAY FOR EQUAL WORK
EQUALITY.
EQUILIBRIUM (ECONOMICS).
EXCHANGE.
EXTERNALITIES (ECONOMICS).
FAMILY ALLOWANCES
FERTILITY, HUMAN.
FOOD CONSUMPTION
FOREIGN EXCHANGE PROBLEM
FREE CHOICE OF EMPLOYMENT
FREE TRADE AND PROTECTION.
FUEL
FULL EMPLOYMENT POLICIES.
GENERAL AGREEMENT ON TARIFFS AND
    TRADE.
GENERAL STRIKE.
GENERAL STRIKE, SOUTH AFRICA, 1913.
GENERAL STRIKE, UNITED KINGDOM,
    1926.
GENERAL STRIKE, URUGUAY, 1973.
GEOGRAPHY, ECONOMIC.
GIFTS
GILDS
GOVERNMENT OWNERSHIP
GOVERNMENT PURCHASING
GOVERNMENT SPENDING POLICY
GRIEVANCE PROCEDURES.
GROSS DOMESTIC PRODUCT
GROSS NATIONAL PRODUCT.
HOMOSEXUALITY AND EMPLOYMENT
HOSPITALITY
HOURS OF LABOUR.
HOUSE BUYING.
HOUSING.
HOUSING, RURAL
HOUSING AND HEALTH
HOUSING MANAGEMENT.
HOUSING POLICY.
HOUSING RESEARCH.
HOUSING SUBSIDIES
HOUSING SURVEYS.
HUMAN CAPITAL
INCOME
INCOME DISTRIBUTION.
INCOME MAINTENANCE PROGRAMMES.
INDEX NUMBERS (ECONOMICS).
INDEXATION (ECONOMICS).
INSTITUTIONAL ECONOMICS.
INTEREST AND USURY
INTERINDUSTRY ECONOMICS.
INTERNATIONAL ECONOMIC
    INTEGRATION.
INTERNATIONAL ECONOMIC
    RELATIONS.
INTERNATIONAL LABOUR
    ORGANISATION.
JOB ANALYSIS.
JOB EVALUATION.
JOB SATISFACTION.
JOB VACANCIES
LABOUR AND LABOURING CLASSES.
LABOUR CONTRACT
LABOUR COSTS
LABOUR DISPUTES
LABOUR ECONOMICS.
LABOUR MOBILITY.
LABOUR POLICY
LABOUR SERVICE
LABOUR SUPPLY.
LAISSEZ-FAIRE.
LAND.
LAND, NATIONALIZATION OF
LAND REFORM.
LAND TENURE.
LEAVE OF ABSENCE
LUXURY.

MALTHUSIANISM.
MANPOWER POLICY.
MARXIAN ECONOMICS.
MASS MEDIA AND TRADE UNIONS
MEDICAL CARE, COST OF
MIGRANT LABOUR.
MONOPOLIES.
MULTIPLIER (ECONOMICS).
NOISE POLLUTION.
NON-WAGE PAYMENTS
OLIGOPOLIES.
OPEN AND CLOSED SHOP
PART-TIME EMPLOYMENT
PENSION TRUSTS
PENSIONS
PENSIONS, MILITARY
PICKETING
POLLUTION.
POPULATION.
POPULATION POLICY.
POPULATION RESEARCH.
PRESCRIPTION PRICING
PRICE DISCRIMINATION.
PRICE INDEXES.
PRICE MAINTENANCE.
PRICE POLICY.
PRICE REGULATION
PRICES.
PRODUCTION (ECONOMIC THEORY).
PRODUCTION FUNCTIONS (ECONOMIC
    THEORY).
PROFIT.
PROFIT SHARING.
PROPERTY.
PROTESTANTISM AND CAPITALISM.
PUBLIC HOUSING
PUBLIC LANDS.
REAL PROPERTY
REGIONAL DEVELOPMENT
REGIONAL ECONOMICS.
RENT
RENT CONTROL.
RENT SUBSIDIES
RESTRAINT OF TRADE
RETRAINING, OCCUPATIONAL
RIGHT OF PROPERTY.
RIGHT TO LABOUR.
RISK.
RURAL DEVELOPMENT.
SABOTAGE.
SALARIED EMPLOYEES
SERVICE, COMPULSORY NON-MILITARY
SEX DISCRIMINATION IN EMPLOYMENT.
SHOP STEWARDS
SIT DOWN STRIKES
SKILLED LABOUR
SOCIALIST COMPETITION.
SPACE IN ECONOMICS.
STRIKES AND LOCKOUTS.
SUBSIDIES
SUPPLY AND DEMAND.
SURVIVORS' BENEFITS
SYSTEM ANALYSIS.
TECHNICAL ASSISTANCE.
TECHNICAL ASSISTANCE, AMERICAN.
TECHNICAL ASSISTANCE, BRITISH.
TECHNICAL ASSISTANCE, GERMAN
TECHNICAL ASSISTANCE IN LATIN
    AMERICA.
TECHNOCRACY.
TIME AND ECONOMIC REACTIONS.
TIME AND MOTION STUDY.
TRADE AND PROFESSIONAL
    ASSOCIATIONS
TRADE UNIONS.
TRADE UNIONS, CATHOLIC
TRADE UNIONS AND COMMUNISM.
TRADE UNIONS AND FOREIGN POLICY
TRANSFER PRICING.
TRUSTS, INDUSTRIAL
UNDERDEVELOPED AREAS.
UNEMPLOYED.

UNEMPLOYMENT, TECHNOLOGICAL.
UNFAIR LABOUR PRACTICES
UNITED NATIONS ECONOMIC
    COMMISSION FOR EUROPE.
UNITED NATIONS ECONOMIC
    COMMISSION FOR LATIN AMERICA.
UNSKILLED LABOUR
URBAN ECONOMICS.
UTILITY THEORY.
VALUE.
WAGE PAYMENT SYSTEMS
WAGE SURVEYS.
WAGE-PRICE POLICY.
WAGES.
WAGES AND PRODUCTIVITY
WEALTH.
WELFARE ECONOMICS.
WHITE COLLAR WORKERS.
WOMEN IN TRADE UNIONS
WORK.
WORKS COUNCILS

EDUCATION.

General.

AFRICAN STUDIES
AUDIO-VISUAL EDUCATION
BUSINESS EDUCATION
CATHOLIC SCHOOLS
CHINESE STUDIES
CHURCH SCHOOLS
COLLEGE COSTS
COMMUNISM AND EDUCATION.
COMMUNIST EDUCATION.
COMMUNITY AND SCHOOL.
COMPUTER ASSISTED INSTRUCTION.
DISCRIMINATION IN EDUCATION
DISSERTATIONS, ACADEMIC
EDUCATION.
EDUCATION, COMPARATIVE.
EDUCATION, ELEMENTARY
EDUCATION, HIGHER.
EDUCATION, PRESCHOOL
EDUCATION, RURAL
EDUCATION, SECONDARY
EDUCATION, URBAN
EDUCATION AND STATE
EDUCATION OF ADULTS.
EDUCATION OF WOMEN
EDUCATIONAL ASSISTANCE.
EDUCATIONAL ASSOCIATIONS
EDUCATIONAL EQUALIZATION.
EDUCATIONAL INNOVATIONS.
EDUCATIONAL LAW AND LEGISLATION
EDUCATIONAL PLANNING.
EDUCATIONAL PSYCHOLOGY.
EDUCATIONAL PUBLISHING
EDUCATIONAL RESEARCH.
EDUCATIONAL SOCIOLOGY.
EDUCATIONAL TECHNOLOGY
EDUCATIONAL VOUCHERS
EDUCATORS
EUROPEAN STUDIES.
EVENING AND CONTINUATION SCHOOLS
EXAMINATIONS
FEDERAL AID TO EDUCATION
GRADING AND MARKING (STUDENTS).
GRADUATES
HANDICAPPED CHILDREN
HEALTH EDUCATION.
HOME AND SCHOOL.
HUMANITIES
ILLITERACY
INDIVIDUALIZED INSTRUCTION.
INDUSTRY AND EDUCATION.
INTELLECTUAL LIFE.
INTELLECTUALS.
INTERCULTURAL EDUCATION.
LATIN AMERICAN STUDIES.
LEARNING, PSYCHOLOGY OF.

LIBRARIES, UNIVERSITY AND COLLEGE
LIBRARIES AND EDUCATION
MILITARY EDUCATION.
MORAL EDUCATION.
ORIENTAL STUDIES
PERCEPTUAL-MOTOR LEARNING.
PERSONNEL SERVICE IN EDUCATION
POLITICS AND EDUCATION.
PRIVATE SCHOOLS
SCHOLARLY PUBLISHING
SCHOLARSHIPS
SCHOOL CHILDREN
SCHOOL INTEGRATION
SCHOOL MANAGEMENT AND
    ORGANIZATION
SCHOOL SOCIAL WORK
SCHOOLS
SEGREGATION IN EDUCATION
SEX DISCRIMINATION IN EDUCATION
SEX INSTRUCTION.
SINGAPORE STUDENTS IN IRELAND
    (REPUBLIC).
SINGAPORE STUDENTS IN THE UNITED
    KINGDOM.
SOCIAL WORK EDUCATION.
SOCIALISM AND EDUCATION.
STATE AID TO PRIVATE SCHOOLS
STUDENT AID
STUDENT COUNSELLORS.
STUDENT TEACHERS
STUDENTS
STUDENTS, PART-TIME
STUDENTS, RATING OF
STUDENTS FOR A DEMOCRATIC
    SOCIETY.
STUDENTS' SOCIETIES
STUDENTS' SOCIO-ECONOMIC STATUS
SUBURBAN SCHOOLS
TEACHERS, TRAINING OF
TEACHERS' COLLEGES
TEACHERS' UNIONS
TEACHING.
TEACHING, FREEDOM OF.
TECHNICAL EDUCATION.
UKRAINIAN STUDIES.
UNITED NATIONS EDUCATIONAL,
    SCIENTIFIC AND CULTURAL
    ORGANIZATION
UNIVERSITIES AND COLLEGES.
VOCATIONAL EDUCATION.

Educational institutions.

COIMBRA UNIVERSITY.
COLEGIO DE SANTA CRUZ DE
    TLATELOLCO.
COLUMBIA UNIVERSITY.
DAKAR UNIVERSITY.
DARTINGTON HALL SCHOOL.
EDMONTON GIRLS CHARITY SCHOOL.
ILLINOIS STATE UNIVERSITY.
KAZAN' UNIVERSITY.
LONDON UNIVERSITY.
SUMMERHILL ACADEMY, ABERDEEN.
UNIVERSITY OF THE NORTH.
WARWICK UNIVERSITY.
WILLIAM TYNDALE JUNIOR AND
    INFANTS SCHOOLS.
YENCHING UNIVERSITY.

FINANCE.

General.

AGRICULTURAL CREDIT
BALANCE OF PAYMENTS.
BANK HOLDING COMPANIES
BANK INVESTMENTS
BANK RESERVES
BANKRUPTCY

BANKS AND BANKING.
BANKS AND BANKING, CENTRAL.
BANKS AND BANKING, COOPERATIVE
BANKS AND BANKING, FOREIGN
BANKS AND BANKING, INTERNATIONAL.
BANKS AND BANKING, TRADE UNION
BUDGET.
BUSINESS TAX
CAPITAL.
CAPITAL ASSETS PRICING MODEL.
CAPITAL BUDGET.
CAPITAL GAINS TAX
CAPITAL INVESTMENTS.
CAPITAL LEVY
CAPITAL MOVEMENTS.
COINAGE
COLLEGE COSTS
COMMERCIAL FINANCE COMPANIES
CONSUMER CREDIT
COST ACCOUNTING.
CREDIT.
CUSTOMS ADMINISTRATION
CUSTOMS UNIONS.
DEBTS, EXTERNAL
DEBTS, PUBLIC
DEVELOPMENT BANKS.
DEVELOPMENT CREDIT CORPORATIONS
DISCOUNT
EMIGRANT REMITTANCES
EURODOLLAR MARKET.
EUROPEAN REGIONAL DEVELOPMENT
    FUND.
EXPENDITURES, PUBLIC.
EXPORT CREDIT.
FINANCE.
FINANCIAL INSTITUTIONS
FINANCIAL STATEMENTS
FLOW OF FUNDS
FOREIGN EXCHANGE.
FORWARD EXCHANGE.
FRIENDLY SOCIETIES
GOLD.
GOLD STANDARD.
GOVERNMENT LENDING
GRANTS-IN-AID
INCOME TAX.
INDUSTRIAL DEVELOPMENT BONDS
INFLATION (FINANCE).
INFLATION (FINANCE) AND
    ACCOUNTING.
INFLATION (FINANCE) AND TAXATION
INHERITANCE AND TRANSFER TAX.
INSIDER TRADING IN SECURITIES
INSURANCE.
INSURANCE, ACCIDENT
INSURANCE, AGRICULTURAL
INSURANCE, AUTOMOBILE
INSURANCE, DISABILITY
INSURANCE, EXPORT CREDIT
INSURANCE, GOVERNMENT
INSURANCE, HEALTH
INSURANCE, INDUSTRIAL
INSURANCE, INVESTMENT GUARANTY.
INSURANCE, LIFE
INSURANCE, MARINE
INSURANCE, MATERNITY
INSURANCE, SOCIAL.
INSURANCE, UNEMPLOYMENT
INSURANCE COMPANIES
INTERGOVERNMENTAL FISCAL
    RELATIONS
INTERGOVERNMENTAL TAX RELATIONS
INTERNATIONAL FINANCE.
INTERNATIONAL LIQUIDITY.
INVESTMENT ANALYSIS.
INVESTMENT OF PUBLIC FUNDS.
INVESTMENT TRUSTS
INVESTMENTS.
INVESTMENTS, AMERICAN.
INVESTMENTS, BRITISH
INVESTMENTS, FOREIGN.
INVESTMENTS, GERMAN.

FINANCE(Cont.)

INVESTMENTS, JAPANESE.
INVESTMENTS, SWEDISH
LOCAL FINANCE
LOCAL TAXATION
METROPOLITAN FINANCE
MONETARY POLICY.
MONETARY UNIONS.
MONEY.
MONEY SUPPLY
MORTGAGE LOANS
MORTGAGES
MUNICIPAL FINANCE
NATIONAL INCOME.
NEGATIVE INCOME TAX
PAPER MONEY
PAYMENT
POSTAL SAVINGS BANKS
POUND, BRITISH.
PROFITS TAX
PROGRAMME BUDGETING
PROPERTY TAX.
REAL ESTATE INVESTMENT
REAL PROPERTY TAX
RECONSTRUCTION FINANCE
   CORPORATION.
REVENUE SHARING
RISK (INSURANCE).
SAVING AND INVESTMENT
SECURITIES
SPECIAL ASSESSMENTS
STAMP DUTIES
STOCK EXCHANGE
TARIFFS.
TAX ACCOUNTING.
TAX DEDUCTIONS
TAX PLANNING.
TAXATION.
TURNOVER TAX
WORKING CAPITAL.

Banks, exchanges, etc.

BANCO DE MEXICO.
BANCO DE PORTUGAL.
BANK OF CANADA.
BANK OF THE NETHERLANDS.
BANQUE DE FRANCE.
BANQUE NATIONALE DE BELGIQUE.
CENTRAL AMERICAN BANK FOR
   ECONOMIC INTEGRATION.
EXPORT-IMPORT BANK OF THE UNITED
   STATES.
INTER-AMERICAN DEVELOPMENT BANK.
INTERNATIONAL CENTRE FOR
   SETTLEMENT OF INVESTMENT
   DISPUTES.
INTERNATIONAL MONETARY FUND.
REICHSBANK.
ROYAL BANK OF SCOTLAND.
UGANDA COMMERCIAL BANK.

GEOGRAPHY, GEOLOGY AND METEOROLOGY.

General.

AIR
ANTARCTIC REGIONS.
ANTHROPOGEOGRAPHY.
ARID REGIONS.
ARTESIAN BASINS
ATLASES.
CARTOGRAPHY.
CENTRAL PLACES.
CITIES AND TOWNS.
COASTAL ZONE MANAGEMENT
CONSERVATION OF NATURAL
   RESOURCES.
CONTINENTAL SHELF
DESERTS

DROUGHTS
EARTHQUAKES
ECOLOGY.
ENERGY CONSERVATION.
EUROPEAN ECONOMIC COMMUNITY
   ASSOCIATED COUNTRIES.
GEOGRAPHICAL PERCEPTION.
GEOGRAPHY.
GEOGRAPHY, ECONOMIC.
GEOGRAPHY, MATHEMATICAL.
GEOLOGY
GEOMORPHOLOGY.
GEOPOLITICS.
GLACIAL LANDFORMS
HUMAN ECOLOGY.
HUMAN ENGINEERING.
HYDROGRAPHY
LAND.
LANDSCAPE.
LANDSCAPE PROTECTION
MARINE RESOURCES
MICROCLIMATOLOGY
MINERAL RESOURCES IN SUBMERGED
   LANDS.
MINERAL WATERS
MOUNTAINS
NAMES, GEOGRAPHICAL.
NATIONAL PARKS AND RESERVES
NATURAL RESOURCES.
NATURE CONSERVATION
NEW TOWNS.
PHYSICAL GEOGRAPHY
POLLUTION.
RADIOACTIVE POLLUTION.
REGIONAL PLANNING.
RESIDENTIAL MOBILITY
RIVERS
RURAL GEOGRAPHY.
SOIL MOISTURE
SPRINGS
SURVEYING
UNITED NATIONS ENVIRONMENT
   PROGRAMME.
URBAN RENEWAL.
URBANIZATION.
VOYAGES AND TRAVELS.
WATER
WATER CONSUMPTION
WATER QUALITY MANAGEMENT
WATER RESOURCES DEVELOPMENT
WATER SUPPLY
ZONING

Rocks, minerals, etc.

BAUXITE.
CLAY
FELDSPAR
SLATE
URANIUM ORES

Individual countries and places

Africa

AFRICA.
AFRICA, CENTRAL
AFRICA, EAST
AFRICA, NORTH
AFRICA, SUBSAHARAN
AFRICA, WEST
ALGERIA
ANGOLA
ARAB COUNTRIES.
BOPHUTHATSWANA
BOTSWANA
BURUNDI
CAMEROUN
CHAD
CISKEI

DOUALA
EAST LONDON
EGYPT
EQUATORIAL GUINEA
ETHIOPIA
GABON
GAMBIA
GAZANKULU
GHANA
GUINEA-BISSAU
IVORY COAST
KENYA
KITALE
KWAZULU
LEBOWA
LIBERIA
LIBYA
LUANDA
LUBUMBASHI
MADAGASCAR
MALAWI
MALI (REPUBLIC)
MALINDI
MANIEMA.
MAURITANIA
MAURITIUS
MBAGUTA.
MOROCCO
MOZAMBIQUE
NAIROBI
NIGER VALLEY.
NIGERIA
PORT ELIZABETH
PORTUGUESE GUINEA
RHODESIA
RUFA'A AL-HOI.
RWANDA
SALISBURY, RHODESIA
SAN PEDRO (IVORY COAST)
SÃO TOME E PRINCIPE
SENEGAL
SEYCHELLES
SIERRA LEONE
SOMALI REPUBLIC
SOUTH AFRICA
SOUTH WEST AFRICA.
SOWETO
SPANISH SAHARA
SUDAN
SWAZILAND
TANZANIA
TIMBUKTU
TRANSKEI.
TRANSVAAL
TUNISIA
UGANDA
UPPER VOLTA
VENDA
ZAIRE
ZAMBIA
ZANZIBAR

America, Latin.

AMAZON VALLEY
AMERICA
AMERICA, LATIN
ANDES REGION
ARGENTINE REPUBLIC
BARBADOS
BELIZE
BOLIVIA
BRAZIL
BRITISH VIRGIN ISLANDS
BUENOS AIRES (PROVINCE)
CARACAS (ARCHDIOCESE)
CARIBBEAN AREA
CAUCA VALLEY
CAYMAN ISLANDS
CHILE
CHIMBORAZO

COLOMBIA
CONDOTO
COQUIMBO
CUBA
CUZCO (DEPARTMENT)
DOMINICAN REPUBLIC
DUTCH GUIANA.
ECUADOR
FALKLAND ISLANDS.
GALAPAGOS (PROVINCE).
GRENADA
GUATEMALA
GUAYAS
GUYANA.
HAITI
HONDURAS
JAMAICA
MATO GROSSO
MEXICO
MEXICO CITY
MINAS GERAIS
NANACATLAN, MEXICO
NEW GRANADA (VICEROYALTY)
NICARAGUA
OAXACA
PANAMA
PARAGUAY
PATAGONIA
PERU
PICHINCHA
PUERTO RICO
PUSTUNICH, MEXICO
SANTA FE, ARGENTINA (PROVINCE)
SÃO PAULO (CITY)
TRINIDAD AND TOBAGO
TZINTZUNTZAN.
URUGUAY
VENEZUELA
WEST INDIES

America, North.

ALABAMA
ALASKA
ALBANY
ALBERTA
AMERICA
APPALACHIAN MOUNTAINS
BALTIMORE
BINGHAMTON METROPOLITAN AREA.
BOSTON, MASSACHUSETTS
BRITISH COLUMBIA
CALIFORNIA
CANADA.
CHICAGO
CLEVELAND, OHIO
COLUMBUS, OHIO
GEORGIA (UNITED STATES)
GREENLAND
HARPERS FERRY, WEST VIRGINIA
KENTUCKY
KINGSTON, ONTARIO
LABRADOR
LITTLE LAUREL
LOS ANGELES
LOUISIANA
MARYLAND
MILWAUKEE
MISSISSIPPI VALLEY
MONTREAL
NEW BRUNSWICK
NEW YORK (CITY)
NEW YORK (STATE)
NEWFOUNDLAND
NEWFOUNDLAND AND LABRADOR
NORTH CAROLINA
NORTH WEST TERRITORIES
NOVA SCOTIA
OHIO
OKLAHOMA
ONTARIO

PENNSYLVANIA
PHILADELPHIA
PRINCE EDWARD ISLAND
QUEBEC (PROVINCE)
RHODE ISLAND
SACRAMENTO
ST. JOHN'S
SAN FRANCISCO
SANTA BARBARA, CALIFORNIA
SANTA FE, NEW MEXICO
SASKATCHEWAN
SCHUYLKILL COUNTY
TORONTO
UNITED STATES.
VANCOUVER
VANCOUVER ISLAND
WINNIPEG
YAMASKA BASIN.
YUKON

Asia.

AFGHANISTAN
ARAB COUNTRIES.
ASIA
ASIA, SOUTHEAST
ASSAM
BALUCHISTAN
BANGLADESH.
BENGAL
BENGAL, WEST
BIHAR
BILLITON
BOMBAY (CITY)
BORNEO
BRUNEI
BUKHARA
BURMA
BURYAT REPUBLIC
CALCUTTA
CAMBODIA
CANTON
CHARDZHOU (OBLAST')
CHINA
CYPRUS
DACCA
DELHI (UNION TERRITORY)
EAST (FAR EAST)
EAST (NEAR EAST)
EILAT
GEORGIA
GOA, DAMAN AND DIU
GORNO-ALTAISK (OBLAST')
GUJARAT
HARYANA
HONG KONG
HUNAN, CHINA (PROVINCE)
INDIA.
INDIAN OCEAN REGION
INDOCHINA
INDONESIA
IRAN
IRAQ
ISRAEL
JAPAN.
JAVA
JERUSALEM
JORDAN
KAZAKSTAN
KERALA
KHOREZM PEOPLE'S SOVIET REPUBLIC
KIRGHIZIA
KOREA
KRASNOYARSK (KRAI)
KURGAN (OBLAST')
LEBANON
MADHYA BHARAT
MADRAS
MAHARASHTRA
MALAYA
MALAYSIA

MONGOLIA
MYSORE
NEPAL
OMAN
ORISSA
PAKISTAN
PALESTINE
PAMIR
PARACEL ISLANDS
PERSIAN GULF
PHILIPPINE ISLANDS
PRATAS ISLANDS
PUNJAB (PAKISTAN)
QATAR.
SABAH
SAIGON
SAKHALIN
SAMARKAND
SAR LUK, VIETNAM
SAUDI ARABIA
SAURASHTRA, INDIA (STATE)
SHIWA
SIBERIA
SINGAPORE
SOVIET CENTRAL ASIA
SPRATLY ISLANDS
SRI LANKA.
SUAKIN
SYRIA
TAIWAN
TAJIKISTAN
THAILAND
TURKESTAN
TURKEY
TURKMENISTAN
TUVA
UNITED ARAB EMIRATES.
UTTAR PRADESH
UZBEKISTAN
VIETNAM
YAKUTIA

Australia and Oceania.

AUCKLAND
AUSTRALIA
AUSTRALIAN CAPITAL TERRITORY
BELLONA ISLAND
CANBERRA
DARWIN
FIJI ISLANDS
GILBERT AND ELLICE ISLANDS COLONY
HAWAIIAN ISLANDS
IRIAN BARAT
NEW CALEDONIA
NEW GUINEA
NEW SOUTH WALES
NEW ZEALAND
NORTHERN TERRITORY
PACIFIC, THE
PAPUA NEW GUINEA
PERTH, WESTERN AUSTRALIA
PILBARA
POLYNESIA
PORT MORESBY
QUEENSLAND.
SAMOA
SOLOMON ISLANDS
SOUTH AUSTRALIA
SUNDA ISLANDS
SYDNEY
TASMANIA
TIMOR
TUVALU
VICTORIA, AUSTRALIA
WESTERN AUSTRALIA
WESTERN SAMOA

GEOGRAPHY, GEOLOGY AND METEOROLOGY(Cont.)

Europe.

AALST
ALBANIA
ALESSANDRIA (PROVINCE)
ANDALUSIA
ANTWERP
APULIA
ARNSBERG
ASTORGA
ATHENS
AUSTRIA
AUSTRIA-HUNGARY
AVIGNON.
AZERBAIJAN
BADEN
BAKU
BALKAN STATES
BALTIC STATES
BARCELONA
BASEL-LAND (CANTON)
BASHKIR REPUBLIC
BASQUE PROVINCES
BAVARIA
BELGIUM.
BERLIN
BESSARABIA
BOCHUM
BORDEAUX
BOSNIA
BRANDENBURG (PROVINCE)
BREMEN
BRESCIA
BRITTANY
BRUSON
BUCIUMI.
BULGARIA
CALABRIA
CARINTHIA
CASTILE
CATALONIA
CAUCASUS
COMO (CITY)
COPENHAGEN
CORSICA
CRACOW
CROATIA
CZECHOSLOVAKIA
DAGHESTAN
DALMATIA
DANUBE VALLEY
DENMARK
DIJON
DONAUWOERTH
DUBLIN
DUERO
DUESSELDORF
ESTONIA
EUROPE
EUROPE, EASTERN
EUROPEAN ECONOMIC COMMUNITY
  COUNTRIES
EUROPEAN FREE TRADE ASSOCIATION
  COUNTRIES
FERRARA
FINLAND
FLORENCE
FRANCE.
FRANKFURT AM MAIN
GALICIA (SPAIN)
GENOA
GERMANY
GERMANY, EASTERN
GIBRALTAR
GIETRZWAŁD
GIRONDE
GOEPPINGEN
GOMEL' (OBLAST')
GOR'KII (OBLAST')
GOTHENBURG
GREECE
GREENE, LOWER SAXONY

GUERNICA
HAGUE
HAINAUT
HAMBORN
HAMBURG
HUNGARY
ICELAND
IRELAND (REPUBLIC)
ITALY
KABARDINO-BALKARIAN REPUBLIC
KALMYK REPUBLIC
KARACHAI-CHERKESS AUTONOMOUS
  OBLAST'
KARELIA
KHERSON (OBLAST')
KLAIPEDA
LATVIA
LEIPZIG
LEMGO
LENINGRAD
LIEGE (PROVINCE)
LILLE.
LIMBURG (PROVINCE)
LIMOUSIN
LINZ
LIPPE
LITHUANIA
ŁÓDŹ
LOMBARDY
LORRAINE
LOT VALLEY.
LUBLIN
LUCCA
LUDWIGSBURG
LUND
LUSATIA
LUXEMBOURG
L'VOV
MADEIRA
MADRID
MAJORCA
MALMÖ
MALTA
MARI REPUBLIC
MEDITERRANEAN
MOLDAVIA
MOLDAVIAN REPUBLIC
MONTAILLOU
MOSCOW
MOSCOW (OBLAST')
MUENSTER
MURMANSK (OBLAST')
NANTES
NETHERLANDS
NEUBURG
NEUCHÂTEL (CANTON)
NORD (DEPARTMENT)
NORMANDY
NORRLAND
NORTH OSSETIAN REPUBLIC
NORTH RHINE-WESTPHALIA
NORWAY
NUREMBERG
ODER RIVER.
PARIS
PERPIGNAN.
PISTOIA (PROVINCE)
POLAND
POLESIE
PORTO MARGHERA
PORTUGAL.
POZNAŃ
PRUSSIA
REGENSBURG
REGION CENTRE
REMSCHEID
RHINELAND-PALATINATE
RHÔNE-ALPES
ROMANIA
ROSTOV (OBLAST')
ROTTERDAM
RUHR

RUSSIA
RUSSIA (RSFSR)
RUTHENIA
SAARLAND
SAINT-NAZAIRE
SCANDINAVIA.
SCHLESWIG-HOLSTEIN
SERBIA
SEVILLE
SICILY
SILESIA
SLOVAKIA
SPAIN
SPLIT
STRASBOURG
SWEDEN
SWITZERLAND
SYRACUSE (PROVINCE)
SZCZECIN
SZCZERCÓW
TALLIN
TAMBOV (OBLAST')
TATAR REPUBLIC
TICINO
TIRASPOL
TRENTINO-ALTO ADIGE
TRENTO (PROVINCE)
TREVISO
TRIESTE
TURNHOUT
UKRAINE
UKRAINE, WESTERN
URAL REGION
VALENCIA, SPAIN (REGION)
VENEZIA EUGANEA
VENICE
VERNAMIEGE EN VALAIS
VIENNA
VOLGA BASIN
VORONEZH (OBLAST')
WALLONIA
WARSAW
WHITE RUSSIA
WUPPERTAL
YAROSLAVL (OBLAST')
YUGOSLAVIA
ZAPOROZH'E (OBLAST')
ZIEMIA LUBUSKA.
ZUERICH (CITY)
ZWOLLE

United Kingdom.

ABERDEEN
AFAN VALLEY
ANTRIM (COUNTY)
AVON
AYRSHIRE
BASILDON
BATLEY
BELFAST
BERKSHIRE
BIRMINGHAM
BLACK COUNTRY
BLAENAVON
BOLTON
BRECON BEACONS NATIONAL PARK.
BRISTOL
BUCKINGHAMSHIRE
CAMDEN
CANNING TOWN
CARDIFF
CHESHIRE
CIRENCESTER
CLWYD
CUMBERLAND
DARTMOOR NATIONAL PARK.
DERBYSHIRE
DONEGAL
DORSET
DURHAM (CITY)

DURHAM (COUNTY)
EAST SUSSEX
EDINBURGH
ESSEX
FAROE ISLANDS
GLASGOW
GLOUCESTERSHIRE
GREENWICH
GUERNSEY
HACKNEY
HAMPSHIRE
HARTSOP VALLEY.
HEBRIDES
HUDDERSFIELD
HUMBERSIDE
IRELAND
IRELAND, NORTHERN
ISLE OF MAN
ISLINGTON
KENT
KING'S LYNN
LAMBETH
LANARKSHIRE
LEEDS
LEIGH
LIVERPOOL
LONDON
MANCHESTER
MILTON KEYNES
MONMOUTHSHIRE
NEWCASTLE-UPON-TYNE
NORFOLK
NORTH SHIELDS
NORTHAMPTONSHIRE
NOTTINGHAMSHIRE
OLDHAM
OXFORD
PORTSMOUTH
READING
SALFORD
SCOTLAND
SHEFFIELD
SHETLAND ISLANDS
SHROPSHIRE
SOUTH YORKSHIRE
SOUTHWARK
STRATHCLYDE
SUFFOLK
SURREY
TOWER HAMLETS
TYNE AND WEAR
TYNESIDE
TYRONE
UNITED KINGDOM.
WALES
WEST MIDLANDS
YORKSHIRE

HISTORY.

General.

ARCHAEOLOGY
ARCHAEOLOGY, MEDIEVAL.
ARCHIVES
CHURCH HISTORY.
CITIES AND TOWNS, ANCIENT
CITIES AND TOWNS, MEDIEVAL
CIVILIZATION.
CIVILIZATION, MODERN.
CIVILIZATION, OCCIDENTAL.
EAST AND WEST.
ECONOMIC HISTORY.
EXCAVATIONS (ARCHAEOLOGY)
FEUDALISM.
HISTORIANS
HISTORICAL RESEARCH
HISTORIOGRAPHY.
HISTORY
HISTORY, ANCIENT.
HISTORY, UNIVERSAL.

INQUISITION
LAND SETTLEMENT
LAND TENURE.
MIDDLE AGES
MOHAMMEDAN EMPIRE
PEASANT UPRISINGS
PUBLIC RECORDS
SERFDOM
SOCIAL HISTORY.
TWENTIETH CENTURY.
TWENTY-FIRST CENTURY
WILLS

International (including wars).

BALTIC ENTENTE, 1934- .
CHACO DISPUTE.
CHINESE-JAPANESE WAR, 1894-1895.
CHINESE-JAPANESE WAR, 1937-1945.
EUROPEAN WAR, 1914-1918
FRANCO-GERMAN WAR, 1870-1871.
GENEVA CONVENTIONS.
HAGUE PEACE CONFERENCES.
HOLY ALLIANCE.
ISRAEL-ARAB CONFLICT, 1948- .
ISRAEL-ARAB WAR, 1967
ISRAEL-ARAB WAR, 1973.
ITALO-ETHIOPIAN WAR, 1935-1936.
MOROCCAN CRISIS, 1904-1906.
MOROCCAN CRISIS, 1911.
MUNICH FOUR POWER AGREEMENT,
    1938.
OPERATION OVERLORD.
RAPALLO, TREATY OF, 1922.
RECONSTRUCTION (1914-1939)
RECONSTRUCTION (1939-1951)
RUSSO-FINNISH WAR, 1939-1940.
RUSSO-TURKISH WAR, 1828-1829.
SEVEN YEARS' WAR, 1756-1763.
SOUTH AFRICAN WAR, 1899-1902.
SUEZ CANAL.
TRENT AFFAIR, NOV.8, 1961.
UTRECHT, TREATY OF, 1713.
VENDEAN WAR, 1793-1800.
VERSAILLES, TREATY OF, JUNE 28, 1919
    (GERMANY).
VIETNAMESE WARS, 1945-1975.
WORLD POLITICS.
WORLD WAR, 1939-1945.

African territories.

BOERS.
FULAH EMPIRE.
GENERAL STRIKE, SOUTH AFRICA, 1913.

American territories.

CRISTERO REBELLION, 1926-1929.
FREEDMEN IN JAMAICA.
FREEDMEN IN THE UNITED STATES.
FRONTIER AND PIONEER LIFE
GENERAL STRIKE, URUGUAY, 1973.
INDIAN TERRITORY
RECONSTRUCTION (UNITED STATES).
TACNA-ARICA QUESTION.

Asiatic territories.

EASTERN QUESTION.
EASTERN QUESTION (FAR EAST).
EASTERN QUESTION (NEAR EAST).
HUK REBELLION.
ISRAEL AND THE DIASPORA.
KOREAN REUNIFICATION QUESTION
    (1945-).

European territories.

BERLIN QUESTION (1945-).
BLACK DEATH.
BYZANTINE EMPIRE
CLOSTER-SEVEN, CONVENTION OF, 1757.
CONCORDAT OF 1929 (ITALY).
EASTERN QUESTION (BALKAN).
GERMAN CONFEDERATION, 1815-1866.
GERMAN REUNIFICATION QUESTION
    (1949-).
GREECE, ANCIENT
HANSA TOWNS.
HANSEATIC LEAGUE.
JANSENISTS.
LAUSITZ CULTURE.
MACEDONIAN QUESTION.
MOSCOW TRIALS, 1936-1937.
MOUVEMENTS UNIS DE LA RESISTANCE.
MUDEJARES.
REFORMATION
RENAISSANCE.
ROME, ANCIENT
UPPER SILESIAN QUESTION.

United Kingdom.

CHARTISM.
DOMESDAY BOOK.
GENERAL STRIKE, UNITED KINGDOM,
    1926.
HOME RULE
INCLOSURES.
IRISH QUESTION.
KETT'S REBELLION, 1549.
LEVELLERS.
PARISHES

Colonial companies.

DUTCH EAST INDIA COMPANY.
RUSSIAN-AMERICAN COMPANY.
SOUTH SEA COMPANY.
SYMETAIN.

LANGUAGE, LITERATURE AND THE ARTS.

Language.

ANTHROPOLOGICAL LINGUISTICS.
ARAWAKAN LANGUAGES.
BILINGUALISM.
ENGLISH LANGUAGE
FRENCH LANGUAGE.
FRENCH LANGUAGE IN CANADA.
FUNCTIONAL LOAD (LINGUISTICS).
GENERATIVE GRAMMAR.
GERMAN LANGUAGE
GRAMMAR, COMPARATIVE AND
    GENERAL.
HISTORICAL LINGUISTICS.
IRISH LANGUAGE.
ITALIAN LANGUAGE
JAPANESE LANGUAGE
LANGUAGE AND LANGUAGES.
LANGUAGES
LINGUISTIC CHANGE.
LINGUISTICS.
NEGRO-ENGLISH DIALECTS.
NEUROPSYCHOLOGY.
PSYCHOLINGUISTICS.
ROMANCE LANGUAGES
RUSSIAN LANGUAGE IN KIRGHIZIA.
SEMANTICS.
SEMANTICS, COMPARATIVE.
SEMIOLOGY.
SOCIOLINGUISTICS.
TRANSLITERATION.

WELSH LANGUAGE.
WORDS, NEW

Literature.

AFRICAN DRAMA.
AUSTRIAN PERIODICALS.
AZERBAIJANI NEWSPAPERS.
BELGIAN PERIODICALS.
CHILDREN'S PERIODICALS, CHILEAN.
COMMUNISM AND LITERATURE.
CRITICISM
DUTCH NEWSPAPERS
ENGLISH LITERATURE
ENGLISH NEWSPAPERS.
ENGLISH PERIODICALS.
FRENCH LITERATURE
FRENCH NEWSPAPERS.
FRENCH PERIODICALS.
GERMAN NEWSPAPERS
GERMAN PERIODICALS.
HOMOSEXUALITY AND LITERATURE
HUNGARIAN PERIODICALS
ISRAELI NEWSPAPERS
ISRAELI PERIODICALS
ITALIAN NEWSPAPERS.
JOURNALISM
LITERATURE.
LITERATURE AND MORALS.
LITERATURE AND SOCIETY.
LOVE STORIES.
NEWSPAPERS
NIGERIAN NEWSPAPERS.
POETRY.
POLISH PERIODICALS.
POLITICAL PLAYS
POLITICAL POETRY, ENGLISH.
POLITICS IN LITERATURE.
PRESS
PRISONERS' WRITINGS.
RACE PROBLEMS IN LITERATURE.
RADIO JOURNALISM
ROMANTICISM
RUSSIAN DIARIES.
RUSSIAN LITERATURE.
RUSSIAN NEWSPAPERS
SATIRE, ENGLISH.
SATIRE, FRENCH.
SATIRE, ITALIAN.
SATIRE, RUSSIAN.
SCOTTISH NEWSPAPERS.
SERBIAN LITERATURE
SILESIAN PERIODICALS.
SOCIALISM IN LITERATURE.
SPEECHES, ADDRESSES, ETC.
TATAR PERIODICALS.
UNDERGROUND LITERATURE
VENEZUELAN NEWSPAPERS.
VENEZUELAN PERIODICALS.
WHITE RUSSIAN PERIODICALS.
WOMEN IN LITERATURE.
WOMEN'S PERIODICALS, ENGLISH.

The Arts.

AESTHETICS.
ARCHITECTURE
ARCHITECTURE AND SOCIETY.
ART AND SOCIETY.
ARTS
COMMUNISM AND THE ARTS.
COMMUNIST AESTHETICS.
MUSIC
PERFORMING ARTS
POLITICAL BALLADS AND SONGS,
   ARGENTINIAN.
POLITICAL BALLADS AND SONGS, IRISH.
POLITICS IN MOVING PICTURES.
POPULAR CULTURE.
SOCIALISM AND THE ARTS.

STATE ENCOURAGEMENT OF SCIENCE,
   LITERATURE AND ART
THEATRE

LAW (including INTERNATIONAL LAW).

General.

APPELLATE PROCEDURE
BAIL
BURDEN OF PROOF
CONDUCT OF COURT PROCEEDINGS
CONFIDENTIAL COMMUNICATIONS
COUNTY COURTS
COURT RULES
COURTS
DUE PROCESS OF LAW
EQUALITY BEFORE THE LAW
IDENTIFICATION.
JUDGMENTS
JUDICIAL ERROR
JUDICIAL PROCESS
JUDICIAL REVIEW
JURISPRUDENCE.
JUSTICE.
JUSTICE, ADMINISTRATION OF
JUSTICES OF THE PEACE
JUVENILE COURTS.
LAW.
LAW, COMPARATIVE.
LAW AND ETHICS.
LAW AND SOCIALISM.
LAW ENFORCEMENT
LAW LIBRARIES
LAW REFORM
LAW REPORTS, DIGESTS, ETC.
LEGAL AID
LEGAL RESEARCH
MEETINGS.
NATURAL LAW.
NEWSPAPER COURT REPORTING
PENOLOGY
POWER OF ATTORNEY
PREPAID LEGAL SERVICES
PREROGATIVE, ROYAL.
PUBLICITY (LAW)
RELIGION AND LAW.
REMOTE SENSING SYSTEMS.
RESPONSIBILITY, LEGAL
RULE OF LAW
SEX DISCRIMINATION IN EMPLOYMENT.
SOCIAL LEGISLATION
SOCIOLOGICAL JURISPRUDENCE.
TRIALS

Public law.

ABORTION.
ABUSE OF ADMINISTRATIVE POWER
ADMINISTRATIVE COURTS
ADMINISTRATIVE DISCRETION
ADMINISTRATIVE LAW.
ADMINISTRATIVE REMEDIES
AGRICULTURAL LAWS AND
   LEGISLATION
ALIENS
AMNESTY
ARREST
BIRTH CONTROL.
CITIZENSHIP.
CITY PLANNING AND REDEVELOPMENT
   LAW
COMPENSATION (LAW)
CONSTITUTIONAL COURTS
CONSTITUTIONAL LAW.
DISCIPLINARY POWER
DRUGS
ECONOMIC LEGISLATION.
EDUCATIONAL LAW AND LEGISLATION
ELECTION LAW

EMIGRATION AND IMMIGRATION LAW
EMINENT DOMAIN
ENVIRONMENTAL LAW.
LEGISLATION
LEGISLATIVE AUDITING
MENTAL HEALTH LAWS
MILITARY LAW
NARCOTIC LAWS
NAVAL OFFENCES
POLITICAL QUESTIONS AND JUDICIAL
   POWER
POOR LAWS
PRESS LAW
PUBLIC HEALTH LAWS
PUBLIC INTEREST.
PUBLIC LAW
RELIGIOUS LAW AND LEGISLATION
TREASON
WATER
ZONING LAW

Civil law and procedure.

ACTIONS AND DEFENCES
CHARITABLE USES, TRUSTS AND
   FOUNDATIONS
CIVIL LAW
CIVIL PROCEDURE
COMPENSATION (LAW)
CONVEYANCING
DIVORCE
DOMESTIC RELATIONS.
DOMESTIC RELATIONS COURTS
ESTATE PLANNING
EXECUTIONS (LAW)
EXECUTORS AND ADMINISTRATORS
INHERITANCE AND SUCCESSION
INJUNCTIONS
JURISTIC PERSONS
LAND TITLES
LANDLORD AND TENANT
LIABILITY (LAW)
MARRIAGE LAW
MATRIMONIAL ACTIONS
NEGLIGENCE
OBLIGATIONS (LAW).
PARENT AND CHILD (LAW)
PARTIES TO ACTIONS
PERSONAL PROPERTY
PROBATE RECORDS
REAL PROPERTY
SUPPORT (DOMESTIC RELATIONS)
TORTS
TRESPASS.
TRUSTS AND TRUSTEES

Commercial, industrial and labour laws.

ADVERTISING LAWS
AGENCY (LAW)
ARBITRATION AND AWARD
AUTHORS AND PUBLISHERS
BANKING LAW
BANKRUPTCY
BUSINESS LAW
COMMERCIAL LAW
CONTRACTS
COPYRIGHT
CORN LAWS
CORPORATION LAW.
FACTORY LAWS AND LEGISLATION
INDUSTRIAL LAWS AND LEGISLATION
INSURANCE LAW
INTANGIBLE PROPERTY.
LABOUR LAWS AND LEGISLATION
LIQUIDATION
PARTNERSHIP
PATENT LICENCES.
PATENT SEARCHING.
PETROLEUM LAW AND LEGISLATION

PICKETING
RECEIVERS
STANDARDIZED TERMS OF CONTRACT
SUNDAY LEGISLATION

Criminal law and procedure.

ARREST
CAPITAL PUNISHMENT
COURTS-MARTIAL AND COURTS OF
   INQUIRY
CRIMINAL JUSTICE, ADMINISTRATION
   OF.
CRIMINAL LAW
CRIMINAL PROCEDURE
DRINKING AND ROAD ACCIDENTS
DRUGS AND AUTOMOBILE DRIVERS
EMBEZZLEMENT
FIREARMS.
FORGERY
FRAUD
INDICTMENTS
LARCENY
OBSCENITY (LAW)
OFFENCES AGAINST PROPERTY
OFFENCES AGAINST THE PERSON
PAROLE
PERJURY
PLEAS (CRIMINAL PROCEDURE).
PRELIMINARY EXAMINATIONS
   (CRIMINAL PROCEDURE)
PRISON SENTENCES
SENTENCES (CRIMINAL PROCEDURE)
TRIALS (BLASPHEMY)
TRIALS (ESPIONAGE)
TRIALS (MURDER)
TRIALS (POLITICAL CRIMES AND
   OFFENCES)
TRIALS (TREASON)

Ecclesiastical law.

CANON LAW.

Foreign law.

LAND TENURE (MAORI LAW).

Conflict of laws, civil and criminal.

INTERNATIONAL LAW, PRIVATE.

International law.

AGGRESSION (INTERNATIONAL LAW).
ARBITRATION, INTERNATIONAL.
ARTIFICIAL ISLANDS.
ASYLUM, RIGHT OF.
CIVIL RIGHTS (INTERNATIONAL LAW).
COMMISSIONS OF INQUIRY,
   INTERNATIONAL.
CONTRABAND OF WAR.
CONTRACTS, MARITIME.
COURT OF JUSTICE OF THE EUROPEAN
   COMMUNITIES.
CRIMINAL LIABILITY (INTERNATIONAL
   LAW).
EQUALITY OF STATES.
GENERAL AGREEMENT ON TARIFFS AND
   TRADE.
GENOCIDE.
GUERRILLAS (INTERNATIONAL LAW).
HIJACKING OF AIRCRAFT.
INSURANCE LAW, INTERNATIONAL.
INTERNATIONAL AND MUNICIPAL LAW
INTERNATIONAL LAW.
INTERNATIONAL LAW COMMISSION.

MARINE POLLUTION
MARINE RESOURCES AND STATE.
MARITIME LAW.
OCEAN BOTTOM (MARITIME LAW).
PACIFIC SETTLEMENT OF
   INTERNATIONAL DISPUTES.
RECOGNITION (INTERNATIONAL LAW).
REPATRIATION.
SANCTIONS (INTERNATIONAL LAW).
SPACE LAW.
WAR (INTERNATIONAL LAW).

MATHEMATICS AND STATISTICS.

ALGEBRA, ABSTRACT.
ALGEBRAS, LINEAR.
ALGORITHMS.
ASSEMBLER LANGUAGE (COMPUTER
   PROGRAM LANGUAGE).
AUDITING.
BAYESIAN STATISTICAL DECISION
   THEORY.
CALCULATING MACHINES.
COBOL (COMPUTER PROGRAM
   LANGUAGE).
COMPUTER ASSISTED INSTRUCTION.
COMPUTER GRAPHICS.
COMPUTER INPUT-OUTPUT EQUIPMENT.
COMPUTER NETWORKS.
COMPUTER PROGRAMMING
   MANAGEMENT.
COMPUTER PROGRAMS
COMPUTERS.
CONTROL THEORY.
CORRELATION (STATISTICS).
CRIMINAL STATISTICS
DATA BASE MANAGEMENT.
DATA STRUCTURES (COMPUTER
   SCIENCE).
DATA TRANSMISSION SYSTEMS.
DEBUGGING IN COMPUTER SCIENCE.
DECIMAL SYSTEM.
DEMOGRAPHY.
DIFFERENTIAL GAMES.
DIVORCE
DYNAMIC PROGRAMMING.
ECONOMICS, MATHEMATICAL.
ELECTRONIC DIGITAL COMPUTERS.
ESTIMATION THEORY.
EXPERIMENTAL DESIGN.
FACTOR ANALYSIS.
FILE ORGANIZATION (COMPUTER
   SCIENCE).
FLOW CHARTS.
FUNCTIONS OF REAL VARIABLES.
GAMES, THEORY OF.
GEM (COMPUTER PROGRAM).
GEOGRAPHY, MATHEMATICAL.
GRAPH THEORY.
HIPO TECHNIQUE.
IBM 370 (COMPUTER).
INDUSTRIAL STATISTICS.
INPUT DESIGN, COMPUTER.
LEGOL (COMPUTER PROGRAM
   LANGUAGE).
LINEAR PROGRAMMING.
MACHINE THEORY.
MAN-MACHINE SYSTEMS.
MATHEMATICAL MODELS.
MATHEMATICAL OPTIMIZATION.
MATHEMATICS.
METRIC SYSTEM.
MICROCOMPUTERS.
MINIATURE COMPUTERS.
MORTALITY.
MULTIVARIATE ANALYSIS.
ON-LINE DATA PROCESSING.
OPERATIONS RESEARCH.
POPULATION FORECASTING.
PREDICTION THEORY.
PRIVACY, RIGHT OF

PROBABILITIES.
PROGRAMMING (ELECTRONIC
   COMPUTERS).
PROGRAMMING LANGUAGES
   (ELECTRONIC COMPUTERS).
QUEUEING THEORY.
REGISTERS OF BIRTHS, ETC.
REGRESSION ANALYSIS.
SAMPLING (STATISTICS).
SIMULATION METHODS.
SPATIAL ANALYSIS (STATISTICS).
STATISTICS.
STOCHASTIC DIFFERENTIAL
   EQUATIONS.
STOCHASTIC PROCESSES.
STRUCTURED PROGRAMMING.
SYSTEM ANALYSIS.
SYSTEM THEORY.
SYSTEMS ENGINEERING.
TIME SERIES ANALYSIS.
TIME-SHARING COMPUTER SYSTEMS.
TRANSFER FUNCTIONS.
VITAL STATISTICS.
WEIGHTS AND MEASURES

MILITARY AND NAVAL SCIENCE.

ARMAMENTS.
ARMED FORCES
ATOMIC BOMB
ATOMIC WEAPONS.
BORDER PATROLS
CHEMICAL WARFARE.
DETERRENCE (STRATEGY).
EUROPEAN DEFENCE COMMUNITY.
EXSERVICEMEN
GENERALS
GUERRILLA WARFARE.
INTERCONTINENTAL BALLISTIC
   MISSILES.
MILITARISM.
MILITARY ART AND SCIENCE.
MILITARY ASSISTANCE, AMERICAN.
MILITARY BASES, AMERICAN
MILITARY EDUCATION
MILITARY LAW
MILITARY OCCUPATION.
MILITARY POSTS
MILITARY SERVICE, COMPULSORY
MILITARY SERVICE AS A PROFESSION.
MILITARY TRAINING CAMPS
MUNITIONS.
NAVAL OFFENCES
PENSIONS, MILITARY
PRISONERS OF WAR.
PRISONERS OF WAR, GERMAN.
PSYCHOLOGY, MILITARY.
SEA POWER.
SOCIOLOGY, MILITARY.
TEAR GAS MUNITIONS.
TRANSPORTATION, MILITARY.
WAR.
WOMEN SOLDIERS

PHILOSOPHY AND RELIGION.

Philosophy.

ALIENATION (PHILOSOPHY).
CHRISTIAN ETHICS.
CHRISTIANITY AND EXISTENTIALISM.
COMMUNIST ETHICS.
CONDUCT OF LIFE.
CONSCIOUSNESS.
ENLIGHTENMENT.
ETHICS.
EVOLUTION.
EXISTENTIALISM.
EXPERIENCE.
HOLISM.

HUMANISM
IDEALISM.
IDENTITY.
IDEOLOGY.
KNOWLEDGE, THEORY OF.
LAW AND ETHICS.
LITERATURE AND MORALS.
LOGIC.
LOGIC, SYMBOLIC AND MATHEMATICAL.
MATERIALISM.
METAPHYSICS.
METHODOLOGY.
MIND AND BODY.
MORAL EDUCATION.
PARADOX.
PHENOMENOLOGY.
PHILOSOPHICAL ANTHROPOLOGY.
PHILOSOPHY
PHILOSOPHY, AMERICAN.
PHILOSOPHY, BRITISH.
PHILOSOPHY, GERMAN.
PHILOSOPHY, HUNGARIAN.
PHILOSOPHY, MEDIEVAL.
PHILOSOPHY, MODERN.
PHILOSOPHY, PERSIAN.
PHILOSOPHY, POLISH.
PHILOSOPHY, RUSSIAN.
PHILOSOPHY, SCOTTISH.
PHILOSOPHY, WHITE RUSSIAN.
PLATO.
POSITIVISM.
PRACTICE (PHILOSOPHY).
PRAGMATICS.
RATIONALISM.
REASON.
SEMANTICS (PHILOSOPHY).
SPACE AND TIME.
UTILITARIANISM.

Religion.

ALBIGENSES.
ANABAPTISTS
ANTICLERICALISM
ANTISEMITISM
ATHEISM
BIBLE, NEW TESTAMENT
BOGOMILES.
BUDDHA AND BUDDHISM
CATHOLIC CHURCH.
CATHOLIC CHURCH IN AFRICA.
CATHOLIC CHURCH IN FRANCE.
CATHOLIC CHURCH IN GERMANY.
CATHOLIC CHURCH IN IRELAND.
CATHOLIC CHURCH IN ITALY.
CATHOLIC CHURCH IN POLAND.
CATHOLIC CHURCH IN RWANDA.
CATHOLIC CHURCH IN SCOTLAND.
CATHOLIC CHURCH IN THE UNITED
  KINGDOM.
CATHOLIC EMANCIPATION.
CATHOLIC SCHOOLS
CATHOLICS IN IRELAND.
CATHOLICS IN ITALY.
CATHOLICS IN NORTHERN IRELAND.
CATHOLICS IN THE UNITED KINGDOM.
CHRISTIAN ETHICS.
CHRISTIAN LIFE.
CHRISTIANITY
CHRISTIANITY AND ECONOMICS.
CHRISTIANITY AND EXISTENTIALISM.
CHRISTIANITY AND INTERNATIONAL
  AFFAIRS.
CHRISTIANITY AND POLITICS.
CHURCH.
CHURCH AND LABOUR
CHURCH AND RACE PROBLEMS.
CHURCH AND SOCIAL PROBLEMS
CHURCH AND STATE
CHURCH AND STATE IN AFRICA.
CHURCH AND STATE IN ITALY.

CHURCH AND STATE IN LATIN
  AMERICA.
CHURCH AND STATE IN POLAND.
CHURCH AND STATE IN RUSSIA.
CHURCH AND STATE IN SOUTH AFRICA.
CHURCH AND STATE IN SPAIN.
CHURCH AND STATE IN TANZANIA.
CHURCH AND STATE IN THE ARGENTINE
  REPUBLIC.
CHURCH AND STATE IN THE SUDAN.
CHURCH AND STATE IN THE UNITED
  KINGDOM.
CHURCH AND UNDERDEVELOPED
  AREAS.
CHURCH CHARITIES.
CHURCH HISTORY.
CHURCH LANDS
CHURCH OF ENGLAND
CHURCH OF ENGLAND IN SOUTH
  AFRICA.
CHURCH SCHOOLS
CLERGY
COMMUNISM AND CHRISTIANITY.
COMMUNISM AND ISLAM.
COMMUNISM AND RELIGION.
CONFESSION
DISSENTERS, RELIGIOUS
DOMINICANS
DOMINICANS IN FRANCE.
DRUSES.
EVANGELICALISM.
FRANCISCANS IN MEXICO.
FRANCISCANS IN NEW SPAIN
  (VICEROYALTY).
FRIENDS, SOCIETY OF
GUADELOUPE, NUESTRA SEÑORA DE.
HINDUISM
HOLINESS CHURCHES
IDOLS AND IMAGES
JEHOVAH'S WITNESSES
JESUITS
JIHAD.
JUDAISM.
JUDAISM AND SOCIAL PROBLEMS.
MARY, Virgin
METHODISM.
METHODIST CHURCH IN THE UNITED
  STATES.
MISSIONS
MODERNISM
MOHAMMEDANS IN RUSSIA.
MONASTERIES
MORMONS AND MORMONISM.
NATIONALISM AND RELIGION
OPUS DEI.
PERSECUTION
PROTESTANTISM AND CAPITALISM.
PURITANS.
QUETZALCÓATL.
REFORMATION
RELIGION.
RELIGION AND LAW.
RELIGION AND SCIENCE.
RELIGION AND SOCIOLOGY.
RELIGION AND STATE
RELIGIOUS LAW AND LEGISLATION
RELIGIOUS LIBERTY
RELIGIOUS THOUGHT
ROYAL SUPREMACY (CHURCH OF
  ENGLAND).
SCIENTOLOGY.
SECTS
SERMONS, ENGLISH.
SHAMANISM
SISTERS OF CHARITY.
SOCIALISM, CHRISTIAN.
SOCIALISM AND CATHOLIC CHURCH.
SOCIALISM AND RELIGION.
SOCIOLOGY, CHRISTIAN.
SOUL.
STUNDISTS.
TRANSUBSTANTIATION.

WAR AND RELIGION.
WOMEN IN CHRISTIANITY.

POLITICAL SCIENCE, POLITICS AND GOVERNMENT.

General.

ADMINISTRATION.
ADMINISTRATIVE AGENCIES
ADMINISTRATIVE AND POLITICAL
  DIVISIONS
ADMINISTRATIVE PROCEDURE
ADVERTISING, POLITICAL.
AGENTS PROVOCATEURS
AGRICULTURE AND STATE
ALIENS
AMNESTY
ANARCHISM AND ANARCHISTS.
ANTICOMMUNIST MOVEMENTS
ASSASSINATION
ATOMIC WEAPONS AND DISARMAMENT.
AUTHORITARIANISM.
AUTHORITY.
BALANCE OF POWER.
BALLOT.
BOYCOTT
BRIBERY
BROADSIDES
BUDDHISM AND STATE
BUREAUCRACY.
BUSINESS AND POLITICS
CABINET MINISTERS
CABINET SYSTEM
CAMPAIGN FUNDS.
CENSORSHIP
CENTRE PARTIES
CHILDREN AND POLITICS.
CHRISTIAN DEMOCRACY.
CHRISTIANITY AND INTERNATIONAL
  AFFAIRS.
CHRISTIANITY AND POLITICS.
CHURCH AND STATE
CHURCH AND STATE IN AFRICA.
CHURCH AND STATE IN ITALY.
CHURCH AND STATE IN LATIN
  AMERICA.
CHURCH AND STATE IN POLAND.
CHURCH AND STATE IN RUSSIA.
CHURCH AND STATE IN SOUTH AFRICA.
CHURCH AND STATE IN SPAIN.
CHURCH AND STATE IN TANZANIA.
CHURCH AND STATE IN THE ARGENTINE
  REPUBLIC.
CHURCH AND STATE IN THE SUDAN.
CHURCH AND STATE IN THE UNITED
  KINGDOM.
CITIZENS' ASSOCIATIONS
CITIZENSHIP.
CITIZENSHIP, LOSS OF
CIVICS, RUSSIAN.
CIVIL RIGHTS.
CIVIL SERVICE
CIVIL SERVICE RECRUITING
CIVIL SUPREMACY OVER THE MILITARY.
COALITION GOVERNMENTS.
COLONIES.
COLONIES IN AFRICA.
COLONIES IN WEST AFRICA.
COMMUNICATION IN POLITICS.
COMMUNISM.
COMMUNISM AND CHRISTIANITY.
COMMUNISM AND EDUCATION.
COMMUNISM AND INTELLECTUALS.
COMMUNISM AND ISLAM.
COMMUNISM AND LITERATURE.
COMMUNISM AND MEDICINE.
COMMUNISM AND RELIGION.
COMMUNISM AND THE ARTS.
COMMUNISM AND ZIONISM.
COMMUNIST EDUCATION.

COMMUNIST REVISIONISM.
COMMUNIST SELF-CRITICISM.
COMMUNIST STATE.
COMMUNISTIC SETTLEMENTS.
COMMUNITY LEADERSHIP.
COMMUNITY POWER.
CONCENTRATION CAMPS
CONSCIENTIOUS OBJECTORS.
CONSERVATISM.
CORPORATE STATE.
CORRUPTION (IN POLITICS)
COUPS D'ÉTAT.
DECENTRALIZATION IN GOVERNMENT
DELEGATED LEGISLATION
DEMOCRACY.
DENAZIFICATION.
DESPOTISM.
DETENTE.
DICTATORS.
DIPLOMACY.
DIRECT ACTION.
DISARMAMENT.
DISCRIMINATION
DISMEMBERMENT OF NATIONS.
DISSENTERS
EDUCATION AND STATE
ELECTIONS.
ELITE.
EMPLOYEE-MANAGEMENT RELATIONS
   IN GOVERNMENT
ENDOWMENTS
EQUALITY.
ESPIONAGE, GERMAN
EUROPEAN COOPERATION.
EUROPEAN FEDERATION.
EXECUTIVE ADVISORY BODIES
EXECUTIVE POWER
FASCISM.
FEDERAL GOVERNMENT.
FREEDOM OF ASSOCIATION
FREEDOM OF INFORMATION
FREEDOM OF MOVEMENT
GEOPOLITICS.
GERRYMANDER.
GOVERNMENT, COMPARATIVE.
GOVERNMENT CONSULTANTS.
GOVERNMENT EXECUTIVES
GOVERNMENT INFORMATION
GOVERNMENT PUBLICITY.
GOVERNMENTAL INVESTIGATIONS
GUERRILLAS.
HOME RULE
IMPERIALISM.
INDEPENDENT REGULATORY
   COMMISSIONS
INDUSTRY AND STATE.
INSURGENCY
INTELLIGENCE SERVICE
INTERNAL SECURITY
INTERNATIONAL AGENCIES.
INTERNATIONAL BROADCASTING.
INTERNATIONAL COOPERATION.
INTERNATIONAL ORGANIZATION.
INTERNATIONAL RELATIONS.
INTERNATIONALISM.
JOURNALISM, SOCIALIST
JUDICIAL REVIEW OF ADMINISTRATIVE
   ACTS
KIDNAPPING
KINGS AND RULERS
LAW AND SOCIALISM.
LEADERSHIP.
LEGISLATIVE BODIES
LEGISLATORS
LIBERALISM.
LIBERTY.
LIBERTY OF SPEECH
LIBERTY OF THE PRESS
LIBRARIES, GOVERNMENTAL,
   ADMINISTRATIVE, ETC.
LOBBYING.
LOCAL ELECTIONS

LOCAL GOVERNMENT.
LOCAL GOVERNMENT OFFICIALS AND
   EMPLOYEES
MAJORITIES.
MARXISM.
MAY DAY (LABOUR HOLIDAY).
MAYORS
MEDIATION, INTERNATIONAL.
METROPOLITAN GOVERNMENT
MINORITIES.
MISCONDUCT IN OFFICE
MONARCHY.
MUNICIPAL CORPORATIONS
MUNICIPAL GOVERNMENT.
MUNICIPAL RESEARCH
MUNICIPAL SERVICES.
NATIONALISM.
NATIONALISM AND RELIGION
NATIONALITIES, PRINCIPLE OF.
NEUTRALITY.
NOBEL PRIZES.
NONVIOLENCE.
OLIGARCHY.
OMBUDSMAN
OPPOSITION (POLITICAL SCIENCE).
PACIFIC SETTLEMENT OF
   INTERNATIONAL DISPUTES.
PACIFISM.
PARADOX.
PARISHES
PARLIAMENTARY PRACTICE
PARTY AFFILIATION
PASSIVE RESISTANCE
PATRIOTISM
PATRONAGE, POLITICAL
PEACE.
PEACE SOCIETIES.
PEASANT UPRISINGS
POLICE, POLITICAL AND SECRET
POLICY SCIENCES.
POLITICAL CLUBS.
POLITICAL CONVENTIONS.
POLITICAL CRIMES AND OFFENCES
POLITICAL ETHICS.
POLITICAL PARTICIPATION.
POLITICAL PARTIES.
POLITICAL PLAYS
POLITICAL PRISONERS.
POLITICAL PSYCHOLOGY.
POLITICAL SCIENCE.
POLITICAL SOCIALIZATION.
POLITICAL SOCIOLOGY.
POLITICS, PRACTICAL.
POLITICS AND EDUCATION.
POLITICS IN LITERATURE.
POLITICS IN MOVING PICTURES.
POPULATION TRANSFERS
POPULISM.
PRESS, COMMUNIST
PRESS AND POLITICS.
PRESSURE GROUPS
PRIME MINISTERS.
PROPAGANDA.
PUBLIC SERVICE.
RADICALISM.
RADIO IN POLITICS
RADIO IN PROPAGANDA.
RAILWAYS AND STATE.
RECREATION AND STATE
REFERENDUM
REFUGEES, DANISH.
REFUGEES, GERMAN.
REFUGEES, HUNGARIAN
REFUGEES, RUSSIAN.
REFUGEES, SPANISH.
REFUGEES IN AUSTRIA.
REFUGEES IN FRANCE.
REFUGEES IN GERMANY.
REFUGEES IN INDIA.
REFUGEES IN SWEDEN.
REFUGEES IN SWITZERLAND.
REGIONALISM.

REGIONALISM (INTERNATIONAL
   ORGANIZATION).
RELIGION AND STATE
RELIGIOUS LIBERTY
REPRESENTATION IN ADMINISTRATIVE
   PROCEEDINGS
REPRESENTATIVE GOVERNMENT AND
   REPRESENTATION.
REVOLUTIONISTS.
REVOLUTIONS.
RIGHT AND LEFT (POLITICAL SCIENCE).
ROYAL SUPREMACY (CHURCH OF
   ENGLAND).
SCIENCE AND STATE.
SECESSION.
SECRET SOCIETIES
SECURITY, INTERNATIONAL.
SEDITION
SEPARATION OF POWERS
SOCIAL SCIENCES AND STATE
SOCIALISM.
SOCIALISM, CHRISTIAN.
SOCIALISM AND CATHOLIC CHURCH.
SOCIALISM AND EDUCATION.
SOCIALISM AND RELIGION.
SOCIALISM AND THE ARTS.
SOCIALISM AND YOUTH.
SOCIALISM IN LITERATURE.
SOCIALISTS.
SOVEREIGNTY.
SOVIETS
SPHERES OF INFLUENCE.
STATE, THE.
STATE AID TO PRIVATE SCHOOLS
STATE ENCOURAGEMENT OF SCIENCE,
   LITERATURE AND ART
STATE GOVERNMENTS
STATE SUCCESSION.
STATESMEN
SUBVERSIVE ACTIVITIES.
SUFFRAGE.
SYNDICALISM
TECHNOLOGY AND STATE.
TELEVISION IN POLITICS.
TERRORISM.
TORTURE
TOTALITARIANISM.
TRADE UNIONS AND COMMUNISM.
TRADE UNIONS AND FOREIGN POLICY
TREASON
UTOPIAS.
VIOLENCE.
VOTING.
VOTING RESEARCH
WAR.
WAR AND EMERGENCY POWERS.
WAR AND RELIGION.
WAR AND SOCIALISM.
WOMEN AND SOCIALISM.
WOMEN IN POLITICS.
WOMENS' RIGHTS.
WORLD POLITICS.

**Particular countries, nationalities, parties,
organizations, etc.**

ALIANZA NACIONAL POPULAR.
ALIANZA POPULAR REVOLUCIONARIA
   AMERICANA.
AMERICAN CIVIL LIBERTIES UNION.
AMERICAN PARTY.
ANTINAZI MOVEMENT.
ATLANTIC COMMUNITY.
BLACK PANTHER PARTY.
BLACK POWER
BUND DER KOMMUNISTEN.
CARBONARI.
CARLISTS.
CHINESE YOUTH PARTY.
COMMONWEALTH SECRETARIAT.
COMMUNIST COUNTRIES

COMMUNITY HEALTH SERVICES FOR
  THE AGED
CORPULENCE.
DEATH
DRUGS
EPIDEMICS.
FOOD.
GASES, ASPHYXIATING AND POISONOUS
HANDICAPPED
HAZARDOUS SUBSTANCES
HEALTH EDUCATION.
HEALTH SERVICES ADMINISTRATION
HEALTH SURVEYS
HOSPITAL CARE
HOSPITALS
HOUSING AND HEALTH
HYGIENE, PUBLIC.
IATROGENIC DISEASES.
INDUSTRIAL ACCIDENTS
INDUSTRIAL HYGIENE.
INDUSTRIAL PSYCHIATRY.
INDUSTRIAL SAFETY
INFANTS
LIFE EXPECTANCY.
LONG-TERM CARE OF THE SICK.
LONGEVITY.
MALNUTRITION.
MEDICAL ANTHROPOLOGY.
MEDICAL CARE.
MEDICAL CARE, COST OF
MEDICAL ECONOMICS.
MEDICAL ETHICS.
MEDICAL LAWS AND LEGISLATION.
MEDICAL POLICY
MEDICAL RESEARCH
MEDICAL SOCIAL WORK
MEDICINE
MEDICINE, STATE
MENTAL HEALTH LAWS
MENTAL HYGIENE.
MENTAL ILLNESS.
MENTALLY HANDICAPPED CHILDREN
MERCURY
MORTALITY.
NURSES AND NURSING.
NUTRITION.
OCCUPATIONAL DISEASES.
OLD AGE
PHARMACY
PHYSICAL EDUCATION AND TRAINING
PHYSICALLY HANDICAPPED
PLAY THERAPY.
POLLUTION.
PREGNANCY.
PRESCRIPTION PRICING
PSYCHIATRIC HOSPITALS
PSYCHIATRY.
PSYCHOLOGY, PATHOLOGICAL.
PSYCHOLOGY, PHYSIOLOGICAL.
PUBLIC HEALTH ADMINISTRATION
RABIES.
REFUSE AND REFUSE DISPOSAL
ROAD ACCIDENTS
RURAL HEALTH SERVICES
SELF-MEDICATION.
SICK
SMOKING
SOCIAL MEDICINE.
STERILIZATION (BIRTH CONTROL).
WATER QUALITY MANAGEMENT
WORLD HEALTH ORGANIZATION

SCIENCE AND TECHNOLOGY.

ATOMIC ENERGY.
ATOMIC POWER.
BIOLOGY
BIOMETRY.
CHEMICAL WARFARE.
CHEMISTRY
COMMUNICATION IN SCIENCE.

DIFFUSION OF INNOVATIONS.
EDUCATIONAL TECHNOLOGY
ENGINEERING
FIELD THEORY (PHYSICS).
FORECASTING.
GENETIC COUNSELLING.
GENETICS.
HUMAN ENGINEERING.
HUMAN GENETICS.
HYDRAULIC ENGINEERING
INTERNATIONAL ATOMIC ENERGY
  AGENCY.
PHYSICS
RELIGION AND SCIENCE.
REMOTE SENSING SYSTEMS.
RESEARCH.
SCIENCE.
SCIENCE AND STATE.
SPACE FRAME STRUCTURES.
TECHNOLOGICAL FORECASTING.
TECHNOLOGICAL INNOVATIONS.
TECHNOLOGY
TECHNOLOGY AND CIVILIZATION.
TECHNOLOGY AND STATE.
TECHNOLOGY TRANSFER.

SOCIOLOGY, ANTHROPOLOGY AND ETHNOLOGY.

General.

ABOLITIONISTS.
ACCULTURATION.
ACTION RESEARCH
ADOLESCENCE.
ADOPTION
ALIENATION (SOCIAL PSYCHOLOGY).
ANTHROPOLOGICAL LINGUISTICS.
ANTHROPOLOGISTS, SPANISH.
ANTHROPOLOGY.
ANTHROPOMETRY
ANTIPATHIES AND PREJUDICES
ANTISEMITISM
APARTMENT HOUSES
ARCHITECTURE AND SOCIETY.
ART AND SOCIETY.
ASSOCIATIONS, INSTITUTIONS, ETC.
BEDFORD PRISON.
BEGGING
BIRTH CONTROL.
BLIND
BOYS
BRIGANDS AND ROBBERS
BRITISH BROADCASTING CORPORATION.
BROADCASTING
CAMP SITES, FACILITIES, ETC.
CASTE
CHARITIES.
CHILD DEVELOPMENT.
CHILD WELFARE
CHILDREN.
CHILDREN IN AUSTRIA.
CHILDREN IN MALAYSIA.
CHILDREN OF IMMIGRANTS
CHURCH AND RACE PROBLEMS.
CHURCH AND SOCIAL PROBLEMS
CHURCH CHARITIES.
CITIES AND TOWNS.
CITY PLANNING.
COALITION (SOCIAL SCIENCES).
COLDINGLEY PRISON.
COMMON LAW MARRIAGE
COMMUNES (CHINA).
COMMUNICATION.
COMMUNICATION IN THE SOCIAL
  SCIENCES.
COMMUNISM AND INTELLECTUALS.
COMMUNISTIC SETTLEMENTS.
COMMUNITY.
COMMUNITY AND SCHOOL.
COMMUNITY CENTRES

COMMUNITY DEVELOPMENT.
COMMUNITY HEALTH SERVICES FOR
  THE AGED
COMMUNITY LIFE.
COMMUNITY ORGANIZATION.
CONFLICT OF GENERATIONS.
COUNSELLING.
CRIME AND CRIMINALS.
CRIME PREVENTION.
CRIMINAL STATISTICS
CROWDING STRESS.
CRUELTY TO CHILDREN
CULTURAL PROPERTY, PROTECTION OF
CULTURAL RELATIONS.
CULTURE.
CULTUS.
DAY NURSERIES
DELINQUENT WOMEN.
DIET
DISASTER RELIEF.
DISCRIMINATION IN HOUSING
DRINKING CUSTOMS.
DRUG ABUSE.
DRUG ABUSE AND CRIME
DRUGS AND MASS MEDIA.
DRUGS AND YOUTH.
DWELLINGS
ELITE.
EMIGRATION AND IMMIGRATION.
ENCOMIENDAS (LATIN AMERICA).
EQUALITY.
ETHNIC ATTITUDES.
ETHNICITY.
ETHNOLOGY.
EUGENICS.
EVALUATION RESEARCH (SOCIAL
  ACTION PROGRAMMES).
EXSERVICEMEN
FAMILY.
FAMILY RESEARCH
FAMILY SIZE
FAMILY SOCIAL WORK
FAMINES.
FEMINISM.
FERTILITY, HUMAN.
FIREARMS.
FISHING VILLAGES
FOLK LORE
FOOD.
FOOD HABITS.
FOREIGN NEWS.
FOSTER HOME CARE
FOUNDLINGS
FOX-HUNTING
FREEDMEN IN JAMAICA.
FREEDMEN IN THE UNITED STATES.
FREEMASONS
FRONTIER AND PIONEER LIFE
GENOCIDE.
GLENDAIRY PRISON, BARBADOS.
GOSSIP.
HALFWAY HOUSES
HALLUCINOGENIC DRUGS.
HANDICAPPED
HANDICAPPED CHILDREN
HEROIN.
HOLIDAYS
HOMELESSNESS
HOMOSEXUALITY.
HOMOSEXUALITY AND EMPLOYMENT
HOMOSEXUALITY AND LITERATURE
HONOUR.
HOUSEWIVES.
HOUSING MANAGEMENT.
HUMAN ECOLOGY.
HUMAN EVOLUTION.
ILCHESTER PRISON.
ILLEGITIMACY
IMPRISONMENT
INCOME MAINTENANCE PROGRAMMES.
INDIANS, TREATMENT OF
INDIVIDUALISM.

TELEVISION PROGRAMMES, PUBLIC
  SERVICE.
TEMPERANCE.
TIME ALLOCATION SURVEYS
TRAILS
TRAMPS
TRIADS (SECRET SOCIETIES).
TRIBES AND TRIBAL SYSTEM
UNDERDEVELOPED AREAS.
UNITED NATIONS ENVIRONMENT
  PROGRAMME.
UNIVERSAL NEGRO IMPROVEMENT
  ASSOCIATION.
UNMARRIED COUPLES
UNMARRIED MOTHERS
UNTOUCHABLES.
UPPER CLASSES
URBAN RENEWAL.
URBANIZATION.
VANDALISM.
VICTIMS OF CRIME.
VILLAGE COMMUNITIES
VILLAGES
VIOLENCE.
VIOLENT DEATHS
VOLUNTEER WORKERS IN SOCIAL
  SERVICE
WELFARE STATE.
WIFE BEATING.
WITCHCRAFT
WOMEN.
WOMEN, NEGRO.
WOMEN AND SOCIALISM.
WOMEN IN BUSINESS.
WOMEN IN CHRISTIANITY.
WOMEN IN COMMUNITY DEVELOPMENT.
WOMEN IN LITERATURE.
WOMEN IN MASS MEDIA.
WOMEN IN POLITICS.
WOMEN IN THE MOTION PICTURE
  INDUSTRY.
WOMEN IN THE TELEVISION INDUSTRY.
WOMEN IN TRADE UNIONS
WOMEN SOLDIERS
WOMENS' RIGHTS.
WORTH.
YOUTH.

Particular races, tribes and nationalities.

AFRICANS IN EUROPE.
AGUARUNA INDIANS.
AKWE-SHAVANTE INDIANS.
ALEUTS.
ALGERIANS IN FRANCE.
AMERICANS IN CANADA.
ARAPESH TRIBE.
ARMENIANS.
ASIATICS IN THE UNITED KINGDOM.
AUSTRALIAN ABORIGINES.
BAMBRZY.
BANABANS.
BANGLADESHIS IN FOREIGN
  COUNTRIES.
BANTUS IN ZAIRE.
BASQUES.
BASQUES IN AMERICA.
BASSA (LIBERIAN PEOPLE).
BOERS.
BRITISH IN INDIA.
BRITISH IN PARAGUAY.
BUSHMEN.
CANELOS INDIANS.
CHEROKEE INDIANS.
CHINESE AMERICANS.
CHINESE IN INDONESIA.
CHINESE IN MALAYSIA.
COLOURED PEOPLE (SOUTH AFRICA).
CREOLES (SIERRA LEONE).
CZECHS IN AUSTRIA-HUNGARY.
DASANETCH (AFRICAN PEOPLE).

EAST INDIANS IN FOREIGN COUNTRIES.
EAST INDIANS IN SOUTH AFRICA.
EAST INDIANS IN THE UNITED
  KINGDOM.
EAST INDIANS IN UGANDA.
FILIPINOS IN THE UNITED KINGDOM.
FRENCH CANADIANS.
FRENCH IN RUSSIA.
FULAHS.
GERMAN AMERICANS.
GERMANIC TRIBES.
GERMANS IN CHILE.
GERMANS IN CZECHOSLOVAKIA.
GERMANS IN EASTERN EUROPE.
GERMANS IN LITHUANIA.
GERMANS IN POLAND.
GERMANS IN SILESIA.
GERMANS IN SWITZERLAND.
GIPSIES
GREEKS IN AUSTRALIA.
GRIQUAS.
GURUNGS.
INCAS.
INDIANS.
INDIANS OF CENTRAL AMERICA.
INDIANS OF MEXICO.
INDIANS OF NORTH AMERICA
INDIANS OF SOUTH AMERICA.
IRISH AMERICANS.
ITALIAN AMERICANS.
ITALIANS IN AFRICA.
ITALIANS IN BRAZIL.
JAPANESE AMERICANS.
JAPANESE IN CANADA.
JAPANESE IN SOUTHEAST ASIA.
JEWISH AMERICANS.
JEWS
JEWS IN ARAB COUNTRIES.
JEWS IN BRAZIL.
JEWS IN GERMANY.
JEWS IN GIBRALTAR.
JEWS IN PALESTINE.
JEWS IN POLAND.
JEWS IN RUSSIA.
JEWS IN THE UNITED KINGDOM.
JEWS IN VENEZUELA.
KABYLES.
KEKCHI INDIANS.
KURDS IN SYRIA.
LAPPS IN FINLAND.
MALAYANS IN SINGAPORE.
MAROONS.
MATACO INDIANS.
MAYAS.
MENANGKABAU (INDONESIAN PEOPLE).
MEXICAN AMERICANS.
MNONG (INDOCHINESE TRIBE).
MOPAN INDIANS.
MOROCCANS IN ISRAEL.
NAGAS.
NAIRS
NEGRO CHILDREN.
NEGRO RACE.
NEGROES.
NEGROES IN AFRICA
NEGROES IN LATIN AMERICA.
NEGROES IN SOUTH AFRICA.
NEGROES IN THE UNITED KINGDOM.
PAKISTANIS IN FOREIGN COUNTRIES.
PAKISTANIS IN THE UNITED KINGDOM.
PALESTINIAN ARABS.
PANARE INDIANS.
PENNSYLVANIA GERMANS.
POLES IN CANADA.
POLES IN LATIN AMERICA.
POLES IN THE UNITED STATES.
PORTUGUESE IN BELGIUM.
RUSSIANS IN ALASKA.
RUSSIANS IN CHINA.
RUSSIANS IN FOREIGN COUNTRIES.
RUSSIANS IN FRANCE.
RUSSIANS IN KOREA.

RUSSIANS IN SIBERIA.
RUSSIANS IN VIETNAM.
SERBS IN HUNGARY.
SERBS IN THE UNITED STATES
SLOVENES IN CARINTHIA.
SPANIARDS IN GERMANY.
SWISS IN AUSTRALIA.
TAMILS.
TAPIRAPE INDIANS.
TARASCO INDIANS.
TATARS.
TINNE INDIANS.
TZOTZIL INDIANS
WELSH IN PATAGONIA.
WELSH IN THE UNITED STATES.
WEST INDIANS IN CANADA.
WEST INDIANS IN THE UNITED
  KINGDOM.
YANKTON INDIANS.
YANOAMA INDIANS.
YECUANA INDIANS.
ZAPOTEC INDIANS.

TRANSPORT AND COMMUNICATIONS.

General.

AERONAUTICS, COMMERCIAL
AERONAUTICS AND STATE.
AIR CHARTER CONTRACTS.
AIR LINES
AIRPORTS
ARTIFICIAL SATELLITES IN
  TELECOMMUNICATION.
AUTOMOBILES
BARGES.
BILLS OF LADING.
CANALS
COMMERCIAL VEHICLES.
COMMUNICATION AND TRAFFIC
COMMUTING
CONCRETE BOATS.
DANGEROUS GOODS
DRINKING AND ROAD ACCIDENTS
DRUGS AND AUTOMOBILE DRIVERS
FREIGHT AND FREIGHTAGE.
HARBOURS
INLAND NAVIGATION
INLAND WATER TRANSPORTATION
LOCAL TRANSIT
MERCHANT MARINE.
MOTOR BUS LINES
MOTOR BUSES
MOTOR TRUCKS
MOTOR VEHICLES
PERSONAL RAPID TRANSIT
POSTAL SERVICE
RADIO BROADCASTING.
RAILWAYS
RAILWAYS AND STATE.
ROAD ACCIDENTS
ROAD CONSTRUCTION
ROAD PLANNING
ROADS
SHIPPING.
SHIPPING BOUNTIES AND SUBSIDIES.
SHIPPING CONFERENCES.
SPEED LIMITS
STEAMBOAT LINES
TELECOMMUNICATION.
TELEPHONE.
TOLL ROADS
TRADE ROUTES.
TRAFFIC ESTIMATION
TRAFFIC SURVEYS
TRAILS
TRAMWAYS
TRANSPORTATION.
TRANSPORTATION, AUTOMOTIVE.
TRANSPORTATION, MILITARY.
TRANSPORTATION AND STATE.

TRANSPORTATION PLANNING
UNITIZED CARGO SYSTEMS.
URBAN TRANSPORTATION.
URBAN TRANSPORTATION POLICY.

Individual undertakings, etc.

BAIKAL-AMUR RAILWAY.
CANADIAN PACIFIC RAILWAY.
CHANNEL TUNNEL.
GREAT WESTERN RAILWAY.
PORT OF LONDON AUTHORITY.
SOUTHERN RAILWAY.
STOCKTON AND DARLINGTON RAILWAY.